Greek Testament, With English Notes, Critical, Philological, And Exegetical

Ἡ ΚΑΙΝΗ ΔΙΑΘΗΚΗ.

THE

GREEK TESTAMENT,

WITH

ENGLISH NOTES,

CRITICAL, PHILOLOGICAL, AND EXEGETICAL,

PARTLY

SELECTED AND ARRANGED FROM THE BEST COMMENTATORS, ANCIENT AND MODERN,

BUT CHIEFLY ORIGINAL.

THE WHOLE BEING ESPECIALLY ADAPTED TO THE USE OF

ACADEMICAL STUDENTS, CANDIDATES FOR THE SACRED OFFICE, AND MINISTERS:

THOUGH ALSO INTENDED AS A MANUAL EDITION FOR THE USE OF

THEOLOGICAL READERS IN GENERAL.

BY THE

RÉV. S. T. BLOOMFIELD, D.D. F.S.A.

VICAR OF BISBROOKE, RUTLAND.

FIFTH AMERICAN FROM THE SECOND LONDON EDITION.

IN TWO VOLUMES.

VOL. I.

PHILADELPHIA:
PUBLISHED BY PERKINS & PURVES.
BOSTON: BENJAMIN PERKINS.
1843.

T. K. & P. G. COLLINS, PRINTERS, PHILA.

PREFACE

TO THE

AMERICAN EDITION.

The design of the Publishers in reprinting Dr. Bloomfield's Greek Testament with English Notes, is to furnish the American public with a book, which is well adapted to aid the critical student of the New Testament Scriptures. Dr. Bloomfield is extensively known in England, and to some extent in this country, as an editor of the text of Thucydides, accompanied by a translation and learned notes. The first edition of his Greek Testament was sold off in about three years after its publication; and, a copy of the second edition having by special effort been very early procured, the American publishers have made such unexpected progress in their reprint of it, that it comes before the public many months sooner than was anticipated.

The plan of Dr. Bloomfield's work may be briefly described to the reader. The *text* is formed on the *basis* of the last edition of Robert Stephens, adopted by Mill, and differing slightly from the vulgate text which originated in the Elzevir edition of the New Testament in 1624. In a very few cases, as the editor states, alterations of this text have been admitted, which are supported by the united authority of MSS., ancient versions, and fathers, and also the early printed editions. All *conjectural* emendations have been carefully excluded. Before words where the reading has been altered, an asterisk is uniformly placed, and some notice is taken of the alteration in the Notes. Brackets designate such portions of the text as are suspected of being an interpolation; brackets and a line drawn over the words designate such words or phrases as are probably or certainly spurious. Other marks are used by the editor to indicate suspected words, or such as probably need emendation. The important readings admitted by Wetstein, Matthæi, Griesbach, or Scholz, are noticed when not admitted; as is also any difference between the vulgate text and that of Stephens, adopted by the editor.

Dr. Bloomfield states, that he has bestowed great labour and care upon the division of the text into paragraphs, and also upon its punctuation. The Annotations, he says, are in a very considerable degree original; and where they are not so, they are derived from consulting all the sources of exegetical literature which are at present accessible.

In the second edition, which is here reprinted, the editor states that he has embodied the results of an attentive study of the reformers, Luther, Calvin, and Melancthon; that he has carefully revised the punctuation, and the marginal parallel references; that he has discussed more amply the claims and merits of various readings, and also various Greek and Hellenistic idioms, and introduced a far greater number of illustrations of phraseology from classical writers, and from Philo Judæus and Josephus. He has also given more regular and copious introductions to all the books of the New Testament. Some of the earlier annotations have been entirely rewritten, and many others on the more difficult passages have been greatly enlarged.

The condensation in the mode of printing has made room for all this additional matter, without enlarging the size or the price of the book; and, in this condensed form, the American publishers now proffer the work to the public.

Dr. Bloomfield published, some time since, a work entitled *Recensio Synoptica*, which exhibits the results of ancient and modern criticism on the New Testament in a very abridged form. The labour necessary to perform such a work, was well adapted to prepare him for the present one; to which he must have come, furnished with an extensive knowledge of what had been done by his predecessors in the business of interpretation.

Under these circumstances, and possessed of a sound and sober judgment and a discriminating mind, and having long been conversant with a wide field of classical Greek study, it was to be expected that Dr. B. would exhibit a commentary, which should be a kind of *multum in parvo;* and such is the fact. The reader will find, in most places of the New Testament, at least a hint of the most important opinions that have been maintained in respect to the meaning of them. I have had occasion to follow Dr. B. through two epistles which are among the longest, and I have rarely found an exception to the tenor of the above remark.

As a convenient manual for the study of the New Testament, which furnishes the student with much important information and many useful hints, I can commend this work to our religious public, and have recommended it to the publishers. But in doing this, it is not to be understood, that I pledge myself to all the results of Dr. B.'s exegetical study. He holds the rights of conscience and private judgment too high, not to concede very cheerfully to others the liberty of differing from him; and especially so, as to the sense of difficult and doubtful passages. I cannot subscribe to some of the views in this work, which have a polemic aspect in defence of the hierarchy of the English church, because, after long and patient investigation of the New Testament and of early Christian writers, I do not find any satisfactory evidence of such a modelling of the early church, either in the one or in the other of these sources. Still less can I hold with Dr. B., that διὰ λουτροῦ παλιγγενεσίας, in Tit. iii. 5, expresses the sentiment that regeneration accompanies the external rite of baptism. But cases of such a nature are very unfrequent in his book; and, for the most part, the expression of his opinions is managed with a kind, courteous, and candid spirit. His zeal for the hierarchy and warm attachment to his national church seem to be the strongest temptations that beset him, in the otherwise gentle and even tenor of his way.

The Notes will be found most deficient on the Apocalypse,—a book about the plan and object of which Dr. B. does not appear yet to have wholly satisfied his own mind.

Those who may differ from the author of the Notes in these volumes, in some respects, will be just and generous enough, I would hope, not to reject the good which the work contains on this account. An effort like this, to aid in the study of the New Testament original, and to promote critical and exegetical knowledge among the ministers of the gospel, deserves approbation and patronage, even from those who cannot give to all the sentiments which the work contains, their unqualified approbation.

Dr. B. has expressed great solicitude in his letters to me, that the work should come before the American public in as neat and accurate a manner as possible. To this his request, so natural and reasonable, all possible attention has been paid.

As to the care bestowed on the printing, the work will speak for itself. It has been executed at the University Press, Cambridge; and those who are acquainted with the character of the gentlemen who have the control of this establishment, will be slow to believe that the mother country itself can furnish superintendents and correctors, who are more skilled and accurate than those who conduct this business. So far as I have examined, I think Dr. B. himself will be satisfied with the accuracy which has been attained.

May this, and every attempt to promote the knowledge of the divine word, be blessed of Him who gave that word in order that it should shed light upon the path of our duty and salvation!

M. STUART.

Andover Theol. Seminary, October 1st, 1836.

PREFACE.

In laying before the Public a *fourth* Work, — not less elaborate than any of those in which he has been previously engaged, — the Author feels that the approbation, with which his *former* labours have been received, may well remove from his mind much of that anxiety which he would otherwise have felt as to the reception of the *present*.

It is obviously proper, in sending forth a new Edition of the New Testament, — as it would be in editing *any other* ancient writings, — as well to point out to the reader the principal *deficiencies*, which such Edition is intended to supply, as to state the particular *purposes* which it is intended to answer.

As far as regards the *Text* of the New Testament, the present Editor is not disposed to deny, that amongst the various Editions hitherto published, sufficient evidence is afforded to enable any person competently imbued with Learning and Criticism, to ascertain the true reading. Yet what are called the *Standard Texts* differ considerably; especially that of Griesbach, as compared with the *textus receptus*, and even with that of Matthæi, or of Scholz. And it is not to be supposed that students, — or indeed readers of the New Testament in general, — have at command *all* the chief Standard Texts, or ordinarily possess the ability to decide between their diversities. It, therefore, seemed desirable, that such persons should be supplied with a text so constructed, that the *variations* from the *textus receptus* should be, as far as might be practicable, distinctly marked in the *Text itself*; and, as much as possible, not left to be learned from the Notes: and further, that the *state of the evidence*, in all important cases, should be laid before the reader, — together with the *reasons* which had induced the Editor to adopt any variation from the *textus receptus;* so that the Student might thence learn to judge for himself; for (as Seneca justly observes), "longum iter est per *præcepta*, breve et efficax per *exempla*." But a *new recension* of the text, formed on such a plan, — however desirable, and even necessary, — was not to be found in this country; nor, indeed, in any other, — based on sound principles of Criticism; the Texts for Academical and general use, on the Continent, being little more than *reprints* of that of Griesbach; of which the imperfections (as will appear from what is said in these pages, and in the course of the following work) are very considerable.

And if thus great was the want of a *Text* fitted for such uses, how much greater was that of a consistent and suitable *body of Annotation!* The earliest modern Commentaries on the New Testament were little more than unconnected *Scholia* on passages where there seemed a "dignus vindice nodus." And no wonder; since they were formed chiefly on the model of the *Scholiasts* on the Classical writers; whose labours, at the revival of literature, were the only aids to the understanding of those writings. This method was, in many respects, *convenient* to the earlier Commentators on the Scriptures; who, not intending to form what is now called a *perpetual Commentary*, proposed merely to explain or illustrate such points as especially needed it, and such as they felt most able to explain. And, not unfrequently, the passages which they chose to discuss were made rather the means of displaying their own learning or reading, than of explaining the sense of their author. Indeed, even those Theologians who most successfully cultivated this branch of learning, (as Valla, Vatablus, Luther, Calvin, Melancthon, Beza, Erasmus, Strigelius, Lucas Brugensis, Zegerus, Drusius, Castalio, Scaliger, Casaubon, Capellus, Grotius, Cameron, and Priceus,) and who, in general, interpreted the New Testament in a Grammatical and Critical manner, without introducing doctrinal discussions, fell, in different degrees, into the error of only explaining what it was *convenient* for them to explain, and did not aim at forming a regular *Commentary*.[1] This system,—if system it may be called,—continued to a late period, and may be traced, more or less, in almost all the Commentators of the seventeenth century, even in Grotius himself. There were, indeed, a few exceptions, as in the case of Calvin, Luther, and Crellius; but in those instances the Commentaries were extended to so immoderate a length, as effectually to preclude their being *read;* and to this day they are chiefly used for reference. The very same error was committed, though by a different process, towards the close of the seventeenth century, by Cocceius and others of his school,—as Lampe, Gerdes., Wessel., and other Dutch Theologians; in whose hands the *Analytical* method became as pernicious, and unfavourable to the discovery of truth, as had been the *Logical* and *Grammatical* in the hands of Crellius, Schliting, and others of that School; in whose writings may be discovered the very same *abuse*, from excess, of what is

[1] [Indeed, it was, at that early period, scarcely possible that any *one* man should form a COMMENTARY; which, as Samuel Johnson observes, "must arise from the fortuitous discoveries of many men in many devious walks of literature·" and such fortuitous circumstances can only be expected to occur in the lapse of a considerable portion of time.]

N. B. The Notes within brackets have been added in the Second Edition.

good in itself, as that which is justly complained of in the Heterodox class of the Foreign Expositors of the present age. The Commentaries of our own countrymen, during the seventeenth, and part of the eighteenth century (though valuable in themselves, and of perpetual importance) partake of the same fault as those of Grotius and others in the Critici Sacri, — in being too prolix and desultory in some parts, and unsatisfactorily brief in others; no approach being made to any thing like a connected COMMENTARY. *This* state of things, both here and on the Continent, also long continued; and the first attempt at any thing like a regular and connected Grammatical Commentary, formed to be *redd through*, and not to be used for *reference* only — for Academical and general use, and not for that of the learned only — was made by the erudite and acute KOPPE, who in 1778 commenced an Edition of the New Testament with a corrected text, short Critical Notes, and rather copious philological and exegetical Annotations, serving to establish the literal and grammatical sense; all doctrinal discussions being excluded. The learned Editor only lived to publish two Volumes, containing the Epistles to the Romans, Galatians, Ephesians, and Thessalonians; and after his death the work was continued by Heinrichs and Pott; who, however, so altered the original plan (which was excellent), as to spoil it for the purposes especially had in view by Koppe. Moreover, the principles maintained by those Editors are so heterodox, that — whatever may be the learning and ability occasionally displayed — their interpretations ought to be received with the greatest distrust and caution. Koppe himself, indeed, was not wholly free from that leaven of heterodoxy, which has worked so extensively and perniciously in the greater part of the German Commentators, for the last half century, from Semler downwards. As to the literary merits and *defects* of Koppe's work, the Editor cannot better express his opinion, than in the words of the learned and judicious PELT, Proleg. on Thess. p. 47, "Jejunam haud raro simplicitatem nimio coëmit pretio, profundioribus scilicet cogitationum rejectis rationibus; in multis tamen præclare sensum attigit, quamquam philologicæ etiam subtilitati non semper, ut decebat, operam dederit." To omit such decidedly heterodox works as are better passed over in silence, the Commentaries of ROSENMUELLER and KUINOEL have (especially the latter) much valuable matter. The work of the former, however, (besides that its principles are very objectionable) is almost wholly a *compilation*. Far more valuable is that of the latter; its principles, too, are better; though what are called Neologian views not unfrequently discover themselves; and the work, being too often interlarded with some of the most pestilent dogmas of Semler, Paulus, and others, though accompanied with refutations by the Editor, is very unfit to come into the hands of Students. *Both* the foregoing works are, moreover, somewhat faulty in the Critical and Philological departments; being occasionally deficient in accuracy, and in an acquaintance with the principles of the great Critics of the illustrious School of BENTLEY and HEMSTERHUSIUS, PORSON and HERMANN. In Fritzsche, indeed, we see a disciple worthy of his master, the great HERMANN, and an accomplished Philologist; but besides that the prolixity, and, still more, excursiveness of his Commentary, render it unfit for Academical or general use, we may say of this, as of the *foregoing* works, and also of Dindorf's and Morus's Annotations, and Iaspis's Version (or rather Paraphrase) with Notes, — πολλὰ μὲν ἐσθλὰ μεμιγμένα, πολλὰ δὲ λυγρά [1]. In the exegetical works of Ernesti, Storr, Carpzov, Staudlin, Knapp, Borger, Tittmann, Winer, Heydenreich, Laurmann, Tholuck, Emmerling, Bornemann, and Pelt, there is, for the most part, little which is really objectionable in *principle;* but they are more or less characterised by prolixity, obscurity, and above all, the want of a clear and well-digested arrangement. In short, as it has been truly observed by the learned Pelt, in the Preface to his Commentary on Thessalonians, — "Quis neget, omnes fere N. T. libros novâ indigere eâque accuratiore, et ad nostri temporis necessitates accommodatâ expositione; quæ grammaticis, historicis, Criticis, aliisque rationibus quæ in commentario conficiendo in censum venire solent, satisfaciat [2]?"

Hence it is abundantly apparent, that an Edition of the New Testament, with Critical and exegetical apparatus, formed with a due regard to the advanced state of Biblical science at the present day,[3] and in other respects

[1] How can we fail to lament, that while we see the learned Critics *acknowledging* the sense, which the immutable laws of Verbal Criticism compel us to assign to Scripture, we should also see *him* caught in the toils of that miserable sophistry, which entangles the ordinary and half-learned sciolists and sceptics of his country!

[I say *half-learned;* for, as Mr. Rose truly observes, "Rationalism is laughed to scorn by the real philologists of Germany, as the emptiness of their religious theories by genuine philosophers. The Rationalists *have* learning on subjects to which they have applied themselves, — the illustration of manners and customs, or the investigation of antiquities; whatever, in fact, relates to the mere exterior in which Scriptural truth is covered."]

[2] The same want had been before perceived by the acute and learned Winer, as may be seen in his Oratio de emendandâ Interpretatione Nov. Test. Lips. 1823, 8vo, and in his preface to an useful edition of the Epistle to the Galatians, intended to be a specimen of what he thought was proper to be done on the whole of the New Testament.

[3] [That Biblical science has greatly advanced within the lifetime of those who have mainly contributed to produce that advance, is undeniable. That such should be the case is not surprising, since (as Dr. Hey has observed) "there is no kind of mental improvement which does not improve *Criticism.*" Polite arts *refine* our *taste;* and science *ripens* our *judgment*, and strengthens our understanding. And not only has Biblical science advanced and is advancing, but the safety of the religion itself requires that it should continue to advance. "Let then (to use the words of the great Cudworth) no man, in pursuit of the name of an applied *sobriety*, imagine that we can go too far or be too well read in the book of God's DIVINITY, or in the book of God's *works*, PHILOSOPHY; but rather let men awaken themselves, and vigorously pursue an endless progress of proficiency in

adapted for Academical and general use as a Manual, is still a *Desideratum.* The older exegetical works of the English School are confessedly insufficient of themselves for the purposes which they were originally intended to serve; and the later and elementary works (besides being for the most part very superficial and unscientific) are so modelled on the older ones, as to be little promotive of their professed object. In fact, in *all* didactic works intended for Academical and for general use, it is now indispensable, that the matter contained in them should not only be as *complete* as possible in *itself*, but should fully attain to the standard of knowledge actually reached in the works of those who have most advanced the science therein treated of.

This acknowledged want it has been the endeavour of the present Editor to supply; with what degree of success, he leaves to the learned and candid reader to determine; and he will now proceed to unfold the *plan* of the present Work, to state the *principles* of Criticism and Interpretation by which he has been guided, and the *purposes* which it is especially intended to answer.

The Text has been formed (after long and repeated examinations of the whole of the New Testament for that purpose solely) on the *basis* of the last Edition of R. Stephens, adopted by Mill, whose text differs very slightly from, but is admitted to be preferable to, the *common* Text, which originated in the Elzevir Edition of 1624. From this there has been no deviation, except on the most preponderating evidence; critical conjecture being wholly excluded[1]; and such alterations only introduced, as rest on the united authority of MSS., ancient Versions and Fathers, and the early-printed Editions,—but especially upon the *invaluable* Editio Princeps; and which had been already adopted in one or more of the *Critical* Editions of Bengel, Wetstein, Griesbach, Matthæi, and Scholz. And here the Editor must avow his total dissent, though not from the *Canons of Criticism* professedly acted upon by Griesbach in his Edition of the New Testament, yet altogether from the *system of Recensions* first promulgated by him, and founded, as the Editor apprehends, upon a misapplication of those

both." How necessary it is, in times like the present, that the standard of Biblical study should be raised, has been evinced, with his usual ability, by the Bishop of London; and also by Mr. Prebendary Raikes, in his instructive little work, entitled "Remarks on Clerical Education."]

1 [*Conjectural* emendations, indeed, are at once *unnecessary* (with so many MSS.) and *presumptuous; nay foolish*, as often founded on ignorance of the contents and true character of the Book, on which the Conjecturers have chosen to try their ingenuity. To this effect, it is well observed by the learned Editor of the New Testament recently published at Bâle, "Sponte patet, multis in locis Sacri Codicis nec Hemsterhusianas nec Gronovienses emendationes esse ferendas, si isti viri, dum vel maximo acumine et doctrinæ subtilitate pollerent, *Spiritu illo vivifico, quo sacros Scriptores concitatos intelligimus, expertes forent.* Nec enim in Scriptoribus, qui dicuntur, profanis, res critica absque ingenii quodam cum auctore consortio confici poterit."]

canons. The perpetual, and, for the most part, needless cancellings,[1] and alterations of all kinds, introduced by Griesbach, evince a temerity which would have been highly censurable even in editing a *profane* writer, but, when made in the Sacred Volume, they involve also a charge of *irreverence* for the Book which was intended to make men "wise unto salvation[2]." In most respects the Editor coincides with the views of Matthæi (whose Edition of the N. T. is pronounced by Bp. Middleton to be by far the best yet seen), and, in a great measure, with those of the learned and independent Scholz.

Further, the present Editor has so constructed his TEXT, that the reader shall possess the advantage of having before him both the Stephanic text and also the corrected text formed on the best MS. ancient Versions and early Editions. To advert to the various kinds of *alterations* of the common text, as they arise from the *omission* or the *insertion* of words, or from a *change of one word into another*,—nothing whatever has been *omitted* which has a place in the Stephanic Text; such words only as are, by the almost universal consent of Editors and Critics, regarded as *interpolations*, being here placed within *brackets*, more or less inclusive, according to the degree of suspicion attached to them. Nothing has been *inserted* but on the same weighty authority; and even *those* words are pointed out *as insertions* by being expressed in a smaller character. All *altered* readings have *asterisks* prefixed, the old ones being invariably indicated in the Notes. And such readings as, though left untouched, are by eminent Critics thought to need alteration, have a ‡ prefixed. [Such words (very few in number) as are, on good grounds, supposed to be corrupt readings, though the MSS. supply not the means of emendation, are designated by an *obelus*.] As to *Various Readings*, the most important are noticed; chiefly those which, though not admitted into the text of the present Edition, have been adopted by one or more of the four great Editors, Wetstein, Matthæi, Griesbach, and Scholz, or are found in the Editio Princeps; or those wherein the

[1] In justification of these, it has generally been urged, that the words, phrases, or clauses, so thrown out are glossematical, and therefore spurious. On this point, however, the present Editor is entirely at issue with the Griesbachian School; and he has much pleasure in referring his readers to a masterly Commentatio by C. C. Tittmann de Glossematis N. T. rectè investigandis, (at p. 501 sqq. of his Opusc. Theolog. Lips. 1803.); as also an able and instructive Dissertation of Bornemann de Glossematis N. T. cautè dijudicandis, Lips. 1830, who there completely refutes the rash assertions of Wassenbergh, in a Dissertation de Glossis appended to Valck. Scholia ad N. T., and ably distributes these pretended Glosses under *five Classes*.

[2] Thus it is well observed by the profoundly learned Valckenaer in his Schol. in N. T. Tom. II. p. 360. "Qui talia in Auctoribus *profanis* periclitari vellet, omnium sibilis exciperetur, nedum talia tentare licet in Sacris, ubi Critica exercenda sobria et modesta, ut a superstitione quidem libera, sic tamen multo magis a temeritate."

common Text differs from that of Stephens. In such cases, the *reasons* for non-adoption are usually adduced. And this has always been done in the case of *alterations* of the Text, however minute. The CRITICAL NOTES are almost entirely original, and chiefly serve to give *reasons* for the methods pursued in forming the Text. Such Notes would have been brought forward more frequently, had not their introduction been forbidden by the brevity necessary to be preserved in a work of this nature. It also seemed to the Editor more advisable to treat fully and (he trusts) satisfactorily on a comparatively small number of controverted passages, than to introduce frequent, though brief, and therefore unsatisfactory, Critical remarks.

The division of the Text, not into *verses* (though these are expressed in the inner margin), but *paragraphs*, is agreeable to the custom of the most eminent Editors, from Wetst. downwards, and can need no justification. Certain it is that scarcely any thing could have had a more unfavourable effect on the interpretation of the New Testament than H. Stephens's breaking up the whole into verses; thus, occasionally, dissevering clauses which are closely connected in sense.

The *Punctuation* has been throughout most carefully corrected and adjusted, from a comparison of all the best Editions, from the Editio Princeps to that of Scholz. To each verse is subjoined, in the outer margin, a select body of the most apposite *Parallel References*, as adopted by Bp. Lloyd from Curcellæus. The citations from the Old Testament are expressed as such by being *spaced out;* and the words of any speaker are indicated by an appropriate mode of punctuation, and by the use of a Capital letter to designate the commencement of those words.

To advert to the EXEGETICAL NOTES: — These are, for the most part, of the kind found in the best Critical Editions of the Greek *Classical* writers; being intended to comprise whatever respects the *interpretation*, and tends to the establishment of the *Grammatical sense:* and in order thereto, great pains have been taken to trace the *connexion* and *scope* of the passage under discussion[1]. And here, together with the greatest *comprehensiveness*, there has been adopted the utmost *compression* consistent with perspicuity; so as to form *an Epitome of exegetical and philological annotation.* The method systematically adopted by the present Annotator, in order to ascer-

[1] In this department of his labours the Editor has availed himself of the valuable assistance (though that not unfrequently failed him) of Chrysostom, Theophylact, Euthymius, and Theodoret; of Calvin, Grotius, Crellius, Carpzov, Koppe, Pott, Heinrichs, Rosenmueller, Kuinoel, and others of the more recent Foreign Commentators; as also, of our own divines, Hammond, Whitby, Locke, Peirce, Benson, Doddridge, Chandler, Newcome, Campbell, Macknight; and finally, Dr. A. Clarke and Mr. Scott, to the various merits and general excellence of whose elaborate Commentary the Editor (widely as he differs from that pious writer on a few points of doctrine, and some matters of doubtful disputation) bears most decided testimony.

tain the sense of passages of very doubtful or disputed meaning, has been this; to seek their illustration. 1. From parallel passages of the N. T., or passages where the same, or a similar phrase, occurs either in the writer himself, or in the other writers of the N. T. or the O. T.; thus making Scripture its own Interpreter. 2. From passages of the Septuagint (including the Apocrypha), Josephus, and Philo. 3. From the Apostolical Fathers. 4. From Apocryphal writings of undoubted antiquity; and which, whatever may be their claims to *inspiration*, are, at least, of considerable utility, as indicating the Theological opinions of the times when they were written, whatever those might be, whether *earlier* or *later* than the N. T.; in the former case, showing the opinions of the Jews previous to the promulgation of the Gospel; in the latter, contributing, in various ways, to the interpretation of the N. T., and often establishing its authenticity and uncorrupted preservation. 5. From Rabbinical writers of unquestionable antiquity. 6. From the Fathers in general, Greek and Latin, of the first four centuries, including the Greek Commentators, Theodoret, Theophylact, Euthymius, and Œcumenius. 7. From the Greek Classical writers, especially those who lived after the formation of the Alexandrian and Hellenistic, Common or popular dialect. The illustrations derived from this last source are generally original; and when not specifically ascribed to any commentator or critic, may, in almost all cases, be so considered.

The Annotations have been partly derived, with due acknowledgment, wherever practicable, from the most eminent Commentators, ancient and modern; but they are *in a very considerable degree* original. In their general character, they are elementary, and introductory to the larger Commentaries; and they especially and systematically indicate and establish what the Editor conceives to be the *true* interpretation of disputed passages.[1]

In the present work, the editor has (as in his Recensio Synoptica) seen reason continually to search out the fountain-heads of interpretation; as found in Chrysostom, and other eminent Greek Fathers, Commentators, Scholiasts, and Glossographers. And if he be thought by some to have employed

[1] [The Editor has endeavoured, on controverted passages, to ascertain the one true, and therefore *only* sense, namely, that intended by the sacred writer. For, in opposition to the notion of certain Theologians (as Doddridge), that the words of Scripture mean all that they *may* mean, (formed on the Canon of Cocceius, "Verba SS. tantum semper valere quantum valere possunt,") the Editor contends that there is only *one* true sense—*that in the mind of the sacred writer*. In the words of the learned Becher, Præf. ad Tittmann de Synonymis, P. II., "Falsa est quævis interpretatio, quæ in verbis quærit aliam sententiam, quam scriptor ipse in animo habuit, et verbis suis cogitari ab aliis voluit." Indeed, Doddridge, in thus adopting the above Canon, ought to have attended to the words there following, which were meant to limit it, and would make its use comparatively safe: "Et esse in omni eo sensu accipienda, quem significare possunt, juxta emphasin verborum, usitatam rationem phraseos ἀκολουθίαν rerum, et ἀναλογίαν scripturæ."]

unnecessary pains in ascertaining the *antiquity* of interpretations, he would beg them to ponder the weighty observation of Bp. Middleton, who remarks, that "Theologians would do well to notice the *antiquity* of the opinions which they defend, because that antiquity is sometimes no inconsiderable evidence of truth." He has, however, carefully repressed any undue prepossession either in favor of *antiquity*, or of *novelty*[1], and we may say, in the words of Strabo, *βούλομαι τὸ ἀληθὲς, ἄν τε παλαιὸν ἄν τε νέον.* He has everywhere endeavoured to combine simple and solid *old* views with ingenious and learnéd *new* ones; ever bearing in mind (with due restriction) the profound remark of Thucydides, when speaking of the union of youth with age in deliberation and counsel, *νομίσατε νεότητα μὲν καὶ γῆρας ἄνευ ἀλλήλων μηδὲν δύνασθαι· ὁμοῦ δὲ τό τε φαῦλον καὶ τὸ μέσον καὶ τὸ πάνυ ἀκριβὲς ἂν ξυγκραθὲν μάλιστ' ἂν ἰσχύειν.*

It has been the Author's fortune *sometimes* to justify and confirm, by the suffrage of antiquity, what had been unjustly distrusted, and rejected as mere *novelty;* but *far more frequently* to show the solid grounds of interpretations, which it had been too long the fashion to reject, merely *because they were common;* though, from their antiquity and general reception, they might have been *presumed to be true;* for, to use the words of Cicero, "Opinionum commenta delet dies, Naturæ ac veritatis judicia confirmat."

In ascertaining the true interpretation, the Editor has always aimed especially at settling the *Grammatical* and *literal* sense[2] of any disputed passage; mindful of the pithy dictum of the great Scaliger, "that all controversies in Theology arose from mistakes in *Grammar*," meaning thereby, in an extended sense, *Philology in general.* Thus the immortal Luther (as appears from Tittmann de Synonymis, p. 41.) was accustomed to assert, "optimum Grammaticum, eum etiam optimum Theologum esse[3]." Indeed, as Bp. Middleton well observes, "when we consider how many there are, who seek to warp the Scriptures to their own views and prepossessions, *Verbal Criticism* seems to be the *only barrier* that can be opposed successfully against heresy and schism."

1 Thus it is profoundly observed by the illustrious Bacon, Nov. Org. I. 56, "Reperiuntur ingenia alia in admirationem Antiquitatis, alia in amorem et amplexum Novitatis effusa; pauca vero ejus temperamenti sunt, ut modum tenere possint, quin aut quæ rectè posita sunt ab Antiquis convellant, aut ea contemnant quæ rectè afferuntur a Novis. Hoc vero magno scientiarum et Philosophiæ detrimento fit, quum studia potius sint Antiquitatis et Novitatis, quam judicia: Veritas autem non a felicitate temporis alicujus, quæ res varia est; sed a lumine Naturæ et Experientiæ, quod æternum est, petenda est." The folly of an excessive fondness for *either* is ably pointed out by the same great writer De Augm. Scient. L. II.

2 [On this see Becher's Preface (pp. x. & xi.) to P. II. of Tittmann de Synon.]

3 [*Melancthon*, too, used to say, "non posse evadere bonum *Theologum*, qui non antea fuerit bonus *Interpres;* neque posse Scripturam intelligi theologicè, nisi antea intellecta sit grammaticè."]

The present Annotator has, moreover, especially kept in view *simplicity* of sense, in opposition to *contort*, however erudite, interpretations[1]. On which subject it was well observed by the acute Maldonati, "Verior aliquando Vulgi quam sapientum sententia est, quod dum simplicius veritatem quærit, facilius invenit." Words and phrases must not be taken in some *recondite* sense, which men of learning and ingenuity, in support of an hypothesis, may devise; but in the ordinary sense of the words, wherein the persons addressed, whether by preaching or writing, would be likely to understand them.

It is an admirable remark of Bp. Middleton, Gr. Ar. p. 539: "It is better to understand phrases according to their obvious import, even though we should be compelled to leave the proof of their fitness to more fortunate inquiry. When once we begin to withhold from words their ordinary and natural signification, we must not complain, if Infidels charge our Religion with mysticism, or its expositors with fraud."

The editor would further state, that all *pretended* Pleonasms, Hebraisms, &c. are in the present work discountenanced, as well as all other Philological devices to dilute, pare down, or explain away the sense[2]. Above all, care has been taken not to lower the dignity of certain portions of the New Testament by ill judged attempts at explanation, where all explanation must fall short. [However, in such a case, as Dr. Hey well observes, "Men may be said to understand any subject, when they see all that can be seen of it by man."]

As to the much controverted subject of the *style of the New Testament*, the present editor is opposed to the opinions alike of those who regard the Greek as pure, and even elegant; and, of those who pronounce it barbarous and ungrammatical. To maintain the *former*, after the labours of so many eminent writers from Vorstius downwards, were a vain attempt: and as to the *latter*, it surely does not follow that, because some words are found nowhere else, they were *coined* by the Sacred writers, or were *barbarous*; since there is great reason to suppose, that the Classical authors preserved to us do not contain a tenth part of the Greek language, as it existed at the beginning of the Christian æra. The words or phrases then *may* have

[1] See the excellent Dissertation of Tittmann de Simplicitate in Interpretatione N. T. and another de Causis contortarum Interpret. N. T. p. 239—281. de Synon. N. T.

[2] See Deyling's Dissertation de Amplitudine Sensus Biblici non Coarctandâ, Op. Sacr. P. v.

[Accordingly, he has carefully noted those *enumerations* of vices which not unfrequently occur in the New Testament (especially in St. Paul's writings), and which the generality of Commentators (especially the recent foreign Expositors) usually consider as merely put *κατὰ συνάθροισιν*, as a *congeries* of all sorts of vice; thus avoiding the trouble of explanation. Whereas the Editor has, he trusts, succeeded, in every such case, in tracing a *plan*, and showing the *distinctive meaning* of the terms. For examples, the reader is referred to Rom. i. 29. sqq. Galat. v. 19—21. 2 Tim. ii. 5.]

been used by the best writers; or they may have formed part of the provincial or popular[1], colloquial and domestic phraseology, not preserved in any of the remains of antiquity. As to the *non-observance of the rules laid down by the Greek Grammarians*, sometimes imputed as a fault to the writers of the N. T., it is an excellent distinction of Tittmann de Syn. p. 231, "Scriptores sacri grammaticas quidem leges servarunt, non autem grammaticorum[2]."

But to return, it has been the uniform practice of the present Editor fairly to avow, and fully to meet, the innumerable difficulties to be found in the N. T., especially in the Epistles, those best interpreters of the Gospels. But, in order to find space, within the narrow limits of a *manual* Edition, for occasionally dilating on passages of acknowledged difficulty[3],—he has systematically excluded all such remarks as seemed trite and obvious, or likely to occur to an attentive reader; and such as might well be derived from *Lexicons* and *Dictionaries* of all kinds; as also from works

1 [This is a matter of more consequence than it would, at first sight, appear to be; since there can be no doubt that very great mistakes concerning the sense of Scripture (and some even involving *doctrines*) have arisen from not bearing in mind the *popular* cast of the style of the New Testament. Insomuch that it is the opinion of Dr. Hey (in his Lect. p. 5.) that "the chief difficulty as to expressions in Divinity arises from not considering them as popular." And so Tittmann de Synon. p. 216. "Ea est orationis Scriptorum sacrorum natura, ut ad vitæ communis loquendi consuetudinem quàm proximè accedat. Sed hujus consuetudinis (quâ indocti pariter ac docti utuntur) ea indoles est, ut syntaxeos, quantum legibus illis non necessariis constat, vincula ægerrime patiatur. Unde fit, ut sermo vitæ communis fere omnes loquendi formas habeat, quibus idiomata constant, et schemata orationis. Non est igitur mirandum, apud sacros scriptores *mixtum* illud dicendi genus reperiri, cujus causas qui optime perspectas habuerit, eum non dubitamus quin optimum illorum interpretem esse dicamus."]

2 See the Dissertation of the same writer, "de Scriptorum N. T. Diligentiâ Grammaticâ rectè æstimandâ."

[There are not wanting expressions in the New Testament which are *rejected* by some rash Critics, on the score of being formed *contrary to analogy*. But there are few of the most perfect Classical writers which might not furnish some such instances. As an example of which, may be noted, a form of expression occurring in one of the most finished compositions of antiquity—the Phœnissæ of Euripides, v. 405. καὶ τοῦτο λυπρὸν, ξυνασοφεῖν τοῖς μὴ σοφοῖς. Now here ξυνασ. is rejected by many Critics, (as Valcknaer and Pierse,) on the ground of *being formed contrary to all analogy*. Porson, however, prudently forbears to make any alteration; "since, (says he,) Euripides may have violated the usual rules for the sake of a stronger antithesis." Thus, in a similar manner, may we usually account for such violations of analogy in the *New Testament:* e. gr. Phil. ii. 30. on the disputed question παραβουλεύεσθαι; where see Note.

3 The difficulties of Scripture, as they must not be underrated, so neither are they to be magnified beyond due bounds. "From either extreme," says the learned Bp. Van Mildert, in his Bampt. Lect. p. 217, "evil consequences may arise: from the one, carelessness or presumption; from the other, blind submission to spiritual guides, or a morbid indisposition to rational inquiry. In either case, encouragement will be given to the dissemination of error; and Romanism, on the one hand, or Fanaticism, on the other, may be favoured; and the privilege of using the Word may be arrogantly monopolized by the Ministers, or irreverently assumed by such as are wholly destitute of the acquirements necessary for the Interpreter."

introductory to the study of the N. T., — and especially from Mr. Horne's invaluable INTRODUCTION; which the Editor considers quite indispensable to every Student, and reader of this work, who would hope to use it with full advantage.

To some persons the remarkable *diversity of interpretations* may appear unaccountable. Yet this is no proof that the sense of Scripture is too uncertain to be ascertained; but merely that Exegetical science was for a long time, and has been, until a comparatively late period, in a very imperfect state.[1] The same diversities, indeed, occur, though in a less degree, in the Annotations on other ancient writers. And it is well accounted for, both from the great difficulty of the Books of the N. T., and also from the manifest insufficiency, as Critics and Philologists, of by far the greater part of those who have taken upon themselves to determine the sense of Scripture; few of whom have employed that *accurate* and *scientific* mode of interpretation, found in the Annotations of the great Critics and Philologists of the seventeenth, eighteenth, and nineteenth centuries on the Greek Classical writers. To *introduce* this into the interpretation of the N. T. has been, in the present work, (as in his Recensio Synoptica,) the especial aim of the Editor; in fact, to accomplish that for the *New Testament* which he had already, in his two preceding works, effected for *Thucydides*.

The Editor may be permitted to observe, that one principal motive which first induced him seriously to apply himself to the Critical study of the New Testament, was, — that he might be enabled to prove to infidels that the Sacred Volume is *not*, as they aver, *unintelligible*, but that it can be shown to be everywhere susceptible of a rational and consistent sense; if only the same means be taken to *ascertain* that sense, which have been bestowed on other ancient writings, — nay, even on some modern ones[2].

[1] Thus it is justly observed by the learned Tittmann, "Tirones hodie discunt ac norunt, quæ doctissimi olim viri vix mente divinarunt." This is especially the case with respect to the Greek Article, Greek Syntax, Etymology, the nature of language in general, and especially that of the diction of the New Testament writers.

[2] [This involves an interesting inquiry, — namely, whether the *same principles* must govern the interpretation of the New Testament, as those which are used in explaining other ancient writings. Now, PLANCK, in his Introduction to Sacred Philology, says, that the *very same* principles must be acted on. But PROFESSOR TURNER of New York, in his Translation of that Work, judiciously modifies the rule as follows: "It cannot be denied, that the same principles must govern the interpretation of Scripture as are used in explaining other writings. And yet, the peculiar character of certain portions of Scripture is such as to allow, and very reasonably too, an interpretation, which could not with certainty be elicited, without conceding such a view of their character as cannot be pretended to apply to that of any other writings extant. I refer to whatever portions of the Old Testament are really typical of events connected with the New Dispensation; and also to those portions

Finally, the Editor has made it his particular care to give a new literal version of, or close paraphrase on, all passages of more than ordinary difficulty, and a regular series of glossarial Notes on all words and phrases which required it. In the latter he has endeavoured, in some instances, to combine and arrange what is scattered in the works of various Lexicographers and Philologists, and in others to supply their deficiencies. In all terms of dubious import he has endeavoured not only to *fix* the sense, but (in the words of Johnson) "to mark the progress of their meaning, and show by what gradations of intermediate sense, they have passed from their primitive to their remote and accidental signification."

The Editor cannot conclude without expressing his feelings of devout thankfulness for that Gracious Aid from above, by which, under the pressure of various and formidable difficulties, and with such slender means only, as an inconsiderable benefice in an obscure situation could supply, he has been enabled to complete two such arduous, and, he trusts, not unimportant Theological works as his Recensio Synoptica and the present Edition of the New Test.; works which, as a faithfully attached Son of the Church of England[1], he has the highest satisfaction in reflecting are so strongly confirmatory of her doctrines, discipline, and principles. May she derive that accession of *support* from the contents of the present work, which it is calculated to supply! *Then* indeed, unsparing as have been the sacri-

of the *prophecies*, which, while they declare truths and facts in immediate connection with that religious system under which the authors lived, do also announce other facts of a subsequent age, and identified with doctrines and realities belonging to the Gospel. This is not the place to discuss the whole subject connected with this remark, but the scriptural fact on which it was founded constitutes a striking difference between some portions of Scripture and ordinary writings. In such cases, therefore, the allowed principles by which writings in general are explained, are not of themselves sufficient. The comment on the New Testament, which can in no case be proved to be incorrect, must be regarded by the Christian expositor in the light of a principle beyond the ordinary principles of interpretation, and must become an additional aid to him in eliciting the true meaning. Compare Ps. viii. with Heb. ii. 6—9." In confirmation and illustration of the above view, may be added an important remark of Servius, in his Catena on Job, thus translated by Bp. Warburton, Works, Vol. v. p. 378: "It is fit we should understand names according to the nature of the subject matter, and not mould and model the truth of things on the abusive signification of *words*." Now, the rock on which the German Commentators split, is the attending to *words* only, and neglecting *things*. The *usus loquendi* can but show what *may* be the sense. It is the scope of the composition and the intent of the author, the *series orationis* and the nature of the Gospel system, that can elicit what *is* the sense. Finally, no interpretation that introduces any inconsequence of reasoning into the Divine Word is to be admitted; since it is infinitely more credible that error should be in the exposition of the interpreter, than incoherence in the sacred writer's discourse.]

1 [And thus, in effect, the Church of Christ. For, to use the words of my old and revered friend the late Dr. Samuel Parr, "the Church of England has not ceased to be the Church of Christ, because, in one sense of the expression, it is the religion of the State. Whatever ideas men may entertain upon the subject of Christian liberty, no clear and satisfactory evidence has been adduced from which it appears that *national* religion is inconsistent either with the express commands or the vital spirit of Christianity."]

fices of *health*, *fortune*, *comfort*, — and *whatever renders life desirable*, — which he has so long made in her service, — he will not, under any circumstances, think that he "has laboured in vain and spent his strength for nought;" but, looking forward to that *final* "recompense of reward," which he humbly hopes to receive at the great day of Account from the CHIEF SHEPHERD, and LORD OF THE VINEYARD, he will ever say, in the words of the Apostle, Ἐν τούτῳ χαίρω καὶ χαρήσομαι!

PREFACE

TO THE

SECOND EDITION.

It is with feelings of no ordinary satisfaction, that the Author sits down to again address himself to the Public, in a *second Edition*, — after so short a period, as that which has elapsed, since he laid before them the *first*. That a very large impression, of a *newly introduced* work, should have been thus exhausted in little more than three years from the publication, — is a testimony of the public approbation, of which the Writer may justly feel proud. Nevertheless he did not allow the voice of public approbation, testified from a *very early period*, to relax his diligence in future; — but rather found in it the strongest incentive to increased exertions, in order still further to *merit* that approbation. He was, moreover, aware that the work, notwithstanding the labour and pains already employed in its construction, was susceptible of considerable *improvement*: nay, he well knew that it would have been far superior to what it was, — but for certain unfavourable circumstances (*hereafter adverted to*) under which it was formed. Though, at the same time, he was sensible that no *first* Edition of a work, on a plan so new and extensive, had any chance of being what it ought to be, and might afterwards become. Accordingly, not long after the publication of the first Edition, and as soon as there seemed a probability of a second being called for, — he thought it essential for him to ascertain the *points of improvement*, of which the work was susceptible. In doing this, he did not allow himself to be guided solely by his *own* judgment; — but availed himself of the councils of several eminent Biblical Scholars, both in this and in foreign countries. He also occupied a considerable time in searching the great Public Libraries of London and Cambridge, for the purpose of examining such scarce Exegetical books, on the New Testament, the use of which could not otherwise be obtained; and he diligently sought after, and for the most part procured, such other works of rarity and value, British and Foreign, as had not heretofore formed part of his collection. And as he had before carefully traced the fountain-heads of interpretation, — as found in the early Fathers and the ancient Commentators, Scholiasts, and Glossographers,—so he now thought it expedient to turn his especial attention to a class of writers which had been almost wholly neglected by Expositors,—the great **Reformers**, both of the continent and of this country,—especially Luther, Calvin, and Melancthon; and not in their Expository writings only, but in their Theological works in general: and in respect to ***English*** Theology, he did not confine himself to the ***Reformers***, but extended his examination to those mighty "Masters in Israel," who succeeded our Reformers, and flourished from the age of Elizabeth down to the middle of the last century. These he carefully went through, in order to bring forward such matter as seemed especially important, at this day, to the interpretation of the New Testament. After a diligent use of all the works above mentioned, the Editor applied himself to an examination of the interpretation of the whole N. T. anew; employing therein the important aids derived from those many valuable works; but, at the same time, freely exercising his own judgment, and again putting in the balance the various interpretations of controverted passages proposed by different Expositors. With what ***success*** he has ***carried into execution*** the extensive ***plan*** of improvement which, after mature deliberation, he had laid down, will appear from an examination of the work itself. And in order that the reader may the better understand the ***points of difference*** between the former Edition and the present, the following ***specification*** of the ***nature*** and ***extent*** of the various alterations introduced into the latter, may be not unacceptable. These may be distributed into ***two*** classes,—1. ***external***, as regards the ***form*** and ***appearance*** of the work; 2. ***internal***, as respects its intrinsic merits. As to the ***former***, since, in the first Edition, the size of the page of letter-press was so unusually wide in form, as to leave far too small a margin,—the Author directed that in the ***present***, the margin should be enlarged by a small diminution of the width of the typographical form, yet so as not to diminish the quantity of matter in a line. As to the ***typography***, that of the first Edition could not easily be surpassed; yet, notwithstanding the Editor's diligence, from various causes, not necessary to be detailed, many more errors of the press remained in the Notes, than he could have wished. In the ***present*** Edition the greatest exertions have been made by the Editor to secure the utmost possible accuracy: in the furtherance of which important object, he has been much aided by the truly respectable Establishment of Messrs. Gilbert and Rivington, especially the latter, whose sound Classical learning and unwearied vigilance secured such an attention to the Author's corrections in proof, as to render a ***second*** Revise (which the shortness of the time forbade) almost unnecessary; and thus materially to lessen the disadvantages of his very great distance from the

Press. Insomuch that, upon the whole, a degree of accuracy, the Author trusts, has been attained in the present work, somewhat unusual, at least in this country.

To pass on to the *internal* alterations, and, it is hoped, amendments,—*first*, the PUNCTUATION of the Text (a matter of no small importance) has been every where most carefully revised, and, the Editor hopes, *very considerably improved*. In adjusting this, it was his aim to steer a due medium between the two *extremes*,—*one* (into which the earlier Editors fell), that of placing *too many* stops; and the other (that of the recent Foreign Scholars) of employing *too few*. Thus (to descend to particulars) the *colon* has been frequently used, where the earlier Editors had employed the *period;* thereby, too often, breaking up the continuity of the discourse; which is above all things to be avoided, especially in the Epistles of St. Paul. It is, indeed, a no small deficiency in the system of Greek Punctuation, that it is unprovided with the *semicolon*. To lessen that want, the Editor has occasionally employed the *period* followed by a *small* (instead of a *capital*) letter, as answering to our *colon;* and the Greek colon, correspondently to our *semicolon*. The period followed by a *capital* he has employed for the purpose of marking the *semi-sections*. In the use of the *comma* he has, (after the example of all the recent foreign Scholars of eminence,) deviated still more from the early and ordinary mode of punctuation,—which, by loading a long sentence with commas, and needlessly breaking it up into minute portions, throws an obscurity over the whole passage, and accordingly tends rather to *impede* than to *aid* the understanding of the sense. The Editor, however, has very rarely introduced any material change of punctuation, except on the authority of one or more of the great Editors, from the time of Wetstein downwards; or sometimes that of Robert Stephens, in the rare and valuable Edition called the "*O mirificam.*" And in all cases he has been careful to adapt the *punctuation* to what, in the Notes, has been, he trusts on good grounds, shown to be the *true interpretation*.

The MARGINAL PARALLELS have been carefully examined, and some errors in figures have been discovered and corrected. Of these so called *Parallels*, derived from Curcellæus, the Editor has ventured to reject a few, which were by no means parallel. In the first three Gospels they have been all of them transferred from the outer Margin to the Notes, where they are printed in Italics, within brackets. The place they formerly occupied has been assigned to what, the Editor is persuaded, the reader will find *singularly useful;* and for which feature of the work he was indebted to the recent Foreign Edition of the New Testament, for Academi cal use, by PROF. VATER. Thus, in each of the first three Gospels, the reader will find placed before him *at one view*, in *immediate juxta-position*, references to all the portions of the other two, parallel, in subject and words, to any portion of the one under perusal. And where no such marginal parallels are found opposite to any portion, it may be presumed that that portion is *peculiar* to the Gospel in which it is contained.

To pass on to the TEXT itself, — it will be found, with a few exceptions, the same as in the preceding Edition; and with reason; — since the Editor's opinions, as to the origin and character of the Griesbachian text, are, after much further research, precisely the same as before. He is still firmly persuaded, that the most *ancient* MSS., of the Western and Alexandrian Family, do not present so pure a text, as that of some comparatively modern ones, of the Constantinopolitan Family; and represented, with few exceptions, in the invaluable EDITIO PRINCEPS, for which we are indebted to the munificence of CARDINAL XIMENES. In short, he has no doubt that the texts of the first mentioned MSS. were systematically *altered*, for various reasons, by the early Biblical Critics: thus exemplifying what Lord Bacon says (de Augm. Scient. i. 9.), that "the most corrected copies are commonly the least correct[1]." In deference, however, to the opinions of other scholars, the Editor has, in the present Edition, more frequently introduced the mark ‡ expressive of doubt.

Of the ANNOTATIONS, *Critical and Exegetical*, the former, discussing the *true reading* of passages, will be found, in the present Edition, far more numerous; and several of those contained in the preceding, will in *this* be found enlarged, or in some respects, it is hoped, more or less *improved*, and not a few re-written. The same may be said of *another* class of notes closely connected in their nature with those, — namely, *Critical discussions on the Greek idioms*, especially respecting the Hellenistic dialect found in the Alexandrian and later writers, as compared with the phraseology of the earlier and purer authors. But the most extensive and important additions will be found, — where they were most needed, — in the EXEGETICAL notes. Now these, in the former Edition, were not so much in *continuity* as seemed desirable; there being too often a want of that *connecting thread* which *binds all together*. This, and occasionally the passing over of certain matters, which to some persons required elucidation, — or *others* which seemed too extensive to be treated of in a work

[1] On this important subject the Author refers his readers, for proofs and particulars, to the learned *Prolegomena* of PROF. SCHOLZ, to his Critical Edition of the New Testament with various readings, now in progress, and on the point of being completed, — the result of a quarter of a century's unwearied labours in collating MSS. in every part of Europe. A monument of diligence and erudition rarely surpassed, and by which he has laid the Christian world under greater obligations than any Critical Editor since the time of the illustrious WETSTEIN. See also the able and instructive Prolegomena to Bagster's Polyglott, by Professor Lee.

of this nature, — had almost entirely arisen from the Annotator's fear of overrunning the limits prescribed to the work. In the present Edition, these deficiencies have been studiously supplied, and the connexion and course of argument regularly traced; and no topics have been avoided merely from their extensiveness, — except such as respect matters of *Chronology* and the *Harmony* of the Gospels (on which he begs to refer his readers to the elaborate works of Dr. Hales, Mr. Townsend, and Mr. Greswell), or of *Biblical Antiquities*, on which he refers them to Mr. Horne's invaluable Introduction. The *general sense*, too, of a whole passage will in this be found far more frequently laid down than in the former Edition: a procedure agreeable to good taste and propriety. For since, by his Critical examination of the construction of a passage, and the import of words and phrases contained therein, the Commentator has, as it were, to *take it in pieces*, in order to point out the structure and import; so, by a neat *paraphrastic version*, conveying the *full* sense, he is enabled to put it together again, and present it as a *whole*. Moreover, a far greater number of *illustrations* of the phraseology or sense from the *Classical writers*, and likewise from Josephus and Philo Judæus, (for the most part *original*,) are now adduced: as also a still more regular series of *glossarial notes* on words or phrases involving any difficulty.

Another important feature of the present Edition is, that regular Introductions are given to *all* the Books of the New Testament; whereas, in the former Edition, there were only a *few*, (and those somewhat slight,) from about the middle of the second Volume. These Introductions are, indeed, some of them comparatively brief; but they will, in such a case, it is hoped, be found to comprehend the discussion of all points of any material importance. In drawing them up, the Author carefully *thought out* the subjects; and, occasionally, they will be found to contain views which had not occurred to former inquirers; and which may, it is hoped, contribute not a little to the settling of questions which have been long disputed; as, for instance, on the *sources of the first three Gospels*, — and on the *writer of the Epistle to the Hebrews*.

Finally, on the Quotations from the Old Testament a great deal *more* will be found accomplished in this than in the former Edition; though, at the same time, the Author is ready to admit that not a little still *remains* to be done, (and especially various minute *details* requiring a separate work, are necessary to be entered into,) in order to place in a clearer point of view the *amount of discrepancy* between the accounts in the New Testament and those of the Septuagint, or the Hebrew originals respectively; and, as founded thereupon, the best mode of *removing*, or of *accounting* for it.

In order to encounter successfully the difficulties which embarrass this subject, it is indispensably necessary to form correct notions, as to that most delicate perhaps of all points in exegetical science, — the *legitimate use and due extent of the principle of* ACCOMMODATION, so grievously misapplied by German Theologians in general; but on which the Editor can, with confidence, refer his readers, to p. 277, sq. of an excellent little work lately brought out by Prof. Turner, of New York; being a translation of Planck's Introduction to Sacred Philology and Interpretation, with many judicious Notes by the learned Translator. It has been recently reprinted in that very useful publication the *Biblical Cabinet.*

To advert to the *details* of enlargement in the Annotations, considerable additions and alterations will be found, more or less, on *all* the Books of the New Testament, but especially on the Gospel of St. Matthew, (on which the Annotatory matter, — which, from the plan of the work not being, at that early stage, sufficiently developed, was incomplete, — has been two-thirds of it re-written,) and the Epistles to the ROMANS, 1st and 2d CORINTHIANS, GALATIANS, EPHESIANS, and, above all, on the Epistle to the HEBREWS, where, even after the long-continued labours of that distinguished Biblical Critic (the Father of Exegetical science in the new world), PROF. STUART, not a little was still requisite to fully clear the sense of that most difficult composition. On the Gospels of St. *Mark* and St. *Luke* the fewest additions have been introduced, because there they were least requisite; the reader being supposed to regularly refer to the Notes on the parallel passages of St. *Matthew.* On St. *John's Gospel*, and on the *Acts of the Apostles*, they will be found very frequent; as also, more or less, on all the Epistles not before specified. The Editor is, indeed, not aware of *any* one passage of real difficulty, which has not received such an ample discussion, as may, to *most* inquirers, appear sufficient to enable them to ascertain the true sense. On certain portions, indeed, far *more* than ordinary labour has been bestowed; so as to almost entitle the Notes to the name of *Excursuses*[1].

[1] As, for instance, at MATT. i. 1 and MARK i. 1, on *the sources of the first three Gospels;* viii. 28, on the readings Γεργεσηνῶν, Γαδαρηνῶν, and Γερασηνῶν, and the site of the ancient city of *Gergesha;* xii. 31, on the *Blasphemy against the Holy Ghost;* xiii. 1, on *Parables, and the parabolical mode of instruction;* xvi. 18, 19, on the power of the *Keys* delivered to Peter, and the foundation of the Christian Church; xx. 28, *δοῦναι τὴν ψυχὴν αὐτοῦ λύτρον ἀντὶ πολλῶν*; on the *Atonement* and *Universal* Redemption; xviii. 19, on *Christian Baptism;* MARK vii. 21; classification and distinct sense in enumeration of vices; ix. 44, *ὅπου ὁ σκώληξ αὐτῶν οὐ τελευτᾷ*, &c.; on the *eternal punishment* of the wicked x. 29, 30, *οὐδείς ἐστιν ὃς ἀφῆκεν οἰκίαν — ζωὴν αἰώνιον*; LUKE vii. 29, *ἐδικαίωσαν*; JOHN iii. 1—21, on our Lord's *Discourse with Nicodemus;* v. 2—5, on the *healing at the Pool of Bethesda;* ix. 1—11, on the *authenticity of the narration of the woman taken in adultery;* viii. 44, *ὅτι ψεύστης ἐστὶν καὶ ὁ πατὴρ αὐτοῦ*; x. 8, *πάντες ὅσοι πρὸ ἐμοῦ ἦλθον κλέπται εἰσὶ καὶ λῃσταί*, to show the persons meant, and why called κλ. κ. λ.; xxi. 18—23, on the *scope and exact sense, and on the authenticity of vv. 24, 25;* ACTS ii. 30, on the *authenticity of the words τὸ κατὰ σάρκα — Χριστόν*; vii, 1, on the

But, while the Editor has constantly exerted himself to clear up satisfactorily matters of a difficult and recondite nature, — he has been anxious to make himself understood by any attentive and tolerably well-informed reader. He has, accordingly, everywhere *simplified* what seemed unnecessarily recondite, and made perspicuous what had been left obscure; generally, where his aim at brevity had produced, as it often does, obscurity: he moreover sometimes corrected trifling misstatements arising from inadvertence, or too exclusive attention to matters of higher moment; for, as JOHNSON has observed, "he who is searching for rare and remote things, will neglect those which are obvious and familiar. Thus it happens that in things *difficult* there is danger from ignorance; and in things *easy*, from confidence or inadvertence." Accordingly, while he was anxious to put forth his whole strength, where it was most called for, — on those numerous points, of great intricacy and doubt, "de quibus adhuc sub judice lis est," yet he has been, he trusts, never inattentive to minor matters.

The Editor has, also (agreeably to a very generally expressed wish), introduced far more of *original* matter than before; and, in all cases which involved any doubt or difficulty, given his own opinion on the subject in question. At the same time he has, for the most part, stated his *reasons*

nature and scope of the Apologetical Speech of Stephen. In the course of the chapter are considered and accounted for the discrepancies between St. Stephen and the writers of the Old Testament; x. 11, *τέσσαρσιν ἀρχαῖς δεδεμένον*; xi. 20, on the *reading* (namely, whether Ἕλληνας or Ἑλληνιστάς) and the *interpretation*; xiii. 18, on the *reading* (namely, whether *ἐτροφοφόρησεν* or *ἐτροποφόρησεν*) and *sense*; xiii. 48, *ἐπίστευσαν ὅσοι ἦσαν τεταγμένοι εἰς ζωήν*; xv. 20, *ἀλισγημάτων καὶ τῆς πορνείας*; xvi. 12, *πρώτη — τῆς Μακ. πόλις*; xvii. 23, on the inscription 'ΑΓΝΩΣΤΩι ΘΕΩι; xx. 28, *τὴν ἐκκλησίαν τοῦ* [*Κυρίου καὶ*] Θεοῦ (on the *reading*); xxii. 25, *προέτεινεν αὐτὸν τοῖς ἱμᾶσιν*; xxvii. on the whole of this chapter much has been done, especially on the nautical terms — and the very difficult and disputed words, (v. 14.) Εὐροκλύδων, (v. 17.) *βοηθείαις ἐχρ. ὑποζωννύντες τὸ πλοῖον. χαλ. τὸ σκεῦος* and (v. 40.) *τὸν ἀρτέμονα*; ROMANS i. 17, *δικαιοσύνη γὰρ Θεοῦ — πίστιν*, *sense*; i. 29, sqq., on the *classification* and *distinct sense* of the various terms in this enumeration of vices; v. 15 — 19, *οἱ πολλοὶ — πάντες*; vi. 12, 13, on the *reading* and *sense*; viii. 19, *ἡ ἀποκ. τῆς κτίσεως*, &c. *sense*; ix. 5, *ὁ ὢν ἐπὶ πάντων Θεὸς εὐλογητὸς εἰς τοὺς αἰῶνας*, *reading* and *sense*; 1 COR. vi. 2, *οἱ ἅγιοι τὸν κόσμον κρινοῦσι*; xi. 4, 5, xi. 10, *ἐξουσίαν ἔχειν ἐπὶ τῆς κεφαλῆς διὰ τοὺς ἀγγέλους*, *sense*; xii. & xiv., throughout, on the reality, *nature, and distinctive import* of the SPIRITUAL GIFTS; xv., throughout, especially on that portion which is read at our *Burial Service*, of which the scope and course of argument are especially examined in an *Introduction* to the chapter; 2 COR. i. 6, on the *reading* and *sense*; Gal. iii. 20, *ὁ δὲ μεσίτης ἑνὸς οὐκ ἔστιν· ὁ δὲ Θεὸς εἷς ἐστιν*, *true sense*; iv. 24, *ἅτινά ἐστιν ἀλληγορούμενα*; v. 19 — 21, on the *classification* and *distinct sense* in the enumeration of vices there; EPH. v. 16, *ἐξαγοραζόμενοι τὸν καιρόν*, *sense*; PHIL. ii. 6, *ὃς ἐν μορφῇ Θεοῦ — ἴσα Θεῷ*, *sense* and *doctrine*; iii. 16, *reading* and *interpretation*; 2 THESS. ii. 3, seqq., on the *great Apostasy* and the *Man of Sin*; 1 TIM. iii. 15, 16, *ἥτις ἐστὶν ἐκκλησία — Θεὸς ἐφανερώθη ἐν σαρκὶ — ἐν δόξῃ*, *reading*, *sense* and *doctrine*; 2 TIM. ii. 5, *distinct sense* of the terms in this enumeration of vices; HEB. viii., *Introduction*, in which the *Pauline origin* is evinced; ix. 1, *τό τε Ἅγιον κοσμικόν*, nature and sense of *κοσμ.*; ix. 15 — 18, *καὶ διὰ τοῦτο διαθήκης καινῆς μεσίτης ἐστὶν*, &c. — *ὅτε ζῇ ὁ διατιθέμενος*; x. 34, *reading* and *sense*; x. 38, *ὁ δὲ δίκαιος ἐκ πίστεως ζήσεται· καὶ ἐὰν ὑποστείληται*, &c., *true sense* and *doctrine*: 2 PET. i. 5 — 8, incl. *ἐπιχορηγήσατε ἐν τῇ πίστει — τὴν ἀγάπην*, on the distinct sense of the terms in this *series of virtues*, and on the scope of the whole; i. 19 — 21, *καὶ ἔχομεν βεβαιότερον τὸν προφητικὸν — ἰδίας ἐπιλύσεως οὐ γίνεται*, *sense* of this dark passage.

for such: not meaning, however, to assume that he has always fixed on the *true* interpretation. Though, in cases where he has missed it, he has, he trusts, placed within the reader's power sufficient means for arriving at the truth. At any rate, he trusts he has materially facilitated the labours of *others*, — and, in the words of a great scholar, "pontem struxerit aliis transituris ad veriora [1]."

The difficulty, however, was, how to *introduce* this immense quantity of additional matter, without either increasing the number of volumes, or injuring, in some measure, the matter which already occupied them. This required all the advantages derived by the experience of more than ten years in carrying his various works through the press; but at length the object was so effectually attained, that the pages of the present Edition only exceed those of the former (with the exception of the additional prefatory matter, and the Indexes) by about 110 pages. The remainder was provided for, partly by filling the pages even fuller than before, — but chiefly, 1. by the *omission* of various remarks, which seemed sufficiently obvious to occur of themselves to any attentive reader, or concerning things which had been before explained. 2. By the careful *condensation* of all such of the matter retained, as admitted thereof; in doing which, the Author never hesitated to *re-write* an article, if he could thereby effect any very material condensation. This, indeed, was the more necessary, since he sometimes found it advisable to *sacrifice* room, by using *more* words than before; for clearness sake breaking up and separating matter, which had been thrown too much into masses. Of this, he trusts, the reader will find the advantage, in increased perspicuity, and greater ease of finding any exposition of a word or phrase, of which he may be in search. And this leads the Author to observe, that it will be found not the *least useful* feature of this new Edition, that Indexes (both of Greek *words and phrases* explained, and of *matters* treated of in the Annotations) have been drawn up with the greatest care, so as to make them *practically* serviceable; and to which the reader is earnestly requested to recur, whenever he is in want of any explanation of a word or phrase, and does not find it in the Notes: since, in order to save room for more important purposes, the Editor has, in general, been content to give an explanation *only once*, and afterwards to leave it to

1 The Author takes this opportunity of saying, that, wherever he has seen reason, on more mature consideration, to change his opinion respecting any matter in dispute (whether of *reading* or of *interpretation*) he has never dissembled such change, nor hesitated to alter what he had before written, or, if necessary, to re-write an article: for he felt (with Prof. Hey, Lect. Vol. i. p. 4.) that "since, from the *progressive* nature of mental acquirements, nothing is more probable than that we should, on repeated examination, discern truth where we had before not discovered it; so no one need be ashamed to retract an opinion, or acknowledge an error." In short, in the quaint but expressive words of one of our great early Divines, "He that is overcome of the truth parteth victory with him that overcometh, and hath the best share for his part."

be reverted to by the reader, either with a reference in the Notes, or (as such references would have occupied too much room) *without* it, when it might readily be found by the aid of the Indexes.

Thus much may suffice to point out the *nature* and *extent* of the various additions and alterations in the work now again submitted by the Author to the candour of the Public: and he trusts they will be found such as to render his labours not unworthy of a *continuance* of that approbation, which they have hitherto experienced. One thing he can with truth say, that he has diligently exerted himself to *merit* it. Whatever may be found imperfect, is not so for want of care, but (as SAMUEL JOHNSON says) "because care will not always be successful; and recollection or information come too late for use." And although he cannot hope, that in a work of such great extent, and so multifarious in its matter, he has entirely avoided mistakes; yet, he can with truth say, that it has been his anxious study to *mislead* no one, but ὀρθοτομεῖν τὸν λόγον τῆς ἀληθείας[1].

Much, it is true, of what has been accomplished in this second Edition, *might* have been effected in the *first*. But that was rendered impracticable, by the very great disadvantages, difficulties, and hindrances (including ill-health), under which it was formed; and the too short space of time allowed (from certain peculiar circumstances, not necessary to be here adverted to) for its completion. Above all, it was the Author's *great misfortune*, that his Biblical labours should, in this work as well as in his RECENSIO SYNOPTICA (as also in his Translation and Edition of THUCYDIDES), have been carried on in a situation as unfavourable as can well be imagined; — one of the obscurest nooks in the kingdom[2], (which his old friend, the late Dr. SAMUEL PARR, used to call the *Ultima Thule*; "quæ a cultu atque humanitate civitatis longissimè abest,") at 112 miles distance from the Metropolis, and consequently exposed to perpetual delays and disappointments

1 Accordingly he has endeavoured to keep his mind free from any *party* bias, and has aimed at preserving the *strictest impartiality* in adjusting the interpretation of those passages which involve doctrines, whereon any difference of opinion subsists among the various denominations of professing Christians. At any rate, he has studiously avoided treating on any such passage *polemically*, or *controversially*. So far, indeed, from aggravating the bitterness of the *odium Theologicum*, that *party-spirit* in Religion, which (in the words of the excellent Dr. Hutcheson) "seeks to cantonize men into sects, for trifling causes," he would rather sound an *Irenicum* to his Ministerial brethren of every denomination, and warn them against *rending the seamless vest of Christ*, their common Lord and Master. Earnestly would he entreat them not to "fall out by the way," but to "agree to differ;" "in id unum intenti," (to use the words of the learned and pious Lampe) "ut, junctis manibus et animis, fissuras Zionis, nimium quantum patentes, compingerent:" ever remembering the maxim of a great ancient Father, "In rebus necessariis *unitas*, in dubiis *libertas*, in omnibus CARITAS." "If any man," says one of the greatest ornaments of our own Church, "differs from me in opinion, I am not troubled at it; but tell him that truth is in the understanding, and charity is in the will; and is, or ought to be, there before either his or my opinion on those matters can enter; and therefore that we ought to *love* alike, though we do not *understand* alike." (Jer. Taylor.)

2 Tugby, in Leicestershire.

in communicating with the Press, and where only *one Revise* was practicable. In this *most ungenial* spot (fit only to be a sort of *ergastulum literarium*), it was impossible for him to hold any communication with learned or enlightened society; or to have access to libraries. And though he had expended, in a manner, a *fortune*, in the formation of a very extensive collection, provided with most of the best works in Classical and Biblical literature, — yet many still remained, which, however requisite, were beyond his power *at once* to procure. These were, — as the Author found opportunity and means, — sought out and procured for the use of the second Edition.

The Editor cannot conclude without expressing his sense of the handsome treatment which his work has received at the hands of the Reviewers in the Critical Journals, both in the Established Church and *out* of it — among professing Christians of various denominations, the most widely separated — especially those very respectable Journals, the ECLECTIC REVIEW and the CHRISTIAN REMEMBRANCER. He begs to return his best thanks for the suggestions offered by his learned Reviewers in *general*, for the improvement of the work in a second Edition; and he trusts they will be found *all* of them to have been attended to. He will be happy to receive any *further* suggestions, or remarks, either from them or others, especially Ministers[1]: nor will even the strictures of any who may, in the spirit of candour, point out errors, be otherwise than thankfully received. In the words of the illustrious Grotius, "*non illi promptius me monebunt errantem, quam ego monentes sequar.*"

The Author has only to add, that having fairly *done his best*, he commits his work to the candour of the Public, with some confidence, — at least from the consciousness of having *endeavoured well:* and, though he shrinks not from any fair or candid criticism, — yet it might disarm the ruthlessness of even a thorough-paced Critic, if he could know the *extent* of the difficulties, of all sorts, with which the Author had continually to struggle, in his progress through this work. In the prosecution of which he has not only had constantly upon him the charge of two Parishes (and thus was continually obliged to carry forward his labours *ἐν παρέργῳ*[2]), but has suffered under the continual pressure of those carking cares, that drag down the mind to earth, necessarily involved in scanty, precarious, and continually decreasing resources. The Author is induced (*most unwillingly*) thus to allude to matters of private and personal concern — as feeling it due to the purchasers of the work in its *first* Edition, to give

1 Who may communicate them to the Author through the medium of Messrs. Rivington.

2 And yet in the words of the great Grecian Historian, *οὐκ ἐνδέχεται ὅταν τύχῃ, ἐκ παρέργου μελετᾶσθαι· ἀλλὰ μᾶλλον μηδὲν ἐκείνῳ πάρεργον ἄλλο γίγνεσθαι.* — Thucydides, L. 1.

this explanation of the causes (beyond his control) which occasioned what, under other circumstances, might have seemed strange and difficult to be accounted for. It is true that the same, — nay even *greater* — difficulties impeded the Author in his labours on this *second* Edition: but what may not the *labor improbus* of several years, under Divine blessing, accomplish? And, in fact, when great literary undertakings are to be carried forward, under signal disadvantages, — whatever *is* accomplished cannot be done *at once*; but only *by stages*, just as the labourer may, after some breathing-time, gain fresh vigour to work withal; and as the cares necessary to provide for the passing day, may give him opportunity to employ it. In truth, the Author was resolved to put forth his whole strength, while he had yet the *power* to make the performance what it ought to be. He was anxious to "work while it was yet day," — aware that "the night" could not be far off "when no man can work." Should he, however, be spared to *complete*, what he has further ventured, in subservience to the Divine will, to mark out as the *extent* of his labours in the service of the Sanctuary, — he shall, he hopes, be ready, under Divine Grace, to deliver up an account of "that which hath been committed to his trust;" content, under *all* circumstances, that "*his cause is with the Lord, and his work with his* God." Nor can he dismiss the present performance, without expressing a deeply thankful sense of the Gracious Aid and support from above, which have been mercifully vouchsafed him during his long and anxious labours thereon. And he desires to offer up his fervent prayers to "the Father of lights," that it may be blessed to the right understanding of those Holy Scriptures, which are alone "able to make us wise unto salvation," "through Faith, which is in Christ Jesus."

EXPLANATION OF CHARACTERS

USED IN THE WORK. (See Preface, p. xii.)

* denotes an altered reading.

‡ ..... a reading thought to need alteration.

[ ] ..... a reading considered, with *some* probability, as an interpolation.

[ ] ..... a reading *most probably*, or *certainly*, an interpolation.

† ..... a reading, probably a corruption of the Text, though the MSS. offer no variation of reading, nor the means of emendation.

The small type in the Text is used to denote that the word or words are not found in the *common* Text; but have been *inserted* on competent authority.

ΤΟ ΚΑΤΑ ΜΑΤΘΑΙΟΝ

ΕΥΑΓΓΕΛΙΟΝ.

1 I. [a] *ΒΙΒΛΟΣ γενέσεως Ἰησοῦ Χριστοῦ, υἱοῦ Δαυῒδ, υἱοῦ Ἀβραάμ.* a Luke 3. 23, &c.
2 [b] *Ἀβραὰμ ἐγέννησε τὸν Ἰσαάκ· Ἰσαὰκ δὲ ἐγέννησε τὸν Ἰακώβ· Ἰακὼβ* Acts 13. 23. b Gen. 21. 2. et 25. 24. et 29. 35.

C. I. This is almost universally acknowledged to have been the first written of the Gospels; but the exact time when, is a question which has been long agitated, and not yet determined. It has been assigned to various years, from A. D. 37 or 38, to 63 or 64, but the arguments in favor of an *early* date, I apprehend, greatly preponderate. These are founded, 1. on *external testimony*; 2. on *internal evidence*. As to the former, the *testimony of antiquity* has considerable weight. But that is decidedly in favor of an *early* date. In fact, the passage of Irenæus Adv. Hæres. iii. 1. (cited by Euseb. Eccl. Hist. v. 8.), is the *only* testimony of antiquity in favor of a *late* date; and that is not decisive, since the language is so vague, that the maintainers of the *contrary* hypothesis understand it in a sense by no means unfavorable to their view. And, considering that we have no certain information as to where Peter abode from A. D. 46 to 63, the arguments depending upon *implication* are inconclusive: and probably the good Father did not intend to speak with historical exactness. At all events, whatever weight may be assigned to that passage, it is overbalanced by the testimony of *Eusebius*, Eccl. v. 24. where it is strongly implied, that Matthew wrote his Gospel *very early*. Which, indeed, is confirmed by Eusebius' own *positive testimony* in his *Chronicum;* where he assigns the 3d year of the reign of Caligula, i. e. A. D. 41. (8 years after Christ's ascension), as the period when Matthew published his Gospel. And this is confirmed by the suffrages of Chrys., Euthym., and Theophylact. *Internal evidence* also preponderates in favor of an early date. For while the arguments for a *late* date are rather specious than solid, those for an early one are, for the most part, exceedingly cogent. The principal one (probably outweighing *all* on the other side) is, that it is not probable the followers of Christ should have been left, for nearly 30 years after his ascension, without a written history of his ministry.

This question is closely connected with *another*, and more important one, — namely, as to the *language* in which this Gospel was written; some contending that it was in the *Hebrew* of St. Matthew's time (i. e. Syro-Chaldee); others, in *Greek*. Now here, while the *internal* evidence seems to be equal on both sides, the *external*, as resting on the testimony of antiquity, is decidedly in favor of a *Hebrew* original. Besides the passages of Papias and Origen, cited by Eusebius, those of Eusebius and Irenæus, above referred to (as also Euseb. Eccl. Hist. v. 10.), bear the strongest testimony thereto. Yet as they are both of them, I apprehend, in a corrupt state, I will cite them for the purpose of emendation. The first is L. v. 8. where, according to all our copies, the words are: *ὁ μὲν δὴ Ματθαῖος ἐν τοῖς Ἑβραίοις τῇ ἰδίᾳ αὐτῶν διαλέκτῳ καὶ γραφὴν ἐξένεγκεν εὐαγγελίου, τοῦ Πέτρου καὶ τοῦ Παύλου ἐν Ῥώμῃ εὐαγγελιζομένων, καὶ θεμελιούντων τὴν Ἐκκλησίαν.* But the use of *καὶ* there is unprecedented, and will by no means bear the sense assigned by Dr. Hales. And *γραφὴν* is not to be endured. For who ever heard of such a phrase as "published a *scripture of* the Gospel"? The passage stands not in need, as Dr. Hales imagined, of "critical *translation*," but critical *emendation*. I would cancel the *καί*, and read *γραφῇ*, and *εὐαγγέλιον*. The mistake originated thus: The N arose from the E following; and the *καὶ* arose from this being noted as a var. lect. in the margin; for the χ for *γράφεται* and the ϗ are often interchanged. The above emendation is placed beyond doubt by the other passage at iii. 24, where *γραφῇ παραδοὺς τὸ εὐαγγ.* exactly answers to *γραφῇ ἐξένεγκεν εὐαγγέλιον*. But, in the latter part of the passage, there is evidently a corruption; for the sense assigned by Reading and Dr. Hales, cannot be elicited from the words without exceedingly straining the sense of *παρουσίᾳ*. Rather than do which, I would prefer supposing the true reading to be *απουσία* (and render *τῇ αὐτοῦ ἀπ.*, 'by his departure'). The

c Gen. 38. 27, &c. 1 Chr. 2. 5, 9.

δὲ ἐγέννησε τὸν Ἰούδαν καὶ τοὺς ἀδελφοὺς αὐτοῦ. [c] Ἰούδας δὲ ἐγέν-
3 νησε τὸν Φαρὲς καὶ τὸν Ζαρὰ ἐκ τῆς Θαμάρ· Φαρὲς δὲ ἐγέννησε τὸν

words *παρουσία* and *ἀπουσία* are not unfrequently confounded; on which see Wesseling on Diod. Sic. Vol. ii. 274.

But to return, it is not too much to say, that the existence of a Hebrew original was held by the Fathers almost unanimously. And when Dr. Burton affirms that "no ancient writer can be proved to have *seen* the document in question," he demands such a proof of its existence as, from the very nature of the case, it is unreasonable to ask; for as the *Hebrew* original must, after the dispersion of the Jews, and from the universal prevalence of the Greek language, have soon become almost *useless;* so, at an early period it would become obsolete, or be only partially retained, as forming the basis of the very early *fabrications* (adapted to the taste of the judaizing Christians), the *Gospel of the Ebionites*, the *Gospel of the Nazarenes*, and *the Gospel according to the Hebrews*, cited by Origen, Epiphanius, and Jerome. It is quite enough to prove the existence of the document *as long as it was in use*, on the testimony of writers who, though they could not have *seen*, what was then *lost*, were well able to weigh the evidence of its *former* actual existence. But while the existence of the Gospel in Hebrew may be considered as resting on such a strong foundation, that it can scarcely be rejected without impairing the credit of all ancient testimony; it must not be denied, that arguments scarcely less cogent are adduced in favor of our present *Greek* Gospel; which has many internal marks of being an *original* writing; for otherwise how can we account for the interpretation of Hebrew names — the citation of the parallel passages of the O. T. not from the *Hebrew*, but from the *Sept.* — and for the versions being all adapted so closely to the *Greek?* Add to this, that Eusebius, and the other Fathers of his time, evidently consider the Greek Gospel as an *original:* not to mention *numerous* instances of verbal agreement between Matthew and the other Evangelists, which, on the supposition of a *Hebrew* original, are hard to be accounted for. After all, however, the main point (as Dr. Hales observes) is, whether the present Greek Gospel is entitled to the *authority* of an original, or not. This, I apprehend, can be shown beyond all dispute. But that will not at all invalidate the former existence of a *Hebrew* original, which is demanded by the evidence of antiquity, and is in itself very probable; for a *Hebrew* Gospel must, in the first age of Christianity (when almost confined to *Judæa)*, have been as requisite as a *Greek* one was afterwards. And there is in the book itself, even in its present state, internal testimony of its being written, at first, especially for the use of the *Jewish* nation; since those circumstances are particularly dwelt on, which were adapted to establish the faith of such as believed, and to sway the minds of those who were disbelievers in the Divine mission of Jesus Christ. And in vain is it to seek to impugn the existence of the Gospel in Hebrew, by urging, as is done, that the Gospel, as we now have it, bears no marks of being a *translation*, but has every appearance of being an *original.* For surely it has far more marks of being a translation, and has far less of the air of an original than *Josephus's History of the Jewish War*, which is confessedly a translation from a Hebrew original. Yet the circumstances under which the Greek both of Josephus and St. Matthew's Gospel were respectively brought out, are such as not to warrant us in regarding either one or the other, as strictly speaking, a *translation.* There is, indeed, reason to think that Josephus made considerable *alterations* in his work, when he brought it out for the use of the *Greeks and Romans.* And there is not less reason to suppose that St. Matthew made *some* alterations; especially in the interpretation of Hebrew names, and in the adaptation of the quotations from the O. T. to the *Sept.* version. And as to the ancient versions being all formed from the *Greek* Gospel, that will not invalidate the existence of a *Hebrew edition* (so to speak), for it is admitted by all, that the *Hebrew* Gospel had become obsolete, before even the earliest of the versions was formed.

In short, all the difficulties which have so long embarrassed this question will vanish; and every thing which seems at first sight strange, be accounted for, by supposing (as Whitby, Benson, and Hales have done), that there were two *originals* (or rather, I should say, two *editions)*, one in Hebrew and the other in Greek; but both written by St. Matthew. I cannot, however, agree with those eminent men in fixing the date of the Greek edition to so late a period as they do — 58, 60, or even 64. The true date seems to be that assigned by Eusebius, in his *Chronicum*, — namely, A. D. 41; probably not long after St. Matthew had departed from Judæa to evangelize the Gentile nations. This necessarily carries back the publishing of the *Hebrew* edition to some period not a little anterior to that date. And when we consider how necessary it was that Christians should *not long* be left without any authentic history of our Saviour's ministry, we shall not, I think, err in assigning the date of the *Hebrew* edition to A. D. 37 or 38, four or five years after Christ's ascension.

With respect to the *authenticity* of this Gospel, it is established by the most irrefragable evidence, in a long and unbroken chain of writers citing or alluding to various parts of it, from St. Barnabas downwards, to the time of Theophylact and Photius. And as to the genuineness of the *two first chapters*, which has been recently called in question by the Unitarians, that too has been established most triumphantly; these two chapters being cited or alluded to perhaps *more than the rest.* And, besides the harshness of supposing the Gospel to commence with two words evidently pointing to something that preceded, ἐν δὲ ταῖς ἡμέραις ἐκείναις (and which we *find* at Chap. ii.), and the fact, that there are *other* passages which evidently refer to passages in those chapters; not to say, that the want of a *genealogy* in a work, written at first especially for Jewish Christians, would be a great *deficiency*, we may defy the Unitarians to produce any *unmutilated* MS. or ancient version (though the Peschito Syriac and the Italic Vulgate carry us back to a period nearly coeval with the formation of the canon of the N. T.) which is without those chapters. As to the *separation* of the genealogy, i. 1 — 18. in some Latin MSS., that by no means implies the *spuriousness* of even the portion in question. And although one very modern Greek MS. (the Cod. Ebner.) is without the genealogy, yet that was doubtless owing to the genealogy being, in the

4 Ἐσρώμ. Ἐσρὼμ δὲ ἐγέννησε τὸν Ἀράμ· [d] Ἀρὰμ δὲ ἐγέννησε τὸν [d] Numb. 7. 12. 1 Chr. 2. 10.
Ἀμιναδάβ. Ἀμιναδὰβ δὲ ἐγέννησε τὸν Ναασσών· Ναασσὼν δὲ ἐγέν- [e] Ruth. 4. 17. 1 Chr. 2. 10, 11, 12.
5 νησε τὸν Σαλμών. [e] Σαλμὼν δὲ ἐγέννησε τὸν Βοὸζ ἐκ τῆς Ῥαχάβ. [f] 1 Sam. 16. 1. & 17. 12.
Βοὸζ δὲ ἐγέννησε τὸν Ὠβὴδ ἐκ τῆς Ῥούθ. Ὠβὴδ δὲ ἐγέννησε τὸν 2 Sam. 12. 24.
6 Ἰεσσαί· [f] Ἰεσσαὶ δὲ ἐγέννησε τὸν Δαυῒδ τὸν βασιλέα. Δαυῒδ δὲ ὁ [g] 1 Kings 11. 43. & 14. 31. & 15. 8.
7 βασιλεὺς ἐγέννησε τὸν Σολομῶνα ἐκ τῆς τοῦ Οὐρίου. [g] Σολομὼν δὲ 1 Chr. 3. 10. 2 Chr. 14. 1.

archetype, separated from the rest, and negligently passed over by the scribe.

Against this mass of *positive evidence* for the genuineness of these chapters, Unitarians, indeed, oppose a show of arguments, partly external and partly internal. But these have been triumphantly refuted by Mosheim, Bishop Horsley, Abps. Magee and Laurence, Dr. Pye Smith, and others.

With respect to the *title* of this Gospel, *Εὐαγγέλιον κατὰ Ματθαῖον*, the word *εὐαγγέλιον* (from *εὖ* and *ἀγγελία*) in the *Classical* writers, signifies, in general, *good news*, sometimes the *reward* given to the bearer of it. In the *Septuagint* and the *New Testament* it almost always has the *former* signification, corresponding to the Heb. בְּשֹׂרָה. In the New Testament it specially imports the good tidings of the Messiah's Advent, who should deliver man from sin and death, through his merits and intercession; and of the foundation of that spiritual and eternal kingdom predicted in the Prophets, and fulfilled by the incarnation of Jesus Christ. Hence the term at length became merely a name for *the dispensation;* or (as in the Ecclesiastical writers), by metonymy, the *History* of the circumstances which accompanied the promulgation of that dispensation. Our English word *Gospel*, from the Saxon *God* (good), and *spel* (news), well expresses the force of the Greek *εὐαγγέλιον*. The *κατὰ* must not be rendered *secundum*, *according to;* for (by an idiom found in the later Greek writers), *κατὰ* with the Accusative, has simply the force of a Genitive, i. e. *τοῦ Ματθαίου*.

V. 1. *Βίβλος γενέσεως.*] Some suppose an ellipsis of *ἥδ' ἐστί*. (See Mark i. 1.) But that is not necessary, *βίβλος*, like the Heb. סֵפֶר, denotes any sort of writing, whether long or short. See Mark x. 4.

This verse forms a preface to chap. i. and a title to the *genealogy* contained in the first sixteen verses; for *βίβλος* (like the Hebrew סֵפֶר), denotes a roll or writing, whether long or short. See Taylor's Calmet v. *Book*.

On the following *genealogy* not a few difficulties exist; 1. As to discrepancies from the Old Testament history in names, which might easily arise from errors in *transcription*, especially as some of the names bear a great similarity, and it was not unusual for the same person to have more than one name. 2. As to the *reconciling* this genealogy with that of St. Luke; which is best done by supposing that St. *Matthew* gives the genealogy of *Joseph;* and St. *Luke* that of *Mary*. And therefore the former (who wrote principally for the *Jews*) traces the pedigree from Abraham to David; and so, through Solomon's line, to Joseph, the *legal* father of Jesus. And it must be remembered that, among the Jews, legal descent was always reckoned in the *male* line. While St. Luke, who wrote for the *Gentiles*, traces the pedigree upwards from Heli, the father of Mary, to David and Abraham, and thence to Adam, the common father of all mankind. Finally, whatever difficulties, even after all the diligence of learned inquirers, shall exist on certain matters connected with this genealogy, we may rest assured, that if these genealogies of Christ, which must be understood to have been derived from the public records in the temple, had not been agreeable thereto, the deception would have been instantly detected. And thus, whether Christ's pedigree be traced through the line of *Joseph* or of *Mary*, it was undeniable that Jesus was descended from David and Abraham; agreeably to the ancient promises and prophecies, that the Messiah should be of their seed.

— *Δαυῒδ.*] So Matthæi, Griesb. Knapp. Vater, Fritz. and Scholz edit., here and elsewhere, with the almost universal consent of the MSS. for *Δαβίδ*.

— *υἱοῦ Ἀβραάμ.*] *υἱοῦ* is for *ἀπογόνου*, after the custom of the Hebrew, in which the correspondent word signifies *any lineal descendant*, however far removed: the idiom, however, is also found in Homer. Thus the general sense is "a descendant of David and Abraham;" which is what the Evangelist now proceeds to prove. That the Jews expected the Messiah to be such, is clear from Matt. xii. 23. xxi. 9. and xxii. 44. David is mentioned first, as being nearer in time to their age.

2. *ἐγέννησε.*] The repetition of this word throughout the genealogy is said to be Hebraic. But it is common to all languages in *genealogies*, which, like law writings, must be very particular and plain, and therefore cannot but deal much in repetition.

— *καὶ τοὺς ἀδελφοὺς αὐτοῦ.*] Why these should be mentioned, though not the Messiah's progenitors, various reasons have been alleged (see Lightfoot, Whitby, and Wetst.), which, however, need not be anxiously debated, since there is every reason to regard the genealogy as no more than a transcript from the public registers.

3. *τὸν Φαρὲς καὶ τ. Ζ.*] *Both* are mentioned as being twin brothers, and striving for primogeniture, and also to identify Phares.

5. *Ῥαχάβ.*] It has been debated, whether this was the harlot of Jericho, mentioned at Josh. ii. 1. and whose faith is so commended at Heb. xi. 31, or some other person of the same name. Theophyl. of the ancient, and many modern commentators, are of the latter opinion. See Lightfoot and Whitby.

6. *Σολομῶνα.*] So almost all the editions from Wets. downwards, on the authority of the best MSS. The common reading, *Σολομῶντα*, is equally agreeable to propriety (as in *Ξενοφῶν*), but it is deficient in MS. authority.

— *ἐκ τῆς τοῦ Οὐρίου.*] The commentators suppose an ellipse of *γυναικὸς* and of *ποτέ*. The former may be admitted, but the latter is not, properly speaking, an ellipse at all; but merely an instance of the suppression of something supposed to be well known to the person addressed.

ἐγέννησε τὸν Ῥοβοάμ. Ῥοβοὰμ δὲ ἐγέννησε τὸν Ἀβιά· Ἀβιὰ δὲ ἐγέν-
h 1 Kings 15. 24. νησε τὸν Ἀσά. [h] Ἀσὰ δὲ ἐγέννησε τὸν Ἰωσαφάτ· Ἰωσαφὰτ δὲ ἐγέν- 8
2 Kings 8. 16, 24. νησε τὸν Ἰωράμ. Ἰωρὰμ δὲ ἐγέννησε τὸν Ὀζίαν· [i] Ὀζίας δὲ ἐγέννησε 9
2 Chr. 17. 1. & 21. 1. τὸν Ἰωάθαμ. Ἰωάθαμ δὲ ἐγέννησε τὸν Ἄχαζ. Ἄχαζ δὲ ἐγέννησε τὸν
i 2 Kings 15. 7, 38. & 16. 20. Ἐζεκίαν. [k] Ἐζεκίας δὲ ἐγέννησε τὸν Μανασσῆ· Μανασσῆς δὲ ἐγέν- 10
2 Chr. 26. 23. & 27. 9. & 28. 27. νησε τὸν Ἀμών. Ἀμὼν δὲ ἐγέννησε τὸν Ἰωσίαν· [l] Ἰωσίας δὲ ἐγέννησε 11
k 2 Kings 20. 21. & 21. 18, 24. 1 Chr. 3. 14, &c. τὸν Ἰεχονίαν καὶ τοὺς ἀδελφοὺς αὐτοῦ, ἐπὶ τῆς μετοικεσίας Βαβυλῶνος.
2 Chr. 32. 33. & 33. 20, 25. [m] Μετὰ δὲ τὴν μετοικεσίαν Βαβυλῶνος, Ἰεχονίας ἐγέννησε τὸν Σαλαθιήλ. 12
l 2 Kings 23. 30, 34. & 24. 6. 1 Chr. 3. 15, 16. Σαλαθιὴλ δὲ ἐγέννησε τὸν Ζοροβάβελ· Ζοροβάβελ δὲ ἐγέννησε τὸν Ἀβι- 13
2 Chr. 36. 1, 4, 8. m 1 Chr. 3. οὐδ. Ἀβιοὺδ δὲ ἐγέννησε τὸν Ἐλιακείμ· Ἐλιακεὶμ δὲ ἐγέννησε τὸν Ἀζώρ.
17, 19. 1 Esdr. 5. 2. & 5. 2, et Ἀζὼρ δὲ ἐγέννησε τὸν Σαδώκ· Σαδὼκ δὲ ἐγέννησε τὸν Ἀχείμ. Ἀχεὶμ 14
Hagg. 1. 1. δὲ ἐγέννησε τὸν Ἐλιούδ· Ἐλιοὺδ δὲ ἐγέννησε τὸν Ἐλεάζαρ. Ἐλεάζαρ 15
δὲ ἐγέννησε τὸν Ματθάν· Ματθὰν δὲ ἐγέννησε τὸν Ἰακώβ. Ἰακὼβ 16
δὲ ἐγέννησε τὸν Ἰωσὴφ τὸν ἄνδρα Μαρίας, ἐξ ἧς ἐγεννήθη ἸΗΣΟΥΣ
ὁ λεγόμενος Χριστός.

Πᾶσαι οὖν αἱ γενεαὶ ἀπὸ Ἀβραὰμ ἕως Δαυῒδ, γενεαὶ δεκατέσσαρες· 17
καὶ ἀπὸ Δαυῒδ ἕως τῆς μετοικεσίας Βαβυλῶνος, γενεαὶ δεκατέσσαρες·
καὶ ἀπὸ τῆς μετοικεσίας Βαβυλῶνος ἕως τοῦ Χριστοῦ, γενεαὶ δεκατέσσαρες.

n Luke 1. 27, 34, 35. [n] ΤΟΥ δὲ Ἰησοῦ Χριστοῦ ἡ γέννησις οὕτως ἦν. μνηστευθείσης γὰρ 18
τῆς μητρὸς αὐτοῦ Μαρίας τῷ Ἰωσὴφ, πρὶν ἢ συνελθεῖν αὐτοὺς, εὑρέθη

8. *Ἰ. ἐγένν. τὸν Ὀζίαν.*] *Ἐγένν.* must here be taken in an extended sense, founded on the Jewish custom, by which the children of children were reputed the children not only of their immediate parents, but of their ancestors; who are said to have begotten those removed several generations from them (see Is. xxxix. 7); for, by an omission not uncommon in Jewish genealogies, three kings are here omitted—Uzziah being the great-grandson of Joram. The most probable reason for this omission is the curse denounced against the idolatry of the house of Ahab, to which those princes belonged.

11. *ἐπὶ τῆς μετοικ.*] *Ἐπὶ* in this use signifies *about*, i. e. a little over or under, an idiom also found in the Latin *circa* and *sub*. *Μετοικεσία*, *transmigration*, is an Hellenistic word applied, *quasi per meiosin*, to denote the removal of the Jews from their own country to Babylonia (see 2 Kings xviii. 32), and correspondent to a Hebrew word which expressed the full force of the thing by *captivity*.

12. *μετὰ τὴν μετοικ.*] Some (as Kuinoel) render it "*at* the time of the transmigration." But the common signification *after* may very well be retained; indeed Fritzsche denies that μετὰ has ever any other. And at Joseph. Ant. I. 12. 2. *εὐθὺς μετ' ὀγδόην ἡμέραν περιτέμνουσι* he translates *exactâ die octavâ*. Although of the ancestors of Jesus in this and the following verses, no mention is made in the O. T., yet this does not derogate from the authority of what is here recorded.

16. *ὁ λεγόμενος*] "who is known by the name of," or "is accounted and *is* Christ." This idiom is not confined to Hellenistic, but is also found in Classical Greek, at least in the kindred term *κεκλῆσθαι*, which is, however, almost confined to the Poets. So Hom. Il. B. 260.

—*Ἰησοῦς*] from the Hebrew יְהוֹשׁוּעַ, a Saviour; a title applied by the Jews, as *σωτὴρ* was by the Greeks, to any public benefactor, and applied to the Messiah *κατ' ἐξοχήν*. *Χριστὸς* is properly an appellative, derived from the Hebrew: מָשִׁיחַ signifying *anointed*, and employed with allusion to the regal, sacerdotal, and prophetical offices; since kings, priests, and prophets, among the Jews, were inaugurated into their respective offices by anointing. But, at length, by frequent application to one individual only, it came to supply the place of a proper name, and thus needed not the article.

17. *γενεαί.*] This use of *γενεὰ*, to denote a succession of persons one after another, is found not only in the Old Testament, but in the best Classical writers.

—*δεκατέσσαρες.*] The Jews were accustomed to divide their genealogical reckonings into classes, doubtless to aid the memory. Here, however, the classification is important, since in each class a change is denoted.

18. *οὕτως*] "in the manner following." Thus the Classical writers perpetually use adjectives and adverbs of a similar sense.

—*μνηστευθείσης γάρ.*] Said to be Genit. absol. for Nomin. with verb. But that is unnecessary; and the force of the Gen. absol. notes time more exactly. This use of *γὰρ* in the sense *nempe*, or *scilicet*, at the beginning of a narration, is frequent in the Classical writers, and may be said to be both inchoative and explanatory. See Hoogev. Part. p. 100. 8.

—*πρὶν ἢ συνελθεῖν.*] On the use of *πρὶν ἢ* with an Infin., for *πρὶν* (said to be middle Attic,) see Viger. p. 442, and Buttmann, G. G. p. 265. (Engl. Transl.) It seems to have arisen from *πρὶν* including a sort of indirect *comparison*. *Συνελθ.* is by some taken to mean removal to the

19 ἐν γαστρὶ ἔχουσα ἐκ Πνεύματος ἁγίου. [o] Ἰωσὴφ δὲ ὁ ἀνὴρ αὐτῆς, [o] Deut. 24. 1.
δίκαιος ὢν, καὶ μὴ θέλων αὐτὴν παραδειγματίσαι, ἐβουλήθη λάθρα
20 ἀπολῦσαι αὐτήν. ταῦτα δὲ αὐτοῦ ἐνθυμηθέντος, ἰδοὺ, ἄγγελος Κυρίου
κατ᾽ ὄναρ ἐφάνη αὐτῷ λέγων· Ἰωσὴφ υἱὸς Δαυῒδ, μὴ φοβηθῇς παραλαβεῖν Μαριὰμ τὴν γυναῖκά σου· τὸ γὰρ ἐν αὐτῇ γεννηθὲν ἐκ
21 Πνεύματός ἐστιν ἁγίου. [p] τέξεται δὲ υἱὸν, καὶ καλέσεις τὸ ὄνομα αὐτοῦ [p] Luke 1. 31. & 2. 21. Acts 4.
Ἰησοῦν· αὐτὸς γὰρ σώσει τὸν λαὸν αὐτοῦ ἀπὸ τῶν ἁμαρτιῶν αὐτῶν. 12. & 10. 43. & 13. 38, 39.

husband's house; by others, sexual intercourse, by an ellipsis of εἰς εὐνὴν, suppressed *verecundiæ gratiâ*. The latter is perhaps the better founded interpretation, as being more agreeable to the context, and supported by numerous Classical examples adduced by the Philological Commentators. The difference between this and the Classical use is, that in the latter a *Dative* almost always follows.

— εὑρέθη ἐν γαστρὶ ἔχουσα.] Sub. βρέφος, or ἔμβρυον. Examples both of the elliptical and plenary phrase are adduced by the Philological Commentators. Εὑρ. ἔχ. is almost universally taken for ἦν ἔχουσα, i. e. εἶχε. And εὑρίσκεσθαι is, indeed, sometimes so used by the Classical writers. Yet so to take it *here* would enervate the sense. The ancients (as it appears from Euthymius) took the word, in its full force, for ἐφάνη, or ἐμφανὴς ἐγένετο. Nay, there *may* be (as Harenberg thinks) a reference to that examination by midwives, which in such a case was usual with the Jews. But there rather seems an allusion to Joseph's discovery of her pregnancy; probably on her return from her visit of three months to Elizabeth.

— ἐκ Πνεύματος ἁγίου.] Bp. Middleton has here an excellent Note, in which he fully exposes Wakefield's mistranslation of the phrase, "by *a* holy Spirit," and concludes with giving the following admirable summary of the various senses of the important term πνεῦμα. There are six meanings — 1. *Breath*, or wind; in which sense it rarely occurs: Matt. xxvii. 50. John iii. 8. Rev. xiii. 15. — 2. The *intellectual* or *spiritual* part of man, as distinguished from σὰρξ, his *carnal* part. — 3. *Spirit*, as abstracted from *body* or *matter*; whence is deduced the idea of *immaterial* agents. Compare Luke xxiv. 34. John iv. 24. Acts xxiii. 9. The πνεύματα of the demoniacs belong to this head. — 4. The *Spirit*, κατ᾽ ἐξοχὴν; i. e. the Third Person in the Trinity; in which acceptation, except in anomalous cases like the present, it is never used without the article. It may be observed, however, that in all the passages where *personal acts* are attributed to the πνεῦμα ἅγιον, and which are, therefore, adduced to prove the personality of the Holy Spirit, the article is invariably prefixed. See Matt. xxviii. 19. Mark i. 10. Luke iii. 22. John i. 31. Acts i. 16. xx. 28. — 5. The *influence*, not the *Person* of the Spirit; in which sense, except in cases of reference, or *renewed* mention, the article never appears. — 6. The *effects* of the *Spirit*.

19. δίκαιος.] This is by some ancients and many moderns explained in the sense *merciful, lenient*; as we say a *worthy good* man. And so the Heb. צדיק and the Latin *æquus*, as the Commentators have proved by many examples. It is not, however, necessary to resort to this idiom *here*; since the usual acceptation is not less apposite, as denoting a *lover of justice*, and a *man of uprightness and integrity*. Being such, he determined to put her away by *law*; and yet, with that mercy which ever accompanies true justice, he wished not to make her a *public* example, but to put her away privately; i. e. with only the two witnesses required to attest the delivery of the bill of divorce; which did not necessarily state the *reason* for the divorcement.

— παραδειγματίσαι.] This word, found only in the Sept. and the later Greek writers, properly signifies to bring into public notice; but, in use, it is generally employed *in malam partem*, to denote *exposure to public ignominy*.

— ἐβουλήθη.] This denotes, not *will*, or *counsel*, as it is rendered; but inclination of will. See Fritzsche. Ἀπολῦσαι, *to divorce*; as in Matt. v. 31. and 32. Mark x. 4. Luke xvi. 18, and the Heb. שלח in Jerem. iii. 8.

— λάθρα, *privately*; inasmuch as that permitted the suppression of the *cause*.

20. ἐνθυμηθέντος.] The word is here used in its *primitive* signification, which is, *to turn any thing in mind, to reflect, meditate*.

— ἰδού.] This, like the Heb. הנה, and Latin *ecce*, is often employed, as here, to prepare the reader or hearer for something unexpected and wonderful. It is rare in the Classical writers; but an example occurs in Eurip. Herc. Fur. 1066.

— ἄγγελος Κυρ.] Camp. and Middlet. observe, that ἄγγελος is used both as an appellative, denoting *office*, (to be rendered *messenger*) and as the title of a particular class of beings; when it becomes almost a proper name. and should be rendered *Angel*.

— κατ᾽ ὄναρ.] In the times of patriarchism, as well as the earlier ages of Judaism, God often revealed his will by *dreams*, not only to his own people, but to the nations at large. And the ancients in general put great faith in them; and rules for their interpretation were formed, both among Jews and Gentiles. There is, however, reason to think, that *prophetical* dreams had, except in the case of Simon the Just, ceased after the time of the last of the prophets, Malachi. *Now*, however, this channel of communication between God and man, in addition to that of direct revelation, became re-opened in the *prophetic dream of Joseph*.

— παραλαβεῖν.] Scil. εἰς οἰκίαν, supplied in Lucian, Timon 17. The παρα refers to the parents, from whom the bride was received. Τὴν γυν. σου (velut) tuam uxorem.

— τὸ γεννηθέν.] The neuter is commonly used of the fœtus in utero, since its sex is unknown.

21. τὸ ὄνομα αὐτοῦ.] Commonly explained as put for αὐτὸν, and usually accounted a Hebraism; but the idiom sometimes occurs in the early Greek writers. See Matt. G. G. p. 594. It is not, however, *properly* put for αὐτόν. See Fritz.

— σώσει — αὐτῶν.] Dr. Maltby (Serm. Vol.

(*Τοῦτο δὲ ὅλον γέγονεν, ἵνα πληρωθῇ τὸ ῥηθὲν ὑπὸ τοῦ Κυρίου διὰ* 22
q Isai. 7. 14. *τοῦ προφήτου λέγοντος· q Ἰδοὺ, ἡ παρθένος ἐν γαστρὶ ἕξει,* 23
καὶ τέξεται υἱὸν, καὶ καλέσουσι τὸ ὄνομα αὐτοῦ Ἐμ-
μανουήλ. ὅ ἐστι μεθερμηνευόμενον, μεθ' ἡμῶν ὁ Θεός.)
Διεγερθεὶς δὲ ὁ Ἰωσὴφ ἀπὸ τοῦ ὕπνου, ἐποίησεν ὡς προσέταξεν αὐτῷ 24
ὁ ἄγγελος Κυρίου· καὶ παρέλαβε τὴν γυναῖκα αὐτοῦ, καὶ οὐκ ἐγί- 25
νωσκεν αὐτὴν, ἕως οὗ ἔτεκε τὸν υἱὸν αὐτῆς τὸν πρωτότοκον, καὶ ἐκά-
λεσε τὸ ὄνομα αὐτοῦ ἸΗΣΟΥΝ.

a Luke 2. 4, 6, 7. II. a *ΤΟΥ δὲ Ἰησοῦ γεννηθέντος ἐν Βηθλεὲμ τῆς Ἰουδαίας, ἐν ἡμέ-* 1
ραις Ἡρώδου τοῦ βασιλέως, ἰδοὺ, μάγοι ἀπὸ ἀνατολῶν παρεγένοντο εἰς

II. 546.) distributes the significations of the important term *σώζειν* into the four following heads. "1. To preserve generally, from any evil or danger whatsoever. 2. To preserve from sickness, or any bodily disorder; *to heal*. This sense is the most easy to distinguish; yet it has not been duly attended to in every instance by our Translators. 3. To preserve from the temporal anger of the Almighty, such as was manifested in the destruction of Jerusalem. This notion, he remarks, appears to have been originally founded upon expressions in the Jewish Prophets. 4. To give future salvation in Heaven. It might (he continues) have been desirable to have confined the use of the word *save* to those passages which come under the fourth class. Those in the third might have been interpreted to *put in the way*, or into a *state* of salvation." The preservation *here* meant, is, I apprehend, a deliverance, both from the punishment of sin, by his atonement, and from the *dominion* of sin (Rom. vi. 14.) by procuring for men the grace of the Holy Spirit, to *enable* them to resist it successfully.

22. *ἵνα πληρωθῇ*.] These are not the words of the *angel*, as some have supposed, but an observation of the *Evangelist*; and the *τοῦτο δὲ ὅλον* refers not only to what has been mentioned in the preceding narrative, but also to all other circumstances connected with the transaction there recorded. The *ἵνα* denotes, as Campbell says, no more than that there was as exact a conformity between the event and the passage quoted, as there could have been, if the former had been effected merely for the accomplishment of the latter. "God (continues Campbell) does not bring about an event, because some prophet had foretold it; but the prophet was inspired to foretell it, because God had previously decreed the event." The particles *ἵνα* and *ὅπως* must therefore not be too rigorously interpreted; since they often express not the cause, or design, but the event only, and the phrase *ἵνα πληρωθῇ* should then be translated, "So that thus was fulfilled."

23. *ἡ παρθένος*.] The earlier Translators seem to have thought the Article pleonastic. But the researches of later Philologists have shown that it is very rarely such, though its sense cannot always be expressed. Here it is used *κατ' ἐξοχὴν*, and denotes (as Dr. Owen and Bp. Middlet. observe) that *particular* virgin, who was prophesied of from the beginning, and whose seed was to bruise the serpent's head.

— *καλέσουσι*] scil. *ἄνθρωποι*, i. e. his name shall be called, or *be*: for the fulfilment of the prophecy depends not upon Christ's *literally* having borne the name Emmanuel, but upon his *being* such, which he clearly was as God-man. Thus the Evangelist has interpreted both Emmanuel and Jesus, to show that the prophecy was fulfilled, not in the names, but in their *signification* or *application*.

24. *διεγερθεὶς ἀπὸ τοῦ ὕπνου*.] Simil. Herodot. i. 34. *ὁ δ' ἐπεί τ' ἐξηγέρθη, καταῤῥωδήσας τὸν ὄνειρον*, &c.

25. *οὐκ ἐγίνωσκεν*.] A common euphemism, like that of *cognoscere* in Latin.

— *ἕως οὗ ἔτεκε*.] "This (says Campbell) does not necessarily imply his knowledge of her afterwards, though it suggests the *affirmative* rather than the *negative*." The quotations produced on the contrary side are, as Whitby has shown, not quite to the point. The suffrage, indeed, of antiquity (which speaks in the negative) is not lightly to be set aside. Yet even that was not constant and without dissent. The term *πρωτότοκος*, it is urged, will not determine the case in the *affirmative*, because it was used, whether there were any more children or not; but the contrary is ably maintained by Fritz. who shows that *ἕως οὗ ἔτεκε* suggests only the *affirmative*. The question, however, is one of mere curiosity; and we may safely say, with St. Basil (cited by Bp. Taylor) that "though it was necessary for the completion of the prophecy, that the mother should continue a virgin until she had brought forth her first-born, yet what she was afterwards, it is idle to discuss, since that is of no manner of concern to the mystery."

II. 1. *τοῦ δὲ Ἰησοῦ γεννηθέντος*] "(some time) after the birth of Jesus." On the chronology of the visit of the Magi, and the nativity, see Benson's Chronology of the Life of Christ, p. 74; and Dr. Hales; the former of whom refutes the arguments of those who fix the visit of the Magi at a considerable distance of time after the nativity; and he offers good reasons for supposing that it took place between the 39th and 42d day after the birth of Jesus, about February 13th, J. P. 4710. This is confirmed by Justin Dial. cum Tryph., (who says, the event was *ἅμα τοῦ γεννηθῆναι αὐτὸν*), and is agreeable to the impression naturally suggested by the air of the narrative.

— *μάγοι*.] The term adopted in our Translation, *wise men*, is not sufficiently definite, since the persons were a particular caste, as distinguished by their peculiarities as any of the Grecian *sects* of philosophers. The word is better left untranslated, as in the Syriac, Arabic, Latin, and Italian versions. It is of Persian origin, (Mogh) and designated throughout the East (and especially Persia, the original seat of this class of persons),

2 Ἱεροσόλυμα, λέγοντες· Ποῦ ἐστιν ὁ τεχθεὶς βασιλεὺς τῶν Ἰουδαίων;
εἴδομεν γὰρ αὐτοῦ τὸν ἀστέρα ἐν τῇ ἀνατολῇ, καὶ ἤλθομεν προσκυνῆ-
3 σαι αὐτῷ. Ἀκούσας δὲ Ἡρώδης ὁ βασιλεὺς ἐταράχθη, καὶ πᾶσα Ἱερο-
4 σόλυμα μετ' αὐτοῦ· καὶ συναγαγὼν πάντας τοὺς ἀρχιερεῖς καὶ γραμματεῖς τοῦ λαοῦ, ἐπυνθάνετο παρ' αὐτῶν, ποῦ ὁ Χριστὸς γεννᾶται.
5 οἱ δὲ εἶπον αὐτῷ· Ἐν Βηθλεὲμ τῆς Ἰουδαίας· οὕτω γὰρ γέγραπται

the *priests, philosophers*, and *men of letters*, in general; who devoted themselves to the study of divine and human science, especially medicine and astronomy, or rather astrology. Their doctrines are said to have been derived from *Abraham*, or at least purified by him from Zabian idolatry. They again became corrupted, and were again purified by *Zoroaster*, who is supposed to have been a descendant of the Prophet Daniel; deriving from him that intimate knowledge of the Mosaic writings, which his religion evinces. From whence the persons in question derived their information, whether, as some suppose, from a prediction of Zoroaster (whom they believed to have been divinely inspired), or from a prophecy of the Arabian prophet *Balaam*, is uncertain. Be that as it may, a general expectation then prevailed in the East, that a most extraordinary person was about to be born, who should be Sovereign of the world. Vide Menag. ad Diog. Laert. i. 1. Porphyr. de Abstin. iv. 16. Perizon. ad Ælian. Var. Hist. ii. 17. Hyde de Relig. Vet. Pers. 31. et Brisson de Princ. Pers. 179. Ἀπὸ ἀνατολῶν must not be taken with παρεγένοντο, but with μάγοι. The passages here cited by the recent Commentators are few of them apposite, because the phrase is associated with an *Article*. The only kindred passage is Matt. xxvii. 57. ἄνθρωπος πλούσιος ἀπὸ Ἀριμαθαίας. Nor is the sense *Magi Orientales*. There is rather an ellipse of ἐλθόντες, or something equivalent.

2. αὐτοῦ τὸν ἀστέρα.] It would be out of place here to detail the various opinions which have been promulgated concerning this star; especially as the only probable one is, that it was a *luminous meteor;* exceedingly brilliant, as we learn from Ignat. ad Ephes. xix. called a *star* from its resemblance thereto, and formed, and its motion regulated, *preternaturally*. The course the Magi were to take, was probably suggested to them by revelation — or rather they had learned it from some old tradition of the Jews, that a new star would appear at the coming of the Messiah. Numerous Classical citations are adduced by Wets., showing the general belief, that new stars appeared at the birth or death of celebrated personages, and otherwise had some undefined connection with the most important events of their lives.

— προσκυνῆσαι αὐτῷ.] This construction with the Dative, is almost confined to the later writers; the earlier and purer ones using the Accus. With respect to the *sense*, it is not possible to define the exact nature of this προσκύνησις; because in the East (though never in the West) the prostration of the body to the very earth (which this word imports) was paid alike to monarchs and to gods. Whether, therefore, it was *adoration* or *reverential homage*, is doubtful; though, if we consider the Divine revelation vouchsafed to them, the Magi could scarcely but view the new born exalted personage as one far above any earthly monarch; and, if at all acquainted with the Prophecies of the Old Testament (which we cannot doubt), they might very well expect far more in the *Messiah* than the human nature. προσκυνεῖν *properly* signifies to kiss one's hand to any one (equivalent to kissing any one's hands); a form of respectful salutation. *This*, however, has reference wholly to the Greek and Roman customs. In *Scripture* the expression has probably never that sense; and to perceive its force there, see Dr. J. P. Smith, Scrip. Testimony to the Messiah, Vol. II. p. 270.

3. ἐταράχθη.] The perturbation was occasioned by the prevalent persuasion, that the reign, then supposed to be near at hand, would be ushered in by a long train of national calamities. Πᾶσα has reference to ἡ πόλις, *understood* as Ἱεροσ.

4. τοὺς ἀρχιερεῖς καὶ γραμματεῖς.] A formula denoting all the members of the Sanhedrim. By ἀρχ. we are to understand not only the ἀρχιερεύς, and his deputy (the Sagan), but all those who had passed the office, and still by courtesy enjoyed the title; and who seem to have worn an Archieratical robe: also the heads of the 24 courses. The γραμματεῖς were persons employed either in transcribing, or in explaining the Sacred books, and were distributed into two orders, Civil and Ecclesiastical. Among them were the νομικοί (or lawyers), mentioned in the New Testament, who were, indeed, the only persons occupied in teaching the law and religion to the people

— γεννᾶται.] This is by some taken for γεννηθήσεται, or μέλλει γεννᾶσθαι. Others say it is the Fut. mid. contract. (Atticè) with the force of Fut. Pass. But it is very doubtful whether this idiom has place in the New Testament. It is better to regard it as a present, and, with Elsn. and Kuinoel, suppose it put for the Fut.; or rather to take it as used *populariter* to signify *is to be* born.

5. διὰ τοῦ προφήτου.] The words following correspond neither to the Heb. nor to the Sept.; and therefore the priests are supposed to have given the *sense* rather than the *words* of the Prophet. And, as it is not professed to be a *citation*, but only a statement of the *sense*, literal agreement is not to be required. Several recent interpreters, indeed, take the words of the Prophet in the Hebrew and Sept. *interrogatively;* which will be equivalent to a strong negation. But as this is, with reason, objected to by Fritz. and others, it may be best to allege, that there is only a discrepancy in words, not in reality — the scope of the Prophet and the Evangelist (for I would suppose the passage adduced by *Matthew* and not by the Sanhedrim) is the same — namely, to state that though Bethlehem be one of the smallest cities of Judah, yet it will not be the smallest (i. e. will be the greatest) in celebrity — since out of it, &c.

b Micah 5. 2. & John 7. 42. διὰ τοῦ προφήτου· [b] Καὶ σὺ Βηθλεέμ, γῆ Ἰούδα, οὐδα- 6
μῶς ἐλαχίστη εἶ ἐν τοῖς ἡγεμόσιν Ἰούδα· ἐκ σοῦ γὰρ
ἐξελεύσεται ἡγούμενος, ὅστις ποιμανεῖ τὸν λαόν μου
τὸν Ἰσραήλ. Τότε Ἡρώδης λάθρα καλέσας τοὺς μάγους, ἠκρί- 7
βωσε παρ᾽ αὐτῶν τὸν χρόνον τοῦ φαινομένου ἀστέρος· καὶ πέμψας 8
αὐτοὺς εἰς Βηθλεέμ, εἶπε· Πορευθέντες ἀκριβῶς ἐξετάσατε περὶ τοῦ
παιδίου· ἐπὰν δὲ εὕρητε, ἀπαγγείλατέ μοι, ὅπως κἀγὼ ἐλθὼν προσ-
κυνήσω αὐτῷ. Οἱ δὲ ἀκούσαντες τοῦ βασιλέως, ἐπορεύθησαν. καὶ, 9
ἰδοὺ, ὁ ἀστὴρ, ὃν εἶδον ἐν τῇ ἀνατολῇ, προῆγεν αὐτοὺς, ἕως ἐλθὼν
ἔστη ἐπάνω οὗ ἦν τὸ παιδίον. Ἰδόντες δὲ τὸν ἀστέρα, ἐχάρησαν χαρὰν 10
c Psal. 72. 10. Isai. 60. 6. μεγάλην σφόδρα· [c] καὶ ἐλθόντες εἰς τὴν οἰκίαν, *εἶδον τὸ παιδίον 11
μετὰ Μαρίας τῆς μητρὸς αὐτοῦ, καὶ πεσόντες προσεκύνησαν αὐτῷ, καὶ
ἀνοίξαντες τοὺς θησαυροὺς αὐτῶν, προσήνεγκαν αὐτῷ δῶρα, χρυσὸν καὶ
λίβανον καὶ σμύρναν. Καὶ χρηματισθέντες κατ᾽ ὄναρ μὴ ἀνακάμψαι 12
πρὸς Ἡρώδην, δι᾽ ἄλλης ὁδοῦ ἀνεχώρησαν εἰς τὴν χώραν αὐτῶν.

6. *γῆ Ἰούδα.*] Almost all Commentators regard *γῆ* as used in the sense *πόλις*; of which they adduce many examples from the Greek Tragedians. But in them, if *γῆ* be put for *πόλις*, it is only by *πόλις* having the sense a *country*, or *state;* for Seidler on Eurip. Troad. 4. and Fritzsche in loc. rightly deny that *γῆ* is ever so used. There is, however, no reason to resort to the conjecture proposed by Fritzsche, *τῆς Ἰουδαίας*. It is better to read (as did our English Translators and Lightfoot), *γῆ* or rather *γῇ*, taking it for *ἐν γῇ*. Though indeed the common reading may very well be tolerated, if *γῆ* be taken in the sense *district, canton*, as in Hesiod Opp. 161. *ἐφ᾽ ἑπταπύλῳ Θήβῃ, Καδμηΐδι γαίῃ*, where there is the same *opposition*, in which the Particip. of the verb subst. is to be understood, equivalent to a relative pronoun and a verb.

—*ἐν τοῖς ἡγ.*] Sept. *χιλιάσιν*· Heb. אַלְפֵי. For as the Jews divided their tribes into thousands, i. e. companies of 1000 families, so the term was sometimes taken to denote the district where they resided. And here *τοῖς ἡγεμόσιν* is put figuratively, for *ταῖς ἡγεμόνισιν*, scil. *χώραις*, the masculine being used dignitatis gratiâ.

—*ποιμανεῖ.*] This metaphorical use of *ποιμ.* to denote *govern*, is found in Homer and the early Greek writers, and seems to be a vestige of ancient simplicity. It is, moreover, very suitable to the *pastoral* nature of Christ's kingdom, so often dwelt on in the Gospel of St. John.

7. *ἠκρίβωσε.*] for *ἀκριβῶς ἀνέμαθεν*, "procured from them exact information."

—*φαινομένου.*] This is not put for *φανέντος*, as Kuin. supposes; but the Particip. present is meant either to denote *beginning*, as Glass maintains, or *continuity*, as Grot. This construction with the Genit. was probably in *popular* use, q. d. "the time when the star would begin to shine, or be shining."

8. *πορευθέντες ἀ. ἐξετάσατε.*] This use of the Particip. is supposed to be pleonastic. But there may be a faint notion of *speed* intended; or rather it has in general an *intensive* force, especially with Imperatives. See Matthiæ G. G. § 55.

9. *ἀκούσαντες.*] The *sense* is, "so having received the King's command." *ἐν τῇ ἀνατ.* should be rendered "in its rising." See Fritz.

—*εἶδον.*] So almost all the MSS. Versions and Fathers, with the Editio Princeps and other ancient editions; which has been received by Mill, Wets., Griesb., and Matth. And as it is sanctioned by the most certain of Critical canons, it may be supposed the true reading. The common one *εὗρον* was first brought forward by Erasm. in his fifth Edition, and adopted, together with almost the whole of the Text of that Edition, by H. Steph. in his *third* edition.

10. *ἐχάρησαν — σφόδρα.*] A stronger expression than this cannot easily be met with. The addition of a cognate substantive to any verb is found also in the Classical writers (See Matth. G. G. p. 597.). The addition, too, of *σφόδρα* to *μέγας*, is a relique of early antiquity, when the superlative was formed (as in the Northern languages), not by a termination, but by the addition of *particles*, usually put *after* the adject.

11. *ἐλθόντες εἰς τ. ο.*] This is not for *εἰσελθ.*, as some say; but it signifies "having gone to *the* house which they sought."

—*θησαυρούς.*] Campb. rightly renders *caskets:* though *θησαυρὸς* (as also the Latin Thesaurus) signifies "any receptacle (as a box or bag) for valuables."

—*προσήνεγκαν — δῶρα.*] Agreeably to the Oriental custom (even yet retained), of never appearing before a King, or any great personage, without offering him gifts; usually the choicest productions of the country of the giver. Markland ap. Bowyer, p. 50. observes, that this expression occurs seven times more in the New Testament, and is constantly used in a religious sense, of offerings to God. Δῶρα, *by way of presents*. This is put in apposition. *χρυσὸν καὶ λίβ. καὶ σμύρναν*. From the nature of the presents it has been usually supposed that the Magi came from Arabia. But that is very doubtful. See Fritzsche in loc.

12. *Χρηματισθέντες.*] This word, properly, and in the Classical writers, signifies 1. to despatch business; 2. to debate on it; as in Thucyd. *ἐχρημάτισε περὶ φιλίας τοῖς Ἀθηναίοις*; 3. to give audience and return answers. Hence the transition is easy to the sense found in the New Testament,

13 Ἀναχωρησάντων δὲ αὐτῶν, ἰδοὺ, ἄγγελος Κυρίου φαίνεται κατ᾽ ὄναρ
τῷ Ἰωσὴφ, λέγων· Ἐγερθεὶς παράλαβε τὸ παιδίον καὶ τὴν μητέρα
αὐτοῦ, καὶ φεῦγε εἰς Αἴγυπτον, καὶ ἴσθι ἐκεῖ, ἕως ἂν εἴπω σοί· μέλλει
14 γὰρ Ἡρώδης ζητεῖν τὸ παιδίον, τοῦ ἀπολέσαι αὐτό. Ὁ δὲ ἐγερθεὶς
παρέλαβε τὸ παιδίον καὶ τὴν μητέρα αὐτοῦ νυκτὸς, καὶ ἀνεχώρησεν
15 εἰς Αἴγυπτον· [d] καὶ ἦν ἐκεῖ ἕως τῆς τελευτῆς Ἡρώδου· ἵνα πληρωθῇ [d] Hos. 11. 1.
τὸ ῥηθὲν ὑπὸ τοῦ Κυρίου διὰ τοῦ προφήτου λέγοντος· Ἐξ Αἰγύ-
16 πτου ἐκάλεσα τὸν υἱόν μου. Τότε Ἡρώδης ἰδὼν ὅτι ἐνεπαίχθη

the Sept. and Joseph. Ant. iii. 8, 8, and xi. 8. 4. to impart Divine warnings, and, in the Pass. to *receive* them; the term being used either absolutely (as Heb. viii. 5., xi. 7., and xii. 25.), or with the additions ὑπὸ τοῦ πνεύματος τοῦ ἁγίου, as Luke ii. 26., or ὑπὸ ἀγγέλου ἁγίου, as Acts x. 22. Thus κατ᾽ ὄναρ in the present passage suggests the notion of *Divine* admonition, since dreams were believed to be occasionally sent from God. Ἀνακάμψαι, *bend back their course, return.* The Classical writers usually subjoin πάλιν.

13. Αἴγυπτον.] A better place of refuge could not be found, from its proximity to Bethlehem, and complete independence on Herod. And as there were many Jews settled there, who enjoyed both civil protection and religious toleration, it would be at once a safe and comfortable place of residence.

— ἴσθι.] "continue, remain." Ἕως ἂν εἴπω σοί, namely, "what thou must do further." Μέλλει, &c. "For Herod is about to seek the child, for the purpose of destroying him." The τοῦ is not, as some say, pleonastic; but the Genit. denotes *purpose*, as often in the Classical writers. Ἕνεκα is here commonly supplied, though objected to (together with most other ellipses) by our present philologists.

14. νυκτός.] *By night;* to conceal his departure; and *the very night* of his receiving the vision, to show his ready obedience.

15. τῆς τελευτῆς.] Scil. τοῦ βίου; like *finis* for finis vitæ in Latin. The plena locutio occurs in Homer, Herodotus, and others of the more ancient writers.

— ἵνα πληρωθῇ.] "So that thus was fulfilled."

— ἐξ Αἰγύπτου — μου.] "These words (from Hos. xi. 1.) are not cited merely by way of *accommodation;* but, referring primarily to the deliverance of the children of Israel out of Egypt, they were secondarily and figuratively fulfilled in the person of Christ. That Israel was a type of Christ, appears from Exod. iv. 22. where he is called by God *his son;* his *first born:* whence also *Israel* is put for *Christ*, Isa. xlix. 3. Now as a prophetical prediction is then fulfilled, when what was foretold is come to pass, so a type is then fulfilled, when that is done in the *antitype* which was before done in the *type*. It is no objection that the remainder of the prophecy does not belong to Christ, as Matthew only notices the resemblance between the type and antitype, in that both were called out of Egypt." — *Whitby.* A somewhat different and perhaps juster view is taken by a learned reviewer (of Bp. Wilson's Evidences of Christianity) in the British Critic, for 1832, who regards it as an allusion or adaptation. q. d. "So that the figurative declaration of God in Hosea, ἐξ Αἰγ. — μου, became, in this instance, a literal fact." Similarly Epiphan., (cited by Heinsius,) when combating the *opposite* error of the Antidicomarcionites, or the Collyridians — says, Ὡς κἀκεῖνο τὸ παρά τισι τῶν ἔξωθεν φιλοσόφων ᾀδόμενον, καὶ ἐν αὐτοῖς πληρώσασθαι ἐν τῷ λέγειν, Αἱ ἀκρότητες ἴσανται. "So that the current saying of one of the heathen philosophers, *extremes meet*, was fulfilled in these."

16. ἐνεπαίχθη.] "Was deceived;" literally, was trifled with. A use similar to that of *illudere*, in Latin.

— ἀποστείλας.] The commentators say there is an ellipsis of τινὰς or ἀγγέλους. It is not, however, necessary to suppose ellipsis at all, any more than in the Latin *mittere*, which is similarly used. When the Accus. is *expressed* (as sometimes in Herodot. and other early writers), it is of more definite sense than the above. There is no pleonasm in ἀποστείλας, but merely a vestige of primitive verbosity. Τοὺς παῖδας, "the male children;" for though the masculine is sometimes used with nouns of the common gender, in reference to the whole species, both male and female, yet that is chiefly in the Classical writers, and where the context and subject suggest the right application.

— ὁρίοις αὐτῆς, its district, or territory.

— ἀπὸ διετοῦς καὶ κατωτέρω.] There are few phrases that have been less understood than this. It has been usually regarded as an elliptical expression for ἀπὸ διετοῦς χρόνου, or, as formed from τὸ διετὲς, *biennium*. But the latter expression is quite destitute of authority; and the former is very rarely found, and only *in plenâ locutione*. And neither of the two is suitable in signification. It is rightly observed by Fischer de Vit. Lexx. N. T. that a *masculine sense* is required. But when he supposes a *neuter form*, he takes for granted what does not exist. The word has a masculine *form* as well as a masculine sense; and no wonder; for it is, in fact, an adjective, with the substantive παιδὸς, being left to be supplied from the context, and, in the present case, τοὺς παῖδας preceding. The singular is used for the plural, as being taken in a generic sense. Thus it is the same as if there were written ἀπὸ διετῶν. This view of the phrase is confirmed by similar ones in Pollux ii. 2. νήπιος διετής. ii. Paral. xxxi. 16. ἀπὸ τριετοῦς καὶ ἐπάνω. i. Paral. xxvii. 23. ἀπὸ εἰκοσιέτους καὶ κάτω. See also Ezr. iii. 8. Numb. i. 45. As to the opinion of several recent Commentators, that διετὴς may denote *a year* old, it is wholly unsupported by authority. For as to that of *Hesych.* Διετής· δι᾽ ὅλου ἔτους, it is nothing to the purpose, for we must there read either, with the editors, δι᾽ ἔτους, or rather διετήσιος, from Suid. and Pollux, the Gloss being borrowed from the Schol. on Thucyd. ii. 38. ἀγῶσι — διετησίοις νομίζοντες, who explains διετ. by δι᾽ ὅλου τοῦ ἔτους. But such a sense would be quite inapplicable to the present passage. And that the children were

ὑπὸ τῶν μάγων, ἐθυμώθη λίαν, καὶ ἀποστείλας ἀνεῖλε πάντας τοὺς παῖδας τοὺς ἐν Βηθλεὲμ καὶ ἐν πᾶσι τοῖς ὁρίοις αὐτῆς, ἀπὸ διετοῦς καὶ κατωτέρω, κατὰ τὸν χρόνον ὃν ἠκρίβωσε παρὰ τῶν μάγων. Τότε ἐπληρώθη 17
e Jer. xxxi. 15. τὸ ῥηθὲν ὑπὸ Ἱερεμίου τοῦ προφήτου, λέγοντος· ᵉ Φωνὴ ἐν Ῥαμᾶ 18
ἠκούσθη, θρῆνος καὶ κλαυθμὸς καὶ ὀδυρμὸς πολύς· Ῥαχὴλ κλαίουσα
τὰ τέκνα αὐτῆς· καὶ οὐκ ἤθελε παρακληθῆναι, ὅτι οὐκ εἰσί. Τελευτή- 19
σαντος δὲ τοῦ Ἡρώδου, ἰδοὺ, ἄγγελος Κυρίου κατ' ὄναρ φαίνεται τῷ
Ἰωσὴφ ἐν Αἰγύπτῳ, λέγων· Ἐγερθεὶς παράλαβε τὸ παιδίον καὶ τὴν 20
μητέρα αὐτοῦ, καὶ πορεύου εἰς γῆν Ἰσραήλ· τεθνήκασι γὰρ οἱ ζητοῦντες τὴν ψυχὴν τοῦ παιδίου. Ὁ δὲ ἐγερθεὶς παρέλαβε τὸ παιδίον 21
καὶ τὴν μητέρα αὐτοῦ, καὶ ἦλθεν εἰς γῆν Ἰσραήλ. ἀκούσας δὲ, ὅτι 22
Ἀρχέλαος βασιλεύει ἐπὶ τῆς Ἰουδαίας ἀντὶ Ἡρώδου τοῦ πατρὸς αὐτοῦ,
ἐφοβήθη ἐκεῖ ἀπελθεῖν· χρηματισθεὶς δὲ κατ' ὄναρ, ἀνεχώρησεν εἰς
f Judg. 13. 5. τὰ μέρη τῆς Γαλιλαίας. ᶠ Καὶ ἐλθὼν κατῴκησεν εἰς πόλιν λεγομένην 23
MK. LU. Ναζαρέτ· ὅπως πληρωθῇ τὸ ῥηθὲν διὰ τῶν προφητῶν, Ὅτι Ναζω-
1. 3. ραῖος κληθήσεται.
a III. ἘΝ δὲ ταῖς ἡμέραις ἐκείναις παραγίνεται Ἰωάννης ὁ βαπτιστὴς 1

of *one* year old, is opposed to all Ecclesiastical History.

17. τότε ἐπληρώθη, &c.] The words may be paraphrased, "Then that happened whereby was more fully completed, &c.; or rather, as the citation is only an accommodation of Jerem. xxxi. 15., "Such another catastrophe took place as that recorded by Jeremiah;" a manner of speaking familiar to the writers of the New Testament. See Matth. xv. 7. & 8., compared with Isaiah xxix. 13. and Matth. xiii. 14. compared with Is. vi. 9. Matth. xiii. 34. & 35. compared with Ps. lxxvii. 22. According to this mode any thing may truly be said to be *fulfilled*, if it admits of being properly *applied*.

18. θρῆνος — πολύς.] A most pathetic accumulation of terms, expressing bitter grief, with which Wets. compares a similar one in Plato. ὀδυρμοὺς δὲ καὶ στεναγμοὺς καὶ θρήνους καὶ ἀλγηδόνας κ. τ. λ. The words (Kuin. observes,) are to be understood of the *Bethlehemites*.

— κλαίουσα.] Sub. ἦν. A fine figure, whereby Rachel is supposed to be bewailing the slaughter, and weeping for her children, as Ephraim is, in the same chapter, as lamenting himself. Ὅτι οὐκ εἰσὶ, must be taken, not with παρακλ., but with κλαίουσα. In the passage of the Prophet, the words must mean "are gone (into captivity)."

20. οἱ ζητοῦντες.] A use of plural for singular, common both to the Scriptural and the Classical writers, especially in speaking of Kings and Princes. See 1 Kings i. 33. 43., compared with Matth. ix. 8. The expression ζητεῖν τὴν ψυχήν τινος, is said by Vorst. and Leusd. to be formed from the Heb. את־נפש בקש in 1 Sam. xxiii. 15. The use of ψυχὴν for ζωὴν, though, no doubt, derived by the sacred writers from the Hebrew, is likewise found in Herodot. and the other early Greek writers.

22. βασιλεύει.] Taken impropriè for ἄρχει, since Archelaus was not a βασιλεὺς, but an ἐθνάρχης. Ἐκεῖ, for ἐκεῖσε.

23. κατῴκησεν εἰς] "fixed his abode at;" in contradiction to παρῴκησεν. Εἰς is for ἐν, *at*; as 2 Chron. xix. 4. κατῴκησεν εἰς Ἱερουσαλήμ. A signification common in the later Classical writers.

— Ναζ. κληθ.] Κληθήσεται is by some taken to mean "shall *be*." But to that sense it is here unnecessary, nay injudicious, to have recourse; for that Jesus was so *called*, in contempt, is well known from many passages of the Gospels. Bp. Middlet. renders Ναζ. "*the* Nazarene;" "since the Art. could not be inserted, the noun being preceded by the nuncupative verb κληθήσεται." Nazareth was proverbially a despised place, as is clear from Nathanael's question, "Can there be any good thing come out of Naz." Thus Ναζωραῖος became among the Jews a proverbial term for a despised and rejected character. Thus the meaning is, "that Jesus should be despised and dishonored." Διὰ τῶν προφητῶν is said because (as is rightly observed by Jerome) no *particular* prophet is meant, but the *substance* of what occurs in all those passages of the Old Testament which were supposed to refer to the contempt with which the Messiah should be treated.

III. 1. ἐν δὲ ταῖς ἡμέραις ἐκ.] This phrase, for ἐν τούτῳ τῷ χρόνῳ, is a customary mode of commencing a narrative, both in the Scriptural and Classical writers. The difference is, that the latter use it *strictly*, when only a *brief* period is interposed between the occurrence to be narrated, and some other event before mentioned; whereas the former use it with greater latitude, when there is a considerable interval; as here of many years: yet always with a reference to some previously mentioned time. And the time adverted to, is that of the residence of Joseph at Nazareth. The transition may, indeed, seem abrupt, but not more so than many things in the Scriptures, or even the *Classics*, as Thucyd. The reason why Matthew passes over the period of Christ's infancy is, that he had little certain information, and it was too, not his purpose to narrate aught but what was connected with the establishment of the Messiah's kingdom. He therefore is silent on the events of Jesus's infan-

MK. LU.

2 κηρύσσων ἐν τῇ ἐρήμῳ τῆς Ἰουδαίας, καὶ λέγων· Μετανοεῖτε! ἤγγικε 1. 3.
3 γὰρ ἡ βασιλεία τῶν οὐρανῶν. Οὗτος γάρ ἐστιν ὁ ῥηθεὶς ὑπὸ Ἡσαΐου 2 4
τοῦ προφήτου λέγοντος· Φωνὴ βοῶντος ἐν τῇ ἐρήμῳ, Ἑτοι- 3
μάσατε τὴν ὁδὸν Κυρίου! εὐθείας ποιεῖτε τὰς τρί-
4 βους αὐτοῦ! Αὐτὸς δὲ ὁ Ἰωάννης εἶχε τὸ ἔνδυμα αὐτοῦ ἀπὸ 6
τριχῶν καμήλου, καὶ ζώνην δερματίνην περὶ τὴν ὀσφὺν αὐτοῦ· ἡ δὲ
τροφὴ αὐτοῦ ἦν ἀκρίδες καὶ μέλι ἄγριον.

cy and earlier years, and passes on to the uprise of his great *Forerunner*. The Section is omitted in some MSS. of the Alexandrian recension, later versions and Fathers: but its *omission* can far better be accounted for (partly from commencing an Ecclesiastical *Section*, and partly from the difficulty of expressing the same in the Oriental versions) than its *insertion*. It has a transitive sense, like the Latin *autem*. Παραγίνεται κηρύσσων, is for παραγίνεται καὶ κηρύσσει. Παραγίνεσθαι, like παριέναι and παρέρχεσθαι in Thucyd. and other writers, has the sense *accedere, prodire;* as said properly of those who come forward to *deliver an oration*. Now, κηρύσσω properly signifies to proclaim; and 2dly. to publicly teach *vivâ voce, to preach*. It moreover includes a notion of earnestness and vehemence.

— ὁ βαπτιστής.] A name of office, equivalent to ὁ βαπτίζων, Mark vi. 14., and employed by the sacred writers, to distinguish him from John the *Evangelist*. Baptism is universally admitted to have been in use with the Jews, as a part of the ceremony for the admission of proselytes; (as indeed it was, with the Persians and other Oriental nations). This appears both from the Talmud, and from allusions which occur in the Classical writers. It was believed that the administration of this rite would form part of the office of the Messiah. Nay, the *mode* in which the word is here introduced by Matthew, without any explanation, shows that the ceremony alluded to was familiar to them.

— ἐν τῇ ἐρήμῳ.] Sub. χώρᾳ, by which, however, is to be understood, not an absolutely desert tract; but one comparatively so; as being thinly inhabited, unenclosed by fences, and not in tillage but pasture; like the *steppes* of Asia, the *llanos* of S. America, and the extensive *commons* lately existing in this country. This indeed is adverted to in the Heb. מדבר, literally, *a place to drive cattle upon.*

2. μετανοεῖτε.] The word properly signifies *to take after thought*, as opposed to προνοεῖν. 2dly. to change one's opinion. 3dly. in a religious sense, to so change one's views as to reform one's life. Μετάνοια properly and primarily signifies a change of mind or purpose. But it is so rare in this sense, that no Commentator on the N. T. nor *Steph. Thesaurus* has adduced an example. The following may therefore be acceptable. Joseph. Bell. I. 4. 4. οἱ δὲ μᾶλλον ἐμίσουν τὴν μετάνοιαν αὐτοῦ, καὶ τοῦ τρόπου τὸ ἀνώμαλον. In a religious sense, it denotes such a change of mind as to the commission of any previous actions, as shall induce us to forsake the practices, from a conviction that they are opposed to the will of God, and are contrary to our true happiness here and hereafter.

— ἡ βασ. τῶν οὐρ.] This formula and ἡ βασ. τοῦ Θεοῦ, are synonymous, and frequently occur in the N. T. They denote, 1. the abodes of eternal felicity in heaven, and the state of things there; 2. (with allusion to the prophecies of the O. T.) They represent the spiritual *reign of Christ*, the *Gospel dispensation*, as here and at Matt. ii. 7. x. 7. Luke x. 9. xvii. 21., and various other passages. In some others it is doubtful which of these two senses is to be adopted. Nor are there wanting those where *both* seem to be combined.

3. οὗτος.] Some would take this δεικτικῶς. But though that use is not unfrequently found in the Classical writers; yet it very rarely occurs in the Scriptural ones, and would not here be very suitable. It is more natural to regard the words as the *Evangelist's*. — Ἡσαΐου τοῦ προφήτου. The words which follow convey the *sense*, though they do not follow the exact *terms* either of the Hebrew or Sept. [*Comp.* Isa. 40. 3. John i. 23.]

— φωνὴ, &c.] "[There is heard] the voice of one preaching in the wilderness, and exclaiming, Ἑτοιμάσατε τὴν, &c." An image borrowed from the practice of Eastern monarchs, who, on taking a journey, or going on a military expedition, used to send forward persons to level the eminences, smoothen the unevennesses, fill up the hollows, &c., so as to *form a road*. To this purpose Wets. cites Sueton. Calig. 37. Joseph. B. J. iii. 5, 1. and Justin ii. 10. Plut. 837. Ovid Amat. ii. 16, 51. See my note on Thucyd. ii. 97 & 100.

4. τὸ ἔνδυμα — καμήλου.] Some take this to mean the camel's pelt, with the hair on, as sheepskins were worn by the Hebrew prophets. See Zechar. xiii. 14. Others, however, more justly, suppose that it was the shaggier camel's hair, spun into coarse cloth, like our drugget. And we find from the Talmud, that camel's hair garments were much worn by the Jews. Joseph. Bell. i. 17. speaks of ἐσθὴς ἐκ τριχῶν πεποιημένη, probably the σάκκος τρίχινος, of Revel. vi. 12. Nor were they unknown to the Heathens. Thus the Schol. on Eurip. Phœn. 329. mentions τὰ τρίχινα ἐνδύματα. Those, however, were probably made of the finer camel's hair, like a manufacture formerly made in this country, and called *camlets*. Garments similar to the Baptist's are still worn (or rather a manufacture of wool and camel's hair) in the East by the poor, or those who affect austerity. John wore this garment in imitation of the prophets, especially Elijah. See 2 Kings i. 8. whom he also imitated in the austerity of his life. Indeed, it was his prophetical habit and mode of life, that was chiefly instrumental (in connection with the prevailing expectation of the Messiah's advent) to drawing the attention of the Jews to his ministry, in which the *spirit of prophecy*, which had been lost to Israel for 400 years, was in some measure restored.

— ζώνην δερμ.] So of Elijah, 2 Kings i. 8. ζώνην δερματίνην περιεζωσμένος τὴν ὀσφὺν αὐτοῦ.

MK. LU.
1. 3. Τότε ἐξεπορεύετο πρὸς αὐτὸν Ἱεροσόλυμα, καὶ πᾶσα ἡ Ἰουδαία, καὶ 5
5 πᾶσα ἡ περίχωρος τοῦ Ἰορδάνου· καὶ ἐβαπτίζοντο ἐν τῷ Ἰορδάνῃ ὑπ' 6
αὐτοῦ, ἐξομολογούμενοι τὰς ἁμαρτίας αὐτῶν. Ἰδὼν δὲ πολλοὺς τῶν 7
7 Φαρισαίων καὶ Σαδδουκαίων ἐρχομένους ἐπὶ τὸ βάπτισμα αὐτοῦ, εἶπεν
αὐτοῖς· Γεννήματα ἐχιδνῶν! τίς ὑπέδειξεν ὑμῖν φυγεῖν ἀπὸ τῆς
8 μελλούσης ὀργῆς; Ποιήσατε οὖν *καρπὸν *ἄξιον τῆς μετανοίας· Καὶ 8

The austerity consisted in the *materials*; for otherwise these *girdles* formed a regular part of the dress; and were of linen, silk, or even gold and silver, according to the circumstances. See the references in Wets. or Recens. Synop.

— ἡ τροφὴ — ἀκρίδες.] That locusts (of which Bochart reckons ten species) were *permitted* to be eaten, appears from Levit. xi. 22.; that they formed a *customary* food in the East is plain from Agatharch. v. 27. Strabo. xvi. p. 1118. Plin. vi. 30. &c. (Wets.) From Aristoph. Ach. 1116. and the Schol., it appears that the *Greeks* also ate of them, but that they were accounted a mean food. That they are at the present day a common diet among the poor, throughout most of the countries of Asia and Africa, which they infest, we learn from the concurrent testimony of modern travellers.

— μέλι ἄγριον.] This is by some taken to denote a sort of *saccharine matter* exuding from palm, date, or olive trees. See Diodor. Sic. xix. 104., (who calls it by this very name μέλι ἄγριον) Joseph. B. J. iv. 27. Plin. N. H. xxiii. 4. and the Rabbinical writers, who mention *palm honey* and *fig honey*. The more common opinion, however, is, that we are to understand honey procured from hollow trees and clefts of rocks, deposited there by swarms of wild bees. See 1 Sam. xiv. 26. Judg. xiv. 8. and Ps. lxxxi. 16.

5. καὶ πᾶσα.] The καὶ is by Fritzsche not ill rendered *nempe*. Πᾶσα, like πάντες in Mark i. 6., is to be taken, in a restricted sense, for *very many*.

6. ἐβαπτίζοντο.] That baptismal ablution or lustrations had been, even among the heathens, thought necessary for admission to religious ceremonies, and for the expiation of offences, the Classical citations here adduced by Wets. and others, fully prove and illustrate. That they were in use, too, among the *Jews*, we find both from the Old Testament, the Rabbinical writers, and Josephus. See B. J. ii. 8. 7. But the baptism here meant is one solemn ablution, never to be repeated, comprehending the wives and children likewise of the proselytes; and founded partly on the ceremony which (as the Jewish theologians inform us) took place immediately previous to the promulgation of the Law, at Mount Sinai, and partly on the Jewish baptism of proselytes; though essentially differing from it. The one involving an obligation to perform the whole law; the other, an obligation to reformation, and faith in the Messiah about to appear — the one founded on a system of justification by works, the other one on faith in Christ. The custom, however, is believed not to have been introduced until after the return from the Babylonish captivity; and that to provide a less revolting mode of initiation into the Jewish church than circumcision. The Jews must have understood the ceremony as significant of a change of religion, and of introduction into a dispensation different from that of Moses. And that they should have expressed no surprise at this, need not be thought strange; since they were taught by the predictions of the prophets, and the instructions of their most eminent teachers, that at the advent of the Messiah (which was now universally expected), the face of things would be entirely changed, and a new religion be introduced by Baptism. (Wets., Bengel, Kuin., and Rosenm.)

— ἐξομολογούμενοι.] This is not so much put for the simple verb, as it is a *stronger* expression, of which examples (chiefly from Joseph. and Philo.) are adduced by Elsner and Wets. This must be understood not of a particular and individual, but a *general* confession of sins, and renunciation of justification by works.

7. Φαρισαίων καὶ Σαδδουκαίων.] On these Sects see Recensio Synopt., or Horne's Introduction. Ἐρχομένους — αὐτοῦ. The sense is well expressed by the Persic and Syriac versions, "coming for the purpose of being baptized." So Luke iii. 7. ἐκπορευομένοις βαπτισθῆναι ὑπ' αὐτοῦ. Of this signification of ἐπὶ examples are given by Wets. and Krebs.

— γεννήματα ἐχιδνῶν.] "brood of vipers!" So they are likewise called by Christ himself, Mark xii. 34. Infr. 23. 33. Τίς ὑπέδειξεν ὑμῖν, &c. The interrogative here does not, as some suppose, imply a strong negation; but the τίς rather imports *exclamation* (as in Galat. iii. 1.), namely, from excessive surprise at seeing persons of such dissimilar opinions and characters (Sadducees and Pharisees, men of the world and votaries of pleasure mixed with precise formalists, not to say hypocrites), unite in confessing their sins, in making declarations of repentance, and vows of reformation. The motives of the *generality* in coming thither, must have been corrupt (see Whitby and Mack.), or so severe an expression would not have been employed; and no wonder; for the Jews were then immersed in moral depravity and religious error.

— ὀργῆς.] This is to be taken, by metonymy, for *punishment*, of which use examples are adduced by the Philologists. [*Comp.* Infr. 12. 34, & 23. 33. Rom. 5. 9. 1 Thess. I. 10.]

8. καρπὸν ἄξιον.] So Ed. Pr. and Steph. 1., with almost all the MSS., which is received by Wets., Matth., Gries. and Scholz. The common reading καρποὺς ἀξίους was introduced by Erasm. on very slight authority, and received, together with all his other alterations, by Steph. in his 3d edition; and thus was introduced into the textus receptus. The phrase ποιεῖν καρπὸν is said to be a Hebraism; but some examples have been adduced from the classical writers, as Plut. ii. 1117. C. οὐ μέντοι τὸ θεράπευμα τοῦτο ἔσχε καρπὸν ἄξιον. Arist. de Plant. i. 4. τῶν φυτῶν τινὰ μὲν ποιοῦσι καρπόν. Both passages defend the reading adopted in the text. Wets. paraphrases thus: "If ye really repent, show forth not merely the *leaves* of *profession*, but the *fruits* of *performance*.

MK. LU.

9 μὴ δόξητε λέγειν ἐν ἑαυτοῖς· Πατέρα ἔχομεν τὸν Ἀβραάμ. λέγω γὰρ 1. 3.
ὑμῖν, ὅτι δύναται ὁ Θεὸς ἐκ τῶν λίθων τούτων ἐγεῖραι τέκνα τῷ
10 Ἀβραάμ· ἤδη δὲ καὶ ἡ ἀξίνη πρὸς τὴν ῥίζαν τῶν δένδρων κεῖται·
πᾶν οὖν δένδρον μὴ ποιοῦν καρπὸν καλὸν ἐκκόπτεται, καὶ εἰς πῦρ 9
11 βάλλεται. Ἐγὼ μὲν βαπτίζω ὑμᾶς ἐν ὕδατι, εἰς μετάνοιαν· ὁ δὲ 7 16
ὀπίσω μου ἐρχόμενος ἰσχυρότερός μου ἐστίν· οὗ οὐκ εἰμὶ ἱκανὸς τὰ
ὑποδήματα βαστάσαι· αὐτὸς ὑμᾶς βαπτίσει ἐν πνεύματι ἁγίῳ καὶ
12 πυρί. Οὗ τὸ πτύον ἐν τῇ χειρὶ αὐτοῦ· καὶ διακαθαριεῖ τὴν ἅλωνα 17

9. μὴ δόξητε λέγειν.] This is thought to be a pleonasm for μὴ λέγητε, but it is, in fact, a stronger expression. As to the Greek Classical idiom concerning δοκεῖν, it is here inapplicable. The phrase seems to be rather a *popular* expression (though it occurs in the Talmud) founded on a blending of two phrases. Λέγειν ἐν ἑαυτῷ is thought to be a Hellenistic phrase, occurring also in Esth. vi. 6., equivalent to διανοεῖν, *secretly think*, and answering to the Hebr. אמר בלבו. Yet it occurs in a passage of Chrysippus cited by Wets.

—Πατέρα ἔχομεν τὸν Ἀβ.] "We have Abraham for our father, and therefore, as his descendants, cannot but be accepted by God." Ἐκ τῶν λίθων κ. τ. λ. Here there is either a comparison of the surrounding multitude to stocks and stones, by a common metaphor; g. d. "God can effect that these *stones*, now lying in Jordan" (compare Joseph. Ant. 4. 3.), i. e. men as unfit for useful purposes as these stones, "shall become children unto Abraham," and imitate the virtues of Abraham. Or (according to others) the words are meant to strongly show the omnipotence of God, who can raise up instruments to effect his own wise and benevolent purposes from the meanest subjects. [*Comp.* John viii. 39. Acts xiii. 26.]

10. ἡ ἀξίνη.] i. e. the axe of judgment and punishment. Ῥίζαν hints at utter destruction; and the ἤδη at what shall shortly happen. In the Scriptures men are often compared to *trees*; and sometimes (as Eccles. x. 15. and Dan. iv. 20 and 23.) their punishment to the *felling* of trees. [*Comp.* Infr. vii. 19. John xv. 16.]

11. ἐν ὕδατι.] The ἐν is thought redundant; and Commentators adduce examples from the Classical writers. It rather, however, denotes the *instrument*, as Luke xiv. 34. and often.

—εἰς μετάνοιαν.] The εἰς denotes *purpose*. So ἐπὶ supra v. 7. This is a *brief* phrase, adverting to the solemn engagement entered into by the baptized, to "cease to do evil, and learn to do well." This, indeed, was so closely associated with baptism, that it is called by Mark i. 4. the baptism of repentance.

—ὁ ὀπίσω μου ἐρχόμενος.] Kuin. renders it *successor*. But that conveys a wrong idea. The Present is here used as at ver. 10. We may paraphrase: "There is one coming who will be after me in time, but who will be far greater than I." There is an *allusion* to the expression ὁ ἐρχόμενος, [*he who is coming*,] by which the *Messiah was* then, from the opinion of his speedy appearance, designated; as in John's inquiry, σὺ εἶ ὁ ἐρχόμενος. The expression is a *brief* one, requiring ἄνωθεν, or ἐκ τοῦ οὐρανοῦ, to be supplied, as elsewhere. Ἱκανὸς is equivalent to the ἄξιος of St. John, as in Herodotus viii. 36. and elsewhere.

—τὰ ὑποδήματα βαστάσαι.] Ὑπόδημα in Hellenistic phraseology is equivalent to σανδάλιον. Βαστάζειν is synonymous with κομίζειν in a passage of Plutarch which I have adduced in Rec. Syn. Markland says it signifies to *carry off* or *away*. But that is only *implied* in the general sense, which is *to have charge of*. From Lucian in Herod. 5. cited by Wets. ὁ δέ τις μάλα δουλικῶς ἀφαιρεῖ τὸ σανδάλιον ἐκ τοῦ ποδὸς (to which may be added Hor. Epist. i. 13, 15: Soleas portat: and Æschyl. Agam. 917.) and other passages adduced by the Commentators, it appears that this was by the ancients (both Orientals and Occidentals) accounted among the most servile of offices. Yet we find from the Rabbinical writers, that it was rendered by the disciple to the master; and from Eusebius, that this descended, with other observances towards the Rabbins, to the first Christian teachers.

—βαπτίσει—πυρί.] There has been no little difference of opinion as to the force of βαπτίσει and πυρί. The most probable opinion is that of Chrys. and others of the ancients, that βαπτίζειν here, in the sense *obruere aliquem re*, has reference to the *exuberant abundance* of those extraordinary spiritual gifts soon to be imparted to the first converts. With respect to καὶ πυρί, Glass would suppose an Hendiadys, and take it for *ignito*: Eslner regards the καὶ as *exegetical*, (in the sense *even*) as representing the Symbol of the Holy Spirit. In either case, there may be an allusion to the miraculous descent of the Holy Ghost in *fiery tongues*; which view is supported by Chrys. Others, however, as Wets., maintain that by the symbol of fire is meant the *severest punishment*, or moral purgation. [*Comp.* John i. 26. Acts i. 5. ii. 4. xi. 16. xix. 4.]

12. οὗ τὸ πτύον—αὐτοῦ.] The οὗ is *not* redundant, as Grot., Wets., and others suppose; for, as Fritz. observes, if it were taken away, there would be no connection with the preceding. And he rightly renders, "cujus (erit) ventilabrum (nempe) in ejus manu." Πτύον signifies, not *fan* (which is expressed by λικμὸς in Amos ix. 9. and was something like our *boulting* machine, to raise wind by a sort of fan-like sail;) but a *winnowing shovel*, which, from Hesych., seems to have been, in the lower part of it, shaped like a Δ. The word is derived from πτύειν, *to toss away*. Διακαθαριεῖ is for διακαθαρίσει, Atticè.

—τὴν ἅλωνα.] The word signifies properly the elevated area formed in a field, after harvest, of soil hardened by the use of a cylinder, (See Paulsen ap. Fritz.) where the corn in the sheaf was trodden by oxen, and winnowed; which latter operation was performed by tossing the rough and broken straw away with a fork; and then by stirring up the compound of grain and chaff with the πτύον; when the chaff was delivered to the wind, and the grain left in a heap. After which the rough straw was collected and burnt, so

MK. LU.
1. 3. αὐτοῦ, καὶ συνάξει τὸν σῖτον αὐτοῦ εἰς τὴν ἀποθήκην· τὸ δὲ ἄχυρον
κατακαύσει πυρὶ ἀσβέστῳ.
Τότε παραγίνεται ὁ Ἰησοῦς ἀπὸ τῆς Γαλιλαίας ἐπὶ τὸν Ἰορδάνην πρὸς 13
9 21 τὸν Ἰωάννην, τοῦ βαπτισθῆναι ὑπ' αὐτοῦ. Ὁ δὲ Ἰωάννης διεκώλυεν 14
αὐτὸν, λέγων· Ἐγὼ χρείαν ἔχω ὑπὸ σοῦ βαπτισθῆναι, καὶ σὺ ἔρχῃ
πρός με; ἀποκριθεὶς δὲ ὁ Ἰησοῦς εἶπε πρὸς αὐτόν· Ἄφες ἄρτι· 15
οὕτω γὰρ πρέπον ἐστὶν ἡμῖν πληρῶσαι πᾶσαν δικαιοσύνην. τότε
10 ἀφίησιν αὐτόν. Καὶ βαπτισθεὶς ὁ Ἰησοῦς ἀνέβη εὐθὺς ἀπὸ τοῦ ὕδα- 16
22 τος. καὶ ἰδοὺ, ἀνεῴχθησαν αὐτῷ οἱ οὐρανοὶ, καὶ εἶδε τὸ Πνεῦμα τοῦ
11 Θεοῦ καταβαῖνον ὡσεὶ περιστερὰν, καὶ ἐρχόμενον ἐπ' αὐτόν. Καὶ ἰδοὺ, 17
φωνὴ ἐκ τῶν οὐρανῶν, λέγουσα· Οὗτός ἐστιν ὁ Υἱός μου ὁ ἀγαπητὸς,
ἐν ᾧ εὐδόκησα.

doubt, for manure. *Here*, however, ἅλων seems to signify the above compound of grain and chaff to be winnowed; a sense often occurring in the Sept.

By τὴν ἀποθήκην is meant a repository where any thing, as here corn, ἀποτίθεται; chiefly in the East, subterraneous, or partly so, but covered down and thatched over. By the ἄχυρον is denoted, not the chaff, but the rough and broken pieces of straw, separated from the corn by the above process. [*Comp.* infr. xiii. 30.]

13. τότε.] The particle, the Commentators think, does not mark the exact time when the baptism of Christ took place, but only points to the time when John was baptizing.

— παραγίνεται τοῦ βαπτ.] Christ condescended to be baptized, and it was administered to him by John, upon the very same principles on which the priests were dedicated to their office. See Heb. ii. 17. and Ex. viii. 6. It was necessary to justify the counsels of Divine Wisdom in framing the law of Moses, that the Messiah should recognise its Divine institution, and sanction its ordinances, by observing its rites in his own person. And the selection of John to perform the ceremony would answer many important purposes, and especially tend to the establishment, by a voice from heaven, of the authority both of Christ and his Forerunner. See more in Whitby and Mackn. Τοῦ βαπτισθῆναι is, as Fritzsche says, the Genit. of *cause*, and the expression is equivalent to εἰς τὸ βαπτισθῆναι.

14. διεκώλυεν] "was hindering, would have hindered." A not unfrequent sense of the Imperf., on which see my Note on Thucyd. iv. 44, 45.

— ἐγὼ χρείαν, &c.] A refined way of saying, "I am very far inferior to thee, and yet dost thou come to me, as to a superior?" For (as Grot. observes) "he who binds another by baptism, seems to be superior to him who is bound."

15. ἄφες ἄρτι] Rosenm. and Schleus. explain *permitte quæso;* comparing the ἄρτι with δὴ and the Heb. נָא. But the interpretation "for the present," is far preferable. Indeed, the former mode would destroy the *emphasis*, which has been with reason supposed to exist in the word. The meaning is, that John must suffer him for the *present* to be baptized with the baptism of *water*, for that baptism of his with the *Spirit* was yet to be exhibited. At ἄφες sub., not με, but τοῦτο εἶναι, which is confirmed by Chrys. Τὴν δικαιοσύνην is for δικαίωμα, *institution*, as often in the Sept. So, at Deut. vi. 24, πληροῦν τὴν δικαιοσύνην is equivalent to ποιεῖν τὰ δικαιώματα.

16. εὐθύς.] There is here a transposition (such as that in Mark i. 29. and xi. 2.), found also in the Classical writers, by which εὐθὺς must be taken, not with ἀνέβη, but (as Grot. and others have seen) with ἀνεῴχθ. Fritz., indeed, makes objections to εὐθὺς being taken with ἀνεῴχθ.; and would join it, by a similar transposition, with βαπτισθ. But though that method is less harsh, the sense thence arising is somewhat frigid.

— ἀνεῴχθησαν οἱ οὐρανοί.] This is explained by most foreign recent Interpreters of *lightning* of the most vivid sort, "by which, as it were, the heavens seem cleft asunder." "So (they add) we find *scindere* and *findere cœlum* in the Roman writers. Such language being adapted to the common opinion of the ancients, that the sky was a solid mass, and that fire from thence burst through the vast convex of the firmament." But this seems to be a mere device to pare down the marvellous, in order to make it more credible. We have good reason to suppose the light to have been *preternatural*, and to have accompanied the Divine Spirit; such a light as accompanied Jesus, on being visibly revealed to St. Paul, at his conversion. Αὐτῷ is by some referred to *Jesus*, as a Dat. commodi; by others, to *John;* by which the sense will be, "to his view," namely, John's.

— ὡσεὶ περιστεράν.] There is an ambiguity in this circumstance, which has occasioned a variety of interpretation. Some understand by it the descent of a *material dove*, as a symbol of the Spirit, and with allusion to the innocence and meekness of Christ. Others, with more probability, take ὡσεὶ περ. to refer to the *mode* in which the Spirit, in some visible form (probably of a flame of fire), descended; namely, with that peculiar *hovering motion* which distinguishes the descent of a dove, and which is adverted to by Virg. Æn. v. 216. cited by Wets. Otherwise it would have been ὡσεὶ περιστερᾶς, as ὡσεὶ πυρὸς, Acts ii. 3. [*Comp.* John i. 33.]

17. φωνὴ ἐκ τῶν οὐρ.] Wets., Rosenm., Kuin., and Schleus., take this of *thunder;* which, however, involves absurdity; for (as Mr. Rose on Parkhurst Lex. p. 491. observes), "if *articulate words* were heard, λέγουσα simply tells us that the very words which follow were used, and the thunder is a gratuitous supposition. If it is meant that *no uttered words were heard*, only a stroke of thunder, which *was to be understood as*

MK. LU.
1 IV. *Τότε ὁ Ἰησοῦς ἀνήχθη εἰς τὴν ἔρημον ὑπὸ τοῦ πνεύματος,* 1. 4.
2 *πειρασθῆναι ὑπὸ τοῦ Διαβόλου. Καὶ νηστεύσας ἡμέρας τεσσαράκοντα* 12 1
3 *καὶ νύκτας τεσσαράκοντα, ὕστερον ἐπείνασε. Καὶ προσελθὼν αὐτῷ* 13 2
ὁ πειράζων, εἶπεν· Εἰ Υἱὸς εἶ τοῦ Θεοῦ, εἰπὲ, ἵνα οἱ λίθοι οὗτοι 3
4 *ἄρτοι γένωνται. Ὁ δὲ ἀποκριθεὶς εἶπε· Γέγραπται· Οὐκ ἐπ' ἄρτῳ* 4
μόνῳ ζήσεται ἄνθρωπος, ἀλλ' ἐπὶ παντὶ ῥήματι ἐκπο- 3.
5 *ρευομένῳ διὰ στόματος Θεοῦ. Τότε παραλαμβάνει αὐτὸν ὁ* 4

declaring that Jesus, &c., reasoning is idle; for language could hardly have been used less appropriate to convey this idea."

— ἀγαπητός.] For ὁ *μονογενής*. Applied here, and xiii. 8, and Luke ix. 35, xx. 13, to the Messiah. It is taken from the Sept.; as in Gen. xxii. 2; Jer. vi. 26; Amos viii. 10; Zach. xii. 10.—This use occurs in Hom. Il. vi. 401, and Hesiod, referred to by Pollux, iii. 2.

— ἐν ᾧ εὐδόκησα.] The use of the ἐν in this phrase is a Hebraism, occurring also in the Septuagint. The Aorist is *not* (as some suppose) put for the *present*, but has the sense of *custom*, which is frequent in that tense. See Matth. Gr. Gr. § 503. [*Comp.* infr. xii. 18. xvii. 5; Isa. xlii. 1; Ps. ii. 7; Luke ix. 35; 2 Pet. i. 17; Col. i. 13.]

IV. 1. ἀνήχθη — Διαβόλου.] Ἀνήχ. must not be taken, with some recent Commentators, for ἤχθη, but the ἀνα may refer to the high and mountainous country of which the *desert* here mentioned (whether what is now called *Quarantania*, a rugged mountain range; or, as others think, the desert of Mount Sinai), consisted, as compared with the low ground about Jordan. The ἀνα may, however, be intensive; and thus ἀν— will be for ἀπ—. By τοῦ πνεύματος is here denoted the influence of the Holy Spirit.

— πειρασθῆναι ὑ. τ. Δ.] We are now advanced to the record of a most awful and mysterious transaction, consequently encompassed with difficulties, defying the human understanding: to avoid which, several eminent persons, both ancient, and modern, have thought that a *visionary scene*, not a *real event*, is here narrated. But there is not the slightest intimation in the narrative, that the temptation was such. The air of the narrative produces an impression the contrary; and there are many strong reasons why such a view cannot be admitted. On the other hand, in favor of the common mode, we may safely maintain, that there is nothing in the circumstances, which involves any strong improbability: but rather what is quite agreeable to the analogy of God's methods, in other points, in his dispensations to man. So Bishop Porteus, and Mr. Townson, trace several points of striking similitude to the *temptation of Adam and Eve in Paradise*. And others have compared the character and design thereof with those of the *Crucifixion*, and have recognised in both a vicarious transaction. As to the confident assertion of the *Unitarians*, that the very form of expression, ἀνήχθη ὑπὸ τοῦ πν. shows that it is only a visionary scene, referring for similar expressions to Rev. i. 10. Acts xi. 5, the latter of these has nothing in common with this of St. Matthew; and the former, though it bears some verbal resemblance to the parallel passage of Luke iv. 1, is really of quite another character. Similar *expressions* do indeed occur at Matth. xii. 28. Lu. ii. 27. Acts viii. 29. and x. 19. But no one ever imagined the actions *there* described to be merely *imaginary*.

— τοῦ Διαβόλου] Διάβολος, properly *a slanderer*. It is sometimes in the N. T. an *appellative*; but mostly denotes, with the Art., *the* great *enemy* of God and man; thus exactly answering to the Heb. שָׂטָן. This arises from the close connection between the senses of *hater* and *enemy*. And though it be not often found so used, yet the *verb* διαβάλλεσθαι occurs in Herodot. and other writers, and is used in the sense *to be hated*; and διαβάλλεσθαί τινι, in Thucyd. iii. 109, iv. 21, viii. 83, signifies, "to be set against any one, to hate him." See my Note there.

3. ὁ πειράζων.] Particip. for substantive verbal; an idiom found both in the Scriptural and the Classical writers.

— Υἱὸς τοῦ Θεοῦ.] Not, "*a* son of God," as Campb. and Wakef. render. For it has been proved by Bp. Middl. that υἱὸς τοῦ Θεοῦ,' or υἱὸς Θεοῦ are never taken in a lower sense than ὁ υἱὸς τοῦ Θεοῦ, which is always to be understood in the *highest* sense. Thus in Mark i. 1. Υἱὸς τοῦ Θεοῦ is spoken by the Evangelist himself of Jesus. In John x. 36. the same phrase is employed by Christ himself of himself: and in Matth. xxvii. 40. it is used by those who well knew Christ's pretensions. Neither is υἱὸς Θεοῦ, without either of the Articles, to be taken in an inferior sense; for, not to examine all the places in which it occurs, we have Matt. xxvii. 43, where the crime laid to Christ is, that he said, "I am the son of God."

— εἰπέ.] "order." This is no Hebraism, but occurs in Thucyd. and the best Classical writers. As *dic* in the Latin.

— ἄρτοι.] *Loaves*. "Ἄρτος, used indefinitely, is rightly translated *bread*; but when joined with εἷς, or any other word limiting the signification in the singular number, ought to be rendered *loaf*; in the plural it ought always to be rendered *loaves*." (Campb.)

4. ἐπ' ἄρτῳ — ζήσεται.] The quotation agrees with the Heb. and Sept. For, although the Vatican text has τῷ, yet many of the best MSS. and several fathers omit it. Ὁ is placed before ἄνθρωπος in several MSS. of the Alex. recension, and has been introduced into the text by Griesb., Knapp, and Fritz.; but I think without sufficient authority. Vater and Scholz have not admitted it. The Pres. is here put for the Fut., or rather may be taken of what is *customary*. The ἐπὶ signifies *upon* or *by*.

— ἐπὶ παντὶ — Θεοῦ.] This explained allegorically, will signify the spiritual life imparted by the Word of God, like the Heb. דָּבָר, a mode of interpretation confirmed by the authority of the Fathers. Yet as ῥῆμα (to which, however, there is no word corresponding in the Heb.) may be rendered *thing*, as well as word; so the best modern Commentators are justified in explaining

MK. LU.

1. 3. *Διάβολος εἰς τὴν ἁγίαν πόλιν, καὶ ἵστησιν αὐτὸν ἐπὶ τὸ πτερύγιον τοῦ*
9 *ἱεροῦ· καὶ λέγει αὐτῷ· Εἰ Υἱὸς εἶ τοῦ Θεοῦ, βάλε σεαυτὸν κάτω·* 6
10 *γέγραπται γὰρ, ὅτι τοῖς ἀγγέλοις αὐτοῦ ἐντελεῖται περὶ*
11 *σοῦ· καὶ ἐπὶ χειρῶν ἀροῦσί σε, μήποτε προσκόψῃς*
πρὸς λίθον τὸν πόδα σου. Ἔφη αὐτῷ ὁ Ἰησοῦς· Πάλιν γέ- 7
12 *γραπται· Οὐκ ἐκπειράσεις Κύριον τὸν Θεόν σου. Πά-* 8
5 *λιν παραλαμβάνει αὐτὸν ὁ Διάβολος εἰς ὄρος ὑψηλὸν λίαν, καὶ δείκνυ-*
6 *σιν αὐτῷ πάσας τὰς βασιλείας τοῦ κόσμου καὶ τὴν δόξαν αὐτῶν, καὶ* 9
λέγει αὐτῷ· Ταῦτα πάντα σοι δώσω, ἐὰν πεσὼν προσκυνήσῃς μοι.
7 *Τότε λέγει αὐτῷ ὁ Ἰησοῦς· Ὕπαγε ὀπίσω μου, Σατανᾶ· γέγραπται* 10
8 *γάρ· Κύριον τὸν Θεόν σου προσκυνήσεις, καὶ αὐτῷ*

it, "whatever is ordained by God." "The temptation (observes Campb.) is repelled by a quotation from the O. T. purporting that, when the sons of Israel were in the like perilous situation in a desert, without the ordinary means of subsistence, God supplied them with food, by which their lives were preserved, to teach us that no strait, however pressing, ought to shake our confidence in him." With this sentiment comp. Wisd. xvi. 26. *οὐχ αἱ γενέσεις τῶν καρπῶν τρέφουσιν ἄνθρωπον, ἀλλὰ τὸ ῥῆμά σου τοὺς σοὶ πιστεύοντας διατηρεῖ.* [*Comp.* Deut. 8. 3.]

5. As to the difference in the *order* of the temptations recorded by Matthew, as compared with that in Luke (who transposes the last two) the discrepancy (if, indeed, it can be called such) is not to be removed by any "device for the nonce;" such as supposing the temptation to idolatry to have taken place *twice;* or the order in Luke to have been disturbed by transcribers. Mr. Townsend accounts for the difference in order by ascribing it to *difference of purpose* in the Evangelists. But it is better to attribute it to a difference of purpose in *narrating* the temptation; and to suppose, that while Matthew intended to fix the *order of the circumstances,* (which is plain by his having employed the definite terms *τότε* and *πάλιν,*) Luke did not mean to be so very exact, but merely to record the transaction in a *general way;* and thus the ordinary conjunction was sufficient for his purpose.

—*παραλαμβάνει*] *Παραλαμβάνειν* often signifies, both in the Scriptural and Classical writers, to take any one along with us (*παρα*) as a companion. Neither this term nor *ἵστησιν* gives the least countenance to the vulgar notion, that the Devil transported our Lord through *the air.* The latter is admitted to have the sense, *prevailed upon him to take his station.* So xviii. 2. and Gen. xliii. 9. *στήσω αὐτὸν ἐναντίον σου.*

—*ἁγίαν πόλιν.*] So called *κατ᾽ ἐξοχὴν,* as having the holy Temple and its worship. Thus the inscription on their coins was "Jerusalem the holy." Indeed, the Heathens called those cities *holy,* which were accounted the special residence of any of their deities.

—*πτερύγιον*] On the sense of this term Commentators are not agreed. One thing is admitted, that it cannot mean *pinnacle;* for there would have been no Article. And for the sense *pinnacled battlement,* (assigned by Grot., Hammond, and Doddr.) there is no authority. Unluckily we have no other example of *πτερύγιον* used of a *building.* But as the primitive *πτερὸν* has been proved by Wets. to denote the *roof of a temple,* so this is supposed by Krebs, Middlet., Schleus., and Fritz., to denote the pointed roof of some part of the temple, and as they are inclined to think, the *great Eastern porch.* The most probable opinion, however, is, that of Wets., Michaelis, Rosenm., and Kuin., that it referred to what was called *the King's Portico,* which overhung the precipice at the S. and E. of the temple (see Joseph. Ant. xv. 11 and 5.); and was perhaps so called from the spire-like figure which the end of the building presented from below. [*Comp.* Psalm xci. 11.]

6. *γέγραπται γὰρ, ὅτι κ. τ. λ.*] The former was a temptation to *presumption* from trust in himself; this, to *distrust* in God's Providence. The *Scripture quotation* with which the Devil subtilely tries to effect his purpose, is perverted; for the promise of protection there given is limited to those only, who endure the evils which *meet them* in the path of duty; not in such as they *bring upon themselves* by rashly presuming on God's protection. The metaphor in *ἐπὶ χειρῶν ἀροῦσί σε,* is, as Kuin. remarks, taken from *parents,* who, in travelling over rough ways, lift up and carry their children over the stones in their path, lest they should trip and stumble upon them.

7. *οὐκ ἐκπειράσεις,* &c.] *Ἐκπειράζειν* (where the *ἐκ* is intensive) signifies to make trial of any one's power generally; and here, of any one's power *to save.* The Commentators, however, are divided in opinion whether Christ is warning against *presumption* or *distrust.* The *former* is the more probable. [*Comp.* Deut. vi. 16.]

8. *δείκνυσιν — κόσμον.*] *Δεικνύναι* sometimes imports not absolutely to *exhibit to the sight,* but merely to *point out;* and here may serve to *indicate* the several kingdoms. Yet there is a difficulty as concerns *τοῦ κόσμου,* in the term of Luke iv. 5. *τῆς οἰκουμένης.* To obviate this, the best modern Commentators are agreed, that the terms must be taken in a restricted sense, to denote *Palestine* only. And indeed undoubted examples of this signification have been adduced, as Rom. iv. 13. Luke ii. 1. Rom. i. 8. From this lofty mountain (supposed to have been Nebo) a prospect would be afforded (as formerly to Moses) of nearly the whole of Palestine; and its provinces might be styled *kingdoms,* just as their tetrarchs or ethnarchs were called kings. See Matt. ii. 22.

9. *προσκυνήσῃς.*] The word here implies, not merely *homage,* but *adoration,* i. e. religious worship. The manner of rendering both was in the East the same, namely, by prostration to the earth.

MK. LU.
11 μόνῳ λατρεύσεις. Τότε ἀφίησιν αὐτὸν ὁ Διάβολος· καὶ ἰδοὺ, 1. 3.
ἄγγελοι προσῆλθον καὶ διηκόνουν αὐτῷ. 13
12 ΑΚΟΥΣΑΣ δὲ ὁ Ἰησοῦς, ὅτι Ἰωάννης παρεδόθη, ἀνεχώρησεν εἰς τὴν 14 14
13 Γαλιλαίαν· καὶ καταλιπὼν τὴν Ναζαρὲτ, ἐλθὼν κατῴκησεν εἰς Καπερ-
14 ναοὺμ τὴν παραθαλασσίαν, ἐν ὁρίοις Ζαβουλὼν καὶ Νεφθαλεὶμ· ἵνα 15
15 πληρωθῇ τὸ ῥηθὲν διὰ Ἡσαΐου τοῦ προφήτου λέγοντος· Γῆ Ζαβουλὼν καὶ γῆ Νεφθαλεὶμ, ὁδὸν θαλάσσης, πέραν
16 τοῦ Ἰορδάνου, Γαλιλαία τῶν ἐθνῶν, ὁ λαὸς ὁ καθή-

10. λατρεύσεις.] Λατρεύειν signifies properly to *render service* to any one; but in the Sept. and N. T. it is generally confined to *religious* service. [*Comp.* Deut. vi. 13, and x. 20.]

11. διηκόνουν αὐτῷ.] Διακονεῖν properly signifies to *be an attendant on* any one; but here and at Matt. xxvii. 55. and Mark i. 13 and 15 and 41. it signifies (like *ministrare* in Latin) to *wait at table*, and, by implication, to *supply with food.* So Eur. Cycl. 31. Κύκλωπι δειπνῶν διάκονος.

12. παρεδόθη.] Sub. εἰς φυλακὴν, which is usually *expressed*, as in Acts viii. 3. and xxii. 4. and Diodor. Sic. cited by Munthe. Or it may be (with Fritz.) regarded as an *indefinite* form of expression, (left so, in order to avoid mentioning what is unpleasant) signifying "to be delivered up into any one's power, for harm." [*Comp.* Luke iii. 19. John iv. 43.]

13. τὴν παραθαλασσίαν] "which is on the coast of the sea," or lake of Gennesareth. So called to distinguish it from *another* Capernaum. [*Comp.* Luke iv. 16. 30, 31.]

15. Νεφθαλεὶμ.] Drusius would read Νεφθαλεὶ, from the Hebrew. But the present reading seems better to correspond to the Syro-Chaldee, which was spoken by the Apostles; and, according to whose peculiarities of termination proper names of the O. T. would be likely to be conformed.

15, 16. The words agree neither with the Sept. nor the Hebrew; yet the discrepancy is by no means so great as would at first sight appear. The Heb., indeed, is in our Common version wrongly translated; and the Sept. is very corrupt. If the mistakes of the one be rectified, and the corruptions of the other be amended, the discrepancy will almost vanish; especially if we consider the *purpose* of the Evangelist; who did not mean to cite the *whole* prophecy contained in Is. ix. 1 and 2, but that *part* of it which sufficed for his purpose. *Why* he did not cite the whole, was, I apprehend, for this reason — that the Sept. was then, as it is now, throughout these verses exceedingly corrupt, and that the Hebrew was very obscure. The Evangelist, however, perceived that the general scope of the *former* of the two verses was the same as that of the *latter;* and that this latter presented only a fuller statement of what was contained in the former. The sense of both being this, that "in the former time he debased (or permitted to be debased) the land of Zebulon, and the land of Naphthali; the maritime district; the country beyond Jordan, called Galilee of the Gentiles; but in the latter time he hath made (or shall make) it glorious." Such being the case, the Evangelist rightly judged, that the *substance* of the two verses might be blended into one; omitting, in the former verse, the obscure words of the Hebrew, and the corrupt ones of the Greek; and retaining the rest, with the slight change (adopted from the Sept.) of making γῆ Ζαβ. &c. *nominative* instead of *accusative* cases, followed by ὁ λαὸς ὁ καθήμενος put in apposition with, as explanatory of, the preceding, and pointing out the *nature* of the glory, to which that country was destined. The country here meant by ὁδὸν θαλάσσης is that circumjacent to the sea of Galilee; for that is the θαλ. here intended. Ὁδὸν θαλ. is elliptically expressed for ἡ χώρα καθ' ὁδόν. So Æschyl. Prom. Vinct. 2. init. Χθονὸς μὲν εἰς τηλουρὸν ἥκομεν πέδον, Σκύθην ἐς οἶμον. where the Schol. explains οἶμον by ὁδὸν meaning *tract* or *country.* Thus the words will be found a most graphical description of the country afterwards called Galilee, divided into its districts, as it was in the time of the Prophet; in which Γῆ Ζαβ. and γῆ Νεφ. denote the whole of the tribes of Zebulon and Naphthali, except a tract of country bordering on the lake, the same I imagine as that which, in mentioning the divisions of Galilee, the Rabbins call *valley.* The two next clauses, πέραν Ἰορ., Γαλιλ. τῶν ἐθνῶν denote, I apprehend, the *same* district; the latter being only another appellation of the former. The country meant is that district, between Mount Hermon and the river, which skirts the E. side of Jordan, in its course from Mount Libanus to where it enters the sea of Galilee, in which were situated Chorazin and other places frequented by our Lord. As to the discrepancies which seem to subsist between the Sept. and S. Matthew, I apprehend that, in the time of the Evangelists, the text of the Sept. very nearly agreed with that which we now find in his Gospel; and it ran, I conceive, as follows: χώρα Ζαβ., ἡ γῆ Νεφ. ὁδὸν θαλάσσης [καὶ τὴν παραλίαν [οἰκοῦντες] καὶ πέραν τοῦ Ἰορ., Γαλ. τῶν ἐθνῶν, ὁ λαὸς ὁ πορ. ἐν σκότει εἶδε τὸ φῶς μέγα. οἱ καθ. ἐν χ. [καὶ] σκ. θαν. φῶς ἔλαμψε ἐπ' αὐτούς. Most of the deviations from the present text are, more or less, supported by MSS. The words λοιποὶ οἱ in the common text are evidently from the margin, as also οἰκοῦντες, which is found in some MSS. As to τὴν παραλίαν, the true reading, I have no doubt, is τῆς παραλίας. But I suspect that even *that* came originally from the *margin;* where it was meant to *explain* ὁδὸν θαλ. In the Alex. and some other MSS. we have *both* ὁδὸν θαλ. and its *gloss;* which, as is often the case, by degrees expelled the original reading. Εἶδε τὸ, for the textual ἴδετε, or εἴδετε, is found in several of the best MSS. The error is such as often occurs; and here led to the rash alteration of αὐτοὺς into ὑμᾶς. The reading of the Sept., οἱ οἰκοῦντες, strongly supports that found in the Codex Cant. and several of the best MSS. of the early Italic Version, οἱ καθήμενοι. This is confirmed by the Hebrew, which is well rendered by Rosenm., "et qui Cimmerias regiones colebant, iis sol affulgebit." However ungrammatical the idiom

MK. LU.
1. 4. μενος ἐν σκότει εἶδε φῶς μέγα· καὶ ‡τοῖς ‡καθημέ-
νοις ἐν χώρᾳ καὶ σκιᾷ θανάτου φῶς ἀνέτειλεν αὐτοῖς.
15 Ἀπὸ τότε ἤρξατο ὁ Ἰησοῦς κηρύσσειν καὶ λέγειν· Μετανοεῖτε· 17
16 ἤγγικε γὰρ ἡ βασιλεία τῶν οὐρανῶν. Περιπατῶν δὲ [ὁ Ἰησοῦς] παρὰ 18
τὴν θάλασσαν τῆς Γαλιλαίας, εἶδε δύο ἀδελφούς, Σίμωνα τὸν λεγόμενον Πέτρον, καὶ Ἀνδρέαν τὸν ἀδελφὸν αὐτοῦ, βάλλοντας ἀμφίβληστρον
17 εἰς τὴν θάλασσαν· ἦσαν γὰρ ἁλιεῖς. καὶ λέγει αὐτοῖς· Δεῦτε ὀπίσω 19
18 μου, καὶ ποιήσω ὑμᾶς ἁλιεῖς ἀνθρώπων. οἱ δὲ εὐθέως ἀφέντες τὰ 20
19 δίκτυα, ἠκολούθησαν αὐτῷ. Καὶ προβὰς ἐκεῖθεν, εἶδεν ἄλλους δύο 21
ἀδελφούς, Ἰάκωβον τὸν τοῦ Ζεβεδαίου, καὶ Ἰωάννην τὸν ἀδελφὸν αὐτοῦ,
20 ἐν τῷ πλοίῳ μετὰ Ζεβεδαίου τοῦ πατρὸς αὐτῶν, καταρτίζοντας τὰ
δίκτυα αὐτῶν· καὶ ἐκάλεσεν αὐτούς. οἱ δὲ εὐθέως ἀφέντες τὸ πλοῖον 22
καὶ τὸν πατέρα αὐτῶν, ἠκολούθησαν αὐτῷ.

a Mark 1. 23. Luke 4. 31. infr. 9. 35.

[a] Καὶ περιῆγεν ὅλην τὴν Γαλιλαίαν ὁ Ἰησοῦς, διδάσκων ἐν ταῖς 23
συναγωγαῖς αὐτῶν, καὶ κηρύσσων τὸ εὐαγγέλιον τῆς βασιλείας, καὶ
θεραπεύων πᾶσαν νόσον καὶ πᾶσαν μαλακίαν ἐν τῷ λαῷ. Καὶ ἀπῆλ- 24
θεν ἡ ἀκοὴ αὐτοῦ εἰς ὅλην τὴν Συρίαν· καὶ προσήνεγκαν αὐτῷ πάντας τοὺς κακῶς ἔχοντας, ποικίλαις νόσοις καὶ βασάνοις συνεχομένους,

may seem, it is very agreeable to the character of the Hellenistic Greek, and is not unfrequently found in the Apocalypse.

16. *καθήμενος ἐν σκότει.*] Καθῆσθαι sometimes signifies, as here, to *live* or *be*; of which sense the Commentators adduce examples, as Judith v. 3. 1 Macc. ii. 1. and 29. Sir. xxxvii. 18. Herodot. i. 45. *ἐν πένθει καθ.* and Dionys. Hal. Ant. p. 502. To which may be added Aristoph. Pac. 642. *ἡ πόλις γὰρ ὠχριῶσα κἀν φόβῳ καθημένη.* As, however, the word, in this sense, is almost always connected with terms importing *grief* or *calamity*, there may be an *allusion* to *sitting*, as being the posture of mourners. Σκότος and φῶς are, in Scripture, used to denote respectively the ignorance of irreligion, and the light of the Gospel. But here φῶς, (abstract for concrete,) signifies an *enlightener*, or *teacher*; of which sense Wets. adduces numerous examples, as Hom. Il. π. 39. *φόως Δαναοῖσι γένωμαι.* Eurip. El. 449. Ἑλλάδι φῶς.

— *ἐν χώρᾳ καὶ σκιᾷ θανάτου.*] This is to be taken, like the Sept. *ἐν χώρᾳ σκιᾷ θανάτου* for *ἐν χώρᾳ σκοτεινῇ*, similar to which is the *mortis umbra* of Ovid and Virg.

— *ἀνέτειλεν.*] We have here a continuation of the metaphor. So the Classical writers speak of the coming of some public benefactor as *a light sprung up in the midst of darkness*, (see Æschyl. Pers. 239. and Agam. 505.) and ἀνατέλλω properly denotes the rising of the sun. Αὐτοῖς is redundant; not by Hebraism, but according to the *popular* use in almost all languages. [*Comp.* Isa. xlii. 7.]

17. *ἀπὸ τότε.*] Sub. *χρόνου*, i. e. from the time that Jesus settled at Capernaum. Ἤρξατο κηρύξειν for ἐκήρυξε; by a redundancy, say the Commentators, common to both the Heb. and Latin. But it may be doubted whether there is any real pleonasm in the expression. [*Comp.* supr. iii. 2. et infr. x. 7.]

18. *ἀμφίβληστρον.*] This is properly an adjective with δίκτυον understood. The word is used by Hesiod, Herodo., and other authors, and appears, from its use, (see Herodo. i. 141.) to have denoted a *large drag-net*; as δίκτυον, from δίκω, usually *a small casting-net*. [*Comp.* Luke v. 2, et John i. 42.]

19. *δεῦτε ὀπίσω μου.*] Δεῦτε is usually considered as a mere particle of exhortation, like ἄγε or ἄγετε and the Heb. לך or לכן. But it is here and at xi. 28. xxii. 4. Mark i. 17. vi. 31. used in its proper sense, to denote *venite*, or *adeste*. Buttm. rightly derives it from δεῦρ' ἴτε. The ὀπίσω μου has reference to the custom for disciples to follow their master, and the expression is equivalent to "Be my disciple." So Diog. Laert. ii. 48. Socrates is said to have thus *called* Xenophon: *ἕπου τοίνυν καὶ μάνθανε.*

— *ἁλιεῖς ἀνθρώπων.*] i. e. able to draw men over to the Gospel. So Plato in his *Sophista*, compares the teacher of wisdom to a fisher. And in Stob. Serm. p. 313. (cited by Palairet) Solon says: Ἐγὼ μὴ ἀνασχῶμαι ἵνα ἄνθρωπον ἁλιεύσω. Indeed, as Kuin. remarks, terms of hunting and fishing are often used by the Classical writers of conciliating friends, or gaining disciples.

21. *ἐν τῷ πλοίῳ.*] This is wrongly rendered by some "in the *boat*." Πλοῖον, indeed, is a general term to denote a *vessel* of any size; but it must here denote *the ship*, i. e. their ship.

23. *περιῆγεν*] *obiit, peragravit.* Act. for mid., by the ellip. of ἑαυτόν. Αὐτῶν is used with reference to the plural *implied* in the preceding Γαλιλαίαν, by a common idiom, on which see Matt. Gr. Gr. § 435.

— *νόσον καὶ πᾶσαν μαλ.*] Kuin. regards the terms as synonymous, which they sometimes are, but not here. Νόσος rather denotes *a thoroughly formed disorder*, whether acute or chronic; *μαλακία*, an *incipient indisposition*, or temporary malady. See Euthym. and Markland in Bowyer.

24. *αὐτοῦ.*] Genit. of object, for περὶ αὐτοῦ; as in Joseph. p. 786. 45. ἀφίκετο ἀγγελία περὶ αὐτοῦ.

— *ἀκοὴ*] *fame*; as in Thucyd. i. 20. So the Latin *auditio* for *fama*.

— *βασάνοις συνεχομένους.*] Βάσανος signifies 1. a

καὶ δαιμονιζομένους, καὶ σεληνιαζομένους, καὶ παραλυτικούς· καὶ
25 *ἐθεράπευσεν αὐτούς. Καὶ ἠκολούθησαν αὐτῷ ὄχλοι πολλοὶ ἀπὸ τῆς*
Γαλιλαίας καὶ Δεκαπόλεως, καὶ Ἱεροσολύμων καὶ Ἰουδαίας, καὶ πέραν
τοῦ Ἰορδάνου.

touchstone; 2. *examination*, or trial, *by torture*; 3. *torture* itself; 4. any *tormenting malady*; of which signification examples are adduced by Wets. Συνέχεσθαι is often used with a Dative of some disorder; and has reference to such as *confine* the patients to their bed.

— *καὶ δαιμονιζομένους, καὶ σεληνιαζομένους*.] Notwithstanding the learning and talent which have been so profusely expended in support of the hypothesis of Mede, that these δαιμονιζόμενοι were merely *persons afflicted with lunacy*, it is, I conceive, utterly untenable. The disorders could *not* be the *same*; that of those possessed with demons being precisely *distinguished*, not only from natural diseases of the worst sort, but from lunacy in particular. It is true, that among both Heathens and Jews, lunacy and epilepsy were ascribed to the agency of *demons* (the spirits of dead men, or other evil beings); and it must be granted, that there are some passages of Scripture (as Matt. xvii. 11 and 15. John vii. 20. viii. 48 and 52. x. 2.) which prove that the terms *σελην.*, *ἐπιληπ.*, and *δαιμ.* were *sometimes* used synonymously. But that will not prove that they were not *properly* distinct from each other. And surely *when* distinguished, their being *sometimes* used synonymously ought not to affect their *proper acceptation*. The great preponderance, too, of the latter over the former seems to evince an intention, on the part of the sacred writers, to prevent the false conclusions which might be drawn from the diseases having many symptoms in common, by marking those cases of *possession* which Jesus relieved by some circumstances *not* equivocal, and which could never accompany an imaginary disorder. And when it is urged, that the Evangelists merely adopted the popular phraseology of their countrymen, without any *belief* in the *superstitions* connected therewith, (as with us the use of the term *bewitched* implies no belief in witchcraft,) that is taking for granted the very thing to be proved, and confounds a distinction, that between *popular phraseology* and *doctrine*. Mr. Mede was led into the view adopted by him, from having "observed it to be God's gracious method, in the course of his revealed dispensations, to take advantage of men's habitual prejudices, to support his truth, and keep his people attached to his ordinances." But the learned writer should have known how to distinguish between *rites* and *doctrines*. They were *rites* only, of which the Almighty availed himself, for the benefit of his servants: in matters of *doctrine*, the like compliance could not be indulged them without violating material truths; and therefore Scripture affords us no example of *such* a condescension. And surely, to support a false and supposititious opinion concerning diabolic possessions would have been contaminating the purity of the Christian faith. Moreover, when it is urged, that no reason can be given why there should have been demoniacal possessions at the time of *our Lord*, and not at the *present day*, we reply, that these *possessions* might then be permitted to be far more frequent than at any other period, in order that the power of Christ over the world of spirits might be more evidently shown, and that He who came to destroy the works of the Devil might obtain a manifest triumph over him. Mede, Farmer, and others, indeed, insist much on the highly figurative character of Oriental style, and compare those passages of Matt. viii. 26. Mark iv. 39. and Luke viii. 24., where Jesus, it is said, "rebuked the winds," and another where it is said he "rebuked a *fever*." But as to the former expression, it is, in fact, only equivalent to the *motus componere fluctus* of Virgil: and the expression *rebuking the fever* is but a strongly figurative one, to denote *repressing its violence*. And when it is urged, that in the demoniacs no symptoms are recorded which do not coincide with those of epilepsy or insanity at the present day, we may ask, if an evil spirit were permitted to disturb men's vital functions, have we any conception how this could be done *without* occasioning some or other of the symptoms which accompany natural disease?

It must, moreover, be borne in mind, that these demoniacal possessions have an intimate relation to the doctrine of *redemption*, and were, therefore, reasonably to be *expected* at the promulgation of the Gospel. The doctrines of *demoniacal possessions* and of a *future state* were equally supported by the acts and preaching of Jesus and his Disciples; and are equally woven into the substance of the Christian faith; the doctrines of the *Fall* and of the *Redemption* being the two cardinal hinges on which our holy Religion turns. To form a right judgment of the matter in question, it should be considered what part the Devil bore in the œconomy of grace. Now, in the history of the Fall, Satan is represented as instigating the first man to disobedience; for which his punishment by the *second* Adam (who restored man to his lost inheritance) is, at the time of the fall, denounced in the terms of "*bruising his head* by the *seed of the woman*." When, therefore, we find this restoration was procured by the death of Christ, we may reasonably *expect* to find *that punishment* on the tempter which was predicted in the history of the *Fall*, recorded in the history of the *Restoration*. And so, indeed, we find it. See Luke x. 18. Had the *first Adam* stood in the rectitude of his creation, he had been immortal, and beyond the reach of natural and moral evil. His fall to mortality brought *both* into the world. The office of the *second Adam* was to restore us to that happy state. But as the immortality purchased for us by the Son of God was not like that forfeited by Adam, to commence in *this* world, but is reserved for the reward of the *next*, both *physical* and *moral* evil were to endure for a season. Yet to manifest that they were, indeed, to receive their final doom from the Redeemer, it was but fit that, in the course of his ministry, he should give a *specimen* of his power over them. One part, therefore, of his God-like labors was taken up in curing all kinds of *natural diseases*. But had he stopped there, in the midst of his victories over *physical* evil, the proof of his dominion over both worlds had remained defective. He was, therefore, to display his sover-

V. Ἰδὼν δὲ τοὺς ὄχλους, ἀνέβη εἰς τὸ ὄρος· καὶ καθίσαντος αὐτοῦ, 1
προσῆλθον αὐτῷ οἱ μαθηταὶ αὐτοῦ· καὶ ἀνοίξας τὸ στόμα αὐτοῦ, 2
a Luke 6. 20. ἐδίδασκεν αὐτοὺς, λέγων· [a] Μακάριοι οἱ πτωχοὶ τῷ πνεύματι· ὅτι 3
b Luke 6. 21. Isa. 61. 2. αὐτῶν ἐστιν ἡ βασιλεία τῶν οὐρανῶν. [b] μακάριοι οἱ πενθοῦντες· ὅτι 4
c Psal. 37. 11. αὐτοὶ παρακληθήσονται. [c] μακάριοι οἱ πρᾳεῖς· ὅτι αὐτοὶ κληρονομή- 5
d Luke 6. 21. σουσι τὴν γῆν. [d] μακάριοι οἱ πεινῶντες καὶ διψῶντες τὴν δικαιοσύνην· 6

eignty over *moral evil* likewise. And this could not be clearly evinced, as it was over *natural* evil, but by a sensible victory over Satan, through whose temptation *moral evil* was brought into the world, and by whose wiles and malice it was sustained and increased. For evil is represented in Scripture as having been introduced by a Being of this description, who, in some manner, not intelligible to us, influenced the immaterial principle of man. The continuance of evil in the world is often ascribed to the continual agency of the same being. Our ignorance of the *manner* in which the mind may be controlled by the agency in question ought not to induce us to reject the doctrine itself.

In short, the hypothesis that the demoniacs were merely lunatic persons, with the semblance of *simplicity*, involves far greater *difficulties* than the common view. How otherwise are we to account for the fact, that the *demoniacs* everywhere address Jesus as the Messiah? which was not the case with those who only labored under *bodily* disorders. And when we find mention made of the *number* of demons in particular possessions, *actions* ascribed to them, and actions so expressly *distinguished* from those of the possessed—conversations held by the former in regard to the disposal of them after their expulsion, and accounts given how they *were* actually disposed of—when we find desires and passions ascribed peculiarly to them, and similitudes taken from the conduct which they usually observe, —it is impossible for us to deny their existence. In acquiescing in which, where we cannot *understand*, we may and ought to bow our reason to the Giver of reason. On one side, we have the wonderful doctrine, that it pleased the Almighty to permit invisible and evil beings to possess themselves, in some incomprehensible manner, of the bodies and souls of men; and for purposes which we can partly see, and are partly left to conjecture. On the other, we have Christ, the *revealer of truth*, establishing *falsehood*, sanctioning error and deception, and consequently being answerable for future and gross impositions, such as have been practised in latter ages! We have the Evangelists inconsistent with themselves; and a narrative acknowledged to be inspired, and intended for the unlearned, unintelligible to the learned and even involving falsehood! The hands, too, of Infidels are greatly strengthened by any such concession; and various other awkward consequences arise, which are ably stated by Bp. Warburton, in L. ix. of his Divine Legation, and in a Sermon on this text, to which I have been much indebted in forming the above article.

Ch. V. 1. The subjoined table, from Bishop Marsh's Dissertation on the first three Gospels, represents the parallel passages, as they are scattered throughout the Gospel of St. Luke, on the three following chapters.

MATTHEW.	LUKE.	MATTHEW.	LUKE.
v. 3—6.	vi. 20, 21.	vi. 19—21.	xii. 33, 34.
11, 12.	22, 23.	22, 23.	xi. 34—36.
15.	xi. 33.	24.	xvi. 13.
18.	xvi. 17.	25—33.	xii. 22—31.
25, 26.	xii. 58, 59.	vii. 1—5.	vi. 37—42.
32.	xvi. 18	7—11.	xi. 9—13.
39—42	vi. 29, 30.	12.	vi. 31.
44.	27, 28.	13.	xiii. 24.
45.	35.	16—21.	vi. 43—46
46, 47.	32, 33.	22, 23.	xiii. 25—27.
48.	36.	24—27	vi. 47—49.
vi. 9—13.	xi. 2—4.		

— ἰδὼν τοὺς ὄχλους.] "Seeing so great a concourse," &c.

— τὸ ὄρος.] As the Article does not allude to any before mentioned or definite mountain, it is by many Commentators regarded as indefinite, like the Heb. הַר, or put for τί. The principle, however, is unsound, both as respects the Greek and the Hebrew. See Fritz. We must leave the Art. its definite force, and with Middl. suppose τὸ ὄρος to denote *the mountain district*, as distinguished from the *other two*; as Gen. xix. 17. and Josh. ii. 22. He is of opinion that our Lord would not lead the multitude to Mount *Tabor*, (which has been commonly supposed the scene of the discourse) since part of the ridge lay much nearer to Capernaum.

— καθίσαντος αὐτοῦ] for καθίσαντι αὐτῷ, says Kuin. This, however, is unnecessary. The construction here adopted is found in Herodot. and other writers. Καθ. has reference to the *posture* in which the Jewish doctors taught; the master *sitting*, while the disciples stood.

2. ἀνοίξας τὸ στόμα αὐτοῦ.] This is usually esteemed an Hebraism; but Wets. has adduced similar expressions from the Greek Classics; and the expression may rather be considered as a vestige of the redundancy of primitive phraseology; afterwards retained with verbs of speaking, and on occasions of more than usual importance. See Winer's Gr. § 54. 2, a. Sometimes it is used *instead* of a verb of speaking, as in Ps. lxxviii. 12. ἀνοίξω τὸ στόμα μου ἐν παραβολαῖς.

3. μακάριοι οἱ πτωχοὶ τῷ πνεύματι.] The sense here partly depends upon the *construction*, on which Commentators are not agreed. Many of the moderns join τῷ πνεύματι with μακ.; while the greater number, and nearly all the ancient, construe it with πτωχοί. And this seems preferable; for the former method, though it yields a tolerable sense, is too harsh, and breaks that uniformity of expression, which runs through the several μακαρισμοί. Πτωχοὶ τῷ πν. is well explained by Euthym. οἱ ταπεινοὶ τῇ προαιρέσει those of a humbler disposition. See Is. lxvi. 2. Here τῷ πνεύματι is added, in order to determine the sense.

4. οἱ πενθοῦντες.] This is by some explained. "those who bear afflictions with resignation." But it is better, with Chrys. and some moderns.

7 ὅτι αὐτοὶ χορτασθήσονται. [e] μακάριοι οἱ ἐλεήμονες· ὅτι αὐτοὶ ἐλεηθή- e Infra 6. 14. Mark 11. 25. Jam. 2. 13.
8 σονται. [f] μακάριοι οἱ καθαροὶ τῇ καρδίᾳ· ὅτι αὐτοὶ τὸν Θεὸν ὄψον- f Psal. 24. 4. Heb. 12. 14.
9 ται. μακάριοι οἱ εἰρηνοποιοί· ὅτι αὐτοὶ υἱοὶ Θεοῦ κληθήσονται. 1 Cor. 13. 12. 1 John 3. 2.
10 [g] μακάριοι οἱ δεδιωγμένοι ἕνεκεν δικαιοσύνης· ὅτι αὐτῶν ἐστιν ἡ βα- g 1 Pet. 3. 14. 2 Tim. 2. 12.
11 σιλεία τῶν οὐρανῶν. [h] μακάριοί ἐστε, ὅταν ὀνειδίσωσιν ὑμᾶς καὶ h Luke 6. 22. 1 Pet. 4. 14.
διώξωσι, καὶ εἴπωσι πᾶν πονηρὸν ῥῆμα καθ' ὑμῶν ψευδόμενοι, ἕνεκεν
12 ἐμοῦ. [i] Χαίρετε καὶ ἀγαλλιᾶσθε! ὅτι ὁ μισθὸς ὑμῶν πολὺς ἐν τοῖς i Luke 6. 23. Jam. 1. 2.
οὐρανοῖς· οὕτω γὰρ ἐδίωξαν τοὺς προφήτας τοὺς πρὸ ὑμῶν. Acts 7. 52. infr. 23. 34, &c.
13 [k] Ὑμεῖς ἐστε τὸ ἅλας τῆς γῆς· ἐὰν δὲ τὸ ἅλας μωρανθῇ, ἐν τίνι k Mark 9. 50. Luke 14. 34. & 35.

as Kuin. and others, to interpret, "those who mourn [for their sins."] See Isa. lvii. 18. and James iv. 9.

—παρακληθήσονται] "they shall be comforted;" namely, with the hope of final acceptance and salvation.

5. οἱ πρᾳεῖς] "the meek and forgiving." It is not *apathy* which is enjoined, but a regulation of passion. See Ephes. iv. 26. The blessing here promised (taken from Ps. xxxvii. 11.) is primarily an earthly, but terminates in a heavenly one; conferring not a temporal, but an eternal inheritance.

6. οἱ πεινῶντες—δικαιοσύνην] i. e. those who ardently pursue, and, as naturally, seek after it, as men do to satisfy hunger and thirst. By δικαιοσύνην is denoted the performance of all the duties which God has enjoined.

—χορτασθήσονται.] The Interpreters variously supply what is here wanting to complete the sense. The best method seems to be that of Chrys. and Euthym. who simply supply παντὸς ἀγαθοῦ, i. e. with every good, both in this world, and in the next. Χορταζ. is properly used of *animals*, but is, in the later writers, applied to *men*.

7. ἐλεηθήσονται] "shall experience mercy and compassion;" namely, always from God, in pardon and acceptance; and (as seems to be also implied) usually from man. See Chrys. and comp. Prov. xi. 25.

8. οἱ καθαροὶ τῇ καρδίᾳ] i. e. "the pure in heart," as contradistinguished from those who, like the Pharisees, only aimed at an outward and ceremonial purity. So the Heb. בַר לֵבָב and תָם לֵבָב, as Ps. xxiv. 4. and Gen. xx. 50. Many parallel sentiments are adduced by Wets. from the Classical writers. I add Aristoph. Ran. γνώμῃ καθαρεύειν.

—τὸν Θεὸν ὄψονται.] A phrase occurring also at Heb. xii. 14, which is best explained as indicating the *favour of God* here, and his *final acceptance*, by salvation, hereafter. In the East, where monarchs were seldom seen, and seldomer approached by their subjects, it is no wonder that *introduction to them* should have been an image of high honour and happiness.

9. εἰρηνοποιοί] i. e. not only those who are peaceably inclined, but also who study to preserve peace among others.

—υἱοὶ Θεοῦ] namely, as imitating and bearing resemblance to God, who is styled the God of peace. See Rom. xv. 20. and 2 Cor. xiii. 11. So Philo de Sacr. οἱ τὸ ἀρεστὸν τῇ φύσει καὶ τὸ καλὸν, υἱοί εἰσι τοῦ Θεοῦ. Similar expressions, too, occur in the Pagan Philosophers, who are supposed to have borrowed them from the Scriptures. It is here *implied* that they will be loved and blessed with a truly paternal affection.

10. δεδιωγμένοι ἕνεκεν δικαιοσύνης.] Διώκειν signifies, 1. *to follow after*; 2. *to pursue any one for apprehension*; 3. in a metaphorical sense, *to pursue with acts of enmity, to persecute*, as in the present passage, which is similar to 1 Pet. iii. 14. ἀλλ' εἰ καὶ πάσχοιτε διὰ δικαιοσύνην, μακάριοι. In *both* the sense of δικ. is, "virtue and true religion."

11. ὅταν ὀνειδίσωσιν] for εἰ ὀνειδίσουσι. Sub. ἄνθρωποι, by an ellipsis common to most languages. On this use of the subjunct. see Winer's Gr. Some of the best Commentators are of opinion, that, having in the former verse touched on persecution *generally*, our Lord here descends to *particulars*; and notices one special act of it, namely, prosecution before human tribunals, on account of religion. Διώκειν is a well known forensic term to denote *prosecute*; and the other expressions in this sentence may have reference to judicial insult and gross abuse, as well as injustice. It may, however, be taken here in the same sense as in the preceding verse, the sense there being only further developed here.

—ψευδόμενοι] Particip. for adv., as in a similar passage of Joseph. Ant. vii. 11. 1. τοὺς πλουσιωτάτους τῶν Ἰουδαίων ἔλεγε, καταψευδόμενος, διδασκάλους εἶναι αὐτῷ τοῦ βουλεύματος γεγονέναι.

—ἕνεκεν ἐμοῦ] "in my cause."

12. χαίρετε καὶ ἀγαλλιᾶσθε.] The words are *not*, as Kuin. supposes, synonymous; but the latter is a stronger term than the former. The sense of μισθὸς need not here be pressed on, since it must signify a reward assigned of mere grace. See Rom. iv. 4.

13. ἐστε] "are, or are [to be]" "should consider yourselves as." Τῆς γῆς is for τῶν ἀνθρώπων.

—τὸ ἅλας τ. γ.] So Livy, cited by Grot. calls Greece the *sal gentium*; salt being a common symbol of wisdom. The meaning is, "What salt is to food, by seasoning and by preserving it, so ought ye to be to the rest of men. Others are to learn from you, and ye are to be examples to others."

—μωρανθῇ] "becomes insipid" ἄναλον γένηται, as Mark ix. 50. This sense is derived from that signification of μωρὸς, by which (like the Latin *fatuus*, and the Heb. תָּפֵלָה, as applied to objects of taste) it denotes *insipid*. The word is properly cognate with μαυρὸς, *debilis*. Thus we use *faint* in the sense *insipid*. It is certain that *rock* salt may lose its savour; but probably not *sea* salt. And as the allusion is somewhat remote, most recent Commentators have (with Schoettg.) supposed that a *bituminous* salt is here meant, procured from the lake Asphaltites, and which, having a fragrant odour, was strewn over the sacrifices in the temple, to counteract the smell of the burning flesh. Now as large quantities

ἁλισθήσεται; εἰς οὐδὲν ἰσχύει ἔτι, εἰ μὴ βληθῆναι ἔξω, καὶ καταπα-
l Philip. 2. 15. τεῖσθαι ὑπὸ τῶν ἀνθρώπων. [l] Ὑμεῖς ἐστε τὸ φῶς τοῦ κόσμου. οὐ 14
m Mark 4. 21. Luke 8. 16. & 11. 33. δύναται πόλις κρυβῆναι ἐπάνω ὄρους κειμένη. [m] οὐδὲ καίουσι λύχνον 15
καὶ τιθέασιν αὐτὸν ὑπὸ τὸν μόδιον, ἀλλ᾽ ἐπὶ τὴν λυχνίαν· καὶ λάμπει
n 1 Pet. 2. 12. πᾶσι τοῖς ἐν τῇ οἰκίᾳ. [n] Οὕτω λαμψάτω τὸ φῶς ὑμῶν ἔμπροσθεν τῶν 16
ἀνθρώπων, ὅπως ἴδωσιν ὑμῶν τὰ καλὰ ἔργα, καὶ δοξάσωσι τὸν πατέ-
ρα ὑμῶν τὸν ἐν τοῖς οὐρανοῖς.

Μὴ νομίσητε, ὅτι ἦλθον καταλῦσαι τὸν νόμον ἢ τοὺς προφήτας· οὐκ 17
o Luke 16. 17. ἦλθον καταλῦσαι, ἀλλὰ πληρῶσαι. [o] Ἀμὴν γὰρ λέγω ὑμῖν· ἕως ἂν 18

were laid up in the temple for this use, it would often spoil by exposure to the sun and atmosphere, and was then, we learn, scattered over the pavement, to prevent the priests from slipping, in wet weather. This, then, is thought to be an allusion to the temple service. There is here only a case *supposed*, which does sometimes, though rarely, occur. But this method is not necessary to be adopted, and seems at variance with the parallel passage at Luke xiv. 35.

— ἐὰν δὲ τὸ — ἁλισθήσεται.] "Our Lord has here supported a *particular truth* on a *general principle*. The particular truth is, that the loss of the salt, or genuine spirit of Christianity, cannot be supplied by any expedient whatsoever: and it is supported on this general principle; that every thing has its salt, or essential quality, which makes it to be what it is; and without which it is no longer the same; having degenerated into another thing." (Warburton).

— εἰ μὴ βληθ. ἔξω] "a sort of rustic proverb, signifying to be good for nothing." Markl. on Luke xiv. 34.

14. τὸ φῶς τοῦ κόσμου] i. e. the means by which God is pleased to enlighten the minds of men with true religion, as the globe is enlightened by the rays of the sun; which is, in the *proper* sense, τὸ φῶς τοῦ κόσμου. The term was applied by the Jews to their Rabbins, as among the Greeks and Romans celebrated persons were called *lights of the world*.

— οὐ δύναται πόλις κρυβῆναι, &c.] It is commonly supposed that this being connected with ver. 16., which contains the *application* of the similitude, namely, οὕτω λαμψάτω, &c., there is an ellip. of καθώς; as Is. lv. 9. and Jer. iii. 20. But it is better to suppose that in these words is *implied* the corresponding clause, "So neither can *you* remain in secret; the eyes of all being turned upon you." Then ver. 16. will supply an *admonition* founded on what is said in the two preceding verses.

— πόλις — ἐπάνω ὄρους.] This part of the simile may, as some suppose, have been suggested to Jesus by the city Bethulia, a little N. of Mt. Tabor; and clearly visible from the situation where the discourse was pronounced.

15. καίουσι] for the more Classical ἅπτουσι, which is used by Lu. viii. 16. xi. 33. Yet examples of it have been adduced, chiefly from the later writers, and in the *passive*. The sentence contains a proverbial saying, to express depriving any thing of its utility, by putting it to a use the farthest from what it was intended for. The words λύχνον and μόδιον have Articles, because they are *monadic* nouns, as denoting things of which there is usually *one* only in a house. See Middlet. and Campb.

16. τὸ φῶς ὑ.] i. e. the light of your *example* in a holy life.

— ἴδωσιν—καὶ δοξάσωσι.] For ἰδόντες δοξ. Δοξάζειν in the sense *praise*, *glorify*, is Hellenistic. In Classical Greek it signifies to *suppose*.

17. καταλῦσαι] "to abrogate, to annul." A sense as applied to laws or institutions of any kind, often occurring in the Classical writers. Our Lord here anticipates an objection; namely, that his doctrines differed, in many respects, from the Mosaic; and that therefore his system could not but *destroy* that promulgated by God to Moses, and borne testimony to by the Prophets. And yet it was not to be imagined, that the all-wise Being would lay down a law, as a *rule* of life, under *one* dispensation, which should be at variance with what he had promulgated under *another*. By τὸν νόμον must be meant in some sense, the law of Moses; that being the invariable sense of the word in the Gospels and Acts. Some, however, understand the *ceremonial*, others the *moral* law. Each, indeed, may be said to be meant. For the *ceremonial* law was completed by our Lord, in answering the types and fulfilling the prophecies, after which it was to cease, the *shadow* being supplied by the *substance*; the *moral*, by his exalting its precepts to a spirituality before unknown, and purifying it from the corruptions of the Jewish teachers: for it is plain from the whole of Scripture, that the ceremonial law alone was abrogated, while the moral law was left, as of perpetual obligation. And thus, in either case the law was meant to be, as St. Paul terms it, our παιδαγωγὸς, or conductor to, and preparer for, the Gospel, and to cease when it had answered the purpose for which it was originally designed, as a *part* of the great plan of Divine wisdom and mercy, for the salvation of man. This assurance of our Lord was made, to correct the false opinion of the Jews; that the Messiah would raise the Mosaic law to the greatest perfection, and *literally* fulfil the happy predictions of the Prophets.

18. ἀμὴν.] A word derived from the Heb., and used either at the beginning, or the end of a sentence. In the former case it has the affirmative sense, *verily*, and is equivalent to ναί, or ἀληθῶς; in the latter, it is put for γένοιτο, "*so be it!*" Ἕως ἂν παρέλθῃ οὐρ. is a proverbial phrase, often occurring in Scripture, and sometimes in the Classics, to denote that a thing can *never* happen. (So Ps. cxix. 46, Job xi. 9. Luke xvi. 17. Matt. xxiv. 35. Is. v. 10. Jer. xxxiii. 20. 21. Job. xiv. 12.) Dio. Cass. cited by Wets. εἰπόντας θᾶσσον ἂν τὸν οὐρανὸν συμπεσεῖν, ἢ Πλεντίανόν τι ὑπὸ Σεβήρου παθεῖν. Dionys. Hal. vi. 95. where it is agreed in a treaty, that there shall be peace μέχρις ἂν οὐρανός τε καὶ γῆ τὴν αὐτὴν στάσιν ἔχωσι.

παρέλθῃ ὁ οὐρανὸς καὶ ἡ γῆ, ἰῶτα ἓν ἢ μία κεραία οὐ μὴ παρέλθῃ
19 ἀπὸ τοῦ νόμου, ἕως ἂν πάντα γένηται. [p] ὃς ἐὰν οὖν λύσῃ μίαν τῶν p Jam. 2. 10. supr. ver. 3,
ἐντολῶν τούτων τῶν ἐλαχίστων, καὶ διδάξῃ οὕτω τοὺς ἀνθρώπους, ἐλά-
χιστος κληθήσεται ἐν τῇ βασιλείᾳ τῶν οὐρανῶν. ὃς δ᾽ ἂν ποιήσῃ καὶ
20 διδάξῃ, οὗτος μέγας κληθήσεται ἐν τῇ βασιλείᾳ τῶν οὐρανῶν. [q] Λέγω q Luke 11. 39. infr. 23. 25. 26. 27.
γὰρ ὑμῖν, ὅτι ἐὰν μὴ περισσεύσῃ ἡ δικαιοσύνη ὑμῶν πλεῖον τῶν γραμ-
ματέων καὶ Φαρισαίων, οὐ μὴ εἰσέλθητε εἰς τὴν βασιλείαν τῶν οὐρα-
21 νῶν. [r] Ἠκούσατε ὅτι ἐῤῥέθη τοῖς ἀρχαίοις· "Οὐ φονεύσεις· ὃς δ᾽ r Exod. 20. 13. Deut. 5. 17.
22 ἂν φονεύσῃ, ἔνοχος ἔσται τῇ κρίσει." [s] Ἐγὼ δὲ λέγω ὑμῖν, ὅτι πᾶς s 1 John 3. 15.
ὁ ὀργιζόμενος τῷ ἀδελφῷ αὐτοῦ εἰκῆ, ἔνοχος ἔσται τῇ κρίσει· ὃς δ᾽ ἂν

The words ὁ οὐρανὸς καὶ ἡ γῆ, form a periphrasis for *the universe*; which the Jews supposed was never utterly to perish, but would be constantly renewed. See Baruch iii. 32. and i. 11. So Phil. Jud. 656. says, that the laws of Moses may be expected to remain ἕως ἂν ἥλιος καὶ σελήνη, καὶ ὁ σύμπας οὐρανός τε καὶ κόσμος ᾖ. Something very similar is cited by Wets. from a Rabbinical writer.

—ἰῶτα—κεραία.] Ἰῶτα denoted *properly*, the letter *Jod* [י] (as being the smallest of the letters in the Hebrew alphabet,) and *figuratively*, any thing very small: κεραία, the points, or corners, which distinguished similar letters of the Hebrew alphabet, but were used figuratively to denote the minutest parts of any thing. Similar sentiments are cited from the Rabbinical writers. Thus our Lord means to express, in addition to the *eternal obligation*, the *boundless extent* of the moral law, as demanding the utmost purity of *thought*, as well as innocence of action.

—ἕως ἂν πάντα γένηται.] "until all shall come to pass," i. e. be accomplished, namely, by the fulfilment of the legal types and prophecies, and the complete establishment of the moral law.

19. λύσῃ.] "Shall neglect, or transgress." A sense common in the Classical writers, and here required by the antithetical term ποιεῖν.

—μίαν τῶν ἐλαχίστων.] Render "One of the least of these commandments." Here there is an allusion to the practice of the Pharisees, who, agreeably to their own lax notions of morality, divided the injunctions of the law into the *weightier* and the *lighter*. Any transgression of the latter they held to be very venial. And, by their own arbitrary classification of the former, they evaded the *spirit*, while they pretended to fulfil the *letter* of the law.

—ἐλάχιστος κληθήσεται.] Said *per meiosin* for, "he shall be farthest from attaining heaven," i. e. "he shall not attain it at all." By the antithesis μέγας must be taken for μέγιστος, of which the Commentators adduce examples, to which may be added Plato ap. Matth. G. G. § 266. *Here* only a high degree of the positive can be meant. Μέγας κληθήσεται, "he shall be great," i. e. in high favour; on which sense see my note on Thucyd. i. 138. By τῇ βασ. τ. οὐρ. is meant, the kingdom of Christ on earth, the Gospel dispensation.

20. περισσεύσῃ, &c.] "shall excel." Here our Lord fully declares his meaning; openly *naming* those whom he had before only *hinted* at. The sentence is, as it were, an answer to a question; q. d. "What, will not the righteousness of the law, as exhibited in the lives of such holy persons as the Pharisees, save us?" "No such thing—for I plainly tell you, that unless," &c. Δικαιοσύνη must here denote, like the Heb. צדקה, piety and virtue, as evinced in a life spent agreeably to the Divine commands, especially in the cultivation of the moral virtues.

—οὐ μὴ εἰσέλθ.] "Ye shall by no means enter." On this syntax see Winer's Gr. p. 161. m.

21. τοῖς ἀρχαίοις.] It is matter of dispute whether this should be rendered "*by*, or *to* them of old time." The former is maintained by most of the Commentators from Beza downward; the latter, by the Fathers and the ancient translators, and a few modern Commentators, as Doddr. Campb., Bp. Jebb, and Rosenm. So Joseph. Antiq. viii. 2. 4. "God gave to Solomon wisdom, ὥστε τοὺς ἀρχαίους ὑπερβάλλειν ἀνθρώπους." Upon the whole, the former interpretation seems to deserve the preference; as being most suitable to the context, and confirmed by the usage of the later writers, especially the Sept. and the N. T. And the words will thus be akin to a Talmudic saying, which may be rendered, εἰρήκασιν οἱ ἀρχαῖοι ἡμῶν. By οἱ ἀρχαῖοι Kuin. understands the *Jewish teachers* not long before the age of the Gospel. And Fritz. observes that the notion of ἀρχαῖος is *relative*. Be that as it may, certain it is that in that age the moral law had been utterly perverted; and that our Lord meant to *allude* to that corruption, is plain from what follows.

—ἔνοχος ἔσται τῇ κρίσει] "will be liable to the judgment." So Plato, cited by Wets., ἔνοχος ἔστω νόμοις ὁ τοῦτο δράσας. By τῇ κρίσει is meant an inferior Court of Judicature, consisting (as the Rabbins say) of twenty-three, or according to Joseph. Bell. i. 20. 5. and Ant. iv. 8. 14., of *seven* judges.

22. τῷ ἀδελφῷ] for ἑτέρῳ, *any one*. An idiom arising from the Jews being accustomed to regard all Israelites as brethren.

—εἰκῆ] "without sufficient cause;" implying also *above measure*. For such a person, to use the words of Aristot. cited by Wets. is angry, οἷς οὐ δεῖ, καὶ ἐφ᾽ οἷς οὐ δεῖ, καὶ μᾶλλον ἢ δεῖ. Critics are divided in opinion as to the genuineness of the word, which is rejected by Erasm., Bengel, Mill, and Fritz., but received by Grot., Wets., Griesb., Matthæi, Tittm., Vater, Knapp., and Scholz. The authority of MSS. for its omission is next to nothing; and that of *versions* slender. And although that of the Fathers be considerable, yet far inferior to that *for* the word—Not to say that the *universal consent* of Fathers would not counterbalance such strong external evidence

εἴπῃ τῷ ἀδελφῷ αὐτοῦ· ῥακὰ, ἔνοχος ἔσται τῷ συνεδρίῳ· ὃς δ᾽ ἂν
εἴπῃ· μωρὲ, ἔνοχος ἔσται εἰς τὴν γέενναν τοῦ πυρός. Ἐὰν οὖν προσ- 23
φέρῃς τὸ δῶρόν σου ἐπὶ τὸ θυσιαστήριον, κἀκεῖ μνησθῇς ὅτι ὁ ἀδελφός σου ἔχει τὶ κατὰ σοῦ· ἄφες ἐκεῖ τὸ δῶρόν σου ἔμπροσθεν τοῦ 24
θυσιαστηρίου, καὶ ὕπαγε, πρῶτον διαλλάγηθι τῷ ἀδελφῷ σου, καὶ
t Luke 12. 58. τότε ἐλθὼν πρόσφερε τὸ δῶρόν σου. [t] Ἴσθι εὐνοῶν τῷ ἀντιδίκῳ σου 25
ταχὺ, ἕως ὅτου εἶ ἐν τῇ ὁδῷ μετ᾽ αὐτοῦ· μήποτέ σε παραδῷ ὁ ἀντί-
δικος τῷ κριτῇ, καὶ ὁ κριτής σε παραδῷ τῷ ὑπηρέτῃ, καὶ εἰς φυλακὴν
βληθήσῃ. Ἀμὴν λέγω σοι, οὐ μὴ ἐξέλθῃς ἐκεῖθεν, ἕως ἂν ἀποδῷς 26
u Exod. 20. 14. Deut. 5. 18. τὸν ἔσχατον κοδράντην. [u] Ἠκούσατε ὅτι ἐῤῥέθη [τοῖς ἀρχαίοις]· Οὐ 27
x Job. 31. 1. μοιχεύσεις. [x] Ἐγὼ δὲ λέγω ὑμῖν, ὅτι πᾶς ὁ βλέπων γυναῖκα πρὸς τὸ 28

as that *for* the word. Internal evidence, too, *for* the word, far preponderates. In short, I quite agree with Matthæi, who pithily remarks, "*Asceticè*, non Criticè, disputatum est contra hoc vocabulum."

— ἔνοχος ἔσται τῇ κρίσει] i. e. is liable to such a punishment in the other world as may be paralleled with that which the Court of seven inflicts. Ῥακά. A term of strong reproach, equivalent to "*a vile, worthless fellow.*"

— μωρέ.] A term expressive of the greatest abhorrence, equivalent to "*thou impious wretch,*" for, in the language of the Hebrews, *folly* is equivalent to "*impiety.*"

— γέενναν τοῦ πυρός.] Γέεννα is formed from the Hebr. גיא הנם (the valley of Hinnom) a place S. E. of Jerusalem, called Γαίεννα at Josh. xviii. 16. (and probably a deep dell; φάραξ as it is rendered at Josh. xv. 8.) where formerly children had been sacrificed by fire to Moloch; and which long afterwards was held in such abomination, that the carcasses of animals, and dead bodies of malefactors, were thrown into it; which, in so hot a climate, needing to be consumed by fire, which was constantly kept up, it obtained the name γέεννα τοῦ πυρός. Both from its former and its present use, it was no unfit emblem of the place of torment reserved for the wicked, and might well supply the term to denote it. Of course, the sense is, that the latter offence would incur as much greater a punishment than the former as burning alive was more dreadful than stoning, &c.

23. As the former verse forbids *ill timed* and *excessive anger and hatred*, so this and the following enjoin *love to our neighbour*, and a *placable spirit.* And since the Pharisees reckoned anger, hatred, and reviling among the slighter offences; and thought that they did not incur the wrath of God, if sacrifices and other external rites were accurately observed; so here we are taught, that external worship is not pleasing in the sight of God, unless it is accompanied by a meek and charitable spirit.

— δῶρον.] Whatever was brought to the altar, was so called.

ἔχει τὶ κατὰ σοῦ.] It is not necessary with most Commentators, to *supply* ἔγκλημα, cause of complaint; since that is implied by the context. The same expression occurs at Mark xi. 25. and Rev. ii. 4.

24. διαλλάγηθι] "(do thy endeavour to) be reconciled with;" namely either by asking pardon, or by *granting* it. Thus Philo de sacrificiis p. 841. says, that when a man had injured his brother, and, repenting of his fault, *voluntarily acknowledged it*, he was first to make restitution, and then to come into the temple, presenting his sacrifice, and asking pardon. Thus we are taught that vain is all external worship of the Deity, if the duties towards our fellow creatures be neglected.

25. Here is inculcated the *general maxim* of speedy reconciliation with an adversary. And this is illustrated by an example derived *è re pecuniariâ.* Ἴσθι εὐνοῶν, "be friends with." This is not so much a *periphrasis* for εὐνόησον, as a stronger expression. So Luke xix. 17. ἴσθι ἐξουσίαν ἔχων.

— τῷ ἀντιδίκῳ.] The word signifies properly an *opponent in a suit at law*; but here a *creditor*, who is about to become a plaintiff, in Art. by suing his debtor at law.

— ἐν τῇ ὁδῷ] "in the way," namely to the Court, or to the Judge. For from Heinecc. Antiq. Rom. iv. 16. 18. we find that sometimes the plaintiff and defendant used to settle their affair *by the way*; and then the latter, who had been summoned to trial, was dismissed.

— ὑπηρέτῃ] "the person who carried into execution the sentence of the Judge," whether corporal punishment or fine, called by Lu. xii. 58. πράκτωρ, probably the more exact term.

27. τοῖς ἀρχαίοις.] These words have been rightly rejected by all the later Editors, since they are found in few of the MSS., are not in the Ed. Print., and are sanctioned by scarcely any Versions or Fathers; and we can far better account for their insertion than their omission.

28. γυναῖκα] i. e. a *married woman*; which sense is required by the context and almost general use of μοιχεύω and μοιχεία in the Scriptures. Βλέπων is for ἐπιβλέπων, passionately "*gazing upon.*" So ἐποφθαλμιᾷν. Our Lord means to say, that it is not only the *act*, but the *unchaste desire*, also, (what is called at 2 Pet. ii. 14. the "adulterous eye") which is included in the commandment. Ἐπιθυμία may (with Whitby) be defined "such a desire as gains the full consent of the will, and would certainly terminate in action, did not impediments from other causes arise;" thus making the essence of the vice to be in the *intention.* So also thought many of the sages of Greece and Rome, from whom citations are adduced by Wets., as Juven. Sat. xiii. 208., "Scelus intra se tacitum qui cogitat ullum *Facti crimen habet*;" to which I add Max. Tyr. Diss. 33, 4., who says that, to prevent criminal *action*, the only safe expedient is στῆσαι τὰς πηγὰς, καὶ ἀποφράξαι τῶν ἡδονῶν γένεσιν. Indeed, the an-

29 ἐπιθυμῆσαι αὐτῆς, ἤδη ἐμοίχευσεν αὐτὴν ἐν τῇ καρδίᾳ αὐτοῦ. [y] Εἰ [y] Infr. 18. 8. Mark 9. 43, 45, 47.
δὲ ὁ ὀφθαλμός σου ὁ δεξιὸς σκανδαλίζει σε, ἔξελε αὐτὸν καὶ βάλε ἀπὸ
σοῦ· συμφέρει γάρ σοι ἵνα ἀπόληται ἓν τῶν μελῶν σου, καὶ μὴ ὅλον
30 τὸ σῶμά σου βληθῇ εἰς γέενναν. Καὶ εἰ ἡ δεξιά σου χεὶρ σκανδαλίζει σε, ἔκκοψον αὐτὴν καὶ βάλε ἀπὸ σοῦ· συμφέρει γάρ σοι ἵνα
ἀπόληται ἓν τῶν μελῶν σου, καὶ μὴ ὅλον τὸ σῶμά σου βληθῇ εἰς
γέενναν.
31 [z] Ἐῤῥέθη δὲ, ὅτι ὃς ἂν ἀπολύσῃ τὴν γυναῖκα αὐτοῦ, δότω αὐτῇ [z] Deut. 24. 1. infr. 19. 7. Mark 10. 4.
32 ἀποστάσιον. Ἐγὼ δὲ λέγω ὑμῖν, ὅτι ὃς ἂν ἀπολύσῃ τὴν γυναῖκα αὐ- Luke 16. 18. 1 Cor. 7. 10.
τοῦ, παρεκτὸς λόγου πορνείας, ποιεῖ αὐτὴν μοιχᾶσθαι· καὶ ὃς ἐὰν

tient philosophers maintained, that there was a *moral defilement* adhering to lascivious *thoughts*. So Eurip. Hippol. 317. makes Phædra exclaim, χεῖρες μὲν ἁγναί, φρὴν δ' ἔχει μίασμά τι. Similar sentiments, too, but with far less of guarded delicacy, are found in the Rabbinical writers.

29. εἰ δὲ ὁ ὀφθαλμός—σκανδαλίζει σε.] "If thy right eye prove a stumbling block to thee," "occasion thee to stumble," "lead thee into sin." Kuin. observes that the Hebrews were accustomed to compare lusts and evil passions with members of the body; for example, an evil eye denoted envy. Thus to pluck out the eye and cut off the hand, is equivalent to *crucify the flesh*, Gal. v. 24., and *mortify your members*, Col. iii. 5. The sense therefore is: "deny thyself what is even the most desirable and alluring, and seems the most necessary, when the sacrifice is demanded by the good of thy soul." Some think that there is an allusion to the amputation of diseased members of the body, to prevent the spread of any disorder. Why the *right* eye should be mentioned, the Commentators have not told us. The reason must be, as I have observed in Rec. Syn., that the *right* eye was essentially necessary to the purposes of *war*, as it was then carried on. The sentiments contained in this passage are illustrated by Wets. from various passages of the Classical writers; Phil. Jud. Vol. i. 241, 19. Διόπερ ἑλέσθαι ἂν μὲν δοκοῦσιν οἱ μὴ τελείως εὐπαίδευτοι πεπηρῶσθαι μᾶλλον ἢ τὰ μὴ προσήκονθ' ὁρᾷν· κεκωφῶσθαι μᾶλλον ἢ βλαβερῶν ἀκούειν λόγων· καὶ ἐκτετμῆσθαι γλῶτταν ὑπὲρ τοῦ μηδὲν τῶν ἀῤῥήτων ἐκλαλῆσαι. Seneca Ep. 51. "Projice quæcunque cor tuum laniant; quæ si aliter extrahi nequirent, *cor cum illis evellendum erat.*" In this, and numerous other such like passages, scattered up and down in the Philosophers who lived *after* the promulgation of the Gospel, we may see a higher tone of morals than had been before maintained; and which can be ascribed to nothing but the silent effect of the Gospel, (as is the case in every age,) even on those who refused to receive it.

31. ὃς ἂν ἀπολύσῃ, &c.] We are to bear in mind, that the Jews were permitted to divorce wives without assigning any cause; also that Jesus neither here nor at Matt. xix. 3. meant to give *political* directions; and that he, moreover, did not contradict Moses, who not even himself approved of the arbitrary divorces of his times (See xix. 8.); finally, that the Jewish Doctors in the age of Christ were not agreed on the sense of the passage of Deut. xxiv. 1, which treats of divorce. Those of the school of *Hillel* said that the wife might not only be divorced for some great offence, but על כל דבר κατὰ πᾶσαν αἰτίαν, for any cause however slight, so that a writing of divorcement were given to her. Of which document see the usual form in Lightfoot H. Heb. On the other hand, that of *Shammai* contended that ערות דבר, the term in Deut. xxiv. 1., which was the subject of the dispute, and which the school of *Hillel* understood of any defect of person, or of disposition, could only mean *something criminal*, as adultery. See Selden de Ux. Heb. iii. 18. Lightf. Hor. Heb. &c. From the words of Christ, xix. 3., compared with Matt. x. 2. seq., it is clear that Moses meant the words to be taken as those of the school of Hillel interpreted them; and yet it is plain from Matt. xix. 8. & Gen. ii. 24, that Moses did not approve of arbitrary divorce. The Jewish Doctors, however, changed a *moral precept* into a *civil institution*. [To speak in plainer terms, Many things which Moses had *tolerated* in civil life, in order to avoid a greater evil (See Matt. xix. 8. and note), the Pharisees determined to be *morally right*; as in the case of retaliation. Edit.] Jesus, therefore, who did not intend to give political directions, here teaches in what case, *salvâ religione et conscientiâ*, a wife might be divorced. (Kuin.) The word ἀποστάσιον (equivalent to βιβλίον ἀποστασίου at xix. 7.) is not found in the Classical writers. But we may compare διστάσιον.

32. πορνείας.] The Commentators and Jurists are much divided in opinion as to the exact sense of this term. It is generally interpreted *adultery*. That, however, would seem to require μοιχείας; and as adultery was a *capital* offence, it would appear unnecessary to denounce *divorce* against such as were found guilty of it. Some understand by it *fornication before marriage*; others *incest*, or vice generally; and Mr. Morgan, in his work on Marriage, Adultery, and Divorce, *religious apostasy*, or *idolatry*. It is strange that so learned and diligent an inquirer should have profited so little by his laborious examination of "all the passages in which the word occurs in the Scriptures, the Sept., and Josephus," as to assert, that "it is derived from πόῤῥω νεύειν, and that its *primitive* signification is *religious apostasy!*" The truth is, πόρνη is from πέπορνα, pret. mid. of περνάω, which is derived from περάω, which signifies primarily to transfer or *give up*. And although πορνεία sometimes signifies idolatry, or religious apostasy, both in the Sept. and the N. T., yet it is only in the Prophets and the Apocalypse. Indeed, to suppose so highly figurative a signification to be employed in a passage intended to give a most important

a Lev. 19. 12. Exod. 20. 7. Deut. 5. 11. & 23. 23. Num. 30. 3.
b Jas. 5. 12.
c Ps. 48. 2.
d Exod. 21. 24. Deut. 19. 21. Lev. 24. 20.

ἀπολελυμένην γαμήσῃ, μοιχᾶται. [a] Πάλιν ἠκούσατε ὅτι ἐῤῥέθη τοῖς 33
ἀρχαίοις· Οὐκ ἐπιορκήσεις, ἀποδώσεις δὲ τῷ Κυρίῳ τοὺς ὅρκους σου.
[b] Ἐγὼ δὲ λέγω ὑμῖν μὴ ὀμόσαι ὅλως· μήτε ἐν τῷ οὐρανῷ, ὅτι θρό- 34
νος ἐστὶ τοῦ Θεοῦ· [c] μήτε ἐν τῇ γῇ, ὅτι ὑποπόδιόν ἐστι τῶν ποδῶν 35
αὐτοῦ· μήτε εἰς Ἱεροσόλυμα, ὅτι πόλις ἐστὶ τοῦ μεγάλου βασιλέως.
μήτε ἐν τῇ κεφαλῇ σου ὀμόσῃς, ὅτι οὐ δύνασαι μίαν τρίχα λευκὴν 36
ἢ μέλαιναν ποιῆσαι. Ἔστω δὲ ὁ λόγος ὑμῶν· ναὶ ναί, οὒ οὔ· τὸ 37
δὲ περισσὸν τούτων ἐκ τοῦ πονηροῦ ἐστιν. [d] Ἠκούσατε ὅτι ἐῤῥέθη· 38

regulation for all future ages, is like supposing a law to be couched in a riddle. The very same objection lies equally against all the *other* new interpretations. On such an occasion as the present (and that when the words of Matt. xix. 9. were pronounced), the term *must* be taken in its ordinary signification. Πόρνη (like the corresponding term in our own language, from the A. S. pÿpan denotes one who yields up the person, whether for hire, or for the purposes of sensuality; and, by implication, *unlawfully*. And consequently, the term *πορνεία*, as applied to females, denotes unlawful commerce with the other sex. But *that*, in a *married* woman, will involve *adultery;* and therefore the term may well be used in that sense. Thus, at Rom. i. 29., *πορνεία* must include adultery; as also at Amos vii. 17., *ἡ γυνή σου ἐν τῇ πόλει πορνεύσῃ*. The corresponding term in our own language is used in this very sense. See Todd's Johnson. In short, the very use of the word to denote apostasy or idolatry could only have arisen from this sense of *πορν.* And as to the objection, which has seemed so formidable to many as to set them upon devising new interpretations, namely, that adultery was punished by the Jewish law with *death*—that involves no real difficulty at all; for our Lord, in pronouncing on this deeply important matter, was legislating for all future ages, and therefore could have no reference to the Mosaic law, especially as it was now on the point of being abolished. It was sufficient for us to be informed, that adultery may authorize the *divorcement* of the offending party. Whether and *how far* the offence should be punishable by the *Magistrate*, was a question of *policy*, with which our Lord did not interfere, and with which Religion has nothing to do. At λόγου there is no such redundancy, *per Hebraismum*, as many Commentators suppose. This use of the word (which is found also in the Classical writers) is taken from *drawing up accounts*. So we say *on the score of.*

33. The Pharisees distributed oaths into the *weightier*, and the *slighter;* and forbade perjury only when the name of God was contained in the oath; but if it was *omitted*, they held it none, or a very slight offence; as also mental prevarication, by swearing with the lips, and disavowing the oath with the heart. A standard of morality even below that of the heathens. See Hom. Il. i. 312. Now it is this use of vain oaths, which directly led to *perjury*, that Jesus here means to prohibit. He is, therefore, not to be understood as forbidding *judicial* oaths; but (as appears from the examples he subjoins) such oaths as are introduced in common conversation, and on ordinary occasions.

—*οὐκ ἐπιορκήσεις.*] Ἐπιορκεῖν may mean either to *swear falsely*, and not *ex animo;* or, *to violate one's oath* Both however are here to be understood. The words *ἀποδώσεις δὲ ... σου* are to be taken (like *ὃς δ' ἂν φονεύσῃ*, &c. at ver. 19.) as an *interpretation* of the Jewish Doctors. Thus there will be an easier connexion between the doctrine of the Pharisees, expressed in these words, and the opposite one of Christ. (Kuin.)

34. seq.] Here are *instanced* the oaths most frequently used by the Jews. From the examples adduced by Wets. it appears that the heathens used oaths very similar to those of the Hebrews.

—*ἐν.*] Heb. ב. per, by. The difference between the Classical and the Hellenistic construction of *ὄμνυμι* is, that in the former it takes an Accus. or Genit. with *κατά;* the latter a Dat. with *ἐν*, and sometimes, though very rarely, *εἰς* with an Accus., as at ver. 35.

35. *τοῦ μεγάλου βασιλέως*] i. e. *Dei Optimi Maximi;* as Ps. xlvii. 3. xlviii. 2. & 3. xcv. 3. Job xiii. 9. &c. "The antient Arabs, (says Schulz,) called God simply THE KING."

36. *ἐν τῇ κεφ. σου.*] This was a practice common to both Greeks and Romans.

—*οὐ δύνασαι—ποιῆσαι.*] There is something here at which many Interpreters have stumbled; and some would *read*, from conjecture, *μίαν τρίχα λευκὴν ποιῆσαι μέλαιναν.* Others attempt to remove the difficulty by *interpretation*, thus: "thou canst not produce, or bring forth, one hair, white or black." This, however, is doing violence to the position of the words, and yields a somewhat jejune sense. I see no reason to abandon the interpretation of the antient, and most of the modern Interpreters, who understand it of *change of colour*. There is an ellipsis of *εἶναι*. The sense is, "thou hast no power even over the colour of thy hair; to make one hair otherwise than what it is; whether white or black." This is seemingly a proverbial expression.

37. *ναὶ ναί· οὒ οὔ.*] Most Commentators regard this passage as a kindred one to that in James v. 12; and take the first *ναί* and *οὐ* to signify the *promise*, or assertion, the second *ναί* and *οὐ* its *fulfilment;* construing: *ὁ λόγος ὑμῶν ὁ ναί, ἔστω ναί· ὁ λόγος δ' οὔ, ἔστω οὔ.* And they compare Rev. i. 7. and 2 Cor. i. 18. & 19. See also Maimonid. cited by Wets. Thus the adverb will be converted into a noun; which is frequent both in the Scriptural and Classical writers. The above method, however, does violence to the construction; and the passages cited are of another kind. It is therefore better (with Chrysostom. Kuin. and Fritz.) to suppose, that the *ναί* and *οὐ* are repeated, by way of expressing seriousness and gravity; q. d. "be content with a solemn and serious affirmation, or negation."

—*τοῦ πονηροῦ.*] It is debated whether the sense be, "the evil one." or "evil." The Ar-

39 “Ὀφθαλμὸν ἀντὶ ὀφθαλμοῦ, καὶ ὐδόντα ἀντὶ ὀδόντος.” [e] Ἐγὼ δὲ [e] Prov. 20. 22. & 24. 29.
λέγω ὑμῖν μὴ ἀντιστῆναι τῷ πονηρῷ· ἀλλ᾽ ὅστις σε ῥαπίσει ἐπὶ τὴν Luke 6. 29. Rom. 12. 17, 19. 1 Cor. 6. 7.
40 δεξιάν σου σιαγόνα, στρέψον αὐτῷ καὶ τὴν ἄλλην· καὶ τῷ θέλοντί σοι 1 Thess. 5. 15. 1 Pet. 3. 9.
41 κριθῆναι, καὶ τὸν χιτῶνά σου λαβεῖν, ἄφες αὐτῷ καὶ τὸ ἱμάτιον· καὶ
ὅστις σε ἀγγαρεύσει μίλιον ἕν, ὕπαγε μετ᾽ αὐτοῦ δύο. [f] Τῷ αἰτοῦντί [f] Deut. 15. 8, 10.
σε δίδου· καὶ τὸν θέλοντα ἀπὸ σοῦ δανείσασθαι μὴ ἀποστραφῇς. Luke 6. 35.
43 [g] Ἠκούσατε ὅτι ἐῤῥέθη· Ἀγαπήσεις τὸν πλησίον σου, καὶ [g] Lev. 19. 18. Exod. 34. 12.
44 μισήσεις τὸν ἐχθρόν σου. [h] Ἐγὼ δὲ λέγω ὑμῖν· ἀγαπᾶτε τοὺς ἐχθροὺς Deut. 7. 2. [h] Luke 6. 27. &c.
ὑμῶν, εὐλογεῖτκ τοὺς καταρωμένους ὑμᾶς, καλῶς ποιεῖτε * τοῖς * μι- Rom. 12. 14, 20.

ticle will here (as Middlet. observes) determine nothing, because the neuter adject. may be used as a substantive; and so τὸ πονηρὸν at Rom. xii. 9. Yet as the former sense is supported by the words of Christ himself at Joh. viii. 44, and in the Lord's Prayer; and as there is every reason to think it was adopted by the antients, it deserves the preference. We may render "springs from the temptation of the Devil."

38. ὀφθαλμὸν—ὀδόντος.] The Commentators here generally suppose an ellipsis of δώσεις. But that is too arbitrary; and εἶναι, with an accommodation of sense, is preferable. There is a reference to the *lex talionis*, which, according to the law and the customs of the Jews, was left, in some measure, with individuals. A similar, and even more severe law, had existed in the very early periods of Greece and Rome, as in all barbarous stages of society; but the right of avengement was afterwards transferred to the magistrate.

39. ἀντιστῆναι τῷ πονηρῷ.] As ἀντίστασθαι, like the Syr. and Arab. חלף, not only signifies to *withstand*, but (from the adjunct) to *retaliate upon*, we may, with Kuin. and Schleus. adopt that sense here. But I prefer it, with others, to explain ἀντιστῆναι, "to set oneself in a posture of hostile opposition," [in order to retaliate.] Τῷ πονηρῷ means the *injurious person*, the *injurer*, as the Sept. render רשע by ἀδικῶν as well as πονηρός. Moral maxims similar to the above are adduced from the Heathen Philosophers. That the commands in this and the following verses are not to be taken literally, as enjoining the particular actions here specified, but the *disposition* of forgiveness is apparent, not only from its being usual in the East to put the action for the disposition, but from the manner in which the precepts are introduced. See Horne's Introd. II. 452, seq.

—ῥαπίσει.] The word corresponds to our *rap* or *slap*; and was chiefly, as here, used of striking on *the face*; which was regarded as an affront of the worst sort; and was severely punished both by the Jewish and Roman laws. The expression here used was, no doubt, a proverbial one; and like most such, must be understood *cum grano salis*; as a similar expression which occurs in the Latin writers *ora præbere contumeliis*. It has reference also, in a great measure, to resistance to a *superior* force.

40. θέλοντί σοι κριθῆναι.] Kuin. and others think that κριν. is here taken to be in a figurative sense, of quarrelling, disputing, &c. And they cite Hesych. κρινώμεθα· ἀντὶ τοῦ μαχώμεθα καὶ διαλεγώμεθα. Read μαχώμεθα· καὶ διαλυώμεθα. So Thucyd. I. 140. διαλύεσθαι τὰ ἐγκλήματα, and I. 145. δίκῃ ἑτοῖμοι εἶναι διαλύεσθαι περὶ τῶν ἐγκλημάτων. But this amounts to no *proof*. And the use of κρίνεσθαι in the Sept. for ריב and דין is but a weak one. It is better, with almost all Interpreters, antient and modern, to take κριθῆναι in its proper sense, as a *forensic* term signifying "*to be impleaded at law*;" as in a similar expression of Thucyd. i. 39. δίκῃ ἐθελῆσαι κρίνεσθαι, where see my note. Θέλοντι is said by the Commentators to be redundant; but the word is scarcely ever such, and here means "should wish." By χιτῶνα is denoted the *under* garment; and by ἱμάτιον the *upper*: usually more valuable than the former. Λαβεῖν is said to be for αἱρεῖν. But if κριθῆναι be taken in a forensic sense, that will be unnecessary.

41. ἀγγαρεύσει, &c.] This verb is taken from the term ἄγγαρος, i. e. a *King's Courier*; who had authority to press horses and carriages, either for the post, or for the public service; and, when necessary, (especially in the latter case,) could compel the personal attendance of the owners. See Herodot. viii. 98. Xen. Cyr. viii. 6, 17. Joseph. Antiq. xiii. 3. The term was derived from the Persians, who first introduced the use of Couriers, to transmit intelligence, which was employed among the Romans, (who exacted this service from the provincials,) and is yet retained by the Turks.

—μίλιον.] On this, and the other Latinisms of the N. T. see Horne's Introd. II. 29.

42. δανείσασθαι.] The word signifies to borrow, with or without usury. Here the latter must be meant, because usury was forbidden by the Jewish law. It does not, however, (as Kuin. supposes) imply the non-payment of the sum borrowed; for, in that case, it would have been said, not *lend*, but *give*.

43. τὸν πλησίον.] The term was by the Jews used exclusively to denote their own people. And although in the passage of Scripture here alluded to (Levit. xix. 18.) it is not expressly added "thou shall hate thine enemy," yet the Jews thought it *deducible* from the words ἀγαπήσεις τὸν πλησίον, and countenanced by various precepts in Scripture, concerning the idolatrous nations around them; which precepts they extended to *all* heathens; whom, it seems, they emphatically termed *their enemies*. On the enmity (almost proverbial) bornè by the Jews to all other nations see the Classical citations in the Recens. Synop.

44. ἀγαπᾶτε τοὺς ἐχθροὺς ὑμῶν] "bear good will towards your enemies;" implying a disposition to do them good; not indeed as *enemies*, but as being *fellow creatures*. See Chrys. and Tittm. de Syn. N. T. III. p. 5. The words following are meant to explain and exemplify what is meant by ἀγαπᾶτε.

—εὐλογεῖτε.] This is generally interpreted

1 Pet. 3. 9. Luke 23. 34. Acts 7. 60. 1 Cor. 4. 13. σοῦσιν ὑμᾶς, καὶ προσεύχεσθε ὑπὲρ τῶν ἐπηρεαζόντων ὑμᾶς, καὶ διω-
κόντων ὑμᾶς· ὅπως γένησθε υἱοὶ τοῦ πατρὸς ὑμῶν τοῦ ἐν οὐρανοῖς· 45
ὅτι τὸν ἥλιον αὐτοῦ ἀνατέλλει ἐπὶ πονηροὺς καὶ ἀγαθοὺς, καὶ βρέχει
i Luke 6. 32. ἐπὶ δικαίους καὶ ἀδίκους. [i] Ἐὰν γὰρ ἀγαπήσητε τοὺς ἀγαπῶντας 46
ὑμᾶς, τίνα μισθὸν ἔχετε; οὐχὶ καὶ οἱ τελῶναι τὸ αὐτὸ ποιοῦσι; Καὶ 47
ἐὰν ἀσπάσησθε τοὺς ‡ ἀδελφοὺς ὑμῶν μόνον, τί περισσὸν ποιεῖτε;
k Lev. 11. 44. & 19. 2. & 20. 7, 26. 1 Pet. 1. 15, 16. οὐχὶ καὶ οἱ ‡ τελῶναι οὕτω ποιοῦσιν; [k] Ἔσεσθε οὖν ὑμεῖς τέλειοι, 48
ὥσπερ ὁ πατὴρ ὑμῶν ὁ ἐν τοῖς οὐρανοῖς τέλειός ἐστι.

VI. Προσέχετε τὴν ‡ ἐλεημοσύνην ὑμῶν μὴ ποιεῖν ἔμπροσθεν τῶν 1

"wish them all manner of good." But that sense cannot well be extracted from the word. It is better explained by others "bene precamini iis." But the simplest interpretation is that of Kuin., "bene iis dicite," "give them good words." Καταρᾶσθαι may very well be understood of reviling in general. So at 1 Cor. iv. 12. λοιδορεῖν and εὐλογεῖν are similarly opposed. There seems, indeed, to be a climax in the clauses of this verse.

— τοῖς μισοῦσιν.] This all the Editors from Mill downwards are agreed is the true reading. It is found in the Edit. Princ., and almost all the MSS., and has been received into the text by Griesb., Matth., Fritz., Vater, and Scholz., and rightly, for the common reading, τοὺς μισοῦντας. It is one of the Hellenistic idioms, to use the dative after καλῶς ποιεῖν for the *accus.*, which is the Classical usage. See Winer's Gr. Gr. § 24. 1. 6. The same difference subsists with respect to ἐπηρεάζειν.

— ἐπηρεαζόντων.] The Old Commentators tells us, that ἐπηρεάζειν signifies to injure any one either by words or deeds. But *insult* is the leading sense of the term. And when it denotes injury by *deeds*, it is injury accompanied with insult. The recent Commentators are almost universally of opinion, that it denotes injury by *deeds*, as passing from injury by words. Perhaps, however, it is best to take it of insult and abuse, (see my note on Thucyd. i. 26. 6. ἐκέλευον κατ' ἐπήρειαν,) and to suppose *injurious action* included in the general term διώκω.

45. υἱοὶ τοῦ πατρὸς] i. e. "assimilated to him by conformity of disposition," as children usually are to their parents. See John viii. 44. 1 John iii. 10.

— ἀνατέλλει.] The word is here used in a Hiphil sense, for "*causeth to rise.*" An idiom not unfrequent in the Classical writers, on which see Winer's Gr. and Schl. Lex. Many parallel sentiments are adduced by Wets. and others from the Classical writers; some possibly borrowed, directly or indirectly, from the New Testament.

— βρέχει.] It is agreeable to the Classical usage to join ὁ Θεὸς or Ζεὺς to ὕει, and sometimes other words of similar signification, as those denoting to *thunder* or *lighten*.

46. ἀγαπήσητε τοὺς ἀγ.] Here there is the very frequent ellipsis of μόνον.

— ἔχετε.] This is not put for ἕξετε, as Kuin. and others say; but the sense is, "have ye laid up in the word of God." See v. 12. & vi. 1. And so Thucyd. i. 129. κεῖταί σοι εὐεργεσία.

47. ἀσπάσησθε.] This includes (species for genus) the exercise of all the offices of kindness and affection.

— ἀδελφοὺς] i. e. your countrymen. Almost all the MSS., with the Edit. Princ. and other early Editions, together with many ancient Versions and Fathers, have φίλους, which is preferred by Wets., and received into the text by Matth. The common reading was adopted, from the Erasmian Editions, by Steph., on slender MS. authority. Yet it is so strongly supported by Critical probability, that it *requires* little; φίλους being, as Grot. and others have seen, evidently a gloss. However, it is found in many ancient and good MSS., and all the best Versions.

— τί περισσὸν] "what that is superior," "or extraordinary." Comp. ver 20. Æschin. Socr. Dial. iii. 6. opposes τὰ περιττὰ to τὰ κοινά. Thus also Thucyd. iii. 55. οὐδὲν ἐκπρεπέστερον ὑπὸ ἡμῶν—ἐπάθετε, and ἔξω τοῦ πρέποντος.

For τελῶναι some MSS., Versions, and Fathers have ἐθνικοὶ, which is edited by Knapp, Griesb., Fritz., and Tittm. And indeed the *antithesis* favours it; and that this was a maxim among them, appears from Wetstein's citations, to which I have in Rec. Syn. added an interesting passage from Themist. which shows that Socrates *almost* anticipated the doctrine of Christ, on bearing goodwill to our enemies. However ἐθνικοὶ *might* arise from a wish to strengthen the antithesis; and probably *did*; as the two or three MSS. which have it are full of such *emendations*. I have, therefore, with Wets. and Matth., retained the common reading; the *MS.* evidence for the new one being next to nothing and that of the Fathers slender, for *Chrys.* reads τελῶναι.

48. ἔσεσθε.] Fut. for Imperat., say the Commentators. Nay, Abresch. affirms that ἔσεσθε is equally imperative with ἔστε. But it is more correct to say that it *bears an affinity* to the Imperat., and (as Fritz. has suggested) is a delicate way of signifying what is directed to be done. Nor is this a Hebraism; but it is found both in Greek, Latin, and English. See Matth. Gr. Gr. § 404. The sense is, "you are required to be τέλειοι." It is obvious that the precept must be taken with limitation; the meaning being, that we are to *aim* at that perfection, especially in acts of benevolence to our fellow creatures, (here especially had in view, as appears from the parallel passage at Luke vi. 36.) which pre-eminently characterizes the Deity. Nor is this limitation arbitrary; but is suggested by ὥσπερ; which, like some other adverbs of comparison, does not denote *equality* in the things compared; (e. g. Matth. xix. 19. ἀγαπήσεις τὸν πλησίον ὡς σεαυτόν.) but *similarity*; q. d. "in the same *manner*, though not in the same degree."

VI. 1. προσέχετε.] Sub. τὸν νοῦν; as we say "*mind that*," &c. At μὴ ποιεῖν supply ὥστε.

— ἐλεημοσύνην.] All the recent Editors except Matth. are agreed in reading δικαιοσύνην, instead

ἀνθρώπων, πρὸς τὸ θεαθῆναι αὐτοῖς· εἰ δὲ μήγε, μισθὸν οὐκ ἔχετε
2 *παρὰ τῷ πατρὶ ὑμῶν τῷ ἐν τοῖς οὐρανοῖς.* [a] *ὅταν οὖν ποιῇς ἐλεημο-* a Rom. 12. 8.
σύνην, μὴ σαλπίσῃς ἔμπροσθέν σου, ὥσπερ οἱ ὑποκριταὶ ποιοῦσιν ἐν
ταῖς συναγωγαῖς καὶ ἐν ταῖς ῥύμαις, ὅπως δοξασθῶσιν ὑπὸ τῶν ἀν-
3 *θρώπων. ἀμὴν λέγω ὑμῖν ἀπέχουσι τὸν μισθὸν αὐτῶν. σοῦ δὲ*
ποιοῦντος ἐλεημοσύνην, μὴ γνώτω ἡ ἀριστερά σου τί ποιεῖ ἡ δεξιά
4 *σου·* [b] *ὅπως ᾖ σου ἡ ἐλεημοσύνη ἐν τῷ κρυπτῷ· καὶ ὁ πατήρ σου* b Luke 14. 14.
5 *ὁ βλέπων ἐν τῷ κρυπτῷ, αὐτὸς ἀποδώσει σοι ἐν τῷ φανερῷ. Καὶ*
ὅταν προσεύχῃ, οὐκ ἔσῃ ὥσπερ οἱ ὑποκριταί· ὅτι φιλοῦσιν ἐν ταῖς

of *ἐλεημ.*, which has indeed the appearance of a gloss. Our Lord, it is urged, first lays down a *general precept;* and then specifies the *particulars.* But strong reasons are urged by Wets. and Matth. why this reading cannot be admitted, especially this; (Qui justè vivit, dicitur *δικαιοσύνην ποιεῖν* non vero *ποιεῖν τὴν δικαιοσύνην*,) and it is so very deficient in authority, being found in only three or four MSS. with Wets. Matth. and Scholz. It were strange that a *gloss* should creep into almost every MS. Besides the quarter from whence we receive this reading is one fruitful in corruption under the guise of emendation. May we not, then, suspect that an alteration was made to *introduce* the very regularity above adverted to; though it is little agreeable to the unstudied style which so generally prevails in the N. T.— The phrase *ἐλεημοσύνην ποιεῖν* occurs in Sirach vii. 10. Tob. xii. 10. and Sapient. xxxv. 2.

— *εἰ δὲ μήγε.*] Scil. *προσέξετε μὴ ποιεῖν.* See Matth. ix. 17. 2 Cor. xi. 16. Though there can scarcely be said to be an *ellipsis*, since in use, writers seem to have had in mind *otherwise.*— *Ἔχετε* is *not* put for the Fut., but is to be taken as at v. 46. where see Note.

2. *μὴ σαλπίσῃς.*] The common notion, that this has reference to the pharisees having a trumpet sounded before them, when they distributed their alms, is justly exploded by the best Commentators; since there is no vestige of such a custom in the Rabbinical writings. We may, (with Chrys., Euthym., and Theophyl.,) simply take the verb in a metaphorical sense, of *ostentation* in giving; with reference to the custom common to all the ancient nations, of making proclamation, &c., by sound of trumpet. It was probably a proverbial saying. It is well observed by Bp. Warburton, Sermon xxxi. on this text, that, "we are not to understand the precept to be an *exclusive direction* how and in what manner the duty of alms-giving shall be performed: (as that its merit consists in being done *in secret*,) but only an *information* given by way of direction, concerning the disposition of mind necessary to make the giver's alms acceptable before God. q. d. Be not as the *hypocrites*, who, devoid of all benevolence, and actuated either by superstition, self-interest, or vain-glory, seek only the praise of men, and therefore, as it were, sound a trumpet before them, to proclaim their alms-giving.

— *οἱ ὑποκριταί.*] The word properly denotes 1. an *actor;* and, (as such wore *masks*,) 2. *one who acts under a mask*, a *dissembler*.

—*συναγωγαῖς.*] Grot., Wolf, Elsn., Kuin., and others take the word of places of public concourse, to the *exclusion* of synagogues. But those must surely be *included*, as being the places where alms were especially distributed.

— *ἀπέχουσι.*] It is not for *ἀφέξουσι* as many Commentators explain; but the Present is used of what is *customary*. It is moreover, for *ἀπολαβοῦσι*; a use found also at Phil. iv. 18. Luke vi. 24. and often in the later Greek writers, always with an Accusat., or at least in an active sense. Some render "fall short of." But that sense would require the *Genit.* Fritz. thinks there is here an intensive force in *ἀπέχουσι*; q. d. "they have the *whole* of their reward." But the sense is, "they receive their reward, all that they seek, or will ever have." So Luke vi. 24. *ἀπέχετε τὴν παράκλησιν ὑμῶν*.

3. *μὴ γνώτω — σοῦ.*] A proverbial saying, importing such secrecy, as to escape, if possible, the observation even of ourselves. Several similar sayings are cited from the Rabbinical and Classical writers. Of the latter the most apposite is a passage of Epictet. iii. 2. where the Philosopher, exposing the folly of one who does nothing but out of regard to the public view, adds (possibly, with this passage in his mind): *ἀπέχεις ἅπαντα*.

4. *ἐν τῷ φανερῷ*] sub. *τόπῳ*, for *φανερῶς*, namely in the presence of saints and angels, at the resurrection of the just. The words are not found in a few MSS., Versions, and Fathers, here and at v. 6. And they are cancelled in one or other of the passages by some critics; but defended by others. There is, I conceive, far too little external evidence to authorize *cancelling* them in either of the *first two* passages: and internal evidence is very strong for the *former*. And, as to the latter, it is surely less probable, that they were *inserted* by those who wished to complete the Antithesis, than that they were *cancelled* by those who stumbled at the *repetition*. In removing which, some cancelled the words at v. 4., others at v. 6.; and others, at v. 18.: and as the point was a doubtful one, and the marks of doubt probably left in all the passages, some bold or blundering scribes omitted them in all three; which was better than to cancel, as Griesb. has done, the first and third, and leave the *second.*— However, as external evidence (both in MSS., Versions, and Fathers) is decidedly against the words at v. 18., and as internal evidence is unfavourable to them, I have, for critical consistency, felt bound, while I defend them here and at v. 6. to *bracket* them at v. 18.; though I am far from being certain that they are not genuine even *there*. May the repetition have been *purposely* adopted, (as often) by our Lord, in order that what he had to say might be impressed more deeply on the minds of his hearers? I need only refer to Mark ix. 44., 46., 48., where the words *ὅπου ὁ σκώληξ οὐ τελευτᾷ, καὶ τὸ πῦρ οὐ σβέννυται* occurring in all three verses, are omitted in

συναγωγαῖς καὶ ἐν ταῖς γωνίαις τῶν πλατειῶν ἑστῶτες προσεύχεσθαι,
ὅπως ἂν φανῶσι τοῖς ἀνθρώποις. ἀμὴν λέγω ὑμῖν, ὅτι ἀπέχουσι τὸν
μισθὸν αὐτῶν. Σὺ δὲ ὅταν προσεύχῃ, εἴσελθε εἰς τὸ ταμιεῖόν σου, 6
καὶ κλείσας τὴν θύραν σου, πρόσευξαι τῷ πατρί σου τῷ ἐν τῷ κρυ-
πτῷ· καὶ ὁ πατήρ σου, ὁ βλέπων ἐν τῷ κρυπτῷ, ἀποδώσει σοι ἐν τῷ
φανερῷ. Προσευχόμενοι δὲ μὴ βαττολογήσητε, ὥσπερ οἱ ἐθνικοί· 7
δοκοῦσι γὰρ, ὅτι ἐν τῇ πολυλογίᾳ αὐτῶν εἰσακουσθήσονται. μὴ οὖν 8
ὁμοιωθῆτε αὐτοῖς· οἶδε γὰρ ὁ πατὴρ ὑμῶν, ὧν χρείαν ἔχετε, πρὸ τοῦ
c Luke 11. 2. ὑμᾶς αἰτῆσαι αὐτόν. [c] Οὕτως οὖν προσεύχεσθε ὑμεῖς· Πάτερ ἡμῶν 9
ὁ ἐν τοῖς οὐρανοῖς, ἁγιασθήτω τὸ ὄνομά σου· ἐλθέτω ἡ βασιλεία σου· 10
γενηθήτω τὸ θέλημά σου, ὡς ἐν οὐρανῷ καὶ ἐπὶ τῆς γῆς. τὸν ἄρτον 11

the first and second by certain MSS., (mostly those which omit the words at v. 4. and 6. here.) And yet no Critic has been bold enough to cancel them *there*.

5. ἑστῶτες.] Most Commentators take this for ὄντες, but it appears from Scripture and the Rabbinical writers, that the Jews used to pray standing. See Horne iii. 327. There is, however, no stress to be laid upon ἑστῶτες, and we might render: "they love to stand praying," &c.— Γωνίαις τῶν πλατειῶν, i. e. the place where streets meet at angles; where there is a broader space, and greater concourse of passengers. So the Jerusalem Talmud: "I observed Rabbi Jannai standing and praying in the street of Trippor; and repeating an additional prayer at each of the *four corners*."

6. ταμιεῖον.] This is explained by Kuin. "an upper chamber," sometimes called ὑπερῷον, corresponding to Hebr. עליה, appropriated to retirement and prayer. Fritz., however, with reason, thinks the two should not be confounded, and that by ταμιεῖον is denoted a yet more retired and secret place. See Vitringa de Synag. Jud. p. 151.

7. βαττολογήσητε.] The word does not occur in the Classical writers; but from what follows, and from the cognate term βαττολογία, occurring in Suid., Hesych., Eustath., and explained by them πολυλογία, we ascertain it to be the using of prolix useless speech, a dealing in vain repetition. Οἱ ἐθνικοί, corresponding to גויים, *strangers*, as opposed to עם, the people of God.

— ἐν τῇ πολυλογίᾳ.] We have very few examples of the Heathen prayers. But if we may judge by their *hymns*, as we find those of Homer, Orpheus (or Pseudo-Orpheus), and Callimachus, they were so stuffed up with synonymes, epithets, and prerogatives of the Deity, as to justify these expressions βαττολογέω and πολυλογία.— Ἐν, for διὰ or ἕνεκα, ב; a use not confined to the Hellenistic, but sometimes occurring in the Classical style.

9. οὕτως] "in this manner, after this model." This being, as Euthym. says, the *fountain* of prayer, whence we may draw precatory thoughts. Surely due reverence for a prayer, which (as Wets. observes) contains all things that can be asked of God, together with an acknowledgment of his Divine majesty and power, and our subjection requires that we should always *include* it in our prayers; especially as the words of Luke xi. 2. "when ye pray, say, Our Father," &c. seem to contain an express command. Comp. also Numb. vi. 23. (Sept.) and v. 16. There is every reason to think it always formed a part of the devotions of the first Christains. See Acts i. 24. ii. 42. iv. 24. This prayer, as we learn from Luke xi. 2., was uttered at the request of one of Christ's disciples; who entreated that a *form* of prayer might be given them, such as John had delivered to his disciples; which, indeed, was commonly done by the Jewish Masters. It consists of a *preface*, six *petitions*, and a *doxology*. The whole of it, with the exception of the clause "as we forgive our debtors," is, in substance, found in the nineteen prayers of the Jewish Liturgy. On the whole, see Horne's Introd. ii. 563.

— πάτερ — οὐρανοῖς.] This address, (frequent in the Jewish form of prayer,) is expressive of the deepest reverence; and the ἐν τοῖς οὐρανοῖς implies all the attributes of that glorious Being, who inhabiteth heaven, — but whom the Heaven of Heavens cannot contain; — namely, his omnipresence, omniscience, omnipotence, and infinite holiness. He is styled "our Father," as being such by right of creation and preservation, adoption, and grace.

— ἁγιασθήτω — σοῦ,] for δοξασθήτω, as Chrys. explains. Imperat. for Optat. to strengthen the sense. Ὄνομα is here, as often in Scripture, put for the *person* himself. This is accounted a Hebraism; but *some* examples are adduced from the Classical writers.

10. ἐλθέτω ἡ βασιλεία σοῦ.] Here we pray that the Christian dispensation may be diffused over the whole earth, by the conversion of both Jews and Gentiles; so that all, being members of God's kingdom on earth, may finally be partakers of his kingdom of glory in Heaven. See more in note on Matt. iii. 2.

—γενηθήτω τὸ θέλημα — γῆς] "may the dispensations of thy Providence be acquiesced in by us on earth with the same willing alacrity as they are obeyed in heaven." From this view of the sense, I have, with Fritz. accented the σοῦ, since it is emphatic, and cannot therefore be an enclitic; and so also just before. At ἐπὶ τῆς γῆς there is thought to be an ellipsis of οὕτως, which is frequent both in the Scriptural and Classical writers. Fritz., however, and Winer deny that there is any ellipsis, the οὕτω being, they say, suggested by the καὶ, *etiam*.

11. ἄρτον.] This word, like the Hebr. לחם, denotes, by a noriental figure, the necessaries of life, including, by implication, clothing; and it is synonymous with τὰ ἐπιτήδεια τοῦ σώματος, at James ii. 16.

12 ἡμῶν τὸν ἐπιούσιον δὸς ἡμῖν σήμερον. καὶ ἄφες ἡμῖν τὰ ὀφειλήματα
13 ἡμῶν, ὡς καὶ ἡμεῖς ἀφίεμεν τοῖς ὀφειλέταις ἡμῶν. [d] καὶ μὴ εἰσενέγκῃς [d] Infr. 13. 19.
ἡμᾶς εἰς πειρασμὸν, ἀλλὰ ῥῦσαι ἡμᾶς ἀπὸ τοῦ πονηροῦ. [ὅτι σοῦ
ἐστιν ἡ βασιλεία καὶ ἡ δύναμις καὶ ἡ δόξα εἰς τοὺς αἰῶνας. ἀμήν.]

— ἐπιούσιον.] On the sense of this term, Commentators are by no means agreed; the difficulty being increased by the word being not found in the Classical writers, and occurring nowhere else in the Scriptural ones, except in the parallel passage of Luke xi. 3. Hence we are compelled to seek its sense, somewhat precariously, from its *etymology*. The only two interpretations that have any semblance of truth are the following: 1. That of Salmas., Grot., Kuster. Fischer, Valck., Michaelis, and Fritzsche; who take it for τῆς ἐπιούσης ἡμέρας, and as equivalent to εἰς αὔριον.—And this view is confirmed by the word, which answers to ἐπιούσιος in the Nazarene Gospel, namely, לקחר. The derivation however, on which it is founded, is irregular, and the word contrary to analogy; not to say that it seems at variance with our Lord's command at v. 25 & 34., "to take no thought for the morrow," and yields a sense somewhat jejune, and even far-fetched. Greatly preferable is that of the antient Fathers and Commentators in general, and the Syriac Version; and, of the moderns, Beza, Mede, Toup, Kuin., Schleus., Whal., Rosenm., and Matthæi, which, deriving the term from οὐσία, assign as the sense, "sufficient for our support;" the ἐπι denoting *belonging to, fit*, or *needful for*. This interpretation is ably maintained in two learned Dissertations by Pfeiffer and Stolberg, in the 2d Volume of the Thesaurus Theol. appended to the Dutch Edition of the Critici Sacri, and another by Kirkmaier in Vol. ii. 189. seqq. of the *Novus* Thes. Theolog. a *second* appendix to the same.

12. τὰ ὀφειλήματα.] Answering to ἁμαρτίας in the parallel passage of Luke. This usage of the word (with which the Commentators compare the Heb. חוב *to owe*, and *to sin*, as the Greeks say ὀφείλειν δίκην, *pœnas debere*) arises from this; that obedience being a debt we owe to God, any one who commits sin, thereby contracts a kind of obligation, to be paid by suffering the punishment awarded to it. And ἀφιέναι signifies to remit the penalty, to forgive. Τοῖς ὀφειλ. ἡμῶν signifies those who sin against us. So Luke in the parallel passage, παντὶ ὀφείλοντι ἡμῖν, and Luke xiii. 4., ὀφειλέται παρὰ πάντας ἀνθρώπους.

— ὡς ἀφίεμεν.] The best modern Commentators are of opinion that ὡς here signifies *for*, or *since;* a signification frequent in the Classical writers, and confirmed, they think, by the parallel passage in Luke. But that is not decisive; since the prayer is supposed to have been delivered on *two* occasions, with a slight variation. However, I cannot approve of regarding, with the generality of Interpreters, the ὡς as conditional. It mostly, as Grot. observes, "marks *similitude*." So Tyndale well renders "even as."

13. μὴ εἰσενέγκῃς — πειρασμόν.] The best Commentators are of opinion, that this expression imports: "Suffer us not to be led into, abandon us not unto, temptation," i. e. (by *implication*) so as to be *overcome* by it.

— τοῦ πονηροῦ.] It is debated whether the sense here be *evil*, or the *evil one*, SATAN, q. d. "from [the temptation of] Satan." The evidence for the latter sense preponderates; particularly as it is found in the Jewish formularies, from whence this clause was taken. See, however, Lampe on John, Vol. iii. p. 442.

— ὅτι σοῦ &c.] The genuineness of this doxology has, to most Critics, appeared doubtful: and, with the exception of Matthæi, all the more eminent ones from Erasm. and Grot. down to Scholz, have rejected it. It is, indeed, supported by almost all the MSS., by both the Syriac, and some other Oriental Versions, and by some Greek Fathers. But, on the other hand, it is not found in at least eight MSS., all of very high antiquity, and in others is marked as doubtful; nor has it any place in the Italic, Vulgate, and some other Versions, and many of the Greek and all the Latin Fathers. And as doxologies of this kind were much in use among the Jews and early Christians, there is great reason to suppose that it was interpolated from the antient liturgies, in which we know it formed the response of the people; the *prayer* alone being pronounced by the priest. It is far more likely to have been *introduced from the Liturgies*, than that it should have been *removed from* the passage because of its not being contained in the parallel one of St. Luke. It is, indeed, argued, that the Greek Church would never have presumed to add from their liturgies, to a form of prayer by Christ himself. But it may be replied, that they never did formally add it; the doxology being introduced gradually, and, no doubt, at first written in a different character, or in red ink, and in the margin, as found in several MSS. And when it is argued, that the Latin Fathers purposely omitted the clauses, to remove a discrepancy between St. Matthew and St. Luke; that is only taking for granted what cannot be proved, and what should not be believed except on the strongest proof, as involving the credit of those venerable persons. Besides, there was a far more serious discrepancy involved in the clause immediately preceding; that not being found in the Vulgate and Italic Versions, nor in the Fathers in question. But they did not attempt to remove *that* discrepancy. Why then *this?* Moreover, this doxology materially interrupts the connexion between the ὡς καὶ ἡμεῖς ἀφίεμεν and the admonition founded on it at v. 14. And although the omission of the clause does not entirely remove, yet it greatly *lessens* the harshness of the interruption. As to the argument founded on the sublimity, beauty, and appropriateness of the clause in question, it is very inconclusive; for the antient Liturgies, both Greek and Latin, being chiefly founded on Scripture, abound in passages of great sublimity. And as to the *appropriateness*, that is quite consistent with the clause being insititious: for such alone could *cause* it to be introduced here. And a *spurious* passage may be fitted to any context, as well as a genuine one. Its being found, too, in the Peschito-Syriac Version will not absolulely prove its genuineness, unless we could be sure that we have that Version in its original purity. And especially it will not prove that it was not introduced from the liturgies above mentioned; for those liturgies, ascending to the time of St. Bar-

e Mark 11. 25. Ecclus. 28. 2. f Infr. 18. 35.

[e] Ἐὰν γὰρ ἀφῆτε τοῖς ἀνθρώποις τὰ παραπτώματα αὐτῶν, ἀφήσει καὶ 14
ὑμῖν ὁ Πατὴρ ὑμῶν ὁ οὐράνιος· [f] ἐὰν δὲ μὴ ἀφῆτε τοῖς ἀνθρώποις 15
τὰ παραπτώματα αὐτῶν, οὐδὲ ὁ Πατὴρ ὑμῶν ἀφήσει τὰ παραπτώματα
ὑμῶν. Ὅταν δὲ νηστεύητε, μὴ γίνεσθε ὥσπερ οἱ ὑποκριταὶ, σκυθρω- 16
ποί· ἀφανίζουσι γὰρ τὰ πρόσωπα αὐτῶν, ὅπως φανῶσι τοῖς ἀνθρώποις νηστεύοντες. ἀμὴν λέγω ὑμῖν, ὅτι ἀπέχουσι τὸν μισθὸν αὐτῶν.
Σὺ δὲ νηστεύων ἄλειψαί σου τὴν κεφαλὴν, καὶ τὸ πρόσωπόν σου 17
νίψαι· ὅπως μὴ φανῇς τοῖς ἀνθρώποις νηστεύων, ἀλλὰ τῷ Πατρί σου 18
τῷ ἐν τῷ κρυπτῷ· καὶ ὁ Πατήρ σου, ὁ βλέπων ἐν τῷ κρυπτῷ, ἀποδώσει σοι [ἐν τῷ φανερῷ.]

g Infr. 19. 21. Luke 12. 33.

[g] Μὴ θησαυρίζετε ὑμῖν θησαυροὺς ἐπὶ τῆς γῆς, ὅπου σὴς καὶ βρῶσις 19

nabas and St. Clemens, were far more antient than the highest antiquity ever *claimed* for the Peschito-Syriac Version. Not to say, that there are passages where that Version is admitted to be interpolated, probably from the later Syriac Versions. And where should we sooner expect it than in a passage like the present, of which the interpolation (if such there be) was confined to the East? for the MSS. which support it are almost wholly of the Constantinopolitan or the Eastern class. And as to what Matthæi says, that "if we *reject* this clause, then we must *receive* that at 1 John v. 5. with both hands," since "utriusque loci eadem est crisis," that by no means follows. For although it be true, as he says, that "the *external* evidence for the latter passage is almost entirely of the Latin Church, and that it is supported chiefly by *internal* evidence," yet the two cases are by no means the same; internal evidence here being *more against* the clause than it is *there in its favour*. And surely it does not follow, that we *must receive* the passage of 1. Joh., if we *reject* this; since there may be equal consistency in rejecting *both*. At all events, if we reject this, we must reject it on the ground, that, as Bp. Marsh observes, (Lect. P. vi. p. 27.) internal evidence may show that a passage is *spurious*, though external evidence is in its favour. And if we *reject that*, we must reject it on the ground, that (in the words of the same learned Prelate) "no external evidence can prove a passage to be spurious, when internal evidence is decidedly against it." However, I mean not to say that the state of the evidence is here such as to authorize us to *cancel* the clause (for nothing but internal evidence of the most conclusive kind, opposed to such strong external evidence as exists, could warrant that): and I have therefore felt justified in merely placing it within *single* brackets.

14, 15. *ἐὰν γὰρ ἀφῆτε* &c.] In order to more impressively recommend the virtue just mentioned, our Lord, in the Hebrew manner, (see Is. iii. 9. xxxviii. 1. Jer. xxix. 11. Deut. ix. 7.) propounds the same sentiment both affirmatively and negatively. (Kuin.) We are not, however, to understand hereby that the practice of this, or of any other single duty, can obtain God's favour, where other Christian virtues are neglected: for, though negative precepts are absolute, yet affirmative promises admit of this limitation, "if no other condition of salvation be wanting."

16. *ὅταν δὲ νηστεύητε.*] This is meant, not of public and enjoined, but of private and voluntary fasting. On both which see Horne's Introd. Vol. iii. p. 324. note, and p. 378.

— *μὴ γίνεσθε — σκυθρωποί*] "do not put on a morose countenance." Σκυθρωπὸς properly signifies *scowling*, as opposed to ἱλαρός. The words ὑποκριταὶ and σκυθρωποὶ are conjoined in some passages cited by Wets. and others.

— *ἀφανίζουσι*] "they disfigure." Ἀφανίζειν signifies 1. to *cause to disappear*; 2. to *change the appearance of, deform*. The term has reference, partly, to the squalid appearance which the Pharisees affected, by the sprinkling of ashes or earth on their heads, and letting their beards and hair grow; and partly to the sour countenance into which their faces were screwed up by a semblance of penitence. See Chrys. And so Æschyl. Agam. 766. says of persons affecting "to rejoice with those that rejoice;" Συγχαίρουσιν ὁμοιοπρεπεῖς ἀγέλαστα πρόσωπα, β ι α ζ ό μ ε ν ο ι.

— *ὅπως φανῶσι — νηστ.*] Φανῶσι has the middle force, "that they may appear unto men to fast;" and *τοῖς ἀνθρώποις* is not, as some say, for *ὑπὸ τῶν ἀνθρώπων*. Simil. Aristoph. Ran. 1095., cited by Wets., *ῥάκι' ἀμπισχών, ἵν' ἐλεεινοὶ τοῖς ἀνθρώποις φαίνωντ' εἶναι*. On fasting as a Christian duty, see Whitby and Mackn.

17. *ἄλειψαι — νίψαι*] i. e. appear as usual; for the Jews, like the Greeks, regularly washed and and anointed, except at times of mourning and public humiliation.

18. *ἐν τῷ φανερῷ.*] See note supra, v. 4.

19. Μὴ *θησαυρίζετε* &c.] *Θησαυρὸς* properly signifies a *repository for valuables*; but sometimes, as here, the *treasure itself*; i. e. such precious *moveables* as are usually treasured up; e. gr. gold, silver, &c., (either in the mass, or worked up into vessels); and *costly apparel*, in which the riches of the antients chiefly consisted. So Thucyd. ii. 98. *χωρὶς δὲ ὅσα ὑφαντά τε καὶ λεῖα καὶ ἡ ἄλλη κατασκευή*, where see my note. To these two last the words following chiefly allude; for *βρῶσις* (commonly understood of rust and canker, but by Rosenm. and Kuin. of the *curculio* or corn-worm, thus making it refer to grain stored up) may be best taken in its most extensive sense, (with Chrys., Euthym., and Fritz.) to denote that *corruption* to which moveables of *every* kind are subject. Simil. Jerem. in Epist. v. 9. says of the heathen gods; *οὗτοι δὲ οὐ διασώζονται ἀπὸ ἰοῦ καὶ βρωμάτων*. and Sappho, *κεῖνον*, (scil. *χρυσὸν*) *οὐ σὴς οὐδὲ κὶς δάπτει*. With the sentiment I would compare Philostr. Vit. Apoll. v. 36. *πλοῦτον ἡγοῦ μὴ τὸν ἀπόθετον· τί γὰρ ἂν βελτίων οὗτος τῆς ὁπόθεν συναχθείσης ψάμμου*; Vide et seqq. See also

20 ἀφανίζει, καὶ ὅπου κλέπται διορύσσουσι καὶ κλέπτουσι· θησαυρίζετε 1 Tim. 6. 6, 9, 18, 19.
δὲ ὑμῖν θησαυροὺς ἐν οὐρανῷ, ὅπου οὔτε σὴς οὔτε βρῶσις ἀφανίζει, Heb. 13, 5.
21 καὶ ὅπου κλέπται οὐ διορύσσουσιν οὐδὲ κλέπτουσιν. ὅπου γάρ ἐστιν
22 ὁ θησαυρὸς ὑμῶν, ἐκεῖ ἔσται καὶ ἡ καρδία ὑμῶν. [h] Ὁ λύχνος τοῦ h Luke 11. 34.
σώματός ἐστιν ὁ ὀφθαλμός. ἐὰν οὖν ὁ ὀφθαλμός σου ἁπλοῦς ᾖ, ὅλον
23 τὸ σῶμά σου φωτεινὸν ἔσται· ἐὰν δὲ ὁ ὀφθαλμός σου πονηρὸς ᾖ,
ὅλον τὸ σῶμά σου σκοτεινὸν ἔσται. εἰ οὖν τὸ φῶς τὸ ἐν σοὶ σκότος
24 ἐστὶ, τὸ σκότος πόσον! [i] Οὐδεὶς δύναται δυσὶ κυρίοις δουλεύειν· ἢ i Luke 16. 13.
γὰρ τὸν ἕνα μισήσει, καὶ τὸν ἕτερον ἀγαπήσει· ἢ ἑνὸς ἀνθέξεται, καὶ
τοῦ ἑτέρου καταφρονήσει. οὐ δύνασθε Θεῷ δουλεύειν καὶ * μαμωνᾷ.
25 [k] Διὰ τοῦτο λέγω ὑμῖν· μὴ μεριμνᾶτε τῇ ψυχῇ ὑμῶν, τί φάγητε καὶ k Luke 12. 22. Phil. 4. 6.
τί πίητε· μηδὲ τῷ σώματι ὑμῶν, τί ἐνδύσησθε. Οὐχὶ ἡ ψυχὴ πλεῖόν 1 Tim. 6. 8. 1 Pet. 5. 7. Psal. 55. 22.
26 ἐστι τῆς τροφῆς, καὶ τὸ σῶμα τοῦ ἐνδύματος; [l] Ἐμβλέψατε εἰς τὰ l Job 38. 41. Psal. 147. 9.
πετεινὰ τοῦ οὐρανοῦ· ὅτι οὐ σπείρουσιν, οὐδὲ θερίζουσιν, οὐδὲ συνά- Luke 12. 24.
γουσιν εἰς ἀποθήκας· καὶ ὁ πατὴρ ὑμῶν ὁ οὐράνιος τρέφει αὐτά.
27 οὐχ ὑμεῖς μᾶλλον διαφέρετε αὐτῶν; Τίς δὲ ἐξ ὑμῶν μεριμνῶν δύνα-

Philo. p. 116. A. cited by me in Rec. Syn.— Ἀφανίζει is for διαφθείρει.

— διορύσσουσι] scil. τὸν τοῖχον, which word, or οἰκίαν, is generally *supplied*. The walls in the East being chiefly of hardened clay, the houses are very liable to be thus broken into. On the general scope and interpretation of vv. 19 and 20, see Horne's Introd. iii. 406. 383. and 452.

22. ὁ λύχνος τοῦ σώματος &c.] It has been usual to interpret ὀφθαλμὸς ἁπλοῦς "a liberal person;" and ὀφθαλμὸς πονηρὸς, "a covetous eye;" which has been thought to be required by the preceding and following words. And several phrases in the Sept. the N. T., and the Rabbinical writers are adduced, to countenance this mode of interpretation. Yet it involves some confusion; and the words ἐὰν οὖν — φῶς may be better taken, (with Chrysost., Theophyl., Euthym., and others among the antients, and most of the recent Commentators) in their *proper* sense; so that ἁπλοῦς be interpreted *sanus, integer, clear*, and πονηρὸς, depraved, sickly, dim; of which signification many examples are adduced by Kypke, and Elsner. By τὸ φῶς ἐν σοὶ is meant the light of conscience.— So, among the passages cited by the Commentators, Philo, ὅπερ νοῦς ἐν ψυχῇ, τοῦτο ὀφθαλμὸς ἐν σώματι, borrowed from Aristot. Topic. i. 14.— Hence may be defended and illustrated a supposed corrupt, and certainly obscure, expression in Æschyl. Eumen. 520. Schutz. Τίς δὲ μηδὲν ἐν φάει Καρδίας ἀνατρέφων, Ἢ πόλις βροτὸς θ', ὁμοίως ἔτ' ἂν σέβοι δίκαν; so the passage should be pointed. It has been well observed by Olearius, that the whole passage is *adagial*; of which the *first* part forms the *adage* itself: "The eye is the light of the body." 2. The *deduction*, by consequence; "If then thine eye be healthy and clear," &c. 3. The *application*: "If therefore the light (or what *should* be so) in thee be darkness, how great must be that darkness."

24. οὐδεὶς — δουλεύειν.] It is *implied* by the context, that the two masters are of contrary dispositions, and give contrary orders. The words μισεῖν and ἀγαπᾷν may be taken in a qualified sense, as denoting to *love less*, or *love more*; of which there are many examples both in the Sept. and the N. T. Ἀντέχεσθαι is a stronger term than ἀγαπᾷν, as denoting close connection and strict attachment. The difference here between the Classical and Scriptural use is, that in the former ἀντέχεσθαι is used with a Genit. of *thing*, not as here of *person*. The reason assigned by Middlet. for the omission of the Article at ἑνὸς is inadmissible. It seems to have been omitted simply because, having been employed in the other clause of the antithesis, it might be omitted without occasioning mistake. This could not have been done at τοῦ ἑτέρου, for a reason which will apply to the English as well as the Greek.

— μαμωνᾷ.] This reading is found in most of the MSS. and many Greek Fathers; the Edit. Prin. and several early Editions; and is confirmed by the parallel passage of Luke, and by its derivation from the Chaldee and Syriac ממונא. It has been received by Wets., Griesb., Matthæi, Vater, Fritz., and Scholz. The word in Chaldee and Syriac signifies *riches*; but, like the Greek πλοῦτος, is here *personified*. As to its being a god of the Chaldees, corresponding to the Greek Plutus, that has been rather *asserted* than *proved*.

25. μὴ μεριμνᾶτε.] Not, "take no thought;" but, "take no anxious thought," "be not anxiously solicitous;" as Phil. iv. 6. μηδὲν μεριμνᾶτε, "be anxious about nothing." And so in the parallel passage of Luke μὴ μετεωρίζεσθε, "be not tossed with anxious cares." ψυχῇ and σώματι are datives *of cause*. The argument is: "If God has given us life and bodies, surely he will not deny us the lesser blessings of food and clothing."

26. τὰ πετεινὰ τοῦ οὐρανοῦ] עוף השמים. This is supposed to be a Hebraism; since to the names of animals the Hebrews were accustomed to subjoin the places in which they usually lived. It was not, however, *confined* to the Hebrew, but occurs in the earliest Greek phraseology. So Hom. Il. p. 675. ὑπουρανίων πετεινῶν. and Eurip. Elect. 897. ἢ σκῦλον οἰωνοῖσιν αἰθέρος τέκνοις.

— καί, *and yet*, is called a Hebraism; but is also a Grecism. It my, however, here have the more usual force of *but*. Μᾶλλον is not redundant, but an emphatic addition. So Thucyd. iv. 3. χωρίον διάφορον (*excellent*,) μᾶλλον ἑτέρου.

ται προσθεῖναι ἐπὶ τὴν ἡλικίαν αὐτοῦ πῆχυν ἕνα; Καὶ περὶ ἐνδύμα- 28
τος τί μεριμνᾶτε; καταμάθετε τὰ κρίνα τοῦ ἀγροῦ, πῶς αὐξάνει· οὐ
κοπιᾷ, οὐδὲ νήθει· λέγω δὲ ὑμῖν, ὅτι οὐδὲ Σολομὼν ἐν πάσῃ τῇ δόξῃ 29
αὐτοῦ περιεβάλετο ὡς ἓν τούτων. Εἰ δὲ τὸν χόρτον τοῦ ἀγροῦ, σήμε- 30
ρον ὄντα καὶ αὔριον εἰς κλίβανον βαλλόμενον, ὁ Θεὸς οὕτως ἀμφιέννυ-
σιν, οὐ πολλῷ μᾶλλον ὑμᾶς, ὀλιγόπιστοι; Μὴ οὖν μεριμνήσητε, λέ- 31
γοντες· τί φάγωμεν, ἢ τί πίωμεν, ἢ τί περιβαλώμεθα; πάντα γὰρ 32
ταῦτα τὰ ἔθνη ἐπιζητεῖ· οἶδε γὰρ ὁ πατὴρ ὑμῶν ὁ οὐράνιος ὅτι
m Luke 12. 33. χρῄζετε τούτων ἁπάντων. [m] Ζητεῖτε δὲ πρῶτον τὴν βασιλείαν τοῦ Θεοῦ 33
καὶ τὴν δικαιοσύνην αὐτοῦ, καὶ ταῦτα πάντα προστεθήσεται ὑμῖν.
Μὴ οὖν μεριμνήσητε εἰς τὴν αὔριον· ἡ γὰρ αὔριον μεριμνήσει τὰ 34
a Luke 6. 37, 38. Psal. 41. 2. Rom. 2. 1. & 14. 3, 4, 10, 13. 1 Cor. 4. 3, 4, 5. James 4. 11, 12. Mark 4. 24. b Luke 6. 41.
ἑαυτῆς. ἀρκετὸν τῇ ἡμέρᾳ ἡ κακία αὐτῆς.
VII. [a] ΜΗ κρίνετε, ἵνα μὴ κριθῆτε. ἐν ᾧ γὰρ κρίματι κρίνετε, 1
κριθήσεσθε· καὶ ἐν ᾧ μέτρῳ μετρεῖτε, * μετρηθήσεται ὑμῖν. [b] Τί δὲ 2
βλέπεις τὸ κάρφος τὸ ἐν τῷ ὀφθαλμῷ τοῦ ἀδελφοῦ σου, τὴν δὲ ἐν 3

27. ἡλικίαν.] The antient Commentators, and most modern ones, take this to mean, *stature*; which sense is ably maintained by Beza, Grot., Elsn., and Fritz. Yet they only prove that it *might* be so taken, if a better sense were not at hand; namely, that of *ætatis mensura*. Now this is surely more appropriate; for the admonition is directed against excessive anxiety about food and clothing; which, though necessary to the preservation of life, have nothing in common with *stature*. And πῆχυς, like other measures of extent, is not unfrequently applied to duration of *time*. Those, however, who support this interpretation are not agreed as to the *nature of the metaphor*. Most think there is an allusion to the allegorical fable of the Parcæ; while Wets. supposes it alludes to a *stadium* or race-course, of which, as consisting of several hundred cubits, *one* cubit might not unaptly be termed ἐλάχιστον.

28. καταμάθετε] "attentively survey." The κατὰ is intensive, as in κατανοήσατε, Luke xii. 27. Κοπιᾷ and νήθει refer to the occupations of males and of females respectively.

29. δόξῃ] "splendour." A sense frequent in the Sept. and New Testament; but scarcely ever occurring in the Classical writers.

30. χόρτον.] The Hebrews divided all vegetables into two sorts, עץ and עשב, *trees*, and plants or herbs; the former of which were by the Hellenists called ξύλον; the latter, χόρτος; comprehending both grass and corn, and likewise *flowers*, including the lilies just mentioned, supposed to be the plant called the Crown Imperial.—From scarcity of fuel, all the withered stalks, even of the herbage, are in the East employed for that purpose. (Grot. and A. Clarke.)

31. τὰ ἔθνη ἐπιζητεῖ.] A kind of argument often made use of in the O. T., in order, as it were, to *shame* the Israelites into virtue, by showing them that they lived no better than the unenlightened heathens. That *they* should have eagerly sought after such things, was not wonderful; since they had no belief in, or dependence on the Providence of God; and in their labours, or their prayers to the gods, solely regarded *temporal* blessings; as we find from Juvenal, Sat. x.

— οἶδε γὰρ — ἁπάντων.] Our Lord here argues from God's *knowledge*, to his *goodness*. Your heavenly Father *knoweth*, and therefore will bestow them; i. e. on the supposition that ye *ask* for them, and are not otherwise *unfit* to receive them. (Markland.)

33. τὴν βασιλείαν τοῦ Θεοῦ] i. e. the religion promulgated by God, its promises and blessedness. On the full sense of this comprehensive expression, see a Dissertation of Storr, translated into English, and inserted in Vol. I. of the American Biblical Repository.

— τὴν δικαιοσύνην α.] i. e. that mode of justification which he hath revealed, and the righteousness and holiness which it requires; not that righteousness or system of morality which the Jews had devised, consisting chiefly of ceremonies and mere externals.

34. εἰς τὴν αὔριον.] Sub. ἡμέραν. Most Commentators take εἰς τὴν αὔριον for τὰ εἰς τὴν αὔριον. But that is unnecessary. The εἰς may very well denote *object*. Αὔριον is taken for time to come in general.

— ἀρκετὸν — αὐτῆς.] These, like the words immediately preceding, have the air of an adage, similar to some adduced by Vorst. and Schoettg. The neuter in ἀρκετὸν is put, by an idiom common both to the Greek and Latin. And χρῆμα or πρᾶγμα is understood. See Matth. Gr. Gr. § 439.

— τῇ ἡμέρᾳ.] Some Commentators supply ἑκάστῃ. But it is better to suppose the Article used with reference to παρούσῃ, "*the* (present) day." Κακία is well explained by Chrys. κάκωσις. ταλαιπωρία; a sense found in the Sept., but not in the Classical writers.

VII. 1. μὴ κρίνετε — κριθῆτε.] Almost all Commentators take κρίνετε for κατακρίνετε, chiefly because in the parallel passage of Luke vi. 37. μὴ καταδικάζετε καὶ οὐ μὴ καταδικασθῆτε is added. But Fritz. (perhaps with reason) perfers the interpertation of Chrysost., by which κρίνετε is taken of sitting in judgment over others acting as severe censors of their faults. And καταδικάζω may be understood in the same way, but only in a stronger sense. One thing is certain, that *forensic* judgment cannot here be included.

2. ἐν ᾧ γὰρ κρίματι.] The ἐν is thought to be redundant. But it rather answers to the

4 τῷ σῷ ὀφθαλμῷ δοκὸν οὐ κατανοεῖς; Ἢ πῶς ἐρεῖς τῷ ἀδελφῷ σου·
Ἄφες, ἐκβάλω τὸ κάρφος ἀπὸ τοῦ ὀφθαλμοῦ σου. καὶ ἰδοὺ, ἡ δοκὸς
5 ἐν τῷ ὀφθαλμῷ σου; Ὑποκριτά! ἔκβαλε πρῶτον τὴν δοκὸν ἐκ τοῦ
ὀφθαλμοῦ σοῦ, καὶ τότε διαβλέψεις ἐκβαλεῖν τὸ κάρφος ἐκ τοῦ ὀφθαλ-
6 μοῦ τοῦ ἀδελφοῦ σου. Μὴ δῶτε τὸ ἅγιον τοῖς κυσί· μηδὲ βάλητε
τοὺς μαργαρίτας ὑμῶν ἔμπροσθεν τῶν χοίρων· μήποτε καταπατήσωσιν
7 αὐτοὺς ἐν τοῖς ποσὶν αὐτῶν, καὶ στραφέντες ῥήξωσιν ὑμᾶς. [c] Αἰτεῖτε, c Infr. 21. 22. Mark 11. 24.
καὶ δοθήσεται ὑμῖν· ζητεῖτε, καὶ εὑρήσετε· κρούετε, καὶ ἀνοιγήσεται Luke 11. 9. John 14. 13.
8 ὑμῖν. πᾶς γὰρ ὁ αἰτῶν λαμβάνει, καὶ ὁ ζητῶν εὑρίσκει, καὶ τῷ κρού- & 15. 7. & 16. 23. James 1. 5, 6.
9 οντι ἀνοιγήσεται. [d] Ἢ τίς ἐστιν ἐξ ὑμῶν ἄνθρωπος, ὃν ἐὰν αἰτήσῃ 1 John 3. 22. d Luke 11. 11.
10 ὁ υἱὸς αὐτοῦ ἄρτον, μὴ λίθον ἐπιδώσει αὐτῷ; καὶ ἐὰν ἰχθὺν αἰτήσῃ,
11 μὴ ὄφιν ἐπιδώσει αὐτῷ; Εἰ οὖν ὑμεῖς, πονηροὶ ὄντες, οἴδατε δόματα e Luke 6. 31.
ἀγαθὰ διδόναι τοῖς τέκνοις ὑμῶν, πόσῳ μᾶλλον ὁ πατὴρ ὑμῶν ὁ ἐν Tob. 4. 15. Matt. 22. 40. Rom. 13. 8, 10.
12 τοῖς οὐρανοῖς, δώσει ἀγαθὰ τοῖς αἰτοῦσιν αὐτόν! [e] Πάντα οὖν ὅσα Gal. 5. 14. 1 Tim. 1. 5.

Heb. ב, or, as Fritz. thinks, is to be taken in the sense *per*. See Matth. Gr. Gr. p. 842. Instead of ἀντιμετρηθήσεται, μετρηθ. is received by the unanimous consent of all Editors from Mill to Fritz. and Scholz. The other was doubtless derived from the parallel passage of Luke.

3. τί δὲ βλέπεις] I would render "*how* beholdest thou," "how is it that thou," &c. See ante supra, v. 25, and a Rabbinical writer cited by Wets. on Luke vi. 19. Nearly the same with πῶς in the next verse. Κάρφος is rightly explained by Grot., Brug., Kuin., and others on (the authority, of Hesych. and Suid,) *splinter*. So the Latin tuberæ and verrucæ, as we say *straws*, opposed to δοκὸν, *beam*. There is reference to a proverb of frequent use with the Jews, against those who, severe upon the slight offences of others, were-insensible of their own crimes. Many similar sayings are adduced both from the Rabbinical and Classical writers. See Horat. Sat. i. 3. 25.

4. ἄφες, ἐκβάλω.] The commentators usually supply ἵνα. To this, however, Fritz. with reason objects, as unnecessary; and compares the Latin *permitte, eximam*. The Article in ἡ δοκὸς refers to the beam, as just mentioned. See Winer's Gr. § 53. and compare Æschyl. Eum. 78, and Agam. 243, cited and explained by me on Thucyd. ii. 39. *Transl.*

6. μὴ δῶτε—χοίρων.] Lest any one should suppose *all* liberty taken away of judging even concerning matters the most manifest, Christ subjoins a precept fraught with that prudence, which he elsewhere directs to be joined with simplicity. (Grot.) Here again we have two adagial sayings. Similar ones are adduced from the Rabbinical, and even the Classical writers, to which may be added the following from Aristot. ap. Themist. p. 234. μήτε ῥίψαι σοφίαν εἰς τοὺς τριόδους. By *dogs* and *swine* are meant those profane and sensual persons, who were so refractory, and devoted to the lusts of the flesh, that so far from receiving the truth, when proposed to them, they resisted and blasphemed it, and impeded the prevalence of it. By τὸ ἅγιον is meant *the doctrine of the Gospel*. From the Rabbinical writers it appears, that the Jews called the precepts of wisdom *pearls*. And our Lord more than once compares the truths (especially the more recondite ones) of the Gospel to the same. See Matt. xiii. 46.

—μήποτε καταπατήσωσιν—ὑμᾶς.] Many Commentators take καταπ. of the *swine*, and στραφέντες ῥήξωσιν of the *dogs*, per Chiasmum. This, however, is so harsh, that it is better, with Erasm., Pric., Wets., and Fritz.) to refer *both* to the swine; στραφέντες having reference to the *oblique* direction in which hogs make their attack. Ἐν τοῖς ποσὶν αὐτῶν is usually rendered *inter pedes, under foot*; but by Fritz., "suis pedibus."

7. αἰτεῖτε—ὑμῖν.] The same thing is expressed in three seemingly proverbial forms. At κρούετε sub. τὴν θύραν, in which term as well as ἀνοίγειν the ellipsis was common.

8. ὁ αἰτῶν.] Namely, *aright*. ὁ ζητῶν, i. e. what is expedient and proper. Τῷ κρούοντι, i. e. who earnestly, and with faith addresses himself in prayer. Ἀνοιγήσεται, "It will be opened." The sense here nearly that of the *present*, used to denote *custom*.

9. ἢ τίς—ἄνθρωπος.] The ἢ is thought by Fritz. to denote *contrariety*, but it has rather the *illustrative* force; when what follows is meant to illustrate the foregoing by *another* view of the subject As to the τίς, Elsn. and Fritz. rightly suppose an *anacoluthon*, by which two interrogations are blended; thus "an quis est e vobis homo, quem, si filius panem poposcerit, num forte lapidem ei porrigat?" Ἄνθρωπος (the best Commentators, ancient and modern, are agreed) is *emphatical*, "making (as Campb. says) the illustration of the goodness of the celestial Father, from the conduct of even human fathers, with all their imperfections, much more energetic."

11. πονηροί.] The ancients, and, of the moderns, Grot., Elsn., and Schoettg., explained this *evil, corrupt*; the recent Commentators, *avaricious*. But for the latter sense there is little or no authority, nor indeed propriety. The term is used by way of *comparison* with the celestial Father.

—οἴδατε διδόναι.] Almost all the recent Commentators take this as said, *per periphrasin*, for δίδοτε; and they adduce several passages of the Classical writers, which, however, are not quite to the purpose. It seems better to regard it as a Hebraism, and a stronger expression.

12. πάντα οὖν—προφῆται.] A golden precept,

ἂν θέλητε ἵνα ποιῶσιν ὑμῖν οἱ ἄνθρωποι, οὕτω καὶ ὑμεῖς ποιεῖτε
αὐτοῖς· ‡ οὗτος γάρ ἐστιν ὁ νόμος· καὶ οἱ προφῆται.
f Luke 13. 24. [f] Εἰσέλθετε διὰ τῆς στενῆς πύλης· ὅτι πλατεῖα ἡ πύλη, καὶ εὐρύ- 13
χωρος ἡ ὁδὸς ἡ ἀπάγουσα εἰς τὴν ἀπώλειαν· καὶ πολλοί εἰσιν οἱ
εἰσερχόμενοι δι᾽ αὐτῆς. * Τί στενὴ ἡ πύλη, καὶ τεθλιμμένη ἡ ὁδὸς 14
ἡ ἀπάγουσα εἰς τὴν ζωήν· καὶ ὀλίγοι εἰσὶν οἱ εὑρίσκοντες αὐτήν!
g Micah 3. 5. 2 Tim. 3. 5. [g] Προσέχετε δὲ ἀπὸ τῶν ψευδοπροφητῶν, οἵτινες ἔρχονται πρὸς ὑμᾶς 15
ἐν ἐνδύμασι προβάτων, ἔσωθεν δέ εἰσι λύκοι ἅρπαγες. Ἀπὸ τῶν καρ- 16
πῶν αὐτῶν ἐπιγνώσεσθε αὐτούς. μήτι συλλέγουσιν ἀπὸ ἀκανθῶν στα-
h Luke 8. 9. 6. 43, 44. infr. 12. 33. φυλὴν, ἢ ἀπὸ τριβόλων σῦκα; [h] Οὕτω πᾶν δένδρον ἀγαθὸν καρποὺς 17
καλοὺς ποιεῖ· τὸ δὲ σαπρὸν δένδρον καρποὺς πονηροὺς ποιεῖ. Οὐ 18
δύναται δένδρον ἀγαθὸν καρποὺς πονηροὺς ποιεῖν, οὐδὲ δένδρον σα-
i Supr. 3. 10. John. 15. 2, 6. πρὸν καρποὺς καλοὺς ποιεῖν. [i] (Πᾶν δένδρον μὴ ποιοῦν καρπὸν κα- 19
λὸν ἐκκόπτεται, καὶ εἰς πῦρ βάλλεται.) ἄραγε ἀπὸ τῶν καρπῶν αὐτῶν 20
ἐπιγνώσεσθε αὐτούς.

familiar to the Jews, and not unknown to the Gentiles, as the Philological Commentators have shown. The οὖν is by some thought *transitive*; by others *resumptive*. To ὅσα ἂν θέλητε οὕτω Fritz. strongly objects; urging that οὕτω would require ὡς ἄν; and he cancels the οὕτως. Here, however, we have *popular* diction; to alter which were uncritical. More may be said for the οὕτως, which he edits, with Matth., (from the Edit. Princ., and some MSS. and Versions) for οὗτος, just after. Yet the cannon of preferring the more difficult reading must induce us to retain οὗτος. The sense is, "This is the sum and substance of what is contained in the law and the prophets on the relative duties of men."

13. εἰσέλθετε] "strive to enter," (as in the parallel passage at Luke xiii. 24.) namely, εἰς τὴν ζωήν. The course of human action is *often* called in Scripture דרך ὁδός; and consequently, from the restraints and difficulties of virtue, its road is termed *strait*; as that of vice, *broad*. Here, however, the comparison is to a *gate* opening into a *road* leading up to a citadel. Similar comparisons and parallel sentiments are found in the Heathen writers, as cited by Wets. See also Recens. Synop. The τῆς implies *another* gate, leading to the broad road, which we are not to enter. The sense of the passage is this: "Aim at entering in at *the strait* gate: though there be a gate that is wide, and the way to it broad, and many are travelling along it; yet it leads to perdition; therefore take it not. And though there be a gate that is strait, and the way to it narrow, and few are they that travel thereto; yet take it, for it leads to life and eternal happiness."

14. τί στενή.] It is scarcely possible to imagine stronger evidence than what there is for this reading; which has been received by all the most eminent Editors. The common reading ὅτι may, indeed, be tolerated, in the sense *sed*; but Erasmus, from whom Stephens derived it, had little or no authority for it. Whereas τί is supported by the great body of the MSS., all the best Versions, Chrys., Theophyl., and Euthym., and the Ed. Princ. The sense, then, is, "How narrow is the gate!" Ἀπάγουσα. Ἄγειν is the regular term; yet ἀπαγ. occurs in a similar passage of Cebes, p. 14.

— οἱ εὑρίσκοντες.] Schleusn. explains *consequuntur*: a frequent use of the word. The expression seems meant to suggest the difficulty and exertion necessary to attain it.

15. προσέχετε δὲ ἀπὸ τῶν ψευδοπροφητῶν.] The full meaning is, "I have exhorted you to enter in by the strait gate. But beware of false guides." (Newcome.) Προσέχειν, when followed by ἀπό τινος (with which Kuin. compares the Heb. שמר מן) is equivalent to φοβεῖσθαι ἀπό τινος. It occurs several times in the Sept., but never in the Classical writers. Ἑαυτοῖς seems to be understood, which is *expressed* at Luke xvii. 3.

— ψευδοπροφ.] This is variously understood; but it is best taken for ψευδοδιδάσκαλοι. See 2 Pet. ii. 1. Προφήτης and προφητεύειν, in the sense *teacher* and *teach*, being common. Some think the ψευδ. in ψευδοπροφ. has reference to their *doctrines*; others, to their *lives*. *Both* may be supposed.

— ἐν ἐνδύμασι προβάτων.] Ἐν, like the Hebr. ב and the Latin *in*, and our in, is often used with verbs of clothing, to denote the *material* of which the clothing is formed. Ἐνδύμασι προβάτων has reference to the μηλωτὴ (sheep-skin, or sometimes a cloak made of the fleece roughly worked up) with which the false prophets clothed themselves, and, as it seems, the false teachers among the Pharisees.

16. καρπῶν] i. e. "manners and actions." A frequent figure. See Matt. iii. 8. I would compare Thucyd. v. 26. τοῖς γὰρ ἔργοις ἀθρήσει καὶ εὑρήσει. In μήτι συλλέγουσιν, &c. there is a sort of adagial illustration, found also in Theogn. 537.

17. σαπρόν.] The word denotes *primarily* what is *decayed* and *rotten*; but 2dly, by metonymy, what is *refuse* and *worthless*, (as old vessels, and small fishes) also, when applied to trees or fruit, what is of a *bad quality*. The passages adduced by Wets. will illustrate all these senses.

19. Some Critics are of opinion that this verse is introduced, by interpolation, from Matt. iii. 10. The objection, however, that it impedes the course of reasoning, will be lessened, if we consider it as an awful admonition incidentally thrown in. See Newcome.

20. ἄραγε.] Some Commentators take it for πάντως, *profecto*. But there is no reason to aban

21 [k] Οὐ πᾶς ὁ λέγων μοι, Κύριε, Κύριε, εἰσελεύσεται εἰς τὴν βασιλείαν k Hos. 8. 2. Luke 6. 46.
τῶν οὐρανῶν· ἀλλ᾽ ὁ ποιῶν τὸ θέλημα τοῦ πατρός μου τοῦ ἐν οὐρα- Rom. 2. 13. James 1. 22.
22 νοῖς. Πολλοὶ ἐροῦσί μοι ἐν ἐκείνῃ τῇ ἡμέρᾳ· Κύριε, Κύριε, οὐ τῷ
σῷ ὀνόματι προεφητεύσαμεν, καὶ τῷ σῷ ὀνόματι δαιμόνια ἐξεβάλομεν,
23 καὶ τῷ σῷ ὀνόματι δυνάμεις πολλὰς ἐποιήσαμεν; [l] Καὶ τότε ὁμολο- l Luke 13. 26, 27.
γήσω αὐτοῖς· ὅτι οὐδέποτε ἔγνων ὑμᾶς· ἀποχωρεῖτε ἀπ᾽ ἐμοῦ οἱ ἐργα- 1 Cor. 13. 2. infr. 25. 12, 41.
24 ζόμενοι τὴν ἀνομίαν. [m] Πᾶς οὖν ὅστις ἀκούει μου τοὺς λόγους τού- m Luke 6. 47.
τους, καὶ ποιεῖ αὐτούς, ὁμοιώσω αὐτὸν ἀνδρὶ φρονίμῳ, ὅστις ᾠκοδό-
25 μησε τὴν οἰκίαν αὐτοῦ ἐπὶ τὴν πέτραν· καὶ κατέβη ἡ βροχὴ, καὶ
ἦλθον οἱ ποταμοὶ, καὶ ἔπνευσαν οἱ ἄνεμοι, καὶ προσέπεσον τῇ οἰκίᾳ
26 ἐκείνῃ, καὶ οὐκ ἔπεσε· τεθεμελίωτο γὰρ ἐπὶ τὴν πέτραν. Καὶ πᾶς
ὁ ἀκούων μου τοὺς λόγους τούτους καὶ μὴ ποιῶν αὐτούς, ὁμοιωθήσεται ἀνδρὶ μωρῷ, ὅστις ᾠκοδόμησε τὴν οἰκίαν αὐτοῦ ἐπὶ τὴν ἄμμον·
27 καὶ κατέβη ἡ βροχὴ, καὶ ἦλθον οἱ ποταμοὶ, καὶ ἔπνευσαν οἱ ἄνεμοι,
καὶ προσέκοψαν τῇ οἰκίᾳ ἐκείνῃ, καὶ ἔπεσε· καὶ ἦν ἡ πτῶσις αὐτῆς
28 μεγάλη. [n] Καὶ ἐγένετο, ὅτε συνετέλεσεν ὁ Ἰησοῦς τοὺς λόγους τούτους, n Mark. 1. 22. Luke 4. 32.
29 ἐξεπλήσσοντο οἱ ὄχλοι ἐπὶ τῇ διδαχῇ αὐτοῦ· ἦν γὰρ διδάσκων αὐτοὺς
ὡς ἐξουσίαν ἔχων, καὶ οὐχ ὡς οἱ Γραμματεῖς.

don the common interpretation, *itaque, ergo*. The Particle is *conclusive*, as in Matt. xvii. 26. xi. 18. The ἄρα is *illative*, and the γε *limitative*. See Herm. on Viger, p. 821 & 825.

21. οὐ πᾶς.] This is taken by the Commentators to mean *no one*. But though that interpretation is sanctioned by Chrys. and Euthym., there seems no sufficient reason to abandon the usual sense of οὐ πᾶς. We have only to suppose the common ellipsis of μόνον with ὁ ποιῶν. The sense is, "Not all, who with the lips acknowledge me as their Lord, will be admitted to the blessings which I come to bestow; but those only who likewise perform what my Father enjoins." Κύριος is here and often elsewhere used for διδάσκαλος, being the name given by the Jews to their Rabbis.

22. ἐν ἐκείνῃ τῇ ἡμέρᾳ] i. e. the day *implied* in the foregoing words; namely, at the period when there will be a final admission or rejection of all persons. In some other passages, however, as Matt. xi. 24, and Luke x. 12, the pronoun may be understood as referring to some day well known; that expression being, as appears from the Rabbinical writers, used emphatically of *the day of judgment*.

—τῷ σῷ ὀνόματι] "by thy power and authority." See Luke ix. 39.

—προεφητεύσαμεν] "have taught and preached the Gospel;" not, however, excluding the ordinary sense *prophesied*; for there is reason to think, that miracles were permitted by God to be worked by men whose lives were at variance with the precepts of the Gospel.

23. ὁμολογήσω αὐτοῖς.] "I will tell them openly and plainly." A signification of which examples are adduced from Ælian, Var. Hist. ii. 4. Herodo. iii. 6.

—οὐδέποτε ἔγνων ὑμᾶς] i. e. "I never recognised you as my servants, or approved you." This is considered a Hebraism; ידע having the sense *approve*. But some examples are adduced by Wets. from Greek writers; not, however, quite to the point. Far more apposite is the example from Isæus adduced by me in Recens Synop. Σὺ δὲ τίς εἶ; σοὶ δὲ τί προσήκει θάπτειν; οὐ γινώσκω σε, (I do not recognise you) οὐ μὴ εἰσίῃς τὴν οἰκίαν.

—ἐργαζόμενοι τὴν ἀνομίαν.] The purity of the Greek is established by a passage of Themist. adduced in Recens. Synop. i. e. οἱ ἐργαζόμενοι ἀρετήν. Ἐργ. is a far stronger term than ποιεῖν, and signifies to do any thing studiously and habitually, to *make a trade of it*. The *Art.* here has an intensive force; q. d. all kinds of iniquity. See Middlet. Gr. A. v. § 2.

24. πᾶς οὖν—αὐτούς.] This is regarded as a Hebrew construction for πάντα οὖν ἀκούοντα—ὁμοιώσω ἀνδρί. But it may be better called a *popular* construction, and a relique of primitive simplicity of diction. Thus it is found in Herodotus, and all unstudied writers and speakers, in every language. The same may be said of ποιεῖ αὐτούς, scil. λόγους, which is a *popular* phrase, to denote "performing my precepts." Ὁμοιώσω is for ὁμοιωθήσεται; or, "I will, may, compare him." Φρονίμῳ, prudent, provident; as in Xen. Œcon. xi. 8. cited by Wets.

—ἐπὶ τὴν πέτραν.] Upon the force of the Art. here and at ἐπὶ τὴν ἄμμον (which, however, cannot well be expressed in a translation) see Middlet. in loc.

25. ἡ βροχή.] This denotes, like the Heb. גשם, a heavy *gush of rain*, and the Art. is used, as commonly with the great objects of nature, both in Greek and English. Ποταμοί, floods or torrents. So χείμαρροι ποταμοί in Homer.

26, 27. Many similar sentiments, especially one of Rabbi Elisha, are adduced by Wets. from the Rabbinical writers.

28. καὶ ἐγένετο ὅτε.] Like the Hebr. ויהי.

—τῇ διδαχῇ.] The word may denote either the *doctrine taught*, or the *manner of teaching*. But the former seems to be the principal sense intended; the latter being only secondary and implied.

29. ἦν διδάσκων] for ἐδίδασκε, as the Commenta-

VIII. *Καταβάντι δὲ αὐτῷ ἀπὸ τοῦ ὄρους, ἠκολούθησαν αὐτῷ* 1
a Mark 1. 40. Luke 5. 12. *ὄχλοι πολλοί·* [a] *καὶ ἰδοὺ, λεπρὸς ἐλθὼν προσεκύνει αὐτῷ λέγων· Κύ-* 2
ριε, ἐὰν θέλῃς, δύνασαί με καθαρίσαι. Καὶ ἐκτείνας τὴν χεῖρα, ἥψατο 3
αὐτοῦ ὁ Ἰησοῦς λέγων· Θέλω, καθαρίσθητι. καὶ εὐθέως ἐκαθαρίσθη
b Lev. 14. 3, 4, 10. *αὐτοῦ ἡ λέπρα.* [b] *Καὶ λέγει αὐτῷ ὁ Ἰησοῦς· Ὅρα μηδενὶ εἴπῃς·* 4
ἀλλ' ὕπαγε, σεαυτὸν δεῖξον τῷ ἱερεῖ, καὶ προσένεγκε τὸ δῶρον ὃ προσ-
έταξε Μωσῆς, εἰς μαρτύριον αὐτοῖς.
c Luke 7. 1. [c] *Εἰσελθόντι δὲ αὐτῷ εἰς Καπερναοὺμ προσῆλθεν αὐτῷ ἑκατόνταρχος* 5
παρακαλῶν αὐτὸν καὶ λέγων· Κύριε, ὁ παῖς μου βέβληται ἐν τῇ οἰκίᾳ 6
παραλυτικὸς, δεινῶς βασανιζόμενος. Καὶ λέγει αὐτῷ ὁ Ἰησοῦς· Ἐγὼ 7

tors say. But the sense seems to be: "he had been teaching," or, "he was teaching then," in reference to the customary and general character of his teaching. See Beza.

— *ὡς ἐξουσίαν ἔχων*] scil. *τοῦ διδάσκειν*, "as one having authority to teach," i. e. self-derived power; not as the Scribes, who rested only on that of their Doctors; as not the *interpreter*, but the *maker* of the law. Several illustrations of the phrase have been adduced by Wets. and others.

VIII. 1. *δέ.*] The particle has here the *transitive* sense, and *αὐτῷ* is redundant, *populariter*.

2. *προσεκύνει.*] This is not, says Whitby, to be taken as denoting an acknowledgment of the Divinity of our Lord; for the term was one expressive of *civil* adoration, and only paid to him as the Messiah, or a prophet sent from God.

— *κύριε.*] A form of address used by the Jews to those with whom they were unacquainted, (see Joh. iv. 19. xii. 21. xx. 15.) as *domine* with the Latins, of which see examples in Wets. Yet as it was used by scholars, when addressing their masters, and was doubtless applied to *Rabbis*, so it may here be taken.

— *ἐὰν θέλῃς, δύνασαι.*] This appears from the examples in Wets. to have been a form of earnest and respectful address, much used by those who sought for relief, especially from physicians.

— *καθαρίσαι.*] A word used peculiarly of healing leprosy, and which has reference to the *legal impurity* supposed to be incurred by the disease, which could only be removed by the cure of the disorder.

3. *ἐκτείνας τὴν χεῖραν.*] There is here neither pleonasm nor Hebraism, as is commonly supposed. Nor is the expression devoid of force; though it may be regarded as a relique of the circumstantiality of antient diction.

— *ἥψατο αὐτοῦ*] i. e. *more Medicorum*, says Wets., who adduces many examples of a similar use of the word. But our Lord seems to have touched the leper, both to inspire him with confidence, (as conceiving that unless with the *power* as well as will to heal him, he would have incurred pollution, and possibly infection) and also to make the bystanders see that the cure was effected by his touch. Our Lord, in most cases, condescended to accompany his words by corresponding actions. As to Jesus's violation of the law, it must be remembered that works performed by Divine virtue were exempted from the ritual precepts.

4. *μηδενὶ εἴπῃς.*] The best Commentators are agreed that the order was only meant to extend to the period when he had presented himself to the Priests, for examination. Considering the great multitude of bystanders, it was impossible to prevent the transaction from being made public; so that the object of the injunction must have been, to keep the officiating priest ignorant of the transaction, that he might not maliciously deny the leper to be perfectly clean; which would disappoint the benevolent object of the miracle. It has been supposed (and not without reason) by some (as Lightf. and Newcome) that this transaction is placed here by the Evangelist (for certain reasons) out of its proper chronological order.

— *εἰς μαρτύριον αὐτοῖς.*] It has been debated whether *αὐτοῖς* has reference to the *priest* (i. e. the priests; *ἱερεῖ* being taken distributively) or to the *people*. Though there is some harshness in the latter mode, (since the antecedent does not exist in the preceding context); yet propriety requires it; for the offering could be no testimony to the *priests*. It may, however, be understood of *both*.

5. *προσῆλθεν αὐτῷ ἑκατόνταρχος.*] The best Commentators are agreed that, from the striking similarity of circumstances between this transaction and that recorded at Luke vii. 1., they must be the same. The points of difference, they think, are very reconcilable; *παῖς* being both in the Classical and Hellenistic Greek often used for *δοῦλος*, servant; like *puer* in Latin, and used because such kind of services as are performed by our *footmen* or *valets*, was originally rendered by *boys*. Hence the name was afterwards retained, when a change was made in the person. And as to the Centurion here being said to solicit for *himself* what in Luke he entreats through the medium of his *friends*, it may be observed, that the Jews, and in some measure the Greeks and Romans, were accustomed to represent what was done by any one for another, as done by the person himself. See Mark x. 15. compared with Matt. xx. 20. And though Matthew does not tell us that he was a proselyte (as does Luke), yet he says nothing to the contrary. See Grot., Lightf., Kuin., and Fritz.

6. *βέβληται.*] A term appropriate to sick persons confined to their couch. Whether it be rendered *decubuit*, with Kuin., or *lecto affixus est*, with Fritz., the sense is the same.

— *βασανιζόμενος.*] It is debated whether this should be rendered *tortured* or *afflicted*. For palsies, whether attended with contraction, or remission of the nerves, do not, they say, occasion any great pain. Yet it has been proved that, in *one* stage of the disorder, the patient suffers great agony; as also when it passes into apoplexy. The word is rarely found beyond the Scriptural writers, except in Joseph. and Philo.

8 ἐλθὼν θεραπεύσω αὐτόν. [d] Καὶ ἀποκριθεὶς ὁ ἑκατόνταρχος ἔφη· [d Luke 18. 10, 21.]
Κύριε, οὐκ εἰμὶ ἱκανὸς ἵνα μου ὑπὸ τὴν στέγην εἰσέλθῃς· ἀλλὰ μόνον LU.
9 εἰπὲ λόγῳ, καὶ ἰαθήσεται ὁ παῖς μου. καὶ γὰρ ἐγὼ ἄνθρωπός εἰμι 7.
ὑπὸ ἐξουσίαν, ἔχων ὑπ᾽ ἐμαυτὸν στρατιώτας· καὶ λέγω τούτῳ· Πορεύθητι, καὶ πορεύεται· καὶ ἄλλῳ· Ἔρχου, καὶ ἔρχεται· καὶ τῷ δούλῳ
10 μου· Ποίησον τοῦτο, καὶ ποιεῖ. Ἀκούσας δὲ ὁ Ἰησοῦς ἐθαύμασε, 9
καὶ εἶπε τοῖς ἀκολουθοῦσιν· Ἀμὴν λέγω ὑμῖν· οὐδὲ ἐν τῷ Ἰσραὴλ
11 τοσαύτην πίστιν εὗρον. Λέγω δὲ ὑμῖν, ὅτι πολλοὶ ἀπὸ ἀνατολῶν καὶ
δυσμῶν ἥξουσι, καὶ ἀνακλιθήσονται μετὰ Ἀβραὰμ καὶ Ἰσαὰκ καὶ
12 Ἰακὼβ ἐν τῇ βασιλείᾳ τῶν οὐρανῶν· οἱ δὲ υἱοὶ τῆς βασιλείας ἐκβλη-
θήσονται εἰς τὸ σκότος τὸ ἐξώτερον· ἐκεῖ ἔσται ὁ κλαυθμὸς καὶ ὁ
13 βρυγμὸς τῶν ὀδόντων. Καὶ εἶπεν ὁ Ἰησοῦς τῷ * ἑκατοντάρχῃ· Ὕπαγε, 10

8. ἱκανὸς] for ἄξιος, as in Joh. i. 27. and Matt. iii. 11. The full force of this expression will depend upon whether he was a proselyte, or a heathen. It is not, however, necessary to refine so much as the Commentators have done. We may regard the words as constituting a formula expressive of profound humility.

—λόγῳ.] On this reading and αὐτοῦ, all the Editors from Mill downwards are, with reason, agreed. The two readings are found in the best and greater part of the MSS., Versions, Fathers, and the earliest Editions. As to the vulg. τὸν λόγον and τῷ Ἰησοῦ, they were introduced on slender authority by Erasm. The τῷ Ἰ. is evidently from the margin; and τὸν λόγον arose partly from a confusion of the ν and ι adscript; and partly from an ignorance of the phrase εἰπεῖν λόγῳ, which is like the Latin *verbo dicere*, and our *say at a word*; here, *give order by a word*. Finally εἰπεῖν λόγῳ occurs in the parallel passage of Luke.

9. ἄνθρωπός εἰμι ὑπὸ ἐξουσίαν.] Sub. τασσόμενος, which is *expressed* at Luke vii. 8. and Diod. Sic. cited by Munthe. The sense is *not* what some Commentators maintain, "I am a man *holding* authority;" (for that would require ἐπ᾽ ἐξουσίας,) but (as the parallel passage of Luke requires) "I am a man placed under authority," viz. the authority of my superior officer. See Lennep, cited by Scheid. Etymol. 771. This is an argument *a minori ad majus*; q. d. "I who hold but a subordinate office, can order my soldiers and servants, who obey *at a word*; much *more* canst thou, who hast supernatural power, cure disorders at thy fiat." The words following are highly appropriate, and even graphical.

10. ἐν τῷ Ἰσραὴλ] i. e. "the people of Israel;" as often in the Scriptures. But there is not, as some suppose, an *ellipsis* of λαῷ, or οἴκῳ.

—πίστιν.] The word here denotes faith in its general sense; namely, a firm reliance on the *power* of Jesus to work the miracle in question; a persuasion supposed to have originated in the cure of the nobleman's son, at Cana, only a day's journey distant.

11. πολλοί.] Namely the Gentiles; for they were such, as compared with the υἱοὶ τῆς βασιλείας, the Jews.

—ἀπὸ ἀνατολῶν καὶ δυσμῶν.] Luke adds ἀπὸ Βοῤῥᾶ καὶ Νότου. The expression (denoting from all parts of the world) is frequent both in the Scriptural and Classical writers. Grot. thinks that there is a reference to the promise made to Jacob, Gen. xxviii. 14.

—ἀνακλιθήσονται.] A convivial term, like ἀνακεῖσθαι, κατακεῖσθαι, κατακλίνεσθαι, and others, adapted to the Oriental custom of *reclining*, not *sitting*, at table; on which see Horne's Intr. Both the Scriptural, Rabbinical, and Classical writers (adapting their language to the ordinary conceptions of men) represent the joys of heaven under the image of a *banquet*; and consequently with imagery suited thereto. [*Comp.* Luke xiii. 28, 29. Mal. i. 11.]

12. υἱοὶ τῆς βασιλείας.] Scil. τοῦ Θεοῦ, i. e. the Israelites, for whom the happiness of that kingdom was especially destined; and who had arrogated to themselves a place there, to the exclusion of other nations. Kuin. remarks that υἱὸς like the Heb. בן, is used to denote a person holding some kind of property in the thing signified by the noun in the Genit., with which it is joined; as Luke x. 6. υἱὸς τῆς εἰρήνης. See also Joh. xvii. 12. and Lu. x. 6.

—σκότος τὸ ἐξώτερον.] Compar. for superl. The expression denotes darkness the most remote from light, and is employed in opposition to the brilliant lights, which are figuratively supposed to be burning in the banqueting room. Some however think that there is an allusion to the dark and squalid subterranean dungeons, into which the worst malefactors were thrust. This I can confirm from Joseph. Bell. iii. 8, 5., where, speaking of suicides, he says, τούτων μὲν ᾅδης δέχεται τὰς ψυχὰς σκοτιώτερος. See also Dion. Hal. Antiq. viii. p. 522. sub fin., and Horne's Intr. iii. 427. But thus we should have rather had μυχιαίτερον.

—ἐκεῖ ἔσται—ὀδόντων.] The force of the Art. is expressed by Middlet. thus: "*there shall* they *weep and gnash* their *teeth*;" the Art. having reference to the persons just mentioned. Ὀδόντων is *not*, as some say, pleonastic; though the word is sometimes omitted in this phrase. Wets. compares Juv. Sat. v. 157. To which I add Soph. Trach. 1074. βέβρυχα κλαίων. [*Comp.* Infr. xxi. 43. xiii. 42. 50. xxii. 13. xxiv. 51. xxv. 30. Luke xiii. 28.]

13. ἑκατοντάρχῃ.] In this reading, Wets. Matth., Griesb., Vater, and Fritz. agree, for the common ἑκατοντάρχῳ; and with reason, since it is supported by the greater number of MSS., and is more agreeable to *later* Grecism. See Poppo's Proleg. on Thucyd. p. 220.

—ἐν τῇ ὥρᾳ ἐκείνῃ] "at that very instant!" for ὥρα sometimes signifies, as the Chaldee and Syr.

MK. LU.
1. 4. καὶ ὡς ἐπίστευσας γενηθήτω σοι. καὶ ἰάθη ὁ παῖς αὐτοῦ ἐν τῇ ὥρᾳ
ἐκείνῃ.
29 38 Καὶ ἐλθὼν ὁ Ἰησοῦς εἰς τὴν οἰκίαν Πέτρου, εἶδε τὴν πενθερὰν 14
30 39 αὐτοῦ βεβλημένην καὶ πυρέσσουσαν· καὶ ἥψατο τῆς χειρὸς αὐτῆς, καὶ 15
31 ἀφῆκεν αὐτὴν ὁ πυρετός· καὶ ἠγέρθη καὶ διηκόνει * αὐτῷ. Ὀψίας δὲ 16
32 40 γενομένης προσήνεγκαν αὐτῷ δαιμονιζομένους πολλούς· καὶ ἐξέβαλε τὰ
34 41 πνεύματα λόγῳ, καὶ πάντας τοὺς κακῶς ἔχοντας ἐθεράπευσεν· ὅπως 17
πληρωθῇ τὸ ῥηθὲν διὰ Ἡσαΐου τοῦ προφήτου λέγοντος· Αὐτὸς
τὰς ἀσθενείας ἡμῶν ἔλαβε, καὶ τὰς νόσους ἐβά-
4. 8. στασεν.
35 22 Ἰδὼν δὲ Ἰησοῦς πολλοὺς ὄχλους περὶ αὐτὸν, ἐκέλευσεν ἀπελθεῖν εἰς 18
9. τὸ πέραν. καὶ προσελθὼν εἷς γραμματεὺς εἶπεν αὐτῷ· Διδάσκαλε, 19
57
58 ἀκολουθήσω σοι, ὅπου ἐὰν ἀπέρχῃ. Καὶ λέγει αὐτῷ ὁ Ἰησοῦς· Αἱ 20

שעה and Hebr. רגע, not *hour*, but a point of time, *time*.

14. Πέτρου.] On the several particulars of Peter's life, see Horne's Introd. iv. 438—442.

15. ἥψατο.] *More medicorum*, says Wets., who adduces examples from the Classical writers.—But see note supra. v. 3. Ἀφίημι is a usual term to denote the departure of a disorder. (See Foesii Œcon. Hippocr.) The miracle here recorded did not consist in the cure of an incurable disorder, but in the *mode* of cure, instantly and by a touch.

—διηκόνει] *waited*, or attended upon him. Camp. "entertained him." Others, "waited upon him at table." It seems better, however, to preserve the *general sense*; which is required by the context. This διακονία is evidently recorded as a proof of the *completeness* of cure.—See note supra. iv. 11.

αὐτῷ.] On this reading, for the common one αὐτοῖς, almost all the Editors are agreed. It has every support from MSS., Versions, and Fathers, is found in the Edit. Princ. and the two first of Stephens, and is received by Scholz. Fritz., indeed, defends αὐτοῖς, and it is retained by Griesbach, but upon insufficient grounds.

16. ὀψίας.] The Hebrews reckoned two ὀψίαι, the *early*, from the ninth hour to our six o'clock, or sunset, and the *late*, from sunset to nightfall. From Mark i. 32. it appears that the *later* one is here meant; namely, after sunset. (Grot. Kuin., and Fritz.) Thus the sabbath (for we find by Mark i. 21. that it was a sabbath day) had ended when the sick were brought.

—λόγῳ, "at a word."] Fritz. render "solâ Imperii vi." So the Latin *verbo*. See vii. 9. and note.

17. αὐτὸς—ἐβάστασεν.] The words are from Isa. liii. 4., where are described the propitiatory sufferings of Christ for the sins of the world.—And they are supposed, by some Commentators, to be applied by way of *accommodation*. Yet, since the Jews considered dangerous diseases as the temporal punishment of sin, and our Lord often addressed those whom he healed, "*thy sins be forgiven thee*," it may be granted that the prophecy had a *double fulfilment*; first in the removal of corporeal maladies, and secondly in the remission of our sins, by the sacrifice on the cross. See 1 Pet. ii. 24. The verbal variation here between St. Matthew and the Sept. is ably reconciled by Abp. Magee on the Atonement, Vol. i. p. 415. seqq., who refers ἀσθενείας and the corresponding Hebrew word to *bodily* maladies (a signification not unfrequent in the Classics, ex. gr. Thucyd. ii. 49.) νόσους and its corresponding Hebrew term to diseases of the *mind*; the former clause signifying Christ's removing the sicknesses of men by miraculous cures, the latter, his bearing their sins on the cross. The Unitarian perversion of the passage, whereby it is made to relate to the removal of dieases only, without any reference to a propitiatory sacrifice, is completely refuted by Abp. Magee ubi supra. "It is not surprising (he observes) that so distinguishing a character of the Messiah, as that of his *healing all manner of diseases with a word*, (a character, too, which Isaiah himself has depicted so strongly at ch. xxx. 5. that our Lord (Matt. xi. 4.) quotes the words in proof of his Messiahship), should be introduced by the Prophet in a passage, where his main object was to represent the plan of our redemption by means of Christ's sufferings; especially as the Jews so connected the ideas of sin and disease, that an allusion to one must suggest suggest the other."

At ἔλαβε (נשא) sub. ἐφ' ἑαυτῷ; or take ἔλαβε for ἀνέλαβε. This use of the word is frequent in the Sept. As to ἐβάστ., it cannot, as corresponding to the Heb. סבל, demote *cared*, without great violence. And to this Fritz. (a witness in *this* respect omni exceptione major) bears the strongest testimony. Besides, the interpretation in question passes over the important word αὐτὸς, *himself*. I would not, indeed, deny that βαστάζειν might signify to remove or *cure* [a disorder] (for a passage of Galen cited by Wets., and another of Diog. Laert. iv. 59., (see also Huet on Origen. Comm. on Matt. xi. 9.) seem to prove this); but I see not how it can, in the passage of the *Prophet*, be so taken; while the language of the *Evangelist* may be taken in the manner above mentioned.

18. ἰδὼν—ἐκέλευσεν κ. τ. λ.] This was not so much because he was incommoded by the number of applicants for cure, as because Christ systematically avoided keeping a multitude long together, to prevent any supicion of encouraging sedition. See Le Clerc. On εἰς τὸ πέραν see my Note on Thucyd. i. 111.

19. εἷς for τίς.] A use thought by some to be a Hebraism; but it is adduced (as well as *unus* in Latin) from several of the *later* Greek writers.

MK. LU

ἀλώπεκες φωλεοὺς ἔχουσι, καὶ τὰ πετεινὰ τοῦ οὐρανοῦ κατασκηνώσεις· 4. 9.
21 ὁ δὲ Υἱὸς τοῦ ἀνθρώπου οὐκ ἔχει, ποῦ τὴν κεφαλὴν κλίνῃ. Ἕτερος 59
δὲ τῶν μαθητῶν αὐτοῦ εἶπεν αὐτῷ· Κύριε, ἐπίτρεψόν μοι πρῶτον
22 ἀπελθεῖν καὶ θάψαι τὸν πατέρα μου. Ὁ δὲ Ἰησοῦς εἶπεν αὐτῷ· 60
Ἀκολούθει μοι, καὶ ἄφες τοὺς νεκροὺς θάψαι τοὺς ἑαυτῶν νεκρούς. 8.
23 Καὶ ἐμβάντι αὐτῷ εἰς τὸ πλοῖον ἠκολούθησαν αὐτῷ οἱ μαθηταὶ αὐ- 36 23
24 τοῦ. Καὶ ἰδοὺ, σεισμὸς μέγας ἐγένετο ἐν τῇ θαλάσσῃ, ὥστε τὸ πλοῖον 37
25 καλύπτεσθαι ὑπὸ τῶν κυμάτων· αὐτὸς δὲ ἐκάθευδε. Καὶ προσελθόν- 38 24
τες οἱ μαθηταὶ [αὐτοῦ] ἤγειραν αὐτὸν, λέγοντες· Κύριε, σῶσον ἡμᾶς·
26 ἀπολλύμεθα! Καὶ λέγει αὐτοῖς· Τί δειλοί ἐστε, ὀλιγόπιστοι; Τότε 39
ἐγερθεὶς ἐπετίμησε τοῖς ἀνέμοις καὶ τῇ θαλάσσῃ, καὶ ἐγένετο γαλήνη 41 5
27 μεγάλη. οἱ δὲ ἄνθρωποι ἐθαύμασαν λέγοντες· Ποταπός ἐστιν οὗτος!
ὅτι καὶ οἱ ἄνεμοι καὶ ἡ θάλασσα ὑπακούουσιν αὐτῷ.

20. *αἱ ἀλώπεκες—κλίνῃ.*] This was meant to warn him of the difficulties he would have to encounter in following so destitute a master; and may lead us to suppose that the scribe was desirous of becoming Christ's disciple, from interested motives only. Φωλεοὺς denotes *dens*, or *lairs*, and κατασκηνώσεις, not *nests*, (which would be νοσσιαὶ) but *places of shelter*, such as those where birds settle and perch.

— ὁ Υἱὸς τοῦ ἀνθρώπου.] This title, taken from Dan. vii. 13, where everlasting dominion is ascribed to the *Messiah* under that title, and now first assumed by Christ, occurs 61 times in the Gospels, and is always used by Christ himself, never by any other person. It occurs once in The Acts, (vii. 56.) and is employed by the martyr Stephen. On the origin and nature of the appellation there are various opinions, which see detailed in Recens. Synop. One thing is clear, that from the corresponding term ὁ Υἱὸς τοῦ Θεοῦ, this title belongs to Christ κατ' ἐξοχὴν; and that *both* taken together decidedly prove that Christ, in some manner unknown to us, united in his person both the human and the divine nature, "was very man and very God;" thus negativing the opposite tenets of Socinians and of Gnostics. Bp. Middleton observes, that "in a variety of places in which our Saviour calls himself the Son of man, the allusion is either to his present humiliation, or to his future glory." "Now if (continues he) this remark be true, we have, though an indirect, yet a strong and perpetual declaration, that the human nature did not originally belong to him, and was not properly his own."—John v. 27. iii. 13. vi. 62.

— οὐκ ἔχει—κλίνῃ.] A proverbial expression, to denote being destitute of any fixed place of residence, of which sense see two examples adduced in Horne's Introd. p. 409, sqq. See also Wetstein's examples.

21. ἕτερος] for ἄλλος, i. e. either one of the twelve, or of the disciples in general; said by tradition to be Philip. His father was, if not dead, probably at the point of death.

— ἐπίτρεψόν κ. τ. λ.] A request (implying that he had been *called* by our Lord) in itself reasonable. Thus Elijah permitted Elisha to go and bid adieu to his parents: and it was regarded as the bounden duty of children to take care of the funerals of their parents; but which Christ here was pleased to refuse, for reasons unknown to us, and which doubtless arose from circumstances peculiar to the case. Though we are taught the important lesson, that when we are called to the promotion of religion, either in others or ourselves, we should not allow any temporal business, which may be as well done by men of the world, to prevent us from applying to the work. (See the illustrations in Wets.) Ἀκολούθει μοι.—Equivalent to, "become my disciple."

22. ἄφες—νεκρούς.] A sententia paradoxa *per antanaclasin*, (probably proverbial) turning on the double sense of νεκρούς; which may mean not only the *naturally*, but the *spiritually dead*; i. e. insensible to the concerns of the soul or eternity, dead in trespasses and sins. A metaphor familiar to the Jews, not unknown to the Greeks, (as appears from the examples and illustrations adduced by the Commentators) and frequent in the N. T. Τοὺς ἑαυτῶν νεκροὺς is well explained by Euthym. τοὺς προσήκοντας αὐτοῖς νεκρούς. So Thucyd. ii. 34. καὶ ἐπιφέρει τῷ ἑαυτῷ νεκρῷ (sub. σώματι) ἕκαστος ἤν τι βούλεται.

24. σεισμός.] The word properly denotes *terræ motus*; but sometimes, as here, stands for *maris commotio*, λαῖλαψ, (a *hurricane*) which is the term used by Mark and Luke. Καλύπτεσθαι, "was being covered." Ἀπολλύμεθα, "we are perishing."

25. αὐτοῦ.] This is not found in most of the best MSS., some versions and early Edit. and Theophylact, and is cancelled by Mill., Wets., Griesb., Vater, and Scholz.—rightly, for, besides the preponderance of *external* evidence, *internal* evidence is against it; since we can far better account, for its addition than omission. It is not needed, because the *article* carries with it the sense of the pronoun possessive.

26. ὀλιγόπιστοι.] viz. in not confiding in his power to save, as well asleep as awake.

— ἐπετίμησε—θαλάσσῃ.] A highly figurative expression, signifying, he restrained its fury, as Luke iv. 39. ἐπ. τῷ πυρετῷ. So Ps. cvi. 9. ἐπετίμησε τῇ ἐρυθρᾷ θαλάσσῃ. and lxviii. 31. xviii. 16. civ. 7. Neh. i. 4. 2 Macc. ix. 8. ὁ δὲ ἄρτι δοκῶν τοῖς τῆς θαλάσσης κύμασιν ἐπιτάσσειν. These nouns ἄνεμος and θάλασσα have the Art., as denoting some of the great objects of nature. See Middlet. Gr. A. iii. 1, 5. The *suddenness* of the perfect calm is a proof of the reality of the miracle; for after a storm, the sea is never perfectly smooth, until some time has elapsed.

27. ποταπός.] Qualis quantusque sit. The men

MK. LU.
5. 8. Καὶ ἐλθόντι αὐτῷ εἰς τὸ πέραν, εἰς τὴν χώραν τῶν * Γαδαρηνῶν, 28
1 26 ὑπήντησαν αὐτῷ δύο δαιμονιζόμενοι, ἐκ τῶν μνημείων ἐξερχόμενοι,

might well regard our Lord as super-human; since to "still the raging of the sea," was always reckoned among the operations of God, insomuch that in Ps. lxv. 7, it forms as it were a designation of the Deity.

28. Γαδαρηνῶν.] The reading has here been thought doubtful; the MSS. fluctuating between Γεργεσηνῶν, Γαδαρηνῶν, and Γερασηνῶν. The weight of authority, as far as regards *number* of MSS., is in favour of the first-mentioned, which is the *common* reading: but those MSS. are chiefly of an inferior kind, and of *one class*; while Γαδαρηνῶν is supported by a not inconsiderable number of MSS. of great antiquity and *different recensions*, by the Pesch., Syr., and Persic Versions, and some Fathers; as Euseb., Epiphan., and Chrysostom. As to Γερασηνῶν, it is supported almost solely by the Vulg. and a few inferior Versions. Now if *external* evidence were alone to be considered, we must prefer Γεργ. But *internal* evidence is to be taken into the account; and that, as we shall see, is strongly in favour of Γαδ. And when some seek to reconcile the discrepancy between St. Matthew and the other Evangelists, who have Γαδαρ., by maintaining that Gergesa was in the immediate vicinity of Gadara, so that the limits belonging to one city were so included within the limits of the other, that one Evangelist might say "the country of the Gadarenes," and another, "the country of the Gergesenes," with equal truth; that is but *taking for granted* what ought to be *proved*. Upon the whole, there is great reason to think that the reading Γεργ. originated merely in the *conjecture of Origen* (as is plain from his own words, T. iv. p. 140.) He rejected the reading Γαδαρ. because, he says, "there were no cliffs nor sea at Gadara." But he forgot that the Evangelists are speaking not of the *city*, but of the *territory*, which, as we shall see, extended down to the Sea of Galilee. But the site is *not*, as the maps place it, at *Oomkeis*; and that for *two* reasons. 1. Because that is contrary to what Pliny affirms, who says (L. v. 16.) that it was situated "præfluente Hieromace." And 2. Because it runs counter to the testimony of the *coins of the city*, which bear the representation of a *trireme with rowers*; which shows, that it must have been in the immediate vicinity of the sea of Galilee, and that its territory must have reached to it. Besides, the *hot-baths* which Origen and others attest were in the vicinity of Gadara, are found, not on the *left*, but on the *right* bank of the Hieromax: for the baths in question undoubtedly correspond to those now called *Hammet el Sheik*, plainly the ancient חמת, Ἄμμαθα, or *Amathia*. In fact, the true situation of Gadara is very nearly pointed out in a passage of Eusebius, in his Onomasticum, v. Γάδαρα. His words are: Πόλις ὑπὲρ τὸν Ἰορδάνην, ἀντικρὺ Σκυθοπόλεως καὶ Τιβεριάδος πρὸς ἀνατολαῖς, ἐν τῷ ὄρει, οὗ πρὸς ὑ π ο υ ρ γ ί α ι ς (I would read ὑπωρείαις. for the common reading makes nonsense) τὰ τῶν θερμῶν ὑδάτων παράκειται. Now *the* mountain at whose foot are the hot-baths, is *Hippos*. And as the situation of Amathia must correspond to *Hammet el Sheik*, we may approximate to that of Gadara. It was, I conceive, near the termination of Hippos, where it runs out into a sort of promontory. The exact situation, however, may pretty exactly be determined from a passage of the Itinerary of Antoninus the Martyr, cited in Reland's Palestine, p. 775, and which I will cite in order to emend.

"Venimus in civitatem quæ vocatur Gaddi, quæ dicitur Gabaon (I conjecture Gaddor, גדור, the Hebrew name of the city.) In parte ipsius civitatis sunt aquæ calidæ, milliario III. (I conjecture II., the two marks being often interchanged) quæ appellantur Thermæ *Heliæ*, (I conjecture *Haliæ*, from ἅλαι, *salinæ*, *salt-springs*.) Ibi (i. e. at Thermæ) est etiam fluvius calidus, (I conjecture *gelidus*, a not unfrequent epithet of a river) qui dicitur Gadarra, et descendit torrens, et intrat in Jordanem."

Thus it appears, that the true situation of Gadara is at about two miles from the Hot-baths, from whence to the Lake of Genesaret are three miles; which agrees with what Josephus says of the distance.

But to return, it seems quite clear that the reading Γεργ. either arose from the conjecture of Jerome, or, if he adopted it from others, was derived from those who saw that Γεργασηνῶν was inadmissible, (because Gerasa was situated in quite another part of the country,) and therefore might with no slight probability conjecture Γεργ. For I mean not to deny (as does Fritz.) that there ever was such a city as *Gergesa*; or that it was situated on the E. coast of the lake. There is no proof that Origen speaks from *report* only (as Fritz. *takes for granted*); nay, his words seem to show that he speaks from his own knowledge. Yet, though he mentions it as πόλις ἀρχαία, we are not, I think, authorised to conclude that it was *then in being*; but only to understand by it the *ruins* of that city. The question, however, is, *at what part* of the E. coast was Gergesa situated? I apprehend, we may nearly fix its site. Epiphanius adv. Hær. L. i. p. 131, relates, that in the neighbourhood of Gadara there were "caves cut out of the rocks, burying-grounds, and tombs." Now it is plain that these were the reliques of some ancient and very considerable city; and what could it be but *Gergesa*, which I suspect was a little to the N. N. E. of Gadara, and itself situated on the brow of the mountain? Thus, though Gadara and Gergesa were near to each other, yet the cliff over which the swine rushed was, it seems, nearer to the latter than the former. This is plain from the words of Origen, which show that it was probably opposite to Old Gergesa: and from what he says, it appears that the site of the miracle was then pointed out by the people of the country. That, however, was no reason why St. Matthew should have written Γεργ.; for the Gergashites had long ceased to exist. And, therefore, that could not, as some Commentators have imagined, be the general name of the country in which Gadara was situated. In short, the city of Gergesa had been destroyed as long ago as the war of the Israelites with the inhabitants, (so Josephus i. 6, 2, says: "the cities of the Gergashites were destroyed," &c.,) who, the Rabbins tell us, went in a body to Africa; permission, by proclamation, being made by Joshua that they should go whither they would. From that time we hear no more of the Gergashites. And, as the inhabitants were removed from the country, it must have soon ceased to bear their name; and at the time of Christ, (as we learn from Josephus in Vita, 69,) Gadara, which

MK. LU.

χαλεποὶ λίαν, ὥστε μὴ ἰσχύειν τινὰ παρελθεῖν διὰ τῆς ὁδοῦ ἐκείνης. 5. 8.
2 27
29 Καὶ ἰδοὺ, ἔκραξαν λέγοντες· Τί ἡμῖν καὶ σοὶ, Ἰησοῦ, Υἱὲ τοῦ Θεοῦ; 3
30 ἦλθες ὧδε πρὸ καιροῦ βασανίσαι ἡμᾶς; Ἦν δὲ μακρὰν ἀπ᾽ αὐ- 7 26
31 τῶν ἀγέλη χοίρων πολλῶν βοσκομένη. Οἱ δὲ δαίμονες παρεκάλουν 11 32
αὐτὸν, λέγοντες· Εἰ ἐκβάλλεις ἡμᾶς, ἐπίτρεψον ἡμῖν ἀπελθεῖν εἰς τὴν 12
32 ἀγέλην τῶν χοίρων. καὶ εἶπεν αὐτοῖς· Ὑπάγετε. Οἱ δὲ ἐξελθόντες 13 33
ἀπῆλθον εἰς τὴν ἀγέλην τῶν χοίρων· καὶ ἰδοὺ, ὥρμησε πᾶσα ἡ ἀγέλη
τῶν χοίρων κατὰ τοῦ κρημνοῦ εἰς τὴν θάλασσαν, καὶ ἀπέθανον ἐν
33 τοῖς ὕδασιν. Οἱ δὲ βόσκοντες ἔφυγον, καὶ ἀπελθόντες εἰς τὴν πόλιν, 14 34
34 ἀπήγγειλαν πάντα, καὶ τὰ τῶν δαιμονιζομένων. Καὶ ἰδοὺ, πᾶσα ἡ 35
πόλις ἐξῆλθεν εἰς συνάντησιν τῷ Ἰησοῦ. καὶ ἰδόντες αὐτὸν, παρεκάλε- 16
σαν ὅπως μεταβῇ ἀπὸ τῶν ὁρίων αὐτῶν.

1 IX. Καὶ ἐμβὰς εἰς τὸ πλοῖον, διεπέρασε, καὶ ἦλθεν εἰς τὴν ἰδίαν 2. 5.
3 18
2 πόλιν. Καὶ ἰδοὺ, προσέφερον αὐτῷ παραλυτικὸν ἐπὶ κλίνης βεβλημέ- 5 20
νον. καὶ ἰδὼν ὁ Ἰησοῦς τὴν πίστιν αὐτῶν, εἶπε τῷ παραλυτικῷ·
3 Θάρσει τέκνον, ἀφέωνται σοὶ αἱ ἁμαρτίαι σου. Καὶ ἰδοὺ, τινὲς τῶν 6 7 21
4 γραμματέων εἶπον ἐν ἑαυτοῖς· Οὗτος βλασφημεῖ. Καὶ ἰδὼν ὁ Ἰησοῦς 8 22

was the capital of Peræa, and, I suspect, had arisen out of the ruins of Gergesa, had a pretty considerable district, including several towns or villages, (doubtless amongst these, the ruined Gergesa and its vicinity); and, consequently, its inhabitants would *not* be called *Gergesenes*, but *Gadarenes*. I have, therefore, with Fritz. and Scholz, edited Γαδαρηνῶν.

— μνημείων.] Tombs were not only among the Jews, but the Gentiles, very spacious; and usually subterranean. Hence they often served as places of shelter to the houseless wanderer; or such poor wretches as lepers, or demoniacs, who were driven from human habitations; places, indeed, which might seem not unsuitable to the latter, since the ancients supposed that evil demons hovered about sepulchres.

— χαλεποί.] The word properly denotes (like ἄπορος and some other words, see my note on Thucyd. iv. 32. 4.) "what brings one into difficulty and peril;" and is applied both to things inanimate and *animate;* as brutes, or brutal persons; and then signifies *savage, fierce.* Of all these uses examples may be seen in Wets.

29. τί ἡμῖν καὶ σοί.] An idiom frequent both in Hellenistic and Classical Greek, (of which see examples in Wets. and Matth. Gr. Gr. § 385. 10.) in which there is an ellipsis either of κοινὸν. (*expressed* by Ach. Tat. and Leon. Tar. ap. Wets.) or πρᾶγμα, supplied in passages of Demosth. and Nichomachus cited in Recens. Syn. The sense of the phrase somewhat varies with the context; but it usually implies *troublesome* or *unauthorised interference.* Here it seems to be, "what authority hast thou over us?" q. d. what have we to do with thee (as subjects)? Ἰησοῦ before υἱὲ τοῦ Θεοῦ is omitted in some MSS., and cancelled by Griesb.; but rashly: for, as Matth. suggests, "sigla Ἰησοῦ ante υἱὲ facile negligebatur."

— πρὸ καιροῦ] "before the appointed time," i. e. the day of judgment, against which evil spirits "are reserved to be chained in torments in the pit of destruction." See 2 Pet. ii. 4. Jude 6.

30. μακράν.] "a good way off." So our Comm. Vers. Better "at some distance," as Newcome and Campb. render, for μακρὸς, like all such words, is only a *comparative* term. If the above mode of explanation be rejected, we may here and at Luke xviii. 13. μακρόθεν, and some other passages (including examples of the Latin *procul*, adduced by Wets., Munthe, &c.), suppose the word to mean *off, opposite to,* implying a short distance.

31. ἐπίτρεψον ἡμῖν.] Griesb. edits, from *four* MSS. and some inferior Versions, ἀπόστειλον ἡμᾶς. But his reasons are, though specious, not to be balanced against the strong external evidence for the common reading.

32. κατὰ τοῦ κρημνοῦ] "down the steep." This sense of κατὰ is frequent in the best Classical writers, examples from whom are adduced by Wets., Munthe, &c. The readings, ἀπόστειλον ἡμᾶς ἀπελθεῖν for ἐπίτρεψον ἡ. ἀπ. and τοὺς χοίρους for τὴν ἀγέλην, are received into the text by Griesb., but wrongly; for *external* evidence is almost entirely against them, and *internal* by no means in their favour. See Fritz.

IX. 1. τὸ πλοῖον] i. e. either the vessel which had brought them over, or the ferry boat.

— ἰδίαν πόλιν.] So εἰς τὴν πόλιν αὐτοῦ in 1 Sam. viii. 22. This expression denoted not only the place of any one's *birth*, but *residence;* and, according to the Jewish laws, a year's residence gave citizenship.

2. ἰδὼν τὴν πίστιν.] That this was great, appears from the trouble which (as we find by Mark ii. 4. and Luke v. 19) they had taken to bring the man.

— ἀφέωνται.] The sense is, "thy sins are [hereby] forgiven thee." It was usual with the Jews, in accordance with the language of the O. T., to regard diseases as the effects of sin. On the phrase ἀφιέναι τὰς ἁμαρτίας, see a Dissertation of Vitringa, vol. i. p. 199.

3. εἶπον ἐν ἑαυτοῖς.] A popular form of expression, like one in our own language, answering to διαλογιζόμενοι ἐν ταῖς καρδίαις in Mark and Luke.

— βλασφημεῖ.] Though in the Classical writers the word almost always denotes, in its prop-

MK. LU.
2. 5. τὰς ἐνθυμήσεις αὐτῶν, εἶπεν· Ἱνατί ὑμεῖς ἐνθυμεῖσθε πονηρὰ ἐν
9 23 ταῖς καρδίαις ὑμῶν; τί γάρ ἐστιν εὐκοπώτερον, εἰπεῖν· Ἀφέωνταί 5
10 24 * σου αἱ ἁμαρτίαι· ἢ εἰπεῖν· Ἔγειραι καὶ περιπάτει; Ἵνα δὲ εἰδῆτε, 6
ὅτι ἐξουσίαν ἔχει ὁ Υἱὸς τοῦ ἀνθρώπου ἐπὶ τῆς γῆς ἀφιέναι ἁμαρ-
11 τίας — Τότε λέγει τῷ παραλυτικῷ· Ἐγερθεὶς ἆρόν σου τὴν κλίνην,
12 25 καὶ ὕπαγε εἰς τὸν οἶκόν σου. Καὶ ἐγερθεὶς ἀπῆλθεν εἰς τὸν οἶκον 7
26 αὐτοῦ. Ἰδόντες δὲ οἱ ὄχλοι ἐθαύμασαν, καὶ ἐδόξασαν τὸν Θεὸν τὸν 8
δόντα ἐξουσίαν τοιαύτην τοῖς ἀνθρώποις.

14 27 Καὶ παράγων ὁ Ἰησοῦς ἐκεῖθεν, εἶδεν ἄνθρωπον καθήμενον ἐπὶ 9
28 τὸ τελώνιον, Ματθαῖον λεγόμενον, καὶ λέγει αὐτῷ· Ἀκολούθει μοι.
καὶ ἀναστὰς ἠκολούθησεν αὐτῷ. Καὶ ἐγένετο, αὐτοῦ ἀνακειμένου ἐν 10
15 29 τῇ οἰκίᾳ, καὶ ἰδού, πολλοὶ τελῶναι καὶ ἁμαρτωλοὶ ἐλθόντες συνανέ-
16 30 κειντο τῷ Ἰησοῦ καὶ τοῖς μαθηταῖς αὐτοῦ. Καὶ ἰδόντες οἱ Φαρισαῖοι 11
εἶπον τοῖς μαθηταῖς αὐτοῦ· Διατί μετὰ τῶν τελωνῶν καὶ ἁμαρτωλῶν
17 31 ἐσθίει ὁ διδάσκαλος ὑμῶν; Ὁ δὲ Ἰησοῦς ἀκούσας εἶπεν αὐτοῖς· Οὐ 12
χρείαν ἔχουσιν οἱ ἰσχύοντες ἰατροῦ, ἀλλ' οἱ κακῶς ἔχοντες. Πορευθέν- 13

er sense, to *calumniate*; yet in Scripture it almost invariably has the religious sense, *to speak impiously respecting God*. The persons in question *took for granted* (and hence are reproached as ἐνθυμούμενοι πονηρὰ unjustly) that Jesus was *not* sent from God; and hence falsely concluded, that by professing to be a Divine Legate, he was blasphemous and injurious towards God.

4. ἰδὼν] for εἰδώς, which is found in Luke vi. 8. and xi. 17. and some writers, especially Philo and Josephus.

— ἱνατί.] "The origin of the expression (says Fritz.) is to be explained by *ellipsis*. The complete phrase, after the *present* tense, is ἵνα τί γένηται, 'ut quid fiat,'" after the Preterite, ἵνα τί γένοιτο, "ut quid fieret?" See Herm. on Vig. p. 849.

5 & 6. There is in these vv. an irregularity of construction, which has perplexed the Commentators; most of whom are of opinion, that the words τότε λέγει τῷ παραλυτικῷ are parenthetical; and they suppose a transition in the address; ἵνα εἰδῆτε, &c. being directed to the *lawyers*, and ἐγερθεὶς, &c. to the *paralytic*. But this parenthesis is somewhat harsh; and we should *thus* expect ἀφέωνταί σοι αἱ ἁμαρτίαι rather than Ἐγερθεὶς, &c. Other modes of taking the words are resorted to by Heins., Kuin., and Fritz., all liable to objection. It should seem best *not* to suppose a parenthesis; but to consider the words ἵνα εἰδῆτε — ἁμαρτίας as said per *anantapodoton*, vel *aposiopesin*. Thus the sense of the whole passage may be expressed, in paraphrase, as follows. "It was as easy for me to pronounce, Thy sins are forgiven thee, as to say [i. e. with *effect*] Rise and walk. But that ye may know that the Son of man hath power on earth to forgive sins, [I have done what I have done.] Then, addressing the paralytic, he said, Arise," &c. Campb. well observes, that "although both, and *with effect*, were equally easy to our Lord, yet in the *former* case the effect was invisible, and might be questioned by the multitude; whereas the immediate consequence of the *latter* was an ocular demonstration of the power with which it was accompanied: and to say the one with effect, which effect was *visible*, was a manifest proof that the other was said also with effect, though the effect was invisible." Σου for σοι is in most of the best MSS., and the Ed. Princ., and is adopted by almost all the Editors.

8. τοῖς ἀνθρώποις.] This is usually considered as Plur. for Sing.; but, as Grot. and Fritz. remark, the Plural has place *in sententia generali*.

9. παράγων.] Παράγειν properly signifies to *pass by*, or *away*; and here, to *go away*, *withdraw*, like the Heb. עָבַר.

— τὸ τελώνιον] "the toll-house;" a sort of hut, in which the collector sat. The word is sometimes written τελωνεῖον, and seems to be properly an adjective, with the ellipse of οἴκημα.

— ἠκολούθησεν αὐτῷ.] He had no hesitation in doing this, as being, doubtless, well acquainted with the character of Jesus. It is generally agreed, from the great similarity of the narrations, that the *Matthew* here and the *Levi* of Mark ii. 14. and Luke v. 29. are names of the same individual, especially as it was usual with the Jews to bear two names. The Evangelist follows the custom of the ancient historians in general; who, on having occasion to speak of themselves, use the third person, to avoid egotism.

10. ἐν τῇ οἰκίᾳ] "in *his* house," i. e. of Matthew, as appears from Mark ii. 15, and Luke v. 29, if indeed the feast was the same; which, however, Greswell denies; without reason, I think. It is better to suppose the mention of the feast *anticipated*; for Newc. has shown, that a period of nearly six months intervened between the call of Matt. and this feast. The καὶ before ἰδοὺ seems harsh; but may be best considered with Fritz., as used (like the Heb. ו in 1 Sam. xxviii. 1. and 2 Sam. xiii. 1.) in the sense *nempe*.

— ἁμαρτωλοί.] The word here, and generally elsewhere in the Gospels, denotes *heathens*, or such Jews as associated with them, and were considered on a footing with them. On which see Lightf. and A. Clarke.

11. διατί — ἐσθίει.] From the passages cited by Wets. and others, it appears that the *Heathens* as well as the Jews, accounted it a pollution to eat with the impious.

12. οὐ χρείαν ἔχοντες.] This appears, from the

MK. LU.
τες δὲ μάθετε τί ἐστιν· Ἔλεον θέλω, καὶ οὐ θυσίαν· οὐ 2. 5.
γὰρ ἦλθον καλέσαι δικαίους, ἀλλ᾽ ἁμαρτωλοὺς, [εἰς μετάνοιαν.] 32
14 Τότε προσέρχονται αὐτῷ οἱ μαθηταὶ Ἰωάννου, λέγοντες· Διατί 18 33
ἡμεῖς καὶ οἱ Φαρισαῖοι νηστεύομεν πολλὰ, οἱ δὲ μαθηταί σου οὐ
15 νηστεύουσι; καὶ εἶπεν αὐτοῖς ὁ Ἰησοῦς· Μὴ δύνανται οἱ υἱοὶ τοῦ 19 34
νυμφῶνος πενθεῖν, ἐφ᾽ ὅσον μετ᾽ αὐτῶν ἐστιν ὁ νυμφίος; ἐλεύσονται
δὲ ἡμέραι, ὅταν ἀπαρθῇ ἀπ᾽ αὐτῶν ὁ νυμφίος, καὶ τότε νηστεύσουσιν. 20 35
16 Οὐδεὶς δὲ ἐπιβάλλει ἐπίβλημα ῥάκους ἀγνάφου ἐπὶ ἱματίῳ παλαιῷ· 21 36
αἴρει γὰρ τὸ πλήρωμα αὐτοῦ ἀπὸ τοῦ ἱματίου, καὶ χεῖρον σχίσμα γί-
17 νεται. Οὐδὲ βάλλουσιν οἶνον νέον εἰς ἀσκοὺς παλαιούς· εἰ δὲ μήγε, 22 37
ῥήγνυνται οἱ ἀσκοὶ, καὶ ὁ οἶνος ἐκχεῖται, καὶ οἱ ἀσκοὶ ἀπολοῦνται·
ἀλλὰ βάλλουσιν οἶνον νέον εἰς ἀσκοὺς καινοὺς, καὶ ἀμφότεροι συντηροῦνται.

Classical citations adduced by Wets., Fritz., and myself, to have been a proverbial expression, employed to rebut such like reproaches as the present.

13. The connection is thus traced by Kuin. "You Pharisees severely censure *me* for associating with persons such as tax-gatherers, whom you call sinners. I therefore remind *you* of the word of God, as found in the Prophet, &c."

— *πορευθέντες.*] This is *not*, as the Commentators usually say, redundant; but is put for the *verb* with *καὶ*; q. d. "Go and apply yourselves to learn." So the phrase cited by Schoettg. צא ולמד *go and learn*, as used by Rabbis when they wished to refer their disciples to the Scriptures. The *indefinite* mode of citation here employed was, as Surenhus. says, usual with the Rabbis, and, in some measure, with all the ancient writers. See Valckn. on Herodo. iv. 131.

— *Ἔλεον.*] The word here denotes *φιλανθρωπία*, universal benevolence. The ולא of the Hebr. and the *καὶ οὐ* here denote, not a simple and absolute, but *comparative* negation, and may be rendered *non tam — quam;* an idiom common to both Hebrew and Greek. Passages similar in sentiment are adduced from the Rabbinical writers by Wets. and Scheid, and from the Classical writers by Kypke and Munthe. *Θυσία* is taken, by synecdoche, for the whole of the ceremonial law.

— *οὐ γὰρ ἦλθον*, &c.] These words are, rightly, thus explained by the ancients and most moderns: "Not you who, like the Pharisees, *fancy* yourselves righteous, but you who acknowledge yourselves sinners, and seek a method of expiation." Dr. Burton, however, thinks "it matters not whether we take *δικαίους* ironically, or *not*." But surely it *does* matter whether we destroy the antithesis, (which requires *both* terms to be understood in a modified sense,) and take away the spirit of this pungent retort, or not. The words *εἰς μετάνοιαν* are not found in several MSS., Versions, and Latin Fathers, (both here and at Mark ii. 17,) are disapproved by Mill, Bengel, Knappe, and Vater, and are cancelled by Griesb. They are, however, defended by Whitby, Wets., Matthæi, Fritz., and Scholz; and the MS. authority for them is so strong, that they must be retained. Indeed, as Fritz. observes, they seem quite necessary to the course of argument, and yet cannot well be thought left to be *understood*. [*Comp.* infra, xii. 7. Hos. vi. 6. 1. Tim. i. 15.]

14. *νηστεύομεν.*] We are not to understand this of *public* but *private* fasts, upon various extraordinary occasions.

15. *μὴ δύνανται — νυμφίος.*] A most delicate form of expressing by *conjecture*, what is meant to be strongly denied. *Δύνανται* is not redundant, (as Kuin. and others say.) but, by the ellipse of some words (such as here, "consistently with the nature of a marriage feast," which Fritz. supplies) may be rendered *debent*, or *decent*.

— *οἱ υἱοὶ τοῦ νυμφῶνος*] i. e. (by a Hebraism whereby בן prefixed denotes *distinction* or *participation*) those who were admitted into the bride chamber; namely (the friends of the bride groom, the *παράνυμφοι, pronubi*), who formed the marriage procession, and were invited to a participation of the seven days' matrimonial feasting. See Horne's Introd. iii. 410.

— *πενθεῖν.*] Mark and Luke have *νηστεύειν*. Yet *πενθεῖν* may be taken per synecdochen; for fasting was among the signs of grief. In *ὁ νυμφίος* there is a reference to the title given by the ancient Hebrews to Christ. *Νηστεύσουσι*, they will, or may fast.

16. *οὐδεὶς ἐπιβάλλει*, &c.] "no one clappeth a patch of undressed cloth," &c., i. e. rough from the weaver, and which has not yet passed through the hands of the fuller. Thus the expression answers to the *καινὸν* of Luke. *Ἐπίβλημα* is Hellenistic for *ἐπίρῥαμμα*.

— *αἴρει γὰρ — γίνεται.*] By this it is meant that the two substances being dissimilar, (one rigid and the other supple) will never wear well together, but the rigid will tear away part of the supple. The comparison is *popular;* and the *application* suggested by this and the metaphor in the next verse is, the inexpediency of imposing too grievous burthens on them, during their weakness and imperfection, as new converts.

17. *βάλλουσιν*] Scil. *ἄνθρωποι*. *Βάλλειν* is used to signify *infundere*, both in the Scriptural and Classical writers.

— *ἀσκοὺς*] flasks made of goat or sheep skins, used in all the ancient nations, and still employed in the Southern parts of Europe. Now these, as they are not so easily distended when they grow old and stiff, so they are liable to burst by the fermentation of the liquor.

— *ἀμφότεροι.*] On this reading all the Editors are agreed, from Mill to Scholz. It is found in almost all the MSS., the Edit. Princ., and some other early Edd.: as also in the parallel passage of Luke. As to the common reading

MK. LU.
5. 8. *Ταῦτα αὐτοῦ λαλοῦντος αὐτοῖς, ἰδοὺ, ἄρχων εἷς ἐλθὼν προσεκύνει* 18
22 41 *αὐτῷ λέγων· Ὅτι ἡ θυγάτηρ μου ἄρτι ἐτελεύτησεν· ἀλλὰ ἐλθὼν*
23 42 *ἐπίθες τὴν χεῖρά σου ἐπ' αὐτὴν, καὶ ζήσεται. Καὶ ἐγερθεὶς ὁ Ἰησοῦς* 19
24 *ἠκολούθησεν αὐτῷ, καὶ οἱ μαθηταὶ αὐτοῦ.*
25 43 *Καὶ ἰδοὺ, γυνὴ αἱμοῤῥοοῦσα δώδεκα ἔτη, προσελθοῦσα ὄπισθεν,* 20
28 *ἥψατο τοῦ κρασπέδου τοῦ ἱματίου αὐτοῦ· ἔλεγε γὰρ ἐν ἑαυτῇ· ἐὰν* 21
34 48 *μόνον ἅψωμαι τοῦ ἱματίου αὐτοῦ, σωθήσομαι. Ὁ δὲ Ἰησοῦς ἐπιστρα-* 22
φεὶς καὶ ἰδὼν αὐτὴν, εἶπε· Θάρσει θύγατερ· ἡ πίστις σου σέσωκέ σε.
38 *Καὶ ἐσώθη ἡ γυνὴ ἀπὸ τῆς ὥρας ἐκείνης. Καὶ ἐλθὼν ὁ Ἰησοῦς* 23
εἰς τὴν οἰκίαν τοῦ ἄρχοντος, καὶ ἰδὼν τοὺς αὐλητὰς καὶ τὸν ὄχλον
39 52 *θορυβούμενον, λέγει αὐτοῖς· Ἀναχωρεῖτε· οὐ γὰρ ἀπέθανε τὸ κορά-* 24
40 53 *σιον, ἀλλὰ καθεύδει. καὶ κατεγέλων αὐτοῦ. Ὅτε δὲ ἐξεβλήθη ὁ ὄχλος,* 25
41 54 *εἰσελθὼν ἐκράτησε τῆς χειρὸς αὐτῆς, καὶ ἠγέρθη τὸ κοράσιον. καὶ* 26
ἐξῆλθεν ἡ φήμη αὕτη εἰς ὅλην τὴν γῆν ἐκείνην.

ἀμφότερα, it may, indeed, be defended (in the sense "both things);" but it probably either arose from accident, (οι and α being perpetually confounded), or from the alteration of those who wished to remove the harshness connected with ἀμφότεροι.

18. ἄρχων] Scil. τῆς συναγωγῆς, which is *expressed* in Luke viii. 41. He is by Mark v. 22, called ἀρχισυνάγωγος, and named Jairus. The εἷς after ἄρχων is found in most of the MSS., the Edit. Princ., and the best of the Versions; which is with reason adopted by Wets., Griebs., Matth., Fritz., and Scholz.

— ἄρτι ἐτελεύτησεν] "is by this time dead," or "*as it were* dead." This is agreeable to Mark's ἐσχάτως ἔχει and not irreconcileable with Luke's ἀπέθνησκεν, which may be rendered "was dying." And certain it is, that ἀποθνήσκω like the Heb. מות, was used of those at the point of death.

— ἐπίθες τὴν χεῖρα.] "According (says Grot.) to the custom of our Lord, as it had been also of the prophets; who, in praying for the benefit of any person, used to put their hands upon him." See Numb. xxvii. 18. 2 Kings v. 11. Matt. xix. 13. Acts iv. 30.

— ζήσεται.] The interpretation of this word must depend upon the sense assigned to the former ἐτελεύτησε: but in the *popular* acceptation it is susceptible of either the signification *to be restored to life*, or *to continue to live*, which must imply recovery from her sickness.

20. αἱμοῤῥοοῦσα.] It is not clear whether, by this we are to understand a flux from the *os sacrum*, or the *os matricis*. The former seems the more probable. See Mead cited in Rec. Syn. I would add, that Levit. xv. 33. seems to favour the latter opinion. One thing is certain, that a flux of blood of *either* kind is the least curable of all distempers.

— τοῦ κρασπέδου.] Not so much the *hem*, as the *tassel*, (i. e. one of the lower tassels) of the garment; which had four corners, called πτερύγια, from each of which was suspended a tassel of threads or strings, called κράσπεδον. To touch the lower ones, was regarded as a mark of profound respect. This, however, is not to be regarded as exclusively a *Jewish* custom; for I have, in Recens. Synop., adduced three examples (from Arrian, Athenæus, and Plutarch) of heathens touching or kissing the fringe of a great man's robe as a mark of respect, and to gain his good will and favour. It is still retained in the East. The secrecy and delicacy here employed may be attributed to the *nature* of the disorder, which was considered unclean.

21. σωθήσομαι.] "I shall be restored to health." The word is not unfrequent in this sense, as used of recovery from a dangerous disorder.

23. τοὺς αὐλητάς.] The antiquity of the custom of wailing for the dead, and expressing grief by tearing the hair and mangling the flesh, appears from various parts of the O. T.: it was common to both Greeks and Romans, and still continues in some barbarous or half civilized nations. Besides these offices of *relations*, other persons were hired to join in the howling, and to sing dirges, accompanied by various wind instruments.

— θορυβούμενον.] This would properly mean *tumultuantem*; but the word must here include the sense of *lamentation*, namely, such tumultuary responses as the *preficæ* would make in concert.

24. οὐκ ἀπέθανε — καθεύδει.] We are not to infer from this that the girl was not *dead*. For that is contrary to the whole tenor of the narration. The best Commentators are agreed that the sense is, "she is not *so* departed, as not to return to life," (which was the idea associated with death;) and that by καθεύδει is meant, "is, as it were, asleep." To explain ἀπέθανε with Dr. Burton, "*she was not dying* at the time *when her father thought her dying*," would be exceedingly harsh and frigid.

25. ἐξεβλήθη] "was dismissed," or, required to withdraw. This and many such terms in both Hellenistic and Classical writers are not to be strained, but to be understood *populariter*. Our Lord excluded the people, in order that those whom he wished to be spectators of the miracles (as the parents, and Peter, James, and John, see Mark v. 37—40.) might view what was done without interruption.

— ἐκράτησε τῆς χειρός.] Not as a form of raising any one, nor through courtesy, or *more medicorum* as many Commentators say; but, as usual, to accompany the miracle with some *act*, as that of touching.

27 Καὶ παράγοντι ἐκεῖθεν τῷ Ἰησοῦ ἠκολούθησαν αὐτῷ δύο τυφλοὶ,
28 κράζοντες καὶ λέγοντες· Ἐλέησον ἡμᾶς, υἱὲ Δαυΐδ! Ἐλθόντι δὲ εἰς
τὴν οἰκίαν προσῆλθον αὐτῷ οἱ τυφλοὶ, καὶ λέγει αὐτοῖς ὁ Ἰησοῦς·
Πιστεύετε ὅτι δύναμαι τοῦτο ποιῆσαι; λέγουσιν αὐτῷ· Ναὶ, Κύριε.
29 Τότε ἥψατο τῶν ὀφθαλμῶν αὐτῶν, λέγων· Κατὰ τὴν πίστιν ὑμῶν
30 γενηθήτω ὑμῖν. Καὶ ἀνεῴχθησαν αὐτῶν οἱ ὀφθαλμοί. καὶ ἐνεβριμή-
31 σατο αὐτοῖς ὁ Ἰησοῦς λέγων· Ὁρᾶτε μηδεὶς γινωσκέτω. Οἱ δὲ ἐξελθόντες διεφήμισαν αὐτὸν ἐν ὅλῃ τῇ γῇ ἐκείνῃ.
32 Αὐτῶν δὲ ἐξερχομένων, ἰδοὺ, προσήνεγκαν αὐτῷ ἄνθρωπον κωφὸν,
33 δαιμονιζόμενον. Καὶ ἐκβληθέντος τοῦ δαιμονίου, ἐλάλησεν ὁ κωφός·
καὶ ἐθαύμασαν οἱ ὄχλοι λέγοντες· [ὅτι] Οὐδέποτε ἐφάνη οὕτως ἐν τῷ
34 Ἰσραήλ! Οἱ δὲ Φαρισαῖοι ἔλεγον· Ἐν τῷ ἄρχοντι τῶν δαιμονίων
ἐκβάλλει τὰ δαιμόνια.
35 [a] Καὶ περιῆγεν ὁ Ἰησοῦς τὰς πόλεις πάσας καὶ τὰς κώμας, διδά- a Mark 6. 6. Luke 13. 22. supr. 4. 23.
σκων ἐν ταῖς συναγωγαῖς αὐτῶν, καὶ κηρύσσων τὸ εὐαγγέλιον τῆς βασι-
λείας, καὶ θεραπεύων πᾶσαν νόσον καὶ πᾶσαν μαλακίαν [ἐν τῷ λαῷ.] b Mark 6. 34.
36 [b] Ἰδὼν δὲ τοὺς ὄχλους, ἐσπλαγχνίσθη περὶ αὐτῶν, ὅτι ἦσαν ἐσκυλμένοι Num. 27. 17. Zach. 10. 2.

27. υἱὲ Δαυΐδ.] As that was one of the titles then ascribed by the Jews to the Messiah, the use of it was an unequivocal acknowledgment of Jesus's Messiahship. And that use must have been founded on their reliance on the testimony of others who had seen his miracles.

30. ἀνεῴχθησαν αὐτῶν οἱ ὀφθαλμοί] "they were restored to sight," or, "received the faculty of sight." This is thought to be a Hebraism; but it is rather a *popular* form of expression. Thus it is found also in the *Classical* writers.

— ἐνεβριμήσατο] "strictly enjoined them." The expression, notwithstanding its etymology, only imports earnestness, not passion.

31. διεφήμισαν αὐτόν.] The verb is rarely used except of *things;* when used of *persons*, it signifies "to make any one known or celebrated."

32. κωφὸν, δαιμονιζόμενον.] So I point, with Vater and Fritz. For, as Fritz. observes, the latter word is explanatory of the former; q. d. "who was such, by demoniacal influence." And this Rosenm. and Kuin. admit is the sense intended by St. Matthew and St. Luke. Yet, with a strange perversity, they choose to ascribe the dumbness to *disorder*. Only, they say, "the Evangelists thought proper to retain the common expression." But this would be inconsistent with the character of *honest men*, much less messengers from God. See note supra iv. 24. and at variance with the firm belief of demoniacal possession, elsewhere so apparent in their writings. Besides, the truth and dignity of the miracle will *not*, as is alleged, remain the same. It would not be the *same miracle;* and the *dignity* would be far less. For though Dr. Mead expresses his surprise "that divines should contend so eagerly for demoniacal possession, as if something were wanting to demonstrate Christ's power, when exercised only over natural diseases;" yet what has been said supra iv. 24, (and in Bp. Warburton's 27th Sermon,) will abundantly prove that something *would* have been wanting to demonstrate if not the *power*, yet the assumed *character* of Jesus, had it been exercised only over natural diseases. Assured we may be, that, in proportion as the soul exceeds in dignity the body, so must the suppression of evil from superhuman agents, exceed that of evil produced in the regular course of nature. Besides, the very terms employed shew, that the removal of the dumbness was occasioned by the expulsion of the dæmon. Not to say, that the amazement of the people necessarily *supposes* the cure of *demoniacal possession*, not that of *disease;* for the latter *had* been very frequently seen in Israel, and evinced by the *Prophets;* nay, even so far as to raise the dead. [*Comp.* Luke xi. 14.]

33. οὐδέποτε ἐφάνη οὕτως.] An elliptical form of expression, in which τοῦτο, or τοιοῦτό τι, and γενόμενον are usually said to be understood. Fritz., indeed, objects to the uncommonness of the ellipsis; but without reason, for this seems to have been a *popular* form of expression. Mill, Wets., Griesb., Matth., and Scholz, are agreed that ὅτι before οὐδέποτε which is found in very few MSS., must be cancelled.

34. ἐν τῷ ἀρχ.] per Heb. ב. This, however, is not a Hebraism. To the examples adduced by Schleus. Lex. may be added another from Thucyd. iii. 42. Οὐκ ὠφελεῖται ἐν τῷ τοιῷδε. [*Comp.* infr. xii. 24. Mark iii. 23. Luke xi. 15.]

35. ἐν τῷ λαῷ.] These words are not found in several MSS., the Edit. Princeps, almost all the ancient Versions, and some Greek Fathers They are therefore rejected by Mill, cancelled by Griesb., Fritz., and Scholz, and bracketed by Knapp. and Vater; though retained by Matthæi. They were probably derived from iv. 23.

36. ἐσπλαγχνίσθη] "was moved with compassion." The word occurs neither in the Sept. nor the Classical writers, and seems to have been formed by the New-Testament writers from σπλάγχνα, bowels; for *there* the Jews placed the seat of sympathy; by a metaphor taken from that *yearning* which is felt in pity, or the other kindly affections. The verb is construed sometimes with περὶ, with or without a Genit., others with ἐπὶ and an Accus.

— ἐσκυλμένοι.] It is almost impossible to imagine stronger authority, internal and external,

c Luke 10. 2. John 4. 35.

καὶ ἐῤῥιμμένοι, ὡσεὶ πρόβατα μὴ ἔχοντα ποιμένα. ᶜ Τότε λέγει τοῖς 37
μαθηταῖς αὐτοῦ· Ὁ μὲν θερισμὸς πολὺς, οἱ δὲ ἐργάται ὀλίγοι·
MK. LU. δεήθητε οὖν τοῦ κυρίου τοῦ θερισμοῦ, ὅπως ἐκβάλῃ ἐργάτας εἰς τὸν 38
6. 9. θερισμὸν αὐτοῦ.

7 1 X. Καὶ προσκαλεσάμενος τοὺς δώδεκα μαθητὰς αὐτοῦ, ἔδωκεν αὐ- 1
τοῖς ἐξουσίαν πνευμάτων ἀκαθάρτων, ὥστε ἐκβάλλειν αὐτὰ, καὶ θεραπεύειν πᾶσαν νόσον καὶ πᾶσαν μαλακίαν. Τῶν δὲ δώδεκα ἀποστόλων 2
τὰ ὀνόματά ἐστι ταῦτα· πρῶτος Σίμων ὁ λεγόμενος Πέτρος, καὶ Ἀνδρέας ὁ ἀδελφὸς αὐτοῦ· Ἰάκωβος ὁ τοῦ Ζεβεδαίου, καὶ Ἰωάννης
ὁ ἀδελφὸς αὐτοῦ· Φίλιππος, καὶ Βαρθολομαῖος· Θωμᾶς, καὶ Ματ- 3
θαῖος ὁ τελώνης· Ἰάκωβος ὁ τοῦ Ἀλφαίου, καὶ Λεββαῖος ὁ ἐπικληθεὶς Θαδδαῖος· Σίμων ὁ Κανανίτης, καὶ Ἰούδας [ὁ] Ἰσκαριώτης, 4
ὁ καὶ παραδοὺς αὐτόν.

Τούτους τοὺς δώδεκα ἀπέστειλεν ὁ Ἰησοῦς, παραγγείλας αὐτοῖς, 5
λέγων· Εἰς ὁδὸν ἐθνῶν μὴ ἀπέλθητε, καὶ εἰς πόλιν Σαμαρειτῶν μὴ

than exists for this reading, which has been approved by almost every Commentator, and received by all the Editors from Wets. downwards. As to the common reading, ἐκλελυμένοι, it is plainly a gloss. The sense of ἐσκυλμένοι is *harassed*, *vexed*, *troubled*. It does *not* denote properly, (as is commonly said) to *tear the hair*, but to *claw*, as applied to dogs and other animals: so Æschyl. Pers. 583. γναπτόμενοι σκύλλονται. The words occurs also at Mark v. 35. and Luke viii. 44. 3 Macc. iii. 25. iv. 6.

— ἐῤῥιμμένοι] i. e. not *scattered*, as some render, but *tossed aside*, abandoned, unprotected. See Wets. Similar pastoral images occur in 1 Kings xxii. 17. and Judith xi. 19.

37. ὁ μὲν θερισμὸς — ὀλίγοι.] Probably a proverbial saying, including an agricultural comparison, like many others in Scripture. Indeed, ἔργον and its compounds are peculiarly applied to the labours of husbandry. Schoettg. observes, that in the Rabbinical writings teachers are figured as *reapers*, and their work of instruction as the *harvest*.

38. ἐκβάλῃ] "would speedily send forth."

X. 1. ἐξουσίαν πνευμάτων ἀ.] Most Commentators here supply κατὰ, which, however, though found in several MSS., is only an ancient *gloss*. The πνευμ. is rightly regarded by Kuin. as a *Genit. of object*; as in Ecclus. x. 4. ἐξουσία τῆς γῆς. John xvii. 2. Rom. ix. 21, and several passages of the Classical writers cited by Raphel and Palairet. [*Comp.* Mark iii. 14.]

2. ἀποστόλων.] This important term properly denotes ὁ ἀπεσταλμένος, one sent by another, on some important business, as in Herodo. i. 21, where it signifies a *herald*, and 1 Kings xiv. 6. But (in imitation of the name given to an officer sent by the High-priest and Sanhedrim to the distant and foreign Jews, to collect the tribute levied for the support of the Temple) it is, in the N. T., almost always used to denote "*persons employed to convey the message of salvation from God to man*," and especially the *twelve Apostles*; who were peculiarly so called, as being at first especially sent out by Christ, and commissioned to preach the Gospel in Judæa; and who afterwards, with Paul and Barnabas, (who were supernaturally selected for the work) received full and extraordinary authority, not only to promulgate his religion throughout the world, but to found and regulate the Christian Church; and especially to ordain teachers and pastors, who should hereafter govern it by *ordinary* authority.

— πρῶτος — Πέτρος] i. e. first in *order*, as being first called, not in *dignity*; for Christ seems not to have authorised any difference in rank. If he had done so, the Evangelists would have observed it; but they have *not*; for the names are recited by them in different order. Judas, however, is always named last, and Peter first; and John and his brother James third and fourth, or fourth and fifth. Certainly these three were especially esteemed by Christ, perhaps for their docility, attachment, and mental endowments. (Rosenm.) It is a most satisfactory, and, in opposition to the pretensions of the Bishops of Rome, a sufficient explanation of πρῶτος, that Peter was *first called* to the ministry. So Theophyl. Προτίθησι δὲ Πέτρον καὶ Ἀνδρέαν διότι καὶ πρωτόκλητοι.

4. ὁ Ἰσκαριώτης.] The ὁ was brought into the text by the Elzevir Editor, and has been retained by Wets. and all the recent Editors except Matthæi, who cancelled it. Bishop Middleton is of opinion, that the presence or the absence of the Art. depends upon whether Ἰσκαριώτης be a *surname*, or an *epithet* significant of *place of birth* or residence. If, as Chrys. and some others say, it is derived from *Carioth*, Judas's birth-place, the Art., he thinks, is required; and if it be a mere surname, it should not have it. Yet as, on other occasions, the Art. is often omitted where in propriety it ought to be inserted, because it is *implied*; (as when a cognomen passes into a simple name) so it may be *here*; and therefore that will determine nothing as to the *reading*. But, since *external* evidence is decidedly in *favour* of the Article, and *internal* equally balanced, it ought not to have been cancelled by Matth. and Valpy. Ὁ καὶ παραδοὺς α. Not, "who also betrayed," (that would require προδοὺς) but "who even delivered him up" [to his enemies.] Vulg. tradidit. See Campb. and Fritz.

5. εἰς ὁδὸν ἐθν.] for εἰς ὁδὸν ἣ ἄγει εἰς τὰ ἔθνη, the Genit. here being a Genit. of motion, as in Gen.

MK. LU.

6 εἰσέλθητε. *Πορεύεσθε δὲ μᾶλλον πρὸς τὰ πρόβατα τὰ ἀπολωλότα* 6. 9.
7 οἴκου Ἰσραήλ. *Πορευόμενοι δὲ κηρύσσετε λέγοντες· Ὅτι ἤγγικεν* 2
8 ἡ βασιλεία τῶν οὐρανῶν. *Ἀσθενοῦντας θεραπεύετε, λεπροὺς καθαρί-*
ζετε, [νεκροὺς ἐγείρετε,] δαιμόνια ἐκβάλλετε· δωρεὰν ἐλάβετε, δωρεὰν
9 δότε. *Μὴ κτήσησθε χρυσὸν, μηδὲ ἄργυρον, μηδὲ χαλκὸν, εἰς τὰς ζώνας* 8 9 3
10 ὑμῶν· μὴ πήραν εἰς ὁδὸν, μηδὲ δύο χιτῶνας, μηδὲ ὑποδήματα, μηδὲ
11 ‡ ῥάβδον· ἄξιος γὰρ ὁ ἐργάτης τῆς τροφῆς αὐτοῦ ἐστιν. *Εἰς ἣν δ'*
ἂν πόλιν ἢ κώμην εἰσέλθητε, ἐξετάσατε τίς ἐν αὐτῇ ἄξιός ἐστι· κἀκεῖ 10 4
12 μείνατε, ἕως ἂν ἐξέλθητε. *Εἰσερχόμενοι δὲ εἰς τὴν οἰκίαν, ἀσπάσασθε*

iii. 24. the way of the tree of life, and Jer. ii. 18. ἡ ὁδὸς Αἰγύπτου. (Kuin. and Fritz.) Εἰς πόλιν, sub. τινά; for it is *wrongly* taken by Kuin. of "the city of Samaria;" which would require the Art.

6. [*Comp.* infr. xv. 24. Acts xiii. 46.]

7. [*Comp.* Luke ix. 2. Supr. iii. 2. iv. 17.]

8. νεκροὺς ἐγείρετε.] Editors are much divided in opinion as to the authenticity of these words; which are rejected by the generality of Critics, but defended by Whitby, Griesb., and Fritz. The internal evidence *for* and *against* is nearly balanced; but the latter somewhat preponderates. (See Grot., Mill, Campb., and Matthæi.) The *external* is most decidedly against them. See Scholz, who has, with Matthæi cancelled the words. If they be retained, we may suppose that, like some few other passages in this discourse respecting events which did not immediately take place, they have reference to the period comprehended under the more extensive commission the Apostles received after Christ's resurrection. See John xx. 21. I have not followed the change of position adopted by Griesb. from some MSS. and Versions, because that would remove one principal cause which may be assigned for the *omission* of the words, namely, the *homœoteleuton.* The *change of position* might well arise from *omission*, afterwards supplied in the margin.

— δωρεὰν — δότε.] This (which is a sort of proverbial saying) must, as appears from Luke x 7, be confined to what went just before; namely, the dispensing of miraculous gifts; and therefore cannot be drawn into an argument against the maintenance of Christian ministers. All that is meant is, that they were not to make *a trade* of their miraculous gifts, as the Jewish exorcists did of their pretended power to cast out devils.

9. μὴ κτήσησθε] "ye must not provide, or furnish yourselves with:" a signification common in the best Classical writers.

— εἰς τὰς ζώνας ὑμῶν.] The words (to which μὴ κτήσησθε χρυσὸν, μηδὲ ἄργ. μηδὲ χαλκὸν must be all referred) signify, "for your purses," i. e. for your travelling expenses. ζώνας signifies properly *girdles*. But the Oriental nations, (and even the Greeks and Romans) used the belt, with which their flowing garments were confined, as purses — a custom still subsisting in the East, and in Greece. [*Comp.* Luke xxii. 35.]

10. πήραν.] A sort of wallet, generally of leather, used by shepherds and travellers, for the reception of provisions, mentioned both in the O. T. and in Homer. Yet as εἰς ὁδὸν "for the use of the journey," is here associated with it, it may mean, by a common figure, the *provisions themselves*.

— δύο χιτῶνας.] This, (as Fritz. rightly remarks) does not forbid the *wearing* of two coats, (for the ancients generally wore two on a journey) but a *change* of coats.

— ὑποδήματα.] A sort of strong shoes, for *long* journeys. On other occasions *sandals* were worn. These ὑποδήματα they were not to provide, but (as Mark more clearly expresses it) to use sandals only. 'Ράβδους is found in most of the MSS., the Copt., Arm., and later Syriac Versions, Theophyl., Ed. Princ., Steph. Ed. 1 & 2, and is adopted by Grotius, Beza, Whitby, Wets., and Scholz. But it is quite at variance with Mark vi. 8; for, as to its meaning "a change of staves," that is an attempt to remove the discrepany (as Fritz. says) "risu quam refutatrone dignior." Besides, we can far better account for the change of ῥάβδον into ῥάβδους, than the contrary. The scribes stumbling at a *singular* noun, after several *plural* ones, changed the singular into a plural; which they might more easily do, since the abbreviations for ον and ους are not very dissimilar. And vain will it be to urge, that in Luke ix. 3. we have ῥάβδους; for there ῥάβδον, on very strong evidence, both external and internal, is adopted by all the best Editors. Thus it appears, that the *external* evidence for ῥάβδον (including several ancient MSS. and the best Versions, as the Pesh. Syr.) is nearly equal to that for ῥάβδους. And the *internal* evidence is almost wholly on its side. Under these circumstances, I have thought proper (with Mill, Griesb., Matth., Tittm., Vater, and Fritz.) to retain ῥάβδον. The sense will thus be quite reconcileable with Mark vi. 8; the injunction that they should not *provide* themselves with a staff. almost implying that they might *take* one, if they *had* it.

— ἄξιος γὰρ &c.] A proverbial expression occurring also in Levit. xix. 13. Deut. xxiv. 14. 15. q. d. 'You may cheerfully trust the providence of God to take care of you while engaged in such a cause; and you may reasonably expect to find sustenance among those for whose benefit you labor.' The expression τροφὴ means both food and raiment. "They are forbidden to encumber themselves with any articles of raiment besides what they were wearing, or with money to purchase more, because they would be entitled to a supply from those on whom their labours were bestowed, and money would be but an encumbrance."

11. ἄξιος] scil. παρ' ᾧ μείναιτ' ἄν, "of your company." Some other ellipses which have been supposed are too arbitrary. Nay, the *absolute* use, which is found both in the Scriptural and Classical writers, and supported by the ancient interpreters, may possibly be preferable.

MK. LU.
6. 9. αὐτήν. Καὶ ἐὰν μὲν ᾖ ἡ οἰκία ἀξία, ἐλθέτω ἡ εἰρήνη ὑμῶν ἐπ᾽ αὐ- 13
11 5 τήν· ἐὰν δὲ μὴ ᾖ ἀξία, ἡ εἰρήνη ὑμῶν πρὸς ὑμᾶς ἐπιστραφήτω. Καὶ 14
ὃς ἐὰν μὴ δέξηται ὑμᾶς, μηδὲ ἀκούσῃ τοὺς λόγους ὑμῶν, ἐξερχόμενοι
τῆς οἰκίας ἢ τῆς πόλεως ἐκείνης, ἐκτινάξατε τὸν κονιορτὸν τῶν ποδῶν
a Inf. 11. 24. ὑμῶν. [a] Ἀμὴν λέγω ὑμῖν ἀνεκτότερον ἔσται γῇ Σοδόμων καὶ Γομόῤῥων 15
ἐν ἡμέρᾳ κρίσεως, ἢ τῇ πόλει ἐκείνῃ.
b Luke 10. 3. Rom. 16. 19. [b] Ἰδού, ἐγὼ ἀποστέλλω ὑμᾶς ὡς πρόβατα ἐν μέσῳ λύκων· γίνεσθε 16
οὖν φρόνιμοι ὡς οἱ ὄφεις, καὶ ἀκέραιοι ὡς αἱ περιστεραί. Προσέχετε 17
δὲ ἀπὸ τῶν ἀνθρώπων· παραδώσουσι γὰρ ὑμᾶς εἰς συνέδρια, καὶ ἐν
c Mark 13. 11. Luke 12. 11. Acts 12. 1. & 25. 23. 2 Tim. 4. 22. ταῖς συναγωγαῖς αὐτῶν μαστιγώσουσιν ὑμᾶς. [c] καὶ ἐπὶ ἡγεμόνας δὲ 18
καὶ βασιλεῖς ἀχθήσεσθε, ἕνεκεν ἐμοῦ, εἰς μαρτύριον αὐτοῖς καὶ τοῖς
d Luke 12. 12. & 21. 14, 15. ἔθνεσιν. [d] Ὅταν δὲ παραδιδῶσιν ὑμᾶς, μὴ μεριμνήσητε πῶς ἢ τί λα- 19
λήσητε· δοθήσεται γὰρ ὑμῖν ἐν ἐκείνῃ τῇ ὥρᾳ, τί λαλήσετε· οὐ γὰρ 20
ὑμεῖς ἐστε οἱ λαλοῦντες, ἀλλὰ τὸ πνεῦμα τοῦ πατρὸς ὑμῶν τὸ λαλοῦν
e Micah 7. 5, 6. Luke 21. 16. ἐν ὑμῖν. [e] Παραδώσει δὲ ἀδελφὸς ἀδελφὸν εἰς θάνατον, καὶ πατὴρ 21
τέκνον· καὶ ἐπαναστήσονται τέκνα ἐπὶ γονεῖς, καὶ θανατώσουσιν αὐ-
f Mark 13. 13. Luke 21. 17. infr. 24. 13. τούς. [f] Καὶ ἔσεσθε μισούμενοι ὑπὸ πάντων διὰ τὸ ὄνομά μου· ὁ δὲ 22
ὑπομείνας εἰς τέλος, οὗτος σωθήσεται. Ὅταν δὲ διώκωσιν ὑμᾶς ἐν τῇ 23

13. ἐλθέτω.] This, and ἐπιστραφήτω just after, are commonly regarded as examples of Imperat. for Future. But it is better, with Fritz., to take the sense to be "*volo* pacem vestram," &c. Εἰρήνη means the benefit of your peace, &c. or blessing. Πρὸς ὑμᾶς ἐπιστραφήτω. This is used in a popular sense, to signify, "become void and ineffectual." So Isaiah lv. 11. οὕτως ἔσται τὸ ῥῆμά μου, ὃ ἐὰν ἐξέλθῃ ἐκ τοῦ στόματός μου, οὐ μὴ ἀποστραφῇ, ἕως ἂν τελεσθῇ ὅσα ἂν ἠθέλησα. See also Ps. xxxiv. 6. and vii. 16.

14. καὶ ὃς ἐάν.] This is *not* (as is commonly said) for ἐὰν δέ τις; but ἐὰν is for ἄν. The construction is *popular*, and involves an *antapodoton* of frequent occurrence; moreover, ἐκείνης is for ἐκείνου, per synesin. The Genit. ποδῶν is governed by the ἐκ in ἐκτινάξατε. Shaking off the dust from the feet at persons was a symbolical action, disclaiming all intercourse with them.—[*Comp.* Acts. xiii. 51. xviii. 6.]

15. ἐν ἡμέρᾳ κρίσεως.] "in the day of judgment." Some Commentators understand this of the *destruction of the Jewish nation*. But *that* is rather, as Whitby observes, styled the day of *vengeance*; and is otherwise, (as the same Commentator has proved) inapplicable here. The expression, then, must, notwithstanding the omission of the Article (on which see Bp. Middl.), be understood of the day of *final judgment*.

16. γίνεσθε — περιστεραί.] We have here two beautiful and appropriate similes (common in the Classical writers), which hint at the dangers to which they would be exposed, and the best means of avoiding them. Similar sentiments are adduced from the Rabbinical writers.

18. εἰς μαρτύριον αὐτοῖς] namely, of the truth of the Gospel, by your endurance of persecution in behalf of it.

19. μὴ μεριμνήσητε] i. e. be not anxiously solicitous. Πῶς ἢ τί λαλήσητε, "how or what you *may* speak."

20. οὐ γάρ.] The Commentators regard this as a comparative negation, like *non tam — quam*; of which there are many examples in the Scriptural and Classical writers. But Winer, in his Gr. N. T. p. 139., seems right in denying this qualified sense to have place in οὐ followed by ἀλλά; and after discussing several passages where the formula is found (as Acts. v. 4. and 1 Thess. iv. 8. 1 Cor. i. 17. and the present passage), he shows that the sentiment is enfeebled when the οὐ is translated *non tam*. *Here*, he observes, the reference is not to the physical act of speaking, but to the sentiment uttered; which was to be really imparted to the Apostles by the Holy Spirit. Newcome very well supplies "in effect and ultimately." Ἐστε is Pres. for Fut.: or it may stand for *are to be*, populariter.—The sense is: "for you are not to be the speakers, but the Spirit of your Father [is to be] that which speaketh [or, the speaker] in you.

21. ἐπαναστήσονται.] Kuin., Rosenm., and others, take this as a forensic terms, to signify *they shall rise up as witnesses*. And they appeal to Matt. xii. 41. But there ἐν τῇ κρίσει is added.—There seems no reason to abandon the usual interpretation, as referred to *hostility*, *attack*, and *persecution*, which is well supported by Wets., Kypke, and Fritz. Here may be compared a very similar passage of Thucyd. iii. 83. καὶ γὰρ πατὴρ παῖδα ἀπέκτεινε, "used to put to death."

22. πάντων.] This is commonly taken for *many*; but better by Euthym., for *most*, *quasi omnibus*.

— εἰς τέλος.] This does not denote the destruction of Jerusalem; nor σωθήσεται just after, a temporary preservation, as Hamm., Wets., and Rosenm. explain; but τέλος is by the antient and most modern Commentators rightly interpreted, "the end [of their troubles] whether by death or deliverance;" and σωθήσεται, "salvation in heaven."

23. τῇ — τήν.] Bp. Middlet. observes that the Art. is not without meaning; serving to mark the opposition between οὗτος and ἄλλος, "*two* cities only being supposed.

πόλει ταύτῃ, φεύγετε εἰς τὴν ἄλλην. Ἀμὴν γὰρ λέγω ὑμῖν· οὐ μὴ
τελέσητε τὰς πόλεις τοῦ Ἰσραὴλ, ἕως ἂν ἔλθῃ ὁ Υἱὸς τοῦ ἀνθρώπου.
24 [g] Οὐκ ἔστι μαθητὴς ὑπὲρ τὸν διδάσκαλον, οὐδὲ δοῦλος ὑπὲρ τὸν κύ- g Luke 6. 40. John 13. 16.
25 ριον αὐτοῦ. [h] Ἀρκετὸν τῷ μαθητῇ, ἵνα γένηται ὡς ὁ διδάσκαλος αὐ- & 15. 20. h infr. 12. 24.
τοῦ, καὶ ὁ δοῦλος ὡς ὁ κύριος αὐτοῦ. εἰ τὸν οἰκοδεσπότην ‡ Βεελζε- Mark 3. 22. Luke 11. 15.
26 βοὺλ ‡ ἐκάλεσαν, πόσῳ μᾶλλον τοὺς οἰκιακοὺς αὐτοῦ; [i] Μὴ οὖν φο- i Mark 3. 22. Luke 8. 17.
βηθῆτε αὐτούς· οὐδὲν γάρ ἐστι κεκαλυμμένον, ὃ οὐκ ἀποκαλυφθήσεται· & 12. 2.
27 καὶ κρυπτὸν, ὃ οὐ γνωσθήσεται. Ὃ λέγω ὑμῖν ἐν τῇ σκοτίᾳ, εἴπατε
ἐν τῷ φωτί· καὶ ὃ εἰς τὸ οὖς ἀκούετε, κηρύξατε ἐπὶ τῶν δωμάτων.
28 Καὶ μὴ ‡ φοβηθῆτε ἀπὸ τῶν ἀποκτεινόντων τὸ σῶμα, τὴν δὲ ψυχὴν
μὴ δυναμένων ἀποκτεῖναι· φοβήθητε δὲ μᾶλλον τὸν δυνάμενον καὶ
29 ψυχὴν καὶ σῶμα ἀπολέσαι ἐν γεέννῃ. Οὐχὶ δύο στρουθία ἀσσαρίου
30 πωλεῖται; καὶ ἓν ἐξ αὐτῶν οὐ πεσεῖται ἐπὶ τὴν γῆν ἄνευ τοῦ πατρὸς k Luke 21. 18.
31 ὑμῶν. [k] Ὑμῶν δὲ καὶ αἱ τρίχες τῆς κεφαλῆς πᾶσαι ἠριθμημέναι εἰσί. Acts 27. 34. 2 Sam. 14. 11.

—τελέσητε τὰς πόλεις] for τελ. (τὴν ὁδὸν διὰ) τὰς πόλεις. The ellipsis is frequent in the Classical writers, as Thucyd. iv. 78. ἐς Φάρσαλον ἐτέλεσε, where see my note.

—ἕως—ἀνθρώπου,] until, or unto, up to the time when, &c. The words are by the best Commentators referred to the destruction of Jerusalem.

24. οὐκ ἔστι—διδάσκαλον] "no disciple is above his master." Mid. A proverbial saying, which imports, that he cannot expect better treatment than his master.

25. Βεελζεβοὺλ.] Several Editors and Critics would read Βεελζεβοὺβ, which Jerome adopted into the Vulg., under the idea that it is the same with the Ekronite idol called at 2 Kings i. 2. בעל זבוב, *the Lord of flies*; and that the change of β into λ was made agreeably to the genius of the Greek language, which admits no word to end in β. But besides that for Βεελζεβοὺβ, there is scarcely the authority of *one* MS. (as Grot., Lightf., Wets., and others remark), the title was one of *honour*; like the Ζεὺς Ἀπομυῖος, *banisher of flies*, given to Hercules. Whereas the name here evidently is one of *contempt*. Hence the best Commentators, with reason, suppose that the name is indeed the same with that of the above-mentioned; but, (according to a custom among the Jews, of *altering the names* of idols, to throw contempt on them (changed to Βεελζεβοὺλ, i. e. Lord of *dung*, i. e. metaphorically, idolatry, or, according to others, the "Lord of *Idols*." Hence it was afterwards given by the Jews to the Prince of dæmons.

—ἐκάλεσαν.] Wets., Griesb., Kuin., Vater, Fritz., and Scholz edit. ἐπεκάλεσαν; which indeed has very strong authority from MSS., Editions, and Fathers. Yet as the MSS. fluctuate between this and *three* other readings, we may suspect *alteration*; and *then* the simplest reading is to be preferred. Thus, in the present case, ἐκάλεσαν might give birth to all the rest. I have, therefore, (with Matthæi) retained the common reading.

26. μὴ οὖν φοβηθῆτε κ. τ. λ.] The sense here is disputed; but it seems to be: "Fear not your persecutors and calumniators, nor be alarmed for the success of the Gospel; for your innocence shall be made as clear as the light, and your doctrine shall enlighten the whole world." The words following contain a proverb usual among the Heathens, importing that the truth cannot be extinguished; as in the well-known "Magna est veritas, et prævalebit."

27. ὃ λέγω—δωμάτων.] Of the phrases λέγειν ἐν φωτὶ and ἀκούειν τι (λεγόμενον) εἰς οὖς, as also of δῶμα in the sense, house-top, see the Classical examples in Wets. and Recens. Synop. They are all metaphorical, and the last adagial.

28. φοβηθῆτε.] Wets., Griesb., Matth., Vat., and Scholz, edit. φοβεῖσθε, from very many MSS., the Edit. Princ., and some Fathers. But, though external evidence be, perhaps, in *favour* of φοβεῖσθε, yet internal is, I apprehend, *against* it, since it occurs before and after in the context, and φοβηθῆτε was more likely to be changed into φοβεῖσθε than the contrary, to retain the common reading, which, indeed, is found without var. lect. in the parallel passage at Lu. xii. 4.

—ἀπὸ τῶν ἀποκτεινόντων.] Though there be considerable authority for ἀποκτενόντων, which is preferred by nearly all the great Editors; yet there seems no sufficient reason for change; since the common reading is more suitable in sense, is found in at least as many MSS., and is confirmed by the parallel passage at Luke xii. 4. See also Matth. xxiii. 37. The construction at φοβ. with ἀπὸ is called a Hebraism. But it may be paralleled with our "feeling apprehension *of*," or *from*.

29. ἓν ἐξ αὐτῶν οὐ] for οὐδὲν, say the Commentators and Winer in his Gr. Gr. § 20. 1. But perhaps there is more *emphasis* in the present position; the sense being nearly the same as in οὐδὲ ἓν, *not even one*. In fact, in all the examples adduced by Winer (as Eph. v. 5. and iv. 29. 2 Pet. i. 20.) there is an intensity of sense.

—πεσεῖται ἐπὶ τὴν γῆν.] An idiom common in the Scriptural, and not unexampled in the Classical writers, for ἀπολεῖται.

—ἄνευ τοῦ πατρὸς ὑ.] "without the counsel and providence of;" as Thucyd. ii. 70. ὅτι ἄνευ αὐτῶν (scil. τῆς γνώμης) ξυνέβησαν. With respect to the *sentiment*, which inculcates the superintending care of Providence even over the meanest works of the creation, the Commentators adduce many parallels from the Classical, and the Rabbinical writers.

30. καὶ αἱ τρίχες—εἰσί.] Another proverbial saying (similar to many in the O. T. and the

l Mark 8. 38. Luke 9. 26. & 12. 8. 2 Tim. 2. 12. Rev. 3. 5.
m Luke 12. 49, 51.
n Micah 7. 6.
o Luke 14. 26.
p Infr. 16. 24. Mark 8. 34. Luke 9. 23.
q Infr. 16. 25. Mark 8 35. Luke 9. 24. & 17. 33. John 12. 25.
r Infr. 18. 5. Luke 10. 16. John 13. 20.
s Mark 9. 41.

Μὴ οὖν φοβηθῆτε· πολλῶν στρουθίων διαφέρετε ὑμεῖς. [l] Πᾶς οὖν ὅστις 32
ὁμολογήσει ἐν ἐμοὶ ἔμπροσθεν τῶν ἀνθρώπων, ὁμολογήσω κἀγὼ ἐν
αὐτῷ ἔμπροσθεν τοῦ πατρός μου τοῦ ἐν οὐρανοῖς. Ὅστις δ' ἂν ἀρνή- 33
σηταί με ἔμπροσθεν τῶν ἀνθρώπων, ἀρνήσομαι αὐτὸν κἀγὼ ἔμπρο-
σθεν τοῦ πατρός μου τοῦ ἐν οὐρανοῖς. [m] Μὴ νομίσητε, ὅτι ἦλθον 34
βαλεῖν εἰρήνην ἐπὶ τὴν γῆν· οὐκ ἦλθον βαλεῖν εἰρήνην, ἀλλὰ μάχαιραν.
Ἦλθον γὰρ διχάσαι ἄνθρωπον κατὰ τοῦ πατρὸς αὐτοῦ, καὶ θυγατέρα κα- 35
τὰ τῆς μητρὸς αὐτῆς, καὶ νύμφην κατὰ τῆς πενθερᾶς αὐτῆς. [n] Καὶ ἐχθροὶ 36
τοῦ ἀνθρώπου οἱ οἰκιακοὶ αὐτοῦ. [o] Ὁ φιλῶν πατέρα ἢ μητέρα ὑπὲρ ἐμὲ 37
οὐκ ἔστι μου ἄξιος· καὶ ὁ φιλῶν υἱὸν ἢ θυγατέρα ὑπὲρ ἐμὲ οὐκ ἔστι μου
ἄξιος. [p] Καὶ ὃς οὐ λαμβάνει τὸν σταυρὸν αὐτοῦ καὶ ἀκολουθεῖ ὀπίσω 38
μου, οὐκ ἔστι μου ἄξιος. [q] Ὁ εὑρὼν τὴν ψυχὴν αὐτοῦ ἀπολέσει αὐτήν· καὶ 39
ὁ ἀπολέσας τὴν ψυχὴν αὐτοῦ, ἕνεκεν ἐμοῦ, εὑρήσει αὐτήν. [r] Ὁ δεχόμενος 40
ὑμᾶς ἐμὲ δέχεται· καὶ ὁ ἐμὲ δεχόμενος δέχεται τὸν ἀποστείλαντά με. 41
Ὁ δεχόμενος προφήτην εἰς ὄνομα προφήτου μισθὸν προφήτου λήψεται·
καὶ ὁ δεχόμενος δίκαιον εἰς ὄνομα δικαίου μισθὸν δικαίου λήψεται. 42
[s] Καὶ ὃς ἐὰν ποτίσῃ ἕνα τῶν μικρῶν τούτων ποτήριον ψυχροῦ μόνον, εἰς
ὄνομα μαθητοῦ, ἀμὴν λέγω ὑμῖν· οὐ μὴ ἀπολέσῃ τὸν μισθὸν αὐτοῦ.

Rabbinical writers) importing that the very smallest of our concerns are under the care of God.

32. *ὁμολογήσει ἐν ἐμοί.*] A Hebrew and Hellenistic construction for *ὁμολ. ἐμὲ*, as at Lu. xii. 8. Rom. x. 9. The sense of the word is literally, "to make profession in conformity to any one." In the other member of the sentence it stands for *agnoscere, to recognise, approve.*

33. *ἀρνήσηταί με.*] A *popular* expression denoting to *reject a profession by my name.* In the clause following it signifies to *cast off.*

34. *μὴ νομίσητε — μάχαιραν.*] This is (as Wets. and Campb. remark) "a forcible and indeed Oriental mode of expressing the *certainty* of a foreseen consequence of any measure, by representing it as the *purpose* for which the measure was adopted." See also Whitby. Dr. Parr, in a Sermon on this text, ably traces the true meaning of this passage; and rescues the words from the misconceptions of ignorance, and the misrepresentations of infidelity, by showing that they were intended only to *predict*, not to *justify*, the evils of which Christianity has been eventually productive. By *μάχαιρα* is here meant both *war* (namely, the Jewish war which soon followed), and civil commotion; which is supported by what follows, and by the parallel passage in Lu. xii. 51.

35. *διχάσαι — κατά.*] *Διχάζειν* signifies properly *to divide into two parts;* but here it denotes to *separate and set at variance;* in which there is a mixture of two constructions. This and the verse following are formed on Micah vii. 6.

36. *τοῦ ἀνθρώπου.*] Bp. Middlet. considers this equivalent to *παντὸς ἀνθρώπου*, *every man*, or, men generally. This is confirmed by the words of Micah; where for *ἐχθροὶ πάντες ἀνθρώπου*, Bp. Middlet. rightly conjectures *παντὸς*, which, indeed, is required by the Hebrew. *Ὑπὲρ ἐμὲ* is a Hebraism, as in Gen. xlviii. 2. Judg. ii. 19.

38. *λαμβάνει τὸν σταυρόν.*] There is here an allusion to the Roman custom, of compelling a malefactor going to crucifixion to bear his cross. As crucifixion was not a Jewish punishment, in this mention of it our Lord may seem to have alluded to his *own* crucifixion; and consequently the passage is, in a certain sense, prophetical.

— *ἀκολουθεῖ ὀπίσω μου.*] This is not a Hebraism, but is found in Classical writers. See Wets. It is a construction which at first involved an addition of sense, but at length became a pleonasm. See Winer's Gr. Gr. p. 175. and Robinson's note there.

39. *ὁ εὑρὼν — ἀπολέσει αὐτήν.*] This is supposed to be an *acutè dictum*, or Oxymoron, including a Paronomasia between the two senses of *ψυχή*, namely, *life* and *soul*. There is also a *dilogia* in the words *ἀπολέσει* and *εὑρήσει*. Life is an Hebrew image of *felicity*, and in this sense the word ought to be taken in the words *ἀπολέσει αὐτὴν* and *εὑρήσει αὐτὴν* following.

40. *ὁ δεχόμενος ὑμᾶς, ἐμὲ δέχεται*] "and consequently he that receiveth *not* you, receiveth not me." The treatment shown to an ambassador is in fact shown to his sovereign.

41. *εἰς ὄνομα προφήτου*] for *ὡς προφ.*, "for being such." By *προφ.* seems to be meant a *teacher* of the Gospel; and by *δίκαιον*, a pious *professor of it.*

42. *μικρῶν.*] Not, "men of mean station;" or "very young persons," as some explain: but, as the antient and the best modern Interpreters take the expression, *disciples*, as opposed to *teachers;* either because *μαθητῶν* may be understood at *μικρῶν*, from the context, or be taken substantively, as answering to (what it seems was in the original Hebrew) קטנים, and being, as we find from the Rabbinical writings) the name given to disciples. *Ποτίζειν ποτήριον* is for *ποτίζειν*. At *ψυχροῦ* sub. *ὕδατος*, an ellipsis, (also found after *θερμὸν*) which, like *frigida* and *gelida* in Latin, is not unfrequent in the Classical writers. It is *supplied* in Mark ix. 41. To give a cup of cold water was proverbial for giving the smallest thing.

LU. 7.

1 XI. *Καὶ ἐγένετο, ὅτε ἐτέλεσεν ὁ Ἰησοῦς διατάσσων τοῖς δώδεκα μα-*
θηταῖς αὐτοῦ, μετέβη ἐκεῖθεν, τοῦ διδάσκειν καὶ κηρύσσειν ἐν ταῖς
πόλεσιν αὐτῶν.

2 *Ὁ ΔΕ Ἰωάννης ἀκούσας ἐν τῷ δεσμωτηρίῳ τὰ ἔργα τοῦ Χριστοῦ,* 18
3 *πέμψας δύο τῶν μαθητῶν αὐτοῦ, εἶπεν αὐτῷ· Σὺ εἶ ὁ ἐρχόμενος, ἢ* 19
4 *ἕτερον προσδοκῶμεν; Καὶ ἀποκριθεὶς ὁ Ἰησοῦς εἶπεν αὐτοῖς· Πορευ-* 22
5 *θέντες ἀπαγγείλατε Ἰωάννῃ, ἃ ἀκούετε καὶ βλέπετε. τυφλοὶ ἀναβλέ-*
πουσι, καὶ χωλοὶ περιπατοῦσι· λεπροὶ καθαρίζονται, καὶ κωφοὶ ἀκού-
6 *ουσι· νεκροὶ ἐγείρονται, καὶ πτωχοὶ εὐαγγελίζονται. καὶ μακάριός ἐστιν* 23
7 *ὃς ἐὰν μὴ σκανδαλισθῇ ἐν ἐμοί. Τούτων δὲ πορευομένων, ἤρξατο* 24
ὁ Ἰησοῦς λέγειν τοῖς ὄχλοις περὶ Ἰωάννου· Τί ἐξήλθετε εἰς τὴν ἔρημον
8 *θεάσασθαι; κάλαμον ὑπὸ ἀνέμου σαλευόμενον; Ἀλλὰ τί ἐξήλθετε* 25

XI. 1. *διατάσσων*] "giving directions," or injunctions.

—*αὐτῶν*.] It is not clear to *whom* this refers. Chrys. and Euthym. understand the *disciples;* other antients, the *Jews;* most modern Commentators, the *Galilæans;* according to the Hebrew idiom of using a pronoun where its antecedent is not expressed, but must be understood from the context. See Winer's Gr. Gr. § 15. 3.

3. *σὺ εἶ — προσδοκῶμεν*.] "Art thou he who should come, or must we look for another?" Few questions have been more debated than the purpose of John's sending this message to Jesus. Some antients and many moderns think that he sent in order to satisfy certain doubts which had occurred to his mind during his confinement. But surely his view of the descent of the Holy Ghost at Christ's baptism, the testimony he then heard from heaven, the divine impulse by which he recognised Jesus as "the Lamb of God that taketh away the sin of the world," and his own reiterated testimonies forbid such a supposition: and to imagine that John's *confinement* should have affected the strength of his resolves, or drawn from him the language of fretful remonstrance, or peevish complaint, would do great injustice to so noble a character. In short, the opinion has been shown to be utterly untenable by Chrys., Euthym., Theophyl., and Greg., of the antients; and of the moderns, Hamm., Whitby, Doddr., Bp. Atterbury, and Mr. Benson (Hulsean Lectures, 1820. pp. 60—67.); who maintain, that John sent for the satisfaction of *his disciples*, who, mortified at seeing their master imprisoned for preaching the coming of the Messiah; and disappointed that He whom he testified to be such, should make no such claim; nor make any attempt to deliver his Forerunner: stumbling, too, at the humbleness of Jesus's birth, and the lowliness of his station; and offended at his difference in character from their own ascetic master, had entertained doubts as to his Messiahship. Against *them*, therefore, and not against *John*, the rebuke is levelled. It should seem that for *their* satisfaction John had sent; and as they would not heed his repeated endeavours to remove their doubts, he resolved to refer them to *Christ himself*, for the removal of their scruples: and that our Lord, well aware of his intention, took the surest means of fixing the wavering minds of his disciples, by displaying such supernatural endowments as should completely answer to the predicted character of the Messiah; and then sent them to their master for the *application*.

With respect to the *reply itself*, both the *manner* and the *matter* of it are highly deserving of attention. As to the former, it is, as Bp. Atterbury observes, not direct and positive, but so ordered only, as to give them an occasion of answering the question themselves, which they had proposed to Christ. As to the latter, the learned Prelate, with his usual taste, ably points out the *gradation* to be observed in the particulars, and the appositeness of it in relation to the inquiries. So that the words, "Go show John," &c. may mean, "You come to learn of me whether I am the Messiah. Your master has often told you I am He, but you will not believe *him*. To him you should have gone as my forerunner: to *me* it belongs not so properly to proclaim my own titles, which might excite your suspicion. Behold therefore the testimony *of God!* for the works which I am doing before your eyes bear witness that the Father hath sent me." The description of the works in question is so framed as to be taken from a prophecy of Isaiah lxi. 1. and xxxv. 5, 6. of the Messiah. Thus it is as if our Lord had said, "Ye believe not the *Baptist's* testimony, that I am He who should come. Yet surely Isaiah, whom ye so reverence, and upon whose authority ye have received the Baptist himself, will obtain credence with you; and he has thus prophesied of me."

5. *πτωχοὶ εὐαγγελίζονται*.] A peculiar feature of Christianity, as distinguished from Judaism and Heathenism, whose priests and philosophers courted the rich, and contemned the poor. See John vii. 49.

6. *σκανδαλισθῇ ἐν ἐμοί*] "stumble in faith, disbelieve and fall from faith in my Messiahship." *Σκάνδαλον* signifies *a stumbling block*, and, in a spiritual sense, what obstructs us in our Christian course, and causes us to fall away from the faith.

7. *κάλαμον ὑπὸ ἀνέμου σαλευόμενον*.] The Commentators are not agreed whether the words should be taken in the *natural* sense, meaning, that it was not the sight of any *trifling* thing, such as reeds (with which the wilderness abounded), tossed about by the wind, but, &c., or the *metaphorical*, as figuratively descriptive of levity and inconstancy — a wavering man. The former view is adopted by Grot., Beza, Campb., Wets., Rosenm., Schleus., and Fritz.; the latter by the ancients generally, and, of the moderns, by Whitby,

LU.
7. ἰδεῖν; ἄνθρωπον ἐν μαλακοῖς ἱματίοις ἠμφιεσμένον; ἰδοὺ, οἱ τὰ μαλα-
26 κὰ φοροῦντες ἐν τοῖς οἴκοις τῶν βασιλέων εἰσίν. Ἀλλὰ τί ἐξήλθετε 9
27 ἰδεῖν; προφήτην; ναὶ, λέγω ὑμῖν, καὶ περισσότερον προφήτου. Οὗτος 10
γάρ ἐστι περὶ οὗ γέγραπται· Ἰδοὺ, ἐγὼ ἀποστέλλω τὸν ἄγγελόν μου πρὸ προσώπου σου, ὃς κατασκευάσει τὴν
28 ὁδόν σου ἔμπροσθέν σου. Ἀμὴν λέγω ὑμῖν· οὐκ ἐγήγερται 11
ἐν γεννητοῖς γυναικῶν μείζων Ἰωάννου τοῦ βαπτιστοῦ· ὁ δὲ μικρότερος
ἐν τῇ βασιλείᾳ τῶν οὐρανῶν μείζων αὐτοῦ ἐστιν. Ἀπὸ δὲ τῶν ἡμε- 12
ρῶν Ἰωάννου τοῦ βαπτιστοῦ ἕως ἄρτι, ἡ βασιλεία τῶν οὐρανῶν βιάζεται, καὶ βιασταὶ ἁρπάζουσιν αὐτήν. Πάντες γὰρ οἱ προφῆται καὶ 13
ὁ νόμος ἕως Ἰωάννου προεφήτευσαν· καὶ, εἰ θέλετε δέξασθαι, αὐτός 14

Mackn., and Kuin. The latter, indeed, is more pointed and significant, but the former is more simple, and not less agreeable to the context.

8. ἀλλὰ τί] for ἢ τί, says Kuin. But Fritz. more rightly regards this use of ἀλλὰ after interrogations, as meant to deny anything as corresponding to the objective *at*, q. d. If ye deny that ye went with that view, for what purpose *did* ye go? Μαλακοῖς, denotes soft, and therefore fine; whether of silk, linen, or other materials.

— βασιλέων.] Very many MSS. have βασιλείων, which is edited by Matth. and Scholz, but wrongly, for internal evidence is quite against it, inasmuch as it would produce an idle circumlocution, in the place of an expression whose simplicity and Oriental air attest its truth. The error arose from a mistake of the abbreviation for ων and ειων.

9. περισσότερον προφήτου.] The full sense is, 'a prophet, and something more exalted than a prophet,' namely, as bearing more important commissions. On the points of superiority, see Grot., Lightf., Whitby, and Mackn.

10. Quoted from Mal. iii. 1. The words, however, differ not only from the Heb. but the Sept., in one or both of which Drs. Owen and Randolph suppose a corruption, but without cause. Ἐπιβλέψεται is only a *free* version of פנה, which scarcely admits of a *literal* one. Indeed, some MSS. have ἑτοιμάσει, and no doubt others in the time of Christ, ἐπισκευάσει, which is a correct version of the Heb. πρὸ προσ. μου in both Sept. and the Evangelists, are a literal version of the Heb. לפני, instead of which the English V. has *me*. Thus the only real difference in the Evangelists, is the supplying (for better illustration of the sense) *one* which is implied in another *expressed*; and in changing, for better application to this present purpose, μου into σου.

11. οὐκ ἐγήγερται] Ἐγείρεσθαι, like the Hebrew קום is especially applied to the birth of eminent persons. (Grot. and Kuin.) Μικρότερος, for μικρότατος. See Winer's Gr. Gr. p. 87.

12. ἡ βασιλεία — βιασταί.] Few passages have been more variously interpreted than the present. Whatever may be obscure, one thing is plain — that the two clauses are closely connected with each other; so that whatever can be shown to be the sense of the former, will fix the sense of the latter. And as there is not a little difficulty, it is of the more importance to attend to the *general scope;* which (as in all this portion, v. 9—14.) is, to show the *high dignity* of the Baptist. But to advert to the interpretations in question; most of them will be found either contrary to the *scope* or to the *connexion* just pointed out. Among these are those which are founded on the attributing an *active* sense to βιαζ. Leaving, therefore, to βιάζεται its natural force, (as a *passive*,) it will be best interpreted (with almost all the ancient and the best modern Commentators) as put for βιαίως κρατεῖται, "*impetu quodam et cupidè excipitur Messiæ regnum.*." But if *this* sense be admitted, it will fix that of οἱ βιασταί, which cannot, as Hamm., Wets., and Bp. Middl., imagine, mean "those who had lived by rapine," as the publicans, soldiers, and the meaner crowd. This is at variance with the connexion, and yields a forced and frigid sense; such indeed as Middl. would never have adopted, had he not been induced to do so, rather than admit that one of his canons on the Article is broken. From the context, βιασταί must denote "persons who engage in any thing impetuously and eagerly." So in the parallel passage of Luke xvi. 16, (which has been too little attended to.) ὁ νόμος καὶ οἱ προφῆται ἕως Ἰωάννου· ἀπὸ τότε ἡ βασιλεία τοῦ θεοῦ εὐαγγελίζεται, καὶ πᾶς εἰς αὐτὴν βιάζεται.

13. πάντες — προεφήτευσαν.] The γὰρ is causal, and has reference to v. 11., for v. 12. is, as it were, parenthetical, and the scope of it is, to point out the dignity of John; from the time of whose appearance the message of the Gospel was received with delight, and its truths were embraced with eagerness by those whose minds were earnestly bent on forcing their way through the strait gate. The sense (which is obscure from brevity) will be made clearer by regarding προεφ. as put *emphatically*. We may paraphrase: "*For* all the prophets, and other sacred writers of the law (i. e. revelation) of God, and its expounders up to the time of John, did but *foreshow* and treat of as *far off*, the dispensation, which should hereafter be promulged: whereas John announced it as *at hand*.

14. εἰ θέλετε δέξασθαι] An impressive formula, like ὁ ἔχων — ἀκουέτω just afterwards, the one soliciting *patient attention*, the other *implicit faith*. This sense of δέχεσθαι, (hearken, believe,) both with the Accus., and used, as here, *absolutely*, is frequent in the Classical writers.

— αὐτός ἐστιν Ἡλίας,] i. e. this is the person meant by Malachi iv. 5. and designated under that name. What is said is not at variance with the *disavowal* of the Baptist himself, John i. 21.; since it is manifest that he was not Elias according to the *sense* in which Elias was expected by the Jews, i. e. the *same person*. He only *bore the name*, by figurative adoption, as being the anti-

LU.
15 ἐστιν Ἠλίας ὁ μέλλων ἔρχεσθαι. Ὁ ἔχων ὦτα ἀκούειν, ἀκουέτω. Τίνι 7
16 δὲ ὁμοιώσω τὴν γενεὰν ταύτην; Ὁμοία ἐστὶ * παιδίοις ἐν ἀγοραῖς 31 32
17 καθημένοις, καὶ προσφωνοῦσι τοῖς ἑταίροις αὐτῶν, καὶ λέγουσιν· Ηὐλήσαμεν ὑμῖν, καὶ οὐκ ὠρχήσασθε· ἐθρηνήσαμεν ὑμῖν, καὶ οὐκ ἐκό-
18 ψασθε. Ἦλθε γὰρ Ἰωάννης μήτε ἐσθίων μήτε πίνων· καὶ λέγουσι· 33
19 Δαιμόνιον ἔχει. ἦλθεν ὁ Υἱὸς τοῦ ἀνθρώπου ἐσθίων καὶ πίνων· καὶ 34
λέγουσιν· Ἰδοὺ, ἄνθρωπος φάγος καὶ οἰνοπότης, τελωνῶν φίλος καὶ 35
20 ἁμαρτωλῶν. Καὶ ἐδικαιώθη ἡ σοφία ἀπὸ τῶν τέκνων αὐτῆς. Τότε
ἤρξατο ὀνειδίζειν τὰς πόλεις, ἐν αἷς ἐγένοντο αἱ πλεῖσται δυνάμεις αὐ- 10.
21 τοῦ, ὅτι οὐ μετενόησαν. Οὐαί σοι, Χοραζίν! οὐαί σοι, ‡ Βηθσαϊδάν! 13
ὅτι εἰ ἐν Τύρῳ καὶ Σιδῶνι ἐγένοντο αἱ δυνάμεις αἱ γενόμεναι ἐν ὑμῖν,
22 πάλαι ἂν ἐν σάκκῳ καὶ σποδῷ μετενόησαν. Πλὴν λέγω ‡ ὑμῖν· Τύρῳ 14

type to Elias, who was the *type* of what the Baptist would be in after times. So in Sirach 48. 10. he is represented as ὁ καταγραφεὶς ἐν ἐλεγμοῖς εἰς καίρους, &c., where for ἐλ. (variously written in MSS.) I conjecture ἐλεγμῷ. The ι arose from the ι adscript, and the ς from the ε following. That the figurative adoption of a *name* does not imply an *identity*, is admitted by the Rabbins themselves; most of whom acknowledge that the prophecy in question regards the *Messiah*. The *typical* character of Elias is clear from the Gospel; for as the angel (alluding to this prophecy) told Zacharias that his son would be endued with the *spirit* and *power* of Elias; so these qualifications were communicated to John in the same manner as the spirit of Moses was given to Elijah by the Holy Ghost. The resemblance between the Prophet and the Baptist is conspicuous; not only in mode of life, manners, and dress, but still more in *spirit*, (with which he was exceedingly jealous for the Lord of Hosts, 1 Kings xix. 10.) and in *power*, whereby he "turned many to the Lord their God," Luke i. 16.

15. ὁ ἔχων — ἀκουέτω.] A formula (conveying an appeal to the understanding) often used to solicit attention to something of great importance; and chiefly occurring after parabolic or prophetic declarations figuratively expressed.

16. τίνι δὲ ὁμοιώσω.] A form of introducing a parable frequent in the Scriptures and the Talmud.

— παιδίοις.] In this reading all the Editors from Wets. to Scholz acquiesce, instead of the common one παιδαρίοις, which has very little authority. Ὁμοία ἐστὶ only denotes that there is a *general* similarity, by which the two things compared may be mutually illustrated. Ἀγοραῖς denotes not only market-places, but those *broad places* in the streets, (especially where they intersect each other) which are places of concourse, *like* market-places. Hence the words ἀγοραὶ and πλατεῖαι are often in the Sept. used indifferently to express the same Heb. word. Καθῆσθαι is said to be, like the Heb. ישב, used in the sense *versari*, *esse*. Yet it may allude to the *posture*, so suitable to Eastern manners.

17. ηὐλήσαμεν — ἐκόψασθε] Seemingly a proverbial expression; in which there is a reference to the *dramatic* sports of children; who, to use their phraseology, "play at" (i. e. represent) some action or character. So the Pharisees are compared to wayward children, who will participate in no play which their companions propose; since they neither would admit the severe precepts of John, nor approve the mild requisitions of Christ. On the use of musical wind instruments both at funerals and at feasts, in airs adapted, in character, to each respectively, see Grot., Mackn., and Horne's Introd. iii. 480, and 524.

18. ἦλθε.] This is *not* redundant, as some Commentators suppose, but signifies, "came forward as a teacher and prophet." Μήτε ἐσθίων μήτε πίνων, is an hyperbolical expression, well characterizing the ascetic austerity of John. By the force of the opposition ἐσθίων καὶ πίνων, must denote the *contrary*, namely, the living like other men.

19. καὶ ἐδικαιώθη — αὐτῆς.] There is scarcely any passage in the N. T. that has been more variously expounded. The most probable interpretations are the following.—1. understanding σοφία to apply to the counsels and plans of John and Christ respectively, we may regard the sentence as a reflection of our Lord on the Pharisees, thus: q. d. "But [when the perverseness of men has done its utmost in aspersing the preachers of true religion] *wisdom and virtue* will still vindicate themselves." 2. We may understand by σοφία the counsels of God for the conversion of the Jews; and by τέκν. those who embrace those counsels. And, in this view, the sentence has been thus paraphrased:—"The conduct of John the Baptist and myself, however different, are alike conformable to the Divine wisdom; and those who are enlightened by this wisdom will justify both;" i. e. will vindicate the propriety of both, as the result of different circumstances. The first interpretation seems preferable, as more agreeable to the context. In either case the καὶ is for ἀλλὰ, as often, and ἀπὸ means, "on the part of, or in the case of."

21. οὐαί σοι.] "Alas for thee!"

— Βηθσαϊδάν.] Βηθσαϊδὰ is found in many MSS., Versions, and Fathers; and is adopted or preferred by every Editor from Mill to Fritz., except Griesb. and Scholz, who retain the common reading; and rightly, for external evidence is against Βηθσαϊδὰ, and internal by no means in its favour; Βηθσαϊδὰν being the more *difficult* reading, and therefore more probably genuine. It is not, as some imagine, in the accusative case, but is a nominative of Chaldee form.

— πάλαι.] This signifies not so much *diu* as *jamdiu*.

LU.
10. καὶ Σιδῶνι ἀνεκτότερον ἔσται ἐν ἡμέρᾳ κρίσεως ἢ ὑμῖν. Καὶ σὺ, 23
15 Καπερναοὺμ, ἡ ἕως τοῦ οὐρανοῦ ὑψωθεῖσα, ἕως ᾅδου καταβιβασθήσῃ·
ὅτι εἰ ἐν Σοδόμοις ἐγένοντο αἱ δυνάμεις αἱ γενόμεναι ἐν σοὶ, ἔμειναν
ἂν μέχρι τῆς σήμερον. Πλὴν λέγω ὑμῖν, ὅτι γῇ Σοδόμων ἀνεκτότερον 24
21 ἔσται ἐν ἡμέρᾳ κρίσεως ἢ σοί. Ἐν ἐκείνῳ τῷ καιρῷ ἀποκριθεὶς 25
ὁ Ἰησοῦς εἶπεν· Ἐξομολογοῦμαί σοι, πάτερ, κύριε τοῦ οὐρανοῦ καὶ τῆς
γῆς, ὅτι ἀπέκρυψας ταῦτα ἀπὸ σοφῶν καὶ συνετῶν, καὶ ἀπεκάλυψας
αὐτὰ νηπίοις. Ναὶ, ὁ πατὴρ, ὅτι οὕτως ἐγένετο εὐδοκία ἔμπροσθέν 26
22 σου! Πάντα μοι παρεδόθη ὑπὸ τοῦ πατρός μου· καὶ οὐδεὶς ἐπιγι- 27
νώσκει τὸν υἱὸν, εἰ μὴ ὁ πατήρ· οὐδὲ τὸν πατέρα τίς ἐπιγινώσκει, εἰ
μὴ ὁ υἱὸς, καὶ ᾧ ἐὰν βούληται ὁ υἱὸς ἀποκαλύψαι. Δεῦτε πρός με 28
πάντες οἱ κοπιῶντες καὶ πεφορτισμένοι, κἀγὼ ἀναπαύσω ὑμᾶς. Ἄρατε 29
τὸν ζυγόν μου ἐφ' ὑμᾶς, καὶ μάθετε ἀπ' ἐμοῦ· ὅτι πρᾷός εἰμι καὶ

—σάκκῳ,] from the Hebrew שַׂק, a coarse cloth, of linen or rough wool, worn for humiliation; as ashes were sprinkled on the head in token of sorrow. See Horne's Introd. vol. iii. p. 523.

23. ἡ ἕως—καταβιβασθήσῃ.] These are hyperbolical expressions, figuratively representing the height of prosperity, and the depth of adversity: ᾅδου signifying the lower parts of the earth. Simil. Antholog. i. 80. 15. ad Fortunam. Τοὺς δ' ἀπὸ τῶν νεφελῶν εἰς ἀΐδην κατάγει.

24. Comp. Sup. x. 15.

25. ἀποκριθεὶς εἶπεν.] This expression is here, as sometimes elsewhere, used, where nothing has gone before to which an answer could be supposed; in which most Commentators (as Kuin,) imagine a pleonasm of ἀποκριθεὶς; others a Hebraism, עָנָה being sometimes so used. There must, however, be some *reason* for the use of either term; and Whitby seems right in supposing, that there is usually a *relation* to something; i. e. to something which is passing in the mind either of the speaker or hearer, i. e. (as Fritz. says) "either to some supposed question, suppressed from brevity, to which this is an answer; (See Math. xxii. 1. Luke v. 22. vii. 39. sq.) or to some question which might arise from certain actions." See Mark ix. 38. Luke i. 60; xxii. 51.

—ἐξομολογοῦμαί σοι.] This verb properly signifies to *acknowledge*, with an ellipsis of χάριν *(obligation)*; and, *è consequenti*, to *return thanks*, to *praise*, and *glorify*. This secondary sense it carries, when followed by a Dative; and often occurs in the Sept., where the same Hebrew word is rendered by ἐξομολογεῖσθαι, αἰνεῖν, and ὑμνεῖν.

—ὅτι ἀπέκρυψας—νηπίοις.] The best Commentators, ancient and modern, are agreed that the sense is, "because, having permitted these things to be hidden to the wise and sagacious, thou hast revealed them unto children in knowledge." For God is said in Scripture to *do* what he is pleased to *permit* to be done, and what he foresees *will* be done under the circumstances in which his creatures are placed; though their wills are held under no constraint. With respect to the *former* idiom, it occurs in Rom. vi. 17. Is. xii. 1. Exod. vii. 4. and 5. 2 Sam. xii. 11. and 12; and often elsewhere; nay, sometimes in the Classical writers. See Fritz. The σοφοὶ and the συνετοὶ are thought to have reference to the Hebrew חכמים and נבונים, different orders of Jewish teachers of the law. Perhaps, however, that is too fanciful; σοφοὶ, it should seem, has reference to *acquired* knowledge, and συνετοὶ to *natural* talents: while νηπ., by the force of the opposition, denotes persons of plain understanding, with no pretensions to peculiar ability.

26. ὁ πατήρ.] Nomin. for Vocat. An idiom chiefly occurring in Heb. and Hellenistic Greek, but occasionally in the Classical writers, Greek and Latin. The ὅτι is *emphatical*. We may render: "Yea [I do thank thee], O Father, because it was thy good pleasure that so [it should be.]"

27. πάντα.] On the *subject* of the discourse here, the Commentators are not agreed; some understand it of *things*, and explain it generally, of all *power*. Others understand it not of *things*, but of *persons*. The *former*, however, is more probable; but the context requires that we should, with some of the best Commentators, take πάντα to mean all things relating to the counsels of God for the salvation of man.

—παρεδόθη] "were communicated and taught." So John vii. 16. ἡ ἐμὴ διδαχὴ οὐκ ἔστιν ἐμὴ ἀλλὰ τοῦ πέμψαντός με. And Comp. John xvii. 7. and 8. This doctrine of a certain subordination of the Son to the Father, and the origination of the attributes of Divinity with the Father, comp. infra 28. 13. John iii. 35. xiii. 3. and xvii. 2. when connected with what we elsewhere learn of their equality and majesty co-eternal, (See John i. 18. vi. 46. and x. 15.) and that which follows, of the reciprocal knowledge of the same Persons, involve a mystery which the human understanding cannot penetrate. See Chrys., Grot., and Doddr.

28. οἱ κοπιῶντες καὶ πεφορτισμένοι.] Some understand these words of the *Jews*, with reference to the burdens of the ceremonial law; and the additional injunctions of the Rabbis, called φορτία βαρέα, δυσβάστακτα, Matth. xxiii. 4. Others refer them to the burdens of *temptation* and *sin*. Thus, there might be reference both to the Jews and Gentiles. And indeed it seems best to take them, with Chrys., Origen, and Theophyl., of both Jews and Gentiles, and meant to apply as the case might be; to the Jews, in *both* senses, to the Gentiles in the *latter*; and ἀναπαύσω will be interpreted accordingly.

29. ἄρατε—ἐμοῦ.] These words are exegetical of the preceding; and the sense "become my

MK. LU.
30 ταπεινὸς τῇ καρδίᾳ· καὶ εὑρήσετε ἀνάπαυσιν ταῖς ψυχαῖς ὑμῶν. Ὁ 2. 6.
γὰρ ζυγός μου χρηστὸς, καὶ τὸ φορτίον μου ἐλαφρόν ἐστιν.
1 XII. Ἐν ἐκείνῳ τῷ καιρῷ ἐπορεύθη ὁ Ἰησοῦς τοῖς σάββασι διὰ τῶν 23 1
σπορίμων· οἱ δὲ μαθηταὶ αὐτοῦ ἐπείνασαν, καὶ ἤρξαντο τίλλειν στά-
2 χυας καὶ ἐσθίειν. Οἱ δὲ Φαρισαῖοι ἰδόντες εἶπον αὐτῷ· Ἰδοὺ, οἱ 24 2
3 μαθηταί σου ποιοῦσιν, ὃ οὐκ ἔξεστι ποιεῖν ἐν σαββάτῳ. Ὁ δὲ εἶπεν 25 3
αὐτοῖς· Οὐκ ἀνέγνωτε τί ἐποίησε Δαυῒδ, ὅτε ἐπείνασεν, [αὐτὸς] καὶ
4 οἱ μετ' αὐτοῦ; πῶς εἰσῆλθεν εἰς τὸν οἶκον τοῦ Θεοῦ, καὶ τοὺς ἄρ- 26 4
τους τῆς προθέσεως ἔφαγεν, οὓς οὐκ ἐξὸν ἦν αὐτῷ φαγεῖν, οὐδὲ τοῖς
5 μετ' αὐτοῦ, εἰ μὴ τοῖς ἱερεῦσι μόνοις; Ἢ οὐκ ἀνέγνωτε ἐν τῷ νόμῳ,
ὅτι τοῖς σάββασιν οἱ ἱερεῖς ἐν τῷ ἱερῷ τὸ σάββατον βεβηλοῦσι, καὶ
6 ἀναίτιοί εἰσι; λέγω δὲ ὑμῖν, ὅτι τοῦ ἱεροῦ * μεῖζόν ἐστιν ὧδε. Εἰ δὲ
7 ἐγνώκειτε τί ἐστιν, "Ἔλεον θέλω καὶ οὐ θυσίαν," οὐκ ἂν κατεδικάσατε

disciples," is expressed in metaphors familiar to the Jews, and not unfrequent with the Gentiles; whereby a law or precept is called a *yoke*, by a metaphor taken from oxen which are in harness. See Zach. ix. 9. Jer. vi. 16. Phil. ii. 7. and 8., and Recens. Synop. Πρᾶος denotes "gentle, unassuming, and condescending;" as opposed to the tyranny and haughtiness of the Scribes and Pharisees. The clause πρᾶος—καρδίᾳ is, in some measure, parenthetical; and meant by our Lord to recommend himself to their choice as a teacher. Ἀνάπαυσις denotes not only relief from the burdens of the Jewish ceremonial law, but relief from the sense of unforgiven sin; including all the comforts and blessings of the Gospel, both in this world and in the next.

30. χρηστός.] As spoken of a *burden*, the word denotes what is convenient, and suitable to the strength of the bearers, εὔφορον. [*Comp.* 1 John v. 3.]

XII. 1. ἐν ἐκείνῳ τῷ καιρῷ.] An indefinite phrase, signifying *about* that time, not necessarily connecting what follows with the preceding. The exact time is indicated by Luke vi. 1.

—σάββασι.] This term (by the usage of both the Sept. and the N. T.) has only the force of a singular. Τίλλειν conjoined with ἐσθίειν, *implies* what Luke expresses by ψώχοντες. It appears from Deut. xxiii. 25. that it was allowed by the law, to pluck ears of corn with the hand in another's field.

2. ὃ οὐκ ἔξεστι κ. τ. λ.] That, however, was a disputed point; for though Moses had forbidden all *servile* work on the Sabbath day; it was a controverted point what was, and what was not such. *Reaping* was admitted to fall under the former class; and plucking of ears, being a sort of reaping, was forbidden by the more rigid Rabbis. That, however, especially when the action was done from necessity, was contrary to the *spirit* of the law. See Exod. xii. 16. But our Lord only meets the accusation, by urging, that the thing was not done purposely, but from necessity; on the score of which, or for the performance of a work of charity, he shews that the ceremonial law may be dispensed with.

3. αὐτός.] This has no place in many of the MSS., and some Versions; and has been thrown out, or disapproved, by almost all the Editors from Mill to Scholz, but is retained by Matthæi and Fritz.: rightly, I think, for not only external but internal evidence, is in favor of the word, which, as Fritz. observes, is necessary to the connection: αὐτὸς — αὐτοῦ being said, κατ' ἐπανόρθωσιν, of which he adduces several examples, as Acts xi. 14. ὃς λαλήσει ῥήματα πρός σε ἐν οἷς σωθήσῃ σὺ καὶ πᾶς ὁ οἶκός σου.

4. οἶκον τοῦ Θεοῦ.] Not the *Temple*, (which was not then built,) but the court of the *Tabernacle*, which preceded it. See Horne's Introduction. Εἰ μὴ is for ἀλλὰ when a negative has preceded; which is called a Hebraism, but it is occasionally found in the Classical writers. See Recens. Synop. Homberg and Fritz., however, make εἰ μὴ dependent upon ἐξὸν, assigning an *exceptive*, not an *adversative* force. [*Comp.* 1 Sam. xxi. 6. Exod. xxv. 30. Levit. xxiv. 6. viii. 31.]

5. ἐν τῷ νόμῳ.] See Numb. xxviii. 9.

—βεβηλοῦσι.] Not really so, but κατὰ τὸ ῥητόν: as those may be said to violate a law, by doing what, unless the worship of God had excused it, it would not have been lawful for them to do. So the Rabbis speak, when they say that the Sabbath is *lawfully violated* by doing such and such sacerdotal works, and that "there it no Sabbatism in the Temple."

6. τοῦ ἱεροῦ — ὧδε.] Our Lord here anticipates an objection; q. d. "But *you* are no Priest, nor is your work for the benefit of the Temple." To which he does not directly reply, "*I* am one greater than the Temple;" but, modestly and delicately, "here is something, i. e. one, greater than the Temple." Thus those engaged in his service, may be allowed an equal liberty with the priests, especially as works of necessity, or of mercy, are to be preferred before ritual observances. Μεῖζον, which is preferred by nearly all the Editors and Commentators, and edited by Matth., Fritz., and Scholz, is evidently the true reading, being found in the greater part of the MSS., the Edit. Princ., and many of the Greek Fathers. The sense is the same as ver. 41.: καὶ ἰδοὺ, πλεῖον Ἰωνᾶ ὧδε (ἐστι). and 42. πλεῖον Σολομῶνος, and Lu. xi. 31.

7. εἰ δὲ ἐγνώκειτε τί ἐστιν.] A delicate mode, (as supr. ix. 13.,) of asserting the excellency of thing. The passage cited is Hos. vi. 6., before adduced at ix. 13. Ἔλεον and θυσ. stand, respectively, for the virtues of charity and benevolence, and the works of the ceremonial law.

MK LU.
2 6. τοὺς ἀναιτίους. Κύριος γάρ ἐστι [καὶ] τοῦ σαββάτου ὁ Υἱὸς τοῦ 8
28 5 ἀνθρώπου.
3. Καὶ μεταβὰς ἐκεῖθεν, ἦλθεν εἰς τὴν συναγωγὴν αὐτῶν. Καὶ ἰδού, 9
2 7 ἄνθρωπος ἦν τὴν χεῖρα ἔχων ξηράν. καὶ ἐπηρώτησαν αὐτὸν, λέγοντες, 10
εἰ ἔξεστι τοῖς σάββασι θεραπεύειν; ἵνα κατηγορήσωσιν αὐτοῦ. Ὁ δὲ 11
εἶπεν αὐτοῖς· Τίς ἔσται ἐξ ὑμῶν ἄνθρωπος, ὃς ἕξει πρόβατον ἓν, καὶ
ἐὰν ἐμπέσῃ τοῦτο τοῖς σάββασιν εἰς βόθυνον, οὐχὶ κρατήσει αὐτὸ καὶ
2. ἐγερεῖ; Πόσῳ οὖν διαφέρει ἄνθρωπος προβάτου! ὥστε ἔξεστι τοῖς 12
5 10 σάββασι καλῶς ποιεῖν. Τότε λέγει τῷ ἀνθρώπῳ· Ἔκτεινον τὴν χεῖρά 13
σου. καὶ ἐξέτεινε· καὶ ἀποκατεστάθη ὑγιὴς ὡς ἡ ἄλλη. Οἱ δὲ Φαρι- 14
σαῖοι συμβούλιον ἔλαβον κατ᾽ αὐτοῦ ἐξελθόντες, ὅπως αὐτὸν ἀπολέσωσιν. ὁ δὲ Ἰησοῦς γνοὺς ἀνεχώρησεν ἐκεῖθεν. Καὶ ἠκολούθησαν αὐτῷ 15
ὄχλοι πολλοὶ, καὶ ἐθεράπευσεν αὐτοὺς πάντας· καὶ ἐπετίμησεν αὐτοῖς, 16
ἵνα μὴ φανερὸν αὐτὸν ποιήσωσιν. Ὅπως πληρωθῇ τὸ ῥηθὲν διὰ 17
Ἡσαΐου τοῦ προφήτου, λέγοντος· Ἰδοὺ, ὁ παῖς μου, ὃν ᾑρέτι- 18

8. Κύριος — ἀνθρώπου.] Grot. and many other eminent Commentators maintain that ὁ υἱὸς τοῦ ἀνθρώπου here signifies *man* generally; which may seem to be countenanced by the parallel passage of Mark ii. 28. But in all the other 87 passages of the N. T. where it occurs, the expression signifies the Son of man, *the Messiah*; which sense also the *Article* requires: whereas υἱὸς τοῦ ἀνθρώπου without the Art. as invariably denotes *a* son of man, a man. Neither does the ὥστε at Mark xi. 28. compel us to take the phrase to denote *man*; since it may be *continuative*, introductory of a new argument, and signify *moreover;* on which sense see examples in Hoogev. Part. See more in Hamm., Whitby, and Doddr. As to the γὰρ of the present passage, it may refer to something not expressed, but merely what is passing in the mind of the speaker; an idiom very frequent in all writers, Scriptural and Classical. And here the suppression is evidently from the same cause that produced the use of μεῖζον for μείζων. It will clear the construction to consider ver. 7. as parenthetical, and to refer the γὰρ to some clause connected with ver. 6.; q. d. "There is one here greater than the Temple (and his sanction will warrant the breach of any such ceremonial institution as that of the Sabbath); for the Son of man," &c. The καὶ before τοῦ σαββάτου, is not found in the great body of the MSS., nor in several of the Greek Fathers; and is cancelled by Matth., Griesb., Knapp, Vater, Fritz., and Scholz; as having probably been introduced from the parallel passages of Mark and Luke. Here it sould seem rather to darken and perturb the sense.

9. αὐτῶν] i. e. of the people to whom he had now come.

10. χεῖρα ξηράν.] This is not to be understood of "a *partial paralysis*," as some suppose; but according to the most accurate inquirers, an *atrophy of the limb*, occasioned by an evaporation of the vital juices, involving an inability to move the nerves and muscles; which must also be the sense at 1 Kings xii. 4.

— εἰ ἔξεστι, &c.] A modest form of negation. Not so the ruler of the synagogue on a similar occasion, recorded at Luke xiii. 14. See also John ix. 16. From the Rabbinical citations, it appears that it had been decided unlawful to heal any one on the Sabbath day, unless he were in imminent peril of life. Yet it appears from Luke xiv. 3, that Christ at length made the Pharisees almost ashamed to advance the principle. At ἐὰν ἐμπέσῃ there is a Hebrew or Hellenistic construction. Some, too, suppose an anacoluthon at οὐχὶ κρατήσει. But this is rightly rejected by Fritz. Ἐγερεῖ, "will pull it out." A rare sense of the word, of which, however, the Commentators adduce an example from Philo. This was allowed by the earlier Rabbis, but forbidden by the later ones.

13. ἀποκατεστάθη.] The word properly signifies to bring any thing back to its former situation, or state; and figuratively, to restore to health, as in the Sept. and some later writers.

17. ὅπως πληρωθῇ,] See Note supra i. 22.

18. ἰδοὺ, ὁ παῖς μου, &c.] This prophecy, (from Is. xlii. 1.) differs somewhat from the Hebrew, and yet more from the Sept.; which is supposed to have been corrupted; and the words Ἰακὼβ and Ἰσραὴλ (of which there are no traces in the Heb.,) to have been inserted *by the Jews*, that the passage might not be applied to the Messiah; but without reason. The words, I suspect, were, at first, noted in the *margin* of some very antient Archetypes; and then were introduced, inadvertently, into the *text* by the scribes; who thought the words were to be *added*. Thus Eusebius testifies that the words were, in his time, *obelized* in the Sept., and were not expressed in the other Greek Versions; that is, not even that of Aquila the Jew, which is certainly very adverse to the above suspicion. In short, in the first two verses (at least as far as οὐ σβέσει), there is very little variation from the Hebrew, certainly none of any importance and where there *is* any at all, it is justified by the Sept. And as to the variation of the Sept. from the *Evangelist*, it is not (up to the above words) any greater diversity than that of a *free* version as compared with a *literal* one — that is, if the words of the Sept. be corrected from MSS., and a *great corruption*, which at present exists, be removed. For such I consider ἀνήσει, which gives a sense directly the reverse to that which is required by the context. I have no doubt but that the true reading is ἀνάψει, *will*

LU.
σα· ὁ ἀγαπητός μου, εἰς ὃν εὐδόκησεν ἡ ψυχή μου. 11.
Θήσω τὸ πνεῦμά μου ἐπ᾽ αὐτὸν, καὶ κρίσιν τοῖς ἔθ-
19 νεσιν ἀπαγγελεῖ. Οὐκ ἐρίσει, οὐδὲ κραυγάσει· οὐδὲ
20 ἀκούσει τις ἐν ταῖς πλατείαις τὴν φωνὴν αὐτοῦ. Κάλαμον συντετριμμένον οὐ κατεάξει, καὶ λῖνον τυφό-
μενον οὐ σβέσει· ἕως ἂν ἐκβάλῃ εἰς νῖκος τὴν κρί-
21 σιν. Καὶ [ἐν] τῷ ὀνόματι αὐτοῦ ἔθνη ἐλπιοῦσι.
22 Τότε προσηνέχθη αὐτῷ δαιμονιζόμενος, τυφλὸς καὶ κωφὸς, καὶ 14
ἐθεράπευσεν αὐτόν· ὥστε τὸν τυφλὸν καὶ κωφὸν καὶ λαλεῖν καὶ βλέ-
23 πειν. Καὶ ἐξίσταντο πάντες οἱ ὄχλοι, καὶ ἔλεγον· Μήτι οὗτός ἐστιν

exclaim. The word occurs in Theocritus Id. iv. 37. and elsewhere. The abbreviation for αυ is sometimes confounded with η. Bp. Randolph thinks the Evangelist here followed some old translation different from the Sept. But that is too hypothetical: whether there *was* any such version so early as the time of St. Matthew may be doubted. It should rather seem, that the Evangelist, observing the Sept. not to give a faithful representation of the original, *corrected* it agreeably thereto, and, as I conjecture, conformably to what had appeared in the *Syro-Chaldee* Edition of his Gospel.

The greatest difficulty, however, connected with this passage rests on the words ἕως ἂν ἐκβάλῃ — ἐλπιοῦσι. There is here a considerable variation from both the Sept. and the Hebrew; though I think it will be found to involve no real discrepancy. Let us, however, first examine the variation between the *Hebrew* and the *Sept.* The translators by ἔθνη thought proper to give the *meaning* intended by the Prophet, rather than the *literal expression;* which would have required νῆσοι. The sense is, the "most remote nations, not only the Jews, but the Gentiles." As to the diversity in ὀνόματι, (for the Heb. תורתו means *law* or *doctrine,*) we may *either*, with Schleus., suppose ὀνόματι to be used in the sense *law* or doctrine, as in various passages of the N. T., which he so explains in his Lex. Nov. Test.; *or* we may suppose the true reading to be νόμῳ. So in Ps. cxx. 4. instead of ὀνόματος several MSS. have νόμου, which is required by the Hebrew, and was edited by Grabe. However, as both methods seem somewhat precarious, I should prefer supposing that the Sept. here, as before, chose to express the *general sense* in a *very free* version; and that the Evangelist followed the Sept. as far as he thought it sufficiently faithful and to his purpose.

But there yet remains one diversity to be discussed; which is, I apprehend, quite irreconcilable, namely, ἀναλάμψει. I have no doubt that the Sept. wrote ἀνακάμψει; and also that a negative particle has here (as occasionally in all authors) slipped out. Thus οὐκ ἀνακ., "he will not give way or desist," (See Cebes cited by Steph. Thes. in v.) expresses the true sense of the Heb. לא יכהה. Finally, to advert to the difference between the *Hebrew* and the *Evangelist*, this consists, 1. in the omission of several words, and 2. in the *change* of others. But neither, I apprehend, involves any real *discrepancy;* for the sense, as will be seen, is precisely the same. The Evangelist seems to have purposely omitted *part* of the words, because they were not very apposite to his purpose; and probably were even then very corrupt in the Sept.: and in expressing the sense of the *others*, he chose (as is often done in Scripture) to *blend* together the two clauses לאמת יוציא משפט and ישים בארץ משפט into one, and expresses the SUBSTANCE of them. So that the sense of the words ἕως ἐκβάλῃ (answering to ἐξοίσει in the Sept.) εἰς νῖκος τὴν κρίσιν is this: ["And thus will it be] until he send forth [over the whole earth] his Rule of life, [the Gospel] conquering and to conquer:" literally for conquest. On this sense of κρίσις see Schleusn. and Wahl., and Bp. Lowth on Is. xlii. 4. The article is, as often, put for the pronoun possessive; as the later Syriac translator saw, and also the early interpreters; for to *them* we may attribute the αὐτοῦ which is added in several MSS. The Evangelist has shown the true *application* of the prophecy; the chief import of which is centred in the second verse. The whole has reference to the *quiet* and *unostentatious* mode in which Christ promulgated his religion; not resorting to violence or clamour, or offering resistance to oppression; but employing the mildest means: by which, however, it would at length be spread over all the nations of the universe.

— ᾑρέτισα.] The verb denotes properly to *choose*, and from thence, as here, to *love* and *favour*. [*Comp.* sup. 3, 17. infra 17. 5.]

20. κάλαμον — σβέσει.] These are lively figures of extreme weakness, importing profound humility and contrition. And here, (as often in the Classical writers,) by the negation of one thing is implied the affirmation of the contrary: q. d. "he will *strengthen* wavering faith, and will *rekindle* nearly extinct piety."

21. καὶ ἐν — ἐλπιοῦσι.] "In him (in his Gospel) shall the Gentiles trust (for instruction and salvation.") The ἐν is omitted in various MSS. the Edit. Princ., and some Fathers, is marked for omission by Wets. and Vater, and is cancelled by Matthæi, Griesb., and Scholz. But as both the Heb. and Sept. have a preposition, it should seem probable, that the Evangelist, in adopting this image from the Sept., would take the *preposition* as well as the words; which indeed can scarcely be dispensed with, since its omission destroys the construction.

23. ἐξίσταντο.] The word properly signifies, by an ellips. of τοῦ νοῦ, to be stirred out of one's mind, and secondly, to *be greatly astonished;* by the same metaphor as we say to be frightened *out of one's wits.* Μήτι must be rendered *num*, not *nonne;* for, as Campb. remarks, the former implies that *disbelief* preponderates; the latter,

MK. LU.
3. 11. ὁ υἱὸς Δαυΐδ; Οἱ δὲ Φαρισαῖοι ἀκούσαντες, εἶπον· Οὗτος οὐκ ἐκβάλ- 24
22 23 15 17 λει τὰ δαιμόνια, εἰ μὴ ἐν τῷ Βεελζεβοὺλ ἄρχοντι τῶν δαιμονίων. Εἰδὼς 25
24 δὲ ὁ Ἰησοῦς τὰς ἐνθυμήσεις αὐτῶν, εἶπεν αὐτοῖς· Πᾶσα βασιλεία μερισθεῖσα καθ᾽ ἑαυτῆς ἐρημοῦται· καὶ πᾶσα πόλις ἢ οἰκία μερισθεῖσα
26 18 καθ᾽ ἑαυτῆς οὐ σταθήσεται. Καὶ εἰ ὁ Σατανᾶς τὸν Σατανᾶν ἐκβάλλει, 26
19 ἐφ᾽ ἑαυτὸν ἐμερίσθη· πῶς οὖν σταθήσεται ἡ βασιλεία αὐτοῦ; Καὶ εἰ 27
ἐγὼ ἐν Βεελζεβοὺλ ἐκβάλλω τὰ δαιμόνια, οἱ υἱοὶ ὑμῶν ἐν τίνι ἐκβάλλουσι; Διὰ τοῦτο αὐτοὶ ὑμῶν ἔσονται κριταί. Εἰ δὲ ἐγὼ ἐν πνεύματι 28
20 Θεοῦ ἐκβάλλω τὰ δαιμόνια, ἄρα ἔφθασεν ἐφ᾽ ὑμᾶς ἡ βασιλεία τοῦ Θεοῦ.
27 21 Ἢ πῶς δύναταί τις εἰσελθεῖν εἰς τὴν οἰκίαν τοῦ ἰσχυροῦ, καὶ τὰ 29
σκεύη αὐτοῦ διαρπάσαι, ἐὰν μὴ πρῶτον δήσῃ τὸν ἰσχυρόν; καὶ τότε
23 τὴν οἰκίαν αὐτοῦ διαρπάσει; Ὁ μὴ ὢν μετ᾽ ἐμοῦ κατ᾽ ἐμοῦ ἐστι· 30
28 καὶ ὁ μὴ συνάγων μετ᾽ ἐμοῦ σκορπίζει. Διὰ τοῦτο λέγω ὑμῖν· πᾶσα 31

belief. The multitude seems to have spoken thus modestly, to avoid offending the Pharisees: By υἱὸς Δ. is meant the promised Messiah. See note sup. i. 1.

24. ἄρχοντι τῶν δαιμονίων.] Not only was an hierarchy of *good* angels held, but a subordination and headship was believed to exist among the *evil* ones. And this not only by the *Incantatores* and *Exorcistæ*, &c., but by the Rabbis, and even the Philosophers.

25. πᾶσα βασιλεία—ἐρημοῦται.] A proverbial saying, (similar to many cited from the Classical and Rabbinical writers,) in which there is (as Kuin. observes) an argumentum ab absurdo; q. d. "The safety of a *state* or a *family* is promoted by concord, and is destroyed by dissensions. If Satan were to assist me in expelling his demons from the bodies of men, whither he has empowered them to enter, he would be at discord with himself, would act foolishly, and his authority could not continue." The argument then is briefly this: that it were absurd to suppose Satan acting against himself, by casting out his own agents of evil.

26. καὶ εἰ ὁ Σατανᾶς.] The καὶ is taken by Beza for ἀλλά; by Kuin. in the sense *quodsi*. But it is better to render it [*so*] *also*.

27. ἐν Βεελζεβοὺλ.] That there were persons among the Jews who professed to cast out demons by exorcisms, and invocation of the God of Abraham, Isaac, and Jacob, we learn both from the Scriptures (see Luke ix. 49. Acts xix. 13. Mark ix. 38.) and from Joseph. Ant. viii. 2, 5. vii. 6, 3, also from the early Fathers, (as Justin Martyr, Irenæus, Origen, Tertullian, and others) and Lucian Trag. p. 171. The argument therefore, is, "If those who cast out demons prove themselves to be leagued with Satan, then must *your disciples* be *also* leagued with him; and the censure will apply to *them* as well as unto me." It affects not the argument whether the demons were really expelled by such exorcism (though it might *sometimes* happen, by the permission of God); it is sufficient for the *argumentum ad hominem*, that the Pharisees *thought* they were expelled, and did not attribute it to the agency of Satan. Υἱοί, by an idiom derived from the customs of the Jews, denotes *disciples*. See 1 Kings xx. 35. 2 Tim. i. 2.

28. ἐν πνεύματι Θεοῦ] "by divine co-operation;" as in Luke xi. 20. ἐν δακτύλῳ Θεοῦ. See Middlet. G. A. p. 168. The reasoning is this: "But if I cast out dæmons by *divine* power, I perform *miracles* by the aid of God: hence it follows, that I am *sent* from God. But if I be sent from God, you should believe me, when I announce to you the kingdom of God."

—ἔφθασεν.] Schmid and Fritz. take this to be a strong expression, signifying "is come upon you before you are aware." Perhaps it rather means "is *already* come upon you." The ἢ may be rendered, with Erasm., *alioqui*; or, with Fritz., "*vel*, (ut aliter vobis occurram)."

29. The purpose of this verse is to show the *folly* of supposing that he acts by a power from, and consequently *under* Satan; since he evinces *superiority* over him, by overpowering him, and despoiling him of his authority. "And if (as all must confess) he who binds another is stronger than he who is bound by him, you will easily perceive that I must be far more *powerful* than the Prince of demons."

30. ὁ μὴ ὢν, &c.] Here we have another proverb; of which the *converse holds* equally true, (and is used by Christ at Luke ix. 50,); as often in adages. (See Prov. xxvi. 4 & 5,) each being applicable, according to *circumstances*. The scope of the reasoning here seems to be this; that there can be no *collusion* between Satan and himself—since they are, and must necessarily be, in opposition to each other; agreeably to the proverb, &c. Of the above propositions (both of them true, but in a different view), Bp. Taylor, in his Works, xiv. 300, marks out the distinct measures and proper import of each. In συνάγων, &c. there is *not*, as Kuin. supposes, an allusion to the amassing of money, on the one hand, and its dissipation, on the other; but it is an agricultural, or possibly a pastoral, metaphor, taking from forking together hay or corn, or gathering and folding sheep.

31. διὰ τοῦτο.] There is scarcely any point in the interpretation of the N. T. which has been more debated than the nature of the BLASPHEMY AGAINST THE HOLY SPIRIT, of which it is here said, that "it shall *not be forgiven*." It would be a waste of time to *read*, still more to detail and review, the far greater part of the interpretations propounded by Theologians, ancient and modern, of this verse. These may, however, be seen in the Critici Sacri, Pol. Syn. Suicer's Thesaur. i. 69. 8, Wolf, Koecher, Kuinoel, and

ἁμαρτία καὶ βλασφημία ἀφεθήσεται τοῖς ἀνθρώποις· ἡ δὲ τοῦ Πνεύ- MK. 3.
32 *ματος βλασφημία οὐκ ἀφεθήσεται τοῖς ἀνθρώποις. Καὶ ὃς ἂν εἴπῃ* 29
λόγον κατὰ τοῦ Υἱοῦ τοῦ ἀνθρώπου, ἀφεθήσεται αὐτῷ· ὃς δ' ἂν

lastly in Bingham's Antiquities of the Christian Church, L. xvi. ch. 7. In order to ascertain the true sense, it is of importance to attend carefully to the *connection*, and to gather what help we can from the parallel passages. Now the *connection* should seem to be decided by the formula διὰ τοῦτο, which introduces what is said; and has reference not so much to what has *just preceded*, as to the *whole* of the foregoing matter; and especially points at the diabolical calumny which had been uttered by the Scribes, in attributing the undisputed miracles of Christ to the agency of the Devil; as is certain from Mark iii. 28. 30. *ὅτι ἔλεγον· πνεῦμα ἀκάθαρτον ἔχει*, of which the full sense is ["this denunciation was uttered] because they said," &c. Of the almost innumerable interpretations which have been propounded, there are only *two* which deserve notice. The main question on which the whole hinges is, whether it was the conduct of the Pharisees *on this particular occasion*, that is meant, or that of the same persons, soon *afterwards*, by *similarly calumniating* the supernatural gifts of the Spirit, shortly afterwards poured forth, after the resurrection and ascension of Christ. The latter view is strenuously and ably maintained by Whitby, (after Baxter and Hamm.) Doddr., and Mack., whose arguments may be stated in the words of Mr. Holden, as follows: "1. It is declared, that whosoever speaketh a word against the Son of man, it shall be forgiven him;" and, therefore, the Pharisees, in calumniating his miracles, were not guilty of the unpardonable sin. "2dly. The sin against the Holy Ghost could not be committed during our Saviour's abode on earth, as the Holy Ghost was not given till after his ascension, John vii. 39. xvi. 7. Acts ii. 1, seq. 3dly. In St. Luke xii. 10, our Saviour makes the same declaration respecting this sin, when no calumny against him was uttered." These arguments, however, are by no means conclusive. As to the 1st and 3d reasons, they are utterly *groundless*; for blasphemy *could* be committed during our Saviour's lifetime — since, though the Holy Ghost was not given to men until after Christ's ascension, and even then only occasionally and limitedly, to Christ it was given *perpetually*, and *without measure*.

This is plain from John iii. 34. *οὐ γὰρ ἐκ μέτρου δίδωσιν ὁ Θεὸς τὸ Πνεῦμα*, where compare the context. The 3d argument has not the least cogency; since in St. Luke the *order* of the events is very little observed, and the occasions when things were said, is often only hinted, not noted. The only one of any weight that has been urged, is, — that the Pharisees present could not be thought utterly inexcusable, since the crowning evidence of Christ's Messiahship, by his resurrection and the subsequent effusion of the Holy Spirit, had not yet been afforded. But that argument is more specious than solid; and involves a sitting in judgment on our God's proceedings: in the words of St. Paul, it is *ὑπερφρονεῖν παρ' ὃ δεῖ φρονεῖν*. The crime of the Pharisees was assuredly, all things considered, *greater* than that committed by those who afterwards spoke evil of the supernatural gifts of the Holy Spirit. It was, as Archbp. Secker observes, "the greatest and most wilful obstinacy in wrong that can be imagined, when they and all around them saw the most illustrious and beneficial miracles done in confirmation of the most holy and benevolent doctrines, to stand out in opposition to both; to insist that the Devil conspired against himself, rather than own the finger of God, where it was so exceedingly visible; not only to oppose, but to revile, the strongest evidence laid before them in the fullest manner, and that, very probably, against the secret conviction of their own hearts; such behaviour manifests the most hardened and desperate wickedness." In short, when we consider the extreme harshness of supposing, that what was said in immediate connection with the conduct of the Pharisees, and introduced by a formula *confining* it to that, was meant not to be understood of *that*, but of another offence, which bore an affinity to it — we shall see that the interpretation in question is really untenable. There is the more reason to warn Biblical students against adopting it; since it was the adoption of it by the Latin and some Greek Fathers, and the subsequent extension of it to speaking evil of the *operations* of the Holy Spirit *generally*, even of his *graces*, which opened a door to the grevious errors into which those Theologians, of the ancient and earlier modern School fell, who almost made the *Sin* (as they inaccurately term it) *against the Holy Spirit*, to consist in a wilful opposition to the teaching of the Spirit, in respect to what such men persuade themselves is alone the truth, as it is in Jesus. Hence the passage has been quoted by Romanists against Protestants, and Protestants against Romanists; by orthodox Protestants against heterodox Protestants; and *might* be adduced by the *maintainers* of the lying miracles of the day against those who *reject* them. Nay, it has been explained of *obstinate resistance* to the *graces* of the Holy Spirit by invincible hardness of heart and impenitence; or of *apostasy*, or of *falling into mortal sins after the grace of the Holy Spirit in baptism*. Yet those who maintain these various views are constrained to, *virtually* at least, admit the crime to be pardonable; which seems contrary to our Saviour's words. Besides, it could not be the design of our Lord to utter what should prove, as it were, a trap for the consciences of men; and should operate to fill timid, though sincerely pious persons, with vain alarm; or to furnish arms for Church polemics to wield one against another *ad infinitum*. I mean not, by what has been said, to aver, that the crime in question was committed *alone* by the Pharisees, who had ascribed the miracles of Christ to the power of the Devil, or that our Lord meant to *confine* the denunciation to *that* blasphemy. It was, I apprehend, meant to apply *also* to those who should *hereafter* ascribe the miracles worked by the Apostles, or by their immediate successors in the government of the Church, to the agency of the evil spirit. At the same time, it must be remembered that most of the offences which have been thought to *constitute* the blasphemy against the Holy Spirit, *bear some affinity* thereto; being, if not *blasphemy* against the Holy Spirit, *sin* against the Holy Spirit, "doing despite to the Spirit of Grace, and bringing swift *destruction* on those who commit them."

LU.
11. εἴπῃ κατὰ τοῦ Πνεύματος τοῦ ἁγίου, οὐκ ἀφεθήσεται αὐτῷ οὔτε ἐν
‡ τούτῳ ‡ τῷ αἰῶνι οὔτε ἐν τῷ μέλλοντι. Ἢ ποιήσατε τὸ δένδρον 33
καλὸν, καὶ τὸν καρπὸν αὐτοῦ καλόν· ἢ ποιήσατε τὸ δένδρον σαπρὸν, καὶ
τὸν καρπὸν αὐτοῦ σαπρόν· ἐκ γὰρ τοῦ καρποῦ τὸ δένδρον γινώσκεται.
Γεννήματα ἐχιδνῶν! πῶς δύνασθε ἀγαθὰ λαλεῖν, πονηροὶ ὄντες; ἐκ 34
γὰρ τοῦ περισσεύματος τῆς καρδίας τὸ στόμα λαλεῖ. Ὁ ἀγαθὸς ἄν- 35
θρωπος ἐκ τοῦ ἀγαθοῦ θησαυροῦ [τῆς καρδίας] ἐκβάλλει [τὰ] ἀγα-
θά· καὶ ὁ πόνηρὸς ἄνθρωπος ἐκ τοῦ πονηροῦ θησαυροῦ ἐκβάλλει
πονηρά. Λέγω δὲ ὑμῖν, ὅτι πᾶν ῥῆμα ἀργὸν, ὃ ἐὰν λαλήσωσιν οἱ 36
ἄνθρωποι, ἀποδώσουσι περὶ αὐτοῦ λόγον ἐν ἡμέρᾳ κρίσεως. Ἐκ γὰρ 37
τῶν λόγων σου δικαιωθήσῃ, καὶ ἐκ τῶν λόγων σου καταδικασθήσῃ.

Τότε ἀπεκρίθησάν τινες τῶν Γραμματέων καὶ Φαρισαίων λέγοντες· 38
Διδάσκαλε, θέλομεν ἀπὸ σοῦ σημεῖον ἰδεῖν. Ὁ δὲ ἀποκριθεὶς εἶπεν 39
29 αὐτοῖς· Γενεὰ πονηρὰ καὶ μοιχαλὶς σημεῖον ἐπιζητεῖ· καὶ σημεῖον

32. *οὔτε ἐν τούτῳ — μέλλοντι.*] According to a common proverb importing *never*. See the Rabbinical citations in Recens. Synop. For *presumptuous* sins, like this, no expiation was provided, even under the Jewish law.

— *τούτῳ τῷ.*] The greater part of the MSS. and many early Editions have *τῷ νῦν*, which is confirmed by 1 Tim. vi. 17. 2. Sam. iv. 10. Tit. iv. 10, is preferred by Wets., and edited by Matthæi and Scholz. And this I should have received, had it not been liable to some suspicion of having arisen *ex interpretatione*.

33. *ἢ ποιήσατε*, &c.] '*ponite*, suppose, consider.' A Latinism for *τίθετε*. There is here a *return* to the course of argument, interrupted by the solemn warning at vv. 31 & 32. And the words, which have the air of an adage, may, with some Expositors, be applied to the *Pharisees*. And this is supported by the parallel passages at Matt. vii. 17, and Luke vi. 44. But from the context, they seem better referred, (with the best Commentators,) to our *Lord himself*. q. d. Account the tree as good which produces good fruit; or the tree bad, which produces bad fruit. The goodness of my doctrine argues its *divine* origin, as good fruit a good tree. [*Comp.* supr. vii. 17. Luke vi. 44.]

34. *πῶς δύνασθε ἀγ. λαλεῖν.*] A popular idiom importing that it is scarcely possible. On *γενν. ἐχιδ.* see Note supra, iii. 7. A yet stronger expression occurs at xxiii. 33.

— *ἐκ γὰρ τοῦ περισσεύματος*, &c.] A proverbial expression, with which Wets. compares Menand. *ἀνδρὸς χαρακτὴρ ἐκ λόγων γνωρίζεται.* Aristid. *οἷος ὁ τρόπος, τοιοῦτος καὶ ὁ λόγος.*

35. *ἐκβάλλει.*] For *προφέρει*. It is not, however, a Hebraism, as some say; for examples are adduced from the best Greek writers. The sense is, "The good man, from the treasure of his kind affections, brings forth candid opinions, and equitable decisions; the wicked man has within him a store of pride, enmity; and malice, which he pours forth in slanderous and unjust language."

— *τῆς καρδίας*] is omitted in the greater part of the MSS., the Edit. Princ., and several Versions and Fathers; and is cancelled, or rejected by all the Editors from Mill downwards. It was, no doubt, inserted from the preceding verse, or the parallel passage in Luke vi. 45. The *τὰ* before *ἀγαθὰ* I have bracketed, as having no place in very many MSS., the Edit. Princ., Matthæi and Scholz, and liable to the strong objections stated by Middlet. Some, indeed, as Raphel, Wets., and Fritz., seek a peculiar sense arising from the addition of the Art. to *ἀγαθὰ*, and its rejection after *πονηρά*. But on the sense itself they widely differ; and the principle on which they go is too fanciful to be admitted.

36. *ἀργόν.*] On the sense of this word there has been no little difference of opinion. Some explain it *rash, vain, unedifying*. And there is something to countenance this in the use of the Heb. בטל. But although that sense (which is ably supported by Wets.) may be not inapposite, yet it is not so apt as that of *useless, pernicious*, propounded by others; in which there is a *litotes* common to many words of similar signification. The scope of the passage, however, is most in favour of the interpretation of Chrys., Whitby, and Campb., *false*; though there may probably be a reference to falsehood combined with *calumny*, such as the Pharisees were guilty of. With respect to the construction, there is here what is called a Nom. absolute, occasioned by the abandonment of the construction.

38. *θέλομεν — ἰδεῖν.*] This was a demand often made. (See infra xvi. 1. Mark viii. 11. Luke xi. 16,) and probably founded on the prophecy of Daniel vii. 13, which describes the Son of man as coming in the clouds of heaven. Insomuch that it was almost a characteristic of the Jews to ask a sign. So St. Paul, 1 Cor. i. 22, says: *οἱ Ἰουδαῖοι σημεῖον αἰτοῦσι.* We find from Luke xi. 16, that the sign they asked was one *from heaven*. They had witnessed several *δυνάμεις* or ordinary miracles, on earth; and they seem to demand the appearance of some *celestial* one, which would be the strongest test of Jesus's pretensions. Our Lord, however, knowing that the demand was made from bad motives, refused to comply with it.

39. *μοιχαλίς.*] This is by some understood of *spiritual* adultery; i. e. idolatry. But of *that* there is no reason to think the Jews of that age were guilty. Others would take it to denote *degeneracy* from the piety of their ancestors. But that is harsh and unauthorized. The term *may* be taken of adultery in the proper sense, which was then exceedingly prevalent. But it rather denotes spiritual adultery, — of godlessness and

MK. LU.

40 οὐ δοθήσεται αὐτῇ, εἰ μὴ τὸ σημεῖον Ἰωνᾶ τοῦ προφήτου. Ὥσπερ 3. 11.
γὰρ ἦν Ἰωνᾶς ἐν τῇ κοιλίᾳ τοῦ κήτους τρεῖς ἡμέρας καὶ τρεῖς νύκτας· 30
οὕτως ἔσται ὁ Υἱὸς τοῦ ἀνθρώπου ἐν τῇ καρδίᾳ τῆς γῆς τρεῖς ἡμέ-
41 ρας καὶ τρεῖς νύκτας. Ἄνδρες Νινευῖται ἀναστήσονται ἐν τῇ κρίσει 32
μετὰ τῆς γενεᾶς ταύτης, καὶ κατακρινοῦσιν αὐτήν· ὅτι μετενόησαν εἰς
42 τὸ κήρυγμα Ἰωνᾶ· καὶ ἰδοὺ πλεῖον Ἰωνᾶ ὧδε. Βασίλισσα νότου 31
ἐγερθήσεται ἐν τῇ κρίσει μετὰ τῆς γενεᾶς ταύτης, καὶ κατακρινεῖ αὐ-
τήν· ὅτι ἦλθεν ἐκ τῶν περάτων τῆς γῆς ἀκοῦσαι τὴν σοφίαν Σολομῶ-
43 νος· καὶ ἰδοὺ, πλεῖον Σολομῶνος ὧδε. Ὅταν δὲ τὸ ἀκάθαρτον πνεῦμα 24
ἐξέλθῃ ἀπὸ τοῦ ἀνθρώπου, διέρχεται δι᾽ ἀνύδρων τόπων, ζητοῦν ἀνά-
44 παυσιν, καὶ οὐχ εὑρίσκει. Τότε λέγει· Ἐπιστρέψω εἰς τὸν οἶκόν μου,
ὅθεν ἐξῆλθον. καὶ ἐλθὸν εὑρίσκει σχολάζοντα, σεσαρωμένον καὶ κεκο- 25
45 σμημένον. Τότε πορεύεται καὶ παραλαμβάνει μεθ᾽ ἑαυτοῦ ἑπτὰ ἕτερα 26
πνεύματα πονηρότερα ἑαυτοῦ, καὶ εἰσελθόντα κατοικεῖ ἐκεῖ· καὶ γίνεται τὰ ἔσχατα τοῦ ἀνθρώπου ἐκείνου χείρονα τῶν πρώτων. Οὕτως
ἔσται καὶ τῇ γενεᾷ ταύτῃ τῇ πονηρᾷ. 8.
46 Ἔτι δὲ αὐτοῦ λαλοῦντος τοῖς ὄχλοις, ἰδοὺ, ἡ μήτηρ καὶ οἱ ἀδελφοὶ 31 19
47 αὐτοῦ εἱστήκεισαν ἔξω, ζητοῦντες αὐτῷ λαλῆσαι. εἶπε δέ τις αὐτῷ· 32 20
Ἰδοὺ, ἡ μήτηρ σου καὶ οἱ ἀδελφοί σου ἔξω ἑστήκασι, ζητοῦντές σοι
48 λαλῆσαι. Ὁ δὲ ἀποκριθεὶς εἶπε τῷ εἰπόντι αὐτῷ· Τίς ἐστιν ἡ μήτηρ 33 21
49 μου; καὶ τίνες εἰσὶν οἱ ἀδελφοί μου; Καὶ ἐκτείνας τὴν χεῖρα αὐτοῦ 34
ἐπὶ τοὺς μαθητὰς αὐτοῦ, εἶπεν· Ἰδοὺ, ἡ μήτηρ μου καὶ οἱ ἀδελφοί

practical infidelity. For the marriage covenant, which the Jewish nation was typified as having entered into with God, might be broken by *godlessness* as much as by idolatry.

— σημ. οὐ δοθ. εἰ μὴ τὸ σημ. Ἰωνᾶ] q. d. the *proof* of my divine legation shall be an event no other than what happened to Jonah. See Jonah ii. 1, 2.

40. τοῦ κήτους.] This, it is now generally agreed, denotes not the whale, but another large fish called *Lamia*. See Horne's Introd. ii. 560. This is, however, denied by Bp. Jebb, Sacr. Lit. Ἐν τῇ καρδίᾳ τῆς γῆς is said to be a Hebraism for ἐν τῇ γῇ; but a similar expression occurs in our own and most other languages.

41. ἄνδρες Νινευῖται.] This pleonasm of ἄνδρες is common in the Greek writers, and may be considered a vestige of the wordiness of primitive phraseology. Ἀναστήσονται — κατακρινοῦσιν αὐτήν. There is something refined, and perhaps Oriental, in the turn of this and the next verse, by which the Ninevites and the Queen of the South are supposed to bear testimony against the Jews, as to the transactions here mentioned; and by that testimony, be the means of increasing the condemnation of the Jews by the contrast. On μετεν. εἰς τὸ κήρ. Ἰ. see Jonah iii. 5.

42. περάτων τῆς γῆς.] A usual phrase to denote a *remote country;* such as was Sheba: (See 1 Kings x. 1. 2 Chron. ix. 1.) of which examples are adduced by Wets.; and others may be seen in Recens. Synop.

43—45. The difficulty of this passage is not in itself, but in its *connection*, to determine whether it belongs to the verse immediately preceding, viz. vv. 38—42, or to the whole narration, v. 22—42. If the *former*, it is meant as a warning to those who had been demanding a sign. And then the most probable interpretation will be that of Kaufmann, cited by Kuin.; q. d. "Though I were to give you a sign from heaven, yet the effect would be but momentary; the demon of infidelity and obstinacy would return, and, seizing you with greater violence, would but increase your final condemnation." This, however, is somewhat harsh and forced. It is better to suppose (with others) that the application is to the whole of the above portion, and meant, 1. as a retort on his base calumniators; and, 2. as a warning to those who had been seeking a sign; in short, to the Jewish nation in general. In this view the sense is well expressed by Lightf. and Whitby. The parable, however, is susceptible of a *general* application, suited to all nations and ages; on which see Dr. Hales. With respect to the minor circumstances of the parable, they are merely meant for ornament, and accommodated to the notions of the Jews, as to the haunts and habits of demons, who, they supposed, chiefly abode ἐν τοῖς ἀνύδροις, in the deserts.

44. σχολάζοντα] i. e. ready for his reception. The word is elsewhere almost always used of a *person*. Τὰ ἔσχατα — πρώτων. A proverbial expression. [*Comp.* 2 Pet. ii. 20, 21. Heb. vi. 4. x. 26.]

46. οἱ ἀδελφοί] i. e. either *brethren*, or *kinsmen*, i. e. cousins; for it is disputed whether these were the sons of Joseph and Mary, or of Joseph by a former wife; or of Mary's sister, the wife of Cleophas. The last is the ancient and more general opinion; and of this use of the term *brother* the Scriptures furnish many examples. Yet not a few modern Commentators maintain

MK. LU.
3. μου. Ὅστις γὰρ ἂν ποιήσῃ τὸ θέλημα τοῦ πατρός μου τοῦ ἐν οὐρα- 50
35 νοῖς, αὐτός μου ἀδελφὸς καὶ ἀδελφὴ καὶ μήτηρ ἐστίν.
4. 8. XIII. Ἐν δὲ τῇ ἡμέρᾳ ἐκείνῃ ἐξελθὼν ὁ Ἰησοῦς ἀπὸ τῆς οἰκίας, 1
1 4 ἐκάθητο παρὰ τὴν θάλασσαν· καὶ συνήχθησαν πρὸς αὐτὸν ὄχλοι 2
πολλοὶ, ὥστε αὐτὸν εἰς τὸ πλοῖον ἐμβάντα καθῆσθαι· καὶ πᾶς ὁ ὄχλος
2 5 ἐπὶ τὸν αἰγιαλὸν εἱστήκει. Καὶ ἐλάλησεν αὐτοῖς πολλὰ ἐν παραβολαῖς, 3

that the word must be taken in the usual sense. See Note supra i. 25. Εἱστήκεισαν has the termination of a Pluperf. but the sense of a Perf., of which examples are adduced by Wets.

50. μου ἀδελφὸς, &c.] The Commentators notice the ellips. of ὡς, *quasi*, and compare a similar one of the Heb. כ; also adducing examples of a similar idiom in the Greek and Latin. But, as Fritz. has rightly remarked, no such ellip. must here be supposed, which would destroy the force of the address.

XIII. 1. ἐν τῇ ἡμέρᾳ ἐκείνῃ] "at that time." See Lu. v. 17.

2. τὸ πλοῖον.] The Art. may denote either the vessel kept for Jesus, or one belonging to the Apostles; or, indeed, both. See Middlet.

3. παραβολαῖς.] The word παραβολὴ, in its general sense denotes, 1. a *juxta-position* of one thing with another; 2. a *comparison* of one with the other, in point of similarity or dissimilarity; 3. an *illustration* of any thing, resulting from a comparison of it with another thing. In *Rhetoric* it is defined, "that species of the *genus* ALLEGORY, which consists of a continued narration of real or fictitious events, applied, by way of simile, to the illustration of moral truth." In *Scripture*, it may be defined *generally* as a *similitude*, derived from natural things, in order to instruct men in things spiritual. In the O. T. it sometimes denotes merely a *proverb*, or *pithy apophthegm* (Heb. מָשָׁל), and sometimes means a weighty truth, couched under ænigma or figure. In the N. T. it generally denotes a *fable* or *apologue*; namely, a narration applied, with more or less of ænigma, by way of simile, to the illustration of moral or religious truths. In this use, the parable consists of two parts: 1. the *Protasis*, conveying merely the LITERAL SENSE; 2. the *Apodosis*, which presents the *thing signified* by the similitude, the EXPLANATION, containing the *mystical* sense couched therein. The *second* part may be dispensed with, and was often omitted by our Lord, from the causes adverted to infra v. 13. The Parables of Christ were of two sorts: 1. such as contained illustrations of moral doctrines, and the duties of man to man; 2. what signified, though obscurely and *sub involucris*, the nature of the Gospel, and the future state of the Church. *These* could not be understood without the previous comprehension of things which required to be cleared by our Lord himself, or by the Holy Spirit, who was promised to guide them to all truth. For the *right explanation* of the Parables (especially when they are without the Apodosis), we must, 1. ascertain their *general scope* or design; which is to be collected from the context, and the occasion on which the parable was spoken; 2. we must first explain the *literal* or external sense, and then the *mystical* or internal; 3. we must avoid a too minute scrupulosity, by *pressing* on single words: nor must we aim at accommodating every part to the general spiritual intent of the parable; since few correspond in every part to the thing compared, many circumstances being introduced which serve only (like drapery) for ornament. They may *suggest*, but they rarely *establish*, some *collateral* truth. They more frequently only serve to illustrate the general meaning, and invigorate the general effect. For this reason, no doctrine of any great moment should ever be extorted from particular passages in parables. Lastly, an attention to *historical* circumstances, as well as an acquaintance with the nature and properties of the things whence the similitudes are taken, the peculiar genius of the composition itself, and the local and national circumstances of the hearers — all these are of great importance to the interpretation of parables.

To advert briefly to the *reasons* why parabolic instruction was resorted to by our Lord, in preference to a more regular mode:—1. As it was the most antient mode of instruction, so it was the *customary* one throughout the East, and was well adapted to the character of the Eastern nations, where it is prevalent to this day. 2. It had many *advantages*, both to the *hearers* and to the *speaker*, because, as Mrs. H. More well observes, "it is naturally adapted to engage the attention, and is level with the capacity of all; and conveys moral or religious truths in a more vivid and impressive manner than the dry didactic mode; and by laying hold of the imagination, insinuates itself into the understanding and affections, and, while it opens the doctrine it professes to conceal, it gives no alarm to men's prejudices." So Maimonid. Port. Mos. p. 84. (cited by Wets.) "Non potest doceri vulgus. nisi per ænigmata et parabolas, ut ita communis sit ista docendi ratio mulieribus etiam puerisque et parvulis, quo, cum perfecti evaserint intellectus ipsorum, parabolarum istarum sensus dignoscunt." Nor was it so very *obscure* to attentive and inquiring auditors. And as to such as would neither exercise attention and thought, nor seek elucidation from the speaker,—they must be presumed to be *indisposed* to receive the instruction, and consequently *unworthy* of it. This mode had also the advantage, as far as it was really obscure, of exercising, and consequently invigorating, the understanding. And it was never the intention of God that man should attain *heavenly* knowledge any more than *earthly*, without pains and attention. Parabolical instruction was therefore adopted, among other reasons, in order, (to use the words of Justin Martyr cited by Grot.) ὥστε καὶ πονῆσαι τοὺς ζητοῦντας εὑρεῖν καὶ μαθεῖν. And it is well remarked by Artemidor. 4. 70. p. 386., cited by me in Rec. Syn., Καὶ γὰρ εἰκὸς τοὺς Θεοὺς τὰ πολλὰ δι' αἰνιγμάτων λέγειν, ἐπειδὴ, σοφώτεροι ὄντες ἡμῶν αὐτῶν, οὐδὲν ἡμᾶς ἀβασανίστως βούλονται μανθάνειν. "To the *teacher* this mode had the advantage of being well adapted to veil unwelcome truths or hard sayings, till the hearers should be able to bear them;" and, in the case of our *Lord*, to

MK. LU.

4 λέγων· Ἰδοὺ ἐξῆλθεν ὁ σπείρων τοῦ σπείρειν. Καὶ ἐν τῷ σπείρειν 4. 8.
αὐτὸν, ἃ μὲν ἔπεσε παρὰ τὴν ὁδόν· καὶ ἦλθε τὰ πετεινὰ καὶ κατέφα- 3 4
5 γεν αὐτά. Ἄλλα δὲ ἔπεσεν ἐπὶ τὰ πετρώδη, ὅπου οὐκ εἶχε γῆν πολλήν· 5 6
6 καὶ εὐθέως ἐξανέτειλε, διὰ τὸ μὴ ἔχειν βάθος γῆς· ἡλίου δὲ ἀνατεί- 6
7 λαντος, ἐκαυματίσθη, καὶ, διὰ τὸ μὴ ἔχειν ῥίζαν, ἐξηράνθη. Ἄλλα δὲ 7 7
ἔπεσεν ἐπὶ τὰς ἀκάνθας· καὶ ἀνέβησαν αἱ ἄκανθαι καὶ ἀπέπνιξαν
8 αὐτά. Ἄλλα δὲ ἔπεσεν ἐπὶ τὴν γῆν τὴν καλήν· καὶ ἐδίδου καρπὸν, 8 8
9 ὃ μὲν ἑκατὸν, ὃ δὲ ἑξήκοντα, ὃ δὲ τριάκοντα. Ὁ ἔχων ὦτα ἀκούειν, 9
10 ἀκουέτω! Καὶ προσελθόντες οἱ μαθηταὶ εἶπον αὐτῷ· Διατί ἐν παρα- 10 9
11 βολαῖς λαλεῖς αὐτοῖς; Ὁ δὲ ἀποκριθεὶς εἶπεν αὐτοῖς· Ὅτι ὑμῖν δέ- 11 10
δοται γνῶναι τὰ μυστήρια τῆς βασιλείας τῶν οὐρανῶν, ἐκείνοις δὲ οὐ
12 δέδοται. Ὅστις γὰρ ἔχει, δοθήσεται αὐτῷ, καὶ περισσευθήσεται· ὅστις
13 δὲ οὐκ ἔχει, καὶ ὃ ἔχει, ἀρθήσεται ἀπ᾽ αὐτοῦ. Διὰ τοῦτο ἐν παρα-

shield him from the malice of the Scribes and Pharisees; who would have laid hold on any *express* declarations which they could turn to his prejudice.

— ὁ σπείρων.] The Art. (as Middlet. remarks) here gives the participle the nature of a substantive, i. e. σπορεὺς, which was unknown to the LXX. This is not a Hebraism, but is frequent in the Greek Classical writers. See Matth. Gr. Gr. § 269.

5. τὰ πετρώδη.] Sub. χωρία, (which is *expressed* in Thuc. iv. 9.), "stony or rocky ground."

6. ἐκαυματίσθη.] In Palestine, during the seed time (which is in November), the sky is generally overspread with clouds. The seed *then* springs up even in *stony* places; but when the sun dissipates the clouds, having outgrown its strength, it is quickly dried away. (Rosenm.)

7. ἐπὶ τὰς ἀκάνθας] "among thorns;" or rather, upon thorny ground. So Polyæn. p. 615. χωρίον ἀκανθῶδες. Bp. Middlet. has not said any thing on the force of the Art. in this and the following verse. It may be considered an insertion in *reference;* and that reference should seem to be the thorny ground, and the good ground, as parts of a whole, namely of the field to be sown.

8. ἐδίδου] "gave, yielded." This sense of δίδωμι is frequent in the Classical writers.

— ἑκατόν.] This immense produce is not unexampled. See Rec Syn. It is not, however, necessary to *press* on the expression, since a *most abundant* harvest is all that is required to be supposed.

11. μυστήρια.] This does not mean things entirely beyond the reach of the human understanding. The word (from μύειν, to shut up) properly denotes something hidden, withheld, and therefore unknown, either wholly or partly. For all mystery has been well said to be imperfect knowledge. Here, and elsewhere in the N. T., it denotes something disclosed only to certain persons, and not revealed to the multitude; namely, in the present case, the things concerning the plan of salvation, which had not yet been revealed, and were partly opened out in our Lord's *explanations* of his parables. Thus we are to understand this (as Walch, cited by Koecher, observes) not so much of the doctrines of the Christian religion as "de statu fatisque ecclesiæ sub œconomiâ Novi Fœderis futuris." So that there may be (as Dr. A. Clarke supposes) a reference to the *prophetic* declarations concerning the *future* state of the Christian Church, expressed in the following and other parables. Of course, the rejection of the Jews, and the calling of the Gentiles, are *included* in these *mysteries;* and those were gradually disclosed to the disciples, "as they could bear them," first by our Lord, and then by the Spirit, which was sent to guide them into all truth. These were things not in themselves obscure, nor withheld from any desire to conceal necessary truth; but only because the things in question were, for various reasons, not proper to be then communicated to all; but reserved, in their complete explication, for the οἱ ἐσωτερικοί of the disciples.

12. ὅστις γὰρ ἔχει — αὐτοῦ.] This adage partaking of the *oxymoron* (which has a twofold application), properly (and as it was, no doubt, commonly used) has reference to *worldly riches;* for οἱ ἔχοντες and οἱ οὐκ ἔχοντες, (scil. χρήματα) is a frequent phrase in the Classical writers to denote the *have-somethings*, and the *have-nothings*, the rich and the poor. And, in this view, the adage can little need explication. *Here*, however, it is transferred to *spiritual riches;* and under it is couched the lesson, — that he who hath considerable religious knowledge, and takes that care to improve it, with which men are observed to increase their *wealth*, will find it increase; while those who have but little, and manage it, as the poor are often observed to do, imprudently, will find it come to nought. The little he hath learned will slip out of his memory; he will be deprived of it, and, in that sense, it will be taken from him.

13. διὰ τοῦτο — λαλῶ.] The Jews, as we have seen, were addressed in parables, because their hardened wickedness and blind obstinacy had *indisposed* them to receive instruction of a more explicit kind. For we are by no means to understand from this and v. 15. μήποτε ἴδωσι τοῖς ὀφθαλμοῖς &c. that our Lord spake in parables, *in order* to cause the blindness and obstinacy, and therefore *occasion* the final condemnation of the Jews. The words, when properly interpreted, involve nothing incompatible with the justice and mercy of the All Good and Perfect Being; the true sense being, that the hearts of the men were so hardened by a long course of wilful and presumptuous sin, that, according to the regular operation of moral causes and effects, they,

MK. LU.
4. 8 βολαῖς αὐτοῖς λαλῶ· ὅτι βλέποντες οὐ βλέπουσι, καὶ ἀκούοντες οὐκ
12 ἀκούουσιν, οὐδὲ συνιοῦσι. Καὶ ἀναπληροῦται [ἐπ᾽] αὐτοῖς ἡ προφη- 14
τεία Ἡσαΐου ἡ λέγουσα· Ἀκοῇ ἀκούσετε, καὶ οὐ μὴ συνῆτε·
καὶ βλέποντες βλέψετε, καὶ οὐ μὴ ἴδητε. Ἐπαχύνθη 15
γὰρ ἡ καρδία τοῦ λαοῦ τούτου, καὶ τοῖς ὠσὶ βαρέως
ἤκουσαν, καὶ τοὺς ὀφθαλμοὺς αὐτῶν ἐκάμμυσαν·
μήποτε ἴδωσι τοῖς ὀφθαλμοῖς, καὶ τοῖς ὠσὶν ἀκούσωσι, καὶ τῇ καρδίᾳ *συνῶσι, καὶ ἐπιστρέψωσι, καὶ
ἰάσωμαι αὐτούς. Ὑμῶν δὲ μακάριοι οἱ ὀφθαλμοὶ, ὅτι βλέπουσι· 16
καὶ τὰ ὦτα ὑμῶν, ὅτι ἀκούει! Ἀμὴν γὰρ λέγω ὑμῖν, ὅτι πολλοὶ 17
προφῆται καὶ δίκαιοι ἐπεθύμησαν ἰδεῖν ἃ βλέπετε, καὶ οὐκ εἶδον· καὶ
ἀκοῦσαι ἃ ἀκούετε, καὶ οὐκ ἤκουσαν. Ὑμεῖς οὖν ἀκούσατε τὴν παρα- 18
βολὴν τοῦ σπείροντος. Παντὸς ἀκούοντος τὸν λόγον τῆς βασιλείας, 19
15 12 καὶ μὴ συνιέντος, ἔρχεται ὁ πονηρὸς καὶ ἁρπάζει τὸ ἐσπαρμένον ἐν τῇ
16 13 καρδίᾳ αὐτοῦ· οὗτός ἐστιν ὁ παρὰ τὴν ὁδὸν σπαρείς. Ὁ δὲ ἐπὶ τὰ 20
πετρώδη σπαρεὶς, οὗτός ἐστιν ὁ τὸν λόγον ἀκούων, καὶ εὐθὺς μετὰ
17 χαρᾶς λαμβάνων αὐτόν· οὐκ ἔχει δὲ ῥίζαν ἐν ἑαυτῷ, ἀλλὰ πρόσκαιρός 21
ἐστι· γενομένης δὲ θλίψεως ἢ διωγμοῦ διὰ τὸν λόγον, εὐθὺς σκανδα-

though *seeing*, in fact, did not see; and though hearing, yet, in fact, did not hear, nor harken, and consequently could not understand. The expression is a proverbial one, common to both the Scriptural and the Classical writers, and used of those who employ not to advantage the faculties of seeing or perceiving, hearing or understanding, and laying to heart. Thus the general sense of the passage of Isaiah now adduced is, that the Jews would hear indeed the doctrines of the Gospel, but not *understand* them; would see the miracles wrought in confirmation of its truth, but not be *convinced* thereby. Not that the evidences themselves were insufficient to establish its truth, but because their hearts were too corrupt to allow them to see the force of those evidences.

14. *καὶ ἀναπληροῦται*] i. e. 'is again fulfilled,' by the similar blind obstinacy of the same people. This is by some regarded as what Spanh. calls the secondary and improper use of the formula, by analogy, or example, when a thing happens similar to one that has formerly been done, said, or predicted. There is, however, no reason why it may not be understood of a second fulfilment.

—*ἀκοῇ ἀκούσετε*.] This is called a Hebraism, though examples have been adduced from the Greek Classical writers. The idiom almost always carries emphasis. Ἐπὶ before ἀκ. is marked for omission, or cancelled, by almost all the Editors; and on the strongest grounds, it being omitted in most MSS. and Versions.

15. *ἐπαχύνθη*] Παχὺς and its derivatives (like *pinguis* in Latin) are often used of *stupidity*, from a notion common to all ages, that fat tends to mental dulness. But as with us *stupidity* is colloquially used in the sense *obstinacy*, so here both senses seem to be meant.

—*ἐκάμμυσαν*.] Καμμύειν is for *καταμύειν*, and means, to *close the eyelids*; literally, to shut down the eyelids, in order to avoid seeing a thing. The word is confined to the later writers, the earlier ones using the uncontracted form, either with or without ὀφθαλμούς. Of course, the eye of the *understanding* is here meant. So Philo p. 589. cited by Loesn. καμμ. τὸ τῆς ψυχῆς ὄμμα. The figurative closing of the ears (adverted to in the corresponding words of the following clause) is here *implied*. That would require the term ἔβυσαν. So in a very ancient life of St. Luke we have (probably with allusion to this passage) Πρὸς δὲ τὴν ἀληθινὴν διδασκαλίαν τὰ τῆς καρδίας ἔβυον ὦτα, καὶ τὰ τῆς διανοίας ὄμματα. See also Euthymius. Μήποτε, for ἵνα μή; *adeo non*, in the eventual sense, as in John xii. 40. It is implied, in the following words that this blindness would continue till the destruction of the Jewish state. Συνῶσι. This is found in very many MSS., and is edited by Matth., Griesb., Vater, and Fritz.

16. *μακάριοι οἱ ὀφθαλμοί*.] A mode of speaking common to the poetic or the pathetic and spirited style, in every language. See Lu. xi. 27. x. 23. Matt. xvi. 17.

18. *ἀκούσατε τὴν παραβολήν*.] "or attend ye, therefore, to the (explanation) parable."

19. *μὴ συνιέντος*] i. e. and does not lay it to heart so as to understand it; by metonymy of cause for effect. This signification is of frequent occurrence in the Sept. Παντὸς ἀκούοντος may, with Fritz., be rendered "quicunque audit." Perhaps, however, it is a Hebraism.

—*ὁ—σπαρείς*.] He who is such may metaphorically be called a man sown by the way-side. A man may be termed sown (σπαρεὶς) on the same principle that we call a field sown, which receives the seed. We may render, "he who is sown on the way-side." For (as appears from the next verse) the man is compared to the *field*, not to the seed.

20. [*Comp.* Isai. lviii. 2. John v. 35.]

21. *οὐκ ἔχει ῥίζαν*.] It is properly the *word* that hath no root in itself. Comp. Col. ii. 7. Eph. iii. 18. But, *per hypallagen*, it is transferred to the *person*. We may paraphrase, "but he does

MK. LU.

22 λίζεται. Ὁ δὲ εἰς τὰς ἀκάνθας σπαρεὶς, οὗτός ἐστιν ὁ τὸν λόγον ἀκού- 4. 8.
ων· καὶ ἡ μέριμνα τοῦ αἰῶνος τούτου, καὶ ἡ ἀπάτη τοῦ πλούτου 18 14
23 συμπνίγει τὸν λόγον, καὶ ἄκαρπος γίνεται. Ὁ δὲ ἐπὶ τὴν γῆν τὴν 20 15
καλὴν σπαρεὶς, οὗτός ἐστιν ὁ τὸν λόγον ἀκούων καὶ συνιῶν· ὃς δὴ
καρποφορεῖ, καὶ ποιεῖ ὁ μὲν ἑκατὸν, ὁ δὲ ἑξήκοντα, ὁ δὲ τριάκοντα.
24 Ἄλλην παραβολὴν παρέθηκεν αὐτοῖς, λέγων· Ὡμοιώθη ἡ βασιλεία
τῶν οὐρανῶν ἀνθρώπῳ σπείροντι καλὸν σπέρμα ἐν τῷ ἀγρῷ αὐτοῦ·
25 ἐν δὲ τῷ καθεύδειν τοὺς ἀνθρώπους, ἦλθεν αὐτοῦ ὁ ἐχθρὸς καὶ
26 ἔσπειρε ζιζάνια ἀνὰ μέσον τοῦ σίτου, καὶ ἀπῆλθεν. Ὅτε δὲ ἐβλάστη-
27 σεν ὁ χόρτος, καὶ καρπὸν ἐποίησε, τότε ἐφάνη καὶ τὰ ζιζάνια. Προσελθόντες δὲ οἱ δοῦλοι τοῦ οἰκοδεσπότου, εἶπον αὐτῷ· Κύριε, οὐχὶ
καλὸν σπέρμα ἔσπειρας ἐν τῷ σῷ ἀγρῷ; πόθεν οὖν ἔχει [τὰ] ζιζάνια;
28 Ὁ δὲ ἔφη αὐτοῖς· Ἐχθρὸς ἄνθρωπος τοῦτο ἐποίησεν. Οἱ δὲ δοῦλοι
29 εἶπον αὐτῷ· Θέλεις οὖν ἀπελθόντες συλλέξωμεν αὐτά; Ὁ δὲ ἔφη·
Οὔ· μήποτε συλλέγοντες τὰ ζιζάνια, ἐκριζώσητε ἅμα αὐτοῖς τὸν σῖτον.
30 Ἄφετε συναυξάνεσθαι ἀμφότερα μέχρι τοῦ θερισμοῦ· καὶ ἐν [τῷ]
καιρῷ τοῦ θερισμοῦ ἐρῶ τοῖς θερισταῖς· Συλλέξατε πρῶτον τὰ ζιζάνια,
καὶ δήσατε αὐτὰ εἰς δέσμας, πρὸς τὸ κατακαῦσαι αὐτά· τὸν δὲ σῖτον
συναγάγετε εἰς τὴν ἀποθήκην μου. 13.
31 Ἄλλην παραβολὴν παρέθηκεν αὐτοῖς, λέγων· Ὁμοία ἐστὶν ἡ βασι- 31 19
λεία τῶν οὐρανῶν κόκκῳ σινάπεως, ὃν λαβὼν ἄνθρωπος ἔσπειρεν ἐν
32 τῷ ἀγρῷ αὐτοῦ· ὃ μικρότερον μέν ἐστι πάντων τῶν σπερμάτων· ὅταν 32
δὲ αὐξηθῇ, μεῖζον τῶν λαχάνων ἐστὶ, καὶ γίνεται δένδρον, ὥστε ἐλθεῖν
τὰ πετεινὰ τοῦ οὐρανοῦ, καὶ κατασκηνοῦν ἐν τοῖς κλάδοις αὐτοῦ.
33 Ἄλλην παραβολὴν ἐλάλησεν αὐτοῖς· Ὁμοία ἐστὶν ἡ βασιλεία τῶν 21
οὐρανῶν ζύμῃ, ἣν λαβοῦσα γυνὴ ἐνέκρυψεν εἰς ἀλεύρου σάτα τρία, ἕως
οὗ ἐζυμώθη ὅλον.

not suffer it to take deep root in his mind." Πρόσκαιρος, scil. μόνον, "is but a temporary and unstable disciple." Σκανδαλίζεται, "takes offence at, and falls off from the Gospel."

22. ἡ μέριμνα] "anxious care." So called because μερίζει τὸν νοῦν, it distracts the mind with worldly cares, and so dissipates the attention, as not to leave us (in the words of Gray) "leisure to be wise," or to attend to the concerns of the soul.

23. ὁ δὲ — σπαρεὶς]. "He who is represented as one that received seed into the good ground." Ὃς καρποφορεῖ is to be referred, not to the *word*, but to the *person* in whose heart the word is sown. Thus is adumbrated the different effect of the Gospel on different hearts.

25. τοὺς ἀνθρώπους.] Euthym., Whitby, Beng., and Wakef. understand this to denote "the men whose duty it was to take care of the field." But that is very harsh; neither was it customary to keep watch in fields, except when the corn was far advanced to maturity. It is, therefore, better to suppose, with Grot., that ἐν τ. καθ. ἀ. is meant for a description of night.

— ζιζάνια.] The Commentators are not agreed *what* plant is here intended. It is with most probability supposed to be the *darnel*, or *lolium temulentum* of Linnæus, which grows among corn, and has, in the ear, much resemblance to wheat; but is of a deleterious quality, and therefore deserves the epithet *infelix*, given by Virgil.

27. τὰ ζιζάνια.] The Art. is not found in many MSS. and some Versions and Fathers, and is cancelled by almost all the Editors from Wets. to Scholz.

30. τῷ.] This is not found in many MSS. and early Editions with the Syr. Vers. and Epiphanius, and is cancelled by Wets., Matth., Griesb., Knapp., Vater, and Scholz. Middlet. and Fritz., however, disapprove of the omission; though on different grounds, and each resting too much on Grammatical niceties, to which the Sacred writers were little attentive.

32. ὃ μικρότερον.] This, the Commentators say, is for μικρότατον; as just after μεῖζον is for μέγιστον, by an idiom familiar to the Evangelists, and probably derived from Hebraism. Fritz., however, remarks that this principle has been of late exploded. The phrase was proverbial with the Jews to denote a very small thing.

33. ζύμη] i. e. leaven, or sour dough, which assimilates to its own nature the mass with which it is mixed. Thus is represented the nature of

MK. 4. Ταῦτα πάντα ἐλάλησεν ὁ Ἰησοῦς ἐν παραβολαῖς τοῖς ὄχλοις· καὶ 34
33 34 χωρὶς παραβολῆς οὐκ ἐλάλει αὐτοῖς. Ὅπως πληρωθῇ τὸ ῥηθὲν διὰ 35
τοῦ προφήτου λέγοντος· Ἀνοίξω ἐν παραβολαῖς τὸ στόμα μου· ἐρεύξομαι κεκρυμμένα ἀπὸ καταβολῆς κόσμου.

Τότε ἀφεὶς τοὺς ὄχλους, ἦλθεν εἰς τὴν οἰκίαν ὁ Ἰησοῦς· καὶ προσ- 36
ῆλθον αὐτῷ οἱ μαθηταὶ αὐτοῦ, λέγοντες· Φράσον ἡμῖν τὴν παραβολὴν
τῶν ζιζανίων τοῦ ἀγροῦ. Ὁ δὲ ἀποκριθεὶς εἶπεν αὐτοῖς· Ὁ σπείρων 37
o Gen. 3. 15. John. 8. 44. Acts 13. 10. 1 John 3. 8. τὸ καλὸν σπέρμα ἐστὶν ὁ Υἱὸς τοῦ ἀνθρώπου· °ὁ δὲ ἀγρὸς ἐστιν ὁ 38
κόσμος· τὸ δὲ καλὸν σπέρμα, οὗτοί εἰσιν οἱ υἱοὶ τῆς βασιλείας· τὰ δὲ
p Rev. 14. 15. Joel 3. 13. ζιζάνια, εἰσὶν οἱ υἱοὶ τοῦ πονηροῦ. ᵖὉ δὲ ἐχθρὸς ὁ σπείρας αὐτά 39
ἐστιν ὁ Διάβολος· ὁ δὲ θερισμὸς συντέλεια τοῦ αἰῶνός ἐστιν· οἱ δὲ
θερισταὶ ἄγγελοί εἰσιν. Ὥσπερ οὖν συλλέγεται τὰ ζιζάνια καὶ πυρὶ 40
* καίεται· οὕτως ἔσται ἐν τῇ συντελείᾳ τοῦ αἰῶνος τούτου. Ἀποστελεῖ 41
ὁ Υἱὸς τοῦ ἀνθρώπου τοὺς ἀγγέλους αὐτοῦ· καὶ συλλέξουσιν ἐκ τῆς
βασιλείας αὐτοῦ πάντα τὰ σκάνδαλα, καὶ τοὺς ποιοῦντας τὴν ἀνομίαν·
q Supr. 8. 12. ᵠ καὶ βαλοῦσιν αὐτοὺς εἰς τὴν κάμινον τοῦ πυρός. ἐκεῖ ἔσται ὁ κλαυθ- 42
r Wisd. 3. 7. Dan. 12. 3. supr. ver. 9. μὸς καὶ ὁ βρυγμὸς τῶν ὀδόντων. ʳ Τότε οἱ δίκαιοι ἐκλάμψουσιν, ὡς 43
ὁ ἥλιος, ἐν τῇ βασιλείᾳ τοῦ πατρὸς αὐτῶν. Ὁ ἔχων ὦτα ἀκούειν,
ἀκουέτω!

Πάλιν ὁμοία ἐστὶν ἡ βασιλεία τῶν οὐρανῶν θησαυρῷ κεκρυμμένῳ 44
ἐν τῷ ἀγρῷ. ὃν εὑρὼν ἄνθρωπος ἔκρυψε, καὶ ἀπὸ τῆς χαρᾶς αὐτοῦ
ὑπάγει καὶ πάντα ὅσα ἔχει πωλεῖ, καὶ ἀγοράζει τὸν ἀγρὸν ἐκεῖνον.

the influence of the Gospel on the minds of men, as in the preceding parable is shadowed forth the wide propagation of the Gospel from the very smallest beginnings.

34. χωρὶς παραβολῆς, &c.] This is by some restricted to *that time*, and the auditors *then* with Christ. By others it is, with more probability, regarded as importing, in a general way, that our Lord used parables very frequently.

35. ἀνοίξω — κόσμου.] From Ps. lxxvii. (78) 2., but not exactly agreeing either with the Hebrew or Greek. Though ἐρεύξομαι might then be in the text of the Sept.; and φθέγξομαι, the present reading, may be a gloss. The words are admitted to be not quoted by the Evangelist as a prophecy, but to be accommodated to the present purpose. Ἐρεύγεσθαι is properly used of the gushing forth of fluids, but metaphorically, of free and earnest speech.

— ἀπὸ καταβολῆς.] The term is properly used of the founding of buildings, but applied occasionally by the Classical writers to the beginning of any thing. It was especially used of the *world*, because, according to the common notion of ancient times, the world was thought to be an immense *plain surface*, resting on foundations.

36. τὴν οἰκίαν] i. e. the house he had left, at Capernaum.

38. τὸ δὲ καλὸν σπέρμα, &c.] "as to the good seed." Οὗτοι is accommodated in construction to υἱοί, though referring to σπέρμα. Perhaps, however, σπέρμα is considered as a noun of multidude.

40. καίεται.] Such is the reading of almost all the MSS. and early Editions, and is adopted by almost every Editor from Wets. downwards. The common reading κατακαίεται was probably derived from the Scholiasts.

— ἐν τῇ συντελείᾳ τοῦ αἰῶνος.] This is by some interpreted of the *end of the age*, i. e. the Jewish polity and state. But though that sense of the phrase has place elsewhere, the context must here limit it to the *final consummation of things*. The *other* sense may, however, be *included*.

41. σκάνδαλα.] Σκάνδαλον signifies a stumbling block, either naturally or metaphorically, i. e. whatever occasions any one to err, in his principles or practice. Here, however, as it is joined with τοὺς ποιοῦντας, it must denote, not *things*, but *persons*, i. e. false teachers, such as are censured by Peter and Jude; who, under the semblance of Christian liberty, inculcated doctrines repugnant to moral virtue, and held vice to be among the ἀδιάφορα, or things indifferent.

42. βαλοῦσιν — πυρός.] An allusion to the Oriental custom of burning alive, mentioned in Dan. iii. 10. The expression is equivalent to γέεννα τοῦ πυρός, Matth. v. 22.

43. ἐκλάμψουσιν — αὐτῶν.] Our Lord seems to have had in mind Dan. xii. 3. Comp. Wisd. iii. 7. Eccles. ix. 11. 1 Mac. ii. 62. 1 Pet. v. 4. (Mackn.)

44. θησαυρῷ κεκρυμμένῳ] i. e. such valuables as, in the insecurity of society in ancient times, men were accustomed to bury in the earth, on the expectation of invasion from an enemy. From the present passage, and one cited by Wets. from the Mischna, it appears that the Jewish law adjudged all treasure found on land to be the right of the then proprietor of the land.

— ἔκρυψε] i. e. either, "covers it up (again)," or, conceals (his good fortune). Bp. Midd.

45 *Πάλιν ὁμοία ἐστὶν ἡ βασιλεία τῶν οὐρανῶν ἀνθρώπῳ ἐμπόρῳ ζη-*
46 *τοῦντι καλοὺς μαργαρίτας· ὃς εὑρὼν ἕνα πολύτιμον μαργαρίτην, ἀπελ-*
θὼν πέπρακε πάντα ὅσα εἶχε, καὶ ἠγόρασεν αὐτόν.
47 *Πάλιν ὁμοία ἐστὶν ἡ βασιλεία τῶν οὐρανῶν σαγήνῃ βληθείσῃ εἰς*
48 *τὴν θάλασσαν, καὶ ἐκ παντὸς γένους συναγαγούσῃ· ἥν, ὅτε ἐπληρώθη,*
ἀναβιβάσαντες ἐπὶ τὸν αἰγιαλὸν, καὶ καθίσαντες συνέλεξαν τὰ καλὰ εἰς
49 *ἀγγεῖα, τὰ δὲ σαπρὰ ἔξω ἔβαλον.* [s] *Οὕτως ἔσται ἐν τῇ συντελείᾳ τοῦ* [s Infr. 25. 32.]
αἰῶνος. ἐξελεύσονται οἱ ἄγγελοι, καὶ ἀφοριοῦσι τοὺς πονηροὺς ἐκ μέσου
50 *τῶν δικαίων·* [t] *καὶ βαλοῦσιν αὐτοὺς εἰς τὴν κάμινον τοῦ πυρός. ἐκεῖ* [t Sup. ver. 42.]
51 *ἔσται ὁ κλαυθμὸς καὶ ὁ βρυγμὸς τῶν ὀδόντων. Λέγει αὐτοῖς ὁ Ἰη-*
52 *σοῦς· Συνήκατε ταῦτα πάντα; λέγουσιν αὐτῷ· Ναὶ, κύριε. Ὁ δὲ*
εἶπεν αὐτοῖς· Διὰ τοῦτο πᾶς γραμματεὺς μαθητευθεὶς εἰς τὴν βασι-
λείαν τῶν οὐρανῶν ὅμοιός ἐστιν ἀνθρώπῳ οἰκοδεσπότῃ, ὅστις ἐκβάλλει
ἐκ τοῦ θησαυροῦ αὐτοῦ καινὰ καὶ παλαιά.
53 *Καὶ ἐγένετο, ὅτε ἐτέλεσεν ὁ Ἰησοῦς τὰς παραβολὰς ταύτας, μετῆρεν*
54 *ἐκεῖθεν·* [u] *καὶ ἐλθὼν εἰς τὴν πατρίδα αὐτοῦ, ἐδίδασκεν αὐτοὺς ἐν τῇ* [u Mark 6. 1, 2. Luke 4. 16.]
συναγωγῇ αὐτῶν· ὥστε ἐκπλήττεσθαι αὐτοὺς καὶ λέγειν· Πόθεν τού-
55 *τῳ ἡ σοφία αὕτη καὶ αἱ δυνάμεις;* [x] *Οὐχ οὗτός ἐστιν ὁ τοῦ τέκτονος* [x John 6. 42. supr. 12. 46. Mark 6. 3.]
υἱός; οὐχὶ ἡ μήτηρ αὐτοῦ λέγεται Μαριὰμ, καὶ οἱ ἀδελφοὶ αὐτοῦ Ἰά-
56 *κωβος καὶ Ἰωσῆς καὶ Σίμων καὶ Ἰούδας; καὶ αἱ ἀδελφαὶ αὐτοῦ οὐχὶ*

would, from some MSS., cancel the Art. at τῷ ἀγρῷ. And indeed it is not easy to see what sense it can have. It must not, however, be *cancelled* on such slender authority; and idioms, though difficult to be accounted for, are not therefore to be swept away.

45. ἀνθρώπῳ ἐμπόρῳ] "a merchant." Such as those found in the East, who travel about buying or exchanging jewels, pearls or other valuables; a custom illustrated by the citations in Wets. The ἀνθρώπῳ added is agreeable to an idiom found chiefly in the earliest writers, but not unfrequent in Hellenistic Greek, by which the substantive is treated as an adjective. And ἐμπ. was originally an adjective.

—μαργαρίτας.] With respect to the *origin* of this word, it is justly remarked by Bp. Marsh, that as pearls are the produce of the East, it is more reasonable to suppose that the Greeks borrowed the word from the Orientalists, than the contrary, which is the common opinion. The great value of pearls appears from what is said by Pliny.

47. σαγήνῃ] verriculum, a drag net, which, when sunk, and dragged to the shore, sweeps as it were the bottom. The word occurs in Ez. xxvi. 5 & 14. for the Heb. חֵרֶם. and in Æschyl., Ælian, Artemid., and other later writers. At ἐκ παντὸς γένους sub. τινά or τί: not, however, understanding, with Kuin., other things besides fish, but supplying ἰχθύδια or ἰχθύδιον.

48. τὰ σαπρὰ] "the refuse." A vox sol. de h. re. See vii. 17. and Note. Ἔξω has no reference, as Kuin. and others suppose, to the *baskets*; but simply denotes *away*.

49. ἐκ μέσου.] This is thought to be redundant. But see Fritz.

52. διὰ τοῦτο.] The Commentators regard this either as redundant, or, which is much the same thing, as a *formula transitionis*. But it rather seems to denote an *inference* from what has preceded, and may be rendered *Wherefore then, since that is the case;* thus ushering in an admonition to *use* the knowledge they have.

—γραμματεὺς.] The term properly denotes a doctor of the Jewish law, but here, a teacher of the Gospel; the name being transferred, from similarity of office. See Vitringa de Synag.

—μαθητευθεὶς εἰς τὴν βασιλ. τ. ο.] Griesb., Knapp, and Vater, and Fritz. edit. τῇ βασιλείᾳ; but on too slight authority. The phrase may be rendered, "discipled into the kingdom of heaven, or, "admitted by discipleship into the Christian society." See xxiii. 34. xxviii. 19. Acts xiv. 21. and an admirable Visitation Sermon of Bp. Blomfield on this text. If however, τῇ βασιλείᾳ *be* the true reading, the sense will be, "instructed for," "disciplined to," i. e. completely acquainted with the nature and purposes of the Gospel. At καινὰ and παλαιὰ we *may* sub. βρώματα or σκεύη. It is, however, not necessary to too much scrutinize these words; which simply denote such provisions, or other necessaries, as the householder may think suitable to the wants of his family; both what he has long laid up, and what he has recently provided. The application, in reference to the Christian teacher, is obvious. See Rec. Synop.

54. πατρίδα] scil. πόλιν, i. e. Nazareth, the place where he had been brought up, and which was therefore, in a certain sense, his country.

55. οὗτος.] The use of this pronoun here, as often in the Classical writers, implies contempt, like the Heb. זֶה; and Latin *iste*.

—τοῦ τέκτονος.] The word τέκτων denotes an artificer, or artisan, as opposed to a *laborer;* and, according to the term accompanying it, may denote any artificer, whether in wood, stone, or metal. But when it stands alone, it always denotes a *carpenter*, (as *faber* and חָרָשׁ) in the

y Mark 6. 4. Luke 4. 24. John 4. 44.
z Mark 6. 5.

πᾶσαι πρὸς ἡμᾶς εἰσι; πόθεν οὖν τούτῳ ταῦτα πάντα; [y] Καὶ ἐσκαν- 57
δαλίζοντο ἐν αὐτῷ. Ὁ δὲ Ἰησοῦς εἶπεν αὐτοῖς· Οὐκ ἔστι προφήτης
ἄτιμος, εἰ μὴ ἐν τῇ πατρίδι αὐτοῦ, καὶ ἐν τῇ οἰκίᾳ αὐτοῦ. [z] Καὶ οὐκ 58
MK. LU.
6. 9. ἐποίησεν ἐκεῖ δυνάμεις πολλὰς διὰ τὴν ἀπιστίαν αὐτῶν.

14 7 XIV. ἘΝ ἐκείνῳ τῷ καιρῷ ἤκουσεν Ἡρώδης ὁ τετράρχης τὴν ἀκοὴν 1
Ἰησοῦ, καὶ εἶπε τοῖς παισὶν αὐτοῦ· Οὗτός ἐστιν Ἰωάννης ὁ βαπτιστής· 2
αὐτὸς ἠγέρθη ἀπὸ τῶν νεκρῶν, καὶ διὰ τοῦτο αἱ δυνάμεις ἐνεργοῦσιν
17 ἐν αὐτῷ. Ὁ γὰρ Ἡρώδης κρατήσας τὸν Ἰωάννην, ἔδησεν αὐτὸν καὶ 3
ἔθετο ἐν φυλακῇ, διὰ Ἡρωδιάδα τὴν γυναῖκα Φιλίππου τοῦ ἀδελφοῦ
18 αὐτοῦ. Ἔλεγε γὰρ αὐτῷ ὁ Ἰωάννης· Οὐκ ἔξεστί σοι ἔχειν αὐτήν. Καὶ 4
19 θέλων αὐτὸν ἀποκτεῖναι, ἐφοβήθη τὸν ὄχλον, ὅτι ὡς προφήτην αὐτὸν 5
21 εἶχον. Γενεσίων δὲ ἀγομένων τοῦ Ἡρώδου, ὠρχήσατο ἡ θυγάτηρ τῆς 6
23 Ἡρωδιάδος ἐν τῷ μέσῳ, καὶ ἤρεσε τῷ Ἡρώδῃ· ὅθεν μεθ᾽ ὅρκου ὡμο- 7
24 λόγησεν αὐτῇ δοῦναι ὃ ἐὰν αἰτήσηται. Ἡ δὲ προβιβασθεῖσα ὑπὸ τῆς 8
μητρὸς αὐτῆς· Δός μοι, φησὶν, ὧδε ἐπὶ πίνακι τὴν κεφαλὴν Ἰωάννου
26 τοῦ βαπτιστοῦ. Καὶ ἐλυπήθη ὁ βασιλεύς· διὰ δὲ τοὺς ὅρκους καὶ 9

Scriptural, and, almost always, in the Classical writers. (Campb.) That such is the sense here intended, cannot reasonably be doubted; especially as it is supported by the concurrent testimony of ancient ecclesiastical writers.

57. οὐκ ἔστι προφήτης — αὐτοῦ.] A proverbial sentiment, importing, that one whose endowments enable him to instruct others, is, no where so little held in honor, as among his townsmen and immediate connexions.

58. οὐκ ἐποίησεν — αὐτῶν.] "Christ did not judge it suitable to obtrude his miracles upon them, and so could not properly perform them."

XIV. 1. τὴν ἀκοὴν Ἰησοῦ, i. e. περὶ τοῦ Ἰ.

2. παισίν.] This, by a use frequent in the Sept., is supposed to denote *friends*. But it rather signifies *ministers*, *officers* (namely of his Court.)

— αἱ δυνάμεις ἐνεργ. ἐν α.] To account for the Art. here, Bp. Middlet. would render "the powers, or spirits, are active in him." But the arguments he adduces are rather specious than solid; and there seems to be no reason to abandon the common interpretation of δυνάμεις, *miracles*. Ἐνεργ. *may* be taken, with most expositors, for ἐνεργοῦνται, "miracles are effected by him." But perhaps it is better, with Beza, Wakef., Schleusn., and Fritz., to retain the *active* sense, and take δυνάμεις of the power of working miracles, as in Acts vi. 8. x. 38., by which the Art. may very well be accounted for.

3—13. In this Episodical digression, recounting the imprisonment and death of John the Baptist, the Aorists must be rendered as Pluperfects. On which see Winer. and Alts. Grammars of the N. T.

4. ἔχειν] for γαμεῖν. A use frequent in the Classical writers, like that of *habere* in Latin.

6. γενεσίων ἀγομένων.] The Commentators are not agreed, whether this expression should be understood of the *birthday* festival of Herod, or that in *commemoration* of his accession. That the latter was observed as a feast, is certain from Joseph. Ant. xv. 11. 3. (of Herod) and 1 Kings i. 8 & 9. Hos. vii. 5. Since, however, no examples of this sense of the word γενέσια have been adduced, the common interpretation is the safer; and that the antients, both Jews and Gentiles, kept their birthdays as days of great rejoicing, is certain from a variety of passages cited by Wets. At γενεσίων some supply συμποσίων; others, ἡμερῶν. The *latter* is preferable, as in the phrase ἄγειν ἑορτήν. Yet no ellips. is necessary, or indeed proper, since γενέσια, and also ἐγκαίνια and γενέθλια, (which is the term used by the earlier writers,) are in fact *nouns*. At least there is no *plena locutio* hitherto produced, which will determine what was originally the noun employed with them.

— ὠρχήσατο.] Most Commentators (as Grot. and Kuin.,) here understand a pantomimic and lascivious dance, recently introduced into Judæa, such as that so severely censured by Juven. Sat. vi. 63. and Hor. Od. iii. 6, 21. Yet that Herod should have permitted, and even been gratified with, a lascivious dance by his *daughter-in-law*, would argue incredible indecorum and depravity. It is therefore better, with Lightf., Mich., and Fritz., to suppose that the dance was a decorous one, expressive of rejoicing, but from the extreme elegance with which it was performed, such as attracted admiration.

8. προβιβασθεῖσα] '*adducta*, urged, instigated.' A signification occurring in the Sept. and also Xen. Mem. i. 2. 17. προβιβ. λόγῳ. Πίνακι, a broad and flat plate or dish, not a *basin*, as Campb. renders; for from its origin (namely πίνος, a board) the word commonly denotes what is *flat*, or nearly so. Dr. Walsh, in his Travels in Turkey, informs us, that the head of the celebrated Ali Pacha, after being cut off, and sent to Constantinople, was publicly exposed on *a dish*.

9. ἐλυπήθη.] This is by Kuin. and Wahl. interpreted 'was angry;' of which sense they adduce examples from the Classical and Scriptural writers. But some of them are exceptionable; and here there seems no reason to deviate from the usual signification of the word, to be sorry. Though it *might* be rendered "he was chagrined." The feeling was doubtless a mixed one; *sorrow* (on his own account chiefly) and *chagrin*, not

MK. LU.

10 τοὺς συνανακειμένους, ἐκέλευσε δοθῆναι. Καὶ πέμψας ἀπεκεφάλισε τὸν 6. 9.
11 Ἰωάννην ἐν τῇ φυλακῇ. Καὶ ἠνέχθη ἡ κεφαλὴ αὐτοῦ ἐπὶ πίνακι, καὶ 27 28
12 ἐδόθη τῷ κορασίῳ· καὶ ἤνεγκε τῇ μητρὶ αὐτῆς. Καὶ προσελθόντες 29
οἱ μαθηταὶ αὐτοῦ ἦραν τὸ σῶμα, καὶ ἔθαψαν αὐτό· καὶ ἐλθόντες ἀπ- 32
13 ήγγειλαν τῷ Ἰησοῦ. Καὶ ἀκούσας ὁ Ἰησοῦς, ἀνεχώρησεν ἐκεῖθεν ἐν
πλοίῳ εἰς ἔρημον τόπον κατ' ἰδίαν· καὶ ἀκούσαντες οἱ ὄχλοι, ἠκολού- 33
θησαν αὐτῷ πεζῇ ἀπὸ τῶν πόλεων.
14 Καὶ ἐξελθὼν ὁ Ἰησοῦς εἶδε πολὺν ὄχλον, καὶ ἐσπλαγχνίσθη ἐπ' 34 11
15 * αὐτοῖς, καὶ ἐθεράπευσε τοὺς ἀῤῥώστους αὐτῶν. Ὀψίας δὲ γενομένης, 35 12
προσῆλθον αὐτῷ οἱ μαθηταὶ αὐτοῦ, λέγοντες· Ἔρημός ἐστιν ὁ τόπος,
καὶ ἡ ὥρα ἤδη παρῆλθεν· ἀπόλυσον τοὺς ὄχλους, ἵνα ἀπελθόντες εἰς
16 τὰς κώμας, ἀγοράσωσιν ἑαυτοῖς βρώματα. Ὁ δὲ Ἰησοῦς εἶπεν αὐτοῖς· 37 13
17 Οὐ χρείαν ἔχουσιν ἀπελθεῖν· δότε αὐτοῖς ὑμεῖς φαγεῖν. Οἱ δὲ λέγουσιν αὐτῷ· Οὐκ ἔχομεν ὧδε, εἰ μὴ πέντε ἄρτους καὶ δύο ἰχθύας. Ὁ 38
18 δὲ εἶπε· Φέρετέ μοι αὐτοὺς ὧδε. Καὶ κελεύσας τοὺς ὄχλους ἀνακλι- 39 14
θῆναι ἐπὶ τοὺς χόρτους, [καὶ] λαβὼν τοὺς πέντε ἄρτους καὶ τοὺς δύο 41 16
ἰχθύας, ἀναβλέψας εἰς τὸν οὐρανὸν, εὐλόγησε· καὶ κλάσας ἔδωκε τοῖς
20 μαθηταῖς τοὺς ἄρτους, οἱ δὲ μαθηταὶ τοῖς ὄχλοις· καὶ ἔφαγον πάντες, 42 17
καὶ ἐχορτάσθησαν· καὶ ἦραν τὸ περισσεῦον τῶν κλασμάτων δώδεκα 43
21 κοφίνους πλήρεις. Οἱ δὲ ἐσθίοντες ἦσαν ἄνδρες ὡσεὶ πεντακισχίλιοι, 44

without *anger*, at being thus taken advantage of; and even *fear*; —for he could not but feel apprehensive of the consequences of so unpopular an action. His chagrin may also, as Hammond thinks, have been increased by a superstitious dread of any ill omened occurrence on his birthday. So Martial Epigr. X. 87. "Natalem colimus, tacete lites." In short, great must have been the fluctuation of Herod's mind, occasioned by various contending passions and feelings in his bosom; which is well described by Grotius. Διὰ τοὺς ὅρκους, i. e. "out of a scruple to break his oath before his guests;" for at entertainments there was a delicacy in refusing requests.

10. πέμψας] scil. τινα. That this is not a Hebraism, (as Rosenm. says) is plain from two Classical examples adduced in Rec. Synop.

13. ἀκούσας.] Namely, of John's death, and Herod's opinion of himself. On both which accounts, and also to avoid the imputation of blame for any disturbances which might be expected to follow such an atrocity, and likewise (as we learn from Mark) to refresh himself and his Apostles after their fatigue, our Lord sought retirement. Πεζῇ. Not "on foot," but "by land," as opposed to ἐν πλοίῳ. See Campb. This signification is frequent in the Classical writers, and sometimes has place where there is no opposition expressed or even implied.

—ἀκούσαντες] i. e. having heard [where he was]. [*Comp.* Lu. ix. 10.]

14. αὐτοῖς.] On this reading all the Editors are agreed. The common one αὐτοὺς is proved to have been a mere typographical error of Stephens's third Edition. On this narration *Comp.* Jo. vi. 5. seqq.

15. ὀψίας γενομένης] i. e. the *first* evening, which commenced at three o'clock. Nor, considering the aptitude of the place, and the time of year, a little before the Passover, is this inconsistent with the expression of Lu. ix. 12. ἡ δὲ ἡμέρα ἤρξατο κλίνειν, for the day is there quite on the wane. That mentioned further on at v. 23. is the *second* evening, which commenced at sun set.

—ἡ ὥρα ἤδη παρῆλθεν] "the day is far spent." Ὥρα, like the Latin *hora*, has often this sense. Fritz. understands it of the proper time for healing and instructing the people. But that is harsh.

19. [καί.] This is rejected or cancelled by almost all Editors, as not found in the greater part of the MSS., early Editions, and Fathers. Rightly, for *internal* evidence is as much against it as external.

—εὐλόγησε.] Sub. τὸν Θεόν. The word is elsewhere interchanged with εὐχαριστεῖν, as synonymous. See Matth. xv. 36. Mark viii. 6. Luke i. 64. ii. 28. xxiv. 53. John vi. 11 & 23. Acts xxvii. 35. Jam. iii. 5. When a noun denoting *food*, or *sacrifice*, is expressed, there is an ellips. for εὐλογεῖν τὸν Θεὸν ὑπὲρ τὴν θυσίαν.

—κλάσας.] The Jewish loaves were in fact *cakes*; broad, thin, and brittle, like our biscuits; and therefore required to be *broken* rather than cut, and thus would leave very many fragments; which accounts for the great quantity thereof gathered up.

20. ἦραν] scil. οἱ ἀπόστολοι. And at τὸ περισσεῦον sub. μέρος. Κλασμάτων, i. e. not only the fragments, which would arise from *breaking up* loaves for so great a multitude, but (as appears from John vi. 13.) those also which each person would make in eating. The words following δώδεκα — πλήρεις are in apposition with and exegetical of the preceding; q. d. namely, twelve baskets full.

—κοφίνους.] This word has occasioned more discussion among the Commentators than might have been imagined; especially from these co-

MK.
6. χωρὶς γυναικῶν καὶ παιδίων. Καὶ εὐθέως ἠνάγκασεν [ὁ Ἰησοῦς] 22
45 τοὺς μαθητὰς αὐτοῦ ἐμβῆναι εἰς τὸ πλοῖον, καὶ προάγειν αὐτὸν εἰς
46 τὸ πέραν, ἕως οὗ ἀπολύσῃ τοὺς ὄχλους. Καὶ ἀπολύσας τοὺς ὄχλους, 23
ἀνέβη εἰς τὸ ὄρος κατ᾽ ἰδίαν προσεύξασθαι. Ὀψίας δὲ γενομένης,
47 μόνος ἦν ἐκεῖ. Τὸ δὲ πλοῖον ἤδη μέσον τῆς θαλάσσης ἦν, βασανιζό- 24
48 μενον ὑπὸ τῶν κυμάτων· ἦν γὰρ ἐναντίος ὁ ἄνεμος. Τετάρτῃ δὲ φυ- 25
λακῇ τῆς νυκτὸς ἀπῆλθε πρὸς αὐτοὺς ὁ Ἰησοῦς, περιπατῶν ἐπὶ τῆς
49 θαλάσσης. Καὶ ἰδόντες αὐτὸν οἱ μαθηταὶ ἐπὶ τὴν θάλασσαν περιπα- 26
τοῦντα, ἐταράχθησαν, λέγοντες· Ὅτι φάντασμά ἐστι· καὶ ἀπὸ τοῦ
50 φόβου ἔκραξαν. Εὐθέως δὲ ἐλάλησεν αὐτοῖς ὁ Ἰησοῦς λέγων· Θαρσεῖτε· 27
ἐγώ εἰμι, μὴ φοβεῖσθε. Ἀποκριθεὶς δὲ αὐτῷ ὁ Πέτρος εἶπε· Κύριε, 28
εἰ σὺ εἶ, κέλευσόν με πρός σε ἐλθεῖν ἐπὶ τὰ ὕδατα. Ὁ δὲ εἶπεν· 29
Ἐλθέ. καὶ καταβὰς ἀπὸ τοῦ πλοίου ὁ Πέτρος, περιεπάτησεν ἐπὶ τὰ
ὕδατα, ἐλθεῖν πρὸς τὸν Ἰησοῦν. Βλέπων δὲ τὸν ἄνεμον ἰσχυρὸν, 30
ἐφοβήθη· καὶ ἀρξάμενος καταποντίζεσθαι, ἔκραξε λέγων· Κύριε, σῶσόν
με. εὐθέως δὲ ὁ Ἰησοῦς ἐκτείνας τὴν χεῖρα, ἐπελάβετο αὐτοῦ, καὶ 31
λέγει αὐτῷ· Ὀλιγόπιστε, εἰς τί ἐδίστασας; Καὶ ἐμβάντων αὐτῶν εἰς 32
51 τὸ πλοῖον, ἐκόπασεν ὁ ἄνεμος. Οἱ δὲ ἐν τῷ πλοίῳ, ἐλθόντες προσεκύ- 33
νησαν αὐτῷ, λέγοντες· Ἀληθῶς Θεοῦ Υἱὸς εἶ!

phini being in Juven. Sat. iii. 14. and vi. 512. connected with *hay*, which has been a mote in the eyes of the Commentators. The most rational opinion is, that the κοφ. in question were either (as Buxt. thinks) such baskets as had, from the earliest period, been a part of the household utensils of the Jews; (See Deut. xxviii. 5.) or (as Reland, Schleus., and Kuin. suppose) were such portable flag-baskets, as were commonly used by the Jews in travelling through Heathen countries, to convey their provisions, in order to avoid the pollution of unclean food. The hay, it is supposed, they took with them, to make a bed. Yet these baskets could not have held any quantity sufficient for that purpose. It is more probable that the cophini *here* meant carried no hay; and that those mentioned by Juvenal were of a much larger sort, like our *hampers*, used for containing various articles of pedlary, such as the foreign Jews, even then, there is reason to think, used to deal in.

22 ἠνάγκασεν.] From this term many have inferred the unwillingness of the disciples to depart; influenced by ambitious views, and thinking that, from the multitude being so desirous to make Jesus a King, now would be the time for him to set up his earthly kingdom. The verb, however, like others in Greek and Latin of similar import, is often used of *moral persuasion*. See Thucyd. viii. 41. and vii. 37. Nay, by an idiom frequent in our own language, it may only mean he *caused* them to enter, &c.

23. *Comp.* John vi. 16. τὸ ὄρος should not be rendered *a* mountain, but the mountain — namely, that on the back of Bethsaida, a part of that range by which the Lake is encircled on all sides.

24. μέσον.] Sub. κατά; unless it be, as Fritz. says, a *Nomin.* Βασανιζόμενον simply signifies "violently tossed;" as in Polyb. i. 48. 2. a stormy wind is said πύργους βασανίζειν.

25. περιπατῶν ἐπὶ τῆς θαλ.] Thus our Saviour evinced his Divine power; for this is in Job. ix. 8. made a property of the Deity; ὁ τανύσας τὸν οὐρανὸν, καὶ περιπατῶν, ὡς ἐπ᾽ ἐδάφους, ἐπὶ θαλάσσης, and Horapollo Hierogl. i. 58, says, that the Egyptian hieroglyphic for expressing impossibility was "a man's feet walking on the sea."

27. ἐγώ εἰμι] "it is I." Literally, I am the person! A somewhat rare idiom.

28. κέλευσον, &c.] Under *bid* is also implied *enable* me to, &c.; for Peter wished a miracle to be worked, to prove that it was really Jesus.

31. ἐδίστασας] The word properly signifies to stand in *bivio*, undetermined which way to take; as Eurip. Or. 625. διπλῆς μερίμνης διπτύχους ἰὼν ὁδούς.

32. ἐκόπασεν] "was lulled, or hushed." Sub. ἑαυτόν. Examples are adduced by the Commentators from Herodo. and Ælian.

33. Θεοῦ Υἱὸς εἶ.] Bishop Middleton has proved that the want of the Art. will not authorize us to translate "a son of God," or "son of a God." For, as to the former in the sense *prophet*, there is no proof that prophets were so called. And as to the latter, which is thought suitable to the ideas of *Pagans*, there is no proof that these men *were* such; or, if so, they might adopt the language of the Apostles on this extraordinary occasion: and though it be urged, that the disciples were not yet acquainted with the divinity of our Lord; yet even *that* must be received with some limitation: that the Messiah would be *the son of God*, was a Jewish doctrine; and, therefore, if they acknowledged him as *the Christ*, they must have regarded him as the Son of God, a title which they had repeatedly heard him claim to himself. And what they themselves heard, they would be likely to impart to the mariners; whose exclamation may thus be understood in the highest sense. Ἀληθῶς, too, *implies* as much as, "Thou art really [the character which thou claimest and art said to be], the Son of God."

MK.

34 Καὶ διαπεράσαντες, ἦλθον εἰς τὴν γῆν Γεννησαρέτ. καὶ ἐπιγνόντες 6.
35 αὐτὸν οἱ ἄνδρες τοῦ τόπου ἐκείνου, ἀπέστειλαν εἰς ὅλην τὴν περίχωρον 53 54
36 ἐκείνην, καὶ προσήνεγκαν αὐτῷ πάντας τοὺς κακῶς ἔχοντας· καὶ παρε- 55
κάλουν αὐτὸν, ἵνα μόνον ἅψωνται τοῦ κρασπέδου τοῦ ἱματίου αὐτοῦ· 56
καὶ ὅσοι ἥψαντο, διεσώθησαν. 7.
1 XV. Τότε προσέρχονται τῷ Ἰησοῦ οἱ ἀπὸ Ἱεροσολύμων γραμματεῖς 1
2 καὶ Φαρισαῖοι, λέγοντες· Διατί οἱ μαθηταί σου παραβαίνουσι τὴν 5
παράδοσιν τῶν πρεσβυτέρων; οὐ γὰρ νίπτονται τὰς χεῖρας αὐτῶν, ὅταν
3 ἄρτον ἐσθίωσιν. Ὁ δὲ ἀποκριθεὶς εἶπεν αὐτοῖς· Διατί καὶ ὑμεῖς πα- 9
4 ραβαίνετε τὴν ἐντολὴν τοῦ Θεοῦ διὰ τὴν παράδοσιν ὑμῶν; Ὁ γὰρ Θεὸς 10
ἐνετείλατο, λέγων· Τίμα τὸν πατέρα [σου] καὶ τὴν μητέρα·
καὶ ὁ κακολογῶν πατέρα ἢ μητέρα, θανάτῳ τελευτά-
5 τω· ὑμεῖς δὲ λέγετε· Ὃς ἂν εἴπῃ τῷ πατρὶ ἢ τῇ μητρί· Δῶρον ὃ ἐὰν 11
ἐξ ἐμοῦ ὠφεληθῇς καὶ οὐ μὴ τιμήσῃ τὸν πατέρα αὐτοῦ ἢ τὴν μητέρα 12

XV. 1. *οἱ ἀπὸ Ἱεροσολύμων.*] "Those of," or belonging to "Jerusalem." An idiom occurring in numerous passages of the Scriptural and Classical writers referred to by the Commentators. — *Those of Jerusalem* were the most learned of the Pharisaical sect, and, as such, were entitled to deliver instruction wherever they went. They were probably sent by the chief of the Pharisees, and as probably came with insidious intentions.

2. *τὴν παράδοσιν τῶν πρεσβυτέρων.*] Παράδ. signifies a precept, or body of precepts, not written, but handed down by tradition. So Joseph. Ant. xiii. 10, 6, says, *ὅτι νόμιμα πολλά τινα παρέδοσαν τῷ δήμῳ οἱ Φαρισαῖοι ἐκ πατέρων διαδοχῆς, ἅπερ οὐκ ἀναγέγραπται ἐν τοῖς Μωϋσέως νόμοις.* These *νόμιμα* were afterwards digested into one body, and called the *Talmud*; divided into the *Mischna* (or Text) and the *Gemara* (or Commentary), on which see Horne's Introd. ii. 417, seqq. By *τῶν πρεσβυτέρων* are meant, not the members of the Sanhedrim, but the most celebrated doctors.

3. *διατί καὶ ὑμεῖς — ὑμῶν.*] Our Lord confutes them from their own positions; ably opposing the *παράδοσις*, &c. to the *ἐντολὴ τοῦ Θεοῦ*; and before he disputes respecting the tradition to which they referred, he uproots the very foundation on which their whole reasoning was erected, and shows, by a manifest example, how often this was at variance with the Divine Laws.

4. *τίμα τὸν πατέρα.*] Exod. xx. 12. This was understood to comprehend, under *obedience* and dutiful *respect*, taking *care of* and *supporting*. See Numb. xxii. 17. xxiv. 1. Judg. xiii. 17. Deut. v. 16. Eph. vi. 2. So Eccles. iii. 8. *ἐν ἔργῳ καὶ λόγῳ τίμα πατέρα.* Thus also *κακολογεῖν*, answering to Heb. קלל, denoted slighting, *neglecting* [to support.] Such, too, was the mode of interpretation sanctioned by their own Canonists. See Lightf. and Wets. See Exod. xxi. 17. Comp. Deut. xxi. 18. Σου after *πατέρα* is cancelled or rejected by all the best Editors, as indeed of little or no authority. Θανάτῳ is *not* a mere pleonasm, but a strong expression, importing a capital punishment of the worst sort. Or *θαν. τελ.* may mean, "let him be put to death without mercy," Hebrew מות יומת to which our common phrases bear a little affinity.

5. *δῶρον*] Scil. *ἔστω*. From the parallel passage of Mark, it is evident that *δῶρον* is here simply the interpretation of the Heb. קרבן denoting any thing devoted — namely, to the service of God. But, as it was often employed in making a vow against using any article, it came, at length, to denote any thing *prohibited*; and, if spoken with reference to any particular person, the phrase imported, that the vower obliged himself *not to give* any thing to the person in question; and thus, if that person were the father of the vower, he was held *prohibited* from relieving his necessities. Such is the view taken of the term by Lightf., Grot., Campb., Kuin., and most recent Commentators. Yet it seems more natural, with the ancient Fathers, and some modern Commentators, to take *δῶρον* simply of something *consecrated*, or *supposed* to be consecrated, to pious uses, by a collusion between the sons and the priests, so as to leave the father destitute. For (to use the words of Bp. Jebb, Sacr. Lit. p. 246, who has elegantly illustrated v. 3—6.) "when the Jews wished to evade the duty of supporting their parents, they made a *pretended*, or at least an *eventual* dedication of their property to the sacred treasury; or rather a dedication of all that *could* or *might* have been given by them to their parents, saying, Be it *Corban*. From that moment, though at liberty to expend such property on any *selfish* purpose, they were *prohibited* from bestowing it on their parents." To say, therefore, to a parent, *Be it a gift*, was an aggravated breach of the commandment, and was virtually *κακολογεῖν πατέρα, ἢ μητέρα.*

— *καὶ οὐ μὴ τιμήσῃ*, &c.] Euthym., not without reason, complains of the difficulty of the construction, in which some suppose an *apodosis* to be wanting, suppressed *per aposiopesin*; either *ἠλευθέρωται*, or *ἀναίτιός ἐστι*, or the like. Others suppose an *ellipsis* of some word, as *ὀφείλει*. Kuin. and others regard the *καὶ* as a mere expletive, (as often the Hebrew ו) and render "he need not honour." But this removal of a difficulty by *silencing* a word is too violent a procedure. And as to the other methods abovementioned, there is certainly no *aposiopesis*; nor any *ellipsis*, properly so called; nor finally is an apodosis wanting; for, as Bp. Jebb, *ubi supra*, observes, the context has within itself the full meaning, "Whosoever shall say, *Corban*, &c.

MK.
7. αὐτοῦ. καὶ ἠκυρώσατε τὴν ἐντολὴν τοῦ Θεοῦ διὰ τὴν παράδοσιν ὑμῶν. 6
13 6 ὑποκριταί! καλῶς προεφήτευσε περὶ ὑμῶν Ἡσαΐας, λέγων· Ἐγγίζει 7
μοι ὁ λαὸς οὗτος τῷ στόματι αὐτῶν, καὶ τοῖς χείλεσί 8
με τιμᾷ· ἡ δὲ καρδία αὐτῶν πόῤῥω ἀπέχει ἀπ' ἐμοῦ· 9
μάτην δὲ σέβονταί με, διδάσκοντες διδασκαλίας, ἐν-
14 τάλματα ἀνθρώπων. Καὶ προσκαλεσάμενος τὸν ὄχλον, εἶπεν 10
15 αὐτοῖς· Ἀκούετε καὶ συνίετε! Οὐ τὸ εἰσερχόμενον εἰς τὸ στόμα 11
κοινοῖ τὸν ἄνθρωπον· ἀλλὰ τὸ ἐκπορευόμενον ἐκ τοῦ στόματος, τοῦτο
17 κοινοῖ τὸν ἄνθρωπον. Τότε προσελθόντες οἱ μαθηταὶ αὐτοῦ εἶπον 12
αὐτῷ· Οἶδας, ὅτι οἱ Φαρισαῖοι ἀκούσαντες τὸν λόγον, ἐσκανδαλίσθη-
σαν; Ὁ δὲ ἀποκριθεὶς εἶπε· Πᾶσα φυτεία, ἣν οὐκ ἐφύτευσεν ὁ 13

must also not honour" [better, must *even not* honour, Edit.] i. e. he is under an obligation *not* to do so. So in the parallel passage of Mark vii. 12. οὐκέτι ἀφίετε αὐτὸν οὐδὲν ποιῆσαι τῷ πατρί.

7. προεφήτευσε]. From the use of this term, the early Commentators in general regarded the passage which follows as a real *prophecy*. Others considered it as a prediction of what would afterwards happen, veiled under a rebuke to the persons addressed. But the employment of the above expression does not necessarily imply that the words are to be considered as a *prophecy;* for προφητεύειν may, and, I think, ought, here to be taken in the very frequent sense of speaking or writing under Divine inspiration. And there is a peculiar propriety in the use of the term here; the words purporting to be the words of God himself. That Chrys., Theophyl., and Euthym. did not regard the passage as a *prophecy*, is certain; and that they viewed προεφ. in this very light, is highly probable from their expositions. As to περὶ ὑμῶν, that may very well be taken *populariter*, for (ὡς) περὶ ὑμῶν; the sense being, that Isaiah spoke, under divine inspiration, of the Jews, as if he had been speaking of you. So Euthym.: Ἄγει τὸν προφήτην πάλαι κατηγοροῦντα αὐτῶν ἃ νῦν οὗτος κατηγορεῖ. Thus the passage may, with the best Commentators, be regarded as an accommodation or application, by way of illustration, of what was said of the Jews of Isaiah's time, to those of the time of Christ. It may, therefore, be classed among *quotations in the way of illustration*, which are allowed not to be, properly speaking, prophecies; though they are sometimes said to be *fulfilled*, i. e. in a *qualified* and peculiar sense of the word, whereby any thing may be said to be *fulfilled*, which can be *pertinently applied;* on which see Note supra ii. 17 & 18. In such cases, the sacred writers did not intend it to be understood, that the passages they were citing from the O. T. were to be considered as real predictions; but only that there was a *con-similarity* of cases and incidents; so that the words of the Prophets in the Old Testament were as applicable to the transactions recorded by the Apostles, as they were suitable to denote the events of their own times.

8. ἐγγίζει μοι, and τῷ στόματι αὐτῶν καί.] These words, omitted in a few MSS., and some Versions and Fathers, are double bracketed by Vater, and cancelled by Griesb. But the evidence in question will scarcely warrant *suspicion*. The words of the quotation in this and the next verse, exactly correspond to the Sept., except that in the Sept. there is a καὶ between διδασκαλίας and ἐντ., which, however, has nothing corresponding to it in the Heb., and doubtless arose from the mistake either of scribes or sciolists. In v. 9, both the Sept. and St. Matthew differ not a little from the Heb.; and the discrepancy is such as cannot be removed, unless by resorting to so considerable an alteration (without sufficient authority) of the Hebrew text, as sober criticism will not permit. For though there is no doubt, that for ותהי the Sept. read ותהו, and for מלמדה read מלמדם; yet, although these *are* slight alterations, they ought not to be admitted. on authority far greater than that of *any Version*, or indeed *all* the Versions; because they break up the construction of the whole sentence, the יען כי, *(inasmuch as,)* at the begining of the 13th verse corresponding to לכן, *(therefore,)* at the beginning of v. 14. The words of the Prophet may be rendered, "Their worship of me is [only] a taught commandment of men;" i. e. the religion rests only on the precepts of men's teaching, i. e. according to the tradition of the elders, and the interpretation of the Scribes. So that, upon the whole, though their be a discrepancy in *words*, their is none in *sense*. [*Comp.* Isai. xxix. 13.]

9. διδασκαλίας] "as, or by way of, commandments." See Middlet.

— ἐντάλ. ἀνθρώπων.] "The term (says Campb.) is here and at Mark ix. 7. and Col. ii. 2. contrasted, by implication, with the commands of *God*, which are in the N. T. called, not ἐντάλματα, but ἐντολαί.

11. οὐ τὸ εἰσερχόμενον — ἄνθρωπον.] Our Lord did not hereby intend to abrogate the distinction between clean and unclean things for food. His meaning was only this, — that nothing was naturally and *per se* impure (and therefore such as could defile the mind of man); but was only so *ex instituto*. Or his words may be understood *comparatè;* q. d. forbidden meats do not pollute so much as impure thoughts and intentions. Bp. Middlet. observes, that the Art. at τὸν ἄνθρωπον is necessary, because, as in the case of regimen, the definiteness of a part supposes the definiteness of the whole.

13. φυτεία.] The word properly signifies "a planting," or plant; but metaphorically denotes the doctrines, or traditions in question, by an allusion to the *mind as soil*, and *precepts as plants*. Comp. John xv. 2. A comparison familiar both to the Hebrews and Greeks. See Matt. xiii. 29 & 38. John xv. 2. 1 Cor. iii. 6.

MK.
14 πατήρ μου ὁ οὐράνιος, ἐκριζωθήσεται. Ἄφετε αὐτούς· ὁδηγοί εἰσι 7.
τυφλοὶ τυφλῶν· τυφλὸς δὲ τυφλὸν ἐὰν ὁδηγῇ, ἀμφότεροι εἰς βόθυνον
15 πεσοῦνται. Ἀποκριθεὶς δὲ ὁ Πέτρος εἶπεν αὐτῷ· Φράσον ἡμῖν τὴν
16 παραβολὴν ταύτην. Ὁ δὲ Ἰησοῦς εἶπεν· Ἀκμὴν καὶ ὑμεῖς ἀσύνετοί
17 ἐστε; Οὔπω νοεῖτε, ὅτι πᾶν τὸ εἰσπορευόμενον εἰς τὸ στόμα εἰς τὴν 18 19
18 κοιλίαν χωρεῖ, καὶ εἰς ἀφεδρῶνα ἐκβάλλεται; Τὰ δὲ ἐκπορευόμενα ἐκ 20
τοῦ στόματος, ἐκ τῆς καρδίας ἐξέρχεται, κἀκεῖνα κοινοῖ τὸν ἄνθρωπον.
19 Ἐκ γὰρ τῆς καρδίας ἐξέρχονται διαλογισμοὶ πονηροὶ, φόνοι, μοιχεῖαι, 21
20 πορνεῖαι, κλοπαὶ, ψευδομαρτυρίαι, βλασφημίαι. Ταῦτά ἐστι τὰ κοινοῦν- 23
τα τὸν ἄνθρωπον· τὸ δὲ ἀνίπτοις χερσὶ φαγεῖν οὐ κοινοῖ τὸν ἄνθρωπον.
21 Καὶ ἐξελθὼν ἐκεῖθεν ὁ Ἰησοῦς, ἀνεχώρησεν εἰς τὰ μέρη Τύρου καὶ 24
22 Σιδῶνος. Καὶ ἰδοὺ, γυνὴ Χαναναία ἀπὸ τῶν ὁρίων ἐκείνων ἐξελθοῦ- 25
σα ἐκραύγασεν αὐτῷ λέγουσα· Ἐλέησόν με, κύριε, υἱὲ Δαυΐδ! ἡ θυ- 26
23 γάτηρ μου κακῶς δαιμονίζεται. Ὁ δὲ οὐκ ἀπεκρίθη αὐτῇ λόγον. καὶ
προσελθόντες οἱ μαθηταὶ αὐτοῦ ἠρώτων αὐτὸν λέγοντες· Ἀπόλυσον
24 αὐτὴν, ὅτι κράζει ὄπισθεν ἡμῶν. Ὁ δὲ ἀποκριθεὶς εἶπεν· Οὐκ
25 ἀπεστάλην εἰ μὴ εἰς τὰ πρόβατα τὰ ἀπολωλότα οἴκου Ἰσραήλ. Ἡ δὲ
26 ἐλθοῦσα προσεκύνει αὐτῷ, λέγουσα· Κύριε, βοήθει μοι. Ὁ δὲ ἀποκριθεὶς εἶπεν· Οὐκ ἔστι καλὸν λαβεῖν τὸν ἄρτον τῶν τέκνων, καὶ 27
27 βαλεῖν τοῖς κυναρίοις. Ἡ δὲ εἶπε· Ναὶ, κύριε· καὶ γὰρ τὰ κυνάρια 28

14. *Comp.* infra xxiii. 16. Luke vi. 39.

— τυφλὸς δὲ τυφλὸν—πεσοῦνται.] A proverbial saying, common to both the Hebrews, Greeks, and Romans. Βόθυνον signifies, not *ditch*, but *pit*, such as was dug for the reception of rain water.

15. παραβολὴν] i. e. "maxim, or weighty apophthegm." It is not that Peter did not *understand* the maxim; (which was by no means obscure, insomuch that our Lord says καὶ ὑμεῖς ἀσύνετοί ἐστε;) but that his prejudices darkened his understanding. Indeed, he could scarcely believe his ears that a distinction of meats availed not; and therefore asks an explanation.

16. ἀκμὴν] Put adverbially for ἔτι, as not unfrequently in the Classical writers. *Comp.* infra xvi. 9. Mr. Rose on Parkh., p. 26, says the meaning is, Yet still after so many miracles, are ye without understanding?

17. ἀφεδρῶνα.] A word of the Macedonian dialect. From its etymon (ἀπὸ and ἕζομαι) it signifies a place *apart*, and thence a *privy*.

18. *Comp.* James iii. 6. Gen. vi. 5, and viii. 21. The meaning is, that evil principles, being seated in the *heart*, and therefore governing the conversation and conduct, especially defile a man. So a great poet well says,

"Our outward act is prompted from within,
And from the sinner's *mind* proceeds the sin."

21. εἰς τὰ μέρη.] As Christ seems not to have actually entered the Gentile territories, we must here (with Grot.) interpret εἰς *versus*, *towards*, and so the Syriac, and the Hebrew ה local, like our *ward* in *toward*. Mark, indeed, has εἰς τὰ μεθόρια Τύρου: but μεθόριον is a word of dubious signification; and denoted a strip of land which was between two countries, but properly belonging to neither. So it is explained by the Gloss. Vet. *inter fines*.

22. γυνὴ Χαναναία.] Called by Mark Ἑλληνὶς Συροφοίνισσα, i. e. a Gentile dwelling on the confines of Phœnicia. She was therefore a Gentile by birth, though probably not a proselyte, as some have supposed. Yet it does not follow, that she was an idolatress; for many Gentiles in those parts were believers in one true God, and felt much respect for Judaism, though they did not profess it. She might easily, therefore, have learnt both the doctrine of a Messiah, and the appellation, from the Jews. For a particular explanation of this narration, and a correct view thereof, showing the peculiar propriety of our Lord's conduct, in making the manner in which he complied with the request of the Greek heathen (ordained by the providence of God to be one of the first *Pagan* proselytes), a type of the mode in which the Gentiles should be received, see two admirable Sermons of Dr. Jortin and Bp. Horsley on this text.]

23. ἠρώτων] "asked, besought him." An usage confined to the N. T. and Sept.

— ἀπόλυσον] i. e. "dispatch her business;" i. e. as it is implied, "with the grant of the favour she asks," as appears from vv. 24 & 26.

24. *Comp.* supr. x. 5 & 6. Acts xiii. 46. Rom. xv. 8.

26. κυναρίοις.] The word was adopted after the manner of the Jews in speaking of the Gentiles, though it was also a term of reproach in common use with both.

27. ναὶ κύριε.] The Commentators are not agreed as to the force of this formula. Most modern expositors (after Scalig. and Casaub.) assign to it the sense "obsecro te," as in Rev. xxii. 20, and sometimes in the Classical writers. And

MK.
7. ἐσθίει ἀπὸ τῶν ψιχίων τῶν πιπτόντων ἀπὸ τῆς τραπέζης τῶν κυρίων
29 αὐτῶν. Τότε ἀποκριθεὶς ὁ Ἰησοῦς εἶπεν αὐτῇ· Ὦ γύναι, μεγάλη 28
30 σου ἡ πίστις! γενηθήτω σοι ὡς θέλεις. Καὶ ἰάθη ἡ θυγάτηρ αὐτῆς
ἀπὸ τῆς ὥρας ἐκείνης.
31 Καὶ μεταβὰς ἐκεῖθεν ὁ Ἰησοῦς, ἦλθε παρὰ τὴν θάλασσαν τῆς Γαλι- 29
λαίας· καὶ ἀναβὰς εἰς τὸ ὄρος, ἐκάθητο ἐκεῖ. Καὶ προσῆλθον αὐτῷ 30
ὄχλοι πολλοὶ ἔχοντες μεθ' ἑαυτῶν χωλοὺς, τυφλοὺς, κωφοὺς, κυλλοὺς,
καὶ ἑτέρους πολλούς· καὶ ἔῤῥιψαν αὐτοὺς παρὰ τοὺς πόδας τοῦ Ἰησοῦ,
καὶ ἐθεράπευσεν αὐτούς· ὥστε τοὺς ὄχλους θαυμάσαι, βλέποντας κω- 31
8. φοὺς λαλοῦντας, κυλλοὺς ὑγιεῖς, χωλοὺς περιπατοῦντας, καὶ τυφλοὺς
1 βλέποντας· καὶ ἐδόξασαν τὸν Θεὸν Ἰσραήλ. Ὁ δὲ Ἰησοῦς προσκαλε- 32
2 σάμενος τοὺς μαθητὰς αὐτοῦ εἶπε· Σπλαγχνίζομαι ἐπὶ τὸν ὄχλον,
ὅτι ἤδη * ἡμέραι τρεῖς προσμένουσί μοι, καὶ οὐκ ἔχουσι τί φάγωσι·
3 καὶ ἀπολῦσαι αὐτοὺς νήστεις οὐ θέλω, μήποτε ἐκλυθῶσιν ἐν τῇ ὁδῷ.
Καὶ λέγουσιν αὐτῷ οἱ μαθηταὶ αὐτοῦ· Πόθεν ἡμῖν ἐν ἐρημίᾳ ἄρτοι 33
5 τοσοῦτοι, ὥστε χορτάσαι ὄχλον τοσοῦτον; Καὶ λέγει αὐτοῖς ὁ Ἰησοῦς· 34
Πόσους ἄρτους ἔχετε; οἱ δὲ εἶπον· Ἑπτὰ, καὶ ὀλίγα ἰχθύδια. Καὶ 35
6 ἐκέλευσε τοῖς ὄχλοις ἀναπεσεῖν ἐπὶ τὴν γῆν. Καὶ λαβὼν τοὺς ἑπτὰ 36
ἄρτους καὶ τοὺς ἰχθύας, εὐχαριστήσας ἔκλασε, καὶ ἔδωκε τοῖς μαθηταῖς
8 αὐτοῦ, οἱ δὲ μαθηταὶ τῷ ὄχλῳ. Καὶ ἔφαγον πάντες, καὶ ἐχορτάσθη- 37
9 σαν. καὶ ἦραν τὸ περισσεῦον τῶν κλασμάτων, ἑπτὰ σπυρίδας πλήρεις.
Οἱ δὲ ἐσθίοντες ἦσαν τετρακισχίλιοι ἄνδρες, χωρὶς γυναικῶν καὶ 38
παιδίων.
10 Καὶ ἀπολύσας τοὺς ὄχλους ‡ ἐνέβη εἰς τὸ πλοῖον, καὶ ἦλθεν εἰς τὰ 39

so the Heb. אָנָּ. The ancients, and some moderns (as Grot., Le Clerc, Elsn., Schleus., and others) take it to import *assent*, which, indeed, is most agreeable to the answer. And though ἀλλὰ does not follow, as it properly should; yet, in such pathetic sentences, regularity is overlooked. *Here* (as often) γὰρ has reference to a short clause omitted, to be thus supplied: "True, Lord! [but extend a small portion of thy help and mercy towards me]; for even (καὶ) the dogs," &c.

29. εἰς τὸ ὄρος] not "to *a* mountain," but to *the* mountain, namely, the mountainous ridge, which skirts the lake on all sides.

30. κυλλοὺς.] It is by no means clear what is meant by this term, and how it differs from χωλοὺς. See Recens. Syn. I have there conjectured, that κυλλὸς (which Hesych. explains by κάμπυλος) meant "a person with a distorted limb," as a foot; exactly answering to our expressions *bow-leg*, and *bow-legged*. Such persons are not, in a proper sense, *lame*; yet they sometimes labour under more inconveniences than would be occasioned by the loss of a limb. And therefore we need not wonder that such should present themselves as objects of our Lord's mercy; and surely the cure of such a radical *malformation* must give the most exalted idea of our Lord's power.

31. κωφοὺς] i. e. deaf and dumb; since those born deaf are naturally dumb also.

32. ἡμέραι τρεῖς.] The reading here is dubious. Most of the ancient MSS., and some Fathers have ἡμέραι, which has been received by almost all Editors from Wets. downward; and justly, since the common reading ἡμέρας plainly arose from an alteration of the more difficult reading. Yet this leaves a construction of unprecedented harshness; which Fritz. would remove by inserting, from a few MSS., Versions, and Fathers, εἰσιν, καί. The authority, however, is so slight, and the words so evidently from the margin, that I cannot venture to follow the example. It is strange that none should have seen that the difficulty may better be removed by simply altering the accent of προσμένουσι to προσμενοῦσι, thus taking it for a particip. Dat. plur. — a kind of error not unexampled. Thus, in Thucyd. iii. 31, I have shown, that for ἐφορμῶσιν, the true reading is, ἐφορμοῦσιν; and the sentence (similar to the present) is καὶ ἅμα ἢν ἐφορμοῦσιν αὐτοῦ σφίσι δαπάνη γίγνηται. *Thus* the ellipse of εἰσι will be very regular, and the construction usual: q. d. "there are three days to them staying with me;" i. e. they have stayed with me three days. The words following, καὶ οὐκ ἔχουσι, &c, "signify, "and [now] they have nothing [left] to eat."

39. ἐνέβη.] Almost all the Editors from Wets. to Fritz. adopt or prefer ἀνέβη, from several MSS., Versions, and Fathers, with the Edit. Princ. and the two first of Steph. And this may possibly be the true reading. But as I cannot remember any instance of that word being used of *embarking*, (whereas ἐμβαίνω is often so used, both in the N. T. and Sept., see viii. 23. ix. 1. xiii. 2. xiv. 22 & 32, and in the parallel passages), I have scrupled to receive it.

MK

1 ὅρια Μαγδαλά. XVI. *Καὶ προσελθόντες οἱ Φαρισαῖοι καὶ Σαδ-* 8.
δουκαῖοι, πειράζοντες ἐπηρώτησαν αὐτὸν σημεῖον ἐκ τοῦ οὐρανοῦ ἐπι- 11
2 *δεῖξαι αὐτοῖς. Ὁ δὲ ἀποκριθεὶς εἶπεν αὐτοῖς· Ὀψίας γενομένης,*
3 *λέγετε· Εὐδία· πυῤῥάζει γὰρ ὁ οὐρανός· Καὶ πρωΐ· Σήμερον*
χειμών· πυῤῥάζει γὰρ στυγνάζων ὁ οὐρανός. Ὑποκριταί! τὸ μὲν
πρόσωπον τοῦ οὐρανοῦ γινώσκετε διακρίνειν, τὰ δὲ σημεῖα τῶν καιρῶν
4 *οὐ δύνασθε; Γενεὰ πονηρὰ καὶ μοιχαλὶς σημεῖον ἐπιζητεῖ· καὶ σημεῖ-* 12
ον οὐ δοθήσεται αὐτῇ, εἰ μὴ τὸ σημεῖον Ἰωνᾶ τοῦ προφήτου. Καὶ 13
καταλιπὼν αὐτοὺς ἀπῆλθε.
5 *Καὶ ἐλθόντες οἱ μαθηταὶ αὐτοῦ εἰς τὸ πέραν, ἐπελάθοντο ἄρτους* 14
6 *λαβεῖν. Ὁ δὲ Ἰησοῦς εἶπεν αὐτοῖς· Ὁρᾶτε καὶ προσέχετε ἀπὸ τῆς* 15
7 *ζύμης τῶν Φαρισαίων καὶ Σαδδουκαίων. Οἱ δὲ διελογίζοντο ἐν ἑαυτοῖς* 16
8 *λέγοντες· Ὅτι ἄρτους οὐκ ἐλάβομεν. Γνοὺς δὲ ὁ Ἰησοῦς, εἶπεν [αὐ-* 17
τοῖς·] Τί διαλογίζεσθε ἐν ἑαυτοῖς, ὀλιγόπιστοι, ὅτι ἄρτους οὐκ ἐλά-
9 *βετε; Οὔπω νοεῖτε, οὐδὲ μνημονεύετε τοὺς πέντε ἄρτους τῶν πεντακισ-* 18 19
10 *χιλίων, καὶ πόσους κοφίνους ἐλάβετε; οὐδὲ τοὺς ἑπτὰ ἄρτους τῶν* 20
11 *τετρακισχιλίων, καὶ πόσας σπυρίδας ἐλάβετε; Πῶς οὐ νοεῖτε, ὅτι οὐ* 21
*περὶ * ἄρτων εἶπον ὑμῖν προσέχειν ἀπὸ τῆς ζύμης τῶν Φαρισαίων καὶ*

XVI. 1. ἐπηρώτησαν.] Here is the same idiom as that by which we say, to *ask* (i. e. request) any person to do a thing. On the thing itself see supra xii. 38.

2. εὐδία] Sub. ἔσται. The Jews, and indeed the ancients in general, were attentive observers of all prognostics of weather, fair or foul; and many similar sayings are adduced from both the Rabbinical and Classical writers by the Commentators.

3. στυγνάζων] for καὶ στυγνάζει. The Commentators and Lexicographers say, that στυγνάζειν signifies properly to *grieve*, and thence *to be gloomy*. The very reverse, however, is the truth. The verb (which is rarely met with, except in the N. T. and Sept.) is derived from στύγος, *thick*, and that from στίω, *to stuff up*.

— τὸ μὲν πρόσωπον, &c.] "From this reproof it appears, that the refusal of the Jews to acknowledge the Messiahship of Christ, was owing neither to the want of evidence, nor to the want of capacity to judge of that evidence. The accomplishment of the ancient prophecies (Gen. xlix. 10. Is. xi. 1; xxxv. 5. Deut. ix. 24.) and the miracles which he performed, were proof sufficient, and much more easily discernible than the signs of the seasons." (Mackn.) As to the opinions of the Jews concerning the MESSIAH, they are admirably summed up by Bp. Blomfield (Traditional Knowledge, p. 106), as follows:—"They considered him to be the *Word of God*. (See on Joh. i. 1—3.) They believed that all God's transactions with mankind were carried on through the medium of his *Word*, the *Messiah*; who they thought, delivered the Israelites from Egypt, and brought them into Canaan. They believed, that the Spirit of the Lord would be upon him, and manifest itself by the working of miracles. (See Matt. xii. 28.) They supposed that the Messiah would appear, not in a *real* human body, but in the *semblance* of one. They expected that he would not be subject to death. Yet they thought that he would offer, in his own person, an expiatory sacrifice for their sins. (Joh. i. 49.) He was, they thought, to restore the Jews to freedom; (see Luke i. 68. xxiv. 21. 2 Esdr. xii. 34.) to restore a pure and perfect form of worship; (Luke i. 73. Joh. iv. 25.) to give remission of sins; (Luke i. 76. Matt. i. 21.) to work miracles; (Jo. vii. 31.) to descend into *Hades*, and to bring back to earth the souls of the departed Israelites, united to their glorified bodies. This was to be the first resurrection. (See Ephes. iv. 8, 9. 1 Pet. iii. 18, 19.) After which the Devil was to be cast into hell for a thousand years. Then was to begin the Messiah's kingdom, which was to last a thousand years. At the end of that time, the Devil was to be released, and to excite great troubles; but he was to be conquered, and again to be imprisoned for ever. Thereupon the second and general resurrection was to take place, followed by the judgment. The world was then to be renewed; and new heavens, a new earth, and a new Jerusalem were to appear. Lastly, the Messiah, having fulfilled his office, was to deliver up the kingdom to God, at whose right hand he was to sit for evermore." See more in Dr. Pye Smith's Scripture Testimony to the Messiah, vol. i. p. 464 seqq.

4 & 5. Vide supra xii. 39.

6. ὁρᾶτε καὶ προσέχετε.] An emphatical phrase, signifying mind and *studiously attend to*. It is not so much a Hebraism, as an idiom common to the simple and colloquial style in all languages. Ζύμης, i. e. their doctrines, as διδαχὴ imports both doctrines and ordinances. See Lightfoot. [*Comp.* Luke xii. 1.]

7. λέγοντες· ὅτι] Sub. εἶπε or the like. See Grot. and Glass.

9. *Comp.* supr. xiv. 17. and John vi. 9.

10. *Comp.* supr. xv. 34.

11. ἄρτων.] So, for ἄρτου, all the most eminent Editors from very many MSS., of various families, and some versions.

MK. LU.
8. 9. Σαδδουκαίων; Τότε συνῆκαν, ὅτι οὐκ εἶπε προσέχειν ἀπὸ τῆς ζύμης 12
τοῦ ἄρτου, ἀλλ᾽ ἀπὸ τῆς διδαχῆς τῶν Φαρισαίων καὶ Σαδδουκαίων.
27 18 Ἐλθὼν δὲ ὁ Ἰησοῦς εἰς τὰ μέρη Καισαρείας τῆς Φιλίππου, ἠρώτα 13
τοὺς μαθητὰς αὐτοῦ, λέγων· Τίνα [με] λέγουσιν οἱ ἄνθρωποι εἶναι
28 19 τὸν Υἱὸν τοῦ ἀνθρώπου; Οἱ δὲ εἶπον· Οἱ μὲν Ἰωάννην τὸν Βα- 14
πτιστήν· ἄλλοι δὲ Ἠλίαν· ἕτεροι δὲ Ἱερεμίαν, ἢ ἕνα τῶν προφητῶν.
29 20 Λέγει αὐτοῖς· Ὑμεῖς δὲ τίνα με λέγετε εἶναι; Ἀποκριθεὶς δὲ Σίμων 15
Πέτρος εἶπε· Σὺ εἶ ὁ Χριστὸς, ὁ Υἱὸς τοῦ Θεοῦ τοῦ ζῶντος. Καὶ 16
ἀποκριθεὶς ὁ Ἰησοῦς εἶπεν αὐτῷ· Μακάριος εἶ, Σίμων βὰρ Ἰωνᾶ, 17
ὅτι σὰρξ καὶ αἷμα οὐκ ἀπεκάλυψέ σοι, ἀλλ᾽ ὁ Πατήρ μου ὁ ἐν τοῖς
οὐρανοῖς. Κἀγὼ δὲ σοὶ λέγω, ὅτι σὺ εἶ Πέτρος· καὶ ἐπὶ ταύτῃ τῇ 18

13. *τίνα με λέγουσι* &c.] Bp. Middleton has shown that the interpretation of Beza and others, which supposes a double interrogation ["whom do men say that I am? the Son of man?"] would involve an intolerable harshness, not to say solecism. Yet, as the common reading and construction is liable to no little objection, he thinks the conjecture of Adler probable; that the received reading was made up of *two*, viz.: *τίνα με λέγουσιν οἱ ἄνθρωποι εἶναι* (which is the reading of Mark and Luke) and of *τίνα λέγουσιν οἱ ἄνθρωποι εἶναι τὸν υἱὸν τοῦ ἀνθρώπου*, which is the supposed true reading of St. Matthew. The *με* is omitted in the Vatican MS. and several Versions and Fathers.

14. The meaning of this verse will depend upon that assigned to the preceding. If *με* be there removed, the sense here may be, that some thought John the Baptist to be the *Son of man;* others, Elijah, &c. meaning by *υἱὸς τοῦ ἀνθρώπου*, the person who should be Forerunner to, and usher in the Υἱὸς τοῦ Θεοῦ.

16. ὁ Υἱὸς — ζῶντος]. Whitby supposes that there was this difference between ὁ Χριστὸς, and ὁ Υἱὸς τοῦ Θεοῦ, that the former referred to his *office*, the latter to his Divine *original;* though he admits that neither Nathanael (John i. 49.) nor the other Jews, nor even the Apostles, used it in that *sublime* sense in which Christians always take it. Ζῶντος denotes the (only) living and true [God], as distinguished from *εἴδωλα ἄψυχα*, (Wisd. xiv. 29), and fictitious deities; and because he alone hath life in himself, and is the Giver of life. [*Comp.* Joh. vi. 69. Acts viii. 37. ix. 20; 1 John iv. 15; v. 5.]

17. *σὰρξ καὶ αἷμα*] i. e. according to the sense of the expression in the N. T. and the Rabbinical writers, *Man*, as composed of flesh and blood; by a circumlocution, which (as Fritz. observes) always contains the idea of weakness and frailty. The sense is, Man [in his greatest wisdom], (alluding to the Scribes) hath not taught thee this, but God [by whose Providence thou becamest my disciple]. We are not, however, by this to understand any particular communication, by revelation, to Peter; but only the effect of that *conviction*, which resulted from the evidence afforded by the miracles, and the precepts and doctrines taught by Christ. It is remarkable that this phrase should not occur in the Septuagint.

18, 19. We are now advanced to a passage on which, as the Church of Rome mainly rests its doctrines of the supremacy and infallibility of the Pope, and the power of the Church, we are bound to discuss the sense with especial care. Let us, then, examine the words and clauses in order, as they offer themselves. First, from the very *form of expression* in Κἀγὼ δὲ σοὶ λέγω it is plain, that what is here said by Christ is meant to *correspond* to what had been just said by *Peter*. As *he* had declared to Jesus: Σὺ εἶ — ζῶντος, so *Jesus* says to him: Κἀγὼ δὲ σοὶ λέγω, the sense of which is: "Moreover *I also* say to *thee*." In the next clause ὅτι σὺ εἶ Πέτρος, we are to bear in mind that *Peter* was not the *original* name of this disciple; but a *surname*, given to him (as was customary with the Jewish *Rabbis* at the baptism of proselytes) at his *conversion*. And as those names were often given with allusion to some peculiar quality or disposition; so, in the case of Simon, it had reference to that *zeal* and *firmness* which he displayed; as well in first making this confession of faith in Christ, as in afterwards building up the Church and establishing the Religion of Christ. For examples of this kind of *Paronomasia* in giving names, see Gen. xvii. 5. xxxii 27. and compare Gen. xxvii. 36. Eurip. Phœn. 645. Æschyl. Prom. 472. Theb. 401. Agam. 670. So also Christ in like manner, surnamed James and John *Boanerges*, sons of thunder. Moreover Peter, or rather *Cephas*, (for Πέτρος is only the name Grecized,) means, not *stone*, (as some affirm,) but *Rock*, as Cephas often does, and *πέτρος* not unfrequently in the Classical writers, as Herodo. ix. 55. Soph. Œd. T. 334. Callim. Hymn in Apoll 22. So Juvencus Hist. Ev. iii. 275. must have understood it, who well expresses the sense thus: "Tu nomen *Petri* dignâ virtute tueris. Hac in mole mihi, *Saxique* in robore ponam Semper mansuras æternis mœnibus ædes." Moreover, *σὺ εἶ* may be rendered "thy name denotes." So Mark iii. 17. Βοανεργὲς ὅ ἐστιν, υἱοὶ βροντῆς.

But to proceed. Commentators, both ancient and modern, are not agreed as to what is meant by ἐπὶ ταύτῃ τῇ πέτρᾳ. Now *that* depends upon the *reference;* which some suppose to be the *confession of faith* just made by Peter, while others (and indeed almost every modern expositor of any note,) refer it to *Peter himself:* and with reason; for certainly, as is observed by Bp. Marsh (Comp. View, App. p. 27.), "it would be a desperate undertaking to prove that Christ meant any other person than Peter." In fact, they can indicate no other, consistently with the rules of correct exegesis; for, not to mention that the profession had not been Peter's only, but in making it, he spoke not for himself alone, but for all the Apostles (and in *that* quality returned answer to a question which had been addressed to *them collectively:* "Whom say *ye* that I am?" &c.) the *connection* subsisting in the *reason* given for the

πέτρᾳ οἰκοδομήσω μου τὴν ἐκκλησίαν· καὶ πύλαι ᾅδου οὐ κατισχύ-
19 σουσιν αὐτῆς. Καὶ δώσω σοι τὰς κλεῖς τῆς βασιλείας τῶν οὐρανῶν·

surname which had been bestowed on Simon, *confines* it to that alone; as also does the *parallelism* between Christ's reply to Peter and the answer which he had given. And when the Expositors above alluded to conjecture that, in pronouncing the words, Christ pointed to *himself*, (as the great foundation) they argue upon a wholly gratuitous and very improbable supposition. Moreover, the words following καὶ σοὶ δώσω imply that there had been some *previous* gift or distinction. In short, the sense is: "Thou art by *name Rock*; (i.e. thy name *means* ROCK) and suitably to that will be thy work and office; for upon *thee* (i. e. upon thy preaching, as upon a rock) shall the foundation of the Church be laid." It may, indeed, seem strange, that so natural and well-founded an interpretation should have been passed over by any. But that may be attributed *partly*, to the causeless fears into which Protestants have been betrayed; lest, by admitting it, they should give a countenance to the Papal claim of supremacy; and *partly*, to an idea, that such a sense would be contrary to what is elsewhere said in Scripture,— namely, that Christ *is the only foundation*. See 1 Cor. iii. 11. But as to the *first*, the fear is groundless: it being (as Bp. Middlet. observes) "difficult to see what *advantage* could be gained; unless we could evade the meaning of δώσω σοι τὰς κλεῖς, which follows." And as to the *latter* fear, it is equally without foundation; since the two expressions are employed in two very *different* senses. In St. Peter's case, it was very applicable: for as he was the first Apostle called to the ministry so he was the first who preached the Gospel to the Jews, and also the first who preached it to the Gentiles. So that, to use the words of Bp. Pearson on the Creed, "the promise made here was punctually fulfilled, by Christ's using Peter's ministry in laying the foundation of the Christian Church among both Jews and Gentiles; and in his being the first preacher to them of that faith which he here confesses, and making the first proselytes to it: for St. Peter laid the first foundations of a church among the Jews, by the conversion of 3000 souls, Acts ii. 41., who, when they gladly had embraced St. Peter's doctrine, where all baptized; and then, ver. 47., we first find mention of a Christian Church. St. Peter also laid the first foundation of a Church among the *Gentiles*, by the conversion of Cornelius and his friends, Acts x." "If (says Bp. Taylor) St. Peter was chief of the Apostles, and head of the Church, he might fairly enough be the representative of the whole college of Apostles, and receive this promise in their right, as well as his own;— that promise, I say, which did not pertain to Peter principally and by origination, and to the rest by communication, society, and adherence; but that promise which was made to Peter first; yet not for himself, but for all the college, and for all their successors: and then made a second time to them all, without representation, but in diffusion, and performed to all alike in presence, except St. Thomas." In fact, the *Apostles generally* are in other parts of the N. T. called the *foundation* on which the Church is built, as in Eph. ii. 20. and Rev. xxi. 14., as being the persons employed in erecting the Church by their preaching. And what they all, more or less did, Peter *commenced* the doing thereof, and might therefore be said to be the *first foundation;* though in matters of doctrine, the Christian Church rests on the testimony, not of one but of *all*.

But to proceed to the clause καὶ πύλαι ᾅδου οὐ κατισχύσουσιν αὐτῆς, here there is the same debate as to the reference in αὐτῆς; some referring it to πέτρα, by which it must mean Peter's confession of faith; and not a few to the rock of *the Gospel*. Both methods are alike harsh and gratuitous, and in violation of the laws of exegesis. Almost all expositors of note are agreed in referring it to ἐκκλησίαν, both as it is the *nearer* antecedent, and because there thus arises a better sense. As to what is urged, that "the *grammatical construction* is against it," the persons who make this assertion show that they know as little of *grammar* as of criticism. And when they urge that the sense yielded by ἐκκλ. is wholly untenable on the ground of historical fact — this proceeds wholly upon a misconception of the *force* of ἐκκλ., on which see Bp. Pearson on the Creed. Art. ix., where he explains the different modes of using the word. In connection with this promise, the force of πύλαι ᾅδου is to be attended to. Now certain plausible senses have been propounded: but, besides that they are far-fetched, the constant import of the phrase, both in the Greek Classical, the Old Testament, and the Rabbinical writers (where it constantly means the grave, or the entrance to it, the state of the dead), must determine it to mean simply *death* (i. e. the entrance into a new state of being). Thus the clause which we are considering contains a promise, *either* of perpetual stability to the Church Catholic, on which see Bp. Horsley, in D'Oyly and Mant, and Vitringa de Synag. p. 86., *or*, (taking ἐκκ., as the best Commentators direct, to denote the *members* of it *individually*,) that not even death shall prevail over the [faithful] members of it: but that they shall be raised to a happy resurrection. Let us now proceed to examine the true import of the words which contain the *second* privilege conferred on St. Peter; namely, δώσω — οὐρανῶν. These words appear to be a *continuation* of the image by which the Church was compared to an edifice founded on a rock. And they seem intended to *further explain* what was meant by founding the Church upon Peter, as a foundation; and they *figuratively* denote, that Peter should be the person by whose instrumentality the kingdom of heaven (the Gospel dispensation) should be first opened to both Jews and Gentiles; which was verified by the event. See Acts ii. 41. x. 44. compared with xv. 7. and Joh. xx. 23. seq. It is clear, that this cannot be supposed to give Peter any supremacy over the rest of the Apostles (because the keys were, in the same sense, afterwards given to *them* also), much less to the whole Church of Christ in after ages. As to the expression, "the keys," it may also refer to the *power* and *authority* for the said work; especially as a key was antiently an usual symbol of authority (see Is. xxii. 22.); and presenting with a key was a common form of investing with authority; insomuch that it was afterwards worn as a badge of office.

The words ὃ ἐὰν λύσῃς — οὐρανοῖς are explanatory of the former. Yet it should seem that the image taken from the *keys* is not continued here; but that they are a *fuller developement* of the ideas

MK. LU.
8. 9. καὶ ὃ ἐὰν δήσῃς ἐπὶ τῆς γῆς, ἔσται δεδεμένον ἐν τοῖς οὐρανοῖς· καὶ
30 21 ὃ ἐὰν λύσῃς ἐπὶ τῆς γῆς, ἔσται λελυμένον ἐν τοῖς οὐρανοῖς. Τότε 20
διεστείλατο τοῖς μαθηταῖς αὐτοῦ, ἵνα μηδενὶ εἴπωσιν, ὅτι αὐτός ἐστιν
[Ἰησοῦς] ὁ Χριστός.
31 22 Ἀπὸ τότε ἤρξατο ὁ Ἰησοῦς δεικνύειν τοῖς μαθηταῖς αὐτοῦ, ὅτι δεῖ 21
αὐτὸν ἀπελθεῖν εἰς Ἱεροσολύμα, καὶ πολλὰ παθεῖν ἀπὸ τῶν πρεσβυτέρων καὶ ἀρχιερέων καὶ γραμματέων, καὶ ἀποκτανθῆναι, καὶ τῇ τρίτῃ
32 ἡμέρᾳ ἐγερθῆναι. Καὶ προσλαβόμενος αὐτὸν ὁ Πέτρος, ἤρξατο ἐπιτι- 22
33 μᾷν αὐτῷ, λέγων· Ἵλεώς σοι, κύριε! οὐ μὴ ἔσται σοι τοῦτο. Ὁ δὲ 23
στραφεὶς εἶπε τῷ Πέτρῳ· Ὕπαγε ὀπίσω μου, Σατανᾶ! σκάνδαλόν
μου εἶ· ὅτι οὐ φρονεῖς τὰ τοῦ Θεοῦ, ἀλλὰ τὰ τῶν ἀνθρώπων. Τότε 24
34 23 ὁ Ἰησοῦς εἶπε τοῖς μαθηταῖς αὐτοῦ· Εἴ τις θέλει ὀπίσω μου ἐλθεῖν,

of *trust* and *power* of which keys form a symbol; and that the power here meant is of a more extended kind. Not a little diversity, however, of interpertation *here* exists (see Recens. Synop.); though there is little doubt but that the view taken by lightfoot, Selden, Hamm., Whitby, Kuin., and most recent Commentators, is the true one; who shew that δέειν signifies to *forbid*, not only in the Rabbinical writings, but in Dan. vi. 8. ix. 11, 16., as also in the Chaldee Pharaphrase on Numb. xi. 28.; and that λύειν Heb. הַתִּיר and שְׁרָה) denotes to *pronounce lawful*, *concede*, *permit*, *direct*, *constitute*, &c. The sense will, then be: "Whatsoever thou shalt forbid to be done, or whatsoever thou shalt *declare lawful*, and constitute in the Church, shall be ratified, and hold good with God; including all the measures necessary for the establishment and government of the Church. (See Vitringa de Synag. p. 754. seq.) That the above powers were exercised by Peter, in conjunction with the other Apostles, is indisputable. We need only advert to the decisions of the Council held at Jerusalem; when nearly the whole of the Mosaic ritual law was *loosed*, given up, and abrogated, while *part* of it was *bound* and still held obligatory. (See also Acts x. 28. & xxi. 24.) The words of our Lord at Joh. xx. 23. confer a similar privilege as to *persons* as that of the keys here imports as to *things*, viz. doctrines and institutions.

It is here observable that this sense of the words δέειν and λύειν is directly contrary to that which prevails among the Classical writers, in whom λύειν (νόμον) is synonymous with καταλύειν (νόμον), to *abrogate*, &c.; but nowhere, I believe, in the sense *concede*, *permit*, except in Diod. Sic. i. 27. (cited by Selden.) ὅσα ἐγὼ δήσω οὐδεὶς δύναται λύσαι. But even *that* is the *literal* Greek version of an *Oriental inscription*, and therefore is likely to follow the Eastern idiom. In fact, the phrase δέειν νόμον has never been produced from any Classical writer. I have, however, met with a passage which *approaches* to it in Soph. Antig. 40. εἰ τάδ'— ἐγὼ λύουσ' ἂν ἢ 'φάπτουσα προσθείμην πλέον. where the Schol. explains τάδε ἐφάπτουσα by βεβαιοῦσα τὸν νόμον.

Whatever may be thought of the dignity thus conferred, it will certainly by no means justify the assertion of any peculiar prerogative to the *Roman Pontiff*; nor affect the question at issue between Protestants and Romanists upon the *power of the Church*. Whatever foundation Peter might be to the Church, it is clear that the very image excludes all notion of a *succession* of persons similarly circumstanced. Nor, if the superiority of *Peter* had *been* permanent, could it afford a shadow of reason for deducing from it the supremacy of the first Bishop of Rome *in the persons of his successors*. At the same time, it must be observed that the authority of *binding* and *loosing*, first communicated to St. Peter and the other Apostles, was exercised by their immediate successors; and indeed has been continued, as far as altered circumstances would permit, by their *successors*, the Bishops of the Church to the present day.

20. The most eminent Critics are agreed, that Ἰησοῦς, found in the common text, is to be cancelled, on the authority of 54 MSS. and several Versions and Fathers.

21. On the connexion of the remaining portion of the Chapter, see Mackn., Porteus, and Townsend.

— πρεσβυτέρων] the members of the great Sanhedrim. See xxvi. 3. Acts iv. 8. xxv. 15. At Lu. xxii. 66. they are called πρεσβυτέριον.

22. προσλαβόμενος αὐτόν.] This controverted expression may mean "taking him aside," but is best interpreted, "taking him by the hand;" an action naturally accompanying advice, remonstrance, or censure. Schleus. adduces an example of this sense from Plutarch; to which I add another from Aristoph. Lysist. 1128. λαβοῦσα δ' ὑμᾶς, λοιδορῆσαι βούλομαι. Ἐπιτιμάω here only denotes affectionate chiding.

— Ἵλεώς σοι.] Sub. Θεὸς εἴη. Equivalent to our "God forbid," and common in the Sept., Philo, and Josephus. The words following, οὐ μὴ ἔσται σοι τοῦτο are exegetical of Ἵλεώς σοι, and Grot. regards them as equivalent to the Classical μὴ γένοιτο; while Fritz., more properly, makes *this* distinction between them,—that the former is a formula *malum omen avertentis*; the latter, *precantis et valde sperantis* rem aliter eventuram esse; i. e. Di meliora, domine; non credo hoc tibi accidet. There is an ellipsis of ὁ Θεὸς εἴη, *supplied* in 1 Chron. xi. 19. Sept. Ἵλεώς μοι ὁ Θεὸς, τοῦ ποιῆσαι τὸ ῥῆμα τοῦτο.

23. Σατανᾶ.] The word here signifies either an adversary, or an evil counsellor. Σκάνδαλον, &c. is exegetical of the preceding, and signifies, "thou art an obstacle to the great work of atonement by my death;" namely, by fostering that natural horror of his painful and ignominious death, which occasionally harassed our Saviour.

— οὐ φρονεῖς.] Φρονεῖν τί τινος signifies "to

MK. LU.

ἀπαρνησάσθω ἑαυτὸν, καὶ ἀράτω τὸν σταυρὸν αὐτοῦ, καὶ ἀκολουθείτω 8. 9.
25 μοι. Ὃς γὰρ ἂν θέλῃ τὴν ψυχὴν αὐτοῦ σῶσαι, ἀπολέσει αὐτήν· ὃς 35 24
26 δ' ἂν ἀπολέσῃ τὴν ψυχὴν αὐτοῦ ἕνεκεν ἐμοῦ, εὑρήσει αὐτήν. (Τί γὰρ 36 25
ὠφελεῖται ἄνθρωπος, ἐὰν τὸν κόσμον ὅλον κερδήσῃ, τὴν δὲ ψυχὴν
αὐτοῦ ζημιωθῇ; ἢ τί δώσει ἄνθρωπος ἀντάλλαγμα τῆς ψυχῆς αὐτοῦ;)
27 Μέλλει γὰρ ὁ Υἱὸς τοῦ ἀνθρώπου ἔρχεσθαι ἐν τῇ δόξῃ τοῦ Πατρὸς
αὐτοῦ μετὰ τῶν ἀγγέλων αὐτοῦ· καὶ τότε ἀποδώσει ἑκάστῳ κατὰ 9.
28 τὴν πρᾶξιν αὐτοῦ. Ἀμὴν λέγω ὑμῖν, εἰσί τινες τῶν ὧδε ‡ ἑστηκότων, 1 27
οἵτινες οὐ μὴ γεύσωνται θανάτου, ἕως ἂν ἴδωσι τὸν Υἱὸν τοῦ ἀνθρώπου ἐρχόμενον ἐν τῇ βασιλείᾳ αὐτοῦ.
1 XVII. ΚΑΙ μεθ' ἡμέρας ἓξ παραλαμβάνει ὁ Ἰησοῦς τὸν Πέτρον καὶ 2 28

be well affected to any one, to take his side." Here it denotes *caring for, being devoted to*, as 1 Macc. x. 20.

24. ἀπαρνησάσθω ἑαυτὸν] "let him neglect his preservation, not value his life." Comp. Luke xiv. 26., and see note on Matt. x. 38. sq.

26. τί γὰρ ὠφελεῖται—ψυχῆς αὐτοῦ;] This seems to be, like the following τί δώσει, &c., a *proverbial* expression; but transferred by Jesus from temporal to spiritual application; there being an allusion to the two meanings of ψυχὴ,—*life* and *soul*. If we think an earthly and temporary life cheaply bought, at whatever price, how much *more* a heavenly and eternal one." At ζημιωθῇ τὴν ψυχὴν sub. εἰς, which is sometimes *expressed* in the Classical writers, though they *generally* use the *Dative*. Τί δώσει, &c. Another proverbial expression, with which Wets. compares several others. I add a saying of Socrates, preserved by Libanius, in which he says, τιμιώτατον τῷ ἀνθρώπῳ ψυχὴν εἶναι· δεύτερον δὲ τὸ σῶμα, τρίτον τὰ χρήματα. [*Comp*. John xii. 25.]

27. μέλλει γὰρ &c.] The Commentators are not agreed as to the *reference* in this and the next verse. The antient and the earlier modern ones in general refer the former of them to the *final* advent of Christ at the day of judgment; the latter, to the second advent of Christ at the destruction of Jerusalem, about 40 years afterwards. Most recent Expositors, however, since the time of Whitby, refer the *former* verse also to the second advent of Christ. And indeed they make out, as far as regards the connection with the preceding verses, a tolerably good case. Not so, as regards the words and phrase of the verse itself; which, though they be not wholly unsuitable to the *first* advent, yet are far more naturally to be understood (according to their use elsewhere) of the *final* advent. And as to the *connection*, the γὰρ may be referred, not to the verses immediately preceding, but to the injunction at v. 24.; vv. 25. & 26. being parenthetical. Nor is the course of argument injured; which may be preserved by supplying mentally a few words of connection between v. 27 & 28., q. d. [Of his power and determination to judge and punish the impenitent, he will ere long give a specimen on the unbelieving and persecuting Jews]; for "verily I say," &c. And as this second coming ἐν βασιλ. (i. e., as Fritz. rightly explains, in medio regni splendore) is elsewhere described in terms bearing a strong resemblance to those which designate Christ's *final* advent, there was the greater propriety in introducing them as a just ground to expect and prepare for it. And although it has been urged that it would be harsh to understand the τινες of *one* person; and St John alone of the bystanders is known to have lived to see the destruction of Jerusalem, yet that argument is very inconclusive; for it is highly probable that others of the by-standers, as well as St. John, might live forty years. And certainly the air of the words suggests a *distant* event, not one close at hand; as would be the case, if we take this, with Mackn. and others, of the *Transfiguration*, or of Christ's assuming his mediatorial kingdom after his ascension. As to the first of those two interpretations, it has not a shadow of probability; since the words of this verse bear no affinity to those used in describing that awful transaction. As to the *second*, it is not permitted by the connection; since there is no allusion to Christ's coming to judgment. Perhaps, however, as the two events in question formed part of one transaction, the two interpretations may be united. And then the sense will be, that some then present should live to see Christ enter upon and finally establish his mediatorial reign; at the completion of which he will come in the glory of his Father to reward every man according to his works.

28. ἑστηκότων] Many MSS. and some Fathers have ἑστώτων, which is edited by Matth., Griesb., Knapp., Vater, and Scholz. Others have ἑστῶτες, which is adopted by Wets., and edited by Fritz., as being the more *difficult* reading. But it seems to have come from the margin, and to have been a conjecture of those who proposed to read εἰσί τινες ὧδε ἑστῶτες. As to the first mentioned reading, it *may* be the true one; but the evidence is not so strong as to demand any change in the text; and the common reading is defended by Mark ix. 1. and Luke ix. 27.

—γεύεσθαι θανάτου is a Hebraism (like θεωρεῖν θαν., Joh. viii. 51., ἰδεῖν θαν., Luke ii. 26.) by which verbs of sense are used in the metaphorical signification to *experience*, not unfrequent in the *Classical* writers; where it is joined not, indeed, with θανάτου, but with nouns denoting *trouble*.

XVII. 1. We are now arrived at the narration of a most awful and mysterious transaction—such as draws back for a moment the veil from the invisible world: on the circumstances, *manner*, and *probable purposes*, of which a brief notice must here suffice. For further particulars, the reader is referred to Bp. Hall's Contemplations, Whitby, Mackn., Porteus, and Townsend; and, above all, to the masterly Dissertation of Witsius,

MK. LU.
9. 9. Ἰάκωβον καὶ Ἰωάννην τὸν ἀδελφὸν αὐτοῦ, καὶ ἀναφέρει αὐτοὺς εἰς
29 ὄρος ὑψηλὸν κατ᾽ ἰδίαν. Καὶ μετεμορφώθη ἔμπροσθεν αὐτῶν, καὶ 2
ἔλαμψε τὸ πρόσωπον αὐτοῦ ὡς ὁ ἥλιος, τὰ δὲ ἱμάτια αὐτοῦ ἐγένετο
3 4 30 λευκὰ ὡς τὸ φῶς. Καὶ ἰδοὺ, ὤφθησαν αὐτοῖς Μωσῆς καὶ Ἠλίας, 3
μετ᾽ αὐτοῦ συλλαλοῦντες. Ἀποκριθεὶς δὲ ὁ Πέτρος εἶπε τῷ Ἰησοῦ· 4
5 33 Κύριε, καλόν ἐστιν ἡμᾶς ὧδε εἶναι. εἰ θέλεις, ποιήσωμεν ὧδε τρεῖς
34 σκηνάς· σοὶ μίαν, καὶ Μωσῇ μίαν, καὶ μίαν Ἠλίᾳ. Ἔτι αὐτοῦ λα- 5
7 35 λοῦντος, ἰδοὺ, νεφέλη φωτεινὴ ἐπεσκίασεν αὐτούς· καὶ ἰδοὺ, φωνὴ ἐκ

in the Meletemata Leidensia, or the abstract of it in Townsend. The transaction itself may be considered as a *figurative representation* of Christ's final advent in glory to judgment. To advert to some of the *particulars*,—why *three* disciples and no *more* were admitted, seems to have been, because that number was the number of witnesses necessary to establish legal proof of any transaction. The three particular disciples taken were selected as being the most attached and confidential of the disciples. That the presence of Moses and Elias was a bodily, and not, as some say, a *visionary* appearance, there is no reason to doubt; especially as it involves no difficulty, but such as Omnipotence will vanquish at the general Resurrection, though the *nature* of the change in question is incomprehensible to us, with our present faculties. As to supposing, with some sceptical foreign Theologians, the *whole* to have been a vision, that is still *less* defensible; for though the disciples had been asleep (or rather *heavy for* sleep,) the transaction, it seems, taking place in the night (see Luke ix. 32.), they are distinctly said to have been *awake* when they *saw* and *heard* Moses and Elias conversing with Jesus. With respect to the *purposes* of this transaction, it seems to have been intended, 1. to loosen the prejudices of the Apostles as to the performance of the Mosaic Law, by a figurative and symbolical representation of the expiration of the Jewish, and the commencement of the Christian dispensation: 2. to reconcile their minds to the sufferings and death of Christ: 3. to strengthen their faith; affording an *additional* proof, as it were, by a *sign* from heaven, of the Divine mission of *Jesus*. For it is probable that as the Jews supposed the Messiah would, at his coming, be seen literally descending from the heavens, and arrayed in glory; so our Lord was pleased to give his *Apostles* this decisive proof of his Messiahship, by showing himself in his glory, such as that with which he would appear at the final Advent. The representation was, no doubt, *also* intended to comfort and support the Apostles under their present and future trials and tribulations, by a prospect of the *glory* which should be revealed in their Saviour, and, through him, in themselves.

—ὄρος.] This mountain is, from antient tradition, supposed to have been *Tabor*. Lightf., however, questions the truth of the tradition: but, as far as respects the distance of the mountain from Cæsarea Philippi, on insufficient grounds; for it is only about 45 miles from that place, a distance easily accomplished in *six days*. But neither, on the other hand, will the words of v. 22. and Mark ix. 30., as is alleged, *prove* what those who maintain that the mountain was Tabor, aver; namely, that a journey was taken through Galilee just before the Transfiguration. As to the former passage, see the note there; and as to the latter, it only proves that a journey to *Capernaum*, was taken *after* the Transfiguration: and therefore it is highly improbable that there should have been so long a journey taken just *before* it. And although the expressions used by St. Matthew and Mark do not specify any *particular mountain*, yet the context evidently points at some mountain in the neighbourhood of Cæsarea. And this probability is converted into certainty by the words of St. Luke, ἀνέβη εἰς τὸ ὄρος (as it is found in all the MSS., confirmed by the Pesch. Syr. Version), where the Article limits the sense to *some* mountain, which might be called *the* mountain in respect to Cæsarea; and that cannot well be any other than some part of the ridge of *Hermon*; most probably that part of it which runs out into the plain of the Jordan, within six miles of Cæsarea, called the *Mons Paneum*. The tradition above mentioned seems to have arisen from a confounding of the *two* Mounts Hermon; one very near Tabor, the other near Cæsarea. It should seem that after it had been preserved by antient tradition, that Mount Hermon was the scene of the Transfiguration, those who lived in later ages supposed the Hermon to be that near Tabor, as was natural; since the two were often associated. So Ps. lxxxix. 12. "Tabor and Hermon shall rejoice in Him;" and others afterwards fixed on *Tabor itself*, on account of its very close contiguity, and its being most κατ᾽ ἰδίαν, in their mistaken view of the expression, referring it to the *mountain*; for Mr. Maundrell, in his Travels, remarks that it stands "apart:" and all travellers describe it as being of a conical form, detached from the neighbouring mountain, and terminating in a point.

2. μετεμορφώθη] "was transfigured." The word (which sometimes imports a change of substance) here denotes only a change in external appearance (as in Ælian V. H. i. 1.), agreeably to the sense of its primitive μορφὴ in the Old and New Testament. Thus, in the plainer words of Luke ix. 29. τὸ εἶδος τοῦ προσώπου αὐτοῦ ἕτερον ἐγένετο.

4. σκηνὰς] Namely booths composed of branches of trees, such as were hastily raised for temporary purposes by travellers, and such as were reared at the feast of tabernacles. (Campb.)

5. φωτεινὴ] Griesb. and Fritz. edit φωτὸς on account of its being the more difficult reading. But that Critical canon has its exceptions; and *one* is, when the reading involves a violation of the norma loquendi. Now νεφ. φωτὸς, as Knittel and Fritz. remark, "repugnantiam quandam continent, (Comp. Mark ix. 7.) nec facile dici potest," whereas φωτεινὴ is supported by vi. 22. See xi. 34 & 36. *Another* is, when the external evidence for reading is exceedingly slight; which is the case here; for it is found only in five or six inferior MSS. The cloud here mentioned,

MK. LU.

τῆς νεφέλης, λέγουσα· Οὗτός ἐστιν ὁ Υἱός μου ὁ ἀγαπητὸς, ἐν ᾧ 9. 9.
6 εὐδόκησα· αὐτοῦ ἀκούετε. Καὶ ἀκούσαντες οἱ μαθηταὶ, ἔπεσον ἐπὶ
7 πρόσωπον αὐτῶν, καὶ ἐφοβήθησαν σφόδρα. Καὶ προσελθὼν ὁ Ἰησοῦς
8 ἥψατο αὐτῶν, καὶ εἶπεν· Ἐγέρθητε, καὶ μὴ φοβεῖσθε. Ἐπάραντες 8 36
δὲ τοὺς ὀφθαλμοὺς αὐτῶν, οὐδένα εἶδον, εἰ μὴ τὸν Ἰησοῦν μόνον.

9 Καὶ καταβαινόντων αὐτῶν ‡ ἀπὸ τοῦ ὄρους, ἐνετείλατο αὐτοῖς ὁ Ἰη- 9
σοῦς, λέγων· Μηδενὶ εἴπητε τὸ ὅραμα, ἕως οὗ ὁ Υἱὸς τοῦ ἀνθρώπου 11
10 ἐκ νεκρῶν ἀναστῇ. Καὶ ἐπηρώτησαν αὐτὸν οἱ μαθηταὶ αὐτοῦ, λέγον-
τες· Τί οὖν οἱ Γραμματεῖς λέγουσιν, ὅτι Ἠλίαν δεῖ ἐλθεῖν πρῶτον;
11 ὁ δὲ Ἰησοῦς ἀποκριθεὶς εἶπεν αὐτοῖς· Ἠλίας μὲν ἔρχεται πρῶτον, 12
12 καὶ ἀποκαταστήσει πάντα· λέγω δὲ ὑμῖν, ὅτι Ἠλίας ἤδη ἦλθε· καὶ 13
οὐκ ἐπέγνωσαν αὐτόν· ἀλλ᾽ ἐποίησαν ἐν αὐτῷ ὅσα ἠθέλησαν· οὕτω
13 καὶ ὁ Υἱὸς τοῦ ἀνθρώπου μέλλει πάσχειν ὑπ᾽ αὐτῶν. Τότε συνῆκαν
οἱ μαθηταὶ, ὅτι περὶ Ἰωάννου τοῦ Βαπτιστοῦ εἶπεν αὐτοῖς.

14 Καὶ ἐλθόντων αὐτῶν πρὸς τὸν ὄχλον, προσῆλθεν αὐτῷ ἄνθρωπος 14 37
15 γονυπετῶν αὐτὸν, καὶ λέγων· Κύριε, ἐλέησόν μου τὸν υἱὸν, ὅτι σελη- 17 38
νιάζεται, καὶ κακῶς πάσχει· πολλάκις γὰρ πίπτει εἰς τὸ πῦρ, καὶ 18
16 πολλάκις εἰς τὸ ὕδωρ. Καὶ προσήνεγκα αὐτὸν τοῖς μαθηταῖς σου, 40

called at 2 Pet. i. 17. the "excellent glory," is supposed to have been the Shechinah, in which the Divine Majesty often appeared to the Jews.

—ἐπεσκίασεν.] Not, *overshadowed*, but *surrounded*. An Hellenistic use found in the Sept. The αὐτοὺς may be understood of *all present*.

—φωνὴ, &c.] This is one of the *three* instances in the Gospels, of God's personally interposing and bearing testimony in favour of his Son. Αὐτοῦ is to be taken *emphatically*, "him alone," and no longer Moses and the Prophets. Comp. supra iii. 17. 2 Pet. i. 17. Mark i. 11. John i. 34. Is. xlii. 1.

6. ἔπεσον ἐπὶ πρόσωπον.] A posture generally and naturally assumed by those to whom visions were made; and to be accounted for not merely on a principle of *fear*, (it being the general persuasion that the sight of a supernatural being must destroy life) but of *reverence*. [*Comp*. Dan. viii. 18, ix. 21. x. 10 & 18.]

9. ἀπὸ τοῦ ὄρους] i. e. that mentioned, supra xvi. 20. For ἀπὸ Matth., Griesb., Fritz., and Scholz edit ἐκ, from very many MSS., early Editions, and Fathers. But there is no sufficient reason for alteration; especially as καταβ. ἀπὸ ὄρους is often used in the N. T.; καταβ. ἐκ τοῦ ὄρους *never*.

—τὸ ὅραμα] "what they had seen," ἃ εἶδον, as Mark phrases it. This term quite excludes the notion that it was a mere vision.

10. τί οὖν οἱ Γραμματεῖς—πρῶτον] Conf. supra xi. 14. there is here a difficulty, arising from the obscurity of the connection, and the brevity of the enunciation. The sense is most probably as follows: "How can the declaration of the scribes (grounded on the prophecy of Malachi iv. 5.) hold good,—that Elias must precede the Messiah, to announce his coming, and restore all things, &c., when we see the Messiah already come, and no Elias performing any of the offices in question?"

11. Ἠλίας μὲν—πάντα.] The sense (which has been causelessly disputed) is plainly as follows: "Elias is indeed first to come, and will restore all things;" i. e. be the means of introducing a mighty moral change and reformation. There is thought to be an allusion to the words of Malachi iv. 5, 6. Sept., what is there said *specially*, being here applied *generally*. The *future* tense is used, because Jesus here merely uses the language which was generally applied to the Messiah; q. d. "So then, it seems Elias," &c. Ἀποκαταστήσει is said by some to be taken of *design* rather than effect. But what John was to do, which was only to act an introductory part, *was* accomplished, and ἀποκατ. must be explained with a reference thereto. If this be not admitted, the way in which the words were said will sufficiently justify the use of the term.

12. οὐκ ἐπέγνωσαν αὐτὸν] "knew him not;" "did not recognise him as such;" there being much disagreement as to his real character.

—ἐν αὐτῷ.] This is thought to be a Hebraism; but it is rather a *popular* idiom, similar to one in our own language. Ποιεῖν is adapted to denote *treatment* of every kind, whether good or bad. Ὅσα ἠθέλησαν is a *popular* idiom, which usually implies violence. See Luke xxiii. 25. and Mark ix. 13.

14. αὐτόν.] So all the Editors from Wets. downwards read, for αὐτῷ, on the strongest evidence both of MSS. and Fathers, and the usage of Scripture, as Mark i. 40. x. 17.

—γονυπετῶν.] The force of the term is well illustrated in Horne's Introd. iii. 328.

15. σεληνιάζεται] literally, "he is moonstruck." From the symptoms mentioned here and at Mark ix. 18. this disorder is supposed to have been *epilepsy*; under whose paroxysms those afflicted with it are deprived of all sense, bodily and mental, and nearly all articulation. And as we find, in the ancient medical writers, epileptic patients said to be *moonstruck*, agreeably to the common notion, of the influence of the moon in producing the disorder, it is very possible that the disorder in question was epilepsy. Be that, how-

MK. LU.
9. 9. καὶ οὐκ ἠδυνήθησαν αὐτὸν θεραπεῦσαι. Ἀποκριθεὶς δὲ ὁ Ἰησοῦς 17
19 41 εἶπεν· Ὦ γενεὰ ἄπιστος καὶ διεστραμμένη! ἕως πότε ἔσομαι μεθ᾽
27 42 ὑμῶν; ἕως πότε ἀνέξομαι ὑμῶν; φέρετέ μοι αὐτὸν ὧδε. Καὶ ἐπετί- 18
μησεν αὐτῷ ὁ Ἰησοῦς, καὶ ἐξῆλθεν ἀπ᾽ αὐτοῦ τὸ δαιμόνιον· καὶ
28 ἐθεραπεύθη ὁ παῖς ἀπὸ τῆς ὥρας ἐκείνης. Τότε προσελθόντες οἱ 19
μαθηταὶ τῷ Ἰησοῦ κατ᾽ ἰδίαν, εἶπον· Διατί ἡμεῖς οὐκ ἠδυνήθημεν
ἐκβαλεῖν αὐτό; Ὁ δὲ Ἰησοῦς εἶπεν αὐτοῖς· Διὰ τὴν ἀπιστίαν ὑμῶν. 20
ἀμὴν γὰρ λέγω ὑμῖν· ἐὰν ἔχητε πίστιν ὡς κόκκον σινάπεως, ἐρεῖτε
τῷ ὄρει τούτῳ· Μετάβηθι ἐντεῦθεν ἐκεῖ, καὶ μεταβήσεται· καὶ οὐ-
29 δὲν ἀδυνατήσει ὑμῖν. Τοῦτο δὲ τὸ γένος οὐκ ἐκπορεύεται, εἰ μὴ ἐν 21
προσευχῇ καὶ νηστείᾳ.

Ἀναστρεφομένων δὲ αὐτῶν ἐν τῇ Γαλιλαίᾳ, εἶπεν αὐτοῖς ὁ Ἰησοῦς· 22
31 44 Μέλλει ὁ Υἱὸς τοῦ ἀνθρώπου παραδίδοσθαι εἰς χεῖρας ἀνθρώπων·
45 καὶ ἀποκτενοῦσιν αὐτόν, καὶ τῇ τρίτῃ ἡμέρᾳ ἐγερθήσεται. καὶ ἐλυπή- 23
θησαν σφόδρα.

Ἐλθόντων δὲ αὐτῶν εἰς Καπερναούμ, προσῆλθον οἱ τὰ δίδραχμα 24
λαμβάνοντες τῷ Πέτρῳ, καὶ εἶπον· Ὁ διδάσκαλος ὑμῶν οὐ τελεῖ τὰ
δίδραχμα; λέγει· Ναί. Καὶ ὅτε εἰσῆλθεν εἰς τὴν οἰκίαν, προέφθα- 25

ever, as it may, the symptoms are all reconcile-able with dæmoniacal influence.

17. *ὦ γενεὰ ἄπιστος.*] *Who* are the persons here meant, has been much debated. Some understand the *father* and the *relations*. Others, the *Jews*, i. e. the *Scribes* who might be present on the occasion. Others, again, the *disciples*; which seems from the context to be the most probable. But it is better (with Doddr., Kypke, Kuin., &c.) to suppose the reproof meant for *all* present, each as they deserved it. Γενεὰ ἄπιστος may be referred to the *disciples*, and perhaps the *father*; διεστρ. to the *Scribes*; the first ὑμῶν to the *disciples* and the second to the *scribes*.

— διεστραμμένος signifies, literally, *crooked*, *perverse*, and, metaphorically, *bad*; whether in body, or in mind or morals. There is a similar metaphor in our word *wrong*, from the part. past *wrung*, from *wringen*, to twist. In both terms there is a tacit reference to what is *straight*.

— ἕως πότε — ὑμῶν] render, "How long must I be with you," i. e. "how long must my presence be necessary to you?"

18. *καὶ ἐπετίμησεν — δαιμόνιον.*] Some refer the αὐτῷ to the sick person; others, far more correctly, to the *dæmon*. In fact, the passage is to be taken as if written καὶ ἐπετίμησε τῷ δαίμονι, καὶ ἐξῆλθε.

20. *ὡς κόκκον σινάπεως*] i. e. even in the smallest degree; for this was, as we find from the Rabbinical citations in Wets., a proverbial expression to denote any thing exceedingly small, (the σίναπι being the smallest of all seeds) just as to *remove mountains* was an adagial hyperbole to denote the accomplishment of any thing apparently impossible. [*Comp.* Mark xi. 23. Luke xvii. 6.]

21. *τοῦτο τὸ γένος.*] Here almost all Commentators supply δαιμονίων. But that would suppose *different kinds* of dæmons, which, though a possible fact, yet must not be admitted into revelation *per ellipsin*. The truth is, that (as Chrys., Euthym., and some modern Commentators have seen,) the sense is: "this kind *of beings*," namely, dæmons. Similar expressions might be adduced both from the Greek, Latin, and modern languages.

— *ἐν προσευχῇ καὶ νηστείᾳ.*] viz., says Campb., as necessary to the attainment of that faith, without which the dæmons could not be expelled; and, therefore, prayer and fasting might be said to be the *cause*, as being *the cause of the cause*.

22. *παραδίδοσθαι.*] Not betrayed, but delivered up.

— *ἀναστρεφομένων ἐν τῇ Γ.*] This should not be rendered, "while they abode in Galilee;" nor, "while they returned to Galilee;" nor, as some interpret, "while they passed through." For though it may seem to be required by Mark ix. 30. παρεπορεύοντο διὰ τῆς Γαλιλαίας, yet there is no authority for such a sense; nor do the words of St. Mark require it; for ἐπορ. there means, "they passed along through" (as in ii. 23.) i. e. travelled through. And that is the very sense of ἀναστρέφω, here of which signification Wets. will supply examples. Render, "as they were travelling in in Galilee," i. e., as we find from v. 24, on their way to Capernaum; and, as we learn from supra xvi. 21, on their journey to Jerusalem.

24. *τὰ δίδραχμα*] "the didrachmas." A collective name for the *tax* so called. The plural is used with reference to the many persons from whom it was collected, each paying one. Thus there is no need to read (as Pisc. proposes) τὸ δ. And the Art. has reference to the *customary* payment. The noun is declined τὸ δίδραχμον, τοῦ διδράχμου; consequently, δίδραχμα is the accus. plural, which I should scarcely have thought worth mentioning, had not some Commentators of eminence, through ignorance of this minute grammatical point, fallen into error. The tax was doubtless the half shekel, the sacred tribute.

25. *ὅτε εἰσῆλθεν εἰς τὴν οἰκίαν*] *Who* is here meant, is not clear. Almost all the Commentators suppose, *Jesus*. We may, however, understand it, with Euthym., L. Brug., and Kuin., (supported by the Syr.) of *Peter*. The sense

MK. LU.

σεν αὐτὸν ὁ Ἰησοῦς, λέγων· Τί σοι δοκεῖ, Σίμων; οἱ βασιλεῖς τῆς 9. 9.
γῆς ἀπὸ τίνων λαμβάνουσι τέλη ἢ κῆνσον; ἀπὸ τῶν υἱῶν αὐτῶν, ἢ
26 ἀπὸ τῶν ἀλλοτρίων; Λέγει αὐτῷ ὁ Πέτρος· Ἀπὸ τῶν ἀλλοτρίων.
27 Ἔφη αὐτῷ ὁ Ἰησοῦς· Ἄραγε ἐλεύθεροί εἰσιν οἱ υἱοί. Ἵνα δὲ μὴ σκανδαλίσωμεν αὐτούς, πορευθεὶς, εἰς τὴν θάλασσαν βάλε ἄγκιστρον, καὶ
τὸν ἀναβάντα πρῶτον ἰχθὺν ἆρον· καὶ ἀνοίξας τὸ στόμα αὐτοῦ, εὑ-
ρήσεις στατῆρα· ἐκεῖνον λαβὼν δὸς αὐτοῖς ἀντὶ ἐμοῦ καὶ σοῦ.
1 XVIII. Ἐν ἐκείνῃ τῇ ὥρᾳ προσῆλθον οἱ μαθηταὶ τῷ Ἰησοῦ, λέ- 46
2 γοντες· Τίς ἄρα μείζων ἐστὶν ἐν τῇ βασιλείᾳ τῶν οὐρανῶν; Καὶ 36 47
προσκαλεσάμενος ὁ Ἰησοῦς παιδίον, ἔστησεν αὐτὸ ἐν μέσῳ αὐτῶν·
3 καὶ εἶπεν· Ἀμὴν λέγω ὑμῖν· ἐὰν μὴ στραφῆτε καὶ γένησθε ὡς τὰ
4 παιδία, οὐ μὴ εἰσέλθητε εἰς τὴν βασιλείαν τῶν οὐρανῶν. Ὅστις οὖν
‡ ταπεινώσῃ ἑαυτὸν ὡς τὸ παιδίον τοῦτο, οὗτός ἐστιν ὁ μείζων ἐν τῇ
5 βασιλείᾳ τῶν οὐρανῶν. Καὶ ὃς ἐὰν δέξηται παιδίον τοιοῦτον ἓν ἐπὶ 37 48
6 τῷ ὀνόματί μου, ἐμὲ δέχεται· Ὃς δ᾽ ἂν σκανδαλίσῃ ἕνα τῶν μικρῶν
τούτων τῶν πιστευόντων εἰς ἐμέ, συμφέρει αὐτῷ, ἵνα κρεμασθῇ μύλος

may be thus expressed: "When Peter had entered into the house, [whither Jesus had already gone, while the tax-gatherers were applying to Peter for the contribution,] and was just about to ask him wether he would not pay the contribution, Jesus was beforehand with his question, by asking *him* one, namely, Τί σοι, &c. Υἱῶν, i. e. those of their own family, as opposed to ἀλλοτ., those not of their own family.

26. ἄρα γε ἐλεύθεροί ε. οἱ υἱοί.] Though there has been some question raised as to what is meant by these words, yet, after all, the simplest and truest interpretation is that of Chrysost. and Euthym. (approved by Fritz.), namely, "that this tribute, paid to God for his temple, I ought not to pay, inasmuch as I am his *Son.*" There is an argument *à fortiori*. "If such be the case with an earthly king's son, how much more," &c.

27. ἵνα μὴ σκανδαλίσωμεν αὐτοὺς] i. e. that we may not make them suppose, that we undervalue the temple; which might cause them to stumble at, and reject my pretensions.

— τὸν ἀναβάντα ἰχθὺν] "that which rises to, or meets the hook." As to the piece of money here mentioned, we need not, with Schmidt, suppose it created on purpose; but that it had fallen into the sea, and been swallowed by the fish. Many instances are on record of jewels, coins, &c. being found in the bellies of fishes.

XVIII. 1. ἐν ἐκείνῃ τῇ ὥρᾳ] "at that time" (ὥρα for καιρὸς, as xi. 25.) and probably on the same day with the events just recorded, namely the transfiguration, and the payment of the didrachma by our Lord for himself and Peter. On the discrepancy respecting the mode in which this transaction took place, see Michaelis, as cited by Mr. Townsend, Vol. i. p. 307. Τίς ἄρα μείζων &c. This inquiry, no doubt, arose from a dispute, which had arisen of late from the preference just shown by Jesus to Peter, John, and James; and which had excited some envy in the rest of the disciples, and prehaps some pride in the bosoms of those preferred.

— μείζων] for μέγιστος, say the Commentators. But the disciples seem to have desired to know, not who should be *the greatest*, but who should be *great*, and fill the *more considerable* posts in the Court of the Messiah. The notion (common to all the Jews) that the Messiah would erect a temporal kingdom, they yet clung to; and never laid aside till fully enlightened at the descent of the Holy Spirit.

2. ἔστησεν αὐτὸ — αὐτῶν] Thus employing a method of instruction always prevalent in the East; namely, that by emblems and symbolical actions. See Joh. xiii. 4. & 14. xx. 22. xxi. 19.

3. ὡς τὰ παιδία] Namely, in respect to unambitiousness, humility, docility, and absence of a worldly-minded spirit, dispositions the very reverse to those which they were then indulging. Comp. infra xix. 14. 1 Cor. xiv. 26. Our Lord proceeds to show that he who evinces the dispositions thus enjoined shall be distinguished in the spiritual kingdom which he comes to establish.

4. ταπεινώσῃ] Lachm. and Scholz edit, from many ancient MSS., ταπεινώσει. But there is not sufficient evidence to justify any change. If the propriety of the Greek be objected to, we might answer, with Matthæi, in N. T., non Græcitas sed Codices valent. However, the propriety has been learnedly supported by Fritz.

5. καὶ ὃς ἐὰν δέξηται &c.] The preceding verse is evidently directed to the *Apostles*; while this and the following seem not suitable to them; but were probably addressed to some *bystanders*, for to the people at large it would be very suitable.

6. μικρῶν] i. e. disciples generally without reference to age or quality. The words τῶν πιστευόντων are exegetical of the preceding.

— συμφέρει αὐτῷ.] Some supply μᾶλλον, i. e. rather than he should commit such a crime. But that is not necessary, it being *implied*.

— μύλος ὀνικὸς.] Same Commentators understand by this the *upper of the two mill-stones*, called in Heb. רכב, as *riding* on the other: others, *a mill-stone turned by an ass*, and consequently larger than that turned by the hand. Be that as it may, the expression συμφέρει — καταποντισθῇ seems to be proverbial. The punishment in question, though not in use among the Jews themselves, was so

MK. LU.
9. 15. ὀνικὸς ‡ ἐπὶ τὸν τράχηλον αὐτοῦ, καὶ καταποντισθῇ ἐν τῷ πελάγει τῆς
θαλάσσης. Οὐαὶ τῷ κόσμῳ ἀπὸ τῶν σκανδάλων! ἀνάγκη γάρ ἐστιν 7
ἐλθεῖν τὰ σκάνδαλα· πλὴν οὐαὶ τῷ ἀνθρώπῳ ἐκείνῳ, δι᾽ οὗ τὸ σκάν-
43 δαλον ἔρχεται! Εἰ δὲ ἡ χείρ σου ἢ ὁ πούς σου σκανδαλίζει σε, 8
ἔκκοψον αὐτὰ καὶ βάλε ἀπὸ σοῦ· καλόν σοι ἐστὶν εἰσελθεῖν εἰς τὴν
ζωὴν χωλὸν ἢ κυλλὸν, ἢ δύο χεῖρας ἢ δύο πόδας ἔχοντα, βληθῆναι
47 εἰς τὸ πῦρ τὸ αἰώνιον. Καὶ εἰ ὁ ὀφθαλμός σου σκανδαλίζει σε, ἔξελε 9
αὐτὸν, καὶ βάλε ἀπὸ σοῦ· καλόν σοι ἐστὶ μονόφθαλμον εἰς τὴν ζωὴν
εἰσελθεῖν, ἢ δύο ὀφθαλμοὺς ἔχοντα, βληθῆναι εἰς τὴν γέενναν τοῦ πυρός. Ὁρᾶτε μὴ καταφρονήσητε ἑνὸς τῶν μικρῶν τούτων· λέγω γὰρ 10
ὑμῖν, ὅτι οἱ ἄγγελοι αὐτῶν ἐν οὐρανοῖς διὰ παντὸς βλέπουσι τὸ πρόσωπον τοῦ Πατρός μου τοῦ ἐν οὐρανοῖς. Ἦλθε γὰρ ὁ Υἱὸς τοῦ ἀν- 11
4 θρώπου σῶσαι τὸ ἀπολωλός. Τί ὑμῖν δοκεῖ; ἐὰν γένηταί τινι ἀν- 12
θρώπῳ ἑκατὸν πρόβατα, καὶ πλανηθῇ ἓν ἐξ αὐτῶν· οὐχὶ ἀφεὶς τὰ

among the surrounding nations: where it was inflicted on criminals of the worst sort.

— πελάγει τῆς θαλάσσης] A somewhat rare phrase, which preserves the primitive sense of πέλαγος, namely *a depth*. For ἐπὶ before τὸν τράχ. very many MSS. have εἰς, which is edited by Wets., Matth., Griesb., Vater, Fritz., and Scholz: perhaps upon just grounds. With this and ver. 7. comp. Luke xvii. 1 & 2.

7. σκανδάλων] Namely, those just adverted to, arising from the calamities and persecutions that awaited the professors of Christianity; and which are supposed to have been present to the mind of our Lord and his Apostles.

— ἀνάγκη γὰρ &c.] The necessity here mentioned is *conditional*; and we may paraphrase this, and the parallel passage of Luke, as follows: "it cannot but happen that offences, (σκάνδαλα) circumstances which obstruct the reception, or occasion the abandonment of the faith, should occur; whether occasioned by persecution, denial of the common offices of humanity, contempt, &c. The argument is, that though, from the corruption of human nature, and the abuse of men's free agency, offences must needs arise, yet so terrible are the consequences of those offences, that it is better to endure the greatest deprivations, or corporeal pain, than occasion them. On this subject see Bp. Taylor's Works, Vol. iii. 221. sq.

8. Compare ch. v. 30. sq. and Notes. With respect to the *connection*, Kuin. denies that there is any. But it should seem that, together with cautions against the σκάνδαλα which draw *others* into sin, our Lord mixes one (intended for his disciples) against throwing any σκάνδαλον in our *own* way, either by giving way to worldly-mindedness, or to sensuality, and inordinate affection. In short, the best commentary on these verses are those of 1 John ii. 15 & 16., probably written with a view to this admonition of Christ: Μὴ ἀγαπᾶτε τὸν κόσμον &c. ὅτι πᾶν τὸ ἐν κόσμῳ, ἡ ἐπιθυμία τῆς σαρκὸς, καὶ ἐπιθυμία τῶν ὀφθαλμῶν, &c.

10. ὁρᾶτε μὴ καταφρονήσητε &c.] Reverting back to the subject before treated at 6 & 7, our Lord from *persecution* in general proceeds to warn his hearers against *pride* and *contempt* towards the persons in question. And this admonition is urged from two reasons. 1. The care with which God, by his angels, watches over his meanest servants; 2. the love of Christ shown equally unto *them*, by his laying down his life for their sakes, as well as their more honoured brethren. It is plain that *this* admonition is meant for such as were become disciples. As to the *first* reason, it is an *argumentum ad hominem*, adverting to the general belief of the Jews (retained among the early Christians, and professed by several of the Fathers), that every person, or at least the *good*, had his attendant angel. These are said at Heb. i. 14. to be "ministering spirits to those who shall be heirs of salvation." This angelic attendant they regarded as the representative of the person; and even as bearing a personal resemblance to him: nay, standing in the same favour with God as the person himself.

— βλέπουσι τὸ πρόσωπον &c.] "they enjoy the favour of," &c., in accordance with the Oriental custom, by which none were allowed to see the monarch but those who were in especial favour with him. [*Comp.* 1 Kings x. 8.]

11. ἦλθε γὰρ — ἀπολωλός.] The connection here is not quite certain; but it seems to be with the *former* part of the preceding verse, q. d. "Despise not any fellow-Christians, however humble; for the Son of Man came to *save ruined men*, without exception or distinction." The verse is rejected by Kuin., and cancelled by Griesb. and Lachm.; but rashly: for *external* evidence is quite in its favour; it being only omitted in 5 MSS. and 3 inferior Versions: and *internal* decidedly so; for it is far easier to account for its omission than its insertion from Luke xix. 10. It is omitted in so few MSS., that we might almost suppose the omission to have been from the negligence of the scribes. But I rather suspect that the slashing Alexandrian Critics (who throughout the whole of the N. T. took such unwarrantable liberties with the text) here threw out the verse for no better reason. than that they could not trace its *connection*. But the very difficulty of tracing that connection is the best of all reasons why we should not suppose the verse to be an insertion; for the kind of persons who used to insert clauses from one Gospel into another would never have thought of making the insertion here.

12. The connection seems to be this: "[You may figure to yourselves the grief and anger which the Almighty feels at *one* of his faithful being se-

I.U.
13 ἐννενηκονταεννέα ἐπὶ τὰ ὄρη, πορευθεὶς ζητεῖ τὸ πλανώμενον; Καὶ 15.
ἐὰν γένηται εὑρεῖν αὐτὸ, ἀμὴν λέγω ὑμῖν, ὅτι χαίρει ἐπ' αὐτῷ μᾶλλον, 6
14 ἢ ἐπὶ τοῖς ἐννενηκονταεννέα τοῖς μὴ πεπλανημένοις. Οὕτως οὐκ ἔστι
θέλημα ἔμπροσθεν τοῦ Πατρὸς ὑμῶν τοῦ ἐν οὐρανοῖς, ἵνα ἀπόληται 7
15 εἷς τῶν μικρῶν τούτων. Ἐὰν δὲ ἁμαρτήσῃ εἰς σὲ ὁ ἀδελφός σου,
ὕπαγε, καὶ ἔλεγξον αὐτὸν μεταξὺ σοῦ καὶ αὐτοῦ μόνου. Ἐάν σου
16 ἀκούσῃ, ἐκέρδησας τὸν ἀδελφόν σου· ἐὰν δὲ μὴ ἀκούσῃ, παράλαβε
μετὰ σοῦ ἔτι ἕνα ἢ δύο· ἵνα ἐπὶ στόματος δύο μαρτύρων ἢ
17 τριῶν σταθῇ πᾶν ῥῆμα. Ἐὰν δὲ παρακούσῃ αὐτῶν, εἰπὲ τῇ
ἐκκλησίᾳ· ἐὰν δὲ καὶ τῆς ἐκκλησίας παρακούσῃ, ἔστω σοι ὥσπερ
18 ὁ ἐθνικὸς καὶ ὁ τελώνης. Ἀμὴν λέγω ὑμῖν· ὅσα ἐὰν δήσητε ἐπὶ
τῆς γῆς, ἔσται δεδεμένα ἐν τῷ οὐρανῷ· καὶ ὅσα ἐὰν λύσητε ἐπὶ τῆς
19 γῆς, ἔσται λελυμένα ἐν τῷ οὐρανῷ. Πάλιν λέγω ὑμῖν, ὅτι ἐὰν δύο
ὑμῶν συμφωνήσωσιν ἐπὶ τῆς γῆς περὶ παντὸς πράγματος, οὗ ἐὰν
αἰτήσωνται, γενήσεται αὐτοῖς παρὰ τοῦ Πατρός μου τοῦ ἐν οὐρανοῖς.
20 Οὗ γάρ εἰσι δύο ἢ τρεῖς συνηγμένοι εἰς τὸ ἐμὸν ὄνομα, ἐκεῖ εἰμὶ ἐν
μέσῳ αὐτῶν.
21 Τότε προσελθὼν αὐτῷ ὁ Πέτρος εἶπε· Κύριε, ποσάκις ἁμαρτήσει
22 εἰς ἐμὲ ὁ ἀδελφός μου, καὶ ἀφήσω αὐτῷ; ἕως ἑπτάκις; Λέγει αὐτῷ
ὁ Ἰησοῦς· Οὐ, λέγω σοι, ἕως ἑπτάκις, ἀλλ' ἕως ἑβδομηκοντάκις ἑπτά.

duced away, by the joy which he feels at the *recovery* of one that had gone astray;] which is like that of the shepherd," who, &c. *Τί ὑμῖν δοκεῖ* (in which words the ὑμῖν is emphatic) is a formula, showing that the thing is illustrated by what takes place with *themselves*, and in the *ordinary occurrences of life*. At τὸ πλανώμενον here, as at τὸ ἀπολωλὸς in the verse preceding, sub. πρόβατον.

15. Kuin. thinks there is here no connection with the preceding verses, and that what is now introduced was pronounced at another time. A recent English Commentator imagines that from the *offended*, our Lord proceeds to the *offending* party. But it is directly the *reverse;* and the purpose is not, as he says, how to reclaim a sinner. "but to bring to a better mind one who has wilfully injured us;" a sense of ἁμαρτ. frequent in the best writers. Comp. Luke xvii. 3 & 4. There is an allusion to the custom of the Mosaic law, on which the canons of the primitive Church were founded. Ἐκέρδησας *may* be understood, either with Euthym., of gaining him over. and recovering him to *brotherhood;* or, with Grot. and most expositors, of recovering him to a right state of mind, and to the path of duty and the road to salvation.

17. εἰπὲ τῇ ἐκκλησίᾳ] This must mean, "to the particular congregation to which you both respectively belong;" namely, in order that he may be publicly admonished to lay aside his inimical and injurious spirit.

17. ἔστω σοι — τελώνης] i. e. "account him as a person whose intercourse is to be avoided, as that of heathens and publicans." Simil. Rom. xvi. 17. ἐκκλίνατε ἀπ' αὐτῶν. See also 2 Thess. iii. 14.

18. ὅσα ἐὰν δήσητε &c.] On the sense of these words see Note supra xvi. 19. It must not, however, be *here* taken in the same extent as there; but (as the best Commentators are agreed) be limited by the connection with the preceding context, and the circumstances of the case in question. We may thus paraphrase: "Whatever ye shall determine and appoint respecting such an offender, whether as to his removal from the Christian society, if obdurate and incorrigible, or his readmission into it on repentance, I will ratify; and whatever guidance ye ask from heaven in forming those determinations, shall be granted you; so that there be two or three who unite in the determination, or in the prayer." Hence it is obvious that, in their primary and strict sense, the words and the promise have reference to the Apostles alone; however they may, in a qualified sense, apply to Christian teachers of every age.

19. περὶ παντὸς πράγματος] *de quacunque re;* a Hebraism. *Comp.* 1 John iii. 22. v. 14.

20. εἰς τὸ ἐμὸν ὄνομα] said to be for ἐν τῷ ὀνόματί μου. But the sense is, "on my behalf, in the service of me and my religion."

— δύο ἢ τρεῖς] i. e. very few. A certain for an uncertain, but very small, number. So the Rabbinical writers say that wherever two are sitting conversing on the law, there the Shechinah is among them. Ἐν μέσῳ αὐτῶν, viz. spiritually by my assistance to speed their petitions.

21. ποσάκις ἁμαρτήσει] This comes under Winer's rule, (Gr. Gr. Nov. Test. § 39. 5.) "Two finite verbs are sometimes so connected, that the first one is to be taken as a *participle*. Matt. xviii. 21. xvii. 20:" which is accounted a *Hebraism;* but is, in fact, common to all languages, in the early periods, and in the *popular* style.

— ἑπτάκις.] The number seven was called the complete or full number, and therefore was commonly used to denote *multitude* or *frequency*.

22. ἑβδομηκοντάκις ἑπτά] A high certain, for an uncertain and unlimited number. The meaning is, "as often as he offend, and truly repent."

MK.
10. *Διὰ τοῦτο ὡμοιώθη ἡ βασιλεία τῶν οὐρανῶν ἀνθρώπῳ βασιλεῖ, ὃς* 23
ἠθέλησε συνᾶραι λόγον μετὰ τῶν δούλων αὐτοῦ. Ἀρξαμένου δὲ αὐτοῦ 24
συναίρειν, προσηνέχθη αὐτῷ εἷς ὀφειλέτης μυρίων ταλάντων. Μὴ 25
ἔχοντος δὲ αὐτοῦ ἀποδοῦναι, ἐκέλευσεν αὐτὸν ὁ κύριος αὐτοῦ πραθῆ-
ναι, καὶ τὴν γυναῖκα αὐτοῦ καὶ τὰ τέκνα, καὶ πάντα ὅσα εἶχε, καὶ
ἀποδοθῆναι. Πεσὼν οὖν ὁ δοῦλος προσεκύνει αὐτῷ, λέγων· Κύριε, 26
μακροθύμησον ἐπ' ἐμοὶ, καὶ πάντα σοι ἀποδώσω. Σπλαγχνισθεὶς δὲ 27
ὁ κύριος τοῦ δούλου ἐκείνου, ἀπέλυσεν αὐτὸν, καὶ τὸ δάνειον ἀφῆκεν
αὐτῷ. Ἐξελθὼν δὲ ὁ δοῦλος ἐκεῖνος, εὗρεν ἕνα τῶν συνδούλων αὐτοῦ, 28
ὃς ὤφειλεν αὐτῷ ἑκατὸν δηνάρια· καὶ κρατήσας αὐτὸν ἔπνιγε, λέγων·
*Ἀπόδος μοί * εἴ τι ὀφείλεις. Πεσὼν οὖν ὁ σύνδουλος αὐτοῦ εἰς τοὺς* 29
πόδας αὐτοῦ, παρεκάλει αὐτὸν, λέγων· Μακροθύμησον ἐπ' ἐμοὶ, καὶ
[πάντα] ἀποδώσω σοι. Ὁ δὲ οὐκ ἤθελεν, ἀλλὰ ἀπελθὼν ἔβαλεν αὐ- 30
τὸν εἰς φυλακὴν, ἕως οὗ ἀποδῷ τὸ ὀφειλόμενον. Ἰδόντες δὲ οἱ σύν- 31
δουλοι αὐτοῦ τὰ γενόμενα, ἐλυπήθησαν σφόδρα· καὶ ἐλθόντες διεσά-
φησαν τῷ κυρίῳ αὐτῶν πάντα τὰ γενόμενα. Τότε προσκαλεσάμενος 32
αὐτὸν ὁ κύριος αὐτοῦ λέγει αὐτῷ· Δοῦλε πονηρέ! πᾶσαν τὴν ὀφειλὴν
ἐκείνην ἀφῆκά σοι, ἐπεὶ παρεκάλεσάς με· οὐκ ἔδει καὶ σὲ ἐλεῆσαι 33
τὸν σύνδουλόν σου, ὡς καὶ ἐγώ σε ἠλέησα; καὶ ὀργισθεὶς ὁ κύριος 34
αὐτοῦ, παρέδωκεν αὐτὸν τοῖς βασανισταῖς, ἕως οὗ ἀποδῷ πᾶν τὸ
ὀφειλόμενον αὐτῷ. Οὕτω καὶ ὁ Πατήρ μου ὁ ἐπουράνιος ποιήσει 35
ὑμῖν, ἐὰν μὴ ἀφῆτε ἕκαστος τῷ ἀδελφῷ αὐτοῦ ἀπὸ τῶν καρδιῶν ὑμῶν
τὰ παραπτώματα αὐτῶν.

1 XIX. *Καὶ ἐγένετο, ὅτε ἐτέλεσεν ὁ Ἰησοῦς τοὺς λόγους τούτους,* 1

23. *διὰ τοῦτο*] This is *not* (as Kuin. thinks) a mere formula transitionis, but is to be considerod as put elliptically; q. d. "Wherefore [because pardon of injuries is to be unlimitedly granted to the repentant] the Gospel Dispensation, and the conduct of God therein, may be compared with that of a King in the following parable. *Συνᾶραι λόγον*, like *rationes conferre*, in Latin, signifies to bring together and close, or settle accounts. So *συλλογίζεσθαι* in Levit. xxv. 50.

— *δούλων*.] Not *slaves*, but ministers, or officers in the receipt or disbursement of money; of what sort, is not certain.

24. *μυρίων ταλάντων*] i. e. of silver; for in all numbers occurring in ancient authors, *gold* is never to be supposed, unless *mentioned*. The Commentators need not have troubled themselves to calculate the amount in English money, since there is no doubt but (as Origen, De Dieu, and Fritz. have seen) *μυρ.* denotes a very great, but no particular number of talents. The common mode of interpretation destroys the *vraisemblance*.

25. *πραθῆναι* &c.] According to the custom of all the nations of early antiquity. Among the Jews, however, this bondage only extended to *six* years.

26. *μακροθύμησον ἐπ' ἐμοὶ*] This is well rendered in E. V. "have patience with me," as the Latin *indulge*, *expecta*. So Artemid. Onir. iv. 12. *μακροθυμεῖν κελεύει καὶ μὴ κενοσπουδεῖν*. The word occurs also with *ἐπὶ* in Ecclus. xxv. 18.

28. *κρατήσας ἔπνιγε*] "he seized him by the throat." As *πνίγειν* here, so *ἄγχειν* often occurs, in the Classical writers, of the seizing of debtors by creditors, to drag them before a magistrate, in order to compel them to pay a debt.

— *εἴ τι*.) There is the strongest evidence, both external and internal, for this reading; which is preferred by almost every Editor and Commentator of note. The common one, *ὅ τι* is doubtless a gloss. The *sense* is the very same, for the *εἰ* is not conditional. Of this phrase there are many examples in the Classical writers, as Diog. Laert. cited by Wets. *εἴ τι μοι ὀφείλει ἀφίημι αὐτῷ*. See my Note on Thucyd. II. 72.

29. *πάντα*] There is very strong evidence in MSS., early Editions, Versions, and Fathers, against this word, which is rejected by Mill and Wets., and cancelled by Matth., Griesb., and Scholz. Yet it is found in the old Syriac Version, and its genuineness is well defended by Fritz.

31. *ἐλυπήθησαν*] The word imports a mixture of grief and indignation.

34. *βασανισταῖς*.] I have shown in Recens. Synop. that the sense is not *tormentors*, but *jailors*, *δεσμοφύλακες*, Acts xvi. 23 & 24; for *βάσανος* sometimes signifies a *jail*. Thus it is literally correctors — as we say *a house of correction*.

35. *τὰ παραπτώματα αὐτῶν*.] These words are cancelled by Griesb. and others, but on slender authority; and, indeed, as Schultz. and Fritz. have proved, they are necessary to the sense.

MK.
μετῆρεν ἀπὸ τῆς Γαλιλαίας, καὶ ἦλθεν εἰς τὰ ὅρια τῆς Ἰουδαίας, πέ- 10.
2 ραν τοῦ Ἰορδάνου. Καὶ ἠκολούθησαν αὐτῷ ὄχλοι πολλοί· καὶ
3 ἐθεράπευσεν αὐτοὺς ἐκεῖ. Καὶ προσῆλθον αὐτῷ οἱ Φαρισαῖοι πειρά- 2
ζοντες αὐτὸν καὶ λέγοντες αὐτῷ, εἰ ἔξεστιν ἀνθρώπῳ ἀπολῦσαι τὴν
4 γυναῖκα αὐτοῦ κατὰ πᾶσαν αἰτίαν. Ὁ δὲ ἀποκριθεὶς εἶπεν αὐτοῖς·
Οὐκ ἀνέγνωτε, ὅτι ὁ ποιήσας ἀπ' ἀρχῆς ἄρσεν καὶ θῆλυ ἐποίησεν 6
5 αὐτούς, καὶ εἶπεν· Ἕνεκεν τούτου καταλείψει ἄνθρωπος 7
τὸν πατέρα καὶ τὴν μητέρα, καὶ προσκολληθήσεται
τῇ γυναικὶ αὐτοῦ· καὶ ἔσονται οἱ δύο εἰς σάρκα 8

XIX. 1. *εἰς τὰ ὅρια — Ἰορδάνου.*] There is here a difficulty; for, according to the sense at first offering itself, it would be tantamount to making the country beyond the Jordan a *part* of Judæa; which we know it was not. As to Joseph. Hist. xii. 5. (which passage has been adduced in proof,) it proves rather the *contrary*: for there a comma ought to be placed after Ἰουδαίας. Otherwise the Article τῆς would have been repeated before πέραν. Some attempt to remove this difficulty, by supposing the πέραν to mean, "on *this* side," or *alongside* of: both interpretations alike *contra linguam*, and at variance with Mark x. 1. The best mode of removing the difficulty is to take πέραν τοῦ Ἰ. for διὰ τοῦ πέραν, thus: καὶ ἦλθεν πέραν τοῦ Ἰ. εἰς τὰ ὅρια τῆς Ἰ. Fritz., indeed, denies this to be Greek. And he proposes to connect πέραν τοῦ Ἰ with μετῆρεν α. τ. Γ. (taking the words as put, *per attractionem*, for "movens a Galilæâ, transiit fluvium.") Thus regarding the words καὶ ἦλθεν εἰς τὰ ὅρια τῆς Ἰ. as parenthetical. But the *violence* thus done to the *construction* is more objectionable than the *liberty* supposed to be taken with the *usus loquendi*, as the words stand: for to say it is *not Greek*, is surely too hypercritical, and is making no distinction between Attic and Hellenistic Greek. The former mode is therefore preferable; which, indeed, is required by the passage of Mark x. 1. κἀκεῖθεν ἀναστὰς, ἔρχεται εἰς τὰ ὅρια τῆς Ἰουδαίας διὰ τοῦ πέραν τοῦ Ἰορδάνου, i. e. 'having passed through the country beyond Jordan,' as Fritz. himself there interprets; where, in like manner, exception *might* be taken to the Greek, though the *sense* is clear. Jesus, it seems, purposely chose the longer course through the country beyond Jordan, to the shorter through Samaria.

3. In λέγοντες αὐτῷ, εἰ, &c. there is a blending of the oratio *directa* and *indirecta*: on which see Winer's Gr. Gr. p. 182. and other examples in Luke xiii. 23. Acts i. 6. xxi. 37. Genesis xvii. 17.

— *εἰ ἔξεστιν*, &c.] The insidious motive of this question is apparent by a comparison of this with the parallel passage in Luke xvi. 18. where the judgment of Christ respecting the unlawfulness of divorce is given in illustration of his assurance that the law should endure for ever. The interrogators hoped, by inducing Jesus to again deliver his judgment on this point, to embroil him with the school of Hillel, which taught that divorces were allowable even on trivial grounds. But Christ's wisdom frustrated their cunning, and thwarted their aims by an appeal to their great Lawgiver.

— *κατὰ*] "propter." This is no Hebraism, since examples of this signification are found not only in the Sept., but in the best Greek writers from Homer to Pausanias.

— *πᾶσαν*] "any whatever." A use of πᾶς occurring in Rom. iii. 20. Gal. ii. 16. 1 Cor. x. 25. but very rarely in the Classical writers.

— *αἰτίαν.*] The word here simply means *cause*, (which, indeed, is its primitive signification) not *fault*, as some Commentators explain; a misconception productive of the *gloss* (for such it is) which in some MSS. was introduced in the place of αἰτίαν, namely, ἁμαρτίαν.

4. *ὁ ποιήσας.*] The Commentators take this as a Participle for Noun, i. e. the Creator; a frequent idiom in Scripture, but not necessary to be supposed here; since (as I observed in Recensio Synoptica, and since that time Fritz. in loc.) ἄνθρωπον in a collective sense (in reference to which we have αὐτοὺς just after) must be supplied from the preceding ἀνθρώπῳ. However, ἐποίησεν and εἶπεν are to be closely connected; for the inference against divorce is founded on *what God* said (by Adam.) Thus the sense is, "Have ye not read what the Creator, after having at the first made them male and female, said," &c. To clear the sense, I have, with Schott, transferred the mark of interrogation to the end of the sentence. The argument is strengthened by ἀπ' ἀρχῆς, and ἄρσεν καὶ θῆλυ (sub. γένος and κατά); the latter of which, meaning *man* and *woman*, implying that only two persons, *one* male and *one* female, were created, plainly intimates the intention of God, that marriage should be in pairs, and indissoluble except by death or adultery. See more in a passage from Bradford's Boyle Lectures cited in Recens. Synop.

5. *προσκολληθήσεται*] "shall be closely connected," as by glue. A forcible metaphor often occurring in the N. T., and sometimes in the Classics, and also found in the Heb. דבק, and the Latin *agglutinare*. The var. lect. κολληθήσεται, (found in many MSS. and Fathers, and edited by Fritz. and Scholz) *may* be the true reading. But there is not sufficient evidence to authorize any change. For both external and internal evidence are in favour of the old reading, which is supported by Ephes. v. 31. and the Septuagint, from which the citation is made.

— *εἰς σάρκα μίαν.*] A Hebraism for σὰρξ μία, (See Winer's Gr. Gr. § 22. 3.) i. e. one and the same *person*. So Plato says ὥστε δύο ὄντας ἕνα γεγονέναι. It has been thought remarkable, that there is nothing corresponding to οἱ δύο in the Hebrew. Insomuch that Mr. Horne (Introd. ii. 264 & 287.) is persuaded that "it *ought to be inserted* in the Hebrew text." But nothing could be more uncritical than to insert it. In short, it is quite plain that the Septuagint Translators supplied οἱ δύο to strengthen the sense by the aid of antithesis. And, indeed, in the Hebrew something is left to be supplied mentally, such as

MK. LU.
10. 18. *μίαν;* Ὥστε οὐκέτι εἰσὶ δύο, ἀλλὰ σὰρξ μία· ὃ οὖν ὁ Θεὸς συνέ- 6
9 3 ζευξεν, ἄνθρωπος μὴ χωριζέτω. Λέγουσιν αὐτῷ· Τί οὖν Μωϋσῆς 7
4 ἐνετείλατο δοῦναι βιβλίον ἀποστασίου, καὶ ἀπολῦσαι αὐτήν; Λέγει 8
5 αὐτοῖς· Ὅτι Μωϋσῆς πρὸς τὴν σκληροκαρδίαν ὑμῶν ἐπέτρεψεν ὑμῖν
11 ἀπολῦσαι τὰς γυναῖκας ὑμῶν· ἀπ᾿ ἀρχῆς δὲ οὐ γέγονεν οὕτω. Λέγω 9
δὲ ὑμῖν, ὅτι ὃς ἂν ἀπολύσῃ τὴν γυναῖκα αὐτοῦ, [εἰ] μὴ ἐπὶ πορνείᾳ,
καὶ γαμήσῃ ἄλλην, μοιχᾶται· καὶ ὁ ἀπολελυμένην γαμήσας μοιχᾶται.
12 Λέγουσιν αὐτῷ οἱ μαθηταὶ αὐτοῦ· Εἰ οὕτως ἐστὶν ἡ αἰτία τοῦ ἀν- 10
θρώπου μετὰ τῆς γυναικὸς, οὐ συμφέρει γαμῆσαι. Ὁ δὲ εἶπεν αὐ- 11
τοῖς· Οὐ πάντες χωροῦσι τὸν λόγον τοῦτον, ἀλλ᾿ οἷς δέδοται. Εἰσὶ 12
γὰρ εὐνοῦχοι, οἵτινες ἐκ κοιλίας μητρὸς ἐγεννήθησαν οὕτω· καὶ εἰσιν
εὐνοῦχοι, οἵτινες εὐνουχίσθησαν ὑπὸ τῶν ἀνθρώπων· καὶ εἰσιν εὐνοῦχοι, οἵτινες εὐνούχισαν ἑαυτοὺς διὰ τὴν βασιλείαν τῶν οὐρανῶν. Ὁ δυνάμενος χωρεῖν χωρείτω.
13 15 Τότε προσηνέχθη αὐτῷ παιδία, ἵνα τὰς χεῖρας ἐπιθῇ αὐτοῖς καὶ 13
14 16 προσεύξηται· οἱ δὲ μαθηταὶ ἐπετίμησαν αὐτοῖς. Ὁ δὲ Ἰησοῦς εἶπεν· 14

"the man and his wife." Had it ever *been* in the Hebrew text, how could we account for its omission?

6. ὃ οὖν.] There seems to be a tacit reference to *γένος* before implied.

— συνέζευξεν.] The sense is "*arctissimè consociavit;*" by a metaphor taken from the yoking of oxen, and common to both the Greek and Latin, nay, perhaps all languages.

7. ἐνετείλατο, &c.] Moses does not command them to divorce their wives; but, when they *do* divorce them, to give them a writing of divorcement. An objection is here proposed: "If the bond of matrimony be perpetual, why did Moses permit divorce, and why did he permit her that was divorced to be married again?" Answ. "But every thing *permitted* by the law of the land is not just and equitable." On this and the two following verses see Notes on Matt. v. 31. seq.

8. Μωϋσῆς] i. e. not God; so that it is, as Jerome says, a *consilium hominis*, not *imperium Dei*. "Moses (observes Grotius) is named as the promulgator, not of a common, primæval, and perpetual law, but of one only Jewish, given in reference to the times." The sum of Christ's words, Theophylact observes, is this: "Moses wisely restrained by civil regulations your licentiousness, and permitted divorce only under certain conditions, and that because of your brutality, lest you should perpetrate something worse, namely, make away with them by sword or poison." See Whitby on this and the preceding verse.

— πρὸς τὴν σκληροκαρδίαν] *pertinaciæ vestræ ratione habitâ*, with reference to your unyielding, unforgiving spirit.

— εἰ μή.] The *εἰ* is not found in very many ancient MSS. and several early Versions, and is cancelled by Griesb., Vater, Matth., and Fritz.; but retained by Scholz; whose caution I have imitated, although the genuineness of the word may be strongly suspected.

10. ἡ αἰτία — γυναικός] "the *case* or *condition* of men with their wives." Both words have the Article, as being *Correlatives*. (Middlet.) This use of *αἰτία* is *forensic*, and akin to that of the Latin *causa*.

11. χωροῦσι] χωρεῖν properly signifies *capax esse*; but it is sometimes used metaphorically of *capability*, whether of *mind*, or (as here) of *action*. Thus the sense is, "all are not capable of practising this maxim," or, as the best Commentators render, "this thing." [*Comp.* 1 Cor. vii. 2 & 7. ix. 17.]

— οἷς δέδοται.] scil. ἐκ Θεοῦ, as in 1 Cor. vii. 7. Yet not without the co-operation of man, as appears from the words following.

12. εὐνούχισαν ἑ.] A strongly figurative expression, (akin to that of ἐκκόπτειν τὴν δεξιὰν, v. 29 & 30. xviii. 8. & 9.) found also in the Rabbinical writers, and meant of the suppression of the desire — said with reference to those who, from a desire to further the interests of religion, live in celibacy. The Commentators compare a similar expression from Julian, to which may be added Max. Tyr. Diss. 34. ἄφελε τὴν αἰδοίων ἐπιθυμίαν, καὶ διέκοψας τὸ θηρίον.

— χωρείτω] "qui capere, h. e. viribus suis sustinere possit, sustineat." Here the Imperative has rather the force of *permission* than *injunction*; or, at any rate, the admonition must, like that of 1 Cor. vii. 26. have reference chiefly to the *circumstances* under which it was delivered.

13. ἵνα τὰς χεῖρας ἐπιθῇ.] Imposition of hands was a rite which from the earliest ages; see Gen. xlviii. 14, had been in use among the Jews on imploring God's blessing upon any person, and was especially employed by the Prophets, (Numb. xxvii. 18. 2 Kings v. 11.) but sometimes by elders, or men noted for piety. These children, therefore, were brought to Christ for his blessing; and, it should seem, to be admitted into his Church. That they were not brought to be healed of any disorder, but to obtain spiritual blessings, is plain; and that they were not only considered *capable* of receiving them by the people, but also by our Lord himself, is equally clear. By αὐτοῖς is meant τοῖς προσφέρουσι.

MK. LU.

Ἄφετε τὰ παιδία, καὶ μὴ κωλύετε αὐτὰ ἐλθεῖν πρός με· τῶν γὰρ τοι- 10. 18.
15 ούτων ἐστὶν ἡ βασιλεία τῶν οὐρανῶν. Καὶ ἐπιθεὶς αὐτοῖς τὰς χεῖρας, 16
ἐπορεύθη ἐκεῖθεν.
16 Καὶ ἰδοὺ, εἷς προσελθὼν εἶπεν αὐτῷ· Διδάσκαλε ἀγαθὲ, τί ἀγα- 17 18
17 θὸν ποιήσω, ἵνα ἔχω ζωὴν αἰώνιον; Ὁ δὲ εἶπεν αὐτῷ· Τί με λέγεις 18 19

14. τῶν τοιούτων] namely, such as have these *dispositions* — i. e. humility, docility, and simplicity. For Christ meant what he said for his disciples — namely, to inculcate the same lesson as he had done a little before (supra xviii. 3.) when in answer to an inquiry of the disciples, which of them should be greatest in the kingdom of heaven, he placed a young child in the midst. See also the note on Luke xviii. 15.

15. ἐκεῖθεν] i. e. from that part of Peræa, or Judæa, where he had been stopping on his road to Jerusalem. See Mark x. 17. and supra v. 1.

16. εἷς] for τις. This was, as we find from v. 22., a young man; and, as we learn from Luke xviii. 18., a ruler; by which is probably meant a ruler of the Synagogue. His conduct seems to have been dictated by a real desire to be put into the way of salvation, and a sincere intention of following Christ's injunctions; which, however, proved too hard for a disposition in which avarice prevailed over piety.

— τί ἀγαθὸν — αἰώνιον.] This question is thought to have reference to the Pharisaical division of the precepts of the law into the *weighty*, and the *light*. The young man, it seems, was puzzled by the nice distinctions which were made in classing those precepts; and wished to have some clear information as to what was pre-eminently promotive of salvation.

17. τί με λέγεις ἀγαθόν; οὐδεὶς, &c.] In this and the preceding verse there are some remarkable varr. lectt. In 6 MSS., some later Versions, and some Fathers, the ἀγαθὲ at v. 16. and the ὁ Θεὸς at v. 17. are not found; and for τί με λέγεις ἀγαθὸν, we have τί με ἐρωτᾷς περὶ τοῦ ἀγαθοῦ; these readings were preferred by Erasm., Grot., Mill, and Bengel, and were received into the text by Griesb. and Lachman; but utterly without reason. The *external* evidence for them is very slender; and the internal, I apprehend, by no means strong. Besides, the answer of our Lord would thus be deprived of all its *simplicity*, and nearly all its *propriety*. It would in fact, be *no* answer to the inquiry; for the young man did not (as appears from the words following, εἰ δὲ θέλεις — ἐντολὰς) inquire what was *naturally*, or *essentially good*, but what good should be *done* by him. And if the words be, as Griesb. directs, referred to what *follows*, there is, as Fritz. proves, quite as great an inconsistency. Thus that the readings in question are false, is plain. *How* they *originated*, is not so obvious. Matthæi thinks that they arose from the conjecture of Origen. But that, as Fritz. has shown, involves a great improbability. At all events, it is more important to inquire *what* induced the persons (whoever they were) to make the alterations in question. Matthæi and Nolan (Gr. Vulg. p. 474.) ascribe it to a groundless fear lest the words should be brought forward against the divinity of Christ. Such charges, however, are not rashly to be made, nor lightly to be credited. *If* the alterations were *all* introduced *designedly*, it is *more* probable that, as Wets. suggests, they arose from those who thought that the answer would be more suitably made to the QUESTION *itself* ("what good thing shall I do"), than to the *title* "good master." Yet how could any persons who had sufficient influence to materially alter the text, fail to see that the answer to the *question* itself *is* given in the words *following?* There seems far more reason to suppose, with Fritz., that no original intention existed to alter the passage, from any scruples doctrinal or otherwise; but that the alterations arose at first from accident; namely, in the omission of ἀγαθὲ (propter homœoteleuton.) Whereupon the words of the next verse, τί με λέγεις having become quite unsuitable, would, he says, be altered to τί με ἐρωτᾷς περὶ τοῦ ἀγαθοῦ; I am, however, inclined to think that the alteration was not made *all at once*; but that, at first, a suitable sense was endeavoured to be elicited, by taking λέγεις for ἐρωτᾷς (as in the Sept. and elsewhere in the N. T. See Schl. Lex. in v. § 5.) and then by the slight alteration ἀγαθοῦ, and supposing an ellipsis of περὶ. Comp. Mark i. 30. with Luke iv. 38. And, indeed, ἀγαθοῦ *without* the Article is cited by Origen himself, at p. 664, C. Thus would be generated a gloss, or marginal Scholium, τί με ἐρωτᾷς περὶ ἀγ. or τοῦ ἀγ.; which, it seems, was admitted into the text in six MSS., and possibly those which were used by the framers of the ancient Versions above mentioned. I say *possibly*, since it is extremely doubtful whether the reading was in their MSS.; for their chief aim is to give the *sense*; and, therefore, in passages of great difficulty or obscurity, the ancient Versions afford no certain evidence as to the readings of their MSS. Thus the genuineness of the common reading is, I trust, immovably established. The *propriety* of the answer, according to that reading, is quite as demonstrable. The young man accosts our Lord by a title usually employed by the Jews to their most eminent Rabbis, and of which they were very proud. Hence, before he replies to his inquiry, he takes occasion to indirectly censure the adulation of the persons *addressing*, and the arrogance of those *addressed*. At the same time he *proceeds upon* the notion entertained of him by the young man; who evidently only regarded him in the light of an *eminent teacher*. Moreover, when our Lord adds, οὐδεὶς ἀγαθὸς, εἰ μὴ ὁ Θεὸς, we are to understand with Bps. Pearson and Bull, the sense to be, that there is no being originally, essentially, and independently good, but God. Thus the Father, being the fountain of the whole *Deity*, must, in some sense, be the fountain of the goodness of the Son. Accordingly, the Ante-Nicene Fathers were generally agreed, that ἀγαθὸς essentially and strictly applied only to God the Father; and to Christ only by reason of the goodness derived to him as being *very God of very God*. This use of ἀγαθὸς will establish and illustrate the *ratio significationis* of the expressive word employed, with slight variations, by all the Northern nations, to denote the Supreme Being, GOD. Finally, something very similar to the present, both in thought and expression, occurs in a passage of Pseudo-Phocylides, Frag. xiii. 47.

MK. LU.
10. 18. ἀγαθόν; οὐδεὶς ἀγαθὸς, εἰ μὴ εἷς ὁ Θεός. Εἰ δὲ θέλεις εἰσελθεῖν εἰς
19 20 τὴν ζωὴν, τήρησον τὰς ἐντολάς. Λέγει αὐτῷ· Ποίας; ὁ δὲ Ἰησοῦς εἶπε· 18
Τό· οὐ φονεύσεις· οὐ μοιχεύσεις· οὐ κλέψεις· οὐ
ψευδομαρτυρήσεις· τίμα τὸν πατέρα [σου] καὶ τὴν 19
μητέρα· καὶ ἀγαπήσεις τὸν πλησίον σου ὡς σεαυ-
20 21 τόν. Λέγει αὐτῷ ὁ νεανίσκος· Πάντα ταῦτα ἐφυλαξάμην ἐκ νεότη- 20
21 22 τός μου· τί ἔτι ὑστερῶ; Ἔφη αὐτῷ ὁ Ἰησοῦς· Εἰ θέλεις τέλειος 21
εἶναι, ὕπαγε, πώλησόν σου τὰ ὑπάρχοντα καὶ δὸς πτωχοῖς· καὶ ἕξεις
22 23 θησαυρὸν ἐν οὐρανῷ· καὶ δεῦρο ἀκολούθει μοι. Ἀκούσας δὲ ὁ νεα- 22
νίσκος τὸν λόγον, ἀπῆλθε λυπούμενος· ἦν γὰρ ἔχων κτήματα πολλά.
23 24 Ὁ δὲ Ἰησοῦς εἶπε τοῖς μαθηταῖς αὐτοῦ· Ἀμὴν λέγω ὑμῖν ὅτι 23
25 25 δυσκόλως πλούσιος εἰσελεύσεται εἰς τὴν βασιλείαν τῶν οὐρανῶν. Πά- 24
λιν δὲ λέγω ὑμῖν· εὐκοπώτερόν ἐστι κάμηλον διὰ τρυπήματος ῥαφί-

Edit. Gaisf. Μὴ γαυροῦ σοφίῃ, μήτ' ἀλκῇ, μήτ' ἐνὶ (I conjecture ἐπὶ) πλούτῳ. Εἷς Θεός ἐστι σοφὸς, δυνατός θ' ἅμα, καὶ πολύολβος.

— τὰς ἐντολάς] namely, of God, as comprehended in the Decalogue; for though our Lord adduces his instances only from the laws of the *second* table, yet he virtually confirms *all* of them.

18. ποίας] for τίνας, as often in the Sept.

— τό· οὐ φονεύσεις.] Though the *whole* law is meant, yet, as often in the N. T. (see Rom. xiii. 8. and James ii. 8.) the commandments of the *second* table alone are adduced in *exemplification*; not that they are of greater importance than those of the first table; but because there is a necessary connection between the duties towards God, and those towards man; and because the latter are not so easily *counterfeited* as the former. That the terms of salvation here offered are not at all different from those stated in other parts of Scripture, has been evinced by the Commentators. See Lightf., Whitby, and Mackn. On the use of the Article, thus employed with reference to a whole clause, see Matth. Gr. Gr. § 279.

— τί ἔτι ὑστερῶ;] At τί sub. κατὰ, "In what am I yet behindhand, or wanting?" This readiness to undertake more than he had yet done, showed that he was well disposed, and caused Jesus, as we learn from Mark, to be pleased with him. So a Rabbinical writer, cited by Wets.: "There is a Pharisee who says, 'What ought I to do, and I will do it.' That is good. But there is also a Pharisee who says, 'What ought I to do *besides*, and I will do it.' That is *better*."

21. τέλειος.] The term is here used not only in the *moral* sense, by which God is said to be perfect, but in that *comparative* sense by which a thing is perfect so far as the constitution of it permits. It therefore denotes a true Christian, and such as will be accepted by God. See note, supra v. 48. and Luke xii. 33. Rom. xii. 2. Phil. iii. 13. Col. i. 28. & iv. 12. James iii. 2. Some, however, think that Christ had referred to the Pharisaical notion of perfection in that respect. See Lightf. There may have been an *allusion* to it, but no more.

— πώλησόν σου τὰ ὑπάρχοντα] q. d. "show your love to God and obedience to me his Messenger, by selling your goods and following my cause." *Comp.* supra vi. The injunction, meant to lower the pride, and try the sincerity of the convert, was only binding on the *individual* thus addressed, or on those similarly circumstanced, as in the Apostolic age; and has no relation to Christians of the present or any other period. See Lightf., Whitby, and Mackn.

The use of ὕπαγε just before, is like that at xviii. 15. Mark x. 21. and is said by some Commentators to be pleonastic. But it rather carries an intensive force, and may be rendered "*begone!*"

— δεῦρο.] This is explained by the Commentators as put for ἐλθέ; whereas the truth is, there is an ellipsis of ἐλθὲ or the like, which is *supplied* in Hom. Od. p. Δεῦρο Μοῦσ' ἐλθέ.

22. ἦν ἔχων] "he was in possession." Or the sense may be, "he chanced to possess." See Matth. Gr. Gr. 559. 9.

23. δυσκόλως] for χαλεπῶς. He will scarcely be persuaded to become a Christian.

— πλούσιος.] That is, if he place his trust in his riches, and make them his summum bonum; a necessary limitation, as appears from the parallel passage at Mark x. 23. At the same time, considering how many impediments to good, and how many incitements to evil attend riches; how the cares of the world, and the deceitfulness of riches choke the word (see 1 Tim. vi. 9.) this limitation scarcely lessens the difficulty; since it is the very nature and effect of riches to *cause* men to *trust* in them, and to seek their happiness in them. Hence both pride is fostered, and selfishness increased. So that although the words of this and the next verse primarily referred to the extreme difficulty (represented by a proverbial mode of expressing what is next to impossible) with which the rich would be converted; yet they are applicable to, and were doubtless intended to supply an awful warning of, the danger of trusting in uncertain riches, and the necessity of a true coversion: without which men do not really belong to the kingdom of Christ on earth, and therefore will not be admitted to his kingdom in heaven.

24. κάμηλον.] Some ancient and modern Commentators would read κάμιλον, a *cable rope*; or take κάμηλον in that sense. But for the former there is little or no manuscript authority; and for the latter no support from the *usus loquendi*. That the common reading and interpretation must be retained, all the best Commentators are agreed.

MK. LU.
δος ‡ διελθεῖν, ἢ πλούσιον εἰς τὴν βασιλείαν τοῦ Θεοῦ εἰσελθεῖν. 10. 18.
25 Ἀκούσαντες δὲ οἱ μαθηταὶ [αὐτοῦ,] ἐξεπλήσσοντο σφόδρα, λέγοντες· 26 26
26 Τίς ἄρα δύναται σωθῆναι; ἐμβλέψας δὲ ὁ Ἰησοῦς εἶπεν αὐτοῖς· 27 27
Παρὰ ἀνθρώποις τοῦτο ἀδύνατόν ἐστι, παρὰ δὲ Θεῷ πάντα δυνατά
[ἐστι.]
27 Τότε ἀποκριθεὶς ὁ Πέτρος εἶπεν αὐτῷ· Ἰδού, ἡμεῖς ἀφήκαμεν 28 28
28 πάντα, καὶ ἠκολουθήσαμέν σοι· τί ἄρα [ἔσται] ἡμῖν; ὁ δὲ Ἰησοῦς
εἶπεν αὐτοῖς· Ἀμὴν λέγω ὑμῖν, ὅτι ὑμεῖς οἱ ἀκολουθήσαντές μοι, ἐν
τῇ παλιγγενεσίᾳ, ὅταν καθίσῃ ὁ Υἱὸς τοῦ ἀνθρώπου ἐπὶ θρόνου

— διελθεῖν.] For this many MSS., several Versions, and some Fathers, read *εἰσελθεῖν*, which is preferred by Wets., and edited by Matthæi, Knapp, Griesb., Vater, and Scholz.; though the common reading is retained by Tittm. and Fritz. But though the evidence of MSS. and Versions is somewhat in favour of the new reading, yet internal evidence is rather in favour of the common one, which is found in Mark x. 25. and several MSS., in Luke xviii. 25.

— ῥαφίδος.] Later Greek for *βελόνης* from *ῥάπτω*. The word signifies literally a *sewing tool*.

25. αὐτοῦ.] This is omitted in many MSS. of various Recensions, and some Versions of Fathers, and is cancelled by Griesb., Fritz., and Scholz, perhaps rightly.

— τίς δύναται σ.] This is generally interpreted, "who then can be saved? [since all men are either rich, or desire to be so."] But that is a harsh mode of interpretation; and therefore it is better, with Euthym. and Markl., to suppose an ellipsis, and interpret, "what [rich man,] then, can be saved?" There is, however, properly speaking, no *ellipsis*; but the *τις* is supposed to be mentally referred to *πλούσιος* which preceded. And the Apostles may have meant to express by inference the *difficulty* with which *men in general*, as well as the rich, would be saved.

26. ἐμβλέψας] "fixing his eyes upon them." There is a similar use at Mark x. 21 & 27. xiv. 67. Luke xx. 17. and elsewhere; in which places the word must not, (with many recent Commentators,) be regarded as merely pleonastic, or as having the sense *turning towards*, but must retain its full force; signifying extreme earnestness, as in Mark x. 21. 27. Luke xx. 17. John i. 36, and Xenoph. Cyrop. i. 3. 2. *ἐμβλέπων αὐτῷ ἔλεγε*. also Acts. xvi. 18. *ἐπιστρέψας εἶπε*.

— παρὰ ἀνθρώποις.] This use of *παρὰ* is said to be Hebraic, and the Commentators tell us that the Greeks use the simple dative with *δυνατὸν* or *ἀδύνατόν ἐστι*. But the meaning is somewhat different, and we may render, "as far as concerns (the power of.)"

— ἀδύνατον.] Le Clerc ap. Elsley, and most recent Commentators, as Kuin. and Fritz., take the word in the qualified sense, *extremely difficult*, as also at Luke xviii. 27. and Heb. vi. 4. But I agree with Mr. Rose on Parkhurst, p. 16. a., that "the affixing of this sense to passages [like this] *containing a doctrine*, which is altered by the translation, is improper." We are therefore to leave the *full sense*; as intimating that, in the work of salvation, human nature is quite insufficient of itself, and stands in great need of the aids of Divine grace.

Ἐστὶ is omitted in very many MSS. of various recensions, and is cancelled by Griesb., Tittm., Fritz., and Scholz.

27. ἡμεῖς ἀφήκαμεν — ἡμῖν;] This inquiry does not appear to have been suggested by *disappointment*, but simply from the wish of ascertaining the reward, which he and the other Apostles would have for giving up their all in the cause of the Gospel. That all was indeed slender; but it was yielded up unhesitatingly. And hence our Lord, who did not estimate their value from the *amount* of the sacrifices, but from the *mind* and *disposition* with which they had been made, kindly cherished their hopes; pointing to the fruition of them in an immortality of bliss.

— τί ἄρα ἔσται ἡμῖν;] "what, then, shall be our reward?" namely, in heaven. Said with reference to the preceding *ἕξεις θησαυρὸν ἐν οὐρανῷ*.

28. ἐν τῇ παλιγγενεσίᾳ] On the *sense* contained in these words, a wonderful diversity of opinion exists. Now this, it will be observed, depends much upon the *construction*. Some, as the early modern Commentators in general, construe the words with the *preceding* οἱ ἀκολουθ. μοι, understanding by παλ. the great change of manners and doctrines which arose from the preaching of John the Baptist, or from the moral regeneration consequent upon the *first* preaching of the Gospel. This, however, is harsh and forced; and it is plain that the words following contain a fuller description of this *παλιγγενεσία*, and relate not to time *past*, but to *future*. Indeed, it is now generally admitted, that the words must be referred to what *follows*; though Expositors are not agreed as to the *nature* of the promise, or the *time* of its fulfilment. Whitby fixes the time at the *close of the world*, and after the fall of Antichrist; and he understands, by παλιγγ., not a resurrection of their *persons*, but a revival of their *spirit*, by admitting the Gospel to govern their faith and practice. Adopting this view, others consider the time in question to be the *Millennium*. But the whole of this edifice is built on a sandy foundation, and is utterly untenable. Far better founded is the view adopted by Lightf., Hamm., and others, who understand παλιγγ. to refer either to the *renovation*, or *new state of things*, which took place at the promulgation of Christianity, after the ascension and resurrection of Christ; or, to the *regeneration* which was then effected by the Gospel. And they understand "the throne of his glory" to apply to his *mediatorial* kingdom. And the *sitting on thrones*, and judging, &c. they interpret of the *ministerial* authority with which the Apostles had been invested by our Lord. Thus they take the general sense to be, that the Apostles were to rule the Christian Church by the laws of the Gospel, which they were authorized and inspired to

MK. LU.
10. 18. δόξης αὐτοῦ, καθίσεσθε καὶ ὑμεῖς ἐπὶ δώδεκα θρόνους, κρίνοντες τὰς
29 29 δώδεκα φυλὰς τοῦ Ἰσραήλ. Καὶ πᾶς ὃς ἀφῆκεν οἰκίας, ἢ ἀδελφοὺς ἢ 29
30 30 ἀδελφὰς, ἢ πατέρα ἢ μητέρα, ἢ γυναῖκα ἢ τέκνα, ἢ ἀγροὺς, ἕνεκεν τοῦ
ὀνόματός μου, ἑκατονταπλασίονα λήψεται, καὶ ζωὴν αἰώνιον κληρονομήσει.
31 Πολλοὶ δὲ ἔσονται πρῶτοι ἔσχατοι, καὶ ἔσχατοι πρῶτοι. XX. Ὁμοία 30
γάρ ἐστιν ἡ βασιλεία τῶν οὐρανῶν ἀνθρώπῳ οἰκοδεσπότῃ, ὅστις ἐξῆλθεν 1
ἅμα πρωῒ μισθώσασθαι ἐργάτας εἰς τὸν ἀμπελῶνα αὐτοῦ. Συμφω- 2

preach, and by the infallible decisions respecting faith and practice which he enabled them to give." Yet this interpretation, however specious, will no more bear examination than the foregoing one. For though we may grant that παλιγγ. admits of either of these senses, yet the words following cannot, without great violence, be made to yield any sense at all suitable thereto. Not to say that what they assign as the sense would not be sufficiently suitable to the purposes for which the words were pronounced; namely, to hold out to the disciples an ample *compensation* for all their sacrifices and sufferings in the cause of the Gospel. Under these circumstances, I cannot hesitate to adopt, in preference to all others, the sense assigned to the passage by the ancient Expositors in general (and of the modern ones by Kuin. and Fritz.), confirmed by the Syriac, Persic, Arabic, Æthiopic, and Italic Versions; understanding παλιγγ. of the *resurrection to judgment*, and a new state of existence. This is very agreeable to, nay, is required by what follows, ὅταν καθίσῃ — ἐπὶ θρόνου δόξης αὐτοῦ, for in the only other passage where Christ is so spoken of (Matt. xxv. 31.), the words relate indisputably to the *day of judgment*. And as regards the term itself, it is, from the nature of the context, far more likely to have been used in its physical sense and ordinary acceptation, than in any *figurative* one whatsoever. While, at the same time, it was likely that the *adjunct* to this substantial and definite assurance in the form of *promise* should be denoted by a figurative expression to signify high exaltation and supreme felicity. See 1 Cor. vi. 2. Luke xxii. 30. On the purposes of such *involucra*, see my remarks in Rec. Syn.

Of the truth of this interpretation there cannot be a stronger proof than the fact, that the most powerful supporters of the other are compelled to *engraft* this, and so include both. Nay Campb. grants, that "the *principal* completion of the promise will be at the *general resurrection*." If, however, the other interpretation be at all admitted, it can only be as a kind of subordinate adjunct, by way of allusion, to the principal idea. Compare Acts iii. 21. ἄχρι χρόνων ἀποκαταστάσεως πάντων.

29. ὃς] Several MSS. have ὅστις, which is received by Knapp, Tittm., Vat., and Griesb. in his two first Editions, though it has been rejected in his third. The common reading is retained by Fritz. and Scholz; and rightly, since ὅστις, though better Greek, seems to be a *correction* of the Alexandrian critics. It is, moreover, confirmed by Luke xii. 8. & 10. and Acts ii. 21.

— ἑκατ. λήψ.] This is by most Commentators understood of a *temporal* recompense, as that suggested in the parallel passage of Mark, namely in the support and comfort they would receive at the hands of their richer brethren. But there is no reason here so to limit the term ἑκατ., which is only a strong mode of expressing that they shall, on the *whole*, receive back very far *more* in value than they parted with. And although it is not expressly said whether that is to be *temporal* or *spiritual*, yet notwithstanding that what follows in the next verse seems to fix it to *temporal* blessings, still we are justified in *including spiritual* ones; even the inward satisfactions of a good conscience, and the inexpressible consolations of the Gospel (far exceeding in value all that is most precious of earthly goods, however great), which would be their support under all persecutions and troubles. Comp. 2 Cor. vi. 8. seqq., which passage affords both a comment upon our Lord's declaration, and a fulfilment of the prediction contained in it.

30. πολλοὶ δὲ — πρῶτοι.] A sort of proverbial mode of expression, often employed by our Lord to check the presumption of the Apostles; the sense of which is, that many of the Jews, to whom the blessings of Christ's kingdom were first offered, would be the last to partake of them; and that many of the Gentiles, to whom they were to be offered after the Jews, would be the first to enjoy them. In illustration of this, our Lord subjoined the parable at the beginning of the next chapter; in which, however, as I have shewn in Rec. Synop., the application is not to be limited to the Jews, but left general; being meant for the instruction of all Christians of all ages.

XX. 1. Ὁμοία γὰρ, &c.] The sense is: "The same thing will take place in the Christian Dispensation, which occurred in the management of a certain master of a family." The γὰρ may be rendered "thus for example."

The Commentators remark on the *pleonasm* in ἀνθρώπῳ, of which there are many similar examples in Scripture, and which they regard as a *Hebraism*. But there are instances of it in the Greek Classical writers, especially Herodotus. It may, therefore, better be regarded as a vestige of the wordiness of primitive diction. It must be remembered, too, that the idiom in question is almost wholly confined to words which were originally *adjectives*.

This Parable is found, though with a widely extended application, in the Jerusalem Talmud. "*Here* it is meant (as observes Waterland) to represent God's dealings with mankind in respect to their outward call to the means of grace, as well as to the retribution in a state of glory." In this Parable, as in many others, some parts of the simile do not correspond; namely, those which only respect the ornament, and do not affect the *scope* of the parable; as the labourers waiting to be hired, and the murmurings, &c. of the labourers after the distribution of the wages. The main point of similarity is the rejection of those who were first, and the admission of those who seemed last.

— ἅμα πρωΐ.] This is regarded by the Commentators as an elliptical expression, for ἅμα σὺν π.

νήσας δὲ μετὰ τῶν ἐργατῶν ἐκ δηναρίου τὴν ἡμέραν, ἀπέστειλεν αὐ-
3 τοὺς εἰς τὸν ἀμπελῶνα αὐτοῦ. Καὶ ἐξελθὼν περὶ [τὴν] τρίτην ὥραν,
4 εἶδεν ἄλλους ἑστῶτας ἐν τῇ ἀγορᾷ ἀργούς· κἀκείνοις εἶπεν· Ὑπάγετε
5 καὶ ὑμεῖς εἰς τὸν ἀμπελῶνα, καὶ ὃ ἐὰν ᾖ δίκαιον, δώσω ὑμῖν. Οἱ δὲ
ἀπῆλθον. πάλιν ἐξελθὼν περὶ ἕκτην, καὶ ἐννάτην ὥραν, ἐποίησεν
6 ὡσαύτως. Περὶ δὲ τὴν ἑνδεκάτην ὥραν ἐξελθὼν, εὗρεν ἄλλους ἑστῶτας
ἀργοὺς, καὶ λέγει αὐτοῖς· Τί ὧδε ἑστήκατε ὅλην τὴν ἡμέραν ἀργοί;
7 Λέγουσιν αὐτῷ· Ὅτι οὐδεὶς ἡμᾶς ἐμισθώσατο. λέγει αὐτοῖς· Ὑπάγετε καὶ ὑμεῖς εἰς τὸν ἀμπελῶνα, καὶ ὃ ἐὰν ᾖ δίκαιον, λήψεσθε.
8 Ὀψίας δὲ γενομένης, λέγει ὁ κύριος τοῦ ἀμπελῶνος τῷ ἐπιτρόπῳ αὐ-
τοῦ· Κάλεσον τοὺς ἐργάτας, καὶ ἀπόδος αὐτοῖς τὸν μισθὸν, ἀρξά-
9 μενος ἀπὸ τῶν ἐσχάτων ἕως τῶν πρώτων. Καὶ ἐλθόντες οἱ περὶ τὴν
10 ἑνδεκάτην ὥραν ἔλαβον ἀνὰ δηνάριον. Ἐλθόντες δὲ οἱ πρῶτοι, ἐνό-
μισαν ὅτι πλείονα λήψονται. καὶ ἔλαβον καὶ αὐτοὶ ἀνὰ δηνάριον.
11 Λαβόντες δὲ ἐγόγγυζον κατὰ τοῦ οἰκοδεσπότου λέγοντες· Ὅτι οὗτοι
12 οἱ ἔσχατοι μίαν ὥραν ἐποίησαν, καὶ ἴσους ἡμῖν αὐτοὺς ἐποίησας τοῖς
13 βαστάσασι τὸ βάρος τῆς ἡμέρας καὶ τὸν καύσωνα. Ὁ δὲ ἀποκριθεὶς
εἶπεν ἑνὶ αὐτῶν· Ἑταῖρε, οὐκ ἀδικῶ σε· οὐχὶ δηναρίου συνεφώνησάς

But that phrase occurs in the Sept., not in the Greek Classical writers. Whereas ἅμα and similar words are of frequent occurrence with nouns of time. I know of no example with πρωΐ, which may be regarded (with Scheid on Lennep), as properly a *Dative* of the old noun πρωΐς, as the Latin *heri* from *heris*.

2. ἐκ δηναρίου] "at or for a denarius." This mode of denoting price (which occurs also at Matt. xxvii. 7.) is rarely found in the Classical writers, and only in the later ones. The earlier and best writers use the *Genitive simply*. The *denarius*, which was equivalent to the Greek drachma, was then the usual wages of a labourer, and the pay of a soldier.

3. τὴν] This is omitted in very many of the MSS., including all the most ancient ones, and some Fathers. It is cancelled by Wets., Matth., Griesb., Knapp, Tittm., Fritz., and Scholz; and rightly; for in such common phrases the Article was usually omitted. Indeed ordinals are usually anarthrous.

— ἑστῶτας — ἀργούς.] The very place where (from its being used for buying and selling, and all public business) the greatest number of persons assembled, especially the idle or unemployed. So Ælian, V. H. xix. 25. (cited by Grot.) μετεπέμπετο τοὺς ἐν ταῖς ἀγοραῖς ἀποσχολάζοντας. The time here mentioned was equivalent to what was called the πλήθουσα ἀγορά.

4. ἐὰν] for ἄν. In which use with the Subjunctive (rare in the Classical writers) it answers to the Latin *cunque* and our *soever*.

— δίκαιον,] i. e. not what was legally due, but what was equitable, or *reasonable*.

6. ἀργούς.] This is cancelled by Griesb. and Vater; but there is very little authority for its omission; and it is well defended by Fritz., as being necessary to the sense.

8. τῷ ἐπιτρόπῳ] A servant nearly answering to the Roman *procurator* and our *bailiff*, and entrusted with the whole domestic economy.

— ἀρξάμενος — πρώτων.] The construction of this passage has been mistaken by Kypke and Kuin., but is thus rightly laid down by Fritz.: ἀπόδος αὐτοῖς τὸν μισθὸν ἕως τῶν πρώτων, ἀρξάμενος ἀπὸ τῶν ἐσχάτων.

9. ἀνὰ] This is said by the Commentators to be put adverbially; and they refer to a *plena locutio* in Rev. xxii. 21. ἀνὰ εἷς ἕκαστος. There is, in fact, an ellipse of ἕκαστον.

12. ἐποίησαν,] Some render it *confecerunt*, *spent*. But although examples are adduced proving this sense of ποιεῖν and the Latin *facere* with nouns of time; yet it is better, with most recent Commentators, to take it for εἰργάσαντο, by an Hebraism formed on עָשָׂה, as in Ruth ii. 19. Matth. xxi. 28. And so *facere agrum* in Columella.

— ἴσους] for ἰσομοίρους, of which Wets. gives examples.

— καύσωνα.] Καύσων (which is of the same form with δώσων, φώσων, σείσων, ἄξων, μύξων, &c.) literally signifies *the burner*, the burning (wind) *Eurus*; and is often to be found in the Sept. Here it may be explained simply *heat*, as in Genes. xxxi. 40. ἐγενόμην τῆς ἡμέρας συγκαιόμενος τῷ καύσωνι, where in the Heb. it is חֹרֶב, i. e. the *shriveller*, the *drier*. It is to be remembered that, in the East, though the air be cool in the early part of the day; yet during the remainder of it, the heat of the sun is exceedingly scorching. I would compare Liban. Epist. 245: περὶ ἣν οὗτος πολὺ καῦμα, πολὺν δὲ καπνὸν ἠνέσχετο.

13. ἑταῖρε] An idiom found in the Heb. רֵעַ, the Greek ὦ ἀγαθὲ, or φίλε, and the Latin *bone vir*. It was a familiar form of address, and consequently often used to inferiors, and sometimes to strangers or indifferent persons.

— οὐκ ἀδικῶ σε·] Wets. and Waterland task their ingenuity in endeavouring to find a *reason why* all the labourers should have had the same wages. But such *incidental* circumstances as this we are not to *press* in the application, much less to draw doctrinal inferences. It is enough to conclude that, though there be some things in the Gospel dispensation different from what we should

MK. LU.
10. 18. μοι; Ἆρον τὸ σὸν καὶ ὕπαγε. θέλω τούτῳ τῷ ἐσχάτῳ δοῦναι ὡς 14
καὶ σοί. Ἢ οὐκ ἔξεστί μοι ποιῆσαι ὃ θέλω ἐν τοῖς ἐμοῖς; ἢ ὁ ὀφθαλ- 15
μός σου πονηρός ἐστιν, ὅτι ἐγὼ ἀγαθός εἰμι; Οὕτως ἔσονται οἱ 16
ἔσχατοι πρῶτοι, καὶ οἱ πρῶτοι ἔσχατοι· πολλοὶ γάρ εἰσι κλητοὶ, ὀλίγοι
δὲ ἐκλεκτοί.

32 31 Καὶ ἀναβαίνων ὁ Ἰησοῦς εἰς Ἱεροσόλυμα, παρέλαβε τοὺς δώδεκα 17
33 μαθητὰς κατ' ἰδίαν ἐν τῇ ὁδῷ, καὶ εἶπεν αὐτοῖς· Ἰδοὺ, ἀναβαίνομεν 18
εἰς Ἱεροσόλυμα, καὶ ὁ Υἱὸς τοῦ ἀνθρώπου παραδοθήσεται τοῖς ἀρχιε-
32 ρεῦσι καὶ γραμματεῦσι· καὶ κατακρινοῦσιν αὐτὸν θανάτῳ, καὶ παρα- 19

expect, yet the whole is agreeable to strict justice.

14. θέλω δ.] "It is my pleasure: I choose to give."

15. ἢ ὁ ὀφθαλμός σου πονηρός ἐ.] A figurative expression, importing "art thou envious?" Fritz. well explains the nature of the metaphor thus: "Nam invidentiæ, ut aliarum animi perturbationum, indices oculi sunt. Hinc factum, ut Hebraici hominem invidum appellarent רַע עַיִן."

16. οὕτως] i. e. as it was in the case of the labourers last hired by the master.

—πολλοὶ γὰρ—ἐκλεκτοί.] On the important terms κλητοὶ and ἐκλεκτοὶ, it may be proper to offer a few observations. These are supposed to have been originally Jewish forms of expression, applied (like many others) by Christ to similar distinctions in the Gospel Dispensation. In the Sept., κλητοὶ often denotes those *chosen* to receive especial favours, or *called* to execute peculiar trusts. Hence it is, both in the O. and N. T., applied to the *Jews*; who had been *chosen* from the nations, and *called* to peculiar privileges. Thus at Ps. cv. 6. they are called ἐκλεκτοί. In the N. T., κλῆσις is often used to denote the *peculiar favour* first vouchsafed to the *Jews*. More frequently, however, both κλητοὶ and κλῆσις are used of that shewn to *Christians*. As to ἐκλεκτοὶ, it may be questioned whether it ever be (as some say) *synonymous* with κλητοὶ, at least in the N. T. The terms are properly *distinct*, and have reference to two different stages in the Christian course. Thus, in the present passage, and at xxii. 14. they are put in opposition; and in the former, by κλητοὶ are denoted those who have been *invited* into, and have *entered* into, the service of Christ; and by ἐκλ., those who have *approved* themselves therein. In the latter, κλ. means those who are *invited* to the blessings and privileges of the Gospel; and ἐκλ. those who, having *accepted* the invitation, *approve* themselves worthy of their high calling in Christ. It is true that in *both* these parables, by the κλητοὶ are especially designated the *Jews*, who were invited to the marriage feast of the Gospel, but who almost wholly rejected the invitation (see Luke xiv. 18.); by the ἐκλ., those of them who accepted it, and who are termed by St. Paul, Rom. xi. 6, 7. "the remnant κατ' ἐκλογήν." However, the saying admits of, and was doubtless intended for, a *general* application; by which κλ. will denote those who have *accepted* the invitation, and are professedly members of the Christian Church; ἐκλ., those who have *approved* themselves not unworthy of the blessing, and have not "received the grace of God in vain." Thus κλ. is often used in the Epistles of St. Paul and the other Apostles in this general sense; but *sometimes* merely as an appellation of Christianity. There seems to be a reference to this saying of our Lord, in its *general* application, at Rev. xvii. 14. οἱ μετ' αὐτοῦ κλητοὶ καὶ ἐκλεκτοὶ καὶ πιστοί; where the common punctuation leads to a very objectionable sense, and caused Hammond to suppose that *three different degrees* of Christians were meant: a notion wholly unsupported by Scripture. All will be right if the κλ. be construed with οἱ, and be referred to what preceded, καὶ τὸ Ἀρνίον νικήσει, and νικήσουσι be supplied from thence; the words ὅτι Κύριος—βασιλέων being taken as parenthetical. Thus the words may be rendered: "And the Lamb shall conquer them (for he is King of kings and Lord of lords), and the Saints who are with him, both approved and trusty." Thus κλ. will be, like ἅγιοι, a designation of true Christians, as in Rom. i. 6. and Jude 1. τοῖς ἐν Θεῷ κλητοῖς, and more fully in Rom. i. 7. κλητοῖς ἁγίοις. As to the πιστοὶ, it is in some measure exegetical of ἐκλ., equivalent to οἱ τετηρημένοι in Jude 1.

17. ἀναβαίνων εἰς Ἰ.] Said with reference to the elevated situation of Jerusalem. Thus similar expressions occur in Homer, as Od. α. 210., and frequently in Joseph. and the Sept. How ancient this custom was, we find from its mention in Ps. cxxii. 3 & 4.

—εἶπεν αὐτοῖς, &c.] By this we are, I think, to understand that Jesus spoke *out*, as we say, and positively; though, from the time when he made a distinct avowal of his Messiahship, at Peter's confession, he had, as we find from supra xvi. 22. *begun* to disclose.

18. κατακρινοῦσιν αὐτὸν θανάτῳ,] This is to be taken impropriè (for the Jews had no power of life and death), and is more definitely expressed by Mark xiv. 64. κατέκριναν αὐτὸν εἶναι ἔνοχον θανάτου: which words have reference to the sentence ἔνοχος θανάτου ἐστί. Fritz. says that the sense of κατακρίνειν τινὰ θανάτῳ is, "*to devote any one to death.*" But the expression rather signifies, by a blending of two senses, to condemn any one, *so that* he shall be delivered to death. By ἔθνεσι the *Romans* are plainly meant; for crucifixion was a *Roman* punishment. The minute particularity of this prediction is astonishing; and, as Doddr. observes, is a remarkable proof of the prophetic spirit with which Christ was endued; for, humanly speaking, it was far more probable that he should have been either *assassinated*, in a transport of popular fury, or *stoned*, by the orders of the Sanhedrim; especially as Pilate had given them permission to judge him according to their own law. But "all this was done that the Scripture might be fulfilled."

MK. LU.

δώσουσιν αὐτὸν τοῖς ἔθνεσιν εἰς τὸ ἐμπαῖξαι καὶ μαστιγῶσαι καὶ 10. 18.
σταυρῶσαι· καὶ τῇ τρίτῃ ἡμέρᾳ ἀναστήσεται. 34 33
20 Τότε προσῆλθεν αὐτῷ ἡ μήτηρ τῶν υἱῶν Ζεβεδαίου, μετὰ τῶν υἱῶν 35
21 αὐτῆς, προσκυνοῦσα καὶ αἰτοῦσά τι παρ' αὐτοῦ. Ὁ δὲ εἶπεν αὐτῇ· 36
Τί θέλεις; Λέγει αὐτῷ. Εἰπὲ ἵνα καθίσωσιν οὗτοι οἱ δύο υἱοί μου,
22 εἷς ἐκ δεξιῶν σου καὶ εἷς ἐξ εὐωνύμων σου, ἐν τῇ βασιλείᾳ σου. Ἀπο- 37 38
κριθεὶς δὲ ὁ Ἰησοῦς εἶπεν· Οὐκ οἴδατε τί αἰτεῖσθε. δύνασθε πιεῖν
τὸ ποτήριον, ὃ ἐγὼ μέλλω πίνειν, καὶ τὸ βάπτισμα, ὃ ἐγὼ βαπτίζομαι,
23 βαπτισθῆναι; λέγουσιν αὐτῷ· Δυνάμεθα. Καὶ λέγει αὐτοῖς· Τὸ 39
μὲν ποτήριόν μου πίεσθε, καὶ τὸ βάπτισμα, ὃ ἐγὼ βαπτίζομαι, βαπτι-
σθήσεσθε· τὸ δὲ καθίσαι ἐκ δεξιῶν μου καὶ ἐξ εὐωνύμων μου, οὐκ ἔστιν 40
24 ἐμὸν δοῦναι, ἀλλ' οἷς ἡτοίμασται ὑπὸ τοῦ Πατρός μου. Καὶ ἀκού- 41
25 σαντες οἱ δέκα, ἠγανάκτησαν περὶ τῶν δύο ἀδελφῶν. ὁ δὲ Ἰησοῦς 42

19. εἰς τὸ ἐμπαῖξαι] This, (as Grot. remarks) is to be taken ἐκβατικῶς: q. d. The consequence of which will be, that, &c. *Comp.* Joh. xviii. 33.

20. ἡ μήτηρ, &c.] Namely, Salome, mother of James and John, Mark v. 40. & xvi. 1. She had doubtless followed him from Galilee, with other pious women who attended on our Lord in his journeys. The request she made seems to have originated in the promise just before given to the Apostles of sitting on twelve thrones, &c.

— μετὰ τῶν υἱῶν α.] This shows that they participated in the petition; and, indeed, though they preferred it through the medium of their mother, yet it should seem that *they* were the principal movers of the affair. Thus Mark is justified in representing *them* as asking it. And indeed that Jesus *regarded* them as the principals, is clear from his addressing the answer to *them*.

— αἰτοῦσά τι παρ' αὐτοῦ] or, as it is more clearly stated by St. Mark, they said, θέλομεν, ἵνα ὃ ἐὰν αἰτήσωμεν, ποιήσῃς ἡμῖν.

21. εἷς ἐκ — ἐξ εὐωνύμων] Said in allusion to the Eastern custom, by which sitting next to the throne denotes the next degree of dignity; and consequently the first situations on the right and left denote the highest dignities. See 1 Kings ii. 19. Ps. xliv. 9. and the Classical Illustrators.

— σου.] This is added in almost all the best MSS., and Versions, and is, with reason, received by Wets., Matth., Griesb., Knapp, Tittm., Vat., Fritz., and Scholz.

22. οὐκ οἴδατε τί αἰτεῖσθε.] i. e. ye do not comprehend the nature of my kingdom; which will rather call you to suffer with me than to enjoy honour or temporal advantage under me. Rochefoucault well observes, "Nous desirerions peu de choses avec ardeur, si nous connaissions parfaitement ce que nous desirons."

— δύνασθε πιεῖν — πίνειν.] An image frequent with the Hebrews; who thus compared whatever was dealt out to men by the Almighty (whether good or evil) to a cup of wine. See John xviii. 11. Ps. xvi. 5. xxiii. 5. Nor was this confined to the Hebrews; for, as it was customary among the ancients in general to assign to each guest at a feast a particular *cup* as well as dish; and since by the quality and quantity of the liquor contained in it, the respect of the entertainer was expressed; hence *cup* came in general to signify a *portion assigned*, whether of pleasure or sorrow (as Hom. Il. ω. 524, where see Heyne); though, for an obvious reason, the expression was more frequently used of *evil* than of *good*.

— καὶ τὸ βάπτισμα — βαπτισθῆναι;] This metaphor, of immersion in water, as expressive of being overwhelmed by affliction, is frequent both in the Scriptural and Classical writers; with this difference, however, that in the latter there is usually added some word expressive of the evil or affliction. The words καὶ τὸ βάπτισμα — βαπτισθῆναι and καὶ τὸ βάπτισμα — βαπτισθήσεσθε are not found in some MSS., Versions, and Fathers; and are rejected by Grot. and Mill, and are cancelled by Griesb. and Fritz. But the external evidence against the words is very slender. And therefore, though the internal be very unfavourable to them (because it is far more probable that they should have been introduced from Mark, than accidentally omitted in the MSS.), yet they ought not to be cancelled.

23. οὐκ ἔστιν ἐμὸν] Sub. ἔργον, which is sometimes *supplied*. See Bos Ell. p. 95. So the Latin *non est meum*.

— ἀλλ' οἷς ἡτοίμασται] The early Commentators and Translators (misled by some of the antient Versions) here supposed an ellipsis of δοθήσεται, which would afford some colour to the Arian and Socinian doctrines; since, as Whitby and Campb. observe, "in the distribution of future rewards, Christ might seem to acknowledge his inferiority to the Father, inasmuch as there would be some power reserved by the Father to himself, and not committed to the Son." Others of the ancients supposed an ellipsis of ἐκείνων ἐστὶν, interpreting the clause οὐκ ἐμὸν δοῦναι, not with relation to our Lord's *power*, but with respect to his *justice* and *equity*; or referring the phrase only to his *human* nature. Others again understand, from the context, ὑμῖν, which even crept into the text of the Vulgate. And thus, indeed, all difficulty is removed; but in a manner little warrantable. In fact, all these ellipses are very irregular and inadmissible. It is better to suppose no ellipsis at all; but only to take ἀλλὰ in the somewhat unusual sense of εἰ μὴ, as in Mark ix. 8. (where ἀλλὰ corresponds to εἰ μὴ in Matt. xvii. 8.) Examples from the *Classical* writers are by no means rare. (See Rec. Synop.) The *converse*, εἰ μὴ for ἀλλὰ, is frequent, and occurs in Rom. xiv. 14. This mode of interpretation is supported by the an-

MK.
10. προσκαλεσάμενος αὐτοὺς εἶπεν· Οἴδατε, ὅτι οἱ ἄρχοντες τῶν ἐθνῶν
43 κατακυριεύουσιν αὐτῶν, καὶ οἱ μεγάλοι κατεξουσιάζουσιν αὐτῶν. Οὐχ 26
οὕτως [δὲ] ἔσται ἐν ὑμῖν· ἀλλ' ὃς ἐὰν θέλῃ ἐν ὑμῖν μέγας γενέσθαι,
44 ἔστω ὑμῶν διάκονος· καὶ ὃς ἐὰν θέλῃ ἐν ὑμῖν εἶναι πρῶτος, ἔστω ὑμῶν 27
45 δοῦλος· ὥσπερ ὁ Υἱὸς τοῦ ἀνθρώπου οὐκ ἦλθε διακονηθῆναι, ἀλλὰ 28
διακονῆσαι, καὶ δοῦναι τὴν ψυχὴν αὐτοῦ λύτρον ἀντὶ πολλῶν.

thority of the Pesh. Syr., Arabic, Persic, and Æthiopic Versions; and, of Commentators, is adopted by Casaub., Grot., Gatak., Gusset, Hackspan, Koecher, Starck, Raphel, Palairet, Bengel, Rosenm., and Kuin. Indeed, it may be observed, the Sept. sometimes render the Heb. כי אם by ἀλλά. Thus our *but*, in this use, has the very same origin, being derived (as Horne Tooke shows) from the Saxon Be-utan, from Beonutan, to *be out*; as when we say "all *but* (i. e. except) one." Thus ἀλλὰ has the two senses of our *but*, indicated in H. Tooke's Div. of P. I. p. 135. 190. 325. seqq. *How* ἀλλὰ comes to have this sense, seems to be from its being thus put for ἀλλ' ἤ, *otherwise than*. Thus all difficulty, both as regards words and things, is entirely removed; for, as observes Whitby, "the expression argues no defect in the *power* of Christ, but merely a perfect conformity to the will of his Father." "Our Lord (says Bp. Horsley, Serm. V. v. p. 281.) does not deny his power to give, but only declares who they are who shall receive this honour. His answer, far from intimating any thing of that kind, concludes as strongly *against* it as a negative argument can be supposed to do. Thus the meaning is, 'I cannot arbitrarily give happiness, but must bestow it on those alone for whom, in reward of holiness and obedience, it is prepared, according to God's just decrees.'"

25. οἱ ἄρχοντες — αὐτῶν,] Erasm., Grot., Wets., Rosenm., and Fritz. take the κατακ. and κατεξ. to denote *tyrannical and arbitrary power*, of course hinting a *censure* thereon; in which sense the words do occur in the Sept. But as it is scarcely to be supposed that the governors in question were always tyrants; and as the *simple* verbs are used in Luke, it is better, with many good Commentators, to suppose the sense to be, "exercise authority over." Thus the κατὰ is not so much *intensive*, as it promotes definiteness. The Commentators thus adverted to, with even *less* reason, suppose the first αὐτῶν to refer to the *people*, the second to the *kings*; which is harsh, and inconsistent with the parallel passage in Luke. There is, in fact, a repetition of the same sentiment in different words (as also at ver. 27.) for greater emphasis. See Bp. Jebb's Sacr. Lit. p. 288 seqq.

26. δέ.] This is omitted in many MSS., some Versions, and Theophyl., and was cancelled by Griesb., Knapp, Tittm., Vat., and Scholz; but restored by Fritz.; and rightly; for, it is supported not only by high authority here and in Mark, but is so suitable to the passage, that it can hardly be dispensed with. The cause of the omission (which was accidental) seems to have been this: that after it had been originally written ΟΥΤΩΔΕ in MS., without stops, the Δ was taken with Ω, and mistaken, as not unfrequently, for an N, and then the E would be absorbed by the E following.

— διάκονος — δοῦλος.] There is properly a difference between these terms; the former signifying a *servant* like our *footman*, or *valet*, and usually a free man; the latter, a servant for all work, and also a *slave*. They were, however, sometimes interchanged. So Aristid. Vol. iii. 360. — οὕτω φαῦλος ἦν τοὺς τρόπους, καὶ αὐτόχρημα διάκονος. The use *here*, and the general sense are plain.

28. δοῦναι — ἀντὶ πολλῶν.] In order to determine the sense of this passage (so important in its connection with the distinguishing doctrine of the Gospel, the ATONEMENT), it is proper carefully to attend to its *scope*, and then to ascertain the force of its principal *terms* λύτρον, ἀντὶ, and πολλῶν. The scope of the passage evidently is, to point out the *purpose* of Christ's coming into the world. It was δοῦναι — πολλῶν. On the sense of ψυχὴ here there has never been any doubt. — It plainly signifies (as often in the Scriptures, and even the Classical writers) *life*. He came to give up his life as a λύτρον. Now λύτρον properly denotes the *ransom* paid, in order to deliver any one from *death*, or its equivalent, *captivity*, or *punishment* in general. Thus in Exod. xxi. 30. the word answers to כֹּפֶר. More frequently it denotes the *piacular victim*, כֹּפֶר, sometimes expressed by ἐξίλασμα; which Hesych. explains ἀντίλυτρον. It has been abundantly proved that, among both the Jews and the Gentiles, *piacular victims* were accepted as a ransom for the life of an offender, and to atone for his offence. The heathens believed that no atonement was so complete or effectual as that whereby the piacular victim should be a *human* being; whose life was thus given ἀντὶ *instead* of the life of the other. Hence such victims were called ἀντίψυχοι, and the atonement made by them an ἀντίλυτρον. And Aristides, Sacr. v. has an oracular response, where, with allusion to this, there is demanded ψυχὴ ἀντὶ ψυχῆς. So also Eurip. Phœn. 1012. — ψυχὴν δὲ δώσω τήνδ' ὑπερθανεῖν χθονός. Indeed, on the further notion, that the life of one person was, in some cases, to be given and accepted for the life of another, the whole of the Alcestis of Euripides is founded. The *true* notion, indeed, of atonement was unknown to the Heathens; though they felt the necessity for it. See Horne's Introd. Vol. i. 8. & 146, 147. The very term ἀντὶ, it may also be observed, is the strongest that can be imagined; it being derived from the ancient word ἄνς, which signifies change. The ἀντὶ is for ἐν ἀντὶ, *in mutatione*, per mutationem.

The sense, then, of this passage, can be no other than that which has been assigned to it by every Interpreter of any consideration in every age, (including, of the recent foreign Commentators, Kuinoel and Fritz.) namely, that our Lord was to give up his life as a piacular victim, a ransom for mankind, that they might not suffer spiritual death. And thus it harmonizes with the doctrine of Scripture elsewhere. So in Dan. ix. 24. it is predicted, that the Messiah shall make reconciliation for iniquity; whence he is called by the Jewish Rabbins איש כפר, literally ἀνὴρ

MK. LU.

29 *Καὶ ἐκπορευομένων αὐτῶν ἀπὸ Ἱεριχὼ, ἠκολούθησεν αὐτῷ ὄχλος* 10. 18.
30 *πολύς. Καὶ ἰδοὺ, δύο τυφλοὶ καθήμενοι παρὰ τὴν ὁδὸν, ἀκούσαντες* 46 35 36
31 *ὅτι Ἰησοῦς παραγει, ἔκραξαν λέγοντες· Ἐλέησον ἡμᾶς, Κύριε, υἱὸς* 47 48 37 38
Δαυΐδ! Ὁ δὲ ὄχλος ἐπετίμησεν αὐτοῖς, ἵνα σιωπήσωσιν· οἱ δὲ μεῖζον 39
32 *ἔκραζον, λέγοντες· Ἐλέησον ἡμᾶς, Κύριε υἱὸς Δαυΐδ. Καὶ στὰς* 49 40
33 *ὁ Ἰησοῦς ἐφώνησεν αὐτοὺς καὶ εἶπε· Τί θέλετε ποιήσω ὑμῖν; Λέ-* 51 41
34 *γουσιν αὐτῷ· Κύριε, ἵνα ἀνοιχθῶσιν ἡμῶν οἱ ὀφθαλμοί. σπλαγ-* 52 42
χνισθεὶς δὲ ὁ Ἰησοῦς ἥψατο τῶν ὀφθαλμῶν αὐτῶν· καὶ εὐθέως ἀνέ- 43
βλεψαν αὐτῶν οἱ ὀφθαλμοὶ, καὶ ἠκολούθησαν αὐτῷ.

λύτρον. Comp. Matt. xxvi. 28. John xi. 52. Eph. v. 2. 1 Tim. ii. 6. Heb. ix. 14 & 28. (and the Notes on those passages,) all declaring the same doctrine, that Christ's death was a sacrifice for the sins of mankind; even that true and substantial sacrifice, which those of the law but faintly shadowed forth in types, symbols and figures.

I cannot, however, leave this passage without removing a stumbling-block, which has been found here by serious, but misjudging or timid believers, who have been too ready to conclude that from πολλῶν it may be implied that redemption is not *universal*. But utterly without reason; for the best Expositors, ancient and modern, are agreed, that πολλῶν is here to be taken for πάντων; of which they adduce many examples.—And although not a few of them are inapposite, yet some others fully establish the point; ex. gr. Comp. Dan. xii. 2. with John v. 28. sq. and Rom. v. 12. 15. 18 & 19. with 1 Cor. xv. 22. not to mention *some* examples in the Classical writers. Yet, even in these instances, it may be doubted whether πολλοὶ can ever be said to be, strictly speaking, *put for* πάντες. It should seem that, in such cases, an idiom subsists, which has been, I apprehend, unperceived by Philologists; where there is, by an apposition, either *expressed* or *implied*, a comparison of πολλοὶ with some other *very* small number (usually *one*), which remains after deducting it from a *total*. In such a case, πολλοὶ may be said to be *equivalent* to πάντες; being, *in a manner*, the whole of the number in question; though it cannot strictly be said to *signify* that; the literal sense being the remainder of a large number, after a very small one has been subtracted. This principle will apply to all the passages alleged in proof that πολλοὶ is used for πάντες. I mean to all that are *justly* alleged; for Matt. xx. 16. has quite another bearing (see the note there); and in places like 1 Cor. x. 33. where the ARTICLE is used, the principle cannot be admitted. There the meaning is, either "the *majority*," or "the *rest*." And such is the case in almost all the passages adduced from the Classical writers; where the sense is, "very many," or "ever so many." The Commentators might also have cited a passage of Thucyd. i. 133. where τοῖς πολλοῖς, as appears from a comparison with 134. § 5. must mean [all] the rest. So also at i. 38. we have τοῖς πλέοσιν (for πολλοῖς) opposed to τοῖσδε μόνοις. As examples of the *tacit* comparison above adverted to, I would specify Rom. viii. 29. εἰς τὸ εἶναι αὐτὸν πρωτότοκον ἐν πολλοῖς ἀδελφοῖς, (where the εἷς is implied in πρωτ.) Matt. xxvi. 28. and Mark xiv. 24. τοῦτο γάρ ἐστι τὸ αἷμά μ ο υ, τό τῆς καινῆς διαθήκης, τὸ περὶ πολλῶν ἐκχυνόμενον εἰς ἄφεσιν ἁμαρτιῶν. (where τὸ περὶ πολλῶν is for τὸ ἑνὸς περὶ πολλῶν, with allusion to the μου just before) Heb. ix. 28. οὕτως ὁ Χριστὸς ἅπαξ προσενεχθεὶς εἰς τὸ πολλῶν ἀνενεγκεῖν ἁμαρτίας, &c. The same principle will also apply to *some* passages where the Article *is found*, namely, where it does not exert its definite force. So Rom. xii. 5. οὕτως οἱ πολλοὶ, ἓν σῶμά ἐσμεν ἐν Χριστῷ. And in Rom. v. 15. 18 & 19. the Article is used both to εἷς and πολλοί. the Articles there coming under the head of "*Insertions in reference* (See Middl. in loc.), and *renewed mention*;" the reference being to v. 12. where ὥσπερ δι' ἑνὸς ἀνθρώπου is opposed to εἰς π ά ν τ α ς ἀνθρώπους. Upon the whole, in such a case we may most correctly render "*all the rest*." And this may be done in the only two Classical passages *not* having the Article that are here apposite, namely, Eurip. Hec. 284. Ἥδ' ἀντὶ πολλῶν ἐστί μοι παραψυχή, and Virgil Æn. v. 815. UNUM PRO MULTIS DABITUR CAPUT.

30. δύο τυφλοὶ, &c.] There is a considerable variation in the accounts of this miracle by the three Evangelists. *Mark* and *Luke* notice only one blind man, *Matthew* two; *Luke* represents the miracle as performed "when Jesus was drawing nigh to Jericho," before he entered it; *Matthew* and *Mark*, after he had left Jericho. The joint testimony, however, of Matthew and *Mark*, as to the time, seems to outweigh that of Luke, who is not so observant of chronological order; and as all agree, that Christ was then attended by a "*multitude*," who "*led the way*," and who "*followed him*" towards *Jerusalem*, it is more probable that the incident took place after he left Jericho, where this multitude seems to have been collected. For He came privately from Ephraim to Jericho, attended only by the twelve. (Hales.) The minute discrepancies in this narrative, compared with those of Mark and Luke, involve no contradiction; since, though those Evangelists mention *one* blind man as healed, yet they do not say that *only* one was healed; and Mark and Luke in mentioning one, might mean to point out that one who was the more known. Again, the apparent difference between Matthew and Mark, as compared with Luke, with regard to the *place* where the miracle was performed, may, it is thought, be removed by reading in Luke "when, or while, Jesus was near Jericho." If, however, the trifling discrepancies adverted to were really irreconcileable, still they would not weaken the credit of the Evangelists, being such as are found in the best historians; nay, they may be rather thought to strengthen their authority as independent witnesses.

31. ἐπετίμησεν, ἵνα.] Campb. translates "charged them, that," &c. But though that be sometimes the signification of the term at Matt. xii. 16. yet it is here unnecessary to deviate from the import,

MK. LU.
11. 19. XXI. Καὶ ὅτε ἤγγισαν εἰς Ἱεροσόλυμα, καὶ ἦλθον εἰς Βηθφαγῆ 1
1 20 πρὸς τὸ ὄρος τῶν ἐλαιῶν, τότε ὁ Ἰησοῦς ἀπέστειλε δύο μαθητάς, λέ-
2 30 γων αὐτοῖς· Πορεύθητε εἰς τὴν κώμην τὴν ἀπέναντι ὑμῶν· καὶ εὐ- 2
θέως εὑρήσετε ὄνον δεδεμένην, καὶ πῶλον μετ᾽ αὐτῆς· λύσαντες ἀγά-
3 31 γετέ μοι. Καὶ ἐάν τις ὑμῖν εἴπῃ τι, ἐρεῖτε· Ὅτι ὁ κύριος αὐτῶν 3
χρείαν ἔχει· εὐθέως δὲ ‡ ἀποστελεῖ αὐτούς. Τοῦτο δὲ ὅλον γέγονεν, 4
ἵνα πληρωθῇ τὸ ῥηθὲν διὰ τοῦ προφήτου λέγοντος· Εἴπατε τῇ 5
θυγατρὶ Σιών· Ἰδού, ὁ βασιλεύς σου ἔρχεταί σοι
πραΰς, καὶ ἐπιβεβηκὼς ἐπὶ ὄνον, καὶ πῶλον υἱὸν

"*rebuke*," which is indeed more suitable. The most probable reason assigned for the rebuke is, that they were unwilling that Jesus's course should be interrupted, or his discourse broken off, or rendered inaudible. Thus it should seem that the people only blamed the importunity, as being unseasonable; as in a kindred passage at xii. 16. ἐπετίμησεν αὐτοῖς, ἵνα μή, &c.

XXI. 1. εἰς Βηθφαγῆ.] Mark xi. 1. and Luke xix. 29. add καὶ Βηθανίαν. We may therefore suppose that the territories of the two villages were contiguous; yet that Bethphage came *first* in travelling from Jericho to Jerusalem. Hence Calmet and others are wrong in describing Bethphage as being a village *between* Bethany and Jerusalem. So Epiphan. adv. Hæres. p. 340. cited by Reland Palæst. 629. testifies that there was an old road to Jerusalem from Jericho through Bethphage and Bethany, and the Mount of Olives. Nay, Calmet himself describes Bethany as situated at the foot of the Mount of Olives (and so all accounts represent it—see Reland); but from the words πρὸς τὸ ὄρος τ. ἐλ. being here conjoined with Βηθφ., it is probable that Bethphage was situated on some part of the lower ridge, or ἀκρώρεια, of the mountain, and Bethany just below it, at the *foot* of it: and, consequently, it could not be between Bethany and Jerusalem. This is supported by the testimony of Jerome and Origen, the former of whom describes Bethphage as "sacerdotum viculus, situs in monte Oliveti." And the latter, in his Annot. on Matt., says it was situated on Mount Olivet.

2. πῶλον] "a colt." Mark and Luke add, "on which no man had ever sat." Animals which had never borne the yoke, or been employed for ordinary purposes, were (by a custom common to all the ancients, whether Jews or Gentiles) employed for sacred uses. See Deut. xxi. 3. 1 Sam. vi. 7. Horat. Epod. 9. 22. Ovid. Met. 3. 11. Virg. Georg. 4. 540. 551. Mark and Luke mention the sending for the *colt* only, as being that whereon alone our Lord *rode*; not mentioning the *ass*, though *also* brought (agreeable to the prophecy of Zecharias), because they do not mention that prophecy. There is plainly in the latter representation no negation of the former. Whitby notices the minuteness of the matters predicted, and rightly infers from thence Christ's supernatural prescience.

3. εἴπῃ τι.] A *popular* mode of expression equivalent to, "if he shall make objection."

— ὁ κύριος] i. e. not "the Lord," which involves great improbability, but "the master," Rabbi, as at vii. 21. and viii. 25. John xi. 12. xiii. 13 & 14. See Doddr., Campb., and Schleusn.

— ἀποστελεῖ.] Many MSS., Versions, and Fathers, have ἀποστέλλει, which is preferred by Mill and Wets., and edited by Matth., Griesb., Knapp, Tittm., and Scholz, but without reason. In so minute a variation *manuscript* authority is of little weight; and yet there is far more of it for the old reading than for the new one; which cannot be admitted without violating the norma loquendi; for the Present cannot (as Kuin. imagines) be *here* taken for the Future. The common reading is rightly defended by Schulz. (who observes that the new reading arose from an error of pronunciation) and restored to the text by Fritz.

4. ὅλον.] This is suspected not to be genuine by Griesb. and Grotz., and is cancelled by Lachm.; but wholly without cause, for external evidence is *almost entirely* in favour of the word, and internal nearly as much so, since it is almost necessary to the sense *(tota hæc res)*, and was more likely to have been omitted, by accident, in three or four MSS., than have been foisted into the text of nearly as many hundreds. Besides, the word occurs without any var. lect. in passages exactly similar, supr. i. 22. xxvi. 56.

5. τῇ θυγατρὶ Σιών] i. e. *Jerusalem*, by a poetical personification usual in the prophetical writings. Jerusalem might be called the daughter of Sion, being situated at the foot, and, as it were, under the wing of that fortified mount. The quotation is from Zech. ix. 9. (with the exception of the introductory words, which are from Is. lxii. 11.), and agrees, at least all that is meant to be taken (for a short clause is omitted, as being not to the present purpose), with both the Sept. and the Hebrew. For עָנִי, the true reading, is thought by Dr. Randolph to be ענו. But there is no occasion for any such change; since עָנִי may mean *lowly*, and is so interpreted by Gesenius in his Lexicon. There is, indeed, a variation in the last words between Matthew and the Sept. But there is some reason to think, that formerly the Sept. was read nearly as in Matthew. At least the Evangelist's text closely agrees with the Hebrew.

— ὄνον καὶ πῶλον.] Several eminent Commentators would render the καὶ *even*. But this is doing violence to the plain sense expressed, and would really destroy the *coincidence* as to fulfilment of prophecy. Certainly there is no necessity for it in order to reconcile the Evangelists; for St. Matthew does not say that our Lord *rode* on the ass, but only that it was *prepared* for him. Neither will it follow from our Lord's saying, "thus was fulfilled." For the prophecy was sufficiently fulfilled by the ass and colt being both *got ready*. Not to say, that even the words of the *Prophet* are not inconsistent with this view; for any one who goes on horseback, accompanied by a *led* horse (to use when he pleases),

MK. LU.
6 ὑποζυγίου. Πορευθέντες δὲ οἱ μαθηταὶ, καὶ ποιήσαντες καθὼς 11. 19.
7 προσέταξεν αὐτοῖς ὁ Ἰησοῦς, ἤγαγον τὴν ὄνον καὶ τὸν πῶλον, καὶ 4 7 32 35
ἐπέθηκαν ἐπάνω αὐτῶν τὰ ἱμάτια αὐτῶν, καὶ ‡ ἐπεκάθισεν ἐπάνω
8 αὐτῶν. Ὁ δὲ πλεῖστος ὄχλος ἔστρωσαν ἑαυτῶν τὰ ἱμάτια ἐν τῇ ὁδῷ· 8 36
ἄλλοι δὲ ἔκοπτον κλάδους ἀπὸ τῶν δένδρων, καὶ ἐστρώννυον ἐν τῇ
9 ὁδῷ. Οἱ δὲ ὄχλοι οἱ προάγοντες καὶ οἱ ἀκολουθοῦντες ἔκραζον λέ- 9 37
γοντες· Ὡσαννὰ τῷ υἱῷ Δαυΐδ! εὐλογημένος ὁ ἐρχόμενος ἐν 10 38
ὀνόματι Κυρίου! Ὡσαννὰ ἐν τοῖς ὑψίστοις!
10 Καὶ εἰσελθόντος αὐτοῦ εἰς Ἱεροσόλυμα, ἐσείσθη πᾶσα ἡ πόλις,
11 λέγουσα· Τίς ἐστιν οὗτος; Οἱ δὲ ὄχλοι ἔλεγον· Οὗτός ἐστιν Ἰησοῦς
ὁ προφήτης, ὁ ἀπὸ Ναζαρὲτ τῆς Γαλιλαίας.
12 Καὶ εἰσῆλθεν ὁ Ἰησοῦς εἰς τὸ ἱερὸν τοῦ Θεοῦ, καὶ ἐξέβαλε πάντας τοὺς 15 45
πωλοῦντας καὶ ἀγοράζοντας ἐν τῷ ἱερῷ, καὶ τὰς τραπέζας τῶν κολλυβιστῶν

may be, not improperly, described as ἐπιβεβηκὼς, with respect to *both*, and thus be said to ride both, like the ἀμφιπποι, or *desultores*, mentioned in several ancient writers, a sort of cavalry, where every man had two horses, which he rode in rotation (the ἀμφι in this term being for ἀμφοτερῶθεν); on which subject see my Note on Thucyd. x. 57.

— ὑποζυγίου.] Scil. κτήνους. The word properly signifies any *beast of burden*. (See my note on Thucyd. ii. 3.) But as the ass was commonly so used, it came of itself to denote an ass.

7. ἐπεκάθισεν.] The reading here is not a little controverted. Ἐπεκάθισεν is the reading of all the early Edd.; which was altered by the Elzevir Editor, from several MSS. to ἐπεκάθισαν. But ἐπεκάθισαν has been restored by Wets., Matth., Knapp, Griesb., Tittm., Fritz., and Scholz. Ἐπεκάθισαν, moreover, is supported by St. Luke's ἐπεβίβασαν. It is also preferred by several Commentators, as Beza, Camerar., Pisc., Wakef., and Schleus.; and if we were to follow the *proprietas linguæ*, it ought to be adopted. Yet as the verb is often in the Sept. used in the sense "*to sit*," or "*ride*," so the reading ἐπεκάθισεν seems to deserve the preference, especially as it is supported by the parallel passage of Mark. If ἐπεκάθισαν be read, αὐτῶν will, if understood of the ass and the colt, be unsuitable; and if of the *garments*, it will be very jejune. We might indeed, conjecture αὐτὸν, supposing ἐπάνω to be taken absolutely for thereon. This will be confirmed by the parallel passage of St. Luke, and not be at variance with that of St. Mark. But the mention of the ass and colt at v. 2. and 7. greatly supports the reading αὐτῶν. The people would put the trappings on both the ass and the colt, to do the more honour to Jesus; and as not knowing on which he would ride. On the *ellip.* of αὐτὸν, see Winer's Gr. Gr. § 16. 1. Thus, though there is a minute diversity in Matthew and Mark, as compared with Luke, yet it is no real discrepancy, since it does not involve any contradiction. Matthew (as is observed by the British Crit. and Quart. Theol. II. 371) tells us, *all* that happened, because he saw and knew all: Mark and Luke received the facts at second-hand, and mentioned only the material fact. As to the αὐτῶν, it must not, with many Commentators, be taken, per enallagen, as plural for singular; or τινὸς be supplied, with others; but, with Euthym., Theophyl., Beza, Hombergh, Schleus., Wahl., and Fritz., must be referred to the *garments*, not the ass and colt.

8. ὁ πλεῖστος ὄχλος] "the bulk of the people," consisting of those going to keep the passover, and of those who, after Lazarus's resurrection, had come out of the city to meet Christ. See John xii. 9.

— ἔστρωσαν ἑαυτῶν τὰ ἱμάτια.] An Oriental custom employed on the public entry of kings, yet in use among the Greeks also. See examples in Recens. Synop. and Horne's Introd. iii. 397.

— ἔκοπτον κλάδους.] Meant as a symbol of joy, employed at the feast of tabernacles and other public rejoicings among the Jews. Yet the custom was in use also among the Greeks and Romans.

9. Ὡσαννὰ] Heb. הוֹשִׁיעָה נָּא, *Save us now*, or *we beseech thee!* from Ps. cxvii. 25.

— ὁ ἐρχόμενος.] A title of the Messiah, as also υἱοῦ Δαυΐδ.

— Ὡσαννὰ ἐν τοῖς ὑψίστοις!] *Comp.* Psal. cxviii. 24. and see Horne's Introd. iii. 316. Kuin. thinks there is an ellipse of ὁ ὢν; and Grot. takes the ἐν τοῖς ὑψίστοις adverbially, for *summè*. But it is better, with others, to supply μέρεσι, taking it as a periphrasis for ἐν οὐρανοῖς. Thus in Heb. i. 3. and viii. 1. ἐν ὑψηλοῖς, is interchanged with ἐν οὐρανοῖς. As to the ellipse after Ὡσαννὰ, it is rather ἔστω; Ὡσαννὰ being regarded as a noun. Thus Fritz. well renders, "eadem lætantium gratulatio *in cælo* obtineat."

10. ἐσείσθη] "was in commotion," agitated with hope, fear, wonder, or disapprobation, according as each person was affected.

11. ὁ προφήτης.] The force of the Article is, the [celebrated] prophet.

12. τὸ ἱερόν.] A general name for the whole edifice, with all its courts: as distinguished from the ναὸς, or temple properly so called; which comprehended only the vestibule, the sanctuary, and the holy of holies. See Horne's Introd. iii. 236. sqq.

— ἐξέβαλε — ἱερῷ.] It appears from Mark xi 11. that Jesus did not do this *on the day of his entry* into Jerusalem, (though it is there said that he entered into the temple, and looked round the whole of it,) but the *day after*; spending the night at Bethany, and returning to Jerusalem in the morning; and in the way thither working the miracle of the fig-tree. As Mark is so positive and particular in his account, and as Matth. does

MK. LU.
11. 19. κατέστρεψε, καὶ τὰς καθέδρας τῶν πωλούντων τὰς περιστεράς· καὶ λέγει 13
17 46 αὐτοῖς· Γέγραπται, Ὁ οἶκός μου οἶκος προσευχῆς κληθή-
σεται· ὑμεῖς δὲ αὐτὸν ἐποιήσατε σπήλαιον λῃστῶν. Καὶ προσῆλθον αὐ- 14
τῷ τυφλοὶ καὶ χωλοὶ ἐν τῷ ἱερῷ· καὶ ἐθεράπευσεν αὐτούς. Ἰδόντες δὲ 15
οἱ ἀρχιερεῖς καὶ οἱ γραμματεῖς τὰ θαυμάσια ἃ ἐποίησε, καὶ τοὺς παῖδας
κράζοντας ἐν τῷ ἱερῷ καὶ λέγοντας· Ὡσαννὰ τῷ υἱῷ Δαυΐδ! ἠγανάκτησαν, καὶ εἶπον αὐτῷ· Ἀκούεις τί οὗτοι λέγουσιν; Ὁ δὲ Ἰησοῦς λέγει αὐ- 16
τοῖς· Ναί. οὐδέποτε ἀνέγνωτε, Ὅτι ἐκ στόματος νηπίων καὶ
12 θηλαζόντων κατηρτίσω αἶνον; Καὶ καταλιπὼν αὐτοὺς, 17
ἐξῆλθεν ἔξω τῆς πόλεως εἰς Βηθανίαν, καὶ ηὐλίσθη ἐκεῖ.

Πρωΐας δὲ ἐπανάγων εἰς τὴν πόλιν, ἐπείνασε· καὶ ἰδὼν συκῆν 18
13
14 μίαν ἐπὶ τῆς ὁδοῦ, ἦλθεν ἐπ' αὐτὴν, καὶ οὐδὲν εὗρεν ἐν αὐτῇ, εἰ 19
μὴ φύλλα μόνον· καὶ λέγει αὐτῇ· Μηκέτι ἐκ σοῦ καρπὸς γένηται
21 εἰς τὸν αἰῶνα. καὶ ἐξηράνθη παραχρῆμα ἡ συκῆ. Καὶ ἰδόντες οἱ 20
22 μαθηταὶ ἐθαύμασαν, λέγοντες· Πῶς παραχρῆμα ἐξηράνθη ἡ συκῆ!
23 Ἀποκριθεὶς δὲ ὁ Ἰησοῦς εἶπεν αὐτοῖς· Ἀμὴν λέγω ὑμῖν· ἐὰν ἔχητε 21
πίστιν καὶ μὴ διακριθῆτε, οὐ μόνον τὸ τῆς συκῆς ποιήσετε, ἀλλὰ κἂν

not *expressly* connect our Lord's driving out the traders with the events of the day, we ought, it should seem, to adopt Mark's account. To do which, there cannot be a greater inducement than the consideration, that those who adopt the other hypothesis are compelled to suppose that the circumstances in question happened *twice* on *two successive* days. Nay, *thrice;* for our Lord had done much the same thing in the first year of his ministry (John ii. 14.) The reason why he did not *then* do it, is suggested by the words of Mark, ὀψίας δὲ γενομένης, i. e. because, it being evening, the buyers and sellers had most of them retired. That it should then be *evening*, was likely enough, considering the events of the day, which must have occupied a considerable time.

— κολλυβιστῶν] from κόλλυβος, a petty coin, signifies those who exchanged foreign coin into Jewish, or the larger into the smaller coin, for the convenience of the purchasers of the commodities sold in the temple. See Horne's Intr. iii. 184.

13. γέγραπται, &c.] This quotation is from Isa. lvi. 7. where it exactly agrees with the Sept. and Hebrew. In the latter clause of the sentence there is not, as the Commentators suppose, a quotation, but only the saying is formed on a similar one at Jerem. vii. 11. Μὴ σπήλαιον λῃστῶν ὁ οἶκός μου; where there is an allusion to the custom (common to all countries) for robbers to make their abode in caves.

— λῃστῶν.] Perhaps, not literally thieves, but extortioners and cheats, at least persons devoted to base lucre. An interpretation which seems required by the expression of John οἶκος ἐμπορίου. Though our Lord's assertion might be justified in its full sense by what is found in Joseph. B. J. v. 9, 4.

16. ἐκ στόματος — αἶνον;] an application to the present case of a passage of Ps. viii. 2. Sept. (which speaks of the existence and providence of God, as so clearly appearing from the works of nature, that even the most simple must see) where the Hebrew is rendered "thou hast ordained strength;" the Sept. "thou hast perfected praise," i. e. accomplished a grand effect by weak means; for the divine praise is perfected even by the silence of the suckling, and the artless cry of the babe. Thus there is no real discrepancy in sentiment, though there be a diversity in expression, between the Heb. and the Sept. That the whole Psalm has a prophetic reference to the Messiah, is plain by there being three other passages in the N. T. where it is applied to him. 1. Cor. xv. 27. Eph. i. 22. Heb. ii. 6.

17. ηὐλίσθη ἐκεῖ] "*lodged* or *spent the night there.*" A sense found in 3 Esdr. ix. 2. Eccl. xxiv. 7. Jesus left the city, and returned to Bethany for the night; not so much, we may suppose, to avoid the snares that might be laid for his life, as to avoid all suspicion of affecting temporal power; the night being a season favourable for popular commotion. See Thucyd. ii. 3. 4. φυλάξαντες νύκτα, where see my note.

18. πρωΐας δὲ ἐπανάγων, &c.] On the chronology of the Passion Week, the reader is referred to Townson, Hales, Townsend, and Greswell.

19. μήκετι — αἰῶνα.] This was emblematical and figurative; according to the usual custom of the sages of the East to express things by symbolical actions. It was also prophetic. Our Lord intended to prove that his power to punish the disobedient was as great as that to confer benefits. It was, moreover, to prefigure the destruction of the perverse Jews, because in the *time of fruits* they had borne none (see ver. 33—41.); and, likewise, to read a very important lesson to all his disciples of every age, — that if the opportunities God gives for the approving themselves virtuous be neglected, nought will remain but to be withered by the fiat which shall consign them to everlasting destruction.

21. καὶ μὴ διακριθῆτε,] Kuin. observes that this negative expression is the very same with the positive one ἐὰν ἔχητε πίστιν, the two being united for the sake of emphasis, as at xiii. 34. and elsewhere. In διακρ. in this sense (to hesitate) there

MK. LU.
τῷ ὄρει τούτῳ εἴπητε· Ἄρθητι καὶ βλήθητι εἰς τὴν θάλασσαν, γε- 11. 20.
22 νήσεται. Καὶ πάντα ὅσα ἂν αἰτήσητε ἐν τῇ προσευχῇ, πιστεύοντες, 24
λήψεσθε.
23 Καὶ ἐλθόντι αὐτῷ εἰς τὸ ἱερὸν, προσῆλθον αὐτῷ διδάσκοντι οἱ ἀρ- 27 1
χιερεῖς καὶ οἱ πρεσβύτεροι τοῦ λαοῦ, λέγοντες· Ἐν ποίᾳ ἐξουσίᾳ ταῦ- 28 2
24 τα ποιεῖς; καὶ τίς σοι ἔδωκε τὴν ἐξουσίαν ταύτην; Ἀποκριθεὶς δὲ 29 3
ὁ Ἰησοῦς εἶπεν αὐτοῖς· Ἐρωτήσω ὑμᾶς κἀγὼ λόγον ἕνα· ὃν ἐὰν
25 εἴπητέ μοι, κἀγὼ ὑμῖν ἐρῶ ἐν ποίᾳ ἐξουσίᾳ ταῦτα ποιῶ. Τὸ βά- 4
πτισμα Ἰωάννου πόθεν ἦν; ἐξ οὐρανοῦ, ἢ ἐξ ἀνθρώπων; Οἱ δὲ διελογίζοντο, παρ' ἑαυτοῖς λέγοντες· Ἐὰν εἴπωμεν· ἐξ οὐρανοῦ, ἐρεῖ
26 ἡμῖν· Διατί οὖν οὐκ ἐπιστεύσατε αὐτῷ; ἐὰν δὲ εἴπωμεν· ἐξ ἀν- 31
θρώπων, — φοβούμεθα τὸν ὄχλον· πάντες γὰρ ἔχουσι τὸν Ἰωάννην 32 6
27 ὡς προφήτην. Καὶ ἀποκριθέντες τῷ Ἰησοῦ εἶπον· Οὐκ οἴδαμεν. 33 7 8
ἔφη αὐτοῖς καὶ αὐτός· Οὐδὲ ἐγὼ λέγω ὑμῖν ἐν ποίᾳ ἐξουσίᾳ ταῦτα
28 ποιῶ. Τί δὲ ὑμῖν δοκεῖ; Ἄνθρωπος εἶχε τέκνα δύο· καὶ προσελ-

is the same metaphor as in διστάζω and the Latin *diffido*.

— τὸ τῆς συκῆς.] An elliptical expression for τὸ περὶ τῆς συκῆς γεγονὸς ἔργον.

— τῷ ὄρει τούτῳ.] Spoken δεικτικῶς, with reference, it is supposed, to the Mount of Olives. For *mountain*, Luke says *sycamore tree*. But there is, in fact, no discrepancy; because Jesus might, and, no doubt, did, make use of *both* examples. On the force of these adagial sayings see Note on Matt. xvii. 20. The construction of the passage is, according to Fritz., as follows: ἀλλὰ καὶ γενήσεται, ἐὰν τῷ ὄρει εἴπητε &c.

22. [*Comp.* Supr. vii. 7. Luke xi. 9. John xv. 7. 1 John iii. 22. v. 14.]

23. ἐλθόντι αὐτῷ.] These are Datives for Genitives of consequence.

— ἐν ποίᾳ ἐξουσίᾳ.) Ἐν, Heb. ב, "by virtue of." This they were privileged to ask, because they had the power of inquiring into the pretensions of a prophet; nay, since the authority of preaching in the temple was derived from them. The interrogators expected, no doubt, that he would answer, "By virtue of my right as Messiah," and thus enable them to fix upon him the charge of blasphemy. But Jesus forbore to directly answer his malevolent interrogators; not through *fear* (as appears from the boldness evinced in the parables immediately following), but on purpose; and according to a method familiar to Hebrew, nay to Grecian disputants (see the citations of Schoettgen and Wets.), he answers by interrogation, replying to question by question, and that propounded with consummate wisdom; for while the Pharisees were not disposed, nay, were even afraid, to dispute John's claim to be a prophet, they would thereby, on their own principles, admit the claims of *Jesus*, to whose divine mission John had borne repeated and unequivocal testimony. Schoettg. remarks that, among the Jews, if any proposed a captious question to another, the other had a right to propose one in turn, and not to answer the first till he had received a reply to his.

25. τὸ βάπτισμα — ἦν;] The sense is, "whence had John authority to baptize?" Βάπτισμα is put, by synecdoche, for the whole ministry of John to preach repentance, and the doctrines he taught; because baptism was its most prominent feature, being a symbol of the purity which he enjoined. See Campbell.

— ἐξ οὐρανοῦ,] for ἐκ Θεοῦ, or οὐράνιον, of heavenly origin; a use which sometimes occurs in the LXX., but rarely in the Classical writers.

— διατί οὖν οὐκ ἐπ. α.] "why, then, have ye not believed him?" i. e. in his testimony of me.

26. φοβούμεθα] This is not (as Kuin. and other Philologists suppose,) of the middle voice, signifying *to terrify oneself*, but a deponent formed from what had originally been of the passive voice; just as our neuter or deponent verb, *to be afraid*, was formed from the old passive *to be afear'd*, to be struck with fear. Fritz. ably remarks on that *brachylogia* in the present passage, by which a clause is omitted after ἐξ ἀνθρώπων (equivalent to "that will not be for our good"), to which the γὰρ following refers, and which γὰρ is put for two γὰρ's. I have edited as the sense seems to require, ἐξ ἀνθρώπων, — *per aposiopesin*.

— ὡς προφήτην.] Ὡς is wrongly taken by Kuin. as put for ὄντως; though ὄντως is found in the parallel passage of Mark. It is either elegantly pleonastic (by which the expression will be equivalent to that of Luke) or somewhat diminishes the force of the assertion.

27. οὐκ οἴδαμεν.] Hence (says Wets.) Jesus rightly infers their unfitness to be judges in this matter, or to claim to have their authority reverenced.

28. τί δὲ ὑμῖν δοκεῖ;] "What think you? give me your opinion of what I am about to say."

— ἄνθρωπος — δύο·] By ἄνθρ. is plainly meant *God*; but it is not so clear what is meant by τέκνα δύο, on which there has been some diversity of opinion. The best Commentators, however, are agreed that the words designate two different classes of the Jewish nation; 1. *the profane and irreligious* generally, but who were brought to repentance by John, and to reformation by Christ; 2. *the Scribes and Pharisees*, whether priests or laymen, who, though professedly anxious to do the will of God, were, in reality, the greatest enemies to religion, and especially that of the Gospel.

MK. LU.
12. 20. θὼν τῷ πρώτῳ, εἶπε· Τέκνον, ὕπαγε σήμερον ἐργάζου ἐν τῷ ἀμπε-
λῶνί μου. Ὁ δὲ ἀποκριθεὶς εἶπεν· Οὐ θέλω· ὕστερον δὲ μετα- 29
μεληθεὶς, ἀπῆλθε. Καὶ προσελθὼν τῷ ‡ δευτέρῳ εἶπεν ὡσαύτως. 30
Ὁ δὲ ἀποκριθεὶς εἶπεν· Ἐγὼ, κύριε· καὶ οὐκ ἀπῆλθε. Τίς ἐκ τῶν 31
δύο ἐποίησε τὸ θέλημα τοῦ πατρός; Λέγουσιν αὐτῷ· Ὁ πρῶτος.
Λέγει αὐτοῖς ὁ Ἰησοῦς· Ἀμὴν λέγω ὑμῖν, ὅτι οἱ τελῶναι καὶ αἱ
πόρναι προάγουσιν ὑμᾶς εἰς τὴν βασιλείαν τοῦ Θεοῦ. Ἦλθε 32
γὰρ πρὸς ὑμᾶς Ἰωάννης ἐν ὁδῷ δικαιοσύνης, καὶ οὐκ ἐπιστεύσατε αὐτῷ· οἱ δὲ τελῶναι καὶ αἱ πόρναι ἐπίστευσαν αὐτῷ. ὑμεῖς δὲ
ἰδόντες οὐ μετεμελήθητε ὕστερον, τοῦ πιστεῦσαι αὐτῷ.
1 9 Ἄλλην παραβολὴν ἀκούσατε. Ἄνθρωπός [τις] ἦν οἰκοδεσπότης, 33
ὅστις ἐφύτευσεν ἀμπελῶνα, καὶ φραγμὸν αὐτῷ περιέθηκε, καὶ ὤρυξεν
ἐν αὐτῷ ληνὸν, καὶ ᾠκοδόμησε πύργον· καὶ ἐξέδοτο αὐτὸν γεωργοῖς,
2 10 καὶ ἀπεδήμησεν. Ὅτε δὲ ἤγγισεν ὁ καιρὸς τῶν καρπῶν, ἀπέστειλε 34
τοὺς δούλους αὐτοῦ πρὸς τοὺς γεωργοὺς, λαβεῖν τοὺς καρποὺς αὐτοῦ.
3 Καὶ λαβόντες οἱ γεωργοὶ τοὺς δούλους αὐτοῦ, ὃν μὲν ἔδειραν, ὃν δὲ 35
4 11 ἀπέκτειναν, ὃν δὲ ἐλιθοβόλησαν. Πάλιν ἀπέστειλεν ἄλλους δούλους 36

30. *δευτέρῳ*] Many MSS. and some Versions and Fathers have *ἑτέρῳ*, which was approved by Mill and Bengel, and has been adopted by Wets., Griesb., Knapp, Tittm., Vater, and Scholz. But Matth. and Fritz. retain the common reading; and rightly, for it is supported by greater authority, and the other reading is evidently a correction. The two words, however, are often confounded; a remarkable example of which occurs in Thucyd. iii. 49., where see my note.

— *ἐγὼ, κύριε*] The best Commentators are agreed that this phrase, (for which *ἔγωγε* is used in the Classics) answers to the Heb. הִנֵּנִי, which is, by ellipse, a phrase of responsive assent, rendered by the LXX. *ἰδοὺ ἐγὼ*, in 1 Sam. iii. 4. Numb. xiv. 14. See also Luke i. 38. and Acts ix. 10. "The Hebrews (observe Vatab., Erasm., and Brug.) answer by pronouns, where the Latins use verbs and adverbs, as *etiam* Domine." It may be paralleled by our own idiom, "*aye*, sir." Indeed our *aye* and the *eja*, *ja*, or *ya*, of the Northern languages, seem to be cognate with *ἐγώ*.

31. *οἱ τελῶναι καὶ αἱ πόρναι*] i. e. even the worst of those profane and dissolute persons.

— *προάγουσι*.] Glass explains this "lead on;" and Schleus. and Wahl assign still less admissible senses. There seems no reason to abandon the common interpretation, "go before," precede: render, "are preceding you."

32. *ἐν ὁδῷ δικ.*] A Hebrew form of expression for "he came to you in the practice of, i. e. practising righteousness;" and, by implication, leading others into the same course.

— *τοῦ πιστεῦσαι*] for *εἰς τὸ πιστ.*, i. e. *ὥστε πιστ.*

33. *τις*] This is not found in many of the best MSS. and some Versions and Fathers, and was cancelled by Griesb.. Knapp, Vat., Tittm., Fritz., and Scholz. It was retained by Wets. and Matthæi; but, if we may judge from supra ver. 28., without reason. Nay, Fritz. thinks that even the *construction* requires its absence. But that is somewhat hypercritical, and is judging of Hellenistic and popular style by the rules of Classical writing.

— *ὤρυξεν — ληνόν*.] The *ληνὸς* properly denoted the large vat (called the wine-press) into which the grapes were thrown, to be expressed; in which sense it often occurs in the Sept. But as this vessel had connected with it on the side, or under it (to check, by the coolness of the situation, too great fermentation) a *cistern*, into which the expressed juice flowed; so, by synecdoche, *ληνὸς* came to denote (as here) that cistern; which, as it was necessarily subterranean, and sometimes *under the vat*, so it was often called *ὑπολήνιον*, as in the parallel passages in Mark and Is. xvi. 10. These cisterns (which are even yet in use in the East), bore some resemblance to the *λάκκοι* of the Greeks, which the Scholiast on Aristoph. Eccl. 154. (cited by Wets.) explains *καὶ ὀρύγματα εὐρύχωρα, καὶ στρογγύλα τετράγωνα*, (I conjecture *καὶ στρογγύλα καὶ τετράγωνα*) *καὶ ταῦτα κονιῶντες* (plastering) *οἶνον ὑπεδέχοντο καὶ ἔλαιον εἰς αὐτά*.

— *πύργον*.] This was built partly as a place of abode for the occupier, while the produce was collecting; and partly for security to the servants stationed there as guards over the place. Grot. observes, that in the application of the parable, such circumstances as this are to be considered as only serving for ornament; or, only express generally, that every thing was provided both for pleasure and security.

— *ἐξέδοτο*] for *ἐξεμίσθωσε*, as in Polyb. vi. 17. 2. Herodian i. 6. 8. cited by the Commentators; to which I add Thucyd. iii. 68. *τὴν γῆν ἀπεμίσθωσαν ἐπὶ δέκα ἔτη*, the earliest record of letting *on lease* I have ever met with. The word may here be rendered "let it out," understanding, however, the rent to be not in *money*, but (agreeably to the most ancient usage, yet retained in the East, and even in some parts of the West) in a certain portion of the *produce*. Thus *τοὺς καρποὺς* just after should be rendered "his fruit, or produce, the portion which fell to him."

34. *καιρὸς τῶν καρπῶν*,] "the time for gathering the fruits." So Mark xi. 15.

35. *ἔδειραν*,] *Δέρειν* signifies properly to *flay* or

MK. LU.

37 πλείονας τῶν πρώτων· καὶ ἐποίησαν αὐτοῖς ὡσαύτως. Ὕστερον δὲ 12. 20.
ἀπέστειλε πρὸς αὐτοὺς τὸν υἱὸν αὐτοῦ, λέγων· Ἐντραπήσονται τὸν 6 13
38 υἱόν μου. Οἱ δὲ γεωργοὶ ἰδόντες τὸν υἱὸν, εἶπον ἐν ἑαυτοῖς· Οὗτός 7 14
ἐστιν ὁ κληρονόμος· δεῦτε, ἀποκτείνωμεν αὐτὸν, καὶ κατάσχωμεν τὴν
39 κληρονομίαν αὐτοῦ. Καὶ λαβόντες αὐτὸν, ἐξέβαλον ἔξω τοῦ ἀμπελῶνος, 8 15
40 καὶ ἀπέκτειναν. Ὅταν οὖν ἔλθῃ ὁ κύριος τοῦ ἀμπελῶνος, τί ποιήσει 9
41 τοῖς γεωργοῖς ἐκείνοις; Λέγουσιν αὐτῷ· Κακοὺς κακῶς ἀπολέσει 16
αὐτούς· καὶ τὸν ἀμπελῶνα ἐκδόσεται ἄλλοις γεωργοῖς, οἵτινες ἀπο-
42 δώσουσιν αὐτῷ τοὺς καρποὺς ἐν τοῖς καιροῖς αὐτῶν. Λέγει αὐτοῖς ὁ
Ἰησοῦς· Οὐδέποτε ἀνέγνωτε ἐν ταῖς γραφαῖς; Λίθον ὃν ἀπεδο- 10 17
κίμασαν οἱ οἰκοδομοῦντες, οὗτος ἐγενήθη εἰς κε-
φαλὴν γωνίας. παρὰ Κυρίου ἐγένετο αὕτη, καὶ ἔστι 11
43 θαυμαστὴ ἐν ὀφθαλμοῖς ἡμῶν. Διὰ τοῦτο λέγω ὑμῖν, ὅτι
ἀρθήσεται ἀφ᾽ ὑμῶν ἡ βασιλεία τοῦ Θεοῦ, καὶ δοθήσεται ἔθνει
44 ποιοῦντι τοὺς καρποὺς αὐτῆς. Καὶ ὁ πεσὼν ἐπὶ τὸν λίθον τοῦτον, 18
45 συνθλασθήσεται· ἐφ᾽ ὃν δ᾽ ἂν πέσῃ, λικμήσει αὐτόν. Καὶ ἀκούσαν- 19
τες οἱ ἀρχιερεῖς καὶ οἱ Φαρισαῖοι τὰς παραβολὰς αὐτοῦ, ἔγνωσαν ὅτι

skin; but as words denoting great violence come at length, through *abuse*, to bear a milder sense, it was at length used to signify *beat severely*.

37. *ἐντραπήσονται*] "they will treat with reverence." Ἐντρέπεσθαι signifies, 1. to turn upon oneself; 2. *ex adjuncto*, to be afraid; 3. to regard with reverence. The expression is, as Grot. observes, to be understood θεοπρεπῶς, not to exclude prescience, but to denote that the contingency of an event is viewed in its causes.

38. *Comp.* infr. xxvi. 3. xxvii. 1. John xi. 53.

41. κακοὺς κακῶς ἀπ.] Camp. renders, "he will bring these wretches to a wretched death." This phrase (in which the Paronomasia is remarkable,) occurs very frequently in the Greek writers from Homer downwards. It is worthy of observation that by *Luke* the words are ascribed to Christ himself, and draw from the scribes the exclamation, *μὴ γένοιτο!* Of the many methods proposed for removing this apparent discrepancy, the best seems to be that of Doddr., who supposes that Christ in the *first instance* drew their own condemnation from the Sanhedrim, and then soon afterwards repeated their words, by way of confirmation. There is nothing to stumble at in the Priests pronouncing their own destruction, since they seem not at first to have understood Christ's drift in the parable.

— ἀποδώσουσιν — αὐτῶν.] This (as I have before observed) was the most ancient mode of paying RENT (which term signifies what is *rendered* for occupancy), namely, by rendering a certain proportion of the produce; of which I have adduced several examples with illustrations in Recens. Synop. The most apposite is Plato de Legg. viii. *γεωργίαι δὲ ἐκδεδομέναι δούλοις, ἀπαρχὴν τῶν ἐκ τῆς γῆς ἀποτελοῦσιν.* See my note on Thucyd. vi. 20. *ἀπαρχὴ ἐσφέρεται.*

42. λίθον — γωνίας.] Taken from Ps. cxvii. 22. Sept., to which there is also a reference in other passages of Scripture; all of which show that the words, though very applicable to David, are, in their highest sense, to be referred to the Messiah; as the Jews themselves acknowledge. Λίθον ὃν for λίθος ὃν is not (as Glass. imagines) a Hebraism; but is a construction frequent both in the Greek and Latin. See Matth. Gr. Gr. § 474. c.

— κεφαλὴν γωνίας.] Both the Jewish and Christian dispensations are often designated by the figure of a *building*; and of the latter Christ is represented as the *corner*-stone, and, by its importance in sustaining and defending the building, the *head*-stone. See 1 Cor. iii. 11. Eph. ii. 21. However, the *nature* of the metaphor is not very obvious, nor is it very plain what this κεφ. γων. was. Bp. Middlet., with reason, thinks that, from this passage, it appears to have been, 1. something which might be added when the building was complete; 2. that it was so situated, that a passer by might fall against it; and, 3. that it might fall upon him. So that, says he, "it exactly answers to an upright stone or buttress, added for the purpose of protecting the corner of a building, where it is most exposed to external violence."

— αὕτη — θαυμαστὴ] Feminines for neuters, Hebraicè. An idiom often adopted by the LXX. See Winer's Gr. Gr. p. 84. fin. The construction ἐγενήθη εἰς is Hebraic, as also is θαυμαστὴ ἐν ὀφθ. ἡμῶν; for, notwithstanding that the Commentators adduce many examples of the phrase ἐν ὀφθ. with a *verb*, yet they produce not one with an *adjective*.

43. ἔθνει] i. e. as Euthym. explains, τῷ γένει τῶν Χριστιανῶν. Rosenm. and Kuin. very well paraphrase thus: "Because ye have rejected this stone, the benefits of the Messiah's kingdom and religion shall not be communicated to *you*; but imparted to a nation, or race of persons (whether Jews or Gentiles), all obedient followers of Jesus, who shall, &c. i. e. the Jewish nation shall no longer be the peculiar people of God; but that nation or race shall be so, which (of whatever country) embraces the plan of salvation now promulgated."

44. καὶ ὁ πεσὼν — αὐτόν.] Almost all Critics are agreed that this verse should properly follow ver. 42. (as, they think, the connection indicates), and that it has probably no place here, but was introduced from the parallel passage of Luke. The MSS. and Versions, however, give not the slight-

MK. 12. 12
περὶ αὐτῶν λέγει· καὶ ζητοῦντες αὐτὸν κρατῆσαι, ἐφοβήθησαν τοὺς 46
ὄχλους· ἐπειδὴ ὡς προφήτην αὐτὸν εἶχον.

XXII. ΚΑΙ ἀποκριθεὶς ὁ Ἰησοῦς πάλιν εἶπεν αὐτοῖς ἐν παραβολαῖς, 1
a Luke 14. 16. Rev. 19. 7, 9. λέγων· [a] Ὡμοιώθη ἡ βασιλεία τῶν οὐρανῶν ἀνθρώπῳ βασιλεῖ, ὅστις 2
ἐποίησε γάμους τῷ υἱῷ αὐτοῦ· καὶ ἀπέστειλε τοὺς δούλους αὐτοῦ 3
καλέσαι τοὺς κεκλημένους εἰς τοὺς γάμους· καὶ οὐκ ἤθελον ἐλθεῖν.
b Prov. 9. 2. [b] Πάλιν ἀπέστειλεν ἄλλους δούλους, λέγων· Εἴπατε τοῖς κεκλημένοις· 4
Ἰδοὺ, τὸ ἄριστόν μου ἡτοίμασα, οἱ ταῦροί μου καὶ τὰ σιτιστὰ τεθυμένα, καὶ πάντα ἕτοιμα· δεῦτε εἰς τοὺς γάμους. Οἱ δὲ ἀμελήσαντες 5
ἀπῆλθον, ὁ μὲν εἰς τὸν ἴδιον ἀγρὸν, ὁ δὲ εἰς τὴν ἐμπορίαν αὐτοῦ.
Οἱ δὲ λοιποὶ κρατήσαντες τοὺς δούλους αὐτοῦ, ὕβρισαν καὶ ἀπέκτειναν. 6
‡ Καὶ ἀκούσας ὁ βασιλεὺς ἐκεῖνος, ὠργίσθη· καὶ πέμψας τὰ στρατεύ- 7

est countenance to the *first* surmise; and the *second* is very slenderly supported. I cannot but think that all is as it was left by the Evangelist; and I am gratified to find my opinion ably supported by that of Fritz., whom see.

With respect to the *nature* of the metaphor, there is an allusion to Is. viii. 14 & 15.; and the verbs are terms denoting *greater* or *less* degrees of injury: the first being to bruise and crush; the second, to beat to pieces, and destroy utterly. Wets. and others think that there is an allusion to the different modes of stoning among the Jews. And they paraphrase thus: "Whosoever shall stumble at and reject me as the Messiah, shall encounter misery; yet they *may* repent and be healed. But on whomsoever this rock (the Messiah, which might have been their defence) shall fall, it will crush them in utter ruin."

46. ὡς προφ.] The ὡς is thought to be put for ὄντως, *verè*. Comp. Mark xi. 32. and Luke xx. 6. But however this sense may have place in other passages, it would here seem sufficient to render *utpote*.

XXII. 1. ἐν παραβολαῖς,] It is clear that this is put for the more elegant διὰ παραβολῶν, as in Aristoph. Ran. 61. σοὶ δι' αἰνιγμῶν ἐρῶ. The ἀποκριθεὶς may here simply denote *addressing*; unless there is, as some suppose, an *answer* to the *thoughts* of the Pharisees.

2. ἡ βασιλ. τῶν οὐρανῶν] the administration of the heavenly kingdom, or Dispensation. Ὡμοιώθη, i. e. the same thing will take place as that represented in the parable of a King, &c. The *primary* object of this parable is to represent the invitation given to the Jews to embrace the Gospel; the rejection of that offer, the severe punishment to be inflicted on them for their disobedience, and the admission of the Gentiles, in their stead, to the privileges of Christianity. Such parts of the similitude as are not referrible to these *heads*, are to be considered as merely introduced for ornament, or to complete the *vraisemblance*. There is, however, a *secondary* intent to be noticed, which is, to inculcate a truth needful to be kept in mind in every age; namely, that the *rewards* held out by the Gospel are not to be conferred on *mere professors*, but upon those only who cultivate the dispositions and habits enjoined by its precepts. There is a peculiar propriety in the comparison itself, since in Scripture the *Jewish* Covenant, as well as the Christian, is represented under the figure of a *marriage contract* between God and his people. See Is. liv. 5. Jerem. iii. 8. and, in the N. T., see Matt, xxv. 5. John iii. 29. 2 Cor. xi. 2. Revel. xix. 7—9.

— γάμους] This is by most Commentators taken to signify *a marriage feast*; though, as the word (correspondently to the Heb. משתה) often signifies a *feast* in general, some Commentators assign that sense here; agreeably, as they think, to the moral purport of the parable. Many, however, of the recent Commentators (as Michael., Rosenm., Kuin., and Schleus.) understand an *inauguration feast*, when the Oriental kings were considered as it were *affianced* to their country. See Luke xii. 36. xiv. 8. Esth. ii. 18. ix. 22. 1 Kings i. 5—9. There seems no reason, however, to abandon the common interpretation. Whichever be the sense, the plural may be considered as having reference to the continuance of those feasts for several days.

3. καλέσαι] generally signifies "to invite;" like the Latin *vocare* and the Heb. קרא. So Theophr. Char. 12. κεκλημένος εἰς γάμους. Here, however, it rather denotes to *summon*; for Luc., Brug., Grot., and Kuin. have shown that, among the ancients, guests were first *invited* some time before; and then *summoned*, within a short time of the feast, that they might be ready.

4. τὸ ἄριστον] This was, in early times, the name given to *breakfast*: afterwards it denoted the *noonday meal*; and, at length, it was applied to the *chief meal*, taken at the close of the day. Hence it came to signify a *banquet* in general. See Kypke on John xxi. 12. and Mureti Var. Lect. IV. 12.

— τὰ σιτιστὰ] The term properly denotes animals put up to fatten; and as here we have had mention made just before of ταῦροι, it must denote calves, sheep, &c., with the exception of bullocks.

— τεθυμένα.] Θύω properly signifies *suffio* (whence θύος and θύωμα); and *at first* signified to make those offerings of incense, fruits, and flowers, for which sacrifices of animals were afterwards substituted. And as θύειν still continued to be used, it then denoted to *sacrifice*; and at length generally to *slaughter* for eating; a process found in the Heb. זבח (Grot. and Hemsterh.).

5. τὸν ἴδιον] for αὐτοῦ. Ἀγρὸν, properly *land*; but here *farm*, or (as the words following require) *farming business*; for ἐμπορίαν, from the antithesis, must denote other sorts of business, as trade or manufactures.

7. καὶ ἀκούσας — ὠργίσθη.] There are on this

ματα αὐτοῦ, ἀπώλεσε τοὺς φονεῖς ἐκείνους, καὶ τὴν πόλιν αὐτῶν ἐνέ-
8 *πρησε. Τότε λέγει τοῖς δούλοις αὐτοῦ· Ὁ μὲν γάμος ἕτοιμός ἐστιν,*
9 *οἱ δὲ κεκλημένοι οὐκ ἦσαν ἄξιοι. πορεύεσθε οὖν ἐπὶ τὰς διεξόδους*
10 *τῶν ὁδῶν, καὶ ὅσους ἂν εὕρητε, καλέσατε εἰς τοὺς γάμους. Καὶ*
ἐξελθόντες οἱ δοῦλοι ἐκεῖνοι εἰς τὰς ὁδοὺς, συνήγαγον πάντας, ὅσους
εὗρον, πονηρούς τε καὶ ἀγαθούς· καὶ ἐπλήσθη ὁ γάμος ἀνακειμέ-
11 *νων.* [c] *Εἰσελθὼν δὲ ὁ βασιλεὺς θεάσασθαι τοὺς ἀνακειμένους, εἶδεν* c 2 Cor. 5. 3. Ephes. 4. 24.
12 *ἐκεῖ ἄνθρωπον οὐκ ἐνδεδυμένον ἔνδυμα γάμου· Καὶ λέγει αὐτῷ·* Coloss. 3. 10, 12.
Ἑταῖρε, πῶς εἰσῆλθες ὧδε μὴ ἔχων ἔνδυμα γάμου; Ὁ δὲ ἐφιμώθη. Rev. 3. 4. & 16. 15. & 19. 8. d Supr. 8. 12.
13 [d] *Τότε εἶπεν ὁ βασιλεὺς τοῖς διακόνοις· Δήσαντες αὐτοῦ πόδας καὶ χεῖρας,* & 13. 42. infr. 25. 30.
ἄρατε αὐτὸν καὶ ἐκβάλετε εἰς τὸ σκότος τὸ ἐξώτερον· ἐκεῖ ἔσται ὁ
14 *κλαυθμὸς καὶ ὁ βρυγμὸς τῶν ὀδόντων.* [e] *Πολλοὶ γάρ εἰσι κλητοὶ,* e Supr. 20. 16. MK. LU.
ὀλίγοι δὲ ἐκλεκτοί. 12. 20.
15 *Τότε πορευθέντες οἱ Φαρισαῖοι, συμβούλιον ἔλαβον ὅπως αὐτὸν* 13 20
16 *παγιδεύσωσιν ἐν λόγῳ. Καὶ ἀποστέλλουσιν αὐτῷ τοὺς μαθητὰς αὐτῶν*
μετὰ τῶν Ἡρωδιανῶν, λέγοντες· Διδάσκαλε, οἴδαμεν ὅτι ἀληθὴς εἶ, 14 21

clause several varieties of reading. Many MSS., Versions, and Fathers, have ἀκούσας δὲ, and after βασιλεὺς add ἐκεῖνος. And so Matt., Griesb., and Scholz edit. I cannot venture to imitate their example; because, although there is considerable *external* evidence for the readings in question, yet *internal* evidence is, I apprehend, quite against them; and Fritz. has shewn how they originated. In short, all the FIVE varieties of reading here found in the MSS. present no more than so many different ways by which the passage was tampered with by the early critics. And as the common reading is plainly the *parent* of all the other readings, it ought, according to one of the most certain of critical canons, to be preferred.

9. τὰς διεξόδους τῶν ὁδῶν,] Most Commentators explain this "*compita viarum*," "places where many streets or roads meet," and therefore of public concourse. Fisch. and Fritz. explain it "*vias rusticas.*" The former interpretation is preferable; and yet it is difficult to extract such a sense from the word. I would therefore, with Bois ap. Wolf., rather suppose it to mean the great thoroughfares of the city, and outlets into the country—the great trunks, as it were, of communication; and which, in the great ancient cities, were made to terminate at the gates. Such would be places of the greatest concourse. See Thucyd. iii. 98.

10. πονηρούς τε καὶ ἀγαθούς.] By this it is intimated, that the *bad* as well as the good would form part of the *visible Church*; though the privileges of the Gospel would belong to the latter, while its threatenings, denounced against the wicked, would fall on the former.

11. θεάσασθαι τοὺς ἀνακειμένους] As was then usual with grandees and others who made great feasts.

— ἔνδυμα γάμου·] An appropriate dress, with which those who attended were expected to be clothed. This custom was common alike to the Hebrews, Greeks, and Romans; and something like it yet prevails in the East. In *this*, therefore, consisted the offence of the delinquent,—that he had neglected to *provide himself* with the appropriate dress. By this wedding garment some think that *faith* is represented: but that was *implied* in the act of attending the supper; and it should rather seem (as Euthym., Grot., Le Clerc, and most recent Commentators take it), to mean adorning our Christian profession by a suitable conduct. See Eph. iv. 1. 2 Pet. i. 10. compared with Rev. xix. 7. The whole, indeed, hinges upon this: whether we are to suppose the garment provided by the *guests*, or by the *king*. If the *latter*, then, indeed, neither of the above interpretations can well be admitted; and we must rather understand the gifts of the Holy Spirit,—grace, faith, and sanctification; as Irenæus, Hilary, Menochius, and Gerard interpret. This, however, does not agree with the scope of the parable; and it may be observed, that the supposition on which it rests, of the garment being provided by the *king*, is deficient in *ancient* authority, the examples adduced being almost entirely from modern travellers. It is therefore best to suppose the garment or rather *dress*) to have been provided by the *guests*. And such is the opinion of Chrys. and Euthym. Thus in two similar parables cited by Wets. from Rabbinical writers, those who washed themselves, cleansed their garments, and otherwise prepared themselves for the banquet, are contrasted with those who made no preparation; but went on with their occupations, and thus entered the palace "*in turpitudine suâ*," in their mean, ordinary dress.

12. ἐφιμώθη.] "was mute." Φιμοῦν signifies properly to *muzzle*, and metaphorically to *silence*.

13. σκότος τὸ ἐξώτερον] i. e. darkness the most dense and extreme, as being the furthest removed from the light of the banquet.

14. πολλοὶ—ἐκλεκτοί.] See the long and able annotation of Hammond in Recens. Synop., and a fine observation of Theophyl. cited by Parkhurst, Lex. v. ἐκλεκτός.

15. παγιδεύσωσιν] "that they might ensnare him." The term is properly used of snaring birds; but, like ἀγρεύειν, employed by Mark xii. 12. and the Latin *irretire* and *illaqueare*, is used of plotting any one's destruction.

16. τῶν Ἡρωδιανῶν.] From the slight mention of these persons in the N. T., and the silence of

MK. LU.
12. 20. καὶ τὴν ὁδὸν τοῦ Θεοῦ ἐν ἀληθείᾳ διδάσκεις, καὶ οὐ μέλει σοι περὶ
22 οὐδενός· οὐ γὰρ βλέπεις εἰς πρόσωπον ἀνθρώπων. Εἰπὲ οὖν ἡμῖν· 17
15 23 τί σοι δοκεῖ; ἔξεστι δοῦναι κῆνσον Καίσαρι, ἢ οὔ; Γνοὺς δὲ ὁ 18
Ἰησοῦς τὴν πονηρίαν αὐτῶν, εἶπε· Τί με πειράζετε, ὑποκριταί;
16 24 Ἐπιδείξατέ μοι τὸ νόμισμα τοῦ κήνσου. οἱ δὲ προσήνεγκαν αὐτῷ 19
δηνάριον. Καὶ λέγει αὐτοῖς· Τίνος ἡ εἰκὼν αὕτη καὶ ἡ ἐπιγραφή; 20
17 25 Λέγουσιν αὐτῷ· Καίσαρος. τότε λέγει αὐτοῖς· Ἀπόδοτε οὖν τὰ 21
26 Καίσαρος Καίσαρι, καὶ τὰ τοῦ Θεοῦ τῷ Θεῷ. Καὶ ἀκούσαντες ἐθαύ- 22
μασαν· καὶ ἀφέντες αὐτὸν ἀπῆλθον.
18 27 Ἐν ἐκείνῃ τῇ ἡμέρᾳ προσῆλθον αὐτῷ Σαδδουκαῖοι, οἱ λέγοντες μὴ 23
19 28 εἶναι ἀνάστασιν, καὶ ἐπηρώτησαν αὐτὸν, λέγοντες· Διδάσκαλε, Μωϋσῆς 24

Josephus, nothing *certain* with respect to them can be determined; but the prevailing and best-founded opinion seems to be, that they did not form any distinct *religious sect* (though probably Sadducees in doctrine, as was Herod), but were rather a *political party*, composed of the courtiers, ministers, domestics, and partisans and adherents generally of Herod; who maintained, with Herod, that the dominion of the Romans over the Jews was lawful, and ought to be submitted to; and that under the present circumstances, the Jews might, allowably, resort to Gentile usages and customs. This opinion is confirmed by the *termination* of the word, *ιανοι*, which was in that age appropriated to denoting political partisans, such as *Cæsariani*, *Pompeiani*, *Ciceroniani*, &c.

—*ἀληθὴς*] "upright," neither practising simulation nor dissimulation.

—*οὐ μέλει — ἀνθρώπων.*] The expressions *οὐ μέλει σοι περὶ οὐδενὸς*, and *οὐ βλέπεις εἰς πρόσωπον ἀνθ.* (of which the former is a Greek phrase, the latter a Hebraism) are generally thought to be of the same sense. But Fritz., with others, denies this, and lays down the connection as follows: "tu per neminem a veritate te abduci sinis; neque enim homines curas, quos si curares, a vera via facile aberrares, sed Deum." Thus he thinks that *πρόσωπον ἀνθρ.* is put, by an unusual circumlocution, for *ἀνθρώπους*. To this, however, I cannot assent; for the *πρόσ.* adverts to the *external* condition of men, with allusion to its being no more a part of the man than the *πρόσωπον*, or actor's mask.

18. *πονηρίαν.*] This signifies like the Latin malitia, *craft*. The other Evangelists use the more definite terms *πανουργίαν* and *ὑπόκρισιν*.

19. *τὸ νόμισμα τοῦ κήνσου.*] "nummum ex eo genere quo census exigi solebat." (Fritz.)

20. *τίνος — ἐπιγραφή;*] The inscription was ΚΑΙΣΑΡ ΑΥΓΟΥΣΤ: ΙΟΥΔΑΙΑΣ ΕΑΛΩΚΥΙΑΣ. "Our Lord here baffles the malignant proposers of the question, by taking advantage of their own concession, that the denarius bore the emperor's image and superscription, and also of the determination of their own schools, that wherever any king's coin was current, it was a proof of that country's subjection to that government. He significantly warns these turbulent and seditious demagogues, the Pharisees, *to render unto Cæsar the dues of Cæsar*, which they resisted; and these licentious and irreligious courtiers, the Herodians, *to render unto God the dues of God*, which they neglected; thus publicly reproving both, but obliquely, in a way that they could not take any hold of." (Dr. Hales.)

"Though the right of Cæsar to demand tribute of the Jews may seem to be undecided by the answer, yet the precept at ver. 22 is decisive, and being united with the preceding verses by *οὖν*, it inculcates that duty of submission to established governments which is a leading feature of the Christian religion." (Whitby.) [*Comp.* Rom. xiii. 7.]

23. *μὴ εἶναι ἀνάστασιν.*] Campb. maintains that the sense is, "no future life;" for *ἀνάστασις*, he says, when applied to the dead, properly denotes no more than a *renewal* of life to them, in whatever manner. The Sadducees, he observes, denied not merely the resurrection of the *body*, but the immortality of the soul, and a future state of retribution. "They had (continues he) no notion of spirit, and were consequently obliged to make use of terms which properly relate to the body, when they spoke of a future state, which therefore came at length to be denoted simply by the word *resurrection*." (Comp. Acts xxiii. 8.) Now that the *Pharisees*, continues he, *themselves* did not universally mean by this term the re-union of soul and body, is evident both from Josephus's account of their doctrines, and from passages in the Gospels. To say, therefore, of the Sadducees, that they denied the resurrection, would give a very defective account of their tenets. It is plain from Josephus and other Jewish writers, as also Acts xxiii. 8., that they denied the existence of angels, and *all* separate bodies. Thus going much further than the Pagans, who did, indeed, deny the *resurrection of the body*, but believed in a state after death, wherein the *souls* of the departed exist in a state of happiness or misery, according to their deeds on earth. It is plain, from our Lord's answer, that the Sadducees denied not merely the *resurrection of the body*, but the *immortality of the soul*. They had, it seems, no notion of *spirit*, and were consequently obliged to make use of terms which properly relate to the body, when they spoke of a future state; which, therefore, came at length to be denoted simply by the word *resurrection*. Compare Acts xxiii. 8." The above contains a just representation of the opinions of the Sadducees (on which see Horne's Introd., Vol. III. 327. and note), but is, I apprehend, no proof that our common version, is as Dr. C. maintains, inaccurate. Nay, on the contrary, his own version is (properly speaking) no version at all, but merely an *explanation*. The learned Commentator does not sufficiently bear in mind, that *popular* phraseology (such as is generally that of the N. T.) must be interpreted *as such*. There is little doubt but that the phrase *ἀνάστασις τῶν νε-*

MK. LU.

εἶπεν· Ἐάν τις ἀποθάνῃ μὴ ἔχων τέκνα, ἐπιγαμβρεύ- 12. 20.
σει ὁ ἀδελφὸς αὐτοῦ τὴν γυναῖκα αὐτοῦ, καὶ ἀναστή-
25 σει σπέρμα τῷ ἀδελφῷ αὐτοῦ. Ἦσαν δὲ παρ' ἡμῖν ἑπτὰ 20 29
ἀδελφοί· καὶ ὁ πρῶτος γαμήσας ἐτελεύτησε· καὶ μὴ ἔχων σπέρμα,
26 ἀφῆκε τὴν γυναῖκα αὐτοῦ τῷ ἀδελφῷ αὐτοῦ. Ὁμοίως καὶ ὁ δεύτερος, 21 22 30 31
27 καὶ ὁ τρίτος, ἕως τῶν ἑπτά. Ὕστερον δὲ πάντων ἀπέθανε καὶ ἡ γυνή. 32
28 Ἐν τῇ οὖν ἀναστάσει τίνος τῶν ἑπτὰ ἔσται γυνή; πάντες γὰρ ἔσχον 23 33
29 αὐτήν. Ἀποκριθεὶς δὲ ὁ Ἰησοῦς εἶπεν αὐτοῖς· Πλανᾶσθε μὴ εἰδό- 24 34
30 τες τὰς γραφὰς, μηδὲ τὴν δύναμιν τοῦ Θεοῦ. Ἐν γὰρ τῇ ἀναστάσει 25 35
οὔτε γαμοῦσιν, οὔτε ἐκγαμίζονται· ἀλλ' ὡς ἄγγελοι τοῦ Θεοῦ ἐν 36
31 οὐρανῷ εἰσι. Περὶ δὲ τῆς ἀναστάσεως τῶν νεκρῶν, οὐκ ἀνέγνωτε τὸ 26 37
32 ῥηθὲν ὑμῖν ὑπὸ τοῦ Θεοῦ, λέγοντος· Ἐγώ εἰμι ὁ Θεὸς Ἀ- 27 38
βραὰμ, καὶ ὁ Θεὸς Ἰσαὰκ, καὶ ὁ Θεὸς Ἰακώβ; οὐκ ἔστιν
33 ὁ Θεὸς Θεὸς νεκρῶν, ἀλλὰ ζώντων. Καὶ ἀκούσαντες οἱ ὄχλοι ἐξεπλήσσοντο ἐπὶ τῇ διδαχῇ αὐτοῦ.
34 Οἱ δὲ Φαρισαῖοι ἀκούσαντες ὅτι ἐφίμωσε τοὺς Σαδδουκαίους, συνή- 28

κρῶν, or ἀνάστασις, denoted, in common parlance, and agreeably to the general doctrines of the Pharisees, the resurrection of the *soul* as well as of the body, and the re-union of both in a future state. Though, at the same time, the ideas of the Pharisees *themselves* (and still more the people at large) as to the *nature* of that future life, were very vague, and occasionally founded on the notions of the heathens. So that our Lord's reply was, in wisdom, so framed as not only to refute the *Sadducæan* doctrines, but remove the misconceptions of the *Pharisees*; and thus to benefit not only the *unbelievers* of the doctrine of the resurrection, but the *misbelievers*.

24. This is not a regular quotation, nor does it profess to be such — but correctly represents the sense of the injunction of the law. On the *intent* of which see Dr. A. Clarke.

— ἐπιγαμβρεύσει.] Ἐπιγαμβρεύω (which occurs also in the Sept.) denotes to marry a widow by right of affinity.

— σπέρμα.] This word, like the Heb. זֶרַע, denotes offspring or progeny, whether one or more children; though in Scripture it is almost confined to the *latter*. On the contrary, in the *Classical* writers it is generally used of the former. So Soph. El. 1510. and Œd. Tyr. 1087. and a Delphic oracle in Thucyd. v. 16. Διὸς υἱοῦ ἡμιθέου τὸ σπέρμα — ἀναφέρειν. There are, however, examples in the Classical writers of σπέρμα in a *plural* sense. Thus Soph. Trach. 304. Eurip. Med. 798. ἀλλὰ κτανεῖν τὸ σπέρμα τολμήσεις, γύναι.

28. ἐν τῇ ἀν.] "in the future state following the resurrection."

29. πλανᾶσθε — Θεοῦ] i. e. ye deceive yourselves by assuming a false hypothesis — namely, that if there be a future state it must be like the present, and by your ignorance of the true sense of the Scriptures; not considering the *omnipotence* of God, to whom renewal of existence can require no more exertion of power than original creation; nor reflecting that God is able to raise up the dead without their former passions.

30. οὔτε ἐκγαμίζονται.] On this point there was much difference of opinion among the Jewish Rabbins. Some maintaining that there is marrying in heaven; others that there is not. The general opinion was, that the dead would be raised either in their former or with other bodies. And it was the common notion, that the offices of the new bodies would be precisely the same with those of the former ones. The wiser few, however, were of quite another opinion. But of these some went into the *other* extreme — and maintained that the raised would have no bodies. (so Maimonides de Pœnit. viii. 3.) in the future state.

— ὡς ἄγγελοι.] Luke says ἰσάγγελοι. Though neither expression imports *equality*, but only *similarity*. This similarity must chiefly by the context be referred to the point in question; i. e. the not being subject to the appetites of the body; although, upon the whole, εἰσὶν ὡς seems, as Fritz. suggests, to denote *condition* generally. At all events, it does not follow, because angels are, as is supposed, composed of spirit only, that the righteous shall, at the resurrection, have *spirits only*. That they will also have bodies of some sort or other, is certain from 1 Cor. xvi. 42. seq.

32. ἐγώ εἰμι ὁ Θεὸς, &c.] From this passage the doctrine of the resurrection is proved, *more Judaico*, and that inferentially and by legitimate consequence from what has been said. The argument (as stated by Mr. Holden after Mr. Horne) is as follows: "Abraham, Isaac, and Jacob had been long dead when these words were spoken wherein God says, 'I am,' not I was, 'the God of Abraham,' &c.; and as He is not 'the God of the dead, but of the living,' these patriarchs must have been existing in some sense when this declaration was made; for it implies a relationship between God and them, which could not be if they were not existing. The patriarchs, therefore, though dead to us, are alive to God; which proves a future state." This mode of argumentation, it may be added, was peculiarly *Jewish*. So a Rabbinical writer, cited by Wets., proves the resurrection of the dead from the very same passage, and almost in the very same words.

MK. LU.
12. 20. χθησαν ἐπὶ τὸ αὐτὸ, καὶ ἐπηρώτησεν εἷς ἐξ αὐτῶν, νόμικὸς, πειράζων 35
29 αὐτὸν καὶ λέγων· Διδάσκαλε, ποία ἐντολὴ μεγάλη ἐν τῷ νόμῳ; ὁ δὲ 36
30 Ἰησοῦς * ἔφη αὐτῷ· Ἀγαπήσεις Κύριον τὸν Θεόν σου, ἐν 37
ὅλῃ τῇ καρδίᾳ σου, καὶ ἐν ὅλῃ τῇ ψυχῇ σου, καὶ ἐν
ὅλῃ τῇ διανοίᾳ σου. Αὕτη ἐστὶ πρώτη καὶ μεγάλη ἐντολή. 38
31 Δευτέρα δὲ ὁμοία αὐτῇ· Ἀγαπήσεις τὸν πλησίον σου ὡς 39
σεαυτόν. Ἐν ταύταις ταῖς δυσὶν ἐντολαῖς ὅλος ὁ νόμος καὶ οἱ 40
προφῆται κρέμανται.

35 41 Συνηγμένων δὲ τῶν Φαρισαίων, ἐπηρώτησεν αὐτοὺς ὁ Ἰησοῦς, λέγων· 41
Τί ὑμῖν δοκεῖ περὶ τοῦ Χριστοῦ; τίνος υἱός ἐστι; λέγουσιν αὐτῷ· 42

35. νομικός.] Mark xii. 28. calls him εἷς τῶν γραμματέων; from which it has been by some thought that νομικὸς and γραμματεὺς were synonymous terms: while others supposed that a *distinction* existed, as that the γραμματεῖς were the public expounders of the law, while the νομικοὶ were the private expounders and teachers of it. This, however, rests on mere conjecture. One thing alone seems certain, that the νομικοὶ were expounders of the law, whether publicly or privately. So Epict. i. 13. has νομικὸν, ἐξηγούμενον τὰ νόμιμα.

—πειράζων αὐτόν.] Some modern Interpreters assign to πειράζων the *good* sense, *explorans*, *trying*, viz. his skill in Scripture; which seems to be countenanced by Mark. But most of them adopt the bad one, *tempting;* and there seems no sufficient reason for abandoning the common interpretation. The truth seems to be (as Chrys. and Theophyl. suppose) that the man came with an evil intention, but departed better disposed.

36. ποία ἐντολὴ μεγάλη.] Here ποία is for τίς; and μεγάλη for μεγίστη, by Hebraism; on which account it has the privilege of a superlative, in dispensing with the Article. Superlatives do so, from the affinity which they bear to ordinals. See Middlet. Gr. Art. vi. § 3 & 4. and Winer's Gr. § 29. 1. But to turn from words to *things*, the question involved a matter of no little controversy among the Jewish Doctors; as to the comparative importance of different precepts; some maintaining the pre-eminence of one, some of another. Only while they distinguished the Divine precepts (which they numbered 613) into *great* and *small*, they constantly gave the preference to the *ceremonial* ones. Christ, however, decided in favour of the *moral* law, yet not to the neglect of the *ceremonial*.

37. ἔφη.] This reading, which is found in the greater part of the best MSS., is preferred by Mill and Bengel; and is edited by Matth., Griesb., Knapp, Tittm., Vat., and Scholz, instead of the common one εἶπεν.

—ἐν ὅλῃ τῇ καρδίᾳ, &c.] These are formulas nearly equivalent, and united for intensity of sense (as in a passage of Philo cited by Wets.) importing, not that perfection in degree, or elevation in kind contended for by some, but that we must assign to God the *first* place in our affections, and consecrate to him the united powers and faculties with which he hath endued us.

38. πρώτη καὶ μεγ. ἐντ.] How and in what respect this was such, see Bp. Taylor's Works, vol. iii. p. 7. and Bps. Sherlock and Porteus in D'Oyly and Mant; also compare Luke x. 27. Rom. xiii. 9. Gal. v. 14. 1 Tim. i. 5. and James ii. 8.

39. ὁμοία αὐτῇ] i. e. similar in kind, though not in degree; springing out of it, and closely connected with it.

—τὸν πλησίον.] The term here, as often in the N. T., has a very extensive import, including every person with whom we have to do. [*Comp.* Rom. xiii. 8.]

—ὡς σεαυτόν.] We are not here commanded to love; i. e. benefit our fellow creatures *as much as* ourselves (which were inconsistent with the strong principle of *self*-love, which the Almighty has implanted in us, for our preservation); for ὡς (like the Heb. כ) imports, not equality in *degree*, but *similarity* in *kind*. Thus the precept corresponds to that of our Lord at Matt. vii. 12. And we are commanded not only to avoid injuring him, as we avoid injuring ourselves; but to treat him in the same manner as we might, if exchanging situations with him, fairly claim to be treated.

40. ἐν ταύταις — κρέμανται.] This is generally thought to be a metaphor taken from the Jewish custom, of suspending the tables of the laws from a nail or peg. But the metaphor is common to almost all languages, as used of things closely connected, and springing from the same origin. There is, however, a Hebraism in the use of ἐν for ἐκ. Or the ἐν should have been followed by ἀνακεφαλαιοῦνται, or πληροῦνται, as in Rom. xiii. 9. On the full sense see Dr. Paley and Archbp. Sharp, in D'Oyly and Mant.

42. τί ὑμῖν — υἱός ἐστι;] This question was proposed by our Lord to the Pharisees, to show them how little they knew the true nature and dignity of the Messiah. Bp. Bull, in his Jud. Eccl. Cath. i. 12. observes, that "although the Prophets had not obscurely signified that Christ would be God as well as man; and though the wiser few of the Jews saw that, yet that the generality embraced the abject notion that he would be a mighty conqueror, and a glorious monarch (like Cyrus, Alexander, or Cæsar), who would subdue all the nations of the earth, and make Jerusalem the metropolis of the world. And as a *mere man* might, under God's providence, effect all this; where is the wonder that the Jews supposed the Messiah would be *no more*." He adds that, had the Pharisees held the *divinity* of the Messiah, they might easily have solved the proposed enigma, by replying that Christ would indeed be David's Son *quod ad carnem attinet*, but his Lord as regarded his *divine* nature.

MK. LU.
43 Τοῦ Δαυῒδ. Λέγει αὐτοῖς· Πῶς οὖν Δαυῒδ ἐν πνεύματι κύριον αὐ- 12. 20.
44 τὸν καλεῖ; λέγων· Εἶπεν ὁ Κύριος τῷ κυρίῳ μου· Κά- 36 42
θου ἐκ δεξιῶν μου, ἕως ἂν θῶ τοὺς ἐχθρούς σου 43
45 ὑποπόδιον τῶν ποδῶν σου. Εἰ οὖν Δαυῒδ καλεῖ αὐτὸν 37 44
46 κύριον, πῶς υἱὸς αὐτοῦ ἐστι; Καὶ οὐδεὶς ἐδύνατο αὐτῷ ἀποκριθῆναι
λόγον· οὐδὲ ἐτόλμησέ τις ἀπ᾽ ἐκείνης τῆς ἡμέρας ἐπερωτῆσαι αὐτὸν
οὐκέτι.
1 XXIII. Τότε ὁ Ἰησοῦς ἐλάλησε τοῖς ὄχλοις καὶ τοῖς μαθηταῖς 38 45
2 αὐτοῦ, λέγων· Ἐπὶ τῆς Μωϋσέως καθέδρας ἐκάθισαν οἱ Γραμματεῖς
3 καὶ οἱ Φαρισαῖοι. Πάντα οὖν ὅσα ἂν εἴπωσιν ὑμῖν τηρεῖν, τηρεῖτε
καὶ ποιεῖτε· κατὰ δὲ τὰ ἔργα αὐτῶν μὴ ποιεῖτε· λέγουσι γὰρ,
4 καὶ οὐ ποιοῦσι. [a] Δεσμεύουσι γὰρ φορτία βαρέα καὶ δυσβάστακτα,
καὶ ἐπιτιθέασιν ἐπὶ τοὺς ὤμους τῶν ἀνθρώπων· τῷ δὲ δακτύλῳ
5 αὐτῶν οὐ θέλουσι κινῆσαι αὐτά. [b] πάντα δὲ τὰ ἔργα αὐτῶν ποιοῦσι

a Luke 11. 46. Acts 15. 10. Gal. 6. 13.
b Supr. 6. 1, 2, 5, 16. Num. 15. 38. Deut. 6. 8. & 22. 12.

43. *ἐν πνεύματι*] scil. *ἁγίῳ*, which is *expressed* in the parallel passage of Mark. This is plainly the sense, notwithstanding the attempts of some recent Commentators to explain the term away. Indeed, the writers of the O. T. are always *supposed* by our Lord to have written under the inspiration, more or less plenary, of the Holy Spirit.

— *κύριον*.] "This word, corresponding with the Heb. אָדוֹן, *adon*, signifying *Lord* or *Master*, was a term implying an acknowledgment of superiority in the person to whom it was addressed, and therefore never given to *inferiors*, though sometimes, perhaps, out of courtesy, to *equals*. Upon this, then, our Lord's argument turns. An independent monarch, such as David, acknowledged no Lord or Master but God; far less would he bestow that title upon a son, or descendant; and, consequently, the Messiah, being so called by him, under the influence of the Spirit, and therefore acknowledged as his superior, must be Divine." — (Campbell.)

44. *κάθου ἐκ δεξιῶν*.] A comparison taken from *kings*, on whose *right* hand sat the heir, or he who was next in dignity, and on the left hand he that was immediately below him in rank. But sitting on the right *implied* also a *participation* in the regal power and authority. Hence *συμβασιλεύειν* is interpreted by St. Paul, 1 Cor. xv. 25. *βασιλεύειν*.

— *ἕως ἂν θῶ*] "whilst I make." The image is derived from the custom of conquerors putting their foot on the neck of a vanquished enemy, as a mark of subjugation. How the words are to be understood of the *Messiah*, appears from 1 Cor. xv. 25. sq. On this use of *ἂν* with the Subjunct., see Winer's Gr. § 36. 2. a., and Alt's Gr. p. 147.

45. *εἰ οὖν — ἐστι*;] Some of the best Commentators regard this as an *inversion of construction*, as in Mark ii. 23. But since the sense is the same either way, there is no necessity to resort to any such supposition.

46. *τις*] "any one," namely, of the class of persons whom he had just silenced. By *ἐπερωτῆσαι* we are to understand the putting such sort of captious ensnaring questions as those above-mentioned.

XXIII. 1. *τότε*] i. e. after he had put the Pharisees and Sadducees to silence.

2. *καθέδρας*.] This alludes to the *sitting* posture in which the Jewish doctors taught. See Vitringa de Synag., p. 166. They, i. e. the Chief Priests, are said to sit in Moses' seat, by having succeeded to him in the office of teachers of religion. In *ἐκάθισαν* we may, with Fritz., suppose the Aorist used in the sense of *custom*.

3. *πάντα — ποιεῖτε*] This must be taken *restrictively*; (as in Col. iii. 20. 22. Ephes. v. 24.) i. e. all things which they read from the Law and the Prophets, and whatever they taught agreeably thereunto. Bp. Warb., in an able Sermon on this text, points out the magnanimity of this conduct of our Lord, and shows how different it was from what would have been pursued by an *impostor*, who had a *new* system to introduce upon one *established*, but shaken by the immorality of its teachers, who would have improved so favourable a circumstance to his own advantage. Our Lord, on the contrary, reproves the popular prejudice, and, endeavouring to reconcile the people to their teachers, his inveterate enemies, instructs them to distinguish between the *public* and *private* character of the teacher: showing them that though men who "say, and do not," should not be followed for *examples*, yet that as *ministers of religion*, who are invested with authority to teach the Law, they are to be attended to as *instructors* when officially enforcing the ordinances of God.

— *τηρεῖν*,] Some Editors cancel this word, which is omitted in 7 MSS., some Versions, and Latin Fathers. But that is very slender testimony; since Versions are, in a case like this, of little authority; and the MSS. are all of the Alexandrian recension, and such as abound with alterations arising from ill-judged fastidiousness.

4. *δεσμεύουσι*] "they bind [on] loads," as a bundle or bale, on a pack-horse. By these *burdens* are meant the traditions of the elders.

— *τῷ δὲ δακτύλῳ — κινῆσαι*] i. e. "they will not take upon their *own* shoulders the burdens which they lay on those of others," nor even stir them with their finger ends; a proverbial expression (common both to Greek and Latin writers) to denote "being quite indisposed to exert oneself in any labour."

πρὸς τὸ θεαθῆναι τοῖς ἀνθρώποις. πλατύνουσι δὲ τὰ φυλακτήρια
c Mark 12. 38. Luke 11. 43. & 20. 46. 3 John 9. αὐτῶν, καὶ μεγαλύνουσι τὰ κράσπεδα τῶν ἱματίων αὐτῶν· [c] φιλοῦσί 6
τε τὴν πρωτοκλισίαν ἐν τοῖς δείπνοις, καὶ τὰς πρωτοκαθεδρίας ἐν
ταῖς συναγωγαῖς, καὶ τοὺς ἀσπασμοὺς ἐν ταῖς ἀγοραῖς, καὶ καλεῖσθαι 7
ὑπὸ τῶν ἀνθρώπων ῥαββὶ, ῥαββί. ὑμεῖς δὲ μὴ κληθῆτε ῥαββί.
d James 3. 1. [d] εἷς γάρ ἐστιν ὑμῶν ὁ ‡ καθηγητὴς, [ὁ Χριστός·] πάντες δὲ ὑμεῖς 8
e Mal. 1. 6. ἀδελφοί ἐστε. [e] Καὶ πατέρα μὴ καλέσητε ὑμῶν ἐπὶ τῆς γῆς· εἷς 9
f Supr. 20. 26, 27. γάρ ἐστιν ὁ Πατὴρ ὑμῶν, ὁ ἐν τοῖς οὐρανοῖς. Μηδὲ κληθῆτε κα- 10
g Luke 14. 11. & 18. 14. θηγηταί· εἷς γὰρ ὑμῶν ἐστιν ὁ καθηγητὴς, ὁ Χριστός. [f] Ὁ δὲ 11
Job 22. 29. Prov. 29. 23. μείζων ὑμῶν ἔσται ὑμῶν διάκονος. [g] Ὅστις δὲ ὑψώσει ἑαυτὸν, τα- 12
James 4. 6. 1 Pet. 5. 5. πεινωθήσεται· καὶ ὅστις ταπεινώσει ἑαυτὸν, ὑψωθήσεται.
h Mark. 12. 40. Luke 20. 47. [h] Οὐαὶ δὲ ὑμῖν, Γραμματεῖς καὶ Φαρισαῖοι, ὑποκριταί! ὅτι κα- 13

5. πλατύνουσι.] Christ does not censure the *wearing* of those, or of the fringes, but the doing it ostentatiously, by making them very large. These phylacteries, (of which see a description in Horne's Introd.), took their rise from a *literal* instead of a spiritual interpretation of Deut. vi. 8. That these were, as the Commentators inform us, also regarded as *amulets*, or charms to preserve from evil, may be very true; but when they would hence deduce the *name itself*, we may hesitate; for the name may quite as well imply that they were thereby *reminded* to *keep* the law. See a passage of Plutarch cited by Kypke.

6. πρωτοκλισίαν] "the first seat at banquets." That, among the Jews, was probably at the *top* of the table, as with us; though among the Greeks and Romans the *middle* place at a triclinium was the most honourable.

— πρωτοκαθεδρίας,] i. e. on the seats of the seniors and the learned; who sat immediately under, with their backs to the pulpit of the reader; their faces being turned towards the people. See Vitringa de Synag. p. 191.

8, 9, 10.] In these three verses there is essentially the same sentiment, but with some variation of terms; resorted to in order to favour the *repetition*, which is meant to give energy to an earnest warning, forbidding the assumption, on the one hand, or the admission, on the other, of such a sort of absolute domination as that assumed by the Scribes over men, without authority from God. It is only meant, therefore, to warn them against that unlimited veneration for the decisions of men, or implicit reliance on any human teacher, which was so common among the Jewish devotees. Such being the purport, this passage cannot be supposed to forbid Christian teachers bearing such accustomed appellations as appertain to superiority of office, of station, or of talent; but only admonishes not to use them as the Scribes did, for the purposes of pride and ostentation, and to exercise a spiritual tyranny over the faith and consciences of their Christian brethren, or pretend to such infallibility and supreme authority as is due to Christ alone. See more in a masterly Sermon of Bp. Warburton, vol. ix. pp. 190—206.

The three terms here employed, ῥαββὶ, πατὴρ, and καθηγ. were, as we learn from the Rabbinical writers, appellations such as were ordinarily assumed by and given to their principal Teachers; and not only all *three* were, we find, sometimes employed, but each twice; which is alluded to in the preceding verse.

8. μὴ κληθῆτε] "suffer not yourselves to be called."

— καθηγητής.] There is some doubt as to the reading here. Many of the best Commentators would read διδάσκαλος, which is found in several MSS., Versions, and Fathers, but is received by no Editor except Fritz.: doubtless because it would seem a gloss on καθηγ. But διδάσκ. is so much preferable, from its being more correspondent to the Heb. רבי, and such an offensive tautology and confusion of terms is thereby removed, that it can scarcely be doubted but that it is the true reading.

— ὁ Χριστός.] This is omitted in several ancient MSS., and some Versions and Fathers; is rejected by Mill and Beng., cancelled by Griesb., and Fritz., and bracketed by most other Editors. It probably crept in from ver. 10.

9. πατέρα — γῆς·] "style no man on earth *your Father*." There is an ellipsis of τίνα.

12. ὅστις δὲ — ὑψωθήσεται] A sentiment very often introduced by our Lord; and indeed a frequent maxim among the Jews, and sometimes occurring in the Classical writers. By Christ, however, it is employed in a *spiritual* sense; i. e. "him *God* will exalt."

13, 14.] These verses are *transposed* in the *textus vulgatus* and most of the MSS.; but are placed in the present order in the best MSS.; confirmed by several Versions, Fathers, and early Editions, approved, with reason, by all the most eminent Commentators, and restored by Mill, Wets., Matth., Knapp, Fritz., and Scholz. Ver. 13. is omitted in several MSS. of the Alexandrian recension, with some Versions and Latin Fathers. But there is no good ground for rejecting it. It should seem that the text above adopted presents the true reading and order; probably *accidentally* changed by the eyes of the transcribers being carried from the *first* οὐαὶ δὲ — ὑποκριταί! to the *second*, by which the words ὅτι κατεσθίετε — κρίμα were omitted, and afterwards inserted, either by the *scribes* (perceiving their mistake), or by the *correctors*, but in the wrong place.

— κατεσθίετε.] Of this use of the word examples occur frequently in the Greek Classical writers; and the same is the case with the correspondent term in Latin, and indeed in the modern languages. Οἰκίας means, goods, property, as οἶκος is often used in the Classical writers. Both the above

τεσθίετε τὰς οἰκίας τῶν χηρῶν, καὶ προφάσει μακρὰ προσευχόμενοι·
14 διὰ τοῦτο λήψεσθε περισσότερον κρίμα. [i] Οὐαὶ ὑμῖν, Γραμματεῖς [i] Luke 11. 52.
καὶ Φαρισαῖοι, ὑποκριταί! ὅτι κλείετε τὴν βασιλείαν τῶν οὐρανῶν
ἔμπροσθεν τῶν ἀνθρώπων. ὑμεῖς γὰρ οὐκ εἰσέρχεσθε, οὐδὲ τοὺς
15 εἰσερχομένους ἀφίετε εἰσελθεῖν. Οὐαὶ ὑμῖν, Γραμματεῖς καὶ Φαρισαῖοι, ὑποκριταί! ὅτι περιάγετε τὴν θάλασσαν καὶ τὴν ξηρὰν, ποιῆσαι ἕνα προσήλυτον· καὶ ὅταν γένηται, ποιεῖτε αὐτὸν υἱὸν γεέννης
16 διπλότερον ὑμῶν. [k] Οὐαὶ ὑμῖν, ὁδηγοὶ τυφλοί! οἱ λέγοντες· Ὃς ἂν [k] Supr. 15. 14. & 5. 33, 34.
ὀμόσῃ ἐν τῷ ναῷ, οὐδέν ἐστιν· ὃς δ᾽ ἂν ὀμόσῃ ἐν τῷ χρυσῷ τοῦ
17 ναοῦ, ὀφείλει. Μωροὶ καὶ τυφλοί! τίς γὰρ μείζων ἐστὶν, ὁ χρυσὸς,
18 ἢ ὁ ναὸς ὁ ἁγιάζων τὸν χρυσόν; καί· ὃς ἐὰν ὀμόσῃ ἐν τῷ θυσι-
αστηρίῳ, οὐδέν ἐστιν· ὃς δ᾽ ἂν ὀμόσῃ ἐν τῷ δώρῳ τῷ ἐπάνω αὐτοῦ,
19 ὀφείλει. [l] Μωροὶ καὶ τυφλοί! τί γὰρ μεῖζον, τὸ δῶρον, ἢ τὸ θυ- [l] Exod. 29. 37.
20 σιαστήριον τὸ ἁγιάζον τὸ δῶρον; Ὁ οὖν ὀμόσας ἐν τῷ θυσιαστη-
21 ρίῳ ὀμνύει ἐν αὐτῷ, καὶ ἐν πᾶσι τοῖς ἐπάνω αὐτοῦ. [m] Καὶ ὁ ὀμόσας [m] 1 Kings 8. 13. 2 Chron. 6. 2.
22 ἐν τῷ ναῷ ὀμνύει ἐν αὐτῷ, καὶ ἐν τῷ κατοικήσαντι αὐτόν. [n] Καὶ [n] Supr. 5. 34.
ὁ ὀμόσας ἐν τῷ οὐρανῷ ὀμνύει ἐν τῷ θρόνῳ τοῦ Θεοῦ, καὶ ἐν τῷ
καθημένῳ ἐπάνω αὐτοῦ.
23 [o] Οὐαὶ ὑμῖν, Γραμματεῖς καὶ Φαρισαῖοι, ὑποκριταί! ὅτι ἀποδεκα- [o] Luke 11. 42.

metaphors are found in Hom. Od. β. 237. κατέδουσι βιαίως Οἶκον Ὀδυσσῆος. This "eating up" was done by various subtle artifices. After making them devotees, they devised various means of laying them under contribution; or caballed with the children to deprive the widow of a portion of her dowry, for some return, either in hand, or in expectation.

—προφάσει] Sub. ἐπὶ, "under a pretext," namely, of religion; for it was but a mask to conceal their avarice.

—μακρά.] Sometimes, it is said, these prayers occupied nine hours a day.

14. κλείετε ἔμπροσθεν τῶν ἀνθ.] For the more Classical κλείειν ἀπὸ or ἀποκλείειν. It may be compared with our phrase, *to shut the door in the face of.* In the words of the parallel passage of Luke, ἤρατε τὴν κλεῖδα τῆς γνώσεως, there is an allusion to locking a door against any, and preventing them from entering by carrying off the key. The metaphor has reference to the hindering men from embracing Christianity; which they effected by misinterpreting the prophecies, and by other methods.

15. περιάγετε — ξηρὰν,] A proverbial expression, frequent both in Greek and Latin, importing the greatest activity and exertion. The zeal, indeed, of the Jews for proselytism was, itself, proverbial among the Heathens (see Hor. Sat. i. 4.) insomuch that at length it was forbidden by the *Constitutiones Imperatorum.*

—υἱὸν γεέννης] i. e. by Hebraism, "deserving of, or doomed to, hell." So 1 Sam. xx. 31. 2 Sam. xii. 5. υἱὸς θανάτου, "devoted to death." It is strange that Kypke, Rosenm., and some others, should take διπλ. to signify *dolosum.* The grammatical objection to the common interpretation, on the ground that the word never occurs in the *comparative,* has no force, for I have myself in Rec. Syn. adduced two examples. Moreover, διπλότερον, here and in the other two passages where it occurs, is not an adjective, but an *adverb.*

16. In this and the seven following verses Christ condemns the subtle distinctions of the Pharisees concerning oaths, and points out the sanctity and obligation of an oath. See Notes on Matt. v. 33. sqq.

—τῷ χρυσῷ τοῦ ναοῦ.] By this some understand the *gold which adorned the Temple;* others, *the sacred utensils;* others again, *the money set apart for sacred purposes.* As no particular gold is mentioned, it may be understood of any or *all* of the above.

17. ὁ ἁγιάζων] "makes it sacred and apart from common use." The money was holy, because it was subservient to the uses of the Temple, and other sacred purposes, like the ἀνάθηματα among the Greeks, and the *donaria* among the Romans. — (Rosenm.)

21. κατοικήσαντι.] This is read, for the common κατοικοῦντι, in the greater part of the MSS. and the Ed. Prin.; and it has been, with reason, edited by Matth., Griesb., Tittm., Vat., Fritz., and Scholz.

23. ἀποδεκατοῦτε — κύμινον.] The Pharisees were scrupulously exact in paying tithes, not only of the fruits of the earth, but even of such insignificant herbs as those here specified, as ἡδύοσμον, the garden mint, ἄνηθον, *dill;* (on which see Dioscor. iii. 461.) and κύμινον, *cummin,* a disagreeable pungent herb, and so little esteemed, that it was proverbially employed to express worthlessness. That the above are only meant as *examples* of insignificant herbs, is plain from Luke having "mint and *rue,*" with the addition of καὶ πᾶν λάχανον. Ἀποδεκατεύειν is a word not used by the Classical writers, and only found in the Sept.; where it expresses the Heb. עִשֵּׂר, which signifies both to *take* tithe and to *pay* tithe. Our Lord, it must be observed, does not censure them for paying tithes of these herbs; but, after performing

τοῦτε τὸ ἡδύοσμον καὶ τὸ ἄνηθον καὶ τὸ κύμινον· καὶ ἀφήκατε τὰ
βαρύτερα τοῦ νόμου, τὴν κρίσιν καὶ τὸν ἔλεον καὶ τὴν πίστιν· ταῦτα
ἔδει ποιῆσαι, κἀκεῖνα μὴ ἀφιέναι. Ὁδηγοὶ τυφλοί· οἱ διϋλίζοντες 24
p Luke 11. 39. supr. 15. 20. Mark 7. 4. τὸν κώνωπα, τὴν δὲ κάμηλον καταπίνοντες. [p] Οὐαὶ ὑμῖν, Γραμματεῖς 25
καὶ Φαρισαῖοι, ὑποκριταί! ὅτι καθαρίζετε τὸ ἔξωθεν τοῦ ποτηρίου
καὶ τῆς παροψίδος, ἔσωθεν δὲ γέμουσιν ἐξ ἁρπαγῆς καὶ * ἀδικίας.
Φαρισαῖε τυφλέ! καθάρισον πρῶτον τὸ ἐντὸς τοῦ ποτηρίου καὶ τῆς 26
παροψίδος, ἵνα γένηται καὶ τὸ ἐκτὸς αὐτῶν καθαρόν.
q Luke 11. 44. [q] Οὐαὶ ὑμῖν, Γραμματεῖς καὶ Φαρισαῖοι, ὑποκριταί! ὅτι παρομοιά- 27
ζετε τάφοις κεκονιαμένοις, οἵτινες ἔξωθεν μὲν φαίνονται ὡραῖοι, ἔσωθεν δὲ γέμουσιν ὀστέων νεκρῶν καὶ πάσης ἀκαθαρσίας. Οὕτω καὶ 28
ὑμεῖς ἔξωθεν μὲν φαίνεσθε τοῖς ἀνθρώποις δίκαιοι, ἔσωθεν δὲ μεστοί
r Luke 11. 47. ἐστε ὑποκρίσεως καὶ ἀνομίας. [r] Οὐαὶ ὑμῖν, Γραμματεῖς καὶ Φαρισαῖοι, 29
ὑποκριταί! ὅτι οἰκοδομεῖτε τοὺς τάφους τῶν προφητῶν, καὶ κοσμεῖτε
τὰ μνημεῖα τῶν δικαίων, καὶ λέγετε· Εἰ * ἤμεθα ἐν ταῖς ἡμέραις 30

these minute observances, for omitting the weightier matters of the Law. This applies to all the subjects of the woes in this Chapter, as is plain from the words *ταῦτα ἔδει ποιῆσαι, κἀκεῖνα μὴ ἀφιέναι*.

— *ἀφήκατε*] "ye neglect." The word is often applied to the neglect of Divine precepts.

— *κρίσιν, ἔλεον, καὶ τὴν πίστιν.*] Render "justice, charity, (or humanity) and faith," or trust in God, as the proper foundation of our love; not *fidelity*, as some explain; though that sense may be *included*. Thus it will be agreeable to Luke's *τὴν ἀγάπην τοῦ Θεοῦ*. The passage seems to be taken from Micah vi. 8. and may be compared with Pind. Olymp. xiii. 6, 11. and Hor. Od. i. 24, 6.

24. *διϋλίζοντες τὸν κώνωπα.*] Not "strain *at*," (which was a mere typographical blunder of the first Edition of our common Version) but strain *out*. There is an allusion to the custom of the Jews (prevalent also among the Greeks and Romans) of passing their wines (which in the southern countries might easily receive gnats, and indeed breed *insects*) through a strainer. See Amos vi. 6. The Jews did it from religious scruples, (the *κώνωψ* or *culex vinarius* being unclean,) the Gentiles, from cleanliness. The ratio significationis arises as follows. The term signifies to *pass any liquid through a strainer*, (*ὀθονίον*. See Dioscor. iii. 9. & v. 82.) *to separate it from the* *ὕλη*; or material particles, (gnats, or aught else) that they may be passed *out* and *off*. With respect to *κάμηλον*, it signifies, not a *cable*, nor a *beetle*, (as some would take it) but a *camel*. To make the opposition as strong as may be, two things are selected as opposite as possible, the *smallest insect*, and the *largest animal*. This sort of expression was in use both with the Jewish and the Grecian writers. *Καταπίνω* is used not of *liquids* only, but also of *solids*, as here. In the former case it may be rendered to *gulp down*; in in the latter, to *bolt down*.

25. *καθαρίζετε — παροψίδος.*] On the purification of domestic utensils see Horne's Introd. vol. iii. p. 337. *Παροψὶς* is a word found only in the later writers, and signifies a *platter*, *dish*, or, as some think, *sauce-boat*.

— *ἀδικίας.*] This, for the common reading *ἀκρασίας*, is found in the greater part of the MSS., and many Versions and Fathers; and is edited by Matth., Griesb., Knapp; Tittm., Fritz., and Scholz. The internal evidence for it, too, is as strong as the external; for it suits far better with the *character* of the Pharisees, who (as Campb. observes) are never accused of *intemperance*, though often of *injustice*.

27. *κεκονιαμένοις.*] On the exact force of *κονιάω* see my Note in Rec. Synopt. The tombs were annually *whitewashed*, that their situation might be known, and the pollution of touching them avoided. This whitening, we learn, extended as far on the surface of the ground as the vault reached under ground. The sense is, that the Pharisees were so polluted with vice, that they defiled all who had communication with them, and were to be avoided like sepulchres. In the parallel passage of Luke xi. 44. they are likened to *μνημεῖα ἄδηλα*, (see Note in loc.); but there is, in fact, no discrepancy, but reference is had to the *contagion* they spread around them.

— *ἀκαθαρσίας.*] Very apposite to the present purpose is a passage adduced by me in Recens. Synop. from the Schol. on Soph. Phil., who explains the words *ῥάκη βαρείας νοηλείας πλέα* by *πεπληρωμένα — τῆς ἐκ νόσου ἀκαθαρσίας*, i. e. *pus* and bloody matter.

28. *μεστοί — ἀνομίας.*] *Μεστὸς* is almost always used cum genitivo *mali*.

29. *οἰκοδομεῖτε — κοσμεῖτε.*] 'Both the Jews and the Heathens alike showed their respect for the illustrious dead, by repairing and beautifying, and, when necessary, rebuilding their tombs. See the proofs and illustrations in Rec. Syn. "This," as Kuin. observes, "our Lord did not mean to censure, but to expose the hypocrisy of the Pharisees in pretending a respect for the Prophets which they did not feel."

30. *ἤμεθα.*] This reading (for the common one *ἦμεν*) is found in most of the best MSS., in some Fathers, and in the Ed. Princ.; and was, with reason, edited by Matth., Griesb., and others down to Scholz. *Ἤμην*, found also in John xi. 15. Acts x. 30. and elsewhere, was the usual Imperfect in the Alexandrian dialect, though it was by the later Greeks changed into the Attic form *ἦν*. See Alt's Gr. N. T. p. 21.

τῶν πατέρων ἡμῶν, οὐκ ἂν * ἤμεθα κοινωνοὶ αὐτῶν ἐν τῷ αἵματι
31 τῶν προφητῶν. Ὥστε μαρτυρεῖτε ἑαυτοῖς, ὅτι υἱοί ἐστε τῶν φονευ-
32 σάντων τοὺς προφήτας. Καὶ ὑμεῖς πληρώσατε τὸ μέτρον τῶν πατέ-
33 ρων ὑμῶν. [s] Ὄφεις! γεννήματα ἐχιδνῶν! πῶς φύγητε ἀπὸ τῆς [s] Supr. 3. 7.
34 κρίσεως τῆς γεέννης; [t] Διὰ τοῦτο ἰδοὺ, ἐγὼ ἀποστέλλω πρὸς ὑμᾶς [t] Luke 11. 49. Acts 5. 40.
προφήτας καὶ σοφοὺς καὶ γραμματεῖς· καὶ ἐξ αὐτῶν ἀποκτενεῖτε καὶ & 22. 19. 2 Cor. 11. 24, 25.
σταυρώσετε, καὶ ἐξ αὐτῶν μαστιγώσετε ἐν ταῖς συναγωγαῖς ὑμῶν, καὶ
35 διώξετε ἀπὸ πόλεως εἰς πόλιν· [u] ὅπως ἔλθῃ ἐφ᾽ ὑμᾶς πᾶν αἷμα [u] Gen. 4. 8. Heb. 11, 4.
δίκαιον ἐκχυνόμενον ἐπὶ τῆς γῆς, ἀπὸ αἵματος Ἄβελ τοῦ δικαίου, ἕως 2 Chron. 24. 21, 22.
τοῦ αἵματος Ζαχαρίου, υἱοῦ Βαραχίου, ὃν ἐφονεύσατε μεταξὺ τοῦ ναοῦ

31. ὥστε μαρτυρεῖτε ἑ., &c.] "ye have the same blood-thirsty disposition (thus they are elsewhere called γενεὰ ἀποκτείνουσα), and ye thus show approbation of your fathers' crimes, by pursuing the same course; as is *expressed* in the parallel passage of Luke xi. 48. ἄρα μαρτυρεῖτε καὶ συνευδοκεῖτε τοῖς ἔργοις τῶν πατέρων ὑμῶν, where the ὅτι must not be rendered *although* (as some translate), but has the sense *quatenus*. See Schleus. Lex. in v. § 5. which, as he observes, "*habet vim restringendi et specificandi.*"

We are now prepared to see the *inferential* force of ὥστε, which is as follows: So then [by this conduct, so similar to that of your fathers], ye bear testimony respecting yourselves, that ye are *true sons* of your fathers, who murdered the prophets. On the force of which expression see Notes on Matt. v. 45. and John viii. 44. Most recent Commentators explain μαρτυρ. ἑαυτοῖς, "ye bear testimony against yourselves." But there is no sufficient reason to deviate from the common version *unto*, i. e. *respecting* yourselves.

32. πληρώσατε τὸ μέτρον τ. π. ὑ.] This may, with many of the best Commentators, ancient and modern, be accounted an *ironical concession*, or *permission*, often occurring in Scripture; such as indignantly leaves the persons addressed to experience the consequences of their wilfulness. For, in the words of Bp. Taylor, "they still continued in the same malice towards those sent from God to reform them; but painted it over with a pretence of *piety*, and of disavowing their father's sins." On this "*measure unfulfilled*," see the remarks of Grotius, and the illustrations of Wets., who shew that the language seems to imply that there is a certain height to which the iniquity of *nations* and individuals is permitted by God to rise, and that when that measure is full, the punishment is inflicted; and that though the vengeance of the Almighty be slow, it is always sure, compensating for long-delayed vengeance by the severity of the stroke. See the fine Tract of Plutarch de Serâ Numinis Vindictâ.

33. ὄφεις — ἐχιδνῶν.] See iii. 7. and on τῆς γεέννης, see Note on ver. 15. Φύγητε. The best Commentators think that this is put for φεύξεσθε; the latter writers imitating the Poetic idiom of using the Subjunctive for the Future, which is generally thought a solecism, though defended by Fritz. in loc.

34. διὰ τοῦτο.] On the force of this formula the Commentators are divided in opinion. Most recent Expositors consider it as merely *a form of transition*; as ἐν τούτῳ or ἐπὶ τούτῳ in Matt. xiii. 52. xxii. 29. Mark xii. 24. Yet, as that principle is somewhat precarious, we may, with Euthym. and Fritz., refer it to ver. 32. διότι (says Euthym.) μέλλετε πληρῶσαι τὸ μέτρον τῆς κακίας τῶν πατέρων ὑμῶν.

— προφήτας — γραμματεῖς.] Our Lord here applies to his Apostles and their successors the titles given by the Jews to their Doctors; signifying that *his messengers* (so called in Luke xi. 49.), would be as entitled to the appellation προφήτας (in the sense, Divine Legates and *inspired interpreters of the will of God*) as were the prophets of old; and would likewise be entitled to the appellations σοφοὺς, חכמים, and γραμματεῖς, ספרים, as being thoroughly conversant in the Scriptures and Divine learning.

— ἐξ αὐτῶν] Sub. τινάς. Ἀποκτενεῖτε. See Acts vii. 59. & xii. 2.

— σταυρώσετε.] Though there is no evidence of the *crucifixion* of any Christian teacher much before the destruction of Jerusalem; yet the *silence* of history (so exceedingly brief as it has come down to us) is no proof that there were none such. It is better to rest on *this*, than to suppose, with some, that Christ here includes *himself*; or to take σταυρ. in sensu improprio for "*to put to a cruel death.*"

— μαστιγώσετε.] See x. 17. and Acts xxii. 19.

35. ὅπως] This should be rendered, not *ita ut*, but, as Hoogev. suggests, *ut*, or *hoc modo ut*. Fritz. well expresses the sense of the passage thus: "Vos omnino ita agetis, ut videamini in id unicè intenti, ut omnis sanguinis justi atque insontis culpam soli sustineatis." Ἐκχυνόμενον is, as Fritz. remarks, to be taken *generally*, so as to include both past, present, and future.

— Ζαχαρίου — Βαραχίου.] There has been much dispute as to the *person* here meant by our Lord. The various opinions are detailed and reviewed by Kuin. and Fritz. The two alone worthy of remark are, 1. that it was Zechariah, one of the Minor Prophets. But as there is no historical testimony that he was murdered, most of the recent Commentators are of opinion that the person meant is that Zacharias, the *High Priest*, who, for his having reproved the iniquities of the Jewish people, was, by the order of King Joash, slain between the sanctuary and the altar of whole burnt offerings. See 2 Chron. xxiv. 20, 21. And though this Joash be called son of *Jehoiada*, yet it was not unfrequent among the Jews to bear *two* names; especially when, as in the present case, the names were of the same meaning.

— θυσιαστηρίου.] "the altar for holocausts, or

καὶ τοῦ θυσιαστηρίου. Ἀμὴν λέγω ὑμῖν, ὅτι ἥξει ταῦτα πάντα ἐπὶ τὴν 36
x Luke 13. 34, 35. 2 Esdr. 1. 30. γενεὰν ταύτην. x Ἱερουσαλὴμ, Ἱερουσαλὴμ! ἡ ἀποκτείνουσα τοὺς 37
προφήτας, καὶ λιθοβολοῦσα τοὺς ἀπεσταλμένους πρὸς αὐτὴν, ποσάκις
ἠθέλησα ἐπισυναγαγεῖν τὰ τέκνα σου, ὃν τρόπον ἐπισυνάγει ὄρνις τὰ
νοσσία ἑαυτῆς ὑπὸ τὰς πτέρυγας, καὶ οὐκ ἠθελήσατε; Ἰδοὺ, ἀφίεται 38
y Ps. 118. 26. supr. 21. 9. ὑμῖν ὁ οἶκος ὑμῶν ἔρημος. y Λέγω γὰρ ὑμῖν· Οὐ μή με ἴδητε 39
MK. LU. ἀπ᾽ ἄρτι, ἕως ἂν εἴπητε· Εὐλογημένος ὁ ἐρχόμενος ἐν ὀνόματι
13. 21. Κυρίου.
1 5 XXIV. ΚΑΙ ἐξελθὼν ὁ Ἰησοῦς ἐπορεύετο ἀπὸ τοῦ ἱεροῦ· καὶ 1
2 6 προσῆλθον οἱ μαθηταὶ αὐτοῦ ἐπιδεῖξαι αὐτῷ τὰς οἰκοδομὰς τοῦ ἱεροῦ.
Ὁ δὲ Ἰησοῦς εἶπεν αὐτοῖς· Οὐ βλέπετε πάντα ταῦτα; ἀμὴν λέγω 2
ὑμῖν, οὐ μὴ ἀφεθῇ ὧδε λίθος ἐπὶ λίθον, ὃς οὐ [μὴ] καταλυθήσεται.

burnt sacrifices," which, Grot. shews, was *in subdiali*, in the Court of the Priests.

36. ὅτι] This is found in most of the best MSS. and some Versions and Fathers, with the Ed. Princ., and has been adopted by almost every Editor from Beng. to Scholz.

—ἥξει—ταύτην.] By ταῦτα πάντα are meant "all these crimes;" and ἥκειν, or, as in the former verse, ἐλθεῖν ἐπί τινα here signifies "to come upon any one," "to be visited upon any one," namely, to bring down punishment on his head.

37. ἡ ἀποκτείνουσα] Erasm. well points out the *permanent action* (as referring alike to past, present, and future) denoted by this use of the present tense.

—αὐτὴν,] for ἑαυτὴν or σεαυτήν. So I read, instead of the Stephanic αὑτὴν, with the Edit. Princ., Beza, Schmid, Griesb., and Fritz. There is no occasion to bring in the figure by which a transition is made from the second to the third person; which would here be very awkward.

—τέκνα.] The word is often used thus, figuratively, of the *inhabitants* of a city, both in the Scriptural and the Classical writers.

—ἐπισυναγαγεῖν.] The ἐπι is not, as the Commentators imagine, pleonastic, but signifies *to.* Thus the term signifies to draw together *to any one.*

—ἠθελήσατε.] The plural here has reference to the plural *implied* in Ἱερουσαλὴμ, which means *inhabitants* of Jerusalem, an idiom frequent both in the Scriptural and Classical writers.

38. ἀφίεται] Prophetic present put for future.

—οἶκος.] The Commentators are not agreed whether this is to be taken of the *Temple*, or of the *whole Jewish nation*, especially its *metropolis*; as the Latin writers use *domus* for *patria*. The former sense is, indeed, applicable, but somewhat too *weak*; not to say that Θεοῦ would thus require to be added: and therefore the latter is preferable.

39. οὐ μή με ἴδητε—Κυρίου.] Many are the modes of interpretation offered of this perplexing passage. Some Commentators think that our Lord meant to predict his removal from them, until the destruction of Jerusalem; which is in the next Chapter designated under the name of "the coming of the Lord." And they render the words ἕως ἂν εἴπητε, "until ye might say." "would have reason to say." There is indeed something to countenance this view in the actual state of Judæa at that period, as recorded by the accurate Josephus, Bell. J. vii. 36. But such a sense of ἕως ἂν εἴπητε is strained; and the interpretation is otherwise liable to some serious objections. Greatly preferable is that of Chrysost. and others, who take the *coming* here spoken of to mean the *second* coming of our Lord to judgment at the end of the world. Thus by *ye* will be meant the *Jewish nation.* That the great bulk of the Jews will, ere that awful catastrophe, be brought to acknowledge that Messiah whom their ancestors rejected, we are taught by the sure word of prophecy. See Grot., Doddr., and Scott. Those who adopt this interpretation maintain that ἀπ᾽ ἄρτι should be rendered "after a while," i. e. after the ascension. But that sense is destitute of proof, and indeed unnecessary, if ἴδητε be taken (with Koecher) of *familiar intercourse* as a teacher; for our Lord had with the present address closed his *public* ministry. Εὐλογημένος, &c. was the form by which the Messiah (usually styled ὁ ἐρχόμενος, &c.) was to be addressed in his coming.

XXIV. 1. ἐπιδεῖξαι αὐτῷ τὰς οἰκοδ.] The disciples were pointing with wonder and pride at their stateliness, and seemed to say, "Is it possible that such a magnificent edifice should be *utterly* destroyed?" Indeed, the destruction of the Temple was, in the minds of the Jews, viewed as coeval only with the *end of the world*; or at least that modification in its constitution, which they supposed would take place at the coming of the Messiah.

2. οὐ βλέπετε.] Several MSS. and Versions are without the οὐ, which is marked as probably to be omitted by Griesb. and others, and cancelled by Fritz. But the MS. evidence *for* it is incomparably stronger than that *against* it; and had it not been in the text from the first, who would have thought of inserting it? for, when away, the same sense arises. But why (it may be asked) should the οὐ have been *removed?* I answer, because it is not employed agreeably to the Classical usage, and because it is not found in the parallel passage of Mark.

—οὐ μὴ ἀφεθῇ—λίθον] A proverbial and hyperbolical expression, denoting utter destruction, but in this instance almost fulfilled to the letter; as we learn from Joseph. B. J. vii. 1, 1. Euseb., and the Rabbinical writers. Simil. Luke xix. 43 & 44. The words ὃς οὐ καταλυθήσεται are added, to strengthen the preceding. See Soph. Antig. 441. and Hom. Il. xxi. 50. referred to by Fritz. The μὴ is omitted in almost all the best MSS., and several Fathers, and the early Editions. It is rejected

MK. LU.
3 Καθημένου δὲ αὐτοῦ ἐπὶ τοῦ ὄρους τῶν ἐλαιῶν, προσῆλθον αὐτῷ οἱ 13. 21.
μαθηταὶ κατ᾿ ἰδίαν, λέγοντες· Εἰπὲ ἡμῖν, πότε ταῦτα ἔσται; καὶ τί 3 4 7
4 τὸ σημεῖον τῆς σῆς παρουσίας, καὶ τῆς συντελείας τοῦ αἰῶνος; Καὶ 5 8
ἀποκριθεὶς ὁ Ἰησοῦς εἶπεν αὐτοῖς· Βλέπετε μή τις ὑμᾶς πλανήσῃ.
5 Πολλοὶ γὰρ ἐλεύσονται ἐπὶ τῷ ὀνόματί μου, λέγοντες· Ἐγώ εἰμι ὁ 6
6 Χριστός· καὶ πολλοὺς πλανήσουσι. Μελλήσετε δὲ ἀκούειν πολέμους

by Mill, Beng., and Wets., and cancelled by Matth., Griesb., Knapp, Tittm., Fritz., and Scholz; and justly, for scarcely any authority could justify so gross a barbarism. The μὴ arose from the οὐ μὴ just before. Καταλυθήσεται (Krueg. observes) has reference to the *dissolution* of the *coagmentatio lapidum.*

3. πότε ταῦτα ἔσται — τοῦ αἰῶνος.] The Commentators are much divided in opinion as to the intent of this inquiry: and not less than four different hypotheses of interpretation have been propounded. The 1st, confines the inquiry to the approaching destruction of Jerusalem. The 2d, extends it to *two* questions, and includes the *second* advent of Christ in the regeneration, according to the Jewish expectation. The 3d, instead of the *second*, substitutes the *last* advent of Christ at the end of the world, and the general judgment. The 4th, (to use the words of Dr. Hales, who adopts it) "unites all the preceding into *three questions;* the 1st, relating to the destruction of Jerusalem; the 2d, to our Lord's second appearance in glory at the restitution of all things, Acts iii. 21; the 3d, to the general judgment at the end of the world." "the inquiry (continues he) involves three questions: 1. *When* shall these (things) be? and the *sign* when they shall happen? 2. And what the sign of thy presence? and 3. What the sign when all these things shall be concluded, or of the conclusion of the world?" Mr. Townsend (in common with Chrys., Euthym., and many ancient Interpreters, and also the most eminent modern ones), embraces the first (or rather *second)* hypothesis. "From their question (he says) it appears that the disciples viewed the coming of Christ and the end of the world or age, as events nearly related, and which would indisputably take place together [and used the expression, συντέλεια τοῦ αἰῶνος to designate *both*. — Edit.]; they had no idea of the dissolution of the Jewish polity, as really signified by, or included in, either of these events. They imagined, perhaps, a great and awful change in the physical constitution of the universe, which they probably expected would occur within the term of their own lives; but they could have no conception of what was really meant by the expression which they employed, the coming of Christ. The coming of Christ, and the end of the world, being therefore only different expressions to denote the same period as the destruction of Jerusalem, the purport of the disciples' question plainly is, When shall the destruction of Jerusalem be — and what shall be the signs of it? The latter part of the question is the first answered, and our Saviour foretells, in the clearest manner, the *signs* of his coming, and the destruction of Jerusalem. He then passes on to the other part of the question, concerning the *time* of his coming."

It is no easy matter to decide on the comparative claims of these two views, which are manifestly the soundest of the four. If we were to advert simply to the *intent* of the inquiry of the Apostles, and trace the remarkable *fulfilment* of the following predictions, even in minute circumstances, we could scarcely, I think, fail to give the preference to the *latter*. But Dr. Hales's has much to recommend it, in the strong bearing which very many passages have on the *last* advent and the final judgment; while Mr. Townsend's is too limited, by making our Lord's words only an answer to the inquiries of the Apostles; indeed scarcely so much: since their *third* question must, by *implication*, be understood to have reference to that regeneration, renovation, or restitution of all things, according to their views. See Note on παλιγγενεσία supra xix. 28., and comp. Acts iii. 21. and Rom. viii. 19. Whereas there is no difficulty in supposing that our Lord, finding that the disciples had pointed to the Temple, to draw from him some more explicit declaration respecting the utter destruction, and in their questions had *wished* for more information than they ventured directly to ask, was pleased not only to answer their question, but to give them such further information on an awful topic closely connected with that of their inquiry, as would be most important for them to know, and, through them, his diciples of every age. So that, as the prediction concerning the destruction of the Temple arose naturally out of the train of passing circumstances, so, it should seem, did the awful predictions in this and the next Chapter arise out of the limited interrogatories of the Apostles. It may be observed, that the information as to the *last advent* and general judgment being *superadded* to the information in reply to their question, is, as might be expected, in a great degree, given *last* (xxv. 31—46); yet there are many allusions to it in the *preceding* matter, which *chiefly* concerns the event of the second advent *to judgment;* and in some passages the two predictions are so closely interwoven together, and the expressions and imagery are so applicable to the day of judgment, that we might almost say that a kind of secondary sense must be admitted; which as Mr. Horne has observed, is not unfrequently found in the prophetical writings, where two subjects, a principal and a subordinate one, are carried on together. This principle, will, if I mistake not, afford a sure clue to guide us in our greatest difficulties as to the interpretation of this sublime portion of Scripture.

4. βλέπ. μή τις πλαν.] A form of earnest caution, as in Eph. v. 6. Col. ii. 8. 2 Thes. ii. 3.

5. ἐπὶ τῷ ὀνόματί μου] i. e. assuming the name and character of Messiah. Between these and the false *prophets* at ver. 11, a distinction must be made. Of the former were Simon Magus and Dositheus, and perhaps those adverted to by Joseph. B. J. i. 2. Of the latter were Theudas, Barchochebas the Egyptian, and many other impostors mentioned by Josephus.

6. πολέμους.] Wets. cites, in illustration, Joseph. Ant. 18, 9, 1, and on ἀκοὰς πολ. Joseph. Ant. 20, 3,

MK. LU.
13. 21. καὶ ἀκοὰς πολέμων· ὁρᾶτε, μὴ θροεῖσθε· δεῖ γὰρ πάντα γενέσθαι·
8 10 ἀλλ᾽ οὔπω ἐστὶ τὸ τέλος. Ἐγερθήσεται γὰρ ἔθνος ἐπὶ ἔθνος, καὶ 7
βασιλεία ἐπὶ βασιλείαν· καὶ ἔσονται λιμοὶ καὶ λοιμοὶ καὶ σεισμοὶ
9 11 κατὰ τόπους. Πάντα δὲ ταῦτα ἀρχὴ ὠδίνων. Τότε παραδώσουσιν 8
12 ὑμᾶς εἰς θλίψιν, καὶ ἀποκτενοῦσιν ὑμᾶς· καὶ ἔσεσθε μισούμενοι ὑπὸ 9
13 17 πάντων τῶν ἐθνῶν διὰ τὸ ὄνομά μου. Καὶ τότε σκανδαλισθήσονται 10
πολλοί· καὶ ἀλλήλους παραδώσουσι, καὶ μισήσουσιν ἀλλήλους· καὶ 11
πολλοὶ ψευδοπροφῆται ἐγερθήσονται, καὶ πλανήσουσι πολλούς· καὶ 12
διὰ τὸ πληθυνθῆναι τὴν ἀνομίαν, ψυγήσεται ἡ ἀγάπη τῶν πολλῶν·

3, & 4, 2; Bell. Jud. 2, 16, & 1, 1, 2. [*Comp.* Jer. iv. 27; v. 10, 18.]

— ὁρᾶτε, μὴ θροεῖσθε·] So Fritz. rightly points (with Steph.), remarking that ὁρᾶτε μὴ would signify *videte, ne*, and require θροῆσθε.

— δεῖ — γενέσθαι.] This is referred by the earlier modern Commentators to the *counsel* of God, who permits evil. to educe good therefrom. But it is better, with most recent Interpreters, to take the expression as only denoting the *certainty* of the events predicted. Τὸ τέλος is equivalent to συντέλεια τοῦ αἰῶνος at ver. 3. Wets. compares Hom. Il. β. 122. τέλος δ' οὔπω τι πέφανται.

7. ἐγερθήσεται — ἔθνος.] This is referred by Grot., Wets., and Kypke, to those various wars and civil commotions with which most parts of the civilized world were then convulsed.

— λιμοὶ καὶ λοιμοί.] The words are often found joined in a context similar to the present; and no wonder, pestilence usually succeeding famine, (to the citations from Quint. Curt. ix. 10, and Hesiod. Op. 240, adduced by Wets., may be added Thucyd. i. 28,) insomuch that κατὰ λιμὸν λοιμὸς grew to a proverb. See Thucyd. ii. 54. Λιμὸς is well derived by Hemsterh. from λειμμὸς (and that from λέλειμμαι.) Yet I suspect that λιμὸς and λοιμὸς are of common origin, having the same general idea of *pining*, *wasting away*, &c. Wets. adduces ample historical proofs of both these visitations.

— σεισμοί.] This must not be taken, with some, metaphorically, of *civil commotions*, but be understood literally; for it appears from the passages adduced by Wets. and Kuin., that earthquakes were then very prevalent, and were always by the ancients regarded as portents, presaging public calamity and distress. See Joel iii. 3 & 4. Sil. Ital. v. 615.

— κατὰ τόπους.] The earlier Commentators interpret "in divers places;" but the recent ones, after Beza, "every where," by an ellips. of ἑκάστους. And this method is supported by some of the ancient Versions. Perhaps, however, the true sense is, "in various places." The words are (with some ancient Commentators, and Wets. and Fritz.) to be referred not to σεισμοὶ only, but also to λιμοὶ and λοιμοί.

8. πάντα δὲ — ὠδίνων.] We must here suppose an ellipse of μόνον as well as the usual one ἐστι; "these are only the prelude of sorrows." So Eurip. Med. 60, ἐν ἀρχῇ πῆμα, κοὐδέπω μεσοῖ. Ὠδὶν is here (as often in the Sept. and Classical writers) used of severe affliction, whether bodily or mental.

9. τότε.] This may (as Rosenm. suggests) be taken in a lax sense for *circa ista tempora*; since the events which follow happened partly *before* the above mentioned calamities, and partly at the *same time* with them.

— παραδώσουσιν ὑ. εἰς θλίψιν.] Θλίψις properly signifies *compression*, and figuratively constraint, oppression, affliction, and persecution. The construction is the same as in a kindred passage of Jerem. xv. 4. παραδ. εἰς ἀνάγκας. [*Comp.* sup. x. 17.]

— μισούμενοι ὑπὸ πάντων τῶν ἐθνῶν] i. e. "ye shall be generally objects of hatred." The feeling of the Gentiles to Christians is plain from various passages of the Classical writers. The true reason for this Bp. Warburton (Div. Leg. Vol. II. L. II. § 6.) has well pointed out, namely, that while the different *Pagan* religions sociably agreed with each other, the Gospel taught Christians not only, like the Jews, to bear their testimony to the falsehood of them all, but also zealously and earnestly to urge on men the renunciation of them as a matter of absolute necessity, and as requiring them under the most tremendous penalties, to embrace the Christian religion.

— τῶν ἐθνῶν.] The τῶν is omitted in the common text; but it has place in very many MSS. and all the Edd. up to the Elzevir (in which Wets. thinks it was omitted by a typographical error), and has been restored by Beng., Wets., Matth., Griesb., Knapp, Tittm., Fritz., and Scholz; rightly, I think: for *internal* as well as *external* evidence is in its favour; since it was more likely to be wrongly *omitted* than to have been *added*. Διὰ τὸ ὄνομά μου, "for the sake of [their profession of] my religion." Comp. Jo. xv. 20. xvi. 2. The correspondence of the expressions in this and the following verses up to ver. 13., to facts recorded in History, has been evinced by Wets. and others.

10. Of the expressions in this verse, σκανδ. must be understood of *apostasy*, and παραδ. of the betraying of their former partners in the faith. Μισήσ. ἀλλ. seems to have reference to that *hatred* which would be borne by the apostates to their former companions, even when they did not betray them.

11. ψευδοπροφ.] namely, in the *primary* application, persons pretending to a Divine commission to preach deliverance and freedom from the Roman yoke; in the *secondary*, false teachers. See supra vii. 11.

12. διὰ τὸ πληθυνθῆναι τὴν ἀνομίαν,] I would render, "and because of the prevalence of iniquity and lawlessness of every kind." It seems better to assign this *general* sense to ἀνομίαν, than any of those *special* ones which are given by one or other of the Commentators. This sense of the word is very frequent both in the N. T. and the Sept. There is something very similar in Ezr. ix. 6. ὅτι αἱ ἀνομίαι ἡμῶν ἐπληρώθησαν.

MK. LU.

13 ὁ δὲ ὑπομείνας εἰς τέλος, οὗτος σωθήσεται. Καὶ κηρυχθήσεται τοῦτο 13. 21.
14 τὸ εὐαγγέλιον τῆς βασιλείας ἐν ὅλῃ τῇ οἰκουμένῃ, εἰς μαρτύριον πᾶσι 10 19
15 τοῖς ἔθνεσι· καὶ τότε ἥξει τὸ τέλος. Ὅταν οὖν ἴδητε τὸ βδέλυγμα 14 20
τῆς ἐρημώσεως, τὸ ῥηθὲν διὰ Δανιὴλ τοῦ προφήτου, ἑστὼς ἐν τόπῳ
16 ἁγίῳ· (ὁ ἀναγινώσκων νοείτω·) τότε οἱ ἐν τῇ Ἰουδαίᾳ φευγέτωσαν 21
17 ἐπὶ τὰ ὄρη· ὁ ἐπὶ τοῦ δώματος μὴ καταβαινέτω, ἆραι * τὰ ἐκ τῆς 15

— ψυγήσεται ἡ ἀγ. τ. π.] "the love of the greater part shall grow cold." By ἀγ. some understand the love of God and zeal for religion; others, mutual love. The latter is generally adopted by the ancient and some eminent modern Commentators, and is certainly more agreeable to the *usus loquendi;* but the former is so strongly supported by the context, that it deserves the preference. That the ardour of many in the cause of Christianity was abated, is plain from Rev. ii. and iii.; and we may infer it from the fact of the defection in several Churches, attested in Gal. iii. 1. seq. 2 Thess. iii. 1. seq. 2 Tim. i. 15. Heb. x. 25. It should seem, however, that the fulfilment of this prediction is chiefly to be sought in the circumstances which shall precede the *second* advent of our Lord to judgment. There can be no doubt that it has been fulfilling for the last century, in the increase of infidelity and heresy. See an excellent Sermon of Bp. Warburton on this text (No. xxxiii.), in which he shews, from considerations drawn, 1. from the nature of things, 2. from the experience of our times, how truly iniquity is assigned as the cause of that general apostasy predicted to be the character of these latter days.

13. ὁ δὲ ὑπομείνας εἰς τέλος.] This many recent Commentators understand of the destruction of Jerusalem, rendering, "he who endureth unto the destruction, shall be saved,"—namely, from the ruin which shall overwhelm its inhabitants. And indeed Ecclesiastical history informs us, that few or no Christians perished in Jerusalem at that catastrophe, they having timely abandoned the city. But this seems a strained mode of interpretation; and it is better, with the ancient and early modern Commentators, and some eminent recent ones, (as Rosenm., Kuin., and Fritz.) to take ὑπομ. εἰς τέλος of continual perseverence in Christian faith and practice; and σωθ. of salvation in heaven. It should seem, that the *secondary* application alone has place here.

14. ἐν ὅλῃ τῇ οἰκουμένῃ.] Most Commentators understand this of the *Roman* world; i. e. the Roman Empire; for which signification of οἰκουμένη there is valid authority. (See Recens. Synop.) But as this is scarcely reconcileable with the words following, πᾶσι τοῖς ἔθνεσι, and since there is reason to think that Christianity had, at the period in question, been promulgated in countries which formed no part of the Roman Empire, (see Whitby and Doddr.) it may be better to retain the ordinary sense of the expression; understanding, by a slight hyperbole, *the greater part of the then known world.* [*Comp.* Rom. i. 8. & x. 18.]

— εἰς μαρτύριον πᾶσι τοῖς ἔθνεσι] namely, as some Commentators explain, "that the offer of salvation had been made to the Jews;" by the rejection of which they had drawn down vengeance on their heads: or, according to others, "in order that all nations may know and be able to testify;" that the Jews had filled up the measure of their iniquity and obstinacy by rejecting the proffered salvation, both spiritual and temporal. These two explanations merge into each other, and may be combined. But as far as the prediction has reference to the *second* advent of Christ, it will require another sense, on which see the Commentaries in Poole's Syn. Τὸ τέλος, "the end of the Jewish state, and the consummation of God's judgments against it."

15. τὸ βδέλυγμα τῆς ἐρημώσεως.] Dan. ix. 27; xii. 11. Here βδέλ. has (by Hebraism) the force of an adjective; as in Luke i. 48. ταπείνωσις τῆς δούλης, for δούλη ταπεινή. The sense is, "the abominable desolation;" i. e. the Roman army; always abominable, as composed of heathens, and carrying idolatrous standards; but then abominably *desolating*, as being invaders and destroyers.

— ἐν τόπῳ ἁγίῳ.] Most Commentators, from Grot. downwards, explain this "on holy ground." But Bp. Middlet. has shown that this interpretation is ungrounded; for the phrase occurs elsewhere in the N. T. only at Acts vi. 13. xxi. 28, where it can alone be understood of the *Temple*. In the Sept. it is often used, and always of the Temple, sometimes the *Sanctum Sanctorum*. There is therefore no reason to abandon the ancient and common interpretation, "in the Holy place," [properly so called,] which is required by the parallel passage in Mark xiii. 14, and is confirmed by the history of the completion of the prophecy in Josephus.

— ὁ ἀναγινώσκων ν.] These words are by most supposed to be our *Lord's*, and meant to fix the attention of his hearers. But the best recent Commentators, with reason, consider them as a parenthetical admonition of the *Evangelist*, and perhaps founded on Daniel ix. 25. καὶ γνώσῃ καὶ διανοηθήσῃ. Νοεῖν signifies properly to *turn in mind*, and, from the adjunct, *to attend.*

16. τότε] "when these things take place." Οἱ ἐν τῇ Ἰουδαίᾳ, i. e. the inhabitants of Judæa, as opposed to those of Jerusalem.

— τὰ ὄρη.] Not only as being natural strongholds, (often used as such, as we find from Josephus,) but because they abounded in large caverns; wherein the Jews, at times of public danger, took refuge.

17. ἐπὶ τοῦ δώματος, &c.] In this and the two following verses we have some proverbial (and somewhat hyperbolical) forms of expression, denoting the imminency of the danger, and the necessity of the speediest flight. It has ever been customary in the East to build the houses with flat roofs, provided with a staircase both inside and outside. By the latter way (or, as others suppose, over the roofs of the neighbouring houses, and so to the city wall) their flight is recommended to be taken.

— τά.] This (instead of the common reading τί), is found in all the best MSS. and the ancient Edd. confirmed by the Syr. and Coptic Versions and many Fathers. It has also been approved by almost all the recent Editors. and received from Matth. down to Scholz: with reason, for the

MK. LU.
13. 21. οἰκίας αὐτοῦ· καὶ ὁ ἐν τῷ ἀγρῷ μὴ ἐπιστρεψάτω ὀπίσω, ἆραι τὰ 18
16 17 23 ἱμάτια αὐτοῦ. Οὐαὶ δὲ ταῖς ἐν γαστρὶ ἐχούσαις καὶ ταῖς θηλαζούσαις 19
18 ἐν ἐκείναις ταῖς ἡμέραις. Προσεύχεσθε δὲ ἵνα μὴ γένηται ἡ φυγὴ 20
19 ὑμῶν χειμῶνος, μηδὲ [ἐν] σαβ6άτῳ. Ἔσται γὰρ τότε θλίψις μεγάλη, 21
20 οἵα οὐ γέγονεν ἀπ' ἀρχῆς κόσμου ἕως τοῦ νῦν, οὐδ' οὐ μὴ γένηται.
Καὶ εἰ μὴ ἐκολοβώθησαν αἱ ἡμέραι ἐκεῖναι, οὐκ ἂν ἐσώθη πᾶσα 22
21 σάρξ· διὰ δὲ τοὺς ἐκλεκτοὺς κολοβωθήσονται αἱ ἡμέραι ἐκεῖναι.
Τότε ἐάν τις ὑμῖν εἴπῃ· Ἰδοὺ, ὧδε ὁ Χριστὸς, ἢ ὧδε· μὴ πιστεύ- 23
22 σητε. Ἐγερθήσονται γὰρ ψευδόχριστοι καὶ ψευδοπροφῆται, καὶ δώ- 24
σουσι σημεῖα μεγάλα καὶ τέρατα, ὥστε πλανῆσαι, εἰ δυνατὸν, καὶ τοὺς
23 ἐκλεκτούς. Ἰδοὺ, προείρηκα ὑμῖν. Ἐὰν οὖν εἴπωσιν ὑμῖν· Ἰδοὺ, ἐν 25
τῇ ἐρήμῳ ἐστί· μὴ ἐξέλθητε· Ἰδοὺ, ἐν τοῖς ταμείοις· μὴ πιστεύ- 26

common reading arose from ignorance of the nature of the more recondite expression τὰ ἐκ τ. ο., which (as Fritz. well remarks), is put for ἆραι τὰ ἐν τῇ οἰκίᾳ ἐκ τῆς οἰκίας αὐτοῦ. The ἐπὶ in ἐπιστρεψάτω has reference to οἰκίαν, which may be taken from the preceding οἰκίας. By τὰ ἱμάτια are meant the upper garments; (the cloak and coat) which husbandmen of the Southern countries have ever, when at work, laid aside, or left at home: who are then said to be γυμνοί. So Hesiod. Op. ii. 9. (cited by Elsn.) Γυμνὸν σπείρειν, γυμνὸν δὲ βοωτεῖν, Γυμνὸν δ' ἀμᾶσθαι. Virg. Georg. i. 299. Nudus ara, sere nudus.

19. οὐαὶ δὲ — ἡμέραις.] It was unnecessary for Grot. and Wolf. to detail the *jus belli* as to women so situated; for our Lord only, while he predicts, deplores (a fine trait of his benevolence) the miserable lot of such persons. This *woe* was (as the records of history testify) amply fulfilled.

20. χειμῶνος.] The Commentators supply ὄντος. But διὰ is preferable. No ellipse, however, is necessary to be supposed.

— μηδὲ σαββάτῳ.] Because that would be a material hindrance; since no traveller was permitted by the Jewish Law (which was acted on by the Christians in Judæa long after the time of the destruction of Jerusalem) to proceed further than five furlongs on that day, and the gates of all towns were strictly closed.

The ἐν is not found in the greater part of the MSS., the Edit. Princ., and some Fathers; and is cancelled or rejected by almost every Editor from Bengel to Scholz; perhaps rightly, for internal as well as external evidence, is against it. Yet it is defended by xii. 2.

21. οἵα οὐ γέγονεν — νῦν.] The best Commentators agree in considering this as a somewhat hyperbolical, and perhaps proverbial mode of expressing what is *exceedingly great*, as Exod. x. 14; xi. 6. Dan. xii. 1. Joel ii. 2. Yet such were the atrocities and horrors of the siege of Jerusalem (never to this day paralleled) that the words may admit of the most literal acceptation. We may observe the triple negative, as most strongly emphatic. So Heb. xiii. 5. οὐ μή σε ἀνῶ, οὐδ' οὐ μή σε ἐγκαταλίπω. See also Rev. xiii. 14. At ἕως τοῦ νῦν sub., not κόσμου, with Fritz., but χρόνου. Νῦν for τότε is a rare use; but it is, I apprehend, the primary force of the word; which, being derived from νέω (cognate with νύσσω) signifies, 1. a point [of time], 2. time (as καιρὸς from κάω.). So the Heb. עת (whence the Latin *æt-as)* though it properly denotes *time*, sometimes signifies *now*.

22. εἰ μὴ ἐκολ.] Κολυβοῦν, from κόλυβος, a cripple, signifies to amputate, and, as applied to time, to *shorten*. So Malela, p. 237. (cited by Wets.) τοῦ αὐτοῦ μηνὸς τὰς ἡμέρας ἐκολλίβησαν. *How* they were shortened, we find from Joseph., from whom we learn that many incidental causes combined towards bringing about that event, and the deliverance.

— τοὺς ἐκλεκτοὺς] meaning, no doubt, the Jewish Christians then in Judæa. See Note supra xx. 16. Grot., Markl., Kuin., and Fritz. observe, that there is here an allusion to the very ancient opinion, that in some cases of national calamity, public destruction is averted by Providence, lest the righteous should suffer with the wicked.

23. Simil. Luke xvii. 23; xxi. 8.

24. ψευδόχριστοι καὶ ψευδοπροφ.] Such as Theudas, the son of Judas the Galilean, and others mentioned by Josephus.

— δώσουσι σημεῖα μεγ. καὶ τέρ.] An interesting question here arises, whether these σημεῖα and τέρατα were really performed, or merely *professed*. The ancient and early modern Commentators, together with some recent ones, adopt the *former* opinion; ascribing the deeds to dæmoniacal agency. The *latter* view is taken by most recent Commentators; who refer to a similar use of διδόναι in Deut. xiii. 2. 1 Kings xiii. 3 & 5. These σημεῖα and τέρατα (between which terms there need not be any such distinction made as in the Classical writeIs) are supposed to have been various sleights of pretended magic produced by optical deception, simulated cures of disorders founded in artful collusion, &c.; also, as far as there might be *reality*, wonders performed by dæmoniacal agency, such (in the words of 2 Thess. ii. 9.) as were produced κατ' ἐνέργειαν τοῦ Σατανᾶ, ἐν πάσῃ δυνάμει, καὶ σημείοις καὶ τέρασι ψεύδους.

— εἰ δυνατόν.] This expression does not imply *impossibility*. but only *extreme difficulty* in the performance of what is possible. (So Matt. xxvi. 39. Acts xx. 16. Rom. xii. 18.) and therefore this text ought never to have been adduced to prove the doctrine of the perseverance of the elect.

26. ἐστί·] i. e. αὐτὸς (q. d. you know who) is, namely, the Messiah. There is something *graphic* in this use of the pronoun for the appellative; which, though it had been long generally adopted of *that* great Personage, who was the object of universal expectation, yet in this case it was employed by the lurking adherents of false Christs.

— ἐν ἐρήμῳ.] The very place where (as we find

MK. LU.

27 σητε. Ὥσπερ γὰρ ἡ ἀστραπὴ ἐξέρχεται ἀπὸ ἀνατολῶν, καὶ φαίνεται 13. 21.
ἕως δυσμῶν, οὕτως ἔσται καὶ ἡ παρουσία τοῦ Υἱοῦ τοῦ ἀνθρώπου.
28 Ὅπου γὰρ ἐὰν ᾖ τὸ πτῶμα, ἐκεῖ συναχθήσονται οἱ ἀετοί. Εὐθέως 24 25
29 δὲ μετὰ τὴν θλίψιν τῶν ἡμερῶν ἐκείνων ὁ ἥλιος σκοτισθήσεται, καὶ ἡ 25
σελήνη οὐ δώσει τὸ φέγγος αὐτῆς, καὶ οἱ ἀστέρες πεσοῦνται ἀπὸ τοῦ 26
30 οὐρανοῦ, καὶ αἱ δυνάμεις τῶν οὐρανῶν σαλευθήσονται. Καὶ τότε 26 27
φανήσεται τὸ σημεῖον τοῦ Υἱοῦ τοῦ ἀνθρώπου ἐν τῷ οὐρανῷ· καὶ

from Joseph.) these impostors usually appeared and abode.

— *ἐν τοῖς ταμείοις.*] This is not to be taken, with most Commentators, as plural for singular; but, as Schleus. and Fritz. rightly observe, the term is to be considered as denoting a *genus*, q. d. He is in the kind of places called *ταμιεῖα* (i. e. secret apartments) namely, in one or other of them.

27. *ὥσπερ γὰρ ἡ ἀστραπὴ — οὕτως*, &c.] By this exquisite simile is represented the suddenness, the celerity, and, as some think, the conspicuousness of Christ's advent to take vengeance on the Jews. At *ἀπὸ ἀνατολῶν* (in which expression both Classical and Scriptural writers use the plural) sub. *ἡλίου*, which is *expressed* in Soph. Œd. C. 1245. *αἱ μὲν, ἀπ' ἀελίου δυσμᾶν, αἱ δ' ἀνατέλλοντος.*

28. *ὅπου γὰρ — ἀετοί.*] The connection of this verse with the preceding is variously traced. But the *γὰρ* must not be too rigorously interpreted; or it may be thought to have reference to a clause omitted. In this figurative language (which seems founded on Job xxxix. 40. *οὗ δ' ἂν ὦσι τεθνεῶτες παραχρῆμα εὑρίσκονται*, scil. *οἱ ἀετοί*, from ver. 27. and was perhaps proverbial) there seems an allusion to the *certainty* as well as suddenness of the destruction. By the *eagles* are meant the *Romans;* and as eagles very rarely feed on dead carcasses, so (the best Commentators are agreed) the bird here meant is the *Vultur percnopterus*, or *γυπαετὸς*, which was by the ancients referred to the eagle genus. By the *πτῶμα* is meant the *Jewish nation*, as lying, like the fabled Prometheus, a miserable *prey* to the foes who were tearing out her vitals.

29. *εὐθέως δὲ*, &c.] On these and the following verses the opinions of Commentators are much divided. The ancients and early moderns understand the expressions, *literally;* and refer the whole to the awful events which shall precede the final catastrophe of our globe, and the day of judgment; especially as in the next Chap., and other parts of Scripture, the same signs are mentioned as ushering in the last great day. But the *connection* here (which is even *stronger* in the parallel places of Mark and Luke) and the assurance contained in them *all*, "this generation shall not pass away till all be fulfilled," has induced the most eminent modern Commentators to refer the passage to *the signs accompanying the destruction of Jerusalem and the Jewish nation.* They consider the language as highly figurative, understanding by the darkening of the sun, &c. the ruin of states and great personages. The appearance of the sign of the Son of man they take to denote the subversion of the Jewish state; and the gathering together of his elect they refer to the gathering of the Christian Church out of all nations. "In ancient Hieroglyphic writings (observes Bp. Warburton) the sun, moon, and stars were used to represent states and empires, kings, queens, and nobility; their eclipse or extinction denoted temporary disasters, or entire overthrow. So, continues he, the Prophets in like manner call kings and empires by the names of the heavenly luminaries. Stars falling from the firmament are employed to denote the destruction of the nobility and other great men; insomuch that, in reality, the prophetic style seems to be a speaking hieroglyphic." See also Whitby and Doddr., who refer to Is. xiii. 10. li. 6. Ez. xxxii. 7. Dan. viii. 10. Esth. viii. 16. Jer. xv. 9. Joel xi. 31. iii. 15. Amos viii. 9. And many examples have been adduced of similar figurative language in the Classical writers. Yet as the expressions admit of explanation according to *each* of the above hypotheses; it may be safer to unite both interpretations; one as the *primary* the other as a *secondary* sense, or by way of allusion.

— *οἱ ἀστέρες πεσοῦνται ἀπὸ τοῦ ο.*] This admits of two explanations, according to the two views just mentioned. If the *former* be adopted, it must be understood of the falling of the heavenly bodies from the apparent concave sphere in which they are fixed; of course producing "darkness which may be felt." According to the *latter*, it will denote, in conjunction with the foregoing phrases, those great *obscurations* of the light of the heavenly bodies which, Josephus tells us, took place during the siege of Jerusalem, and which, we learn from Humboldt, attend earthquakes. Similar expressions are cited from Herodot. vii. 37. Statius x. and other authors. *Αἱ δυνάμεις τοῦ οὐρανοῦ* is an expression frequent in the Sept. to denote the heavenly bodies. There is no vain repetition, but a strong emphasis intended by the expression of the same thing in other words; or there may be a *hysteron proteron* q. d. "they will be tossed to and fro, and will then fall." *Σαλεύεσθαι* is used properly of the tossing to and fro of ships at anchor. See Thucyd. i. 137. where see my note.

30. *τὸ σημεῖον τοῦ Υἱοῦ τοῦ ἀνθ.*] Wolf, Rosenm., and Kuin. think that *τὸ σημεῖον* is put pleonastically, since it is omitted by Mark and Luke. But though it might be dispensed with, it adds something to the sense. Some supposed an allusion to the *sign from heaven* required. See supra xvi. 1. But it should rather seem that *τὸ σημεῖον* merely means the *visible appearance:* q. d. "then shall be seen the visible appearance of the Son of Man," i. e. then shall the Son of Man visibly appear agreeably to what the Jews understood from the prophecy in Dan. vii. 13.), and shall give manifest evidences of his power, by taking vengeance on the Jews. The *secondary* application is obvious.

By *αἱ φυλαὶ τῆς γῆς* is meant, as the best modern Commentators, and also Chrysost. are agreed, the inhabitants of Judæa; who would have cause enough to lament. See Luke xxiii. 28. There is a reference to Zech. xii. 12. And St. John in the Apoc. i. 7., certainly had in mind these words of our Lord. In *ἐρχόμενον ἐπὶ τῶν νεφελῶν* we have

MK. LU.
13. 21. τότε κόψονται πᾶσαι αἱ φυλαὶ τῆς γῆς, καὶ ὄψονται τὸν Υἱὸν τοῦ
ἀνθρώπου ἐρχόμενον ἐπὶ τῶν νεφελῶν τοῦ οὐρανοῦ μετὰ δυνάμεως καὶ
δόξης πολλῆς. Καὶ ἀποστελεῖ τοὺς ἀγγέλους αὐτοῦ μετὰ σάλπιγγος 31
φωνῆς μεγάλης· καὶ ἐπισυνάξουσι τοὺς ἐκλεκτοὺς αὐτοῦ ἐκ τῶν
τεσσάρων ἀνέμων, ἀπ' ἄκρων οὐρανῶν ἕως ἄκρων αὐτῶν.
28 29 30 Ἀπὸ δὲ τῆς συκῆς μάθετε τὴν παραβολήν· ὅταν ἤδη ὁ κλάδος 32
αὐτῆς γένηται ἁπαλὸς, καὶ τὰ φύλλα ἐκφυῇ, γινώσκετε ὅτι ἐγγὺς τὸ
29 31 θέρος. Οὕτω καὶ ὑμεῖς, ὅταν ἴδητε πάντα ταῦτα, γινώσκετε ὅτι 33
30 32 ἐγγύς ἐστιν ἐπὶ θύραις. Ἀμὴν λέγω ὑμῖν· οὐ μὴ παρέλθῃ ἡ γενεὰ 34
31 33 αὕτη, ἕως ἂν πάντα ταῦτα γένηται. Ὁ οὐρανὸς καὶ ἡ γῆ παρελεύ- 35
σονται, οἱ δὲ λόγοι μου οὐ μὴ παρέλθωσι. Περὶ δὲ τῆς ἡμέρας 36

splendid imagery, assimilated to the character of *Hebrew poetry*, to designate majesty of approach.

31. *καὶ ἀποστελεῖ τοὺς ἀγγέλους*, &c.] Here again there is much diversity of interpretation; which, however, might have been avoided, had the Commentators considered the *two-fold* application of the whole of this most interesting portion of Scripture; which even those, who elsewhere recognise it before, seem here to forget. The application of the words to the *final* advent of our Lord is too obvious to need pointing out. (Compare, in this view, the sublime description in 1 Cor. xv.) But neither ought the advent of our Lord to *the destruction of Jerusalem* to have been unperceived by any; for in that application the words have great propriety; *τοὺς ἀγγέλους* denoting (as the best Commentators admit) the preachers of the Gospel, announcing the message of salvation, and gathering those who should accept its offer from every quarter of the globe into one society under Christ, their common head. That God's prophets and ministers, both in the O. and the N. T., are often called his ἄγγελοι, is certain. The words *μετὰ σάλπιγγος φωνῆς* (where the construction, unperceived by many, is *μετὰ μεγάλης φωνῆς σάλπιγγος*) are supposed by most Commentators to have a reference to *preaching*, as compared to the sound of a trumpet, as Is. lviii. 1. Jer. vi. 17. Ez. xxxiii. 3—6. Rom. x. 18. But in both the above applications there seems a reference to the method of convoking solemn assemblies among the Jews and Gentiles, namely, by sound of trumpet. The words are therefore, *not*, as Kuin. imagines, introduced merely *ad ornatum*. In *ἐπισυνάξουσι*, the *ἐπὶ* (which has been misunderstood) has reference to the *place* (heaven), or the *society* into which the faithful followers of Christ are gathered. The words *ἐκ τῶν τεσσ. ἀνέμων* are a Hebrew form, denoting "from all quarters of the globe;" for the Jews not only took the *winds* to denote the *cardinal points* of the heavens; but employed them to mark the *regions* which lay in the direction of any of them. The words *ἀπ' ἄκρων — αὐτῶν* are also an Hebrew form, serving as an emphatic repetition of the same thing; where *ἄκρων* denotes those parts of the world where the earth and heaven (according to the vulgar notion) were supposed to border upon each other. [*Comp.* supra xiii. 41. 1 Cor. xv. 52. 1 Thess. iv. 16.]

32. *ἀπὸ δὲ τῆς συκῆς — παραβολήν.*] This is a reply to the inquiry at ver. 3., respecting the *time* of this destruction; which, our Lord intimates, will be as plainly indicated by the signs before mentioned, as the approach of Summer is by the early buds of the fig-tree. I have, with H. Steph., Matth., Fritz., and Lachm., edited *ἐκφυῇ* instead of the common reading. It is found in several ancient MSS., confirmed by the Syr. Ital. Vulg. and Ethiopic Versions. Fritz. indicates the origin of the error, and remarks, "Subjectum est *τὰ φύλλα*, ut ante *ὁ κλάδος*." As to the propriety, Matth. well observes, "Arbor dicitur *φύειν* et *ἐκφύειν φύλλα, ὄζους*. Homer Il. α. 234. Sed *τὰ φύλλα* dicuntur etiam *ἐκφύεσθαι, ἐκφυῆναι*." Bp. Middl. well observes, that the article at *τὰ φ.* shews that it is the Nomin. *ἐκφ.*, not the *Accus.*

— *τὸ θέρος*,] i. e. rather *Spring* than Summer, by an imitation of the Hebrew; in which language there are no terms to denote Spring and Autumn; the former being included under קיץ, (the Summer), the latter under חרף (the Winter). The cause of this idiom is generally sought for in the temperature of the East; but as it occurs in the Western languages also, it is probably a vestige of the simplicity and poverty of the primitive speech. The phrase *ἐγγὺς ἐπὶ θύραις* is formed from two phrases blended together for emphasis, and therefore denotes the closest proximity. Comp. James v. 9. The nominative at *ἐστι* is to be supplied from the preceding context; and therefore can be no other than *ὁ Υἱὸς τοῦ ἀνθρώπου*, or *ἡ παρουσία τοῦ Υἱοῦ τοῦ ἀνθρώπου*.

34. *ἡ γενεὰ αὕτη*.] Notwithstanding the dissent of some, the phrase can only mean "this very generation," "the race of men now living."

36. *περὶ δὲ τῆς ἡμέρας*, &c.] This verse is by many Commentators referred solely to the *final* advent of Christ, the day of judgment, but without sufficient reason; since there is here no closer allusion to the day of judgment than in the preceding verses; and as the verses *following* undoubtedly relate to the destruction of Jerusalem, so must this, at least primarily. Ἡ *ἡμέρα ἐκείνη* is used of the destruction of Jerusalem in various passages. *Τῆς* is not found in many MSS. of both the Constant. and Alexandrian families, and is cancelled by Matth., Griesb., Knapp, Tittm., Vater, and Scholz; but wrongly: for, as Bp. Middleton observes, the article is required by *ἐκείνης*, which is *understood* from the preceding. It is also confirmed by Matt. xxv. 13. Mark xiii. 32. The Pesch. Syr. Version (though the Editors and Commentators fail to notice it, *perhaps because the Latin Version does not shew it*) renders so that the Translator must not only have had the article, but *ἐκείνης* repeated; for he uses the emphatic] to the word corresponding to *ὥρας*, but

LU.
ἐκείνης καὶ τῆς ὥρας οὐδεὶς οἶδεν, — οὐδὲ οἱ ἄγγελοι τῶν οὐρανῶν — 17.
37 εἰ μὴ ὁ πατήρ μου μόνος. Ὥσπερ δὲ αἱ ἡμέραι τοῦ Νῶε, οὕτως 26
38 ἔσται καὶ ἡ παρουσία τοῦ Υἱοῦ τοῦ ἀνθρώπου. Ὥσπερ γὰρ ἦσαν ἐν
ταῖς ἡμέραις ταῖς πρὸ τοῦ κατακλυσμοῦ τρώγοντες καὶ πίνοντες, γα- 27
μοῦντες καὶ ἐκγαμίζοντες, ἄχρι ἧς ἡμέρας εἰσῆλθε Νῶε εἰς τὴν κιβωτὸν,
39 καὶ οὐκ ἔγνωσαν, ἕως ἦλθεν ὁ κατακλυσμὸς καὶ ἦρεν ἅπαντας· οὕτως
ἔσται καὶ ἡ παρουσία τοῦ Υἱοῦ τοῦ ἀνθρώπου.
40 Τότε δύο ἔσονται ἐν τῷ ἀγρῷ· ὁ εἷς παραλαμβάνεται, καὶ ὁ εἷς 35
41 ἀφίεται. δύο ἀλήθουσαι ἐν τῷ μυλῶνι· μία παραλαμβάνεται, καὶ μία
ἀφίεται.
42 Γρηγορεῖτε οὖν, ὅτι οὐκ οἴδατε ποίᾳ ὥρᾳ ὁ κύριος ὑμῶν ἔρχεται. 12.
43 Ἐκεῖνο δὲ γινώσκετε, ὅτι εἰ ᾔδει ὁ οἰκοδεσπότης ποίᾳ φυλακῇ ὁ κλέ- 39
πτης ἔρχεται, ἐγρηγόρησεν ἂν, καὶ οὐκ ἂν εἴασε διορυγῆναι τὴν οἰκίαν
44 αὐτοῦ. διὰ τοῦτο καὶ ὑμεῖς γίνεσθε ἕτοιμοι· ὅτι, ᾗ ὥρᾳ οὐ δοκεῖτε, 40
45 ὁ Υἱὸς τοῦ ἀνθρώπου ἔρχεται. Τίς ἄρα ἐστὶν ὁ πιστὸς δοῦλος καὶ 42

subjoins the demonstr. pronoun ܗܝ in the *feminine* one, answering to the *masc.* ܗܘ just before adapted to the masc. noun ܝܘܡܐ. Μου is omitted in several MSS., and is cancelled by Griesb.; but rashly: since it is defended by vii. 21. x. 32. seq. xi. 27. xii. 50. xv. 13. xvi. 17., and others adduced by Schulz. It seems to have been omitted for no better reason than *euphony*. It is indeed not found in the text of the Pesch. Syr. Version; but I suspect that ܐ was an error of the Scribes, for ܝ, which will express *my*, while the ܐ, which usually terminates the word, is regularly cast off before a pronominal suffix. The εἰ μὴ is imperfect, and needs to be supplied, namely from Mark. That the Son should not know the precise time of the destruction of Jerusalem, or of the end of the world, ought not to be drawn by the Unitarians to prove the *mere* humanity of Christ; for the expression has reference solely to his *human* nature; since, though as Son of God, he was omniscient, as Son of man he was not so.

37. ὥσπερ δὲ, &c.] The sense is, "the same shall happen at the advent of Christ, as did in the time of Noah," namely, the calamity shall be sudden and unexpected. This general sentiment is unfolded in ver. 37—41. [*Comp.* Luke xvii. 26. seqq. 1 Pet. iii. 20.] (Kuin.)

38. τρώγοντες — ἐκγαμίζοντες] There is no reason to put any strong emphasis on the words τρώγοντες and πίνοντες; still less to take γαμ. and ἐκγαμ. of unlawful lusts; and indeed the best Commentators are of opinion, that the words are meant to express no more than the *security* and *levity* with which they pursued the usual employments and amusements of life, when on the brink of destruction. Yet considering the solemn warning subjoined to ver. 35, at Luke xxi. 34, it is *implied*, that the antediluvians were guilty of gross sensuality.

39. οὐκ ἔγνωσαν] i. e. by a common Hebraism in ידעו, They did not attend or consider, did not make use of their knowledge. This sense is, however, sometimes found in the Classical writers. Ἦρεν, "swept away." The Classical writers say αἴρειν ἐκ μέσου may be rendered. Thus αἴρειν answers to the Heb. נשא necare, in Job xxxii. 22. 1 Macc. v. 2.

40. τότε δύο ἔσονται, &c.] The scope of this and the following verse is not clear. Some take it to denote that the destruction will be as *general* as it will be unexpected; so that no two persons employed together shall escape. Others, with more reason, suppose it to mean that some of both sexes shall escape, while others shall perish; implying a providential distinction.

41. δύο ἀλήθουσαι.] The μύλων was a hand-mill with two stones turned by two persons, generally females. See my Note on Thucyd. ii. 78.

42. γρηγορεῖτε] Γρηγορεῖν has *two* senses: 1. to be wakeful; 2. to be watchful, as here.

Some of the best Commentators, ancient and modern, are agreed that our Lord's discourse as far as regards the destruction of Jerusalem terminates at ver. 41., and that what follows, (which is peculiarly applicable to the *final* advent of our Lord) forms, as it were, the *moral* of the prophecy, and its practical application to his disciples of *every age*. Many of the above Commentators, too, think that it was spoken at another time, and upon another occasion, since Luke places it (xii. 39.) in another connection. But as the portion in question is applicable in both connections, there is no reason why we should not suppose that our Lord employed so solemn a warning *twice*.

43. φυλακῇ] for ὥρα, which is read in some MSS., but by gloss. The sense is, "at what particular time." The warning to vigilance is *pointed* by the use of a familiar allusion quite adapted to the country, and the state of society in Judæa; and therefore also employed by St. Paul, St. Peter, and St. John. [*Comp.* 1 Thess. v. 2. 2 Pet. iii. 10. Rev. iii. 3. and xvi. 15.]

44. διὰ τοῦτο] i. e. "because ye are in the same situation as the householder."

45. τίς ἄρα ἐστίν.] The Commentators have been perplexed with τίς, which some take in the sense *qualis* or *quantus*; but others regard as put hypothetically, for εἴ τις, of which usage they adduce

LU.
12. φρόνιμος, ὃν κατέστησεν ὁ κύριος αὐτοῦ ἐπὶ τῆς θεραπείας αὐτοῦ, τοῦ
43 διδόναι αὐτοῖς τὴν τροφὴν ἐν καιρῷ; Μακάριος ὁ δοῦλος ἐκεῖνος, ὃν 46
44 ἐλθὼν ὁ κύριος αὐτοῦ εὑρήσει ποιοῦντα οὕτως. Ἀμὴν λέγω ὑμῖν, ὅτι 47
45 ἐπὶ πᾶσι τοῖς ὑπάρχουσιν αὐτοῦ καταστήσει αὐτόν. Ἐὰν δὲ εἴπῃ 48
ὁ κακὸς δοῦλος ἐκεῖνος ἐν τῇ καρδίᾳ αὐτοῦ· Χρονίζει ὁ κύριός μου
ἐλθεῖν· καὶ ἄρξηται τύπτειν τοὺς συνδούλους αὐτοῦ, * ἐσθίῃ δὲ καὶ 49
46 * πίνῃ μετὰ τῶν μεθυόντων· ἥξει ὁ κύριος τοῦ δούλου ἐκείνου ἐν 50
z Supr. 8. 12. & 13. 42. infr. 25. 30. ἡμέρᾳ ᾗ οὐ προσδοκᾷ, καὶ ἐν ὥρᾳ ᾗ οὐ γινώσκει· z καὶ διχοτομήσει 51
αὐτὸν, καὶ τὸ μέρος αὐτοῦ μετὰ τῶν ὑποκριτῶν θήσει. ἐκεῖ ἔσται
ὁ κλαυθμὸς καὶ ὁ βρυγμὸς τῶν ὀδόντων.

XXV. Τότε ὁμοιωθήσεται ἡ βασιλεία τῶν οὐρανῶν δέκα παρθέ- 1
νοις, αἵτινες λαβοῦσαι τὰς λαμπάδας αὐτῶν, ἐξῆλθον εἰς ἀπάντησιν
τοῦ νυμφίου. Πέντε δὲ ἦσαν ἐξ αὐτῶν φρόνιμοι, καὶ αἱ πέντε μωραί. 2

examples. Those, however, are not applicable, because (as Fritz. remarks, in nearly all of them the interrogation is suitable and applicable: and thus the Article will have no force. I agree with him in regarding this (like some of those in the examples adduced) as an interrogation conjoined with exclamation. The sense may be thus expressed: "Who then is that faithful and attentive servant (i. e. I should much wish to *know* him) whom, &c. This interpretation is confirmed by the authority of Chrys., who observes that the *τίς* is meant to express how rare and valuable such servants are. *Τῆς θεραπείας*, "household," for *τῶν θεραπόντων*; abstract for concrete; on which idiom see Matth. Gr. Gr. This idiom is almost confined to words signifying *service*. *Ἐν καιρῷ*, i. e. as appears from what is said by Casaub. and Le Clerc, *monthly*.

47. *πᾶσι — καταστήσει αὐτόν*] i. e. from being dispenser, or *οἰκόνομος*, he will promote him to *ἐπίτροπος*, treasurer, or steward.

48. *ὁ κακὸς δ. ἐκεῖνος*] It is not easy to see what *ἐκεῖνος* has to do here; the *bad* servant not having been yet mentioned: and there is plainly no regular opposition between the two. Fritz. has cancelled the word, as having been introduced from ver. 46. But it is almost impossible that it should have found its way into *all* the MSS.: and yet none countenance the omission. The word must therefore be retained, and explained as it may. And, unless it be a Hellenistic pleonasm, it may serve to strengthen the Article *ὁ*, which may be thought to require it: for, throughout this parable, the Article is subservient to the purpose of *hypothesis*. See Middlet. Gr. A. ch. iii. § 2. And as in such cases the Article was considered by the ancient Grammarians to be used *indefinitely*, so it might seem to *need* the assistance of *ἐκεῖνος*, to give it some definiteness.

49. *αὐτοῦ*] This word is inserted, from several of the best MSS., Versions and Fathers, by Griesb., Knapp., Tittm., Fritz., and Scholz. All the best Editors from Wets. to Scholz are agreed on the emendation *ἐσθίῃ καὶ πίνῃ*, for *ἐσθίειν* and *πίνειν*; which has the strongest evidence of MSS., Versions, and Fathers, and is required by one of the most certain of critical canons.

51. *διχοτομήσει αὐτὸν*] On the interpretation of *διχοτ.* there has been no little difference of opinion. See Recens. Synop. The versions, "will turn him away," or "will confiscate his goods," are alike unauthorized and frigid; nay, inconsistent with the parallel passage of Luke. Most Commentators explain the word *literally*, of the ancient punishment of *being sawn asunder*. But as the sufferer seems, in the words following, represented *as surviving* the punishment, this cannot well be admitted. Heumann, Doddr., Rosenm., and Kuin. take *διχ.* in a figurative sense, to denote the infliction of a *most severe flagellation*; by a figure common to most languages ancient and modern. So Hist. Susannæ, v. 55. *σχίσει σε μέσον*. & 39. *πρίσαι σε μέσον*. When it is said *τὸ μέρος αὐτοῦ μετὰ τῶν ὑποκριτῶν θήσει* (by which is meant, "will place him in the same situation with hypocrites") we must understand, "when he survives his punishment;" which many would *not*. There is an allusion to the general treatment of delinquent slaves, whose miseries are well expressed by *κλαυθμὸς καὶ ὁ βρυγμὸς τῶν ὀδόντων*.

After all, however, the objection, that the sufferer is afterwards mentioned as *alive*, may not be fatal to the *literal* interpretation of *διχ.*; for I agree with Fritz., that in the words following *καὶ τὸ μέρος — θήσει*, the similitude is blended with the thing signified. Yet it is not *necessary* to adopt that interpretation, since the other is equally well founded. Thus, however, is avoided the difficulty which otherwise embarrasses the word *ὑποκριτῶν*, which the Commentators vainly endeavour to remove by various devices in translation. The sense seems to be, "As he will miserably scourge him, and consign him to the woeful abode of incorrigible criminals; so will the Lord consign the wilfully disobedient disciple to the abode of hypocrites," i. e. (as the Jews universally acknowledged) to *Hell*. In the parallel passage of Luke there is *not* this blending; the *τῶν ἀπίστων* being applicable to the servant.

XXV. 1. *τότε ὁμοιωθήσεται* &c.] The scope of this parable (to which one very similar is adduced from a Rabbinical tract) and the various circumstances are fully illustrated in Recens. Synop. It is meant to intimate the necessity of continued vigilance, constant prayer, and perseverance in every good work; and is especially designed to discourage all trust in a late repentance.

— *δέκα*.] Some *certain* number was likely to be used; and from this parable and a passage of a Rabbinical writer cited by Wets., we may infer that ten was a favourite number with the Jews.

2. *φρόνιμοι*] "prudent, cautious." Αἱ πέντε,

3 Αἵτινες μωραὶ, λαβοῦσαι τὰς λαμπάδας αὐτῶν, οὐκ ἔλαβον μεθ᾽ ἑαυτῶν
4 ἔλαιον· αἱ δὲ φρόνιμοι ἔλαβον ἔλαιον ἐν τοῖς ἀγγείοις αὐτῶν μετὰ τῶν
5 λαμπάδων αὐτῶν. Χρονίζοντος δὲ τοῦ νυμφίου, ἐνύσταξαν πᾶσαι, καὶ
6 ἐκάθευδον. Μέσης δὲ νυκτὸς κραυγὴ γέγονεν. Ἰδοὺ, ὁ νυμφίος ἔρχε-
7 ται! ἐξέρχεσθε εἰς ἀπάντησιν αὐτοῦ! Τότε ἠγέρθησαν πᾶσαι αἱ
8 παρθένοι ἐκεῖναι, καὶ ἐκόσμησαν τὰς λαμπάδας αὐτῶν. Αἱ δὲ μωραὶ
ταῖς φρονίμοις εἶπον· Δότε ἡμῖν ἐκ τοῦ ἐλαίου ὑμῶν, ὅτι αἱ λαμπά-
9 δες ἡμῶν σβέννυνται. Ἀπεκρίθησαν δὲ αἱ φρόνιμοι, λέγουσαι· Μήποτε οὐκ ἀρκέσῃ ἡμῖν καὶ ὑμῖν· πορεύεσθε [δὲ] μᾶλλον πρὸς τοὺς
10 πωλοῦντας, καὶ ἀγοράσατε ἑαυταῖς. [a] Ἀπερχομένων δὲ αὐτῶν ἀγοράσαι, a Luke 13. 25.
ἦλθεν ὁ νυμφίος· καὶ αἱ ἕτοιμοι εἰσῆλθον μετ᾽ αὐτοῦ εἰς τοὺς γά-
11 μους· καὶ ἐκλείσθη ἡ θύρα. Ὕστερον δὲ ἔρχονται καὶ αἱ λοιπαὶ παρ-
12 θένοι, λέγουσαι· Κύριε, κύριε, ἄνοιξον ἡμῖν. [b] Ὁ δὲ ἀποκριθεὶς b Supr. 7. 23.
13 εἶπεν· Ἀμὴν λέγω ὑμῖν, οὐκ οἶδα ὑμᾶς. [c] Γρηγορεῖτε οὖν, ὅτι οὐκ οἴ- c Supr. 24. 42. Mark 13. 33, 35.
δατε τὴν ἡμέραν οὐδὲ τὴν ὥραν, [ἐν ᾗ ὁ Υἱὸς τοῦ ἀνθρώπου ἔρχεται.] Luke 21. 36. 1 Cor. 16. 13. 1 Pet. 5. 8.
14 [d] Ὥσπερ γὰρ ἄνθρωπος ἀποδημῶν ἐκάλεσε τοὺς ἰδίους δούλους, καὶ Rev. 16. 15. d Luke 19. 12.
15 παρέδωκεν αὐτοῖς τὰ ὑπάρχοντα αὐτοῦ· καὶ ᾧ μὲν ἔδωκε πέντε τά-
λαντα, ᾧ δὲ δύο, ᾧ δὲ ἕν· ἑκάστῳ κατὰ τὴν ἰδίαν δύναμιν· καὶ ἀπε-
16 δήμησεν εὐθέως. Πορευθεὶς δὲ ὁ τὰ πέντε τάλαντα λαβὼν, εἰργάσατο

"the other five." Such is the force of the Article.

3. αἵτινες μωραὶ] "such as were foolish." The phraseology is *Hellenistic*, to which Fritz. has without reason taken exception. Αὐτῶν. This is edited by Scholz, from many of the best MSS.

5. ἐνύσταξαν, καὶ ἐκάθευδον] "they nodded, and [then] fell asleep."

7. ἐκόσμησαν] for κατεσκεύασαν, which is used in the Sept.; though the same Hebrew word הֵיטִיב is by the Sept. used both for κοσμεῖν and ἐπισκευάζειν. The sense is, "put them in order," "made them fit for use." I am not, however, aware that the word is elsewhere used with λαμπάδα, and therefore I suspect that it is one of the phrases of *common life*, not found in the Classical writers.

9. μήποτε οὐκ ἀρκέσῃ, &c.] Here there is plainly something to be supplied. Several Commentators, as Rosenm., and Kuin., would supply οὕτω, and take μήποτε in the sense *perhaps*. But the proof is weak, and the sense somewhat lame. It is better, with Erasm., Wolf, and Elsn., to suppose an ellipsis of σκοπεῖτε, or ὁρᾶτε, or (what Fritz. proposes), φοβούμεθα or δεδίαμεν. After all, the best founded ellipse may be that of the negative particle, or some negative phrase (as in Gen. xx. 11.), which is adopted in E. V. and preferred by Hoogev., and is also supported by Euthym. The negative, is, I conceive, omitted *verecundiæ gratiâ*; for the ancients attached some sort of *shame* to denying a request.

— πορεύεσθε — ἑαυταῖς.] This seems to have been a common mode of expression, used to those who asked what could not be spared; and, of course, forms an ornamental circumstance. It is amazing that this passage should have been adduced to support the Romish doctrine of *works of supererogation*; since the circumstance, whether regarded as essential, or ornamental, puts a negative on the doctrine. See Chrys. and Euthym. in Recens. Synop. The δὲ before μᾶλλον is cancelled by Griesb. and Scholz, from several MSS.; but wrongly, since the current of authority runs the other way, and the *usus loquendi* of Scripture is adverse; for Fritz. truly says "ubique N. T. loca hujusmodi etiam δὲ habent, non μᾶλλον solum." See x. 6, 28. Luke x. 20.

10. αἱ ἕτοιμοι] "those who were ready." This absolute use of ἕτοιμος with *persons* is rare, with *things* not unfrequent.

12. οὐκ οἶδα ὑμᾶς.] The best Commentators are agreed that the sense is, as supr. vii. 23., "I do not recognize you as among those who accompanied me and my spouse;" or, regarding it as a common form of repulsion, "I know nothing about you."

13. ἐν ᾗ ὁ Υἱὸς — ἔρχεται.] These words are omitted in several good MSS., most of the Versions, and some Fathers, and are cancelled by Griesb., Fritz., and Scholz. They have certainly the air of an addition to fill up the sense, perhaps from supr. xxiv. 42 & 44.

14. ὥσπερ γὰρ ἄνθρωπος, &c.] To this parable (which is not the same with the very similar one in Luke xix. 12.) the apodosis is wanting, i. e. "As that person did, so will the Son of Man do;" or rather there is an *anacoluthon*, arising from inattention to the construction. Ἀποδημῶν, "on taking his departure." Or it may, with Fritz., be taken for ἀποδημεῖν θέλων.

15. κατὰ τὴν ἰδίαν δύναμιν] "according to each one's particular capacity, and ability to employ the money to advantage." Thus it seems that masters sometimes (as is still the case in the East, and in Russia) committed to their slaves some capital, to be employed in traffic; for the improvement of which they were to be accountable to them.

16. εἰργάσατο ἐν αὐτοῖς] scil. χρήματα, which is almost always *expressed* in the Classical writers. This use of ἐν is Hellenistic. A Classical writer would have used ἐπί. In this use ἐργάσασθαι sig-

ἐν αὐτοῖς, καὶ ἐποίησεν ἄλλα πέντε τάλαντα. Ὡσαύτως καὶ ὁ τὰ δύο 17
ἐκέρδησε καὶ αὐτὸς ἄλλα δύο. Ὁ δὲ τὸ ἓν λαβὼν, ἀπελθὼν ὤρυξεν 18
ἐν τῇ γῇ, καὶ ἀπέκρυψε τὸ ἀργύριον τοῦ κυρίου αὐτοῦ. Μετὰ δὲ 19
χρόνον πολὺν ἔρχεται ὁ κύριος τῶν δούλων ἐκείνων, καὶ συναίρει μετ᾽
αὐτῶν λόγον. Καὶ προσελθὼν ὁ τὰ πέντε τάλαντα λαβὼν προσήνεγκεν 20
ἄλλα πέντε τάλαντα, λέγων· Κύριε, πέντε τάλαντά μοι παρέδωκας·
e Supr. 24. 47. Luke 22. 29, 30. ἴδε, ἄλλα πέντε τάλαντα ἐκέρδησα ἐπ᾽ αὐτοῖς. e Ἔφη [δὲ] αὐτῷ 21
ὁ κύριος αὐτοῦ· Εὖ, δοῦλε ἀγαθὲ καὶ πιστὲ, ἐπὶ ὀλίγα ἦς πιστὸς,
ἐπὶ πολλῶν σε καταστήσω· εἴσελθε εἰς τὴν χαρὰν τοῦ κυρίου σου.
Προσελθὼν δὲ καὶ ὁ τὰ δύο τάλαντα λαβὼν εἶπε· Κύριε, δύο τά- 22
λαντά μοι παρέδωκας· ἴδε, ἄλλα δύο τάλαντα ἐκέρδησα ἐπ᾽ αὐτοῖς.
Ἔφη αὐτῷ ὁ κύριος αὐτοῦ· Εὖ, δοῦλε ἀγαθὲ καὶ πιστὲ, ἐπὶ ὀλίγα 23
ἦς πιστὸς, ἐπὶ πολλῶν σε καταστήσω· εἴσελθε εἰς τὴν χαρὰν τοῦ
κυρίου σου. Προσελθὼν δὲ καὶ ὁ τὸ ἓν τάλαντον εἰληφὼς εἶπε· 24
Κύριε, ἔγνων σε ὅτι σκληρὸς εἶ ἄνθρωπος, θερίζων ὅπου οὐκ ἔσπειρας, καὶ συνάγων ὅθεν οὐ διεσκόρπισας· καὶ φοβηθεὶς, ἀπελθὼν 25
ἔκρυψα τὸ τάλαντόν σου ἐν τῇ γῇ· ἴδε, ἔχεις τὸ σόν. Ἀποκριθεὶς δὲ 26
ὁ κύριος αὐτοῦ εἶπεν αὐτῷ· Πονηρὲ δοῦλε καὶ ὀκνηρὲ, ᾔδεις ὅτι
θερίζω ὅπου οὐκ ἔσπειρα, καὶ συνάγω ὅθεν οὐ διεσκόρπισα; Ἔδει 27

nifies to invest capital, or to *make money*. Ἐποίησεν, "acquired by traffic;" a use chiefly found in the later Greek, the earlier writers employing κερδῆσαι.

18. ὤρυξεν] scil. ὄρυγμα, which is implied. See Herodot. iv. 71.

21. ἔφη δὲ] The δὲ is omitted in many good MSS. and some Versions, and is cancelled by Griesb., Tittm., Fritz., and Scholz. Εὖ for εὖγε, which was used like our *bravo!* and therefore often employed at the public games by the multitude in the expression of applause. At ἐπὶ ὀλίγα, sub. κατασταθεὶς. The syntax with the *Accus.* (which is rare) occurs also at Heb. ii. 7.

— τὴν χαράν.] Some of the best Commentators are of opinion, that in order to keep the *story* apart from the *application*, we should here take χαρ., by a metonomy of the adjunct, in the sense *banquet*. It is scarcely necessary, however, to abandon the common interpretation, which, as Chrys. and Euthym. observe, denotes τὴν ἅπασαν μακαριότητα. The *Synchysis* in question is not unusual in the antient writers.

24. ἔγνων σε ὅτι.] On this construction, which depends on *attraction*, see Winer's Gr. Gr. p. 186.

— σκληρὸς,] hard-hearted, griping. The expressions following are formulas, probably in common use with agricultural persons, and expressive of the habits of such persons. Though some similar ones are found in the Classical writers, nor are they wanting in our own language. We may render, "reaping where thou hast not sown, and harvesting where thou hast not scattered (namely the seed)." Thus διασκορπίζειν signifies to *sow* in Is. xxviii. 29. (Aquila) where the Sept. has σπείρειν. So Schleus. and others explain διασκορπ. I would, however, prefer to take it of *turning* the corn, to prepare it for *carrying*, which is the meaning of συνάγων.

25. φοβηθεὶς] i. e. fearing lest, if I should lose the money, thou wouldst severely exact it of me, by taking away all my substance. (Kuin.) This was evidently a mere excuse; but, as Euthym. observes, the parable puts a *weak* excuse into the mouth of the slothful servant, in order to show that in such a case *no reasonable* apology can be made.

— ἴδε, ἔχεις τὸ σόν.] Formula nihil ultra debere se profitentis. (Grot.) We have a similar one in English. So also xx. 14. ἆρον τὸ σόν.

26. πονηρὲ καὶ ὀκνηρὲ] Campb. has here an able note on the distinction between words nearly, but not quite, synonymous, as exemplified in κακὸς, πονηρὸς, ἄνομος, ἄδικος. "Though such words (says he) are sometimes used promiscuously, yet there is a difference. Thus ἄδικος properly signifies *unjust*; ἄνομος, lawless, criminal; κακὸς, vicious; πονηρὸς, malicious. Accordingly, κακὸς is opposed to ἐνάρετος, or δίκαιος; πονηρὸς, to ἀγαθός. Κακία, is *vice*; πονηρία, malice or malignity. This is the use of the words in the Gospel. Thus the negligent, riotous, debauched servant in ch. xxiv. 48. is denominated κακὸς δοῦλος, a vicious servant. Here the bad servant is not debauched, but slothful, and, to defend his sloth, abusive. Thus in xx. 32. the inexorable master is called πονηρός. A malignant, that is, an envious, eye is πονηρὸς, not κακὸς ὀφθαλμός. The disposition of the Pharisees is termed κακὸς, and the devil is termed ὁ πονηρὸς, not ὁ κακός." See more in Tittm. de Syn. N. T.

— ᾔδεις, &c.] This is said (as Euthym. and Grot. observe) by the figure *Synchoresis*: "Be it as you say, that I am, &c. then ought you to have taken the more care not to deprive me of what is really my own. Though it were *true*, as you say, that I reap where I sow not, and you durst not risk the money in merchandize; you ought to have put it out to the public money-changers to interest; some exertions should have been made." This, however, will not be necessary, if the words are taken *interrogatively*. I have, therefore, with Griesb. and Fritz., placed the mark of interrogation.

οὖν σε βαλεῖν τὸ ἀργύριόν μου τοῖς τραπεζίταις· καὶ ἐλθὼν ἐγὼ
28 ἐκομισάμην ἂν τὸ ἐμὸν σὺν τόκῳ. Ἄρατε οὖν ἀπ' αὐτοῦ τὸ τάλαντον,
29 καὶ δότε τῷ ἔχοντι τὰ δέκα τάλαντα. [f] Τῷ γὰρ ἔχοντι παντὶ δοθή- f Supr. 13. 12. Mark 4. 25.
σεται, καὶ περισσευθήσεται· ἀπὸ δὲ τοῦ μὴ ἔχοντος καὶ ὃ ἔχει Luke 8. 18. & 19. 26.
30 ἀρθήσεται ἀπ' αὐτοῦ. [g] Καὶ τὸν ἀχρεῖον δοῦλον ἐκβάλλετε εἰς τὸ g Supr. 8. 12. & 13. 42. & 22.
σκότος τὸ ἐξώτερον. ἐκεῖ ἔσται ὁ κλαυθμὸς καὶ ὁ βρυγμὸς τῶν 13.
ὀδόντων.
31 [h] Ὅταν δὲ ἔλθῃ ὁ Υἱὸς τοῦ ἀνθρώπου ἐν τῇ δόξῃ αὐτοῦ, καὶ πάν- h Zach. 14. 5. supr. 16. 27.
τες οἱ [ἅγιοι] ἄγγελοι μετ' αὐτοῦ· τότε καθίσει ἐπὶ θρόνου δόξης 1 Thess. 4. 16. 2 Thess. 1. 7. Jude ver. 14.
32 αὐτοῦ, [i] καὶ συναχθήσεται ἔμπροσθεν αὐτοῦ πάντα τὰ ἔθνη· καὶ Rev. 1. 7. i Rom. 14. 10.
ἀφοριεῖ αὐτοὺς ἀπ' ἀλλήλων, ὥσπερ ὁ ποιμὴν ἀφορίζει τὰ πρόβατα 2 Cor. 5. 10. Ezech. 20. 38. & 34. 17. 20.
33 ἀπὸ τῶν ἐρίφων· καὶ στήσει τὰ μὲν πρόβατα ἐκ δεξιῶν αὐτοῦ, τὰ δὲ
ἐρίφια ἐξ εὐωνύμων.
34 Τότε ἐρεῖ ὁ βασιλεὺς τοῖς ἐκ δεξιῶν αὐτοῦ· Δεῦτε, οἱ εὐλογημένοι
τοῦ πατρός μου, κληρονομήσατε τὴν ἡτοιμασμένην ὑμῖν βασιλείαν ἀπὸ

27. βαλεῖν] for διδόναι, as in Luke xix. 23., or the more Classical θέσθαι.

— τραπεζίταις.] These discharged not only the offices of our *bankers*, in receiving and giving out money, in taking or giving interest upon it; but also in exchanging coins, and distinguishing genuine from forged money.

— τόκῳ.] "interest;" for the word only imports what is *produced* by, as we say, turning money, which, indeed, was *originally* the sense of *usury*, i. e. the profit allowed to the lender for the use of borrowed money. But, indeed, if the τόκῳ were taken in the worst sense that was ever ascribed to *usury*, it would not imply Christ's *approbation*, since the whole (as has been before observed) is said κατὰ συγχώρησιν. Κομίζεσθαι signifies to *carry off*; and it is generally implied that the thing was before in our possession.

28. ἄρατε οὖν, &c.] These words (says Kuin.) merely serve as a *finish to the picture*.

29. τῷ γὰρ ἔχοντι, &c.] On this proverb see Matth. xiii. 12. and Note. We may here paraphrase with Kuin., "When any one does not properly use gifts bestowed, or benefits received, even *these* are taken from him. But to him who rightly employs them, *more* are given, as rewards of his good management." On the μὴ in τοῦ μὴ ἔχοντος it may be observed, that this is used in preference to οὐκ. because a *supposition* is implied (see Herman. Vig. p. 805.); as is the case with participles taken generally, and corresponding to *quicunque*, or *siquis*, as Matt. ix. 36. John v. 23. Rom. xiv. 3. 1 Cor. vii. 30.

30. ἀχρεῖον.] Literally, "good for nothing, bad." This *meiosis* extends to many other words of similar signification, as ἄχρηστος, ἀξύμφορος, &c. See Rec. Syn.

— σκότος τὸ ἐξώτερον.] Corresponding to the *Tartarus* of the Heathen Mythology. Of the same kind is the expression at 2 Pet. ii. 17. ζόφος τοῦ σκότους.

31. ὅταν δὲ ἔλθῃ, &c.] After pressing the warnings inculcated in the preceding parables, our Lord now proceeds to advert to the *great day of retribution* itself, in a description which (Doddr. observes) is "one of the noblest instances of the true sublime any where to be found." It represents, 1. the *extent* of the judgment; 2. the *methods* with which it will be carried on; 3. the *place and circumstances*.' The imagery is partly derived from the pompous mode of administering justice in the East (see Ps. ix. 5—9. Zach. xiv. 3. Is. vi. 1. lxvi. 1. Dan. vii. 9. 1 Thess. iv. 16.), and partly it is a pastoral metaphor (frequent in Scripture) adverting to the antient Eastern custom of keeping separate the sheep and the goats. And, besides the respective dispositions of the two animals, as sheep were more valuable than goats, they would, in an allegory wherein the Messiah and those whom he was to guide, are compared to a Shepherd and his sheep, fitly represent the former, the *accepted*, and the latter, the *rejected*.

— ἐπὶ θρόνου δόξης αὐτοῦ] "upon his glorious throne." The ἅγιοι before ἄγγελοι is omitted in several MSS., and is cancelled by Griesb. and Fritz., as having been introduced from the parallel place of Mark; but is retained by Wets., Matth., and Scholz. The point is doubtful, but the quarter from whence the omission comes is suspicious.

32. πάντα τὰ ἔθνη] i. e. both Jews and Gentiles, both quick and dead.

34. ὁ βασιλεύς.] So called, the Commentators say, as then exercising the highest act of kingly power. And indeed the kingly and judicial authority were then closely united. But perhaps the term is merely used in accordance with the preceding Regal imagery.

— τοῦ πατρός.] Some supply ὑπό; but the Genit. may of itself note the efficient cause; not to say, with Fritz., that οἱ εὐλογημένοι is in some measure a *noun*.

— ἡτοιμασμένην ὑμῖν, &c.] Similar is the passage of Tobit vi. 17. ὅτι σοὶ αὕτη ἡτοιμασμένη ἦν ἀπὸ τοῦ αἰῶνος.

— ἀπὸ καταβολῆς κόσμου.] This has been thought to countenance the doctrines of *absolute decrees*. But the expression is merely a Hebraism; and it is clear from the context that the true meaning is, that the kingdom of heaven was *all along* prepared for those, who should approve themselves worthy of acceptance by the performance of those good works (a specimen of which is subjoined) which invariably spring from a true faith. The κληρονομήσατε shows the *certainty* of the thing, as *due* by the promise of God.

k Isa. 58. 7. Ezech. 18. 7. Eccl. 7. 39. James 1. 27. καταβολῆς κόσμου. [k] ἐπείνασα γάρ, καὶ ἐδώκατέ μοι φαγεῖν· ἐδίψησα, 35
καὶ ἐποτίσατέ με· ξένος ἤμην, καὶ συνηγάγετέ με· γυμνὸς, καὶ 36
περιεβάλετέ με· ἠσθένησα, καὶ ἐπεσκέψασθέ με· ἐν φυλακῇ ἤμην,
καὶ ἤλθετε πρός με. Τότε ἀποκριθήσονται αὐτῷ οἱ δίκαιοι, λέγοντες· 37
Κύριε, πότε σὲ εἴδομεν πεινῶντα, καὶ ἐθρέψαμεν; ἢ διψῶντα, καὶ
ἐποτίσαμεν; πότε δέ σε εἴδομεν ξένον, καὶ συνηγάγομεν; ἢ γυμνὸν, 38
καὶ περιεβάλομεν; πότε δέ σε εἴδομεν ἀσθενῆ, ἢ ἐν φυλακῇ, καὶ 39
l Prov. 19. 17. Heb. 6. 10. ἤλθομεν πρός σε; [l] Καὶ ἀποκριθεὶς ὁ βασιλεὺς ἐρεῖ αὐτοῖς· Ἀμὴν 40
λέγω ὑμῖν· ἐφ' ὅσον ἐποιήσατε ἑνὶ τούτων τῶν ἀδελφῶν μου τῶν
ἐλαχίστων, ἐμοὶ ἐποιήσατε.

m Supr. 7. 23. Luke 13. 27. Psalm 6. 8. [m] Τότε ἐρεῖ καὶ τοῖς ἐξ εὐωνύμων· Πορεύεσθε ἀπ' ἐμοῦ, οἱ κατ- 41
ηραμένοι, εἰς τὸ πῦρ τὸ αἰώνιον τὸ ἡτοιμασμένον τῷ Διαβόλῳ καὶ τοῖς
ἀγγέλοις αὐτοῦ. Ἐπείνασα γάρ, καὶ οὐκ ἐδώκατέ μοι φαγεῖν· ἐδί- 42
ψησα, καὶ οὐκ ἐποτίσατέ με· ξένος ἤμην, καὶ οὐ συνηγάγετέ με· 43
γυμνὸς, καὶ οὐ περιεβάλετέ με· ἀσθενὴς καὶ ἐν φυλακῇ, καὶ οὐκ ἐπεσκέψασθέ με. Τότε ἀποκριθήσονται [αὐτῷ] καὶ αὐτοὶ, λέγοντες· 44
Κύριε, πότε σὲ εἴδομεν πεινῶντα, ἢ διψῶντα, ἢ ξένον, ἢ γυμνὸν, ἢ
ἀσθενῆ, ἢ ἐν φυλακῇ, καὶ οὐ διηκονήσαμέν σοι; Τότε ἀποκριθήσεται 45
αὐτοῖς, λέγων· Ἀμὴν λέγω ὑμῖν· ἐφ' ὅσον οὐκ ἐποιήσατε ἑνὶ τού-
n John 5. 29. Dan. 12. 2. των τῶν ἐλαχίστων, οὐδὲ ἐμοὶ ἐποιήσατε. [n] Καὶ ἀπελεύσονται οὗτοι 46
MK. 14. LU. 22. εἰς κόλασιν αἰώνιον· οἱ δὲ δίκαιοι εἰς ζωὴν αἰώνιον.
1 1 XXVI. Καὶ ἐγένετο, ὅτε ἐτέλεσεν ὁ Ἰησοῦς πάντας τοὺς λόγους 1
τούτους, εἶπε τοῖς μαθηταῖς αὐτοῦ· Οἴδατε ὅτι μετὰ δύο ἡμέρας τὸ 2
πάσχα γίνεται· καὶ ὁ Υἱὸς τοῦ ἀνθρώπου παραδίδοται εἰς τὸ σταυ-

35. συνηγάγετε] scil. εἰς τὸν οἶκον. The *complete* phrase occurs in 2 Sam. ii. 27. and Judg. xix. 18. The difference between the Classical and Hellenistic use is this, that in the latter it is used of *one only*, in the former of *more than one*.

36. γυμνός.] The term here (like the corresponding one in most languages, ancient and modern) does not denote absolutely *naked*, but "without some of one's garments," or generally *ill* clothed.

— ἐπεσκέψασθε.] The word signifies 1st, to *look at*, survey; 2d, to *look after*, implying attendance, care, and relief. Thus it is used of both the attendance of a physician, and of a nurse or friend. Ἤλθετε πρός με, like the Latin *adire*, implies solace and comfort.

38. πότε δέ.] Raphelius observes that the δὲ is not adversative, but copulative. It is not, however, simply such, but may be rendered *moreover*, or *again*.

40. ἐμοὶ ἐποιήσατε] "ye, as it were, did it unto me, as doing it by my order." Our Lord is pleased to regard what is done to his disciples, whether for good or evil, as done to himself. See Matt. x. 12. and Acts xiv. 4.

41. αἰώνιον.] Considering the opinions of the Jews, and indeed of the ancients in general, our Lord's hearers could not fail to understand this word in the usual sense *everlasting*, and not (as some ancient and modern Commentators contend) in that of a very long, but *limited* duration. And this seems to me one of the strongest arguments against an interpretation which has no solid foundation. The inferences which have been drawn from the use of δεῦτε and πορεύεσθε ἀπ' ἐμοῦ, and of ἡτοιμασμένον τῷ Διαβ. καὶ τοῖς ἀγγέλοις αὐτοῦ, that hell was not originally designed for men, and that they are the authors of their own miseries, are quite unfounded; because δεῦτε *could* not have been used to the rejected, and among the οἱ ἄγγελοι τοῦ Διαβόλου may be included the incorrigibly bad of every age.

44. αὐτῷ.] This is not found in most of the best MSS. and Versions, and some Fathers; nor has it any place in the Ed. Princ. It was cancelled by Beng., Wets., Matth., and Scholz.

XXVI. 2. γίνεται.] Said to be for ἄγεται, "is to be celebrated," (a frequent sense of the present tense;) which, however, is not only a Hebraism, but (as Raphelius shows) a Grecism also.

— πάσχα] the paschal feast. The word is derived from the Heb. פֶּסַח, *a passing by*, from פָּסַח, to pass, pass by. And in the Sept. and the N. T. τὸ πάσχα signifies 1. the *paschal lamb*; 2. the *paschal feast*.

— καὶ ὁ Υἱός.] The καὶ presents some difficulty, which can only be removed by taking it *in sensu χρονικῷ*, for καὶ τότε. It is often used for ὅτε, which may admit of being resolved into καὶ τότε. That his death was near at hand, our Lord had repeatedly apprised his disciples; but he had not until now told them the exact time.

MK. LU.
3 ῥωθῆναι. Τότε συνήχθησαν οἱ ἀρχιερεῖς καὶ οἱ γραμματεῖς καὶ οἱ 14. 22.
πρεσβύτεροι τοῦ λαοῦ εἰς τὴν αὐλὴν τοῦ ἀρχιερέως τοῦ λεγομένου 2
4 Καϊάφα· καὶ συνεβουλεύσαντο ἵνα τὸν Ἰησοῦν κρατήσωσι δόλῳ καὶ
5 ἀποκτείνωσιν. Ἔλεγον δέ· Μὴ ἐν τῇ ἑορτῇ, ἵνα μὴ θόρυβος γένηται 2
ἐν τῷ λαῷ.
6 Τοῦ δὲ Ἰησοῦ γενομένου ἐν Βηθανίᾳ ἐν οἰκίᾳ Σίμωνος τοῦ λε- 3
7 προῦ, προσῆλθεν αὐτῷ γυνὴ ἀλάβαστρον μύρου ἔχουσα βαρυτίμου, καὶ
8 κατέχεεν ἐπὶ τὴν κεφαλὴν αὐτοῦ ἀνακειμένου. Ἰδόντες δὲ οἱ μαθηταὶ 4
9 αὐτοῦ, ἠγανάκτησαν, λέγοντες· Εἰς τί ἡ ἀπώλεια αὕτη; ἠδύνατο 5
γὰρ τοῦτο [τὸ μύρον] πραθῆναι πολλοῦ, καὶ δοθῆναι τοῖς πτωχοῖς.
10 Γνοὺς δὲ ὁ Ἰησοῦς, εἶπεν αὐτοῖς· Τί κόπους παρέχετε τῇ γυναικί; 6
11 ἔργον γὰρ καλὸν εἰργάσατο εἰς ἐμέ. Πάντοτε γὰρ τοὺς πτωχοὺς ἔχετε 7
12 μεθ᾽ ἑαυτῶν· ἐμὲ δὲ οὐ πάντοτε ἔχετε. Βαλοῦσα γὰρ αὕτη τὸ μύρον 8
13 τοῦτο ἐπὶ τοῦ σώματός μου, πρὸς τὸ ἐνταφιάσαι με ἐποίησεν. Ἀμὴν 9

3. *τότε*] i. e. on the second day before the Passover. Οἱ *ἀρχιερεῖς — λαοῦ*. A periphrasis for *τὸ συνέδριον*, as that assembly is called in John x. 47, and whose office it was to sit in judgment on false prophets.

— *αὐλήν*.] The word signifies, 1. *an open enclosure*; 2. *an area*, or *court yard*, such as was before the *vestibule* of a large house; 3. *an interior court*, such as is in the middle of Oriental houses; 4. by synecdoche, *an edifice provided with such an αὐλή*; and was a name given to the residences of kings or great persons, denoting *mansion* or *palace*.

4. *δόλῳ*.] The Commentators supply *ἐν* or *σύν*. But no ellipsis is necessary, as the Dative form of itself will express the instrument or means.

5. *μὴ ἐν τῇ ἑορτῇ*] scil. *γενέσθω τοῦτο*. By *ἑορτῇ* is meant, not the *feast-day*, but the whole paschal *festival*. The three great festivals, indeed, were periods when notorious malefactors were usually executed, for the sake of more public example. This, however, the Sanhedrim would have waived; but having so fair an offer from Judas, they embraced the opportunity.

6. *Σίμωνος τοῦ λεπροῦ*.] So called by surname, because he *had been* a leper, and had probably been cured by Christ. So Matthew was called the *Publican*, as having been such. [*Comp.* John xi. 2; xii. 3.]

7. *προσῆλθεν αὐτῷ γυνή*, &c.] There has been no little debate on the question, whether the transaction related here and in Mark xiv. 3—9, be the same with that recorded in John xii. 2, or a different one. The reader is therefore referred, on the latter hypothesis, to Lightfoot and Pilkington; on the former, to Doddr., Michaelis, Recens. Synop., Fritz., and especially Townsend Ch. Arr. i. 387, with whom I entirely agree. There is no great weight in the allegations of *discrepancies* between the two stories; while their *points of agreement* are so remarkable, that they cannot well be regarded as two different transactions; but have every appearance of being two statements by two different eye-witnesses of the same transaction. It cannot, indeed, be denied, that one or other of the two narratives must be inserted out of the strict chronological order; which, it should seem, there is greater reason to think is observed by John, than by Matthew and Mark.

— *ἀλάβαστρον μύρου*.] This simply denotes a cruse of ointment, which (as we learn from the writers on Antiquities) was much of the form of our oil-flasks, with a long and narrow neck. The utensil was so called, because it had been first, and was always generally made of a sort of marble called *onyx*, from being of the color of a human nail; and also *alabaster*, not from the Arabic *Bet straton*, as some imagine, but I conceive, from the *extreme smoothness*, and consequently difficulty of handling articles made of it. Thus the utensil came to be called *ἀλάβαστρον*, which it is probable was originally an *adjective* with the ellip. of *σκεῦος*. Afterwards, however, it came to be manufactured of *any* materials, as glass, metal, stone, and even wood. In the phrase *ἀλάβαστρον μύρου* (which is found in Herodot. iii. 20, and Athen. 268), there is the same ellipse of *πλέων*.

Mark and John call this *μύριον*, *nard*, which, as appears from Heyn. on Tibull. ii. 27, was rather an *oil* than an unguent, and therefore (especially as the term *κατέχεεν* just after demands this) we may suppose that such is the sense of *μύρ.* here.

— *βαρυτίμου*.] A word used by the later Greek writers, equivalent to *πολύτιμος*, which is used by John, or *πολυτελής*, used by Mark.

— *κατέχεεν ἐπὶ τὴν κεφ.*] The *Classical* construction is *κατέχ. κατά τινος*, or *κατέχ. τινος*. This was an usual mark of *respect* from hosts towards their guests, both among Jews and Gentiles.

8. *ἀπώλεια*.] So *φθόρος ἀργυρίου* in Theocr. Id. xv. 18, and *ἀπόλλυμι* in Theophr. Ch Eth. xv. and Plutarch i. 869. At *εἰς τί* sub. *ἐστι*, or *γέγονε*, which is *expressed* in Mark.

9. *τὸ μύρον*.] The words are wanting in several of the best MSS., besides several Versions and Fathers; and are cancelled by Griesb., Fritz, and Scholz. They seem to have come from the margin, where they were intended to supply a substantive to which *τοῦτο* might be referred, and were introduced from John xii. 5.

10. *τί κόπους παρέχετε*.] Παρέχειν is not unfrequently used with an Accus. of a noun, importing *labour* or *exertion*; but almost always in the *singular*, with the exception of *πρᾶγμα*, which always has the *plural*.

11. *πάντοτε γάρ*, &c.] "The good work which was to be done soon or never, was preferable to that of which the opportunities were continual." [*Comp.* supra 18, 20, infra 28, 20. John xii. 8.]

12. *πρὸς τὸ ἐντ. ἐποίησεν*.] Ἐνταφιάζειν signifies

MK. LU.
14. 22. λέγω ὑμῖν· ὅπου ἐὰν κηρυχθῇ τὸ εὐαγγέλιον τοῦτο ἐν ὅλῳ τῷ κόσμῳ,
λαληθήσεται καὶ ὃ ἐποίησεν αὕτη εἰς μνημόσυνον αὐτῆς.
10 3 Τότε πορευθεὶς εἷς τῶν δώδεκα, ὁ λεγόμενος Ἰούδας Ἰσκαριώτης, 14
4 πρὸς τοὺς ἀρχιερεῖς, εἶπε· Τί θέλετέ μοι δοῦναι, κἀγὼ ὑμῖν παρα- 15
11 6 δώσω αὐτόν; οἱ δὲ ἔστησαν αὐτῷ τριάκοντα ἀργύρια· καὶ ἀπὸ 16
τότε ἐζήτει εὐκαιρίαν ἵνα αὐτὸν παραδῷ.
12 7 9 Τῇ δὲ πρώτῃ τῶν ἀζύμων προσῆλθον οἱ μαθηταὶ τῷ Ἰησοῦ, λέγον- 17

to make preparation for burying, by such observances (namely, washing, laying out, anointing, and embalming) as were used previously thereto. The best Commentators, from Grot. downward, are agreed that πρὸς τὸ has reference not to the intention of the *woman*, but rather of *Providence*. There *may* be, as some think, simply an ellipse of ὡσεὶ, (which is confirmed by the Syriac Version,) i. e. she has done it, *as if* for my burial. For (as Grot. remarks) it is not unfrequent in Hebrew for any one to be said to do a thing for this or that end; which, however, is not really *intended* by him; only his act is consequent upon it *aliunde:* as 1 Kings xvii. 18. Prov. xvii. 19. In either view, the words must be regarded as suggesting the nearness of his death; and (as Grot. says) justifying what had been done by an argument *a pari:* that, had she expended this on his *dead* body, they who used such ointments could not reasonably object to it; and had, therefore, no ground now to do so, as he was so near death and burial.

13. ἐν ὅλῳ τῷ κόσμῳ.] This clause is by some, as Kuin. and Fritz., construed with the *following* word λαληθήσεται; but it is usually, and more properly, taken with the *preceding* ὅπου, and is well rendered by Casaub. "in toto, inquam, mundo." So also the Syr. Version. By εὐαγγ. is meant religion. Εἰς μνημόσυνον αὐτῆς, "for her [honourable] remembrance," since μνημόσυνον, as well as its kindred terms, is almost always meant for praise.

14. τότε.] The sense *may* be "about that time;" for this particle is of very indefinite signification, and is used with considerable latitude. The particle, however, may have reference to ver. 3, and be resumptive, and the narration of the anointing parenthetical. The τότε does not at all events, denote (as Kuin. and others imagine) "when they had resolved to apprehend him," but rather "when they were yet unresolved whether to apprehend him *then*, or not."

15. ἔστησαν αὐτῷ.] On the interpretation of ἔστησαν Commentators are divided. Some ancient and many modern ones explain it "weighed out," i. e. paid; by a reference to the ancient custom of paying the precious metals by *weight;* which continued, or at least the mode of expression, even after the introduction of *coined* money. This signification of ἱστάναι is frequent in the Sept., and in the Classical writers from Homer downward. Others, however, induced by a seeming discrepancy from the accounts of Mark and Luke; the former of whom says ἐπηγγείλαντο αὐτῷ ἀργύριον; the latter συνέθεντο ἀργύριον δ., would take it to mean *promised* to give. But that would be exceedingly harsh; and the testimony of the ancient Versions will afford no confirmation, since they rather give the sense *appointed* than promised. Nor is the discrepancy in question so material as to *need* being got rid of in so violent a manner. For, without resorting to the arbitrary supposition of Michaelis and Rosenm., that the money in question was only an *earnest* of more; the term used by Mark, (which means *engaged* to to give,) and that used by Luke, (which means *agreed*,) may either of them be said, in such a case, to *imply* immediate payment at the treasury. That the money *was* paid, we find from Matt. xxvii. 3—5.

17. τῇ δὲ πρώτῃ τῶν ἀζύμων.] We are here brought to the consideration of a question on which Commentators are much divided in opinion; namely, whether our Lord celebrated the Passover before his crucifixion, and if so, at *what time?* There are expressions in the Evangelists which seem, at first sight, contradictory. John appears to differ from the rest respecting the time that the Jews partook of the Passover; and supposes that they did not eat it on the same evening as our Saviour; yet all the Evangelists agree, that the night of the day in which he ate what was called the passover, was *Thursday*. He is also said to command his disciples to prepare the passover, and he tells them he had earnestly desired to eat this Passover with them. Yet we find that on the day after that on which he had thus celebrated it, the Jews would not go into the judgment hall, lest they should be defiled, but that they might eat the passover. Now the law required that all should eat it *on the same day*. The principal solutions which have been propounded of this puzzling question are as follows: 1. *That our Lord did not eat the Passover at all*. Of those who adopt this opinion some contend that it is only a *common* supper that is spoken of; others, that Jesus (like the Jews of the present day) celebrated only a *memorative*, not a *sacrificial* Passover. 2. That he *did eat* the Passover, and on the *same day* with the Jews. 3. That he ate it, but *not on the same day* with the Jews; *anticipating* it by one day. Of these solutions, the first, in both its forms, is alike inconsistent with the plain words of Scripture, φάγειν τὸ πάσχα, and θύειν τὸ πάσχα. That our Lord did *not* eat the Passover, rests merely on conjecture; and the place, the preparation, and the careful observance of the Paschal feast, alike forbid the notion of a *common*, or of a *memorative* supper. As to the second solution, it is equally inadmissible, since, on that hypothesis (as Mr. Townsend says), "if our Lord ate it the same hour in which the Jews ate theirs, he certainly could not have died that day, as they ate the passover on Friday, about six o'clock in the evening. If he did *not*, he must have been crucified on *Saturday*, the Jewish sabbath, and could not have risen again on the first day of the week, as the Evangelists testify, but on Monday." The third solution (which has been adopted by Scaliger, Casaub., Capell., Grot., Bochart, Hamm., Cudw., Carpzov, Kidder, Ernesti, Michaelis, Rosenm., Kuin., Bens., A. Clarke, Townsend, and many other eminent Commentators) has the strongest claims to be preferred;

		MK.	LU.
18	τες αὐτῷ· Ποῦ θέλεις ἑτοιμάσωμέν σοι φαγεῖν τὸ πάσχα; ὁ δὲ	14.	22.
	εἶπεν· Ὑπάγετε εἰς τὴν πόλιν πρὸς τὸν δεῖνα, καὶ εἴπατε αὐτῷ· Ὁ	13 14	10 11
	διδάσκαλος λέγει· Ὁ καιρός μου ἐγγύς ἐστι· πρός σε ποιῶ τὸ πά-		
19	σχα μετὰ τῶν μαθητῶν μου. Καὶ ἐποίησαν οἱ μαθηταὶ ὡς συνέταξεν	16	13
	αὐτοῖς ὁ Ἰησοῦς· καὶ ἡτοίμασαν τὸ πάυχα.		
20	Ὀψίας δὲ γενομένης, ἀνέκειτο μετὰ τῶν δώδεκα. Καὶ ἐσθιόντων	17	14
21	αὐτῶν, εἶπεν· Ἀμὴν λέγω ὑμῖν, ὅτι εἷς ἐξ ὑμῶν παραδώσει με. Καὶ	18	
22	λυπούμενοι σφόδρα ἤρξαντο λέγειν αὐτῷ ἕκαστος αὐτῶν· Μήτι ἐγώ	19	23
23	εἰμι, κύριε; Ὁ δὲ ἀποκριθεὶς εἶπεν· Ὁ ἐμβάψας μετ᾽ ἐμοῦ ἐν	20	

since it is most consistent with the language of the Evangelists, and best reconciles any seeming discrepancies. The Passover was to commence on the first full moon in the month Nisan; but, from the inartificial and imperfect mode of calculation by reckoning from the first appearance of the moon's phasis, a doubt might exist as to the day; and this doubt afforded ground, occasionally, for an observance of different days; which, it is said, the Rabbinical writings recognize. And as the Pharisees and Sadducees, and also the *Karæi*, (on whom See Horne's Introd.) differed on so many *other* points, so it is likely that they should on the present. And this disagreement would, it is obvious, make a day's difference in the calculation; which difference would extend throughout the whole month; so that what would to one party be the 14th day, would to the other be the 13th. Of course, the error in this diversity of observance must rest, not with our Lord, but with the Pharisees who differed from the order which he adopted. They might *defer*, but our Lord would not *anticipate* the day ἐν ᾗ ἔδει θύεσθαι τὸ πάσχα. Thus, while Christ celebrated this his last Passover, one day earlier than the Traditionarii, the ruling party among the Jews; yet he might be said equally to observe the ritual command of eating on the 14th of Nisan. See more in Rec. Syn. This is not a mere novel notion, but was adopted by Euthym., and probably Chrysostom.

Thus every real difficulty, as far as the subject admits of it, is solved.

18. τὸν δεῖνα.] This expression was used both by the Classical and Hellenistic writers (as we say Mr. *Such-a-one*, and the Spaniards *fullano)* in speaking of a person whose name one does not recollect, or think it worth while to mention, but who is well known to the person addressed. Many reasons have been imagined for Jesus's suppressing the name, which, has been variously recorded by Ecclesiastical tradition. It was a person who, our Lord knew, would be ready to accommodate him with a room, and with whom he had, no doubt, previously arranged the matter.

— ὁ καιρός μου.] Schmid., Rosenm., Kuin., and some others, take καιρὸς to denote the *time of keeping the passover;* and the μου, they think, refers to the different day on which Jesus, with the Karæi and others, kept it, from that of the Pharisees. But though this interpretation may seem countenanced by the words following, yet it presents so frigid a sense, that there is no reason to abandon the usual interpretation, by which καιρὸς is explained the time of Christ's passion and death. So Ps. xxxi. 15, "my time is in thine hand." Thus the full sense will be, "The time for my departure is near; previous to which it is necessary that I should celebrate the Passover, which I will do at thy house." This use of ποιεῖν, like *facere* in Latin, is found also in the Classical writers.

19. ἡτοίμασαν τὸ πάσχα.] This is usually rendered, "they prepared the paschal lamb." But it rather seems to signify, "they made ready for the paschal meal;" with reference to such preliminaries as examining the lamb, slaying, skinning, and roasting it. On the ceremonies with which the Passover was celebrated, see an admirable summary (from Lightfoot) in Horne's Introd. iii. 310—312.

20. ἀνέκειτο.] Though the Passover was directed to be eaten standing, (Exod. xii. 11.) yet the Doctors had introduced the *reclining* posture, (which had been usual at meals from ancient times,) accounting it a symbolical action, typifying that *rest* and freedom to which, at the institution of the rite, they were tending, but had now attained.

22. μήτι ἐγώ εἰμι] sub. ὁ παραδώσων σε, omitted through delicacy.

23. ὁ ἐμβάψας, &c.] The Commentators are not agreed whether this was meant to *designate* the betrayer; or whether it was only a prophetical application of a proverbial saying; indicating that one of his familiar companions would betray him, and not meant to be applied particularly, except by the person himself intended. The latter opinion is preferable. Indeed it is plain, from Mark xiv. 20., that Christ did not mean to particularly designate him, since he says εἷς τῶν δώδεκα ὁ ἐμβ., &c. See also Luke xii. 21. Theophyl. and Grot. are of opinion that Judas reclined near Christ; so that, though there were more dishes on the table, of which every one dipped his bread into the one nearest to him, yet he helped himself from the *same* dish. Thus would Jesus more easily (and without the others hearing) answer the interrogation of Judas by the words "thou hast said;" and thus John would more unobservedly (on asking who the traitor should be) receive the sign from Jesus. The disciples (except *John*, see John xiii. 26.), it should seem, did not, until Judas's departure, understand who was meant. They only knew, at the time, that *some* one of the twelve, who had been helping himself from the same dish with Jesus, would betray him. It should seem, the question, Is it I? was asked by Judas immediately after he had received the sop from Jesus, and that the question asked by John, *who it should be?* was asked immediately after Jesus had made the public declaration, "One of the twelve, who has been dipping his hand in the same dish, and whose hand is on the same table with me, will betray me."

The custom of several taking food with the

MK. LU.
14. 22. τῷ τρυβλίῳ τὴν χεῖρα, οὗτός με παραδώσει. Ὁ μὲν Υἱὸς τοῦ ἀν- 24
21 21 22 θρώπου ὑπάγει, καθὼς γέγραπται περὶ αὐτοῦ· οὐαὶ δὲ τῷ ἀνθρώπῳ ἐκείνῳ, δι' οὗ ὁ Υἱὸς τοῦ ἀνθρώπου παραδίδοται· καλὸν ἦν
αὐτῷ, εἰ οὐκ ἐγεννήθη ὁ ἄνθρωπος ἐκεῖνος. Ἀποκριθεὶς δὲ Ἰούδας 25
ὁ παραδιδοὺς αὐτὸν, εἶπε· Μήτι ἐγώ εἰμι, ῥαββί; λέγει αὐτῷ· Σὺ
εἶπας.
22 19 Ἐσθιόντων δὲ αὐτῶν, λαβὼν ὁ Ἰησοῦς τὸν ἄρτον, καὶ * εὐχαριστήσας 26
ἔκλασε, καὶ ἐδίδου τοῖς μαθηταῖς, καὶ εἶπε· Λάβετε, φάγετε· τοῦτό

hand from the same dish, has ever been in use in the East.

Ὁ ἐμβάψας should be rendered "he who has dipped" (or rather dived): for we need not suppose, with Dr. Shaw, and some of the Commentators, that this was merely dipping the hand into liquid, like soup; but of diving the hand into a deep dish (like a soup-tureen) in order to transfer the *meat*, already torn up into pieces. So Major Taylor, cited by me in Rec. Syn. "The hearty way in which our friend *dived* his hand into a large dish, and transferred its contents to our plates, formed a contrast to the delicacy of European manners." See also an extract from Jackson's Morocco, in Rec. Syn. Hence it appears that ἐμβάψας is for ἐμβαλὼν, which occurs in a fragment of Anacreon, χεῖρά τ' ἐν τηγάνῳ βαλεῖν. This idiom is so rare, that no example, I believe, has ever been adduced by any Philologist; and I have myself only met with *one*, namely in Philostr. de Sophist. Vitis, xxi. 3., where, speaking of a party of harvest-men sitting at dinner under an oak-tree, and suddenly killed by lightning, he says, οἱ θερισταὶ, ἐφ' οὗπερ ἕκαστος ἔτυχε πράττων, οὕτως ἀπέθανεν (I conjecture ἀπέθανον). Ὁ μὲν γὰρ κύλικα ἀναιρούμενος (render, not *sustinens*, but *in manus sumens*: so Hesiod. Theog. 553. χερσὶν ὅγ' ἀμφοτέρησιν ἀνείλετο λευκὸν ἄλειφαρ), ὁ δὲ πίνων, ὁ δὲ βάπτων (I conjecture ὁ δ' ἐμβ.), ὁ δ' ἐσθίων, ὁ δέ τι ποιῶν (I conj. ὁ δ' ὅ, τι π.), τὰς ψυχὰς ἀφῆκαν.

24. ὑπάγει] "is going." The present tense is u ·d to denote the nearness of the things predicted. There is, too, an euphemism, "is going (unto death)," such as is common to most languages, in words denoting *to depart*; and of which the Commentators adduce examples both from the Sept. and the Classical writers. In the Anthol. Gr. vii. 169., we have the *complete* phrase εἰς ἀΐδην ὑπάγω.

— καθὼς γέγραπται π. α.] Namely, in the Ps. xxii. 1—3. Is. liii. 8. Dan. ix. 26. Zach. xii. 10. & xiii. 7. Καλὸν—ἐγεννήθη is a form of expression employed by the antients to express a condition the most miserable; of which examples are adduced by Lightf., Schoettg., Wets., and Kypke. The most apposite is Schemoth R. § 40. p. 135. "He that knoweth the Law, and doeth it not, it were better for him that he had not come into the world."

25. σὺ εἶπας.] A form of full assent, and serious affirmation, found not only in Hebrew, but sometimes in Greek and Latin.

26. ἐσθιόντων αὐτῶν.] Some of the best Commentators render, "when they had eaten;" which sense seems to be required by 1 Cor. xi. 25. μετὰ τὸ δειπνῆσαι. But ἐσθιόντων scarcely admits of that sense; and the seeming discrepancy may be removed by a mutual accommodation, rendering the former expression "while they were [yet] eating," (i. e., as Rosenm. *translates*, towards the end of the supper) and the latter, "as they had just finished the paschal feast."

— τὸν ἄρτον.] Bp. Middlet., on the authority of some MSS., would cancel the τόν: an alteration which he thinks called for by the absence of the τὸν in the parallel passages of Mark and Luke. But it is more probable that the τὸν was cancelled by those who wished to conform the text of Matthew to that of the other Evangelists; which, however, is not necessary; since, though the sense *with* the Article is more definite (i. e. *the* loaf, or rather cake, thin and hard, and fitter to be broken than cut), yet it would be intelligible without it. That *two* cakes of unleavened bread were provided for the Passover, all the accounts testify; though as only *one* was broken by our Lord, it is no wonder that in the new ordinance founded on the Jewish rite, only *one* (and that large or small in proportion to the probable number of communicants) should be provided.

— εὐχαριστήσας.] It is not easy to imagine stronger authority of MSS., Versions, Fathers, and early Editions, than that which exists for this reading (instead of the common one εὐλογήσας), which has been with reason adopted by Wets., Matth., and Scholz. Nevertheless, the common one is retained and defended by Griesb. and Fritz.; whose reasons, however, seem light, when weighed against such predominant external evidence. From the term εὐχαριστήσας, the rite afterwards took its name; especially as the service was a sacrifice of praise and thanksgiving. Indeed it was customary among the Jews never to take food or drink without returning thanks to God the giver, in prayer, by which it became sanctified.

— ἔκλασε.] Namely, as a type of the breaking of the body of our Redeemer on the cross.

— ἐστι.] All the best Commentators are agreed that the sense of ἐστι is, *represents*, or *signifies*; an idiom common in the Hebrew, which wanting a more distinctive term, made use of the verb substantive; a simple form of speech, yet subsisting in the common language of most nations. See Gen. xl. 12. xli. 26. Dan. vii. 23. viii. 21. 1 Cor. x. 4. Gal. iv. 24. Thus the Jews answered their children, who asked respecting the Passover, what is this? This *is* the body of the lamb which our fathers ate in Egypt. See Bp. Marsh's Lectures, p. 332—335. Wets. truly observes, that "while Christ was distributing the bread and wine, the thought could not but arise in the minds of the disciples, What can this mean, and what does it denote? They did not inquire, whether the bread which they saw were *really bread*, or whether another body lay unconspicuously hid in the interstices of the bread, but *what this action signified?* of what it was a *representation* or memorial?"

MK. LU.
27 ἐστι τὸ σῶμά μου. Καὶ λαβὼν τὸ ποτήριον, καὶ εὐχαριστήσας, ἔδωκεν 14. 22.
28 αὐτοῖς λέγων· Πίετε ἐξ αὐτοῦ πάντες· τοῦτο γάρ ἐστι τὸ αἷμά μου, 23 24 20
τὸ τῆς καινῆς διαθήκης, τὸ περὶ πολλῶν ἐκχυνόμενον εἰς ἄφεσιν ἁμαρ-
29 τιῶν. Λέγω δὲ ὑμῖν, ὅτι οὐ μὴ πίω ἀπ' ἄρτι ἐκ τούτου τοῦ γεννή- 25 18
ματος τῆς ἀμπέλου, ἕως τῆς ἡμέρας ἐκείνης, ὅταν αὐτὸ πίνω μεθ'
ὑμῶν καινὸν ἐν τῇ βασιλείᾳ τοῦ πατρός μου.

27. τὸ ποτήριον.] Some few MSS. have not the τό. But the evidence, both external and internal, for the Article is so strong, that it must be retained. See Bp. Middlet. Hence it should seem that *one* cup only was used; for (as observes Middlet.) "though four cups of wine were to be emptied at different times during the ceremony, a single cup four times filled was all that the occasion required." *Which* of the four is here meant, Commentators are not agreed. It is generally supposed to have been the *third*, or the *cup of blessing*; which was regarded as the most important of the four. That the wine was mixed with water, all are agreed; and this custom the Romanists still scrupulously retain; though they boldly violate the next injunction, πίετε ἐξ αὐτοῦ πάντες, by confining the cup to the Clergy (as if the words were meant for the *Apostles* only), notwithstanding that this view is utterly forbidden by the *reason* subjoined *why all* are to drink of it; and in spite of the strong authority of Antiquity, in the practice of the Church up to a comparatively recent period.

28. τοῦτο γάρ — διαθήκης] "For this is my blood, by which the new covenant is ratified." So Luke: τοῦτο τὸ ποτήριον ἡ καινὴ διαθήκη ἐν τῷ αἵματί μου, "By the administration of this cup I institute a new Religion, to be ratified by my blood." In the *federal* sacrifices of the ancients it was (as Grot. and Hamm. show) usual to receive the blood in a vessel; which was *itself drunk* by the more barbarous nations; but by the more civilized *wine* was substituted for it; to which the *colour* (the wine of the East being red) would contribute: and indeed wine is by poets called the *blood* of the grape. Hence our Lord is by some thought to have had a reference to this.

— ἐκχυνόμενον εἰς ἄφ. ἁμ.] Here (as Grot. remarks) there is a transition from the idea of *federal* to that of *piacular* sacrifices; in which the *victim* was offered up in the place of the *man*, who had deserved death. Ἐκχυν. is, as Grot. remarks, Present for Proximate future, "now being (i. e. to *be*) shed." Of this examples are frequent. Περὶ is here put for ὑπὲρ, as in Matt. ix. 36.; and the πολλῶν is equivalent to πάντων, as Matt. xx. 28. See the Note there. *Comp.* Rom. v. 15. Διαθήκης is to be rendered, not *testament*, but *covenant*.

29. οὐ μὴ πίω — πατρός μου.] On the sense of these words there is much diversity of opinion, chiefly occasioned by the various senses assigned to ἐν τῇ βασιλείᾳ τοῦ πατρός μου, which some think equivalent to ἐν οὐρανῷ, the Gospel dispensation; while others refer the words to Christ's mediatorial kingdom; and others, again, his *Millenian* reign. But for the last-mentioned interpretation, there is as little reason or evidence as can well be imagined; and as to the one before (which supposes that our Lord merely intended to announce the abrogation of the Jewish Passover, and the substitution of the Christian Lord's Supper in its place) it is based on a sandy foundation; for it does not appear that our Lord here had any reference to the discontinuance of the Passover. The truth, I think, may be found in one or other of the first-mentioned interpretations, of which the former (adopted by many recent Expositors), bears a considerable semblance of truth, being very suitable to the context, and supported by the parallel passage of Luke, where the expression is ἐν τῇ βασιλείᾳ τοῦ Θεοῦ, which often denotes the Gospel dispensation. Thus καινὸν will be put adverbially for ἐν καινῷ τρόπῳ, "in a new manner," i. e. a spiritual one, namely at the virtual presence of Christ, at the celebration of the Sacrament. Yet specious as this may appear, there is something unsound in principle; for it is *pressing* too much on the καινόν. Besides, when, we may ask, was it fulfilled? At the commencement of Christ's kingdom after his resurrection, when he ate and drank with his disciples, say the above Commentators, who adduce Luke xxiv. 30, 45. John xxi. 13. Acts i. 4. x. 41. But we do not learn that he drank at all, much less that he drank wine. He merely ate a little of some fish and honey-comb, which his disciples set before him (and that merely to convince them that he was really risen from the dead, and no phantom), and then probably presented the rest to his disciples. And so, indeed, several MSS. and Versions (including the two later Syr. and Vulg.) say *in words*. It appears, therefore, that this interpretation is untenable; and the *fourth* is alone such as can be safely adopted, by which βασ. τοῦ πατρός μου is taken for ἐν τῇ βασ. τῶν οὐρανῶν supra viii. 11. Luke xiii. 29. The general sense couched under this strong metaphor is, that his departure from them was nigh at hand, and would prevent his again participating in any future solemnity of the kind, unto the end of the world. The καινὸν has a reference to the *spiritual* nature of that kingdom emphatically termed "the kingdom of my Father," even the *new* Jerusalem, that "city not made with hands," "eternal in the heavens." The expression γεννήματος τοῦ ἀμπέλου is a periphrasis for *wine*, occurring not only in the Sept., but (at least with a slight change) in the Classical writers; e. gr. Pind. Nem. ix. 23. ἀμπέλου παῖς. Anacr. Od. I. 7. γόνος ἀμπέλου. Instead of γεννήματος, many MSS. have ἐπιγεννήματος, which is edited by Matthæi, on the ground of greater propriety, and the general usage of the Scriptural writers; where γέννημα is used of men and animals; ἐπιγέννημα, of the fruits of the earth. He acknowledges, however, that there is, even in the Classical writers, some diversity of reading. I have not ventured to follow the learned Editor here, because I feel doubtful whether a minute propriety like this would be observed, or be even known to those, (like the Evangelists,) writing in a foreign language. Besides, the general character of the MSS. which have ἐπιγεν. is such as rather to strengthen a suspicion that it arose, like thousands of other readings of the same MSS., *ex emendatione*.

MK. LU.
14. 22. *Καὶ ὑμνήσαντες, ἐξῆλθον εἰς τὸ ὄρος τῶν ἐλαιῶν. Τότε λέγει* 30
26 27 39 *αὐτοῖς ὁ Ἰησοῦς· Πάντες ὑμεῖς σκανδαλισθήσεσθε ἐν ἐμοὶ ἐν τῇ νυκτὶ* 31
ταύτῃ. γέγραπται γάρ· Πατάξω τὸν ποιμένα, καὶ δια-
28 *σκορπισθήσεται τὰ πρόβατα τῆς ποίμνης. Μετὰ δὲ τὸ* 32
29 *ἐγερθῆναί με, προάξω ὑμᾶς εἰς τὴν Γαλιλαίαν. Ἀποκριθεὶς δὲ ὁ* 33
Πέτρος εἶπεν αὐτῷ· Εἰ [καὶ] πάντες σκανδαλισθήσονται ἐν σοί, ἐγὼ
30 *οὐδέποτε σκανδαλισθήσομαι. Ἔφη αὐτῷ ὁ Ἰησοῦς· Ἀμὴν λέγω σοι,* 34
ὅτι ἐν ταύτῃ τῇ νυκτὶ, πρὶν ἀλέκτορα φωνῆσαι, τρὶς ἀπαρνήσῃ με.

30. ὑμνήσαντες] "having sung a hymn;" i. e. either, as some think, one adapted to the rite which Christ had just instituted (so the Christian hymn mentioned at Acts iv. 24) *or*, as most Commentators suppose, the usual Paschal hymn called κατ' ἐξοχὴν, the *Hallel*, which comprised the 113th and four following Psalms. Whether it was sung, or recited, has been doubted; but from the Rabbinical researches of Buxtorf and Lightf., the *former* is the more probable.

31. σκανδαλισθήσεσθε] i. e. (as Euthym. explains) σαλευθήσεσθε τὴν εἰς ἐμὲ πίστιν, ἤγουν φεύξεσθε, ye shall fall away from, forsake me.

— πατάξω — ποίμνης] From Zach. xiii. 7., though with a slight, but very unimportant, variation from the Heb. and Sept. It is indeed there said of an *evil* shepherd; but, as Whitby remarks, our Lord applies the passage to himself rather as an argument *à fortiori* than a prediction. Most recent Commentators (from Grot.) think that this is a *proverbial* expression, of which they adduce examples. But those will only show that there *was* a similar proverbial expression, not that *this* is such; which is inconsistent with the ὡς γέγραπται, by which is indicated a quotation from the O. T. The true reading in the Sept. is, no doubt, πάταξον (found in many of the best MSS.) But as the terminations ω and ον are very similar (especially in MSS.), so probably πατάξω was a frequent, perhaps the *common*, reading in the time of Christ. This is much better than supposing, with Owen and Randolph, that the *Hebrew* is corrupted; for, although the *first* person is not inapplicable in the *Evangelist*, yet it is quite unsuitable in the *Prophet*.

32. προάξω ὑμᾶς] Here there is a continuation of the *pastoral* metaphor of the preceding verse; and the force of the figure is clear by bearing in mind the Oriental custom, of the shepherd not following, but *leading* the sheep; which is alluded to in John x. 4. Rosenm. and Kuin. think that the sense of προάξω must not be pressed on, since all that is meant is, "I will see you again in Galilee, expect me in Galilee." There is, however, something lax and precarious in this sort of interpretation; and I prefer supposing, that the sense (which is, as in other predictions of our Lord at this period, briefly and obscurely worded) is as expressed by the following paraphrase (founded on Fritz.) "On returning to life, I shall precede you into Galilee;" i. e. I shall first be present in Galilee, where, if you follow me, you will recover your shepherd and leader.

33. εἰ καὶ πάντες] The καὶ is absent from most of the best MSS. and some Versions, and was rejected by Mill and Beng., and cancelled by Wets., Matth., Griesb., Tittm., and Scholz; but restored by Fritz.; whose reasons, however, are more specious than solid. After all, there is more reason to suppose it was introduced from Mark, in a great part of the MSS., than that it should have been accidentally omitted in so many as form the remainder. For no one would ever designedly omit it, since no *Critic* would be ignorant of the sense, *even*. Whereas some might think that they should *strengthen* the sense by inserting the καὶ, which at all events might make others prefer εἰ καὶ to the καὶ εἰ of Mark; which, however, is more agreeable to propriety. So Hom. Il. ν. 316. καὶ εἰ μάλα καρτερός ἐστιν. Indeed καὶ is occasionally, from various causes, foisted in by scribes or sciolists; insomuch that I should probably have done right in more decidedly rejecting the καὶ in Thucyd. iii. 27. 3. καὶ εἴ τι ἐβεβλωσήκει.

34. πρὶν ἀλέκτορα φωνῆσαι] The Schol. on Theocrit. says that φωνεῖν is properly used of the voice of birds. Yet it is perhaps never used, in any Classical writer, of *cocks*; but ᾄδειν, κεκραγέναι, φθέγγεσθαι. As the Rabbinical writers have told us that cocks were forbidden to be kept in Jerusalem, because of the "holy things," it has been objected that Peter could not hear one crow. But (without *cutting* the knot by resorting to any unusual sense of ἀλέκτωρ, or disallowing the testimony of the Talmud) we may, with Reland, maintain that the cock might crow *outside* of the city; and yet, in the stillness of night, be heard by Peter from the house of Caiaphas, which was situated near the city-wall. But perhaps the best mode of removing the difficulty would be to render, "before cock crowing." So Aristoph. Eccl. 391. ὅτε τὸ δεύτερον ὡ'λεκτρυὼν ἐφθέγγετο. Whether cocks were kept, or not, in Jerusalem, they, no doubt, were in the vicinity: and this phrase, like the correspondent one in Latin, depends upon *general custom*. [*Comp.* John xiii. 38.]

It has been thought a contradiction, that *Mark* xiv. 30. says, πρὶν ἢ δὶς φωνῆσαι. But there will be none, if it be considered that the heathens reckoned *two* cock crowings; of which the *second* (about day-break) was the more remarkable, and was that called κατ' ἐξοχὴν the cock-crowing. Thus the sense is, "before that time of night, or early morn, which is called the cock-crowing, (namely, the *second* time which bears that name) thou shalt deny me thrice." Mark relates the thing more circumstantially; but there is no real discrepancy between the two accounts. In Mark the expression καὶ ἀλέκτωρ ἐφώνησε may be rendered, "and it was cock-crowing-time;" in Luke and John the expression οὐ μὴ ἀλέκτωρ φωνήσει, "it shall not be cock-crowing time." G. Wakefield here well remarks on the *climax* in this verse, and the emphatical nature of the expressions. Our Lord assures his presumptuous disciple, that he will not only *fall off*, and *forsake* his Master, but will *deny* having any knowledge of him; and that not *once* only, but *thrice;* and on that *very night*."

MK. LU.

35 Λέγει αὐτῷ ὁ Πέτρος· Κἂν δέῃ με σὺν σοὶ ἀποθανεῖν, οὐ μή σε 14. 22.
ἀπαρνήσομαι. ὁμοίως δὲ καὶ πάντες οἱ μαθηταὶ εἶπον. 31
36 Τότε ἔρχεται μετ' αὐτῶν ὁ Ἰησοῦς εἰς χωρίον λεγόμενον Γεθσημανῆ, 32
καὶ λέγει τοῖς μαθηταῖς· Καθίσατε αὐτοῦ, ἕως οὗ ἀπελθὼν προσεύ-
37 ξωμαι ἐκεῖ. Καὶ παραλαβὼν τὸν Πέτρον καὶ τοὺς δύο υἱοὺς Ζεβεδαίου, 33
38 ρξατο ἤ λυπεῖσθαι καὶ ἀδημονεῖν. Τότε λέγει αὐτοῖς ὁ Ἰησοῦς· Περί- 34
λυπός ἐστιν ἡ ψυχή μου ἕως θανάτου· μείνατε ὧδε, καὶ γρηγορεῖτε
39 μετ' ἐμοῦ. Καὶ ‡ προελθὼν μικρὸν, ἔπεσεν ἐπὶ πρόσωπον αὐτοῦ, 35 41
προσευχόμενος καὶ λέγων· Πάτερ μου, εἰ δυνατόν ἐστι, παρελθέτω 36 42

35. *κἂν δέῃ με σ. σ. ἀποθανεῖν*] A strong form of expression, of such frequent occurrence in the Classical writers, that it may be regarded as almost proverbial. On the use of *οὐ μὴ* with the Fut. Indic., see Winer's Gr. Gr. p. 160.

— *ὁμοίως δέ.*] The δὲ, which is not found in the textus receptus, is supported by most of the best MSS. and some Versions, Fathers, and early Editions; and it has been restored by Wets., Matth., Griesb., Tittm., Fritz., and Scholz. It is, indeed, required by the *proprietas linguæ*.

36. *Γεθσημανῆ.*] Heb. גַּת שְׁמָנָא, "place of oil presses." It was situated at the foot of the Mount of Olives. This is improperly, by some Commentators, supposed to have been the *village* in which the produce of the Mount of Olives was prepared for use; for the term *χωρίον* can only mean a *field* or *close;* as, indeed, is plain from the very *ratio significationis* of the word, which is from *χωρίω* cognate with *χωρίζω*, to set apart, take in, or enclose; whence *χωρὶς*, *apart*. They were, I imagine, deceived by this *χωρίον* having a *name* assigned to it. Yet that *fields* had names, we find from 2 Kings xviii. 17. "the fuller's field." 2 Sam. ii. 16. "the field of strong men;" and Acts i. 19. "Aceldama, the field of blood;" and, what is still more to the purpose, Ps. xlix. 11. "call the lands after their own names;" and finally, what is most to the purpose, Thucyd. i. 108. *μάχῃ ἐν Οἰνοφύταις*, where the Editors fell into the same error of thinking it to be a *town*. The word *χωρίον* is used in the same sense also at Thucyd. i. 106. and Pausan. i. 29. 2. In fact, we find by Maundrell, that the very close in question Γεθσημ. still remains; and the Missionary Herald for 1824, p. 66., attests that there are still several antient olive-trees in the place.

37. *παραλαβὼν τὸν Πέτρον — Ζεβ.*] The same whom he had taken as witnesses of his transfiguration. In *λυπεῖσθαι καὶ ἀδημονεῖν* there is a sort of climax; for the latter is a much stronger term than the former, and signifies to be so overwhelmed, as to become insensible. [*Comp.* sup. iv. 21. John xii. 27.

38. *ὁ Ἰησοῦς.*] This is introduced by Wets., Griesb., Matth., Fritz., and Scholz, from the best MSS., Versions, and Fathers. *Περίλυπός — μου*, for *περίλ. εἰμι*; which is accounted a Hebraism: but it is found in most languages. In *περίλυπος*, the *περὶ* is *intensive*, as in the words *περιχαρὴς*, *περίφοβος*, *περιδεὴς*, and *περιαλγής*. It is well observed by the great Valckn., "Postremum illud *περίλυπος* apte adhibuerunt Evangelistæ, de Jesu, in horto Gethsemanis, quando, sub forma hominis, Deum tegens, et peccatorum humanorum pondere *pressus pœne opprimeretur*." Ἕως θανάτου is a not unfrequent addition to the phrase. So Jonas iv. 9. *λελύπημαι ἕως θανάτου*. See also Ps. cxiv. 3. As to the *nature* of this *agony* of our Lord in the garden of Gethsemane, much has been written, but nothing certainly determined. To so awfully mysterious a subject we cannot approach too reverently. That this *cup* was not simply *death*, (which some of the antient interpreters understood) we may be very certain. That the agony was occasioned (as some suppose) through the *divine wrath*, by our Redeemer thus bearing the sins of the world, is liable to many objections; as is also the opinion, that our Lord had then a severe spiritual conflict with the great enemy of mankind. The deadly horror was, no doubt, produced by a variety of causes arising from his peculiar situation and circumstances, and which it were presumptuous too minutely to scan. At the same time, however, we may rest assured that our Lord's agony was, in some mysterious way, connected with the offering of himself as a sacrifice for the sins of the world, and the procuring the redemption of mankind.

39. *προελθὼν*] Many of the best MSS. have *προσελθὼν*, which is received into the text by Matth. and Scholz, and strenuously defended by them; but on precarious grounds. The common reading has been justly restored by Griesb. and Fritz.; for it is in vain to urge MS. authority in words perpetually confounded, and none are more so than *προ* and *προς* in composition. But even were that waived, and MSS. were in favour of *προς*, yet the testimony of Versions and Fathers, *all* of them on the side of *προ*, would here turn the scale in favour of the common reading. Besides, *προς* is capable of no tolerable sense, except by a most harsh ellipse.

— *εἰ δυνατόν ἐ.*] "We are here (says Grot.) to distinguish between what is impossible *per se*, and what is impossible *hoc vel illo pacto*. Now *per se* nothing is impossible with God, except such things as are in themselves inconsistent, or else are repugnant to the Divine nature. The sense, therefore, is, 'if it be consistent with the counsels and methods of thy Providence for the salvation of men.'" Thus the words are perfectly reconcileable with those of the parallel passage of Mark iv. 36. *πάντα δυνατά σοι*. Similar sentiments are quoted from the Classical writers. In *παρελθέτω — τὸ ποτήριον* there is (as appears from the Classical citations) a figure derived from a cup being carried *past* any one at a feast. So Anacreon, *παρέρχεται; μὴ κάτεχε*. We may remark the bold figure involved in *ποτήριον*, similar to what occurs in Isaiah li. 17., "who hast drunk at the hand of the Lord the cup of his fury; hast drunken the dregs of the cup of trembling:" with which I would compare a very sublime passage of Æschyl. Agam. 1367. *τάδ' ἂν δικαίως ἦν*,

MK. LU.
14. 22. ἀπ' ἐμοῦ τὸ ποτήριον τοῦτο· πλὴν οὐχ ὡς ἐγὼ θέλω, ἀλλ' ὡς σύ.
37 45 Καὶ ἔρχεται πρὸς τοὺς μαθητάς, καὶ εὑρίσκει αὐτοὺς καθεύδοντας, καὶ 40
λέγει τῷ Πέτρῳ· Οὕτως οὐκ ἰσχύσατε μίαν ὥραν γρηγορῆσαι μετ'
38 46 ἐμοῦ; γρηγορεῖτε καὶ προσεύχεσθε, ἵνα μὴ εἰσέλθητε εἰς πειρασμόν. 41
39 Τὸ μὲν πνεῦμα πρόθυμον, ἡ δὲ σὰρξ ἀσθενής. Πάλιν ἐκ δευτέρου 42
ἀπελθὼν προσηύξατο, λέγων· Πάτερ μου, εἰ οὐ δύναται τοῦτο τὸ
ποτήριον παρελθεῖν ἀπ' ἐμοῦ, ἐὰν μὴ αὐτὸ πίω, γενηθήτω τὸ θέλημά
40 σου. Καὶ ἐλθὼν εὑρίσκει αὐτοὺς πάλιν καθεύδοντας· ἦσαν γὰρ 43
αὐτῶν οἱ ὀφθαλμοὶ βεβαρημένοι. Καὶ ἀφεὶς αὐτούς, ἀπελθὼν πάλιν 44
41 προσηύξατο ἐκ τρίτου, τὸν αὐτὸν λόγον εἰπών. Τότε ἔρχεται πρὸς τοὺς 45
μαθητὰς αὐτοῦ, καὶ λέγει αὐτοῖς· Καθεύδετε τὸ λοιπὸν καὶ ἀναπαύ-
εσθε·—ἰδού, ἤγγικεν ἡ ὥρα, καὶ ὁ Υἱὸς τοῦ ἀνθρώπου παραδίδοται
42 εἰς χεῖρας ἁμαρτωλῶν.—Ἐγείρεσθε! ἄγωμεν! ἰδού, ἤγγικεν ὁ παρα- 46
διδούς με.
43 47 Καὶ ἔτι αὐτοῦ λαλοῦντος, ἰδού, Ἰούδας, εἷς τῶν δώδεκα, ἦλθε, καὶ 47
μετ' αὐτοῦ ὄχλος πολὺς μετὰ μαχαιρῶν καὶ ξύλων, ἀπὸ τῶν ἀρχιερέων

ὑπερδίκως μὲν οὖν Τοσῶνδε κρατῆρ' ἐν δόμοις κακῶν ὅδε Πλήσας ἀραίων, αὐτὸς ἐκπίνει μολών.

40. οὕτως] "*itane? siccine?*" This, like εἶτα and some other particles, is so used with interrogations, as to denote wonder mixed with censure. Wets. cites Hom. Il. β. 23. & Od. ε. 204. From the *natural* sense of the term, our Lord now passes to the *metaphorical*, and engrafts upon it an exhortation to *Christian watchfulness*; on which subject see an excellent Sermon on this text by Dr. South, Vol. vi. 353., where, after observing that, in the Christian warfare, the two great defensives against temptation are *watching* and *prayer*, he remarks, I. that *watching* imports, in the first place, a sense of the greatness of the evil we contend against: 2dly, a diligent survey of the power of the enemy, compared with the weakness and treachery of our own hearts; 3dly, a consideration of the ways by which temptation has prevailed on ourselves or others; 4thly, a continual *attention* to the danger, in opposition to *remissness*; 5thly, a constant and severe temperance. II. That *Prayer* is rendered effectual, 1st, by fervency or importunity; 2dly, by constancy or perseverance. III. That *Watching* and *Prayer* must be always *united*; the first without the last being but *presumption*; the last without the first a *mockery*.

41. εἰσέλθητε.] Εἰσελθεῖν is here used, like ἐμπίπτειν in 1 Tim. vi. 9., to denote *fall under, succumb*. Our Lord does not direct them to pray to God that no temptation might befall them; but that they might not be *overcome* by the temptations in which they must be involved; and to pray for extraordinary spiritual assistance under them.

— τὸ μὲν πνεῦμα — ἀσθενής.] This is meant not as an excuse for their frailty, but as an incentive to greater vigilance, together with prayer.

42. πάλιν ἐκ δευτέρου.] Some would refer πάλιν to ἀπελθών, and ἐκ δευτ. (scil. χρόνου) to προσηύξατο. But the Classical examples adduced by the Commentators show that the words must be taken together: in which there is not (as some imagine) a *pleonasm*, but a *stronger expression*.

43. βεβαρημένοι.] Sub. ὕπνῳ; though the ellipse is rarely supplied. Βαρύνεσθαι is often used of the heaviness of *sleep*.

45. καθεύδετε τὸ λοιπόν.] This seems so inconsistent with the subsequent exhortation ἐγείρεσθε! ἄγωμεν! that many Commentators take the sentence interrogatively; q. d. "do ye yet sleep?" But this is doing violence to the construction, and is contrary to the *usus loquendi* (as Fritz. shows); which will not permit τὸ λοιπὸν to be taken in any other sense than "*in ceterum tempus*." It is better with Chrysost., Euthym., Erasm., Beza, Grot., and some recent Commentators (as Schmid. and Fritz.), to suppose a kind of slightly *ironical rebuke*; q. d. ["Since you have thus far failed to watch] sleep on the remainder of the time, and take your rest [if you can]." But, if irony be thought unsuitable to the occasion, (though Campb. pronounces it very natural) we may, with Theophyl., Rosenm., and Kuin., take the imperatives *permissively*, "I no longer desire you to watch;" "you can no longer render me service." I have endeavoured by punctuation, to, in some degree, represent the abruptness of the phraseology. I would further observe, that it is in vain to allege that the foregoing punctuation is required by the words of Luke xxii. 46. τί καθεύδετε. Nothing forbids us to suppose, that the address recorded by Luke took place as well as that mentioned by Matth., that of the former *preceding* that of the latter.

— ἡ ὥρα.] Scil. τῆς παραδόσεως, as Euthym. rightly supplies. The καὶ following signifies *when*, or *in which*, by what some call a Hebraism; though it is found in Herodot., Thucyd., and others.

— ἁμαρτωλῶν.] i. e. the Romans, as being heathens. Others, less probably, take it of the *Jews*. It may, however, be understood of *both*.

47. ξύλων] "lignorum," clubs and such like *tumultuary* weapons. Such, however, would scarcely have been borne by Roman soldiers; though John xviii. 3. speaks of a Roman σπεῖρα. that expression, however, must be understood in a more general sense of *less* than a cohort. And these might be stationed at some little distance, to aid the civil power, which was *likely* to be accompanied by a considerable mob.

MK. LU.
48 καὶ πρεσβυτέρων τοῦ λαοῦ. Ὁ δὲ παραδιδοὺς αὐτὸν ἔδωκεν αὐτοῖς 14. 22.
49 σημεῖον, λέγων· Ὃν ἂν φιλήσω, αὐτός ἐστι· κρατήσατε αὐτόν. Καὶ 44
εὐθέως προσελθὼν τῷ Ἰησοῦ, εἶπε· Χαῖρε, ῥαββί· καὶ κατεφίλησεν
50 αὐτόν. Ὁ δὲ Ἰησοῦς εἶπεν αὐτῷ· Ἑταῖρε, ἐφ' ‡ ᾧ πάρει; Τότε 46
προσελθόντες ἐπέβαλον τὰς χεῖρας ἐπὶ τὸν Ἰησοῦν, καὶ ἐκράτησαν αὐτόν.
51 Καὶ ἰδοὺ, εἷς τῶν μετὰ Ἰησοῦ, ἐκτείνας τὴν χεῖρα, ἀπέσπασε τὴν μά- 47 50
χαιραν αὐτοῦ, καὶ πατάξας τὸν δοῦλον τοῦ ἀρχιερέως, ἀφεῖλεν αὐτοῦ
52 τὸ ὠτίον. Τότε λέγει αὐτῷ ὁ Ἰησοῦς· Ἀπόστρεψόν σου τὴν μάχαιραν
εἰς τὸν τόπον αὐτῆς· πάντες γὰρ οἱ λαβόντες μάχαιραν ἐν μαχαίρᾳ
53 ἀπολοῦνται. Ἢ δοκεῖς ὅτι οὐ δύναμαι ἄρτι παρακαλέσαι τὸν πατέρα
54 μου, καὶ παραστήσει μοι πλείους ἢ δώδεκα λεγεῶνας ἀγγέλων; Πῶς
οὖν πληρωθῶσιν αἱ γραφαὶ, ὅτι οὕτω δεῖ γενέσθαι;
55 Ἐν ἐκείνῃ τῇ ὥρᾳ εἶπεν ὁ Ἰησοῦς τοῖς ὄχλοις· Ὡς ἐπὶ λῃστὴν 48 52
ἐξήλθετε μετὰ μαχαιρῶν καὶ ξύλων, συλλαβεῖν με; Καθ' ἡμέραν πρὸς 49 53
ὑμᾶς ἐκαθεζόμην διδάσκων ἐν τῷ ἱερῷ, καὶ οὐκ ἐκρατήσατέ με.

48. φιλήσω.] Agreeably to the customary mode of *salutation* in ancient times, especially in the East; which is still retained in Spain and some parts of Italy and France.

49. κατεφίλησεν.] In the Classical writers the κατα is usually *intensive*; but in the Sept. both the simple and compound are used indifferently.

50. ἑταῖρε.] This is best regarded as a common form of address, though generally implying some degree of contempt, or, as here, reproach.

— ἐφ' ᾧ.] Most of the best MSS., together with some Fathers and early Edd., have ἐφ' ὃ, which is edited by Matthæi, Griesb., Tittm., Fritz., and Scholz. It is scarcely possible to determine the true reading, because the signification of *purpose* is expressed both by the *Dative* and the *Accus*. Yet, if the phrase occurred in a *Classical* writer, I should not hesitate to edit ἐφ' ᾧ; for I am not aware of any unimpeachable examples of the simple ὃς in this sense used in the *Accus*., but many of the *Dative*. See my Note on Thucyd. i. 134. ἐφ' ᾧ ἐχώρει. Πάρει is wrongly rendered by Erasmus, by a very common error in all translators. I shall fully discuss the point in a note on Josephus Bell. i. 12. 4. The case is different with respect to the compounds ὅστις, ὅσπερ, &c. *There* Classical use employs alone the *Accus*.

51. ἀπέσπασε.] This is Hellenistic Greek for ἔσπασε, or ἐσπάσατο, and occurs elsewhere only in the LXX. Μάχαιραν, or *cutlass*, such as travellers in Judæa used to carry for security against the robbers, who infested the country. Ἀφεῖλε is for ἀπέτεμε; an Alexandrian or Hellenistic use; for except the N. T. and LXX., it has only been adduced from Polyænus. It is, however, found in the Latin *auferre*, and in the common dialect of our own language.

— τὸ ὠτίον.] This certainly signifies the whole ear, and not the *tip* of it (as Grot. thinks); for that is inconsistent with the οὖς in the parallel passage of Luke. Besides, ὠτίον is not unfrequently used in the LXX. for οὖς. And, (as Lobeck on Phryn. p. 211, observes,) the common dialect calls most parts of the body by diminutives, as τὰ ῥινία, τὸ ὀμμάτιον. Rosenm. and Kuin. remark that the sense of ἀφεῖλε must not be *pressed on*, since from the language of Luke we may infer that the ear hung by the skin. And certainly such kind of hyperbolical idioms are common in every language. [*Comp*. John xviii. 10.]

52. πάντες γὰρ — ἀπολοῦνται.] Some ancient and several modern Commentators consider these words as a *prediction* of the destruction of the Jews who took up the sword unjustly against Christ and his disciples. But this, though countenanced by Rev. xiii. 10, is a somewhat harsh interpretation; and it seems better to adopt that of Elsn., Campb., Kuin., and Fritz., who consider it as a proverbial saying against repelling force by force, and the exercise of private vengeance; importing that those who shall defend themselves by the sword, will, or may, perish by the sword. Of course, it must be taken with restriction, as it regarded the *disciples*, and be here applied to those who take up the sword against the magistrate. Perhaps, however, a double sense may have been intended, 1st for *caution* (including *admonition*, that swords were not the weapons by which the Messiah's cause was to be defended); and 2dly, by way of *prediction*, which would suggest the best argument for non-resistance. [*Comp*. Gen. ix. 6. Rev. xiii. 10.]

53. ἢ δοκεῖς, &c.] The connection seems to be this: "Or, [if that argument will not avail, take *this*, that I *need* not thy assistance, for] thinkest thou," &c. The argument in this and the following verse is, that such conduct implied both distrust in Divine Providence, and ignorance of Scripture. The term ἄρτι is very significant, and denotes *even in this crisis*. Καὶ παραστήσει, "and he would bring to my aid." As to the *number* which follows, it is better, (with some of the best Commentators,) not to dwell upon it, much less deduce any inferences from it, since it only denotes *a very great number*.

54. ὅτι.] Supply αἱ λέγουσαι. Or, as this ellipse is harsh, with Fritz., take ὅτι in the sense *nam*. Thus there should be a mark of interrogation after γραφαὶ, and a period after γενέσθαι. [*Comp*. Isa. liii. 7, 8, 10.]

MK. LU.
14. 22. Τοῦτο δὲ ὅλον γέγονεν, ἵνα πληρωθῶσιν αἱ γραφαὶ τῶν προφητῶν. 56
50 Τότε οἱ μαθηταὶ πάντες ἀφέντες αὐτὸν ἔφυγον.
53 54 Οἱ δὲ κρατήσαντες τὸν Ἰησοῦν ἀπήγαγον πρὸς Καϊάφαν τὸν ἀρχιε- 57
54 ρέα, ὅπου οἱ γραμματεῖς καὶ οἱ πρεσβύτεροι συνήχθησαν. Ὁ δὲ Πέ- 58
55 τρος ἠκολούθει αὐτῷ ἀπὸ μακρόθεν, ἕως τῆς αὐλῆς τοῦ ἀρχιερέως·
55 καὶ εἰσελθὼν ἔσω ἐκάθητο μετὰ τῶν ὑπηρετῶν, ἰδεῖν τὸ τέλος. Οἱ δὲ 59
56 ἀρχιερεῖς καὶ οἱ πρεσβύτεροι καὶ τὸ συνέδριον ὅλον ἐζήτουν ψευδομαρτυρίαν κατὰ τοῦ Ἰησοῦ, ὅπως θανατώσωσιν αὐτόν· καὶ οὐχ εὗρον· καί, 60
57 πολλῶν ψευδομαρτύρων προσελθόντων, οὐχ εὗρον. Ὕστερον δὲ προσελ-
58 θόντες δύο ψευδομάρτυρες εἶπον· Οὗτος ἔφη· Δύναμαι καταλῦσαι 61
60 τὸν ναὸν τοῦ Θεοῦ, καὶ διὰ τριῶν ἡμερῶν οἰκοδομῆσαι αὐτόν. Καὶ 62
ἀναστὰς ὁ ἀρχιερεὺς εἶπεν αὐτῷ· Οὐδὲν ἀποκρίνῃ; τί οὗτοί σου
61 καταμαρτυροῦσιν; Ὁ δὲ Ἰησοῦς ἐσιώπα. καὶ ἀποκριθεὶς ὁ ἀρχιερεὺς 63
εἶπεν αὐτῷ· Ἐξορκίζω σε κατὰ τοῦ Θεοῦ τοῦ ζῶντος, ἵνα ἡμῖν εἴπῃς,

56. τοῦτο δὲ — προφητῶν.] Some (as Erasm.) ascribe this observation to the *Evangelist;* but others, more properly, (as appears from Mark xiv. 49,) attribute it to our Lord. [*Comp.* John xviii. 12 & 24.]

57. ἀπήγαγον πρὸς K.] i. e. "after having been *first* taken to Annas, (as we learn from John xviii. 13,) in order, it should seem, to do him honour, and while the Sanhedrim was collecting. Ἀπάγειν is a term appropriate to leading any one to trial or execution. Kuin. ,observes, that πρὸς is often joined with Accusative cases of pronouns and persons, to indicate the place in which the person is whose name follows.

58. τῆς αὐλῆς] the inner court of the palace.

59. ἐζήτουν ψευδομαρτυρίαν.] We are not, I think, warranted in supposing, (as has been generally done,) that they suborned false witnesses. Had they done this, (for which, indeed, there was then no *time*, in the hurry with which their determination to take Jesus' life was acted on), they would have tutored their witnesses better than to be rejected even by *themselves*. But the meaning seems to be, that, though they *professed* to seek *true* testimony, yet they readily entertained *any* whether true or false, that might criminate Jesus. Nay, they studiously sought and encouraged the latter; whilst, on the other hand, all testimony in his *favour* was (by the Jewish law) rejected; for, though it was permitted to say any thing true or false *against* false prophets, or persons suspected of idolatry, no man was permitted to appear in their *behalf*. Dr. Hales, indeed, adduces an extract from Buxtorf's Talmudic Lexicon, containing a citation from a Rabbinical writer, admitting, as he thinks, the *subornation* of false witnesses against Christ, describing the *mode*, and justifying it on the ground that idolaters and false prophets are to be proved guilty by whatever means. The passage is certainly curious; but Dr. Hales has mistaken, and consequently mis-stated its purport. It only authorizes their being *entrapped* into a discovery of their guilt, as Pausanias was by the Ephori (see Thucyd. i. 134); not the *subornation* of false witnesses against them. In short the passage is merely curious as showing a tradition prevalent among the Jews of *unfair dealing* in the present instance. But to return to the words in question, the best view that can be taken of them is, that the *judgment* of the Evangelist is blended with his *narrative;* a sort of *synchysis* not unfrequent in ancient writers. So it is well remarked by L. Brugensis: "*Falsum* dicit Matthæus; quamvis simularent se quærere verum." This is plain, too, from the passage of St. Mark, where, instead of ψευδομαρτυρίαν, we have simply μαρτυρίαν. Thus, just after, at οὐχ εὗρον, we must supply μαρτυρίαν (taken from ψευδομαρτυρίαν), by which is to be understood μαρτυρίαν ἱκανὴν, or, as Mark expresses it, ἴσην.

60. οὐχ εὗρον.] These words are wanting in some MSS., Versions, and a few Fathers; are rejected by Campb., and cancelled by Griesb., but retained by Fritz. and Scholz, rightly, since internal as well as external evidence is in their favour.. As to the authority of the Versions, it is slender in a point of *this* kind. And we have here not a *mere* repetition, (as the ancient Critics, who cut the words out, supposed,) but a repetition for *emphasis*. The Evangelist here, and at the next verse, calls them false witnesses, as Calvin justly remarks, "non qui mendacium de nihilo conflatum proferunt, sed qui calumniosè pervertunt rectè dicta, et ad crimen detorquent."

61. δύναμαι — αὐτόν.] This was, (as appears, from Mark xiv. 58, and John ii. 19), in effect a falsity, by the suppression of *some* words of Christ, with the action which explained them, and adding others. By *this temple* our Lord plainly meant his body. If it *could* have been proved that Jesus had spoken irreverently of the temple, by predicting its destruction, that would have afforded ground for a charge of blasphemy, which was a capital offence. The High-Priest, however, finding that even this testimony could scarcely afford matter for the charge, artfully changed his ground.

63. ἐξορκίζω σε, &c.] This seems to have been the most solemn form of administering an oath. Ὁρκίζειν and ἐξορκ. are used in the LXX. to express the Heb. הִשְׁבִּיעַ, "to make to swear, to swear" *in*, as we say of a witness. The syntax takes an Accus. of the person sworn, (whether witness or criminal,) and a Genit. with κατὰ, or sometimes an Accus., without a preposition, of the Deity sworn by. As this *oath of adjuration* brought an obligation, under *the curse of the Law*,

MK. LU.

64 εἰ σὺ εἶ ὁ Χριστὸς, ὁ Υἱὸς τοῦ Θεοῦ. λέγει αὐτῷ ὁ Ἰησοῦς· Σὺ 14. 22.
εἶπας. Πλὴν λέγω ὑμῖν· ἀπ᾽ ἄρτι ὄψεσθε τὸν Υἱὸν τοῦ ἀνθρώπου 62
καθήμενον ἐκ δεξιῶν τῆς δυνάμεως, καὶ ἐρχόμενον ἐπὶ τῶν νεφελῶν τοῦ
65 οὐρανοῦ. Τότε ὁ ἀρχιερεὺς διέῤῥηξε τὰ ἱμάτια αὐτοῦ, λέγων, ὅτι 63
ἐβλασφήμησε· τί ἔτι χρείαν ἔχομεν μαρτύρων; ἴδε, νῦν ἠκούσατε τὴν
66 βλασφημίαν αὐτοῦ. τί ὑμῖν δοκεῖ; Οἱ δὲ ἀποκριθέντες εἶπον· 64
67 Ἔνοχος θανάτου ἐστί. Τότε ἐνέπτυσαν εἰς τὸ πρόσωπον αὐτοῦ, καὶ 65
68 ἐκολάφισαν αὐτόν· οἱ δὲ ἐῤῥάπισαν, λέγοντες· Προφήτευσον ἡμῖν,
Χριστὲ, τίς ἐστιν ὁ παίσας σε;
69 Ὁ δὲ Πέτρος ἔξω ἐκάθητο ἐν τῇ αὐλῇ, καὶ προσῆλθεν αὐτῷ μία 66 56
70 παιδίσκη, λέγουσα· Καὶ σὺ ἦσθα μετὰ Ἰησοῦ τοῦ Γαλιλαίου. Ὁ δὲ 68 57
71 ἠρνήσατο ἔμπροσθεν πάντων, λέγων· Οὐκ οἶδα τί λέγεις. Ἐξελθόντα 69 58

it imperatively claimed a reply, when the adjuration accompanied an interrogation; and the answer thus returned was regarded as an answer on oath; in which falsity was accounted perjury. Thus our Lord, who had before disdained to reply to an unfounded, and even absurd charge, (especially before judges who had predetermined to find him guilty) now thought himself bound to answer, as an example to others of reverence towards such a solemn form.

— ὁ Χριστὸς, ὁ Υἱὸς τοῦ Θεοῦ.] Grot. and Whitby remark, that from this and other passages, (as Matt. xvi. 16,) it is clear that the Jews expected their Messiah to be *Son of God;* (interpreting the 2d Psalm as said of him) which title, it is certain, they understood as implying divinity, otherwise the High-Priest could not have declared the assumption of it to be blasphemy. See more in Bp. Blomfield's Dissertation on the knowledge of a Redeemer before the advent of our Lord, p. 115. See Note supra 25.

64. σὺ εἶπας.] Ἀπ᾽ ἄρτι is for ἀπὸ τοῦ νῦν, (used by Luke), which, by a slight accommodation, may mean μετὰ μικρὸν, as Euthym. here explains. The words following have reference to the sublime imagery descriptive of the Messiah's advent in Dan. vii. 13 & 14. See Matt. xxiv. 30, and Note.

— τῆς δυνάμεως] for τοῦ Θεοῦ; literally, the Power, abstract for concrete, as we say "the Almighty;" (see Heb. i. 3; viii. 1. 1 Pet. iv. 14,) an idiom founded on the Jewish mode of expressing the Deity, הַגְּבוּרָה, Hagburch, equivalent to ὁ δυνατὸς, i. e. κατ᾽ ἐξοχήν. Thus, in Luke xxii. 69, and sometimes in Philo Jud. τοῦ Θεοῦ is added, as it were, to *determine* the sense. Hence the expression is not ill rendered in the Peshito. Syr. by ܕܚܝܠܐ; though it is wrongly translated by Schaaf *virtutis*. Rather, *numinis* or *Dei*, as in 2 Thess. ii. 4. The *advent* here meant signifies, *primarily* at least, the coming of Christ to take vengeance on the Jews at the destruction of Jerusalem; and secondarily, but chiefly, his coming to judge the world.

65. διέῤῥηξε τὰ ἱμάτια.] It was a custom among the ancients to express the more violent passions, especially *grief* and *indignation*, by rending the garments, either partly, or from top to bottom, but sometimes from bottom to top.

— ἴδε.] Said by the Commentators to be put for ἴδετε But it is better to consider it as an adverb like ἰδού. So John xix. 14. ἴδε, ὁ βασιλεύς.

66. ἔνοχος θανάτου.] Ἔνοχος (derived from the preterite middle of ἐνέχω) is equivalent to ἐνεχόμενος, and signifies, 1. "held fast" by, bound to; 2. being subject, or liable to. In this last sense it is used properly with the Dative (as in the LXX., N. T., and the Classical writers. See Matth. Gr. Gr. § 347); but sometimes with the *Genit.*, as in the present passage and Mark iii. 29, and occasionally in the Classical writers; in which syntax there is commonly thought to be an ellipse of κρίματι. But it should rather seem that the construction (which occurs also in the Classical writers) is like to that of Plato. Apolog. p. 83. τιμᾶταί μοι ὁ ἀνὴρ θανάτου.

67. ἐνέπτυσαν — αὐτοῦ.] A mode of expressing the deepest contempt and abhorrence, common both to ancient and modern times. On this and the other marks of contumely accumulated on the head of our Redeemer, see Horne's Introd. iii. 161, sqq.

— ἐκολάφισαν.] Between κολαφίζω and ῥαπίζω there is the same difference in signification, as in our *thump* and *slap*. [*Comp.* infra xxvii. 20 Isa. 1. 6.]

68. προφήτευσον ἡμῖν, &c.] To understand this, it is proper to bear in mind, (what we learn from Mark and Luke,) that Christ was blindfolded when these words were pronounced; in which there was a taunt on his arrogating the title of Messiah, and a play on the double sense of προφητεύειν, which (as also μαντεύεσθαι) is often used in a sense corresponding to our *divine*, or guess.

69. ἔξω] i. e. without the place where Jesus was examined by the council, which was the *vestibule*, called by Matthew πυλὼν, by Mark προαύλιον.

— παιδίσκη.) The word properly signifies a *girl;* but, as in our own language, it is often in later Greek, used to denote a *maid servant*. She is by John xviii. 17. styled ἡ θυρωρός. And, indeed, the office of porter, though among the Greeks and Romans it was confined to *men*, was among the Jews generally exercised by women. Καὶ σὺ, &c. may be rendered, "Thou too wert one of the party with Jesus;" for εἶναι μετά τινος often denotes to be on any one's side.

70. οὐκ οἶδα τί λέγεις.] A form expressive of strong denial. So Soph. Aj. 270. οὐ κάτοιδ᾽ ὅπως λέγεις. For reconciliations of the minute *seeming*

MK. LU.
14. 22. δὲ αὐτὸν εἰς τὸν πυλῶνα εἶδεν αὐτὸν ἄλλη, καὶ λέγει τοῖς ἐκεῖ· Καὶ
70 οὗτος ἦν μετὰ Ἰησοῦ τοῦ Ναζωραίου· καὶ πάλιν ἠρνήσατο μεθ' 72
69 ὅρκου, ὅτι οὐκ οἶδα τὸν ἄνθρωπον. Μετὰ μικρὸν δὲ προσελθόντες οἱ 73
ἑστῶτες εἶπον τῷ Πέτρῳ· Ἀληθῶς καὶ σὺ ἐξ αὐτῶν εἶ· καὶ γὰρ ἡ
71 60 λαλιά σου δῆλόν σε ποιεῖ. Τότε ἤρξατο ‡ καταναθεματίζειν καὶ ὀμνύ- 74
72 61 ειν, ὅτι οὐκ οἶδα τὸν ἄνθρωπον. καὶ εὐθέως ἀλέκτωρ ἐφώνησε. Καὶ 75
ἐμνήσθη ὁ Πέτρος τοῦ ῥήματος τοῦ Ἰησοῦ εἰρηκότος αὐτῷ, ὅτι πρὶν
ἀλέκτορα φωνῆσαι, τρὶς ἀπαρνήσῃ με· καὶ ἐξελθὼν ἔξω ἔκλαυσε
πικρῶς.

a Mark 15. 1. Luke 22. 66. & 23. 1. John 18. 28.

XXVII. [a] ΠΡΩΙΑΣ δὲ γενομένης, συμβούλιον ἔλαβον πάντες οἱ 1
ἀρχιερεῖς καὶ οἱ πρεσβύτεροι τοῦ λαοῦ κατὰ τοῦ Ἰησοῦ ὥστε θανατῶσαι αὐτόν· καὶ δήσαντες αὐτὸν ἀπήγαγον, καὶ παρέδωκαν αὐτὸν 2
Ποντίῳ Πιλάτῳ τῷ ἡγεμόνι.

Τότε ἰδὼν Ἰούδας ὁ παραδιδοὺς αὐτὸν, ὅτι κατεκρίθη, μεταμεληθεὶς 3
ἀπέστρεψε τὰ τριάκοντα ἀργύρια τοῖς ἀρχιερεῦσι καὶ τοῖς πρεσβυτέροις,
λέγων· Ἥμαρτον παραδοὺς αἷμα ἀθῶον. Οἱ δὲ εἶπον· Τί πρὸς 4

discrepancies in various parts of the narrative, see Recens. Synop., Grot., Mackn., and Kuin.

72. ὅτι οὐκ οἶδα.] Ὅτι, like the Hebrew particles כי and אכן, after verbs of *swearing* and *affirming*, denotes *profecto*, ἦ μὴν, ὄντως. Thus I Kings i. 30, where the Sept. has ὅτι, and Gen. xxii. 17; xlii. 16, where in the Sept. for כי is ἦ μήν. But in Gen. xxviii. 16, the Sept. expresses אכן by ὅτι; and Sym. by ὄντως. In Gen. xliv. 28, the Hebrew אך is rendered by the Sept. ὅτι. (Kuin.) It should rather seem that there is an ellipsis of λέγων, which is *implied* in ἠρνήσατο.

73. ἡ λαλιά σου δῆλόν σε ποιεῖ.] "thy talk, or dialect, bewrayeth thee." Καταφωρᾷ would have been a more definite term, as in Thucyd. viii. 87. καταφωρᾷ δὲ μάλιστα καὶ ἣν εἶπε πρόφασιν. Different provinces of the same country have usually their distinct idioms, accent, &c., which in the remoter parts are more strongly marked. That this was the case with Galilee, we learn from the Rabbinical writers, who tell us that the speech of the Galilæans was broad and rustic.

74. καταναθεματίζειν.] Nearly all the best, and by far the greater part of the MSS., have καταθεματίζειν, which was preferred by Mill. Beng., and Wets., and has been adopted by Matth., Griesb., Tittm., and Scholz. But it is not easy to see how καταθεματίζειν can be reconciled to analogy, or yield any sense suitable to the context; for it can only mean *deponere*, or possibly be synonymous with καταναθεματίζειν. It is, besides, destitute of any *authority* beyond the present passage, except that of the Ecclesiastical writers, who plainly took it from their MSS. of the N. T. And as ἀνὰ might easily slip out, or be lost, by an inattention to a mark of abbreviation, the authority of MSS. has far less weight than the *usus linguæ*. I have, therefore, thought proper, with Vater and Fritz., to retain the common reading.

XXVII. 1. πρωΐας δὲ γεν.] The meeting of the Sanhedrim could not be held till the *morning*, since the courts of the Temple were never opened by night: nor, if they had been then held, could judgment have been pronounced; for among the Jews justice was required to be administered in the *day time*, and in public.

2. δήσαντες.] This word is, on account of John xviii. 12. (whence it appears that Christ had been bound *before)* by most Commentators supposed to be put for δεδεμένον. That, however, is too violent a way of removing the discrepancy. It is better, with Elsn. and Fritz., to suppose that our Lord's bonds had been removed during examination, and were now again put on him.

—ἡγεμόνι.] So he is sometimes styled by Josephus also; though, properly speaking. Pilate was only an ἐπίτροπος, or procurator, as Joseph. and Philo often call him. He is styled ἡγεμὼν, because he (as was not unusual in the *lesser* provinces) had entrusted to him the *authority* of ἡγεμὼν, as if *President*, (which included the administration of justice, and the power of life and death); in subordination, however, to the President of Syria.

3. μεταμεληθείς.] On this is chiefly founded the opinion of some of the antient Fathers, as well as many eminent modern Commentators, (as Whitby, Rosenm., Kuin., and A. Clarke), that Judas was partly induced to betray his Master by the expectation that. as Messiah, he could not suffer death; but would no doubt deliver himself from their hands, in some such way as he had done aforetime. But the language of our Lord (see supra xxvi. 24. and John xvii. 12.), and of Peter, Acts i. 25., forbids us to suppose that his repentance was sincere, or aught but the remorse of an upbraiding conscience. Indeed, we have every reason to suppose that, as he was originally actuated solely by *avarice*, so was he now possessed wholly with *despair*. He could not bear the stings of remorse sharpened as they would be by the contempt and abhorrence of all good men, whether Christ's disciples, or not; for it is acutely remarked by Elsn., "apud improbos conscientia vigilare non solet, nisi quum *res sit conclamata.*"

—ἀπέστρεψε] returned. An Hellenistic use of the word.

4. αἷμα ἀθῶον] "an innocent person." A signification found in the LXX. and Philo, p. 839. οὔτ' αἵματος ἀθῴου προσήψατο. The word ἀθῶος

5 ἡμᾶς; σὺ ὄψει. Καὶ ῥίψας τὰ ἀργύρια ἐν τῷ ναῷ, ἀνεχώρησε· καὶ
6 ἀπελθὼν ἀπήγξατο. [b] Οἱ δὲ ἀρχιερεῖς λαβόντες τὰ ἀργύρια εἶπον· [b Acts 1. 18.]
Οὐκ ἔξεστι βαλεῖν αὐτὰ εἰς τὸν κορβανᾶν, ἐπεὶ τιμὴ αἵματός ἐστι.
7 Συμβούλιον δὲ λαβόντες ἠγόρασαν ἐξ αὐτῶν τὸν ἀγρὸν τοῦ κεραμέως,
8 εἰς ταφὴν τοῖς ξένοις. [c] Διὸ ἐκλήθη ὁ ἀγρὸς ἐκεῖνος Ἀγρὸς αἵματος [c Acts 1. 19.]
9 ἕως τῆς σήμερον. [d] Τότε ἐπληρώθη τὸ ῥηθὲν διὰ Ἱερεμίου τοῦ προφή- [d Zach. 11. 12.]

properly, and always in the Classical writers, signifies *impunis*, the not being liable to punishment. Αἷμα ἀθ. is in Hellenistic Greek often (as here) taken to denote an innocent person; αἷμα thus exactly corresponding to the expression σὰρξ καὶ αἷμα. So it occurs in the Sept. and Philo Jud. There is in ἀθῶον also a deviation from Classical usage, by which (as Matthæi observes) the word has alone the sense *cui non nocetur, qui non læditur.* Yet the Hellenistic usage is not only defensible, but more agreeable to the primary signification of the word, which has, with reason, been supposed to be *impunis*, and the not being liable to θωὴ, or punishment. Τί πρὸς ἡμᾶς; Sub. τοῦτ' ἐστι.

—σὺ ὄψει.] 'thou wilt, or ought to see to that; be that thy care.' A Latinism from *tu videris*, for which the Greek Classical writers used σοὶ μελέτω, or employed the *Imperative*.

5. ἀπελθὼν ἀπήγξατο.] The plain import of the words would seem to be, "he went and hanged himself;" for many examples of the phrase have been adduced both from the LXX. and the Classical writers. And this sense is supported by the ancient Versions. Since, however, it has been thought inconsistent with the account given by Peter (Acts i. 18.) of the death of Judas, many methods of interpretation have been devised, to reconcile this discrepancy. See Recens. Synop. I am still of opinion that there is nothing to authorize us to desert the common signification of ἀπάγχεσθαι (wherein the *reflected* sense is to be noticed, on which see Thucyd. iii. 81. and my Note there), nor any reason to suppose but that Judas *hanged* himself. It is very probable that he selected that mode of suicide, since it was frequent; and of the expression itself, ἀπελθὼν ἀπήγξατο, &c. several examples have been adduced. And, as we shall see further on, it involves no real discrepancy with St. Luke's account. Whereas the other interpretations are (as I have shown in Recens. Synop.) open to many objections. Thus even that which assigns the sense "was suffocated," (literally, suffocated himself,) introduces a signification which cannot with certainty be established; for though in Herod. ii. 131. ἡ παῖς ἀπήγξατο ὑπὸ ἄχεος *may*, with Perizon., be rendered "was suffocated with grief" (an effect of mental agony which is known to sometimes occur), yet it seems far better to render the expression, with the Editors in general, "hanged herself;" a sense occurring also at vii. 232. of the same writer: λέγεται — ἄλλον ἄγγελον — ὡς ἠτίμωτο, ἀπάγξασθαι. Besides, the context, and the use of the expression ἀπελθὼν, point to an *action*, not to any thing of so *passive* a nature as *dying of grief*. The best mode of reconciling the apparent discrepancy is, to suppose (with Casaub., Raphel., Krebs., Kuinoel, Schleusn., and Fritz.) that after he had suspended himself, the rope breaking, or giving way (from the noose slipping, or otherwise), he fell down headlong, and burst asunder, so that his bowels protruded. Thus in a Rabbinical writer cited by Wets. on Acts i. 18. quidam de tecto in plateam decidit, et *ruptus est venter*, et *viscera ejus effluxerunt.* Πρηνὴς in the passage of Acts may be taken, like our *headlong*, simply of falling down from a high place, as in the examples adduced in Recens. Synop. And this view is confirmed by the expression, which *implies* falling from on high. Thus, according to the above Commentators, the narration in the Gospel is completely reconciled with that in the Acts, by supposing that in the former is recorded the *kind of death by which* Judas *sought* destruction; and in the latter, that by which *he made his final exit;* and which, at least, was the *event* or result of the other.

6. κορβανᾶν,] The word is Syriac, and signifies 1st, *something offered, an offering;* and, by use, *an offering to the sacred treasury:* 2dly, the place, or *treasury* itself, which consisted of chests placed in the Court of the Women.

7. τὸν ἀγρὸν τοῦ κεραμέως,] The Article τοῦ expresses a *particular* field known by that name; so called from having been occupied by a potter: no doubt to dig clay for his wares. Thus several villages in England have the prefix, *Potter:* probably from part of the ground having been formerly occupied for potteries; for example, Pottersbury, in Northamptonshire. So the field at Athens, appropriated as a cemetery for those who fell in the service of the country, was called Ceramicus, from having been formerly used for brick-making. This, of course, would make a field unfit for *tillage;* though good enough for a burying ground. And thus the smallness of the price may be accounted for.

— τοῖς ξένοις.] It is debated by the Commentators whether by these we are to understand *foreign Jews*, sojourning at Jerusalem for religious or other purposes, or *Gentile foreigners.* The latter, for the reasons which I have assigned in Recens. Synop., is by far the most probable.

9. τὸ ῥηθὲν διὰ Ἱερ.] The following passage is not found in *Jeremiah;* but something very like it, and, as it seems, the very prophecy, occurs in *Zach.* xi. 13; which has induced some to suppose a corruption of the names, arising from MS. abbreviations. Other *less* probable opinions may be seen in Recens. Synop. The best solution of the difficulty is to suppose, either that Matthew simply wrote διὰ τοῦ προφήτου, omitting, as he often does, the *name* of the prophet (and indeed Ἱερ. *is* omitted in a few MS. and several of the antient Versions); or, since Mede and Bp. Kidder have shown it to be highly probable that *Jeremiah* wrote the Chapter from which these words are taken, as well as the two former, to suppose that the Evangelist wrote from that opinion. The mode adopted by Griesb., Paulus, and Fritz., which supposes an *error of memory* on the part of the Evangelist, for Ζαχαρίου, would remove all difficulty. But it proceeds upon an objectionable principle. To return, however, to the words before us, every grammatical machine has been

MK. LU.
15. 23. του λέγοντος· Καὶ ἔλαβον τὰ τριάκοντα ἀργύρια, τὴν
τιμὴν τοῦ τετιμημένου, ὃν ἐτιμήσαντο ἀπὸ υἱῶν
Ἰσραήλ· καὶ ἔδωκαν αὐτὰ εἰς τὸν ἀγρὸν τοῦ κε- 10
ραμέως· καθὰ συνέταξέ μοι Κύριος.
2 3 Ὁ δὲ Ἰησοῦς ἔστη ἔμπροσθεν τοῦ ἡγεμόνος: καὶ ἐπερώτησεν αὐτὸν 11
ὁ ἡγεμὼν, λέγων· Σὺ εἶ ὁ βασιλεὺς τῶν Ἰουδαίων; Ὁ δὲ Ἰησοῦς
3 2 ἔφη αὐτῷ· Σὺ λέγεις. Καὶ ἐν τῷ κατηγορεῖσθαι αὐτὸν ὑπὸ τῶν ἀρ- 12
4 χιερέων καὶ τῶν πρεσβυτέρων οὐδὲν ἀπεκρίνατο. Τότε λέγει αὐτῷ ὁ 13
5 Πιλάτος· Οὐκ ἀκούεις πόσα σου καταμαρτυροῦσι; Καὶ οὐκ ἀπε- 14
κρίθη αὐτῷ πρὸς οὐδὲ ἓν ῥῆμα· ὥστε θαυμάζειν τὸν ἡγεμόνα λίαν.
6 Κατὰ δὲ ἑορτὴν εἰώθει ὁ ἡγεμὼν ἀπολύειν ἕνα τῷ ὄχλῳ δέσμιον, 15
7 ὃν ἤθελον. εἶχον δὲ τότε δέσμιον ἐπίσημον, λεγόμενον Βαραββᾶν. 16
8 Συνηγμένων οὖν αὐτῶν, εἶπεν αὐτοῖς, ὁ Πιλάτος· Τίνα θέλετε ἀπολύ- 17
9 σω ὑμῖν; Βαραββᾶν, ἢ Ἰησοῦν τὸν λεγόμενον Χριστόν; Ἤιδει γὰρ, 18
10 ὅτι διὰ φθόνον παρέδωκαν αὐτόν. Καθημένου δὲ αὐτοῦ ἐπὶ τοῦ 19
βήματος, ἀπέστειλε πρὸς αὐτὸν ἡ γυνὴ αὐτοῦ, λέγουσα· Μηδέν σοὶ

put in motion to reconcile them with those of the Hebrew and Sept., but all in vain. Much trouble, however, might have been spared, had it been considered, that we have not a *citation*, but an *application* of the words of the prophecy or vision; which was, no doubt, intended to presignify the train of events recorded by the Evangelists. So little *other* application has it, that the Jews themselves have always referred the words to the Messiah.

As to the *mode* in which the words in question are to be taken, there is no reason to abandon the common interpretation, confirmed by Euthym., according to which τινὲς must be supplied at ἀπὸ υἱῶν 'I. It indeed involves a somewhat harsh ellipse, but not *so* harsh as the method Fritz. has adopted in its place, namely, to take the words of *Judas*. Besides, that makes ὃν ἐτιμήσαντο a most offensive pleonasm. Whereas, according to the common interpretation, the words ὃν ἐτιμήσαντο — 'Ισρ. are exegetical of the preceding. It is well observed by Vater, "latet τινὲς in v. ἀπὸ, ut alibi in v. ἐκ. Conf. Matth. xxiii. 24." There may seem some difficulty in καθὰ — κύριος; the best way of removing which is to suppose, that these words (corresponding to ויאמר יהוה אלי of the Hebrew) are left by the Evangelist *unaccommodated*. Campb. and others would take ἔλαβον as the *first* person, and read ἔδωκα. Thus we *might* render, "I took the thirty shekels (the price of him that was valued, whom they valued), from the sons of Israel (and they gave them for the potter's field), as the Lord appointed me." But this is destitute of manuscript authority, and does such violence to the words, that no dependence can be placed on the sense thus *extorted*. With respect to τοῦ τετιμημένου, the best Commentators regard it as taken, *per metalepsin*, in the sense *purchased*, referring to Thucyd. i. 33. πρὸ πολλῶν χρημάτων — ἐτιμήσασθε. But perhaps τιμᾶσθαι may here be used in the sense *to have a price set on one's head*. Now when it is said that the Priests agreed with Judas for 30 pieces of silver, it is *implied* that they *offered* him that sum; which, indeed, might be expected from his inquiry, What will ye give me?

— καθὰ] an adverb formed from κατ' [ἐκεῖνα] ἃ.

11. σὺ εἶ ὁ βασ. τῶν 'I.] i. e. "dost thou claim to be king of the Jews?" To this the σὺ λέγεις following is a form of solemn asseveration. See Note on xxvi. 64. Pricæus compares the *dixti* of Plautus. Hence may be seen the true force of our affirmatives *aye* and *yes*, which are both derived from the old French *ayez*. The sense therefore is, "You say right, (I am a king)." From John xviii. 36. it appears that this declaration was made after our Lord had said that his kingdom was not of this world, i. e. not temporal. On the *order of the events* recorded in this and the following verses, see Euthym. and Kuinoel (cited and translated in Rec. Syn.) who have skilfully adjusted the harmony, and illustrated the connection and mutual bearing of the circumstances. [*Comp.* John xviii. 33. 37. 1 Tim. vi. 13.]

14. οὐδὲ ἕν.] A stronger expression than οὐδέν.

15. κατὰ δὲ ἑορτὴν, &c.] The Commentators are not agreed whether by καθ' ἑορτὴν we are to understand "at feast time," or, "at the *paschal* feast." The latter opinion is thought to be proved by John xviii. 39. And though that passage be not decisive, yet, according to propriety of language, this would seem to be the best founded opinion. See Middlet. There will be little difficulty in supposing, that as ἑορτὴ would of itself, without addition, most readily suggest the idea of the *paschal* feast, so καθ' ἑορτὴν would mean at the *paschal* feast. Indeed, I find καθ' ἑορτὴν used precisely in this way in Joseph. B. 7. i. 11. 5. and ἐνστάσης ἑορτῆς Antiq. xiv. 11. 5. Whether the custom here mentioned was *old*, or *new*, has been debated; but has, with some certainty, been proved to be the *latter*. It was probably derived either from their neighbours the Syrians, or from the Greeks and Romans; the former of whom had such a custom at their Thesmophoriæ, the latter at their Lectisternia.

16. ἐπίσημον.] 'Επίσημος signifies, 1. *signatus*, bearing a stamp; 2. *notabilis*, in a good sense; 3. *notabilis*, in a bad sense, as in the Latin *famosus*.

19. τοῦ βήματος.] See Recens. Synop. or Horne's Introd. vol. iii. p. 131. Μηδὲν σοὶ — ἐκείνῳ. Sub.

MK. LU.
καὶ τῷ δικαίῳ ἐκείνῳ· πολλὰ γὰρ ἔπαθον σήμερον κατ' ὄναρ δι' 15. 23.
20 αὐτόν. Οἱ δὲ ἀρχιερεῖς καὶ οἱ πρεσβύτεροι ἔπεισαν τοὺς ὄχλους, ἵνα 11
21 αἰτήσωνται τὸν Βαραββᾶν, τὸν δὲ Ἰησοῦν ἀπολέσωσιν. Ἀποκριθεὶς δὲ 12 20
ὁ ἡγεμὼν εἶπεν αὐτοῖς· Τίνα θέλετε ἀπὸ τῶν δύο ἀπολύσω ὑμῖν;
22 οἱ δὲ εἶπον· Βαραββᾶν. Λέγει αὐτοῖς ὁ Πιλάτος· Τί οὖν ποιήσω
Ἰησοῦν τὸν λεγόμενον Χριστόν; λέγουσιν αὐτῷ πάντες· Σταυρωθή-
23 τω. Ὁ δὲ ἡγεμὼν ἔφη· Τί γὰρ κακὸν ἐποίησεν; οἱ δὲ περισσῶς
24 ἔκραζον, λέγοντες· Σταυρωθήτω. Ἰδὼν δὲ ὁ Πιλάτος ὅτι οὐδὲν ὠφε- 14 21
λεῖ, ἀλλὰ μᾶλλον θόρυβος γίνεται, λαβὼν ὕδωρ ἀπενίψατο τὰς χεῖρας
ἀπέναντι τοῦ ὄχλου, λέγων· Ἀθῶός εἰμι ἀπὸ τοῦ αἵματος τοῦ δικαίου
25 τούτου· ὑμεῖς ὄψεσθε. Καὶ ἀποκριθεὶς πᾶς ὁ λαὸς εἶπε· Τὸ αἷμα
26 αὐτοῦ ἐφ' ἡμᾶς καὶ ἐπὶ τὰ τέκνα ἡμῶν! Τότε ἀπέλυσεν αὐτοῖς τὸν 15 25
Βαραββᾶν· τὸν δὲ Ἰησοῦν φραγελλώσας παρέδωκεν ἵνα σταυρωθῇ.
27 Τότε οἱ στρατιῶται τοῦ ἡγεμόνος, παραλαβόντες τὸν Ἰησοῦν εἰς τὸ 16

γενέσθω. On the nature of the idiom see Note on Matt. viii. 20.

— κατ' ὄναρ.] It has been much debated whether this dream was natural, or supernatural. The latter view is maintained by the Fathers and the earlier Commentators; the former, by most of the recent Interpreters. And, indeed, we may so well account for the thing from natural causes, (especially as History has recorded many similar cases) that we are not required — perhaps scarcely warranted, to call in the supernatural. Πολλὰ, *much;* as often with verbs signifying to *suffer.* So Athen. p. 7. B. πολλὰ κακοπαθήσας. Σήμερον may mean, as Commentators explain, "[early] this morning." And morning dreams were supposed to be most veracious and ominous.

21. [*Comp.* Acts iii. 14.]

23. τί γὰρ κακὸν ἐπ.] The γὰρ is not, as some imagine, redundant; but has reference to a clause omitted, expressing, or implying a refusal of the punishment demanded, q. d. "Not so, or why so, *for,* &c." See Middlet, Grot., and Krebs. That this is not a Hebraism, (as some have thought) is evident from the Classical examples which have been adduced by Krebs.

24. ὅτι οὐδὲν ὠφελεῖ] "se nihil proficere," that he is doing no good, effecting nothing.

— ἀπενίψατο τὰς χεῖρας.] A symbolical action, to express being guiltless of the thing; washing the hands being probably a usual mode, among the Jews, of any one's solemnly attesting his innocence of any particular crime; and, doubtless, founded on the precept of Deut. xxi. 6 & 7, where, in case of murder of which the perpetrator is unknown, the elders of the nearest town are commanded to *wash their hands,* in testimony of their innocence, over the victim which was sacrificed for expiation of the crime. So also Ps. xxvi. 6. "I will wash my hands in [testimony of my] innocency." It has, indeed, been disputed among Commentators, whether Pilate here followed *Jewish* or *Gentile* custom. But, considering the *purpose* of the action, — namely, to testify his innocence to the people, the *former* is the more probable. Besides, there has never been any *proof* adduced that such a custom subsisted among the *Gentiles.* For the Gentile custom to which Commentators appeal, was only that of washing the hands, not to *attest innocence,* but to *expiate crime,* though involuntary; one being for *expiation,* the other for *attestation.* It is not, indeed, impossible that the use of this symbolical action existed among the Gentiles (though it is strange that no *allusion* to it should have been found); but if so, it was probably rather (according to the import of the phrase with us) to express that "one will have no participation in any thing, nor be answerable for the blame incurred thereby. It is plain, however, from Pilate's *words,* and the answer made to them by the people, that *more* than *this* was meant; namely, to solemnly attest his innocence, and to cast on *them* the guilt of the crime. And as Pilate had lived long enough in Judæa to become thoroughly acquainted with Jewish customs, and would be more likely to adopt a *Jewish form,* for the satisfaction of the Jewish *people,* no doubt can well be entertained but that the action was done according to *Jewish,* not Gentile custom.

— ἀπὸ τοῦ αἱμ.] The ἀπὸ is added by Hebraism; on which see Fritz.

— δικαίου is here (as supra ver. 19.) taken by Casaub., Le Clerc, Campb., and others, in a *forensic* sense, i. e. innocent of the crime laid to his charge. But perhaps the forensic and ordinary senses are combined; q. d. this innocent man and just person. To the *latter* Pilate bore testimony in a despatch sent to the Emperor Tiberius. Ὑμεῖς ὄψεσθε, "you must look to that;" q. d. "you must take the blame."

25. τὸ αἷμα — ἡμᾶς] scil. ἐλθέτω, as it is finely rendered by Juvencus, "Nos, nos, cruor iste sequatur, Et genus in nostrum scelus hoc, et culpa redundet!" Elsn. and Wets. have proved that it was usual among the Greeks for witnesses, on whose testimony any were put to death, to devote themselves, and even their children, to curses, if they bore false testimony. The antiquity of the custom is plain from 2 Kings ii. 37. Similar forms of imprecation are adduced both from the Rabbinical and the Classical writers.

26. φραγελλώσας.] A word derived from the Latin *flagellare.* The *flagella* were so sharp, that they are termed by Horace *Horribilia.* Scourging either with flagella (as in the case of slaves), or, (as in that of free persons) with rods, was among the Romans a prelude to capital punishment: and it was in use by the Greeks in the earliest ages.

27. τὸ πραιτώριον] The word here denotes, not

MK. LU.
15. 23. *πραιτώριον, συνήγαγον ἐπ' αὐτὸν ὅλην τὴν σπεῖραν. Καὶ ἐκδύσαντες* 28
17 *αὐτὸν, περιέθηκαν αὐτῷ χλαμύδα κοκκίνην. καὶ πλέξαντες στέφανον* 29
ἐξ ἀκανθῶν, ἐπέθηκαν ἐπὶ τὴν κεφαλὴν αὐτοῦ, καὶ κάλαμον ἐπὶ τὴν
18 *δεξιὰν αὐτοῦ· καὶ γονυπετήσαντες ἔμπροσθεν αὐτοῦ ἐνέπαιζον αὐτῷ,*
19 *λέγοντες· Χαῖρε, ὁ βασιλεὺς τῶν Ἰουδαίων! Καὶ ἐμπτύσαντες εἰς* 30
20 *αὐτὸν, ἔλαβον τὸν κάλαμον, καὶ ἔτυπτον εἰς τὴν κεφαλὴν αὐτοῦ. Καὶ* 31
ὅτε ἐνέπαιξαν αὐτῷ, ἐξέδυσαν αὐτὸν τὴν χλαμύδα, καὶ ἐνέδυσαν αὐτὸν
21 26 *τὰ ἱμάτια αὐτοῦ· καὶ ἀπήγαγον αὐτὸν εἰς τὸ σταυρῶσαι. Ἐξερχόμενοι* 32
δὲ εὗρον ἄνθρωπον Κυρηναῖον ὀνόματι Σίμωνα· τοῦτον ἠγγάρευσαν,
ἵνα ἄρῃ τὸν σταυρὸν αὐτοῦ.

22 33 *ΚΑΙ ἐλθόντες εἰς τόπον λεγόμενον Γολγοθᾶ, * ὅ ἐστι, [* λεγόμενον,]* 33

that part of the *camp* so called, but a magnificent *edifice* in the upper part of Jerusalem, which had formerly been Herod's Palace, and was afterwards the abode of the Roman Procurators when they *sojourned* at Jerusalem; for their *residence* was at Cesarea.

28. *χλαμύδα*] This was a kind of round cloak, confined on the right shoulder by a clasp, so as to cover the left side of the body, and worn over the other garments. It was used alike by officers and privates; but, of course, with a difference in texture and dyeing. What is here called *κοκκίνη* is by Mark denominated *πορφύρα*, and by John *πορφυροῦν*. Yet there is no real discrepancy; for though the colours are, properly speaking, different, yet *πορφυροῦς* denoted sometimes a *bright red;* and hence the words *κοκκίνη* and *πορφύρα* were sometimes interchanged. The robe here mentioned was, no doubt, a cast-off *sagum* of some general officer.

29. *στέφανον ἐξ ἀκανθῶν.*] There has been no little debate as to the *nature* and *materials* of this crown; some contending that as this, like all the rest of what was done by the soldiers, was merely in mockery of Jesus' regal pretensions, there could be no motive to *cruelty:* and they propose to take the word *ἀκανθῶν* as the Genit. plural not of *ἄκανθα* but of *ἄκανθος*, i. e. the *bear's foot*, which is rather a smooth than a thorny plant, and would be more convenient to plait. Those, on the other hand, who defend the common version, reply that both *ἄκανθα* and *ἀκάνθινος* often occur in the N. T. and Sept., and always in the sense *thorn* and *thorny;* and that the ancient versions all confirm that version, as well as some ancient Fathers, as Tertullian and Clem. Alexandrinus. It should seem that the latter interpretation is the best founded. Indeed there is (as I observed in Recens. Synop.) the highest probability opposed to mere conjecture. There is, however, great reason to think (with Theophyl. and Budæus) that the crown was not of mere *thorns*, but of some prickly shrub (probably *acacia*), as in a kindred passage cited by Wets. "in capite corona subito exstitit, ex *asperis herbis*," especially since those fit to make a fillet are such. So also Pliny Hist. xxi. 10. vilissimam coronam, *spineolam*. Finally, Hesych. cited by Wets.: *Ἔφυγον κακὸν, εὗρον ἄμεινον. Νόμος ἦν Ἀθήνησιν ἀμφιθαλῆ παῖδα ἀκάνθης, μετὰ δρυΐνων στεφάνων, στέφεσθαι.*

— *χαῖρε, ὁ βασιλ.*] A usual salutation to Emperors, as *Cæsar, ave!* In *ὁ βασιλ.*, the Nominative is put for the vocative, as Mark ix. 25. and Luke viii. 54. See Winer's Gr. Gr. § 22. 2.

30. [*Comp.* Isai. 50. 6. sup. 26. 67.]

31. *ἀπήγαγον.*] A usual term for *leading away* a criminal to execution.

32. *ἐξερχόμενοι*] "as they were going out [of the city];" for executions were, both among the Jews and Gentiles, conducted outside of the cities.

— *ἄνθρωπον Κ.*] This use of *ἄνθρωπος* with nouns of *country*, *business*, or *office* (see Matth. Gr. Gr. § 430. 7.), is thought to be pleonastic, but is in reality only a vestige of the wordiness of antique phraseology. *Ἠγγάρευσαν*, "compelled;" literally, *impressed*, which implies compulsion (see Note on Matth. v. 41.); though it was customary for the criminal *himself* to carry his cross, which was of the form of a T, and was denominated *σταυρὸς*, from *σταίω*, cognate with *στάω to fix*, namely in the ground, as our *stake* comes from the past participle of *to stick*. About the middle of it was fixed a piece of wood, on which the crucified person sat, or rather rode; and into which he sometimes, in bravado, leaped. For the heighth of the cross was (contrary to the common opinion) such as to admit of this, being only such as to raise the feet of the crucified person a yard from the ground. The hands were fastened to the cross-piece with nails, but the feet were only tied to the post with ropes. Crucifixion can be traced back to as early a period as the age of Semiramis; and was a punishment chiefly inflicted on slaves, or free persons convicted of the most heinous crimes. That the corpses were left as a prey to ravenous birds, appears from Artemidorus iv. 49.

33. *Γολγοθᾶ.*] From the Chaldee *gol-goltha*, the second λ being omitted, for euphony, as in *Babel* for *Balbel*. The place in question was a sort of *knoll*, and so called from being strewed with the skulls of executed malefactors, like the Ceadas at Sparta, on which see my note on Thucyd. i. 134. [*Comp.* John xix. 17.]

Instead of the common reading ὅς, ὃ is found in many of the best MSS., some ancient Versions, and early Edd., and is edited by Beng., Matth., Griesb., Knapp, Tittm., Fritz., and Scholz: with reason; for ὃ deserves the preference, as being the more difficult reading. The common reading *λεγόμενος*, just after, can only be defended by the precarious principle of *Hypallage*. Hence, some MSS. change its place, several omit it, and Fritz. cancels it. But it is better to *heal* than to amputate: and I doubt not but that *λεγόμενον* is the true reading; which is found in not a few MSS., and is confirmed by the readings *μεθερμηνευόμενον*, and *καλούμενον*, and also by the Syriac, Arabic, Persic, and Æthiopic Versions, which must have read

MK. LU.
34 κρανίου τόπος, ἔδωκαν αὐτῷ πιεῖν ὄξος μετὰ χολῆς μεμιγμένον· καὶ 15. 23.
35 γευσάμενος οὐκ ἤθελε πιεῖν. Σταυρώσαντες δὲ αὐτὸν, διεμερίσαντο τὰ 23 24 34
ἱμάτια αὐτοῦ, βάλλοντες κλῆρον· [ἵνα πληρωθῇ τὸ ῥηθὲν
ὑπὸ τοῦ προφήτου· Διεμερίσαντο τὰ ἱμάτιά μου
ἑαυτοῖς, καὶ ἐπὶ τὸν ἱματισμόν μου ἔβαλον κλῆρον.]
36 καὶ καθήμενοι, ἐτήρουν αὐτὸν ἐκεῖ. Καὶ ἐπέθηκαν ἐπάνω τῆς κεφα- 25
37 λῆς αὐτοῦ τὴν αἰτίαν αὐτοῦ γεγραμμένην, ΟΥΤΟΣ ΕΣΤΙΝ ΙΗΣΟΥΣ 26
38 Ο ΒΑΣΙΛΕΥΣ ΤΩΝ ΙΟΥΔΑΙΩΝ. Τότε σταυροῦνται σὺν αὐτῷ δύο 27
λῃσταὶ, εἷς ἐκ δεξιῶν καὶ εἷς ἐξ εὐωνύμων.
39 Οἱ δὲ παραπορευόμενοι ἐβλασφήμουν αὐτὸν, κινοῦντες τὰς κεφαλὰς 29 35
40 αὐτῶν καὶ λέγοντες· Ὁ καταλύων τὸν ναὸν καὶ ἐν τρισὶν ἡμέραις
οἰκοδομῶν, σῶσον σεαυτόν. εἰ Υἱὸς εἶ τοῦ Θεοῦ, κατάβηθι ἀπὸ τοῦ 30
41 σταυροῦ. Ὁμοίως δὲ καὶ οἱ ἀρχιερεῖς ἐμπαίζοντες, μετὰ τῶν γραμμα- 31
42 τέων καὶ πρεσβυτέρων, ἔλεγον· Ἄλλους ἔσωσεν, ἑαυτὸν οὐ δύναται
σῶσαι. εἰ βασιλεὺς Ἰσραήλ ἐστι, καταβάτω νῦν ἀπὸ τοῦ σταυροῦ, καὶ
43 πιστεύσομεν ἐπ' αὐτῷ. Πέποιθεν ἐπὶ τὸν Θεόν· ῥυσάσθω νῦν αὐ- 32

λεγόμενον, or μεθερμηνευόμενον. Λεγόμενος arose from the vicious reading ὃς preceding. Render "which word *is* (i. e. signifies) when interpreted, *Skull-place.*" This sense of λέγεσθαι is found also in John xx. 16. Ῥαββουνί· ὃ λέγεται διδάσκαλε. Thus in a kindred passage of Matth. i. 23. ὅ ἐστι, μεθερμηνευόμενον, μεθ' ἡμῶν ὁ Θεός. See also Mark v. 41. xv. 22. & 34. John i. 42. Acts iv. 36. In short, the thing is so certain, that I have ventured to *edit* λεγόμενον.

34. ὄξος — μεμιγμ.] Mark xv. 23. mentions a potion administered to Christ, but he calls it ἐσμυρνισμένον οἶνον. Now in order to remove the discrepancy, the best Commentators suppose that it was the *same drink* under different *names;* since ὄξος is used to denote wine (especially the poorer kinds); and χολὴ, though properly signifying *wormwood*, yet sometimes in the Sept. denotes *any bitter infusion*. Others are of opinion, that the potions mentioned by the two Evangelists were *distinct mixtures;* the vinegar mingled with gall being, they think, offered in derision; and the myrrhed wine, the *medicated cup* usually administered to criminals about to suffer a painful death. The *former* interpretation, however, seems to be preferable; and it is confirmed by the ancient *gloss* which has crept into many of the best MS., and all the best of the ancient Versions, οἶνον. [*Comp.* Ps. lxix. 22.]

35. ἵνα πληρωθῇ — κλῆρον.] These words are found in comparatively few MSS., have no place in the ancient Versions, and several Fathers, nor the Edit. Princ. They have been cancelled by every Editor of note from Wets. to Scholz. [*Comp.* Ps. xxii. 19. John xix. 23.]

37. αἰτίαν αὐτοῦ.] Namely, the τίτλον, or ἐπιγραφὴν τῆς αἰτίας, his crimination, the crime laid to his charge: This was engraven on a metal plate, in black characters on a white ground. The trifling discrepancy in the words of this inscription may very well have arisen from the language in which it was written.

38. δύο λῃσταί] i. e. "highway robbers," with which, and banditti of all sorts, Judæa then swarmed; an evil which has been ascribed to various causes — excessive population (arising from frequency of divorce), misplaced lenity towards offenders, the impatience of the Jews under the Roman yoke, and the crafty policy of the governors in encouraging such offenders. [*Comp.* Is. liii. 12.

39. κινοῦντες τὰς κεφαλάς.] A mark of derision common to all the nations of antiquity, and here a fulfilment of prophecy. See Ps. xxii. 7.

40. ὁ καταλύων, &c.] The ὁ refers to Σὺ understood; and καταλύων and οἰκοδομῶν signify *populariter*, "who undertook to destroy." See Glass Phil. [*Comp.* supra xxvi. 61. John ii. 19.]

41. καὶ πρεσβυτέρων.] Many of the best MSS. add καὶ Φαρισαίων, which is adopted by Wets., Matth., Fritz., and Scholz.

42. ἄλλους — σῶσαι.] Beza, Beng., Pearce, and some others, would take the words *interrogatively;* which makes them, they think, more cuttingly sarcastic. But this does violence to the contour of the passage, and destroys the antithesis, which, as Fritz remarks, is strengthened by the Asyndeton. In further confirmation, I have in Recens. Syn. adduced the following apt examples. Aristid. iii. 430. B. (of Palamedes) πάσας τὰς ἄλλας εὑρίσκων μηχανὰς, μίαν οὐχ εὗρεν, ὅπως σωθήσεται. Æschyl. Prom. V. 482—5. κακὸς δ' ἰατρὸς ὥς τις, εἰς νόσον Πεσὼν ἀθυμεῖς, καὶ σεαυτὸν οὐκ ἔχεις Εὑρεῖν ὁποίοις φαρμάκοις ἰάσιμος. [*Comp.* Wisd. ii. 18.]

— βασιλεὺς, &c.] We may remark the *distinctive* taunts of the Jews and the Romans; the former of whom adverted to Jesus's claim to be *King of Israel* (i. e. Messiah); the latter, to his assuming the title of *King of the Jews*, which, however, many of the Romans understood as equivalent to Messiah. The ἐπ' is inserted by almost every Editor from Wets. to Scholz, on the authority of nearly all the best MSS., and several Versions and Fathers.

43. πέποιθεν ἐπὶ τὸν Θ.] The Commentators are at a loss to know what the railers here allude to; perhaps, they think, to his declaration at Matth. xxvi. 53. But that was delivered *aside* to his disciples. There is rather a reference to that *fearlessness* with which Jesus yielded himself to the soldiers sent to apprehend him; and which might

MK. LU.
15. 23. τὸν, εἰ θέλει αὐτόν. εἶπε γάρ· Ὅτι Θεοῦ εἰμι Υἱός. Τὸ δ᾽ αὐτὸ 44
39 καὶ οἱ λῃσταὶ οἱ συσταυρωθέντες αὐτῷ ὠνείδιζον * αὐτόν.
33 44 Ἀπὸ δὲ ἕκτης ὥρας σκότος ἐγένετο ἐπὶ πᾶσαν τὴν γῆν ἕως ὥρας 45
34 ‚ ἐννάτης. Περὶ δὲ τὴν ἐννάτην ὥραν ἀνεβόησεν ὁ Ἰησοῦς φωνῇ μεγάλῃ, 46
λέγων· Ἠλὶ, Ἠλὶ, λαμὰ σαβαχθανί; τοῦτ᾽ ἔστι· Θεέ μου, Θεέ μου,

very well be thought to imply *confidence* in the Divine aid for deliverance. The railers, however, in this taunt unwittingly fulfilled a remarkable prophecy of the Messiah, Ps. xxii. 8.

— *εἰ θέλει αὐτόν.*] Θέλειν here, after the manner of the Heb. חָפֵץ, denotes to *delight in*.

44. *οἱ λῃσταὶ — αὐτόν.*] Or rather *one* of them, as is stated in the more *exact* account of Luke. This trifling discrepancy may, however, be removed; not, indeed, by supposing an *enallage*, nor by introducing the figure *Amplification*, which cannot here apply, but by supposing that the Evangelist speaks *generally*. See Winer Gr. 21. Αὐτὸν (for the common reading αὐτῷ) is found in almost all the best MSS., and is adopted by Wets., Griesb., Matth., Vater, Tittm., Fritz., and Scholz.

45. *σκότος — πᾶσαν τὴν γῆν.*] There are here two points, which have occasioned no small perplexity to the Commentators; 1. the *darkness* here recorded; and 2. the *distance* to which it extended. On the former subject, they are not agreed as to the *nature* of the darkness, and its *cause*. The recent Commentators in general seek to account for it in the ordinary course of nature; while the antient, and most modern ones regard it as preternatural. That it could not be produced by a *total eclipse of the sun* is certain; for that can only happen at a *change* of the moon; whereas it was now *full moon*. Besides, a total eclipse never continues beyond a quarter of an hour. Some ascribe it to a mist arising from sulphureous vapours, such as precede or accompany *earthquakes*. This, the naturalists tell us, may extend to a semi-diameter of ten miles from any spot. Those who adopt this view of the subject appeal to the words of ver. 51. *καὶ ἡ γῆ ἐσείσθη*, &c. But can such a haze as that be *all* that is here meant? Taking the whole of the circumstances into the account, it should seem that both the darkness and the earthquake may be regarded as *preternatural*; something in the manner of a portentous *natural* meteoric phenomenon described by Ebn Batuta, in his travels, who mentions a certain spot as being "enveloped by a dense black cloud so close to the earth, that it might be almost touched with the hand." The darkness, which, it may be observed, is not said to have been *total* (nor, indeed, from the circumstances which are recorded as accompanying it, *could* it be such), was *probably* (for who shall dare to go beyond conjecture) produced (as Elsner supposes) by a preternatural accumulation of the densest clouds, enveloping the whole atmosphere; such as that mentioned at Exod. x. 21—3., brought preternaturally, at the stretching forth of the hand of Moses, over the whole land of Egypt, except that portion occupied by the children of Israel, and which was meant to portend the calamities that should soon overwhelm the Jewish nation."

But to turn to the *second* question: the *extent* of this darkness. Most of the antient interpreters regard it as extending over the *whole earth*; though *some* of them, as Origen, and the most eminent modern ones, confine it to *Judæa*; while those who hold the hypothesis of a thick *haze*, such as precedes earthquakes, necessarily to *the vicinity of Jerusalem*. The *second* is, I apprehend, the true view. For, 1st, there is nothing in the words of the original that compels us to suppose *universality*; and it is more natural to take the expression of *Judæa*, the place of the transactions recorded. So, in a kindred passage of Luke iv. 25., *ἐγένετο λιμὸς ἐπὶ πᾶσαν τὴν γῆν*. The Fathers, indeed, and some modern Commentators (especially Grot.) allege, in proof of its universality, passages of Phlegon, Thallus, and Dionys. the Areopagite. But they are not agreed on the nature of *Phlegon's* testimony: indeed, *nothing* which they ascribe to him has any direct bearing on this event. As to the passage adduced from *Thallus*, cited by Jul. Africanus, who mentions a darkness over all the world, and an earthquake which overturned many houses in Judæa and elsewhere; there is no reason to think that Thallus lived *before* Christ; and as the more *ancient* Fathers quote him for *other* matters, but never for *this*, no weight can be attached to the passage in question. As to the story told of Dionys. the Areopagite, it is entitled to still *less* attention, since Dr. Lardner has proved that all the writings attributed to him are spurious. Besides, there was surely (if we may venture to pronounce on the inscrutable purposes of Almighty Providence) a peculiar propriety in the darkness being *confined to Judæa*; — as indicating the wrath of God on that country for the enormity then perpetrating; and presenting an apt emblem of the spiritual darkness in which that benighted region was involved. Finally, by adopting this view, and not needlessly exaggerating the intensity of the obscuration, we are enabled satisfactorily to account for the silence of the Pagan Historians, and even Josephus, without supposing in the latter a wilful suppression of truth. Indeed, that writer has passed by *other* occurrences which we should as little think he would omit as this.

46. *Ἠλὶ — σαβαχθανί.*] This is, with the exception of *σαβ.* (which is Syro Chaldaic), taken from Ps. xxii. 1. Mark writes Ἐλωΐ and λαμμᾶ, making it all Syro Chaldaic, which was the dialect then prevalent in Judæa, and, no doubt, used by our Lord. It is of more consequence to consider the *purpose* for which the words were pronounced. They must not be allowed to express (what some have ventured to ascribe to them) *impatience*, *faintheartedness*, and *despair*. We are not, however, to preclude this by giving them, as some do, a very different sense to that which would otherwise be ascribed to them. It is better to suppose that, by citing the verse, and applying it to himself, our Lord meant to turn the attention of his disciples to the *whole* Psalm; and to signify to them that he was now *accomplishing* what is there *predicted* of the Messiah. It has indeed been thought by some, that the words are too expressive of extreme mental suffering to admit of such an explanation. They would regard them as "the natural effusions of

MK. LU.
47 ἱνατί με ἐγκατέλιπες; Τινὲς δὲ τῶν ἐκεῖ ἑστώτων ἀκούσαντες, ἔλεγον· 15. 23.
48 Ὅτι Ἠλίαν φωνεῖ οὗτος. καὶ εὐθέως δραμὼν εἷς ἐξ αὐτῶν, καὶ λαβὼν 35 36
49 σπόγγον, πλήσας τε ὄξους καὶ περιθεὶς καλάμῳ, ἐπότιζεν αὐτόν. οἱ
δὲ λοιποὶ ἔλεγον· Ἄφες, ἴδωμεν εἰ ἔρχεται Ἠλίας σώσων αὐτόν.
50 Ὁ δὲ Ἰησοῦς πάλιν κράξας φωνῇ μεγάλῃ, ἀφῆκε τὸ πνεῦμα. 37 46
51 Καὶ ἰδού, τὸ καταπέτασμα τοῦ ναοῦ ἐσχίσθη εἰς δύο ἀπὸ ἄνωθεν 38
52 ἕως κάτω· καὶ ἡ γῆ ἐσείσθη, καὶ αἱ πέτραι ἐσχίσθησαν· καὶ τὰ
μνημεῖα ἀνεῴχθησαν, καὶ πολλὰ σώματα τῶν κεκοιμημένων ἁγίων
53 ἠγέρθη, καὶ ἐξελθόντες ἐκ τῶν μνημείων, μετὰ τὴν ἔγερσιν αὐτοῦ,
εἰσῆλθον εἰς τὴν ἁγίαν πόλιν, καὶ ἐνεφανίσθησαν πολλοῖς.

mental torture, scarce conscious of the complaints it uttered." But this is not a sufficiently reverent view. In short, *no* interpretation must be admitted which implies any expression of querulousness, or distrust in the favour and support of God. Moreover, on a subject so awfully mysterious as this, and that of the agony in the garden, it is better to abstain from all prying speculation, and learn, in the words of the Philosopher, σωφρονεῖν ἐν τῇ σοφίᾳ.

47. Ἠλίαν φωνεῖ.] These were not, as some imagine, Roman soldiers; for *they* could know nothing about Elias. The best Commentators are of opinion that they were Hellenistic Jews, who either mistook Christ's words, or intentionally and maliciously perverted them, in derision of his claim to be the Messiah, and with reference to a common opinion, that Elias would return to life at the coming of the Messiah, and prepare the way for his kingdom.

48. καὶ εὐθέως—ἐπότιζεν αὐτόν.] Namely, in consequence of what Jesus had just before said (as recorded by John xix. 28.) διψῶ.

—καλάμῳ.] Some render *reed;* Campb. *stick.* But I prefer, with Markl. "*a stalk;*" a not unfrequent, and perhaps the primary, sense of the word. Thus Matthew and John will be reconciled; for the ὑσσώπῳ of the latter is equivalent to καλάμῳ ὑσσώπου. The stalk of the hyssop is, in the East, so long, that it might easily reach our Lord on the cross; especially since it was by no means so high as is commonly supposed. Περιθεὶς may be rendered, "winding, or fastening it round." With πλήσας ὄξους, I would compare the Schol. on Aristoph. σπόγγους πεπληρωμένους μέλιτος. [*Comp.* Ps. lxix. 22.]

49. ἄφες, ἴδωμεν.] Sub. ἵνα. This use of ἄφες and ἄφετε is not pleonastic (as some imagine), but hortatory, like our *come!*

50. κράξας φωνῇ μεγάλῃ.] Gruner (a German Physician, author of a learned Tract to prove the death of Christ real, and not, as some sceptics have pronounced, a mere *syncope)* and Kuin. take this to indicate a loud *outcry* from *pain;* as in the case of persons oppressed with an excessive congestion of blood about the heart—the precursor of suffocation. But that does not here apply; for this was not a mere *outcry* but an *exclamation* in *words*, (as is clear from Luke xxiii. 46. and John xix. 30.) namely, τετέλεσται—πάτερ. This sense of κράζειν is frequent in Scripture, especially as used of exclamations in precatory addresses to God. See Rom. viii. 15. Gal. iv. 6. James v. 4.

—ἀφῆκε τὸ πνεῦμα.] Many ancient and some modern Commentators suppose something *preternatural* in Christ's death, as being the effect of his *volition*. But there is nothing in the words of Scripture to countenance such an opinion; though our Saviour's volition must be *supposed* to accompany his offering himself for the sins of the world. The term is no other than such as is frequently used, both in the Sept. and the Classical writers, of *expiration*, either with πνεῦμα or ψυχήν. From the comparative shortness of time during which our Lord survived his crucifixion, some Commentators have supposed an especial interposition of the Deity. But it may very well be accounted for from natural causes, as is shown by Gruner, in the above-mentioned Tract de morte Christi verâ, from which copious extracts may be seen in Recens. Synop.

51. καταπέτασμα τοῦ ναοῦ.] This expresion designates the *interior* of the two veils, which separated the Holy of Holies from the Sanctuary; and which is called by that name in the Sept., Philo, and Josephus. On the form and materials of this veil, see the authors referred to in Recens. Synop. From a most interesting passage of Pausan. v. 12, 12, which I have there adduced, it appears, that exactly *such* a veil (of woollen, richly embroidered, and in colour purple) was used at the Temple of Diana at Ephesus, and that of Jupiter at Olympia. It reached from the roof to the ground, and was drawn up and down by ropes.

At εἰς δύο there is the common ellipse of μέρη. This *rending* of the veil, must, like all the other occurrences of this awful scene, be regarded as preternatural. For, though some recent Interpreters ascribe it to the *earthquake* just after recorded, certain it is, that no *earthquake* could rend a veil of 60 feet long, so exceedingly thick as, from its size and purpose, it must have been. Besides, the earthquake is plainly *distinguished* from the rending of the veil. It was, beyond doubt, supernatural; and on the symbolical intent of it see Recens. Synop.

—καὶ ἡ γῆ ἐσείσθη.] This also must be regarded as preternatural; for though an earthquake be not of itself such, yet when we consider the circumstances which accompanied the one here described, we cannot but regard it as produced by the *direct* agency of the Author of nature, and, therefore, so far preternatural.

Of this earthquake vestiges still remain, in *immense fissures*, which attest the violence of the rending, and show the significancy and propriety of the words καὶ αἱ πέτραι ἐσχίσθησαν. [*Comp.* xxvi. 31; 2 Chron. iii. 14.]

52. καὶ τὰ μνημεῖα ἀνεῴχθησαν.] An effect not unfrequently attributed to earthquakes in the ancient writers. See Recens. Synop. In τῶν κεκοιμημένων there is not, as some imagine, an Hebraism, for the idiom occurs in the Classical writers.

53. καὶ ἐξελθόντες—εἰσῆλθον, &c.] In this nar-

MK. LU.
15. 23. Ὁ δὲ ἑκατόνταρχος καὶ οἱ μετ' αὐτοῦ τηροῦντες τὸν Ἰησοῦν, ἰδόντες 54
39 47 τὸν σεισμὸν καὶ τὰ γενόμενα, ἐφοβήθησαν σφόδρα, λέγοντες· Ἀληθῶς
Θεοῦ Υἱὸς ἦν οὗτος.
40 49 Ἦσαν δὲ ἐκεῖ γυναῖκες πολλαὶ ἀπὸ μακρόθεν θεωροῦσαι, αἵτινες 55
ἠκολούθησαν τῷ Ἰησοῦ ἀπὸ τῆς Γαλιλαίας, διακονοῦσαι αὐτῷ· ἐν αἷς 56
ἦν Μαρία ἡ Μαγδαληνὴ, καὶ Μαρία ἡ τοῦ Ἰακώβου καὶ Ἰωσῆ μήτηρ,
καὶ ἡ μήτηρ τῶν υἱῶν Ζεβεδαίου.
42 Ὀψίας δὲ γενομένης, ἦλθεν ἄνθρωπος πλούσιος ἀπὸ Ἀριμαθαίας 57
43 50 52 τοὔνομα Ἰωσὴφ, ὃς καὶ αὐτὸς ἐμαθήτευσε τῷ Ἰησοῦ. Οὗτος προσελ- 58
θὼν τῷ Πιλάτῳ, ᾐτήσατο τὸ σῶμα τοῦ Ἰησοῦ. τότε ὁ Πιλάτος ἐκέλευ-
46 53 σεν ἀποδοθῆναι τὸ σῶμα. καὶ λαβὼν τὸ σῶμα ὁ Ἰωσὴφ, ἐνετύλιξεν 59
αὐτὸ σινδόνι καθαρᾷ, καὶ ἔθηκεν αὐτὸ ἐν τῷ καινῷ αὐτοῦ μνημείῳ, 60
ὃ ἐλατόμησεν ἐν τῇ πέτρᾳ· καὶ προσκυλίσας λίθον μέγαν τῇ θύρᾳ

rative there are *three* points which demand our attention. 1. *Who* were the οἱ κεκοιμημένοι. 2. What was the *purpose* of their being raised from the dead. 3. What was the *time* at which it took place. They were *holy persons*, whether Jews, (as old Simeon), or such as had *lately* died in the the faith of Christ. They must have been persons *not long dead*, or they would not have been recognised by their contemporaries. The *purpose* is, with most probability, supposed to have been, to show that the power of the grave was destroyed, by *life* and *immortality* being brought to light by the Gospel; and thus a pledge given of the general resurrection. As to the *time* — that will depend on whether the phrase μετὰ τὴν ἔγερσιν αὐτοῦ be taken with the *preceding*, or the *following* words; on which Interpreters, ancient and modern, are divided in opinion. The *former* method seems the best founded. We need not, however, suppose, with some who adopt this view, that the resurrection in question was *gradual*, *begun* at the rending open of the graves, and *accomplished* after the resurrection of Christ. That would be too hypothetical; nor is it required by the declaration of the Apostle at Col. i. 18, and 1 Cor. xv. 20, that "Jesus was the first born from the dead, and the first fruits of them that slept." It is better to suppose (with some ancient, and a few modern Commentators), that the words are inserted somewhat out of place, and perhaps belong to ἠγέρθη. As to the hypothesis of the sceptical school in Germany, that the verses are spurious, it is destroyed by the *fact*, that the words are found in *all* the MSS. and Versions, and are so alluded to by the early Fathers as to show their existence in *their* time: and interpolation at an *earlier* period was next to impossible.

54. ἀληθῶς — οὗτος.] I have proved at large in Recens. Synop. that Θεοῦ Υἱὸς cannot mean, as Grot., Markl., Campb. Rosenm., and Kuin. maintain, "an innocent and just man." or *a* son of *a* God, (i. e. a demigod); but *the* Son of God, the Messiah. The soldiers could not but know Jesus's pretensions to be such; and the import of the phrase must have been familiar to them. And seeing the awful and preternatural circumstances which accompanied his death, it was natural that they should exclaim, *some* of them, This was truly an innocent and just person! and *others*, This was truly the personage he affirmed himself to be — the Son of God!

57. ἀπὸ Ἀρ.] scil. ὤν. This sense of ἀπὸ (for which ἐκ is sometimes used) corresponds to the Latin *ex*, the Welsh *ap*, and our *of*. The riches and honourable station of Joseph are mentioned, to show the fulfilment of Isa. liii. 9. The best Commentators are agreed that Joseph was one of the Sanhedrim; for βουλευτὴς may be taken *improprie* for ἄρχων.

— ἐμαθήτευσε] for μαθητὴς ἦν. Of this instransitive sense examples are adduced by Wets. and Kypke from Plutarch and Jamblichus.

58. ᾐτήσατο τὸ σῶμα.] Though the bodies of crucified persons were not *interred* by the Romans, yet they were generally given, on application, to their friends for burial. This would be more especially done in Judæa; because the custom of the country (founded on the Scriptural command, Deut. xxi. 23) required the bodies to be buried before sun-set; and particularly in the present case, on account of the approaching festival.

59. ἐνετύλιξεν — σινδόνι.] Similar language is found in Herodot. ii. 86. in his account of embalmment. The σινδὼν was a *web*, or wrapper of fine linen, which was used for the same purposes as our *sheets*; (see Thucyd. ii. 49. and my Note there), and also employed to roll around a corpse, previously to interment or embalming, being then secured by linen bandages. The word is derived by some from Sidon, where this linen was made. But it was chiefly manufactured in *Egypt*, and is therefore best derived from a similar word in the Coptic. Though I suspect that it *there* had its name (as in the case of our *nankeen* and *muslin*, so denominated from Nanking and Masulipatam) from the article being originally brought from *Sind*, (i. e. Hindoostan), by that trade which, from a period anterior to all history, subsisted between Egypt and the East.

60. ἐν τῷ καινῷ αὐτοῦ μν.] These *two* circumstances are mentioned, to show the *honour* paid to our Lord by Joseph (as Dio says Augustus buried Agrippa in his *own tomb*); and to preclude any cavil of the Pharisees; as if the corpse had been resuscitated by touching the bones of some prophet; see 2 Kings xiii. 21. On the general evidence for the reality of the resurrection, see Horne's Introd. [*Comp.* Isa. liii. 9.]

— τῇ πέτρᾳ.] The Article here is very significant, and has reference to the rockiness of the country; on which we have the testimony of

MK. LU.
61 τοῦ μνημείου, ἀπῆλθεν. Ἦν δὲ ἐκεῖ Μαρία ἡ Μαγδαληνὴ, καὶ ἡ 15. 23.
ἄλλη Μαρία, καθήμεναι ἀπέναντι τοῦ τάφου. 47 55
62 Τῇ δὲ ἐπαύριον, ἥτις ἐστὶ μετὰ τὴν παρασκευὴν, συνήχθησαν οἱ
63 ἀρχιερεῖς καὶ οἱ Φαρισαῖοι πρὸς Πιλάτον, λέγοντες· Κύριε, ἐμνήσθη-
μεν ὅτι ἐκεῖνος ὁ πλάνος εἶπεν ἔτι ζῶν· Μετὰ τρεῖς ἡμέρας ἐγείρο-
64 μαι. Κέλευσον οὖν ἀσφαλισθῆναι τὸν τάφον ἕως τῆς τρίτης ἡμέρας·
μήποτε ἐλθόντες οἱ μαθηταὶ αὐτοῦ [νυκτὸς] κλέψωσιν αὐτὸν, καὶ
εἴπωσι τῷ λαῷ· Ἠγέρθη ἀπὸ τῶν νεκρῶν· καὶ ἔσται ἡ ἐσχάτη
65 πλάνη χείρων τῆς πρώτης. Ἔφη δὲ αὐτοῖς ὁ Πιλάτος· Ἔχετε κουστω-
66 δίαν· ὑπάγετε, ἀσφαλίσασθε ὡς οἴδατε. Οἱ δὲ πορευθέντες ἠσφαλίσαντο τὸν τάφον, σφραγίσαντες τὸν λίθον, μετὰ τῆς κουστωδίας. 16. 24.
1 XXVIII. ὈΨΕ δὲ σαββάτων, τῇ ἐπιφωσκούσῃ εἰς μίαν σαββάτων, 1 1
ἦλθε Μαρία ἡ Μαγδαληνὴ, καὶ ἡ ἄλλη Μαρία, θεωρῆσαι τὸν τάφον.

Strabo and Josephus, confirmed by modern travellers.

— προσκυλίσας λ.] The Commentators remark, that it was an Oriental custom thus to guard the entrances of caves, and also of subterraneous sepulchres. This was, however, not confined to the East, but extended to the West; as appears from the Classical passages adduced by Grot. and by myself in Recens. Synoptica; whence it appears that in the early ages stones were generally used in the place of doors to caves or vaults. The stone panelled doors which close many of the Egyptian monuments, were an invention midway between the *block of stone* of the primitive times, and the *wooden door* of after ages.

62. τὴν παρασκευήν.] Παρασκευὴ denoted *the day preceding any sabbath or festival*, as being that on which the *preparation* for its celebration was to be made. See Horne's Introd.

— συνήχθησαν πρὸς Π.] "convenerunt ad Pilatum." There is a *significatio prægnans* for, they went to and assembled at, i. e. they went in a body to.

63. πλάνος.] This word, like the Latin *planus*, signified properly a *vagabond*, and, from the adjunct, a *cheat, impostor*, &c. Μετὰ τρεῖς ἡμέρας, i. e. within three days, equivalent to the third day. See Note on Matt. xvi. 21. That the Jews so understood it, is plain from the next verse. "A most amazing instance of God's providence (observes Markland) to make Jesus' greatest enemies bear witness, that before his death he had foretold his resurrection within three days." To *which* of the prophecies (whether that at Matt. xii. 40, or at Matt. xxvi. 61,) they alluded, is not clear. Certain it is, however, that our Lord's declaration, that he should rise from the dead, was publicly known.

64. καὶ ἔσται ἡ ἐσχάτη πλάνη, &c.] A proverbial saying, importing that it would be worse if the whole people should acknowledge him as Messiah, and thus rise up in rebellion. Νυκτὸς after αὐτοῦ is wanting in most of the best MSS., Versions, and some Fathers, and is cancelled by Griesb., Fritz., and Scholz. Yet it is defended by xxviii. 13.

65. ἔχετε κουστωδίαν.] The Commentators are not agreed whether ἔχετε should be taken in the Indicative, or in the Imperative. Either method is admissible; but as no example has been adduced of such a sense of ἔχειν as *to take*, though found in the corresponding term of modern languages; and especially as the sense thus yielded is not so suitable to what follows, the *former* method (which is confirmed by some ancient and the best modern Commentators) seems preferable. Render, "ye *have* a guard;" namely, that stationed in the Castle of Antonia, and which was meant to quell any tumult in the city.

— ὡς οἴδατε.] The sense of this expression too is controverted; but the best rendering seems to be that of Grot. Schleus., Rosenm., Kuinoel, Fritz., and others, "quantum potestis." In fact, there is an ellipsis of ἀσφαλέστατα, to be supplied from ἀσφαλίσασθε. The literal sense is, "as safely as ye *know how*," i. e. as ye are able.

66. σφραγίσαντες.] A mode of security in use from the earliest times; (as we find from Daniel vi. 17.), when it supplied the place of locks. See the Classical citations adduced by Wets. and myself in Rec. Synop. In the present case, the sealing material (no doubt with Pilate's seal) is supposed to have been affixed to the two ends of a cord or band brought round the stone. Μετὰ τῆς κουστωδίας may either (by such a transposition as that supra ver. 53,) be referred (with Raphel., Kypke, and Kuin.) to ἠσφαλίσαντο τὸν τάφον; or rather the words may be taken (with Fritz.) as a *brachylogia* for μετὰ τοῦ προσθεῖναι τὴν κουστωδίαν, "together with (a setting of) the guard," i. e. at this same time that they set the guard.

XXVIII. 1. ὀψὲ δὲ σαββ.] This must, with Krebs, Wahl., Tittm., Kuin., and Fritz., be explained, "after the sabbath," i. e. as Mark more clearly expresses it διαγενομένου τοῦ σαββάτου, which must determine the sense here. Of this signification the Commentators adduce examples from Philostr., Plut., Ælian, and Xenophon.

— τῇ ἐπιφωσκούσῃ.] An elliptical expression for ἅμα τῇ ἡμέρᾳ ἐπιφ. The complete one occurs in Herodot. iii. 86, and ix. 44. The word is said by Casaub. to be used properly of the first appearing of the heavenly bodies. It may be paralleled by our verb to *dawn*. Μίαν is for πρώτην; by an idiom often found in the Sept., and derived from the *Hebrew*; though it exists, more or less, in most languages. On the evidence for our Lord's resurrection the reader is referred, for a *general view* of the subject and the arguments establishing the credibility thereof, to Horne's

MK. LU.
16. 24. *Καὶ ἰδού, σεισμὸς ἐγένετο μέγας· ἄγγελος γὰρ Κυρίου καταβὰς ἐξ* 2
οὐρανοῦ, προσελθὼν ἀπεκύλισε τὸν λίθον ἀπὸ τῆς θύρας, καὶ ἐκάθητο
ἐπάνω αὐτοῦ. Ἦν δὲ ἡ ἰδέα αὐτοῦ ὡς ἀστραπὴ, καὶ τὸ ἔνδυμα αὐ- 3
τοῦ λευκὸν ὡσεὶ χιών. Ἀπὸ δὲ τοῦ φόβου αὐτοῦ ἐσείσθησαν οἱ τη- 4
6 *ροῦντες, καὶ ἐγένοντο ὡσεὶ νεκροί. Ἀποκριθεὶς δὲ ὁ ἄγγελος εἶπε ταῖς* 5
γυναιξί· Μὴ φοβεῖσθε ὑμεῖς· οἶδα γὰρ ὅτι Ἰησοῦν τὸν ἐσταυρωμέ-
6 *νον ζητεῖτε. Οὐκ ἔστιν ὧδε· ἠγέρθη γὰρ, καθὼς εἶπε. δεῦτε ἴδετε τὸν* 6
7 *τόπον ὅπου ἔκειτο ὁ Κύριος. Καὶ ταχὺ πορευθεῖσαι εἴπατε τοῖς* 7
μαθηταῖς αὐτοῦ, ὅτι ἠγέρθη ἀπὸ τῶν νεκρῶν· καὶ ἰδοὺ, προάγει
8 *ὑμᾶς εἰς τὴν Γαλιλαίαν· ἐκεῖ αὐτὸν ὄψεσθε. ἰδοὺ, εἶπον ὑμῖν. Καὶ* 8
9 *ἐξελθοῦσαι ταχὺ ἀπὸ τοῦ μνημείου μετὰ φόβου καὶ χαρᾶς μεγάλης,*
ἔδραμον ἀπαγγεῖλαι τοῖς μαθηταῖς αὐτοῦ. Ὡς δὲ ἐπορεύοντο ἀπαγ- 9
γεῖλαι τοῖς μαθηταῖς αὐτοῦ, καὶ ἰδοὺ ὁ Ἰησοῦς ἀπήντησεν αὐταῖς,
λέγων· Χαίρετε. Αἱ δὲ προσελθοῦσαι ἐκράτησαν αὐτοῦ τοὺς πόδας,

Introd. vol. i. p. 239. 260. For a *harmony* of the various narratives, to Mr. West and Dr. Townson, and especially to Mr. Townsend (Chron. Arr.), and Mr. Greswell. On the important point of the *change of the Sabbath* from the seventh to the first day of the week, which arose out of our Lord's resurrection on the latter, the reader is referred to Horne's Introd. to a pamphlet of Dr. Millar of Armagh, and especially to an elaborate Sermon with Notes by Professor Lee of Cambridge, 1833. From which works it appears, that there is sufficient warrant in Scripture for the change of the Sabbath, without recurring to the Romish doctrine of *independent tradition*; and also that there is great reason to think the Patriarchal Sabbath coincided with our *Sunday*; also that, as it was thrown back to *Saturday*, in order to commemorate the Jewish Exodus; so that the *return* to the original Sabbath, when the purpose for which the new one had been appointed was answered, was just as reasonable as its former *change*. In short, to use the words of Professor Lee, *ubi supra*, "As the original sabbath had been sacred from the beginning, and had lost nothing of its primitive sanctions by having been accommodated to the times of the egress; and, as that system had come to an end, that day would now necessarily recur, by virtue of the precept which at first sanctified and set it apart. There would, consequently, be no necessity for any new commandment, in the New Testament, again to sanction it for the future observance of the Church." Nay, Professor Lee is further of opinion (and *gives good reasons for supposing*) that the heathens took this day, with its observances, from the Patriarchs; and that, as nothing ever occurred which could have induced the heathens to interrupt the recurrence of this as *the seventh* day, its observance must have come down to us from times as ancient as those under which the first appointment of a sabbath was kept.

2. *καὶ ἰδοὺ σεισμὸς*, &c.] I have in Recens. Synop. shown that the interpretation of *σεισμὸς* propounded by some Interpreters (namely, a *tempest* or *whirlwind)* cannot be admitted: still less that of "trembling" or "fear." Not merely absurd, but irreverent, is the interpretation of *ἄγγελος* by the Sceptical School of Theologians in Germany, by which it is made to mean, not a *person*, but a *thing*; i. e. lightning or flames, which often accompany earthquakes.

3. *ἰδέα*] form, figure, or appearance; a signification frequent in the best Classical writers.

—*λευκὸν ὡσεὶ χιών*.] A simile of frequent occurrence in writers of every nation. "Whiteness (says Grot.) having ever been a symbol of purity and sanctity." See Dan. vii. 9. Apoc. iii. 4; vi. 11; vii. 9 and 13. Hence among all the nations of antiquity, it was customary for those who were celebrating divine worship to be clothed in white. But to this whiteness of garment there was, in these *angels*, superadded an undefinable and peculiar splendour, something like what is attributed to Christ in the transfiguration. (xvii. 2.) So Luke says they were *ἐν ἐσθήσεσιν ἀστραπτούσαις*, a sign of celestial glory, such as Herod presumptuously affected. See Acts xii. 22.

4. *ἀπὸ τοῦ φόβου*.] Ἀπὸ here denotes the *origin* and cause of the fear; an idiom common to both Greek and Latin. Ἐγένοντο ὡσεὶ νεκροὶ is an hyperbolical phrase common to all ages and all languages.

6. *τόπον*.] The word here denotes the cavity, or *cell*, hollowed out in the vault; and in which was deposited the corpse. [*Comp.* supra xii. 40, xvi. 21. xvii. 23.]

8. *μνημείου*.] The *μνημεῖον*, or *monumentum*, amongst the Greeks and Romans, and perhaps the Jews, consisted of the cave, מערה, *σπήλαιον*, and חצר, *τὸ ὕπαιθρον*, a small inclosure in the same ground around it. This whole *μνημεῖον* was also itself situated in a larger space of ground, outside of the inclosure, called by the Romans *tutela monumenti*; and here corresponding to the cultivated garden.

—*μετὰ φόβου καὶ χαρᾶς*.] The phraseology (with which Wets. compares several passages from the Classical writers) strongly expresses the mingled sensations of *fear* (or rather *awe)* at the appearance of the angel, and *joy* at the good news be announced.

9. *χαίρετε*.] This is wrongly rendered by Campb. "rejoice." It is a common form of salutation. So the Syriac renders, "Pax vobis!" Our *Hail!* best represents the sense; since *hail*, in the language of our ancestors, denoted health, prosperity, and good of every kind.

—*ἐκράτησαν πόδας*] i. e. in the manner of sup-

10 καὶ προσεκύνησαν αὐτῷ. [a] Τότε λέγει αὐταῖς ὁ Ἰησοῦς· Μὴ φοβεῖ- a John 20. 17. Acts 1. 3.
σθε· ὑπάγετε, ἀπαγγείλατε τοῖς ἀδελφοῖς μου, ἵνα ἀπέλθωσιν εἰς τὴν
Γαλιλαίαν· κἀκεῖ με ὄψονται.
11 Πορευομένων δὲ αὐτῶν, ἰδού, τινὲς τῆς κουστωδίας ἐλθόντες εἰς τὴν
12 πόλιν, ἀπήγγειλαν τοῖς ἀρχιερεῦσιν ἅπαντα τὰ γενόμενα. Καὶ συνα-
χθέντες μετὰ τῶν πρεσβυτέρων, συμβούλιόν τε λαβόντες, ἀργύρια ἱκανὰ
13 ἔδωκαν τοῖς στρατιώταις, λέγοντες· Εἴπατε, ὅτι οἱ μαθηταὶ αὐτοῦ
14 νυκτὸς ἐλθόντες ἔκλεψαν αὐτὸν, ἡμῶν κοιμωμένων. Καὶ ἐὰν ἀκουσθῇ
τοῦτο ἐπὶ τοῦ ἡγεμόνος, ἡμεῖς πείσομεν αὐτὸν, καὶ ὑμᾶς ἀμερίμνους
15 ποιήσομεν. Οἱ δὲ λαβόντες τὰ ἀργύρια, ἐποίησαν ὡς ἐδιδάχθησαν.
Καὶ διεφημίσθη ὁ λόγος οὗτος παρὰ Ἰουδαίοις μέχρι τῆς σήμερον.
16 [b] Οἱ δὲ ἕνδεκα μαθηταὶ ἐπορεύθησαν εἰς τὴν Γαλιλαίαν, [εἰς τὸ b Supr. 26. 32.
17 ὄρος] οὗ ἐτάξατο αὐτοῖς ὁ Ἰησοῦς. Καὶ ἰδόντες αὐτὸν προσεκύνησαν

pliants; who used to prostrate themselves, and embrace the feet of those from whom they sought protection. Brug., Lightf., and Rosenm., take it to mean "*kissed* his feet;" a custom also prevalent in the East, from whence it afterwards passed to the West. But the words will not admit such a sense. And, indeed, the deep *awe* which inspired their *adoration* (on which see Note on Matt. ii. 2,) seems to have scarcely permitted an action rather importing *affection* than any more reverential feeling.

10. κἀκεῖ με ὄψονται] i. e., as Fritz. says, καὶ ἀπαγγ. ὅτι ἐκεῖ με ὄψονται.

12. ἀργύρια ἱκανὰ] ἱκ. for πολλά; which use is frequent when the word occurs with nouns signifying *many*. The Commentators regard ἀργ. as plural for singular. In fact, ἀργύριον denotes 1. *silver in bullion*; 2. *silver coined*; in which sense it is chiefly used in the singular; 3. *silver coins*; but chiefly the stater, tetradrachma, or shekel; in which sense it is generally used in the plural, mostly accompanied with numerals, or words that imply number, as *many*, *few*, &c. 4. In the plural it denotes *money*, as here.

13. ἔκλεψαν αὐτὸν] "took him away clandestinely." In this sense κλέπτω occurs in 2 Sam. xix. 41. Several examples from the Classical writers are adduced by the Commentators, but not any quite apposite. One, however, exists in Thucyd. vii. 85.

14. ἐπὶ τοῦ ἡγεμόνος.] Here ἐπὶ is not for ὑπὸ, as some maintain; but is used in the sense *apud*, *coram*, as the Syr. takes it, with the approbation of Grot. and Fritz.

— πείσομεν αὐτὸν] "we will appease (his wrath), conciliate his pardon and favour; namely, by entreaties or gifts." There is, however, no *ellipse* of χρήμασι, as some recent English Commentators suppose. The *means* of persuasion are left to be *imagined*. 'Αμερίμνους ποιήσομεν is a phrase corresponding to the Latin *indemnem* vel *securum præstare*, (scil. a malo), to make one safe and sure [from harm].

15. ὁ λόγος οὗτος] i. e. this story, about the stealing of the body, which was put into the mouths of the soldiers. That it was studiously disseminated by the Jews, we learn from a passage of Justin Martyr cited by the Commentators: indeed, traces of it are found in the Rabbinical writings

16. εἰς τὸ ὄρος οὗ, &c.] Since neither by himself, in his *prophetic declaration* at Matt. xxvi. 32, nor in his *promise*, supra v. 10, nor by the angel, v. 4, is *any mountain* specified as the place of meeting between Christ and his disciples, it is argued by Whitby, Mackn., and other English Commentators, that the words οὗ ἐτάξατο must be referred, not to ὄρος, but to Γαλιλαίαν. This, however, would be doing such violence to the construction, that it cannot be admitted. At the same time, there is little doubt that the Apostles *did* assemble for that purpose on a *mountain* (for the same reason that *our Lord* chose mountains for prayer, &c.); and probability and ecclesiastical tradition concur in pointing out *Tabor* as the place. Are we, then, to suppose that there is, in the passage before us, a *reference* to a *particular spot* of meeting, which, nevertheless, has not been mentioned by the Evangelist, where one might have expected it, supra v. 10? Had Kuin. and Fritz. thought so, they would, no doubt, have imputed it to the "hasty negligence with which," they say, "the Evangelist speeds to the conclusion of his Gospel." But far be such irreverence from serious believers! Besides, neither do the other Evangelists, who have *supplied* what St. Matthew here omits, make mention of this circumstance; which yet would not be *likely* to be omitted. And it is scarcely probable that our Lord would appoint the *place*, and not fix the *time*: since any long continuance in so wild and desert a place as Mount Tabor, must have been very inconvenient to the disciples. I cannot help suspecting, that the words εἰς τὸ ὄρος (which ought to be rendered, not "into a mountain," but "unto the mountain,") are not genuine. They are not found in six MSS., and therefore I have thought proper to place them within brackets. They seem to have arisen from a *marginal remark* of those who were well aware of the Ecclesiastical tradition, that this transaction took place at *Mount Tabor*; whence it seems others afterwards introduced them into the *text*, as thinking them required by the ου, and as serving to make the thing more definite. By their *removal* the difficulty in question will vanish; since the οὗ will thus refer to Γαλιλαίαν just before, and the reference to v. 9 will be more distinct; vv. 11—15 being, as Dr. A. Clarke saw, in some measure parenthetical. The οὗ is thus used for οἷ, *whither*, as at Luke x. 1. ἀπέστειλεν αὐτοὺς εἰς πᾶσαν πόλιν — οὗ ἔμελλεν αὐτὸς ἔρχεσθαι, and xxiv. 28. ἤγγισαν εἰς τὴν κώμην, οὗ ἐπορεύοντο. 1 Cor. xvi. 6.

The above Commentators are of opinion, that

c Supr. 11. 27. John 3. 35. & 13. 3. & 17. 2. Heb. 1. 2. & 2. 8. d Mark 16. 15. Luke 24. 47.

αὐτῷ· οἱ δὲ ἐδίστασαν. [c] Καὶ προσελθὼν ὁ Ἰησοῦς ἐλάλησεν αὐτοῖς, 18
λέγων· Ἐδόθη μοι πᾶσα ἐξουσία ἐν οὐρανῷ καὶ ἐπὶ γῆς. [d] Πορευ- 19
θέντες [οὖν] μαθητεύσατε πάντα τὰ ἔθνη, βαπτίζοντες αὐτοὺς εἰς τὸ

although the Evangelist does not mention more than the *Eleven*, yet that we may suppose there were many more witnesses; namely, the *Seventy* and other recently converted disciples, so that the number may coincide with the 500 mentioned by St. Paul, 1 Cor. xv. 6. But thus what is said v. 19. πορευθέντες μαθητ. κ. τ. λ. would have to be referred to the *whole;* which cannot be meant. Besides, St. Paul there expressly *distinguishes* the appearance to the *Apostles* (the Twelve or Eleven) from that to the 500 (meaning the disciples at large).

17. οἱ δὲ ἐδίστασαν.] There has been some difficulty raised both as to the *construction*, and the *persons* meant by οἱ δέ. As to the former, there can be no doubt but that the οἱ δὲ is rightly taken, by some ancient and several of the best modern Commentators, for τινὲς δέ; of which many examples are adduced. But the latter difficulty is not so easily removed. To resort to conjectural alteration, with Beza, is to *cut* the knot. To take ἐδίστασαν, with Grot., Doddr., and Fritz., as a pluperfect, ("had doubted,") is harsh, and too much like a device for the nonce. In Recens. Syn. and the first Edition of this work, I gave the preference to the interpretation of Whitby, West, Owen, and Kuin., who refer the words to the *seventy disciples*, some of whom might have scruples remaining, and who would probably attend together with the Eleven. But I am now persuaded that that view is inadmissible; not so much because it has no countenance from St. Matthew, as because it is contradicted by the express words of St. Paul. Nor are we compelled to take the οἱ δὲ of *one only*, Thomas; for we may suppose, that although he alone *expressed* his doubts, yet there might be at least one more besides, who felt distrust, doubting the *bodily* presence of the Lord. The construction is elliptical, for καὶ ἰδόντες αὐτὸν, οἱ μὲν προσεκύνησαν αὐτὸν, οἱ δὲ ἐδ., or οἱ δέ τινες. So Thucyd. vi. 15. οἱ μὲν πλεῖστοι στρατεύειν παρῄνουν, οἱ δέ τινες καὶ ἀντέλεγον.

Διστάζειν properly signifies to stand *in bivio*, not knowing or determining which road to take. The metaphor may be illustrated from the following elegant passage of Eurip. Orest. 625. διπλῆς μερίμνης διπτύχους ἰὼν ὁδούς.

18. ἐδόθη μοι πᾶσα ἐξ.] "all power of every kind," the highest authority (δόξα προαιώνιος, John xvii. 5. and 24.) These words have been by some so explained as to derogate from the *Divinity* of Christ. But, when properly understood, they will by no means lead to any such conclusion. It is justly argued by Whitby and Mede, that as in his *Divine* nature our Lord doubtless had this power from all eternity, so, if this declaration be supposed to be made with respect to his *Divine nature*, it must be understood of him as being *God of God*, deriving his being and essence by an eternal generation from the Father. But he was also perfect *man*, as well as perfect *God;* and therefore the words may have been spoken in reference to his state of *humiliation*, now about to terminate in glory at the right hand of God; before which time he could not *exercise* the power, though he had before received it. In short, such unlimited power could neither be received nor exercised by any Being less than *God*. *Christ therefore is* GOD.

— πορευθ. οὖν μαθητ., &c.] The connexion here is ably traced by Bp. Beveridge, thus, — "I have now all power, &c. conferred upon me; *by virtue of which* therefore I empower and commission *you* to enlarge, settle, and govern the Church which I have founded." Thus we have here that great *commission* granted by Christ to his Apostles and their successors, with respect to all nations (both Jews and Gentiles) embracing three particulars, μαθητεύειν, βαπτίζειν, and διδάσκειν, i. e. 1. to disciple them, or convert them to the faith; 2. to initiate them into the Church by baptism; 3. to instruct them when baptized, in the doctrines and duties of a Christian life. From the present passage we may infer three things, 1. the necessity of baptism; 2. the lawfulness of *Infant* baptism; 3. the doctrine of the *Trinity:* since we are baptized in (or unto) the Father, Son, and Holy Ghost, without any mention of difference, distinction, or superiority. And with respect to the *second* point, "no argument can," as Dr. Doddridge says, "be drawn from these words to the prejudice of infant baptism," because, though especially *adapted* to *adults*, as necessarily forming the bulk of the first converts; yet it need not be thought to exclude *infants*, who cannot be expected to have faith in order to be baptized. And this inference would necessarily be *drawn* by the Jews, since they were accustomed to see infants baptized; and would naturally conclude, that as no *alteration* was announced, the *mode* of admission into covenant remained the same. The *propriety* of infant baptism may be inferred from the analogy which the rite bears to *circumcision*, and the *baptism of proselytes*, which included their *children* as well as themselves. There is precisely the same reason why the children of *Christians* should be admitted from their infancy into the Christian covenant, as why the infants of Jewish parents should be admitted into the Mosaic Covenant. Infants being as capable of covenanting in the one case as in the other. And if God did not consider their *age* any objection against even *circumcision*, or the baptism of the children of Jewish proselytes; we have no reason to urge it as an objection against being received to Christian baptism. In short, it may be confidently pronounced, that Infant Baptism has subsisted from the times of the Apostles to the present day. Timothy was brought up a Christian ἀπὸ βρέφους, as multitudes of others must, when whole families were baptized. So also Justin Martyr, Apol. i. says that there were then many of both sexes, 60 or 70 years of age, οἳ ἐκ παίδων ἐμαθητεύθησαν τῷ Χριστῷ, ἄφθοροι διαμένουσι. And certain it is, that in Tertullian's day, the practice was general. In fact, had infant baptism *not* subsisted in the time of the Apostles, what, (as Wets. observes) would have been done with the infants or male children of Christians? Were they to be *circumcised?* certainly not. Were they then to be brought up in neither Judaism nor Christianity, but with their minds *a tabula rasa?* certainly not. "Bring them up," says St. Paul, "in the fear and nurture of the *Lord*." Otherwise they would have been in a worse condition than if their parents had never been Christians. And though nothing is said in Scripture to *enjoin* infant baptism, it was not ne-

20 ὄνομα τοῦ Πατρὸς καὶ τοῦ Υἱοῦ καὶ τοῦ ἁγίου Πνεύματος, διδάσκοντες
αὐτοὺς τηρεῖν πάντα ὅσα ἐνετειλάμην ὑμῖν. Καὶ ἰδοὺ, ἐγὼ μεθ᾽
ὑμῶν εἰμι πάσας τὰς ἡμέρας, ἕως τῆς συντελείας τοῦ αἰῶνος. Ἀμήν.

cessary that it should be expressly enjoined; just as neither the age nor sex of those admitted to the Lord's Supper is mentioned or prescribed. On the other hand, there was a good reason why that should *not* be done; namely, lest superstitious persons should stick at the *bark* only of the doctrines, and give their chief attention to what is *ceremonial*, to the neglect of what is *essential*." See more in Wets., who also well observes, that whatever may be thought of *other* passages, certainly in *this*, which contains the institution of baptism, a *mild and liberal* exposition of μαθητεύειν is to be preferred to a rigid interpretation. Such, indeed, as there is no doubt was adopted by the *Apostles*. On this subject see more in the able Notes of Lightf. and Whitby, and especially an elaborate annotation of Wets. translated and given entire in Rec. Syn. The reader is also referred to an able pamphlet by the learned and candid Professor Stuart (of America), on the Mode of Baptism, who after having at large considered the subject of *sprinkling* as compared with *immersion*, and proved that the former is equally as proper as the latter, as sufficiently expressing the same intention, concludes with the following remark on *Infant* Baptism. "I have only to say that I believe in both the propriety and expediency of the rite thus administered; and therefore accede to it *ex animo*. Commands, or plain and certain examples, in the New Testament relative to it, I do not find. Nor, with my views of it, do I need them. If the subject had respect to what is *fundamental*, or *essential*, in Christianity, then I must find either the one or the other, in order to justify adopting or practising it. But as the case now is, the *general analogy* of the ancient dispensation; the *enlargement* of privilege under the Gospel; the silence of the New Testament on the subject of receiving children into a special relation to the church, by the baptismal rite, which shows, at least, that there was no dispute in early ages relative to this matter; the certainty that in Tertullian's day the practice was general; all these considerations put together — united with the conviction that baptism is *symbol* and *dedication*, and may be so in the case of infants as well as adults; and that it brings parents and children into a peculiar relation to the church, and under peculiarly recognized obligation — serve to satisfy me fully, that the practice may be, and should be continued."

ΤΟ ΚΑΤΑ ΜΑΡΚΟΝ

ΕΥΑΓΓΕΛΙΟΝ.

I. ᾿ΑΡΧΗ τοῦ εὐαγγελίου Ἰησοῦ Χριστοῦ, Υἱοῦ τοῦ Θεοῦ ὡς γέ- 1
γραπται ἐν [Ἡσαΐᾳ] * τῷ * προφήτῃ· Ἰδού, ἐγὼ ἀποστέλλω τὸν 2

C. I. The writer of this Gospel is almost universally admitted to have been John, surnamed Mark, who was sister's son to Barnabas, and son of Mary, a pious woman, at whose house the first Christians usually assembled at Jerusalem. This is, indeed, denied by Grotius, and, after him, by Dr. Burton; but the objections of the former have been overruled by Fritz. And as to what is urged by the latter, that "if the Evangelist died, as we are told by Eusebius, in the 8th year of Nero (i. e. A. D. 61 or 62), he could not be mentioned in the 2d Epistle to Timothy, which was not written till, at the earliest, A. D. 64;" we are surely not authorized to reject, on so slender a ground, what is founded in high probability, supported by the earliest Ecclesiastical tradition, on a point where it could scarcely fail to preserve the truth. It is more reasonable to suppose, either that Euseb. was *misinformed* as to the exact date; or rather that there is some mistake of the scribes *in the figure*. Probably for Η we should read ΙΓ (13).

Mark was not an Apostle, nor probably one of the Seventy disciples, especially as St. Peter (1 Pet. v. 13.) calls him his *son* [namely, in the faith], i. e. his convert. For the outlines of the Evangelist's history traced from the N. T. and the early Ecclesiastical writers, the reader is referred to Mr. Horne's Introduction. The *time* when this Gospel was written is much disputed, and cannot be fixed with certainty; but it is with most probability fixed at A. D. 66 or 67., and a little after the time when St. *Luke* published his Gospel: certainly not till after the death of St. Peter, and probably St. Paul. This matter is, however, closely connected with another question, of far greater importance,—whether, in writing his Gospel, Mark made use of the Gospel of Matthew? On this the opinions of the learned are at the antipodes; some maintaining that Mark's Gospel is only an abridgement of Matthew's; others, that Mark made no use of that Gospel—nay, was totally unacquainted with it: indeed, that the Gospels were *all* of them formed without knowledge of, and independently of each other. Now here, if ever, "in medio tutissimus ibis." The instances of verbal coincidence are so striking (nearly the whole of the Gospel being found in Matthew) as to forbid the *latter* supposition. And as to the *former*, it may, with equal confidence, be maintained, that this Gospel is *not* a mere abridgement of St. Matthew's, since it differs from it (as we shall see) in many important respects. The question whether St. Mark made use of St. Luke's Gospel, is of more difficult determination. Dr. Hales thinks that Griesbach has, by an elaborate process, furnished strong internal evidence of the priority of Luke's Gospel to Mark's. In using these Gospels, Dr. Hales thinks that Mark in general rather adopted the *language* of Matthew, but the *order* of Luke; yet neither *implicitly*. Besides, he is more circumstantial and correct than either of them in the relation of joint facts. Now, Dr. Hales argues, had *Luke* followed *Mark* (as is the common opinion), it is not credible that he would have omitted *all* those; since even John has used *some*. And this priority of Luke to Mark is not only maintained by many eminent moderns, but confirmed by the authority of Clemens Alex., who attests that Gospels, with the genealogies, were first written, and by Julian, who mention them in the order—*Matthew, Luke, Mark, and John*. We can, as Dr. Hales observes, account *thus* for the order in which they at present stand. "From the time that the notion prevailed that Mark's Gospel was an abridgement of St. Matthew's, it was natural to place it *next* to St. Matthew's." This (I would add) might take place even on the opinion that Mark *chiefly* followed Matthew. Thus, also, when Tertullian ranges the Gospels of Matthew, John, Luke, and Mark, he classifies them into *original*, and, in some degree, compilatory compositions. To advert to a yet more important subject—it may be thought surprising, that persons of acknowledged ability should have adopted opinions so diametrically

ἄγγελόν μου πρὸ προσώπου σου, ὃς κατασκευάσει
3 τὴν ὁδόν σου [ἔμπροσθέν σου,] Φωνὴ βοῶντος ἐν

opposite to each other, as to the *origin*, or sources, and *nature* of the Gospels. But the truth is, that the existence of such striking *verbal coincidences* between Matthew, Mark, and Luke, when coupled with the remarkable *variations*, and almost *discrepancies* in their respective accounts, presents a most perplexing phenomenon. Hence men of talent have set themselves to devise such *hypotheses*, as to the origin of the Gospels, as may satisfactorily *account for* these phenomena; and, as might be expected, they have, to a *certain degree*, met with success. Of the many that have been propounded, FOUR *alone* deserve any attention. 1. That *one* or *two* of the three Gospels were taken from the *third*. 2. That *all three* were derived from some *original document*, Greek or Hebrew, common to all three. 3. That they were derived from *detached narratives* of parts of the history of Christ, communicated by the Apostles to the first converts. 4. That they were derived from *oral tradition*. Now as to the *traditionary* hypothesis, suffice it to say that, besides proceeding on a wholly gratuitous *assumption* (as to the existence of *verbal Gospels*), and taking for granted other things (as to the *length of time* which elapsed before a Gospel was committed to writing, &c. &c.) it only brings upon us new and *real* difficulties in the place of *alleged* ones (especially as to the *uniformity* of such tradition), and is utterly inconsistent with the striking *verbal coincidences* found in the Gospels. As to the *documentary* hypothesis, even in its most modified and least objectionable form (No. 3.), it is liable to the same objections as No. 2., of *complexity* and *artificialness*; and that fatal one, the *silence of all Ecclesiastical antiquity* as to the existence of any such primary document, or documentary narratives. In short, of all these three hypotheses, (namely 2, 3, 4) we may truly say, that, while they are such as by no means to command our credence, they detract not a little from the *authority* of the first three Gospels as inspired compositions. Whatever may be the *modifications* with which either the *documentary* or the *traditionary* hypotheses be brought forward — whatever may be the *refinements* resorted to — they are insufficient to elude the plain inference, implied in each and all, that the Evangelists are scarcely to be regarded as *regular*, much less as *inspired* historians. There is, indeed, the less excuse for resorting to these hypotheses, since it is wholly *unnecessary* so to do; as will appear from an examination of the *first*-mentioned hypothesis, which has been held, with various modifications, by many of the most eminent Theologians and Commentators, ancient and modern. Even to *this* view, indeed, objections may, and have been made, which are thus summed up by Mr. Horne, Vol. I. 494 & 496: "1. The Evangelists could have no *motive* for copying from each other. 2. It does not appear that any of the ancient Christian writers had a suspicion that either of the first three Evangelists had seen the other Gospels before he wrote his own. 3. It is not suitable to the character of any of the Evangelists, that they should abridge or transcribe another historian. 4. It is evident, from the nature and design of the first three Gospels, that the Evangelists had not seen any *authentic* written history of Jesus Christ. 5. All the first three Evangelists have several things peculiar to themselves; which show that they did not borrow from each other, and that they were all well acquainted with the things of which they undertook to write a history." On a close examination, however, of these objections, some, it is conceived, will be found groundless, others to proceed from *misapprehension*, or *taking for granted* what has not, and cannot be *proved*: in short, that all put together have not weight enough to decide even a doubtful case. That there should have been such various *modifications* of the hypothesis now under consideration, is no proof, as the objectors to it allege, that it is wholly unfounded. *Extremes have in all ages produced extremes.* From the strong verbal coincidences between this Gospel and that of St. Matthew, many, from the time of Augustine downwards, have regarded Mark as a mere epitomizer of Matthew. Now this is at variance with the universal testimony of early antiquity, and is forbidden by the *alterations* in the order of time and the arrangement of facts, and the *addition* of much matter not found in Matthew. The strong coincidences may serve to prove that he often *followed* Matthew; but his frequent *deviations* from Matthew show that he was by no means an abridger. But, on the other hand, that the *succeeding* Evangelists did not see each the Gospel of his predecessor, is, as Dr. Hales observes, "a *negative* which cannot be *proved*. Whereas the *affirmative* is highly probable, from the intimate connection and correspondence between them, and appears to be sufficiently established from *internal evidence*." Upon the whole, there seems no good reason to reject the first-mentioned hypothesis; which will, I apprehend, have only to be duly *modified*, and properly *limited*, to free it from all reasonable objection. The state of the evidence as to the verbal coincidences is, as we have seen, such as to utterly *exclude* the notion (otherwise improbable) that the Evangelists who followed the *first* did not know, much less make use of, their predecessors' works. The case seems to have been this: 1. That the Gospels of Matthew and Luke were original and independent narratives (except that Luke probably made some use of the Hebrew original of St. Matthew). 2. That Mark's Gospel appeared after those two; and that the Evangelist freely used the matter contained in one or the other, according as it suited his purpose, and was agreeable to his plan. 3. That such parts as are not found in Matthew or Luke, were either derived from St. Peter (under whose sanction and direction he wrote), or at least from the testimony of "eye-witnesses, and ministers of the word." As to the *discrepancies* (which, however, have been much exaggerated) between his Gospel and that of St. Matthew, they will (as Dr. Hales observes) "not prove that he could not have known of it, or used the Gospel; but only that he felt himself authorised to claim the character of an original historian; which, considering his many advantages for arriving at the truth, and the countenance and direction of St. Peter, he might well do." This view, while it satisfactorily accounts for the verbal coincidences, cannot, when properly understood, be justly thought to derogate from the credit of St. Mark's Gospel, as a Canonical work, or one written under Divine inspiration. See Dr. Hales' judicious remarks on the

MT. LU.

3. 3. τῇ ἐρήμῳ, Ἑτοιμάσατε τὴν ὁδὸν κυρίου, εὐθείας ποι-
3 4 εῖτε τὰς τρίβους αὐτοῦ· ἐγένετο Ἰωάννης βαπτίζων ἐν τῇ 4

inspiration of the Evangelists. Vol. iii. pp. 26—30. To advert to the *purpose* of this Gospel, "A brief and plain account (to use the words of the same writer) of the grounds of the Christian religion was, even after the Gospels of Matthew and Luke, wanted for plain and unlettered persons. And this Mark, under the sanction and with the occasional assistance of St. Peter, undertook to draw up, at the request (as we learn from early Ecclesiastical writers) of the Christian converts of Rome, who had attended on St. Peter's preaching. In compliance with their request, Mark most judiciously selected, and sometimes *enlarged*, the more important parts of Matthew and Luke, and adapted them to his peculiar purpose; which was to give a *succinct* history of our Lord's ministry, commencing from the preaching of the Baptist to his *Ascension*, and concluding with the preaching of the Apostles every where throughout the world. Hence we are enabled to account for his *omission* of certain portions of their Gospels either entirely or partially; on the same principle that *John* coming after him, omits *considerably more*, so as to form a *distinct* Gospel, which may be considered as a *supplement to the rest* [See, however, Intr., to St. John's Gospel. Ed.], with only the insertion of so much matter common to the former, as to connect his Gospel with theirs."

There are indeed not wanting those who, strenuously contending for the Gospels being formed independently of each other, are of opinion that these coincidences in the writings of the Evangelists may be sufficiently accounted for without having recourse to the supposition that the later Gospels were, in some degree, formed on the preceding ones. According to this view, the verbal coincidences are ascribed to the *uncommon attention* with which Christ's sayings were treasured up in the memories of his hearers, and the supernatural aid promised to "bring all things to their remembrance, whatever he had said unto them." (John xiv. 26.) See Bp. Gleig and Archdeacon Nares cited by Mr. Horne. But this, it should seem, is ascribing more to *memory* than, even under the most favourable circumstances, can be safely done. At all events, it is not well judged to bring in the principle of strict *verbal inspiration*, in direct opposition to the strongest internal evidence of one Gospel, at least, being partly formed from the other two. There is nothing, it is apprehended, in the above view derogatory of the true claims of either Evangelist; especially of Luke, as will appear from his own preface to his Gospel; on which see the Notes *in loco*. Inspiration, as far as it was *needed*, was, we may believe, so far granted; and to suppose it to have proceeded *beyond* that, is to run counter to the usual course of God's operations, whether in the *natural* or the *moral* world, in which a beautiful *economy* is observable. The Deity, we may be assured, adapts both the ordinary and the extraordinary dispensations of his Providence to the actual circumstances of the moral world in different places, ages, or countries.

The *authenticity* of this Gospel (which, indeed, has scarcely been disputed) is established on an unbroken chain of testimony, commencing from the time even of St. Clement, in the first century, down to the 4th century. As to the *date* of this Gospel and St. Luke's, it appears, from Irenæus, that neither was published till after the death of St. Peter and St. Paul. Hence we cannot assign an *earlier* date than 65 to either of the Gospels, nor a *later* one than 68 (both being confessedly written before the destruction of Jerusalem), and probably Luke's Gospel and Acts were published in 66, and Mark's Gospel in 67.

I take this opportunity of offering some further remarks on the state of the evidence, as concerns the date of publication of St. *Matthew's* Greek Gospel. On a more mature consideration of the various arguments advanced in favour of an *early*, and those of a *later* date, I must confess that the evidence for the *latter* seems to preponderate. That of *antiquity* is stronger for it; and the complete silence of the writers of the Apostolical Epistles as to any *written* Gospels, tends to the same conclusion. A late period, too, was, as Dr. Hales observes, the fittest of all; for whilst the eye-witnesses and ministers of the word were executing their commission of "discipling all nations, by *preaching* the Gospel every where," they had scarcely *leisure* for *writing*. But when they were "*finishing* their course," in order to supply the place of their *oral* instructions, after their decease, *writing* became necessary. *This* induced Peter to write his Epistles to the Jewish converts, Paul his Epistles to the Hebrews, James and John their general Epistles, and likewise the Evangelists their Gospels. The marvellous difference of opinion as to the date of Matthew's Gospel, has been chiefly occasioned by the conflicting testimonies of *Irenæus*, as quoted by Eusebius v. 8., and of Eusebius himself, in his *Eccl. Hist.* iii. 24. and his *Chronicon*. Yet the discrepancy may be reconciled, by supposing that the time mentioned by Eusebius, namely the 3d year of the reign of Caligula (i. e. some time in A. D. 40.), is to be understood of the *Hebrew*, not the *Greek* Gospel. This, indeed, is plain from that writer's own words; where he says that, having spread the Gospel *by word of mouth*, the Evangelist, on leaving Judæa to go and preach Christianity to the Gentiles, left his countrymen his Gospel for their information, written πατρίῳ γλώττῃ, which last circumstance Mr. Horne, iv. 257. (or his authorities) omits to state, in noticing this passage. And as to what is said by *Irenæus*, cited by Euseb. Eccl. Hist. v. 8. as quoted in English by Mr. Horne, namely, that Matthew put forth a Gospel among the Hebrews, while Peter and Paul were preaching Christianity at Rome; there would seem to be no difficulty in supposing, as Mr. Horne *does*, in order to reconcile this discrepancy, that the words of Irenæus are to be understood of St. Matthew's *Greek* Gospel; and thereby, its date will pretty nearly be fixed. But then, in the *translation*, literal as it professes to be, which Mr. Horne (or the *authors* by him followed) gives of the passage, there is again (through inadvertence) a passing over of the important words τῇ ἰδίᾳ αὐτῶν διαλέκτῳ. Now this would seem to put an end to the *reconcilement* of the discrepancy between Irenæus and Eusebius, and oblige us to suppose that Irenæus was *misinformed*; which, considering his opportunities of gaining the necessary information, is by no means probable. It may rather be suspected that the words are *corrupt* (as, indeed, they have long

MT. LU.

5 ἐρήμῳ, καὶ κηρύσσων βάπτισμα μετανοίας εἰς ἄφεσιν ἁμαρτιῶν. Καὶ 3. 3.
ἐξεπορεύετο πρὸς αὐτὸν πᾶσα ἡ Ἰουδαία χώρα, καὶ οἱ Ἱεροσολυμῖται· 5

been acknowledged to be); and the best way, I would suggest, to emend them is simply by reading γραφῇ for γραφὴν, and for εὐαγγελίου, reading εὐαγγέλιον: point the passage thus: ὁ μὲν δὴ Ματθ. ἐν τοῖς Ἑβραίοις, τῇ ἰδίᾳ αὐτῶν διαλέκτῳ, καὶ γραφῇ, (in their own tongue, and in *writing*, as opposed to preaching,) ἐξήνεγκεν εὐαγγέλιον, τοῦ Πέτρου καὶ τοῦ Παύλου ἐν Ῥώμῃ εὐαγγελιζομένων, καὶ θεμελιούντων τὴν ἐκκλησίαν. These emendations are indispensable to make any tolerable sense, and are confirmed by the words of Eusebius, v. 24. in a passage *entirely founded* on this of Irenæus (of which see a citation in the Introduction to St. Matthew). But if we understand the words, as we must, of St. Matthew's *Hebrew* Gospel, we are compelled to assign to it a much later period than probability, or the words of Eusebius himself in his Chronicon will justify. For which reason I cannot help suspecting that there *yet* remains some corruption; for Peter was very little at *Rome*, and certainly not till A. D. 63, a short time before his martyrdom. Instead of Ῥώμῃ, the true reading, I apprehend, is ῥώμῃ, the words being often confounded. See my Note on Thucyd. ii. 81. The sense will then be, "with zeal and ardour." So in Eurip. Rhes. 64. χρῆσθαι τ' εὐτυχεῖ ῥώμῃ θεοῦ. Thus there will no longer be any discrepancy; for the labours of St. Peter and St. Paul in evangelizing and founding the Christian Church commenced (even in the case of St. *Paul*) as early as the year 40 or 41. Of course, the passage has no bearing, as it has been supposed, on the date of the publication of the *Greek* Gospel. Nor do I know of any passage that has, in any writer of sufficient antiquity to deserve credit. It was probably published about A. D. 60, a little before the Epistle of St. James, and meant for the same persons.

In conclusion, to advert to the *style* of the present Gospel, it is well adapted to the purpose of the writer, being plain, simple, and concise; though not wanting in energy. And however it may occasionally be deficient in the *linguæ proprietas* of exact composition, and contain many Hebraisms, and even Latinisms, yet its *authenticity* is thereby the more strongly confirmed; it being plainly the work of a Jew, chiefly conversant with the Syro-Chaldee, and who had learnt his Greek chiefly from the Septuagint and the Alexandrian writers. As to the *persons* for whom this Gospel was intended, the truth here, as often, will be found to lie *in medio*. It should seem to have been written chiefly, though not exclusively, for the Gentile converts, especially of the West.

V. 1. ἀρχὴ τοῦ εὐαγγελίου — Θεοῦ.] In this Gospel we encounter a difficulty at the very threshold; for the Commentators are by no means agreed on the *construction* of the first four verses, and consequently differ as to their sense. Some (as Euthym., Theophyl., Grot., and others) place a comma after Θεοῦ, and lay down the sense as follows: "The beginning of the Gospel of Jesus the Messiah, thus happened, as it was written in the prophet." But thus (as Fritz. remarks) the Article would be required at ἀρχὴ, a particle (γὰρ, or the like) at ἐγένετο, and οὕτως and a verb would have to be supplied. It is better with Le Clerc, Wets., Beza, Campb., Rosemn., and Kuin., to regard verse 1. as a separate sentence, forming a kind of *title* to the work. "It was not unusual (says Campb.) with authors to prefix a short sentence, to serve both as a title to the book, and to signify that the beginning immediately followed. So Hosea i. 1." In this view they quote the commencing sentence of the History of Herodotus, to which I have, in Recens. Synop., added the Proems of *Thucyd.*, *Procop.*, *Ocell.*, *Luc.*, *Timæus*, and some other writers. Thus the ὡς, which may be rendered *sicut*, refers to verse 4, as the *completion* of the prophecies mentioned. It is, however, not necessary (with Kuin. and others) to supply ἥδε ἐστι at ἀρχὴ, since (as Fritz. observes) the pronoun is never required in *a title*, because the very *situation* of the title prefixed to a book, shows it to *belong* to the book to which it is prefixed. For the same reason the *Article* is not wanted at ἀρχή. After all, however, there is something weak in the proofs supporting this mode of interpretation; for not one of the passages cited from the beginnings of the Historians above mentioned and Hosea are quite to the purpose. And as to the customs (to which Campb. appeals), of scribes placing *incipit* at the beginning, and *explicit* at the end of their transcripts, it is nothing to the purpose. I would therefore adopt the mode of taking the passage proposed by Erasm., Zeger, Markland, and Fritz. To this interpretation there is nothing to object on the score of *grammatical propriety*; and though this suspension of the sense is somewhat awkward, yet the style of the Evangelist is occasionally rough and harsh. The *sense* thus arising is excellent; for that from the preaching of John arose the commencement of the Gospel, is certain from Luke xvi. 16. See also Note on Luke ii. 2.

2. ἐν Ἡσαΐᾳ τ. πρ.] This is the reading of several of the best MSS., and all the most important of the ancient Versions, and it is preferred by some of the most eminent Commentators, and is edited by Griesb., Knapp, Tittm., and Scholz. the superior weight of MS. authority for the common reading ἐν τοῖς προφήταις being overbalanced by critical reasons. Yet even thus the passage may be considered as not quite emended. There is surely as great reason to think that Ἡσαΐᾳ came from the margin, as there is to suppose τοῖς προφήταις to have arisen *ex emendatione*. It is not found in some ancient MSS. and the Syr., Pers., Goth., Vulg., and Ital. Versions; and is cancelled by Fritz.; rightly, I think; for, as Dr. Mill remarked, there is every reason to think, that the original reading was ἐν τῷ προφήτῃ, from which the other two arose — namely, from those who took upon themselves to supply, in two different ways, what seemed to them a deficiency.

The first passage is taken from Malachi iii. 1., the second from Is. xl. 3. The neglect of the *formula citationis*, before the second passage, is agreeable to a not unfrequent custom of Jewish writers, on which Fritz. refers to Surenh. βιβλ καταλλ. p. 45.

— ἔμπροσθέν σου] These words are omitted in a few ancient MSS., some Versions, and Origen and Victor, and are cancelled by Griesb., Fritz., and Scholz., who suppose them to have been introduced from Matth. xi. 10. and Luke vii. 27. Fritz. sees no reason why they should have been cancelled, if they had been written by the Evan-

MT. LU.
3. 3. καὶ ἐβαπτίζοντο πάντες ἐν τῷ Ἰορδάνῃ ποταμῷ ὑπ' αὐτοῦ, ἐξομολογού-
4 μενοι τὰς ἁμαρτίας αὐτῶν. Ἦν δὲ Ἰωάννης ἐνδεδυμένος τρίχας καμή- 6
λου, καὶ ζώνην δερματίνην περὶ τὴν ὀσφὺν αὐτοῦ, καὶ ἐσθίων ἀκρίδας
11 16 καὶ μέλι ἄγριον. Καὶ ἐκήρυσσε λέγων· Ἔρχεται ὁ ἰσχυρότερός μου 7
ὀπίσω μου, οὗ οὐκ εἰμὶ ἱκανὸς κύψας λῦσαι τὸν ἱμάντα τῶν ὑποδημάτων αὐτοῦ. Ἐγὼ μὲν ἐβάπτισα ὑμᾶς ἐν ὕδατι, αὐτὸς δὲ βαπτίσει 8
ὑμᾶς ἐν Πνεύματι ἁγίῳ. Καὶ ἐγένετο ἐν ἐκείναις ταῖς ἡμέραις, ἦλθεν 9
13 Ἰησοῦς ἀπὸ Ναζαρὲτ τῆς Γαλιλαίας, καὶ ἐβαπτίσθη ὑπὸ Ἰωάννου εἰς
21 τὸν Ἰορδάνην. Καὶ εὐθέως ἀναβαίνων ἀπὸ τοῦ ὕδατος, εἶδε σχιζομέ- 10
22 νους τοὺς οὐρανούς, καὶ τὸ Πνεῦμα ‡ ὡσεὶ περιστερὰν καταβαῖνον ἐπ'
17 αὐτόν· καὶ φωνὴ ἐγένετο ἐκ τῶν οὐρανῶν· Σὺ εἶ ὁ Υἱός μου 11
4. 4. ὁ ἀγαπητός, ἐν ‡ ᾧ εὐδόκησα. Καὶ εὐθὺς τὸ Πνεῦμα αὐτὸν 12
1 1 ἐκβάλλει εἰς τὴν ἔρημον. Καὶ ἦν ἐκεῖ ἐν τῇ ἐρήμῳ ἡμέρας τεσσαρά- 13
2 2 κοντα, πειραζόμενος ὑπὸ τοῦ Σατανᾶ, καὶ ἦν μετὰ τῶν θηρίων· καὶ
11 οἱ ἄγγελοι διηκόνουν αὐτῷ.

gelist. But as the number of MSS. in which they are omitted is very small, we may suppose them to have been omitted *propter homœoteleuton.* [*Comp.* John i. 15, 23]

5. καὶ οἱ Ἰ.] The καὶ is not a mere *copula*, but the sense is, as Fritz. remarks, "and (what is remarkable)." Griesbach's alteration ἐξεπορεύετο is alike unnecessary, and devoid of authority; and the changing the place of πάντες, and putting it after Ἱεροσ., is even less defensible. That position is only found in *six* MSS. and some *Versions;* which, however, are no great authority on points which respect the *order* of words. Besides, the reading in question would be (as Fritz. has shown) inadmissible, from its yielding a sense not at all satisfactory. The meaning is, that *very many* (of them) were baptized, &c. So Matth. x. 22. ἔσεσθε μισούμενοι ὑπὸ πάντων.

7. οὐκ εἰμὶ ἱκανὸς] Literally, "I am unfit."

— κύψας.] This expresses the *posture* in which the action was done. And, indeed, as the sandals were fastened to the foot by very complicated straps, they could not be loosed without some trouble. This was therefore esteemed a menial office, and was usually committed to slaves. John i. 27. has λῦσαι — τοῦ ὑποδήματος.

8. [*Comp.* Acts i. 5. ii. 4. xi. 16. xix. 4.]

9. καὶ ἐγένετο — ἦλθεν] A construction frequent in the Gospels, and derived from the Hebrew. See Genes. xiv. 1. & 2. Most Commentators supply ὅτι. But it is justly observed by Fritz., that the construction may be considered as *bimembris;* wherein the first member is *explained* by the second; which is added *per asyndeton*, and may, in translation, be introduced by *nempe*. The more usual form of the idiom is when the ἐγένετο is followed by a καί.

— ἐν ἐκείναις ταῖς ἡμέραις.] Namely, when John was preaching in the desert the baptism of repentance. Τῆς Γαλιλαίας is added to Nazareth, to determine its situation, since it was an obscure place. Εἰς is *not* here for ἐν, as most Commentators imagine, who adduce examples which are quite inapposite. The sense of ἐβαπτ. εἰς is, "*was dipped*," or *plunged into*. Or we may suppose, that, as in the phrase λούεσθαι εἰς βαλανεῖον, there is a *significatio prægnans*, for "to be washed (by being plunged) into a bath;" so the sense here may be, "He underwent the rite of baptism (by being plunged) into the water." [*Comp.* John i. 32.]

10. εὐθέως] Lightf. and Wets. remarks on the very frequent, and sometimes unnecessary, use of εὐθέως and εὐθὺς by Mark. But, as Fritz observes, they are never used unnecessarily; though they may seem to be so, by being construed with the wrong word; for they are often, as here, put *per hyperbaton*. Thus here εὐθέως must be construed with εἶδε, which must, with the best Commentators, be referred to *Jesus*, not *John*, with others.

— σχιζομένους] Elsn. and Wets. adduce numerous passages in which mention is made of the heavens being *cleaved* with *lightning*. But it is truly remarked by Fritz, that they are all dissimilar; for (to use his own words) "hic cœlum dehiscit, ut divinus spiritus, relicto domicilio, ad Jesum desuper possit allabi." So Matth. iii. 16. ἀνεῴχθησαν οἱ οὐρανοί.

— ὡσεὶ] Many MSS., and indeed most of the ancient ones, have ὡς, which is edited by Griesb., Fritz., and Scholz, who think that the common reading was derived from the other Gospels. There is not, however, sufficient authority to warrant any change. The expression does not define the *form of appearance* (though it was, as we learn from Luke iii. 22., in a *bodily form*), but the *manner of its descent*, namely, like the *rapid gliding* of a dove.

11. ἐν ᾧ] Several antient MSS., and almost all the Versions have ἐν σοὶ, which is confirmed by Luke iii. 22., and is edited by Griesb. and Fritz. This *may* be the true reading; but there is not sufficient authority to warrant any change, especially since *internal* evidence is, I apprehend, against σοί. For ᾧ was more likely to be changed into the more *definite* σοὶ than the contrary. [*Comp.* infr. ix. 7. Ps. ii. 7. Is. xlii. 1. Matt. iii. 17. xvii. 5. 2 Pet. i. 17.]

12. ἐκβάλλει.] This is not well rendered by Grot. and others, "discedere jubet," or "emisit sine vi." For the word must here be taken of the strong and efficacious (though not overpowering) influence of the Holy Ghost.

13. καὶ ἦν μετὰ τῶν θηρίων.] These words describe the *scene* of the temptation, which was one of the

MT. LU.

14 Μετὰ δὲ τὸ παραδοθῆναι τὸν Ἰωάννην, ἦλθεν ὁ Ἰησοῦς εἰς τὴν 4. 4.
15 Γαλιλαίαν, κηρύσσων τὸ εὐαγγέλιον τῆς βασιλείας τοῦ Θεοῦ, καὶ λέ- 12
γων· Ὅτι πεπλήρωται ὁ καιρὸς, καὶ ἤγγικεν ἡ βασιλεία τοῦ Θεοῦ·
μετανοεῖτε, καὶ πιστεύετε ἐν τῷ εὐαγγελίῳ. 17
16 Περιπατῶν δὲ παρὰ τὴν θάλασσαν τῆς Γαλιλαίας, εἶδε Σίμωνα καὶ 18
Ἀνδρέαν τὸν ἀδελφὸν αὐτοῦ ‡ βάλλοντας ἀμφίβληστρον ἐν τῇ θαλάσσῃ·
17 ἦσαν γὰρ ἁλιεῖς. Καὶ εἶπεν αὐτοῖς ὁ Ἰησους· Δεῦτε ὀπίσω μοῦ, 19
18 καὶ ποιήσω ὑμᾶς γενέσθαι ἁλιεῖς ἀνθρώπων. Καὶ εὐθέως ἀφέντες 20
19 τὰ δίκτυα αὐτῶν, ἠκολούθησαν αὐτῷ. Καὶ προβὰς ἐκεῖθεν ὀλίγον, 21
εἶδε Ἰάκωβον τὸν τοῦ Ζεβεδαίου, καὶ Ἰωάννην τὸν ἀδελφὸν αὐτοῦ,
20 καὶ αὐτοὺς ἐν τῷ πλοίῳ καταρτίζοντας τὰ δίκτυα. Καὶ εὐθέως ἐκά- 22
λεσεν αὐτούς· καὶ ἀφέντες τὸν πατέρα αὐτῶν Ζεβεδαῖον ἐν τῷ πλοίῳ
μετὰ τῶν μισθωτῶν, ἀπῆλθον ὀπίσω αὐτοῦ. 7.
21 Καὶ εἰσπορεύονται εἰς Καπερναούμ· καὶ εὐθέως τοῖς σάββασιν 31
22 εἰσελθὼν εἰς τὴν συναγωγὴν ἐδίδασκε. Καὶ ἐξεπλήσσοντο ἐπὶ τῇ δι- 29 32
δαχῇ αὐτοῦ· ἦν γὰρ διδάσκων αὐτοὺς ὡς ἐξουσίαν ἔχων, καὶ οὐχ ὡς
23 οἱ γραμματεῖς. Καὶ ἦν ἐν τῇ συναγωγῇ αὐτῶν ἄνθρωπος ἐν πνεύ- 33
24 ματι ἀκαθάρτῳ, καὶ ἀνέκραξε, λέγων· Ἔα, τί ἡμῖν καὶ σοὶ, Ἰησοῦ 34
Ναζαρηνέ; ἦλθες ἀπολέσαι ἡμᾶς; οἶδά σε τίς εἶ, ὁ ἅγιος τοῦ

wildest parts of the desert; like that in Virg. Æn. iii. 646. (cited by Wets.) Quam vitam in silvis *inter deserta ferarum Lustra* domosque traho.

14. [*Comp.* John iv. 43.]

15. πεπλήρωται] "adest, מלא." Time is said πληροῦσθαι, partly when it is *gone*, partly when any definite period *approaches*. So John vii. 8. Luke xxi. 24. Wets. compares Joseph. Ant. vi. 4. 1. ἐξεδέχετο τὸν καιρὸν γενέσθαι· πληρωθέντος δὲ αὐτοῦ κ.τ.λ. Acts vii. 23, 30. "The time here spoken of (says Campb.) is that which, according to the predictions of the Prophets, was to intervene between their days, or between any period assigned by them, and the appearance of the Messiah. This had been revealed to Daniel, as consisting of what, in prophetic language, is denominated seventy weeks, that is (every week being seven years), 490 years; reckoning from the order issued to rebuild the Temple at Jerusalem. However much the Jews misunderstood many of the *other* prophecies relating to the reign of this extraordinary personage, what concerned both the time and the place of his first appearance seems to have been pretty well apprehended by the bulk of the nation. From the N. T., as well as from the other accounts of that period still extant, it is evident that an expectation of this great deliverer was then general among them."

— μετανοεῖτε.] See Note on Matt. iii. 2. Πιστεύετε ἐν τῷ εὐαγγελίῳ. The distinction made by some Commentators between πιστεύειν ἐν τῷ εὐαγγ. and πιστ. τῷ εὐαγγ. is unfounded. The only difference is, that the former is the Hellenistic, the latter the Classical form. The sense here is, "be brought to a true faith in the Gospel."

16. βάλλοντας] Most of the antient MSS. have ἀμφιβάλλοντας, which is edited by Griesb., Fritz., and Scholz. But as no example has been adduced of the compound in this phrase (where the ἀμφι is rendered by Fritz. *huc illuc*), there seems no sufficient authority to alter the common reading; and probably the ἀμφι originated in a mere error of the scribes, from the word following.

19. καταρτίζοντας] Καταρτίζειν signifies, 1. to restore to its former state what has been disarranged or broken: 2. to repair; and it is used of ships, nets, walls, &c. &c. Καὶ αὐτούς. This expression is (as Fritz. thinks) used, because James and John were employed on the same *kind* of business; namely, what was connected with fishing.

21. τοῖς σάββασιν] This clause, as some imagine, alludes to our Lord's custom of attending the Synagogue every Sabbath day. But it should rather, with some ancient and most modern Commentators, be taken of one particular Sabbath, *the next Sabbath*, as is plain from the εὐθέως, and what follows. On this use of τὰ σάββατα (which Fritz. thinks originated from the Chaldee singular form in emphasis שבתא), see Schleus. Lex.

22. ὡς ἐξουσίαν ἔχων] See Note on Matt. vii. 28.

23. ἐν πνεύματι ἀκαθάρτῳ] Some take the ἐν for σὺν; but for this there is no sufficient authority. Others, more properly, render, "in the power of an unclean spirit," or, "occupied by an unclean spirit," "having an unclean spirit," as Luke says. The man must have had lucid intervals, or he would not have been admitted to the Synagogue. His disorder seems to have been epilepsy brought on by Dæmoniacal agency.

24. ἔα] An interjection derived from the Imperative of ἐᾷν, and signifying, *let us alone!* It expresses indignation, or extreme surprise. Τί ἡμῖν καὶ σοὶ, scil. κοινὸν, which is sometimes *supplied* in the Classical writers. [*Comp.* Matt. 8, 29.]

— ἦλθες ἀπολέσαι ἡμᾶς] The Commentators are not agreed whether this clause should be taken interrogatively, or declaratively. The recent Editors mostly prefer the latter mode. But there is more point and spirit, and perhaps more propriety, in the former. By ἀπολέσαι is *not* meant (as most of the Commentators imagine) βασανίσαι,

MT. LU
8. 4. Θεοῦ. Καὶ ἐπετίμησεν αὐτῷ ὁ Ἰησοῦς, λέγων· Φιμώθητι, καὶ ἔξελθε 25
35 ἐξ αὐτοῦ. Καὶ σπαράξαν αὐτὸν τὸ πνεῦμα τὸ ἀκάθαρτον, καὶ κράξαν 26
36 φωνῇ μεγάλῃ, ἐξῆλθεν ἐξ αὐτοῦ. Καὶ ἐθαμβήθησαν πάντες, ὥστε 27
συζητεῖν πρὸς αὐτοὺς, λέγοντες· Τί ἐστι τοῦτο; τίς ἡ διδαχὴ ἡ
καινὴ αὕτη; ὅτι κατ᾽ ἐξουσίαν καὶ τοῖς πνεύμασι τοῖς ἀκαθάρτοις
37 ἐπιτάσσει, καὶ ὑπακούουσιν αὐτῷ! Ἐξῆλθε δὲ ἡ ἀκοὴ αὐτοῦ εὐθὺς 28
εἰς ὅλην τὴν περίχωρον τῆς Γαλιλαίας.

14 38 Καὶ εὐθέως ἐκ τῆς συναγωγῆς ἐξελθόντες, ἦλθον εἰς τὴν οἰκίαν 29
Σίμωνος καὶ Ἀνδρέου, μετὰ Ἰακώβου καὶ Ἰωάννου. Ἡ δὲ πενθερὰ 30
Σίμωνος κατέκειτο πυρέσσουσα· καὶ εὐθέως λέγουσιν αὐτῷ περὶ
39 αὐτῆς. Καὶ προσελθὼν ἤγειρεν αὐτὴν, κρατήσας τῆς χειρὸς αὐτῆς· 31
15 καὶ ἀφῆκεν αὐτὴν ὁ πυρετὸς εὐθέως, καὶ διηκόνει αὐτοῖς. Ὀψίας δὲ 32
16 40 γενομένης, ὅτε ἔδυ ὁ ἥλιος, ἔφερον πρὸς αὐτὸν πάντας τοὺς κακῶς
ἔχοντας, καὶ τοὺς δαιμονιζομένους· καὶ ἡ πόλις ὅλη ἐπισυνηγμένη ἦν 33
πρὸς τὴν θύραν. Καὶ ἐθεράπευσε πολλοὺς κακῶς ἔχοντας ποικίλαις 34
41 νόσοις, καὶ δαιμόνια πολλὰ ἐξέβαλε· καὶ οὐκ ἤφιε λαλεῖν τὰ δαιμόνια,
ὅτι ᾔδεισαν αὐτόν.

42 Καὶ πρωῒ, ἔννυχον λίαν, ἀναστὰς ἐξῆλθε, καὶ ἀπῆλθεν εἰς ἔρημον 35
τόπον, κἀκεῖ προσηύχετο. Καὶ κατεδίωξαν αὐτὸν ὁ Σίμων καὶ οἱ 36
μετ᾽ αὐτοῦ. καὶ εὑρόντες αὐτὸν, λέγουσιν αὐτῷ· Ὅτι πάντες ζητοῦσί- 37

the term used by Matthew; but rather, as Euthym. explains (in a popular sense), "to destroy our power," by expelling us from earth; so *βασανίσαι* expresses the *final* end of them, namely, being consigned to hell torments. By *ἡμᾶς*, is evidently meant his *colleagues*. Ὁ ἅγιος τοῦ Θεοῦ signifies, by the force of the Article, the *Messiah*, as being such *κατ' ἐξοχήν*.

26. *σπαράξαν*] Σπαράσσειν properly signifies *to tear, to lacerate*; but here and in Luke xix. 39., it signifies *to bring on violent convulsions* and *spasms*, such as accompany epilepsy, and which are sometimes called *σπαραγμοὶ*, though usually *σπασμοὶ* by the Greek Medical writers.

27. *πρὸς αὐτοὺς*] for *πρὸς ἀλλήλους*, *inter se*.

— *τί ἐστι — αὕτη*] Chrys. and Euthym., of the ancients, and Maldon. and Fritz., of the moderns, have alone seen the true scope of this clause; which expresses not so much *interrogation* as *admiration*. The whole may be rendered thus: "What is this? of what sort is this *new* (i. e. extraordinary) mode of teaching? for [the teacher] gives his order authoritatively to the unclean spirits, and they obey him'" Of this sense of *νέος*, examples are found in Acts xvii. 19. and Thucyd. v. 50. Κατ' ἐξουσίαν imports self-derived and independent authority, supposed to be opposed to that of the Jewish *exorcists*.

28. *τὴν περίχωρον τῆς Γ.*] The Commentators are not agreed whether this denotes "the country round about Galilee," or, "the *region of Galilee*." If the former method be adopted, the sense must be, as Beza represents it, "not only throughout Galilee itself, but the circumjacent regions." But this is at variance with the parallel passage of Luke iv. 37. *εἰς πάντα τόπον τοῦ περιχώρου*, and it would require *καὶ τὴν περίχ.* Thus the latter interpretation is preferable: Render "the surrounding country of Galilee." This signification is often found in the Sept., and also the N. T., as Matt. xiv. 35. *ἀπέστειλαν εἰς ὅλην τὴν περίχωρον ἐκείνην*. See also Mark vi. 55. Luke iii. 3. & iv. 37.

30. *κατέκειτο*] Κατακεῖσθαι, like the Latin *jacere*, is a term appropriate to one who is *confined* by sickness. Ἤγειρεν κρατήσας τ. χ. must be considered in the same light as the *ἥψατο τῆς χειρὸς αὐτῆς*, namely, as an instance of Christ accompanying his words (Be thou healed, or the like) by a *corresponding action*; either simply touching the hand, or raising the person from his couch, as symbolical of recovery. Insomuch that *ἐγείρω* sometimes denotes *to heal*. In Matth. viii. 15. *καὶ ἠγέρθη*, there is a *signif. prægnans*; the sense being, "she rose up well."

32. *ὅτε ἔδυ ὁ ἥλιος*] They waited till that time (which was the end of the Sabbath) before they would bring their sick: since even to seek medical assistance, in the *day*, unless in extreme danger, was thought a breach of the Sabbath.

34. *πολλοὺς*] Matth. says, *πάντας*. But the one term is not inconsistent with the other. Jesus healed *many*, even *all* who were brought to him. [*Comp.* Acts xvi. 17, 18.]

— *οὐκ ἤφιε — αὐτόν*] scil. *τὸν Χριστὸν εἶναι*, as is *expressed* in many MSS. and in Luke iv. 41. The sense is, "He would not suffer them to speak, because they knew, and would address him as Messiah;" a title to which our Lord as yet made no public claim, lest he should excite tumult among the people. Ἤφιε is a form of later Grecism for *ἠφίει*.

36. *κατεδίωξαν*] This word not only signifies *persequi*, but *insequi*. See Hos. ii. 7. It here implies the *ardent desire* which Simon had of finding and accompanying his Master.

— *ζητοῦσί σε*] The Ed. Pr. and very many MSS. have *σε ζητοῦσι*, which was edited by Griesb.,

MT. LU.

38 σε. *Καὶ λέγει αὐτοῖς· Ἄγωμεν εἰς τὰς ἐχομένας κωμοπόλεις, ἵνα καὶ* 8. 4.
39 *ἐκεῖ κηρύξω· εἰς τοῦτο γὰρ ἐξελήλυθα. Καὶ ἦν κηρύσσων ἐν ταῖς* 43 44
συναγωγαῖς αὐτῶν εἰς ὅλην τὴν Γαλιλαίαν, καὶ τὰ δαιμόνια ἐκβάλλων. 5.
40 *Καὶ ἔρχεται πρὸς αὐτὸν λεπρός, παρακαλῶν αὐτὸν καὶ γονυπετῶν* 2 12
41 *αὐτόν, καὶ λέγων αὐτῷ· Ὅτι, ἐὰν θέλῃς, δύνασαί με καθαρίσαι. Ὁ* 3 13
δὲ Ἰησοῦς σπλαγχνισθεὶς, ἐκτείνας τὴν χεῖρα, ἥψατο αὐτοῦ, καὶ λέγει
42 *αὐτῷ· Θέλω, καθαρίσθητι! Καὶ εἰπόντος αὐτοῦ, εὐθέως ἀπῆλθεν*
43 *ἀπ᾽ αὐτοῦ ἡ λέπρα, καὶ ἐκαθαρίσθη. Καὶ ἐμβριμησάμενος αὐτῷ,*
44 *εὐθέως ἐξέβαλεν αὐτόν, καὶ λέγει αὐτῷ· Ὅρα μηδενὶ μηδὲν εἴπῃς·* 4 14
ἀλλ᾽ ὕπαγε, σεαυτὸν δεῖξον τῷ ἱερεῖ, καὶ προσένεγκε περὶ τοῦ καθα-
45 *ρισμοῦ σου ἃ προσέταξε Μωϋσῆς, εἰς μαρτύριον αὐτοῖς. Ὁ δὲ ἐξελθὼν,* 15
ἤρξατο κηρύσσειν πολλὰ καὶ διαφημίζειν τὸν λόγον, ὥστε μηκέτι αὐτὸν
δύνασθαι φανερῶς εἰς πόλιν εἰσελθεῖν· ἀλλ᾽ ἔξω ἐν ἐρήμοις τόποις
ἦν, καὶ ἤρχοντο πρὸς αὐτὸν πανταχόθεν.
1 II. *Καὶ * εἰσῆλθε πάλιν εἰς Καπερναοὺμ δι᾽ ἡμερῶν· καὶ ἠκούσθη*
2 *ὅτι εἰς οἶκόν ἐστι. Καὶ εὐθέως συνήχθησαν πολλοὶ, ὥστε μηκέτι* 9.
3 *χωρεῖν μηδὲ τὰ πρὸς τὴν θύραν· καὶ ἐλάλει αὐτοῖς τὸν λόγον. Καὶ* 2 18
ἔρχονται πρὸς αὐτὸν παραλυτικὸν φέροντες αἰρόμενον ὑπὸ τεσσάρων.
4 *Καὶ μὴ δυνάμενοι προσεγγίσαι αὐτῷ, διὰ τὸν ὄχλον, ἀπεστέγασαν τὴν* 19

Matth., Fritz., and Scholz. But there seems no sufficient reason for change. *External* evidence is greatly in favour of the received reading; and internal scarcely less so: for it should seem that the ancient Critics changed the position, in order that the sentence might have a better termination. It is far less likely (considering the *sigmatism* which prevails in even the best writers) that they should have made the alteration for *the sake of euphony*.

38. *τὰς ἐχομένας*] "neighbouring." This signification of the word thus arises. Ἔχεσθαί τινος signifies properly to *hold oneself* by any thing; then, *to adhere to* it; *keep close* to it; to *be close to it, be near it, be neighbouring*.

— *κωμοπόλεις*] is a rare word, and occurs elsewhere only in Strabo, Ptolemy, J. Malela, and Isidore; and signifies a place between a city and a village, i. e. a country town, such as Joseph. Bell. i. 3, 2. says there were many in Galilee. These were mostly, though not always, unwalled, and may be supposed, like those cities of the early ages described by Thucyd. i. 5., as being *κατὰ κώμας οἰκουμένας*.

For *κἀκεῖ* I have edited *καὶ ἐκεῖ*, with Griesb., Fritz., and Scholz, from very many MSS. and many early editions: not merely, however, on account of MS. authority, but because the *καὶ* is *emphatical*; and wherever it is so, no crasis can be admitted. Ἐξελήλυθα is a stronger term than ἐλήλυθα, and signifies, "I am come forth (as a teacher)."

39. *ἐν ταῖς συν.*] Griesb., Knapp., Tittm., Vat., and Scholz, edit *εἰς τὰς συναγωγὰς*, from a few MSS., as being the more *difficult* reading. But the Critical canon preferring such, has its exceptions; one of which is when (as here) it introduces what is contra linguæ consuetudinem. For the use of *εἰς* for *ἐν* will not here apply. There is little doubt but that the *εἰς* was a mere error of the scribes (arising from the *εἰς* just after); which would afterwards cause the noun to be accommodated to it in case. Fritz. sees this matter in the true light, and has restored the common reading, which, indeed, the ancient Versions all support.

43. *ἐμβριμησάμενος*] "having given him a strict charge." See on Matt. ix. 30. Ἐξέβαλεν α. for ἀπέλυσε, despatched him quickly.

44. See Levit. xiv. 2.

45. *κηρ. π. καὶ διαφ.*] Here the latter term *διαφ.* (which occurs in the Classics) is intended to strengthen the former. The sense is, "to publicly proclaim and divulge the thing." Λόγον is used as at Matt. iv. 8, and elsewhere in Hebraism, since דבר is so employed.

II. 1. *δι᾽ ἡμερῶν.*] Euthym. and Theoph. rightly take this for *διελθουσῶν ἡμερῶν τινῶν*, "after some days had intervened." This sense of *διὰ* (mostly in *composition)* occurs both in the N. T. and the Sept., and in the best Classical writers. For *πάλιν εἰσῆλθεν* we have *εἰσῆλθε πάλιν* in many MSS., with the Syr. and other ancient Versions, some Fathers, and the Edit. Princ. It is rightly edited by Matth., Fritz., and Scholz.

— *εἰς οἶκον*] *domi*, at home, namely, in the house in which he sojourned. This is regarded as an example of the use of *εἰς* for *ἐν*. But there seems to be rather a blending of two forms of expression, namely, "He has gone *to* his house and is *in* it."

2. *ὥστε μηκέτι χωρεῖν, &c.*] Τὰ πρὸς θύραν for τὸ πρόθυρον, the vestibule. The sense of the passage is, "So that there was no longer place for them in the vestibule [much less the house itself]."

— *τὸν λόγον.*] Used *κατ᾽ ἐξοχὴν* for *τὸν λόγον τοῦ Θεοῦ*, or *τῆς βασιλείας*, the doctrine of the Gospel.

3. *αἰρόμενον ὑπὸ τεσσ.*] "carried by four persons;" namely, on a litter." Φέροντες, bringing. The construction is, *καὶ ἔρχ.* (scil. *ἄνθρωποι φέροντες πρὸς αὐτόν*; namely, to be healed) *παραλυτικὸν αἰρόμενον ὑπὸ τ.*; namely, as we learn from Matt. and Luke, on a litter carried by them.

MT. LU.
9. 5. στέγην ὅπου ἦν· καὶ ἐξορύξαντες χαλῶσι τὸν κράββατον, ἐφ᾽ ᾧ ὁ πα-
20 ραλυτικὸς κατέκειτο. Ἰδὼν δὲ ὁ Ἰησοῦς τὴν πίστιν αὐτῶν, λέγει τῷ 5
2 21 παραλυτικῷ· Τέκνον, ἀφέωνταί σοι αἱ ἁμαρτίαι σου. Ἦσαν δέ τινες 6
τῶν Γραμματέων ἐκεῖ καθήμενοι, καὶ διαλογιζόμενοι ἐν ταῖς καρδίαις
αὐτῶν· Τί οὗτος οὕτω λαλεῖ βλασφημίας; τίς δύναται ἀφιέναι 7
4 22 ἁμαρτίας, εἰ μὴ εἷς ὁ Θεός; Καὶ εὐθέως ἐπιγνοὺς ὁ Ἰησοῦς τῷ 8
πνεύματι αὐτοῦ, ὅτι οὕτως αὐτοὶ διαλογίζονται ἐν ἑαυτοῖς, εἶπεν αὐτοῖς·
5 23 τί ταῦτα διαλογίζεσθε ἐν ταῖς καρδίαις ὑμῶν; Τί ἐστιν εὐκοπώτερον, 9
εἰπεῖν τῷ παραλυτικῷ· Ἀφέωνταί * σου αἱ ἁμαρτίαι, ἢ εἰπεῖν·
6 24 * Ἔγειρε [καὶ] ἆρόν σου τὸν κράββατον, καὶ περιπάτει; Ἵνα δὲ 10
εἰδῆτε, ὅτι ἐξουσίαν ἔχει ὁ Υἱὸς τοῦ ἀνθρώπου * ἐπὶ τῆς γῆς ἀφιέναι

4. *ἀπεστέγασαν τὴν στέγην*, &c.] In the interpretation of this passage there are some difficulties; which have appeared to many Commentators so formidable, that they have endeavoured to remove them by resorting to various methods, almost all of them (as I have shown in Recens. Synop.) at variance with the meaning of the terms *ἀπεστέγασαν*, *στέγην*, and *ἐξορύξαντες*. The interpretation of Lightf., Whitby, Kuin., and Winer is the *least* liable to objection; which supposes that the bearers brought the paralytic to the flat roof of the house by the stairs on the outside, or along the top from an adjoining house; and then forced open the trap-door which led downwards, to the *ὑπερῷον*. But that *forcing open the trap-door* has nothing to countenance it; nay, (as Fritz. remarks,) the words *ἀπεστέγασαν τὴν στέγην ὅπου ἦν* can only mean that the *bearers tore off the tiles in the very place under which they knew Jesus to be.* We may suppose that, not able to approach Jesus in the room where he was, (probably an upper room,) they ascended to the flat roof by the outer stairs, and having uncovered the roofing, (whether tiles or thatching), and dug through the lath and plaster, *about the place where they understood Jesus to be*, they let the couch down through the orifice. No *other* method could have effectually attained the *object;* namely, of bringing the litter to Jesus without having to pass through the crowd.

Ἐξορ. has here a *significatio prægnans*, i. e. *digging through* and *scooping out.*

—*χαλῶσι*] "let, or lower [down]." So Acts ix. 25. *χαλάσαντες αὐτὸν ἐν σπυρίδι.* and xxvii. 17. 2 Cor. xi. 33. Jerem. xxxviii. 6. The word does not in this sense occur in the best Classical writers.

5. *σοί.*] Griesb., Tittm., and Fritz. edit *σοῦ*, omitting the *σοῦ* following, from some MSS., confirmed as they think, by ver. 9. But those MSS. are too few to have much weight; and ver. 9. can have *none;* for supposing *σοῦ* there to *be* the true reading, yet what is so likely as that when a formula, such as *ἀφέωνταί σοι αἱ ἁμαρτίαι σου*, is not employed directly, but put hypothetically, that it should be *shortened.*

6. *οὕτω.*] This is omitted in some MSS., and is cancelled by Fritz. But it must be retained, as being very significant. The sense is, "Why, or how, does that man [dare to] so speak blasphemies!"

7. *εἰ μὴ εἷς ὁ Θεός.*] Some point *εἰ μὴ εἷς, ὁ Θεός*, in the sense, "but one — that is God." And they adduce as examples Matt. xix. 17, and Mark x. 18. But in *those* passages the common punctuation and interpretation adopted in *this* passage, by which *εἷς* is taken in the sense *only* (answering to the use of the Heb. אחד in Exod. xxxiii. 5. Judg. xxi.) is even more required than in the present; and in all of these it is confirmed by the ancient Versions. Besides, it is here required by the parallel passage of Luke. [*Comp.* Job xiv. 4. Isa. xliii. 25.]

8. *τῷ πνεύματι αὐτοῦ.*] Some ancient and early modern Commentators take this to designate Christ's divine nature, which consequently imparted omniscience. Others interpret it, "by the Spirit," i. e. the Holy Spirit, which, as man, our Lord had received. But of these two interpretations the former is destitute of proof; and the latter is negatived by the *αὐτοῦ* added. *Preferable* is a third, supported by the most recent Commentators, as Rosenm., Kuin., and Fritz., "in his mind," i. e. in *himself.* This, however, seems a curtailment of the sense, which, I think, is, "by his own spirit." Thus *spirit* will be used emphatically, for the spirit of wisdom, or understanding; and the *αὐτοῦ* is very significant, since, (as Campb. remarks) "the intention of the sacred writer was to signify, that our Lord, in this case, did not, as others do, derive his knowledge from the ordinary and outward methods of discovery which are open to all men, but from peculiar powers he possessed independently of every thing external." See John ii. 25.

—*αὐτοί.*] This word (as also the reading *σοῦ* for *σοί* just after) is found in a great majority of the MSS., several Versions, Theophyl., and the Edit. Princ. It has been admitted by Wets., Matth., Griesb., Vat., Fritz., and Scholz.

9. *ἔγειρε.*] So Matth., Griesb., Tittm., Vat., Fritz., and Scholz, edit. with several of the best MSS. and some early Editions, for *ἔγειραι.* which is a very irregular form, and, Fritz. thinks, cannot be defended. Yet it *may* have been *a popular* form, like some others used by Mark; and the reading is, in all the passages to which they appeal, doubtful. The *καὶ* following is omitted in several of the best MSS. and some Versions, and is cancelled by almost all Editors from Griesb. to Scholz; but on scarcely sufficient evidence.

10. *ἐπὶ τῆς γῆς ἀφιέναι.*] This position, instead of the common one *ἀφ. ἐπὶ τῆς γῆς* is found in a very great number of MSS. and Versions, and is adopted by Matth., Griesb., Tittm., Vat., Fritz., and Scholz.

12. *ἐναντίον*] "coram." This is not a mere Hebraism, but is a use found in the Classical writers. At *οὕτως* Heupel would supply *τι* and *γενόμενον.* Fritz. maintains that it signifies *hoc modo*, equivalent to *ut hæc res est.*

MT. LU.

11 ἁμαρτίας·—λέγει τῷ παραλυτικῷ· Σοὶ λέγω, ἔγειρε [καὶ] ἆρον τὸν 9. 5.
12 κράββατόν σου, καὶ ὕπαγε εἰς τὸν οἶκόν σου. Καὶ ἠγέρθη εὐθέως, 7 25
καὶ ἄρας τὸν κράββατον, ἐξῆλθεν ἐναντίον πάντων· ὥστε ἐξίστασθαι 8 26
πάντας, καὶ δοξάζειν τὸν Θεὸν λέγοντας· Ὅτι οὐδέποτε οὕτως εἴδομεν.
13 Καὶ ἐξῆλθε πάλιν παρὰ τὴν θάλασσαν· καὶ πᾶς ὁ ὄχλος ἤρχετο
14 πρὸς αὐτὸν, καὶ ἐδίδασκεν αὐτούς. Καὶ παράγων εἶδε Λευῒν τὸν τοῦ 9 27
Ἀλφαίου καθήμενον ἐπὶ τὸ τελώνιον, καὶ λέγει αὐτῷ· Ἀκολούθει μοι. 28
15 Καὶ ἀναστὰς ἠκολούθησεν αὐτῷ. Καὶ ἐγένετο ἐν τῷ κατακεῖσθαι 10 29
αὐτὸν ἐν τῇ οἰκίᾳ αὐτοῦ, καὶ πολλοὶ τελῶναι καὶ ἁμαρτωλοὶ συνανέ-
κειντο τῷ Ἰησοῦ καὶ τοῖς μαθηταῖς αὐτοῦ· ἦσαν γὰρ πολλοὶ, καὶ
16 ἠκολούθησαν αὐτῷ. Καὶ οἱ Γραμματεῖς καὶ οἱ Φαρισαῖοι, ἰδόντες 11 30
αὐτὸν ἐσθίοντα μετὰ τῶν τελωνῶν καὶ ἁμαρτωλῶν, ἔλεγον τοῖς μαθηταῖς αὐτοῦ· Τί ὅτι μετὰ τῶν τελωνῶν καὶ ἁμαρτωλῶν ἐσθίει καὶ
17 πίνει; Καὶ ἀκούσας ὁ Ἰησοῦς λέγει αὐτοῖς· Οὐ χρείαν ἔχουσιν οἱ 12 31
ἰσχύοντες ἰατροῦ, ἀλλ᾽ οἱ κακῶς ἔχοντες. οὐκ ἦλθον καλέσαι δικαίους, 13 32
18 ἀλλὰ ἁμαρτωλοὺς [εἰς μετάνοιαν.] Καὶ ἦσαν οἱ μαθηταὶ Ἰωάννου 14
καὶ οἱ τῶν Φαρισαίων νηστεύοντες· καὶ ἔρχονται καὶ λέγουσιν αὐτῷ·
Διατί οἱ μαθηταὶ Ἰωάννου καὶ οἱ τῶν Φαρισαίων νηστεύουσιν, οἱ δὲ 33
19 σοὶ μαθηταὶ οὐ νηστεύουσι; Καὶ εἶπεν αὐτοῖς ὁ Ἰησοῦς· Μὴ δύ- 15 34
νανται οἱ υἱοὶ τοῦ νυμφῶνος, ἐν ᾧ ὁ νυμφίος μετ᾽ αὐτῶν ἐστι,
νηστεύειν; ὅσον χρόνον μεθ᾽ ἑαυτῶν ἔχουσι τὸν νυμφίον οὐ δύνανται
20 νηστεύειν. Ἐλεύσονται δὲ ἡμέραι ὅταν ἀπαρθῇ ἀπ᾽ αὐτῶν ὁ νυμφίος· 35
21 καὶ τότε νηστεύσουσιν ἐν ‡ ἐκείναις ταῖς ἡμέραις. Καὶ οὐδεὶς ἐπιβλη- 16 36

15. *ἦσαν γὰρ—αὐτῷ.*] These words have been variously rendered, and indeed admit of more than one sense. Most Commentators, (after Grot.) take the *καὶ* for the relative *οἳ*, and render, "for there were many, who had followed Levi, and had sat down to table with him." But this involves a needless repetition, and it should rather seem, that the *αὐτῷ* is to be referred to *Jesus*, and that the sense is, what Fritz. assigns, "for there were many present [in Levi's house] and they had followed Jesus into the house."

16. *τί ὅτι.*] The sense of this idiom (which occurs both in the Scriptural and Classical writers) is, "What is [the cause] that," "How is it that." In the Classical writers a particle is generally interposed.

17. *εἰς μετάνοιαν.*] These words are wanting in many of the best MSS., in nearly all the Versions, and in some Fathers; and are cancelled by Griesb., Fritz., and Scholz, being supposed to have been introduced from Luke v. 31. [*Comp.* 1 Tim. i. 15.]

18. *οἱ τῶν Φαρισαίων.*] Mill and Beng. would read *οἱ Φαρισαῖοι*, from most of the best MSS. and Versions, which is edited by Griesb., Tittm., Vat., and Scholz. But there is scarcely sufficient authority for the alteration.

—*σοὶ μαθηταί.*] It is strange that almost all Commentators should take this *σοὶ* as a Dative for Genit. For although the Dative is used for the Genit., both in the Sciptural and Classical writers, yet only under certain circumstances, which here do not exist. Fritz. rightly remarks, that many such passages are either corrupt, or wrongly understood. And he adds, that unless a Dative can depend on the *notion* of the substantive, or be inserted *by the bye*, or be a *Dativus commodi*, or the like, it cannot be coupled with a substantive. He, very properly, takes the *σοὶ* as the Nominative plural of *σὸς, σὴ, σὸν*.

19. *μὴ δύνανται οἱ υἱοὶ τοῦ ν.*] Campb. well observes, that "on a subject such as this, relating to the ordinary manners and customs which obtain in a country, it is usual to speak of a thing which *is never* done, as of what *cannot* be done." Whitby remarks, that the term is used on any reasonable hindrance, though far short of improbability. I. If the actions be incongruous or improper, as Luke xi. 7. II. If the thing violates any rule of law or equity, as Deut. xii. 17. Acts x. 47. III. If it be not agreeable to the Divine counsels, as Matt. xxvi. 42. IV. If any inconvenience arises, or other employment impedes it, as Mark iii. 20. V. If there is any defect or fault in the object, as "Christ *could* do no mighty works because of their unbelief," Mark vi. 5. VI. If there is a disposition adverse to it, Gen. xxxvii. 4. John xiv. 17.

20. *ἐν ἐκείναις ταῖς ἡμέραις.*] Several ancient MSS. and Versions have *ἐν ἐκείνῃ τῇ ἡμέρᾳ*, which is preferred by Mill and Beng., and edited by Griesb., Vat., and Scholz; but without good reason; for, as Fritz. observes, it can on no account be admitted, since the plural refers to the preceding *ἡμέραι*. I would remark, too, that the testimony of the *Versions* is not of much weight,

MT. LU.
9. 5. μα ῥάκους ἀγνάφου ἐπιῤῥάπτει ἐπὶ ἱματίῳ παλαιῷ· εἰ δὲ μὴ, αἴρει
τὸ πλήρωμα αὐτοῦ τὸ καινὸν τοῦ παλαιοῦ, καὶ χεῖρον σχίσμα γίνεται.
17 37 Καὶ οὐδεὶς βάλλει οἶνον νέον εἰς ἀσκοὺς παλαιούς· εἰ δὲ μὴ, ῥήσσει 22
ὁ οἶνος ὁ νέος τοὺς ἀσκοὺς, καὶ ὁ οἶνος ἐκχεῖται, καὶ οἱ ἀσκοὶ ἀπο-
12. 6. λοῦνται· ἀλλὰ οἶνον νέον εἰς ἀσκοὺς καινοὺς βλητέον.
1 1 Καὶ ἐγένετο παραπορεύεσθαι αὐτὸν ἐν τοῖς σάββασι διὰ τῶν σπο- 23
ρίμων, καὶ ἤρξαντο οἱ μαθηταὶ αὐτοῦ ὁδὸν ποιεῖν τίλλοντες τοὺς
2 2 στάχυας. Καὶ οἱ Φαρισαῖοι ἔλεγον αὐτῷ· Ἴδε, τί ποιοῦσιν ἐν τοῖς 24
3 3 σάββασιν, ὃ οὐκ ἔξεστι; Καὶ αὐτὸς ἔλεγεν αὐτοῖς· Οὐδέποτε ἀνέγνω- 25
τε τί ἐποίησε Δαυῒδ, ὅτε χρείαν ἔσχε καὶ ἐπείνασεν, αὐτὸς καὶ οἱ
4 4 μετ᾽ αὐτοῦ; πῶς εἰσῆλθεν εἰς τὸν οἶκον τοῦ Θεοῦ ἐπὶ Ἀβιάθαρ 26
τοῦ ἀρχιερέως, καὶ τοὺς ἄρτους τῆς προθέσεως ἔφαγεν, οὓς οὐκ ἔξεστι
φαγεῖν, εἰ μὴ τοῖς ἱερεῦσι, καὶ ἔδωκε καὶ τοῖς σὺν αὐτῷ οὖσι; Καὶ 27
ἔλεγεν αὐτοῖς· Τὸ σάββατον διὰ τὸν ἄνθρωπον ἐγένετο, οὐχ ὁ ἄν-

since in some of them the singular might be taken of *time in general*, and therefore be a free translation of the *plural*. As little reason is there for cancelling the καὶ just after, as is done by Griesb., Vat., Tittm., and Scholz, from many of the best MSS.; for the copula (as Fritz. observes) cannot be dispensed with. On this and the two next verses see Notes on Matt. ix. 16, 17.

21. αἴρει — παλαιοῦ.] The construction is, τὸ πλήρωμα αὐτοῦ τὸ καινὸν αἴρει (τὶ) (ἀπὸ) τοῦ παλαιοῦ, "its new supplement taketh (something) from the old (garment)." That the ancients supplied ἀπὸ, is plain from its appearing in the MSS. in various positions in the passage, but, no doubt, always from the margin. Πλήρωμα is for ἀναπλήρωμα, *the supplementary portion*, as it is explained by Hesych. On the full sense of these two verses, see Markl. in Recens. Synop.

23. ἐν σάββ.] Luke vi. 1. says more definitely, ἐν σαββάτῳ δευτεροπρώτῳ, where see Note.

— παραπορεύεσθαι — σπορίμων.] Παραπ. is not here put (as many imagine) for πορεύεσθαι; nor is the sense of παραπ. διὰ τῶν σπ. what Abr., Pal., and Krebs say, "to pass by *near* the corn-fields." The full sense is, "to pass along (i. e. through) the corn-fields." See Deut. xxiii. 25.

— ἤρξαντο ὁδὸν ποιεῖν τίλλοντες τ. σ.] This is (as Beza and Schleusn. remark) an *interchanged collocation*, (the *primary notion* being seated in the *participle* instead of the verb), for ἤρξαντο ὁδὸν ποιοῦντες τίλλειν, &c., as xi. 5, and Acts xxi. 13. Ὁδὸν ποιεῖν is Hellenistic Greek (with some tincture of Latinism) for ὁδὸν ποιεῖσθαι; the distinction between the Active and Middle voice being, in the later writers, often neglected.

24. ἴδε, τί — ἔξεστι] "See! why, or how, are they doing on the Sabbath what is not lawful to be done?"

25. ὅτε χρείαν ἔσχε] "when he was in great straits," "was pressed by necessity." See 1 Sam. xxi. 6. It is not merely synonymous (as many suppose) with the ἐπείνασε following.

— αὐτὸς — αὐτοῖς·] This is said κατ᾽ ἐπανόρθωσιν. See note on Matt. xii. 3. I have pointed accordingly.

26. ἐπὶ Ἀβιάθαρ τοῦ ἀρχ.] The sense of this disputed passage *seems* to be, "during the High-priesthood of Abiathar." But from the passage of the O. T. alluded to (1 Sam. xxi. 6.), it appears that, at the period when the circumstance here adverted to took place, *Ahimelech* was High-Priest; and other passages show that Abiathar was *son* of Ahimelech. To remove this difficulty, many methods have been proposed. Some would cut the passage out altogether; others admit that it was an error of memory in the Evangelist — methods alike inadmissible. Others endeavour to remove the difficulty by *modifying* the usual signification of ἐπὶ, or adopting other senses. But that is too precarious, and indeed *inefficient* a mode to deserve attention. Several recent Commentators suppose that the Evangelist has followed the *Rabbinical* mode of citation; which consists in selecting some principal word out of each section, and applying the name to the section itself. So Rom. xi. 2. ἐν Ἠλίᾳ. and Mark xii. 26. ἐπὶ τῆς Βάτου. Thus the sense will be, "In that portion of the book of Samuel where the History of Abiathar is related." But this is not permitted by the collocation of the words; nor will ἐπὶ with the Genit. admit of such a signification. Neither is Abiathar called a High-Priest in 1 Sam. xxi. 2. seq. Others, again, think that father and son had two names, and that the father was *also* called Abiathar. But this solution is too manifestly made "for the nonce," and is grounded on no proof whatever. Equally gratitous is the supposition of some, that Abiathar was the Sagan, or Deputy to his father Ahimelech, and is therefore styled High-Priest. This, indeed, vanishes before the severe historical touchstone applied by Fritz. Finally, Bp. Middlet. thinks that a great deal of learning and ingenuity have been employed to remove a difficulty which *does not exist*. This, he says, has arisen from imagining that the words of St. Mark, explained in the obvious way, would mean, "in the priesthood of Abiathar," a sense which, indeed, they will not admit. *Without* the Article, indeed (continues he), such would have been the meaning, as in 1 Macc. xiii. 42. Luke iii. 2. ἐπ᾽ ἀρχιερέων Ἄννα καὶ Καϊάφα. Demosth. i. 250. Thucyd. ii. 2. In fact nothing is more common in the Classical writers. "Now (argues the learned Prelate) in these examples the *Article* would imply, as in the case of Abiathar, that these persons were *afterwards* distinguished by their respective offices from others of the same name. And that the name Abiathar was not an uncommon one among the Jews, is certain. And this might render the addition τοῦ

MT LU.
28 θρωπος διὰ τὸ σάββατον. Ὥστε κύριός ἐστιν ὁ Υἱὸς τοῦ ἀνθρώ- 12 6.
που καὶ τοῦ σαββάτου. 8 5
1 III. ΚΑΙ εἰσῆλθε πάλιν εἰς τὴν συναγωγὴν, καὶ ἦν ἐκεῖ ἄνθρω- 9 6
2 πος ἐξηραμμένην ἔχων τὴν χεῖρα, καὶ παρετήρουν αὐτὸν, εἰ τοῖς σάβ- 10 7
3 βασι θεραπεύσει αὐτὸν, ἵνα κατηγορήσωσιν αὐτοῦ. καὶ λέγει τῷ 8
ἀνθρώπῳ τῷ ἐξηραμμένην ἔχοντι τὴν χεῖρα· Ἔγειρε εἰς τὸ μέσον.
4 καὶ λέγει αὐτοῖς· Ἔξεστι τοῖς σάββασιν ἀγαθοποιῆσαι, ἢ κακο- 9
5 ποιῆσαι; ψυχὴν σῶσαι, ἢ ἀποκτεῖναι; οἱ δὲ ἐσιώπων. καὶ περιβλε- 12 10
ψάμενος αὐτοὺς μετ᾽ ὀργῆς, συλλυπούμενος ἐπὶ τῇ πωρώσει τῆς
καρδίας αὐτῶν, λέγει τῷ ἀνθρώπῳ· Ἔκτεινον τὴν χεῖρά σου. καὶ 13
6 ἐξέτεινε, καὶ ἀποκατεστάθη ἡ χεὶρ αὐτοῦ ὑγιὴς [ὡς ἡ ἄλλη.] Καὶ 14 1
ἐξελθόντες οἱ Φαρισαῖοι εὐθέως μετὰ τῶν Ἡρωδιανῶν συμβούλιον
ἐποίουν κατ᾽ αὐτοῦ, ὅπως αὐτὸν ἀπολέσωσι.

ἀρχ. natural, if not absolutely necessary. Thus the sense will be, that this action of David was in the time of Abiathar, *the* noted person who was *afterwards* High-Priest. So Luke iv. 27. ἐπὶ Ἐλισσαίου τοῦ προφήτου. This method (which had before occurred to Zegerus and Wets.) seems entitled to the preference; but I must frankly confess that it is not such as to be quite satisfactory to my own mind. [*Comp.* Exod. xxix. 32. Levit. viii. 31.]

28. ὁ Υἱὸς τοῦ ἀνθρώπου] Grot., Campb., Wakef., Kuin., and Fritz., strenuously contend that the sense here is not "*the* Son of Man," which is the general interpretation, but a son of *man*. "For (says Campb.) as the last words are introduced as a *consequence* from what has been advanced, the *Son of man* here must be equivalent to *men* in the preceding, otherwise a term is introduced into the conclusion which was not in the premises." But this savours too much of the sophistry of Scotch dialectics; and the interpretation is liable to very serious objections. Suffice it to say, 1. that such a signification of Υἱὸς τοῦ ἀνθ. is unfounded in the N. T.; and 2. that such a sense of κύριος no where exists in the Sept., the writers of later Greek, or the N. T. In short, the interpretation can by no means be admitted, as introducing, without sufficient ground, a very strong expression; which leads to a laxity of opinion and practice as to the observance of the Sabbath, such as our Lord could not mean to inculcate. Nor is it *necessary* so to interpret; for (as I have observed on Matt. xii. 8.), the ὥστε here may be not *illative*, but *continuative;* of which uses examples may be seen in Steph. Thes. and Hoogev. Partic. Or, with Maldon., it may be considered as *completive*. This view is strongly confirmed by the manner in which St. Luke introduces the words. Besides the new interpretation is negatived by the καὶ *(even)* of the present passage; which has great force, and implies (as Doddr. justly observes) that "the Sabbath was an institution of high importance, and may perhaps also refer to that signal authority which Christ, by the ministry of his Apostles, should exert over it, in changing it from the *seventh* to the *first day of the week*." We may add, that this was a delicate way of claiming to be the MESSIAH, as in the words uttered by our Lord on another occasion, "There is here *something* greater than the Temple."

In short, the reasoning seems to be this: that as the Sabbath was an institution meant for the good of man, the relaxation of the strict observance of it might, in some extreme cases, be justified, as in that of David, and in this of his disciples. Besides, if that were not the case, that *His* countenance and permission were a sufficient authority, for the Messiah is Lord, &c.

III. 2. παρετήρουν] Παρατηρεῖν signifies, 1. to keep one's eyes fixed beside or close to (παρὰ) any person or thing. 2. to watch, whether for a *good*, or (as generally) for an *evil* purpose.

4. ἔξεστι — κακοποιῆσαι] Almost all recent English Commentators introduce here a Note of Campb. inculcating that "in Scripture, a negation is often expressed by an affirmation of the contrary." But it does not appear what bearing such a trite remark has on the present passage. Here there is an *interrogation;* which our Lord introduces, as being more spirited than a mere *declarative* sentence. He leaves *themselves* to decide the point. By the expression ἀγαθοποιῆσαι, he adverts to his healing the cripple: and by κακοποιῆσαι, to the designs against his life, which the Pharisees were plotting even on the *Sabbath*.

5. μετ᾽ ὀργῆς] It is not necessary here to discuss, with Commentators, the question, whether Christ really felt anger, or not; or what is the true definition of anger; for the word ὀργὴ does not here denote *anger*, but (as sometimes in the Classical writers) *commotio animi, indignation;* which may be defined, with Whitby, "a displeasure of the mind, arising from an injury done or intended to ourselves or others, with a desire to remove the injury." This view is established by the word following συλλυπούμενος, being grieved in mind, which was, no doubt, meant to qualify and explain ὀργῆς. Πωρώσει (from πῶρος, a hard piece of skin) signifies callousness, perversity.

— ὡς ἡ ἄλλη] These words which are omitted in several MSS., most of the Versions, and some Fathers, are rejected by most Critics, and cancelled by almost all the Editors from Griesb. to Scholz, being supposed to be introduced from Matth. xii. 13., which seems very probable. Ἀποκαθιστάναι signifies to restore any thing to its former place or state, and is, in the Passive, by Hippocr. and the late Greek writers, and also the Sept., used of restoration from sickness to health. So Hippocr. Epidem. p. 1222. ἡ γλῶσσα ἀπεκαθίστατο εἰς ταὐτό.

6. [*Comp.* Matt. xxii. 16.]

MT. LU.
12. 6. Καὶ ὁ Ἰησοῦς ἀνεχώρησε μετὰ τῶν μαθητῶν αὐτοῦ πρὸς τὴν θά- 7
15 17 λασσαν· καὶ πολὺ πλῆθος ἀπὸ τῆς Γαλιλαίας ἠκολούθησαν αὐτῷ, καὶ
ἀπὸ τῆς Ἰουδαίας, καὶ ἀπὸ Ἱεροσολύμων, καὶ ἀπὸ τῆς Ἰδουμαίας, καὶ 8
πέραν τοῦ Ἰορδάνου· καὶ οἱ περὶ Τύρον καὶ Σιδῶνα, πλῆθος πολὺ,
ἀκούσαντες ὅσα ἐποίει, ἦλθον πρὸς αὐτόν. Καὶ εἶπε τοῖς μαθηταῖς 9
αὐτοῦ, ἵνα πλοιάριον προσκαρτερῇ αὐτῷ, διὰ τὸν ὄχλον, ἵνα μὴ θλί-
19 βωσιν αὐτόν. Πολλοὺς γὰρ ἐθεράπευσεν· ὥστε ἐπιπίπτειν αὐτῷ, ἵνα 10
18 αὐτοῦ ἅψωνται, ὅσοι εἶχον μάστιγας. Καὶ τὰ πνεύματα τὰ ἀκάθαρτα, 11
ὅταν αὐτὸν ἐθεώρει, προσέπιπτεν αὐτῷ, καὶ ἔκραζε, λέγοντα· Ὅτι σὺ
εἶ ὁ Υἱὸς τοῦ Θεοῦ! Καὶ πολλὰ ἐπετίμα αὐτοῖς, ἵνα μὴ αὐτὸν φα- 12
12 νερὸν ποιήσωσι. Καὶ ἀναβαίνει εἰς τὸ ὄρος, καὶ προσκαλεῖται οὓς 13
13 ἤθελεν αὐτός· καὶ ἀπῆλθον πρὸς αὐτόν. Καὶ ἐποίησε δώδεκα, ἵνα 14
ὦσι μετ᾽ αὐτοῦ, καὶ ἵνα ἀποστέλλῃ αὐτοὺς κηρύσσειν, καὶ ἔχειν ἐξου- 15
σίαν θεραπεύειν τὰς νόσους, καὶ ἐκβάλλειν τὰ δαιμόνια· [πρῶτον] Σιμῶνα,
14 (καὶ ἐπέθηκε τῷ Σίμωνι ὄνομα Πέτρον·) καὶ Ἰάκωβον τὸν τοῦ Ζε- 16
βεδαίου, καὶ Ἰωάννην τὸν ἀδελφὸν τοῦ Ἰακώβου· (καὶ ἐπέθηκεν αὐ- 17

7. [*Comp.* Matt. iv. 25.]

8. οἱ περὶ Τύρον καὶ Σιδῶνα] Grot. rightly observes, that these are not the Tyrians and Sidonians, but those who inhabited the confines of Tyre and Sidon. See vii. 24.

9. εἶπε τοῖς μαθηταῖς] "he directed his disciples." Προσκαρτερῇ αὐ., "should attend upon him." Προσκαρτερεῖν signifies, 1. to persevere in, and continue *intent on any thing*. 2. to *attend on any person*. So Acts viii. 13. βαπτισθεὶς ἦν προσκαρτερῶν τῷ Φιλίππῳ, and also in several Classical passages cited by the Commentators. Fritz. thinks it very strange that the phrase should here be used of a *thing*. But, in fact, the *thing* is put for a *person*—the *rowers* for the *boat*, as in a kindred passage of Thucyd. iv. 120, where see my Note, also infra iv. 36. ἄλλα δὲ πλοιάρια ἦν μετ᾽ αὐτοῦ, i. e. with Jesus's vessel, where see Note.

10. ἐθεράπευσε] Brug., Newc., Kuin., and Fritz. rightly observe, that "this must have a *pluperfect* sense," "had healed." Μάστιγας denotes "grievous disorders." The word properly signifies *a scourge*, but metaphorically any *torturing affection*, especially disease.

11. πνεύματα τὰ ἀκάθαρτα—προσέπιπτεν] Camer., Rosenm., and Kuin. take πνεύματα to denote the *persons* who were troubled with dæmons. But, as Fritz. justly remarks, there is here ascribed to dæmons, what the persons possessed by them did, because those persons were not their own masters, but were governed by the dæmons.

—ὅταν αὐτὸν ἐθεώρει] The sense is, "as often as they saw him," which Fritz. pronounces to be solœcistic, unless we write ὅτ᾽ ἂν ἐθ. But there can be no difficulty in supposing that the Evangelist so wrote, or, at least, so considered the conjunction in his mind. Poppo on Thucyd. perpetually so edits.

14. ἐποίησε] "appointed." So Apoc. i. 6. καὶ ἐποίησεν ἡμᾶς βασιλεῖς καὶ ἱερεῖς τῷ Θεῷ, and sometimes in the later Classical writers. So the Heb. עָשָׂה in 1 Sam. xii. 6. and sometimes the Latin *facere*, as in Cicero pro Plancio, 4.

15. ἐξουσίαν] The word here signifies rather *power* than authority.

16. πρῶτον Σιμῶνα] Beza, Schmid, Glass, Schott, and Fritz., introduced this addition, on the authority of at least *four* MSS., as being necessarily required to complete the sense. And so Newc., Wakef., and Campb. translate. There is, indeed (as Matthæi admits), a manifest *lacuna*. And though that is supplied in various ways, in the MSS., yet in none so satisfactorily as in the above manner. Indeed, De Dieu and Kuin. defend the common reading, and maintain that it is a *concisa et hians oratio*, of which the sense is, "And he appointed Simon, whom he (afterwards) called Peter." But let the style of the Evangelist be as unstudied as they please, yet *this* would be an unparalleled negligence. Far better is it to suppose a *lacuna*. To the above addition, however, a strong objection has been made; namely, that it may be supposed to be introduced from Matt. x. 2. But that passage, as Fritz. observes, is very dissimilar. I cannot, however, help suspecting that the πρῶτον was derived from that source; and I have little doubt but that the true reading is Σιμῶνα without πρῶτον. So in the parallel passage of Luke vi. 14. (which Mark seems to have had in view), ἐκλεξάμενος ἀπ᾽ αὐτῶν δώδεκα, οὓς καὶ ἀποστόλους ὠνόμασε· Σίμωνα (ὃν καὶ ὠνόμασε Πέτρον) καὶ Ἀνδρέαν, &c. Besides, it is far more probable that *one* word should have slipped out than two. And *thus* we are enabled to *account* for the omission, on the principle of homœteleuton, or rather *general similarity*; for in Manuscript characters Σίμωνα is very like Δαιμόνια. That would cause the omission in some MSS.; though I have no doubt but that, in others, the omission of Σίμωνα was occasioned by its standing by itself, and seeming to form no part of the construction; though it belongs to the preceding ἐποίησε δώδεκα, inserted in the Cod. Vatic. In four other MSS. πρῶτον was inserted (though probably not in the Archetypes), because it softens the seeming harshness; which, however, is less, if we consider that the words preceding ἵνα ὦσι—δαιμόνια are, in some measure, parenthetical.

The words καὶ ἐπέθηκε—Πέτρον are here added parenthetically; because, in fact, this surname was not given to Simon on the *Mount*, but afterwards. See Matt. xvi. 18.

MT. LU.

18 τοῖς ὀνόματα Βοανεργὲς, ὅ ἐστιν, υἱοὶ βροντῆς·) καὶ Ἀνδρέαν, καὶ 12. 6.
Φίλιππον, καὶ Βαρθολομαῖον, καὶ Ματθαῖον, καὶ Θωμᾶν, καὶ Ἰάκω- 15
19 βον τὸν τοῦ Ἀλφαίου, καὶ Θαδδαῖον, καὶ Σίμωνα τὸν Κανανίτην, καὶ
Ἰούδαν Ἰσκαριώτην, ὃς καὶ παρέδωκεν αὐτόν.
20 Καὶ ἔρχονται εἰς οἶκον· καὶ συνέρχεται πάλιν ὄχλος, ὥστε μὴ δύ-
21 νασθαι αὐτοὺς μήτε ἄρτον φαγεῖν. Καὶ ἀκούσαντες οἱ παρ' αὐτοῦ, 11.
22 ἐξῆλθον κρατῆσαι αὐτόν· ἔλεγον γὰρ, ὅτι ἐξέστη. Καὶ οἱ Γραμμα- 24 15
τεῖς οἱ ἀπὸ Ἱεροσολύμων καταβάντες ἔλεγον· Ὅτι Βεελζεβοὺλ ἔχει, καὶ
23 ὅτι ἐν τῷ ἄρχοντι τῶν δαιμονίων ἐκβάλλει τὰ δαιμόνια. Καὶ προσκαλεσάμενος αὐτοὺς, ἐν παραβολαῖς ἔλεγεν αὐτοῖς· Πῶς δύναται Σατανᾶς 26 17
24 Σατανᾶν ἐκβάλλειν; Καὶ ἐὰν βασιλεία ἐφ' ἑαυτὴν μερισθῇ, οὐ δύναται
25 σταθῆναι ἡ βασιλεία ἐκείνη· καὶ ἐὰν οἰκία ἐφ' ἑαυτὴν μερισθῇ, οὐ
26 δύναται σταθῆναι ἡ οἰκία ἐκείνη· καὶ εἰ ὁ Σατανᾶς ἀνέστη ἐφ' 26 18
27 ἑαυτὸν καὶ μεμέρισται, οὐ δύναται σταθῆναι, ἀλλὰ τέλος ἔχει. Οὐ 29 21
δύναται οὐδεὶς τὰ σκεύη τοῦ ἰσχυροῦ, εἰσελθὼν εἰς τὴν οἰκίαν αὐτοῦ,
διαρπάσαι, ἐὰν μὴ πρῶτον τὸν ἰσχυρὸν δήσῃ· καὶ τότε τὴν οἰκίαν 22
28 αὐτοῦ διαρπάσει. Ἀμὴν λέγω ὑμῖν, ὅτι πάντα ἀφεθήσεται τὰ ἁμαρ- 31
τήματα τοῖς υἱοῖς τῶν ἀνθρώπων, καὶ αἱ βλασφημίαι, ὅσας ἂν βλα-

17. Βοανεργὲς] With this word the Commentators are much perplexed. One thing is certain, that it does not correctly represent the Syro-Chaldee term. *What* that was, the Commentators are not agreed. Most think, with Jerome, that the true word is Βενερεεὶμ, from the Heb. בני רעם, for in Hebrew רעם continually signifies *thunder*. But this varies too much from the *vestigia literarum*. Others derive it from the Heb. בני רעש. But that deviates *further*, and only signifies "sons of *noise*," or sound. The best derivation seems to be that of Caninius, De Dieu, and Fritz., בני רגש; for *Reges*, in Syriac and Arabic signifies *thunder*. Thus the word βοανεργὲς seems to be a slight corruption for βοανὲρεγες. The reason for this appellation has been variously conjectured. See Horne's Introd.

20. μήτε ἄρτον φαγεῖν] i. e. not even to take food (by a common Hebraism); much less to attend to any thing else.

21. καὶ ἀκούσαντες—αὐτόν] There are few passages on which Commentators are more divided in opinion than this. Several questions are involved in the discussion of the sense: 1. who are the οἱ παρ' αὐτοῦ? 2. to what report may ἀκούσαντες be thought to have reference? 3. what is the sense of ἐξῆλθον and of κρατῆσαι? 4. who those are that are represented as saying ἐξέστη? On these points I see no reason to abandon the opinions which I propounded in Recens. Synop. Fritz., after a very long and minute discussion, determines (as I had myself done) that the best interpretation is that of the ancient and many eminent modern Commentators (Grot., Beza, Kypke, Campb., Wets., Valckn., and Kuin.), as follows: "When Jesus' kinsfolk (i. e. his mother and brothers, see ver. 31.) had heard (that he was at Capernaum), they went out from their house, in order that they might lay hands on him; for, said they, he is surely beside himself." Fritz. remarks that the Greeks say εἶναι παρά τινος, in the sense "to be of any one's nation or family;" of which he adduces examples. That from Susanna ver. 33. ἔκλαιον δὲ οἱ παρ' αὐτῆς, is quite decisive. Ἀκούσαντες signifies "having heard of his being at Capernaum, and what was going on in the house." Κρατῆσαι signifies "to lay hands on and hold fast;" yet it does not necessarily imply *violence*, but sometimes *friendly intentions*, as in 2 Kings iv. 8. and Mark ix. 27. Ἐξέστη, sub. τοῦ νοῦ or γνώμης, is to be taken in a figurative sense for "he is transported too far." The word is often used in the Classical writers of vehement commotion or perturbation; and we have there both the complete and the elliptical phrase.

22. Βεελζ. ἔχει] i. e. he is possessed of Beelzebub. [*Comp.* John vii. 20. viii. 48. x. 20.]

23—29. In these verses are shown, 1. the *absurdity* of the charge; and 2. the *wickedness* of it; it being of so deep a dye, that it will never be forgiven.

24. ἐφ' ἑαυτὴν μερ.] Μερίζεσθαι signifies properly to *be separated* into parts, or parties; and, from the adjunct, to be *at variance*, and *in opposition*. In which case it carries with it the regimen of verbs signifying *opposition*.

26. καὶ εἰ ὁ Σ.] The καὶ is said by Kuin. to be for οὕτως. But Fritz. shows that it retains the usual force.

27. οὐ δύναται οὐδεὶς] A great number of MSS., some Versions, and the Edit. Princ., have οὐδεὶς δύναται, which is edited by Griesb., Matth., and Scholz; but injudiciously: for the common reading, as being the more difficult, is to be preferred, and is very properly retained by Tittm., Vat., and Fritz. This idiom of the double negative is frequent in Scripture (as Luke ix. 2. John vi. 63. ix. 33.), though it was generally stumbled at, more or less, by the scribes. Τοῦ ἰσχυροῦ. The force of the Article here is that of *insertion* in Hypothesis. See Middlet. Gr. Art. C. iii. § 2. 1.

28. καὶ αἱ] Thus several of the best MSS. read for καί. And so Griesb., Tittm., Fritz., and Scholz edit; and very properly: since it is far easier to account for the omission than for the insertion of the αἱ. Besides, the article is here

MT. LU.

12. 8. σφημήσωσιν· ὃς δ᾿ ἂν βλασφημήσῃ εἰς τὸ Πνεῦμα τὸ ἅγιον, οὐκ ἔχει 29
ἄφεσιν εἰς τὸν αἰῶνα, ἀλλ᾿ ἔνοχός ἐστιν αἰωνίου κρίσεως. ὅτι ἔλεγον· 30
46 19 πνεῦμα ἀκάθαρτον ἔχει. Ἔρχονται οὖν ‡ οἱ ἀδελφοὶ καὶ ἡ μήτηρ ‡ 31
αὐτοῦ, καὶ ἔξω ἑστῶτες ἀπέστειλαν πρὸς αὐτὸν, φωνοῦντες αὐτόν. Καὶ 32
47 20 ἐκάθητο ὄχλος περὶ αὐτόν· εἶπον δὲ αὐτῷ· Ἰδοὺ, ἡ μήτηρ σου καὶ
48 21 οἱ ἀδελφοί σου ἔξω ζητοῦσί σε. Καὶ ἀπεκρίθη αὐτοῖς, λέγων· Τίς 33
49 ἐστιν ἡ μήτηρ μου, ἢ οἱ ἀδελφοί μου; Καὶ περιβλεψάμενος κύκλῳ 34
τοὺς περὶ αὐτὸν καθημένους, λέγει· Ἴδε, ἡ μήτηρ μου καὶ οἱ ἀδελφοί
50 μου. Ὃς γὰρ ἂν ποιήσῃ τὸ θέλημα τοῦ Θεοῦ, οὗτος ἀδελφός μου, 35
13. καὶ ἀδελφή μου, καὶ μήτηρ ἐστί.
2 4 IV. ΚΑΙ πάλιν ἤρξατο διδάσκειν παρὰ τὴν θάλασσαν· καὶ συνή- 1
χθη πρὸς αὐτὸν ὄχλος πολὺς, ὥστε αὐτὸν ἐμβάντα εἰς τὸ πλοῖον, καθῆσθαι ἐν τῇ θαλάσσῃ· καὶ πᾶς ὁ ὄχλος πρὸς τὴν θάλασσαν ἐπὶ τῆς
3 γῆς ἦν. Καὶ ἐδίδασκεν αὐτοὺς ἐν παραβολαῖς πολλὰ, καὶ ἔλεγεν αὐ- 2
5 τοῖς ἐν τῇ διδαχῇ αὐτοῦ· Ἀκούετε· ἰδοὺ, ἐξῆλθεν ὁ σπείρων τοῦ 3
4 σπεῖραι· καὶ ἐγένετο ἐν τῷ σπείρειν, ὃ μὲν ἔπεσε παρὰ τὴν ὁδὸν, καὶ 4
5 6 ἦλθε τὰ πετεινὰ [τοῦ οὐρανοῦ] καὶ κατέφαγεν αὐτό. Ἄλλο δὲ ἔπεσεν 5
ἐπὶ τὸ πετρῶδες, ὅπου οὐκ εἶχε γῆν πολλήν· καὶ εὐθέως ἐξανέτειλε,
6 διὰ τὸ μὴ ἔχειν βάθος γῆς· ἡλίου δὲ ἀνατείλαντος ἐκαυματίσθη, καὶ, 6
7 7 διὰ τὸ μὴ ἔχειν ῥίζαν, ἐξηράνθη. Καὶ ἄλλο ἔπεσεν εἰς τὰς ἀκάνθας· 7
8 8 καὶ ἀνέβησαν αἱ ἄκανθαι, καὶ συνέπνιξαν αὐτὸ, καὶ καρπὸν οὐκ ἔδωκε.
Καὶ ἄλλο ἔπεσεν εἰς τὴν γῆν τὴν καλήν· καὶ ἐδίδου καρπὸν ἀναβαί- 8
νοντα καὶ αὐξάνοντα, καὶ ἔφερεν ἓν τριάκοντα, καὶ ἓν ἑξήκοντα, καὶ ἓν
9 ἑκατόν. Καὶ ἔλεγεν [αὐτοῖς]· Ὁ ἔχων ὦτα ἀκούειν ἀκουέτω. Ὅτε 9

as much required as at ἁμαρτ. just before. [Comp. 1 John 5. 16.

29. βλασφ. εἰς τὸ Πνεῦμα τὸ ἅγ.] See Note on Matt. xii. 31.

— κρίσεως.] The ἁμαρτήματος (or ἁμαρτίας), which Grot., Mill, Griesb., Rosenm., and Kuin. would read, is a mere *emendation* of the common reading to improve the antithesis; which, however, is unnecessary. See Matt. and Fritz.

30. ὅτι ἔλεγον — ἔχει] These are (as Beza, Casaub., Grot., Kuin., and Fritz. rightly observe) the words of the *Evangelist*, not of our Lord.

31. ἔρχονται οὖν] The οὖν is here, as often (like *ergo* sometimes in Latin), *resumptive*, taking up the thread of the narrative from ver. 21. Instead of οἱ ἀδελφοὶ καὶ ἡ μήτηρ, a few ancient MSS., and most of the Versions, have ἡ μήτηρ καὶ οἱ ἀδελφοί, which is edited by Griesb., Tittm., Vat., and Scholz. But there is no sufficient authority for the change; which may, with Wets. and Fritz., be accounted for from a wish to do honour to the mother of Christ. By ἔξω is meant, not outside of the *house*, but outside of the *crowd*.

32. καὶ οἱ ἀδελφοί σου] Many MSS. and the Edit. Princ. add καὶ αἱ ἀδελφαί σου, which words are edited by Matth., Griesb., Tittm., Vat., and Scholz; but are, with more reason, rejected by Kuin. and Fritz.

IV. 1. ἤρξατο διδάσκειν] for ἐδίδαξε, say most Commentators. But, as Fritz. shows, the phrase may have its full force. The sense is, "He began to teach by the sea;" and then, by the increasing crowd of auditors, he was compelled to embark on board the boat (mentioned supra iii. 9.), and there to teach the people, seated on shipboard at sea.

2. ἐν τῇ διδαχῇ for ἐν τῷ διδάσκειν] a mode of expression peculiar to Mark.

4. τοῦ οὐρανοῦ] Omitted in very many MSS., most of the Versions, and the Edit. Princ.; and rejected by Mill, Beng., Wets., Matth., Griesb., Tittm., Vat., Fritz., and Scholz; as being introduced from the other Gospels.

7. τὰς ἀκάνθας] The Article is here found, as being employed, in a *general* sense, for *thorny ground*.

— καρπὸν οὐκ ἔδωκε] "did not yield fruit." This was not necessary to be said of the former seed sown; but *here* it was with reason expressed, since the first growth justly afforded some hope of a prosperous increase. (Rosenm.)

8. ἀναβαίνοντα καὶ αὐξάνοντα] "which sprung up and increased." Αὐξ. is for αὐξανόμενον, which is found in some ancient MSS.; but, doubtless, from a gloss. The active is used by the later, and especially the Hellenistic writers; the middle by the earlier. Ἔφερεν ἕν. This use of ἕν, serving to *enumeration*, is Hebraic. See 1 Sam. x. 3 Exod. xviii. 3, 4.

9. αὐτοῖς.] The word is omitted in very many MSS., nearly all the Versions, and the early Editions, and is cancelled by almost every Editor from Wets. to Scholz.

MT. LU.

10 δὲ ἐγένετο καταμόνας, ἠρώτησαν αὐτὸν οἱ περὶ αὐτὸν σὺν τοῖς δώδεκα 13. 8.
11 τὴν παραβολήν. καὶ ἔλεγεν αὐτοῖς· Ὑμῖν δέδοται γνῶναι τὸ μυστή- 10 11 9 10
ριον τῆς βασιλείας τοῦ Θεοῦ, ἐκείνοις δὲ τοῖς ἔξω ἐν παραβολαῖς τὰ
12 πάντα γίνεται· ἵνα βλέποντες βλέπωσι, καὶ μὴ ἴδωσι· καὶ ἀκούον- 13
τες ἀκούωσι, καὶ μὴ συνιῶσι· μήποτε ἐπιστρέψωσι, καὶ ἀφεθῇ
13 αὐτοῖς τὰ ἁμαρτήματα. Καὶ λέγει αὐτοῖς· Οὐκ οἴδατε τὴν παραβο-
14 λὴν ταύτην; καὶ πῶς πάσας τὰς παραβολὰς γνώσεσθε; Ὁ σπείρων 19 12
15 τὸν λόγον σπείρει. Οὗτοι δέ εἰσιν οἱ παρὰ τὴν ὁδὸν, ὅπου σπείρεται
ὁ λόγος· καὶ ὅταν ἀκούσωσιν, εὐθέως ἔρχεται ὁ Σατανᾶς, καὶ αἴρει
16 τὸν λόγον τὸν ἐσπαρμένον ἐν ταῖς καρδίαις αὐτῶν. Καὶ οὗτοί εἰσιν 20 13
ὁμοίως οἱ ἐπὶ τὰ πετρώδη σπειρόμενοι, οἳ ὅταν ἀκούσωσι τὸν λόγον,
17 εὐθέως μετὰ χαρᾶς λαμβάνουσιν αὐτόν· καὶ οὐκ ἔχουσι ῥίζαν ἐν 21
ἑαυτοῖς, ἀλλὰ πρόσκαιροί εἰσιν· εἶτα, γενομένης θλίψεως, ἢ διωγμοῦ
18 διὰ τὸν λόγον, εὐθέως σκανδαλίζονται. Καὶ οὗτοί εἰσιν οἱ εἰς τὰς 22 14
19 ἀκάνθας σπειρόμενοι, [οὗτοί εἰσιν] οἱ τὸν λόγον ἀκούοντες· καὶ αἱ
μέριμναι τοῦ αἰῶνος τούτου, καὶ ἡ ἀπάτη τοῦ πλούτου, καὶ αἱ περὶ

10. *καταμόνας*] Sub. *χώρας*, *apart*, what is in a manner "at [a separate] part." The expression occurs both in the Scriptural and Classical writers. Οἱ *περὶ αὐτὸν* means "those that were about him." By which expression are designated the stated attendants on our Lord's ministry, his regular disciples, probably (as Euthym. thinks) the *Seventy* disciples. So Jamblich. Vit. Pyth. 17. *οἱ περὶ τὸν ἄνδρα* means Pythagoras's disciples. The construction *ἐρωτᾷν τινά τι* is remarkable.

11. *δέδοται*] "it is granted" [by Divine grace]; not *obtigit*, as Wets. renders; which is an unjustifiable curtailment of the sense. By *τοῖς ἔξω*, is meant to those who are most removed from intimate connection with me, and acceptance of my religion. This name the Jews used to give to the Heathens, as being removed from covenant with God. Our Lord, therefore, as Whitby remarks, seems to hint to them, that in a short time the kingdom of God would be taken from them, and they themselves be the *οἱ ἔξω*. This mode of speaking is also found in the Rabbinical writers. See Lightf.

12. *ἵνα βλέπ. βλέπωσι*] The Commentators have almost universally taken the *ἵνα* for *ὅτι*, *qui*, or *ita ut*. But Fritz. more correctly explains it *eo consilio, ut*. Our Lord means that the prophetical saying of Isaiah will be made good. The sense is, "To the multitude all things are propounded by the intervention of parables; with the intent that (as the prophet says), since they have eyes and ears perfect, and yet see not, not understand, they may not repent and obtain forgiveness of their sins." The expression *βλέπ. καὶ μὴ ἴδωσι* is (as Le Clerc observes) a proverbial one, and relates to those who might see, if they would use their faculties, that which they now overlook, through inattention and folly. So Æschyl. Prom. Οἳ *πρῶτα μὲν βλέποντες ἔβλεπον μάτην, Κλύοντες οὐκ ἤκουον.* [*Comp*. John xii. 40. Acts xxviii. 26. Rom. xi. 8.]

The words *καὶ ἀφεθῇ αὐτοῖς τὰ ἁμ.* the Commentators consider as an explanation of those of Isaiah *καὶ ἰάσωμαι αὐτούς*; the Hebrews viewing all severe disorders as the punishment of sin. And that those were really such under the Mosaic dispensation, Abp. Magee (on Atonement, vol. i. p. 433,) thinks we may fairly infer from John v. 14. But the Hebrew is ורפא לו, "ne gens salva evadat." For, as Fritz. observes, the Heb. רפא, (as also the Chaldee אסא), to *heal*, often signifies to *forgive*, offences being compared with wounds and disorders.

13. *καὶ πῶς*.] "And how then!" Among the other significations of *καὶ* when prefixed to interrogations, is that of *drawing a consequence*, as in Matt. iii. 14, and here. By *πάσας* is meant, not "all [other]," but, "all [such as it behoves you to know]."

14. *ὁ σπείρων — σπείρει*.] A brief and popular form of expression, of which the sense is, "The sower [mentioned in the parable] is to be considered as one sowing the Word [of God]."

15. *οἱ παρὰ τὴν ὁδὸν*] scil. *σπειρόμενοι*, or *σπαρέντες*. or Ὅπου is for *οἷς*, *whom*, which is, indeed, found in some MSS. and the Syr., but is doubtless a gloss. So the Latin *ubi* for *in quo*.

16. *ὁμοίως*] "by a similar mode of explanation."

18. *οὗτοί εἰσιν*.] These words are omitted in many MSS., the Ed. Princ. and Beng., several Versions, and some Fathers, and are cancelled by Wets., Matth., Tittm., Vat., and Fritz., which last Editor proves that this is the true way of reading the passage, though others are offered by the MSS.

19. *τούτου*.] Griesb. and Fritz. cancel this word, on the authority of some MSS., as being introduced from the other Gospels. But the sense will scarcely dispense with the word, and the custom of the N. T. requires it. It is, besides, absent from so very few MSS. that the omission may be thought accidental, or introduced elegantiæ gratiâ, for the passage reads better without it. Fritz. adduces Matt. xiii. 39. as an example of the absence of the pronoun; but it may be better dispensed with *there*, since the same expression with the *τούτου* had occurred a little before.

— *ἡ ἀπάτη τοῦ πλούτου*.] Some recent Interpreters take *ἀπάτη* for *τέρψις*. But there is no reason to abandon the common interpretation, "the fallaciousness of riches," expressive of those various *deceits*, which accompany riches, pro-

MT. LU.
13. 8. τὰ λοιπὰ ἐπιθυμίαι, εἰσπορευόμεναι συμπνίγουσι τὸν λόγον, καὶ
23 15 ἄκαρπος γίνεται. Καὶ οὗτοί εἰσιν οἱ ἐπὶ τὴν γῆν τὴν καλὴν σπα- 20
ρέντες, οἵτινες ἀκούουσι τὸν λόγον καὶ παραδέχονται· καὶ καρποφο-
16 ροῦσιν, ἓν τριάκοντα, καὶ ἓν ἑξήκοντα, καὶ ἓν ἑκατόν. Καὶ ἔλεγεν 21
αὐτοῖς· Μήτι ὁ λύχνος ἔρχεται, ἵνα ὑπὸ τὸν μόδιον τεθῇ ἢ ὑπὸ
17 τὴν κλίνην; οὐχ ἵνα ἐπὶ τὴν λυχνίαν ἐπιτεθῇ; Οὐ γάρ ἐστί τι 22
κρυπτὸν, ὃ ἐὰν μὴ φανερωθῇ· οὐδὲ ἐγένετο ἀπόκρυφον, ἀλλ᾽ ἵνα
εἰς φανερὸν ἔλθῃ. Εἴτις ἔχει ὦτα ἀκούειν, ἀκουέτω. Καὶ ἔλεγεν 23
18 αὐτοῖς· Βλέπετε, τί ἀκούετε. Ἐν ᾧ μέτρῳ μετρεῖτε, μετρηθήσεται 24
ὑμῖν, καὶ προστεθήσεται ὑμῖν τοῖς ἀκούουσιν. ὃς γὰρ ἂν ἔχῃ, δοθή- 25
σεται αὐτῷ· καὶ ὃς οὐκ ἔχει, καὶ ὃ ἔχει ἀρθήσεται ἀπ᾽ αὐτοῦ.
Καὶ ἔλεγεν· Οὕτως ἐστὶν ἡ βασιλεία τοῦ Θεοῦ, ὡς ἐὰν ἄνθρωπος 26

ducing disappointment, and throwing a veil over the heart, as to *real* happiness here and hereafter. See 1 Tim. vi. 17.

—αἱ περὶ τὰ λ. ἐπιθ.] The sense seems to be, "the desires *exercised* about the rest of the *gaudes* of life" (to use an old English term). Λοιπὰ has reference to τοῦ πλούτου, and alludes to honours and sensual gratifications; what are called by St. Paul the τῆς σαρκὸς ἐπιθυμίαι, and by Luke viii. 14. ἡδοναὶ τοῦ βίου. There may however be (as Grot. suggests) an *euphemism*, since sensuality of every kind is adverted to.

20. παραδέχονται] "receive and entertain it, assent to it." Ἓν τριάκοντα, &c. There is something harsh in this, instead of which we should expect εἷς. The best way of accounting for it is to suppose, (with Grot. and Fritz.), that the Evangelist suddenly returns back from the *thing*, and the *explication*, to the *parable*.

21. αὐτοῖς] i. e. the *disciples*, not the people at large. Compare vv. 21, 24, 26, and Luke viii. 16—18. And although vv. 21—25 are brought forward in another sense in Matt. v. 15; x. 26; vii. 2 & 13, yet proverbial *sententiæ* like this are (as Grot. observes) applicable in various views. It is (to use the words of Whitby) as if Christ had said: "I give you a clear light by which you may discern the import of this and other parables; but this I do, not that you may keep it to yourselves, and hide it from others, but that it may be beneficial to you, and by you be made beneficial to others; and that having thus learned, you may instruct them how they ought to hear, and to receive the word heard in good and honest hearts, ver. 20. And though I give you the knowledge of these mysteries of the kingdom of God (καταμόνας) privately, I do it not that you may keep them so; for there is nothing thus hid, which should not be made manifest, neither was any thing made secret by me, but that it should afterwards come abroad."

—μήτι] "num quid." An adverb sometimes involving affirmation, sometimes negation, (as here,) in which latter case Hoogev. considers it as emphatic. Ἔρχεται, for φέρεται, is "brought." Neuter for passive, by an idiom common to both Greek and Latin, as spoken of *letters*; though occurring also in *other* cases, as Thucyd. i. 137. ἦλθε γὰρ (i. e. money) αὐτῷ ὕστερον ἐκ τῶν Ἀθηνῶν.

For ἐπιτεθῇ several MSS. (some of them ancient,) and Theophylact have τεθῇ, which was proposed by Mill, and edited by Griesb., Knapp, and Fritz. But there is not sufficient authority for the alteration, which seems to be a mere *emendation* of the Alexandrian school. As little ground is there for the omission of the τι just afterwards by the same Editors. The τι could scarcely be dispensed with in the plain style of the Evangelist, though it might more elegantly be omitted. It was therefore cancelled by the *emendatores*, and *carelessly omitted*, on account of the preceding τι in ἐστί, by the scribes of the ordinary MSS.

By κλίνην must be understood the *couch* (like our sofa), which, as Grot. observes, had such a cavity as to admit of a *candelabrum* being put under it; nay, it seems, any thing much larger; indeed, from the citations adduced by Wets., it appears to have been used by the ancients as a common hiding-place. [*Comp.* Matt. v. 15. Luke viii. 16. xi. 33.]

22. οὐδὲ ἐγένετο ἀπόκρυφον, ἀλλ᾽ ἵνα, &c.] An elliptical form for οὐδὲ ἐγένετο ἀπόκ. (ἀλλ᾽ ἐγένετο ἀπόκρυφον) ἵνα, &c. Thus there is no reason to adopt any one of the *various readings*, which have sprung from ignorance of the nature of the expression. [*Comp.* Matt. x. 26. Luke viii. 17. xii. 2.]

24. βλέπετε τί — ἀκούουσιν.] There is an obscurity about this verse; which has given rise to several readings, and induced Editors to adopt various expedients to remove it. Griesb. and Tittm. expunge the clause καὶ προστεθήσεται — ἀκούουσιν, with a few MSS.; and Vater, from some MSS., cancels the τοῖς ἀκ. But it has been fully shown by Fritz. that *neither* emendation can be received; and he himself edits βλέπετε, τί ἀκούετε, καὶ προστεθήσεται ὑμῖν τοῖς ἀκούουσιν. Ὧι μέτρῳ μετρεῖτε, μετρηθήσονται ὑμῖν. By this emendation the thought is expressed more logically, and the sense more neatly expressed. But as there is no *direct* authority for the change, and as the Evangelist is by no means characterized by *neatness* and *exact correspondence* of the members of a sentence, it ought not to have been introduced into the text.

The τί here answers to the πῶς of Luke. Euthym. well paraphrases thus: Ἐν ᾧ μέτρῳ μετρεῖτε τὴν προσοχὴν, ἐν τῷ αὐτῷ μετρηθήσεται ὑμῖν ἡ γνῶσις. [*Comp.* Matt. xiii. 12, & xxii. 29. Luke vii. 18, & xix. 26.]

26. Fritz. well observes, that in ver. 26—32, there is a continuation of our Lord's discourse, which is now addressed to the people at large. The following parable is recorded only by Mark. On its bearing and application Commentators

MT. LU.

27 βάλῃ τὸν σπόρον ἐπὶ τῆς γῆς, καὶ καθεύδῃ καὶ ἐγείρηται νύκτα καὶ 13. 13.
ἡμέραν, καὶ ὁ σπόρος βλαστάνῃ καὶ μηκύνηται, ὡς οὐκ οἶδεν αὐτός.
28 Αὐτομάτη γὰρ ἡ γῆ καρποφορεῖ· πρῶτον χόρτον, εἶτα στάχυν, εἶτα
29 πλήρη σῖτον ἐν τῷ στάχυϊ. Ὅταν δὲ παραδῷ ὁ καρπὸς, εὐθέως
ἀποστέλλει τὸ δρέπανον, ὅτι παρέστηκεν ὁ θερισμός.
30 Καὶ ἔλεγε· Τίνι ὁμοιώσωμεν τὴν βασιλείαν τοῦ Θεοῦ; ἢ ἐν ποίᾳ 31 18
31 παραβολῇ παραβάλωμεν αὐτήν; Ὡς ‡ κόκκῳ σινάπεως, ὅς, ὅταν 19
σπαρῇ ἐπὶ τῆς γῆς, μικρότερος πάντων τῶν σπερμάτων ἐστὶ τῶν ἐπὶ 32
32 τῆς γῆς· καὶ ὅταν σπαρῇ, ἀναβαίνει, καὶ γίνεται πάντων τῶν λαχάνων μείζων, καὶ ποιεῖ κλάδους μεγάλους, ὥστε δύνασθαι ὑπὸ τὴν
33 σκιὰν αὐτοῦ τὰ πετεινὰ τοῦ οὐρανοῦ κατασκηνοῦν. Καὶ τοιαύταις 34

differ; some, as Whitby and Fritz., referring it to the seed which fell on good ground, in the preceding parable of the sower. But others, as Mackn., think the correspondence in many respects fails; and they are of opinion, that it should be taken in connection with the preceding verses, and was intended to prevent the Apostles from being dispirited, when they did not see their labours attended with success.

27. *καθεύδῃ καὶ ἐγείρηται*, &c.] This expression is like that of Ps. iii. 6. *ἐκοιμήθην καὶ ὕπνωσα, ἐξηγέρθην*, and is an image of security and confidence.

28. *αὐτομάτη*.] The word properly signifies *self-moved*, and is here, as often in the Classical writers, used of that energy of nature, which is independent of human aid. *Καρποφορεῖ* is generally taken for *φέρει*; the *καρπὸ* being inert, as in Diod. Sic. p. 137. *ἄμπελος — καρποφορεῖ τὸν οἶνον.* But Beza, Pisc., and Fritz. more properly give it the full sense *fruges fert*, and take *φέρει* from it in the next clause.

— *χόρτον*] "blade." For want of some such *definite* term, the Greeks and Romans were obliged to use the same word as denoted *grass*. The words *χόρτον* and *στάχυν* are put in the singular, because they are used in a *general* sense, which, however, implies plurality. *Στάχυς* denotes the ear in its green state, and it is so called from the peculiarly *erect* form it then has. *Πλήρη σῖτον*, the complete, perfect, and mature *grain*. So Gen. xli. 7. *σταχύες πλήρεις*.

29. *ὅταν δὲ παραδῷ ὁ καρπός*.] With this passage the ancient Translators were so perplexed, that they either gave versions which wander from the sense; or else they expressed the sense in a general way by, "when the crop is ripe." The best mode of removing the difficulty is, (with Beza, Heupel, Wolf, Kuin., and Fritz.,) to suppose an ellipsis of *ἑαυτὸν*, as in the case of many other active verbs to which use imparted a reciprocal sense; *κρύπτειν, κείθειν, ἀποῤῥίπτειν, ἀναλαμβάνειν, παρέχειν, ἱφιέναι, ἐνδιδόναι, ἐπιδιδόναι*, and finally *παραδοῦναι*· which, though it does not occur in the Classical writers, is found in Hellenistic Greek; e. gr. Josh. xi. 19. *οὐκ ἦν πόλις, ἥτις οὐ παρέδωκε* (surrender) *τοῖς υἱοῖς Ἰσραήλ*. 1 Pet. ii. 23. *παρεδίδου δὲ τῷ κρίνοντι δικαίως*. The question, however, is, to *whom* the fruit is to be understood to yield itself up, and deliver its increase? To the *reaper*, say the Commentators generally. But I prefer, with Fritz., to refer it to *τῷ ἀνθρώπῳ*, taken from the preceding. Thus also *ὁ ἄνθρωπος* must be understood at *ἀποστέλλει*. As to *ἀποστέλλει τὸ δρέπανον*, it is put, by a seemingly *popular* metonomy, for "he sendeth those who may put in the sickle;" i. e. the reapers. So, in a very similar passage of Joel iii. 13. *ἐξαποστείλατε δρέπανα, ὅτι παρέστηκεν ὁ τρυγητός*. See also Rev. xiv. 15. 19.

31. *κόκκῳ*.] The greater part of the MSS., together with the ancient Editions, and some Versions and Fathers, have *κόκκον*, which is adopted by Mill and Wets., and edited by Matth., Griesb., and others down to Scholz; except that Fritz. retains the common reading; I think rightly; for (as he shows) it is otherwise scarcely possible to justify the construction. And although *κόκκον* may seem to be the more difficult reading, yet (as it appears from the Greek Commentators) there is reason to think that *κόκκῳ* was altered into *κόκκον ex interpretatione*. Besides, it may be added, as the words are so very much alike, (the *ι adscript* and the *ν* being perpetually confounded,) MS. authority will here have but little weight. On the subject of this *Sinapi*, for the purpose of removing what has been thought a great difficulty, (namely, how to reconcile what is here said about the size of the seed and of the plant with the *sinapis* nigra, or common mustard plant,) Mr. Frost has propounded the hypothesis, that the sinapi of the N. T. does not designate any species of the genus we call *Sinapis*, but a species of the *Phytolacca* called the *Phytolacca dodecandra*, which is a tree common in North America; and, Mr. Frost *says*, grows abundantly in Palestine, and has properties exactly corresponding to those here ascribed to the *κόκκος*. But the learned Botanist has adduced no *authentication* of these statements from the works of eastern travellers. Indeed, the hypothesis is not only probably devoid of *proof*, but is *unnecessary* for the commendable purpose in view. Every enlightened Interpreter will see how uncritical it were to *press*, so much as Mr. Frost has done, on the expression "least of all seeds." It is sufficient if the smallest mustard seed be *among* the very least of seeds known *in Palestine*; for it is plain that the *tobacco* could not be here contemplated, since it was unknown till the discovery of America. And the *Foxglove* was probably not known in *Palestine*. It is plain, too, that *πάντων* must not be pressed upon; for the Heb, כל is often similarly pleonastic. Thus it is omitted in the parallel passage of St. Matthew.

Again, *γίνεται δένδρον* may very well be taken, by a popular hyperbole, for "it becomes, *as it were*, a tree;" especially as from a comparison of the parallel words of Matthew, *ποιεῖ κλάδους μεγάλους*, it is plain that the sense must be, "*that which branches out widely*, LIKE *a tree*." Thus, in the

MT. LU.
8. 8. *παραβολαῖς πολλαῖς ἐλάλει αὐτοῖς τὸν λόγον, καθὼς ἠδύναντο ἀκούειν.*
χωρὶς δὲ παραβολῆς οὐκ ἐλάλει αὐτοῖς· κατ᾽ ἰδίαν δὲ τοῖς μαθηταῖς 34
αὐτοῦ ἐπέλυε πάντα.

18 22 *Καὶ λέγει αὐτοῖς ἐν ἐκείνῃ τῇ ἡμέρᾳ, ὀψίας γενομένης· Διέλθωμεν* 35
εἰς τὸ πέραν. Καὶ ἀφέντες τὸν ὄχλον, παραλαμβάνουσιν αὐτὸν, ὡς 36
24 23 *ἦν, ἐν τῷ πλοίῳ· καὶ ἄλλα δὲ πλοιάρια ἦν μετ᾽ αὐτοῦ. Καὶ γίνεται* 37
λαῖλαψ ἀνέμου μεγάλη· τὰ δὲ κύματα ἐπέβαλλεν εἰς τὸ πλοῖον, ὥστε
αὐτὸ ἤδη γεμίζεσθαι. Καὶ ἦν αὐτὸς ἐπὶ τῇ πρύμνῃ, ἐπὶ τὸ προσκε- 38
25 24 *φάλαιον καθεύδων· καὶ διεγείρουσιν αὐτὸν, καὶ λέγουσιν αὐτῷ· Δι-*
26 *δάσκαλε, οὐ μέλει σοι ὅτι ἀπολλύμεθα; Καὶ διεγερθεὶς ἐπετίμησε τῷ* 39
ἀνέμῳ, καὶ εἶπε τῇ θαλάσσῃ· Σιώπα, πεφίμωσο. καὶ ἐκόπασεν ὁ
25 *ἄνεμος, καὶ ἐγένετο γαλήνη μεγάλη. Καὶ εἶπεν αὐτοῖς· Τί δειλοί* 40
27 *ἐστε οὕτω; πῶς οὐκ ἔχετε πίστιν; Καὶ ἐφοβήθησαν φόβον μέγαν,* 41

parallel passage of Luke, for *δένδρον* some MSS. have *ὡς δένδρον*, where, though the *ὡς* evidently came from the margin, yet it shows the mode in which the word was taken by the Glossographer. Besides the statements of Lightf., Scheuchzer, and Dr. A. Clarke, make it certain, that this plant sometimes grows to a height which may very well allow it to be a shelter for birds. Thus the above celebrated botanist mentions a species of the plant several feet high, which presents a *tree-like* appearance. As to what Mr. F. calls "the impossibility of an *annual plant* becoming a shrub, much less a *tree*," it is too formal and far-fetched an objection to deserve the least attention. Besides, Mr. Frost's own argument cannot but be fatal to his own hypothesis, since it must be negatived by the words *ὅταν δὲ αὐξηθῇ, γίνεται πάντων τῶν λαχάνων μείζων*, for surely the term *λαχ.*, *plant*, is not applicable to a *tree*. That some properties are common to the *Sinapi* and to the *phytolacca dodecandra* is clearly insufficient to establish Mr. Frost's position.

33. *καθὼς ἠδύναντο ἀκούειν*] i. e. "as they had the ability and capacity to understand them; and in such a way as they could profit by them."

34. *ἐπέλυε πάντα*] "gave solutions and explanations of every thing" [that was obscure to them.] *Ἐπιλύειν*, (as the Heb. פתר and the Latin *solvere)* often has this sense. Its primary signification is to *untie a knot*. The Hebrew term seems to be derived from פתח to *open* or loose what is shut or bound, whence מפתח, *a key*, literally an *opener*.

36. *παραλαμβάνουσιν—ἐν τῷ πλοιῳ.*] On the interpretation of this passage Commentators are by no means agreed. Most take *ἐν τῷ πλοίῳ* as put for *εἰς τὸ πλοῖον*, in this sense: "After he had dismissed the multitude, his disciples took him, just as he was, (i. e. unprepared as he was, and without delay,) on board the ship." An interpretation ably supported by Rosenm. and Kuin. But as this taking of *ἐν* for *εἰς* is here somewhat harsh, I should be rather inclined to agree with Euthym. and some other ancients, together with several of the modern Commentators, in joining *ἐν τῷ πλοίῳ* with *ὡς ἦν*, which renders any *enallage* unnecessary. Thus the sense will be, that on the dismissal of the multitude, they carried him off, just as he sat in the boat [out of which he had been teaching]." Yet this reference to the boat mentioned supra v. 1. is somewhat harsh, and the sense rather jejune. *Ἦν* is too little significant a term to have *ἐν τῷ πλοίῳ* joined with it; which words are plainly joined in construction with *παραλαμβάνουσι*. Then *ἐν τῷ πλ.* is, strictly speaking, not used for *εἰς τὸ πλοῖον*, but is a *phrasis prægnans* (and hence the *Dative* is used for the Accus.) denoting, they took him *on board*, and carried him in the bark [namely, that mentioned supra v. 1.] As to *ὡς ἦν*, there is no need to suppose it to mean *just as he was*, without waiting for refreshment, or accommodations for the passage; a sense somewhat jejune and forced. And surely no great *preparations* would be necessary for a passage of a few miles across a lake. We must here, as in very many places of the best writers, take it simply to mean *εὐθὺς*, quam celerrimè. (See my note on Thucyd. iii. 30. *ὥσπερ ἔχομεν.*) This was agreeably to their Lord's *injunction*, and because probably the evening was coming on. See Fritz., who aptly compares Lucian Asin. C. 24. *κάτω ἀφῆκαν ὡς ἦν τῷ δέσμῳ.*

—*μετ᾽ αὐτοῦ*] i. e. as Fritz. explains, with Jesus's vessel. And he cites many examples of this figure, by which the vessel is put for the crew, or the crew for the vessel. One, however, still more to the purpose, occurs in Thucyd. iv. 120. 2. *ὁ Βρασίδας διέπλευσε νυκτὸς ἐς τὴν Σκιώνην, τριήρει μὲν φιλίᾳ προπλεούσῃ, αὐτὸς δὲ ἐν κελητίῳ ἄποθεν ἐφεπόμενος, ὅπως εἰ μέν τινι τοῦ κέλητος μείζονι πλοίῳ περιτυγχάνοι, ἡ τριήρης ἀμύνοι αὐτῷ.*

37. *λαῖλαψ*] a whirlwind, hurricane; for the ancient Lexicographers explain it by *συστροφή*, and Aristot. de Mundo, *πνεῦμα βίαιον, καὶ εἱλούμενον κάτωθεν ἄνω*. It seems derived from *λαι*, *very*, and *λάπτειν*, to *snatch*, take off, carry away. *Ἐπέβαλλε* is to be taken in an intransitive sense for *se injecerunt*, *irruebant*. *Γεμίζεσθαι*, scil. *ἐκ τῶν κυμάτων*, to be supplied from the preceding.

38. *τῇ πρύμνῃ*] i. e. the place where the steersman sat, and the most commodious one for a passenger. *Τὸ προσκεφ.* must be rendered, not *a* pillow, but *the* pillow. The Article has a peculiar force, as pointing to a particular part of the furniture of the ship. This seems to have been the *leather-stuffed cushion*, which was used as a pillow.

39. *σιώπα, πεφ.*] The *asyndeton* here is very suitable to the gravity of the address, and the dignity of the occasion. If Valckn. had had the taste to perceive this, he would have suppressed his conjecture, that *σιώπα* is a gloss. Besides, the

MT. LU.

καὶ ἔλεγον πρὸς ἀλλήλους· Τίς ἄρα οὗτός ἐστιν, ὅτι καὶ ὁ ἄνεμος 8. 8.
καὶ ἡ θάλασσα ὑπακούουσιν αὐτῷ;
1 V. ΚΑΙ ἦλθον εἰς τὸ πέραν τῆς θαλάσσης, εἰς τὴν χώραν τῶν 28 26
2 Γαδαρηνῶν. Καὶ ἐξελθόντι αὐτῷ ἐκ τοῦ πλοίου εὐθέως ἀπήντησεν 27
3 αὐτῷ ἐκ τῶν μνημείων ἄνθρωπος ἐν πνεύματι ἀκαθάρτῳ, ὃς τὴν κα-
τοίκησιν εἶχεν ἐν τοῖς μνήμασι· καὶ οὔτε ἁλύσεσιν οὐδεὶς ἠδύνατο
4 αὐτὸν δῆσαι, διὰ τὸ αὐτὸν πολλάκις πέδαις καὶ ἁλύσεσι δεδέσθαι, 29
καὶ διεσπᾶσθαι ὑπ' αὐτοῦ τὰς ἁλύσεις, καὶ τὰς πέδας συντετρίφθαι·
5 καὶ οὐδεὶς αὐτὸν ἴσχυε δαμάσαι. Καὶ διαπαντὸς, νυκτὸς καὶ ἡμέρας,
ἐν τοῖς * μνήμασι καὶ ἐν τοῖς ὄρεσιν ἦν, κράζων καὶ κατακόπτων
6 ἑαυτὸν λίθοις. Ἰδὼν δὲ τὸν Ἰησοῦν ἀπὸ μακρόθεν, ἔδραμε καὶ 28
7 προσεκύνησεν αὐτῷ, καὶ κράξας φωνῇ μεγάλῃ εἶπε· Τί ἐμοὶ καὶ σοὶ, 29
Ἰησοῦ Υἱὲ τοῦ Θεοῦ τοῦ ὑψίστου; ὁρκίζω σε τὸν Θεὸν, μή με βα-
8 σανίσῃς. ἔλεγε γὰρ αὐτῷ· Ἔξελθε τὸ πνεῦμα τὸ ἀκάθαρτον ἐκ τοῦ
9 ἀνθρώπου. καὶ ἐπηρώτα αὐτόν· Τί σοι ὄνομα; καὶ ‡ ἀπεκρίθη 30

use of *two terms*, however seemingly synonymous, *strengthens* the sense. Thus even in the form with which cryers, or heralds, commenced their addresses, Ἄκουε, σίγα.

41. ἔλεγον] Not the disciples only, but the mariners also.

V. 1. Γαδαρηνῶν.] See Note on Matt. viii. 28.

2. ἄνθρωπος ἐν πν. ἀκ.] Sub. ὤν. So ver 25. γυνή τις οὖσα ἐν ῥύσει αἵματος. There is no such *hypallage*, as some Commentators suppose; nor do Grot. and Fritz. rightly take the ἐν for σύν. Indeed ὢν with ἐν is equivalent to ἐνεχόμενος, "*laboring under*."

3. τὴν κατοίκησιν] The Article refers to αὐτοῦ understood; and the force of the Imperfect in εἶχεν is that of *use* and *habit*. Μνήμασι, instead of the common reading μνημείοις, is read in a great part of the MSS., the Edit. Princ., and Beng. It was with reason preferred by Mill, adopted by Wets., and edited by Matth., Griesb., Tittm., Vat., Fritz., and Scholz. The common reading arose, no doubt, from ver. 2. The sepulchral monuments of the ancients, especially in the East, were tolerably roomy vaults, and would be no indifferent shelter for maniacs. Indeed, from Diog. Laert. 4x. 38. ἐρημάζων ἐνίοτε, καὶ τοῖς τάφοις ἐνδιατρίβων, we find that they formed no contemptible *habitations*, and were sometimes used as such.

5. ἐν τοῖς — ἦν] This punctuation I have adopted with the Vulg., Syr., E. V., Doddr., Winer, and Fritz, as being required by propriety. To place the comma after κράζων, as is generally done, would yield a false sense. See Winer's Gr. Gr. § 39. The position ἐν τοῖς μν. καὶ ἐν τοῖς ὄρεσιν for the common reading ἐν τοῖς ὄρεσιν καὶ ἐν τοῖς μν., is found in many of the best MSS., and almost all the Versions, and is edited by Griesb., Tittm., Fritz., and Scholz.

The circumstance of cutting himself with sharp *stones*, instead of a knife (which, of course, would not be granted him), is quite agreeable to the usual custom of *maniacs;* who tear their flesh, and cut it with whatever they can lay their hands on; of which Wets. adduces examples. Here, however, this was manifestly the result of dæmoniacal possession.

7. Θεοῦ τοῦ ὑψίστου] The epithet ὁ ὕψιστος as applied to God, occurs no where else in the Gospels, and only once out of them; namely, Heb. vii. 1., taken from Genes. xiv. 22. It corresponds to the Heb. עליון. The expressions seem to have been at first given with reference to the exalted abode of God, i. e. in Heaven. See Isa. lxvi. 1. The appellations may also refer to the *supreme majesty* of the Deity; and correspondent terms are found in the Theology of all the *Pagan* nations of antiquity. In the O. T., however, עליון is almost always used to distinguish the Deity from those who were *called* Gods.

— ὁρκίζω σε τὸν Θεὸν] This formula usually denotes to *put any one on his oath*. See Note on Matt. xxvi. 63. But here (as Grot., Rosenm., and Kuin. have shown) it has the force of *oro, obtestor te per Deum*, and thus is equivalent to the δέομαί σου of Luke xviii. 28.

— μή με βασανίσῃς] Namely, as some ancient and modern Commentators explain, "by compelling me to depart from the man." But this interpretation, however agreeable to the context, is somewhat harsh, and is not permitted by the parallel passages of Matthew and Luke; from whence it appears that the word is to be taken of the *mode* of torment, which was supposed to be apportioned to dæmons compelled to come out of possessed persons, namely, the being compelled (as Luke expresses it) εἰς τὴν ἄβυσσον ἀπελθεῖν (see 2 Pet. ii. 4. and Apoc. ix. 1 & 2, xi. 7, &c.), a term applied by the Greeks to their Tartarus. The words of ver. 10, καὶ παρεκάλει — ἔξω τῆς χώρας may, indeed, seem to favor the first-mentioned interpretation. But they are equally suitable to the other. The dæmons entreat that if they *must* depart from the man, they may at least not be compelled to leave the *country;* which was but another form of preferring the first-mentioned request, that he would not send them away to the place of torment.

9. ἀπεκρίθη λέγων] Many MSS. (some of them ancient) and most of the Versions read λέγει αὐτῷ, which is preferred by Beng., and edited by Griesb., Tittm., Vat., Fritz., and Scholz. But there is no sufficient reason for the alteration.

— τί σοι ὄνομα] Spirits, both good and evil, are

MT. LU.

8. 8. ‡ λέγων· Λεγεὼν ὄνομά μοι, ὅτι πολλοί ἐσμεν. καὶ παρεκάλει αὐτὸν 10
30 31 32 πολλὰ, ἵνα μὴ αὐτοὺς ἀποστείλῃ ἔξω τῆς χώρας. ἦν δὲ ἐκεῖ πρὸς 11
31 * τῷ ὄρει ἀγέλη χοίρων μεγάλη βοσκομένη· καὶ παρεκάλεσαν αὐτὸν 12
[πάντες] οἱ δαίμονες λέγοντες· Πέμψον ἡμᾶς εἰς τοὺς χοίρους, ἵνα
32 εἰς αὐτοὺς εἰσέλθωμεν. Καὶ ἐπέτρεψεν αὐτοῖς εὐθέως ὁ Ἰησοῦς. καὶ 13
33 ἐξελθόντα τὰ πνεύματα τὰ ἀκάθαρτα, εἰσῆλθον εἰς τοὺς χοίρους· καὶ
ὥρμησεν ἡ ἀγέλη κατὰ τοῦ κρημνοῦ εἰς τὴν θάλασσαν (ἦσαν δὲ ὡς
33 34 δισχίλιοι), καὶ ἐπνίγοντο ἐν τῇ θαλάσσῃ. Οἱ δὲ βόσκοντες τοὺς 14
χοίρους ἔφυγον, καὶ * ἀπήγγειλαν εἰς τὴν πόλιν καὶ εἰς τοὺς ἀγρούς.
34 35 καὶ ἐξῆλθον ἰδεῖν τί ἐστι τὸ γεγονός. Καὶ ἔρχονται πρὸς τὸν Ἰη- 15
σοῦν, καὶ θεωροῦσι τὸν δαιμονιζόμενον καθήμενον, καὶ ἱματισμένον
36 καὶ σωφρονοῦντα, τὸν ἐσχηκότα τὸν λεγεῶνα· ἐφοβήθησαν. καὶ διη- 16
γήσαντο αὐτοῖς οἱ ἰδόντες, πῶς ἐγένετο τῷ δαιμονιζομένῳ, καὶ περὶ
37 τῶν χοίρων. καὶ ἤρξαντο παρακαλεῖν αὐτὸν ἀπελθεῖν ἀπὸ τῶν ὁρίων 17
38 αὐτῶν. Καὶ ἐμβάντος αὐτοῦ εἰς τὸ πλοῖον, παρεκάλει αὐτὸν ὁ δαι- 18
μονισθεὶς ἵνα ᾖ μετ' αὐτοῦ. Ὁ δὲ [Ἰησοῦς] οὐκ ἀφῆκεν αὐτὸν, 19

always represented in Scripture, as *having names*: assumed, as Commentators think, in accommodation to human infirmity. Be that as it may, our Lord did not ask the name through ignorance, but (as Euthym. suggests) to thereby elicit an answer; that the bystanders might have the more occasion to admire the stupendous power by which the miracle was wrought.

—Λεγεὼν] This word (from the name of a well-known Roman body of troops) was often used by the Jews to denote a *great number*. That the term has that sense here, and not that of *Chief of the Legion*, is plain from the words following, and those of vv. 10 & 12.

10. αὐτοὺς] i. e. himself and his fellows, who called themselves by the name Legion.

11. πρὸς τῷ ὄρει] This reading, for πρὸς τὰ ὄρη is found in the greater part of the MSS., nearly the whole of the Versions (confirmed by Luke viii. 32. ἐν τῷ ὄρει), and is adopted by Wets., Beng., Matth., Griesb., Vat., Tittm., Fritz., and Scholz. Yet the common reading is not, as Fritz. affirms, *inepta*; for the πρὸς might mean *in*, *at*, or *by*, as in many passages, which see in Schleusn. or Wahl. Πάντες is omitted in very many MSS., and all the best Versions, and is cancelled by Griesb., Vat., Tittm., Fritz., and Scholz.

13. καὶ ἐπνίγοντο] "were suffocated," i. e. by drowning. So that it might be rendered "were drowned," as in a passage of Plutarch cited by Wets. Indeed our *drown* comes from the Saxon *Druncnian*, to choke. But that sense is inherent in the added words ἐν τῇ θαλάσσῃ. Those who adopt the hypothesis which supposes the demoniacs to have been *lunatics*, are here involved in inextricable difficulties; for the words of Mark (as Fritz. truly observes) can be no otherwise understood than as asserting that the dæmons ejected from the man really entered into the bodies of such of the swine as they chose.

14. οἱ δὲ βόσκοντες.] The participle has here the force of a substantive, as Matt. viii. 28. Luke viii. 34. vii. 14. Ἀπήγγειλαν (instead of the common reading ἀνήγγ.) is found in several MSS., and is edited by Griesb., Titt., Vat., Fritz., and Scholz. I long hesitated to receive this reading; because, though strict propriety requires ἀπήγγ., not ἀνήγγ., yet in such a writer as Mark, that is not decisive; and there are in the N. T. a few instances of ἀναγγ. for ἀπαγγ., a signification which is noticed by Hesych. Yet I know none followed, as here, by εἰς with an Accusative of thing for person; in which case ἀπαγγ. (which is a stronger term) seems requisite.

By τὴν πόλιν is meant the city of Gadara, and by τοὺς ἀγροὺς, the country around it.

—ἰδεῖν τί ἐστι τὸ γεγ.] This seems to be a *popular* mode of expression, meaning to examine into the reality of any reported occurrence.

15. θεωροῦσι τὸν—λεγεῶνα] There is no reason to adopt any of the changes here found in MSS. and supported by Critics; not even the cancelling of καὶ before ἱματισμένον, for it tends to strengthen the sense. And although there may seem an unnecessary addition in τὸν ἐσχηκότα τὸν λεγεῶνα after τὸν δαιμονιζόμενον, yet the latter is far more significant; and there is a sort of climax. Render "They see the demoniac seated; both clothed and in his right mind; him (I say) who had been possessed by the demons who called themselves Legion." The being *seated* is mentioned, as a mark of sanity of mind, since maniacs rarely *sit*. Ἐφοβήθησαν is by most Commentators understood of *fear* lest they might suffer a *greater* calamity; but it rather denotes awe at the stupendous miracle.

17. καὶ ἤρξαντο παρακ.] "whereupon they fell to beseeching him," &c. This sense of καὶ like that of the Heb. ו is frequent in Scripture, and sometimes occurs in the Classical writers. Τῶν ὁρίων α., "their district." See Note on Matt. viii. 28. [*Comp.* Acts xvi. 39.]

18. ἵνα ᾖ μετ' αὐτοῦ] "might accompany him." This was, as many Commentators suppose, from fear lest the demons should again enter into him. But a better motive may be imagined.

19. οὐκ ἀφῆκεν αὐτόν.] The reasons which influenced our Lord's refusal have been variously conjectured; (see Theophyl., Euthym., Grot., Kuin., and Fritz.,) any, or indeed all of which combined, may have had effect. Τοὺς σοὺς, scil. οἰκείους to be taken from οἶκον.

MT. LU.

ἀλλὰ λέγει αὐτῷ· Ὕπαγε εἰς τὸν οἶκόν σου πρὸς τοὺς σοὺς, καὶ 9. 8.
ἀνάγγειλον αὐτοῖς, ὅσα σοι ὁ Κύριος *πεποίηκε, καὶ ἠλέησέ σε. 39
20 Καὶ ἀπῆλθε καὶ ἤρξατο κηρύσσειν ἐν τῇ Δεκαπόλει ὅσα ἐποίησεν
αὐτῷ ὁ Ἰησοῦς· καὶ πάντες ἐθαύμαζον.
21 ΚΑΙ διαπεράσαντος τοῦ Ἰησοῦ ἐν τῷ πλοίῳ πάλιν εἰς τὸ πέραν, 1 40
22 συνήχθη ὄχλος πολὺς ἐπ᾽ αὐτόν· καὶ ἦν παρὰ τὴν θάλασσαν. Καὶ 18 41
ἰδοὺ, ἔρχεται εἷς τῶν ἀρχισυναγώγων ὀνόματι Ἰάειρος· καὶ ἰδὼν αὐ-
23 τὸν, πίπτει πρὸς τοὺς πόδας αὐτοῦ, καὶ παρεκάλει αὐτὸν πολλὰ, 42
λέγων· Ὅτι τὸ θυγάτριόν μου ἐσχάτως ἔχει· ἵνα ἐλθὼν ἐπιθῇς
24 αὐτῇ τὰς χεῖρας, ὅπως σωθῇ· καὶ ζήσεται. Καὶ ἀπῆλθε μετ᾽ αὐ- 19
τοῦ· καὶ ἠκολούθει αὐτῷ ὄχλος πολὺς, καὶ συνέθλιβον αὐτόν.
25 Καὶ γυνή τις οὖσα ἐν ῥύσει αἵματος ἔτη δώδεκα, καὶ πολλὰ 20 43
26 παθοῦσα ὑπὸ πολλῶν ἰατρῶν, καὶ δαπανήσασα τὰ παρ᾽ αὐτῆς πάντα, καὶ μηδὲν ὠφεληθεῖσα, ἀλλὰ μᾶλλον εἰς τὸ χεῖρον ἐλθοῦσα,
27 ἀκούσασα περὶ τοῦ Ἰησοῦ, ἐλθοῦσα ἐν τῷ ὄχλῳ ὄπισθεν, ἥψατο τοῦ 44

— *πεποίηκε.*] This reading (instead of the common one *ἐποίησε*) is found in the greater part of the MSS., some Fathers, and the Edit. Princ.; and is, with reason, adopted by Beng., Wets., Matth., Griesb., Tittm., Vat., Fritz., and Scholz. Propriety, indeed, as well as MS. authority, would seem to require the preterite; for (as Fritz. observes) "in the dispossessed person, the effect of the things which the Lord had done remained; but the compassion (denoted by *ἠλέησέ σε*) is a thing which would be transient." Yet *ἐποίησε* occurs in the parallel place of Luke, from which it was probably introduced here. In *καὶ ἠλέησέ σε* there is no occasion to insert *ὅτι*, with Beza. It is better to suppose, with Grot., that these words are suspended on the preceding, so that *ὅσα* may be repeated. Perhaps, however, Fritz. is right in accounting this a *variation of construction*.

21. *ἐπ᾽ αὐτὸν*] Fritz. observes that the *ἐπὶ* corresponds to the German *nach*, and that the sense here is, "ut eum indipisceretur."

22. *εἷς τῶν ἀρχισ.*] Ἀρχισυνάγωγος properly signifies the president of a synagogue. But there was but one synagogue at Capernaum; and from the expression *εἷς τῶν ἀρχισυν.*, taken in conjunction with Acts xiii. 15. and what we learn from the Rabbinical writers, we may infer, that in a synagogue there was not only *one* who was properly President; but *others*, consisting of the more respectable members, who also *bore the title*; either as having exercised the office of President, or because they occasionally discharged the duties of the office; which were to preserve decorum and the proper forms of worship, and to select and invite those who should read or speak in the congregation.

23. *ἐσχάτως ἔχει*] "in ultimis est," "is at the last stage of the disease." The phrase *ἐσχάτως ἔχειν*, which occurs only in the latter Greek writers, is equivalent to the more classical *ἐσχάτως εἶναι*, or *διακεῖσθαι*.

— *ἵνα ἐλθὼν ἐπιθῇς*, &c.] There is here a difficulty of construction, which some attempt to remove by supposing an *hyperbaton*. This, however, would involve an unprecedented harshness. It is better, with the Syr. and Vulg., Kypke, Kuin., and Fritz., to regard the expression as a *circumlocution*, for the *Imperative*; *ἵνα* with a Subjunctive being put for the Imperative, as in Ephes. v. 23. Thus the sense is, "Come, and lay thy hands upon her." Yet some verb must be supplied at *ἵνα*; either *δέομαι*, as is generally thought, or rather *παρακαλῶ*, taken in the *sense* of *δέομαι*.

25. *οὖσα ἐν ῥύσει αἵματος.*] This construction is thought by Winer Gr. Gr. p. 134. a Hebraism; by others, a Latinism; but it is common to both Hebrew, Greek, and Latin. Thus the Greeks say *εἶναι ἐν νόσῳ*, (Soph. Aj. 270.,) and the Romans *in morbo esse*.

26. *πολλὰ παθοῦσα.*] The expression is a strong one (like the "diu a medicis *vexatos*" of Celsus); yet when we consider the ignorance of Jewish physicians, and the various nostrums prescribed in such a case, (on which see Lightf.), many of which would be nauseous and strong, and all of them injurious to a habit of body so languid as in this disease, we may conceive that her sufferings would be great. There *may* be something *sarcastic* in the word *πολλῶν*, with which the Commentators compare the saying of Menander, *πολλῶν ἰατρῶν εἴσοδός μ᾽ ἀπώλεσαν*.

— *αὐτῆς.*] This (for *ἑαυτῆς*), is read in most of the best MSS. and Theophyl., and rightly edited by Matth., Griesb., Tittm., Fritz., and Scholz; since the common reading arose from an attempt at emendation produced by seeming difficulty. The phrase may (as Fritz. suggests), be best explained, by regarding it as one of those in which the *παρὰ* with a Genit. does not in *sense* differ from a simple Genitive.

— *εἰς τὸ χεῖρον ἐλθοῦσα.*] Literally, "having come into a worse condition." This use of *εἰς* or *ἐπὶ* with adjectives of the Comparative degree, importing "for the better" or "for the worse," is frequent in the best writers.

On the construction in ver. 25—27. (which is somewhat anomalous), Fritz. well remarks, that the Participles *ἀκούσασα* and *ἐλθοῦσα* have nothing to do with the preceding ones *οὖσα* and *ἐλθοῦσα*, but are put *ἀσυνδέτως*. The difficulty may, however, he thinks, be removed by considering the words *οὖσα ἐν ῥύσει — εἰς τὸ χεῖρον ἐλθοῦσα* as *quasi parentheticæ*, and showing the nature of the disease. Thus *καὶ γυνή τις* will connect with *ἀκούσασα περὶ τοῦ Ἰ., ἐλθοῦσα*, for *ἦλθε καὶ*, &c. This, how-

MT LU.
9. 8. ἱματίου αὐτοῦ· ἔλεγε γάρ· Ὅτι κἂν τῶν ἱματίων αὐτοῦ ἅψωμαι, 28
21 σωθήσομαι. Καὶ εὐθέως ἐξηράνθη ἡ πηγὴ τοῦ αἵματος αὐτῆς, 29
45 καὶ ἔγνω τῷ σώματι ὅτι ἴαται ἀπὸ τῆς μάστιγος. Καὶ εὐθέως ὁ Ἰη- 30
σοῦς ἐπιγνοὺς ἐν ἑαυτῷ τὴν ἐξ αὐτοῦ δύναμιν ἐξελθοῦσαν, ἐπιστραφεὶς
46 ἐν τῷ ὄχλῳ, ἔλεγε· Τίς μου ἥψατο τῶν ἱματίων; καὶ ἔλεγον αὐτῷ 31
οἱ μαθηταὶ αὐτοῦ· Βλέπεις τὸν ὄχλον συνθλίβοντά σε, καὶ λέγεις·
Τίς μου ἥψατο; καὶ περιεβλέπετο ἰδεῖν τὴν τοῦτο ποιήσασαν. Ἡ δὲ 32
47 γυνὴ, φοβηθεῖσα καὶ τρέμουσα, εἰδυῖα ὃ γέγονεν ἐπ' αὐτῇ, ἦλθε καὶ 33
22 48 προσέπεσεν αὐτῷ, καὶ εἶπεν αὐτῷ πᾶσαν τὴν ἀλήθειαν. Ὁ δὲ εἶπεν 34
αὐτῇ· Θύγατερ, ἡ πίστις σου σέσωκέ σε· ὕπαγε εἰς εἰρήνην, καὶ
49 ἴσθι ὑγιὴς ἀπὸ τῆς μάστιγός σου. Ἔτι αὐτοῦ λαλοῦντος, ἔρχονται 35
ἀπὸ τοῦ ἀρχισυναγώγου λέγοντες· Ὅτι ἡ θυγάτηρ σου ἀπέθανε· τί

ever, is so like *re-writing* the sentence, that it is perhaps better to consider the whole as one of the many examples of *anacoluthon*, which occur not only in the N. T. but also in the best Classical writers.

28. *ἔλεγε γάρ.*] Several MSS. and some Latin Versions add *ἐν ἑαυτῇ*, which Fritz. thinks so indispensable to the sense that he receives the words into the text; utterly disallowing the examples which have been adduced of a similar brevity of expression in *λέγειν* and the Heb. אמר. But, whatever *propriety* may dictate, and the usage of the best writers confirm; certain it is, that, in the popular and familiar phraseology of most languages, the idiom is found; though it rarely, if ever, occurs, except when, from the circumstances of the case, no mistake can arise from the omission in question.

29. *ἐξηράνθη ἡ πηγὴ τ. α.*] Campb. translates "the source of her distemper." But this is neither a correct version, nor a good paraphrase. *Πηγὴ* must be taken in a physical sense, though not in that proposed by Fritz. Nor is it much to the purpose that the Philological Commentators heap up examples of *δακρύων πηγή*. Kuin. and Fritz. rightly observe, that *ἡ πηγὴ τοῦ αἵματος αὐτῆς* must be closely kept together, and that *πηγὴ τοῦ αἱμ.* is for *ῥύσις τοῦ αἱμ.*, answering to the Heb. מקר דמים in Levit. xii. 7. and xx. 18., a bloody flux. This is placed beyond doubt by the expression of Luke *ἔστη ἡ ῥύσις τοῦ αἵματος αὐτῆς*.

—*τῷ σώματι*] i. e., as Euthym. well explains, *διὰ τοῦ σώματος, μηκέτι ῥαινομένου τοῖς σταλαγμοῖς*. It is plain (as Fritz. observes) that the woman was then suffering under the disorder in its greatest violence. Ἴαται, "that she had been healed;" for it is the *preterite*, not the *present* (*ἰᾶται*). Ἔγνω is a very significant term, and denotes *full conviction from actual experience*. Hence, too, we may see the stupendous nature of the miracle: for, as Grot. observes, "no one can, naturally, all at once recover from an inveterate malady; but vestiges of the disorder, in its gradual retreat, will long remain."

30. *ἐπιγνοὺς — ἐξελθοῦσαν.*] These words are thought to involve some perplexity. One thing is plain, namely, that from hence, and from Luke vi. 9, it appears that the power of performing miracles was not, with our *Saviour*, as in the case of the Prophets and Apostles, *adventitious*, (in consequence of which they ascribed their miracles to God,) but *inherent* in him by his Divine nature. This, however, is but an *inference* from the words; in discussing the sense of which, even the best Commentators have much (but vainly) perplexed themselves and their readers. It is needless to advert to the unhallowed speculations of those who refer them to *animal magnetism*: nor can those be commended who ascribe the cure to an *effluvium*, or *emanation*; though Fritz., after a long examination of the force of the words, thinks that they mean, "Jesus knowing *vim salubrem effluxisse é corpore*." It is best to suppose the words not meant to be taken in a *physical* sense; or to teach us the *mode* whereby the miracle was performed. They are rather to be considered as a popular manner of expression, (like *διὰ τῶν χειρῶν*, often used of the working of miracles); and, therefore, not to be *rigorously* interpreted, or bound down to philosophical precision; but only importing, that Christ was fully aware that a miracle had been worked by his power and efficacy. The sentence is, however, obscured by ellipsis and hyperbaton. The construction is, *ἐπιγνοὺς ἐν ἑαυτῷ τὴν δύναμιν ἐξελθοῦσαν ἐξ αὐτοῦ*; where at *τὴν δύν.* must be supplied *ἐν αὐτῷ οὖσαν* from *ἐξ αὐτοῦ ἐξελθ.*, "knowing that the power of working miracles, which was inherent in him, had gone out of him," as it were by the performance of a miracle *through* him. This force of *δύναμιν* is indicated by the *article*, from inattention to which many of the best Commentators take *τὴν δύναμιν* to simply signify "a miracle;" which obliges them to interpret *ἐξελθ.* in the far-fetched sense, "*vim exercuisse*."

32. *περιεβλέπετο*] for *περιέβλεπε*, by a use peculiar to the N. T.

33. *πᾶσαν τὴν ἀλ.*,] i. e. as Middlet. explains, "the whole truth respecting the affair in question." In this *absolute* use of the phrase, (with which Fritz. compares Demosth. *πάντα γὰρ εἰρήσεται τἀληθῆ πρὸς ὑμᾶς*), there is an ellipse of *τοῦ ἔργου*, or the like. But when it is *not* absolute, the ellipse is unnecessary, being supplied in the words following; as in Thucyd. vi. 87. *εἰρήκαμεν δ' ὑμῖν πᾶσαν τὴν ἀλήθειαν περὶ ὧν ὑποπτευόμεθα.*

34. *ὕπαγε εἰς εἰρήνην.*] This and the kindred phrases *πορεύεσθαι*, and *βαδίζειν εἰς εἰρήνην* were founded on the Heb. לכי לשלום, and were forms of affectionate or condescending valediction; and mean, as Fritz. explains, "I secundo omine," "go in God's name."

35. *ἀπὸ τοῦ ἀρχισ.*] literally, "from the President's, i. e. his house, (for he was now with Jesus.)

MT. LU.

36 ἔτι σκύλλεις τὸν διδάσκαλον; Ὁ δὲ Ἰησοῦς, εὐθέως ἀκούσας τὸν 9. 8.
λόγον λαλούμενον, λέγει τῷ ἀρχισυναγώγῳ· Μὴ φόβου, μόνον πίστευε. 50
37 Καὶ οὐκ ἀφῆκεν οὐδένα αὐτῷ συνακολουθῆσαι, εἰ μὴ Πέτρον καὶ
38 Ἰάκωβον καὶ Ἰωάννην τὸν ἀδελφὸν Ἰακώβου. Καὶ ἔρχεται εἰς τὸν 23 51
οἶκον τοῦ ἀρχισυναγώγου, καὶ θεωρεῖ θόρυβον, κλαίοντας καὶ ἀλαλά- 52
39 ζοντας πολλά. Καὶ εἰσελθὼν λέγει αὐτοῖς· Τί θορυβεῖσθε καὶ 24
40 κλαίετε; τὸ παιδίον οὐκ ἀπέθανεν, ἀλλὰ καθεύδει. Καὶ κατεγέλων 53
αὐτοῦ. Ὁ δὲ ἐκβαλὼν * πάντας, παραλαμβάνει τὸν πατέρα τοῦ 25 54
παιδίου καὶ τὴν μητέρα, καὶ τοὺς μετ᾽ αὐτοῦ, καὶ εἰσπορεύεται,
41 ὅπου ἦν τὸ παιδίον ἀνακείμενον. Καὶ κρατήσας τῆς χειρὸς τοῦ
παιδίου λέγει αὐτῇ· Ταλιθὰ κοῦμι· ὅ ἐστι μεθερμηνευόμενον, Τὸ
42 κοράσιον, σοὶ λέγω· ἔγειρε. Καὶ εὐθέως ἀνέστη τὸ κοράσιον καὶ 55
περιεπάτει (ἦν γὰρ ἐτῶν δώδεκα), καὶ ἐξέστησαν ἐκστάσει μεγάλῃ.
43 καὶ διεστείλατο αὐτοῖς πολλὰ, ἵνα μηδεὶς γνῷ τοῦτο· καὶ εἶπε δο- 56
θῆναι αὐτῇ φαγεῖν. 13. 4.
1 VI. ΚΑΙ ἐξῆλθεν ἐκεῖθεν, καὶ ἦλθεν εἰς τὴν πατρίδα αὐτοῦ· 54 16
2 καὶ ἀκολουθοῦσιν αὐτῷ οἱ μαθηταὶ αὐτοῦ. καὶ γενομένου σαββάτου, ἤρξατο ἐν τῇ συναγωγῇ διδάσκειν· καὶ πολλοὶ ἀκούοντες ἐξεπλήσσοντο, λέγοντες· Πόθεν τούτῳ ταῦτα; καὶ τίς ἡ σοφία ἡ δο-
θεῖσα αὐτῷ, ὅτι καὶ δυνάμεις τοιαῦται διὰ τῶν χειρῶν αὐτοῦ γίνονται;
3 Οὐχ οὗτός ἐστιν ὁ τέκτων, ὁ υἱὸς Μαρίας, ἀδελφὸς δὲ Ἰακώβου καὶ 55

So John xviii. 28. ἄγουσιν οὖν τὸν Ἰησοῦν ἀπὸ τοῦ Καϊάφα. The idiom is found both in Greek and Latin, and indeed in modern languages.

38. κλαίοντας καὶ ἀλ.] These words are exegetical of θόρυβον. Ἀλαλάζειν from ἄλαλα, (whence our *halloo)* seems to be akin to the Heb. הילל, from whence came ἐλελίζειν. Both denoted the *shout* uttered by the soldiers of all the ancient nations, previous to battle. Ἀλαλάζειν, however, was sometimes used of any shrill vociferation, especially of grief, as in Jerem. xxv. 34 & 47, and Eurip. Elect. 843. ἤσπαιρεν, ἠλάλαξε. [*Comp.* John xi. 1.]

40. ἐκβαλὼν πάντας.] This merely means, "having ordered all to be removed." Jesus retained just *so many* as were sufficient to prove the reality of the cure. To have permitted the presence of *more* might have savoured of ostentation. For ἅπαντας, πάντας is found in very many MSS. and the Edit. Princ., and is adopted by Beng., Wets., Mill, Griesb., Tittm., Vat., Fritz., and Scholz. The difference is, that πάντας signifies *omnes*, ἅπαντας *cunctos*.

43. ἵνα μηδεὶς γνῷ τοῦτο.] A *popular* form of expression, importing, "that nothing of this should be made known." The order, however, could not be meant to enjoin *perpetual* secrecy, but *present suppression;* in order to avoid drawing together a concourse and raising a tumult. Εἶπε δοθῆναι αὐτῇ φαγεῖν. Εἶπε is for διέταξε. On the syntax see Winer's Gr. Gr. § 38. With respect to the thing itself, it is rightly remarked by Grot., that the order was given that it might be apparent that the maid was not only restored to *life*, but to *health*.

VI. 1. πατρίδα αὐτοῦ] "the place where he was brought up," namely, Nazareth.

2. καὶ γενομένου σαββ.] The sense (on which the Commentators are not quite agreed) seems to be, "on the Sabbath day;" γεν, being for ὄντος. This is confirmed by the readings (glosses though they be) of the Cod. Cantab. and some other ancient MSS. Ἀκούοντες, "on hearing him." Fritz. renders it *auditores*. But that would require the Article. Ἐξεπλήσσοντο, scil. ἐπὶ τῇ διδαχῇ αὐτοῦ, which is added in Matthew. Πόθεν τούτῳ ταῦτα; Sub. εἰσὶ, in the sense *contigerunt*. A *fuller* account of this transaction is given by Luke iv. 16. seqq. Τίς ἡ σοφία ἡ δοθ. αὐτῷ; scil. ὑπὸ τοῦ Θεοῦ. The τίς signifies *quænam*. The ὅτι just after is omitted in the greater part of the MSS. (or ἵνα put in its place), and is cancelled by Matth., Griesb., Tittm., and Scholz. It is, however, retained and ably defended by Fritz.; who remarks, that "all the various readings are only so many *corrections* of *librarii*, who did not comprehend the argumentation from *miracles* to prove *divine wisdom;* which is well pointed out by Grot." The sense is, "Whence have these talents fallen to the lot of this man; and what is this wisdom given him from above; that [not only he teaches us the way of salvation, but] even such *miracles* [as we have heard related] are performed by him?" Διὰ τῶν χειρῶν, by Hebraism (like ביד) for δι' αὐτοῦ.

3. ὁ τέκτων.] Some MSS. have ὁ τοῦ τέκτονος υἱός. But this is rejected by all the Editors, *except Fritz.*, who are, with reason, agreed that it was introduced from St. Matthew, and sprung from those who wished to consult the dignity of our Lord. That our Lord, however, was a carpenter, is (notwithstanding the denial of Origen) testified by nearly all the MSS., confirmed by general tradition, and the authority of the Fathers; of whom Justin Martyr says that Christ εἰργάζετο

MT. LU.
13. 4. Ἰωσῆ καὶ Ἰούδα καὶ Σίμωνος; καὶ οὐκ εἰσὶν αἱ ἀδελφαὶ αὐτοῦ
56 57 ὧδε πρὸς ἡμᾶς; Καὶ ἐσκανδαλίζοντο ἐν αὐτῷ. Ἔλεγε δὲ αὐτοῖς ὁ 4
Ἰησοῦς· Ὅτι οὐκ ἔστι προφήτης ἄτιμος, εἰ μὴ ἐν τῇ πατρίδι αὐτοῦ,
58. καὶ ἐν τοῖς συγγενέσι, καὶ ἐν τῇ οἰκίᾳ αὐτοῦ. Καὶ οὐκ ἠδύνατο ἐκεῖ 5
οὐδεμίαν δύναμιν ποιῆσαι· εἰ μὴ ὀλίγοις ἀῤῥώστοις ἐπιθεὶς τὰς χεῖρας ἐθεράπευσε. Καὶ ἐθαύμαζε διὰ τὴν ἀπιστίαν αὐτῶν· καὶ περιῆ- 6
10. 9. γε τὰς κώμας κύκλῳ διδάσκων.
1. 1. ΚΑΙ προσκαλεῖται τοὺς δώδεκα, καὶ ἤρξατο αὐτοὺς ἀποστέλλειν δύο 7
δύο· καὶ ἐδίδου αὐτοῖς ἐξουσίαν τῶν πνευμάτων τῶν ἀκαθάρτων.
9 3 Καὶ παρήγγειλεν αὐτοῖς, ἵνα μηδὲν αἴρωσιν εἰς ὁδὸν, εἰ μὴ ῥάβδον 8
10 μόνον· μὴ πήραν, μὴ ἄρτον, μὴ εἰς τὴν ζώνην χαλκόν· ἀλλ' ὑπο- 9
11 4 δεδεμένους σανδάλια, καὶ μὴ ‡ ἐνδύσασθαι δύο χιτῶνας. Καὶ ἔλεγεν 10
αὐτοῖς· Ὅπου ἐὰν εἰσέλθητε εἰς οἰκίαν, ἐκεῖ μένετε ἕως ἂν ἐξέλθητε
14 5 ἐκεῖθεν. Καὶ ὅσοι ἂν μὴ δέξωνται ὑμᾶς, μηδὲ ἀκούσωσιν ὑμῶν, ἐκ- 11
πορευόμενοι ἐκεῖθεν, ἐκτινάξατε τὸν χοῦν τὸν ὑποκάτω τῶν ποδῶν

ἄροτρα καὶ ζυγά. That our Lord should have been taught *some* handicraft occupation the Jewish law required, and the poverty of Joseph would render necessary. And what was so likely, as that he should bring him up to his father's trade; which, though lowly, was not degrading? See more in Bp. Middleton. [*Comp.* John vi. 42.]

— ὧδε πρὸς ἡμᾶς] "hic apud nos." Fritz. observes, that both the Scriptural writers and the Classical ones (at least the poets), so place πρὸς with an Accusative, *adjecto verbo quietis*, which is equivalent to παρὰ with a Dative.

4. [*Comp.* John iv. 44.]

5. καὶ οὐκ ἠδύνατο — ποιῆσαι.] These words, in their common acceptation, present a seeming difficulty, which has perplexed the Commentators, and to avoid which, some (as Wolf and Kuin.) suppose a pleonasm, taking οὐκ ἠδύνατο ποιῆσαι for οὐκ ἐποίησε. But (as Fritz. has shown) this pleonasm is *factitious*, and the passages adduced in support of it admit of a better explanation without it. Others take οὐκ ἠδύνατο for *noluit*. This, however, Fritz. shows, is even more destitute of foundation than the former sense. The true interpretation seems to be that of many ancient Commentators as Chrysost., Euthym., and Theophyl.), and, of the moderns, Grot., Whitby, Le Clerc, Bentley, and Fritz. "Our Saviour *could* not (says Theophyl.), not because he wanted *power;* but that the subjects of it were unbelieving, and therefore (as Whitby says) wanted the *condition* on which alone it was fit he should heal them. Christ could not, consistently with the rules on which he invariably acted in performing miracles, (namely, to require faith in his Divine mission) perform them. The Commentators observe, that it is conformable to the *Hebrew* manner of speaking, to say, that that *cannot* be, which *shall* not, or *ought not* to be. But abundance of examples of this have been adduced from both the Greek and Latin Classical writers; and the idiom is found even in modern languages.

6. ἐθαύμαζε.] Schleusn., Kuin., and others, take the word rather of *indignation* than *wonder;* a signification, indeed, not unfrequent in the *Classical* writers, but perhaps not found in the N. T. Far simpler, and more satisfactory is the common interpretation, "he wondered at their want of faith," and perverseness, in rejecting his claims on such unreasonable grounds. This construction, however, of θαυμάζειν is very rare, the usual one being θαυμάζ. ἐπί τινι, or περί τινος. Of the examples adduced by Wets., Munth, and Heupel, the following alone are apposite. Isocr. ὥστε καὶ τοὺς εἰδότας — θαυμάζειν διὰ τὴν καρτερίαν ταύτην. and John vii. 21. ἓν ἔργον ἐποίησα, καὶ πάντες θαυμάζετε διὰ τοῦτο. [*Comp.* Luke xiii. 22.]

Κύκλῳ must (as Fritz. says) be joined περιῆγε, κώμας; and he shows that κύκλῳ is by the Classical writers often subjoined to verbs compounded with περι.

7. δύο δύο] "by twos." An idiom found in the Hebrew, in which distributives are wanting. It is, however, not confined to the Hebrew, but found, though very rarely, in the Classical writers. So in Æsch. Pers. 915. we have μυρία μυρία for κατὰ μυριάδας. [*Comp.* Matt. x. 1. Luke vi. 13.]

9. καὶ μὴ ἐνδύσασθαι.] This is the reading of the common text, and it is supported by the great body of the MSS. But ἐνδύσησθε is found in some of the *best*, and in the Syr., Vulg., Goth., and Coptic Versions, as also in the Edit. Princ. and Steph. 1. & 2.; and it has been edited by Mill, Beng., Matth., Griesbach, and all other Editors down to Scholz, except Fritz., who has recalled the common reading ἐνδύσασθαι; and, I think, on good grounds. He shows that ἐνδύσησθε would involve an unprecedented anacoluthon, and an extreme harshness; and, after a long and learned discussion, decidedly prefers ἐνδύσασθαι; by which there will be either an *anacoluthon*, or a *variation* by means of two constructions. Thus, after ἀλλ', from the words ἵνα μηδὲν αἴρ. εἰς ὁδὸν. we must supply ἰέναι, or βαδίζειν. This interpretation is also supported by Grot., Heupel, Campb., and Kuin.; and, as being alike satisfactory in sense and construction, it deserves the preference.

11. ἐκτινάξατε τὸν χοῦν, &c.] Besides the parallel passage, comp. Luke x. 10, 11. Acts xiii. 51. The words Ἀμὴν λέγω — ἐκείνῃ are not found in some ancient MSS., and the Italic, Vulgate, Arabic, Coptic, Persic, and Armenian Versions. They were rejected, as not genuine, by Erasmus, Beza, Zeg., and Mill, were bracketed by Griesb., Knapp, Tittm., and Vater, and cancelled by Lachm. But, as Matth. and Fritz. show, without

MT. LU.

ὑμῶν, εἰς μαρτύριον αὐτοῖς. Ἀμὴν λέγω ὑμῖν· ἀνεκτότερον ἔσται 14. 9.
12 Σοδόμοις ἢ Γομόῤῥοις ἐν ἡμέρᾳ κρίσεως, ἢ τῇ πόλει ἐκείνῃ. Καὶ 6
13 ἐξελθόντες ἐκήρυσσον ἵνα μετανοήσωσι· καὶ δαιμόνια πολλὰ ἐξέβαλλον·
καὶ ἤλειφον ἐλαίῳ πολλοὺς ἀῤῥώστους καὶ ἐθεράπευον.
14 Καὶ ἤκουσεν ὁ βασιλεὺς Ἡρώδης, φανερὸν γὰρ ἐγένετο, τὸ ὄνομα 1 2. 7
αὐτοῦ, καὶ ἔλεγεν· Ὅτι Ἰωάννης ὁ βαπτίζων ἐκ νεκρῶν ἠγέρθη, καὶ
15 διὰ τοῦτο ἐνεργοῦσιν αἱ δυνάμεις ἐν αὐτῷ. Ἄλλοι ἔλεγον, Ὅτι Ἠλίας 8
ἐστίν· ἄλλοι δὲ ἔλεγον· Ὅτι προφήτης ἐστὶν, [ἢ] ὡς εἷς τῶν προ-
16 φητῶν. Ἀκούσας δὲ ὁ Ἡρώδης εἶπεν· Ὅτι ὃν ἐγὼ ἀπεκεφάλισα 9
17 Ἰωάννην, οὗτός ἐστιν· αὐτὸς ἠγέρθη ἐκ νεκρῶν. Αὐτὸς γὰρ ὁ Ἡρώδης 3
ἀποστείλας ἐκράτησε τὸν Ἰωάννην, καὶ ἔδησεν αὐτὸν ἐν [τῇ] φυλακῇ,
διὰ Ἡρωδιάδα τὴν γυναῖκα Φιλίππου τοῦ ἀδελφοῦ αὐτοῦ, ὅτι αὐτὴν
18 ἐγάμησεν. Ἔλεγε γὰρ ὁ Ἰωάννης τῷ Ἡρώδῃ· Ὅτι οὐκ ἔξεστί σοι 4
19 ἔχειν τὴν γυναῖκα τοῦ ἀδελφοῦ σου. Ἡ δὲ Ἡρωδιὰς ἐνεῖχεν αὐτῷ, καὶ 5

reason. Certainly the authority of about *seven* MSS. (abounding with all sorts of daring alterations) and some second-rate Versions, generally treading in others' steps, and coinciding with those altered MSS., cannot be considered as authority for the *cancelling* of any clause, even when internal evidence may be *unfavourable* to it. Which is *not* the case here; for *good reasons* may be given why it should have been *omitted*. As to the *Versions*, the clause being found in the *three Syriac Versions* far more than overbalances the whole authority *against* it.

13. ἤλειφον ἐλαίῳ.] It appears from various passages of the Medical and Rabbinical writers cited by Wets. and Lightf., that *oil* (which in the Eastern and Southern countries is of a peculiarly mild quality) was used by the ancients, both Jews and Gentiles, as a medical application. And that it was so employed by the Apostles; and that the sense is, "they anointed many with oil, and thereby cured their diseases," is the opinion of almost all the recent Commentators. But surely this circumstance, that the Apostles had *successfully made use of a well-known medicine*, would ill comport with the gravity and dignity of the preceding words, which, I think, compel us to suppose, with all the ancient and early modern Commentators, that the healing was as much miraculous as the casting out of demons. The anointing was only employed as a *symbolical action*, typical of the *oil of gladness* and grace to be imparted by Divine assistance. See Euthym. and Theophyl. For the first Christians, being accustomed to represent, in visible signs, the allegorical allusions in Scripture, used oil not only, as the Jews had done, as a *remedy*, which had from high antiquity become *sacred*; but (from that sacredness) as a *religious rite* at baptism, confirmation, and prayers for the sick. Thus it may be regarded as one of those *significant actions* by which both the Prophets of the O. T. and the Apostles (after their Lord's example) with indulgence to human weakness, accompanied their supernatural and miraculous cures. See James v. 14. In all which cases, the *methods* adopted in those actions (which were various) contributed nothing to the cure; that being effected by means of which we can have no conception.

14. ἤκουσεν ὁ βασιλεὺς] There is here, seemingly, a want of the *Subject* to the verb. With this the early Critics have, indeed, furnished us, supplying τὴν ἀκοὴν τοῦ Ἰησοῦ, which Beza approves, and Fritz., with his usual rashness, inserts in the *text*. And it is surely better to retain a harshness, than to get rid of it by such means. Grot. proposes to put φανερὸν γὰρ ἐγένετο into a parenthesis. But this would involve a very harsh transposition. The best mode is, either to take τὸ ὄνομα αὐ. twice, or to supply the subject αὐτὸν from the context, which is *suggested* in τὸ ὄνομα αὐτοῦ.

15. ὅτι προφήτης — προφητῶν] There has been much discussion on the reading and sense of these words. If the testimony of MSS. and ancient Versions can prove any thing, it is certain that the true reading is ὅτι προφ. ἐστὶν ὡς εἷς τῶν προφ., of which the sense can only be, "he is a prophet resembling one of the prophets [of old times.]" The ἢ before ὡς is of little or no authority, being omitted in almost every MS. of consequence, nearly all the Versions, and early Editions; and cancelled by Beng., Wets., Matth., Griesb., Tittm., Vat., and Scholz. The above reading, indeed, involves some harshness; yet the sense of τῶν προφ. is not ill suggested by the *Article*.

16. ὃν ἐγὼ — ἐστιν.) This sort of *attraction* is frequent both in the Scriptural and Classical writers; but it is here adopted to give greater strength to the asseveration. The ἐγὼ also seems to be emphatical.

17. ἐν τῇ φυλακῇ] The τῇ is omitted in several MSS. and the Ed. Princ.; and is cancelled by Beng., Matth., Griesb., Tittm., and Scholz; but is retained by Fritz.: and with reason; for the number of MSS. is not such as to warrant its being *cancelled;* and we can more easily account for its *omission* that its *insertion*.

19. ἐνεῖχεν αὐτῷ.] Not, "had a quarrel with," as E. V.; nor "resented this," as Campb.; nor, as Wakef. and some recent Commentators explain, "was enraged against him;" but, "bore a grudge against him." Ἐνέχειν, (equivalent to ἐγκοτεῖν) signifies to harbour (literally, "have in mind") κότον, a grudge or resentment against any one. The *complete* phrase occurs in Herodot. i. 118. vi. 119. and viii. 27., the elliptical one in Luke xi. 53. Genes. xlix. 23. (answering to שטם) and Job xvi. 9. So Hesych. ἐνέχει· μνησικακεῖ, and ἐνεῖχον· ἐχόλουν.

MT.
14. ἤθελεν αὐτὸν ἀποκτεῖναι· καὶ οὐκ ἠδύνατο. Ὁ γὰρ Ἡρώδης ἐφο- 20
βεῖτο τὸν Ἰωάννην, εἰδὼς αὐτὸν ἄνδρα δίκαιον καὶ ἅγιον, καὶ συνετήρει αὐτόν· καὶ ἀκούσας αὐτοῦ, πολλὰ ἐποίει, καὶ ἡδέως αὐτοῦ ἤκουε.
6 Καὶ, γενομένης ἡμέρας εὐκαίρου, ὅτε Ἡρώδης τοῖς γενεσίοις αὐτοῦ 21
δεῖπνον ἐποίει τοῖς μεγιστᾶσιν αὐτοῦ καὶ τοῖς χιλιάρχοις καὶ τοῖς
πρώτοις τῆς Γαλιλαίας, καὶ εἰσελθούσης τῆς θυγατρὸς αὐτῆς τῆς 22
Ἡρωδιάδος, καὶ ὀρχησαμένης, καὶ ἀρεσάσης τῷ Ἡρώδῃ καὶ τοῖς συν-
7 ανακειμένοις, εἶπεν ὁ βασιλεὺς τῷ κορασίῳ· Αἴτησόν με ὃ ἐὰν θέλῃς,
καὶ δώσω σοι· καὶ ὤμοσεν αὐτῇ, Ὅτι ὃ ἐάν με αἰτήσῃς, δώσω σοι, 23
8 ἕως ἡμίσους τῆς βασιλείας μου. Ἡ δὲ ἐξελθοῦσα εἶπε τῇ μητρὶ αὐτῆς· 24
Τί αἰτήσομαι; ἡ δὲ εἶπε· Τὴν κεφαλὴν Ἰωάννου τοῦ βαπτιστοῦ.
Καὶ εἰσελθοῦσα εὐθέως μετὰ σπουδῆς πρὸς τὸν βασιλέα, ᾐτήσατο 25
λέγουσα· Θέλω ἵνα μοι δῷς ἐξαυτῆς ἐπὶ πίνακι τὴν κεφαλὴν Ἰωάν-
9 νου τοῦ βαπτιστοῦ. Καὶ περίλυπος γενόμενος ὁ βασιλεὺς, διὰ τοὺς 26
10 ὅρκους καὶ τοὺς συνανακειμένους οὐκ ἠθέλησεν αὐτὴν ἀθετῆσαι. Καὶ 27
εὐθέως ἀποστείλας ὁ βασιλεὺς σπεκουλάτωρα, ἐπέταξεν ἐνεχθῆναι τὴν
κεφαλὴν αὐτοῦ. Ὁ δὲ ἀπελθὼν ἀπεκεφάλισεν αὐτὸν ἐν τῇ φυλακῇ, 28
11 καὶ ἤνεγκε τὴν κεφαλὴν αὐτοῦ ἐπὶ πίνακι, καὶ ἔδωκεν αὐτὴν τῷ κο-
12 ρασίῳ· καὶ τὸ κοράσιον ἔδωκεν αὐτὴν τῇ μητρὶ αὐτῆς. Καὶ ἀκού- 29
σαντες οἱ μαθηταὶ αὐτοῦ, ἦλθον καὶ ἦραν τὸ πτῶμα αὐτοῦ, καὶ
ἔθηκαν αὐτὸ ἐν [τῷ] μνημείῳ.

20. ἐφοβεῖτο τὸν Ἰ.] The term here imports a mixture of awe and reverence. There is much difference of opinion as to the sense of συνετήρει. The Vulg., L. Brug., Hamm., Le Clerc, Wets., Campb., Kuin., Schleusn., Wahl, and most Commentators, take it in the sense, "preserved him," i. e. from the malice of Herodias. But there is no authority for this signification. Greatly preferable is that assigned by the Syr., Arabic, Italic, and English Versions, and adopted by Erasm., Grot., Lamy, Whit., Wakef., Rosemn., and Fritz., "observabat eum," "observantiâ prosecutus est," "magni eum faciebat." So Diog. Laert. φίλους συντηρεῖν, paid him respect. This signification seems to arise from that of keeping any one in our mind. Καὶ ἀκούσας αὐτοῦ, "and when he had heard him," i. e. his admonitions. Πολλὰ ἐποίει, "did many things [which were suggested by him.]" [*Comp.* Matt. xiv. 5; xxi. 26.]

21. ἡμέρας εὐκ.] Here again the Interpreters are divided in opinion; the ancient and early modern Commentators rendering it, "an opportune season," namely, for working on the mind of Herod, and obtaining his order for the execution of John. But almost all since the time of Glass and Hamm. take it to signify "a festival day." The expression, however, as Fritz. proves, can only mean "a *leisure* day." And thus it exactly answers to our term *holiday*. So εὐκαίρως at xiv. 11. and 1 Tim. iv. 2.

— τοῖς μεγιστᾶσιν.] A word only occurring in the later writers, (as Joseph. and the Sept.), and formed from μέγιστος, as νεᾶν from νέος. It denotes the *magnates*, or great men of a country, by whose counsel and assistance the monarch is aided.

— τοῖς πρώτοις.] This is by Grot. and Kuin. taken to denote the principal magistrates. But it should rather be understood (with Fritz.) of the principal persons for wealth or consequence of those in a private station. So Joseph. Ant. vii. 9, 8. οἱ τῆς χώρας πρῶτοι.

23. ἕως ἡμίσους τῆς βασ.] Many Commentators supply μέρους. But there is perhaps no ellipse; for ἥμισυ seems to have been as much a substantive as our *half*. The promise involved a sort of hyperbole, and was, as appears from the Classical citations of Wets., a not unusual manner of expression with Kings.

25. μετὰ σπουδῆς] Heb. בחפזון For ἐν σπουδῇ, i. e. σπουδαίως, promptly, with alacrity. Ἐξαυτῆς is for παραυτίκα, *forthwith*. The earlier authors generally write ἐξ αὐτῆς scil. ὥρας. There will be no occasion for the ellipse of ἀλλὰ, which Kuin, and others suppose, before τοὺς ὅρκους, if περίλυπος γενόμενος be rendered "although he was very sorry."

26. ἀθετῆσαι] "to set her at nought;" namely, by refusing her request. This sense is chiefly confined to the later writers, especially the Sept. and Joseph., who use the word either absolutely, or with an Accusative of *person*, sometimes accompained with εἰς; more rarely with an Accus. of *thing*.

27. σπεκουλάτωρα.] This term, from the Latin *speculator*, denotes one of the body-guards, who were so called, because their principal duty was that of *sentinels*: for I rather agree with Casaub., Wets., and Fritz., that they had their name from their office *speculari*, and not, quasi *spiculatores*, from spiculum; because the former points to their chief business. They had, however, other confidential duties, and among these, that of acting, like the Turkish soldiers of the present day, as executioners.

29. τῷ μνημείῳ.] The τῷ is rejected by all the

MT. LU.

30 Καὶ συνάγονται οἱ ἀπόστολοι πρὸς τὸν Ἰησοῦν, καὶ ἀπήγγειλαν 14. 9.
31 αὐτῷ πάντα, καὶ ὅσα ἐποίησαν καὶ ὅσα ἐδίδαξαν. καὶ εἶπεν αὐτοῖς· 10
Δεῦτε ὑμεῖς αὐτοὶ κατ' ἰδίαν εἰς ἔρημον τόπον, καὶ ἀναπαύεσθε
ὀλίγον. ἦσαν γὰρ οἱ ἐρχόμενοι καὶ οἱ ὑπάγοντες πολλοὶ, καὶ οὐδὲ
32 φαγεῖν ηὐκαίρουν. Καὶ ἀπῆλθον εἰς ἔρημον τόπον τῷ πλοίῳ κατ'
33 ἰδίαν. Καὶ εἶδον αὐτοὺς ὑπάγοντας [οἱ ὄχλοι,] καὶ ἐπέγνωσαν αὐτὸν 13
[πολλοὶ] οἱ ὄχλοι· καὶ πεζῇ ἀπὸ πασῶν τῶν πόλεων συνέδραμον ἐκεῖ, 11
34 καὶ προῆλθον αὐτοὺς, καὶ συνῆλθον πρὸς αὐτόν. Καὶ ἐξελθὼν εἶδεν 14
ὁ Ἰησοῦς πολὺν ὄχλον, καὶ ἐσπλαγχνίσθη ἐπ' αὐτοῖς, ὅτι ἦσαν ὡς
πρόβατα μὴ ἔχοντα ποιμένα· καὶ ἤρξατο διδάσκειν αὐτοὺς πολλά.
35 Καὶ ἤδη ὥρας πολλῆς γενομένης, προσελθόντες αὐτῷ οἱ μαθηταὶ αὐτοῦ, 15 12
36 λέγουσιν· Ὅτι ἔρημός ἐστιν ὁ τόπος, καὶ ἤδη ὥρα πολλή· ἀπόλυσον
αὐτοὺς, ἵνα, ἀπελθόντες εἰς τοὺς κύκλῳ ἀγροὺς καὶ κώμας, ἀγοράσωσιν
37 ἑαυτοῖς ἄρτους· τί γὰρ φάγωσιν οὐκ ἔχουσιν. Ὁ δὲ ἀποκριθεὶς εἶπεν

Editors from Matth. to Scholz; and with reason; for it is, as Markl. has shown, liable to objection on the score of propriety; it is found in scarcely any MS. but Cod. D., being introduced, perhaps inadvertently, by Stephens, in his 3d Edit.

31. ὑμεῖς αὐτοί.] This must be rendered not "vos ipsi," or "vos quoque," with most Commentators, but (with Erasm., Schleus.. Kuin., and Fritz.] "vos soli," on which use of αὐτὸς see Schleus., or Wahl. Lex. On ηὐκαίρουν comp. supra iii. 20.

32. [*Comp.* John vi. 16.]

33. καὶ εἶδον — πρὸς αὐτόν.] There are few passages of the N. T. where a greater diversity of readings exist than in the present. Editors and Commentators are alike agreed that it has suffered grievously from transcribers; and the unusual diversity of readings, has here (as in many other cases) led Critics too readily to take *interpolation for granted:* and, in order to relieve the plethora, *pruning* has been employed with considerable effect by the recent Editors. Griesb. edits thus: καὶ εἶδον αὐτοὺς ὑπάγοντας· καὶ ἐπέγνωσαν πολλοί· καὶ πεζῇ ἀπὸ πασῶν τῶν πόλεων συνέδραμον ἐκεῖ. But for this, and most of the alterations that have been made, there is little authority. Indeed, I see no good grounds except for the cancelling of οἱ ὄχλοι, which is, indeed, found in scarcely any MS. of account, and has no place in the early Editions, except of Erasm., 4. and 5., from which it was introduced into Steph. 3. It has been, with reason, rejected by Mill and Wets., and cancelled by Matth., Griesb., Vat., Tittm., Fritz., and Scholz. Thus πολλοὶ becomes the *subject* of the verbs εἶδον and ἐπέγνωσαν. To this, however, there is great objection. It is frigid as regards εἶδον, and as concerns ἐπέγν. *inapposite*, for, as Campb. remarks, "the historian would not be likely to say that *many* knew him, since, after being so long occupied in teaching and healing them, there would be comparatively few who did *not* know him." I cannot, therefore, but suspect (though it seems not to have occurred to any of the Editors and Commentators) that πολλοί, though the authorities for its omission are but slender, should not be here. Yet it does not, I suspect, stand here *for nothing;* but, as it is scarcely possible for us to dispense with a *subject*, and as the parallel passages of Matthew and Luke both have οἱ ὄχλοι, I strongly suspect that under this suspicious πολλοὶ is concealed that very reading; which I have therefore ventured to introduce in *smaller character*. In this I am supported not only by Critical probability, (for the words πολλοὶ and ὄχλοι are frequently confounded) but by the authority of the other Evangelists; and, indeed, of all those numerous MSS. which contain οἱ ὄχλοι, since *they* may be considered as *authority* for the reading in question; there being little doubt but that in their *Archetypes* the reading οἱ ὄχλοι was written in the margin, and intended as a correction of the textual πολλοί. I have left the received readings throughout the rest of the verse, because no tolerable case of interpolation, or of corruption, has been established against them. The clause καὶ προῆλθον αὐτοὺς is indeed cancelled by Griesb. and Fritz.; but on very slender authority. The objection on the score of *false construction*, as if αὐτῶν were required, is frivolous; for the very same construction is found in almost every good MS. in *Luke* xxii. 47., and is rightly edited by Matth., Griesb., and Scholz. Besides, the circumstance is surely so *natural*, that *internal evidence* is greatly in its favour. One may easily imagine *how* the people who saw our Lord and the Apostles (no doubt, *on board ship;* which removes Campbell's objection), might be so circumstanced in respect of them, as to be enabled to get before them to the place whither they were bound. They would easily see, by the course in which the vessel was directed, the spot where it was meant to land. As to ἦλθον, edited by Griesb. and Fritz. for συνῆλθον, it has scarcely the support of a single MS., and is, no doubt, a mere *correction*. The common reading must be preferred, as being the more *difficult*. It has a *significatio prægnans;* and the πρὸς with the Accusative is equivalent to a *Dative*, which latter construction is found in xiv. 53, and Luke xxiii. Συνέρχεσθαι is often used in this sense in the N. T.

Ἐκεῖ denotes εἰς τὸν ἔρημον, and πεζῇ signifies not *on foot*, but *by land*, which sense occurs elsewhere in the N. T.

34. [*Comp.* Matt. ix. 36. Jerem. xxiii. 1. Ezek. xxxiv. 2.]

35. ἤδη ὥρας πολλῆς γεν.] Almost all Commentators take the sense to be, "it was now late in

MT. LU.
14. 9. αὐτοῖς· Δότε αὐτοῖς ὑμεῖς φαγεῖν. Καὶ λέγουσιν αὐτῷ· Ἀπελθόντες
16 13 ἀγοράσωμεν διακοσίων δηναρίων ἄρτους, καὶ δῶμεν αὐτοῖς φαγεῖν;
17 Ὁ δὲ λέγει αὐτοῖς· Πόσους ἄρτους ἔχετε; ὑπάγετε καὶ ἴδετε. Καὶ 38
19 14 γνόντες λέγουσι· Πέντε, καὶ δύο ἰχθύας. Καὶ ἐπέταξεν αὐτοῖς ἀνα- 39
κλῖναι πάντας, συμπόσια συμπόσια, ἐπὶ τῷ χλωρῷ χόρτῳ. Καὶ ἀνέ- 40
πεσον πρασιαὶ πρασιαί, ἀνὰ ἑκατὸν καὶ ἀνὰ πεντήκοντα. Καὶ λαβὼν 41
τοὺς πέντε ἄρτους καὶ τοὺς δύο ἰχθύας, ἀναβλέψας εἰς τὸν οὐρανὸν
εὐλόγησε· καὶ κατέκλασε τοὺς ἄρτους, καὶ ἐδίδου τοῖς μαθηταῖς αὐ-
20 17 τοῦ, ἵνα παραθῶσιν αὐτοῖς· καὶ τοὺς δύο ἰχθύας ἐμέρισε πᾶσι. Καὶ 42
ἔφαγον πάντες, καὶ ἐχορτάσθησαν· καὶ ἦραν κλασμάτων δώδεκα κο- 43
21 24 φίνους πλήρεις, καὶ ἀπὸ τῶν ἰχθύων. Καὶ ἦσαν οἱ φαγόντες τοὺς 44
22 ἄρτους ὡσεὶ πεντακισχίλιοι ἄνδρες. Καὶ εὐθέως ἠνάγκασε τοὺς μαθη- 45
τὰς αὐτοῦ ἐμβῆναι εἰς τὸ πλοῖον, καὶ προάγειν εἰς τὸ πέραν πρὸς
23 Βηθσαϊδάν, ἕως αὐτὸς ἀπολύσῃ τὸν ὄχλον. Καὶ ἀποταξάμενος αὐτοῖς, 46
24 ἀπῆλθεν εἰς τὸ ὄρος προσεύξασθαι. Καὶ ὀψίας γενομένης, ἦν τὸ 47
πλοῖον ἐν μέσῳ τῆς θαλάσσης, καὶ αὐτὸς μόνος ἐπὶ τῆς γῆς. Καὶ 48
εἶδεν αὐτοὺς βασανιζομένους ἐν τῷ ἐλαύνειν· ἦν γὰρ ὁ ἄνεμος
25 ἐναντίος αὐτοῖς. Καὶ περὶ τετάρτην φυλακὴν τῆς νυκτὸς ἔρχεται πρὸς
αὐτούς, περιπατῶν ἐπὶ τῆς θαλάσσης· καὶ ἤθελε παρελθεῖν αὐτούς.
26 Οἱ δὲ ἰδόντες αὐτὸν περιπατοῦντα ἐπὶ τῆς θαλάσσης, ἔδοξαν φάντα- 49
σμα εἶναι, καὶ ἀνέκραξαν· πάντες γὰρ αὐτὸν εἶδον, καὶ ἐταράχθησαν. 50
27 Καὶ εὐθέως ἐλάλησε μετ᾽ αὐτῶν, καὶ λέγει αὐτοῖς· Θαρσεῖτε· ἐγώ
32 εἰμι· μὴ φοβεῖσθε. Καὶ ἀνέβη πρὸς αὐτοὺς εἰς τὸ πλοῖον, καὶ ἐκό- 51
πασεν ὁ ἄνεμος· καὶ λίαν ἐκ περισσοῦ ἐν ἑαυτοῖς ἐξίσταντο καὶ

the day." Yet they adduce no better proof than examples of the *Latin* phrase *in multam noctem*, or *diem*. But that sense would require διαγεν. Render, "et quum jam tempus multum effluxisset [ex quo docere cœperat]." Unless, therefore, this be a *Latinism*, we may explain the phrase, with Fritz., "when much of the day was now past." [*Comp.* John vi. 5.]

37. ἀπελθόντες — φαγεῖν.] The best Commentators, ancient and modern, are of opinion this sentence contains an interrogation implying admiration, and perhaps indignation. It may be rendered: "What must we go and buy?" &c. There is reason to think that the sum in question was a proverbial one, for a sum of money exceeding the inconsiderable; as we say, *a good round sum*.

38. [*Comp.* John vi. 9.]

39. συμπόσια συμπόσια] i. e. κατὰ συμπόσια, in a distributive sense; an idiom common in Hebrew. See Note supra, ver. 7. Συμπόσιον signifies properly *a drinking together*, or a *common entertainment*; and then, by a metonymy common in our own language, it designates the *party* assembled.

— χλωρῷ χόρτῳ.] Casaub. and Wets. say that χλωρῷ is added because χόρτος properly signifies *hay*. It simply, however, means *fodder*; and though in the Classical writers it almost always denotes *dry* fodder, yet in the N. T. it as constantly signifies *herbage* of any kind, both of grass and corn.

40. Πρασιὰ properly signifies a *plot* of ground, such as in gardens are employed for the growth of vegetables. It is strange that the latest Commentators should adopt the derivation of Hesych. from πέρας, "quasi περασιαί," when the Etym. Mag. and Zonaras' Lex. offer so much better a one; — namely, from πράσον, an old word signifying a leek or onion. Thus the term denotes properly *an onion-bed*, and then any plot of ground of a regular form, as square or parallelogram. See my Note on Thucyd. ii. 56. It here denotes *regular* and equal *companies*, like squadrons of troops. From Luke we find that each was composed of 50 persons. This method was, no doubt, adopted, to let the multitude know their own number.

45. [*Comp.* John vi. 17.]

46. ἀποταξάμενος αὐτοῖς] "having bid them (i. e. the multitude) farewell." The phrase ἀποτάσσεσθαί τινι, in this sense, is (as Fritz. observes) not Attic Greek, but that of Philo, Joseph., and the later writers, especially the N. T. ones. [*Comp.* John vi. 16, 17.]

48. ἐν τῷ ἐλαύνειν] scil. τὴν ναῦν. The ellipsis is sometimes supplied, but at other times κώπην is used. Βασανιζομένους, laborantes, distressed.

— ἤθελε παρελθεῖν αὐτούς.] The laboured Annotations of Grot., Fritz., and others here are little to the purpose; and much trouble might have been spared by considering the phrase as a *popular* one, for "he would (i. e. he was about to) pass by them;" or, "he made as though he would have passed by them." So of Jesus it is

MT.
52 ἐθαύμαζον. Οὐ γὰρ συνῆκαν ἐπὶ τοῖς ἄρτοις· ἦν γὰρ ἡ καρδία 14.
αὐτῶν πεπωρωμένη.
53 ΚΑΙ διαπεράσαντες ἦλθον ἐπὶ τὴν γῆν Γεννησαρέτ, καὶ προσωρμί- 34
54 σθησαν. Καὶ ἐξελθόντων αὐτῶν ἐκ τοῦ πλοίου, εὐθέως ἐπιγνόντες
55 αὐτὸν, περιδραμόντες ὅλην τὴν περίχωρον ἐκείνην, ἤρξαντο ἐπὶ τοῖς 35
κραββάτοις τοὺς κακῶς ἔχοντας περιφέρειν, ὅπου ἤκουον ὅτι ἐκεῖ ἐστι.
56 Καὶ ὅπου ἂν εἰσεπορεύετο εἰς κώμας ἢ πόλεις ἢ ἀγροὺς, ἐν ταῖς
ἀγοραῖς ἐτίθουν τοὺς ἀσθενοῦντας, καὶ παρεκάλουν αὐτὸν, ἵνα κἂν τοῦ 36
κρασπέδου τοῦ ἱματίου αὐτοῦ ἅψωνται· καὶ ὅσοι ἂν ἥπτοντο αὐτοῦ
ἐσώζοντο. 15.
1 VII. ΚΑΙ συνάγονται πρὸς αὐτὸν οἱ Φαρισαῖοι, καί τινες τῶν 1
2 Γραμματέων, ἐλθόντες ἀπὸ Ἱεροσολύμων. Καὶ ἰδόντες τινὰς τῶν
μαθητῶν αὐτοῦ κοιναῖς χερσὶ, (τοῦτ᾽ ἔστιν ἀνίπτοις) ἐσθίοντας ἄρτους,
3 [ἐμέμψαντο·] (οἱ γὰρ Φαρισαῖοι καὶ πάντες οἱ Ἰουδαῖοι, ἐὰν μὴ

said, Luke xxiv. 28. Καὶ αὐτὸς προσεποιεῖτο πορρωτέρω πορεύεσθαι.

52. οὐ γὰρ συνῆκαν ἐπὶ τοῖς ἄρτοις.] By the ἄρτοις is meant, as Krebs observes, τῷ θαύματι τοῖς ἄρτοις γενομένῳ. That Commentator, however, and Kuin., with some other recent Interpreters, seem wrong in assigning to ἐπὶ the sense *post*. I myself still continue of the same opinion as in Recens. Synop., that the true sense is *per*, *by*, denoting the efficient cause; as in Matt. iv. 4. And this is confirmed by Fritz. in his Note, who renders: "Non enim per prioris portenti opportunitatem quidquam intellexerant, sed erant callo obductâ mente."

53. προσωρμίσθησαν] scil. ἐκεῖ. Προσορμίζειν signifies to bring a ship πρὸς ὅρμον, to a port; or, as here, to a station or place fit for landing or drawing a ship ashore.

54. ἐπιγνόντες αὐτὸν] Some MSS. and Versions have added οἱ ἄνδρες τοῦ τόπου ἐκείνου; words, no doubt, derived from Matt. xiv. 13. It may seem harsh that the *subject* of the verb should be suppressed; to soften which, Fritz. would take the words ἐπιγνόντες—ἤρξαντο as put impersonally. But it will be more satisfactory to suppose an ellipsis of the subject; namely, the common one, corresponding to the *man* of the Germans and our *men*, which will here denote the *inhabitants* of that country. This obscurity is perhaps meant to be somewhat cleared up by the ἐκείνην following, which is equivalent to ἐκείνου τόπου.

55. For περιφέρειν some MSS. have φέρειν; others, ἐπιφέρειν; and others, again, προσφέρειν, which Fritz. edits; but wrongly; for the varr. lectt. arose from the librarii stumbling at the use of περιφέρειν here, which has a *significatio prægnans*, *including* the senses expressed by the above various readings; q. d. "they carried them about, (i. e. up and down) and brought them to those places where they heard he was."

—ὅπου] This must not be taken for *quoniam* (with Palairet and Schleusn.), but rather (with Beza, Grot., Wets., Kuin., and Winer) the words ὅπου—ἐκεῖ must be closely connected, corresponding to the Heb. אשר־שם, in the sense *ubi*. Thus ἐκεῖ is said to be redundant. Fritz., however, makes well-founded objections to this combination of the words, and to the supposing the redundancy of them; because the words ὅτι ἐκεῖ ἐστι are an independent clause. And he, very properly, limits the above-mentioned idiom to passages where the words occur in the *same clause*. He would therefore render ἐστι *adest*. But it may be better to regard the sentence as an abbreviation of the fuller mode of expression of primitive times; when it would have been phrased "carried them to the place of which they had heard it said, 'he *is there*.'" Compare 1 Kings xviii. 10. Thus ἐκεῖ is least of all pleonastic.

56. παρεκάλουν αὐτὸν] It is not clear whether this is to be understood of *those who laid the sick persons down*, or of the *sick persons themselves*. The former method is more suited to the construction; but the latter (which is adopted by Abp. Newcome) is more agreeable to probability.

—ὅσοι ἂν ἥπτ.] The ἂν is not without force, denoting, as Winer thinks (Gr. N. T. p. 117.), the uncertainty of the number. I would render, "as many as might have touched."

VII. 2. κοιναῖς] It was quite in the Jewish idiom to oppose *common* and *holy*, the most usual signification of the latter word in the Old Testament being separated from common, and devoted to sacred use. Their meals were (as the apostle expressed it, 1 Tim. iv. 5.) *sanctified by the word of God and prayer*. They were, therefore, not to be touched with unhallowed hands. The superficial Pharisee, who was uniform (wherever religion was concerned) in attending to the letter, not to the spirit of the rule, understood this as implying solely that they must wash their hands before they eat. (Campb.) Κοινὸς here (as often in Joseph.) signifies what is ritually impure: thus, as regarded the *hands*, it denoted that they were not washed ritually, i. e. just before the meal; though they might otherwise be clean.

—ἐμέμψαντο] This word is omitted in several MSS. and some Versions, is rejected by Mill and Beng., and is cancelled by Griesb., Tittm., and Scholz, but retained and defended by Fritz. strenuously, but not, it should seem, very successfully. No tolerable reason has ever been given why, supposing it to have been originally in the text, it should have been thrown out. On the other hand, it is easy to see how it should have been *added*, namely, by those who were not aware of the true construction of the whole passage, and did not see that vv. 3 & 4 are parenthetical.

MT.
15. πυγμῇ νίψωνται τὰς χεῖρας, οὐκ ἐσθίουσι, κρατοῦντες τὴν παράδοσιν
τῶν πρεσβυτέρων· καὶ ἀπὸ ἀγορᾶς, ἐὰν μὴ βαπτίσωνται, οὐκ ἐσθί- 4
ουσι· καὶ ἄλλα πολλά ἐστιν, ἃ παρέλαβον κρατεῖν, βαπτισμοὺς πο-
τηρίων καὶ ξεστῶν καὶ χαλκίων καὶ κλινῶν·) ἔπειτα ἐπερωτῶσιν αὐτὸν 5
2 οἱ Φαρισαῖοι καὶ οἱ Γραμματεῖς· Διατί οἱ μαθηταί σου οὐ περιπατοῦσι κατὰ τὴν παράδοσιν τῶν πρεσβυτέρων, ἀλλὰ ἀνίπτοις χερσὶν
3 ἐσθίουσι τὸν ἄρτον; Ὁ δὲ ἀποκριθεὶς εἶπεν αὐτοῖς· Ὅτι καλῶς 6
προεφήτευσεν Ἡσαΐας περὶ ὑμῶν τῶν ὑποκριτῶν, ὡς γέγραπται·
8 Οὗτος ὁ λαὸς τοῖς χείλεσί με τιμᾷ, ἡ δὲ καρδία αὐ-
9 τῶν πόῤῥω ἀπέχει ἀπ' ἐμοῦ. Μάτην δὲ σέβονταί 7
με, διδάσκοντες διδασκαλίας, ἐντάλματα ἀνθρώπων.
Ἀφέντες γὰρ τὴν ἐντολὴν τοῦ Θεοῦ, κρατεῖτε τὴν παράδοσιν τῶν 8
ἀνθρώπων, βαπτισμοὺς ξεστῶν καὶ ποτηρίων· καὶ ἄλλα παρόμοια
3 τοιαῦτα πολλὰ ποιεῖτε. Καὶ ἔλεγεν αὐτοῖς· Καλῶς ἀθετεῖτε τὴν 9
4 ἐντολὴν τοῦ Θεοῦ, ἵνα τὴν παράδοσιν ὑμῶν τηρήσητε. Μωϋσῆς γὰρ 10
εἶπε· Τίμα τὸν πατέρα σου καὶ τὴν μητέρα σου· καὶ
ὁ κακολογῶν πατέρα ἢ μητέρα, θανάτῳ τελευτάτω·
5 ὑμεῖς δὲ λέγετε· Ἐὰν εἴπῃ ἄνθρωπος τῷ πατρὶ ἢ τῇ μητρί· Κορ- 11

3. πάντες] i. e. all those who observed the traditions; for the Sadducees and a few others (comparatively a small part of the nation) rejected this custom.

— πυγμῇ] There are few expressions on which the Commentators are more divided in opinion than this. The early Versions show that the ancients were as much perplexed with it as the moderns. The Vulg. and some other Versions give the sense *sæpe;* whence it has been supposed, that they read πυκνῇ, which might be taken for πυκνά, and that for πυκνῶς. But (as Fritz. observes) there is no proof of the existence of any such *adverb* as πυκνῇ; and the sense *sæpe* would be inapposite. To advert to the *interpretations* of those who *retain the common reading;* several Commentators, ancient and modern, take πυγμῇ to mean "up to the elbow." But even though πυγμὴ should be proved to have the signification *elbow;* yet such a one as "*up to*" in the Dative, cannot be tolerated. For the same reason, the interpretation of Lightf., Hamm., Schoettg., and Heupel, "up to the *wrist*," must be rejected. Others, as Wets., Pearce, Campb., and Rosenm., endeavor to remove the difficulty by taking πυγμῇ to mean "a handful of water," such as the contracted palm will contain; or rather a *quartarius*, the smallest measure allowed for washing the hands. And this mode of interpretation Campb. supports very ingeniously, but not convincingly; for that sense would require πυγμῇ ὕδατος. In short, πυγμῇ can only mean the *doubled* or *closed fist*, in which sense the word is here taken by Scalig., Beza, Grot., and Fritz.; who, however, are not agreed as to the *manner* of the action. The most probable view is that of Beza and Fritz., who render "unless they have first washed their hands with the fist;" which explanation is confirmed by the customs of the Jews, as preserved in the Rabbinical writers, and even yet in use. Thus the rendering of the Syr. *diligenter* may be admitted as a free translation, as also those of *studiosè*, or *sedulò*, adopted by some moderns: indeed (as Leigh says) almost all the interpretations imply diligent care in washing.

— κρατοῦντες] "carefully, pertinaciously adhering to, and observing." Such is the full sense of the word, which is so used in 2 Thess. ii. 15.

4. ἀπὸ ἀγορᾶς] Sub. ἐλθόντες, or γενόμενοι; of which ellipse the Commentators adduce many examples, as also of the complete phrase.

— ἐὰν μὴ βαπτ.] This is best explained, "unless they wash their bodies" (in opposition to the washing of the *hands* before mentioned); in which, however, is not implied *immersion;* which was never used, except when some *actual*, and not *possible* pollution, had been incurred.

— ἃ παρέλαβον κρατεῖν.] The full sense is, "which they had received from their ancestors, that they may firmly keep them." Ξεστῶν, from ξέστης, a liquid measure, of wood, holding a pint and a half. The word is frequent in the later writers, and is from the Latin *Sextus*. Χαλκίων, copper or brazen vessels. *Earthen* vessels are not mentioned, because those, if supposed to be polluted, were at once broken. See Levit. xv. 12.

7. [*Comp.* Coloss. ii. 18. seqq. Tit. i. 14.]

9. καλῶς ἀθετεῖτε] The best Commentators (as Euthym., Beza, Casaub., Glass, Cameron, Heupel, Campb., Rosenm., Kuin., Schleusn., Fritz., and Scott) are agreed that this is to be taken as an ironical reproof. Thus the καλῶς corresponds to our *finely;* a use frequent in the Classical writers. Some Commentators, who are averse to imputing irony to our Lord, devise other modes of interpretation; all of them, however, either open to strong objections, or *closely bordering* on irony.

11. ἐὰν εἴπῃ — ὠφεληθῇς] Something seems wanting in this sentence, to supply which, Pisc., Beza, and Casaub. understand *insons erit*. But it is better to resort to that idiom by which the Greeks leave in a sentence some verb of a contrary signification to be repeated from the preceding sentence: and thus, with Krebs, Kuin., and Fritz., we may here repeat μὴ θανάτῳ τελευτάτω, "he shall

MT.

12 δῶρον (ὅ ἐστι, δῶρον), ὃ ἐὰν ἐξ ἐμοῦ ὠφεληθῇς· καὶ οὐκέτι ἀφίετε 15.
13 αὐτὸν οὐδὲν ποιῆσαι τῷ πατρὶ αὐτοῦ ἢ τῇ μητρὶ αὐτοῦ, ἀκυροῦντες
τὸν λόγον τοῦ Θεοῦ τῇ παραδόσει ὑμῶν ᾗ παρεδώκατε· καὶ παρόμοια 9
14 τοιαῦτα πολλὰ ποιεῖτε. Καὶ προσκαλεσάμενος πάντα τὸν ὄχλον, ἔλεγεν 10
15 αὐτοῖς· Ἀκούετέ μου πάντες καὶ συνίετε. Οὐδέν ἐστιν ἔξωθεν τοῦ 11
ἀνθρώπου εἰσπορευόμενον εἰς αὐτὸν, ὃ δύναται αὐτὸν κοινῶσαι· ἀλλὰ
τὰ ἐκπορευόμενα ἀπ᾽ αὐτοῦ, ἐκεῖνά ἐστι τὰ κοινοῦντα τὸν ἄνθρωπον.
16 Εἴ τις ἔχει ὦτα ἀκούειν, ἀκουέτω. Καὶ ὅτε εἰσῆλθεν εἰς οἶκον ἀπὸ
17 τοῦ ὄχλου, ἐπηρώτων αὐτὸν οἱ μαθηταὶ αὐτοῦ περὶ τῆς παραβολῆς. 15
18 Καὶ λέγει αὐτοῖς· Οὕτω καὶ ὑμεῖς ἀσύνετοί ἐστε; οὐ νοεῖτε, ὅτι 16
πᾶν τὸ ἔξωθεν εἰσπορευόμενον εἰς τὸν ἄνθρωπον, οὐ δύναται αὐτὸν 17
19 κοινῶσαι; ὅτι οὐκ εἰσπορεύεται αὐτοῦ εἰς τὴν καρδίαν, ἀλλ᾽ εἰς τὴν
κοιλίαν· καὶ εἰς τὸν ἀφεδρῶνα ἐκπορεύεται, καθαρίζον πάντα τὰ
20 βρώματα. Ἔλεγε δέ· Ὅτι τὸ ἐκ τοῦ ἀνθρώπου ἐκπορευόμενον, ἐκεῖνο 18
21 κοινοῖ τὸν ἄνθρωπον. Ἔσωθεν γὰρ, ἐκ τῆς καρδίας τῶν ἀνθρώπων, 19

not suffer the punishment denounced." Or we may suppose an *Aposiopesis*, of some such words as "It shall be allowed to him so to do."

12. καὶ οὐκέτι ἀφίετε, &c.] The sense is, "and, while thus abrogating the Divine precept, ye permit him not any longer to," &c., namely, out of the money so consecrated; because the devotion of it was made with an imprecation against the devotee, if he employed the money to *any other* purpose.

13. ᾗ παρεδ.] This is not, as some think, pleonastic, but signifies "*quæ propagare soletis*," as Fritz. renders. The ᾗ is, by attraction, for ἥν.

15. [*Comp.* Acts x. 15. Rom. xiv. 17, 20. Tit. i. 15.]

19. καθαρίζον πάντα τὰ β.] In this passage there is much variety of reading, and diversity of interpretation. The varr. lectt. however, are, as Fritz. has shown, of such a nature as to afford no reason to call in question the common reading; they being either *slips of the pen*, or *glosses*. And the conjectures of Critics are entitled to no attention; unless it can be shown that the common reading is incapable of any tolerable explanation; which is not the case. For although most of the *many* modes of interpretation adopted are quite inadmissible, and some even ludicrously absurd, yet a tolerably good sense may be extracted from the words. Such, I conceive, is that which I have, with some hesitation, propounded in Recens. Synop., where καθαρίζον is taken as a Nominative absolute, and rendered "purifying by removal." This I find confirmed by the authority of Fritz., who, after a minute discussion of the sense, adopts that view. Of course, the Participle with ὃ and χρῆμα understood, must be considered as standing for ὃ and a verb in the Indicative, i. e. ὃ καθαρίζει; q. d. "which circumstance (namely, that the meats are cast into the jakes) makes them all alike pure." This use of the Participle, which *often* takes place in παρὸν, προσῆκον, δόξαν, &c., I have more than once illustrated in Thucyd.

21. ἔσωθεν γὰρ, &c.] This passage involves not a few difficulties, and has therefore been variously interpreted. In order to determine its complete sense, it is proper to ascertain its *scope*. Now that undoubtedly is, to *illustrate* the foregoing principle,—that vice and corruption spring from *within* a man. And this is done by first pointing to evil *thoughts*, as the fountain whence spring evil *actions* (see Matt. xii. 34.); and then *exemplifying* this truth by adverting to the principal and leading vices, *murder*, *adultery* and *fornication*, *theft*, (including rapaciousness in general) *blasphemy*, and *evil speaking*, both in general and in particular. In these *enumerations* of vices, occasionally occurring in the N. T., the Commentators have, almost universally, recognised mere *lists*, devoid of all order or arrangement, and only presenting a *congeries* of whatever is bad. I trust that I shall be enabled to prove that, though there may sometimes seem "a maze," it is "not without a plan;" and in most cases to show *what* that *is*; though there may, occasionally, on some details, exist uncertainty, as to the interpretation of terms of very extensive application. We are here, I think, especially bound to suppose *classification*, and thus it is proper to pay attention to the parallel passage of Matthew, where we have only the grand outlines of the picture; here in a great measure filled up. But, to consider more particularly the terms in question, I was long of opinion that there are three classes of vices here intended, namely, 1. μοιχεῖαι, πορνεῖαι, φόνοι, κλοπαί; 2. πλεονεξίαι — πονηρός; 3. βλασφ., ὑπερ., ἀφρ. And this view I find confirmed by the authority of Fritz. Yet, on mature reflection, I cannot help thinking this is too artificial and arbitrary a mode; and am now of opinion, that there is here little more of *classification* than we find in the passage of St. Matthew; but that we have here *filled* up what are there only the *outlines* of the picture. This will furnish a clue to ascertaining the sense of more than one controverted term. Thus, I apprehend, πλεον. and δόλος denote only lesser degrees of theft; namely, rapacity, and artful overreaching in a bargain (see Thucyd. iii. 45, 6. and 82. 2.). So Xenoph. Cyr. 1. 6, 28. not dissimilarly enumerates κακουργίαι καὶ ἀπαται, καὶ δολώσεις, καὶ πλεονεξίαι. Πονηρ. is by the earlier Commentators, interpreted *vice*, or wickedness; and by the later, *malignity* or malevolence; the latter of which senses is preferable, if we here suppose another *class* of vices intended. But that is discountenanced by the parallel passage; and it would be somewhat out of place. It should

MT.
15. οἱ διαλογισμοὶ οἱ κακοὶ ἐκπορεύονται· μοιχεῖαι, πορνεῖαι, φόνοι, κλο- 22
παὶ, πλεονεξίαι, πονηρίαι, δόλος, ἀσέλγεια, ὀφθαλμὸς πονηρὸς, βλασφη-
20 μία, ὑπερηφανία, ἀφροσύνη. Πάντα ταῦτα τὰ πονηρὰ ἔσωθεν ἐκπο- 23
ρεύεται, καὶ κοινοῖ τὸν ἄνθρωπον.
21 Καὶ ἐκεῖθεν ἀναστὰς ἀπῆλθεν εἰς τὰ μεθόρια Τύρου καὶ Σιδῶνος. 24
καὶ εἰσελθὼν εἰς [τὴν] οἰκίαν, οὐδένα ἤθελε γνῶναι· καὶ οὐκ ἠδυνή-
θη λαθεῖν. Ἀκούσασα γὰρ γυνὴ περὶ αὐτοῦ, ἧς εἶχε τὸ θυγάτριον 25
αὐτῆς πνεῦμα ἀκάθαρτον, ἐλθοῦσα προσέπεσε πρὸς τοὺς πόδας αὐτοῦ,
22 (ἦν δὲ ἡ γυνὴ Ἑλληνὶς, Συροφοίνισσα τῷ γένει·) καὶ ἠρώτα αὐτὸν 26
ἵνα τὸ δαιμόνιον ἐκβάλῃ ἐκ τῆς θυγατρὸς αὐτῆς. Ὁ δὲ Ἰησοῦς εἶπεν 27
26 αὐτῇ· Ἄφες πρῶτον χορτασθῆναι τὰ τέκνα· οὐ γὰρ καλόν ἐστι λα-
27 βεῖν τὸν ἄρτον τῶν τέκνων, καὶ βαλεῖν τοῖς κυναρίοις. Ἡ δὲ ἀπεκρίθη 28
καὶ λέγει αὐτῷ· Ναὶ, Κύριε· καὶ γὰρ τὰ κυνάρια ὑποκάτω τῆς

therefore seem that πονηρ. and δολ. denote two *species* of the *genus*, rapacity; of which the former may be supposed to mean *trickery*, something like our *swindling*. This view of the sense of δόλος and πον. is confirmed by Jerem. ix. 1—6. where the Israelites are described in nearly the colours of the picture here: e. gr. πάντες μοιχῶνται, σύνοδος ἀθετούντων, ἐνέτειναν τὴν γλῶσσαν αὐτῶν ὡς τόξον· ψεῦδος, καὶ οὐ πίστις ἐνίσχυσεν ἐπὶ τῆς γῆς. πᾶς φίλος δολίως πορεύσεται.—τόκος ἐπὶ τόκῳ, καὶ δόλος ἐπὶ δόλῳ.

To these evil *actions* and *habits* are subjoined the cognate evil *dispositions*, ἀσέλγεια and ὀφθαλμὸς πονηρός; the former of which expressions denotes that spirit of craving which never cries hold! enough! that desire of one's neighbour's goods which leads us to look on his wealth with the eye of desire, grudging him his possessions. So Prov. xxiii. 6. "eat not the bread of him that hath an evil (i. e. grudging) eye," and xxviii. 22. "He that hasteth to be rich hath an evil eye." That ἀσελγ. must here have the sense of excessive desire for wealth (auri sacra fames) is plain from its situation in the sentence, which forbids it to be taken in the usual one *lascivia* or *insolentia*, *injuria*, as Kuin. explains. Indeed ἀσελγὴς seems primarily to mean *extreme*, *excessive*. So Ælian ap. Suid. in ἀσέλγεια says of a *wind*: πολὺς καὶ ἀσελγὴς τίκτεται ἐκεῖθι. namely, in deep dells through which it is conveyed as through a funnel. Or ἀσέλγεια may here denote *profligacy*, the being devoid of principle, snatching at gain in any way. This is confirmed by the derivation of the word, which seems to be from an *intensive* and σέλγης, which I suspect came from the Heb. שלח, to let loose, q. d. *abandoned* to vice, lost to all principle.

To advert to the last three terms, which will, I apprehend, be found to have an affinity to each other. Βλασφ., as appears from the parallel passage, means, not *blasphemy*, but *calumny*. In determining the force of the two other terms, it is proper to consider the *scope*, which I conceive is, to designate the vices which engender calumny. And as Solomon says, (Prov. xiii. 10.), "only by pride cometh contention," so only by pride and vanity cometh evil speaking and slanderous words. So in Prov. viii. 13. "Pride, and arrogance, and the tongue of perversity do I hate;" where by *perversity* is, I apprehend, meant *slander*. So Prov. xvii. 20. "the perverse in his tongue ונהפך בלשונו (i. e. he who perverts the truth) shall fall into evil." Which is the reason why, at x. 18., it is said, "He that uttereth a slander is a *fool*." Finally, the remaining term is capable of several senses, and has been variously interpreted. But as it seems to be closely connected with the preceding term ὑπερηφ., it may denote (as Fritz. explains) that thoughtless levity and rashness in speaking, which produces evil speaking more frequently than deliberate malice.

24. τὰ μεθόρια Τ. καὶ Σ.] This is by most Commentators taken to mean, that tract of country which *divided* Palestine from Tyre and Sidon. But Fritz. thinks the meaning is, that our Lord entered *into* the territory of Tyre and Sidon. In fact, the district in question was a strip of anciently debateable *border land*, (like the *Thyreatis* between Argolis and Laconia, and some other tracts in Greece); but afterwards ceded by Solomon to the King of Tyre: though it long afterwards retained its original name of the *border land*.

— τήν.] This is omitted in very many MSS., and nearly all the early Edd. and is cancelled by almost every Editor from Bengel to Scholz. The Article can (as Middlet. says) have no place here. Γνῶναι, namely, that he was there. It seems to be a *popular* form of expression. Καὶ οὐκ ἠδ. The καὶ signifies *but*.

26. Ἑλληνὶς] a Gentile, or pagan, (called in Matthew Χαναναία) for the distinction is one not of country, but religion. The Heathens had, for a long time, been called by the name of *Greeks*, because many of those with whom the Jews held commerce were either such, or at least used the Grecian language.

— Συροφοίνισσα.] A woman of the country called Syria-Phœnicia, which lay between Syria and Phœnicia. Συροφ. too is said because there were Λιβυφοίνικες, i. e. Carthaginians. Many MSS. here have Συροφοινίκισσα, which is received by Matth., Griesb., Vat., Tittm., and Scholz. But the common reading is retained and ably defended by Fritz.

— ἐκβάλῃ.] This (for the common reading ἐκβάλλῃ), is found in very many of the best MSS. and the Ed. Princ., and adopted by Wets., Griesb., Tittm., Vat., Fritz., and Scholz. It is (as Fritz. shows) required by the correspondence of tenses found in the Greek idiom.

27. ἄφες πρῶτον—κυναρίοις] q. d. "Do not ask me *before the time* to confer benefits upon you, nor act like servants who would be fed before the *children* are satiated." (Fritz.)

28. ναὶ, Κύριε] Sub. καλόν ἐστι, &c. "True,

MT.
29 τραπέζης ἐσθίει ἀπὸ τῶν ψιχίων τῶν παιδίων. Καὶ εἶπεν αὐτῇ· 15.
Διὰ τοῦτον τὸν λόγον, ὕπαγε· ἐξελήλυθε τὸ δαιμόνιον ἐκ τῆς θυ- 28
30 γατρός σου. Καὶ ἀπελθοῦσα εἰς τὸν οἶκον αὐτῆς, εὗρε τὸ δαιμόνιον
ἐξεληλυθὸς, καὶ τὴν θυγατέρα βεβλημένην ἐπὶ τῆς κλίνης.
31 ΚΑΙ πάλιν ἐξελθὼν ἐκ τῶν ὁρίων Τύρου καὶ Σιδῶνος, ἦλθε πρὸς
τὴν θάλασσαν τῆς Γαλιλαίας, ἀνὰ μέσον τῶν ὁρίων Δεκαπόλεως. Καὶ 29
32 φέρουσιν αὐτῷ κωφὸν μογιλάλον, καὶ παρακαλοῦσιν αὐτὸν, ἵνα ἐπιθῇ
33 αὐτῷ τὴν χεῖρα. Καὶ ἀπολαβόμενος αὐτὸν ἀπὸ τοῦ ὄχλου κατ᾽ ἰδίαν,
ἔβαλε τοὺς δακτύλους αὐτοῦ εἰς τὰ ὦτα αὐτοῦ, καὶ πτύσας, ἥψατο τῆς
34 γλώσσης αὐτοῦ· καὶ ἀναβλέψας εἰς τὸν οὐρανὸν, ἐστέναξε, καὶ λέγει
35 αὐτῷ· Ἐφφαθὰ, ὅ ἐστι διανοίχθητι. Καὶ εὐθέως διηνοίχθησαν αὐτοῦ αἱ ἀκοαί· καὶ ἐλύθη ὁ δεσμὸς τῆς γλώσσης αὐτοῦ, καὶ ἐλάλει
36 ὀρθῶς. Καὶ διεστείλατο αὐτοῖς, ἵνα μηδενὶ εἴπωσιν· ὅσον δὲ αὐτὸς

Lord, it is right." Καὶ γάρ, [But do it] for even, &c.

29. ὕπαγε.] This does not import *begone*, but implies a granting of the request, q. d. "go in God's name." Διὰ τοῦτον τὸν λόγον, "because of this speech [so full of humility and faith]."

30. βεβλημένην ἐπὶ τῆς κλ.] i. e. lying tranquil and composed on a bed; not, as before, running up and down, or lying on the ground. Vide supra v. 15.

32. κωφὸν μογιλάλον.] There is some difference of opinion on the sense of these words. Some ancient Translators, and early modern Commentators take μογιλάλον to denote one *dumb;* which they seek to establish by the use of the word in the Sept. at Isa. xxxv. 5. But that version is *erroneous*, and therefore cannot afford any proof. In vain, too, do they appeal to Matt. ix. 33. and Luke xi. 14, for there is every reason to suppose this miracle a different one from that there recorded. Besides, the words used of the man after his cure (ἐλάλει ὀρθῶς) concur with the proper signification of the term, (namely, *one who speaks with difficulty*,) to show that the person was not *dumb by nature*, nor, probably, *deaf by nature*; otherwise it would have been needless to call him dumb (for such persons always *are so*); but was one who, having early lost his *hearing*, gradually lost much of his *speech*, and had become a stammerer. Such an impediment is either *natural*, arising from what is called a *bos*, or ulcer, by which any one is, as we say, *tongue-tied*, (of which Wets. adduces some examples from the Classical writers, and I have myself, in Recens. Synop., added others more apposite, from Artemid. and Philostratus,) or brought on, when, from an early loss of hearing, the membrane of the tongue becomes rigid and unable to perform its office. That the *former* was the case of this poor sufferer, would seem to appear from the expression at ver. 35. ἐλύθη ὁ δεσμὸς τῆς γλώσσης. But even *that* may be taken figuratively, (as in some of the passages cited by Wets.,) and the latter view is probably the true one. This sense of μογιλάλος is adopted by the Syriac Translator, and also by Beza, Grot., and almost all of the recent Commentators; who answer the argument of their opponents, that at ver. 37 we have καὶ τοὺς ἀλάλους λαλεῖν, by replying that that is either a *general* expression, and not limited to *this* sense; or that ἄλαλος is used by a common *hyperbole*.

33. ἀπολαβόμενος—ἰδίαν] "taking him aside and apart from the multitude," not, away from them, or out of their sight. This was probably done for the same reason as that which influenced our Lord in the miracle recorded supra, v. 40.

—ἔβαλε—τὰ ὦτα αὐτοῦ.] Since this, and the other action mentioned, could contribute nothing to the cure (though we find such used on other occasions, as viii. 23, and John ix. 6.) it has been asked *why* our Lord used them. Such inquiries are often rash, and we are not bound in all cases to give a reason (since our Saviour's *adoption* of an action shows its *fitness*); yet here we can be at no loss. The reason was, no doubt, that assigned by Grot. and Whitby, and adopted by most recent Commentators, as Kuin. and Fritz.; namely, that Christ was pleased, in condescension to human weakness, to use external actions significant of the cure to be performed; and thereby to strengthen the faith and confirm the hopes of the sick persons, and those who brought them; and, moreover, to show that the power he was about to exert resided *in himself*. Our Lord adopted *these* actions, and *also* the usual one of laying his hands on the sick, in order to show that he was not confined to any one particular mode. [*Comp.* John ix. 6. Infra viii. 23.]

34. καὶ ἀναβλ., &c.] [*Comp.* John xi. 41; xvii. 1.]

—ἐστέναξε] "he groaned;" in sympathy with human calamity. [*Comp.* Heb. iv. 15.]

—ἐφφαθά.] Syro Chaldee, and the Imperative of the passive conjugation Ethpael. Διανοίχθητι, i. e. Have the use of thine ears. Λύεσθαι would seem a more proper term as applied to the tongue; but διανοίγεσθαι is adopted as being applicable to the removal of *both* obstructions. For in Hebrew phraseology *to open any one's eyes* or *ears* denotes imparting to him the faculty of sight or speech. Grot. observes, that such words are usually interchanged, "*per abusionem.*" But the reason rather is, that in words indicative of the deprivation of any natural faculty there is *one common idea*. Thus our words *dumb, blind*, and *deaf*, are all derived from past participles of verbs signifying to *stop up*. And the same might be shown in almost all the correspondent words of other languages.

36. ὅσον] for καθ' ὅσον, say most Commentators; who also at μᾶλλον supply τοσούτῳ. But

MT.
15. αὐτοῖς διεστέλλετο, μᾶλλον περισσότερον ἐκήρυσσον. Καὶ ὑπερπερισσῶς 37
ἐξεπλήσσοντο, λέγοντες· Καλῶς πάντα πεποίηκε· καὶ τοὺς κωφοὺς
ποιεῖ ἀκούειν, καὶ τοὺς ἀλάλους λαλεῖν.

VIII. ἘΝ ἐκείναις ταῖς ἡμέραις, παμπόλλου ὄχλου ὄντος, καὶ μὴ 1
32 ἐχόντων τί φάγωσι, προσκαλεσάμενος [ὁ Ἰησοῦς] τοὺς μαθητὰς αὐτοῦ, 2
λέγει αὐτοῖς· Σπλαγχνίζομαι ἐπὶ τὸν ὄχλον· ὅτι ἤδη * ἡμέραι τρεῖς
προσμένουσί μοι, καὶ οὐκ ἔχουσι τί φάγωσι. Καὶ ἐὰν ἀπολύσω αὐ- 3
τοὺς νήστεις εἰς οἶκον αὐτῶν, ἐκλυθήσονται ἐν τῇ ὁδῷ· τινὲς γὰρ
33 αὐτῶν μακρόθεν ἥκουσι. Καὶ ἀπεκρίθησαν αὐτῷ οἱ μαθηταὶ αὐτοῦ· 4
34 Πόθεν τούτους δυνήσεταί τις ὧδε χορτάσαι ἄρτων ἐπ᾽ ἐρημίας; Καὶ 5
35 ἐπηρώτα αὐτούς· Πόσους ἔχετε ἄρτους; οἱ δὲ εἶπον· Ἑπτά. Καὶ 6
36 παρήγγειλε τῷ ὄχλῳ ἀναπεσεῖν ἐπὶ τῆς γῆς· καὶ λαβὼν τοὺς ἑπτὰ
ἄρτους, εὐχαριστήσας ἔκλασε, καὶ ἐδίδου τοῖς μαθηταῖς αὐτοῦ, ἵνα
παραθῶσι· καὶ παρέθηκαν τῷ ὄχλῳ. Καὶ εἶχον ἰχθύδια ὀλίγα· καὶ 7
37 εὐλογήσας, εἶπε παραθεῖναι καὶ αὐτά. Ἔφαγον δὲ, καὶ ἐχορτάσθησαν· 8
38 καὶ ἦραν περισσεύματα κλασμάτων, ἑπτὰ σπυρίδας. Ἦσαν δὲ οἱ φαγόν- 9
τες ὡς τετρακισχίλιοι· καὶ ἀπέλυσεν αὐτούς.

39 Καὶ εὐθέως ἐμβὰς εἰς τὸ πλοῖον μετὰ τῶν μαθητῶν αὐτοῦ, ἦλθεν 10
16.
1 εἰς τὰ μέρη Δαλμανουθά. Καὶ ἐξῆλθον οἱ Φαρισαῖοι, καὶ ἤρξαντο 11
συζητεῖν αὐτῷ, ζητοῦντες παρ᾽ αὐτοῦ σημεῖον ἀπὸ τοῦ οὐρανοῦ, πει-
4 ράζοντες αὐτόν. Καὶ ἀναστενάξας τῷ πνεύματι αὐτοῦ, λέγει· Τί ἡ 12
γενεὰ αὕτη σημεῖον ἐπιζητεῖ; Ἀμὴν λέγω ὑμῖν· εἰ δοθήσεται τῇ
γενεᾷ ταύτῃ σημεῖον! Καὶ ἀφεὶς αὐτοὺς, ἐμβὰς πάλιν εἰς τὸ πλοῖον, 13
ἀπῆλθεν εἰς τὸ πέραν.

5 Καὶ ἐπελάθοντο λαβεῖν ἄρτους. καὶ εἰ μὴ ἕνα ἄρτον οὐκ εἶχον 14
6 μεθ᾽ ἑαυτῶν ἐν τῷ πλοίῳ. καὶ διεστέλλετο αὐτοῖς λέγων· Ὁρᾶτε, 15

Fritz., with reason, rejects both ellipses, and simply renders the words *quantum*—and *magis*. There is not (as some suppose) any pleonasm in μᾶλλον περ.; but as Fritz. observes, the μᾶλλον adds weight and intensity to the following comparative περισσότερον. He compares Aristoph. Eccl. 1131. μᾶλλον ὀλβιώτερος.

VIII. 2. ἡμέραι.] This (for the common reading ἡμέρας) is found in very many MSS., most of them ancient, and is preferred by Mill, Beng., and Wets., and edited by Matth., Griesb., Tittm., Vat., Fritz., and Scholz. See Note on Matt. xv. 32. Fritz., indeed, points ὅτι, ἤδη ἡμέραι τρεῖς, προσμ. μ. remarking, "temporum notationes illo pacto haud raro a veteribus reliquæ orationi interponi;" adducing, as an example, Lucian. Dial. Mer. i. 4. οὐ γὰρ ἑώρακα, πολὺς ἤδη χρόνος, αὐτόν. But of that idiom not a single example, I believe, can be adduced from the *Scriptures*, with whose style it totally disagrees.

3. νήστεις.] Sub. κατὰ, "fasting;" from νῆστις, literally, "at fasting;" or, in our ancient phraseology, *a* "*fasting*." So *a* "*cold*," &c. &c. Thus it came at length to have the force of an adjective. And the number (sing. or plur.) is accommodated to that of the *subject* of the assertion. Such seems to be the true nature of the idiom, neglected by Commentators and Philologists. For ἥκουσι some would read, from several MSS., ἥκασι. But Fritz. shows that the use of the preterite ἧκα, however it may be found in the Sept., Joseph., and Liban., cannot be proved to have been adopted by the writers of the N. T. Besides, there is no *need* of the change, since the Present of ἥκω has often the sense of the Preterite. Thus we may render "are come," or "had come."

11. συζητεῖν αὐτῷ] "to enter into argument with him." The word *properly* signifies "*to use mutual inquiry and discussion.*" The construction of this verse (which is somewhat rough) is thus adjusted by Fritz. "ζητοῦντες—ἀπὸ τοῦ οὐρανοῦ has regard to ἤρξαντο συζ. αὐτῷ, but πειράζοντες αὐτὸν to the whole sentence ἤρξαντο—ἀπὸ τοῦ οὐρανοῦ." [*Comp.* John vi. 30.]

12. ἀναστενάξας τῷ πν.] The ἀνα is intensive, and signifies what is *deep*; (for the notions of *height* and *depth* concur,) i. e. "having fetched a deep groan or sigh from the very heart."

—εἰ δοθήσεται, &c.] The εἰ is not (as some imagine) put for οὐ; but (as the best Commentators are agreed) this is a form of solemn asseveration (common in the O. T., but rarely, if ever, found in the Classical writers), in which there is implied an *imprecation*; which, however, is omitted *per aposiopesin et gravitatis ergo*. The nature of the imprecation ("may I not live!" or the like) will depend upon the subject, and the speak-

MT.
16 βλέπετε ἀπὸ τῆς ζύμης τῶν Φαρισαίων, καὶ τῆς ζύμης Ἡρώδου. Καὶ 16.
17 διελογίζοντο πρὸς ἀλλήλους, λέγοντες· Ὅτι ἄρτους οὐκ ἔχομεν. Καὶ 8
γνοὺς ὁ Ἰησοῦς λέγει αὐτοῖς· Τί διαλογίζεσθε· ὅτι ἄρτους οὐκ
ἔχετε; Οὔπω νοεῖτε, οὐδὲ συνίετε; ἔτι πεπωρωμένην ἔχετε τὴν 9
18 καρδίαν ὑμῶν; Ὀφθαλμοὺς ἔχοντες οὐ βλέπετε; καὶ ὦτα ἔχοντες
19 οὐκ ἀκούετε καὶ οὐ μνημονεύετε; Ὅτε τοὺς πέντε ἄρτους ἔκλασα εἰς
τοὺς πεντακισχιλίους, πόσους κοφίνους πλήρεις κλασμάτων ἤρατε; λέ-
20 γουσιν αὐτῷ· Δώδεκα. Ὅτε δὲ τοὺς ἑπτὰ εἰς τοὺς τετρακισχιλίους, 10
πόσων σπυρίδων πληρώματα κλασμάτων ἤρατε; οἱ δὲ εἶπον· Ἑπτά.
21 Καὶ ἔλεγεν αὐτοῖς· Πῶς οὐ συνίετε;
22 ΚΑΙ ἔρχεται εἰς Βηθσαϊδάν· καὶ φέρουσιν αὐτῷ τυφλὸν, καὶ
23 παρακαλοῦσιν αὐτὸν, ἵνα αὐτοῦ ἅψηται. Καὶ ἐπιλαβόμενος τῆς χειρὸς
τοῦ τυφλοῦ, ἐξήγαγεν αὐτὸν ἔξω τῆς κώμης. Καὶ πτύσας εἰς τὰ
ὄμματα αὐτοῦ, ἐπιθεὶς τὰς χεῖρας αὐτῷ, ἐπηρώτα αὐτὸν εἴ τι βλέπει;
24 Καὶ ἀναβλέψας ἔλεγε· Βλέπω τοὺς ἀνθρώπους, ὡς δένδρα, περιπα-
25 τοῦντας. Εἶτα πάλιν ἐπέθηκε τὰς χεῖρας ἐπὶ τοὺς ὀφθαλμοὺς αὐτοῦ,
καὶ ἐποίησεν αὐτὸν ἀναβλέψαι· καὶ ἀποκατεστάθη, καὶ ἐνέβλεψε
26 τηλαυγῶς ἅπαντας. Καὶ ἀπέστειλεν αὐτὸν εἰς τὸν οἶκον αὐτοῦ, λέγων·
Μηδὲ εἰς τὴν κώμην εἰσέλθῃς, μηδὲ εἴπῃς τινὶ ἐν τῇ κώμῃ.

er. This is *supplied* at Ezek. xiv. 16. Sept. The Classical writers use the complete form, but only, I think, with εἰ μή.

15. βλέπετε ἀπό.] Equivalent to the προσέχετε of Matthew and the φυλάσσεσθε of Luke. This use is Hellenistic. Καὶ τῆς ζύμης Ἡ. *Matthew* joins the *Sadducees* with the Pharisees, and makes no mention of *Herod*. But there is no real discrepancy, since Herod and the Herodians (i. e. his adherents and courtiers) were, no doubt, Sadducees, and there is every reason to think that their doctrines and morals were such as to justify the caution of our Lord. Ζύμη, by a striking metaphor, denotes the *infection* of *false doctrines*, (so Matt. xvi. 12,) as well as of corrupt morals.

19. πέντε ἄρτους ἔκλασα εἰς τοὺς π.] It is well observed by Fritz. that there is here a *prægnans constructio*, in which is included the two senses, to *break* the loaves, and to *distribute* them to the multitude. This idiom is indeed frequent both in the Scriptural and Classical writers.

22—26. This miracle is recorded only by Mark; though it has several circumstances which render it worthy of particular attention. [*Comp.* vii. 32.]

23. ἐξήγαγεν—κώμης] i. e., as most Commentators say, because he thought those who had seen so many miracles in vain, were not worthy to see more. The reason, however, seems rather to have been, that our Lord never chose to perform a miracle with a crowd pressing about him. See supra iii. 10. & v. 28.

—πτύσας εἰς τὰ ὄμματα]. Our Lord was here again pleased to *vary* the mode of the external action: and that the one adopted on this occasion was not unusual with those who *pretended* to cure blindness, or dimness of sight, we may suppose from the same thing occurring in an account of a *pretended* miracle narrated in Suet. Vesp. 7. Our Lord was also pleased to vary the *operation*, and cause that it should not be instantaneous, but gradual.

24. καὶ ἀναβλέψας] Ἀναβλέπειν signifies not only to *look up*, but "to recover the sight," which latter signification many Commentators (after Erasm.) here adopt. That, however (as Campb. observes), only has place where a *complete* recovery is denoted; which was not the case here, the *perfection* of it being marked by the words ἀποκατεστάθη, καὶ ἐνέβλεψε τηλαυγῶς ἅπαντας. The best Commentators, ancient and modern, are agreed on the *former* signification *to look up*. He looked up in order to ascertain whether he had recovered his sight.

—βλέπω τοὺς ἀνθρώπους—περιπατοῦντας] These words have occasioned somewhat of perplexity. There is, as might be expected, great variety of readings; for several MSS. and early Edd. read βλέπω τοὺς ἀνθρώπους· ὅτι ὡς δένδρα ὁρῶ περιπ. And this was edited by Schmid, Mill, Beng., and Matth. But Fritz. has shown that this reading yields no tolerable sense; and he (in common with Griesb., Tittm., Vat., and Scholz) edits the words without the ὅτι and ὡς, as in the *textus receptus*. This, too, is found in the Edit. Pr. and the great body of MSS., confirmed by almost every one of the ancient Versions: and it is doubtless to be preferred. The other seems to have arisen, as Fritz. remarks, e διττογραφίᾳ, i. e. βλέπω and ὁρῶ; and ὅτι and ὡς. The words ὡς δένδρα are to be referred to the τοὺς ἀνθ., not περιπ.; and the sense is, "I see men, as trees, walking;" i. e. I can distinguish men from trees only by their walking; a result of imperfect vision; since a *confusion of vision* in the objects is, as Plato observes, the first sign of returning sight, which, as he says, τῆς αἰσθήσεως σημεῖα παραλλάττει. This view of the sense is confirmed by Victor, who, no doubt, derived it from the Fathers. From the above it is plain that the person was not *born* blind, but had lost his sight from disease.

26. μηδὲ εἰς τὴν—κώμῃ] On these words there has been a needless scruple raised, the best way

MT. LU.
16. 9. *Καὶ ἐξῆλθεν ὁ Ἰησοῦς καὶ οἱ μαθηταὶ αὐτοῦ εἰς τὰς κώμας Και-* 27
13 18 *σαρείας τῆς Φιλίππου· καὶ ἐν τῇ ὁδῷ ἐπηρώτα τοὺς μαθητὰς αὐτοῦ,*
14 19 *λέγων αὐτοῖς· Τίνα με λέγουσιν οἱ ἄνθρωποι εἶναι; Οἱ δὲ ἀπεκρίθη-* 28
σαν· Ἰωάννην τὸν βαπτιστήν· καὶ ἄλλοι Ἠλίαν· ἄλλοι δὲ ἕνα τῶν
15 20 *προφητῶν. καὶ αὐτὸς λέγει αὐτοῖς· Ὑμεῖς δὲ τίνα με λέγετε εἶναι;* 29
ἀποκριθεὶς δὲ ὁ Πέτρος λέγει αὐτῷ· Σὺ εἶ ὁ Χριστός. Καὶ ἐπετί- 30
20 21 *μησεν αὐτοῖς, ἵνα μηδενὶ λέγωσι περὶ αὐτοῦ.*
21 22 *ΚΑΙ ἤρξατο διδάσκειν αὐτούς, ὅτι δεῖ τὸν Υἱὸν τοῦ ἀνθρώπου πολ-* 31
λὰ παθεῖν, καὶ ἀποδοκιμασθῆναι ἀπὸ τῶν πρεσβυτέρων καὶ ἀρχιερέων
καὶ γραμματέων, καὶ ἀποκτανθῆναι· καὶ μετὰ τρεῖς ἡμέρας ἀναστῆναι.
22 *καὶ παῤῥησίᾳ τὸν λόγον ἐλάλει. Καὶ προσλαβόμενος αὐτὸν ὁ Πέτρος,* 32
23 *ἤρξατο ἐπιτιμᾷν αὐτῷ. Ὁ δὲ ἐπιστραφεὶς καὶ ἰδὼν τοὺς μαθητὰς αὐ-* 33
τοῦ, ἐπετίμησε τῷ Πέτρῳ, λέγων· Ὕπαγε ὀπίσω μου, σατανᾶ· ὅτι οὐ
φρονεῖς τὰ τοῦ Θεοῦ, ἀλλὰ τὰ τῶν ἀνθρώπων.
24 *Καὶ προσκαλεσάμενος τὸν ὄχλον σὺν τοῖς μαθηταῖς αὐτοῦ εἶπεν* 34
23 *αὐτοῖς· Ὅστις θέλει ὀπίσω μου ἐλθεῖν ἀπαρνησάσθω ἑαυτόν, καὶ*
25 24 *ἀράτω τὸν σταυρὸν αὐτοῦ, καὶ ἀκολουθείτω μοι. Ὃς γὰρ ἂν θέλῃ* 35
τὴν ψυχὴν αὐτοῦ σῶσαι, ἀπολέσει αὐτήν· ὃς δ' ἂν ἀπολέσῃ τὴν
26 25 *ψυχὴν αὐτοῦ, ἕνεκεν ἐμοῦ καὶ τοῦ εὐαγγελίου, οὗτος σώσει αὐτήν. Τί* 36
γὰρ ὠφελήσει ἄνθρωπον, ἐὰν κερδήσῃ τὸν κόσμον ὅλον, καὶ ζημιωθῇ
τὴν ψυχὴν αὐτοῦ; ἢ τί δώσει ἄνθρωπος ἀντάλλαγμα τῆς ψυχῆς 37
26 *αὐτοῦ; Ὃς γὰρ ἂν ἐπαισχυνθῇ με καὶ τοὺς ἐμοὺς λόγους ἐν τῇ* 38
γενεᾷ ταύτῃ τῇ μοιχαλίδι καὶ ἁμαρτωλῷ, καὶ ὁ Υἱὸς τοῦ ἀνθρώπου
ἐπαισχυνθήσεται αὐτόν, ὅταν ἔλθῃ ἐν τῇ δόξῃ τοῦ πατρὸς αὐτοῦ μετὰ
28 27 *τῶν ἀγγέλων τῶν ἁγίων.* IX. *Καὶ ἔλεγεν αὐτοῖς· Ἀμὴν λέγω* 1
ὑμῖν, ὅτι εἰσί τινες τῶν ὧδε ἑστηκότων, οἵτινες οὐ μὴ γεύσωνται θανά-
17. *του, ἕως ἂν ἴδωσι τὴν βασιλείαν τοῦ Θεοῦ ἐληλυθυῖαν ἐν δυνάμει.*
1 28 *Καὶ μεθ' ἡμέρας ἓξ παραλαμβάνει ὁ Ἰησοῦς τὸν Πέτρον καὶ τὸν* 2
Ἰάκωβον καὶ τὸν Ἰωάννην, καὶ ἀναφέρει αὐτοὺς εἰς ὄρος ὑψηλὸν κατ'
2 29 *ἰδίαν μόνους· καὶ μετεμορφώθη ἔμπροσθεν αὐτῶν· καὶ τὰ ἱμάτια* 3
αὐτοῦ ἐγένετο στίλβοντα, λευκὰ λίαν ὡς χιών, οἷα γναφεὺς ἐπὶ τῆς γῆς
3 30 *οὐ δύναται λευκᾶναι. Καὶ ὤφθη αὐτοῖς Ἠλίας σὺν Μωϋσεῖ· καὶ* 4
4 33 *ἦσαν συλλαλοῦντες τῷ Ἰησοῦ. Καὶ ἀποκριθεὶς ὁ Πέτρος λέγει τῷ* 5
Ἰησοῦ· Ῥαββί, καλόν ἐστιν ἡμᾶς ὧδε εἶναι· καὶ ποιήσωμεν σκηνὰς
τρεῖς· σοὶ μίαν, καὶ Μωϋσεῖ μίαν, καὶ Ἠλίᾳ μίαν. Οὐ γὰρ ᾔδει τί 6
5 34 *λαλήσῃ· ἦσαν γὰρ ἔκφοβοι. Καὶ ἐγένετο νεφέλη ἐπισκιάζουσα αὐτοῖς·* 7

of avoiding which is to consider them as expressing this sense: "Do not go into the village and tell them what has happened."

31. ἀποδοκιμασθῆναι] An allusion to Ps. cxviii. 22. And the word implies *contumely* with rejection.

32. παῤῥησίᾳ] i. e. "plainly." So Euthym. φανερῶς καὶ ἀπαρακαλύπτως, i. e. without any figure of speech, as John expresses it.

35. [*Comp.* John xii. 25.]

38. [*Comp.* Rom. i. 16. 2 Tim. ii. 12. 1 John ii. 23.]

IX. 3. γναφεὺς from γνάφος, a tool with which the ancients used to raise the nap of worn cloth. This was one of the employments of an artisan called γναφεύς: and with it were united that of cleansing soiled garments, and restoring them to their original state; either by dyeing them, or, by the use of fullers' earth and alkali, restoring their whiteness.

7. ἐπισκιάζουσα αὐτοῖς.] This construction with the *Dative* is rare; (that with the *Accusative* being the usual one) but it is found also in Acts v. 15, and Ps. xc. 3, Sept., and ἐπισκιάζειν τινὶ may there

MT. LU.
καὶ ἦλθε φωνὴ ἐκ τῆς νεφέλης· [λέγουσα·] Οὗτός ἐστιν ὁ Υἱός 17. 9.
8 μου ὁ ἀγαπητός· αὐτοῦ ἀκούετε! Καὶ ἐξάπινα περιβλεψάμενοι, 8 36
9 οὐκέτι οὐδένα εἶδον, ἀλλὰ τὸν Ἰησοῦν μόνον μεθ᾽ ἑαυτῶν. Καταβαινόν- 9
των δὲ αὐτῶν ἀπὸ τοῦ ὄρους, διεστείλατο αὐτοῖς, ἵνα μηδενὶ διηγή-
σωνται, ἃ εἶδον, εἰ μὴ ὅταν ὁ Υἱὸς τοῦ ἀνθρώπου ἐκ νεκρῶν ἀναστῇ.
10 Καὶ τὸν λόγον ἐκράτησαν, πρὸς ἑαυτοὺς συζητοῦντες, τί ἐστι τό· ἐκ
11 νεκρῶν ἀναστῆναι. Καὶ ἐπηρώτων αὐτὸν λέγοντες· *Ὅ τι λέγουσιν 10
12 οἱ γραμματεῖς, ὅτι Ἠλίαν δεῖ ἐλθεῖν πρῶτον; ὁ δὲ ἀποκριθεὶς εἶπεν
αὐτοῖς· Ἠλίας μὲν ἐλθὼν πρῶτον, ἀποκαθιστᾷ πάντα· [καὶ] * κα- 11
θὼς γέγραπται ἐπὶ τὸν Υἱὸν τοῦ ἀνθρώπου, ἵνα πολλὰ πάθῃ καὶ

be rendered, "to be a shade to," or over "any one;" the Dative (which is *not*, as Fritz. imagines, a Dativus commodi) being suspended on the ἐπί.

— λέγουσα.] This is omitted in many MSS., some Versions, and Theophyl.; and is cancelled by Matth., Griesb., and Fritz., as having been introduced from the other Gospels. [*Comp.* Matt. iii. 17. Luke iii. 22. 2 Pet. i. 17.]

8. ἐξάπινα.] This rather rare form is a neuter plural, taken adverbially, of the old epic adjective ἐξάπινος; whence the Ionic ἐξαπίνης, contracted by the Attics to ἐξαίφνης. Yet the old adverb had been retained by the Macedonians, occurs sometimes in the later writers, and is frequent in the LXX. Ἀλλὰ τὸν Ἰ. This is generally taken as put for εἰ μή. Fritz., however, supposes the ἀλλά as put with reference to the negative in οὐκέτι, and supplies a *verb* of seeing; namely, ἑώρων, from the preceding participle. Yet the former mode is defended and illustrated by our *but*, which has often the sense *except*. The fact is, that in this case, ἀλλά is for ἀλλ᾽ ἤ, *otherwise than*.

10. τὸν λόγον ἐκράτησαν, &c.] The sense (much disputed) of these words, will chiefly depend upon the *construction*. Some construe them with the words *following*, πρὸς ἑαυτούς; others take them with the *preceding*, συζητοῦντες. The former method is preferred by some of the ancient, and the earlier modern Commentators; but the latter is adopted by almost all the later Expositors; and with reason; for such a construction as the former would be unprecedented. They are, however, not agreed on the sense of ἐκράτησαν; some rendering it "reticuerunt," others, "animo exceperunt;" others, again, "animo retinuerunt." To *all* of these interpretations, however, objections are made by Fritz.; who himself renders "sermonem (Jesu) firmiter tenuerunt." This version perhaps deserves the preference; but the *reticuerunt* of Schleus. and others *may* be the true sense. Τί ἐστι — νεκρῶν, quidnam esset è mortuis redire,— "what Jesus meant by speaking of rising from the dead." They did not question the general resurrection, which all but the Sadducees believed: but they could not reconcile this language with what they had learnt in the law,—that Christ should live for ever, and hold an everlasting kingdom. Hence their slowness in comprehending the assurances, so often reiterated to them, by Christ, of his death and resurrection. Insomuch that when the Lord was dead, their hopes died with him, and only revived at his resurrection.

11. ὅ τι λέγουσιν.] Almost all Commentators take ὅτι in the sense *why*. Fritz., with reason, rejects, as unfounded, this signification. He would read τί οὖν from some Latin Versions. But this reading is of slender authority, and the οὖν was doubtless derived from Matt. xvii. 10. If the common reading be correct, the best mode of interpretation will be, to supply τί ἐστι τοῦτο here and infra ver. 28, which is confirmed by the Armenian Version. But as this is a very harsh ellipse, we may suspect some corruption in the text. Perhaps the true reading is that of one or two MSS. τί for διὰ τί. This is confirmed even by those MSS. which are quoted in favor of τί οὖν; and perhaps by the Versions which are adduced in support of πῶς οὖν. The ο might easily arise from the ς preceding. The authority, however, is too weak; and the reading is probably no more than a *conjecture* to remove the difficulty; which may more effectually and quite as allowably, be done by reading ὅ τι, which I have ventured to edit here and infra v. 28. This signification is not frequent; yet instances *do* occur. Steph. Thes. furnishes *three*; Hom. Il. κ. 142. Odyss. τ. 463, where Eustath. rightly explains it by τί or διὰ τί, both in interrogation; of which Stephens gives one example from Isocrates, to which I am enabled to add the following. Thucyd. i. 90, fin. καὶ ὁπότε τις αὐτὸν ἔροιτο τῶν ἐν τέλει ὄντων ὅ τι οὐκ ἐπέρχεται, &c. (So Bekker and Poppo rightly edited, instead of the common reading ὅτι.) Xenoph. Ephes. iv. 2, fin. ἐκέλευσε ἐπιμέλειαν ἔχειν πᾶσαν, ἕως, ἔφη, μάθωμεν ὅστις ὁ ἄνθρωπος ἐστιν, καὶ ὅ τι ὄντως αὐτοῦ μέλει θεοῖς. where ὅ τι was rightly emended instead of the common reading ὅτι. In such a case ὅ τι is for διότι. It is no wonder that the Scribes or Critics should have altered ὅ τι into τί, from ignorance of its meaning. The same has happened elsewhere. Thus in Lucian Contempl. § 18. πρὸς ἐμαυτὸν ἐννοῶ τί τὸ ἡδὺ αὐτοῖς παρὰ βίον. some MSS. have ὅτι; but the true reading, as Hemsterhus. saw, is ὅ τι, which, he observes, is often used for τι. Here the ο was absorbed by the ω preceding.

12. Ἠλίας μὲν — πάντα.] Here there is *not* any irony, (as some imagine,) but rather a Synchoresis. Render, "Elias is, indeed, first to come, and is to restore things to their former state."

— καὶ καθὼς γέγραπται, &c.] There are few passages which have more perplexed the Commentators than this. Various are the attempts which have been made to assign a satisfactory sense to the words of the common text καὶ πῶς. But all have failed; being more or less defective, either in sense or construction, or both. This being the case, the most eminent Commentators have been long agreed, that the passage is corrupt; and various modes of emendation have been proposed. Mere *conjectures* merit little attention. As to the *various readings of* MSS,. not one is deserv-

MT. LU.
17. 9. ἐξουδενωθῇ —· ἀλλὰ λέγω ὑμῖν, ὅτι καὶ Ἠλίας ἐλήλυθε, καὶ 13
12 ἐποίησαν αὐτῷ ὅσα ἠθέλησαν. [καθὼς γέγραπται ἐπ᾽ αὐτόν.]
37 Καὶ ἐλθὼν πρὸς τοὺς μαθητὰς, εἶδεν ὄχλον πολὺν περὶ αὐτοὺς, καὶ 14
Γραμματεῖς συζητοῦντας αὐτοῖς. Καὶ εὐθέως πᾶς ὁ ὄχλος ἰδὼν αὐτὸν 15
ἐξεθαμβήθη, καὶ προστρέχοντες ἠσπάζοντο αὐτόν. Καὶ ἐπηρώτησε τοὺς 16
14 38 Γραμματεῖς· Τί συζητεῖτε πρὸς αὐτούς; Καὶ ἀποκριθεὶς εἷς ἐκ τοῦ 17
ὄχλου εἶπε· Διδάσκαλε, ἤνεγκα τὸν υἱόν μου πρός σε, ἔχοντα πνεῦμα
15 39 ἄλαλον. Καὶ ὅπου ἂν αὐτὸν καταλάβῃ, ῥήσσει αὐτόν· καὶ ἀφρίζει, 18
16 40 καὶ τρίζει τοὺς ὀδόντας αὐτοῦ, καὶ ξηραίνεται. Καὶ εἶπον τοῖς μα-
17 41 θηταῖς σου, ἵνα αὐτὸ ἐκβάλωσι, καὶ οὐκ ἴσχυσαν. Ὁ δὲ ἀποκριθεὶς 19
[* αὐτοῖς] λέγει· Ὦ γενεὰ ἄπιστος! ἕως πότε πρὸς ὑμᾶς ἔσομαι;

ing of notice, except that for the vulg. *καὶ πῶς*, several ancient MSS., with the latter Syr. Version and Euthym. and Victor, read *καθώς*. But even this will not render much service. Some, therefore, (as Beza, Campb., and Bp. Marsh,) have resorted to the mild conjecture *καὶ καθώς*. The sense assigned by Bp. Marsh is, "And that, as it is written of the Son of man, he (John the Baptist) may suffer many things and be set at nought." But this is too mild a medicine to be effectual. Hence some recent Commentators, Grot., Schulz., and Fritz., have attempted to restore the corruption by stronger methods. And as it appears that in this passage (as in the parallel one of Matt. vii. 12 & 13.) the fate of John Baptist and of Christ are meant to be paralleled, so they conceive that the substance of the two verses have been, by some accident, transposed; and propose that the clause *καθὼς γέγραπται — ἐξουδενωθῇ* should be transposed, and placed after *ὅσα ἠθέλησαν*; the words *καθὼς γέγραπται ἐπ᾽ αὐτὸν* being cancelled, as a *double reading* of the former. Thus the passage will stand as follows: Ἠλίας μὲν ἐλθὼν πρῶτον ἀποκαθιστᾷ πάντα· ἀλλὰ λέγω ὑμῖν, ὅτι καὶ Ἠλίας ἐλήλυθε· καὶ ἐποίησαν αὐτῷ ὅσα ἠθέλησαν, καθὼς γέγραπται ἐπὶ τὸν Υἱὸν τοῦ ἀνθρώπου, ἵνα πολλὰ πάθῃ καὶ ἐξουδενωθῇ. This yields an excellent sense, and the transposition is countenanced by the parallel passage of Matt. xvii. 12 & 13. But as there is not the slightest authority for it, either in MSS. or Versions, it cannot be adopted in the text, nor ought it to be introduced into any Version. Indeed it may, after all, be unnecessary; for, adopting as I have ventured to do, the reading, *καὶ καθὼς*, &c., we may *supply* after *ἐξουδενωθῇ* the short corresponding clause (which is often, in such cases, left to be understood from the context) *οὕτω πάσχει*, "thus *he* (i. e. John Baptist) is to suffer." This is strongly confirmed by the *οὕτω καὶ* of Matthew. The words *καθὼς — αὐτὸν*, at the end of the verse, are merely a *διττογραφία* of the former, and therefore stand for nothing. Yet they strongly confirm the reading *καθὼς*, which is so indispensable to the emendation of the passage,) especially as they are found in every one of the MSS. The omission of *καὶ* before *καθ.* is very frequent in the MSS. of all writers. The Dative at *ἐποίησαν αὐτῷ* is a Dativus commodi, as in Isocr. Nic. 613. ἃ πάσχοντες ὑφ᾽ ἑτέρων ὀργίζεσθε τοῖς ἄλλοις μὴ ποιεῖτε. [*Comp.* Luke i. 17.]

15. *ἐξεθαμβήθη.*] The word implies a mixture of admiration, veneration, and awe.

17. *ἤνεγκα — πρός σε.*] The state of the case was, that the man had brought his son to Jesus to be healed by him. But our Lord not being immediately at hand, or the man not being willing to trouble Him, he presented his son to the *Apostles* for cure; since it was known that they had healed many such poor wretches.

— *ἔχοντα — ἄλαλον.*] Notwithstanding what some recent Commentators urge, who adopt Mede's hypothesis on the Demoniacs, this can only signify, as Fritz. acknowledges, "whose body was in the power of a dæmon who made him dumb." So in Luke xi. 14. a deaf dæmon (i. e. one who causes deafness) is mentioned. Here Wets. compares Plut. T. ii. p. 438. (speaking of the Pythian priestess) *ἀλάλου καὶ κακοῦ πνεύματος οὖσα πλήρης.*

18. *ὅπου — καταλάβῃ.*] Wets. and others render, "and wherever, or whenever, it may attack him;" for the verb *καταλαμβάνειν*, they say, is often used of the *attack* of any disorder, especially of *epilepsy*. But the context demands that we should take *καταλάβῃ* of the *dæmon;* and the sense is, "wherever, or whenever, it lights on him;" a signification often found in Thucyd.

— *ῥήσσει αὐτόν.*] Beza and others, with E. V., render it "tears him." But the true sense is that of the ancient Versions and Commentators, and most modern ones, "dashes him on the ground;" of which signification many examples from the Classical writers and the Sept. are adduced by the Commentators.

— *τρίζει τοὺς ὀδ. α.*] "grinds his teeth." So Theophyl. Sim. p. 91. C. *χαλεπαίνων καὶ τετριγὼς τοὺς ὀδόντας*. Aristoph. Ran. 926. *μὴ πρίε τοὺς ὀδόντας*. These and the other particulars in this verse and ver. 22, are, indeed, all symptoms of *epilepsy*. But if we even should suppose that the man *was* an epileptic; it would not follow that the disorder was not induced by demoniacal influence.

— *ξηραίνεται.*] Some antient and several modern Commentators explain, "faints away," "falls into a swoon." But however this may be a symptom of epilepsy, the word will not bear that sense, and can only mean "pines away." I agree with Fritz. that the word denotes, not so much what happens during the dæmon's attack, as it is a *general consequence* from thence. Thus Celsus says of epilepsy, "hominem *consumit!*"

19. *αὐτοῖς.*] For Vulg. *αὐτῷ* many MSS. and Versions have *αὐτοῖς*, which is edited by Griesb., Tittm., and Scholz rightly, as far as regards suitableness to the context. But as the MSS. in general fluctuate between *αὐτῷ* and *αὐτοῖς*, while some others have neither one nor the other,

MT. LU.

20 ἕως πότε ἀνέξομαι ὑμῶν; φέρετε αὐτὸν πρός με. Καὶ ἤνεγκαν αὐ- 17. 9.
τὸν πρὸς αὐτόν. καὶ ἰδὼν αὐτὸν, εὐθέως τὸ πνεῦμα ἐσπάραξεν αὐτόν· 42
21 καὶ πεσὼν ἐπὶ τῆς γῆς ἐκυλίετο ἀφρίζων. Καὶ ἐπηρώτησε τὸν πατέρα
αὐτοῦ· Πόσος χρόνος ἐστὶν, ὡς τοῦτο γέγονεν αὐτῷ; Ὁ δὲ εἶπε·
22 Παιδιόθεν. καὶ πολλάκις αὐτὸν καὶ εἰς τὸ πῦρ ἔβαλε καὶ εἰς ὕδατα,
ἵνα ἀπολέσῃ αὐτόν. ἀλλ', εἴ τι δύνασαι, βοήθησον ἡμῖν σπλαγχνισθεὶς
23 ἐφ' ἡμᾶς. Ὁ δὲ Ἰησοῦς εἶπεν αὐτῷ τό· εἰ δύνασαι πιστεῦσαι—·
24 πάντα δυνατὰ τῷ πιστεύοντι. Καὶ εὐθέως κράξας ὁ πατὴρ τοῦ παιδίου, μετὰ δακρύων ἔλεγε· Πιστεύω, κύριε· βοήθει μου τῇ ἀπιστίᾳ!

I cannot help suspecting that *both* are from the margin.

20. ἰδὼν αὐτὸν—ἐσπάραξεν.] Most Commentators take ἰδὼν for ἰδόντα. But that is a false view of the construction, which Fritz. rightly regards as an *anacoluthon*. The Evangelist meant to say καὶ ἰδὼν (ὁ παῖς) αὐτὸν, εὐθέως ὑπὸ τοῦ πνεύματος ἐσπαράσσετο, but then changed the construction; of which see another example in Acts xx. 3. Wets. and Vater take ἰδὼν as a Nominative absolute, supplying αὐτός.

21. ὡς] for ἐξ οὗ, or ἀφ' οὗ, ("since the time) when."

—παιδιόθεν.] This form, and the kindred, but more elegant one παιδόθεν, are of later Grecism. The earlier purer writers employed ἐκ παιδὸς, or ἐκ παιδίου.

22. τὸ πῦρ.] The Article (absent from Vulg.) is found in many ancient MSS., and is adopted by Matth., Griesb., Fritz., and Scholz, and confirmed by Matt. xvii. 15. John xv. 6. Acts xxviii. 5, and other passages. Propriety, indeed, would seem to require this, since it falls under that canon of Middlet. by which all those utensils or substances in a house, of which there is ordinarily but *one*, take the Article. Thus when πῦρ signifies the fire in any house, it requires the Article; when it signifies any other, or fire in general, it rejects it. But whether, even in the former case, the Article was not occasionally, in the common dialect, omitted in phrases of frequent occurrence, is more than I would venture to affirm. Besides, the word may here be taken in a general sense; and if so, it *needs* no Article. Fritz. inserts the Article even before ὕδατα; but purely from conjecture; and very wrongly: for the word is used in a generic sense. So we speak of accidents "by fire and flood."

—ἀλλ', εἴ τι δύνασαι.] This use of ἀλλ' is said to be *supplicatory*; but it is rather hortatory; and the idiom results, as Fritz. observes, from the *Imperative*, with which the particle is, in such a case, united. As to the εἴ τι δύνασαι, some Commentators there recognise a doubt; while others deny that there is any; neither of which views seems well founded. Fritz. rightly regards it as a *formula obtestationis*, entreating help. He cites Soph. Aj. 326. More apposite, however, is the passage Dio Chrysost. p. 81, adduced by me in Recens. Synop.: ἐκείνης δεομένης τοῦ πατρὸς, εἴ τι δύναιτο, βοηθεῖν. See also Thucyd. vi. 25. and Herodot. viii. 57. Of course, the very nature of this formula implies *some* doubt of the power of the person whose help is implored.

23. εἰ δύνασαι—πιστεύοντι.] With this sentence Commentators have been somewhat perplexed; partly from the brevity and indefiniteness of the phraseology, and partly from the peculiar use of the τό. The *conjectures* that have been hazarded are very inefficient, and indeed unnecessary. Some would remove the difficulty as regards the τὸ by taking it for τοῦτο. But that is a long exploded principle; and to supply κατὰ, as they do, is absurd. The best recent Commentators are, with reason, agreed that the τὸ is here meant to be applied to the sentence following, by a use common in the Classical writers: where it is often applied to a *whole sentence*. See Winer's Gr. Gr. p. 54. Krebs, Rosemn., and Kuin. would extend the force of the τὸ to πιστεύοντι. But to produce the sense which they extract, they are obliged to insert an εἶναι after πάντα, and supply at the end of the sentence βοηθήσω σοι, or εὖ ἔχει. But *thus* εἶναι could *not but* have been expressed; and the other ellipsis is harsh. The only satisfactory solution of the difficulty is that propounded in Recens. Synop. (and which has been since adopted by Fritz.) namely, to suppose that after πιστεῦσαι is to be supplied (what our Lord, from modesty, *suppressed*) βοηθήσω σοι, or εὖ ἔχει. From the same feeling, ἐμοὶ is omitted after δύνασαι. The δύνασαι, at which so many Critics stumble, is used with reference to the δύνασαι of the *question*, to which this is an answer. And the best way of accounting for the use of the τὸ is, to suppose, either that this mode of speaking was not unusal to our Lord, in cases where his help was entreated with any sort of doubt; or that the answer returned was well known. Thus the sense will be, "*the* (well known answer.") All the best Commentators are agreed that τῷ πιστεύοντι is a Dativus commodi. Render, "All things are possible [to be done] for him who believeth." [*Comp.* Luke xvii. 6.]

24. πιστεύω, κύριε.] Κύριε is not found in about seven MSS. and some Versions, and is cancelled by Griesb., Vater, and Scholz; but with singular rashness. For, as Fritz. observes, "*Nihil* hâc voce, in humili et supplici patris observatione, fingi potest aptius.

But how came it, some may ask, that a word so proper and suitable should have been omitted? I answer, it may, as the MSS. are so few, have been omitted inadvertently by those scribes who did not see its force; yet not, as Fritz. supposes, "ob ἔλεγε quod præcedit." I rather suspect it to have been omitted from *design*. The Alexandrian critic who first struck it out, no doubt thought there was more *gravity* in making the clause terminate with the most important word; which itself conveyed the answer. So thought our English Translators, who render, "*Lord, I believe*." And the Greek critic would probably have emended κύριε, π., had it not been forbidden by the *linguæ proprietas* to commence an ad-

MT. LU.

17. 9. Ἰδὼν δὲ ὁ Ἰησοῦς ὅτι ἐπισυντρέχει ὄχλος, ἐπετίμησε τῷ πνεύματι τῷ 25
ἀκαθάρτῳ, λέγων αὐτῷ· Τὸ πνεῦμα τὸ ἄλαλον καὶ κωφὸν, ἐγώ σοι
18 42 ἐπιτάσσω· ἔξελθε ἐξ αὐτοῦ, καὶ μηκέτι εἰσέλθῃς εἰς αὐτόν. Καὶ 26
κράξαν καὶ πολλὰ σπαράξαν αὐτὸν, ἐξῆλθε. καὶ ἐγένετο ὡσεὶ νεκρός·
ὥστε πολλοὺς λέγειν ὅτι ἀπέθανεν. Ὁ δὲ Ἰησοῦς κρατήσας αὐτὸν τῆς 27
χειρὸς, ἤγειρεν αὐτόν· καὶ ἀνέστη.
19 Καὶ εἰσελθόντα αὐτὸν εἰς οἶκον οἱ μαθηταὶ αὐτοῦ ἐπηρώτων αὐτὸν 28
21 κατ᾿ ἰδίαν, † Ὅ τι ἡμεῖς οὐκ ἠδυνήθημεν ἐκβαλεῖν αὐτό; Καὶ εἶπεν 29
αὐτοῖς· Τοῦτο τὸ γένος ἐν οὐδενὶ δύναται ἐξελθεῖν, εἰ μὴ ἐν προσευχῇ
καὶ νηστείᾳ.
22 ΚΑΙ ἐκεῖθεν ἐξελθόντες παρεπορεύοντο διὰ τῆς Γαλιλαίας· καὶ οὐκ 30
ἤθελεν ἵνα τὶς γνῷ. Ἐδίδασκε γὰρ τοὺς μαθητὰς αὐτοῦ, καὶ ἔλεγεν 31
23 44 αὐτοῖς· Ὅτι ὁ Υἱὸς τοῦ ἀνθρώπου παραδίδοται εἰς χεῖρας ἀνθρώπων,
καὶ ἀποκτενοῦσιν αὐτόν· καὶ ἀποκτανθεὶς, τῇ τρίτῃ ἡμέρᾳ ἀνα-
45 στήσεται. Οἱ δὲ ἠγνόουν τὸ ῥῆμα, καὶ ἐφοβοῦντο αὐτὸν ἐπερωτῆσαι. 32
18. Καὶ ἦλθεν εἰς Καπερναούμ· καὶ ἐν τῇ οἰκίᾳ γενόμενος, ἐπηρώτα 33
46 αὐτούς· Τί ἐν τῇ ὁδῷ πρὸς ἑαυτοὺς διελογίζεσθε; Οἱ δὲ ἐσιώπων· 34
1 πρὸς ἀλλήλους γὰρ διελέχθησαν ἐν τῇ ὁδῷ, τίς μείζων. Καὶ καθίσας 35
ἐφώνησε τοὺς δώδεκα, καὶ λέγει αὐτοῖς· Εἴ τις θέλει πρῶτος εἶναι,
2 47 ἔσται πάντων ἔσχατος καὶ πάντων διάκονος. Καὶ λαβὼν παιδίον, 36
ἔστησεν αὐτὸ ἐν μέσῳ αὐτῶν· καὶ ἐναγκαλισάμενος αὐτὸ, εἶπεν αὐτοῖς·
4 48 Ὃς ἐὰν ἓν τῶν τοιούτων παιδίων δέξηται ἐπὶ τῷ ὀνόματί μου, ἐμὲ 37
δέχεται· καὶ ὃς ἐὰν ἐμὲ δέξηται, οὐκ ἐμὲ δέχεται, ἀλλὰ τὸν ἀποστείλαντά με.
49 Ἀπεκρίθη δὲ αὐτῷ [ὁ] Ἰωάννης λέγων· Διδάσκαλε, εἴδομέν τινα 38
[ἐν] τῷ ὀνόματί σου ἐκβάλλοντα δαιμόνια, ὃς οὐκ ἀκολουθεῖ ἡμῖν·
50 καὶ ἐκωλύσαμεν αὐτὸν, ὅτι οὐκ ἀκολουθεῖ ἡμῖν. Ὁ δὲ Ἰησοῦς εἶπε· 39
Μὴ κωλύετε αὐτόν. οὐδεὶς γάρ ἐστιν ὃς ποιήσει δύναμιν ἐπὶ τῷ ὀνόματί μου, καὶ δυνήσεται ταχὺ κακολογῆσαί με. Ὃς γαρ οὐκ ἔστι καθ᾿ 40

dress with a vocative case. And it seems they had not the good taste to feel the propriety of making the profession of faith be accompanied by an address so adapted to entreaty.

— βοήθει μου τῇ ἀπιστίᾳ.] By ἀπιστίᾳ, as Grot. rightly observes, is here meant, not a total want of faith, but a deficient or wavering faith. The sense is, "I have a faith, but it is infirm; supply its deficiency, regard it as complete, and heal my son accordingly."

25. ἐπισυντρέχει.] "were running together towards him." The τὸ at τὸ πνεῦμα, &c. is authoritatively emphatical.

28. ὅ τι] I have, at the Note supra, v. 14, sufficiently justified this deviation from all the editors, instead of the vulg. ὅτι. The various readings of the MSS., namely, διὰ τί, or τί ὅτι, are manifestly *glosses*.

30. παρεπορεύοντο] "passed along;" namely, the Lake and the Jordan. See Note on Mark ii. 23. Οὐκ ἤθελεν — γνῷ. A *popular* mode of speaking, like that at vii. 23. οὐδένα ἤθελε γνῶναι, signifying like that he wished to travel in a private character.

31. παραδίδοται] "is being delivered; i. e. is shortly to be delivered."

36. ἐναγκαλισάμενος.] Kypke, Elsn., and Wets. observe, that as the child was of somewhat advanced years, the signification here is not strictly "*to take up into the arms*," but to *embrace*.

37. [*Comp.* John xiii. 20.]

38. ἐν τῷ ὀν.] The ἐν of the text. recept. is absent from several MSS., and is cancelled by Mill, Wets., Matth., Griesb., Vater, and Scholz. But I think, wrongly. It is defended by xi. 9. x. 16.; and 7. Jam. v. 10. The early Critics, it seems, stumbled at the Hebraistic idiom; and hence either cancelled the ἐν, or changed it into ἐπὶ, which last reading (slenderly supported by MS. authority) ought not to have been edited by Fritz.

39. οὐδεὶς γάρ ἐστιν, &c.] The sense is, "nemo enim meâ auctoritate miraculum edet, et poterit illico mihi conviciari." This construction (similar to that at 1 Cor. vi. 5.) is quite agreeable to *Classical* usage. So Plato Menex. p. 71. A. οὐδεὶς ὅστις οὐ γελάσεται καὶ ἐρεῖ. Thucyd. ii. 51.

MT.
41 ‡ ἡμῶν, ὑπὲρ ‡ ἡμῶν ἐστιν. Ὃς γὰρ ἂν ποτίσῃ ὑμᾶς ποτήριον ὕδα- 18.
τος ἐν [τῷ] ὀνόματί [μου,] ὅτι Χριστοῦ ἐστὲ, ἀμὴν λέγω ὑμῖν, οὐ μὴ
42 ἀπολέσῃ τὸν μισθὸν αὐτοῦ. Καὶ ὃς ἂν σκανδαλίσῃ ἕνα τῶν μικρῶν 6
τῶν πιστευόντων εἰς ἐμὲ, καλόν ἐστιν αὐτῷ μᾶλλον, εἰ περίκειται λίθος
μυλικὸς περὶ τὸν τράχηλον αὐτοῦ, καὶ βέβληται εἰς τὴν θάλασσαν.
43 Καὶ ἐὰν σκανδαλίζῃ σε ἡ χείρ σου, ἀπόκοψον αὐτήν· καλόν σοι ἐστὶ 8
κυλλὸν εἰς τὴν ζωὴν εἰσελθεῖν, ἢ τὰς δύο χεῖρας ἔχοντα ἀπελθεῖν εἰς
44 τὴν γέενναν, εἰς τὸ πῦρ τὸ ἄσβεστον· ὅπου ὁ σκώληξ αὐτῶν
45 οὐ τελευτᾷ, καὶ τὸ πῦρ οὐ σβέννυται. Καὶ ἐὰν ὁ πούς

ἀπορίᾳ τοῦ θεραπεύσαντος. Δυνήσεται ταχὺ signifies, "will readily bring himself to," &c. (Fritz.)

40. Instead of the text. recept. ἡμῶν—ἡμῶν, many MSS. and Versions have ὑμῶν—ὑμῶν, which is found in most of the early editions; and edited by Mill, Matth., Griesb., Vater, and Scholz. But, I think, without reason: for in external evidence the reading is not superior to the received one, (and if it were, *Manuscript* authority is of little weight in respect to words perpetually confounded in the MSS.) and in *internal*, greatly inferior; for, as Fritz. truly remarks, both here and at Luke ix. 50. "de Jesu agitur, non de Apostolis. Et potuit Jesus includere simul discipulos, se excludere non potuit." He also observes that this verse contains a *fresh* reason why no molestation should be given to the person in question. [*Comp.* also Matt. xii. 30.]

41. ἐν [τῷ] ὀν.—ἐστέ.] The words in brackets are not found in very many MSS. Versions and Early editions, and were thrown out of the text by Griesb., Vater, Fritz., and Scholz, rightly, I think; for we may more easily account for the *insertion* than the *omission* of the words: especially as the force of the somewhat rare phrase ἐν ὀνόματι ὅτι hoc nomine vel titulo, "on account of," was likely to be unknown to the scribes. See Thucyd. iv. 60. 1. At the same time, it is not impossible, that the common reading may be the true one. At least the reasons alleged *against* it by Fritz. (that it is pleonastic; that the epexegesis in ὅτι τοῦ Χρ. ἐ. is languid; and that for ἐν τῷ ὀν. ought to have been written ἐπὶ for consistency's sake. *Comp.* v. 38.) are not of any great weight; they might rather lead us to suspect *alterations*, to get rid of what was offensive,—did we not remember that the Critics in question were not persons likely to have devised so neat an emendation.

—ὅτι Χριστοῦ ἐστέ.] It has been debated whether Χριστὸς in the N. T. be a *proper name*, or an *appellative*. That it was originally an appellative descriptive of office and dignity (like ὁ Βαπτιστὴς, seems certain; and so frequent is this use in the N. T., that some contend that it is never employed otherwise. But in Rom. v. 6. 1 Cor. i. 12. and 23. 2 Cor. iii. 3. Col. iii. 24. 1 Pet. i. 11. to render "the anointed," or even "the Messiah," would be harsh. Hence Middlet. maintains that in all those passages Χριστὸς is merely a proper name; and he contends that even during our Saviour's life, it had become such. Compare Matt. xxvii. 17. and 20. with Matt. x. 2. Campb., however, is of opinion that this use of the word was not introduced until after the resurrection. With the present passage Middlet. aptly compares a kindred one at 1 Cor. iii. 23. ὑμεῖς δὲ Χριστοῦ, Χριστὸς δὲ Θεοῦ. The same phrase εἶναί τινος, to be devoted to any one, occurs elsewhere in the N. T., and sometimes in the Classical writers.

43. τὰς δύο χεῖρας] "both of your hands." The article has here the force of the possessive pronoun.

44. ὅπου—σβέννυται.] The words are derived from Is. lxvi. 24., where the punishment to be inflicted, in this life, on those who are rebellious towards God, are vividly depicted, by the representation of their carcasses being subject to the continual gnawing of worms, and the devouring of an unextinguishable fire, so as to be objects of detestation to all future generations. The words are here applied to represent the *eternal misery* of another world, by images derived from Γέεννα in this world; on which, as a frequent emblem of torment, see Note at Matt. v. 22. The true rendering seems to be, "where the worm is never to die, nor the fire to be quenched." So the Sept. well renders, ὁ γὰρ σκώληξ αὐτῶν οὐ τελευτήσει, καὶ τὸ πῦρ αὐτῶν οὐ σβεσθήσεται. Similar figures are found in Ecclus. vii. 17. ἐκδίκησις ἀσεβοῦς πῦρ καὶ σκώληξ. and Judith xvi. 17. Κύριος παντοκράτωρ ἐκδικήσει αὐτοὺς ἐν ἡμέρᾳ κρίσεως, δοῦναι πῦρ καὶ σκώληκας εἰς σάρκας αὐτῶν, καὶ κλαύσονται ἐν αἰσθήσει ἕως αἰῶνος. Some difference of opinion, however, exists as to the *nature* of the punishments here designated by ὁ σκώληξ αὐτῶν καὶ τὸ πῦρ (scil. αὐτῶν, i. e. of the wicked) namely, whether they are to be regarded as *actual* and *positive* inflictions, or as *figuratively representing* the gnawing of remorse and self-condemnation, and the torture of unavailing reproach, for having brought on themselves their own destruction. *Many* have been inclined to think that, though the *fire* be taken in a physical sense, the *worm* is *figurative*. On which interpretation it is truly observed by Fritz. that "what holds good of one clause of the sentence, must of the other; for a confusion of the physical with the metaphorical in the same sentence is not to be tolerated." And he would have *both* taken in the literal sense. But there seems no reason why both terms should not be regarded as *figurative*, yet designating, under these figures, *real inflictions* as dreadful to the then frame, as the gnawing of worms, or the burning of fire, to our present. See a recent Tract by the learned and excellent Professor Stuart, entitled "Exegetical Essays," on some words of Scripture relative to future punishment, namely, αἰὼν, and αἰώνιος, שְׁאוֹל, ᾅδης and γέεννα, and especially Sect. 3., which treats on the nature and manner of using figurative language in respect to the objects of a future world. The able writer there shows how it happens (namely, by the weakness of our nature, and the poverty and inadequateness of human language) that we are compelled, in speaking of the Deity, or of the things of *another* world,

MT.
18. σου σκανδαλίζῃ σε, ἀπόκοψον αὐτόν· καλόν ἐστί σοι εἰσελθεῖν εἰς
τὴν ζωὴν χωλὸν, ἢ τοὺς δύο πόδας ἔχοντα βληθῆναι εἰς τὴν γέενναν,
εἰς τὸ πῦρ τὸ ἄσβεστον, ὅπου ὁ σκώληξ αὐτῶν οὐ τελευτᾷ, καὶ τὸ πῦρ 46
9 οὐ σβέννυται. Καὶ ἐὰν ὁ ὀφθαλμός σου σκανδαλίζῃ σε, ἔκβαλε αὐτόν· 47
καλόν σοι ἐστὶ μονόφθαλμον εἰσελθεῖν εἰς τὴν βασιλείαν τοῦ Θεοῦ, ἢ
δύο ὀφθαλμοὺς ἔχοντα βληθῆναι εἰς τὴν γέενναν τοῦ πυρὸς, ὅπου ὁ 48
σκώληξ αὐτῶν οὐ τελευτᾷ, καὶ τὸ πῦρ οὐ σβέννυται. Πᾶς γὰρ πυρὶ 49
ἁλισθήσεται, καὶ πᾶσα θυσία ἁλὶ ἁλισθήσεται. Καλὸν τὸ ἅλας· ἐὰν 50
δὲ τὸ ἅλας ἄναλον γένηται, ἐν τίνι αὐτὸ ἀρτύσετε; Ἔχετε ἐν ἑαυτοῖς
ἅλας, καὶ εἰρηνεύετε ἐν ἀλλήλοις.

to make use of terms which have a reference to *this* world. "Thus," continues he, "Heaven is represented as a *paradise*, i. e. a *pleasure garden*; as a city with magnificent walls and structures; as a place of perpetual feasting and delight; as a land of rest and overflowing plenty; as a magnificent palace, in which the guests appear adorned with princely robes and splendid crowns, and are admitted to the immediate presence of the great King of kings. *Hell* is represented as an *abyss*; a *bottomless pit*; a *lake* that burneth with fire and brimstone, the smoke of which ascendeth up for ever and ever; a *Gehenna*, where the worm dieth not, and the fire is not quenched; as a place of outer darkness; as a loathsome dungeon; as a place of torture and anguish unspeakable: a place of banishment from God, on which all the vials of his wrath are poured out; and by other such tremendous images all drawn from natural objects of terror and distress. That none of these descriptions are to be *literally understood*, seems to be exceedingly obvious; for if any one is to be *literally* understood, *which* is the one? Who will determine this question? If then, there are no particular grounds for making any such determination, we must either construe all of them *figuratively*, or all of them *literally*. Not the latter, because then the Bible must be made to contradict itself, beyond all possibility of reconciliation. It must also be made to contradict the nature of the *spiritual* and invisible world. The former, therefore is the only principle which can be admitted.

Not only does the language under our consideration express torment, the acutest in kind, but *eternal in duration*. So in the parallel passage of Matthew, are the expressions *εἰς γέενναν τοῦ πυρὸς* and *εἰς πῦρ τὸ αἰώνιον*, the latter qualifying and completing the idea in the former. And therefore the notions of those who from the time of Origen have dared to *limit* this duration, are both groundless and presumptuous. So Prof. Stuart, at § 17. of the before-mentioned work, after considering at large the bearing which the use of the terms *αἰὼν* and *αἰώνιος* in Scripture, have on the subject of future punishment, comes to this conclusion (awful, indeed, but not to be suppressed) that it does most plainly and indubitably follow, that *if the Scriptures have not asserted the* ENDLESS punishment of the wicked, neither have they asserted the ENDLESS *happiness of the righteous, nor the* ENDLESS *glory and existence of the Godhead*. The one is equally certain with the other. Both are laid in the same balance. They must be tried by the same tests. And if we give up the one, we must, in order to be consistent, give up the other also." When it can be shown, that there is *deliverance* from "the lake of fire," which is "*the second death*," then something will be done to affect the question under consideration. Until then, I see not how we can avoid the conclusion, that the smoke of future torment will ascend up *for ever and ever!* So Bp. Jer. Taylor, in his matchless Discourse, entitled "The Foolish Exchange," after showing the distinction to be made between the language of the Prophet, which represents the utter and everlasting destruction of the Jewish nation, and observing that the worm stuck close to the Jewish nation, and the fire of God's wrath flamed out till it produced its perdition; adds, that this, being transferred to signify the state of accursed souls, whose dying is a continual perishing, who cannot cease to be, must mean an eternity of duration, in a proper and natural signification. So that as the worm, when it signifies a temporal infliction, means a worm that never ceases giving torment till the body is consumed; so when it is transferred to an immortal state, it must signify as much in that proportion. That "eternal," that "everlasting," hath no end at all; because the soul cannot be killed in the natural sense, but is made miserable and perishing for ever; that is, "the worm shall not die" so long as the soul shall be unconsumed, or "the fire shall not be quenched" till the period of an immortal nature comes. And that this shall be absolutely for ever, without any restriction, appears unanswerable in this, because the same "for ever" that is for the blessed souls, the same "for ever" is for the accursed souls. So that this undying worm, this unquenchable fire of Hell have no period at all; but shall last as long as God lasts, or the measure of a proper eternity." That this was the universal sentiment of the Fathers (with the exception of Origen), is shown by Whitby, on Heb. vi. 2. That the doctrine is consonant to *reason*, as well as Scripture, appears from its having been held by Greeks, Romans, and Jews, and indeed the ancients universally.

49. *πᾶς γὰρ — ἁλισθήσεται.*] There is perhaps no passage in the N. T. which has so perplexed the Commentators, or so defied all efforts to assign to it any certain interpretation, as this. It is impossible here to *detail*, much less *review*, even a *tenth* of the interpretations which have been proposed. It must suffice (omitting all mere conjectures, or interpretations proceeding on a strained sense of the words) to notice those expositions only which have any semblance of truth. It is a material previous question, whether the words are to be considered with reference to what *went before*, or taken as a *separate dictum*. The latter is the view taken by some, especially Kuin.; who maintains, that this and the next verse are out of place, and belong to some other

MT.
1 X. *ΚΑΚΕΙΘΕΝ* ἀναστὰς ἔρχεται εἰς τὰ ὅρια τῆς Ἰουδαίας, διὰ 19.
τοῦ πέραν τοῦ Ἰορδάνου· καὶ συμπορεύονται πάλιν ὄχλοι πρὸς αὐτὸν, 1
2 καὶ, ὡς εἰώθει, πάλιν ἐδίδασκεν αὐτούς. Καὶ προσελθόντες οἱ Φα- 3
ρισαῖοι ἐπηρώτησαν αὐτὸν, εἰ ἔξεστιν ἀνδρὶ γυναῖκα ἀπολῦσαι· πειρά-
3 ζοντες αὐτόν. Ὁ δὲ ἀποκριθεὶς εἶπεν αὐτοῖς· Τί ὑμῖν ἐνετείλατο
4 Μωϋσῆς; οἱ δὲ εἶπον, Μωϋσῆς ἐπέτρεψε βιβλίον ἀποστασίου γράψαι, 7
5 καὶ ἀπολῦσαι. Καὶ ἀποκριθεὶς ὁ Ἰησοῦς εἶπεν αὐτοῖς· Πρὸς τὴν 8
6 σκληροκαρδίαν ὑμῶν ἔγραψεν ὑμῖν τὴν ἐντολὴν ταύτην· ἀπὸ δὲ ἀρχῆς
7 κτίσεως ἄρσεν καὶ θῆλυ ἐποίησεν αὐτοὺς ὁ Θεός. Ἕνεκεν τούτου 4

part of the Gospel. This, however, is a gratuitous supposition; which has, moreover, the disadvantage of depriving us of all *benefit of a context*, to shed some glimmer of light on this deep obscurity. Yet those who admit that the passage has a connexion with and reference to what precedes, are not agreed as to the precise nature of that connexion. Many refer it to the words immediately preceding; so that either a *reason* may be supposed given *why* the wicked in Hell will be tormented unto eternal life, or that ver. 49. may be considered as a further explication, or illustration, of what was said in ver. 48.; for γάρ has often the sense of *nempe*. But the great objection to this mode of interpretation is, that it compels them to assign such a sense to πᾶς as cannot be justified on any principle of correct exegesis, namely, "every *wicked man*," or, "every one *(of those condemned to Hell)*." Quite as objectionable is the sense of πᾶσα θυσία, assigned by some of these Commentators, "every one consecrated to God;" by which the *salt* is taken to mean the salt of *grace*. Many other interpretations are grounded upon this hypothesis, that the words have reference to those which immediately *precede;* every one of which, however, (as Fritz. has proved) is liable to very strong objections.

Let us now examine the *other* class of interpretations, namely, those which proceed on the principle, that the words have reference to ver. 47. Thus πᾶς will denote "every one of you," "every Christian." But what is the meaning of πυρὶ ἁλισθήσεται? Here, as in the former class, we have a multitude of precarious and even absurd interpretations. Indeed, only two can be adduced, which deserve any attention. 1. That of those who take πυρὶ ἁλισθ. to mean "shall be purified by the *Holy Ghost*." See Matt. iii. 11. Acts iii. 3. They render: "For every Christian will be seasoned with the fire [of the Holy Ghost]," as (in the old Law) the precept was, every sacrifice shall be seasoned with salt; q. d. "As (καὶ for ὡς, as often) every sacrifice, under the Old Law, was to be seasoned with *salt*, so in the New, every Christian shall have a portion of the Holy Spirit." But to assign such a sense to πυρὶ is harsh, and we can scarcely suppose the Evangelist would word the sentence so enigmatically. In fact, the difficulty is chiefly centred in the interpretation of πυρί; which is best taken by the ancients generally, and some moderns (as Beza, Rosenm., Kuin., and Fritz.), to mean "the fiery trials of life." They are not, however, agreed on the sense of ἁλισθήσεται. Beza and others take the meaning to be, "Every Christian is purified by the fiery trials of life, *as* every sacrifice is salted with salt." But as ἁλισθ. will not admit of such a sense, I prefer the interpretation of ἁλ. proposed by Bos, Muzel, and Fritz.; especially as it is confirmed by the ancient *gloss* δοκιμασθήσεται, namely, "shall be put to the proof." They well remark, that the reference of this verse is not to ver. 47 only, but likewise to ver. 43—7. For, as Fritz. truly observes, "since Jesus has there thrice expressed the sentiment, that a loss even of the members of the body, nay, of those most useful, is to be encountered, rather than to yield to the seductions of vice; that so being tried and approved, we may attain the prize of our high calling;" nothing can be expected but that we should show that such sort of trials (like those of athletes) are either very useful, or absolutely necessary." By πᾶς must be understood *all persons*, all *Christians*, since to them ver. 43—48. belong. Πῦρ designates those fiery trials, in encountering which the self-denial and fortitude is compared to that of suffering the loss of a limb. Πυρὶ ἁλ. may be interpreted, "will be tried and prepared by such fiery trials [for the enjoyment of eternal felicity]." There is here a metaphor taken from victims, which were prepared for sacrifice by the imposition of the *mola salsa*. The words of the next clause καὶ πᾶσα θυσία ἁλὶ ἁλισθήσεται are founded on Levit. ii. 13. καὶ πᾶν δῶρον θυσίας (i. e. every sacrifice) ὑμῶν ἁλὶ ἁλισθήσεται. And the καὶ is to be rendered *sicuti*, *as*, like the Heb. ו.

Here is a paronomasia on the double sense of salt; for the word is first used, at ver. 49, in its *proper* sense; then, at ver. 50, in its *figurative* one; where it denotes, as some say, the salt of *friendship;* but rather, we may suppose, with others, the salt of *wisdom*. See Coloss. iv. 6. *Comp.* Matt. v. 13. Luke xiv. 84. Rom. xii. 18. Heb. xii. 14. After recommending the study of *wisdom*, our Lord enjoins the cultivation of *peace* one with another.

X. 2. οἱ Φαρ.] There are many MSS. here that have not the Article; which is cancelled by Griesb., Vater, and Scholz. But, I apprehend, without any good reason. The Article (found in the parallel passage) can scarcely be dispensed with; and the sense is, "the persons who were of *the* sect of the Pharisees in the surrounding country." It will, perhaps, be said, that the sense is, "some Pharisees," &c. But that would require Φαρ. τινες. Besides, it is easier to account for the *omission* than for the *addition* of the οἱ, which Fritz., with more than his usual discretion, retains and defends. It is true, that some MSS. are without the οἱ in the parallel passage. But they are very few in number, and *almost all of them such as omit it here.*

6. ἀπὸ δὲ ἀρχῆς κτίσεως.] In this rare phrase κτίσις signifies "the things created," the world or

MT. LU.
19. 18. καταλείψει ἄνθρωπος τὸν πατέρα αὐτοῦ καὶ τὴν μη-
5 τέρα· καὶ προσκολληθήσεται πρὸς τὴν γυναῖκα αὐτοῦ, καὶ ἔσονται οἱ δύο εἰς σάρκα μίαν. Ὥστε οὐκέτι 8
6 εἰσὶ δύο, ἀλλὰ μία σάρξ. Ὃ οὖν ὁ Θεὸς συνέζευξεν ἄνθρωπος μὴ 9
χωριζέτω. Καὶ ἐν τῇ οἰκίᾳ πάλιν οἱ μαθηταὶ αὐτοῦ περὶ τοῦ αὐτοῦ 10
9 ἐπηρώτησαν αὐτόν. Καὶ λέγει αὐτοῖς· Ὃς ἐὰν ἀπολύσῃ τὴν γυναῖκα 11
αὐτοῦ καὶ γαμήσῃ ἄλλην, μοιχᾶται ἐπ' αὐτήν· καὶ ἐὰν γυνὴ ἀπολύσῃ 12
τὸν ἄνδρα αὐτῆς καὶ γαμηθῇ ἄλλῳ, μοιχᾶται.

13 15 Καὶ προσέφερον αὐτῷ παιδία, ἵνα ἅψηται αὐτῶν· οἱ δὲ μαθηταὶ 13
ἐπετίμων τοῖς προσφέρουσιν. Ἰδὼν δὲ ὁ Ἰησοῦς ἠγανάκτησε, καὶ εἶπεν 14
14 16 αὐτοῖς. Ἄφετε τὰ παιδία ἔρχεσθαι πρός με, [καὶ] μὴ κωλύετε αὐτά·
17 τῶν γὰρ τοιούτων ἐστὶν ἡ βασιλεία τοῦ Θεοῦ. Ἀμὴν λέγω ὑμῖν· ὃς 15
ἐὰν μὴ δέξηται τὴν βασιλείαν τοῦ Θεοῦ ὡς παιδίον, οὐ μὴ εἰσέλθῃ
15 εἰς αὐτήν. Καὶ ἐναγκαλισάμενος αὐτά, τιθεὶς τὰς χεῖρας ἐπ' αὐτά, 16
ηὐλόγει αὐτά.

16 Καὶ ἐκπορευομένου αὐτοῦ εἰς ὁδὸν, προσδραμὼν εἷς καὶ γονυπετήσας 17
18 αὐτὸν, ἐπηρώτα αὐτόν· Διδάσκαλε ἀγαθὲ, τί ποιήσω, ἵνα ζωὴν αἰώνιον
17 19 κληρονομήσω; Ὁ δὲ Ἰησοῦς εἶπεν αὐτῷ· Τί με λέγεις ἀγαθόν; οὐ- 18
18 20 δεὶς ἀγαθὸς, εἰ μὴ εἷς ὁ Θεός. Τὰς ἐντολὰς οἶδας· Μὴ μοιχεύ- 19
σῃς· μὴ φονεύσῃς· μὴ κλέψῃς· μὴ ψευδομαρτυρήσῃς·
μὴ ἀποστερήσῃς· τίμα τὸν πατέρα σου καὶ τὴν μητέ-

universe, as xiii. 19. 2 Pet. iii. 4. Sap. v. 18, & xvi. 24. The argument meant to be urged in this and the verse following is, that God at the beginning of the world created man and woman that they should live together in the greatest union; and that hence married persons are to be regarded not as two, but one, and therefore, by the Divine law, no divorce can be permitted.

10. *ἐν τῇ οἰκίᾳ.*] This seems to designate some private lodging, which they occupied on the road; and the expression is here used in contradistinction to the *public place* where our Lord had been arguing with the Pharisees.

11, 12. In these two vv. there is a marvellous diversity of readings, none of which, however, authorise any change in the text. There may be some want of neatness in the phraseology, nay, of precision in the use of one of the terms employed — namely, ἀπολύσῃ in ver. 12. But if the whole be taken as expressed *populariter*, there will be nothing to stumble at. It is true that, strictly speaking, a Jewish wife could not divorce her husband; for as to the examples of Salome and others, *their* actions were done in defiance of all law, and in imitation of Roman licentiousness. Ἀπολύσῃ, therefore, at ver. 12, may, with many of the best Commentators, be considered as used with some license, on account of the antithesis, for ἐξέλθῃ ἀπὸ τοῦ ἀνδρός; which, indeed, is found in some MSS. and Versions, and is *edited* by Fritz.; but is plainly a gloss. There is the same catachresis at 1 Cor. vii. 12 & 13, (where the Apostle may be supposed to have had this passage in mind) in the use of μὴ ἀφιέτω αὐτήν, and μὴ ἀφιέτω αὐτόν. Perhaps, too, this term is used with reference to the customs of the *Gentiles* rather than the Jews, and seems to be meant to give a rule to the Apostles for *general* application, and which should put both sexes on the same footing.

The αὐτὴν is by some referred to the *repudiated wife;* by others, to the *newly married* one. Either may be admitted; but in the former case the sense of ἐπὶ will be, "to the injury of;" in the latter, "in respect of;" i. e. in his connection with. [*Comp.* Matt. v. 32. Luke xvi. 18. 1 Cor. vii. 10. seq.]

14. [*Comp.* Matt. xviii. 3. 1 Cor. xiv. 20. 1 Pet. ii. 2.]

— *καὶ μὴ κωλ.*] The *καὶ* is not found in many MSS., and is rejected by Mill, and cancelled by Griesb., Matth., and Scholz; while Fritz. objects that such an *Asyndeton* is unknown in *Scripture*. Perhaps, however, that is being *hypercritical*. And when he says that the *καὶ* is necessary to the sense, he writes inconsiderately; for in admitting the Asyndeton *any where*, he admits that it may be left to be implied. In the parallel passage of Matthew, indeed, the *καὶ* is found in perhaps all the MSS. But there the order of the words is different, and it could scarcely be dispensed with.

— *τῶν τοιούτων*, &c.] Render, "for to them belongeth," &c.

15. [*Comp.* supra ix. 36.]

17. *ἐκπορευομένου — ὁδὸν*] "as he was departing (from thence) on his way."

18. [*Comp.* Exod. xx. 13. xxi. 12. Deut. v. 17. Rom. xiii. 9.]

19. *μὴ ἀποστερήσῃς.*] Many Commentators are of opinion that ἀποστερεῖν is used in Scripture in a very extensive sense, so as to denote committing injustice of any kind; and to be nearly synonymous with ἀδικεῖν. But ἀποστερεῖν has properly a more *special* signification, denoting to deprive any one of his property, whether by actual

MT. LU.

20 ρα. Ὁ δὲ ἀποκριθεὶς εἶπεν αὐτῷ· Διδάσκαλε, ταῦτα πάντα ἐφυλα- 19. 18.
21 ξάμην ἐκ νεότητός μου. Ὁ δὲ Ἰησοῦς ἐμβλέψας αὐτῷ ἠγάπησεν αὐτὸν, 19 20 21
καὶ εἶπεν αὐτῷ· Ἕν σοι ὑστερεῖ· ὕπαγε, ὅσα ἔχεις πώλησον, καὶ δὸς 21 22
[τοῖς] πτωχοῖς, καὶ ἕξεις θησαυρὸν ἐν οὐρανῷ· καὶ δεῦρο ἀκολούθει
22 μοι ἄρας τὸν σταυρόν. Ὁ δὲ στυγνάσας ἐπὶ τῷ λόγῳ, ἀπῆλθε λυπού- 22 23
23 μενος· ἦν γὰρ ἔχων κτήματα πολλά. Καὶ περιβλεψάμενος ὁ Ἰησοῦς, 23 24
λέγει τοῖς μαθηταῖς αὐτοῦ· Πῶς δυσκόλως οἱ τὰ χρήματα ἔχοντες εἰς
24 τὴν βασιλείαν τοῦ Θεοῦ εἰσελεύσονται. Οἱ δὲ μαθηταὶ ἐθαμβοῦντο
ἐπὶ τοῖς λόγοις αὐτοῦ. Ὁ δὲ Ἰησοῦς πάλιν ἀποκριθεὶς λέγει αὐτοῖς·
Τέκνα, πῶς δύσκολόν ἐστι τοὺς πεποιθότας ἐπὶ τοῖς χρήμασιν εἰς τὴν
25 βασιλείαν τοῦ Θεοῦ εἰσελθεῖν! Εὐκοπώτερόν ἐστι κάμηλον διὰ τῆς 24 25
τρυμαλιᾶς [τῆς] ῥαφίδος ‡ διελθεῖν, ἢ πλούσιον εἰς τὴν βασιλείαν τοῦ
26 Θεοῦ εἰσελθεῖν! Οἱ δὲ περισσῶς ἐξεπλήσσοντο, λέγοντες πρὸς ἑαυ- 25 26
27 τούς· Καὶ τίς δύναται σωθῆναι; Ἐμβλέψας δὲ αὐτοῖς ὁ Ἰησοῦς λέ- 26 27
γει· Παρὰ ἀνθρώποις ἀδύνατον, ἀλλ᾿ οὐ παρὰ τῷ Θεῷ· πάν-
28 τα γὰρ δυνατά ἐστι παρὰ τῷ Θεῷ. Καὶ ἤρξατο ὁ Πέτρος λέγειν αὐτῷ· 27 28

and open robbery, or by secret fraud, as denying a debt, cheating in the quality of goods sold, or overreaching in the bargain. Be that as it may, the words have not (as Wets. and others imagine) reference to the *ninth* and *tenth* Commandments, but, as Heupel observes, to the *seventh*, μὴ κλέψῃς, on which this is a sort of paraphrase, to show the extent of the injunction. Indeed, the Jews were accustomed, in ordinary discourse, and even in writing, to recite the precepts of the Decalogue not in the very words in which they are expressed, but in other equivalent terms.

21. ἠγάπησεν αὐτόν.] On the sense of ἠγάπ. there is much difference of opinión; which has been occasioned by the fact, that the young man did not *follow* our Lord's admonition. Some would adopt a sense of ἀγαπᾷν by which it denotes to *be content with*. But the syntax is then very different. And it is used of *things*, not *persons*, and is construed either with a Dative of object, or with a Participle, or an Infinitive. The other interpretations are divided into such as respect good will generally, "he was kindly disposed towards him," or (as that has been by many supposed not sufficient) such as imply good will by some outward gesture or action. H. Steph. and Lightf, interpret, "he kissed him;" while Casaub., Grot., Wets., Heum., Kuin., and Fritz. interpret "he accosted him kindly;" both significations alike destitute of authority. The interpretation, "he felt kindly disposed towards him," (which is supported by the ancient Commentators,) is the most natural and probable.

21. τοῖς πτωχοῖς.] The Article is not found in very many MSS. and the Edit. Princ., and is cancelled by Beng., Matth., Fritz. and Scholz. The chief reason, it should seem, why these Editors have cancelled the τοῖς, is because it is not found in the parallel passages of Matthew and Luke. But *granting*, as Fritz. alleges, that "such expressions admit of the Article, and also may dispense with it;" yet is not a writer to be allowed to choose which he will? And as Mark *uses* the Article in precisely the same case at ch. xiv. 5 & 7, it is surely proper to leave it to him here. And certainly we may far better account for the *omission* than the *insertion* of it here; namely, from a wish to make the phrase tally with Matthew and Luke. On this verse compare Matt. vi. 19. Luke xii. 33. xvi. 9.

22. στυγνάσας.] This may be referred either to the *countenance* or to the *mind*. In the *former* case it will denote that *contraction of the countenance*, which is produced by hearing any thing which displeases one: in the latter, it will signify *perturbation*. Thus, however, the term would be nearly the same with λυπούμενος just after. The former interpretation, therefore, is preferable; especially as it is confirmed by a passage of Nicetas ap. Schleus. Lex. οἱ δὲ κατηφιῶντες καὶ στυγνάζοντες ἐβίωσκον.

24. [*Comp.* Job xxxi. 24. Ps. lxii. 10. 1 Tim. vi. 17.]

25. τῆς τρυμαλιᾶς τῆς ῥαφίδος.] The Articles are omitted in several MSS. most of them ancient. Middlet. thinks them spurious; and Fritz. cancels them. Certainly, propriety requires that ῥαφὶς, as it denotes a needle in general, should not have the Article. And then propriety alike requires that if *that* be omitted, the *other* too shall be left out. Since, however, the latter propriety is of too refined a kind to be likely to have been known to the Evangelist; and as the idiom is found in our own language, it may be safer to *retain* the Article in question. Τρυμαλιὰ is from τρύω, *tero*, and is of the same form with ἁρμαλιά.

— διελθεῖν.] Very many MSS., and some Fathers, have εἰσελθεῖν, which is adopted by Wets. and Matth. But it would require much *stronger* evidence to establish so glaring a violation of propriety; for which Schulz. in vain alleges Matt. vii. 13, because (as Fritz. truly observes) at εἰσέλθετε διὰ τῆς στενῆς πύλης should be supplied εἰς τὴν ζωήν.

26. καὶ τίς δύναται σωθ.] As Matt. xix. 25. has τίς ἄρα, this has by many been regarded as a Hebraism. But καὶ thus prefixed to τίς is frequent in the Classical writers, as appears from the examples adduced by Bos, Elsn., and Wets. The καὶ in this use may be rendered "*aut* (but)." There is perhaps an ellipse of ἄρα. By the τίς must be understood πλούσιος.

27. [*Comp.* Job xlii. 2. Jer. xxxii. 17. Luke i. 37.]

28. καὶ ἤρξατο.] The καὶ is not found in very

MT. LU.
19. 18. Ἰδού, ἡμεῖς ἀφήκαμεν πάντα, καὶ ἠκολουθήσαμέν σοι. ‡ Ἀποκριθεὶς 29
28
29 29 δὲ ὁ Ἰησοῦς εἶπεν· Ἀμὴν λέγω ὑμῖν· οὐδείς ἐστιν, ὃς ἀφῆκεν οἰκίαν,
ἢ ἀδελφοὺς, ἢ ἀδελφὰς, ἢ πατέρα, ἢ μητέρα, ἢ γυναῖκα, ἢ τέκνα, ἢ ἀγροὺς,
30 ἕνεκεν ἐμοῦ καὶ τοῦ εὐαγγελίου, ἐὰν μὴ λάβῃ ἑκατονταπλασίονα νῦν ἐν τῷ 30
καιρῷ τούτῳ, (οἰκίας καὶ ἀδελφοὺς καὶ ἀδελφὰς καὶ μητέρας καὶ τέκνα

many MSS., and is cancelled by Griesb., Vat., and Scholz. But I think, wholly without reason. For it is obvious, and acknowledged by Fritz., that some particle is necessary; and he edits ἤρξατο δέ. But for that reading there is not sufficient *authority;* and besides, there would thus appear no *reason* for the omission of the particle. Whereas the καὶ would be likely to be omitted, as being used in a manner never found in the Classical writers. At ver. 29, the true reading, I suspect, is καὶ ἀπ. ὁ Ι., as found in many MSS. and early Editions, and edited by Fritz. and Scholz. Those many MSS. which have neither particle nor the other, are in favour of this reading. For the Critics, it seems, were content with expelling the καὶ, and introduced nothing in its stead.

29. ἕνεκεν ἐμοῦ καὶ τ. εὐαγγ.] Very many MSS. have ἕνεκα also before τοῦ εὐαγγ., which is edited by Griesb., Matth., and Scholz. I have not ventured to follow their example: yet not because I think (as does Fritz.) that the word is *better away;* but because it appears to me, (especially considering the reading of the parallel passage) that it was more likely to have been *inserted* than omitted. Besides, the very same expression occurs supra viii. 35, with only *one* ἕνεκα.

29, 30. There are marvellous *diversities* of *reading* in these verses (especially the latter), and no slight difficulties have been started as to the *interpretation* of the words as they now stand. Two scruples have been raised, one as to the *promise* itself; the other as to its *limitation*, μετὰ διωγμῶν. With respect to the former, Campb. objects that in ver. 30. the words οἰκίας — ἀγροὺς seem to signify that the compensation shall be *in kind*, in *this life;* which, he says, could only mislead instead of enlightening. Besides, that some things are mentioned at ver. 29. of which a man can have but *one*, as father and mother. And yet at ver. 30. we have the *plural* — mothers. *Wife* is mentioned at ver. 29, but not *wives* at ver. 30. According to rule (he adds) if *one* was repeated, *all* should have been repeated. And the construction required the *plural* number in all. In short, it is plain that he regarded the passage (with Pearce, Owen, and others) as an *interpolation*. But the consent of all the MSS. and early Versions utterly discountenances such a notion. And as to the objections of Campb., though they have been adopted and strenuously urged by Fritz., they have, in reality, little or no force. We may safely maintain (with several Commentators, ancient and modern) that the promise even as regarded *this* world was (considering that ἑκατονταπλασίονα must be taken for πολλαπλασίονα, which indeed is *read* in the parallel passage of Luke, and in some MSS. of that of Matthew) fulfilled literally in the Apostolic age. For the disciples, as they travelled about, or were driven by persecutions, experienced every where the most unbounded hospitality from their brethren; insomuch that the advantages they had lost might be said to be amply made up to them. There is even less force in the other objections. The *strict regularity*, which Campb. and Fritz. desiderate, is by no means a characteristic of the Scriptural writers, (indeed of few ancient ones) and least of all of St. Mark. The irregularities they complain of are indeed, *all* of them, *removed* in one or other of the MSS., and those alterations are all *received into the text* by Fritz., though in defiance of every principle of true Criticism. As to the *plural* number being required throughout ver. 30, it surely makes no great difference whether the plural or the singular be adopted. We might, indeed, say that the *singular* in things of which men have but one should have been used. Hence I have sometimes thought that μητέρα should be read, from several MSS. The plural, however, may be tolerated, as referring to Christians at large. For though the declaration is commenced with οὐδεὶς, yet that is evidently *intended of many*. And though grammatical propriety confined the Evangelist to the use of the *singular* as to the things just adverted to in the *first* verse, yet in the second and more minute enumeration he abandons it. Then again, though three particulars are omitted in ver. 30, which have place in ver. 29, (i. e. πατέρας, μητέρας and γυναῖκας), yet μητέρας might, in some measure, *include* the other; or, as there is very good authority for it in MSS. and Versions, and strong support in a well known critical principle, we might be justified in introducing καὶ πατέρας into the text after καὶ μητέρας. As to the omission of γυναῖκας, it is not difficult to account for that; for not only delicacy forbade the introduction of this particular, but, in reality, it was a kind of loss which, in the nature of things, did not *admit* of being made up.

As to the *spiritual recompense* in this life, mentioned by Campb. (and anxiously sought for by many pious Commentators), "the joy and peace in believing," which would more than counterbalance their losses, *that*, it should seem, was not here adverted to by our Lord. And though it may seem but *little* that temporal remuneration should be mentioned to the *Apostles*, yet *that* might be especially meant for the *disciples at large*. Thus Chrysostom in his Homily on Matt. xix. 27, & seqq. p. 405. 40. acutely and truly observes: Ἵνα γὰρ μή τινες, ἀκούσαντες τὸ, ὑμεῖς [ὡς] ἐξαίρετον τῶν μαθητῶν εἶναι τοῦτο νομίσωσι, (λέγω δὴ τὸ τῶν μεγίστων καὶ πρωτείων ἐν τοῖς μέλλουσιν ἀπολαβεῖν) ἐξέτεινε τὸν λόγον, καὶ ἥπλωσε τὴν ὑπόσχεσιν ἐπὶ τὴν γῆν ἅπασαν· καὶ ἀπὸ τῶν παρόντων καὶ τὰ μέλλοντα πιστοῦται. In the words ἐξέτεινε —— τὴν γῆν ἅπασαν there is a reference to ver. 31, πολλοὶ — πρῶτοι, which Chrys. rightly said, are *here* applied by Christ, with reference to *worldly condition*, as at ix. 35.; the sense being, that many of those who are accounted first in this world, will be found last in the world to come. The οἱ before is absent from many MSS., and is cancelled by Griesb., Matth., and Fritz., perhaps rightly. See Bp. Middlet. on Matt. xix. 30.

Proceed we to consider the *other* difficulty viz. that found in the qualifying words, μετὰ διωγμῶν; which, taken in conjunction with a promise of

MT. LU.
καὶ ἀγρούς, μετὰ διωγμῶν) καὶ ἐν τῷ αἰῶνι τῷ ἐρχομένῳ ζωὴν αἰώνιον. 19. 18.
31 Πολλοὶ δὲ ἔσονται πρῶτοι, ἔσχατοι· καὶ [οἱ] ἔσχατοι, πρῶτοι. 30 20.
32 ἮΣΑΝ δὲ ἐν τῇ ὁδῷ, ἀναβαίνοντες εἰς Ἱεροσόλυμα καὶ ἦν προά- 17
γων αὐτοὺς ὁ Ἰησοῦς· καὶ ἐθαμβοῦντο, καὶ ἀκολουθοῦντες ἐφοβοῦντο.
Καὶ παραλαβὼν πάλιν τοὺς δώδεκα, ἤρξατο αὐτοῖς λέγειν τὰ μέλλοντα 31
33 αὐτῷ συμβαίνειν· Ὅτι, ἰδοὺ ἀναβαίνομεν εἰς Ἱεροσόλυμα, καὶ ὁ Υἱὸς 18
τοῦ ἀνθρώπου παραδοθήσεται τοῖς ἀρχιερεῦσι καὶ [τοῖς] γραμματεῦσι· 32
καὶ κατακρινοῦσιν αὐτὸν θανάτῳ, καὶ παραδώσουσιν αὐτὸν τοῖς ἔθνεσι, 19
34 καὶ ἐμπαίξουσιν αὐτῷ, καὶ μαστιγώσουσιν αὐτὸν, καὶ ἐμπτύσουσιν αὐ- 33
τῷ, καὶ ἀποκτενοῦσιν αὐτόν· καὶ τῇ τρίτῃ ἡμέρᾳ ἀναστήσεται.
35 Καὶ προσπορεύονται αὐτῷ Ἰάκωβος καὶ Ἰωάννης οἱ υἱοὶ Ζεβεδαίου 20
λέγοντες· Διδάσκαλε, θέλομεν ἵνα ὃ ἐὰν αἰτήσωμεν, ποιήσῃς ἡμῖν.
36 Ὁ δὲ εἶπεν αὐτοῖς· Τί θέλετε ποιῆσαί με ὑμῖν; Οἱ δὲ εἶπον αὐτῷ· 21
37 Δὸς ἡμῖν, ἵνα εἷς ἐκ δεξιῶν σου καὶ εἷς ἐξ εὐωνύμων σου καθίσωμεν
38 ἐν τῇ δόξῃ σου. ὁ δὲ Ἰησοῦς εἶπεν αὐτοῖς· Οὐκ οἴδατε τί αἰτεῖσθε· 22
δύνασθε πιεῖν τὸ ποτήριον ὃ ἐγὼ πίνω, καὶ τὸ βάπτισμα ὃ ἐγὼ βα-
39 πτίζομαι, βαπτισθῆναι; Οἱ δὲ εἶπον αὐτῷ· Δυνάμεθα. ὁ δὲ Ἰησοῦς εἶπεν αὐτοῖς· Τὸ μὲν ποτήριον, ὃ ἐγὼ πίνω, πίεσθε· καὶ τὸ 23
40 βάπτισμα, ὃ ἐγὼ βαπτίζομαι, βαπτισθήσεσθε· τὸ δὲ καθίσαι ἐκ δεξιῶν μου καὶ ἐξ εὐωνύμων μου οὐκ ἔστιν ἐμὸν δοῦναι, ἀλλ᾽ οἷς ἡτοί-
41 μασται. Καὶ ἀκούσαντες οἱ δέκα, ἤρξαντο ἀγανακτεῖν περὶ Ἰακώβου 24
42 καὶ Ἰωάννου. Ὁ δὲ Ἰησοῦς προσκαλεσάμενος αὐτοὺς, λέγει αὐτοῖς· 25
Οἴδατε ὅτι οἱ δοκοῦντες ἄρχειν τῶν ἐθνῶν, κατακυριεύουσιν αὐτῶν·

things merely temporal, has been thought by many to have been *illusory*; insomuch that they have sought either to alter the reading διωγμῶν into διωγμὸν, or to take μετὰ in the sense *after*. But there is no authority for either change. The ancient Commentators, and several modern ones (as Beza, Zeger, Heupel, Wolf, Winer, and Fritz.), rightly explain the sense to be "under persecutions," i. e. "even amidst persecutions;" for where tribulation abounded, consolation should much more abound. Upon the whole, this remarkable passage may be regarded as one of those sayings of our Lord which were at once *declarations* and *prophecies*. And the fulfilment of it in the latter view is strikingly manifest, both from Scripture and from the Ecclesiastical History of the first Century.

31. [*Comp.* Matt. xx. 16. Luke xiii. 30.]

32. ἐθαμβοῦντο, &c.] On the *origin* and *nature* of these feelings of the Apostles, the Commentators are divided in opinion. Some, as Heum., Rosenm., and Kuin., attribute them to the prediction, which Christ now delivers of his death and passion. So Euthym., Beza, and others, suppose that the cause of their *fear* was our Lord's going to Jerusalem, notwithstanding the Sanhedrim were seeking to apprehend him; and dread of the evils which he had said at ver. 31. & ix. 31. impended over him. Since, however, they did not understand their Lord on that occasion, and were probably not then aware of the designs of the Sanhedrim, this view cannot well be admitted. Fritz. thinks it was a sort of involuntary presentiment of evil. This is, I conceive, the *truth*; but not the *whole* truth; because it accounts for ἀκολουθοῦντες ἐφοβοῦντο, but not for ἐθαμβοῦντο. *That* must be referred (as I suggested in Recens. Synop,) to a certain *undefinable awe*, with which the Apostles, since the Transfiguration, had begun more and more to contemplate their Lord; and which, besides his many miracles, the increasing air of majesty and authority which he more and more assumed, as his hour drew so near, was well calculated to inspire.

On the remaining part of this verse, compare supra viii. 31. Matt. xvi. 21.

38. [*Comp.* Luke xii. 50.]

40. ἐξ εὐωνύμων μου.] Μου is omitted in many MSS. and Versions, and is cancelled by Matth., Griesb., Vat., and Scholz; but is retained by Tittm. and Fritz.: rightly, I think; for not only external, but *internal* evidence is quite in favour of the word, which, it is more probable, was *cancelled* by the fastidious Alexandrian critics, to remove tautology, than *added* by the *librarii* of later times. It may, indeed, be thought to have been introduced from Matthew. But let us remember *why* the σοῦ was thrown out at Matt, xx. 22., and *by whom restored*; by those very Editors who here cancel the μου, merely on *surmise*. On this verse comp. Matt. xxv. 34.

42. οἱ δοκοῦντες ἄρχειν] The old Commentators regard the participle as *redundant*. And to this opinion the most recent English Expositors cling, adducing from them a cloud of examples, most of them not to the purpose. I have myself always objected to the unnecessary introduction of the above figure, whether in the Scriptural or the Classical writers; which view I find supported by the authority of Fritz., who pronounces that

MT. LU.

20. 18. καὶ οἱ μεγάλοι αὐτῶν κατεξουσιάζουσιν αὐτῶν. Οὐχ οὕτω δὲ ἔσται ἐν 43
26 ὑμῖν· ἀλλ' ὃς ἐὰν θέλῃ γενέσθαι μέγας ἐν ὑμῖν, ἔσται διάκονος ὑμῶν·
27 καὶ ὃς ἂν θέλῃ ὑμῶν γενέσθαι πρῶτος, ἔσται πάντων δοῦλος. Καὶ 44
28 γὰρ ὁ Υἱὸς τοῦ ἀνθρώπου οὐκ ἦλθε διακονηθῆναι, ἀλλὰ διακονῆσαι, 45
καὶ δοῦναι τὴν ψυχὴν αὐτοῦ λύτρον ἀντὶ πολλῶν.

29 35 Καὶ ἔρχονται εἰς Ἱεριχώ· καὶ ἐκπορευομένου αὐτοῦ ἀπὸ Ἱεριχὼ, καὶ 46
30 τῶν μαθητῶν αὐτοῦ, καὶ ὄχλου ἱκανοῦ, υἱὸς Τιμαίου, Βαρτίμαιος ὁ
36 τυφλὸς, ἐκάθητο παρὰ τὴν ὁδὸν προσαιτῶν. Καὶ ἀκούσας ὅτι Ἰησοῦς 47
37 38 ὁ Ναζωραῖός ἐστιν, ἤρξατο κράζειν καὶ λέγειν· Ὁ υἱὸς Δαυῒδ Ἰησοῦ,
31 39 ἐλέησόν με! Καὶ ἐπετίμων αὐτῷ πολλοὶ, ἵνα σιωπήσῃ· ὁ δὲ πολλῷ 48
μᾶλλον ἔκραζεν· Υἱὲ Δαυῒδ, ἐλέησόν με! Καὶ στὰς ὁ Ἰησοῦς εἶπεν 49
32 40 αὐτὸν φωνηθῆναι· καὶ φωνοῦσι τὸν τυφλὸν, λέγοντες αὐτῷ· Θάρσει,
ἔγειραι· φωνεῖ σε. Ὁ δὲ ἀποβαλὼν τὸ ἱμάτιον αὐτοῦ, ἀναστὰς ἦλθε 50
41 πρὸς τὸν Ἰησοῦν. Καὶ ἀποκριθεὶς λέγει αὐτῷ ὁ Ἰησοῦς· Τί θέλεις 51
33 ποιήσω σοι; ὁ δὲ τυφλὸς εἶπεν αὐτῷ· Ῥαββουνὶ, ἵνα ἀναβλέψω.
34 42 Ὁ δὲ Ἰησοῦς εἶπεν αὐτῷ· Ὕπαγε· ἡ πίστις σου σέσωκέ σε. καὶ 52
43 εὐθέως ἀνέβλεψε, καὶ ἠκολούθει τῷ Ἰησοῦ ἐν τῇ ὁδῷ.

21. 19. XI. ΚΑΙ ὅτε ἐγγίζουσιν εἰς Ἱερουσαλὴμ, εἰς Βηθφαγὴ καὶ Βηθα- 1
1 29 νίαν πρὸς τὸ ὄρος τῶν Ἐλαιῶν, ἀποστέλλει δύο τῶν μαθητῶν αὐτοῦ,
2 30 καὶ λέγει αὐτοῖς· Ὑπάγετε εἰς τὴν κώμην τὴν κατέναντι ὑμῶν· καὶ 2
εὐθέως εἰσπορευόμενοι εἰς αὐτὴν εὑρήσετε πῶλον δεδεμένον, ἐφ' ὃν
3 31 οὐδεὶς ἀνθρώπων κεκάθικε· λύσαντες αὐτὸν ἀγάγετε. Καὶ ἐάν τις 3
ὑμῖν εἴπῃ· Τί ποιεῖτε τοῦτο; εἴπατε, ὅτι ὁ κύριος αὐτοῦ χρείαν ἔχει·

the word is *no where* pleonastic. That it is not so *here*, will appear from the numerous examples which I have adducéd from the Classical writers in Recens. Syn., which will confirm the rendering of Grot., "qui imperare censentur;" or that of Fritz., "qui sibi imperare videntur." [*Comp.* Luke xxii. 25.]

— οἱ μεγάλοι αὐτῶν] The sense is, "the great ones (magnates) among them." Fritz. calls this a *mira dictio*. He might better have termed it dictio *popularis*. Κατεξουσιάζουσιν, i. e. as Casaub. renders, imperium in eorum nomine exercent.

44. [*Comp.* supra ix. 35. 1 Pet. v. 3.]

45. [*Comp.* John xiii. 14. Phil. ii. 7. Eph. i. 7. Col. i. 14. 1 Tim. ii. 6.]

46. Βαρτίμαιος] Some take this for a *patronymic*, or *explication* of ὁ υἱὸς Τιμαίου. Others, with more reason, consider it as a *real name*, and think the person was called Βαρτίμαιος and was the son of Timæus. So Βαρθολομαῖος and Βαριησοῦς. and Thucyd. i. 29, Ἰσαρχίδας ὁ Ἰσάρχου. In such cases the patronymic has been converted into a regular appellative. There is some resemblance to those names which have the *form* only, without the signification; on which see my Note on Thucyd. i. 1.

— προσαιτῶν] The προς is not (as some imagine) without force; but it cannot signify, as some suppose, *besides*, but rather denotes *to* or *for*, render "asking for himself." So in πρόσοδος and προσκαλεῖσθαι. Supply τὸ χρῆμα.

48. πολλοὶ] Not "the multitude," for that sense would require οἱ πολλοί; but *many*, namely, of those who accompanied Jesus.

49. φωνηθῆναι] "to be called or summoned."

50. ἀποβαλὼν τὸ ἱμάτιον] Namely, through joy, and in order to reach Jesus the sooner. A *graphic trait*, evidently proceeding from an eye-witness, like that in John vi. 10. "Now there was much grass in the place."

51. Ῥαββουνὶ] "great master." The reading ουνι for ονι is found in most of the best MSS., and is edited by Matth., Griesb., Vat., Tittm., Fritz., and Scholz; with reason. The ι is, as Fritz. says, paragogic, and the whole termination is, the Talmudists tell us, augmentative. See John xx. 16. and Lampe in loc.

XI. 1. καὶ ὅτε ἐγγίζουσιν — Ἐλαιῶν] There is here much diversity of reading, owing to the antient Critics stumbling at the close brevity and roughness of the phraseology, and, as usual, taking the liberty to expand and polish. The *sense*, indeed, is what those MSS. represent: namely, "and when they had approached to Jerusalem, and were come to the [vicinity of] Bethphage and Bethany [even] to the Mount of Olives." But we are not warranted in *receiving* those readings, as Fritz. has done.

2. κεκάθικε] "has sate." Doddr. and others have well remarkéd here on our Lord's prescience even as to the most minute and fortuitous particulars, viz. 1. Ye shall find a colt; 2. on which no man ever sat; 3. bound with his mother; 4. where two ways meet; 5. as ye enter into the village; 6. the owners of which will at first seem unwilling that you should unbind him; 7. but when they hear that I have need of him, they will let him go. "Many such things (adds Doddr.) occurred a little before his death. Com-

MT. LU.
4 καὶ εὐθέως αὐτὸν ἀποστελεῖ ὧδε. Ἀπῆλθον δέ, καὶ εὗρον [τὸν] πῶ- 21. 19.
λον δεδεμένον πρὸς τὴν θύραν ἔξω ἐπὶ τοῦ ἀμφόδου· καὶ λύουσιν 6 32
5 αὐτόν. Καί τινες τῶν ἐκεῖ ἑστηκότων ἔλεγον αὐτοῖς· Τί ποιεῖτε λύ- 33
6 οντες τὸν πῶλον; Οἱ δὲ εἶπον αὐτοῖς καθὼς ἐνετείλατο ὁ Ἰησοῦς· 34
7 καὶ ἀφῆκαν αὐτούς. Καὶ ἤγαγον τὸν πῶλον πρὸς τὸν Ἰησοῦν, καὶ 7 35
8 ἐπέβαλον αὐτῷ τὰ ἱμάτια αὐτῶν· καὶ ἐκάθισεν ἐπ' αὐτῷ. Πολλοὶ 8 36
δὲ τὰ ἱμάτια αὐτῶν ἔστρωσαν εἰς τὴν ὁδόν· ἄλλοι δὲ στοιβάδας ἔκο-
9 πτον ἐκ τῶν δένδρων, καὶ ἐστρώννυον εἰς τὴν ὁδόν. Καὶ οἱ προάγοντες
καὶ οἱ ἀκολουθοῦντες ἔκραζον, λέγοντες· Ὡσαννά! εὐλογημένος ὁ 9 37
10 ἐρχόμενος ἐν ὀνόματι Κυρίου! εὐλογημένη ἡ ἐρχομένη βασιλεία [ἐν 38
ὀνόματι Κυρίου,] τοῦ πατρὸς ἡμῶν Δαυΐδ· Ὡσαννὰ ἐν τοῖς ὑψίστοις!
11 Καὶ εἰσῆλθεν εἰς Ἱεροσόλυμα ὁ Ἰησοῦς, καὶ εἰς τὸ ἱερόν· καὶ περιβλεψάμενος πάντα, ὀψίας ἤδη οὔσης τῆς ὥρας, ἐξῆλθεν εἰς Βηθανίαν 17
μετὰ τῶν δώδεκα.
12 Καὶ τῇ ἐπαύριον, ἐξελθόντων αὐτῶν ἀπὸ Βηθανίας, ἐπείνασε. Καὶ 18
13 ἰδὼν συκῆν μακρόθεν ἔχουσαν φύλλα, ἦλθεν, εἰ ἄρα εὑρήσει τὶ ἐν 19
αὐτῇ· καὶ ἐλθὼν ἐπ' αὐτήν, οὐδὲν εὗρεν εἰ μὴ φύλλα. οὐ γὰρ ἦν
14 καιρὸς σύκων. Καὶ ἀποκριθεὶς [ὁ Ἰησοῦς] εἶπεν αὐτῇ· Μηκέτι ἐκ

pare Matth. xxvi. 31—35. Mark xiv. 15 & 16. Luke xxii. 11—13."

3. ἀποστελεῖ] Very many MSS., several Versions, and the Edit. Princ. have ἀποστέλλει, which is adopted by Wets., Matth., Griesb., Vat., Tittm., and Scholz. But Fritz., more judiciously, retains the common reading; and gives good reasons for so doing. As for the authority of MSS., it is of little avail in such minutiæ as λ and λλ.

4. ἐπὶ τοῦ ἀμφόδου] This is wrongly rendered by some "*in bivio*." The word properly denotes a *passage*, but in the Sept. and N. T. signifies a *street*, Heb. חוּץ. as here.

7. [*Comp.* John xii. 14. 2 Kings ix. 13.]

8. στοιβάδας] The word (which is in the Classical authors written στιβὰς) denotes properly *something strewed on the ground*; whether straw, hay, stubble, rushes, reeds, leaves, or the twigs of trees; of *all* which examples may be seen in Wets. Here, however, from a comparison with Matth. xxi. 8., it appears to denote *frondes*, the leafy twigs of trees, such as were used for low couches.

9. [*Comp.* Ps. cxviii. 25, 26. Matt. xxiii. 39.]

10. The words ἐν ὀν. Κυρ. are omitted in some MSS., and cancelled by Griesb., Vater, Fritz., and Scholz, but without any sufficient reason.

11. [*Comp.* John ii. 14.]

13. οὐ γὰρ ἦν καιρὸς σύκων] There are few passages that have occasioned greater perplexity than the present. The difficulty of reconciling the words with our Lord's *expectation* of finding figs on the tree, or with his subsequent cursing of it, is obvious. Some have given up the solution in despair; others have suspected the passage to be corrupt, and propounded various conjectures; *all of them inadmissible*, since the MSS. discountenance any *alteration*, still more any *cancelling* of words. The present reading must be retained, and the difficulty be removed by *interpretation*. Almost all the methods, however, which have been propounded, are either founded on unauthorized senses of καιρὸς, or are inapposite. One thing seems clear, — that we must (with Kidder, Markl., Pearce, Campb., Wolf, Doddr., Wets., Wakef., Rosenm., Kuin., Schleusn., and Wahl) take καιρὸς σύκων as corresponding to the καιρὸς τῶν καρπῶν at Matt. xxi. 34., and the καιρὸς τοῦ θερισμοῦ at Matt. xiii. 30., as also the ὁ τῶν σύκων καιρὸς at Athenæus, p. 65. And this sense is very rational; for what (as Pearce and Campb. say) can *the time* of any fruit be, but the time of its maturity and *gathering*? But the declaration contained in οὐ γὰρ ἦν καιρὸς σύκων cannot (as the order of the words would induce us to suppose) be meant to offer the *reason why* there was nothing but leaves on the tree; for the fig is of that class of trees wherein the fruit is developed *before* the *leaves* appear. Now some would place the words καὶ ἐλθὼν — φύλλα in a parenthesis; for which, however, there seems no place. Others suppose a *trajectio* per *synchysin* (as at xvi. 3 & 4. Τίς ἀποκυλίσει ἡμῖν τὸν λίθον ἐκ τῆς θύρας τοῦ μνημείου; καὶ ἀναβλέψασαι θεωροῦσιν ὅτι ἀποκεκύλισται ὁ λίθος· ἦν γὰρ μέγας σφόδρα.) by which the words οὐ γάρ, &c. though coming immediately after καὶ ἐλθών, &c. are to be referred to the more remote ἦλθεν εἰ ἄρα εὑρήσει τὶ ἐν αὐτῇ, thus: seeing a fig-tree afar off having leaves, he came, to see if haply he might find any fruit thereon; for fig-gathering was not yet come: and therefore, if the tree had produced any figs, some, however unripe, might be expected to be growing on it. But when he came to it, he found nothing but leaves; and thus, his disappointment could only have proceeded from the barrenness of the tree. Unripe figs, it has been observed, may be eaten for allaying hunger. And though this might seem early for figs, yet, in Judæa, the fig-tree bears twice in the year; the first crop being at the beginning of the summer. Not to say that a few forward and vigorous trees will ripen their fruit several weeks before the generality.

MT. LU.
21. 19. σοῦ εἰς τὸν αἰῶνα ‡ μηδεὶς καρπὸν φάγοι! καὶ ἤκουον οἱ μαθηταὶ
12 45 αὐτοῦ. Καὶ ἔρχονται εἰς Ἱεροσόλυμα· καὶ εἰσελθὼν ὁ Ἰησοῦς εἰς τὸ 15
ἱερὸν, ἤρξατο ἐκβάλλειν τοὺς πωλοῦντας καὶ ἀγοράζοντας ἐν τῷ ἱερῷ·
καὶ τὰς τραπέζας τῶν κολλυβιστῶν καὶ τὰς καθέδρας τῶν πωλούντων
τὰς περιστερὰς κατέστρεψε· καὶ οὐκ ἤφιεν ἵνα τὶς διενέγκῃ σκεῦος 16
13 46 διὰ τοῦ ἱεροῦ. Καὶ ἐδίδασκε, λέγων αὐτοῖς· Οὐ γέγραπται, ὅτι ὁ 17
οἶκός μου οἶκος προσευχῆς κληθήσεται πᾶσι τοῖς
ἔθνεσιν; ὑμεῖς δὲ ἐποιήσατε αὐτὸν σπήλαιον λῃστῶν. Καὶ ἤκουσαν 18
47 οἱ γραμματεῖς καὶ οἱ ἀρχιερεῖς, καὶ ἐζήτουν πῶς αὐτὸν ἀπολέσουσιν·
48 ἐφοβοῦντο γὰρ αὐτὸν, ὅτι πᾶς ὁ ὄχλος ἐξεπλήσσετο ἐπὶ τῇ διδαχῇ
αὐτοῦ.

Καὶ ὅτε ὀψὲ ἐγένετο, ἐξεπορεύετο ἔξω τῆς πόλεως. Καὶ πρωῒ παρα- 19
πορευόμενοι, εἶδον τὴν συκῆν ἐξηραμμένην ἐκ ῥιζῶν. Καὶ ἀναμνη- 20
σθεὶς ὁ Πέτρος λέγει αὐτῷ· Ῥαββὶ, ἴδε, ἡ συκῆ, ἣν κατηράσω, 21
21 ἐξήρανται. Καὶ ἀποκριθεὶς ὁ Ἰησοῦς λέγει αὐτοῖς· Ἔχετε πίστιν 22
Θεοῦ. ἀμὴν γὰρ λέγω ὑμῖν, ὅτι ὃς ἂν εἴπῃ τῷ ὄρει τούτῳ· Ἄρθητι, 23
καὶ βλήθητι εἰς τὴν θάλασσαν· καὶ μὴ διακριθῇ ἐν τῇ καρδίᾳ αὐτοῦ,
22 ἀλλὰ πιστεύσῃ, ὅτι ἃ λέγει γίνεται· ἔσται αὐτῷ ὃ ἐὰν εἴπῃ. Διὰ 24
τοῦτο λέγω ὑμῖν· Πάντα ὅσα ἂν προσευχόμενοι αἰτεῖσθε, πιστεύετε
ὅτι λαμβάνετε· καὶ ἔσται ὑμῖν. Καὶ ὅταν στήκητε προσευχόμενοι, 25
ἀφίετε εἴ τι ἔχετε κατά τινος· ἵνα καὶ ὁ πατὴρ ὑμῶν ὁ ἐν τοῖς οὐρανοῖς ἀφῇ ὑμῖν τὰ παραπτώματα ὑμῶν· εἰ δὲ ὑμεῖς οὐκ ἀφίετε, 26
20. οὐδὲ ὁ πατὴρ ὑμῶν ὁ ἐν τοῖς οὐρανοῖς ἀφήσει τὰ παραπτώματα ὑμῶν.
23 1 ΚΑΙ ἔρχονται πάλιν εἰς Ἱεροσόλυμα· καὶ, ἐν τῷ ἱερῷ περιπατοῦν- 27
τος αὐτοῦ, ἔρχονται πρὸς αὐτὸν οἱ ἀρχιερεῖς καὶ οἱ γραμματεῖς καὶ
2 οἱ πρεσβύτεροι, καὶ λέγουσιν αὐτῷ· Ἐν ποίᾳ ἐξουσίᾳ ταῦτα ποιεῖς· 28
24 3 καὶ τίς σοι τὴν ἐξουσίαν ταύτην ἔδωκεν, ἵνα ταῦτα ποιῇς; Ὁ δὲ 29

14. μηδεὶς] This reading (for vulg. οὐδεὶς) is found in very many MSS., some Fathers, and several of the early Editions; and is received by Wets., Griesb., Matth., Fritz., Tittm., and Scholz. Strict *grammatical propriety* requires it, but that Mark so wrote is by no means certain.

15. ἤρξατο ἐκβάλλειν] This is not, as most Commentators imagine, for ἐξέβαλε; but the sense is, "he proceeded to cast out." [*Comp.* John ii. 14.]

16. διενέγκῃ σκεῦος] This is usually understood to mean any *vessel*, namely, devoted to profane uses, and by which any gain was made. But the word σκεῦος, which in the Sept. corresponds to the Heb. כְּלִי, has, like that word, a considerable latitude of signification, and denotes, like the Latin *vas*, or *instrumentum*, a *utensil* (whether for sacred or profane use), or *piece of furniture*, or *dress*, and, in a general sense, an *article*, whether for use or traffic.

In doing this our Lord upheld the Jewish Canons (founded on Levit. xix. 30. and Deut. xii. 5.), which, as we find from the Rabbinical writers, define the reverence of the Temple (i. e. the outer Court) to mean, that none should go into it with his staff, shoes, or purse, or with dust upon his feet; and that none should make it a thoroughfare. The irregularities which our Lord rebukes, had, it is supposed, originated in, or been increased by the proximity of the Castle of Antonia; to which there would be a constant resort of various persons, (so Joseph. B. J. i. 3. 5. παριόντα διὰ τοῦ ἱεροῦ.) and that the Priests, having an interest in, connived at them.

17. [*Comp.* 1 Kings viii. 29. Is. lvi. 7. Jer. vii. 11.]

18. [*Comp.* John vii. 19.]

22. ἔχετε πίστιν Θεοῦ] Some take this to mean, "have a strong faith;" by a common Hebraism, whereby the genitive of "God" subjoined to substantives, denotes greatness or excellence. But there is no reason to abandon the common interpretation, by which Θεοῦ is a Genitive of *object* or *end*, as in Rom. iii. 22. Gal. ii. 20. iii. 22., where it is also found with πίστις. Of course it is *implied*, that the faith which is reposed in God shall be firm and undoubting, as the words following suggest and illustrate.

23. [*Comp.* Matt. xvii. 20. Luke xvii. 6.]

24. ἔσται ὑμῖν] This, like ἔσται αὐτῷ just before, is a Dative of *possession*, "shall be yours." [*Comp.* Matt. vii. 7. Luke xi. 9. John xiv. 13. James i. 5, 6. 1 John iii. 22. v. 14.]

25. [*Comp.* Matt. vi. 14. Eph. iv. 32. Col. iii: 13. Eccl. xxviii. 2.]

28. [*Comp.* Exod. ii. 14. Acts iv. 7. vii. 27.]

MT. LU.
Ἰησοῦς ἀποκριθεὶς εἶπεν αὐτοῖς· Ἐπερωτήσω ὑμᾶς κἀγὼ ἕνα λόγον, 21. 20
30 καὶ ἀποκρίθητέ μοι· καὶ ἐρῶ ὑμῖν ἐν ποίᾳ ἐξουσίᾳ ταῦτα ποιῶ. Τὸ 25 4
βάπτισμα Ἰωάννου ἐξ οὐρανοῦ ἦν, ἢ ἐξ ἀνθρώπων; ἀποκρίθητέ μοι.
31 Καὶ ἐλογίζοντο πρὸς ἑαυτοὺς, λέγοντες. Ἐὰν εἴπωμεν· Ἐξ οὐρανοῦ, 5
32 ἐρεῖ· Διατί οὖν οὐκ ἐπιστεύσατε αὐτῷ; ἀλλ᾽ ἐὰν εἴπωμεν· Ἐξ ἀν- 26 6
θρώπων, ἐφοβοῦντο τὸν λαόν· ἅπαντες γὰρ εἶχον τὸν Ἰωάννην ὅτι
33 ὄντως προφήτης ἦν. Καὶ ἀποκριθέντες λέγουσι τῷ Ἰησοῦ· Οὐκ οἴ- 27 7
δαμεν. Καὶ ὁ Ἰησοῦς ἀποκριθεὶς λέγει αὐτοῖς· Οὐδὲ ἐγὼ λέγω ὑμῖν 8
ἐν ποίᾳ ἐξουσίᾳ ταῦτα ποιῶ.
1 XII. ΚΑΙ ἤρξατο αὐτοῖς ἐν παραβολαῖς λέγειν· Ἀμπελῶνα ἐφύ- 33 9
τευσεν ἄνθρωπος, καὶ περιέθηκε φραγμὸν, καὶ ὤρυξεν ὑπολήνιον, καὶ
2 ᾠκοδόμησε πύργον, καὶ ἐξέδοτο αὐτὸν γεωργοῖς, καὶ ἀπεδήμησε. Καὶ 34 10
ἀπέστειλε πρὸς τοὺς γεωργοὺς τῷ καιρῷ δοῦλον, ἵνα παρὰ τῶν γεωργῶν
3 λάβῃ ἀπὸ τοῦ καρποῦ τοῦ ἀμπελῶνος. Οἱ δὲ λαβόντες αὐτὸν ἔδειραν, 35
4 καὶ ἀπέστειλαν κενόν. Καὶ πάλιν ἀπέστειλε πρὸς αὐτοὺς ἄλλον δοῦ- 36 11
λον· κἀκεῖνον λιθοβολήσαντες ἐκεφαλαίωσαν, καὶ ἀπέστειλαν ἠτιμωμέ-
5 νον. Καὶ πάλιν ἄλλον ἀπέστειλε· κἀκεῖνον ἀπέκτειναν. καὶ πολλοὺς 12
6 ἄλλους, τοὺς μὲν δέροντες, τοὺς δὲ ἀποκτείνοντες. Ἔτι οὖν ἕνα υἱὸν 37 13
ἔχων ἀγαπητὸν αὐτοῦ, ἀπέστειλε καὶ αὐτὸν πρὸς αὐτοὺς ἔσχατον, λέ-
7 γων· Ὅτι ἐντραπήσονται τὸν υἱόν μου. Ἐκεῖνοι δὲ οἱ γεωργοὶ εἶπον 38 14
πρὸς ἑαυτούς· Ὅτι οὗτός ἐστιν ὁ κληρονόμος· δεῦτε ἀποκτείνωμεν
8 αὐτὸν, καὶ ἡμῶν ἔσται ἡ κληρονομία. Καὶ λαβόντες αὐτὸν ἀπέκτειναν, 39 15
9 καὶ ἐξέβαλον ἔξω τοῦ ἀμπελῶνος. Τί οὖν ποιήσει ὁ κύριος τοῦ ἀμπε- 40
λῶνος; ἐλεύσεται καὶ ἀπολέσει τοὺς γεωργοὺς, καὶ δώσει τὸν ἀμπε- 41 16
10 λῶνα ἄλλοις. Οὐδὲ τὴν γραφὴν ταύτην ἀνέγνωτε; Λίθον ὃν 42 17
ἀπεδοκίμασαν οἱ οἰκοδομοῦντες, οὗτος ἐγενήθη εἰς
11 κεφαλὴν γωνίας. παρὰ Κυρίου ἐγένετο αὕτη· καὶ
12 ἔστι θαυμαστὴ ἐν ὀφθαλμοῖς ἡμῶν. Καὶ ἐζήτουν αὐ- 46 19

32. ἐξ ἀνθρώπων· ἐφοβοῦντο τὸν λαόν.] The Scribes and the Commentators alike stumble at this construction, and endeavour to remove the irregularity by various methods, all of them fruitless and indeed *unnecessary*. For there is no need to supply, with some, τί γενήσεται ἡμῖν, or κακῶς ἕξει· There is, as Kypke and Fritz. say, an *anacoluthon*, (frequent in the best writers,) by which the Evangelist passes from the *very words* of the persons spoken of, to a *narration of what was said;* a sort of idiom similar to that by which there is a transition from the oratio *directa* to the *obliqua*. Thus ἐφοβοῦντο τὸν λαὸν is for φοβούμεθα τὸν λαὸν, which is found in Matt. xxi. 26. [*Comp.* supra vi. 20; and Matt. xiv. 5.]

XII. 1. ἐν παραβολαῖς.] Beza rightly regards this as denoting the *genus* orationis, and as equivalent to παραβλήδην; for our Lord probably spoke *several*, though the Evangelist has recorded only *one*.

— ἀμπελῶνα ἐφύτ.] *Comp.* Ps. lxxx. 8. Is. v. 1. Jer. ii. 21. xii. 10.

4. λιθοβολήσαντες ἐκεφαλ.] On the sense of ἐκεφαλ. the Commentators are divided in opinion. But almost all the interpretations proposed are objectionable; either as straining the sense by arbitrary ellipses, or as assigning significations which either are not inherent in the word, or are frigid and unsuitable. The true sense seems to be that expressed by the Syr., Vulg., and other Versions, and some modern Translations, (as E. V.,) and adopted by Beza, Pisc., Casaub., Heupel, Rosenm., Schleus., Kuin., and Fritz., "wounded him in the head." Thus λιθοβολ. will denote the *manner* and *means;* i. e. "by pelting him with stones." This interpretation is moreover confirmed by the τραυματίζειν of Luke. And although this signification of the verb is perhaps without example, yet it is strongly supported by the analogy of the language, as in the verbs γναθοῦν, γυιοῦν, γαστρίζειν, μηρίζειν. Ἠτιμωμένον, "ignominiously treated." This form (ἀτιμάω for ἀτιμάζω) is of very rare occurrence. But the Evangelist has many such peculiarities, derived, probably, from the language of common life.

7. [*Comp.* Ps. ii. 8. Matt. xxvi. 3. John xi. 53. Gen. xxxvii. 18.]

10. [*Comp.* Ps. cxviii. 22. Isaiah xxviii. 16. Acts iv. 11. Rom. ix. 33. 1 Pet. ii. 7.]

MT. LU.
22. 20. τὸν κρατῆσαι, καὶ ἐφοβήθησαν τὸν ὄχλον· ἔγνωσαν γὰρ ὅτι πρὸς
αὐτοὺς τὴν παραβολὴν εἶπε· καὶ ἀφέντες αὐτόν, ἀπῆλθον.
16 20 Καὶ ἀποστέλλουσι πρὸς αὐτόν τινὰς τῶν Φαρισαίων καὶ τῶν Ἡρω- 13
διανῶν, ἵνα αὐτὸν ἀγρεύσωσι λόγῳ. Οἱ δὲ ἐλθόντες λέγουσιν αὐτῷ· 14
21 Διδάσκαλε, οἴδαμεν ὅτι ἀληθὴς εἶ, καὶ οὐ μέλει σοι περὶ οὐδενός· οὐ
γὰρ βλέπεις εἰς πρόσωπον ἀνθρώπων, ἀλλ' ἐπ' ἀληθείας τὴν ὁδὸν
17 22 τοῦ Θεοῦ διδάσκεις. ἔξεστι κῆνσον Καίσαρι δοῦναι ἢ οὔ; δῶμεν, ἢ
18 23 μὴ δῶμεν; Ὁ δὲ εἰδὼς αὐτῶν τὴν ὑπόκρισιν εἶπεν αὐτοῖς· Τί με 15
19 24 πειράζετε; φέρετέ μοι δηνάριον, ἵνα ἴδω. Οἱ δὲ ἤνεγκαν. Καὶ λέγει 16
20 αὐτοῖς· Τίνος ἡ εἰκὼν αὕτη καὶ ἡ ἐπιγραφή; οἱ δὲ εἶπον αὐτῷ·
21 25 Καίσαρος. Καὶ ἀποκριθεὶς ὁ Ἰησοῦς εἶπεν αὐτοῖς· Ἀπόδοτε τὰ Καί- 17
22 26 σαρος Καίσαρι, καὶ τὰ τοῦ Θεοῦ τῷ Θεῷ. καὶ ἐθαύμασαν ἐπ' αὐτῷ.
23 27 Καὶ ἔρχονται Σαδδουκαῖοι πρὸς αὐτόν, οἵτινες λέγουσιν ἀνάστασιν 18
24 28 μὴ εἶναι· καὶ ἐπηρώτησαν αὐτόν, λέγοντες· Διδάσκαλε, Μωϋσῆς 19
ἔγραψεν ἡμῖν, ὅτι ἐάν τινος ἀδελφὸς ἀποθάνῃ, καὶ καταλίπῃ γυναῖκα,
καὶ τέκνα μὴ ἀφῇ, ἵνα λάβῃ ὁ ἀδελφὸς αὐτοῦ τὴν γυναῖκα αὐτοῦ, καὶ
25 29 ἐξαναστήσῃ σπέρμα τῷ ἀδελφῷ αὐτοῦ. Ἑπτὰ ἀδελφοὶ ἦσαν· καὶ ὁ 20
26 30 πρῶτος ἔλαβε γυναῖκα, καὶ ἀποθνήσκων οὐκ ἀφῆκε σπέρμα· καὶ ὁ 21
δεύτερος ἔλαβεν αὐτήν, καὶ ἀπέθανε, καὶ οὐδὲ αὐτὸς ἀφῆκε σπέρμα·
31 καὶ ὁ τρίτος ὡσαύτως. Καὶ ἔλαβον αὐτὴν οἱ ἑπτά, καὶ οὐκ ἀφῆκαν 22
27 28 32 33 σπέρμα. Ἐσχάτη πάντων ἀπέθανε καὶ ἡ γυνή. Ἐν τῇ οὖν ἀναστάσει, 23
ὅταν ἀναστῶσι, τίνος αὐτῶν ἔσται γυνή; οἱ γὰρ ἑπτὰ ἔσχον αὐτὴν
29 34 γυναῖκα. Καὶ ἀποκριθεὶς ὁ Ἰησοῦς εἶπεν αὐτοῖς· Οὐ διὰ τοῦτο 24
30 35 πλανᾶσθε, μὴ εἰδότες τὰς γραφὰς μηδὲ τὴν δύναμιν τοῦ Θεοῦ; ὅταν 25
γὰρ ἐκ νεκρῶν ἀναστῶσιν, οὔτε γαμοῦσιν, οὔτε γαμίσκονται, ἀλλ' εἰσὶν
31 37 ὡς ἄγγελοι [οἱ] ἐν τοῖς οὐρανοῖς. Περὶ δὲ τῶν νεκρῶν, ὅτι ἐγείρονται, 26
οὐκ ἀνέγνωτε ἐν τῇ βίβλῳ Μωϋσέως, ἐπὶ ‡ τῆς βάτου, ὡς εἶπεν αὐτῷ
32 ὁ Θεὸς λέγων· Ἐγὼ ὁ Θεὸς Ἀβραάμ, καὶ ὁ Θεὸς Ἰσαάκ,
38 καὶ ὁ Θεὸς Ἰακώβ; οὐκ ἔστιν ὁ Θεὸς νεκρῶν, ἀλλὰ Θεὸς ζών- 27
των· ὑμεῖς οὖν πολὺ πλανᾶσθε.

13. ἀγρεύσωσι.] This verb, like the Heb. צוד, properly signifies *to make spoil of, catch, take*, as said of beasts, birds, and fishes; but as that implies circumvention, so it metaphorically denotes *to lay snares for any one*, either by words or deeds, and may then be rendered *to ensnare*. Matth. uses the more *special* expression παγιδεύσωσι.

17. [*Comp.* Matt. xvii. 25. Rom. xiii. 7.]

18. [*Comp.* Acts xxiii. 8.]

19. [*Comp.* Deut. xxv. 5, 6.]

— ἔγραψεν ἡμῖν.] Γράφειν is, both in the Classical and Scriptural writers, used as applied to *legislation*, and then denotes to *prescribe*, *enact*.

24. οὐ διὰ — Θεοῦ.] The interrogation here implies a strong affirmation.

26. ἐπὶ τῆς βάτου.] This is usually taken as if there were a *transposition* for ὡς εἶπεν αὐτῷ ὁ Θεὸς ἐπὶ τῆς βάτου. But Wolf, Mich., Rosenm., and Kuin., more properly, adopt the view taken by Beza and Jablonski; who regard this as a *form of citing Scripture* usual, in that age, with the Jewish Doctors; namely, of referring to any particular part of Scripture by naming some remarkable circumstance therein narrated. Thus the sense will be, "in the section which treats of the burning bush." So in Rom. xi. 2. ἢ οὐκ οἴδατε ἐν Ἡλίᾳ τί λέγει ἡ γραφή. And, I would add, the ancient Critics cite various parts of *Homer* in a similar manner; e. gr. ἐν Καταλόγῳ — ἐν Τάφῳ Πατρόκλου, ἐν Νεκυομαντείᾳ. Nay, Thucydides i. 9. himself refers to Homer ἐν τοῦ σκήπτρου τῇ Παραδόσει.

On the present verse compare Exod. iii. 6. Acts vii. 32. Heb. xi. 16.

With respect to the *Article*, it is not certain whether τῆς be the true reading, or τοῦ. But although τοῦ is found in very many of the best MSS., and is received by Matth., Griesb., and Scholz; yet, as the masculine is found only in the earlier Classical writers, not in the *later* ones, who use the feminine, I have, with Fritz., retained the common reading.

27. Θεὸς ζώντων.] Many MSS., some Versions,

MT. LU.

28 Καὶ προσελθὼν εἷς τῶν γραμματέων, ἀκούσας αὐτῶν συζητούντων, 22. 20.
εἰδὼς ὅτι καλῶς αὐτοῖς ἀπεκρίθη, ἐπηρώτησεν αὐτόν· Ποία ἐστὶ 34 35
29 πρώτη ‡ πασῶν ἐντολή; ὁ δὲ Ἰησοῦς ἀπεκρίθη αὐτῷ· Ὅτι πρώτη 36
πασῶν τῶν ἐντολῶν· Ἄκουε, Ἰσραήλ· Κύριος ὁ Θεὸς 37
30 ἡμῶν Κύριος εἷς ἐστι· καὶ ἀγαπήσεις Κύριον τὸν
Θεόν σου ἐξ ὅλης τῆς καρδίας σου, καὶ ἐξ ὅλης τῆς
ψυχῆς σου, καὶ ἐξ ὅλης τῆς διανοίας σου, καὶ ἐξ ὅλης 38 39
31 τῆς ἰσχύος σου. Αὕτη πρώτη ἐντολή. Καὶ δευτέρα ὁμοία, ‡ αὕτη. Ἀγαπήσεις τὸν πλησίον σου ὡς σεαυτόν. μείζων 40
32 τούτων ἄλλη ἐντολὴ οὐκ ἔστι. Καὶ εἶπεν αὐτῷ ὁ γραμματεύς· Καλῶς, διδάσκαλε, ἐπ᾽ ἀληθείας εἶπας, ὅτι εἷς ἐστι· [Θεὸς,] καὶ οὐκ
33 ἔστιν ἄλλος πλὴν αὐτοῦ. Καὶ τὸ ἀγαπᾷν αὐτὸν ἐξ ὅλης τῆς καρδίας,
καὶ ἐξ ὅλης τῆς συνέσεως, καὶ ἐξ ὅλης τῆς ψυχῆς, καὶ ἐξ ὅλης τῆς
ἰσχύος, καὶ τὸ ἀγαπᾷν τὸν πλησίον ὡς ἑαυτὸν, πλεῖόν ἐστι πάντων τῶν
34 ὁλοκαυτωμάτων καὶ [τῶν] θυσιῶν. Καὶ ὁ Ἰησοῦς ἰδὼν αὐτὸν ὅτι νουνεχῶς ἀπεκρίθη, εἶπεν αὐτῷ· Οὐ μακρὰν εἶ ἀπὸ τῆς βασιλείας τοῦ
Θεοῦ. Καὶ οὐδεὶς οὐκέτι ἐτόλμα αὐτὸν ἐπερωτῆσαι.

35 Καὶ ἀποκριθεὶς ὁ Ἰησοῦς ἔλεγε, διδάσκων ἐν τῷ ἱερῷ· Πῶς λέ- 41 41
36 γουσιν οἱ γραμματεῖς, ὅτι ὁ Χριστὸς υἱός ἐστι Δαυΐδ; αὐτὸς γὰρ 43 42
Δαυΐδ λέγει ἐν [τῷ] πνεύματι [τῷ] ἁγίῳ· Εἶπεν ὁ Κύριος τῷ 44

with Euthym. and Theophyl., omit Θεός; which is cancelled, perhaps without good reason, by Griesb., Fritz., and Scholz.

28. [*Comp.* Luke x. 25.]

—πασῶν.] Very many MSS. have here, and just after, πάντων; which is preferred by Mill and Beng., and edited by Matth., Griesb., Tittm., Fritz., and Scholz. But with the idiom by which, in certain formulas, πάντων (in the neuter) is put in the sense all *things* (as Thucyd. iv. 52.) rare even in the Classical writers, it is unlikely that the Evangelist should have been acquainted; and I have seen no example where πάντων is thus brought into immediate concurrence with the Genit feminine. That, indeed, is generally omitted. Perhaps, as the authority for the *former* πάντων is greatly superior to that for the *latter*, Mark may have written in this verse πρώτη πάντων ἐντολή; and in the next, πρώτη πασῶν τῶν ἐντολῶν, which the scribes would be likely to alter into πάντων, in order to adapt it to the former passage. Certainly πάντων cannot (as some imagine) be a *masculine*, and have reference to νόμων.

29. Κύριος—ἐστι.] See Deut. vi. 4. x. 12. Luke x. 27. Vitringa and Campb. take the words as forming two sentences. "The Lord (i. e. Jehovah) is our God: the Lord is one." But, though the verb substantive be admitted in the Hebrew, yet the idiom of that language will not permit the separation of the words אלהינו and יהוה; and the construction in *Greek* will as little permit of it.

31. ὁμοία αὕτη.] See Levit. xix. 18. Luke x. 27. Rom. xiii. 9. Gal. v. 14. James ii. 8. There is here a variation in reading: some MSS. and Versions, with Euthym. and Victor, having ὁμοία αὐτῇ; others, ὁμοία αὐτῆς; others, again, ὁμοία ταύτῃ. The first seems preferable, was approved by Mill and Heupel, and is edited by Fritz. But as the evidence for it is *very slight*, (for that of the *Versions* is scarcely to be admitted,) and as all the varr. lectt. seem to be *so many ways of removing the difficulty* of the common reading, it ought not to have been *received into the text;* it was probably derived from St. Matthew. The sense is, "The second is like [unto it; i. e. in importance]; namely, this." Fritz., indeed, scruples at this *absolute* use of ὅμοιος; but it is found in the Classical writers; and though it may not occur elsewhere in the *Scriptural* ones, that might be by accident, especially as it does not often occur *any where*.

32. καλῶς—εἶπας.] Render, "Of a truth, Master, thou hast spoken well." Θεὸς before εἷς ἐστι is not found in a considerable portion of the best MSS., several Versions, and the Ed. Princ. It seems to be from the margin; and is rightly cancelled by Wets., Matth., Griesb., Tittm., Vat., Fritz., and Scholz. Πλὴν αὐτοῦ is omitted in some MSS., but is defended by many Classical passages cited by the Commentators; to which may be added one more apposite than any of them, from Aristoph. Plut. 106. οὐ γάρ ἐστιν ἄλλος, πλὴν ἐγώ. See my Note on Thucyd. ii. 9. No. 5.

33. συνέσεως.] This is not, as Schleus. and Wahl imagine, for ψυχῆς, but for διανοίας.

34. ἰδὼν—ἀπεκρίθη.] Put by *attraction* for ἰδὼν ὅτι, &c., "perceiving that he had answered wisely." Νουνεχῶς is later Greek for the earlier νουνεχόντως.

36. τῷ πνεύματι τῷ ἁγίῳ.] See Ps. cx. 1. Acts ii. 34. 1 Cor. xv. 25. Heb. i. 13. The *Articles* are omitted in many of the best MSS., and several early Editions; and cancelled by Griesb., Matth., Tittm., Vat., Fritz., and Scholz; rightly, I think, because the omission is not only confirmed by the Var. lect. in Matt. xxii. 43, but by the context, which, says Middlet., requires the *influence* of the Holy Spirit.

I have, just before, with Fritz., edited λέγει, for εἶπεν; for though the direct evidence for it be but

MT. LU.
22. 20. κυρίῳ μου· Κάθου ἐκ δεξιῶν μου, ἕως ἂν θῶ τοὺς
45 43 44 ἐχθρούς σου ὑποπόδιον τῶν ποδῶν σου. Αὐτὸς οὖν Δαβὶδ 37
λέγει αὐτὸν κύριον καὶ πόθεν υἱὸς αὐτοῦ ἐστι; Καὶ ὁ πολὺς ὄχλος
ἤκουεν αὐτοῦ ἡδέως.

46 Καὶ ἔλεγεν αὐτοῖς ἐν τῇ διδαχῇ αὐτοῦ· Βλέπετε ἀπὸ τῶν γραμ- 38
23. ματέων, τῶν θελόντων ἐν στολαῖς περιπατεῖν, καὶ ἀσπασμοὺς ἐν ταῖς
6 7 ἀγοραῖς, καὶ πρωτοκαθεδρίας ἐν ταῖς συναγωγαῖς, καὶ πρωτοκλισίας ἐν 39
14 47 τοῖς δείπνοις. Οἱ κατεσθίοντες τὰς οἰκίας τῶν χηρῶν, καὶ προφάσει 40
24. 21. μακρὰ προσευχόμενοι· οὗτοι λήψονται περισσότερον κρίμα.
1 Καὶ καθίσας ὁ Ἰησοῦς κατέναντι τοῦ γαζοφυλακίου, ἐθεώρει πῶς ὁ 41
ὄχλος βάλλει χαλκὸν εἰς τὸ γαζοφυλάκιον· καὶ πολλοὶ πλούσιοι ἔβαλλον
2 πολλά. καὶ ἐλθοῦσα μία χήρα πτωχὴ ἔβαλε λεπτὰ δύο, ὅ ἐστι κοδράν- 42
3 της. Καὶ προσκαλεσάμενος τοὺς μαθητὰς αὐτοῦ, λέγει αὐτοῖς· Ἀμὴν 43
λέγω ὑμῖν, ὅτι ἡ χήρα αὕτη ἡ πτωχὴ πλεῖον πάντων βέβληκε τῶν βα-
4 λόντων εἰς τὸ γαζοφυλάκιον. Πάντες γὰρ ἐκ τοῦ περισσεύοντος αὐτοῖς 44
ἔβαλον· αὕτη δὲ, ἐκ τῆς ὑστερήσεως αὐτῆς, πάντα ὅσα εἶχεν ἔβαλεν,
ὅλον τὸν βίον αὐτῆς.

1 5 XIII. ΚΑΙ ἐκπορευομένου αὐτοῦ ἐκ τοῦ ἱεροῦ, λέγει αὐτῷ εἷς τῶν 1
μαθητῶν αὐτοῦ· Διδάσκαλε, ἴδε, ποταποὶ λίθοι, καὶ ποταπαὶ οἰκο-
2 6 δομαί! Καὶ ὁ Ἰησοῦς ἀποκριθεὶς εἶπεν αὐτῷ· Βλέπεις ταύτας τὰς 2

slight, yet the *indirect* is very strong; since (as Fritz. observes) it is found in the parallel passages of Mark and Luke, and is confirmed by the λέγει, at ver. 37. I would add, that the λέγει of very numerous MSS. and Editions for εἶπεν, in the next clause (which, therefore, Matth., Griesb., and Scholz receive into the text, though at variance with the Sept. and the parallel passages of Matthew and Luke) is, I doubt not, meant for *this*; a sort of mistake frequent in all authors. Indeed, propriety would seem to require that λέγειν should be used of a *man* (as David), and εἰπεῖν of *God*, the latter being a more significant and authoritative term.

38. στολαῖς.] The στολὴ was an Oriental garment, descending to the ancles, and worn by persons of distinction, as Kings (1 Chron. xv. 27. John iii. 6), Priests (3 Esdr. i. 1. v. 81), and honourable persons: (see Xen. Cyr. i. 4. 26. ii. 4, 1. Luke xv. 22.) and were affected by the Jurists of the Pharisaical sect.

40. οἱ κατεσθίοντες, &c.] This is by most Commentators esteemed a *solecism*; but similar constructions are found in the Classical writers. It is *better* regarded by some recent Commentators as an example of *anacoluthon*. Fritz., however, objects to that principle, as unsuitable to the simplicity of construction in the passage; and he would take the whole sentence as *exclamatory*, "these devourers!" &c., these shall receive, &c. I prefer, however, with Grot., to suppose an *Asyndeton*, and render, "those who devour," &c., "those shall receive," &c.; which method involves the *least* difficulty. [*Comp.* 2 Tim. iii. 6. Tit. i. 11.]

41. [*See* 2 Kings xii. 9.]

42. λεπτά.] The λεπτὸν was a very minute coin, the half of a *quadrans* or farthing. It is in our common translation rendered *mite*; which word comes from *minute*, as *farthing* from *fourthing*, formed in imitation of *quadrans*.

43. πλεῖον] i. e. more in proportion to her substance. [*Comp.* 2 Cor. viii. 12.]

44. ἐκ τοῦ περισσεύοντος αὐτοῖς] for ἐκ τοῦ περισσεύματος, which is found in some MSS. here and at Matthew and Luke, but is doubtless a correction. Τὸν βίον αὐτῆς, "her means of living;" a signification of βίος common both in the Classical writers and the Sept.

XIII. 1. ποταποὶ λίθοι.] These were indeed stupendous; in proof of which the Commentators adduce Joseph. Ant. xv. 11, 3. Bell. v. 5, 6, (from which passages it is said that the stones of the temple were some of them 45 cubits in length, 5 in depth, and 6 in breadth. It is strange, however, they did not see that the latter account, as far as it regards the dimensions of the stones, makes the former one seem almost incredible. For it represents them as only about 25 cubits long, 8 in height, and about 12 in depth. It is not so much the excessive *length* spoken of (for in Bell. i. 21, 6. Josephus speaks of the stones of Strato tower as some of them 50 *feet* long, 9 high, and 10 broad) as the *disproportion in breadth*, which affords room for suspicion. And as this account differs so materially from the *other* in Josephus, I cannot but suspect that for μ′ we should read κ′, which will make the number *twenty-five*. Thus both accounts will exactly tally. I cannot omit to add, that though I have carefully examined almost all the accounts which the ancients have left us as to the dimensions of stones used for building, I have never found any to exceed 35 *feet*. The exclamation of the Apostles here is illustrated by what Josephus says at Bell. v. 5, 6. namely, that the whole of the exterior of the Temple, both as regarded stones and workmanship, was calculated to excite astonishment (ἔκπληξιν.) [*Comp.* 1 Kings ix. 7.]

MT. LU.
μεγάλας οἰκοδομάς; Οὐ μὴ ἀφεθῇ λίθος ἐπὶ λίθῳ, ὃς οὐ μὴ κατα- 24. 21.
3 λυθῇ. Καὶ, καθημένου αὐτοῦ εἰς τὸ ὄρος τῶν Ἐλαιῶν κατέναντι τοῦ 3
ἱεροῦ, ἐπηρώτων αὐτὸν κατ' ἰδίαν Πέτρος καὶ Ἰάκωβος καὶ Ἰωάννης 7
4 καὶ Ἀνδρέας· Εἰπὲ ἡμῖν, πότε ταῦτα ἔσται; καὶ τί τὸ σημεῖον ὅταν
5 μέλλῃ πάντα ταῦτα συντελεῖσθαι; Ὁ δὲ Ἰησοῦς ἀποκριθεὶς αὐτοῖς 4
6 ἤρξατο λέγειν· Βλέπετε μή τις ὑμᾶς πλανήσῃ. Πολλοὶ γὰρ ἐλεύσον- 5
ται ἐπὶ τῷ ὀνόματί μου, λέγοντες· Ὅτι ἐγώ εἰμι· καὶ πολλοὺς πλανή-
7 σουσιν. Ὅταν δὲ ἀκούσητε πολέμους καὶ ἀκοὰς πολέμων, μὴ θροεῖσθε· 9
8 δεῖ γὰρ γενέσθαι· ἀλλ' οὔπω τὸ τέλος. Ἐγερθήσεται γὰρ ἔθνος ἐπὶ 7 10
ἔθνος, καὶ βασιλεία ἐπὶ βασιλείαν· καὶ ἔσονται σεισμοὶ κατὰ τόπους, 11
9 καὶ ἔσονται λιμοὶ καὶ ταραχαί. ἀρχαὶ ὠδίνων ταῦτα. Βλέπετε δὲ 8
ὑμεῖς ἑαυτούς· παραδώσουσι γὰρ ὑμᾶς εἰς συνέδρια, καὶ εἰς συνα- 9 12
γωγὰς δαρήσεσθε, καὶ ἐπὶ ἡγεμόνων καὶ βασιλέων σταθήσεσθε ἕνεκεν
10 ἐμοῦ, εἰς μαρτύριον αὐτοῖς. Καὶ εἰς πάντα τὰ ἔθνη δεῖ πρῶτον κη- 14 13
11 ρυχθῆναι τὸ εὐαγγέλιον. Ὅταν δὲ ἀγάγωσιν ὑμᾶς παραδιδόντες, μὴ 14
προμεριμνᾶτε τί λαλήσητε, μηδὲ μελετᾶτε· ἀλλ', ὃ ἐὰν δοθῇ ὑμῖν ἐν 15
ἐκείνῃ τῇ ὥρᾳ, τοῦτο λαλεῖτε· οὐ γάρ ἐστε ὑμεῖς οἱ λαλοῦντες, ἀλλὰ
12 τὸ Πνεῦμα τὸ ἅγιον. Παραδώσει δὲ ἀδελφὸς ἀδελφὸν εἰς θάνατον, 16
καὶ πατὴρ τέκνον· καὶ ἐπαναστήσονται τέκνα ἐπὶ γονεῖς, καὶ θανατώ-
13 σουσιν αὐτούς. Καὶ ἔσεσθε μισούμενοι ὑπὸ πάντων διὰ τὸ ὄνομά 9
μου· ὁ δὲ ὑπομείνας εἰς τέλος οὗτος σωθήσεται. 13 19
14 Ὅταν δὲ ἴδητε τὸ βδέλυγμα τῆς ἐρημώσεως, τὸ ῥηθὲν ὑπὸ Δανιὴλ 15 20
τοῦ προφήτου, ἑστὼς ὅπου οὐ δεῖ, [ὁ ἀναγινώσκων νοείτω·] τότε οἱ 21
15 ἐν τῇ Ἰουδαίᾳ φευγέτωσαν εἰς τὰ ὄρη· ὁ δὲ ἐπὶ τοῦ δώματος μὴ 17
καταβάτω εἰς τὴν οἰκίαν, μηδὲ εἰσελθέτω ἆραί τι ἐκ τῆς οἰκίας αὐτοῦ·
16 καὶ ὁ εἰς τὸν ἀγρὸν ὢν μὴ ἐπιστρεψάτω εἰς τὰ ὀπίσω ἆραι τὸ ἱμάτιον 18
17 αὐτοῦ. Οὐαὶ δὲ ταῖς ἐν γαστρὶ ἐχούσαις καὶ ταῖς θηλαζούσαις ἐν 19 23
18 ἐκείναις ταῖς ἡμέραις! προσεύχεσθε δὲ, ἵνα μὴ γένηται ἡ φυγὴ ὑμῶν 20
19 χειμῶνος. Ἔσονται γὰρ αἱ ἡμέραι ἐκεῖναι θλῖψις, οἵα οὐ γέγονε 22
τοιαύτη ἀπ' ἀρχῆς κτίσεως, ἧς ἔκτισεν ὁ Θεὸς, ἕως τοῦ νῦν, καὶ οὐ
20 μὴ γένηται. Καὶ εἰ μὴ Κύριος ἐκολόβωσε τὰς ἡμέρας, οὐκ ἂν ἐσώθη 22
πᾶσα σὰρξ, ἀλλὰ διὰ τοὺς ἐκλεκτοὺς, οὓς ἐξελέξατο, ἐκολόβωσε τὰς
21 ἡμέρας. Καὶ τότε ἐάν τις ὑμῖν εἴπῃ· Ἰδοὺ, ὧδε ὁ Χριστὸς, ἤ· 23
22 ἰδοὺ, ἐκεῖ· μὴ πιστεύσητε. Ἐγερθήσονται γὰρ ψευδόχριστοι καὶ ψευ- 24
δοπροφῆται· καὶ δώσουσι σημεῖα καὶ τέρατα, πρὸς τὸ ἀποπλανᾷν, εἰ
23 δυνατὸν, καὶ τοὺς ἐκλεκτούς. Ὑμεῖς δὲ βλέπετε· ἰδοὺ, προείρηκα 25
24 ὑμῖν πάντα. Ἀλλ' ἐν ἐκείναις ταῖς ἡμέραις, μετὰ τὴν θλῖψιν ἐκείνην, 29 25
25 ὁ ἥλιος σκοτισθήσεται, καὶ ἡ σελήνη οὐ δώσει τὸ φέγγος αὐτῆς· καὶ
οἱ ἀστέρες τοῦ οὐρανοῦ ἔσονται ἐκπίπτοντες, καὶ αἱ δυνάμεις αἱ ἐν

11. *μελετᾶτε.*] Μελετᾷν, in the Classical writers, is used of the *fore-thought*, *study*, and *elaboration* of Orations, in opposition to *extemporary* oratory. Thus the declamations of the Rhetoricians were called μελέται. [*Comp.* Matt. x. 19. Luke xii. 11.]

13. [*Comp.* Matt. x. 22. Rev. ii. 7. 10.]

14. [*Comp.* Dan. ix. 27. xii. 11.]

21. [*Comp.* Luke xvii. 23.]

22. [*Comp.* Deut. xiii. 1. 2 Thess. ii. 11.]

24. [*Comp.* Is. xiii. 10. Ezek. xxxii. 7. Joel ii. 10, 31. Rev. vi. 12.]

25. *οἱ ἀστέρες τοῦ οὐρανοῦ ἔσ. ἐκπ.*] This passage is inadequately represented by all Translators. The sense is, "the stars of heaven shall be wan-

MT. LU.
24. 21. τοῖς οὐρανοῖς σαλευθήσονται. Καὶ τότε ὄψονται τὸν Υἱὸν τοῦ ἀνθρώ- 26
30 26 27 που ἐρχόμενον ἐν νεφέλαις μετὰ δυνάμεως πολλῆς καὶ δόξης. Καὶ 27
31 τότε ἀποστελεῖ τοὺς ἀγγέλους αὐτοῦ, καὶ ἐπισυνάξει τοὺς ἐκλεκτοὺς
αὐτοῦ ἐκ τῶν τεσσάρων ἀνέμων, ἀπ' ἄκρου γῆς ἕως ἄκρου οὐρανοῦ.
32 29 Ἀπὸ δὲ τῆς συκῆς μάθετε τὴν παραβολήν· ὅταν αὐτῆς ἤδη ὁ 28
30 κλάδος ἁπαλὸς γένηται, καὶ ἐκφυῇ τὰ φύλλα, γινώσκετε ὅτι ἐγγὺς τὸ
33 31 θέρος ἐστίν· οὕτω καὶ ὑμεῖς, ὅταν ταῦτα ἴδητε γινόμενα, γινώσκετε 29
34 32 ὅτι ἐγγύς ἐστιν ἐπὶ θύραις. Ἀμὴν λέγω ὑμῖν, ὅτι οὐ μὴ παρέλθῃ ἡ 30
35 33 γενεὰ αὕτη, μέχρις οὗ πάντα ταῦτα γένηται. Ὁ οὐρανὸς καὶ ἡ γῆ 31
παρελεύσονται· οἱ δὲ λόγοι μου οὐ μὴ παρέλθωσι.
36 Περὶ δὲ τῆς ἡμέρας ἐκείνης ἢ τῆς ὥρας, οὐδεὶς οἶδεν· οὐδὲ οἱ 32
ἄγγελοι οἱ ἐν οὐρανῷ, οὐδὲ ὁ Υἱός· εἰ μὴ ὁ Πατήρ.
Βλέπετε, ἀγρυπνεῖτε καὶ προσεύχεσθε· οὐκ οἴδατε γὰρ πότε ὁ καιρός 33
ἐστιν. Ὡς ἄνθρωπος ἀπόδημος ἀφεὶς τὴν οἰκίαν αὐτοῦ, καὶ δοὺς τοῖς 34
δούλοις αὐτοῦ τὴν ἐξουσίαν καὶ ἑκάστῳ τὸ ἔργον αὐτοῦ, καὶ τῷ θυρωρῷ ἐνετείλατο ἵνα γρηγορῇ. Γρηγορεῖτε οὖν· οὐκ οἴδατε γὰρ πότε ὁ 35
κύριος τῆς οἰκίας ἔρχεται· ὀψὲ, ἢ μεσονυκτίου, ἢ ἀλεκτοροφωνίας, ἢ
πρωΐ· μὴ ἐλθὼν ἐξαίφνης, εὕρῃ ὑμᾶς καθεύδοντας. Ἃ δὲ ὑμῖν λέγω, 36
26. 22. πᾶσι λέγω· Γρηγορεῖτε. 37
2 1 XIV. ΗΝ δὲ τὸ πάσχα καὶ τὰ ἄζυμα μετὰ δύο ἡμέρας· καὶ 1
3 2 ἐζήτουν οἱ ἀρχιερεῖς καὶ οἱ γραμματεῖς, πῶς αὐτὸν ἐν δόλῳ κρατήσαν-
4 τες ἀποκτείνωσιν. Ἔλεγον δέ· Μὴ ἐν τῇ ἑορτῇ, μήποτε θόρυβος 2
5 ἔσται τοῦ λαοῦ. Καὶ ὄντος αὐτοῦ ἐν Βηθανίᾳ, ἐν τῇ οἰκίᾳ Σίμωνος 3
6
7 τοῦ λεπροῦ κατακειμένου αὐτοῦ, ἦλθε γυνὴ ἔχουσα ἀλάβαστρον μύρου

ing;" i. e. shall gradually lose their light. On the use of *εἰμὶ* and the participle, for some verb, see Winer's Gr. Gr. § 39. 2. All the difference here between the Evangelists is, that Mark is more graphically minute than Matthew and Luke.

26. [*Comp.* Dan. vii. 13. Rev. i. 7. 1 Thess. iv. 16. 2 Thess. i. 10.]

28. *ἐκφυῇ*] See Note on Matt. xxiv. 32.

31. [*Comp.* Ps. cii. 27. Is. xl. 8. Heb. i. 11.]

32. *ἢ*] This (for the common reading *καὶ*) is found in most of the ancient MSS., Versions, and Fathers, and is received by almost every Editor from Wets. to Scholz. Here comp. Acts i. 7.

33. [*Comp.* Luke xii. 40. 1 Thess. v. 6.]

XIV. [*Comp.* John xi. 55. xiii. 1.]

3. [*Comp.* Luke vii. 37. John xi. 2.]

— *πιστικῆς*] With this word the Commentators have been not a little perplexed; and hence their opinions are very various. Besides conjectural alterations, and derivations from some name of place, which are alike inadmissible, there are *three interpretations* worthy of notice. 1. That of Camer., Beza, Grot., Wets., and Rosenm., who think that *πιστικῆς* is put, per metathesin, for *σπικάτου*, as supra vii. 4. *ξέστη* for *sextario*. And this is somewhat confirmed by the Vulgate *Spicati*. But there is little other authority for it, or indeed, *probability*; for why (as Fritz. remarks) should not St. Mark have at once used *σπικάτου*, as Galen often does? 2. Others, as Erasm., Luther, Vatabl., Suic., Capell., Casaub., Salmas., Scalig., Le Clerc, Beng., Kypke, Heum., Kuin., Tittm., and Wahl, derive the word from *πίστις* (as from *μάντις, μαντικός*; from *πρᾶξις, πρακτικός*; from *κρίσις, κριτικὸς*), and take it to signify *pure, genuine, unadulterated*. For that nard was often *adulterated*, appears from Pliny and Diosc., the former of whom mentions a *pseudo*-nardus. Fritz., however, objects, that then *πιστικὸς* would be *qui fidem vel facere vel habere potest*, a signification plainly unsuitable to nard. And to derive the term from *πιστὸς*, would lead to a like result. 3. Pisc., H. Steph., Schmid, Schwartz, Heupel, Fischer, Schneider, Schleusn., and Fritz. derive it from *πίνειν* or *πιεῖν* (or, as Fritz. maintains, *πιπίσκειν*: thus *πιπίσκω, πίσω, ἔπισα, πέπισμαι, πιστὸς, πιστικός*: for adjectives in —*ικός* are often derived from verbals in —*τός*.), and they take it to mean *liquid*. Fritz., however, explains *potable*; and he shews, from some passages of Athenæus, that unguents were sometimes *drunk* by the ancients. Upon the whole, however, he has better succeeded in proving that the interpretation *liquid* or *potable* is *probably true*, than that the sense, *genuine*, is *certainly false*. The trifling *abuse* he complains of will not be fatal to that interpretation; for it may very well be, that Mark here (as occasionally elsewhere) uses a term of the common Greek dialect; and as the interpretation is strongly supported by the ancient Versions and Fathers, I see no reason to abandon it. So Eusebius Apod. i. 9. (cited by Fritz.) calls the Gospel *τὸ πιστικὸν τῆς καινῆς διαθήκης κρᾶμα*.

MT. LU.

νάρδου πιστικῆς πολυτελοῦς· καὶ συντρίψασα τὸ ἀλάβαστρον, κατέχεεν 26. 22.
4 αὐτοῦ κατὰ τῆς κεφαλῆς. Ἦσαν δέ τινες ἀγανακτοῦντες πρὸς ἑαυτούς, 8
5 καὶ λέγοντες· Εἰς τί ἡ ἀπώλεια αὕτη τοῦ μύρου γέγονεν; Ἠδύνατο 9
γὰρ τοῦτο πραθῆναι ἐπάνω τριακοσίων δηναρίων, καὶ δοθῆναι τοῖς
6 πτωχοῖς· καὶ ἐνεβριμῶντο αὐτῇ· Ὁ δὲ Ἰησοῦς εἶπεν· Ἄφετε αὐτήν· 10
7 τί αὐτῇ κόπους παρέχετε; καλὸν ἔργον εἰργάσατο ἐν * ἐμοί. πάν- 11
τοτε γὰρ τοὺς πτωχοὺς ἔχετε μεθ᾽ ἑαυτῶν, καὶ, ὅταν θέλητε, δύνασθε
8 αὐτοὺς εὖ ποιῆσαι· ἐμὲ δὲ οὐ πάντοτε ἔχετε. Ὃ ἔσχεν αὕτη, ἐποίησε. 12
9 Προέλαβε μυρίσαι μου τὸ σῶμα εἰς τὸν ἐνταφιασμόν. Ἀμὴν λέγω 13
ὑμῖν· ὅπου ἂν κηρυχθῇ τὸ εὐαγγέλιον τοῦτο εἰς ὅλον τὸν κόσμον,
10 καὶ ὃ ἐποίησεν αὕτη λαληθήσεται εἰς μνημόσυνον αὐτῆς. Καὶ ὁ Ἰού- 14 3
δας ὁ Ἰσκαριώτης, εἷς τῶν δώδεκα, ἀπῆλθε πρὸς τοὺς ἀρχιερεῖς, ἵνα
11 παραδῷ αὐτὸν αὐτοῖς. Οἱ δὲ ἀκούσαντες ἐχάρησαν καὶ ἐπηγγείλαντο 4
αὐτῷ ἀργύριον δοῦναι· καὶ ἐζήτει πῶς εὐκαίρως αὐτὸν παραδῷ. 15 5
16 6
12 ΚΑΙ τῇ πρώτῃ ἡμέρᾳ τῶν ἀζύμων, ὅτε τὸ πάσχα ἔθυον, λέγουσιν 17 7
αὐτῷ οἱ μαθηταὶ αὐτοῦ· Ποῦ θέλεις ἀπελθόντες ἑτοιμάσωμεν ἵνα 8
13 φάγῃς τὸ πάσχα; Καὶ ἀποστέλλει δύο τῶν μαθητῶν αὐτοῦ, καὶ 8
λέγει αὐτοῖς· Ὑπάγετε εἰς τὴν πόλιν· καὶ ἀπαντήσει ὑμῖν ἄνθρωπος 18 10
14 κεράμιον ὕδατος βαστάζων· ἀκολουθήσατε αὐτῷ, καὶ ὅπου ἐὰν εἰσέλθῃ, εἴπατε τῷ οἰκοδεσπότῃ, ὅτι ὁ διδάσκαλος λέγει· Ποῦ ἐστι τὸ 11
15 κατάλυμα, ὅπου τὸ πάσχα μετὰ τῶν μαθητῶν μου φάγω; Καὶ αὐ- 12
τὸς ὑμῖν δείξει ‡ ἀνώγεον μέγα ἐστρωμένον ἕτοιμον· ἐκεῖ ἑτοιμάσατε
16 ἡμῖν. Καὶ ἐξῆλθον οἱ μαθηταὶ αὐτοῦ· καὶ ἦλθον εἰς τὴν πόλιν, καὶ 19
εὗρον καθὼς εἶπεν αὐτοῖς· καὶ ἡτοίμασαν τὸ πάσχα. 13
17 Καὶ ὀψίας γενομένης, ἔρχεται μετὰ τῶν δώδεκα· καὶ ἀνακειμένων 20 14
18 αὐτῶν καὶ ἐσθιόντων, εἶπεν ὁ Ἰησοῦς· Ἀμὴν λέγω ὑμῖν, ὅτι εἷς ἐξ 21

—*καὶ συντρίψασα*] Here, again, the Commentators are at issue on the sense of *συντρίψασα*. Some take it to mean "having broken it in pieces;" others, "having shaken it up." But the former would be unnecessary, and unsuitable to the purpose in view; and the latter interpretation proceeds too much upon hypothesis, and is utterly repugnant to the sense of the word; as is that of others, "rubbing it in." The true interpretation is, no doubt, that of Drus., De Dieu, Krebs, Rosenm., Kuin., Schleusn., Wahl, Bretschn., and Fritz., who take it to mean "*diffracto orificio*, alabastrum aperuit." The term was, it seems, used of the *opening* of flasks of oil or liquid ointment; which was, by knocking off the tip end of the narrow neck, where the orifice was sealed up, to preserve the contents. Now this, plainly, might be done without wasting the contents. The above view of the sense is confirmed by the ancient Versions, which express the general signification "*aperuerunt*."

6. *ἐν ἐμοί.*] This (for *εἰς ἐμὲ*) is found in almost all the best MSS. and early Editions; is adopted by Wets. and edited by Beng., Matth., Vat., Tittm., Fritz., and Scholz; no doubt, rightly; for its Hebrew character and greater difficulty attest its genuineness. [*Comp.* Deut. xv. 11.]

8. *ἔσχεν*] i. e. *ἐδύνατο*; a sense of *ἔχειν*, like that of *habere* in Latin, common in the Classical writers. Προέλαβε, i. e. *προέφθασε*, "anticipated," pre-occupied.

12. See Exod. xii. 17. Deut. xvi. 5.

13. *ἄνθρωπος*] From the word being opposed to *οἰκοδεσπότης* in the following verse, and from the servile nature of the occupation, it may be inferred that this was a domestic.

—*κεράμιον*] The Commentators concur in recognizing here an ellipse of *σκεῦος*, or *ἀγγεῖον*; and they produce examples both of the elliptical and the complete phrase. But the examples of the *latter* have *κεραμεῖον*, which is, *beyond doubt*, an adjective, whereas *κεράμιον*, as Fritz. shows, was always considered as a *substantive*.

14. *κατάλυμα*] See note on Luke ii. 15. 7.

15. *ἀνώγεον*] An upper room, used by the Jews for the same purposes as those to which our dining-rooms and parlours are applied. Griesb., Fritz., and Scholz edit, from the best MSS., *ἀνώγαιον*. But the thing is not so certain as to warrant a change. Ἐστρωμένον has a reference to the preparation of beds, couches, or sofas, carpets, pillows, stools, &c., such as among the Oriental nations, supply the place of chairs, tables, and indeed almost all the other furniture of a room.

17. See John xiii. 21.

18. [*Comp.* Ps. xli. 9. Acts i. 16.]

MT. LU.
26. 22. ὑμῶν παραδώσει με ὁ ἐσθίων μετ᾽ ἐμοῦ. Οἱ δὲ ἤρξαντο λυπεῖσθαι, 19
22 23 καὶ λέγειν αὐτῷ, εἷς καθ᾽ εἷς· Μήτι ἐγώ; καὶ ἄλλος· Μήτι
23 ἐγώ; Ὁ δὲ ἀποκριθεὶς εἶπεν αὐτοῖς· Εἷς ἐκ τῶν δώδεκα, ὁ ἐμβα- 20
24 21 πτόμενος μετ᾽ ἐμοῦ εἰς τὸ τρυβλίον. ὁ μὲν Υἱὸς τοῦ ἀνθρώπου ὑπάγει, 21
καθὼς γέγραπται περὶ αὐτοῦ· οὐαὶ δὲ τῷ ἀνθρώπῳ ἐκείνῳ, δι᾽ οὗ
ὁ Υἱὸς τοῦ ἀνθρώπου παραδίδοται. καλὸν ἦν αὐτῷ, εἰ οὐκ ἐγεννήθη
ὁ ἄνθρωπος ἐκεῖνος.
26 Καὶ ἐσθιόντων αὐτῶν, λαβὼν ὁ Ἰησοῦς ἄρτον, εὐλογήσας ἔκλασε, καὶ 22
ἔδωκεν αὐτοῖς καὶ εἶπε· Λάβετε φάγετε. τοῦτό ἐστι τὸ σῶμά μου.
27 Καὶ λαβὼν τὸ ποτήριον εὐχαριστήσας ἔδωκεν αὐτοῖς· καὶ ἔπιον ἐξ 23
28 αὐτοῦ πάντες. καὶ εἶπεν αὐτοῖς· Τοῦτό ἐστι τὸ αἷμά μου, τὸ τῆς 24
29 καινῆς διαθήκης, τὸ περὶ πολλῶν ἐκχυνόμενον. Ἀμὴν λέγω ὑμῖν, ὅτι 25
οὐκέτι οὐ μὴ πίω ἐκ τοῦ γεννήματος τῆς ἀμπέλου, ἕως τῆς ἡμέρας
ἐκείνης, ὅταν αὐτὸ πίνω καινὸν ἐν τῇ βασιλείᾳ τοῦ Θεοῦ.
30 39 Καὶ ὑμνήσαντες, ἐξῆλθον εἰς τὸ ὄρος τῶν Ἐλαιῶν. καὶ λέγει αὐτοῖς 26
31 ὁ Ἰησοῦς· Ὅτι πάντες σκανδαλισθήσεσθε ἐν ἐμοὶ ἐν τῇ νυκτὶ ταύτῃ· 27
ὅτι γέγραπται· Πατάξω τὸν ποιμένα, καὶ διασκορπισθήσεται τὰ πρό-
32 βατα. ἀλλὰ μετὰ τὸ ἐγερθῆναί με, προάξω ὑμᾶς εἰς τὴν Γαλιλαίαν 28
33 Ὁ δὲ Πέτρος ἔφη αὐτῷ· Καὶ εἰ πάντες σκανδαλισθήσονται, ἀλλ᾽ οὐκ 29
34 ἐγώ. Καὶ λέγει αὐτῷ ὁ Ἰησοῦς· Ἀμὴν λέγω σοι, ὅτι σὺ σήμερον ἐν 30
35 τῇ νυκτὶ ταύτῃ, πρὶν ἢ δὶς ἀλέκτορα φωνῆσαι, τρὶς ἀπαρνήσῃ με. ὁ δὲ 31
ἐκ περισσοῦ ἔλεγε μᾶλλον· Ἐάν με δέῃ συναποθανεῖν σοι, οὐ μή σε
ἀπαρνήσομαι. ὡσαύτως δὲ καὶ πάντες ἔλεγον.
36 40 ΚΑΙ ἔρχονται εἰς χωρίον, οὗ τὸ ὄνομα Γεθσημανῆ· καὶ λέγει τοῖς 32
37 μαθηταῖς αὐτοῦ· Καθίσατε ὧδε ἕως προσεύξωμαι. Καὶ παραλαμβά- 33
νει τὸν Πέτρον καὶ τὸν Ἰάκωβον καὶ Ἰωάννην μεθ᾽ ἑαυτοῦ. καὶ ἤρξα-
38 το ἐκθαμβεῖσθαι καὶ ἀδημονεῖν. Καὶ λέγει αὐτοῖς· Περίλυπός ἐστιν 34
ἡ ψυχή μου ἕως θανάτου· μείνατε ὧδε καὶ γρηγορεῖτε. Καὶ προελ- 35
39 41 θὼν μικρὸν, ἔπεσεν ἐπὶ τῆς γῆς, καὶ προσηύχετο, ἵνα εἰ δυνατόν ἐστι,
42 παρέλθῃ ἀπ᾽ αὐτοῦ ἡ ὥρα· καὶ ἔλεγεν· Ἀββᾶ ὁ πατὴρ, πάντα 36
δυνατά σοι. παρένεγκε τὸ ποτήριον ἀπ᾽ ἐμοῦ τοῦτο· ἀλλ᾽ οὐ τί ἐγὼ
40 45 θέλω, ἀλλὰ τί σύ. καὶ ἔρχεται καὶ εὑρίσκει αὐτοὺς καθεύδοντας, καὶ 37
46 λέγει τῷ Πέτρῳ· Σίμων, καθεύδεις; οὐκ ἴσχυσας μίαν ὥραν γρηγορῆ-

19. εἷς καθ᾽ εἷς] A Hebrew idiom for καθ᾽ ἕνα, as the Commentators say; but it is found also in other writers, though, indeed, almost wholly those who formed their style on the N. T. Fritz. has proved that the κατὰ cannot be taken, as some suppose, for καὶ εἶτα.

22. [*Comp.* 1 Cor. xi. 24.]

27. Πατάξω, &c.] See Zach. xiii. 7.

28. [See infra xvi. 7.]

29. [See John xiii. 37.]

30. σύ.] This is found in almost all the ancient MSS. and the early Edd., confirmed by most of the ancient Versions, and has been, with reason, received by Wets., Matth., Griesb., Knapp, Vater, Tittm., Fritz., and Scholz. It was, no doubt, absorbed by the σή following. The word is emphatical.

32. [*Comp.* John xviii. 1.]

34. [*Comp.* Luke xxii. 44. John xii. 27.]

36. [*Comp.* John vi. 38.]

— Ἀββᾶ ὁ πατήρ.] There has been no little difference of opinion as to the reason for this seeming pleonasm, and the exact force of the idiom. The ancient Greek Interpreters, several early modern ones (as Beza, Lightf., and Leigh), and most of the later Commentators (as Newcome, Campb., Wakef., Fisch., Schleus., Rosenm., and Kuin.), think that ὁ πατὴρ is added, agreeably to a custom by which the Jews used to call a person or thing by two names, one Hebrew and the other Greek. But I rather agree with others (as Fritz.), that the latter is an *interpretation* or *explication* of the former, as in Rom. viii. 15. Gal. iv. 6. As to Ἀββᾶ, it is (as Fritz. observes) used agreeably to the custom (found even in the

MT. LU.

38 σαι; Γρηγορεῖτε καὶ προσεύχεσθε, ἵνα μὴ εἰσέλθητε εἰς πειρασμόν. 26. 22.
39 τὸ μὲν πνεῦμα πρόθυμον, ἡ δὲ σὰρξ ἀσθενής. Καὶ πάλιν ἀπελθὼν 41 42
40 προσηύξατο, τὸν αὐτὸν λόγον εἰπών. Καὶ ὑποστρέψας εὗρεν αὐτοὺς 43
πάλιν καθεύδοντας· ἦσαν γὰρ οἱ ὀφθαλμοὶ αὐτῶν βεβαρημένοι, καὶ
οὐκ ᾔδεισαν τί αὐτῷ ἀποκριθῶσι.
41 Καὶ ἔρχεται τὸ τρίτον, καὶ λέγει αὐτοῖς· Καθεύδετε τὸ λοιπὸν καὶ 45
ἀναπαύεσθε. ἀπέχει! ἦλθεν ἡ ὥρα· ἰδού, παραδίδοται ὁ Υἱὸς τοῦ
42 ἀνθρώπου εἰς τὰς χεῖρας τῶν ἁμαρτωλῶν.—Ἐγείρεσθε! ἄγωμεν! 46
ἰδού, ὁ παραδιδούς με ἤγγικε.
43 Καὶ εὐθέως, ἔτι αὐτοῦ λαλοῦντος, παραγίνεται Ἰούδας, εἷς ὢν τῶν 47 47
δώδεκα, καὶ μετ᾽ αὐτοῦ ὄχλος πολὺς μετὰ μαχαιρῶν καὶ ξύλων, παρὰ
44 τῶν ἀρχιερέων καὶ τῶν γραμματέων καὶ τῶν πρεσβυτέρων. Δεδώκει δὲ 48
ὁ παραδιδοὺς αὐτὸν σύσσημον αὐτοῖς, λέγων· Ὃν ἂν φιλήσω, αὐτός
45 ἐστι· κρατήσατε αὐτόν, καὶ ἀπαγάγετε ἀσφαλῶς· Καὶ ἐλθών, εὐθέως 49 48
46 προσελθὼν αὐτῷ λέγει· Ῥαββί, ῥαββί· καὶ κατεφίλησεν αὐτόν. Οἱ 50
δὲ ἐπέβαλον ἐπ᾽ αὐτὸν τὰς χεῖρας αὐτῶν, καὶ ἐκράτησαν αὐτόν.
47 Εἷς δέ τις τῶν παρεστηκότων σπασάμενος τὴν μάχαιραν, ἔπαισε τὸν 51 50
48 δοῦλον τοῦ ἀρχιερέως, καὶ ἀφεῖλεν αὐτοῦ τὸ ὠτίον. Καὶ ἀποκριθεὶς 55 52
ὁ Ἰησοῦς εἶπεν αὐτοῖς· Ὡς ἐπὶ λῃστὴν ἐξήλθετε μετὰ μαχαιρῶν καὶ
49 ξύλων, συλλαβεῖν με; Καθ᾽ ἡμέραν ἤμην πρὸς ὑμᾶς ἐν τῷ ἱερῷ 53
διδάσκων, καὶ οὐκ ἐκρατήσατέ με· ἀλλ᾽ ἵνα πληρωθῶσιν αἱ γραφαί.
50 Καὶ ἀφέντες αὐτὸν πάντες ἔφυγον. Καὶ εἷς τις νεανίσκος ἠκολούθει
51 αὐτῷ, περιβεβλημένος σινδόνα ἐπὶ γυμνοῦ· καὶ κρατοῦσιν αὐτὸν

Lord's prayer) of commencing with the word *Father*.

38. [*Comp*. Gal. v. 17.]

41. ἀπέχει] The Commentators are not agreed on the force of this expression. Of the various interpretations propounded, there are only two which have any claim to attention. 1. That of most of the recent Commentators, *abest*, scil. transiit animi mei angor. But this is liable to insuperable objections, both Grammatical and others. 2. That of Luther, Beza, H. Steph., Hamm., Gatak., Raph., Heup., and Fritz., "*sufficit*," it is enough;" "I no longer need your vigils." This is strongly confirmed by the ancient Versions, and the Glosses of the Scholiasts, and yet more by the ἱκανόν ἐστι of Luke. And although the sense be rare, yet there have been *two* other examples adduced; one from Anacreon xxviii. 33. ἀπέχει· βλέπω γὰρ αὐτήν. and another from Cyril. Thus ἀπέχει is an impersonal, and to be taken, as the simple ἔχειν and many of its compounds frequently are, in a *neuter* sense.

43. [*Comp*. John xviii. 3.]

44. σύσσημον.] An Alexandrian term for the Attic σημεῖον. Αὐτὸς is for οὗτος, by an Hellenistic use often found in the N. T.

—ἀσφαλῶς.] This is not (as some Commentators imagine) to be taken with κρατήσατε, and rendered *sine periculo*; but with ἀπαγάγετε, and rendered "*caute ac diligenter*." So in Acts xvi. 23. the jailer is ordered ἀσφαλῶς τηρεῖν. and in ver. 24. ἀσφαλίζεσθαι is used of securely keeping the prisoners.

45. [*Comp*. 2 Sam. xx. 9.]

47. εἷς δέ τις.] Almost all the Commentators account this a *pleonasm*, of which they adduce examples both from Scriptural and Classical writers. But it is, in fact, no pleonasm, and Fritz. truly observes, that εἷς τις signifies *unus aliquis*, *some one*. The expression is generally used of one whose name we know not, or do not care to mention. The reason for suppressing the name *here* is obvious. That for using the same indefinite expression further on at ver. 51., seems to have been from the Evangelist not *knowing* the person's name. For though many conjectures thereupon have been hazarded, yet not one of them has even probability to recommend it, except this, that he was a young man of the Roman soldiery; especially as again, in this very verse, the Article points to a particular part of the company; which could only have been the soldiery.

49. [*Comp*. Ps. xxii. 7. lxix. 10. Is. liii. 12.]

50. [*Comp*. Job xix. 13. Ps. lxxxviii. 8.]

51. σινδόνα.] See Note on Matt. xxvii. 59. The sense, however, *here* is somewhat different. For as the word primarily denoted a web of cloth, so it came to mean a *wrapper*, such as was often used for a night-vest; of which Wets. adduces examples from Herodot. and Galen, and Schleusn. another from D. Kimchi. This is doubtless the sense *here*, though the word sometimes denoted those webs of cloth which, as we find from Oriental travellers, are still used as a *day* dress, like our Highland plaids, and called *Hyks*.

—ἐπὶ γυμνοῦ.] Almost all Commentators suppose an ellipse of σώματος. But Fritz. would take it as a Genitive of the *neuter noun*, τὸ γυμνόν, the naked body. That, however, would require

MT. LU.
26. 22. οἱ νεανίσκοι. Ὁ δὲ καταλιπὼν τὴν σινδόνα, γυμνὸς ἔφυγεν ἀπ' 52
αὐτῶν.
57 54 Καὶ ἀπήγαγον τὸν Ἰησοῦν πρὸς τὸν ἀρχιερέα· καὶ συνέρχονται 53
58 αὐτῷ πάντες οἱ ἀρχιερεῖς καὶ οἱ πρεσβύτεροι καὶ οἱ γραμματεῖς. Καὶ 54
ὁ Πέτρος ἀπὸ μακρόθεν ἠκολούθησεν αὐτῷ ἕως ἔσω εἰς τὴν αὐλὴν
55 τοῦ ἀρχιερέως· καὶ ἦν συγκαθήμενος μετὰ τῶν ὑπηρετῶν, καὶ θερ-
59 μαινόμενος πρὸς τὸ φῶς. Οἱ δὲ ἀρχιερεῖς καὶ ὅλον τὸ συνέδριον 55
ἐζήτουν κατὰ τοῦ Ἰησοῦ μαρτυρίαν, εἰς τὸ θανατῶσαι αὐτόν· καὶ
60 οὐχ εὕρισκον. Πολλοὶ γὰρ ἐψευδομαρτύρουν κατ' αὐτοῦ, καὶ ἴσαι αἱ 56
μαρτυρίαι οὐκ ἦσαν. Καί τινες ἀναστάντες ἐψευδομαρτύρουν κατ' αὐ- 57
61 τοῦ, λέγοντες· Ὅτι ἡμεῖς ἠκούσαμεν αὐτοῦ λέγοντος· Ὅτι ἐγὼ κα- 58
ταλύσω τὸν ναὸν τοῦτον τὸν χειροποίητον, καὶ διὰ τριῶν ἡμερῶν ἄλλον
ἀχειροποίητον οἰκοδομήσω. Καὶ οὐδὲ οὕτως ἴση ἦν ἡ μαρτυρία αὐτῶν. 59
62 Καὶ ἀναστὰς ὁ ἀρχιερεὺς εἰς τὸ μέσον, ἐπηρώτησε τὸν Ἰησοῦν, λέγων· 60
63 Οὐκ ἀποκρίνῃ οὐδέν; Τί οὗτοί σου καταμαρτυροῦσιν; Ὁ δὲ ἐσιώ- 61
πα, καὶ οὐδὲν ἀπεκρίνατο. Πάλιν ὁ ἀρχιερεὺς ἐπηρώτα αὐτὸν, καὶ
64 λέγει αὐτῷ· Σὺ εἶ ὁ Χριστὸς ὁ Υἱὸς τοῦ εὐλογητοῦ; ὁ δὲ Ἰησοῦς 62
εἶπεν· Ἐγώ εἰμι. καὶ ὄψεσθε τὸν Υἱὸν τοῦ ἀνθρώπου καθήμενον
ἐκ δεξιῶν τῆς δυνάμεως, καὶ ἐρχόμενον μετὰ τῶν νεφελῶν τοῦ οὐρανοῦ.
65 Ὁ δὲ ἀρχιερεὺς, διαῤῥήξας τοὺς χιτῶνας αὐτοῦ, λέγει· Τί ἔτι χρείαν 63
66 ἔχομεν μαρτύρων; ἠκούσατε τῆς βλασφημίας· τί ὑμῖν φαίνεται; Οἱ 64
67 δὲ πάντες κατέκριναν αὐτὸν εἶναι ἔνοχον θανάτου. Καὶ ἤρξαντό τινες 65
ἐμπτύειν αὐτῷ, καὶ περικαλύπτειν τὸ πρόσωπον αὐτοῦ καὶ κολαφίζειν
68 αὐτὸν, καὶ λέγειν αὐτῷ· Προφήτευσον· καὶ οἱ ὑπηρέται ῥαπίσμασιν
αὐτὸν ἔβαλλον.

the Article, and the existence of the word must not be admitted without some authority more valid than the use of τὰ γυμνά, "*the unprotected parts of the body;*" for in that expression there is an ellipse of μέρη as well as of τοῦ σώματος. The phrase is plainly for ἐπὶ τοῦ γυμνοῦ τοῦ σώματος, and the very elliptical form it assumes, shows that it was much in use; probably in the phraseology of common life. It was probably a provincial idiom.

— οἱ νεανίσκοι.] This, by the force of the Article, must denote the Roman soldiers just mentioned. Examples are adduced by Rosenm., and Kuin. of this sense in Greek, and also of *juventutes* and *adolescentes*, in Latin. Nay, it even extends to the Hebrew.

53. [*Comp.* John xviii. 13, 24.]

54. πρὸς τὸ φῶς] for πρὸς τὸ πῦρ. So Luke xxii. 56. καθήμενον πρὸς τὸ φῶς. This has been proved to be a Hebraism, such as often occurs in the Sept., and corresponds to אוּר. For though the purity of the Greek has been maintained by many Commentators, yet they only adduce passages where the word signifies *fulgor*, rather than *ignis*; or, in one or two instances, a *blaze*, such as arises from kindled wood. Thus, by a metonymy of effect for cause, φῶς is transferred to all objects which emit *light*, though it may be accompanied with *heat* likewise.

55. [*Comp.* Acts vi. 13.]

56. ἴσαι.] The Commentators are not agreed on the sense. By the ancient Versions and most early modern Commentators, it is taken to mean *convenientes*, '*such as tally.*' So E. V. "agreed not together." Erasm., Grot., Hamm., Whitby, Heup., and Campb., render it, "non idonea erant," "were insufficient to establish the charges against him." But, as Beza and Fritz. observe, the *usus loquendi* will not permit this sense; and the difficulty which drove the above Commentators to adopt so forced un interpretation is really by no means formidable: see Recens. Synop. Lightf. observes, that the Jewish Canons divided testimonies into three kinds, 1. a *vain* or discordant testimony; 2. a *standing* or presumptive testimony; 3. an *even* consistent testimony.

58. χειροποίητον] i. e. "the work of man." This was added (says Grot.) lest Christ should seem to have spoken parabolically. Of the word χειροπ. examples are adduced by Wets., to which may be added a passage of Thucyd. ii. 77. yet more apposite, where φλὸξ χειροποίητη is opposed to ἀπὸ ταυτομάτου πῦρ. Our Lord alluded to Is. xvi. 12. See Note on Acts vii. 48, and compare infra xv. 29. John ii. 19.

61. [*Comp.* Is. liii. 7. Acts viii. 32.]

62. καὶ ὄψεσθε, &c.] *Comp.* Dan. vii. 10. John vi. 62. Acts i. 11. 1 Thess. iv. 16. 2 Thess. i. 10. Rev. i. 7.

65. [*Comp.* John xvi. 10, 11. Is. l. 6. John xix. 3. xviii. 16, 17.]

MT. LU.

66 Καὶ ὄντος τοῦ Πέτρου ἐν τῇ αὐλῇ κάτω, ἔρχεται μία τῶν παιδισκῶν 26. 22.
67 τοῦ ἀρχιερέως, καὶ ἰδοῦσα τὸν Πέτρον θερμαινόμενον, ἐμβλέψασα αὐτῷ 69 56
68 λέγει· Καὶ σὺ μετὰ τοῦ Ναζαρηνοῦ Ἰησοῦ ἦσθα. Ὁ δὲ ἠρνήσατο, 70 57
λέγων· Οὐκ οἶδα οὐδὲ ἐπίσταμαι τί σὺ λέγεις. καὶ ἐξῆλθεν ἔξω εἰς
69 τὸ προαύλιον· καὶ ἀλέκτωρ ἐφώνησε. Καὶ ἡ παιδίσκη ἰδοῦσα αὐτὸν 71 58
πάλιν, ἤρξατο λέγειν τοῖς παρεστηκόσιν· Ὅτι οὗτος ἐξ αὐτῶν ἐστιν.
70 Ὁ δὲ πάλιν ἠρνεῖτο. Καὶ μετὰ μικρὸν πάλιν οἱ παρεστῶτες ἔλεγον τῷ 72 59
Πέτρῳ· Ἀληθῶς ἐξ αὐτῶν εἶ· καὶ γὰρ Γαλιλαῖος εἶ, καὶ ἡ λαλιά 73
71 σου ὁμοιάζει. Ὁ δὲ ἤρξατο ἀναθεματίζειν καὶ ὀμνύειν· Ὅτι οὐκ 74 60
72 οἶδα τὸν ἄνθρωπον τοῦτον ὃν λέγετε. Καὶ ἐκ δευτέρου ἀλέκτωρ ἐφώνησε. καὶ ἀνεμνήσθη ὁ Πέτρος τοῦ ῥήματος οὗ εἶπεν αὐτῷ ὁ Ἰησοῦς· 75
Ὅτι πρὶν ἀλέκτορα φωνῆσαι δὶς, ἀπαρνήσῃ με τρίς. καὶ ‡ ἐπιβαλὼν
ἔκλαιε. 27. 23.

1 XV. ΚΑΙ εὐθέως ἐπὶ τὸ πρωῒ συμβούλιον ποιήσαντες οἱ ἀρχιερεῖς 1
μετὰ τῶν πρεσβυτέρων καὶ γραμματέων, καὶ ὅλον τὸ συνέδριον, δήσαν- 1
2 τες τὸν Ἰησοῦν ἀπήνεγκαν καὶ παρέδωκαν τῷ Πιλάτῳ. καὶ ἐπηρώτησεν 11 3
αὐτὸν ὁ Πιλάτος· Σὺ εἶ ὁ βασιλεὺς τῶν Ἰουδαίων; Ὁ δὲ ἀποκρι-
3 θεὶς εἶπεν αὐτῷ· Σὺ λέγεις. Καὶ κατηγόρουν αὐτοῦ οἱ ἀρχιερεῖς 12
4 πολλά. Ὁ δὲ Πιλάτος πάλιν ἐπηρώτησεν αὐτὸν, λέγων· Οὐκ ἀπο-
5 κρίνῃ οὐδέν; ἴδε, πόσα σου καταμαρτυροῦσιν. Ὁ δὲ Ἰησοῦς οὐκέτι 14
οὐδὲν ἀπεκρίθη· ὥστε θαυμάζειν τὸν Πιλάτον.

68. οὐκ—λέγεις.] This is rightly regarded by Wets. as an idiomatical form of negation. In οὐκ οἶδα οὐδὲ ἐπίσταμαι there seems a stress laid upon ἐπιστ.; and hence the student may attend to the observation of Matth. Gr. Gr. § 233, who rightly observes, that it is properly the mid. voice of ἐφίστημι, with the subaudition of τὸν νοῦν, in which the Ionic form is retained. It therefore signifies, "to set one's mind to any thing," as we say, enter into it, comprehend it. Wets. subjoins many examples, both from the Classical and Rabinical writers. On the seeming discrepancy with the accounts of the other Evangelists, see Horne's Introd. iv. 285.

69. [*Comp.* John xviii. 25.]

72. καὶ ἐκ δευτέρου, &c.] *Comp.* John xiii. 38. xviii. 27.

—ἐπιβαλών.] With this word the Commentators have been exceedingly perplexed; and hence their interpretations are marvellously discordant. To omit conjectural alterations, and manifestly false interpretations, many Commentators, ancient and modern, take ἐπιβάλλειν in the sense *begin;* and regard ἐπιβαλὼν ἔκλαιε as standing for κλαίειν ἐπέβαλε, either in the sense "began to weep," or "proceeded to weep," as in Acts xi. 4. ἀρξάμενος—ἐξετίθετο for ἤρξατο—ἐκτίθεσθαι. That passage, however, has quite another sense. Besides, though the above signification of ἐπιβάλλειν does exist in the later writers, yet of the *hypallage* in these words no example has been adduced. Besides, the sense is so feeble, and even frigid, that, although it is supported by most of the ancient Versions, it cannot, I think, be admitted. In fact, there should seem rather to be an *ellipsis*, though to determine with certainty what was originally the *plena locutio*, is perhaps impossible; some would take ἐπιβαλὼν to mean "having rushed out of doors;" a sense not unsuitable, and supported by the parallel passages. Yet such a signification of ἐπιβάλλειν has never been established, the passages cited being not to the purpose. There seems little doubt but that the truth lies with one or other of the two following interpretations. 1. That of Casaub., Bois, Heupel, Kypke, Wets., Koecher, Campb., and others, "having reflected thereon;" which is a very suitable sense. And abundant examples are adduced, both of the complete phrase ἐπιβάλλειν τὸν νοῦν, and even of the elliptical ones. Yet, as Fritz. remarks, the latter is only found where the *context suggests* the notion of *attention;* which is not the case here. He, therefore, after a minute discussion of the merits of all the interpretations, decides in favour of that of Chrysost., Theophyl., and other Greek Fathers, and to which several eminent modern Commentators have inclined, (as Salmas., Suic., Elsn., Heum., Krebs, and Fischer), by which ἐπιβαλὼν is taken as equivalent to ἐπικαλυψάμενος, "having covered his head (with his vest)." But here, again, decisive authority is wanting; for though the complete phrase ἐπιβάλλειν ἱμάτιον is very frequent, yet not one example has been adduced of the elliptical one, τινι, not even if ἐπιβάλλειν ἱμάτιον τῇ κεφαλῇ. To this, indeed, Fritz. answers that, from the great frequency of the phrase, no additional word was *necessary* to decide the sense; which is (he remarks) the case with other terms, as ὑποδησάμενος and περιῤῥηξάμενος. That the action is suitable to extreme grief, none can doubt; and that it was in use among the ancients, is proved by a cloud of examples.

XV. 1. [*Comp.* Ps. ii. 2. John xviii. 28. Acts iii. 13.]

2. [*Comp.* John xviii. 33.]

4. [*Comp.* John xix. 10.]

MT. LU.

27. 23. Κατὰ δὲ ἑορτὴν ἀπέλυεν αὐτοῖς ἕνα δέσμιον, ὅνπερ ᾐτοῦντο· Ἦν δὲ 6
15 16 17 19 ὁ λεγόμενος Βαραββᾶς μετὰ τῶν συστασιαστῶν δεδεμένος, οἵτινες ἐν 7
17 τῇ στάσει φόνον πεποιήκεισαν. Καὶ ἀναβοήσας ὁ ὄχλος ἤρξατο αἰτεῖ- 8
σθαι, καθὼς ἀεὶ ἐποίει αὐτοῖς. Ὁ δὲ Πιλάτος ἀπεκρίθη αὐτοῖς, λέ- 9
γων· Θέλετε ἀπολύσω ὑμῖν τὸν βασιλέα τῶν Ἰουδαίων; ἐγίνωσκε γὰρ 10
20 18 ὅτι διὰ φθόνον παραδεδώκεισαν αὐτὸν οἱ ἀρχιερεῖς. Οἱ δὲ ἀρχιερεῖς 11
21 20 ἀνέσεισαν τὸν ὄχλον, ἵνα μᾶλλον τὸν Βαραββᾶν ἀπολύσῃ αὐτοῖς. Ὁ δὲ 12
22 Πιλάτος ἀποκριθεὶς πάλιν εἶπεν αὐτοῖς· Τί οὖν θέλετε ποιήσω, ὃν λέ-
21 γετε βασιλέα τῶν Ἰουδαίων; οἱ δὲ πάλιν ἔκραξαν· Σταύρωσον αὐτόν. 13
23 22 ὁ δὲ Πιλάτος ἔλεγεν αὐτοῖς· Τί γὰρ κακὸν ἐποίησεν; Οἱ δὲ περισ- 14
26 23 24 σοτέρως ἔκραξαν· Σταύρωσον αὐτόν. Ὁ δὲ Πιλάτος βουλόμενος τῷ 15
25 ὄχλῳ τὸ ἱκανὸν ποιῆσαι, ἀπέλυσεν αὐτοῖς τὸν Βαραββᾶν· καὶ παρέδωκε τὸν Ἰησοῦν, φραγελλώσας, ἵνα σταυρωθῇ.

27 Οἱ δὲ στρατιῶται ἀπήγαγον αὐτὸν ἔσω τῆς αὐλῆς, (ὅ ἐστι πραιτώ- 16
28 ριον,) καὶ συγκαλοῦσιν ὅλην τὴν σπεῖραν· καὶ ἐνδύουσιν αὐτὸν πορ- 17
29 φύραν, καὶ περιτιθέασιν αὐτῷ πλέξαντες ἀκάνθινον στέφανον, καὶ 18
30 ἤρξαντο ἀσπάζεσθαι αὐτόν· Χαῖρε, βασιλεῦ τῶν Ἰουδαίων. Καὶ ἔτυ- 19
πτον αὐτοῦ τὴν κεφαλὴν καλάμῳ, καὶ ἐνέπτυον αὐτῷ, καὶ τιθέντες τὰ
31 γόνατα προσεκύνουν αὐτῷ. Καὶ ὅτε ἐνέπαιξαν αὐτῷ, ἐξέδυσαν αὐτὸν 20
τὴν πορφύραν, καὶ ἐνέδυσαν αὐτὸν τὰ ἱμάτια τὰ ἴδια· καὶ ἐξάγουσιν
32 26 αὐτὸν, ἵνα σταυρώσωσιν αὐτόν. Καὶ ἀγγαρεύουσι παράγοντά τινα 21
Σίμωνα Κυρηναῖον, ἐρχόμενον ἀπ᾽ ἀγροῦ (τὸν πατέρα Ἀλεξάνδρου καὶ
Ῥούφου), ἵνα ἄρῃ τὸν σταυρὸν αὐτοῦ.

33 33 Καὶ φέρουσιν αὐτὸν ἐπὶ Γολγοθᾶ τόπον, ὅ ἐστι, μεθερμηνευόμενον, 22
34 Κρανίου τόπος. Καὶ ἐδίδουν αὐτῷ πιεῖν ἐσμυρνισμένον οἶνον· ὁ δὲ 23
35 οὐκ ἔλαβε. Καὶ σταυρώσαντες αὐτὸν, * διαμερίζονται τὰ ἱμάτια αὐ- 24
34 τοῦ, βάλλοντες κλῆρον ἐπ᾽ αὐτὰ, τίς τί ἄρῃ. ἦν δὲ ὥρα τρίτη, καὶ 25

6. ἀπέλυεν] "used to release;" as in Matt. εἰώθει ἀπολύειν. [*Comp.* John xviii. 39.]

8. At αἰτεῖσθαι supply ποιεῖν αὐτόν. [*Comp.* John xviii. 40. Acts iii. 14.]

11. ἀνέσεισαν] "instigated." Some MSS. have ἀνέπεισαν, and others ἔσεισαν. The one is a gloss, and the other derived from the parallel passage of Matthew. The textual reading, which is a stronger term, is confirmed by Luke xxiii. 5. and, this use of the word, by the examples produced from Diod. Sic. by Elsner and Munthe, to which may be added Eurip. Orest. 612. and Dionys. Hal. viii. 81.

14. τί γὰρ κακόν.] The γὰρ refers to a clause suppressed, "Why should I crucify him, for," &c.

15. τῷ ὄχλῳ τὸ ἱκανὸν ποιῆσαι] "to satisfy the wishes of the people," or, as Grot. explains it, agreeably to the usage of *satis facere* in Latin writers, to remove all cause of complaint on their part. [*Comp.* John. xix. 1.]

16. [*Comp.* John xix. 1.]

19. τιθέντες τὰ γόνατα] for γονυπετήσαντες, which is used by Matth. The phrase signifies to place the knees (i. e. on the ground).

21. Ἀλεξ. καὶ Ῥ.] Persons probably well known, and then living at Rome; since Paul, Rom. xvi. 13. salutes *Rufus* there.

22. [*Comp.* John xix. 17.]

24. διαμερίζονται.] This (for διεμέριζον) is found in nearly all the best MSS., and is adopted by every Editor from Wets. to Scholz. It is indeed not only required by the *linguæ proprietas*, but, what is more, is confirmed by the parallel passages of Matt. and Luke. The error seems to have arisen from the ται being absorbed by the τα following. [*Comp.* Ps. xxii. 18. John xix. 23.]

25. ἦν δὲ ὥρα τρίτη καὶ ἐσταύρωσαν α.] *Comp.* John xix. 14. A difficulty is here started by some Commentators, namely, that the crucifixion is twice described by Mark as taking place. To avoid which, some would take the καὶ for ἐξ οὗ. But that signification is quite unauthorized. Others endeavour to remove the difficulty by a change of punctuation. But that involves a most harsh construction. It is better, with others (among whom is Fritz.) to take ἐσταύρωσαν as an Aorist with a Pluperfect sense (on which use see Winer's Gr. Gr. p. 106.), thus: "It was the third hour when they had crucified him." Even this, however, is unnecessary, if σταυρώσαντες in the preceding verse be taken, as it may, in a *present* tense (and indeed the Cod. Vatic. *has* the present tense), thus: "and on proceeding to crucify him, they divided his garments." Now *this* indicates the commencement of action, namely, the *stripping of our Lord.* The *next verse* denotes the *com-*

MT. LU.

26 ἐσταύρωσαν αὐτόν. Καὶ ἦν ἡ ἐπιγραφὴ τῆς αἰτίας αὐτοῦ ἐπιγεγραμ- 27. 23.
27 μένη, Ὁ ΒΑΣΙΛΕΥΣ ΤΩΝ ἸΟΥΔΑΙΩΝ. Καὶ σὺν αὐτῷ σταυροῦσι 37 38
28 δύο λῃστάς, ἕνα ἐκ δεξιῶν καὶ ἕνα ἐξ εὐωνύμων αὐτοῦ. Καὶ ἐπληρώθη
29 ἡ γραφὴ ἡ λέγουσα· Καὶ μετὰ ἀνόμων ἐλογίσθη. Καὶ 39 35
οἱ παραπορευόμενοι ἐβλασφήμουν αὐτὸν, κινοῦντες τὰς κεφαλὰς αὐτῶν
καὶ λέγοντες· Οὐά! ὁ καταλύων τὸν ναὸν καὶ ἐν τρισὶν ἡμέραις
30 οἰκοδομῶν, σῶσον σεαυτὸν, καὶ κατάβα ἀπὸ τοῦ σταυροῦ. Ὁμοίως 41
31 [δὲ] καὶ οἱ ἀρχιερεῖς ἐμπαίζοντες πρὸς ἀλλήλους, μετὰ τῶν γραμματέων,
32 ἔλεγον· Ἄλλους ἔσωσεν, ἑαυτὸν οὐ δύναται σῶσαι. Ὁ Χριστὸς ὁ 42
βασιλεὺς τοῦ Ἰσραὴλ καταβάτω νῦν ἀπὸ τοῦ σταυροῦ, ἵνα ἴδωμεν καὶ
33 πιστεύσωμεν. καὶ οἱ συνεσταυρωμένοι αὐτῷ ὠνείδιζον αὐτόν. Γενομέ- 44 39
νης δὲ ὥρας ἕκτης, σκότος ἐγένετο ἐφ᾽ ὅλην τὴν γῆν, ἕως ὥρας ἐννάτης· 45 44
34 καὶ τῇ ὥρᾳ τῇ ἐννάτῃ ἐβόησεν ὁ Ἰησοῦς φωνῇ μεγάλῃ, λέγων· Ἐλωΐ 46
Ἐλωΐ, λαμμᾶ σαβαχθανί; ὅ ἐστι, μεθερμηνευόμενον, Ὁ Θεός
35 μου ὁ Θεός μου, εἰς τί με ἐγκατέλιπες; Καὶ τινὲς τῶν παρεστηκότων 47
36 ἀκούσαντες, ἔλεγον· Ἰδοὺ, Ἡλίαν φωνεῖ. Δραμὼν δὲ εἷς, καὶ γεμίσας 48
σπόγγον ὄξους, περιθείς τε καλάμῳ, ἐπότιζεν αὐτὸν, λέγων· Ἄφετε,
ἴδωμεν εἰ ἔρχεται Ἡλίας καθελεῖν αὐτόν.
37 Ὁ δὲ Ἰησοῦς ἀφεὶς φωνὴν μεγάλην, ἐξέπνευσε. Καὶ τὸ καταπέτα- 50 46
38 σμα τοῦ ναοῦ ἐσχίσθη εἰς δύο, ἀπὸ ἄνωθεν ἕως κάτω. Ἰδὼν δὲ ὁ 51 45
39 κεντυρίων ὁ παρεστηκὼς ἐξ ἐναντίας αὐτοῦ, ὅτι οὕτω κράξας ἐξέπνευ- 54 47
40 σεν, εἶπεν· Ἀληθῶς ὁ ἄνθρωπος οὗτος Υἱὸς ἦν Θεοῦ! ἦσαν δὲ καὶ 55 49
γυναῖκες ἀπὸ μακρόθεν θεωροῦσαι, ἐν αἷς ἦν καὶ Μαρία ἡ Μαγδαλη- 56
νὴ, καὶ Μαρία ἡ τοῦ Ἰακώβου τοῦ μικροῦ καὶ Ἰωσῆ μήτηρ, καὶ Σα-

pletion of action, and therefore fixes the *time when* it took place. In short, *σταυρώσαντες αὐτὸν*, simply means, '*and, on crucifying him.*'

With respect to the seeming discrepancy between Mark and John, as to the *hour of the crucifixion*, various methods have been proposed for its removal. See Recens. Synop. Now although such discrepancies "are (as Fritz. observes) rather to be patiently borne, than removed by rash measures," yet here we are, it should seem, not reduced to any great straits. For though the mode of reconciling the two accounts by a sort of *management* is not to be commended; yet surely, when we have the testimony of several of the ancient Fathers, that an early *corruption of number* in one of these two passages had taken place by a confusion of the Γ and ϛ, we cannot hesitate to adopt so simple and natural a mode of removing the discrepancy. See more in Note on John xix. 14.

26. [*Comp.* John xix. 19.]

28. [*Comp.* Is. liii. 12.] This ver. is marked for omission by Griesb. and cancelled by Fritz.; but injudiciously; for there is no reason why so remarkable a fulfilment of prophecy, mentioned by the other Evangelists, should not also be recorded by *Mark*. Besides, the number of MSS. in which it is omitted is so comparatively small, that it is very probable it was inadvertently passed over by the scribes; which might arise from this and the next ver. both beginning with a *καί*.

29. *οὐά*.] An interjection of derision and insult, like the Latin *vah*, and our hoa! oho! ah-ah! which, however, are used, like all interjections, with much latitude of signification, and are adapted to express most of the violent emotions. [*Comp.* Ps. xxii. 8. lxix. 20. Supra xiv. 58. John ii. 19.]

31. *δέ*.] This is absent from many good MSS., and is cancelled by Matth., Griesb., Tittm., Vat., Fritz., and Scholz.

36. *καθελεῖν*.] A vox solennis de hac re,—like the Latin *refigere*. [See my Note on Thucyd. ii. 14.] [*Comp.* Ps. lxix. 22. John xix. 29.]

37. *ἀφεὶς φωνὴν μεγ.*] Φωνὴν ἀφιέναι signifies to send forth a voice, whether articulate or inarticulate. [See Note on Matt. xxvii. 50. John xix. 30.]

39. *ὅτι οὕτω κράξας*.] This does not mean (as many explain) that he had cried with such a loud voice; nor that the Centurion felt admiration at his being so soon released from his torments, but that, on hearing *such* words as those at ver. 34. pronounced, as it were from the bottom of the heart, by the crucified person; and that he should so immediately after be *released* from his torments,—the Centurion thence felt assured, that he was not only a *righteous person*, but had the character which he claimed; namely, that of being ὁ Υἱὸς τοῦ Θεοῦ: on the force of which expression see Note on Matt. xxvii. 54.

40. [*Comp.* Ps. xxxviii. 12.]

41. [*Comp.* Luke viii. 2, 3.]

42. *προσάββατον*.] A very rare word, only occurring elsewhere in Judith viii. 6., and by which,

MT. LU.
27. 23. λώμη, αἳ καὶ, ὅτε ἦν ἐν τῇ Γαλιλαίᾳ, ἠκολούθουν αὐτῷ, καὶ διηκόνουν 41
αὐτῷ· καὶ ἄλλαι πολλαὶ αἱ συναναβᾶσαι αὐτῷ εἰς Ἱεροσόλυμα.
57 54 Καὶ ἤδη ὀψίας γενομένης, (ἐπεὶ ἦν παρασκευὴ, ὅ ἐστι προσάββατον,) 42
51 * ἐλθὼν Ἰωσὴφ ὁ ἀπὸ Ἀριμαθαίας, εὐσχήμων βουλευτὴς, ὃς καὶ αὐτὸς 43
58 52 ἦν προσδεχόμενος τὴν βασιλείαν τοῦ θεοῦ· τολμήσας εἰσῆλθε πρὸς
Πιλάτον, καὶ ᾐτήσατο τὸ σῶμα τοῦ Ἰησοῦ. Ὁ δὲ Πιλάτος ἐθαύμασεν 44
εἰ ἤδη τέθνηκε· καὶ προσκαλεσάμενος τὸν κεντυρίωνα, ἐπηρώτησεν
αὐτὸν εἰ πάλαι ἀπέθανε· καὶ γνοὺς ἀπὸ τοῦ κεντυρίωνος, ἐδωρήσατο 45
59 53 τὸ σῶμα τῷ Ἰωσήφ. Καὶ ἀγοράσας σινδόνα, καὶ καθελὼν αὐτὸν, 46
60 ἐνείλησε τῇ σινδόνι, καὶ κατέθηκεν αὐτὸν ἐν μνημείῳ, ὃ ἦν λελατομη-
μένον ἐκ πέτρας· καὶ προσεκύλισε λίθον ἐπὶ τὴν θύραν τοῦ μνημείου.
61 55 Ἡ δὲ Μαρία ἡ Μαγδαληνὴ καὶ Μαρία Ἰωσῆ ἐθεώρουν ποῦ τίθεται. 47
28. 24.
1 1 XVI. ΚΑΙ διαγενομένου τοῦ σαββάτου, Μαρία ἡ Μαγδαληνὴ καὶ 1
Μαρία ἡ τοῦ Ἰακώβου καὶ Σαλώμη ἠγόρασαν ἀρώματα, ἵνα ἐλθοῦσαι
ἀλείψωσιν αὐτόν. Καὶ λίαν πρωῒ τῆς μιᾶς σαββάτων ἔρχονται ἐπὶ τὸ 2
μνημεῖον, ἀνατείλαντος τοῦ ἡλίου. Καὶ ἔλεγον πρὸς ἑαυτάς· Τίς 3

as he was writing for Gentiles, Mark explains the Jewish sense of παρασκευή; meaning by προσ. the time which preceded the commencement of the Sabbath, which began at the sunset of Friday. [*Comp*. John xix. 33.]

43. εὐσχήμων] "respectable, honourable." The word properly signifies *of good presence*, then *decorous, dignified*, &c. It is never used in *this* sense by the Classical writers; but is so employed in Joseph. de Vitâ 9. ἀνδρῶν εὐσχημόνων. By βουλευτὴς is meant, if not *one of the Sanhedrim*, at least *one of the council of the High Priest*. See Note on Matth.

— ἐλθών.] For the common reading ἦλθεν is found in many of the best MSS. and some Versions and Fathers; and was edited by Matth., Fritz., and Lachm., rightly, I think; for the common reading, as Fritz. observes, involves an intolerable *Asyndeton*: and for the addition of καὶ before τολμήσας, which would make all right, there is very little authority; and it was only an *emendation* of the Critics. Fritz. thinks that ἦλθεν partly arose from Matt. xxvii. 57, and partly from the Greek Interpreters (as we find from Euthym.) terminating the sentence at Θεοῦ; and having changed ἐλθὼν into ἦλθεν, and added καὶ before τολμ. So much trouble was occasioned by the awkward insertion (at least *here*) of εὐσχήμων — Θεοῦ. Thus τολμήσας will be taken for the adverb τολμηρῶς; a frequent construction in the N. T., as Fritz. testifies. I would observe, that ἐλθὼν and ἦλθεν are so much alike in MSS., that one might *inadvertently* be confounded with the other. However, I would not venture to deny that it is *possible* ἐλθὼν may be the *emendation*, and ἦλθεν the original reading. But then the καὶ before τολμ. is indispensable. And as we must, in either case, take what *may* have proceeded from emendation, it seems prudent to give the preference to *number* and *excellence of MSS.*

44. ἐθαύμασεν εἰ.] Beza and others wrongly render the εἰ by *an*, as if there were a *doubt*; whereas εἰ is used with θαυμάζειν, as the Latin *si* with *mirari* (indeed with all verbs of *wonder*) to express what is not *doubted*, but *wondered* at: Thus we may here render, "*that* he were already dead!" The πάλαι is wrongly rendered in E. V. "long." Much mistake in the interpretation of the word might have been avoided by adverting to its primary sense. The word (as Valckn. and Lennep. show) comes from πάλω (or πάλλω), to violently shake any thing, and so turn it over. It is a Dative case of the old noun πάλα; and thus when used of *time* (to which it was early *appropriated*) denotes ὁ χρόνος ὁ ἐπὶ πάλαι, tempus, *quod retro est*, time which has been thrown back, got rid of, *past*; whether recently elapsed, or long gone by, in both which significations it occurs in the Classical writers. Thus the Latin *olim* is from ὄλις (and that from ὄλω, *volvo*), and properly denotes χρόνος ὁ (κατ') ὄλιν: (so πάλιν for κατὰ πάλιν) time which has rolled past and gone. Thus in the words of Pilate there is a repetition of the foregoing question, with the adoption of a more precise term.

46. μνημείῳ ὃ ἦν, &c.] *Comp*. Matt. xii. 40. xxvi. 12. John xix. 41. Wolf, Salmas., Krebs., Schleus., and others are mistaken in taking these words to denote a monument constructed of hewn and polished stone, as appears from Matt. xxvii. 60. ὃ ἐλατόμησεν ἐν τῇ πέτρᾳ. It was, no doubt, a *cave* hewn out in the rock; that being the custom of the country, and of most of the Eastern nations. Many thousands of such μνημεῖα still remain, and are noticed by travellers.

— θύραν] Not "*door*," but "*entrance*."

XVI. 1. διαγενομένου] "being elapsed," or past: a sense of the word frequent in the Classical as well as Scriptural writers.

— ἠγόρασαν] Not "had bought," but "bought." So the Vulg. "emerunt," a translation supposed to have been adopted to reconcile this passage with Luke xxiii. 56, where it is said that the spices were prepared upon the evening of the Sabbath. But, as Mr. Townsend observes, "it is only by a scrupulous adherence to the plain sense of Scripture that all difficulties are ever removed." And the researches of recent Harmonists and Interpreters have established the fact, which had escaped the earlier Commentators, namely, that there were *two* parties of women, to whom the two Evangelists refer respectively. Thus also we are enabled satisfactorily to remove

MT. LU.

4 ἀποκυλίσει ἡμῖν τὸν λίθον ἐκ τῆς θύρας τοῦ μνημείου; καὶ ἀνα- 27. 24.
βλέψασαι θεωροῦσιν ὅτι ἀποκεκύλισται ὁ λίθος· ἦν γὰρ μέγας σφό- 2
5 δρα. Καὶ εἰσελθοῦσαι εἰς τὸ μνημεῖον, εἶδον νεανίσκον καθήμενον ἐν 3 3
6 τοῖς δεξιοῖς περιβεβλημένον στολὴν λευκήν· καὶ ἐξεθαμβήθησαν. Ὁ 4
δὲ λέγει αὐταῖς· Μὴ ἐκθαμβεῖσθε. Ἰησοῦν ζητεῖτε τὸν Ναζαρηνὸν 5 5 6
τὸν ἐσταυρωμένον· ἠγέρθη, οὐκ ἔστιν ὧδε· ἴδε, ὁ τόπος ὅπου ἔθη-
7 καν αὐτόν. Ἀλλ᾽ ὑπάγετε, εἴπατε τοῖς μαθηταῖς αὐτοῦ καὶ τῷ Πέτρῳ, 7 6
ὅτι προάγει ὑμᾶς εἰς τὴν Γαλιλαίαν· ἐκεῖ αὐτὸν ὄψεσθε, καθὼς εἶπεν 16
8 ὑμῖν. Καὶ ἐξελθοῦσαι [ταχὺ] ἔφυγον ἀπὸ τοῦ μνημείου. εἶχε δὲ 8 9
αὐτὰς τρόμος καὶ ἔκστασις· καὶ οὐδενὶ οὐδὲν εἶπον, ἐφοβοῦντο γάρ.
9 Ἀναστὰς δὲ πρωῒ πρώτῃ σαββάτου, ἐφάνη πρῶτον Μαρίᾳ τῇ Μαγ-
10 δαληνῇ, ἀφ᾽ ἧς ἐκβεβλήκει ἑπτὰ δαιμόνια. Ἐκείνη πορευθεῖσα ἀπήγ-
11 γειλε τοῖς μετ᾽ αὐτοῦ γενομένοις, πενθοῦσι καὶ κλαίουσι. Κἀκεῖνοι,
12 ἀκούσαντες ὅτι ζῇ καὶ ἐθεάθη ὑπ᾽ αὐτῆς, ἠπίστησαν. Μετὰ δὲ ταῦτα
δυσὶν ἐξ αὐτῶν, περιπατοῦσιν, ἐφανερώθη ἐν ἑτέρᾳ μορφῇ, πορευομένοις
13 εἰς ἀγρόν. Κἀκεῖνοι ἀπελθόντες ἀπήγγειλαν τοῖς λοιποῖς· οὐδὲ ἐκεί-

a difficulty which had embarrassed the old Commentators; namely, to reconcile *ἀνατείλαντος τοῦ ἡλίου* at ver. 2. with the *πρωῒ σκοτίας ἔτι οὔσης* at John xx. 1.

4. *ἦν γὰρ μέγας σφόδρα.*] The Commentators have been not a little perplexed with this clause, because it cannot be referred to what immediately precedes. To remove this difficulty, some would take *γὰρ* in the sense of *δή*. But it is *better*, with others, to suppose that the words have reference, not to the clause which immediately preceded, but to the *one before* that, *τίς — μνημείου*; the intermediate words being regarded as parenthetical. Yet the construction at *καὶ ἀναβλέψασαι* will not admit of the *parenthesis;* and thus the difficulty remains in its full force; and it would seem impossible to remove it, except by *transposing* the words, as is done by Newcome and Wakef. But for *that* there is little authority: and what may be allowable in forming *translations*, is not so in *editing* the words of an original. I cannot but think that the *γὰρ* has reference to some clause omitted; not, indeed, that which Whitby, Grot., and Rosenm. *ad libitum* suppose, "and this happened luckily for them;" but to something which may be supplied from *both the preceding sentences*, thus: "[And well might they say, Who will roll, &c., and behold, doubtless with surprise, its removal;] *for* it was very great." Thus the words at ver. 7. *καθὼς εἶπεν ὑ.* are, with Fritz., to be referred, not to the clause which immediately precedes, but to the one before that.

5. [*Comp.* John xx. 12.]

7. *τοῖς μαθηταῖς α.*] Many recent Commentators understand, by this expression, Christ's followers in general. But the older ones (and lately Fritz.) seem right in taking it to denote the *Apostles*, by a frequent figure of speech, whereby a part is put for the whole; and of which examples are adduced by Grot.

The *καὶ* just after is best rendered, "et (præsertim)," as put for *καὶ μάλιστα*; a signification often occurring in the Classical writers from Homer downwards. On the reason why *Peter* is here named, the Commentators differ in opinion; though they are in general agreed that it was not from any pre-eminence which he had over the rest of the Apostles. The several reasons they assign may perhaps be *conjoined*. Peter was, it seems, named both for his consolation and assurance, and also from the permanent regard which his singular affection towards his Master had created. See supra xiv. 28. Matt. xxvi. 32. Acts i. 3. xiii. 31. 1 Cor. xv. 5.

8. *ταχύ.*] This is omitted in most of the best MSS., and is cancelled by almost every Editor from Wets. to Scholz. It was, no doubt, introduced from Matt. xxviii. 8. The words *οὐδενὶ οὐδὲν εἶπον* must (as appears from the *ἐφοβοῦντο* just after) be understood of the time during their return, or shortly after; and of the persons whom they might then meet with. [*Comp.* John xx. 18.]

9. The authenticity of the remainder of this Gospel has been impugned by several Critics, but defended by more. See a statement of the arguments on both sides in Recens. Synop. To what is there said it may be added, that Scholz, after all his researches (extended to MSS. nearly half as numerous again as Griesbach's), has never been able to find this portion omitted in more than *one* MS. (and that one in which great liberties have been taken) and *a single Version.*

9. *ἑπτὰ δαιμόνια*] Many of the recent Foreign Commentators stumble at the *ἑπτά*. But it has no difficulty, except to those who adopt Mede's hypothesis with respect to the Demoniacs. Why should not this poor wretch have been possessed with *seven* devils as well as another was with a *legion?* i. e. very many. [*Comp.* John xx. 14. 16. Luke viii. 2.]

12. *ἐν ἑτέρᾳ μορφῇ*] Some interpret *μορφῇ* of *dress;* but the authority for that signification is very slender. Others, more properly, understand by it, *visage* and *general appearance.* Whatever the alteration in appearance might be, it was such as also to prevent our Lord's being immediately recognised by the two disciples who were going into the country. See Luke xxiv. 13.

13. *οὐδὲ ἐκείνοις ἐπίστευσαν*] This seems to be at variance with Luke xxiv. 34., who says, that before they approached, Jesus had appeared to Simon, and that he had related it to the assembly.

a John 20. 19. 1 Cor. 15. 5, 7.
b John 15. 16.
c Luke 10. 17. Acts 5. 16. & 8. 7. & 16. 18. & 2. 4. & 10. 46. 1 Cor. 12. 10, 28.
d Luke 10. 19. Acts 28. 3, 6.

νοις ἐπίστευσαν. [a] Ὕστερον ἀνακειμένοις αὐτοῖς τοῖς ἕνδεκα ἐφανερώ- 14
θη· καὶ ὠνείδισε τὴν ἀπιστίαν αὐτῶν καὶ σκληροκαρδίαν, ὅτι τοῖς
θεασαμένοις αὐτὸν ἐγηγερμένον οὐκ ἐπίστευσαν. [b] Καὶ εἶπεν αὐτοῖς· 15
Πορευθέντες εἰς τὸν κόσμον ἅπαντα, κηρύξατε τὸ εὐαγγέλιον πάσῃ
τῇ κτίσει. Ὁ πιστεύσας καὶ βαπτισθεὶς σωθήσεται· ὁ δὲ ἀπιστήσας 16
κατακριθήσεται. [c] Σημεῖα δὲ τοῖς πιστεύσασι ταῦτα παρακολουθήσει· 17
ἐν τῷ ὀνόματί μου δαιμόνια ἐκβαλοῦσι· γλώσσαις λαλήσουσι καιναῖς·
[d] ὄφεις ἀροῦσι· κἂν θανάσιμόν τι πίωσιν, οὐ μὴ αὐτοὺς βλάψει· ἐπὶ 18
ἀῤῥώστους χεῖρας ἐπιθήσουσι, καὶ καλῶς ἕξουσιν.
Ὁ μὲν οὖν Κύριος, μετὰ τὸ λαλῆσαι αὐτοῖς, ἀνελήφθη εἰς τὸν οὐρα- 19
νὸν, καὶ ἐκάθισεν ἐκ δεξιῶν τοῦ Θεοῦ. Ἐκεῖνοι δὲ ἐξελθόντες ἐκήρυξαν 20
πανταχοῦ, τοῦ κυρίου συνεργοῦντος, καὶ τὸν λόγον βεβαιοῦντος διὰ τῶν
ἐπακολουθούντων σημείων.

For even *this* they had not fully credited, nay, even when Jesus had come up, Luke adds, ἔτι ἀπιστούντων αὐτῶν. All this, however, tends to make us repose a firmer confidence in the testimony of those who themselves so slowly and cautiously admitted belief. (Grot.) In the passage of Luke, the Apostles and Disciples are indeed spoken of, but λαλοῦντες does not denote *all* the Apostles and Disciples gathered together, but only some of them. Passages of this sort, in which what seems spoken of *all* is to be understood only of some, are not unfrequent in the N. T. There is therefore *no decrepancy* between Mark and Luke. *Some* of the assembly (as Luke tells us) believed that Jesus had returned to life; *all the rest* denied implicit credit to the narrations concerning that event. Hence even when Jesus appeared to them, they fancied they saw a *phantasm*; from all which we may conclude that they were by no means *credulous*. (Kuin.)

15. πάσῃ τῇ κτίσει] i. e. to all human creatures, both Jews and Gentiles, to *all nations*, as Matthew expresses it.

16. ὁ πιστεύσας — κατακριθήσεται.] By comparing this with the commission given the Apostles, Matt. xxviii. 20, and Luke xxiv. 47, it is plain that not only *faith*, but *repentance* and *obedience* were to be preached in the name of Christ, the sense being, that he who by true and lively faith embraces Christianity, and engages, in baptism, to obey its injunctions, and faithfully fulfil his engagements, shall obtain everlasting salvation. With respect to κατακριθήσεται whether it be rendered "damned," or "condemned," matters but little as to the ultimate sense; since, upon the *lowest* meaning that has been affixed to σωθήσεται (namely, the being put into a state of salvation), the contrary cannot but imply a state of *present reprobation*; which, if continued in, must assuredly terminate in *perdition*: and the *condemnation*, to take place at the day of Judgment, cannot but imply the being consigned to the curse, and the eternal woe consequent upon it. By "not believing," is meant either obstinately refusing assent to the evidence of the truth of the Gospel, however satisfactory; or not so believing the Gospel as to *obey* it, and thus holding the truth in unrighteousness. In the former case, he who believeth not must be condemned to eternal misery, because he rejects the only means whereby he can be saved. That reason requires us to limit the denunciation here to *wilful* disbelief, and not extend it to *involuntary*, is shown by Dr. Campb. and Dr. Maltby, cited by me in Recens. Synop. And that it is confirmed by the word of God, is plain from John iii. 18. compared with v. 36.

17. σημεῖα δὲ, &c.] [*Comp*. Luke x. 17. Acts v. 16. & viii. 7. xvi. 18. ii. 4. x. 46. 1 Cor. xii. 10, 28.] On the several particulars of our Lord's promise, so as to show their full force and exact fulfilment, much valuable matter may be found in Recens. Synop. The exercise of the *first* gift, namely, the casting out of devils, is proved by the early Fathers, Justin Martyr, Clemens Alex., Origen, Irenæus, Tertullian, &c. Of the *second*, namely, *speaking with new tongues*, which must be understood, in its *full* sense, of the miraculous communication of the faculty of speaking with tongues never previously learned, (on which I have copiously treated in the Note at Acts ii. 4.), we have abundant proof, both from Scripture, and the testimonies of the earliest Fathers. The same may be said of the next two particulars, the "*taking up of serpents*," and the "*drinking of poison without injury*." The former was in that age regarded as a decisive test of supernatural protection; though we find that this power was sometimes pretended to by impostors. As to the *latter*, that faculty (as Doddr. observes) would be especially necessary in an age when the art of poisoning was brought to such cursed refinement. As to the *fifth* particular, *healing the sick* supernaturally, the Scriptures and early Ecclesiastical writers are full of examples. Upon the whole, there is abundant evidence for the fulfilment of all the promises which the above expressions, in their plain and full sense, imply; and for their chief purposes, namely, of miraculous attestation to their Divine mission, and supernatural protection under all the evils which they should have to encounter in the exercise of their ministry.

ΤΟ ΚΑΤΑ ΛΟΥΚΑΝ

ΕΥΑΓΓΕΛΙΟΝ.

---

1 I. Ἐ*ΠΕΙΔΗΠΕΡ* πολλοὶ ἐπεχείρησαν ἀνατάξασθαι διήγησιν περὶ
2 τῶν πεπληροφορημένων ἐν ἡμῖν πραγμάτων, [a] καθὼς παρέδοσαν ἡμῖν [a] Heb. 2. 3. 1 John 1. 1.

Of this Evangelist (as of St. Mark) little is known with certainty, except what is learned from the N. T. The traditions of the early Fathers are few and slight; and those of the later ones merit little attention. They, and the older Commentators in general, are of opinion that he was a *Jew;* but their proofs are by no means strong. It is *more probable* that (as many recent Expositors suppose) he was descended from Gentile parents, but had in his youth embraced Judaism, from which he had been converted to Christianity. Yet whether even this be true, may be doubted; for there is great reason to think that Luke was but a very young man when converted to *Christianity;* and it is not likely that he had, before that time, passed over from Paganism to Judaism. It may rather be supposed that he was born of *Jewish* parents; or at least (as in the case of Timothy) of parents, the father a gentile, and the mother a Jewess. The Hebrew-Greek style of his writings and the accurate knowledge shewn in them of the Jewish religion, make it probable that the writer was not a *Jewish Proselyte,* but a *Jew,* on the *mother's* side, though a Greek on the father's. Thus also we are enabled to account for the power of Greek style which he occasionally evinces. For it was likely that he would by his *father* be competently instructed in Greek literature. That he should be *so far* a Jew, is not at all inconsistent with his bearing a *Greek* name, which he would derive from his father. There is, I apprehend, nothing in the N. T. which militates against this hypothesis (by which all seeming discrepancies are reconciled), but much to confirm it; for surely he was more likely to be reckoned among *Jews* (see Acts xxi. 27. compared with xxi. 15 & 17.), if he were *Jew-born* by the mother's side, and brought up a Jew, than if he had been merely a *Proselyte* from Gentilism. As to the argument founded on Col. iv. 11 & 14, it is by no means cogent; since the *opposition* there alleged between Arist., Marcus, and Justus, and Luke and Demas, cannot be shown to exist.

The first mention of Luke in the N. T. is at Acts xvi. 10 & 11, where he is said to have been with Paul at Troas; from whence he attended him to Jerusalem, and having continued with him in his troubles, accompanied him on his voyage from Cæsarea to Rome, and stayed with him during his two years' confinement there. The time of Luke's death we cannot ascertain from any precise information. We only know that it was after that of St. Peter and of St. Paul. With this is closely connected *another* question, — as to the *date* of the publication of his Gospel; which I have considered at large in the Introd. to Mark's Gospel, when treating on the sources of the first three Gospels. Of the *genuineness and authenticity* of this Gospel, there has never been any doubt entertained. It is quoted or alluded to by writers, in an unbroken chain, from the Apostolical Fathers down to the time of Chrysostom. To its *Canonical authority,* indeed (as well as that of St. Mark's Gospel), objections have been made by *Michaelis.* These, however, have been satisfactorily answered, especially by Professor Alexander (of America) on the Canon of the N. T. p. 202 — 210, whose remarks may be seen in Mr. Horne's Introduction. As to the authenticity of the first two Chapters, which has been recently called in question by those who impugn the miraculous conception of Christ, — suffice it to say, that those Chapters are found in *all the MSS.* of the Gospel, of which we have any knowledge, and in *all the Versions.* And to this complete *external evidence* may be added *internal evidence* of the strongest kind: for while there is no Critical reason imaginable *against* the Chapters, there is the strongest reason to suppose them *genuine,* since the 1st is connected with the 2d, and the 2d with the 3d, in exactly the same manner as the 1st and 2d Chapters of Matthew are connected with the 3d. In fact, the only argument even *specious,* that has been urged against their authenticity is, that they were not found in the copies used by *Marcion* in the second century. But Dr. Lardner has shewn, that if he used

οἱ ἀπ' ἀρχῆς αὐτόπται καὶ ὑπηρέται γενόμενοι τοῦ λόγου· [b] ἔδοξε

b Acts 1. 1. κἀμοὶ, παρηκολουθηκότι ἄνωθεν πᾶσιν ἀκριβῶς, καθεξῆς σοὶ γράψαι, 3

St. Luke's Gospel at all, he so mutilated and altered it, that even he did not allow it to be called *Luke's* Gospel. Indeed, several of the most distinguished Critics of the last half century (as Semler, Eichhorn, Griesb., Loeffler, Bp. Marsh, and Dr. Pye Smith) have shown that there is no good reason for supposing that he used St. Luke's Gospel at all. That this Gospel was written for the benefit of *Gentile converts*, is quite plain from the contents, and is confirmed by the unanimous voice of antiquity. On which see Dr. Townson's Works, Vol. I. pp. 181—196, or Horne's Introduction, Vol. IV. 296. sq. On the difficulty which has been found (or rather *made*) in the Proem, and what was the general purpose of the Evangelist in drawing up this Gospel, the reader is referred to the Notes on the Proem. St. Luke's Gospel is, both in plan and character, different from those of St. Matthew and St. Mark; having many peculiarities, and especially this, that, while Matthew and Mark generally relate the facts they record *chronologically*, Luke has mostly not done so, but narrated them according to a *classification* of events; a plan pursued by writers of the greatest eminence, as Livy, Suetonius, Florus, and, to a certain degree, Plutarch in his Lives.

With respect to the *style* of this Gospel, it is purer and more fluent than that of the others; as might be expected from one who, as a Physician, must have had a tolerably good education, and have been, in some degree, a man of letters. There is one peculiarity which deserves attention, namely, that (as Dr. Campb. has remarked) "while each of the Evangelists has a number of words used by none but himself, in St. Luke's Gospel the number of such words is greater than that of all the others put together; and in the *Acts* very far more." For further information on this subject, the reader is referred to Schleiermacher's Critical Essay on the Gospel of St. Luke; and especially to a valuable Critique on it by Dr. Burton in the British Critic for 1827, also Bp. Cleaver's Discourse on the style of St. Luke's Gospel. Suffice it to say that, as there is more of the finish of composition in this Gospel, there is less of nature and simplicity than in the other three. The writer also approaches nearer to the regular historian, by giving, as it were, his *own opinion and judgment* combined with his narrative. See vi. 11. vi. 16. xvi. 4. xi. 53. iii. 20. In recording the moral instructions given by our Lord, especially in the *Parables*, he is surpassed by no other writer for simplicity and pathos.

I. 1. ἐπειδήπερ—διήγησιν.] There is a similar commencement to Justin's History; "Cum multi ex Romanis—res Romanas Græco peregrinoque sermone contulissent, &c.;" and to Isocrat. ad Demon., p. 2. Ὅσοι μενοῦν τοὺς προτρεπτικοὺς λόγους συγγράφουσι, καλὸν ἔργον ἐπιχειροῦσι, &c. See also the commencement to Josephus's Jewish Antiq. *Who* are meant by these "*many*" has been much discussed; but it is now agreed that the *Gospels of Matthew and Mark* could not be intended to be included in those writings; St Matthew being one τῶν ἀπ' ἀρχῆς αὐτόπτων, and the Gospel of Mark not yet written. The narratives in question were probably the compositions of pious and well-meaning persons; but, as we may infer, without the necessary information, or qualifications for writing a Gospel History. They were not intentionally false, but necessarily erroneous and defective. It is certain that we are not to understand what are called the *Apocryphal Gospels* (as they have been collected by Fabricius), since very few, if any, of those can be proved to have been then in being. It is, however, probable that a portion of them would be incorporated into those Apocryphal Gospels, and thus have been preserved. "It is (as Wets. observes) not surprising that the minds of men, strongly excited as they were by the mighty *moral revolution* which had taken place, should have been deeply interested about the origin and nature of a Religion so novel in its character, and promulgated in a manner so widely different from all that had preceded it." And that several should have applied themselves to satisfy this rational curiosity; professing, indeed, to derive their relations from credible, but all of them, more or less, erroneous and defective testimonies. That they were in some degree defective or erroneous, is implied in the very act of St. Luke's undertaking to supply Theophilus with more certain information. For the use of the term ἐπιχειρεῖν will not, as the ancient and some modern Commentators have supposed, supply any such inference; since the word merely means to *undertake* any thing, whether the attempt be accomplished, or *fail*: and therefore, as the Evangelist certainly means not to speak invidiously of the compositions in question; we may, with the most eminent modern Commentators, suppose that there is here no reference to either *success* or *failure*.

Ἀνατάξασθαι has been wrongly supposed by some to signify *re-arranging what is already written*. For the sense of *repetition* in the word, though frequent, is not perpetual. Nor need we, with some, suppose that the preposition here loses its proper force. It is better to take it to denote, not indeed, *repetition*, but *succession*, as of one thing after another, which implies *setting in order*. Thus ἀνατάξασθαι will be equivalent to συντάξασθαι, and that, in a figurative sense, may very well denote *contexere, componere*.

—πεπληροφορημένων] Πληροφορέω signifies, 1st, *to carry a full measure*, to *be full*, or *make full*. 2dly, *to render fully certain*, either as spoken, 1. of *persons*, or, 2. (as here and in 2 Tim. iv. 17.) of *things*, which are thus said to be fully confirmed and established, and are therefore received as *certain truths*, with full assurance of faith.

2. καθὼς παρέδοσαν] Some difficulty attaches to these words (though English Commentators almost universally fail to notice it); for if they be referred, with most Interpreters, to *the narratives before mentioned*, there would seem to be no *reason* why St. Luke should undertake a work which would appear to be superfluous; the information in those being supplied by the persons best qualified to give it. But though that reference *may*, according to the construction, be made, it is certain that such could not be St. Luke's meaning, otherwise he would have said, not ἡμῖν, but αὐτοῖς. What, then, is the reference? Shall we suppose it to be the present Gospel? thus understanding an *hyperbaton*, and making the clause καθὼς, &c. come in after ἀκριβῶς? A method pursued by the learned Capellus. This, however, I have not ventured to adopt, since it is at once too violent and arbitrary. Neither, indeed, is it necessary;

4 κράτιστε Θεόφιλε, ἵνα ἐπιγνῷς περὶ ὧν κατηχήθης λόγων τὴν ἀσφάλειαν.
5 [c] Ἐγένετο ἐν ταῖς ἡμέραις Ἡρώδου τοῦ βασιλέως τῆς Ἰουδαίας ἱερεύς c Matt. 2. 1. 1 Chron. 24. 10, 19. Neh. 12. 4, 17.
τις ὀνόματι Ζαχαρίας ἐξ ἐφημερίας Ἀβιά· καὶ ἡ γυνὴ αὐτοῦ ἐκ τῶν
6 θυγατέρων Ἀαρών, καὶ τὸ ὄνομα αὐτῆς Ἐλισάβετ. Ἦσαν δὲ δίκαιοι

for if, with Koecher, Rosenm., and Kuin. (and I think Grot.), the καθὼς, &c. be referred to τῶν πεπληροφορημένων ἐν ἡμῖν πραγμάτων; (these words being understood to assign the *ground* of that firm conviction) thus καθὼς will have (as not unfrequently in the N. T.) the sense *inasmuch as, quatenus*. By ἡμῖν will be meant "us Christians," i. e. all Christians.

— ἀπ' ἀρχῆς] This is by some supposed to refer to the period at which St. Luke commences his narration: by others, to the commencement of Christ's ministry. The former view is manifestly erroneous; and the latter far from well founded, since the expression must (like that at Matt. xix. 10.) refer to the *primordia* of the thing in question; namely, the *Christian dispensation*, which had its origin in the birth of Christ. So 1 John i. 1. ὃ ἦν ἀπ' ἀρχῆς, ὃ ἀκηκόαμεν, ὃ ἑωράκαμεν — ἀπαγγέλλομεν ὑμῖν (a passage admirably illustrative of the present). Comp. also Heb. ii. 3. And so often in St. John's Gospel and Epistles. See Benson's examples on the above passage. It is probable, however, that by ἀρχὴ St. *Luke* means the *remote origin* of the Christian dispensation in the *birth of the Forerunner* of its Author, namely, John the Baptist; which the Evangelist commences with narrating. Thus also St. Mark i. 1. says that the Gospel had its origin in the preaching of John the Baptist, as prophesied of by Isaiah.

— τοῦ λόγου.] Many of the best Commentators take this to mean "the thing in question, i. e. the Gospel." And ὑπηρέται they interpret "associates in the matter," namely, Christ's relatives, disciples, and friends. Of this sense of λόγος, examples are adduced from Acts xiii. 5, 15, 26. 1 Cor. iv. 1. Wisd. vi. 4. and several from the Classical writers. There is, however, no good reason to abandon the common interpretation, by which τοῦ λόγου is taken to mean τοῦ λόγου τοῦ Θεοῦ, *the Gospel*; a signification frequent in this Gospel and the Acts of the Apostles, and derived from that frequent idiom, by which the Jews applied the phrase, "the word of God;" or, elliptically, "the word," to whatever is revealed by God to men for their instruction. Thus, too, we obtain a more significant expression, and one more agreeable to *facts*; since Luke received his information, both from those who had attended on the ministry of Christ while on earth, and from those who, after his ascension, were preëminently ministers for the propagation of his Gospel throughout the world; especially Saint Paul.

3. παρηκολουθηκότι — ἀκριβῶς.] Render: "having accurately investigated every thing from the very first." Παρακολουθεῖν signifies properly to *follow up, trace*, &c. Many examples have been adduced from the Classical writers, both of the natural and the figurative sense. Ἄνωθεν cannot mean (as some imagine) "by inspiration;" since the context requires the usual sense "from the very first." Thus it is equivalent to ἀπ' ἀρχῆς just before, and has reference to the period at which the Gospel commences (namely, from the conception of John the Baptist), a period earlier than that of Matthew and Mark.

— καθεξῆς.] This denotes, not so much order of *time*, as of *events*, with reference to the *regular disposition*, and *orderly classification* which especially distinguish this Gospel. See the Introd.

— Θεόφιλε.] The notion of some of the older Commentators, that this is only a feigned name, expressive of *any Christian*, and not that of a real person, is now generally exploded. It would indeed be the only instance in the N. T. of a feigned name. Κράτιστε *may* be (as it is regarded by the best Commentators) a title of respect and civility addressed to persons of rank and consequence. So Acts xxiii. 26. τῷ κρατίστῳ Φήλικι. and xxiv. 3. κράτιστε Φῆλιξ. But reference to *title* would be out of place here, and not agreeable to the manner of Scripture. The sense therefore seems to be that of our word *excellent*, defined by Johnson as "said of a person of great virtue and worth." So Ps. xviii. 3. 2 Macc. iv. 12. Thucyd. ii. 40. κράτιστοι δ' ἂν τὴν ψυχὴν δικαίως κριθεῖεν. To suppose it (with some) used like the Roman "vir præstantissime, vir optime," i. e. as a *civil compliment*, is forbidden by the character of an Evangelist to his convert. In fact, the above sense assigned to κράτιστε proceeds upon the *supposition*, purely gratuitous, that Theophilus was a person of high rank and elevated station; a circumstance, to say the least, doubtful. It is probable that he had been converted by Luke, and that he lived out of Palestine.

4. ἵνα ἐπιγνῷς] The ἐπι is here intensive, and the sense of the verb is to *ascertain and be thoroughly informed of* any thing. Κατηχήθης does not import what is now meant by *Catechetical instruction*, but merely denotes that instruction (elementary and chiefly *vivâ voce*), which preceded and followed up admission by baptism into the Christian Church. By λόγων are, I conceive, meant, as the *subject* of the κατηχ., both the *statements* made of the facts which had taken place respecting the origin of the new religion, and the *doctrines* which it revealed. It is remarked by Kuin., that τὴν ἀσφάλειαν glances at the opposite qualities in the narrations just adverted to; as do also the preceding terms ἄνωθεν, ἀκριβῶς, and καθεξῆς.

5. ἐφημερίας.] This word (from ἐπὶ and ἡμέριος, a poetic form for ἡμερινὸς) signifies properly a *daily* service, as was that of the Jewish priests in the temple; and since that was performed by the priests, in turn, for a *week* alternately, it came to denote (as here), by metonymy, *the class* (and there were 24 classes) that took that weekly service in rotation. This is mentioned, to show that John was of *honourable* birth. Zacharias was not, however (as has been supposed), the High Priest; since τις is added, and the High Priest was of no class at all. The offering of incense was, no doubt, only the daily offering, which would fall to his lot as an ordinary priest in his course.

6. δίκαιοι] "persons of uprightness and integrity." Ἐνώπιον τοῦ Θεοῦ is an Hebraic adjunct importing *reality*; for whatever *is* what it *is*, *in the sight of an omniscient God*, must be *really so*. The words following are exegetical and illustra-

ἀμφότεροι ἐνώπιον τοῦ Θεοῦ, πορευόμενοι ἐν πάσαις ταῖς ἐντολαῖς καὶ
δικαιώμασι τοῦ Κυρίου ἄμεμπτοι. Καὶ οὐκ ἦν αὐτοῖς τέκνον, καθότι 7
ἡ Ἐλισάβετ ἦν στεῖρα, καὶ ἀμφότεροι προβεβηκότες ἐν ταῖς ἡμέραις
αὐτῶν ἦσαν. Ἐγένετο δὲ, ἐν τῷ ἱερατεύειν αὐτὸν ἐν τῇ τάξει τῆς 8
d Exod. 30. 7. Lev. 16. 17. Heb. 9. 6. ἐφημερίας αὐτοῦ ἔναντι τοῦ Θεοῦ, [d] κατὰ τὸ ἔθος τῆς ἱερατείας, 9
ἔλαχε τοῦ θυμιάσαι, εἰσελθὼν εἰς τὸν ναὸν τοῦ Κυρίου· καὶ πᾶν τὸ 10
πλῆθος τοῦ λαοῦ ἦν προσευχόμενον ἔξω τῇ ὥρᾳ τοῦ θυμιάματος.
e Exod. 30. 1. [e] Ὤφθη δὲ αὐτῷ ἄγγελος Κυρίου ἑστὼς ἐκ δεξιῶν τοῦ θυσιαστηρίου 11
τοῦ θυμιάματος. καὶ ἐταράχθη Ζαχαρίας ἰδὼν, καὶ φόβος ἐπέπεσεν 12
f Infr. ver. 60. ἐπ' αὐτόν. [f] Εἶπε δὲ πρὸς αὐτὸν ὁ ἄγγελος· Μὴ φοβοῦ, Ζαχαρία· 13
διότι εἰσηκούσθη ἡ δέησίς σου, καὶ ἡ γυνή σου Ἐλισάβετ γεννήσει
g Infr. ver. 58. υἱόν σοι, καὶ καλέσεις τὸ ὄνομα αὐτοῦ Ἰωάννην. [g] Καὶ ἔσται χαρά 14
σοι καὶ ἀγαλλίασις, καὶ πολλοὶ ἐπὶ τῇ ‡ γεννήσει αὐτοῦ χαρήσονται.

tive; and πορευόμενοι is figuratively used of *habitual action.* Δικαιώμασι and ἐντολαῖς, denoting the *ordinances* and *commandments*, are nearly synonymous; but the former may (as some suppose) denote the *moral*, the latter the *ceremonial* law. Ἄμεμπτοι (irreproachable) expresses their good repute with men, as δικ. their piety towards God. So Ovid (cited by Wets.) says similarly of Deucalion and Pyrrha, "innocuos ambos, cultores numinis ambos.

7. καθότι] "inasmuch as," "seeing that."

— προβεβηκότες ἐν ταῖς ἡμ.] This is said to be a Hebraism: but it is only such by the use of ἡμέραις for ἡλικίᾳ, and in the use of ἐν; the Classical writers (as is shown by the examples in Recens. Synop.) using the phrase προβαίνειν τῇ ἡλικίᾳ, or κατὰ τὴν ἡλικίαν. The expression exactly corresponds to our *elderly*, and the Greek ὠμογέρων. So Suid. explains προβεβηκόσι by παλαιοτέροις. This, in the present case, could not *exceed* 50, since after that time a priest was superannuated.

8. ἱερατεύειν.] The word is only found in the later writers; the earlier ones using ἱερᾶσθαι.

9. ἔλαχε τοῦ θυμιάσαι] Sub. κλῆρον, scil. μέρος, which is *expressed* in Acts i. 17; though perhaps the Accus. may be the λάχος included in the verb. Among the various offices thus distributed by lot, the most honourable was this, — of *burning incense.* So much so, indeed, that no priest was allowed to perform it more than *once.* Τὸν ναὸν τοῦ Κ.; i. e., the *Sanctuary*, in which was the altar of incense, as distinguished from the *temple at large*, in which the people were praying, v. 10.

10. For τοῦ λαοῦ ἦν several MSS. have ἦν τοῦ λαοῦ, which is adopted by almost every Editor from Matth. to Scholz; but wrongly, I conceive; for the authority is too weak to establish the existence of so great a harshness as the separation of a Genit. so closely connected with its Nomin. as τοῦ λαοῦ with πλῆθος. This harshness, and the small number of MSS. in favour of the new reading, induce me to suspect that it arose from a mere error of the scribes; who first omitting τοῦ λαοῦ (which, indeed, would not seem very necessary) and then, observing the error, inserted the ἦν *after* τοῦ λαοῦ. The same kind of mistake has occasioned many thousands of corruptions in the Classical writers. For a description of the sacred rite then performing see Lightf. in Rec. Syn. and compare Ecclus. l. 15, and seqq.

11. ἐκ δεξιῶν] scil. μερῶν. This was considered as a good omen by the ancients. And such angelic appearances are occasionally mentioned in *Scripture*, as Judg. xiii. 22, and Dan. x. 8.

13. On the *circumstances* connected with the births of John the Baptist and of Christ, see Lightf., Whitby, and Mackn., and especially Dr. Bell on the mission of John the Baptist; who ably evinces the genuineness of this part of the sacred history, and shows, that "the whole train of events here said to have taken place, are of a nature so entirely beyond the power of man to produce, that, if they really happened as they are said to have happened, the authority of any fact founded on them becomes unquestionable." He further shows, that "whatever circumstance one may select with the endeavour to fix *imposture*, it can be evinced that any such supposition involves absurdities of the grossest sort; in fact, that in general, the supposed imposture is not only *morally*, but almost *physically* impossible. And, in short, that whether the character, circumstances, and condition of the persons concerned, or the nature of the supposed *plot* and its chances of success be considered, the whole affair is completely immersed in absurdity, and runs counter to the ordinary principles of human action."

— εἰσηκούσθη.] A Hellenistic use of the word, in which the εἰς signifies *leaning towards*, which implies *favour*, &c.

— ἡ δέησίς σου.] Some think the prayer adverted to was a prayer for offspring; addressed either then or formerly. Many specious arguments have been urged *for*, and not a few weighty reasons *against* this supposition. Besides that the apparent impossibility of the thing may be supposed to have produced acquiescence in the will of God; the pious priest would be unlikely to mingle private concerns with public devotions: and it is, therefore, more probable that he was praying for the advent of Him whose coming many signs announced to be near at hand, even the Messiah.

14. ἔσται χαρά σοι.] Literally, "he shall be joy to thee," i. e. occasion of joy; said in allusion to the name Ἰωάννης, which signifies "the grace and mercy of God." Ἀγαλλίασις is a stronger term, and denotes *exultation.* Instead of γεννήσει, Griesb. and many others down to Scholz edit, from very many MSS., γενέσει, which is, indeed, agreeable to the *proprietas linguæ*; but of such minutiæ the sacred writers are little observant, and the former was more likely to be changed into the latter than the contrary.

15 [h] Ἔσται γὰρ μέγας ἐνώπιον τοῦ Κυρίου· καὶ οἶνον καὶ σίκερα οὐ μὴ b Num. 6. 3. Jud. 13. 4.
πίῃ· καὶ Πνεύματος ἁγίου πλησθήσεται ἔτι ἐκ κοιλίας μητρὸς αὐτοῦ. Jer. 1. 5. Gal. 1. 15.
16 [i] Καὶ πολλοὺς τῶν υἱῶν Ἰσραὴλ ἐπιστρέψει ἐπὶ Κύριον τὸν Θεὸν αὐτῶν. i Mal. 4. 5. Matt. 11. 14.
17 [k] Καὶ αὐτὸς προελεύσεται ἐνώπιον αὐτοῦ ἐν πνεύματι καὶ δυνάμει k Mal. 4. 6. Matt. 3. 1. Mark 9. 12.
Ἡλίου· ἐπιστρέψαι καρδίας πατέρων ἐπὶ τέκνα καὶ ἀπειθεῖς ἐν φρο-
18 νήσει δικαίων, ἑτοιμάσαι Κυρίῳ λαὸν κατεσκευασμένον. [l] Καὶ εἶπε l Gen. 17. 17.
Ζαχαρίας πρὸς τὸν ἄγγελον· Κατὰ τί γνώσομαι τοῦτο; ἐγὼ γάρ
εἰμι πρεσβύτης, καὶ ἡ γυνή μου προβεβηκυῖα ἐν ταῖς ἡμέραις αὐτῆς.
19 [m] Καὶ ἀποκριθεὶς ὁ ἄγγελος εἶπεν αὐτῷ· Ἐγώ εἰμι Γαβριὴλ ὁ παρ- m Dan. 8. 16. & 9. 21.
εστηκὼς ἐνώπιον τοῦ Θεοῦ· καὶ ἀπεστάλην λαλῆσαι πρός σε, καὶ Matt. 18. 10.
20 εὐαγγελίσασθαί σοι ταῦτα. Καὶ ἰδού, ἔσῃ σιωπῶν καὶ μὴ δυνάμενος
λαλῆσαι ἄχρι ἧς ἡμέρας γένηται ταῦτα, ἀνθ᾽ ὧν οὐκ ἐπίστευσας τοῖς
21 λόγοις μου, οἵτινες πληρωθήσονται εἰς τὸν καιρὸν αὐτῶν. Καὶ ἦν ὁ
λαὸς προσδοκῶν τὸν Ζαχαρίαν· καὶ ἐθαύμαζον ἐν τῷ χρονίζειν αὐτὸν

15. *μέγας ἐνώπιον τοῦ Κυρίου*] i. e. *μέγας παρὰ Θεῷ*, in the sight of the Lord or Jehovah. Though some take *Κυρίου* of *Christ*, yet Middlet. has shown that the use of the Article with *Κυρ.* requires us to understand it of *Jehovah*.

—*οἶνον — πίῃ.*] A Nazaritic injunction. So Numb. vi. 3, it is said of him who has vowed a vow of Nazareth: *ἀπὸ οἴνου καὶ σίκερα ἁγνισθήσεται.* *Σίκερα* is derived from the Heb. שכר, *to inebriate*, and denotes generally any intoxicating drink; but was chiefly applied to what we call *made* wines; or fermented drink, such as ale, or spirit of aniseed, &c. The words *ἐκ κοιλίας μητρὸς αὐτοῦ* contain a Hebrew hyperbole, denoting "from the earliest period." See Is. xlviii. 8; xlix. 1 & 5. Ps. lxxi. 6. Yet something very similar occurs in the Anthol. Græc. v. 25. The Classical writers use the phrases *ἐκ παιδὸς*, or *βρέφους*, or *νηπίων*. The *ἔτι* is for *ἤδη*.

16. *ἐπιστρέψει ἐπὶ Κύρ.*] "will convert to the true worship of God," as Acts xi. 21; xiv. 15. 2 Cor. iii. 16.

17. *αὐτοῦ.*] A difference of opinion exists as to what this is to be referred. Some, as Kuin., regard it as put *emphatically* for *Christ*, and compare Luke v. 17. I John ii. 6 & 12. But *there* the reference is not, as here, clear and determinate, the *αὐτοῦ* being closely connected with *Κύριον τὸν Θεὸν*, i. e. *Jehovah*. The allusion in *προελεύσεται ἐνώπιον αὐτοῦ* is clear from Matt. iii. 3. where see Note. *Πνεύματι* signifies disposition, and *δυνάμει* zeal, energy, or mighty endowments. On Elias, as a type of the Baptist, see Note on Matt. xi. 14. In *ἐπιστρέψαι*, &c. there is plainly an allusion to Mal. iv. 6, (compare also Ecclus. xlviii. 10,) but on the exact import of the words Commentators are not agreed. The most natural mode of interpretation, and that most suitable to the words of the Prophet, is to regard them as denoting that reconciliation of discordant sects and political feuds, by a common repentance and reformation, and general cultivation of philanthropy, which it was the purpose of the Gospel to promulgate and enjoin on men.

—*καὶ ἀπειθεῖς ἐν φρονήσει δικ.*] There is some difference of opinion as to the sense of these words. Many Commentators construe them with the words *following*, and render: "And by the wisdom of the righteous (or of righteousness) to render the disobedient a people well-disposed for the Lord, i. e. furnished for the Lord, or formed for him." This, however, does violence to the construction of the sentence; and therefore it is better, with most Commentators, (supported by the authority of Valckn.,) to take the words as a separate and independent clause. Thus *ἐν φρονήσει* will be for *εἰς φρόνησιν*, and the sense will be, "to reform the disobedient and unrighteous to the comprehension and embracing of righteousness." The true construction seems to be this: *καὶ ἐπιστρέψαι ἀπειθεῖς (ὥστε εἶναι) ἐν φ. δ.*, "so that they may be of the disposition of the righteous."

The sense of *ἑτοιμάζειν Κυρίῳ λαὸν κατεσκευασμένον* is, "to make ready a people prepared or fitted for [the service of] the Lord." Thus all is plain. The two first clauses state the *particular* purposes of the Baptist's mission; namely, to introduce concord, philanthropy, and reformation of mind and practice. The third states the *general purpose*, or perhaps the *result* of the former.

18. *κατὰ τί.*] Sub. *σημεῖον*, which is *expressed* in a similar passage of Gen. xv. 8. So also *ἐν τινὶ* at Judg. vi. 15, and 1 Sam. xxix. 4. Grot. here remarks on the difference in the cases of Abraham and Zechariah, as to the *same action*. The former did not ask for a sign, from *distrust* in the promise of God, but for *confirmation of his faith*; whereas the latter had no faith at all. Hence, though a sign was given to him, it was a *punishment* likewise, though wisely ordained to be such, as should fix the attention of the Jews on the promised child. See more in Rec. Syn.

19. *παρεστηκὼς ἐνώπιον τοῦ Θεοῦ.*] An image borrowed from Oriental custom in courts. See Rec. Syn. and Note on 1 Thess. iii. 6.

20. *ἔσῃ — λαλῆσαι.*] This is not a mere pleonasm; but the latter phrase is meant to explain and strengthen the force of the former. Thus in Acts: *ἔσῃ τυφλὸς, μὴ βλέπων τὸν ἥλιον.* The Commentators who refer this to the idiom by which the affirmation of a thing is joined with a denial of its contrary, confound two distinct idioms.

21. The people might well wonder that Zech. should stay so long; for it appears to have been customary for the priest *not* to tarry long, on account of the people waiting in the outer court; who would fear lest some harm had befallen him, from negligence in the duty, or otherwise; which might be *ominous of evil* to the people at large.

ἐν τῷ ναῷ. Ἐξελθὼν δὲ οὐκ ἠδύνατο λαλῆσαι αὐτοῖς· καὶ ἐπέγνω- 22
σαν ὅτι ὀπτασίαν ἑώρακεν ἐν τῷ ναῷ· καὶ αὐτὸς ἦν διανεύων αὐτοῖς,
καὶ διέμενε κωφός. Καὶ ἐγένετο, ὡς ἐπλήσθησαν αἱ ἡμέραι τῆς λει- 23
τουργίας αὐτοῦ, ἀπῆλθεν εἰς τὸν οἶκον αὐτοῦ. Μετὰ δὲ ταύτας τὰς 24
ἡμέρας συνέλαβεν Ἐλισάβετ ἡ γυνὴ αὐτοῦ, καὶ περιέκρυβεν ἑαυτὴν
n Gen. 30. 23. Isa. 4. 1. μῆνας πέντε, λέγουσα· n Ὅτι οὕτω μοι πεποίηκεν ὁ Κύριος ἐν ἡμέραις 25
αἷς ἐπεῖδεν, ἀφελεῖν τὸ ὄνειδός μου ἐν ἀνθρώποις.
ἘΝ δὲ τῷ μηνὶ τῷ ἕκτῳ ἀπεστάλη ὁ ἄγγελος Γαβριὴλ ὑπὸ τοῦ 26
o Matt. 1. 18. Θεοῦ εἰς πόλιν τῆς Γαλιλαίας ᾗ ὄνομα Ναζαρὲτ, o πρὸς παρθένον 27
μεμνηστευμένην ἀνδρὶ ᾧ ὄνομα Ἰωσὴφ, ἐξ οἴκου Δαυΐδ· καὶ τὸ ὄνομα
τῆς παρθένου Μαριάμ. Καὶ εἰσελθὼν ὁ ἄγγελος πρὸς αὐτὴν, εἶπε· 28
Χαῖρε, κεχαριτωμένη· ὁ Κύριος μετὰ σοῦ· εὐλογημένη σὺ ἐν γυναιξίν! Ἡ δὲ ἰδοῦσα διεταράχθη ἐπὶ τῷ λόγῳ αὐτοῦ, καὶ διελογίζετο 29
ποταπὸς εἴη ὁ ἀσπασμὸς οὗτος. Καὶ εἶπεν ὁ ἄγγελος αὐτῇ· Μὴ 30

When Zechariah at length appeared, and was evidently deprived of the faculty of utterance, the people would be likely to conjecture that *something extraordinary* had happened to him, and naturally asked, whether he had seen *ὀπτασίαν*, as we say, *apparition*.

22. *λαλῆσαι αὐτοῖς*] i. e. to give them the accustomed benediction, as most Commentators explain; though the thing is not certain. *Ἦν διανεύων αὐτοῖς*, scil. *τοῦτο*, i. e. nodding *assent* to the inquiry, whether he had seen a vision. *Διανεύειν* signifies to express one's meaning by nods, or becks. See Recens. Synop. *Κωφὸς* here signifies *both deaf and dumb*, as may be imagined from what has been observed on a former occasion.

23. *λειτουργίας*.] *Λειτουργία* is derived from the old word *λήϊτος*, *publicus*; and signifies properly *any public service*, whether civil or military. But in the Scriptures it is applied to the public offices of *religion*; 1. that of the *Priests and Levites*, under the Mosaic Law; 2. that of *Christian Ministers* of every sort, under the Gospel Dispensation.

24. *συνέλαβεν*.] Sub. *ἔμβρυον*.

—*περιέκρυβεν ἑ*.] The import of this expression has been much disputed. Some Commentators, ancient and modern, take it to mean, she *concealed her situation*. To which it has been justly objected, that there could be no *reason* for such concealment. Indeed, the word cannot *signify* any such thing; and it is not necessarily *implied* in the context: not to say that that sense would be scarcely of sufficient moment. It should, therefore, seem best to take *περιέκ. ἑαυτὴν* in the sense, "she kept herself retired." This she would be induced to do, throughout her whole pregnancy, not only through motives of *delicacy*, (considering her advanced years,) but still more from an anxiety to preserve herself from such accidents, as might either endanger the *safety* of the precious embryo, or impart any *defilement* to it; (See Lightf., and comp. Judg. xiii. 14.) and lastly, she would feel herself bound, considering the signal favour she had received at the hands of the Almighty, (by which was removed from her the reproach that barrenness was thought to convey) to employ the period of her pregnancy for the purposes of more than ordinary devotion. It is frivolous to debate *which five months* are here meant; for the *last* five are not permitted by the *context*, which manifestly points to the *first* five. But the words *ἐν τῷ μηνὶ τῷ ἕκτῳ ἀπεστάλη* will not, (as it has been thought,) oblige us to suppose that she kept retired *only* the *first* five. There was more reason, on every account, for the *next four*; and, therefore, we are warranted in extending that privacy (with Lightf.) to the *whole* period of Elizabeth's gestation.

25. *ἐπεῖδεν*] "looked upon me," i. e. (by implication) with favour. A signification found in the Heb. רָאָה, the Gr. Class. *ἐσιδεῖν*, and the Latin *respicere*. *Ὄνειδος* is one of those words which, though in the later Grecism having a *bad* sense, yet in the *earlier* one were of *middle* signification; as Eurip. Bacch. 640. *κάλλιστον ὄνειδος*. So *δόξα*, and the Latin *fama*, &c. This is only the case with words which from their *origin admit* of a middle signification: not so with those which, from their derivation, *must* have a *bad* one. So *ψόγος*, from *ψέω*, cogn. with *ψάω*, rado, to *rub*, and, in a metaphorical sense, to be rough upon, rub hard upon, *reprove*.

26—39. On the miraculous conception here treated of, see Townsend's Chron. Arr. of N. T., p. 32, sqq.

27. *μεμνηστευμένην*] "betrothed, contracted;" without which no woman was ever married, among the Jews, and probably the Gentiles also, from the earliest ages. See Hom. Il. Z. 245.

28. *κεχαριτωμένη*.] This is not well rendered "beloved," or "favourite of heaven," as in Campbell's version. Better (as in the Vulg.) "gratiâ plena," "highly favoured." For (as Valckn. observes) all verbs of this form, as *αἱματόω*, *θαυματόω*, &c. have a sense of *heaping up*, or *rendering full*. *Χαριτόω* is rare, and only found, in the Classical writers, once in Liban. It occurs, however, in Ecclus. ix. 8; xviii. 17, and Ps. xviii. 26. Symm. Ὁ *Κύριος μετὰ σοῦ*. Sub. *ἔστω*. A frequent form of salutation. See Ruth ii. 4. Judg. vi. 12.

—*εὐλογημένη ἐν γυναιξίν*.] This is said to be a Hebrew form of expressing the superlative; but it is found also in both the Greek and the Latin Classical writers. Suffice it to refer to the Horatian "Micat *inter omnes* Julium sidus, velut *inter ignes* Luna minores."

29. *ποταπὸς εἴη ὁ ἀσπ. οὗτος*.] A popular form of expression, equivalent to "what these remarkable addresses might mean."

31 φοβοῦ, Μαριάμ· εὗρες γὰρ χάριν παρὰ τῷ Θεῷ. [p] καὶ ἰδού, συλ- p Isa. 7. 14. infr. 2. 21.
λήψῃ ἐν γαστρὶ καὶ τέξῃ υἱόν, καὶ καλέσεις τὸ ὄνομα αὐτοῦ Ἰησοῦν. Matt. 1. 21.
32 [q] Οὗτος ἔσται μέγας, καὶ Υἱὸς ὑψίστου κληθήσεται· καὶ δώσει αὐτῷ q Isa. 9. 6. & 16. 5.
33 Κύριος ὁ Θεὸς τὸν θρόνον Δαυΐδ τοῦ πατρὸς αὐτοῦ, [r] καὶ βασιλεύσει & 54. 5. 2 Sam. 7. 12.
ἐπὶ τὸν οἶκον Ἰακὼβ εἰς τοὺς αἰῶνας, καὶ τῆς βασιλείας αὐτοῦ οὐκ Psal. 132. 11. r Dan. 2. 44. & 7. 14, 27.
34 ἔσται τέλος. Εἶπε δὲ Μαριὰμ πρὸς τὸν ἄγγελον· Πῶς ἔσται τοῦτο, Mich. 4. 7. Isa. 9. 7.
35 ἐπεὶ ἄνδρα οὐ γινώσκω; Καὶ ἀποκριθεὶς ὁ ἄγγελος εἶπεν αὐτῇ· 1 Chron. 22. 10. Psal. 45. 6. & 89. 36.
Πνεῦμα ἅγιον ἐπελεύσεται ἐπὶ σέ, καὶ δύναμις ὑψίστου ἐπισκιάσει σοι· Jer. 23. 5. 1 Cor. 15. 24.
36 διὸ καὶ τὸ γεννώμενον ἅγιον κληθήσεται Υἱὸς Θεοῦ. Καὶ ἰδού, Ἐλισά- Heb. 1. 8.
βετ ἡ συγγενής σου καὶ αὐτὴ συνειληφυῖα υἱὸν ἐν γήρει αὐτῆς· καὶ
37 οὗτος μὴν ἕκτος ἐστὶν αὐτῇ τῇ καλουμένῃ στείρᾳ. [s] Ὅτι οὐκ ἀδυνατή- s Job 42. 2. Jer. 32. 17.
38 σει παρὰ τῷ Θεῷ πᾶν ῥῆμα. Εἶπε δὲ Μαριάμ· Ἰδού, ἡ δούλη Zach. 8. 6. Matt. 19. 26. infr. 18. 27.
Κυρίου· γένοιτό μοι κατὰ τὸ ῥῆμά σου. καὶ ἀπῆλθεν ἀπ᾽ αὐτῆς ὁ
ἄγγελος.
39 Ἀναστᾶσα δὲ Μαριὰμ ἐν ταῖς ἡμέραις ταύταις ἐπορεύθη εἰς τὴν
40 ὀρεινὴν μετὰ σπουδῆς εἰς πόλιν † Ἰούδα· καὶ εἰσῆλθεν εἰς τὸν οἶκον
41 Ζαχαρίου, καὶ ἠσπάσατο τὴν Ἐλισάβετ. Καὶ ἐγένετο, ὡς ἤκουσεν ἡ
Ἐλισάβετ τὸν ἀσπασμὸν τῆς Μαρίας, ἐσκίρτησε τὸ βρέφος ἐν τῇ κοιλίᾳ
42 αὐτῆς· καὶ ἐπλήσθη Πνεύματος ἁγίου ἡ Ἐλισάβετ, καὶ ἀνεφώνησε
φωνῇ μεγάλῃ καὶ εἶπεν· Εὐλογημένη σὺ ἐν γυναιξί, καὶ εὐλογημένος
43 ὁ καρπὸς τῆς κοιλίας σου! καὶ πόθεν μοι τοῦτο, ἵνα ἔλθῃ ἡ μήτηρ

30. *εὗρες χάριν.*] This is not a Hebraism. So Thucyd. i. 58. *εὕροντο οὐδὲν ἐπιτήδειον*, and v. 35. *εὕροντο τὰς σπονδάς*. The *middle* form, however, is always used by the Classics.

32. *κληθήσεται*] "shall be." The Unitarian mistranslation of *υἱὸς ὑψίστου*, "*a* son of the most high God," is completely refuted by Bp. Middlet. The force of the expression is also ably pointed out by Bp. Bull, Jud. Eccl. Cath., p. 37, and his Defens. Fid. Nic., p. 242.

35. *δύναμις ὑψίστου ἐπ.*] These words are exegetical of the preceding clause. Ἐπισκιάζειν signifies, 1. to overshadow; 2. to surround; 3. to defend, or assist; 4. as here, to exert a power or influence in, like *ἐπισκήνωσῃ* in 2 Cor. xii. 9.

36. *γήρει.*] This (for *γήρᾳ*) is found in almost all the best MSS. and the early Edd., and is, with reason, adopted by Wets., Matth., Griesb., Tittm., Vater, and Scholz.

—*ἕκτος ἐστὶν—στείρᾳ.*] On this idiom I have fully treated in Recens. Synop., and on Thucyd. i. 13, and iii. 2.

37. *οὐκ ἀδυνατήσει—ῥῆμα.*] A proverbial form of expression, similar to one in Gen. xviii. 14. *μὴ ἀδυνατήσει παρὰ τῷ Θεῷ ῥῆμα*. Here *ῥῆμα*, like the Heb. דָּבָר, signifies *thing*, as often; and the Future has the force of the Present.

38. *ἰδοὺ—Κυρίου.*] An expression of pious acquiescence.

39. *τὴν ὀρεινήν.*] Scil. *χώραν*, called at v. 65. *τῇ ὀρεινῇ τῆς Ἰουδαίας*; by which is meant, I conceive, the hilly country about Hebron So Joseph. Antiq. xii. 1, 1. *ἀπὸ τῆς ὀρεινῆς* (scil. *χώρας*) *τῆς Ἰουδαίας*. This is placed beyond doubt by Joseph. B. J., p. 1200. Huds. *Κεῖται δὲ* (scil. *Χέβρων*) *κατὰ τὴν ὀρεινήν*, and Bell. J. i. 1. 5. *ἐμβάλλει διὰ τῆς Ἰουδαίας εἰς τὴν ὀρεινήν*.

—*πόλιν Ἰούδα.*] *What* city is here meant, has been much debated. Some think *Jerusalem*: others, *Hebron*. It is now, however, agreed, that it cannot have been the *former*; since it was not in the *Highland* district. Whereas *Hebron*, it is urged, was not only a Sacerdotal city, but was situated in the Highlands. But why, then, it may be asked, did not the Evangelist at once *say* Hebron? It should seem scarcely probable, too, that he would mention the *metropolis* of the tribe in so very indefinite a manner. What writer ever speaks of the capital of a province as *a city in* it? Not to say, that, (as Reland observes,) from the air of the context, we should expect the name of some *certain* city. Hence many have suspected that there is here an error in the *reading*. And Reland, Palæst., p. 870, conjectures, with great probability, that the true reading is Ἰούτα, itself also a sacerdotal city, and in the Highlands, a few miles east of Hebron, mentioned in Josh. xv. 55; xxi. 16. This conjecture is embraced by Vales., Michaelis, Rosenm., and Kuin., who truly observe, that the scribes might easily mistake the comparatively little known Ἰούτα with the well known Ἰούδα: or that Ἰούτα, may have been changed in pronunciation into Ἰούδα, in the time of St. Luke. As confirmatory of the above, I would add, that one Edition of the Sept in the passage of Joshua has Ἰεδδὰ, plainly by an error of the scribes, for Ἰουδδά.

41. *ἐσκίρτησε ἐν τῇ κοιλίᾳ α.*] Σκιρτᾷν properly signifies to bound, like young animals; but is sometimes, like *salire* in Latin, applied to denote the leaping of the fœtus in utero. So Gen. xxv. 22. *ἐσκίρτων τὰ παιδία ἐν αὐτῇ*, and Nonn. Dionys. viii. 224. This is not uncommon in the advanced stages of pregnancy; and is usually occasioned by sudden perturbation.

43. *πόθεν μοι τοῦτο.*] Sub. *τὸ πρᾶγμα γέγονε*.

τοῦ Κυρίου μου πρός με; ἰδοὺ γὰρ, ὡς ἐγένετο ἡ φωνὴ τοῦ ἀσπα- 44
σμοῦ σου εἰς τὰ ὦτά μου, ἐσκίρτησεν ἐν ἀγαλλιάσει τὸ βρέφος ἐν τῇ
t Infr. 11. 28. κοιλίᾳ μου. ᵗ Καὶ μακαρία ἡ πιστεύσασα· ὅτι ἔσται τελείωσις τοῖς 45
λελαλημένοις αὐτῇ παρὰ Κυρίου.

u 1 Sam. 1. 11. Καὶ εἶπε Μαριάμ· Μεγαλύνει ἡ ψυχή μου τὸν Κύριον, καὶ ἠγαλ- 46
Gen. 30. 13. x Gen. 17. 7. λίασε τὸ πνεῦμά μου ἐπὶ τῷ Θεῷ τῷ σωτῆρί μου· ᵘ ὅτι ἐπέβλεψεν 47
Exod. 20. 6. Psal. 103. 17. ἐπὶ τὴν ταπείνωσιν τῆς δούλης αὐτοῦ. Ἰδοὺ γὰρ, ἀπὸ τοῦ νῦν μακα- 48
y Isa. 29. 15. & 51. 9. & 52. 10. ριοῦσί με πᾶσαι αἱ γενεαί· ὅτι ἐποίησέ μοι μεγαλεῖα ὁ Δυνατὸς, καὶ 49
Ps. 33. 10. 1 Pet. 5. 5. ἅγιον τὸ ὄνομα αὐτοῦ· ˣ Καὶ τὸ ἔλεος αὐτοῦ εἰς γενεὰς γενεῶν τοῖς 50
z 1 Sam. 2. 7, 8. Ps. 113. 7. φοβουμένοις αὐτόν. ʸ Ἐποίησε κράτος ἐν βραχίονι αὐτοῦ· διεσκόρπισεν 51
Job 5. 11. & 12. 18, 19, 21. ὑπερηφάνους διανοίᾳ καρδίας αὐτῶν. ᶻ Καθεῖλε δυνάστας ἀπὸ θρόνων, 52

This manner of speaking is a form expressive of admiration at any unexpected honour done, and is not unfrequent in the Classical writers.

44. ἐσκίρτησεν ἐν ἀγαλλ.] i. e. by a popular manner of speaking, as it *were* leaped for joy; for the fœtus was incapable of any sensation. Her knowledge that Mary was to be the mother of the Messiah, as well as her immediate belief in the promise of the angel, was doubtless imparted by a Divine revelation. Instead of ἐσκίρτησεν ἐν ἀγαλλ. τὸ βρέφος very many MSS. have ἐσκίρτησε τὸ βρέφος ἐν ἀγαλλ., which is edited by Matth., Griesb., and Scholz; but wrongly; for the reading seems to have arisen merely from an accidental omission of ἐν ἀγαλλ. (which is awkwardly interposed between the Nominat. and the verb), and then to have been inserted, but in the wrong place. Besides, the reading in question involves, in ἐν ἀγαλλ. ἐν τῇ κοιλ., a greater irregularity than can be found any where else in St. Luke's writings.

45. ἡ πιστεύσασα· ὅτι, &c.] Some join ὅτι closely with πιστ. But this construction, though sanctioned by the usage of Scripture, pares down the sense, while that proposed by Kuin. is unnecessarily tortuous.

46. It is observable, that most of the phrases in this noble effusion are borrowed from the O. T.; especially from the song of Hannah, to which it bears a strong resemblance, and in which there were so many phrases remarkably suited to Mary's own case.

— μεγαλύνει ἡ ψυχή μου.] This use of ψυχὴ is not a mere Hebraism, but is very emphatic, and implies the greatest earnestness and intensity of feeling. Μεγαλύνειν, in this precatory use, (of which there are instances in the *Classical* writers) signifies to *extol*. Ταπείνωσις signifies not *humility*, but *lowly condition*, as in Gen. xxix. 32, and elsewhere; though the former may be included as a secondary sense.

48. μακαριοῦσι] "shall esteem me happy;" namely, in giving birth to the Saviour of the world. In this absolute use the word occurs in James v. 11; but in the Classical writers it is usually accompanied with a Genitive of thing, stating the *cause*, or *origin*.

49. μεγαλεῖα.] The Commentators supply ἔργα. But it is better to say that, in such a case as this, the adjective is used substantively. Nor is μεγ. to be rendered, with some, "*miracles*;" but ἐποίησέ μοι μεγ. may be translated, "hath conferred upon me very great benefits;" for μεγαλεῖος signifies more than μέγας. The expression is founded on Ps. lxx. 19. (Sept.) ἃ ἐποίησας μοι μεγαλεῖα. See Deut. x. 21. 1 Sam. xii. 16. Tobit xi. 15. There seems to be an antithesis between μεγαλεῖα here, and μεγαλύνει at ver. 46. The expression ὁ Δυνατὸς, formed on the Heb. גבור, designates κατ' ἐξοχὴν (as in Ps. xxiv. 8. Sept.) *the Almighty*. At ἅγιον — αὐτοῦ supply ἐστι, render "holy and to be reverenced is his name." This is formed on Ps. cxi. 3.

50. τοῖς φοβ.] for πρὸς τοὺς φοβουμένους; a syntax frequent in the LXX. See Exod. xx. 6. Ps. lxxxviii. 2. Sept.

51. Here we have a celebration of God's power; and the general declaration ἐποίησε κράτος ἐν βραχίονι αὐτοῦ (where the Aorist denotes *custom*) is then illustrated by *examples*. Βραχ. denotes, by an usual Hebrew figure, the mighty power of God, as shown most signally; for (as a Commentator remarks), "the *great* power of God is represented by his *finger*; his *greater* by his *hand*; and his *greatest* by his *arm*." By ἔλεος is meant, as often in the Sept., the *benignity* of God. Instead of εἰς γενεὰς γενεῶν several MSS. have ἐ. γενεὰν καὶ γενεάν; which reading is edited by Matthæi. But wrongly; for that and the other *three* various readings, are no more than so many various modes of explaining, or simplifying a rather unusual expression, yet founded on the Hebrew idiom. The use, too, of ποιεῖν throughout the passage is Hebraic.

— διεσκόρπισεν] "he utterly discomfits." A metaphor derived from putting to flight a defeated enemy. The word not unfrequently occurs in the LXX. (and in this very sense, in Ps. lviii. 11.), but very rarely in the Classical writers, though one example is adduced by Kuin., from Ælian, Var. Hist. xiii. 46. τοὺς μὲν διεσκόρπισεν, οὓς (read τοὺς) δὲ ἀπέκτεινε.

Διανοίᾳ is governed by ἐπὶ understood, and may be understood to denote their inmost thoughts and devices. The full sense of the passage is well expressed by Mr. Norris, in the following paraphrase: "He scatters the imaginations of the proud, perplexes their schemes, disturbs their politics, breaks their measures, sets those things far asunder which they had united in one system, and so disperses the broken pieces of it, that they can never put them together again. And by this he turns their wisdom into folly, their imaginary greatness into contempt, and their glory into shame; so overruling their counsels, in his wise government of the world, as to make all turn to *his*, not *their*, *praise*."

52. καθεῖλε δυνάστας.] Καθαίρω signifies properly to *pull down*, as applied to *things*; but it is not unfrequently used of *persons*. The passage is formed on Ecclus. x. 14. See my Note on

53 καὶ ὕψωσε ταπεινούς. [a] Πεινῶντας ἐνέπλησεν ἀγαθῶν, καὶ πλουτοῦντας [a] Psal. 34. 10. 1 Sam. 2. 5.
54 ἐξαπέστειλε κενούς. [b] Ἀντελάβετο Ἰσραὴλ παιδὸς αὐτοῦ, μνησθῆναι [b] Isa. 30. 18. & 41. 8.
55 ἐλέους ([c] καθὼς ἐλάλησε πρὸς τοὺς πατέρας ἡμῶν) τῷ Ἀβραὰμ καὶ τῷ & 54. 5. Jer. 31. 3, 20. [c] Gen. 17. 19.
56 σπέρματι αὐτοῦ εἰς τὸν αἰῶνα. Ἔμεινε δὲ Μαριὰμ σὺν αὐτῇ ὡσεὶ & 22. 18. Ps. 132. 11.
μῆνας τρεῖς· καὶ ὑπέστρεψεν εἰς τὸν οἶκον αὐτῆς.
57 Τῇ δὲ Ἐλισάβετ ἐπλήσθη ὁ χρόνος τοῦ τεκεῖν αὐτὴν, καὶ ἐγέννησεν
58 υἱόν. [d] Καὶ ἤκουσαν οἱ περίοικοι καὶ οἱ συγγενεῖς αὐτῆς, ὅτι ἐμεγά- [d] Supr. v. 14.
59 λυνε Κύριος τὸ ἔλεος αὐτοῦ μετ᾽ αὐτῆς· καὶ συνέχαιρον αὐτῇ. [e] Καὶ [e] Gen. 17. 12. Lev. 12. 3.
ἐγένετο, ἐν τῇ ὀγδόῃ ἡμέρᾳ ἦλθον περιτεμεῖν τὸ παιδίον· καὶ ἐκάλουν
60 αὐτὸ, ἐπὶ τῷ ὀνόματι τοῦ πατρὸς αὐτοῦ, Ζαχαρίαν [f] Καὶ ἀποκριθεῖ- [f] Supr. v. 13.
61 σα ἡ μήτηρ αὐτοῦ εἶπεν· Οὐχὶ, ἀλλὰ κληθήσεται Ἰωάννης. Καὶ
εἶπον πρὸς αὐτήν· Ὅτι οὐδείς ἐστιν ἐν τῇ συγγενείᾳ σου, ὃς καλεῖται
62 τῷ ὀνόματι τούτῳ. Ἐνένευον δὲ τῷ πατρὶ αὐτοῦ, τὸ τί ἂν θέλοι
63 καλεῖσθαι αὐτόν. [g] Καὶ αἰτήσας πινακίδιον, ἔγραψε λέγων· Ἰωάννης [g] Supr. v. 13.
64 ἐστὶ τὸ ὄνομα αὐτοῦ. καὶ ἐθαύμασαν πάντες. Ἀνεῴχθη δὲ τὸ στόμα
αὐτοῦ παραχρῆμα καὶ ἡ γλῶσσα αὐτοῦ· καὶ ἐλάλει εὐλογῶν τὸν Θεόν.
65 Καὶ ἐγένετο ἐπὶ πάντας φόβος τοὺς περιοικοῦντας αὐτούς καὶ ἐν ὅλῃ
66 τῇ ὀρεινῇ τῆς Ἰουδαίας διελαλεῖτο πάντα τὰ ῥήματα ταῦτα. Καὶ ἔθεντο

Thucyd. vi. 83. Δυνάστας (potentates) denotes, not kings only, but all who are invested with political power, in Recens. Synop. Wets. aptly compares Hesiod Ἔργ. i. 5. Ῥεῖα μὲν γὰρ βριάει, ῥέα δὲ βριάοντα χαλέπτει. Ῥεῖα δ' ἀρίζηλον μινύθει, καὶ ἄδηλον ἀέξει.

53. Ἀγαθῶν is a term savouring of the simplicity of common life and Oriental plainness, denoting the *subsidia vitæ*.

54. ἀντελάβετο Ἰ.] Ἀντιλαμβάνειν denotes properly "*to lay hold of any thing*," or person, by the hand, in order to support it when it is likely to fall; but it is here, as often in the Classical writers, used metaphorically, for "to protect," "support."

—μνησθῆναι.] Sub. ὥστε or εἰς τὸ, as v. 72. and frequently elsewhere. The construction will be plain from the punctuation which I have adopted, and it is confirmed by Ps. xcvii. 3. LXX. With respect to the full sense of μνησθῆναι. God (as I explained in Rec. Synop.) is said to be *mindful* of his people, when he exerts his power for their support, and confers on them the benefits he promised.

56. ὡσεὶ μῆνας τρεῖς] i. e., as Theophyl., Euthym., and Grot. show, till very near the time of Elizabeth's delivery. That she left her at so critical a time was probably from motives of delicacy; since such were periods of great bustle, by the extraordinary resort of company to congratulate the mother.

59. ἐκάλουν] "they were calling," "were going to call it." A frequent sense of the Imperfect.

60. οὐχί.] This paragogic form of οὐ is intensive, signifying *nay, by no means*. So Luke xii. 51. xiii. 3. 5.

62. ἐνένευον] "they intimated by becks and signs." See Note supra v. 22. At τὸ τί sub. κατὰ, *as to*. It is not necessary, however, to take the τὸ for τοῦτο. It belongs to the whole of the clause following; nor is there any pleonasm in the word, as some imagine.

63. πινακίδιον.] This is supposed to mean the *small square writing board, whitened over*, which is even yet in use in the East. Λέγων, "expressing." A sense occurring also in the Classical writers, and derived from the unexact phraseology of common life.

64. ανεῴχθη—γλῶσσα α.] This is, by the best Commentators, rightly referred to one of those idioms, by which a verb is joined with *two* nouns of cognate sense; to *one* only of which it is *properly* applicable. So Hom. σῖτον καὶ οἶνον ἔδοντες. and 1 Cor. iii. 2. Γάλα ὑμᾶς ἐπότισα καὶ οὐ βρῶμα. So also Æschyl. Prom. 21. οὔτε φωνὴν, οὔτε μορφὴν βροτῶν ὄψει. Besides, the term ἀνοίγεσθαι may not unaptly be applied to *setting free* the tongue. Thus (as De Rhoer observes) Sophocles and Themistius speak of the tongue being *shut*, and of the *door* of the tongue. Now surely there is no more impropriety in speaking of the tongue being *opened*. Moreover, the Heb. פתח, to which ἀνοίγειν answers, signifies not only to *open*, but to *loose*, as in Gen. xxiv. 32. Is. v. 27. See Note on Mark vii. 34. Thus there will be no occasion to supply (with most Commentators) ἐλύθη, or διηρθρώθη, which is *supplied* in some few copies, no doubt from the margin.

I have in Recens. Synop. shewn that the hypothesis by which the loss and the recovery of Zacharias' speech is attributed to *natural* causes cannot be admitted, because we learn from the Evangelist that it was a judicial infliction. The presumption as well as folly of making this, in common with many similar narrations of the N. T., a mere *myth*, cannot be too severely reprobated.

65. φόβος.] This imports here a mixed feeling of *wonder* and *awe*.

66. ἔθεντο ἐν τῇ καρδίᾳ] scil. ταῦτα, namely, (says Euthym.), ὡς ἀξιόλογα. This phrase is rare in the Classical writers. We may compare the Homeric μῦθον ἐντίθεσθαι θυμῷ. and the Latin *reponere*, or *condere mente*. The τί, which is for τίς, expresses *admiration*; and the ἄρα is *ratiocinative*. Ren-

πάντες οἱ ἀκούσαντες ἐν τῇ καρδίᾳ αὐτῶν, λέγοντες· Τί ἄρα τὸ
παιδίον τοῦτο ἔσται; καὶ χεὶρ Κυρίου ἦν μετ᾿ αὐτοῦ. Καὶ Ζαχα- 67
ρίας ὁ πατὴρ αὐτοῦ ἐπλήσθη Πνεύματος ἁγίου, καὶ προεφήτευσε,
h Infr. 2. 30. Matt. 1. 21. λέγων· [h] Εὐλογητὸς Κύριος ὁ Θεὸς τοῦ Ἰσραὴλ, ὅτι ἐπεσκέψατο, καὶ 68
i Ps. 132. 17, 18. ἐποίησε λύτρωσιν τῷ λαῷ αὐτοῦ· [i] καὶ ἤγειρε κέρας σωτηρίας ἡμῖν, 69
k Psal. 72. 12. Jer. 23. 6. & 30. 10. ἐν τῷ οἴκῳ Δαυῒδ τοῦ παιδὸς αὐτοῦ· ([k] καθὼς ἐλάλησε διὰ στόματος 70
Dan. 9. 27. τῶν ἁγίων τῶν ἀπ᾿ αἰῶνος προφητῶν αὐτοῦ,) σωτηρίαν ἐξ ἐχθρῶν 71
ἡμῶν, καὶ ἐκ χειρὸς πάντων τῶν μισούντων ἡμᾶς· ποιῆσαι ἔλεος μετὰ 72
l Gen. 22. 16. Ps. 105. 9. Jer. 31. 33. τῶν πατέρων ἡμῶν, καὶ μνησθῆναι διαθήκης ἁγίας αὐτοῦ· [l] ὅρκον 73
Heb. 6. 13. m Heb. 9. 14. ὃν ὤμοσε πρὸς Ἀβραὰμ τὸν πατέρα ἡμῶν, τοῦ δοῦναι ἡμῖν, [m] ἀφό- 74

der, "What sort of man, now, will this child become?"

—καὶ χεὶρ Κυρίου ἦν μετ᾿ αὐτοῦ.] These words are by some supposed to be a part of the speech; by others, more rightly, an observation of the Evangelist; and part of the narrative. The καὶ is not for γὰρ, as some suppose; but signifies *et sanè, and indeed.*

67. προεφήτευσε.] Many learned Commentators think that the term here, and occasionally elsewhere, merely denotes to praise God in fervent and exalted strains, *like* those of a prophet. And indeed such a sense in προφήτης is found in the Classical writers; but not in the Scriptural ones; much less in προφητεύειν. It may indeed be with truth affirmed, that in the N. T., at least, there are but two significations of προφητεύειν; 1. to *prophesy, predict future events;* the other to *speak under the impulse of divine inspiration.* Now the hymn of Zacharias was both inspired and prophetical.

68. ἐπεσκέψατο] scil. τὸν λαὸν, "hath visited with his mercy and favour." The metaphor (which occurs also in ver. 78. and vii. 16. Acts xv. 14. Heb. ii. 6.) is derived either, as is commonly supposed, from the custom of princes, to visit the provinces of their kingdom, in order to redress grievances, and confer benefits; or rather from the visiting of the distressed by the benevolent. Zacharias' language was permitted by the Holy Spirit to be accommodated to the opinion of the speaker, and, indeed, at that time, of all Jews; who supposed the Messiah was to be manifested for the deliverance and benefit of the *Jews* only, not to be a blessing to the whole human race.

69. κέρας σωτηρίας.] On the exact nature of the metaphor, Commentators are not agreed. Noesselt supposes an allusion to the *iron horns* which were sometimes fastened to the helmets of the ancients. Fischer and others to the *four horns of the altar,* which were among the Hebrews (as the *aræ* and *foci* among the Greeks and Romans) places of refuge for suppliants. Thus Christ will be regarded as a new refuge of safety to those who embrace his religion. This, however, seems rather ingenious than solid. Far more natural is the common interpretation (adopted by the ancients and most moderns, and ably supported by Kuin.) which derives the metaphor from *horned animals,* whose strength is in their horns. Hence *horn* is a term perpetually used to denote *strength,* and is thus a symbol of power and principality. Thus κέρας σωτηρίας is put for βασιλέα καὶ σωτῆρα ἰσχυρὸν, a royal and powerful deliverer and helper.

70. τῶν ἁγίων—προφ.] The second τῶν is not found in some ancient MSS., and is suspected not to be genuine by Gersdorf and Vater, "because," say they, "the Article is no where else so used *præcedente adjectivo.*" Yet on that very account they ought to have been less ready to cancel the Article, than to inquire whether the preceding word is *really* an adjective. Now Bp. Jebb and Rosenm. think it is *not* an adjective, but a *substantive,* as very often elsewhere. So Deut. xxxiii. 2. 3. 1 Sam. ii. 9. 2 Chron. vi. 41. Job xv. 15. Ps. xxx. 4. xxxiii. 29. That the Patriarchs, from Adam downwards, were God's *saints,* though not *all* of them his *prophets,* is certain: and why they might be so called, appears from Levit. xx. 7. So xix. 2. and xxi. 8. This view I should have adopted, but for the very similar passage of St. Luke himself, Acts iii. 25. ἄχρι χρόνων ἀποκαταστάσεως πάντων, ὧν ἐλάλησεν ὁ Θεὸς διὰ στόματος [πάντων] ἁγίων αὐτοῦ προφητῶν ἀπ᾿ αἰῶνος. where Griesb. and others insert τῶν before ἁγίων; which, however, Bp. Middlet. thinks unnecessary. Yet here it is found in all the MSS.: and if the Article be used with the *adjective,* it cannot be dispensed with in the *substantive.* And that the writer meant it so to be taken in the passage of Acts is clear; because ἁγίων αὐτοῦ προφ. can only mean, "of his holy prophets:" and τῶν ἁγ. πρ. could mean *no more.* This indeed is confirmed by 2 Pet. iii. 2. μνησθῆναι τῶν πρ. ῥημάτων ὑπὸ τῶν ἁγίων προφητῶν. and Rev. xxii. 6. ὁ Θεὸς τῶν πνευμάτων τῶν ἁγίων προφητῶν.

—ἀπ᾿ αἰῶνος.] This phrase, which often occurs in the Hellenistic writers, and sometimes in the Classical, (who, however, prefer ἀπ᾿ ἀρχῆς), means, "from the most ancient times."

71. σωτηρίαν] i. e. a means of salvation, for σωτῆρα; a frequent idiom in the Scriptures.

72. ποιῆσαι ἔλεος μετὰ τῶν π. ἡ.] Sub. ὥστε. The sense is: "in order to show his mercy and kindness to," &c.; for the phrase does not imply any *promise;* but ποιῆσαι τὸ ἔλεος μετά τινος corresponds to the Heb. עשה חסד עם in Genes. xxi. 23. and signifies "to deal mercifully and kindly with, to exercise kindness to," as Acts xv.

73. ὅρκον ὃν ὤμοσε.] The difficulty here in syntax cannot be removed by resorting to the principle of *apposition;* nor even by supposing the antecedent as put in the same case with the relative, because that does violence to the construction; but rather by supplying κατὰ, with Camer. and others. Thus the sense will be, "*by* (i. e. confirmed by the oath," &c.

—τοῦ δοῦναι.] Sub. περὶ, or take τ. δ. for ἐν τῷ δοῦναι, Hellenisticè. This and the next ver. contain the *substance* of the oath unto Abraham, on which see Recens. Synop. The Prophets of the O. T., in describing the times of the Messiah, and the spiritual worship which was to succeed

75 ἕως ἐκ χειρὸς τῶν ἐχθρῶν ἡμῶν ῥυσθέντας λατρεύειν αὐτῷ [n] ἐν n 1 Pet. 1. 15.
ὁσιότητι καὶ δικαιοσύνῃ ἐνώπιον αὐτοῦ πάσας τὰς ἡμέρας [τῆς ζωῆς]
76 ἡμῶν. [o] Καὶ σὺ, παιδίον, προφήτης ὑψίστου κληθήσῃ· προπορεύσῃ o Mal. 3. 1. & 4. 5.
77 γὰρ πρὸ προσώπου Κυρίου, ἑτοιμάσαι ὁδοὺς αὐτοῦ, [p] τοῦ δοῦναι supr. v. 17. p Infr. 3. 3.
78 γνῶσιν σωτηρίας τῷ λαῷ αὐτοῦ, ἐν ἀφέσει ἁμαρτιῶν αὐτῶν, [q] διὰ q Mal. 4. 2. Zach. 3. 8.
σπλάγχνα ἐλέους Θεοῦ ἡμῶν, ἐν οἷς ἐπεσκέψατο ἡμᾶς ἀνατολὴ ἐξ & 6. 12.
79 ὕψους, [r] ἐπιφᾶναι τοῖς ἐν σκότει καὶ σκιᾷ θανάτου καθημένοις, τοῦ r Isa. 9. 1. & 42. 7.
80 κατευθῦναι τοὺς πόδας ἡμῶν εἰς ὁδὸν εἰρήνης. [s] Τὸ δὲ παιδίον ηὔξανε & 43. 8. & 49. 9. & 60. 1.
καὶ ἐκραταιοῦτο πνεύματι· καὶ ἦν ἐν ταῖς ἐρήμοις, ἕως ἡμέρας ἀνα- Matt. 4. 16. s Infr. 2. 40.
δείξεως αὐτοῦ πρὸς τὸν Ἰσραήλ.

1 II. ἘΓΕΝΕΤΟ δὲ ἐν ταῖς ἡμέραις ἐκείναις, ἐξῆλθε δόγμα παρὰ
2 Καίσαρος Αὐγούστου, ἀπογράφεσθαι πᾶσαν τὴν οἰκουμένην. (αὕτη ἡ

to the ceremonial observances of the Law, use the very same language as this Divine Hymn; though neither the Jews, nor even the prophets themselves, understood those prophecies as we, (informed by history, and enlightened by the Gospel), are enabled to do. Ἀφόβως must be taken not with ῥυσθέντας, but with λατρεύειν, which is required by the construction, and yields a sense most in unison with the nature of the Gospel, as alluding to the absence of the "spirit of bondage," mentioned Rom. viii. 15. Ὁσιότητι denotes the observances rendered to *God*; δικαιοσύνῃ, the duties to *men*. Compare Eph. iv. 24. Τῆς ζωῆς is omitted in many of the best MSS., all the most important Versions, and some Fathers, and is cancelled by Griesb., Vat., Tittm., and Scholz; and rightly, for we can far better account for its *insertion* than its *omission*.

77. At τοῦ δ. sub. διά. Γνῶσιν σωτηρίας. This under the Law, was by *legal righteousness*; under the Gospel, by *remission of sins*.

78. διὰ σπλάγχνα ἐλέους.] With this Comp. σπλ. οἰκτιρμῶν at Col. iii. 12 Each is a stronger expression than either noun would be, taken simply. See Tittm. de Syn. p. 68., who observes that as σπλ. properly denotes the *viscera nobiliora*, the heart, lungs, &c., hence the term is used of all the more vehement affections of the mind, as we say of those destitute of them, that they are *heartless*. Ελ. is, he observes, a stronger term than οἰκτ.; the latter signifying only the *pain we feel at the misery of others*; the former, the *desire of relieving that misery*, with an adjunct notion of *beneficence*.

— ἀνατολὴ ἐξ ὕψους.] On the interpretation of this phrase there has been some diversity of opinion. Many eminent Commentators take ἀνατολὴ to signify a budding branch, and figuratively a *son*, like the Heb. צֶמַח. But the metaphor is so harsh, and leads to such a confusion, (taken in conjunction with the words following), that I see no reason to abandon the common interpretation, "the dawn from on high," with allusion to those passages of the O. T. which describe the Messiah under the metaphor of the *light*, and the *sun*. See Mal. iv. 2. To this interpretation, indeed, it is objected by Wets. and others, that thus ἐξ ὕψους will not be proper — because the sun *when he ascends* is always in the *horizon*, and not *over head*. This, however, is hypercritical criticism, and proceeds on the *error* of tying popular language down to the rules of strict philosophical propriety. The expression may very well denote that *moderate elevation* which the sun soon attains after its rise. However, ἐξ ὕψους may be taken, with Kuin., Tittm., and Wahl, for ἄνωθεν, i. e. from heaven. So Virgil, Ecl. iv. 7., from the Sibylline oracles, "Jam nova progenies cœlo demittitur alto." The terms which follow indeed seem to require this interpretation. The whole passage represents the Messiah as coming, like the rising sun, to dispel the darkness which covered the world, bringing life and immortality to light through the Gospel.

79. The same metaphor is continued. Compare Ps. xliii. 3. cxix. 105. and on εἰς ὁδὸν βαβ., Eurip. Med. 740. and Æsch. Ag. 170.

80. πνεύματι] "in mind," and wisdom, as opposed to bodily growth.

— ἐν ταῖς ἐρήμοις.] Whether by this is meant the *Hill country* where he was born, or the *Desert* properly so called, the Commentators are not agreed. The latter may be considered pretty certain. The *period* of his retirement is with probability supposed to have been at the age of puberty, when he would have strength of body and mind to bear that solitude, which for him was so necessary and so beneficial. For thus he would not be warped by the prejudices of the Jewish teachers, and would, in that seclusion, approach near unto God, and seek that guidance of the Holy Spirit which was necessary to enable him to be the Herald of the Gospel. Sweet, too, are the uses of *solitude* (as well as *adversity*), as the greatest of men have experienced. So Josephus spent some years of his early youth in the desert; and Chrysostom many of those of his mature age in a *cave*, (as it is said), diligently studying the Scriptures; and framing his immortal Homilies.

— ἀναδείξεως.] The word is often used of admission to any office unto which a person has been appointed; and here denotes "entrance on his ministry;" as x. 1. and Acts i. 24.

II. 1. ἐν ταῖς ἡμέραις ἐκείναις.] This does not refer to the last verse, but to ver. 36. seqq. of the preceding Chapter. Ἐξῆλθε δόγμα, "an edict or decree was issued," or promulgated, neuter for passive. This sense of ἐξέρχεσθαι occurs in the LXX. at Dan. ii. 13. ix. 25. and Esth. i. 19., where it answers to the Heb. יָצָא. Δόγμα in this forensic sense occurs both in Hellenistic and Classical Greek.

— ἀπογράφεσθαι πᾶσαν τὴν οἰκ.] Winer, Gr. Gr. § 38. 3., takes ἀπογρ. to be in apposition with the preceding. But it is better to suppose an ellipsis

ἀπογραφὴ πρώτη ἐγένετο ἡγεμονεύοντος τῆς Συρίας Κυρηνίου.) καὶ 3
t Mich. 5. 2. John 7. 42. 1 Sam. 16. 4. Matt. 1. 1. et seqq. ἐπορεύοντο πάντες ἀπογράφεσθαι, ἕκαστος εἰς τὴν ἰδίαν πόλιν. [t] Ἀνέβη 4
δὲ καὶ Ἰωσὴφ ἀπὸ τῆς Γαλιλαίας ἐκ πόλεως Ναζαρὲτ, εἰς τὴν Ἰουδαίαν,
εἰς πόλιν Δαυΐδ, ἥτις καλεῖται Βηθλεέμ, διὰ τὸ εἶναι αὐτὸν ἐξ οἴκου
καὶ πατριᾶς Δαυΐδ, ἀπογράψασθαι σὺν Μαριὰμ τῇ μεμνηστευμένῃ 5
αὐτῷ γυναικὶ, οὔσῃ ἐγκύῳ. Ἐγένετο δὲ, ἐν τῷ εἶναι αὐτοὺς ἐκεῖ, ἐπλή- 6
u Matt. 1. 25. σθησαν αἱ ἡμέραι τοῦ τεκεῖν αὐτήν· [u] καὶ ἔτεκε τὸν υἱὸν αὐτῆς 7
τὸν πρωτότοκον καὶ ἐσπαργάνωσεν αὐτὸν καὶ ἀνέκλινεν αὐτὸν ἐν τῇ
φάτνῃ· διότι οὐκ ἦν αὐτοῖς τόπος ἐν τῷ καταλύματι.

of ὥστε, (i. e. εἰς τὸ) in the sense of *purpose*, of which examples are frequent. By τὴν οἰκ., scil. γῆν, it is now generally admitted, cannot be meant, *the whole world*. Most of the Commentators take it to mean *the Roman world*, i. e. empire; this expression (like *orbis terrarum* in Latin) being then in general use. See Acts xxiv. 5. Apoc. iii. 10. xvi. 14. Since, however, no historian notices such a general census of the whole empire; and since it is improbable that *had there been* one, it would have been mentioned in connection with the Proprætor of Syria, we may rather suppose (with Keuchen, Bynæus, Wolf, Lardner, Pearce, Fischer, Rosenm., and Kuin., and others), that *Judæa only* is meant, as in Acts xi. 28. and Luke iv. 3. and perhaps xxi. 20. Indeed the Jews called Judæa *the earth* of all the earth. See Ruth i. 1. 2 Sam. xxiv. 8. and Mr. Rose's Parkh. in v.

As to the sense of ἀπογράφεσθαι, which is rendered in E. V. "*taxed*," we have the testimony of Josephus that no tax was levied from Judæa till many years after this period, and the use of the word rather requires us to adopt the interpretation of almost all modern Commentators, "*registered*;" understanding the ἀπογραφὴ as a *census* of the *population*. Of this many examples are adduced by Wets., and others are added in Recens. Synop.; to which I must beg to refer for information on the next verse, as concerns αὕτη ἡ ἀπογραφὴ πρώτη — Κυρηνίου, into the discussion of which the nature of this work will not permit me to enter. The reader is likewise referred to Townsend, Chr. Arr. i. 51.

4. ἐξ οἴκου καὶ πατριᾶς Δ.] Grot., Kypke, and others, have rightly observed, that the πατριὰ was a part of the οἶκος; the latter comprehending the collateral branches, and even servants (οἰκογενεῖς), the former being confined to the direct line of descent; very similar to the distinction, among the Romans, of *gentes* and *familiæ*. After the many separations which had taken place of the Jews, any such census as the above would have been impossible, unless each went to the place which had formerly been the lot of his clan or family. The only reason which the Commentators can imagine for Mary's attendance is, that she was an *heiress*; for otherwise *women* were not registered. But it does not follow, from the words of the Evangelist, that Mary went to *be registered*; for σὺν may very well mean, "accompanied by."

5. μεμνηστευμένῃ] "who had been betrothed (and was then married)." That such must be the sense, appears from Matt. i. 25.

6. ἐπλήσθησαν αἱ ἡμ.] Simil. Gen. xxv. 24. (Sept.) καὶ ἐπληρώθησαν αἱ ἡμέραι τοῦ τεκεῖν αὐτήν. Ἡμ. is here put for *time*; which use is frequent in Scripture, and is here called a Hebraism; but it occurs in Thucyd. vi. 65. αἱ ἡμέραι ἐν αἷς ξυνέθεντο ἥξειν ἐγγὺς ἦσαν.

7. ἐσπαργάνωσεν.] Σπαργανόω scarcely ever occurs in the Classical writers, though σπάργανον often does. We find it, however, in Ezra xvi. 4. These σπάργανα were not only in use *then*, but even until very late in modern times, as a preventive to distortion.

— ἀνέκλινεν α. ἐν τῇ φάτνῃ.] Ἀνακλίνω is often used absolutely; the *place* of laying being left to be supplied from the context, or the subject. Here it is a *vox signata de h. re*, and may be rendered "*cradled*." It is not so easy to fix the sense of φάτνη. It is commonly taken to denote "*a manger*." But, although such would seem no unfit receptacle for a new born child, yet, as *mangers* are not *now* in use in the East, but *hair cloth bags* instead, this interpretation has been thought groundless. Yet it has never been established that mangers were *not* used by the ancients; nay, there has been tolerable proof adduced, from Homer and Herodotus, that they *were*; namely, of the form of our *cribs*. See Is. xxxix. 9. and Job xxxix. 9. The common interpretation, however, seems to be untenable on another and more serious ground. For if the φάτνη (as Wets. observes) was a part of the stable, and the stable a part of the inn; it follows that he who had a place in the stable, had one in the inn. Yet the Evangelist says "there was no room for them in the inn." It is (as Bp. Middlet. observes) plain from the whole context, that φάτνῃ was not merely the place in which the babe was laid, but the place also in which he was born and swaddled. The words ἐν τῇ φάτνῃ surely belong as much to ἔτεκεν as to ἀνέκλινεν, for else where should the delivery take place? Not in the κατάλυμα, for *there* there was no room, not merely for the *child*, but for "*them*." It is plain, therefore, that we must adopt the interpretation of Wets., Rosen., Middlet., Kuin., and many others; who by φάτνῃ understand some *place of lodging*, though less convenient than the κατάλυμα. Many think it was an enclosed space, either in front of or behind the house, paled in like our *farm yards*; which is, indeed, very agreeable to the primary sense of the word. Such, however, would seem but indifferent shelter for one in Mary's situation, and therefore others adopt the signification "*stable*," which latter sense is thought to be confirmed by the authority of many of the early Fathers, who call the place of Christ's nativity a *cave*. Those writers, however, expressly distinguish between the cave and the φάτνῃ. It is, I think, plain that they took φάτνῃ to mean a *crib*, and equally so that they read ἐν φάτνῃ, which is found in some ancient MSS. But the authority is insufficient to establish that reading; which seems to have originated from the

8 *Καὶ ποιμένες ἦσαν ἐν τῇ χώρᾳ τῇ αὐτῇ ἀγραυλοῦντες, καὶ φυλάσ-*
9 *σοντες φυλακὰς τῆς νυκτὸς ἐπὶ τὴν ποίμνην αὐτῶν. Καὶ ἰδοὺ, ἄγγελος*
Κυρίου ἐπέστη αὐτοῖς, καὶ δόξα Κυρίου περιέλαμψεν αὐτούς· καὶ ἐφο-
10 *βήθησαν φόβον μέγαν. Καὶ εἶπεν αὐτοῖς ὁ ἄγγελος· Μὴ φοβεῖσθε·*
ἰδοὺ γὰρ, εὐαγγελίζομαι ὑμῖν χαρὰν μεγάλην, ἥτις ἔσται παντὶ τῷ λαῷ·
11 *ὅτι ἐτέχθη ὑμῖν σήμερον σωτὴρ, ὅς ἐστι Χριστὸς Κύριος, ἐν πόλει*
12 *Δαυΐδ. Καὶ τοῦτο ὑμῖν τὸ σημεῖον· εὑρήσετε βρέφος ἐσπαργανω-*
13 *μένον κείμενον ἐν [τῇ] φάτνῃ.* [x] *Καὶ ἐξαίφνης ἐγένετο σὺν τῷ ἀγγέ-* x Dan. 7. 10. Rev. 5. 11.
λῳ πλῆθος στρατιᾶς οὐρανίου, αἰνούντων τὸν Θεὸν, καὶ λεγόντων· y Infr. 19. 38. Isa. 57. 19.
14 [y] *Δόξα ἐν ὑψίστοις Θεῷ, καὶ ἐπὶ γῆς εἰρήνη· ἐν ἀνθρώποις εὐδοκία!* Eph. 2. 17. Rom. 5. 1.

alteration of Critics, who took φάτ. in the sense *manger* or *crib*; a sense, however, for which there is no good authority in *Scripture*, where the word invariably signifies a stall [for cattle] or a stable [for horses]. See infra xiii. 15. As to the choice between the above two interpretations, *neither* seems to be correct. The φάτνη appears to have been neither a *mere inclosure*, nor a *regular building*, like our *stable*. It was indeed exactly like the *hovels* and *sheds*, covered over head, but open on one side, which are found round our *farm yards*, or *home stalls*. And this would be, in a climate like that of Judæa, no bad shelter for the *houseless*. Sheds like this were so easily constructed, and so convenient, that it is not probable a *cave* should have been used; which would have been in many respects less comfortable. On the Jewish καταλύματα, see Rec. Syn.

8. ἀγραυλοῦντες.] The word properly signifies to abide in the fields *sub dio*, whether by night or day, but usually the former. It is not certain, however, that these shepherds abode in the *open air*. They might be in *huts*; for Kypke cites from Diod. Sic. ἀγαυλία, to denote a military encampment. And Busbequius, Epist. i. 58, speaks of "wandering flocks" (like the Spanish Merinos) tended day and night by the shepherds, who carry their wives and children with them in waggons, and for themselves, he adds, "*exigua tabernacula tendunt*," no doubt, such as the *bird-boy's hut of sods and boughs* so graphically described by Robert Bloomfield in his Farmer's Boy. Yet these shepherds were probably not *Nomades*, but Bethlehemites, whose "watch over their flocks by night" may be best expressed by the modern term *bivouac*, which comes from the A. Saxon bepacian, *vigilare*. Τῆς νυκτὸς is for νυκτερινάς; and φυλάσσ. φυλ. τ. ν. may be rendered, "keeping the night watches;" the plural having reference to the various turns, or reliefs, by which the watch was kept.

9. ἐπέστη αὐτοῖς.] Ἐφιστάναι denotes *to come upon the sight suddenly*, and, as appears from the examples in Wets., is especially used of *supernatural* appearances. Δόξα Κυρίου is explained by many recent Commentators "a bright glory or splendour," by a well known idiom alluding to the name of the Deity. But it is better, with Euthym., Whitby, Schoettg., and Wahl, to take it here, and at Acts vii. 55, (as also in Exod. xxiv. 16. xl. 34.. 1 Kings viii. 11. 2 Chr. vii. 1. Heb. כבוד יהוה) of that Θεῖον φῶς, or extreme splendour, in which the Deity is represented as appearing to men; and sometimes called the Shechinah, an appearance frequently attended, as in this case, by a company of angels.

10. χαράν.] By metonymy, for "cause of joy," as James i. 2. and Aristoph. Plut. 637. λέγεις μοι χαράν.

11. σωτήρ.] Wets. has here and on i. 79. incontestably proved (after Bp. Pearson), by a vast assemblage of citations, that the terms σωτὴρ, Κύριος, Θεὸς, and ἐπιφανὴς, so often applied in Scripture to Jesus Christ, prove him to have been of an origin far more august than the human; the terms being only applicable to a *Deus præsens*, *The Son of God*, *and* God.

12. τῇ φάτνῃ.] The τῇ is not found in very many of the best MSS., and early Edd.; and has been, with reason, cancelled by the Editors from Wets. to Scholz.

14. ἐν ὑψίστοις.] Sub. either τόποις scil. οὐρανοῖς, (the plural being used with reference to the Heb. שמים, which only occurs in the plural), or rather οὐρανοῖς, required by that dogma of Jewish Theology, which reckoned *three* heavens, the *aerial*, the *starry*, and the *highest*, or the seat of God and the angels. The phrase occurs also in Matt. xxi. 9. Mark xi. 10. Luke xix. 38. Job xvi. 19.

— δόξα — εὐδοκία.] There are few sentences so short, with which Commentators have been more perplexed than this. Hence some read εὐδοκίας, and others *conjecture* εὐδοκία. But the former seems to be merely an ancient *conjecture*, and is as little to be attended to as the latter, which is professedly such. No greater notice is due to those who change the *doxology* into a kind of *proverb*, by taking εὐδοκία ἐν ἀνθρώποις as the *predicate*, and the rest of the words as the *subject* of the sentence. Various methods of interpretation have been propounded by Commentators of the last half century; all liable more or less to objection. In this strait, a recent English Commentator comes to our aid, and proposes to extricate us from the embarrassment by a simple expedient. "The whole difficulty (says he) seems to have arisen from dividing the verse into *three* clauses. That it consists only of *two* is evident to demonstration, from the apposition of ἐν ὑψίστοις and Θεῷ in the one, to ἐπὶ γῆς and ἐν ἀνθρώποις in the other. Hence also the following order: Θεῷ ἐν ὑψίστοις δόξα (ἐστὶ,) καὶ ἐν ἀνθρώποις ἐπὶ γῆς εἰρήνη, εὐδοκία." But so far from this being "evident to demonstration," the sentence, even *after* it has been put on the bed of Procrustes, still remains (*mirabile dictu*) the same — i. e. *trimembris*; for at εὐδοκία must necessarily be repeated ἐστι; and ἐν ἀνθρώποις must *also* be repeated, otherwise there will be no sense. Besides, the *order* here proposed does violence to the plain structure of the sentence; and that by the above mentioned unnatural procedure. The "*apposition*" supposed

Καὶ ἐγένετο, ὡς ἀπῆλθον ἀπ᾽ αὐτῶν εἰς τὸν οὐρανὸν οἱ ἄγγελοι, καὶ 15
οἱ ἄνθρωποι, οἱ ποιμένες, εἶπον πρὸς ἀλλήλους· Διέλθωμεν δὴ ἕως
Βηθλεέμ, καὶ ἴδωμεν τὸ ῥῆμα τοῦτο τὸ γεγονὸς, ὃ ὁ Κύριος ἐγνώ-
ρισεν ἡμῖν. Καὶ ἦλθον σπεύσαντες, καὶ ἀνεῦρον τήν τε Μαριὰμ καὶ 16
τὸν Ἰωσὴφ, καὶ τὸ βρέφος κείμενον ἐν τῇ φάτνῃ. Ἰδόντες δὲ διεγνώ- 17
ρισαν περὶ τοῦ ῥήματος τοῦ λαληθέντος αὐτοῖς περὶ τοῦ παιδίου τούτου. Καὶ πάντες οἱ ἀκούσαντες ἐθαύμασαν περὶ τῶν λαληθέντων ὑπὸ 18
τῶν ποιμένων πρὸς αὐτούς. Ἡ δὲ Μαριὰμ πάντα συνετήρει τὰ ῥήματα 19
ταῦτα, συμβάλλουσα ἐν τῇ καρδίᾳ αὐτῆς. καὶ * ὑπέστρεψαν οἱ ποιμέ- 20
νες, δοξάζοντες καὶ αἰνοῦντες τὸν Θεὸν ἐπὶ πᾶσιν οἷς ἤκουσαν καὶ
εἶδον, καθὼς ἐλαλήθη πρὸς αὐτούς.

a Gen. 17. 12. Lev. 12. 3. supr. 1. 31. Matt. 1. 21. John 7. 22.

[a] ΚΑΙ ὅτε ἐπλήσθησαν ἡμέραι ὀκτὼ τοῦ περιτεμεῖν * αὐτὸν, καὶ 21
ἐκλήθη τὸ ὄνομα αὐτοῦ Ἰησοῦς, τὸ κληθὲν ὑπὸ τοῦ ἀγγέλου πρὸ τοῦ
συλληφθῆναι αὐτὸν ἐν τῇ κοιλίᾳ.

a Lev. 12. 2. et seqq.

[a] ΚΑΙ ὅτε ἐπλήσθησαν αἱ ἡμέραι τοῦ καθαρισμοῦ αὐτῶν, κατὰ τὸν 22
νόμον Μωϋσέως, ἀνήγαγον αὐτὸν εἰς Ἱεροσόλυμα, παραστῆσαι τῷ Κυρίῳ, ([b] καθὼς γέγραπται ἐν νόμῳ Κυρίου· Ὅτι πᾶν ἄρσεν 23
διανοῖγον μήτραν ἅγιον τῷ Κυρίῳ κληθήσεται·) [c] καὶ 24
τοῦ δοῦναι θυσίαν, κατὰ τὸ εἰρημένον ἐν νόμῳ Κυρίου, ζεῦγος
τρυγόνων ἢ δύο νεοσσοὺς περιστερῶν.

b Exod. 13. 2. & 22. 29. & 34. 19. Num. 3. 13. & 8. 16, 17.
c Lev. 12. 6, 8.

is *not such*, but an *antithetical apodosis*. The sentence, I repeat, is grammatically *trimembris*. For though some eminent Commentators recognize only *two* members *and a corollary*, that is conceding the very point in dispute, the corollary clause constituting a *third*. That third indeed is in some measure exegetical of the preceding; ἐν ἀνθρώποις corresponding to ἐπὶ γῆς (which corresponds to ἐν ὑψίστοις of the first member), and εὐδοκία to εἰρήνη. At the second member, Θεῷ must be supplied from the first, and be taken for πρὸς τὸν Θεόν. It must also be supplied in the third from the second. Εὐδοκία signifies a state of acceptance. The omission of the copula before the clause ἐν ἀνθρώποις εὐδ. may be accounted for on the principle suggested by Doddr.; namely, that "such exclamatory sentences are usually broken up into short elliptic clauses." It should seem, however, that εὐδοκία is in apposition with, and explanatory of ἐπὶ γῆς εἰρήνη. Thus the sentence is *grammatically* trimembris, but *in sense* bimembris. In *such* cases of apposition ὅ ἐστι is understood, and thus no copula is necessary. It is plain that we must supply in the two last clauses not ἔστω, as many do; but ἐστι. The 2d and 3d clauses assign the *cause* and *ground* of the δόξα.

15. καὶ οἱ ἄνθρωποι, οἱ ποιμένες, &c.] The καὶ is, as often, redundant, after the manner of the Heb. ו. As to the next words, there is *not*, as the Commentators suppose, any pleonasm; for the use of the Article before each word forbids us to take it as the common idiom ἄνθρωπος μάντις; but the latter term is in apposition with, and exegetical of the former; q. d. the men, i. e. the shepherds.

—τὸ ῥῆμα.] The Commentators here take ῥῆμα for πρᾶγμα, as in several other passages. As to the Heb. דבר, and the Greek Classical ἔπος and λόγος. There is, however, generally a sort of significatio *prægnans*, the word denoting a *thing spoken* of. Here τὸ γεγονὸς is added by way of explanation.

16. ἐν τῇ φ.] Render "in the home-stall."

19. συμβάλλουσα.] Some explain this "endeavouring to comprehend." But the proof is imperfect. Others, with Elsn., "forming conjectures respecting," i. e. by comparing past with present events. But far more natural and agreeable to the context is the common interpretation, "pondering, revolving," as in many passages of the Classical writers. So διαλογίζεσθαι ἐν ταῖς καρδίαις in Mark ii. 6. and Luke v. 22. Ἐν τῇ καρδίᾳ belongs both to συνετήρει and συμβάλλουσα. So Dan. vii. 28. καὶ τὸ ῥῆμα ἐν τῇ καρδίᾳ μου συνετήρησαν.

20. ὑπέστρεψαν.] This reading, for the Vulg. ἐπέστρ., is found in almost all the MSS. and early Edd., confirmed by numerous passages from this Gospel and the Acts. And it is adopted by every Critical Editor from Wets. to Scholz.

21. αὐτόν] This (for the Vulg. τὸ παιδίον) is found in almost all the best MSS. and Versions, and early Edd.; and is adopted by Matt., Griesb., Tittm., Vat., and Scholz: rightly, for the common reading is plainly a *correction*.

22. παραστῆσαι.] The term is used κατ' ἐξοχὴν, of victims brought to the altar, and of offerings *consecrated* to God. So the Latin *admonere* and *sistere*. There is here no little variety of reading. Some copies have αὐτοῦ, others αὐτῆς, but the great majority αὐτῶν. For the first two readings there is little or no authority. Αὐτῆς is justly suspected to be a παραδιόρθωσις, and to have proceeded (as did the omission of αὐτῶν) from the superstition of those who were scandalized at the idea of impurity being ascribed to Jesus. But they should have considered that the impurity was only *external* and *ceremonial*, not *moral*, it being merely an obligation and restraint laid on

25 *Καὶ ἰδοὺ, ἦν ἄνθρωπος ἐν Ἱερουσαλὴμ, ᾧ ὄνομα Συμεών· καὶ ὁ*
ἄνθρωπος οὗτος δίκαιος καὶ εὐλαβὴς, προσδεχόμενος παράκλησιν τοῦ
26 *Ἰσραὴλ, καὶ Πνεῦμα ‡ ἅγιον ἦν ἐπ' αὐτόν· καὶ ἦν αὐτῷ κεχρηματισμένον*
ὑπὸ τοῦ Πνεύματος τοῦ ἁγίου, μὴ ἰδεῖν θάνατον, πρὶν ἢ ἴδῃ
27 *τὸν Χριστὸν Κυρίου. Καὶ ἦλθεν ἐν τῷ Πνεύματι εἰς τὸ ἱερόν· καὶ*
ἐν τῷ εἰσαγαγεῖν τοὺς γονεῖς τὸ παιδίον Ἰησοῦν, τοῦ ποιῆσαι αὐτοὺς
28 *κατὰ τὸ εἰθισμένον τοῦ νόμου περὶ αὐτοῦ, καὶ αὐτὸς ἐδέξατο αὐτὸ εἰς* d Gen. 46. 30.
29 *τὰς ἀγκάλας αὐτοῦ, καὶ εὐλόγησε τὸν Θεὸν καὶ εἶπε·* [d] *Νῦν ἀπολύεις* Phil. 1. 23. e Ps. 98, 2.
30 *τὸν δοῦλόν σου, δέσποτα, κατὰ τὸ ῥῆμά σου, ἐν εἰρήνῃ,* [e] *ὅτι εἶδον* Isa. 52. 10. infr. 3. 6.
31 *οἱ ὀφθαλμοί μου τὸ σωτήριόν σου, ὃ ἡτοίμασας κατὰ πρόσωπον πάν-* f Isa. 42. 6. & 49. 6.
32 *των τῶν λαῶν·* [f] *φῶς εἰς ἀποκάλυψιν ἐθνῶν, καὶ δόξαν λαοῦ σου Ἰσ-* Acts 13. 47. & 28. 28. supr. 1. 88.

women newly brought to bed, till after the performance of certain rites.

25. *δίκαιος καὶ εὐλαβής.*] Of these terms the former is explained by the Commentators to denote one who observes the outward ceremonies of the Law; the latter one who cultivates the *inward* devotion. But this view appears too much squared by Jewish notions. There is no reason why *δίκ.* should not mean (in the usual sense) a person of integrity and uprightness, discharging faithfully his duties towards *men;* and *εὐλ.*, one pious and devout, circumspectly and scrupulously performing his duties towards *God;* thus denoting rather more than *εὐσεβής*. See Acts x. 22. Nor is this sense without examples in the Classical writers from Plato downwards. See Wets. or Recens. Syn.

—*παράκλησιν τ.* 'Ι.] i. e. by metonymy of abstract for concrete, *παράκλητον*, the Consoler, a name, by the Jews of that age and long afterwards, used to designate the expected Messiah, with reference to the language of the Prophets, which would then be brought peculiarly to mind by the oppression under which they were groaning from the Gentiles. *Πνεῦμα ἅγ.*, i. e. "the influence of the Holy Spirit." See Middlet. For *ἅγιον ἦν* very many MSS. have *ἦν ἅγιον* which is edited by Matth., Griesb., Vat., and Scholz.

26. *ἦν αὐτῷ κεχρ.*] The more usual construction would be *κεχρηματισμένος ὑπὸ τοῦ Πν.*, as in Matt. ii. 12. Acts x. 22. and elsewhere. *Χρηματίζειν* signifies to give a *χρῆμα* (anciently synonymous with *χρησμὸς*), or oracular and Divine admonition. In *what manner* this was in the present case conveyed; whether by oral communication, dream, or otherwise, cannot with certainty be determined. *Ἰδεῖν θάνατον* is a Hebraism answering to ראות מות. It never occurs in the Classical writers; though *ᾅδην ἰδεῖν* and *εἰσιδεῖν* are cited from the Poets.

27. *ἐν τῷ Πν.*] "under the influence of the Spirit." *Ἐν*, like the Heb. ב, *by*, is often synonymous with *διὰ*, denoting *the moving cause*. *Τὸ εἰθισμένον*, for *τὸν ἐθισμὸν*, or *τὸ ἔθος*, which, like *δικαίωμα*, denoted the *rites of the Law*. Thus the Hebrew משפט is rendered *ἐθισμὸς* 1 Kings xviii. 28.

29. *ἀπολύεις.*] *Ἀπολύειν* signifies properly "to loose, let go from any place (or figuratively from any state, which implies coercion) to any other place," as home, &c.; and it is used either with *εἰς τὴν οἰκίαν* or *absolutely;* and sometimes, as here, it is employed figuratively, and by euphemism, of *death*, with the addition of *τοῦ σώματος*, or of *τοῦ ζῆν*, as is usual in the *Classical* writers, though in the *Scriptural* ones without it, as here and in Num. xx. 29. and Gen. xv. 2. See more in Recens. Synop. The result of the diligent researches of the Philological Illustrators is, that the term was by the Classical writers used partly of deliverance from confinement to liberty; partly of deliverance from labours and anxieties of various kinds, not only by the being eased of laborious duties, but by removal from them by death; thus attesting "a hope full of immortality;" inasmuch as, amidst various metaphors, the body is supposed to enchain the soul, and detain it from its native home. The sense of the passage is, "Now, Lord, thou dost (by this sight) dismiss me to the grave, as thou promisedst, in peace and tranquillity, because mine eyes have seen my salvation," i. e. the *author* of it. There is no occasion to suppose, with many, that *ἀπολύεις* is for *ἀπολύσεις*. The aged saint, by a beautiful figure, takes this sight of his Redeemer, as *a dismissal* from the burden of life, a sort of *Go in peace.* So Statius in his Theb. vii. 366. cited by Wetstein, Et fessum vitâ dimittite, Parcæ! I add Æschyl. Agam. 520, where the herald, out of joy, on again seeing his native country, exclaims, *τεθνάναι δ' οὐκ ἀντερῶ θεοῖς*. It is strange that so many Commentators should have failed to see that *ὅτι* after *ἐν εἰρήνῃ* is to be closely connected therewith, and rendered not "*for*" but "*because.*" Now this construction is common when a *verb* or *adjective* precedes; why, then, should it not be allowed after an *adjectival phrase?* The other signification requires much unauthorized subaudition to make out any construction, as may be seen by consulting the Paraphrasts. *Δεσπότης* is in Scripture used of the supreme Lord, i. e. God; but in the Classical writers the highest sense it has, is when used of Sovereigns.

30. *εἶδον οἱ ὀφθ.*] In *οἱ ὀφθ.* there is an *emphasis*, as in Gen. xlv. 11. Job xix. 27. xlii. 5. 1 John i. 1. *Τὸ σωτήριον*, Neut. adjective for substantive, as in Luke ii. 30. Eph. iii. 6. Psal. xcviii. 2. See Matth. Gr. Gr. § 627.

32. *φῶς — ἐθνῶν.*] This is an apposition with *τὸ σωτήριον σὸν* at ver. 30. Grot. observes, that the passage has reference to Is. xlii. 6. and Psal. xcviii. 2. from which it should seem that there is here a transposition, for *φῶς ἐθνῶν, εἰς ἀποκάλυψιν*. But *εἰς ἀποκ.* does not, I conceive, mean (as Grot. and others suppose) "for a revelation of the righteousness of God;" but is better explained by Euthym. *εἰς ἀνάβλεψιν τῶν ἐθνῶν* scil. *τετυφλωμένων τῇ πλάνῃ*.

ῥαήλ. Καὶ ἦν Ἰωσὴφ καὶ ἡ μήτηρ αὐτοῦ θαυμάζοντες ἐπὶ τοῖς λαλου- 33
g Isa. 8. 14. Matt. 21. 44. Rom. 9. 32, 33. 1 Pet. 2. 8. 1 Cor. 1. 23, 24. & 2 Cor. 2. 16. Acts 28. 22. h John 19. 25. μένοις περὶ αὐτοῦ. [g] Καὶ εὐλόγησεν αὐτοὺς Συμεὼν, καὶ εἶπε πρὸς 34
Μαριὰμ τὴν μητέρα αὐτοῦ· Ἰδοὺ, οὗτος κεῖται εἰς πτῶσιν καὶ ἀνά-
στασιν πολλῶν ἐν τῷ Ἰσραὴλ, καὶ εἰς σημεῖον ἀντιλεγόμενον· ([h] καὶ 35
σοῦ δὲ αὐτῆς τὴν ψυχὴν διελεύσεται ῥομφαία·) ὅπως ἂν ἀποκαλυ-
φθῶσιν ἐκ πολλῶν καρδιῶν διαλογισμοί.

Καὶ ἦν Ἄννα προφῆτις, θυγάτηρ Φανουὴλ, ἐκ φυλῆς Ἀσήρ· αὕτη 36
προβεβηκυῖα ἐν ἡμέραις πολλαῖς, ζήσασα ἔτη μετὰ ἀνδρὸς ἑπτὰ ἀπὸ
i 1 Sam. 1. 22. 1 Tim. 5. 5. τῆς παρθενίας αὐτῆς. [i] Καὶ αὕτη χήρα ὡς ἐτῶν ὀγδοηκοντατεσσάρων, 37
ἣ οὐκ ἀφίστατο ἀπὸ τοῦ ἱεροῦ, νηστείαις καὶ δεήσεσι λατρεύουσα νύ-
κτα καὶ ἡμέραν· καὶ αὕτη αὐτῇ τῇ ὥρᾳ ἐπιστᾶσα ἀνθωμολογεῖτο τῷ 38
Κυρίῳ, καὶ ἐλάλει περὶ αὐτοῦ πᾶσι τοῖς προσδεχομένοις λύτρωσιν ἐν
Ἱερουσαλήμ. Καὶ ὡς ἐτέλεσαν ἅπαντα τὰ κατὰ τὸν νόμον Κυρίου, 39
k Supr. 1. 80. infr. ver. 52. ὑπέστρεψαν εἰς τὴν Γαλιλαίαν εἰς τὴν πόλιν αὐτῶν Ναζαρέτ. [k] Τὸ δὲ 40

33. ἦν] "*per syncopen*, for ἦσαν, *Doricè*," say the Commentators. It was not, however, peculiar to the *Doric*. It was rather an *ancient* usage, but could not well arise from *Syncope*; though it was caught up, (together with many other syncopated words,) by the Poets, to suit their convenience. I suspect it to have been a *very* old form, as old as the time when, in the simplicity of early diction (which yet lingers in the popular dialect), a distinction of number in the *verb* was unattended to; and that it afterwards continued in use in the *common* dialect.

34. οὗτος κεῖται, &c.] The imagery is supposed to be taken from Is. viii. 14. & xxviii. 16, which passages are applied to the Messiah in Rom. ix. 33. See Grot., Wolf, Le Clerc, and Wets.; who remark, that under the figure of a stone lying in a path, on which heedless persons may trip, Christ is designated as a *rock of stumbling* to those who reject him, but a *rock of support* to those who avail themselves of his aid. Κεῖσθαι εἰς is not, however, to be regarded as implying *fatality*, but to be taken in a popular acceptation, for *to be ordained* or *appointed* for any thing, as in Phil. i. 17. and 1 Thess. iii. 3. Πτῶσιν and ἀνάστασιν are to be taken figuratively, of sin and misery,—and of reformation and happiness; namely, that he should be the occasion of sin to many, who would reject him; and be the occasion of many being raised, from the bondage of sin, to repentance, faith, and salvation through him.

— εἰς σημεῖον, scil. εἶναι.] On the sense of σημεῖον Commentators are not agreed. Beza, L. Brug., Mald., Mackn., and Doddr., think it is a figure intimating the deliberate malice of Christ's persecutors. And though no example of σημεῖον so used has been adduced, yet several have been noted of the corresponding Latin term *signum*. The sense, however, thus arising is somewhat *jejune*; and since this whole passage is founded (though the Commentators have failed to notice it) on Isaiah viii. 14—18, it is certain that the sense must be (as Grot. and most of the best Expositors since his time have seen), that "He should be a signal example of virtue calumniated, and beneficence basely requited." Ἀντιλεγόμενον is to be taken nearly as equivalent to ἀντιλεχθησόμενον. The Pesch. Syr. Tr. freely, but not unfaithfully, renders, "a mark for contradiction or calumny." The best comment is supplied by the words of Heb. xii. 3. written, as also ii. 13, with this passage of the prophet in mind: Ἀναλογίσασθε τὸν τοιαύτην ὑπομεμενηκότα ὑπὸ τῶν ἁμαρτωλῶν εἰς αὐτὸν ἀντιλογίαν, ἵνα μὴ κάμητε, ταῖς ψυχαῖς ὑμῶν ἐκλυόμενοι.

35. καὶ—δὲ] "quia—imo." Σοῦ αὐτῆς, for σεαυτῆς; perhaps by a popular idiom. In τὴν ψυχ. δ. ῥομφαία is figurative language, similar to what we find in the Poetic parts of the O. T., and indeed in the *Classical* Poets, by which men's minds are said to be wounded, as the body is transfixed with arrows, swords, &c. See Prov. xii. 18, and Rec. Syn. We can be at no loss to imagine the many ways in which this prophecy was fulfilled, (since the calumnies shot at her *Son* must have pierced her to the heart, without supposing, with some, that Mary should *suffer martyrdom*.

— ὅπως ἂν — διαλογ.] Διαλογισμὸς is a vox mediæ significationis, denoting the *course* of thought and reflection, whether good or evil. The sense is, "in order that the real disposition of every one as [to truth and virtue] may be disclosed."

36. προφῆτις.] Of the various senses which have been here assigned to this term, the best founded is that of the ancients and Grot., adopted by Schleus., "one endued with the χάρισμα, or Spiritual grace, of uttering Divine revelations." Προβεβηκυῖα ἐν ἡμέραις πολλαῖς is, *per hypallagen*, for πολὺ προβ. Ἔτη ἑπτὰ, scil. μόνα. At χήρα sub. γύνη, which is sometimes expressed, especially in the earlier writers. The very long widowhood of Anna is particularly mentioned, since virtuous widowhood was held in great honour among the Jews, and even Gentiles. See Joseph. Ant. xviii. 6, 6, and Val. Max. ii. 1, 3.

37. οὐκ ἀφίστατο — νύκτα καὶ ἡμέραν.] An hyperbolical expression, importing that she *assiduously attended* at all the stated periods of public worship, both day and night, (for there were occasionally night-services of sacred music); and perhaps that she spent most of her time in the temple, engaged in prayer and holy meditation.

38. ἐπιστᾶσα] "coming up." Αὐτῇ τῇ ὥρᾳ, i. e. at the time that Simeon uttered the above words. Ἀνθωμολογεῖτο τῷ Κ. This is by some rendered, "returned thanks." That sense, however, is confined to the Classical writers; and even in them has χάριν added, and is accompanied by no Dative. It is better to adopt the sense which

παιδίον ηὔξανε, καὶ ἐκραταιοῦτο πνεύματι, πληρούμενον σοφίας· καὶ
χάρις Θεοῦ ἦν ἐπ' αὐτό.
41 [l] ΚΑΙ ἐπορεύοντο οἱ γονεῖς αὐτοῦ κατ' ἔτος εἰς Ἱερουσαλὴμ τῇ ἑορ- l Deut. 16. 1. Exod. 23. 15,
42 τῇ τοῦ πάσχα. Καὶ ὅτε ἐγένετο ἐτῶν δώδεκα, ἀναβάντων αὐτῶν εἰς 17. & 34. 23. Lev. 23. 5.
43 Ἱεροσόλυμα κατὰ τὸ ἔθος τῆς ἑορτῆς, καὶ τελειωσάντων τὰς ἡμέρας, ἐν
τῷ ὑποστρέφειν αὐτοὺς, ὑπέμεινεν Ἰησοῦς ὁ παῖς ἐν Ἱερουσαλήμ· καὶ
44 οὐκ ἔγνω Ἰωσὴφ καὶ ἡ μήτηρ αὐτοῦ. Νομίσαντες δὲ αὐτὸν ἐν τῇ
συνοδίᾳ εἶναι, ἦλθον ἡμέρας ὁδὸν, καὶ ἀνεζήτουν αὐτὸν ἐν τοῖς συγ-
45 γενέσι καὶ ἐν τοῖς γνωστοῖς· καὶ μὴ εὑρόντες αὐτὸν, ὑπέστρεψαν εἰς
46 Ἱερουσαλὴμ ζητοῦντες αὐτόν. Καὶ ἐγένετο, μεθ' ἡμέρας τρεῖς εὗρον
αὐτὸν ἐν τῷ ἱερῷ, καθεζόμενον ἐν μέσῳ τῶν διδασκάλων, καὶ ἀκούοντα
47 αὐτῶν καὶ ἐπερωτῶντα αὐτούς. [m] Ἐξίσταντο δὲ πάντες οἱ ἀκούοντες m Matt. 7. 28 Mark 1. 22.
48 αὐτοῦ ἐπὶ τῇ συνέσει καὶ ταῖς ἀποκρίσεσιν αὐτοῦ. Καὶ ἰδόντες αὐτὸν Infr. 4. 22. 32. John 7. 15, 46
ἐξεπλάγησαν· καὶ πρὸς αὐτὸν ἡ μήτηρ αὐτοῦ εἶπε· Τέκνον, τί ἐποίησας
49 ἡμῖν οὕτως; ἰδοὺ, ὁ πατήρ σου κἀγὼ ὀδυνώμενοι ἐζητοῦμέν σε. Καὶ
εἶπε πρὸς αὐτούς· Τί ὅτι ἐζητεῖτέ με; οὐκ ᾔδειτε ὅτι ἐν τοῖς τοῦ

the word bears in some kindred passages of the LXX. (as Ps. lxxix. 13,) and render, "returned praises to the Lord." The two significations, however, merge into each other. Λύτρωσιν here seems to include the notions of *deliverance* and *redemption*. Most of the Jews thought only of the *temporal*, the wiser few took it in the *spiritual* sense.

40. χάρις Θεοῦ, &c.] Raphel., Wets., Campb., and Wakef., take these words, by an idiom connected with the oblique cases of Θεὸς, to denote *greatness* or *excellence*, and by a common signification of χάρις *(grace)* to denote that he was of extraordinary comeliness. But there is no example of χάρις in the N. T. in any *nearer* sense than gracefulness of *speech;* which cannot here apply. Besides, χάρις τοῦ Θεοῦ is of such frequent occurrence in the N. T., (especially in St. Luke's works,) that the Evangelist would never have ventured on introducing such an idiom of Θεὸς as that just adverted to, in *this* case, since misapprehension would be sure to arise. In fact, χάρις Θεοῦ, except in a few passages where it has reference to the *miraculous gifts of the Holy Spirit*, always denotes in the N. T. the *favour of God to men*. And that it is so taken here is placed beyond doubt by a kindred passage, infra ver. 52.

41. ἐπορεύοντο.] All the males were required to attend at the three festivals at Jerusalem; and females, though not commanded, yet used often to attend, especially at the Passover.

42. ἀναβάντων αὐτῶν.] The αὐτῶν includes *Jesus;* which, indeed, is implied in the preceding words ὅτε ἐγένετο ἐ. δ.; for the age of 12 years (which was considered the age of puberty, and was that when the children were put to learn some trade) was, as appears from the Rabbinical writers, that at which the above obligation was thought binding; when too they were solemnly introduced into the Church, and initiated in its doctrines and ceremonies.

44. ἐν συνοδίᾳ.] The word properly denotes "*a journeying together*," and then, by metonymy, *a company* of fellow travellers. The Orientals express this by *Caravan*.

— ἀνεζήτουν] "sought him out," i. e. diligently; for the ἀνα is intensive. So Thucyd. ii. 8. πάντα ἀνεζητεῖτο.

— τοις γνωστοῖς] "acquaintance." The word very rarely occurs as a substantive, (being properly a participle or adjective) though it is found in Ps. lxxviii. 9.

46. μεθ' ἡμ. τρεῖς] i. e. on the 3d day. The 1st. was spent in their journey; the 2d. in their return to Jerusalem; and on the 3d. they found him.

— ἐν τῷ ἱερῷ.] By this is meant a *court* in which (as we learn from the Rabbinical writers) the doctors sat, for the purpose of public instruction. It is not necessary to press on the sense of ἐν μέσῳ, which may be taken to mean "*among* them;" viz. in the centre of an area round which the benches of the doctors were raised semicircularly. Nor are we from ἐπερωτῶντα αὐτοὺς to suppose any thing like *disputation*, but modest interrogation. — See Doddr. Indeed, it is plain from the Rabbinical citations in Lightf., that the Jewish doctors used such a plan of instruction as dealt much in interrogation, both on the part of the teachers and the taught. Something very similar I have noted in the following account given by Josephus of his boyhood, Life, § 2: — Ἐγὼ δὲ συμπαιδευόμενος, εἰς μεγάλην παιδείας προὔκοπτον ἐπίδοσιν, μνήμῃ τε καὶ συνέσει δοκῶν διαφέρειν. Ἔτι δ' ἄρα παῖς ὤν, περὶ τεσσαρεσκαιδέκατον ἔτος, διὰ τὸ φιλογράμματον ὑπὸ πάντων ἐπῃνούμην, συνιόντων ἀεὶ τῶν ἀρχιερέων καὶ τῶν τῆς πόλεως πρώτων, ὑπὲρ τοῦ παρ' ἐμοῦ περὶ τῶν νομίμων ἀκριβέστερόν τι γνῶναι.

47. τῇ συνέσει] "intelligence," "natural sagacity." So Thucyd. i. 138. φύσεως ἰσχὺν δηλώσας· οἰκείᾳ γὰρ ξυνέσει, &c. In τῇ συνέσει καὶ ταῖς ἀποκ. there is no Hendiadys (as Kuin. imagines) but ἐν ταῖς ἀποκρ. is added, to show in what that σύνεσις especially consisted.

49. ἐν τοῖς τοῦ πατρός μου.] Commentators are perplexed with this elliptical expression; in which there was perhaps a *studied* ambiguity. Some supply πράγμασι, others οἰκήμασι. The former is well supported by Classical examples, and if this were a Classical author, it might deserve the preference; but in an Hellenistic one it cannot be admitted. Besides, the answer, according to

n Infr. 9. 45. & 18. 34. πατρός μου δεῖ εἶναί με; ⁿ Καὶ αὐτοὶ οὐ συνῆκαν τὸ ῥῆμα, ὃ ἐλάλη- 50
σεν αὐτοῖς. Καὶ κατέβη μετ' αὐτῶν, καὶ ἦλθεν εἰς Ναζαρέτ· καὶ ἦν 51
ὑποτασσόμενος αὐτοῖς. Καὶ ἡ μήτηρ αὐτοῦ διετήρει πάντα τὰ ῥήματα
o 1 Sam. 2. 26. supr. 1. 80. & 2. 40. ταῦτα ἐν τῇ καρδίᾳ αὐτῆς. ° Καὶ Ἰησοῦς προέκοπτε σοφίᾳ καὶ ἡλι- 52
κίᾳ, καὶ χάριτι παρὰ Θεῷ καὶ ἀνθρώποις.

III. ἘΝ ἔτει δὲ πεντεκαιδεκάτῳ τῆς ἡγεμονίας Τιβερίου Καίσαρος, 1
ἡγεμονεύοντος Ποντίου Πιλάτου τῆς Ἰουδαίας, καὶ τετραρχοῦντος τῆς Γαλι-
MT. MK. λαίας Ἡρώδου, Φιλίππου δὲ τοῦ ἀδελφοῦ αὐτοῦ τετραρχοῦντος τῆς Ἰτου-
3. 1. ραίας καὶ Τραχωνίτιδος χώρας, καὶ Λυσανίου τῆς Ἀβιληνῆς τετραρχοῦντος, 2
1 ἐπ' ἀρχιερέων Ἄννα καὶ Καϊάφα, ἐγένετο ῥῆμα Θεοῦ ἐπὶ Ἰωάννην τὸν
2 [τοῦ] Ζαχαρίου υἱὸν ἐν τῇ ἐρήμῳ· καὶ ἦλθεν εἰς πᾶσαν τὴν περίχωρον 3
3 2 τοῦ Ἰορδάνου, κηρύσσων βάπτισμα μετανοίας εἰς ἄφεσιν ἁμαρτιῶν· ὡς 4
γέγραπται ἐν βίβλῳ λόγων Ἡσαΐου τοῦ προφήτου, λέγοντος· Φωνὴ
βοῶντος ἐν τῇ ἐρήμῳ· ἑτοιμάσατε τὴν ὁδὸν Κυρίου,
εὐθείας ποιεῖτε τὰς τρίβους αὐτοῦ. πᾶσα φάραγξ 5
πληρωθήσεται, καὶ πᾶν ὄρος καὶ βουνὸς ταπεινωθή-
σεται· καὶ ἔσται τὰ σκολιὰ εἰς εὐθεῖαν, καὶ αἱ τρα-
χεῖαι εἰς ὁδοὺς λείας. καὶ ὄψεται πᾶσα σὰρξ τὸ σω- 6
7 τήριον τοῦ Θεοῦ. Ἔλεγεν οὖν τοῖς ἐκπορευομένοις ὄχλοις βα- 7
πτισθῆναι ὑπ' αὐτοῦ· Γεννήματα ἐχιδνῶν! τίς ὑπέδειξεν ὑμῖν φυγεῖν
8 ἀπὸ τῆς μελλούσης ὀργῆς; Ποιήσατε οὖν καρποὺς ἀξίους τῆς μετα- 8
9 νοίας· καὶ μὴ ἄρξησθε λέγειν ἐν ἑαυτοῖς· Πατέρα ἔχομεν τὸν
Ἀβραάμ· λέγω γὰρ ὑμῖν, ὅτι δύναται ὁ Θεὸς ἐκ τῶν λίθων τούτων

that sense, would scarcely be suitable to the question. It is therefore better, with the ancient, and a great majority of the modern Commentators, to supply *οἰκήμασι*, of which ellipsis Wets. has adduced abundance of examples, both from the Classical and Scriptural writers. So Gen. xli. 51. Ecclus. xlii. 10.

51. *ἦν ὑποτασσόμενος αὐτοῖς.*] Ὑποτάσσεσθαι is used not only of forcible and compulsatory, but voluntary, subjection, as that of wives and of children. Ῥήματα may here mean both sayings and doings.

52. *προέκοπτε*] "advanced." In this sense there is (as I observed in Recens. Synop.) a metaphor taken from the felling of trees, or clearing of thickets, to effect a passage. Ἡλικίᾳ is by some interpreted "stature;" by others, "age." The latter is *possibly* true; but it would rather have required a double *καὶ* before *σοφίᾳ*; and the former is more suitable to the context. *Both* may have been in the mind of the Evangelist.

III. 1. On the chronological questions connected with this passage, the reader is referred to Dr. Hales, Mr. Benson, and Mr. Townsend.

2. *ἐπ' ἀρχ. Ἄ. καὶ Κ.*] [*Comp.* Acts iv. 6.] There has been much perplexity occasioned by the use, in the Gospels and also in Joseph., of phraseology expressing or implying plurality, where the Law recognised but *one*. In strict propriety there could be but *one* high priest at a time, who held the office for life. But, after the reduction of Judæa to the Roman yoke, great changes were made; and the occupants of an office, which had enjoyed almost regal authority, were changed at the will of the conquerors. Hence some have supposed that the office had been made annual; and that Annas and Caiaphas occupying it *by turns*, each, or both, might be said to be the High Priest. This, however, is a wholly gratuitous supposition, and overturned by what is said in Joseph. Ant. xviii. 2, 2. Others think that Caiaphas was the High Priest, and Annas his Sagan, or Deputy; a title given to him by Joseph. Ant. xviii. 6, 24. And great was the dignity of the Sagan; who was allowed, upon occasion, to perform the most sacred functions of the High Priest. Others, again, imagine that the *title* is given to Annas, as being the chief of Aaron's family then alive, and being regarded as the rightful High Priest by the Jews, though Caiaphas held the *office* by appointment of the Roman Governor. These last two methods *also* proceed on supposition, and although there is nothing which *contradicts* either, there is no reason for giving a preference to either.

— *ἐγένετο ῥῆμα Θ. ἐπὶ Ἰ.*] "the command of the Lord was issued to John." A formula implying Divine authority, which occurs also in Jer. i. 2.

3. *καὶ ἦλθεν.*] "And he (accordingly) went."

4. See Is. xl. 3. John i. 23.

5. The Evangelist, it may be observed, cites this passage of the Prophet further on than Matthew and Mark, because he was writing especially for Gentile converts; and the latter part of the question was necessary to assure them, that the "salvation of God," and the participation in the privileges of the Gospel, extended to *them* as well as the Jews.

6. See Ps. xcviii. 3.

MT. MK.

9 ἐγεῖραι τέκνα τῷ Ἀβραάμ. Ἤδη δὲ καὶ ἡ ἀξίνη πρὸς τὴν ῥίζαν τῶν 3. 1.
δένδρων κεῖται· πᾶν οὖν δένδρον μὴ ποιοῦν καρπὸν καλὸν ἐκκόπτε- 10
ται καὶ εἰς πῦρ βάλλεται.
10 Καὶ ἐπηρώτων αὐτὸν οἱ ὄχλοι, λέγοντες· Τί οὖν ποιήσομεν; Ἀπο-
11 κριθεὶς δὲ λέγει αὐτοῖς· Ὁ ἔχων δύο χιτῶνας μεταδότω τῷ μὴ ἔχοντι·
12 καὶ ὁ ἔχων βρώματα ὁμοίως ποιείτω. Ἦλθον δὲ καὶ τελῶναι βαπτι-
13 σθῆναι, καὶ εἶπον πρὸς αὐτόν· Διδάσκαλε, τί ποιήσομεν; Ὁ δὲ εἶπε
πρὸς αὐτούς· Μηδὲν πλέον παρὰ τὸ διατεταγμένον ὑμῖν πράσσετε.
14 Ἐπηρώτων δὲ αὐτὸν καὶ στρατευόμενοι, λέγοντες· Καὶ ἡμεῖς τί ποιήσομεν; Καὶ εἶπε πρὸς αὐτούς· Μηδένα διασείσητε, μηδὲ συκοφαν-
τήσητε· καὶ ἀρκεῖσθε τοῖς ὀψωνίοις ὑμῶν.
15 Προσδοκῶντος δὲ τοῦ λαοῦ, καὶ διαλογιζομένων πάντων ἐν ταῖς καρ-
16 δίαις αὐτῶν περὶ τοῦ Ἰωάννου, μήποτε αὐτὸς εἴη ὁ Χριστός, ἀπεκρίνατο 11 7
ὁ Ἰωάννης ἅπασι, λέγων· Ἐγὼ μὲν ὕδατι βαπτίζω ὑμᾶς· ἔρχεται
δὲ ὁ ἰσχυρότερός μου, οὗ οὐκ εἰμὶ ἱκανὸς λῦσαι τὸν ἱμάντα τῶν ὑπο- 8
δημάτων αὐτοῦ· αὐτὸς ὑμᾶς βαπτίσει ἐν Πνεύματι ἁγίῳ καὶ πυρί.
17 οὗ τὸ πτύον ἐν τῇ χειρὶ αὐτοῦ, καὶ διακαθαριεῖ τὴν ἅλωνα αὐτοῦ· 12
καὶ συνάξει τὸν σῖτον εἰς τὴν ἀποθήκην αὐτοῦ, τὸ δὲ ἄχυρον κατα-
18 καύσει πυρὶ ἀσβέστῳ. Πολλὰ μὲν οὖν καὶ ἕτερα παρακαλῶν εὐηγγε-
19 λίζετο τὸν λαόν. Ὁ δὲ Ἡρώδης ὁ τετράρχης, ἐλεγχόμενος ὑπ' αὐτοῦ
περὶ Ἡρωδιάδος τῆς γυναικὸς [Φιλίππου] τοῦ ἀδελφοῦ αὐτοῦ, καὶ

10. [*Comp.* Acts ii. 37.]

11. αὐτοῖς.] And to the Pharisees more especially, as we learn from Matt. iii. 7. *Charity* is here enjoined, as a prominent part of that moral virtue in which *they* were so notoriously deficient. [*Comp.* 1 John iii. 17. iv. 20.]

12. The Future in ποιήσομεν here and just before is to be rendered by *must* rather than *shall*; a Hebraism. The ποιήσωμεν of many ancient MSS., edited by Scholz, is only a gloss. It is well observed by Bornemann: 'Neutrum est falsum, sed exquisitius futurum, quod in subsequentibus mutare librarii desierunt. Eadem est scribendi diversitas,' John vi. 5. πόθεν ἀγοράσομεν ἄρτους;

13. μηδὲν πλέον — πράσσετε.] This use of πράσσειν, as said of *taxes*, (like *perficere* in Latin), is frequent in the Classical writers. The sense was either *to exact*, or *to collect*; the former was the idea of the payer, the latter of the receiver. The *original* sense intended seems to have been "to manage." The difference between the active and middle forms is this: the active signifies to collect *for another's use*, the middle to collect for one's *own*. Διατάσσειν is a *vox signata*, used of legal enactments, especially such as relate to laying on taxes. See Duker on Thucyd. iii. 70. The παρὰ after a comparative, or a word which *implies* comparison (especially μείζων or κρείττων), is used for ἤ, both in the Scriptural and Classical writers. The literal sense of παρὰ in this use is "*alongside of*;" and juxtaposition almost implies comparison. Our Lord does not, we see, condemn their profession, but only the *abuse* of the power it gave them.

14. στρατευόμενοι.] Michaelis thinks that this denotes the "men under arms, or going to battle;" for he imagines that Herod's war with Aretas had already commenced; and that there is here reference to the troops engaged in that service. A *chronological* reason, however, may be opposed to overturn this supposition; and, moreover, the *Article* would thus be indispensable.

— μηδένα διασείσητε.] This is by many Commentators taken to mean, "do not harass;" a signification found in the Classical writers. But some more *special* sense seems to be intended. It is therefore best explained as equivalent to, and indeed formed from, the Latin *concutere*, which has been proved to have the signification "to extort money by dint of threats." Διασείειν imports extortion by threats of *violence*; συκοφαντεῖν that by threats of unjust accusation, false information, &c.

— ἀρκεῖσθε τοῖς ὀψωνίοις.] In the early ages a soldier's pay consisted chiefly in a *supply of food*: and was called ὀψώνιον, from ὄψον, *meat*. In process of time an equivalent in money was substituted for the supply of food; and then ὀψώνιον, which had originally meant *support*, came to denote *pay*; though still *some* allowances *in kind* were left the soldier; which probably opened a way to the extortion alluded to.

15. προσδοκῶντος τοῦ λ.] i. e. as the people were waiting and in suspense; so Acts xxviii. 6.

16. ἅπασι] i. e. both those there, and those at Jerusalem, who (we learn from John ii. 18.) had sent a message of inquiry. On this verse comp. John i. 26. Acts i. 5. xi. 16. xiii. 25. Is. xliv. 3. Joel ii. 28. Acts ii. 4.

18. εὐηγγ. τὸν λαόν] "he evangelized the people," proclaimed to them the Gospel; as Acts viii. 25. Gal. i. 9.

19. Φιλίππου.] This is omitted in very many MSS., and almost all the early Editions, and has been with reason cancelled by almost every Ed-

MT. MK.

3. 1. περὶ πάντων ὧν ἐποίησε πονηρῶν ὁ Ἡρώδης, προσέθηκε καὶ τοῦτο 20
ἐπὶ πᾶσι, καὶ κατέκλεισε τὸν Ἰωάννην ἐν τῇ φυλακῇ.
16 10 Ἐγένετο δὲ, ἐν τῷ βαπτισθῆναι ἅπαντα τὸν λαὸν, καὶ Ἰησοῦ βα- 21
πτισθέντος καὶ προσευχομένου, ἀνεῳχθῆναι τὸν οὐρανὸν, καὶ καταβῆναι 22
17 11 τὸ Πνεῦμα τὸ ἅγιον σωματικῷ εἴδει, ὡσεὶ περιστερὰν, ἐπ᾽ αὐτὸν, καὶ
φωνὴν ἐξ οὐρανοῦ γενέσθαι, λέγουσαν· Σὺ εἶ ὁ υἱός μου ὁ ἀγαπητός, ἐν σοὶ ηὐδόκησα. Καὶ αὐτὸς ἦν ὁ Ἰησοῦς ὡσεὶ ἐτῶν τριάκοντα 23
ἀρχόμενος· ὢν, ὡς ἐνομίζετο, υἱὸς Ἰωσὴφ, τοῦ Ἡλὶ, τοῦ Ματθὰτ, τοῦ 24
Λευῒ, τοῦ Μελχὶ, τοῦ Ἰαννὰ, τοῦ Ἰωσὴφ, τοῦ Ματταθίου, τοῦ Ἀμὼς, 25
τοῦ Ναοὺμ, τοῦ Ἐσλὶ, τοῦ Ναγγαὶ, τοῦ Μαὰθ, τοῦ Ματταθίου, τοῦ 26
Σεμεῒ, τοῦ Ἰωσὴφ, τοῦ Ἰούδα, τοῦ Ἰωαννᾶ, τοῦ Ῥησὰ, τοῦ Ζοροβάβελ, 27
τοῦ Σαλαθιὴλ, τοῦ Νηρὶ, τοῦ Μελχὶ, τοῦ Ἀδδὶ, τοῦ Κωσὰμ, τοῦ Ἐλ- 28
μωδὰμ, τοῦ Ἢρ, τοῦ Ἰωσὴ, τοῦ Ἐλιέζερ, τοῦ Ἰωρεὶμ, τοῦ Ματθὰτ, τοῦ 29
Λευῒ, τοῦ Συμεὼν, τοῦ Ἰούδα, τοῦ Ἰωσὴφ, τοῦ Ἰωνὰν, τοῦ Ἐλιακεὶμ, τοῦ 30 31
Μελεᾶ, τοῦ Μαϊνὰν, τοῦ Ματταθὰ, τοῦ Ναθὰν, τοῦ Δαυῒδ, τοῦ Ἰεσ- 32
σαὶ, τοῦ Ὠβὴδ, τοῦ Βοὸζ, τοῦ Σαλμὼν, τοῦ Ναασσὼν, τοῦ Ἀμιναδὰβ, 33
τοῦ Ἀρὰμ, τοῦ Ἐσρὼμ, τοῦ Φαρὲς, τοῦ Ἰούδα, τοῦ Ἰακὼβ, τοῦ 34
Ἰσαὰκ, τοῦ Ἀβραὰμ, τοῦ Θάρα, τοῦ Ναχὼρ, τοῦ Σεροὺχ, τοῦ Ῥαγαῦ, 35
τοῦ Φάλεκ, τοῦ Ἐβὲρ, τοῦ Σαλὰ, τοῦ Καϊνὰν, τοῦ Ἀρφαξὰδ, τοῦ Σὴμ, 36
τοῦ Νῶε, τοῦ Λάμεχ, τοῦ Μαθουσάλα, τοῦ Ἐνὼχ, τοῦ Ἰαρὲδ, τοῦ 37
4. Μαλελεὴλ, τοῦ Καϊνὰν, τοῦ Ἐνὼς, τοῦ Σὴθ, τοῦ Ἀδὰμ, τοῦ Θεοῦ. 38
1 IV. ἸΗΣΟΥΣ δὲ Πνεύματος ἁγίου πλήρης, ὑπέστρεψεν ἀπὸ τοῦ 1
12 13 Ἰορδάνου· καὶ ἤγετο ἐν τῷ Πνεύματι εἰς τὴν ἔρημον ἡμέρας τεσσαρά- 2

itor from Wets. to Scholz. [*Comp.* Matt. xiv. 3. Mark vi. 17.]

21. βαπτ. καὶ προσ.] [*Comp.* John i. 32.] The words καὶ προσ., which are added by St. Luke, merit attention. Our Lord, who was content to be obedient unto the Law for man, underwent the rites and performed the ceremonies of the Mosaic Law; and on the same principle underwent this baptism, because, as we find from St. Matthew, he wished to set an example to others of fulfilling all righteousness. With respect to the use of *prayer*, it was doubtless to set an example to others of the indispensable necessity of prayer, to make any external rites effectual. See Bp. Taylor, vol. ii. 190.

22. [*Comp.* Is. xlii. 1. Mark ix. 7. 2 Pet. i. 17.]

23. αὐτὸς ἦν ὁ Ἰησοῦς — ἀρχόμενος.] These words have occasioned much perplexity, not only to modern Commentators, but, (as appears from the Varr. Lectt.) to the ancient Interpreters. The phraseology is rugged; yet the harshness must not be removed by cancelling any word (for the consent of MSS. will not permit that); nor even by *silencing* it. Some seek to remove the difficulty by connecting ὢν with ἀρχ. But this is doing violence to the construction, and yields a feeble and frigid sense. Upon the whole, no interpretation involves so little difficulty as that of the ancient and the best modern Commentators, by which ἦν is construed with ἀρχ., and εἶναι understood after ἀρχ. The sense, then, is, "Jesus was beginning to be of about 30 years," i. e. he had nearly completed his 30th year. I grant that this is somewhat anomalous phraseology; but it is not more so than some other modes of expression to be found in Scripture; and was probably formed on the *popular* mode of speaking. There must not be an ἀπὸ supplied before ἐτῶν, (with some recent Commentators), for in this sense εἶναι carries the Genit. *alone*. See Matth., Gr. Gr. p. 519. Obs. 2.

— ὡς ἐνομίζετο.] This evidently alludes to his Divine origin.

— τοῦ Ἡλί.] This must mean the *son-in-law* of Heli, for Jacob was the father of Joseph. So Matt. i. 16. Thus this genealogy must be considered as the lineage of *Mary, the daughter of Heli*. On the mode of reconciling the seeming discrepancy in the genealogies, see Dr. Hales.

35. Σερούχ.] This (for Σαρούχ) is found in almost all the best MSS., Versions, and early Editions, and is received by almost every Editor from Wets. to Scholz.

IV. 2. ἡμέρας τεσσαράκοντα.] These words would seem to connect with the πειραζόμενος following, as some Editors take them. But St. Matthew describes the temptation as taking place at the *close* of that period. Most recent Commentators attempt to remove the discrepancy by supposing the meaning to be. not that Jesus was tempted 40 days *in succession*, but that, at *various times during* those days, he was exposed to temptations, *besides* those which the Evangelist now proceeds to enumerate. This method, however, cannot well be admitted. At least it is better, with some ancient and modern Commentators, to connect the words with the *preceding*. [*Comp.* Exod. xxxiv. 28. 1 Kings xix. 8.] Πειραζόμενος, however, is not, I conceive, put for πειρασθῆναι,

MT. MK.

κοντα πειραζόμενος ὑπὸ τοῦ Διαβόλου. Καὶ οὐκ ἔφαγεν οὐδὲν ἐν ταῖς 4. 1.
3 ἡμέραις ἐκείναις· καὶ, συντελεσθεισῶν αὐτῶν, ὕστερον ἐπείνασε. Καὶ 2
εἶπεν αὐτῷ ὁ Διάβολος· Εἰ Υἱὸς εἶ τοῦ Θεοῦ, εἰπὲ τῷ λίθῳ τούτῳ, 3
4 ἵνα γένηται ἄρτος. καὶ ἀπεκρίθη Ἰησοῦς πρὸς αὐτὸν, λέγων· Γέ- 4
γραπται, ὅτι οὐκ ἐπ' ἄρτῳ μόνῳ ζήσεται [ὁ] ἄνθρω-
5 πος, ἀλλ' ἐπὶ παντὶ ῥήματι Θεοῦ. Καὶ ἀναγαγὼν αὐτὸν 8
ὁ Διάβολος εἰς ὄρος ὑψηλὸν, ἔδειξεν αὐτῷ πάσας τὰς βασιλείας τῆς
6 οἰκουμένης ἐν στιγμῇ χρόνου· καὶ εἶπεν αὐτῷ ὁ Διάβολος· Σοὶ δώσω 9
τὴν ἐξουσίαν ταύτην ἅπασαν, καὶ τὴν δόξαν αὐτῶν· ὅτι ἐμοὶ παραδέ-
7 δοται, καὶ ᾧ ἐὰν θέλω, δίδωμι αὐτήν. Σὺ οὖν ἐὰν προσκυνήσῃς
8 ἐνώπιόν μου, ἔσται σοῦ * πᾶσα. Καὶ ἀποκριθεὶς αὐτῷ εἶπεν ὁ Ἰη- 10
σοῦς· Ὕπαγε ὀπίσω μου, Σατανᾶ· γέγραπται [γάρ]· Προσκυνήσεις Κύριον τὸν Θεόν σου, καὶ αὐτῷ μόνῳ λα-
9 τρεύσεις. Καὶ ἤγαγεν αὐτὸν εἰς Ἱερουσαλὴμ, καὶ ἔστησεν αὐτὸν ἐπὶ 5
τὸ πτερύγιον τοῦ ἱεροῦ, καὶ εἶπεν αὐτῷ· Εἰ [ὁ] Υἱὸς εἶ τοῦ Θεοῦ, 6
10 βάλε σεαυτὸν ἐντεῦθεν κάτω· γέγραπται γάρ· Ὅτι τοῖς ἀγγέλοις αὐτοῦ ἐντελεῖται περὶ σοῦ, τοῦ διαφυλάξαι σε·
11 καὶ [ὅτι] ἐπὶ χειρῶν ἀροῦσί σε, μή ποτε προσκό-
12 ψῃς πρὸς λίθον τὸν πόδα σου. Καὶ ἀποκριθεὶς εἶπεν
αὐτῷ ὁ Ἰησοῦς· Ὅτι εἴρηται· Οὐκ ἐκπειράσεις Κύριον 7
13 τὸν Θεόν σου. Καὶ συντελέσας πάντα πειρασμὸν ὁ Διάβολος, 11
ἀπέστη ἀπ' αὐτοῦ ἄχρι καιροῦ.
14 ΚΑΙ ὑπέστρεψεν ὁ Ἰησοῦς ἐν τῇ δυνάμει τοῦ Πνεύματος εἰς τὴν
Γαλιλαίαν· καὶ φήμη ἐξῆλθε καθ' ὅλης τῆς περιχώρου περὶ αὐτοῦ. 12 14
15 Καὶ αὐτὸς ἐδίδασκεν ἐν ταῖς συναγωγαῖς αὐτῶν δοξαζόμενος ὑπὸ πάν-
16 των. [a] Καὶ ἦλθεν εἰς τὴν Ναζαρὲτ, οὗ ἦν τεθραμμένος· καὶ εἰσῆλ- a Matt. 2. 23. & 13. 54.
θε, κατὰ τὸ εἰωθὸς αὐτῷ, ἐν τῇ ἡμέρᾳ τῶν σαββάτων εἰς τὴν συνα- Mark 6. 1. John 4. 43. Neh. 8. 5, 6.
17 γωγὴν, καὶ ἀνέστη ἀναγνῶσαι. Καὶ ἐπεδόθη αὐτῷ βιβλίον Ἡσαΐου

but is a *nominativus pendens*, for Genit. absolute. This mode of taking the passage is confirmed by Mark i. 12. who here follows Luke: καὶ ἦν ἐν τῇ ἐρήμῳ ἡμέρας τεσσαράκοντα, πειραζόμενος ὑπὸ τοῦ Σατανᾶ. Moreover, at πειραζόμενος is implied τότε from the context. *That*, however, will not, as in the case of διὰ ἡμ. τεσσ., involve any contradiction; since what takes place at *the close* of any period of time is understood, *populariter*, to fall *within* that term. I must further observe, that in ἤγετο just before, there seems to be included (per significationem prægnantem) καὶ ἦν scil. ἐκεῖ, which is *expressed* by Mark.

4. ὁ ἄνθρ.] The ὁ is omitted in very many of the best MSS., and cancelled by Matth., Griesb., and Scholz. But there is not sufficient authority to *cancel* it. [*Comp.* Deut. viii. 3.]

6. καὶ τὴν δόξαν αὐτῶν] scil. βασιλειῶν. We may paraphrase, "and the glory which will proceed from the government of them."

7. πᾶσα.] This (for the common reading πάντα) is found in almost all the best MSS., with several Versions, Fathers, and early Edd. It has also been received by Wets., Matth., Griesb., and others, down to Scholz, to whose authority I have yielded. Indeed, as being the more *difficult* reading, it seems to deserve the preference. Yet πάντα may be defended, as being more natural, and agreeable to the popular style; though *propriety* requires πᾶσα as referred to ἐξουσίαν.

8. γάρ.] See Deut. vi. 13. 1 Sam. vii. 3. This and the ὁ in the next verse are omitted in the best MSS., and cancelled by almost all the recent Editors.

10. See Ps. xci. 11.

11. The ὅτι is not found in very many MSS., early Edd., and Versions, and is cancelled by Matthæi. It seems to have come from the margin, and to have originated from those Critics who read γέγραπται γὰρ ὅτι — ἐντελεῖται; thus regarding the words as not strictly speaking a *quotation*, but only a *report* of the *sense*. And thus the ὅτι would require to be repeated. But it should seem that there *is* an actual quotation, and therefore the ὅτι is pleonastic; on which see Wahl's Clavis by Robinson.

12. See Deut. vi. 16.

14. ἐν τῇ δυνάμει τοῦ Πν.] "under the influence of the Spirit." Καθ' ὅλης, *throughout*, *over all*. This sense occurs also in Acts ix. 31, and is sometimes found in the *later* Classical writers.

15. δοξαζόμενος] for ἐν δόξῃ ὤν.

τοῦ προφήτου· καὶ ἀναπτύξας τὸ βιβλίον εὗρε τὸν τόπον οὗ ἦν
b Isa. 61. 1, 2. Matt. 11. 5. Isa. 42. 7. γεγραμμένον· [b] Πνεῦμα Κυρίου ἐπ' ἐμέ· οὗ εἵνεκεν 18
ἔχρισέ με * εὐαγγελίσασθαι πτωχοῖς, ἀπέσταλκέ
με ἰάσασθαι τοὺς συντετριμμένους τὴν καρδίαν·
κηρύξαι αἰχμαλώτοις ἄφεσιν, καὶ τυφλοῖς ἀνάβλε-
c Lev. 25. 10. ψιν· ἀποστεῖλαι τεθραυσμένους ἐν ἀφέσει· [c] κηρύ- 19
ξαι ἐνιαυτὸν Κυρίου δεκτόν. Καὶ πτύξας τὸ βιβλίον, 20
ἀποδοὺς τῷ ὑπηρέτῃ ἐκάθισε· καὶ πάντων ἐν τῇ συναγωγῇ οἱ ὀφθαλμοὶ ἦσαν ἀτενίζοντες αὐτῷ. Ἤρξατο δὲ λέγειν πρὸς αὐτούς· Ὅτι 21
d Isa. 50. 4. Matt. 13. 54. Mark 6. 2, 3. sup. 2. 47. John 6. 42. σήμερον πεπλήρωται ἡ γραφὴ αὕτη ἐν τοῖς ὠσὶν ὑμῶν. [d] Καὶ πάντες 22
ἐμαρτύρουν αὐτῷ, καὶ ἐθαύμαζον ἐπὶ τοῖς λόγοις τῆς χάριτος τοῖς
ἐκπορευομένοις ἐκ τοῦ στόματος αὐτοῦ, καὶ ἔλεγον· Οὐχ οὗτός ἐστιν

17. βιβλίον.] The βιβλία of the Hebrews, and indeed of the ancients in general, were *rolls* fastened to two laths with handles; by holding which in his hand, the reader could roll, or unroll the book at his pleasure.

18. ἔχρισέ με εὐαγγ.] This portion, taken from Is. lxi. 1, was selected by Jesus, in order to draw the attention of the people, and to show its fulfilment in himself: as also with allusion to the *reason* why he was called Christ, and his Religion termed the Gospel. Its application to the Messiah is acknowledged by the best Jewish Expositors. Indeed, the prophecy throughout admits of a *spiritual* interpretation, and an application to all times and all people.

— ἔχρισε.] This term signifies, not so much being *anointed*, as *inaugurated*, *introduced* into an office; which, in the case of eminent persons (as kings, prophets, priests, &c.) was always conferred by *unction*.

— εὐαγγελίσασθαι.] Very many MSS. and early Edd. have the common reading εὐαγγελίζεσθαι. But the other is preferred by almost all Editors from Matth. to Scholz.

— ἰάσασθαι — καρδίαν.] These words are omitted in a few MSS., Versions, and Fathers, and have been rejected by Grot. and Mill, and cancelled by Griesb. and others; but most rashly, since they are found both in the Heb. and LXX., and, as they are only omitted in *six* MSS., we may impute the omission merely to the carelessness of the Scribes. The words probably formed *one line* of the Archetype; and on that account might be the more easily omitted; especially as the line before began with a word of the same ending as that which commenced this; namely, εὐαγγελίσασθαι. From the same cause have arisen thousands of *lacunæ* in the Classical writers. Moreover, the words are required by the *parallelism*; in which πτωχοῖς and συντετρ. τὴν καρδίαν correspond to each other, the latter signifying the afflicted, or *contrite*, the former the distressed or *poor in spirit*; according as the *literal* or the *spiritual* sense be adopted. Συντ. is occasionally found even in the Classical writers, in a metaphorical sense, of mental sorrow.

The correspondent terms which follow, αἰχμαλώτοις, τυφλοῖς, and τεθραυσμένους, have likewise a double sense. Ἄφεσις, in the sense of *deliverance from captivity*, is found also in the Classical writers. With respect to τυφλοῖς, the sense of the *Hebrew*, "those who are bound," is greatly preferable, though the other may be justified, by taking the term to denote those who are as it were blind with long confinement in dark dungeons. In the spiritual sense, αἰχμ. will denote those who are bound with the chain of sin; and τυφλοῖς those who are blinded by sin and Satan; namely, the "blind people that have eyes," (Is. xliii. 8,) or those that "seeing, see not." (Matt. xiii. 13.) The next clause ἀποστεῖλαι — ἀφέσει is not found in either the Heb. or LXX. in *this* passage, though it is at C. 58. It was, no doubt, inserted, in reading, from that passage, as illustrative. As to the conjecture of Owen, that the words are a gloss, it is unfounded; and as to that of Randolph, that the Hebrew formerly contained a clause to this effect, is too hypothetical. Ἐν ἀφέσει is not, as most Commentators imagine, for εἰς ἄφεσιν; but may be rendered "in freedom," a *phrase* for the *adjective* free.

19. κηρύξαι — δεκτόν.] This sums up the whole of the above, in words which contain an allusion to *the year of Jubilee*; when, by sound of trumpet, was proclaimed deliverance, and restoration of every kind. Thus it is meant, that *the Gospel* is to *the Law* what the Jubilee year was as compared to all others. In the application, ἐνιαυτὸς will denote *time* generally. Δεκτὸν is for ἀρεστὸν, as 2 Cor. vi. 2. καιρὸς δεκτός. The word is not found in the Classical writers.

20. ἐκάθισε.] As those did, who proceeded to address some instruction to the people, after having read the portion of Scripture. See Vitringa de Syn. Jud., p. 899.

21. ἐν τοῖς ὠσὶν ὑμῶν.] E. V. "in your hearing." And so most Commentators take it. But that involves a very harsh *catachresis*, and it is better (with the Syr., Beng., De Dieu, and Campb.) to render, "which ye have heard;" literally, "which is now in your ears." Thus we must suppose an ellipsis of the relative. But this, however frequent in *Hebrew*, is very rare in *Greek*; and would *here* be so harsh, that I would rather suppose an ἣ had slipped out after αὕτη. The ἡ twice occurring just before would make this the more easily absorbed. The Syriac Translator certainly had it in his copy.

22. ἐμαρτύρουν α.] Μαρτυρεῖν with a Dative signifies "to bear testimony to, or for," and almost always implies *in favor of*. The word here expresses *commendation* on the grounds afterwards mentioned. Ἐθαύμαζον ἐπὶ, &c. is exegetical of the preceding. This syntax of θαυμάζειν with ἐπὶ, *(at)* occurs also in Mark xii. 17, and sometimes in the Classical writers. Διὰ or ἐν is more usual.

23 ὁ υἱὸς Ἰωσήφ; [e] Καὶ εἶπε πρὸς αὐτούς· Πάντως ἐρεῖτέ μοι τὴν e Matt. 4. 13. & 13. 54.
παραβολὴν ταύτην· Ἰατρὲ θεράπευσον σεαυτόν· ὅσα ἠκούσαμεν γε-
νόμενα ἐν τῇ Καπερναοὺμ, ποίησον καὶ ὧδε ἐν τῇ πατρίδι σου.
24 [f] Εἶπε δέ· Ἀμὴν λέγω ὑμῖν, ὅτι οὐδεὶς προφήτης δεκτός ἐστιν ἐν τῇ f Matt. 13. 57. Mark 6. 4.
25 πατρίδι αὐτοῦ. [g] Ἐπ᾽ ἀληθείας δὲ λέγω ὑμῖν· πολλαὶ χῆραι ἦσαν ἐν John 4. 44. g 1 Kings 17. 7.
ταῖς ἡμέραις Ἠλίου ἐν τῷ Ἰσραὴλ, ὅτε ἐκλείσθη ὁ οὐρανὸς ἐπὶ ἔτη τρία Jam. 5. 17.
26 καὶ μῆνας ἕξ, ὡς ἐγένετο λιμὸς μέγας ἐπὶ πᾶσαν τὴν γῆν· καὶ πρὸς
οὐδεμίαν αὐτῶν ἐπέμφθη Ἠλίας, εἰ μὴ εἰς Σάρεπτα τῆς Σιδῶνος πρὸς
27 γυναῖκα χήραν. [h] Καὶ πολλοὶ λεπροὶ ἦσαν ἐπὶ Ἐλισσαίου τοῦ προ- h 2 Kings 5. 14.
φήτου ἐν τῷ Ἰσραήλ· καὶ οὐδεὶς αὐτῶν ἐκαθαρίσθη, εἰ μὴ Νεεμὰν ὁ
28 Σύρος. Καὶ ἐπλήσθησαν πάντες θυμοῦ ἐν τῇ συναγωγῇ, ἀκούοντες
29 ταῦτα. Καὶ ἀναστάντες ἐξέβαλον αὐτὸν ἔξω τῆς πόλεως· καὶ ἤγαγον
αὐτὸν ἕως [τῆς] ὀφρύος τοῦ ὄρους, ἐφ᾽ οὗ ἡ πόλις αὐτῶν ᾠκοδόμητο,
30 εἰς τὸ κατακρημνίσαι αὐτόν· αὐτὸς δὲ διελθὼν διὰ μέσου αὐτῶν, MK.
ἐπορεύετο. 1.
31 ΚΑΙ κατῆλθεν εἰς Καπερναοὺμ πόλιν τῆς Γαλιλαίας· καὶ ἦν δι- 21
32 δάσκων αὐτοὺς ἐν τοῖς σάββασι. Καὶ ἐξεπλήσσοντο ἐπὶ τῇ διδαχῇ 22
33 αὐτοῦ· ὅτι ἐν ἐξουσίᾳ ἦν ὁ λόγος αὐτοῦ. Καὶ ἐν τῇ συναγωγῇ ἦν 23
ἄνθρωπος ἔχων πνεῦμα δαιμονίου ἀκαθάρτου, καὶ ἀνέκραξε φωνῇ
34 μεγάλῃ, λέγων· Ἔα· τί ἡμῖν καὶ σοὶ, Ἰησοῦ Ναζαρηνέ; ἦλθες 24
35 ἀπολέσαι ἡμᾶς; οἶδά σε τίς εἶ· ὁ ἅγιος τοῦ Θεοῦ. Καὶ ἐπετίμησεν 25
αὐτῷ ὁ Ἰησοῦς, λέγων· Φιμώθητι, καὶ ἔξελθε ἐξ αὐτοῦ. Καὶ ῥίψαν
αὐτὸν τὸ δαιμόνιον εἰς [τὸ] μέσον, ἐξῆλθεν ἀπ᾽ αὐτοῦ, μηδὲν βλάψαν 26
36 αὐτόν. Καὶ ἐγένετο θάμβος ἐπὶ πάντας· καὶ συνελάλουν πρὸς ἀλλή- 27
λους, λέγοντες· Τίς ὁ λόγος οὗτος; ὅτι ἐν ἐξουσίᾳ καὶ δυνάμει

Τῆς χάριτος is a Genit. of a substantive put for an adjective (graceful and eloquent.)

23. ποίησον ὧδε] i. e. as a full proof that thou art the personage foretold by Isaiah.

24. οὐδεὶς προφ., &c.] This is the *first* argument in answer to the objection *supposed* at v. 23.

25. This and the next two verses form (as Mr. Holden observes) our Lord's *next argument:* namely, that God has a right, and will dispense his extraordinary favours as he pleases, and this he does in a way which sometimes appears strange to men's judgment, but is consistent with perfect wisdom and equity; as in the instance which Jesus cites from 1 Kings xvii. 9, and 2 Kings v. 1—14. [*Comp.* James v. 17.]

—ἐπ᾽ ἀληθείας] for ἐν ἀληθείᾳ, i. e. ἀληθῶς or ἀμὴν, as elsewhere in the N. T. and sometimes in the Classical writers. Ἔτη—ἕξ. Our Lord is here showing by examples, that God most frequently communicates his extraordinary benefits to those who are capable of receiving them, passing over the unworthy. In ἐκλείσθη we have a metaphor occurring also in Rev. xi. 6. and Ecclus. xlviii. 3. Ὡς, for ὥστε, as with the same syntax (the Indicative) in Mark iv. 27, and Heb. iii. 11.

26. εἰ μὴ εἰς Σάρ.] On this use of εἰ μὴ preceded by a negative sentence, and involving an ellipsis in which the verb is repeated, see Viger, p. 510, and Wahl. Γυναῖκα χήραν is *not* a pleonasm, but a primitive *oratio plena*, like the *old* Latin *vidua mulier* in Terence, and our *widow woman.*

29. ἐξέβαλον] "drove or hurried him." Καὶ ἤγαγον should be rendered, "and they were leading or taking him," &c. &c.

—ὀφρύος.] This was one of the terms denoting parts of the body (others are μαστὸς, δειρὰς, ποὺς, πτέρνα, and the Latin *dorsum, venter, caput, pes),* but applied to describe various objects in nature, especially hills. The τῆς before ὀφρύος is not found in very many MSS. and the early Edd., and is cancelled by most recent Editors.

—κατακρημνίσαι.] This was, indeed, as among the Romans, a death sometimes adjudged by the law; but, in the present case, it would have been a tumultuary proceeding, like the stoning of Stephen.

30. διελθὼν διὰ μέσου αὐτῶν.] Whether by any supernatural power, is not said, but it seems to be *implied.* Though most *recent* Commentators (and Tertullian of old) discountenance that idea. They think that διελθὼν may denote "gliding through them." See John ix. 59, and Note.

33. πνεῦμα δαιμονίου ἀκ.] This is a blending of two synonymous expressions, for the sake of greater significancy.

35. τό.] The word is omitted in most of the ancient MSS., and almost all the early Edd., and is cancelled by Wets., Matth., Griesb., and other Editors, down to Scholz. Μηδὲν βλάψαν α., "after having done him no hurt."

36. θάμβος] i. e. a mingled feeling of amazement and awe.

MT. MK.
8. 1. ἐπιτάσσει τοῖς ἀκαθάρτοις πνεύμασι, καὶ ἐξέρχονται. Καὶ ἐξεπορεύετο 37
28 ἦχος περὶ αὐτοῦ εἰς πάντα τόπον τῆς περιχώρου.
14 29 Ἀναστὰς δὲ ἐκ τῆς συναγωγῆς, εἰσῆλθεν εἰς τὴν οἰκίαν Σίμωνος. 38
30 [ἡ] πενθερὰ δὲ τοῦ Σίμωνος ἦν συνεχομένη πυρετῷ μεγάλῳ. Καὶ
31 ἠρώτησαν αὐτὸν περὶ αὐτῆς. Καὶ ἐπιστὰς ἐπάνω αὐτῆς, ἐπετίμησε τῷ 39
15 πυρετῷ, καὶ ἀφῆκεν αὐτήν. παραχρῆμα δὲ ἀναστᾶσα διηκόνει αὐτοῖς.
16 32 Δύνοντος δὲ τοῦ ἡλίου, πάντες ὅσοι εἶχον ἀσθενοῦντας νόσοις ποικί- 40
34 λαις, ἤγαγον αὐτοὺς πρὸς αὐτόν· ὁ δὲ ἑνὶ ἑκάστῳ αὐτῶν τὰς χεῖρας
ἐπιθεὶς, ἐθεράπευσεν αὐτούς. Ἐξήρχετο δὲ καὶ δαιμόνια ἀπὸ πολλῶν, 41
κράζοντα καὶ λέγοντα· Ὅτι σὺ εἶ ὁ Χριστὸς ὁ Υἱὸς τοῦ Θεοῦ. καὶ
ἐπιτιμῶν οὐκ εἴα αὐτὰ λαλεῖν, ὅτι ᾔδεισαν τὸν Χριστὸν αὐτὸν εἶναι.
35 Γενομένης δὲ ἡμέρας ἐξελθὼν ἐπορεύθη εἰς ἔρημον τόπον, καὶ οἱ 42
36 37 ὄχλοι ἐπεζήτουν αὐτὸν, καὶ ἦλθον ἕως αὐτοῦ· καὶ κατεῖχον αὐτὸν,
38 τοῦ μὴ πορεύεσθαι ἀπ᾽ αὐτῶν. Ὁ δὲ εἶπε πρὸς αὐτούς· Ὅτι καὶ 43
ταῖς ἑτέραις πόλεσιν εὐαγγελίσασθαί με δεῖ τὴν βασιλείαν τοῦ Θεοῦ·
39 ὅτι εἰς τοῦτο ἀπέσταλμαι. Καὶ ἦν κηρύσσων ἐν ταῖς συναγωγαῖς τῆς 44
Γαλιλαίας.

a Matt. 13. 22. Mark 4. 1. V. [a] ΕΓΕΝΕΤΟ δὲ ἐν τῷ τὸν ὄχλον ἐπικεῖσθαι αὐτῷ τοῦ ἀκούειν 1
τὸν λόγον τοῦ Θεοῦ, καὶ αὐτὸς ἦν ἑστὼς παρὰ τὴν λίμνην Γεννησαρέτ.
b Matt. 4. 18. Mark 1. 16. [b] Καὶ εἶδε δύο πλοῖα ἑστῶτα παρὰ τὴν λίμνην· οἱ δὲ ἁλιεῖς ἀποβάν- 2
τες ἀπ᾽ αὐτῶν, ἀπέπλυναν τὰ δίκτυα. Ἐμβὰς δὲ εἰς ἓν τῶν πλοίων, 3
ὃ ἦν τοῦ Σίμωνος, ἠρώτησεν αὐτὸν ἀπὸ τῆς γῆς ἐπαναγαγεῖν ὀλίγον·
c John 21. 6. καὶ καθίσας ἐδίδασκεν ἐκ τοῦ πλοίου τοὺς ὄχλους. [c] Ὡς δὲ ἐπαύσατο 4
λαλῶν, εἶπε πρὸς τὸν Σίμωνα· Ἐπανάγαγε εἰς τὸ βάθος, καὶ χαλά-
σατε τὰ δίκτυα ὑμῶν εἰς ἄγραν. Καὶ ἀποκριθεὶς ὁ Σίμων εἶπεν 5
αὐτῷ· Ἐπιστάτα, δι᾽ ὅλης τῆς νυκτὸς κοπιάσαντες, οὐδὲν ἐλάβομεν·

38. ἡ πενθ.] The ἡ is not found in most of the ancient MSS. and in the Ed. Princ., and other early Edd., and is cancelled by Wets., Matth., Griesb., Tittm., Vat., and Scholz.

39. ἐπετίμ. τῷ πυρετῷ.] A highly figurative expression, signifying he put a stop to the violence of the fever.

41. σὺ εἶ.] *Comp.* Mark iii. 11. Why the demons here confess the power of their Conqueror, and proclaim him to be the promised MESSIAH, was in order to impede his ministry. On which account Jesus checks them, and commands them to be silent. See Bp. Warburton Serm. Vol. X. p. 145.

V. What is related in the 11 first vv. of this Ch. agrees with what is narrated at Matt. v. 18. 22. (where see Note) and Mark i. 16—20. On which Dr. Townson observes, that the Evangelists vary only in the *number*, or choice of *circumstances*; and wrote from the same idea of the *fact* which they lay before us.

2. ἑστῶτα] i. e. as opposed to being in motion. Compare viii. 38. The Greeks used στῆναι, and the Latins *stare*, to express the situation of ships, whether at *anchor* or fastened *on shore*. See Recens. Synop. Ἀπέπλυναν, "had washed," i. e. had been washing. The ἀπ in ἀπέπλ. signifies *off*, with respect to the filth of the fish, &c. Δίκτυον, Valckn. remarks, is from δέδικται, preterite of δίκω, *jacio*, q. d. a casting net.

3. ἐπαναγαγεῖν.] Sub. ναῦν. I have in Recens. Synop. compared Herodot. vii. 100. τὰς δὲ νέας οἱ ναύαρχοι ἀναγαγόντες ὅσον τε (I conjecture γε) τέσσερα πλέθρα ἀπὸ τοῦ αἰγιαλοῦ. The ἐπὶ is equivalent to our *ward* in composition. On this term, and on ἀγαγεῖν and κατάγειν, which signify to *bring to land*, see my Note on Thucyd. Vol. I. p. 52. Transl.

4. ἐπανάγαγε—καὶ χαλάσατε.] This change from the singular to the plural, Bornemann accounts for thus: "In altum enim navigat, qui eo gubernaculum dirigit, h. l. Simon, sed ad retia projicienda pluribus hominibus opus erat, qui in navi versabantur." Χαλᾷν is a vox sol. de hac re, though καθιέναι and ῥίπτειν are also used. Ἄγρα signifies the *prey* taken or caught, like *captura* in Pliny, cited by Kuin. So also Lucian Pisc. § 47. Ἁλιεύσειν διέγνωκας; σιώπησον, καὶ τὴν ἄγραν περίμενε.

5. ἐπιστάτα.] Ἐπιστάτης properly denotes one who is set over any *persons* or *business*, as here that of instruction; and is thus equivalent to *master* or *teacher*, διδάσκαλος, used by the other Evangelist. The latter sense is rather rare in the Classical writers; when it *does* occur, it denotes a *professor* of any art, as opposed to a novice. Ῥήματι, *command*. So the Heb. מצוה. This is

6 ἐπὶ δὲ τῷ ῥήματί σου χαλάσω τὸ δίκτυον. Καὶ τοῦτο ποιήσαντες,
συνέκλεισαν πλῆθος ἰχθύων πολύ· διεῤῥήγνυτο δὲ τὸ δίκτυον αὐτῶν,
7 καὶ κατένευσαν τοῖς μετόχοις τοῖς ἐν τῷ ἑτέρῳ πλοίῳ, τοῦ ἐλθόντας
συλλαβέσθαι αὐτοῖς· καὶ ἦλθον, καὶ ἔπλησαν ἀμφότερα τὰ πλοῖα,
8 ὥστε βυθίζεσθαι αὐτά. Ἰδὼν δὲ Σίμων Πέτρος, προσέπεσε τοῖς γό-
νασι τοῦ Ἰησοῦ, λέγων· Ἔξελθε ἀπ᾽ ἐμοῦ ὅτι ἀνὴρ ἁμαρτωλός εἰμι,
9 Κύριε. Θάμβος γὰρ περιέσχεν αὐτὸν καὶ πάντας τοὺς σὺν αὐτῷ ἐπὶ
10 τῇ ἄγρᾳ τῶν ἰχθύων ᾗ συνέλαβον. [d] Ὁμοίως δὲ καὶ Ἰάκωβον καὶ d Jer. 16. 16. Ezek. 47. 9.
Ἰωάννην υἱοὺς Ζεβεδαίου, οἳ ἦσαν κοινωνοὶ τῷ Σίμωνι. Καὶ εἶπε πρὸς Matt. 4. 19. Mark 1. 17.
τὸν Σίμωνα ὁ Ἰησοῦς· Μὴ φοβοῦ· ἀπὸ τοῦ νῦν ἀνθρώπους ἔσῃ e Matt. 4. 20.
11 ζωγρῶν. [e] Καὶ καταγαγόντες τὰ πλοῖα ἐπὶ τὴν γῆν, ἀφέντες ἅπαντα & 19. 27. Mark 10. 28. infr. 18. 28.
ἠκολούθησαν αὐτῷ. MT. MK.
12 ΚΑΙ ἐγένετο ἐν τῷ εἶναι αὐτὸν ἐν μιᾷ τῶν πόλεων, καὶ ἰδοὺ ἀνὴρ 8. 1.
πλήρης λέπρας· καὶ ἰδὼν τὸν Ἰησοῦν, πεσὼν ἐπὶ πρόσωπον ἐδεήθη 2 40
13 αὐτοῦ, λέγων· Κύριε, ἐὰν θέλῃς, δύνασαί με καθαρίσαι. Καὶ ἐκτείνας 3 41
τὴν χεῖρα ἥψατο αὐτοῦ, εἰπών· Θέλω, καθαρίσθητι. Καὶ εὐθέως ἡ
14 λέπρα ἀπῆλθεν ἀπ᾽ αὐτοῦ. Καὶ αὐτὸς παρήγγειλεν αὐτῷ μηδενὶ εἰπεῖν· 4 44
ἀλλὰ ἀπελθὼν δεῖξον σεαυτὸν τῷ ἱερεῖ, καὶ προσένεγκε περὶ τοῦ κα-
15 θαρισμοῦ σου, καθὼς προσέταξε Μωϋσῆς, εἰς μαρτύριον αὐτοῖς· Διήρ- 45
χετο δὲ μᾶλλον ὁ λόγος περὶ αὐτοῦ· καὶ συνήρχοντο ὄχλοι πολλοὶ
ἀκούειν, καὶ θεραπεύεσθαι ὑπ᾽ αὐτοῦ ἀπὸ τῶν ἀσθενειῶν αὐτῶν·
16 αὐτὸς δὲ ἦν ὑποχωρῶν ἐν ταῖς ἐρήμοις, καὶ προσευχόμενος.
17 Καὶ ἐγένετο ἐν μιᾷ τῶν ἡμερῶν, καὶ αὐτὸς ἦν διδάσκων· καὶ ἦσαν
καθήμενοι Φαρισαῖοι καὶ νομοδιδάσκαλοι, οἳ ἦσαν ἐληλυθότες ἐκ πάσης

not, however, merely a Hebraism, since it is found in a monumental inscription in Herodot. vii. 228. *κείμεθα, τοῖς κείνων ῥήμασι πειθόμενοι.*

6. *συνέκλεισαν.*] This and the Latin *concludere* are terms appropriate to hunting and fishing; of which examples are cited by Wets. The reading *πλῆθος ἰχθύων* for *ἰχθύων πλῆθος* is found in all the best MSS. and early Edd., and is adopted by the most eminent Editors.

— *διεῤῥήγνυτο*] "was breaking," had begun to break, or had well nigh broke.

7. *κατένευσαν.*] Literally, made signs with their hands, beckoned. See Note supra i. 22. *Τοῦ ἐλθόντας.* Sub. *ἕνεκα*, for *ἵνα* with a Subjunctive. *Συλλαβέσθαι*, to take hold of with, i. e. help them. The verb has, in *complete* construction, a *Dative of the person* governed of the *σὺν* in composition, a *Genitive of the thing* dependent upon *περὶ* understood, and an Accusative of the thing dependent on *κατὰ* understood. But in the best Greek writers the Accus. is found almost always omitted; not unfrequently the Genit.; and sometimes *all three*. *Ὥστε βυθίζεσθαι*, "so that they were sinking;" i. e. ready to sink. The Infinitive present sometimes corresponds to the Imperfect rather than the Present.

8. *Ἔξελθε ἀπ᾽ ἐμοῦ.*] Valckn. takes this to be a popular phrase for "depart from my ship;" *εἰσελθεῖν εἴς τινα* and *ἐξελθεῖν ἀπό τινος* being used to denote entrance to, or departure from, any one's house; as Luke i. 28. *εἰσελθὼν πρὸς αὐτήν.* Acts xvi. 40. *εἰσῆλθον εἰς τὴν Λυδίαν.* This proof, however, as regards the phrase *ἐξελθεῖν ἀπὸ* is defective, and the sense in question would here be frigid. But it is of more importance to advert to the *object* of this request. To refer it, with most modern Commentators, to Peter's *superstitious fears of death* or some heavy calamity, as having seen a supernatural being, is neither doing justice to the Apostle, nor is warranted by the context; which requires the more judicious view taken by Euthym., Capell., Grot., Lightf., Doddr., Rosenm., and Kuin., who regard it as an exclamation indicative of profound humility and deep reverence, as of one unworthy to appear in the presence of so great a personage. Thus his casting himself at Jesus' feet may be regarded as adoration to a Divine person. The *θάμβος* which follows imports, not (as Kuin. explains) *horror*, but a *mixed feeling* of *amazement* and *awe*.

9. *περιέσχεν*·] "possessed," as 2 Macc. iv. 16 Compare Homer, *θάμβος δ᾽ ἔχεν εἰσορόωντας.*

10. *ἀνθρώπους ἔσῃ ζωγρῶν.*] A most apt and lively metaphor. Though, indeed, terms of hunting and fishing are, by the Greek and Hebrew writers, sometimes used of those who attach men to themselves, or others; as I have in Recens. Synop. proved and illustrated by numerous original examples from Xenoph., Diog. Laert., Plut., Ælian, and others. The words are well rendered by Dr. Parr, Serm., "[Ye have been catching *fish*, to *destroy* them;] henceforth ye shall catch *men*, to *save* them."

14. *ἀλλὰ ἀπελθὼν δεῖξον.*] This change of the construction from the *indirecta* to the *directa oratio* is sanctioned by the usage of the best Classi-

MT. MK.
9. 2. κώμης τῆς Γαλιλαίας καὶ Ἰουδαίας καὶ Ἱερουσαλήμ· καὶ δύναμις
2 3 Κυρίου ἦν εἰς τὸ ἰᾶσθαι αὐτούς. Καὶ ἰδοὺ, ἄνδρες φέροντες ἐπὶ 18
κλίνης ἄνθρωπον, ὃς ἦν παραλελυμένος· καὶ ἐζήτουν αὐτὸν εἰσενεγκεῖν
4 καὶ θεῖναι ἐνώπιον αὐτοῦ· καὶ μὴ εὑρόντες [διὰ] † ποίας εἰσενέγκω- 19
σιν αὐτὸν, διὰ τὸν ὄχλον, ἀναβάντες ἐπὶ τὸ δῶμα, διὰ τῶν κεράμων
καθῆκαν αὐτὸν σὺν τῷ κλινιδίῳ εἰς τὸ μέσον ἔμπροσθεν τοῦ Ἰησοῦ.
5 Καὶ ἰδὼν τὴν πίστιν αὐτῶν, εἶπεν αὐτῷ· Ἄνθρωπε, ἀφέωνταί σοι αἱ 20
3 6 ἁμαρτίαι σου. Καὶ ἤρξαντο διαλογίζεσθαι οἱ Γραμματεῖς καὶ οἱ Φα- 21
7 ρισαῖοι, λέγοντες· Τίς ἐστιν οὗτος, ὃς λαλεῖ βλασφημίας; τίς δύναται
4 8 ἀφιέναι ἁμαρτίας, εἰ μὴ μόνος ὁ Θεός; Ἐπιγνοὺς δὲ ὁ Ἰησοῦς τοὺς 22
διαλογισμοὺς αὐτῶν, ἀποκριθεὶς εἶπε πρὸς αὐτούς· Τί διαλογίζεσθε
5 9 ἐν ταῖς καρδίαις ὑμῶν; τί ἐστιν εὐκοπώτερον, εἰπεῖν· Ἀφέωνταί σοι 23
6 10 αἱ ἁμαρτίαι σου· ἢ εἰπεῖν· Ἔγειρε καὶ περιπάτει; ἵνα δὲ εἰδῆτε ὅτι 24
ἐξουσίαν ἔχει ὁ Υἱὸς τοῦ ἀνθρώπου ἐπὶ τῆς γῆς ἀφιέναι ἁμαρτίας,
11 (εἶπε τῷ παραλελυμένῳ·) Σοὶ λέγω· ἔγειρε, καὶ ἄρας τὸ κλινίδιόν
7 12 σου, πορεύου εἰς τὸν οἶκόν σου. Καὶ παραχρῆμα ἀναστὰς ἐνώπιον 25
αὐτῶν, ἄρας ἐφ' ᾧ κατέκειτο, ἀπῆλθεν εἰς τὸν οἶκον αὐτοῦ δοξάζων
8 τὸν Θεόν. Καὶ ἔκστασις ἔλαβεν ἅπαντας, καὶ ἐδόξαζον τὸν Θεὸν, καὶ 26
ἐπλήσθησαν φόβου, λέγοντες· Ὅτι εἴδομεν παράδοξα σήμερον.
9 13 Καὶ μετὰ ταῦτα ἐξῆλθε, καὶ ἐθεάσατο τελώνην ὀνόματι Λευΐν καθή- 27
14 μενον ἐπὶ τὸ τελώνιον, καὶ εἶπεν αὐτῷ· Ἀκολούθει μοι. Καὶ κατα- 28
10 15 λιπὼν ἅπαντα, ἀναστὰς ἠκολούθησεν αὐτῷ. Καὶ ἐποίησε δοχὴν μεγάλην 29
[ὁ] Λευΐς αὐτῷ ἐν τῇ οἰκίᾳ αὐτοῦ· καὶ ἦν ὄχλος τελωνῶν πολὺς καὶ
ἄλλων, οἳ ἦσαν μετ' αὐτῶν κατακείμενοι. Καὶ ἐγόγγυζον οἱ Γραμμα- 30
11 16 τεῖς αὐτῶν καὶ οἱ Φαρισαῖοι πρὸς τοὺς μαθητὰς αὐτοῦ, λέγοντες·
12 17 Διατί μετὰ τελωνῶν καὶ ἁμαρτωλῶν ἐσθίετε καὶ πίνετε; Καὶ ἀποκρι- 31
θεὶς ὁ Ἰησοῦς εἶπε πρὸς αὐτούς· Οὐ χρείαν ἔχουσιν οἱ ὑγιαίνοντες

cal writers. It may be regarded as a relic of the inartificial simplicity of primitive diction. [*Comp.* Levit. xiii. 2. xiv. 2, 21, 22.]

17. καὶ δύναμις — αὐτούς.] Render, "and the power of the Lord was (exerted) to heal them." By Κυρίου some understand *God*. But that would require μετ' αὐτοῦ (i. e. Christ) to be supplied; an ellipse which can by no means be admitted. By αὐτοὺς must, (as the recent Commentators have seen) be understood, not the Pharisees, but the sick. Thus (Kuin. observes) the Hebrews use the pronoun relative when there is no antecedent noun, though it may be easily be understood from the context. This is very true, and the idiom is by no means confined to the *Hebrew* writers; but it is here not applicable, for αὐτοὺς plainly has reference to the αὐτῶν (i. e. ἀσθενῶν) at ver. 15.

19. διά.] This is omitted in very many MSS. and early Edd., and is cancelled by Matth., Griesb., Vat., Tittm., Scholz; and with reason; for it is plainly an addition of the Scholiasts, as infra xiv. 4. Since, however, the *ellipse* of διὰ is harsh, I am inclined to suspect that ποίας is not the true reading, but ποίᾳ, sub. ὁδῷ, which, though not noted from any of the MSS., seems to have been read by the Italic and Vulgate Translators, who render "quâ parte." The ς might easily have arisen from the ε following. My conjecture is confirmed by the opinion of Bornem., who cites Schaefer on Apoll. Rhod. i. 934. in proof that ποίᾳ (sub. μέριδι vel ὁδῷ) may mean, "quânam parte?" And there is little doubt but that, in the common dialect, the word was also used *extra interrogationem*, for *quâ* parte.

26. ἔκστασις ἔλαβεν ἅπ.] So Hom. Il. λ. 402. φόβος ἔ λ λ α β ε πάντας. Mangey conjectures that one of the two words φόβος and ἔκστασις is a gloss on the other. But the ideas are (as Grot., observes) very different. They were struck with *wonder* at the thing done, and full of *reverence* at the Divine power. ἔκστασις signifies, exceeding great wonder. So Menander in Stobæi Serm. cxi. p. 556. 25. πάντα δὲ τὰ μὴ προσδοκώμεν ἔκστασιν φέρει. Παράδοξα. This denotes what is παρὰ δόξαν, *beyond one's expectation*, and, from the adjunct, *unusual*, *wonderful*.

29. δοχὴν] "an entertainment;" from δέχεσθαι. to receive or entertain guests. Ὁ Λευΐς. The ὁ is omitted in many MSS. and early Edd. and is cancelled by Wets., Matth., Griesb., Tittm.; and Scholz. Yet its insertion is agreeable to the strictest propriety of the language.

30. αὐτῶν.] i. e. the persons present, the Capernaumites. Some MSS. and the Edit. Princ. have τῶν before τελωνῶν, which is received by Matth., Griesb., and Scholz.

MT. MK.

32 ἰατροῦ, ἀλλ᾽ οἱ κακῶς ἔχοντες. οὐκ ἐλήλυθα καλέσαι δικαίους, ἀλλὰ 9. 2
33 ἁμαρτωλοὺς εἰς μετάνοιαν. Οἱ δὲ εἶπον πρὸς αὐτόν· Διατί οἱ μαθηταὶ 14 18
Ἰωάννου νηστεύουσι πυκνὰ καὶ δεήσεις ποιοῦνται, ὁμοίως καὶ οἱ τῶν
34 Φαρισαίων· οἱ δὲ σοὶ ἐσθίουσι καὶ πίνουσιν; Ὁ δὲ εἶπε πρὸς
αὐτούς· Μὴ δύνασθε τοὺς υἱοὺς τοῦ νυμφῶνος, ἐν ᾧ ὁ νυμφίος μετ᾽ 15 19
35 αὐτῶν ἐστι, ποιῆσαι νηστεύειν; Ἐλεύσονται δὲ ἡμέραι [καὶ] ὅταν 20
ἀπαρθῇ ἀπ᾽ αὐτῶν ὁ νυμφίος, τότε νηστεύσουσιν ἐν ἐκείναις ταῖς
36 ἡμέραις. Ἔλεγε δὲ καὶ παραβολὴν πρὸς αὐτούς· Ὅτι οὐδεὶς ἐπίβλημα 16 21
ἱματίου καινοῦ ἐπιβάλλει ἐπὶ ἱμάτιον παλαιόν· εἰ δὲ μήγε, καὶ τὸ
καινὸν σχίζει, καὶ τῷ παλαιῷ οὐ συμφωνεῖ τὸ ἐπίβλημα τὸ ἀπὸ τοῦ
37 καινοῦ. Καὶ οὐδεὶς βάλλει οἶνον νέον εἰς ἀσκοὺς παλαιούς· εἰ δὲ 17 22
μήγε, ῥήξει ὁ νέος οἶνος τοὺς ἀσκούς, καὶ αὐτὸς ἐκχυθήσεται, καὶ οἱ
38 ἀσκοὶ ἀπολοῦνται· ἀλλὰ οἶνον νέον εἰς ἀσκοὺς καινοὺς βλητέον, καὶ
39 ἀμφότεροι συντηροῦνται. Καὶ οὐδεὶς πιὼν παλαιὸν εὐθέως θέλει νέον·
λέγει γάρ· Ὁ παλαιὸς χρηστότερός ἐστιν. 12.
1 VI. ἘΓΕΝΕΤΟ δὲ, ἐν σαββάτῳ δευτεροπρώτῳ διαπορεύεσθαι αὐ- 1 23
τὸν διὰ τῶν σπορίμων· καὶ ἔτιλλον οἱ μαθηταὶ αὐτοῦ τοὺς στάχυας,
2 καὶ ἤσθιον, ψώχοντες ταῖς χερσί. τινὲς δὲ τῶν Φαρισαίων εἶπον αὐ- 2 24
3 τοῖς· Τί ποιεῖτε ὃ οὐκ ἔξεστι ποιεῖν ἐν τοῖς σάββασι; Καὶ ἀπο- 3 25
κριθεὶς πρὸς αὐτοὺς εἶπεν ὁ Ἰησοῦς· Οὐδὲ τοῦτο ἀνέγνωτε, ὃ ἐποίησε

31. *οὐ χρείαν ἔχουσιν*, &c.] See Note on Matt. ix. 12. To the parallel sentiments adduced by the Commentators, I add a very apposite one (applied to Diogenes) from Dio Chrys. Orat. viii. p. 131. Morell. Ἑώρα γὰρ ὅτι πλεῖστοι ἄνθρωποι ἐκεῖ (i. e. Corinth) συνίασι διὰ τοὺς λιμένας καὶ τὰς ἑταίρας· δεῖν οὖν φρόνιμον ἄνδρα, ἥπερ τὸν ἀγαθὸν ἰατρὸν, ὅπου πολλοὶ νοσοῦσιν, ἐκεῖσε ἰέναι βοηθήσοντα, οὕτως ὅπου πλεῖστοι εἰσὶν ἀφρονέστεροι, ἐκεῖ μάλιστα ἀποδημεῖν, ἐξελέγχοντα καὶ κολάζοντα τὴν ἄνοιαν αὐτῶν.

34. See Is. lxii. 5. 2 Cor. xi. 2.

35. *καὶ ὅταν ἀπ.*] The *καὶ* is omitted in several MSS. and the greater part of the Versions; and in *most* of those it is inserted before *τότε*, exactly as in the parallel passages of Matthew and Mark, and as, I conceive, the Evangelist wrote; for it is difficult to account for a *καὶ* here. To call it a *Hebrew pleonasm* is but to shuffle over the difficulty. And yet it cannot well be rendered *nempe*, with some, or *et quidem* with others. To construe it with *τότε* (as do Homberg and Abresch.) is doing utter violence to the construction. It should seem that the *καὶ* was first omitted by accident, then written in the margin as to *be* inserted, and finally brought in *at a wrong place*.

— *τότε — ἐν ἐκ. τ. ἡμέραις.*] Bornem. compares a similar pleonasm from Demosth. de Cor. p. 288. *τότε τοίνυν κατ᾽ ἐκεῖνον τὸν καιρόν.* However, such are not properly called *pleonasms*, since the *verbosity*, as he calls it, is *intensive*.

36. *ἐπίβλημα.*] This is omitted in many MSS. and is cancelled by Wets., Mill, Markl., Matth., and Tittm., but retained by Scholz and Gratz, though with a mark of probable expunction. Certainly to cancel it is very objectionable. It would be harsh, and inconsistent with the plain style of Scripture to *supply* a noun from such a distance. Besides, the word is found in *all* the Versions, except two later ones of little authority, and more than 3-4ths of the MSS., including some of the most ancient. I cannot therefore but suspect that the omission was accidental. The cause of it will immediately appear, if we consider that many MSS. and Edd. have *τὸ ἐπίβλημα*; for it is obvious how easily the word *ἐπίβλημα* might be lost by means of the two *τὸ*'s. Thus those very MSS. in which this word is omitted bear testimony of the existence of the first *τὸ* in their Archetype. I have therefore admitted it into the text.

39. Of this illustration, (which is confined to Luke,) the scope, as the best ancient and modern Commentators agree, is of a piece with the preceding doctrine; namely, that all things should be suited to *circumstances*, and that as use forms the taste, so men's long accustomed modes are not speedily to be changed, nor can they be suddenly initiated into austerities.

VI. 1. *ἐν σαββάτῳ δευτ.*] It is impossible for me to notice, much less review, the very numerous interpretations which have been propounded of this obscure expression; nor is it *necessary*; since the only one that has any semblance of truth is that of Theophyl. and Euthym., among the ancients, and Scaliger, Lightf., Casaub., Whitby, Schleus., Kuin., &c. of the moderns, namely, that the sense is the *first* Sabbath *after the second day of unleavened bread*; namely, that on which the *wave sheaf* was commanded to be offered up, and from which, and not the *first* day of the Passover, the fifty days were reckoned to the Pentecost. Hence it is no wonder that all the Sabbaths from the Passover to the Pentecost, should have taken their appellation *ἀπὸ τῆς δευτέρας τοῦ πάσχατος*.

— *ψώχοντες.*] This word is of rare occurrence, Yet it is adduced from Nicand. Ther. 590 and 629, aud *καταψ.* from Herodot. iv. 75

MT. MK.
12. 2. *Δαυΐδ, ὁπότε ἐπείνασεν αὐτὸς καὶ οἱ μετ' αὐτοῦ ὄντες; ὡς εἰσῆλθεν* 4
4 26 *εἰς τὸν οἶκον τοῦ Θεοῦ, καὶ τοὺς ἄρτους τῆς προθέσεως ἔλαβε καὶ*
ἔφαγε, καὶ ἔδωκε καὶ τοῖς μετ' αὐτοῦ· οὓς οὐκ ἔξεστι φαγεῖν εἰ μὴ
8 28 *μόνους τοὺς ἱερεῖς; Καὶ ἔλεγεν αὐτοῖς· Ὅτι κύριός ἐστιν ὁ Υἱὸς τοῦ* 5
3. *ἀνθρώπου καὶ τοῦ σαββάτου.*
9 1 *ἘΓΕΝΕΤΟ δὲ, καὶ ἐν ἑτέρῳ σαββάτῳ εἰσελθεῖν αὐτὸν εἰς τὴν συ-* 6
ναγωγὴν καὶ διδάσκειν· καὶ ἦν ἐκεῖ ἄνθρωπος, καὶ ἡ χεὶρ αὐτοῦ ἡ
2 *δεξιὰ ἦν ξηρά. Παρετήρουν δὲ [αὐτὸν] οἱ Γραμματεῖς καὶ οἱ Φαρι-* 7
σαῖοι, εἰ ἐν τῷ σαββάτῳ θεραπεύσει· ἵνα εὕρωσι κατηγορίαν αὐτοῦ.
3 *Αὐτος δὲ ᾔδει τοὺς διαλογισμοὺς αὐτῶν, καὶ εἶπε τῷ ἀνθρώπῳ τῷ ξη-* 8
4 *ρὰν ἔχοντι τὴν χεῖρα· Ἔγειραι καὶ στῆθι εἰς τὸ μέσον. ὁ δὲ ἀναστὰς*
ἔστη. Εἶπεν οὖν ὁ Ἰησοῦς πρὸς αὐτούς· Ἐπερωτήσω ὑμᾶς τι· ἔξεστι 9
5 *τοῖς σάββασιν ἀγαθοποιῆσαι, ἢ κακοποιῆσαι; ψυχὴν σῶσαι, ἢ ‡ ἀπο-*
13 *λέσαι; Καὶ περιβλεψάμενος πάντας αὐτοὺς, εἶπεν * αὐτῷ· Ἔκτεινον* 10
14 6 *τὴν χεῖρά σου· ὁ δὲ ἐποίησεν οὕτω. καὶ ἀποκατεστάθη ἡ χεὶρ αὐτοῦ*
[ὑγιὴς] ὡς ἡ ἄλλη. Αὐτοὶ δὲ ἐπλήσθησαν ἀνοίας· καὶ διελάλουν 11
πρὸς ἀλλήλους, τί ἂν ποιήσειαν τῷ Ἰησοῦ.
13 *Ἐγένετο δὲ ἐν ταῖς ἡμέραις ταύταις, ἐξῆλθεν εἰς τὸ ὄρος προσεύξα-* 12
σθαι· καὶ ἦν διανυκτερεύων ἐν τῇ προσευχῇ τοῦ Θεοῦ. Καὶ ὅτε 13

4. *μόνους τοὺς ἱ.*] Several MSS. have *μόνοις τοῖς ἱ.* as in Matt. and Mark. But that reading is *ex emendatione*. The syntax with the Dative is most usual, but that with the Accus. sometimes occurs. In which case there is an ellipse of *ὥστε* with the foregoing infinitive repeated. [*Comp.* Exod. xxix. 32, 33. Levit. viii. 31.]

7. *αὐτόν.*] This is omitted in very many MSS. and early Edd., and also in some Versions; and is cancelled by Wets., Matth., Griesb., Tittm., Vat., and Scholz. But it is found in the parallel passage of Mark, and is so agreeable to the style of the N. T., that we may rather suspect the word to have been cancelled by some over-nice ancient critics. The testimony of *Versions* is, in a case of this kind, of little weight.

— *κατηγορίαν α.*] "an accusation against him." This is an example of what Grammarians call the *Genitive of object*, — as Acts iv. 9. *εὐεργεσία ἀνθρώπου*. See Alt's Gram. N. T. § 26. p. 45.

9. *ἐπερωτήσω ὑ.*] "I will ask *you* a question." For *ἀπολέσαι* very many MSS. and early Edd. have *ἀποκτεῖναι*; which is received by Matth., Griesb., Tittm., Vat., and Scholz; but without sufficient reason; for the new reading has every appearance of being a *gloss*.

— *ἐπερ. ὑ. τί.*] There are two ways in which the *τι* may be taken; 1. declaratively for *πότερον*, *ecquid*, either with the preceding or following (as Matt. xxi. 31.) And so the Syr. and many Commentators. 2. Interrogatively, for *Quid*, What? as Theophyl. and Gratz interpret. Each of these modes has much to recommend it; and the latter is thought to communicate peculiar *spirit* to the address. Yet this sort of *δεινότης*, however common in the Classical writers, is little suitable to the style of *Scripture*. The usual punctuation, therefore, is preferable, by which the *τι* is construed with the *preceding*; and that on account of its greater simplicity, and because it is confirmed by a similar mode of expression at Matt. xxi. 24. Luke xx. 3.

10. *αὐτῷ.*] This (for the common reading *τῷ ἀνθρώπῳ*) is found in a very great number of MSS., the Ed. Princ., and the principal Versions; and has been edited by Wets., Griesb., Matth., Tittm., Vat., and Scholz. The common reading is probably from the margin.

— *ἐποίησεν οὕτω.*] The *οὕτω* is omitted in very many MSS., and is cancelled by Matth., Griesb., Tittm., and others; but injudiciously: for a great part of those MSS. have *ἐξέτεινεν* for *ἐποίησεν*, and with that the *οὕτω* is inconsistent. To *ἐποίησεν* the *οὕτω* is almost indispensable, and it is confirmed by a similar use in ix. 15. xii. 45. Acts xii. 8. Luke ii. 48. iii. 11. vi. 31. x. 37. Ὑγιὴς is omitted in very many MSS., and is cancelled by most Editors. See, however, the Note on Matt. xii. 13. and Mark iii. 5. and compare Acts xiv. 10. Bornem. remarks on this *usus proleptictus*, in *ὑγιής*.

11. *ἀνοίας*] "fury, rage;" a signification found in Thucyd. iii. 48, and elsewhere. A similar idiom occurs in our own language.

12. *ἦν διανυκτερεύων ἐν τῇ προσευχῇ τ. θ.*] On the interpretation of *τῇ προσευχῇ τοῦ θεοῦ* there has been some difference of opinion. The ancients, and most moderns, take it to mean, "*prayer to God*;" while some of the early modern Commentators and others of the more recent ones, as Markl., Wets., Doddr., and Campb., maintain that it signifies a *proseucha*, or *oratory*. And that there were Jewish places of worship so called is undoubted. But whether that sense is *here* to be assigned is another question. Those Commentators adduce, indeed, several reasons why the *common* interpretation cannot be admitted. They urge that *προσευχὴ τοῦ Θεοῦ*, in the sense, *prayer to God*, is abhorrent from the simplicity of Scriptural expression, and subversive of analogy; and that *διανυκτερεύειν* properly respects some *place where* the night is spent. But *διανυκτερεύειν* is not only used of *places where* but of *things*, (i. e. *business*) in which the night is occupied, as in

MK.
ἐγένετο ἡμέρα, προσεφώνησε τοὺς μαθητὰς αὐτοῦ· καὶ ἐκλεξάμενος 3.
14 ἀπ' αὐτῶν δώδεκα, οὓς καὶ ἀποστόλους ὠνόμασε· Σίμωνα, ὃν καὶ 14 16
ὠνόμασε Πέτρον, καὶ Ἀνδρέαν τὸν ἀδελφὸν αὐτοῦ, Ἰάκωβον καὶ Ἰωάν- 17
15 νην, Φίλιππον καὶ Βαρθολομαῖον, Ματθαῖον καὶ Θωμᾶν, Ἰάκωβον τὸν 18
16 τοῦ Ἀλφαίου καὶ Σίμωνα τὸν καλούμενον Ζηλωτὴν, Ἰούδαν Ἰακώβου 19
17 καὶ Ἰούδαν Ἰσκαριώτην, ὃς καὶ ἐγένετο προδότης. [a] Καὶ καταβὰς μετ' a Matt. 4. 25. Mark 3. 7.
αὐτῶν, ἔστη ἐπὶ τόπου πεδινοῦ· καὶ ὄχλος μαθητῶν αὐτοῦ, καὶ πλῆ-
θος πολὺ τοῦ λαοῦ ἀπὸ πάσης τῆς Ἰουδαίας καὶ Ἱερουσαλὴμ, καὶ τῆς
παραλίου Τύρου καὶ Σιδῶνος, οἳ ἦλθον ἀκοῦσαι αὐτοῦ, καὶ ἰαθῆναι
18 ἀπὸ τῶν νόσων αὐτῶν· καὶ οἱ ὀχλούμενοι ‡ ὑπὸ πνευμάτων ἀκαθάρ-
19 των· καὶ ἐθεραπεύοντο. [b] Καὶ πᾶς ὁ ὄχλος ἐζήτει ἅπτεσθαι αὐτοῦ· b Matt. 14. 36. Mark 5. 30.
ὅτι δύναμις παρ' αὐτοῦ ἐξήρχετο, καὶ ἰᾶτο πάντας.
20 [c] Καὶ αὐτὸς ἐπάρας τοὺς ὀφθαλμοὺς αὐτοῦ εἰς τοὺς μαθητὰς αὐ- c Matt. 5. 2, &c.
τοῦ, ἔλεγε· Μακάριοι οἱ πτωχοί· ὅτι ὑμετέρα ἐστὶν ἡ βασιλεία τοῦ
21 Θεοῦ. [d] Μακάριοι οἱ πεινῶντες νῦν· ὅτι χορτασθήσεσθε. μακάριοι d Isa. 55. 1. & 61. 3. & 65. 13.
22 οἱ κλαίοντες νῦν· ὅτι γελάσετε. [e] Μακάριοί ἐστε, ὅταν μισήσωσιν & 66. 10. e Matt. 5. 11.
ὑμᾶς οἱ ἄνθρωποι, καὶ ὅταν ἀφορίσωσιν ὑμᾶς, καὶ ὀνειδίσωσι, καὶ 1 Pet. 2. 19. & 3. 14.
ἐκβάλωσι τὸ ὄνομα ὑμῶν ὡς πονηρὸν, ἕνεκα τοῦ Υἱοῦ τοῦ ἀνθρώπου. & 4. 14.

the examples cited in Recens. Synop. And as to *simplicity* of expression, it is no more violated here than in numerous other cases, where the use of the Genitive falls under that Rule of Winer's Gr. N. T. § 23. 1. p. 71. "The Genitive after nouns which indicate feeling, speech, or action in respect to any thing, is sometimes to be understood as indicating the *relation* which that feeling, speech, or action has toward that thing;" e. gr. Matt. xiii. 18. Luke vi. 7. Acts iv. 9. See also Matthiæ Gr. Gr. § 313. In such cases the Genit. has the force of an Accus. with πρός.

Wholly unfounded are the other objections of Campb. As to *subversion* of *analogy*, analogy must not be sought by placing on the bed of Procrustes whatever deviates from it; and *variety* is quite the characteristic of ancient writings. The rest of his objections proceed on a confusion of ancient with modern modes of expression. See Recens. Synop. As to that which respects the employment of the *Article* here, it has been fully answered by Bp. Middlet.; who has shown that it is not uncommon with προσευχὴ in the sense of *prayer*. See Matt. xxi. 22 Acts i. 14. 1 Cor. vii. 5. and *comp.* Matt. xiv. 23.

By *prayer* we are here to understand not prayer alone; but holy meditation, and devout thoughtfulness, which ought to precede and follow prayer. Even a heathen (Artemidorus Onir. iii. 53.) testifies of heathens. Οὐδεὶς ἄπεισιν εἰς προσευχὴν, μὴ οὐχὶ φροντίζων σφόδρα.

15. I have pointed as I have in this and the next verse, with Schulz., Scholz, and Gratz, because the Apostles are here evidently meant to be distributed into pairs. That they were so sent forth to evangelize, is certain, from Mark vi. 7.

17. τόπου πεδινοῦ.] To reconcile this with the description in Matthew (for the discourse here recorded is substantially the same with that), we may suppose that it was a sort of high, but level, *table-land*.

18. ὀχλούμενοι ὑπὸ πν. ἀκ.] Ὀχλεῖσθαι and ἐνοχλ. signify "to be troubled or vexed, whether by irksome business, or by such sickness as hinders any one from pursuing his occupation;" of which senses abundant examples, both with νόσου expressed, and understood, are adduced by Wets and others. In the N. T. and LXX., however, the latter is never found, but only that of *being vexed, or troubled*, as said of *demoniacal possession*. So Acts v. 16. ὀχλουμένους ὑπὸ πνευμάτων ἀκαθάρτων. and Tob. vi. 7. ἐάν τινα ὀχλῇ δαιμόνιον, καὶ πνεῦμα πονηρὸν, &c. And such is plainly the sense here, and not that assigned by those who advocate the hypothesis of Mede. For the *sick* and *the demoniacs* are here plainly *distinguished*.

For ὑπὸ many MSS. have ἀπὸ, which is edited by Matth., Griesb., Tittm., Vat., and Scholz. But it does not appear that ἀπὸ in this sense is ever used in the N. T. after a verb passive; while ὑπὸ frequently is, both in the N. T. and the Classical writers; and, indeed, this sense (of *origin* or cause) is not strong enough to suit the Passive. So in this very phrase we have ὑπὸ, at Acts v. 16. Compare, also, Acts x. 38. and xiii. 4. As to MS. authority, it is of little weight in words so perpetually confounded as ἀπὸ and ὑπό.

19. δύναμις παρ' αὐτοῦ ἐξήρχετο.] This will not, any more than Mark v. 30., prove the notion that the power by which the sick were healed was exerted by a sort of efflux, or effluvium from his body. See Note on Mark v. 30. The best Commentators, ancient and modern, are agreed that ἐξέρχεσθαι here, like the Heb. יָצָא in Ruth i. 13., simply means *se exercebat*.

22. ἀφορίσωσιν.] This was the *first* degree of excommunication among the Jews. On which see Vitringa de Synag. and other authorities referred to in Recens. Synop.

— ἐκβάλωσι — πονηρόν.] On the sense of this expression Commentators are not agreed. Now ἐκβάλλειν signifies generally to *cast out*, both in a civil and in a military sense; i. e. either "to *banish*." or "to *cashier*." It also signifies "to *displace officers*," or "*reject actors*." Hence many

f Acts 5. 41. & 7. 51. * [f] *Χάρητε ἐν ἐκείνῃ τῇ ἡμέρᾳ, καὶ σκιρτήσατε! ἰδοὺ γάρ, ὁ μισθὸς* 23
ὑμῶν πολὺς ἐν τῷ οὐρανῷ· κατὰ ταῦτα γὰρ ἐποίουν τοῖς προφήταις
g Amos 6. 1, 8. Eccl. 31. 8. *οἱ πατέρες αὐτῶν.* [g] *Πλὴν οὐαὶ ὑμῖν τοῖς πλουσίοις· ὅτι ἀπέχετε τὴν* 24
h Isa. 65. 13. James 4. 9. & 5. 1. *παράκλησιν ὑμῶν.* [h] *οὐαὶ ὑμῖν, οἱ ἐμπεπλησμένοι· ὅτι πεινάσετε.* 25
οὐαὶ ὑμῖν, οἱ γελῶντες νῦν· ὅτι πενθήσετε καὶ κλαύσετε. Οὐαὶ 26
[ὑμῖν], ὅταν καλῶς ὑμᾶς εἴπωσι [πάντες] οἱ ἄνθρωποι· κατὰ ταῦτα
γὰρ ἐποίουν τοῖς ψευδοπροφήταις οἱ πατέρες αὐτῶν.

i Exod. 23. 4. Prov. 25. 21. Matt. 5. 44. Rom. 12. 14, 20. 1 Cor. 4. 12. [i] *Ἀλλ' ὑμῖν λέγω τοῖς ἀκούουσιν· Ἀγαπᾶτε τοὺς ἐχθροὺς ὑμῶν·* 27
καλῶς ποιεῖτε τοῖς μισοῦσιν ὑμᾶς· [k] *εὐλογεῖτε τοὺς καταρωμένους ὑμῖν·* 28
k Infr. 23. 34. Acts 7. 60. *[καὶ] προσεύχεσθε ὑπὲρ τῶν ἐπηρεαζόντων ὑμᾶς.* [l] *Τῷ τύπτοντί σε* 29
l Matt. 5. 39. 1 Cor. 6. 7. *ἐπὶ τὴν σιαγόνα πάρεχε καὶ τὴν ἄλλην· καὶ ἀπὸ τοῦ αἴροντός σου τὸ*
m Deut. 15. 7. Matt. 5. 42. *ἱμάτιον καὶ τὸν χιτῶνα μὴ κωλύσῃς.* [m] *Παντὶ δὲ τῷ αἰτοῦντί σε δί-* 30
n Matt. 7. 12. Tob. 4. 16. *δου· καὶ ἀπὸ τοῦ αἴροντος τὰ σὰ μὴ ἀπαίτει.* [n] *Καὶ καθὼς θέλετε* 31
o Matt. 5. 46. *ἵνα ποιῶσιν ὑμῖν οἱ ἄνθρωποι, καὶ ὑμεῖς ποιεῖτε αὐτοῖς ὁμοίως.* [o] *Καὶ* 32
εἰ ἀγαπᾶτε τοὺς ἀγαπῶντας ὑμᾶς, ποία ὑμῖν χάρις ἐστί; καὶ γὰρ οἱ
ἁμαρτωλοὶ τοὺς ἀγαπῶντας αὐτοὺς ἀγαπῶσι. Καὶ ἐὰν ἀγαθοποιῆτε 33
τοὺς ἀγαθοποιοῦντας ὑμᾶς, ποία ὑμῖν χάρις ἐστί; καὶ γὰρ οἱ ἁμαρ-
p Matt. 5. 40. Deut. 15. 8. *τωλοὶ τὸ αὐτὸ ποιοῦσι.* [p] *Καὶ ἐὰν δανείζητε παρ' ὧν ἐλπίζετε ἀπολα-* 34
βεῖν, ποία ὑμῖν χάρις ἐστί; καὶ γὰρ οἱ ἁμαρτωλοὶ ἁμαρτωλοῖς δανεί-
q Matt. 5. 44. *ζουσιν, ἵνα ἀπολάβωσι τὰ ἴσα.* [q] *Πλὴν ἀγαπᾶτε τοὺς ἐχθροὺς ὑμῶν* 35
καὶ ἀγαθοποιεῖτε, καὶ δανείζετε μηδὲν ἀπελπίζοντες· καὶ ἔσται ὁ μι-

here assign the sense "to reject with scorn and ignominy;" which is preferable to the sense "*to banish*," adopted by Kuinoel, or "*to defame*," supported by Campbell: though the signification is wholly unauthorized. Wolf regards it as a fuller expression of the sense contained in *ἀφορίσωσι*. But it seems rather to advert to the treatment which they would experience at the hands of the *heathens*, as *ἀφορίσωσι* to that from the *Jews*. How covered with obloquy and contempt were the primitive Christians by the Heathens, we have abundant evidence, both in Scripture and in the writings of the first Christian Apologists.

23. *χάρητε.*] This (for *χαίρετε*) is found in almost all the best MSS., and is adopted by Wets., Griesb., Matth., Tittm., Vat., and Scholz. On which use of the Subjunctive in an Imperative or hortatory sense, see Buttm., Matth., and Herm. on Vig.

25. *οὐαὶ ὑμῖν.*] Campb., in a long and able Note (which see in Recens. Synop.), shows, as Euthym. had long ago done, that *οὐαὶ* here is not *imprecative*, but *declarative:* "Woe is unto you! alas for you!"

26. *οὐαί, ὅταν καλῶς, &c.*] This was meant primarily for the *Apostles* and *first teachers of the Gospel*, but mutatis mutandis for their successors. Grot. has appositely cited a narration respecting Phocion, recorded by Plut. T. ii. 187. F., where we are told, that when, in his orations, he had particularly pleased the multitude, he used to ask his friends whether any thing wrong had escaped him in his address. *Ὑμῖν* and *πάντες* are omitted in almost all the best MSS. and several Versions and Fathers, and are cancelled by nearly all Editors from Griesb. to Scholz. The same may be said of the *καὶ* at ver. 28, where the Asyndeton much increases the gravity of the injunction.

30. The expressions in this and the foregoing verse are not to be too rigorously interpreted; being merely intended to inculcate a spirit of forbearance and meekness under injuries or deprivations. At *τὰ σὰ* subaud. *χρήματα*; and at *κωλύσῃς* sub. *ἀπὸ τοῦ αἴρειν*.

32. *χάρις*] put for *εὐεργεσία* and its consequent *μισθός*. So Dionys. Hal. A. vi. 86. *τίς ἐστιν ἡ σὴ χάρις ἡμῖν καὶ ὠφέλεια*. In this and the following verses, *μόνον* is to be supplied after *ὑμᾶς*.

35. *καὶ δανείζετε μηδὲν ἀπελπ.*] On the sense of *μηδὲν ἀπελπ.* the Commentators are not agreed. Some take it to mean "nothing despairing." But though *ἀπελπίζειν* often signifies to despair, yet that it cannot have that sense here is plain from the words of the preceding verse, *παρ' ὧν ἐλπίζετε ἀπολαβεῖν*. Others take *ἀπελπ.* in an *active* sense of *causing* despair. But that sense of the word is unauthorized, and here unsuitable. The true interpretation seems to be the one generally assigned by ancient and modern Commentators, "hoping for nothing again;" a sense which, however deficient in Classical authority, is very agreeable to analogy; for as *ἀπολαβεῖν* is used for *λαβεῖν ἀπό τινος*, so *ἀπελπίζειν* may be for *ἐλπίζειν ἀπό τινος*. So Athen. p. 649. *ἀπεσθίειν* for *ἐσθίειν ἀπό τινος*. The sense, therefore, is: "Lend to those from whom there is little hope of receiving back your money." From numerous passages of the Classical writers which I have adduced in Recens. Synop., it appears that the heathens sometimes used to lend money to respectable persons brought to unmerited distress. Insomuch that the words might seem to have reference to that kind of beneficial *collection* in aid of distress, which the Greeks called *ἐρανισμός*. If any one, for instance, had lost a considerable part of his property by shipwreck, fire, or any other calamity,

σθὸς ὑμῶν πολὺς, καὶ ἔσεσθε υἱοὶ [τοῦ] ὑψίστου. ὅτι αὐτὸς χρηστός
36 ἐστιν ἐπὶ τοὺς ἀχαρίστους καὶ πονηρούς. [r] Γίνεσθε οὖν οἰκτίρμονες, [r] Matt. 5. 48.
37 καθὼς καὶ ὁ πατὴρ ὑμῶν οἰκτίρμων ἐστί. [s] Καὶ μὴ κρίνετε, καὶ οὐ [s] Matt. 7. 1. Rom. 2. 1.
μὴ κριθῆτε· μὴ καταδικάζετε, καὶ οὐ μὴ καταδικασθῆτε· ἀπολύετε, 1 Cor. 4. 5.
38 καὶ ἀπολυθήσεσθε. [t] Δίδοτε, καὶ δοθήσεται ὑμῖν· μέτρον καλὸν, πε- [t] Prov. 10. 22. & 19. 17.
πιεσμένον καὶ σεσαλευμένον καὶ ὑπερεκχυνόμενον δώσουσιν εἰς τὸν κόλ- Matt. 7. 2. Mark. 4. 24.
πον ὑμῶν. τῷ γὰρ αὐτῷ μέτρῳ ᾧ μετρεῖτε, ἀντιμετρηθήσεται ὑμῖν.
39 [u] Εἶπε δὲ παραβολὴν αὐτοῖς· Μήτι δύναται τυφλὸς τυφλὸν ὁδη- [u] Isa. 42. 19. Matt. 15. 14.
40 γεῖν; οὐχὶ ἀμφότεροι εἰς βόθυνον πεσοῦνται; [x] Οὐκ ἔστι μαθητὴς [x] Matt. 10. 24. John 13. 16.
ὑπὲρ τὸν διδάσκαλον αὐτοῦ· κατηρτισμένος δὲ πᾶς ἔσται ὡς ὁ διδά- & 15. 20.
41 σκαλος αὐτοῦ. [y] Τί δὲ βλέπεις τὸ κάρφος τὸ ἐν τῷ ὀφθαλμῷ τοῦ [y] Matt. 7. 3.
ἀδελφοῦ σου, τὴν δὲ δοκὸν τὴν ἐν τῷ ἰδίῳ ὀφθαλμῷ οὐ κατανοεῖς;
42 [z] Ἢ πῶς δύνασαι λέγειν τῷ ἀδελφῷ σου· Ἀδελφὲ, ἄφες ἐκβάλω τὸ [z] Prov. 18. 17.
κάρφος τὸ ἐν τῷ ὀφθαλμῷ σου, αὐτὸς τὴν ἐν τῷ ὀφθαλμῷ σου δοκὸν
οὐ βλέπων; Ὑποκριτὰ, ἔκβαλε πρῶτον τὴν δοκὸν ἐκ τοῦ ὀφθαλμοῦ
σου, καὶ τότε διαβλέψεις ἐκβαλεῖν τὸ κάρφος τὸ ἐν τῷ ὀφθαλμῷ τοῦ

it was not unusual for his friends to supply him with money, not to be paid back by *any certain day*, but when *convenient*. This, however, they scarcely ever did, except to those who, they had some hope might, (by a more prosperous turn of fortune), some time or other, not only repay the money, but *return the favour*, which they termed ἀντεφανίζειν. Whereas our Lord enjoins his hearers to do this good (in the words of Thucyd. ii. 40.) "not with the narrow calculations of self-interest, but in the confidence of liberality;" a confidence reposed in Him who is the poor man's surety.

— υἱοὶ τ. ὑψ.] i. e. either "beloved of God," (as in Ecclus. iv. 10. γίνου ὀρφανοῖς ὡς πατὴρ — καὶ ἔσῃ ὡς υἱὸς ὑψίστου) or, "you will be like unto God, as being animated with a spirit of benevolence similar to that of the Deity." The Art. is omitted in many MSS. and the Ed. Princ., and is cancelled by Matth., Griesb., Tittm., Vat., and Scholz; agreeably to the usage of Luke. See i. 32. 35. 76.

— ὅτι αὐτὸς — πονηρούς.] This is not, as Kuin. asserts, "the same sentiment, in other words, as that at Matth. v. 45." For there the injunction is only to shew kindness even to our *enemies*; here we are also enjoined to shew beneficence to our *fellow-creatures*. And when we are commanded to imitate God, who is beneficent even to the ungrateful; — this is said to anticipate an objection, — that the persons whom we may benefit are almost sure to prove *ungrateful*. To which the answer is, But yet benefit them, for God, &c. In the next verse, οἰκτ. should be rendered, not "*merciful*," but *compassionate*; pitying and relieving, according to your power, the distresses of others.

37. καταδικάζετε.] This word and κριν. and ἀπολ. are properly forensic terms; the former signifying to condemn, the other to acquit. They are, however (as Grot. and other good Commentators have seen) to be accommodated to private use. The three clauses advert, the 1st to sitting in judgment on the faults of others; the 2d to passing condemnation on them. The 3d enjoins a contrary spirit, that of judging for the best, acquitting our neighbour of such charges as are not manifestly well founded.

38. δίδοτε, &c.] With *candour in judging* is united *liberality in giving*, as being a kindred virtue. Insomuch that, at the end of the verse, the words τῷ γὰρ αὐτῷ — ὑμῖν are employed to enjoin the exercise of the virtue mentioned in the preceding ver., by a metaphor derived from the imagery in this; in which the καλὸν (*fair* and full) is further illustrated by the terms πεπιεσμένον, σεσαλευμένον, and ὑπερεκχυνόμενον; which have reference to the three principal modes of giving abundant measure among the Jews; for, as Buxt. observes, there were many: such as the *supernatans*, the *abrasa*, the *accumulata*, *pressa*, *agitata*, *operta*. Of these the *abrasa* corresponds to *our* mode of measuring corn, by upheaping the measure, and cutting off the cumulus with a lath. The *cumulata* and *operta* were still larger than the *abrasa*; but the *pressa*, *agitata*, and *supernatans*, corresponding to the three here mentioned, were the amplest. Ὑπερεκχ. is not to be taken (with almost all Commentators) of a measure of *liquids* (for that is inconsistent with its being "poured into the lap," as just after), but (with Euthym. and Beza) of a measure of *solids*, by an idiom common to all languages. Thus there is a climax; for the ὑπερεκχ. *supposes* that the measure has been already pressed down and shaken together. In δώσουσιν εἰς τὸν κόλπον ὑμῶν there is an allusion to the Oriental custom, of receiving a measure of corn or other dry articles *in the bosom* or the *lap* of their flowing vests, the former of which they made use of like our *pockets*. See 2 Kings iv. 39. Prov. xv. 33. And so also among the Greeks and Romans, e. gr. Herodot. vi. 125. τὸν κόλπον πάντα πλησάμενος χρυσοῦ. Hor. Sat. ii. 3. 71. nucesque ferre *sinu laxo*. The expression is proverbial, and expressive of what *generally* takes place. Similar ones are cited by the Commentators from the Rabbinical and the Classical writings.

40. The purport of the words in their *present* application (for it is sometimes different) is this: "The disciple is not usually above his teacher; but every one who is, or would be, a thoroughly instructed person, a finished scholar, must be, i. e. must aim at being, as perfect as his teacher."

a Matt. 7. 17. & 12. 33. ἀδελφοῦ σου. [a] Οὐ γάρ ἐστι δένδρον καλὸν, ποιοῦν καρπὸν σαπρόν· 43
b Matt. 7. 16. οὐδὲ δένδρον σαπρὸν, ποιοῦν καρπὸν καλόν. [b] Ἕκαστον γὰρ δένδρον 44
ἐκ τοῦ ἰδίου καρποῦ γινώσκεται· οὐ γὰρ ἐξ ἀκανθῶν συλλέγουσι σῦκα,
c Matt. 12. 34, 35. οὐδὲ ἐκ βάτου τρυγῶσι σταφυλήν. [c] Ὁ ἀγαθὸς ἄνθρωπος ἐκ τοῦ ἀγα- 45
θοῦ θησαυροῦ τῆς καρδίας αὐτοῦ προφέρει τὸ ἀγαθόν· καὶ ὁ πονηρὸς
ἄνθρωπος ἐκ τοῦ πονηροῦ θησαυροῦ τῆς καρδίας αὐτοῦ προφέρει τὸ
πονηρόν· ἐκ γὰρ τοῦ περισσεύματος τῆς καρδίας λαλεῖ τὸ στόμα αὐτοῦ.
d Mal. 1. 6. Matt. 7. 21. & 25. 11. infr. 13. 25. Rom. 2. 13. James 1. 22. e Matt. 7. 24. [d] Τί δέ με καλεῖτε Κύριε, Κύριε· καὶ οὐ ποιεῖτε ἃ λέγω; [e] Πᾶς 46
ὁ ἐρχόμενος πρός με καὶ ἀκούων μου τῶν λόγων καὶ ποιῶν αὐτοὺς, 47
ὑποδείξω ὑμῖν τίνι ἐστὶν ὅμοιος. Ὅμοιός ἐστιν ἀνθρώπῳ οἰκοδομοῦντι 48
οἰκίαν, ὃς ἔσκαψε καὶ ἐβάθυνε, καὶ ἔθηκε θεμέλιον ἐπὶ τὴν πέτραν.
πλημμύρας δὲ γενομένης, προσέῤῥηξεν ὁ ποταμὸς τῇ οἰκίᾳ ἐκείνῃ, καὶ
οὐκ ἴσχυσε σαλεῦσαι αὐτήν· τεθεμελίωτο γὰρ ἐπὶ τὴν πέτραν. Ὁ δὲ 49
ἀκούσας, καὶ μὴ ποιήσας, ὅμοιός ἐστιν ἀνθρώπῳ οἰκοδομήσαντι οἰκίαν
ἐπὶ τὴν γῆν χωρὶς θεμελίου· ᾗ προσέῤῥηξεν ὁ ποταμὸς, καὶ εὐθέως
MT. ἔπεσε, καὶ ἐγένετο τὸ ῥῆγμα τῆς οἰκίας ἐκείνης μέγα.
8. VII. ἘΠΕΙ δὲ ἐπλήρωσε πάντα τὰ ῥήματα αὐτοῦ εἰς τὰς ἀκοὰς 1
5 τοῦ λαοῦ, εἰσῆλθεν εἰς Καπερναούμ. Ἑκατοντάρχου δέ τινος δοῦλος 2
κακῶς ἔχων ἤμελλε τελευτᾷν, ὃς ἦν αὐτῷ ἔντιμος. Ἀκούσας δὲ περὶ 3
τοῦ Ἰησοῦ, ἀπέστειλε πρὸς αὐτὸν πρεσβυτέρους τῶν Ἰουδαίων, ἐρωτῶν
αὐτὸν ὅπως ἐλθὼν διασώσῃ τὸν δοῦλον αὐτοῦ. Οἱ δὲ, παραγενόμενοι 4
πρὸς τὸν Ἰησοῦν, παρεκάλουν αὐτὸν σπουδαίως, λέγοντες· Ὅτι ἄξιός
ἐστιν ᾧ παρέξει τοῦτο· ἀγαπᾷ γὰρ τὸ ἔθνος ἡμῶν, καὶ τὴν συναγω- 5
γὴν αὐτὸς ᾠκοδόμησεν ἡμῖν. ὁ δὲ Ἰησοῦς ἐπορεύετο σὺν αὐτοῖς. Ἤδη 6
δὲ αὐτοῦ οὐ μακρὰν ἀπέχοντος ἀπὸ τῆς οἰκίας, ἔπεμψε πρὸς αὐτὸν ὁ
8 ἑκατόνταρχος φίλους, λέγων αὐτῷ· Κύριε, μὴ σκύλλου· οὐ γάρ εἰμι
ἱκανὸς ἵνα ὑπὸ τὴν στέγην μου εἰσέλθῃς· διὸ οὐδὲ ἐμαυτὸν ἠξίωσα 7
9 πρός σε ἐλθεῖν· ἀλλὰ εἰπὲ λόγῳ, καὶ ἰαθήσεται ὁ παῖς μου. Καὶ 8
γὰρ ἐγὼ ἄνθρωπός εἰμι ὑπὸ ἐξουσίαν τασσόμενος, ἔχων ὑπ᾽ ἐμαυτὸν
στρατιώτας, καὶ λέγω τούτῳ· Πορεύθητι, καὶ πορεύεται· καὶ ἄλλῳ·
Ἔρχου, καὶ ἔρχεται· καὶ τῷ δούλῳ μου, Ποίησον τοῦτο, καὶ ποιεῖ.
10 ἀκούσας δὲ ταῦτα ὁ Ἰησοῦς ἐθαύμασεν αὐτόν. Καὶ στραφεὶς τῷ ἀκο- 9

Thus, as the disciple generally follows his master's example, so if you neglect your duty to God, neither will your hearers observe theirs. The connection of the verses following is obvious.

43. οὐ γάρ ἐστι, &c.] Render "for that is not a good tree which brings forth bad fruit."

46. καλεῖτε.] The word has here a sensus prægnans, and signifies, "Why do you address me, saying Lord?"

48. ἔσκαψε καὶ ἐβάθυνε] by Hendiadys, for βαθέως ἔσκαψε; a kind of expression found both in the Classical and the Hellenistical writers. So Judg. xiii. 10. ἐτάχυνε καὶ ἔδραμε, for ταχέως ἔδραμε. See Winer's Gr. Gr. § 47. 3. The moral (as Grot. observes) is, that the study of piety should not be superficial, but a principle well grounded and deeply rooted in the heart, so as to resist the assaults of passion, temptation, &c.

— πλημμύρας.] The word denotes a *swell* or inundation of any kind.

VII. 2. ὃς ἦν αὐτῷ ἔντιμος] "who was much esteemed by him." Of this signification examples are adduced by Wets.

3. πρεσβυτέρους τῶν Ἰ.] Perhaps the elders of the synagogue which he had built.

4. ἄξιός ἐστιν ᾧ παρέξει.] If the phrase be not a Latinism, ἄξιος must be taken in the *absolute* sense, of which I have adduced numerous examples in Recens. Synop. Παρέξει is Attic for παρέξῃ (on which see Matth. Gr. Gr. § 197. and 496. and Winer's Gr. Gr. § 7. 2.) one of the many Atticisms in this Gospel: Ὅτι, as often, introduces the exact words of the speaker.

5. τὴν συναγωγὴν — ἡμῖν.] Render: "And he it is who hath built for us the synagogue." This

λουθοῦντι αὐτῷ ὄχλῳ εἶπε· Λέγω ὑμῖν, οὐδὲ ἐν τῷ Ἰσραὴλ τοσαύτην
10 πίστιν, εὗρον. Καὶ ὑποστρέψαντες οἱ πεμφθέντες εἰς τὸν οἶκον, εὗρον τὸν ἀσθενοῦντα δοῦλον ὑγιαίνοντα.
11 ΚΑΙ ἐγένετο ἐν τῇ ἑξῆς, ἐπορεύετο εἰς πόλιν καλουμένην Ναΐν· καὶ
12 συνεπορεύοντο αὐτῷ οἱ μαθηταὶ αὐτοῦ ἱκανοὶ, καὶ ὄχλος πολύς. Ὡς
δὲ ἤγγισε τῇ πύλῃ τῆς πόλεως, καὶ ἰδοὺ ἐξεκομίζετο τεθνηκὼς υἱὸς
μονογενὴς τῇ μητρὶ αὐτοῦ· καὶ αὐτὴ χήρα. καὶ ὄχλος τῆς πόλεως
13 ἱκανὸς ἦν σὺν αὐτῇ. καὶ ἰδὼν αὐτὴν ὁ Κύριος, ἐσπλαγχνίσθη ἐπ᾿
14 αὐτῇ, καὶ εἶπεν αὐτῇ· Μὴ κλαῖε. [f] καὶ προσελθὼν ἥψατο τῆς σο- [f] Acts 9. 40.
ροῦ· οἱ δὲ βαστάζοντες ἔστησαν· καὶ εἶπε· Νεανίσκε, σοὶ λέγω,
15 ἐγέρθητι. καὶ ἀνεκάθισεν ὁ νεκρὸς, καὶ ἤρξατο λαλεῖν· καὶ ἔδωκεν
16 αὐτὸν τῇ μητρὶ αὐτοῦ. [g] ἔλαβε δὲ φόβος ἅπαντας, καὶ ἐδόξαζον τὸν [g] Mark 7. 37. infr. 24. 19.
Θεὸν, λέγοντες· Ὅτι προφήτης μέγας ἐγήγερται ἐν ἡμῖν· καὶ ὅτι John 4. 19. & 6. 14.
17 ἐπεσκέψατο ὁ Θεὸς τὸν λαὸν αὐτοῦ. καὶ ἐξῆλθεν ὁ λόγος οὗτος ἐν & 9. 17. supr. 1. 68.
ὅλῃ τῇ Ἰουδαίᾳ περὶ αὐτοῦ καὶ ἐν πάσῃ τῇ περιχώρῳ. MT.
18 ΚΑΙ ἀπήγγειλαν Ἰωάννῃ οἱ μαθηταὶ αὐτοῦ περὶ πάντων τούτων. 11.
19 Καὶ προσκαλεσάμενος δύο τινὰς τῶν μαθητῶν αὐτοῦ ὁ Ἰωάννης ἔπεμψε 2
πρὸς τὸν Ἰησοῦν, λέγων· Σὺ εἶ ὁ ἐρχόμενος, ἢ ἄλλον προσδοκῶμεν; 3
20 Παραγενόμενοι δὲ πρὸς αὐτὸν οἱ ἄνδρες εἶπον· Ἰωάννης ὁ βαπτιστὴς
ἀπέσταλκεν ἡμᾶς πρός σε, λέγων· Σὺ εἶ ὁ ἐρχόμενος, ἢ ἄλλον προσ-
21 δοκῶμεν; (ἐν αὐτῇ δὲ τῇ ὥρᾳ ἐθεράπευσε πολλοὺς ἀπὸ νόσων καὶ

was not unusual in an individual. The person was, no doubt, a proselyte.

7. εἰπὲ λόγῳ] "give thy fiat at a word," or by word of mouth.

9. ἐθαύμασεν] held him in admiration. A use of θαυμάζειν somewhat rare.

12. ἐξεκομίζετο.] Ἐκκομίζειν is a funeral term like the Latin *efferre*; for the custom of interring the dead outside of cities or towns, was common to all the ancients; to the *Jews*, because dead bodies were among them unclean; and to the *Gentiles*, in order to prevent infection. (Grot.)

— τῇ μητρί.] Dative of possession for the Genit., as Matt. ii. 18. and not unfrequently in the Scriptural, and also Classical writers. See Matth. Gr. Gr. § 392. 3. and Winer's Gr. Gr. § 25. 6. Note 3. One cannot but remark the simple pathos of the story, with which I have in Recens. Synop. compared Eurip. Alc. 305. μόνος γὰρ αὐτοῖς ἦσθα, and 925. κόρος ἀξιοθρῆνος ᾤχετ᾿ ἐν δόμοισι μονόπαις.

At καὶ αὐτὴ χήρα there is something like an Anantapodoton. Some MSS., indeed, have αὐτῇ χήρᾳ. But that is a mere *emendation*, and moreover unnecessary; for we have only to supply ἦν, agreeably to the tense of the preceding verb, especially as it would be in some measure *anticipated* from the following ἦν; for a repetition of ἦν within so short a space would have been offensive. The ἦν just after is, indeed, omitted in many MSS., early Edd., and Versions. And it is cancelled by almost all the Editors. Yet it cannot well be dispensed with. I suspect that its omission partly arose from a mistake originating in a confounding of this ἦν with the one just before. The MSS. in which it is not found are comparatively few; and the Versions can have no weight, since those which here omit the ἦν *insert* it just before, and they could not well express it in both places.

14. ἥψατο τῆς σοροῦ.] Meaning thereby to stop the bearers. Σορὸς *generally* denotes a *coffin*, of marble or other materials. But as such were not in use among the *Jews*, the word must here denote the *bier*, or *funeral couch* on which the dead of the higher classes were carried forth. See the references in Recens. Synop. and my Note on Thucyd. ii. 34.

17. ἐν ὅλῃ τῇ Ἰ.] Here and at Matt. ix. 31. the Commentators take ἐν for διά. But that is so harsh that it is better to suppose ἐν used for εἰς, (as often) in the sense *unto*, which implies *over* and *throughout*.

18. δύο τινάς.] The τις indefinite is simply used with a numeral at Acts xxiii. 23. & xix. 14. And the Philologists think that the addition of the τις renders the number indefinite; which is frequently the case in the Classical writers; and the τις may be there expressed by our *some*; but whether it has that force in the N. T., I doubt. It is unsuitable to the sacred writers, and can hardly have place in numbers so small as *two*. Besides, Matthew mentions positively *two*. It rather seems to have the usual sense *certain*: q. d. certain persons, two in number.

21. ἐθεράπευσε.] This is not well rendered "*cured*," or "was curing." It should rather seem that the Aorist is put for the Pluperfect, as often in narration; as Mark iii. 10.

— νόσων καὶ μαστ. καὶ πν. π.] Here we see *demoniacal possession* studiously distinguished from *disorders*, and that by a Physician. The disorders are also distinguished into the ordinary and milder ones, (νόσοι), or the more grievous and painful μάστιγες; (as Mark iii. 10. and v. 29. and Ps. xxxii. 10.) so called, because such were regarded

MT.
11. μαστίγων καὶ πνευμάτων πονηρῶν, καὶ τυφλοῖς πολλοῖς ἐχαρίσατο τὸ
4 βλέπειν·) Καὶ ἀποκριθεὶς ὁ Ἰησοῦς εἶπεν αὐτοῖς· Πορευθέντες 22
5 ἀπαγγείλατε Ἰωάννῃ, ἃ εἴδετε καὶ ἠκούσατε· ὅτι τυφλοὶ ἀναβλέπουσι,
χωλοὶ περιπατοῦσι, λεπροὶ καθαρίζονται, κωφοὶ ἀκούουσι, νεκροὶ ἐγεί-
6 ρονται, πτωχοὶ εὐαγγελίζονται. καὶ μακάριός ἐστιν, ὃς ἐὰν μὴ σκαν- 23
7 δαλισθῇ ἐν ἐμοί. Ἀπελθόντων δὲ τῶν ἀγγέλων Ἰωάννου, ἤρξατο λέγειν 24
πρὸς τοὺς ὄχλους περὶ Ἰωάννου· Τί ἐξεληλύθατε εἰς τὴν ἔρημον θεά-
8 σασθαι; κάλαμον ὑπὸ ἀνέμου σαλευόμενον; Ἀλλὰ τί ἐξεληλύθατε 25
ἰδεῖν; ἄνθρωπον ἐν μαλακοῖς ἱματίοις ἠμφιεσμένον; ἰδοὺ, οἱ ἐν
9 ἱματισμῷ ἐνδόξῳ καὶ τρυφῇ ὑπάρχοντες ἐν τοῖς βασιλείοις εἰσίν. Ἀλλὰ 26
τί ἐξεληλύθατε ἰδεῖν; προφήτην; ναὶ λέγω ὑμῖν, καὶ περισσότερον
10 προφήτου. Οὗτός ἐστι περὶ οὗ γέγραπται· Ἰδοὺ ἐγὼ ἀποστέλ- 27
λω τὸν ἄγγελόν μου πρὸ προσώπου σου, ὃς κατασκευάσει τὴν ὁδόν σου ἔμπροσθέν σου. Λέγω γὰρ ὑμῖν· 28
μείζων ἐν γεννητοῖς γυναικῶν προφήτης Ἰωάννου τοῦ βαπτιστοῦ οὐδείς ἐστιν. ὁ δὲ μικρότερος ἐν τῇ βασιλείᾳ τοῦ θεοῦ μείζων αὐτοῦ
ἐστι. Καὶ πᾶς ὁ λαὸς ἀκούσας καὶ οἱ τελῶναι ἐδικαίωσαν τὸν Θεὸν, 29

as peculiar *scourges* from God. Ἐθεράπευσε is used *propriè* of the νόσοι and μάστιγες, and *impropriè* of the dispossessions. However, in *that* case there was almost always a *disorder* cured at the same time that a demon was ejected. Ἐχαρίσατο τ. β., "he bestowed sight." The τὸ, which is omitted in several MSS., and which some Editors are inclined to cancel, is very necessary to the sense. Τὸ βλ. signifies *the faculty of sight*.

22. See Is. xxix. 18. xxxv. 5.

25. Τρυφῇ is by most recent Commentators, supposed to mean sumptuous *dress*; to which it is sometimes applied in the Classical writers, as in Eurip. Phœn. 1505. στολίδα κροκόεσσαν ἀνεῖσα τρυφᾶς. Thus it would stand for τρυφερῷ. That, however, would be too poetic for plain prose; and there is no reason to abandon the interpretation *luxury*, i. e. a *luxurious life*. Thus in a kindred passage of Artemid. iii. 60. τοῖς ἐν τρυφῇ διάγουσι. The ὑπάρχ. must be accommodated in sense to *each* of the nouns with which it is connected. See also 2 Pet. ii. 13. Besides, *both* circumstances are necessary to designate the luxurious. See Luke xvi. 19.

27. See Malachi iii. 1. Mark i. 2.

29. ἐδικαίωσαν.] On the signification of this word the Commentators are not agreed. The versions "honoured," "obeyed," and others, are but *paraphrases*. It is best to suppose a significatio prægnans, and to adopt the primary sense, and that espoused by many of the best Commentators, *acknowledged* and *commended* the justice of God (i. e. of his purpose in calling them to repentance by John) and were accordingly baptized. This interpretation is required by the antithetical formula in the next verse, τὴν βουλὴν (counsel) τοῦ Θεοῦ ἠθέτησαν, &c. A disputed point, however, still remains, — namely, whether this and the verse following are to be considered as the words of *our Lord*, (which is the common opinion) or whether (as some eminent Interpreters maintain) the words of the *Evangelist*, containing a remark, that in consequence of what our Lord then said concerning John, the people immediately resorted to his baptism. And it must be granted that such remarks do occasionally occur in the N. T But, (as is justly urged by Campb.), such cannot be the sense; because John was then in prison, where he remained till his death. An objection so serious, that Bornem., who strenuously maintains the words to be the *Evangelist's*, is compelled, in stating their sense, to pass over all mention of the people being baptized by John. And then, as if distrusting his own view, "he sees no reason why the Aorists ἐδικαίωσαν and ἠθέτησαν should not be taken as Pluperfects." But, pace viri doctissimi, there *is* a reason; namely, that it may be doubted, whether the Aorist ever is, strictly speaking, put for the Pluperfect; most of the passages adduced by Philologists being not at all to the purpose. And Winer and Alt have shown under *what circumstances* alone this can be said to be the case. *Here*, however, no such circumstances exist. Prof. Robinson, indeed, on Winer, p. 106, thinks the Aorist is simply put for the Pluperfect at John iv. 1. ὡς οὖν ἔγνω ὁ Κύριος ὅτι ἤκουσαν οἱ Φαρ. ὅτι, &c. But *there*, it may be observed, the Aorist is used *suitably* to the use of the *Present* instead of the Imperfect, in the verbs following in this clause, ποιεῖ and βαπτίζει. Our authorized Version, indeed, renders ἤκ. in the Pluperfect; but only because it renders the other verbs in the *past tense*. In short, had the writer meant to express a Pluperfect *sense*, why should he not have used the Pluperfect *tense*? As to what is urged by Bornem. that the words, regarded as those of *Christ*, are languid and frigid; that is a mere question of *taste*. But if we allow these to be frigid, it would not be difficult to prove the words which follow this same verse, in Matt. xi. 12., to be so also. And yet even Bornem. must acknowledge *those* to be Christ's. Finally, the words under consideration *can* be no other than Christ's, because they are evidently of the very same nature with that verse, and related to the same *conversation* of our Lord. For as πᾶς ὁ λαὸς means the people at large, the populace, (called at John vii. 49. ὁ ὄχλος ὁ μὴ γινώσκων τὸν νόμον.) as opposed to the Rulers and Pharisees, so also the best Commentators interpret the ex-

MT.
30 βαπτισθέντες τὸ βάπτισμα Ἰωάννου· οἱ δὲ Φαρισαῖοι καὶ οἱ νομικοὶ 11.
τὴν βουλὴν τοῦ Θεοῦ ἠθέτησαν εἰς ἑαυτούς, μὴ βαπτισθέντες ὑπ᾿ αὐ-
31 τοῦ. [εἶπε δὲ ὁ Κύριος·] Τίνι οὖν ὁμοιώσω τοὺς ἀνθρώπους τῆς 16
32 γενεᾶς ταύτης; καὶ τίνι εἰσὶν ὅμοιοι; Ὅμοιοί εἰσι παιδίοις τοῖς ἐν
ἀγορᾷ καθημένοις, καὶ προσφωνοῦσιν ἀλλήλοις καὶ λέγουσιν. Ηὐλή- 17
σαμεν ὑμῖν, καὶ οὐκ ὠρχήσασθε· ἐθρηνήσαμεν ὑμῖν, καὶ οὐκ ἐκλαύ-
33 σατε. Ἐλήλυθε γὰρ Ἰωάννης ὁ βαπτιστὴς μήτε ἄρτον ἐσθίων μήτε 18
34 οἶνον πίνων· καὶ λέγετε· Δαιμόνιον ἔχει. Ἐλήλυθεν ὁ Υἱὸς τοῦ ἀν- 19
θρώπου ἐσθίων καὶ πίνων· καὶ λέγετε· Ἰδού, ἄνθρωπος φάγος καὶ
35 οἰνοπότης, τελωνῶν φίλος καὶ ἁμαρτωλῶν. Καὶ ἐδικαιώθη ἡ σοφία
ἀπὸ τῶν τέκνων αὐτῆς πάντων.

36 [h] Ἠρώτα δέ τις αὐτὸν τῶν Φαρισαίων, ἵνα φάγῃ μετ᾿ αὐτοῦ· καὶ h Matt. 26. 6. Mark 14. 3. John 11. 2. & 12. 3.
37 εἰσελθὼν εἰς τὴν οἰκίαν τοῦ Φαρισαίου, ἀνεκλίθη. Καὶ ἰδού, γυνὴ ἐν
τῇ πόλει, ἥτις ἦν ἁμαρτωλός, ἐπιγνοῦσα ὅτι ἀνάκειται ἐν τῇ οἰκίᾳ τοῦ

pression *βιασταὶ* at Matt. xi. 12. of the meaner crowd.

To advert to what may be considered as principally leading to the opinion of these verses being from the *Evangelist*—namely, the words which introduce the verse following, *εἶπε δὲ ὁ Κύριος*; these are now universally admitted to be not genuine. And vain is it that Bornem. seeks to build even upon this an argument for the preceding being those of the Evangelist. Nothing, surely, is more improbable than that the words should have originated in any such desire to prevent mistake in the words following; for no one could fail to see that they were *Christ's*. In short, it is plain that the words originated from the *Lectionaries*, since the verse commences an *ἀνάγνωσις* or Reading, and which required to be *introduced* by some such words. Thus Scholz attests that they are found, not only in the Lectionaries, but in the margin of those MSS. *textus perpetui*, which always mark the commencement of the Readings in the margin. It may, moreover, be urged, that the *οὖν* at v. 3., which is found in all the MSS., evidently has reference to what was said at v. 29, 30.

Lastly, there is another reason why the verses under consideration cannot but be from our *Lord*—namely, that they are evidently adverted to by Him at v. 35. *καὶ ἐδικαιώθη ἡ σοφία ἀπὸ τῶν τέκνων αὐτῆς πάντων*. And thus we are there supplied with an *authentic interpretation* of one of the most variously expounded passages in all the N. T. By *σοφία* is meant the wise counsel of God for bringing men to the Gospel, by what was a preparation thereto, namely, thoroughly repenting of their former sins, and being baptized by John. By the *children* of wisdom are meant, those who recognized that wisdom, and approved it by acting conformably thereto, and who were therefore (by the same metaphor) children of God.

The passage may be rendered thus: "And now the great body of the people who have heard him,—and even the publicans,—have acknowledged and fulfilled the purpose of God, by being baptized by John: but the Pharisees and Lawyers have set at nought the purpose of God respecting themselves, having not been baptized by John." *Εἰς ἑαυτοὺς* is by some interpreted "against themselves," "to their own injury." But although this sense of *εἰς* is supported alike by Classical and Scriptural authority, and would here give a good sense, it is better (with Camer., Grot., Hamm., Wolf, Whitby, Wets., Campb., Rosenm., and Kuin.) to suppose a slight transposition, and connect *εἰς ἑαυτοὺς* with *βουλὴν τοῦ Θεοῦ*, in the sense "*in regard to* themselves." This use of *εἰς* is very frequent. See the Lexicons.

33. {*Comp.* Matt. iii. 4. Mark i. 6.]

37. *καὶ ἰδού, γυνή*, &c.] It has been a much disputed question whether this story be the same with that narrated at Matt. xxvi. 6. Mark xiv. 3. John xii. 3., or not. The *former* is maintained by some ancient and most early modern Commentators, especially Lightf. and Grot. The latter by Theophyl. and Euthym. (from Chrysost.), and by many of the best modern Commentators, as Buxt., Hamm., Whitby, Wolf, Markl., Michaelis, Rosenm., Kuin., Deyling, and Lampe, (the substance of whose arguments may be found stated in Recens. Synop.) The points of *dissimilarity* between the two narrations, and between the Mary here mentioned, and Mary Magdalene, are striking. As to the *similarity*,—the *action* (anointing) was not unusual, the name of the vessel common, and the name of the Pharisee one of those most frequently met with. This is quite independent of the sense to be assigned to *ἁμαρτωλός*, whether *sinner* or *Gentile*. Of the *latter* sense there is perhaps not one undoubted example in the *singular*: and even with the *plural* it requires the Article, unless united with *τελῶναι*. Though, therefore, that interpretation may have been adopted by several good Commentators, the *former*, which is espoused by most Commentators, is greatly preferable. But when they assign to the word the sense *harlot*, or *adulteress*, they adduce no proof of that signification from the Classical writers. Nor is it necessary to suppose any such *particularity*. There is no reason why it may not be taken in the *general* sense of a *vicious person*; in which signification the singular is frequent, e. gr. Luke v. 8. *ὅτι ἁμαρτωλός εἰμι*. Thus we are enabled to get rid of the harshness of taking *ἦν* in a *pluperfect* tense, (very rarely met with) which all the Commentators do who assign to *ἁμαρτωλὸς* the signification *harlot*. The woman, it seems, was then a sinner: however, a sinner under conviction of sin, and having the sincere desire of amendment.

Φαρισαίου, κομίσασα ἀλάβαστρον μύρου. Καὶ στᾶσα παρὰ τοὺς πόδας 38
αὐτοῦ ὀπίσω κλαίουσα, ἤρξατο βρέχειν τοὺς πόδας αὐτοῦ τοῖς δάκρυσι,
καὶ ταῖς θριξὶ τῆς κεφαλῆς αὐτῆς ἐξέμασσε· καὶ κατεφίλει τοὺς πόδας
¹ Infr. 15. 2. *αὐτοῦ, καὶ ἤλειφε τῷ μύρῳ.* ¹ *Ἰδὼν δὲ ὁ Φαρισαῖος ὁ καλέσας αὐτὸν,* 39
εἶπεν ἐν ἑαυτῷ, λέγων· Οὗτος εἰ ἦν προφήτης, ἐγίνωσκεν ἂν τίς καὶ
ποταπὴ ἡ γυνὴ, ἥτις ἅπτεται αὐτοῦ· ὅτι ἁμαρτωλός ἐστι.
Καὶ ἀποκριθεὶς ὁ Ἰησοῦς εἶπε πρὸς αὐτόν· Σίμων, ἔχω σοί τι 40
εἰπεῖν. ὁ δέ φησι· Διδάσκαλε, εἰπέ. Δύο χρεωφειλέται ἦσαν δα- 41
νειστῇ τινι· ὁ εἷς ὤφειλε δηνάρια πεντακόσια, ὁ δὲ ἕτερος πεντήκοντα.
Μὴ ἐχόντων δὲ αὐτῶν ἀποδοῦναι, ἀμφοτέροις ἐχαρίσατο. Τίς οὖν αὐ- 42
τῶν, εἰπέ, πλεῖον αὐτὸν ἀγαπήσει; Ἀποκριθεὶς δὲ ὁ Σίμων εἶπεν· 43
Ὑπολαμβάνω ὅτι ᾧ τὸ πλεῖον ἐχαρίσατο. Ὁ δὲ εἶπεν αὐτῷ· Ὀρθῶς
ἔκρινας. Καὶ στραφεὶς πρὸς τὴν γυναῖκα, τῷ Σίμωνι ἔφη· Βλέπεις 44
ταύτην τὴν γυναῖκα; Εἰσῆλθόν σου εἰς τὴν οἰκίαν· ὕδωρ ἐπὶ τοὺς
πόδας μου οὐκ ἔδωκας· αὕτη δὲ τοῖς δάκρυσιν ἔβρεξέ μου τοὺς πό-
δας, καὶ ταῖς θριξὶ [τῆς κεφαλῆς] αὐτῆς ἐξέμαξε. Φίλημά μοι οὐκ 45
ἔδωκας· αὕτη δὲ ἀφ' ἧς ‡ εἰσῆλθον, οὐ διέλιπε καταφιλοῦσά μου
τοὺς πόδας. Ἐλαίῳ τὴν κεφαλήν μου οὐκ ἤλειψας· αὕτη δὲ μύρῳ 46
ἤλειψέ μου τοὺς πόδας. Οὗ χάριν, λέγω σοι, ἀφέωνται αἱ ἁμαρτίαι 47
αὐτῆς αἱ πολλαὶ, ὅ τι ἠγάπησε πολύ. ᾧ δὲ ὀλίγον ἀφίεται, ὀλίγον

38. *στᾶσα ὀπίσω.*] Jesus, it seems, was reclining at table on a couch, leaning on his left elbow, his head and countenance turned towards the table; and his naked feet (the sandals being taken off before the meal) turned the contrary way, towards that which the servants bearing the dishes were waiting on the triclinium or table. (Maldon. & Kuin.)

— *κατεφίλει.*] The *κατα* is intensive; and this action implied the deepest reverence and most profound humility; as the bathing his feet with her tears did earnest supplication. The anointing of the feet was a mark of profound respect, retained even in modern times.

39. *προφήτης.*] i. e. a Divine legate, and consequently endued with supernatural knowledge. Yet, as Grot. observes, not even the *Prophets* knew all things, but only such things as God was pleased to reveal to them.

41. *ὁ εἷς — ὁ δὲ ἕτερος.*] Ὁ *μὲν* — ὁ *δὲ* is the more elegant mode of expression; but the other is more pointed.

44. This and the following verses advert to the customs in use among the Jews to guests who were made very welcome. 1. Their sandals were unloosed, and their feet washed and carefully wiped, and, if the person were of high rank, anointed. 2. A kiss was the usual salutation on entrance, or as soon as the person was made comfortable. 3. The head was usually anointed with aromatic oils or unguents. The words *τῆς κεφαλῆς* are omitted in many MSS. and Versions, and have been cancelled by Griesb., Vat., Scholz, and others; but on insufficient grounds. The MSS. are comparatively few; Versions are, in a case like the present, no sure testimony; and better reasons may be given for the *omission* than for the *insertion* of the words.

45. *εἰσῆλθον.*] The chief Editors and Commentators agree in preferring *εἰσῆλθεν*, which is the reading of some MSS. and Versions. The evidence, however, for it is so slender, that, small as the difference is, an Editor is scarcely warranted in receiving it; especially as it cannot be proved that the common reading is positively wrong; for we have only to regard the language as partaking of the same hyperbolical cast, which is so characteristic of Oriental phraseology. Besides, it is probable that the woman came in very soon after our Lord was seated, and thus supplied those observances which Simon had neglected. Indeed, there is something *feeble* in the sense of *εἰσῆλθεν*. That *εἰσῆλθον* is as proper *in grammar* as *εἰσῆλθεν*, is plain from a kindred passage of Liban. which I have cited in Recens. Synop.: *ὁ δὲ ἄνθρωπος ἐκεῖνος, ἀφ' οὗπερ ἧκον, οὐ διέλιπε βάλλων· εἰ δὲ οὐκ ἐπήγνυτο τὰ βέλη.*

— *οὐ διέλιπε καταφιλοῦσα.*] On the Participle for Infinitive after verbs signifying *repeated action*, see Winer's Gr. Gr. § 39. 1.

47. *αἱ πολλαί.*] Sub. *οὖσαι*, which is *expressed* in a similar passage of Philostratus Vit. Ap. i. 13. *μετεῤῥύθμισε τῶν ἁμαρτημάτων πολλῶν ὄντων.*

— *ὅ τι ἠγάπησε πολύ.*] On the sense of the *ὅτι* here Commentators are not agreed. The ancient and early modern ones interpret *ὅτι* (according to its usual acceptation) *for* or *because*. But all the most eminent of the recent Expositors, regarding this sense as repugnant to the scope of the parable; which, say they, represents the gratuitous forgiveness of sins as the *cause of the love*, not the *love*, the *cause of the forgiveness*; an effect, they remark, at v. 50. ascribed to faith) and they render the *ὅτι therefore*. Since, however, this signification is deficient in authority, others (as Parkhurst) suppose that the love of the woman is adduced as the *sign*, not the *cause* of her pardon, and that *οὗ χάριν* expresses an inference from the antecedent to the consequent; "Wherefore [since she has shown so great a regard for me] I

48 ἀναπᾷ. [k] Εἶπε δὲ αὐτῇ· [l] Ἀφέωνταί σου αἱ ἁμαρτίαι. [l] Καὶ ἤρξαντο
49 οἱ συνανακείμενοι λέγειν ἐν ἑαυτοῖς· Τίς οὗτός ἐστιν ὃς καὶ ἁμαρτίας
50 ἀφίησιν; [m] Εἶπε δὲ πρὸς τὴν γυναῖκα· Ἡ πίστις σου σέσωκέ σε·
πορεύου εἰς εἰρήνην.

k Matt. 9. 2. l Matt. 9. 3. Mark 2. 7. m Matt. 9. 22. Mark 5. 34. & 10. 52. infr. 8. 48. & 18. 42.

1 VIII. ΚΑΙ ἐγένετο, ἐν τῷ καθεξῆς, καὶ αὐτὸς διώδευε κατὰ πόλιν
καὶ κώμην κηρύσσων καὶ εὐαγγελιζόμενος τὴν βασιλείαν τοῦ Θεοῦ· καὶ
2 οἱ δώδεκα σὺν αὐτῷ, [n] καὶ γυναῖκές τινες, αἳ ἦσαν τεθεραπευμέναι
ἀπὸ πνευμάτων πονηρῶν καὶ ἀσθενειῶν, Μαρία ἡ καλουμένη Μαγδα-
3 ληνὴ, ἀφ᾽ ἧς δαιμόνια ἑπτὰ ἐξεληλύθει, καὶ Ἰωάννα γυνὴ Χουζᾶ ἐπιτρόπου Ἡρώδου, καὶ Σουσάννα, καὶ ἕτεραι πολλαὶ, αἵτινες διηκόνουν ‡
αὐτῷ ἀπὸ τῶν ὑπαρχόντων αὐταῖς.

n Matt. 27. 55, 56. Mark 16. 9. John 19. 25.

MT. 13. MK. 4.

4 [o] Συνιόντος δὲ ὄχλου πολλοῦ, καὶ τῶν κατὰ πόλιν ἐπιπορευομένων 2 1
5 πρὸς αὐτὸν, εἶπε διὰ παραβολῆς· Ἐξῆλθεν ὁ σπείρων τοῦ σπεῖραι τὸν 3 3
σπόρον αὐτοῦ· καὶ ἐν τῷ σπείρειν αὐτὸν, ὃ μὲν ἔπεσε παρὰ τὴν 4 4
ὁδόν· καὶ κατεπατήθη, καὶ τὰ πετεινὰ τοῦ οὐρανοῦ κατέφαγεν αὐτό.
6 Καὶ ἕτερον ἔπεσεν ἐπὶ τὴν πέτραν· καὶ φυὲν ἐξηράνθη, διὰ τὸ μὴ 5 6 6 6
7 ἔχειν ἰκμάδα. Καὶ ἕτερον ἔπεσεν ἐν μέσῳ τῶν ἀκανθῶν· καὶ συμ- 7 7
8 φυεῖσαι αἱ ἄκανθαι ἀπέπνιξαν αὐτό. Καὶ ἕτερον ἔπεσεν εἰς τὴν γῆν 8 8
τὴν ἀγαθήν· καὶ φυὲν ἐποίησε καρπὸν ἑκατονταπλασίονα. ταῦτα
9 λέγων ἐφώνει· Ὁ ἔχων ὦτα ἀκούειν, ἀκουέτω. Ἐπηρώτων δὲ αὐτὸν 9 10 9 10

say unto you, [it is plain that] her many sins are forgiven, for, or because, she loved much." Yet even this method is open to no little objection: and the ancient interpretation, being the most simple and involving the least difficulty, deserves the preference. And as to what has been alleged, that it represents *love* as the *meritorious cause* of the remission of sins, that is by no means the case. Although faith is afterwards said to have saved her, yet as it was faith working by love, and veneration, the latter might be said, in a popular sense, to be the *cause* of her salvation. The meaning of ὅτι ἠγάπησε πολὺ may be expressed by "inasmuch as she hath given full evidence of her love and attachment." Now that *implied faith* in the Messiah-ship of Jesus, and may be presumed to have sprung from true repentance. "Wherefore (saith our Lord) [since she hath so great a regard for me] her sins, her many sins, are forgiven; as she hath loved much, i. e. as her sins have been great, so is the forgiveness she shall have, great in proportion. Read ὅ τι, standing for καθ᾽ ὅτι, as ὅ τι is often used for διότι, or διὰ τί. See Note on Mark ix. 11.

The words which follow, ᾧ δὲ ὀλίγον — ἀγαπᾷ are not to be too much pressed. They were meant to glance at Simon, for his comparatively little attention.

48. ἀφέωνταί σου αἱ ἁμ.] "thy sins are (hereby) forgiven thee." Many Commentators say that this is doubtless a repetition of the consolatory assurance which Christ had on some previous occasion given to the woman. But this may be considered utterly unfounded. We have merely a *formal* pronunciation of that forgiveness which the foregoing words *implied*. So Euthym.: εἶπε αὐτῇ, ἵνα πληροφορηθῇ.

VIII. 1. κατὰ πόλιν.] Wets. rightly distinguishes between this expression and κατὰ τὴν πόλιν, the latter being said of *one*, the former of more than one. In fact, the κατὰ has the *distributive* sense, which takes place not only in numerals, but also in words which are not so, by an ellipsis, as the Grammarians think, of ἕκαστος. The sense is, "city by city."

2. Μαγδαληνή.] The best Commentators are agreed that there is no authority in Scripture for supposing *this* Mary to have been a harlot; nay, it should seem that she was a person of some consequence. Ἐξεληλύθει, "had been expelled." Neut. for passive, as often in the Gospels and Acts. Many recent Commentators take the ἑπτὰ as signifying "*many*," definite for indefinite, as in Matt. xii. 45. and xii. 26. But that idiom is not to be introduced unnecessarily; and here it is not very suitable.

3. ἐπιτρόπου.] The Commentators are not agreed on the exact office designated by ἐπίτροπος; which, as it denotes generally one who has an office committed to his charge, is of very extensive signification, and may denote Guardian, or Lieutenant of a province, or Treasurer, or house or land Steward, agent and manager. So Xen. Œcon. xii. 2. ἔχω ἐπιτρόπους ἐν τοῖς ἀγροῖς.

3. διηκόνουν] "supplied with the necessaries of life;" as Matth. iv. 11. xxvii. 35. Mark i. 13. xv. 41. This signification occurs also in Theophr. Char. ii. 4. For αὐτῷ a great number of MSS. and many Versions have αὐτοῖς, which is edited by Matth. and Scholz. But both external and internal evidence are rather in favour of the common reading.

8. εἰς.] This reading (for ἐπὶ) is found in many MSS. and Versions, and is adopted by almost every Editor from Wets. to Scholz, being the more difficult reading; whereas the other seems to be derived from Matth. and Mark. Εἰς occurs again in this sense infra xiv. 9.

MT. MK.
13. 4. οἱ μαθηταὶ αὐτοῦ, λέγοντες· τίς εἴη ἡ παραβολὴ αὕτη. Ὁ δὲ εἶπεν· 10
11 13 11 Ὑμῖν δέδοται γνῶναι τὰ μυστήρια τῆς βασιλείας τοῦ Θεοῦ· τοῖς δὲ
12 λοιποῖς ἐν παραβολαῖς· ἵνα βλέποντες μὴ βλέπωσι, καὶ ἀκούοντες μὴ
18 13 14 συνιῶσιν. Ἔστι δὲ αὕτη ἡ παραβολή· ὁ σπόρος ἐστὶν ὁ λόγος τοῦ 11
19 15 Θεοῦ· οἱ δὲ παρὰ τὴν ὁδὸν εἰσὶν οἱ ἀκούοντες· εἶτα ἔρχεται ὁ Διά- 12
βολος καὶ αἴρει τὸν λόγον ἀπὸ τῆς καρδίας αὐτῶν, ἵνα μὴ πιστεύσαν-
20 16 τες σωθῶσιν. Οἱ δὲ ἐπὶ τῆς πέτρας, οἳ, ὅταν ἀκούσωσι, μετὰ χαρᾶς 13
17 δέχονται τὸν λόγον· καὶ οὗτοι ῥίζαν οὐκ ἔχουσιν, οἳ πρὸς καιρὸν
22 18 πιστεύουσι, καὶ ἐν καιρῷ πειρασμοῦ ἀφίστανται. Τὸ δὲ εἰς τὰς ἀκάν- 14
19 θας πεσὸν, οὗτοί εἰσιν οἱ ἀκούσαντες, καὶ ὑπὸ μεριμνῶν καὶ πλούτου
καὶ ἡδονῶν τοῦ βίου πορευόμενοι συμπνίγονται, καὶ οὐ τελεσφοροῦσι.
23 20 Τὸ δὲ ἐν τῇ καλῇ γῇ, οὗτοί εἰσιν, οἵτινες ἐν καρδίᾳ καλῇ καὶ ἀγαθῇ 15
ἀκούσαντες τὸν λόγον κατέχουσι, καὶ καρποφοροῦσιν ἐν ὑπομονῇ.
21 Οὐδεὶς δὲ λύχνον ἅψας, καλύπτει αὐτὸν σκεύει, ἢ ὑποκάτω κλίνης 16
τίθησιν. ἀλλ' ἐπὶ λυχνίας ἐπιτίθησι, ἵνα οἱ εἰσπορευόμενοι βλέπωσι
22 τὸ φῶς. Οὐ γάρ ἐστι κρυπτὸν, ὃ οὐ φανερὸν γενήσεται· οὐδὲ ἀπό- 17
24 κρυφον ὃ οὐ γνωσθήσεται, καὶ εἰς φανερὸν ἔλθῃ. Βλέπετε οὖν πῶς 18
12 25 ἀκούετε· ὃς γὰρ ἂν ἔχῃ, δοθήσεται αὐτῷ· καὶ ὃς ἂν μὴ ἔχῃ, καὶ
12. 3. ὃ δοκεῖ ἔχειν, ἀρθήσεται ἀπ' αὐτοῦ.
46 31 Παρεγένοντο δὲ πρὸς αὐτὸν ἡ μήτηρ καὶ οἱ ἀδελφοὶ αὐτοῦ, καὶ οὐκ 19
47 32 ἠδύναντο συντυχεῖν αὐτῷ διὰ τὸν ὄχλον. Καὶ ἀπηγγέλη αὐτῷ, λεγόντων· 20
Ἡ μήτηρ σου καὶ οἱ ἀδελφοί σου ἑστήκασιν ἔξω, ἰδεῖν σε θέλοντες.
48 50 33 35 Ὁ δὲ ἀποκριθεὶς εἶπε πρὸς αὐτούς· Μήτηρ μου καὶ ἀδελφοί μου 21
οὗτοί εἰσιν οἱ τὸν λόγον τοῦ Θεοῦ ἀκούοντες καὶ ποιοῦντες αὐτόν.
8. 4. Καὶ ἐγένετο, ἐν μιᾷ τῶν ἡμερῶν, καὶ αὐτὸς ἐνέβη εἰς πλοῖον καὶ οἱ 22
18 35 μαθηταὶ αὐτοῦ, καὶ εἶπε πρὸς αὐτούς· Διέλθωμεν εἰς τὸ πέραν τῆς
24 37 λίμνης· καὶ ἀνήχθησαν. Πλεόντων δὲ αὐτῶν ἀφύπνωσε. καὶ κατέβη 23

9. *τίς εἴη ἡ παραβολὴ α.*] i. e. what might be the meaning of this parable. See Winer's Gr. Gr. § 35. 3. So Cebes Tab. *διήγησαι ἡμῖν — τί πότε ἐστιν ὁ μῦθος;*

10. [*Comp.* Matt. xi. 25, 26. 2 Cor. iii. 5. 14. Is. vi. 9. Ezek. xii. 2. Rom. xi. 8.]

14. *πορευόμενοι συμπνίγονται.*] Πορ. is best explained "in their progress through life," "as they proceed in life." So Euthym. *πολιτευόμενοι*. See Luke i. 6. In *ὑπὸ μεριμνῶν καὶ πλούτου* the sense (which is imperfectly developed) seems to be, "by the cares of poverty and the anxieties of riches." These are illustrated by passages of Theocrit. Idyl. xxi. and Eurip. Med. 599. adduced in Recens. Synop.

— *οὐ τελεσφοροῦσι.*] The word is used of trees or plants bringing fruit to maturity, and almost always with an Accus.

15. *καλῇ καὶ ἀγαθῇ.*] Beza and Grot. regard this as an expression *ex adytis Philosophiæ;* and they compare the expression of the Classical writers *καλὸς κἀγαθὸς* as said of one who is endowed with all the advantages of body, mind, fortune, &c. But the expression here simply designates a "thoroughly good heart," the *καλῇ* being used merely with reference to the thing compared, namely, the *ground* just before. So Xenophon often used the word of land or soil naturally fertile. Ἐν ὑπομονῇ is by some rendered "with patience;" by others, "with perseverance." Both senses may have place.

18. *ὃ δοκεῖ ἔχειν.*] *Δοκεῖ* is *not* (as many Commentators imagine) redundant here, and perhaps in very few of the many passages which they adduce. Luke has expressed something *more* than Matthew and Mark; namely, that what such a person yet retains is likely to be so soon lost, that he can hardly be said to have it. [*Comp.* infra xix. 26.]

20. *ἀπηγγέλη — λεγόντων.*] Most Commentators supply *τινῶν*, or *αὐτῶν*. But the construction of Genitive absolute is here harsh, and it should rather seem that *ἀπὸ* is to be fetched from the verb, or *ὑπὸ* supplied, together with *αὐτῶν* referring to *ὄχλον*, which is a noun of multitude. Ἰδεῖν is for *συντυχεῖν*, i. e. *λαλῆσαι*, as in Matth. (antecedent for consequent). So in Thucyd. iv. 125. and Xen. Cyr. iv. 6, 2.

21. [*Comp.* John xv. 14. 2 Cor. v. 16.]

23. *ἀφύπνωσε*] obdormivit. A rare sense, *ἀφυπνόω* and *ἀφυπνίζω* signifying in the Classical writers to raise oneself from sleep, to awake. The other occurs, however, in the LXX. (Judg. v. 27.) in Ignat. Martyr. § 7., and is noticed in the Glossaria Gr. Lat. Markl. thinks it was an Antioch-

MT. MK.

λαῖλαψ ἀνέμου εἰς τὴν λίμνην, καὶ συνεπληροῦντο, καὶ ἐκινδύνευον. 8. 4.
24 Προσελθόντες δὲ διήγειραν αὐτὸν, λέγοντες· Ἐπιστάτα, ἐπιστάτα, 25 38
ἀπολλύμεθα. Ὁ δὲ ἐγερθεὶς ἐπετίμησε τῷ ἀνέμῳ καὶ τῷ κλύδωνι τοῦ 26 39
25 ὕδατος· καὶ ἐπαύσαντο, καὶ ἐγένετο γαλήνη. Εἶπε δὲ αὐτοῖς· Ποῦ 40
ἐστιν ἡ πίστις ὑμῶν; Φοβηθέντες δὲ ἐθαύμασαν, λέγοντες πρὸς 27 41
ἀλλήλους· Τίς ἄρα οὗτός ἐστιν, ὅτι καὶ τοῖς ἀνέμοις ἐπιτάσσει καὶ
τῷ ὕδατι, καὶ ὑπακούουσιν αὐτῷ; 5.
26 Καὶ κατέπλευσαν εἰς τὴν χώραν τῶν Γαδαρηνῶν, ἥτις ἐστὶν ἀντιπέ- 28 1
27 ραν τῆς Γαλιλαίας. Ἐξελθόντι δὲ αὐτῷ ἐπὶ τὴν γῆν ὑπήντησεν αὐτῷ 2
ἀνήρ τις ἐκ τῆς πόλεως, ὃς εἶχε δαιμόνια ἐκ χρόνων ἱκανῶν, καὶ
ἱμάτιον οὐκ ἐνεδιδύσκετο, καὶ ἐν οἰκίᾳ οὐκ ἔμενεν, ἀλλ᾽ ἐν τοῖς μνή-
28 μασιν. Ἰδὼν δὲ τὸν Ἰησοῦν, καὶ ἀνακράξας, προσέπεσεν αὐτῷ, καὶ 3 6
φωνῇ μεγάλῃ εἶπε· Τί ἐμοὶ καὶ σοί, Ἰησοῦ, Υἱὲ τοῦ Θεοῦ τοῦ ὑψί- 29 7
29 στου; δέομαί σου, μή με βασανίσῃς. Παρήγγειλε γὰρ τῷ πνεύματι 8
τῷ ἀκαθάρτῳ ἐξελθεῖν ἀπὸ τοῦ ἀνθρώπου· πολλοῖς γὰρ χρόνοις συνηρ-
πάκει αὐτὸν, καὶ ἐδεσμεῖτο ἁλύσεσι καὶ πέδαις φυλασσόμενος, καὶ
διαῤῥήσσων τὰ δεσμὰ, ἠλαύνετο ὑπὸ τοῦ δαίμονος εἰς τὰς ἐρήμους.
30 Ἐπηρώτησε δὲ αὐτὸν ὁ Ἰησοῦς, λέγων· Τί σοι ἐστὶν ὄνομα; ὁ δὲ 9
31 εἶπε· Λεγεών· ὅτι δαιμόνια πολλὰ εἰσῆλθεν εἰς αὐτόν. Καὶ παρε- 10
32 κάλει αὐτὸν ἵνα μὴ ἐπιτάξῃ αὐτοῖς εἰς τὴν ἄβυσσον ἀπελθεῖν. Ἦν δὲ
ἐκεῖ ἀγέλη χοίρων ἱκανῶν βοσκομένων ἐν τῷ ὄρει· καὶ παρεκάλουν 30 11
αὐτὸν ἵνα ἐπιτρέψῃ αὐτοῖς εἰς ἐκείνους εἰσελθεῖν. καὶ ἐπέτρεψεν αὐ- 31 12
33 τοῖς. Ἐξελθόντα δὲ τὰ δαιμόνια ἀπὸ τοῦ ἀνθρώπου εἰσῆλθεν εἰς τοὺς 32 13
χοίρους· καὶ ὥρμησεν ἡ ἀγέλη κατὰ τοῦ κρημνοῦ εἰς τὴν λίμνην, καὶ
34 ἀπεπνίγη. Ἰδόντες δὲ οἱ βόσκοντες τὸ ‡ γεγενημένον ἔφυγον, καὶ 33 14

ism. But it rather seems to have been a *popular* use of the word.

25. κατέβη.] Stormy gusts are often said καταβαίνειν, or κατιέναι. So Thucyd. ii. 25. ἀνέμου κατιόντος, et sæpe. Plut. ap. Steph. Thes. Pausan. xi. 34. 3. κατιόντος ἔτι τοῦ πνεύματος. Pollux i. 103. κατιόντος τοῦ ἀνέμου.

—συνεπληροῦντο.] A popular catachresis, by which what happens to the *ship* is ascribed to the *sailors*. Examples are found in the best writers.

29. πολλοῖς χρόνοις.] Grot. and Rosenm. take this for πολλάκις. But as in ver. 27. we find ἐκ χρόνων ἱκανῶν, so Loesn. and Kuin. here take χρόνοις for *inde a pluribus annis*. And indeed that sense is frequent in the Classical writers, and sometimes occurs in the Sept. Loesn. cites Diod. Sic. xliv. A. and Wets. Plut. de Educ. xiv. 26. ἐν δεσμωτηρίῳ πολλοὺς κατεσάπη χρόνους. I add Thucyd. i. 96. τούτων — τοῖς χρόνοις οὐκ ἀκριβῶς ἐπεμνήσθη.

31. τὴν ἄβυσσον] scil. χώραν, i. e. Tartarus, that part of Hades in which the souls of the wicked were supposed to be confined. See 2 Pet. i. 14. Apoc. xx. 1. So also Eurip. Phœn. 1632. Ταρτάρου ἀβύσσου χάσματα. See Professor Stuart's instructive Essays on the words relating to Future Punishment, especially on שאול, ᾅδης, and τάρταρος. "Sheol (says he) was considered as a vast and wide domain or region, of which the grave seems to have been as it were only a part, or a kind of entrance way. It appears to have been regarded as extending deep down into the earth, even to its lowest abysses. It may also be remarked, that, as in the O. T. Sheol is a place to which the righteous go, as well as the wicked; and as our Saviour, subsequently to his death, is represented as being in Hades, Ps. xvi. 10. Acts ii. 27, 31; so it is not improbable that the general conception of Hades, as meaning *the region of the dead*, comprised both an *Elysium* and a *Tartarus* (to speak in Classical language), or a state of happiness and a state of misery." It is plain that by ἄβυσσος is meant this Tartarus. So 2 Pet. ii. 4, we have the expression ταρταρώσας. I would further observe that the etymology of the Heb. שאול need not have so perplexed Philologists. Notwithstanding the doubts of Gesenius, it is certainly derived (as Parkh. and others supposed) from שאל; yet not from the signification, to *seek*; nor has it any sense in common with ᾅδης. I suspect that the primitive physical signification of שאל was to *dig deep*, to *scoop out*, to *hollow*; and as men dig deep only in *search* of something, so the verb came to mean, figuratively, *search* or *seek* for. So Job iii. 21. "and dig for (i. e. anxiously seek) death more than for hidden treasures." Thus the word was originally merely the past participle of שאל, and denoted a pit thus dug. Indeed, the words *hell* and the *grave* (called in German Hölle) were originally only past participles of verbs meaning to *dig out*, to *hollow*.

34. τὸ γεγενημένον.] Many MSS. have τὸ γεγε-

MT. MK.
8. 5. [ἀπελθόντες] ἀπήγγειλαν εἰς τὴν πόλιν καὶ εἰς τοὺς ἀγρούς. Ἐξῆλθον 35
34 15 δὲ ἰδεῖν τὸ γεγονός· καὶ ἦλθον πρὸς τὸν Ἰησοῦν, καὶ εὗρον καθήμενον τὸν ἄνθρωπον, ἀφ᾽ οὗ τὰ δαιμόνια ἐξεληλύθει, ἱματισμένον καὶ
16 σωφρονοῦντα παρὰ τοὺς πόδας τοῦ Ἰησοῦ· καὶ ἐφοβήθησαν. Ἀπ- 36
17 ήγγειλαν δὲ αὐτοῖς καὶ οἱ ἰδόντες, πῶς ἐσώθη ὁ δαιμονισθείς. Καὶ 37
ἠρώτησαν αὐτὸν ἅπαν τὸ πλῆθος τῆς περιχώρου τῶν Γαδαρηνῶν ἀπελθεῖν ἀπ᾽ αὐτῶν· ὅτι φόβῳ μεγάλῳ συνείχοντο. αὐτὸς δὲ ἐμβὰς εἰς
18 τὸ πλοῖον ὑπέστρεψεν. Ἐδέετο δὲ αὐτοῦ ὁ ἀνήρ, ἀφ᾽ οὗ ἐξεληλύθει 38
τὰ δαιμόνια, εἶναι σὺν αὐτῷ. Ἀπέλυσε δὲ αὐτὸν ὁ Ἰησοῦς, λέγων·
19 Ὑπόστρεφε εἰς τὸν οἶκόν σου, καὶ διηγοῦ ὅσα ἐποίησέ σοι ὁ Θεός. 39
20 καὶ ἀπῆλθε, καθ᾽ ὅλην τὴν πόλιν κηρύσσων ὅσα ἐποίησεν αὐτῷ ὁ
9. Ἰησοῦς.
1 21 ἘΓΕΝΕΤΟ δὲ, ἐν τῷ ὑποστρέψαι τὸν Ἰησοῦν, ἀπεδέξατο αὐτὸν ὁ 40
ὄχλος· ἦσαν γὰρ πάντες προσδοκῶντες αὐτόν.
18 22 Καὶ ἰδοὺ, ἦλθεν ἀνὴρ ᾧ ὄνομα Ἰάειρος, καὶ αὐτὸς ἄρχων τῆς συνα- 41
γωγῆς ὑπῆρχε, καὶ πεσὼν παρὰ τοὺς πόδας τοῦ Ἰησοῦ, παρεκάλει
23 αὐτὸν εἰσελθεῖν εἰς τὸν οἶκον αὐτοῦ· ὅτι θυγάτηρ μονογενὴς ἦν αὐτῷ 42
24 ὡς ἐτῶν δώδεκα, καὶ αὕτη ἀπέθνησκεν. ἐν δὲ τῷ ὑπάγειν αὐτὸν οἱ
20 25 ὄχλοι συνέπνιγον αὐτόν. Καὶ γυνὴ οὖσα ἐν ῥύσει αἵματος ἀπὸ ἐτῶν 43
26 δώδεκα, ἥτις * ἰατροῖς προσαναλώσασα ὅλον τὸν βίον, οὐκ ἴσχυσεν ὑπ᾽
27 οὐδενὸς θεραπευθῆναι, προσελθοῦσα ὄπισθεν, ἥψατο τοῦ κρασπέδου 44
τοῦ ἱματίου αὐτοῦ· καὶ παραχρῆμα ἔστη ἡ ῥύσις τοῦ αἵματος αὐτῆς.
29 30 Καὶ εἶπεν ὁ Ἰησοῦς· Τίς ὁ ἁψάμενός μου; ἀρνουμένων δὲ πάντων, 45
31 εἶπεν ὁ Πέτρος καὶ οἱ μετ᾽ αὐτοῦ· Ἐπιστάτα, οἱ ὄχλοι συνέχουσί σε
καὶ ἀποθλίβουσι, καὶ λέγεις· Τίς ὁ ἁψάμενός μου; ὁ δὲ Ἰησοῦς 46
εἶπεν· Ἥψατό μου τίς· ἐγὼ γὰρ ἔγνων δύναμιν ἐξελθοῦσαν ἀπ᾽ ἐμοῦ.
33 Ἰδοῦσα δὲ ἡ γυνὴ ὅτι οὐκ ἔλαθε, τρέμουσα ἦλθε, καὶ προσπεσοῦσα 47
αὐτῷ, δι᾽ ἣν αἰτίαν ἥψατο αὐτοῦ ἀπήγγειλεν αὐτῷ ἐνώπιον παντὸς
22 34 τοῦ λαοῦ, καὶ ὡς ἰάθη παραχρῆμα. Ὁ δὲ εἶπεν αὐτῇ· Θάρσει θύ- 48
35 γατερ, ἡ πίστις σου σέσωκέ σε· πορεύου εἰς εἰρήνην. Ἔτι αὐτοῦ 49
λαλοῦντος, ἔρχεταί τις παρὰ τοῦ ἀρχισυναγώγου λέγων αὐτῷ· Ὅτι
36 τέθνηκεν ἡ θυγάτηρ σου· μὴ σκύλλε τὸν διδάσκαλον. Ὁ δὲ Ἰησοῦς 50
ἀκούσας, ἀπεκρίθη αὐτῷ, λέγων· Μὴ φοβοῦ· μόνον πίστευε, καὶ
23 37 σωθήσεται. [Εἰσ]ελθὼν δὲ εἰς τὴν οἰκίαν, οὐκ ἀφῆκεν εἰσελθεῖν οὐ- 51
δένα, εἰ μὴ Πέτρον καὶ * Ἰωάννην καὶ Ἰάκωβον, καὶ τὸν πατέρα τῆς

νὸς, which is received by Griesb. and Scholz; but without any reason. Ἀπελθόντες before ἀπήγγ. is rightly cancelled by all Editors, being absent from almost all MSS., and, no doubt, introduced from Matt. viii. 33.

37. [*Comp.* Acts xvi. 39.]

40. ἀπεδέξατο] "joyfully received him." A sense inherent in the ἀπὸ, and found in the Classical as well as the Scriptural writers.

42. ἀπέθνησκεν] "was (as it were) dying," "was near unto death." Συνέπνιγον, for συνέθλιβον, which is used by Mark.

43. οὖσα ἐν ῥύσει.] This use of εἶναι with ἐν, denoting to *labour under* a disorder, occurs elsewhere in Scripture. We may compare ἄνθρωπος ἐν πνεύματι ἀκαθάρτῳ in Mark v. 2. In either case the ἐν is for σὺν. For εἰς ἰατροὺς is written ἰατροῖς in almost all the best MSS., which is adopted by all Editors from Wets. to Scholz.

51. εἰσελθών.] Many MSS. have ἐλθὼν, which is received by Wets., Griesb., and Scholz. Καὶ Ἰωάννην καὶ Ἰάκωβον (for Ἰάκ. καὶ Ἰωάνν.) is found in all the best MSS. and Versions, and Theophyl., and is edited by Wets., Matth., Griesb., Tittm., and Scholz, who are probably right in so doing, as the mistake might easily arise from the καὶ — καί. Yet the common reading might be defended.

MT. MK

52 παιδὸς καὶ τὴν μητέρα. ἔκλαιον δὲ πάντες, καὶ ἐκόπτοντο αὐτήν. Ὁ 9. 5.
53 δὲ εἶπε· Μὴ κλαίετε· οὐκ ἀπέθανεν, ἀλλὰ καθεύδει. Καὶ κατεγέ- 24 38 39
54 λων αὐτοῦ, εἰδότες ὅτι ἀπέθανεν. Αὐτὸς δὲ ἐκβαλὼν ἔξω πάντας, καὶ 25 40
55 κρατήσας τῆς χειρὸς αὐτῆς, ἐφώνησε, λέγων· Ἡ παῖς, ἐγείρου. Καὶ 41 42
ἐπέστρεψε τὸ πνεῦμα αὐτῆς, καὶ ἀνέστη παραχρῆμα· καὶ διέταξεν
56 αὐτῇ δοθῆναι φαγεῖν. Καὶ ἐξέστησαν οἱ γονεῖς αὐτῆς· ὁ δὲ παρήγ- 43
γειλεν αὐτοῖς μηδενὶ εἰπεῖν τὸ γεγονός. 10. 6.
1 IX. ΣΥΓΚΑΛΕΣΑΜΕΝΟΣ δὲ τοὺς δώδεκα [μαθητὰς αὐτοῦ,] 1 7
ἔδωκεν αὐτοῖς δύναμιν καὶ ἐξουσίαν ἐπὶ πάντα τὰ δαιμόνια, καὶ νό-
2 σους θεραπεύειν· καὶ ἀπέστειλεν αὐτοὺς κηρύσσειν τὴν βασιλείαν τοῦ 7
3 Θεοῦ, καὶ ἰᾶσθαι τοὺς ἀσθενοῦντας. Καὶ εἶπε πρὸς αὐτούς· Μηδὲν 9 8
αἴρετε εἰς τὴν ὁδόν· μήτε ‡ ῥάβδους, μήτε πήραν, μήτε ἄρτον, μήτε 10
4 ἀργύριον· μήτε ἀνὰ δύο χιτῶνας ἔχειν. Καὶ εἰς ἣν ἂν οἰκίαν εἰσέλ- 11 10
5 θητε, ἐκεῖ μένετε, καὶ ἐκεῖθεν ἐξέρχεσθε. Καὶ ὅσοι ἂν μὴ δέξωνται 14 11

52. ἐκόπτοντο αὐτήν] "bewailed her." Κόπτεσθαι properly signifies to *beat* or *strike oneself*; and then, because that is the usual accompaniment of extreme grief, to *bewail*, *grieve for any one*. It answers to the Heb. ספר, which is followed by ל, *for*, or על, *over*, and has sometimes in the Sept. (as here) simply an Accusative, thus becoming a Deponent.

54. ἡ παῖς.] Nomin. for Vocat., which occurs also at vi. 25. x. 21. xii. 32. xviii. 11. and Mark v. 41., and sometimes in the Classical writers, especially the Attic ones. The words ἐκβαλὼν ἔξω πάντας καὶ are not found in some very ancient MSS. and Versions, are rejected by Schulz. and Bornem., and cancelled by Lachm. They certainly *may* have been introduced from the parallel passage of Mark. But as the MSS. are so very few (only about 8), may we not rather suspect an *accidental omission*?

IX. 1. μαθητὰς αὐτοῦ.] These words are omitted in very many of the best MSS., several Versions, and some Fathers; and are cancelled by almost every Editor from Wets. to Scholz. Some MSS. and those Versions which have not μαθ. αὐτοῦ have ἀποστόλους αὐτοῦ. Nothing, therefore, can be plainer than that *both* are from the margin. It may be said, indeed, that these words are confirmed by Matth. x. 1. But it is more probable that they have been introduced from thence. Better reasons may be imagined for their *insertion* than for their *omission*. The elliptical expression οἱ δώδεκα, for *the Twelve Apostles*, is frequent in the N. T., though, as might be expected, there are generally some MSS. which have ἀπόστολοι added. I cannot but here animadvert on the bad criticism and disingenuous spirit evinced by the supporters of the system which considers the Dæmoniacs as merely lunatics. For though dæmoniacs and lunatics would in this verse seem to be as plainly distinguished as words can make them, yet the persons in question seek to neutralize this by foisting an *alios* in their versions, as if ἄλλους were found in the text.

—καὶ νόσους θεραπεύειν.] This is, as Bornem. remarks, an elliptical form of expression for καὶ ἐξουσίαν θερ. νόσους, of which he adduces an apposite example from Xen. Anab. i. 2. 27. Σ. ἔδωκε Κύρῳ χρήματα πολλά, Κῦρος δ' ἐκείνῳ δῶρα — καὶ τὴν χώραν μηκέτι ἀφαρπάζεσθαι, τὰ δὲ ἡρπασμένα ἀνδράποδα ἀπολαμβάνειν. See Matth. Gr. Gr. § 532. a.

2. ἀπέστειλεν, &c.] *Comp.* Matt. x. 7. In the foregoing verse it is said, that he gave them power to cast out dæmons and to heal disorders. In this the sense is, that they had a commission to go forth and *exercise* that power, in conjunction with the preaching of the Gospel-Dispensation.

3. ῥάβδους.] Many MSS. have ῥάβδον, which is preferred by almost all the recent Editors. See Note on Matt. x. 10. Ἀνά, a-piece. So Matt. xx. 9. ἔλαβον ἀνὰ δηνάριον, and John ii. 6. ἀνὰ μετρητὰς δύο ἢ τρεῖς. On this *distributive* sense, see Bornem. and Matth. Gr. Gr. § 579. 3. The Commentators and Grammarians, however, seem wrong in supposing that in this idiom the numeral and noun belong to the ἀνά. They are rather to be referred to the *verb*; and the preposition is to be taken as put *absolutely* (thus becoming, as it were, an *adverb*) by an ellipsis of ἕκαστον, which is sometimes *expressed*, though generally left to be understood. Our word *apiece* well expresses the force of the idiom; being for *at-piece* (as it was formerly written) where piece coming from the Ital. pezzo (which is from the Germ. beissen, to bite; for piece and bit have the same origin), exactly answers to ἕκαστον, as well it may; since the idea of *separation* is quite as inherent in ἕκαστος as in *pezzo*, both, in fact, being originally *passive verbals*, signifying *broken off*, *separated*.

—ἔχειν.] This is usually explained as Infin. for Imperat. ἔχετε: a not unfrequent idiom, to lessen the harshness of which Philologists generally suppose an ellipse of an *Imperative of wish*, or of δεῖ. But it is better, with Herm. on Vig. p. 591, to suppose the idiom to be a relique of ancient simplicity of language, when a wish was expressed simply by a verb in the Infinitive. Of this there is a confirmation in the use of the Hebrew verb. The principle, however, cannot apply to the phraseology of later Greek writers, especially prose writers. It will usually be found that the Infinitive has a reference to some verb which has preceded, and to which the writer, inadvertently, *accommodates the construction*. Thus the idiom falls under the head of *Anantapodoton*; e. gr. here ἔχειν is used *as if* αἴρειν (referred to εἶπε, *bade*) had preceded, and not αἴρετε.

MT. MK.
10. 6. ὑμᾶς, ἐξερχόμενοι ἀπὸ τῆς πόλεως ἐκείνης· καὶ τὸν κονιορτὸν ἀπὸ τῶν
12 ποδῶν ὑμῶν ἀποτινάξατε, εἰς μαρτύριον ἐπ' αὐτούς. Ἐξερχόμενοι 6
13 δὲ διήρχοντο κατὰ τὰς κώμας, εὐαγγελιζόμενοι καὶ θεραπεύοντες παν-
14. ταχοῦ.
1 14 Ἤκουσε δὲ Ἡρώδης ὁ τετράρχης τὰ γινόμενα ὑπ' αὐτοῦ πάντα· 7
2 καὶ διηπόρει, διὰ τὸ λέγεσθαι ὑπό τινων, ὅτι Ἰωάννης ἐγήγερται ἐκ
15 νεκρῶν· ὑπό τινων δὲ, ὅτι Ἠλίας ἐφάνη· ἄλλων δὲ, ὅτι προφήτης 8
16 εἷς τῶν ἀρχαίων ἀνέστη. καὶ εἶπεν [ὁ] Ἡρώδης· Ἰωάννην ἐγὼ ἀπε- 9
κεφάλισα· τίς δέ ἐστιν οὗτος, περὶ οὗ ἐγὼ ἀκούω τοιαῦτα; καὶ ἐζήτει ἰδεῖν αὐτόν.

30 Καὶ ὑποστρέψαντες οἱ ἀπόστολοι διηγήσαντο αὐτῷ ὅσα ἐποίησαν. 10
31 Καὶ παραλαβὼν αὐτοὺς, ὑπεχώρησε κατ' ἰδίαν εἰς τόπον ἔρημον πόλεως
14 32 33 καλουμένης Βηθσαϊδά. Οἱ δὲ ὄχλοι γνόντες, ἠκολούθησαν αὐτῷ· καὶ 11
34 δεξάμενος αὐτοὺς, ἐλάλει αὐτοῖς περὶ τῆς βασιλείας τοῦ Θεοῦ, καὶ τοὺς
15 35 χρείαν ἔχοντας θεραπείας ἰᾶτο. Ἡ δὲ ἡμέρα ἤρξατο κλίνειν· προσελ- 12
36 θόντες δὲ οἱ δώδεκα εἶπον αὐτῷ· Ἀπόλυσον τὸν ὄχλον, ἵνα ἀπελθόντες εἰς τὰς κύκλῳ κώμας καὶ τοὺς ἀγροὺς καταλύσωσι, καὶ εὕρωσιν
16 37 ἐπισιτισμόν· ὅτι ὧδε ἐν ἐρήμῳ τόπῳ ἐσμέν. Εἶπε δὲ πρὸς αὐτούς· 13
17 Δότε αὐτοῖς ὑμεῖς φαγεῖν. οἱ δὲ εἶπον· Οὐκ εἰσὶν ἡμῖν πλεῖον ἢ
πέντε ἄρτοι καὶ * ἰχθύες δύο· εἰ μή τι πορευθέντες ἡμεῖς ἀγοράσωμεν
εἰς πάντα τὸν λαὸν τοῦτον βρώματα· ἦσαν γὰρ ὡσεὶ ἄνδρες πεντα- 14
19 39 κισχίλιοι. Εἶπε δὲ πρὸς τοὺς μαθητὰς αὐτοῦ· Κατακλίνατε αὐτοὺς
40 κλισίας, ἀνὰ πεντήκοντα· καὶ ἐποίησαν οὕτω, καὶ ἀνέκλιναν ἅπαντας. 15
41 Λαβὼν δὲ τοὺς πέντε ἄρτους καὶ τοὺς δύο ἰχθύας, ἀναβλέψας εἰς τὸν 16
οὐρανὸν, εὐλόγησεν αὐτοὺς, καὶ κατέκλασε, καὶ ἐδίδου τοῖς μαθηταῖς
20 42 43 παρατιθέναι τῷ ὄχλῳ. Καὶ ἔφαγον καὶ ἐχορτάσθησαν πάντες· καὶ 17
16. 8. ἤρθη τὸ περισσεῦσαν αὐτοῖς κλασμάτων κόφινοι δώδεκα.
13 27 ΚΑΙ ἐγένετο, ἐν τῷ εἶναι αὐτὸν προσευχόμενον καταμόνας, συνῆσαν 18
αὐτῷ οἱ μαθηταὶ, καὶ ἐπηρώτησεν αὐτοὺς, λέγων· Τίνα με λέγουσιν

5. *καὶ τὸν κον.*] Bornem. well renders the *καὶ adeo*, even; and he and Scholz have rightly removed the comma after *ἐκείνης*, as the construction of the sentence required; with which Bornem. compares Aristoph. Av. 1735. *διὰ σὲ τὰ πάντα κρατήσας καὶ* (even) *πάρεδρον Βασιλείαν ἔχει Διός*.

7. *διηπόρει*] "he was in doubt and perplexity," namely, what to think.

10. *πόλεως*] "of the city," or the district of Bethsaida.

12. *ἡμέρα ἤρξατο κλίνειν*.] *Κλίνειν* and its compounds are often used with *ἥλιος* of the declination of the sun to the horizon. Sometimes, as here, *ἡμέρα* is used instead of *ἥλιος*. On the present transaction, comp. John vi. 5. At *τὰς κύκλῳ* sub. *ἐν*, and *οὔσας*, or *κειμένας*. The ellips. is frequent in the Classical writers.

—*ἵνα καταλύσωσι*] "that they may seek *καταλύματα*, or lodgings;" as xix. 7. and Gen. xxiv. 23. (Sept.) The figure is derived (like that in our *stage* for *stayage*) from travellers unloading their beasts and ungirding themselves.

13. *ἰχθύες δύο*.] This, instead of *δύο ἰχθύες*, is found in a very great number of MSS., and is received by Wets., Matth., Griesb., Tittm., Knapp, and Scholz.

—*εἰ μή τι*.] There is here some obscurity, the sense being not fully developed. Hence Beza, Grot., Pisc., and Wolf suppose an ellipsis of *οὐ δυνατόν ἐστι*, or *οὐ δυνάμεθα*. But this is so harsh, that Kypke, Kuin., and others seek to remove the difficulty by taking *εἰ μή τι* for *num quid*, and making the sentence interrogative. For that signification, however, they adduce no sufficient authority. It is better, therefore, to adhere to the usual signification of *εἰ μὴ*, i. e. *unless*; and suppose (with the Syriac Translator, Casaub., Valckn., Schleus., and Wahl) that the *τι* has what Hoogev. calls the *vis στοχαστική*, and signifies *fortasse*, or perhaps *forsooth*. It should seem that the apostles, through delicacy, do not fully express their meaning, which was probably this: "We have no more than, &c. unless, forsooth, we should go and purchase [sufficient food] for all this multitude."

14. *κλισίας*.] Sub. *κατά*. The word is very rare in the Classical writers, but is found in Josephus.

MT. MK.

19 οἱ ὄχλοι εἶναι; Οἱ δὲ ἀποκριθέντες εἶπον· Ἰωάννην τὸν βαπτιστήν· 16. 8.
ἄλλοι δὲ Ἠλίαν· ἄλλοι δὲ, ὅτι προφήτης τις τῶν ἀρχαίων ἀνέστη. 14 28
20 Εἶπε δὲ αὐτοῖς· Ὑμεῖς δὲ τίνα με λέγετε εἶναι; ἀποκριθεὶς δὲ [ὁ] 15 29
21 Πέτρος εἶπε· Τὸν Χριστὸν τοῦ Θεοῦ. Ὁ δὲ ἐπιτιμήσας αὐτοῖς, 20 30
22 παρήγγειλε μηδενὶ εἰπεῖν τοῦτο· εἰπὼν, ὅτι δεῖ τὸν Υἱὸν τοῦ ἀνθρώ- 21 31
που πολλὰ παθεῖν, καὶ ἀποδοκιμασθῆναι ἀπὸ τῶν πρεσβυτέρων καὶ
ἀρχιερέων καὶ γραμματέων, καὶ ἀποκτανθῆναι, καὶ τῇ τρίτῃ ἡμέρᾳ
ἐγερθῆναι.
23 Ἔλεγε δὲ πρὸς πάντας· Εἴ τις θέλει ὀπίσω μου ἐλθεῖν, ἀπαρνη- 24 34
σάσθω ἑαυτὸν, καὶ ἀράτω τὸν σταυρὸν αὐτοῦ [καθ᾽ ἡμέραν,] καὶ
24 ἀκολουθείτω μοι. Ὃς γὰρ ἂν θέλῃ τὴν ψυχὴν αὐτοῦ σῶσαι, ἀπολέσει 25 35
αὐτήν· ὃς δ᾽ ἂν ἀπολέσῃ τὴν ψυχὴν αὐτοῦ ἕνεκεν ἐμοῦ, οὗτος σώσει
25 αὐτήν. Τί γὰρ ὠφελεῖται ἄνθρωπος κερδήσας τὸν κόσμον ὅλον, ἑαυ- 26 36
26 τὸν δὲ ἀπολέσας ἢ ζημιωθείς; Ὃς γὰρ ἂν ἐπαισχυνθῇ με καὶ τοὺς 38
ἐμοὺς λόγους, τοῦτον ὁ Υἱὸς τοῦ ἀνθρώπου ἐπαισχυνθήσεται, ὅταν
ἔλθῃ ἐν τῇ δόξῃ αὐτοῦ καὶ τοῦ Πατρὸς καὶ τῶν ἁγίων ἀγγέλων. 9.
27 Λέγω δὲ ὑμῖν ἀληθῶς· εἰσί τινες τῶν ὧδε ἑστηκότων, οἳ οὐ μὴ γεύ- 28 1
σονται θανάτου, ἕως ἂν ἴδωσι τὴν βασιλείαν τοῦ Θεοῦ. 17.
28 Ἐγένετο δὲ μετὰ τοὺς λόγους τούτους ὡσεὶ ἡμέραι ὀκτὼ, καὶ παρα- 1 2
λαβὼν [τὸν] Πέτρον καὶ Ἰωάννην καὶ Ἰάκωβον, ἀνέβη εἰς τὸ ὄρος
29 προσεύξασθαι. Καὶ ἐγένετο, ἐν τῷ προσεύχεσθαι αὐτὸν, τὸ εἶδος τοῦ 2 3
προσώπου αὐτοῦ ἕτερον, καὶ ὁ ἱματισμὸς αὐτοῦ λευκὸς ἐξαστράπτων.

20. ὁ Π.] The ὁ is omitted in many good MSS., and is cancelled by Matth. and Scholz.

22. The alteration in punctuation which I have adopted in τοῦτο· εἰπὼν, ὅτι seems called for by propriety, and is confirmed by the parallel passages of Matthew and Mark. This *narrative* sense of εἰπεῖν is very frequent.

23. καθ᾽ ἡμέραν.] The Editors and Critics are in doubt as to the genuineness of this expression. It is *rejected* by Wets., Matth., and Scholz, but *retained* by Griesb., Knapp., Tittm., and Vat. External evidence is pretty equally balanced; the Alexandrian recension and almost all the Versions having it, and the Constant., with the other Versions, and several Fathers, being without it. Griesb. thinks it was removed by the *librarii*, as not being in the other Gospels. But he adduces no example of a similar curtailment from the same cause. Matthæi, on the contrary, thinks it was *introduced* from the Fathers and Interpreters; who had perhaps in view 1 Cor. xv. 31. And of this he adduces some strong proofs. I entirely agree with him; and would add that the same *asceticism*, which induced several of the Fathers to *throw out* the εἰκῇ at Matt. v. 22, *may* have induced them to *introduce* καθ᾽ ἡμέραν here. But I rather think that they only brought it forward to complete the *sense*, not the *text*; and that having been taken from them by the *Scholiasts*, it was occasionally marked in the *margin* of copies, and then was introduced into the text of the *transcripts*. It was not, however, I conceive, introduced *directly* from the Fathers, or the Interpreters. It was, no doubt, at first borrowed by the *Scholiasts*; and from them was marked in the *margin* of copies, from whence careless scribes introduced it into the text.

24. [*Comp.* Matthew x. 39. xvi. 25. John xii. 25.]

25. ζημιωθείς.] Repeat ἑαυτὸν in the sense ἑαυτοῦ ψυχήν. Herodot. vii. 39. has τὴν ψυχὴν ζημιώσεται.

26. [*Comp.* infra xii. 9. Matt. x. 33.]

28. ἐγένετο — ὀκτώ.] There is here something seemingly anomalous in the construction; to remove which, some recur to the idiom whereby in Hebrew and Hellenistical phraseology verbs singular are united with nouns plural. But that principle is inapplicable here. And as to ἐγένοντο, which some would read, it is a mere conjecture. The truth is, that ἐγένετο is not the true verb to ἡμέραι, but, together with δὲ, constitutes (by an ellipse of τοῦτο) a *formula*, frequent in St. Luke, which merely serves to introduce some new narration. Thus ἐγένετο δὲ, &c. will be connected with καὶ παραλαβών; and consequently ὡσεὶ ἡμέραι ὀκτὼ will be a *parenthetical epanorthosis* of the preceding μετὰ τ. λ. τ. As to those nouns denoting time, when put in the Nominative, (among which we may reckon ὅσαι ἡμέραι for ὁσημέραι, which occurs in the common text of Thucyd. viii. 64,) there is manifestly an ellipsis of a verb in the plural, either εἰσι or ἦσαν, according to the context. See Hom. Od. ξ. 93. However, the expression sometimes (as in the case of ὅσαι ἡμέραι) becomes an *adverbial phrase*, and afterwards an adverb. Τὸν is omitted in very many MSS. and early Editions, and is cancelled by Matth., Griesb., and Scholz, perhaps without sufficient reason.

29. λευκὸς ἐξ.] "very dazzling white." The ἐξ. is intensive.

MT. MK.
17. 9. *Καὶ ἰδοὺ, ἄνδρες δύο συνελάλουν αὐτῷ, οἵτινες ἦσαν Μωϋσῆς καὶ* 30
3 4 *Ἠλίας· οἳ, ὀφθέντες ἐν δόξῃ, ἔλεγον τὴν ἔξοδον αὐτοῦ, ἣν ἔμελλε πλη-* 31
ροῦν ἐν Ἱερουσαλήμ. Ὁ δὲ Πέτρος καὶ οἱ σὺν αὐτῷ ἦσαν βεβαρημένοι 32
ὕπνῳ· διαγρηγορήσαντες δὲ εἶδον τὴν δόξαν αὐτοῦ, καὶ τοὺς δύο ἄν-
δρας τοὺς συνεστῶτας αὐτῷ. Καὶ ἐγένετο, ἐν τῷ διαχωρίζεσθαι αὐ- 33
4 5 *τοὺς ἀπ᾽ αὐτοῦ, εἶπεν ὁ Πέτρος πρὸς τὸν Ἰησοῦν. Ἐπιστάτα, καλόν*
ἐστιν ἡμᾶς ὧδε εἶναι· καὶ ποιήσωμεν σκηνὰς τρεῖς, μίαν σοὶ, καὶ
5 6 * *μίαν Μωϋσεῖ, καὶ μίαν Ἠλίᾳ· μὴ εἰδὼς ὃ λέγει. Ταῦτα δὲ αὐτοῦ* 34
7 *λέγοντος, ἐγένετο νεφέλη καὶ ἐπεσκίασεν αὐτούς· ἐφοβήθησαν δὲ ἐν τῷ*
ἐκείνους εἰσελθεῖν εἰς τὴν νεφέλην· καὶ φωνὴ ἐγένετο ἐκ τῆς νεφέλης, 35
λέγουσα· Οὗτός ἐστιν ὁ Υἱός μου ὁ ἀγαπητός· αὐτοῦ ἀκούετε. καὶ, 36
ἐν τῷ γενέσθαι τὴν φωνὴν, εὑρέθη ὁ Ἰησοῦς μόνος. καὶ αὐτοὶ ἐσίγησαν,
καὶ οὐδενὶ ἀπήγγειλαν ἐν ἐκείναις ταῖς ἡμέραις οὐδὲν ὧν ἑωράκασιν.
Ἐγένετο δὲ ἐν τῇ ἑξῆς ἡμέρᾳ, κατελθόντων αὐτῶν ἀπὸ τοῦ ὄρους, 37
συνήντησεν αὐτῷ ὄχλος πολύς. Καὶ ἰδοὺ, ἀνὴρ ἀπὸ τοῦ ὄχλου ἀνεβό- 38
*ησε, λέγων· Διδάσκαλε, δέομαί σου * ἐπιβλέψαι ἐπὶ τὸν υἱόν μου, ὅτι*
μονογενής ἐστί μοι· καὶ ἰδοὺ, πνεῦμα λαμβάνει αὐτὸν, καὶ ἐξαίφνης 39
κράζει, καὶ σπαράσσει αὐτὸν μετὰ ἀφροῦ, καὶ μόγις ἀποχωρεῖ ἀπ᾽
αὐτοῦ, συντρῖβον αὐτόν. Καὶ ἐδεήθην τῶν μαθητῶν σου, ἵνα ἐκβά- 40
λωσιν αὐτὸ, καὶ οὐκ ἠδυνήθησαν. Ἀποκριθεὶς δὲ ὁ Ἰησοῦς εἶπεν· 41
Ὦ γενεὰ ἄπιστος καὶ διεστραμμένη! ἕως πότε ἔσομαι πρὸς ὑμᾶς,
καὶ ἀνέξομαι ὑμῶν; προσάγαγε τὸν υἱόν σου ὧδε. Ἔτι δὲ προσερ- 42
χομένου αὐτοῦ, ἔῤῥηξεν αὐτὸν τὸ δαιμόνιον καὶ συνεσπάραξεν· ἐπε-
τίμησε δὲ ὁ Ἰησοῦς τῷ πνεύματι τῷ ἀκαθάρτῳ, καὶ ἰάσατο τὸν παῖδα·
καὶ ἀπέδωκεν αὐτὸν τῷ πατρὶ αὐτοῦ. ἐξεπλήσσοντο δὲ πάντες ἐπὶ τῇ 43
μεγαλειότητι τοῦ Θεοῦ. Πάντων δὲ θαυμαζόντων ἐπὶ πᾶσιν, οἷς ἐποί-

30. *ὀφθέντες ἐν δ.*] "appearing with a resplendent light." See supra ii. 9.

31. *τὴν ἔξοδον.*] This word often signifies a *military expedition*, both in the Scriptural and Classical writers. Hence some have imagined that it here figuratively represents the *contest* our Lord was afterwards to maintain against the rebellious Jews, on his advent at the destruction of Jerusalem. But this is neither warranted by the words, nor permitted by the context. The best Commentators since the time of Grot. are agreed, that *ἔξοδος* is here used to denote *death*; by a euphemism common both in the Scriptural and Classical writers, and indeed found in every language; and which is justly considered among the allusions that have preserved that most ancient of traditions, the immortality of the soul.

32. [*Comp.* Dan. viii. 18. x. 9.]

33. *μίαν Μωϋσεῖ.*] This, instead of *Μωϋσεῖ μίαν*, is found in almost all the best MSS. and Versions, with the Edit. Princ.; and has been rightly edited by Matth., Griesb., Vat., and Scholz.

35. [*Comp.* Matt. iii. 17. Mark i. 11. 2 Pet. i. 17.]

38. *ἐπιβλέψαι.*] The *textus receptus* has *ἐπίβλεψον*. But almost all the best MSS. have *ἐπιβλέψαι*, which has been accordingily edited by Matth., Griesb., Vater, Tittm., and Scholz. Bornem., however, makes well founded objections to that reading, as being in opposition to the *usus loquendi* of St. Luke, and he would read *ἐπιβλέψαι*, from some MSS., confirmed by a similar idiom in Acts xxv. 3. I have received this, because the Scribes of the other MSS. might easily mistake in so small a matter.

40. *ἐκβάλωσιν.*] This, for *ἐκβάλλ.*, is edited by Matth., Griesb., and Scholz.

41. *πρὸς ὑμᾶς*] *apud vos.* Equivalent to the *μεθ᾽ ὑμῶν* of Matthew. The same signification is found in John i. 1. *Ἀνέξομαι ὑμῶν*, "shall I bear with you." This sense is frequent in the N. T., and sometimes occurs in the Classical writers, though with the *Accusative*.

— *τὸν — ὧδε.*] This (instead of *ὧδε τὸν υἱόν σου*) is found in almost all the best MSS., and the Ed. Pr., and is received by Matth., Griesb., Vat., and Scholz.

43. *ἐπὶ τῇ μεγ. τοῦ Θεοῦ*] "at the mightiness of God as manifested in Christ." *Μεγαλειότης* is a word which, in Scripture, is almost appropriated to designating *Divine* power. So it is used in Acts xix. 27. of Diana; and in 2 Pet. i. 16. of *Christ*, thus showing Peter's belief in the divinity of our Lord.

44. *θέσθε — ὦτα ὑμῶν.*] Equivalent to *θέσθε εἰς τὰς καρδίας*, which occurs in Luke xxi. 14. "Let these sayings sink into your ears," i. e. attend to and lay them to heart.

44 ησεν ὁ Ἰησοῦς, εἶπε πρὸς τοὺς μαθητὰς αὐτοῦ· [a] Θέσθε ὑμεῖς εἰς a Matt. 16. 21. & 17. 22.
τὰ ὦτα ὑμῶν τοὺς λόγους τούτους· ὁ γὰρ Υἱὸς τοῦ ἀνθρώπου μέλλει Mark 9. 31. infr. 18. 32. Acts 1. 23.
45 παραδίδοσθαι εἰς χεῖρας ἀνθρώπων. [b] Οἱ δὲ ἠγνόουν τὸ ῥῆμα τοῦτο, b Supr. 2. 50. infr. 18. 34.
καὶ ἦν παρακεκαλυμμένον ἀπ᾽ αὐτῶν, ἵνα μὴ αἴσθωνται αὐτό· καὶ Mark 9. 32.
ἐφοβοῦντο ἐρωτῆσαι αὐτὸν περὶ τοῦ ῥήματος τούτου.
46 [c] Εἰσῆλθε δὲ διαλογισμὸς ἐν αὐτοῖς, τὸ, τίς ἂν εἴη μείζων αὐτῶν. c Matt. 18. 1. Mark 9. 33. infr. 22. 24.
47 Ὁ δὲ Ἰησοῦς ἰδὼν τὸν διαλογισμὸν τῆς καρδίας αὐτῶν, ἐπιλαβόμενος
48 παιδίου, ἔστησεν αὐτὸ παρ᾽ ἑαυτῷ, [d] καὶ εἶπεν αὐτοῖς· Ὃς ἐὰν δέξη- d Matt. 18. 5. Mark 9. 37.
ται τοῦτο τὸ παιδίον ἐπὶ τῷ ὀνόματί μου, ἐμὲ δέχεται· καὶ ὃς ἐὰν ἐμὲ infr. 10. 16. John. 13. 20.
δέξηται, δέχεται τὸν ἀποστείλαντά με. Ὁ γὰρ μικρότερος ἐν πᾶσιν Matt. 23. 11. infr. 14. 11. & 18. 14.
ὑμῖν ὑπάρχων, οὗτος ἔσται μέγας.
49 [e] Ἀποκριθεὶς δὲ ὁ Ἰωάννης εἶπεν· Ἐπιστάτα, εἴδομέν τινα ἐπὶ τῷ e Mark 9. 38.
ὀνόματί σου ἐκβάλλοντα [τὰ] δαιμόνια· καὶ ἐκωλύσαμεν αὐτὸν, ὅτι
50 οὐκ ἀκολουθεῖ μεθ᾽ ἡμῶν. [f] Καὶ εἶπε πρὸς αὐτὸν ὁ Ἰησοῦς· Μὴ f Matt. 12. 30. Mark. 9. 40. infr. 11. 23.
κωλύετε· ὃς γὰρ οὐκ ἔστι καθ᾽ ἡμῶν, ὑπὲρ ἡμῶν ἐστιν.
51 [g] ἘΓΕΝΕΤΟ δὲ ἐν τῷ συμπληροῦσθαι τὰς ἡμέρας τῆς ἀναλήψεως g Mark 16. 19. Acts 1. 2.
αὐτοῦ, καὶ αὐτὸς τὸ πρόσωπον αὐτοῦ ἐστήριξε τοῦ πορεύεσθαι εἰς Ἱε-
52 ρουσαλήμ. Καὶ ἀπέστειλεν ἀγγέλους πρὸ προσώπου αὐτοῦ· καὶ
πορευθέντες εἰσῆλθον εἰς κώμην Σαμαρειτῶν, ὥστε ἑτοιμάσαι αὐτῷ.

45. ἵνα μὴ αἰσθ.] The best Commentators are agreed, that ἵνα is for ὥστε, *adeo ut*, *insomuch that*, a very frequent sense. The sense is: "And it was hidden (i. e. obscure) to them, so that they did not understand it." "They understood (says Kuin.) the *words* of Christ, but were at a loss how to reconcile them with their preconceived opinion, (founded on their own traditions) that the Messiah should *live for ever*, or with the great things they expected from him." These prejudices, in after ages, led to the *distinction* made by the Rabbins between *Messiah Ben Joseph*, who was to die, and *Messiah Ben David*, who was to triumph and live for ever. See Whitby. Some recent Commentators have endeavoured (after Campb.) to revive the interpretation of the early Translators; who take ἵνα in the ordinary sense *to the end that*, as expressing something *intentional*. And it is not to be denied, that predictions were sometimes intentionally expressed darkly, that they might not be thoroughly understood. But that principle must not be unnecessarily called in. Campb. justly admits, that "if the Evangelists had employed an *adjective* (as κρυπτὰ) for the past participle, ἵνα might better have been interpreted *so that*." If, however, no *better* reason can be given for the other interpretation than *that*, it cannot stand; for what is so common as the use of a past participle for an adjective? Are there not hundreds of past participles in both the ancient and modern languages used as adjectives, and a still greater number of adjectives which were once past participles, but have ceased to be such, and have become purely adjectives?

46. τὸ, τίς, &c.] This use of τὸ, in reference not to a *noun*, but to a *sentence*, or part of a sentence, is almost peculiar to St. Luke, though it occurs also in Matt. xix. 18, and Mark ix. 23. (Campb.) In fact, the neuter Article (to use the words of Winer, Gr. Gr. p. 54.) "stands before all propositions which are cited as proverbs, or maxims, or which on account of their importance require to be made distinctly prominent."

49. τά.] This is omitted in very many MSS., and is cancelled by Matth., Griesb., and Scholz. But the case is doubtful; for Critical reasons may be adduced both ways.

— οὐκ ἀκολουθεῖ μεθ' ἡμῶν.] The sense is, "does not belong to our company of disciples," "is not our fellow disciple." The phrase is supposed to have been formed from the custom of the Jewish Doctors (like that of the Greek Philosophers), of being accompanied by their disciples wherever they went. But it is found also in the Classical writers. See Lobeck on Phrynicus, p. 353, sq.

50. ὃς γὰρ — ἡμῶν.] See Note on Mark ix. 40.

51. συμπλ. τὰς ἡμέρας τῆς ἀναλ. α.] Συμπληροῦσθαι, when used of *time*, denotes such a completion of a period between two given periods as that the latter is *fully come*. Here it is, as often, taken *populariter*; an event being thus spoken of as *come*, when it is *very near at hand*. On the sense of ἀναλήψεως the Commentators are not agreed. Some take it to signify a *removal*, others a *lifting up*, i. e. on the cross: interpretations alike inadmissible. The true one is, no doubt, that of the Syr. and Arab., Euthym., Beza, De Dieu, Grot., and others down to Rosenm., Kuin., Schleus., and Wahl, who understand it of our Lord's *ascension into heaven*. The *noun*, indeed, does not elsewhere occur either in the N. T. or the LXX except in 2 Kings ii. 11. of the *translation* of Enoch; but the *verb* ἀναλαμβάνειν is often used to denote Christ's ascension, ex. g. Acts i. 2; ii. 23. 1 Tim. iii. 16. An ἀνάληψις occurs in Test. xii. Patr. in Fabric. Cod. Pseud. i. p. 585, and in the name of a Treatise, called ἀνάληψις Μωϋσέως.

— τὸ πρόσωπον α. ἐστήριξε.] This is best explained as a Hobraism formed from שום פנים, which often in the Sept. denotes to firmly determine and resolve. So the Pers. Vers. renders "positum

h John 4. 4, 9. [h] Καὶ οὐκ ἐδέξαντο αὐτὸν, ὅτι τὸ πρόσωπον αὐτοῦ ἦν πορευόμενον εἰς 53
i 2 Kings 1. 10, 12. Ἱερουσαλήμ. [i] Ἰδόντες δὲ οἱ μαθηταὶ αὐτοῦ Ἰάκωβος καὶ Ἰωάννης 54
εἶπον· Κύριε, θέλεις εἴπωμεν πῦρ καταβῆναι ἀπὸ τοῦ οὐρανοῦ, καὶ
ἀναλῶσαι αὐτοὺς, ὡς καὶ Ἠλίας ἐποίησε; στραφεὶς δὲ ἐπετίμησεν αὐ- 55
k John 3. 17. & 12. 47. τοῖς, καὶ εἶπεν· Οὐκ οἴδατε οἵου πνεύματός ἐστε ὑμεῖς; [[k] ὁ γὰρ 56
Υἱὸς τοῦ ἀνθρώπου οὐκ ἦλθε ψυχὰς ἀνθρώπων ἀπολέσαι, ἀλλὰ σῶσαι.]
MT. 8. καὶ ἐπορεύθησαν εἰς ἑτέραν κώμην.
19 Ἐγένετο δὲ, πορευομένων αὐτῶν ἐν τῇ ὁδῷ, εἶπέ τις πρὸς αὐτόν· 57
Ἀκολουθήσω σοι ὅπου ἂν ἀπέρχῃ, κύριε. Καὶ εἶπεν αὐτῷ ὁ Ἰησοῦς· 58
20 Αἱ ἀλώπεκες φωλεοὺς ἔχουσι, καὶ τὰ πετεινὰ τοῦ οὐρανοῦ κατασκηνώ-
σεις· ὁ δὲ Υἱὸς τοῦ ἀνθρώπου οὐκ ἔχει ποῦ τὴν κεφαλὴν κλίνῃ.
21 Εἶπε δὲ πρὸς ἕτερον· Ἀκολούθει μοι. ὁ δὲ εἶπε· Κύριε, ἐπίτρεψόν 59
22 μοι ἀπελθόντι πρῶτον θάψαι τὸν πατέρα μου. Εἶπε δὲ αὐτῷ ὁ Ἰη- 60
σοῦς· Ἄφες τοὺς νεκροὺς θάψαι τοὺς ἑαυτῶν νεκρούς· σὺ δὲ ἀπελ-
l 1 Kings 19. 20. θὼν διάγγελλε τὴν βασιλείαν τοῦ Θεοῦ. [l] Εἶπε δὲ καὶ ἕτερος· Ἀκο- 61
λουθήσω σοι, κύριε· πρῶτον δὲ ἐπίτρεψόν μοι ἀποτάξασθαι τοῖς εἰς
τὸν οἶκόν μου. Εἶπε δὲ πρὸς αὐτὸν ὁ Ἰησοῦς· Οὐδεὶς ἐπιβαλὼν τὴν 62
χεῖρα αὐτοῦ ἐπ᾽ ἄροτρον, καὶ βλέπων εἰς τὰ ὀπίσω, εὔθετός ἐστιν εἰς
τὴν βασιλείαν τοῦ Θεοῦ.

X. ΜΕΤΑ δὲ ταῦτα ἀνέδειξεν ὁ Κύριος καὶ ἑτέρους ἑβδομήκοντα, 1
καὶ ἀπέστειλεν αὐτοὺς ἀνὰ δύο πρὸ προσώπου αὐτοῦ, εἰς πᾶσαν πόλιν

firmum fecit;" and Valckn., "firmiter animo destinavit."

53. ὅτι τὸ πρόσωπον αὐ. ἦν πορευόμενον, &c.] This phrase is Hebraic (so in 2 Sam. xvii. 11. ופניך הלכים בקרב, which is rendered by the LXX. καὶ τὸ πρόσωπόν σου πορευόμενον ἐν μέσῳ αὐτῶν), and the sense is, "when they knew that he was travelling to Jerusalem."

54. ἀναλῶσαι] "to destroy." This signification is common both in the Scriptural and Classical writers, and is applied to destruction by *fire*, in Gen. xli. 30. Ez. v. 12. On the wide difference between the case adverted to by the Apostles and their *own*, see Grot. and Whitby.

55. οὐκ οἴδατε — ἐστε.] Most recent Commentators take this sentence *interrogatively*, rendering, "know ye not with what spirit and disposition ye ought to be actuated [as my disciples]?" The ancient and the earlier modern ones take it *declaratively*, "Ye know not with what disposition ye are actuated [and whither it would hurry you];" ye do not consider the unsuitableness of what you propose. The latter interpretation is preferable; for the former certainly does some violence to the words by making ἐστε mean "ye ought to be." The whole clause, and the introductory words καὶ εἶπεν are omitted in many MSS., Versions, and Fathers, and are suspected by some Editors not to be genuine; but without cause. There is no more reason to suspect the genuineness of *this* clause than of the preceding. The MSS. in which the *latter* is not found, are, with very few exceptions, the same as omit the former. And there is little doubt but that in these MSS. the words were *omitted* by the carelessness of the Scribes; whose blunder, I suspect, was occasioned by the two καί's, each of which probably commenced a line in the very ancient originals of the Uncial MSS.

61. ἀποτάξασθαι τοῖς, &c.] Heins. and Doddr. apply the words to the man's *possessions*, supposing an ellipse of κτήμασι; and they take the sense to be, "to arrange and settle my affairs." But this is very harsh. The common interpretation, by which τοῖς εἰς τὸν οἶκον is taken for τοῖς οἰκείοις, yields a sense so simple and natural, that we cannot doubt its truth. And of the sense *to bid farewell* in ἀποτ. abundant examples have been adduced by Kypke.

62. οὐδεὶς ἐπιβαλὼν — Θεοῦ.] We have here an admonition couched under a figure derived from the *ploughman;* who must keep his eyes intent on his work, and not permit them to be turned away to any other object, otherwise his labour will be fruitless. See Hesiod. Op. D. ii. 61. and Theocr. Id. 10. init. Ἐπιβάλλειν χεῖρά τινι is often used of undertaking any work. The ἀπόδοσις (as Grot. remarks) is here (as often) mingled with the comparison. *Turning back* implies *inattention*, or preference to some other employment than that we are engaged in. So Lucian. Catapl. cited by Wets. ἐπιστρέφονται γοῦν εἰς τὰ ὀπίσω, ὥσπερ οἱ δυσέρωτες. Similar is the Pythagorean maxim in Simplic. on Epict. 332. cited by Grot. εἰς τὸ ἱερὸν ἀπερχόμενος μὴ ἐπιστρέφου.

X. 1. ἀνέδειξεν — καὶ ἑτέρους] "appointed seventy others also," i. e. besides the Apostles. Some few MSS., Versions, and Fathers, read ἑβδ. δύο. But their authority is weak; and I suspect that the B was derived from the K following. Those two letters are in MSS. written in the uncial character, frequently confounded. Some, however, are of opinion that 70 is a round number for 72, the number, they say, of the Elders

2 καὶ τόπον οὗ ἔμελλεν αὐτὸς ἔρχεσθαι. [m] Ἔλεγεν οὖν πρὸς αὐτούς· m Matt. 9. 37. John 4. 35. 2 Thess. 3. 1.
Ὁ μὲν θερισμὸς πολὺς, οἱ δὲ ἐργάται ὀλίγοι· δεήθητε οὖν τοῦ κυ-
ρίου τοῦ θερισμοῦ, ὅπως ἐκβάλῃ ἐργάτας εἰς τὸν θερισμὸν αὐτοῦ.
3 [n] Ὑπάγετε· ἰδοὺ ἐγὼ ἀποστέλλω ὑμᾶς ὡς ἄρνας ἐν μέσῳ λύκων. n Matt. 10. 16.
4 [o] Μὴ βαστάζετε βαλάντιον, μὴ πήραν, μηδὲ ὑποδήματα· καὶ μηδένα o Matt. 10. 9, 10. supr. 9. 3. & 22. 35. Mark 6. 8. 2 Kings 4. 29.
5 κατὰ τὴν ὁδὸν ἀσπάσησθε. [p] Εἰς ἣν δ᾽ ἂν οἰκίαν εἰσέρχησθε, πρῶ-
6 τον λέγετε· Εἰρήνη τῷ οἴκῳ τούτῳ. καὶ ἐὰν [μὲν] ᾖ ἐκεῖ [ὁ] p Matt. 10. 12. Mark 6. 10.
υἱὸς εἰρήνης, ἐπαναπαύσεται ἐπ᾽ αὐτὸν ἡ εἰρήνη ὑμῶν· εἰ δὲ μήγε,
7 ἐφ᾽ ὑμᾶς ἀνακάμψει. [q] Ἐν αὐτῇ δὲ τῇ οἰκίᾳ μένετε, ἐσθίοντες καὶ q Lev. 19. 13. Deut. 24. 14. & 25. 4.
πίνοντες τὰ παρ᾽ αὐτῶν· ἄξιος γὰρ ὁ ἐργάτης τοῦ μισθοῦ αὐτοῦ ἐστι. Matt. 10. 10. 1 Cor. 9. 4. et seqq.
8 μὴ μεταβαίνετε ἐξ οἰκίας εἰς οἰκίαν. Καὶ εἰς ἣν δ᾽ ἂν πόλιν εἰσέρ- 1 Tim. 5. 18.
9 χησθε, καὶ δέχωνται ὑμᾶς, ἐσθίετε τὰ παρατιθέμενα ὑμῖν, [r] καὶ θερα- r Matt. 3. 2. & 4. 17.
πεύετε τοὺς ἐν αὐτῇ ἀσθενεῖς, καὶ λέγετε αὐτοῖς· Ἤγγικεν ἐφ᾽ ὑμᾶς
10 ἡ βασιλεία τοῦ Θεοῦ. [s] Εἰς ἣν δ᾽ ἂν πόλιν εἰσέρχησθε, καὶ μὴ δέ- s Matt. 10. 14. Mark 6. 11. sup. 9. 5.
11 χωνται ὑμᾶς, ἐξελθόντες εἰς τὰς πλατείας αὐτῆς, εἴπατε· Καὶ τὸν Acts 13. 51. & 18. 6.
κονιορτὸν τὸν κολληθέντα ἡμῖν ἐκ τῆς πόλεως ὑμῶν ἀπομασσόμεθα
ὑμῖν. Πλὴν τοῦτο γινώσκετε, ὅτι ἤγγικεν ἐφ᾽ ὑμᾶς ἡ βασιλεία τοῦ MT.
12 Θεοῦ. Λέγω [δὲ] ὑμῖν, ὅτι Σοδόμοις ἐν τῇ ἡμέρᾳ ἐκείνῃ ἀνεκτότερον 11.
13 ἔσται, ἢ τῇ πόλει ἐκείνῃ. Οὐαί σοι, Χοραζίν! οὐαί σοι, Βηθσαϊδά! 21
ὅτι εἰ ἐν Τύρῳ καὶ Σιδῶνι ἐγένοντο αἱ δυνάμεις αἱ γενόμεναι ἐν ὑμῖν,

selected by Moses as his colleagues in the government of the people, and of the Jewish Sanhedrim, as also the Translators of the Sept. But in the first case *seventy* was the number; and of the rest there is reason to think that not 72, but 70, was the real number.

2. οὖν.] Some ancient MSS. read δὲ, which is thought to be confirmed by most of the Versions, and it is placed in the inner margin by Griesb., and received into the text by Lachmann. But rashly — for it is a mere *alteration* of the Alexandrian school. The Critics stumbled, it seems, at this rather unusual sense of οὖν, by which it has a *resumptive*, or *continuative* force, and may be rendered *porro*, as in 1 Cor. viii. 4. See Schleus. Lex. in v. § 3.

— ἐκβάλῃ.] This, for ἐκβάλλῃ, is found in very many MSS. and early Edd., and is received by almost all Editors from Matth. to Scholz. On the *sense* see Note on Matt. ix. 38.

4. μὴ — ἀσπάσησθε] i. e. do not indulge in merely complimentary or courteous addresses, to the neglect of the weightier concerns of your sacred office.

6. μὲν.] This is omitted in most of the ancient MSS., and in several Versions, Fathers, and early Edd., and is cancelled by Wets., Matth., Griesb., Tittm., Vat., and Scholz. It was probably inserted to complete the apodosis. The Article ὁ is omitted in almost all the best MSS., some Fathers, and nearly all the early Edd. I suspect that it crept, by an error of the press, into the 5th edition of Erasmus, and consequently was introduced into the 3d of Stephens, where it is found. Therefore, it could not, as some imagine, be a mere conjecture of Beza. It is true he considered the Article as indispensable: in which he was so far mistaken, that the Article can by no means be tolerated; the regimen (as Middl. observes) not permitting it, this being one of those numerous cases, in which υἱὸς (by Hebraism) is put before a Genitive to indicate the relation of *possession*, or *resemblance*, *participation*, &c., as in Luke xvi. 8. υἱοὶ τοῦ αἰῶνος τούτου. Matt. xxiii. 15. υἱοὶ τῆς γεέννης. 1 Thess. v. 5. υἱοὶ τοῦ φωτὸς, &c. The sense is, "one deserving of your blessing."

7. τὰ παρ᾽ αὐτῶν] scil. παρατιθέμενα. See Bos Ell. Ἄξιος γὰρ — ἐστι. The full sense is, "[And this ye may freely do,] for the labourer is worthy of his hire;" as much as to say, "ye will earn your support by your labour for the spiritual good of your hosts." Μὴ μεταβαίνετε — οἰκίαν, literally, "do not change your lodgings, by going from house to house."

11. ἀπομασσόμεθα ὑμῖν.] Render, "we wipe off unto you," i. e. we return it back to you; a form of giving up all intercourse. Ἐφ᾽ ὑμᾶς is by almost all Commentators supposed to mean, "against you," "to your harm." But that sense cannot be admitted. All that is meant seems to be this, that the same solemn message is to be delivered unto them, whether they will hear, or whether they will forbear. Render, "But (or however) know ye this, (i. e. receive this our testimony) that the kingdom," &c. Griesb. indeed cancels ἐφ᾽ ὑμᾶς, from some MSS. But they are so few in number, as to have little weight. Nay, we might suspect the words to be omitted by *accident*; but that it seems more probable that they were cancelled by the *Critics*, from mere fastidiousness, in order to remove what *they* thought a tautological repetition.

12. δὲ.] This is omitted in very many MSS., most of them ancient, and several Versions, and early Edd., and is cancelled by Matth., Griesb., Tittm., and Scholz. But the formula is almost always accompanied with some conjunction. And *perspicuity* here would require one.

MT. 11. πάλαι ἂν ἐν σάκκῳ καὶ σποδῷ καθήμεναι μετενόησαν. Πλὴν Τύρῳ 14
22 23 καὶ Σιδῶνι ἀνεκτότερον ἔσται ἐν τῇ κρίσει, ἢ ὑμῖν. Καὶ σὺ, Καπερ- 15
ναοὺμ, ἡ ἕως τοῦ οὐρανοῦ ὑψωθεῖσα, ἕως ᾅδου καταβιβασθήσῃ. Ὁ 16
ἀκούων ὑμῶν ἐμοῦ ἀκούει, καὶ ὁ ἀθετῶν ὑμᾶς ἐμὲ ἀθετεῖ· ὁ δὲ ἐμὲ
ἀθετῶν ἀθετεῖ τὸν ἀποστείλαντά με. Ὑπέστρεψαν δὲ οἱ ἑβδομήκοντα 17
μετὰ χαρᾶς, λέγοντες· Κύριε, καὶ τὰ δαιμόνια ὑποτάσσεται ἡμῖν ἐν
t Rev. 12. 8, 9. τῷ ὀνόματί σου. [t] Εἶπε δὲ αὐτοῖς· Ἐθεώρουν τὸν Σατανᾶν ὡς ἀστρα- 18
u Mark 16. 18. Acts 28. 5. πὴν ἐκ τοῦ οὐρανοῦ πεσόντα. [u] Ἰδοὺ, δίδωμι ὑμῖν τὴν ἐξουσίαν τοῦ 19
x Exod. 32. 32. Isa. 4. 3. πατεῖν ἐπάνω ὄφεων καὶ σκορπίων, καὶ ἐπὶ πᾶσαν τὴν δύναμιν τοῦ
Dan. 12. 1. Phil. 4. 3. Rev. 13. 8. ἐχθροῦ· καὶ οὐδὲν ὑμᾶς οὐ μὴ ἀδικήσῃ. [x] Πλὴν ἐν τούτῳ μὴ χαί- 20
MT. 11. ρετε, ὅτι τὰ πνεύματα ὑμῖν ὑποτάσσεται· χαίρετε δὲ [μᾶλλον] ὅτι
25 τὰ ὀνόματα ὑμῶν ἐγράφη ἐν τοῖς οὐρανοῖς. Ἐν αὐτῇ τῇ ὥρᾳ ἠγαλλι- 21
άσατο τῷ πνεύματι ὁ Ἰησοῦς καὶ εἶπεν· Ἐξομολογοῦμαί σοι, Πάτερ,
Κύριε τοῦ οὐρανοῦ καὶ τῆς γῆς, ὅτι ἀπέκρυψας ταῦτα ἀπὸ σοφῶν
26 καὶ συνετῶν, καὶ ἀπεκάλυψας αὐτὰ νηπίοις. ναὶ, ὁ Πατὴρ, ὅτι οὕτως
27 ἐγένετο εὐδοκία ἔμπροσθέν σου. [y] Πάντα παρεδόθη μοι ὑπὸ τοῦ 22
y Psal. 8. 7. Heb. 2. 8. Πατρός μου· καὶ οὐδεὶς γινώσκει τίς ἐστιν ὁ Υἱὸς, εἰ μὴ ὁ Πατὴρ,
Matt. 11. 27. & 28. 18. John 3. 35. καὶ τίς ἐστιν ὁ Πατὴρ, εἰ μὴ ὁ Υἱὸς, καὶ ᾧ ἐὰν βούληται ὁ Υἱὸς
& 17. 2. 1 Cor. 15. 27. ἀποκαλύψαι. [z] Καὶ στραφεὶς πρὸς τοὺς μαθητὰς κατ᾽ ἰδίαν εἶπε· 23
Eph. 1. 21, 22. Phil. 2. 9. Μακάριοι οἱ ὀφθαλμοὶ οἱ βλέποντες ἃ βλέπετε. λέγω γὰρ ὑμῖν, ὅτι 24
John 4. 18. & 6. 46. & 14. 8, 9. πολλοὶ προφῆται καὶ βασιλεῖς ἠθέλησαν ἰδεῖν ἃ ὑμεῖς βλέπετε, καὶ οὐκ
z Matt. 13. 16. 1 Pet. 1. 10. εἶδον· καὶ ἀκοῦσαι ἃ ἀκούετε, καὶ οὐκ ἤκουσαν.

a Matt. 22. 35. Mark 12. 28. [a] Καὶ ἰδοὺ, νομικός τις ἀνέστη, ἐκπειράζων αὐτὸν, καὶ λέγων· Δι- 25
b Deut. 6. 5. & 10. 12. & 30. 6. δάσκαλε, τί ποιήσας ζωὴν αἰώνιον κληρονομήσω; Ὁ δὲ εἶπε πρὸς 26
Lev. 19. 18. Rom. 13. 9. αὐτόν· Ἐν τῷ νόμῳ τί γέγραπται; πῶς ἀναγινώσκεις; [b] Ὁ δὲ 27
Gal. 5. 14. James 2. 8. ἀποκριθεὶς εἶπεν· Ἀγαπήσεις Κύριον τὸν Θεόν σου ἐξ

13. *ἐν σάκκῳ — καθήμεναι.*] This posture of mourning and repentance was in use not only among the Eastern, but the Western nations of antiquity. See Kypke in Recens. Syn.

18. *ἐθεώρουν τὸν Σ., &c.*] The best Commentators are agreed that this is a bold and figurative mode of expression, anticipating the future triumph of the Gospel over the powers of darkness. So Bp. Warburton, Serm. xxvii. says "it is a lively picture of the sudden precipitation of the *Prince of the air*, where he had so long held his empire; and hung, like a pestilential meteor, over the sons of men;" and that, as being *exalted to heaven* imports widely spread dominion, so *falling from heaven* denotes a fall from eminence and power. A kindred expression occurs in Is. xiv. 12. See also John xii. 31. Ephes. vi. 12. Nor is it without example in the Classical writers. Thus Cicero Epist. Att. ii. says of Pompey, "ex astris decidisse."

19. I would not, with many recent Commentators, regard this as merely a *figurative mode of expression*, importing that they should be delivered, by Divine assistance, from the greatest perils; but take it in the literal acceptation. See Note on Mark xvi. 17. Some Commentators here recognise *another figure* expressive of *safety* from men as deadly in their hostility as serpents and scorpions. See more in Recens. Synop. In *Καὶ οὐδὲν — ἀδικήσῃ* there is an *intensive* accumulation of negatives. See Matt. xxiv. 21. and Note. Something similar occurs in Lucian Pisc. § 19. *οὐδὲν οὐ μὴ γένηται ἄδικον, Δικαιοσύνης συμπαρούσης.*

20. *πλὴν*] *attamen.* *Ὅτι τὰ ὀνόματα, &c.* The best Commentators are agreed that there is here an allusion to the methods of *human* polity; future life being represented under the image of a temporal *πολίτευμα*; in which the names of *citizens* were inscribed in a *book*, from which were occasionally expunged the names of those persons who were thought unworthy, and who thereby lost the *jus civitatis*. The same image is frequent in the O. T., and sometimes occurs in the N. T.; nor is it rare in the Classical writers.

Μᾶλλον is omitted in very many MSS., Versions, Fathers, and early Edd., and is cancelled by almost all Editors, rightly, I think.

21. *ἠγαλλιάσατο τῷ πν.*] Here we have the same rapturous expressions of praise and thanksgiving, as on the return of the twelve Apostles from executing the same commission. See Note on Matt. xi. 25, 27. and xiii. 16. and *comp.* Is. xxxix. 14. 1 Cor. i. 19. 26.

25. et seqq. See Grot., Whitby, and Doddr., and the notes on a kindred narration in Matt. xxii. 36.

27. *ἐξ ὅλης τῆς καρδίας — διανοίας.*] Vorst. considers these as *Hellenistic* phrases: while Valckn.

ὅλης τῆς καρδίας σου καὶ ἐξ ὅλης τῆς ψυχῆς σου, καὶ
ἐξ ὅλης τῆς ἰσχύος σου καὶ ἐξ ὅλης τῆς διανοίας σου·
28 καὶ τὸν πλησίον σου ὡς σεαυτόν. [c] Εἶπε δὲ αὐτῷ· Ὀρθῶς c Lev. 18. 5. Ezek. 20. 11, 13.
29 ἀπεκρίθης· τοῦτο ποίει, καὶ ζήσῃ. Ὁ δὲ θέλων δικαιοῦν ἑαυτὸν, εἶπε
30 πρὸς τὸν Ἰησοῦν· Καὶ τίς ἐστί μου πλησίον; Ὑπολαβὼν δὲ ὁ Ἰησοῦς
εἶπεν· Ἄνθρωπός τις κατέβαινεν ἀπὸ Ἱερουσαλὴμ εἰς Ἱεριχὼ, καὶ
λῃσταῖς περιέπεσεν· οἳ καὶ ἐκδύσαντες αὐτὸν καὶ πληγὰς ἐπιθέντες
31 ἀπῆλθον, ἀφέντες ἡμιθανῆ τυγχάνοντα. Κατὰ συγκυρίαν δὲ ἱερεύς τις
32 κατέβαινεν ἐν τῇ ὁδῷ ἐκείνῃ· καὶ ἰδὼν αὐτὸν, ἀντιπαρῆλθεν. Ὁμοίως
δὲ καὶ Λευΐτης, γενόμενος κατὰ τὸν τόπον, ἐλθὼν καὶ ἰδὼν ἀντιπαρ-

and Bornem. endeavour to prove that they are *Classical*, by adducing examples from Arrian Dissert. on Epictetus. The truth seems to be that they were expressions of *late Grecism*, such as are not unfrequently found in the writers of the N. T., in common with Arrian in his Philosophical writings.

29. θέλων δικ.] i. e. wishing to excuse himself from the imputation of not having attended to the Law he taught. For the Pharisee wished to show that he had not proposed a slight, or easily solvable question; but one of importance, and difficult determination. And since πλησίον is a term of extensive application, he takes occasion, from that ambiguity, to put the question καὶ τίς ἐστί μου πλησίον; Jesus, however, returns an answer quite contrary to the expectation of the lawyer; and by teaching that (after the example of the Samaritan who had deserved so well of the Jew) even to *strangers*, *foreigners*, and *enemies*, were to be extended the offices of humanity and kindness, he left the Pharisee nothing to answer." (Kuin.)

— τίς ἐστί μου πλησίον;] literally, who is near to me, i. e. neighbour. Bp. Middl. has shown *how* it is, that the Article can here be dispensed with; namely, from the vicinity of the same word *with* the Article, and in the sense *neighbour*. This use of ὁ πλησίον has before been illustrated in the Notes on Matt. and Mark. And the expression may, in this sense, be defined, any one of our *fellow-creatures*, with whom we are in any way connected, whether in respect of country, religion, or political institutions.

"HOMO SUM: nihil humani a me alienum puto."

30. ὑπολαβὼν] Sub. τὸν λόγον, which ellipse is *supplied* in Herodot. iii. 146. Render, "taking him up," i. e. "answering;" a signification common both to the Scriptural and Hellenistical, and also to the Classical writers. So the Latin *excipere* and *suscipere*. It is well observed by Kuin., that in the best Classical writers ὑπολαβὼν is *joined to* ἔφη, when any one interrupts the speaker, and so answers him as to take exception at, reprehend, or at least circumscribe, or correct, any position laid down by the other; in which case the word is *not redundant*. Thus it here seems to convey, by implication, an intimation that he had *not*, as he thought, thoroughly kept the moral law. It was, indeed, (as Gilpin says), the impossibility of doing this, which made a Saviour necessary. Wakef. and Campb. connect ἄνθρωπος closely with ἀπὸ Ἱερ., remarking, that the whole energy of the story depends on the opposition between the Jew and the Samaritan. But such a transposition would be very harsh, and indeed unnecessary; since, considering how very little Judæa was frequented by foreigners, it might very well be *implied*, that a person travelling from Jerusalem to Jericho would be a *Jew*. He could not be a *Samaritan*, because Samaritans were never allowed to go to Jerusalem. Κατέβαινεν has reference to the *situation* of Jericho as compared with Jerusalem, the latter being on a hill, and the former on low ground. Περιπίπτειν signifies 1. to *fall on*. 2. to happen upon, fall in with, generally of *things*, but sometimes of *persons*; and almost always implying *evil*.

The phrase πληγὰς ἐπιθεῖναι is found also in Acts xvi. 23., and occasionally in the Fathers; but never in the Classical writers; so that it is supposed to be a Latinism formed from the phrase *imponere plagas*. Yet we find in 2 Maccab. iii. 26. πολλὰς ἐπιῤῥιπτοῦντες αὐτῷ πληγάς. Ἡμιθανὴς is the *ordinary* Greek form for the Attic ἡμιθνής. Yet I suspect that it was the more ancient form. and the other an Attic contraction.

31. κατὰ συγκυρίαν.] The Classical writers not unfrequently use κατὰ συντυχίαν; but never κατὰ συγκυρίαν; and indeed they rarely use συγκυρία. Insomuch that we might suppose it to be entirely Hellenistic, did it not occur several times in Hippocrates. Hence it appears to have been a very ancient word; and the phrase κατὰ συγκυρίαν was probably early in use, but afterwards supplanted by κατὰ συντυχίαν. Yet it maintained, it seems, a place in the *popular* diction even to the time of Eustathius.

31. ἀντιπαρῆλθεν.] The exact sense of this term is not clear. It cannot well be that commonly assigned to it, "passed by on the other or farther side," i. e. by getting out of the road. Most recent Commentators consider the ἀντι as *pleonastic*. But that is *declining* the difficulty. I should be inclined to think with Grot., that it might mean, "passed by going the contrary way," i. e. from Jerusalem to Jericho. But *that* is forbidden by the κατέβαινεν; neither would that circumstance be to the purpose. It should seem that ἀντι here means *over against*, which, indeed, I believe to be its *original* sense; it being, no doubt, for [ἐν] ἀντι, from the old word ἄνς, whence the common term ἔναντι. Thus the sense is, "He passed by *right over against* him," and not *at some distance off*, as travellers might do, for in such a desert as that whole tract was, it is not likely that there should be any regular inclosed road. The term ἀντιπαρέρχομαι occurs also in the LXX. once.

32. ἐλθὼν καὶ ἰδών.] The ἐλθὼν is *not* redundant, but shows that the Levite did more than the

ἦλθε. Σαμαρείτης δέ τις, ὁδεύων, ἦλθε κατ᾽ αὐτὸν, καὶ ἰδὼν αὐτὸν 33
ἐσπλαγχνίσθη. καὶ προσελθὼν κατέδησε τὰ τραύματα αὐτοῦ, ἐπιχέων 34
ἔλαιον καὶ οἶνον, ἐπιβιβάσας δὲ αὐτὸν ἐπὶ τὸ ἴδιον κτῆνος, ἤγαγεν
αὐτὸν εἰς πανδοχεῖον, καὶ ἐπεμελήθη αὐτοῦ. Καὶ ἐπὶ τὴν αὔριον ἐξ- 35
ελθὼν, ἐκβαλὼν δύο δηνάρια ἔδωκε τῷ πανδοχεῖ, καὶ εἶπεν αὐτῷ· Ἐπιμε-
λήθητι αὐτοῦ· καὶ ὅ τι ἂν προσδαπανήσῃς, ἐγὼ ἐν τῷ ἐπανέρχεσθαί με
ἀποδώσω σοι. Τίς οὖν τούτων τῶν τριῶν δοκεῖ σοι πλησίον γεγονέναι 36
τοῦ ἐμπεσόντος εἰς τοὺς λῃστάς; Ὁ δὲ εἶπεν· Ὁ ποιήσας τὸ ἔλεος 37
μετ᾽ αὐτοῦ. Εἶπεν οὖν αὐτῷ ὁ Ἰησοῦς· Πορεύου καὶ σὺ ποίει ὁμοίως.
d John 11. 1. & 12. 2, 3. [d] ἘΓΕΝΕΤΟ δὲ, ἐν τῷ πορεύεσθαι αὐτοὺς, καὶ αὐτὸς εἰσῆλθεν εἰς 38
κώμην τινά· γυνὴ δέ τις ὀνόματι Μάρθα ὑπεδέξατο αὐτὸν εἰς τὸν
e Acts 22. 3. οἶκον αὐτῆς. [e] Καὶ τῇδε ἦν ἀδελφὴ καλουμένη Μαρία, ἣ καὶ παρα- 39
καθίσασα παρὰ τοὺς πόδας τοῦ Ἰησοῦ ἤκουε τὸν λόγον αὐτοῦ. Ἡ 40
δὲ Μάρθα περιεσπᾶτο περὶ πολλὴν διακονίαν· ἐπιστᾶσα δὲ εἶπε·
Κύριε, οὐ μέλει σοι ὅτι ἡ ἀδελφή μου μόνην με κατέλιπε διακονεῖν;
εἰπὲ οὖν αὐτῇ ἵνα μοι συναντιλάβηται. Ἀποκριθεὶς δὲ εἶπεν αὐτῇ 41
ὁ Ἰησοῦς· Μάρθα Μάρθα, μεριμνᾷς καὶ τυρβάζῃ περὶ πολλά· ἑνὸς 42

Priest. The latter only cast a passing glance; the former also went towards him.

34. κατέδησε.] A *surgical* term, occurring also in Xen. Cyr. v. and Ecclus. xxvii. 31., and signifying to *apply bandages* to hold down the lips of a wound. The use of oil and wine, both separately, and as a mixture called οἰνέλαιον, is established by the citations of Wets. from the ancient Medical writers. Here, however, they may be best understood as used *separately*; the *wine* to wash the wound and staunch the blood, and the *oil* to allay the pain. The oil (which in that country is very generous) was, no doubt, intended for *anointing*; and the antiquity of the custom of carrying oil on a journey is (as Schoettg. observes) shown by the case of Jacob in the O. T.

— κτῆνος.] This corresponds to our general term *beast*, whether horse, mule, or ass. It was probably an ass. Πανδοχεῖον denotes a *public hostelry*, such as are still known in the East by the name *khan*. The word is said to occur only in the later writers; yet I find something very much like it in Æschyl. Choeph. 649. Σκοτεινόν· ὥρα δ᾽ ἐμπόρους μεθιέναι ἄγκυραν ἐν δόμοισι πανδόκοις ξένων.

35. ἐκβαλὼν] "having cast down, *put down*, or disbursed." The *two denaria* were (as I have observed in Recens. Synop.) equivalent to two days' wages of a labourer. See Matt. xx. 9. Ἐπιμελεῖσθαι was a term appropriated to the *nursing* and *care* of the sick and wounded, as distinct from medical or surgical attendance.

37. ὁ ποιήσας—αὐτοῦ] "he who exercised benevolence towards him." A Hebraism. See Notes on Luke i. 58 & 72.

38. κώμην τ.] namely, Bethany. See John xii. 1. In the phrase ὑποδέχεσθαι εἰς οἶκον is implied hospitable entertainment. The words εἰς τὸν οἶκον are very rarely added in the Classical writers; yet in Hom. Od. xvi. 70. we have the equivalent phrase ὑποδέχομαι οἴκῳ.

39. καὶ] also, i. e. as well as the disciples. Παρακαθίσασα, "having seated herself." That the phrase itself, and the custom of *sitting* as a posture of instruction, was not unknown to the *Greeks* and *Romans*, as well as the Jews, is clear from the citations adduced by Wets.

40. περιεσπᾶτο.] Περισπᾷν signifies properly to *draw around*, *draw aside*, *draw out of course*. Thus those are, by an elegant metaphor, said περισπᾶσθαι, who are distracted; and whose minds are drawn aside in various directions by anxious cares. So Diod. Sic. p. 82. A. ἀπῆλθε περισπασθεὶς ὑπὸ βιωτικῆς χρείας. Hor. Sat. viii. 6, 7. Omni sollicitudine *districtum*.

Διακονεῖν here denotes the preparation of the meal, and other services required by hospitality. Συναντιλαβέσθαι signifies to lend a hand with one, to help in any work.

41. τυρβάζῃ] "thou art troubled," (or, "thou distractest thyself with") a multiplicity of cares. Τυρβάζειν is said by some Commentators to properly signify to *raise the mud*. But it comes from τύρβη, which does not signify *mud*; but is equivalent to our old English Substantive a *stir*. Ang. Sax. *stour*, which is probably cognate with τύρβη, *turba*; and that comes from τύρειν (cognate with τάρειν and ταράσσειν), to *stir*, which is the *same word*, for σ is often prefixed to words, as τέγος, στέγος. Though, indeed, the true nature of such *inceptive* letters seems to be this — that they were originally part of the word, and were, in process of time, dropped, *euphoniæ gratiâ*.

42. ἑνός.] On the *reference* in this word, Commentators are not agreed. Several ancient and some modern Interpreters suppose an ellipsis of βρώματος here, and of βρωμάτων at πολλά, thus conveying a moral *gnome*, that *one* dish is sufficient for any reasonable person. But surely such a commendation of temperance and frugality were worthy rather of a second-rate Heathen Philosopher, than the lips of Him who "spake as never man spake." Indeed, the ellipsis in question is most irregular. Others are of opinion that we have here a kind of *adage*, spiritually applied, *knowledge* being often compared to *food*. But that sense is very frigid. There can be no doubt that by ἑνὸς (in which there is in reality *no ellip-*

MT.

δέ ἐστι χρεία. Μαρία δὲ τὴν ἀγαθὴν μερίδα ἐξελέξατο, ἥτις οὐκ 6.
ἀφαιρεθήσεται ἀπ' αὐτῆς.

1 XI. *ΚΑΙ* ἐγένετο, ἐν τῷ εἶναι αὐτὸν ἐν τόπῳ τινὶ προσευχόμενον,
ὡς ἐπαύσατο, εἶπέ τις τῶν μαθητῶν αὐτοῦ πρὸς αὐτόν· Κύριε, δίδαξον ἡμᾶς προσεύχεσθαι, καθὼς καὶ Ἰωάννης ἐδίδαξε τοὺς μαθητὰς
2 αὐτοῦ. Εἶπε δὲ αὐτοῖς· Ὅταν προσεύχησθε λέγετε· Πάτερ ἡμῶν ὁ 9
ἐν τοῖς οὐρανοῖς, ἁγιασθήτω τὸ ὄνομά σου· ἐλθέτω ἡ βασιλεία σου· 10
3 γενηθήτω τὸ θέλημά σου ὡς ἐν οὐρανῷ καὶ ἐπὶ τῆς γῆς. Τὸν ἄρτον
4 ἡμῶν τὸν ἐπιούσιον δίδου ἡμῖν τὸ καθ' ἡμέραν· καὶ ἄφες ἡμῖν τὰς 11
ἁμαρτίας ἡμῶν, καὶ γὰρ αὐτοὶ ἀφίεμεν παντὶ ὀφείλοντι ἡμῖν· καὶ μὴ 12
εἰσενέγκῃς ἡμᾶς εἰς πειρασμόν, ἀλλὰ ῥῦσαι ἡμᾶς ἀπὸ τοῦ πονηροῦ. 13
5 [f] Καὶ εἶπε πρὸς αὐτούς· Τίς ἐξ ὑμῶν ἕξει φίλον, καὶ πορεύσεται πρὸς [f] Infr. 18.1, &c.
αὐτὸν μεσονυκτίου, καὶ εἴπῃ αὐτῷ· Φίλε, χρῆσόν μοι τρεῖς ἄρτους·
6 ἐπειδὴ φίλος μου παρεγένετο ἐξ ὁδοῦ πρός με, καὶ οὐκ ἔχω ὃ παρα-

sis) is meant (as is commonly understood) the *care of the soul, contrasted with that of the body.*

— *μερίδα.*] Grot., Elsn., Kypke, Kuin., and almost all recent Commentators, are of opinion that *μερὶς* here signifies *business*, or *occupation*; as in Xen. Cyr. iii. 3. 5. Anab. vii. 6. 25. So the Latin *pars* in Cic. Quint. Frat. So Julian, p. 253. (cited by Elsn.) *οὐ μικρᾶς μερίδος ὁ Φιλόσοφος προέστηκεν*, i. e. non exiguo muneri præfectus est Philosophus. This, however, I cannot but consider a stiff and frigid view of the sense. It should rather seem that the term *μερίδα* is chosen with allusion to any one's taking his part of any thing left him to choose from. Our Lord appears to have had in mind Ps. xvii. 14. and perhaps Ps. xvi. 5.

XI. 1. *δίδαξον ἡμᾶς προσ.*] We are not to suppose but that our Lord had given them instructions on prayer, both as to the manner and matter. But it was the custom of the Rabbis to give their disciples some brief *form* of prayer.

2. seqq. On the interpretation here see Notes on Matt. vi. 9. seqq. I cannot but advert to the marvellous *omissions* which are found in some few MSS., Versions, and Fathers, and which are almost invariably adopted by Griesb. and some other Editors. The words *ἡμῶν ὁ ἐν τοῖς οὐρ.* are not found in about 8 MSS., with the Vulg. and Pers. Versions. But that authority is too slender to claim any attention. The reason for the omission may readily be *conceived;* though it were vain to imagine reasons for *all* the innumerable alterations which were introduced by the *Alexandrian biblical Aristarchs.*

The words *γενηθήτω — γῆς* are omitted in nearly the same MSS. and Versions as the preceding *ἡμῶν — οὐρανοῖς*, and, of course, there is no greater attention due in this than in the former case. But the omission *here* cannot well be considered as otherwise than *unintentional*. And not only the very small number of MSS. (about six) warrants us to suppose this; but there is a *palæographical* principle which increases the probability thereof; namely, that as *this* clause begins with 4 words. 2 of them the same, and the other 2 of the same *termination* with the former clause *ἁγιασθήτω τὸ θέλημά σου*; so it is likely that these each formed *a line* in the very ancient Archetype or Archetypes; and thus (as in a thousand other cases) the scribes' eyes might be deceived, and they inadvertently omit the second of those clauses.

Again, the words *ἀλλὰ ῥῦσαι — πονηροῦ* are omitted in about the same number of MSS. and Versions as the before-mentioned clauses; with the addition of three or four others, and *Origen;* and are cancelled even by Scholz. *Here* the omission cannot be accounted for on the same principle as at *γενηθήτω — σου*; yet the testimony is too weak, and the quarter whence it comes so suspicious, as to destroy all confidence. And far more probable is it, that the words were omitted by the above-mentioned critics for some speculative doctrinal reasons than that in *all* the MSS. except about ten, the clause should have been introduced from Matthew. This last reason will also apply to the *other* omissions; especially as the *doxology*, which is found in almost all the MSS. of *Matthew*, is here found in *not one*. Is it likely that those who introduced *three* interpolations, should *all* of them omit to introduce the *fourth*.

4. *καὶ γὰρ αὐτοὶ*, &c.] These words may seem to confirm the interpretation of those who render the *ὡς* in Matthew vi. 10. by *for, forasmuch as*. But it is not *necessary* to resort to that sense; and there is no real discrepancy; since in *Luke* that duty is *taken for granted* as indispensable, which in *Matthew* is made the *condition*, or *measure* of the forgiveness that we implore. Thus there is surely no discrepancy between "Give us *this* day," and "Give us *day by day*."

5. *τίς.*] The best Commentators are of opinion that *τίς* is for *εἴ τις*, as in 1 Cor. vii. 18. and James v. 13. Thus the sense would be, "Should any one of you," &c. But this seems a wrong view, and I agree with Fritz. on Matth. p. 726. and Bornemann in loco, that the true sense in such cases is *quisnam?* where the interrogation, as Fritz. says, expresses "*animi commotionem;*" though (as Bornemann remarks) in some passages referred to this idiom, we must call in the principle of a blending of two constructions. At *εἴπῃ* the proper construction is abandoned for another which is not unsuitable.

6. *ἐξ ὁδοῦ.*] Valckn. and Campb. construe this with *παρεγένετο*, and render, "is come out of his road." This sense, however, is forced, and the construction harsh; and it is better, with others, to connect *παρεγένετο* with *πρός με*; a very fre-

MT.
7. θήσω αὐτῷ· κἀκεῖνος ἔσωθεν ἀποκριθεὶς εἴπῃ· Μή μοι κόπους 7
παρεχε· ἤδη ἡ θύρα κέκλεισται, καὶ τὰ παιδία μου μετ᾽ ἐμοῦ εἰς
τὴν κοίτην εἰσίν· οὐ δύναμαι ἀναστὰς δοῦναί σοι. Λέγω ὑμῖν· εἰ 8
καὶ οὐ δώσει αὐτῷ ἀναστὰς διὰ τὸ εἶναι αὐτοῦ φίλον· διά γε τὴν
7 ἀναίδειαν αὐτοῦ, ἐγερθεὶς δώσει αὐτῷ ὅσων χρῄζει. Κἀγὼ ὑμῖν λέγω· 9
Αἰτεῖτε, καὶ δοθήσεται ὑμῖν· ζητεῖτε, καὶ εὑρήσετε· κρούετε, καὶ
8 ἀνοιγήσεται ὑμῖν. Πᾶς γὰρ ὁ αἰτῶν λαμβάνει· καὶ ὁ ζητῶν εὑρί- 10
9 σκει· καὶ τῷ κρούοντι ἀνοιγήσεται. Τίνα δὲ ὑμῶν τὸν πατέρα αἰτήσει 11
ὁ υἱὸς ἄρτον, μὴ λίθον ἐπιδώσει αὐτῷ; * ἢ καὶ ἰχθὺν, μὴ ἀντὶ
10 ἰχθύος ὄφιν ἐπιδώσει αὐτῷ; ἢ καὶ ἐὰν αἰτήσῃ ᾠὸν, μὴ ἐπιδώσει 12
11 αὐτῷ σκορπίον; Εἰ οὖν ὑμεῖς, πονηροὶ ὑπάρχοντες, οἴδατε ἀγαθὰ 13
δόματα διδόναι τοῖς τέκνοις ὑμῶν, πόσῳ μᾶλλον ὁ Πατὴρ ὁ ἐξ οὐρα-
12. νοῦ, δώσει πνεῦμα ἅγιον τοῖς αἰτοῦσιν αὐτόν;
22 Καὶ ἦν ἐκβάλλων δαιμόνιον, καὶ αὐτὸ ἦν κωφόν· ἐγένετο δὲ, τοῦ 14
23 δαιμονίου ἐξελθόντος, ἐλάλησεν ὁ κωφός· καὶ ἐθαύμασαν οἱ ὄχλοι.
24 Τινὲς δὲ ἐξ αὐτῶν εἶπον· Ἐν Βεελζεβοὺλ ἄρχοντι τῶν δαιμονίων ἐκ- 15
38 βάλλει τὰ δαιμόνια. Ἕτεροι δὲ πειράζοντες σημεῖον παρ᾽ αὐτοῦ ἐζήτουν 16
25 ἐξ οὐρανοῦ. Αὐτὸς δὲ, εἰδὼς αὐτῶν τὰ διανοήματα, εἶπεν αὐτοῖς· 17
Πᾶσα βασιλεία ἐφ᾽ ἑαυτὴν διαμερισθεῖσα ἐρημοῦται, καὶ οἶκος ἐπὶ
26 οἶκον πίπτει. Εἰ δὲ καὶ ὁ Σατανᾶς ἐφ᾽ ἑαυτὸν διεμερίσθη, πῶς στα- 18
θήσεται ἡ βασιλεία αὐτοῦ; ὅτι λέγετε ἐν Βεελζεβοὺλ ἐκβάλλειν με τὰ
27 δαιμόνια. Εἰ δὲ ἐγὼ ἐν Βεελζεβοὺλ ἐκβάλλω τὰ δαιμόνια, οἱ υἱοὶ 19
28 ὑμῶν ἐν τίνι ἐκβάλλουσι; διὰ τοῦτο κριταὶ ὑμῶν αὐτοὶ ἔσονται. Εἰ 20
δὲ ἐν δακτύλῳ Θεοῦ ἐκβάλλω τὰ δαιμόνια, ἄρα ἔφθασεν ἐφ᾽ ὑμᾶς ἡ
29 βασιλεία τοῦ Θεοῦ. Ὅταν ὁ ἰσχυρὸς καθωπλισμένος φυλάσσῃ τὴν 21

quent construction, especially in Luke. The ἐξ ὁδοῦ depends on ὢν understood, and the sense is, "who is just come off a journey." On κόπους πάρ. see Note at Matt. xxvi. 10.

7. εἰς τὴν κοίτην.] Newcome and Middl. would take κοίτην to mean *bed-chamber*. But for that signification there is no authority. The interpretation was probably adopted to avoid the difficulty of supposing that all were in the same bed, since κοίτην has the Article. But that does not necessarily involve such a sense; for the Article may here have the force of the pronoun possessive, and μετ' ἐμοῦ may mean (as Pearce and Campb. render) "as well as myself." Εἰς τὴν κοίτην is best rendered by our old adverb *a-bed* (for *at bed*).

8. ἀναίδειαν] "importunity which will not be repressed." See ἀναιδὴς in Homer Il. Δ. 521.

9. κἀγὼ ὑμῖν.] The comparison is not *à simili*, but *à majori*, q. d. "If the *importunate teazer* obtains so much from men, what will not he that offers up fervent and assiduous prayers obtain from his Father in heaven?" [*Comp.* Mark xi. 24. John xiv. 13. xv. 7. xvi. 23. James i. 5. 1 John iii. 22.]

11. ὑμῶν.] Many MSS., Versions, and Fathers prefix ἐξ, which is adopted by Griesb., and Scholz, but it seems to come from the margin. See infra xiv. 5. Ἤ, instead of εἰ, is found in a great number of the best MSS., in most of the Versions, several Fathers, and the Ed. Princ.; and is adopted by Wets., Matth., Griesb., Tittm., Vat., and Scholz. The words are perpetually confounded in the MSS., but ἢ seems to be required by the context.

13. ἐξ οὐρανοῦ] for οὐρανοῖς, as often. By πνεῦμα ἅγιον are meant the ordinary aids of the Holy Spirit. So Euthym. χάριν πνευματικήν.

14. κωφόν.] This is said to be put by metonymy, for what *causes* deafness, as Mark ix. 25. But it may mean *dumb*, as often elsewhere.

15. [*Comp.* Matt. xii. 24.]

16. [*Comp.* Matt. xvi. 1.]

— ἐζήτουν.] Bornem. would read ἐζήτουν, which would indeed be more Classical; but the common reading is *Hellenistic* Greek.

17. καὶ οἶκος — πίπτει.] Campbell's version, "one family is falling after another," yields an unsatisfactory sense, and is irreconcileable with the parallel passages of Matth. and Mark. The common version well expresses the sense, while it preserves the construction. The sentence contains a *parallelism*; and (as Valckn. saw) διαμερ. in the former member is to be repeated, with an adaptation of gender, in the latter. This mode of taking the passage is confirmed by the parallel ones in Matthew and Mark, and is adopted by almost all the ancient and the best modern Commentators, who illustrate the *sentiment* both from the Classical and Rabbinical writers. [*Comp.* John ii. 25. Mark iii. 24.]

21. ὁ ἰσχυρός.] The Article here falls under Middleton's canon, of *insertions in Hypothesis*.

MT.
22 ἑαυτοῦ αὐλὴν, ἐν εἰρήνῃ ἐστὶ τὰ ὑπάρχοντα αὐτοῦ. Ἐπὰν δὲ ὁ ἰσχυ- 12.
ρότερος αὐτοῦ ἐπελθὼν νικήσῃ αὐτὸν, τὴν πανοπλίαν αὐτοῦ αἴρει, ἐφ᾽
23 ᾗ ἐπεποίθει, καὶ τὰ σκύλα αὐτοῦ διαδίδωσιν. Ὁ μὴ ὢν μετ᾽ ἐμοῦ 30
24 κατ᾽ ἐμοῦ ἐστι· καὶ ὁ μὴ συνάγων μετ᾽ ἐμοῦ σκορπίζει. Ὅταν τὸ 43
ἀκάθαρτον πνεῦμα ἐξέλθῃ ἀπὸ τοῦ ἀνθρώπου, διέρχεται δι᾽ ἀνύδρων
τόπων ζητοῦν ἀνάπαυσιν· καὶ μὴ εὑρίσκον, λέγει· Ὑποστρέψω εἰς
25 τὸν οἶκόν μου, ὅθεν ἐξῆλθον. Καὶ ἐλθὸν εὑρίσκει σεσαρωμένον καὶ 44
26 κεκοσμημένον. Τότε πορεύεται καὶ παραλαμβάνει ἑπτὰ ἕτερα πνεύματα
πονηρότερα ἑαυτοῦ, καὶ εἰσελθόντα κατοικεῖ ἐκεῖ· καὶ γίνεται τὰ
ἔσχατα τοῦ ἀνθρώπου ἐκείνου χείρονα τῶν πρώτων.
27 Ἐγένετο δὲ, ἐν τῷ λέγειν αὐτὸν ταῦτα, ἐπάρασά τις γυνὴ φωνὴν ἐκ
τοῦ ὄχλου, εἶπεν αὐτῷ· Μακαρία ἡ κοιλία ἡ βαστάσασά σε, καὶ μα-
28 στοὶ οὓς ἐθήλασας! Αὐτὸς δὲ εἶπε· Μενοῦνγε μακάριοι οἱ ἀκούοντες
29 τὸν λόγον τοῦ Θεοῦ, καὶ φυλάσσοντες αὐτόν. Τῶν δὲ ὄχλων ἐπαθροι- 39
ζομένων, ἤρξατο λέγειν· Ἡ γενεὰ αὕτη πονηρά ἐστι· σημεῖον ἐπιζητεῖ,
καὶ σημεῖον οὐ δοθήσεται αὐτῇ, εἰ μὴ τὸ σημεῖον Ἰωνᾶ τοῦ προφήτου.
30 Καθὼς γὰρ ἐγένετο Ἰωνᾶς σημεῖον τοῖς Νινευΐταις, οὕτως ἔσται καὶ ὁ 40
31 Υἱὸς τοῦ ἀνθρώπου τῇ γενεᾷ ταύτῃ. Βασίλισσα νότου ἐγερθήσεται ἐν 42
τῇ κρίσει μετὰ τῶν ἀνδρῶν τῆς γενεᾶς ταύτης, καὶ κατακρινεῖ αὐτούς·
ὅτι ἦλθεν ἐκ τῶν περάτων τῆς γῆς ἀκοῦσαι τὴν σοφίαν Σολομῶνος· 41
32 καὶ ἰδοὺ, πλεῖον Σολομῶνος ὧδε. Ἄνδρες Νινευῒ ἀναστήσονται ἐν τῇ
κρίσει μετὰ τῆς γενεᾶς ταύτης, καὶ κατακρινοῦσιν αὐτήν· ὅτι μετενόη- MT.
σαν εἰς τὸ κήρυγμα Ἰωνᾶ· καὶ ἰδοὺ, πλεῖον Ἰωνᾶ ὧδε. 5.
33 Οὐδεὶς δὲ λύχνον ἅψας εἰς κρύπτην τίθησιν, οὐδὲ ὑπὸ τὸν μόδιον, 15
ἀλλ᾽ ἐπὶ τὴν λυχνίαν, ἵνα οἱ εἰσπορευόμενοι τὸ φέγγος βλέπωσιν. 6.
34 Ὁ λύχνος τοῦ σώματός ἐστιν ὁ ὀφθαλμός· ὅταν οὖν ὁ ὀφθαλμός σου 22
ἁπλοῦς ᾖ, καὶ ὅλον τὸ σῶμά σου φωτεινόν ἐστιν· ἐπὰν δὲ πονηρὸς ᾖ, 23
35 καὶ τὸ σῶμά σου σκοτεινόν. Σκόπει οὖν μὴ τὸ φῶς τὸ ἐν σοὶ σκότος

The force of it is "he who [is]." Thus also ὁ ἰσχυρότερος is "he who (is) stronger." The reasoning at ver. 22. is, that when another attacks, conquers, and spoils any one's property, it is plain that the other is more powerful than he.

22. τὰ σκῦλα.] Many eminent modern Commentators take σκ. to signify "*effects*," corresponding to the σκεύη of Matthew. This they confirm from the Heb. שָׁלָל, which, though it properly signifies *spoil*, often denotes *goods*, as in Esth. iii. 13. That sense, however, is not established on any Classical authority; nor, indeed, is it necessary to resort to it, since the common version *spoils*, denoting the *goods made a spoil of*, includes the other sense. [*Comp.* Is. liii. 12. Col. ii. 15.]

26. [*Comp.* John v. 14. 2 Pet. ii. 20. Heb. vi. 4. x. 26.]

27. μακαρία, &c.] With this exclamation the Commentators compare several from the Classical and the Rabbinical writers. Κοιλία and μαστοὶ are put for μήτηρ.

28. μενοῦνγε] "imo vero, yea indeed," as Rom. ix. 20. x. 18. Phil. iii. 8. So Euthym. explains it ἀληθῶς. Μενοῦνγε is a stronger expression than μενοῦν, and is used at the *beginning* of a sentence; which the other is *not*. The γε is used as in καίτοι γε, μήτιγε, &c.

32. πλεῖον Σολ.] See Note on Matt. xii. 6.

33. εἰς κρύπτην.] Here we may supply χώραν, or take εἰς κρυπτὴν as put for εἰς κρυπτὸν (which, is, indeed, found in a few MSS. and Editions, even to that of Mill, but is evidently from the margin). Bornem. denies that there is any ellipsis at all, and compares the expressions εἰς μακρὰν, εἰς μίαν, and τὴν ταχίστην. Probably, however, those are of a different nature from the present: and to suppose κρυπτ. to stand for εἰς κρυπτὸν, or ἐν κρυπτῷ, is objectionable, inasmuch as a *Substantive* is required, to suit the parallelism. It is better, therefore, to suppose, with Schleusn., that κρυπτὴν is a *substantive*, especially as examples of this use, though rare, are occasionally found; one being adduced from Athen. p. 205. A., another from Heraclides de Civit. p. 73. Indeed, in the sense *vault* the word occurs not unfrequently in the writers of late Grecism, and gave birth to the Latin *crypta* and our *Croft*. That, however, is, I apprehend, not the sense here, but rather such as is found in the passage of Heraclides. What is here meant seems to be, *a dark hole or corner*, in which articles are stowed out of the way. The

ἐστίν. Εἰ οὖν τὸ σῶμά σου ὅλον φωτεινὸν, μὴ ἔχον τὶ μέρος σκοτεινὸν, 36
ἔσται φωτεινὸν ὅλον, ὡς ὅταν ὁ λύχνος τῇ ἀστραπῇ φωτίζῃ σε.
MT. Ἐν δὲ τῷ λαλῆσαι, ἠρώτα αὐτὸν Φαρισαῖός τις, ὅπως ἀριστήσῃ παρ᾽ 37
23. αὐτῷ· εἰσελθὼν δὲ ἀνέπεσεν. Ὁ δὲ Φαρισαῖος ἰδὼν ἐθαύμασεν, ὅτι 38
25 οὐ πρῶτον ἐβαπτίσθη πρὸ τοῦ ἀρίστου. εἶπε δὲ ὁ Κύριος πρὸς αὐτόν· 39
Νῦν ὑμεῖς οἱ Φαρισαῖοι τὸ ἔξωθεν τοῦ ποτηρίου καὶ τοῦ πίνακος
26 καθαρίζετε, τὸ δὲ ἔσωθεν ὑμῶν γέμει ἁρπαγῆς καὶ πονηρίας. Ἄφρο- 40
νες! οὐχ ὁ ποιήσας τὸ ἔξωθεν καὶ τὸ ἔσωθεν ἐποίησε; Πλὴν τὰ 41
23 ἐνόντα δότε ἐλεημοσύνην· καὶ ἰδοὺ, πάντα καθαρὰ ὑμῖν ἐστιν. Ἀλλ᾽ 42

above appears so certain, that I have ventured, with Schleus., to accent κρύπτην.

36. In order to remove what they call an *irregularity* and *tautology*, several Commentators devise various *conjectures*, all of them unauthorized, and indeed unnecessary. There is, properly speaking, no tautology at all; nor any greater irregularity, than is often elsewere found in Scripture, and sometimes in the Classical writers. This section, vv. 33—36, forms one of the many independent and separate sayings of our Lord, which St. Luke has put together, in a miscellaneous form, without attention to time or place, from ch. xi. to xviii. 14. And therefore it is uncertain whether there be any connection between this section and the preceding one, vv. 27—32. What is here said by Christ does, indeed, appear in *another connection* at Matt. v. 15. Mark iv. 21. supra iii. 6. But our Lord might choose to introduce it *twice*, under different circumstances; meaning to caution his hearers against that *prejudice*, which blinded the eyes of their understanding to the evidence of his Messiahship, and demanded a *sign*. Accordingly, he exhorts them to profit by the light of reason and conscience, illumined by the truths of the Gospel. He means to say (v. 33.) that as he who lights a lamp does it that it may give light to all around, so the faculty of reason and the gift of conscience should not be allowed to lie hid and be useless. And that (v. 34.) as the eye, when the vision is sound, directs a man's steps aright; so the *mental* eye of reason and conscience, is a valuable guide, when *not perverted*. Therefore, they are warned (v. 35.) to take heed that this internal and spiritual light be not obscured [for otherwise, it is said in St. Matthew, great indeed will be that darkness.] Then at v. 36. is a *further illustration* of the great importance of preserving and cultivating this light; and that introduced in a *familiar* and *popular* manner with the not unusual intermixture of the *comparison* and the *thing compared*. "Though (observes Bp. Middl.) nothing more than the body has been mentioned, yet the soul is evidently the object which our Saviour has in view: and to this, probably, by a tacit inference, the application is to be made. In v. 35. the analogy between external and internal light had been established: in the present, the complete illumination described in the concluding clause, though intended of the mind, is affirmed only of the body, the application, after what had been said, being supposed to be obvious." Οὖν has here the *continuative* sense *inquam, quippe, certum, porro*, (as was perceived by the Pesch. Syr. Translator) on which use see Schleus. Lex. in v. § 3. Finally, there is, in reality, no tautology at all; for the clause μὴ ἔχον τι μέρος σκοτεινὸν is intended *to strengthen* what was said in the preceding; and the clause ἔσται φωτεινὸν ὅλον is meant to *illustrate* what was just before said, by a reference to the figure employed at v. 33. of the lamp; and the ὅλον (which is here to be taken adverbially for καθ᾽ ὅλον) is put after φωτ., the better to connect with the comparison ὡς ὅταν, &c. The word ἀστραπὴ almost always elsewhere denotes the *lightning*, but here, as sometimes in the Sept., it signifies, in a general sense, a *bright flame* or *lustre*.

37. ἀνέπεσεν] This simply means "he seated himself at table;" the word only having reference to that *reclining* posture adopted at meals. Ἐλθὼν signifies "on entering," i. e. immediately on entering; which is required by what follows; where the sense is meant to be *strongly marked* by πρῶτον and πρό. Of ἐβαπτίσθη, Pass. for Middl., the sense is the same as at Mark vii. 4, where see Note.

38. [*Comp.* Mark vii. 3.]

39. νῦν.] In the interpretation of this particle, the Commentators generally run into the extremes, either of regarding it as *expletive*, or of *pressing on* the sense. It is best, with Schleus. and Wahl, to consider it as an affirmative particle, signifying, '*sane, profecto*,' as in Acts xxii. 16. So we sometimes use Now! or *aye, now!* Kuin. and others think there is a *transposition* of ὑμῶν, which they construe with ἁρπαγῆς. But that is at variance with the context; and the passages adduced in proof are not to the purpose. We have only to suppose (with Bornem.) a *brevity* of construction, for τὸ δὲ ἔσωθεν ὑμῶν οὐ καθαρίζετε· γέμει γὰρ ἁρπαγῆς, &c. The interpretation of Elsn. and Kuin., however learned and ingenious, is too far-fetched, and depends too much on an insufficiently established sense of ποιεῖν, to be received. The common interpretation by which τὸ ἔξωθεν (scil. μέρος) is taken to denote *the body*, and τὸ ἔσωθεν the *mind*, bears, in its simplicity, the stamp of truth. [*Comp.* Tit. i. 15.]

41. τὰ ἐνόντα.] The ancient and most modern Commentators consider this as an elliptical phrase, and supply κατὰ and χρήματα, in the sense "according to your ability," or your substance; as Tobit iv. 7. ἐκ τῶν ὑπαρχόντων σοι ποίει ἐλεημοσύνην. Of each signification examples have been adduced, and the ellip. is not unfrequent in τὰ δυνατά. Other Commentators, however, (as Raphel. Heum., Kypke, and Wets.) think that the sense would require ἐκ τῶν ἐνόντων. And they take τὰ ἐνόντα to signify "what is within the cup," or dish, i. e. its contents, q. d. "Be not anxious about the outward part; [or its brightness] but [rather] attend to its contents, and do but give alms therefrom, and then food and every thing else shall be pure to you." Thus ἐλεημοσύνην will be in apposition with and exegetical of τὰ ἐνόντα. Upon the

MT.
οὐαὶ ὑμῖν τοῖς Φαρισαίοις, ὅτι ἀποδεκατοῦτε τὸ ἡδύοσμον καὶ τὸ 23.
πήγανον καὶ πᾶν λάχανον, καὶ παρέρχεσθε τὴν κρίσιν καὶ τὴν ἀγάπην
43 τοῦ Θεοῦ. Ταῦτα ἔδει ποιῆσαι, κἀκεῖνα μὴ ἀφιέναι. Οὐαὶ ὑμῖν τοῖς 6
Φαρισαίοις, ὅτι ἀγαπᾶτε τὴν πρωτοκαθεδρίαν ἐν ταῖς συναγωγαῖς, καὶ
44 τοὺς ἀσπασμοὺς ἐν ταῖς ἀγοραῖς. Οὐαὶ ὑμῖν, Γραμματεῖς καὶ Φαρι- 7
σαῖοι, ὑποκριταί! ὅτι ἐστὲ ὡς τὰ μνημεῖα τὰ ἄδηλα· καὶ οἱ ἄνθρω- 27
45 ποι οἱ περιπατοῦντες ἐπάνω οὐκ οἴδασιν. Ἀποκριθεὶς δέ τις τῶν
46 νομικῶν λέγει αὐτῷ· Διδάσκαλε, ταῦτα λέγων καὶ ἡμᾶς ὑβρίζεις. ὁ
δὲ εἶπε· Καὶ ὑμῖν τοῖς νομικοῖς οὐαί! ὅτι φορτίζετε τοὺς ἀνθρώ- 4
πους φορτία δυσβάστακτα, καὶ αὐτοὶ ἑνὶ τῶν δακτύλων ὑμῶν οὐ προσ-
47 ψαύετε τοῖς φορτίοις. Οὐαὶ ὑμῖν! ὅτι οἰκοδομεῖτε τὰ μνημεῖα τῶν 29
48 προφητῶν, οἱ δὲ πατέρες ὑμῶν ἀπέκτειναν αὐτούς. Ἄρα μαρτυρεῖτε 31
καὶ συνευδοκεῖτε τοῖς ἔργοις τῶν πατέρων ὑμῶν· ὅτι αὐτοὶ μὲν ἀπέ-
49 κτειναν αὐτοὺς, ὑμεῖς δὲ οἰκοδομεῖτε αὐτῶν τὰ μνημεῖα. Διὰ τοῦτο καὶ 34
ἡ σοφία τοῦ Θεοῦ εἶπεν· Ἀποστελῶ εἰς αὐτοὺς προφήτας καὶ ἀπο-
50 στόλους, καὶ ἐξ αὐτῶν ἀποκτενοῦσι καὶ ἐκδιώξουσιν· ἵνα ἐκζητηθῇ τὸ 35
αἷμα πάντων τῶν προφητῶν, τὸ ἐκχυνόμενον ἀπὸ καταβολῆς κόσμου,
51 ἀπὸ τῆς γενεᾶς ταύτης, ἀπὸ τοῦ αἵματος Ἄβελ ἕως τοῦ αἵματος Ζαχαρίου τοῦ ἀπολομένου μεταξὺ τοῦ θυσιαστηρίου καὶ τοῦ οἴκου. ναὶ
52 λέγω ὑμῖν· ἐκζητηθήσεται ἀπὸ τῆς γενεᾶς ταύτης. Οὐαὶ ὑμῖν τοῖς 36
νομικοῖς, ὅτι ἤρατε τὴν κλεῖδα τῆς γνώσεως· αὐτοὶ οὐκ εἰσήλθετε, καὶ 13
53 τοὺς εἰσερχομένους ἐκωλύσατε. Λέγοντος δὲ αὐτοῦ ταῦτα πρὸς αὐτοὺς,
ἤρξαντο οἱ Γραμματεῖς καὶ οἱ Φαρισαῖοι δεινῶς ἐνέχειν, καὶ ἀποστο-

whole, this interpretation is so strongly confirmed by Matt. xxiii. 26. that it probably deserves the preference. [*Comp.* Is. lviii. 7. Dan. iv. 27. infra xii. 33.]

42. [*Comp.* 1 Sam. xv. 22. Hos. vi. 6. Mich. vi. 8. Matt. ix. 13.]

44. *οἴδασιν.*] At this word the preceding *περιπατοῦντες* is to be repeated. The sense is, "The men who walk over know not [that they are walking over them.]"

46. *καὶ ὑμῖν τ. ν.*] Some recent Commentators (as Rosenm. and Kuin.) take the *καὶ* in the sense *præsertim*. And indeed the *νομικοὶ* were, in dignity, superior to the Scribes and Pharisees, as being their *teachers*. But it seems harsh to suppose a sense of *καὶ* so very rare,—nay, which Bornem. asserts is found only with adjectives or adverbs in the superlative. There is no reason to abandon the common interpretation, which assigns to *καὶ* a sense at once usual and equally agreeable to the context; for si ce the Scribes and Pharisees, and the *νομικοὶ*, or Jurists, were closely connected as instructors and instructed, he who spoke to the prejudice of the one, spoke so of the other also. [*Comp.* Is. x. 1.]

47. *ὅτι οἰκοδομεῖτε.*] On the omission of *μὲν*, see Matthæi's Gr. § 284. 4. Winer's Gr. § 13. 2.

48. *ὅτι — μνημεῖα.*] Bornem. rightly renders, *quod, dum majores vestri prophetas necarunt, vos horum monumenta instaurastis.* And remarks that the Greeks often put a *primary* sentiment in the *second* place, and a *secondary* one in the first place in the sentence. See note on Matt. xxiii. 29, 30, sq.

49. *ἡ σοφία τοῦ Θεοῦ.*] Several ancient Commentators (as Euthym.), and some modern ones, as Brug. and Wolf, take this to mean the *Λόγος*, or Son of God, i. e. Christ himself, who is called in 1 Cor. i. 24. the Wisdom of God. And this interpretation is strongly confirmed by the *ἐγὼ* of Matthew in the parallel passage. And Dr. Burton in his Bampton Lectures, p. 364. observes that there seems reason to conclude, that the Jews were in the habit of using the term *wisdom* in a personal sense. However, there is more reason to think, with the generality of modern Commentators, that *ἡ σοφία τοῦ Θεοῦ* is abstract for concrete for *ὁ Θεὸς ὁ σοφός*. [*Comp.* Acts viii. 10. Matt. x. 16. xxiii. 34. supra x. 3. John xvi. 2. Acts vii. 51. Heb. xi. 35.]

51. [See Gen. iv. 8. 2 Chron. xxiv. 21.]

52. *ἤρατε τὴν κλεῖδα τῆς γ.*] The Christian doctrine is here compared to an edifice; which, when the key is taken away, becomes inaccessible. The sense is the same as Matt. xxiii. 13, i. e. ye both reject the Gospel dispensation yourselves, and hinder others from embracing it. Matt. xvi. 19.

53. *δεινῶς ἐνέχειν*] i. e. *ἐγκοτεῖν*, on which sense see Note on Mark vi. 19. Ἀποστοματίζειν is properly a Rhetorical term, and signifies to repeat *memoriter*, to bring forward any thing from memory, or *ex tempore*. See Tim. Lex. Plat., and especially Suid. and Hesych. So *λέγειν ἀπὸ στόματος* and *ἀποστοματίζειν*; of which numerous examples are given by Wets. Sometimes, however, it is used in an active or transitive sense, "*to make any one speak memoriter*," of which examples are produced from Plato 216. C. & 217. A. This is

MT.
16. *ματίζειν αὐτὸν περὶ πλειόνων, ἐνεδρεύοντες αὐτόν· [καὶ] ζητοῦντες* 54
θηρεῦσαί τι ἐκ τοῦ στόματος αὐτοῦ, ἵνα κατηγορήσωσιν αὐτοῦ.
XII. *ἘΝ οἷς ἐπισυναχθεισῶν τῶν μυριάδων τοῦ ὄχλου, ὥστε κατα-* 1
6 *πατεῖν ἀλλήλους, ἤρξατο λέγειν πρὸς τοὺς μαθητὰς αὐτοῦ· πρῶτον*
10. *προσέχετε ἑαυτοῖς ἀπὸ τῆς ζύμης τῶν Φαρισαίων, ἥτις ἐστὶν ὑπόκρισις.*
26 *Οὐδὲν δὲ συγκεκαλυμμένον ἐστὶν, ὃ οὐκ ἀποκαλυφθήσεται· καὶ κρυ-* 2
27 *πτὸν, ὃ οὐ γνωσθήσεται. Ἀνθ᾽ ὧν ὅσα ἐν τῇ σκοτίᾳ εἴπατε, ἐν τῷ* 3
φωτὶ ἀκουσθήσεται· καὶ ὃ πρὸς τὸ οὖς ἐλαλήσατε ἐν τοῖς ταμείοις,
28 *κηρυχθήσεται ἐπὶ τῶν δωμάτων. Λέγω δὲ ὑμῖν τοῖς φίλοις μου· Μὴ* 4
φοβηθῆτε ἀπὸ τῶν ‡ ἀποκτεινόντων τὸ σῶμα, καὶ μετὰ ταῦτα μὴ ἐχόν- 5
των περισσότερόν τι ποιῆσαι. Ὑποδείξω δὲ ὑμῖν τίνα φοβηθῆτε. φο-
βήθητε τὸν μετὰ τὸ ἀποκτεῖναι ἐξουσίαν ἔχοντα ἐμβαλεῖν εἰς τὴν γέενναν·
29 *ναὶ, λέγω ὑμῖν, τοῦτον φοβήθητε. Οὐχὶ πέντε στρουθία πωλεῖται ἀσ-* 6
σαρίων δύο; καὶ ἓν ἐξ αὐτῶν οὐκ ἔστιν ἐπιλελησμένον ἐνώπιον τοῦ
30 *Θεοῦ· ἀλλὰ καὶ αἱ τρίχες τῆς κεφαλῆς ὑμῶν πᾶσαι ἠρίθμηνται. μὴ* 7
31 32 *οὖν φοβεῖσθε· πολλῶν στρουθίων διαφέρετε. Λέγω δὲ ὑμῖν· Πᾶς ὃς* 8
ἂν ὁμολογήσῃ ἐν ἐμοὶ ἔμπροσθεν τῶν ἀνθρώπων, καὶ ὁ Υἱὸς τοῦ ἀνθρώ-
33 *που ὁμολογήσει ἐν αὐτῷ ἔμπροσθεν τῶν ἀγγέλων τοῦ Θεοῦ. Ὁ δὲ* 9
12. *ἀρνησάμενός με ἐνώπιον τῶν ἀνθρώπων, ἀπαρνηθήσεται ἐνώπιον τῶν*
32 *ἀγγέλων τοῦ Θεοῦ. Καὶ πᾶς ὃς ἐρεῖ λόγον εἰς τὸν Υἱὸν τοῦ ἀνθρώ-* 10
31 *που, ἀφεθήσεται αὐτῷ· τῷ δὲ εἰς τὸ ἅγιον Πνεῦμα βλασφημήσαντι*
10. 19 *οὐκ ἀφεθήσεται. Ὅταν δὲ προσφέρωσιν ὑμᾶς ἐπὶ τὰς συναγωγὰς καὶ* 11
τὰς ἀρχὰς καὶ τὰς ἐξουσίας, μὴ μεριμνᾶτε πῶς ἢ τί ἀπολογήσησθε, ἢ
20 *τί εἴπητε· τὸ γὰρ ἅγιον Πνεῦμα διδάξει ὑμᾶς ἐν αὐτῇ τῇ ὥρᾳ, ἃ* 12
δεῖ εἰπεῖν.
Εἶπε δέ τις αὐτῷ ἐκ τοῦ ὄχλου· Διδάσκαλε, εἰπὲ τῷ ἀδελφῷ μου 13
μερίσασθαι μετ᾽ ἐμοῦ τὴν κληρονομίαν. Ὁ δὲ εἶπεν αὐτῷ· Ἄνθρωπε, 14

plainly the sense of the word in the present passage. The Pharisees strove to draw from Jesus unpremeditated effusions, in order that they might catch up something hastily and inconsiderately uttered, whence they might elicit matter for public accusation.

54. *καί.*] This is omitted in almost all the ancient MSS., several of the Versions, and almost all the early Edd., and is cancelled by Wets., Matth., Griesb., Tittm., Vat., and Scholz. It came, no doubt, from the margin.

XII. 1. *ἐν οἷς.*] Most Commentators interpret "*interea.*" Thus there will be an ellip. of *χρόνοις*. But the true ellip., I conceive, is *πράγμασι*, "during which proceedings." *Μυριάδων* (as Kuin. observes) stands for *an exceedingly great number*, as often the Heb. רבבות. The idiom, however, is common to all languages.

— *πρῶτον.*] This may be taken either with the preceding *ἤρξατο λέγειν*, or the following *προσέχετε*. The former construction is adopted by the earlier, and the latter by the recent Translators and Commentators. The *Editors*, almost without exception, point according to the *former*. Yet the *latter* seems by far the better founded: and thus *πρῶτον* signifies *inprimis*, as in Matt. vi. 33. Rom. i. 8; iii. 2, and in Joseph. Ant. x. 10. 5. *πρῶτον αὐτοῖς προστάξας*. [*Comp.* Mark viii. 15.]

2. [*Comp.* Job xii. 22. Mark iv. 22.]

4. *ἀποκτεινόντων.*] Several MSS. and early Edd. have *ἀποκτενόντων*, which is edited by Wets., Matth., Griesb., Vat., and Scholz. But there is no sufficient reason for the change. If any *were* made, I should prefer, with Bornem., *ἀποκτεννόντων*, or *ἀποκτενούντων*, or *ἀποκτιννύντων*. But as so many readings *may* be true, while it is difficult to prove which of them is *the* true one, it is better to adhere to the *common* text. The various readings seem to be only *so many* ways of removing the harshness of having two participles on one verb.

7. [*Comp.* 1 Sam. xiv. 45. 2 Sam. xiv. 11. 1 Kings, i. 52. Infra xxi. 18. Acts xxvii. 34.]

10. [*Comp.* Mark iii. 28. Heb. x. 26. 1 John v. 16.]

11. *τὰς ἀρχὰς καὶ τὰς ἐξουσίας.*] Of these words *conjoined*, examples are cited by Wets., to which may be added Onosand. p. 104. The latter denotes *magistrates*, the former *rulers* and *governors*. In this sense *ἀρχὴ* is almost always found in the *plural*. I have, however, in Recens. Synop., adduced examples of the *singular* from Thucyd. iv. 53 Theogn. 1941. Liban. Orat. p. 369. [*Compare* Matt. x. 19. Mark xiii. 11. Infra xxi. 14.]

13. *μερίσασθαι μετ᾽ ἐμοῦ.*] This use of *μετὰ* im-

15 τίς με κατέστησε δικαστὴν ἢ μεριστὴν ἐφ' ὑμᾶς; Εἶπε δὲ πρὸς αὐ-
τούς· Ὁρᾶτε καὶ φυλάσσεσθε ἀπὸ τῆς πλεονεξίας· ὅτι οὐκ ἐν τῷ
16 περισσεύειν τινὶ ἡ ζωὴ αὐτοῦ ἐστιν ἐκ τῶν ὑπαρχόντων αὐτοῦ. Εἶπε
δὲ παραβολὴν πρὸς αὐτούς, λέγων· Ἀνθρώπου τινὸς πλουσίου εὐφό-
17 ρησεν ἡ χώρα· καὶ διελογίζετο ἐν ἑαυτῷ, λέγων· Τί ποιήσω; ὅτι
18 οὐκ ἔχω ποῦ συνάξω τοὺς καρπούς μου; Καὶ εἶπε· Τοῦτο ποιήσω·
καθελῶ μου τὰς ἀποθήκας, καὶ μείζονας οἰκοδομήσω, καὶ συνάξω
19 ἐκεῖ πάντα τὰ γεννήματά μου καὶ τὰ ἀγαθά μου· καὶ ἐρῶ τῇ ψυχῇ
μου· Ψυχή, ἔχεις πολλὰ ἀγαθὰ κείμενα εἰς ἔτη πολλά· ἀναπαύου,
20 φάγε, πίε, εὐφραίνου. Εἶπε δὲ αὐτῷ ὁ Θεός· Ἄφρων, ταύτῃ τῇ
νυκτὶ τὴν ψυχήν σου ἀπαιτοῦσιν ἀπὸ σοῦ· ἃ δὲ ἡτοίμασας, τίνι ἔσται;
21 Οὕτως ὁ θησαυρίζων ἑαυτῷ, καὶ μὴ εἰς Θεὸν πλουτῶν.

ports *participation*. The sense is, so "to divide as to admit me to my share." On the thing itself see Grot., Whitby, and Recens. Syn.

14. τίς με—ἐφ' ὑμᾶς.] In allusion to Exod. ii. 14. The difference between δικαστὴς and μεριστὴς, I had myself thought to be this; that the former signifies an arbitrator, or referee in general; the latter such a one as has power to adjust conflicting claims, by *apportioning* to all parties their proper share. Thus ἢ μερ. may be said to be exegetical of δικ., as in a kindred passage of Appian. T. i. 64. 96. μήτε ἡγεῖσθαι Ῥωμαίοις δικαστὴν ἢ διαιτητήν. And Menander, Εἴ τις δικαστὴς ἢ διαιτητὴς θεῶν. Valckenaer, however, has pronounced an opinion, which, though it somewhat differs from the above, and from that of all other Commentators, may probably serve to decide the question. He maintains, that by δικ. is meant a judge *publicly appointed*; and by μεριστὴς, a *privately* appointed judge, an arbitrator, one authorised to determine conflicting claims, and apportion what is right to all, usually called a διαιτητής. And what Luke calls μεριστὰς, Plato de Legg. p. 915, first calls αἱρετοὺς δικαστὰς, and then διαιτητάς.

15. αὐτοὺς] i. e. "the bystanders, his hearers in general."

— ὁρᾶτε καὶ φυλ.] "Mind and carefully guard against." So Heliod. cited by Wets. ὅρα δὲ οὖν, φυλάττου. The construction φυλ. ἀπὸ often occurs in the LXX., and sometimes in the Classical writers. Πλεονεξία here denotes an excessive desire of increasing one's substance; and it is the scope of the subsequent parable to show how little such a spirit avails, whether to produce happiness, or procure longevity. See a masterly discourse on this subject, from this text, by Dr. South, vol. iv. 415. seqq. With this admonition the Commentators compare many moral lessons of the Heathen Philosophers, to which I have in Recens. Synop. added others, the most apposite of which is an answer of the Pythian oracle, preserved by Liban. Orat. φυλάττεσθαι τὴν φιλοχρήματον ὡς ὄλεθρον ἔχουσαν, where I would emend the manifest corruption by reading τὸ φιλ. and ἔχον, or φιλοχρηματίαν, retaining ἔχουσαν. Dr. South pithily remarks, that "there are many more whom riches have made covetous, than covetousness made rich."

— οὐκ ἐν τῷ περισσεύειν, &c.] On the sense, and still more the *construction*, of this passage, Commentators are not agreed. Kuin. maintains that ἐν τῷ περισσεύειν τινὶ signifies, "when there is abundance to any one," i. e. "when he has abundance." Οὐκ, he says, is to be referred to ἐστι, which is to be joined with ἐκ τῶν ὑπαρχ. αὐτοῦ. Schleus., Wahl, and Bornem., rightly take ζωὴ for "the *comfort* of life (*happiness*, "our being's end and aim"), as in Acts ii. 28. Rom. viii. 6, and 1 Pet. iii. 10. Thus the sense will be: "In whatever affluence a man may be, his happiness depends not on his possessions. Bornem., however, takes well founded exception to the above *construction*; and gives the following version and paraphrase: "*Non in abundantiâ cuiquam felicitas versatur* [parta] *ex opibus ejus*; i. e. nemini, propterea quod abunde habet, felicitas *paratur ex opibus quas possidet*." And he adduces an example of ἐκ in this sense from Xenoph. Conv. iv. 57.

16. εὐφόρησεν ἡ χώρα.] I have, in Recens. Synop., shown that χώρα here denotes *farm*; a signification found in the LXX., Joseph., and the Classical writers. Εὐφόρησεν, "bore well," yielded abundant produce. The word is rare, but it occurs in Joseph. Bell. i. 2. 43.

18. π. τ. γεννήματα] all the *produce* of my lands]: a sense occurring also infra xxii. 18, and in the later Greek writers, and the LXX. Τὰ ἀγαθὰ may mean goods *generally*, as just after; or such *produce* as might not fall under the name of γεννήματα, as wool, &c.

19. τῇ ψυχῇ μου.] Euthym., Brug., and Kuin. seem right in taking this to mean "*to myself*," as in Matt. x. 39. [*Comp.* Eccles. xi. 9. Ecclus. xi. 19. 1 Cor. xv. 32. James v. 5.]

— εὐφραίνου.] This denotes, in a general way, the *sensual delight* resulting from the *animal gratifications* just mentioned: not the least of which in the East, and in all hot countries, is the ἀναπαύεσθαι, the "*far niente*," of the Italians. Simil. Tobit vii. 9. φάγε, πίε, καὶ ἡδέως γίνου.

20. εἶπε.] Not in direct words addressed to the man, but by a silent decree. See Prov. i. 26. [*Comp.* Job xx. 22. Ps. lii. 7. Jer. xvii. 11.]

— ἀπαιτοῦσι.] The Commentators are not agreed as to what is the Nominat. here. Most think it alludes to those *angels*, who, as the Jews thought, accompanied the angel of death to require *the debt of life*, which is inherent in ἀπαιτεῖν. But it seems better to suppose (with the best modern Commentators) that by an idiom common to both Hebrew and Greek, the noun is suppressed, and to be supplied from the context. Or, ἀπαιτοῦσι may be regarded as an *impersonal* form, "it shall be required;" of which idiom there are many examples. See Winer's Gr.

21. οὕτως] i. e. "such is the case with," such the folly of. Ἑαυτῷ, "for himself (only)." On

MT.
6. *Εἶπε δὲ πρὸς τοὺς μαθητὰς αὐτοῦ· Διὰ τοῦτο ὑμῖν λέγω· μὴ* 22
25 *μεριμνᾶτε τῇ ψυχῇ ὑμῶν, τί φάγητε· μηδὲ τῷ σώματι, τί ἐνδύσησθε.*
26 *Ἡ ψυχὴ πλεῖόν ἐστι τῆς τροφῆς, καὶ τὸ σῶμα τοῦ ἐνδύματος. Κατα-* 23
νοήσατε τοὺς κόρακας, ὅτι οὐ σπείρουσιν, οὐδὲ θερίζουσιν· οἷς οὐκ 24
ἔστι ταμεῖον οὐδὲ ἀποθήκη· καὶ ὁ Θεὸς τρέφει αὐτούς. πόσῳ μᾶλ-
27 *λον ὑμεῖς διαφέρετε τῶν πετεινῶν; Τίς δὲ ἐξ ὑμῶν μεριμνῶν δύναται* 25
προσθεῖναι ἐπὶ τὴν ἡλικίαν αὐτοῦ πῆχυν ἕνα; Εἰ οὖν οὔτε ἐλάχιστον 26
28 *δύνασθε, τί περὶ τῶν λοιπῶν μεριμνᾶτε; Κατανοήσατε τὰ κρίνα πῶς* 27
29 *αὐξάνει· οὐ κοπιᾷ, οὐδὲ νήθει· λέγω δὲ ὑμῖν· οὐδὲ Σολομῶν ἐν*
30 *πάσῃ τῇ δόξῃ αὐτοῦ περιεβάλετο ὡς ἓν τούτων. Εἰ δὲ τὸν χόρτον ἐν* 28
τῷ ἀγρῷ σήμερον ὄντα καὶ αὔριον εἰς κλίβανον βαλλόμενον ὁ Θεὸς
31 *οὕτως ἀμφιέννυσι· πόσῳ μᾶλλον ὑμᾶς, ὀλιγόπιστοι; Καὶ ὑμεῖς μὴ* 29
32 *ζητεῖτε τί φάγητε ἢ τί πίητε· καὶ μὴ μετεωρίζεσθε. ταῦτα γὰρ πάν-* 30
τα τὰ ἔθνη τοῦ κόσμου ἐπιζητεῖ· ὑμῶν δὲ ὁ πατὴρ οἶδεν ὅτι χρῄζετε
33 *τούτων. Πλὴν ζητεῖτε τὴν βασιλείαν τοῦ Θεοῦ· καὶ ταῦτα πάντα* 31
προστεθήσεται ὑμῖν. Μὴ φοβοῦ, τὸ μικρὸν ποίμνιον· ὅτι εὐδόκησεν 32
ὁ πατὴρ ὑμῶν δοῦναι ὑμῖν τὴν βασιλείαν. Πωλήσατε τὰ ὑπάρχοντα 33
20 *ὑμῶν, καὶ δότε ἐλεημοσύνην. ποιήσατε ἑαυτοῖς βαλάντια μὴ παλαιού-*

the sense of *εἰς Θεὸν πλουτῶν* there is some difference of opinion. Certain Expositors take the meaning to be, "he who is rich for the honour and glory of God," which is the benefit of man. Thus Kypke compares Lucian Epist. Saturn. 24. *ἐς τὸ κοινὸν πλουτεῖν.* and Philo. Byzant. *πλουτεῖν εἰς θεῶν κόσμον.* More simple, and perhaps nearer the truth, is the interpretation of the ancient and many modern Commentators (as Grot., Beza, Elsn., Wolf, Rosenm., and Kuin.,) who take *πλουτεῖν εἰς τὸν Θεὸν* for *θησαυρίζειν παρὰ Θεῷ*, in the sense, "to lay up riches with God;" namely, by works of charity, benevolence, and virtue in general.

22. *διὰ τοῦτο*] i. e. as I am treating on this subject.

23. *πλεῖον*] "a greater gift;" and consequently authorizing and enjoining you to depend upon God for the supply of the *lesser*.

24. *τοὺς κόρακας.*] "The Divine Providence (remark Grot. and Bochart) is especially shown in the case of the ravens; [the corvus corax of the Zoologists] for though (as we learn from Aristotle and Ælian) the old ones very soon expel their young from the nests, and Philo says that they often abandon both nest and young; yet, by a wise Providence, they instinctively heap up in their nests whatever creates worms, whereby their abandoned young are preserved." See Ps. cxlvii. 9, and Job xxxviii. 41.

— *ταμεῖον.*] Campb. wrongly renders this "*cellar.*" The word scarcely differs in sense from *ἀποθήκη*. The difference, if any, seems to be this; that *ταμεῖον* denoted a regularly built *barn*, and *ἀποθ.* merely one of those temporary subterranean *depositaries* for grain which are common in the East. Or if *ἀγαθὰ* be had in view, *ταμ.* may denote one of those large *storehouses*, in which whatever was necessary for domestic use was laid up, and thence dispensed.

29. *μὴ μετεωρίζεσθε.*] The full sense (missed by most Commentators) is, "Be not anxiously fluctuating between hope and fear [of a livelihood.]" *Μετεωρίζεσθαι* signifies properly to be lifted on high; and, among other things, it is used of *vessels tossed aloft at sea;* which are in time depressed to the depths of the sea (as the Psalmist finely describes); an apt figure of *anxiety*, whence the signification in question is derived. That *μετεωρίζεσθαι* should have this sense is no wonder, since *μετέωρος* not unfrequently has the signification *dubious*, *fluctuating*. (See my Note in Recens. Synop. and on Thucydides ii. 8.)

30. *ἔθνη τοῦ κόσμου.*] This is a plena locutio for the more frequent *ἔθνη*, Heb. גוים, denoting "the [other] nations of the world, (besides the Jewish)."

32. *τὸ μικρὸν ποίμνιον.*] The Article supplies the place of the Vocative, *Hellenistice:* This double diminutive has great emphasis; and Commentators compare the expressions *μικρὸν ἀργυρίδιον, μικρὰ πολίχνια, μικρὸν γήδιον.* But there is this difference, that here the double dimin. (like the diminutive forms in Italian, and indeed in most languages), is expressive of tenderness and affection.

— *εὐδόκησεν*] "hath thought good." This verse is connected with the preceding, and also with the following, and that connection is well expressed by Dr. Burton in the following paraphrase. "I told you to seek the kingdom of God: and I now say, that God *intends* to GIVE you this kingdom. Do not, therefore, value your worldly possessions, but prepare for the world to come."

33. To the followers of Christ in those times of persecution and peril, the possession of riches would prove but an incumbrance. Better, therefore, were it to resign them at once, as mariners battling with a dangerous sea, lighten the vessel of all superfluous burdens. [*Comp.* Matt. xix. 21. Acts ii. 45. Infra xvi. 9.]

— *βαλάντια.*] This is said, by metonymy, for the *money contained in the purse.* The word signifies the same as *θησαυρὸς* in the other member of the sentence, except that by *θησαυρὸς* is meant a greater, and by *βαλ.* a lesser portion of wealth.

μενα, θησαυρὸν ἀνέκλειπτον ἐν τοῖς οὐρανοῖς, ὅπου κλέπτης οὐκ ἐγ- MT. 6.
34 γίζει, οὐδὲ σὴς διαφθείρει. Ὅπου γάρ ἐστιν ὁ θησαυρὸς ὑμῶν, ἐκεῖ καὶ 21
35 ἡ καρδία ὑμῶν ἔσται. Ἔστωσαν ὑμῶν αἱ ὀσφύες περιεζωσμέναι, καὶ
36 οἱ λύχνοι καιόμενοι· καὶ ὑμεῖς ὅμοιοι ἀνθρώποις προσδεχομένοις τὸν
κύριον ἑαυτῶν, πότε ἀναλύσει ἐκ τῶν γάμων· ἵνα, ἐλθόντος καὶ κρού-
37 σαντος, εὐθέως ἀνοίξωσιν αὐτῷ. Μακάριοι οἱ δοῦλοι ἐκεῖνοι, οὓς ἐλθὼν
ὁ κύριος εὑρήσει γρηγοροῦντας. Ἀμὴν λέγω ὑμῖν, ὅτι περιζώσεται καὶ
38 ἀνακλινεῖ αὐτούς, καὶ παρελθὼν διακονήσει αὐτοῖς. Καὶ ἐὰν ἔλθῃ ἐν
τῇ δευτέρᾳ φυλακῇ, καὶ ἐν τῇ τρίτῃ φυλακῇ ἔλθῃ, καὶ εὕρῃ οὕτω, μακά-
39 ριοί εἰσιν οἱ δοῦλοι ἐκεῖνοι. Τοῦτο δὲ γινώσκετε, ὅτι εἰ ᾔδει ὁ οἰκοδεσπότης ποίᾳ ὥρᾳ ὁ κλέπτης ἔρχεται, ἐγρηγόρησεν ἄν, καὶ οὐκ ἂν ἀφῆκε 24.
40 διορυγῆναι τὸν οἶκον αὐτοῦ. Καὶ ὑμεῖς οὖν γίνεσθε ἕτοιμοι· ὅτι ᾗ ὥρᾳ 44
41 οὐ δοκεῖτε, ὁ Υἱὸς τοῦ ἀνθρώπου ἔρχεται. Εἶπε δὲ αὐτῷ ὁ Πέτρος·
Κύριε, πρὸς ἡμᾶς τὴν παραβολὴν ταύτην λέγεις, ἢ καὶ πρὸς πάντας;
42 Εἶπε δὲ ὁ Κύριος· Τίς ἄρα ἐστὶν ὁ πιστὸς οἰκονόμος καὶ φρόνιμος, ὃν 45
καταστήσει ὁ κύριος ἐπὶ τῆς θεραπείας αὐτοῦ, τοῦ διδόναι ἐν καιρῷ τὸ
43 σιτομέτριον; Μακάριος ὁ δοῦλος ἐκεῖνος, ὃν ἐλθὼν ὁ κύριος αὐτοῦ εὑρή- 46
44 σει ποιοῦντα οὕτως. Ἀληθῶς λέγω ὑμῖν, ὅτι ἐπὶ πᾶσι τοῖς ὑπάρχουσιν 47
45 αὐτοῦ καταστήσει αὐτόν. Ἐὰν δὲ εἴπῃ ὁ δοῦλος ἐκεῖνος ἐν τῇ καρδίᾳ αὐτοῦ· 48
Χρονίζει ὁ κύριός μου ἔρχεσθαι· καὶ ἄρξηται τύπτειν τοὺς παῖδας καὶ 49
46 τὰς παιδίσκας, ἐσθίειν τε καὶ πίνειν καὶ μεθύσκεσθαι· ἥξει ὁ κύριος τοῦ 50
δούλου ἐκείνου ἐν ἡμέρᾳ ᾗ οὐ προσδοκᾷ, καὶ ἐν ὥρᾳ ᾗ οὐ γινώσκει·
καὶ διχοτομήσει αὐτόν, καὶ τὸ μέρος αὐτοῦ μετὰ τῶν ἀπίστων θήσει.
47 Ἐκεῖνος δὲ ὁ δοῦλος ὁ γνοὺς τὸ θέλημα τοῦ κυρίου ἑαυτοῦ, καὶ μὴ
48 ἑτοιμάσας μηδὲ ποιήσας πρὸς τὸ θέλημα αὐτοῦ, δαρήσεται πολλάς· ὁ

(Rosenm.) Ἀνέκλ. is a rare word, but it occurs in the LXX., and occasionally in Diod. Sic. and other later writers.

35. αἱ ὀσφύες περιεζ.] There is here an allusion to what must be done before the *long-robed* inhabitants of the East can engage in any active employment, civil or military. The custom, however, extended to the West, as appears from many passages of the Classical writers. [*Comp.* Eph. vi. 14. 1 Pet. i. 3.]

36. ἀνθρώποις] "men (servants)." An idiom common to the Hebrew, Greek, and Latin, and even modern languages, especially when any word corresponding to *master* is in the context.

— ἀναλύσει] shall return. A sense derived from a nautical metaphor, and used both in the LXX. and Classical writers. Γάμος in the plural is here, as often, used to denote a feast generally.

37. περιζ. καὶ ἀνακλ.] Many Commentators compare this with what took place at the Roman *Saturnalia*, and the Cretan *Hermæa*. But, as Kuin. remarks, such was common to *all* servants, good and bad. *Here* the subject is the reward assigned to *diligent* and *faithful* servants. The image (as he observes) only imports, that *as* the master will treat such servants with unusual condescension and kindness, *so* will your heavenly Master, of his free bounty, reward your diligence and fidelity with rewards as disproportionate.

39. [*Comp.* 1 Thess. v. 2. 2 Pet. iii. 10. Rev. iii. 3. xvi. 15.]

42. τίς ἄρα, &c.] Jesus does not answer to the question proposed by Peter *directly*, but by *implication*. For, from the following parable, it is manifest that what is said, though applicable to *all*, is meant *especially* for the *Apostles*; who are compared to *house-stewards*, such as in large families used to dispense the allotted portion of food to the servants. Τῆς θεραπείας, for τῶν θεραπευόντων, abstract for concrete, as frequently, both in the Scriptural and Classical writers. See my Note on Thucyd. v. 23.

47. καὶ μὴ ἑτοιμάσας — αὐτοῦ.] This is, *per Synchysin*, for μὴ ἑτοιμ. [ἑαυτὸν πρὸς] [τὸ ποιεῖν] μηδὲ ποιῆσαι, &c. [*Compare* James iv. 17.]

48. δαρήσεται ὀλίγας.] Here and just before there is said to be an ellipse of κατά. But as the complete phrase has never been produced, while the elliptical one is common, this may be reckoned among those *false ellipses* which have been swept away, by the enlightened researches of Hermann, Schaefer, and others.

To inflict any stripes upon a man for not performing his Lord's will, when he had no *knowledge* of it, would be manifestly unjust. So Thucyd. iii. 40. puts even in the mouth of the stony-hearted *Cleon* the sentiment ξύγγνωμον δ' ἐστὶ τὸ ἀκούσιον (where see my Note), and Eurip. Hippol. 1331. τὴν δὲ σὴν ἁμαρτίαν τὸ μὴ εἰδέναι ἐκλύει κάκης (guilt). Hence some would restrict the words to the knowing the Lord's will *by special revelation*, and the not knowing it by that means. But it is

MT.
10. δὲ μὴ γνοὺς, ποιήσας δὲ ἄξια πληγῶν, δαρήσεται ὀλίγας. Παντὶ δὲ ᾧ
ἐδόθη πολὺ, πολὺ ζητηθήσεται παρ' αὐτοῦ· καὶ ᾧ παρέθεντο πολὺ,
περισσότερον αἰτήσουσιν αὐτόν. Πῦρ ἦλθον βαλεῖν εἰς τὴν γῆν· καὶ 49
τί θέλω, εἰ ἤδη ἀνήφθη; βάπτισμα δὲ ἔχω βαπτισθῆναι· καὶ πῶς 50
34 συνέχομαι ἕως οὗ τελεσθῇ. Δοκεῖτε ὅτι εἰρήνην παρεγενόμην δοῦναι 51
ἐν τῇ γῇ; οὐχὶ, λέγω ὑμῖν, ἀλλ' ἢ διαμερισμόν. Ἔσονται γὰρ ἀπὸ 52
τοῦ νῦν πέντε ἐν οἴκῳ ἑνὶ διαμεμερισμένοι, τρεῖς ἐπὶ δυσὶ καὶ δύο ἐπὶ
35 τρισί. Διαμερισθήσεται πατὴρ ἐφ' υἱῷ καὶ υἱὸς ἐπὶ πατρί· μήτηρ 53
ἐπὶ θυγατρὶ καὶ θυγάτηρ ἐπὶ μητρί· πενθερὰ ἐπὶ τὴν νύμφην αὐτῆς
καὶ νύμφη ἐπὶ τὴν πενθερὰν αὐτῆς.

Ἔλεγε δὲ καὶ τοῖς ὄχλοις· Ὅταν ἴδητε τὴν νεφέλην ἀνατέλλουσαν 54
ἀπὸ δυσμῶν, εὐθέως λέγετε· Ὄμβρος ἔρχεται· καὶ γίνεται οὕτω.
16. Καὶ ὅταν νότον πνέοντα, λέγετε· Ὅτι καύσων ἔσται· καὶ γίνεται. 55
3 Ὑποκριταί! τὸ πρόσωπον τῆς γῆς καὶ τοῦ οὐρανοῦ οἴδατε δοκιμάζειν, 56
τὸν δὲ καιρὸν τοῦτον πῶς οὐ δοκιμάζετε; Τί δὲ καὶ ἀφ' ἑαυτῶν οὐ 57

better to understand them *comparatively*, of one who knew it more perfectly, as compared with one who knew it less perfectly. And this view has the advantage of *including* the other. The full sense of the passage is ably pointed out by Bp. Jebb, Sacr. Lit. p. 201.

— παντί.] This is not, as Winer imagines, a Dative absolute, but is put for παντὸς, being *accommodated*, by *attraction*, to ᾧ.

— παντὶ δὲ ᾧ ἐδόθη — παρ' αὐτοῦ.] Bishop Sanderson, Serm. ad Pop. iv. p. 191, observes, the very *distribution* of God's gifts lays on us the necessity of *using* them. Where God *bestoweth*, he *bindeth*; and to whom any thing is *given*, of him something shall be *required*.

49. πῦρ ἦλθον βαλ.] "From the necessity of Christian vigilance, our Lord is led to consider those times of persecution, when it would be especially needed; and the *fire* of which would be kindled soon after his death and passion; which are represented under the figure of baptism." (Grot.) Fire is an image of discord and violence.

— τί θέλω — ἀνήφθη.] This clause partakes of that obscurity which is generally inherent in what is uttered amidst extreme mental agitation. And hence Commentators are at issue on its meaning. Grot., Whitby, and others assign to the εἰ the sense "*O that*," and render, "And what do I wish? O that it were already kindled!" But though εἰ be sometimes used for εἴθε, as in Luke xix. 42. & xxii. 42., it is in a very different construction from the present. Rosenm. and Kuin. take the τί for πῶς, and the εἰ for *ut*, like the Heb. אם, rendering, "And how much I wish that it were already accomplished?" But both significations, in such a context as the present, are precarious. It is *better*, with Le Clerc and Campb. to render the *Vulgate*, "Quid volo, nisi ut accendatur." But to take εἰ for εἰ μὴ is unauthorized. We must retain the usual signification of εἰ, and we may take θέλω for θέλοιμι, with the Syr. Version, q. d. "And what should I (have to) wish, if it were but already kindled?" the very sense expressed by the Vulg., but thus elicited without any violence. There is, however, scarcely a shade of difference between this and the first-mentioned interpretation.

50. βάπτισμα δὲ ἔχω βαπτισθῆναι] i. e. I have to suffer many things. See Note on Matt. xx. 22. and comp. Mark x. 38.

— καὶ πῶς — τελεσθῇ] "And how am I distressed till it be accomplished!" Συνέχεσθαι signifies properly "to be *hemmed in*," and is used with a Dative, denoting disease, or calamity, either expressed or implied. The term here merely denotes an *anxious longing*. The general sense of this pathetic exclamation is well expressed by Mr. Holden thus: "I am come to deliver a doctrine which, through the wickedness of man, will be the cause of persecutions and sufferings, with which I must be overwhelmed; yet what do I wish, except that they already took place, since they will be abundantly repaid by the propagation of the Gospel."

51. ἀλλ' ἤ.] The best Commentators render this *imo potius*. But of such a sense no proof has been adduced. There will be no occasion to deviate from the usual signification of ἤ, if the ἀλλ' be taken, not for ἀλλὰ, but ἄλλο, and an ellipsis be supposed, or rather a repetition from the context after ὑμῖν, of οὐ[δὲν] παρεγενόμην δοῦναι ἐν τῇ γῇ. Buttmann, in his Larger Gr. Gr. p. 408. (Engl. Transl.) after illustrating this use of οὐδὲν ἄλλο and οὐδὲν ἄλλ', shews how the expression, by the progress of ellipse, came at length to be considered equivalent to εἰ μή· as Aristoph. Ran. 1106. Οὐκ ἠπίσταντ' ἀλλ' ἢ μᾶζαν καλέσαι. Though he acknowledges that in most cases there is an abbreviation of the thought before this ἀλλ' ἤ, which it is impossible to supply in words. Here, however, it is, as we have seen, very possible. On the present passage comp. Micah vii. 6.

54. τὴν νεφέλην] i. e. "*the* cloud;" alluding to a well-known phænomenon regarded as a certain prognostic of rainy weather. We learn both from the Scriptures (see 1 Kings xviii. 4.) and from the travellers in the East, that a small cloud like a man's hand is often the forerunner of violent storms of wind and rain. See Horne's Introd. vol. iii. 32.

57. τί δὲ — δίκαιον.] On the connection of these words some difference of opinion exists. The older Commentators almost universally refer them to what *precedes*; most recent Interpreters, as Pott and Kuin., to what *follows*. Both may be said to be, in a certain sense, right. The *gram-*

MT.
58 κρίνετε τὸ δίκαιον; Ὡς γὰρ ὑπάγεις μετὰ τοῦ ἀντιδίκου σου ἐπ᾽ ἄρ- 5.
χοντα, ἐν τῇ ὁδῷ δὸς ἐργασίαν ἀπηλλάχθαι ἀπ᾽ αὐτοῦ· μήποτε κατα- 25
σύρῃ σε πρὸς τὸν κριτήν, καὶ ὁ κριτής σε παραδῷ τῷ πράκτορι, καὶ
59 ὁ πράκτωρ σε βάλλῃ εἰς φυλακήν. Λέγω σοι· οὐ μὴ ἐξέλθῃς ἐκεῖθεν, 26
ἕως οὗ καὶ τὸ ἔσχατον λεπτὸν ἀποδῷς.
1 XIII. ΠΑΡΗΣΑΝ δέ τινες ἐν αὐτῷ τῷ καιρῷ ἀπαγγέλλοντες αὐτῷ
περὶ τῶν Γαλιλαίων, ὧν τὸ αἷμα Πιλάτος ἔμιξε μετὰ τῶν θυσιῶν αὐ-
2 τῶν. Καὶ ἀποκριθεὶς ὁ Ἰησοῦς εἶπεν αὐτοῖς· Δοκεῖτε ὅτι οἱ Γαλιλαῖοι

matical connection is with the *following*, *as* appears from the ὡς γάρ: but there is a connection of *thought* with the *preceding*; these words, in fact, forming the *vinculum* between two sentiments. At the end of the next verse the *conclusion* of the argument is, as often, left to be *supplied* by the attentive hearer or reader, and the sense is well expressed by Dr. Burton.

58. δὸς ἐργασίαν.] A Latinism for "*da operam.*" Ἀπαλλάττεσθαι ἀπό τινος signifies either "to be rid of any thing," or "to be dismissed, or let go by any person," and "is used (says Schleusn.) in a *forensic* sense, either of a criminal who is set at liberty when an adversary does not follow up an accusation; or of a debtor, who receives an acquittance from his creditor, by paying the money due, or making a composition." [*Comp.* Prov. xxv. 8.]

— πράκτορι.] Πράττειν and εἰσπράττειν signify "to exact the payment of a mulct, or of its equivalent in corporal punishment;" and accordingly πράκτωρ denotes the *exactor pœnæ* (as in Æschyl. Eum. iii. 13. πράκτορες αἵματος), and, in a general sense, the executioner of a magistrate's sentence.

XIII. 1. παρῆσαν] "came up," as in Matt. xxvi. 50. This signification is found in the *Classical* writers; though, in the earlier and purer ones, followed by εἰς and a proper name. In the *later*, the word is, as here, used absolutely. So Diod. Sic. xvii. 8. παρῆσάν τινες ἀπαγγέλλοντες, &c.

— περὶ τῶν Γαλ. ὧν, &c.] To *what* circumstance in the history of that time this incident is to be referred, Commentators are not agreed. Those which they mention (as the *sedition of the Samaritans* on Mount Gerizim, or the *rebellion set on foot by the followers of Judas of Galilee*) are liable to insuperable objections. The affair is doubtless one (like the murder of the babes at Bethlehem) passed over by Josephus. Though nothing is more probable than that something of this sort should have happened; for the Galilæans were the most seditious people in Judæa, and Pilate not the most merciful of Governors. Josephus has not, indeed, mentioned any Galilæans slain in the Temple by *Pilate*; but we learn from various parts of his history (see Ant. xv. 4. & 7. xvii. 9. 3. & vi. 17. 10.) that tumults often arose at the festivals, and sometimes battles took place even in the Temple. For which reason Herod erected the fortress of Antonia, in the immediate vicinity, and garrisoned it with a strong military force. So Joseph. Ant. xvii. 11. 6 μάλιστα δὲ τὴν σφαγὴν τῶν περὶ τὸ ἱερὸν ἐδεῖναν — ὡς ἑορτῆς τε ἀνεστηκυίας, καὶ ἱερείων ἐν τρόπῳ σφαχθοῖεν. Josephus relates that *Archelaus* put to death 300 Galilæans *in the Temple* in the act of sacrificing. It is therefore likely that a similar insurrection of Galilæans, also at a *festival*, happened in the government of *Pilate*, and was repressed in the same manner.

With respect to the phraseology, there is in τῶν θυσιῶν an ellipse of αἵματος, to be supplied from αἷμα; an idiom found both in the Greek and Latin writers. The complete expression occurs in Philo. ii. 315, (cited by Wets.,) where, giving a reason why God commanded that a homicide who had fled for refuge to an altar should be delivered up to justice; for otherwise, says he, αἵματι ἀνδροφόνων αἷμα θυσιῶν ἀνακραθήσεται. I add Theophyl. Simoc. p. 127. Οἱ μὲν οὖν ἐκκεντήσαντες τὸν B. ἀνεῖλον· ἀναμεμιγμένου τοίνυν τοῦ δείπνου καὶ αἵμασιν. It is a boldly figurative way of saying, that they were slain while attending the sacrifice How atrocious it was thought to slay any one at an altar is well known. The circumstance in question was, it seems, mentioned as being the effect of a Divine judgment on the sufferers. And our Lord's answer is meant to remove the erroneous notion of considering *that*, or *such like* calamities, as marks of Divine vengeance; and moreover to predict a similar fate to those who would not repent; a prediction which ere long attained its full completion, — when, in the very Temple, innumerable multitudes of Jews were slain, and their blood was literally mingled with the blood of the victims.

This passage, as Bp. Warburton observes, has been usually regarded as a reproof of the opinion which ascribes the general calamities effected by natural or civil causes to God's displeasure against sin; but incorrectly: that opinion being founded in the very essence of religion. What the text condemns is the superstitious *abuse* of it, which uncharitably concludes that the *sufferers* in a calamity are greater sinners than other men. This view the learned Prelate ably maintains, 1. from the *character of the speaker*; 2. from the *state and circumstances of the hearers*; and, 3. from the words of the text itself. For, "1. He who attempts to instruct others in the knowledge of God, must needs conceive that the Moral Governor of the universe, who leaves himself not without witness, doth frequently employ the physical and civil operations of our world to reform the moral. In man's state here, natural and civil events are the proper instruments of moral government. The teacher, therefore, of religion will be naturally led to inculcate this truth, that general calamities, though events merely physical or civil, were ordained for the scourge of moral disorders. 2. This is clear from the *condition* of the hearers; for the Jews, of all people on earth, were best justified in ascribing national calamities to the anger of offended Heaven. They had been accustomed to receive rewards and punishments through the instrumentality of *nature*, and of a religion which more exactly dispensed them. 3. The very words of the reproof ['except ye repent, ye shall all likewise perish'] *imply* that, among the many ends effected in the administra-

οὗτοι ἁμαρτωλοὶ παρὰ πάντας τοὺς Γαλιλαίους ἐγένοντο, ὅτι τοιαῦτα
πεπόνθασιν; οὐχὶ, λέγω ὑμῖν· ἀλλ᾽, ἐὰν μὴ μετανοῆτε, πάντες ὡσαύ- 3
τως ἀπολεῖσθε. Ἢ ἐκεῖνοι οἱ δέκα καὶ ὀκτὼ, ἐφ᾽ οὓς ἔπεσεν ὁ πύργος 4
ἐν τῷ Σιλωὰμ καὶ ἀπέκτεινεν αὐτοὺς, δοκεῖτε ὅτι οὗτοι ὀφειλέται ἐγένοντο παρὰ πάντας ἀνθρώπους τοὺς κατοικοῦντας ἐν Ἱερουσαλήμ;
οὐχὶ, λέγω ὑμῖν· ἀλλ᾽, ἐὰν μὴ μετανοῆτε, πάντες ὁμοίως ἀπολεῖσθε. 5
a Isa. 5. 2. Matt. 21. 19. [a] Ἔλεγε δὲ ταύτην τὴν παραβολήν· Συκῆν εἶχέ τις ἐν τῷ ἀμπελῶνι 6
αὐτοῦ πεφυτευμένην· καὶ ἦλθε ζητῶν καρπὸν ἐν αὐτῇ, καὶ οὐχ εὗρεν.
Εἶπε δὲ πρὸς τὸν ἀμπελουργόν· Ἰδοὺ, τρία ἔτη ἔρχομαι ζητῶν καρπὸν 7
ἐν τῇ συκῇ ταύτῃ, καὶ οὐχ εὑρίσκω· ἔκκοψον αὐτὴν, ἱνατί καὶ τὴν γῆν
καταργεῖ; Ὁ δὲ ἀποκριθεὶς λέγει αὐτῷ· κύριε, ἄφες αὐτὴν καὶ τοῦτο 8
τὸ ἔτος, ἕως ὅτου σκάψω περὶ αὐτὴν, καὶ βάλω * κόπρια· κἂν μὲν 9
ποιήσῃ καρπόν, — εἰ δὲ μήγε, εἰς τὸ μέλλον ἐκκόψεις αὐτήν.
Ἦν δὲ διδάσκων ἐν μιᾷ τῶν συναγωγῶν ἐν τοῖς σάββασι· καὶ ἰδοὺ, 10
γυνὴ ἦν πνεῦμα ἔχουσα ἀσθενείας ἔτη δέκα καὶ ὀκτὼ, καὶ ἦν συγκύ- 11
πτουσα καὶ μὴ δυναμένη ἀνακύψαι εἰς τὸ παντελές. Ἰδὼν δὲ αὐτὴν ὁ 12

tion of Nature, this was one, — to express God's displeasure at human iniquities, in order to bring men to *repentance*. But if the belief of a moral end in these calamities be a principle of religion proper to be inculcated, what was it, you will ask, that deserved so severe a reproof as this? It was that *superstition* which so often accompanies, and so fatally infects this principle of religion — that of ascribing public calamities, not to God's displeasure against sin in general, but to his vengeance on the persons of the sufferers, whom this superstition concludes to be greater sinners than other men." The learned Prelate then proceeds to shew, that this superstitious notion *deserved* the severity of our Lord's censure, "1. because it implied *gross ignorance* in the nature of the punishment, and betrayed *malignity of heart*; 2. from its extreme *uncharitableness*; and 3. because it has a direct tendency to defeat the very end of the chastisement, whereby exemplary warnings become lost, and every fresh gleam of Divine mercy only serves to ripen them into the speedy objects of God's justice; as was probably the case with the Jews then, whose day of grace was past, their doom pronounced, and the Imperial Eagle, scenting the carcass from afar, came down to the extermination of this devoted people." Next the admirable writer fully evinces that the doctrine which ascribes the *general* calamities arising from natural causes to God's displeasure against sin, is agreeable both to reason and religion, displaying God's glory in the fairest colours, and establishing man's peace and happiness on the most solid foundation. The very same view is taken by Dr. Waterland (Works, vol. iv.)

2. παρὰ] "beyond," as Luke iii. 13. and elsewhere. The origin of which sign is shewn by Winer, Gr. Gr. p. 149.

4. ἐν τῷ Σιλ.] The sense is, "at," i. e. *by* "Siloam." This tower was probably one of the towers of the city walls, and was, I imagine, the one at the S. E. angle of the walls. Thus the fountain is correctly noted by Milton as being "*fast by the Oracle of God.*" Ὀφειλέται, sinners. A Chaldee idiom, by which debts and sins, and debtors and sinners, are interchanged.

7. τρία ἔτη.] At which time from planting, the Naturalists tell us, those that bear at all will produce fruit. Καταργεῖ is for ἀργὸν ποιεῖ, "makes it unproductive," as in Ezra iv. 21. The term is mostly figuratively employed to denote *abrogating a law*.

— ἱνατί καὶ τ. γ. κ.] The καὶ here is so far from being, as some say, redundant, that it is almost emphatic, denoting that the tree not only bore no fruit itself, but hindered the growth of it in others.

9. κόπρια.] This, instead of κοπρίαν, is found in a great number of MSS. and early Edd., and is adopted by Wets., Matth., Griesb., Vat., Tittm., and Scholz.

11. πνεῦμα ἔχουσα ἀσθ.] "laboured under weakness." The recent Commentators mostly regard πν. ἀσθ. as a periphrasis, for ἀσθένειαν, as denoting simply a *disease*. But the passages of the Classical writers which they adduce are of a different nature. The words of our Lord at ver. 16. ἣν ἔδησεν ὁ Σατανᾶς show that πνεῦμα is very significant; and, considering the very frequent use of the word in the sense δαιμονίου, it cannot be doubted but that the sense is (as the ancient and most modern Commentators suppose) "having a dæmon which inflicts disease and infirmity." So Acts xvi. 16. πνεῦμα Πύθωνος, where see Note. It was, indeed, the Jewish notion, and indeed that of the Gentiles, that diseases, especially the severely acute and tediously chronic ones, were inflicted by dæmons. But the peculiarity of the present expression, and the words of our Lord himself, oblige us to suppose a real dæmoniacal possession. Euthym. well explains πν. ἀσθ. by δαιμόνιον ἀῤῥωστίας, μὴ ἐῶν αὐτὴν ὑγιαίνειν.

— καὶ ἦν συγκ.] "she was bowed together." This, however, is not simply an *active in a passive sense*; for the word may be taken in a *neuter* sense for σύγκυφος εἶναι; from which the transition to a passive one is easy. The disorder called κύφωσις is seated in the whole of the spine, and extends to the loins; inducing a total inactivity of the vertebræ: so that the patient is necessarily *bowed together*, from utter weakness of the parts. And therefore the disease might very well be

Ἰησοῦς προσεφώνησε καὶ εἶπεν αὐτῇ· Γύναι, ἀπολέλυσαι τῆς ἀσθενείας
13 σου. Καὶ ἐπέθηκεν αὐτῇ τὰς χεῖρας· καὶ παραχρῆμα ἀνωρθώθη, καὶ
14 ἐδόξαζε τὸν Θεόν. [b] Ἀποκριθεὶς δὲ ὁ ἀρχισυνάγωγος, ἀγανακτῶν ὅτι b Exod. 20. 9. Deut. 5. 13.
τῷ σαββάτῳ ἐθεράπευσεν ὁ Ἰησοῦς, ἔλεγε τῷ ὄχλῳ· Ἓξ ἡμέραι εἰσὶν Ezek. 20. 12.
ἐν αἷς δεῖ ἐργάζεσθαι· ἐν ταύταις οὖν ἐρχόμενοι θεραπεύεσθε, καὶ
15 μὴ τῇ ἡμέρᾳ τοῦ σαββάτου. [c] Ἀπεκρίθη οὖν αὐτῷ ὁ Κύριος, καὶ c Exod. 23. 5. Deut. 22. 4.
εἶπεν· Ὑποκριτὰ, ἕκαστος ὑμῶν τῷ σαββάτῳ οὐ λύει τὸν βοῦν αὐτοῦ Matt. 12. 1, 11. Mark 3. 2. supra 6. 7.
16 ἢ τὸν ὄνον ἀπὸ τῆς φάτνης, καὶ ἀπαγαγὼν ποτίζει; ταύτην δὲ, θυ- infra 14. 5. John 7. 23.
γατέρα Ἀβραὰμ οὖσαν, ἣν ἔδησεν ὁ Σατανᾶς ἰδοὺ δέκα καὶ ὀκτὼ ἔτη,
οὐκ ἔδει λυθῆναι ἀπὸ τοῦ δεσμοῦ τούτου τῇ ἡμέρᾳ τοῦ σαββάτου;
17 Καὶ ταῦτα λέγοντος αὐτοῦ, κατῃσχύνοντο πάντες οἱ ἀντικείμενοι αὐτῷ·
καὶ πᾶς ὁ ὄχλος ἔχαιρεν ἐπὶ πᾶσι τοῖς ἐνδόξοις τοῖς γινομένοις ὑπ' MT.
αὐτοῦ. 13.
18 Ἔλεγε δέ· Τίνι ὁμοία ἐστὶν ἡ βασιλεία τοῦ Θεοῦ; καὶ τίνι ὁμοι- 31
19 ώσω αὐτήν; Ὁμοία ἐστὶ κόκκῳ σινάπεως, ὃν λαβὼν ἄνθρωπος ἔβαλεν
εἰς κῆπον ἑαυτοῦ· καὶ ηὔξησε καὶ ἐγένετο εἰς δένδρον μέγα, καὶ τὰ 32
20 πετεινὰ τοῦ οὐρανοῦ κατεσκήνωσεν ἐν τοῖς κλάδοις αὐτοῦ. [Καὶ] 33
21 πάλιν εἶπε· Τίνι ὁμοιώσω τὴν βασιλείαν τοῦ Θεοῦ; Ὁμοία ἐστὶ
ζύμῃ, ἣν λαβοῦσα γυνὴ ἐνέκρυψεν εἰς ἀλεύρου σάτα τρία, ἕως οὗ ἐζυμώθη ὅλον.
22 ΚΑΙ διεπορεύετο κατὰ πόλεις καὶ κώμας διδάσκων, καὶ πορείαν
23 ποιούμενος εἰς Ἱερουσαλήμ. Εἶπε δέ τις αὐτῷ· Κύριε, εἰ ὀλίγοι οἱ 7.
24 σωζόμενοι; Ὁ δὲ εἶπε πρὸς αὐτούς· Ἀγωνίζεσθε εἰσελθεῖν διὰ τῆς 13
στενῆς πύλης· ὅτι πολλοὶ, λέγω ὑμῖν, ζητήσουσιν εἰσελθεῖν, καὶ οὐκ
25 ἰσχύσουσιν, ἀφ' οὗ ἂν ἐγερθῇ ὁ οἰκοδεσπότης, καὶ ἀποκλείσῃ τὴν

called ἀσθένεια. The words *εἰς τὸ παντελὲς* are a *phrase* for the *adverb* παντελῶς, as Heb. vii. 25. and sometimes in the later Classical writers.

12. ἀπολέλυσαι.] Both the Hebrew and Greek writers used to compare disorders to *chains* and *ropes*, by which men are, as it were, held bound. Of this Kypke and Wets. produce examples.

15. οὐ λύει, &c.] Christ refutes their cavil by a reference to their *own practice:* for that it was considered allowable to attend to the *necessary care of animals* on the Sabbath, is clear from many passages of the Rabbinical writers, cited by Schoettg. Nay, even *Pagan* superstition permitted various employments of husbandry even on the solemn festivals.

18. [*Comp.* Mark iv. 30.]

22. [*Comp.* Matt. ix. 35. Mark vi. 6.]

23. εἰ ὀλίγοι οἱ σωζ.] It has been a disputed point, what is the exact *import* of this inquiry, and the *spirit* which dictated it. Some understand σωζ. of *temporal* deliverance, namely, being preserved from the approaching destruction of the Jewish state. But that is surely supposing a kind of *ænigma* little suitable to a simple *inquiry*. More probable is the opinion of many eminent Interpreters, from Hamm. to Kuin., that σωζ. is to be understood of preservation from the general unbelief of Christ and his religion; of which sense they adduce examples from the N. T. and Ignatius' Epistles to Polycarp. Those, however, are rather proofs of the *sense* "being put into the way of salvation." It is far more natural to understand the word (with most Interpreters, ancient and modern,) of *salvation* — properly so called: q. d. Are there few who will attain salvation? A sense which seems *required* by the terms of our Lord's *reply*. Whether the question was a *captious* one or not (though the latter is the more probable opinion), certain it is (as appears from Lightf. and Schoettg.) that the point was a disputed one in the Jewish schools; some maintaining *universal salvation*, others limiting it to a few *elect*. Now to a question of such minor importance as this, (for it rather concerns us, as Grot. observes, to know *what sort* of persons will be saved, than *how few*) our Lord (agreeably to his custom of never answering questions of *mere curiosity*) was pleased to return no answer; but makes his words an answer to the question which *ought rather* to have been asked, — namely, "*how* salvation is to be attained." Ἀγωνίζεσθαι is a very significant term, founded on an agonistic allusion. The sense is, "strain every nerve." This use of εἰ for πότερον in *direct* address is rare; in *indirect* address it is not unfrequent either in the Scriptural or Classical writers. The best mode of viewing the former idiom is to consider it as a blending of the *oratio directa* with the *indirecta*.

25. ἀφ' οὗ.] Sub. χρόνου, "from the time," "when once." I have preferred the punctuation adopted by the Bâle Editor, and approved by Bornemann, because it seems most agreeable to

MT.
7. θύραν, καὶ ἄρξησθε ἔξω ἑστάναι καὶ κρούειν τὴν θύραν, λέγοντες·
22 23 Κύριε, Κύριε, ἄνοιξον ἡμῖν· καὶ ἀποκριθεὶς ἐρεῖ ὑμῖν· Οὐκ οἶδα
ὑμᾶς πόθεν ἐστέ. Τότε ἄρξεσθε λέγειν· Ἐφάγομεν ἐνώπιόν σου καὶ 26
ἐπίομεν, καὶ ἐν ταῖς πλατείαις ἡμῶν ἐδίδαξας. Καὶ ἐρεῖ· Λέγω ὑμῖν, 27
8. οὐκ οἶδα ὑμᾶς πόθεν ἐστέ· ἀπόστητε ἀπ᾽ ἐμοῦ, πάντες οἱ ἐργάται
12 τῆς ἀδικίας. Ἐκεῖ ἔσται ὁ κλαυθμὸς καὶ ὁ βρυγμὸς τῶν ὀδόντων, 28
ὅταν ὄψησθε Ἀβραὰμ καὶ Ἰσαὰκ καὶ Ἰακὼβ καὶ πάντας τοὺς προ-
11 φήτας ἐν τῇ βασιλείᾳ τοῦ Θεοῦ, ὑμᾶς δὲ ἐκβαλλομένους ἔξω. Καὶ 29
19. ἥξουσιν ἀπὸ ἀνατολῶν καὶ δυσμῶν, καὶ ἀπὸ βοῤῥᾶ καὶ νότου· καὶ
30 ἀνακλιθήσονται ἐν τῇ βασιλείᾳ τοῦ Θεοῦ. Καὶ ἰδοὺ, εἰσὶν ἔσχατοι, 30
οἳ ἔσονται πρῶτοι· καὶ εἰσὶ πρῶτοι, οἳ ἔσονται ἔσχατοι.

Ἐν αὐτῇ τῇ ἡμέρᾳ προσῆλθόν τινες Φαρισαῖοι, λέγοντες αὐτῷ· 31
Ἔξελθε καὶ πορεύου ἐντεῦθεν, ὅτι Ἡρώδης θέλει σε ἀποκτεῖναι. Καὶ 32
εἶπεν αὐτοῖς· Πορευθέντες εἴπατε τῇ ἀλώπεκι ταύτῃ· Ἰδοὺ, ἐκβάλλω
δαιμόνια καὶ ἰάσεις ἐπιτελῶ σήμερον καὶ αὔριον, καὶ τῇ τρίτῃ τελειοῦ-
23. μαι. Πλὴν δεῖ με σήμερον καὶ αὔριον καὶ τῇ ἐρχομένῃ πορεύεσθαι· 33
37 —ὅτι οὐκ ἐνδέχεται προφήτην ἀπολέσθαι ἔξω Ἱερουσαλήμ. Ἱερουσα- 34
λήμ! Ἱερουσαλήμ! ἡ ἀποκτείνουσα τοὺς προφήτας, καὶ λιθοβολοῦσα
τοὺς ἀπεσταλμένους πρὸς αὐτὴν, ποσάκις ἠθέλησα ἐπισυνάξαι τὰ τέκνα
σου, ὃν τρόπον ὄρνις τὴν ἑαυτῆς νοσσιὰν ὑπὸ τὰς πτέρυγας; καὶ οὐκ

the context to connect this ver. (as the Syr. Transl. and Beza did) with the *preceding* rather than the *following*, according to which we may best suppose the *apodosis* to be at τότε ver. 26. Ἐγερθῇ is not (as some imagine) redundant, but is a part of the imagery of the story, and signifies, "has risen from his seat."

26. ἐνώπιόν σου] "in thy presence and company." This mode of address is a form of *rousing any one's recollection* of a person; as denoting familiar intercourse.

27. οὐκ οἶδα ὑ. π. ἐ.] This seems to be a familiar mode of expressing that we desire to have nothing to do with the person, as Matt. vii. 23. xxv. 12. So Lucian, Pisc. 50. i. 617, makes Aristotle, when brought back to life, say of one who pretends to be a true follower of Aristotle, and is not such, ἀγνοῶ γὰρ ὅστις ἐστίν.

—ἐργάται τῆς ἀδικίας.] Grot. well explains the ἐργ. as denoting *habit* and devotedness to. So Bp. Sanderson, Serm. ad Aulam, p. 216, observes, that the wicked are so termed in Scripture because they do, *hoc agere*, make it their work, business, or trade. Schleus. compares Xen. Mem. ii. 1. 27. καλῶν καὶ σεμνῶν ἐργάτης. To which I would add 2 Macc. iii. 6. οἱ ἐργάται τῆς ἀδικίας. Menand. Hist. i. 145. A. χαλεπῶν ἔργων καὶ ἀνοσίων ἐργάται.

29. [*Comp.* Is. ii. 2, 3. Mal. i. 11.]

32. τῇ ἀλώπεκι τ.] Our Lord did not use this appellation by way of contumely, but to show his intimate knowledge of his disposition and secret policy. (Wets.) However the use of it confirms the opinions of those who think that these persons had been sent to intimate to Jesus, a *pretended* design of the Tetrarch to kill him, and that to get rid of him out of his dominions:—for the same reason, probably, that the Gadarenes at Matt. viii. 34. desire Jesus to depart from their coasts.

—ἐκβάλλω δαιμόνια, &c.] The course of reasoning in this verse seems to be this: "I am employed innocently, and even highly meritoriously, nor shall I long weary him with my presence, but soon take my departure; why then should he seek my life?" Σήμερον καὶ αὔριον is a sort of proverbial form, denoting any short interval of time, as in a kindred passage of Arrian Epict. iv. 10. and Hos. vi. 2. cited by Wets. On the import of τελειοῦμαι the Commentators are not agreed. Some recent ones take it to mean, "I shall be sacrificed;" but of this sense they adduce no valid proof. It is better, with the ancient and most modern Interpreters, to explain it, "I shall be brought to the end of my course, and then shall die." So Phil. iii. 12. οὐχ ὅτι ἤδη τετελείωμαι. Almost all Commentators consider the word as an *Attic contract form* for τελειώσομαι, and that as put for τελειωθήσομαι. But Bornem., with reason, objects that the penult of this verb is *long*; and notices similar errors in the forms of other verbs in the Classics. *Here* certainly the Present may be tolerated; nay, is *required*, by the correspondent verbs foregoing, ἐκβάλλω and ἐπιτελῶ; though the *sense* be, "I am being brought to my end;" which involves a notion of what is scarcely *future*, as very shortly to take place.

33. πλὴν—πορεύεσθαι.] The sense seems (as Kuin. suggests) to be, "However, I must for this short time go on in my usual course or ministry; for πορεύεσθαι, (like the Heb. הלך) denotes habitual action or regular business. πορεύεσθαι cannot, as Hammond thinks, have reference to the counsel of the Pharisees, v. 31. for then some words denoting, "after working my miracles," will have to be supplied—and the ellipsis which he lays down is both harsh, and the reasoning inconsequent. There is, in fact, not so much an *ellipsis*, as an *aposiopesis*, to be supplied from

MT.
35 ἠθελήσατε. Ἰδοὺ, ἀφίεται ὑμῖν ὁ οἶκος ὑμῶν ἔρημος. ἀμὴν δὲ λέγω 23.
ὑμῖν, ὅτι οὐ μή με ἴδητε, ἕως ἂν ἥξῃ ὅτε εἴπητε· Εὐλογημένος ὁ 38 39
ἐρχόμενος ἐν ὀνόματι Κυρίου.

1 XIV. *ΚΑΙ ἐγένετο, ἐν τῷ ἐλθεῖν αὐτὸν εἰς οἶκόν τινος τῶν ἀρχόν-*
των τῶν Φαρισαίων σαββάτῳ φαγεῖν ἄρτον, καὶ αὐτοὶ ἦσαν παρατη-
2 *ρούμενοι αὐτόν. Καὶ ἰδοὺ, ἄνθρωπός τις ἦν ὑδρωπικὸς ἔμπροσθεν*
3 *αὐτοῦ· [a] καὶ ἀποκριθεὶς ὁ Ἰησοῦς εἶπε πρὸς τοὺς νομικοὺς καὶ Φαρι-* [a] Matt. 12. 10.
4 *σαίους, λέγων· Εἰ ἔξεστι τῷ σαββάτῳ θεραπεύειν; οἱ δὲ ἡσύχασαν.*
5 *Καὶ ἐπιλαβόμενος ἰάσατο αὐτὸν καὶ ἀπέλυσε. [b] καὶ ἀποκριθεὶς πρὸς* [b] Exod. 23. 5. Deut. 22. 4. supra 13. 15.
αὐτοὺς εἶπε· Τίνος ὑμῶν ὄνος ἢ βοῦς εἰς φρέαρ ἐμπεσεῖται, καὶ οὐκ
6 *εὐθέως ἀνασπάσει αὐτὸν ἐν τῇ ἡμέρᾳ τοῦ σαββάτου; Καὶ οὐκ ἴσχυ-*
σαν ἀνταποκριθῆναι αὐτῷ πρὸς ταῦτα.

7 *Ἔλεγε δὲ πρὸς τοὺς κεκλημένους παραβολὴν, ἐπέχων πῶς τὰς πρω-*
8 *τοκλισίας ἐξελέγοντο, λέγων πρὸς αὐτούς· [c] Ὅταν κληθῇς ὑπό τινος* [c] Prov 25. 6, 7.
εἰς γάμους, μὴ κατακλιθῇς εἰς τὴν πρωτοκλισίαν· μήποτε ἐντιμότερός
9 *σου ᾖ κεκλημένος ὑπ' αὐτοῦ, καὶ ἐλθὼν ὁ σὲ καὶ αὐτὸν καλέσας ἐρεῖ*
σοι· Δὸς τούτῳ τόπον· καὶ τότε ἄρξῃ μετ' αἰσχύνης τὸν ἔσχατον
10 *τόπον κατέχειν. Ἀλλ' ὅταν κληθῇς, πορευθεὶς ἀνάπεσον εἰς τὸν ἔσχα-*
τον τόπον· ἵνα ὅταν ἔλθῃ ὁ κεκληκώς σε, εἴπῃ σοι· Φίλε, προσανά-
βηθι ἀνώτερον· τότε ἔσται σοι δόξα ἐνώπιον τῶν συνανακειμένων σοι.

what went before—as follows "[I shall, I say, finish this course in spite of Herod, and shall *not* be killed in *Galilee*] *for* it cannot be," &c.

—οὐκ ἐνδέχεται—Ἱερουσαλήμ.] These words contain one of the most cutting reproaches imaginable. Of course, οὐκ ἐνδέχεται must be understood with the usual limitation in such sort of *acutè dicta*; i. e. "*it can scarcely be*;" for John the Baptist and others had been put to death out of Jerusalem.

35. ἀφίεται ἔρημος.] I cannot agree with Griesbach and Scholz in cancelling ἔρημος; because it is indispensably necessary to the sense; and ὑμῖν would thus be worse than useless. There is an allusion to land or territory which is *thrown up*, as no longer worth cultivating.

XIV. 1. φαγεῖν ἄρτον.] This phrase, the Commentators say, is formed from the Hebrew אכול לחם; which though it properly signifies no more than "to take food," yet often denotes to feast, to make good cheer. But that sense, I apprehend, is never found, except when the meal is one to which guests are invited; and then it may be *supposed* that the cheer is better than that of an ordinary domestic meal. But then this is never the *signification* of the phrase, and is only *implied* in the context. Such a meal, no doubt, was the present. Indeed, it appears from what Lightf., Wets., and others, have copiously adduced from the Rabbinical writers, that it was usual with the Jews to provide better cheer on the Sabbath than on other days. Also that they used to make feasts and give entertainments especially on that day.

By τινο τῶν ἀρχ. τῶν Φαρ. is meant (as Grot., Hamm., Whitby, Pearce, and Campb., have shown) one of the rulers [of a synagogue] who was a Pharisee. Comp. John iii. 1. That *all* such rulers were not Pharisees, appears from John viii. 48.

2. ἔμπροσθεν αὐτοῦ] "in his view;" having probably so placed himself, though he did not dare to ask for cure, it being the Sabbath day.

5. τίνος ὑμῶν—καὶ οὐκ, &c.] Bornemann rightly renders, "*Cujusnam vestrum asinus aut bos in puteum incidet, et quis non statim eum extrahet?*"

—ὄνος.] Many good MSS., Versions, and some Fathers and early Edd. have υἱὸς, which is adopted by Wets., Matth., and Scholz; but without sufficient reason; for the canon of preferring the more difficult reading does not apply in cases where that would involve an exceeding harshness, and violate the usage of the language, or where the words are *very similar*. Such is the case here. In these sort of sayings *an ass and an ox* are put for *any domestic animal*, as being in the most common use.

7. παραβολὴν.] The word here seems to bear the sense of an *important* moral precept, on which see Note on Matt. xiii. 2.

—ἐπέχων.] Some imagine here an ellipse of τοὺς ὀφθαλμούς. But as they adduce examples only of the *complete* phrase ἐπέχειν ὀφθ. τινι, not of the elliptical one, this cannot be admitted. Others, more properly, supply τὸν νοῦν, both here and at Acts iii. 5. But even that is so seldom found supplied, that it is better to suppose no ellipse at all, as in 1 Tim. iv. 16. ἔπεχε σεαυτῷ. Thus ἐπέχων will simply denote "*observing*."

9. δὸς τόπον] "give place, seat, situation." The phrase often occurs in the later Greek Classical writers, and was probably founded on the Latin *locum dare*. From Schoettg. it appears that this was the phrase used on such occasions by the Jews, who (as well as the Greeks and Romans) had frequent disputes about the chief seats at feasts.

d Job 22. 29. Prov. 29. 23. Matt. 23. 12. supra. 1. 51. infra 18. 14. James 4. 6, 10. 1 Pet. 5. 5.
e Neh. 8. 12. Tob. 4. 7. Prov. 3. 9, 28.

d Ὅτι πᾶς ὁ ὑψῶν ἑαυτὸν, ταπεινωθήσεται· καὶ ὁ ταπεινῶν ἑαυτὸν 11
ὑψωθήσεται.
e Ἔλεγε δὲ καὶ τῷ κεκληκότι αὐτόν· Ὅταν ποιῇς ἄριστον ἢ δεῖπνον, 12
μὴ φώνει τοὺς φίλους σου, μηδὲ τοὺς ἀδελφούς σου, μηδὲ τοὺς συγγενεῖς σου, μηδὲ γείτονας πλουσίους· μήποτε καὶ αὐτοί σε ἀντικαλέ-
σωσι, καὶ γένηταί σοι ἀνταπόδομα. Ἀλλ' ὅταν ποιῇς δοχὴν, κάλει 13
πτωχοὺς, ἀναπήρους, χωλοὺς, τυφλούς· καὶ μακάριος ἔσῃ· ὅτι οὐκ 14
ἔχουσιν ἀνταποδοῦναί σοι· ἀνταποδοθήσεται γάρ σοι ἐν τῇ ἀναστάσει
τῶν δικαίων.
Ἀκούσας δέ τις τῶν συνανακειμένων ταῦτα, εἶπεν αὐτῷ· Μακάριος 15
ὃς φάγεται ἄρτον ἐν τῇ βασιλείᾳ τοῦ Θεοῦ. f Ὁ δὲ εἶπεν αὐτῷ· 16
Ἄνθρωπός τις ἐποίησε δεῖπνον μέγα, καὶ ἐκάλεσε πολλούς. g Καὶ 17
ἀπέστειλε τὸν δοῦλον αὐτοῦ τῇ ὥρᾳ τοῦ δείπνου εἰπεῖν τοῖς κεκλημέ-
νοις· Ἔρχεσθε, ὅτι ἤδη ἕτοιμά ἐστι πάντα. Καὶ ἤρξαντο ἀπὸ μιᾶς 18
παραιτεῖσθαι πάντες. Ὁ πρῶτος εἶπεν αὐτῷ· Ἀγρὸν ἠγόρασα, καὶ
ἔχω ἀνάγκην ἐξελθεῖν καὶ ἰδεῖν αὐτόν· ἐρωτῶ σε, ἔχε με παρῃτημένον. Καὶ ἕτερος εἶπε· Ζεύγη βοῶν ἠγόρασα πέντε, καὶ πορεύομαι 19
δοκιμάσαι αὐτά· ἐρωτῶ σε, ἔχε με παρῃτημένον. Καὶ ἕτερος εἶπε· 20
Γυναῖκα ἔγημα, καὶ διὰ τοῦτο οὐ δύναμαι ἐλθεῖν. Καὶ παραγε- 21
νόμενος ὁ δοῦλος ἐκεῖνος ἀπήγγειλε τῷ κυρίῳ αὐτοῦ ταῦτα. Τότε
ὀργισθεὶς ὁ οἰκοδεσπότης εἶπε τῷ δούλῳ αὐτοῦ· Ἔξελθε ταχέως

f Isa. 25. 6. Matt. 22. 2. Rev. 19. 9.
g Prov. 9. 2, 5.

11. *πᾶς ὁ ὑψῶν — ὑψωθήσεται.*] Probably an adage. Similar sentiments occur in the Rabbinical writers.

12. *μὴ φώνει τοὺς φίλους, &c.*] The best Commentators are of opinion, that the negative particle must here be taken with limitation, and rendered *non tam, quam potius*, as in many passages of the O. and N. T. This idiom, however, Winer and Bornem. say, is *properly* confined to cases where the two particles are employed in the same sentence; not, as here, in two different ones, and they lay down the sense as follows: "Noli beneficia in alios conferre eo consilio, ut acceptam tibi gratiam referant, sed ut comproberis Deo." But this is an unjustifiable refinement. The plain intent of what is said, being to inculcate, that charity is a duty far more obligatory than hospitality.

This sense of *φωνεῖν* is very rare, and is founded on that more frequent one by which the word denotes to *hail* any one; and, from the adjunct, to summon or call him to us.

14. *ὅτι οὐκ — ἀντ. γάρ, &c.*] The full sense is, "because, though they can make thee no return, a return will be made thee," &c.

— *ἀναστάσει τῶν δικαίων.*] So *ἀναστ. τῆς ζωῆς* in John v. 29. where it is opposed to *ἀναστ. κρίσεως*. The Pharisees believed in a resurrection of *the just*, but imagined that there would be *two* resurrections; the first to take place at the coming of the Messiah, who would thus establish an earthly kingdom, to which the Pharisee here evidently alludes. (See Grot. and Pearce.)

18. *ἀπὸ μιᾶς.*] some supply *ὥρας*; others *γνώμης*; others, again, *φωνῆς*. which is *expressed* in Joseph. ii. 509. and Diod. Sic. 515. D. But the true ellipse seems to be *γνώμης* (on which see Bos.): from one and the same [bad] principle. *Παραιτεῖσθαι* here signifies *to excuse themselves*, as is clear from the following *ἔχε με παρῃτημένον*, which is a Latinism formed on the *excusatum me habeas rogo*, which occurs in Martial.

— *ἀγρὸν ἠγόρασα.*] Since we cannot suppose that a man would buy land without seeing it; or that having bought it, the going to see it should be a matter of such urgency; most recent Commentators take the sense of *ἠγόρασα* to be, *I intend to buy*. But this can by no means be admitted. Others suppose that the purchase was *conditional*. But of such a mode of purchasing *land*, (i. e. on *warrant*), there is no proof, and thus the interpretation is altogether *hypothetical*. The best method of interpretation seems to be that proposed in Recens. Synop., namely, to take the Aorist in the sense (on which idiom see Matth. Gr. Gr. § 506. and Win. Gr. Gr. § 34. Note 3.) "I have been purchasing," i. e. "been in treaty for;" which well accounts for the *going and seeing* the land, agreeably to the *going and proving* the oxen just after mentioned.

19. *ζεύγη βοῶν ἠγόρασα.*] Here again I would render *ἠγόρασα*, "I am, or have been, in treaty for," because though, in a passage of a Rabbinical writer, mention is made of some oxen being sold on warranty, and subject to subsequent proof, yet we may readily imagine that such cases were rare.

20. *γυναῖκα — οὐ δύναμαι ἐλθεῖν.*] This was the most specious excuse; for, by the laws and customs of most nations, any omission in the *duties*, much less the *etiquette* of life, was thought excusable in newly married persons; hence even soldiers had usually a furlough for a year.

MT.
εἰς τὰς πλατείας καὶ ῥύμας τῆς πόλεως, καὶ τοὺς πτωχοὺς καὶ ἀναπή- 10.
22 ρους καὶ χωλοὺς καὶ τυφλοὺς εἰσάγαγε ὧδε. Καὶ εἶπεν ὁ δοῦλος·
23 κύριε, γέγονεν ὡς ἐπέταξας· καὶ ἔτι τόπος ἐστί. Καὶ εἶπεν ὁ κύριος
πρὸς τὸν δοῦλον· Ἔξελθε εἰς τὰς ὁδοὺς καὶ φραγμοὺς, καὶ ἀνάγ-
24 κασον εἰσελθεῖν, ἵνα γεμισθῇ ὁ οἶκός μου. Λέγω γὰρ ὑμῖν, ὅτι
οὐδεὶς τῶν ἀνδρῶν ἐκείνων τῶν κεκλημένων γεύσεταί μου τοῦ δείπνου.
25 Συνεπορεύοντο δὲ αὐτῷ ὄχλοι πολλοί· καὶ στραφεὶς εἶπε πρὸς αὐ- 37
26 τούς· Εἴτις ἔρχεται πρός με, καὶ οὐ μισεῖ τὸν πατέρα ἑαυτοῦ καὶ
τὴν μητέρα, καὶ τὴν γυναῖκα καὶ τὰ τέκνα, καὶ τοὺς ἀδελφοὺς καὶ τὰς
ἀδελφὰς, ἔτι δὲ καὶ τὴν ἑαυτοῦ ψυχὴν, οὐ δύναταί μου μαθητὴς εἶναι.
27 Καὶ ὅστις οὐ βαστάζει τὸν σταυρὸν αὐτοῦ καὶ ἔρχεται ὀπίσω μου, οὐ 38
28 δύναταί μου εἶναι μαθητής. Τίς γὰρ ἐξ ὑμῶν θέλων πύργον οἰκοδομῆσαι, οὐχὶ πρῶτον καθίσας ψηφίζει τὴν δαπάνην, εἰ ἔχει [τὰ] ‡ πρὸς
29 ἀπαρτισμόν; ἵνα μήποτε, θέντος αὐτοῦ θεμέλιον καὶ μὴ ἰσχύοντος
ἐκτελέσαι, πάντες οἱ θεωροῦντες ἄρξωνται ἐμπαίζειν αὐτῷ· λέγοντες·
30 Ὅτι οὗτος ὁ ἄνθρωπος ἤρξατο οἰκοδομεῖν, καὶ οὐκ ἴσχυσεν ἐκτελέσαι.
31 Ἢ τίς βασιλεὺς πορευόμενος συμβαλεῖν ἑτέρῳ βασιλεῖ εἰς πόλεμον, οὐχὶ
καθίσας πρῶτον βουλεύεται εἰ δυνατός ἐστιν ἐν δέκα χιλιάσιν ἀπαντῆ-
32 σαι τῷ μετὰ εἴκοσι χιλιάδων ἐρχομένῳ ἐπ᾽ αὐτόν; εἰ δὲ μήγε, ἔτι
πόῤῥω αὐτοῦ ὄντος, πρεσβείαν ἀποστείλας ἐρωτᾷ τὰ πρὸς εἰρήνην.
33 Οὕτως οὖν πᾶς ἐξ ὑμῶν, ὃς οὐκ ἀποτάσσεται πᾶσι τοῖς ἑαυτοῦ ὑπάρ- 5.
34 χουσιν, οὐ δύναταί μου εἶναι μαθητής. Καλὸν τὸ ἅλας· ἐὰν δὲ τὸ 13
35 ἅλας μωρανθῇ, ἐν τίνι ἀρτυθήσεται; Οὔτε εἰς γῆν, οὔτε εἰς κοπρίαν εὔθετόν ἐστιν· ἔξω βάλλουσιν αὐτό. ὁ ἔχων ὦτα ἀκούειν ἀκουέτω.

21. *ῥύμας*] "lanes;" a signification only found in the later writers, and, as appears from Lobeck on Phryn., first employed as a *comic* appellation. Τοὺς πτωχοὺς — τυφλοὺς, i. e. the most wretched and miserable objects.

23. *φραγμοὺς.*] The Commentators all take this to mean, "places fenced off." But that sense is quite unsatisfactory. From the connexion of the term with ὁδοὺς, it is plain that some *kind of road* is meant; and as φραγμὸς signifies what we call in the country a *dead fence* (i. e. one made with faggots) so the sense here must be, "a fenced path," such as would be necessary across vineyards, orchards, &c.

— *ἀνάγκασον.*] All the best Commentators have been long agreed, that this can only denote the *moral compulsion* of *earnest persuasion.*

25. [*Comp.* Deut. xiii. 6. xxxiii. 9.]

26. *μισεῖ*] i. e. comparatively, namely, "*minus amat*," as appears from Matt. vi. 24. x. 37.

28. By these parabolical comparisons, Christ counsels them, (and *all* of *us* of future ages) before we enter on the Christian life, to seriously weigh the *difficulties* of the *duties* required of us, the *sacrifices* to be made, and the *temptations* to be resisted: so that we may not afterwards be moved by them to abandon our Christian course.

— *πύργον*] Doddr. supposes this to be such a tower as was built in the vineyards of the East, for the temporary accommodation of those who guarded the produce. But the *costliness* implied in calculating its expense indicates a *permanent mansion* of the higher class; such, it seems, as was called πύργος, by a similar figure to the Latin *turris*, as denoting a turreted house; and, by implication, a considerable edifice. We are however, to understand a *country house*, or *seat*, in which sense turris occurs in Livy xxxiii. 48., where Duker gives other examples. I find from Arundel's Travels in Asia Minor, vol. ii. 335, that πύργος even yet designates a country house, usually surrounded by gardens and groves.

— *τὰ πρὸς ἀπ.*] Several MSS. have τὰ εἰς, and some εἰς without the τὰ, which is cancelled by Griesb. and Scholz; rightly, if the construction be what Bornem. affirms, εἰ ἔχει τὴν δαπάνην εἰς ἀπ.

— *καθίσας.*] This is used *graphicè*, and is merely *ad ornatum.* ψηφίζειν signifies, 1. to count by dropping pebbles; a primitive mode of calculation still preserved among barbarous nations; 2. to calculate, reckon.

31. *συμβαλεῖν*] The construction συμβάλλειν εἰς πόλεμον, or μάχην τινι, is frequent in the Classical writers. Such adjuncts are *exegetical.* Καθίζειν and the Latin *sedere* are often used in expressions denoting *to take counsel.*

32. *ἐρωτᾷ τὰ πρὸς εἰρ.*] By τὰ πρὸς εἰρήνην is meant what *tends* to peace, i. e. proposals for peace, conditions of peace. So Wets. appositely cites τὰ πρὸς τὰς διαλύσεις from Polyb.

33. *ἀποτάσσεται*] "renounces, forsakes." Ἀποτάσσειν signifies, 1. to range into parts. 2. (in the middle voice) to *take part* with *one*, which implies a *renouncing the other.* This last sense of the word is Alexandrian Greek, and only found in Joseph. and other later writers.

a Matt. 9. 10. Supra 5. 29. XV. [a] ΗΣΑΝ δὲ ἐγγίζοντες αὐτῷ πάντες οἱ τελῶναι καὶ οἱ ἁμαρ- 1
τωλοὶ, ἀκούειν αὐτοῦ. Καὶ διεγόγγυζον οἱ Φαρισαῖοι καὶ οἱ Γραμ- 2
ματεῖς, λέγοντες· Ὅτι οὗτος ἁμαρτωλοὺς προσδέχεται, καὶ συνεσθίει
b Matt. 18. 12. αὐτοῖς. Εἶπε δὲ πρὸς αὐτοὺς τὴν παραβολὴν ταύτην, λέγων· [b] Τίς 3
ἄνθρωπος ἐξ ὑμῶν ἔχων ἑκατὸν πρόβατα, καὶ ἀπολέσας ἓν ἐξ αὐτῶν, 4
οὐ καταλείπει τὰ ἐννενηκονταεννέα ἐν τῇ ἐρήμῳ, καὶ πορεύεται ἐπὶ τὸ
ἀπολωλὸς, ἕως εὕρῃ αὐτό; Καὶ εὑρὼν ἐπιτίθησιν ἐπὶ τοὺς ὤμους 5
c 1 Pet. 2. 25. ἑαυτοῦ χαίρων· [c] καὶ ἐλθὼν εἰς τὸν οἶκον συγκαλεῖ τοὺς φίλους καὶ 6
τοὺς γείτονας, λέγων αὐτοῖς· Συγχάρητέ μοι, ὅτι εὗρον τὸ πρόβατόν
d Supra. 5. 32. μου τὸ ἀπολωλός. [d] Λέγω ὑμῖν, ὅτι οὕτω χαρὰ ἔσται ἐν τῷ οὐρανῷ 7
ἐπὶ ἑνὶ ἁμαρτωλῷ μετανοοῦντι, ἢ ἐπὶ ἐννενηκονταεννέα δικαίοις, οἵτινες
οὐ χρείαν ἔχουσι μετανοίας. Ἢ τίς γυνὴ δραχμὰς ἔχουσα δέκα, ἐὰν 8
ἀπολέσῃ δραχμὴν μίαν, οὐχὶ ἅπτει λύχνον, καὶ σαροῖ τὴν οἰκίαν, καὶ
ζητεῖ ἐπιμελῶς, ἕως ὅτου εὕρῃ; καὶ εὑροῦσα συγκαλεῖται τὰς φίλας 9
καὶ τὰς γείτονας, λέγουσα· Συγχάρητέ μοι, ὅτι εὗρον τὴν δραχμὴν ἣν
ἀπώλεσα. Οὕτω, λέγω ὑμῖν, χαρὰ γίνεται ἐνώπιον τῶν ἀγγέλων τοῦ 10
Θεοῦ ἐπὶ ἑνὶ ἁμαρτωλῷ μετανοοῦντι.
Εἶπε δέ· Ἄνθρωπός τις εἶχε δύο υἱούς· καὶ εἶπεν ὁ νεώτερος αὐ- 11
τῶν τῷ πατρί· Πάτερ, δός μοι τὸ ἐπιβάλλον μέρος τῆς οὐσίας. καὶ 12
διεῖλεν αὐτοῖς τὸν βίον. Καὶ μετ᾽ οὐ πολλὰς ἡμέρας συναγαγὼν 13
ἅπαντα ὁ νεώτερος υἱὸς, ἀπεδήμησεν εἰς χώραν μακρὰν, καὶ ἐκεῖ δι-

34. The connection here is obscure, and disputed. It is, with most probability, laid down as follows: "Ye see, then, the necessity of counting the cost and hazard of becoming my disciples. For if ye engage inconsiderately, ye may either apostatize altogether, or become mere *professors*, *hearers* of the word, and not *doers*.

XV. 1. The Pharisees regarded heathens and gross sinners as equally unworthy of being conversed with; even though with the intention of converting them. They therefore calumniated Christ for too much familiarity with these persons; not considering, that he conversed with them not as their companion, but their physician of the soul. Hence our Lord employs the following parables to show them how *inhuman*, and how different from God's merciful disposition to *them* was such conduct. See Note on Matt. xviii. 12—14.

2. *προσδέχεται.*] Προσδέχεσθαι implies admission to any one's acquaintance; and *συνεσθίειν*, to his intimacy. See 1 Cor. v. 11. Gal. ii. 12. and Ps. ci. 5.

4. *ἐπὶ* joined with verbs of motion indicates the *purpose* of the action. Kypke compares Diog. Laert. i. 10. 2. *πεμφθεὶς — ἐπὶ πρόβατον.* I add Thucyd. iv. 13. *ἐπὶ ξύλα — παραπέμπειν.*

5. *ἐπιτίθησιν — ὤμους.*] It *may* have been, as some say, a *custom* with the Jewish shepherds to carry their sheep on their shoulders. But this passage will not *prove* it; for a lost *sheep* far from home must by shepherds of *all* countries be *carried*, since a single sheep cannot be *driven*.

7. *ἢ*] for *μᾶλλον ἤ*, as in the best writers. See Winer's Gr. § 28. who traces the idiom to Hebraism. Bornem. refers it to the construction being moulded as if *πότερον εἰ* had preceded: citing Ecclus. 22. 15. But that is refining too much, *more Hermanni*. There can be no doubt that the *Scriptural* use originated in Hebraism. See Schulz. By *μετάνοια* is not meant that sorrow for sin which is continually required even of the best men, but that thorough *reformation*, which is indispensably necessary to the true conversion of the habitual sinner.

8. *τίς γυνή.*] With this parable the Commentators compare a very similar one in the Rabbinical writings. And Wets. cites from Theophrast. Char. 10. *τῆς γυναικὸς ἀποβαλούσης τρίχαλκον, οἷος μεταφέρειν τὰ σκεύη, καὶ τὰς κλίνας, καὶ τὰς κιβωτοὺς, καὶ διφᾶν τὰ καλύμματα.*

— *ἅπτει λύχνον.*] There would be this need; since (as we find from the remains of Herculaneum and Pompeii) the houses of the lower classes, in ancient times, either had no windows, or what were rather like the loop-holes of our barns.

12. *τὸ ἐπιβάλλον μέρος.*] Sub. *μοι* from the preceding, "the portion which falleth to me." This use of *ἐπιβάλλειν* is found in the best writers from Herodot. downwards. The Jewish law did not, any more than the Roman, permit to a father the arbitrary disposal of his *whole* property. It was entailed on the children, after his death, in equal portions; except that the first-born had a double share. Such distribution, however, was, as I have shewn in Recens. Synop., *sometimes* made by an indulgent parent to his children during his lifetime, with a reservation of what was necessary to the support of himself and his wife, if alive.

13. *συναγαγὼν ἅπαντα.*] The sense is, "having converted the whole into money," as is clear from two passages cited by Wets. from Plutarch, p. 772. and Quintil. Dial. v. There is, however, no *ellipsis* of *εἰς ἀργύριον*; but only that circumstance is implied in *συναγ.*, which seems to have been a form of expression used in common life.

14 σκόρπισε τὴν οὐσίαν αὐτοῦ ζῶν ἀσώτως. Δαπανήσαντος δὲ αὐτοῦ πάντα, ἐγένετο λιμὸς ἰσχυρὸς κατὰ τὴν χώραν ἐκείνην, καὶ αὐτὸς ἤρξατο
15 ὑστερεῖσθαι. Καὶ πορευθεὶς ἐκολλήθη ἑνὶ τῶν πολιτῶν τῆς χώρας
ἐκείνης· καὶ ἔπεμψεν αὐτὸν εἰς τοὺς ἀγροὺς αὐτοῦ βόσκειν χοίρους.
16 Καὶ ἐπεθύμει γεμίσαι τὴν κοιλίαν αὐτοῦ ἀπὸ τῶν κερατίων, ὧν ἤσθιον
17 οἱ χοῖροι· καὶ οὐδεὶς ἐδίδου αὐτῷ. Εἰς ἑαυτὸν δὲ ἐλθὼν εἶπε·
Πόσοι μίσθιοι τοῦ πατρός μου περισσεύουσιν ἄρτων, ἐγὼ δὲ λιμῷ
18 ἀπόλλυμαι! Ἀναστὰς πορεύσομαι πρὸς τὸν πατέρα μου, καὶ ἐρῶ αὐ-
19 τῷ· Πάτερ, ἥμαρτον εἰς τὸν οὐρανὸν καὶ ἐνώπιόν σου· [καὶ] οὐκέτι
εἰμὶ ἄξιος κληθῆναι υἱός σου· ποίησόν με ὡς ἕνα τῶν μισθίων σου.
20 [e] Καὶ ἀναστὰς ἦλθε πρὸς τὸν πατέρα ἑαυτοῦ. Ἔτι δὲ αὐτοῦ μακρὰν e Acts 2. 39. Eph. 2. 13, 17.
ἀπέχοντος, εἶδεν αὐτὸν ὁ πατὴρ αὐτοῦ, καὶ ἐσπλαγχνίσθη· καὶ δρα-
21 μὼν ἐπέπεσεν ἐπὶ τὸν τράχηλον αὐτοῦ καὶ κατεφίλησεν αὐτόν. Εἶπε δὲ
αὐτῷ ὁ υἱός· Πάτερ, ἥμαρτον εἰς τὸν οὐρανὸν καὶ ἐνώπιόν σου, καὶ οὐ-
22 κέτι εἰμὶ ἄξιος κληθῆναι υἱός σου. Εἶπε δὲ ὁ πατὴρ πρὸς τοὺς δούλους
αὐτοῦ· Ἐξενέγκατε τὴν στολὴν τὴν πρώτην καὶ ἐνδύσατε αὐτόν, καὶ
δότε δακτύλιον εἰς τὴν χεῖρα αὐτοῦ καὶ ὑποδήματα εἰς τοὺς πόδας·

— διεσκόρπισε] "dissipated." A metaphor taken from winnowing.

— ἀσώτως] i. e. τρόπῳ ἀσώτου. Ἄσωτος originally denoted *one who cannot be saved;* but was afterwards used, in an *active* sense, to denote "one who cannot save [himself]," a *prodigal*, a *dissolute person*, whom (as I think Alexis ap. Athenæum says) "the Goddess of Salvation herself could not save." Some Commentators, however, maintain a *passive* sense, referring to Aristot. Eth. iv. 1. But that passage supplies no certain proof. And it is plain that Aristotle considered the word as having an *active* sense, since he just after explains it by ἀκρατῶς καὶ εἰς ἀκολασίαν δαπανηρούς; the most accurate definition that has ever yet been given of the word.

15. ἐκολλήθη] "connected himself with," i. e. bound or engaged himself to. The verb has properly a *passive* sense, but is always used in a reflected or reciprocal one. Βόσκειν χοίρους. An employment considered by all the ancient nations, even where *no* religious prejudices subsisted, as among the vilest. How degrading, then, to a *Jew*.

16. καὶ ἐπεθύμει γεμίσαι — αὐτῷ.] The sense which several Translators and Commentators assign to ἐπεθύμει, *desired*, is far from satisfactory. Campb. strenuously maintains that the expression cannot denote *desire ungratified* ("for the young man," says he, "had surely the power, and would scarcely scruple to satisfy his hunger on the husks"); and that it is in vain to support this view by *taking for granted* circumstances which do not appear from the story." This is true, but little to the purpose. It will only hold good against supplying κερατίων at ἐδίδου αὐτῷ. And why, it may be asked, should οὐδεὶς be here said? for surely *none* could give him, even of the κεράτια, but his master. In vain does Campb. urge that ἐπεθ. "cannot signify desire *ungratified.*" It certainly *does* signify it. The poor wretch desired to satisfy his hunger with the food of *men*, if he could; but of that he could buy very little, and no man *gave* him aught. And as to the *swine's husks*, he could not satisfy his hunger with so small a quantity as his stomach would bear. Consequently ἐπεθ. *does* denote desire ungratified. Campb., indeed, takes ἐπιθυμεῖν here for ἀγαπᾷν, to be fain, i. e. content. But that sense has never been established on any certain proof, either in the Scriptural or Classical writers. Now the difference between I *was* fain, and I *would* fain, is worthy of remark. The former signifies "I was glad" (*fain* coming from the Ang. Sax. *feagen, glad)*, which implies a sort of κειθανάγκη, or compulsion for fear of worse; the latter (in which *fain* is an *adverb)* signifies "I would gladly do," or have done, a thing, if permitted. And though the former sense would certainly be *apt*, both here and at Luke xvi. 21, yet, considering how deficient it is in authority, it cannot with propriety be adopted. It is better, therefore, to retain the common version, "he would fain have filled his belly, &c. And no one gave him aught, namely, such food as is eaten by human beings;" (at αὐτῷ supplying τι scil. φαγεῖν.) This latter clause, we may observe, contains a pathetic *representation* of extreme distress.

By the κερατ., Commentators are now agreed, is meant (as Sir Tho. Brown first proved) the fruit of the *ceratonia siliquosa*, or *carob-tree*, common in the Southern and Eastern countries, and still used for feeding swine, nay, occasionally eaten by the poorer class of people, as were the *siliquæ* among the Romans.

19. καί.] This is omitted in very many of the best MSS. and Versions, and is rightly cancelled by almost all Editors. The *Asyndeton* is intensive.

21. πάτερ, &c.] The prodigal commences the confession he had meditated, notwithstanding he had the embrace of forgiveness; yet he does not finish his intended speech; being, we may suppose, interrupted in uttering the last words ποίησον — σου by the words of his father.

22. ἐξενέγκατε, &c.] The articles called for are such whose use denoted *freedom* and dignity; nay, the robe is to be *the best.* This use of πρῶτος,

καὶ ἐνέγκαντες τὸν μόσχον τὸν σιτευτὸν θύσατε, καὶ φαγόντες εὐφραν- 23
θῶμεν· ὅτι οὗτος ὁ υἱός μου νεκρὸς ἦν, καὶ ἀνέζησε· καὶ ἀπολω- 24
λὼς ἦν, καὶ εὑρέθη. καὶ ἤρξαντο εὐφραίνεσθαι. Ἦν δὲ ὁ υἱὸς αὐτοῦ 25
ὁ πρεσβύτερος ἐν ἀγρῷ· καὶ ὡς ἐρχόμενος ἤγγισε τῇ οἰκίᾳ, ἤκουσε
συμφωνίας καὶ χορῶν· καὶ προσκαλεσάμενος ἕνα τῶν παίδων, ἐπυν- 26
θάνετο τί εἴη ταῦτα; Ὁ δὲ εἶπεν αὐτῷ· ὅτι ὁ ἀδελφός σου ἥκει· 27
καὶ ἔθυσεν ὁ πατήρ σου τὸν μόσχον τὸν σιτευτὸν, ὅτι ὑγιαίνοντα αὐτὸν ἀπέλαβεν. Ὠργίσθη δὲ, καὶ οὐκ ἤθελεν εἰσελθεῖν. Ὁ οὖν πατὴρ 28
αὐτοῦ ἐξελθὼν παρεκάλει αὐτόν. Ὁ δὲ ἀποκριθεὶς εἶπε τῷ πατρί· 29
Ἰδοὺ, τοσαῦτα ἔτη δουλεύω σοι, καὶ οὐδέποτε ἐντολήν σου παρῆλθον·
καὶ ἐμοὶ οὐδέποτε ἔδωκας ἔριφον, ἵνα μετὰ τῶν φίλων μου εὐφρανθῶ.
Ὅτε δὲ ὁ υἱός σου οὗτος, ὁ καταφαγών σου τὸν βίον μετὰ πορνῶν, 30
ἦλθεν, ἔθυσας αὐτῷ τὸν μόσχον τὸν σιτευτόν. Ὁ δὲ εἶπεν αὐτῷ· 31
Τέκνον, σὺ πάντοτε μετ᾽ ἐμοῦ εἶ, καὶ πάντα τὰ ἐμὰ σά ἐστιν. Εὐ- 32
φρανθῆναι δὲ καὶ χαρῆναι ἔδει· ὅτι ὁ ἀδελφός σου οὗτος νεκρὸς ἦν
καὶ ἀνέζησε· καὶ ἀπολωλὼς ἦν καὶ εὑρέθη.

XVI. ἜΛΕΓΕ δὲ καὶ πρὸς τοὺς μαθητὰς αὐτοῦ· Ἄνθρωπός τις 1
ἦν πλούσιος, ὃς εἶχεν οἰκονόμον· καὶ οὗτος διεβλήθη αὐτῷ ὡς δια-
σκορπίζων τὰ ὑπάρχοντα αὐτοῦ. Καὶ φωνήσας αὐτὸν εἶπεν αὐτῷ· Τί 2
τοῦτο ἀκούω περὶ σοῦ; ἀπόδος τὸν λόγον τῆς οἰκονομίας σου· οὐ
γὰρ δυνήσῃ ἔτι οἰκονομεῖν. Εἶπε δὲ ἐν ἑαυτῷ ὁ οἰκονόμος· Τί ποιή- 3
σω, ὅτι ὁ κύριός μου ἀφαιρεῖται τὴν οἰκονομίαν ἀπ᾽ ἐμοῦ; σκάπτειν

is rarely found except in the Scriptures. The only apposite examples adduced from the Classics are Athen. V. p. 197. *Ταύταις δ' ἀμφίταποι ἁλουργεῖς ὑπέστρωντο τῆς πρώτης ἐρέας.* Joseph. Ant. xiii. 5. 4. *τὰ πρῶτα μύρα χριόμενοι.*

23. *τὸν μόσχον τὸν σιτ.*] such as we may suppose most opulent rustic families would be usually provided with, for any extraordinary call on their hospitality; as with us *poultry.* Moreover *veal* was by the ancients reckoned a delicacy. Θύσατε, butcher, see Note on Matt. xxii. 4.

24. *νεκρὸς ἦν καὶ ἀνέζησε.*] This must, notwithstanding the dissent of Herman and Rosenm., be taken in a metaphorical sense, of *spiritual* death and coming to life again by repentance; a sense often occurring in Scripture, and not unfrequent in the Classical writers. See Rec. Syn.

25. *ἤκουσε συμφωνίας καὶ χορῶν.*] It was a very ancient and *Oriental* custom to have concerts of music at entertainments. See Hom. Od. xvii. 358.

27. *ὑγιαίνοντα*] "safe and sound." So the Greeks say *σῶν καὶ ὑγιῆ*, as Herodot. iii. 124. Thucyd. iii. 34. Yet the *figurative* sense *inculcated* at ver. 24. may be here *united* with the physical one. So Plutarch, cited by Kypke, *ἵνα μὴ τοῦ ὑγιαίνοντος καὶ τεταγμένου* (orderly) *βίου καταφρονήσωσι.*

29. *δουλεύω.*] The present tense here denotes *continuity*, "I have been and am serving thee."

30. *ὁ καταφαγὼν—βίον.*] This metaphor, to denote prodigality, is common in the Classical writers from Homer downwards. See Rec. Syn.

31. *πάντα τὰ ἐμὰ σά ἐστιν*] i. e. "*is to be thine as my* HEIR," *κύριος πάντων* (for his brother had forfeited all title to *inheritance*). Such a person the Romans called *Herus minor.*

XVI. 1. *ἄνθρωπός τις ἦν κλ.*] On the scope of this Parable the Commentators widely differ. (See Recens. Synop.) It is, however, generally admitted to have an affinity to the foregoing one; and, like that, to have been meant for the instruction of Christ's followers in general; for *μαθηταὶ* is often taken in this extended sense. And as that represents the consequences of living without God in the world, so this seems to have been meant to teach men the true use of riches; and how they may be employed, so that being in this world rich towards God, they may attain eternal happiness in the world to come. A parable very similar to this is cited by Lightf. and A. Clarke from D. Kimchi on Isaiah xl. 21.

—*οἰκονόμον.*] The *οἰκονόμος* was a domestic, generally a freedman, who discharged duties corresponding with those of our *house-stewards* and of our *house-keepers.* Διεβλήθη, "was accused." This use of the word, of a *true* and not of a calumnious charge, is chiefly found in the Sept. and the later Greek writers.

2. *τί*] for *διατί*, how! or what! importing expostulation and anger.' *τὸν λόγον*, "the account," viz. which you are bound to give. So Plato Phæd. § 8. *ὑμῖν δὲ τοῖς δικασταῖς βούλομαι τὸν λόγον ἀποδοῦναι.* Δυνήσῃ is *not* redundant, but signifies *must;* i. e. "unless thou give a *satisfactory* account." The not attending to this point has occasioned some misconceptions in the interpretation of the Parable.

3. *σκάπτειν οὐκ ἰσχύω.*] The sense is, "I have

4 οὐκ ἰσχύω, ἐπαιτεῖν αἰσχύνομαι. Ἔγνων τί ποιήσω· ἵνα ὅταν μετα-
5 σταθῶ τῆς οἰκονομίας, δέξωνταί με εἰς τοὺς οἴκους αὐτῶν. Καὶ
προσκαλεσάμενος ἕνα ἕκαστον τῶν χρεωφειλετῶν τοῦ κυρίου ἑαυτοῦ,
6 ἔλεγε τῷ πρώτῳ· Πόσον ὀφείλεις τῷ κυρίῳ μου; ὁ δὲ εἶπεν· Ἑκατὸν βάτους ἐλαίου· καὶ εἶπεν αὐτῷ· Δέξαι σου τὸ γράμμα, καὶ
7 καθίσας ταχέως γράψον πεντήκοντα. Ἔπειτα ἑτέρῳ εἶπε· Σὺ δὲ
πόσον ὀφείλεις; ὁ δὲ εἶπεν· Ἑκατὸν κόρους σίτου. καὶ λέγει αὐτῷ·
8 Δέξαι σου τὸ γράμμα καὶ γράψον ὀγδοήκοντα. [a] Καὶ ἐπῄνεσεν ὁ κύ- [a] Eph. 5. 8. 1 Thess. 5. 5.
ριος τὸν οἰκονόμον τῆς ἀδικίας, ὅτι φρονίμως ἐποίησεν. ὅτι οἱ υἱοὶ
τοῦ αἰῶνος τούτου φρονιμώτεροι ὑπὲρ τοὺς υἱοὺς τοῦ φωτὸς εἰς τὴν

not strength to work as a day labourer;" of which occupation *digging*, as being the most laborious and servile, is put, a *part* for the *whole*. So Phocyl. *εἰ δέ τις οὐ δέδαε τέχνην, σκάπτοιτο δικέλλῃ.* and Aristoph. Av. 1432. *τί γὰρ πάθω, σκάπτειν γὰρ οὐκ ἐπίσταμαι.*

4. *ἔγνων.*] Kuin. and others explain, "I understand or see, a thought occurs to me." But this is destitute of authority, and limits the sense, which seems to include this, and the common version "I am (or have) resolved." So Bishop Sanderson, (in an admirable Sermon on ver. 8, p. 209.) "He casteth about this way and that way and every way; and, at last, bethinketh himself of a course, and resolveth upon it."

—*μετασταθῶ.*] *Μεθίστημι* is often used of removal from office. In *δέξωνται* we have antecedent for consequent *(support)*, as in John xix. 27. *Δέξ. may* (as Kuin. directs) be taken *impersonally*: but, on account of the *αὐτῶν* following, it is better to suppose an ellipse of *ἄνθρωποι*; or rather there seems to be a reference to *certain persons* in the mind of the steward; namely, his master's debtors.

5. *τῷ πρώτῳ.*] One or two cases are mentioned as *examples* of what was said to all.

6. *δέξαι τὸ γράμμα*, &c.] There is some doubt as to the sense of *γράμμα*. The almost invariable opinion of Commentators, ancient and modern, is that it signifies a *bond*, or *engagement*; of which sense Kypke adduces four examples from Josephus and Libanius. And Grot. has proved that *γράμμα*, like the Latin *literæ*, had the signification of *syngrapha*, or *chirographa* (so we say a note of *hand*) and *cautio*. These *bonds*, he shews, were kept in the hands of the steward. Dr. A. Clarke thinks that "this *γράμμα* was a writing in which the debt was specified, together with the obligation to pay so much, at such and such times. This," continues he, "appears to have been in the *hand-writing* of the debtor, and probably signed by the steward; and this precluded imposition on each part. To prevent all appearance of forgery in this case, *he* is desired to write it over again, and cancel the whole engagement." That it was in the *hand-writing* of the debtor, is very probable. Yet such a *note of hand* could not require the *steward's signature*. It is more probable that (according to the explanation given by Dr. Mackn.) the *γράμμα* denotes a *contract* (probably on lease) for *rent*. However, the common interpretation *may* be, and I think ought to be, *united*, to represent the true sense. These *γράμματα* were, it should seem, both *bonds* and *contracts*. Those who took land were, we may suppose, required, previously to occupancy, to execute and sign an *engagement*, binding them to pay as rent a certain portion of the produce to the proprietor. This was, no doubt, countersigned by the proprietor or his steward, with an *acceptance* of the rent, (thus ratifying the contract,) of which a *copy*, also signed by the steward, was given to the occupier for his security. Thus the writing in question being both an *engagement* and a *contract*, was rightly styled a *γράμμα*, in whichever sense that word may be taken. Now this alteration of *contract* would be a more *lasting* advantage to the tenants, and, of course, would entitle the steward to a proportionably greater degree of their gratitude.

8. *κύριος.*] This denotes the "master (of the steward)," not, as it is commonly interpreted, "*the Lord*," i. e. Christ.

—*ἐπῄνεσεν*] "commended him," not for his *fraud*; but, besides his *prudence* in securing his future subsistence, for the *dexterity* with which he had effected it (as, in Terent. Heauton. iii. 2, 26, Chremes praises a knavish servant: "Syrus. Eho! *laudas*, quæso, qui heros fallerent? Chremes. *In loco* ego verò *laudo*."); for a *blundering* fraud would merit both censure and contempt. *Τὸν οἰκ. τῆς ἀδικίας* is for *τὸν οἰκ. τὸν ἄδικον*, (Hebraicè) the fraudulent steward. (So v. 9. *μαμωνᾶ τῆς ἀδικίας* for *τοῦ μ. ἀδίκου*.)

—*ὅτι οἱ υἱοὶ — εἰσι.*] The best Commentators are agreed that these are the words, not of the *master*, but of *Christ*, suggesting an important admonition. The force of the expression *υἱοὶ τοῦ α. τ.* and *υἱοὶ τοῦ φωτὸς* is fully and ably discussed by Bp. Sanderson in a Sermon on this text. Both phrases are found in the Rabbinical writers.

The words *εἰς τὴν γενεὰν τὴν ἑαυτῶν* admit of various explanations, and have been variously interpreted. The older Commentators take it for *ἐν τῇ γενεᾷ*, and assign to *γεν.* various metaphorical senses alike unauthorized. But a *literal* acceptation is to be preferred; namely, that of their own race, people like-minded with themselves. Nor is there any occasion to take the *εἰς* for *ἐν*. It may be rendered *quod attinet ad*, as far as respects the judgments and ideas of persons of their own kind. Bp. Sanderson, in his Sermon on this text, enumerates the various respects in which they are wiser. "1. As being more sagacious and provident to forethink what they ought to do, and forecast how it ought to be done; to weigh all probable and possible obstructions to their designs, and endeavour to remove them. 2. More industrious and diligent in pursuing what they have designed. 3. More cunning and close. 4. More united, holding all together." He then

b Matt. 6. 19. & 19. 21. 1 Tim. 6. 19. γενεὰν τὴν ἑαυτῶν εἰσι. [b] Κἀγὼ ὑμῖν λέγω· ποιήσατε ἑαυτοῖς φίλους 9
ἐκ τοῦ μαμωνᾶ τῆς ἀδικίας, ἵνα ὅταν ἐκλίπητε, δέξωνται ὑμᾶς εἰς τὰς
c Infr. 19. 17. αἰωνίους σκηνάς. [c] Ὁ πιστὸς ἐν ἐλαχίστῳ καὶ ἐν πολλῷ πιστός ἐστι· 10
καὶ ὁ ἐν ἐλαχίστῳ ἄδικος καὶ ἐν πολλῷ ἄδικος ἐστιν. Εἰ οὖν ἐν τῷ 11
ἀδίκῳ μαμωνᾷ πιστοὶ οὐκ ἐγένεσθε, τὸ ἀληθινὸν τίς ὑμῖν πιστεύσει;
καὶ εἰ ἐν τῷ ἀλλοτρίῳ πιστοὶ οὐκ ἐγένεσθε, τὸ ὑμέτερον τίς ὑμῖν δώσει; 12

shows how Christians should emulate the worldling's wisdom in all those particulars, so as to be wise in their *own* way, and in the sight of God. He moreover considers the *limitation* implied in εἰς τὴν γεν., rendering it "in *genere suo*," in their kind of wisdom, namely, in worldly *things*, for *worldly ends*. "Simply and absolutely considered (continues he) the child of light is the wiser man, since true wisdom can be learned only from the word of God. That godliness is the only wisdom, and that there is no fool but the sinner, will appear as follows:—1. He is all for the present, and never considers what *mischiefs* or *inconveniences* will follow thereupon *afterwards*. 2. When, *both* are permitted to *his choice*, he hath not the wit to prefer that which is eminently *better*, but chooseth that which is *extremely worse*. 3. He proposes to himself base and *unworthy ends*. 4. For the attaining even of those *poor ends*, he makes choice of such *means* as are neither *proper* nor *probable* thereunto. 5. He goes on in *bold enterprise* with great confidence of success, upon very *slender grounds* of assurance. And lastly, where his own wit will not serve him, *refuseth to be advised* by those that are *wiser* than himself, what he wanteth in *wit*, making up in *will*. No wise man, I think, can take a person of this character for any other than a *fool*. And every *worldly* or *ungodly man* is all this, and more; and every *godly man* the contrary."

9. ποιήσατε—σκηνάς.] On the whole of this verse there is no little diversity of interpretation. With respect to μαμωνᾶ τῆς ἀδικίας, it is plainly put for μαμωνᾶ ἀδίκου, by a common Hebraism. But the force of the epithet here is not so clear. Some take μαμωνᾶ τῆς ἀδ. to denote *riches acquired by injustice*. But this cannot *here* be admitted, because it would lead to a sense which would inculcate a doctrine unworthy of the Gospel; as if the wrath of God for ill-gotten gain could be appeased by giving alms to the poor. It is *better* to suppose, with the best modern Commentators, that ἀδικία is here to be taken in the sense *deceitful*, *unstable*, as opposed to ἀληθινὸς, as at ver. 11. Of this sense they adduce many examples from the LXX. and the Classical writers, and a few from the N. T. But these last are not to the purpose; and the others are *doubtful* as taken from *poetic* phraseology. I therefore prefer, with some antient and several modern Commentators, to suppose that the epithet has reference, in a general sense, to the *means* whereby riches are often acquired. And I would suggest, that ἀδικία sometimes is used of *harsh and griping conduct*, and taking unfair advantages, without which *great* riches, it is to be feared, are rarely amassed. See Matth. xxv. 24. At ἐκλίπητε there is an ellipse of τὸν βίον, which is generally *expressed* in the Classical writers, though in the LXX. always omitted.

As to the *persons* meant in δέξωνται, many ancient and modern Commentators understand the *angels appointed to receive departed spirits*. And for this there is some countenance in Matth. xxiv. 31. Luke vi. 38. and especially xii. 20. τὴν ψυχήν σου ἀπαιτοῦσιν ἀπὸ σοῦ. But there the ἀπαιτ. may be taken as an *impersonal*: so indeed almost all recent Commentators take the δέξωνται in the present passage, q. d. "that ye may be received." However, it would seem most natural to refer δέξωνται to the φίλους before; and this is strongly confirmed by the foregoing parable, of which this is an application. And thus the sense *may* be, as Scott and Le Bas suppose, "Make to yourselves friends, by relieving the poor and destitute, that those whom you have thus befriended may, by their prayers and intercessions, be a means of your being received into heaven," i. e. may contribute to your reception. And in αἰωνίους σκηνὰς there is meant to be an *opposition*, namely of solid and lasting houses ["not made with hands"] to the temporary and frail *tents* of this world. The above view is supported by Bp. Sanderson, who after remarking that these words contain the *application* of the Parable, says, "it has two *parts*. 1. More *general* respecting the *end*; that as he was careful to provide *maintenance* for the preservation of his *natural life*, so we should be careful to make provision for *our souls*, that we may attain to *everlasting life*. 2. More *special*, respecting *the means*; that as he provided for himself out of his *master's goods*, by disposing the same into *other hands*, and upon *several persons*; so we should *lay up for ourselves a good foundation* towards the attainment of everlasting life out of the *unrighteous mammon* wherewith God hath intrusted us, by being *rich in good works*, communicating and distributing some of that in our hands towards *the necessities* of others."

10. ὁ πιστὸς—ἐστιν.] This is an adagial saying, to be understood only of what *generally* happens; and adverting to the principle on which masters act; who, after proving the fidelity of servants in *small* matters, at length confide more important business to their care. Our Lord, however, proceeds to give it an application as respects the comparative importance of the riches of this world and those of heaven; q. d. As he who is faithful in small matters, &c., so he who has misapplied the riches committed to his stewardship, &c.

11. τίς.] By implication, *no one*, q. d. God will not. Τὸ ἀληθινὸν, "the true riches," i. e. the favour of God and admission to the mansions of eternal bliss. So said in opposition to the riches of the world, which are but a vain show, and promise what they never perform.

12. εἰ ἐν τῷ ἀλλοτρίῳ—δώσει.] This is only another mode of expressing the same thing viewed in another light. By τὸ ἀλλότριον are meant the goods of this life only; which are so called, because they are, strictly speaking, not our own, but only committed to us as stewards. So Clem. Rom. ii. 5. cited by Wets., enjoins us τὰ κοσμικὰ ταῦτα ὡς ἀλλότρια ἡγεῖσθαι, καὶ μὴ ἐπιθυμεῖν αὐτῶν. By τὸ ὑμέτερον are meant the riches of an eternal inheritance in heaven, called *our own*, because,

MT.
13 Οὐδεὶς οἰκέτης δύναται δυσὶ κυρίοις δουλεύειν· ἢ γὰρ τὸν ἕνα μισή- 6.
σει, καὶ τὸν ἕτερον ἀγαπήσει· ἢ ἑνὸς ἀνθέξεται, καὶ τοῦ ἑτέρου κατα- 24
φρονήσει. οὐ δύνασθε Θεῷ δουλεύειν καὶ μαμωνᾷ.
14 Ἤκουον δὲ ταῦτα πάντα καὶ οἱ Φαρισαῖοι, φιλάργυροι ὑπάρχοντες,
15 καὶ ἐξεμυκτήριζον αὐτόν. Καὶ εἶπεν αὐτοῖς· Ὑμεῖς ἐστε οἱ δικαιοῦντες ἑαυτοὺς ἐνώπιον τῶν ἀνθρώπων· ὁ δὲ Θεὸς γινώσκει τὰς καρδίας
ὑμῶν· ὅτι τὸ ἐν ἀνθρώποις ὑψηλὸν βδέλυγμα ἐνώπιον τοῦ Θεοῦ 11.
16 [ἐστιν]. Ὁ νόμος καὶ οἱ προφῆται ἕως Ἰωάννου· ἀπὸ τότε ἡ βα- 13 12
17 σιλεία τοῦ Θεοῦ εὐαγγελίζεται, καὶ πᾶς εἰς αὐτὴν βιάζεται. Εὐκοπώτε- 5.
ρον δέ ἐστι τὸν οὐρανὸν καὶ τὴν γῆν παρελθεῖν, ἢ τοῦ νόμου μίαν 18
18 κεραίαν πεσεῖν. Πᾶς ὁ ἀπολύων τὴν γυναῖκα αὐτοῦ καὶ γαμῶν ἑτέραν 32
μοιχεύει· καὶ πᾶς ὁ ἀπολελυμένην ἀπὸ ἀνδρὸς γαμῶν μοιχεύει.
19 Ἄνθρωπος δέ τις ἦν πλούσιος, καὶ ἐνεδιδύσκετο πορφύραν καὶ βύσσον,
20 εὐφραινόμενος καθ᾽ ἡμέραν λαμπρῶς. πτωχὸς δέ τις ἦν ὀνόματι Λά-
21 ζαρος, ὃς ἐβέβλητο πρὸς τὸν πυλῶνα αὐτοῦ, ἡλκωμένος καὶ ἐπιθυμῶν
χορτασθῆναι ἀπὸ τῶν ψιχίων τῶν πιπτόντων ἀπὸ τῆς τραπέζης τοῦ

1st, the possession of it is secured to us on certain conditions; 2dly, it will be wholly our own, and not to be shared with others.

14. ἐξεμυκτήριζον α.] "sneered at him." Μυκτηρίζειν (from μυκτὴρ, the nose) properly signifies to *turn up the nose*; a metaphor used in most languages to designate *derision*. [*Comp.* Matt. xxiii. 14.]

15. δικαιοῦντες ἑ.] This expression (which is variously interpreted) most probably designates their arrogating to themselves a virtue and sanctity not really theirs. Thus δικαιόω is taken, like the Hiphil conjugation in Hebrew, for "to *make* [*one seem*] *just*." Βδέλυγμα is for βδελυκτὸν, *abstract* for *concrete*. Of course, this enunciation must be restricted to what went before, and denote the pomp of ceremonious observances, which served as a cloak to vice. [*Comp.* Ps. vii. 9. 1 Sam. xvi. 7.]

16—18. On these verses, see Note on Matt. xi. 12 & 13. v. 18 & 32. and on the connection with the preceding, see Whitby, Doddr., Kuin., and Vat.

17. [*Comp.* Ps. cii. 26. Is. xl. 8. 2 Pet. iii. 7.]

19. ἄνθρωπος δέ τις, &c.] It has been disputed, both among ancient and modern Commentators, whether the following narration be a real history, or merely a story, or something composed of both, i. e. founded on fact, but adorned with colouring and imagery. The best Commentators, both ancient and modern, with reason consider it as *a parable*; since all the circumstances seem parabolical, and a story very similar to it is found in the Babylonian Gemara. Its scope is too obvious to need explanation.

— πορφύραν.] The use of purple vestments was originally confined to *Kings*, but had gradually extended itself to the noble and rich. On this, and the nature and species of Byssus among the ancients, see Recens. Synop.

20. πτωχός.] Not so much a *beggar*, as a *poor destitute person*. Ἐβέβλητο, "was stretched out at." See Note on Matt. viii. 6. The portal of a rich man was, for many reasons, a frequent resort of the needy. In which view Wets. cites Hom. Od. ρ. 336. and Il. κ. 25. This still continues to be the case in Italy and elsewhere. It would seem to have been the *usual* place where Lazarus was laid. See Note on Acts iii. 2.

21. ἐπιθυμῶν χορτ.] It has been much debated among the Commentators whether ἐπιθυμῶν signifies *desiring, (who desired)*, or *who was glad*, or *fain*. The former interpretation has been generally maintained by ancient and modern Commentators; but the latter has been adopted by Elsn., Parkh., Campb., and others, whose reasons, however, are insufficient. For ἀγαπᾷν, though used in this sense by the *Classical* writers, is never found in the Scriptural ones; and ἐπιθυμεῖν nowhere occurs in that sense in the Classical, nor, I believe, in the Scriptural writers; for as to Luke xv. 16, see the Note there. Our common Translators have, I think, done right in adopting the sense "he would fain" in *that* passage; and have as rightly retained the ordinary signification in the present. *Here* it is simply *desire*, or *wish* that is expressed. His desire, in being laid there, was to be fed, &c. The taking his post there was a sort of *begging by action*. That this his desire was, as some represent, *not fulfilled*, is not only not implied in the term itself, but is, as Campb. shows, inconsistent with the circumstances of the narrative.

— τῶν ψιχίων, &c.] Not, the crumbs which fell from, &c. but the "*scraps* which *chanced* to be sent from the table." By the same metaphor, Pythagoras (cited by D'Outrin) enjoined τὰ πίπτοντα ἀπὸ τῆς τραπέζας μὴ ἀναιρεῖσθαι, i. e. not to gather up the scraps or leavings, but let them alone for the poor. This whole context is well illustrated by Homer Odyss. ρ. 220. (omitted by all the Commentators), Πτωχὸν ἀνιηρὸν, δαιτῶν ἀπολυμαντῆρα, Ὃς πολλῇσι φλιῇσι παραστὰς φλίψεται ὤμους, Αἰτίζων ἀκόλους. where ἀπολυμ. is explained by the Schol. τὸν καθάρματα ἀποφερόμενον. The 2d line illustrates the custom of mendicants taking their station at a rich man's portal; and the expression denoting *continuance* there, though homely, is strong. The 3d and 1st lines are illustrated by a kindred passage at the Hymn in Cer. 115. Αἰτίζων ἀκόλους τε καὶ ἔκβολα λύματα δαιτός.

πλουσίου· ἀλλὰ καὶ οἱ κύνες ἐρχόμενοι ἀπέλειχον τὰ ἕλκη αὐτοῦ.
Ἐγένετο δὲ ἀποθανεῖν τὸν πτωχὸν, καὶ ἀπενεχθῆναι αὐτὸν ὑπὸ τῶν 22
ἀγγέλων εἰς τὸν κόλπον [τοῦ] Ἀβραάμ. ἀπέθανε δὲ καὶ ὁ πλούσιος
καὶ ἐτάφη. Καὶ ἐν τῷ ᾅδῃ ἐπάρας τοὺς ὀφθαλμοὺς αὐτοῦ, ὑπάρχων 23
ἐν βασάνοις, ὁρᾷ τὸν Ἀβραὰμ ἀπὸ μακρόθεν, καὶ Λάζαρον ἐν τοῖς κόλ-
d Isa. 66. 24. Zach. 14. 12. Mark 9. 44. ποις αὐτοῦ. [d] Καὶ αὐτὸς φωνήσας εἶπε· Πάτερ Ἀβραὰμ, ἐλέησόν με, 24
καὶ πέμψον Λάζαρον, ἵνα βάψῃ τὸ ἄκρον τοῦ δακτύλου αὐτοῦ ὕδατος,
καὶ καταψύξῃ τὴν γλῶσσάν μου· ὅτι ὀδυνῶμαι ἐν τῇ φλογὶ ταύτῃ.
e Job. 21. 13. [e] Εἶπε δὲ Ἀβραάμ· Τέκνον, μνήσθητι ὅτι ἀπέλαβες [σὺ] τὰ ἀγαθά 25
σου ἐν τῇ ζωῇ σου, καὶ Λάζαρος ὁμοίως τὰ κακά· νῦν δὲ ‡ ὅδε παρα-

— ἀλλὰ καὶ οἱ κύνες, &c.] This must not, with some, be considered as meant to note an *alleviation* of Lazarus' sufferings; though the tongue of a dog is known to be healing; but only (as Euthym. and Doddr. remark), to represent his helpless and miserable condition (with his ulcers neither bound up, nor mollified with ointment); and consequently the *uncharitable neglect of the rich man.*

22. ἀπενεχθῆναι αὐτὸν ὑπὸ τῶν ἀγγ., &c.] The elder Commentators take these words literally; the more recent ones think that the simple idea of Lazarus being removed to supreme felicity in heaven, is adorned with imagery agreeable to the opinions of the Jews; which are stated and illustrated by Wets., Schoettg., and others, cited or referred to in Recens. Synop., from which it appears that the same notions prevailed among the Greeks and Romans. Now if there had been only the circumstance of his being carried by the angels to the place of eternal bliss, — *that*, however agreeable to the notions of the Jews, would have had some countenance for it in our Lord's words; especially, "as this office (Doddr. remarks) would be suitable to their benevolent natures, and to the circumstances of a departed spirit." But when we consider the many *other* circumstances connected with it; as the ἀπενεχθῆναι αὐτὸν εἰς τὸν κόλπον τοῦ Ἀβ. (which has reference to the Oriental custom of *reclining* at table, by which the head of a person sitting next him who was at the top of the triclinium was brought almost in his lap (See Note on John vi. 11.); and that, according to the Jewish opinions, angels were employed to convey the bad to hell, as well as the good to heaven, it should seem that the former view is the most correct. Yet it is to be borne in mind, that no *responsibility* on our Lord's part is involved in this case, as in that of the *Dæmoniacs*; for our best Commentators and Theologians are agreed, that *in parabolical narrations*, provided the doctrines inculcated be strictly true, the terms in which they are expressed may be adapted to the prevailing notions of those to whom they are addressed. See Grot., Doddr., and Mackn.

23. ἐν ᾅδῃ.] So Note on Matt. xi. 23. Here, indeed, it is commonly supposed that the word denotes *Hell*, the *place of torment*. And even Professor Stuart, in his Exegetical Essays on Words denoting future punishment, assigns this sense; though he admits that this is the only passage where the word carries that import. Wets., Rosenm., and Campb., however, take it in the usual signification to denote the place of departed souls, *Sheol*, or Hades, which the Jews as well as the Greeks supposed to be divided into two parts, *Paradise* and *Gehenna*, contiguous to each other, but separated by an impassable chasm [thus Hor. Carm. ii. 13. 23. "sedesque *discretas* piorum"], so narrow, however, that there was a *prospect* of one from the other; nay, such that their respective inmates could converse with each other. Thus both the rich man and Lazarus would be equally in Hades, though in different parts. This view seems preferable, because it is better to avoid supposing any such unusual signification as the above. Indeed, if ἐν τοῖς βασάνοις be meant as Kuin. (who retains the common signification) says, to qualify ἐν τῷ ᾅδῃ, that of itself decidedly proves that ᾅδης must be taken in the usual sense, — otherwise, according to the signification *Hell*, no such qualification could have been necessary. In fact, ἐν τοῖς βασάνοις ὑπάρχων is equivalent to ἐν τῷ ταρτάρῳ ὤ. as St. Peter speaks more definitely, 2 Pet. ii. 4. σειραῖς ζόφου ταρταρώσας. and Joseph. cont. Ap. ii. 33. ἐν ταρτάρῳ δεδεμένους. The *parabolical* representation is, indeed, accommodated to Jewish ideas, and the invisible state is described by images derived from the *senses*. But it is going too far to say, with Dr. Jortin (in D'Oyly and Mant) that "we are only to infer the doctrine of a future state of rewards and punishments." For unless we suppose the great source of all truth to sanction *error*, we cannot but infer that there is an *intermediate state* before the general resurrection; since that is too prominent a feature of the representation to be numbered with circumstances merely *ornamental*.

25. ὅδε.] Very many MSS., Versions, Fathers, and early Edd., have ὧδε, which is edited by Matth. and Scholz. But, though this may seem agreeable to a well-known canon; yet that does not apply to words exceedingly similar and often confounded; in which case manuscript authority is small. *Propriety* must, *then*, decide; and that here requires ὅδε.

— σύ.] This is omitted in several MSS., Versions, and Fathers, and is cancelled by Griesb., Tittm., and Scholz; but without reason; for besides that the antithesis requires the σὺ, and the insufficiency of the evidence for cancelling it, (that of *Versions* being in a case like this but slender), we can account for its *omission* in *two* ways; for its insertion, in *one* only, and that not a very probable one.

— μνήσθητι ὅτι — ὀδυνᾶσαι.] The words are excellently paraphrased by Bp. Sanderson. Serm. ad Populum, p. 151. "If thou hadst any thing good in thee, remember thou hast had thy reward in earth already; and now there remaineth for thee nothing but the *full punishment* of thine ungodli-

26 καλεῖται, σὺ δὲ ὀδυνᾶσαι. Καὶ ἐπὶ πᾶσι τούτοις, μεταξὺ ἡμῶν καὶ
ὑμῶν χάσμα μέγα ἐστήρικται· ὅπως οἱ θέλοντες διαβῆναι ἔνθεν πρὸς
27 ὑμᾶς μὴ δύνωνται, μηδὲ οἱ ἐκεῖθεν πρὸς ἡμᾶς διαπερῶσιν. Εἶπε δέ·
Ἐρωτῶ οὖν σε, πάτερ, ἵνα πέμψῃς αὐτὸν εἰς τὸν οἶκον τοῦ πατρός
28 μου· ἔχω γὰρ πέντε ἀδελφούς· ὅπως διαμαρτύρηται αὐτοῖς, ἵνα μὴ
29 καὶ αὐτοὶ ἔλθωσιν εἰς τὸν τόπον τοῦτον τῆς βασάνου. [f] Λέγει αὐτῷ f Isa. 8. 20. & 34. 16. John 5. 39, 45. Acts 15. 21. & 17. 11.
Ἀβραάμ· Ἔχουσι Μωϋσέα καὶ τοὺς προφήτας· ἀκουσάτωσαν αὐτῶν.
30 Ὁ δὲ εἶπεν· Οὐχὶ, πάτερ Ἀβραάμ· ἀλλ᾽ ἐάν τις ἀπὸ νεκρῶν πο-
31 ρευθῇ πρὸς αὐτοὺς, μετανοήσουσιν. Εἶπε δὲ αὐτῷ· Εἰ Μωϋσέως καὶ
τῶν προφητῶν οὐκ ἀκούουσιν, οὐδὲ, ἐάν τις ἐκ νεκρῶν ἀναστῇ, πει- MT.
σθήσονται. 18.
1 XVII. ΕΙΠΕ δὲ πρὸς τοὺς μαθητάς· Ἀνένδεκτόν ἐστι τοῦ μὴ ἐλ- 7
2 θεῖν τὰ σκάνδαλα· οὐαὶ δὲ δι᾽ οὗ ἔρχεται. Λυσιτελεῖ αὐτῷ, εἰ μύλος 6
ὀνικὸς περίκειται περὶ τὸν τράχηλον αὐτοῦ, καὶ ἔῤῥιπται εἰς τὴν θά-
3 λασσαν, ἢ ἵνα σκανδαλίσῃ ἕνα τῶν μικρῶν τούτων. προσέχετε ἑαυτοῖς. 15
Ἐὰν δὲ ἁμάρτῃ εἰς σὲ ὁ ἀδελφός σου, ἐπιτίμησον αὐτῷ· καὶ ἐὰν μετα-
4 νοήσῃ, ἄφες αὐτῷ. Καὶ ἐὰν ἑπτάκις τῆς ἡμέρας ἁμάρτῃ εἰς σὲ, καὶ
ἑπτάκις τῆς ἡμέρας ἐπιστρέψῃ [ἐπὶ σὲ,] λέγων· Μετανοῶ· ἀφήσεις αὐτῷ.

ness there in *Hell*. But as for Lazarus, he hath had the chastisement of his infirmities on earth already; and now remaineth for him nothing but *the full reward* of his godliness here in *Heaven*."

26. ἔνθεν.] This (for the common reading ἐντεῦθεν) is found in many MSS. and the Ed. Princ. and was rightly adopted by Wets., Matth., Griesb., and Scholz; the common reading plainly having arisen from a marginal gloss. In the later Grecism (see the Critics cited by Bornem.) ἔνθεν was used for ἐντεῦθεν. However, this was no innovation; since it is found in Hom. Il. xiii. 13. It had probably always been retained in the *common* dialect, though, in the more refined diction, ἐντεῦθεν was early substituted. Yet ἔνθεν is found in Thucyd. and Xenophon. What is more, ἔνθεν καὶ ἔνθεν occurs frequently in the Sept.; ἐντεῦθεν very rarely, as Numb. xxii. 24. φραγμὸς ἐντεῦθεν καὶ φραγμὸς ἐντεῦθεν. And Thucyd., in a similar passage, has ἔνθεν, vii. 81. ὁδὸς δὲ ἔνθεν τε καὶ ἔνθεν.

28. διαμαρτύρηται.] Render, warn, or *seriously admonish, by bearing witness of these truths.*

29. Μωϋσέα καὶ τοὺς προφ.] meaning the sacred books of the Jews (as in Matt. xvii. 5.); all revealing, more or less clearly, the doctrine of a future life, and a state of rewards and punishments.

30. οὐχί.] The construction is elliptical. We must supply ἀκούσουσιν, "they will not attend to them, they will slight them," as I did.

31. εἰ Μωϋσέως — πεισθήσονται.] The Jews themselves confessed that the Law was delivered to them by God, and confirmed by manifest and signal miracles; the report of which, as handed down to them from their ancestors, they had received. Yet they led a life contrary to the plain injunctions of the law. Nothing, therefore, hindered their reformation but a perverse mind, unwilling to embrace, as true, what they could not prove to be false. (Rosenm.) The passage may be thus paraphrased: "Occasions of repentance and reformation are not wanting to them. If, therefore, they will not embrace *these*; not even *miracles* could move their perverse and stubborn wills." For, as it is well expressed by Dr. South (Serm. vol. i.), "where a strong inveterate love of sin has made any doctrine or proposition wholly unsuitable to the heart, no argument or demonstration, no nor miracle, whatsoever, will be able to bring the heart cordially to close with or receive it. See more in Doddr. and Campb., and also a Discourse by Bp. Atterbury, vol. ii. Serm. 2, and Bp. Sherlock, vol. ii. Serm. 15.

XVII. 1. ἀνένδεκτόν ἐστι] for οὐκ ἐνδέχεται, which occurs in Luke xiii. 33, and denotes what necessarily must happen, from the condition of man. See Matt. xviii. 7. and Note. The τοῦ inserted before μὴ ἐλθεῖν from many MSS., Fathers, and early Edd., and adopted by Matth., Griesb., Vater, and Scholz, is probably genuine, being certainly agreeable to the usage of St. Luke. And thus we may render literally, "it is impossible for offences not to come."

In the following portions there is no occasion to perplex ourselves about the *connection*; since, as the best Commentators have observed, the discourse is formed of detached admonitions, and consequently no connection is *intended*.

2. λυσιτελεῖ.] Here there is the frequent ellipse of μᾶλλον.

3. προσέχετε ἑαυτοῖς.] These words may be referred either to what *precedes*, or to what *follows*. And here Expositors are divided in opinion. The *former* view seems preferable, since this *solemn formula* of warning is certainly most suitable to what has just preceded. The δὲ, too, just after, which here (as very often) marks the transition to a new subject, rather shews that the words belong to the preceding. However, it *may* be meant for *both*. See Whitby and Gilpin. On what follows, *comp*. Levit. xix. 17. Prov. xvii. 9. Ecclus. xix. 13.

4. [*Comp*. Matt. xviii. 21.]

— ἑπτάκις] for πολλάκις; a frequent Hebrew idiom. The ἐπὶ σὲ after ἐπιστρέψῃ is omitted in

MT.
17. *Καὶ εἶπον οἱ ἀπόστολοι τῷ Κυρίῳ· Πρόσθες ἡμῖν πίστιν. Εἶπε* 5
20 *δὲ ὁ Κύριος· Εἰ εἴχετε πίστιν ὡς κόκκον σινάπεως, ἐλέγετε ἂν τῇ* 6
συκαμίνῳ ταύτῃ· Ἐκριζώθητι, καὶ φυτεύθητι ἐν τῇ θαλάσσῃ· καὶ
ὑπήκουσεν ἂν ὑμῖν. Τίς δὲ ἐξ ὑμῶν δοῦλον ἔχων ἀροτριῶντα ἢ ποι- 7
μαίνοντα, ὃς εἰσελθόντι ἐκ τοῦ ἀγροῦ ἐρεῖ· Εὐθέως παρελθὼν ἀνά-
πεσαι· ἀλλ' οὐχὶ ἐρεῖ αὐτῷ· Ἑτοίμασον τί δειπνήσω, καὶ περιζωσά- 8
μενος διακόνει μοι, ἕως φάγω καὶ πίω· καὶ μετὰ ταῦτα φάγεσαι καὶ
πίεσαι σύ; Μὴ χάριν ἔχει τῷ δούλῳ ἐκείνῳ, ὅτι ἐποίησε τὰ διατα- 9
χθέντα [αὐτῷ]; οὐ, δοκῶ. Οὕτω καὶ ὑμεῖς, ὅταν ποιήσητε πάντα 10
τὰ διαταχθέντα ὑμῖν, λέγετε· Ὅτι δοῦλοι ἀχρεῖοί ἐσμεν· ὅτι ὃ
ὠφείλομεν ποιῆσαι πεποιήκαμεν.

ΚΑΙ ἐγένετο, ἐν τῷ πορεύεσθαι αὐτὸν εἰς Ἱερουσαλήμ, καὶ αὐτὸς 11
διήρχετο διὰ μέσου Σαμαρείας καὶ Γαλιλαίας. Καὶ εἰσερχομένου αὐ- 12
τοῦ εἴς τινα κώμην, ἀπήντησαν αὐτῷ δέκα λεπροὶ ἄνδρες, οἳ ἔστησαν
πόῤῥωθεν· καὶ αὐτοὶ ἦραν φωνὴν, λέγοντες· Ἰησοῦ ἐπιστάτα, ἐλέησον 13
a Lev. 13. 2. & 14. 2. Matt. 8. 4. supr. 5. 14. *ἡμᾶς! [a] Καὶ ἰδὼν εἶπεν αὐτοῖς· Πορευθέντες ἐπιδείξατε ἑαυτοὺς τοῖς* 14
ἱερεῦσι. Καὶ ἐγένετο, ἐν τῷ ὑπάγειν αὐτοὺς, ἐκαθαρίσθησαν. Εἷς δὲ 15
ἐξ αὐτῶν, ἰδὼν ὅτι ἰάθη, ὑπέστρεψε μετὰ φωνῆς μεγάλης δοξάζων τὸν
Θεόν· καὶ ἔπεσεν ἐπὶ πρόσωπον παρὰ τοὺς πόδας αὐτοῦ, εὐχαριστῶν 16

very many MSS., Versions, and Fathers, and is cancelled by Wets., Matth., Griesb., Tittm., Vat., and Scholz. But the evidence for it is so strong, that it is more probable the words were omitted by some over nice Critics, to remove what seemed an offensive repetition, than that it should have been brought in to complete the sense. Such sort of tautology as this *strengthens* the sense, and is found in the best writers. The Editors have chiefly been induced to cancel the words, because they thought the existence of two readings, ἐπὶ σὲ and πρὸς σὲ, shewed that *both were from the margin*. But there are exceptions to that, as well as most other Critical Canons. And one is, where a phrase or clausula is such as the Critics, from over fastidiousness, would be likely to object to and alter. For, in such a case, there may be *several* ways by which the alleged imperfection might be removed; which may *all* be resorted to by the Critics. And yet that will not prove that the readings are all alike not genuine. Certainly the existence of the words in the Pesch. Syr. Versions attests their high antiquity.

6. συκαμίνῳ] i. e. the *ficus sycamorus* of Linnæus; a tree whose leaves resemble those of the mulberry, and its fruit that of the fig-tree. It is found in Egypt and Palestine, and is so called as resembling the *fig-tree* in its fruit, and the *mulberry* in its leaf.

8. φάγεσαι καὶ πίεσαι.] These are, as Wets. observes, 2 pers. Fut. Mid. for φάγῃ and πίῃ, according to the early usage (which, it seems, continued in the common dialect to a late period), whereby φάγομαι and πίομαι were used for φαγοῦμαι and πιοῦμαι. See Matth. Gr. Gr. § 197. 1. and Buttm. Gr. Gr. p. 244. ἀλλὰ οὐχὶ ἐρεῖ with most for καὶ ο. The doctrine contained in ver. 7—10 is plainly this, that the rewards held out to Christian obedience are not of merit, but purely of grace. On which I would refer the reader to a powerful Sermon of Dr. South on Job xxii. 20, entitled "The Doctrine of merit stated, and the impossibility of Man's meriting of God."

9. μὴ χάριν ἔχει.] Kuin. renders, "num gratiam habere debet," which is approved by Bornem., who gives several examples of this sense, and refers to various Critics.

—αὐτῷ.] This is not found in nearly all the best MSS., and in several Fathers and early Edd., and is with reason cancelled by almost every Editor from Beng. to Scholz.

11. διήρχετο διὰ μέσου Σ.] On the exact force of this expression the Commentators are in doubt, since Samaria and Galilee seem to be mentioned in a manner the reverse of their geographical position. But it should rather seem that no notice is *meant* of that position; and that Grot., De Dieu, Wets., Campb., and others, have rightly supposed that our Lord did not proceed by the *direct* way (namely, through Samaria) to Jerusalem; but that, upon coming to the confines of Samaria and Galilee, he diverged to the east; so as to have Samaria on the right, and Galilee on the left. Thus he seems to have passed the Jordan at Scythopolis (where there was a bridge), and to have descended along the bank on the Peræan side, until he again crossed the river, when he came opposite to Jericho. The reason which induced our Lord to take this circuitous route, was probably both to avoid any molestation from the Samaritans, and at the same time to impart to a greater number of Jews the benefits of his Gospel.

12. εἰσερχομένου αὐτοῦ] "as he was entering," i. e. about to enter. Πόῤῥωθεν. No doubt, within the distance, whatever it was (for on that the Rabbins are not agreed), at which lepers were obliged to stand apart from others.

14. τοῖς ἱερεῦσι.] This is either meant (as Grot. and others think) to be taken in a *collective* sense; or, with Wets., we may suppose the priests of

17 αὐτῷ. καὶ αὐτὸς ἦν Σαμαρείτης. Ἀποκριθεὶς δὲ ὁ Ἰησοῦς εἶπεν·
18 Οὐχὶ οἱ δέκα ἐκαθαρίσθησαν; οἱ δὲ ἐννέα ποῦ; Οὐχ εὑρέθησαν
19 ὑποστρέψαντες δοῦναι δόξαν τῷ Θεῷ, εἰ μὴ ὁ ἀλλογενὴς οὗτος. [b] Καὶ b Matt. 9. 22. Mark 5. 34. & 10. 52.
εἶπεν αὐτῷ· Ἀναστὰς πορεύου· ἡ πίστις σου σέσωκέ σε. supra 7. 50. & 8. 48.
20 Ἐπερωτηθεὶς δὲ ὑπὸ τῶν Φαρισαίων, πότε ἔρχεται ἡ βασιλεία τοῦ infra 18. 42.
Θεοῦ, ἀπεκρίθη αὐτοῖς καὶ εἶπεν· Οὐκ ἔρχεται ἡ βασιλεία τοῦ Θεοῦ
21 μετὰ παρατηρήσεως· οὐδὲ ἐροῦσιν· Ἰδοὺ ὧδε, ἤ ἰδοὺ ἐκεῖ· ἰδοὺ γὰρ
22 ἡ βασιλεία τοῦ Θεοῦ ἐντὸς ὑμῶν ἐστιν. Εἶπε δὲ πρὸς τοὺς μαθητάς· MT.
Ἐλεύσονται ἡμέραι, ὅτε ἐπιθυμήσετε μίαν τῶν ἡμερῶν τοῦ Υἱοῦ τοῦ 24.
23 ἀνθρώπου ἰδεῖν, καὶ οὐκ ὄψεσθε. Καὶ ἐροῦσιν ὑμῖν· Ἰδοὺ ὧδε, ἤ 23
24 ἰδοὺ ἐκεῖ· μὴ ἀπέλθητε, μηδὲ διώξητε. ὥσπερ γὰρ ἡ ἀστραπὴ ἡ 27
ἀστράπτουσα ἐκ τῆς ὑπ' οὐρανὸν εἰς τὴν ὑπ' οὐρανὸν λάμπει· οὕτως
25 ἔσται [καὶ] ὁ Υἱὸς τοῦ ἀνθρώπου ἐν τῇ ἡμέρᾳ αὐτοῦ. Πρῶτον δὲ
δεῖ αὐτὸν πολλὰ παθεῖν, καὶ ἀποδοκιμασθῆναι ἀπὸ τῆς γενεᾶς ταύτης.
26 Καὶ καθὼς ἐγένετο ἐν ταῖς ἡμέραις [τοῦ] Νῶε, οὕτως ἔσται καὶ ἐν 37
27 ταῖς ἡμέραις τοῦ Υἱοῦ τοῦ ἀνθρώπου. Ἤσθιον, ἔπινον, ἐγάμουν, ἐξε- 38
γαμίζοντο, ἄχρι ἧς ἡμέρας εἰσῆλθε Νῶε εἰς τὴν κιβωτὸν, καὶ ἦλθεν
28 ὁ κατακλυσμὸς καὶ ἀπώλεσεν ἅπαντας. Ὁμοίως καὶ ὡς ἐγένετο ἐν ταῖς
ἡμέραις Λώτ· ἤσθιον, ἔπινον, ἠγόραζον, ἐπώλουν, ἐφύτευον, ᾠκοδό-
29 μουν· ᾗ δὲ ἡμέρᾳ ἐξῆλθε Λὼτ ἀπὸ Σοδόμων, ἔβρεξε πῦρ καὶ θεῖον
20 ἀπ' οὐρανοῦ καὶ ἀπώλεσεν ἅπαντας. κατὰ ταῦτα ἔσται ᾗ ἡμέρᾳ ὁ
31 Υἱὸς τοῦ ἀνθρώπου ἀποκαλύπτεται. Ἐν ἐκείνῃ τῇ ἡμέρᾳ, ὃς ἔσται ἐπὶ 17
τοῦ δώματος καὶ τὰ σκεύη αὐτοῦ ἐν τῇ οἰκίᾳ, μὴ καταβάτω ἆραι αὐτά·
32 καὶ ὁ ἐν τῷ ἀγρῷ ὁμοίως μὴ ἐπιστρεψάτω εἰς τὰ ὀπίσω. Μνημονεύετε

both Jews and Samaritans. But the former is far more probable.

17. See a masterly Sermon on this text by Dr. Parr, entitled, *On the sin of ingratitude*.

18. ἀλλογενής.] Such the Samaritans were esteemed by the Jews; and Josephus calls them ἀλλοεθνεῖς. Whether they were to be regarded as *Gentiles*, was a disputed question among the Rabbins. That they were not *heathens*, was certain; but the Jews took advantage of some approach to idolatry, in the worship at Mount Gerizim, to regard them as such.

20. μετὰ παρατηρήσεως.] On the sense of this expression Commentators are not agreed. The word παρατ. is indeed rare; but four examples are adduced from the later writers, in which the sense is, *attention, observation*. But as that signification does not seem suitable here, many recent Commentators render it *splendour, pomp, parade;* which, however, is rather an *interpretation* than a *version*. It may be best taken, by metonymy, to denote *what attracts observation*.

21. ἐντὸς ὑμῶν ἐ.] for ἐν ὑμῖν, "is among you." q. d. the kingdom of the Messiah has even *commenced* among you (i. e. in your own country, and among your own people), though ye do not see it. So xi. 20. ἔφθασεν ἐφ' ὑμᾶς ἡ βασιλεία τοῦ θεοῦ. On this interpretation the best Commentators are agreed, and adduce examples of this use of ἐντός. The common interpretation, which takes it of the *internal* and *spiritual* principle, yields a good *sense* (see Rom. xiv. 17.), but is forbidden by the *context*.

25. [*Comp*. Matt. xvi. 21. xvii. 22. xx. 18. Mark viii. 31. supra ix. 22. 26.]

26. [*Comp*. 1 Pet. iii. 20. Gen. vi. 2.]

28. ὁμοίως καὶ ὡς ἐγ.] A somewhat unusual mode of expression, which is learnedly discussed by Bornem., who, however, is wrong in referring these words to what *precedes*. It should seem to be a *stronger* expression than either ὁμοίως ἐγένετο or οὕτως ἐγέν. would have been. And we may suppose an *ellipsis*, thus to be supplied: "the circumstances of that age, and the consequent catastrophe, took place also in a similar manner as they did in the days of Lot." [*Comp*. Gen. xix. 14.]

29. ἔβρεξε.] Sub. Θεός; a frequent ellips., but *supplied* in Gen. xix. 24. Πῦρ denotes lightning; and such is the *proper* signification of θεῖον, i. e. *divine fire*. Thus places struck with lightning were said to be θεῖα, and were separated from human use. Since, however, in such places there are (to use the words of Lucret. vi. 219.) *inusta vapore Signa notæque, graves halantes sulphuris auras;* and since lightning has a sulphurous smell, hence it is often used for *sulphur*, as here and in Apoc. xiv. 10. xix. 20. Therefore, by πῦρ καὶ θεῖον is denoted a sulphurous fire, meaning that of lightning.

32. μνημ. τῆς γυν. Λώτ.] See Gen. 19. 26. Whatever may be the view taken of the occurrence in question, — whether Lot's wife was *literally* turned to a pillar of salt, or *figuratively* so, by being suffocated, and the corpse indurated by the salsiginous vapour, — the warning is equally

MT.
16. τῆς γυναικὸς Λώτ. Ὃς ἐὰν ζητήσῃ τὴν ψυχὴν αὐτοῦ σῶσαι, ἀπολέσει 33
25 αὐτήν· καὶ ὃς ἐὰν ἀπολέσῃ αὐτὴν, ζωογονήσει αὐτήν. Λέγω ὑμῖν· 34
24. ταύτῃ τῇ νυκτὶ ἔσονται δύο ἐπὶ κλίνης μιᾶς· ὁ εἷς παραληφθήσεται,
41 καὶ ὁ ἕτερος ἀφεθήσεται. δύο ἔσονται ἀλήθουσαι ἐπὶ τὸ αὐτό· ἡ 35
40 μία παραληφθήσεται, καὶ ἡ ἑτέρα ἀφεθήσεται. [δύο ἔσονται ἐν τῷ 36
ἀγρῷ· ὁ εἷς παραληφθήσεται, καὶ ὁ ἕτερος ἀφεθήσεται.] Καὶ ἀπο- 37
κριθέντες λέγουσιν αὐτῷ· Ποῦ, Κύριε; ὁ δὲ εἶπεν αὐτοῖς· Ὅπου
28 τὸ σῶμα, ἐκεῖ συναχθήσονται οἱ ἀετοί.

a Eccl. 18. 22. Rom. 12. 12. Eph. 6. 18. Col. 4. 2. 1 Thess. 5. 17. supra 11. 5. & 21. 36.

XVIII. [a] ΕΛΕΓΕ δὲ καὶ παραβολὴν αὐτοῖς πρὸς τὸ δεῖν πάντοτε 1
προσεύχεσθαι, καὶ μὴ ἐκκακεῖν, λέγων· Κριτής τις ἦν ἔν τινι πόλει τὸν 2
Θεὸν μὴ φοβούμενος, καὶ ἄνθρωπον μὴ ἐντρεπόμενος. Χήρα δὲ [τις] 3
ἦν ἐν τῇ πόλει ἐκείνῃ, καὶ ἤρχετο πρὸς αὐτὸν, λέγουσα· Ἐκδίκησόν
με ἀπὸ τοῦ ἀντιδίκου μου. Καὶ οὐκ ἠθέλησεν ἐπὶ χρόνον· μετὰ δὲ 4
ταῦτα εἶπεν ἐν ἑαυτῷ· Εἰ καὶ τὸν Θεὸν οὐ φοβοῦμαι, καὶ ἄνθρωπον
οὐκ ἐντρέπομαι· διά γε τὸ παρέχειν μοι κόπον τὴν χήραν ταύτην ἐδικήσω 5
αὐτὴν, ἵνα μὴ εἰς τέλος ἐρχομένη ὑπωπιάζῃ με. Εἶπε δὲ ὁ Κύριος· 6
b Rev. 6. 10. Ἀκούσατε τί ὁ κριτὴς τῆς ἀδικίας λέγει. [b] Ὁ δὲ Θεὸς οὐ μὴ ποιήσει τὴν 7

forcible against the sin of disbelieving these awful predictions, and against a love of the world, or other carnal dispositions.

33. ὃς ἐὰν, &c.] Comp. supra ix. 24. Mark viii. 25. John xii. 25. and Matt. x. 39., where see note. *Here* the application is somewhat different, referring to what *precedes*. This sense of ζωογονεῖν (namely to *preserve*) is never found in the Classical writers; but it is not unfrequent in the LXX.

36. This verse is omitted in a great number of the best MSS., some Versions, and several early Edd.; and is cancelled by almost all recent Editors, as an interpolation from Matthew. But as it is found in some MSS. and almost every Version of antiquity and credit, it should rather seem to be genuine, and only omitted accidentally, *propter homœoteleuton*.

37. ποῦ, Κύριε] scil. ταῦτα ἔσται vel γενήσεται; i. e. *where* shall these things come to pass? Not, as Kuin. explains, *by what means* shall, &c. For thus the words of our Lord in reply would be no answer to the question. And thus, even granting (what perhaps could not be *proved*) that ποῦ is *ever* used for πῶς, it could not be shewn to have that sense *here*. Our Lord, indeed, we may well suppose, was not, neither intended to be, understood *then*; but he was *afterwards*; and therefore this partakes of the nature of a prophecy, to be understood completely only by the *event*, and when fulfilled.

XVIII. 1. πρὸς τὸ δεῖν] "on the subject of the duty of," &c. See supra ix. 18. and note. Of this sense of πρὸς with verbs of speaking and writing, Kypke adduces an example from Plutarch. Πάντοτε signifies *constantly, perseveringly*, in opposition to that intermission of regular duty, which arises from weariness or despondency. "This (observes Dr. Barrow, Serm. i. 75.) imports, as the ensuing discourse shews, restless importunity in prayer, so often enjoined by the phrases μὴ ἐκκακεῖν, μὴ παλύεσθαι, προσκαρτερεῖν, ἀγωνίζεσθαι, προσμένειν, ἀγρυπνεῖν ἐν προσκαρτερήσει." See the whole of his Sermons, vi. and vii., on 1 Thes. v. 17. Ἐκκακεῖν signifies properly "to abandon any thing from cowardice, laziness, or despondency." The commencement of this chapter is plainly connected in subject with the close of the preceding. For an attention to the duties of prayer, patience, and perseverance would be their best support in the hour of tribulation and distress, under the evils which would precede the destruction of Jerusalem.

2. τὸν Θεὸν — ἐντρεπόμενος.] A proverbial form, denoting the most daring and unblushing wickedness; of which many examples are given by Elsn. and Wets.; to which I have added many others in Rec. Syn. All may have originated from Hom. Od. x. 39.

3. ἐκδίκησον] almost all English Commentators agree in censuring the *avenge* of our Common version, and render "do me justice upon." But the change is unncessary, since *avenge* in our early writers has this very sense; namely, "to take satisfaction for an injury from or upon the injurer." So far from *revenge* forming any part of the idea, in the minds of the Translators, even the word itsolf is frequently used by our old writers in the sense of taking retribution, justice by law.

4. ἐπὶ χρόνον] scil. τινα, as Acts xxviii. 6. 1 Cor. vii. 39. and Hom. Il. β. 299.

5. εἰς τέλος.] An Hellenistic phrase (formed on the Hebr. לנצח) for the Classical one διὰ τέλους, and signifying *perpetually, constantly*. So ἀεὶ is used in a kindred passage of Herodot. iii. 119. which I have adduced in Recens. Synop. Δι' ὅλου, Euthym. Ὑπωπιάζειν is properly a *pugilistic* term. It signifies 1. to bruise under the eyes; 2. to bruise generally. 3. It figuratively denotes to stun any one by dinning in his ears, and consequently to weary him. So Euthym. ἐνοχλῇ. See Joseph. Bell. i. 1, 2. No certain example of this sense has been adduced from the Classical writers; but it is frequent in the correspondent Latin term *obtundere*; so that this is probably a Latinism.

ἐκδίκησιν τῶν ἐκλεκτῶν αὐτοῦ τῶν βοώντων πρὸς αὐτὸν ἡμέρας καὶ
8 νυκτὸς, καὶ μακροθυμῶν ἐπ' αὐτοῖς; λέγω ὑμῖν ὅτι ποιήσει τὴν ἐκδίκησιν αὐτῶν ἐν τάχει. Πλὴν ὁ Υἱὸς τοῦ ἀνθρώπου ἐλθὼν ἆρα εὑρήσει τὴν πίστιν ἐπὶ τῆς γῆς;
9 Εἶπε δὲ καὶ πρός τινας τοὺς πεποιθότας ἐφ' ἑαυτοῖς ὅτι εἰσὶ δί-
10 καιοι, καὶ ἐξουθενοῦντας τοὺς λοιποὺς, τὴν παραβολὴν ταύτην. Ἄνθρωποι δύο ἀνέβησαν εἰς τὸ ἱερὸν προσεύξασθαι· ὁ εἷς Φαρισαῖος,
11 καὶ ὁ ἕτερος τελώνης. ᶜ ὁ Φαρισαῖος σταθεὶς πρὸς ἑαυτὸν ταῦτα c Isa. 1. 15. & 58. 2. Rev. 3. 17.
προσηύχετο· Ὁ Θεὸς, εὐχαριστῶ σοι, ὅτι οὐκ εἰμὶ ὥσπερ οἱ λοιποὶ
τῶν ἀνθρώπων, ἅρπαγες, ἄδικοι, μοιχοί· ἢ καὶ ὡς οὗτος ὁ τελώνης.
12 Νηστεύω δὶς τοῦ σαββάτου, ἀποδεκατῶ πάντα ὅσα κτῶμαι. Καὶ ὁ
13 τελώνης μακρόθεν ἑστὼς οὐκ ἤθελεν οὐδὲ τοὺς ὀφθαλμοὺς εἰς τὸν οὐρανὸν ἐπᾶραι· ἀλλ' ἔτυπτεν εἰς τὸ στῆθος αὐτοῦ, λέγων· Ὁ Θεὸς,

7. *ἐκδίκησιν ποιήσει* is for *ἐκδικήσει*.

—*τῶν ἐκλεκτῶν*] "his choice and approved servants." *Βοώντων* is to be understood of loud and earnest entreaty. The figure is often found in the Classical writers, but always of reproach or expostulation. There is a difficulty attendant on *οὐ μὴ*, which most Commentators do not face. Bornem. offers an able solution, by taking the passage as if written thus: *ἀλλ' οὐ φοβητέον, μὴ καὶ μακροθυμῶν ὁ Θεὸς ποιήσει τῶν ἐκλ. α.* &c. This method is strongly confirmed by the context.

—*καὶ μακροθυμῶν ἐ. α.*] If, with most Expositors, *μακροθυμεῖν*, according to its general sense in the N. T., be taken of God's *long suffering*, consequently *αὐτοῖς* must be referred to those who *aggrieve the righteous*. That, however, would involve an unprecedented harshness, since such a sense cannot be elicited even from the context, much less any word of the text. *Αὐτοῖς* cannot, without violence, be referred to any other word than to *ἐκλεκτοῖς*. We must therefore suppose some other sense of *μακροθυμεῖν*. And as the word signifies properly to be slow-minded, it may very well denote to be slow in avenging or affording assistance. And in this sense the word occurs in a kindred sentiment at Ecclus. xxxii. 18. Sept. *καὶ ὁ Κύριος οὐ μὴ βραδύνει, οὐδὲ μὴ μακροθυμήσει ἐπ' αὐτοῖς*. This interpretation (which alone suits the scope of the parable) is adopted by almost all recent Commentators, and is confirmed by Euthym.

8. *πλὴν ὁ Υἱὸς — τῆς γῆς.*] The Commentators are not agreed whether this coming of our Lord adverts to his *final* advent, or to his advent at the *destruction of Jerusalem*. But may not *both* views be admitted? as in chap. xxv. & xxvi. of St. Matthew. The former may be maintained; but the latter is so confirmed by the account which we have of the time in question, in the Epistles of James, Peter, and Paul, that it can scarcely be doubted but it is the true interpretation. Of course, *τῆς γῆς* must be taken, as often, of the land of Judæa. See the notes of Wets., Doddr., Campb., Rosenm., and Kuin., or the abstract in Rec. Syn. The interrogation implies a strong negation.

It is strange that Markl. and Campb. should suppose *τὴν πίστιν* to mean "the belief of this truth," namely, that God will avenge his elect; for that would require *τὴν πίστιν ταύτην*. The true force of the Article is well pointed out by Bornem.

9. *εἶπε δὲ πρὸς κτλ.*] The best Commentators are agreed that *πρὸς* here and at v. 1. means *concerning*, as supra xii. 41. infra xix. 9., and sometimes in the Classical writers. This the Commentators exemplify from Plutarchi Op. p. 394. *πρὸς ὃν δὲ Πίνδαρος εἴρηκε.* I add Thucyd. iii. 42. *πρὸς τὰ μέγιστα λέγειν.*

11. *πρὸς ἑαυτόν.*] There has been some doubt as to the construction of these words; which some Expositors connect with *σταθεὶς*, in the sense "*apart*, by himself;" others with *προσηύχετο*. The latter mode is preferable; for the former proceeds on a confusion of *πρὸς ἑαυτὸν* with *καθ' ἑαυτόν*. *Πρὸς ἑαυτὸν* can only denote "with himself;" and is not unfrequently joined with verbs of speaking or thinking; of which the Commentators adduce examples both from the N. T. and the later Classical writers. Wets. renders it *secum tacitus*, and compares the Horatian "labra movet metuens audiri." The illustration is better than the Version, for it is not, as some have thought (for instance, Bulkeley and Dr. Maltby) *mental* prayer that is meant; but *secret* prayer, when the words are pronounced by the lips, but not so as to be heard by a bystander. *Σταθεὶς* is is by some rendered *consistens*; by others is considered as added for ornament. But (as I suggested in Recens. Synop.) it has reference to the posture of prayer among the Jews — namely, *standing*: insomuch that it was not permitted to pray in any other posture.

—*ἅρπαγες.*] *Ἅρπαξ* denotes one who *injures* another by *force*; *ἄδικος*, one who *over-reaches* him by *fraud*, or under a semblance of justice.

12. *δὶς τοῦ σαββ.*] viz. on the 2d and 5th days, as appears from Epiphanius and the Rabbins, cited by Wets. By these are meant not *public*, but *private* and voluntary fasts. On *ἀποδεκ.* see Note on Matt. xxiii. 23.

13. *μακρόθεν ἑστώς.*] Namely, in the court of the Gentiles, if he was a Pagan; or, if a Jew, placed far apart from the Pharisees.

—*οὐκ ἤθελεν — ἐπᾶραι.*] Schoettg. remarks that it was a maxim of the Rabbins, that he who prays should cast down his eyes, but raise his heart to God; contrary to the custom of the Greeks and Romans, which was to lift up the eyes and hands in prayer. Yet in this picture of real contrition and genuine humility we must suppose every thing *unstudied*.

—*ἔτυπτεν εἰς τὸ στῆθος.*] An action suited to

d Job. 22. 29. Prov. 29. 23. supra 14. 11. Matt. 23. 12. James 4. 6, 10. 1 Pet. 5. 5.

ἱλάσθητί μοι τῷ ἁμαρτωλῷ. [d] Λέγω ὑμῖν, κατέβη οὗτος δεδικαιωμένος 14
εἰς τὸν οἶκον αὐτοῦ, ‡ ἢ ἐκεῖνος. ὅτι πᾶς ὁ ὑψῶν ἑαυτὸν ταπεινωθή-
σεται· ὁ δὲ ταπεινῶν ἑαυτὸν ὑψωθήσεται.

MT. MK.
19. 10. Προσέφερον δὲ αὐτῷ καὶ τὰ βρέφη, ἵνα αὐτῶν ἅπτηται· ἰδόντες 15
13 13 δὲ οἱ μαθηταὶ ἐπετίμησαν αὐτοῖς. Ὁ δὲ Ἰησοῦς προσκαλεσάμενος αὐτὰ, 16
14 14 εἶπεν· Ἄφετε τὰ παιδία ἔρχεσθαι πρός με, καὶ μὴ κωλύετε αὐτά· τῶν
15 γὰρ τοιούτων ἐστὶν ἡ βασιλεία τοῦ Θεοῦ. Ἀμὴν λέγω ὑμῖν, ὃς ἐὰν 17
μὴ δέξηται τὴν βασιλείαν τοῦ Θεοῦ ὡς παιδίον, οὐ μὴ εἰσέλθῃ εἰς
αὐτήν.

16 17 Καὶ ἐπηρώτησέ τις αὐτὸν ἄρχων, λέγων· Διδάσκαλε ἀγαθὲ, τί ποι- 18
17 18 ήσας ζωὴν αἰώνιον κληρονομήσω; Εἶπε δὲ αὐτῷ ὁ Ἰησοῦς· Τί με 19
18 19 λέγεις ἀγαθόν; οὐδεὶς ἀγαθὸς, εἰ μὴ εἷς, ὁ Θεός. Τὰς ἐντολὰς οἶ- 20
δας· Μὴ μοιχεύσῃς· μὴ φονεύσῃς· μὴ κλέψῃς· μὴ
ψευδομαρτυρήσῃς· τίμα τὸν πατέρα σου καὶ τὴν μη-
19 20 τέρα σου. Ὁ δὲ εἶπε· Ταῦτα πάντα ἐφυλαξάμην ἐκ νεότητός μου. 21

grief, remorse, &c., and common to all nations; as appears from the many passages adduced by Wets. and others: among which, however, I find none sufficiently similar in the *construction*; which appears Hellenistical, and consists in the omission of the pronoun; though the phrase, even *with a personal pronoun*, is rare.

— μοι τῷ ἁμ.] Wets. and others think that the Article is emphatical, and used κατ' ἐξοχήν. But its force is better indicated by Bp. Middlet. thus: "Whenever an *attributive* noun is placed in opposition with a personal pronoun, such attributive has the Article prefixed. Thus in Luke vi. 24. ὑμῖν τοῖς πλουσίοις. xi. 46. ὑμῖν τοῖς νομικοῖς. We have the same form of speech also in Herodot. ix. p. 342. μὲ τὴν ἱκέτιν. Plut. Conv. vii. Sap. p. 95. ἐμὲ τὸν δύστηνον. See also Soph. Elect. 282. Eurip. Ion. 348. Aristoph. Av. 5. Acharn. 1154. Eccles. 619. Of the usage in question the ground is sufficiently obvious. The Article here, as elsewhere, marks the assumption of its predicate; and the strict meaning of the publican's prayer is, "Have mercy on me, who am *confessedly* a sinner;" or, "seeing that I am a sinner, have mercy on me."

14. κατέβη εἰς τὸν οἶκον αὐτοῦ.] Said with reference to the *lower* situation of the city with respect to the Temple. So ver. 10. ἀνέβησαν. But in fact the expression is nearly equivalent to "went back," ἀπεχώρει, as in Thucyd. iii. 42. ἀξυνετώτερος ἂν δόξας εἶναι ἀπεχώρει. By δεδικαιωμένος is meant *accepted, approved*, considered *as* just. See Schoettg.

— ἢ ἐκεῖνος.] There is thought to be here the common ellipse of μᾶλλον. But it is better (with Euthym., Rosenm., and Kuin.) to suppose that, as the Hebrews often express a simple negation by a *comparative*, (as in Gen. xxxviii. 26. and 1 Sam. xxiv. 17.) so here the sense is, that the Publican went away justified; but not the Pharisee.

For ἢ most of the MSS. and almost all the early Edd. have ἢ γὰρ, which is approved by Mill, and adopted by almost every Editor from Wets. to Scholz. But though the more difficult is usually to be considered the preferable reading, yet that principle does not extend to manifest violations of the propriety of the language. And, notwithstanding what those Editors say, this use of γὰρ cannot be defended; as appears from the vain attempts made to explain it. For to render it *sane*, or *nimirum*, or to consider it as having reference to a clause omitted, is alike inadmissible. And as ἢ γὰρ differs so slightly from another reading, namely ἤπερ, found in some MSS. and Basil, we may suspect the ἢ γὰρ to be an error of the scribes, who had ἤπερ in their originals. Whether, indeed, *that* be the true reading, I doubt. It seems to have been a very early *correction* of Luke's Greek. For elegance of style would require ἤπερ, rather than ἤ. It may be added, too, that every ancient Version of credit represents ἢ or ἤπερ, not ἢ γάρ. How περ might be confounded with γὰρ (especially by those who did not consider the construction) is obvious from the strong similarity between π and ſ and α and ε. I suspect, however, that of those who wrote γὰρ many had in their originals παρ' ἐκεῖνον, which is found in several very ancient MSS. and the Pesch. Syr. Version; and that παρ' had arisen from περ. Then ἐκεῖνος would easily be altered to ἐκεῖνον. Thus it appears that the original reading was ἢ, from which arose ἤπερ, and ἢ γάρ. Now it is one of the most certain of Critical Canons, that, among several readings of a word or passage, that from which all the rest might easily have originated is to be preferred. Moreover, that ἢ, rather than ἤπερ, is the true reading, is probable from the former occurring in a similar construction, supra xv. 7. *sine var. lect.*

15—17. This section is introduced here in a very different connection than it is by Matthew and Mark. By *them* it is brought forward after the narration of the inquiry made by the Pharisees as to the lawfulness of divorce; and that simply because it took place immediately *after*. St. Luke, however, introduces it *here*, as intending to *classify* things according to their subjects; and indeed the connection here is very suitable.

15. τὰ βρέφη] i. e. the children of the persons who resorted to him. Render, "their children." On the rest of the Chap. see the Notes on the parallel passages.

16. [*Comp.* Matt. xviii. 3. 1 Cor. xiv. 20. 1 Pet. ii. 2.]

MT. MK.

22 Ἀκούσας δὲ ταῦτα ὁ Ἰησοῦς εἶπεν αὐτῷ· Ἔτι ἕν σοι λείπει· πάντα 19. 10.
ὅσα ἔχεις πώλησον, καὶ διάδος πτωχοῖς, καὶ ἕξεις θησαυρὸν ἐν οὐρανῷ· 20 21 21
23 καὶ δεῦρο ἀκολούθει μοι. Ὁ δὲ ἀκούσας ταῦτα περίλυπος ἐγένετο· ἦν 22 22
24 γὰρ πλούσιος σφόδρα. Ἰδὼν δὲ αὐτὸν ὁ Ἰησοῦς περίλυπον γενόμενον, 23 23
εἶπε· Πῶς δυσκόλως οἱ τὰ χρήματα ἔχοντες εἰσελεύσονται εἰς τὴν βα-
25 σιλείαν τοῦ Θεοῦ. Εὐκοπώτερον γάρ ἐστι, κάμηλον διὰ τρυμαλιᾶς ῥαφί- 25
26 δος εἰσελθεῖν, ἢ πλούσιον εἰς τὴν βασιλείαν τοῦ Θεοῦ εἰσελθεῖν. Εἶπον 25 26
27 δὲ οἱ ἀκούσαντες· καὶ τίς δύναται σωθῆναι; Ὁ δὲ εἶπε· Τὰ ἀδύ- 26 27
28 νατα παρὰ ἀνθρώποις δυνατά ἐστι παρὰ τῷ Θεῷ. Εἶπε δὲ [ὁ] Πέτρος· 27 28
29 Ἰδοὺ, ἡμεῖς ἀφήκαμεν πάντα καὶ ἠκολουθήσαμέν σοι. Ὁ δὲ εἶπεν 28 29
αὐτοῖς· Ἀμὴν λέγω ὑμῖν, ὅτι οὐδείς ἐστιν ὃς ἀφῆκεν οἰκίαν, ἢ γονεῖς,
30 ἢ ἀδελφοὺς, ἢ γυναῖκα, ἢ τέκνα, ἕνεκεν τῆς βασιλείας τοῦ Θεοῦ, ὃς 30
οὐ μὴ ἀπολάβῃ πολλαπλασίονα ἐν τῷ καιρῷ τούτῳ, καὶ ἐν τῷ αἰῶνι
τῷ ἐρχομένῳ ζωὴν αἰώνιον. 20.
31 ΠΑΡΑΛΑΒΩΝ δὲ τοὺς δώδεκα, εἶπε πρὸς αὐτούς· Ἰδοὺ, ἀναβαί- 17 32
νομεν εἰς Ἱεροσόλυμα, καὶ τελεσθήσεται πάντα τὰ γεγραμμένα διὰ τῶν 18 33
32 προφητῶν τῷ Υἱῷ τοῦ ἀνθρώπου. Παραδοθήσεται γὰρ τοῖς ἔθνεσι, 19 34
33 καὶ ἐμπαιχθήσεται καὶ ὑβρισθήσεται καὶ ἐμπτυσθήσεται· καὶ μαστιγώ-
34 σαντες ἀποκτενοῦσιν αὐτόν· καὶ τῇ ἡμέρᾳ τῇ τρίτῃ ἀναστήσεται. Καὶ
αὐτοὶ οὐδὲν τούτων συνῆκαν, καὶ ἦν τὸ ῥῆμα τοῦτο κεκρυμμένον ἀπ᾽
αὐτῶν, καὶ οὐκ ἐγίνωσκον τὰ λεγόμενα.
35 Ἐγένετο δὲ ἐν τῷ ἐγγίζειν αὐτὸν εἰς Ἱεριχὼ, τυφλός τις ἐκάθητο παρὰ 29 46
36 τὴν ὁδὸν προσαιτῶν· ἀκούσας δὲ ὄχλου διαπορευομένου, ἐπυνθάνετο 30
37 τί εἴη τοῦτο. Ἀπήγγειλαν δὲ αὐτῷ, ὅτι Ἰησοῦς ὁ Ναζωραῖος παρέρ-
38 χεται. καὶ ἐβόησε λέγων· Ἰησοῦ Υἱὲ Δαυῒδ, ἐλέησόν με! Καὶ οἱ 47
39 προάγοντες ἐπετίμων αὐτῷ ἵνα σιωπήσῃ· αὐτὸς δὲ πολλῷ μᾶλλον ἔκρα- 31 48
40 ζεν· Υἱὲ Δαυῒδ, ἐλέησόν με. Σταθεὶς δὲ ὁ Ἰησοῦς ἐκέλευσεν αὐτὸν 32 49
41 ἀχθῆναι πρὸς αὐτόν· ἐγγίσαντος δὲ αὐτοῦ, ἐπηρώτησεν αὐτον, λέγων· 33 51
42 Τί σοι θέλεις ποιήσω; ὁ δὲ εἶπε· Κύριε, ἵνα ἀναβλέψω. καὶ ὁ 34 52
43 Ἰησοῦς εἶπεν αὐτῷ· Ἀνάβλεψον· ἡ πίστις σου σέσωκέ σε. Καὶ παραχρῆμα ἀνέβλεψε, καὶ ἠκολούθει αὐτῷ δοξάζων τὸν Θεόν· καὶ πᾶς ὁ
λαὸς ἰδὼν, ἔδωκεν αἶνον τῷ Θεῷ.

22. [*Comp.* Matt. vi. 19. 1 Tim. vi. 19.]

28. ἀφήκαμεν πάντα.] MSS. A. & B. have ἀφέντες τὰ ἴδια, and D. τὰ ἴδια ἀφήκ. The former of which, Bornem. thinks, is the true reading: 1. because of the weight of testimony in its favour; 2. from the expression being "*exquisitior;*" 3. because the common reading might have been formed after the model of Matt. xix. 27. Mark x. 28. Luke v. 11; whereas the other has nothing similar to it in Scripture. But the learned Critic is, I apprehend, quite wrong. The *external* testimony for the *common* reading is almost as strong as can be expected for any reading. All the MSS. (300 in number) except *three*, have it. And the *internal* evidence is, when properly considered, strongly in favour of the common reading. It is surely far more likely that in MSS. so notorious for being *dressed up* by Alexandrian Critics, a reading somewhat plain and homely, should have been altered into one *exquisitioris* Græcismi, than that a somewhat elegant reading should have been altered *all but* universally into a *plain* one. Not, indeed, that it is absolutely *homely;* for the term is such as Xenophon himself might have used. But fastidiousness is the characteristic of all Critics of a certain calibre in every age. And as to what Bornem. urges, as *gravissimum argumentum*, that the common reading *might* be formed from other passages, while the new one has nothing like it in the Gospels — it is hardly possible to imagine any argument more futile. If the learned Critic had examined the varr. lect. more carefully, he would have found *another* reading; which, though it has no claims to be thought the *true* one, might have prevented him from thus rashly adopting one so little authorized as the above-mentioned, namely, ἀφήκαμεν πάντα τὰ ἴδια. Now nothing can be more evident than

XIX. *ΚΑΙ εἰσελθὼν διήρχετο τὴν Ἱεριχώ· καὶ ἰδοὺ, ἀνὴρ ὀνό- 1
ματι καλούμενος Ζακχαῖος, καὶ αὐτὸς ἦν ἀρχιτελώνης· καὶ οὗτος ἦν 2
πλούσιος· καὶ ἐζήτει ἰδεῖν τὸν Ἰησοῦν τίς ἐστι, καὶ οὐκ ἠδύνατο ἀπὸ 3
τοῦ ὄχλου, ὅτι τῇ ἡλικίᾳ μικρὸς ἦν. καὶ προδραμὼν ἔμπροσθεν, ἀνέ- 4
βη ἐπὶ συκομορέαν, ἵνα ἴδῃ αὐτόν· ὅτι [δι'] † ἐκείνης ἤμελλε διέρχεσθαι. Καὶ ὡς ἦλθεν ἐπὶ τὸν τόπον, ἀναβλέψας ὁ Ἰησοῦς εἶδεν αὐτὸν, 5
καὶ εἶπε πρὸς αὐτόν· Ζακχαῖε, σπεύσας κατάβηθι· σήμερον γὰρ ἐν
τῷ οἴκῳ σου δεῖ με μεῖναι. Καὶ σπεύσας κατέβη, καὶ ὑπεδέξατο αὐτὸν 6
χαίρων. Καὶ ἰδόντες ἅπαντες διεγόγγυζον, λέγοντες· Ὅτι παρὰ ἁμαρ- 7
a Supra. 3. 14. τωλῷ ἀνδρὶ εἰσῆλθε καταλῦσαι. [a] Σταθεὶς δὲ Ζακχαῖος εἶπε πρὸς τὸν 8
Κύριον· Ἰδοὺ, τὰ ἡμίση τῶν ὑπαρχόντων μου, Κύριε, δίδωμι τοῖς
b Supra 13. 16. πτωχοῖς. καὶ εἴ τινός τι ἐσυκοφάντησα, ἀποδίδωμι τετραπλοῦν. [b] Εἶπε 9
δὲ πρὸς αὐτὸν ὁ Ἰησοῦς· Ὅτι σήμερον σωτηρία τῷ οἴκῳ τούτῳ ἐγέ-
c Matt. 10. 6. & 15. 24. & 18. 11. Acts 13. 46. νετο· καθότι καὶ αὐτὸς υἱὸς Ἀβραάμ ἐστιν. [c] ἦλθε γὰρ ὁ Υἱὸς τοῦ 10
ἀνθρώπου ζητῆσαι καὶ σῶσαι τὸ ἀπολωλός.*

*ἈΚΟΥΟΝΤΩΝ δὲ αὐτῶν ταῦτα, προσθεὶς εἶπε παραβολὴν, διὰ τὸ 11
ἐγγὺς αὐτὸν εἶναι Ἱερουσαλὴμ, καὶ δοκεῖν αὐτοὺς ὅτι παραχρῆμα μέλλει
ἡ βασιλεία τοῦ Θεοῦ ἀναφαίνεσθαι. Εἶπεν οὖν· Ἄνθρωπός τις 12
εὐγενὴς ἐπορεύθη εἰς χώραν μακρὰν, λαβεῖν ἑαυτῷ βασιλείαν καὶ ὑπο-*

that τὰ ἴδια came from the *Scholiasts* and the *Margin*, and that ἀφέντες was but something framed by the *Alexandrian Aristarchs*.

XIX. 1. διήρχετο] "was passing through." So Campb. and Wakef., confirmed by the Syr.

2. ἀρχιτελώνης.] This signifies a sort of *receiver-general* of the taxes of a district, in which several inferior collectors were employed. That Zacchæus was a Jew, and not, as some imagine, a Gentile, is pretty certain from ver. 9. The occurrence of οὗτος after αὐτὸς may seem harsh, but examples from the Classics are adduced by Bornem. Indeed it will appear less so, if we consider the words καὶ οὗτος ἦν πλούσιος as in some measure a parenthetical clause. It may be rendered "and the man was rich."

3. ἐζήτει — τίς ἐστι.] On this idiom see Viger and Matth. Gr. Gr. § 295. 3. Τίς signifies *qualis*, what sort of person. The use of ἀπὸ before τοῦ ὄχλου is Hellenistic, and formed on the Heb. מ, *on account of*.

4. προδραμὼν ἔμπ.] The Commentators adduce similar pleonasms from the Classical writers. Yet it may be doubted whether there is ever, strictly speaking, a pleonasm at all. There is almost always a *strengthening of the sense*.

— ἐκείνης.] Sub. ὁδοῦ, and indeed διὰ, which, though it is found in the common text, and in very many MSS., yet is omitted in most of the *ancient* MSS., and cancelled by almost every recent Editor. The ellip., however, is harsh; and not to be defended by a similar one at v. 19, for, as Bornem. remarks, and I had myself long conjectured, there can be little doubt that the true reading there is ποίᾳ, and here ἐκείνῃ.

5. εἶδεν αὐτὸν, &c.] The ancient, and the most judicious modern Commentators rightly refer our Lord's knowledge of the name and circumstances of Zacchæus to his Divine omniscience.

— μεῖναι] "to sojourn." See Note on Matt. x.

7. καταλῦσαι.] See Note on Luke ix. 12.

8. σταθεὶς — εἶπε.] Construe: σταθεὶς δὲ πρὸς τὸν Κύριον εἶπε· (πρὸς αὐτὸν) namely after Zacchæus had been introduced into the presence of Jesus (and had thereby an opportunity of addressing him), he said, &c. So Acts v. 20. σταθέντες λαλεῖτε, and xxvii. 22.

— δίδωμι.] Grot., Wets., Campb., Whitby, and others take this as *Present* for *Future*, to denote *firmness of purpose*. But it is better to suppose (with Euthym., Theophyl., and Vater) the sense to be, "I do [hereby] give;" agreeably to which Christ says, *This day* is salvation come unto thee and thy family, &c. [*Comp.* John iv. 53. Acts x. 2. and the Note on Matt. xxviii. 19.]

9. εἶπε δὲ πρὸς α.] The πρὸς is by some rendered *concerning*. But though that signification does occur, yet never after the phrase εἶπε δέ. And although Zacchæus is just after spoken of in the third person, yet we have only to suppose that the latter clause was addressed to the *bystanders*, and the former to *Zacchæus*, whose declaration required some reply. I have pointed accordingly.

— καθότι.] The Particle thus denotes *cause*, and, as is often the case with γὰρ, the use here is elliptical; q. d. [Yes I do this] because, or inasmuch as, &c.

11. δοκεῖν αὐτοὺς, &c.] Our Lord's words just before declared his Messiahship, and the Apostles no doubt supposed them to imply his speedy entrance upon his reign, and assumption of the character of liberator of the Jewish nation. This erroneous opinion our Lord corrects in the following parable, on which see Notes on Matt. xxv. 14. seqq. and Dr. Hales.

12. λαβεῖν ἑαυτῷ βασ.] Whitby, Campb., and Schleus. have shown, that the phrase signifies "to receive institution to a kingdom, procure for him-

MT.
13 στρέψαι. Καλέσας δὲ δέκα δούλους ἑαυτοῦ, ἔδωκεν αὐτοῖς δέκα μνᾶς, 25.
14 καὶ εἶπε πρὸς αὐτούς· Πραγματεύσασθε ἕως ἔρχομαι. Οἱ δὲ πολῖται 14
αὐτοῦ ἐμίσουν αὐτὸν, καὶ ἀπέστειλαν πρεσβείαν ὀπίσω αὐτοῦ, λέγοντες·
15 Οὐ θέλομεν τοῦτον βασιλεῦσαι ἐφ᾽ ἡμᾶς. Καὶ ἐγένετο, ἐν τῷ ἐπαν-
ελθεῖν αὐτὸν λαβόντα τὴν βασιλείαν, καὶ εἶπε φωνηθῆναι αὐτῷ τοὺς
δούλους τούτους, οἷς ἔδωκε τὸ ἀργύριον, ἵνα γνῷ τίς τί διεπραγμα-
16 τεύσατο. Παρεγένετο δὲ ὁ πρῶτος, λέγων· κύριε, ἡ μνᾶ σου προσειρ- 20
17 γάσατο δέκα μνᾶς. Καὶ εἶπεν αὐτῷ· Εὖ, ἀγαθὲ δοῦλε· ὅτι ἐν ἐλα-
18 χίστῳ πιστὸς ἐγένου, ἴσθι ἐξουσίαν ἔχων ἐπάνω δέκα πόλεων. Καὶ
19 ἦλθεν ὁ δεύτερος, λέγων· κύριε, ἡ μνᾶ σου ἐποίησε πέντε μνᾶς. Εἶπε
20 δὲ καὶ τούτῳ· Καὶ σὺ γίνου ἐπάνω πέντε πόλεων. Καὶ ἕτερος ἦλθε,
λέγων· κύριε, ἰδοὺ ἡ μνᾶ σου, ἣν εἶχον, ἀποκειμένην ἐν σουδαρίῳ.
21 ἐφοβούμην γάρ σε, ὅτι ἄνθρωπος αὐστηρὸς εἶ· αἴρεις ὃ οὐκ ἔθηκας, 24
22 καὶ θερίζεις ὃ οὐκ ἔσπειρας. Λέγει δὲ αὐτῷ· Ἐκ τοῦ στόματός σου 26
κρινῶ σε, πονηρὲ δοῦλε· Ἤιδεις ὅτι ἐγὼ ἄνθρωπος αὐστηρός εἰμι,
23 αἴρων ὃ οὐκ ἔθηκα, καὶ θερίζων ὃ οὐκ ἔσπειρα· καὶ διατί οὐκ ἔδω- 27
κας τὸ ἀργύριόν μου ἐπὶ τὴν τράπεζαν, καὶ ἐγὼ ἐλθὼν σὺν τόκῳ ἂν
24 ἔπραξα αὐτό; Καὶ τοῖς παρεστῶσιν εἶπεν· Ἄρατε ἀπ᾽ αὐτοῦ τὴν 28
25 μνᾶν, καὶ δότε τῷ τὰς δέκα μνᾶς ἔχοντι. Καὶ εἶπον αὐτῷ· κύριε,
26 ἔχει δέκα μνᾶς. Λέγω γὰρ ὑμῖν, ὅτι παντὶ τῷ ἔχοντι δοθήσεται· ἀπὸ 29

self royalty," as was the case with Archelaus and Herod. [*Comp.* Mark xiii. 34.]

13. δέκα δ. ἑ.] "ten of his servants." This is merely (as Euthym. remarks) a round number. Πραγματεύσασθε. The word signifies literally and in the Classical writers, "to be engaged in business; but here it is used as a deponent, in the sense "to do business with by investment in trade." Thus πραγματευτὴς is used both in the Classical writers and the LXX. to denote a *merchant*. The term in Matthew is ἐργάζεσθαι.

14. οὐ θέλομεν, &c.] The earlier Commentators are of opinion that this adverts to the case of Archelaus. But that view is liable to objections; and therefore it is better, with most recent Commentators, to regard the circumstance as introduced *ad ornatum;* though undoubtedly it forms an interesting feature of the story.

16. προσειργάσατο.] In this use of ἐργάζεσθαι there is the same metaphor as that by which we say "to *make* money," viz. by investment in trade. Money so employed was said to be ἔνεργον; on the contrary, what was allowed to lie dormant was said to be ἀργόν.

17. ἴσθι ἐξ. ἔχων.] This idiom is found in the Classical writers as well as the Scriptural ones.

— ἐπάνω.] This sense, as denoting *authority over*, is rare in the Classical writers, and only occurs in the later ones. There is here (as I remarked in Recens. Synop.) an allusion to the ancient Oriental custom of assigning the government and revenues of a certain number of cities to a meritorious officer. See the examples in proof of this in Recens. Synop. and especially in my Note on Thucyd. i. 138. [*Comp.* supra xvi. 10.]

20. σουδαρίῳ.] The word is of Latin origin, and denotes such a cloth as was among the ancients generally used as a *kerchief*, but sometimes as a *napkin*. And from the Rabbinical writers it appears that such were sometimes used to wrap money in and lay it by.

21. αὐστηρός.] The word primarily (as applied to *feeling)* signifies *dry*, *harsh;* and, as applied to the *taste*, *sour* and *crabbed*. In a metaphorical sense it signifies *severe* and *cynical;* or, in another view, *severe* and *griping*, which is the sense here, and Dio Chrys. Orat. 12. p. 207. ἄνδρα αὐστηρόν. So Hor. Ep. i. 7. 91. *Durus* nimis attentusque videris esse mihi.

— αἴρεις ὃ οὐκ ἔθηκας.] A proverbial expression, like Matt. xxv. 24. Kypke observes, that αἴρω is used of taking up and carrying off any thing which has been found; and mentions a law of Solon ἃ μὴ ἔθου, μὴ ἀνέλῃ· εἰ δὲ μὴ, θάνατος ἡ ζημία. From other passages cited by him and Wets. it is clear that the pure Greek idiom requires ἀναιρεῖσθαι. And as no example is adduced of αἴρειν in the sense of carrying off and appropriating, it may be regarded as Hellenistic, though an idiom exactly corresponding to it is found in the Ang. Sax. and old English *Hlifian*, to *lift* i. e. to carry off, appropriate by theft.

22. [*Comp.* Matt. xii. 37. 2 Sam. i. 16.]

23. τράπεζαν.] The word denotes, 1. a table; 2. a money-table or counter, on which the money-changers did their business. But as those counters were, no doubt, provided with *desks* or *tillers*, for the deposit of money, so τράπεζα came to mean, 3. *a place for the investment of money*, just as our *bank*, derived from ἄβαξ, originally only denoted a *counter*.

Many MSS. and Edd. here omit the Article. But there is no proof that the phrase had become so common, that the Article, which is properly *requisite*, could be dispensed with.

— ἔπραξα.] This sense of πράσσειν for *exigere* is found also in the Classical writers, but generally in the middle voice.

26. The Commentators are not agreed whether

MT. MK.
21. 11. δὲ τοῦ μὴ ἔχοντος, καὶ ὃ ἔχει ἀρθήσεται ἀπ᾽ αὐτοῦ. Πλὴν τοὺς 27
ἐχθρούς μου ἐκείνους, τοὺς μὴ θελήσαντάς με βασιλεῦσαι ἐπ᾽ αὐτοὺς,
ἀγάγετε ὧδε καὶ κατασφάξατε ἔμπροσθέν μου. Καὶ εἰπὼν ταῦτα 28
ἐπορεύετο ἔμπροσθεν, ἀναβαίνων εἰς Ἱεροσόλυμα.

ΚΑΙ ἐγένετο, ὡς ἤγγισεν εἰς Βηθφαγὴ καὶ Βηθανίαν, πρὸς τὸ ὄρος 29
2 2 τὸ καλούμενον Ἐλαιῶν, ἀπέστειλε δύο τῶν μαθητῶν αὐτοῦ εἰπών· 30
Ὑπάγετε εἰς τὴν κατέναντι κώμην· ἐν ᾗ εἰσπορευόμενοι εὑρήσετε πῶλον
δεδεμένον, ἐφ᾽ ὃν οὐδεὶς πώποτε ἀνθρώπων ἐκάθισε· λύσαντες αὐτὸν
3 3 ἀγάγετε. Καὶ ἐάν τις ὑμᾶς ἐρωτᾷ· Διατί λύετε; οὕτως ἐρεῖτε αὐτῷ· 31
6 4 Ὅτι ὁ Κύριος αὐτοῦ χρείαν ἔχει. Ἀπελθόντες δὲ οἱ ἀπεσταλμένοι εὗ- 32
5 ρον, καθὼς εἶπεν αὐτοῖς. Λυόντων δὲ αὐτῶν τὸν πῶλον, εἶπον οἱ κύ- 33
6 ριοι αὐτοῦ πρὸς αὐτούς· Τί λύετε τὸν πῶλον; οἱ δὲ εἶπον· Ὁ Κύ- 34
7 7 ριος αὐτοῦ χρείαν ἔχει. Καὶ ἤγαγον αὐτὸν πρὸς τὸν Ἰησοῦν· καὶ 35
ἐπιῤῥίψαντες ἑαυτῶν τὰ ἱμάτια ἐπὶ τὸν πῶλον, ἐπεβίβασαν τὸν Ἰησοῦν.
8 8 Πορευομένου δὲ αὐτοῦ, ὑπεστρώννυον τὰ ἱμάτια αὐτῶν ἐν τῇ ὁδῷ. 36
9 9 Ἐγγίζοντος δὲ αὐτοῦ ἤδη πρὸς τῇ καταβάσει τοῦ ὄρους τῶν Ἐλαιῶν, 37
ἤρξαντο ἅπαν τὸ πλῆθος τῶν μαθητῶν χαίροντες αἰνεῖν τὸν Θεὸν φωνῇ
10 μεγάλῃ περὶ πασῶν ὧν εἶδον δυνάμεων, λέγοντες· Εὐλογημένος ὁ 38
ἐρχόμενος βασιλεὺς ἐν ὀνόματι Κυρίου· εἰρήνη ἐν οὐρανῷ, καὶ δόξα
ἐν ὑψίστοις! Καί τινες τῶν Φαρισαίων ἀπὸ τοῦ ὄχλου εἶπον πρὸς 39
αὐτόν· Διδάσκαλε, ἐπιτίμησον τοῖς μαθηταῖς σου. Καὶ ἀποκριθεὶς 40
εἶπεν αὐτοῖς· Λέγω ὑμῖν, ὅτι ἐὰν οὗτοι σιωπήσωσιν, οἱ λίθοι κεκράξονται. Καὶ ὡς ἤγγισεν, ἰδὼν τὴν πόλιν, ἔκλαυσεν ἐπ᾽ αὐτῇ, λέγων· 41
Ὅτι εἰ ἔγνως καὶ σὺ, καί γε ἐν τῇ ἡμέρᾳ σου ταύτῃ, τὰ πρὸς εἰρήνην 42

these are the words of our Lord, or of the King. According to the former interpretation, they may be supposed to be a *parenthetical admonition* to the disciples. This, however, would be harsh, and make the next verse exceedingly so. The latter interpretation is therefore preferable; especially since it is required by the parallel passage in Matth. Yet even this is not unattended with difficulty; which is not diminished by placing (as many Editors do) ver. 25 in a parenthesis. Besides, the words are plainly *not* parenthetical. To remove this difficulty, many Commentators suppose an ellip. of *ὁ δὲ κύριος εἶπε· δότε*. But that is too arbitrary. Nor indeed can *ellipsis* apply to this case; which is one of those numerous instances in which *γὰρ* is used in answers, and where it has, indeed, a *causative* force, but with reference to something which has preceded, or *might* have preceded, as belonging to the subject. See Acts ii. 15. & xvi. 37. Here *δότε* may be supposed to be referred to, to be repeated from the context. [Give, I say,] *for*, &c. [*Comp.* supra viii. 18. Matt. xiii. 12. Mark iv. 25.]

27. *ἀγάγετε — μου.*] A custom derived, no doubt, from the barbarous ages, but (as appears from the Classical citations in Wets.) long retained by the most civilized nations of antiquity. It even yet continues in the East; which has ever been the seat of peculiar atrocity in the punishment of criminals, and the treatment of captured enemies.

28. [*Comp.* Mark x. 32.]

33. *οἱ κύριοι αὐτοῦ.*] I have shown in Recens. Synop. that the sense is, "those who had a power over it," including the *servants* of the owner.

35. [*Comp.* John xii. 14. 2 Kings ix. 13.]

38. [*Comp.* Ps. cxviii. 26. Supra ii. 14.]

40. *οἱ λίθοι κεκράξονται*] Grot. and Wets. have shown that this is a proverbial form of expression, denoting that *it is a moral impossibility for a thing to be otherwise than it is*; the meaning being *here*, that if those should be checked, God would, even by a miracle, animate the very *stones* to celebrate his triumph. In addition to the examples from Greek and Latin writers, adduced by those Commentators, I would compare Æschyl. Agam. 36. *οἶκος δ' αὐτὸς, εἰ φθογγὴν λάβοι, Σαφέστατ' ἂν λέξειεν.* Joseph. Bell. i. 10. 2. *περὶ τῆς εὐνοίας — οὐκ ἔφη δεῖν αὐτῷ· κεκραγέναι γὰρ τὸ σῶμα* (his body) *σιωπῶντος* scil. *αὐτοῦ*, "if he should be silent." Our Lord had probably in view Habakkuk ii. 11, where see the examples adduced by Jerome in his Comm.

42. *εἰ ἔγνως.*] On the force of the phraseology, Commentators are divided in opinion. Some take *εἰ* for *εἴθε*, "would that thou hadst considered;" a use sometimes found both in the Scriptural and Classical writers. Others, with more reason, suppose an ellipsis, *per aposiopesin*, of *εὖ ἂν ἔχοι* or the like. *Both* the above methods come to the same thing. The *εἰ* may popularly be rendered *utinam*; but there is, in fact, an ellipsis, per aposiopesin, which will vary with the subject. The aposiopesis is frequent in language dictated by grief, or any of the violent passions. Grot. has here shown that our Lord's weeping, while

MT. MK.

43 σου· νῦν δὲ ἐκρύβη ἀπὸ ὀφθαλμῶν σου· ὅτι ἥξουσιν ἡμέραι ἐπὶ σὲ, 21. 11.
καὶ περιβαλοῦσιν οἱ ἐχθροί σου χάρακά σοι, καὶ περικυκλώσουσί σε,
44 καὶ συνέξουσί σε πάντοθεν, καὶ ἐδαφιοῦσί σε καὶ τὰ τέκνα σου ἐν σοὶ,
καὶ οὐκ ἀφήσουσιν ἐν σοὶ λίθον ἐπὶ λίθῳ· ἀνθ᾽ ὧν οὐκ ἔγνως τὸν
καιρὸν τῆς ἐπισκοπῆς σου.
45 Καὶ εἰσελθὼν εἰς τὸ ἱερὸν, ἤρξατο ἐκβάλλειν τοὺς πωλοῦντας ἐν αὐτῷ 12 15
46 καὶ ἀγοράζοντας, λέγων αὐτοῖς· Γέγραπται· Ὁ οἶκός μου οἶκος 13 17
προσευχῆς ἐστιν· ὑμεῖς δὲ αὐτὸν ἐποιήσατε σπήλαιον
λῃστῶν.
47 Καὶ ἦν διδάσκων τὸ καθ᾽ ἡμέραν ἐν τῷ ἱερῷ· οἱ δὲ ἀρχιερεῖς καὶ 18
48 οἱ γραμματεῖς ἐζήτουν αὐτὸν ἀπολέσαι, καὶ οἱ πρῶτοι τοῦ λαοῦ· καὶ
οὐχ εὕρισκον τὸ τί ποιήσωσιν, ὁ λαὸς γὰρ ἅπας ἐξεκρέματο αὐτοῦ
ἀκούων.
1 XX. ΚΑΙ ἐγένετο ἐν μιᾷ τῶν ἡμερῶν ἐκείνων, διδάσκοντος αὐτοῦ 23 27
τὸν λαὸν ἐν τῷ ἱερῷ, καὶ εὐαγγελιζομένου, ἐπέστησαν οἱ ἀρχιερεῖς καὶ
2 οἱ γραμματεῖς σὺν τοῖς πρεσβυτέροις, καὶ εἶπον πρὸς αὐτὸν, λέγοντες· 28
Εἰπὲ ἡμῖν ἐν ποίᾳ ἐξουσίᾳ ταῦτα ποιεῖς, ἢ τίς ἐστιν ὁ δούς σοι τὴν
3 ἐξουσίαν ταύτην; Ἀποκριθεὶς δὲ εἶπε πρὸς αὐτούς· Ἐρωτήσω ὑμᾶς 24 29
4 κἀγὼ ἕνα λόγον, καὶ εἴπατέ μοι· Τὸ βάπτισμα Ἰωάννου ἐξ οὐρανοῦ 25 30
5 ἦν, ἢ ἐξ ἀνθρώπων; Οἱ δὲ συνελογίσαντο πρὸς ἑαυτοὺς, λέγοντες· 31
Ὅτι ἐὰν εἴπωμεν· Ἐξ οὐρανοῦ· ἐρεῖ· Διατί οὖν οὐκ ἐπιστεύσατε αὐτῷ;
6 ἐὰν δὲ εἴπωμεν· Ἐξ ἀνθρώπων· πᾶς ὁ λαὸς καταλιθάσει ἡμᾶς· πε- 26 32
7 πεισμένος γάρ ἐστιν Ἰωάννην προφήτην εἶναι. Καὶ ἀπεκρίθησαν μὴ
8 εἰδέναι πόθεν. Καὶ ὁ Ἰησοῦς εἶπεν αὐτοῖς· Οὐδὲ ἐγὼ λέγω ὑμῖν ἐν 27
ποίᾳ ἐξουσίᾳ ταῦτα ποιῶ. 33

it evinces his extreme sensibility and benevolence, does not derogate from, but enhances, his dignity.

— νῦν δὲ ἐκρύβη, &c.] The words may be paraphrased thus: "But now, by an inexcusable ignorance, thou rejectest light offered and pressed upon thee: and therefore perish thou must."

— ἐν τῇ ἡμέρᾳ σου ταύτῃ] "at this thy *time*, so opportune for thy repentance and salvation." Wetstein appositely cites Polyb. 17, 18. βασιλεῦ, φεύγουσιν οἱ πολέμιοι· μὴ παρῇς τὸν καιρόν· οὐ μενοῦσιν ἡμᾶς οἱ βάρβαροι· σὴ νῦν ἐστιν ἡμέρα, σὸς ὁ καιρός.

— καὶ σύ.] "wast then the metropolis of the country to which I was especially sent.'

43. χάρακα] "a rampart." So called from the χάρακες, or *strong pales*, which were driven down to preserve the *agger*, or mound of earth, in due form. There is here a manifest prediction, and indeed lively description of the siege of Jerusalem; and the *accumulation of terms*, περικυκλώσουσι and συνέξουσι, designate the closeness of the blockade, to which Josephus attests.

44. ἐδαφιοῦσι — σοί.] The best Commentators are agreed that there is here a *syllepsis*, of demolishing the building, and of dashing the inhabitants against the stones. Both senses are found in use, and both here seem to be meant. On this passage *comp.* 1 Kings ix. 7, 8. Micah iii. 12. Matt. xxiv. 1, 2. Mark xiii. 2.

— τὸν καιρὸν τῆς ἐπισκοπῆς σου.] There has been some difference of opinion on the sense of ἐπισκοπὴ here, which, as being a word of *middle* signification, admits both of a good and a bad sense. Some Commentators take it here in the *latter*; which may be defended, and that sense is elsewhere found. But *the former* seems more apposite; and is adopted both by Theophyl. and Euthym., and the best modern Commentators; and this sense occurs in Job x. 12. [*Comp.* 2 Cor. vi. 2.]

46. [See 1 Kings viii. 29. Is. lvi. 7. Jer. vii. 11.]

47. [*Comp.* John vii. 19; viii. 37.]

48. ἐξεκρέματο] "hung on his words," i. e. heard him with deep interest. Of this sense of ἐκκρεμᾶσθαι, and the Latin *pendere*, examples are adduced by the Commentators, to which I add Thucyd. vii. 75. Virg. Æn. iv. 79.

XX. 6. καταλιθάσει ἡμᾶς.] The Priests had themselves accustomed the people to that violence. When they could not legally convict their enemies, they incited the populace to stone them, by what was called the *judicium zeli*. See John x. 31. Acts xiv. 19. (Grot.) Stoning was indeed enjoined in the Law of Moses as a punishment for idolatry, blasphemy, incest, and other heinous offences; and its execution was committed to the people at large. Yet it appears from Exod. viii. 23. that such sort of irregular and tumultuary vengeance was in use *before* the Law. Nor was this confined to the Jews; for we find

MT. MK.
21. 12. Ἤρξατο δὲ πρὸς τὸν λαὸν λέγειν τὴν παραβολὴν ταύτην· Ἄνθρωπός 9
[τις] ἐφύτευσεν ἀμπελῶνα, καὶ ἐξέδοτο αὐτὸν γεωργοῖς, καὶ ἀπεδήμησε
34 2 χρόνους ἱκανούς. Καὶ ἐν καιρῷ ἀπέστειλε πρὸς τοὺς γεωργοὺς δοῦλον, 10
35 3 ἵνα ἀπὸ τοῦ καρποῦ τοῦ ἀμπελῶνος δῶσιν αὐτῷ. Οἱ δὲ γεωργοὶ δεί-
36 4 ραντες αὐτὸν ἐξαπέστειλεν κενόν. Καὶ προσέθετο πέμψαι ἕτερον δοῦ- 11
λον· οἱ δὲ κἀκεῖνον, δείραντες καὶ ἀτιμάσαντες, ἐξαπέστειλαν κενόν.
5 Καὶ προσέθετο πέμψαι τρίτον· οἱ δὲ καὶ τοῦτον τραυματίσαντες ἐξέ- 12
37 6 βαλον. Εἶπε δὲ ὁ κύριος τοῦ ἀμπελῶνος· Τί ποιήσω; πέμψω τὸν 13
38 7 υἱόν μου τὸν ἀγαπητόν· ἴσως τοῦτον ἰδόντες ἐντραπήσονται. Ἰδόντες 14
δὲ αὐτὸν οἱ γεωργοὶ, διελογίζοντο πρὸς ἑαυτοὺς, λέγοντες· Οὗτός ἐστιν
ὁ κληρονόμος· δεῦτε ἀποκτείνωμεν αὐτὸν, ἵνα ἡμῶν γένηται ἡ κλη-
39 8 ρονομία. Καὶ ἐκβαλόντες αὐτὸν ἔξω τοῦ ἀμπελῶνος ἀπέκτειναν. Τί 15
40 9
41 οὖν ποιήσει αὐτοῖς ὁ κύριος τοῦ ἀμπελῶνος; ἐλεύσεται καὶ ἀπολέσει 16
τοὺς γεωργοὺς τούτους, καὶ δώσει τὸν ἀμπελῶνα ἄλλοις. Ἀκούσαντες
42 10 δὲ εἶπον· Μὴ γένοιτο! Ὁ δὲ ἐμβλέψας αὐτοῖς εἶπε· Τί οὖν ἐστι 17
τὸ γεγραμμένον τοῦτο· Λίθον ὃν ἀπεδοκίμασαν οἱ οἰκο-
44 δομοῦντες, οὗτος ἐγενήθη εἰς κεφαλὴν γωνίας; πᾶς 18
ὁ πεσὼν ἐπ᾽ ἐκεῖνον τὸν λίθον, συνθλασθήσεται· ἐφ᾽ ὃν δ᾽ ἂν πέσῃ,
45 12 λικμήσει αὐτόν. Καὶ ἐζήτησαν οἱ ἀρχιερεῖς καὶ οἱ γραμματεῖς ἐπιβα- 19
λεῖν ἐπ᾽ αὐτὸν τὰς χεῖρας ἐν αὐτῇ τῇ ὥρᾳ, καὶ ἐφοβήθησαν τὸν λαόν·
46 ἔγνωσαν γὰρ ὅτι πρὸς αὐτοὺς τὴν παραβολὴν ταύτην εἶπε.
22.
15 13 Καὶ παρατηρήσαντες ἀπέστειλαν ἐγκαθέτους, ὑποκρινομένους ἑαυτοὺς 20
δικαίους εἶναι· ἵνα ἐπιλάβωνται αὐτοῦ λόγου, εἰς τὸ παραδοῦναι αὐτὸν
16 14 τῇ ἀρχῇ καὶ τῇ ἐξουσίᾳ τοῦ ἡγεμόνος. Καὶ ἐπηρώτησαν αὐτὸν, λέγον- 21
τες· Διδάσκαλε, οἴδαμεν ὅτι ὀρθῶς λέγεις καὶ διδάσκεις· καὶ οὐ λαμ-
17 15 βάνεις πρόσωπον, ἀλλ᾽ ἐπ᾽ ἀληθείας τὴν ὁδὸν τοῦ Θεοῦ διδάσκεις. Ἔξε- 22
στιν ἡμῖν Καίσαρι φόρον δοῦναι, ἢ οὔ; Κατανοήσας δὲ αὐτῶν τὴν 23
18 πανουργίαν, εἶπε πρὸς αὐτούς· Τί με πειράζετε; ἐπιδείξατέ μοι δη- 24
19 16 νάριον. Τίνος ἔχει εἰκόνα καὶ ἐπιγραφήν; ἀποκριθέντες δὲ εἶπον·
20 17 Καίσαρος. Ὁ δὲ εἶπεν αὐτοῖς· Ἀπόδοτε τοίνυν τὰ Καίσαρος Καίσαρι, 25
21 καὶ τὰ τοῦ Θεοῦ τῷ Θεῷ. Καὶ οὐκ ἴσχυσαν ἐπιλαβέσθαι αὐτοῦ ῥή- 26

allusions to it in Hom. Il. γ. 56. and Thucyd. v. 60.

9. [*Comp.* Is. v. 1. Jer. ii. 21. xii. 10.]

11. προσέθετο πέμψαι.] This expression (as also that at xix. 11. προσθεὶς εἶπε) is an Hellenistic idiom formed on the Hebrew, and found in Gen. viii. 21; xviii. 29, & Job xix. 1.

13. ἴσως.] This is commonly rendered "*it may be*, or *perhaps*." But Pearce, Campb., and Schleus. object, that that sense can have no place in the *Scriptures*, since the Spirit of truth could be under no doubt. Hence they would render it *surely*, adducing examples of that sense from the LXX. and the Classical writers, and referring to several Notes of Critics. But the difficulty started is perhaps imaginary; for the term occurs in a *parable;* and may be supposed to be used per anthropatheism, and to keep up the *verisimilitude* of the story. If this be not admitted, we must, with Bornem., take the ἴσως for οἶμαι *sane;* which he proves by references to Schaefer and Hermann.

14. [*Comp.* Ps. ii. 1. 8. Gen. xxxvii. 18. Matt. xxvi. 3. John xi. 53. Heb. i. 2.]

17. [See Ps. cxviii. 22. Is. viii. 14; xxviii. 16. 1 Pet. ii. 4. 7.]

18. [See Is. viii. 15. Zech. xii. 3.]

20. ἐγκαθέτους.] The word properly denotes one who is stationed in a lurking place, to watch another's motions; either for attacking him, or otherwise; and, in a metaphorical sense, denotes one set as a spy, whether of words or actions.

21. λαμβάνεις πρόσωπον.] A phrase formed on the Heb. נשׂא פנים, and denoting "to show partiality to any one." It occurs frequently in the LXX.

23. κατανοήσας τὴν πανουργίαν.] Two MSS. have ἐπιγνοὺς τὴν πονηρίαν; plainly from emendation. But though the first expression is the more elegant, the second is less proper. The following

MT. MK.

μάτος ἐναντίον τοῦ λαοῦ· καὶ θαυμάσαντες ἐπὶ τῇ ἀποκρίσει αὐτοῦ 22. 12.
ἐσίγησαν.
27 Προσελθόντες δέ τινες τῶν Σαδδουκαίων, οἱ ἀντιλέγοντες ἀνάστασιν 23 18
28 μὴ εἶναι, ἐπηρώτησαν αὐτὸν, λέγοντες· Διδάσκαλε, Μωϋσῆς ἔγραψεν 24 19
ἡμῖν· ἐάν τινος ἀδελφὸς ἀποθάνῃ ἔχων γυναῖκα, καὶ οὗτος ἄτεκνος
ἀποθάνῃ, ἵνα λάβῃ ὁ ἀδελφὸς αὐτοῦ τὴν γυναῖκα, καὶ ἐξαναστήσῃ
29 σπέρμα τῷ ἀδελφῷ αὐτοῦ. Ἑπτὰ οὖν ἀδελφοὶ ἦσαν· καὶ ὁ πρῶτος 25 20
30 λαβὼν γυναῖκα, ἀπέθανεν ἄτεκνος· καὶ ἔλαβεν ὁ δεύτερος τὴν γυναῖκα, 26 21
31 καὶ οὗτος ἀπέθανεν ἄτεκνος· καὶ ὁ τρίτος ἔλαβεν αὐτὴν, ὡσαύτως
32 δὲ καὶ οἱ ἑπτά· [καὶ] οὐ κατέλιπον τέκνα, καὶ ἀπέθανον· ὕστερον 22
33 δὲ πάντων ἀπέθανε καὶ ἡ γυνή. Ἐν τῇ οὖν ἀναστάσει, τίνος αὐτῶν 27 28 23
34 γίνεται γυνή; οἱ γὰρ ἑπτὰ ἔσχον αὐτὴν γυναῖκα. Καὶ ἀποκριθεὶς 29 24
εἶπεν αὐτοῖς ὁ Ἰησοῦς· Οἱ υἱοὶ τοῦ αἰῶνος τούτου γαμοῦσι καὶ ἐκγαμί-
35 σκονται· οἱ δὲ καταξιωθέντες τοῦ αἰῶνος ἐκείνου τυχεῖν, καὶ τῆς ἀνα- 30 25
36 στάσεως τῆς ἐκ νεκρῶν, οὔτε γαμοῦσιν οὔτε ἐκγαμίσκονται· οὔτε γὰρ
ἀποθανεῖν ἔτι δύνανται· ἰσάγγελοι γάρ εἰσι, καὶ υἱοί εἰσι τοῦ Θεοῦ,
37 τῆς ἀναστάσεως υἱοὶ ὄντες. Ὅτι δὲ ἐγείρονται οἱ νεκροὶ καὶ Μωϋσῆς 31 26
ἐμήνυσεν ἐπὶ τῆς Βάτου, ὡς λέγει Κύριον, τὸν Θεὸν Ἀβραὰμ καὶ τὸν 32
38 Θεὸν Ἰσαὰκ καὶ τὸν Θεὸν Ἰακώβ. Θεὸς δὲ οὐκ ἔστι νεκρῶν, ἀλλὰ 27
39 ζώντων· πάντες γὰρ αὐτῷ ζῶσιν. Ἀποκριθέντες δέ τινες τῶν γραμ-
40 ματέων εἶπον· Διδάσκαλε, καλῶς εἶπας. οὐκ ἔτι δὲ ἐτόλμων ἐπερωτᾷν
αὐτὸν οὐδέν.
41 Εἶπε δὲ πρὸς αὐτούς· Πῶς λέγουσι τὸν Χριστὸν υἱὸν Δαυΐδ εἶναι; 42 35
42 καὶ αὐτὸς Δαυΐδ λέγει ἐν βίβλῳ Ψαλμῶν· Εἶπεν ὁ Κύριος τῷ 43 36

examples may suffice. Xenoph. Anab. vii. 5. 11. ὁ δὲ γνοὺς τοῦ Ἡ. τὴν πανουργίαν. Joseph. Ant. x. 12. 6. συνιδὼν τὴν κακουργίαν αὐτῶν.

27. οἱ ἀντιλέγοντες ἀνάστ. μὴ εἶναι.] On this idiom, by which verbs containing *denial* add μὴ to the Infinitive, see Matth. Gr. Gr. § 533. Obs. 3. To the examples adduced may be added another from Thucyd. iii. 41. ἀντέλεγε μὴ ἀποκτεῖναι.

28. [See Deut. xxv. 5.]

31: οὐ κατέλιπον — ἀπέθανον.] Ne mireris prothysteron; "Primaria enim sententia secundariæ præmissa est," ut v. 28. et Joan xv. 6. (Bornemann.) Many MSS. and some Edd. have not the καὶ before οὐ, which is cancelled by almost all the recent Editors — rashly, I think: for it seems to have been thrown out by the early Critics, to avoid the too frequent repetition of the word.

35. οἱ καταξιωθέντες — τυχεῖν.] Of this turn of expression examples are adduced by Wets., to which I would add a very apposite one from Æschyl. Prom. 239. θνητοὺς δ' ἐν οἴκτῳ προθέμενος, τούτου τυχεῖν οὐκ ἠξιώθην αὐτός. where ἀξιόω is for καταξιόω, as in Pind. Nem. x. 73. where the Schol. explains ἀξιωθείην by καταξιωθείην.

36. οὔτε γὰρ — δύνανται.] By this our Lord meant to impugn the Pharisaical notion of a *metempsychosis*. I would compare Artemid. iii. 13. ἀθάνατοι οἱ ἀποθανόντες, ἐπεὶ μηκέτι τεθνήξοντες. See 1 John iii. 2.

- ἰσάγγελοι.] The Commentators are agreed that since ἰσάγγελος is formed after the model of ἰσόθεος, it should be rendered, not *equal to the angels*, but *like unto* the angels; (viz. in respect of immortality and the nature of their bodies), as in Matt. xxii. 30. ὡς ἄγγελοι. The word ἰσάγγελος is rare; but one example is adduced by Bulkley from Hierocles: σέβειν ὁ λόγος παραινεῖ τοὺς ἰσοδαίμονας καὶ ἰσαγγέλους. See also Œcumen. on Acts, p. 74. The angels are called *sons of God* on account of their participation in Divine felicity and glory, as υἱοὶ τῆς ἀναστ. denotes those who are partakers in the resurrection and the future life. On which sense of υἱὸς, see Note on Matt. viii. 12; xi. 19, and an example of the phrase from a Rabbinical writer in Schoettg. on 1 Cor. xv. 42.

37. [See Exod. iii. 6. Acts vii. 32. Heb. xi. 16.]

38. πάντες γὰρ αὐτῷ ζῶσιν.] On the sense of these words Commentators are divided in opinion. Some (as Beza, Wets., and Doddr.) regard them as giving the consequence of our Lord's argument; in the sense, that "all, however dead to us, are still living, as regards God, to whom things future are as present." Others, as Kypke and Campb., consider the γὰρ as not *causal* but *illative*, and confirmatory of the proposition; q. d. "He is not a God of the dead, but of the living, for all (who are alive) live unto him; since death does not terminate our connection with Him, inasmuch as He can recall us to life, and make that life immortal." See some interesting passages, illustrative of this sentiment, cited and referred to in Recens. Synop.

MT. MK.
22. 12. Κυρίῳ μου, Κάθου ἐκ δεξιῶν μου, ἕως ἂν θῶ τοὺς 43
44 45 37 ἐχθρούς σου ὑποπόδιον τῶν ποδῶν σου. Δαυὶδ οὖν 44
38 Κύριον αὐτὸν καλεῖ· καὶ πῶς υἱὸς αὐτοῦ ἐστιν; Ἀκούοντος δὲ 45
παντὸς τοῦ λαοῦ, εἶπε τοῖς μαθηταῖς αὐτοῦ· Προσέχετε ἀπὸ τῶν 46
23. γραμματέων τῶν θελόντων περιπατεῖν ἐν στολαῖς, καὶ φιλούντων ἀσπα-
6 39 σμοὺς ἐν ταῖς ἀγοραῖς, καὶ πρωτοκαθεδρίας ἐν ταῖς συναγωγαῖς, καὶ
14 40 πρωτοκλισίας ἐν τοῖς δείπνοις· οἳ κατεσθίουσι τὰς οἰκίας τῶν χηρῶν, 47
καὶ προφάσει μακρὰ προσεύχονται. οὗτοι λήψονται περισσότερον
κρίμα.
41 XXI. ἈΝΑΒΛΕΨΑΣ δὲ εἶδε τοὺς βάλλοντας τὰ δῶρα αὐτῶν 1
42 εἰς τὸ γαζοφυλάκιον πλουσίους· εἶδε δὲ καί τινα χήραν πενιχρὰν 2
43 βάλλουσαν ἐκεῖ δύο λεπτά, καὶ εἶπεν· Ἀληθῶς λέγω ὑμῖν, ὅτι ἡ χήρα 3
44 ἡ πτωχὴ αὕτη πλεῖον πάντων ἔβαλεν· ἅπαντες γὰρ οὗτοι ἐκ τοῦ 4
περισσεύοντος αὐτοῖς ἔβαλον εἰς τὰ δῶρα τοῦ Θεοῦ, αὕτη δὲ ἐκ τοῦ
24. 13. ὑστερήματος αὐτῆς ἅπαντα τὸν βίον ὃν εἶχεν ἔβαλε.
1 1 ΚΑΙ τινων λεγόντων περὶ τοῦ ἱεροῦ, ὅτι λίθοις καλοῖς καὶ ἀναθή- 5
2 2 μασι κεκόσμηται, εἶπε· Ταῦτα [ἃ] θεωρεῖτε, ἐλεύσονται ἡμέραι ἐν αἷς 6
3 οὐκ ἀφεθήσεται λίθος ἐπὶ λίθῳ, ὃς οὐ καταλυθήσεται. Ἐπηρώτησαν 7
4 δὲ αὐτὸν, λέγοντες· Διδάσκαλε, πότε οὖν ταῦτα ἔσται; καὶ τί τὸ
σημεῖον ὅταν μέλλῃ ταῦτα γίνεσθαι;
4 5 Ὁ δὲ εἶπε· Βλέπετε μὴ πλανηθῆτε· πολλοὶ γὰρ ἐλεύσονται ἐπὶ 8
5 6 τῷ ὀνόματί μου, λέγοντες· Ὅτι ἐγώ εἰμι· καὶ ὁ καιρὸς ἤγγικε. μὴ
6 7 οὖν πορευθῆτε ὀπίσω αὐτῶν. Ὅταν δὲ ἀκούσητε πολέμους καὶ ἀκατα- 9
στασίας, μὴ πτοηθῆτε· δεῖ γὰρ ταῦτα γενέσθαι πρῶτον, ἀλλ᾽ οὐκ
7 8 εὐθέως τὸ τέλος. Τότε ἔλεγεν αὐτοῖς· Ἐγερθήσεται ἔθνος ἐπὶ ἔθνος, 10
καὶ βασιλεία ἐπὶ βασιλείαν· σεισμοί τε μεγάλοι κατὰ τόπους καὶ λιμοὶ 11
καὶ λοιμοὶ ἔσονται, φόβητρά τε καὶ σημεῖα ἀπ᾽ οὐρανοῦ μεγάλα ἔσται.

43. [See Ps. cx. 1. Acts ii. 34. 1 Cor. xv. 25. Heb. i. 13. x. 13.]
46. [See supra xi. 43.]
47. [*Comp.* 2 Tim. iii. 6. Tit. i. 11.]

XXI. 5. ἀναθήμασι.] Ἀνάθημα signifies, 1. any thing laid up or apart; 2. any thing separated, dedicated, consecrated to God. These ἀναθήματα were usually displayed conspicuously in the temple either by being hung up, or otherwise serving to adorn it. These the devotees used to bring thither, not only in the hope of future blessings from heaven, but from their gratitude for past benefits. The offerings varied according to the taste, intention, or the ability of the giver; consisting of crowns, golden or silver vases, pictures, arms, &c.

6. ταῦτα.] Sub. κατὰ, "as for these things;" or suppose, with Bornem., an accusative absolute; though the parallel passages strongly countenance the opinion of Rinck. Lucubr. Crit. p. 334, that ἃ is to be cancelled on the authority of several MSS. and Versions, and a mark of interrogation placed after θεωρεῖτε.

—ἐλεύσονται ἡμέραι, &c.] See supra xix. 44. 1 Kings ix. 7, 8. Micah iii. 12. Wets. appositely compares Hom. Il. δ. 164. ἔσσεται ἦμαρ, ὅταν ποτ᾽ ὀλώλῃ Ἴλιος ἱρή.

9. ἀκαταστασίας.] Ἀκαταστασία denotes that *unsettled state*, which arises from sedition and faction; wherein the laws cease to have any force and things are carried on by force and violence. The word is only found in the later Greek writers and in the LXX.

—μὴ πτοηθ.] Bornem. compares a passage of Plutarch. Moral. π. 451, where πτοῖαι and φόβοι are combined. He also adduces a learned remark of Wyttenb., that πτοία *properly* denotes percussionem animi subitam, et *initium* perturbationum; and then comes to mean, "permanentem a subita percussione profectam perturbationem, sive cum cupiditate sive timore conjunctam." A very accurate representation. Yet *how*, it may be asked, comes the word to mean *percussion*. I answer, πτοίω must not, with Lennep, be supposed derived from πίπτω and πτάω. But πτοίω comes from πτόω, which is cognate with πτύω; and both are onomatop. simply signifying, and the same word with, our verb to *puff*. Now a puff of wind implies a *percussion of the air*: and πτοία came, by a usual figure, to denote percussion simply; and, by use, *percussion of the mind*.

10. φόβητρα] objects of terror, terrific prodigies. The meaning is plain from what follows, σημεῖα ἀπ᾽ οὐρανοῦ, where by σημ. are denoted aerial phænomena.

MT. MK.

12 Πρὸ δὲ τούτων * πάντων ἐπιβαλοῦσιν ἐφ' ὑμᾶς τὰς χεῖρας αὐτῶν καὶ 24. 13.
διώξουσι, παραδιδόντες εἰς συναγωγὰς καὶ φυλακὰς, ἀγομένους ἐπὶ βα- 9 9
13 σιλεῖς καὶ ἡγεμόνας, ἕνεκεν τοῦ ὀνόματός μου· ἀποβήσεται δὲ ὑμῖν εἰς
14 μαρτύριον. Θέσθε οὖν εἰς τὰς καρδίας ὑμῶν μὴ προμελετᾷν ἀπολο- 11
15 γηθῆναι. ἐγὼ γὰρ δώσω ὑμῖν στόμα καὶ σοφίαν, ᾗ οὐ δυνήσονται
16 ἀντειπεῖν οὐδὲ ἀντιστῆναι πάντες οἱ ἀντικείμενοι ὑμῖν. Παραδοθή- 12
σεσθε δὲ καὶ ὑπὸ γονέων καὶ ἀδελφῶν καὶ συγγενῶν καὶ φίλων· καὶ
17 θανατώσουσιν ἐξ ὑμῶν· καὶ ἔσεσθε μισούμενοι ὑπὸ πάντων διὰ τὸ
18 ὄνομά μου· καὶ θρὶξ ἐκ τῆς κεφαλῆς ὑμῶν οὐ μὴ ἀπόληται. Ἐν τῇ
19 ὑπομονῇ ὑμῶν ‡ κτήσασθε τὰς ψυχὰς ὑμῶν. Ὅταν δὲ ἴδητε κυκλου- 13 14
20 μένην ὑπὸ στρατοπέδων τὴν Ἱερουσαλὴμ, τότε γνῶτε ὅτι ἤγγικεν ἡ 15
21 ἐρήμωσις αὐτῆς. Τότε οἱ ἐν τῇ Ἰουδαίᾳ φευγέτωσαν εἰς τὰ ὄρη, καὶ 16
οἱ ἐν μέσῳ αὐτῆς ἐκχωρείτωσαν· καὶ οἱ ἐν ταῖς χώραις μὴ εἰσερχέσθωσαν 18 18
22 εἰς αὐτήν. ὅτι ἡμέραι ἐκδικήσεως αὗταί εἰσι, τοῦ ‡ πληρωθῆναι πάν-
23 τα τὰ γεγραμμένα. Οὐαὶ δὲ ταῖς ἐν γαστρὶ ἐχούσαις καὶ ταῖς θηλα- 19 17
ζούσαις ἐν ἐκείναις ταῖς ἡμέραις· ἔσται γὰρ ἀνάγκη μεγάλη ἐπὶ τῆς
24 γῆς, καὶ ὀργὴ [ἐν] τῷ λαῷ τούτῳ. Καὶ πεσοῦνται στόματι μαχαί-
ρας, καὶ αἰχμαλωτισθήσονται εἰς πάντα τὰ ἔθνη· καὶ Ἱερουσαλὴμ ἔσται
25 πατουμένη ὑπὸ ἐθνῶν, ἄχρι πληρωθῶσι καιροὶ ἐθνῶν. Καὶ ἔσται 29 24

12. πάντων.] This, for the common reading ἁπάντων, is received, from very many MSS. by almost all Editors. On the present passage compare John xvi. 2. Rev. ii. 10. Acts iv. 3. v. 18. xii. 4.

13. εἰς μαρτύριον.] Sub. αὐτοῖς, (which is *expressed* in the parallel passage of Mark,) the sense being "that they shall not be able to say at the judgment, We never heard of these things."

14. [*Comp.* Matt. x. 19. supra xii. 12.]

15. [*Comp.* Exod. iv. 12. Is. liv. 17. Acts vi. 10.]

— στόμα καὶ σοφίαν.] This, by a mixture of metonymy and hendiadys, is used for the faculty of speaking wisely and ably. It is not a mere Hebraism, since στόμα is sometimes, though rarely, used in the Greek Classical writers, as *os* in the Latin. See Dr. South's Serm. on this text vol. v. 433.

18. [See Matt. x. 30. 1 Sam. xiv. 45. 2 Sam. i. 11. 1 Kings i. 5.]

19. ἐν τῇ ὑπομονῇ—ὑμῶν.] The sense is, "by your persevering endurance ye will preserve your lives." For the Imperative, say the Commentators, has the force of a Future. See Glass. Phil. Sac. p. 286, who adduces several examples of this idiom, proceeding, he thinks, from the Prophets. But the passages cited are of a different nature: so that we may rather suppose the true reading here is κτήσεσθε; which is found in several of the best MSS., and no doubt will be found in more, if carefully examined. For the difference is so small as to often escape the eye. Hence the terminations are perpetually confounded. As all the best ancient Versions, too, use the *future*, there is little doubt, considering how *literal* those Versions are, that the Translators had κτήσεσθε in their copies, which is also in several of the early Fathers.

22. πληρωθῆναι.] Very many MSS. have πλησθῆναι, which is received by several Editors. On this passage compare Dan. ix. 26, 27. Zech. xi. 1.

23. ἀνάγκη.] This, like the Hebr. צָרָה, is put for θλῖψις, which is found in the parallel passage of Matth. This sense of the word occurs not only in the Sept., but also in the best Classical writers.

— ἐν τῷ λαῷ τ.] The ἐν is omitted in most MSS. and is cancelled by the recent Editors. But the common reading admits of a good sense; which is well expressed by Lord Bacon, Essays, vol. i. p. 347.

24. στόματι μαχ.] Στόμα μαχ. is thought to be a Hebraism for פִּי חֶרֶב, as in Deut. xx. 13. Yet Wets. and Elsn. adduce some examples from the Classical writers, to which may be added Theophyl. Simoc. p. 129. A. [*Comp.* Rom. xi. 25.]

— πατουμένη.] Some take this to mean "*occupied*," and (consequently) *profaned*. So Apoc. xi. 2. 1 Macc. iii. 52. τὰ ἅγιά σου καταπεπάτηται καὶ βεβήλωται. And sometimes in the Classical writers. Others explain, "shall be ignominiously treated." So Cic. ad Attic. viii. 11. cited by Wets. *Conculcari* miseram Italiam videbis proxima æstate, et quati utriusque vi. To which I add Æschyl. Eum. 110. καὶ πάντα ταῦτα λὰξ ὁρῶ πατούμενα, and Choeph. 639. The significations merge into each other.

— ἄχρι πληρωθῶσι καιροὶ ἐθνῶν.] Commentators are not agreed on the sense of these words. Some take it to be, "the times when the Gentiles shall be visited for their sins." See Jer. xxvii. 7. Ezek. xxi. 25; xxii. 3 & 4; xxx. 3. But that would be supposing the words to be quite ænigmatical. It is *better*, with the ancient and earlier modern Commentators, to interpret, "the time when the number of Gentiles to be called to God shall be complete." That, however, may be thought to be negatived by Rom. xi. 12, seqq. So that some of the best Commentators, from

MT. MK.
24. 13. σημεῖα ἐν ἡλίῳ καὶ σελήνῃ καὶ ἄστροις, καὶ ἐπὶ τῆς γῆς συνοχὴ ἐθνῶν
ἐν ἀπορίᾳ, ἠχούσης θαλάσσης καὶ σάλου· ἀποψυχόντων ἀνθρώπων ἀπὸ 26
25 φόβου καὶ προσδοκίας τῶν ἐπερχομένων τῇ οἰκουμένῃ· αἱ γὰρ δυνάμεις
30 26 τῶν οὐρανῶν σαλευθήσονται. καὶ τότε ὄψονται τὸν Υἱὸν τοῦ ἀνθρώ- 27
που ἐρχόμενον ἐν νεφέλῃ μετὰ δυνάμεως καὶ δόξης πολλῆς.
Ἀρχομένων δὲ τούτων γίνεσθαι, ἀνακύψατε καὶ ἐπάρατε τὰς κεφαλὰς 28
ὑμῶν· διότι ἐγγίζει ἡ ἀπολύτρωσις ὑμῶν.

Lightf., Whitby, and Newton downwards, are, with reason, of opinion, that the words refer to a period when the Jews shall be restored; i. e. when the times of the four great kingdoms, predicted by Daniel, shall have expired, and the fifth, or *kingdom of Christ*, shall be set up in their place; when the scattered sheep of Israel shall be again collected, and become one fold under one shepherd, as citizens of the New Jerusalem. However, after all, the simplest and best representation of the sense may be that offered by Bp. Pearce, who paraphrases it, "until those Gentiles have done all which God has decreed that they should do." Thus the words will have reference to the *primary* import of our Lord's prophecy, and probably were meant to be *confined* to that. See Note on Matt. xxiv. 29.

25. On this verse compare 2 Pet. iii. 10. 12. Is. xiii. 10. Ezek. xxxii. 7. Joel ii. 10. Rev. vi. 12.

—*ἐν ἀπορίᾳ*.] Not "*with* perplexity," but "*amidst* perplexity." Συνοχὴ, like the Latin *angustia*, denotes such *anxiety*, as holds the mind, as it were, enchained. See Gray's Ode to Adversity, sub. init. So 2 Cor. ii. 4. θλίψεως καὶ σ. καρδίας. Hence it is often associated with nouns denoting distress. So Job xxx. 3. συνοχὴν καὶ ταλαιπωρίαν. And see Artemid. in Rec. Syn. Ἀπορία denotes *inopia consilii*, the not knowing what to do. Σάλος denotes the *tossing* of the sea, and figuratively *civil commotion*. See Soph. Œd. Tyr. v. 22, seqq. The reading ἤχους θαλάσσης, received by Griesb., 3d Edit., is a mere emendation of the ancient Critics, proceeding on a misunderstanding of the passage. See Matthæi and Scholz.

—*ἠχούσης θαλάσσης καὶ σάλου*.] These words are, in the present context, not without their difficulty; which has occasioned both variety of reading and diversity of interpretation. To advert first to the *former*, several ancient MSS., and and the Syr., Pers., Arab., Vulg., Italic, and Slav. Versions have ἤχους θαλ., which is approved by Bengel and Kuin., and edited by Griesb. (in his *third* Edition) and Lachm. But without any good reason; for the sense thus arising is very harsh and frigid, and would ill comport with the other imagery of this sublime description. The reading in question seems to have arisen from the *ancient Critics*, who stumbled at the intermixture of circumstances denoting *physical* with those of *moral* agitation. Such, however, is frequent in the O. T., and by no means rare in the N. T., especially in the Apocalypse; nay, it is found in the Classical writers, for example, Æschylus. Yet it is not necessary, nor will it be *proper here*, to take the words in *sensu physico*. They may, and ought to be taken in a metaphorical sense, as belonging to the same description as that at Matt. xxiv. 29. and Mark xiii. 24, 25. At σάλου supply ἠχοῦντος, taken from ἠχούσης preceding; or there may be a sort of Hendiadys. It is well remarked by Grot., that in the Prophetical books "*Mare* significat statum mundi variis casibus turbidum; *Sonus*, excitatos inde tumultus." By the σάλου ἠχ. or κινουμένου are, as Kypke rightly notices, designated ἀκαταστασίαι et turbulentæ harum commotiones et tumultus. There seems, too, an allusion to Psalm lxv. 7., where it is given as an attribute of God, that he "stilleth the raging of the sea, and the noise of its waves, and the tumult of the people;" in which passage Aquila well renders, καταστέλλων ἦχον θαλάσσης, θόρυβον κυμάτων αὐτῆς. For (as Pisc. rightly observes) what is there meant by *strepitus maris* is explained by the following *fremitus nationum*. Nor is this without example in the *Classical* writers. Thus Soph. Œd. Tyr. 23. πόλις γὰρ Ἤδη σαλεύει· κἀνακουφίσαι κάρα Βυθῶν ἔτ' οὐχ οἵα τε φοινίου σάλου. And Plut. Fab. Max. 37. ἡγεμονίαν πολλῷ σάλῳ σεισθεῖσαν ὤρθωσε πάλιν. See also Romul. 24. Theophyl. Simoc. p. 72 & 749. and comp. Pind. Pyth. iv. 484.

The words at v. 26. αἱ δυνάμεις τῶν οὐρανῶν σαλευθήσονται have the same sense as at Matt. xxiv. 29. (where see Note). In fact, the present passage, Matt. xxiv. 29. and Mark xiii. 24, 25. are of the very same nature, and relate to the very same events; i. e. *primarily*, to the destruction of *Jerusalem* and the Jewish state; but *secondarily*, to the destruction of *the world*. Moreover, the imagery (though the Commentators have omitted to notice it) is evidently formed upon Is. xiii. 10 & 13. (which treats of the destruction of Babylon) where Bp. Lowth remarks, "that, when the Hebrews intend to express *happiness*, *prosperity*, the instauration and advancement of states, kingdoms, and potentates, they make use of images taken from the most striking parts of nature, from the heavenly bodies, from the sun, moon, and stars; which they describe as shining with increased splendour, and never setting; the moon becomes like the meridian sun, and the sun's light is augmented seven-fold (see Is. xxx. 26.); new heavens and a new earth are created, and a brighter age commences. On the contrary, the overthrow and destruction of kingdoms is represented by opposite images: the stars are obscured, the moon withdraws her light, and the sun shines no more; the earth quakes, and the heavens tremble; and all things seem tending to their original chaos. See Joel ii. 10. iii. 15, 16. Amos viii. 9." See also Sir Isaac Newton on Is. xiii. 13. (in D'Oyly and Mant) and compare Ps. lix. 2. Sept.

26. *φόβου καὶ προσδοκίας*.] There is a Hendiadys, for "a fearful expectation;" or καὶ may be *exegetical*, for *even*. Ἀποψυχόντων is by many Commentators explained of *death*; but it seems only to mean (like ἐκθνήσκειν) to *die away* with fear. Προσδοκία is often used of such an expectation as is associated with fear. So Thucyd. says, ἐλπὶς τοῦ φόβου.

28. *ἀνακύψατε*.] Ἀνακύπτειν is intransitive, and

MT. MK.

29 Καὶ εἶπε παραβολὴν αὐτοῖς· Ἴδετε τὴν συκῆν καὶ πάντα τὰ δένδρα. 24. 13.
30 ὅταν προβάλωσιν ἤδη, βλέποντες ἀφ᾽ ἑαυτῶν γινώσκετε ὅτι ἤδη ἐγγὺς 32 28
31 τὸ θέρος ἐστίν. οὕτω καὶ ὑμεῖς ὅταν ἴδητε ταῦτα γινόμενα, γινώσκετε 33 29
32 ὅτι ἐγγύς ἐστιν ἡ βασιλεία τοῦ Θεοῦ. Ἀμὴν λέγω ὑμῖν, ὅτι οὐ μὴ 34 30
33 παρέλθῃ ἡ γενεὰ αὕτη, ἕως ἂν πάντα γένηται. ὁ οὐρανὸς καὶ ἡ γῆ 35 31
34 παρελεύσονται, οἱ δὲ λόγοι μου οὐ μὴ παρέλθωσι. Προσέχετε δε ἑαυτοῖς, μή ποτε ‡ βαρυνθῶσιν ὑμῶν αἱ καρδίαι ἐν κραιπάλῃ καὶ μέθῃ
καὶ μερίμναις βιωτικαῖς· καὶ αἰφνίδιος ἐφ᾽ ὑμᾶς ἐπιστῇ ἡ ἡμέρα ἐκεί-
35 νη. ὡς παγὶς γὰρ ἐπελεύσεται ἐπὶ πάντας τοὺς καθημένους ἐπὶ πρό-
36 σωπον πάσης τῆς γῆς. Ἀγρυπνεῖτε οὖν ἐν παντὶ καιρῷ, δεόμενοι ἵνα
καταξιωθῆτε ἐκφυγεῖν ταῦτα πάντα τὰ μέλλοντα γίνεσθαι, καὶ σταθῆναι
ἔμπροσθεν τοῦ Υἱοῦ τοῦ ἀνθρώπου.
37 Ἦν δὲ τὰς ἡμέρας ἐν τῷ ἱερῷ διδάσκων· τὰς δὲ νύκτας ἐξερχόμενος
38 ηὐλίζετο εἰς τὸ ὄρος τὸ καλούμενον Ἐλαιῶν. Καὶ πᾶς ὁ λαὸς ὤρθριζε
πρὸς αὐτὸν ἐν τῷ ἱερῷ ἀκούειν αὐτοῦ. 26. 14.
1 XXII. ἬΓΓΙΖΕ δὲ ἡ ἑορτὴ τῶν ἀζύμων, ἡ λεγομένη πάσχα· καὶ 2 1
2 ἐζήτουν οἱ ἀρχιερεῖς καὶ οἱ γραμματεῖς, τὸ, πῶς ἀνέλωσιν αὐτόν· ἐφο- 4
βοῦντο γὰρ τὸν λαόν.
3 Εἰσῆλθε δὲ [ὁ] Σατανᾶς εἰς Ἰούδαν τὸν ἐπικαλούμενον Ἰσκαριώτην,
4 ὄντα ἐκ τοῦ ἀριθμοῦ τῶν δώδεκα· καὶ ἀπελθὼν συνελάλησε τοῖς ἀρ- 14 10
5 χιερεῦσι καὶ τοῖς στρατηγοῖς, τὸ, πῶς αὐτὸν παραδῷ αὐτοῖς. Καὶ 15 11

denotes to *raise up the body*, as opposed to συγκύπτειν in Luke xiii. 11. Wets. compares Joseph. Bell. Jud. vi. 8. 5. ὀλίγον ἐκκύψαντες ἐκ τοῦ δέους. See Rom. viii. 23.

30. ὅταν προβ.] Supply καρπὸν, or φύλλα. Grot. cites from Dioscorid. προβάλλειν ἄνθος. So the Hebr. שלח is used of the budding and shooting forth of trees.

33. [*Comp.* Ps. cii. 26, 27. Is. li. 6. Heb. i. 11. 2 Pet. iii. 7. 10.]

34. [*Comp.* Rom. xiii. 13. 1 Thess. v. 6. 1 Pet. iv. 7.]

34. κραιπάλῃ καὶ μέθῃ.] The latter term denotes the drunkenness itself, and the former the headache and stupid feeling which supervenes, and indispose the mind for all serious reflection. Βαρυνθῶσιν. Very many MSS. and early Edd. have βαρηθῶσιν, which is adopted by Wets., Matth., and others down to Scholz. But I suspect that the η arose from a confusion with υν, the abbreviations being very similar. It is a great confirmation of the common reading, that the Sept. translators very often used βαρύνεσθαι; never, I believe, βαρεῖσθαι. They have indeed the very phrase ἐβαρύνθη ἡ καρδία at Exod. viii. 15. ix. 7 & 31. x. 1, and at Sapient. Sol. ix. 15, what is here to the purpose, φθαρτὸν γὰρ σῶμα βαρύνει ψυχήν. So Horace Sat. II. ii. 79. Quin *corpus* onustum Hesternis vitiis animum quoque *prægravat* una, Atque *affigit humo* divinæ particulam auræ.

35. ὡς παγὶς γὰρ ἐπελ.] i. e. shall come on unexpectedly. Παγὶς and σκάνδαλον are frequent images expressive of calamity (as the Heb. רשת in Ps. lvii. 6. and 1 Macc. i. 35. v. 4.) especially such as is sudden and unexpected (as here and in Rom. xi. 9.), by which men are taken (like a beast in a trap) before they are aware. Καθημένους. The word here denotes merely *existing*. There is a reference to Jer. xxv. 29. [*Comp.* 1 Thess. v. 2. 2 Pet. iii. 10. Rev. iii. 3. & xvi. 15.]

36. σταθῆναι.] This may be used, as in Luke xix. 8., of being *introduced to*, as a mark of honour and acceptance; or, as it is a judicial term, it may denote to be absolved or acquitted. [*Comp.* supra xii. 40. xviii. 1. 1 Thess. v. 6.]

37. [*Comp.* John viii. 1, 2.]

38. ὤρθριζε πρὸς α.] Ὀρθρίζειν denotes properly to rise early; 2ndly, to go about any business early; 3dly, and when followed by a preposition denoting motion towards, it denotes to go or resort to any place or person. In which sense it occurs here, and occasionally in the Sept.

XXII. 2. [*Comp.* Ps. ii. 2. John xi. 47. Acts iv. 27.]

3. εἰσῆλθε δὲ ὁ Σ.] The best Commentators are agreed that this does not imply a *physical* entry of Satan into Judas; but it is to be understood of mental influence and instigation. As those who obey the divine motions are said to *receive* the Spirit as a divine guest; so Satan is said to *enter into* those who consent unto criminal suggestions. See John xiii. 2. Acts v. 3. Ephes. ii. 2. Consult the Notes on Matth. iii. 16. iv. 1. Luke ii. 27. This view does not at all negative the personality of Satan; since that is *implied*.

The Article before Σατ. is omitted in many MSS. and early Edd., and is cancelled by Griesb., Vat., Tittm. and Scholz; but perhaps without reason; for though the word, as partaking of the nature both of a *proper name*, and an *appellative*, may either admit, or reject it; yet as here three-fourths of the MSS. have it, and as it is *almost always* found in the N. T. with Σατ., except in the *vocative* case, it is best to retain it here.

4. στρατηγοῖς] scil. τοῦ ἱεροῦ. On the meaning

MT. MK.

26. 14. ἐχάρησαν, καὶ συνέθεντο αὐτῷ ἀργύριον δοῦναι. Καὶ ἐξωμολόγησε· 6
16 καὶ ἐζήτει εὐκαιρίαν τοῦ παραδοῦναι αὐτὸν αὐτοῖς ἄτερ ὄχλου.
17 12 Ἦλθε δὲ ἡ ἡμέρα τῶν ἀζύμων, ἐν ᾗ ἔδει θύεσθαι τὸ πάσχα· καὶ 7
18 13 ἀπέστειλε Πέτρον καὶ Ἰωάννην, εἰπών· Πορευθέντες ἑτοιμάσατε ἡμῖν 8
τὸ πάσχα, ἵνα φάγωμεν. Οἱ δὲ εἶπον αὐτῷ· Ποῦ θέλεις ἑτοιμάσω- 9
μεν; Ὁ δὲ εἶπεν αὐτοῖς· Ἰδού, εἰσελθόντων ὑμῶν εἰς τὴν πόλιν, 10
συναντήσει ὑμῖν ἄνθρωπος κεράμιον ὕδατος βαστάζων· ἀκολουθήσατε
14 αὐτῷ εἰς τὴν οἰκίαν, οὗ εἰσπορεύεται· καὶ ἐρεῖτε τῷ οἰκοδεσπότῃ τῆς 11
οἰκίας· Λέγει σοι ὁ διδάσκαλος· Ποῦ ἐστι τὸ κατάλυμα, ὅπου τὸ
15 πάσχα μετὰ τῶν μαθητῶν μου φάγω; Κἀκεῖνος ὑμῖν δείξει ‡ ἀνώγεον 12
19 μέγα ἐστρωμένον· ἐκεῖ ἑτοιμάσατε. Ἀπελθόντες δὲ εὗρον, καθὼς εἴρη- 13
κεν αὐτοῖς· καὶ ἡτοίμασαν τὸ πάσχα.

Καὶ ὅτε ἐγένετο ἡ ὥρα, ἀνέπεσε, καὶ οἱ δώδεκα ἀπόστολοι σὺν αὐ- 14
τῷ. καὶ εἶπε πρὸς αὐτούς· Ἐπιθυμίᾳ ἐπεθύμησα τοῦτο τὸ πάσχα 15
φαγεῖν μεθ᾽ ὑμῶν πρὸ τοῦ με παθεῖν· Λέγω γὰρ ὑμῖν, ὅτι οὐκέτι 16
οὐ μὴ φάγω ἐξ αὐτοῦ, ἕως ὅτου πληρωθῇ ἐν τῇ βασιλείᾳ τοῦ Θεοῦ.
Καὶ δεξάμενος ποτήριον, εὐχαριστήσας εἶπε· Λάβετε τοῦτο καὶ δια- 17
29 25 μερίσατε ἑαυτοῖς· Λέγω γὰρ ὑμῖν, ὅτι οὐ μὴ πίω ἀπὸ τοῦ γεννήματος 18
26 22 τῆς ἀμπέλου, ἕως ὅτου ἡ βασιλεία τοῦ Θεοῦ ἔλθῃ. Καὶ λαβὼν ἄρτον 19
εὐχαριστήσας ἔκλασε, καὶ ἔδωκεν αὐτοῖς, λέγων· Τοῦτό ἐστι τὸ σῶμά
μου, τὸ ὑπὲρ ὑμῶν διδόμενον· τοῦτο ποιεῖτε εἰς τὴν ἐμὴν ἀνάμνη-
27 23 σιν. Ὡσαύτως καὶ τὸ ποτήριον μετὰ τὸ δειπνῆσαι, λέγων· Τοῦτο τὸ 20
28 24 ποτήριον, ἡ καινὴ διαθήκη ἐν τῷ αἵματί μου, τὸ ὑπὲρ ὑμῶν ἐκχυνόμε-
23 20 νον. Πλὴν ἰδού, ἡ χεὶρ τοῦ παραδιδόντος με μετ᾽ ἐμοῦ ἐπὶ τῆς τρα- 21
24 21 πέζης. Καὶ ὁ μὲν Υἱὸς τοῦ ἀνθρώπου πορεύεται, κατὰ τὸ ὡρισμένον· 22

of this expression Commentators vary in opinion. But I agree with Bp. Middlet. on Acts iv. 1. that the most probable view is that of Lightf., who has shewn from the Jewish writers, that in various parts of the Temple, bodies of Levites constantly mounted guard: and that the persons commanding these several parties were called *στρατηγοί*; but that, besides these, there was an officer, who had the supreme authority over all of them; and that this is he whom we may suppose is called, by way of eminence, *ὁ στρατηγὸς τοῦ ἱεροῦ* at Acts iv. 1.

6. *ἐξωμολόγησε.*] The word properly signifies to say the same thing with any one; and 2dly, as here, to agree with, assent to, what he proposes; a signification found also in the best writers.

— *ἄτερ ὄχλου.*] From the use of *ἄτερ* and such terms, certainly not employed in the common speech, and only found in the best writers, especially the Poets, Valcknaer thinks we may reasonably infer that Luke was conversant with the Classical authors.

11. *οἰκοδεσπότῃ τῆς οἰκίας.*] Bornem. compares *οἰκοφύλαξ δόμων, αἰπόλια αἰγῶν, συβόσια συῶν, τὰ βουκόλια τῶν βοῶν* and other similar pleonasms.

15. *ἐπιθυμίᾳ ἐπεθύμησα.*] A Hebrew idiom, as in Gen. xxxi. 30. *ἐπιθυμίᾳ γὰρ ἐπεθύμησας ἀπελθεῖν εἰς τὸν οἶκον τοῦ πατρός.* Blackwall, Winer, and Bornem., produce what they call similar phrases from the Greek writers; but which are *not quite similar*. For in Hebrew this idiom has a strongly *intensive* force; but scarcely ever so in the Greek Classics. As to *δρόμῳ θεῖν*, cited from Xenoph. by Bornem., it does not fall under this class.

16. *ἕως ὅτου — τοῦ Θεοῦ.*] The expression (which seems a Hebraism) imports, that our Lord would have no further society with them on earth. The thing to be completed was the work of human redemption by the sacrifice of Christ. Examples of a similar association of negatives are adduced by Bornem.

19. *τοῦτο ποιεῖτε*, &c.] Do this; namely, which I have done — break bread, &c. See Bornem., who also gives examples of passages where, as here, the pronoun dem. is to be referred *ad remotiora*, and where *ἐμὸς* is used for *ἐμοῦ*. Schoettg. cites various Rabbinical passages, which prove that the ancient Jewish Church in celebrating the Paschal feast, always had in view the sufferings of the Messiah. [*Comp.* 1 Cor. xi. 23, 24.]

24. *τοῦτο τὸ — ἐκχυνόμενον*] Bornem., after a minute discussion of the sense, lays it down as follows: "*Hoc poculum, quod vestram in salutem effunditur, signum est novi fœderis per sanguinem meum sanciendi.*"

21. *ἡ χεὶρ — τραπέζης.*] An Oriental mode of saying "the person is at the table with me." [*Comp.* John xiii. 21.]

22. [*Comp.* John xiii. 18. Psal. xli. 9. Acts i. 16.]

MT. MK.
23 πλὴν οὐαὶ τῷ ἀνθρώπῳ ἐκείνῳ δι' οὗ παραδίδοται. Καὶ αὐτοὶ ἤρξαν- 26. 14.
το συζητεῖν πρὸς ἑαυτοὺς, τὸ, τίς ἄρα εἴη ἐξ αὐτῶν ὁ τοῦτο μέλλων 22 19
24 πράσσειν. Ἐγένετο δὲ καὶ φιλονεικία ἐν αὐτοῖς, τὸ, τίς αὐτῶν δοκεῖ 20. 10.
25 εἶναι μείζων. Ὁ δὲ εἶπεν αὐτοῖς· Οἱ βασιλεῖς τῶν ἐθνῶν κυριεύου- 25 42
26 σιν αὐτῶν, καὶ οἱ ἐξουσιάζοντες αὐτῶν εὐεργέται καλοῦνται. Ὑμεῖς δὲ 26 43
οὐχ οὕτως· ἀλλ' ὁ μείζων ἐν ὑμῖν γενέσθω ὡς ὁ νεώτερος· καὶ ὁ
27 ἡγούμενος, ὡς ὁ διακονῶν. Τίς γὰρ μείζων, ὁ ἀνακείμενος ἢ ὁ διακονῶν; οὐχὶ ὁ ἀνακείμενος; ἐγὼ δέ εἰμι ἐν μέσῳ ὑμῶν ὡς ὁ διακο-
28 νῶν. Ὑμεῖς δέ ἐστε οἱ διαμεμενηκότες μετ' ἐμοῦ ἐν τοῖς πειρασμοῖς 19. 14.
29 μου· κἀγὼ διατίθεμαι ὑμῖν καθὼς διέθετό μοι ὁ πατήρ μου βασιλεί- 28
30 αν, ἵνα ἐσθίητε καὶ πίνητε ἐπὶ τῆς τραπέζης μου ἐν τῇ βασιλείᾳ μου·
καὶ * καθίσεσθε ἐπὶ θρόνων, κρίνοντες τὰς δώδεκα φυλὰς τοῦ Ἰσραήλ.
31 Εἶπε δὲ ὁ Κύριος· Σίμων, Σίμων, ἰδού, ὁ Σατανᾶς ἐξῃτήσατο ὑμᾶς,
32 τοῦ σινιάσαι ὡς τὸν σῖτον· ἐγὼ δὲ ἐδεήθην περὶ σου, ἵνα μὴ ἐκλείπῃ
ἡ πίστις σου· καὶ σύ ποτε ἐπιστρέψας στήριξον τοὺς ἀδελφούς σου. 26.
33 Ὁ δὲ εἶπεν αὐτῷ· Κύριε, μετὰ σοῦ ἕτοιμός εἰμι καὶ εἰς φυλακὴν καὶ 33 29
34 εἰς θάνατον πορεύεσθαι. Ὁ δὲ εἶπε· Λέγω σοι, Πέτρε, οὐ μὴ φω- 34 30
35 νήσει σήμερον ἀλέκτωρ, πρὶν ἢ τρὶς ἀπαρνήσῃ μὴ εἰδέναι με. Καὶ
εἶπεν αὐτοῖς· Ὅτε ἀπέστειλα ὑμᾶς ἄτερ βαλαντίου καὶ πήρας καὶ
36 ὑποδημάτων, μή τινος ὑστερήσατε; οἱ δὲ εἶπον· Οὐδενός. Εἶπεν
οὖν αὐτοῖς· Ἀλλὰ νῦν ὁ ἔχων βαλάντιον ἀράτω, ὁμοίως καὶ πήραν·

24. *ἐγένετο δὲ καὶ φιλονεικία*, &c.] From the difference of circumstances, notwithstanding the identity of the thing itself, some Commentators maintain, that this represents an occurrence distinct from that recorded at Matt. xx. 20. and Mark x. 35. But (as Doddr. remarks) "we cannot suppose such a contention for superiority should have occurred immediately after so affecting a lesson of humility;" accordingly he and some other eminent Commentators are of opinion that this is the same circumstance with that mentioned by Matthew and Mark; but here brought in out of the regular order; of which Luke is less observant than the other Evangelists. However, as Matthew and Mark tell us that the contention took place *in the way*, before they came to Jerusalem, or even Jericho, *ἐγένετο* must be taken in a *pluperfect* sense, "there *had been*," viz. on the road to Jericho.

25. *εὐεργέται καλοῦνται.*] Εὐεργέτης was among the Greeks a title of honour, assigned to all who had deserved well of the monarch or state, defended its liberties, or increased its honour. See my note on Thucyd. i. 129. *κεῖταί σοι εὐεργ.*

26. *οὐχ οὕτως.*] Sub. *ποιεῖτε*. or with Bornem. *ἔσεσθε*, or *ἐστί*. [*Comp.* supra ix. 48. 1 Pet. v. 3.]

— *ὁ μείζων.*] From the antithetical word *νεώτ.* this has been by some supposed to denote "one who is elder," like the Latin *major*. But from the parallel passage of Matthew it is plain that *νεώτ.* is rather to be accommodated to *μείζων* than vice versâ; and Kypke has adduced many Classical authorities for *νεώτερος* in the sense of an *inferior*. He shows that the expressions employed throughout have reference to *office*, or *station* in the kingdom of Christ.

27. *τίς γὰρ*, &c. [*Comp.* John xiii. 14. Phil. ii. 7.]

28. *πειρασμοῖς*] "trials, afflictions."

29. *διατίθεμαι ὑ.*] The best Interpreters, ancient and modern, are of opinion that the sense of *διατίθ.* *here* is *engage for*, or *promise*; but that just after it must have the further removed sense of *grant* or *bestow*. The former is found in the Sept., the latter sprang from the usual sense of *covenanting*, which implies something *granted*. [*Comp.* supra xii. 32. Matt. xxiv. 47.]

30. *καθίσεσθε.*] So for *καθίσησθε*., many of the best MSS., and some early Edd.; which is received by Wets., Matth., Griesb., and others; and rightly, for, as Born. observes, the Future was more likely to be changed into the Subj. than the contrary. And that it is *meant* to be construed with *ἵνα* is probable from a similar construction at John xv. 8.

31. *ἐξῃτήσατο ὑμᾶς*] Ἐξαιτεῖσθαι signifies to require any one to be delivered up to us, whether for *good* or for *evil*. See examples in Recens. Synop. The sense here is simply, "Satan desires to get you into his power;" a strongly figurative form of expression, used with allusion to the narrative of Job's temptation, recorded in Job. ii. 6.

— *τοῦ σινιάσαι.*] Σινιάζειν, from *σινίον*, *a sieve*, signifies to *sift*, or *winnow*; and as that implies agitation, commotion, and separation, so most Commentators think it denotes to *perturb*, *loosen*, undermine, and overthrow your fidelity. But the sense suggested by our common version is more apt,—namely, *sift* you, *scrutinize*, or try your fidelity, and constancy. [*Comp.* 1 Pet. v. 8.]

32. *ἐπιστρέψας*] neuter for reciprocal. The sense is, "Having recovered thyself [namely from that lapse, which will happen to thee] by a sincere repentance."

35. [*Comp.* Matt. x. 9. Mark vi. 8. supra ix. 3. x. 4.]

MT. MK.
26. 14. *καὶ ὁ μὴ ἔχων πωλησάτω τὸ ἱμάτιον αὐτοῦ καὶ ἀγορασάτω μάχαιραν.*
Λέγω γὰρ ὑμῖν, ὅτι ἔτι τοῦτο τὸ γεγραμμένον δεῖ τελεσθῆναι ἐν ἐμοί, 37
τό· Καὶ μετὰ ἀνόμων ἐλογίσθη· καὶ γὰρ τὰ περὶ ἐμοῦ
τέλος ἔχει. Οἱ δὲ εἶπον· Κύριε, ἰδοὺ μάχαιραι ὧδε δύο. ὁ δὲ εἶπεν 38
αὐτοῖς· Ἱκανόν ἐστι.
36 32 *ΚΑΙ ἐξελθὼν ἐπορεύθη, κατὰ τὸ ἔθος, εἰς τὸ ὄρος τῶν Ἐλαιῶν·* 39
ἠκολούθησαν δὲ αὐτῷ καὶ οἱ μαθηταὶ αὐτοῦ. Γενόμενος δὲ ἐπὶ τοῦ 40
39 35 *τόπου, εἶπεν αὐτοῖς· Προσεύχεσθε μὴ εἰσελθεῖν εἰς πειρασμόν. Καὶ* 41
αὐτὸς ἀπεσπάσθη ἀπ᾽ αὐτῶν ὡσεὶ λίθου βολήν· καὶ θεὶς τὰ γόνατα
36 *προσηύχετο, λέγων· Πάτερ, εἰ βούλει παρενεγκεῖν τὸ ποτήριον τοῦτο* 42
ἀπ᾽ ἐμοῦ·—πλὴν μὴ τὸ θέλημά μου, ἀλλὰ τὸ σὸν γενέσθω. ὤφθη 43
δὲ αὐτῷ ἄγγελος ἀπ᾽ οὐρανοῦ ἐνισχύων αὐτόν. Καὶ γενόμενος ἐν 44
ἀγωνίᾳ ἐκτενέστερον προσηύχετο. ἐγένετο δὲ ὁ ἱδρὼς αὐτοῦ ὡσεὶ

36. *πωλησάτω—μάχαιραν.*] Some Commentators stumble at these words; not being able to reconcile them with our Lord's pacific admonitions elsewhere, and his own non-resistance when apprehended by the soldiers. Hence they resort either to novel conjectures, or new interpretations; alike unnecessary,—since (as Grot., Wets., and other eminent modern Commentators have seen) this and the preceding phrases contain nothing more than a prediction of *impending perils*; which are opposed to the *quiet* and *security* of former times. The Prophets (they observe) are accustomed to metaphorically signify perilous times by representing what men then commonly do, in order to guard against danger. So also Euthym. observes, that our Lord signifies that the time for combat is at hand—merely meaning that their enemies are close upon them.

The expression *πωλησάτω τὸ ἱμ.* is a proverbial form, by which a thing is counselled to be done *at any rate*. It is strange the Commentators should have adduced no examples of this mode of speaking. I have noted some from the purest Attic writers; e. gr. Thucyd. viii. 81. *οὐδ᾽, ἢν δέῃ, τελευτῶντα τὴν ἑαυτοῦ στρωμνὴν ἐξαργυρῶσαι.* Xen. Anab. vii. 5, 5. *καὶ προσδανεισάμενος, εἰ μήγ᾽ ἄλλως ἐδύνω, καὶ ἀποδόμενος τὰ σαυτοῦ ἱμάτια.*

37. [*Comp.* Is. liii. 12. Mark xv. 28.] Grot. paraphrases the verse thus: "After the many other evils endured by me, the last now remains, namely, that I should be brought to an ignominious death. And my lot will extend to you also; for the ignominy and hatred encountered by the master, will be visited on you his disciples." *Τέλος ἔχει* is synonymous with *τελεσθῆναι*, and is used by the best Classical writers of the completion of predictions. Wets. and Kypke cite many examples, as Dionys. Ital. Ant. ix. 12. *τέλος εἶχε τοῖς T. τὰ μαντεύματα.*

38. *ἰδοὺ μάχαιραι ὧδε δύο.*] Render, "See here are *two* swords." How it happened that they had the swords, and for what purpose, has been variously accounted for. Euthym. thinks that they had taken them to sacrifice the Paschal lamb. Grot., more rationally, supposes that as the road from Galilee to Jerusalem was infested with robbers, many (and especially the Galilæans) took swords. This is very probable; since Schoett. has shown that at that time, in Judæa, even the Priests were armed when on a journey.

—*ἱκανόν ἐστι.*] On the sense of this expression there is a difference of opinion. Some take *ἱκανόν* to mean, "sufficient for a symbol of hostility." But that would suppose the words almost enigmatical. Others think there is an *irony*; which, however, would be suitable neither to the period nor the season. The best Commentators, ancient and modern, are generally agreed, that *ἱκανόν ἐστι* is here used in a sense not unfrequent in that and similar expressions in all languages; and which is employed on occasions when we do not care to rectify a stupid misapprehension; but dismiss both the person and the thing with "It is very well:" "that will do." Of this idiom they adduce many examples, both from the Classical and the Rabbinical writers.

41. *ἀπεσπάσθη.*] Many Commentators render *proripuit se*. But the more eminent, both ancient and modern, are of opinion that no impetuosity is implied; observing, that both the Hebrews, Greeks, and Romans used many words which properly have a notion of violence with a considerable diminution, and sometimes an entire abandonment thereof. They render "he withdrew himself from them;" adducing several examples, the most apposite of which is 2 Macc. xii. 10. To which I add Thucyd. vii. 80. *ἀπεσπάσθη*, "separated, parted from." See Hemsterh. on Lucian i. 256. and Wakefield's Silv. Cr. v. 70.

—*λίθου βολήν.*] A rough mode of estimating distance, which originated in the simplicity of primitive times, and was afterwards retained in the common dialect, and even found its way into the best writers. Wets. adduces examples of the phrase, but not one to the purpose. The following may therefore be not unacceptable. Procop. p. 236, 17. *διειστήκει γὰρ αὐτοῦ ὅσον λίθου βολήν.*

42. *εἰ βούλει—ἀπ᾽ ἐμοῦ.*] There is thought by the Commentators to be here an ellipsis; and the most probable one is *παρένεγκε*, on which Bornem. refers to Matth. Gr. § 617. p. 124, 8. But it should seem that this is rather an example of *Aposiopesis*. Such is a modest way of making a request. By *παρ.* is here meant, as Bornem. shews, præterire *sinere*. [*Comp.* John vi. 38.]

43, 44. These verses are rejected by some Critics. But as the external evidence for their omission is next to nothing, and the *internal* very slender and precarious; and as their omission is far easier to account for than their insertion, they may justly be regarded as genuine. [*Comp.* John xii. 27. Heb. v. 7.]

MT. MK.

45 θρόμβοι αἵματος καταβαίνοντες ἐπὶ τὴν γῆν. Καὶ ἀναστὰς ἀπὸ τῆς 26. 14.
προσευχῆς, ἐλθὼν πρὸς τοὺς μαθητὰς αὐτοῦ, εὗρεν αὐτοὺς κοιμωμένους 40 37
46 ἀπὸ τῆς λύπης, καὶ εἶπεν αὐτοῖς· Τί καθεύδετε; ἀναστάντες προσ- 41 38
εύχεσθε, ἵνα μὴ εἰσέλθητε εἰς πειρασμόν.
47 Ἔτι δὲ αὐτοῦ λαλοῦντος, ἰδοὺ ὄχλος, καὶ ὁ λεγόμενος Ἰούδας (εἷς 47 43
τῶν δώδεκα) προήρχετο αὐτοὺς, καὶ ἤγγισε τῷ Ἰησοῦ φιλῆσαι αὐτόν. 48 44
48 Ὁ δὲ Ἰησοῦς εἶπεν αὐτῷ· Ἰούδα, φιλήματι τὸν Υἱὸν τοῦ ἀνθρώπου 49 45
49 παραδίδως; Ἰδόντες δὲ οἱ περὶ αὐτὸν τὸ ἐσόμενον, εἶπον αὐτῷ· Κύ- 50
50 ριε, εἰ πατάξομεν ἐν μαχαίρᾳ; Καὶ ἐπάταξεν εἷς τις ἐξ αὐτῶν τὸν 51 47
51 δοῦλον τοῦ ἀρχιερέως, καὶ ἀφεῖλεν αὐτοῦ τὸ οὖς τὸ δεξιόν. Ἀποκριθεὶς δὲ ὁ Ἰησοῦς εἶπεν· Ἐᾶτε ἕως τούτου! καὶ ἁψάμενος τοῦ ὠτίου
52 αὐτοῦ ἰάσατο αὐτόν. Εἶπε δὲ ὁ Ἰησοῦς πρὸς τοὺς παραγενομένους ἐπ᾽ 55 48
αὐτὸν ἀρχιερεῖς καὶ στρατηγοὺς τοῦ ἱεροῦ καὶ πρεσβυτέρους· Ὡς ἐπὶ
53 λῃστὴν ἐξεληλύθατε μετὰ μαχαιρῶν καὶ ξύλων; καθ᾽ ἡμέραν ὄντος
μου μεθ᾽ ὑμῶν ἐν τῷ ἱερῷ, οὐκ ἐξετείνατε τὰς χεῖρας ἐπ᾽ ἐμέ. ἀλλ᾽
αὕτη ὑμῶν ἐστιν ἡ ὥρα· καὶ ἐξουσία τοῦ σκότους!

—ὡσεὶ θρόμβοι αἵματος.] It has been by many supposed that our Lord's sweat was actually blood, or at least bloody; and examples of this phenomenon have been adduced. But the best Expositors, ancient and modern, are agreed that the sense is, "his sweat became *like* drops of blood." This, they think, the words themselves demand. Comp. Acts ix. 19. Theophylact and Photius Epist. 138. consider it as merely a proverbial mode of expression, by which it is said of those who labour, that they sweat drops of blood. But that view can by no means be admitted. Surely the very existence of the saying in the Greek, as well as in our own and other languages, at least attests the existence of bloody sweats, under excessive perturbation of mind or distress of body. See Lucan. Phars. ix. 809—14. cited in Rec. Syn., where, among other expressions, we have *sudor rubet*. So that, after all, those who understand it of a *sanguineous appearance in the sweat*, may be right; for the numerous authorities adduced or referred to in Rec. Syn., prove that sanguineous sweats *sometimes* have been known to attend extreme agony of mind. And this view is strongly supported by the following citation from a medical writer, *Blainville*, for which I am indebted to the British Critic for 1831. P. i. "On l'a trouvée (la sueur) *colorée en rouge* dans une affection qui a reçu le nom de *Diapédèse*, maladie dans laquelle il n'y a pas une véritable transpiration, mais qui constitue bien plutôt une *hemorragie* par exhalation, comme celle que l'on observe à la surface de membraine pituitaire. Cette *transudation* a lieu dans les cas, où par suite d'une frayeur subite, ou d'une *vive émotion*, il se fait congestion." Other examples of this phenomenon may be seen in Sagittarii Hist. Passionis, Bartholin de Cruce, and other writers cited by *Gruner* in his elaborate *Commentatio de J. Christi morte.*

45. κοιμωμένους ἀπὸ τῆς λύπης.] The force of the expression may best be understood by considering, that extreme grief has a stupefying tendency, and tends to induce a sort of heavy, though unrefreshing sleep; an effect which is alluded to in various passages of the Classical writers cited by Wets.

48. [*Comp.* John xviii. 3.]

49. εἰ πατάξομεν.] Εἰ has the sense *num*, as in Mark viii. 23. where see Note. Ἐν is said by the Commentators to be here put for σύν. But no good writers use σὺν in the sense of *the instrumental cause*; whereas ἐν is sometimes found in that sense, though in the writers of the N. T. it, no doubt, proceeded from Hebraism.

50. [*Comp.* John xviii. 10.]

51. ἐᾶτε ἕως τούτου.] The Commentators are not agreed on the sense of these words; which are, from brevity, obscure, and admit of two different interpretations, according as they are supposed to be addressed to the *multitude* or to the *disciples* Agreeably to the former view, the sense is, "leave me free till I shall have healed the wounded man." That, however, requires many harsh ellipses, and yields a sense liable to much objection. According to the latter, the sense is (by an ellipse of αὐτοὺς after ἐᾶτε), "let them do what they please —desist." Others interpret otherwise. But the ellipse of αὐτοὺς is harsh, as is also that at ἕως τούτου. The true ellipse after ἐᾶτε is τὸ πρᾶγμα. So Matt. xxvii. 49. ἄφες, "let alone." There is also a constructio prægnans, as in Thucyd. i. 71. μέχρι τοῦδε ὡρίσθω ὑμῖν ἡ βραδύτης. The sense, then (as Wets., Ros., Kuin., and Schleusn. explain) is: "let the matter alone [after its having proceeded] thus far! Enough of this."

52. ὡς ἐπὶ λῃστήν.] The construction is: ἐξελ. μετὰ μαχαιρῶν καὶ ξύλων ἐπ' ἐμὲ, ὡς ἐπὶ λῃστήν; The ἐπὶ signifies *against*, for *apprehension*; as in Joseph. Antiq. xiv. 11, 6. ἐξελθεῖν ἐπὶ Μάλιχον παῖδας μετὰ ξιφιδίων. At the parallel passages of Matt. xxvi. 55. and Mark xiv. 48. there is added, to *determine* the sense, συλλαβεῖν με, which is indeed *here* found, in some MSS. But, as the above passage of Josephus proves, they are not absolutely necessary to the sense.

53. ἀλλ' αὕτη — σκότους.] There is here again a certain obscurity, arising from the sense being, from intensity of feeling, but imperfectly developed. Some take the words to mean, "This is

MT. MK.
26. 14. ΣΥΛΛΑΒΟΝΤΕΣ δὲ αὐτὸν ἤγαγον, καὶ εἰσήγαγον αὐτὸν εἰς τὸν 54
57 53 54 οἶκον τοῦ ἀρχιερέως· ὁ δὲ Πέτρος ἠκολούθει μακρόθεν. Ἁψάντων 55
58 δὲ πῦρ ἐν μέσῳ τῆς αὐλῆς, καὶ συγκαθισάντων αὐτῶν, ἐκάθητο ὁ Πέ-
69 66 τρος ἐν μέσῳ αὐτῶν. Ἰδοῦσα δὲ αὐτὸν παιδίσκη τις καθήμενον πρὸς 56
70 67 τὸ φῶς, καὶ ἀτενίσασα αὐτῷ, εἶπε· Καὶ οὗτος σὺν αὐτῷ ἦν. Ὁ δὲ 57
71 68 ἠρνήσατο αὐτὸν, λέγων· Γύναι, οὐκ οἶδα αὐτόν. Καὶ μετὰ βραχὺ 58
72 69 ἕτερος ἰδὼν αὐτὸν ἔφη· Καὶ σὺ ἐξ αὐτῶν εἶ. Ὁ δὲ Πέτρος εἶπεν·
73 70 Ἄνθρωπε, οὐκ εἰμί. Καὶ διαστάσης ὡσεὶ ὥρας μιᾶς, ἄλλος τις διϊσχυ- 59
ρίζετο, λέγων· Ἐπ᾽ ἀληθείας καὶ οὗτος μετ᾽ αὐτοῦ ἦν· καὶ γὰρ
74 71 Γαλιλαῖός ἐστιν. Εἶπε δὲ ὁ Πέτρος· Ἄνθρωπε, οὐκ οἶδα ὃ λέγεις. 60
72 Καὶ παραχρῆμα, ἔτι λαλοῦντος αὐτοῦ, ἐφώνησεν [ὁ] ἀλέκτωρ. Καὶ 61
75 στραφεὶς ὁ Κύριος ἐνέβλεψε τῷ Πέτρῳ· καὶ ὑπεμνήσθη ὁ Πέτρος τοῦ
λόγου τοῦ Κυρίου, ὡς εἶπεν αὐτῷ· Ὅτι πρὶν ἀλέκτορα φωνῆσαι,
ἀπαρνήσῃ με τρίς. Καὶ ἐξελθὼν ἔξω ὁ Πέτρος ἔκλαυσε πικρῶς. 62
67 65 Καὶ οἱ ἄνδρες οἱ συνέχοντες τὸν Ἰησοῦν ἐνέπαιζον αὐτῷ, δέροντες· 63
καὶ περικαλύψαντες αὐτὸν, ἔτυπτον αὐτοῦ τὸ πρόσωπον, καὶ ἐπηρώτων 64
68 αὐτὸν, λέγοντες· Προφήτευσον, τίς ἐστιν ὁ παίσας σε; καὶ ἕτερα 65
27. 15. πολλὰ βλασφημοῦντες ἔλεγον εἰς αὐτόν.
1 1 Καὶ ὡς ἐγένετο ἡμέρα, συνήχθη τὸ πρεσβυτέριον τοῦ λαοῦ, ἀρχιερεῖς 66
τε καὶ γραμματεῖς, καὶ ἀνήγαγον αὐτὸν εἰς τὸ συνέδριον αὐτῶν, λέγον- 67
τες· Εἰ σὺ εἶ ὁ Χριστὸς, εἰπὲ ἡμῖν. Εἶπε δὲ αὐτοῖς· Ἐὰν ὑμῖν
εἴπω, οὐ μὴ πιστεύσητε· ἐὰν δὲ καὶ ἐρωτήσω, οὐ μὴ ἀποκριθῆτέ μοι, 68

the time most opportune for your purpose; this is the hour fit for deeds of darkness." An interpretation confirmed by several passages adduced from the Latin Classics. Others explain, "This is the time destined and permitted by God, and this is the power of iniquity," i. e. iniquity has obtained this power; αὕτη ἐστὶ being supplied before ἐξουσία. The latter is greatly preferable; and the interpretation, as far as concerns the *first* clause, is confirmed and illustrated by Matt. xxvi. 45 and 56. The sense of the *second* clause, however, has not been well discerned. It should seem that ἐξουσία τοῦ σκότους is, as it were, a *personification* of the *Prince* of darkness, the Devil (Eph. ii. 2.) And so Ephes. vi. 12. πρὸς τὰς ἀρχὰς, πρὸς τὰς ἐξουσίας, πρὸς τοὺς κοσμοκράτορας τοῦ σκότους. See also Col. i. 13. Indeed ἐξουσία is often used for Ἄρχων, as supra xii. 11. Rom. xiii. 1. 1 Cor. xv. 24. Eph. i. 21. iii. 10. Col. i. 16. ii. 10. Thus the complete sense is, "This is the time when the power to destroy me is granted you by the Providence of God; and in which the Power, or Prince, of darkness is permitted to exercise his rage against me." There is an ellipsis of αὕτη ἐστὶ, to be supplied from the preceding clause.

54. [*Comp.* John xviii. 12, 24.]

56. ἀτενίσασα αὐτῷ.] Ἀτενίζειν signifies "to fix oneself intently;" and, with ὄμμασι or ὀφθαλμοῖς, to fix one's *view* intently. But the words ὄμμασι, or ὀφθαλμοῖς, are almost always left to be understood; and the *object* of view is expressed either by an Accus. with εἰς (as in Acts i. 10. iii. 4.), or with a Dat. without a preposition, as here and in Luke iv. 20.

58. ἕτερος.] Matthew says ἄλλη, *another maid-servant*. But this discrepancy may be removed on the principle suggested by Wets., who observes, that ἕτερος may be used with reference to ἄνθρωπος being understood, which is sometimes applied to a *woman*. Examples of this ellipsis are frequent. Thus Pausan. ii. 21. speaking of two women, τούτους δέ φασιν; and Soph. Elect. 980. τῷδε τῷ κασιγνήτῳ.

— ἄνθρωπε.] This, like the Latin *homo*, and our *man*, is a term of expostulation.

59. διϊσχυρίζετο] "strongly affirmed," as Acts xii. 5, and in passages of Lysias, Ælian, Lucian, and Joseph. cited by the Commentators.

61. [*Comp.* John xiii. 38. xviii. 27.]

66. τὸ πρεσβ. τοῦ λαοῦ.] Luke alone in this passage and Acts xxii. 5. gives this name to the Sanhedrim. At Acts v. 21. he calls it ἡ γερουσία.

67. εἰ σὺ — εἰπὲ ἡμῖν.] These words admit of being rendered in three different ways. 1. "Art thou the Christ? tell us." So our Common Version. 2. "If thou be the Christ, tell us [so]." This is adopted by the Pesch. Syr. and Campb. 3. "Tell us whether thou be the Christ [or not]." The 1st mode has far less to recommend it than the 2d and 3d, of which the latter seems, on account of its greater suitableness to the occasion and the context (especially the words of the answer) to be entitled to the preference.

68. ἐὰν δὲ καὶ ἐρωτήσω.] The Translators and Expositors are here much at fault. So little satisfactory is the ordinary sense of ἐρωτ., that Heinsius would here assign that of *supplicate*. But that signification is ill founded, and the sense arising would here be very objectionable; being, indeed, at variance with the words following οὐ μὴ ἀποκριθῆτέ μοι, by which *interrogation* of some kind is certainly adverted to. As to what Heins. urges,

MT. MK.
69 ἢ ἀπολύσητε. Ἀπὸ τοῦ νῦν ἔσται ὁ Υἱὸς τοῦ ἀνθρώπου καθήμενος 27. 15.
70 ἐκ δεξιῶν τῆς δυνάμεως τοῦ Θεοῦ. Εἶπον δὲ πάντες· Σὺ οὖν εἶ ὁ
Υἱὸς τοῦ Θεοῦ; ὁ δὲ πρὸς αὐτοὺς ἔφη· Ὑμεῖς λέγετε ὅτι ἐγώ εἰμι.
71 Οἱ δὲ εἶπον· Τί ἔτι χρείαν ἔχομεν μαρτυρίας; αὐτοὶ γὰρ ἠκούσαμεν
ἀπὸ τοῦ στόματος αὐτοῦ.
1 XXIII. ΚΑΙ ἀναστὰν ἅπαν τὸ πλῆθος αὐτῶν, * ἤγαγον αὐτὸν 2
2 ἐπὶ τὸν Πιλάτον. Ἤρξαντο δὲ κατηγορεῖν αὐτοῦ, λέγοντες· Τοῦτον
εὕρομεν διαστρέφοντα τὸ ἔθνος, καὶ κωλύοντα Καίσαρι φόρους διδόναι,
3 λέγοντα ἑαυτὸν Χριστὸν βασιλέα εἶναι. Ὁ δὲ Πιλάτος ἐπηρώτησεν 11 2
αὐτὸν, λέγων· Σὺ εἶ ὁ βασιλεὺς τῶν Ἰουδαίων; ὁ δὲ ἀποκριθεὶς
4 αὐτῷ ἔφη· Σὺ λέγεις. ὁ δὲ Πιλάτος εἶπε πρὸς τοὺς ἀρχιερεῖς καὶ
τοὺς ὄχλους· Οὐδὲν εὑρίσκω αἴτιον ἐν τῷ ἀνθρώπῳ τούτῳ.
5 Οἱ δὲ ἐπίσχυον, λέγοντες· Ὅτι ἀνασείει τὸν λαὸν, διδάσκων καθ᾽
6 ὅλης τῆς Ἰουδαίας, ἀρξάμενος ἀπὸ τῆς Γαλιλαίας ἕως ὧδε. Πιλάτος
δὲ ἀκούσας Γαλιλαίαν, ἐπηρώτησεν εἰ ὁ ἄνθρωπος Γαλιλαῖός ἐστι·
7 καὶ ἐπιγνοὺς ὅτι ἐκ τῆς ἐξουσίας Ἡρώδου ἐστὶν, ἀνέπεμψεν αὐτὸν
πρὸς Ἡρώδην, ὄντα καὶ αὐτὸν ἐν Ἱεροσολύμοις ἐν ταύταις ταῖς ἡμέραις.
8 Ὁ δὲ Ἡρώδης ἰδὼν τὸν Ἰησοῦν ἐχάρη λίαν· ἦν γὰρ θέλων ἐξ ἱκανοῦ
ἰδεῖν αὐτὸν, διὰ τὸ ἀκούειν πολλὰ περὶ αὐτοῦ· καὶ ἤλπιζέ τι σημεῖον
9 ἰδεῖν ὑπ᾽ αὐτοῦ γινόμενον. Ἐπηρώτα δὲ αὐτὸν ἐν λόγοις ἱκανοῖς· αὐ-
10 τὸς δὲ οὐδὲν ἀπεκρίνατο αὐτῷ. Εἱστήκεισαν δὲ οἱ ἀρχιερεῖς καὶ οἱ
11 γραμματεῖς εὐτόνως κατηγοροῦντες αὐτοῦ. Ἐξουθενήσας δὲ αὐτὸν ὁ
Ἡρώδης, σὺν τοῖς στρατεύμασιν αὐτοῦ, καὶ ἐμπαίξας, περιβαλὼν αὐτὸν

that Christ had not the power to ask questions of his judges, that is quite supposititious and unauthorized. It is evident, then, that *interrogation* is here meant; — of *what* kind is the question. Certainly not what Bp. Pearce understands *concerning the Christ:* still less what Doddr., "inquiring wherefore they persist in their infidelity." To ask questions, in order to convince, is incongruous. The true force of the expression was alone, I think, seen by *Grotius*, who observes, that "it bears a sense which, united with that of *interrogation*, yet has *another*, namely that of *argumentari*." "The Hebrews (says he) as well as the Greeks used to carry on argument by interrogation." And he adduces an example from Aristotle. He might have added, that this use of the word to signify *quæstionem proponere*, is, as H. Steph. Thes. in v. attests, frequent in the Dialecticians, especially Sextus Empiricus; as also *interrogare* in Latin. The sense, then, may be thus expressed; "If I simply *tell* you that I am the Christ, ye will not believe me: and if I *propose questions in argument*, to support my claim, ye will not answer me, nor, though convinced, will you release me. [However] henceforward shall the Son of Man (meaning himself.) be [seen] sitting," &c. That such is the meaning, is plain from the parallel passages of Matth. and Mark; for there is, in reality, no discrepancy. The πλὴν of Matthew may seem more definite; but there is great force in the *Asyndeton* here. See Note on Matth. xxvi. 64.

69. [*Comp.* Dan. vii. 9. Matt. xvi 27. xxiv. 30. Acts i. 11.]

XXIII. 1. τὸ πλῆθος αὐτῶν] i. e. the chief priests, elders, and Scribes. Πλῆθος *congregatio*, as the Pesch. Syr. renders. The *multitude* of our common Version suggests a wrong meaning, and has misled some Commentators. Ros. and Schl. very well render cœtum. However, the truth is, that πλῆθος has here simply the sense *number*, without reference to great or small. So Thucyd. i. 47. τῶν εἴκοσι νεῶν, ἀπὸ ἐλάσσονος πλήθους, οὐ παρουσῶν, and elsewhere. Ἤγαγον (instead of ἤγαγεν) which is found in almost all the best MSS. and supported by the Ed. Pr., is adopted by most Editors. [*Comp.* John xviii. 28.]

2. τ. εὕρομεν δ.] Εὑρίσκω is here a forensic term, denoting *conviction* on legal examination. [See Matt. xvii. 25. xxii. 21. Mark xii. 17. supra xx. 25. Rom. xiii. 7. Acts xvii. 7.]

4. οὐδὲν εὑρίσκω αἴτιον.] Αἴτιον is properly an adjective neuter, from αἴτιος, denoting *worthy of*, or *the cause of;* and, when used in a judicial sense, signifies *worthy of blame*, and consequently of *punishment*.

7. ἐκ τῆς ἐξουσίας] "ex ditione," the region over which he had held power. Ἀνέπεμψε, "*remisit*," to use the corresponding term in the Roman law. "It was (observes Grot.) the regular practice of the Roman law to remove the prisoner to the governor of the province or district to which he belonged; though Governors had the right of trying all offences within their own province."

8. [*Comp.* supra ix. 7. Matt. xiv. 1.]

9. οὐδὲν ἀπεκρίνατο.] Why he returned no answer, see Euthym. and Kuin. in Rec. Syn.

MT. MK.
27. 15. ἐσθῆτα λαμπρὰν, ἀνέπεμψεν αὐτὸν τῷ Πιλάτῳ. Ἐγένοντο δὲ φίλοι ὅ 12
τε Πιλάτος καὶ ὁ Ἡρώδης ἐν αὐτῇ τῇ ἡμέρᾳ μετ᾽ ἀλλήλων· προϋπῆρχον γὰρ ἐν ἔχθρᾳ ὄντες πρὸς ἑαυτούς. Πιλάτος δὲ συγκαλεσάμενος 13
τοὺς ἀρχιερεῖς καὶ τοὺς ἄρχοντας καὶ τὸν λαὸν, εἶπε πρὸς αὐτούς· 14
Προσηνέγκατέ μοι τὸν ἄνθρωπον τοῦτον, ὡς ἀποστρέφοντα τὸν λαόν.
καὶ ἰδοὺ, ἐγὼ ἐνώπιον ὑμῶν ἀνακρίνας, οὐδὲν εὗρον ἐν τῷ ἀνθρώπῳ
τούτῳ αἴτιον, ὧν κατηγορεῖτε κατ᾽ αὐτοῦ. Ἀλλ᾽ οὐδὲ Ἡρώδης· 15
ἀνέπεμψα γὰρ ὑμᾶς πρὸς αὐτὸν, καὶ ἰδοὺ οὐδὲν ἄξιον θανάτου ἐστὶ
15 6 πεπραγμένον αὐτῷ. Παιδεύσας οὖν αὐτὸν ἀπολύσω. Ἀνάγκην δὲ εἶχεν 16
8 ἀπολύειν αὐτοῖς κατὰ ἑορτὴν ἕνα. Ἀνέκραξαν δὲ παμπληθεὶ, λέγοντες· 17
16 7 Αἶρε τοῦτον, ἀπόλυσον δὲ ἡμῖν τὸν Βαραββᾶν· ὅστις ἦν, διὰ στάσιν 18
22 τινὰ γενομένην ἐν τῇ πόλει καὶ φόνον, βεβλημένος εἰς φυλακήν. 19
Πάλιν οὖν ὁ Πιλάτος προσεφώνησε, θέλων ἀπολῦσαι τὸν Ἰησοῦν. Οἱ 20
25 δὲ ἐπεφώνουν, λέγοντες· Σταύρωσον, σταύρωσον αὐτόν! Ὁ δὲ τρίτον 21
εἶπε πρὸς αὐτούς· Τί γὰρ κακὸν ἐποίησεν οὗτος; οὐδὲν αἴτιον 22
θανάτου εὗρον ἐν αὐτῷ· παιδεύσας οὖν αὐτὸν ἀπολύσω. Οἱ δὲ ἐπέ- 23
κειντο φωναῖς μεγάλαις, αἰτούμενοι αὐτὸν σταυρωθῆναι· καὶ κατίσχυον
15 αἱ φωναὶ αὐτῶν καὶ τῶν ἀρχιερέων. Ὁ δὲ Πιλάτος ἐπέκρινε γενέσθαι 24
26 τὸ αἴτημα αὐτῶν. Ἀπέλυσε δὲ [αὐτοῖς] τὸν διὰ στάσιν καὶ φόνον 25
βεβλημένον εἰς τὴν φυλακὴν, ὃν ᾐτοῦντο· τὸν δὲ Ἰησοῦν παρέδωκε τῷ
θελήματι αὐτῶν.
32 21 Καὶ ὡς ἀπήγαγον αὐτὸν, ἐπιλαβόμενοι Σίμωνός τινος Κυρηναίου 26
[τοῦ] ἐρχομένου ἀπ᾽ ἀγροῦ, ἐπέθηκαν αὐτῷ τὸν σταυρὸν φέρειν
ὄπισθεν τοῦ Ἰησοῦ. Ἠκολούθει δὲ αὐτῷ πολὺ πλῆθος τοῦ λαοῦ, καὶ 27
γυναικῶν, αἳ καὶ ἐκόπτοντο καὶ ἐθρήνουν αὐτόν. Στραφεὶς δὲ πρὸς 28
αὐτὰς ὁ Ἰησοῦς εἶπε· Θυγατέρες Ἱερουσαλὴμ, μὴ κλαίετε ἐπ᾽ ἐμὲ,

11. στρατεύμασιν] *satellites*, i. e. his body-guards, as in Acts xxiii. 10. More than *those* Pilate would not have allowed him to bring.

12. ἐγένοντο φίλοι] "were made friends" See Acts iv. 27. M. Saurin observes that the reconciliation of Herod and Pilate was more wonderful than their enmity. The ænigma, however, is solved by the profound remark of the Stagirite: that "it contributes much to the formation of friendship, or to the recovery of it, to either love or hate the same person; to be engaged, no matter how, as colleagues in the same business." Compare Æschyl. Agam. 659, and see Bp. Sanderson's Sermons ad Aulam, p. 217 in ed.

—ἐν ἔχθρᾳ.] Classical usage would require ἐπ' ἔχθρᾳ, as in Thucyd. i. 69. Schleus. and Kuin. say that προϋπ. has the force of an adverb here and at Acts viii. 9. But, in fact, ὑπάρχ. here follows the construction of τυγχάνειν, and ὄντες could not be dispensed with. For though we may say εἶναι ἐν ἔχθρᾳ, yet not ὑπάρχειν ἐν ἐχθ.

14. ἀποστρέφοντα τὸν λαόν.] Scil. ἀπὸ τοῦ Καίσαρος, "from their allegiance to Cæsar." So Ecclus. xlvi. 13. Καὶ ὅσοι οὐκ ἀπεστράφησαν ἀπὸ Κυρίου.

15. πεπραγμένον αὐτῷ] for πεπ. ὑπ' αὐτοῦ; of which idiom many examples are adduced by Raphel and Wets. from the best writers.

16. παιδεύσας] "having chastized." Παιδεύειν properly signifies to educate a child; and then, by an easy transition, to *correct*, either generally, or in some particular manner, expressed or understood. Here correction by *flagellation* is meant. [*Comp.* John xix. 1.]

17. ἀνάγκην εἶχε.] A phrase very much like the Latin *opus habere*, yet occasionally found in the later Classical writers. The *kind* of necessity will depend upon the context. Here that of *custom* is meant. See Acts iii. 14.

21. ἐπεφώνουν.] Ἐπιφωνεῖν imports responsive shouting, and παμπληθεὶ, "in full chorus." The word is found in Xen., Demosth., and other authors.

23. ἐπέκειντο] "were very pressing and urgent with him." See examples of this sense in Kypke.

24. ἐπέκρινε.] The word denotes the final adjudication or decree of a judge.

25. αὐτοῖς.] This is omitted in many MSS., &c. and is cancelled by Griesb., Knapp, and Scholz; but rashly—for more causes may be imagined for the omission than the insertion of the word. See Rinck. Lucub. Crit. p. 336.

26. τοῦ ἐρχ.] The τοῦ is omitted in most MSS. and early Edd., and is cancelled by almost all Editors. Propriety of language will not admit it, and it seems to have arisen from the του preceding.

27. καὶ γυναικῶν] "even of women."

28. μὴ κλαίετε] "weep not so much for me as," &c. For ἐπ' ἐμὲ some MSS. have ἐπ' ἐμοὶ, which

MT. MK.

29 πλὴν ἐφ' ἑαυτὰς κλαίετε καὶ ἐπὶ τὰ τέκνα ὑμῶν! ὅτι ἰδού, ἔρχονται 27. 15.
ἡμέραι ἐν αἷς ἐροῦσι· Μακάριαι αἱ στεῖραι, καὶ κοιλίαι αἳ οὐκ ἐγέν-
30 νησαν, καὶ μαστοὶ οἳ οὐκ ἐθήλασαν! Τότε ἄρξονται λέγειν τοῖς ὄρεσι·
31 Πέσετε ἐφ' ἡμᾶς! καὶ τοῖς βουνοῖς· Καλύψατε ἡμᾶς! Ὅτι εἰ ἐν
32 τῷ ὑγρῷ ξύλῳ ταῦτα ποιοῦσιν, ἐν τῷ ξηρῷ τί γένηται; Ἤγοντο δὲ
καὶ ἕτεροι δύο κακοῦργοι σὺν αὐτῷ ἀναιρεθῆναι.
33 Καὶ ὅτε ἀπῆλθον ἐπὶ τὸν τόπον τὸν καλούμενον Κρανίον, ἐκεῖ 33 22
ἐσταύρωσαν αὐτόν, καὶ τοὺς κακούργους, ὃν μὲν ἐκ δεξιῶν, ὃν δὲ ἐξ
34 ἀριστερῶν. Ὁ δὲ Ἰησοῦς ἔλεγε· Πάτερ, ἄφες αὐτοῖς· οὐ γὰρ οἴδασι

is supported by Luke xix. 41. and by general Classical usage. Bnt the other is confirmed by that of the LXX.

29, 30. How awfully the predictions contained in these verses were fulfilled at the destruction of Jerusalem, the affecting narrative of the great Jewish Historian abundantly attests. The 1st of these verses alludes to a pathetic circumstance, to which numerous parallels from the ancient writers are adduced by Pricæus, Grot., and Wets. The 2d contains a yet *more touching* feature of this graphic sketch; with which may be compared similar passages in Is. ii. 19. Hos. x. 8. Rev. vi. 16. ix. 6. and some from the ancient Greek writers. In the present passage, however, I cannot, with Kuin. and some recent Commentators, see that "per montes et colles intelliguntur cavernæ et speluncæ." See Matth. xxiv. 16. Indeed, to suppose any *allusion* to the caves as *places of refuge*, would be to mar the magnificent beauty of the thought; which simply expresses, that they would wish for speedy death (caves being used in the East as burial-places) to be rid of their troubles. So M. Laveau, in his Sketch of the ancient history of Moscow, says "that so dreadful were the ravages of the Tartars in the year 1238, that the living envied the dead the repose of the tomb." If there be any *allusion* united with the image in *mountains* or hills, it should rather seem to be, to those immense *barrows* of the early ages, under which sometimes great numbers were buried, and to which the little mount, or tumulus, formed a *monument*.

31. *ἐν τῷ ὑγρῷ — γένηται.*] A proverbial form of expression; for (as we find from Ps. i. 3. Ez. xx. 47. Eccls. vi. 3. and especially the Rabbinical writers) the Hebrews were accustomed to figuratively call the righteous *green trees*, and the wicked *dry* ones. Hence the sense here is: "If the *innocent* and righteous be thus cut off, what may not be expected to befal the *wicked* and disobedient at the day of visitation, which impends over you." Of *ξύλον* in the sense *tree* there are many examples, both in Classical and Hellenistic Greek.

32. It is the opinion of Commentators in general, that Christ is here reckoned among malefactors, agreeably to what was said supra xxii. 37. *καὶ μετὰ ἀνόμων ἐλογίσθη*, and because he was so *considered* by the Jews. Since, however, this involves a considerable harshness, it is better avoided; which it easily may, by regarding *κακοῦργοι*, with many of the best recent Commentators, as not in *concord*, but in *apposition* with *ἕτεροι*; so that it will be the same as if written *οἳ ἦσαν κακοῦργοι*. It will not, however, be necessary to *point off κακοῦργοι*, as those Commentators have done. As examples of this idiom I have noted Aristoph. Ran. 782. & 514. *καὶ γὰρ αὐλητρίς γέ σοι Ἤδ' ἔνδον ἔσθ' ὡραιοτάτη, κὠρχηστρίδες Ἕτεραι δύ' ἢ τρεῖς.* Thucyd. iv. 67. *οἱ δὲ μετὰ τοῦ Δημ. Πλαταιῆς τε ψιλοὶ καὶ ἕτεροι περίπολοι* (for *οἳ ἦσαν π.* See my Note there) *ἐνήδρευσαν*, &c.

By the expression *κακοῦργοι* are not meant, strictly speaking, thieves or robbers, but rebels or insurgents, brigands. It is true that these are called by Matthew and Mark *λῃσταί*. But the terms *λῃσταὶ* and *κακοῦργοι* were, as Kypke and Wets. have shown, convertible; and from the examples they have adduced, it is clear that both terms were applied not only to robbers, but to *plunderers* and ravagers in war. On the word *κακοῦργος* see Thucyd. ii. 67. vii. 4. & 10. ii. 22. iii. 1. vi. 6.; and on *λῃστ.*, iv. 2. viii. 40. and my Notes. The persons in question were, no doubt (as Grot., Kuin. and Bp. Maltby suppose), men who had taken up arms on a principle of resistance to the Roman oppression, and especially to the payment of the tribute-money; but, though professedly opposed to the Romans only, — yet, when engaged in their unlawful courses, made less difference between Romans and Jews than they at first set out with doing.

34. *πάτερ, ἄφες αὐτοῖς*, &c.] Grot. remarks, that much may be pleaded in extenuation of the crime of the *people at large*; especially as regards their ignorance of the real nature of the person whom they so injuriously treated. The Philosophers, he shows, considered ignorance, if not an excuse for crime, an extenuation of the guilt. Thus Aristotle distributes offences into three sorts; *ἀτυχήματα, ἁμαρτήματα*, and *ἀδικήματα*; of which the 1st merits rather *pity*, the 2d requires *reproof and correction*, to the 3d alone belongs *severe punishment*. Now (continues he) as the offence of the Jews was not a mere *ἀτύχημα*, nay exceeded the ordinary sort of *ἁμαρτήματα*, yet it carried with it something of the *ἀτύχημα*, from the ignorance joined with it. To his citations from the Classical writers may be added many others, which I have adduced on the same subject in a Note on Thucyd. iii. 40. (Transl.) For the chief priests and scribes there could indeed be little or no excuse: but then the more magnanimous must our Lord's conduct be considered, who here rose superior in *practice* to what even the most enlightened sages had reached in *theory*; though Menander says, *οὗτος κράτιστος ἔστ' ἀνήρ, ὦ Γοργίαν, ὅστις ἀδικεῖσθαι πλεῖστ' ἐπίσταται βροτῶν.* There can be no doubt but that the *Jews*, as well as the Roman soldiers, were included in this prayer; which must be supposed to import an intercession, that opportunity for repentance might be granted to the guilty, and that pardon might be extended to such as should lay hold on the forbearance of God. That not a few *did* so,

MT. MK.
27. 15. τί ποιοῦσι! Διαμεριζόμενοι δὲ τὰ ἱμάτια αὐτοῦ, ἔβαλον κλῆρον. καὶ 35
39 29 εἱστήκει ὁ λαὸς θεωρῶν. Ἐξεμυκτήριζον δὲ καὶ οἱ ἄρχοντες σὺν αὐτοῖς,
42 31 λέγοντες· Ἄλλους ἔσωσε, σωσάτω ἑαυτὸν, εἰ οὗτός ἐστιν ὁ Χριστὸς ὁ
τοῦ Θεοῦ ἐκλεκτός. Ἐνέπαιζον δὲ αὐτῷ καὶ οἱ στρατιῶται, προσερχό- 36
μενοι καὶ ὄξος προσφέροντες αὐτῷ, καὶ λέγοντες· Εἰ σὺ εἶ ὁ βασιλεὺς 37
37 26 τῶν Ἰουδαίων, σῶσον σεαυτόν. Ἦν δὲ καὶ ἐπιγραφὴ γεγραμμένη ἐπ᾿ 38
αὐτῷ γράμμασιν Ἑλληνικοῖς καὶ Ῥωμαϊκοῖς καὶ Ἑβραϊκοῖς, ΟΥΤΟΣ
ΕΣΤΙΝ Ο ΒΑΣΙΛΕΥΣ ΤΩΝ ΙΟΥΔΑΙΩΝ.
44 32 Εἷς δὲ τῶν κρεμασθέντων κακούργων ἐβλασφήμει αὐτὸν, λέγων· Εἰ 39
σὺ εἶ ὁ Χριστὸς, σῶσον σεαυτὸν καὶ ἡμᾶς. Ἀποκριθεὶς δὲ ὁ ἕτερος 40
ἐπετίμα αὐτῷ λέγων· Οὐδὲ φοβῇ σὺ τὸν Θεὸν, ὅτι ἐν τῷ αὐτῷ κρίματι εἶ; Καὶ ἡμεῖς μὲν δικαίως· ἄξια γὰρ ὧν ἐπράξαμεν ἀπολαμ- 41
βάνομεν· οὗτος δὲ οὐδὲν ἄτοπον ἔπραξε. Καὶ ἔλεγε τῷ Ἰησοῦ· Μνή- 42
σθητί μου, Κύριε, ὅταν ἔλθῃς ἐν τῇ βασιλείᾳ σου. Καὶ εἶπεν αὐτῷ 43
ὁ Ἰησοῦς· Ἀμὴν λέγω σοι, σήμερον μετ᾿ ἐμοῦ ἔσῃ ἐν τῷ παραδείσῳ.
45 33 Ἦν δὲ ὡσεὶ ὥρα ἕκτη, καὶ σκότος ἐγένετο ἐφ᾿ ὅλην τὴν γῆν ἕως 44
ὥρας ἐννάτης. Καὶ ἐσκοτίσθη ὁ ἥλιος, καὶ ἐσχίσθη τὸ καταπέτασμα 45
46 34 τοῦ ναοῦ μέσον· καὶ φωνήσας φωνῇ μεγάλῃ ὁ Ἰησοῦς εἶπε· Πάτερ, 46
50 37 εἰς χεῖράς σου παραθήσομαι τὸ πνεῦμά μου. καὶ ταῦτα εἰπὼν ἐξέπνευ-
54 39 σεν. Ἰδὼν δὲ ὁ ἑκατόνταρχος τὸ γενόμενον, ἐδόξασε τὸν Θεὸν, λέγων· 47
Ὄντως ὁ ἄνθρωπος οὗτος δίκαιος ἦν. Καὶ πάντες οἱ συμπαραγενό- 48

is clear from the Evangelical history contained in the Acts of the Apostles.

40. *οὐδὲ φοβῇ σὺ τὸν Θεὸν, ὅτι*, &c.] The best Commentators are agreed that the *οὐδὲ* must be joined with *σύ*. Bornem. well expresses the sense as follows: "*Ne te quidem vereri Deum, eo magis miror, quod pari es in supplicio.*"

41. *ἄτοπον*.] The word denotes *what has no place*, is *naught*; and therefore may well signify what is *naughty* or evil.

42. *ὅταν ἔλθῃς ἐν τῇ βασιλείᾳ σου*.] Markl. on Lysias i. 572., Reiske, and Kuin. think the sense is, *quando redieris in regno tuo, i. e. Rex, regia potestate præditus.* But though that sense of *ἔρχεσθαι* and *ἥκειν* be found in the Classics, it does not obtain in the Scriptures; and, upon the whole, the interpretation is a *strained* one; so that there is no reason to abandon the common opinion, that *ἐν τῇ βασιλείᾳ* is for *εἰς τὴν βασιλείαν*; especially since this idiom is common in the later Greek writers.

43. *σήμερον — παραδ.*] There has been much discussion, both among ancient and modern Commentators, as to what Christ intended the penitent malefactor to understand by the "*paradise*" promised. Chrys., Euthym., Grot., Wets., and many of the best recent Commentators, are agreed that he could not mean to countenance Jewish fables, or the notions of the Essenes, still less the Pharisaical ones (like the Mahometan) of a *paradise of sensual delights*. Nor must we suppose that by Paradise is meant *heaven*. The word is commonly supposed to be derived from the Persian פרדס, a garden — but, in fact, as Schroeder (Præf. Thes. Ling. Armen. p. 36., referred to by Bornem.) has shown, is derived from the Armenian. Now as great pains were bestowed by the Orientals on their *gardens*, the word easily came to mean a *pleasure*-garden, a place of luxury and enjoyment. In this sense *παράδεισος* often occurs in Xenophon. Hence it is no wonder that the term came to denote, among the later Jews, that *pleasant abode* in Hades appointed for the reception of the pious dead, until they should, after the day of judgment, be again united to their bodies in a future state. See Joseph. Bell. Jud. iii. 8, 4. ii. 8, 11. This, Chrysost. has shown, was the idea entertained of Paradise by all the *Orthodox* believers of his time. The sense, therefore, meant to be expressed was, that the penitent malefactor might hope from the mercy of God for blessings far beyond the imagination of the Jewish doctors; even a secure and quiet retreat for the time which should intervene between death and the resurrection: and also (which was *implied* in the other) an admittance into the regions of that eternal felicity, of which the other was but a foretaste and earnest.

46. [*Comp.* John xix. 38.]

47. *ὄντως — δίκαιος ἦν*.] See Note on Matt. xxvii. 54. by which a method of removing the minute discrepancy between the accounts of the Evangelists will suggest itself. One may observe, how peculiarly suitable *ὄντως* is to this passage of Luke, as *ἀληθῶς* is to those of Matthew and Mark: in the first of which the sense is, "This was truly [what he appeared to be] a just person;" in the 2d and 3d, "This was really the personage he claimed to be — *the Son* of God." On the distinction between *ὄντως* and *ἀληθῶς* see Tittm. de Synom. p. 162.

— *δίκαιος*.] On the distinction between *ἀγαθὸς* and *δίκαιος* see Tittm de Synon. p. 19. sqq. In popular use, however, they are synonymous; especially when as in Æschin. cited by Kuin. they

MT. MK.

μενοι ὄχλοι ἐπὶ τὴν θεωρίαν ταύτην, θεωροῦντες τὰ γενόμενα, τύ- 27. 15.
49 πτοντες ἑαυτῶν τὰ στήθη ὑπέστρεφον. Εἱστήκεισαν δὲ πάντες οἱ γνω- 55 40
στοὶ αὐτοῦ μακρόθεν, καὶ γυναῖκες αἱ συνακολουθήσασαι αὐτῷ ἀπὸ
τῆς Γαλιλαίας, ὁρῶσαι ταῦτα.
50 ΚΑΙ ἰδού, ἀνὴρ ὀνόματι Ἰωσήφ, βουλευτὴς ὑπάρχων, ἀνὴρ ἀγαθὸς 57 43
51 καὶ δίκαιος, (οὗτος οὐκ ἦν συγκατατεθειμένος τῇ βουλῇ καὶ τῇ πράξει
αὐτῶν) ἀπὸ Ἀριμαθαίας πόλεως τῶν Ἰουδαίων, ὃς καὶ προσεδέχετο καὶ
52 αὐτὸς τὴν βασιλείαν τοῦ Θεοῦ· οὗτος προσελθὼν τῷ Πιλάτῳ ᾐτήσατο
53 τὸ σῶμα τοῦ Ἰησοῦ. Καὶ καθελὼν αὐτὸ ἐνετύλιξεν αὐτὸ σινδόνι, καὶ 58
ἔθηκεν αὐτὸ ἐν μνήματι λαξευτῷ, οὗ οὐκ ἦν οὐδέπω οὐδεὶς κείμενος. 59 46
54 Καὶ ἡμέρα ἦν παρασκευή, καὶ σάββατον ἐπέφωσκε.
55 Κατακολουθήσασαι δὲ καὶ γυναῖκες, αἵτινες ἦσαν συνεληλυθυῖαι 61 47
αὐτῷ ἐκ τῆς Γαλιλαίας, ἐθεάσαντο τὸ μνημεῖον, καὶ ὡς ἐτέθη τὸ σῶμα
56 αὐτοῦ. Ὑποστρέψασαι δὲ ἡτοίμασαν ἀρώματα καὶ μύρα· καὶ τὸ μὲν 28. 16.
1 σάββατον ἡσύχασαν κατὰ τὴν ἐντολήν· XXIV. τῇ δὲ μιᾷ τῶν σαβ- 1 1
βάτων, ὄρθρου βαθέος, ἦλθον ἐπὶ τὸ μνῆμα, φέρουσαι ἃ ἡτοίμασαν
ἀρώματα· καί τινες σὺν αὐταῖς.
2 Εὗρον δὲ τὸν λίθον ἀποκεκυλισμένον ἀπὸ τοῦ μνημείου, καὶ εἰσελ- 4
3 θοῦσαι οὐχ εὗρον τὸ σῶμα τοῦ Κυρίου Ἰησοῦ. Καὶ ἐγένετο, ἐν τῷ 5
4 διαπορεῖσθαι αὐτὰς περὶ τούτου, καὶ ἰδού, δύο ἄνδρες ἐπέστησαν αὐ- 2
5 ταῖς ἐν ἐσθήσεσιν ἀστραπτούσαις. Ἐμφόβων δὲ γενομένων αὐτῶν καὶ
κλινουσῶν τὸ πρόσωπον εἰς τὴν γῆν, εἶπον πρὸς αὐτάς· Τί ζητεῖτε τὸν 5 6
6 ζῶντα μετὰ τῶν νεκρῶν; Οὐκ ἔστιν ὧδε, ἀλλ᾽ ἠγέρθη. Μνήσθητε 6
7 ὡς ἐλάλησεν ὑμῖν, ἔτι ὢν ἐν τῇ Γαλιλαίᾳ, λέγων· Ὅτι δεῖ τὸν Υἱὸν
τοῦ ἀνθρώπου παραδοθῆναι εἰς χεῖρας ἀνθρώπων ἁμαρτωλῶν, καὶ
8 σταυρωθῆναι, καὶ τῇ τρίτῃ ἡμέρᾳ ἀναστῆναι. Καὶ ἐμνήσθησαν τῶν
9 ῥημάτων αὐτοῦ· καὶ ὑποστρέψασαι ἀπὸ τοῦ μνημείου ἀπήγγειλαν 8 8
10 ταῦτα πάντα τοῖς ἕνδεκα, καὶ πᾶσι τοῖς λοιποῖς. Ἦσαν δὲ ἡ Μαγδαληνὴ Μαρία καὶ Ἰωάννα καὶ Μαρία Ἰακώβου, καὶ αἱ λοιπαὶ σὺν

are conjoined, and opposed to κακοί. And there are cases when ἀγαθὸς imports not only δίκαιος, but all other virtues. So Aristotle de Republ. iii. 4. says τὸν ἀγαθὸν ἄνδρα φάμεν εἶναι κατ᾽ ἀρετὴν τελείαν, in like manner as Pope's line — "An *honest man's* the noblest work of God."

51. συγκατ. τῇ βουλῇ.] Συγκατατιθέναι signifies properly to *lay down together*, and, in the middle voice, to range oneself with any others, to *act with* them. So that we need not, with most philologists, suppose an ellip. of ψῆφον. The term is used in this sense both in the LXX. and the Classical writers. [See supra ii. 25.]

— προσεδέχετο — τὴν βασ. τοῦ Θεοῦ] "who also himself looked forward to the kingdom which God should establish by the Messiah." [*Comp.* Luke ii. 25.]

54. ἐπέφωσκε] "was just dawning," just drawing on, commencing. As the Sabbath commenced in the evening of the preceding day, the expression ἐπέφωσκε requires to be taken by a metaphor which may seem strange. Kuin., however, (after Wets.) justly observes, that however incongruous it might sound to Greek and Roman ears, when they heard of the evening, or approach of night, expressed by ἐπιφώσκω, yet to Jewish ones it was familiar, and by no means harsh. Campb. rightly accounts for this idiom by attributing it to the confusion of Oriental with Classical ideas and phrases, so likely to occur in a Jew by no means slightly tinctured with Classical erudition.

XXIV. 1. ὄρθρου βαθέος.] Βαθὺς is often used with words denoting *time*, especially evening, night, or the dawn of day. On the true sense of ὄρθρος see my Note on Thucyd. iii. 112. On the order of events connected with the resurrection, see Notes on Matt. xxviii. and Towns. i. 596. sqq. [*Comp.* John xx. 1.]

5. κλινουσῶν τὸ πρόσωπον.] By way of reverence, not adoration. See Doddr. and Wets.

6. See Matt. xvi. 21. xvii. 23.

10. αἱ λοιπαί.] Render *the* other women, by whom are probably meant, as Prof. Scholef. suggests, "that company of women, who along with the two Maries and Joanna are mentioned so frequently and so honorably in this history." See supra viii. 3.

αὐταῖς, αἳ ἔλεγον πρὸς τοὺς ἀποστόλους ταῦτα. Καὶ ἐφάνησαν ἐνώπιον 11
a John 20. 3, 6. αὐτῶν ὡσεὶ λῆρος τὰ ῥήματα αὐτῶν, καὶ ἠπίστουν αὐταῖς. [a] Ὁ δὲ 12
Πέτρος ἀναστὰς ἔδραμεν ἐπὶ τὸ μνημεῖον, καὶ παρακύψας βλέπει τὰ
ὀθόνια κείμενα μόνα· καὶ ἀπῆλθε πρὸς ἑαυτὸν θαυμάζων τὸ γεγονός.
b Mark 16. 12. [b] ΚΑΙ ἰδοὺ, δύο ἐξ αὐτῶν ἦσαν πορευόμενοι ἐν αὐτῇ τῇ ἡμέρᾳ εἰς 13
κώμην ἀπέχουσαν σταδίους ἑξήκοντα ἀπὸ Ἱερουσαλὴμ, ᾗ ὄνομα Ἐμμαούς·
καὶ αὐτοὶ ὡμίλουν πρὸς ἀλλήλους περὶ πάντων τῶν συμβεβηκότων τού- 14
c Matt. 18. 20. infra ver. 36. των. [c] Καὶ ἐγένετο, ἐν τῷ ὁμιλεῖν αὐτοὺς καὶ συζητεῖν, καὶ αὐτὸς ὁ 15
Ἰησοῦς ἐγγίσας συνεπορεύετο αὐτοῖς· οἱ δὲ ὀφθαλμοὶ αὐτῶν ἐκρατοῦντο 16
τοῦ μὴ ἐπιγνῶναι αὐτόν. Εἶπε δὲ πρὸς αὐτούς· Τίνες οἱ λόγοι οὗτοι, 17
οὓς ἀντιβάλλετε πρὸς ἀλλήλους περιπατοῦντες, καί ἐστε σκυθρωποί;
Ἀποκριθεὶς δὲ ὁ εἷς, ᾧ ὄνομα Κλεόπας, εἶπε πρὸς αὐτόν· Σὺ μόνος 18

11. *ἐφάνησαν—ῥήματα α.*] So Lucian Tim. 1. (cited by Wets.) ἅπαντα ταῦτα λῆρος ἤδη ἀναπέφηνε. I have in Recens. Synop. shown that λῆρος is derived from the Anglo Saxon Leepen, as *tale* from Tellen, and that both mean "[something] *told*;" and 2dly, a mere tale, or old saw.

—*ἠπίστουν αὐταῖς.*] Not because they thought they had fabricated the account, but that they considered them as *foolish women*, since, as Thucydides truly observes, vi. 33. οἱ τὰ μὴ πιστὰ δοκοῦντα εἶναι ἀπαγγέλλοντες οὐ μόνον οὐ πείθουσιν, ἀλλὰ καὶ ἄ φ ρ ο ν ε ς δοκοῦσιν εἶναι.

12. *παρακύψας.*] Παρακύπτειν properly signifies to stoop to any thing, and especially to stoop, *look down*, to *look at* any thing; and is usually of those who peep, peer at, or survey any thing attentively. This last is the sense in the present passage: of which I have found an example in Theocr. Id. iii. 7. τοῦτο κατ' ἄντρον παρακύπτοισα.

—*ἀπῆλθε πρὸς ἑ. θ.*] There has been some doubt here raised as to the sense; which will depend upon the *construction*. Πρὸς ἑαυτὸν may be construed either with the *preceding*, ἀπῆλθε, or the *following*, θαυμάζων. Several eminent Commentators, ancient and modern, adopt the *former* mode, adducing several passages from Classical writers, and some from the N. T. But of the latter only one is to the purpose, John xx. 10. ἀπῆλθον οὖν πρὸς ἑαυτοὺς οἱ μαθηταὶ and, at all events, this will only show, that such *may* be the sense, *if the context will permit it*. Yet this it scarcely does; for as to the *sense* which they assign, "he went home to his inn or lodging," it is truly observed by Campb., that "it seems more probable from infra v. 24. and John xx. that Peter did not go *directly* home from the sepulchre, but returned to the place where the Apostles and disciples were assembled." Hence it is better to construe the words with θαυμάζων, as is done by most Expositors, ancient and modern (supported by the authority of all the best ancient Versions and Theophyl.); especially as, from the occurrence of the similar expression διελογίζοντο πρὸς ἑαυτοὺς at xx. 14, it appears to be very suitable to the style of the Evangelist.

13. *δύο ἐξ αὐτῶν.*] These words must be referred to verse 9., where we read ἀπήγγειλαν ταῦτα πάντα τοῖς ἕνδεκα, καὶ πᾶσι τοῖς λοιποῖς. The two persons here mentioned are, with reason, supposed to have been of the number of the Apostles, or at least Seventy disciples. The name of *one* of these persons the Evangelist has recorded; that of the other he has omitted to mention; and has thereby exercised the ingenuity of the Commentators in guessing it; some of whom conjecture *Nathanael*, others, *Bartholomew*, or *Luke himself*.

—*Ἐμμαούς.*] There were *two* places of this name; one a *town*, 160 stadia from Jerusalem; and often mentioned in Josephus, the Books of Maccabees, and the Rabbinical writings; the other (the one here meant) a *village* distant only 70 stadia. These persons probably lived at Emmaus, and were returning thither from the feast of the Passover.

14. *ὡμίλουν πρὸς ἀλλήλ.*] This signification of ὁμ. is rare in the Classical writers, but not unfrequent in the Hellenistic ones.

16. *οἱ δὲ ὀφθαλμοὶ αὐτῶν ἐκρ.*] It is not agreed among the Commentators, whether this *being prevented* proceeded from natural causes, or supernatural ones. The ancients and early moderns take the *latter* view, and attempt to trace the *mode* in which this was effected; adducing several passages of the Classical writers, where a similar effect is ascribed to the influence of some Deity, ex. gr. Soph. Aj. 85. ἐγὼ σκοτώσω βλέφαρα καὶ δεδορκότα. The more recent Commentators ascribe it to *natural* causes, taking the word metaphorically; and refer the hindrance to the inattention of the observers, or to our Lord's being so situated as not to be distinctly seen, as also to the change of apparel mentioned at Mark xvi. 12. In *this* view it is considered as an Oriental and popular mode of expression, importing that they were prevented from recognising, i. e. *failed* to recognise him. But ἐκρατοῦντο, when coupled with διηνοίχθησαν just after, seems to be too strong a term to permit us to suppose aught less than *Divine agency*, on either the body or the mind, or both. Though as there is a marked *economy* in all the preternatural operations of the Deity, it is not for us to pronounce how far that agency *might* be exerted, and how far the natural causes might contribute to the effect in question. Be that as it may, the words ought to be rendered—"their eyes were hindered, that they *did* not see him."

17. *ἀντιβάλλετε.*] The word properly signifies "to toss backwards and forwards," as a ball; but is here used of the reciprocation or interchange of remark in conversing or arguing. So 2 Macc. xi. 3. πρὸς ἑαυτὸν, ἀ., reason with himself. At *καί ἐστε σκυθρωποί*, Kuin. and Bornem. supply τί, *why*, taken from the preceding τίνες.

18. *σὺ μόνος παροικεῖς*, &c.] There has been some difference of opinion as to the exact import of these words. The ancient and earlier modern

παροικεῖς [ἐν] Ἱερουσαλὴμ, καὶ οὐκ ἔγνως τὰ γενόμενα ἐν αὐτῇ ἐν ταῖς
19 ἡμέραις ταύταις; [d] Καὶ εἶπεν αὐτοῖς· Ποῖα; Οἱ δὲ εἶπον αὐτῷ· d Matt. 21. 11. supra 7. 16.
Τὰ περὶ Ἰησοῦ τοῦ Ναζωραίου, ὃς ἐγένετο ἀνὴρ προφήτης, δυνατὸς ἐν John 4. 19. & 6. 14.
20 ἔργῳ καὶ λόγῳ ἐναντίον τοῦ Θεοῦ καὶ παντὸς τοῦ λαοῦ· ὅπως τε
παρέδωκαν αὐτὸν οἱ ἀρχιερεῖς καὶ οἱ ἄρχοντες ἡμῶν εἰς κρίμα θανάτου,
21 καὶ ἐσταύρωσαν αὐτόν. [e] Ἡμεῖς δὲ ἠλπίζομεν ὅτι αὐτός ἐστιν ὁ μέλλων e Acts 1. 6.
λυτροῦσθαι τὸν Ἰσραήλ· ἀλλά γε σὺν πᾶσι τούτοις τρίτην ταύτην ἡμέ-
22 ραν ἄγει σήμερον ἀφ᾽ οὗ ταῦτα ἐγένετο. [f] Ἀλλὰ καὶ γυναῖκές τινες f Matt. 28. 8. Mark 16. 10.
23 ἐξ ἡμῶν ἐξέστησαν ἡμᾶς, γενόμεναι ὄρθριαι ἐπὶ τὸ μνημεῖον· καὶ John 20. 18.
μὴ εὑροῦσαι τὸ σῶμα αὐτοῦ, ἦλθον λέγουσαι καὶ ὀπτασίαν ἀγγέλων
24 ἑωρακέναι, οἳ λέγουσιν αὐτὸν ζῆν. Καὶ ἀπῆλθόν τινες τῶν σὺν ἡμῖν
ἐπὶ τὸ μνημεῖον, καὶ εὗρον οὕτω, καθὼς καὶ αἱ γυναῖκες εἶπον·
25 αὐτὸν δὲ οὐκ εἶδον. Καὶ αὐτὸς εἶπε πρὸς αὐτούς· Ὦ ἀνόητοι καὶ
βραδεῖς τῇ καρδίᾳ τοῦ πιστεύειν ἐπὶ πᾶσιν, οἷς ἐλάλησαν οἱ προ- g Isa. 50. 6. & 53. toto. Phil. 2. 7, &c.
26 φῆται! [g] Οὐχὶ ταῦτα ἔδει παθεῖν τὸν Χριστὸν, καὶ εἰσελθεῖν εἰς τὴν Heb. 12. 2. 1 Pet. 1. 11.

Commentators take the sense to be; "Art thou the only sojourner (or, as others render, 'the only *resident*') in Jerusalem, who art ignorant of these things?" But the best Commentators from Whitby and Wolf downwards, take παροικεῖν in the sense of *being a stranger*, and regard the words as a form of speech applied to those who are ignorant of what is doing around them. Thus the sense will be, "Art thou alone such a stranger in Jerusalem as to be unacquainted with these circumstances? For illustration, Wets. and Kypke adduce several passages of the Classical writers; as Dio Chrys. Or. iii. p. 42. σὺ ἄρα μόνος ἀνήκοος εἶ τούτων, ἃ πάντες ἴσασι.' But I would rather choose to take μόνος for μόνον, and take παροικεῖς for πάροικος εἶς, rendering, "of these things?" i. e. "Art thou [though] but a stranger in Jerusalem, ignorant," &c. The ἐν is omitted in most of the ancient MSS. and the early Edd.; and is cancelled by almost every Editor from Bengel and Wets. to Scholz; but perhaps without good cause; for as there is no example of this signification in the N. T. or the LXX., but many in the best Classical writers, the ἐν would seem to have been suppressed by those ancient *Critics*, who made it their business everywhere to *polish* the style of the N. T.

19. ἀνὴρ προφήτης.] The ἀνὴρ is not, as some imagine, redundant; nor is it, as others suppose, emphatic, and intended as a title of honour; but is merely a vestige of the *verbosity* of primitive times, (thus the idiom is found most in the earliest writers,) when what are now *verbal nouns*, were only *adjectives*, and consequently required ἀνὴρ or some other noun to make them serve for substantives.

— δυνατὸς ἐν ἔργῳ καὶ λόγῳ.] Δυνατὸς properly signifies "having *power*;" but sometimes, *efficacy* or *authority* and influence; and here (as also at Acts vii. 22.) both power and *skill*, or *excellence*. So Thucyd. i. 139. λέγειν τε καὶ πράττειν δυνατώτατος. Here ἔργῳ relates to the *miracles*; and λόγῳ to the *Divine wisdom* of our Lord.

20. ὅπως τε.] Bornem. well remarks that ὅπως τε refers to the οὐκ ἔγνως at v. 18.

21. σὺν πᾶσι.] The σὺν is said to be for ἐπὶ, as often in the Scriptural and Classical writers, like עם for על in Hebrew. But the idiom may better be compared with our adverb *withal*; which was once a *phrase*, i. e. "with all this," or these things. Indeed σύμπασι occurs, in this very sense in Dionys. Hal. i. 59. Ἀλλά γε, just before, is noted by Bornem. as a very rare formula, and to be rendered, *at nimirum*, or *at sane*.

— τρίτην — ἄγει σήμερον] There is something anomalous in this phraseology, which has perplexed the Commentators. Some think that there is a Nominative (as Θεὸς, οὐρανὸς, or ἥλιος) understood. Others suppose ἄγει put for ἄγεται, taken impersonally. Others, again, take σήμερον as a *Nomin.* But all these methods are more or less objectionable. There is more to approve in the method pursued by Beza, Kypke, Middl., and others; who supply Ἰησοῦς, by an idiom, frequent in the best writers; whereby, when it is intended to show that a thing has been done on a certain day, they ascribe what denotes the *day* to the *person*? *Examples* are, indeed, said by Kuin. to be wanting. But examples of the phrase ἄγειν ἡμέραν (like the Latin *agere diem*) are adduced by Wets., and of the idiom in question by the other Commentators; and it would be unreasonable to demand examples of the *two conjoined*.

22. ἐξέστησαν] "have thrown us into amazement." This *active* sense is also found in Acts viii. 9. There is an ellipsis of τοῦ νοῦ. Ὄρθριαι is adject. for adverb, as often, especially in adjectives of *time*, both in Greek and Latin.

25. ἀνόητοι.] Doddr. and Campb. object to the Comm. Vers. "*fools*," and render "*thoughtless*." And indeed that ἀνόητος and similar terms (as μωρὸς and μάταιος) are often in Greek and in all languages used in a milder sense is certain. If *foolish* be thought too harsh, we may render *misjudging*. The word, indeed, denotes either one who *has* not, or who *uses* not the faculty of reason, (the νοῦν) or *uses it not aright*. See Tittm. de Synon. p. 59.

— καὶ βραδεῖς τῇ καρδίᾳ.] Βραδὺς is often opposed to ἀγχίνους, *ready witted*, and is preserved in the Latin *bardus*, from the Æolic βαρδύς. But as here τῇ καρδίᾳ is added, it cannot denote *stupid*, but rather *sluggishly disposed*, *indisposed*; and τοῦ πιστεύειν is for εἰς τὸ πιστεύειν. So James i. 19. βραδὺς εἰς τὸ λαλῆσαι, β. εἰς τὴν ὀργήν.

h Gen. 3. 15. & 22. 18. & 26. 4. & 49. 10. Ps. 16. 8, 9, 10. & 22. toto. & 132. 11. Dan. 9. 24, &c.
i Gen. 19. 3. Acts 16. 15. Heb. 13. 2.

δόξαν αὐτοῦ; [h] Καὶ ἀρξάμενος ἀπὸ Μωϋσέως καὶ ἀπὸ πάντων τῶν 27
προφητῶν, διηρμήνευεν αὐτοῖς ἐν πάσαις ταῖς γραφαῖς τὰ περὶ ἑαυτοῦ. Καὶ ἤγγισαν εἰς τὴν κώμην οὗ ἐπορεύοντο· καὶ αὐτὸς προσε- 28
ποιεῖτο πορρωτέρω πορεύεσθαι. [i] Καὶ παρεβιάσαντο αὐτὸν, λέγοντες· 29
Μεῖνον μεθ᾽ ἡμῶν, ὅτι πρὸς ἑσπέραν ἐστὶ, καὶ κέκλικεν ἡ ἡμέρα. καὶ
εἰσῆλθε τοῦ μεῖναι σὺν αὐτοῖς. Καὶ ἐγένετο, ἐν τῷ κατακλιθῆναι αὐ- 30
τὸν μετ᾽ αὐτῶν, λαβὼν τὸν ἄρτον εὐλόγησε, καὶ κλάσας ἐπεδίδου αὐτοῖς.
Αὐτῶν δὲ διηνοίχθησαν οἱ ὀφθαλμοὶ, καὶ ἐπέγνωσαν αὐτόν· καὶ αὐτὸς 31
ἄφαντος ἐγένετο ἀπ᾽ αὐτῶν. Καὶ εἶπον πρὸς ἀλλήλους· Οὐχὶ ἡ καρδία 32
ἡμῶν καιομένη ἦν ἐν ἡμῖν, ὡς ἐλάλει ἡμῖν ἐν τῇ ὁδῷ, καὶ ὡς διήνοιγεν
ἡμῖν τὰς γραφάς; Καὶ ἀναστάντες αὐτῇ τῇ ὥρᾳ, ὑπέστρεψαν εἰς Ἰε- 33
ρουσαλὴμ, καὶ εὗρον συνηθροισμένους τοὺς ἕνδεκα καὶ τοὺς σὺν αὐτοῖς,
k 1 Cor. 15. 5. [k] λέγοντας· Ὅτι ἠγέρθη ὁ κύριος ὄντως, καὶ ὤφθη Σίμωνι· καὶ 34
αὐτοὶ ἐξηγοῦντο τὰ ἐν τῇ ὁδῷ, καὶ ὡς ἐγνώσθη αὐτοῖς ἐν τῇ κλάσει 35
τοῦ ἄρτου.

l Mark 16. 14. John. 20. 19. [l] Ταῦτα δὲ αὐτῶν λαλούντων, αὐτὸς ὁ Ἰησοῦς ἔστη ἐν μέσῳ αὐτῶν, 36
καὶ λέγει αὐτοῖς· Εἰρήνη ὑμῖν! πτοηθέντες δὲ καὶ ἔμφοβοι γενόμενοι 37

27. ἀρξάμενος ἀπὸ Μ.] Even in the Books of Moses there are *prophecies*, as, for instance, those respecting Esau and Dan, &c. There are also *types* and *symbols*, as of the serpent erected by Moses; and also some connected with the affairs of David, the explanation of which Christ communicated to the Apostles, and the Apostles to us. It seems probable, too, that a similar mystical explication of other prophecies was delivered by Christ, or by the Holy Spirit, and handed down by tradition in the Church. — (Grot.)

28. προσεποιεῖτο πορρωτέρω π.] Προσποιεῖσθαι signifies, "properly to take to oneself, make one's own;" and, in a metaphorical sense, to "*make as though*;" a sense occurring both in the Scriptural (as 1 Sam. xxi. 13. 2 Sam. xiii. 5.) and the Classical writers. See Note on Mark vi. 48. Euthym. well explains it ἐσχηματίζετο, "he made a motion as though." However, there is no ground for founding any charge of *dissimulation* against our Lord; for he would really have gone on, had he not been detained by their *friendly importunity*; which is all that παρεβιάσαντο imports. On which idiom see Note on Matt. xiv. 22. and Mark xiv. 23.

29. πρὸς ἑσπέραν.] Πρὸς with nouns of time denotes the proximity of it, (answering to our *towards*). Thucyd. iv. 135. πρὸς ἔαρ ἤδη. (Wets.)

30. κλάσας α.] This was contrary to the custom of guests; that office belonging to the *host* (as we find from Xenoph., Hom., and Apuleius), except when the host, out of respect, chose to resign it to the guest. (Grot. and Pric.)

31. διηνοίχθησαν οἱ ὀφθαλμοί.] On the hindrance before adverted to being removed, and on a nearer approach, they recognised Christ. See Note supra ver. 16.

— ἄφαντος ἐγένετο ἀ. α.] There has been some difference of opinion as to the exact sense of these words. The best Commentators are, however, agreed that ἄφαντος ἐγένετο ἀ. α. must be equivalent to ἠφανίσθη ἀπ᾽ αὐτῶν; and that we are not to suppose that our Lord vanished as a *spectre* might be imagined to do. Grot., who discusses the *mode* of our Lord's disappearance, confesses that of the *three* ways in which it may have happened, *two* are easier of comprehension, but the third not *impossible*. And he thinks it better, with Basil, not to scrutinize *the how*. A prudence certainly much to be commended, but which here may be thought unnecessary; since, from the passages of the Classical writers adduced by Abresch and Wets. (see also Recens. Synop.) none can doubt but that the sense simply is, "he suddenly or abrubtly withdrew from their company." See more in my Note on Thucyd. viii. 38. ἀποπλέων — ἀφανίζεται. In the whole of the passages adduced there and in Recens. Synop. all that is implied by this use of ἀφανίζεσθαι, or the synonymous expressions ἄφαντος γίνεσθαι, &c. is a notion of *suddenness* or *abruptness* in the action of the verb.

32. καρδία ἡμῶν καιομένη.] Kypke observes that καίεσθαι is often used of the more violent emotions, especially joy; and truly remarks, that the affection here meant was a compound feeling; made up partly of *respectful affection* towards one who had so ably expounded the oracles of the Prophets; of *desire* to longer enjoy his society and instruction; of *joy* — since they anxiously longed that what he had taught them of the resurrection of the Messiah might prove true, and (though with some fluctuation of mind) they rejoiced in the anticipation of that truth.

36. Ἰησοῦς ἔστη ἐν μέσῳ αὐτῶν.] John adds ὀψίας ἐν τῇ ἡμέρᾳ ἐκείνῃ, καὶ θυρῶν κεκλεισμένων, from which words many have inferred that Jesus entered the closed doors without stirring them on their hinges. But thus the words ought to have been διὰ τῶν θυρῶν κεκλεισμένων. Indeed, the last words have solely a reference to the preceding διὰ φόβον τῶν Ἰουδαίων. But (say some) has not John noted that the doors were opened? True: but to such minutiæ as this (namely, whether Jesus himself opened the door, or ordered it to be opened) the Evangelists are not accustomed to descend. Besides, had the disciples from Emmaus also entered by the closed doors? The word ἔστη [which is for ἐπέστη] indicates that Jesus appeared suddenly and unexpectedly. (Kuin.)

37. πτοηθέντες.] This term and ἔμφοβος are sy-

38 ἐδόκουν πνεῦμα θεωρεῖν. Καὶ εἶπεν αὐτοῖς· Τί τεταραγμένοι ἐστέ;
39 καὶ διατί διαλογισμοὶ ἀναβαίνουσιν ἐν ταῖς καρδίαις ὑμῶν; [m] Ἴδετε [m] John 20. 20, 27.
τὰς χεῖράς μου καὶ τοὺς πόδας μου, ὅτι αὐτὸς ἐγώ εἰμι· ψηλαφή-
σατέ με καὶ ἴδετε· ὅτι πνεῦμα σάρκα καὶ ὀστέα οὐκ ἔχει, καθὼς
40 ἐμὲ θεωρεῖτε ἔχοντα. Καὶ τοῦτο εἰπὼν ἐπέδειξεν αὐτοῖς τὰς χεῖρας καὶ
41 τοὺς πόδας. [n] Ἔτι δὲ ἀπιστούντων αὐτῶν ἀπὸ τῆς χαρᾶς, καὶ θαυ- [n] John 21. 10.
42 μαζόντων, εἶπεν αὐτοῖς· Ἔχετέ τι βρώσιμον ἐνθάδε; Οἱ δὲ ἐπέ-
43 δωκαν αὐτῷ ἰχθύος ὀπτοῦ μέρος, καὶ ἀπὸ μελισσίου κηρίου· καὶ
44 λαβὼν ἐνώπιον αὐτῶν ἔφαγεν. [o] Εἶπε δὲ αὐτοῖς· Οὗτοι οἱ λόγοι οὓς [o] Matt. 16. 21. & 17. 22.
ἐλάλησα πρὸς ὑμᾶς ἔτι ὢν σὺν ὑμῖν, ὅτι δεῖ πληρωθῆναι πάντα τὰ & 20. 18. Mark 8. 31.
γεγραμμένα ἐν τῷ νόμῳ Μωϋσέως καὶ Προφήταις καὶ Ψαλμοῖς περὶ & 9. 31. & 10. 33. supra. 9. 22.
45 ἐμοῦ. Τότε διήνοιξεν αὐτῶν τὸν νοῦν, τοῦ συνιέναι τὰς γραφάς· [p] καὶ & 18. 31. & 24. 6.
46 εἶπεν αὐτοῖς· Ὅτι οὕτω γέγραπται, καὶ οὕτως ἔδει παθεῖν τὸν Χρι- [p] Supra v. 26. Psal. 22. 7. Acts 17. 3.
47 στὸν, καὶ ἀναστῆναι ἐκ νεκρῶν τῇ τρίτῃ ἡμέρᾳ, [q] καὶ κηρυχθῆναι ἐπὶ [q] Acts 13. 38. 1 John 2. 12.
τῷ ὀνόματι αὐτοῦ μετάνοιαν καὶ ἄφεσιν ἁμαρτιῶν εἰς πάντα τὰ ἔθνη,
48 ἀρξάμενον ἀπὸ Ἱερουσαλήμ. [r] Ὑμεῖς δέ ἐστε μάρτυρες τούτων. [s] Καὶ [r] Job. 15. 27.
49 ἰδοὺ, ἐγὼ ἀποστέλλω τὴν ἐπαγγελίαν τοῦ πατρός μου ἐφ᾽ ὑμᾶς· ὑμεῖς [s] John 14. 26. & 15. 26.
δὲ καθίσατε ἐν τῇ πόλει Ἱερουσαλὴμ, ἕως οὗ ἐνδύσησθε δύναμιν ἐξ & 16. 7. Acts 1. 4. & 2. toto.
ὕψους.
50 [t] Ἐξήγαγε δὲ αὐτοὺς ἔξω ἕως εἰς Βηθανίαν· καὶ ἐπάρας τὰς χεῖρας [t] Acts 1. 12.

nonymous, but joined for emphasis. On the Jewish notions of spirits, see Rec. Syn. It may be added that our Lord meant not to countenance those notions, but to show his hearers that, according to their *own* notions of spirits, he could not be one.

38. *διαλογισμοὶ ἀναβαίνουσι.*] Of this use of *ἀναβαίνειν* and the Latin *surgere* examples are adduced by Wets., which show that it is not a Hebraism. It is found in all languages.

39. *πνεῦμα — οὐκ ἔχει.*] This was probably spoken agreeably to the general opinion of all nations. See the Note of Grot. and the numerous Classical citations adduced by Wets., many of which (together with others of my own) may be seen in Recens. Synop.

41. *ἀπιστούντων αὐτῶν ἀπὸ τῆς χ.*] This is founded in nature. The disciples yet *doubted*; as is sometimes the case on the occurrence of events very felicitous, which happen suddenly and unexpectedly. We think the news too good to be believed, and fancy we are dreaming. So Ovid. Tarda solet magnis rebus inesse fides.

42. *ἀπὸ μελισσίου κηρίου.*] A frequent food with the ancients, especially those who studied abstemiousness of diet.

44. *οὗτοι οἱ λόγοι* (scil. *εἰσὶ*) *οὓς ἐλ.* &c.] The sense is, "The words uttered by me, when I was with you, imported that all things written of me (my death, burial, and resurrection) should be fulfilled." The *Psalms* are put for the *Hagiographia*, as being the chief book of that division of the O. T. Τὰ γεγρ. "which *are* written."

45. *διήνοιξεν α. τὸν ν.*] This is very distinct in sense from the *explanation of the Scriptures* mentioned supra ver. 27., and imports an enlightening of the mind by assisting the natural powers; and it may include *inclining* and *disposing* the mind to *attend* to the knowledge in question. So Acts xvi. 14. ὁ Κύριος διήνοιξε τὴν καρδίαν προσέχειν τοῖς λαλουμένοις ὑπὸ Π. Plut., cited by Wets., says of the reading of the Poets: προσανοίγει καὶ προσκλίνει τὴν τοῦ νέου ψυχὴν φιλοσοφίας λόγοις.

47. *καὶ κηρυχθῆναι*, &c.] Supply δεῖ from the ἔδει foregoing.

— *ἀρξάμενον ἀπὸ Ἰ.*] Participles, passive or neuter, are sometimes (as here) put impersonally in the neuter gender. The Accus. is used instead of a Genit. of consequence. Thus the sense is "the beginning being made." So Philostr. Epist. Apoll. 3. Ἐπῆλθες ἔθνη — ἀπὸ Συρίας ἀρξάμενος. That the commencement should be made from Jerusalem was according to a sort of ancient prerogative of the Holy city.

48. *τούτων*] Namely (says Whitby) of the events of the life, death, and especially *resurrection* of Christ, as an unequivocal proof of his Divine mission.

49. *ἐπαγγελίαν*] i. e. the thing promised, namely, the gift of the Holy Spirit. Ἐξ ὕψους, i. e. ἐξ οὐρανοῦ, which sense confirms Horne Tooke's derivation of *heaven*, as participle past of heafan to *heave*, *raise*. So the Greek οὐρανὸς comes from ὄρω, to raise.

— *ἐνδύσησθε.*] Ἐνδύεσθαι answers to the Heb. לבש and the Latin *induere*; but, like them, is, both in the Classical and Scriptural writers, used in the sense *to be endued*; i. e. completely furnished with any power; for though περιβάλλεσθαι and ἐνδύεσθαι be used promiscuously in the N. T., yet properly, the former signifies to cast a robe about one, the latter to be involved in a coat or some article of dress; which implies a fully clothing the part, or whole of the body. On this omission of ἂν with the Conjunctive, and on the force in general when expressed, see the masterly Dissertation by Hermann. subjoined to the new edition of Steph. Thes.

50. *ἐξήγαγε — ἔξω.*] That there is here no *ple-*

u Mark 16. 19. Acts 1. 9.

αὐτοῦ εὐλόγησεν αὐτούς. [u] Καὶ ἐγένετο, ἐν τῷ εὐλογεῖν αὐτὸν αὐτοὺς, 51
διέστη ἀπ' αὐτῶν, καὶ ἀνεφέρετο εἰς τὸν οὐρανόν. Καὶ αὐτοὶ προσ- 52
κυνήσαντες αὐτὸν, ὑπέστρεψαν εἰς Ἱερουσαλὴμ μετὰ χαρᾶς μεγάλης·
καὶ ἦσαν διαπαντὸς ἐν τῷ ἱερῷ, αἰνοῦντες καὶ εὐλογοῦντες τὸν Θεόν. 53
ἀμήν.

onasm (as Kuin. fancied), has been shown by Bornem., who adduces several examples from the Classics. On the seeming discrepancy, see Towns.

52. *προσκυνήσαντες αὐτόν.*] The term here must denote the *performance of religious worship*, now first rendered to Christ by the Apostles, and paid to him even though absent and invisible; a decisive proof of the opinion they entertained of his Divinity.

ΤΟ ΚΑΤΑ ΙΩΑΝΝΗΝ

ΕΥΑΓΓΕΛΙΟΝ.

---

1 I. [y] Ἐν ἀρχῇ ἦν ὁ Λόγος, καὶ ὁ Λόγος ἦν πρὸς τὸν Θεὸν, καὶ y 1 John 1. 1, 2. Rev. 19. 13.
2 3 Θεὸς ἦν ὁ Λόγος. Οὗτος ἦν ἐν ἀρχῇ πρὸς τὸν Θεόν. [z] Πάντα δι' infra 10. 28, 30. z Eph. 3. 9.

Of all the Gospels, this may be considered the most important, both as regards the subjects there treated of, and the doctrines thence to be deduced. In no other have we the real person of the Redeemer so fully exhibited. Insomuch that it was called by the Fathers *the Spiritual Volume, the Pectus Christi.* While the other Evangelists chiefly occupy themselves in narrating the *events* which marked our Lord's earthly course, St. John applies himself, almost exclusively, to record the *discourses* of Christ; and whatever, either of words or deeds, was calculated to show forth His Divine majesty and glory, His Divine origin, the nature of the office committed to him by the Father, and the efficacy of his death as an atonement for the sins of the world. The other Evangelists have, indeed, inculcated this fundamental doctrine; but only occasionally and *incidentally;* John professedly and *systematically.* In fact, the purpose of St. John in writing this Gospel differed materially from that of the other Evangelists. It was not to write a *history of the life of Christ*, but to select some of the most remarkable parts of his personal history, in order thereby to introduce some of the most important of his *discourses*, in which he spoke of himself, his person, and his office: intending thereby to demonstrate his *divine nature*, to shew the excellency of his office, and to vindicate the truth against the Jews and Judaizing Christians of those times, and sceptical persons of every age. — who, whether from the influence of error or deep-rooted prejudice, should entertain notions derogatory to the honour of the Saviour. This the Evangelist has done; not by resorting to *subtilty of argument*, but by stating the *evidence of facts*, and urging the authority of our Lord himself. As, then, St. John did not intend to write the *life* of Christ, he commences, not with his birth by the Virgin Mary, but goes back beyond even the creation of the universe, and teaches that our Saviour existed *before that period.* He commences with a PROEME (justly called the *Golden* Proeme), the sum and substance of which, as that is of the whole Gospel, is; that the promised Messiah *existed before* the beginning of the world *with God*, and WAS GOD; that He was Creator of the universe, but was made man, and lived among men, and by words and works manifested himself to be the *Son of God* — the Saviour of mankind. After adverting to the weighty testimony of John the Baptist, and recording the commencing miracles wrought in Cana of Galilee and the Temple of Jerusalem, it seems to have been the intent of the Evangelist to furnish his readers with some *specimens of the Discourses of Christ*, in order thence to establish and illustrate the positions laid down in the Preface. For in each year of Christ's ministry he has narrated certain actions and *miracles*, and recorded certain *discourses* in which our Saviour spoke of his person and office. These *actions* he seems to have related solely with a view to the *discourses* which gave rise to them. As to the *miracles*, it was not (see xx. 31.) his intention to accumulate as many instances as possible of the miraculous powers exerted by Christ; but only those which were best adapted to the purpose of his Gospel. The *later* discourses of our Lord, and the history of his passion, death, and resurrection, St. John has more fully detailed, both that Christians might be assured of the *reality* of his *death* (so great being the efficacy thereof) and that they might be convinced of his *resurrection* and the glory into which, after death, he was received.

To advert to the personal history of the Evangelist himself, suffice it to say that, as being the son of a respectable Master Fisherman, he must have had a tolerable education; and although without pretensions to learning properly so called, could not be termed *illiterate.* He and his brother James had probably received a careful *religious education;* had been well grounded in the Scriptures, if not in the original, yet in the Syro-Chaldee Version, or Paraphrase, and in the Sept.; and were probably not wholly unversed in the Rabbinical learning of the day. From the time that they received their immediate call from Christ,

Col. 1. 17.
Heb. 1. 2.
infra 5. 26.
& 8. 12.
& 9. 5.
& 12. 46.
1 John 5. 11.
a Infra. 3. 19.

αὐτοῦ ἐγένετο, καὶ χωρὶς αὐτοῦ ἐγένετο οὐδὲ ἓν ὃ γέγονεν. Ἐν αὐτῷ 4
ζωὴ ἦν, καὶ ἡ ζωὴ ἦν τὸ φῶς τῶν ἀνθρώπων. ᵃ καὶ τὸ φῶς ἐν τῇ 5
σκοτίᾳ φαίνει, καὶ ἡ σκοτία αὐτὸ οὐ κατέλαβεν.

they became first his *disciples*, then his *constant attendants*, and lastly were appointed with others *as Apostles*. With respect to the *character* and *disposition* of the Evangelist, we have every reason to think that it was at once frank and amiable, uniting suavity with firmness. Hence he became the object of our Lord's peculiar regard and confidence, which he repaid by the most sincere attachment to his Master.

The *genuineness* of the present Gospel is unquestionable; not only as attested by the strongest internal evidence (namely, in the style and manner, the circumstantiality of its details, and the evident marks of the writer's having been an eye-witness of much that he relates), but the strongest *external* evidence, in an unbroken chain of testimonies from writers in the Apostolical age down to that of Epiphanius, Chrys., and Jerome. It was, indeed, never disputed, until lately, by *Bretschneider;* whose doubts, however, have been, as he confesses, entirely removed by the very able writers who came forward to maintain the authenticity of the Gospel. On the genuineness of a particular part of it, namely, the narrative of the woman taken in adultery, ch. viii. 1—11. and also of ch. xxi., see the Notes in loc.

To advert to the *contents* of this Gospel, the Evangelist has a style and manner peculiar to himself, uniting plainness of diction with sublimity of character—not such as results from art, but is engendered by magnitude of conception united with a natural simplicity of expression, and which, coming *from* the heart, speaks *to* the heart. This Gospel is, however, by no means without its difficulties, which may be ascribed, 1. to the abstruseness of the subjects there treated on; 2dly, to the dark cast and manner of the writer; 3dly, to the strongly Hebraic character of the style; and that not only in the acceptation of words, (some of which are peculiar to himself) but in the structure of his sentences, and especially in the use of the Tenses, where *Enallage* of Past, Present, and Future, is not unfrequent. Hence, after all the labor which has been so profusely bestowed upon it by learned and pious Expositors (of whom the most distinguished are Calvin, Beza, Grot., Lampe, Tittm., Kuin., and Tholuck), yet there is not any Book of the N. T. of which the interpretation has been so uncertain and debateable. Accordingly, the Editor of the present work has found it necessary to use every exertion in his power to vanquish the difficulties, and place the interpretation, in some measure, on the same footing of certainty, or something approaching to it, as in the other Gospels.

But to consider the remaining circumstances connected with this Gospel, namely, as to the *place where*, and *time when* it was written: the unanimous voice of antiquity testifies that the *place* was *Ephesus*. And to this all the moderns readily assent. On *the time*, however, considerable difference of opinion exists. It has been the general sentiment, both of ancient and modern inquirers, that it was published about *the close of the first century*. While some of those who are best able to judge of such matters (as Lampe, Lardner, Owen, Tittm., and Kuin.), suppose it to have been written before the destruction of Jerusalem; though they differ as to the exact date. The *former* opinion indeed, is alleged to be most *agreeable to ancient authority*. Yet the testimonies adduced are almost entirely from writers (such as Epiphanius, Theodoret, and Jerome) of a period too far remote from the Apostolic age to have much weight. In fact, the only ancient authority alleged is Irenæus ap. Euseb. Eccl. Hist. v. 8. (where, however, it is merely said that John wrote *after* the other Evangelists) and another passage cited from him by Lardner vi. 187, from which it has been inferred, but *very precariously*, that this Gospel was written *long after* the destruction of Jerusalem. Certainly the evidence is not such as to establish the point in question. And the opinion itself seems to have originated in the notion, prevalent both in ancient and modern times (but destroyed by Tittman, in a masterly Dissertation, *de Vestigiis Gnost. in Evang. Joan. frustra quæsitis)*, that this Gospel was written for the purpose of confuting the Heresies of the Gnostics and others as to the person of Christ. Indeed, if we inquire what *evidence* is alleged for that opinion, several expressions in the *Proeme* are pointed out, and a few others occurring up and down in the Gospel. Yet these cannot, without the aid of strong imaggination, be thought to give any great evidence: and Expositors best acquainted with the contents of this Gospel (as Calvin, Lampe, Tittman, Kuinoel, Tholuck, and Bp. Blomfield in his Lectures) are decidedly of opinion that the notion is unfounded, and that (in the words of Bp. Blomfield) "the design of St. John in writing this Gospel was of a *general nature*, namely to convey to the Christian world just notions of the real nature, character, and office of that great Teacher who came to instruct and to redeem mankind." So long, however, as the opinion prevailed, that the Gospel was a *polemical one*, and written to confute heresies, men were obliged to suppose *as late* a date as the life of the Evangelist would permit, for the publication of the Gospel; since the heresies in question were not prevalent before the latter end of the first century.

To advert to another opinion almost universal, that St. John wrote to supply the deficiencies and omissions of the former Evangelists—for this there is, I apprehend, no foundation in the *Gospel itself*. And when it is attempted to unite this notion with the *late date*, the inconsistency is surely great; for if the date were what those writers allege, and if St. John wrote to supply certain deficiencies in the former Gospels, why are so many things unaccountably *omitted?* as, for instance, the remarkable fulfilment of our Lord's prophecies respecting the destruction of Jerusalem; which would have tended in the highest degree to confirm whatever the Evangelist intends to prove. Moreover, if St. John meant, as *they* say, to supply the omissions and *confirm the authority* of the preceding, is it likely, that he would have suffered 30 or 40 years to elapse without doing either one or the other. Those, indeed, who contend for a late date, ground them not only on *external* testimony, but *internal evidence*, namely in the *contents* of the Gospel. The Evangelist, they allege, considers those whom he is addressing as little

6 [b] Ἐγένετο ἄνθρωπος ἀπεσταλμένος παρὰ Θεοῦ· ὄνομα αὐτῷ Ἰωάν- b Matt. 3. 1. Mar. 1. 2, &c.
7 νης. οὗτος ἦλθεν εἰς μαρτυρίαν, ἵνα μαρτυρήσῃ περὶ τοῦ φωτός, ἵνα Luke 3. 3. & 7. 27. Acts 13. 24.

acquainted with Jewish customs and names; since he gives various explanations even more frequently than St. Mark and St. Luke. The reason of which, they think, was, that, at the time when St. John wrote, many more Gentiles had been converted; and thus it became necessary to explain several circumstances which required no explanation while the Jewish Polity was in existence. These arguments, however, are rather specious than solid. For the very same reasons, in nearly the same degree, might exist 28 or 29 years earlier. Upon the whole, it should seem that there is no conclusive evidence adduced for the *late* date in question. On the other hand, many arguments are urged too far in favour of a date before the destruction of Jerusalem. Suffice it to say, that the arguments in general, though not all of equal weight, yet overbalance those on the contrary side. To advert to a few of both — Lampe, Tittm., and others appeal to ch. v. 2. "there is at Jerusalem by the sheep market, a pool," &c. as a proof that this gospel must have been written before the destruction of Jerusalem; since it recognises the city *as in being* when the words were written. This others attempt to set aside, by remarking, that writers "do not weigh their words so exactly;" and that "the Present there may be put for the Past tense." But the *former* is a frivolous excuse; and as to the *latter*, such a confusion of tenses cannot be admitted in a *narrative*. And when it is suggested that Jerusalem *might*, during a period of 26 or 27 years, have risen from its ruins — yet of that there is no sort of historical evidence; while to its *utter* and total destruction Josephus bears testimony in his Bell. vii. 1. where he says that the whole city was so completely *destroyed and dug up*, ὥστε μηδὲ πώποτ' οἰκισθῆναι πίστιν ἂν ἔτι παρασχεῖν τοῖς προσελθοῦσι. And if, in the course of those, a few houses might have been erected, yet surely not so as to be called a city, and have its streets designated by names. Nor are there wanting, in addition to the above strong *internal* arguments adduced by the Commentators, who maintain the publication *before the destruction of Jerusalem*; which are, however, closely connected with the question as to the *main purpose* of the Evangelist, which, if it was, as it should seem, *general*, evidently points to a date far earlier than the close of the first century. With respect to the above two points, the *date* and the *design* of the Gospel, it appears *most* probable, that it was published not very long after St. John had gone to reside at Ephesus, and only a short period before the destruction of Jerusalem — say A. D. 69. John had probably left Judæa four or five years before, when the troubles were beginning, which ended in the destruction of the Jewish state. Had, indeed, St. John written so late as the close of the first century, he would surely have done *more* towards repressing the heresies of the Gnostics, Cerinthians, Nicolaitans, and others, than barely employ a few expressions intended to repress their dogmas; since in the Apocalypse he has censured them *pointedly, openly*, and *by name*. If, however, the expressions in question should appear to be such as to imply a *settled purpose* in the writer, we have only to suppose that, *together with* the above-mentioned *general* design, there was united a *particular* one, — namely, to encounter those heretical notions, which probably were even then starting up like weeds in the rising corn. And although it cannot be proved that St. John wrote for the *purpose* of supplying the omissions of his predecessors, yet, as he *has*, in some measure, done so, by the insertion of certain particulars, not required by his principal design — we may say that he intended his Gospel to be, in *some* degree, supplementary to, and consequently confirmatory of, theirs.

I. 1. et seqq. On this noble Proeme (which Augustin de Civ. D. x. 29. tells us a Platonic Philosopher said ought to be written in letters of gold, and hung up in all the churches) see an erudite Dissertation of C. Vitringa T. ii. p. 122 — 156.

— ἐν ἀρχῇ] scil. τοῦ κόσμου. The expression answers to the Heb. בראשית, in Gen. i. 1. which the Evangelist seems to have had in mind. On account of the ἦν many Commentators explain the phrase to mean *before* the creation of the world; referring for examples of this sense of ἐν ἀρχῇ to John xvii. 5. Eph. i. 4. and Prov. viii. 23, where it is more exactly defined by the preceding πρὸ τοῦ αἰῶνος, and the following πρὸ τοῦ τὴν γῆν ποιῆσαι. But neither in those passages, nor in the one before us, has ἐν *properly* this sense; nor can it ever have it. It is only *implied* from the context. For what was existing *at* the creation of the world must have existed *before* it. By ἀρχὴ is here meant the origin of all things; and ἐν ἀρχῇ is for ἐπ' ἀρχῆς, and the expression is evidently meant to designate *eternity*. Thus it is by Nonnus expressed by ἄχρονος, *unconnected with time*.

— ἦν ὁ Λόγος.] It is impossible, within the limits of a work of this nature, to do any sort of justice to the important, but most intricate subject of the Logos. I must therefore content myself with referring the reader to my Dissertation in Recens. Synop., also to Tittman, p. 27 — 29. and Townsend N. T. Chron. p. 7. seqq. also Dr. Burton's Bampton Lectures, p. 212 — 24. Whatever may be the source from whence St. John borrowed this term, all the best informed inquirers are agreed (contrary to the Unitarians) that it designates a real subsisting *Being*, and not an *attribute*, — as Wisdom or Reason. Indeed, the personality of the Logos is manifest from the whole of the Proeme.

The reader may consult the summary by Vitringa or Townsend on the substance of the sense contained in this Proem, and the Gnostical heresies which each clause has been *supposed* to encounter.

— πρὸς τὸν Θεόν.] The phrase εἶναι πρὸς τὸν Θεὸν denotes close union and intimate society, and, in the present context, compared with 17, 5. and 1 John i. 1, cannot be thought to mean less than *communion of the Divine nature*, and participation of the Divine glory and majesty, implying a community also of *actions* and *counsels*. This assertion is repeated in the next verse; yet, as Tittm. observes, "not by a Hebrew pleonasm, but in order to more fully explain what is meant by this εἶναι πρὸς τὸν Θεόν, and to shew *how* the Lord used and evinced his majesty, and the Divine power which he had with the Father; and thus to declare his Divine dignity by a new argument."

— καὶ Θεὸς ἦν ὁ Λόγος.] The sense is clearly

c Infra. 8. 12. & 8. 12. & 9. 5. & 12. 46.

πάντες πιστεύσωσι δι᾽ αὐτοῦ. Οὐκ ἦν ἐκεῖνος τὸ φῶς, ἀλλ᾽ ἵνα μαρ- 8
τυρήσῃ περὶ τοῦ φωτός. [c] Ἦν τὸ φῶς τὸ ἀληθινὸν, ὃ φωτίζει πάντα 9

"and the Logos was God." Ὁ Λόγος being the *subject*, and Θεὸς the *predicate*, as in John iv. 24. Πνεῦμα ὁ Θεὸς. and iv. 8. ὁ Θεὸς ἀγάπη ἐστιν. The temerity of Crellius, who, to destroy this irrefragable testimony to the Godhead of Jesus Christ, would alter Θεὸς to Θεοῦ, met with well merited chastisement from Beng. and Wets. Some later Socinians have attempted to compass the same end, by maintaining that as Θεὸς has not the Article, it should be taken in a lower sense, to denote *a* God. But that sophism has been completely refuted by Beng., Campb., Middlet., and Kuin.; the last of whom has proved that, in the present construction, the Article *could* not have been used without producing a position as little accordant with the *Socinian* as with the Trinitarian hypothesis. This criticism is confirmed by the learned Professor Bournoff in his excellent Greek Grammar (in French). His Canon of the Article in question is thus: "En Grec, comme en Français, c'est le nom précédé de l'article qui est le sujet; l'autre est l'attribut. Ex. gr. ἡ ἀρέτη πλοῦτός ἐστι."

3. πάντα — ἐγένετο.] By πάντα is meant *all things in the world* — the *universe*. Ἐγένετο is for ἐκτίζετο, as the usus loquendi permits, and the context requires. See Ps. cxlviii. 33. Many Commentators take διὰ as denoting the *instrumental cause*, as in Hebr. i. 2. But there is no reason to abandon the opinion of almost all the ancient, and the most eminent modern Interpreters, that it denotes the *efficient* and *principal* cause, as in Rom. xi. 36. 1 Cor. i. 9. Gal. i. 1. and often elsewhere. As to the passage of Hebrews, it is of quite a different nature to this of St. John; since in the latter only *one* agent is spoken of, but in the other *two* agents are adverted to. Thus the Logos is described as being "very God" and Creator of the universe; who, on account of his communion with the Divine nature, hath an equal power with the Father; and by his co-operation with the Father, created the world.

The next words, καὶ χωρὶς — γέγονεν, are usually explained as yielding the same sentiment with the foregoing clause; the same thing being expressed both by affirmation and by negation, of which see many examples in Recens. Synop. But *here* we have *not* the *same thing* expressed; but a much stronger sentiment. Even the *dialysis* οὐδὲ ἓν has an intensive force. Indeed Tittm. would understand the words of the *preservation* and *governance* of what had been created.

Here 4 MSS., 3 inferior Versions, and many of the Fathers (chiefly Latin) connect the words ὃ γέγονεν with the sentence following: and this has been adopted by Dr. Burton. But I have not thought proper to follow his example, 1. because *all* the other MSS., all the Versions of any account, and the most judicious of the Fathers (as Chrys., Epiphan., Theophyl., Euthym., Cyprian, Arnob., and Jerome) adhere to the received construction; and, 2. because if, with the ancient Interpreters, we explain, "omne quod creatum est per eum vitam accepit," we have a sense which involves a considerable tautology, and moreover cannot be extracted from the words without violence. And if, with Wets. and Dr. Burton, we suppose the sense to be "*the thing which was made* (i. e. the benefit which was gained for man) *in or through him was life*;" we gain, indeed, a good sense, but one which cannot be proved to exist in the words; and which, indeed, would suppose the words of a passage otherwise plain to be expressed with an almost ænigmatical obscurity. By the common construction, the same sentiment is obtained, without resorting to any such violence.

4. Lightf. observes, that "to the *physical* creation by the Logos is here subjoined a new and *moral* one by the same." Strictly speaking, however, there is here (as Chrys. and Tittm. remark) a *reason* given for what has just been affirmed.

— ἐν αὐτῷ ζωὴ ἦν — φῶς.] It has been not a little disputed, what is meant here by ζωὴ and φῶς. And no wonder, since these are terms of very extensive signification, and there are several senses in which it is equally true, that our Saviour was life and light. And Wets. has adduced numerous passages of ancient writers in which Gods and Heroes are called the life and light of men. By ζωὴ most Expositors think is here meant *author of life and salvation*; and by φῶς, *teacher* and promulgator of its doctrine, the Gospel. But though that sense is very agreeable to the usus loquendi, yet it seems to be not permitted by the *context*; which is elaborately discussed, together with the force of the expressions ζωὴ and φῶς, by Lampe and Tittm.; the latter of whom has shown that, though the senses of ζωὴ and φῶς are often interchangeable, yet that here ζωὴ denotes the *cause*, φῶς the *effect*; the former indicating *vim creatricem et facultatem*, and belonging to *all creatures*; the latter, *salutem ipsam*, and pertaining to *man*. "Thus (he observes) the sense is, 'In eo est vis vivifica,' seu, 'pollet vi, vitam et salutem tribuendi *rebus omnibus, eaque vi utitur in primis ad salutem hominum*.'" It is well observed by Wets., that the ἐν denotes, that the power was *centred* in himself, i. e. *self-derived*, not as was the case with the *Prophets*; and that his power was exerted by a *proper* and *natural*, not an *adventitious, acquired*, or *delegated* force. Thus he is elsewhere said ζωὴν ἔχειν ἐν ἑαυτῷ.

5. καὶ τὸ φῶς — οὐ κατέλαβεν.] Σκοτία is a perpetual image of ignorance, and also the *misery* consequent upon it. See Is. ix. 2. Matth. iv. 16. Acts xxvi. 18., and also the Classical citations in Recens. Synop. Here the word is put (abstract for concrete) in the place of τοῖς ἐσκοτισμένοις τῇ διανοίᾳ (Eph. iv. 18.), namely, persons immersed in ignorance, idolatry, and vice, and consequently far removed from light and virtue, holiness and happiness. Thus the sense is, "And this salvation was offered to wretched, corrupt, and miserable men: but the plan of salvation they did not *comprehend*, much less did they accept and embrace it."

6—8. The scope of these verses (which are in some measure parenthetical) is to prevent misapprehension, and to show the *purpose* of God in *sending John*; and to prove, even on the evidence of John himself, the infinite superiority of Christ to John *q. d.* To bear witness to this light, and further its reception, was John sent from God; not as being himself that light, namely the Messiah, but to bear witness to the Divine mission of Him who was so. Αὐτῷ is for οὗ, by an idiom not confined to the Hebrew, but extending to the *popular* dialect of every language.

7. εἰς μαρτυρίαν, ἵνα μαρτ.] Here there is not so much a repetition of the same thing in plainer

10 ἄνθρωπον ἐρχόμενον εἰς τὸν κόσμον. [d] Ἐν τῷ κόσμῳ ἦν, καὶ ὁ κό- d Heb. 1. 2.
11 σμος δι᾽ αὐτοῦ ἐγένετο, καὶ ὁ κόσμος αὐτὸν οὐκ ἔγνω. εἰς τὰ ἴδια
12 ἦλθε, καὶ οἱ ἴδιοι αὐτὸν οὐ παρέλαβον. [e] Ὅσοι δὲ ἔλαβον αὐτὸν, e Rom. 8. 15. Gal. 3. 26.
ἔδωκεν αὐτοῖς ἐξουσίαν τέκνα Θεοῦ γενέσθαι, τοῖς πιστεύουσιν εἰς τὸ 2 Pet. 1. 4. 1 John 3. 1.
13 ὄνομα αὐτοῦ· [f] οἳ οὐκ ἐξ αἱμάτων, οὐδὲ ἐκ θελήματος σαρκὸς, οὐδὲ f Infra. 3. 5. James 1. 18. 1 Pet. 1. 23.
ἐκ θελήματος ἀνδρὸς, ἀλλ᾽ ἐκ Θεοῦ ἐγεννήθησαν.
14 [g] Καὶ ὁ Λόγος σὰρξ ἐγένετο, καὶ ἐσκήνωσεν ἐν ἡμῖν· καὶ ἐθεασά- g Matt. 1. 16. 17. 2. Luke 1. 31.
μεθα τὴν δόξαν αὐτοῦ, δόξαν ὡς μονογενοῦς παρὰ Πατρὸς, πλήρης & 2. 7. 2 Pet. 1. 17.
χάριτος καὶ ἀληθείας. Col. 1. 19. & 2. 3, 9.

terms, as that ἵνα μαρτ. &c. is an *epanorthosis* upon εἰς μαρτυρίαν τοῦ φωτός. In fact, the *tautologies*, *repetitions*, *pleonasms*, and positions expressed both negatively and affirmatively, in which this Gospel is said by the Commentators to abound, may almost all of them be accounted for on that principle; which itself arose from anxiety on the part of the Evangelist to impress the important truths he had to communicate as forcibly as possible on the minds of his readers.

8. ἐκεῖνος.] The full sense is, "he himself."

9. ἦν τὸ φῶς τὸ ἀληθινὸν] "*that* was the true light;" i. e. he was the true light. Of this use of ἀληθ. with φῶς, examples are adduced by Wets. In the sense of *reality* there is implied *excellence*, as in John vi. 32. xvi. 1. and elsewhere. Φωτίζει is generally taken as put for the Future φωτίσει, or to be taken to mean "who was to enlighten." But it may rather be said to have the sense of the Aorist, by which it denotes what is done at all times; or it may be rendered, "who is to enlighten." By πάντα ἄνθρωπον is meant men of all nations," and not the Jews only; which is intended to oppose the Jewish notion, that the Messiah was to come for the salvation of the *Jews* only.

The next words ἐρχ. εἰς τὸν κόσμον are commonly taken (as indeed would seem more natural) with πάντα ἄνθρωπον. But the best Commentators are agreed that they should be construed with τὸ φῶς: for in the former case, say they, the words would seem unnecessary, and never occur in that sense; whereas in the latter, the phrase is very significant, and applicable to Christ. (*Comp.* xii. 46, and iii. 19.) Besides, ὁ ἐρχόμενος εἰς τὸν κόσμον was a usual phrase to designate the Messiah. See vi. 14; xviii. 37. And finally *that* sense would require the Article. As to the exact force of the declaration, it seems to repeat, somewhat more emphatically, what was said at v. 4. ἡ ζωὴ ἦν τὸ φῶς τῶν ἀνθρώπων.

10. ἐν τῷ κόσμῳ ἦν.] These words designate the appearance and existence of the Logos on earth in a human form. It is well observed by Tittm., that in this and the following verse *ascendit oratio*: q. d. The only and true Saviour came to, and abode in the world,—a world created by him; but which, nevertheless, knew him not, acknowledged him not as such. Nay, though he came to his own people especially, yet even they received him not as the Saviour. Some take τὰ ἴδια to mean *the world at large*. But though it be true, that the whole earth is the Lord's, yet Christ could not be said to be rejected by those to whom he did not reveal himself as Saviour, viz. the Gentiles. Indeed, he professes (Matt. xv. 24.) that "he was not sent but unto the lost sheep of the house of Israel." The best Commentators are therefore, with reason, agreed that τὰ ἴδια, sub. οἰκήματα can only mean his *own country*, or people; a sense of which numerous examples are adduced by Krebs, Wets., and Kypke. The Jews were the peculiar people of God, and consequently of Christ as united in the Godhead. Besides, the Jews might be called Christ's own people, as having been born and having lived among them.

12. ὅσοι δὲ ἔλαβον α.] The reasoning may be completed thus. "His countrymen, as a body, rejected him. Yet his coming was not utterly without effect. Some few did acknowledge him as Messiah. And to such as did, (or hereafter should,) he gave, &c." Ἐξουσία here denotes *privilege*; a signification sometimes occurring in the later Classical writers and the LXX. By τέκνα Θεοῦ is meant *obedient and true worshippers of God*, and, from the adjunct, those who are acknowledged by God as such, and admitted to the privilege of Sonship: to be as happy in this world and the next, as infinite Goodness, under the guidance of infinite Wisdom, can make them. The phrase often occurs in the discourses of our Lord, and in the Epistles of St. Paul and St. John, and is referred by Tittman, as the *fundus locutionis*, to Deut. xiv. 1, 2.

13. οἳ οὐκ—ἐγεννήθησαν.] The sense, as laid down by the best Commentators, is: "Who obtained that Sonship, (υἱοθεσία,) not by virtue of ancestry, nor by any affinity, or connection of human descent, but by a free grant from God." The *plural* is used by adaptation to ἔδωκεν before; but, of course, what is here applied to those who received Jesus as Messiah during his abode on earth, is equally applicable to those who *should*, after his ascension, at any future period receive him as Messiah and embrace his religion. The *plural* αἱμάτων has reference to the *several* ancestors from whom the children of Israel boasted their descent; as Abraham, Isaac, and Jacob. See 2 Cor. xi. 22. sq. I have, in Recens. Synop., compared Eurip. Ion, 693. ἄλλων τραφεὶς ἀφ᾽ αἱμάτων. The plural also occurs in Lycophr. v. 804 & 1249. The two phrases, ἐκ θελ. σαρκ. and ἐκ. θ. ἀνδρὸς, by Hendiadys, designate, *per euphemismum*, the *natural* mode of descent, as opposed to the *spiritual* one proceeding from the adoption of God.

14. καὶ ὁ Λόγος σὰρξ ἐγ.] This is closely connected with ver. 10. ἐν τῷ κόσμῳ ἦν. and is a resumption of what was there said: q. d. "And [accordingly] the Logos was clothed with a human body, and sojourned among us [men]." Σάρκινος ἐ. would have been more Classical Greek. So Artemid. ii. 35. ἐάν τε γὰρ σάρκινοι οἱ Θεοὶ φαίνωνται, &c. This addition of the human nature to the Divine, *implies* that conjunction, by which the same person is both Son of God and Son of man.

—ἐσκήνωσε.] There is no necessity to suppose

h Matt. 3. 11. Mark 1. 7. Luke 3. 16. infra. ver. 26, et seqq. & 3. 31. i Col. 1. 19. & 2. 9. k Exod. 20. 1, &c. Deut. 5. 6, &c.

[h] Ἰωάννης μαρτυρεῖ περὶ αὐτοῦ, καὶ κέκραγε λέγων· Οὗτος ἦν ὃν 15
εἶπον· Ὁ ὀπίσω μου ἐρχόμενος ἔμπροσθέν μου γέγονεν· ὅτι πρῶτός
μου ἦν. [i] Καὶ ἐκ τοῦ πληρώματος αὐτοῦ ἡμεῖς πάντες ἐλάβομεν, καὶ 16
χάριν ἀντὶ χάριτος· [k] ὅτι ὁ νόμος διὰ Μωϋσέως ἐδόθη, ἡ χάρις καὶ 17

(with Lampe and Schoettg.) any reference to the *Schechinah*. The sense is what Wets. lays down: "He who had dwelt in heaven descended from thence, that he might sojourn with men." For, as I have shown by many examples in Recens. Synop., *σκηνοῦν* signifies, "to take up one's quarters, or sojourn." And it is here used in preference to *ζῆν*, with allusion to the life of man *as a sojourn;* and because it better designates that *familiariter vivere* which seems here meant; and suggests such an intercommunity of all the functions of human life, as showed that he was really and truly a *man*.

The next words, *καὶ ἐθεασάμεθα*, &c. seem meant to intimate, that though he was real *man*, yet he was also something far *more;* namely, *Son of God;* implying a community of the *Divine* nature. The terms are such as merit attention. Ἐθεασάμεθα, is very significant, and even emphatic; q. d. "We *distinctly saw* his glory." Now there were many ways in which they saw the *glory* of Christ; namely, in his *miracles*, (see ii. 11,) and not only in acts which evinced *power*, but *wisdom* and *goodness* also, in his ineffable love to men, such as to induce him to suffer death, even the death of the cross, for their salvation. The Apostles themselves, too, (at least St. John and two others) had seen his glory in his *transfiguration* on Mount Tabor. Though these and the other evidences of Christ's glory in his Mediatorial capacity John did not intend to *specify*, content with affirming it to have been *δόξαν ὡς μονογενοῦς παρὰ Πατρὸς*, such a glory as might be expected in a Being the only begotten Son of the Father; who accordingly is, as St. Paul says, the *ἀπαύγασμα τῆς δόξης καὶ χαρακτὴρ τῆς ὑποστάσεως αὐτοῦ*. It is to be noted, that the *ὡς* (as Chrys. and Tittm. remark,) does not express *similitude*, but *identity* and truth; i. e. truly such. On the full sense of *μονογενὴς* see Lampe and Tittm. It is proper to remark the use here of the verbal for the verb, *μονογενὴς* for *μόνος γεννηθεὶς*, which will account for the use of the Genitive with *παρὰ* instead of the simple Genitive. And it is truly observed by Bp. Bull, Judic. Eccl. p. 56. "that *μονογενὴς παρὰ* seems more significantly to express the Divine generation of the Son from the Father, than the simple genitive; the *παρὰ* intimating that the Logos ita Dei Patris unicum filium esse, ut solus revera *ab* atque *ex* ipso Patre genitus fuerit."

As to the *construction* of the passage, many regard the words *καὶ ἐθεασάμεθα — πατρὸς* as parenthetical, referring *πλήρης* to *ἐσκήνωσεν*. But though this makes the syntax regular, it does violence to the structure of the sentence, and deteriorates the sense. It is better, with others, to suppose an enallage, (frequent in St. John,) and regard *πλήρης* as put for *πλήρους*. This is confirmed by an imitation of the passage in Theophyl. Simoc. p. 115. *καὶ ἐθεασάμεθα τὴν δόξαν αὐτῆς πλήρη χάριτος*. *Χάριτος καὶ ἀλ.* is thought to be put, *per Hendiadyn*, for *χάριτος ἀληθινῆς*; and the sense of *πλήρης χάρ. καὶ ἀλ.* to be "most gracious and benignant."

15. Having appealed, in a general way, to the testimony the Baptist bore to Jesus, John now proceeds to mention *what* that testimony was; and by *κέκραγε* he means it was uttered openly, *ex animo*, and *decisively*.

— ὁ ὀπίσω — μου ἦν.] The sense of *ὁ ὀπίσω μου ἐρχόμενος* seems to be, "He who enters (i. e. is to enter) upon his office after me;" in which sense *ἔρχεσθαι* frequently occurs in the N. T., and sometimes in the LXX. The interpretation of *ἔμπροσθέν μου γέγ.*, is doubtful, and may be taken either of *time* or of *dignity*. If the *former* be adopted (as it has been by the later commentators in general, supported by the Latin Versions), the clause *ὅτι πρῶτός μ. ἦν.* must be considered as expressing the same sense as the preceding. And the words may be thus rendered from Tittm.: Hic est ille, quem indigitavi, cum dicerem, me *sequitur*, qui ante extitit, meque prior est." If the *latter*, (which is the mode adopted by the ancient and early modern Expositors, and also Lampe,) the words will express this sense: "This is he of whom I said, He who cometh into the world [or entereth on his office] after me, is become of greater dignity than myself; inasmuch as, by his own Divine nature, he was always before me, more honourable than I." This interpretation seems to deserve the preference, as yielding a sense equally suitable to the context, and more worthy of the Baptist than the other. Of this sense of *ἔμπροσθεν*, somewhat rare in the Scriptural writers, an example occurs in Gen. xlviii. 20.

16—18.] It has been disputed whether these verses are from the *Baptist*, or from the *Evangelist*. The *former* opinion has been adopted by many Interpreters: but (as Tittm. observes) it lies open to the objection, that what is contained in these verses could hardly have been said by John the Baptist of himself, *his own* times, and of his disciples. Lamp. and Tittm. are agreed that they are the words of the *Evangelist;* who, in using the term *πληρώματος* (answering to מלא, which denotes the *sum* of any thing, and also *plenty*) seems to have referred to the expression *πλήρης χάριτος καὶ ἀληθείας* in ver. 14, and meant by it to express the *abundance* of benefits and blessings. Thus *ἐκ τοῦ πληρ. α.* may be rendered, "from his rich store-house of benefits and blessings." *How* these are *in* Christ, appears from the context, and is fully shown by Tittm. in Recens. Synop. *Χάριν ἀντὶ χάριτος* is a periphrasis of the superlative, like the Hebr. חן על חן, an idiom not unknown to the Greek, ex. gr. Theogn. Admon. 344. *δοίης ἀντ' ἀνιῶν ἀνιάς*. Thus the sense is, "benefits upon benefits," abundance of benefits. So Philo i. 354. (cited by Wets.) says the Deity, after giving *τὰς πρώτας χάριτας, εἰσαῦθις, ἑτέρας ἀντὶ ἐκείνων, καὶ τρίτας ἀντὶ τῶν δευτέρων, καὶ ἀεὶ νέας ἀντὶ παλαιοτέρων ἐπιδίδωσι*. This passage was perhaps in the mind of Proclus. Institut. C. p. 131, where he says, that the supreme Deity imparts to the inferior ones, and to men, what he possesses *κατὰ τὸ ὑπερπλῆρες ἑαυτοῦ*. By *πάντες* are meant all Christians of all times and places. Christ, as Tittm. observes, being the perennial fountain of felicity to the whole human race, of every age.

17. *ὅτι ὁ νόμος — ἐγένετο.*] In these words

18 ἡ ἀλήθεια διὰ Ἰησοῦ Χριστοῦ ἐγένετο. [l] Θεὸν οὐδεὶς ἑώρακε πώποτε· l Ex. 33. 20. Deut. 4. 12.
ὁ μονογενὴς Υἱὸς, ὁ ὢν εἰς τὸν κόλπον τοῦ Πατρὸς ἐκεῖνος ἐξηγήσατο. Infra. 6. 46. 1 John 4. 12. 1 Tim. 6. 16.
19 [m] Καὶ αὕτη ἐστὶν ἡ μαρτυρία τοῦ Ἰωάννου, ὅτε ἀπέστειλαν οἱ Ἰου- Matt. 11. 27. Luke 10. 22.
δαῖοι ἐξ Ἱεροσολύμων ἱερεῖς καὶ Λευΐτας, ἵνα ἐρωτήσωσιν αὐτόν· Σὺ m infra 5. 33.
20 τίς εἶ; [n] Καὶ ὡμολόγησε, καὶ οὐκ ἠρνήσατο· καὶ ὡμολόγησεν· Ὅτι n infra 3. 28. Acts 13. 25.
21 οὐκ εἰμὶ ἐγὼ ὁ Χριστός. [o] Καὶ ἠρώτησαν αὐτόν· Τί οὖν; Ἠλίας o Deut. 18. 15.
εἶ σύ; καὶ λέγει· Οὐκ εἰμί. Ὁ προφήτης εἶ σύ; καὶ ἀπεκρίθη·
22 Οὔ. Εἶπον οὖν αὐτῷ· Τίς εἶ; ἵνα ἀπόκρισιν δῶμεν τοῖς πέμψασιν
23 ἡμᾶς· τί λέγεις περὶ σεαυτοῦ; [p] Ἔφη· Ἐγὼ φωνὴ βοῶντος p Isa. 40. 3. Matt. 3. 3.
ἐν τῇ ἐρήμῳ, εὐθύνατε τὴν ὁδὸν Κυρίου! καθὼς εἶπεν Mark 1. 3. Luke 3. 4. supra ver. 15.

(which were meant for the Jews at large) are *exemplified* and *illustrated* the benefits received from Christ by his disciples; and the *grace* of the Gospel is opposed to the *rigour* of the Law. The Law was given *as* a benefit to the *Israelites*; yet it was harsh and burdensome; its blessings scanty, and those confined to one nation: whereas the Gospel imparts its blessings, through Christ, copiously to the whole human race. (Kuin.) Ἡ χάρις καὶ ἡ ἀλ. denotes, *per hendiadyn*, ἡ χάρις ἀληθινὴ, "the true and most excellent grace." See the contrast in *graciousness* between the Law and the Gospel stated more at large by Wets. Both the above Commentators, however, have omitted to notice what is especially adverted to, — the grace of the *Holy Spirit*, in which the Gospel was so superior to the Law. This χάρις Christians receive from the πλήρωμα of Christ; since to him (as is said at iii. 34.) οὐκ ἐκ μέτρου δίδωσιν ὁ Θεὸς τὸ Πνεῦμα. On which subject the reader may profitably consult the 9th, 10th, and 11th chapters of the Dissert. Poster. Harmon. Apost. of Bp. Bull.

18. Θεὸν οὐδεὶς ἑ. π.] This is an illustration of the preceding verse *by example*; and that deduced from the clear knowledge of God communicated by Christ. q. d. [No wonder that the Gospel of Christ should be so superior to the Law of Moses]; for no *man* hath seen (i. e. perfectly known, learned) God; not even Moses and the Prophets. So Ecclus. xliii. 31. τίς ἑώρακεν αὐτὸν, καὶ ἐκδιηγήσεται; This sense of ὁρᾷν, corresponding to the Hebr. ראה is found also in the Classical writers. Thus the passage is by no means in contradiction to Exod. xxxiii. 11, "the Lord spake to Moses face to face." Besides, there is reason to think that it was Christ, the Logos, who appeared as the Jehovah Angel on that and other occasions. On this important point see Bp. Bull, p. 274. sqq. of his matchless Defensio Fidei Nicænæ.

— ὁ ὢν εἰς τὸν κόλπον τ. Π.] Lampe, in a dissertation on these words, has proved that more is denoted, than what the expression means in the *Classical* writers, namely, participation in any one's counsels, — and he lays down the sense as follows: "He who is most intimately connected with the Father, and the dearest to Him." The expression arose from the custom, common to all the ancient nations, of reclining at meals; according to which he who sat next the host (who was at the top of the table) seemed, as it were, to lie in his bosom or lap.

— ἐξηγήσατο] Sub. Θεόν; has distinctly disclosed his nature, attributes, and will. There may be — Wets. thinks there is — reference to the ἐξηγηταὶ, or interpreters of the portents, and directors of religious ceremonies among the Greeks.

19. καὶ αὕτη ἡ μαρτ.] q. d. and this testimony which I have just adduced was borne on the occasion following.

— οἱ Ἰουδαῖοι ἐξ Ἱερ.] "the Jews of Jerusalem;" meaning those who are elsewhere called οἱ ἄρχοντες τῶν Ἰουδαιῶν, had the authority of making inquiry into the pretensions of prophets; namely, the *Sanhedrim*. There is no reason to suppose, with some, that the Evangelist has not given the whole address; for the τίς in the question evidently refers to the *kind* of prophetical character claimed by John; which *implied* an inquiry, 1. whether he was the Christ; 2. whether he was Elias. The form σὺ τίς εἶ was (it appears from Wetstein's citations) not unusual, as addressed by those who demanded to know any one's authority to act in any business. Though the Sanhedrim knew that John's ancestry did not accord with that which had been predicted of Christ; yet, when they bore in mind what had happened to Zacharias in the temple, and that his mother was of the lineage of David, they might think it *possible* that he was the Messiah; especially as it was not absolutely determined among the doctors whether Christ was to be born at Bethlehem or not.

— ὡμολόγησε — καὶ ὡμολόγησεν] These words contain the strongest *asseveration* possible; since the two methods, assertion by affirmation and by negation of the contrary, together with a repetition of the affirmation, are here united.

21. τί οὖν] A *popular* form of expression, for τίς οὖν, yet sometimes found in the best writers. Ἠλίας εἶ σύ; the Jews supposed, from Malachi iv. 5, that Elijah would return from heaven, whither he had been caught up, and would usher in and anoint the Messiah.

— οὐκ εἰμί.] i. e. not in the sense in which the question was asked; though in *another* sense he might be called Elias, as he came in the *spirit* and *power* of Elias. See Matt. xi. 14.

— ὁ προφήτης εἶ σύ;] It is plain that this cannot mean Elijah, since that would involve a vain repetition. The Article shows that it must denote some particular prophet. The best Commentators, ancient and modern, are of opinion that *Jeremiah* is meant, thus the sense will be, "the prophet promised," namely, in Deut. xviii. 15 — 19. See Acts iii. 22.

22. τίς εἶ;] i. e. what sort of person art thou, whether a prophet or not?

23. ἐγὼ φωνὴ, &c.] i. e. as the older Commentators interpret, "I am the person there spoken of;" or, as the later ones, "What the Prophet (namely, Isaiah iv. 3) there says, holds good of

Ἠσαΐας ὁ προφήτης. Καὶ οἱ ἀπεσταλμένοι ἦσαν ἐκ τῶν Φαρισαίων· 24
q Deut. 18. 15. q καὶ ἠρώτησαν αὐτὸν, καὶ εἶπον αὐτῷ· Τί οὖν βαπτίζεις, εἰ σὺ οὐκ 25
r Matt. 3. 11. Mark 1. 7. Luke 3. 16. Acts 1. 5. & 11. 16. & 19. 4. εἶ ὁ Χριστὸς, οὔτε Ἠλίας, οὔτε ὁ προφήτης; r Ἀπεκρίθη αὐτοῖς ὁ 26
Ἰωάννης, λέγων· Ἐγὼ βαπτίζω ἐν ὕδατι· μέσος δὲ ὑμῶν ἕστηκεν, ὃν
ὑμεῖς οὐκ οἴδατε. Αὐτός ἐστιν ὁ ὀπίσω μου ἐρχόμενος, ὃς ἔμπροσθέν 27
μου γέγονεν· οὗ ἐγὼ οὐκ εἰμὶ ἄξιος ἵνα λύσω αὐτοῦ τὸν ἱμάντα τοῦ
ὑποδήματος. Ταῦτα ἐν * Βηθανίᾳ ἐγένετο πέραν τοῦ Ἰορδάνου, ὅπου 28
ἦν Ἰωάννης βαπτίζων.

s Exod. 12. 3. Isa. 53. 7. infra ver. 36. 1 Pet. 1. 19. Acts 8. 32. s Τῇ ἐπαύριον βλέπει ὁ Ἰωάννης, τὸν Ἰησοῦν ἐρχόμενον πρὸς αὐτὸν, 29
καὶ λέγει· Ἴδε ὁ ἀμνὸς τοῦ Θεοῦ ὁ αἴρων τὴν ἁμαρτίαν τοῦ κόσμου.

me; you will find there, what will be a sufficient description of my person and office."

25. τί οὖν βαπτίζεις, &c.] The Pharisees (such as these persons were) thought that the power of baptizing Jews, and thereby forming a new Religion, was confined to the Messiah and his precursors the Prophets; who, they supposed, would return to life for that purpose. The subject of the *nature* and lawfulness of John's baptism is elaborately treated on in a Dissertation of Danzius on the baptism of Proselytes, inserted in Meuschen's Nov. Test. ex Talm. ill. From which the most important passages are translated and introduced in Mr. Townsend's Chron. Arr. N. T., Vol. i. 107. seqq.

26. ἐγὼ βαπτίζω, &c.] The sense of the answer is: "I only baptize with *water*, and collect followers *for the Messiah*, from whom a very different and much more powerful baptism may be expected; even a far more effective means of purifying the people. Moreover, He whom you require (i. e. the Messiah), and by whose authority I do this, is *among* you."

28. Βηθανίᾳ] This reading (instead of the common reading Βηθαβάρα) is found in almost all the best MSS., every Version of credit, many Fathers and ancient Commentators, and almost all the early Editions; and was restored to the text by Wets., Matth., Griesb., Knapp, Vater, Tittm., and Scholz, who are of opinion, that the common reading proceeded from a mere conjecture of Origen; who, because the situation here does not correspond with that of Bethany, where Lazarus and his sisters lived, made the change in question, forgetting that there are in all countries many places of the same name. So in Judæa, Bethsaida, Bethlehem, and Emmaus: and Bethany, from its signification (namely, a ferry-place or passage), was very likely to be one. Besides, *this* seems meant to be distinguished from the other Bethany by the addition πέραν τοῦ Ἰορδάνου, which, I apprehend, denotes on the opposite *bank* of the Jordan: for we may be sure it was on the *river*-side. The *meaning* of the name *Bethabara* is almost exactly the same with that of *Bethany*. Insomuch that many learned men (as Schleusn.) are of opinion that Bethabara and Bethany were only two different names for the same place; which is very probable. We need not, however, suppose, with Schleusn., that the place, in the age of *Christ*, was called *Bethany*, and in a later one, *Bethabara*. It should rather seem that Bethabara is the more *ancient* one. And if, as there is great reason to think, Bethabara here is the same with the Bethabara of Judges vii. 24, what Schl. says could not be the case. The difficulty, however, may be removed by supposing that Bethabara was the original name of the place; but that in the time of Christ it was usually called *Bethania*, as better designating its situation; the original crossing being by *ford*, having now been changed to that by *ferry;* yet that, notwithstanding this, the old name (of which many examples might be adduced) still continued in use, probably among the common people, who are always averse to such changes of names. Insomuch that in the time of Origen, it seems to have been commonly called Bethabara. For he says: Δείκνυσθαι δὲ λέγουσι παρὰ τῇ ὄχθῃ τοῦ Ἰορδάνου τὰ Βηθαβαρᾶ, ἔνθα ἱστοροῦσι τὸν Ἰωάννην βεβαπτικέναι. *Hence* he changed the reading; which others also approved.

29. τῇ ἐπαύριον] This was after the baptism of Jesus: but the expression refers not to the baptism, but to the mission of the priests and Levites.

— ἴδε ὁ ἀμνὸς — κόσμου] In order to rightly understand these words, we must observe, that as often as in Scripture the name Lamb is applied to Christ, so often the subject of what is spoken is his *death* and *passion;* inasmuch as he underwent it for men. And in this view John the Baptist considered Jesus, when he called him *lamb*, namely, as suffering and dying *like a victim*. It is clear that he meant to represent our Lord as one *dying*, and that *in the place of others*. For he has subjoined the words ὁ αἴρων τὴν ἁμαρτίαν τοῦ κόσμου, by way of explication. Now the phrase αἴρειν τὴν ἁμαρτίαν answers to the Hebr. נשא עון or נשא חטאה, which never signifies to *remove* sins, i. e. *extirpate iniquity* from the earth (as some recent Interpreters suppose), but to *forgive* sins (as in Gen. l. 17. Exod. xxxiv. 7. Num. xiv. 19. Ps. xxxii. 1, 5. 1 Sam. xv. 25. xxv. 28.), or to *pay the penalties of sin*, either one's own, or others; as in Exod. xxviii. 38. Lev. v. 1. x. 17, where are conjoined, as synonymous, the formulas to *bear the sin* of the people, and *expiate* and to *atone* the people with God. Therefore the formula to *bear sins* signifies to be punished because of sins, to undergo punishment of sins. Furthermore, as to *bear one's own sins* denotes to be *punished* for one's own sins, so to *bear the sins of others*, must mean to be punished for the sins of others, to undergo the punishment which the sins of others have deserved.

Moreover, Christ is said to bear the sin of the *whole world;* and therefore the interpretation above mentioned can have no place. It must be observed, too, that there is in these formulas a manifest allusion to, and comparison with a *piacular victim*. For such a victim was solemnly

30 [t] Οὗτός ἐστι περὶ οὗ ἐγὼ εἶπον· Ὀπίσω μου ἔρχεται ἀνὴρ, ὃς ἔμπρο- [t Supra ver. 15.]
31 σθέν μου γέγονεν, ὅτι πρῶτός μου ἦν. κἀγὼ οὐκ ᾔδειν αὐτόν· ἀλλ'
ἵνα φανερωθῇ τῷ Ἰσραὴλ, διὰ τοῦτο ἦλθον ἐγὼ ἐν τῷ ὕδατι βαπτίζων.
32 [u] Καὶ ἐμαρτύρησεν Ἰωάννης, λέγων· Ὅτι τεθέαμαι τὸ Πνεῦμα κατα- [u Matt. 3. 16. Mark 1. 10. Luke 3. 21.]
33 βαῖνον ὡσεὶ περιστερὰν ἐξ οὐρανοῦ, καὶ ἔμεινεν ἐπ' αὐτόν. [x] Κἀγὼ [x Matt. 3. 11. Acts 1. 5.]
οὐκ ᾔδειν αὐτόν· ἀλλ' ὁ πέμψας με βαπτίζειν ἐν ὕδατι, ἐκεῖνός μοι
εἶπεν· Ἐφ' ὃν ἂν ἴδῃς τὸ Πνεῦμα καταβαῖνον καὶ μένον ἐπ' αὐτὸν,
34 οὗτός ἐστιν ὁ βαπτίζων ἐν Πνεύματι ἁγίῳ. Κἀγὼ ἑώρακα, καὶ μεμαρτύρηκα ὅτι οὗτός ἐστιν ὁ Υἱὸς τοῦ Θεοῦ.
35 Τῇ ἐπαύριον πάλιν εἱστήκει [ὁ Ἰωάννης,] καὶ ἐκ τῶν μαθητῶν αὐ-
36 τοῦ δύο. [y] καὶ ἐμβλέψας τῷ Ἰησοῦ περιπατοῦντι, λέγει· Ἴδε ὁ ἀμνὸς [y Supra ver. 29.]
37 τοῦ Θεοῦ. Καὶ ἤκουσαν αὐτοῦ οἱ δύο μαθηταὶ λαλοῦντος, καὶ ἠκο-
38 λούθησαν τῷ Ἰησοῦ. Στραφεὶς δὲ ὁ Ἰησοῦς, καὶ θεασάμενος αὐτοὺς
39 ἀκολουθοῦντας, λέγει αὐτοῖς· Τί ζητεῖτε; οἱ δὲ εἶπον αὐτῷ· Ῥαβ-
40 βὶ, (ὃ λέγεται ἑρμηνευόμενον διδάσκαλε) ποῦ μένεις; λέγει αὐτοῖς·
Ἔρχεσθε καὶ ἴδετε. Ἦλθον καὶ εἶδον ποῦ μένει· καὶ παρ' αὐτῷ

brought to the altar, and then the Priest put his hands over the head; which was a *symbolical action*, signifying that the sins committed by the persons expiated were *laid upon the victim*; and, when it was slaughtered, it was then said to *bear* the sins of the expiated; by which it was denoted that the victim paid the penalty of the sins committed, was punished with death in their place, and for the purpose of freeing them from the penalty of sin. Therefore when Christ is called *the lamb bearing* the sins of the world, it is manifest that we must understand one who should take upon himself the sins of men, so as to pay the penalties of their sins, and in their stead, for the purpose of freeing them from those penalties. (Tittm.) On this passage see Recens. Synop., the admirable work of Abp. Magee on the Atonement, and the authors by him referred to. Examine also the Marginal References in Scott's Bible. On the deeply important subject here treated of, I cannot express my sentiments better than in the words of Mr. Townsend, Chron. Arr. i. 103. "In support of the doctrine of the Atonement there is more authority than for any other revealed in the Jewish or Christian Scriptures. It was taught in the beginning of the patriarchal dispensation, the first after the fall, in the words of the promise, and in the institution of sacrifices. It is enforced by the uniform concurrent testimony of the types, prophecies, opinions, customs, and traditions of the Jewish Church. It is the peculiar foundation and principal doctrine of the Christian Church in all ages, which has never deviated from the opinion that the death of Christ on the cross was the full, perfect, and sufficient sacrifice, oblation, and satisfaction for the sins of the whole world."

30—34. John now mentions *how* he obtained this knowledge, that Jesus was the Messiah; namely, by an express revelation from God. Up to the period of his baptism our Lord (such was his humility of deportment) had passed for a mere man. He was first made known as *Messiah* by John at his baptism, and through him to the multitude. Whether John had before any knowledge of Jesus by face, is variously disputed. Certain it is that he did not know him to be *the Messiah*. *That* knowledge he obtained by a Divine revelation, which had given him the *sign* whereby he should recognise the Messiah; namely, the descent of the Holy Spirit, in symbolic figure, upon him. That sign he saw in Jesus, and was therefore sure he was that personage.

Moreover, when it is said, I knew him not [as Messiah], this is not contradictory to the passage of Matt. iii. 14.; for, as Mr. Holden observes, John might have declined the office of baptizing Jesus in consequence of knowing his superior wisdom and sanctity, and perhaps from his believing him a prophet; and yet might not have known him to be the Messiah. All that is here affirmed being, that John was ignorant of the *true* character of Jesus till the time of his baptism. The words ἀλλ' ἵνα φανερ. &c. should be rendered: "But to the end that he should be made manifest to Israel, am I come baptizing with water." It is not said that this was the *sole*, but only that it was the *chief* end.

34. μεμαρτύρηκα.] This is thought to be Preter. for Pres. but the sense is, "have borne, and do bear witness."

35. τῇ ἐπαύριον.[Namely, two days after the mission of the Priests and Levites. See v. 29.

— εἱστήκει] "was standing," i. e. was there. Ὁ Ἰωάννης is omitted in many MSS., Versions, and Fathers, and is cancelled by Matth., Vat., Tittm., Griesb., and Scholz.

39. τί ζητεῖτε;] A popular form of expression, signifying, "What is your business with me?"

— ποῦ μένεις] "where dwellest thou?" Μένειν is used either of a *fixed habitation*, or a *lodging*, as here, and in Luke xix. 5. xxiv. 29. Acts xviii. 3 and 20., and often in the Sept., and sometimes in the Classical writers. So also *manere*, in the Latin. By calling Jesus διδάσκαλε they showed that they sought *instruction*; and by addressing to him the question ποῦ μένεις, they requested *private conversation*; no doubt, on the great doctrine which then occupied the minds of all reflecting Jews.

40.) ἔρχεσθε καὶ ἴδ.[The most correct view of

ἔμειναν τὴν ἡμέραν ἐκείνην· ὥρα [δὲ] ἦν ὡς δεκάτη. [z] Ἦν Ἀνδρέας, 41
ὁ ἀδελφὸς Σίμωνος Πέτρου, εἷς ἐκ τῶν δύο τῶν ἀκουσάντων παρὰ
Ἰωάννου καὶ ἀκολουθησάντων αὐτῷ. Εὑρίσκει οὗτος πρῶτος τὸν ἀδελ- 42
φὸν τὸν ἴδιον Σίμωνα, καὶ λέγει αὐτῷ· Εὑρήκαμεν τὸν Μεσσίαν, (ὅ
ἐστι μεθερμηνευόμενον [ὁ] Χριστός.) [a] καὶ ἤγαγεν αὐτὸν πρὸς τὸν 43
Ἰησοῦν. ἐμβλέψας δὲ αὐτῷ ὁ Ἰησοῦς εἶπε· Σὺ εἶ Σίμων ὁ υἱὸς Ἰωνᾶ·
σὺ κληθήσῃ Κηφᾶς· (ὃ ἑρμηνεύεται Πέτρος.)

Τῇ ἐπαύριον ἠθέλησεν [ὁ Ἰησοῦς] ἐξελθεῖν εἰς τὴν Γαλιλαίαν· καὶ 44
εὑρίσκει Φίλιππον, καὶ λέγει αὐτῷ· Ἀκολούθει μοι. [b] ἦν δὲ ὁ Φίλιπ- 45
πος ἀπὸ Βηθσαϊδὰ, ἐκ τῆς πόλεως Ἀνδρέου καὶ Πέτρου. [c] Εὑρίσκει 46
Φίλιππος τὸν Ναθαναὴλ, καὶ λέγει αὐτῷ· Ὃν ἔγραψε Μωϋσῆς ἐν
τῷ νόμῳ καὶ οἱ προφῆται, εὑρήκαμεν, Ἰησοῦν τὸν υἱὸν τοῦ Ἰωσὴφ τὸν
ἀπὸ Ναζαρέτ. [d] Καὶ εἶπεν αὐτῷ Ναθαναήλ· Ἐκ Ναζαρὲτ δύναταί 47
τι ἀγαθὸν εἶναι; Λέγει αὐτῷ Φίλιππος· Ἔρχου καὶ ἴδε. [e] Εἶδεν ὁ 48
Ἰησοῦς τὸν Ναθαναὴλ ἐρχόμενον πρὸς αὐτὸν, καὶ λέγει περὶ αὐτοῦ·
Ἴδε, ἀληθῶς Ἰσραηλίτης, ἐν ᾧ δόλος οὐκ ἔστι. Λέγει αὐτῷ Ναθαναήλ· 49
Πόθεν με γινώσκεις; ἀπεκρίθη [ὁ] Ἰησοῦς καὶ εἶπεν αὐτῷ· Πρὸ
τοῦ σε Φίλιππον φωνῆσαι, ὄντα ὑπὸ τὴν συκῆν εἶδόν σε. Ἀπεκρίθη 50
Ναθαναὴλ καὶ λέγει αὐτῷ· [e] Ῥαββὶ, σὺ εἶ ὁ Υἱὸς τοῦ Θεοῦ, σὺ εἶ ὁ

z Matt. 4. 18.
a Matt. 16. 18.
b John 12. 21.
c Infra. 21. 2. Gen. 3. 15. & 22. 18. & 49. 10. Deut. 18. 15. 2 Sam. 7. 12. Isa. 7. 14. & 9. 5. & 40. 10, 11. & 53. 1, &c. Jer. 23. 5. & 33. 14. Ezek. 34. 23. & 37. 24. Dan. 9. 24. Mich. 5. 2. Zach. 6. 12. & 9. 9.
d Matt. 2. 23. Luke 2. 4. Infra 7. 41, 42.
e Psal. 32. 2.

the scope of this reply, seems to be that taken by Euthym.; who says that our Lord did not tell them where he abode; but bade them follow him, to inspire them with confidence. Of these disciples one, we learn, was Andrew. The other is generally supposed to have been the Evangelist himself, who usually suppresses his own name: (See xiii. 23. xviii. 15. xix. 26.) but Epiphanius says John or *James*.

— ὥρα δὲ ἦν.] The δὲ is omitted in most of the ancient MSS. and the early Edd., and is cancelled by almost every Editor from Beng. and Wets. to Scholz.

41—43. On the seeming discrepancy here between the Evangelists, see Recens. Syn.

42. ἀδελφὸν τὸν ἴδιον] for ἀδ. αὐτοῦ (like the Heb. ין "his brother." An idiom frequent both in the N. T. and LXX.

— Μεσσίαν, &c.] When a significant name (such as Peter, Thomas, or Tabitha) was given to any one, it was usual to *translate* it, when the person was spoken of in a different language. The Evangelist here follows this custom, both to explain the import of the names *Messiah* and *Cephas* (which the Gentile converts of Asia Minor were not likely to understand) and to prevent his readers from mistaking the persons spoken of for some *other* persons.

44. ὁ Ἰησοῦς.] Very many MSS., Versions, and Fathers omit the ὁ Ἰ. here, but insert it after λέγει; and so Griesb., Matth., and Scholz edit, perhaps rightly.

— ἀκολούθει μοι.] A form of speaking equivalent to "become my disciples," and sometimes used by the Grecian Philosophers.

46. Ναθαναήλ.] This is supposed to have been the same with the *Bartholomew* mentioned by Matthew; that being a *sirname*, as is plain by the occurrence of the name Θολομαῖος twice in Josephus, namely, Antiq. xiv. 8, 1. and Bell. i. 9, 3. It therefore means *Son of* Θολ. or תלמי. Various reasons are there for the above supposition. And 1. that all the *rest* of John's followers mentioned in the chapter were received into the number of the Apostles; 2. since John nowhere makes mention of Bartholomew, nor the rest of the Evangelists of Nathanael; 3. since Luke vi. 14., in his list of the Apostles, puts Bartholomew after Philip, with whom Nathanael was converted.

47. ἐκ Ναζαρὲτ — ἀγαθὸν εἶναι] i. e. τινα ἀγαθόν; it seemed little probable to Nathanael that a *good man*, much less a *prophet*, and least of all the *Messiah*, could come out of *Galilee*, still less from Nazareth, which was but a mean country town, whose inhabitants, as indeed all the Galilæans, were held in contempt by the Jews; the cause for which has been attributed to their being a mixed race, partly of Gentile origin, very corrupt in their morals, and reckoned boorish and stupid, even to a proverb.

— ἔρχου καὶ ἴδε.] A formula equivalent to *Judge for yourself; Seeing is believing*.

48. ἀληθῶς] for ἀληθής. A common permutation. The appellation *true Israelite* (denoting one who imitates the virtues of the Patriarch Israel, see Rom. ix. 6.) was given among the Jews to persons remarkable for probity. In the words ἐν ᾧ δόλος οὐκ ἔστι there is thought to be a reference to what is said of Jacob in Gen. xxv. 27. But it seems rather to have been a phrase borrowed from Ps. xxxii. 2. xiv. 3. (compare 1 Pet. ii. 22.) to designate one who is *integer vitæ scelerisque purus*, a man of thorough integrity, whose profession of religion is not leavened with hypocrisy, one of undoubted integrity towards men, and unfeigned piety towards God; in short, the character of whom a great poet has said—

"An honest man 's the noblest work of God."

50. Nathanael, in his answer, seems to hint that Jesus had been *informed* of his character by his friends. In order, therefore, to remove this

51 βασιλεὺς τοῦ Ἰσραήλ. Ἀπεκρίθη Ἰησοῦς καὶ εἶπεν αὐτῷ· Ὅτι εἶπόν
σοι· Εἶδόν σε ὑποκάτω τῆς συκῆς, πιστεύεις; μείζω τούτων ὄψει.
52 [f] Καὶ λέγει αὐτῷ· Ἀμὴν ἀμὴν λέγω ὑμῖν, ἀπ' ἄρτι ὄψεσθε τὸν οὐρα- f Gen. 28. 12. Matt. 4. 11.
νὸν ἀνεῳγότα, καὶ τοὺς ἀγγέλους τοῦ Θεοῦ ἀναβαίνοντας καὶ κατα- Luke 22. 43. & 24. 4.
βαίνοντας ἐπὶ τὸν Υἱὸν τοῦ ἀνθρώπου. Acts 1. 10.

1 II. ΚΑΙ τῇ ἡμέρᾳ τῇ τρίτῃ γάμος ἐγένετο ἐν Κανᾷ τῆς Γαλιλαί-
2 ας· καὶ ἦν ἡ μήτηρ τοῦ Ἰησοῦ ἐκεῖ. ἐκλήθη δὲ καὶ ὁ Ἰησοῦς καὶ
3 οἱ μαθηταὶ αὐτοῦ εἰς τὸν γάμον. Καὶ ὑστερήσαντος οἴνου, λέγει ἡ
4 μήτηρ τοῦ Ἰησοῦ πρὸς αὐτόν· Οἶνον οὐκ ἔχουσι. Λέγει αὐτῇ ὁ Ἰη-

supposition, and show Nathanael that he knew him not from the information of Philip, or any other person, but from his own knowledge, our Lord mentions what none could know but Philip and Nathanael: Πρὸ τοῦ σε Φίλιππον φωνῆσαι, ὄντα ὑπὸ τὴν συκῆν, εἶδόν σε. Now this circumstance of *sitting under the fig-tree*, Chrysost. and Theophyl., with the best modern Commentators, well illustrate by supposing that Philip had found Nathanael under a *certain fig-tree*; and had then, as often before, *conversed* with him about Christ; and that *now* our Lord mentions this in order to evince his divine power. And no wonder: for there had been a conversation of only *two*, nor was there any one present who could tell what had passed at it. Thus a conversation was alluded to, held at some time previous, and in a particular place, identifying it, and distinguishing it from any other. A proof this of supernatural knowledge, and consequently of a Divine commission. Hence Nathanael, from this display of superhuman knowledge, even of the secrets of the heart, could not but recognise a divine virtue in Jesus. (Tittm.) That conversation, meditation, and even prayer, was carried on under fig-trees, is proved by the Rabbinical citations of Lightf. and Schoettg.

— ὁ Υἱὸς τοῦ Θεοῦ.] By this it is plain Nathanael meant the *Messiah*. And from the term just after, "King of Israel," it is as plain that he thought only of an *earthly* kingdom. Our Lord, however, encourages his faith, imperfect as it was, in the words following, "Dost thou believe," &c.

51, 52. πιστεύεις — Υἱὸν τοῦ ἀνθρώπου.] On the scope of this assurance the Commentators differ; some recognising *reproof*; others, *praise*; which latter view seems best founded. "Our Lord (says Tittm.) at once *commends* and *exhorts*." With respect to the words ἀπ' ἄρτι — Υἱὸν τοῦ ἀνθρώπου, the Commentators are not agreed whether they should be taken *literally*, to signify such angelic manifestations as those recorded at Matt. iv. 11. xxviii. 2. Lu. ii. 9, 13, 22, and 43. Acts i. 10.; or *figuratively*, in the sense, henceforth "you will see me enjoy the especial providence and signal defence of the Almighty; you will see far *greater* works than this, even mighty *miracles* wrought by me; so as to leave no doubt of my Messiahship." The former view is adopted by the ancient and the earlier modern Commentators: the latter, by those of after times, and especially the recent Interpreters; and it seems, upon the whole, to deserve the preference. Yet the literal sense need not be *excluded*; nor is it without reason that most of the older Commentators suppose an allusion to Jacob's vision, Gen. xxviii. 12. Thus the meaning seems to be, that they should henceforward see such a series of *miracles* wrought by Christ, in the course of his ministry, that it should seem as if heaven were opened, and the angels of God were continually (as they appeared in vision to Jacob) ascending and descending upon the Son of Man; hinting that in the Gospel dispensation now commenced, should be *fulfilled* the blessings which had been *figuratively represented* by that vision.

II. 1. τῇ ἡμέρᾳ τῇ τρίτῃ] i. e. on the third day after Christ's arrival in Galilee from Bethany. Γάμος here denotes a marriage-*feast*.

2. ἐκλήθη.] On what ground, whether of *relationship*, or of *acquaintance*, Jesus was invited, is variously conjectured. It is most probable that the bride or bridegroom, or both, were related to his mother, Mary, who, it is supposed, had been προμνηστρία, or νυμφαγωγὸς, and had been already there making arrangements for the feast, since it is plain that she had the chief direction therein. The house is conjectured to have been that of Alpheus or Clopas, who married the sister of Jesus' mother.

3. οἶνον οὐκ ἔχουσι] equivalent to ὑστερεῖ οἶνος; the wine is "falling short." Comp. Gen. xliii. 2. This might very well happen without supposing any excess on the part of the guests; since these festivities lasted a considerable, though not any certain number of days. Besides, Jesus and his disciples were probably not calculated on when the wine was provided; and more than were expected might be attracted to the company by the fame of our Lord. With what intent Mary addressed our Lord, the commentators are not agreed. Some suppose she meant to hint that it was time to depart: and our Lord's answer, they think, imports that it was not yet time to go. That, however, yields a very frigid sense, and supposes something enigmatical in the words: which were no doubt meant to intimate the inability of the host to provide a further supply of wine. And, from the *poverty* of our Lord, it is not probable (as some imagine) that this could be a *hint* to *him* to provide a supply. It seems best to suppose, (with Chrysost., and almost all the earlier modern Commentators,) that Mary had a view to the removal of the want by *miracle*. Indeed, considering the wonderful circumstances of her son's birth and childhood, and the recent testimony to his Divine mission by John the Baptist, she was *warranted* in that expectation. Thus the words may be considered as a hint that it would be proper to commence his Ministry, and prove his Divine mission by a miracle, which should unite a benefit to her friend, together with a manifestation of his own Divine power. Her directions to the servants plainly evince the above expectation. Though that our Lord had been *accustomed* to work miracles in private, for the

σοῦς· Τί ἐμοὶ καὶ σοὶ, γύναι; οὔπω ἥκει ἡ ὥρα μου. Λέγει ἡ μή- 5
g Mark 7. 3. τηρ αὐτοῦ τοῖς διακόνοις· Ὅ τι ἂν λέγῃ ὑμῖν, ποιήσατε. g Ἦσαν δὲ 6
ἐκεῖ ὑδρίαι λίθιναι ἓξ κείμεναι, κατὰ τὸν καθαρισμὸν τῶν Ἰουδαίων,
χωροῦσαι ἀνὰ μετρητὰς δύο ἢ τρεῖς. Λέγει αὐτοῖς ὁ Ἰησοῦς· Γεμί- 7
σατε τὰς ὑδρίας ὕδατος· καὶ ἐγέμισαν αὐτὰς ἕως ἄνω. Καὶ λέγει 8
αὐτοῖς· Ἀντλήσατε νῦν καὶ φέρετε τῷ ἀρχιτρικλίνῳ· καὶ ἤνεγκαν.
Ὡς δὲ ἐγεύσατο ὁ ἀρχιτρίκλινος τὸ ὕδωρ οἶνον γεγενημένον, (καὶ οὐκ 9
ᾔδει πόθεν ἐστίν· οἱ δὲ διάκονοι ᾔδεισαν οἱ ἠντληκότες τὸ ὕδωρ)
φωνεῖ τὸν νυμφίον ὁ ἀρχιτρίκλινος, καὶ λέγει αὐτῷ· Πᾶς ἄνθρωπος 10
πρῶτον τὸν καλὸν οἶνον τίθησι, καὶ ὅταν μεθυσθῶσι, τότε τὸν ἐλάσσω·

support or comfort of his mother (as some imagine), is inconsistent with ver. 11., unless the words there be taken somewhat violently, of *public* miracles.

4. τί ἐμοὶ καὶ σοὶ, γύναι;] These words cannot import (as some Commentators suppose) *strong reprehension*. For that would seem unmerited by the address preceding. As far as the opinion rests on the γύναι, it is utterly unfounded; since this was a form of address used even to the most dignified persons; and employed by Jesus to his *mother* on the most affecting of all occasions. As to the other words, τί ἐμοὶ καὶ σοὶ, they are a *formula* taken from the language of common life; and must be interpreted according to the occasion and the circumstances of the case. It usually denotes impatience of interference, signifying, "What hast thou to do with me?" as appears from numerous passages, both of the Scriptural and Classical writers, adduced by Wets. and others. This would seem to be the sense here; though it was probably modified by the tone of voice, and softened into a mild rebuke for interfering with him in a matter where her parental claim to respect could have no authority over him.

The words following οὔπω—μου evidently mean, "The right time for my doing what you suggest, is not yet come;" which implied that *he* alone was the proper judge of that season, and would seize it when it arrived; thus mixing comfort with mild reproof. The time seems to have been when the wine was *quite* exhausted, and thus the reality of the miracle would be undoubted.

6. ὑδρίαι] i. e. water vats, or butts for domestic purposes, and the various washings prescribed by the Jewish Law. See Luke xi. 39.

— κατὰ τὸν καθ.] Κατὰ here signifies *propter, for the purpose of*; a very rare sense, for which the Classical writers use πρός. Thus, in a kindred passage of Plutarch, which I have adduced in Recens. Synop. Κατὰ τύχην πολλοὶ παρῆσαν ἀγγεῖα, πρὸς τὸ λουτρὸν ὕδατος, διὰ χειρῶν ἔχοντες.

— ἀνὰ μετρ.] On the exact quantity designated by the μετρητὴς Commentators and Antiquaries are not agreed. For the term may designate the Heb. בַּת, to which it answers in the LXX., i. e. a measure containing $7\frac{1}{2}$ gallons; or the *Attic measure Metretes*, consisting of 9 gallons. See Eisenschmid de pond. et mens. iv. 2. The latter is the more probable; though, even according to the former, the quantity of liquor has been cavilled at by sceptics. But the largeness of the quantity would be *requisite* in order to place the miracle beyond dispute. Nor can the quantity be thought enormous for many days' consumption of such a number of guests as had assembled; to which *more* would now be added by the fame of the miracle, and from curiosity to see the worker of it. Not to say that we need not suppose *all* the wine to be consumed. The surplus, if any, would be acceptable to the newly married couple.

7. γεμίσατε—ἕως ἄνω.] These circumstances are *not*, as some fancy, too *minute* to be worthy of introduction. They are mentioned to evince the *truth* and *magnitude* of the miracle; as in that worked by Elijah, 1 Kings xviii. 33—35., the Prophet in like manner exclaims, "Fill four barrels with water, and pour it," &c. "Do it the second time—Do it the third time." The words were, no doubt, pronounced, and the thing done, *publicly*. The order to fill them, which was fully obeyed, rendered all collusion, by procuring and introducing of the wine, impossible. That what the guests saw as water was become wine, was likewise evinced in the plainest manner.

8. ἀρχιτρικλίνῳ] "the director of the feast," i. e. a person (not one of the guests) who was appointed to superintend the preparations for, and management of, a feast; examining the provisions and liquor brought forward, and passing among the guests to see that they were in want of nothing, and giving the necessary orders to the servants. (See Ecclus. xxxii. 1.) This ἀρχιτρίκλινος is to be distinguished from the συμποσιάρχης, βασιλεὺς, or στρατηγὸς, of the Greeks, and the *moderator, arbiter, rex convivii*, of the Romans. This latter was one of the *guests*, chosen sometimes by lot, who presided at the table, and prescribed rules in regard to drinking, &c. (Wahl.) Walch, Lampe, and Kuin., say, that the Architriclinus was a *domestic*. Indeed, if he was the same with the Triclinarches of the Romans, he *was* such. A decisive proof, however, is that Juvencus, in his Hist. Evang., terms the Architriclinus a *summus minister*. The wine was, as usual, handed to the Architriclinus, in order that he might taste, and see if it were worthy of being set before the company.

10. πᾶς ἄνθρωπος—τίθησι.] This denotes wha *it was customary* to do: which is illustrated by the Classical citations in Wets. Μεθύειν is from μέθυ, (probably derived from the Northern word Med or Meth) and signifies to moisten, or be moistened with liquor, and in a figurative sense (like the Latin *madere vino*) *to be saturated with drink*. In *Classical* use it *generally*, but not always implies intoxication. *One* exception I have myself adduced in Recens Synop. from Aristot. ap. Stob. Phys. ii. 312. where the wise man is permitted μεθυσθήσεσθαι κατὰ συμπεριφορῆς. So also Plutarch Alex. 69. (a passage very similar to Gen

11 σὺ τετήρηκας τὸν καλὸν οἶνον ἕως ἄρτι. Ταύτην ἐποίησε τὴν ἀρχὴν
τῶν σημείων ὁ Ἰησοῦς ἐν Κανᾶ τῆς Γαλιλαίας, καὶ ἐφανέρωσε τὴν
δόξαν αὐτοῦ· καὶ ἐπίστευσαν εἰς αὐτὸν οἱ μαθηταὶ αὐτοῦ.
12 Μετὰ τοῦτο κατέβη εἰς Καπερναοὺμ, αὐτὸς καὶ ἡ μήτηρ αὐτοῦ, καὶ
οἱ ἀδελφοὶ αὐτοῦ, καὶ οἱ μαθηταὶ αὐτοῦ· καὶ ἐκεῖ ἔμειναν οὐ πολλὰς
13 ἡμέρας. Καὶ ἐγγὺς ἦν τὸ πάσχα τῶν Ἰουδαίων, καὶ ἀνέβη εἰς Ἱεροσό-
14 λυμα ὁ Ἰησοῦς. [h] Καὶ εὗρεν ἐν τῷ ἱερῷ τοὺς πωλοῦντας βόας καὶ h Matt. 21. 12. Mark 11. 15. Luke 19. 45.
15 πρόβατα καὶ περιστερὰς, καὶ τοὺς κερματιστὰς καθημένους. Καὶ ποιή-
σας φραγέλλιον ἐκ σχοινίων, πάντας ἐξέβαλεν ἐκ τοῦ ἱεροῦ, τά τε πρό-

xliii. 34.) and Menander ap. Athen. p. 364. In the Hellenistic writers, however, as Joseph., Philo, and the LXX., it (like the Heb. שכר) very often only denotes drinking freely, and the hilarity consequent. So in Gen. xliii. 34. it is used of Joseph's brethren. Of the Commentators some adopt the former, some the latter sense. It should seem not very necessary to confine ourselves to either; since the Architriclinus is not speaking of the guests present, but only makes a general observation as to what was *usual*. Τὸν ἐλάσσω, literally, minus nobile, *less* [*good.*]

—σὺ τετήρηκας τὸν καλὸν ο. ἕ. ἄ.] To preclude the suspicion that their taste was vitiated, through excessive drinking, so as not to know water from wine, Jesus orders it first to be carried to the *governor of the feast*, who must have been sober; for those who were entrusted with this office were obliged to observe the strictest sobriety, that they might be able properly to direct the whole business of the entertainment.

11. τῶν σημείων.] Σημεῖον properly denotes 1. a *mark*, seal, or token, by which any thing is known to be what it is, and distinguished from something else; 2. a pledge or assurance, taken in evidence; 3. a *miraculous* sign, A MIRACLE, either 1. in confirmation of the Divine power or legation of the worker of it; or 2. a miracle simply; in which case it is either joined with τέρας, or stands by itself. A miracle may be defined, with Farmer and Dr. Maltby, "Every sensible deviation from, and every *seeming* contradiction to. the laws of nature, *so far as they are known to us*. By thus expressing myself (says Dr. Maltby), I would guard against an objection which has been made to the language employed by some advocates, as well as enemies, of Christianity, when they represent *miracles* as *violations of the laws of nature*." Dr. Brown, a profound metaphysician, and the successor of the celebrated Dugald Stewart, contends that miracles *à priori*. are possible; that they are not violations of the laws of nature, and are capable, under certain circumstances, of being made credible by testimony. "The possibility (says Dr. Brown), of the occasional direct operation of the power which formed the world, in varying the usual course of its events, it would be in the highest degree unphilosophical to deny; nor can we presume to estimate the degree of its probability. The laws of nature, surely, are not *violated* when a new antecedent is followed by a new consequent; they are violated only when the antecedent, being exactly the same, a different consequent is the result. A miracle is *not* a violation of any law of nature. It involves, therefore, primarily, no contradiction, nor physical absurdity. It has nothing in it which is inconsistent with our belief of the most undeviating uniformity of nature; for it is not the sequence of a different event, when the preceding circumstances have been the same: it is an effect that is new to our observation, because it is the result of new and peculiar circumstances. The antecedent has been by supposition different; and it is not wonderful, therefore, that the consequent also should be different. While every miracle is to be considered as the result of an extraordinary antecedent; since it flows directly from a higher power than is accustomed to operate in the common train of events which come beneath our view, the sequence which it displays may be regarded, indeed, as out of the common course of nature, but not as contrary to that course." On this whole subject see Horne's Introduction, vol. i. 205—271.

—καὶ ἐπίστευσαν.] The καὶ may be rendered *and so*, as in Matt. xii. 45. xiii. 22. Luke ix. 39. John x. 11. Acts vii. 10. and sometimes in the Sept.

13. τὸ πάσχα.] The best Commentators, ancient and modern, are generally agreed that St. John mentions *four* Passovers as occurring during Christ's ministry, of which they reckon *this* as the 1st; that mentioned at v. 1. the 2d; that at vi. 4. the 3d; and that at which Christ suffered as the 4th. Thus his ministry will extend to three years and a half.

14. εὗρεν — πωλοῦντας.] The best Commentators, ancient and modern, are generally agreed that this circumstance was prior to, and consequently different from the similar one recorded at Matt. xxi. 12. sq. There seems a great propriety in this symbolical action (which denoted the purification of the Jewish Religion) being used both at the beginning and the close of Christ's ministry.

—βόας.] The number of victims of all sorts, (as we learn from Josephus,) sometimes amounted to 2,500,000; and it is certain from the Rabbinical writers, that immense traffic was carried on in cattle, &c. for victims, and much extortion practised; a great part of the profits of which accrued to the Priests. Even at the best, very great indecorum was involved. The κερμ. here are the same with the κολλυβισταὶ at Matt. xxi. 12, changers of small coin.

15. φραγέλλιον ἐκ σχ.] "a scourge of ropes," or bands made of rushes, &c., such as were used for tying up the cattle. We need not, however, suppose much, if any, *use* made of the φραγέλλιον, except to serve for a *symbolical action*. Besides, there was no need of stripes. The traffickers, conscious of the unlawfulness of their proceedings, and struck by the Divine energy of our Lord, would not hesitate to obey his injunctions,

βατα καὶ τοὺς βόας. Καὶ τῶν κολλυβιστῶν ἐξέχεε τὸ κέρμα, καὶ τὰς
τραπέζας ἀνέστρεψε· καὶ τοῖς τὰς περιστερὰς πωλοῦσιν εἶπεν· Ἄρατε 16
ταῦτα ἐντεῦθεν· μὴ ποιεῖτε τὸν οἶκον τοῦ πατρός μου οἶκον ἐμπο-
i Psal. 69. 9. ρίου. [i] Ἐμνήσθησαν δὲ οἱ μαθηταὶ αὐτοῦ, ὅτι γεγραμμένον ἐστίν· 17
k Matt. 12. 38. & 16. 1. Mark 8. 11. Luke 11. 29. infra. 6. 30. Ὁ ζῆλος τοῦ οἴκου σου ‡ κατέφαγέ με. [k] Ἀπεκρίθησαν οὖν 18
οἱ Ἰουδαῖοι καὶ εἶπον αὐτῷ· Τί σημεῖον δεικνύεις ἡμῖν, ὅτι ταῦτα
l Matt. 26. 61. & 27. 40. Mark 14. 58. & 15. 29. ποιεῖς; [l] Ἀπεκρίθη ὁ Ἰησοῦς καὶ εἶπεν αὐτοῖς· Λύσατε τὸν ναὸν 19
τοῦτον, καὶ ἐν τρισὶν ἡμέραις ἐγερῶ αὐτόν. Εἶπον οὖν οἱ Ἰουδαῖοι· 20
Τεσσαράκοντα καὶ ἓξ ἔτεσιν ᾠκοδομήθη ὁ ναὸς οὗτος· καὶ σὺ ἐν τρισὶν ἡμέραις ἐγερεῖς αὐτόν; Ἐκεῖνος δὲ ἔλεγε περὶ τοῦ ναοῦ τοῦ σώματος 21
m Luke 24. 8. αὐτοῦ. [m] Ὅτε οὖν ἠγέρθη ἐκ νεκρῶν, ἐμνήσθησαν οἱ μαθηταὶ αὐτοῦ 22
ὅτι τοῦτο ἔλεγεν [αὐτοῖς]· καὶ ἐπίστευσαν τῇ γραφῇ καὶ τῷ λόγῳ ᾧ
εἶπεν ὁ Ἰησοῦς. Ὡς δὲ ἦν ἐν Ἱεροσολύμοις ἐν τῷ πάσχα ἐν τῇ ἑορτῇ, 23
πολλοὶ ἐπίστευσαν εἰς τὸ ὄνομα αὐτοῦ, θεωροῦντες αὐτοῦ τὰ σημεῖα ἃ
ἐποίει. Αὐτὸς δὲ ὁ Ἰησοῦς οὐκ ἐπίστευεν ἑαυτὸν αὐτοῖς, διὰ τὸ αὐτὸν 24
n Infra 6. 64. Acts 1. 24. Rev. 2. 23. γινώσκειν πάντας· [n] καὶ ὅτι οὐ χρείαν εἶχεν ἵνα τὶς μαρτυρήσῃ περὶ 25
τοῦ ἀνθρώπου· αὐτὸς γὰρ ἐγίνωσκε τί ἦν ἐν τῷ ἀνθρώπῳ.

especially as the crowd of approving and admiring bystanders would be ready to enforce that obedience.

— κέρμα.] This signifies *small coin*, from κείρω. For the most ancient coins (especially the Oriental) being (like Spanish rials) of a square form, admitted of being *cut*, so as to form the lesser kind of money. Ἐξέχεε is especially suitable to *minute* coin.

— ἀνέστρεψε.] Some would read ἀνέτρεψε, from certain MSS. But though that is more accordant with *Classical* usage, it is, probably, *ex interpretatione*. Ἀναστρέφειν was, it should seem, used in the common dialect for ἀνατρέπειν

17. ὁ ζῆλος — με.] This brought to our Lord's mind the words of Ps. lxix. 9. Κατέφαγε involves an Oriental and emphatical metaphor, appropriate not only to grief or indignation, (as here,) but to other of the more violent passions, which (in the words of Gray) "inly gnaw the heart." See Job xix. 22, and the Classical passages adduced by Lampe and myself in Recens. Synop. Ζῆλος τοῦ οἴκου signifies, not zeal of, but zeal for; and the Aorist κατέφαγε signifies *exedere solet*.

For κατέφαγε, καταφάγεται is found in very many ancient MSS. and early Edd., and is adopted by almost all the recent Editors.

19. λύσατε τὸν ναὸν τ.] An *acutè dictum*, so uttered to draw the attention of the by-standers; the understanding of which, however, might be aided by *action*; our Lord pointing to his own body, the temple of the Logos. Thus the Hebrews used to call the body אהיל, σκῆνος. See Note on 2 Cor. v. 1. Nay, Philo calls it ναός, or ἱερόν, with reference to the dignity of the soul which tenants it. Indeed, δέμας and δομή (found in the sense of *body* in Lycophr. Cass. 783.) both denote a *building*; and St. Paul often speaks of the body of a Christian as being a *temple* of the Holy Spirit. The Imper. has here, as often, a *permissive* sense; q. d. you *may* destroy; which differs little from the *hypothetical* sense, "Be it that you destroy." Our Lord means to say, that his resurrection from the dead will be the especial sign by which his Divine mission shall be declared.

20. τεσσαράκοντα — οὗτος.] The sense is: "Forty and six years hath this Temple been a building." The use of the Aorist will *permit*, and facts *require* this rendering. For it was then the 46th year since the time when Herod commenced the building. He formed it on a dilapidated one originally erected by *Zorobabel*; using the old materials, and sometimes the old foundations. In consequence of which, and especially as it was raised by parts, the old buildings being gradually pulled down, and new ones erected in their place, so the edifice was still called *Zorobabel's*, and the *second* Temple, nay even Josephus so terms it.

22. ἐπίστευσαν τῇ γραφῇ] i. e. by a comparison of those parts of the O. T., which predict the Messiah's rising from the dead, both with Jesus' *words*, and with the *fact* of his resurrection, they thoroughly believed in the inspiration of the Scriptures and the divine mission of Jesus.

23. σημεῖα.] What these were we know not. But from this passage and from iv. 45. and vi. 2. it is certain that Christ worked many miracles not recorded by the sacred writers.

— ἐπίστευσαν εἰς τὸ ὄνομα α.] Their faith, however, it appears from what follows, was only an external and historical, not an internal and vital one. The understanding was convinced, but the will was not subdued to obedience.

24. οὐκ ἐπίστευεν ἑαυτὸν αὐτοῖς.] Some Commentators take this to mean, "he did not trust his person (i. e. his life and safety) to them." But this is frigid; and it is better, with the most eminent Commentators, ancient and modern, to interpret the phrase *figuratively*: "he did not place any implicit confidence in, by imparting his true character as Messiah, — carried himself cautiously and circumspectly towards them." The *complete knowledge* of the hearts of men which is thus ascribed to Christ, is among the other irrefragable proofs of his Divinity; for omniscience is the attribute of *God* alone.

1 III. [o] Ἦν δὲ ἄνθρωπος ἐκ τῶν Φαρισαίων, Νικόδημος ὄνομα [o Infra. 7. 50. & 19. 39.]
2 αὐτῷ, ἄρχων τῶν Ἰουδαίων. [p] οὗτος ἦλθε πρὸς * αὐτὸν νυκτὸς, καὶ [p infr. 9. 16, 33. Acts 10. 38.]
εἶπεν αὐτῷ· Ῥαββὶ, οἴδαμεν ὅτι ἀπὸ Θεοῦ ἐλήλυθας διδάσκαλος·
οὐδεὶς γὰρ ταῦτα τὰ σημεῖα δύναται ποιεῖν ἃ σὺ ποιεῖς, ἐὰν μὴ ᾖ ὁ
3 Θεὸς μετ' αὐτοῦ. [q] Ἀπεκρίθη ὁ Ἰησοῦς καὶ εἶπεν αὐτῷ· Ἀμὴν ἀμὴν [q Tit. 3. 5.]

III. We are now advanced to a most important narrative, — in which, as it has a bearing on one of the most important doctrines of the Gospel, more than usual care should be taken to trace the true scope and intent of the Evangelist in recording this conversation, and to ascertain the real import of the phraseology there employed. Now the *intent* of the sacred historian was here, as in all other parts of his Gospel, to set forth the glory of the Lord; and in the present instance particularly it should seem meant to illustrate his *omniscience*. This is a key to the general import of what is narrated. Another important point is the *true character* and *real motives* of Nicodemus, in seeking this interview. That, however, is a subject involved in much obscurity; since we have there no *direct* information from the Evangelist, but are left to collect both one and the other from the narrative itself; which, while it doubtless contains the *substance*, of what was said *by our Lord*, yet probably records but a *part* of what was said, at least, by *Nicodemus*. Hence no little diversity of opinion exists as to the character and motives of this ruler. Some ascribe to him *integrity*, *candour*, and *diffidence*; united, however, with *timidity*; and they suppose his motives in seeking this interview to have been of the most honourable kind. Others paint his character in very different colours; ascribing his coming to *pride* cloaked under pretended humility, *craftiness*, and *dissimulation*, subservient to a purpose of treachery. Between these opposite views a middle course will probably conduct us nearest to the truth. We may suppose him to have been a proud, timid, and, in a great degree, worldly-minded man: though, at the same time, it should seem that in his character the good preponderated above the evil; and his motives appear, upon the whole, to have been good. If this Nicodemus was, (as is generally thought,) the Nicodemus of whom so much is said in the Rabbinical writers, we may gather some information that will prove important towards ascertaining his real character and views. He is there described as a man of unbounded wealth, even to a proverb, — of magnificent liberality — of piety the most ardent, — insomuch that they ascribe to him the working of miracles. His splendid fortune was, however, they say, attended by a reverse almost as great as that of *Job*. If to this we add what we learn from the Evangelist, — his official character, as a Ruler, and his high renown for learning, as *the* teacher of Israel, — we have the picture complete. Now it is obvious, that a person so circumstanced, — with so much to *lose*, and nothing, in a worldly point of view, to *gain* by any change of religion in the Jewish nation, would be naturally disposed to favour the *present state of things*; and to be tardy in embracing a new religion, and especially one so persecuted and evil spoken of as the Christian. None of his rank in life had hitherto embraced it; and, accordingly, he might think that great caution was necessary on his part. Uneasy doubts had probably long weighed on his mind. His *reason* was, on due inquiry, convinced that the evidence for the Messiahship of Jesus was of the strongest kind: and he could not but consider with alarm what would be his punishment if he neglected so great salvation! But to *yield* to these convictions, and *openly* embrace the Gospel, involved sacrifices of the severest kind, — all that was considered valuable in life, nay, probably life itself. Now Nicodemus was not one of those who are ready to give up *all* for religion's sake. In short, with many prejudices of the mind, was doubtless united a latent unsoundness of *heart*. His convictions of the reality of our Lord's pretensions had probably been gradual, but were now *decided*. Yet he was not prepared to make those unsparing sacrifices which the circumstances of his case demanded. Not venturing openly to avow, what he secretly believed, he resolves, like most timid and selfish men, to steer a *middle* course; and, with the usual expedient of cowardice, seeks to do that *privately* which he was afraid to do *publicly*; and, accordingly, seeks an interview *by night*, in order to be *privately* admitted to his discipleship. From the manner in which that interview was conducted, it is plain that our Lord fully penetrated into his real character. And if we bear in mind the various prejudices and infirmities of the man, in conjunction with his recent and sincere, but not deeply rooted faith in Christ, we shall be enabled to ascertain the real scope of what our Lord addressed to him. It seems to have been the especial intent of our Lord *first* to *humble* his pride of rank, wealth, and talents. That pride had, it seems, induced Nicodemus to think that Jesus would receive *him* as his convert on easier and less humiliating terms than those which he required from *the people* at large; namely, that of submitting to public baptism, and thus owning his need of repentance, and a total change of character. We cannot, of course, ascertain precisely the nature of the *information* for which Nicodemus meant to have applied, had he been allowed to propound all his inquiries. But they were probably on *the nature and properties of true religion; and the way in which those imperfections which he could not fail to discern in the Jewish, might be remedied.* He commences the conversation with a sort of half proud, half flattering compliment, expressive of the conviction of himself and all who weighed the evidence of miracles to prove a divine mission, that Jesus was at least a *teacher sent from God*. Whether Jesus were the Messiah or not, Nicodemus was probably *uncertain*; and perhaps *one* chief purpose of his visit was to ascertain that point, in a close and confidential interview. Fluctuating between hope and fear, doubt and conviction, he was resolved to know how far the doctrines of Jesus, when stated in private and confidential communication, did or did not coincide with the notion which he had formed of the Messiah. See a Discourse of Bp. Heber on the character of Nicodemus.

2. *αὐτόν*.] So many MSS. and some Versions and Fathers, which is adopted by almost all the recent Editors.

λέγω σοι· ἐὰν μή τις γεννηθῇ ἄνωθεν, οὐ δύναται ἰδεῖν τὴν βασι-
λείαν τοῦ Θεοῦ. Λέγει πρὸς αὐτὸν ὁ Νικόδημος· Πῶς δύναται ἄν- 4
θρωπος γεννηθῆναι γέρων ὤν; μὴ δύναται εἰς τὴν κοιλίαν τῆς
μητρὸς αὐτοῦ δεύτερον εἰσελθεῖν καὶ γεννηθῆναι; Ἀπεκρίθη ὁ 5
Ἰησοῦς· Ἀμὴν ἀμὴν λέγω σοι· ἐὰν μή τις γεννηθῇ ἐξ ὕδατος καὶ
πνεύματος, οὐ δύναται εἰσελθεῖν εἰς τὴν βασιλείαν τοῦ Θεοῦ. Τὸ 6
γεγεννημένον ἐκ τῆς σαρκὸς σάρξ ἐστι· καὶ τὸ γεγεννημένον ἐκ τοῦ
πνεύματος πνεῦμά ἐστι. Μὴ θαυμάσῃς ὅτι εἶπόν σοι· Δεῖ ὑμᾶς γεν- 7
r Eccl. 11. 5. 1 Cor. 2. 11. *νηθῆναι ἄνωθεν. [r] Τὸ πνεῦμα ὅπου θέλει πνεῖ, καὶ τὴν φωνὴν αὐτοῦ* 8
ἀκούεις, ἀλλ' οὐκ οἶδας πόθεν ἔρχεται καὶ ποῦ ὑπάγει· οὕτως ἐστὶ

3. *ἀπεκρίθη — ἐὰν μή.* &c.] It is with great probability supposed by Beza, Calvin, Lampe, Tittm., and Kuin., that this reply of our Lord interrupted Nicodemus in his address; and that, in order to increase his faith, by evincing his perfect knowledge of what was passing in the mind of the Jewish teacher, our Lord, without waiting till he should have propounded his inquiries, *anticipated* him by replying to them *in thought*. *What* those inquiries were, however, has been much disputed. The earlier Commentators suppose them to have been on the *mode of attaining eternal salvation*: most recent Commentators, on the *person of the Messiah*, and the *nature of the* salvation to be expected. But there is no reason why both these views may not be united. The question, however, hinges on the force of the expression *γεννηθῇ ἄνωθεν*. Many recent Expositors (as Rosenm. and Kuin.) maintain that it here denotes a total change of *sentiment* and *opinion* as to the Messiah, the nature of his kingdom, and the benefits thereof. But no *proof* has been made out that the expression in question was ever used *merely* of a change of *sentiments* and *views*. Besides, it is plain, from a comparison of these words with those at vv. 5 & 7, that such cannot be the sense here intended. It should seem that our Lord did not intend to advert to any *particular* heads of inquiry meant to be propounded by Nicodemus, but cuts off all such discussions at once, by laying the axe at the root of the prejudices and errors which struggled with his faith, and made him only *half* a believer; declaring that there must be an entire change of heart, disposition, &c., as implied in the sincere embracing of a new and spiritual religion, before he could hope for salvation through the Messiah. The expression *ἄνωθεν γενν.* is plainly equivalent to *ἀναγεννηθῆναι* or *παλιγγενεσία*, which denote properly a *new birth*, but figuratively a *complete alteration* and *reformation*. Our Lord, however, evidently intended *more* than even *that*; as appears v. 5. (where see Note.) That Nicodemus understood his words in the manner above explained, there can be no doubt; for the expression was a common one among the Jews, to signify an *entire change of heart and life*, though it was almost always connected with *baptism* as the *symbol* or pledge of it. The expressions, therefore, of Nicodemus, in his answer v. 4, *γεννηθῆναι* and *δεύτερον γεννηθῆναι*, must not be taken, with many Expositors, in a *physical*, but in a moral and *metaphorical* sense, q. d.; "As it involves not only a physical impossibility, but a moral unfitness, for an aged man to be born again; so it involves as great a moral unfitness for such a person to be figuratively born again, by a total change of mind and heart. He meant, doubtless, to hint that there would be a far greater moral unfitness in *his* case, a man of his great consequence in all respects, such as ought to *exempt him* from ordinary probations and empty ceremonies. To this our Lord replies by simply *repeating* his former assertion; and though he retains the same figure, he varies its form, to set forth the *full extent* of what was required of him. Now the expression *δεύτερον γεννηθῆναι* was one commonly used by the Jews to denote the total change of religion, from heathenism to the worship of the one true God; but it was *also* applied to the entire change of heart and purification of mind *typified* by the ceremony of *baptism*. That the term *ὕδατος* must be understood of *baptism*, is quite plain from Titus iii. 5, and other passages.

The purpose of the next verse (6.) seems to be, to set forth the indispensable *necessity* of this regeneration by water and the Spirit, in order to the attainment of everlasting salvation; for that, as the mere natural or animal life depends on flesh and blood, so does the *spiritual* life depend on the baptism by water and by the Spirit.

8. The argument here is, that however *strange* this two-fold regeneration may seem, it is not to be thought *impossible*, — any more than many wonderful phænomena in the *natural* world; which are obvious to the *senses*, though their *causes* defy all explanation. And in order to illustrate a spiritual truth by something familiar to the senses, our Lord subjoins an example from the *wind*, on the *causes* of which see an interesting extract from Vogler in Recens. Synop. The expressions, however, are not to be interpreted with philosophical subtilty, but according to *popular* ideas; for the investigations of Wolf, Wets., and others, have proved, that both the Hebrews and the ancients in general were accustomed (by a sort of proverb) to signify any thing unknown or obscure by comparing it with *the wind*. The *application* of the figure is, that a man knows that his heart is more interested in religion, that he has a deeper insight and greater relish for spiritual truths: and though he does not perceive the immediate *influence* from which this change proceeded, yet the *effects* he knows by communing with his own heart. And they are of a kind which he must ascribe to the Author of all good, though he cannot trace the *exact process* by which that heavenly agency was employed for that effect; yet he does not the less believe its reality. Here, too, there may be an allusion to the *freedom* of that Divine grace, which, not

9 πᾶς ὁ γεγεννημένος ἐκ τοῦ πνεύματος. [s] ἀπεκρίθη Νικόδημος καὶ [s] Infr. 6. 52, 60.
10 εἶπεν αὐτῷ· Πῶς δύναται ταῦτα γενέσθαι; Ἀπεκρίθη ὁ Ἰησοῦς καὶ
εἶπεν αὐτῷ· Σὺ εἶ ὁ διδάσκαλος τοῦ Ἰσραὴλ, καὶ ταῦτα οὐ γινώσκεις;
11 [t] Ἀμὴν ἀμὴν λέγω σοι, ὅτι ὃ οἴδαμεν λαλοῦμεν, καὶ ὃ ἑωράκαμεν μαρ- [t] Infra. ver. 32. & 7. 16. & 8. 28.
12 τυροῦμεν· καὶ τὴν μαρτυρίαν ἡμῶν οὐ λαμβάνετε. Εἰ τὰ ἐπίγεια & 12. 49. & 14. 24.
εἶπον ὑμῖν, καὶ οὐ πιστεύετε· πῶς, ἐὰν εἴπω ὑμῖν τὰ ἐπουράνια, πι-
13 στεύσετε; [u] Καὶ οὐδεὶς ἀναβέβηκεν εἰς τὸν οὐρανὸν, εἰ μὴ ὁ ἐκ τοῦ [u] Infra. 6. 62. Eph. 4. 9.

confining the blessings of salvation to the *Jews*, extended them to *the whole human* race.

9. On hearing this, Nicodemus, partly perplexed with what seemed obscure, and partly confounded with what, though he *understood*, he was not prepared to *receive*, exclaims, with unfeigned surprise, πῶς δύναται ταῦτα γενέσθαι? — a mode of expression which involves a modest request for further information. Our Lord, however, before he communicated this, was pleased to humble his pride, by adverting to his ignorance of what, as "a teacher of Israel," he might have known, because the Prophets of the O. T. had, though obscurely, intimated these truths. See Isaiah xlix. 21. lxvi. 8. Ezek. xxxvi. 26, 27. xxxvii. 9, 10. His humiliation must have been great indeed if the expression ὁ διδάσκαλος mean, as Bp. Middl., with some reason, supposes it to do, "*the* teacher of Israel;" a title which he aptly compares with those given, in the middle ages, to the great schoolmen; one of whom was called the *Angelic* Doctor; another, the *Admirable*; and a third, the *Irrefragable*.

11. ὃ οἴδαμεν — μαρτυροῦμεν.] The best Commentators are agreed that the plural is here used agreeably to the usage of persons in authority. (See Mark iv. 30.) The next clause ὃ ἑωρ. μαρτ. is still more significant than that which preceded. Both are expressive of that *complete knowledge* which our Lord, as united with God the Father, could not but possess. There is also implied knowledge *by a virtue of his own*, and not by revelation.

12. Having at v. 11. asserted the *authority* with which he was invested, as a teacher come from God; and made his claim to complete truth in every *statement*, and unerring wisdom in every *doctrine*; our Lord here points out the improbability of producing conviction in *greater* matters, when his endeavours to convince upon the less had been thus unsuccessful. "If I have told you earthly things, and ye believe not, how shall ye believe, if I tell you of heavenly things?" as much as to say: The same absence of impartial inquiry and fixed attention — the same disposition to measure every tenet offered to your consideration, by your own confined views, or crooked prepossessions — the same unwillingness to examine the *grounds* upon which, as Teacher of Israel, you have erected your pretensions to superior sagacity and sanctity — these very same causes which prevent you from believing what is more familiar to your memory, and more obvious to your understanding, will have betrayed you into *more* criminal incredulity, when your Teacher expatiates upon a subject of far *greater* difficulty and moment. By τὰ ἐπίγεια are denoted earthly doctrines, such as that of regeneration by water and the Spirit, so called because they are things *done* upon earth, and therefore to be comprehended. By ἐπουράνια is meant the purposes of God for the salvation of man, involving the doctrines mentioned in the subsequent part of this discourse; and also other doctrines, which, though not adverted to in this conversation, were afterwards revealed by the Holy Spirit; namely, the mysterious union of Christ with God, and His being subject unto death not only for the Jews, but for the *Gentiles*; such as are by St. Paul termed μυστήρια. The sense of the whole passage is most learnedly discussed, and the full force of ἐπουράνια ably pointed out, by B. L. Raphelius, in the erudite Preface to his father's Notes on the N. T. He confirms the above explanation of ἐπίγεια by two apposite quotations from Origen and Ammonius, and also the explanation of οὐδεὶς ἀναβέβ., &c. in the next verse.

13. καὶ οὐδεὶς ἀναβέβηκεν — οὐρανῷ.] *Literally* to ascend to heaven could not apply to our Saviour; for his *ascension* had not yet taken place: *figuratively*, it means the investigation of hidden things; and for such investigation Christ, who came down from heaven, was peculiarly qualified. The phrase ἀναβ. εἰς τὸν οὐρανὸν (as Schoettgen and others notice) is used agreeably to the language commonly employed of one who *announced any revelation*, — that he had ascended to heaven and fetched his knowledge from thence. The ὢν is, I conceive, of the Present Indefinite; and ὁ ὢν ἐν οὐρ. means, "whose proper dwelling-place is in heaven." The sense, then, is: "And no one has ever ascended to heaven, to bring down this information from heaven, nor can any one except the *Son of man*, (i. e. the Messiah) reveal the counsels of God for the salvation of man, i. e. "No one knoweth the counsels of God but I who came down from God." Now in Deut. xxx. 11. we read: "This commandment which I command thee this day, it is not hidden from thee, neither is it far off. It is not *in heaven*, that thou shouldst cry, Who shall go over the sea for us, and bring it unto us, that we may hear it, and do it?" Alluding to which passage St. Paul, at Rom. x. 6. says: "The righteousness which is of faith speaketh on this wise, Say not in thine heart, Who shall ascend into heaven? (that is, to bring Christ down from above). But what saith it? The word is nigh thee, even in thy mouth, and in thy heart: that is, the word of faith, which we preach." Meaning, that the Gospel Dispensation is not so hidden, that we must draw it from heaven, or raise it from the abyss; for this were literally the same as if a man were to endeavour to bring down Christ from heaven; it would imply, that having come down from heaven before, he had not in his Gospel sufficiently explained to us the principle of justification and other heavenly things necessary to our salvation. See also Prov. xxx. 4. A similar form of expression occurs in Job xii. 32. and Luke v. 10. (where see Note.) Christ, then, who literally had been in heaven, is metaphorically said to have ascended thither,

x Num. 21. 9. 2 Kings 18. 4. Infra 8. 28. & 12. 32.
y Infra ver. 36. Luke 19. 10. 1 John 5. 10.
z Rom. 5. 8. & 8. 32. 1 John 4. 9.
a Infra 8. 39. & 12. 47. Luke 9. 56. 1 John 4. 14.
b Infra 5. 24. & 6. 40, 47. & 20. 31.

οὐρανοῦ καταβὰς, ὁ Υἱὸς τοῦ ἀνθρώπου ὁ ὢν ἐν τῷ οὐρανῷ. ^x Καὶ 14
καθὼς Μωϋσῆς ὕψωσε τὸν ὄφιν ἐν τῇ ἐρήμῳ, οὕτως ὑψωθῆναι δεῖ τὸν
Υἱὸν τοῦ ἀνθρώπου· ^y ἵνα πᾶς ὁ πιστεύων εἰς αὐτὸν μὴ ἀπόληται, 15
ἀλλ' ἔχῃ ζωὴν αἰώνιον. ^z Οὕτω γὰρ ἠγάπησεν ὁ Θεὸς τὸν κόσμον, 16
ὥστε τὸν Υἱὸν αὐτοῦ τὸν μονογενῆ ἔδωκεν, ἵνα πᾶς ὁ πιστεύων εἰς
αὐτὸν μὴ ἀπόληται, ἀλλ' ἔχῃ ζωὴν αἰώνιον. ^a οὐ γὰρ ἀπέστειλεν ὁ 17
Θεὸς τὸν Υἱὸν αὐτοῦ εἰς τὸν κόσμον, ἵνα κρίνῃ τὸν κόσμον, ἀλλ' ἵνα
σωθῇ ὁ κόσμος δι' αὐτοῦ. ^b Ὁ πιστεύων εἰς αὐτὸν οὐ κρίνεται· ὁ 18
δὲ μὴ πιστεύων ἤδη κέκριται, ὅτι μὴ πεπίστευκεν εἰς τὸ ὄνομα τοῦ

because, being in the bosom of his Father, he had the fulness of knowledge in heavenly things.

14. Let us now trace the *connection* between what is said on heavenly things, and the ascension of Christ into heaven, and the lifting up of the Son of man. Our Lord does not content himself with stating that Nicodemus would not believe, if he told him of heavenly things: he points out his *own peculiar* knowledge of these things, showing that no *mere man* hath so understood these heavenly things as the Son of Man, who came down from heaven to reveal them. Thus there is evidently, though it has been denied, a connection between the declaration about heavenly things, v. 12. and the assertion at v. 13. that they were known to Christ. Indeed, v. 14., which Schmid calls independent even of v. 13., is, in reality, connected with both that and the preceding one. Having asserted that the Jews would not believe him, when he spoke of heavenly things; and declared, that He who was in heaven had therefore contemplated and known them, he selects a particular and most striking *instance* of that which the Jews would not admit, and which he himself knew and came to reveal. He simply lays before Nicodemus two of the purposes of Divine wisdom for the salvation of men, which unassisted reason never could have pointed out — purposes which, till revealed, might well be called *mysteries* — purposes which *having been* revealed, instead of being any longer mysterious to the human mind, became at once level to our apprehensions, credible to our reason, and such as powerfully to interest our affections. They were as follows: — Nicodemus had, in common with other Pharisees, looked for the temporal advantages of the Messiah's kingdom; and his imagination arrayed him in all the pomp of earthly majesty. But what says Christ? "As Moses lifted up the serpent in the wilderness, even so must the Son of man be lifted up." Was not, then, the doctrine of a crucified Redeemer one of those "heavenly things" which Nicodemus and his countrymen were most unlikely to receive. Was it not a doctrine, the knowledge and communication of which was reserved for that exalted Being who came down from heaven. See more in a Sermon of Dr. Samuel Parr, on the Conversation of Christ with Nicodemus.

The doctrine, however, of a *suffering and dying Messiah*, our Lord as yet, from caution, revealed, even to Nicodemus, veiled under figure and ænigma; and though meant to stimulate his attention, it probably was very imperfectly comprehended by him *then*, though he would afterwards bring it to mind, and both see the full truth and recognise a solemn prediction fulfilled. The figurative way of expressing it was this: The Messiah must (it is destined that he should) be suspended on high, as was the brazen serpent in the wilderness. Comp. viii. 28. xii. 22. 32. This is plain from v. 16. It is not, however, agreed on among the Commentators whether this brazen serpent was meant to be a *type* of Christ crucified. Almost all the ancient, and nearly all the modern Commentators up to the middle of the last Century, maintained the affirmative. But the negative has (after Greg. Naz.) been supported by nearly all Commentators since the time of Vitringa, especially by Kuin., A. Clarke, and Tittm., whom see in Recens. Synop. There is, they show, only a *comparison*, namely, as to the *kind* of death, and its *cause*; which consists 1. in Christ's being suspended on the cross *as* the brazen serpent was suspended aloft by Moses; 2. that *as* all who looked with faith upon the serpent were cured of the bite of the fiery serpents, *so* will all who have faith in a crucified Saviour not perish, but have everlasting life.

15. ἵνα πᾶς — αἰώνιον.] Our Lord here adverts to the *causes* and the *effects* of this being lifted up. The *causes* were, 1. to save the human race from that utter perdition, which would have overwhelmed them, from sin, original and actual; 2. to acquire for them eternal salvation. The *effects* were, 1. deliverance from perdition; and 2. restoration to that favour of God, which is "better than life."

16—21. Most of the recent Commentators (as did Erasm. formerly) regard these verses as the words not of Jesus, but of the Evangelist. This they argue from certain *repetitions*, the *style*, and other matters of doubtful disputation. But there is no reason to abandon the common opinion, that they are a continuation of our Lord's discourse. Τὸν κόσμον is, as Grot., Lightf., and Tittm. remark, meant to show that the salvation to be obtained by the Saviour was to be extended to all the nations of the earth, and held out to every individual of the human race, in contradiction to the notion of the Jews, that he would come to bless and save them alone. Comp. 1 John ii. 2. Ἔδωκεν is here equivalent to παρέδωκεν, and signifies "hath delivered him to death;" which implies that he was a *ransom* for a sinful world. Comp. Luke xxii. 19. Rom. viii. 32. Gal. i. 4.

17. Tittm. observes, that what is said from v. 17. to 21. is levelled against the Jewish notion, that the Messiah would come for the benefit of the Jews only, nay, would rather destroy the Gentiles. Κρίνῃ is said to be for κατακρίνῃ, and to have the sense *punish* and *destroy*. We may render: "God sent his Son into the world not to exercise severe *judgment* and inflict *punishment* on any nation of the world, but that every one of

19 μονογενοῦς Υἱοῦ τοῦ Θεοῦ. [c] Αὕτη δέ ἐστιν ἡ κρίσις· ὅτι τὸ φῶς [c Supra 1. 5, 10, 11.]
ἐλήλυθεν εἰς τὸν κόσμον, καὶ ἠγάπησαν οἱ ἄνθρωποι μᾶλλον τὸ σκότος,
20 ἢ τὸ φῶς· ἦν γὰρ πονηρὰ αὐτῶν τὰ ἔργα. [d] Πᾶς γὰρ ὁ φαῦλα [d Job 24. 13, et seqq.]
πράσσων μισεῖ τὸ φῶς, καὶ οὐκ ἔρχεται πρὸς τὸ φῶς, ἵνα μὴ ἐλεγχθῇ
21 τὰ ἔργα αὐτοῦ· [e] ὁ δὲ ποιῶν τὴν ἀλήθειαν ἔρχεται πρὸς τὸ φῶς, ἵνα [e Eph. 5. 3.]
φανερωθῇ αὐτοῦ τὰ ἔργα, ὅτι ἐν Θεῷ ἐστιν εἰργασμένα.
22 [f] Μετὰ ταῦτα ἦλθεν ὁ Ἰησοῦς καὶ οἱ μαθηταὶ αὐτοῦ εἰς τὴν Ἰου- [f Infra 4. 1.]
23 δαίαν γῆν· καὶ ἐκεῖ διέτριβε μετ' αὐτῶν καὶ ἐβάπτιζεν. [g] Ἦν δὲ καὶ [g Matt. 3. 6, 16. Mark. 1 5. Luke 3 7. 1 Sam. 9. 4.]
Ἰωάννης βαπτίζων ἐν Αἰνὼν ἐγγὺς τοῦ Σαλείμ, ὅτι ὕδατα πολλὰ ἦν
24 ἐκεῖ· καὶ παρεγίνοντο καὶ ἐβαπτίζοντο. [h] οὔπω γὰρ ἦν βεβλημένος [h Matt. 14. 3.]
25 εἰς τὴν φυλακὴν ὁ Ἰωάννης. Ἐγένετο οὖν ζήτησις ἐκ τῶν μαθητῶν

them, through his atonement, might be put into the way of salvation." This truth is repeated at v. 18., but so as to show, that there will be no distinction between Jew and Gentile, since *every one*, of whatever nation, will have part in this salvation. Our Lord, however, engrafts upon it *another* sentiment in ἤδη κέκριται; i. e. he is not only doomed to perdition for refusing the offers of salvation, but he is already *as good as punished*, so certain is his condemnation; or, he is already miserable by the slavery of sin, nay, he is self-condemned and past all hope of salvation.

19. αὕτη δέ ἐστιν ἡ κρίσις, &c.] The best Commentators are agreed that by κρίσις is meant not the *punishment itself*, but the ground of the condemnation, as the cause of the punishment. The meaning is, that Christ is not the cause of any evil such men suffer by not listening to his doctrine, but the blame rests solely with *themselves*, who, blinded by passion and prejudice, were indisposed to receive the truth, though coming with the fullest evidence, and spurned the gracious offer of salvation; ἐν οἷς, to use the words of St. Paul, 2 Cor. iv. 4. ὁ Θεὸς τοῦ αἰῶνος τούτου ἐτύφλωσε τὰ νοήματα τῶν ἀπίστων, εἰς τὸ μὴ αὐγάσαι τὸν φωτισμὸν τοῦ εὐαγγελίου τῆς δόξης τοῦ Χριστοῦ.

20, 21. The sentiment at the last clause of v. 19. is here illustrated; and the discourse concludes with a *gnome generalis*, showing the pernicious effect of immorality on all inquiries after truth.

— φαῦλα] The word properly signifies *little, paltry*; and, 2. *worthless* and *vicious*. Ὁ ποιῶν τὴν ἀλήθειαν. The idea of truth here and in some other passages of the N. T. is that of *rectitude and goodness*, as opposed to what is base and vicious. So in 1 Cor. xiii. 6. ἀλήθεια is opposed to ἀδικία. The expression to *do the truth*, is often found in the Rabbinical writings. In ἐν Θεῷ the ἐν corresponds to the Heb. ב, and signifies *agreeably to*; and Θεῷ, "God's will." On ἐλεγχθῇ just before, see Note on Ephes. v. 13. and my Note on Thucyd. vi. 38. No. 15.

22. εἰς τὴν Ἰουδαίαν γῆν.] Not "into Judæa," since any one in *Jerusalem* must necessarily be in *Judæa*; but, as Wolf, Lampe, and Kuin. interpret, "the *territory* of Judæa," as distinguished from its metropolis. So Luke v. 17. vi. 17. and not unfrequently in the Sept., as Josh. viii. 1. I have given into thy power the King of Ai, καὶ τὴν πόλιν αὐτοῦ καὶ τὴν γῆν αὐτοῦ. So Jerusalem and its χώρα (which is the more usual term) are distinguished infra xi. 55. And we say "go into the *country*," as distinguished from the *metropolis*, without reference to any particular *part* of the country. It is not said to what *place* our Lord went to hold his baptism. We may, I think, not improbably conjecture it to have been Bethany or Bethabara, where *John* had been baptizing; on which see Note supra i. 28. The true situation of the place seems to be on the Jordan, about 5 miles from its embouchure into the Dead Sea. This might very well be called the *Ford* or *Ferry town*, since (being situated at the nearest point of the Jordan from Jerusalem), it formed the regular passage from Jerusalem to Peræa and Arabia. It should seem that John had removed from Bethabara to Ænon, in order that the *Samaritans* also might the more conveniently come to his Baptism.

— ἐβάπτιζεν] i. e. through the medium of his disciples; for Christ did not himself baptize. See iv. 2. Thus what a King's servants do is ascribed to himself. Our Lord declined himself baptizing, probably from a dignified modesty; because baptism bound the persons to religious obedience to *himself*, and might therefore with less ostentation be administered by another. Why St. *Paul* baptized few or none, was because of his being always engaged in more important avocations; and that solemn initiatory rite could as well be performed by any other person.

23. ὕδατα πολλὰ] "many streams," i. e. from the adjunct, much water. A sense (perhaps proceeding from Hebraism) often occurring in the Apocalypse. At παρεγίνοντο and ἐβαπτ. sub. ἄνθρωποι.

25. ζήτησις] for συζήτησις, disputation, as in Acts xv. 2. At ἐκ τῶν μαθ. Beza, Grot., Middlet., and Kuin. supply τινὲς; an ellip. not unfrequent after a Genitive; but here not necessary to be resorted to, since ἐκ, like the Heb. מִן, may mean "on the part of," and thus the same sense will arise as if τινὲς had been written; with the additional intimation that the dispute originated with John's disciples. For the common reading Ἰουδαίων, very many Versions and Fathers have Ἰουδαίου, which is preferred by most of the Commentators, and adopted by almost all the Editors from Wets. to Scholz; and with reason; for the ellip. of τινὸς is frequent, whereas that of τινῶν would be anomalous. Besides, the change of Ἰουδαίου into Ἰουδαίων was likely to take place from the *plural* just before. This Jew may be supposed to have been one of those who had been baptized by Christ's disciples.

— περὶ καθαρισμοῦ.] The meaning is not quite clear. Some take it of the comparative merit or efficacy of John's baptism and that of Jesus. But that is a sense which cannot well be elicited from

i Supra 1. 7, 15, 26, 34. Ἰωάννου μετὰ * Ἰουδαίου περὶ καθαρισμοῦ. [i] καὶ ἦλθον πρὸς τὸν 26
Matt. 3. 11. Mark 1. 7. Luke 3. 16. Ἰωάννην καὶ εἶπον αὐτῷ· Ῥαββὶ, ὃς ἦν μετὰ σοῦ πέραν τοῦ Ἰορδάνου,
ᾧ σὺ μεμαρτύρηκας, ἴδε οὗτος βαπτίζει, καὶ πάντες ἔρχονται πρὸς
k 1 Cor. 4. 7. James 1. 17. αὐτόν. [k] Ἀπεκρίθη Ἰωάννης καὶ εἶπεν· Οὐ δύναται ἄνθρωπος λαμ- 27
l Supra 1. 20, 30. βάνειν οὐδὲν, ἐὰν μὴ ᾖ δεδομένον αὐτῷ ἐκ τοῦ οὐρανοῦ. [l] Αὐτοὶ ὑμεῖς 28
Mal. 3. 1. Matt. 11. 10. μοι μαρτυρεῖτε ὅτι εἶπον· Οὐκ εἰμὶ ἐγὼ ὁ Χριστὸς, ἀλλ᾽ ὅτι ἀπε-
Mark 1. 2. Luke 1. 17. & 7. 27. σταλμένος εἰμὶ ἔμπροσθεν ἐκείνου. Ὁ ἔχων τὴν νύμφην νυμφίος ἐστίν· 29
ὁ δὲ φίλος τοῦ νυμφίου, ὁ ἑστηκὼς καὶ ἀκούων αὐτοῦ, χαρᾷ χαίρει διὰ
τὴν φωνὴν τοῦ νυμφίου. Αὕτη οὖν ἡ χαρὰ ἡ ἐμὴ πεπλήρωται. Ἐκεῖ- 30
m Infra 3. 23. 1 Cor. 15. 47. νον δεῖ αὐξάνειν, ἐμὲ δὲ ἐλαττοῦσθαι. [m] Ὁ ἄνωθεν ἐρχόμενος ἐπάνω 31
πάντων ἐστίν· ὁ ὢν ἐκ τῆς γῆς ἐκ τῆς γῆς ἐστι, καὶ ἐκ τῆς γῆς λαλεῖ·
n Infra 5. 20. & 8. 26. ὁ ἐκ τοῦ οὐρανοῦ ἐρχόμενος ἐπάνω πάντων ἐστὶ, [n] καὶ ὃ ἑώρακε καὶ 32
& 12. 49. & 14. 10. ἤκουσε, τοῦτο μαρτυρεῖ· καὶ τὴν μαρτυρίαν αὐτοῦ οὐδεὶς λαμβάνει.

the words. It should seem that the discussion was on the nature and efficacy of *baptismal purification* (as καθαρ. signifies in 2 Pet. i. 9.); which, however, was closely connected with another on the comparative efficacy of the baptism of John and that of Jesus. If the nature of *Christ's* baptism were considered, it might well be thought that that of John was unnecessary. On this, therefore, John's disciples went to consult him.

26. ἦν μετὰ σοῦ.] This expression only denotes Jesus' attendance on John to be baptized. The words ᾧ σὺ μεμαρτ. perhaps have reference, not so much to the testimony borne by John to Jesus, as to the increase of Jesus's celebrity, and credit consequent on it. They thought that John, through excess of modesty, had exaggerated the dignity of Jesus; whom, it is plain, they did not consider as the *Messiah*. However, the οὗτος does not (as Wets. imagines) imply *contempt*, but rather *ill-will*. Πάντες, for οἱ πολλοὶ, *very many*, by an hyperbole usual to those who speak under the influence of passion and prejudice.

27—30. Here the Baptist checks their excessive attachment to himself, and envy at Jesus; first by showing the real nature of Jesus' person, and that couched in a *gnome generalis*, "A man can receive nothing except it be given him from above." By this he means, that he himself can take nothing to himself that God has not given him; nor can Jesus do so: therefore whatever is done by him happens by the providence of God. Then he proceeds to disavow that superior dignity which his disciples ascribed to him; reminding them of his public and private avowal, that he was *not* the MESSIAH, but only his herald, to prepare for his coming. (Tittm.)

29. ὁ ἔχων τὴν νύμφην, &c.] The subject is here illustrated by a similitude derived from common life, in tracing the nature of which some Commentators obscure rather than illustrate the subject by references to Jewish Antiquities. Lampe, Kuin., and Tittm. are rightly agreed that there is merely an illustration by similitude (as in Matt. ix. 15. and Mark ii. 19.), in which John compares Christ to the *bridegroom* at a marriage feast, and himself to the παράνυμφος, or *brideman*; who was a friend that had been employed to negociate the marriage, and had acted as his agent throughout the whole affair. There were, indeed, *two* paranymphs; one on the part of the bridegroom, the other on that of the bride; who afterwards acted as mediators, to preserve peace and harmony between the new-married pair. The allusion at ἑστηκὼς — χαίρει διὰ τὴν φωνὴν τοῦ νυμφίου is variously explained. The words are most probably supposed to allude to the ceremony of the formal interview, previous to marriage, of the betrothed pair, who were brought together by the paranymphs to a private apartment; at the door of which they were themselves stationed, so as to be able to distinguish any elevation of voice on the part of the sponsus addressing the sponsa; from which, and from the *tone* of it, they would easily infer his satisfaction at the choice made for him by them, and feel corresponding joy. The sense, then, may be thus expressed. "As, in the ceremonies pertaining to marriage, the sponsus is the principal person, and his parnymphus willingly cedes to him the preference, and, rejoicing in his acceptance, is content to play an under part; so do I willingly sustain the part of a humble forerunner to Christ." Πεπλήρωται, is complete, consummate.

31. To cut off all future occasion for comparison, John shows that there will be less and less room for it; since the celebrity of the one must increase, that of the other decrease; and so resplendent will be the glory of the former, as to cast that of the latter into the shade, and cause it to fade away like the morning star, or the waning moon at sun-rise. (Tittm. and Euthym.)

31—36. The Commentators are not agreed whether these are to be considered as the words of *the Evangelist*, or of *John the Baptist*. The *former* is the opinion of most recent Commentators, and is grounded on the style and manner being that of the Evangelist. That, however, is a very precarious argument. It is better to adopt (with almost all ancient and most modern Commentators) the *latter* view. For, as Tittm. remarks, "there is a complete connection of these words with the preceding; without the interposition of any expression, from which it could be inferred that what follows is from the Evangelist. Nor is there any reason *why* he should have added these words, and chosen to confirm by his own judgment the testimony of John the Baptist, which must have been to his readers alike remarkable and deserving of credit. On the other hand, there are obvious reasons why this passage should be from John the *Baptist*; for in it he seems to have intended to advert to the reasons confirming

33 [o] Ὁ λαβὼν αὐτοῦ τὴν μαρτυρίαν ἐσφράγισεν ὅτι ὁ Θεὸς ἀληθής ἐστιν. o 1 John 5. 10. Rom. 3. 4.
34 [p] Ὃν γὰρ ἀπέστειλεν ὁ Θεὸς, τὰ ῥήματα τοῦ Θεοῦ λαλεῖ· οὐ γὰρ ἐκ p Supr. 1. 16. Eph. 4. 7.
35 μέτρου δίδωσιν ὁ Θεὸς τὸ Πνεῦμα. [q] Ὁ Πατὴρ ἀγαπᾷ τὸν Υἱὸν, καὶ q Matt. 11. 27. & 28. 18.
36 πάντα δέδωκεν ἐν τῇ χειρὶ αὐτοῦ. [r] Ὁ πιστεύων εἰς τὸν Υἱὸν ἔχει Luke 10. 22. infra 5. 22. & 17. 2.
ζωὴν αἰώνιον· ὁ δὲ ἀπειθῶν τῷ Υἱῷ οὐκ ὄψεται ζωὴν, ἀλλ' ἡ ὀργὴ Heb. 2. 8. r Supra 3. 15, 16. & 6. 47.
τοῦ Θεοῦ μένει ἐπ' αὐτόν. 1 John 5. 11.
1 IV. [s] ΩΣ οὖν ἔγνω ὁ Κύριος, ὅτι ἤκουσαν οἱ Φαρισαῖοι ὅτι Ἰησοῦς s Supra 3. 22, 26.
2 πλείονας μαθητὰς ποιεῖ καὶ βαπτίζει ἢ Ἰωάννης· (καίτοιγε Ἰησοῦς
3 αὐτὸς οὐκ ἐβάπτιζεν, ἀλλ' οἱ μαθηταὶ αὐτοῦ) ἀφῆκε τὴν Ἰουδαίαν, καὶ

what he had said, namely, that the precedence is due, not to *him*, but to *Jesus*. It is, he means to say, only *just* that *his* fame should be spread, and the number of *his* disciples be increased, inasmuch as he was *sent from heaven*, endowed with gifts immeasurably great; nay, was the beloved Son of God, the Lord and promised Saviour of the human race." Indeed the words *cannot* be the *Evangelist's*; for allowing all that can be claimed for the force of the not unfrequent hyperbole in οὐδεὶς (as meaning so few as to be next to none), it would be by no means a correct representation of the state of Christian converts upwards of 60 years after the death of Christ. The first two verses of this portion are very similar in sentiment to supra vv. 11, 12, & 13; and the antithesis between ὁ ἐκ τῆς γῆς and ὁ ἐκ τοῦ οὐρανοῦ necessarily involves the divinity of our Lord Jesus Christ.

We must supply καὶ ἐκ τοῦ οὐρανοῦ λαλεῖ, to correspond to ἐκ τῆς γῆς λαλεῖ. The sense is: "A mere man is not endued with knowledge of divine things, has not that intimate acquaintance with the secret counsels of God, which He possesses who is of celestial origin (to whom God giveth not the Spirit by measure, v. 34.); he, therefore, teacheth, and can teach, only what is earthly, incomplete, and imperfect. But he who is endued by God with a complete knowledge of heavenly things, being thoroughly conversant with the counsels of God, speaketh the words of God: and he is, from his origin, superior to all men in dignity, and far exceeds even the *Prophets* in spiritual knowledge."

With ὁ ὢν—λαλεῖ I would compare Æschyl. ap. Stobæi Serm. Eth. p. 98. τὸ γὰρ βρότειον σπέρμ' ἐφημέρια φρονεῖ. At ὃ ἑώρακε καὶ ἤκουσε we may supply ἐξ αὐτοῦ, i. e. ἐν τῷ οὐρανῷ. The καὶ signifies "and [yet]."

33. The Baptist here corrects the grievous error of undervaluing Jesus, by showing (of course, with an admission of Jesus' Messiahship) that he who believeth or hath faith in Christ, hath it in God. (Tittm.) 'Εσφράγισεν is (as Chrys. says) for ἔδειξεν, and signifies *attests, confirms, professes* his belief; a metaphor taken from deeds *signed* and *sealed*. For as testimonies of contracts, or other engagements, were confirmed by the addition of a seal, any confirmation of truth was called σφραγίς; and as by the imposition of a seal, any thing is rendered *unsuspected of fraud*, sure and certain, therefore, σφραγίζειν came to mean to *confirm*, as here and in Eph. i. 13. 2 Cor. i. 22. Sap. ii. 5.

34. οὐ γὰρ ἐκ μέτρου—Πνεῦμα.] The phrase ἐκ μέτρου with verbs of giving, denotes, by implication, *sparingly, restrictedly*, like provisions in a besieged city. And so the Latin *ad demensum*, tribuere. Οὐκ ἐκ μέτρου, denotes completely. The best Commentators are agreed that there is an allusion to the *Prophets*, the very greatest of them being allowed by the Jewish Rabbis to have only had the gifts of the Holy Spirit ἐκ μέτρου, and that the law itself is only given *ad mensuram*. On the *particulars* of this unbounded power, see Tittm. in Recens. Synop. Δίδωσιν is for δέδωκεν, which occurs just after.

35. πάντα] i. e. whatever is necessary to procure the salvation of man.

36. Here are declared the *consequences* of faith, and also want of faith, in Christ. In the former clause ἔχει is not (as most Commentators imagine) simply for ἕξει, but the Present is used, to show the *certainty* of the thing; "it is laid up for him." By ὁ ἀπειθῶν is meant he who refuseth this faith; though there *may* be, as Doddr. thinks, an allusion to that principle of unreserved obedience to Christ, which can alone make faith available. Οὐκ ὄψεται ζωὴν is a Hebrew phrase denoting, "he shall never possess eternal life." The words following suggest the *reason:* and the descending series (as observes Bp. Jebb) "is magnificently awful: he who, with his heart, *believeth in the Son*, is *already* in possession of eternal life: he, whatever may be his outward profession, whatever his theoretic or historical belief, who *obeyeth not the Son*, not only does not possess *eternal* life, he does not possess any thing worthy to be called life at all; but this is not the whole, for as eternal life is the present possession of the faithful, so the wrath of God is the *present* and *permanent* lot of the disobedient; it *abideth on him*, not being removed by the atoning merits of the Redeemer."

IV. In this Chapter is recorded an important discourse of Christ with a Samaritan woman; for illustrating the *purpose* and *scope* of which, the Evangelist prefaces the narration with some particulars respecting the *occasion* which led to that discourse. Dr. A. Clarke has well pointed out the numerous *internal evidences of truth*, which strike the mind of the attentive reader, in this narrative, which concentrates so much information, that a *Volume* might be filled with its illustrations of the history of the Jews, and the geography of their country. Our Lord, it should seem, left Judæa (perhaps suddenly) in order to avoid every thing that could needlessly excite the indignation of the Ecclesiastical Rulers, and probably for *other* reasons, adverted to by Doddr.

1. μαθητὰς ποιεῖ καὶ βαπτίζει ἢ 'I.] "is making more disciples than John, and is [even] baptizing them." So Grot. or is making more disciples by baptism.

4. Ἔδει δὲ αὐτὸν δ.] It was *so far* necessary, as being a much shorter route than through Peræa.

ἀπῆλθε πάλιν εἰς τὴν Γαλιλαίαν. ˢἜδει δὲ αὐτὸν διέρχεσθαι διὰ τῆς 4
t Gen. 33. 19. & 48. 22. Jos. 24. 32. Σαμαρείας. ᵗἔρχεται οὖν εἰς πόλιν τῆς Σαμαρείας λεγομένην * Συχὰρ, 5
πλησίον τοῦ χωρίου, ὃ ἔδωκεν Ἰακὼβ Ἰωσὴφ τῷ υἱῷ αὐτοῦ. Ἦν δὲ 6
ἐκεῖ πηγὴ τοῦ Ἰακώβ. Ὁ οὖν Ἰησοῦς κεκοπιακὼς ἐκ τῆς ὁδοιπορίας,
ἐκαθέζετο οὕτως ἐπὶ τῇ πηγῇ· ὥρα ἦν ὡσεὶ ἕκτη. Ἔρχεται γυνὴ ἐκ 7
τῆς Σαμαρείας ἀντλῆσαι ὕδωρ. Λέγει αὐτῇ ὁ Ἰησοῦς· Δός μοι πιεῖν
(οἱ γὰρ μαθηταὶ αὐτοῦ ἀπεληλύθεισαν εἰς τὴν πόλιν, ἵνα τροφὰς 8
u Luke 9. 52, 53. ἀγοράσωσι.) ᵘΛέγει οὖν αὐτῷ ἡ γυνὴ ἡ Σαμαρεῖτις· Πῶς σὺ, Ἰου- 9
infra 8. 48. Acts 10. 28. δαῖος ὢν, παρ᾽ ἐμοῦ πιεῖν αἰτεῖς, οὔσης γυναικὸς Σαμαρείτιδος; (οὐ
2 Kings 17. 24. x Isa. 12. 3. γὰρ συγχρῶνται Ἰουδαῖοι Σαμαρείταις.) ˣἈπεκρίθη Ἰησοῦς καὶ εἶπεν 10
infra. 6. 35. & 7. 38, 39. αὐτῇ· Εἰ ᾔδεις τὴν δωρεὰν τοῦ Θεοῦ, καὶ τίς ἐστιν ὁ λέγων σοι·
Δός μοι πιεῖν· σὺ ἂν ᾔτησας αὐτὸν, καὶ ἔδωκεν ἄν σοι ὕδωρ ζῶν.
y Jer. 2. 13. ʸΛέγει αὐτῷ ἡ γυνή· Κύριε, οὔτε ἄντλημα ἔχεις, καὶ τὸ φρέαρ ἐστὶ 11
βαθύ· πόθεν οὖν ἔχεις τὸ ὕδωρ τὸ ζῶν; Μὴ σὺ μείζων εἶ τοῦ 12

So Joseph. Vit. 52. says πάντως ἔδει τοὺς ταχὺ βουλομένους ἀπελθεῖν (namely, from Jerusalem to Galilee) δι᾽ ἐκείνης (Samaria) πορεύεσθαι. He calls it a three days' journey.

5. ἔρχεται εἰς] "comes, came unto, as far as;" for from v. 6. it appears that he took up his quarters *outside* of the city; though his disciples entered it, to procure provisions, and on returning from thence found Jesus talking with a Samaritan woman. Συχάρ. So very many MSS. It is for Vulg. Συχὲμ and received by all the best Editors. Originally called Συχὲμ, from the name of the person of whose family Jacob bought the land, and built an altar. See Gen. xxxiii. 18. The name is supposed to have been altered by the Jews to Συχὰρ, to denote the drunkenness or the idolatry of the inhabitants. But probably it was merely a dialectical change.

6. κεκοπιακώς.] Neut. in a passive sense. On the force of οὕτως the Commentators differ. Some render it *therefore*, others *afterwards*; for neither of which significations is there any authority. The true interpretation seems to be that of the ancients, and several eminent moderns, who take οὕτως for οὕτως ὡς ἦν. or ὡς ἔτυχεν, "*just as he was*, just where it happened, without any pitching of a tent." So Acts xxvii. 17. οὕτως ἐφέροντο, just as it happened, at the mercy of the winds. See also Hor. Od. ii. 11, 13. If this be not approved by the reader, he may (as I suggested in Recens. Synop.) take ἐκαθ. οὕτως as if οὕτως ἐκαθ. had been written; and thus understand οὕτως in the sense *accordingly*, which is better than regarding it, with most recent Commentators, as pleonastic. Lampe thinks, that Jesus stopped there, not only for the sake of rest, but as being a very convenient dining place. So Philostr. V. Ap. ἀριστοποιουμένων δὲ αὐτῶν πρὸς πηγῇ ὕδατος.

7. γυνὴ ἐκ τῆς Σαμ.] This means not a woman from, but *of*, Samaria; and is, by an ellip. of οὖσα, equivalent to γυνὴ Σαμαρεῖτις in the next verse. She had, no doubt, come from Sychar. Δός μοι πιεῖν. The verb is employed as a noun; of which the Greek Classics abound in examples.

9. πῶς σὺ, &c.] She expresses wonder at any favour, however small, being asked by a Jew from a Samaritan. So Raschi, in his Gloss. on the Gemara, says, "it is an abomination to eat the bread or drink the wine of a Samaritan." On the origin and causes of this reciprocal hatred, I have treated at large in Rec. Syn. The *reason* for this the Evangelist subjoins, for the information of his Greek readers, in the words οὐ γὰρ, &c., where συγχ. must be understood of *familiar intercourse and society*; (So Euthym. explains by οὐ κοινωνοῦσι.) for the intercourse of *buying and selling* was still kept up. Συγχρᾶσθαι signifies, properly, "to use any one's co-operation in any thing." The word, however, in this sense occurs only in the later writers, as Polyb. and Arrian; the earlier ones using ἐναλλάσσεσθαι. So Thucyd. i. 120. ἡμῶν δὲ ὅσοι Ἀθηναίοις ἤδε ἐνηλλάγησαν.

10. τὴν δωρεὰν τ. Θ.] i. e. the favour which God graciously vouchsafes to thee, in this opportunity of knowing the Messiah, and receiving the offer of free salvation from himself. Ὕδωρ ζῶν properly means *running water* (as that of fountains and rivers) in opposition to the dead, i. e. stagnant, water of pools or cisterns. It occurs in Gen. xxvi. 19. and Levit. xiv. 5. The Classical writers for ζῶν used the epithets ἀείῤῥυτον, ἀέναον; nay Plato has ἔμψυχον ὕδωρ. In this *physical* sense the woman understood the term. But our Lord employed it *figuratively*, for ζωοποιοῦν. "It being his custom (observes Kuin.) from things corporeal to excite the minds of his hearers to the study and knowledge of things spiritual." It is common in the Scriptures and the Rabbinical writers to liken unto water that which refreshes and blesses the souls of men. See vii. 38. Prov. x. 11. Ecclus. xv. 3. xxiv. 21. And no wonder; since in the hot countries of the East, pure water is the most refreshing of beverages, and is even reckoned among the *blessings* of life.

11. ἄντλημα] "a bucket," such as travellers in the East are accustomed to take with them, and which, by the aid of the rope and wheel provided as *fixtures* at public wells, is sufficient to procure water from the deepest wells.

12. μείζων] "a person of more consequence." This has reference to what Jesus had before said, "If thou hadst known *who it is* that speaketh to thee." The words following are meant to say: It was good enough for our ancestor Jacob, who himself drank of it, &c.; which he would not have done, if he had known a better. If thou canst show us a better, thou wilt, in that respect, be greater than Jacob. Οἱ υἱοὶ, i. e. the family in general, including the servants, as in Gen. xiv.

πατρὸς ἡμῶν Ἰακὼβ, ὃς ἔδωκεν ἡμῖν τὸ φρέαρ, καὶ αὐτὸς ἐξ αὐτοῦ
13 ἔπιε, καὶ οἱ υἱοὶ αὐτοῦ, καὶ τὰ θρέμματα αὐτοῦ; [z] Ἀπεκρίθη [ὁ] z Infra 6. 58.
Ἰησοῦς καὶ εἶπεν αὐτῇ· Πᾶς ὁ πίνων ἐκ τοῦ ὕδατος τούτου διψήσει
14 πάλιν· [a] ὃς δ᾽ ἂν πίῃ ἐκ τοῦ ὕδατος, οὗ ἐγὼ δώσω αὐτῷ, οὐ μὴ a Infr. 6. 27, 35. & 7. 38, 39.
διψήσῃ εἰς τὸν αἰῶνα· ἀλλὰ τὸ ὕδωρ, ὃ δώσω αὐτῷ, γενήσεται ἐν
15 αὐτῷ πηγὴ ὕδατος ἁλλομένου εἰς ζωὴν αἰώνιον. Λέγει πρὸς αὐτὸν ἡ
γυνή· Κύριε, δός μοι τοῦτο τὸ ὕδωρ, ἵνα μὴ διψῶ, μηδὲ ἔρχωμαι
16 ἐνθάδε ἀντλεῖν. Λέγει αὐτῇ ὁ Ἰησοῦς· Ὕπαγε φώνησον τὸν ἄνδρα
17 σου, καὶ ἐλθὲ ἐνθάδε. Ἀπεκρίθη ἡ γυνὴ καὶ εἶπεν· Οὐκ ἔχω ἄνδρα.
18 Λέγει αὐτῇ ὁ Ἰησοῦς· Καλῶς εἶπας· Ὅτι ἄνδρα οὐκ ἔχω· πέντε
γὰρ ἄνδρας ἔσχες· καὶ νῦν ὃν ἔχεις, οὐκ ἔστι σου ἀνήρ· τοῦτο ἀλη- b Infra 6. 14. Luke 7. 16. & 24. 19.
19 θὲς εἴρηκας. [b] Λέγει αὐτῷ ἡ γυνή· Κύριε, θεωρῶ ὅτι προφήτης εἶ c Deut. 12. 5, 11.
20 σύ. [c] Οἱ πατέρες ἡμῶν ‡ ἐν τούτῳ τῷ ὄρει προσεκύνησαν· καὶ ὑμεῖς 1 Kings 9. 3. 2 Chron. 7. 12.

11. This, and the mention of the cattle *enjoined*, is agreeable to the simplicity of early times, and which has, more or less, always prevailed in the East.

13, 14. Our Lord here shows that he does not depreciate Jacob or his well; but intimates that however great was the benefit bestowed by the Patriarch, *he* can bestow a far greater, and thus is superior to Jacob.

— οὐ μὴ διψήσῃ εἰς τὸν α.] i. e. shall have nothing more ever to desire. See Rev. vii. 16. The general meaning of the words, when divested of the figure, is, that such shall be the vivifying effect of the Gospel, as to satisfy the most ardent desires of the soul; which, placing its happiness in God and his worship, no other desire will be thought of. Also, that such is the nature of that doctrine, that it purifies a man from vicious inclinations, and is, as it were, an ever-springing fountain of holy affections, producing comfort here, and everlasting happiness hereafter;" like that good spoken of by an ancient Philosopher, "quod non fiat in dies deterius, quo non melius possit optari." (Seneca Ep.) To *drink*, Lampe observes, signifies to *fully* imbibe Christ's doctrine; and πηγὴ and ἅλλεσθαι involve the idea of perennial abundance.

15. δός μοι, &c.] The Commentators are not agreed whether this was spoken in *simplicity*, or *ironically*. Both may, in some measure, be admitted. Comp. vi. 34. Κύριε, πάντοτε δὸς ἡμῖν τὸν ἄρτον τ.

16. Perceiving that the woman did not yet comprehend him, or perhaps began to trifle with him, our Lord was pleased at once to check her rising freedom, by reminding her of her immoralities; taking care withal *so* to effect this as to prove himself a *Divinely commissioned* Monitor and Teacher.

— φώνησον τὸν ἄνδρα σου.] Our Lord, indeed, knew already, that she had no husband: but he bid her do this, knowing that the answer that would thus be returned, would afford him occasion of showing her his omniscience, and admonish her of her immorality.

17. καλῶς] is not put ironically, but is simply for ἀληθῶς, as is plain from the words following τοῦτο ἀληθὲς εἴρηκας.

18. οὐκ ἔστι σ. ἀ.] "is not [really] thy husband." It appears that the woman had been five times married; but whether those marriages had been dissolved by death or by divorce, does not appear. *Both* might be the case; and as divorce was then shamefully prevalent, this implies no certainty of infidelity on the part of the woman; to represent whom as a *harlot* (as some Commentators do) is unjustifiable, though this is better than the other extreme into which some run (even Tittm.) of representing the woman as free from all blame, by supposing that, though not actually married to this person, she was *espoused* to him. That would require the οὐ to be taken for οὔπω; which is a straining of the sense, and is refuted by the words οὐκ ἔχω ἄνδρα; and as ὃν ἔχεις implies *cohabitation*, she cannot be acquitted of living in *concubinage;* which, however common in the East, and though neither there, nor in the West, *then* accounted very disgraceful by the multitude, yet was held by persons of any pretensions to virtue as sinful and impure, because transgressing the primeval and sacred institution of matrimony.

19. θεωρῶ ὅτι προφήτης εἶ σύ.] The woman is justly amazed that a *stranger* and a *Jew* should be acquainted with the whole tenour of her life; for πάντα may be taken *populariter*, to denote the leading events of her life. Such knowledge she knew could not be acquired but by Divine revelation; and therefore she justly inferred that Jesus must be at least a *prophet;* and, as such, be a proper authority to appeal to for the solution of the controverted question as to the comparative holiness of the Jewish and the Samaritan places of common national worship. To this question our Lord so answers as to give her to understand, that it is not necessary to discuss it at all; since there was at hand such a total change of religious institutions as to render it nugatory.

20. ἐν τούτῳ τῷ ὄρει] i. e. Mount Gerizim, on which the Samaritans maintained that Abraham and Jacob had erected an altar, and offered sacrifices to Jehovah; and, therefore, that the Deity had willed blessing to be pronounced from thence, and an altar to be erected, alleging in proof Deut. xxvii. 2. 12.; and, in order to "make surety doubly-sure," interpolating the text at v. 4. and changing עיבל *Ebal*, into גריזים, *Gerizim*. Hence they called it "the blessed mount," "the holy place." For ἐν τούτῳ τῷ ὄρει very many MSS. and most of the early Editions, have ἐν τῷ ὄρει τούτῳ, which is received by almost every Editor from Wets. to Scholz. I cannot, however, ven-

λέγετε ὅτι ἐν Ἱεροσολύμοις ἐστὶν ὁ τόπος ὅπου δεῖ προσκυνεῖν. Λέγει 21
αὐτῇ ὁ Ἰησοῦς· Γύναι, πίστευσόν μοι, ὅτι ἔρχεται ὥρα, ὅτε οὔτε ἐν
τῷ ὄρει τούτῳ οὔτε ἐν Ἱεροσολύμοις προσκυνήσετε τῷ Πατρί. [d] Ὑμεῖς 22
προσκυνεῖτε, ὃ οὐκ οἴδατε· ἡμεῖς προσκυνοῦμεν, ὃ οἴδαμεν· ὅτι ἡ
σωτηρία ἐκ τῶν Ἰουδαίων ἐστίν. Ἀλλ' ἔρχεται ὥρα, καὶ νῦν ἐστιν, ὅτε 23
οἱ ἀληθινοὶ προσκυνηταὶ προσκυνήσουσι τῷ Πατρὶ ἐν πνεύματι καὶ
ἀληθείᾳ· καὶ γὰρ ὁ Πατὴρ τοιούτους ζητεῖ τοὺς προσκυνοῦντας αὐτόν.
[e] Πνεῦμα ὁ Θεός· καὶ τοὺς προσκυνοῦντας αὐτὸν ἐν πνεύματι καὶ 24
ἀληθείᾳ δεῖ προσκυνεῖν. Λέγει αὐτῷ ἡ γυνή· Οἶδα ὅτι Μεσσίας ἔρ- 25
χεται· (ὁ λεγόμενος Χριστός·) ὅταν ἔλθῃ ἐκεῖνος, ἀναγγελεῖ ἡμῖν

d 2 Kings 17. 29. Isa. 2. 3. Luke 24. 47. Rom. 3. 2. & 9. 4.

e 2 Cor. 3. 17.

ture to admit it, the old reading being superior in *external*, authority; and I think in *internal*, for the new reading seems to be (as the character of several of the MSS. which support it would lead us to suppose) *ex emendatione;* though ungrounded; for ἐν τούτῳ τῷ ὄρει conveys, I conceive, a *stronger* sense (namely, "in this very mountain") than ἐν τῷ ὄρει τούτῳ, which latter is very suitable at v. 21., since *there* we have no emphasis. Grot. and Lampe notice and illustrate the custom (probably ante-diluvial) of worshipping the deity on *mountains*, perhaps as being thought nearer to heaven: or rather, I conceive, from high mountains being more suited to devotion, by their being removed from the din of men. So Milton's Paradise Lost, i. "Sing, heavenly Muse, that on the *secret* top of Horeb or of Sinai," &c.

21. πίστευσόν μοι.] Our Lord here claims, at least, the belief due to a *Prophet*, such as the woman acknowledged him to be. Ἔρχεται, "is coming;" namely, at the destruction of Jerusalem. Προσκυνήσετε is not for προσκυνήσουσι by *Hebraism*, as some Commentators imagine; but is a more *pointed* expression, meaning ye and others. Wets. has shown the exact fulfilment of the prediction, in the overthrow both of the Jewish and Samaritan holy places, by numerous citations from Josephus and the early Fathers.

22. ὑμεῖς — οἴδατε.] There is here somewhat of obscurity; which has occasioned diversity of interpretation. Most Commentators (especially the ancient ones) refer the ὃ to the *Deity*, by the ellips of Θεῖον; meaning that the Samaritans knew not God properly, by confining him to *place*. But this charge, as well as that of idolatry, (which others suppose here alluded to) has been disproved by the researches of Reland, Lampe, and Gesenius; of whom Lampe rightly supposes our Lord to charge them not with *corruption*, but with *ignorance*. See Recens. Synop. But he unjustifiably confines it to ignorance of the *manner* of worship. The more recent Commentators from Beng. and Markl. to Kuin. and Tittm. are of opinion that ὃ denotes not the *object* of the worship, but the *form* of it; and they take ὃ *for* καθ' ὃ, with reference chiefly to the *manner* and *form* of worship, but also, by implication, including *place;* q. d. *Ye* worship according to your ignorance, *we* according to our knowledge; and consequently in the manner and place appointed by Divine command.

In ὅτι ἡ σωτηρία — Ἰουδαίων there is a *reason* suggested why the Jews should best know the mode and the place of the National worship; namely, since from *them* the Messiah (σωτηρία being for σωτήρ) was confessedly to spring.

23. ἐν πνεύματι καὶ ἀληθείᾳ.] I can neither agree with those Commentators who take πν. to denote the *Holy Spirit;* nor with those who take it of the *human mind*. It should seem that these are adverbial phrases, for πνευματικῶς καὶ ἀληθῶς; of which the former involves a tacit contrast of the *letter* of the *Law*, with the *Spirit* of the *Gospel*. See 2 Cor. iii. 6. Rom. ii. 29. Phil. iii. 3., where γράμματι and πνεύματι are opposed, as the λατρεία λογικὴ in Rom. xiii. 1. is opposed to the σαρκική. The ἐν ἀληθείᾳ has reference to the *Law*, as being only (what St. Paul says, Col. ii. 17. and Heb. viii. 5. x. 1.) a *shadow* of good things to come, not the σῶμα.

— καὶ γὰρ ὁ Πατὴρ, &c.] Our Lord now shows by *two reasons* why God is to be so worshipped. 1. From the sovereign *will* of the Deity, to whom spiritual and internal worship is alone acceptable. 2. From the *nature* of the Deity, who is of a *spiritual* nature, far removed from any thing corporeal; and therefore must be worshipped in a spiritual manner, and also *in truth*, since such he requires; and indeed aught else would be a solemn mockery of the God of Truth.

24. Πνεῦμα ὁ Θεός.] By πνεῦμα is meant (as the best Expositors, ancient and modern, are agreed) an immaterial, unconfined, and invisible nature. without parts or passions, and not circumscribed by space or limits, as every thing corporeal must be. The expression, however, also involves the *attributes* and perfections of the Deity, His omniscience, omnipotence, infinite benevolence, &c. That the wiser Jews had tolerably correct ideas of the spirituality of God, is evinced by Schoettg. from various passages of Rabbinical writers.

— καὶ τοὺς προσκυνοῦντας αὐτόν.] In the compass of 3 verses we have 3 variations in the government of the verb προσκυνεῖν. In the N. T. it is used with the Dative, except here and at Matt. iv. 10. Luke iv. 8. The Dative is also used by most of the later Greek writers. The earlier ones invariably have the *Accusative*. This being, as Matthiæ observes, (Gr. Gr. § 407.) one of those many verbs that have an Accusative which does not mark the *passive* object of the action, but that to which an action has only generally an immediate reference. It should, however, seem that the Dative is used with reference to the πρὸς, since verbs which govern an Accus. *out of* composition, when *in* composition, only direct the Subst. to the Dative.

25. The woman here refers the decision of the question to the times of the Messiah, of whose speedy appearance she had probably heard. (Tittm.) The Jews of that age were accustomed to refer the decision of controverted questions to

26 πάντα. [f] Λέγει αὐτῇ ὁ Ἰησοῦς· Ἐγώ εἰμι, ὁ λαλῶν σοι. Καὶ ἐπὶ [f Infra. 9. 37.]
27 τούτῳ ἦλθον οἱ μαθηταὶ αὐτοῦ, καὶ ἐθαύμασαν ὅτι μετὰ γυναικὸς
ἐλάλει· οὐδεὶς μέντοι εἶπε· Τί ζητεῖς; ἢ τί λαλεῖς μετ' αὐτῆς;
28 Ἀφῆκεν οὖν τὴν ὑδρίαν αὐτῆς ἡ γυνὴ, καὶ ἀπῆλθεν εἰς τὴν πόλιν,
29 καὶ λέγει τοῖς ἀνθρώποις· Δεῦτε, ἴδετε ἄνθρωπον, ὃς εἶπέ μοι πάντα
30 ὅσα ἐποίησα· μήτι οὗτός ἐστιν ὁ Χριστός; Ἐξῆλθον οὖν ἐκ τῆς πόλεως, καὶ ἤρχοντο πρὸς αὐτόν.
31 Ἐν δὲ τῷ μεταξὺ ἠρώτων αὐτὸν οἱ μαθηταὶ, λέγοντες· Ῥαββὶ,
32 φάγε. ὁ δὲ εἶπεν αὐτοῖς· Ἐγὼ βρῶσιν ἔχω φαγεῖν, ἣν ὑμεῖς οὐκ
33 οἴδατε. Ἔλεγον [οὖν] οἱ μαθηταὶ πρὸς ἀλλήλους· Μή τις ἤνεγκεν
34 αὐτῷ φαγεῖν; Λέγει αὐτοῖς ὁ Ἰησοῦς· Ἐμὸν βρῶμά ἐστιν, ἵνα ποιῶ
35 τὸ θέλημα τοῦ πέμψαντός με, καὶ τελειώσω αὐτοῦ τὸ ἔργον. [g] Οὐχ [g Matt. 9. 37. Luke 10. 2.]

the coming of future prophets, and especially of the Messiah. And from what has been discovered of the opinions of the Samaritans of that age, (see Gesenius' Comment. de Samaritanis), it should seem that they expected in the Messiah chiefly a great *spiritual* Ruler, and teacher of religion.

The most eminent Critics are agreed that the clause ὁ λεγόμενος Χριστὸς came from the *Evangelist*, not the woman. Ἀναγγ. denoting properly the delivering of a message from one person to another, here involves the idea of what we mean by a *Revelation* from God. See Note infra xvi. 14.

26. ἐγώ εἰμι, ὁ λαλῶν σοι.] The reasons why our Lord revealed himself so much more unreservedly to this woman and the Samaritans than to the Jews, were probably, 1. because the Samaritans were better affected, more sincere, and of greater integrity and moral virtue, and therefore more worthy of unreserved confidence. 2. Because of the reason which induced our Lord to use caution in that respect with the Jews; namely, to avoid giving needless offence to the Rulers, and thereby *anticipating* what he should eventually suffer from them. 3. Because the Samaritans seem to have had more correct ideas of the nature of the Messiah's kingdom, founding their views on Deut. xviii. 15., and therefore would not be likely to abuse what he said to purposes of sedition; besides that they were orderly and quiet in their habits.

27. ἐπὶ τούτῳ.] Sub. ῥήματι. Or it may simply mean "*hereupon*." Ὅτι μετὰ γυν., "with the woman," as being a Samaritan, and in so public a place. See Bp. Middl. and Rec. Syn.

— τί ζητεῖς;] A popular expression, meaning, "what is your purpose or business?"

29. πάντα] i. e. (by an hyperbole natural to her situation, insomuch that she had forgotten to take back her bucket) the *main* events of her life, on which the rest hinged.

— μήτι οὗτός ἐστιν ὁ Χ.] The Commentators are not agreed whether this means, "is this the Christ?" or, "is not this the Christ?" I have in Recens. Synop. shown at large that the latter version cannot be admitted, 1. because there is little or no authority for μήτι in the sense *annon*; 2. because it is less suitable to the case in question. For the woman appears (as Theophyl. notices) to have meant courteously to propose this rather as a question for their *consideration* than to *affirm it*, at least by implication. So also at Matt. xii. 23. μήτι οὗτός ἐστιν ὁ υἱὸς Δαυίδ, should be rendered, "is this the son of David?" a sense supported by the authority of the best ancient Versions, and adopted by the most eminent Expositors. Prof. Scholefield observes, that the μὴ thus joined to the Indicative implies a mixture of *belief*, *doubt*, and *wonder*. Comp. vii. 41. and Acts x. 47.

32. βρῶσιν ἔχω, &c.] Here we trace our Lord's usual endeavour from things corporeal to excite the attention of his disciples to things spiritual. In the Scriptural and Rabbinical phraseology, *that* is said to be any one's *meat* and *drink*, by which one is supported, refreshed, or delighted. Of this Schoettgen subjoins several examples from the Rabbinical writers, and others are adduced by Lampe and Wets. from the Classical writers. The most apposite of which may be seen in Rec. Syn., where I have shown that ἐγὼ is here, as often, emphatic, q. d. Whatever may be the case with *you*, *I* have spiritual enjoyments which ye know not. See two able Discourses of Dr. Parr on this text; in which is well pointed out the force of this figurative language.

33. οὖν.] This is omitted in very many of the best MSS. and some Versions, and is cancelled by almost all the recent Editors.

34. βρῶμα] scil. πνευματικόν. By τὸ ἔργον is meant, not merely that doctrine, but every other part of the work of salvation enjoined by the Father. Comp. xviii. 4.

35. As to the exact force of our Lord's address, Expositors are not agreed whether it is to be taken *figuratively*, or *literally*. The most eminent ones (as Grot., De Dieu, Wolf, Whitby, Rosenm., Tittm., and Kuin.) take λέγετε for λέγουσι, "it is commonly said," and explain the next words to mean: "Is it not a saying among you, that when your seed is sowing, you expect a harvest in four months hence; and thus the husbandman is supported by the distant hope, though yet in the *bud*, of reaping a harvest. Therefore heed not labour, when reward is at hand." This view of the sense may be admitted; but it is open to the objections stated by Doddr. and others, that no example of such a proverb has been adduced, and that the period in question is not *four*, but *six* months. Yet the former objection is by no means fatal; and the latter is of no great weight; for it has been proved, that in the East, scarcely more than four months intervene between the *end* of seed-time and the *beginning* of harvest. Not to mention that it is of the nature of *hope* to *lessen* what lies

ὑμεῖς λέγετε, ὅτι ἔτι * τετράμηνός ἐστι, καὶ ὁ θερισμὸς ἔρχεται; ἰδού,
λέγω ὑμῖν· ἐπάρατε τοὺς ὀφθαλμοὺς ὑμῶν, καὶ θεάσασθε τὰς χώρας,
ὅτι λευκαί εἰσι πρὸς θερισμὸν ἤδη. Καὶ ὁ θερίζων μισθὸν λαμβάνει, 36
καὶ συνάγει καρπὸν εἰς ζωὴν αἰώνιον ἵνα καὶ ὁ σπείρων ὁμοῦ χαίρῃ
καὶ ὁ θερίζων. Ἐν γὰρ τούτῳ ὁ λόγος ἐστὶν ὁ ἀληθινός, ὅτι ἄλλος 37
ἐστὶν ὁ σπείρων, καὶ ἄλλος ὁ θερίζων. Ἐγὼ ἀπέστειλα ὑμᾶς θερίζειν, 38
ὃ οὐχ ὑμεῖς κεκοπιάκατε· ἄλλοι κεκοπιάκασι, καὶ ὑμεῖς εἰς τὸν κόπον
αὐτῶν εἰσεληλύθατε. Ἐκ δὲ τῆς πόλεως ἐκείνης πολλοὶ ἐπίστευσαν εἰς 39
αὐτὸν τῶν Σαμαρειτῶν, διὰ τὸν λόγον τῆς γυναικὸς μαρτυρούσης·
Ὅτι εἶπέ μοι πάντα ὅσα ἐποίησα. Ὡς οὖν ἦλθον πρὸς αὐτὸν οἱ Σα- 40
μαρεῖται, ἠρώτων αὐτὸν μεῖναι παρ᾽ αὐτοῖς· καὶ ἔμεινεν ἐκεῖ δύο
h Infra 17. 8. ἡμέρας. Καὶ πολλῷ πλείους ἐπίστευσαν διὰ τὸν λόγον αὐτοῦ, [h] τῇ τε 41
γυναικὶ ἔλεγον· Ὅτι οὐκέτι διὰ τὴν σὴν λαλιὰν πιστεύομεν· αὐτοὶ 42
γὰρ ἀκηκόαμεν, καὶ οἴδαμεν ὅτι οὗτός ἐστιν ἀληθῶς ὁ σωτὴρ τοῦ
κόσμου, ὁ Χριστός.

i Matt. 13. 57. Mark 6. 4. Luke 4. 24. Μετὰ δὲ τὰς δύο ἡμέρας ἐξῆλθεν ἐκεῖθεν, καὶ ἀπῆλθεν εἰς τὴν 43
Γαλιλαίαν. [i] Αὐτὸς γὰρ [ὁ] Ἰησοῦς ἐμαρτύρησεν, ὅτι προφήτης ἐν τῇ 44

in the way to the attainment of its object. However, the *literal* sense may be the true one; and thus the meaning will be, "Ye are now [perhaps] saying, or may say, it is four months to harvest time; but the *spiritual* harvest of *souls* is already come (though the natural one may not be ready these four months), and therefore ought to commence immediately. See [pointing to the Samaritans coming up] what an Evangelical harvest is approaching?"

— ὑμεῖς λέγετε.] A popular idiom, for λέγετε or λέγουσι scil. ἄνθρωποι, as Matth. xvi. 2. In this address (meant to prepare his disciples for what was about to take place, and to induce them to imitate his example in performing the work of his Father) our Lord uses three arguments to excite their diligence. 1. That the harvest is near. 2. That the fruits to be collected are abundant. 3. That the accomplishment of the whole has been facilitated by others. On the force of τετράμηνος the Commentators are not agreed. Wets. supposes the metaphor to be derived from corn in the blade, of which nothing certain can be pronounced; and this is meant to express hope as yet in the bud. As to the particular time mentioned, though there may sometimes be *six* months between seed time and harvest, yet a Jewish proverb mentions but *four*; and as seed-time and harvest occupy a considerable period, so from the *end* of seed time to the *beginning* of harvest, there may be four months. Others, as Grot., Rosenm., and Tittm., think it is unnecessary to press on the import of τετρ., which is used with *popular* inexactness; and the general sense, they conceive, is: Never heed labour, when the reward is at hand; q. d. As hope calls forth the harvest-man to his work, so be ye also prompt in the accomplishment of the work I commit to you, for the promotion of your own spiritual good and that of others, nay, of the whole human race.

Instead of the common reading τετράμηνον almost all the best MSS. several Fathers, and all the early Editions, except the Erasmian, have τετράμηνος; which is adopted by every ancient Editor from Wets. to Scholz, to whose authority and that of MSS., I have deferred; though, after all, the common reading may be the true one; for τρίμηνον is found in Hebrews xi. 23., and other forms in —ον from derivations of μὴν occur in the later writers.

By λευκαί is meant a white approaching to yellow, such as accompanies maturity. By χώρας are denoted *cultivated fields*; a signification somewhat rare, but occurring in Luke, and occasionally in the Classical writers.

36. καὶ ὁ θερίζων.] Θερίζειν here denotes all sorts of *harvest work*. Here we have (as Rosenm. observes) a blending of the apodosis with the comparison. The sense is: "As the agricultural labourer receives his wages, whether for ploughing and sowing, or for reaping and gathering the corn; so shall ye receive your reward for gathering men unto the kingdom of God; and whether your labour be only preparatory, or such as consummates the spiritual harvest, ye shall alike be blessed with an ample reward."

37. ἐν τούτῳ.] Sub. πράγματι, in this case or instance. Ὁ λόγος, "saying, proverb." The application is, that as Moses and the Prophets, and finally John the Baptist, prepared the minds of men for receiving the Gospel from Christ; so will the Apostles reap the harvest of converts, for which He had prepared.

38. κεκοπιάκατε] "laboured for, worked out." Κοπιᾷν is used of severe toil, such as is required in all the agricultural occupations which precede harvest. Κόπον, i. e. the *fruit* of labour.

41. ἐπίστευσαν] i. e. professed faith in his Messiahship.

42. σωτὴρ τοῦ κόσμου] i. e. not of the Jews only. So much more enlightened, because better disposed, were the Samaritans than the Jews.

44. αὐτὸς γὰρ ὁ Ἰ.] This cannot be meant to offer a *reason* why our Lord went to Galilee. Some have attempted to remove the difficulty by supposing an omission of certain words to which the γὰρ might be suitable, as "Passing by Nazareth," or "but not to Nazareth;" thus distin-

45 ἰδίᾳ πατρίδι τιμὴν οὐκ ἔχει. Ὅτε οὖν ἦλθεν εἰς τὴν Γαλιλαίαν, ἐδέξαντο αὐτὸν οἱ Γαλιλαῖοι, πάντα ἑωρακότες, ἃ ἐποίησεν ἐν Ἱεροσολύ-
46 μοις ἐν τῇ ἑορτῇ· καὶ αὐτοὶ γὰρ ἦλθον εἰς τὴν ἑορτήν. [k] Ἦλθεν οὖν [k Supra 2. 1, 11.]
[ὁ Ἰησοῦς] πάλιν εἰς τὴν Κανᾶ τῆς Γαλιλαίας, ὅπου ἐποίησε τὸ ὕδωρ
οἶνον. Καὶ ἦν τις βασιλικὸς, οὗ ὁ υἱὸς ἠσθένει ἐν Καπερναούμ.
47 Οὗτος ἀκούσας ὅτι Ἰησοῦς ἥκει ἐκ τῆς Ἰουδαίας εἰς τὴν Γαλιλαίαν,
ἀπῆλθε πρὸς αὐτὸν, καὶ ἠρώτα αὐτὸν ἵνα καταβῇ καὶ ἰάσηται αὐτοῦ
48 τὸν υἱόν· ἤμελλε γὰρ ἀποθνήσκειν. [l] Εἶπεν οὖν ὁ Ἰησοῦς πρὸς αὐτόν· [l 1 Cor. 1. 22.]
49 Ἐὰν μὴ σημεῖα καὶ τέρατα ἴδητε, οὐ μὴ πιστεύσητε. Λέγει πρὸς
αὐτὸν ὁ βασιλικός· Κύριε, κατάβηθι πρὶν ἀποθανεῖν τὸ παιδίον μου.
50 Λέγει αὐτῷ ὁ Ἰησοῦς· Πορεύου· ὁ υἱός σου ζῇ. Καὶ ἐπίστευσεν ὁ
51 ἄνθρωπος τῷ λόγῳ ᾧ εἶπεν αὐτῷ ὁ Ἰησοῦς, καὶ ἐπορεύετο. Ἤδη δὲ
αὐτοῦ καταβαίνοντος, οἱ δοῦλοι αὐτοῦ ἀπήντησαν αὐτῷ, καὶ ἀπήγγειλαν
52 λέγοντες, Ὅτι ὁ παῖς σου ζῇ. Ἐπύθετο οὖν παρ' αὐτῶν τὴν ὥραν,
ἐν ᾗ κομψότερον ἔσχε· καὶ εἶπον αὐτῷ· Ὅτι χθὲς ὥραν ἑβδόμην
53 ἀφῆκεν αὐτὸν ὁ πυρετός. Ἔγνω οὖν ὁ πατὴρ ὅτι ἐν ἐκείνῃ τῇ ὥρᾳ,
ἐν ᾗ εἶπεν αὐτῷ ὁ Ἰησοῦς· Ὅτι ὁ υἱός σου ζῇ· καὶ ἐπίστευσεν αὐτὸς
54 καὶ ἡ οἰκία αὐτοῦ ὅλη. Τοῦτο πάλιν δεύτερον σημεῖον ἐποίησεν ὁ Ἰησοῦς, ἐλθὼν ἐκ τῆς Ἰουδαίας εἰς τὴν Γαλιλαίαν.
1 V. [m] ΜΕΤΑ ταῦτα ἦν ἑορτὴ τῶν Ἰουδαίων, καὶ ἀνέβη ὁ Ἰησοῦς [m Lev. 23. 2. Deut. 16. 1.]
2 εἰς Ἱεροσόλυμα. Ἔστι δὲ ἐν τοῖς Ἱεροσολύμοις ἐπὶ τῇ προβατικῇ κο-

guishing *Nazareth* from the *rest* of Galilee. This method, however, is too arbitrary; and may rather be called *cutting* than untying the knot. It is far better (with Alting, Schleusn., Tittm., and Kuin.) to take the γὰρ in the somewhat unusual sense *although*, as in Rom. ix. 15 & 17. Thus the meaning will be, that he returned to Galilee, *though* he had himself borne testimony to the truth of the saying, that a prophet, &c.

45. ἐδέξαντο] gave him a favorable reception.

46. βασιλικός.] On the exact sense of this term Commentators are not agreed. It must denote a *courtier*; but whether holding any office or not, or whether a Jew or a foreigner, is uncertain.

48. ἐὰν μὴ — πιστεύσητε.] This reproof is supposed by Euthym., Doddr., Kuin., and Tittm. to have been meant for the bystanders rather than the nobleman, or rather was directed against the Jews in general. But I am inclined to think that by *ye* is meant *ye Nazarenes*; for we have reason to think the people would not believe without seeing a sign, and consequently our Lord did not vouchsafe a sign, because of their obstinate unbelief. See Matt. xiii. 58. As, however, miracles form the proper evidence of a divine mission, some Commentators think our Lord could not mean the words as a *reproof*. The sense, they say, is: "Except ye see miracles, it cannot be *expected* that ye will believe; therefore I will heal the courtier's son." But that is surely *straining* the sense, and very unnecessarily; for why may we not suppose ἴδητε to be put *emphatically*, and the words be meant as a reproof of those who, like the Nazarenes, refused belief in the authority of numerous miracles established on the most credible evidence; but demanded to see them with their *own* eyes. That surely *was* unreasonable. The proof by miracles could not fairly be demanded to be brought to *every city*, or *individual*.

50. To show that he could do even *more* than the father hoped for, and could heal the sick absent as well as present (and in order thereby to effectually remove any want of faith in the bystanders) Jesus says πορεύου, i. e. "Go in peace: thy business is done." Ζῇ is by the best Commentators interpreted, "is convalescent." So the Heb. הָיָה in Josh. v. 8. and often in the Rabbinical writers. Comp. the well-known "non *vivere*, sed *valere* vita!"

52. κομψότερον ἔσχε.] A popular idiom for βελτιώτερον, or ῥᾴτερον, &c. So the Latin *bellè habere*. Ἀφῆκεν implies the *suddenness* of the cure. See Hippocrates, cited by Triller, ἀφῆκεν αὐτὸν ὁ πυρετός.

54. ἐλθὼν] "after he had returned," &c., πάλιν being construed with ἐλθών.

V. 1. ἑορτὴ] *Which* of the Feasts this was the Commentators are not agreed. Some think it was that of *Purim*, in our March, about a month before the Passover. Others suppose it the *Encænia*, or feast of eight days, about the middle of December. Others, again, the *Feast of Tabernacles*. The most eminent Expositors, however, are of opinion that the *Passover* is meant; which, indeed, seems the most probable. And Bp. Middlet. has shewn that, notwithstanding the absence of the Article, the Passover *may* be, and, on other accounts, probably *is* meant. As an example of a similar omission, he adduces xix. 14. ἦν δὲ παρασκευὴ τοῦ Πάσχα, than which, notwithstanding the omission of the *article*, nothing can be more definite.

2. ἐπὶ τῇ προβ.] There is here an ellips. which is supplied by ἀγορᾷ, or χώρᾳ, or (which is adopt-

λυμβήθρα, ἡ ἐπιλεγομένη Ἑβραϊστὶ Βηθεσδὰ, πέντε στοὰς ἔχουσα.
Ἐν ταύταις κατέκειτο πλῆθος πολὺ τῶν ἀσθενούντων, τυφλῶν, χωλῶν, 3

ed by the most eminent Commentators, as Wolf, Lampe, Campb., Kuin., and Tittm.) πύλῃ. This last is preferable, as being a very frequent ellip. in the best writers from Homer downwards, and is placed beyond doubt by Nehem. iii. 32. xii. 39, who mentions τὴν πύλην τὴν προβατικὴν; whereas there is no evidence of there being any such place as the Sheep-*market*. This is confirmed by the testimony of Sandys, who tells us that "the gate in question (no doubt the gate of St. Stephen) was called in times past the Gate of the Valley, and of the Flock; for that the cattle came in at this gate which were to be sacrificed in the Temple."

Κολυμβήθρα signifies properly *a bathing-pool;* but here it is supposed by the best Commentators to denote not the pool only, but the buildings which had been erected around it, for the accommodation of the bathers. By Ἑβρ. is meant the Syro-Chaldee, then the vernacular tongue in Judæa.

— Βηθεσδά.] The MSS. vary; but there is not the least reason to doubt the accuracy of the common reading, especially as it is confirmed by the derivation from the Hebr. בית and חסדא, "house of mercy," or "charity-hospital." That the bath had medicinal properties, is plain; but whence it derived them, is not so certain. The older Commentators refer them to *supernatural agency;* the more recent ones in general to *natural causes*, for which there may be thought some confirmation in the fact, ascertained from Theophyl., that such was the common notion. But as to the causes to which he says the people ascribed it, namely, the effect produced by the washing at this pool of the entrails of the sheep sacrificed at the Temple, or from the blood and washings from the victims being conveyed hither by pipes (which several learned Physiologists think might impart a medicinal property to the water); there is decided evidence *against* the *former* notion; and the *latter* rests on no proof. Hence the most eminent of the later Commentators prefer to account for the effects by supposing that the water was of itself a medicinal one, deriving its sanative properties from some mineral with which it was impregnated. "This would (says Mead), from the water being perturbed from the bottom by some natural cause (perhaps subterranean heat, or storms) rise upwards and be mingled with it, and so impart a sanative property to those who bathed in it *before the metallic particles had subsided to the bottom.* That it should have done so, κατὰ καιρὸν, is not strange; since Bartholin has, by many examples, shown that it is usual with many medical baths to exert a singular force and sanative power at *stated times*, and at periodical, but *uncertain intervals.*" The learned Physician does not deign to notice the difficulty presented by the words ἄγγελος κατέβαινεν ἐν κολ. καὶ ἐτάρασσε τὸ ὕδωρ; though he doubtless, with most recent Commentators, referred to the *opinion entertained by the Jews*, who, ignorant of natural philosophy, referred such phenomena to a peculiar Divine operation, to whose agency they, as usual, called in the intervention of angels. The Commentators in question, however, distrusting their own solution, with reference to *natural* causes, propose to cancel part of this narration. But all, or the greater part of the words ἐκδεχομένων — τὸ ὕδωρ must be cancelled. And for *that* there is only the authority of 2 MSS., 2 very inferior Versions, and Nonnus. But Nonnus can *here* be *no* authority, since he frequently passes over clauses, and such Versions *very slight.* Besides the *MSS.* are such as abound with all sorts of liberties taken with the text. Insomuch that Rinck. (Lucub. Crit. in loco) though a rash Critic, and too apt to innovate on the authority of a few MSS., frankly admits, "Sed suspectæ fidei in ejusmodi omissionibus censores Alexandrini, qui, veterum exemplorum auctoritate neglectâ, judicio suo nimium indulgentes, quidquid in profanis et Sacris Scriptoribus minus aptè vel sapienter dictum videbatur, obelis notare cœperunt." And even the innovating Lachmann *removes* the brackets, in which Griesb. had included the passage. As to the other varr. lect., they all plainly originated in a desire to *get rid of the difficulty.* In short, the words seem to have been cancelled by them for the *same reason* that some Critics of the present day (who bear a strong resemblance to the Alexandrian *Censores*), wish to *get rid of them.* But that is impracticable; since they are plainly *alluded* to at ver. 7. in the words ὅταν δὲ ταραχθῇ τὸ ὕδωρ, which cannot be explained without them. The words must therefore be retained, and interpreted in the best manner we are able. Kuinoel's mode of explanation *creates* more difficulty than it solves. The plain and obvious meaning (and that recognised by the ancient and all earlier modern Commentators) is, that God had endued the Pool with a preternatural healing quality, and in the communication of it employed one of his ministering spirits; not, however, as we have any reason to think, *visibly.* Certainly the *circumstances* of the narration (as that only the *first* who entered after the commotion of the water was healed; and that *all* disorders — not those only which medicinal waters heal — were cured, and that *instantaneously* and *invariably*) utterly exclude the notion of any thing short of miraculous agency. And if the circumstance of the angel's going down be thought (as it is by Doddridge) to "involve the greatest of all difficulties in the Evangelists" (which, however, is far from being the case), we may (with that Commentator and Bps. Pearce and Mann) suppose, that the sanative property was supernatural, and communicated, during a short period, as typical of the "fountain opened for the purifying of sin, by the atonement of the Messiah (the *prophecy* of Zechariah being thus realized into a *type*), and that the Evangelist, in thus mentioning the descent of the angel, speaks according to the opinion of the Jews; who ascribed all the operations of God's Providence to the ministry of angels." Yet even Doddr. admits that they and St. John "had reason so to do, since it was the *Scripture scheme* that these benevolent *spirits* had been, and frequently are, the invisible instruments of good to men." Surely, then, what was right in *them* cannot but be right in *us;* and the common view is the more to be adhered to, as giving no countenance to a most unsound and dangerous principle, on which I have treated in my Annotation on the *Demoniacs.*

— στοάς.] The best Commentators take these to have been *porticoes* fronting the bath; roofed, but open on the sides, and supported with pillars placed at regular intervals, from which ran side-

4 ξηρῶν, ἐκδεχομένων τὴν τοῦ ὕδατος κίνησιν. Ἄγγελος γὰρ κατὰ καιρὸν
κατέβαινεν ἐν τῇ κολυμβήθρᾳ, καὶ ‡ ἐτάρασσε τὸ ὕδωρ· ὁ οὖν πρῶτος
ἐμβὰς μετὰ τὴν ταραχὴν τοῦ ὕδατος ὑγιὴς ἐγίνετο, ᾧ δήποτε κατείχετο
5 νοσήματι. Ἦν δέ τις ἄνθρωπος ἐκεῖ τριάκοντα καὶ ὀκτὼ ἔτη ἔχων ἐν
6 τῇ ἀσθενείᾳ. Τοῦτον ἰδὼν ὁ Ἰησοῦς κατακείμενον, καὶ γνοὺς ὅτι πολὺν
7 ἤδη χρόνον ἔχει, λέγει αὐτῷ· Θέλεις ὑγιὴς γενέσθαι; Ἀπεκρίθη αὐτῷ
ὁ ἀσθενῶν· Κύριε, ἄνθρωπον οὐκ ἔχω, ἵνα, ὅταν ταραχθῇ τὸ ὕδωρ,
* βάλῃ με εἰς τὴν κολυμβήθραν· ἐν ᾧ δὲ ἔρχομαι ἐγὼ, ἄλλος πρὸ
8 ἐμοῦ καταβαίνει. [n] Λέγει αὐτῷ ὁ Ἰησοῦς· Ἔγειραι, ἆρον τὸν κράβ- n Matt. 9. 6. Mark 2. 11. Luke 5. 24.
9 βατόν σου, καὶ περιπάτει. [o] Καὶ εὐθέως ἐγένετο ὑγιὴς ὁ ἄνθρωπος· o Infra 9. 14.
καὶ ἦρε τὸν κράββατον αὐτοῦ, καὶ περιεπάτει. Ἦν δὲ σάββατον ἐν
10 ἐκείνῃ τῇ ἡμέρᾳ. [p] Ἔλεγον οὖν οἱ Ἰουδαῖοι τῷ τεθεραπευμένῳ· Σάβ- p Exod. 20. 10. Deut. 5. 13.
11 βατόν ἐστιν· οὐκ ἔξεστί σοι ἆραι τὸν κράββατον. Ἀπεκρίθη αὐτοῖς· Neh. 13. 19. Jer. 17. 21, &c.
Ὁ ποιήσας με ὑγιῆ, ἐκεῖνός μοι εἶπεν· Ἆρον τὸν κράββατόν σου, καὶ Matt. 12. 2. Mark 2. 24. Luke 6. 2.
12 περιπάτει. Ἠρώτησαν οὖν αὐτόν· Τίς ἐστιν ὁ ἄνθρωπος ὁ εἰπών
13 σοι· Ἆρον τὸν κράββατόν σου, καὶ περιπάτει; Ὁ δὲ ἰαθεὶς οὐκ
ᾔδει τίς ἐστιν· ὁ γὰρ Ἰησοῦς ἐξένευσεν, ὄχλου ὄντος ἐν τῷ τόπῳ.
14 [q] Μετὰ ταῦτα εὑρίσκει αὐτὸν ὁ Ἰησοῦς ἐν τῷ ἱερῷ, καὶ εἶπεν αὐτῷ· q Matt. 12. 45. infra 8. 11.

walls, separating them from each other; the whole forming a pentagon. This, in so genial a climate as that of Judæa, would be a sufficient shelter by *day*; and at *night* the patients were probably removed.

3. Ἀσθενεῖν is applicable to any *formed* disease; and κατακεῖσθαι, to such chronical ones as confine any one to his bed or room. Ξηρῶν seems to denote those labouring under "pining sickness," such as atrophy or consumption.

4. κατὰ καιρόν.] This only means "at certain unknown intervals of time;" and therefore those who refer it to any stated times, are wrong. Κατείχετο is a stronger term than εἴχετο, and is applied to thoroughly formed, and usually *chronical* disorders. Instead of ἐτάρασσε τὸ ὕδωρ, very many MSS. and several Versions and early Edd. have ἐταράσσετο τὸ ὕδωρ, which was adopted by Bengel and Matthæi, the latter of whom remarks, "facile excidit τὸ ob proximum τό." But it was almost as easy for the τὸ to have been inadvertently *joined with* ἐτάρασσε, especially in MSS. written in Uncials, and without any space between the words. Besides, the common reading is more appropriate, and suitable to the context.

5 ἔχων.] This must be construed with ἦν, not (as is done by many) with τριάκ.; as appears from v. 6. Comp. Luke xiii. 11. viii. 43. John xi. 39. Ἔχων ἐν τῇ ἀσθ. is for ἀσθενὴς ἦν or ἠσθένει. Render, "There was a man there who had been 38 years labouring under sickness." With respect to the disorder, it was probably *paralysis*; for not only was such the constant tradition of the primitive ages; but no less than *six* medical reasons for it are given by Bartholin.

6. ἔχει.] Sub. οὕτως ἐν ἀσθενείᾳ from the preceding.

— θέλεις ὑγ. γ.] "Is it your purpose? are you here with the view of being healed?"

7. βάλῃ.] This, for βάλλῃ, is found in the greater part of the best MSS., and has been received by Wets., Griesb., Matth., Vater, and Scholz.

8. κράββατον.] This was a small mean seat, something like those *portable seats* used by us on ship-board, or elsewhere; and had, it appears, only a skin, rug, or the like, for a covering. See Mark ii. 4, 11. Περιπάτει has reference to the man's former inability to walk, being bedridden: and the order was no doubt given, to evince the completeness of the cure.

9. εὐθέως ἐγένετο ὑγιής.] Thus from an obstinate and incurable disorder he was *immediately* restored to *health*, without that languor which is always observable in those cured by human art

10. οἱ Ἰουδαῖοι.] Not the *bystanders*, but (as Lampe has shown) some who met the healed person on his way home carrying his bed.

— οὐκ ἔξεστι, &c.] This was supposed to be forbidden in Jer. xvii. 21; which passage, however, has reference only to what involves *great labour*; though the lawyers interpreted it as forbidding to carry even the lightest weight. Yet the Rabbinical writers recognize *some* cases, when it was permitted to carry burdens on the Sabbath. If, then, it was lawful for the *Lawyers*, in certain cases, to dispense with the observance of the Sabbath; how much more for *Christ*, the LORD OF THE SABBATH!

11. ὁ ποιήσας, &c.] As the Jews admitted that, by the command of a *prophet*, the Sabbath might be broken, so the man seems to have alluded thereto; accounting (as he justly might) the worker of such a miracle to be a Prophet.

13. οὐκ ᾔδει τίς ἐστιν.] In ᾔδει there seems to be a *significatio prægnans*, for "he knew not [and had not ascertained] who it was, *for* Jesus ἐξένευσε," "had glided away." Ἐκνέω signifies properly to *swim away*; and then, like the Latin *enatare*, and *emergere*, signifies *evadere*, to slip away unobserved. He had probably done this, partly to avoid the admiration of the well-disposed, and partly to cut off the envy of the malicious.

14. ἐν τῷ ἱερῷ.] A frequent place of resort to the Jews, and whither the healed man had probably gone, to return God thanks for his recovery.

Ἴδε, ὑγιὴς γέγονας· μηκέτι ἁμάρτανε, ἵνα μὴ χεῖρόν τί σοι γένηται.
Ἀπῆλθεν ὁ ἄνθρωπος, καὶ ἀνήγγειλε τοῖς Ἰουδαίοις, ὅτι Ἰησοῦς ἐστιν 15
ὁ ποιήσας αὐτὸν ὑγιῆ. Καὶ διὰ τοῦτο ἐδίωκον τὸν Ἰησοῦν οἱ Ἰουδαῖοι, 16
r Infra 14. 10. [καὶ ἐζήτουν αὐτὸν ἀποκτεῖναι,] ὅτι ταῦτα ἐποίει ἐν σαββάτῳ. [r] Ὁ δὲ 17
Ἰησοῦς ἀπεκρίνατο αὐτοῖς· Ὁ Πατήρ μου ἕως ἄρτι ἐργάζεται, κἀγὼ
s Infra 7. 19. & 8. 38. & 9. 4. & 10. 33. Phil. 2. 6. ἐργάζομαι. [s] Διὰ τοῦτο οὖν μᾶλλον ἐζήτουν αὐτὸν οἱ Ἰουδαῖοι ἀπο- 18
κτεῖναι, ὅτι οὐ μόνον ἔλυε τὸ σάββατον, ἀλλὰ καὶ πατέρα ἴδιον ἔλεγε
t Infra ver. 30. & 8. 38. τὸν Θεὸν, ἴσον ἑαυτὸν ποιῶν τῷ Θεῷ. [t] Ἀπεκρίνατο οὖν ὁ Ἰησοῦς καὶ 19
εἶπεν αὐτοῖς· Ἀμὴν ἀμὴν λέγω ὑμῖν· οὐ δύναται ὁ Υἱὸς ποιεῖν ἀφ᾽
ἑαυτοῦ οὐδὲν, ἐὰν μή τι βλέπῃ τὸν Πατέρα ποιοῦντα· ἃ γὰρ ἂν ἐκεῖ-

—*μηκέτι ἁμάρτανε*, &c.] It is not necessary to refer this, with many Commentators, to the Jewish notion, that all violent disorders were the punishment of sin; but we may (with Brug., Grot., and Doddr.) suppose, that the man's disorder had really been brought on by intemperance and vice; and that our Lord meant to give him a proof of his omniscience, by showing his knowledge of that fact.

15. *ἀπῆλθεν*, &c.] There is no reason to suppose (with some Commentators) that his intention in going was a bad one: it was rather from a wish to justify himself for breaking the Sabbath by the command of an undoubted prophet; as also from gratitude to his benefactor, and benevolence to others, by making known the fountain of health. By *τοῖς Ἰουδαίοις* may be meant the influential persons among the Jews, i. e. the Sanhedrim and leading Doctors and Jurists, or (as Tittm. supposes) those Jews whom he met with, as ver. 10.

17. *ἀπεκρίνατο*.] As an *answer* implies a *question*, Grot., Lampe, and others regard the following as a justification of his conduct, pronounced by Jesus before the Rulers, either at public or private examination. No previous *questions*, however, are necessary to be supposed; but we may simply take *ἀπεκρίνατο*, either in the sense *addressed*, or for *ἀπελογήσατο*; on which see Steph. Thes. Our Lord, it seems, intended to refute their calumny by thus addressing them, while standing by at the Temple. The words of his apology are obscure from brevity; and from this, and their abruptness, the best Commentators infer that the Evangelist has not recorded the *whole* of what was then said. But there is something so precarious in that principle, that it ought never to be resorted to, unless in a case of necessity; which does not exist here. It should seem that our Lord comprehended all that was necessary in *one* brief, but pithy, *dictum*, in order to make the more impression on those whom he addressed; especially as it was customary with the Jews to express things, as much as possible, with *apophthegmatical* brevity. Besides, it was not so obscure, but that the Jews readily comprehended the most material part, i. e. his claiming to be *Son of God*, and consequently *equal with God*; from which his right to dispense with the Sabbath would, on the authority even of the Jewish traditions, be undoubted. By *ἐργάζεσθαι* is meant the *operation of* God, as displayed in the preservation and governance of all created beings, which are therefore the works of his omnipotence; and by *ἕως ἄρτι* is expressed the *perpetuity* of that preservation and governance, unremittingly exerted for the safety and welfare of his creatures. Something similar occurs in Philo. i. 44. 29. cited by Wets. *παύεται γὰρ οὐδέποτε ποιῶν ὁ Θεός· ἀλλ᾽ ὥσπερ ἴδιον τὸ καίειν πυρὸς, καὶ χίονος τὸ ψύχειν. οὕτω καὶ Θεοῦ τὸ ποιεῖν.* and i. 46. 49. *ποιῶν ὁ Θεὸς οὐ παύεται· ἀλλ᾽ ἑτέρων γενέσεως ἄρχεται.* By this example of GOD, our Lord intends to rebut their crimination, and to teach them that he imitates God, who hath no Sabbath, but doth His work perpetually. "As my Father doth not cease to benefit men on the Sabbath, neither am I impeded by any such observance." In short, the argument is, that as his Father governed and preserved the world as well on the Sabbath as on other days, so he, as Son, had an equal right so to do. But this involved *equality with his Father*, and consequently essential DIVINITY. But what is more, our Lord professes to do the same *works* which the Father doth; and these not only of benevolence, but of *omnipotence*. He therefore *equals* himself with the Father. And when the Jews, as was natural, understood his words of claiming equality with God, Jesus did not attempt to remove that notion, but confirmed and more expressly asserted it. See Tittman.

18. *πατέρα ἴδιον ἔλ.*] By this is meant calling God *peculiarly* his Father: thus making himself equal to God. See Campb. For they interpreted his words to mean, that being the Son of God and the Messiah, he could, *by his own proper authority*, dispense with the observance of the Sabbath. Now this was contrary to their opinion of the power of the Messiah, which they maintained to be only *delegated*, and in all things *subservient*, and inferior to that of the Father. Hence they understood him as not claiming to be Messiah in the *common* sense, but in a *peculiar* and sublime one, by which he arrogated an authority independent of God; and therefore, in a certain sense, was *equal to Him*.

19. *οὐ δύναται*, &c.] To this charge of the Jews, that he claimed equality with God, by professing to have power, by his *own authority*, to dispense with the observance of the Sabbath, Jesus replies by a fuller explanation of what he had before said. The justification which follows was (as appears from v. 18.) pronounced some little time after the preceding. Here our Lord professes, that he doth nothing of his own will only, but in conformity and conjunction with that of the Father, and that therefore his works are consentaneous to those of the Father; nay, that there is the same will both of Father and Son, with also the same power. That he doth all things after the example of the Father, and therefore can do nothing contrary to His will; in

20 νος ποιῇ, ταῦτα καὶ ὁ Υἱὸς ὁμοίως ποιεῖ. [u] Ὁ γὰρ Πατὴρ φιλεῖ τὸν [u] Supra 3. 35.
Υἱὸν, καὶ πάντα δείκνυσιν αὐτῷ, ἃ αὐτὸς ποιεῖ· καὶ μείζονα τούτων
21 δείξει αὐτῷ ἔργα, ἵνα ὑμεῖς θαυμάζητε. Ὥσπερ γὰρ ὁ Πατὴρ ἐγείρει
τοὺς νεκροὺς καὶ ζωοποιεῖ, οὕτω καὶ ὁ Υἱὸς οὓς θέλει ζωοποιεῖ.
22 [x] Οὐδὲ γὰρ ὁ Πατὴρ κρίνει οὐδένα, ἀλλὰ τὴν κρίσιν πᾶσαν δέδωκε [x] Matt. 11. 27. & 28. 18.
23 τῷ Υἱῷ· [y] ἵνα πάντες τιμῶσι τὸν Υἱὸν, καθὼς τιμῶσι τὸν Πατέρα. supra 3. 35. infra 17. 2. Acts 17. 31.
Ὁ μὴ τιμῶν τὸν Υἱὸν, οὐ τιμᾷ τὸν Πατέρα τὸν πέμψαντα αὐτόν. [y] 1 John 2. 23.
24 [z] Ἀμὴν ἀμὴν λέγω ὑμῖν· ὅτι ὁ τὸν λόγον μου ἀκούων καὶ πιστεύων [z] Supra 3. 18. infra 6. 40, 47. & 8. 51.
τῷ πέμψαντί με ἔχει ζωὴν αἰώνιον· καὶ εἰς κρίσιν οὐκ ἔρχεται, ἀλλὰ Rom. 8. 24.
25 μεταβέβηκεν ἐκ τοῦ θανάτου εἰς τὴν ζωήν. [a] Ἀμὴν ἀμὴν λέγω ὑμῖν· ὅτι Eph. 2. 6. 1 John 3. 2. Luke 23. 43.
ἔρχεται ὥρα, καὶ νῦν ἐστιν, ὅτε οἱ νεκροὶ ἀκούσονται τῆς φωνῆς τοῦ Υἱοῦ [a] Eph. 2. 1, 5. 1 Tim. 5. 6.
26 τοῦ Θεοῦ· καὶ οἱ ἀκούσαντες ζήσονται. ὥσπερ γὰρ ὁ Πατὴρ ἔχει ζωὴν Rev. 3. 1. Rom. 6. 4. Gal. 2. 20.
27 ἐν ἑαυτῷ, οὕτως ἔδωκε καὶ τῷ Υἱῷ ζωὴν ἔχειν ἐν ἑαυτῷ. Καὶ ἐξουσίαν

short, that he cannot depart from the example of the Father, either in doing, or not doing, any thing. Thus there is a comparison of the works of the Father with those of the Son, in universality, identity, and conjunction of will and plan. Hence we are taught the *economical* subordination of the Son to the Father, and yet the co-equality of both: on which see Bp. Bull's Defensio Fidei Nicænæ, Sect. iv. *οὐ δύναται*, as in John iii. 9. 12 & 39, imports not a *physical*, but a moral impossibility, q. d. alienissimum fuerit ab illo. Ἐὰν μὴ is for ἀλλὰ or ἀλλ' ἢν, as in Gal. ii. 16. on which I have before treated.

20. In this verse is expressed in a *popular* and general way (but οἰκονομικῶς) that the Father, out of love to the Son, communicates to him the power of doing *whatever he doth*; nay, will enable him to achieve greater works. Ἵνα is put for ὥστε, denoting simply the *event*. Δεικν. literally signifies to show any one how to do a thing; and, by implication, to enable him to do it. It here, as Doddr. observes, "has reference to the complete knowledge the *Son* hath of the whole of the Father's counsels, in every part of their mutual relations; and expresses the communication of the power to work such wonderful works as God worketh, and even greater, namely, miracles of the most illustrious kind."

21. The portion from ver. 21 to 31. has been variously explained. The question in dispute is, what our Lord meant to be understood by the *resurrection of the dead*, and *judgment*, here mentioned; whether, in a figurative sense, the awakening the men of that generation to a spiritual life; or, in a natural one, the resurrection of *all* men to eternal life: and whether, by *judgment*, he meant the *retribution* to succeed this. The best Expositors are in general agreed in adopting the *second* interpretation, which is, indeed, more agreeable to what *precedes*, and is probably what was *principally* intended. But may it not be here (as in the prophetical declarations of our Lord at Matt. xxiv.), that a two-fold sense was intended: so that under the natural is couched *also* a mystical one. Such a sense, even Tittm. admits, is allowed by the context and the usus loquendi; nay, sometimes seems to be the prominent one, exactly as in the above passage of Matt.

24. *εἰς κρίσιν οὐκ ἔρχεται.*] Ἔρχεται is for ἐλεύσεται, to shew the certainty of the event; and κρ. is for κατάκρισιν or κόλασιν.

—*μεταβέβηκεν—ζωήν.*] These words yield a good sense on either of the above mentioned interpretations, according to the latter of which they will signify, "he hath as it were passed, or he is to pass (on both of which see Win. Gr.) from death to a state of everlasting life and happiness," the Preterite being used to express the *certainty* of the thing; or, according to the former, "he hath passed from a state of death and condemnation unto a state which will terminate in life eternal." The two senses, however, merge into each other.

25, 26. These verses admit of a good sense on either of the foregoing interpretations: and Expositors adopt some one, some the other; not considering that *both* were probably intended. However, the *tropical* and *mystical* should seem to be more prominent than the *literal*. Thus by νεκροὶ will be meant those who are dead in trespasses and sins (Eph. v. 14.), and by ζήσονται, that "they shall be put into the way of obtaining eternal life," namely, by hearkening to the preaching of Christ's Gospel. The full sense of ver. 26. may be thus expressed in paraphrase: "For as the Father hath in himself, as the Fountain of life, the power of giving [the] life or salvation [which had been forfeited by the fall of man in Adam], so hath he communicated to the Son, in like manner, the power to give this eternal life." At ver. 27. there is a transition to the *literal* sense; κρίσιν ποιεῖν meaning to hold judgment. "Ὁ υἱὸς τοῦ ἀνθρώπου has already occurred 70 times, and now for the first time without either of the Articles, from which Beza and others contend that the sense is 'son of a man.' They attempt to defend this on a *Syriasm*, which is rather *against* their conclusion. The omission of the Articles must be explained from *Greek* usage. Now the Articles in the phrase ὁ υἱὸς τοῦ ἀνθρώπου were employed because Christ assumed to himself this appellation, and the very *assumption* forbade him to use the phrase otherwise than as ὁ υἱὸς τοῦ ἀνθρώπου. And the first Article requires the second, for ὁ υἱὸς ἀνθρώπου would offend against *regimen*. Hence the Article is not *materially* and *essentially* necessary, but only accidentally; and consequently it will not be admitted but when *regimen* requires it, i. e. when ὁ υἱὸς pre-

b Dan. 12. 2. 1 Cor. 15. 52. 1 Thess. 4. 16. ἔδωκεν αὐτῷ καὶ κρίσιν ποιεῖν, ὅτι Υἱὸς ἀνθρώπου ἐστί. [b] Μὴ θαυμά- 28
ζετε τοῦτο· ὅτι ἔρχεται ὥρα, ἐν ᾗ πάντες οἱ ἐν τοῖς μνημείοις ἀκού-
c Matt. 25. 46. σονται τῆς φωνῆς αὐτοῦ, [c] καὶ ἐκπορεύσονται· οἱ τὰ ἀγαθὰ ποιή- 29
σαντες εἰς ἀνάστασιν ζωῆς, οἱ δὲ τὰ φαῦλα πράξαντες εἰς ἀνάστασιν
d Supra ver. 19. infra 6. 38. κρίσεως. [d] Οὐ δύναμαι ἐγὼ ποιεῖν ἀπ᾽ ἐμαυτοῦ οὐδέν. καθὼς ἀκούω, 30
κρίνω· καὶ ἡ κρίσις ἡ ἐμὴ δικαία ἐστίν· ὅτι οὐ ζητῶ τὸ θέλημα τὸ
e Infra 8. 14. ἐμὸν, ἀλλὰ τὸ θέλημα τοῦ πέμψαντός με [Πατρός]. [e] Ἐὰν ἐγὼ μαρ- 31
f Isa. 42. 1. Matt. 3. 17. & 17. 5. τυρῶ περὶ ἐμαυτοῦ, ἡ μαρτυρία μου οὐκ ἔστιν ἀληθής. [f] Ἄλλος ἐστὶν 32
ὁ μαρτυρῶν περὶ ἐμοῦ· καὶ οἶδα ὅτι ἀληθής ἐστιν ἡ μαρτυρία, ἣν
g Supra 1. 19. μαρτυρεῖ περὶ ἐμοῦ. [g] Ὑμεῖς ἀπεστάλκατε πρὸς Ἰωάννην· καὶ μεμαρ- 33
τύρηκε τῇ ἀληθείᾳ. Ἐγὼ δὲ οὐ παρὰ ἀνθρώπου τὴν μαρτυρίαν λαμ- 34
βάνω· ἀλλὰ ταῦτα λέγω ἵνα ὑμεῖς σωθῆτε. Ἐκεῖνος ἦν ὁ λύχνος ὁ 35

cedes. Now *here* not ὁ υἱὸς, but υἱὸς follows ἐστὶ, and the phrase could not be otherwise than υἱὸς ἀνθρώπου. Moreover, the sense for which these Commentators contend is equally deducible from the common interpretation; for the title Son of man has everywhere reference to the *incarnation* of Christ, and therefore implies His acquaintance with human infirmity." (Bp. Middl.) In this view of the sense all the ancient Expositors agree, and some of the most eminent modern ones, as Grot., Lampe, Morus, Rosenm., Kuin., and Tittm., who compare a similar use of Υἱὸς ἀνθρώπου at Matt. xiv. 33. and elsewhere. Thus the meaning is, that Christ hath committed to him likewise authority to *hold judgment* at the last day; for his Mediatorial office will not be complete till he hath *judged* the world. There is here a reference to the *incarnation* of Christ, which implies his acquaintance with human infirmity, and consequently his fitness to be our Judge. This is strongly confirmed by Hebr. iv. 15. where the Apostle exhorts his converts κρατεῖν τῆς ὁμολογίας, inasmuch as they have a great High-priest in the heavens, who is at once ὁ Υἱὸς τοῦ Θεοῦ and Υἱὸς τοῦ ἀνθρώπου; the words πεπειρασμένον τῶν ἀσθενειῶν, &c., being only a fuller expression of the idea Son of man. Lampe has here an able note, in which he goes far to prove that there is here an especial reference to Christ's Mediatorial office and acquirement of the gift of salvation by his perfect obedience; and that exercise of judgment pertains to the reward of this obedience. See Is. liii. 12.

28, 29. We have here a *transition* from the *moral* to the *physical* resurrection, and the judgment connected with it. Μὴ θαυμάζετε has reference to what was said at vv. 21. & 25; yet not in the *literal* acceptation of those words, as Kuin. and Tittm. imagine, (for that would yield a very frigid sense, as if it were greater to raise the *buried* than the dead) but the *allegorical* and mystical; q. d. "Wonder not at what I have said of this moral revivification; for," &c. This physical resurrection, though not a work greater in itself, yet was, by the consequences it drew with it, more august and worthy of admiration.

30. οὐ δύναμαι — οὐδέν.] Δύναμαι and ἀπ' ἐμαυτοῦ are to be taken as at v. 19.; only what is there said of *any* action, is here applicable to *judging*. (Euthym.) Our Lord here, as Scott observes, repeats his declaration of the entire coincidence of design and operation between the Father and the Son. It was impossible he should do any thing in his work as Mediator, or as Judge, from any motive, to any end, or by any power, different from those of the Father. Thus what is done by Christ is understood to be done with the full concurrence of the Father, and therefore cannot but be just.

— The words ὅτι οὐ ζητῶ, &c., suggests another reason why his judgment is just; — because he is not biassed by any private interest or passion, as human judges sometimes are, but regards alone his Father's will.

31 ἐὰν ἐγὼ μαρτυρῶ, &c.] Jesus proceeds to show that, from his actions, miracles, and the character of his doctrines, he is proved to be the Messiah; and first anticipates the objection (couched in a proverbial saying) that no one is a fit witness in his own case. Render: "If I were to bear witness of myself, [only], my witness would not be valid;" ἀληθὴς being for πιστός. Thus there will be no discrepancy between what is said here and at viii. 14. Compare viii. 17. There is an ellip. of μόνος; and ἀληθὴς is for πιστός.

32. ἄλλος.] Who is here meant, the Commentators are not agreed. The ancient and early modern ones suppose *John the Baptist*; but some more recent ones, as Kuin. and Lampe, *the Father*. But although they make out a tolerable case, yet the former interpretation is so strongly confirmed by what follows, that I can scarcely doubt but that it is the true one.

33. ὑμεῖς — ἀληθείᾳ] i. e. You yourselves have heard the witness appealed to by a public mission, and he bore testimony concerning us. You *have* therefore *human* testimony. See i. 8. 15. & 26. 3 John 3. 6.

34. ἐγὼ δὲ οὐ, &c.] The sense is: "I say not this through a desire for the honour which human fame can bestow. I want — I *accept* not the testimony of any man. I only appeal to the testimony of John, in order that, believing in me through that testimony, ye may be saved."

35. ὁ λύχνος ὁ καιόμενος.] Render *the "burning and shining light."* "John's ministry (says Campb.) was of a peculiar character; he was the single prophet in whom the old Dispensation had its completion, and by whom the new was introduced; therefore, until our Lord's ministry took place, John may justly be said to have been *the light* of that generation." Bp. Middlet. thinks there is an allusion to some phrase then current to signify an enlightened teacher: which is confirmed not only by what Lightf. says, that "a per-

καιόμενος καὶ φαίνων· ὑμεῖς δὲ ἠθελήσατε ἀγαλλιασθῆναι πρὸς ὥραν
36 ἐν τῷ φωτὶ αὐτοῦ. [h] Ἐγὼ δὲ ἔχω τὴν μαρτυρίαν μείζω τοῦ Ἰωάννου·
τὰ γὰρ ἔργα ἃ ἔδωκέ μοι ὁ Πατὴρ ἵνα τελειώσω αὐτὰ, αὐτὰ τὰ ἔργα
37 ἃ ἐγὼ ποιῶ, μαρτυρεῖ περὶ ἐμοῦ, ὅτι ὁ Πατήρ με ἀπέσταλκε. [i] καὶ ὁ
πέμψας με Πατὴρ αὐτὸς μεμαρτύρηκε περὶ ἐμοῦ. Οὔτε φωνὴν αὐτοῦ
38 ἀκηκόατε πώποτε, οὔτε εἶδος αὐτοῦ ἑωράκατε. καὶ τὸν λόγον αὐτοῦ
οὐκ ἔχετε μένοντα ἐν ὑμῖν· ὅτι ὃν ἀπέστειλεν ἐκεῖνος, τούτῳ ὑμεῖς οὐ
39 πιστεύετε. [k] Ἐρευνᾶτε τὰς γραφὰς, ὅτι ὑμεῖς δοκεῖτε ἐν αὐταῖς ζωὴν
40 αἰώνιον ἔχειν. (καὶ ἐκεῖναί εἰσιν αἱ μαρτυροῦσαι περὶ ἐμοῦ·) καὶ οὐ
41 θέλετε ἐλθεῖν πρός με, ἵνα ζωὴν ἔχητε. Δόξαν παρὰ ἀνθρώπων οὐ
42 λαμβάνω· ἀλλ' ἔγνωκα ὑμᾶς, ὅτι τὴν ἀγάπην τοῦ Θεοῦ οὐκ ἔχετε ἐν

h Matt. 3. 17. & 17. 5. Mark 1. 11. & 9. 7. Luke 3. 22. & 9. 35. supra 1. 33. infra 6. 27. & 8. 18. & 10. 25. & 12. 28. 2 Pet. 1. 17.
i Exod. 33. 20. Deut. 4. 12. 1 Tim. 6. 16. 1 John 4. 12.
k Isa. 8. 20. & 34. 16. Luke 16. 29, & 24. 27. Acts 17. 11. Deut. 18. 15. supra 1. 46.

son famous for light or knowledge was called *a candle*, the *candle of the Law*, the *lamp of light*;" but by a passage of Salomon Jarchi cited by Lampe; and, what is more, by Ecclus. xlviii. 1. Nor is the metaphor unknown in the Classical writers.

— ἠθελ. ἀγαλλ.] The sense is, "Ye were disposed to rejoice greatly in his light, but only *temporarily*, until he reproved their vices, when they said *he had a Devil*." Luke vii. 30. 33.

36. Our Lord now suggests the *reason* why he needs not the testimony of *John*; and that by adducing the infinitely weightier one of the FATHER; appealing to the *works* the Father hath commissioned him to accomplish, and adverting to the testimony of the Prophets of the O. T. By ἔργα are meant especially *miracles*, but not to the exclusion of *other* works suitable to the Messiah. (See xiv. 11, 12.) On the force of the Article (τὴν) here see Middlet. G. A. i. 8. 1.

36, 37. The sense is here somewhat obscure, and consequently controverted. See Rec. Syn. If, however, the declaration and testimony here spoken of may be (as the context requires) limited to bearing witness of Christ; and if the words be supposed closely connected with the preceding, a sense will arise very suitable; as follows: "Nay, the *Father* himself, who hath sent me, hath borne testimony of me; although ye have not heard him audibly, nor seen him in visible form declaring this testimony of me." Such Lampe, Kuin., and Tittm., agree is the sense of the passage. The question, however, is, how the word *although* can be proved to have any place here. The only way to remove this difficulty is to suppose an ellipsis of καίπερ, as in Heb. iv. 1. οὐδὲν διαφέρει δούλου, κύριος πάντων ὤν. It is true we have here not a participle, but a *verb*. Yet this may be regarded as one among the many anomalies to be met with in St. John's writings. The *testimony* of God here meant, is that of the Scriptures of the O. T., spoken of in the next verse, (namely, in its declarations, promises, and prophecies of a Messiah, all fulfilled in Jesus); and that adverted to in the preceding verse, the *power of working miracles* communicated to Christ. Compare vi. 27. Thus it is meant (as Gilpin suggests) that "though the *witness* is invisible, the *testimony* is evident."

The next words (verse 37.) may be rendered, "Yea, ye have not his Word [i. e. the Scriptures] abiding in you," i. e. ye suffer them not to sink into your minds, so as to understand their true import; or perceive their fulfilment in me; as is declared plainly in the next verse.

39. ἐρευνᾶτε τὰς γραφάς.] It has been debated whether ἐρευνᾶτε, ought to be taken as an *Imperative*, or as an *Indicative*. The former method is adopted by almost all the ancient, and a great majority of the modern Commentators; the latter, by the most eminent modern ones (besides whom, see Vitringa de Synag. Jud. p. 671., who illustrates what is meant by ἐρευνᾶτε, and Bp. Bull's Harm. Apost. x. 17.): and with reason; for the Indic. is, as we have seen, far more agreeable to the context, and (as Lampe and Campb. show) is required by the scope of the passage and the course of argument. Nor are the objections which have been advanced against it of any weight: while, on the other hand, the *Imperative* involves a great harshness in reference to the δοκεῖτε just after. That the Jews did use a diligent investigation and study of the Scriptures, is certain from the ancient Rabbinical writings. So Pirke Aboth: "Versa eam [Scripturam] et versa eam." Our Lord *grants* this, and by implication *commends* them for it; but complains that this has not its due effect in bringing them to acknowledge him as their Saviour, and thus to obtain salvation by Him. Thus the very admission that they search the Scriptures involves also a tacit reproof, no less than that (as the Prophet says) "seeing, they see not," being gross-minded, and "slow of heart to believe all that the Prophets foretold of him." The sense may be thus expressed, "Ye indeed search diligently the Scriptures, supposing that in them ye have [revealed] the way of attaining eternal life [but, *atqui*, those are they which bear testimony of me]; and [yet] ye will not come unto me [and become my disciples] that ye may *attain* this life." The general sense is admirably expressed by Bp. Bull, ubi supra, and Lampe.

40. Here is intimated the *cause* of this failure, namely, the want of a disposition to impartially weigh the evidence.

— ἐλθεῖν πρός X. is a phrase occurring also at vi. 35. 37. 44. 45. vii. 37. x. 41. xiv. 6., which signifies to resort to Jesus and accept him as a Teacher and Saviour.

41, 42. Our Lord means to say, that he does not so speak as if he needed their testimony or sanction, but solely to warn them of the awful error in which they were. On this He (at v. 42.) engrafts another sentence, containing the *reason* why they would not receive him as the Messiah; namely, because they had not the love of God (the first and great principle of religion) in their hearts.

ἑαυτοῖς. Ἐγὼ ἐλήλυθα ἐν τῷ ὀνόματι τοῦ Πατρός μου, καὶ οὐ λαμ- 43
βάνετέ με· ἐὰν ἄλλος ἔλθῃ ἐν τῷ ὀνόματι τῷ ἰδίῳ, ἐκεῖνον λήψεσθε.
l Infra 12. 43. Rom. 2. 29. [l] Πῶς δύνασθε ὑμεῖς πιστεῦσαι, δόξαν παρὰ ἀλλήλων λαμβάνοντες, καὶ 44
τὴν δόξαν τὴν παρὰ τοῦ μόνου Θεοῦ οὐ ζητεῖτε; Μὴ δοκεῖτε ὅτι ἐγὼ 45
κατηγορήσω ὑμῶν πρὸς τὸν Πατέρα· ἔστιν ὁ κατηγορῶν ὑμῶν, Μωϋ-
m Gen. 3. 15. & 22. 18. & 49. 10. Deut. 18. 15. σῆς, εἰς ὃν ὑμεῖς ἠλπίκατε. [m] Εἰ γὰρ ἐπιστεύετε Μωϋσῇ, ἐπιστεύετε 46
ἂν ἐμοί· περὶ γὰρ ἐμοῦ ἐκεῖνος ἔγραψεν. Εἰ δὲ τοῖς ἐκείνου γράμ- 47
μασιν οὐ πιστεύετε, πῶς τοῖς ἐμοῖς ῥήμασι πιστεύσετε;

VI. ΜΕΤΑ ταῦτα ἀπῆλθεν ὁ Ἰησοῦς πέραν τῆς θαλάσσης τῆς 1
Γαλιλαίας τῆς Τιβεριάδος· καὶ ἠκολούθει αὐτῷ ὄχλος πολὺς, ὅτι ἑώρων 2
αὐτοῦ τὰ σημεῖα, ἃ ἐποίει ἐπὶ τῶν ἀσθενούντων. Ἀνῆλθε δὲ εἰς τὸ 3
n Exod. 12. 18. Lev. 23. 5. Num. 28. 16. Deut. 16. 1. ὄρος ὁ Ἰησοῦς, καὶ ἐκεῖ ἐκάθητο μετὰ τῶν μαθητῶν αὐτοῦ. [n] ἦν δὲ 4
o Matt. 14. 15. Mark 6. 35. Luke 9. 12. ἐγγὺς τὸ πάσχα ἡ ἑορτὴ τῶν Ἰουδαίων. [o] Ἐπάρας οὖν ὁ Ἰησοῦς τοὺς 5
ὀφθαλμοὺς, καὶ θεασάμενος ὅτι πολὺς ὄχλος ἔρχεται πρὸς αὐτὸν, λέγει
πρὸς τὸν Φίλιππον· Πόθεν ἀγοράσομεν ἄρτους, ἵνα φάγωσιν οὗτοι;
(Τοῦτο δὲ ἔλεγε πειράζων αὐτόν· αὐτὸς γὰρ ᾔδει τί ἔμελλε ποιεῖν.) 6
Ἀπεκρίθη αὐτῷ Φίλιππος· Διακοσίων δηναρίων ἄρτοι οὐκ ἀρκοῦσιν 7
αὐτοῖς, ἵνα ἕκαστος αὐτῶν βραχύ τι λάβῃ. Λέγει αὐτῷ εἷς ἐκ τῶν 8
p 2 Kings 4. 43. μαθητῶν αὐτοῦ, Ἀνδρέας ὁ ἀδελφὸς Σίμωνος Πέτρου· [p] Ἔστι παιδά- 9
ριον ἓν ὧδε, ὃ ἔχει πέντε ἄρτους κριθίνους καὶ δύο ὀψάρια· ἀλλὰ
ταῦτα τί ἐστιν εἰς τοσούτους; Εἶπε δὲ ὁ Ἰησοῦς· Ποιήσατε τοὺς 10
ἀνθρώπους ἀναπεσεῖν. ἦν δὲ χόρτος πολὺς ἐν τῷ τόπῳ. ἀνέπεσον οὖν
q 1 Sam. 9. 13. οἱ ἄνδρες τὸν ἀριθμὸν ὡσεὶ πεντακισχίλιοι. [q] Ἔλαβε δὲ τοὺς ἄρτους 11
ὁ Ἰησοῦς, καὶ εὐχαριστήσας διέδωκε τοῖς μαθηταῖς, οἱ δὲ μαθηταὶ τοῖς
ἀνακειμένοις· ὁμοίως καὶ ἐκ τῶν ὀψαρίων ὅσον ἤθελον. Ὡς δὲ ἐνε- 12
πλήσθησαν, λέγει τοῖς μαθηταῖς αὐτοῦ· Συναγάγετε τὰ περισσεύσαντα
κλάσματα, ἵνα μή τι ἀπόληται. Συνήγαγον οὖν, καὶ ἐγέμισαν δώδεκα 13
κοφίνους κλασμάτων ἐκ τῶν πέντε ἄρτων τῶν κριθίνων, ἃ ἐπερίσσευσε

43. This verse is, I conceive, a further unfolding of the sentiment at verse 41. and the sense is: "I need not human glory, because I came unto you with Divine authority. Yet, so perverse are ye, that if another should come with only his *own* (i. e. human) authority, him ye will admit."

44. Here is suggested the *reason* for this preference, namely, the influence of ambition, vainglory, and worldly-mindedness. The *πῶς δύνασθε*, (which is to be understood comparatè, q. d. How can it be expected but that), as Lampe remarks, implies that the origin of this inability was perversity of will, and such hardness of heart that they *would* not come to Christ.

45. *μὴ δοκεῖτε*, &c.] i. e. Think not that I will accuse you to the Father. This I *need* not do, since Moses and his writings will be sufficient accusers; i. e. ye will be condemned for not believing his writings which testify of me, both by express predictions, and by typical representations. See Vitringa de Synag. J. p. 999.

46. Their pretences for not believing in Christ were these two, their love to God and their reverence for the law of Moses: Christ shows at v. 42. they could have no true *love to God;* and in this verse, that they had no real *faith in Moses;* for if they had, they would have believed on Him. (Drs. Whitby and Hammond.)

— *περὶ ἐμοῦ ἔγραψεν*] i. e. not only showed by what marks a Divine legate might be distinguished from a false prophet, (see Deut. xviii. 15. seqq.) but predicted the coming of the author of a better religion.

47. *πῶς — πιστ.*] how can ye be expected to give credence? See Winer's Gr. § 38. 8. and *Comp.* John xiv. 17.

VI. On v. 1—14. see Matt. xiv. 13—21, and Notes. At v. 6. *πειράζων* is for *δοκιμάζων*.

9. *παιδάριον*] a youth, נַעַר between boyhood and manhood. This was probably a baker's servant, who had been sent to dispose of bread in a place where, from the multitude collected, it was likely to obtain a ready sale.

10. *ἦν δὲ χόρτος — τόπῳ.*] And thus it would be very suitable for the purpose. On these incidental and parenthetical circumstances, which, as Dr. Paley observes, mark an eye-witness; with which I would compare Joseph. Ant. iv. 8. 1. *φοινικόφυτον δέ ἐστι τὸ χωρίον.* Xenoph. Anab. i. 4, 9. *ἐξελαύνει ἐπὶ τὸν Χάλον ποταμὸν, πλήρη ἰχθύων καὶ πραέων.* Æschyl. Pers. 510. Thucyd. iv. 13.

14 τοῖς βεβρωκόσιν. ʳ Οἱ οὖν ἄνθρωποι ἰδόντες ὃ ἐποίησε σημεῖον ὁ r Deut. 18. 15. Luke 7. 16.
Ἰησοῦς, ἔλεγον· Ὅτι οὗτός ἐστιν ἀληθῶς ὁ προφήτης ὁ ἐρχόμενος εἰς & 24. 19. supra 1. 21. & 4. 19.
15 τὸν κόσμον. Ἰησοῦς οὖν γνοὺς ὅτι μέλλουσιν ἔρχεσθαι καὶ ἁρπάζειν infra 7. 40.
αὐτὸν, ἵνα ποιήσωσιν αὐτὸν βασιλέα, ἀνεχώρησε πάλιν εἰς τὸ ὄρος αὐτὸς
16 μόνος. ˢ Ὡς δὲ ὀψία ἐγένετο, κατέβησαν οἱ μαθηταὶ αὐτοῦ ἐπὶ τὴν s Matt. 14. 23. Mark 6. 47.
17 θάλασσαν· καὶ ἐμβάντες εἰς τὸ πλοῖον, ἤρχοντο πέραν τῆς θαλάσσης
εἰς Καπερναούμ. Καὶ σκοτία ἤδη ἐγεγόνει, καὶ οὐκ ἐληλύθει πρὸς
18 αὐτοὺς ὁ Ἰησοῦς· ἥ τε θάλασσα, ἀνέμου μεγάλου πνέοντος, διηγείρετο.
19 Ἐληλακότες οὖν ὡς σταδίους εἰκοσιπέντε ἢ τριάκοντα, θεωροῦσι τὸν
Ἰησοῦν περιπατοῦντα ἐπὶ τῆς θαλάσσης, καὶ ἐγγὺς τοῦ πλοίου γινόμε-
20 νον· καὶ ἐφοβήθησαν. Ὁ δὲ λέγει αὐτοῖς· Ἐγώ εἰμι· μὴ φοβεῖσθε.
21 Ἤθελον οὖν λαβεῖν αὐτὸν εἰς τὸ πλοῖον, καὶ εὐθέως τὸ πλοῖον ἐγένετο
ἐπὶ τῆς γῆς εἰς ἣν ὑπῆγον.
22 Τῇ ἐπαύριον ὁ ὄχλος ὁ ἑστηκὼς πέραν τῆς θαλάσσης, ἰδὼν ὅτι
πλοιάριον ἄλλο οὐκ ἦν ἐκεῖ εἰ μὴ ἓν ἐκεῖνο εἰς ὃ ἐνέβησαν οἱ μαθηταὶ
αὐτοῦ, καὶ ὅτι οὐ συνεισῆλθε τοῖς μαθηταῖς αὐτοῦ ὁ Ἰησοῦς εἰς τὸ
23 πλοιάριον, ἀλλὰ μόνοι οἱ μαθηταὶ αὐτοῦ ἀπῆλθον· (ἄλλα δὲ ἦλθε
πλοιάρια ἐκ Τιβεριάδος ἐγγὺς τοῦ τόπου ὅπου ἔφαγον τὸν ἄρτον, εὐ-
24 χαριστήσαντος τοῦ Κυρίου·) ὅτε οὖν εἶδεν ὁ ὄχλος ὅτι Ἰησοῦς οὐκ
ἔστιν ἐκεῖ, οὐδὲ οἱ μαθηταὶ αὐτοῦ, ἐνέβησαν [καὶ] αὐτοὶ εἰς τὰ πλοῖα,
25 καὶ ἦλθον εἰς Καπερναοὺμ ζητοῦντες τὸν Ἰησοῦν. Καὶ εὑρόντες αὐτὸν t Supra 1. 38. & 4. 14. & 5. 37.
26 πέραν τῆς θαλάσσης, εἶπον αὐτῷ· Ῥαββὶ, πότε ὧδε γέγονας; Ἀπε- infr. ver. 40, 54. & 18. 8.
κρίθη αὐτοῖς ὁ Ἰησοῦς καὶ εἶπεν· Ἀμὴν ἀμὴν λέγω ὑμῖν· ζητεῖτέ Matt. 3. 17. & 17. 5.
με οὐχ ὅτι εἴδετε σημεῖα, ἀλλ᾽ ὅτι ἐφάγετε ἐκ τῶν ἄρτων καὶ ἐχορ- Mark 1. 11. & 9. 7. Luke 3. 22.
27 τάσθητε. ᵗ Ἐργάζεσθε μὴ τὴν βρῶσιν τὴν ἀπολλυμένην, ἀλλὰ τὴν & 9. 35. 2 Pet. 1. 17.

14. On the difference between this miracle and those of Moses see Grot., Lampe, and Rosenm., in Recens. Synop.

16—19.] See Notes on Matt. xiv. 22, sq. and Mark vi. 46, seqq.

18. *διηγείρετο.*] Lampe adduces Pollux i. 9. *κῦμα ἐγειρόμενον, ὑποκινούμενον.*

21. *ἤθελον λαβεῖν αὐτόν.*] To remove a trifling discrepancy with the other Evangelists, the best modern Commentators take the sense to be, "they willingly received," which I have in Recens. Syn. confirmed from several passages of the Classical writers.

22. *ὁ ἑστηκώς*] i. e. who had remained there for the purpose, it seems, of deliberating, whether they should proclaim Jesus as Messiah.

26. Our Lord, observing that the multitude which flocked to him were influenced not by a desire for spiritual improvement, but for worldly advantage, takes occasion from the natural and earthly bread with which he had supplied them, to advert to spiritual and celestial nutriment; showing how much more anxious they ought to be for the acquisition of spiritual than of corporeal nourishment. This portion, from v. 26. to 65. has been the subject of much discussion among Commentators, some of whom (as Kuin.) suppose the obscurity which pervades it to have been occasioned by the Evangelist's *omitting* part of what was then said. This view, however, lies open to serious objection, being hypothetical and unauthorized, and proceeding upon an unsound principle. Much of the difficulty, I apprehend, is to be attributed to the highly figurative cast of the expressions, and the brevity of the phraseology; but most of all by the persons addressed being different in different parts of the discourse. Our Lord sometimes addresses the *higher classes*, who were, more or less, ill-affected to him; at other times, the *lower classes*, who were upon the whole *well-disposed*, but exceedingly dull of comprehension, and quite ignorant of His true character as *Son of God*. Thus we find at vii. 12. these *two classes* at Jerusalem, of which one said of Jesus, "he is a good man;" others, "nay, but he deceiveth the people." Now this will satisfactorily account for the frequent repetitions of the same sentiment, which might otherwise be thought unnecessary. In such cases, either our Lord replies to the objections, or removes the scruples of, the two classes *in separate addresses*: or, in compassion to the ignorance and dulness of the multitude, condescends to repeat the same thing more than once, in order to impress it more strongly on their minds.

27. *ἐργάζεσθε μὴ, &c.*] Ἐργάζεσθαι here, as often in the Classical writers, denotes, together with labour, its *effect* in gain or acquirement. The full sense, then, is: "labour to acquire." Ἀπολλ. denotes what terminates merely in animal life. The metaphor in *βρῶσιν μένουσαν* is such as is common in all languages. The ἀλλὰ is

βρῶσιν τὴν μένουσαν εἰς ζωὴν αἰώνιον, ἣν ὁ Υἱὸς τοῦ ἀνθρώπου ὑμῖν
δώσει· τοῦτον γὰρ ὁ Πατὴρ ἐσφράγισεν ὁ Θεός. Εἶπον οὖν πρὸς 28
u 1 John 3. 23. αὐτόν· Τί ποιοῦμεν, ἵνα ἐργαζώμεθα τὰ ἔργα τοῦ Θεοῦ; [u] Ἀπεκρίθη 29
ὁ Ἰησοῦς καὶ εἶπεν αὐτοῖς· Τοῦτό ἐστι τὸ ἔργον τοῦ Θεοῦ, ἵνα πι-
x Matt. 12. 38. & 16. 1. στεύσητε εἰς ὃν ἀπέστειλεν ἐκεῖνος. [x] Εἶπον οὖν αὐτῷ· Τί οὖν ποιεῖς 30
Mark 8. 11. Luke 11. 29. 1 Cor. 1. 22. σὺ σημεῖον, ἵνα ἴδωμεν καὶ πιστεύσωμέν σοι; τί ἐργάζῃ; [y] Οἱ πατέ- 31
y Exod. 16. 4, 14. ρες ἡμῶν τὸ μάννα ἔφαγον ἐν τῇ ἐρήμῳ, καθώς ἐστι γεγραμμένον·
Num. 11. 7. Psal. 78. 24. Wisd. 16. 20. Ἄρτον ἐκ τοῦ οὐρανοῦ ἔδωκεν αὐτοῖς φαγεῖν. Εἶπεν οὖν 32
1 Cor. 10. 3. αὐτοῖς ὁ Ἰησοῦς· Ἀμὴν ἀμὴν λέγω ὑμῖν· Οὐ Μωϋσῆς δέδωκεν ὑμῖν
τὸν ἄρτον ἐκ τοῦ οὐρανοῦ· ἀλλ' ὁ Πατήρ μου δίδωσιν ὑμῖν τὸν ἄρτον
ἐκ τοῦ οὐρανοῦ τὸν ἀληθινόν. ὁ γὰρ ἄρτος τοῦ Θεοῦ ἐστιν ὁ κατα- 33
βαίνων ἐκ τοῦ οὐρανοῦ, καὶ ζωὴν διδοὺς τῷ κόσμῳ. Εἶπον οὖν πρὸς 34
z Eccl. 24. 29. Isa. 55. 1. αὐτόν· Κύριε, πάντοτε δὸς ἡμῖν τὸν ἄρτον τοῦτον. [z] εἶπε δὲ αὐτοῖς 35
supra 4. 14. infra 7. 37. ὁ Ἰησοῦς· Ἐγώ εἰμι ὁ ἄρτος τῆς ζωῆς· ὁ ἐρχόμενος πρός με οὐ μὴ
πεινάσῃ· καὶ ὁ πιστεύων εἰς ἐμὲ οὐ μὴ διψήσῃ πώποτε. Ἀλλ' εἶπον 36

by most recent Commentators rendered *non tam—quàm*. But that principle in *οὐκ—ἀλλὰ* and *μὴ—ἀλλὰ* has been recently disputed by De Wette, Schulthess, and Winer, Gr. p. 159; and indeed with some reason, especially as concerns *μὴ—ἀλλά*.

—*ἐσφράγισεν*] "confirmed, authorized, commissioned, as it were with a seal, with which contracts and orders were sealed."

28. Here they ask *how* they may obtain these benefits, or gain the approbation of God. By *τὰ ἔργα τοῦ Θεοῦ* are meant the actions which are enjoined by God, as Ps. li. 19. the sacrifices of God.

29. On the full import of the expression *πιστεύειν εἰς Ἰησοῦν* see the elaborate discussion of Tittm., who well explains it Jesum *agnoscere* ac suscipere tanquam salutis humanæ auctorem verissimum et perfectissimum, Servatorem mundi unicum, adeoque ab eo salutem omnem hujus et futuræ vitæ expetere et expectare. The learned Commentator justly remarks, "how important is this passage to evince the necessity of this faith to Christians; also, that it is a thing not *human* but *divine*, as being what God requires from every one, and by which alone he can be acceptable to God." The persons here addressing Jesus were probably of *the higher classes*. Some of them probably had not themselves witnessed the late miracle our Lord had worked, and may have wished to see one worked. However, by adverting to Moses' calling down manna *from heaven*, they seem to have desired, what was by the Jews of that time regarded as the only unequivocal proof of Divine mission, a sign from heaven (such as the calling down manna), something not private, simple, and unostentatious, but public, conspicuous, and striking the senses.

31. *τὸ μάννα*.] Render *the* manna. On the derivation of the word the Commentators are not agreed; whether from the Heb. מן הוא, *what is this?* or from מנה, to *measure*, or *prepare*. The recent Commentators enlarge much in describing the common manna which, in the East, still bedews the ground by night, and is collected in the morning, and made into a kind of cake. The identity, however, of this with the manna of the Israelites, is rather *taken for granted* than proved. There are indeed so many important diversities between the two (pointed out by Deyling in his Obss. S. iii. 7.) as completely to establish the miraculous nature of the transaction, with those who admit the credibility of Moses. It was called "bread from heaven," *bread*—because made up into cakes like the natural manna; and *from heaven*, as being the gift of God.

32. *οὐ Μωϋσῆς—οὐρανοῦ*, &c.] *Τὸν ἄρτον* scil. *ἀληθινόν*. "Our Lord's declaration imports that it is in a subordinate sense only that what dropped from the clouds, and was sent for the nourishment of the body, still mortal, could be called the bread of heaven, being but a type of that which hath descended from the heaven of heavens, for nourishing the immortal soul unto eternal life, and which is therefore, in the most sublime sense, the *bread of heaven*." (Campb.) "Our Lord means that there is as much difference between the food supplied by Moses, and that which his Father would bestow, as between the body and the soul, between temporal and eternal life, earth and heaven." (Tittm.)

33. *ὁ γὰρ ἄρτος*, &c.] Here our Lord, in explanation, shows *what sort* of bread he means, even HIMSELF, as the author of that *Gospel* which nourishes the soul, and leads unto salvation; adverted to in the words *ζωὴν διδοὺς τῷ κόσμῳ*, which allude to the great doctrine of the *Atonement*, by which salvation was given to a world dead in trespasses and sins.

34. *εἶπον*.] The persons who now speak seem to be not the same who had demanded a sign, but the *common* people; who ignorantly supposed that he was speaking of corporeal bread, such as Moses had procured from heaven for their forefathers. In like manner the Samaritan woman, at iv. 15. says, *κύριε, δός μοι τοῦτο τὸ ὕδωρ*.

35. *ἐγώ εἰμι*, &c.] Our Lord now proceeds to the *second* point to be explained in this discourse. q. d. "It is I who am that bread of life, as being the procurer and bestower of salvation; for whosoever becomes my disciple and embraces my doctrine, shall have no desire for any thing further, having all that is necessary to happiness and salvation." See iv. 14. and Note, and here Dr. A. Clarke. *Ὁ ἐρχόμενος πρός με* is equivalent to *ὁ πιστεύων εἰς ἐμὲ* which follows.

36. *ἀλλ' εἶπον—πιστεύετε*.] There is here some

37 ὑμῖν· ὅτι καὶ ἑωράκατέ με, καὶ οὐ πιστεύετε. *Πᾶν ὃ δίδωσί μοι ὁ Πατὴρ,*
38 πρὸς ἐμὲ ἥξει· καὶ τὸν ἐρχόμενον πρός με οὐ μὴ ἐκβάλω ἔξω· [a] ὅτι κατα-
βέβηκα ἐκ τοῦ οὐρανοῦ, οὐχ ἵνα ποιῶ τὸ θέλημα τὸ ἐμὸν, ἀλλὰ τὸ θέλημα a Matt. 26. 39. Mark 14. 36. Luke 22. 42. supra 4. 34. & 5. 30.
39 τοῦ πέμψαντός με. [b] Τοῦτο δέ ἐστι τὸ θέλημα τοῦ πέμψαντός με Πατρὸς,
ἵνα πᾶν ὃ δέδωκέ μοι μὴ ἀπολέσω ἐξ αὐτοῦ, ἀλλὰ ἀναστήσω αὐτὸ ἐν b Infra 10. 28. & 17. 12. & 18. 9.
40 τῇ ἐσχάτῃ ἡμέρᾳ. [c] Τοῦτο ‡ δέ ἐστι τὸ θέλημα τοῦ πέμψαντός με, c 3. 15, 16.
ἵνα πᾶς ὁ θεωρῶν τὸν Υἱὸν καὶ πιστεύων εἰς αὐτὸν, ἔχῃ ζωὴν αἰώνιον,

obscurity, occasioned by brevity. The best Commentators assign this sense: "But, as I have told you before, ye see and know me, yet ye believe not on me." The full meaning, may, however, be better expressed as follows: "But, as I have already told you [and now tell you again], ye have seen me [and my works (including *miracles*) and known my doctrines] and yet ye believe not on me."

37. πᾶν ὃ δίδωσι — ἔξω.] The connection seems to be: [Yet I shall not labour in vain, there will not be wanting those who shall receive my doctrine.] The neuter is here usually considered as put for the masculine, πᾶν ὃ for πᾶς ὃν. Yet perhaps that is, strictly speaking, not the case. It should seem that our Lord first speaks of the number of those given to him *collectively*, and then *individually*. And when taken in conjunction with πᾶν, there is probably (as some eminent Commentators suppose) an obscure allusion to the *calling of the Gentiles*; for they, according to the ancient promise, Ps. ii., were to be *given* to Christ. This is confirmed by what is added at the parallel passage, ver. 45, 46, where it is said that the prophecy is καὶ ἔσονται πάντες διδακτοὶ τοῦ Θεοῦ, synonymous with the πᾶν here is the πάσης σαρκὸς at xviii. 2.; πᾶν ὃ may be meant of the Gentiles *as a body*. And so Tittm. explains it to mean omnes homines, sine discrimine gentium.

But to consider the most important term of this sentence, δίδωσι, as to the sense in which the Father is said to *give* men to Christ, Expositors differ in opinion. The Calvinistic ones, as may be imagined, understand it of being chosen of the Father to eternal salvation by an absolute decree. But to this view see the unanswerable objections of Grot., Hammond, and Whitby, as also of Chrys., who ascribes the dogma to the *Manicheans*. The term therefore (here and at ver. 39 and 65) must signify something compatible with the free agency of man. And there is no difficulty in ascertaining its sense here, because our Lord has himself determined its meaning by the expression which is *substituted for it* in the parallel passage at ver. 44, which is *explanatory* of the present. To *give* men to Christ is evidently equivalent to *draw* them to Christ; and how irreconcileable that is with the *compulsion* implied in the Calvinistic interpretation of *giving*, is obvious. For ἑλκύειν (as has been proved by Tittm.) like the Heb. משך, denotes a power not compulsory, but *strongly suasory*, meaning to *draw* (not *drag*) any one; i. e. to sway the understanding, or incline the will by all moral means and fit motives, as propounded in the Revelation of his will in the Holy Scriptures. See John xii. 32. and Phil. ii. 13. & 14. and the note; as also a Sermon by Dr. Balguy on that text, and one by Dr. Clarke on the present. However, the above is by no means the *whole* of what is meant in these words (though the German Commentators almost universally stop there) but both terms undoubtedly point to a most important doctrine — that of the *preventing grace of God by his Holy Spirit*, indispensably necessary to any one's being given to Christ by God; also the necessity for the *co-operating grace* of that Spirit, after we have been brought to Christ by his preventing grace — proving the truth of what is said in our Article, that "we have no power to do works pleasant and acceptable to God, without the grace of God preventing us, that we may have a good-will, and working with us when we have that good-will." So Phil. ii. 12, 13. μετὰ φόβου καὶ τρόμου τὴν ἑαυτῶν σωτηρίαν κατεργάζεσθε· ὁ Θεὸς γάρ ἐστιν ὁ ἐνεργῶν ἐν ὑμῖν καὶ τὸ θέλειν καὶ τὸ ἐνεργεῖν. (where see Note). Thus δίδωσι adverts to the *thing itself*; and ἑλκ. suggests the *means* by which it is accomplished. At the same time, we know from other parts of Scripture, that these means are not *irresistible*: man *may* receive this grace of God in vain. The truth is that (in the words of Mr. Holden) though God *wills* all men to be saved, he does not *force* them; and though he wills all men to be saved, those only will be saved who have complied with the conditions. Every thing necessary is freely supplied; but men are free agents, and may reject the gracious offer. There is no limitation in the *will* and *mercy* of God, he wills that all whom he has *given* to Christ, or *drawn* to him by the influence of his Spirit, should be saved; yet they may receive this grace of God in vain, and when they are lost, it is not for want of *will* in God, but for want of their own *co-operation* with divine grace: ch xviii. 9.

38. ὅτι καταβέβηκα, &c.] The connection is: "[And] *for* I came down, &c., i. e. for the very purpose of my coming down on earth was, &c. How *should* I repel any who thus come unto me, since I came for the very purpose of saving them."

39. ἐξ αὐτοῦ] scil. παντός. Sub. τι, as at xvi. 17. Apoc. xi. 9. and elsewhere. Μὴ ἀπολέσω, "that I should, as far as depends on me, *suffer* no one to perish." The verb is taken *permissively*. By ἀναστήσω (at which repeat ἵνα, and take ἀναστ. in the Subjunctive) is meant (as almost always in Scripture as well as the Rabbinical writers) the resurrection of the blessed to eternal happiness.

40. This ver. is a plainer expression of the preceding sentiment, importing that every one who discerns him as Messiah, and recognises him as such, shall be both raised to life again, and blessed with everlasting happiness. Instead of δὲ, many MSS., Versions, and Fathers have γὰρ, which is edited by Griesb., Titt., Vater, and Scholz. I suspect, however, that it arose *ex emendatione*, or rather a marginal explanation. The testimony of the Versions, full as it is, only strengthens this suspicion.

καὶ ἀναστήσω αὐτὸν ἐγὼ τῇ ἐσχάτῃ ἡμέρᾳ. Ἐγόγγυζον οὖν οἱ Ἰου- 41
δαῖοι περὶ αὐτοῦ, ὅτι εἶπεν· Ἐγώ εἰμι ὁ ἄρτος ὁ καταβὰς ἐκ τοῦ
d Matt. 13. 55. Mark 6. 3. Luke 4. 22. οὐρανοῦ. [d] καὶ ἔλεγον· Οὐχ οὗτός ἐστιν Ἰησοῦς ὁ υἱὸς Ἰωσήφ, οὗ 42
ἡμεῖς οἴδαμεν τὸν πατέρα καὶ τὴν μητέρα; πῶς οὖν λέγει οὗτος·
Ὅτι ἐκ τοῦ οὐρανοῦ καταβέβηκα; Ἀπεκρίθη [οὖν] ὁ Ἰησοῦς καὶ 43
εἶπεν αὐτοῖς· Μὴ γογγύζετε μετ᾽ ἀλλήλων. Οὐδεὶς δύναται ἐλθεῖν 44
πρός με, ἐὰν μὴ ὁ Πατὴρ ὁ πέμψας με ἑλκύσῃ αὐτόν, καὶ ἐγὼ ἀνα-
e Isa. 54. 13. Jer. 31. 34. Heb. 8. 10. & 10. 16. στήσω αὐτὸν τῇ ἐσχάτῃ ἡμέρᾳ. [e] Ἔστι γεγραμμένον ἐν τοῖς προ- 45
φήταις· Καὶ ἔσονται πάντες διδακτοὶ [τοῦ] Θεοῦ. Πᾶς
[οὖν] ὁ * ἀκούων παρὰ τοῦ Πατρὸς καὶ μαθὼν ἔρχεται πρός με.
f 1. 18. Matt. 11. 27. Luke 10. 22. [f] οὐχ ὅτι τὸν Πατέρα τὶς ἑώρακεν· εἰ μὴ ὁ ὢν παρὰ τοῦ Θεοῦ, οὗτος 46
g Supra 3. 16, 18, 36. ἑώρακε τὸν Πατέρα. [g] Ἀμὴν ἀμὴν λέγω ὑμῖν· ὁ πιστεύων εἰς ἐμὲ 47
h Exod. 16. 15. Num. 11. 7. ἔχει ζωὴν αἰώνιον. Ἐγώ εἰμι ὁ ἄρτος τῆς ζωῆς. [h] Οἱ πατέρες ὑμῶν 48
Ps. 78. 24. 1 Cor. 10. 3. ἔφαγον τὸ μάννα ἐν τῇ ἐρήμῳ, καὶ ἀπέθανον· οὗτός ἐστιν ὁ ἄρτος ὁ 49
Heb. 3. 16, 19. ἐκ τοῦ οὐρανοῦ καταβαίνων, ἵνα τὶς ἐξ αὐτοῦ φάγῃ καὶ μὴ ἀποθάνῃ. 50
i 3. 13. [i] Ἐγώ εἰμι ὁ ἄρτος ὁ ζῶν ὁ ἐκ τοῦ οὐρανοῦ καταβάς· ἐάν τις φάγῃ 51
ἐκ τούτου τοῦ ἄρτου, ζήσεται εἰς τὸν αἰῶνα. Καὶ ὁ ἄρτος δὲ, ὃν ἐγὼ
δώσω, ἡ σάρξ μου ἐστὶν, ἣν ἐγὼ δώσω ὑπὲρ τῆς τοῦ κόσμου ζωῆς.

41. *ἐγόγγυζον.*] This word (an onomatop. similar to *γρύζειν*) imports not only secret discontent, but indignant complaint, though faintly expressed.

44. *ἑλκύσῃ αὐτόν.*] See Note supra ver. 37. Before τῇ ἐσχ. many MSS. insert ἐν, which is received by Matth., Griesb., Tittm., Vat., and Scholz. But I suspect that it arose from the εν preceding, or came from the margin.

45. *καὶ ἔσονται, &c.*] Meaning that these words (taken from Is. liv. 13.) shall be made good. By τοῖς προφήταις is meant (by an idiom common in Jewish citation) in that part of the Sacred Volume called *the Prophets*. Διδακτοὶ is for δεδιδαγμένοι, and there is an ellip. of ὑπό. See Win. Gr. Gr. § 23. 3. 6. Τοῦ before Θεοῦ is omitted in many ancient MSS. and Fathers, and is cancelled by Matth., Griesb., Vat., Tittm., and Scholz, who also edit ἀκούων for ἀκούσας on good grounds.

46. *οὐχ ὅτι — τὸν Πατέρα.*] Kuin. well expresses the sense thus: "What I have said of the teaching of the Father is not to be understood of complete and immediate instruction; *this* hath fallen to the lot of Him only who came down from Heaven, who was sent from the Father, or who hath been with him, and who hath obtained a full knowledge of God and of his will, as being most intimately conjoined with the Father."

47, 48. Here our Lord (to make himself thoroughly understood) *repeats* what he had before said, that he *is*, (i. e. imparts) the food of life, and that whosoever hath faith in him shall receive everlasting life.

49, 50. The scope of these vv. is to illustrate what has been said, by showing, in reply to what was said supra v. 31. on comparison, the superiority of the spiritual bread which Christ bestows, to the corporeal bread procured by Moses. The full sense is: "Your forefathers ate the manna in the wilderness, and [yet] died: that is the bread [of *life*] which descended from heaven, in order that if any eat thereof, he may not die, but live." The phrase φαγεῖν ἐξ ἄρτου denotes to avail themselves of that doctrine, by coming to Jesus, in faith.

51. Here our Lord declares, in literal expressions, what he had in the preceding verse couched in figurative ones. By ζῶν is meant, ζωοποιῶν, denoting (as Tittm. remarks) that he is the author of life, having obtained the power of bestowing it by his death. This is illustrated by the words following, which may be rendered: "And this bread, moreover, which I shall give, is my flesh (i. e. body), which I shall give for the salvation of the world;" where there is plainly a reference to the sacrifice of the death of Christ, and the atonement through his blood. Christ had before called himself the bread, as being the *author* and *bestower* of that spiritual nourishment which preserves the soul unto eternal life, even as corporeal food does the body. Comp. xi. 25. xv. 1. So here he calls himself the *life-giving* bread, as giving his flesh for the life of the world, i. e. to obtain for it eternal life.

It is a disputed point whether in what is said at v. 50. about eating, &c., there is a reference to the *Eucharist*, or not. The *affirmative* was maintained by most ancients and is by most moderns, especially the Romanist Interpreters: while the *negative* has been adopted by many of the most eminent Expositors, of the ancient ones by Tertull., Clem. Alex., Origen, Cyril, Chrys., and Augustine; and, of the moderns, by Grot., Whitby, Wolf, Lampe, Tittm., and Kuin., who show that the *context* will not permit us to take the words of the Eucharist. See Recens. Synop. and Tittm. But though they successfully prove that by eating the flesh and drinking the blood of Christ, must here be meant securing to ourselves the benefits of the sacrifices of Christ by a true and lively faith; yet that will not prove that there is no reference by *allusion* to the Eucharist. Hence I would (with Dr. Hey and Mr. Holden) steer a middle course, and take the passage *primarily* of the propitiatory sacrifice of Christ, and the benefits thence derived by faith; and *secondarily*, as a

52 [k] Ἐμάχοντο οὖν πρὸς ἀλλήλους οἱ Ἰουδαῖοι, λέγοντες· Πῶς δύναται k 3. 9.
53 οὗτος ἡμῖν δοῦναι τὴν σάρκα φαγεῖν; [l] Εἶπεν οὖν αὐτοῖς ὁ Ἰησοῦς· l Matt. 26. 26. 1 Cor. 11.
Ἀμὴν ἀμὴν λέγω ὑμῖν, ἐὰν μὴ φάγητε τὴν σάρκα τοῦ Υἱοῦ τοῦ ἀν- 23, &c.
54 θρώπου, καὶ πίητε αὐτοῦ τὸ αἷμα, οὐκ ἔχετε ζωὴν ἐν ἑαυτοῖς· [m] Ὁ m 4. 14.
τρώγων μου τὴν σάρκα καὶ πίνων μου τὸ αἷμα ἔχει ζωὴν αἰώνιον·
55 καὶ ἐγὼ ἀναστήσω αὐτὸν τῇ ἐσχάτῃ ἡμέρᾳ. ἡ γὰρ σάρξ μου ἀληθῶς
56 ἐστι βρῶσις, καὶ τὸ αἷμά μου ἀληθῶς ἐστι πόσις. Ὁ τρώγων μου
τὴν σάρκα καὶ πίνων μου τὸ αἷμα ἐν ἐμοὶ μένει, κἀγὼ ἐν αὐτῷ.
57 Καθὼς ἀπέστειλέ με ὁ ζῶν Πατὴρ, κἀγὼ ζῶ διὰ τὸν Πατέρα· καὶ ὁ
58 τρώγων με, κἀκεῖνος ζήσεται δι' ἐμέ. [n] Οὗτός ἐστιν ὁ ἄρτος ὁ ἐκ n 3. 13.
τοῦ οὐρανοῦ καταβάς· οὐ καθὼς ἔφαγον οἱ πατέρες ὑμῶν τὸ μάννα,
καὶ ἀπέθανον. Ὁ τρώγων τοῦτον τὸν ἄρτον ζήσεται εἰς τὸν αἰῶνα.
59 Ταῦτα εἶπεν ἐν συναγωγῇ διδάσκων ἐν Καπερναούμ.
60 Πολλοὶ οὖν ἀκούσαντες ἐκ τῶν μαθητῶν αὐτοῦ εἶπον· Σκληρός ἐστιν
61 οὗτος ὁ λόγος· τίς δύναται αὐτοῦ ἀκούειν; Εἰδὼς δὲ ὁ Ἰησοῦς ἐν
ἑαυτῷ, ὅτι γογγύζουσι περὶ τούτου οἱ μαθηταὶ αὐτοῦ, εἶπεν αὐτοῖς·
62 Τοῦτο ὑμᾶς σκανδαλίζει; [o] Ἐὰν οὖν θεωρῆτε τὸν Υἱὸν τοῦ ἀνθρώ- o 3. 13. Mark 16. 19.
63 που ἀναβαίνοντα ὅπου ἦν τὸ πρότερον —. [p] Τὸ πνεῦμά ἐστι τὸ ζωο- Luke 24. 51. Acts 1. 9.
ποιοῦν, ἡ σὰρξ οὐκ ὠφελεῖ οὐδέν· τὰ ῥήματα, ἃ ἐγὼ ‡ λαλῶ ὑμῖν, Eph. 4. 8. p 2 Cor. 3. 6.

prophetic intimation of the advantages to be derived from a worthy participation of the Sacrament of the Lord's Supper; since the two have so close a relation one to the other, that the mention of the one must suggest the other. Thus in speaking of the offspring of his body, our Lord may be supposed to have had reference, by anticipation, to that Sacrament, soon to be instituted, in which, to the end of time, that sacrifice would be typified and its benefits applied.

52. ἐμάχοντο] "altercabant," namely, the two classes before mentioned, the higher class and the one ill affected to Christ, and the multitude, who were well disposed to him; some of whom are here introduced speaking as follows.

53. ἐὰν μὴ φάγητε, &c.] Our Lord, seeing that those whom he addressed, by taking his words in a literal sense, either mistook or misrepresented his meaning, here repeats, with stronger assevoration, what he had before said. At the same time, he expresses himself so particularly, as to show that by eating the flesh and drinking the blood of Christ, he means eating and drinking in a *figurative* and *spiritual* manner; where the expressions signify applying to ourselves the sacrifice of his death, by coming unto Him in faith, and thus participating by faith in the benefits procured by that sacrifice.

56. ἐν ἐμοὶ — αὐτῷ.] These words describe the mystical union by which the faithful are made partakers of the Divine nature. Christ *remains in* any one by loving, aiding, defending, and blessing him, both here and hereafter. The disciple remains *in Christ* by receiving him, and ever accounting him as the author of his salvation, &c. (Tittm.)

57. καθὼς ἀπέστειλε.] The best Commentators here suppose an enallage, and take the sense to be: "As the Father liveth, who sent me." No doubt, the force of the antithesis is in ζῶν, not ἀπέστειλε. By *liveth*, is meant, *hath life in himself.* The full sense of the passage may be thus expressed, with Dr. Burton. "I have life in myself, and have power to give life, because the Father (who dwelleth in me, and I in Him) hath life in himself, and hath power to give life."

58. To prevent all *further* ignorant misapprehension of his meaning, our Lord concludes with inculcating the same truth that he had before done at v. 35. and 48—51., and subjoins the same solemn assurance as at vv. 47. and 51.

60. μαθητῶν.] By these are (as appears from the next verse) meant, not the stated disciples, but the general followers of Christ.

— σκληρός.] Some explain this, "*hard to be understood;*" others, "*ungrateful, offensive.*" Either interpretation may be admitted, and indeed both will be true, as understood of the *two* classes of persons respectively adverted to in the above.

61. In this and the following verses (spoken, not in the Synagogue, but elsewhere, and, no doubt, in private) our Lord condescends to remove the two great stumblingblocks, which even the well disposed, notwithstanding his explanations and assurances, still found; namely, 1. that he had said he had come down from heaven, ver. 42.; and 2. that he was the bread of life, and should give his flesh for the life of the world. In removing the *first* of these, our Lord employs a most energetic form of expression, involving a kind of ellipsis, or rather aposiopesis, suitable to deep emotion. At the end of the verse supply τί ἐρεῖτε. Yet as this would seem harsh in a Version, most Translators supply *Quid (what)* at the beginning of the verse, and place a mark of interrogation at the end. I have, however, pointed in the text according to the true nature of its construction. In τί ἐρεῖτε we have an energetic form of appeal, of very extensive meaning; the force of which is well expressed by Mr. Holden.

63. In this verse is removed the *second* stumblingblock above adverted to; though on the ex

q 2. 25. infra. 13. 11. πνεῦμά ἐστι καὶ ζωή ἐστιν. [q] Ἀλλ' εἰσὶν ἐξ ὑμῶν τινὲς οἳ οὐ πιστεύ- 64
ουσιν. ᾔδει γὰρ ἐξ ἀρχῆς ὁ Ἰησοῦς, τίνες εἰσὶν οἱ μὴ πιστεύοντες,
r v. 44. καὶ τίς ἐστιν ὁ παραδώσων αὐτόν. [r] Καὶ ἔλεγε· Διὰ τοῦτο εἴρηκα 65
ὑμῖν· ὅτι οὐδεὶς δύναται ἐλθεῖν πρός με, ἐὰν μὴ ᾖ δεδομένον αὐτῷ
ἐκ τοῦ Πατρός μου. Ἐκ τούτου πολλοὶ ἀπῆλθον τῶν μαθητῶν αὐτοῦ 66
εἰς τὰ ὀπίσω, καὶ οὐκέτι μετ' αὐτοῦ περιεπάτουν. Εἶπεν οὖν ὁ Ἰη- 67
s Acts 5. 20. σοῦς τοῖς δώδεκα· Μὴ καὶ ὑμεῖς θέλετε ὑπάγειν; [s] Ἀπεκρίθη [οὖν] 68
αὐτῷ Σίμων Πέτρος· Κύριε, πρὸς τίνα ἀπελευσόμεθα; ῥήματα ζωῆς
t Matt. 16. 16. Mark 8. 29. Luke 9. 20. inf. 11. 27. αἰωνίου ἔχεις· [t] καὶ ἡμεῖς πεπιστεύκαμεν καὶ ἐγνώκαμεν, ὅτι σὺ εἶ ὁ 69
Χριστὸς, ὁ Υἱὸς τοῦ Θεοῦ τοῦ ζῶντος. [u] Ἀπεκρίθη αὐτοῖς [ὁ Ἰησοῦς·] 70
u Luke 6. 13. infr. 8. 44. Οὐκ ἐγὼ ὑμᾶς τοὺς δώδεκα ἐξελεξάμην; καὶ ἐξ ὑμῶν εἷς διάβολός
ἐστιν. Ἔλεγε δὲ τὸν Ἰούδαν Σίμωνος Ἰσκαριώτην· οὗτος γὰρ ἤμελλεν 71
αὐτὸν παραδιδόναι, εἷς ὢν ἐκ τῶν δώδεκα.

act import and bearing of the words Commentators are not agreed. Πνεῦμα, the disputed term of this passage, many take of the *Holy Spirit*, others, of *spiritual views*, in contradistinction to the *carnal* ones of the Jews; or, as Bp. Middlet. interprets, the spiritual sense, as opposed to the *literal* one, as πνεῦμα is opposed to γράμμα at 2 Cor. iii. 6. The *first* mentioned interpretation, however, seems excluded by the context and the scope of the passage; the *second* has been ably maintained by Bp. Middl., who assigns the following sense: "But it is the *spiritual* part of Religion, which is of avail in opening the understanding; the mere *letter* is nothing: my words, however, are the spirit and the life of all, which ye have hitherto known only in the literal and carnal sense." Thus the present passage will agree very well with what precedes, meaning that they ought not to stumble at these his sayings, since they were not to be understood in a gross and carnal, but spiritual sense. And, in this view, with σὰρξ οὐκ ὠφελεῖ οὐδὲν may be compared 1 Tim. iv. 8.

Instead of λαλῶ several ancient MSS., Versions, and Fathers, have λελάληκα, which is adopted by Scholz; but wrongly; for it evidently arose *ex emendatione*.

65. Our Lord in these words refers to what was said at v. 37. and 44.: and from a comparison of those verses with this, it is as certain as any thing can well be, that by the Father's *giving* men, is meant His *drawing* them to Him by the strong *moral motives* propounded in His word, and by the sanctifying *influences of the Holy Spirit*. See the Notes on those verses.

66. ἐκ τούτου.] Sub. χρόνου. Ἀπῆλθον ὀπίσω is explained by οὐκέτι μετ' αὐτοῦ περιεπάτουν. Comp. Matt. xvi. 23. Luke iv. 8. Heb. x. 39. Περιπατεῖν is a Hebrew phrase to denote *discipleship;* as Prov. xiii. 20.

67. μὴ καὶ ὑμεῖς.] From the passages of the Classical writers adduced in Recens Synop. (from Wets. and others), it appears that this mode of address was not unfrequently resorted to by monarchs, generals, and philosophers, when about to be abandoned by their adherents.

68. ῥήματα] i. e. "which teach it, and are the medium by which it is conferred." What the ῥήματα are, is plain from v. 63. τὰ ῥήματα — ζωή ἐστιν. Comp. iii. 34. Moses' words, received from the Jehovah. Angels are only called λόγια ζῶντα (see Acts viii. 38.), but Christ's words are called ῥήματα ζωῆς and ζωή, from the infinite superiority, He being himself the Jehovah Angel.

69. The words τοῦ ζῶντος are not found in seven or eight very ancient MSS., nor in the Cop., Sahid., Armenian, Pers., Vulg., and Italic Versions, some Fathers, and Nonnus and Cyrill, and are cancelled by Griesb. and Scholz: but without any good reason; for the common reading is not only supported by *external* evidence of the most decisive kind, but is also equally strong in *internal*, being far more *appropriate* (as better suited to the ardent temperament of Peter) and coinciding with his unequivocal confession of faith, Matt. xvi. 16. Griesb. also, instead of ὁ Υἱὸς, edits ὁ ἅγιος, from a few MSS. and Versions. But that reading is, very properly, rejected by Scholz; since the *external authority* for it is far less, and *internal evidence* is altogether on the side of the common reading; the appellation ἅγιος τοῦ Θεοῦ, as used of our Lord, only occurring once, in the confession of the demoniacs, Mark i. 24. Luke iv. 54. He is, indeed, called ἅγιος παῖς, Acts iv. 27. but not ἅγιος τοῦ Θεοῦ. Whereas the appellation Χριστὸς, ὁ Υἱὸς τοῦ Θεοῦ, frequently occurs in the N. T., and especially in this Gospel, i. 50; xi. 27. See more in Tittm., who proves that the appellations ὁ Χριστὸς and ὁ Υἱὸς τοῦ Θεοῦ were not synonymous; but that the latter has reference to the *Divine* nature of Christ. Hence we may easily conjecture from what quarter came the reading ἅγιος. Moreover, when Scholz rejected that reading, he ought, in consistency, to have rejected the *other*; since the *principal* MSS. are precisely the same for both. And there can be no doubt that the alterations in question came from the *same* quarter, namely, from the *Alexandrian Critics*.

70. οὐκ ἐγὼ — ἐξελεξάμην.] The interrogation (as some of the best Commentators and Editors have seen) terminates at ἐξελ., not at ἐστιν; for the καὶ is, as Euthym. observes, put for καὶ ὅμως. The sense is: Have I not chosen and appointed twelve of you as my legates [and confidants], and one of you is an enemy, and a betrayer or accuser. See Acts xiii. 17. Διάβολός ἐ. The sense is, *an adversary*, one *disaffected* to me. So διαβεβλῆσθαι πρός τινα in the sense of being hostile to, is used in the best Classical writers.

71. ἔλεγε] "he meant:" a sense frequent both in the Classical writers and the N. T.

1 VII. ʼΚΑΙ περιεπάτει ὁ Ἰησοῦς μετὰ ταῦτα ἐν τῇ Γαλιλαίᾳ· οὐ
γὰρ ἤθελεν ἐν τῇ Ἰουδαίᾳ περιπατεῖν, ὅτι ἐζήτουν αὐτὸν οἱ Ἰουδαῖοι
2 ἀποκτεῖναι. [x] Ἦν δὲ ἐγγὺς ἡ ἑορτὴ τῶν Ἰουδαίων ἡ σκηνοπηγία. x Lev. 23. 34.
3 [y] Εἶπον οὖν πρὸς αὐτὸν οἱ ἀδελφοὶ αὐτοῦ· Μετάβηθι ἐντεῦθεν, καὶ y Matt. 12. 46. Mark 3. 31. Acts 1. 14.
ὕπαγε εἰς τὴν Ἰουδαίαν, ἵνα καὶ οἱ μαθηταί σου θεωρήσωσι τὰ ἔργα
4 σου ἃ ποιεῖς· οὐδεὶς γὰρ ἐν κρυπτῷ τὶ ποιεῖ, καὶ ζητεῖ αὐτὸς ἐν
5 παῤῥησίᾳ εἶναι. Εἰ ταῦτα ποιεῖς, φανέρωσον σεαυτὸν τῷ κόσμῳ. [z] οὐδὲ z Mark 3. 21.
6 γὰρ οἱ ἀδελφοὶ αὐτοῦ ἐπίστευον εἰς αὐτόν. Λέγει οὖν αὐτοῖς ὁ Ἰη-
σοῦς· Ὁ καιρὸς ὁ ἐμὸς οὔπω πάρεστιν· ὁ δὲ καιρὸς ὁ ὑμέτερος
7 πάντοτέ ἐστιν ἕτοιμος. [a] Οὐ δύναται ὁ κόσμος μισεῖν ὑμᾶς· ἐμὲ δὲ a 3. 19. & 14. 17. & 15. 18.
μισεῖ, ὅτι ἐγὼ μαρτυρῶ περὶ αὐτοῦ, ὅτι τὰ ἔργα αὐτοῦ πονηρά ἐστιν.
8 [b] Ὑμεῖς ἀνάβητε εἰς τὴν ἑορτὴν ταύτην· ἐγὼ ‡ οὔπω ἀναβαίνω εἰς b Infr. 8. 20.
9 τὴν ἑορτὴν ταύτην, ὅτι ὁ καιρὸς ὁ ἐμὸς οὔπω πεπλήρωται. Ταῦτα δὲ
εἰπὼν αὐτοῖς ἔμεινεν ἐν τῇ Γαλιλαίᾳ.

VII. From hence to ch. x. 2. we have detailed a *fifth* journey of our Lord to Jerusalem, at the Feast of Tabernacles, six months before his death; which is recorded by the Evangelist, as especially suited to the purpose of his Gospel, showing how anxiously our Lord sought to convince the Jews of the supreme dignity of his person and office. Accordingly, after briefly adverting to the *circumstances* which led to, and accompanied the journey, the Evangelist proceeds to detail various *discourses* and addresses (some shorter and others longer) of our Lord to the Jews, at the Festival in question.

1. περιεπάτει] *resided*. This sense occurs also at xi. 54, and is said to be formed on the use of the Heb. הלך. Οὐκ ἤθελεν is wrongly taken by some Commentators for οὐκ ἠδύνατο, since it simply means "was not disposed, did not choose."

3. οἱ ἀδελφοί.] See Note on Matt. xii. 46.

— οἱ μαθηταί.] Sub. ἐκεῖ, "thy disciples *there* [as well as here];" namely, the disciples whom Jesus had made in the first year of his ministry. On the motive with which this advice was offered, see Recens. Synop. The favourable as well as the unfavourable view thereof has been carried too far. His kinsmen probably imagined Jesus to be a *Prophet* — indeed, considering the miracles they had beheld, they could not suppose him less — but had no notion that he was the *Messiah*. They, moreover, conceived Him to be very much actuated by worldly motives; and as *they* looked to personal advantage from his celebrity; they, on finding many disciples in Galilee abandoning him, counselled him to go to Judæa, and confirm the attachment of his faithful followers there, and endeavour to increase their number.

4. οὐδεὶς γὰρ — παῤῥησίᾳ εἶναι.] The general sense is pretty clear from the context: but to show how it exists in the words themselves, is not so easy. Many eminent Expositors (as Wolf, Schleus., and Tittm.) take the καὶ for ἀλλά; thus: "No one doth any thing considerable *in secret*; but he is desirous of coming under the view of the public." This, however, is straining the the sense; and for the above signification of καὶ there is no authority. *Preferable* is the view adopted by the ancient Expositors and many eminent modern ones (as Grot., Lampe, Rosenm., and Kuin.), who regard the καὶ as put for ὃς, by Hebraism; and suppose an inversion of order, thus: "For no one who desires to be famous does great things in secret." Thus the αὐτὸς, they say, is redundant. But how the word can be thus silenced, it is difficult to see: nor is καὶ ever *properly* used for ὃς. The truth is, the αὐτὸς is very necessary to the sense, and ought to be construed with καὶ, which must retain its usual sense. Thus we may consider καὶ αὐτὸς as put for ὃς, not by Hebraism, but by an idiom common to the simple and popular style in all languages. Τὶ here, as often, denotes *something great*. The phrase ἐν παῤῥησίᾳ occurs also at xi. 54, and Col. ii. 15, and in Philo cited by Abresch. Ποιεῖς may mean, "if thou art doing, art engaged in these things," these great designs.

6. ὁ καιρὸς ὁ ἐμός.] By καιρὸς ἐ. is meant, not "the time of my death," as some Commentators take it; but, as others, "the time of my going up to the feast at Jerusalem, and manifesting myself publicly." See v. 8. The words ὁ καιρὸς — ἕτοιμος seem to mean, "Any time and manner will be suitable for *you* to go there; you have no cause for fear." The *reason* is intimated in the verse following; where the natural form of expression (changed into a gnome generalis) would be, "I cannot go thus publicly from that hatred of the multitude which has been incurred by a free reproof of their vices: but they have no such cause to hate *you*." Οὐ δύναται, cannot, in the natural course of things.

8. οὔπω ἀναβαίνω.] Many eminent Commentators and Editors read οὐκ for οὔπω; but on grounds not very solid. The external evidence for οὐκ is only that of *five* MSS. and some inferior Versions. But the authority of *Versions* is, in a case like the present, of no great weight; and the number of MSS. is too small to be entitled to much attention. The reading may be regarded as an *inadvertent alteration*; which is far more probable than that all the other MSS. and ancient Versions should contain a purposed alteration. Besides, οὐκ *cannot* be defended in the usual sense, since it would compromise Christ's *veracity*; and that of οὔπω, which the Commentators inculcate, is not well founded, and *here* could scarcely be supposed to have place without compromising our Lord's *ingenuousness*. The

Ὡς δὲ ἀνέβησαν οἱ ἀδελφοὶ αὐτοῦ, τότε καὶ αὐτὸς ἀνέβη εἰς τὴν 10
c Infra 11. 56. ἑορτὴν, οὐ φανερῶς, ἀλλ᾽ ὡς ἐν κρυπτῷ. [c] Οἱ οὖν Ἰουδαῖοι ἐζήτουν 11
d ver. 40. & 6. 14. & 9. 16. & 10. 19. Matt. 21. 46. Luke 7. 16. e 9. 22. & 12. 42. & 19. 38. αὐτὸν ἐν τῇ ἑορτῇ, καὶ ἔλεγον· Ποῦ ἐστιν ἐκεῖνος; [d] καὶ γογγυσμὸς 12
πολὺς περὶ αὐτοῦ ἦν ἐν τοῖς ὄχλοις. Οἱ μὲν ἔλεγον· Ὅτι ἀγαθός
ἐστιν· ἄλλοι [δὲ] ἔλεγον· Οὔ· ἀλλὰ πλανᾷ τὸν ὄχλον. [e] Οὐδεὶς 13
μέντοι παῤῥησίᾳ ἐλάλει περὶ αὐτοῦ διὰ τὸν φόβον τῶν Ἰουδαίων.
Ἤδη δὲ τῆς ἑορτῆς μεσούσης, ἀνέβη ὁ Ἰησοῦς εἰς τὸ ἱερὸν καὶ 14
ἐδίδασκε. Καὶ ἐθαύμαζον οἱ Ἰουδαῖοι, λέγοντες· Πῶς οὗτος γράμμα- 15
f 8. 28. & 12. 49. & 14. 10, 24. τα οἶδε, μὴ μεμαθηκώς; [f] Ἀπεκρίθη αὐτοῖς ὁ Ἰησοῦς καὶ εἶπεν· Ἡ 16
ἐμὴ διδαχὴ οὐκ ἔστιν ἐμὴ, ἀλλὰ τοῦ πέμψαντός με. Ἐάν τις θέλῃ τὸ 17

sense of *οὔπω ἀναβαίνω* is: "It is not at present my intention to go up," &c. The next words signify: "My time [for going] is not fully come," or at hand, he being then prevented by some hindrance.

The reason why our Lord did not go at first was, we may suppose, because the roads would then be thronged with travellers. And therefore, as privacy was his aim, (as is indicated by the words following, ἀλλὰ ὡς ἐν κρυπτῷ, meaning, as privately as was possible in so public a character,) he chose to go at a time when there would be fewest persons on the road; and, therefore, it is probable, he set off on the first day of the Feast, since he did not *arrive* till the middle of the Feast, which lasted eight days.

11. *οἱ Ἰ. ἐζήτουν.*] Some of the best Commentators take the sense to be, "the principal persons among the Jews (the chief Priests, &c.) sought him, to put him to death." This is countenanced by v. 1, 19 and 25; but the words following demand the sense "Judæi (scil. vulgus) desiderabant eum;" a signification frequent in the N. T., especially St. John's writings. See Calvin, Grot., and Tittm.

12. *γογγυσμός.*] The term has here the sense in which θροῦς is often used in Thucyd. and other writers; namely, a *muttering* or *whispering*, denoting *private discourse.* Δὲ is not found in many MSS., early Editions, and Fathers, and is cancelled by Matthæi, Griesb., and Scholz, perhaps rightly; internal evidence being strongly against it.

13. *οὐδεὶς*] i. e. [of those who thought favourably of him].

—*διὰ τὸν φόβον τῶν Ἰ.*] "through their fear of the Jews;" as xix. 38, and Jer. xxxv. 11. The *Dative* with a preposition would be more Classical Greek. So Thucyd. i. 26. δέει τῶν Κερκυραίων.

14. *ἑορτῆς μεσούσης*] i. e. on one of the days between the 1st and the 7th; which were the most solemn days; namely, the 3d or 4th day.

— *ἀνέβη — ἐδίδασκε.*] See Luke ii. 46, and Note. The Gentile philosophers too were accustomed to deliver their instructions in the *temples*, on account of the sanctity of the place, and the number of persons continually resorting thither. So Philostr. Vit. Ap. v. 26 & 27. *καὶ παρελθὼν εἰς τὸ ἱερόν ποι, ἔφη·* &c.

15. *γράμματα*] *literas*, learning; no doubt, meaning that kind of learning which was alone cultivated in Judæa; namely, the interpretation of the Scriptures, and an acquaintance with Theology in general. Thus the dispute carried on by the Commentators, whether *γράμματα* means *Divine* or *human* learning, is nugatory. Μὴ here seems to be for *οὐ*; though this may perhaps be ranged under that usage of the particle pointed out by Hermann and Wahl, by which is indicated *a softened negation.* Compare 2 Cor. xii. 21.

16. *ἡ ἐμὴ διδαχὴ — με.*] The general import of these words is evident; while the exact sense and application is not so clear but that Expositors differ in opinion. To *determine* that, we must consider the context, the scope, and the literal sense of the terms; especially those on which the sentiment hinges, *διδαχὴ* and *οὐκ — ἀλλά.* To advert to the *scope*, the words were intended to refute the notion of those who, regarding Jesus merely as *αὐτομαθὴς* and *αὐτοδίδακτος*, accounted him (as, we learn from the Rabbinical writers, was customary with the Jews) utterly undeserving of attention — a mere pretender, and no prophet. To which our Lord replies, that his teaching is *not* his own; i. e. that he is not *αὐτοδίδ.*, but *θεοδίδακτος.* This should seem to be the *primary* sense. Yet under it *another* and *secondary* one is also contained, serving to introduce the arguments which follow. Thus *διδαχὴ* is to be taken in the sense *doctrine*; i. e. system of religious instruction. In this sense, too, our Lord asserts that his doctrine, though not derived from their schools, is not therefore false, since it was not devised by himself, but came from the Source of all Truth, *God himself.* Thus the argument here is the same as that *hinted at* by St. Paul, Gal. i. 1. Παῦλος ἀπόστολος *οὐκ ἀπ᾽ ἀνθρώπ. οὐδὲ δι᾽ ἀνθρ., ἀλλὰ διὰ Ἰ. Χ. καὶ Θεοῦ.* Thus it pleased Divine wisdom that the Apostles should be unlearned, in order that the work might not be ascribed to human learning or eloquence. The above view of the sense is supported by the ancient Commentators in general; and, of the modern ones, by Brug., Pisc., Mald., Grot., Calvin, Lampe, and Kuin. In saying this (they remark) our Lord speaks "ex hypothesi Judæorum, secundum captum auditorum," who regarded him as a *mere man.* Some Commentators, however (as Wolf, Pearce, Kypke, and Tittm.), seek to avoid this by supposing that *οὐκ — ἀλλὰ* here involves, not an *absolute*, but a *comparative* negation, to be rendered *non tam — quam.* This is certainly better than, with others, to suppose an ellipsis of *μόνον.* But it is wholly unnecessary, and indeed inadmissible, as being contrary to the *scope* and *context.* See vv. 15 & 17, and compare xiv. 10. Indeed, Winer (Gr. Gr. N. T.) denies that the formula *οὐκ — ἀλλὰ* ever denotes a *comparative* negation: yet wrongly, — for although that principle has been carried too far, still it cannot be denied that it *sometimes* has place, as in Matt. x. 20. *οὐ γὰρ ὑμεῖς ἐστε οἱ λαλοῦντες, ἀλλὰ τὸ Πνεῦμα.*

θέλημα αὐτοῦ ποιεῖν, γνώσεται περὶ τῆς διδαχῆς, πότερον ἐκ τοῦ Θεοῦ
18 ἐστιν, ἢ ἐγὼ ἀπ' ἐμαυτοῦ λαλῶ. [g] Ὁ ἀφ' ἑαυτοῦ λαλῶν τὴν δό- g 5. 41.
ξαν τὴν ἰδίαν ζητεῖ· ὁ δὲ ζητῶν τὴν δόξαν τοῦ πέμψαντος αὐτὸν, οὗ-
19 τος ἀληθής ἐστι, καὶ ἀδικία ἐν αὐτῷ οὐκ ἔστιν. [h] Οὐ Μωϋσῆς δέδω- h Exod. 20. 1. & 24. 3. Acts 7. 53.
κεν ὑμῖν τὸν νόμον; καὶ οὐδεὶς ἐξ ὑμῶν ποιεῖ τὸν νόμον· τί με Matt. 12. 14. Mark 3. 6.
20 ζητεῖτε ἀποκτεῖναι; [i] Ἀπεκρίθη ὁ ὄχλος καὶ εἶπε· Δαιμόνιον ἔχεις· sup. 5. 16, 18. inf. 10. 39. & 11. 53.
21 τίς σε ζητεῖ ἀποκτεῖναι; Ἀπεκρίθη ὁ Ἰησοῦς καὶ εἶπεν αὐτοῖς· Ἓν i 8. 48, 52. & 10. 20.
22 ἔργον ἐποίησα, καὶ πάντες θαυμάζετε [k] διὰ τοῦτο. Μωϋσῆς δέδωκεν k Gen. 17. 10. Lev. 12. 3.

17. *ἐάν τις θέλῃ*, &c.] We have in this and the next ver. two arguments in proof of the preceding position (namely, that his doctrine is from God); 1. *internal*, and deduced from the nature, qualities, and effects of the doctrine itself (v. 17.); the other *external*; namely, that in what he is doing he has in view, not his own honour, but that of God. (Kuin.) Render, "He who is disposed to obey the will of God when revealed, however contrary it may be to his prejudices or carnal affections," shall know, &c. See the Classical citations cited in Rec. Syn. from Lampe; to which I have subjoined one from Hermes ap. Stob. Phys. I. 2. 698. *ὁ δὲ εὐσεβῶν εἴσεται καὶ ποῦ ἐστιν ἡ ἀλήθεια, καὶ τίς ἐκείνη.* By *θέλημα τοῦ Θεοῦ* is meant what he would have us do, both as to belief and practice; and to *do his will* is to embrace that belief, and adopt that course of action. Now the will of God, says St. Paul, is our *sanctification*. This *conforming* of our will implies the abandonment of all the *prejudices* and *passions*, which obscure the judgment and enslave the will (as the eye cannot rightly distinguish colours, when suffused with morbid humours); otherwise what we *wish* to be false, we shall not readily believe to be true: and thus unbelief is more the fault of the *heart* than the understanding. "The Gospel (observes Dr. South) has then only a free admission to the assent of the understanding, when it brings a passport from a rightly disposed *will*. If the heart be but well disposed, the natural goodness of any doctrine will be enough to vouch for the truth: for the suitableness of it will endear it to the will; and thus it will slide into the assent also." See more on this subject in a masterly Sermon of Dr. South on the present text, vol. i. p. 239, in which he discusses very ably the design and purpose of the words, and points out what truths may be supposed to flow from thence, *Γνώσεται*, "he shall know from experience;" namely, by finding that this *doing* the will of God will conduce to his happiness here and *hereafter*, when (as Dr. South says) "persuasion shall pass into knowledge, and knowledge into assurance; and all be at length completed in the beatific vision and full fruition of those joys which are at God's right hand for ever and ever."

18. *ὁ ἀφ' ἑαυτοῦ — ζητεῖ.*] Here our Lord supplies *another* criterion from which to judge whether this doctrine be of God. The false teacher seeks the praise of *men*; but the true legate of *God* seeks the glory of God in the salvation of men.

— *ἀδικία*] "pravum, fucatum." (Calvin.)

19. *οὐ Μωϋσῆς — νόμον.*] There is here thought to be a change of subject; and the recent Commentators (as formerly Calvin) are mostly of opinion that the words have reference to certain remarks (not recorded by the Evangelist) on the part of the rulers present, charging Christ with violating the Sabbath, by healing on that day. But we may well suppose the reference, *if such there be*, made, not to any accusation then advanced, but to what had been and still was occasionally brought forward by them. By *τὸν νόμον* many of the best Commentators understand that part of the Law which enjoins the observance of the Sabbath. But it is better, with Euthym., Beza, Lampe, Calvin, and Tittm., to take it of the *Law generally*, of which the most important injunctions were violated, either in letter or spirit, by the Pharisees. Of this a signal example is then adduced by our Lord, namely, that they are plotting his death; q. d. "You do not even keep the Law of *Moses*, or why plot against my life, in violation of the 6th commandment?"

20. *δαιμόνιον ἔχεις.*] Put for the more Classical term *κακοδαιμονᾷς*; and to be taken, in a popular sense, for "You are out of your senses." The words *τίς σε ζητεῖ ἀποκτεῖναι* are rightly ascribed to the *multitude*; for *they* had no designs on the life of Jesus, and were unconscious of those of the Rulers; therefore they might well feel indignant at what they conceived a false accusation. Jesus, however, notices not their unmerited reproach, nor removes their mistake; but proceeds to trace the malevolence and murderous plots of the principal persons to their true origin, namely, his healing the paralytic on the Sabbath day. He shows that they had no reason to censure him on that account, and justifies his actions from their own practice, and on their own principles.

21. In reply, our Lord practically refutes this charge of madness, by speaking on the matter in question with the words of truth and soberness. He confirms his foregoing assertion by shewing *why* they sought his death, and upon what irrational and unjust grounds they condemned him.

— *ἓν ἔργον ἐποίησα.*] "One [illustrious] work I have done." *Θαυμάζετε* is here not to be taken, (with most Commentators,) in its ordinary sense, but (with the most eminent Commentators, ancient and modern), as at Mark vi. 6. and Gal. i. 6., of that kind of *wonder* which borders on a feeling of disapprobation. This idiom is also found in the Classical writers (on which see my Note on Thucyd. vi. 36.), nor is it unknown in our *own* language.

— *διὰ τοῦτο.*] These words are by most Translators construed with the words *following*. But thus they admit of no suitable sense, and therefore the best Expositors, both ancient and modern, take them with the *preceding*, and render *thereat*; rightly, I think: for *θαυμάζειν* in the above sense is rarely, if ever, put absolutely; but is followed by some *case*, with or without a preposition. So Mark vi. 6. *ἐθαύμαζε διὰ τὴν ἀπιστίαν αὐτῶν*. Revel. xvii. 7.

22. *δέδωκεν ὑ. τὴν περιτ.*] i. e. gave you the com-

ὑμῖν τὴν περιτομήν, (οὐχ ὅτι ἐκ τοῦ Μωϋσέως ἐστὶν, ἀλλ' ἐκ τῶν πατέρων) καὶ ἐν σαββάτῳ περιτέμνετε ἄνθρωπον. Εἰ περιτομὴν λαμβά- 23
νει ἄνθρωπος ἐν σαββάτῳ, ἵνα μὴ λυθῇ ὁ νόμος Μωϋσέως, ἐμοὶ χολᾶτε ὅτι ὅλον ἄνθρωπον ὑγιῆ ἐποίησα ἐν σαββάτῳ; [1] Μὴ κρίνετε 24
κατ' ὄψιν, ἀλλὰ τὴν δικαίαν κρίσιν κρίνατε. Ἔλεγον οὖν τινὲς ἐκ τῶν 25
Ἱεροσολυμιτῶν· Οὐχ οὗτός ἐστιν, ὃν ζητοῦσιν ἀποκτεῖναι; καὶ ἴδε, 26
παῤῥησίᾳ λαλεῖ, καὶ οὐδὲν αὐτῷ λέγουσι. Μήποτε ἀληθῶς ἔγνωσαν

1 Deut. 1. 16, 17. Prov. 24. 23. James 2. 1.

mand to circumcise, enjoined the rite of circumcision.

—οὐχ ὅτι, &c.] Subaud. λέγω. See Bos. Ellip. The sense is: "Not that it was from Moses, but had been established by [Abraham]." It is observed by the Fathers, and also Euthym., and Beng., that thus the dignity of circumcision, as compared with the Sabbath, is meant to be exalted, on the ground of its more ancient institution. On the contrary, Dr. Burton thinks this is meant to prove that the Sabbath was an earlier institution than Circumcision, otherwise the argument would not be valid. Both, however, seem mistaken. There is no *comparison* between the Sabbath and circumcision; but, in the parenthetical clause is merely implied the high antiquity and consequent *dignity* of circumcision. Nor is the argument invalid; since the full sense of καὶ ἐν σαββ. περιτ. ἄνθ is, "and accordingly ye circumcise a man-child, though on the Sabbath." The reason given by the Jews for this was, that circision was an *affirmative* precept, the Sabbath a *negative* one, and therefore the former vacated the latter.

23. εἰ περιτομὴν, &c.] An argumentum a minori ad majus. Thus traced by Lampe, "Illic erat minister Moses, hic Dominus ipse Christus. Illic Lex positiva cedebat positivæ; quanto majus *naturali*." Χολᾶτε; "are ye [justly] angry?" Χολᾷν properly signifies to vent one'e bile (χολήν); and in the later writers it is used either with a Dative, or an Accus. with πρὸς, in the sense to vent one's bile at, i. e. to be very angry with. Ὅλον is by most Commentators and Translators taken as if it belonged to ὑγιῆ, and were put adverbially for καθόλου. But the best ancient and modern Expositors are agreed that it should be taken with ἄνθρωπον, "the whole man," as opposed to the part which was circumcised. Thus arises a stronger sense, and yet one quite justified by facts; for in a violent paralysis the *whole body* is affected. So Hippocr. (cited by Lampe) says, Ὅλος ἄνθρωπος νοσώδης ἐστι. And Aretæus says of a virulent chronical disorder, ὅλῳ τῷ ἀνθρώπῳ ἐνοικεῖ. There *may*, too (as many of those Commentators think) be an *opposition* meant, by allusion to circumcision being confined to a particular *part*, but the healing in question extending to the *whole*. So a Rabbinical writer cited by Wets. says, "Circumcision, which is performed on one of the 248 members of the body, vacates the Sabbath; how much more the *whole body* (i. e. the *healing* of the whole body) of a man [vacates it.]" To fully understand which, and the force of our Lord's reasoning, we must suppose that under *circumcision* is involved the *medical cure* of the wound; and that that, and even medical or surgical aid in all cases of imminent peril, were permitted by the Jurists. So the same writer elsewhere says, fol. v. 1. Periculum vitæ pellit sabbatum; item circumcisio *ejusque sanatio*. Our Lord therefore means to argue that what he had done was justifiable on even stronger ground, inasmuch as circumcision and its medical healing only affected a very small part of the body; *his* cure, the *whole* body.

24. κατ' ὄψιν.] There is some doubt as to the sense of this term. The ancient and most early modern Commentators, also Wolf and Lampe, think it is equivalent to προσωποληπτικῶς, i. e. by partiality or preference; an apt sense, but destitute of proof. It is therefore better (with Erasm., Beza, Wets., Kypke, Kuin., Rosenm., Schleus., and Tittm.) to take it to signify a judging by the outward appearance only, and consequently *superficially* and *precipitately*, which, indeed, *implies* partiality and injustice. Thus in Is. xi. 3 & 4, to judge κατὰ δόξαν is opposed to judging according to truth and equity. Wets. adduces a similar use of ἀπ' ὄψεως, from a kindred passage of Lysias. The force of the argument is, (as it is stated by De Dieu,) "do not condemn in *me* what you approve of in *Moses*; if you allow a man to be circumcised on the Sabbath, because Moses ordered it, but do not allow him to be healed, when I do it, you judge κατ' ὄψιν, according to the person, and not according to justice."

26. μήποτε ἀληθῶς — Χριστός.] The scope of the words is, to suggest a probable reason for their non-molestation of Jesus; namely, that they have really ascertained that he is truly the Christ. The second ἀληθῶς is omitted in many ancient MSS. and Versions, and the Ed. Princ., is rejected by most Critics, and cancelled by Griesb., Vat., and Scholz; but on insufficient grounds: since the *external evidence* is far inferior to that for the common reading; and the *internal* is by no means so strong; for it was more probable that the ancient Critics should stumble at the repetition of ἀληθῶς, and cancel one of the two (thus in some MSS. and Versions the *first* ἀληθῶς is omitted), than that any should foist in what might scarcely seem necessary. And yet, St. John is so fond of the word, that he uses it exactly as many times as all the other writers of the N. T. put together, and yet never once pleonastically. As to the double use of it here, the latter ἀληθῶς is confirmed by John vi. 14. vii. 40. ἀληθῶς ὁ Προφήτης, and Matt. xiv. 33. xxvii. 54; the former by John xvii. 8. ἔγνωσαν ἀληθῶς. Acts xii. 11. οἶδα ἀληθῶς. Hence we see how feeble is the criticism of Bp. Pearce and Dr. Campb. (adopted by Dr. A. Clarke) that the second ἀληθῶς is *unnecessary*, unsuitable to the usual style of the writer, if not inaccurate. The *last* mentioned charge is manifestly unfounded, and the *second* is negatived by positive testimony. The *first*, too, is *groundless*; for how can the word be *unnecessary*, if it *strengthens* the sense? and that it does so, is manifest. Besides, the two are meant of two different classes. "In *primo* (to use the words of the learned Mastricht) veram Sacerdotum cognitionem, in posteriori veritatem Messiæ indicare voluit Evangelista; quæ diversæ

27 οἱ ἄρχοντες, ὅτι οὗτός ἐστιν [ἀληθῶς] ὁ Χριστός ; , [m] ἀλλὰ τοῦτον m Matt. 13. 55. Mark 6. 3. Luke 4. 22.
οἴδαμεν πόθεν ἐστίν· ὁ δὲ Χριστὸς ὅταν ἔρχηται, οὐδεὶς γινώσκει
28 πόθεν ἐστίν. [n] Ἔκραξεν οὖν ἐν τῷ ἱερῷ διδάσκων ὁ Ἰησοῦς, καὶ λέ- n 8. 26, 42, 55. Rom. 3. 4.
γων· Κἀμὲ οἴδατε, καὶ οἴδατε πόθεν εἰμί. καὶ ἀπ' ἐμαυτοῦ οὐκ
29 ἐλήλυθα, ἀλλ' ἔστιν ἀληθινὸς ὁ πέμψας με, ὃν ὑμεῖς οὐκ οἴδατε. [o] Ἐγὼ o Matt. 11. 27. inf. 10. 15.
30 [δὲ] οἶδα αὐτὸν, ὅτι παρ' αὐτοῦ εἰμι, κἀκεῖνός με ἀπέστειλεν. [p] Ἐζή- p 8. 20, 37. Mark 11. 18.
τουν οὖν αὐτὸν πιάσαι· καὶ οὐδεὶς ἐπέβαλεν ἐπ' αὐτὸν τὴν χεῖρα, ὅτι Luke 19. 47. & 20. 19. ver. 19.
31 οὔπω ἐληλύθει ἡ ὥρα αὐτοῦ. [q] Πολλοὶ δὲ ἐκ τοῦ ὄχλου ἐπίστευσαν q 8. 30.
εἰς αὐτὸν, καὶ ἔλεγον· Ὅτι ὁ Χριστὸς ὅταν ἔλθῃ, μήτι πλείονα ση-
32 μεῖα τούτων ποιήσει, ὧν οὗτος ἐποίησεν ; Ἤκουσαν οἱ Φαρισαῖοι τοῦ
ὄχλου γογγύζοντος περὶ αὐτοῦ ταῦτα· καὶ ἀπέστειλαν οἱ Φαρισαῖοι

sunt veritates." That some MSS. and Versions omit *both*, ought only to *strengthen* our persuasion that both were originally written by the Evangelist. The truth seems to be, that the Alexandrian Critics, having decided, pro sapientiâ suâ, that, to prevent tautology, *one* should be omitted, could not agree *which* to remove; and the indications of this doubt were probably expressed in the originals of those MSS. where we find both omitted. Thus the scribes were puzzled which to take, and which to leave; and, as might be expected, omitted *both*.

27. ἀλλὰ τοῦτον, &c.] Tittm. regards these words as not coming from the same persons as the preceding, but from *others*, in reply to those who were inclined to suppose Jesus to be the Messiah. And to this opinion I acceded in the first Edition of this work. But, on further consideration, I have seen reason to abandon that view; since, to suppose so sudden a change of persons in the speakers, without necessity, is surely what cannot well be defended. And unnecessary it certainly *is*; for there is no reason why we should not suppose the *same* persons still speaking; but, as it were, *correcting* their former impression that he might be the Messiah, and seeking an excuse for not believing on him. See the able annotation of Calvin. The ἀλλὰ is better rendered in our common Version *howbeit*, than in any of the others; q. d. However, be that as it may, yet, &c. Of which elliptical use of ἀλλά, see Schleus. Lex. & Wahl's Clavis.

But to advert to the *nature* of the excuse which they made to themselves for not acknowledging Jesus as the Messiah; in the words τοῦτον οἴδαμεν, &c. there is (as we find from the Rabbinical writers) reference to a notion then prevalent, that the parentage, and consequently birth-place, of the Messiah would be unknown — that he would be ἀπάτωρ, ἀμήτωρ, ἀγενεαλόγητος. So that, when he should appear, no one would be able to say whence he had come; for he would appear *suddenly* and *adult*. How these vain notions had arisen, is not clear. See, however, Lampe and Calvin. Be that as it may, they were opposed to Scripture, and were therefore only harboured by *Traditionarii*, the Pharisees and others, not by the *Scripturarii*. The best Commentators, with reason, interpret the πόθεν not so much of *place*, as (like the Latin *unde*) of *origin*. "The Jews (says Tittm.) thought that the origin of the Messiah would be unknown, and that he would be ἀπάτωρ and ἀμήτωρ, or at least born of a 'virgin.'" Perhaps, however, we may, with Markl. and Kuin., take the πόθεν of both place and person. Indeed, this seems required by what follows.

28. ἔκραξεν] palam dixit, professus est. So 1 John i. 15. Rom. ix. 27. Hesych. κέκραγε· φανερῶς διαμαρτύρεται.

— κἀμὲ οἴδατε — εἰμί.] There is a difference of opinion as to the exact sense of these words. Many Commentators, ancient and modern, take them *interrogatively*. But that is negatived by κἀμὲ and the καὶ of the following sentence; and to suppose any clause to be *supplied by ellip.*, would be harsh and arbitrary. They must be taken *declaratively*, in this sense: "Ye do indeed know me and my origin! And yet that will not prove my claim to be false; for I came not of myself, falsely assuming a Divine commission, nor found my claims on self-testimony, but on the testimony of the *God of truth* — but whom ye know not, otherwise ye would have believed his testimony concerning me." Grot. thinks that the words are meant to suggest that the *genuine father* of Jesus was He who sent him; the other, whom they knew, was only "*supposed* to be his father." On ὃν ὑμεῖς οὐκ οἴδατε compare viii. 19. 53.

29. Here Jesus asserts his claim to a Divine original (at least by implication), and to a Divine commission. Δὲ is omitted in very many MSS., Versions, and early Editions, and is cancelled by Matth., Griesb., Tittm., Vat., and Scholz. Internal evidence is certainly against it, and the asyndeton has great force.

30. ἐζήτουν.] The persons here meant, are not those who had been just speaking, but those mentioned at v. 27 & 29. the ἄρχοντες. By ἐζ. is meant they *sought occasion to lay hold on him*, but, for the present, found none. Πιάζειν was an old Doric form for πιέζειν, and signifies properly to *set foot upon*. But in the vulgar dialect it was, by a metaphor taken from beasts, (similar to one in our own language), employed to mean *to lay hands on*, or hold of. Thus it is used both of *apprehending men*, as here and at v. 32 & 44., viii. 20. x. 39. xi. 57. 2 Cor. xi. 32. Ecclus. xxiii. 21., and of *catching fish*, as John xxi. 3 & 10. Rev. xix. 20. It occurs only in the Sept. and the later Greek writers.

— ὥρα] The "full time" appointed for his end.

31. ἐπίστευσαν εἰς αὐτόν.] It was not, however, a firm belief; much less a sound and true faith; for it rested on *miracles* without reference to doctrine, and its very profession was made by implication only, and expressed in a whisper.

32. οἱ Φαρισαῖοι.] i. e. those rulers of the Sanhedrim who were of the Pharisaical party.

r 13. 33. & 16. 16. καὶ οἱ ἀρχιερεῖς ὑπηρέτας, ἵνα πιάσωσιν αὐτόν. [r] Εἶπεν οὖν [αὐτοῖς] 33
ὁ Ἰησοῦς· Ἔτι μικρὸν χρόνον μεθ᾽ ὑμῶν εἰμι, καὶ ὑπάγω πρὸς τὸν
s 8. 21. & 13. 33. πέμψαντά με. [s] ζητήσετέ με, καὶ οὐχ εὑρήσετε· καὶ ὅπου εἰμὶ ἐγὼ, 34
ὑμεῖς οὐ δύνασθε ἐλθεῖν. Εἶπον οὖν οἱ Ἰουδαῖοι πρὸς ἑαυτούς· Ποῦ 35
οὗτος μέλλει πορεύεσθαι, ὅτι ἡμεῖς οὐχ εὑρήσομεν αὐτόν; μὴ εἰς τὴν
διασπορὰν τῶν Ἑλλήνων μέλλει πορεύεσθαι, καὶ διδάσκειν τοὺς Ἕλληνας;
Τίς ἐστιν οὗτος ὁ λόγος ὃν εἶπε· Ζητήσετέ με, καὶ οὐχ εὑρήσετε· καὶ 36
ὅπου εἰμὶ ἐγὼ, ὑμεῖς οὐ δύνασθε ἐλθεῖν;

t 4. 14. & 6. 35. Lev. 23. 36. Isa. 55. 1. Rev. 22. 17. u Isa. 12. 3. & 44. 3. [t] Ἐν δὲ τῇ ἐσχάτῃ ἡμέρᾳ τῇ μεγάλῃ τῆς ἑορτῆς εἱστήκει ὁ Ἰησοῦς, 37
καὶ ἔκραξε λέγων· Ἐάν τις διψᾷ, ἐρχέσθω πρός με καὶ πινέτω. [u] Ὁ 38
πιστεύων εἰς ἐμὲ, καθὼς εἶπεν ἡ γραφὴ, ποταμοὶ ἐκ τῆς κοιλίας

33. [αὐτοῖς.] The word is omitted in very many MSS., Versions, and early Editions, and is rightly cancelled by almost all the Critical Editors; for internal evidence is as much against it as external.

34. Some obscurity here exists, which has occasioned not a little diversity of opinion. See Recens. Synop. But from a comparison of the parallel passages at viii. 21. and xiii. 33., Lampe thinks it clear that this seeking of the Lord is not as if the Jews would seek Jesus as their *helper* at or after the destruction of Jerusalem (according to Chrysost., Theophyl., and Euthym.), or as if they would in vain endeavour to seek Jesus for the purpose of destroying him, after his resurrection, (according to Rupertus), but because they would *seek* the *Messiah* in their own way, according to their own conceptions; which was by implication the same as to seek *Jesus;* since besides *him* no other Messiah was to be expected. They would *seek* him by a scrutiny of the times, by a vain expectation. But by all these attempts they would not *find* him: not in *word*, because the veil of Moses was upon their hearts; not by *vain confidence*, since they *could* not escape the destined destruction; not by seeking after *false Christs*, since they would be miserably deceived by them. I would suggest, that much of the discrepancy in question may be removed by supposing that as our Lord is admitted to have spoken somewhat ænigmatically, so he seems here, as on some other occasions, to have intended a *double* sense, according to the class of persons to whom the words might be referred. So Calvin well remarks: "Christus in ambiguitate verbi significationis ludit." This is especially the case in the second clause. (See Tittm.) And as to the first, though Lampe's view may be admitted, yet neither must that of Chrys. and others, including Calvin, be rejected. "They would seek him then (says Calvin) in another manner, nempe ut miseris suis ac perditis in rebus aliquid opis vel solati invenirent." This is confirmed by viii. 21. In xiii. 33. the application is different.

35. ποῦ οὗτος, &c.] It has been a matter of no little dispute what is meant by τὴν διασπ. τῶν Ἑλλ., by which some understand the *dispersed Jews*, i. e. the Jews dispersed among the Gentiles; as James i. 1. and 1 Pet. i. 1. The first interpretation has no foundation in evidence. And to the *second* it has been objected, that the foreign Jews are nowhere called Ἕλληνες, but Ἑλληνισταί. Hence Salmas., Loesn., Krebs, and Tittm., would take διασπ. for the *place* of dispersion, i. e. where the dispersed Jews inhabit; referring to James i. 1. and 1 Pet. i. 1. But διασπ. there cannot denote the *place*, but only the *persons* dispersed; and the argument above mentioned has no force; for the foreign Jews are not *here* called Ἕλληνες; that word refers only to the *Gentiles*, according to its usual sense in the N. T. And the passages of James and Peter tend to confirm the opinion of Grot., Wets., Rosenm., and Kuin., that by διασπ. τῶν Ἑλλήνων we are here to understand, "the Jews dispersed among the Gentiles," *abstract* for *concrete*, as in 2 Macc. i. 27. ἐπισυνάγαγε τὴν διασπορὰν ἡμῶν, ἐλευθέρωσον τοὺς δουλεύοντας ἐν τοῖς ἔθνεσι. Psalm cxlvi. 2. Sept. τὰς διασπορὰς τοῦ Ἰσραὴλ ἐπισυνάξει. So also Paralip. Jerem. (cited by Wets.) εἴπατε τοῖς υἱοῖς Ἰσραὴλ — ὁ δὲ Βαροὺχ ἀπέστειλεν εἰς τὴν διασπορὰν τῶν ἐθνῶν.

37. The last and *great day* of the festival now drew near; of which the Jews used to say that he who had not seen that day, had seen no rejoicing. It was very solemn, on account of the libations of water then, in great pomp, fetched from Siloam in golden vessels, and brought, amidst the sounds of musical instruments, to the Temple; where the Priest received it at the high altar, mixed it with wine, and poured it on the altar and the victim. This solemnity was not of Divine institution, but had been established by their ancestors in memory of the water so bountifully bestowed on the Israelites in the desert; and, as the Rabbins testify, was meant to be a symbol of the benefits to be sometime poured out and dispensed by the Holy Spirit. This solemn festival our Lord was pleased to consecrate by a most remarkable discourse; the subject of which was suggested to him by the very solemnity itself. He was in the Temple, he stood in a place where he could be seen by every one; and he spake not only openly, but with a loud voice, as if declaring what it was of the utmost consequence should be known by all. (Tittm.) See a full account of all the solemnities of this feast in Rec. Syn., formed from the Notes of Lightf., Vitringa, Surenh., Iken., Lampe, Calmet, and others.

— ἐάν τις διψᾷ] i. e. "if any one ardently desire." Lampe and Tittm. observe, that all such metaphors as this from words denoting *hunger* and *thirst*, imply *need of* as well as *desire for* the things in question. Thus the sense of the passage, after withdrawing the imagery, is: "If any one be desirous of learning, let him commit himself to my instruction, and use aright my doctrine."

38. ὁ πιστεύων, &c.] On the construction of these words some recent Commentators needless-

39 αὐτοῦ ῥεύσουσιν ὕδατος ζῶντος. [x] Τοῦτο δὲ εἶπε περὶ x Joel 2. 28. Acts 2. 17. inf. 16. 7.
τοῦ Πνεύματος, οὗ ἔμελλον λαμβάνειν οἱ πιστεύοντες εἰς αὐτόν. οὔπω
40 γὰρ ἦν Πνεῦμα ἅγιον, ὅτι ὁ Ἰησοῦς οὐδέπω ἐδοξάσθη. [y] Πολλοὶ οὖν y 1. 21. & 4. 42. & 6. 14.
ἐκ τοῦ ὄχλου ἀκούσαντες τὸν λόγον ἔλεγον· Οὗτός ἐστιν ἀληθῶς ὁ Deut. 18. 15. Matt. 21. 46. Luke 7. 16.
41 προφήτης. [z] ἄλλοι ἔλεγον· Οὗτός ἐστιν ὁ Χριστός. ἄλλοι δὲ ἔλεγον· z 1. 46. ver. 52.
42 Μὴ γὰρ ἐκ τῆς Γαλιλαίας ὁ Χριστὸς ἔρχεται; [a] οὐχὶ ἡ γραφὴ εἶπεν, a Ps. 132. 11. Mich. 5. 2. Matt. 2. 5.
ὅτι ἐκ τοῦ σπέρματος Δαυΐδ, καὶ ἀπὸ Βηθλεέμ τῆς κώμης, ὅπου ἦν Luke 2. 4. 1 Sam. 16. 1: 4.
43 Δαυΐδ, ὁ Χριστὸς ἔρχεται; [b] σχίσμα οὖν ἐν τῷ ὄχλῳ ἐγένετο δι᾽ αὐ- b 9. 16. & 10. 19.
44 τόν. Τινὲς δὲ ἤθελον ἐξ αὐτῶν πιάσαι αὐτόν, ἀλλ᾽ οὐδεὶς ἐπέβαλεν
45 ἐπ᾽ αὐτὸν τὰς χεῖρας. Ἦλθον οὖν οἱ ὑπηρέται πρὸς τοὺς Ἀρχιερεῖς
καὶ Φαρισαίους· καὶ εἶπον αὐτοῖς ἐκεῖνοι· Διατί οὐκ ἠγάγετε αὐτόν;
46 Ἀπεκρίθησαν οἱ ὑπηρέται· Οὐδέποτε οὕτως ἐλάλησεν ἄνθρωπος ὡς
47 οὗτος ὁ ἄνθρωπος. Ἀπεκρίθησαν οὖν αὐτοῖς οἱ Φαρισαῖοι· Μὴ καὶ
48 ὑμεῖς πεπλάνησθε; [c] μή τις ἐκ τῶν ἀρχόντων ἐπίστευσεν εἰς αὐτόν, ἢ ἐκ c 12. 42. 1 Cor. 1. 20. & 2. 8.
49 τῶν Φαρισαίων; ἀλλ᾽ ὁ ὄχλος οὗτος ὁ μὴ γινώσκων τὸν νόμον ἐπι- Acts 6. 7.

ly deviate from the common mode, either by connecting ὁ πιστεύων with πινέτω in the preceding sentence, or by taking εἶπε in the sense "*ordered.*" The common construction is well defended by Kuin.; who shows that it is required by the *explanation* of these words at v. 39., and from a kindred sentiment at xiv. 2. There is nothing to stumble at in the Nominative ὁ πιστεύων, which involves an *anacoluthon*, common both in the Scriptural and Classical writers, which may be resolved by *quod attinet ad*, "As to him who," &c. Nor is there any reason to suppose the words after γραφὴ to be the words of *Christ*, not of *Scripture*, because they are not found *totidem verbis* in Scripture. The best Commentators are, indeed, of opinion that no *particular* text of Scripture is meant, but that the substance is given of several passages of Scripture, which refer to the effusion of the Holy Spirit. Surenh. and Schoettg. have, however, shown that there are only *two* passages referred to, namely, Is. lv. 1. lviii. 11.

— ποταμοὶ — ῥεύσουσιν.] Ποτ. is a symbol of abundance; and ῥεύσουσι alludes to the *free* communication of the abundant benefits. The metaphor is frequent in the Jewish writings. So Sohar (ap. Recens. Synop.), "When a man turns to the Lord, he is like a fountain filled with living water, and rivers flow from him to men of all nations and tribes.' Nor is it unknown in the Classical writers. So Philo p. 1140. (cited by Lampe) λόγον δὲ συμβολικῶς ποταμὸν εἶναι φαμὲν, &c. I would add Philostr. Vit. Soph. i. 22, 4. p. 525. δωδεκάκρουνον δοκεῖ τὸ στόμα. Philostr. Vit. Ap. (of the Temple of the Muses at Helicon) λόγων τε κρατῆρες ἵσταντο, καὶ ἠρύοντο αὐτῶν οἱ διψῶντες. Κοιλία, like the Heb. בטן or קרב often, as here, denotes the *heart*, i. e. the *mind*. Thus the sense of the passage is: "Whosoever seeks truth, or desires salvation, must not seek them from Moses or the Jewish Teachers, but have recourse to me, and drink at the fountain of both, which I have opened."

39. τοῦτο δὲ εἶπε — αὐτόν.] Here we have an authentic *explanation* of the allegorical language of the preceding verse. There is not a shadow of reason (with some Critics) to omit ἅγιον and insert δεδομένον; since the latter is plainly from the margin; and the former, if not *expressed*, would be *understood*; for there is no ground to suppose (with some recent Commentators) that πνεῦμα merely denotes the *doctrine* of Christ, and the *knowledge* imparted by him. It is clear that we must understand it, not indeed in the *Personal* sense (which the Unitarians catch up, merely from thence to deduce that the Holy Ghost is not God), but as denoting His *operation* and *influence*, (see Lampe and Tittm.) and, from the adjunct, the *gifts* of the Holy Spirit, by which must be meant (as the occasion and context require) those *extraordinary* and supernatural gifts which were conferred on the Apostles and first converts, for the founding of Christianity; (see Bp. Middlet.) though there may be included those *ordinary* gifts which were then and are still given to every man to profit withal. (See Bp. Warburton's Divine Legation, vol. vi. 317.) By ἐδοξάσθη is meant the resurrection, ascension, and reception to the right hand of God. See xii. 16 — 28. xiii. 31. xiv. 3. and *Comp.* Acts ii. 33.

40. ὁ προφήτης] to be understood as i. 21.

41. μὴ γὰρ, &c.] "What then, does Christ," &c. This use of γὰρ is found in Matt. xxvii. 23. On this force of μὴ, see Note supra vi. 66.

42. ἡ γραφὴ εἶπεν.] There is a reference (by a mode of citation familiar to the Jews) to *several* passages of Scripture which they explained of the Messiah and his birth, as Is. xi 1. Jerem. xxiii. 5. Micah v. 2. Ps. lxxxix. 36.

— ὅπου ἦν Δ.] "where David dwelt." It has been proved by Lampe, that the earlier Jews acknowledged that Christ was of the family of David; and that the Talmudists admitted the Messiah was to be born in Bethlehem.

43. σχίσμα.] The word properly signifies a *rent*; and metaphorically a dissent in opinion, usually attended with angry debate.

46. οὐδέποτε — ὁ ἄνθρωπος.] See Doddr.

48. μή τις ἐκ τῶν ἀρχ. ἐπ.] i. e. the Sanhedrim, whose duty it was to take care that no false doctrines should be promulged; and to hold inquiry concerning those who were making innovations in the Church. (Kuin.) Thus they argue from the example of the *two-fold* authorities, both judicial and magistral.

49. ἀλλ᾽ ὁ ὄχλος — εἰσι.] On the exact force of

d 3. 2.
e Ex. 23. 1. Lev. 19. 15. Deut. 1. 17. & 17. 4, 8. & 19. 15.
f Isa. 9. 1, 2 Matt. 4. 15. supra 1. 46.

κατάρατοί εἰσι. [d] Λέγει Νικόδημος πρὸς αὐτούς, (ὁ ἐλθὼν νυκτὸς 50
πρὸς αὐτὸν) εἷς ὢν ἐξ αὐτῶν· [e] Μὴ ὁ νόμος ἡμῶν κρίνει τὸν ἄνθρω- 51
πον, ἐὰν μὴ ἀκούσῃ παρ' αὐτοῦ πρότερον, καὶ γνῷ τί ποιεῖ; [f] Ἀπε- 52
κρίθησαν καὶ εἶπον αὐτῷ· Μὴ καὶ σὺ ἐκ τῆς Γαλιλαίας εἶ; ἐρεύ-
νησον καὶ ἴδε, ὅτι προφήτης ἐκ τῆς Γαλιλαίας οὐκ ἐγήγερται. Καὶ 53
ἐπορεύθη ἕκαστος εἰς τὸν οἶκον αὐτοῦ.

VIII. Ἰησοῦς δὲ ἐπορεύθη εἰς τὸ ὄρος τῶν Ἐλαιῶν. Ὄρθρου δὲ 1

ἐπικατάρατοι the Commentators are not agreed. Lampe thinks that as the word is used in the LXX. to denote those who by transgression of the Law are doomed to punishment temporal and eternal, it means *execrable*. Kuin. takes it to mean *excommunicated*; but without reason. It is, I think, better interpreted by Schleus. "nullius sunt pretii," as in Plutarch. de Educ.: ἀνθρώπους ἀσήμους καὶ καταράτους. So our *wretched* means 1. cursed and abominable; 2. *vile* and *refuse*. But ἐπικατ. is a stronger term than καταρ., and the sense seems to be: "As to this rabble, who are ignorant of the Law, they are a *parcel of poor wretches!*" The Scribes and Pharisees, it may be observed, entertained the same profound contempt for the multitude which the Heathen Philosophers so liberally indulged in. So Sappho ap. Athen. lx. ὁ δῆμος οὐδὲν οὔτ' ἀκούων οὔθ' ὁρῶν. and Horace, "Odi *profanum vulgus* et arceo."

50. εἷς ὢν ἐξ αὐτῶν.] Being one of the Sanhedrim, he was authorized to speak; and he speaks as one neither justifying nor condemning Jesus, but only objecting to his being condemned unheard.

51. τὸν ἄνθρωπον.] The Translators render *quempiam, a man*. But this does not represent the force of the Article, which involves an ellip. of κρινόμενον "[*the accused*] person," to be taken out of κρίνει.

52. ἐκ τῆς Γαλ.] i. e. of the Galilæan party.

— ὅτι προφήτης, &c.] The ὅτι here, I think, marks not the *cause* but the *proof*. The Commentators are perplexed to reconcile this with the *fact*, — that Galilee had produced, it is said, *four* great Prophets. And most of them resort to the expedient of ascribing this to the ignorance and forgetfulness of the Priests, or the exaggeration of anger. See Doddr. and Campb. But ignorance of the common details of Scripture, or the birth-place of its writers, cannot, with any probability, be imputed to the Sanhedrim; and the other method is not quite satisfactory. Perhaps the difficulty may be best removed by availing ourselves of that latitude, in which the Preterite admits of being taken; and which not unfrequently refers to what is *customary* during a period not very long past. The Prophets of the O. T. in question had all lived upwards of 500 years before. Now the Pharisees, we may suppose, merely advert to what had been *usually* the case at a comparatively *recent* date; namely, since the country had borne the name of Galilee. This sense is well expressed by the gloss (for such it is) ἐγείρεται, found in many MSS. and Nonnus

VIII. 1—11. For a full discussion of the perplexed question as to the *authenticity* of this paragraph, the reader is referred to the Recens. Syn., where he will find a full statement of all the *objections* to its genuineness, together with their *answers*, placed in juxta-position; the evidence being carefully stated, and the decision to be made therefrom suggested. The following is a brief *summary* of the evidence, *external* and *internal* — (the former founded on the ample data recently presented by Scholz); subjoined to which are some remarks on the *nature* of that evidence, and an ἐπίκρισις on the whole question.

1. EXTERNAL *evidence* AGAINST the paragraph. — It is not found in 56 MSS., (in some of which, however, a space is left for it,) in 33 Evangelisteria, and several MSS. of the Syr., Copt., Sahidic, Armenian, and Italic Versions; nor is it treated on by Origen, Apollinar., Theod., Mops., Chrys., Bas., Cosmas., Theophyl., Catenæ, Tertull., Cypr. and Juvenc.; nor is it expressed by Nonnus.

External evidence FOR the Paragraph. — It is found in 284 MSS., and 6 Evangelisteria. In 40 others it is found, but *obelized*. In 15 others it is found with an asterisk: and again in 8 others is placed at the end of the Gospel. Of the remainder of the MSS., not ranged under *either* head, 13 MSS. have not been *examined* on purpose for this Paragraph: and 75 (including 13 Uncial ones) are found *mutilated* in this part by the abstraction of a leaf, or otherwise. And as to its not being contained in *Nonnus's* Version, that proves nothing; for many other omissions are there found equally remarkable. Thus we have a large chasm at vi. 40, and at xi. 55.

Internal evidence against the Paragraph. — This is any thing but decisive; for though the *variety of readings* in those MSS. which have it is great, yet it is scarcely greater than that which exists on some other passages, where there was any thing particularly to stumble at in the matter; as, for instance, part of the 2d, 3d, and 4th verses of the 5th chapter of this Gospel, where some Critics cut out the *whole*, some a *part*, and others contented themselves with endeavouring to alter the *words* on which the objection chiefly rests. This, to a certain degree, is the case *here*. Thus, instead of κατακρίνω at v. 11. some MSS. have κρίνω. In short, the arguments *against* the Paragraph from *internal* evidence resolve themselves into a series of objections, or surmises, founded on misconception; many of them such as might be advanced against *any* passage whose authenticity is undisputed. These may be found, together with, I trust, satisfactory answers, in Rec. Syn. Suffice it here to notice *two* objections which seem very specious; one that the paragraph is but little noticed by the Fathers and ancient Commentators. But this, we may imagine, arose *partly* because there was no *occasion* to advert to it; or because it could not *strengthen* their arguments or dissuasives against adultery — and partly because many persons, however causelessly, *did* stumble at one circumstance of the narration; — wondering why our Lord did not pass a more decided and severe condemnation. Thus the Fathers were apprehensive lest any persons, induced by the seeming im-

2 πάλιν παρεγένετο εἰς τὸ ἱερὸν, καὶ πᾶς ὁ λαὸς ἤρχετο πρὸς αὐτόν·
3 καὶ καθίσας ἐδίδασκεν αὐτούς. Ἄγουσι δὲ οἱ Γραμματεῖς καὶ οἱ Φαρισαῖοι πρὸς αὐτὸν γυναῖκα ἐν μοιχείᾳ κατειλημμένην, καὶ στήσαντες
4 αὐτὴν ἐν μέσῳ, λέγουσιν αὐτῷ· Διδάσκαλε, αὕτη ἡ γυνὴ κατελήφθη
5 ἐπαυτοφώρῳ μοιχευομένη. [g] Ἐν δὲ τῷ νόμῳ Μωϋσῆς ἡμῖν ἐνετείλατο [g] Lev. 20. 10. Deut. 22. 22.
6 τὰς τοιαύτας λιθοβολεῖσθαι· σὺ οὖν τί λέγεις; Τοῦτο δὲ ἔλεγον
πειράζοντες αὐτὸν, ἵνα ἔχωσι κατηγορεῖν αὐτοῦ. Ὁ δὲ Ἰησοῦς κάτω
7 κύψας, τῷ δακτύλῳ ἔγραφεν εἰς τὴν γῆν. [h] Ὡς δὲ ἐπέμενον ἐρωτῶντες [h] Deut. 7. 7.
αὐτὸν, ἀνακύψας εἶπε [πρὸς] ‡ αὐτούς· Ὁ ἀναμάρτητος ὑμῶν πρῶτος

punity of the offence, should be encouraged to the commission of this crime. So Augustin de Conjug. Adult. ii. 7. says, "that many, from a mistaken notion that the passage gave countenance to immorality, or an ill-judged fear lest its tendency should be misunderstood by the ignorant and ill-inclined, removed it from their copies." Hence it was generally passed over in the Homilies and Theological Treatises, and omitted in the Lectionaries. That it should have been passed over by Nonnus, may be imputed to much the same reason; though, indeed, that Paraphrast has omitted several other portions, some as long as this, without any apparent reason. And yet there is nothing in the Paragraph, when properly understood, that militates against the character of Christ, or can give the least encouragement to crime. On the contrary, the whole is perfectly consistent with the gentleness and benevolence of our Lord; while, at the same time, the censure itself is sufficient for the purpose. And if it be objected, that he suffered a guilty woman to go unpunished, it should be remembered: 1. that (according to our Lord's own declarations, John iii. 17; x. 11; 17.) he came not to exercise the office of a judge: and 2. that any such exercise of judicial authority would have been at variance with that deference which he ever inculcated, both by precept and example, to the civil magistrate. As a *sinner* he *morally* condemned her, when he bid her "go and sin no more."

In short, all the arguments put together, founded on internal evidence, *against* the authenticity of this Paragraph, will not counterbalance ONE which may be adduced *for* it, — namely, that, while we can easily imagine why it should have been *omitted*, no tolerable reason can be assigned *why* the story should have been *fabricated at all*, or if so, why fabricated with the present circumstances: and how it could, amidst so many objections, have found its way into five-sixths of the MSS. The *fabricated* stories found in the apocryphal Gospels are quite of a different character, and almost always founded on the most severe and ascetic views. And had this Paragraph been of *that* character, it would, I will venture to say, never have been omitted, or removed by any. To advert to a powerful argument from internal evidence in *favour* of its authenticity, the Paragraph is not denied by any competent judges to have upon it the stamp and impress of truth, in the *profound wisdom* of the answer, "Let him that is without sin cast a stone at her." Insomuch that the most eminent of the Critics who dispute its authenticity (namely, whether it was recorded by *St. John*) are constrained to admit the *truth* of the *narrative itself*, which they think was introduced into the Gospel by Papias, or the disciples of St. John; or else was, at a later period, expressed in the margin of some ancient MSS., and from thence found its way into the rest. But nothing can be imagined more improbable than the *latter* supposition. For there were surely *many* reasons why such a story should *not* have been introduced into the *Text*, and thus propagated into other MSS.; but not one reason why it *should*. And as to the *former*, it is very difficult to imagine how even Papias himself could have been *enabled*, had he *wished* it, to foist in an *interpolation*, especially of *this nature*: and if he had wished to interpolate, why he should have chosen *this alone* of all the *many narrations* which must then have been preserved by tradition, — namely, those πολλὰ ἄλλα, which St. John speaks of at xx. 30, and which he had chosen *not* to record, on the principle that those he *had* recorded were sufficient for the purpose of showing that Jesus was the Messiah. Such being the case, how would Papias dare to introduce *any more?*

4. κατελήφθη ἐπαυτοφώρῳ μοιχευομένη.] Καταλαμβάνεσθαι ἐπαυτοφώρῳ is a phrase properly used of *thieves* caught in the act of theft, or with the property upon them; but more frequently of those detected in the commission of any crime, especially such as is committed furtively. Other verbs of detection, as εὑρίσκω, ἁλίσκω, φωράω, were sometimes used. Ἐπαυτ. may be construed either with κατελ. or with μοιχ.; but the former method is preferable, as being confirmed by the Classical passages cited by the Commentators.

5. λιθοβολεῖσθαι.] On the *mode* of stoning see Note in Recens. Synop.

6. τῷ δακτύλῳ ἔγραφεν εἰς τὴν γῆν.] Some strange notions have been here broached by many ancient and modern Commentators, which may be seen in Lampe. The only correct view seems to be that taken by Euthym., Luther, L. Brug., Grot., Hamm., Lampe, Kypke, Schoettg., and others, that our Lord here employed an action frequent with those who do not choose to answer an improper question, and meant to intimate that they are otherwise engaged. Thus our Lord's action was only a *symbolical* one, though pregnant with meaning, signifying that he cared not to show any attention to what they were saying, or to answer their insidious question. Or it may have implied contempt, or censure, — as if they did not deserve that he should take the trouble to repeat, what he had so often inculcated, that with Juridical questions he had nothing to do; and that they *merited* no other answer than what they had themselves suggested by appealing to the Mosaic precept.

7. πρὸς αὐτούς·] Many Fathers and MSS. read αὐτοῖς.

— ὁ ἀναμάρτητος ὑμῶν.] The Commentators

τὸν λίθον ἐπ' αὐτῇ βαλέτω. Καὶ πάλιν κάτω κύψας ἔγραφεν εἰς τὴν 8
γῆν. Οἱ δὲ ἀκούσαντες, [καὶ ὑπὸ τῆς συνειδήσεως ἐλεγχόμενοι] ἐξήρ- 9
χοντο εἷς καθ' εἷς, ἀρξάμενοι ἀπὸ τῶν πρεσβυτέρων ἕως τῶν ἐσχάτων·
καὶ κατελείφθη μόνος ὁ Ἰησοῦς, καὶ ἡ γυνὴ ἐν μέσῳ * οὖσα. Ἀνακύψας 10
δὲ ὁ Ἰησοῦς, καὶ μηδένα θεασάμενος πλὴν τῆς γυναικὸς, εἶπεν αὐτῇ·
Ἡ γυνὴ, ποῦ εἰσιν ἐκεῖνοι οἱ κατήγοροί σου; οὐδείς σε κατέκρινεν;
Ἡ δὲ εἶπεν· Οὐδεὶς, κύριε. Εἶπε δὲ αὐτῇ ὁ Ἰησοῦς· Οὐδὲ ἐγώ σε 11
κατακρίνω· πορεύου καὶ μηκέτι ἁμάρτανε.
1 1.5, 2. 9. 5. & 12. 46. | Πάλιν οὖν ὁ Ἰησοῦς αὐτοῖς ἐλάλησε, λέγων· Ἐγώ εἰμι τὸ φῶς 12
τοῦ κόσμου· ὁ ἀκολουθῶν ἐμοὶ οὐ μὴ περιπατήσει ἐν τῇ σκοτίᾳ, ἀλλ'

are not agreed on what is here meant by ἀναμάρτητος. Some take it to denote freedom from *adultery;* others, freedom from any *notorious* sin, *like* adultery; others, again, freedom from *sin in general.* But this last interpretation cannot be admitted, since it would be too favourable to the adulteress, and be inconsistent with our Lord's emphatic censure of her crime. Of the other senses, the *former*, which is adopted by the best Commentators, seems alone the true one. It may, however, very well include *fornication, concubinage,* and *lasciviousness of every kind.* To the extreme corruption of morals in his countrymen Josephus bears ample testimony; and that the priests and scribes deeply participated in this corruption there is no reason to doubt; for the Rabbinical writers supply abundant proofs of the lasciviousness of even the most eminent Rabbis. That ἁμαρτάνειν and ἁμαρτία are in the Classical writers often used of *adultery* and *fornication*, is well known. If the word be taken in the above *extensive* sense (which is fully warranted by Scripture) there will be no reason to doubt but that every one of the persons present was, more or less, guilty. As to the objection of Le Clerc and others, that no law demands perfect innocence in its judges, &c., it may be observed, that our Lord is here not speaking *juridically*, but *popularly* and considers the thing *in foro conscientiæ;* as in the passages of Cicero and Synesius compared by Grot. Thus our Lord did by no means absolve the accused, but smote the consciences of the accusers. He neither acquits nor condemns the woman; but tempers his answer with such prudence, that it should neither be contrary to justice, nor inconsistent with mercy; and while it by no means absolved the accused, might smite the consciences of the accusers.

— πρῶτος — βαλέτω.] Render: "let him first cast the stone at her." By *the* stone is meant the fatal stone, which was first cast in form by one of the accusers or witnesses, and served as a signal to the bystanders to commence the stoning.

8. καὶ πάλιν — τὴν γῆν.] The best reason that has been alleged for the repetition of this symbolical action, is that it was meant to give the priests and scribes an opportunity of withdrawing with less confusion. But, in fact, this was a counterpart to the former action.

9. τῆς συνειδήσεως.] This term (like *conscientia*) is employed properly, 1. *generally* to denote the innate light of reason, by which any one possessing in himself the seeds and the rule of truth and falsehood, is *conscious* of his own existence, essence, relation, &c. But it is used more *specially* by the Philosophers, and by the sacred writers, to denote the faculty *consequent* upon it, by which a man exercises right judgment on the goodness or badness of his actions. Hence the office of reproof and conviction is well attributed to it; for, according to the expressive saying of Juven. Sat. xiii. 2. Prima est hæc ultio, quod, *se Judice, nemo nocens absolvitur.* (Lampe.) I add Eurip. Orest. 390. Μεν. Τί χρῆμα πάσχεις; τίς σ' ἀπόλλυσιν νόσος; Ορ. Ἡ ξύνεσις ὅτι σύνοιδα δείν' εἰργασμένος. The words καὶ — ἐλεγχ. are absent from many MSS. and early Editions, and may have been, as Matthæi suspects, from the margin, though it is more probable that they came from the Evangelist, because, as Matth. admits, they are much in his manner, — such ἐπικρίσεις being frequent with him. Instead of the common reading ἑστῶσα very many MSS. Versions and Edd. have οὖσα, which is edited by Matth. and Scholz, and rightly, for *internal* as well as external evidence, is in its favour.

On εἷς καθ' εἷς see Note on Mark xiv. 19. By πρεσβυτέρων (as Keuchen remarks) is here meant the *more honourable*, as by ἐσχάτων the lowest in degree or station. See Mark ix. 35. It is not meant, that they went out, each in seniority, but that they *all* went out, one after another, of every station and age, from first to last.

10. κατέκρινεν] "pronounced sentence on thee."

11. οὐδὲ ἐγώ σε κατακρίνω] "neither do, or will I pass sentence on thee." Πορεύου, &c. We are not to take this as a *remission* of her sins; (which, as supreme Lord, he *might* have pronounced) but simply a declaration that, since his kingdom was not of this world, so he would not assume the office of temporal magistracy. False, therefore, is the conclusion of some, who hence infer that our Lord did not approve of adultery being punished with death. For, upon the same principle they might argue that, when our Lord declined to act as judge between the brothers disputing about an inheritance (see Luke xii. 15.) he did not approve of inheritances being divided: and did not care that the disputes thence arising should be amicably settled. (Lampe.) To prevent any mistake of his meaning, our Lord added μηκέτι ἁμάρτανε.

12. Now follow to the end of the Chapter certain discourses pronounced by our Lord in the Temple, on some other occasion, though *what* that was, is uncertain. The Commentators variously speculate. Tittm. thinks vv. 12—19 are a continuation of the discourse at vii. 38. seqq. The scope of the address he thinks the same; but only that another metaphor is adopted, that of the *Sun.* Thus our Lord is represented as the great *moral Teacher*, and especially the only *Saviour*

13 ἕξει τὸ φῶς τῆς ζωῆς. Εἶπον οὖν αὐτῷ οἱ Φαρισαῖοι· Σὺ περὶ σεαυ-
14 τοῦ μαρτυρεῖς· ἡ μαρτυρία σου οὐκ ἔστιν ἀληθής. [k] Ἀπεκρίθη Ἰησοῦς [k] 5. 31.
καὶ εἶπεν αὐτοῖς· Κἂν ἐγὼ μαρτυρῶ περὶ ἐμαυτοῦ, ἀληθής ἐστιν ἡ
μαρτυρία μου· ὅτι οἶδα πόθεν ἦλθον, καὶ ποῦ ὑπάγω· ὑμεῖς δὲ
15 οὐκ οἴδατε πόθεν ἔρχομαι, καὶ ποῦ ὑπάγω. Ὑμεῖς κατὰ τὴν σάρκα
16 κρίνετε· ἐγὼ οὐ κρίνω οὐδένα. Καὶ ἐὰν κρίνω δὲ ἐγὼ, ἡ κρίσις ἡ
ἐμὴ ἀληθής ἐστιν· ὅτι μόνος οὐκ εἰμὶ, ἀλλ' ἐγὼ καὶ ὁ πέμψας με
17 Πατήρ. [l] Καὶ ἐν τῷ νόμῳ δὲ τῷ ὑμετέρῳ γέγραπται, ὅτι δύο ἀνθρώ- [l] Deut. 17. 6. & 19. 15.
18 πων ἡ μαρτυρία ἀληθής ἐστιν. Ἐγώ εἰμι ὁ μαρτυρῶν περὶ ἐμαυτοῦ, Matt. 18. 16. 2 Cor. 13. 1. Heb. 10. 28.
19 καὶ μαρτυρεῖ περὶ ἐμοῦ ὁ πέμψας με Πατήρ. Ἔλεγον οὖν αὐτῷ· Ποῦ
ἐστιν ὁ πατήρ σου; Ἀπεκρίθη ὁ Ἰησοῦς· Οὔτε ἐμὲ οἴδατε οὔτε τὸν
20 Πατέρα μου· εἰ ἐμὲ ᾔδειτε, καὶ τὸν Πατέρα μου ᾔδειτε ἄν. [m] Ταῦτα [m] Supra 7. 8, 30.
τὰ ῥήματα ἐλάλησεν ὁ Ἰησοῦς ἐν τῷ γαζοφυλακίῳ, διδάσκων ἐν τῷ
ἱερῷ· καὶ οὐδεὶς ἐπίασεν αὐτὸν, ὅτι οὔπω ἐληλύθει ἡ ὥρα αὐτοῦ.
21 [n] Εἶπεν οὖν πάλιν αὐτοῖς ὁ Ἰησοῦς· Ἐγὼ ὑπάγω, καὶ ζητήσετέ με, [n] Supra 7. 34. infra 13. 33.
καὶ ἐν τῇ ἁμαρτίᾳ ὑμῶν ἀποθανεῖσθε· ὅπου ἐγὼ ὑπάγω, ὑμεῖς οὐ

of the world. Indeed the former as well as the latter is an attribute of *Deity;* for the Rabbinical writers speak of *God* as the *light of the world,* and say that the light dwelleth alone with Him. And as *darkness* is often, in this Gospel, used to denote *vice* and *iniquity,* and *life* to signify *virtue* and its concomitant happiness, so φῶς τοῦ κόσμου may very well denote the *Messiah,* who shall enlighten, bless, and save the human race. Indeed this is required by the words following ἕξει τὸ φῶς τῆς ζωῆς.

13. σὺ περὶ σεαυτοῦ μαρτ., &c.] The foregoing lofty claim the Pharisees do not openly reject, but *put aside* by such a sort of argument, as they thought Jesus could not rebut; namely, that self-commendation has no force, and that no one can bear witness in his own case. This our Lord had before admitted, supra v. 31. But he removes the objection by arguing, that though in *common life* the rule holds good, yet an exception to it must be admitted in his own person; who had come down from heaven endued with the fullest Divine knowledge, (see vi. 46) for the purpose of imparting it to men ignorant of celestial things, or what was the true nature of His office. Therefore the words "I know whence I came and whither I go," contain a *periphrasis of Divine legation.* The sense may be thus expressed: "My testimony is perfectly true; for I know with what authority I act, and what commands have been given to me: *you cannot know,* except you learn of me."

15. ὑμεῖς κατὰ τὴν σάρκα κρίνετε.] The sense is; "Ye are used to judge according to the external appearance, warped by passion and prejudice, q. d. τὰ κατὰ πρόσωπον βλέπετε, as St. Paul says, 2 Cor. x. 7.; and thus ye account me a *mere man,* not the Messiah."

—οὐ κρίνω οὐδένα.] The sense is not certain: Lampe contends that it is, "I *as yet* judge no man, being now only a Teacher," while Kuin. and Tittm. supply οὕτως, i. e. as you do, or κατὰ σάρκα.

16—18. Here follows another argument: "I do not alone bear testimony of myself; *God* bears testimony to me by the miracles which I work." (Kuin.) The passage is thus paraphrased by Tittm.: "But even were I to bear the most honourable testimony of myself, yet it would be true, and worthy of credence; for neither am I alone, nor is my testimony solitary, but my Father also who sent me, hath testified of me," namely, by the Prophets. "Our Lord (says Tittm.) employs the same kind of argument here, as at v. 37. seqq. Nay (continues he), it is ordained by your law, that the testimony of two witnesses is worthy of credit." Therefore ought also *my* testimony of myself to be thought worthy of credit; since it is not of myself only, but likewise of my Father, who hath sent me.

19. ποῦ ἐστιν ὁ πατήρ σου.] On the scope of these words the Commentators are not agreed. The best founded opinion seems to be that of Lampe, Kuin., and Tittm., that they were said not from ignorance but by way of insult, q. d. Where is this Father of yours, that we may interrogate him? we do not *see* this other witness. To which our Lord indignantly replies, "Your very question betrays the malignity of your hearts; and shows that you neither truly know, nor care to know, either me or my Father. If you knew me as a Teacher sent from heaven, you would know that it is God who beareth witness of me, though not in a visible way, yet by miracles."

21. πάλιν.] The particle shows that the following discourse was pronounced at another time, and that it has no connexion with the preceding. The sense is: "I am about to depart, and ye shall seek the help of the Messiah, (and therefore of me, who am the Messiah;) but in vain; for having rejected *my* claims, there remaineth no other salvation." Ἐν τῇ ἁμαρτίᾳ ὑμῶν ἀποθ. is a mode of expression taken from Ezek. iii. 19. xviii. 26. xxxiii. 9. 18. Some Commentators render ἐν τῇ ἁμ. ὑ. "in this your sin," i. e. obstinate incredulity and putting Christ to death. But the expression seems *general,* and may therefore be rendered in the *plural.* So Euthym. well paraphrases: "I came to *deliver* you from all your sins; but ye would not; therefore I depart, and ye shall afterwards die in all your sins; inasmuch as ye would not be delivered from them." By ἀποθ. is denoted not so much *temporal* death,

δύνασθε ἐλθεῖν. Ἔλεγον οὖν οἱ Ἰουδαῖοι· Μήτι ἀποκτενεῖ ἑαυτὸν 22
ὅτι λέγει· Ὅπου ἐγὼ ὑπάγω, ὑμεῖς οὐ δύνασθε ἐλθεῖν; καὶ εἶπεν 23
αὐτοῖς· Ὑμεῖς ἐκ τῶν κάτω ἐστὲ, ἐγὼ ἐκ τῶν ἄνω εἰμί· ὑμεῖς ἐκ
τοῦ κόσμου τούτου ἐστὲ, ἐγὼ οὐκ εἰμὶ ἐκ τοῦ κόσμου τούτου. Εἶπον 24
οὖν ὑμῖν, ὅτι ἀποθανεῖσθε ἐν ταῖς ἁμαρτίαις ὑμῶν· ἐὰν γὰρ μὴ
πιστεύσητε ὅτι ἐγώ εἰμι, ἀποθανεῖσθε ἐν ταῖς ἁμαρτίαις ὑμῶν. Ἔλεγον 25
οὖν αὐτῷ· Σὺ τίς εἶ; Καὶ εἶπεν αὐτοῖς ὁ Ἰησοῦς· Τὴν ἀρχὴν ὅ τι
o Supra 7.28. *καὶ λαλῶ ὑμῖν. ° Πολλὰ ἔχω περὶ ὑμῶν λαλεῖν καὶ κρίνειν· ἀλλ᾽ ὁ* 26
πέμψας με ἀληθής ἐστι, κἀγὼ ἃ ἤκουσα παρ᾽ αὐτοῦ, ταῦτα λέγω εἰς
τὸν κόσμον. Οὐκ ἔγνωσαν ὅτι τὸν Πατέρα αὐτοῖς ἔλεγεν. Εἶπεν οὖν 27
αὐτοῖς ὁ Ἰησοῦς· Ὅταν ὑψώσητε τὸν Υἱὸν τοῦ ἀνθρώπου, τότε γνώ- 28
σεσθε ὅτι ἐγώ εἰμι, καὶ ἀπ᾽ ἐμαυτοῦ ποιῶ οὐδέν· ἀλλὰ, καθὼς ἐδίδαξέ
με ὁ Πατήρ μου, ταῦτα λαλῶ. Καὶ ὁ πέμψας με μετ᾽ ἐμοῦ ἐστιν· 29
οὐκ ἀφῆκέ με μόνον ὁ Πατὴρ, ὅτι ἐγὼ τὰ ἀρεστὰ αὐτῷ ποιῶ πάν-
τοτε.

Ταῦτα αὐτοῦ λαλοῦντος, πολλοὶ ἐπίστευσαν εἰς αὐτόν. Ἔλεγεν οὖν 30
ὁ Ἰησοῦς πρὸς τοὺς πεπιστευκότας αὐτῷ Ἰουδαίους· Ἐὰν ὑμεῖς μείνητε 31

(namely, at the destruction of Jerusalem) as eternal death, a state of everlasting woe.

22. *μήτι ἀποκτενεῖ ἑαυτὸν*, &c.] This was a wilful perversion of our Lord's meaning, and a scornful repartee; q. d. What! will he make away with himself, to get away from this our pretended persecution? See vii. 20. This imputation of intended suicide involved, even according to the opinions of the Jews, great criminality; for we find from Josephus, that the Pharisees thought the lowest pit of Hell was reserved for self-murderers.

23. *ὑμεῖς ἐκ τῶν*, &c.] Our Lord does not deign to notice the above absurd and malignant imputation; but points at the *cause* of it, by adverting to their difference in *disposition* as well as origin, from himself; they being of earthly origin and grovelling minds, he of celestial origin and heavenly minded. Compare John iii. 31. He means to intimate, that it is their earthly and corrupt dispositions that hindered them from believing, and would consequently cut them off from salvation.

24. *ὅτι ἐγώ εἰμι.*] Scil. *ἐκεῖνος*, namely, that personage expected and predicted of by the Patriarchs and Prophets. An ellip. found also in a kindred passage at Mark xiii. 6. See also Deut. xxxi. 29. and Acts xiii. 25.

25. *σὺ τίς εἶ;*] The best Commentators are agreed that the question is not one of simple ignorance, seeking information but involving scornful rebuke, q. d. Who art thou who speakest so loftily of thyself, and rebukingly to us? Our Lord, however, was pleased to answer, as if it had been the *former*.

— *τὴν ἀρχὴν — ὑμῖν.*] The sense of these words hinges upon *τὴν ἀρχήν*; where the ancient and older Commentators suppose an ellip. of *κατά*; and take the phrase for *ἀπ᾽ ἀρχῆς*. The *ἀρχὴν* some suppose denotes the *beginning of office*; others, the *beginning of the present address*; which latter opinion is preferable. Thus the expression may simply mean, *dudum*, or *etiam nunc*, as in Gen. xliii. 18. Thus *λαλῶ* will be for *ἐλάλησα*, "I have been telling you."

26. *πολλὰ ἔχω*, &c.] These words are, from brevity, somewhat obscure; but the sense seems to be: ["I could say much more in reference to you, and in reproof of your unbelief;] but I shall content myself with declaring, that as I am sent from the great Father of truth, so what I publicly aver is from Him, and therefore must be true." (See a similar ellip. of *ἀλλὰ* at vii. 28.) *Κρίνειν* is here meant to further define *λαλεῖν*.

27. *οὐκ ἔγνωσαν — ἔλεγεν.*] The sense is: "They did not, or cared not to know that he spake unto them of (i. e. that he meant) his Father," viz. in heaven, *God*.

28. *ὅταν ὑψώσητε*, &c.] These words could not have been understood by his hearers: but they were purposely expressed obscurely, partly from the reserve which prudence induced our Lord then to maintain; and partly because when what was now enigmatical, should be explained by *the event*, there might arise that confirmation of faith which results from the *fulfilment of prophecy*. The same remark applies to the words of our Lord addressed to Peter, respecting John, xxi. 22. *ἐὰν αὐτὸν θέλω μένειν ἕως ἐγὼ ἔρχομαι.* See also iii. 14. xii. 42. Indeed, what is spoken respecting future events, and not intended to be understood until the events themselves have taken place, can be expressed no *otherwise than obscurely*. Here there is an obscure allusion, but plain from the *event*, to the wonderful circumstances attending the crucifixion, and to the events subsequent to it; namely, the resurrection and ascension, the coming of the Holy Spirit, and the working of miracles in the name of Christ, which would so demonstrate Jesus to be the Messiah, that they would all have abundant evidence to see, and many would believe that he was the Christ. At *εἰμι* sub. *ἐκεῖνος*.

It is well remarked by Chrysost., that in *καθὼς — λαλῶ*, our Lord speaks *more humano*. V. 29. is closely connected with the preceding, and the sense is, "who having sent me, leaves me no alone, but aids and supports me, because I thu perform his will in all things."

31. *ἐὰν ὑμεῖς μείνητε*, &c.] "If ye adhere with

32 ἐν τῷ λόγῳ τῷ ἐμῷ, ἀληθῶς μαθηταί μου ἐστέ· καὶ γνώσεσθε τὴν
33 ἀλήθειαν, καὶ ἡ ἀλήθεια ἐλευθερώσει ὑμᾶς. Ἀπεκρίθησαν αὐτῷ·
Σπέρμα Ἀβραάμ ἐσμεν, καὶ οὐδενὶ δεδουλεύκαμεν πώποτε· πῶς σὺ
34 λέγεις· Ὅτι ἐλεύθεροι γενήσεσθε; [p] Ἀπεκρίθη αὐτοῖς ὁ Ἰησοῦς· [p Rom. 6. 16. 2 Pet. 2. 19.]
Ἀμὴν ἀμὴν λέγω ὑμῖν, ὅτι πᾶς ὁ ποιῶν τὴν ἁμαρτίαν, δοῦλός ἐστι
35 τῆς ἁμαρτίας. Ὁ δὲ δοῦλος οὐ μένει ἐν τῇ οἰκίᾳ εἰς τὸν αἰῶνα· ὁ
36 υἱὸς μένει εἰς τὸν αἰῶνα. Ἐὰν οὖν ὁ υἱὸς ὑμᾶς ἐλευθερώσῃ, ὄντως
37 ἐλεύθεροι ἔσεσθε. Οἶδα ὅτι σπέρμα Ἀβραάμ ἐστε· ἀλλὰ ζητεῖτέ με
38 ἀποκτεῖναι, ὅτι ὁ λόγος ὁ ἐμὸς οὐ χωρεῖ ἐν ὑμῖν. Ἐγὼ, ὃ ἑώρακα
παρὰ τῷ Πατρί μου, λαλῶ· καὶ ὑμεῖς οὖν, ὃ ἑωράκατε παρὰ τῷ πατρὶ
39 ὑμῶν, ποιεῖτε. Ἀπεκρίθησαν καὶ εἶπον αὐτῷ· Ὁ πατὴρ ἡμῶν Ἀβραάμ

constancy to my doctrine, and act upon it, in a holy obedience by your lives."

32. *γνώσεσθε τὴν ἀλήθειαν.*] The sense is: "ye shall experimentally find the truth and beneficial effects of my doctrine, as well as the reality of the Divine origin and legation which I claim." Comp. v. 28. vii. 17. Christ adds yet more, *καὶ ἡ ἀλήθεια ἐλευθερώσει ὑμᾶς*; where ἀλ. must mean the true doctrine promulgated by him, *Gospel truth.* Ἐλευθ. signifies "will liberate you from the bondage to sin and Satan, and place you in the glorious liberty of the children of God." (See Rom. viii. 2. 15.) *Servitude* being, by a metaphor common both in the Scriptural and Classical writers, a perpetual symbol of *vice*.

33. *ἀπεκρίθησαν.*] Not the *οἱ πεπιστευκότες* just mentioned, but some bystanders, who here perversely misrepresent Christ's meaning.

— *οὐδενὶ δεδουλεύκαμεν π.*] As the Hebrews had been in slavery not only under the Egyptians and Babylonians, but were subject to the Romans, many Commentators regard this as an impudent *falsehood* uttered in the heat of disputation. But the manner of the speakers indicates not *anger*, but *craftiness*. It is better, with others, to take δεδουλ. in such a restricted sense as the truth of history will justify. Yet I am inclined, with most recent Interpreters, to regard the words as spoken of *themselves* only and their *own age*. And assuredly the Jews, even after they became subject to the Roman Empire, were left in the enjoyment of no inconsiderable liberty, *political* as well as religious. See Notes on Matt. xvii. 24, 27. xv. 26. 60. Our Lord now shows that he meant not political, but *moral* and *spiritual* liberty. Comp. vi. 17. See v. 32.

34. *ποιῶν ἁμ.*] practises it habitually.

35. *ὁ δὲ δοῦλος — αἰῶνα.*] Here we have a *gnome generalis*, and an illustration drawn from what is usual in common life; q. d. "The *Slave* has no claim to remain continually in the same family; but may, at the pleasure of his owner, be sold unto another. Not so the *son*; he cannot be alienated from the family. Thus it is with the *servants of sin*, who may, at any time, be excluded from God's house and favour, into outer darkness. Whereas those who have the liberty of the *sons* of God will abide in it for ever." V. 36. contains *another* view; engrafted on the former, the comparison being the same but with another application. And as, in the foregoing verse there is a comparison between the state of a slave, and that of the son and heir; so in *this* there is, I conceive, one between the freedom communicated by the lord, and that by his son, with the *concurrence* of his Father. For as there may have been cases in which a Proprietor could not manumit without the consent of the son and heir, (or at least a manumission in which the son concurred with the father, might be regarded as being doubly effectual); so the freedom and salvation produced by the conjoint manumission of both Father and Son is most truly effectual. *ὄντως ἐλεύθεροι* has reference, not *merely*, as Wets., Rosenm., and Kuin. suppose, to the freedom from the tyranny of evil passions, but freedom from "the dominion of sin," mentioned by St. Paul. Rom. vi. implying an introduction into "the glorious *liberty* of the *children* of God." Rom. viii. 21. "the adoption, to wit, the redemption, of our bodies." Rom. viii. 23. ix. 4.

37. *οἶδα ὅτι σπέρμα — ἀποκτεῖναι.*] Our Lord grants their assertion; but makes use of it to shew the inconsistency between their boasted claims of ancestry and their present conduct. How degenerate must those descendants of Abraham be who pursue a conduct the reverse of his pure and blameless spirit, by plotting the death of Him to whom both the Patriarchs and Prophets bear witness. Then is suggested the *reason* for that rejection of his doctrine, which made them plot against his person; namely, *ὅτι ὁ λόγος — ὑμῖν*, where the Commentators are not agreed on the exact sense of *χωρεῖ*. The sense "has place," adopted by many eminent ancient and modern Expositors, is destitute of authority, and not definite or significant enough. The best interpretation seems to be that of Nonnus, Grot., De Dieu, Camer., Lampe, Rosenm., Kuin., and Wahl, "does not go into," or penetrate "your hearts," by being received and carried into effect. Ἐν is for εἰς, which is the proper construction, as Matt. xv. 17. The *hypallage* may be accounted for by supposing that there is here a blending of *two* phrases of different constructions.

38. The scope of this verse (which is variously traced by the Commentators) seems to be simply that of drawing a parallel between *His* actions and *theirs*, to *account for* their rejection of Him, God. *He* faithfully delivers the *doctrine* which he has learnt from and with *His father; they do* the *works* which they have learnt from *their father*, even the Devil; as is more clearly signified further on. The account given by Josephus of the Jews of his age fully vindicates our Lord's words from any charge of exaggeration.

— *ἑώρακα.*] Ὁρᾷν has here (as often) not the physical sense to *see*, but the moral sense to *perceive*, i. e. understand, know, learn.

39. *ὁ πατὴρ — ἐστι.*] The scope of the passage

ἐστι. *Λέγει αὐτοῖς ὁ Ἰησοῦς· Εἰ τέκνα τοῦ Ἀβραὰμ ἦτε, τὰ ἔργα*
τοῦ Ἀβραὰμ ἐποιεῖτε [ἄν]. *Νῦν δὲ ζητεῖτέ με ἀποκτεῖναι, ἄνθρωπον* 40
ὃς τὴν ἀλήθειαν ὑμῖν λελάληκα, ἣν ἤκουσα παρὰ τοῦ Θεοῦ· τοῦτο
Ἀβραὰμ οὐκ ἐποίησεν. Ὑμεῖς ποιεῖτε τὰ ἔργα τοῦ πατρὸς ὑμῶν. Εἶ- 41
πον οὖν αὐτῷ· Ἡμεῖς ἐκ πορνείας οὐ γεγεννήμεθα· ἕνα πατέρα ἔχο-
μεν, τὸν Θεόν. Εἶπεν οὖν αὐτοῖς ὁ Ἰησοῦς· Εἰ ὁ Θεὸς πατὴρ ὑμῶν 42
ἦν ἠγαπᾶτε ἂν ἐμέ· ἐγὼ γὰρ ἐκ τοῦ Θεοῦ ἐξῆλθον καὶ ἥκω· οὐδὲ
γὰρ ἀπ' ἐμαυτοῦ ἐλήλυθα, ἀλλ' ἐκεῖνός με ἀπέστειλε. Διατί τὴν λαλιὰν 43
τὴν ἐμὴν οὐ γινώσκετε; ὅτι οὐ δύνασθε ἀκούειν τὸν λόγον τὸν ἐμόν.
q 1 John 3. 8. Jude ver. 6. [q] *Ὑμεῖς ἐκ πατρὸς τοῦ Διαβόλου ἐστὲ, καὶ τὰς ἐπιθυμίας τοῦ πατρὸς* 44

is not well traced by the Commentators. It should seem that the Jews, not knowing that by *their father* Jesus had meant the Devil; and not quite understanding what was meant by their "seeing things with [apud] their father," and regarding it as disrespectful to *Abraham*, take refuge in their former allegation; and simply repeat that Abraham is their father, in whom they trust. To this our Lord objects, that they are not Abraham's sons in the spiritual and real sense; namely, those who closely copy his example, and do his works. This, he shows in the next verse, they are the farthest from doing, by their plotting the murder of one who had told them the whole truth from God.

From the Rabbinical citations adduced by Lightf. and others, it is clear that this figurative sense of *son* was well known to the Jews. Wets. contrasts the belief and practice of *Abraham* (who received every revelation of the will of God and discovery of the truth with unreserved faith), with that of the Jews, who rejected both.

The ἂν after ἐποιεῖτε is omitted in many good MSS. and some Versions and Fathers, together with the early Edd., and is cancelled by Griesb., Tittm., Vater, and Scholz. Internal evidence is indeed against it, yet it is confirmed by ἂν being used in a kindred passage, infra ver. 42.

40. νῦν.] This is, Lampe observes, used *assumptively*, as ix. 41. xviii. 36. Acts xv. 10. And so, I add, it is often taken in Thucyd.

41. πορνείας.] The best Commentators are agreed that the word here, as often, signifies *idolatry*, which was considered by the Jews as a sort of *spiritual* adultery, since so close was the connection of the people of Israel with God, that it was compared to the conjugal union. Compare Judg. ii. 17. 1 Chron. v. 25. Is. i. 21. Hos. i. 2. iv. 12. Their meaning, therefore, is: "If thou art now speaking of our *natural* Father, know that we recognise no other Father than God. To Him we are dear and beloved, like children: Him only do we worship." This argument our Lord rebuts, by again adverting to the *spiritual* sense of Father.

42. ἐξῆλθον καὶ ἥκω.] The sense is: "I proceeded forth from God, and come hither [as his Legate]." The former term has reference to the character of Jesus as the *eternal son of God*; the latter, as *Legate*, *Mediator*, and *Redeemer*. Compare vi. 46. vii. 29. xiii. 3. xvi. 27, 28. xvii. 7. and 25.

43. λαλιάν] for λόγον or λόγους; namely, those which he had just delivered, and such like,—indeed his *doctrine in general*. Γινώσκετε has reference to that *full comprehension* of our Lord's words, which the Jews certainly had not; and the reason of which is suggested in the next words οὐ δύνασθε, &c., where δύν. must be understood of the *moral inability* arising from perversity and indisposition to receive what is said. Compare John vii. 7. and Jerem. vi. 16. Ἀκούειν here, as often, signifies to *hearken*, to *give heed to* what is said.

44. ὑμεῖς — διαβόλου.] Our Lord now speaks more plainly, pointing out their *true* Father, and indicating *two* of the principal characteristics in which their similarity to their Diabolical father consists; namely, *man-slaying* and *lying*. Θέλετε, ye *will*, i. e. ye are resolved. Ἀπ' ἀρχῆς denotes here, as often, "from the beginning of the world." Compare i. 1. and 1 John iii. 8. The expression, however, includes a notion of *continuance* and *perseverance in*. In ἀνθρωποκτόνος there is not, I conceive, a reference (as some imagine) to the murder of Abel, committed at the instigation of Satan; neither, however, must the sense of the word (with others) be *explained away*. It must be taken in its *proper* sense, and be referred to the seduction of our first parents, called ἀνθρωποκτονία, as "bringing death into the world, and all our woe;" the thing being brought about by Satan's machinations. Thus a Rabbinical writer cited by Schoettg. speaks of "children of the old Serpent, who killed Adam and all his posterity." The slaying is also ascribed to the Devil in Wisd. ii. 24.

The words καὶ ἐν τῇ ἀληθείᾳ οὐχ ἕστ. contain a strong affirmation, by a negation of the contrary. And as to *stand* in any action is to steadfastly practise it, so the sense here is, "He has perpetually fallen away from the truth." This is repeated in another mode of expression (occurring also in 1 John i. 8. 2 Macc. vii. 18. and often in the Rabbinical writers), denoting that there is no principle of truth in him. Ἕστηκε has (as almost always) a sense of *present* time, or rather is used indefinitely of *all* times. The idea is further illustrated in the words following, the sense of which will much depend upon the manner in which αὐτοῦ in the next clause is explained; which some ancient and a few modern Translators render, according to the more usual signification of the word, *ipsius*, *his*. Yet this produces so odd a sense,—"for he is a liar, and so is his father," —that almost all Expositors of any eminence, from Erasmus to Tittm., take αὐτοῦ as a *neuter*, rendering *ejus*, *it*; and refer it either to the remote antecedent ψεῦδος, or consider that word as *inherent* in the verbal ψεύστης. As, however, this would seem to involve a *pleonasm* in the article, Bp. Middlet. (after affirming that the article is never pleonastic) ventures to pronounce that all the great scholars who have espoused the com-

ὑμῶν θέλετε ποιεῖν. ἐκεῖνος ἀνθρωποκτόνος ἦν ἀπ' ἀρχῆς, καὶ ἐν τῇ
ἀληθείᾳ οὐχ ἕστηκεν· ὅτι οὐκ ἔστιν ἀλήθεια ἐν αὐτῷ. Ὅταν λαλῇ τὸ
ψεῦδος, ἐκ τῶν ἰδίων λαλεῖ· ὅτι ψεύστης ἐστὶ καὶ ὁ πατὴρ αὐτοῦ.
45 ἐγὼ δὲ ὅτι τὴν ἀλήθειαν λέγω οὐ πιστεύετέ μοι. Τίς ἐξ ὑμῶν ἐλέγχει
46 με περὶ ἁμαρτίας; εἰ δὲ ἀλήθειαν λέγω, διατί ὑμεῖς οὐ πιστεύετέ
47 μοι; r Ὁ ὢν ἐκ τοῦ Θεοῦ τὰ ῥήματα τοῦ Θεοῦ ἀκούει· διὰ τοῦτο r 1 John 4. 6.

mon version, were in error. And, as might be expected, he adopts the *masculine* sense of αὐτοῦ. But, in order to avoid the insuperable objection arising from the sense thus produced, he endeavours to free his criticism from the difficulty in question by changing the *subject* in αὐτοῦ, and rendering, not "the Devil," but his *son*, the *Liar*. This he does by supposing the person at λαλεῖ to be not Διάβολος, but τις understood. And he renders, "when any of you speak that which is false, he speaks after the manner of his kindred (such he takes to be the sense of ἐκ τῶν ἰδίων); for he is a liar, and so also is his father." But to this it is, with reason, objected by Prof. Scholefield, that after describing the man as a liar, it was superfluous to add, "for he is a liar." This difficulty the learned Professor attempts to remove by cancelling the comma, and rendering, "for his father also is a liar;" a sense which he thinks it strange should not have occurred to Bp. Middl. But it probably did occur, and was rejected, as it might with reason; since it does violence to the construction, and introduces a sense not a little jejune,—such as would never suggest *itself*, but would have to be devised for the purpose of removing an objection. But there is a still more formidable objection: for (not to mention that such a sense as "after the manner of his kindred" is very harsh and improbable) this changing the subject *ad libitum*, and *supplying* a nominative, τις at λαλῇ, is surely too arbitrary a method to be justified. The ellipsis in question is, indeed, frequent in the Classical writers; but it is almost confined to the *Attic* ones, being very rarely found in the Alexandrian writers or those of later times, and never in the N. T. or the Sept. For Prof. Scholef. admits that it is unnecessarily supplied at Acts x. 28. And he himself allows that this is a "*questionable* part of the criticism." So questionable, I must think, that it ought to be *rejected*. There is, indeed, no reason to deviate from our common version; for though there may seem something *uncouth* in the *it*, and such as is at first little intelligible, yet the same is observable in many other parts of Scripture. The sentiment too, thus arising is both apposite and natural, and suggests matter for serious reflection. And in a writer like St. John, not tied down to strict rules, when we have arrived at this, we must not be deterred by petty grammatical objections. Thus Markland (who may surely be considered as good a Grecian as Bp. Middl.) observes, supra ver. 33. that "in this Evangelist the sense is more to be regarded than the construction." Now here there is little that can be called irregular. This use of αὐτοῦ in the neuter is indeed not very frequent; yet it is found at Gal. iii. 11. iv. 17. Eph. i. 7. Nor is the use of the article to be called anomalous. The article might indeed be dispensed with. And thus it is used, as is often the Hebr. ה. But, in fact, it is not *without* its force; the sense being "and the originator of it, by the deception of our first parents," Gen. iii. 5. (So Soph. Œd. Tyr. 868. calls Jupiter the πατὴρ νόμων.) Again, instances are abundant of nouns being left to be supplied from a verb preceding (see Glass. Phil. Sacr. 111. 2. 10. and Casaubon); thus there is surely no great harshness in a noun being left to be supplied from a *verbal*, if we consider its true nature, and especially as the very word itself has just preceded. So Koecher says *latet* in ψεύστης.

The above method of exposition is also supported by the suffrage of the earliest antiquity, being adopted by the Pesch. Syriac Translator in the middle of the second century; who renders by ܐܒܘܗ̇ with the *feminine* affin., which therefore cannot be referred to the Devil, and must belong to the preceding *feminine* noun ܟܕܒܘܬܐ, *a lie?* Finally, though I know of no example of ἐκ τῶν ἰδίων in the sense ἰδιώματος, we may suppose it to be a form of expression in the common dialect for ἐκ τοῦ ἰδίου. And so the Pesch. Syr. Translator must have taken it; since he renders in the *singular* ܡܢ ܕܝܠܗ, *de suo*. And as there is something peculiar in St. John's use of τὰ ἴδια at i. 11. & xix. 27; so there is less to scruple at here. 'Ιδ. is for οἰκείων. So Hesych.: ἴδιον· οἰκεῖον. And Lampe adduces Porphyry as saying of demons, τὸ ψεῦδος τούτοις οἰκεῖον.

46. τίς ἐξ ὑμῶν — ἁμαρτίας.] The scope of this address is to convince them of his credibility by another and a popular kind of argument. The best Commentators take ἁμαρτία to denote, not *sin*, according to the common acceptation, but *error*, or falsehood in doctrine, as opposed to the truth mentioned in the next clause. Of this signification many examples are adduced; to which I have in Recens. Synop. added others more apposite; as Æschyl. Agam. 480. φρενῶν ἁμαρτία. Thucyd. i. 32. δόξης ἁμαρτία. & 78. ἐν ἁμαρτίᾳ ὄντες. But it may be better to keep to the general sense, as including both words and actions. 'Ελέγχει must be rendered, not *convinceth*, but *convicteth*. Thus in a kindred passage of Aristoph. Plut. 574. (cited by Eckhard) καὶ σύγ' ἐλέγξαι μ' οὔπω δύνασαι περὶ τούτου.

Jesus appeals to his auditors, whether they can make out any such charge against him, of vice in *action*, or falsehood in *words*, as to warrant his claims to be disregarded; see a similar appeal of Moses to the Israelites, Numb. xvi. Such an interrogatory appeal involves the force of a strong negation. Thus, in the words following, the hearers are *supposed* to have answered, *No one!* The *inference* is manifest. In v. 47. the argument is followed up. "If ye were really, as ye boast, sons of God, ye would hearken to and yield credence to the words of God [from me, His legate]. The very reason why ye hearken not to them is, that ye are not of God;" i. e. sons of God. 'Εκ τοῦ Θεοῦ is for υἱὸς Θεοῦ.

s 7. 20. 10. 20. ὑμεῖς οὐκ ἀκούετε, ὅτι ἐκ τοῦ Θεοῦ οὐκ ἐστέ. s Ἀπεκρίθησαν οὖν 48
οἱ Ἰουδαῖοι καὶ εἶπον αὐτῷ· Οὐ καλῶς λέγομεν ἡμεῖς, ὅτι Σαμαρείτης
εἶ σὺ, καὶ δαιμόνιον ἔχεις; Ἀπεκρίθη Ἰησοῦς· Ἐγὼ δαιμόνιον οὐκ 49
ἔχω, ἀλλὰ τιμῶ τὸν Πατέρα μου, καὶ ὑμεῖς ἀτιμάζετέ με. Ἐγὼ δὲ οὐ 50
ζητῶ τὴν δόξαν μου· ἔστιν ὁ ζητῶν καὶ κρίνων. Ἀμὴν ἀμὴν λέγω 51
ὑμῖν· ἐάν τις τὸν λόγον τὸν ἐμὸν τηρήσῃ, θάνατον οὐ μὴ θεωρήσῃ
εἰς τὸν αἰῶνα. Εἶπον οὖν αὐτῷ οἱ Ἰουδαῖοι· Νῦν ἐγνώκαμεν ὅτι 52
δαιμόνιον ἔχεις. Ἀβραὰμ ἀπέθανε καὶ οἱ προφῆται· καὶ σὺ λέγεις·
Ἐάν τις τὸν λόγον μου τηρήσῃ, οὐ μὴ γεύσεται θανάτου εἰς τὸν αἰῶνα.
Μὴ σὺ μείζων εἶ τοῦ πατρὸς ἡμῶν Ἀβραὰμ, ὅστις ἀπέθανε; καὶ οἱ 53
προφῆται ἀπέθανον· τίνα σεαυτὸν σὺ ποιεῖς; Ἀπεκρίθη Ἰησοῦς· 54
Ἐὰν ἐγὼ δοξάζω ἐμαυτὸν, ἡ δόξα μου οὐδέν ἐστιν· ἔστιν ὁ Πατήρ
μου ὁ δοξάζων με, ὃν ὑμεῖς λέγετε, ὅτι Θεὸς ὑμῶν ἐστι. Καὶ οὐκ 55
ἐγνώκατε αὐτόν· ἐγὼ δὲ οἶδα αὐτόν· καὶ ἐὰν εἴπω ὅτι οὐκ οἶδα
αὐτὸν, ἔσομαι ὅμοιος ὑμῶν, ψεύστης· ἀλλ' οἶδα αὐτὸν, καὶ τὸν λόγον αὐτοῦ τηρῶ. Ἀβραὰμ ὁ πατὴρ ὑμῶν ἠγαλλιάσατο ἵνα ἴδῃ τὴν 56
ἡμέραν τὴν ἐμήν· καὶ εἶδε καὶ ἐχάρη. Εἶπον οὖν οἱ Ἰουδαῖοι πρὸς 57

48. Not being able to *answer* these arguments, the Jews are fain to have recourse to reviling.

— Σαμαρείτης — ἔχεις.] Of these two expressions the latter has been explained at vii. 20. The former appears from the Rabbinical writers, to have been a term of reproach, equivalent to calling any one a *heathen*, or a *heretic*; for the Samaritans were accounted *both*, as well in doctrine as in practice.

49. Here our Lord, with mild dignity, rebuts the insulting charge. Τιμᾷν τὸν Πατέρα here signifies *cum effectu*, the *executing* his Father's injunctions, by delivering his message and doctrine. Compare xvii. 4. This honour to God, he argues, would not be rendered by a *dæmoniac*.

50. ἐγὼ δὲ οὐ ζητῶ, &c.] The full sense is: "However, it is not my part to vindicate my honour; [nor *need* I;] there is a Being who will vindicate it, and hold judgment on men as to their reception of me."

51. ἐάν τις τὸν λόγον, &c.] Here our Lord especially adverts to the happy lot of those who accept his covenant of grace, and observe its requisitions. That they shall never θεωρεῖν θάνατον, which, like ἰδεῖν θάνατον at Luke ii. 26, signifies, "to experience death;" i. e. death spiritual, and eternal. Yet, though it has been proved that the *phrase* as well as the *doctrine* was not unknown to the Jews, the hearers misunderstand or pervert our Lord's words, and endeavour thereby to fasten on him the charge of being possessed with a dæmon. Moreover, as this claim to *confer* immortality implied the *possession* of it himself, the Jews justly interpreted this as virtually an arrogation of superiority over Abraham and the Prophets.

53. καὶ οἱ προφῆται ἀπέθανον.] An abandonment of the construction, for καὶ τῶν προφητῶν οἳ ἀπέθανον. Wets. compares Homer, Il. φ. 107. κάτθανε καὶ Πάτροκλος, ὅσπερ σέο πολλὸν ἀμείνων. See Lucret. iii. 1055. The Jews only stumbled at these claims because they would not acknowledge his Messiahship: for they did not deny that the *Messiah* was to be far superior to all the Patriarchs, Prophets, and even Angels.

54. Here our Lord rebuts the charge of arrogance, by showing that this glory is not *sought* by him, but freely *given* him by the Father.

— δοξάζω ἐμ.] take glory or honour to myself; equivalent to ζητῶ τὴν δόξαν μου, supra 50.

— ὅτι Θεὸς ὑ. ἐ.] is put for Θεὸν ὑμῶν εἶναι; i. e. whose worshippers ye profess to be.

55. καὶ οὐκ ἐγν.] "And [yet] ye do not truly know *Him*, because ye refuse to admit *me*;" for, as Euthym. observes, the keeping of God's commandments is the only sure proof that we know Him.

56. Ἀβραὰμ — ἐχάρη.] Our Lord here contrasts *their* feelings towards Him with that of Abraham, of whom they so boast; and that in order to hint at his Messiahship, and consequently infinite superiority to Abraham.

— ἠγαλλιάσατο ἵνα ἴδῃ.] Render (with Bp. Pearce) "earnestly desired to see;" which sense is confirmed by the Pesch. Syr. Version; "He earnestly wished to see, or know the time when the promise made to him (Gen. xii. 3.) should be fulfilled." He anticipated the period, and exulted as if it were present to him.

Ἵνα seems to be the Accusative (with the ellip. of κατὰ) of ἴς, *a shoot, or fibre*, whatever *issues* from a root; and generally, *issue*. Thus it may well denote the *issue*, or *end*, of *action*. When it denotes *where*, it signifies the issue or end of *motion*, the *place where* it ceases. From the word Fἲς came the Latin *vis*: for as ἴς signifies a fibre, so it might well denote a *nerve* (an animal fibre), and therefore *strength*, (namely, what *stringeth* the nerves, for that is the origin of the word, and the nature of the metaphor.) From this same ἴς (or ἶνς) ἰνὸς may be deduced the Ang. Sax. and Old English *inp, imp, a shoot*, and metaphorically *a son*.

— τὴν ἡμέραν τ. ἐ.] "my time;" i. e. when I the promised Saviour (See Joel ii. 1.) should come into the world." Ἰδεῖν ἡμέραν signifies to live to any time; of which examples are adduced by Elsn., Wets., and Kypke.

— καὶ εἶδε καὶ ἐχάρη] "and he saw it with delight;" i. e. as most recent Commentators ex-

58 αὐτόν· Πεντήκοντα ἔτη οὔπω ἔχεις, καὶ Ἀβραὰμ ἑώρακας; εἶπεν αὐτοῖς ὁ Ἰησοῦς· Ἀμὴν ἀμὴν λέγω ὑμῖν· πρὶν Ἀβραὰμ γενέσθαι, ἐγώ
59 εἰμι. [t] Ἦραν οὖν λίθους, ἵνα βάλωσιν ἐπ' αὐτόν· Ἰησοῦς δὲ ἐκρύβη, [t Infra. 10. 31.]
καὶ ἐξῆλθεν ἐκ τοῦ ἱεροῦ, διελθὼν διὰ μέσου αὐτῶν· καὶ παρῆγεν
οὕτως.

1 IX. Καὶ παράγων εἶδεν ἄνθρωπον τυφλὸν ἐκ γενετῆς. καὶ ἠρώ-

plain, *in Orcus*, or the seat of the righteous dead (see Luke xvi. 23. and Notes). In proof of which they adduce much specious evidence. But, after all, the meaning probably is (as the older Commentators interpret), "he saw it partly by *the eye of faith*, so strong as to be compared to *sight*, (see Heb. xi. 13. 1 Pet. i. 10—12,) and partly by a revelation supposed to be made to him on being commanded to offer up Isaac." At least, Schoettg thinks there is good reason to suppose that he was favoured by the Jehovah Angel with some faint representations of what would take place at the time of the Messiah.

57. πεντήκοντα ἔτη, &c.] The Commentators have been needlessly perplexed with these words; which are best treated on by Beza, Rosenm., and Kuin., who account for this mode of speaking on the principle, that opponents in argument sometimes grant *more* than their antagonists ask, in order to vanquish them in the end more effectually. The number *fifty* is used not (as Grot. supposes) as being a *round* number, (though that might be admitted, if it could be proved that our Lord was then, as Irenæus and some other of the Fathers suppose, about *forty* years of age,) but because among the ancients fifty was considered as the age when any one was past his vigour, and was discharged from severe service, civil or religious. So Philo, p. 24. ἀνὴρ δ' ἄχρις ἑνὸς δέοντος πεντήκοντα. Thus the sense is: "Thou art not yet even πρεσβύτης, much less γέρων."

58. πρὶν Ἀβραὰμ — ἐγώ εἰμι.] This passage is of the highest importance, as illustrating the *supreme majesty* of Christ, by showing his pre-existence long before his birth in this world; and also, by what appears an assumption of the name of Jehovah, of his *Divinity*. There has, however, been some difference of opinion among Commentators on the sense of the words. As to the Unitarian interpretation, which explains the existence not of *nature*, but of *destination*, in this sense: "Before Abraham was [Abraham, the father of many nations, in a mystical sense] I already was destined to be the Messiah;"—it is perhaps the most far-fetched and frigid ever broached even in *that* School. It is utterly inconsistent with the context, and is quite inadmissible, since it introduces an *unauthorized addition* into the sentence. See the unanswerable refutations of Whitby, Lampe, Kuin., and Tittm. Having seen what is *not*, let us examine what *is* the sense. The ancient and most earlier modern Commentators took εἰμὶ to denote the *eternal existence* and consequently *Divinity* of Christ, as bearing the appellation of Deity, "I AM that I am." And this interpretation has been ably supported by Euthym., Glass, Whitby, and especially *Lampe*. Yet Grot., Drus., Heins., Simon, Le Clerc, Wolf, and Wets., and almost all those of the last century, (including Rosenm., Kuin., and Tittm.,) take the *Present* as put for the *Imperfect*, of which a multitude of examples are adduced from the Scriptures. Thus the sense will be: "before Abraham existed, I was in existence;" a doctrine quite agreeable to many other passages of the N. T., especially this Gospel. See i. 1 & 2; iii. 13; vi. 46 & 62; vii. 29; xvii. 5. That idiom, however, (like enallage of every kind) has its limits; and, among other cases, it cannot be admitted where the *sense entirely turns* on the tense; for thus an *uncertainty* would be produced, at variance with the very purpose of language. The fact is, that this peculiar use of εἶναι, if it does not amount to conferring on Christ the *appellation* of DEITY, still may reasonably be thought to intimate, together with *existence prior to a given period*, (which is sufficiently pointed out by the γενέσθαι preceding) *uninterrupted existence since that time*, and, by implication, *existence unconnected with* ANY time:—i. e. *eternal duration*, an attribute of the GODHEAD *alone*. So Ps. xc. 2. πρὶν τὰ ὄρη γεννηθῆναι, σὺ εἶ. Thus the same sense will arise as in the first mentioned interpretation; an *attribute* of Deity being employed for an *appellative*. In this way, it should seem, the Jews must have understood Jesus; otherwise they would not, in exasperation, have attempted to stone him for blasphemy.

59. ἐκρύβη, &c.] In ἐκρ. we have an example of Passive for Middle, on which see Winer's Gr. Gr. p. 101. Most recent Commentators suppose an Hendiadys, in ἐκρύβη καὶ ἐξῆλθεν; or (as Winer, Gr. Gr. § 47. 3.) refer it to the rule by which of two verbs in connection one is to be rendered as an adverb. It is not, however, necessary to resort to that principle here. Jesus, it should seem, hid himself *for the moment*, and soon afterwards went out of the temple. We need not, with the older Commentators, suppose this concealment *miraculously* effected, by vanishing from the sight of the multitude. Not only is nothing *said* to that effect, but the words following rather *discountenance* such a view. See Note on Luke iv. 30. Indeed, the words διελθὼν — οὕτως have been rejected by many of the best Commentators, and are cancelled by Griesb. But there is scarcely evidence sufficient to warrant even any strong *suspicion*; for they are only omitted in *one* MS., (and that one of the most altered,) two or three very recent and inferior Versions, and two or three Fathers. And as the words are not at all essential to the *sense* of the passage, the testimony of Versions, and Fathers cannot here have much weight. All the *most ancient* Versions *have* it; and the Fathers adduced have it, in *other* citations. Finally, it is confirmed by the metrical version of Nonnus. I cannot help suspecting that the Critics who formed the text of the MSS. before mentioned threw out the words for no better reason than to remove *two tautologies*.

IX. This Chapter records other refutations by our Lord, of the objections brought forward by the Pharisees.

1. παράγων] "as he was passing by," or along [the streets]. See Matt. xx. 30. Mark ii. 14. xv. 21.

— τυφλὸν ἐκ γεν.] And consequently incurable by any human art.

τησαν αὐτὸν οἱ μαθηταὶ αὐτοῦ, λέγοντες· Ῥαββὶ, τίς ἥμαρτεν, οὗτος 2
ἢ οἱ γονεῖς αὐτοῦ, ἵνα τυφλὸς γεννηθῇ; Ἀπεκρίθη ὁ Ἰησοῦς· Οὔτε 3
οὗτος ἥμαρτεν οὔτε οἱ γονεῖς αὐτοῦ· ἀλλ' ἵνα φανερωθῇ τὰ ἔργα τοῦ
Θεοῦ ἐν αὐτῷ. Ἐμὲ δεῖ ἐργάζεσθαι τὰ ἔργα τοῦ πέμψαντός με ἕως 4
ἡμέρα ἐστίν· ἔρχεται νὺξ, ὅτε οὐδεὶς δύναται ἐργάζεσθαι. [u] ὅταν 5
ἐν τῷ κόσμῳ ὦ, φῶς εἰμι τοῦ κόσμου. Ταῦτα εἰπὼν ἔπτυσε χαμαὶ 6
καὶ ἐποίησε πηλὸν ἐκ τοῦ πτύσματος, καὶ ἐπέχρισε τὸν πηλὸν ἐπὶ τοὺς
ὀφθαλμοὺς τοῦ τυφλοῦ, καὶ εἶπεν αὐτῷ· Ὕπαγε νίψαι εἰς τὴν κολυμ- 7

[u] 1. 5, 9. & 8. 12. infra 12. 35, 46.

2. *τίς ἥμ. οὗτος ἢ οἱ γο.*] Some of the best Commentators think that there is here a reference to the doctrine of the *προΰπαρξις*, pre-existence of souls; or of the *μετενσωμάτωσις*, or *μετεμψύχωσις*, transmigration of souls into other bodies, by which what a soul had sinned in one body might be punished in another. Others, however, as Lightf., Lampe, and Tittm., deny this; maintaining that it cannot be proved that the Jews in the age of Christ held any such doctrine. But granting that the affirmative cannot be *fully proved*; yet neither can the *negative*; and considering that the doctrine was held in the surrounding nations (especially Egypt), it seems next to impossible, that the disciples of Jesus should not have heard of the doctrine, and felt some interest about it. Indeed Joseph. Ant. xviii. 1. 3. ad Bell. ii. 8. 14. iii. 8. 3. positively affirms, that the Pharisees (whose tenets were generally received by the people, and well known, at least, if not favorably regarded by the Apostles), did hold the Pythagorean doctrine of the *metempsychosis*. Besides, the language is not of *positive belief* seeking for confirmation, but of *doubt* seeking for information. Their question, as to what caused this natural blindness, rested on the common notion (prevalent also among the Heathen), that all dangerous diseases, or grievous calamities, must have been produced by the intervention of some heinous sin, which they were meant to punish. A notion likely to be held by those, who lived under a dispensation, which dwelt much in temporal and corporeal punishment. Now, in applying this to the case of any disease which befel a person in the course of his life, there was reason for perplexity; since it might be referred either to his own sin, or the sin of his parents; for the Jews likewise held, that the sin of parents, when not suffered for by themselves, was visited upon their children in the form of disease or calamity. See Ecclus. xi. 28. But how to apply this to the case of any disease *born with* a person, occasioned no little perplexity. Now for a solution of this difficulty the disciples apply—whether with the dogma of metempsychosis in their minds, or not, cannot be certainly determined. The former, however, is the more probable.

3. *οὔτε οὗτος — αὐτοῦ.*] Repeat *ἵνα τυφλὸς γεννηθῇ*, "This blindness is from no sin, either in his parents or in himself."

— *ἀλλ' ἵνα φανερωθῇ*, &c.] At *ἀλλὰ* supply *τυφλὸς ἐγεννήθη* from *ἵνα τυφλὸς γεννηθῇ*. Our Lord did not vouchsafe to give any *answer* to the *inquiry*, which seems to have been concealed under this interrogatory; but (as when asked, Luke xiii. 23. "Are there few that be saved?") fixes attention on a matter of far greater moment; namely, the truth, that God permits diseases to afflict men for His own wise purposes; *here* for the manifestation of His own glory in the miracle worked by His Messiah; one of whose characteristic miracles (see Is. xxxv. 5.) it was prophesied, should be giving sight to the blind.

4. *ἐμὲ δεῖ ἐργάζεσθαι*, &c.] The connection is best traced by Lampe as follows: "By me [I say] it is necessary that these works should be [now] performed [notwithstanding the objections on the score of prudence]; *now* [I repeat] while there is yet time and opportunity, *for* the night is coming. In *ἔρχεται νὺξ*, &c. there is probably an adage, q. d. The day is the *τὸ ἐνεργὸν*, the time for business; the night is the *tempus inopportunum negotio*. So the German adage, "Die nacht ist niemand's freund." Our Lord meant thereby to intimate, that his continuance with men would be short, and that he should not long either convince them by his miracles, or enlighten them by his doctrines.

5. *ὅταν — ὦ*] "as long as I am," &c. When *ὅταν* has the sense of duration of time, it requires the Subjunctive. *Φῶς τοῦ κόσμου* denotes both the *enlightener* and the *blesser* of the world; *light* being a metaphor both of knowledge and happiness. See Esth. viii. 16. Ps. xcvii. 11. cxii. 4. John i. 5. This sentiment was doubtless suggested by the case of the blind man.

6. *ἔπτυσε — τοῦ τυφλοῦ.*] The reason why this action (by which was meant to be suggested an idea of the *collyrium*, or eye-salve) was employed (though it could in itself contribute nothing to the cure) will appear from the Notes on Mark vii. 33. and viii. 23.

7. *νίψαι*] "wash thyself," probably the eyes only: for *νίπτεσθαι* denotes to wash a part only of the body, while *λούειν* is to wash or bathe the whole body. This distinction is expressly marked infra xiii. 10., where *λελουμένος* is used of him whose whole body is washed, and the verb *νίψασθαι* is joined with *τοὺς πόδας*. (Markl. and Campb.) Cotovicus Itiner. Hieros. p. 292. attests, that this fountain is much reverenced by both Christians and Turks, who use the water to wash the eyes with in certain disorders of that organ. On *κολυμβήθρα* see Note supra v. 2. This order was given to try his faith.

The words *ὃ ἑρμηνεύεται, ἀπεσταλμένος* are by Wassenburgh and Kuin. considered as a *gloss*; but without reason; since they are omitted only in two Oriental Versions. Now Versions are at best but slender evidence for the *omission* of clauses little necessary to the sense; and the omission of the present by those who were writing for the use of Oriental readers may be easily accounted for. There can be no doubt but that it is genuine; for such etymological interpretations of names were then very usual; as might be shown by many examples both from the Scriptural and the Classical writers, especially Thucydides; though such passages have usually proved traps into which ignorant or unwary Critics have

βήθραν τοῦ Σιλωάμ (ὃ ἑρμηνεύεται, ἀπεσταλμένος). ἀπῆλθεν οὖν καὶ
ἐνίψατο, καὶ ἦλθε βλέπων.
8 *Οἱ οὖν γείτονες καὶ οἱ θεωροῦντες αὐτὸν τὸ πρότερον ὅτι* ‡ *τυφλὸς*
9 *ἦν, ἔλεγον· Οὐχ οὗτός ἐστιν ὁ καθήμενος καὶ προσαιτῶν; Ἄλλοι*
ἔλεγον· Ὅτι οὗτός ἐστιν· ἄλλοι δέ· Ὅτι ὅμοιος αὐτῷ ἐστιν. ἐκεῖνος
10 *ἔλεγεν· Ὅτι ἐγώ εἰμι. Ἔλεγον οὖν αὐτῷ· Πῶς ἀνεῴχθησάν σου οἱ*
11 *ὀφθαλμοί; ἀπεκρίθη ἐκεῖνος καὶ εἶπεν· Ἄνθρωπος λεγόμενος Ἰησοῦς*
πηλὸν ἐποίησε, καὶ ἐπέχρισέ μου τοὺς ὀφθαλμούς, καὶ εἶπέ μοι· Ὕπαγε
εἰς τὴν κολυμβήθραν τοῦ Σιλωὰμ καὶ νίψαι. ἀπελθὼν δὲ καὶ νιψά-
12 *μενος, ἀνέβλεψα. Εἶπον οὖν αὐτῷ· Ποῦ ἐστιν ἐκεῖνος; λέγει· Οὐκ*
οἶδα.
13 *Ἄγουσιν αὐτὸν πρὸς τοὺς Φαρισαίους τόν ποτε τυφλόν. Ἦν δὲ*
14 *σάββατον, ὅτε τὸν πηλὸν ἐποίησεν ὁ Ἰησοῦς, καὶ ἀνέῳξεν αὐτοῦ τοὺς*
15 *ὀφθαλμούς. Πάλιν οὖν ἠρώτων αὐτὸν καὶ οἱ Φαρισαῖοι, πῶς ἀνέβλεψεν.*
Ὁ δὲ εἶπεν αὐτοῖς· Πηλὸν ἐπέθηκέ μου ἐπὶ τοὺς ὀφθαλμούς, καὶ
16 *ἐνιψάμην, καὶ βλέπω. Ἔλεγον οὖν ἐκ τῶν Φαρισαίων τινές· Οὗτος ὁ*
ἄνθρωπος οὐκ ἔστι παρὰ τοῦ Θεοῦ, ὅτι τὸ σάββατον οὐ τηρεῖ. ἄλλοι
ἔλεγον· Πῶς δύναται ἄνθρωπος ἁμαρτωλὸς τοιαῦτα σημεῖα ποιεῖν;
17 *καὶ σχίσμα ἦν ἐν αὐτοῖς. Λέγουσι τῷ τυφλῷ πάλιν· Σὺ τί λέγεις*
περὶ αὐτοῦ, ὅτι ἤνοιξέ σου τοὺς ὀφθαλμούς; Ὁ δὲ εἶπεν· Ὅτι προ-

fallen. See Bornem. Dissertat. de Gloss. New Test.

—ἦλθε] for ἀνῆλθε; a frequent signification.

8. τυφλός.] The reading is here uncertain; several ancient MSS., Versions, and some Fathers, having προσαίτης, which is preferred by most Critics, and received by almost every Editor, from Griesb. to Scholz; but, I conceive, on insufficient grounds. Whichever be the true reading, *one* must be an *intentional alteration;* for neither could be a gloss on the other. Now it seems more probable that τυφλ. should be altered into προσαίτης, than προσ. into τυφλ. And I suspect that the former alteration was made by those who took the ὅτι for a *causative conjunction*. Thus it is in the Versions rendered *quia*, or *quod*. And if that were the right interpretation, the sense would rather require προσαίτης than τυφλός. But *thus* οἱ θεωρ. α. τ. πρ. would yield a feeble sense; and ὁρῶντες would be required, not θεωροῦντες. In short, there can be little doubt but that ignorance, or inattention to the *Hellenism* in οἱ θεωροῦντες αὐτὸν ὅτι ἦν for οἱ θεωρ. ὅτι αὐτὸς ἦν, led to the mistake and alteration in question. And surely τυφλ. is far more suitable in sense than προσαίτης. We may render: "And those who had seen, ascertained, and known him to be blind," &c. This is mentioned in order to place the evidence for the miracle in a strong point of view, and show that imposture or collusion was impossible. The Evangelist might, indeed, have written τυφλὸς καὶ προσαίτης, as found in a few MSS. and Latin Versions; but he is not accustomed to be so exact; nor was it *necessary*, for the latter circumstance *comes out* in the subsequent narration. The Critics who formed the text of those MSS., it should seem, were induced to concoct the reading τυφλὸς καὶ προσαίτης because there is reason to think that πτωχὸς τυφλὸς was as common a phrase in Greek, as *cœcus rogator* in Latin; for the blind were almost always beggars.

9. ὅμοιος αὐτῷ ἐ.] For the restoration of sight, and the joy consequent upon it would give a different air to his whole countenance.

11. ἀνέβλεψα.] "I received sight."

13. τοὺς Φαρ.] i. e. the Sanhedrim, the far greater part of whom were Pharisees. That these were the *rulers*, is plain from vv. 22 & 34.

15. μου.] This position of μου instead of that after ὀφθ., is found in most of the best MSS. and early Edd., and is, with reason, received by almost all Editors from Wets. to Scholz.

16. παρὰ τοῦ Θεοῦ] scil. ἀπεσταλμένος, commissioned from God.

— τὸ σάββ. οὐ τηρεῖ.] They still advance the *same* charge that Jesus had before refuted (ch. v. & vii.) since they had no other handle of accusation. But here especially does their *malice* shine through the flimsy gauze of hypocrisy with which they seek to veil it under the guise of *religion*. (Lampe.)

— πῶς δύναται ἄνθρ. ἁμαρτ.] By ἀνθ. ἁμαρτ. is here simply meant an impostor. The argument is, that an impostor would not be endued by God with the power of working miracles; and that if so endued, he was plainly commissioned from on high, and could therefore dispense with any ritual observances.

17. σὺ τί λέγεις — ὅτι ἤνοιξε, &c.] There is no occasion (with Lampe and others) to break up the sentence into two interrogations, "What sayest thou of him? that he hath opened thine eyes!" For though specious reasons may be adduced in favour of that mode, yet *thus* the *second* question would be futile, because it had *before* been put, and the man had manifestly recovered his sight. It is better, with all the ancient and most modern Commentators, to assign the sense:

φήτης ἐστίν· Οὐκ ἐπίστευσαν οὖν οἱ Ἰουδαῖοι περὶ αὐτοῦ, ὅτι τυφλὸς 18
ἦν καὶ ἀνέβλεψεν, ἕως ὅτου ἐφώνησαν τοὺς γονεῖς αὐτοῦ τοῦ ἀναβλέ-
ψαντος· καὶ ἠρώτησαν αὐτούς, λέγοντες· Οὗτός ἐστιν ὁ υἱὸς ὑμῶν, 19
ὃν ὑμεῖς λέγετε ὅτι τυφλὸς ἐγεννήθη; πῶς οὖν ἄρτι βλέπει; Ἀπε- 20
κρίθησαν αὐτοῖς οἱ γονεῖς αὐτοῦ καὶ εἶπον· Οἴδαμεν ὅτι οὗτός ἐστιν
ὁ υἱὸς ἡμῶν, καὶ ὅτι τυφλὸς ἐγεννήθη· πῶς δὲ νῦν βλέπει οὐκ οἴδα- 21
μεν· ἢ τίς ἤνοιξεν αὐτοῦ τοὺς ὀφθαλμούς, ἡμεῖς οὐκ οἴδαμεν· αὐτὸς
x Infra. 12. 42. ἡλικίαν ἔχει, αὐτὸν ἐρωτήσατε· αὐτὸς περὶ αὐτοῦ λαλήσει. [x] Ταῦτα 22
εἶπον οἱ γονεῖς αὐτοῦ, ὅτι ἐφοβοῦντο τοὺς Ἰουδαίους· ἤδη γὰρ συνετέθειντο οἱ Ἰουδαῖοι, ἵνα ἐάν τις αὐτὸν ὁμολογήσῃ Χριστὸν, ἀποσυνάγωγος
γένηται. Διὰ τοῦτο οἱ γονεῖς αὐτοῦ εἶπον· Ὅτι ἡλικίαν ἔχει, αὐτὸν 23
ἐρωτήσατε. Ἐφώνησαν οὖν ἐκ δευτέρου τὸν ἄνθρωπον ὃς ἦν τυφλὸς, 24
καὶ εἶπον αὐτῷ· Δὸς δόξαν τῷ Θεῷ· ἡμεῖς οἴδαμεν ὅτι ὁ ἄνθρωπος οὗτος ἁμαρτωλός ἐστιν. Ἀπεκρίθη οὖν ἐκεῖνος καὶ εἶπεν· Εἰ 25
ἁμαρτωλός ἐστιν, οὐκ οἶδα· ἓν οἶδα, ὅτι τυφλὸς ὢν, ἄρτι βλέπω.
Εἶπον δὲ αὐτῷ πάλιν· Τί ἐποίησέ σοι; πῶς ἤνοιξέ σου τοὺς ὀφθαλ- 26

"What sayest thou (i. e.) what opinion hast thou of him, in that he hath opened thine eyes, or as to his opening thine eyes?"

—προφήτης.] Not "the Prophet foretold by Moses" (as some Commentators suppose), for that (as Bp. Middlet. has observed) would require the *Article;* but a prophet, θεῖος ἀνήρ, as Euthym. explains. It is plain from vv. 31 & 36. that the man considered Jesus only as such: certainly not the Son of God.

18. οἱ Ἰουδαῖοι] i. e. the Φαρισαῖοι before mentioned. Ἐφώνησαν, "had summoned."

19. οὗτος ἐστιν—ἐγεννήθη.] Lampe, Markl., Kuin., and Tittm. think that two questions are here blended into one, i. e. "Is this your son? Do ye say he was born blind?" such would, indeed, be the more *regular* manner of expression? but the present is the more simple, natural, and *characteristic* of the persons; for in their haste to proceed from *interrogation* to *imputation of fraud*, they blurt out the latter (which is implied in λέγετε) *together with* the former. In their answer, the parents *pass over* the imputation, and consider the words as comprehending *two* questions, to which they reply.

21. ἡλικίαν ἔχει.] The sense is, "He is of an age sufficient to enable him to give testimony."

22. συνετέθειντο.] Here we have a *significatio prægnans*. Render, "*de communi consilio decreverant*," as in Acts xxiii. 20. On this use of the Pluperf. Pass. in the Middle or Deponent sense, see Buttm. Gr. p. 234. and Win. Gr. Gr. Ὁμολογήσῃ Χριστόν. Sub. Ἰησοῦν εἶναι.

—ἀποσυνάγωγος γένηται] "should be excommunicated." There were *three* sorts of excommunication (see Rec. Syn.), the *second* of which is supposed to be here meant.

24. δὸς δόξαν τῷ Θεῷ.] This does not signify, what it might seem to import, "Give the praise of thy cure to *God* [and not to this man.]" For the absence of the Article will not permit that sense; and the words are a *form* of expression often employed in the O. T. in order to seriously admonish any one to speak the truth (see Josh. vii. 18 & 19. 1 Sam. vi. 5. Jer. xiii. 16). "For a lie (as Lampe observes) is a denial of the omniscience, holiness, truth, and justice of God: and he who wilfully conceals the truth, or declares a falsehood, insults all those attributes of the Deity." Thus the form was used when a confession of crime was to be wrung from any one. The sense, then, meant to be expressed is, "Confess the truth, dissemble nothing: hast thou been really blind from thy birth, and been healed by this man?" They hoped thus to detect some fraud or collusion; but being disappointed, they resolved to excommunicate the man immediately.

25. εἰ ἁμαρτωλός—οἶδα.] The Commentators are divided in opinion as to the scope and character of these words, in which some recognize *dissimulation*, others *sarcasm:* neither of which views seem well founded. It is *better* (with Brug., Camer., Grot., and Whitby) to take the words to import, that he has no knowledge of what they allege; q. d. "That Jesus is a sinner I know not;" εἰ being put for ὅτι. But the authority for this signification of εἰ is precarious; and I would therefore retain the usual sense *whether*, and take οὐκ οἶδα in a *popular* sense to denote, *I* give no opinion: I have nothing to do with that. This view is confirmed by the words following, ἓν οἶδα, which do not imply knowledge of nothing besides, but of one thing *especially*. Here Wets. aptly compares a similar passage in Aristoph. Av. 1176. τίς τῶν θεῶν; Αγ. οὐκ ἴσμεν· ὅτι δ' εἶχε πτερὰ, τοῦτ' ἴσμεν. And I have myself noticed the following. Arist. Pac. 227. οὐκ οἶδα· πλὴν ἕν, ὅτι (these words being also an answer to a question). Eurip. El. 752. οὐκ οἶδα, πλὴν ἓν—φόνιον οἰμωγὴν κλύω. Soph. Œd. Col. 1161. τί προσχρῄζοντα τῷ θακήματι; Οὐκ οἶδα, πλὴν ἕν, σοῦ γὰρ κ. τ. λ. Eurip. Iph. Taur. ποδαποί; Ἕλληνες, ἓν τοῦτ' οἶδα, κοὐ παραιτέρω. Herc. Fur. 1115. οὐκ οἶδα, πλὴν ἓν—πάντα δυστυχῆ τὰ σά. Thus the man *really gave glory to God*, since he remained constant in bearing testimony to the truth; and would by no threats be induced to dissemble the benefit which he had received.

26, 27. The Sanhedrim now repeat the same question before proposed. A crafty device, by which they hoped to detect some discrepancy in his testimony, which might stamp falsehood on

27 μούς; Ἀπεκρίθη αὐτοῖς· Εἶπον ὑμῖν ἤδη, καὶ οὐκ ἠκούσατε· τί
πάλιν θέλετε ἀκούειν; μὴ καὶ ὑμεῖς θέλετε αὐτοῦ μαθηταὶ γενέσθαι;
28 Ἐλοιδόρησαν οὖν αὐτὸν καὶ εἶπον· Σὺ εἶ μαθητὴς ἐκείνου· ἡμεῖς
29 δὲ τοῦ Μωϋσέως ἐσμὲν μαθηταί. [y] Ἡμεῖς οἴδαμεν ὅτι Μωϋσῇ λελάληκεν [y] Supra 8. 14.
30 ὁ Θεός· τοῦτον δὲ οὐκ οἴδαμεν πόθεν ἐστίν. Ἀπεκρίθη ὁ ἄνθρωπος
καὶ εἶπεν αὐτοῖς· Ἐν γὰρ τούτῳ θαυμαστόν ἐστιν, ὅτι ὑμεῖς οὐκ
31 οἴδατε πόθεν ἐστὶ, καὶ ἀνέῳξέ μου τοὺς ὀφθαλμούς. [z] Οἴδαμεν δὲ ὅτι [z] Prov. 15. 29. & 28. 9. Isa. 1. 15.
ἁμαρτωλῶν ὁ Θεὸς οὐκ ἀκούει· ἀλλ᾽ ἐάν τις θεοσεβὴς ᾖ καὶ τὸ θέλημα
32 αὐτοῦ ποιῇ, τούτου ἀκούει. Ἐκ τοῦ αἰῶνος οὐκ ἠκούσθη, ὅτι ἤνοιξέ
33 τις ὀφθαλμοὺς τυφλοῦ γεγεννημένου. Εἰ μὴ ἦν οὗτος παρὰ Θεοῦ,
34 οὐκ ἠδύνατο ποιεῖν οὐδέν. Ἀπεκρίθησαν καὶ εἶπον αὐτῷ· Ἐν ἁμαρτίαις σὺ ἐγεννήθης ὅλος! καὶ σὺ διδάσκεις ἡμᾶς; καὶ ἐξέβαλον αὐτὸν
35 ἔξω. Ἤκουσεν ὁ Ἰησοῦς, ὅτι ἐξέβαλον αὐτὸν ἔξω· καὶ εὑρὼν αὐτὸν
36 εἶπεν αὐτῷ· Σὺ πιστεύεις εἰς τὸν Υἱὸν τοῦ Θεοῦ; Ἀπεκρίθη ἐκεῖνος
37 καὶ εἶπε· καὶ Τίς ἐστι, κύριε, ἵνα πιστεύσω εἰς αὐτόν; εἶπε δὲ αὐτῷ
ὁ Ἰησοῦς· Καὶ ἑώρακας αὐτὸν, καὶ ὁ λαλῶν μετὰ σοῦ ἐκεῖνός ἐστιν.
38 Ὁ δὲ ἔφη· Πιστεύω, Κύριε· καὶ προσεκύνησεν αὐτῷ. [a] Καὶ εἶπεν [a] Supra 3. 19. infra 12. 47.

the whole; or they hoped that some additional circumstances would transpire, from which they might plausibly reason that the blindness was not *real*, or, at least, not from his birth. The man, however, distinctly perceives their aim; and, no longer able to suppress his indignation, impatiently exclaims, *εἶπον*, &c.

27. *τί*] for *κατὰ τί*, *why*. *Οὐκ ἠκούσατε*, attended not to what I said. The next words are ironical; to which the Sanhedrim reply by gross abuse.

— *ἐλοιδόρησαν καὶ εἶπον*] put for *ἐλοιδ. εἰπόντες*; for they thought it abuse enough to call him the disciple of an impostor. And, in fact, as Basil, cited by Heinsius, well remarks: Πᾶν *ῥῆμα ἐκ διαθέσεως τοῦ ἀτιμάσαι λεγόμενον λοιδορία ἐστι· κἂν μὴ τὸ ῥῆμα δόξῃ εἶναι ὑβριστικόν*.

29. *οὐκ οἰδ. —ἐστίν.*] A popular expression, importing, "We know not his Divine mission, whether his doctrine and miracles proceed from Divine impulse, or dæmoniacal agency." (See viii. 27. Note.)

30. *ἐν τούτῳ*] scil. *μέρει*, in this circumstance. Γὰρ has here, like the Heb. כִּי, the sense *sané*. Ὑμεῖς is *emphatical*. Καὶ, "and yet." The sense is: "This truly is *strange*, that you, who pretend to distinguish true from false prophets, should not be able to discern with *whose* power *he* comes who gives sight to those born blind."

31. *οἴδαμεν*] "it is well known." The following is a sentiment frequent in Scripture (as Ps. lxvi. 18. Is. i. 13.), and found in Hom. Il. *a*. 218. And this and that in the next clause are intended to be especially applied to the case of false prophets asking countenance from God.

32. *ἐκ τοῦ αἰῶνος*] "from the beginning of the world." See Note on Luke i. 70. Τὶς, scil. *ἄνθρωπος*, any mere man. Though communication of sight, in some cases, to those born blind, has of late been effected by the improvements of modern surgical art, yet that does not affect the present case; for the operation in question demands the intervention of the most consummate skill and labour; and it would be equally a *miracle* to restore such persons to sight *without those means*.

34. *ἐν ἁμαρτίαις σὺ ἐγεννήθης ὅλος.*] We need not suppose, with the older Commentators, that there is here any reference to the doctrine of *original sin*. It *may*, as some think, be said on the same principle which prompted the question of the disciples, v. 2. Though the best Commentators, ancient and modern, regard it is an hyperbolical phrase, equivalent to *scutes peccatis*. Perhaps it is a blending of two phrases, *ὅλος ἁμαρτωλὸς εἶς*, and *ἐν ἁμαρτίαις ἐγεννήθης*, formed on Ps. li. 5. which would form the most opprobrious speech that can easily be imagined.

— *ἐξέβαλον αὐτὸν ἔξω.*] The Commentators are not agreed whether this means, "thrust him out of the council chamber," or excommunicated him." The expression must signify the *former*; but the *latter* is *suggested*.

35. *πιστεύεις — Θεοῦ.*] Almost all Commentators regard these words as only importing, "Dost thou believe in the coming of the Messiah?" as all pious Jews did. But the mode of address seems to be directed to the *state of the man's mind*; who, though at the time the miracle was worked upon him, and even when brought before the Sanhedrim, he seems to have regarded Jesus as only a *prophet*; yet, on reflection, and consideration of the wonderful works Jesus had done, began to think that he must be *more* than a prophet; and to wish to be his disciple. His answer seems to comprehend two things; 1st, "Yea, Sir, I *have* that belief;" and 2dly, "Canst thou tell me where, or who that personage is, that I may believe in him, and commit myself to his teaching." The words seem to express a sort of expectation that the extraordinary person whom he was addressing, could *tell* him who and where the Messiah was; or perhaps might himself be that personage. In this view, the words of his answer may be regarded as a refined way of saying, "Art thou that personage? dost thou sustain that character? Tittm. here remarks, that Υἱὸς τοῦ Θεοῦ is, in the discourses of our

ὁ Ἰησοῦς· Εἰς κρίμα ἐγὼ εἰς τὸν κόσμον τοῦτον ἦλθον· ἵνα οἱ μὴ 39
βλέποντες βλέπωσι, καὶ οἱ βλέποντες τυφλοὶ γένωνται. Καὶ ἤκουσαν 40
ἐκ τῶν Φαρισαίων ταῦτα οἱ ὄντες μετ᾽ αὐτοῦ, καὶ εἶπον αὐτῷ· Μὴ
b Infra 15. 22. καὶ ἡμεῖς τυφλοί ἐσμεν; [b] Εἶπεν αὐτοῖς ὁ Ἰησοῦς· Εἰ τυφλοὶ ἦτε, 41
οὐκ ἂν εἴχετε ἁμαρτίαν· νῦν δὲ λέγετε· Ὅτι βλέπομεν· ἡ οὖν ἁμαρ-
τία ὑμῶν μένει.

X. Ἀμὴν ἀμὴν λέγω ὑμῖν· ὁ μὴ εἰσερχόμενος διὰ τῆς θύρας εἰς 1
τὴν αὐλὴν τῶν προβάτων, ἀλλὰ ἀναβαίνων ἀλλαχόθεν, ἐκεῖνος κλέπτης ἐστὶ

Lord and of his Apostles, never a name of office, but of *Divine nature*; yet he thinks that by Υἱὸς τοῦ Θεοῦ the man only understood a divine person, and not the Messiah. I have, with almost all Editors from Wets. to Scholz, inserted καὶ from very many of the best MSS., Versions, Fathers, and early Edd. This omission (of which other examples occur at xiv. 22.) arose from the verse just below.

39. εἰς κρίμα, &c.] These words were (as Doddr. has seen) spoken for the sake of the bystanders. For the very act of worshipping would be likely to draw a crowd of persons about them. On the sense of εἰς κρίμα Commentators are not agreed. Some take it of the *last judgment*. But that is not permitted by the words following; and thus, too, the *Article* would be required. Others think the sense is, "for the purpose of judging [concerning men], showing their condition and pointing out their duties." But that signification is not well established; and the sense yielded would not only be too feeble for the occasion, but deprive the words of that *sting*, which what follows shows they were meant to convey. The true sense seems to be that assigned by Chrysost. and Euthym., and adopted by some eminent modern Commentators, εἰς διάκρισιν καὶ διαχωρισμὸν, "*for distinction and separation*," that men's dispositions may be put to the proof. This is quite agreeable to the primitive signification of κρίνειν, which is *to winnow*, and, in a general way, to *separate*, *divide*, as an army into ranks. See Hom. Il. β. 362. So also Xenoph. Mem. iii. 1, 9. has κρίνειν τοὺς ἀγαθοὺς καὶ τοὺς κακούς.

In the next words the ἵνα is not *causal*, but *eventual*, or rather *consequential*. The general meaning, then, is: "so that the *effect* or consequence of my coming in the world will be, that a discrimination will be made between the true and the false worshippers of God (see iv. 23); so that those who are blind through simple ignorance may see, — i. e. receive sight (by the light of the Gospel, and the illumination of the Holy Spirit), and that those who have the use of sight, and have knowledge, but are blinded by passion and prejudice, — may not see what is before their eyes, but be left judicially to their own blindness." Κρίμα is here used in preference to διαχωρισμὸν, in order to suggest the *result* of that self-discrimination of this world, namely, the final and eternal separation of the two classes at the last award, the κρίμα. See Matt. xxv. 32. compared with Acts xxiv. 25. Heb. vi. 2. By the οἱ βλέποντες are meant the οἱ δοκοῦντες βλέπειν or ἀξυδερκεῖς, those who were thought to have, and thought they had knowledge of Scripture.

41. εἰ τυφλοὶ ἦτε.] Our Lord hints that they labour under a more incurable blindness than that of the common people whom they despised. The full sense is, "If ye were [simply] ignorant, your unbelief might be excusable; but, since ye fancy ye are wise, your unbelief remains [inexcusable]." They had every advantage of coming at the truth, and recognising Jesus as the Messiah; but they resisted conviction, were wilfully blind, and therefore their sin of unbelief could not but rest upon them unexpiated, and sink them in perdition. Ἁμαρτίαν ἔχειν is a phrase signifying to be guilty of any crime, and be liable to punishment for it. It is not a mere Hellenistic idiom; since I find it in Plato iv. p. 70. Bip. ὁ μὴ ἔχων κακίαν καὶ ὁ ἔχων ἀδικίαν.

X. 1 seqq.] Some Commentators think that the discourse in vv. 1—22. was delivered at another time. But the introductory ἀμὴν ἀμὴν λέγω ὑμῖν is never used at the *beginning* of a discourse, but is employed to introduce some further remark or admonition. See John v. 24, 25. vi. 26, 32. viii. 34, &c. And the Evangelist seldom commences any new narrative without *some* kind of preface, however brief. Besides, v. 21. may be supposed to have reference to the blind man. And, moreover, the imputation lately cast upon our Lord, ix. 24. of being an impostor, would induce him to take the first opportunity of *retorting* the charge on his calumniators, and showing that he sought nothing but the benefit of the people. That he was the true Shepherd, *the Messiah*; and that they who called themselves the shepherds of the people, and excommunicated those who acknowledged the Messiah, were the false teachers and impostors: that he himself, so far from seeking, as an impostor would, his own interest, sought nothing but the benefit of the people, and would lay down his life for them. In illustration, our Lord borrows an image from *pastoral* life. He shows, that those teachers alone were worthy of the name of *shepherds*, who, having learnt of HIM, should preach his doctrine. In this, and other of his discourses recorded by St. John, our Lord was pleased to employ expressions not direct, but highly figurative, in order to show the nature of his person and office. Why he was pleased to do this, will appear from what is said in the Note on *Parabolical instruction* at Matt. xiii. 3. Here it is proper to be more than usually attentive to the caution there suggested as to the *application* of Parables; namely, not to press too much on some of the *circumstances*, since they are but ornamental, and form, as it were, the *drapery* to the figure in the pictures. But to advert to the *scope* of the present paragraph, 1—21. Most of the ancient and earlier modern Commentators supposed the *subject* of it to be the *entering upon Ecclesiastical offices*, without being authorized by a commission from those who have such commission regularly transmitted down from the Apostles, and derived consequently from Christ himself. But that such

2 καὶ λῃστής· ὁ δὲ εἰσερχόμενος διὰ τῆς θύρας ποιμήν ἐστι τῶν προ-
3 βάτων. Τούτῳ ὁ θυρωρὸς ἀνοίγει· καὶ τὰ πρόβατα τῆς φωνῆς αὐτοῦ
ἀκούει· καὶ τὰ ἴδια πρόβατα καλεῖ κατ' ὄνομα, καὶ ἐξάγει αὐτά.
4 Καὶ ὅταν τὰ ἴδια πρόβατα ἐκβάλῃ, ἔμπροσθεν αὐτῶν πορεύεται· καὶ
5 τὰ πρόβατα αὐτῷ ἀκολουθεῖ, ὅτι οἴδασι τὴν φωνὴν αὐτοῦ. Ἀλλοτρίῳ
δὲ οὐ μὴ ἀκολουθήσωσιν, ἀλλὰ φεύξονται ἀπ' αὐτοῦ· ὅτι οὐκ οἴδασι
6 τῶν ἀλλοτρίων τὴν φωνήν. Ταύτην τὴν παροιμίαν εἶπεν αὐτοῖς ὁ Ἰη-
σοῦς· ἐκεῖνοι δὲ οὐκ ἔγνωσαν τίνα ἦν, ἃ ἐλάλει αὐτοῖς.
7 Εἶπεν οὖν πάλιν αὐτοῖς ὁ Ἰησοῦς· Ἀμὴν ἀμὴν λέγω ὑμῖν, ὅτι ἐγώ
8 εἰμι ἡ θύρα τῶν προβάτων. Πάντες ὅσοι [πρὸ ἐμοῦ] ἦλθον κλέπται

can be deduced from the present passage, neither the nature of the context, nor the import of the words will, I think, permit us to suppose. The purpose here in view is certainly (according to the opinion of the most eminent of the more recent Commentators) that which has been above detailed. It therefore has reference not to *teachers*, but to *Christians in general*.

1. αὐλήν.] The word means an open hovel, formed by hurdles and wickerwork. By αὐλὴ τῶν προβάτων (Church of the N. T., the kingdom of Christ), is here designated the *Jewish people*, who needed the food of spiritual instruction. See Ezek. xxxiv. 11. Jerem. xxiii. 4. sq. To *enter in by the door*, was probably a proverbial expression, to denote *making a regular ingress*. So Arrian in Epict. finely remarks, Ἀρχὴ φιλοσοφίας παρά γε τοῖς ὡς δεῖ, καὶ κατὰ τὴν θύραν, ἁπτομένοις αὐτῆς, συναίσθησις τῆς αὐτοῦ ἀσθενείας. Christ is called the *door*, as giving an opportunity of entering into heaven. Κλέπτης and λῃστὴς *properly* differ, as our *thief* (or *pilferer*) and *robber*, (or highwayman), the one referring to private stealing, the other to public and violent robbery. Here, however, they have little or no difference, but being *united*, have a force greater than either would bear separately.

3. ὁ θυρωρὸς] i. e. the under-shepherd, in attendance at the door of the αὐλή.

— τῆς φωνῆς α. ἀκούει] i. e. attend to, obey his orders. Φωνῆς denotes those *inarticulate sounds*, as whistling, &c., or certain *words*, such as were addressed to the animals, on which see Recens. Synop. The calling them by their names is illustrated by what Wolf and others adduce; who prove that anciently names were given not only to horses, oxen, dogs, and cats, but also to *sheep*.

4. ἐκβάλῃ] "putteth forth;" for there is no notion of force. So ἐξάγειν and ἐκβάλλειν are indifferently used by the LXX. to express the same Hebrew word.

— ἔμπροσθεν αὐτῶν πορεύεται.] Contrary to the custom which prevails in the West, the Eastern shepherds *precede* their flocks, and lead them by peculiar sounds of the voice. See Ps. xxiii. 2. lxxvii. 20. lxxx. 1. The custom (no doubt introduced by the Moors) still continues in Spain. Yet how ancient was the practice, at least in the *West*, for the sheep to go before, and the shepherd follow, may be inferred from the idea suggested by the Greek word πρόβατον. Probably that custom might have prevailed in the great plains of central Asia, from whence came those early colonists of Greece who introduced the Greek language.

6. παροιμίαν] for παραβολήν; for though the words are *distinguished* in the Classical writers, (the former there signifying a *common saying*, from οἶμος, *via trita*. So our *by-word*) yet they were confounded by the Hellenists.

7. On this and the following passage we may remark that it is entirely *allegorical*. Now all allegory is similitude: but similitude may be considered in various views; and therefore, in one and the same allegory, a person may be considered in many ways. (Rosenm.) There is here not a *mere repetition*, but an explanation or application of the foregoing example. (Kuin. and Tittm.)

Θύρα, like the Heb. פֶּתַח, denotes not only *door*, but *approach*; also, as here, *he who gives it*. Taken in conjunction with what precedes, the primary import of the words must be, that *Christ* is the only way through which mankind can obtain salvation (see ver. 9.); though it may include, in an under sense, that (as Doddr. observes) as a man must observe and pass through the door, in order to his making a regular and unsuspected entrance into a sheep-fold; so he must maintain a proper regard to Christ, in order to his being a true teacher in the Church, and must pass, as it were, through him, or by his authority, into his office. So at xiv. 6, he is called *the way*.

8. πρὸ ἐμοῦ.] These words have perplexed Interpreters of every age. They are *omitted* in very many MSS., Versions, Fathers, and early Edd., and are rejected by Grot. and Campb., and cancelled by Matth.; but on precarious grounds. It is one of the most certain of Critical canons, that an *omission* of words, which have occasioned perplexity to the Commentators, is always to be regarded as suspicious. And there are reasons which make the validity of this Canon stronger in the *Scriptures* than in the Classical writers. The omission might here be officiously made, to save the honour of Moses and the Prophets, especially as the Manichæans denied their Divine legation. *Internal* evidence, therefore, is so strong in favour of these words, as to balance even a *superiority* of external; which, however, does not exist. Besides, the words are almost necessary to make any tolerable sense. They must, then, be regarded as genuine. And the only question is, what is their true *import?* Many ancient and modern Commentators take πρὸ for ἀντὶ, and suppose an ellip. of ἐν τῷ ὀνόματι τοῦ Πατρός μου; understanding it of *false Christs*, as Theudas and Judas of Galilee. This is also maintained by others, who take πρὸ in the usual sense *before*. But the former interpretation is unfounded, and the latter involves an inadmissible ellipsis, and, indeed, an *anachronism;* for, as the best Commentators are agreed, it cannot be proved that there *were* any false Christs previous

εἰσὶ καὶ λῃσταί· ἀλλ᾽ οὐκ ἤκουσαν αὐτῶν τὰ πρόβατα. Ἐγώ εἰμι ἡ 9
θύρα. δι᾽ ἐμοῦ ἐάν τις εἰσέλθῃ, σωθήσεται· καὶ εἰσελεύσεται καὶ
ἐξελεύσεται, καὶ νομὴν εὑρήσει. Ὁ κλέπτης οὐκ ἔρχεται, εἰ μὴ ἵνα 10
κλέψῃ καὶ θύσῃ καὶ ἀπολέσῃ· ἐγὼ ἦλθον, ἵνα ζωὴν ἔχωσι, καὶ περισσὸν

to that time. And if even *one* such could be found, it would not justify the πάντες ὅσοι. One thing is plain, that our Lord could not have meant to include Moses and the Prophets; of whom he every where speaks in terms of the highest reverence. The best solution of this difficulty is supposed to be that of Beng., Rosenm., Campb., and Kuin.; who think that ἦλθον is to be taken of time *recently* past, and up to the present; i. e. "have come;" and that by the term is meant "have lately come in the character of *teachers* of God's people." Now our Lord (say they) throughout this discourse considers himself, viz. as the *supreme* spiritual Shepherd, through whose instruction and grace the under-shepherds must be admitted into his fold, the Church. "In this view (says Campb.) the words are directed chiefly against the Scribes and Pharisees, considered as teachers: whose doctrine was far from breathing the same spirit with his, and whose chief object was not, like that of the good Shepherd, to *feed* and *protect* the flock, but like that of the robber, or of the wolf, to *devour* them." Yet in this there is something not a little harsh: 1. in arbitrarily taking ἦλθον as a kind of Preterite-present; 2. in understanding ἦλθον in the sense "have come, as *teachers*;" for (not to mention that this is inconsistent with the πρὸ ἐμοῦ) our Lord is here not representing himself as a *teacher*, but as *the good Shepherd*; which, as is shewn at ver. 11, must principally involve the idea of *governing*. But how, then, will the parallel hold good between the *Messiah* and the Scribes and Pharisees. In order to remove this difficulty, many have understood οἱ πρὸ ἐμοῦ of *false Christs*. This, however (as we have seen) is at variance with facts. After full and repeated consideration of the words, I am persuaded that the only way to arrive at the truth is to suppose the parallel to be *perfect*, and to keep in view the leading idea in ποιμὴν ὁ καλός. In short, by οἱ πρὸ ἐμοῦ ἦλθον are, I conceive, meant *those who before Christ had come in the character of supreme Shepherd of the people*, and promising access to salvation, as Mediator of the Mosaic covenant. So Gal. iii. 19. the Law is said to have been διαταγεὶς δι᾽ ἀγγέλων ἐν χειρὶ μεσίτου. And at Hebr. viii. 6. ix. 15. xii. 24. the mediator of the new and better covenant is tacitly compared with that of the old and imperfect one. Now that this Mediator under the old Covenant could be no other than the *High Priest* is plain; and is *proved* by the parallel drawn by St. Paul, in his Epistle to the Hebrews, between Christ and the Mediator of the first covenant, the *High Priest*; *first*, between Moses, the original Mediator, and Christ, ch. iii.; and *then* between the successive Mediators, the High Priests for the time being, ch. iv. 15. οὐ γὰρ ἔχομεν ἀρχιερέα μὴ δυνάμενον, &c. ἀλλά, &c. Again, ch. v. 1. it is said, πᾶς γὰρ ἀρχιερεὺς ἐξ ἀνθρώπων λαμβανόμενος; which is exemplified by *Aaron*, the first High Priest. So also at ch. vii. he continues the parallel between these mediators, the High Priests who *die*, and he who is a High Priest *for ever* after the order of Melchisedec, ἀπάτωρ, ἀμήτωρ, ἀγενεαλόγητος: who οὐ κατὰ νόμον ἐντολῆς σαρκικῆς γέγονεν, ἀλλὰ κατὰ δύναμιν ζωῆς ἀκαταλύτου, ver. 16. So also at ver. 23. he contrasts the *High Priests* and the *Messiah* thus: καὶ οἱ μὲν πλείονές εἰσι γεγονότες ἱερεῖς διὰ τὸ θανάτῳ κωλύεσθαι παραμένειν· ὁ δὲ, &c. and ver. 26. τοιοῦτος γὰρ ἡμῖν ἔπρεπεν εἶναι ἀρχιερεὺς, ὅσιος, ἄκακος, ἀμίαντος, &c. See also ver. 27 and 28. At ch. viii. & ix. he proceeds in the parallel, instituting a minute comparison. Thus it is evident that the expression in question, οἱ πρὸ ἐμοῦ ἦλθον may very well mean *those who before Christ had sustained the office of temporary mediators between God and man*, but who were now disannulled by the disannulling of the old covenant, and the coming of a new and better Mediator, the *Lord of the Temple* himself. But how, it may be asked, does this character of κλέπται καὶ λ. correspond to the High Priests? I answer, 1. it has been admitted by almost every Commentator that πάντες may very well be taken to denote πολλοί. 2. It is almost universally agreed, that by κλέπται καὶ λῃσταί we are only to understand *rapacious persons, chiefly intent on gain*. And that most of those under the *second Temple* at least were such, the History of Josephus will abundantly testify: nay, it is clear that almost *all of them* for the last 60 or 70 years had been such; persons who *bought* their office, and then made as much of it as they could, for the short time they were allowed to hold it. The traits of their characters, as delineated by Josephus, exactly correspond to those adverted to in the present comparison, vv. 10, 12, & 13, namely, *avarice* and the most cruel *extortion*, united with the utmost timidity and neglect of *protecting* those under their governance. That our Lord meant *chiefly* the High Priests of a recent period, is plain from the use of the *present* tense εἰσί. Now that the *sheep* should not listen to *their* spiritual admonitions, might be expected; and that they *did* not, is attested by the horrid picture presented by Josephus of the state of society at the time in question, which was even worse than that of Greece just before the Peloponnesian war, so inimitably depicted by Thucydides.

9. ἐάν τις — εὑρήσει.] Commentators are not agreed whether these words are to be referred to *shepherds* (i. e. spiritual pastors) or *sheep*, i. e. their *flock*. Some take one, and some the other, and Tittm. *both*. But if the view taken of the foregoing verse be (as I doubt not it *is*) correct, they can refer only to the people: indeed they could not be referred to *pastors* without great harshness. Ἡ θύρα, i. e. the [only] Mediator, through whom is an access to the Father. See Rom. v. 2. Eph. ii. 18. comp. with Heb. ix. 15. Σωθ. may thus be interpreted: "shall be placed in a state of salvation." And the words εἰσελεύσεται — εὑρήσει form a *pastoral image* expressive of undisturbed enjoyment of the blessings in question.

10. ὁ κλέπτης.] "The false teacher," i. e. "the false teachers;" for this is (as appears from ver. 1.) a singular, being taken for a *genus*; on which see Middlet. Gr. Art. The terms θύσῃ and ἀπολέσῃ are *graphic* (signifying respectively "butcher and destroy"), and describe what was often done by the roving bands of marauders, who then infested Judæa, and who used to *destroy* what they

11 ἔχωσιν. [c] Ἐγώ εἰμι ὁ ποιμὴν ὁ καλός. ὁ ποιμὴν ὁ καλὸς τὴν ψυχὴν c Isa. 40. 11. Ezek. 34. 23. & 37. 24.
12 αὐτοῦ τίθησιν ὑπὲρ τῶν προβάτων· ὁ μισθωτὸς δὲ καὶ οὐκ ὢν ποι-
μήν, οὗ οὐκ εἰσὶ τὰ πρόβατα ἴδια, θεωρεῖ τὸν λύκον ἐρχόμενον, καὶ
ἀφίησι τὰ πρόβατα καὶ φεύγει· καὶ ὁ λύκος ἁρπάζει αὐτά, καὶ σκορ-
13 πίζει τὰ πρόβατα. Ὁ δὲ μισθωτὸς φεύγει, ὅτι μισθωτός ἐστι, καὶ
14 οὐ μέλει αὐτῷ περὶ τῶν προβάτων. Ἐγώ εἰμι ὁ ποιμὴν ὁ καλός·
15 καὶ γινώσκω τὰ ἐμὰ καὶ γινώσκομαι ὑπὸ τῶν ἐμῶν, καθὼς γινώσκει
με ὁ Πατὴρ κἀγὼ γινώσκω τὸν Πατέρα· καὶ τὴν ψυχήν μου τίθημι

could not carry off. See Note on Acts xx. 29. The words περισσὸν ἔχωσιν serve to strengthen the sense of the preceding clause.

11. ἐγὼ—καλός.] The image is here changed, and another confirmation of what was said is introduced, in which our Lord represents himself under the emblem of the *good shepherd*. By ὁ ποιμὴν ὁ καλὸς many Commentators think is simply meant "an enlightened teacher." But this is passing over the article; and to this interpretation it is justly objected by Tittm., that ποιμὴν has no where else the sense *teacher*, but usually involves the idea of *governing*, *protecting*, *taking care of*. Thus in the O. T. *kings* are often called *shepherds*, as also in Homer and Eschylus. So in the N. T. ποιμένες is the name given to the *Curatores* Ecclesiæ, otherwise called ἐπίσκοποι, as Eph. iv. 11.; and in 1 Pet. ii. 25. our Lord is called ποιμὴν καὶ ἐπίσκοπος τῶν ψυχῶν ὑμῶν. And as in Heb. xiii. 20. Paul calls our Lord τὸν ποιμένα τῶν προβάτων τὸν μέγαν, so was he foretold under that character in the prophecies of the O. T. See Is. xl. 11. Ez. xxxiv. 12—33. Zech. xiii. 7. Mic. v. 4.

—ὁ ποιμὴν—προβάτων.] The phrase ψυχὴν τιθέναι answers to the Heb. שׂוּם נֶפֶשׁ, which literally denote *profundere* vitam: but, in use, generally denote only to *hazard* one's life. And this sense is here adopted by many of the most eminent Commentators. By the ancient and most modern Commentators, however, the *former* is assigned; and rightly: for though the *restricted* sense of the phrase is agreeable to the *natural* import of the words, yet the *full* sense is demanded by the *figurative* one as applied to the Redeemer. Our Lord, indeed, here only *hints* at what, at ver. 17, he plainly expresses. The sense, then, is: "As the good shepherd hazards his life for his flock, so does the Messiah, represented by the Prophets under that character, lay down his life for his spiritual flock, the human race."

12. ὁ μισθωτὸς δὲ, &c.] This is said in order to illustrate the character of the good shepherd by contrast with the *bad*; who is called a *hireling*, not because *all* hirelings are unfaithful, but that they are *generally*, more or less, such. Ὁ μισθωτὸς must, like ὁ κλέπτης and ὁ ποιμὴν ὁ καλὸς before, denote a whole class of persons. And Lampe, Kuin., and Tittm. rightly suppose that the Ecclesiastical rulers of that time are meant, as at ver. 8. This sudden transition from one metaphor to another is Hebraic. See Kuin. By the term μισθωτὸς is perhaps *also* denoted their *avarice*, and preference of the honours and emoluments of their office to discharging its duties.

—οὗ οὐκ εἰσὶ τὰ πρόβ.] This shows, that the shepherd is supposed to be also the *owner* of the sheep; such as in Hom. Odyss. iv. 87, is called indifferently ἄναξ (master) and ποιμήν.

14. γινώσκω—ἐμῶν.] These words figuratively designate the mutual love and attachment of the great Shepherd and his spiritual flock. Comp. v. 15 with 17. So Heb. יָדַע. See Amos iii. 2.

15. καθὼς γινώσκει—Πατέρα.] These words are closely connected with the preceding (from which they are unnaturally disjoined by the division of verses), being an illustration by similitude of what was there said, q. d. I both know my sheep, and am known of them, even as the Father knoweth me, and I know the Father. Dr. Burton thinks that the members of this sentence, if properly disposed, would be as follows: Γινώσκω τὰ ἐμὰ, καθὼς γινώσκω τὸν Πατέρα· καὶ γινώσκομαι ὑπὸ τῶν ἐμῶν, καθὼς γινώσκει με ὁ Πατήρ.

—τὴν ψυχὴν—προβάτων.] Our Lord here *applies* what he had already said of a good shepherd, to *himself*; and openly declares that he shall *offer up his life* for men, and for their salvation. By *what means* and *how* that death is available to the salvation of men, we are not clearly informed. We may, however, suppose it to be as follows. Our Lord describes the sheep for whom he lays down his life as being in extreme peril (see vv. 10 & 12); and St. Paul calls those for whom Christ died *weak*, *sinful*, &c., but to be preserved from wrath. Thus in Matth. xx. 28, where our Lord is said δοῦναι τὴν ψυχὴν αὐτοῦ λύτρον ἀντὶ πολλῶν. Now λύτρον denotes the *price* of redemption, i. e. the money given, or the sacrifice offered, by which any one shall be redeemed from peril and punishment,—and what is given, 1. *for* another, in *his place* and in his *stead*: 2. that the other should be liberated from punishment; 3. that it should be sufficient, and not require any *other* price. See Is. liii. 10. Hence it is plain what was the *purpose* of the death of Christ, and for what *causes* he laid down his life. He died, 1. in the place and stead of men: 2. to obtain their liberation from the punishment of sin, or to obtain pardon of their sin; 3. that his death should be sufficient to obtain the pardon of sin. Those therefore are in grievous error, who maintain that Christ died only to confirm the truth of his doctrines, or the certainty of the promises respecting the grace of God, and the pardon of sin; since for neither of these purposes would the death of Christ have been necessary. Nay, the truth and certainty of both are sufficiently established from other proofs; neither does our Lord say that he lays down his life for his *doctrine*, but for his *sheep*. Hence it is clear that our Lord called himself ποιμήν, not inasmuch as he was an enlightened and holy *teacher of religion*; but in a far sublimer sense, namely, inasmuch as by his death he obtained the *pardon of sins*, and the salvation of men. (Tittm.) The lax dogmas of some recent heresiarchs are strongly contrasted with the uncontaminated orthodoxy of an Apostolic Father, as

d Ezek. 37. 22. ὑπὲρ τῶν προβάτων. [d] Καὶ ἄλλα πρόβατα ἔχω, ἃ οὐκ ἔστιν ἐκ τῆς 16
αὐλῆς ταύτης· κἀκεῖνά με δεῖ ἀγαγεῖν, καὶ τῆς φωνῆς μου ἀκούσουσι·
καὶ γενήσεται μία ποίμνη, εἷς ποιμήν. Διὰ τοῦτο ὁ Πατήρ με ἀγαπᾷ, ὅτι 17
ἐγὼ τίθημι τὴν ψυχήν μου, ἵνα πάλιν λάβω αὐτήν. Οὐδεὶς αἴρει αὐτὴν 18
ἀπ' ἐμοῦ· ἀλλ' ἐγὼ τίθημι αὐτὴν ἀπ' ἐμαυτοῦ. ἐξουσίαν ἔχω θεῖναι αὐτήν, καὶ ἐξουσίαν ἔχω πάλιν λαβεῖν αὐτήν. Ταύτην τὴν ἐντολὴν ἔλαβον
παρὰ τοῦ Πατρός μου. Σχίσμα οὖν πάλιν ἐγένετο ἐν τοῖς Ἰουδαίοις διὰ 19
e Supra 7. 20. & 8. 48, 52. τοὺς λόγους τούτους. [e] Ἔλεγον δὲ πολλοὶ ἐξ αὐτῶν· Δαιμόνιον ἔχει καὶ 20
μαίνεται· τί αὐτοῦ ἀκούετε; Ἄλλοι ἔλεγον· Ταῦτα τὰ ῥήματα οὐκ ἔστι 21
δαιμονιζομένου· μὴ δαιμόνιον δύναται τυφλῶν ὀφθαλμοὺς ἀνοίγειν;
f 1 Macc. 4. 59. [f] ΈΓΕΝΕΤΟ δὲ τὰ ἐγκαίνια ἐν [τοῖς] Ἱεροσολύμοις, καὶ χειμὼν ἦν· 22
καὶ περιεπάτει ὁ Ἰησοῦς ἐν τῷ ἱερῷ ἐν τῇ στοᾷ [τοῦ] Σολομῶνος. 23

follows: Ἐν ἀγάπῃ προσελάβετο ἡμᾶς ὁ δεσπότης, διὰ τὴν ἀγάπην, ἣν εἶχεν πρὸς ἡμᾶς, τὸ αἷμα αὐτοῦ ἔδωκεν ὑπὲρ ἡμῶν ὁ Χριστὸς ὁ κύριος ἡμῶν, ἐν θελήματι Θεοῦ, καὶ τὴν σάρκα ὑπὲρ τῆς σαρκὸς ἡμῶν, καὶ τὴν ψυχὴν ὑπὲρ τῶν ψυχῶν ἡμῶν. Clemens Rom. 1 Epist. ad Corinth. § 49.

16. ἄλλα πρόβατα — ταύτης.] The Jews and Gentiles are here represented under the image of two different flocks, inclosed in separate folds. By the ἄλλα πρόβατα are designated the Gentiles; and by τῆς αὐλῆς ταύτης, the *Jews*. Ἀγαγεῖν is for προσαγαγεῖν, bring to [this fold]. Ἄγειν and its derivatives are frequently employed as pastoral terms. Our Lord calls the Gentiles *his sheep, by prolepsis*, because he had marked them as his own, was about to lay down his life for their salvation, and foresaw that many would shortly embrace his religion, which he expresses in the words τῆς φωνῆς μου ἀκούσουσι. "Thus (says Tittm.) our Lord predicts the future admission of the Gentiles to the Christian flock, and the joint participation of them and the Jews in the blessings obtained by him, under one and the same Lord, so that he might be the author of salvation not to *one only*, but to *all* the nations of the universe." Μία, *one only, one and the same*, i. e. in having (whatever may be their diversities) the same common Saviour.

17. ἵνα πάλιν λάβω αὐτήν.] The best Commentators are agreed that the ἵνα is not *causal*, or denoting *end* and *purpose*, but declarative of the future, or the *event*, and is to be rendered *ita tamen ut*.

18. οὐδεὶς αἴρει αὐτὴν ἀπ' ἐμοῦ] "no one taketh it from me" [by force]. We may paraphrase the passage thus: "No one [not even the Father] compelleth me to die for my flock. I have, of my own will undertaken to lay down my life for it. By the same will I shall return again to life." On the voluntary death of Christ see Note on Matt. xvi. 21.

— ταύτην — Πατρός μου] "This charge received I from my Father." In this whole passage our Lord affirms that he is about to undertake death spontaneously; that the malice of those who may plot against his life could avail nothing, even were it *not* decreed that he should undergo death for the salvation of his people; that no force could take away his life, if he were unwilling to part with it; that he freely lays down that life for the salvation of his flock; and that if they shall kill him, it will not be without his own consent. He asserts, moreover, that he lays down his life, so, however, as to receive it back; and therefore that his death is not to be considered as coming under the common law of mortality, by which all that go down to the tomb return to the dust; but that it is altogether peculiar to itself; since, after a few days, he will rise from the sepulchre and return to life. He then affirms that his death happens not by any *fate* or *necessity*, but by the eternal *counsels* of his Father. (Tittm.) Ἐντολὴν is to be understood οἰκονομικῶς, in reference to the mediatorial capacity in which Christ stood.

20. δαιμόνιον — μαίνεται.] See Note on vii. 20.

22. τὰ ἐγκαίνια.] The word answers in the Sept. to the Hebr. חנכה, *handselling* or *initiation*; and in the N. T. denotes the *encænium*, or festival of eight days, occurring in the month Kisleu, instituted by Judas Maccabæus in commemoration of the purification of the Temple from Heathen pollution. Unlike all *other* festivals, which were kept only at *Jerusalem*, this was celebrated throughout the whole of Judæa. And as lights were kept burning in every house throughout each night of the festival, it is called by Josephus, Ant. xii. 7, 7. φῶτα.

— καὶ χειμὼν ἦν.] The best Commentators in general take χειμὼν to denote rainy or wintry weather, as in Matt. xvi. 3. Acts xxvii. 20. Ezra x. 9. But there the sense is, *a storm*, or *tempest*. And the signification *wintry weather*, though it is not unfrequent in the Classical writers, as Thucyd. iv. 6, and vi. 2, yet does not occur in the Scriptures; nor is there any good reason to abandon the common interpretation, "it was winter;" for this circumstance might, as Beng. suggests, be added for the information of those readers who knew not the *time* of the feast.

23. τοῦ Σολ.] Τοῦ is omitted in some MSS. and early Edd., and is cancelled by almost all Editors from Matthæi to Scholz. But the authority is insufficient to warrant that; especially as its absence violates the propriety of language, by which the Article is either prefixed to both the governing and governed nouns, or else is omitted before both. As little reason is there to cancel the τοῖς before Ἱεροσολ. just before, as many Editors have done.

This portico was called *Solomon's*, as having been built by Solomon; being the part of Solomon's temple which had been left undestroyed by the Babylonians, and was therefore allowed to remain, though in a dilapidated state. There were porticos erected all round the temple; but

24 Ἐκύκλωσαν οὖν αὐτὸν οἱ Ἰουδαῖοι, καὶ ἔλεγον αὐτῷ· Ἕως πότε τὴν
25 ψυχὴν ἡμῶν αἴρεις; εἰ σὺ εἶ ὁ Χριστὸς, εἰπὲ ἡμῖν παῤῥησίᾳ. [g] Ἀπε- g Supra 5. 36. Infra ver. 38.
κρίθη αὐτοῖς ὁ Ἰησοῦς· Εἶπον ὑμῖν, καὶ οὐ πιστεύετε. τὰ ἔργα ἃ
ἐγὼ ποιῶ ἐν τῷ ὀνόματι τοῦ Πατρός μου, ταῦτα μαρτυρεῖ περὶ ἐμοῦ.
26 [h] Ἀλλ᾽ ὑμεῖς οὐ πιστεύετε· οὐ γάρ ἐστε ἐκ τῶν προβάτων τῶν ἐμῶν· h Supra 8. 19.
27 καθὼς εἶπον ὑμῖν, τὰ πρόβατα τὰ ἐμὰ τῆς φωνῆς μου ἀκούει, κἀγὼ
28 γινώσκω αὐτά· καὶ ἀκολουθοῦσί μοι, κἀγὼ ζωὴν αἰώνιον δίδωμι
αὐτοῖς· καὶ οὐ μὴ ἀπόλωνται εἰς τὸν αἰῶνα, καὶ οὐχ ἁρπάσει τὶς αὐτὰ
29 ἐκ τῆς χειρός μου. [i] Ὁ Πατήρ μου, ὃς δέδωκέ μοι, μείζων πάντων i Infra 14. 28.
ἐστί· καὶ οὐδεὶς δύναται ἁρπάζειν ἐκ τῆς χειρὸς τοῦ Πατρός μου. k Infra 17. 11, 22.
30 [k] Ἐγὼ καὶ ὁ Πατὴρ ἕν ἐσμεν. [l] Ἐβάστασαν οὖν πάλιν λίθους οἱ l Supra 8. 59.

this fronted the East. Porticos were common in the Heathen temples likewise, and were erected for the accommodation of the priests and worshippers in general; both for walking in inclement weather, (So Cebes, cited by Wets.; ἐτυγχάνομεν περιπατοῦντες ἐν τῷ τοῦ Κρόνου ἱερῷ) and for the purpose of Teachers communicating oral instruction sometimes in walking, to their followers, from which circumstance two principal Sects of Philosophers, namely, the Stoics and the Peripatetics, derived their names.

24. αἴρεις.] Euthym. well explains: αἰωρεῖς, ἀναρτᾷς μεταξὺ πίστεως καὶ ἀπιστίας. The full sense is: "keep us in suspense between hope and fear, belief and disbelief." So Philostr. cited by Blackwall; κἀμὲ πάνυ αἴρει ὁ λόγος ὃν εἴρηκε, and ἐπαίρειν frequently occurs in the sense to *buoy up with hope*.

25. εἶπον ὑ.] "I have told you [who I am]."

— τὰ ἔργα — ἐμοῦ.] The sense is: "[Nay] the works (i. e. the miracles) which I do by the authority of my Father, these bear witness of me [that I am sent by Him]." Of this figurative use of μαρτυρεῖν, Wets. adduces an example from Heraclid. de Deo: Ἔργα δεῖ μαρτυρεῖν, οἷα ἡλίου· νὺξ αὐτῷ καὶ ἡμέρα μαρτυροῦσιν, αὔρα αὐτῷ μαρτυρεῖ, γῆ ὅλη καρποφοροῦσα μάρτυς — οὐρανὸς μαρτυρία. Simil. 19th Psalm· "The Heavens *declare* the glory of God," &c. This *authority* from God, however, our Lord had, not as a mere legate, but as being partaker of the Divine attributes. See v. 17, sq.

26. οὐ γάρ ἐστε, &c.] This suggests the *cause* of their unbelief; namely, that they are not of his flock, will not suffer themselves to be brought into it, nor are willing to acquire the proper dispositions for it. With the words καθὼς εἶπον ὑμῖν Commentators are somewhat perplexed, since Christ had no where before told them that they were not his sheep. To remove this difficulty, it seems, some ancient Critics cancelled the clause; for to no other cause can we well ascribe the omission of it in several ancient, but *altered*, MSS. and some Versions. Nor is it easy to believe (what some modern Critics aver) that the words were foisted in by the Scribes; nay it is incredible that *such* a clause, by no means necessary to the sense, should have crept into nearly all the MSS. As to *Versions*, they are not good authority for *omissions*, and especially of what is perplexing. There can be no doubt that the clause is genuine; and though we find nothing of this kind said in our Lord's preceding discourses, yet may it not have reference to something said, but not *recorded* by St. John? This is preferable to supposing, with some, that it was *indirectly* expressed; i. e. *implied*, in our Lord's words. However, as there can be no doubt that there is a reference to the preceding discourse of the good shepherd, (for our Lord now proceeds to resume the allegory,) and since, though our Lord does *not* there use *these* words, but *does*, in *fact*, say (v. 3.) that "*his sheep* hear his voice;" so it is probable, that καθὼς, &c. belong to those words, and should therefore be joined with the following verse, as in some MSS., Versions, and Euthym., with the approbation of Pearce, Campb., Vat., Tittm.

27. τῆς φωνῆς μου ἀκ.] i. e. give heed to, obey my commands. By τὰ πρόβατα τὰ ἐμὰ are meant such of the sheep as acknowledge their shepherd. Γινώσκω, I acknowledge them as mine, provide for their welfare. See v. 14. Ἀκολουθοῦσί μοι, i. e. in faith and obedience.

28. οὐ μὴ ἀπόλωνται εἰς τὸν αἰῶνα.] Tittm. thus paraphrases: "At no time, neither in this life, nor in death, nor after death, to all eternity, shall any thing happen to them that shall deprive them of salvation." See John viii. 51. The words following καὶ οὐχ ἁρπάσει — μου are *confirmatory* of the above promise; and in the next verse is suggested the *reason why* no one can snatch these faithful disciples from him; namely, that the *Father* hath delivered them to him, in order to be preserved and redeemed; that omnipotent Being in whom are the issues of life and death, both temporal and spiritual. The whole passage bears strong attestation to the Divinity of Christ; but gives, when properly understood, no countenance to the doctrine, that the elect can never fall away and perish; having, in truth, no relation to *personal election*, or *final perseverance*.

30. ἐγὼ — ἐσμεν.] On the exact sense of ἕν ἐσμεν Commentators are not agreed. Some ancient, and most modern ones, understand them of *unity of will, purpose, counsels, and works*. This they support from John xvii. 21—23., and especially from the verse preceding. But so sudden are the transitions, and so excursive the thoughts in our Lord's discourses, as recorded in this Gospel, that the argument drawn from thence is precarious. By far the greater part of the ancient and earlier modern Commentators understand the words of *physical unity of essence*, including *moral* unity. This Lampe has shown, was the opinion of almost every one of the Orthodox Fathers. Tittm., however, while he rejects the first mentioned interpretation, declines embracing the latter; and takes the words of *unity of energy and power*. And indeed this is sup-

Ἰουδαῖοι, ἵνα λιθάσωσιν αὐτόν. Ἀπεκρίθη αὐτοῖς ὁ Ἰησοῦς· Πολλὰ 31
καλὰ ἔργα ἔδειξα ὑμῖν ἐκ τοῦ Πατρός μου· διὰ ποῖον αὐτῶν ἔργον 32
λιθάζετέ με; Ἀπεκρίθησαν αὐτῷ οἱ Ἰουδαῖοι, λέγοντες· Περὶ καλοῦ 33
ἔργου οὐ λιθάζομέν σε, ἀλλὰ περὶ βλασφημίας, καὶ ὅτι σὺ ἄνθρωπος
m Psal. 82. 6. ὢν ποιεῖς σεαυτὸν Θεόν. [m] Ἀπεκρίθη αὐτοῖς ὁ Ἰησοῦς· Οὐκ ἔστι 34
γεγραμμένον ἐν τῷ νόμῳ ὑμῶν, Ἐγὼ εἶπα, θεοί ἐστε; εἰ ἐκείνους εἶπε 35
θεούς, πρὸς οὓς ὁ λόγος τοῦ Θεοῦ ἐγένετο, (καὶ οὐ δύναται λυθῆναι
ἡ γραφή,) ὃν ὁ Πατὴρ ἡγίασε καὶ ἀπέστειλεν εἰς τὸν κόσμον, ὑμεῖς 36
λέγετε· Ὅτι βλασφημεῖς, ὅτι εἶπον· Υἱὸς τοῦ Θεοῦ εἰμι; Εἰ οὐ 37
n Infra 14. 10. 11. & 17. 21, 22. ποιῶ τὰ ἔργα τοῦ Πατρός μου, μὴ πιστεύετέ μοι· [n] εἰ δὲ ποιῶ, κἂν 38
ἐμοὶ μὴ πιστεύητε, τοῖς ἔργοις πιστεύσατε· ἵνα γνῶτε καὶ πιστεύσητε,
ὅτι ἐν ἐμοὶ ὁ Πατὴρ κἀγὼ ἐν αὐτῷ. Ἐζήτουν οὖν πάλιν αὐτὸν πιάσαι· 39
καὶ ἐξῆλθεν ἐκ τῆς χειρὸς αὐτῶν.

ported by the preceding context. For (as Tittm. argues) 1. our Lord at v. 28. attributes the same to himself as to his Father. 2. He shows the reason why nothing can be taken from the Father; namely, *because He is All-mighty*. 3. A reason is added why nothing can be taken from *Him* any more than from his Father, *because they are one*, viz. in the work of *power*, &c. This, Tittm. argues, implies union of *attributes*; and where there is one and the same divine power and attributes, there must be one and the same *Divine nature*. Whichever interpretation be adopted, the words can import no less than a claim to equality with the Father (and consequently prove the Deity *of our Lord*), just as the passage at viii. 58. which, and the present, the Jews must have so understood; otherwise they would not have attempted to stone him for blasphemy, exclaiming, Σὺ ἄνθρωπος ὢν ποιεῖς σεαυτὸν Θεόν. Indeed had he been aught but God, one with the Father, common honour and ingenuousness would have required him to disavow the interpretation they had put upon his words.

31. ἐβάστασαν] "took up." This signification is thought to be Hellenistic; but I have, in Recens. Synop., adduced two examples from Antiphanes and Josephus.

32. πολλὰ καλὰ ἔργα ἔδειξα ὑ.] The sense is: "Many benefits have I conferred upon you." The ἔργα relates not only to the wonderful and salutary *miracles* exhibited by Jesus, but also to his *whole course of action* in promulgating the Gospel of grace. Ἔδειξα may, indeed, seem to have reference most to *miracles*, but it often in the Classical writers simply means, *edere, præstare*, to perform. Of this Wetstein cites examples, to which I have in Recens. Synop. added others. Ἐκ τοῦ Πατρός μ. signifies "in virtue of the powers vested in me by my Father."

34. οὐκ ἔστι γεγραμμένον, &c.] In repelling the charge of blasphemy, our Lord, for reasons which it were irreverent too nicely to scan, was pleased not to *fully* disclose his intimate conjunction with the Father; and why he called God his Father, and himself the Son of God. He contents himself with using a sort of argument quite in the Jewish style; (and therefore adapted to make an impression on his hearers) arguing with them on the ground of what they themselves admitted; namely, that He was a *Prophet* sent from God; and showing that, even on *that* supposition, he had a right to the title which they refused him. Our Lord alludes to Ps. lxxxii. 6. where judges and magistrates are called *Elohim*, sons of the most high God.

35. πρὸς οὓς ὁ λόγος τοῦ Θεοῦ ἐγ.] These words are well explained by Tittm. thus: "to whom was delivered the command mentioned just before, namely, to plead the cause of the destitute, &c. The words καὶ οὐ δύναται λυθῆναι ἡ γραφὴ are to be taken in a restricted sense, to signify, 'And the Scriptures cannot be taken exception to,' cannot be thought wrong."

36. ἡγίασε] "has set apart," as the τὸν ἅγιον τοῦ Θεοῦ; for ἁγιάζειν, like the Heb. קָדַשׁ, signifies to set apart from common use to a sacred purpose. It is justly remarked by Tittm. that our Lord did *not* (as the Socinians say) argue thus, to signify that he was to be called God, and Son of God, in no other sense than that in which those judges were so styled; namely, with respect to *office*; much less to decline the application of the word in the same sense as of the Father; as is evident from what precedes. He merely uses an argument *ab exemplo* (what the Philosophers call an *instance*) and argues *ab concessis*, q. d. *Magistrates* are called divine, and sons of God, without injury to the Deity: nay, God himself hath so called them. May not *I*, then, by a similar right, be so called, whom God hath sent into the world, and to whom he hath committed a charge so salutary to the human race.

37, 38. The sense of the passage (which is expressed *more Judaico*) is simply this: "That I *am* Son of God, the Messiah, and am most closely united with the Deity, my *works* show; q. d. If I had not done the same *works* which my Father doth, ye might refuse credit to my *words*: but since they bear the same stamp, you should at least believe *them*, if you will not believe my *words*; and then you would understand that the Father is in me, and I in the Father." By these words our Lord manifestly declares himself to be Son of God, not in that sense in which the Jewish Rulers were so called, but in a more sublime one; not in respect to the *office* he sustains, but the *nature* which he bears, since he does the same works as the Father. (Tittm.)

The words ἐν ἐμοὶ ὁ Πατὴρ — αὐτῷ plainly (as Tittm. remarks) indicate generally *intimate connexion*, and here, by the force of the context, *conjunction* of one and the same energy. The Father was *in* the Son, the Son *in* the Father;

40 Καὶ ἀπῆλθε πάλιν πέραν τοῦ Ἰορδάνου, εἰς τὸν τόπον ὅπου ἦν
41 Ἰωάννης τὸ πρῶτον βαπτίζων· καὶ ἔμεινεν ἐκεῖ. Καὶ πολλοὶ ἦλθον
πρὸς αὐτὸν, καὶ ἔλεγον· Ὅτι Ἰωάννης μὲν σημεῖον ἐποίησεν οὐδέν·
42 πάντα δὲ ὅσα εἶπεν Ἰωάννης περὶ τούτου ἀληθῆ ἦν. καὶ ἐπίστευσαν
πολλοὶ ἐκεῖ εἰς αὐτόν.

1 XI. ἮΝ δέ τις ἀσθενῶν Λάζαρος ἀπὸ Βηθανίας, ἐκ τῆς κώμης
2 Μαρίας καὶ Μάρθας τῆς ἀδελφῆς αὐτῆς. [o] Ἦν δὲ Μαρία ἡ ἀλείψασα o Infra 12. 3. Matt. 26. 7. Mark 14. 3.
τὸν Κύριον μύρῳ, καὶ ἐκμάξασα τοὺς πόδας αὐτοῦ ταῖς θριξὶν αὐτῆς,
3 ἧς ὁ ἀδελφὸς Λάζαρος ἠσθένει. Ἀπέστειλαν οὖν αἱ ἀδελφαὶ πρὸς
4 αὐτὸν, λέγουσαι· Κύριε, ἴδε, ὃν φιλεῖς, ἀσθενεῖ. Ἀκούσας δὲ ὁ Ιησοῦς
εἶπεν· Αὕτη ἡ ἀσθένεια οὐκ ἔστι πρὸς θάνατον, ἀλλ' ὑπὲρ τῆς δόξης
5 τοῦ Θεοῦ, ἵνα δοξασθῇ ὁ Υἱὸς τοῦ Θεοῦ δι' αὐτῆς. Ἠγάπα δὲ ὁ
6 Ἰησοῦς τὴν Μάρθαν καὶ τὴν ἀδελφὴν αὐτῆς, καὶ τὸν Λάζαρον. Ὡς
οὖν ἤκουσεν ὅτι ἀσθενεῖ, τότε μὲν ἔμεινεν ἐν ᾧ ἦν τόπῳ δύο ἡμέρας.
7 Ἔπειτα μετὰ τοῦτο λέγει τοῖς μαθηταῖς· Ἄγωμεν εἰς τὴν Ἰουδαίαν
8 πάλιν. Λέγουσιν αὐτῷ οἱ μαθηταί· Ῥαββὶ, νῦν ἐζήτουν σε λιθάσαι
9 οἱ Ἰουδαῖοι, καὶ πάλιν ὑπάγεις ἐκεῖ; Ἀπεκρίθη ὁ Ἰησοῦς· Οὐχὶ δώ-
δεκά εἰσιν ὧραι τῆς ἡμέρας; Ἐάν τις περιπατῇ ἐν τῇ ἡμέρᾳ, οὐ

inasmuch as the Son hath the same as the Father, and can do, and doth the same with the Father; Comp. v. 17. See Bulli Opera, p. 39, 40.

39. ἐξῆλθεν] "subduxit se." It is not necessary to press so much, as some Commentators do, on this expression, which simply means, "he escaped out of their hands." See Note on viii. 59.

40. πέραν τοῦ Ἰορδ.] i. e. Bethany, or Bethabara, on the other side of the Jordan. See Note on i. 28.

— ἔμεινεν ἐκεῖ] "abode there;" which, however, does not preclude the supposition of Lampe and Tittm. that he took, during the four months of his sojourn there, some journeys into Peræa.

41. Ἔλεγον, &c.] They reasoned thus: "John worked no *miracle*, yet we believed in his divine mission. And now we see it amply proved by the *miracles* worked by Him to whom John professed to be but a forerunner."

XI. The Evangelist now proceeds to narrate the closing scenes of our Lord's life, what is related in this Chapter having taken place only a few days before the Passover on which he suffered death. The raising of Lazarus being a work of all that Christ had hitherto done the most stupendous, was studiously recorded by the Evangelist, as illustrating the majesty of our Lord. No wonder, therefore, that infidels and sceptics should have used every exertion to destroy its credibility. Their cavils, however, have been triumphantly refuted by Lardner and others, and the quibbling objections of the Rationalists of our own times have been satisfactorily answered by the best Theologians, both British and Foreign.

1. ἀσθενῶν.] The word is used not only of indisposition, but also of dangerous illness, whether acute or chronic; as Xen. Anab. i. 1. Matt. x. 8. Luke iv. 40. vii. 10. The earnest representation sent by the two sisters shows that Lazarus was in imminent danger. Ἀπὸ Βηθ., [an inhabitant] of Bethany. The ἐκ just after is used in a similar way; and the use of *both* where *one* would have sufficed, is characteristic of St. John.

2. ἡ ἀλείψασα.] Said, by anticipation, for who [afterwards] anointed. The figure is not unusual where the action (as here) speedily followed, and is well known. See Matt. xxvi. 13. On this circumstance see Note on Matt. xxvi. 7.

4. οὐκ ἔστι πρὸς θάν.] "is not to be fatal," "will not finally terminate in death." Such is the best interpretation of this dubious expression, which it is better to consider as a *popular form*, than to understand by *death* the *decretory* death by which all must return to earth. The Classical writers use in this sense ἐπὶ θανάτῳ. Ἀλλ' ὑπὲρ, &c. "but is meant to illustrate the glory of God," namely, by the Son being thereby glorified. See ix. 3.

The best Commentators are agreed in considering this verse as the answer sent by our Lord to the sisters. "Our Lord (observes Euthym.) sent this *predictive* answer in order to comfort them. But he himself stayed some time longer, waiting till Lazarus should actually expire and be buried; that no one might say that he had raised him when not yet dead, but only in a fainting fit, or trance."

6. ἔμεινεν — δύο ἡμέρας] i. e. he did not come to Bethany till Lazarus had been dead four days.

7. ἔπειτα μετὰ τοῦτο.] A sort of pleonasm, but of which many examples from the best writers are adduced by Wets. and Kypke. However, we have only εἶτα μετὰ τοῦτο, or ταῦτα, never ἔπειτα, which was probably confined to the *popular* phraseology.

8. καὶ πάλιν ὑπάγεις ἐκεῖ;] The words are (by the expression of wonder) strongly *dissuasive*, and were suggested by some fear for Jesus, notwithstanding their conviction of his divine power to save himself, and also by some apprehension for their own safety.

9. οὐχὶ δώδεκα — ἡμέρας.] The Jews (by a reckoning adopted from the Greeks) divided their day, or the time from sun-rise to sun-set, into

προσκόπτει, ὅτι τὸ φῶς τοῦ κόσμου τούτου βλέπει· ἐὰν δέ τις περι- 10
πατῇ ἐν τῇ νυκτὶ, προσκόπτει, ὅτι τὸ φῶς οὐκ ἔστιν ἐν αὐτῷ. Ταῦτα 11
εἶπε, καὶ μετὰ τοῦτο λέγει αὐτοῖς· Λάζαρος ὁ φίλος ἡμῶν κεκοίμηται·
ἀλλὰ πορεύομαι ἵνα ἐξυπνίσω αὐτόν. Εἶπον οὖν οἱ μαθηταὶ αὐτοῦ· 12
Κύριε, εἰ κεκοίμηται, σωθήσεται. Εἰρήκει δὲ ὁ Ἰησοῦς περὶ τοῦ 13
θανάτου αὐτοῦ· ἐκεῖνοι δὲ ἔδοξαν ὅτι περὶ τῆς κοιμήσεως τοῦ ὕπνου
λέγει. Τότε οὖν εἶπεν αὐτοῖς ὁ Ἰησοῦς παῤῥησίᾳ· Λάζαρος ἀπέθανε· 14
καὶ χαίρω δι' ὑμᾶς, ἵνα πιστεύσητε, ὅτι οὐκ ἤμην ἐκεῖ. ἀλλ' ἄγωμεν 15
πρὸς αὐτόν. Εἶπεν οὖν Θωμᾶς, ὁ λεγόμενος Δίδυμος, τοῖς συμμαθη- 16
ταῖς· Ἄγωμεν καὶ ἡμεῖς, ἵνα ἀποθάνωμεν μετ' αὐτοῦ.
Ἐλθὼν οὖν ὁ Ἰησοῦς, εὗρεν αὐτὸν τέσσαρας ἡμέρας ἤδη ἔχοντα ἐν 17
τῷ μνημείῳ. Ἦν δὲ ἡ Βηθανία ἐγγὺς τῶν Ἱεροσολύμων, ὡς ἀπὸ στα- 18
δίων δεκαπέντε· καὶ πολλοὶ ἐκ τῶν Ἰουδαίων ἐληλύθεισαν πρὸς τὰς 19

twelve hours, of course varying a little according to the season of the year. The words were a sort of adagial maxim, like that at ix. 4, where see Note. On the sense meant to be conveyed by the next words, *ἐάν τις — αὐτῷ*, the Commentators are not agreed. The best view seems to be that taken by Camer., Pearce, and Doddr., and further unfolded by Mor., Rosenm., Kuin., and Tittm.; namely, that the words are a *parabolical ænigma*, in the Eastern manner, but obscurely expressed; the *application* being left to be supplied by the hearers, as in Virg. Ecl. ii. 18. *Alba ligustra cadunt, vaccinia nigra leguntur.* The sense is: "There is a certain and stated time for work; the *day* is that time. Now is *my day:* now my business must be done, while alone it can be done at all."

With respect to the phraseology itself, at *προσκόπτει* sub. *πόδα* (which is *expressed* in Matt. iv. 6.), and also *τινὶ* or some other Dative, which is *supplied* in some passages of Xenoph. and Aristoph. cited in Recens. Synop. *Τὸ φῶς τοῦ κόσμου* is regarded by the Commentators as a periphrasis for *τὸν ἥλιον*. But the expression rather signifies the light which is shed abroad in the world, for *τὸ φῶς τὸ ἐν τῷ κόσμῳ*. *Ὅτι φῶς οὐκ ἔστιν ἐν αὐτῷ* seems to be a *popular* expression, for *φῶς οὐκ ἔστιν αὐτῷ*, "he is destitute of light;" as xii. 35.

11. *κεκοίμηται — ἐξυπνίσω αὐτόν.*] In assigning the *reason* why he must go, Jesus expressed himself first figuratively, and then in plain terms. In *κεκοίμ.* there is a euphemism denoting *death*, common to all languages; but the sacred writers especially used it to adumbrate the death of the righteous. The disciples, however (partly misled by their wishes), misunderstood our Lord.

12. *εἰ κεκοίμηται, σωθ.*] q. d. "if he has gone to sleep, he will recover." Perhaps a sort of adage founded on experience. Thus the Rabbins mention sleep among the six good symptoms in sickness; and many passages are adduced by Wets. from the Classical writers, lauding its beneficial effects in sickness. The disciples seem to have intended to hint, that as Lazarus was likely to recover, there was no occasion for their Lord to hazard himself in Judæa.

14. *Λάζαρος ἀπέθανε.*] Our Lord now declares in plain terms, "Lazarus *is dead.*" The knowledge of which circumstance can be ascribed to nothing but omniscience. In the words following, Jesus *hints at* what he had already plainly *said*, ver. 11; namely, that he was going to raise Lazarus from the dead.

15. *χαίρω δι' ὑμᾶς — ἐκεῖ.*] The words *ἵνα πιστεύσητε* are *not*, as many Commentators suppose, parenthetical; but there is a *transposition* in the construction, for *καὶ χαίρω, ὅτι οὐκ ἤμην ἐκεῖ, δι' ὑμᾶς ἵνα πιστεύσητε.* *Ἤμην* for *ἦν* is a form found only in the later writers. See Lobeck on Phryn. p. 152. *Πιστ.* is here used of that completeness of faith in Christ which, it seems, the disciples had not yet all attained.

16. *ὁ λεγόμενος Δ.*] The best Commentators take this as an *interpretation* of *Θωμᾶς*, i. e. תאום. But some, as Tittm., think it expresses a *cognomen*, as *Σίμων ὁ λεγόμενος Πέτρος*. And this view is confirmed by Nonnus and Sedulius.

— *ἄγωμεν — αὐτοῦ.*] On the sense of these words the Commentators are not agreed. Some would take them *interrogatively*. But that is doing violence to the construction. The only doubt is whether *αὐτοῦ* is to be referred to *Lazarus*, or to *Jesus*. Now many eminent modern Commentators adopt the *former* method; though it does not yield so natural a sense as the *latter*, which is supported by the ancient and many modern Interpreters, as Calvin, Maldon., Lampe, Doddr., Tittm., and Kuin. Thomas, keenly alive to the danger both Jesus and themselves would incur by going into Judæa, exclaims, with characteristic, but well-meant bluntness: "Since our Master *will* expose himself to such peril, let us accompany him, if it be only to share his fate!"

17. *ἐλθὼν*] "having arrived;" not, however, at Bethany itself, but at the *vicinity;* whither Martha, hearing of his approach, had gone to meet him; and had met with him, it seems, not far from the burying-ground, which was always outside of a city or town. *Ἔχειν*, when used, as here, of *time*, signifies *agere, transigere;* an idiom frequent in the Classical writers. The *four* days (observes Lampe) seem to be reckoned from the *burial* of Lazarus; though at ver. 39. the reckoning is made from his *death*. The interval, however, between death and burial among the Jews was very short, generally only a few hours. The 4th day was probably only *begun*, not completed.

18. *ἀπὸ σταδίων δ.*] Sub. *γενομένη*, "it being at about 15 stadia off." The ellip. is *expressed* in Appian, p. 793. Of this absolute use of *ἀπὸ* (which may be compared with our *off*) Kypke adduces examples from several of the later writers.

περὶ Μάρθαν καὶ Μαρίαν, ἵνα παραμυθήσωνται αὐτὰς περὶ τοῦ ἀδελ-
20 *φοῦ αὐτῶν. Ἡ οὖν Μάρθα, ὡς ἤκουσεν ὅτι ὁ Ἰησοῦς ἔρχεται, ὑπήν-*
21 *τησεν αὐτῷ· Μαρία δὲ ἐν τῷ οἴκῳ ἐκαθέζετο. Εἶπεν οὖν ἡ Μάρθα*
πρὸς τὸν Ἰησοῦν· Κύριε, εἰ ἦς ὧδε, ὁ ἀδελφός μου οὐκ ἂν ἐτεθνήκει.
22 *Ἀλλὰ καὶ νῦν, οἶδα ὅτι ὅσα ἂν αἰτήσῃ τὸν Θεὸν, δώσει σοι ὁ Θεός.*
23 *Λέγει αὐτῇ ὁ Ἰησοῦς· Ἀναστήσεται ὁ ἀδελφός σου. [p] Λέγει αὐτῷ* p Supra 5. 29.
24 *Μάρθα· Οἶδα ὅτι ἀναστήσεται ἐν τῇ ἀναστάσει ἐν τῇ ἐσχάτῃ ἡμέρᾳ.*
25 *Εἶπεν αὐτῇ ὁ Ἰησοῦς· Ἐγώ εἰμι ἡ ἀνάστασις καὶ ἡ ζωή. Ὁ πι-*
26 *στεύων εἰς ἐμὲ, κἂν ἀποθάνῃ, ζήσεται· [q] καὶ πᾶς ὁ ζῶν καὶ πιστεύων* q Supra 6. 35.
27 *εἰς ἐμὲ οὐ μὴ ἀποθάνῃ εἰς τὸν αἰῶνα. πιστεύεις τοῦτο; [r] Λέγει* r Matt. 16. 16. supra 4. 42. & 6. 69.
αὐτῷ· Ναὶ, Κύριε· ἐγὼ πεπίστευκα, ὅτι σὺ εἶ ὁ Χριστὸς, ὁ Υἱὸς
28 *τοῦ Θεοῦ, ὁ εἰς τὸν κόσμον ἐρχόμενος. Καὶ ταῦτα εἰποῦσα, ἀπῆλθε*
καὶ ἐφώνησε Μαρίαν τὴν ἀδελφὴν αὐτῆς λάθρα, εἰποῦσα· Ὁ διδά-
29 *σκαλος πάρεστι, καὶ φωνεῖ σε. Ἐκείνη, ὡς ἤκουσεν, ἐγείρεται ταχὺ καὶ*
30 *ἔρχεται πρὸς αὐτόν. Οὔπω δὲ ἐληλύθει ὁ Ἰησοῦς εἰς τὴν κώμην, ἀλλ᾽*
31 *ἦν ἐν τῷ τόπῳ, ὅπου ὑπήντησεν αὐτῷ ἡ Μάρθα. Οἱ οὖν Ἰουδαῖοι*
οἱ ὄντες μετ᾽ αὐτῆς ἐν τῇ οἰκίᾳ καὶ παραμυθούμενοι αὐτὴν, ἰδόντες
τὴν Μαρίαν ὅτι ταχέως ἀνέστη καὶ ἐξῆλθεν, ἠκολούθησαν αὐτῇ, λέγον-
32 *τες· Ὅτι ὑπάγει εἰς τὸ μνημεῖον, ἵνα κλαύσῃ ἐκεῖ. Ἡ οὖν Μαρία ὡς*
ἦλθεν ὅπου ἦν ὁ Ἰησοῦς, ἰδοῦσα αὐτὸν, ἔπεσεν εἰς τοὺς πόδας αὐτοῦ,
λέγουσα αὐτῷ· Κύριε, εἰ ἦς ὧδε, οὐκ ἂν ἀπέθανέ μου ὁ ἀδελφός.

19. Ἰουδαίων.] Chiefly, we may suppose, the *Jerusalemites* from the vicinity. The best Commentators, ancient and modern, are of opinion that *πρὸς τὰς περὶ* M. *καὶ* M. is simply for *πρὸς Μάρθαν καὶ* M. The idiom is common in the Classical writers; but it does not always mean the *person* only, but sometimes includes his relations or near friends. And as at Acts xiii. 13. *οἱ περὶ τὸν Παῦλον* denotes "Paul and his companions," so here it may mean "Martha and Mary with their relations." These visits of condolence were usual among the Jews, and continued to seven days after the funeral. The number of persons going thither became the means of making the miracle generally known, and thereby establishing its reality.

20. *ὡς ἤκουσεν*] "as soon as she had heard;" probably from some travellers on horseback, who had passed Jesus on the road. Ἐν τῷ οἴ. ἐκαθ., "sate at home." Campb. renders, "remained at home." But see ver. 30. the posture was suitable to grief.

22—24. Hence it should seem that Martha had a persuasion that Jesus *could*, and an expectation, though faint, that he *would* raise her brother from the dead.

— *ἐν τῇ ἀναστάσει.*] "at the general resurrection."

25. *ἐγώ εἰμι ἡ ἀνάστασις*, &c.] Here our Lord (by a common figure of the *effect* for the *efficient*) professes that He is the *author* of the resurrection of the dead; and that as he shall sometime raise *all* the dead, so he can and will now raise Lazarus to life. "We have here (says Dr. Jortin), in a few words, the summary of the Gospel; and the sublimity of the language is not less remarkable than the great truths conveyed in the words. Jesus is the *resurrection* to those believers who are departed hence in the Lord; and he is the life to those who are still upon earth; and he will finally be the resurrection and the life to them *both*."

— *ζήσεται*] "shall be raised to a life of felicity and glory." Κἂν ἀποθάνῃ, "though he must die."

26. *πᾶς ὁ ζῶν — τὸν αἰῶνα.*] This seems meant to engraft on the foregoing assurance another, expressed in yet stronger terms, and denoting something *more*, — namely, that the gift shall be not only of life in a figurative, but in a physical sense, and that *never ending*. Ὁ ζῶν *may* signify "while alive;" intimating that the chance for obtaining eternal life is suspended on the issue of the life on earth. But perhaps the best Commentators are right in considering it as a Hebraism; and thus the sense will be, "every person living who believeth," &c.

27. *σὺ εἶ ὁ Χριστὸς — Θεοῦ.*] Martha, it should seem, mentions, in the ardour of her devotion, *both* the titles designating the expected Messiah in Scripture. Tittm. thinks that she understood by the latter something more exalted than the former, — namely, one united in the Godhead, and in whom are centred all the essential attributes of God. Be that as it may, Martha certainly understood by it a term of *nature*, not of *office*.

— *ὁ — ἐρχόμενος*] "who is to come into the world," i. e. who, the Scriptures say, is to come.

28. *λάθρα.*] In thus calling her apart, it appears she had Jesus's directions; though the Evangelist has not recorded it.

29. *ἐγείρεται ταχὺ.*] Not only out of reverence to Jesus, but from her faith being invigorated by the alacrity of her sister.

31. *ἵνα κλαύσῃ ἐκεῖ.*] According to the custom of both Jews and Gentiles, to repair to the cemeteries to weep at the tombs of their relations

Ἰησοῦς οὖν ὡς εἶδεν αὐτὴν κλαίουσαν, καὶ τοὺς συνελθόντας αὐτῇ Ἰου- 33
δαίους κλαίοντας, ἐνεβριμήσατο τῷ πνεύματι καὶ ἐτάραξεν ἑαυτὸν, καὶ 34
εἶπε· Ποῦ τεθείκατε αὐτόν; Λέγουσιν αὐτῷ· Κύριε, ἔρχου καὶ ἴδε.
Ἐδάκρυσεν ὁ Ἰησοῦς. Ἔλεγον οὖν οἱ Ἰουδαῖοι· Ἴδε, πῶς ἐφίλει αὐτόν! 35
s Supra 9. 6. s Τινὲς δὲ ἐξ αὐτῶν εἶπον· Οὐκ ἠδύνατο οὗτος ὁ ἀνοίξας τοὺς ὀφθαλ- 36
μοὺς τοῦ τυφλοῦ ποιῆσαι, ἵνα καὶ οὗτος μὴ ἀποθάνῃ; Ἰησοῦς οὖν 37
πάλιν ἐμβριμώμενος ἐν ἑαυτῷ, ἔρχεται εἰς τὸ μνημεῖον. Ἦν δὲ σπήλαιον, 38
καὶ λίθος ἐπέκειτο ἐπ᾽ αὐτῷ. λέγει ὁ Ἰησοῦς· Ἄρατε τὸν λίθον. Λέ- 39
γει αὐτῷ ἡ ἀδελφὴ τοῦ τεθνηκότος Μάρθα· Κύριε, ἤδη ὄζει· τεταρταῖος γάρ ἐστι. Λέγει αὐτῇ ὁ Ἰησοῦς· Οὐκ εἶπόν σοι, ὅτι ἐὰν πι- 40
στεύσῃς, ὄψει τὴν δόξαν τοῦ Θεοῦ; ἦραν οὖν τὸν λίθον, οὗ ἦν ὁ 41
τεθνηκὼς κείμενος. Ὁ δὲ Ἰησοῦς ἦρε τοὺς ὀφθαλμοὺς ἄνω καὶ εἶπε·
Πάτερ, εὐχαριστῶ σοι ὅτι ἤκουσάς μου. Ἐγὼ δὲ ᾔδειν ὅτι πάντοτέ 42
μου ἀκούεις· ἀλλὰ διὰ τὸν ὄχλον τὸν περιεστῶτα εἶπον, ἵνα πιστεύ-
σωσιν ὅτι σύ με ἀπέστειλας. Καὶ ταῦτα εἰπὼν, φωνῇ μεγάλῃ ἐκραύγασε· 43
Λάζαρε, δεῦρο ἔξω! καὶ ἐξῆλθεν ὁ τεθνηκὼς, δεδεμένος τοὺς πόδας 44
καὶ τὰς χεῖρας κειρίαις· καὶ ἡ ὄψις αὐτοῦ σουδαρίῳ περιεδέδετο.
Λέγει αὐτοῖς ὁ Ἰησοῦς· Λύσατε αὐτὸν καὶ ἄφετε ὑπάγειν.
Πολλοὶ οὖν ἐκ τῶν Ἰουδαίων οἱ ἐλθόντες πρὸς τὴν Μαρίαν, καὶ 45
θεασάμενοι ἃ ἐποίησεν ὁ Ἰησοῦς, ἐπίστευσαν εἰς αὐτόν. Τινὲς δὲ ἐξ 46
αὐτῶν ἀπῆλθον πρὸς τοὺς Φαρισαίους, καὶ εἶπον αὐτοῖς ἃ ἐποίησεν ὁ

33. ἐνεβριμήσατο.] On the sense of this word Commentators are not agreed. The term would, according to its usual acceptation both in the Scriptural and the Classical writers, signify *indignatus est*. And so many eminent Commentators explain it. But (as Tittm. observes) there seems to have been no ground for *censure*. It is better to take the word (with Campb., Rosenm., Schl., and Tittm.) of *violent internal perturbation* excited by *sorrow*, as the Heb. נִכְמַר is used in Gen. xl. 6. and 1 Sam. xv. 11. Indeed βρίμω (from which the word is derived) like its cognate *fremo* simply denotes only the *commotion* of any one of the violent passions, anger, sorrow, &c. The sense assigned by Euthym. and Maldon., "he repressed his spirit or emotion," would deserve attention, were it not for πάλιν ἐμβριμώμενος ἐν ἑαυτῷ at ver. 38, which admits of no other interpretation than the one which I have here adopted, and which is much confirmed by the words following καὶ ἐτάραξεν ἑαυτὸν, which are exegetical of the foregoing, and in which we have an example of reciprocal for passive, as 2 Pet. ii. 8. Thus ἐν τῷ πνεύματι will signify "in his spirit," as it is explained by Middlet. Gr. Art.

38. Ἐπέκειτο does not import, as strict propriety of language would suggest, that the entrance was *from above*, since the researches of Antiquaries show that it was, in the case of the *Jewish* tombs, *from the side*. Hence we may see the suitableness of the Hebrew term to denote the stone which closed up the entrance, namely, גולל, "*the roller*." The same is to be taken of ἄρατε.

39. ὄζει.] Ὄζειν signifies properly to emit an odour, whether *good* (as in Aristoph. ap. Suid.), or *bad*, as here and in other passages in the LXX. and Classical writers adduced by Wets.

— τεταρταῖος γάρ ἐστι.] Of this Greek idiom (by which what properly belongs to the *person* is applied to the *thing*), many examples are adduced by Raphel. and Wets. It seems by these words that Martha thought Jesus meant no more, by ordering the stone to be removed, than to take a last look at the countenance of his friend.

41. εἶπε· Πάτερ, &c.] The words of this prayer are, from high-wrought pathos, very brief, and consequently obscure. Hence their full sense is only to be expressed in a paraphrase. I would propose the following: "Father, I thank thee that thou usest to hear my prayers. I know that thou dost continually hearken to my wishes, [whether expressed, or only mental]; but I have [now] *spoken* [them] because of the multitude present, that [by their seeing the granting of my desire] they may know that thou hast sent me." The best Commentators are agreed, that in ἤκουσας the Aorist expresses, as often, what is *customary*. Ἤδειν in a Present sense is common. The ellipsis after ἀλλὰ is very frequent.

44. δεδεμένος — κειρίαις.] It is not necessary to suppose, with most Commentators, that the whole body was involved in the bandages, (for thus a *second* miracle would be requisite); but, as miracles are not to be supposed without sufficient reason, we may imagine that the sheet, (σινδὼν,) in which the body was wrapped, was not so tightly brought together by the bandages whereby the armlets were kept in their places, but that Lazarus was enabled to *creep forth*.

— σουδαρίῳ] *kerchief*. This did not cover the face, but was brought under the chin.

— λύσατε] i. e. "loosen the bandages." On the credibility of this stupendous miracle, see the able remarks of Tittm. in Rec. Syn.

47 Ἰησοῦς. ᵗ Συνήγαγον οὖν οἱ Ἀρχιερεῖς καὶ οἱ Φαρισαῖοι συνέδριον, καὶ ᵗ Matt. 26. 3. Mark 14. 1. Luke 22. 2.
ἔλεγον· Τί ποιοῦμεν; ὅτι οὗτος ὁ ἄνθρωπος πολλὰ σημεῖα ποιεῖ.
48 Ἐὰν ἀφῶμεν αὐτὸν οὕτω, πάντες πιστεύσουσιν εἰς αὐτόν· καὶ ἐλεύσον-
49 ται οἱ Ῥωμαῖοι καὶ ἀροῦσιν ἡμῶν καὶ τὸν τόπον καὶ τὸ ἔθνος. Εἷς
δέ τις ἐξ αὐτῶν, Καϊάφας, ἀρχιερεὺς ὢν τοῦ ἐνιαυτοῦ ἐκείνου, εἶπεν
50 αὐτοῖς· Ὑμεῖς οὐκ οἴδατε οὐδέν· ᵘ οὐδὲ διαλογίζεσθε, ὅτι συμφέρει ᵘ Infra 18. 14.
ἡμῖν, ἵνα εἷς ἄνθρωπος ἀποθάνῃ ὑπὲρ τοῦ λαοῦ, καὶ μὴ ὅλον τὸ ἔθνος
51 ἀπόληται. τοῦτο δὲ ἀφ' ἑαυτοῦ οὐκ εἶπεν· ἀλλά, ἀρχιερεὺς ὢν τοῦ
ἐνιαυτοῦ ἐκείνου, προεφήτευσεν, ὅτι ἔμελλεν ὁ Ἰησοῦς ἀποθνήσκειν ὑπὲρ
52 τοῦ ἔθνους· καὶ οὐχ ὑπὲρ τοῦ ἔθνους μόνον, ἀλλ' ἵνα καὶ τὰ τέκνα
53 τοῦ Θεοῦ τὰ διεσκορπισμένα συναγάγῃ εἰς ἕν. Ἀπ' ἐκείνης οὖν τῆς

47. *τί ποιοῦμεν.*] "What are we doing?" A popular phrase fitted to deliberation, and implying *also* "What are we *to do?*"

— *σημεῖα.*] They admitted, it seems, the miracles of Jesus, but yet refused faith, on some such groundless pretence as, that they were effected by Diabolical agency.

48. *τόπον.*] Not the *Temple*, as some explain; for that would require *τοῦτον τὸν τόπον*; but the *city* of Jerusalem. Though Kuin. takes it of the *country*. Αἴρειν, like the Hebr. נשׂא, is used of destroying either a city or country.

49. *ὑμεῖς οὐκ οἴδατε οὐδέν.*] These words, and the counsel afterwards given, correspond so little to the foregoing ones, that almost all the best Commentators are of opinion, that something which immediately preceded them in the deliberations has been omitted by the Evangelist. This, however, is a principle always precarious, and is here (as usual) unnecessary. May we not consider the words of the Evangelist, *τί ποιοῦμεν — ἔθνος* as containing *two opinions* pronounced by *two different parties* of the Sanhedrim; *τί ποιοῦμεν — ποιεῖ* by those who were inclined to think *well* of Jesus; and *ἐὰν ἀφῶμεν — ἔθνος* by those who troubled not themselves about the truth or the falsehood of Jesus's pretensions, but viewing the thing solely in a *political* point of view, were alive to the danger of letting him go on; and thought he must be put down, but scrupled at the *means*. Against *these* the rebuke of Caiaphas seems to be directed: q. d. "Ye are foolish and raw! namely, in state craft, by seeing what is *expedient* to be done, and yet scrupling at the means to bring it about." "He seems (observes Campb.) to concede to those who appeared to have scruples, that, though their putting Jesus to death could not be vindicated by strict law or justice, it might be vindicated from expediency and reason of state, or rather from the great law of necessity, the danger being no less than the destruction of their country, and so imminent, that even the murder of an innocent man, admitting Jesus to be innocent, was not to be considered as an evil, but rather as a sacrifice every way proper for the safety of the nation."

50. *συμφέρει — ἀπόληται*] i. e. "It is a frequent maxim of state policy, that the safety of the whole nation is to be preferred to one individual." On the nature of the reasoning, and the cause of the apprehension felt by the Sanhedrim, see Towns. Chron. Arr. i. 384. As to the phraseology, we have here a Positive with *καὶ μὴ* instead of a Comparative with *ἤ*.

51. *προεφήτευσεν.*] The sense "prophesied," generally assigned to the word, has been by most recent Commentators rejected, because the words of Caiaphas were, they say, no *prediction* at all, but only a *politic counsel*, like the Virgilian "Unum pro cunctis dabitur caput." Accordingly, they take *προεφ.* for *quasi* vaticinatus est, ita locutus ut vatic. *videatur*. But C. F. Fritzsche, (*not* the Editor of St. Matthew and Mark) in his learned Tract de Revelationis notione Biblica, p. 63, shrewdly remarks, that he can no more understand the meaning of a *quasi* oraculum in the Gospel, than Cotta (in Cicero de Nat. D. i. 26.) could understand "in Deo quid sit *quasi corpus*, vel quasi *sanguis*." He contends strongly for retaining the usual sense *prophesied*, which he thinks required by the opposition between *ἀφ' ἑαυτοῦ εἶπεν* and *προεφήτευσε*. The meaning, therefore, is, that in saying what he did, (namely, that *one* should die for the people,) he unwittingly uttered a prediction, afterwards fulfilled, that *one*, even Jesus, should die for the people. That Caiaphas, though a bad man, should have been inspired, is not strange, (as will appear by the example of *Balaam*,) since his *office* rather than his person is to be considered; especially as we have some reason to think that the gift of prophecy was occasionally granted to the High Priest. So Philo says expressly: *ὁ δὲ πρὸς ἀλήθειαν ἱερεὺς εὐθὺς ἐστι προφήτης*. Thus Diodati, in his Annotations, well remarks: "God guided the tongue of the High Priest: so that, thinking to utter a speech according to his *own wicked meaning*, he pronounced an oracle according to *God's meaning*: as the High Priest had oftentimes inspirations from God." If this view be thought inadmissible, we may, (and must at least,) with Lampe, Kypke, and Tittm., take *προεφ.* in the sense, "spoke from the impulse of divine inspiration," which comes to the same thing.

52. *καὶ οὐχ ὑπὲρ — εἰς ἕν.*] These words are meant to explain and show the extent of the seeming prediction. And here there is an ellipsis of some words, to be supplied from the preceding clause; q. d. [It was, indeed, decreed that he should die for the nation] and not for the nation only, &c. This is better than (with Kuin. and Tittm.) assigning to *ὅτι* the sense *quoniam*, which is an unusual signification, and here forbidden by the words following *ἔμελλεν ἀποθν.*, which plainly mean, that "he *should* die." *Συναγάγῃ εἰς ἕν*, as it were into one Catholic Church, united in one holy communion, under one common Head. — *Τέκνα τοῦ Θεοῦ.* So called *by anticipation*, in order to show God's gracious designs that they *should* be so.

ἡμέρας συνεβουλεύσαντο, ἵνα ἀποκτείνωσιν αὐτόν. Ἰησοῦς οὖν οὐκ ἔτι 54
παῤῥησίᾳ περιεπάτει ἐν τοῖς Ἰουδαίοις· ἀλλὰ ἀπῆλθεν ἐκεῖθεν εἰς τὴν
χώραν ἐγγὺς τῆς ἐρήμου, εἰς Ἐφραΐμ λεγομένην πόλιν, κἀκεῖ διέτριβε
μετὰ τῶν μαθητῶν αὐτοῦ. Ἦν δὲ ἐγγὺς τὸ πάσχα τῶν Ἰουδαίων· καὶ 55
ἀνέβησαν πολλοὶ εἰς Ἱεροσόλυμα ἐκ τῆς χώρας πρὸ τοῦ πάσχα, ἵνα
ἁγνίσωσιν ἑαυτούς. Ἐζήτουν οὖν τὸν Ἰησοῦν, καὶ ἔλεγον μετ' ἀλλήλων 56
ἐν τῷ ἱερῷ ἑστηκότες· Τί δοκεῖ ὑμῖν; ὅτι οὐ μὴ ἔλθῃ εἰς τὴν ἑορτήν; Δεδώκεισαν δὲ καὶ οἱ Ἀρχιερεῖς καὶ οἱ Φαρισαῖοι ἐντολήν, ἵνα 57
ἐάν τις γνῷ ποῦ ἐστι, μηνύσῃ, ὅπως πιάσωσιν αὐτόν.

x Matt. 26. 6. Mark 14. 3. XII. x Ὁ ΟΥΝ Ἰησοῦς πρὸ ἓξ ἡμερῶν τοῦ πάσχα ἦλθεν εἰς Βηθα- 1
νίαν, ὅπου ἦν Λάζαρος ὁ τεθνηκώς, ὃν ἤγειρεν ἐκ νεκρῶν. Ἐποίησαν 2
οὖν αὐτῷ δεῖπνον ἐκεῖ, καὶ ἡ Μάρθα διηκόνει· ὁ δὲ Λάζαρος εἷς ἦν
y Supra 11. 2. τῶν * ἀνακειμένων σὺν αὐτῷ. y Ἡ οὖν Μαρία λαβοῦσα λίτραν μύρου 3
νάρδου πιστικῆς πολυτίμου, ἤλειψε τοὺς πόδας τοῦ Ἰησοῦ, καὶ ἐξέμαξε
ταῖς θριξὶν αὐτῆς τοὺς πόδας αὐτοῦ· ἡ δὲ οἰκία ἐπληρώθη ἐκ τῆς
ὀσμῆς τοῦ μύρου. Λέγει οὖν εἷς ἐκ τῶν μαθητῶν αὐτοῦ, Ἰούδας Σί- 4
μωνος Ἰσκαριώτης, ὁ μέλλων αὐτὸν παραδιδόναι· Διατί τοῦτο τὸ μύρον 5
z Infra. 13. 29. οὐκ ἐπράθη τριακοσίων δηναρίων, καὶ ἐδόθη πτωχοῖς; z Εἶπε δὲ 6
τοῦτο, οὐχ ὅτι περὶ τῶν πτωχῶν ἔμελεν αὐτῷ· ἀλλ' ὅτι κλέπτης ἦν,

55. *ἵνα ἁγνίσωσιν ἑαυτούς.*] Namely, from such ceremonial defilements as they might have contracted; in order to participation in the Paschal feast. This purification was effected by sacrifices, sprinkling of water, fasting, prayer, and other observances, which lasted from one to six days. This, and the other prescribed rites, brought a great concourse of people together at Jerusalem, before the Festival.

56. *τί δοκεῖ — ἑορτήν.*] These words are by most Expositors supposed to mean, "What think ye, that he should not have come to the Feast." But the Feast was not yet arrived; and therefore that he should not have come, was not surprising. Indeed, from what is said in the next verses, they had little reason to expect him at all. Moreover, the words *τί δοκεῖ ὑμῖν* rather indicate a mutual discussion of what was doubtful and uncertain, whether it would or would not be. I have, therefore, followed the Pesch. Syr., Chrys., Euthym., Lampe, Pearce, Kuin., Tittm., and Campb., in placing a mark of interrogation after *ὑμῖν*; of course taking *ἔλθῃ* in a *future* sense, for *ἐλεύσεται*. The phraseology is, indeed, unusual; but this use of the interrogation with a double negation is intended to represent some one as proposing a question, and himself answering it in the negative. Thus it may be regarded as equivalent to, "Is it *your* opinion [as it certainly is mine] that he will by no means come?" They were warranted in supposing so, since (as we find from the next verse) strict inquiries were made after Jesus, and orders given for his apprehension.

XII. 1. *πρὸ ἓξ ἡμερῶν τοῦ πάσχα.*] A transposition, for *ἓξ ἡμερῶν πρὸ τ. π.*, as in Joseph. Ant. xv. 4. *πρὸ ἡμέρας μιᾶς τῆς ἑορτῆς*, and elsewhere in the later writers. *Ὅπου ἦν Λ. ὁ τεθ.* is rightly rendered by Markland, "where Lazarus was; he who had been dead and raised to life."

2. *ἐποίησαν δ.*] For the Impersonal, "a supper was made." *Διηκόνει* denotes attendance at table, to carve and serve the provisions. The entertainment, however, was, as we find from Matt. xxvi. 6, not in honour of Martha, but a person of the name of Simon, surnamed the Leper, probably a near relative of Mary, who acted as *hostess* on the occasion.

— *ἀνακειμ.*] instead of *συνανακ.*, is found in almost all the best MSS. and the early Edd., and is received by almost every Editor from Wets. to Scholz. Lazarus's presence is mentioned, to show that since his resurrection he had possessed the usual functions of life.

3. *καὶ ἐξέμαξε ταῖς θριξίν.*] This has been thought by Lightf. and Bynæus to denote that Mary had *washed* Jesus' feet before annointing them. If so, there is a remarkable *transposition* in the construction. But as the unguent used was liquid, the wiping would be as suitable to that as to washing. See more in Rec. Syn., in the Notes on Matt. xxvi. 6—11. On *πιστικῆς* see Note on Mark xiv. 3.

— *ἡ δὲ οἰκία — μύρου.*] This is, as Bp. Midd. observes, a figurative mode of expressing the extreme fragrance of the unguent. So Plutarch i. 676. cited by Wets. *ὠδώδει δὴ θεσπέσιον οἷον ἀπὸ ἀρωμάτων καὶ μύρων ὁ οἶκος.*

6. *τὸ γλωσσόκομον.*] This word originally denoted the box in which pipers deposited the mouth pieces of their instruments. Thence it came to denote any box or casket, for holding money, or other valuables. And such is the sense here and in 2 Chron. xxiv. 8. and Plut. p. 1060. cited by Wets. *Βαλλόμενα* is for *εἰσβαλλόμενα*, "what was put therein," as contributions towards a common fund for the support of Christ and his Apostles. According to the common rendering of the passage, the sense proceeds very awkwardly; nor is this to be remedied by that *Θεὸς ἀπὸ μηχανῆς*, a *transposition*, which the Critics call to their aid.

7 καὶ τὸ γλωσσόκομον εἶχε καὶ τὰ βαλλόμενα ἐβάσταζεν. Εἶπεν οὖν
ὁ Ἰησοῦς· Ἄφες αὐτήν· εἰς τὴν ἡμέραν τοῦ ἐνταφιασμοῦ μου τετή-
8 ρηκεν αὐτό. [a] Τοὺς πτωχοὺς γὰρ πάντοτε ἔχετε μεθ᾽ ἑαυτῶν, ἐμὲ δὲ a Deut. 15. 11. Matt. 26. 11. Mark 14. 7.
οὐ πάντοτε ἔχετε.
9 Ἔγνω οὖν ὄχλος πολὺς ἐκ τῶν Ἰουδαίων ὅτι ἐκεῖ ἐστι· καὶ ἦλθον
οὐ διὰ τὸν Ἰησοῦν μόνον, ἀλλ᾽ ἵνα καὶ τὸν Λάζαρον ἴδωσιν, ὃν ἤγειρεν
10 ἐκ νεκρῶν. Ἐβουλεύσαντο δὲ οἱ Ἀρχιερεῖς, ἵνα καὶ τὸν Λάζαρον ἀπο-
11 κτείνωσιν· ὅτι πολλοὶ δι᾽ αὐτὸν ὑπῆγον τῶν Ἰουδαίων, καὶ ἐπίστευον
εἰς τὸν Ἰησοῦν.
12 [b] Τῇ ἐπαύριον ὄχλος πολὺς ὁ ἐλθὼν εἰς τὴν ἑορτὴν, ἀκούσαντες ὅτι b Matt. 21. 8. Mark 11. 7. Luke 19. 35.
13 ἔρχεται ὁ Ἰησοῦς εἰς Ἱεροσόλυμα, [c] ἔλαβον τὰ βαΐα τῶν φοινίκων, καὶ c Psal. 118. 25, 26.
ἐξῆλθον εἰς ὑπάντησιν αὐτῷ, καὶ ἔκραζον· Ὡσαννά· εὐλογημένος ὁ
14 ἐρχόμενος ἐν ὀνόματι Κυρίου ὁ βασιλεὺς τοῦ Ἰσραήλ! Εὑρὼν δὲ ὁ
15 Ἰησοῦς ὀνάριον, ἐκάθισεν ἐπ᾽ αὐτὸ, καθώς ἐστι γεγραμμένον· [d] Μὴ d Zach. 9. 9.
φοβοῦ, θύγατερ Σιών· ἰδοὺ, ὁ βασιλεύς σου ἔρχεται
16 καθήμενος ἐπὶ πῶλον ὄνου. Ταῦτα δὲ οὐκ ἔγνωσαν οἱ μαθηταὶ αὐτοῦ τὸ πρῶτον· ἀλλ᾽ ὅτε ἐδοξάσθη ὁ Ἰησοῦς, τότε ἐμνήσθησαν
‡ ὅτι ταῦτα ἦν ἐπ᾽ αὐτῷ γεγραμμένα, καὶ ταῦτα ἐποίησαν αὐτῷ.
17 Ἐμαρτύρει οὖν ὁ ὄχλος ὁ ὢν μετ᾽ αὐτοῦ, ὅτι τὸν Λάζαρον ἐφώνησεν
18 ἐκ τοῦ μνημείου καὶ ἤγειρεν αὐτὸν ἐκ νεκρῶν. Διὰ τοῦτο καὶ ὑπήντησεν αὐτῷ ὁ ὄχλος, ὅτι * ἤκουσαν τοῦτο αὐτὸν πεποιηκέναι τὸ σημεῖον.
19 Οἱ οὖν Φαρισαῖοι εἶπον πρὸς ἑαυτούς· Θεωρεῖτε ὅτι οὐκ ὠφελεῖτε
οὐδέν; ἴδε, ὁ κόσμος ὀπίσω αὐτοῦ ἀπῆλθεν.

It is plain that the sense commonly assigned to *ἐβάσταζεν* cannot be tolerated; and that of *managed*, proposed by some, is destitute of proof or even probability. Almost all the best Commentators, ancient and modern, are agreed that it must signify *surripuit, intervertit*, (like *ferre* for *auferre* in Latin) of which sense they adduce examples from the later writers, to which I would add the following very apposite one from Joseph. p. 402. 39. Huds. *ὁρμήσαντες εἰς μίαν σκηνὴν, ὡς οὐδένα ἑώρων ἐν μέσῳ, φαγόντες καὶ πιόντες ἐβάστασαν ἐσθῆτα, καὶ πολὺν χρυσὸν κομίσαντες ἔξω τῆς παρεμβολῆς, ἔκρυψαν.* Indeed as at xx. 15. the word denotes to *carry off* by stealth, so it may here very well mean simply to *steal*: a sense required by the *κλέπτης* just before; for thus we learn *why* Judas took exception at the ointment being so employed, and why he is called thief.

7, 8. See on Matt. xxvi. 12.

11. *ὑπῆγον*.] Literally, "drew off," namely, abandoned that attachment to the teaching of the Scribes, which they had formerly had. Not, "withdrew from the Temple service," as some Commentators explain. For (as Campb. observes) no sect of the Jews withdrew from the synagogue. Both Jesus and his Apostles and disciples punctually attending at the Temple service, until they were expelled from the synagogues. The sense of *οἱ Ἰουδ.* for the Scribes and Pharisees occurs often in this Gospel.

13. *βαΐα*.] This is by many Commentators said to be a *Coptic* word, signifying a branch of a palm tree. But it rather comes from *βαιὸς*, *slender*, and thus denotes the *tapering twigs* of the palm-tree. Indeed the Coptic may be *derived* from this, just as there are numerous words in the Rabbinical writers derived from the Greek and Latin. Indeed the Coptic language is filled with words of foreign origin and late introduction.

15. *μὴ φοβοῦ, θύγ. Σ.*] On this prediction of Zech. ix. 9. see Townsend Chron. Arr. i. 395.

16. The first *αὐτῷ* is emphatical, and the words *καὶ* (repeat *ὅτι*) *ταῦτα ἐποίησαν αὐτῷ* mean—and that [the people] had done unto him [in fulfilment of prophecy]. Which last words are suggested by the preceding words.

17. *ὅτι*.] Many MSS., Versions, and early Edd. have *ὅτε*, which was edited by Matth., who remarks that *ὅτι* was introduced into the text by Beza. Be it so—but it is supported by perhaps *stronger* MSS. authority, than *ὅτε*; as *internal* evidence is quite in favour of *ὅτι*; for thus *ἐφώνει*, not *ἐφώνησεν*, would be required. Moreover, the context requires this sense. By *ὁ ὢν μετ᾽ αὐτοῦ* must be meant, "who had been with him," [on the occasion in question.] Thus there is a blending of two clauses into one. The sentence *fully* expressed would run—"The people who had been with him when he raised Lazarus from the dead, attested that he," &c.

18. *ἤκουσαν*.] This, for *ἤκουσε*, is found in most of the best MSS., and early Edd., and is received by almost all Editors from Wets. to Scholz. There is a transposition of *τοῦτο*.

19. *θεωρεῖτε—οὐδέν*;] The best Commentators, ancient and modern, are agreed that these words must be taken interrogatively. See ye, &c.? And thus they have certainly more spirit. The words *ὁ κόσμος—ἀπῆλθεν* are a *popular* form of

Ἦσαν δέ τινες Ἕλληνες ἐκ τῶν ἀναβαινόντων ἵνα προσκυνήσωσιν ἐν 20
τῇ ἑορτῇ· οὗτοι οὖν προσῆλθον Φιλίππῳ τῷ ἀπὸ Βηθσαϊδὰ τῆς 21
Γαλιλαίας, καὶ ἠρώτων αὐτὸν λέγοντες· Κύριε, θέλομεν τὸν Ἰησοῦν
ἰδεῖν. Ἔρχεται Φίλιππος καὶ λέγει τῷ Ἀνδρέᾳ· καὶ πάλιν Ἀνδρέας 22
καὶ Φίλιππος λέγουσι τῷ Ἰησοῦ. ὁ δὲ Ἰησοῦς ἀπεκρίνατο αὐτοῖς, λέ- 23
γων· Ἐλήλυθεν ἡ ὥρα ἵνα δοξασθῇ ὁ Υἱὸς τοῦ ἀνθρώπου. Ἀμὴν 24
ἀμὴν λέγω ὑμῖν· ἐὰν μὴ ὁ κόκκος τοῦ σίτου πεσὼν εἰς τὴν γῆν
ἀποθάνῃ, αὐτὸς μόνος μένει· ἐὰν δὲ ἀποθάνῃ, πολὺν καρπὸν φέρει.
[e]Ὁ φιλῶν τὴν ψυχὴν αὐτοῦ ἀπολέσει αὐτήν· καὶ ὁ μισῶν τὴν ψυχὴν 25
αὐτοῦ ἐν τῷ κόσμῳ τούτῳ εἰς ζωὴν αἰώνιον φυλάξει αὐτήν. [f]Ἐὰν 26
ἐμοὶ διακονῇ τις, ἐμοὶ ἀκολουθείτω· καὶ ὅπου εἰμὶ ἐγὼ, ἐκεῖ καὶ ὁ
διάκονος ὁ ἐμὸς ἔσται· καὶ ἐάν τις ἐμοὶ διακονῇ, τιμήσει αὐτὸν ὁ
Πατήρ.

e Matt. 10. 39. & 16. 25. Mark 8. 35. Luke 9. 24. & 17. 33.
f Infra. 14. 3. & 17. 24. 1 Thess. 4. 17.

speaking, denoting that a teacher has very numerous followers. The hyperbole in κόσμος is frequent in the N. T. and the Rabbinical writers.

20. Ἕλληνες.] It is a much debated question *who* are here to be understood. Some suppose foreign Jews living out of Palestine, and speaking the Greek language. And certainly there were Jews dispersed all over Egypt, Asia Minor, &c., where Greek was the vernacular tongue, and spoken by the sojourning Jews. But that is no reason why they should be *called Greeks;* nor can it, I think, be proved from any passage of the N. T. that they were so called. It is therefore better to suppose (with others) that by Ἕλληνες are to be understood *Gentiles;* for 1. wherever in the N. T. Ἰουδαῖοι and Ἕλληνες are mentioned, by the latter are meant *Gentiles;* 2. because the thing recorded is agreeable to the custom of those times; since the Gentiles worshipped not only the gods of their own country, but of any foreign nation into which they might come, nay they made journeys for the purpose of worship, to the most celebrated foreign temples, especially that of Jerusalem. See the passages of Joseph., Philo, and Sueton., adduced (from Lightf., Wets., and Schoettg.) in Recens. Synop. Nay, many Gentiles were in that age diligent in their search after true religion, and in order thereto, frequented the Jewish Synagogues, though they made no external profession of the Jewish religion, nor were circumcised. Such are in Acts xvii. 4. called οἱ Ἕλληνες σεβόμενοι. Thus though σεβόμενοι be not *here* added, yet it might be *understood*, and these *may* be regarded as a sort of Proselytes. And as it cannot be proved that the Gentiles ever attended at Jerusalem, at the celebration of the *Passover*, these may with most probability be supposed Proselytes *of the gate*, who, however, afterwards made profession of the Mosaic religion. See Lampe and Tittm.

21. ἰδεῖν] "to have an interview with." An idiom common to most languages. There were many reasons why such persons should desire an introduction to so celebrated a person. Their motives, however, in seeking it can only be *conjectured*. And the effect of the application, not being recorded, is also a matter of uncertainty. But it is most probable that they were admitted.

23. ἐλήλυθεν — ἀνθρώπου.] Our Lord may be thought to take occasion from this circumstance to presignify to the two disciples the future progress of the Gospel, when it should be manifested not merely to a few religiously inclined foreigners, but to all the nations of the earth in their own countries. At least, such is the view taken by Noesselt, Kuin., and others, whom see in Recens. Synop. But, notwithstanding that it may seem confirmed by the context, I am inclined to agree with Lampe and Tittm., that the *glory of Christ* here mentioned rather consisted in the resurrection from death, ascension to heaven, and sitting at the right hand of the Father, nay even in the death itself which he suffered for the salvation of the human race, of his own free will, and from the abundant love which he bore towards the Father and towards men. This glory, they add, would be eminently displayed, when it became generally known on earth that he died to save men, — had, moreover, returned from death to life, had ascended to heaven, and was constituted head of the human race, Lord in heaven and earth; and finally, when he should be acknowledged by Jews and Gentiles as the supreme Saviour of all men.

24. ἐὰν μὴ ὁ κόκκος — φέρει.] This is an illustration of what was said in the preceding verse; though the comparison is unaccompanied with application. The sense is: "As a grain of corn cast into the earth, unless it die (i. e. putrify), remains alone, i. e. has no increase; so it must be with *me;* for as *it* must die to yield increase, so must *I* undergo temporal death, in order to be glorified, and produce a great spiritual increase."

25. ὁ φιλῶν τὴν ψυχὴν — αὐτήν.] See Note on Matt. x. 39. Our Lord here teaches, that those of his disciples who desire communion in his glory, must not decline participation in his tribulations. q. d. "He who *so* loveth his life, as to prefer to the loss of it the loss of the advantages of my kingdom, shall not enjoy the felicity destined for those faithful followers, who encounter all perils for mine and the Gospel's sake." Φιλεῖν τὴν ψυχὴν is for φιλοψυχεῖν. The words have indeed immediate reference only to the then state of things and the first Christians; but may, by accommodation, be applied to all times, and Christians of every age.

26. ἐὰν ἐμοὶ διακονῇ τις, ἐμοὶ ἀκολ.] The words may be thus paraphrased: "If any one would dedicate himself to my service, let him imitate my example, submitting cheerfully to all afflictions, nay even death itself, for the advancement of my religion: and (for his encouragement) let him be assured, that where I am, there will be

27 Νῦν ἡ ψυχή μου τετάρακται· καὶ τί εἴπω; Πάτερ, σῶσόν με ἐκ
28 τῆς ὥρας ταύτης; ἀλλὰ διὰ τοῦτο ἦλθον εἰς τὴν ὥραν ταύτην. Πάτερ, δόξασόν σου τὸ ὄνομα. Ἦλθεν οὖν φωνὴ ἐκ τοῦ οὐρανοῦ· Καὶ
29 ἐδόξασα, καὶ πάλιν δοξάσω! ὁ οὖν ὄχλος ὁ ἑστὼς καὶ ἀκούσας, ἔλεγε
30 βροντὴν γεγονέναι. ἄλλοι ἔλεγον· Ἄγγελος αὐτῷ λελάληκεν. Ἀπεκρίθη
ὁ Ἰησοῦς καὶ εἶπεν· Οὐ δι' ἐμὲ αὕτη ἡ φωνὴ γέγονεν, ἀλλὰ δι' ὑμᾶς.
31 [g] Νῦν κρίσις ἐστὶ τοῦ κόσμου τούτου· νῦν ὁ ἄρχων τοῦ κόσμου τού- [g] Infra 16. 11.

be, as partaker of my glory. Moreover, whoever shall serve me faithfully, him will my Father reward with a crown of glory.

27. νῦν ἡ ψυχὴ, &c.] If the common punctuation and interpretation be here adopted, we must suppose that, through perturbation, our Lord first utters, and then retracts a prayer. That, however, is both objectionable and unnecessary; for many of the best ancient and modern Commentators and Editors place a mark of interrogation after ταύτης, thus making *two* interrogations, as follows: What shall I say? [Shall I say] Father, deliver me from this hour? But for this cause came I, for this hour, i. e. to meet this hour. It is well observed by Campb., that "it suited the distress of our Lord's soul to suggest at *first* a petition for deliverance. But in this he is instantly checked by the reflection on the end of his coming. This determines him to cry out, Father, glorify thy name! which was not put as a question, it is what his mind finally and fully acquiesced in. After a short, but severe, struggle, the natural emotions of fear soon subside into *acquiescence* in the will of his Father, whose glory he desires may be promoted by his death."

Ὥρα to denote a time of distress, occurs also on the same subject, in Mark xiv. 35.

28. Π. δόξασόν σ. τ. ὀ.] These (as Dr. Burton observes) are words of *resignation*. q. d. "Cause thy name to be glorified in any manner that seemeth good to thee."

— ἦλθεν οὖν φωνὴ ἐ. τ. ο.] Many recent Commentators understand by φωνὴ here and at Matt. iii. 3. 17. simply *thunder*. They maintain that *no words* were uttered at all; and that the Evangelist did not suppose that there *were* any; but that he only meant to use the words which God, *if he had* expressed His will and intention by human voice, *would have used*. But this is justly accounted by Tittm. an unjustifiable license of interpretation. He observes, that it is inconsistent with the words of v. 30. οὐ δι' ἐμὲ αὕτη ἡ φωνὴ γέγονεν, ἀλλὰ δι' ὑμᾶς. "That a voice *was* (says he) *heard* in *plain words*, from heaven, we are not permitted to doubt, because of the exactly similar circumstances which took place not only in the case of Moses and the children of Israel, (Exod. xix. 19.) and also in that of Samuel, (see 1 Sam. iii. 5. seqq.) but likewise in that of our Lord himself at his baptism, and in his transfiguration on Mount Tabor, which places the thing beyond dispute. For 1. the *words themselves*, which were heard, are expressly mentioned. 2. In the following passage not only are some said to have thought that an angel spoke with Jesus, but our Lord himself says, οὐ δι' ἐμὲ αὕτη ἡ φωνὴ γέγονεν, ἀλλὰ δι' ὑμᾶς. So also St. Peter relates, that he and the rest who were with our Lord on Mount Tabor, heard a *voice* from heaven which *said*, This is my beloved Son. It is true that the by-standers differed in opinion. Some, who perhaps had not been very attentive, and had themselves not heard the words distinctly, said *it thundered*; for the voice had proceeded from the clouds, [and indeed that thunder sometimes accompanied (probably preceded or followed) this voice from heaven, is certain from Exod. xix. 16. 19. Revel. iv. 5. vi. i. x. 3. Edit.] Others, however, had heard them, and immediately supposed that God had spoken by an angel, conformably to the opinion of the Jews, who thought that God never spoke except by the ministry of angels; and therefore they did not doubt whether the words were uttered, but *in what manner*." See Note on Matt. iii. 17. As to the words themselves, the full sense intended, though not *then* expressed, but meant to be understood from *the event*, may be what Dr. Burton expresses in his paraphrase: "I have caused my Name to be glorified by my former dispensations, and now I shall do so again by thy death." On the whole of this important subject, the *Bath Col*, or voice from heaven, see Mr. Townsend's remarks, Chr. Arr. i. 406.

30. δι' ὑμᾶς] for *your* sakes, for the confirmation of your faith.

31. νῦν κρίσις — ἔξω.] There has been much difference of sentiment on the interpretation of these words, which admit of more than one sense. Tittm., after an elaborate discussion of the import, is of opinion that by ἄρχων τοῦ κόσμου is denoted the *genius seculi*, a spirit of unbelief and wickedness, (see Eph. ii. 2. and compare Acts xxvi. 18. with Col. i. 13.) and that by ἄρχων τοῦ κόσμου τούτου we may understand generally the *influence* which unbelief and iniquity exerted over the minds of men, impeding the progress of true religion and happiness. This interpretation, however, is more *ingenious than solid*; and I see no reason to abandon the common one, by which ὁ ἄρχων is taken to mean *Satan*. The full sense of the passage may be expressed thus: "Now is [at hand] the judgment or condemnation of the world," (i. e. now will sentence be passed on this world "which lieth in sin"); "now will the Prince of this world be deposed from his rule." This sense of ἐκβάλλειν is found in the best writers, who use both ἐκβάλλειν βασιλέα ἐκ τῆς ἀρχῆς and simply ἐκβάλλειν. The not discerning the *ratio metaphoræ* has led the Commentators astray. The meaning is, that now is the Prince of this world about to be deposed, and his subjects condemned for sin and unbelief. That the two clauses are very closely connected in sense, is certain from a kindred passage at xvi. 11. compared with v. 6.; where our Lord says that *the Paraclete*, at his coming, ἐλέγξει τὸν κόσμον περὶ κρίσεως, i. e. as it is then explained, ὅτι ὁ ἄρχων τοῦ κόσμου τούτου κέκριται, "is to be condemned," and consequently deposed. See the Note there.

Thus here, by the Ruler of the world being deposed is meant, that his authority is to be abolished, and his empire over the minds of men destroyed; namely, by the abolition of idolatry and

h Supr. 3. 14. του ἐκβληθήσεται ἔξω· [h] κἀγὼ, ἐὰν ὑψωθῶ ἐκ τῆς γῆς, πάντας ἑλκύσω 32
πρὸς ἐμαυτόν. Τοῦτο δὲ ἔλεγε, σημαίνων ποίῳ θανάτῳ ἤμελλεν ἀπο- 33
i 2 Sam. 7. 13. Psal. 89. 29, 36. & 110. 4. Isa. 9. 6, 7. Ezek. 37. 25. Dan. 2. 44. & 7. 14, 27. k Supra 1. 9. θνήσκειν. [i] Ἀπεκρίθη αὐτῷ ὁ ὄχλος· Ἡμεῖς ἠκούσαμεν ἐκ τοῦ νόμου, 34
ὅτι ὁ Χριστὸς μένει εἰς τὸν αἰῶνα· καὶ πῶς σὺ λέγεις· [Ὅτι] δεῖ
ὑψωθῆναι τὸν Υἱὸν τοῦ ἀνθρώπου; τίς ἐστιν οὗτος ὁ Υἱὸς τοῦ ἀνθρώπου; [k] Εἶπεν οὖν αὐτοῖς ὁ Ἰησοῦς· Ἔτι μικρὸν χρόνον τὸ φῶς 35
μεθ᾽ ὑμῶν ἐστι. περιπατεῖτε ἕως τὸ φῶς ἔχετε, ἵνα μὴ σκοτία ὑμᾶς
καταλάβῃ· καὶ ὁ περιπατῶν ἐν τῇ σκοτίᾳ οὐκ οἶδε ποῦ ὑπάγει.
Ἕως τὸ φῶς ἔχετε, πιστεύετε εἰς τὸ φῶς, ἵνα υἱοὶ φωτὸς γένησθε. 36
Ταῦτα ἐλάλησεν ὁ Ἰησοῦς· καὶ ἀπελθὼν ἐκρύβη ἀπ᾽ αὐτῶν.

Τοσαῦτα δὲ αὐτοῦ σημεῖα πεποιηκότος ἔμπροσθεν αὐτῶν, οὐκ ἐπί- 37
l Isa. 53. 1. Rom. 10. 16. στευον εἰς αὐτόν· [l] ἵνα ὁ λόγος Ἡσαΐου τοῦ προφήτου πληρωθῇ, ὃν 38

superstition, and the introduction of true and vital religion.

32. κἀγὼ—ἐμαυτόν.] Here our Lord, I conceive, points out, though obscurely, the *means* by which the great consummation just adverted to would be accomplished, namely, by his *crucifixion, resurrection, ascension, exaltation* to glory, and the commencement of his office as Advocate with the Father, the first work of which would be the sending of the Holy Spirit, and then the mission of those who in every age should preach the Gospel. By these, and by his revealed Word in the N. T., our Lord means to say, he would draw all men to him; would offer such moral inducements and spiritual aids to men as should be sufficient to sway the intellect to assent to the truths of his religion, and the will to obey its moral requisitions. By πάντας may be intimated the *universality* intended in the blessings of redemption; though it *may* also (as Tittm. thinks) mean, that these benefits shall be extended to men of *every* nation, both Jews and Gentiles. Πρὸς ἐμαυτὸν *suggests* the place whither he is going, *Heaven*. Thus at xiv. 2, 3. our Lord says he is going to prepare a place for them; and having prepared it, he will return and *receive them to himself*. Ἐὰν is here and at John vi. 62. xiv. 3. 1 John iii. 2. and elsewhere, and sometimes in the Sept., put for ὅταν, i. e. ὅτ᾽ ἂν, by an ellipsis of ὅτε.

33. σημαίνων.] The word is often used (as here) of things future and obscurely signified, as in oracles, &c. So Plutarch cited by Wets. οὔτε λέγει, οὔτε κρύπτει, ἀλλὰ σημαίνει.

34. τοῦ νόμου] i. e. the Scriptures. See x. 34. Μένει εἰς τὸν αἰῶνα, "is to remain on earth for ever." There are numerous passages of the Prophets, referred to by the Commentators, importing that Christ's kingdom would be everlasting. But by *that* was meant his *Spiritual* kingdom.

—ὑψωθῆναι τὸν Υἱὸν τ. ἀ.] It is plain from hence that the terms Χριστὸς and ὁ Υἱὸς τοῦ ἀνθρώπου were regarded as synonymous. The speakers *take for granted* that Jesus is, what he claims to be, the *Messiah*. The Commentators, however, are wrong in supposing that by ὑψωθῆναι the people understood him to speak of *crucifixion*. It should seem that not even the Apostles comprehended the import of what was said, which was only meant as a *dark prediction* to be *understood after the event*, for the confirmation of their faith. The multitude, as appears from what follows, understood the expression ὑψωθῆναι ἐκ τῆς γῆς only of removal from earth to heaven, whether by death, or otherwise, as in the case of Elijah.

—τίς ἐστιν—ἀνθρώπου.] This is wrongly rendered by our English Translators, "Who is that Son of man?" Τίς is for ποῖος (like *quis* for *qualis* in Latin), as in Mark i. 27. & vi. 2. Luke i. 66. John vii. 36. and often. Render: "What sort of Son of Man is that to be?" To this question our Lord (ver. 35.) only replies *indirectly*, and by allegory, hinting at their erroneous opinions concerning the Messiah, by adverting to that opportunity for obtaining light to dissipate the clouds of error which they must use while they have it, lest they should be overtaken by that spiritual darkness which would disable them from directing their course. Καταλαμβάνειν is often used of the *coming on* of night. At περιπατεῖτε sub. ἐν τῷ φωτὶ, which is explained at ver. 36. by πιστεύετε εἰς τὸ φῶς, "believe in Him who is the great Teacher." By υἱοὶ τοῦ φωτὸς are meant those who should follow the instructions and example of that Teacher. See Luke xvi. 8. Ὁ περιπατῶν ἐν—ὑπάγει must be viewed in the same light as the passage at xi. 10. where see Note, οὐκ οἶδε ποῦ ὑπάγει being a *popular* expression, signifying, "he knows not how to direct his course."

36. ἐκρύβη ἀπ᾽ αὐτῶν] "withdrew himself from them, and kept himself in seclusion, no longer teaching in public."

37—50.] This portion is called by Grot. and Beng. the *Epiphonema*, or *Epicrisis historiæ totius*, containing the remarks of the Evangelist on the *event* (so little successful) of Christ's teaching. In this he treats, 1. of the *miracles* (vv. 37—43.), and 2. of the *doctrine* of Jesus; and shows that *neither* were such as to induce the Jews to believe in him.

38. ἵνα.] The best Commentators, ancient and modern, are agreed that ἵνα here denotes (as often) the *event*, and not the *cause*; "for (as Mr. Holden expresses it) their unbelief did not happen because it was foretold; but it was foretold because it was foreseen that it would happen." For a complete understanding of this abstruse subject, the reader is referred to the able Note of Whitby; and for a learned and able discussion of the phraseology (especially as to its difference from the Hebrew and Sept.), to Tittm. in Recens. Synop. It is shown that the difference is only in words, the sense being precisely the same. q. d. "So that the saying of Isaiah was fulfilled."

εἶπε· Κύριε, τίς ἐπίστευσε τῇ ἀκοῇ ἡμῶν; καὶ ὁ
39 βραχίων Κυρίου τίνι ἀπεκαλύφθη; Διὰ τοῦτο οὐκ ἠδύναν-
40 το πιστεύειν, ὅτι πάλιν εἶπεν Ἡσαΐας· [m] Τετύφλωκεν αὐτῶν τοὺς m Isa. 6. 9. Matt. 13. 14.
ὀφθαλμοὺς, καὶ πεπώρωκεν αὐτῶν τὴν καρδίαν· ἵνα Mark 4. 12. Luke 8. 10.
μὴ ἴδωσι τοῖς ὀφθαλμοῖς, καὶ νοήσωσι τῇ καρδίᾳ, καὶ Acts 28. 26. Rom. 11. 8.
41 ἐπιστραφῶσι, καὶ ἰάσωμαι αὐτούς. Ταῦτα εἶπεν Ἡσαΐας, ὅτε
42 εἶδε τὴν δόξαν αὐτοῦ, καὶ ἐλάλησε περὶ αὐτοῦ· ὅμως μέντοι καὶ ἐκ τῶν
ἀρχόντων πολλοὶ ἐπίστευσαν εἰς αὐτὸν· ἀλλὰ, διὰ τοὺς Φαρισαίους,
43 οὐχ ὡμολόγουν, ἵνα μὴ ἀποσυνάγωγοι γένωνται. [n] ἠγάπησαν γὰρ τὴν n Supra 5. 44.
δόξαν τῶν ἀνθρώπων μᾶλλον ἤπερ τὴν δόξαν τοῦ Θεοῦ.
44 [o] Ἰησοῦς δὲ ἔκραξε καὶ εἶπεν· Ὁ πιστεύων εἰς ἐμὲ, οὐ πιστεύει εἰς o 1 Pet. 1. 21.
45 ἐμὲ, ἀλλ' εἰς τὸν πέμψαντά με· καὶ ὁ θεωρῶν ἐμὲ θεωρεῖ τὸν πέμ-
46 ψαντά με. [p] Ἐγὼ φῶς εἰς τὸν κόσμον ἐλήλυθα, ἵνα πᾶς ὁ πιστεύων p Supra 1. 5, 9. & 3. 19.
47 εἰς ἐμὲ ἐν τῇ σκοτίᾳ μὴ μείνῃ. [q] Καὶ ἐάν τις μου ἀκούσῃ τῶν ῥημά- & 8. 12. & 9. 5.
των καὶ μὴ πιστεύσῃ, ἐγὼ οὐ κρίνω αὐτόν· οὐ γὰρ ἦλθον ἵνα κρίνω q Supra 3. 17. Mark 16. 16.
48 τὸν κόσμον, ἀλλ' ἵνα σώσω τὸν κόσμον. Ὁ ἀθετῶν ἐμὲ καὶ μὴ λαμ-
βάνων τὰ ῥήματά μου ἔχει τὸν κρίνοντα αὐτόν· ὁ λόγος ὃν ἐλάλησα
49 ἐκεῖνος κρινεῖ αὐτὸν ἐν τῇ ἐσχάτῃ ἡμέρᾳ. [r] Ὅτι ἐγὼ ἐξ ἐμαυτοῦ οὐκ r Infra 14. 10.
ἐλάλησα· ἀλλ' ὁ πέμψας με Πατὴρ, αὐτός μοι ἐντολὴν ἔδωκε, τί εἴπω
50 καὶ τί λαλήσω· καὶ οἶδα ὅτι ἡ ἐντολὴ αὐτοῦ ζωὴ αἰώνιός ἐστιν. ἃ
οὖν λαλῶ ἐγὼ, καθὼς εἴρηκέ μοι ὁ Πατὴρ, οὕτω λαλῶ.

— τῇ ἀκοῇ] "our speech," or testimony. A sense of the word derived from the Heb. שְׁמוּעָה, and occurring at Rom. x. 16. Gal. iii. 2. and Jerem. x. 22. Βραχίων signifies *power*; a common metaphor; or rather *power exerted* in *action*. Lampe thinks this has reference to the custom of the warriors of antiquity, to uncover their arms, whether for actual battle, or for giving orders. But there can be no more than an *allusion*, and perhaps not *that*. The interrogation implies a strong negation, q. d. *nemo fere*, *very few*. And although the words might be applicable enough to the times of Isaiah, nay, to almost *all* times, yet (as Tittm. observes) there can be no doubt but that the Prophet had in view our Lord and his age.

39. διὰ τοῦτο] i. e. since they would not hearken to Christ's instructions. Οὐκ ἠδύναντο πιστεύειν. This must, of course, not be understood of physical inability; but we must, with the best Commentators, ancient and modern, take it of *moral* inability, to mean, they *would* not, i. e. literally, *they could not bring themselves to*, &c. See Note on Matt. xiii. 14.

42. ὅμως μέντοι.] An accumulation of synonymous words, to strengthen the sense, as in Herodot. i. 189. On ἀποσυνάγ. γένωνται, see note on ix. 22.

44—50. This forms the *second* part of St. John's discourse above mentioned, namely, on the *doctrines* of Jesus, being a brief summary of them, and in our Lord's own words. See supra i. 15. and Note. The Aorists ἔκραξε (which denotes *public* teaching) and εἶπε must be taken as Pluperfects.

— οὐ — ἀλλ'] Here, as often, this denotes *non tam — quam*, "not [so much] in me as in Him," &c. Or there may be, as Kuin. thinks, an ellip. of μόνον, on which see my Note on Thucyd. iii. 45. and compare Mark ix. 37.

45. ὁ θεωρῶν — με.] This denotes the intimate union of nature, will, counsel, &c. between the Father and the Son. See xiv. 9. and Note.

46. φῶς — ἐλήλυθα.] St. John often styles our Lord φῶς. So i. 9. viii. 12. See Notes.

47. οὐ κρίνω αὐτόν.] The words are commonly taken to mean, "I do not *here* on earth act as judge over him, since I came to be a Saviour, not a Judge." See iii. 17. v. 45. viii. 15. and Notes. Kuin. and Tittm., however, take κρίνειν here in the sense *condemn* and *punish*, q. d. I am not the cause of his condemnation, or that of men, having come not for the ruin, but the salvation, of men. On this verse see iii. 16—19. compared with 2 Pet. iii. 9.

48. ὁ ἀθετῶν — κρ. αὐτόν·] There seems here to be an ἀλλὰ omitted per *Asyndeton*. q. d. [Nevertheless, he will not go unpunished]. He that, &c.

— ὁ λόγος.] By this and the τὰ ῥήματα are meant that part of Christ's teaching which respected his person and office. See iii. 17. and Note. The εἴπω refers to commands; and λαλήσω to oral instruction. It is meant that the unbeliever's inattention and wilful neglect of both will bring down on him condemnation and destruction.

50. Christ here made three declarations: 1. That he had not invented the doctrine himself, but received it from the Father, and that therefore it did not owe its origin to human invention, but was altogether divine. 2. He testified his thorough persuasion, that those things which were committed to him to be delivered, had all no other end but the eternal salvation of men: and that his doctrine points out the way which

a Matt. 26. 1. Mark 14. 1. Luke 22. 1.

1 XIII. ᵃ ΠΡΟ δὲ τῆς ἑορτῆς τοῦ πάσχα, εἰδὼς ὁ Ἰησοῦς ὅτι ἐλήλυθεν αὐτοῦ ἡ ὥρα, ἵνα μεταβῇ ἐκ τοῦ κόσμου τούτου πρὸς τὸν Πατέρα,
ἀγαπήσας τοὺς ἰδίους τοὺς ἐν τῷ κόσμῳ, εἰς τέλος ἠγάπησεν αὐτούς.
2 Καὶ δείπνου γενομένου, (τοῦ Διαβόλου ἤδη βεβληκότος εἰς τὴν καρδίαν
3 Ἰούδα Σίμωνος Ἰσκαριώτου, ἵνα αὐτὸν παραδῷ,) ᵗ εἰδὼς ὁ Ἰησοῦς, ὅτι
πάντα δέδωκεν αὐτῷ ὁ Πατὴρ εἰς τὰς χεῖρας, καὶ ὅτι ἀπὸ Θεοῦ ἐξῆλθε
4 καὶ πρὸς τὸν Θεὸν ὑπάγει· ἐγείρεται ἐκ τοῦ δείπνου, καὶ τίθησι τὰ
5 ἱμάτια, καὶ λαβὼν λέντιον, διέζωσεν ἑαυτόν· εἶτα βάλλει ὕδωρ εἰς τὸν
νιπτῆρα, καὶ ἤρξατο νίπτειν τοὺς πόδας τῶν μαθητῶν, καὶ ἐκμάσσειν

t Matt. 28. 18. Supra 3. 35. Infra 17. 2.

leads to eternal happiness. 3. He affirmed that, in teaching, he had confined himself to the will of his Father; that he had neither added nor suppressed aught, and that therefore his doctrine was pure, complete, and altogether Divine. (Tittm.)

XIII. Having finished the work of *public* instruction, our Lord now devoted the short remainder of his life to the private instruction of his disciples. These he in, chap. xiii., xiv., xv., apprises of his approaching trials, and endeavours to console them by kind assurances, evincing his love both to them and to the whole human race.

1. *πρὸ τῆς ἑορτῆς τοῦ πάσχα.*] See Note on Matt. xxvi. 2.

— *εἰδὼς — ὥρα.*] Of this he was well aware — having frequently conversed with his disciples upon it, and predicted its most minute circumstances.

— *ἵνα μεταβῇ — Πατέρα.*] Christ called his departure *μετάβασις*, as signifying that he had not come on earth as a *mere man*, but as the *Son of God*, who had proceeded from, and would return to God.

— *ἀγαπήσας τοὺς ἰδίους.*] By *τοὺς ἰδ.* almost all Commentators understand *his disciples*. But as the words *τοὺς ἐν τῷ κόσμῳ* are subjoined, Tittm. maintains that the sense must be, "*the whole human race.*" See xvii. 24.

— *ἠγάπησεν.*] Tittm. rightly observes, that this is to be taken, like many other verbs, *declaratively*. By the *tokens* of love evinced by Jesus to his disciples are meant the *symbolical actions* mentioned just afterwards. At *εἰς τέλος* sub. *βίου*; or take *εἰς τέλος ἠγ.* for *διετέλει ἀγαπῶν*, with Grot. and Tittm.

2. *δείπνου γεν.*] Many Commentators render this cœnâ peractâ." But, as at vv. 4 & 12, Christ is said to have risen from supper, and again sat down, others (as Tittm.) with reason take it to mean "cœnâ *instructâ*," "it being supper time," such washing being performed *before*, not *after* a meal. Accordingly, Tittm. thinks that our Lord had sat down to table; but that before he began supper, he arose, to wash his disciples' feet. Then, having sat down again, he held the discourse here recorded. Kuin., on the other hand, takes *γενομένου* for *ὄντος*, and thinks the sense is, "while supper was taking." And he parries the objection, that washing *preceded* the meal, by observing, that this was an *extraordinary* washing, meant as a symbolical action. Yet there were, as we learn from the Rabbinical writers, *two* washings at the Paschal supper. Be that as it may, the symbolical action was meant to inculcate a lesson of humility and affectionate attention to each other's comfort, so much the more seasonable, as the disciples had been disputing *who* were to fill the *chief posts* in the Messiah's temporal kingdom.

— *βεβληκότος εἰς τὴν καρδίαν* Ἰ. Σ.] This and other kindred phrases, with more or less variety, are used in Scripture of suggesting any thought to the mind. Many recent Commentators, indeed, regard this as a popular form of expression, meant only to denote the enormity of the crime meditated. This, however, is founded on a dangerous principle, and the words evidently convey the notion of a *real Being* possessed of an *actual power* over the minds of men. The circumstances of Judas's temptation to betray his Master, and the condescension of that Master, are mentioned together, in order to represent more strongly the baseness of the betrayer.

3. *εἰδὼς ὁ Ἰησοῦς — χεῖρας.*] Tittm. has shown that *ὅτι ἀπὸ Θεοῦ ἐξῆλθε*, taken in conjunction with *πρὸς τὸν Θεὸν ὑπάγει*, can import no less than that Jesus was of celestial origin, and dwelt in heaven before he came upon earth. (See iii. 13; vi. 62; xvii. 5; also i. 1; ii. 18.); also "that *πρὸς τὸν Θεὸν ὑπάγει* must mean, that our Lord would return to the Father, again to reign with Him by equal right." In short, the verse plainly declares the dignity of Christ's person and office — that as he had "come *from*" God (by origination from the Father), and had had the governance of the universe committed to him, so he was going [back] *to* God, to resume the glory he had had with the Father from all eternity. See viii. 42. and Note.

4. *τίθησι*] "lays aside." So *ponere* in Latin. By *ἱμάτια* is meant either the upper garment, the *pallium* (plural for singular, as in the corresponding Hebrew terms), or the *pallium* and *stola*. See Recens. Syn. and Note on Matth. xxiv. 18. *Λέντιον* is a Hellenistic word, from the Latin *linteum*, nearly synonymous with *σινδὼν*, and properly called *σάβανον*, *a towel*. To be thus girded was considered by the ancients in the same light as a person's wearing an *apron* is with us, namely, as indicating the exercise of some servile occupation.

5. *βάλλει — νιπτῆρα.*] Βάλλει is for *ἐμβάλλει*, (or more properly *ἐγχεῖ*) and occurs in this sense in Exod. xxiv. 6. Τὸν νιπ. Bp. Middlt. observes that the *Article* implies that there was *but one* ewer employed for the occasion. This washing which, in the times of primitive simplicity, had been performed by the host or hostess to the guest, was in after ages committed to the servants, and was therefore accounted a servile employment. Thus it is rarely mentioned. At no time had it been done by a *superior* to an *inferior*.

6 τῷ λεντίῳ ᾧ ἦν διεζωσμένος. Ἔρχεται οὖν πρὸς Σίμωνα Πέτρον· καὶ
7 λέγει αὐτῷ ἐκεῖνος· Κύριε, σύ μου νίπτεις τοὺς πόδας; Ἀπεκρίθη
Ἰησοῦς καὶ εἶπεν αὐτῷ· Ὃ ἐγὼ ποιῶ σὺ οὐκ οἶδας ἄρτι, γνώσῃ δὲ
8 μετὰ ταῦτα. Λέγει αὐτῷ Πέτρος· Οὐ μὴ νίψῃς τοὺς πόδας μου εἰς
τὸν αἰῶνα. Ἀπεκρίθη αὐτῷ ὁ Ἰησοῦς· Ἐὰν μὴ νίψω σε, οὐκ ἔχεις
9 μέρος μετ' ἐμοῦ. Λέγει αὐτῷ Σίμων Πέτρος· Κύριε, μὴ τοὺς πόδας
10 μου μόνον, ἀλλὰ καὶ τὰς χεῖρας καὶ τὴν κεφαλήν. [u] Λέγει αὐτῷ ὁ u Infra 15. 3.
Ἰησοῦς· Ὁ λελουμένος οὐ χρείαν ἔχει ἢ τοὺς πόδας νίψασθαι, ἀλλ'
11 ἔστι καθαρὸς ὅλος. Καὶ ὑμεῖς καθαροί ἐστε· ἀλλ' οὐχὶ πάντες. ᾔδει
γὰρ τὸν παραδιδόντα αὐτόν· διὰ τοῦτο εἶπεν· Οὐχὶ πάντες καθαροί
ἐστε.
12 Ὅτε οὖν ἔνιψε τοὺς πόδας αὐτῶν, καὶ ἔλαβε τὰ ἱμάτια αὐτοῦ, ἀνα-
13 πεσὼν πάλιν, εἶπεν αὐτοῖς· Γινώσκετε τί πεποίηκα ὑμῖν; [x] Ὑμεῖς x Matt. 23. 8, 10. 1 Cor. 8. 6.
φωνεῖτέ με· Ὁ διδάσκαλος, καὶ ὁ Κύριος· καὶ καλῶς λέγετε· εἰμὶ
14 γάρ. Εἰ οὖν ἐγὼ ἔνιψα ὑμῶν τοὺς πόδας, ὁ Κύριος καὶ ὁ διδάσκα-
15 λος, καὶ ὑμεῖς ὀφείλετε ἀλλήλων νίπτειν τοὺς πόδας. Ὑπόδειγμα γὰρ
16 ἔδωκα ὑμῖν, ἵνα καθὼς ἐγὼ ἐποίησα ὑμῖν, καὶ ὑμεῖς ποιῆτε. [y] Ἀμὴν y Infra 15. 20. Matt. 10. 24. Luke 6. 40.
ἀμὴν λέγω ὑμῖν· οὐκ ἔστι δοῦλος μείζων τοῦ κυρίου αὐτοῦ, οὐδὲ ἀπό-

6. σύ μου — πόδας.] This sort of interrogation involves a strong negation, and the σὺ and νιπτ. are emphatic.

7. ὃ ἐγὼ ποιῶ, &c.] A popular mode of expression for, "The *meaning* of what I am doing," &c. Μετὰ ταῦτα is often used, as here, of a very short period hence; and then is better rendered afterwards: here it means, "after I have done what I am doing." Our Lord shows the reason at v. 12—17; namely, to set them an example of humility, condescension, and Christian forbearance.

8. ἐὰν μὴ νίψω σε need not be supposed (with Kuin. and others) to mean, "unless thou *sufferest* me to wash thee." The phrase seems to be so worded, to make the thing appear a *privilege* to be conferred by Christ. There is an allusion to the *spiritual* washing away of sin by the blood of Christ. Ἔχειν μέρος μετά τινος is a common phrase denoting conjunction, friendship, and (from the adjunct) communion of benefits.

10. ὁ λελουμένος — ὅλος.] The best Commentators are agreed, that λελ. denotes the washing of the whole body in a bath, as opposed to νίπτεσθαι, which is used of *washing* part of the body. See Acts ix. 37. compared with Homer, Iliad ω. 582. A guest who had gone through the *former*, needed only, on arrival at the house of his host, to have his *feet* washed; which, as the Jews wore no sandals, might be soiled by the way; or, in a hot climate, would need washing after the perspiration occasioned by walking. To offer this was a mark of civility and attention. Thus the sense is: "As he who has bathed has no need of washing himself, except his feet, but is then quite pure, [so] ye need no other washing." Ἢ is for ἀλλ' ἢ, which is of rare occurrence.

— καὶ ὑμεῖς — πάντες.] From the mention of external and ceremonial cleansing, Christ takes occasion to advert to *internal* and *moral purity*; i. e. from evil thoughts and actions; both by way of admonition to the disciples, and to smite the conscience of Judas. The καί, as at ver. 14, may be rendered "and [thus]."

12—17. Here our Lord shews the *intent* of the action he had been performing, admonishing them of the duty it was meant to suggest.

12. τί πεποίηκα ὑμῖν] "the intent of what I have done to you."

13. φωνεῖτέ με· ὁ διδ.] Ὁ διδ. is not (as Campb. supposes) the nominat. for the accus., but rather for the *vocative*, as at Mark v. 41. and elsewhere. See Winer's Gr. § 22, 3. Indeed, here it forms part of the form of address, there being an ellip. of λέγοντες. How frequent, nay perpetual was this mode of address, is proved by the citations adduced from the Rabbinical writers by Schoettgen; which indeed shew that the *proper* name of the Rabbins was almost dropped. Thus in Sanhedrim, fol. 100, 1. we read, "It is Epicureism (or impiety) if any one shall call a Rabbi by his proper name."

14. ὑμεῖς — πόδας.] These words are not to be taken, nor were understood, in the *literal* sense; for neither the Apostles nor the primitive Christians had any such customs. Our Lord here intended an admonition (as Tittm. has shewn at large, see Rec. Syn.) most seasonable to the disciples (in whose bosoms ambition, pride, and other worldly passions had begun to manifest themselves), and, in order to impress it still more on their minds, was pleased to employ a *symbolical* action; a mode of teaching often resorted to by the prophets of the O. T. and by our Lord. By "washing one another's feet," however, he did not mean that they should do this *actually* and according to the *letter*, but that they should behave towards each other with the same *spirit* as that characterized by this symbol of humility and condescension, having a mind weaned from pride, ambition, vain-glory, and ever ready to shew mutual forbearance, condescension, and kindness.

16. ἀπόστολος] for ὁ ἀπεσταλμένος, like the Heb.

στολος μείζων τοῦ πέμψαντος αὐτόν. Εἰ ταῦτα οἴδατε, μακάριοί ἐστε 17
ἐὰν ποιῆτε αὐτά. Οὐ περὶ πάντων ὑμῶν λέγω· ἐγὼ οἶδα οὓς ἐξελε- 18
z Psal. 41. 9. ξάμην· ἀλλ' ἵνα ἡ γραφὴ πληρωθῇ, [z]Ὁ τρώγων μετ' ἐμοῦ
τὸν ἄρτον ἐπῆρεν ἐπ' ἐμὲ τὴν πτέρναν αὐτοῦ. Ἀπ' ἄρτι 19
λέγω ὑμῖν πρὸ τοῦ γενέσθαι, ἵνα ὅταν γένηται, πιστεύσητε ὅτι ἐγώ
a Matt. 10. 40. εἰμι. [a]ἀμὴν ἀμὴν λέγω ὑμῖν· Ὁ λαμβάνων ἐάν τινα πέμψω ἐμὲ 20
λαμβάνει· ὁ δὲ ἐμὲ λαμβάνων λαμβάνει τὸν πέμψαντά με.
b Matt. 26. 21. Mark 14. 18. Luke 22. 21. [b]Ταῦτα εἰπὼν ὁ Ἰησοῦς ἐταράχθη τῷ πνεύματι, καὶ ἐμαρτύρησε καὶ 21
εἶπεν· Ἀμὴν ἀμὴν λέγω ὑμῖν, ὅτι εἷς ἐξ ὑμῶν παραδώσει με. Ἔβλε- 22
c Infra 21. 20. πον οὖν εἰς ἀλλήλους οἱ μαθηταὶ, ἀπορούμενοι περὶ τίνος λέγει. [c]Ἦν 23
δὲ ἀνακείμενος εἷς τῶν μαθητῶν αὐτοῦ ἐν τῷ κόλπῳ τοῦ Ἰησοῦ, ὃν
ἠγάπα ὁ Ἰησοῦς. Νεύει οὖν τούτῳ Σίμων Πέτρος πυθέσθαι τίς ἂν 24
εἴη περὶ οὗ λέγει. Ἐπιπεσὼν δὲ ἐκεῖνος ἐπὶ τὸ στῆθος τοῦ Ἰησοῦ, 25
λέγει αὐτῷ· Κύριε, τίς ἐστιν; Ἀποκρίνεται ὁ Ἰησοῦς· Ἐκεῖνός 26
ἐστιν ᾧ ἐγὼ βάψας τὸ ψωμίον ἐπιδώσω. καὶ ἐμβάψας τὸ ψωμίον, δί-

שלוחו. A similar maxim is cited from the Rabbinical writers.

17. εἰ ταῦτα—αὐτά.] The εἰ may, with Kuin. and others, be rendered *siquidem*, *since*, as at ver. 14. εἰ—ἔνιψα, &c. Acts xi. 17. xvi. 15. xviii. 15. Rom. viii. 31. and elsewhere. See Herm. on Vig. § 312. Matth. Gr. § 508. Buttm. Gr. p. 240. 2. But it may be doubted whether they did really know the truths they had been told; and an *opinion* of knowledge is a frequent cause of ignorance: οἴησις προκοπῆς ἐγκοπή, said the Philosopher. Moreover, as that signification is not to be resorted to unnecessarily, and where it materially alters the sense, so here it is better to retain the ordinary one; and suppose that our Lord here slightly alludes to that self-opinion. q. d. Ye may say that ye know all this very well. If, then, ye do know these things, happy are ye if ye *put them in practice*; for, as Lampe remarks, "knowledge must precede holiness; but it is not of itself sufficient. The *practice* must be added. These two things are inseparably connected: knowledge is the rule of practice, and practice the scope and purpose of knowledge."

18. οὐ περὶ—λέγω] meaning "Of *all* of you I cannot affirm that ye will be happy in the practice of this precept."

—οἶδα οὓς ἐξελεξάμην.] The sense is, "I know the [dispositions of the] persons whom I have chosen [as Apostles]." So xv. 16. ἐγὼ ἐξελεξάμην ὑμᾶς καὶ ἔθηκα ὑμᾶς. At ἀλλ' ἵνα, &c. sub. τοῦτο γίνεται, or the like. The ἵνα has the *eventual* force. Render, "But [such is the case with you] that the words of Scripture are fulfilled:" what was literally meant for Ahithophel being typically intended for, and fulfilled in, Judas.

—ὁ τρώγων—αὐτοῦ.] Ὁ τρ. denotes a familiar friend; the communion of domestic hospitality having in every age been accounted an inviolable pledge of friendship. See Eurip. Hec. 793. Quint. Curt. vii. 4. Ἐπῆρεν, &c. The general sense is, "has turned against me, to overthrow me." A metaphor taken, according to some, from *wrestling*; according to others, from *kicking* animals, which suddenly and treacherously kick at and injure their feeders. This is confirmed by a similar passage at Jerem. ix. 4. πᾶς ἀδελφὸς πτέρνῃ πτερνιεῖ (scil. ἀδελφὸν) καὶ πᾶς φίλος δολίως πορεύσεται.

19. ἀπ' ἄρτι λέγω—πιστεύσητε, &c.] "I tell you this now before it has happened, that when it has taken place, ye may be confirmed in your faith that I am He [whom I professed to be, the Messiah]." There is the same omission at viii. 24. and elsewhere; in which, and many other similar cases, we recognize what we should call genuine *modesty* in a distinguished *human being*; though, in speaking of our Lord, the language even of commendation should be checked by reverential awe. Πιστ. is taken as at ii. 11. and elsewhere; in which an *intension* of the sense denoted by the verb seems meant. Our Lord's purpose was not only to confirm their faith, but calm their perturbation at the perfidy soon to be disclosed, since his words allude to only *one* traitor, as indeed he soon afterwards intimates in express terms.

20. So Matt. x. 40. where see Note. The connexion here is variously traced. The scope of the words seems to be, to fortify them under the tribulations they should endure in the course of their Apostolic office, by the remembrance, that as they sustained the character of *representatives* of their Lord, they should not be troubled at having to suffer, as He had, from the treachery, cowardice, stupidity, and perverseness of those whom they taught.

21. ἐμαρτύρησε καὶ εἶπεν.] For ἐμαρτ. εἰπών. Μαρτυρεῖν denotes open declaration, in contradistinction to the indirect allusion at v. 20.

22. ἔβλεπον εἰς ἀλλ.] This well depicts their *anxiety*, as ἀπορούμενοι their *perplexity* what to think or whom to suspect. See Gen. xlii. 1. and Hom. Il. ω. 480.

24. νεύει.] See Note on Luke i. 22.

25. ἐπιπεσὼν] "leaning upon." Euthym., however, thinks John did not alter his posture, but merely turned his head. That the question was put in a low voice, and answered in the same tone, is plain from vv. 28, 29.

26. ψωμίον.] This is ill rendered *sop*; and not well translated *morsel*, though that signification is sometimes found. As derived from ψάω, it signifies, (like the Heb. פת from פתת to *break*) a

27 δωσιν Ἰούδᾳ Σίμωνος Ἰσκαριώτῃ. Καὶ μετὰ τὸ ψωμίον τότε εἰσῆλθεν εἰς ἐκεῖνον ὁ Σατανᾶς. λέγει οὖν αὐτῷ ὁ Ἰησοῦς· Ὃ ποιεῖς,
28 ποίησον τάχιον. Τοῦτο δὲ οὐδεὶς ἔγνω τῶν ἀνακειμένων πρὸς τί εἶπεν
29 αὐτῷ. [d] τινὲς γὰρ ἐδόκουν, ἐπεὶ τὸ γλωσσόκομον εἶχεν ὁ Ἰούδας, ὅτι d Supra 12. 6.
λέγει αὐτῷ ὁ Ἰησοῦς· Ἀγόρασον ὧν χρείαν ἔχομεν εἰς τὴν ἑορτήν· ἢ
30 τοῖς πτωχοῖς ἵνα τὶ δῷ. Λαβὼν οὖν τὸ ψωμίον ἐκεῖνος, εὐθέως ἐξῆλ-
31 θεν· ἦν δὲ νύξ. Ὅτε [οὖν] ἐξῆλθε, λέγει ὁ Ἰησοῦς· Νῦν ἐδοξάσθη
32 ὁ Υἱὸς τοῦ ἀνθρώπου, καὶ ὁ Θεὸς ἐδοξάσθη ἐν αὐτῷ. Εἰ ὁ Θεὸς e Supra 7. 34. & 8. 21.
ἐδοξάσθη ἐν αὐτῷ, καὶ ὁ Θεὸς δοξάσει αὐτὸν ἐν ἑαυτῷ, καὶ εὐθὺς f Infra 15. 12.
33 δοξάσει αὐτόν. [e] Τεκνία, ἔτι μικρὸν μεθ᾽ ὑμῶν εἰμι, ζητήσετέ με, καὶ Lev. 19. 18. Matt. 22. 39.
καθὼς εἶπον τοῖς Ἰουδαίοις· Ὅτι ὅπου ὑπάγω ἐγὼ, ὑμεῖς οὐ δύνασθε Gal 6. 2. James 2. 8. 1 Pet. 1. 22.
34 ἐλθεῖν· καὶ ὑμῖν λέγω ἄρτι. [f] Ἐντολὴν καινὴν δίδωμι ὑμῖν, ἵνα ἀγα- 1 John 3. 11. & 4. 16, 21.

bit or *piece* of anything. And here probably it denotes a piece of the paschal lamb dipped in the sauce. Such portions were usually distributed by the master. There is no real discrepancy in the statements of the Evangelists. Jesus, it seems, was thus engaged, when John, putting the above question to him, he either helped Judas first, or, in serving out the portions, had come to him in his turn. Judas, then, (perhaps sitting near Jesus, and having heard John's interrogation, or, with the suspicion natural to guilt, supposing that they were speaking of *him*), after receiving the portion, asks in a low voice, Is it I, master? To whom Jesus answers, *σὺ εἶπας, it is thou.* (See Matt. xxvi. 25.) Then in a loud voice he adds ὃ ποιεῖς ποίησον τάχιον, "what thou art to do, do very quickly." Where the Present ποιεῖς is for the Future sense, the Imperative is, as Chrys. remarks, *permissive*.

31. ὅτε [οὖν] ἐξῆλθε.] The MSS., Versions, and Edd., vary as to the *reading*, and still more the *position* of these words; which are in some copies connected with what *precedes*, in others with what *follows*. The Ed. Princ. and Stephen, 1, 2. join them with the *following*, placing a period after νύξ: the Erasmian and Stephen's 3d Ed. connect them with the *preceding*. But the old position was recalled by Beza and the Elzevir Editor; and was thus introduced into the *textus receptus*. Of later Editors, Wets., Matthæi, Knapp, and Vat., join them with the *preceding*; Griesb., Tittm., and Scholz, with the *following*. The determination of this question much depends upon its being decided whether the οὖν should be adopted or rejected. It is found in most of the MSS. (many of them very ancient) in several of the later Versions, and some Fathers; but is *not* found in very many MSS., (some equally ancient), and the earlier and principal Versions; and is rejected by Wets., Matth., Griesb., and Scholz. The point admits not of any certain determination. It might have been thrown out by those who, joining the words with the preceding, thought the οὖν worse than useless: or it might have been inserted by those who, connecting the words with what follows, thought that a particle of *continuation* was wanting. And this seems more probable, and better accounts for the variation of opinion as to the construction of the words. Whether ὅτε — ἐξῆλθε should be taken with the *preceding*, or the *following*, is a matter on which we cannot positively pronounce. I agree, however, rather with those who adopt the *latter* course; by which we gain a better sense; for it surely could not be the intention of the Evangelist to make an insignificant circumstance so very prominent. And if the other mode of position be adopted, there is a great harshness in the next verse beginning so abruptly. This, too, is directly opposed to the great body of the MSS., which have οὖν; for thus the οὖν could not be retained. At ἦν νὺξ the words ὅτε ἐξῆλθε may very well be supplied from the preceding context; and it is *expressed* in Cyril; and we have something equivalent to it in Nonnus.

On the departure of Judas our Lord delivered those most interesting *last discourses* with his disciples, by which he intended to infix in their minds truths, which, ignorant as they were, and labouring under heavy affliction, they could not, indeed, *at that time*, fully comprehend, but which they would *afterwards* understand; and by which, even now, they would be fortified against their impending trials and afflictions. (Tittm.) In ἐδοξάσθη we have the *Prophetic Preterite*, used of what is shortly to happen, to express certainty. See John xi. 23. xv. 6. xvi. 33. and Notes. On this *glory*, both as it regarded our Lord and the Father, see Wets. and Tittm. in Recens. Synop.

32. δοξάσει αὐτὸν ἐν ἑαυτῷ.] It is not easy to say whether ἐν ἑαυτῷ should be referred to *God* or to *Christ*. Rosenm. and others *avoid* the difficulty in their explanation; while Kuin. and others attempt to get rid of it by supposing the words *redundant!* The question is ably discussed by Lampe as follows: "If it be referred to God, God glorifies Christ *in himself* because *by himself*, by his own divine glory, (see Rom. vi. 4.), his perfections all shining in the Son — because he will himself be glorified by the glorification of the Son — because he glorifies his Son *with himself*, giving him a communion and equality of glory, &c. If to the Son, he is glorified *in himself*, because the glory, though given by the Father, *is his own*, and because by the glorification, he possesses an eternal fount, from which the glory of all the elect to the end of the world will be derived."

33. τεκνία.] This appellation was employed in ancient times by masters to their servants, and generally by superiors to inferiors; especially by teachers to their pupils. It is expressive of affection, and may, in several passages of 1 John be rendered, Dear children.

— οὐ δύνασθε ἐλθεῖν] i. e. not *now*, but, as is added further on at xiv. 3., hereafter.

πᾶτε ἀλλήλους· καθὼς ἠγάπησα ὑμᾶς, ἵνα καὶ ὑμεῖς ἀγαπᾶτε ἀλλήλους. Ἐν τούτῳ γνώσονται πάντες ὅτι ἐμοὶ μαθηταί ἐστε, ἐὰν ἀγά- 35
g Infra 21. 18. πην ἔχητε ἐν ἀλλήλοις. [g] Λέγει αὐτῷ Σίμων Πέτρος· Κύριε, ποῦ 36
ὑπάγεις; Ἀπεκρίθη αὐτῷ ὁ Ἰησοῦς· Ὅπου ὑπάγω, οὐ δύνασαί μοι
νῦν ἀκολουθῆσαι· ὕστερον δὲ ἀκολουθήσεις μοι. Λέγει αὐτῷ ὁ Πέ- 37
τρος· Κύριε, διατί οὐ δύναμαί σοι ἀκολουθῆσαι ἄρτι; τὴν ψυχήν
h Matt. 26. 34. Mark 14. 30. Luke 22. 34. μου ὑπὲρ σοῦ θήσω. [h] Ἀπεκρίθη αὐτῷ ὁ Ἰησοῦς· Τὴν ψυχήν σου 38
ὑπὲρ ἐμοῦ θήσεις; ἀμὴν ἀμὴν λέγω σοι, οὐ μὴ ἀλέκτωρ φωνήσει
ἕως οὗ ἀπαρνήσῃ με τρίς.

XIV. Μὴ ταρασσέσθω ὑμῶν ἡ καρδία· πιστεύετε εἰς τὸν Θεόν, 1
καὶ εἰς ἐμὲ πιστεύετε. Ἐν τῇ οἰκίᾳ τοῦ Πατρός μου μοναὶ πολλαί 2
εἰσιν· εἰ δὲ μή, εἶπον ἂν ὑμῖν· πορεύομαι ἑτοιμάσαι τόπον ὑμῖν.

34. ἐντολὴν — ἀλλήλους.] There have been some needless difficulties raised on the sense of these words, and that by pressing too much on the sense of καινήν. In removing these, some of the best Commentators (as Lampe, Kuin., and Knapp) make some rather sophistical distinctions, and especially by laying an undue stress on καθώς. It must, I think, be granted that these words are not to be regarded as a *general precept* of mutual love, though such precepts abound in the N. T. See Eph. v. 2. 1 Thess. iv. 9. James ii. 8. 1 John ii. 8—11. iii. 23. It was very necessary to be then enjoined to the Apostles, as the best alleviation of the trials and tribulations they would have to undergo. Nay, the very Mosaic rule itself (Lev. xix. 18.) was not *universal*, but *particular*, and confined to their countrymen. The injunction here given to the Apostles was, though not absolutely new, yet new to *them*, if we consider the sentiments, opinions, and practice of the age. In their contests for pre-eminence, and selfish preference for themselves, in their worldly, proud and envious spirit, they had forgotten the precept of mutual love. Hence our Lord had before enjoined on them the opposite virtues by an affecting *symbolical action;* and now he enforces one of the most important of these duties by the *present injunction*, which might, Tittm. observes, be called new, if we consider the *standard* to which the duty was raised, καθὼς ἠγάπησα ὑμᾶς. "They were (Tittm. remarks) to show *as* sincere and unfeigned an affection to each other, as fellow labourers in the Gospel, as he had done to them; and by no means to suffer this holy society to be torn asunder by hatred, variance, envy, strife, &c.; but rather to preserve it by mutual concord, and being united in the bonds of sincere affection." It was also so far *new*, as being enforced by new motives, to be performed in a new manner, and made a peculiar characteristic of the Christian Religion, as is suggested in the words ἐν τούτῳ γνώσονται, &c., and which was so observed by the first Christians, that the Heathens used to say, "See how these Christians love one another!"

XIV. Now follow two discourses of Christ: one held at the Eucharistical table, the other on going out of the city. The former is contained in ch. xiv., the latter in ch. xv., xvi.; and may be distributed into three heads:—I. *Consolation* for the impending affliction, vv. 1—5. II. *Exhortation* to faith in Christ, vv. 5—15. III. A *promise* of the Holy Spirit, vv. 16—fin. (Schoettg.) The whole relates primarily to the Apostles only. But it was, no doubt, meant to apply, *mutatis mutandis*, to their successors, all future Teachers of the Gospel.

1. μὴ ταρασσέσθω ὑμῶν ἡ κ., &c.] "Be not troubled in mind at what I have said of my *departure:* only trust in God and in me." The first πιστεύετε admits of being taken either in the *Indicative* or in the *Imperative*. See Note supra, ver. 39. The *former* is adopted in the Vulg. and by the earlier modern Commentators; the *latter*, by many ancient Fathers, the Pesch. Syr. Version, and almost all the modern Commentators from Whitby to Tittm. From the connection of the words, we can scarcely suppose the same word used first in the Indicative, and then in the Imperative, *in the same sentence*. Nothing but a necessity, resulting from the impossibility of otherwise attaining a good sense, could authorize this. We are therefore bound to suppose the Imper. to be meant in the *first* as well as the second πιστ.; especially as it yields a sense not only good in itself, but apposite, and agreeable to the analogy of Scripture.

2. ἐν τῇ οἰκίᾳ — εἰσιν.] This seems meant to wean them from ambition, and console them under present affliction, by a representation of the ample felicity he is going to prepare for them. By ἐν τῇ οἰκίᾳ τοῦ Πατρός μου is expressed κατ' ἀνθρωποπάθειαν, *Heaven*. In the μοναὶ πολλαὶ some suppose an allusion to the *numerous chambers* in the House of his Father on earth, the *Temple;* and others to the custom of Eastern monarchs, of assigning to their courtiers habitations within the precincts of their vast palaces, while others think we may hence infer that there are various degrees of reward in heaven proportioned to men's progress in faith and holiness. But this is very precarious. All that we can with certainty pronounce meant by our Lord is, to console them under affliction, by a view of the glory and boundless felicity in reserve for the faithful servants of God and Christ. The words imply a *participation* in those mansions of bliss which our Lord was going to occupy, and to which he would lead the way to all his disciples. Tittm., too, thinks that by πολλαὶ our Lord *also* meant to intimate that heaven is a *most ample space*, sufficient for the reception of vast numbers, nay, as far as concerns the will of the Father, *all men*. And so also Dr. Burton understands.

— εἰ δὲ μή, εἶπον ἂν ὑμῖν.] "If it had not been

3 [i] Καὶ ἐὰν πορευθῶ καὶ ἑτοιμάσω ὑμῖν τόπον, πάλιν ἔρχομαι καὶ παρα- i Infra ver. 18. & 17. 24. sup. a 12. 26.
λήψομαι ὑμᾶς πρὸς ἐμαυτόν· ἵνα ὅπου εἰμὶ ἐγὼ καὶ ὑμεῖς ἦτε.
4 Καὶ ὅπου ἐγὼ ὑπάγω οἴδατε, καὶ τὴν ὁδὸν οἴδατε. Λέγει αὐτῷ
5 Θωμᾶς· Κύριε, οὐκ οἴδαμεν ποῦ ὑπάγεις· καὶ πῶς δυνάμεθα τὴν
6 ὁδὸν εἰδέναι; Λέγει αὐτῷ ὁ Ἰησοῦς· Ἐγώ εἰμι ἡ ὁδὸς, καὶ ἡ ἀλήθεια, καὶ ἡ ζωή· οὐδεὶς ἔρχεται πρὸς τὸν Πατέρα, εἰ μὴ δι' ἐμοῦ.
7 Εἰ ἐγνώκειτέ με, καὶ τὸν Πατέρα μου ἐγνώκειτε ἄν· καὶ ἀπ' ἄρτι
8 γινώσκετε αὐτὸν, καὶ ἑωράκατε αὐτόν. Λέγει αὐτῷ Φίλιππος· Κύριε,
9 δεῖξον ἡμῖν τὸν Πατέρα, καὶ ἀρκεῖ ἡμῖν. [k] Λέγει αὐτῷ ὁ Ἰησοῦς· k Supra 12. 45. infra ver. 20. & 17. 21, 23.
Τοσοῦτον χρόνον μεθ' ὑμῶν εἰμι, καὶ οὐκ ἔγνωκάς με, Φίλιππε; ὁ
ἑωρακὼς ἐμὲ ἑώρακε τὸν Πατέρα· καὶ πῶς σὺ λέγεις· Δεῖξον ἡμῖν

so, I would have told you so, and not deceived you with vain hopes."

— *πορεύομαι*, &c.] These words contain (as Tittm. observes) a sentence of *particular* application, in confirmation of the foregoing *general* one. "Nay, I go to prepare a place for you there;" namely, by virtue of his sacrifice and intercession; a similitude taken from one who goes before another to some unknown country, to prepare for his reception.

3. *ἐὰν πορευθῶ καὶ ἑτοιμάσω.*] The best Commentators are agreed that the sense is, "When I shall have gone, and shall have prepared a place;" and that *πάλιν ἔρχομαι* (I am to come back) is for *πάλιν ἐλεύσομαι*. They differ, however, on whether this coming of our Lord is to be understood of the *day of judgment* (see vv. 18, 28. xii. 26. Acts i. 11. 1 Thess. iv. 17.), or of *the day of each man's death*. The former interpretation is maintained by most ancient and earlier moderns; the latter by the generality of the recent Commentators. The words are, indeed, a continuation of the foregoing similitude, and derived from the custom of persons, who have gone forward to prepare a residence for their friends, returning to fetch and accompany them thither. But if the latter interpretation be adopted, the words would seem a *mere accommodation*, with little meaning. And even were we to *grant* (what has never yet been proved) that at death the righteous are immediately received up into heaven, yet the maintainers of that doctrine do not assert that Christ *comes to fetch them*. The common interpretation, then, is greatly preferable; and it is placed beyond doubt by 1 Thess. iv. 16, where the language of the Apostle is the best comment on that of his Lord: *ὅτι αὐτὸς ὁ Κύριος ἐν κελεύσματι, ἐν φωνῇ ἀρχαγγέλου, καὶ ἐν σάλπιγγι Θεοῦ καταβήσεται ἀπ' οὐρανοῦ, καὶ οἱ νεκροὶ ἐν Χριστῷ ἀναστήσονται πρῶτον· ἔπειτα ἡμεῖς οἱ ζῶντες, οἱ περιλειπόμενοι, ἅμα σὺν αὐτοῖς ἁρπαγησόμεθα ἐν νεφέλαις εἰς ἀπάντησιν τοῦ Κυρίου εἰς ἀέρα· καὶ οὕτω πάντοτε σὺν Κυρίῳ ἐσόμεθα.* The purpose of *both* passages is the same, namely, the consolation of the persons addressed.

4. The general purport of the ver. may be thus expressed (with Dr. Burton): "Thus ye know that heaven is the place whither I am going; and all my former teaching was suited to shew you the *way* thither."

— *τὴν ὁδὸν*] i. e. the means whereby ye may arrive thither, namely, by faith in Christ. Since, however, the disciples did not thoroughly comprehend his meaning (confounding the terms with notions of an earthly kingdom, and never of the *death* of the Messiah), he makes it clearer at ver. 6; at the same time using a certain boldness of metaphor, in order to impress it in a more lively manner.

6. *ἐγώ εἰμι ἡ ὁδὸς*, &c.] Ὁδὸς is for *ὁδοποιὸς*, or *ὁδηγός*. The other terms *ἡ ἀλήθεια* and *ἡ ζωὴ*, are by the best Commentators supposed to be put, by Hebraism, for the adjectives *ἀληθινὴ* and *ζωοποιός*. See x. 7. compared with ver. 9. xi. 25. But it is rather a more energetic mode of expression, q. d. I am the way, the *true* way [to life], the *author* of life and happiness; the third term being exegetical of the two former. The words following are exegetical of the preceding clause, and by *the coming of the Father* is denoted introduction to the heavenly mansions just before mentioned, alone to be obtained by faith and obedience, through the one true Guide to life and happiness, and by his propitiation.

7—10. In these vv. it is affirmed that he who has seen and heard Christ has, in some way and some sense, seen and heard the Father; which implies an essential union of Father and Son. So intimate is this union, that Christ says, *εἰ ἐγνώκειτε*, &c. Now by the *knowing* Christ is denoted the knowledge of his *attributes*, his infinite wisdom, benevolence, mercy, &c. which, if they be fully known, will be found the same as those of the Father. This *implies* that mysterious *union* of the Father and the Son, which makes the will of the latter essentially the will of the former.

— *καὶ ἀπ' ἄρτι — αὐτόν*.] The best Commentators are agreed that the Present is here (as often) used of what is very *shortly to be*; and that in order to suggest its speedy occurrence. We may therefore render: "Ye will a short time hence know, and, as it were, see him," meaning after Christ's death, and at the sending of the Holy Spirit, to guide them into all truth; or, retaining the usual force of the tenses, the sense may be, "Yea, a short time hence [ye may say that] ye know Him, nay have seen Him;" namely, because ye have known and seen *me*, who am one with Him. This I find confirmed by the learned C. G. G. Thiele in his Notitia Comm. in N. T. p. 7, where, after Luick, he assigns as the full sense (though imperfectly developed) "Nondum intellexistis, verum] *abhinc* intelligitis atque vidistis jam," i. e. intelligetis, quippe jam *auspicati*; [atque ita intelligendi facultatem nacti.]

8. *δεῖξον ἡμῖν τὸν Πατέρα*.] This inquiry seems founded on Philip's erroneously taking *ἑωράκατε* in the *literal* sense.

9. *οὐκ ἔγνωκάς με*] i. e. known who I am, and my true character.

— *ὁ ἑωρακὼς — Πατέρα*] "He who hath seen me

τὸν Πατέρα; Οὐ πιστεύεις ὅτι ἐγὼ ἐν τῷ Πατρὶ, καὶ ὁ Πατὴρ ἐν 10
ἐμοί [ἐστι]; Τὰ ῥήματα ἃ ἐγὼ λαλῶ ὑμῖν ἀπ᾿ ἐμαυτοῦ οὐ λαλῶ·
ὁ δὲ Πατὴρ ὁ ἐν ἐμοὶ μένων, αὐτὸς ποιεῖ τὰ ἔργα. Πιστεύετέ μοι 11
ὅτι ἐγὼ ἐν τῷ Πατρὶ, καὶ ὁ Πατὴρ ἐν ἐμοί· εἰ δὲ μὴ, διὰ τὰ ἔργα
αὐτὰ πιστεύετέ μοι. Ἀμὴν ἀμὴν λέγω ὑμῖν· ὁ πιστεύων εἰς ἐμὲ, τὰ 12
ἔργα ἃ ἐγὼ ποιῶ κἀκεῖνος ποιήσει, καὶ μείζονα τούτων ποιήσει· ὅτι
ἐγὼ πρὸς τὸν Πατέρα μου πορεύομαι· [l] καὶ ὅ τι ἂν αἰτήσητε ἐν τῷ 13
ὀνόματί μου, τοῦτο ποιήσω· ἵνα δοξασθῇ ὁ Πατὴρ ἐν τῷ Υἱῷ. Ἐάν 14
τι αἰτήσητε ἐν τῷ ὀνόματί μου, ἐγὼ ποιήσω.
Ἐὰν ἀγαπᾶτέ με, τὰς ἐντολὰς τὰς ἐμὰς τηρήσατε. καὶ ἐγὼ ἐρωτήσω 15
τὸν Πατέρα, καὶ ἄλλον Παράκλητον δώσει ὑμῖν, ἵνα μένῃ μεθ᾿ ὑμῶν 16,

[l] Infra 15. 16. & 16. 23, 24. Matt. 7. 7. Mark 11. 24.

hath [in effect] seen the Father." The Apostles had seen the sanctity of his life, his contempt of earthly riches and honours, his submission to the lowest state of poverty and misery, his sole desire to promote the salvation of souls. They had, moreover, seen his *majesty*, "the majesty of the only begotten of the Father" (see i. 14.) nay, were shortly to see him *die for the human race*. But in all this, they had, in fact, heard and *seen the Father*, i. e. the image, decrees, counsels, and works of the Father respecting the salvation of men. He who saw Jesus living, acting, and dying, *saw*, in fact, *the Father*, i. e. the image of the Father, and the *effigies* of the Divine nature. There was, therefore, no *need* that our Lord should then show them the Father, and more fully expound his counsels and decrees. They might *already* have sufficiently known them from the words and actions of their Lord, and would shortly know and comprehend them *more fully* by the inspiration of the Holy Spirit. (Tittm.)

10. ὅτι ἐγὼ ἐν τῷ Πατρὶ] scil. εἰμι. The phrase εἶναι ἐν τινι imports *intimate connection and conjunction with*, the nature of which must vary with the subject and the context. Tittm. shows that here (as also at x. 38.) community of *work* and *power* is meant, including also *parity of feelings and counsels*.

— τὰ ῥήματα — οὐ λαλῶ.] These words, and the following, ὁ δὲ Πατὴρ — τὰ ἔργα, are an *illustration* of the *community* just mentioned, as applied both to *words* and to *works*. In the latter clause all will be regular, if we supply, as corresponding to τὰ ῥήματα — λαλῶ, the words τὰ ἔργα ἃ ποιῶ ἐν ὑμῖν ἀπ᾿ ἐμαυτοῦ οὐ ποιῶ. There is a plain *reference* to this omitted clause in the introductory δέ. Here Tittm. draws the following inference: "But since a conjunction not only in respect of *counsel and will*, but in respect of one and the same *energy and power*, subsists between the Father and the Son, it may hence, with certainty, be inferred that there is also between them *a communion of one and the same nature*; and when our Lord affirms, that 'the Father abideth in him,' he has indicated a perpetuity of mutual conjunction, and testifies that it is impossible he should ever do any thing contrary to the mind, counsel, and wishes of the Father."

11. πιστεύετε, &c.] Here Christ not only *repeats* the foregoing assertion, but enjoins them to repose faith in it; telling them (as a *popular* proof of His conjunction with the Father) that His works (i. e. miracles) argue community of mind, energy, and power.

12. ὁ πιστεύων — ποιήσει.] It is evident that this promise appertained solely to the *Apostles*. By τὰ ἔργα ἃ ἐγὼ ποιῶ, Tittm. observes, is meant that *part* of Christ's work which he at xvii. 4. calls *the work committed to him by the Father*, namely, in promulgating the Father's plan of salvation though the Son, in confirming it by miracles, in collecting a community of those who should embrace the plan of salvation, &c. &c. By the *greater* works here mentioned we are to understand not greater *per se*; for, as far as regards the miracles worked by the Apostles, none were *more illustrious* than those performed by our Lord, but only in a *certain degree*, partly as regarded their *office* and *ministry* (which is alone the subject of these words), and partly in respect to the *effects* of those miracles. See more in Tittm. and Whitby.

— ὅτι ἐγὼ — πορεύομαι.] In these words the difficulty is to determine the reference. They seem to have so little bearing on the preceding words, that many Commentators connect them with the following καὶ ὅ τι ἂν αἰτ.; and they render, "because I go to my Father, whatsoever," &c. This, however, is overlooking the καί; and in *because* we have a not very apposite sense. I would render, "For *I* am going to my Father, and [accordingly] whatsoever ye ask," &c. This is confirmed by *facts*; for after our Lord's death, resurrection, and ascension, he sent the Holy Spirit both to guide them into all truth, and to enable them to work all miracles necessary to its confirmation.

13. ὅ τι] i. e. whatsoever, in the furtherance of the work committed to you, which indeed is implied in ἐν τῷ ὀν. Compare this verse with xv. 16. xvi. 23., whence it follows, (as Whitby shows), that "as both Father and Son equally hear and grant the petitions offered up in the name of Christ, both equally possess omniscience and omnipotence." Ἐν τῷ ὀνόμ., "in my cause," "for the furtherance of my cause." Ἐν τῷ υἱῷ, "by and through the Son."

16. ἄλλον Παράκλ. δώσει ὑμῖν.] For their further encouragement, Christ subjoins a *promise*; on the nature of which there has been much difference of opinion. Many of the earlier Commentators assign to παράκ. the sense of *comforter*; others *teacher*; others, again, *helper*: and not a few, *advocate*, or *intercessor*. On due examination, it will, I apprehend, appear, that those of *comforter*, *teacher*, and some others which have been proposed, are *too limited* to reach the *extent* of signification evidently meant by the term, or denote the variety of the gifts imparted by the

17 *εἰς τὸν αἰῶνα· τὸ πνεῦμα τῆς ἀληθείας, ὃ ὁ κόσμος οὐ δύναται λα-*
βεῖν, ὅτι οὐ θεωρεῖ αὐτὸ, οὐδὲ γινώσκει αὐτό· ὑμεῖς δὲ γινώσκετε
18 *αὐτὸ, ὅτι παρ' ὑμῖν μένει, καὶ ἐν ὑμῖν ἔσται. Οὐκ ἀφήσω ὑμᾶς ὀρ-*
19 *φανούς· ἔρχομαι πρὸς ὑμᾶς. Ἔτι μικρὸν, καὶ ὁ κόσμος με οὐκ ἔτι*
20 *θεωρεῖ· ὑμεῖς δὲ θεωρεῖτέ με· ὅτι ἐγὼ ζῶ, καὶ ὑμεῖς ζήσεσθε. Ἐν*
ἐκείνῃ τῇ ἡμέρᾳ γνώσεσθε ὑμεῖς ὅτι ἐγὼ ἐν τῷ Πατρί μου, καὶ ὑμεῖς
21 *ἐν ἐμοὶ, κἀγὼ ἐν ὑμῖν. Ὁ ἔχων τὰς ἐντολάς μου καὶ τηρῶν αὐτὰς,*
ἐκεῖνός ἐστιν ὁ ἀγαπῶν με· ὁ δὲ ἀγαπῶν με ἀγαπηθήσεται ὑπὸ τοῦ
Πατρός μου· καὶ ἐγὼ ἀγαπήσω αὐτὸν, καὶ ἐμφανίσω αὐτῷ ἐμαυτόν.
22 *Λέγει αὐτῷ Ἰούδας (οὐχ ὁ Ἰσκαριώτης)· Κύριε, καὶ τί γέγονεν ὅτι*
23 *ἡμῖν μέλλεις ἐμφανίζειν σεαυτὸν, καὶ οὐχὶ τῷ κόσμῳ; Ἀπεκρίθη ὁ*
Ἰησοῦς καὶ εἶπεν αὐτῷ· Ἐάν τις ἀγαπᾷ με, τὸν λόγον μου τηρήσει·

Holy Spirit. One of the two senses, *Helper* and *Intercessor*, is, I doubt not, the true one; the former of which is adopted by Tittm., Kuin., and almost all recent Commentators; the latter by Bp. Pearson, Lampe, Ernesti, Pearce, Wets., and others. And this (confirmed by most of the ancient Fathers and Commentators) seems to be preferable, especially as it has the peculiar advantage of *including the former*; since, as appears from the passages of the Classical writers, adduced by Lampe, Wets., and Tittm., *παράκλητος* was used not only of a *person called in to plead any one's cause*, but of *one who is a helper in any matter*, or generally a *patron*. And as both these offices are centred in the PARACLETE, so there can be little doubt that both are intended. Nay, even the sense *Comforter* may be *included*.

— *εἰς τὸν αἰῶνα.*] The best Commentators are agreed, that the context here so limits the sense, that the phrase is synonymous with *εἰς τέλος*, "to the end of life."

17. *τὸ πνεῦμα τῆς ἀληθ.*] This may, as the best Commentators explain, denote *the author of all truth*, the *very truth itself* (and *the imparter of it*), *Gospel truth*. There is, however, a reference to the *Holy Spirit* as *being* this Paraclete. See v. 17. 26. From this passage, compared with the following one, and xv. 26. xvi. 13. Matt. x. 20. Acts ii. 18. 33. Rom. viii. 9. Gal. iv. 6. Phil. i. 19. 1 Pet. i. 11., the *Personality* and *Divinity* of the Holy Ghost is manifest, as well as His *procession from* the *Father and the Son*.

— *ὁ κόσμος*] i. e. the sensual, corrupt, and worldly-minded part of it. *Οὐ δύναται λαβεῖν.* i. e. cannot bring themselves to receive it; since, from exclusive attention to worldly things, they neither understand, nor care about spiritual gifts. And thus it happens, as is just afterwards said, that they have neither any perception nor any knowledge of the thing. *Μένει*, "is [soon] to abide."

18. *οὐκ ἀφήσω ὑμᾶς ὀρφ.*, &c.] These words are variously interpreted. Some refer them solely to Christ's reappearance, and society with them, after his resurrection. Others take them, in a *figurative* sense, of Christ's invisible and spiritual presence. But it is best, with Tittm., to unite both interpretations. And this is supported by *facts*. "For (as Tittm. observes) Christ did return *literally* to his disciples, after his resurrection, in a visible manner; and, *metaphorically*, unseen, after his ascension to heaven; when also, as he promised, in departing to heaven (see Matt. xxviii. 20.), he was perpetually *present with* them, by the gracious aid of his omnipotent power, in the discharge of their Evangelical functions. He was always *with* them, and, in fact, gave them, when absent, greater aid than he had done when present.

19. *καὶ*] "and [then]." *Θεωρεῖ*, "is to see, will see." *Θεωρεῖτε*, "ye will see me." *Ζῶ* may be for *ἀναζῶ*, and *ζήσεσθε* for *ἀναζ*. The two terms may be taken, either in a metaphorical sense, of the *spiritual life*, or in the ordinary one of the natural. Nay, both the natural and metaphorical senses may have been intended.

20. *ἐν ἐκ. τῇ ἡμ.*] i. e. when the promise of the sending of the Paraclete shall be fulfilled. *Ἐγὼ ἐν τῷ Πατρί*, &c. On this indissoluble union, see v. 7. and Note.

21. *ὁ ἔχων — ἀγαπῶν με.*] This is a repetition of the sentiment at v. 15. and is meant to limit the declaration in the foregoing verses to those only who evince their *love of God*, by keeping his commandments; *since* to such alone will he manifest himself. See also vv. 23, 24. xv. 14. 1 John ii. 5. iii. 18—24. *Ἔχειν* here, and often elsewhere, denotes *to have in mind*, *be acquainted with*.

— *ἐμφανίσω αὐτῷ ἐμ.*] This is by some understood *literally*, of Christ's personal appearance after his resurrection. But that interpretation (as Kuin. observes) is at variance with the *explanation* of the words at v. 23. It must, therefore, be taken, with others, *metaphorically*, of an invisible and spiritual manifestation. Though as far as regards the *disciples*, both senses may be conjoined, as at v. 18.

22. *Κύριε — κόσμῳ.*] This question, (which, as Lampe observes, displays "*ignorance* proceeding from prejudice, and conjoined with *alarm*"), originated in misapprehension of our Lord's words, arising from the false notions the Apostles entertained of the Messiah's kingdom. "To this, our Lord (observes Tittm.) answered not *directly*, (because they would not have comprehended him) but merely assigns a *reason* for the distinction which he would make between his disciples and the world; or turns their attention to what it *especially* behoved them to know and believe;—namely, that not *He* only, but the FATHER would be perpetually with them by His Holy Spirit, and that *then* they would understand all things necessary for them to know."

Before *τί γέγονεν* I have inserted *καὶ*, from many

καὶ ὁ Πατήρ μου ἀγαπήσει αὐτὸν, καὶ πρὸς αὐτὸν ἐλευσόμεθα καὶ
μονὴν παρ᾽ αὐτῷ ποιήσομεν. ὁ μὴ ἀγαπῶν με τοὺς λόγους μου οὐ 24
τηρεῖ. Καὶ ὁ λόγος ὃν ἀκούετε οὐκ ἔστιν ἐμὸς, ἀλλὰ τοῦ πέμψαντός
με Πατρός.

m Luke 24. 49. infra 15. 26. & 16. 7.

Ταῦτα λελάληκα ὑμῖν παρ᾽ ὑμῖν μένων. [m] ὁ δὲ παράκλητος, τὸ 25
Πνεῦμα τὸ ἅγιον, ὃ πέμψει ὁ Πατὴρ ἐν τῷ ὀνόματί μου, ἐκεῖνος 26
ὑμᾶς διδάξει πάντα, καὶ ὑπομνήσει ὑμᾶς πάντα ἃ εἶπον ὑμῖν. εἰρήνην 27
ἀφίημι ὑμῖν, εἰρήνην τὴν ἐμὴν δίδωμι ὑμῖν· οὐ καθὼς ὁ κόσμος δίδωσιν, ἐγὼ δίδωμι ὑμῖν. μὴ ταρασσέσθω ὑμῶν ἡ καρδία, μηδὲ δειλιά-
τω. [n] ἠκούσατε ὅτι ἐγὼ εἶπον ὑμῖν· Ὑπάγω καὶ ἔρχομαι πρὸς ὑμᾶς. 28
Εἰ ἠγαπᾶτέ με, ἐχάρητε ἂν ὅτι εἶπον· πορεύομαι πρὸς τὸν Πατέρα·

n Supra 10. 29.

of the best MSS., some Versions and Fathers, and the Ed. Princ. It has been received by almost every Editor from Wets. to Scholz. There is a kindred construction at ix. 36. *καὶ τίς ἐστι, Κύριε*, &c., where many inferior MSS. (with the received Text) omit the *καί*. Add 2 Cor. ii. 2. *καὶ τίς ἐστι*, &c. This forms one branch of that *generic construction*, by which *καὶ* is used with particles of interrogation; when it has always an intensive force.

23. *ἐλευσόμεθα καὶ μονὴν κ. α. π.*] The Commentators adduce examples of the phrase *μονὴν ποιεῖν*, which they regard as synonymous with *μένειν*. But it is, in fact, a more significant expression, denoting a *continued* abiding. Of course, it is to be taken in a metaphorical sense, of an invisible and spiritual presence, and (as Kuin. observes) is meant to illustrate the *ἐμφανίσω αὐτῷ ἐμαυτὸν* at v. 21. In the O. T. God is said to *come* to men, when he promises or bestows peculiar benefits on them; also to *dwell* or remain with those whom he especially favours; as also to *leave* and *depart from* those whom he ceases to benefit.

Besides, God and Christ may be said to come by the *Holy Spirit*, whose temple (to use the words of Whitby) is the body of the Saints, (1 Cor. iii. 16; vi. 13.) and by whose indwelling they are made an habitation of God. Eph. ii. 22. *By* this Spirit the Father and Son dwell in all true Christians.

24. *ὁ μὴ ἀγαπῶν — οὐ τηρεῖ.*] This is, I conceive, a *resuming* of what Christ was going to say, when he was interrupted by Judas's question. It is meant to affirm the same truth *negatively;* and consequently there is *implied* the *negative* of the proposition at v. 21; i. e. he will *not* have the love of myself and the Father, the *ἐμφάνεια* and the other benefits resulting from thence. In the words following there must again be something supplied to *complete* the sense; which is rather *intimated* than fully expressed, — namely, "he therefore who rejects me, rejects the Father." Οὐκ ἀλλὰ may here (as often) signify *non tam — quam*, implying no more than community of participation in commanding.

25. *ταῦτα λελάληκα*, &c.] The full sense is: "These instructions and consolations have I given you while present with you. At my departure the Holy Spirit will be your Teacher and Helper."

26. *ἐν τῷ ὀνόμ. μου*] i. e. in my behalf, and in my place. Πάντα, i. e. all things important for you to know, respecting the counsels of God, and the work of Christ for the salvation of men. Ὑπομνήσει, i. e. will bring to mind whatever either having been said had been forgotten, or when said, imperfectly understood and misconceived. Thus the two clauses import the communication of all necessary knowledge, and a rectification of all misconception.

27. *εἰρήνην ἀφίημι — ὑμῖν.*] This is *not*, I conceive (as some Commentators suppose), a *mere form of farewell*, but a solemn and affecting *valediction* and *benediction*, as of a man about to leave his friends for ever. Τὴν ἐμὴν εἰρ. seems added in further explanation and confirmation of the εἰρήνην just before. Ἀφίημι is employed suitably to the *imagery*, and alludes to a dying man as *bequeathing*. The ἐμὴν, taken in reference to the subsequent clause, is *emphatical;* and suggests that this peace is given by Christ alone. The words of that clause are exegetical of the preceding, and suggest a comparison not between the *mode* of giving (for *καθὼς* has often a very lax sense) but between the *kind of gifts;* the *world* (as Gerhard observes) conferring external, empty, and transitory peace; *Christ* bestowing internal and spiritual, stable and solid peace. On the superiority of internal peace to all external advantages the ancient Philosophers often dilate.

28. Our Lord concludes with the same exhortation as that with which he had commenced this affecting address; after which, adverting to what he had said of his departure from them, he urges that their love of Him should make them rather rejoice than grieve thereat. He tells them that he is going, not to some distant region of the world (as some of the disciples fancied, xiii. 36.) but *to the Father*, to resume the majesty and glory he had before the creation of the world; and that from Him he would send to the disciples his Holy Spirit, and be their present and omnipotent aider and helper.

28. *ὅτι ὁ Πατήρ — ἐστι.*] On the true import of these words (which have staggered many orthodox Commentators, and have been abused by the Unitarians to impugn the doctrine of Christ's divinity) I must content myself with *referring* my readers to the invaluable annotatory matter introduced from Lampe, Zanchius, and Tittm. in Rec. Syn.; in which it is shown *in what respects*, and *in what sense*, Christ might be said to be inferior to the Father. The reader will also do well to consult sect. iv. of Bp. Bull's Defensio Fidei Nicænæ; entitled, "De Subordinatione Filii ad Patrem, ut ad sui originem ac principium." Suffice it to remark, that the very mention of the comparison *implies* the fallacy of supposing Christ to have been a *mere man*

29 ὅτι ὁ Πατήρ μου μείζων μου ἐστί. ᵒ Καὶ νῦν εἴρηκα ὑμῖν πρὶν γε- o Supra 13. 19.
νέσθαι· ἵνα ὅταν γένηται, πιστεύσητε.
30 ᵖ Οὐκ ἔτι πολλὰ λαλήσω μεθ᾿ ὑμῶν· ἔρχεται γὰρ ὁ τοῦ κόσμου p Supra 12. 31. Infra 16. 11.
31 [τούτου] ἄρχων, καὶ ἐν ἐμοὶ οὐκ ἔχει οὐδέν. ᵍ Ἀλλ᾿ ἵνα γνῷ ὁ κόσμος, q Supra 10. 18.
ὅτι ἀγαπῶ τὸν Πατέρα, καὶ καθὼς ἐνετείλατό μοι ὁ Πατὴρ, οὕτω ποιῶ.
ἐγείρεσθε, ἄγωμεν ἐντεῦθεν.
1 XV. ἘΓΩ εἰμι ἡ ἄμπελος ἡ ἀληθινὴ, καὶ ὁ Πατήρ μου ὁ γεωργός
2 ἐστι. Πᾶν κλῆμα ἐν ἐμοὶ μὴ φέρον καρπὸν, αἴρει αὐτό· καὶ πᾶν τὸ
3 καρπὸν φέρον, καθαίρει αὐτὸ, ἵνα πλείονα καρπὸν φέρῃ. ʳ Ἤδη ὑμεῖς r Supra 13. 10.
καθαροί ἐστε διὰ τὸν λόγον ὃν λελάληκα ὑμῖν. Μείνατε ἐν ἐμοὶ, κἀγὼ
ἐν ὑμῖν. Καθὼς τὸ κλῆμα οὐ δύναται καρπὸν φέρειν ἀφ᾿ ἑαυτοῦ, ἐὰν

29. *εἴρηκα*] scil. *ταῦτα*; i. e. "his departure and the sending to them of the Paraclete."

30. *οὐκ ἔτι π. λαλ.*] As this is suspended on the words *ἔρχεται γὰρ*, &c., it is plain that the sense requires not *will*, but *shall*; i. e. I shall not *have opportunity* to discourse much with you. On the *ἄρχων τοῦ κόσμου τούτου* see Note on xii. 31. Ἔρχεται is coming upon me. The words *ἐν ἐμοὶ οὐκ ἔχει οὐδὲν* are by the best Commentators admitted to mean, "hath no power;" "will have no effect against me," viz. in frustrating the plan of salvation. Ἐν ἐμοὶ may literally be rendered "*in respect* of me." These words were made good by the event.

Τούτου after *κόσμου* is omitted in very many of the best MSS., Versions, and earlier Fathers, and is cancelled by almost every Editor from Wets. to Scholz, being supposed to have been introduced from xii. 3.

31. *ἀλλ᾿ ἵνα γνῷ*, &c.] Here (as often after *ἀλλὰ*, before *ἵνα* and such particles) something is left to be understood, and may be variously supplied. The full sense seems to be, "But [the Prince of the world is permitted to attack me] that the world may know," &c. This sense of *ἀγαπῶ* is required by the words *καθὼς ἐνετείλατο*, &c.

XV. Commentators are not agreed as to the *place* where the remaining portion (Ch. xv., xvi., xvii.) of Christ's discourse was delivered. Many think it was pronounced somewhere on the way from Jerusalem to Gethsemane. But of this there is no *proof*,—and, from the nature of the discourse, little *probability*. Nay, the words of Ch. xviii. 1. *ταῦτα εἰπὼν ἐξῆλθε — ἦν κῆπος* plainly show that the words cannot have been delivered on the road to Gethsemane; nor, as some, *at* Gethsemane; but (as Glass, Pearce, Lampe. Doddr., Kuin., Knapp, and Tittm. maintain) in *the guest chamber*, after having risen from table, and previous to his departure. In this *resumption* of the foregoing discourse, our Lord, loath to part with his faithful followers, *enlarges* on, and further *illustrates* the same topics.

1. *ἐγώ εἰμι ἡ ἄμπ. ἡ ἀληθ.*] This similitude (probably suggested by the wine on the table, called by Christ, Matt. xxvi. 29. *γέννημα τοῦ ἀμπέλου*) was one not uncommon. It is often used in the O. T. of the Jewish people and Church; and, as appears from the Rabbinical writers, was sometimes taken to designate the *Messiah*. It here represents the vital union between Christ and the *faithful* people in his Church. On the exact import of *ἡ ἀληθ.* Commentators are not agreed. It is best explained by Euthym. *ἡ τὴν ἀλήθειαν καρποφοροῦσα*. The force of the Article here is the same as in *ὁ ποιμὴν ὁ καλὸς*, x. 14. where see Note. In calling God the *γεωργὸς* (i. e. *ἀμπελουργὸς*, genus for species) Christ follows the usage of the O. T. See Is. v. 1—7. Jer. ii. 21. Ps. lxxx. 8—11. Christ is here represented as the *Vine* (i. e. the trunk of the vine) of religious truth,—the Gospel; and his faithful disciples as the *branches* from that vine,—all deriving nourishment, and even life itself, from the trunk.

2. *ἐν ἐμοὶ*] "*belonging* to me;" i. e. considered as the trunk. Sub. *ὂν* for *ὃ ἐστι*, like *φέρον* for *ὃ φέρει*. *Αἴρει*, "cuts it away." Opposed to which, by paronomasia, is *καθαίρει*,—purified the tree; i. e. by ridding it of those useless shoots, which most abound in the best trees. *How* this *spiritual* purification is carried on by the Almighty Vine-dresser, amidst the various dispensations of his Providence, see Lampe in Rec. Syn.

—*πλείονα καρπὸν*] not only *more*, but *better in quality*; for the difference between the works done under the Gospel, and those of mere nature, is like that which exists between the fruit of *wild* trees, and that of *cultivated* ones. So Plutarch. Vit. Arat. similarly speaking of the irregularity of virtue produced independently of philosophy, says, *Τὴν δὲ τοιαύτην ἀνωμαλίαν ἔνδεια λόγου φιλοσόφου περὶ τὰς εὐφυΐας ἀπεργάζεται· τὴν ἀρετὴν, ὥσπερ καρπὸν αὐτοφυῆ καὶ ἀγεώργητον, ἐμφέρουσα δίχα τῆς ἐπιστήμης.*

3. *ἤδη — ὑμῖν.*] From vv. 3—17, Christ now gives the *application* of the comparison; showing to what kind of vine branches they were to be referred, and the duties suitable to that state. (Lampe.) By *καθαρὸς* is here meant freed from ignorance, error, and prejudice; and therefore capable of bearing spiritual fruit. They were *then*, in a great measure, purified; though they were shortly afterwards to be *quite so* by the efficacy of the Holy Spirit soon to be manifested. Hence in the next ver. Christ exhorts them not to break the mutual conjunction between them and himself; but constantly cultivate it, as *He* should on his part preserve it for ever.

4. *μείνατε ἐν ἐμοὶ — ὑμῖν.*] Our Lord here addresses them not so much as *disciples*, as his *future ministers*; and in this capacity exhorts them to zealously *adhere* to him, not only in faith and obedience, but in their Apostolic duties. *Μένειν ἔν τινι* is used, as here, of union of thought, feeling, purpose, and action at 1 John ii. 6, 24, 27, 28. See more in Note supra vi. 56. The next words, *κἀγὼ* (sub. *μενῶ*) *ἐν ὑμῖν*, contain a *promise*, as the following ones do a precept. And the *καὶ* is to

μὴ μείνῃ ἐν τῇ ἀμπέλῳ· οὕτως οὐδὲ ὑμεῖς, ἐὰν μὴ ἐν ἐμοὶ μείνητε.
Ἐγώ εἰμι ἡ ἄμπελος, ὑμεῖς τὰ κλήματα. ὁ μένων ἐν ἐμοὶ, κἀγὼ ἐν 5
αὐτῷ, οὗτος φέρει καρπὸν πολύν· ὅτι χωρὶς ἐμοῦ οὐ δύνασθε ποιεῖν
s Matt. 3. 10. & 7. 19. οὐδέν. [s] Ἐὰν μή τις μείνῃ ἐν ἐμοὶ, ἐβλήθη ἔξω ὡς τὸ κλῆμα, καὶ 6
ἐξηράνθη· καὶ συνάγουσιν αὐτὰ καὶ εἰς τὸ πῦρ βάλλουσι, καὶ καίεται.
t Infra 16. 23. 1 John 3. 22. [t] Ἐὰν μείνητε ἐν ἐμοὶ, καὶ τὰ ῥήματά μου ἐν ὑμῖν μείνῃ, ὃ ἐὰν θέ- 7
λητε αἰτήσεσθε, καὶ γενήσεται ὑμῖν. Ἐν τούτῳ ἐδοξάσθη ὁ Πατήρ μου, 8
ἵνα καρπὸν πολὺν φέρητε· καὶ γενήσεσθε ἐμοὶ μαθηταί. Καθὼς 9
ἠγάπησέ με ὁ Πατήρ, κἀγὼ ἠγάπησα ὑμᾶς· μείνατε ἐν τῇ ἀγάπῃ τῇ
ἐμῇ. Ἐὰν τὰς ἐντολάς μου τηρήσητε, μενεῖτε ἐν τῇ ἀγάπῃ μου· κα- 10
θὼς ἐγὼ τὰς ἐντολὰς τοῦ Πατρός μου τετήρηκα, καὶ μένω αὐτοῦ ἐν
τῇ ἀγάπῃ. Ταῦτα λελάληκα ὑμῖν, ἵνα ἡ χαρὰ ἡ ἐμὴ ἐν ὑμῖν μείνῃ, 11
u Supra 13. 34. Eph. 5. 2. 1 John 3. 11, 16. & 4. 21. 1 Thess. 4. 9. καὶ ἡ χαρὰ ὑμῶν πληρωθῇ. [u] Αὕτη ἐστὶν ἡ ἐντολὴ ἡ ἐμὴ, ἵνα ἀγαπᾶτε 12
ἀλλήλους, καθὼς ἠγάπησα ὑμᾶς. Μείζονα ταύτης ἀγάπην οὐδεὶς ἔχει, 13

be taken for *καὶ οὕτω*, the *οὕτω* being implied in the *apodosis*. The substance of the promise is, that Christ will *abide* in them, importing communion with them by his Holy Spirit, and support and protection to them by the influence of the Paraclete, whom he should send to them from Heaven. See Rom. viii. 9. 1 John iii. 24. iv. 13. The words *καθὼς τὸ κλῆμα — μείνητε* suggest *another* argument to union, deduced from the *highly beneficial effects* of it. As the *branches* receive all their life and vigour from the trunk, so must *they* adhere to Christ and his injunctions, if they would produce spiritual fruit. Ἀφ' *ἑαυτοῦ*, "by its own virtue."

5. *χωρὶς ἐμοῦ*] "apart, separate from me." *Οὐ δύν. ποιεῖν οὐδὲν*, i. e. can do nothing effectual. See 2 Cor. iii. 5. Comp. ver. 4.

6. *ἐβλήθη ἔξω.*] The Aorist is here for the Future, or rather the *Present*, as being used of what is *customary*, or perhaps to represent the thing to be done, as already done. By *τὸ κλῆμα* is meant the branch which has been separated from the trunk. The *καὶ* before *ἐξηράνθη* is not put (as some imagine) for the *relative*, but *αὐτὸ* is understood. *Αὐτὰ* is for *αὐτὸ*, *populariter.*

The *τὸ* before *πῦρ* is found in many MSS. and some early Edd., and is admitted by Matth., Griesb., Knapp, Tittm., Vat., and Scholz. The same phrase, however, occurs *without* the Article at Matt. iii. 10. vii. 19. Luke iii. 9.

7. *ἐὰν μείνητε — γενήσεται ὑμῖν.*] Here is *another* argument for the preservation of this communion; in stating which the foregoing general enunciation (*μένειν ἐν ἐμοὶ*) is further evolved by *καὶ τὰ ῥήματα — μείνῃ*; and as the former denotes continuance in, communion *in general*, so this denotes, *specially*, steadfastness in assenting to and receiving the doctrines and instructions of Christ; especially in the present discourses, wherein he taught them the nature of his person and office. The benefit promised in *ὃ ἐὰν — ὑμῖν* is nearly allied to that at Matt. xxi. 21. The *whatever* must, of course, be limited to whatever is *necessary for the purpose adverted to* in the preceding and following verses, — namely, their bringing forth much fruit, and the promotion thereby of the glory of God.

8. *ἐδοξάσθη.*] The Aorist is here taken as at ver. 6., where see Note. *Ἵνα* is used as *ὅτι*, *quod*, at iii. 23. iv. 17. The *καὶ* is *not*, as most Commentators suppose, for *οὕτω* or *ὅτι*, but we must repeat *ἐν τούτῳ* from the preceding clause. So xiii. 35. *ἐν τούτῳ γνώσονται πάντες ὅτι ἐμοὶ μαθηταί ἐστε.* By *γενήσεσθε* is meant, will *really be*. How, and in what respects the Father is glorified by the disciples of his Son bringing forth the fruits of holiness and virtue, &c. See Tittm. in Recens. Synop.

9—11. *καθὼς ἠγάπησέ με*, &c.] Christ here proceeds to remind them of his own singular love to them, and holds out for their imitation his own *example* in doing the work of the Father. *Καθὼς* and *καὶ* may be rendered *quantopere — tantopere.* (Tittm.) Others, however, as Lampe, take the sense to be *as — so.* Others, again, take the *καθὼς* to signify *since;* and the *καὶ* they regard as a simple copula; which would require a *comma* after *ὑμᾶς*. But the first-mentioned interpretion is preferable. The words *μείνατε — ἐμῇ* are explained by most Commentators, "continue in the love of me," or "to love me." But that sense can only be tolerated by the change of punctuation just mentioned. *Both* methods, however, are liable to much objection. And it is better, with Campb., to suppose the sense to be, "Continue to be beloved by me," "keep your place in my affections."

Then are mentioned the *means* by which they may continue to possess his love, — namely, by keeping *His* commandments, after the example which he had set them by keeping his Father's.

11. *ἵνα ἡ χαρὰ — πληρωθῇ*] i. e. (as the best Commentators explain) "that *my* joy in *you* [at your love, faith, and obedience] may be enduring; and that *your* joy [in continuing in my love] may be complete and perfect." See xvi. 24 & 33. xvii. 13. 1 John i. 4. 2 John 12. *Χαρὰ ἐν ὑμῖν* denotes "joy felt on your account."

12. *αὕτη ἐστὶν — ὑμᾶς.*] These words are meant to show what *sort* of love is evinced by Him to them, and consequently expected in return. A similar argument is used at xiv. 21. See also Matth. xx. 28. Rom. v. 7 & 8. 1 John iii. 16. As instances of this degree of attachment from a friend, Grot. adduces the cases of Pylades and Orestes, and Damon and Pythias. I would add the yet more apposite one of Alcestis, so finely represented in the inimitable drama of Euripides. So ver. 155. *πῶς δ' ἂν μᾶλλον ἐνδείξαιτό τις Πόσιν προτιμῶσ', ἢ θέλουσ' ὑπερθανεῖν.*

14 ἵνα τις τὴν ψυχὴν αὐτοῦ θῇ ὑπὲρ τῶν φίλων αὐτοῦ. Ὑμεῖς φίλοι μου
15 ἐστὲ, ἐὰν ποιῆτε ὅσα ἐγὼ ἐντέλλομαι ὑμῖν. Οὐκέτι ὑμᾶς λέγω δούλους·
ὅτι ὁ δοῦλος οὐκ οἶδε τί ποιεῖ αὐτοῦ ὁ κύριος· ὑμᾶς δὲ εἴρηκα φίλους, ὅτι πάντα ἃ ἤκουσα παρὰ τοῦ Πατρός μου, ἐγνώρισα ὑμῖν.
16 [x] Οὐχ ὑμεῖς με ἐξελέξασθε, ἀλλ᾿ ἐγὼ ἐξελεξάμην ὑμᾶς, καὶ ἔθηκα ὑμᾶς, [x Matt. 28. 19.]
ἵνα ὑμεῖς ὑπάγητε καὶ καρπὸν φέρητε, καὶ ὁ καρπὸς ὑμῶν μένῃ· ἵνα
17 ὅ τι ἂν αἰτήσητε τὸν Πατέρα ἐν τῷ ὀνόματί μου, δῷ ὑμῖν. Ταῦτα
ἐντέλλομαι ὑμῖν, ἵνα ἀγαπᾶτε ἀλλήλους.
18 Εἰ ὁ κόσμος ὑμᾶς μισεῖ, γινώσκετε ὅτι ἐμὲ πρῶτον ὑμῶν μεμίσηκεν.
19 [y] Εἰ ἐκ τοῦ κόσμου ἦτε, ὁ κόσμος ἂν τὸ ἴδιον ἐφίλει· ὅτι δὲ ἐκ τοῦ [y 1 John 4. 5.]
κόσμου οὐκ ἐστὲ, ἀλλ᾿ ἐγὼ ἐξελεξάμην ὑμᾶς ἐκ τοῦ κόσμου, διὰ τοῦτο
20 μισεῖ ὑμᾶς ὁ κόσμος. [z] Μνημονεύετε τοῦ λόγου οὗ ἐγὼ εἶπον ὑμῖν· [z Supra 13. 16. Matt. 10. 24. Luke 6. 40.]
Οὐκ ἔστι δοῦλος μείζων τοῦ κυρίου αὐτοῦ. Εἰ ἐμὲ ἐδίωξαν, καὶ ὑμᾶς
διώξουσιν· εἰ τὸν λόγον μου ἐτήρησαν, καὶ τὸν ὑμέτερον τηρήσουσιν.

14. Here Christ shows *how* that friendship may be evinced; namely, as in the love before mentioned, by keeping his commandments.

15. οὐκέτι ὑμᾶς—ἐγνώρισα.] The sense here is not very clearly developed, and may best be expressed by the following paraphrastic version: "[I say *friends*,] for I no longer style you *servants*, since the servant [differeth from the friend, inasmuch as he] knoweth not what his master doeth" (i. e. his plans of action). But you I call *friends* [and as such I have treated you] since whatsoever I have learned from my Father I have made known to you [thus treating you with the most unreserved confidence]. Some exceptions have indeed been made to the words taken in their ordinary and full acceptation by several recent Commentators; who, because our Lord had before (Luke xii. 4.) called them his *friends*, and had always treated his disciples with affability and kindness, would here take οὐκέτι for οὐκ, and λέγω in the sense of a Preterite, *per Enallagen!* But that is a figure not to be resorted to *ad libitum*, and the use of οὐκέτι for οὐκ is precarious. Lampe's arguments in defence of the common interpretation are sufficient to establish it. Our Lord had, up to this time, (agreeably to the custom of the Jewish Rabbies) *called* them servants; though he had not *treated* them as such. And the term is susceptible of a milder interpretation, considering the connection of disciple with master; and thus it is interchanged with διάκονος at John xii. 26. The words of Luke will only prove that Christ addressed them *as* friends. And certain it is that he had never before *expressly styled them his friends*.

From xvi. 12. it is clear that the πάντα must (as the best Commentators are agreed) be understood *restrictively*, i. e. of all things proper for them then to know. The disciples here present were (as Tittm. observes) the *esoteric*, those *interioris admissionis*, as opposed to the *exoteric*, the οἱ ἔξω. (Compare Matt. xiii. 11. Luke viii. 10.) and therefore favoured with his peculiar confidence.

16. οὐχ ὑμεῖς—ὑμᾶς.] This is meant to excite them to gratitude and obedience, as showing them that the obligation was all on *their* side. Ἐκλέγεσθαι may here (as often) be taken, not so much of *choice*, as of the *love* which it implies; antecedent being put for consequent; as Mark xiii. 20. Acts xiii. 17. 1 Cor. i. 27 & 28. Eph. i. 4. James ii. 5. Τιθέναι, like the Heb. שׂוּם, and the corresponding terms in most languages, has often the sense *appoint*. Ὑπάγητε is regarded by most Commentators as pleonastic. It is not, however, quite so, but conveys a notion of activity in the discharge of their functions as Apostles or Teachers. For that is what is meant by the καρπὸν φέρ. The words καὶ ὁ καρπὸς ὑμῶν μένῃ point at the *ulterior effects* of these labours to succeeding ages; and which, judging by events, we *now know* must endure unto the end of the world. In the words following ἵνα denotes *event*, *result*, or *consequence*. The sense is: "Thus it shall happen, that whatever ye shall ask the Father," &c.

17. In this verse, our Lord, I conceive, means to say, that he has given them the injunctions he has, with the hope and trust that they will *so* fulfil them as to love each other; concord being essential to their spiritual success.

18. From the above injunction of *mutual love*, our Lord passes to a kindred subject,—the *hatred of the world* towards them; forewarning them of the evils they would have to endure in his cause, exhorting them to patient endurance, and consoling them by reminding them of the treatment *He* had experienced in his own case: q. d. "If *my* blameless and most beneficial life could not shield me from the hatred and mortal persecution of the world, (i. e. of the unbelieving and wicked part of it) so neither will yours protect you." Many Commentators take γινώσκετε as an *Imperative*, in the sense *reflect*, *consider*. But the common view, by which it is considered as an *Indicative*, is most natural. Πρῶτον is manifestly an *adverb* for πρότερον, as Campb. has convincingly shown.

19. εἰ ἐκ τοῦ, &c.] Ἐκ τοῦ κόσμου εἶναι signifies "to be conformed to the world." So ἐκ τοῦ Θεοῦ, or διαβόλου, &c. For (as Grot. observes) the ἐκ, as it denotes *descent from*, so it may very well import *affinity to*.

20. οὐκ ἔστι δοῦλος, &c.] Compare Matt. x. 24. John xiii. 16.

— εἰ τὸν λόγον—τηρήσουσιν.] The sense of these words *seems* to be directly contrary to that which the context requires. To remove this difficulty, some would take τηρεῖν for παρατη-

a Infra 16. 3. Matt. 24. 9. [a] Ἀλλὰ ταῦτα πάντα ποιήσουσιν ὑμῖν διὰ τὸ ὄνομά μου, ὅτι οὐκ οἴδασι 21
b Supra 9. 41. τὸν πέμψαντά με. [b] Εἰ μὴ ἦλθον καὶ ἐλάλησα αὐτοῖς, ἁμαρτίαν οὐκ 22
εἶχον· νῦν δὲ πρόφασιν οὐκ ἔχουσι περὶ τῆς ἁμαρτίας αὐτῶν. Ὁ ἐμὲ 23
μισῶν καὶ τὸν Πατέρα μου μισεῖ. Εἰ τὰ ἔργα μὴ ἐποίησα ἐν αὐτοῖς, 24
ἃ οὐδεὶς ἄλλος πεποίηκεν, ἁμαρτίαν οὐκ εἶχον· νῦν δὲ καὶ ἑωράκασι,
c Ps. 35. 19. & 69. 5. καὶ μεμισήκασι καὶ ἐμὲ καὶ τὸν Πατέρα μου. [c] Ἀλλ' ἵνα πληρωθῇ 25
ὁ λόγος ὁ γεγραμμένος ἐν τῷ νόμῳ αὐτῶν, Ὅτι ἐμίσησάν με
d Supra 14. 26. infra 16. 7. Luke 24. 49. δωρεάν. [d] Ὅταν δὲ ἔλθῃ ὁ Παράκλητος, ὃν ἐγὼ πέμψω ὑμῖν παρὰ 26
τοῦ Πατρὸς, τὸ Πνεῦμα τῆς ἀληθείας, ὃ παρὰ τοῦ Πατρὸς ἐκπορεύε-
e Acts 1. 21. & 5. 32. ται, ἐκεῖνος μαρτυρήσει περὶ ἐμοῦ· [e] καὶ ὑμεῖς δὲ μαρτυρεῖτε, ὅτι ἀπ' 27
ἀρχῆς μετ' ἐμοῦ ἐστε.

ρεῖν. But for that sense of the word with τὸν λόγον there is no authority. The same remarks will apply to that method of interpretation (objectionable on other grounds) which is founded on the use of εἰ to signify *as*. The *best* mode of removing the difficulty that has been hitherto propounded is that of Tittm., who assigns the following sense. "If they had admitted and observed my doctrine, they would admit and observe yours. Yet it involves such an anomaly of language as I must hesitate to ascribe to the Evangelist; because, though inattentive to the nicer idioms of the language, yet he nowhere so openly sets all rules at defiance. Not to say that the use of the tenses in the *antithetical* clause forbids this sense. In short, if we would arrive at the truth, on any difficult passage, we must not *tamper* with the sense of any word, nor strain the force of the tenses; but seek some mode of explanation which may not involve any anomaly. In the present instance, this may be done by considering the *affirmative* enunciation as dependent on the *hypothetical* εἰ as meant to *imply* also its *negative*, i. e. "If they have *not* observed my words, neither will they observe yours." On examination, I find that Euthym. and some of the early modern Commentators took the words as *equivalent* to a negative sentence; but *how* this arose, they seem not to have been aware.

21. διὰ τὸ ὄνομά μου] "on my account," "for your attachment to me." And, therefore, what they do to you I regard as done to myself. Οὐκ οἴδασι. This imports not involuntary ignorance, but self-produced blindness as to the true nature of the evidence of a Divine legation.

22. εἰ μὴ ἦλθον, &c.] This verse is exegetical of the preceding, and our Lord (as Lampe observes) "therein encounters a tacit argument, which might be pleaded in excuse of the persons in question, *that they sinned from ignorance*. This he overturns, by showing that their ignorance and perverseness were inexcusable, because sufficient *means* for the attainment of a *knowledge* of the truth had been provided, both by internal and external evidence, in doctrines and in miracles." Ἁμαρτ. must not be taken (with many) of *sin in general*, but of the sin in question, that of rejecting the Messiah. From the antithetical clause νῦν δὲ οὐκ ἔχουσι, &c., it appears that the sense *here* is, "they would have been, comparatively, innocent of the sin," "there would have been some excuse for them."

23. ὁ ἐμὲ μισῶν — μισεῖ.] This is meant to mark, under a *general* assertion, the sinfulness of *their* conduct, in particular: namely, that their hatred and rejection of Him and his mission, and injurious treatment of *Him*, was, in fact, done to his *Father*. v. 24. Here the assertion of v. 22. is resumed, (the words of v. 23. being in some measure parenthetical) and the *proof* of Divine mission from *miracles* is adverted to. Then a conclusion is drawn. Or, as Lampe observes, "we have a *conditional proposition* so assumed, that, from a refutation of the *antecedent*, there results a refutation of the consequent." (See Bp. Warburton's Works, vi. 326.) The sense may be thus expressed: "But now, although these miracles have been wrought before their eyes, yet they have only produced hatred and injurious conduct towards me, a conduct (agreeable to the foregoing assurance) directed against my Father likewise." In this is implied the *consequence* above expressed at v. 22. πρόφασιν οὐκ ἔχουσι περὶ τῆς ἁμαρτίας αὐτῶν.

25. ἀλλ' ἵνα πληρωθῇ.] The older Commentators maintain that the sense is, "But this is come to pass, that the Scripture might be fulfilled;" while the later ones are of opinion that the ἵνα is here, as often, *eventual*, and that the sense is: "Now by this having come to pass the words written in the Law have been made good." Those words were *properly* spoken of the enemies of David: but as David was a type of Christ, so they are *accommodated* to Him.

26. ὅταν δὲ ἔλθῃ ὁ Παράκ.] The scope of the words here is uncertain; but seem to have been spoken with the view of softening an ungrateful communication, by a promise of Divine assistance, and the aid of the Holy Spirit; q. d. "Though rejected by the multitude, I am acknowledged as Messiah by the Father, who, in proof of this, will shortly send you the aids of the Holy Spirit."

— μαρτυρήσει περὶ ἐμοῦ.] This is explained by almost all recent Commentators, of confirming by arguments what has been taught. q. d. "The Holy Spirit will cause that my person, counsels, deeds, and works, shall be more and more known," or, as it is said in xvi. 14. ἐκεῖνος ἐμὲ δοξάσει. The words, however, cannot admit of that sense; and that the usual signification of μαρτυρεῖν is here to be retained, is plain from the next verse; for we can hardly suppose the word used in two such different senses within so short a space. The true interpretation seems to be that of the ancients and earlier moderns, i. e. "the Holy Spirit will bear witness to my Messiahship by the miraculous spiritual gifts with which he will endow believers in me."

27. To the testimony of the *Holy Spirit* Christ

1 XVI. Ταῦτα λελάληκα ὑμῖν, ἵνα μὴ σκανδαλισθῆτε. Ἀποσυναγώ-
2 γους ποιήσουσιν ὑμᾶς· ἀλλ' ἔρχεται ὥρα, ἵνα πᾶς ὁ ἀποκτείνας ὑμᾶς
3 δόξῃ λατρείαν προσφέρειν τῷ Θεῷ. [f] Καὶ ταῦτα ποιήσουσιν [ὑμῖν,] [f] Supra 15. 21.
4 ὅτι οὐκ ἔγνωσαν τὸν Πατέρα οὐδὲ ἐμέ. [g] Ἀλλὰ ταῦτα λελάληκα ὑμῖν, [g] Matt. 9. 15. Mark 2. 19. Luke 5. 34.
ἵνα, ὅταν ἔλθῃ ἡ ὥρα, μνημονεύητε αὐτῶν, ὅτι ἐγὼ εἶπον ὑμῖν. Ταῦτα δὲ
5 ὑμῖν ἐξ ἀρχῆς οὐκ εἶπον, ὅτι μεθ' ὑμῶν ἤμην. Νῦν δὲ ὑπάγω πρὸς τὸν
6 πέμψαντά με· — καὶ οὐδεὶς ἐξ ὑμῶν ἐρωτᾷ με· Ποῦ ὑπάγεις; ἀλλ'
7 ὅτι ταῦτα λελάληκα ὑμῖν, ἡ λύπη πεπλήρωκεν ὑμῶν τὴν καρδίαν. Ἀλλ'
ἐγὼ τὴν ἀλήθειαν λέγω ὑμῖν· συμφέρει ὑμῖν ἵνα ἐγὼ ἀπέλθω. ἐὰν

adds that of the *apostles* and *disciples* themselves; who were, in all respects, qualified to bear unimpeachable testimony to the person, character, and actions of Christ, as having been with him from the beginning of his ministry; a testimony so much the more weighty, since it was,, in the case of some, confirmed by personal miracles, and in others brought forward in writing, by the Gospels.

XVI. 1. ἵνα μὴ σκανδ.] Those were said σκανδαλισθῆναι, who, either stumbling at the external poverty and lowliness of our Lord, formed a wrong judgment of him, and at least *doubted* of his Divine mission; or who, though convinced of it, suffered themselves to be so influenced by the apprehension of evil, as to abandon their Christian profession. (Tittm.)

2. ἀποσυναγώγους π.] See Note on ix. 22. Ἀλλὰ, *quin imò, nay.* Ἵνα for ὅτε, as often.

— λατρείαν προσφέρειν.] Λατρεύειν properly signifies to serve any one as a slave. But in the N. T. and LXX. it is always used to denote the offering of sacrifice, or rendering worship and service of any kind. The sense is: "he will think he is rendering an acceptable service to God." So a Rabbinical writer, cited by Lampe: "Omnis effundens sanguinem improborum æqualis est illi qui sacrificium effert." Doddr. thinks there is here an allusion to such sort of deeds as the assassination of Paul planned by the forty conspirators, (see Acts xxiii. 14. sq.) and in which they gloried: and certain it is that the greatest enormities recorded in Josephus were perpetrated by the *Zelotæ*, who originally were religious zealots.

3. καὶ ταῦτα — ἐμέ.] This is meant to trace such conduct to its original source (namely, ignorance of God and the Son of God, otherwise they would have known how abhorrent from the nature of both is persecution), and to suggest consolation to themselves, as suffering in the cause of God and Christ. See xv. 21. Ὑμῖν after ποιήσ. is not found in very many MSS., Versions, Fathers, and early Edd., and is, with some reason, cancelled by Matth., Griesb., Tittm., Vat., and Scholz.

4. ἡ ὥρα] i. e. the time for suffering such calamities.

— ταῦτα — οὐκ εἶπον.] By ἐξ ἀρχῆς is meant the beginning of Christ's ministry. And in using the expression ὅτι μεθ' ὑμῶν ἤμην, our Lord speaks of himself as *already departed*, since he is on the point of leaving them. Of this there are several examples in the Classical writers; e. gr. Eurip. Alcest. 281. οὐκ ἔτι δὴ μήτηρ σφῶν ἔστιν. 399. ὡς οὐκ ἔτ' οὖσαν οὐδὲν ἂν λέγοις ἐμέ. Heraclid. 9. πλείστων μετέσχον, εἷς ἀνὴρ, Ἡρακλέι, ὅτ' ἦν μεθ' ἡμῶν, νῦν δ' ἐπεὶ κατ' οὐρανὸν Ναίει, κ. τ. λ. Since, however, our Lord *had* apprized his disciples of the persecutions they would have to undergo on account of their Christian profession, many take the οὐκ εἶπον *restrictively*; q. d. I did not *fully* apprize you of, &c. But as ταῦτα may very well mean the things which should befal them after their Lord's departure, and as Christ had nowhere directly adverted on *those* evils, so *that* should seem to be the sense here. This, indeed, is placed beyond doubt by the words following, which suggest the *reason* why Christ did not do it; namely, either because he was then *with* them, to comfort and support them, and himself to bear the brunt of those trials; or, because he was then going to stay with them for some time, and did not wish to pain them *before* the time.

5. νῦν δὲ ὑπάγω, &c.] The Commentators are not agreed on the scope of these words. They are generally considered as introducing a *new subject*, namely, — that of his departure, (see Lampe) and the following sense is assigned: "But now that I am going to Him who sent me, none of you asketh," &c. But thus the καὶ is *silenced*; and the sentiment in the preceding words ταῦτα δὲ — εἶπον is left very deficient. And though δὲ has sometimes a transitive force, yet the context must decide *where* that is to be ascribed. It is better (with Grot., Wakef., Kuin., Tittm., and Vat.) to suppose the words to be connected with the *preceding* clause. Thus the δὲ will be, as often, *adversative*. There is, however, something left, *per aposiopesin*, to be supplied, q. d. "And therefore I have thought it necessary to tell you," or something similar. The καὶ in the words following signifies "And [yet], i. e. though I am going;" a signification frequent in St. John's writings. By ἐρωτᾷ is meant νῦν ἐρωτᾷ; for they had asked *before*. The disciples are, however, I conceive, reproved, not so much for *not then* asking, as for the feeling which occasioned it, namely, *sorrow*; for that profound grief produces silence is undoubted. So Shakspeare:—

"Light sorrows speak; *great grief is dumb*," — imitated from Seneca. *Curæ leves loquuntur, ingentes stupent.* Their sorrow, however, was blameable, as proceeding from *want of reflection* on the *causes* of his departure, the *place* whither he was going, and the *purpose* of it, though these had been before suggested to them. However, our Lord in vv. 7—11. again adverts thereto, and in plainer terms.

7. συμφέρει — ἀπέλθω.] On the highly beneficial effects to the Apostles of Christ's departure, Tittm. remarks thus: "The Holy Spirit effected much more in them than Christ *himself* had done, (see v. 12, 14, & 16.) imparting to them a more complete knowledge of the Saviour, than what He himself could communicate, and also many

γὰρ ἐγὼ μὴ ἀπέλθω, ὁ Παράκλητος οὐκ ἐλεύσεται πρὸς ὑμᾶς· ἐὰν δὲ
πορευθῶ, πέμψω αὐτὸν πρὸς ὑμᾶς. Καὶ ἐλθὼν ἐκεῖνος ἐλέγξει τὸν 8
κόσμον περὶ ἁμαρτίας καὶ περὶ δικαιοσύνης καὶ περὶ κρίσεως. περὶ 9
ἁμαρτίας μὲν, ὅτι οὐ πιστεύουσιν εἰς ἐμέ· περὶ δικαιοσύνης δὲ, ὅτι 10
h Supra 12. 31. πρὸς τὸν Πατέρα μου ὑπάγω, καὶ οὐκ ἔτι θεωρεῖτέ με· [h] περὶ δὲ 11
κρίσεως, ὅτι ὁ ἄρχων τοῦ κόσμου τούτου κέκριται.
i Supra 14, 26. & 15. 26. Ἔτι πολλὰ ἔχω λέγειν ὑμῖν, ἀλλ᾽ οὐ δύνασθε βαστάζειν ἄρτι· [i] ὅταν 12
δὲ ἔλθῃ ἐκεῖνος, τὸ Πνεῦμα τῆς ἀληθείας, ὁδηγήσει ὑμᾶς εἰς πᾶσαν 13

other excellent gifts, necessary for their Apostolic function; supplying to them eloquence irresistible, the power of working the most illustrious miracles, for the confirmation of their testimony concerning Jesus, and rendering their timid minds invincible to all the terrors of their adversaries." "It was (says Euthym.) the pleasure of the Holy Trinity that the Father should *draw* them to the Son, that the Son should *teach* them, and the Holy Spirit *perfect* them. Now the two first things were already completed: but still it was necessary for the *third* to be accomplished, namely, the being *perfected* by the Holy Spirit."

8. ἐλέγξει — κρίσεως.] This is a passage of considerable difficulty, and therefore it is no wonder that the Commentators should not be agreed on its sense. Some take τὸν κόσμον to mean *the world at large*; others, the Jewish world, — the *Jews only*. And according as they adopt one or the other view, they assign to the passage either a *general*, or a *particular* sense. The *former* is supported by Lampe: and the latter by most recent Commentators, especially Kuin. and Tittm., who assign the following as the import: "He will show clearly, 1. the great sin of the Jews in rejecting me, by the conversion of many thousands of Jews through the effusion of the Spirit; 2. that I was really an innocent and just person, by teaching, through the Apostles, that God hath received me into heaven; 3. that the opposition made to me by the rulers of this world is in vain, since my religion will prevail; and that their policy will be judged and condemned." This seems, from the following vv., to be the most correct view: though exception may be taken to some points of the exposition, and others may be doubtful. Thus the sense of ἐλέγξει seems to be mistaken. For since (as Mr. Rose ap. Parkh. in v. observes) "whether *the world* be taken in its unlimited, or in its restricted sense, it is to be its own judge, the sense of ἐλέγξει must be *convince*, not *convict*; those two terms, when applied to a fault, only differing in this, that the individual may be *himself convinced* of his fault, but is *convicted* of it in the judgment of others." *How* this convincement was effected, and to what extent, is taught us in the subsequent book of Scripture, and in the early Ecclesiastical writers. See Acts ii. 4. By ἁμαρτία is meant not only the sin of *unbelief*, but of persecuting and *crucifying* the Lord of life, and endeavouring to suppress the religion sent from God.

With respect to the meaning of περὶ δικαιοσύνης, the best Commentators are agreed that it must belong to Christ; περὶ denoting *quod attinet ad*: and that, taken in conjunction with the words following, δικαιοσύνη can denote no other than the innocence and holiness of Jesus, the Author of justification by his blood. The *proof* of this (adverted to in the words following) was his going to his Father in heaven, evinced by his resurrection, and also by his sending the Holy Spirit with miraculous gifts. See Acts ii. 2. sq. xvii. 31. Rom. i. 4. 1 Cor. xv. 14. sq. In περὶ κρίσεως the περὶ must be taken in the same sense, and the import of the phrase be determined by the words following; which show it to be the *Divine judgment* and condemnation, i. e. the condemnation of the unbelieving part of the world, whether Jews or Heathens. The *certainty* of this is hinted at v. 11., by the mention of the condemnation of ὁ ἄρχων τοῦ κόσμου, which expression, however, does not (as most recent Commentators imagine) denote the body of the Jewish rulers, chief Priests, &c. &c.; but (as the old Commentators thought, and as I have shown is also the sense at xii. 31.) *Satan*. For by the manifestation of the Holy Spirit, in all His miraculous gifts and wonderful effects, the Author of sin was condemned, and his power subverted. And if *he* was condemned, so would his followers, whether Jews or Gentiles; and punishment be executed on them, both in this world and in the next. Such seems to be the sense of this obscure passage; which is adopted and ably supported by Mr. Scott. If τοῦ κόσμου be taken in its *unrestricted* sense, of the *world at large*, the meaning will be what is expressed by Mr. Holden, as follows: "The Comforter will convince the world of the heinous nature and penalty of *sin*, concerning *righteousness* or justification through the death of Christ, as proved by his resurrection and ascension to the Father; and concerning a future *judgment*, in which a final sentence will be passed upon all men."

12. πολλὰ] "many other doctrines," namely, as the Commentators say, the abrogation of the Ceremonial law, the removal of the distinction between Jews and Gentiles. But there seems reference *also* to those more mysterious and spiritual doctrines, such as justification by faith, which the Spirit of truth afterwards revealed by St. Paul. Βαστάζειν, like the Latin *ferre*, often signifies (as here) to *comprehend*; and the same metaphor is found in our *understand*.

13. ἐκεῖνος.] Spoken emphatically, to denote the *Paraclete* before mentioned, v. 7. In τὸ Πνεῦμα τῆς ἀληθ. there is (as Grot. observes) the figure πρὸς τὸ σημαινόμενον It is, however, of more importance to remark on *this* among so many other proofs in this Gospel, of the *personality* of the Holy Spirit, namely, from personal actions being ascribed to him.

— ὁδηγ. ὑμᾶς εἰς πᾶσαν τὴν ἀλ.] In Recens. Synop., I preferred to the common version that of Campb., Wets., and Newc., "into all the truth." This, I have since found, is adopted by Bp. Middlet., who remarks that ἀλήθεια here denotes not *truth universally*, but only in reference to the particular subject. He does not seem,

τὴν ἀλήθειαν· οὐ γὰρ λαλήσει ἀφ' ἑαυτοῦ, ἀλλ' ὅσα ἂν ἀκούσῃ λαλή-
14 σει, καὶ τὰ ἐρχόμενα ἀναγγελεῖ ὑμῖν. Ἐκεῖνος ἐμὲ δοξάσει, ὅτι ἐκ τοῦ
15 ἐμοῦ λήψεται, καὶ ἀναγγελεῖ ὑμῖν. [k] Πάντα ὅσα ἔχει ὁ Πατὴρ, ἐμά [k] Infra 17. 10.
ἐστι· διὰ τοῦτο εἶπον, ὅτι ἐκ τοῦ ἐμοῦ λήψεται, καὶ ἀναγγελεῖ ὑμῖν.
16 Μικρὸν, καὶ οὐ θεωρεῖτέ με· καὶ πάλιν μικρὸν, καὶ ὄψεσθέ με· ὅτι
17 ἐγὼ ὑπάγω πρὸς τὸν Πατέρα. Εἶπον οὖν ἐκ τῶν μαθητῶν αὐτοῦ πρὸς
ἀλλήλους· Τί ἐστι τοῦτο ὃ λέγει ἡμῖν· Μικρὸν, καὶ οὐ θεωρεῖτέ με·
καὶ πάλιν μικρὸν, καὶ ὄψεσθέ με· καί· ὅτι ἐγὼ ὑπάγω πρὸς τὸν
18 Πατέρα; ἔλεγον οὖν· Τοῦτό τί ἐστιν, ὃ λέγει, τὸ μικρόν; οὐκ οἴ-
19 δαμεν τί λαλεῖ. Ἔγνω οὖν ὁ Ἰησοῦς, ὅτι ἤθελον αὐτὸν ἐρωτᾷν· καὶ
εἶπεν αὐτοῖς· Περὶ τούτου ζητεῖτε μετ' ἀλλήλων, ὅτι εἶπον· Μικρὸν
20 καὶ οὐ θεωρεῖτέ με, καὶ πάλιν μικρὸν καὶ ὄψεσθέ με. Ἀμὴν ἀμὴν

however, to have been aware that the force of τὴν ἀλ. had been long ago pointed out by Le Clerc, in his Ars Crit. ii. I. 2., where he adduces other examples from Joseph. Bell. viii. and Plato Apolog. in which Socrates thus addresses his judges: Ὑμεῖς δέ μου ἀκούσεσθε πᾶσαν τὴν ἀλήθειαν. I would render, "the whole truth," i. e. without any thing being kept back, as at present, from circumstances. Our Lord seems to have had in view Ps. xxiv. 5. ὁδήγησόν με ἐπὶ τὴν ἀλήθειάν σου.

—οὐ γὰρ λαλήσει ἀφ' ἑαυτοῦ, &c.] Christ here speaks of the Holy Spirit *after the manner of men*, as of a *Legate*, who ought to say nothing but what he has been instructed by his principal; q. d. "The instruction delivered by the Holy Spirit will not be ἀφ' ἑαυτοῦ, *suo arbitrio*, but agreeably to the injunctions and the will of the Father; and therefore absolutely true and divine. Nay, moreover, he will not only open out to you the whole truth of things *past*, but also, as often as need shall require, "he will tell you things *future*, and of which I have said nothing to you:" (Tittm.) namely, what shall happen either to the world at large, or to the Jewish people, or to the Church. See Acts xi. 28. xx. 23. xxi. 11. 1 Tim. iv. 1. 2 Tim. iii. 1. 2 Pet. i. 14. (Grot.)

14. ἐκεῖνος ἐμὲ δοξ. &c.] The *scope* of the word seems to be, to shew that in all the Holy Spirit shall reveal and teach, he will have in view the glory of Christ; or, that all which he teaches will tend thereto.

15. πάντα ὅσα ἔχει — ἐστι.] These words denote that there is the most intimate connection and perfect community of counsel, will, feeling, energy, and operation between the Father and the Son, and consequently that the cause of the latter is that of God. (Tittm.) This whole passage is excellently adapted to establish the doctrine of the Trinity against the Socinians. "For here are *three persons* expressly distinguished from each other, and yet among them the *closest connection* is said to subsist. The *glory ascribed to them is equal*; and yet this by no means precludes the supposition that the Son is the Heir of the Father, and the Holy Spirit the Legate of both." (Lampe.)

—διὰ τοῦτο εἶπον] i. e. it was in this sense that I said.

16. μικρόν.] Sub. διάστημα χρόνου ἐστὶ or ἔσται, as in Hos. i. 4. Καὶ, for ὅτε, "and [then]." Οὐ θεωρεῖτε. Pres. for Fut. This is a strong, but delicate form of expression to denote *absence by death*. Ὄψεσθέ με is for πάλιν ὄψ., spoken of his visible advent after the resurrection. The next words ὅτι ἐγὼ — Πατέρα are not satisfactorily explained by any Commentator. It should seem to be an elliptical mode of expression, of which the sense is: "[I use this language] because I am going to the Father." Indeed, though speaking of *going away*, and then *coming* shortly, would *suggest* the idea of only a temporary stay, yet it would not do that clearly enough to be understood until *after the event*: which is all that our Lord intended. *Then* it would serve to confirm their faith, as it now cheered their sorrow.

17. τί ἐστι τοῦτο, &c.] It has been thought surprising that the Apostles should have failed to comprehend the words of our Lord. But the thing is easily accounted for, when we consider their conciseness, and remember that they were *predictive*, perhaps *intentionally* obscure, and only to be understood after their fulfilment. Besides, the Apostles' perceptions were clouded by deep-rooted prejudices, as to the temporal nature of Christ's kingdom, and dulled by their excess of sorrow on learning that, whatever might be the full sense of the words, they were, at least, to be deprived of their Lord. Their greatest perplexity, no doubt, was with the words ὅτι ὑπάγω πρὸς τὸν Πατέρα, which they were not likely to understand in the true sense. They might, indeed, comprehend that they were first to be deprived of, and then to receive back their Lord; but as they firmly believed that the Messiah was to come and establish an earthly kingdom, they could make nothing out of the last words. At ver. 18, the sense of τοῦτο — τὸ μικρὸν has been ill represented in most translations, from inattention to the *Article*, which is correctly expressed in the Syriac Version. The construction is: Τί ἐστι τοῦτο ὃ λέγει, τὸ μικρόν; Render, "What meaneth this *little while* which he speaketh of?" Οὐκ οἴδαμεν, &c. "We know not what he is speaking of."

These words of the Apostles to each other are, with reason, supposed by Heumann to have been pronounced *aside*.

19. περὶ τούτου ζητεῖτε, &c.] This sentence is generally regarded as *interrogative*; but by the best Expositors as *declarative*, which is more suitable to our Lord, as knowing all hearts, and being well acquainted both with what they had been saying, and their desire for information, which they dared not ask for. Compare ver. 30. Thus the sense will be, "So then you are debating," &c. However, after all, the interrogative mode (which is supported by the Pesch. Syr. Ver-

λέγω ὑμῖν, ὅτι κλαύσετε καὶ θρηνήσετε ὑμεῖς, ὁ δὲ κόσμος χαρήσεται·
ὑμεῖς δὲ λυπηθήσεσθε, ἀλλ᾽ ἡ λύπη ὑμῶν εἰς χαρὰν γενήσεται. Ἡ 21
γυνὴ ὅταν τίκτῃ λύπην ἔχει, ὅτι ἦλθεν ἡ ὥρα αὐτῆς· ὅταν δὲ γεννήσῃ
τὸ παιδίον, οὐκ ἔτι μνημονεύει τῆς θλίψεως, διὰ τὴν χαρὰν, ὅτι ἐγεννήθη
ἄνθρωπος εἰς τὸν κόσμον. Καὶ ὑμεῖς οὖν λύπην μὲν νῦν ἔχετε· πάλιν δὲ 22
ὄψομαι ὑμᾶς, καὶ χαρήσεται ὑμῶν ἡ καρδία, καὶ τὴν χαρὰν ὑμῶν οὐδεὶς
l Supra 14. 13. & 15. 16. Matt. 7. 7. & 21. 22. Mark 11. 24. Luke 11. 9. James 1. 5. αἴρει ἀφ᾽ ὑμῶν. l Καὶ ἐν ἐκείνῃ τῇ ἡμέρᾳ ἐμὲ οὐκ ἐρωτήσετε οὐδέν. Ἀμὴν 23
ἀμὴν λέγω ὑμῖν, ὅτι ὅσα ἂν αἰτήσητε τὸν Πατέρα ἐν τῷ ὀνόματί μου,
δώσει ὑμῖν. Ἕως ἄρτι οὐκ ᾐτήσατε οὐδὲν ἐν τῷ ὀνόματί μου· αἰτεῖτε, 24
καὶ λήψεσθε, ἵνα ἡ χαρὰ ὑμῶν ᾖ πεπληρωμένη. Ταῦτα ἐν παροιμίαις 25
λελάληκα ὑμῖν· ἀλλ᾽ ἔρχεται ὥρα ὅτε οὐκ ἔτι ἐν παροιμίαις λαλήσω
ὑμῖν, ἀλλὰ παῤῥησίᾳ περὶ τοῦ Πατρὸς ἀναγγελῶ ὑμῖν. Ἐν ἐκείνῃ τῇ 26
ἡμέρᾳ ἐν τῷ ὀνόματί μου αἰτήσεσθε· καὶ οὐ λέγω ὑμῖν, ὅτι ἐγὼ ἐρω-
m Infra 17. 8. 23. τήσω τὸν Πατέρα περὶ ὑμῶν· m αὐτὸς γὰρ ὁ Πατὴρ φιλεῖ ὑμᾶς, ὅτι 27
ὑμεῖς ἐμὲ πεφιλήκατε, καὶ πεπιστεύκατε ὅτι ἐγὼ παρὰ τοῦ Θεοῦ ἐξῆλθον. Ἐξῆλθον παρὰ τοῦ Πατρὸς, καὶ ἐλήλυθα εἰς τὸν κόσμον· πάλιν 28
ἀφίημι τὸν κόσμον, καὶ πορεύομαι πρὸς τὸν Πατέρα.

sion) has more of nature and spirit. q, d. "What, then, are you debating?" &c.

20. ἀμὴν ἀμὴν λέγω ὑμῖν, &c.] Our Lord did not, for the reason above mentioned, give any *explanation*. And thus his silence may be supposed to mean: "Yet it *is* so. What I have said you will find true." However, in order to more deeply impress their minds, he points to the *circumstances* which should accompany the events in question; namely, at first the sorrow of his disciples, and the triumphant exultation of the world; then the grief of the disciples soon afterwards turned into joy: "*quasi post nubila Phœbus.*"

21. Our Lord here illustrates what he has just said by a simile familiar to the Hebrew writers (as Isa. xxi. 3. xxvi. 17. xxxvii. 3. Jer. iv. 31. xxii. 23. xxx. 6.), and not unknown to the Classical ones. See Hom. Iliad, α. 269. Τίκτειν in the Classical writers signifies *to bear children;* but in the Hellenistic ones mostly (as here) to *be in travail*. It is, however, sometimes in Hippocrates interchanged with κύειν. Λύπην ἔχει must, from the context, denote "is in pangs," is suffering pangs. Ὥρα should be rendered, not *hour*, but *time*. Ἄνθρωπος signifies here a human being, without reference to sex. She rejoices (as Grot. expresses it) quod genus humanum novâ prole auxerit. And not only from the thing itself, but its *results* to herself; for as barrenness was thought a reproach, so child-bearing was considered the reverse; not to mention the pleasure anticipated from the duty and affection of the child. So Aristotle observes: οὐ πανὺ εὐδαιμονικὸς ὁ ἄτεκνος.

22. ἔχετε and αἴρει are Presents for Futures. Χαρήσεται ὑμῶν ἡ. κ. A strong expression signifying, "ye shall feel heartfelt joy." By τὴν χαρὰν ὑμῶν οὐδεὶς αἴρει ἀφ᾽ ὑμῶν it is meant that their joy should be uninterrupted and permanent; not liable to be taken away, as all joy founded on human affairs must be.

23. Christ here subjoins, what would tend to repress their anxiety for the explanation, which he had thought fit *not* to give them, by intimating that in that day of joy they would have no *occasion* to put questions on the subject; q. d. "Ye will have nothing to ask me;" for that such is the sense of ἐμὲ οὐκ ἐρωτ. ο. the best Commentators are agreed. On the subject of *putting questions*, Christ engrafts that of *preferring requests;* and shows that whatever else they might have to ask for, in His cause, whether Spiritual illumination, or courage in action, the Father would deny them nothing.

24. ἐν τῷ ὀνόματί μου] i. e. "on my account, for my cause," as many eminent Commentators explain; or, as Hamm. and Lampe, "by my mediation," through me, as Mediator between God and man. But this, which can scarcely be the *direct sense*, is *implied* in the former interpretation.

— αἰτεῖτε — πεπληρ.] i. e. ye have only to ask and receive, that your joy may be complete; meaning their *spiritual* joy, especially that adverted to supra ver. 22.

25. Christ here gives a *reason* why he had spoken ἐν παροιμίαις, darkly and figuratively. See Note on Matt. xiii. 3. To this is opposed ἀναγγέλλειν παῤῥησίᾳ, to speak without the involvements of figurative allusion. I would here compare the words of Æschyl. Agam. 1154. φρενώσω δ' (scil. ὑμᾶς) οὐκ ἔτ' ἐξ αἰνιγμάτων. By ταῦτα is meant all that Christ had said in the preceding discourses. The fulfilment of this promise is alluded to at Luke xxiv. 26—44. and Acts i. 3.

26—28. Here are indicated the *advantages* resulting from this fuller knowledge: "At that time (i. e. when I shall have more fully taught you concerning my Father, his counsels, and decrees) ye shall address your prayers in my name, and shall receive benefits the most precious." (Tittm.)

— καὶ οὐ λέγω — ὑμῶν.] Since Christ has at xiv. 16. promised that he will ask the Father on their behalf; and as we have just after, xvii. 9. seqq. an actual intercession for them, and as Christ is at Rom. viii. 34. Heb. vii. 25. & 1 John ii. 1. said to be continually interceding for his disciples, the sense of the words must be, not what they would at first seem to express, but what has been assigned by the most eminent Interpreters

29 *Λέγουσιν αὐτῷ οἱ μαθηταὶ αὐτοῦ· Ἴδε νῦν παῤῥησίᾳ λαλεῖς, καὶ*
30 *παροιμίαν οὐδεμίαν λέγεις.* [n] *νῦν οἴδαμεν ὅτι οἶδας πάντα, καὶ οὐ* n Infra 17. 8.
χρείαν ἔχεις ἵνα τίς σε ἐρωτᾷ. ἐν τούτῳ πιστεύομεν ὅτι ἀπὸ Θεοῦ
31 *ἐξῆλθες. Ἀπεκρίθη αὐτοῖς ὁ Ἰησοῦς· Ἄρτι πιστεύετε;* [o] *ἰδοὺ, ἔρχεται* o Matt. 26. 31. Mark 14. 27.
32 *ὥρα, καὶ νῦν ἐλήλυθεν, ἵνα σκορπισθῆτε ἕκαστος εἰς τὰ ἴδια, καὶ ἐμὲ*
33 *μόνον ἀφῆτε· καὶ οὐκ εἰμὶ μόνος, ὅτι ὁ Πατὴρ μετ᾽ ἐμοῦ ἐστι. ταῦτα*
λελάληκα ὑμῖν, ἵνα ἐν ἐμοὶ εἰρήνην ἔχητε. ἐν τῷ κόσμῳ θλίψιν ἕξετε·
ἀλλὰ θαρσεῖτε, ἐγὼ νενίκηκα τὸν κόσμον.
1 XVII. [p] *ΤΑΥΤΑ ἐλάλησεν ὁ Ἰησοῦς, καὶ ἐπῆρε τοὺς ὀφθαλμοὺς* p Supra 12. 28.

for the last century, namely, "I need not say that I shall pray the Father for you, since you know I will do *that;* [nay, there is no *need*, in *another* respect] for the Father Himself loveth you." This idiom has the technical name *præteritio*, and is to be found even in the Classical writers. The omission of a clause suspended on *γὰρ* is common in the N. T. Αὐτὸς is for *αὐτόματος*. Πεφιλήκατε and *πεπιστεύκατε* are to be taken as Presents. On the full sense of *ἐξῆλθον παρὰ τοῦ Πατ.* (as denoting not *mission* from, but *procession* from God, implying the being *with God*, and VERY GOD.) Compare iii. 13. 31. vi. 62. viii. 41. and see the Notes of Lampe and Tittm. in Recens. Synop.

30. *νῦν οἴδαμεν*, &c.] We may paraphrase: "Now we experimentally know that to thee all the thoughts, wishes, and desires of men are open, and therefore cannot doubt of thy divine mission." To the Messiah, the Jews always ascribed supernatural knowledge of the thoughts of men.

31. *ἄρτι πιστεύετε;*] Christ here checks their excessive confidence, and inculcates diffidence in their own strength. The interrogation here, as often, involves a strong negation.

32. *καὶ νῦν ἐλήλυθεν*] "nay, is now come." At *ἴδια* sub. *οἰκήματα*. So 1 Macc. vi. 54. *ἐσκορπίσθη ἕκαστος εἰς τὸν τόπον ἑαυτοῦ*. Comp. Hom. Odyss. α. 274. *Μνηστῆρας μὲν ἐπὶ σφέτερα σκίδνασθαι ἄνωχθι.*

—*καὶ οὐκ εἰμὶ*, &c.] The *καὶ* has here, as often, the sense *and yet;* and in *μετ᾽ ἐμοῦ* there is an allusion to the *double* meaning of the phrase. See Note on viii. 29.

33. *ταῦτα.*] The recent Commentators too much limit the force of the word, as if referring only to what was *just said.* Whereas it must, with the ancient, and some eminent modern Commentators, be taken of the whole of what had been said in the preceding discourse; which, it seems, our Lord delivered for the purpose of suggesting grounds of consolation under the evils which they would speedily encounter, and perpetually have to grapple with. See Lampe and Doddr.

—*ἐν ἐμοὶ*] i. e. by faith in me, and reliance on my protection. Εἰρήνην, that tranquillity of mind, consolation, and comfort, which he had so solemnly bequeathed them at xiv. 27, and alone to be attained through Him "who is our Peace." See Eph. ii. 14.

—*νενίκηκα τὸν κόσμον.*] This is, as Kuin. and Tittm. observe, the *prophetic* Preterite, for the Future, namely, when the future event is just about to take place. Νικ. signifies "to foil, and frustrate." Κόσμος here denotes the unbelieving and persecuting part of the world, combined under their leader the *ὁ ἄρχων τοῦ κόσμου τούτου*, to destroy the cause of the Gospel. By saying that *He* hath overcome the world (for the *ἐγὼ* is emphatic) our Lord intimates that by the same all powerful aid (that of the Father, (see v. 32.) and His *own*, and the Holy Spirit's), *they* might also come off more than conquerors in the day of tribulation and persecution. See Rom. viii. 37. 1 Cor. xv. 57. 2 Cor. ii. 14. 1 John iv. 4.

XVII. After concluding the above impressive discourse, Christ addresses himself in *prayer* to God. The prayer is (as Tittm. observes) such, that, "had we no other knowledge of Christ than what was furnished thence, it would be sufficient to show us the supreme dignity of his person, his exalted magnanimity, his ardent love to man, and the momentous consequences of the work He was effecting." The following brief analysis thereof is given by Dr. Hales, vol. iii. 190: "As the Jewish High Priest, on the day of *atonement*, was required to make *annual intercession* for *himself*, for his household, the *Priests* and *Levites*, and for the *whole nation*, Levit. xvi. 17.; so our *all-sufficient* High Priest, *once for all*, Heb. ix. 26. Rom. vi. 10., on this his great day of *atonement*, solemnly *interceded* with God His Father for *himself*, that he might be received into *glory*, his original glory in heaven, xvii. 1—5., for his *household*, the *Apostles* and *Disciples*, that God would preserve them in *his name*, or in the true religion; give them a spirit of *unity* and *concord*, and protect them in and from the *wicked world*, v. 6—19.; and that, finally, they might partake of his glory in heaven, and also be supported by his *love* and *presence* on earth, v. 24—26.; and also for all *future believers*, through their preaching, that they might be endued with the same spirit of unity and concord, and for the *conversion* of the whole world, v. 20—23."

Lampe thinks, that the primary intent of this prayer was, to console the disciples. But it was equally so to *instruct* them, (since, as Dr. Hales observes, it unfolds the grand mystery of the Gospel—the instituted means of salvation by the Father and the Son conjointly, from their love to the world), to set them an example of fortitude and resignation, as well as prayer to God under circumstances of peril, affliction, and distress; finally, to teach Christians of all ages to commit themselves and all their concerns to the Providence of that God who "watcheth over them." This may very well serve to account for the *variation* of *manner* in different parts of the prayer; for though, throughout the whole, Christ speaks as *the Incarnate Son of God*, yet he sometimes supplicates *as Man;* at others he speaks as the *Mediator of his people*, but not unfrequently expresses himself with *Divine* majesty and authority.

1. *ἐπῆρε τοὺς ὀφθαλ. α. ε. τ. ο.*] On this attitude

αὐτοῦ εἰς τὸν οὐρανὸν καὶ εἶπε· Πάτερ, ἐλήλυθεν ἡ ὥρα· δόξασόν
q Matt. 28. 18. supra 5. 27. σου τὸν Υἱόν· ἵνα καὶ ὁ Υἱός σου δοξάσῃ σε· [q] καθὼς ἔδωκας αὐτῷ 2
ἐξουσίαν πάσης σαρκὸς ἵνα πᾶν ὃ δέδωκας αὐτῷ, δώσῃ αὐτοῖς ζωὴν
αἰώνιον. Αὕτη δέ ἐστιν ἡ αἰώνιος ζωή, ἵνα γινώσκωσι σὲ τὸν μόνον 3

of reverent devotion, as well as that of lifting up the *hands*, see Elsn. and Lampe.

— Πάτερ.] On the peculiar sense in which the word is here to be taken, see Lampe in Recens. Synop. Christ is here to be considered as praying according to his *human* nature: for as Schoettg. observes, "in his state of *exinanition*, having emptied himself of his glory, Christ is considered as a *subject* fulfilling the orders of his *Monarch*, namely, God. Therefore to the Triune God, as his Lord and Master, Christ might direct his prayers." Ἐλήλυθεν ἡ ὥρα, i. e. the decisive and appointed time, the time in which the glory both of the Father and the Son should be manifested. ἡ ὥρα is elsewhere so employed in the N. T., and almost always used of a period ushering in calamity.

— δόξασον — δοξάσῃ σε] i. e. "receive Him into the glory He originally had in Heaven." On the *nature* of that glory, *how* it was manifested in Heaven, developed on earth, and revealed to men; how the Father was glorified by the Son, in all His attributes, and in the whole work of salvation, see Lampe and Tittm. in Recens. Synop.

2. καθὼς ἔδωκας — σαρκὸς, &c.] This suggests the *reason* and *cause* of the prayer here offered; our Lord refers both his own glory and that of his Father to the work of salvation committed to him. Καθὼς, "inasmuch as, since."

— ἐξουσίαν πάσης σαρκὸς] "a power over all men." A Hellenistic use of the Genit. Πᾶσα σὰρξ is a frequent Hebraism. Πᾶν is Neut. for masc., by a usage frequent in the Classical writers. It is considered by Kypke and Kuin. as a nom. absol., or an accus. for dat., and αὐτοῖς as redundant, the plural being referred to the sing. πᾶν, by the figure πρὸς τὸ σημαινόμενον. But Lampe, with reason, objects to this pleonasm, and enallage of number. The pleonasm, indeed, is *energetic*, and therefore *no* pleonasm. And the enallage *may* be, as he says, emphatic. It should, however, seem best not too *anxiously* to *press* on such constructions, nor too minutely to discuss them on the principles of Classical construction; but to consider them as *anacolutha*, such as are found in the *popular* phraseology of almost all languages. But, to turn from words to things; on the full *extent* of this *august power* claimed by our Lord, Tittm. shows that it involves the governance of all human affairs, the regulation of the vicissitudes of times, and places, &c. &c.: all in order to accomplish the work of human salvation. A work committed to Him, as the Saviour of men, in order that he who *obtained* that salvation, might be the *giver* of it. Christ might, indeed, be said to give eternal life, by giving and promulgating that Gospel which reveals it. But he emphatically gives it, by the sacrifice of himself to atone for the sins of the whole world.

3. αὕτη δέ ἐστιν — Χριστόν.] In the interpretation of this verse the utmost caution is requisite, since from it senses the *very opposite* have been sought. It has ever been regarded by the Heterodox as one of their strong-holds, and from this they have adventured to impugn the doctrine of the Deity of Christ. In order to effectually frustrate their attempt, many Orthodox Commentators, ancient and modern, lay down such a construction of the sentence, as that the words τὸν μόνον ἀληθινὸν Θεὸν may belong not *only* to the *Father*, but *also* to the *Son*. This they seek to effect in two ways, — 1. by inverting the natural order of the words, thus: "Ut te, et quem misisti Jesum Christum, solum verum Deum agnoscant." 2. by supposing an ellipsis of εἶναι, and after καὶ supplying ἅμα σοι. But the best Commentators have long been agreed, that this arbitrary *transposition* and *supplying of words* involves so much violence, that the interpretation founded thereon is inadmissible. Indeed, as Bp. Middlet. observes, "it could only have originated in a wish to evade the consequences which this text has been supposed to establish." We must not, then, seek here an *assertion of the Deity of Christ*, but content ourselves with proving that Christ *is not* here represented as a *mere Legate*, much less a *mere* MAN. That our Lord did not, *could* not, mean to make such an assertion, is plain both from the passage itself, and from what precedes and follows it.

In the first place, it is proper to ascertain the exact sense of the terms μόνον, ἀληθινὸν, and γινώσκειν. Now this will mainly depend upon the *construction*; about which no little difference of opinion exists. There are *two* classes of Interpreters, who each suppose an ellipsis of εἶναι. But, as Bp. Middlet. has proved, the exposition of the one class is negatived by the presence of the Art. τόν; and that of the other, both by that, and by its involving an unprecedented harshness of construction. It is evident that τὸν μόνον ἀλ. Θ. is in *apposition* with σε: and we may, with Lampe, suppose the τὸν to mean, "who art the," &c.; or, with Bp. Middlet. render, "as being." Of *most* consequence, however, is it to ascertain the *true import* of μόνον ἀληθ. Now many ancient Expositors (as Athanasius, and most of the early Fathers), and, of the moderns, Calvin, Bp. Bull, Wets., Tittm., Hales, and others, suppose the words to recognize in God the Father a superiority, as being such, *principaliter*, and κατ' ἐξοχήν; the Fountain of all Deity; namely, as it is expressed by Athanasius (cited by Bp. Bull) Def. Fid. Nic. p. 264. ὅτι μόνος ἀγέννητος, καὶ μόνος πηγὴ Θεότητος. Yet, however true may be the *doctrine itself*, (which has been established, as on a Rock, by Zanchius and Bp. Bull. in Section iv. of his immortal DEFENSIO *Fidei Nicænæ)*, yet here it should seem to be out of place. Indeed, it may be observed, that one of the arguments which most effectually keep out the *Socinian* interpretation, will go far to exclude *this*. And to those by whom it has been supported, we may, to a certain degree, apply what Bp. Middlet. has said of the Socinian interpreters, who, he observes, "argue as if in *our Saviour's days* there had been the same controversy about the *nature* and *essence* of the One True God, which arose *afterwards*; whereas the dispute then was, whether there were a *plurality* of Gods, or only One; of which the Jews held the latter, and the whole Pagan world, the former opinion." This very circumstance, I would remark, is strongly in favor of an interpretation which has every appearance of be

4 ἀληθινὸν Θεὸν, καὶ ὃν ἀπέστειλας Ἰησοῦν Χριστόν. Ἐγώ σε ἐδόξασα
5 ἐπὶ τῆς γῆς· τὸ ἔργον ἐτελείωσα ὃ δέδωκάς μοι ἵνα ποιήσω· καὶ νῦν
δόξασόν με σὺ, Πάτερ, παρὰ σεαυτῷ, τῇ δόξῃ ᾗ εἶχον πρὸ τοῦ τὸν
6 κόσμον εἶναι παρὰ σοί. Ἐφανέρωσά σου τὸ ὄνομα τοῖς ἀνθρώποις,
οὓς δέδωκάς μοι ἐκ τοῦ κόσμου. Σοὶ ἦσαν, καὶ ἐμοὶ αὐτοὺς δέδωκας·
7 καὶ τὸν λόγον σου τετηρήκασι. Νῦν ἔγνωκαν ὅτι πάντα ὅσα δέδωκάς

ing the true one, and has been adopted by some ancient and many eminent modern Expositors, as Lucas, Brugensis, Maldon, Grot., Whitby, Pearce, Schleus., Bp. Middl., Bp. Burgess, and Archdeacon Pott; according to which, μόνον ἀληθ. is supposed to be meant in opposition to the *false gods* of the Heathens, who have no real entity. Comp. 1 Thess. i. 9. I John ii. 8. Thus the Apostles would be taught that (to use the words of Bp. Middl.) "eternal life is only to be obtained by a knowledge of the *one true God*, and of Jesus Christ; thus directing the mind to the truths both of natural aud revealed religion." This is supported and confirmed by two passages of Josephus, namely, Antiq. viii. 13. 6. προσεκύνουν ἕνα Θεὸν, καὶ μέγιστον καὶ ἀληθῆ μόνον ἀποκαλοῦντες· τοὺς δ' ἄλλους ὀνόματα ὑπὸ φαύλου καὶ ἀνοήτου δόξης πεποιημένα. and Ant. x. 11. 7. where Nebuchadnezzar calls the God of Daniel (Jehovah) τὸν μόνον ἀληθῆ, καὶ τὸ πᾶν κράτος ἔχοντα. i. e. (as Bp. Burgess, in his excellent Tract addressed to Mrs. J. Baillie, p. 77, explains the τὸν μόνον ἀλ.) "greater than all the gods of the heathens." The learned Prelate there well remarks, that "the term *only* does not possess so *exclusive* a sense in Greek, Latin, or English, as is insisted on by Socinians and others, to the exclusion of the Deity of Christ, and that Servius's Note on a passage of Virgil's Georgics, may serve as an illustration: '*Sola*, magna, præcipua, id est, supra alios deos marinos.' The restricted sense of this term, (continues the Bishop), in our own language, may be exemplified from a memorable passage in the Liturgy of our Church: 'Thou *only* art holy,' is said of Christ, but not exclusively of the Holy Spirit; and 'Thou *only* art the Lord,' yet not exclusively of the Father." Thus it is plain that there is no opposition intended between the Father and the Son; and that the Father is no more said to be *the true* God, to the *exclusion* of the Son, than at Is. xliv. 6. xlv. 22. In short (as Bp. Middl. says), "it is perfectly frivolous to introduce this passage into the Trinitarian dispute."

To advert to the import of γινώσκωσι, the term must, in its full force, (which is fully discussed by Lampe and Tittm.) denote such *knowing* and *recognizing* the Father and the Son to be what they have revealed themselves, *cum effectu*, and not in mere speculative knowlege, as shall influence us to worship, serve, and obey them; and to seek salvation from them alone. Thus the general sense may be expressed in paraphrase as follows: "This is the way by which they may attain to eternal salvation, namely, to acknowledge Thee as the only true God, and Jesus Christ whom thou hast sent [as the only true Messiah]." See Note on 1 John v. 20.

4. σε ἐδόξασα.] Jesus glorified the Father by causing him and his attributes to be known and acknowledged on earth. See Lampe and Tittm.

— τὸ ἔργον — ποιήσω.] Not the work of *teaching* only as some recent Commentators suppose, but also (as Grot., Lampe, and Storr have proved) that of *atonement by his death and passion*, which was then commencing. For as they were so very near, this anticipation is very admissible. The words breathe a holy triumph at so goodly a work being nearly completed.

5. δόξασόν με σὺ, &c.] Here again our Lord has predicated of himself things most august, and evincing his Divine majesty. 1. He professes that he had δόξαν, (Heb. כָּבוֹד) i. e. the divine Majesty, embracing the whole compass of the Divine nature, attributes, counsels, and works. (See the Note on i. 14.) 2. He makes the asseveration. "I had this glory παρὰ σοὶ, i. e. with God in Heaven." Therefore he *was in Heaven* before he came into the world, or *was in the bosom of the Father*. (John i. 18.) 3. He professes that he had glory with the Father, *before he came to the earth*; nay, πρὸ τοῦ τὸν κόσμον εἶναι, or (as the Apostles say) πρὸ καταβολῆς κόσμου, and (as St. John expresses it) ἐν ἀρχῇ, i. e. *from eternity*. For by phrases of that sort the Hebrews were accustomed to designate *eternity*. (See the Note on i. 1.) 4. He prays that the glory and majesty which, as *Son of God*, he enjoyed from all eternity, the Father would now invest him with, as *Son of man*, and *Saviour of the human race*. Now, how could he have said this, and *thus* prayed for it from the Father, unless he had been the true and eternal Son of God, such as he is described in this Gospel? (Tittm.) The same learned Commentator and Lampe have completely refuted the Socinian perversion of εἶχον, by which it is understood only of *destination*.

6—14. Christ here speaks of his *disciples*, and commends them to the especial favour and protection of the Father, since they had been his docile followers, and were to be the first planters of his Gospel.

As ὄνομα τοῦ Θεοῦ is often used for Θεὸς, so σου τὸ ὄνομα may denote *Thee*, i. e. thy nature, attributes, and counsels for the salvation of men. See v. 14.

6. οὓς δέδωκάς μοι.] The best Commentators are agreed, that the sense is: "whom, by Thy Providence, thou hast delivered to me, to be taught, and brought unto salvation." By τοῦ κόσμου is meant the world at large, which, as we are elsewhere told, lieth in sin.

— σοὶ ἦσαν] namely, 1. by right of creation and preservation; and 2. by sincere attachment to thee. Δέδωκας, hast given me them as Disciples. Τὸν λόγον σου τετ. means the *doctrine of the Gospel* delivered to them through Christ by God the Father. Τετ. is a very strong term, and imports entire acquiescence in, and adherence to, as a principle of action.

7. ἔγνωκαν] "they assuredly know." By πάντα may be understood both the *words* and *works* enjoined by the Father; but chiefly the former, as appears from the next verse, which is, in some measure, exegetical of the preceding.

8. ὅτι παρὰ σοῦ ἐξῆλθον.] Tittm. observes, that we must be careful to distinguish the *proceeding*

r Supra 16. 27, 30. infra ver. 25. μοι παρά σοῦ ἐστιν· r ὅτι τὰ ῥήματα ἃ δέδωκάς μοι, δέδωκα αὐτοῖς· 8
καὶ αὐτοὶ ἔλαβον, καὶ ἔγνωσαν ἀληθῶς, ὅτι παρὰ σοῦ ἐξῆλθον· καὶ
ἐπίστευσαν ὅτι σύ με ἀπέστειλας. Ἐγὼ περὶ αὐτῶν ἐρωτῶ· οὐ περὶ 9
s Supra 16. 15. τοῦ κόσμου ἐρωτῶ, ἀλλὰ περὶ ὧν δέδωκάς μοι, ὅτι σοί εἰσι. s Καὶ τὰ 10
t Supra 10. 30. infra ver. 21. ἐμὰ πάντα σά ἐστι, καὶ τὰ σὰ ἐμά· καὶ δεδόξασμαι ἐν αὐτοῖς. t Καὶ 11
οὐκ ἔτι εἰμὶ ἐν τῷ κόσμῳ, καὶ οὗτοι ἐν τῷ κόσμῳ εἰσὶ, καὶ ἐγὼ πρός
σε ἔρχομαι. Πάτερ ἅγιε, τήρησον αὐτοὺς ἐν τῷ ὀνόματί σου, ‡ οὓς

of Jesus from God, xvi. 28., and coming to the earth, v. 3., from his being *sent by God*, as the Messiah. It should seem that ἐξῆλθον here includes *both* these particulars: one referring to his *Divine nature*, as SON OF GOD, the other to his office as commissioned from the Father, and sent to redeem mankind. The best comment on this passage is viii. 42. ἐγὼ γὰρ ἐκ τοῦ Θεοῦ ἐξῆλθον καὶ ἥκω (scil. εἰς τὸν κόσμον·) οὐδὲ γὰρ ἀπ' ἐμαυτοῦ ἐλήλυθα, ἀλλ' ἐκεῖνός με ἀπέστειλε.

9. οὐ περὶ τοῦ κόσμου ἐρωτῶ.] Since Christ did elsewhere pray for the world, (see v. 20, 22. Luke xxiii. 34.) nay for his very enemies, Kuin. supposes the sense to be: "I pray especially for thy faithful worshippers; they are worthy of this favour." Others take οὐ — ἀλλὰ for *non tam — quam*, importing that the prayer for His disciples is not to the exclusion of the world from his prayers. But this is *extorting* a sense which is not inherent in the words. The difficulty will, I think, be removed by rendering ἐρωτῶ "I am praying," meaning, I am *now* praying. The nature of the thing did not (as the best Commentators have seen) admit of Christ's *then* praying *for the world*, i. e. the unbelieving part of it, those who had not embraced the Gospel. See v. 20.

— ὅτι σοί εἰσι] i. e. *now* by *adoption* (see 1 John iii. 2.) as heretofore by creation, &c. See note sup. v. 6.

10. καὶ τὰ ἐμὰ — ἐμά.] These words seem meant to *illustrate* the preceding: since from the close communion of will, counsel, and works, of Father and Son, whatever is the one's is also the other's. See xvi. 15. Hence the disciples are sometimes called the *Father's*, and sometimes the *Son's*. The πάντα *may* be taken (as the recent Commentators direct) for the masc. πάντες; but in a *gnome generalis* like this, the neuter may denote both *persons* and *things*.

— καὶ δεδόξασμαι ἐν αὐτοῖς.] These words seem meant to express something *beyond* the preceding, q. d. "they are not only mine, but I am glorified in and through them; therefore they are *effectively* mine." Rosenm. and Tittm. take δεδόξ. in a Future sense, as a *preterite prophetic*. But the glorification in question, namely, by the propagation of his religion, had already taken place, and was taking place. Hence Grot. and Doddr. would take it for a Pres. or Aor. But strict philological propriety will not warrant that. The case seems to be this: The *Perf.* is often put for the *Pres.*, when an action or state is designated, which has commenced in time past, but extends also to the present. See Matth. Gr. Gr. § 503. and Win. Gr. Gr. § 34. 3. a. But the Present, in an action of *continued progression*, like the spreading of the Gospel, is so *intermingled* with the Future, that the Future may also be included. Thus the full sense is: "I have been, am being, and am to be glorified."

11. καὶ οὐκ ἔτι — ἔρχομαι.] These words offer the *reason* why Jesus commends them to the protection of God. See xiv. 18. Render: "I am [as it were] no longer in the world, but they *are* in the world [alone]; while I am going to thee." Yet something is wanting to complete the sense. It should seem that in this verse the words ἐγὼ περὶ αὐτῶν are supposed to be repeated, q. d. "Yea, I do pray for them, as being myself no longer in the world," &c.

— Πάτερ ἅγιε, &c.] Now follows, to the end of the Chapter, the prayer of our Lord for the *disciples*. With Πάτερ ἅγιε the Commentators compare the precatory use of *Sancte Pater!* in the Latin Classical writers.

— τήρησον αὐτοὺς ἐν τῷ ὀν. σ.] On the sense of ἐν τῷ ὀνόμ. σου the Commentators differ. It seems to be best explained by Grot., De Dieu, Kuin., Hales, and Campb., who take it to mean "in the profession of thy doctrine and worship, in the faith and practice of thy religion." "By making known (says Campb.) the name of God to those who enjoyed the old dispensation, is plainly suggested that additional light was conveyed to them, which they could not have derived from it. By manifesting God's name to them, therefore, we must understand the communication of those truths which peculiarly characterize the new dispensation; and as every revelation which God gives tends further to illustrate the divine character, the instructions which our Lord gave to his disciples, relating to life and immortality, and the recovery of sinners through his mediation, may well be called revealing God, or (which, in the Hebrew idiom, is the same) *the name of God* to them."

There is here a remarkable var. lect. Instead of οὓς, very many MSS. (mostly ancient) and several Greek Commentators and early Edd. have ᾧ; which has been received by almost every Editor, except Matthæi, from Beng. and Wets. to Scholz. And this is very agreeable to the Critical Canon, which directs the more difficult reading to be preferred. But that Canon has several limitations and exceptions; and, amongst the rest, where the readings are exceedingly similar in appearance, and where the propriety of the language rejects the more difficult one, or where the context will not permit it. Now *all* these circumstances here concur. For the ᾧ involves an unprecedented harshness; since thus we must take ἐν τῷ ὀνόμ. in the sense "by thy *power*;" a use of ὄνομα nowhere else found in Scripture, or any other writings; and which would be unsuitable to the words following. Besides, the idiom of ᾧ for ὃ is not agreeable to the character of St. John's style, and nowhere occurs in his Gospel or his Epistles. Whereas the above use occurs at ver. 6, 9, and 12, of this prayer. Indeed the common reading is not only greatly superior in *external* evidence (being supported by a decided majority of MSS., some exceedingly ancient, and the earliest Versions and Fathers), but seems to be placed beyond doubt by the *repetition* of

12 δέδωκάς μοι· ἵνα ὦσιν ἓν καθὼς ἡμεῖς. [u]Ὅτε ἤμην μετ᾽ αὐτῶν ἐν τῷ u Infra 18. 9. Ps. 109. 8.
κόσμῳ, ἐγὼ ἐτήρουν αὐτοὺς ἐν τῷ ὀνόματί σου· οὓς δέδωκάς μοι ἐφύλαξα,
καὶ οὐδεὶς ἐξ αὐτῶν ἀπώλετο, εἰ μὴ ὁ υἱὸς τῆς ἀπωλείας, ἵνα ἡ γραφὴ
13 πληρωθῇ. Νῦν δὲ πρός σε ἔρχομαι, καὶ ταῦτα λαλῶ ἐν τῷ κόσμῳ,
14 ἵνα ἔχωσι τὴν χαρὰν τὴν ἐμὴν πεπληρωμένην ἐν αὐτοῖς. Ἐγὼ δέδωκα
αὐτοῖς τὸν λόγον σου· καὶ ὁ κόσμος ἐμίσησεν αὐτοὺς, ὅτι οὐκ εἰσὶν ἐκ τοῦ
15 κόσμου, καθὼς ἐγὼ οὐκ εἰμὶ ἐκ τοῦ κόσμου. Οὐκ ἐρωτῶ ἵνα ἄρῃς αὐτοὺς
16 ἐκ τοῦ κόσμου, ἀλλ᾽ ἵνα τηρήσῃς αὐτοὺς ἐκ τοῦ πονηροῦ. Ἐκ τοῦ κόσμου
17 οὐκ εἰσὶ, καθὼς ἐγὼ ἐκ τοῦ κόσμου οὐκ εἰμί. Ἁγίασον αὐτοὺς ἐν τῇ ἀλη-
18 θείᾳ σου. ὁ λόγος ὁ σὸς ἀλήθειά ἐστι. Καθὼς ἐμὲ ἀπέστειλας εἰς τὸν

the words in the next verse, *ἐγὼ ἐτήρουν αὐτοὺς ἐν τῷ ὀνόματί σου, οὓς δέδωκάς μοι*. I cannot help suspecting that the false interpretation of *ὀνόμ.* and the alteration of *οὓς* to *ᾧ* or *ὃ* (which last is found in several MSS. and Versions), arose chiefly from an inattention to the *transposition*; which, however, is frequent in St. John's writings. Certainly, if the librarii *did* stumble at *ὀνόματι*, (and what was so probable?) they would be likely to alter the reading *οὓς* to *ὃ* or *ᾧ*. Whereas, if we were to suppose *ᾧ* or *ὃ* to have been the *original* reading, it would not be easy to account for the alteration into *οὓς*.

—*ἵνα ὦσιν ἓν καθὼς ἡμεῖς*.] This is a blending of two phrases, *ἵνα ὦσι (καθ᾽) ἓν* and *ἵνα ὦσι καθὼς ἡμεῖς ἐσμεν*; the latter explaining the former: the sense being, "that they may be united in sentiment, affection, and zeal for the dissemination of the Gospel, even as we are united in will and purpose."

12. *ἀπώλετο*.] There seems here to be, as in Ps. ii. 12., an allusion to the case of a traveller, who has, from abandoning his guide, lost the right path, and come to destruction. In the words of the above Psalm, *δράξασθε παιδείας, μήποτε ἀπολεῖσθε ἐξ ὁδοῦ δικαίας*, there is a use of the antecedent for the consequent, as in the present passage.

—*ὁ υἱὸς τῆς ἀπωλείας*.] The sense is not merely, as Rosenm., Kuin., Schleusn., and Tittm. render, *homo nequam, nullius frugis*; but the expression must mean one who is deserving of, and devoted to, perdition. This use of *υἱὸς* with a noun in the Genit. is a Hebraism.

—*ἵνα ἡ γραφὴ πληρωθῇ*.] The best Expositors are agreed that the sense is: "*So that* the Scripture is thus fulfilled;" or, as Bp. Pearce explains, may be *applied* in this case. On the passage here had in view the Commentators are not agreed. Most think there is only a *general reference* to the prophecies concerning the passion of our Saviour. See, however, Ps. 41. 9. and 109, 8. compared with Acts i. 20.

13. *ἵνα ἔχωσι — αὐτοῖς*.] Render: "that they may [by these words] have their joy in me (i. e. of which I am the object) complete and perfect." Now that would shortly be the case at his resurrection, and the sending to them the Holy Spirit.

15. *οὐκ ἐρωτῶ — κόσμου*.] The sense seems to be, "I pray not that thou shouldst remove them from this life." To more fully comprehend the purport of the expression, it is proper to bear in mind a remark of Euthym. and Grot. that "these words are said in *explication* of the preceding, and for the sake of the disciples then present, and within hearing." Our Lord, therefore, meant *indirectly* to warn his disciples, under the bitter persecutions they would be called upon to endure, not to wish or pray for death, since he had important purposes for them to answer, during many years: at the same time suggesting to them motives for constancy and fortitude, in their being *defended* and *preserved* under the sorrows which should surround them.

By *τοῦ πονηροῦ* many eminent Commentators understand *the Evil one*; referring to Matth. vi 13. & 1 John v. 19. But though that interpretation be there suitable, it does not follow that it should *here* be admitted, since the circumstances are different. It is better, with Est., Grotius, Lampe, Campb., Noesselt, Rosenm., and Tittm., to take *τοῦ πονηροῦ* in the *neuter* gender of *evil*, as Rom. xii. 9, and often elsewhere. The sense, too, thence arising is more extensive, and more suitable to the context.

17. *ἁγίασον — ἀλήθειά ἐστι*.] From their *preservation under trials* and calamity, our Lord proceeds to pray for their *preservation in the Evangelical office*. Ἁγιάζειν, like the Heb. קָדַשׁ, signifies properly to separate, set apart to some office, whether civil or Ecclesiastical, i. e. to consecrate to the worship of God, or the concerns of religion. Ἅγιος properly denotes a person so set apart, or consecrated, and is used especially of *Prophets* or *Priests*; both being said *ἁγιάζεσθαι*. It is also used of the appointment by the Father of the Son to the work of human salvation by his incarnation (see x. 36.) and to which our Lord is said to have devoted himself. But how, it may be asked, are we to understand the term, as applied to the *Apostles*? On this Expositors are not agreed. Some assign the sense "Set them apart unto the promulgation of thy truth," i. e. the Word of the Gospel, which is then added, by way of explanation, as the Truth. Others take it to mean, "Sanctify them (namely, by cleansing them from sin, and releasing them from the power of sin, through the operation of the Holy Spirit, unto the promulgation of thy Faith." This latter interpretation seems preferable, as being called for by the *fact*, that the Apostles required far *more* than to be set apart to the ministry: not to say that in the term itself there seems an allusion to the Πνεῦμα ἅγιον. And this use of the word to denote *purify* is of frequent occurrence both in the Sept. and the N. T. as 1 Thess. v. 23. Since, however, the word is sometimes so used in the Sept. (as Gen. ii. 3. *ἡγίασεν ἡμέραν*. and supra x. 36. (of our Lord Jesus Christ) *ὃν ὁ Πατὴρ ἡγίασε*, i. e. *ἀφώρισε*) it may *here* also be admitted; yet only in *conjunction* with the other. And indeed this setting apart and consecrating would be the result of that *cleansing* and *purifying* of which the Apostles then stood much in need.

18. *εἰς τὸν κόσμον*] Namely, for the purpose of *promulgating thy Truth*. See ver. 17.

κόσμον, κἀγὼ ἀπέστειλα αὐτοὺς εἰς τὸν κόσμον· καὶ ὑπὲρ αὐτῶν ἐγὼ ἁγι- 19
άζω ἐμαυτὸν, ἵνα καὶ αὐτοὶ ὦσιν ἡγιασμένοι ἐν ἀληθείᾳ. Οὐ περὶ τούτων 20
δὲ ἐρωτῶ μόνον, ἀλλὰ καὶ περὶ τῶν * πιστευόντων διὰ τοῦ λόγου αὐτῶν εἰς
x Supra 10. 30. & 14. 10. 1 John 1. 3. & 3. 24. ἐμέ· x ἵνα πάντες ἓν ὦσι· καθὼς σὺ, Πάτερ, ἐν ἐμοὶ κἀγὼ ἐν σοὶ, ἵνα καὶ 21
αὐτοὶ ἐν ἡμῖν ἓν ὦσιν· ἵνα ὁ κόσμος πιστεύσῃ ὅτι σύ με ἀπέστειλας. Καὶ 22
ἐγὼ τὴν δόξαν ἣν δέδωκάς μοι δέδωκα αὐτοῖς, ἵνα ὦσιν ἓν καθὼς ἡμεῖς
ἕν ἐσμεν· ἐγὼ ἐν αὐτοῖς, καὶ σὺ ἐν ἐμοί· ἵνα ὦσι τετελειωμένοι εἰς 23
ἓν, καὶ ἵνα γινώσκῃ ὁ κόσμος ὅτι σύ με ἀπέστειλας, καὶ ἠγάπησας αὐ-
y Supra 12. 26. & 14. 3. 1 Thess. 4. 17. supra ver. 5. τοὺς, καθὼς ἐμὲ ἠγάπησας. y Πάτερ, οὓς δέδωκάς μοι, θέλω ἵνα 24
ὅπου εἰμὶ ἐγὼ, κἀκεῖνοι ὦσι μετ᾽ ἐμοῦ· ἵνα θεωρῶσι τὴν δόξαν τὴν
ἐμὴν, ἣν ἔδωκάς μοι, ὅτι ἠγάπησάς με πρὸ καταβολῆς κόσμου· Πάτερ 25
δίκαιε, καὶ ὁ κόσμος σε οὐκ ἔγνω, ἐγὼ δέ σε ἔγνων, καὶ οὗτοι ἔγνωσαν
ὅτι σύ με ἀπέστειλας· καὶ ἐγνώρισα αὐτοῖς τὸ ὄνομά σου, καὶ γνω- 26
z Matt. 26. 36. Mark 14. 32. Luke 22. 39. 2 Sam. 15. 23. ρίσω· ἵνα ἡ ἀγάπη ἣν ἠγάπησάς με ἐν αὐτοῖς ᾖ, κἀγὼ ἐν αὐτοῖς.
XVIII. z ΤΑΥΤΑ εἰπὼν ὁ Ἰησοῦς ἐξῆλθε σὺν τοῖς μαθηταῖς αὐ- 1

19. ἐγὼ ἁγιάζω ἐμαυτόν.] Here, again, some difference of opinion exists as to the sense of the term ἁγιάζειν; though it is generally agreed that it must be explained suitably to the sense adopted at ver. 17. This is, however, by no means necessary, considering the sudden transitions and changes of sense observable in this Gospel. It should seem that the word is here to be taken in the *secondary* sense pointed out at ver. 17; and thus we may render: "I set myself apart, devote myself to my ministry." The ἡγιασμένοι following must be explained in the same manner: "That they also may be devoted to the discharge of *their* sacred office."

20—26. Now commences the *concluding* portion of this sublime prayer, on the scope of which Expositors considerably differ in opinion; not only as to the *persons* who may be supposed to be objects of this prayer, but still more whether what is here said should be referred to Christians of that age, or of *all* ages: according as either of which views be adopted, so the leading terms, δόξαν, &c. are interpreted. One thing is certain — that our Lord here makes some change in the persons the objects of his prayers; namely, from the *Apostles* (then present). And it should seem that by τῶν πιστευόντων (which all the best Editors are agreed is to be read, instead of πιστευσόντων) are meant the *believers in general* of that age, as distinguished from the *Apostles*. For these our Lord prays (ver. 21.) that they may be united to each other and to God, by a union as close as that which subsists between the Father and the Son (see x. 30. and Note), i. e. in being of *one mind, sentiment, will*, and *purpose*, being united to the Father and the Son by the Holy Spirit working in them. And for this, among other reasons: "that the unbelieving part of the world may, by seeing that union and concord, be more led to believe my doctrine to be from God."

At ver. 22, a difference of opinion exists as to *who* are the persons prayed for. Some say, *Christians in general*; others, the *Apostles*. And each class of Expositors interpret the δόξαν there according to their respective views; the former understanding it of the reward laid up in heaven for the righteous. But thus the expression δέδωκα will have to be taken for δώσω; which is the more harsh, as δέδωκας, the next word but one, must thus be taken in a *preterite* sense. Others, therefore, suppose by δόξαν to be meant such a part of Christ's mediatorial glory, imparted to them by the Holy Spirit, as was suitable to the purposes they were to accomplish; including, of course, the *working of miracles* in establishment of the truth of the Gospel. Thus the next words ἵνα ὦσι τετελειωμένοι, &c. advert to the *mode of exercising* such high gifts, namely, with that perfect union with themselves and with the Father and the Son, as exists between the Father and the Son. Then is represented the *purpose*, — namely, that, by being thus τετελειωμένοι (i. e. perfectly united), the world may be brought to believe in the Divine origin of the religion they teach and profess, and in the love and favour of God towards its faithful professors. Ver. 24 seems to have reference, not to the *same persons* only, but to true *believers in general*. The words denote admission to heavenly felicity, and participation in the joy of their Lord. At ver. 25 there is manifestly a transition to the *Apostles*; the οὗτοι being said δεικτικῶς. Our Lord finally commends them to the care and protection of the Father. Οὐκ ἔγνω. See viii. 27 & 28.

25. δίκαιε] most gracious. Ἔγνωσαν, are assured. Ὄνομα, thy counsels, &c. Γνωρίσω, i. e. both in person after my resurrection, and by the Comforter, after my ascension.

26. ἵνα ἡ ἀγάπη — αὐτοῖς] that the love with which thou hast loved me may be in them (i. e. enjoyed by them, that they may be the objects of thy love and Fatherly care, and attain happiness both in this world and in the next), and that I may be in them, namely, by my spiritual presence, that they may remain united with me in the same holy cause, of promoting the salvation of men.

XVIII. 1. The Evangelist now proceeds to record the *Passion* of our Lord, so however as only to touch lightly on what had been recorded by preceding writers; at the same time adding certain circumstances omitted by them; thus strongly confirming the truth of what had been before written, and, in the circumstances which he himself records, plainly taking that truth for granted. (Lampe.)

τοῦ πέραν τοῦ χειμάῤῥου * τοῦ Κέδρων, ὅπου ἦν κῆπος, εἰς ὃν εἰσῆλ-
2 θεν αὐτὸς καὶ οἱ μαθηταὶ αὐτοῦ. Ἤιδει δὲ καὶ Ἰούδας ὁ παραδιδοὺς
αὐτὸν τὸν τόπον· ὅτι πολλάκις συνήχθη ὁ Ἰησοῦς ἐκεῖ μετὰ τῶν μαθη-
3 τῶν αὐτοῦ. [a] Ὁ οὖν Ἰούδας λαβὼν τὴν σπεῖραν, καὶ ἐκ τῶν ἀρχιερέων a Matt. 26. 47. Mark 14. 43.
καὶ Φαρισαίων ὑπηρέτας, ἔρχεται ἐκεῖ μετὰ φανῶν καὶ λαμπάδων καὶ Luke 22. 47. Acts 1. 16.
4 ὅπλων. Ἰησοῦς οὖν εἰδὼς πάντα τὰ ἐρχόμενα ἐπ᾽ αὐτὸν, ἐξελθὼν εἰ-
5 πεν αὐτοῖς· Τίνα ζητεῖτε; Ἀπεκρίθησαν αὐτῷ· Ἰησοῦν τὸν Ναζωραῖον. λέγει αὐτοῖς ὁ Ἰησοῦς· Ἐγώ εἰμι. εἱστήκει δὲ καὶ Ἰούδας ὁ
6 παραδιδοὺς αὐτὸν μετ᾽ αὐτῶν. Ὡς οὖν εἶπεν αὐτοῖς· Ὅτι ἐγώ εἰμι,
7 ἀπῆλθον εἰς τὰ ὀπίσω, καὶ ἔπεσον χαμαί. Πάλιν οὖν αὐτὸς ἐπηρώ-

1. τοῦ Κέδρων.] The reading is here uncertain. Instead of the common reading τῶν Κέδρων, four of the most ancient MSS. and several of the most ancient Versions, with some Fathers, have τοῦ Κεδρῶν, which was preferred by Beza, Casaub., Campb., Cast., Drus., Lightf., Bois, Bynæus, Reland, and others of the best Commentators down to Middleton, Kuinöel, and Tittm.; and has been received by Beng., Griesb., Knapp, Vat., and Scholz. The common reading, however, is strenuously, but not satisfactorily, defended by Lampe and Matthæi. The external evidence for τοῦ may, indeed, *seem* slender; but it is, *in fact*, of the most weighty kind (confirmed also by Josephus), the MSS. being some of the most ancient in existence, and the Versions the most estimable. And internal evidence is quite in favor of τοῦ, since it is far more likely that τοῦ should have been altered by the scribes into τῶν, than τῶν into τοῦ, especially in uncial MSS. Matthæi indeed adduces the authority of Chrys., Cyrill, Theophyl., and Euthym., for the common reading. But the authority of *Commentators* and *Homily-writers*, in *proper names*, which they do not particularly treat on, is but small; especially where the *common* reading is retained. That τῶν Κέδρων occurs twice in the LXX. may seem a strong confirmation of the Vulg. But that would not be *decisive*. Not to say that the very same mistake may there exist. The common reading might, as Bp. Middlet. observes, originate in a mistake of the Copyists (thousands of similar mutations occurring in the Classical writers); or even *design*, since the Greeks were accustomed to Grecize barbarous names. And it would *seem* probable that the name meant "the brook of Cedars." Though Lightf. and Reland have shewn that it is derived from the Heb. קדר; and hence קדרון will denote *the black torrent*. Bp. Middlet. instances a similar corruption in Suid. of Χειμαῤῥοῦς τοῦ Κισσῶ into Χειμ. τῶν Κισσῶν, "the torrent of ivy-trees."

— κῆπος.] This seems to have been a plot of garden ground provided with a sort of cottage.

3. τὴν σπεῖραν.] This word should, I think, be derived from σπίω cognate with σπάω, *to draw* or *twist*, and literally signifies a *band*. Hence it would designate *any* military *corps*; but the best founded opinion, and that supported by all the most eminent Commentators, is that it here denotes either the *Roman cohort*, which garrisoned the castle of Antonia, or the *detachment* of it, which, by order of the Procurator, attended on the Sanhedrim at the great festivals, and kept the peace. Hence the propriety of the *Article*, to denote *the* detachment *then on duty*.

— μετὰ φανῶν καὶ λαμπ.] It is not easy to determine the precise force of these two terms. Bynæus thinks the former means *torches*; the latter, *lamps*. Lampe is of opinion that the latter commonly denoted *torches* (appealing to the λαμπαδοφορία described by Meursius in his Græc. Fer. L. v.), and maintains (from a reference to Athenæus, L. xv. 18.) that the φανοὶ were a more ancient and ruder kind of *torches*, formed of split laths bound into a bundle; but that afterwards torches of other materials, and of a more convenient form (namely, *tapers* and *lanterns*) came into use; though the others still contiued to be employed by the meaner sort of people. That both lanterns and torches were in use among soldiers, appears from Dionys. Hal. ix. (cited by Lampe and Wets.) ἐξέτρεχον ἅπαντες ἐκ τῶν σκηνῶν ἀθρόοι, φανοὺς ἔχοντες καὶ λαμπάδας. It was, indeed (I would add) usual for such corps to carry both arms and lanterns. So Thucyd. iii. 23, speaking of the picket-guard of the Peloponnesians, says, καὶ ἐν τούτῳ οἱ τριακόσιοι αὐτοῖς ἐπεφέροντο λαμπάδας ἔχοντες.

4. ἐρχόμενα ἐπ᾽ αὐτόν.] This phrase is by some accounted a Hebraism. But, as Kypke and Wets. have shown, it is also found in the Classical writers, in whom ἔρχεσθαι signifies to *befall*, and is almost always used of what is *evil*. Ἐξελθών. This is rightly taken by Euthym., Mold., and Pearce for προελθών, namely, from that part of the garden whither Christ had retired for prayer.

6. ἀπῆλθον — ἔπεσον χαμαί.] The earlier and the recent modern Commentators here adopt different views. The former suppose a *miracle*; the latter, with the exception of Titt., recognize none, attributing the circumstance to the awe of the soldiers at the sight of so august a person; of this they adduce what they call parallel instances from the Classical writers. The cases, however, are quite of another kind, and the mode in which those Commentators account for the thing, proceeds almost wholly upon supposition. If we confine ourselves simply to the plain words and the actual circumstances, we shall see that something far surpassing the *ordinary*, and rising to the *preternatural*, is suggested. See the able Notes of Wolf, Lampe, and Tittm. There seems to be no reason to doubt but that some undefineable, but supernatural, power was exercised; as in many similar instances recorded in Holy writ; ex. gr. that of Paul (Acts ix. 3), where he is described as being "*struck to the earth*" as well as struck with *blindness*. Whether *all* fell to the ground (even *Judas*), as the old Commentators maintain, is uncertain, and will by no means alter the case. But we cannot understand less than *very many*.

τησε· Τίνα ζητεῖτε; οἱ δὲ εἶπον· Ἰησοῦν τὸν Ναζωραῖον. ἀπεκρίθη 8
[ὁ] Ἰησοῦς· Εἶπον ὑμῖν, ὅτι ἐγώ εἰμι· εἰ οὖν ἐμὲ ζητεῖτε, ἄφετε
b Supra 17. 12. τούτους ὑπάγειν. [b] Ἵνα πληρωθῇ ὁ λόγος ὃν εἶπεν· Ὅτι οὓς δέδωκάς 9
μοι, οὐκ ἀπώλεσα ἐξ αὐτῶν οὐδένα. Σίμων οὖν Πέτρος ἔχων μάχαιραν, 10
εἵλκυσεν αὐτὴν, καὶ ἔπαισε τὸν τοῦ ἀρχιερέως δοῦλον, καὶ ἀπέκοψεν
αὐτοῦ τὸ ὠτίον τὸ δεξιόν. ἦν δὲ ὄνομα τῷ δούλῳ Μάλχος. εἶπεν οὖν 11
ὁ Ἰησοῦς τῷ Πέτρῳ· Βάλε τὴν μάχαιράν [σου] εἰς τὴν θήκην. τὸ
ποτήριον ὃ δέδωκέ μοι ὁ Πατὴρ, οὐ μὴ πίω αὐτό;

c Matt. 26. 57. Mark 14. 53. Luke 22. 54. [c] Ἡ οὖν σπεῖρα καὶ ὁ χιλίαρχος καὶ οἱ ὑπηρέται τῶν Ἰουδαίων συνέ- 12
d Luke 3. 2. λαβον τὸν Ἰησοῦν, καὶ ἔδησαν αὐτὸν, [d] καὶ ἀπήγαγον αὐτὸν πρὸς Ἄνναν 13
πρῶτον· ἦν γὰρ πενθερὸς τοῦ Καϊάφα, ὃς ἦν ἀρχιερεὺς τοῦ ἐνιαυτοῦ
e Supra 11. 50. ἐκείνου. [e] ἦν δὲ Καϊάφας ὁ συμβουλεύσας τοῖς Ἰουδαίοις, ὅτι συμφέρει 14
f Matt. 26. 58. Mark 14. 54. Luke 22. 54. ἕνα ἄνθρωπον ἀπολέσθαι ὑπὲρ τοῦ λαοῦ. [f] Ἠκολούθει δὲ τῷ Ἰησοῦ 15
Σίμων Πέτρος, καὶ ὁ ἄλλος μαθητής. ὁ δὲ μαθητὴς ἐκεῖνος ἦν γνωστὸς
τῷ ἀρχιερεῖ, καὶ συνεισῆλθε τῷ Ἰησοῦ εἰς τὴν αὐλὴν τοῦ ἀρχιερέως·

8. *εἰ οὖν ἐμὲ — ὑπάγειν.*] A brief manner of speaking, of which the full sense is: "If, then, ye seek to apprehend *me* [take *me*; but] let those [my companions] depart."

9. *ἵνα πληρωθῇ*, &c.] The best Commentators are agreed that the sense is, "Thus was made good, or verified, the words," &c. namely, xvii. 2. By this all difficulty vanishes.

11. *σου.*] This is omitted in very many of the best MSS. and Versions, and is cancelled by almost every Editor from Beng. and Wets. to Scholz; and with reason: for internal evidence is as much against it as external.

— *τὸ ποτήριον — αὐτό.*] See xxvi. 39 & 54. The interrogation, accompanied with a double negation, involves a strong affirmative (so Euthym. well explains *πάνυ μὲν οὖν*), and the whole is expressive of perfect acquiescence in the will of his Father.

12, 13. On the discrepancy which has been supposed to exist in this statement, as compared with the other Evangelists, see the able remarks of Tittm. in Recens. Synop. On the dissimilarity of *matter* in St. John as compared with the other Evangelists, yet coupled with a *similitude of manner*, Dr. Paley has well treated, and especially with reference to the present passage.

15. *καὶ ὁ ἄλλος μαθητής.*] There is no little difficulty here to account for the *Article*. Many eminent Commentators are inclined to think it *redundant*. But Bp. Middl. justly accounts such a device "the refuge of learned ignorance." He admits the difficulty; but rightly maintains that, "though we should not be able to ascertain it, it is better to impute the obscurity to our own want of knowledge, than to attempt to subvert the analogy of language." To *cancel* it with Erasm., Beng., and Vat., is *rash*, because the evidence for its omission is so very slight, only that of four MSS., and that of *Versions* but slender. And, as Bp. Middl. observes, it is far easier to account for the omission of the article in a few of the MSS., supposing it to be authentic, than for its insertion in almost all of them, supposing it to be spurious: for the apparent difficulty which might operate as an inducement in the one case, would be a powerful discouragement in the other. We must therefore explain as we may. Now almost all Commentators, ancient and modern, are agreed that by the *other disciple* the Evangelist means *himself*; and with reason: for though Grot., Lampe, Heum., and Pearce deny this, they are as unsuccessful in proving it *not* to have been St. John, as they are fixing on any *other* disciple. The Evangelist never mentions *himself* by *name*, and yet (as Michaelis shows) he has described the whole of what took place in the hall of Annas, &c. so circumstantially, that we cannot but conclude that he was present, as Ecclesiastical tradition attests. "Supposing, then, (remarks Bp. Middl.) that St. John himself is meant by *ὁ ἄλλος μαθητὴς*, it may not be impossible to assign something like a plausible reason why he should call himself *the other disciple*." "This phrase (continues the learned Prelate) obviously implies the remaining *one of two persons*, who not only were, in common with many others, disciples of Christ, but between whom some still closer relation might be recognized to exist: and if it could be shown that Peter and John stood towards each other in any such relation, the term *the other disciple*, might not unfitly be used, immediately after the mention of Peter, to designate John; especially if, from any cause whatever, John was not to be spoken of by name. Now it does appear that a particular, and even exclusive friendship existed between Peter and John. The same expression, *ὁ ἄλλος μαθ.*, occurs in John xx. 2, 3, 4, 8; from which it may be inferred, that this phrase, when accompanied with the mention of Peter, was readily, in the earliest period of Christianity, understood to signify *John*." Prof. Scholefield, in his Hints, further remarks, that in ch. xx. 2. the words "the other disciple whom Jesus loved" are not to be taken in close connection, so as to imply that Peter and John were *the two* disciples whom he loved; but there must be a kind of break, as if the Evangelist had said, "the other disciple—him, I mean, whom Jesus loved."

— *ὁ δὲ μαθητὴς — ἀρχιερεῖ.*] These words are meant to show *how* it happened that persons of such inferior rank as he and St. Peter should have obtained access to the Hall of the High Priest.

16 ὁ δὲ Πέτρος εἱστήκει πρὸς τῇ θύρᾳ ἔξω. Ἐξῆλθεν οὖν ὁ μαθητὴς ὁ
ἄλλος, ὃς ἦν γνωστὸς τῷ ἀρχιερεῖ, καὶ εἶπε τῇ θυρωρῷ, καὶ εἰσήγαγε
17 τὸν Πέτρον. Λέγει οὖν ἡ παιδίσκη ἡ θυρωρὸς τῷ Πέτρῳ· Μὴ καὶ
σὺ ἐκ τῶν μαθητῶν εἶ τοῦ ἀνθρώπου τούτου; λέγει ἐκεῖνος· Οὐκ
18 εἰμί. Εἱστήκεισαν δὲ οἱ δοῦλοι καὶ οἱ ὑπηρέται ἀνθρακιὰν πεποιηκότες,
ὅτι ψύχος ἦν, καὶ ἐθερμαίνοντο· ἦν δὲ μετ᾽ αὐτῶν ὁ Πέτρος ἑστὼς
19 καὶ θερμαινόμενος. Ὁ οὖν ἀρχιερεὺς ἠρώτησε τὸν Ἰησοῦν περὶ τῶν
20 μαθητῶν αὐτοῦ, καὶ περὶ τῆς διδαχῆς αὐτοῦ. Ἀπεκρίθη αὐτῷ ὁ Ἰη-
σοῦς· Ἐγὼ παῤῥησίᾳ ἐλάλησα τῷ κόσμῳ· ἐγὼ πάντοτε ἐδίδαξα ἐν
[τῇ] συναγωγῇ καὶ ἐν τῷ ἱερῷ, ὅπου * πάντοτε οἱ Ἰουδαῖοι συνέρχον-
21 ται, καὶ ἐν κρυπτῷ ἐλάλησα οὐδέν. Τί με ἐπερωτᾷς; ἐπερώτησον τοὺς
22 ἀκηκοότας, τί ἐλάλησα αὐτοῖς· ἴδε οὗτοι οἴδασιν ἃ εἶπον ἐγώ. Ταῦτα
δὲ αὐτοῦ εἰπόντος, εἷς τῶν ὑπηρετῶν παρεστηκὼς ἔδωκε ῥάπισμα τῷ
23 Ἰησοῦ, εἰπών· Οὕτως ἀποκρίνῃ τῷ ἀρχιερεῖ; Ἀπεκρίθη αὐτῷ ὁ Ἰη-
σοῦς· Εἰ κακῶς ἐλάλησα, μαρτύρησον περὶ τοῦ κακοῦ· εἰ δὲ καλῶς,
24 τί με δέρεις; [g] Ἀπέστειλεν οὖν αὐτὸν ὁ Ἄννας δεδεμένον πρὸς Καϊάφαν g Matt. 26. 57. Mark 14. 53. Luke 22. 54.
τὸν ἀρχιερέα.
25 [h] Ἦν δὲ Σίμων Πέτρος ἑστὼς καὶ θερμαινόμενος· εἶπον οὖν αὐτῷ· h Matt. 26. 69. Mark 14. 69. Luke 22. 55.
Μὴ καὶ σὺ ἐκ τῶν μαθητῶν αὐτοῦ εἶ; ἠρνήσατο ἐκεῖνος, καὶ εἶπεν·
26 Οὐκ εἰμί. Λέγει εἷς ἐκ τῶν δούλων τοῦ ἀρχιερέως, συγγενὴς ὢν οὗ
ἀπέκοψε Πέτρος τὸ ὠτίον· Οὐκ ἐγώ σε εἶδον ἐν τῷ κήπῳ μετ᾽ αὐτοῦ;
27 Πάλιν οὖν ἠρνήσατο ὁ Πέτρος, καὶ εὐθέως ἀλέκτωρ ἐφώνησεν.

18. ἀνθρακιάν.] The word denotes *a mass of live charcoal*, from ἄνθραξ, *a live coal;* and that from ἀνθράσσω, all which come from ἄνθος, whence ἀνθηρὸς, *florid, red, burning*. So Hom. Il. γ. 213. ἀνθρακιὴν στορέσας. Its difference from τέφρα is plain from an adage of Suidas: μὴ τὴν τέφραν φεύγων εἰς ἀνθρακιὰν πέσῃς.

20. πάντοτε.] Instead of the common reading πάντοθεν before οἱ Ἰουδαῖοι, almost all the MSS., with all the Edd. up to Beza's have πάντοτε, which is received by almost every Editor from Wets. to Scholz; and rightly: since the external evidence for παντόθεν is but slender, and its internal far inferior to the other reading. It was, in truth, as Wets. shews, a mere *emendation* of Beza. Both he and the ancient Critics stumbled at the tautology occasioned by the repetition of πάντοτε; the latter, by reading πάντες. At the same time, it cannot be denied that πάντοθεν would have been more suitable. So Joseph. Bell. vi. 4. 3. μὴ γὰρ ἄν ποτε Ἰουδαίους παύσασθαι νεωτερίζοντας τοῦ ναοῦ μένοντος, ἐφ᾽ ὃν οἱ πανταχόθεν συλλέγονται. The τῇ in ἐν τῇ συναγ. is omitted in a great number of the best MSS., and is cancelled by almost all Editors from Beng. and Matthæi to Scholz; and rightly, I conceive: for internal evidence is strong against it; since it would be more likely to be wrongly *inserted*, on account of the ἐν τῷ ἱερῷ, than wrongly *omitted*. And, moreover, when the *singular* is, as here, used in a *generic* sense for the *plural at large*, it rejects the Article.

— ἐν κρυπτῷ ἐλάλησα οὐδέν.] This, as the best Commentators are agreed, must be taken comparatè, and with restriction, i. e. nothing *post sindonem* (like the Heathen mysteries, or the Jewish Cabbala), at variance with any public doctrines, and consequently nothing savouring of sedition.

25—27. Peter, it seems, was exceedingly terrified on beholding such a scene, and especially hearing Jesus examined respecting his *disciples*; from whence he might infer that the Sanhedrim had thoughts of ordering *them* also to be seized. He did not, it appears, return to himself before the cock crew, of which our Lord had spoken; when (as we learn from Luke xxii. 61.) Jesus turned his eyes towards him, and looked him full in the face. Our Lord, by the common decree of the Sanhedrim, had been pronounced worthy of death, since he had professed himself to be the Messiah and the Son of God. In order to carry this sentence into effect, they brought the affair before Pontius Pilate. The council, therefore, rose, and just as the day was dawning, led him *bound*, as one pronounced worthy of death, to the Prætorium. Matt. xxvii. 2., adds, καὶ παρέδωκαν αὐτὸν Ποντίῳ Πιλάτῳ; whence it is evident that it was their counsel and plan that *Pilate* should order him to execution. Thus do these infatuated wretches hurry away the Messiah sent to *them*, and deliver him up to the *Gentiles!* But, it may be asked, why should the Jewish Rulers have delivered Jesus to the Roman Procurator for punishment, and not *themselves* have executed it; and by what right could *Pilate* condemn him to death? On this question the most learned are divided in opinion; some contending that the right of inflicting punishment had been taken away from the Jews; others, that they still retained that right. At least they seem to have exercised it. See Acts vii. 57. xii. 2. xxiii. 27 The discrepancy seems to be best settled by

i Matt. 27. 1. Mark 15. 1. Luke 23. 1. Acts 10. 28. & 11. 3.

[i] ἌΓΟΥΣΙΝ οὖν τὸν Ἰησοῦν ἀπὸ τοῦ Καϊάφα εἰς τὸ πραιτώριον. ἦν 28
δὲ πρωΐα· καὶ αὐτοὶ οὐκ εἰσῆλθον εἰς τὸ πραιτώριον, ἵνα μὴ μιαν-
θῶσιν, ἀλλ' ἵνα φάγωσι τὸ πάσχα. Ἐξῆλθεν οὖν ὁ Πιλάτος πρὸς 29
αὐτούς, καὶ εἶπε· Τίνα κατηγορίαν φέρετε κατὰ τοῦ ἀνθρώπου τούτου;
Ἀπεκρίθησαν καὶ εἶπον αὐτῷ· Εἰ μὴ ἦν οὗτος κακοποιός, οὐκ ἄν σοι 30
παρεδώκαμεν αὐτόν. Εἶπεν οὖν αὐτοῖς ὁ Πιλάτος· Λάβετε αὐτὸν ὑμεῖς, 31
καὶ κατὰ τὸν νόμον ὑμῶν κρίνατε αὐτόν. Εἶπον οὖν αὐτῷ οἱ Ἰουδαῖοι·
Ἡμῖν οὐκ ἔξεστιν ἀποκτεῖναι οὐδένα. [k] Ἵνα ὁ λόγος τοῦ Ἰησοῦ πλη- 32
ρωθῇ, ὃν εἶπε σημαίνων ποίῳ θανάτῳ ἤμελλεν ἀποθνήσκειν. [l] Εἰσῆλ- 33
θεν οὖν εἰς τὸ πραιτώριον πάλιν ὁ Πιλάτος, καὶ ἐφώνησε τὸν Ἰησοῦν,
καὶ εἶπεν αὐτῷ· Σὺ εἶ ὁ βασιλεὺς τῶν Ἰουδαίων; Ἀπεκρίθη αὐτῷ 34
ὁ Ἰησοῦς· Ἀφ' ἑαυτοῦ σὺ τοῦτο λέγεις, ἢ ἄλλοι σοι εἶπον περὶ ἐμοῦ;
Ἀπεκρίθη ὁ Πιλάτος· Μήτι ἐγὼ Ἰουδαῖός εἰμι; τὸ ἔθνος τὸ σὸν καὶ 35
οἱ ἀρχιερεῖς παρέδωκάν σε ἐμοί· τί ἐποίησας; Ἀπεκρίθη ὁ Ἰησοῦς· 36
Ἡ βασιλεία ἡ ἐμὴ οὐκ ἔστιν ἐκ τοῦ κόσμου τούτου· εἰ ἐκ τοῦ κόσμου
τούτου ἦν ἡ βασιλεία ἡ ἐμή, οἱ ὑπηρέται ἂν οἱ ἐμοὶ ἠγωνίζοντο, ἵνα
μὴ παραδοθῶ τοῖς Ἰουδαίοις· νῦν δὲ ἡ βασιλεία ἡ ἐμὴ οὐκ ἔστιν
ἐντεῦθεν. Εἶπεν οὖν αὐτῷ ὁ Πιλάτος, Οὐκοῦν βασιλεὺς εἶ σύ; Ἀπε- 37

k Matt. 20. 19. Mark 10. 33. Luke 18. 32.
l Matt. 27. 11. Mark 15. 2. Luke 23. 3.

those who maintain that a *distinction* must be made between *sacred* and *civil* causes; and that in those pertaining to *religion*, the Jews had yet the power of inflicting capital punishment, [subject, however, to the confirmation of the Procurator. — Edit.] but that in civil causes, and such criminal ones as appertained to the *crimen læsæ majestatis* or treason, (as did sedition) *that* was not conceded to them, the cognizance of all such matters resting solely with the President or Procurator. [On this question see the elaborate discussion in Townsend Chron. Arr. i. 511—18., who decides that the power of life and death had not been formally abrogated by the Romans; but that the grant which secured to the Jews their own rights and privileges, had been gradually *set aside* by the influence of the Roman authority, which had, in some measure, superseded the Jewish magistracy. — Edit.] Now our Lord's cause, at the beginning, did not *seem* to be *civil*; at least the Jewish Rulers had pronounced him worthy of death because he had *professed himself the Messiah*, or *Son of God*; and yet they led him to Pontius Pilate in order that they might cast on *him* the blame of shedding innocent blood. Afterwards, however, when Pilate had declared that he found no fault in him, and seemed to wish to remove from himself the cognizance of the cause, they ventured (as we learn from Luke xxiii. 2.) to bring forward *a two-fold political charge*, namely, that of exciting the populace to rebellion, and of discountenancing the payment of tribute; offences both of them falling within Pilate's jurisdiction, as being ἡγεμὼν of Judæa. (Tittm.)

31. λάβετε αὐτὸν ὑμεῖς.] Take *ye* him and punish him, q. d., *I* cannot do a thing so unheard of in the Roman law as to condemn a person unheard. On ἡμῖν οὐκ ἔξεστιν, &c., see Note on v. 25—27.

32. ἵνα ὁ λόγος — πληρωθῇ, &c.] The best Commentators are of opinion that the sense is: "Thus was made good the words," &c. But it is not necessary to deviate from the usual import of this formula; for as our Lord had predicted the manner of his death (Matt. xx. 19. xxvi. 2. John xii. 32. sq.) so, as Biscoe remarks, the meaning of what is here said seems to be, that the Jews fulfilled this prophecy, when they declined passing sentence on him by their own law; crucifixion being not a *Jewish*, but a Roman punishment.

34. ἀφ' ἑαυτοῦ] "*proprio motu*," from thy own knowledge or suspicion of my having been concerned in seditious practices.

35. μήτι ἐγὼ Ἰουδαῖος, &c.] The full sense is well expressed by Kuin. in the following paraphrase: "No, I have not asked thee of my own thought: I have found nothing hitherto in thee which would afford any colour to such a charge as thine enemies advance: but it does not hence follow that thou art innocent. Of thee and thy case I know nothing. I am not a Jew, to know or care about such things. It is on the representations of thy countrymen and the chief Priests that I examine thee. What hast thou done to afford ground for this accusation?"

36. ἡ βασιλεία, &c.] The sense is: ["I am a King, it is true, but] my kingdom is not a temporal one, but entirely spiritual. If my kingdom had been of this world, I should have collected about me vast numbers of my countrymen. These would have defended me against the attacks of my Jewish adversaries. But as I have done nothing of this sort, it is plain that my kingdom is not of such a nature as at all interferes with earthly governments, or affords any colour for this charge of sedition." (Tittm.)

37. οὐκοῦν βασιλεὺς εἶ σύ;] Some Commentators would have the interrogation removed, — in the sense, So then, thou art a king! This may seem to be more agreeable to what follows; but there is no good authority, for οὐκοῦν is a declarative sentence.

κρίθη ὁ Ἰησοῦς· Σὺ λέγεις ὅτι βασιλεύς εἰμι ἐγώ. ἐγὼ εἰς τοῦτο
γεγέννημαι, καὶ εἰς τοῦτο ἐλήλυθα εἰς τὸν κόσμον, ἵνα μαρτυρήσω τῇ
38 ἀληθείᾳ. πᾶς ὁ ὢν ἐκ τῆς ἀληθείας, ἀκούει μου τῆς φωνῆς. Λέγει
αὐτῷ ὁ Πιλάτος· Τί ἐστιν ἀλήθεια; καὶ τοῦτο εἰπὼν, πάλιν ἐξῆλθε
πρὸς τοὺς Ἰουδαίους, καὶ λέγει αὐτοῖς· Ἐγὼ οὐδεμίαν αἰτίαν εὑρίσκω
39 ἐν αὐτῷ. [m] Ἔστι δὲ συνήθεια ὑμῖν, ἵνα ἕνα ὑμῖν ἀπολύσω ἐν τῷ m Matt. 27. 15. Mark 15. 6.
πάσχα· βούλεσθε οὖν ὑμῖν ἀπολύσω τὸν βασιλέα τῶν Ἰουδαίων; Luke 23. 17.
40 [n] Ἐκραύγασαν οὖν πάλιν πάντες, λέγοντες· Μὴ τοῦτον, ἀλλὰ τὸν n Acts 3. 14.
1 Βαραββᾶν· ἦν δὲ ὁ Βαραββᾶς λῃστής. XIX. [o] Τότε οὖν ἔλαβεν ὁ o Matt. 27. 26. Mark 15. 15.
2 Πιλάτος τὸν Ἰησοῦν, καὶ ἐμαστίγωσε. Καὶ οἱ στρατιῶται πλέξαντες
στέφανον ἐξ ἀκανθῶν, ἐπέθηκαν αὐτοῦ τῇ κεφαλῇ, καὶ ἱμάτιον πορ-
3 φυροῦν περιέβαλον αὐτὸν, καὶ ἔλεγον· Χαῖρε, ὁ βασιλεὺς τῶν Ἰουδαίων·
4 καὶ ἐδίδουν αὐτῷ ῥαπίσματα. Ἐξῆλθεν οὖν πάλιν ἔξω ὁ Πιλάτος, καὶ
λέγει αὐτοῖς· Ἴδε, ἄγω ὑμῖν αὐτὸν ἔξω, ἵνα γνῶτε ὅτι ἐν αὐτῷ οὐδε-
5 μίαν αἰτίαν εὑρίσκω. Ἐξῆλθεν οὖν ὁ Ἰησοῦς ἔξω φορῶν τὸν ἀκάνθινον
στέφανον καὶ τὸ πορφυροῦν ἱμάτιον. καὶ λέγει αὐτοῖς· Ἴδε, ὁ ἄνθρω-
6 πος. Ὅτε οὖν εἶδον αὐτὸν οἱ ἀρχιερεῖς καὶ οἱ ὑπηρέται ἐκραύγασαν,
λέγοντες· Σταύρωσον, σταύρωσον. Λέγει αὐτοῖς ὁ Πιλάτος· Λάβετε
αὐτὸν ὑμεῖς καὶ σταυρώσατε· ἐγὼ γὰρ οὐχ εὑρίσκω ἐν αὐτῷ αἰτίαν.
7 Ἀπεκρίθησαν αὐτῷ οἱ Ἰουδαῖοι· Ἡμεῖς νόμον ἔχομεν, καὶ κατὰ τὸν
νόμον ἡμῶν ὀφείλει ἀποθανεῖν, ὅτι ἑαυτὸν Υἱὸν [τοῦ] Θεοῦ ἐποίησεν.

— *σὺ λέγεις*, &c.] i. e. thou truly sayest that I am a King; it is very true; I am a King. Σὺ λέγεις signifies *it is so*; a phrase of modest assent and affirmation. Our Lord now proceeds to show the *nature* of his kingdom, and in what sense he is a King. He is come not to *reign* but to bear witness to the truth, to promote, confirm, and establish it.

— *ὁ ὢν ἐκ τῆς ἀληθείας*] "he who is studious of the truth," i. e. the truth of the Gospel, true religion. So Rom. ii. 8 *ὁ ἐκ τῆς ἐριθείας*.

38 *τί ἐστιν ἀλήθεια;*] On the exact force of this question Commentators are not agreed. Some take the meaning to be: "What is truth to me? what care I about truth?" But this sense cannot be fairly elicited from the words: nor is it likely that a man in high dignity would speak with such levity. The other interpretations are, as I have shown in Rec. Syn. each in some respects more objectionable. It should seem that Pilate put the question with no design of *insulting* our Lord; but that, knowing the endless disputations of the Philosophers on this subject, and how difficult it was to arrive at any clear notions on the subject, he asked, "What is truth? define it;" as much as to say, "aye, what is truth? that is the great question — but such as YOU are not likely to settle." But our Lord, knowing that the question was put with levity and insincerity, vouchsafed no answer. Nor did Pilate think it worth his while to wait long for the solution of so debated a question from a Jewish peasant. And perceiving that the kingdom claimed by him was purely figurative, (something similar to what the Heathen Philosophers spoke of), and considering him a harmless sort of person, he only thought how he might set him at liberty

XIX. 4, 5. On the motives and intent with which Pilate brought out Jesus, see Recens. Synop.

6. *σταύρωσον, σταύρωσον*.] In very many MSS., Versions, Fathers, and early Edd., is added *αὐτὸν*, which is received by almost every Editor from Wets. to Scholz. But it is so difficult to account for its *omission* in far more than half of the MSS., many of them very ancient, and so easy to account for its *insertion*, that I dare not follow their example. Such kind of exclamations are usually very elliptical, and the pronoun is often omitted. Out of very many examples which I could adduce, one must suffice. Pseudo-Eurip. Rhes. 685. Παῖε, παῖε.

— *λάβετε αὐτὸν ὑμεῖς*, &c. Many understand these words as a *permission*. But Pilate neither said, nor could say this *seriously*; for he well knew that crucifixion was not in use among the Jews; and the Priests had already declared that they could not put him to death, on account of the festival. The words (as Chrysost. long ago saw, and in which light they have been viewed by some modern Commentators, as Lampe) are those of *irritation* and *disgust*; neither does it appear that the Jews regarded them as a *permission*, since they immediately resort to a new charge — that of blasphemy. (Kuin.)

7. *ἡμεῖς νόμον ἔχομεν*, &c.] The sense is: "By our law he has been found guilty of blasphemy; and condemned; but on account of the feast, we could not inflict the punishment; and therefore we had recourse to thee." By *the law*, they meant some passages of the O. T., as Levit. xxiv. 16. Deut. xiii. 1. sq. v. 13 & 20, which denounce death on *pretenders* to Divine mission: for *ἐποίησεν* here means *pretended to be*. On the full purport of the Jewish Law on this head, on the cri-

Ὅτε οὖν ἤκουσεν ὁ Πιλάτος τοῦτον τὸν λόγον, μᾶλλον ἐφοβήθη, 8
καὶ εἰσῆλθεν εἰς τὸ πραιτώριον πάλιν, καὶ λέγει τῷ Ἰησοῦ· Πόθεν 9
εἶ σύ; Ὁ δὲ Ἰησοῦς ἀπόκρισιν οὐκ ἔδωκεν αὐτῷ. Λέγει οὖν αὐτῷ 10
ὁ Πιλάτος· Ἐμοὶ οὐ λαλεῖς; οὐκ οἶδας ὅτι ἐξουσίαν ἔχω σταυρῶσαί
σε, καὶ ἐξουσίαν ἔχω ἀπολῦσαί σε; Ἀπεκρίθη ὁ Ἰησοῦς· Οὐκ εἶχες 11
ἐξουσίαν οὐδεμίαν κατ' ἐμοῦ, εἰ μὴ ἦν σοι δεδομένον ἄνωθεν· διὰ
τοῦτο ὁ παραδιδούς μέ σοι μείζονα ἁμαρτίαν ἔχει. Ἐκ τούτου ἐζήτει 12
ὁ Πιλάτος ἀπολῦσαι αὐτόν. Οἱ δὲ Ἰουδαῖοι ἔκραζον, λέγοντες· Ἐὰν
τοῦτον ἀπολύσῃς, οὐκ εἶ φίλος τοῦ Καίσαρος. πᾶς ὁ βασιλέα αὑτὸν
ποιῶν ἀντιλέγει τῷ Καίσαρι. Ὁ οὖν Πιλάτος ἀκούσας τοῦτον τὸν 13
λόγον, ἤγαγεν ἔξω τὸν Ἰησοῦν, καὶ ἐκάθισεν ἐπὶ τοῦ βήματος, εἰς τόπον

terion of false prophets, and on the kind of death inflicted on such, see the Note of Lampe in Recens. Synop.

The τοῦ before Θεοῦ is omitted in many MSS. and early Edd., and is cancelled by almost every Editor from Wets. to Scholz; a decision approved of by Bp. Midd., who shews that Υἱὸς Θεοῦ may mean *the* Son of God, as well as ὁ Υἱὸς τοῦ Θεοῦ, and proves that Christ, in affirming that he was the Son of God, did, in fact, affirm his Messiahship. See Note on Matt. xiv. 33. and comp. Lu. xxii. 66. with v. 70. Tittm., however (whose Note see in Recens. Synop.) is of opinion that the names *Messiah* and *Son of God* were by no means synonymous, but of very different meaning; the former expressing *office*, the latter *Divine nature*. See i. 14. And that Pilate so *understood* the appellation, he thinks is clear from what follows. Be that as it may, the two appellations by which the Saviour of Israel was called, namely, *Messiah* (which implied, they thought, *Kingship)*, and *Son of God* (which expressed His *Divine nature* and union with God), afforded the chief Priests an opportunity of shifting the charge as they found politic, pressing either that of *sedition*, or of *blasphemy*.

8. μᾶλλον ἐφοβήθη] Namely, to condemn him to be crucified. Pilate's apprehension arose probably from an impression, such as he could not suppress, that Jesus was at least a very extraordinary person, if not the character he claimed to be. Whether this idea was at all mixed up with the notion of a Heathen Demigod (though the most celebrated Commentators ascribe it chiefly to *that)* is very doubtful. The stories of Demigods, &c. were probably by the higher classes regarded in nearly the same light in which *we* view them; namely, as mere *Mythological* fictions, only deserving of attention from their antiquity and poetic elegance.

9. πόθεν εἶ σύ;] This cannot mean, as some Commentators imagine, "of what country art thou?" for Pilate knew him to be a Galilæan; but, as others interpret, "What is your origin and parentage?" So 2 Sam. i. 13. πόθεν εἶ σύ; Josh. ix. 8. πόθεν ἐστέ. For Pilate now knew that Jesus claimed to be of celestial origin (υἱὸς Θεοῦ). To this question our Lord was pleased to make no answer; partly because Pilate's conduct did not *entitle* him to any, and partly because an answer to the interrogation, in the usual acceptation of the words, Pilate could scarcely need; and in any other sense it would have been little intelligible, and have led to *further* questions, all superfluous, since Jesus knew he had resolved to deliver him to the fury of the Jews.

11. οὐκ εἶχες — ἄνωθεν.] The best Commentators, ancient and modern, are agreed that ἄνωθεν signifies "from on high," "from Heaven," i. e. "by Divine Providence," as in iii. 31. James i. 17. and Ælian and Dio Chrys. cited by the Commentators. Instead of ἐξουσίαν ἔχειν, the more Classical phrase is κύριος εἶναι. So in a kindred passage of Dio Cass. p. 398. 1. κύριος καὶ σῶσαι καὶ ἀπολῦσαί τινας. By δεδομένον, Grot. rightly understands, not that *common permission*, which leaves many things to the natural course of events, but something decreed in the Divine counsels.

— διὰ τοῦτο.] With these words the Commentators are perplexed. To suppose it, with Kuin., a mere formula of transition, is very unsatisfactory. The methods proposed by Markl. and Bp. Pearce are too violent and arbitrary. It may, perhaps, be best regarded as a highly *elliptical* expression, and the διὰ τοῦτο need not be too rigorously interpreted. The sense seems to be, "Wherefore [in thus giving me up to the fury of the people] he who put me into thy hands is more in fault than thou."

12. This divining of his thoughts, and this candid judgment of his conduct, seems to have much affected Pilate for the moment; hence he made another effort to save Jesus. The Jews, however, perceiving that Pilate was studying every method of releasing Jesus, and that he paid little attention to their second charge, — of blasphemy, as not falling under his cognizance, — now return to their *first* alleged crime, which especially belonged to the Procurator, namely, that of *sedition*, and *treason against Cæsar*.

— οὐκ εἶ φίλος τ. Κ.] A popular *meiosis*. Ἀντιλέγει is, by a Hellenistic use, put for ἀπειθεῖ or ἀνταίρει. The threat was not to be despised; since, as we learn from Suetonius and Tacitus, Cæsar was most suspicious, and punished with death any offence that bordered on the *crimen læsæ majestatis*.

13. ἐκάθισεν.] A juridical expression signifying *sat for judgment*. Λιθόστρωτον denoted a pavement formed of pieces of marble or stone of various colours: such as were called *vermiculata*, and *tesselata*. A sort of luxury which had arisen in the time of Sylla, and had extended even to the most remote provinces. Julius Cæsar, as we learn from Sueton. Vit. 46, carried about with him in his expeditions such pieces of sawn marble and variegated stone with which to adorn his prætorium. The fashion, as we should call it, seems

14 λεγόμενον Λιθόστρωτον, Ἑβραϊστὶ δὲ Γαββαθᾶ, (ἦν δὲ παρασκευὴ
τοῦ πάσχα, ὥρα δὲ ὡσεὶ † ἕκτη,) καὶ λέγει τοῖς Ἰουδαίοις· Ἴδε, ὁ
15 βασιλεὺς ὑμῶν. Οἱ δὲ ἐκραύγασαν· Ἆρον, ἆρον· σταύρωσον αὐτόν.
λέγει αὐτοῖς ὁ Πιλάτος· Τὸν βασιλέα ὑμῶν σταυρώσω; ἀπεκρίθησαν
16 οἱ ἀρχιερεῖς· Οὐκ ἔχομεν βασιλέα, εἰ μὴ Καίσαρα. [p] Τότε οὖν παρέ- p Matt. 27. 26. Mark 15. 22. Luke 23. 25.
δωκεν αὐτὸν αὐτοῖς, ἵνα σταυρωθῇ.
17 Παρέλαβον δὲ τὸν Ἰησοῦν καὶ ‡ ἀπήγαγον· καὶ βαστάζων τὸν σταυρὸν αὐτοῦ ἐξῆλθεν εἰς τὸν λεγόμενον Κρανίου τόπον, ὃς λέγεται Ἑβραϊ-
18 στὶ Γολγοθᾶ· ὅπου αὐτὸν ἐσταύρωσαν, καὶ μετ᾽ αὐτοῦ ἄλλους δύο
19 ἐντεῦθεν καὶ ἐντεῦθεν, μέσον δὲ τὸν Ἰησοῦν. [q] Ἔγραψε δὲ καὶ τίτλον q Matt. 27. 37. Mark 15. 26. Luke 23. 38.
ὁ Πιλάτος, καὶ ἔθηκεν ἐπὶ τοῦ σταυροῦ· ἦν δὲ γεγραμμένον, ἸΗ-
20 ΣΟΥΣ Ὁ ΝΑΖΩΡΑΙΟΣ Ὁ ΒΑΣΙΛΕΥΣ ΤΩΝ ἸΟΥΔΑΙΩΝ. Τοῦ-
τον οὖν τὸν τίτλον πολλοὶ ἀνέγνωσαν τῶν Ἰουδαίων, ὅτι ἐγγὺς ἦν τῆς
πόλεως ὁ τόπος, ὅπου ἐσταυρώθη ὁ Ἰησοῦς· καὶ ἦν γεγραμμένον
21 Ἑβραϊστί, Ἑλληνιστί, Ῥωμαϊστί. Ἔλεγον οὖν τῷ Πιλάτῳ οἱ ἀρχιερεῖς
τῶν Ἰουδαίων· Μὴ γράφε· Ὁ βασιλεὺς τῶν Ἰουδαίων· ἀλλ᾽ ὅτι
22 ἐκεῖνος εἶπε· Βασιλεύς εἰμι τῶν Ἰουδαίων. Ἀπεκρίθη ὁ Πιλάτος·
23 Ὃ γέγραφα, γέγραφα. [r] Οἱ οὖν στρατιῶται, ὅτε ἐσταύρωσαν τὸν r Matt. 27. 35. Mark 15. 24. Luke 23. 34.
Ἰησοῦν, ἔλαβον τὰ ἱμάτια αὐτοῦ, καὶ ἐποίησαν τέσσαρα μέρη, ἑκάστῳ
στρατιώτῃ μέρος, καὶ τὸν χιτῶνα. ἦν δὲ ὁ χιτὼν ἄῤῥαφος ἐκ τῶν ἄνω-
24 θεν ὑφαντὸς δι᾽ ὅλου. [s] εἶπον οὖν πρὸς ἀλλήλους· Μὴ σχίσωμεν s Psal. 22. 18.
αὐτόν, ἀλλὰ λάχωμεν περὶ αὐτοῦ, τίνος ἔσται· ἵνα ἡ γραφὴ πληρωθῇ
ἡ λέγουσα· Διεμερίσαντο τὰ ἱμάτιά μου ἑαυτοῖς, καὶ
ἐπὶ τὸν ἱματισμόν μου ἔβαλον κλῆρον.
25 Οἱ μὲν οὖν στρατιῶται ταῦτα ἐποίησαν· εἱστήκεισαν δὲ παρὰ τῷ

to have been brought from the East at the Roman conquests in Asia. It had probably long been in use there. So Aristeas ap. Euseb. Præp. Evang. p. 453, says of the Temple at Jerusalem. Τὸ δὲ πᾶν ἔδαφος λιθόστρωτον καθέστηκε. The passage of Suet. throws the strongest light on the passage before us, and shows that by λιθ. is here meant the *Prætorium* of Pilate, paved with variegated marble slabs.

14. παρασκευὴ τοῦ πάσχα.] See Campb.

— ὥρα δὲ ὡσεὶ ἕκτη.] On the seeming discrepancy between this account and that of the other Evangelists, see Recens. Synop. Townsend's Chr. Arr. i. 5. 24. and the Note on Mark xv. 25. There can be no doubt that an error of number has crept in (the Γ being confounded with the ϛ), and that the true reading is Γ, i. e. τρίτη. Indeed, this reading is found in *seven* of the best MSS., some Fathers, as Euseb. (who says it was so written in the autograph), Jerome, Severus, Ammonius, and Theophyl., and some Scholiasts, with Nonnus. In this opinion the best recent Commentators acquiesce. That this clause is not, as Wassenbergh imagined, a *gloss*, is established satisfactorily by Bornm. de Glossis, p. 44.

15. οὐκ ἔχομεν, &c.] A mere pretence, since the Jews always maintained that they owed no allegiance to any earthly monarch, but were subjects of God only.

16. καὶ ἀπήγαγον.] Many MSS. and early Edd., and some Fathers and Commentators have ἤγαγον, which is received by almost every Editor from Wets. to Scholz. But ἀπάγειν (not ἄγειν) is a vox sol. de hac re. The error, I suspect, arose from the contraction κἀπήγαγον, which might easily be mistaken for καὶ ἤγαγον.

19. τίτλον.] On this superscription, see the ingenious dissertation of Dr. Townson in Mr. Towns. Chr. Arr. i. 534.

22. ὃ γέγραφα, γέγραφα] q. d. "as it is written, it shall stand." A *popular* form of expressing a refusal to have it altered.

24. ἵνα ἡ γραφὴ πληρωθῇ.] The best Commentators are of opinion that the sense is: "Thus was fulfilled the Scripture (i. e. Ps. xxii. 19.) which saith." But they are not agreed whether the verse of the Psalm was meant to refer to Christ, or not. Most recent Interpreters think it was *not*; and take the words to relate solely to David, and to have reference to the rebellion of Absalom. They are here only, they think, introduced by application and accommodation to the present purpose. But though it be true that the form ἵνα πληρωθῇ ἡ γραφὴ sometimes means, that such a thing so happened that this or that passage would appear quite suitable to it; yet as this and other passages of the Psalms cannot be proved to have been fulfilled in the case of *David*, whereas this and other parts of the same Psalm were minutely fulfilled in that of *Christ*; and, what is more, as the Evangelist plainly regarded the Psalm as

σταυρῷ τοῦ Ἰησοῦ ἡ μήτηρ αὐτοῦ, καὶ ἡ ἀδελφὴ τῆς μητρὸς αὐτοῦ,
Μαρία ἡ τοῦ Κλωπᾶ, καὶ Μαρία ἡ Μαγδαληνή. Ἰησοῦς οὖν ἰδὼν 26
τὴν μητέρα, καὶ τὸν μαθητὴν παρεστῶτα, ὃν ἠγάπα, λέγει τῇ μητρὶ
αὐτοῦ· Γύναι, ἰδοὺ, ὁ υἱός σου. Εἶτα λέγει τῷ μαθητῇ· Ἰδοὺ, ἡ 27
μήτηρ σου. καὶ ἀπ' ἐκείνης τῆς ὥρας ἔλαβεν αὐτὴν ὁ μαθητὴς ἐκεῖ-
t Psal. 69. 21. νος εἰς τὰ ἴδια. ᵗ Μετὰ τοῦτο εἰδὼς ὁ Ἰησοῦς, ὅτι πάντα ἤδη τετέ- 28
u Matt. 27. 48. λεσται, ἵνα τελειωθῇ ἡ γραφὴ, λέγει· Διψῶ. ᵘ Σκεῦος οὖν ἔκειτο 29
ὄξους μεστόν· οἱ δὲ πλήσαντες σπόγγον ὄξους, καὶ ὑσσώπῳ περιθέντες, προσήνεγκαν αὐτοῦ τῷ στόματι. Ὅτε οὖν ἔλαβε τὸ ὄξος ὁ Ἰησοῦς, 30
εἶπε· Τετέλεσται· καὶ κλίνας τὴν κεφαλὴν παρέδωκε τὸ πνεῦμα.

Οἱ οὖν Ἰουδαῖοι, ἵνα μὴ μείνῃ ἐπὶ τοῦ σταυροῦ τὰ σώματα ἐν τῷ 31
σαββάτῳ, ἐπεὶ παρασκευὴ ἦν· ἦν γὰρ μεγάλη ἡ ἡμέρα * ἐκείνη τοῦ
σαββάτου· ἠρώτησαν τὸν Πιλάτον, ἵνα κατεαγῶσιν αὐτῶν τὰ σκέλη,
καὶ ἀρθῶσιν. Ἦλθον οὖν οἱ στρατιῶται, καὶ τοῦ μὲν πρώτου κατέα- 32
ξαν τὰ σκέλη καὶ τοῦ ἄλλου τοῦ συσταυρωθέντος αὐτῷ· ἐπὶ δὲ τὸν 33
Ἰησοῦν ἐλθόντες, ὡς εἶδον αὐτὸν ἤδη τεθνηκότα, οὐ κατέαξαν αὐτοῦ
τὰ σκέλη· ἀλλ' εἷς τῶν στρατιωτῶν λόγχῃ αὐτοῦ τὴν πλευρὰν ἔνυξε, 34

prophetical, and the words as fulfilled in Christ, the former view is decidedly preferable.

25—27. The incident narrated in these verses is recorded by St. John only. On Clopas, see Recens. Synop.

26. *ἰδοὺ, ὁ υἱός σου*] i. e. regard him as thy son, and just after, *ἰδοὺ ἡ μήτηρ σου*, "regard her as thy mother." Thus commending the two persons whom he most dearly loved to the care and affection of each other.

28. *εἰδὼς — ὅτι πάντα ἤδη τετ.*] On the exact import of *ἤδη τετ.* and *τετέλεσται* at ver. 30, Commentators are not agreed. Many eminent modern ones take the expression to be a popular one for "It is all over with me." "I am about to breathe my last." And they cite from Homer *τὰ δὲ νῦν πάντα τελεῖται*, and other passages less to the purpose. That, however, is a sense *too feeble* to be admitted. The true sense is doubtless that of the ancients and early moderns, "knowing that all things [namely, what he had to do and to suffer] were now accomplished."

—*ἵνα τελειωθῇ — διψῶ.*] Most recent Commentators are of opinion that the passage of the Psalm here alluded to, lxix. 22, was not meant of the Messiah, and consequently not prophetical; but that St. John only *applies* it to Christ by *accommodation*. But that tool of *accommodation* is not very safe in the hands of some who maintain this view, and here it must by no means be employed. It is plain that the Evangelist did *not* mean merely to accommodate the passage; but to shew that it was prophetic of Christ, and was now fulfilled, at least in its principal scope. As to the argument that the *imprecations* at ver. 23 show the Psalm not to be prophetical, it is very weak. For it is not necessary to suppose the *whole* Psalm prophetic of Christ. See Note supra ver. 24.

29. *ὑσσώπῳ περιθέντες.*] On the difficulty connected with *ὑσσώπῳ*, see Note on Matth. xxvii. 50. Suffice it here to say, that there are several species of the hyssop; one of which (and no doubt the one here meant) has a woody, reed-like stalk, of two feet or more in length, and which is mentioned by the Rabbinical writers as bound up in bundles for firing. Ὑσσώπῳ, then, is here put for *καλάμῳ ὑσσώπου* (hence called by Matthew and Mark *καλάμῳ*); and this, if of the length above mentioned, might easily enable a person to reach the mouth of Jesus on the cross, which, as was shown on Matth. xxvii. 32, was so low that the feet of the crucified person were not more than a yard from the ground. Περιθέντες signifies "having wound or fastened it around," or, "having stuck it on." Thus the word is used in the LXX. to express the Hebr. קָשַׁר, to tie to, in Prov. vii. 3. And Aristoph. Thesm. 387. uses *περίθου* for *ἐπίθου*.

30. *παρέδωκε τὸ πνεῦμα.*] This and the *ἀφῆκε τὸ πνεῦμα* of Matthew suggest the idea of a placid, peaceful, and resigned dissolution, and were therefore used by the pious among the Hebrews to denote that the soul is rendered back unto God its original author, to dispose of according to his good pleasure. (Grot. and Kuin.)

31. *μεγ. ἡ ἡμέρα*] "A very solemn festival," namely, as being not only an ordinary *Sabbath*, but the extraordinary one on the 15th of Nisan. For *ἐκείνη*, very many MSS., Versions, and early Edd. have *ἐκείνου*, which is received by most Editors from Wets. to Scholz, with the approbation of Bp. Middl.

—*ἵνα κατεαγῶσιν αὐτῶν τὰ σκέλη.*] Not, as some imagine, to increase their torment, but to accelerate death; as is plain from the passages of the Classical writers cited by Wets. The legs, we learn, were broken, just above the ancle, by an iron mallet.

34. Some difference of opinion exists, 1. as to the *intent* of the Evangelist in this attestation. It has been generally supposed that he meant to establish the fact of Christ's *actual* death; while some (as Dr. Burton) think it was his intent to refute the Docetæ, who held that Jesus had not a real body, but was only a phantom. 2. As to the *phenomenon* itself, the earlier Commenta-

35 καὶ εὐθὺς ἐξῆλθεν αἷμα καὶ ὕδωρ. Καὶ ὁ ἑωρακὼς μεμαρτύρηκε, καὶ
ἀληθινὴ αὐτοῦ ἐστιν ἡ μαρτυρία· κἀκεῖνος οἶδεν ὅτι ἀληθῆ λέγει, ἵνα
36 ὑμεῖς πιστεύσητε. [x] Ἐγένετο γὰρ ταῦτα· ἵνα ἡ γραφὴ πληρωθῇ· [x Exod. 12. 46. Num. 9. 12.]
37 Ὀστοῦν οὐ συντριβήσεται αὐτοῦ. [y] Καὶ πάλιν ἑτέρα γραφὴ [y Zach. 12. 10.]
λέγει· Ὄψονται εἰς ὃν ἐξεκέντησαν.
38 [z] ΜΕΤΑ δὲ ταῦτα ἠρώτησε τὸν Πιλάτον [ὁ] Ἰωσὴφ ὁ ἀπὸ Ἀρι- [z Matt. 27. 57. Mark 15. 42. Luke 23. 50. supra 12. 42.]
μαθαίας, ὢν μαθητὴς τοῦ Ἰησοῦ, (κεκρυμμένος δὲ διὰ τὸν φόβον τῶν
Ἰουδαίων,) ἵνα ἄρῃ τὸ σῶμα τοῦ Ἰησοῦ· καὶ ἐπέτρεψεν ὁ Πιλάτος.
39 Ἦλθεν οὖν καὶ ἦρε τὸ σῶμα τοῦ Ἰησοῦ· [a] ἦλθε δὲ καὶ Νικόδημος, ὁ [a Supra 3. 1.]
ἐλθὼν πρὸς τὸν Ἰησοῦν νυκτὸς τὸ πρῶτον, φέρων μίγμα σμύρνης καὶ
40 ἀλόης * ὡς λίτρας ἑκατόν. Ἔλαβον οὖν τὸ σῶμα τοῦ Ἰησοῦ, καὶ ἔδη-

tors in general regard it as *miraculous*; but the researches of modern Surgery have established the *fact*, that the effusion would have taken place in *any* case, being the *natural* consequence of such a wound; and is, under all circumstances, decisive evidence of the actual death of Christ. Medical writers are, indeed, not quite agreed whether by *αἷμα καὶ ὕδωρ* be meant the small portion of water found in the pericardium, called *lymph*, or (which is more probable) the sanguineous and aqueous liquor found in the cavities of the pleura after a mortal wound, or that follows a stab in the pleura, when the *pericardium* has been pierced, *which is always mortal*; consequently a proof that if Christ had *not* been already dead, this wound would certainly have extinguished the last remains of life; which was doubtless the intent of the soldier. See the learned and convincing Treatise of C. F. F. Gruner (a celebrated German Physician), *de morte Christi verâ, non simulatâ*, Halæ, 1805. The purpose, then, of the Evangelist, in recording this circumstance, was probably both to afford additional evidence of our Lord's actual death, and to refute the notion of the Docetæ, and thus put to silence both infidels and heretics.

35. *καὶ ὁ ἑωρακὼς — ἡ μαρτυρία.*] I would render: "And one who was an eye-witness [to the circumstance] (namely, *John* himself) testifieth to the truth of this, and his testimony is true: yea he is conscious that he speaks the truth, so that ye may rely on his testimony."

36. *ἐγένετο γὰρ ταῦτα.*] The *γὰρ* refers to a clause omitted, q. d. "And *believe* ye well may — for all these things were really done," &c.

— *ὀστοῦν οὐ, &c.*] Many recent Commentators are of opinion that the passages of the O. T. (Exod. xii. 46. Numb. ix. 12.) in which it is enjoined, that "not a bone of the lamb shall be broken," are not *prophetical*, and had no reference to Christ. "There are (say they) no vestiges in the O. T. of the Paschal lamb being considered as a type of Christ: nor did the Evangelist mean to so represent it. He only *applies* the passage to our Lord, and *compares* Christ with the Paschal lamb; intending to denote, that in the institution of the Paschal lamb, something had been enjoined similar to what would, by Divine interposition, take place in the case of Christ; by which Providence, therefore, it happened that his bones were not broken." But that the Evangelist *did* mean to represent the Paschal lamb as a *type* of Christ, and consequently that such must be the only true view, no person who fairly considers the words can doubt. What can offer so probable a reason for the otherwise unaccountable injunction, that not a bone of the Paschal lamb should be broken, as that it might point to the sacrifice of that lamb as a type of the sacrifice of Christ?

There is evidently a correspondence between the *type* and *antetype*. And as the passage noted in the first verse (also alluded to at Rev. i. 7.) is (as Lampe and Tittm. prove) plainly prophetic of the piercing of the Redeemer's side; so we have here both a correspondence of type and antetype, and a fulfilment of prophecy, viz. of the *piercing*. With respect to the circumstance *ὄψονται εἰς*, it was partly fulfilled at the *first* advent of our Lord, at the destruction of Jerusalem and the Jewish state; and will be finally and more signally fulfilled at the last advent, the *day of judgment*, which seems especially alluded to at Rev. i. 7. As to the seeming *discrepancies* in the above two passages, (namely, Exod. xii. 46. Zech. xii. 10.) suffice it to say, that the former is, properly speaking, no citation at all, but only a statement of the *sense*. The other *is* a quotation; and although it differs considerably from the Sept., it agrees with the Versions of Aquila, Theodotian, and Symmachus; and, indeed, with the Hebrew, if, with 36 MSS. and many Critics, we read אליו instead of אלי. And so indeed Abp. Newcome translates. Thus there will be no reason to suppose *a change of person*, for accommodation's sake; which is forbidden by the text of the *Jewish* Translator.

39. *σμύρνης καὶ ἀλόης.*] The *σμύρνα* here mentioned is (as we learn from Dioscorides and Pliny) the juice of a certain tree in Arabia, from which, on the trunk being bored, exudes a kind of gummy liquid, which is caught on mats, &c. The *ἀλόη* is supposed by many Commentators not to be the *herb aloes*, from which a bitter juice is expressed, but an *aromatic tree*, which is also called *agollochum*, and the *hylaloe*, whose wood was likewise employed by the Egyptians for embalming corpses. The best Commentators are of opinion, that we are not to suppose the myrrh and aloes to have been in a *liquid* state, (namely, the distillation from the trees) but to have been the *wood* of those trees *dried* and pulverized. This, indeed, appears by the great *weight* of the spices (100 lb. troy weight.) The body could not have been regularly embalmed, since there was not time sufficient for that; but spices and unguents were brought to wash and anoint the body.

— *ὡς λίτρας ἑκατόν.*] Instead of *ὡσεὶ* not a few MSS. and early Edd. have *ὡς*, which is received by Griesb. and others down to Scholz. I have

σαν αὐτὸ ὀθονίοις μετὰ τῶν ἀρωμάτων, καθὼς ἔθος ἐστὶ τοῖς Ἰουδαίοις ἐνταφιάζειν. Ἦν δὲ ἐν τῷ τόπῳ, ὅπου ἐσταυρώθη, κῆπος, καὶ ἐν 41
τῷ κήπῳ μνημεῖον καινὸν, ἐν ᾧ οὐδέπω οὐδεὶς ἐτέθη. Ἐκεῖ οὖν, διὰ 42
τὴν παρασκευὴν τῶν Ἰουδαίων, ὅτι ἐγγὺς ἦν τὸ μνημεῖον, ἔθηκαν τὸν
Ἰησοῦν.

b Matt. 28. 1. Mark 16. 1. Luke 24. 1. XX. [b] ΤΗι δὲ μιᾷ τῶν σαββάτων Μαρία ἡ Μαγδαληνὴ ἔρχεται 1
πρωῒ, σκοτίας ἔτι οὔσης, εἰς τὸ μνημεῖον· καὶ βλέπει τὸν λίθον ἠρμέ-
νον ἐκ τοῦ μνημείου. Τρέχει οὖν καὶ ἔρχεται πρὸς Σίμωνα Πέτρον 2
καὶ πρὸς τὸν ἄλλον μαθητὴν ὃν ἐφίλει ὁ Ἰησοῦς, καὶ λέγει αὐτοῖς·
Ἦραν τὸν Κύριον ἐκ τοῦ μνημείου, καὶ οὐκ οἴδαμεν ποῦ ἔθηκαν αὐ-
c Luke 24. 12. τόν. [c] Ἐξῆλθεν οὖν ὁ Πέτρος, καὶ ὁ ἄλλος μαθητὴς, καὶ ἤρχοντο εἰς 3
τὸ μνημεῖον. Ἔτρεχον δὲ οἱ δύο ὁμοῦ· καὶ ὁ ἄλλος μαθητὴς προέ- 4
δραμε τάχιον τοῦ Πέτρου, καὶ ἦλθε πρῶτος εἰς τὸ μνημεῖον· καὶ 5
παρακύψας βλέπει κείμενα τὰ ὀθόνια· οὐ μέντοι εἰσῆλθεν. Ἔρχεται 6
οὖν Σίμων Πέτρος ἀκολουθῶν αὐτῷ, καὶ εἰσῆλθεν εἰς τὸ μνημεῖον, καὶ
θεωρεῖ τὰ ὀθόνια κείμενα, καὶ τὸ σουδάριον, ὃ ἦν ἐπὶ τῆς κεφαλῆς 7
αὐτοῦ, οὐ μετὰ τῶν ὀθονίων κείμενον, ἀλλὰ χωρὶς ἐντετυλιγμένον εἰς
ἕνα τόπον. Τότε οὖν εἰσῆλθε καὶ ὁ ἄλλος μαθητὴς ὁ ἐλθὼν πρῶτος 8
εἰς τὸ μνημεῖον, καὶ εἶδε καὶ ἐπίστευσεν· οὐδέπω γὰρ ᾔδεισαν τὴν 9
γραφὴν, ὅτι δεῖ αὐτὸν ἐκ νεκρῶν ἀναστῆναι. Ἀπῆλθον οὖν πάλιν 10
d Mark 16. 5. πρὸς ἑαυτοὺς οἱ μαθηταί. [d] Μαρία δὲ εἱστήκει πρὸς τὸ μνημεῖον κλαί- 11
ουσα ἔξω. Ὡς οὖν ἔκλαιε, παρέκυψεν εἰς τὸ μνημεῖον· καὶ θεωρεῖ 12
δύο ἀγγέλους ἐν λευκοῖς καθεζομένους, ἕνα πρὸς τῇ κεφαλῇ καὶ ἕνα
πρὸς τοῖς ποσὶν, ὅπου ἔκειτο τὸ σῶμα τοῦ Ἰησοῦ. Καὶ λέγουσιν αὐ- 13
τῇ ἐκεῖνοι· Γύναι, τί κλαίεις; λέγει αὐτοῖς· Ὅτι ἦραν τὸν κύριόν

followed their example; though the reading is uncertain, since St. John uses both ὡς and ὡσεὶ in this sense. However, ὡσεὶ is more likely to have been a marginal gloss than ὡς. The Critics could have no reason to alter ὡσεὶ to ὡς, since one is as good Greek as the other. The quantity of spices here mentioned has been thought by some incredibly great; and they propose some other signification of λίτρα. But there is no reason to abandon the common interpretation; for the chamber in which our Lord's body was deposited would, according to the common custom, have to be completely perfumed; and no inconsiderable part would probably be reserved for the *funeral;* since, on such occasions, immense quantities of spices were burnt, especially when great respect was meant to be shown to the dead.

40. ἐνταφ.] The term signifies *to prepare for burial*, whether by embalming or otherwise.

42. διὰ τὴν παρασκευὴν, &c.] Since the day (Friday) was verging to a close, and the Sabbath was at hand, they (for greater despatch) laid Jesus, for the present, in the sepulchre, which was near at hand, that they might observe the Sabbatical rest.

XX. On the harmony of the Resurrection see Notes on Matt. xxviii. 1—10. and Townsend.

2 τὸν ἄλλον μαθ.] See Note on xviii. 15.

4. προέδραμε τάχιον.] Here is a blending of two forms of expression, to strengthen the sense.

5. οὐ μέντοι εἰσῆλθεν.] This was either through fear of the pollution supposed to be imparted by a dead body; or through timidity.

7. χωρὶς ἐντετυλιγμένον ε. ἕ. τ.] The particip. has a signif. prægn., "rolled up and put." The construction is: ἐντετ. εἰς ἕνα τόπον χωρίς. It is excellently remarked by Racine (in his observations on particular passages of Scripture), that the linen clothes thus placed and disposed apart from one another, plainly showed that the body had not been carried away by thieves. Those who steal are not observed to do things in such a quiet orderly manner.

8. ἐπίστευσεν.] Not, the truth of the *resurrection*, as some eminent Commentators explain, (for, as the words following suggest, they did not yet know or fully comprehend the prophecies which predicted Christ's resurrection) but (as most of the best Commentators are agreed) the fact related by Mary, that the body had been removed from the sepulchre.

10. πρὸς ἑαυτούς.] The sense is: "to themselves," i. e. their companions, who then, jointly with them, occupied the same house. So that it comes to mean "to their homes;" of which sense many examples are adduced by the Commentators.

12. ἐν λευκοῖς.] Sub. ἱματίοις, of which ellipsis the Commentators cite several examples. The

14 μου, καὶ οὐκ οἶδα ποῦ ἔθηκαν αὐτόν. [e] Καὶ ταῦτα εἰποῦσα ἐστράφη [e] Matt. 28. 9. Mark 16. 9.
εἰς τὰ ὀπίσω, καὶ θεωρεῖ τὸν Ἰησοῦν ἑστῶτα· καὶ οὐκ ᾔδει ὅτι ὁ
15 Ἰησοῦς ἐστι. Λέγει αὐτῇ ὁ Ἰησοῦς· Γύναι, τί κλαίεις; τίνα ζητεῖς;
Ἐκείνη δοκοῦσα ὅτι ὁ κηπουρός ἐστι, λέγει αὐτῷ· Κύριε, εἰ σὺ ἐβά-
16 στασας αὐτὸν, εἰπέ μοι ποῦ αὐτὸν ἔθηκας· κἀγὼ αὐτὸν ἀρῶ. Λέγει
αὐτῇ ὁ Ἰησοῦς· Μαρία! στραφεῖσα ἐκείνη λέγει αὐτῷ· Ῥαββουνί!
17 (ὃ λέγεται, διδάσκαλε). [f] Λέγει αὐτῇ ὁ Ἰησοῦς· Μή μου ἅπτου· οὔπω [f] Psal. 22. 22.
γὰρ ἀναβέβηκα πρὸς τὸν Πατέρα μου· πορεύου δὲ πρὸς τοὺς ἀδελ-
φούς μου, καὶ εἰπὲ αὐτοῖς· Ἀναβαίνω πρὸς τὸν Πατέρα μου καὶ Πα-
18 τέρα ὑμῶν, καὶ Θεόν μου καὶ Θεὸν ὑμῶν. Ἔρχεται Μαρία ἡ Μαγδαληνὴ ἀπαγγέλλουσα τοῖς μαθηταῖς, ὅτι ἑώρακε τὸν Κύριον, καὶ ταῦτα
εἶπεν αὐτῇ.
19 [g] Οὔσης οὖν ὀψίας, τῇ ἡμέρᾳ ἐκείνῃ τῇ μιᾷ τῶν σαββάτων, καὶ τῶν [g] Mark 16. 14. Luke 24. 36. 1 Cor. 15. 5.
θυρῶν κεκλεισμένων, ὅπου ἦσαν οἱ μαθηταὶ συνηγμένοι, διὰ τὸν φό-
βον τῶν Ἰουδαίων, ἦλθεν ὁ Ἰησοῦς καὶ ἔστη εἰς τὸ μέσον, καὶ λέγει

same occurs in other words *denoting colour*, as κόκκινα, ἄνθινα, λαμπρὰ, &c. "*White* (observes Lampe) has ever been a symbol, 1. of *excellence*, whether of person or office; 2. of *holiness* and *innocence*."

15. ὁ κηπουρός.] This is explained by the best Commentators "*the bailiff*." But there is no reason why it may not denote the *occupier of the plot of garden*. Κύριε. The term is here, as often, merely an appellation of common civility to a person of respectable appearance.

— εἰ σὺ ἐβάστασας α.] i. e. "if thou hast been concerned in its removal." The word βαστάζειν properly signifies to *bear*; 2dly, to *bear away, remove*; the *nature* of the removal being determined by the context. It is, however, (as also ἀναίρειν) especially applied to the removal of a *corpse* for burial. Examples of removal *simply*, and also for *burial*, may be seen in Wets. and Kypke. Mary, it seems, thought the corpse had been removed by some friend, with the knowledge and connivance, if not *assistance*, of the gardener; and she would be anxious to know *where*.

17. μή μου ἅπτου, &c.] On the purpose of this address, and consequently on the exact sense of ἅπτου, Commentators differ; yet the most eminent ones are agreed that the purport of the passage is: "Embrace me not; Let me go; do not waste the time in any demonstrations of affection and respect: you will have an opportunity of showing this *afterwards*; for I am not immediately going to take my departure from earth: but proceed directly to my brethren with this comforting message, — that in a little time I shall ascend to heaven, to God my Father, who is also *your* Father, and *your* God." This sense of ἅπτεσθαι (neglected by the Commentators) I have in Recens. Synop. illustrated from Eurip. Phœn. 910. μὴ ἐπιλαμβάνου. where the Schol. explains μή μου ἅπτου.

What was the action of Mary, interrupted by Christ's words, has been matter of debate among Commentators. It was probably *embracing the knees or feet*, as expressing deep veneration and perhaps adoration. Some Commentators think that Mary's motive in wishing to embrace our Lord was to ascertain whether it was He corporeally, or only a spirit. That may have been *one* of the motives.

In the words following, ἀναβέβηκα is regarded by the best Commentators as a kind of Preterite-Present, q. d. I am not now ascending, i. e going to ascend. The words of the message, ἀναβαίνω πρὸς — ὑμῶν, would inform them that He should stay a *short* time longer with them upon earth, and then ascend — He does not say to *heaven*, but, in order to remind them of the relation in which He stands to God, and they to Him, He says, "to my Father," which would give them to understand, that, for their comfort, He who was from the beginning with God is going to act as their *Mediator* with God; who would now become *their* Father and *their* God, not by creation only, but by the spiritual paternity implied in the Gospel covenant.

19. τῶν θυρῶν κεκλ.] On this passage the ancient, and the recent modern Commentators are at the *antipodes* of opinion; the former maintaining that Jesus penetrated, *by a miracle*, through the closed doors; the latter, that he entered in the ordinary way, after knocking and being admitted. The former view cannot be admitted, 1. because it involves an insuperable Philosophical difficulty, well stated by Whitby and Lampe; 2. because such a sense cannot be shown to exist in the words. Still less, however, is the latter opinion defensible; for no dispassionate person can attentively peruse this passage and the similar one at v. 26. without feeling that something far more than an entry in the ordinary way is meant. In the *latter* passage there would have been no need of the τῶν θυρῶν κεκλ., unless something *more* had been intended; something *supernatural*. (See also v. 30.) But *what*, it may be asked, is that? Not the first-mentioned circumstance, for the reasons above adduced; but (as there is a beautiful œconomy, like that observable in nature, perceptible in our Lord's working of miracles, by which no *more* power is employed than is necessary to accomplish the purpose in view) we may suppose (with the best Commentators, from Calvin, Grot. and Whitby, down to Tittm.) that our Lord caused the doors to preternaturally open of themselves; as the angel did at

αὐτοῖς· Εἰρήνη ὑμῖν! Καὶ τοῦτο εἰπὼν ἔδειξεν αὐτοῖς τὰς χεῖρας καὶ 20
τὴν πλευρὰν αὐτοῦ. Ἐχάρησαν οὖν οἱ μαθηταὶ ἰδόντες τὸν Κύριον.
Εἶπεν οὖν αὐτοῖς ὁ Ἰησοῦς πάλιν· Εἰρήνη ὑμῖν! καθὼς ἀπέσταλκέ 21
με ὁ Πατὴρ, κἀγὼ πέμπω ὑμᾶς. Καὶ τοῦτο εἰπὼν ἐνεφύσησε καὶ 22
h Matt. 16. 19. & 18. 18. *λέγει αὐτοῖς· Λάβετε Πνεῦμα ἅγιον.* [h] *Ἄν τινων ἀφῆτε τὰς ἁμαρτίας,* 23
ἀφίενται αὐτοῖς· ἄν τινων κρατῆτε, κεκράτηνται. Θωμᾶς δὲ, εἷς ἐκ 24
τῶν δώδεκα (ὁ λεγόμενος Δίδυμος) οὐκ ἦν μετ᾽ αὐτῶν, ὅτε ἦλθεν ὁ
Ἰησοῦς. Ἔλεγον οὖν αὐτῷ οἱ ἄλλοι μαθηταί· Ἑωράκαμεν τὸν Κύ- 25
ριον. ὁ δὲ εἶπεν αὐτοῖς· Ἐὰν μὴ ἴδω ἐν ταῖς χερσὶν αὐτοῦ τὸν τύπον
τῶν ἥλων, καὶ βάλω τὸν δάκτυλόν μου εἰς τὸν τύπον τῶν ἥλων, καὶ
βάλω τὴν χεῖρά μου εἰς τὴν πλευρὰν αὐτοῦ, οὐ μὴ πιστεύσω. Καὶ 26
μεθ᾽ ἡμέρας ὀκτὼ πάλιν ἦσαν ἔσω οἱ μαθηταὶ αὐτοῦ, καὶ Θωμᾶς μετ᾽
αὐτῶν. Ἔρχεται ὁ Ἰησοῦς, τῶν θυρῶν κεκλεισμένων, καὶ ἔστη εἰς τὸ
μέσον καὶ εἶπεν· Εἰρήνη ὑμῖν! εἶτα λέγει τῷ Θωμᾷ· Φέρε τὸν 27
δάκτυλόν σου ὧδε καὶ ἴδε τὰς χεῖράς μου· καὶ φέρε τὴν χεῖρά σου καὶ
βάλε εἰς τὴν πλευράν μου· καὶ μὴ γίνου ἄπιστος, ἀλλὰ πιστός. Καὶ 28
ἀπεκρίθη ὁ Θωμᾶς, καὶ εἶπεν αὐτῷ· Ὁ Κύριός μου καὶ ὁ Θεός μου!

Acts v. 19. compared with 23. See also Acts xii. 4. 6. 7. 10. I must not omit to observe, that those who adopt the second interpretation are compelled to make the words τῶν θυρῶν κεκλ. a mere *notatio temporis*, q. d. "at door-shutting time." But for that there is no *authority*; nor *could* it be so taken *here*, since it is closely connected with the following ὅπου ἦσαν, &c.

21. καθὼς ἀπέσταλκε — ὑμᾶς.] As Christ was sent for many most important purposes which could have no parallel with the sending of the Apostles, the καθὼς — καὶ must solely refer to those points which *were* similar; i. e. the being delegated and commissioned by the Father, as His ambassadors, to carry the message of salvation to the world. Just as the Apostles were empowered to hand down their authority to their successors. Thus the Christian Ministry is of Divine ordinance.

22. ἐνεφύσησε.] This we are (with the best Commentators) to regard as a *symbolical action*, by which our Lord was pleased to confirm and illustrate (by a significant sign, comp. sup. iii. 8.) the promise before made: for λάβετε ἅγιον can only be understood as a *present promise* of a *future benefit*, which should very shortly be communicated; namely, on the day of Pentecost, when it was formally and substantially communicated.

23. ἄν τινων, &c.] These words were doubtless meant primarily for the *Apostles*; but they contain a promise which, with due limitation, may be extended to their *successors*. For the privilege given was one of *office*; and as the office was handed down, there is no reason why the *privilege* should not remain. The best Commentators are agreed that ἀφῆτε and κρατῆτε must be taken *declaratively*, i. e. to *pronounce* the remission or retention of sins; which is the general and safest view of the sense: though the more eminent of the recent Commentators (even Tittm.) are of opinion that the sense is, "that they were authorized to declare that pardon of sins and salvation in general will be granted to all who seek it by the appointed means." But see Matt. xvi. 18, 19, and Notes.

25. ἐὰν μὴ ἴδω, &c.] He means to say, that "unless he have the testimony of both sight and touch as to the identity and real bodily presence of Jesus," &c. For Thomas did not so much call in question the *veracity* of the disciples, as he supposed they had been *deceived* by some spirit.

27. ἄπιστος] "unbelieving." This *active* sense is rare in the Classical writers; yet I can myself adduce the following examples in Thucyd. i. 68. 1. Æschyl. Theb. 873. Prov. xxviii. 25. The use of πιστὸς for πιστεύων is still more rare; yet one or two examples are adduced by the Commentators.

28. ὁ Κύριός — μου.] On the sense of these remarkable words there has never been any real doubt, except such as has been raised by Arians and Socinians; who, to avoid this plain recognition of the Divinity of our Lord, have been compelled to resort to the *miserable shift* of taking the words as a mere formula of admiration, as we say *good Lord!* &c., an idiom found also in *other* modern languages, but of which not a vestige is found in the *ancient* ones. Besides, that sense is not permitted by the words following; in which Christ commends the faith of Thomas, though he gently reproves the tardiness with which it was rendered. And, what is more, the words being introduced by an εἶπεν αὐτῷ shows that they cannot be a mere *exclamation of surprise*, but an *address*, which, (to use the words of Bp. Middlet.) "though in the form of an exclamation, amounts to a confession of faith, and was equivalent to a direct assertion of our Saviour's Divinity." See Towns. Chron. Arr. i. 604.

And in vain is it attempted to evade the force of this recognition by assigning a *lower* sense to Θεός; for a refutation of which, and an illustration of the sense in which the Apostles understood it, see Note in Recens. Synop. and Middl. in loc. The testimony is clear, and the authority irrefragable; for by not censuring the Apostles

29 [i] *Λέγει αὐτῷ ὁ Ἰησοῦς· Ὅτι ἑώρακάς με, [Θωμᾶ,] πεπίστευκας· μα-* [i] 1 Pet. 1. 8.
κάριοι οἱ μὴ ἰδόντες, καὶ πιστεύσαντες.
30 [k] *Πολλὰ μὲν οὖν καὶ ἄλλα σημεῖα ἐποίησεν ὁ Ἰησοῦς ἐνώπιον τῶν* [k] Infra 21. 25.
31 *μαθητῶν αὐτοῦ, ἃ οὐκ ἔστι γεγραμμένα ἐν τῷ βιβλίῳ τούτῳ. Ταῦτα*
δὲ γέγραπται, ἵνα πιστεύσητε ὅτι ὁ Ἰησοῦς ἐστιν ὁ Χριστὸς ὁ Υἱὸς τοῦ
Θεοῦ· καὶ ἵνα πιστεύοντες ζωὴν ἔχητε ἐν τῷ ὀνόματι αὐτοῦ.
1 **XXI.** *ΜΕΤΑ ταῦτα ἐφανέρωσεν ἑαυτὸν πάλιν ὁ Ἰησοῦς τοῖς μα-*
2 *θηταῖς ἐπὶ τῆς θαλάσσης τῆς Τιβεριάδος. ἐφανέρωσε δὲ οὕτως. Ἦσαν*
ὁμοῦ Σίμων Πέτρος, καὶ Θωμᾶς ὁ λεγόμενος Δίδυμος, καὶ Ναθαναὴλ ὁ
ἀπὸ Κανᾶ τῆς Γαλιλαίας, καὶ οἱ τοῦ Ζεβεδαίου, καὶ ἄλλοι ἐκ τῶν
3 *μαθητῶν αὐτοῦ δύο. Λέγει αὐτοῖς Σίμων Πέτρος· Ὑπάγω ἁλιεύειν.*
*λέγουσιν αὐτῷ· Ἐρχόμεθα καὶ ἡμεῖς σὺν σοί. Ἐξῆλθον καὶ * ἐνέβη-*

for now *first* applying the name *God* to Him, our Lord *takes it to himself*, thinking it (in the words of the Apostle) "not robbery to be equal with God."

A question, however, still remains as to the *construction*. Many eminent Commentators (as Grot., Wets., Rosenm., Kuin., Tittm., and Middlet.) think that the Κύριος and Θεός are *vocatives*, and that the Article stands for the Classical ὦ. Others (as the ancient Syriac and Persic Translators, and some modern Commentators, from Bp. Pearson downwards) take them as *Nominatives*, with the ellipsis of σὺ εἶ. The *former* method seems to involve the *least* difficulty.

29. Θωμᾶ.] This is omitted in very many MSS. and early Edd., and is cancelled by almost every Editor from Wets. to Scholz.

30. σημεῖα.] By σημεῖα the earlier Commentators understand the *miracles* worked by Christ; while the recent ones in general, take it of the *evidences and proofs* of his resurrection; a sense of the word perhaps found at ii. 18. The former interpretation is manifestly untenable, for the reasons assigned by Kuin. and Tittm. Greatly preferable is the latter, which was adopted by Chrys. and Euthym., and is confirmed and illustrated by a passage of Acts i. 3. παρέστησεν ἑαυτὸν ζῶντα ἐν πολλοῖς τεκμηρίοις. Yet there is some harshness in understanding ταῦτα in the next verse, (which, however, can denote no other than what is denoted by σημεῖα, as is plain from the μὲν corresponding to δέ;) and hence Kuin. and Tittm. suppose by ταῦτα to be meant *the whole of what the Evangelist has recorded of the actions and words of Christ*. But that cannot, from the above connection, be admitted. Ταῦτα may better be taken of the *above evidences of the resurrection;* and assuredly (notwithstanding what Kuin. says) Christ's resurrection being proved, *also* proved him to be the Messiah, since that was the attestation of God. See Acts ii. 24. xiii. 23. Rom. iv. 24. viii. 11. 1 Pet. i. 21. Still there is a harshness in taking σημεῖα to mean *proofs of his resurrection*, because τῆς ἀναστάσεως αὐτοῦ ought thus to have been added. I am therefore persuaded that μὲν οὖν is (as the early Commentators considered it) a *conclusion* from all that has been said: and I would take the σημεῖα to denote evidences of the Messiahship. Nor is there any harshness involved in this *brief* mode of expression: since τοῦ Χριστὸν εἶναι may very well be supplied from the context following.

XXI. Respecting the authenticity of this Chapter, some doubt has been raised by Grot., Le Clerc, and Heumann. But it will clearly appear, from the important matter introduced in Recens. Synop. from Lampe, Kuin., and Tittm., that the opinion is as destitute of all *internal proof* as it is of *external authority*. Granting the Chapter to *be* (as they say) an *Appendix* to the foregoing accounts, "might not (as Tittm. suggests) the Evangelist have had good reason to *add* something to his own work, as St. Paul did to certain of his Epistles; especially that to the Romans?" As to the objection, that the circumstances recorded are not of sufficient consequence,—that has little or no force; indeed, it were presumptuous to sit in judgment on the words of inspiration: and such they must be supposed to be, since not the slightest external evidence has ever been adduced to invalidate their authority. As to some *peculiarities* in this portion of Scripture, we are (as Tittm. suggests) to bear in mind (what is evident from the *other* Gospels as well as St. John's) that our Lord, after his resurrection, no longer held intercourse with his Disciples in the way he had done before his death, nor treated them with the same familiarity; nay, that he bore himself as one already withdrawn from human society, and soon to depart, to enter upon his majesty and glory, at the right hand of the Father; which was done, in order, perhaps, that they might be gradually weaned from his *visible presence*, which they had hitherto enjoyed, and become accustomed to his *invisible presence*.

2. ἦσαν ὁμοῦ] i. e. temporarily, at the period in question. Ἄλλοι ἐκ τῶν μαθητῶν δύο. Whether these were *Apostles*, or of the number of the *Seventy Disciples*, or of *Christ's followers in general*, cannot be determined. It does not, however, follow that because the Evangelist does not mention their names, they were *not* of the number of the *Apostles*.

3. ὑπάγω ἁλιεύειν.] This use of the Present found here in ὑπ. and just after in ἐρχόμεθα, followed by an Infin. of action, denoting *intention* of presently doing a thing, seems to be derived from the *popular* phraseology; though something like it is found in the later Classical writers.

—ἐνέβησαν.] This (for the common reading ἀνέβ.) is found in the best MSS. and earliest Edd., and has been received by almost every Editor from Wets. to Scholz; rightly; for ἀναβαίνειν, in a context like the present, cannot be

σαν εἰς τὸ πλοῖον εὐθὺς, καὶ ἐν ἐκείνῃ τῇ νυκτὶ ἐπίασαν οὐδέν. Πρω- 4
ΐας δὲ ἤδη γενομένης, ἔστη ὁ Ἰησοῦς εἰς τὸν αἰγιαλόν· οὐ μέντοι
ᾔδεισαν οἱ μαθηταὶ ὅτι Ἰησοῦς ἐστι. Λέγει οὖν αὐτοῖς ὁ Ἰησοῦς· 5
Παιδία, μή τι προσφάγιον ἔχετε; ἀπεκρίθησαν αὐτῷ· Οὔ. Ὁ δὲ 6
εἶπεν αὐτοῖς· Βάλετε εἰς τὰ δεξιὰ μέρη τοῦ πλοίου τὸ δίκτυον, καὶ
εὑρήσετε. Ἔβαλον οὖν, καὶ οὐκ ἔτι αὐτὸ ἑλκῦσαι ἴσχυσαν ἀπὸ τοῦ
1 Supra 13. 23. πλήθους τῶν ἰχθύων. [1] Λέγει οὖν ὁ μαθητὴς ἐκεῖνος, ὃν ἠγάπα ὁ 7
Ἰησοῦς, τῷ Πέτρῳ· Ὁ Κύριός ἐστι. Σίμων οὖν Πέτρος, ἀκούσας ὅτι
ὁ Κύριός ἐστι, τὸν ἐπενδύτην διεζώσατο (ἦν γὰρ γυμνὸς), καὶ ἔβαλεν
ἑαυτὸν εἰς τὴν θάλασσαν. Οἱ δὲ ἄλλοι μαθηταὶ τῷ πλοιαρίῳ ἦλθον, 8
(οὐ γὰρ ἦσαν μακρὰν ἀπὸ τῆς γῆς, ἀλλ' ὡς ἀπὸ πηχῶν διακοσίων)
σύροντες τὸ δίκτυον τῶν ἰχθύων. Ὡς οὖν ἀπέβησαν εἰς τὴν γῆν, βλέ- 9
πουσιν ἀνθρακιὰν κειμένην, καὶ ὀψάριον ἐπικείμενον, καὶ ἄρτον· Λέ- 10
γει αὐτοῖς ὁ Ἰησοῦς· Ἐνέγκατε ἀπὸ τῶν ὀψαρίων ὧν ἐπιάσατε νῦν.
Ἀνέβη Σίμων Πέτρος, καὶ εἵλκυσε τὸ δίκτυον ἐπὶ τῆς γῆς, μεστὸν 11
ἰχθύων μεγάλων ἑκατὸν πεντηκοντατριῶν· καὶ τοσούτων ὄντων, οὐκ
ἐσχίσθη τὸ δίκτυον.

tolerated. The words of Mark vi. 51. may be thought to defend it; but that passage is of a different kind.

5. παιδία.] Παιδίον and τεκνίον were terms of kindness or affability used by elderly persons or superiors. Προσφάγιον properly denotes *what is eaten with bread*; as we say *meat*, though (like ὀψάριον) it is generally used of *fish*. The word is only found in the later writers. From Chrys. and Wets. it appears that τί ἔχετε; was a phrase employed by those who inquired of fishers or hunters *what they had taken*.

6. βάλετε εἰς τὰ δεξιὰ μέρη.] An Imperative of *counsel*; proceeding, as they imagined, from one who had some knowledge of their art. (Euthym. and Lampe.) Εὑρήσετε is employed with an ellipsis common to hunters and fishers in all languages. Ἀπὸ, for ὑπὸ, *præ*; a sense usually considered Hebraic, but found also in the Classical writers, especially Thucyd.

7. Ὁ Κύριός ἐστι.] They inferred this from the prodigious draught, and the remembrance of the similar one mentioned at Luke v. 1.

— ἐπενδύτην.] From the researches of Salmas., Lampe, and Fischer, this somewhat obscure word is proved to mean that *upper linen tunic* worn by Greeks, Romans, and Jews, and called by the Romans *superaria*, corresponding to our *coat*, and worn between the inner tunic (the *interula* or *subucula* of the Romans and the χιτωνίσκος or ὑποδύτης of the Greeks) and the *surtout*, upper garment, or cloak. The best description is that of Euthym. in Recens. Synop., from which it seems to have been a common fisherman's coat, consisting of a sort of *full frock without sleeves, reaching only to the knees*, and *bound round the middle by a belt*. The *Article* has here the force of the pronoun possessive; and διεζώσατο has a *significatio prægnans*, for *put on and girded*. Γυμνός. Not absolutely so; but, as we should say, stripped to his shirt and waistcoat. Peter, we may suppose, did not plunge into the sea, in order to swim ashore, (for he could not swim) but only in order to *wade* on shore. In his haste he would not stay to go as the other disciples did, who proceeded more leisurely by the cock-boat belonging to the skiff; at the same time drawing with them to the shore the net of fishes.

8. τὸ δίκτυον τῶν ἰχθύων.] Sub. μεστὸν, which is *expressed* at v. 11. This idiom, in nouns of *capacity*, is found in all languages, chiefly, however, in the popular phraseology.

9. βλέπουσιν ἀνθρακιὰν κειμένην.] Notwithstanding the sophistry of some recent Commentators, who seek to account for this in the *natural* way, there is no doubt, from the air of the passage, but that the fire and food were not only *provided by Christ*, but *miraculously*, as he had just before caused the miraculous draught of fishes. *Both* miracles may have been intended to teach, by symbolical actions, the lesson, that Jesus had both the will and the power to abundantly provide for the comfortable subsistence of his disciples.

— ὀψάριον.] Almost all our Translators render this *fish*, as if there were *many*. But that sense is not well established, and the usage both of the Scriptural and Classical writers shows that it rather denotes *a* fish. And as all the company seem to have made a meal of it, it was, no doubt, *large*, like the fish in the net, which being first called ὀψαρίων, are then said to have been of *great size*. In this sense, indeed, the word often occurs in the Classical writers, as Athen. and Ælian. Hence there is no excusing Wakefield and A. Clarke for rendering "a *small* fish." Even had not the context shown that a *large* fish is meant, Mr. *Wakefield* at least could not have to learn that in Greek (as in other languages) diminutive forms often lose their diminutive sense (so βιβλίον, &c.) as patronymics their patronymic sense. See my Note on Thucyd. i. 1. We may observe that the fish being not only numerous, but *all large*, made the miracle the more conspicuous.

11. ἐσχίσθη.] Not *broken*, as in E. V.; still less *torn*, as Wakef. renders, for that is *exaggerating* the sense (a fault, however, of which that

12 Λέγει αὐτοῖς ὁ Ἰησοῦς· Δεῦτε ἀριστήσατε. οὐδεὶς δὲ ἐτόλμα τῶν
μαθητῶν ἐξετάσαι αὐτόν· Σὺ τίς εἶ; εἰδότες ὅτι ὁ Κύριός ἐστιν.
13 Ἔρχεται οὖν ὁ Ἰησοῦς, καὶ λαμβάνει τὸν ἄρτον καὶ δίδωσιν αὐτοῖς, καὶ
14 τὸ ὀψάριον ὁμοίως. Τοῦτο ἤδη τρίτον ἐφανερώθη ὁ Ἰησοῦς τοῖς μαθηταῖς αὐτοῦ, ἐγερθεὶς ἐκ νεκρῶν.
15 Ὅτε οὖν ἠρίστησαν, λέγει τῷ Σίμωνι Πέτρῳ ὁ Ἰησοῦς· Σίμων
Ἰωνᾶ, ἀγαπᾷς με πλεῖόν τούτων; λέγει αὐτῷ· Ναὶ, Κύριε· σὺ
16 οἶδας ὅτι φιλῶ σε. Λέγει αὐτῷ· Βόσκε τὰ ἀρνία μου. Λέγει αὐτῷ
πάλιν δεύτερον· Σίμων Ἰωνᾶ, ἀγαπᾷς με; λέγει αὐτῷ· Ναὶ, Κύριε·
σὺ οἶδας ὅτι φιλῶ σε. Λέγει αὐτῷ· Ποίμαινε τὰ πρόβατά μου.
17 Λέγει αὐτῷ τὸ τρίτον· Σίμων Ἰωνᾶ, φιλεῖς με; Ἐλυπήθη ὁ Πέτρος,
ὅτι εἶπεν αὐτῷ τὸ τρίτον· Φιλεῖς με; καὶ εἶπεν αὐτῷ· Κύριε, σὺ
πάντα οἶδας· σὺ γινώσκεις ὅτι φιλῶ σε. λέγει αὐτῷ ὁ Ἰησοῦς· Βό-
18 σκε τὰ πρόβατά μου. [m]Ἀμὴν ἀμὴν λέγω σοι· ὅτε ἦς νεώτερος, ἐζώννυ- m 2 Pet. 1. 14.
νυες σεαυτὸν, καὶ περιεπάτεις ὅπου ἤθελες· ὅταν δὲ γηράσῃς, ἐκτενεῖς

Critic is rarely guilty): but, as Campb. translates, *rent*.

12. ἀριστήσατε.] The Commentators and Critics are not agreed whether this should be understood of *dinner*, or of *breakfast*. Most recent Commentators adopt the *latter* interpretation; but Campb. at large maintains the former. If we could be sure that the ancients used (as he asserts) but *two* meals for our *three* (breakfast, dinner, and supper), and that the latter corresponded to our *supper*, he would be right. But I have, on Thucyd. iv. 91, proved that, though, in the early times, but *two* meals were taken, ἄριστον and δεῖπνον, yet that afterwards, even in the time of Thucyd., there were *three*: the ἀκράτισμα, answering to our *breakfast*; the ἄριστον, to our *lunch*, or *early dinner*; and the δεῖπνον to our *later dinner*, or *supper*. If the same custom prevailed in Judæa, then ἄριστον will denote the *second* meal, call it by what name we may. If, however, the Jews (as is not improbable) retained the *primitive* custom of *two* meals a day, then ἄριστον will here mean, as it did in the time of Homer, *breakfast*; and denote (as its *etymon* would suggest) a far more substantial meal than the ἀκράτισμα; which seems to have meant merely a *snack*, caught up by those who could not wait till the ἄριστον, which was taken about an hour before noon.

14. τρίτον] i. e. the third time recorded *in this Gospel*; for it appears from Matth. xxviii. 16 sq. that he had appeared to them *five* times before; or the third time of showing himself to his disciples collectively.

15. πλεῖον τούτων.] By τούτων, Whitby, Pearce, Middl., and others understand "these things;" i. e. the nets, boats, and other implements of his trade: q. d. "dost thou prefer my service to thy temporal occupation?" But there is something frigid in this sense. Besides, as Jortin observes, Peter might love Jesus *more than these*, and yet not love him *much*. The true interpretation seems to be that of the ancient and many of the most eminent modern Commentators, as Lampe, Campb., Kuin. and Tittm., who assign the following sense: "Dost thou love me more than those do?" The question has (as Campb. remarks) a reference to the declaration of Peter, Matth. xxvi. 33, when he seemed to arrogate a superiority above the rest, in zeal for his Master and steadiness in his service. It is proper to observe, that though our Lord asks the question thrice, yet the admonition, which each time follows it up, is not quite the same; for βόσκειν signifies simply to *feed*, provide with pasture; ποιμαίνειν both to *feed* and to *tend*; the former being especially applicable to ἀρνία (meaning young raw professors); and the latter to πρόβατα, or the more advanced and mature professors. As Christ was the ἀρχιποιμὴν (1 Pet. v. 4.), so Peter and the other Apostles were to be ποιμένες. And the notion of *tending* necessarily carries with it that of *guiding* and *governing*. The admonition was *thrice* repeated, either, as Beza supposes, with reference to Peter's *three denials*, the disgrace of which it was just he should wipe away by a triple confession; or, in order that the importance of the injunction might thus be more strongly impressed on the mind of Peter and the other Apostles. So it is said in an ancient writer (Aristoph. Ran. 368.) Τούτοις αὐδῶ, καὖθις ἀπαυδῶ, καὖθις τὸ τρίτον μάλ' ἀπαυδῶ.

17. σὺ πάντα οἶδας.] A recognition of omniscience, and consequently Divinity.

18—23. There is some difficulty connected with these verses, and consequently a difference of opinion, 1. as to the *precise import* of the prediction contained therein. By these words (probably suggested by Peter's girding himself, after having changed his clothes, as he would be likely to do after having come on shore thoroughly wet) our Lord meant, it should seem, to adopt the most impressive mode of signifying to Peter what he would have to undergo in his cause, introductory to the final and solemn *injunction* to *follow his example*. In like manner, at Acts xxi. 10. it is said Agabus, a prophet, took Paul's girdle, and bound his own hands and feet, and said, "Thus saith the Holy Ghost, So shall the Jews at Jerusalem bind the man that owneth this girdle, and shall deliver him into the hands of the Gentiles." To advert to the particular import of the prediction, the words ἐζώννυες σεαυτὸν καὶ περιεπάτεις ὅπου ἤθελες are evidently a figurative mode of expressing youthful vigour and perfect freedom of action. The next words ὅταν δὲ γηράσῃς — θέλεις are

τὰς χεῖράς σου, καὶ ἄλλος σε ζώσει, καὶ οἴσει ὅπου οὐ θέλεις. Τοῦτο 19
δὲ εἶπε, σημαίνων ποίῳ θανάτῳ δοξάσει τὸν Θεόν. καὶ τοῦτο εἰπὼν
n Supra 13. 23. & 1. c. ver. 7. λέγει αὐτῷ· Ἀκολούθει μοι. [n] Ἐπιστραφεὶς δὲ ὁ Πέτρος βλέπει τὸν 20
μαθητὴν, ὃν ἠγάπα ὁ Ἰησοῦς ἀκολουθοῦντα, ὃς καὶ ἀνέπεσεν ἐν τῷ
δείπνῳ ἐπὶ τὸ στῆθος αὐτοῦ, καὶ εἶπε· Κύριε, τίς ἐστιν ὁ παραδιδούς
σε; Τοῦτον ἰδὼν ὁ Πέτρος λέγει τῷ Ἰησοῦ· Κύριε, οὗτος δὲ τί; 21
λέγει αὐτῷ ὁ Ἰησοῦς· Ἐὰν αὐτὸν θέλω μένειν ἕως ἔρχομαι, τί πρὸς 22
σέ; σὺ ἀκολούθει μοι. ἐξῆλθεν. οὖν ὁ λόγος οὗτος εἰς τοὺς ἀδελ- 23
φούς· Ὅτι ὁ μαθητὴς ἐκεῖνος οὐκ ἀποθνήσκει. καὶ οὐκ εἶπεν αὐτῷ

by most Expositors ancient and modern, supposed to allude to *crucifixion;* while several recent Commentators recognize a reference solely to the *helplessness* of age. But that view is surely forbidden by the *οὐ θέλεις*; besides that yields a sense very frigid, and by no means suitable to the occasion. Yet whether the words can fairly be thought to refer to the *crucifixion itself*, may be doubted: for though the expressions ἐκτενεῖς τὰς χεῖράς σου καὶ ἄλλος σε ζώσει be correspondent thereto, since the person would have to stretch out his arms to be nailed to the cross bars; yet that is supposing him to *be already* there, and not have to be *taken* (as the words following express) "where he would not wish to go," namely, to the place of execution. Hence Kuin. and Tittm. maintain that the words only predict that Peter should die a *violent death*. And indeed the words following τοῦτο δὲ — Θεὸν cannot be *proved* to have reference to more than *martyrdom* by whatever death. Yet they, and especially the subsequent admonition ἀκολούθει μοι, rather suggest death by *crucifixion;* and as the universal testimony of antiquity concurs in shewing that Peter suffered martyrdom by *crucifixion*, I am therefore inclined to think, with Casaubon, Scaliger, Amelius, Lampe, Wets., and Ernesti, that there is a reference, not to actual crucifixion, but to the *preparation* for it, by which (as they prove from various examples) the criminal was compelled to put his neck into a furca (of the form Π, called patibulum); his hands being extended and bound to the *transverse horns* (to represent, by a *significant action*, the punishment he was about to suffer); and after being carried, as it were in procession, to the place of execution, he was then *actually* crucified. As to the *obscurity* which this interpretation supposes to exist in the words, that is by no means greater than might be expected in a *prediction*, not intended to be fully understood but by the *event*, when it would prove as great a *support* to the Apostle as it would *before* that time have been a source of alarm and dismay.

Instead of οἴσει, a Classical writer would have said ἀπάξει. And indeed some MSS. have ἀπάξουσι, or ἄξουσι; both evidently *glosses*. From the question put by Peter at ver. 21, it is manifest that he understood his Lord's expressions of a violent death by the executioner; but *what kind* of death he did not understand; and in his 2d Epistle i. 14, though he speaks with uncertainty, yet he plainly alludes to a *violent* death.

19. δοξάσει τὸν Θεόν.] An expression designating martyrdom, on which see Grotius and Tittman.

20. ἐπιστραφείς.] It seems that Peter, though he was aware of the figurative sense intended in ἀκολ., yet thought it safer to observe the direction in the *literal* one, and therefore follows his master. Then, turning about and seeing John also following, and thereby showing his comprehension of the meaning of Jesus, he feels a curiosity to know whether John, his friend and companion, would *also accompany* him in *death*, and therefore asks οὗτος δὲ τί, where must be supplied ποιήσει, which may mean, "What shall he do, i. e. suffer? (for ποιῶ has often the sense of πάσχω) i. e. what shall be his fate?"

22. ἐὰν αὐτὸν θέλω, &c.] Here, again, the sense is obscure, for the very same reason as before, and consequently has led to a great variety of interpretations; all of them, I conceive, more or less erroneous. To ascertain the true sense, the scope of the words, and their natural import, considered separately and conjointly, must first be ascertained. Now it is evident that our Lord intended a *gentle rebuke* to Peter for his curiosity on a subject which did not concern himself, and into which it was not proper for him to pry. Now τί πρὸς σέ was (as appears from the Classical illustrations of Wets. and Kypke) a frequent form of repressing vain curiosity. The *chief* sense, therefore, to be expressed, seems to be that assigned by Euthym., "Do thou mind thine own concerns: mind thy *own* death, and do not too curiously pry into the manner of that of thy companion." As, however, τί πρὸς σέ is followed by ἐὰν αὐτὸν θέλω μ. ἕ. ἔ., something *more* is intended, which, though phrased (for the same reason as the foregoing intimations) somewhat obscurely, yet, when we consider that the force of this kind of phrase is to *put a negative* on any question asked, and that the scope of Peter's inquiry was to know whether John *too* would suffer martyrdom, the words may reasonably be thought to contain, together with a *mild reproof* for the liberty taken, an *obscure intimation* that he would *not* suffer martyrdom, but continue alive up to — what period? — TILL I COME. Now here was an *ænigma*, but such as the Disciples might, with due attention and consideration, understand; and which, therefore, it is strange that so many of the Commentators should have failed to see. They take this coming of Christ to denote his *final advent* to judge the world; as if this were only a *popular* way of expressing, "If I should choose for him not to *die at all*, what would that be to thee?" But that, I apprehend, would be making the expression *more* ænigmatical than its wording will justify. The coming of Christ must rather denote (as many eminent Expositors suppose) the *coming of Christ in power to execute vengeance on the Jewish nation*. That John lived up to, and far beyond, the entire completion of Christ's judgments on the Jewish nation, is well known. As, however, the disciples did not *then* know of

ὁ Ἰησοῦς, ὅτι οὐκ ἀποθνήσκει· ἀλλ'· Ἐὰν αὐτὸν θέλω μένειν ἕως
ἔρχομαι, τί πρὸς σέ;
24 ΟΥΤΟΣ ἐστιν ὁ μαθητὴς ὁ μαρτυρῶν περὶ τούτων, καὶ γράψας
25 ταῦτα· καὶ οἴδαμεν ὅτι ἀληθής ἐστιν ἡ μαρτυρία αὐτοῦ. [o] ἔστι δὲ καὶ [o] Supra 20. 30.
ἄλλα πολλὰ ὅσα ἐποίησεν ὁ Ἰησοῦς ἅτινα ἐὰν γράφηται καθ' ἕν, οὐδὲ
αὐτὸν οἶμαι τὸν κόσμον χωρῆσαι τὰ γραφόμενα βιβλία. Ἀμήν.

this advent of our Lord, but only of the *final* one, it is no wonder that they should have *then* understood it of the *other*, and consequently supposed that he would not die at all.

24, 25. Several eminent Critics and Commentators, even those who receive all the rest of the Chapter, regard these verses as not from the Evangelist, but an addition from another hand,—probably John the Presbyter. This they are induced to suppose, partly from the change of persons in οἴδαμεν, and partly by a fancied dissimilarity to the style in the preceding verse. The latter, however, is but a weak argument, and the former has not much force; though it has been but faintly rebutted by the defenders of the authenticity of the verses; who so distrust their own arguments, as to propose no less than *four conjectures*, all of them without any countenance from the MSS., and two of which introduce bad Greek! It is strange that the impugners of these verses should not have seen, that, if the rest of the Chapter be (as it *certainly is*) from the Evangelist, so *must*, at least, the clause οὗτος—γράψας ταῦτα; for this would be *requisite* to form any *conclusion* (and that these verses, which Kuin. calls a *corollarium*, were meant to do so is pretty clear), and would be a very proper one. But if *that* clause be from St. John, so probably must the *next*, since it is strongly confirmed by an altogether kindred passage at xix. 35. Nor is there any such difficulty in οἴδαμεν as to be fatal to the authority of the clause; since it may be taken, not *per enallagen*, as many contend, for it would rather be οἶδε; but, as some eminent Critics maintain, *communicative*, i. e. to include the disciples and first Christians in general: q. d. "*It is known.*" Indeed, from *whom* can this clause and the next verse have proceeded, if *not* from St. John? The *Bishops of the Churches of Asia*, say the first-mentioned Critics. But St. *John's* assertion could not *need* the support of *their* testimony. Besides, the singular οἶμαι, in the next verse (which cannot be taken for *sanè*, because it is nowhere so used in the Scriptures), forbids this notion. Are we, then, to consider the last verse as an addition by some hand different from that of the preceding clause? That involves a great improbability; for surely there would *seem* to be no need of any addition, at least not to the *reader*; though the *author* might see the thing in a different view. Upon the whole, there is not the slightest reason for supposing that the verse came from any other than the *Evangelist*, who seems to have intended it as a *supplement* to what was said at xx. 30.

The words οὐδὲ αὐτὸν οἶμαι — βιβλία are (as the best Critics and Commentators have been long agreed) an Oriental and hyperbolical mode of expression, to represent that the miracles, the remarkable actions and discourses of Jesus, were exceedingly numerous. Of this kind of speaking many examples are adduced by Bp. Pearce from the Scriptural and the Classical writers. And two are cited by Wets. from the Rabbinical writers, so similar, that one might almost suppose this to have been a common Jewish phrase. To the above I have, in Recens. Synop., added others from Eurip. Hipp. 1248. Æschyl. Pers. 435. and Eurip. Menalipp. frag. 3. οὐδ' ἅπας ἂν οὐρανὸς, Διὸς γραφέντος τὰς βροτῶν ἁμαρτίας, ἐξαρκέσειεν. I would now subjoin Philo Jud. p. 123. D.

It must be observed, that at ver. 24. the τούτων has reference to the events of this Chapter; and the ταῦτα, to those of the rest of the Gospel. At ἄλλα πολλὰ is plainly to be supplied ἃ οὐκ ἔστι γεγραμμένα ἐν τῷ βιβλίῳ τούτῳ. To *these* allusions are occasionally found. Compare Matt. xi. Acts xx. 35; and see a learned tract of Zornius de ἀγράφοις *Christi dictis*. We have, however, reason to acquiesce in the providence of Him who "doeth all things well." Every important purpose, in a work meant for the *people at large* rather than the *learned*, is accomplished by the Gospels in their present state. Had they recorded *all* the words and actions of Christ, or even any considerable part, they would have been, as the Evangelist perhaps means to intimate, too voluminous for a *manual* adapted to ordinary use. Enough is recorded to direct our faith, and regulate our practice: *more* would have been superfluous, and in some respects, have defeated the purpose in view.

ΠΡΑΞΕΙΣ ΤΩΝ ΑΓΙΩΝ

ΑΠΟΣΤΟΛΩΝ.

I. *ΤΟΝ μὲν πρῶτον λόγον ἐποιησάμην περὶ πάντων, ὦ Θεόφιλε,* 1
ὧν ἤρξατο ὁ Ἰησοῦς ποιεῖν τε καὶ διδάσκειν, ἄχρι ἧς ἡμέρας ἐντειλά- 2

This important book forms the grand connecting link of the Gospels with the Epistles, being a sort of *appendix* to the former, and *introduction* to the latter, and is therefore indispensably necessary to a right understanding of *both.* That St. Luke was the author, is plain both from what is said at the commencement, and from the similarity of the style with that of the Gospel; besides the unanimous testimony of early Fathers. Insomuch that some have conjectured that the Gospels and the Acts formed only *two parts* in *one* general work. Of the *genuineness* of the present production we have the amplest proof in the testimonies of the earliest Christian Fathers; insomuch that this has never been disputed. The *time* when it was published we are better enabled to ascertain than that of any other book in the N. T. Considering that the history therein contained is brought down to the second year of St. Paul's imprisonment, it could not have been written before A. D. 63; and as it makes no mention of St. Paul's death, it is most likely to have been written before that event. And learned men in general assign A. D. 63 as the time of its publication. Though, indeed, from the date of the present book depending upon the date of St. Luke's Gospel (on which see the Introduction), and that of St. Paul's death, which is not thoroughly ascertained, — the point admits not of certain determination. It is probable that the latter end of A. D. 65, or the beginning of A. D. 66, is the true date, i. e. if St. Paul perished, not in the persecution which arose immediately after the great fire at Rome, in Oct. A. D. 64, but (as some think, on the testimony of Clemens Rom.) about two years after. If, however, St. Paul perished in the persecution of the autumn of A. D. 64, that will throw back the period; though probably not further than the earlier part of 64. Dr. Burton, indeed, thinks the Acts were written at Rome, during St. Paul's first imprisonment at Rome, between 56 and 58, and published in 58; for otherwise Luke would have said more of St. Paul's history. That, however, will depend upon whether Luke intended to give a history of the evangelical labours of the Apostle.

The *Canonical authority* of this book is connected with that of the *Gospel,* on which see the Introduction, and that to St. Mark. To turn to the *contents,* which will be best appreciated by adverting to the *purpose* of the work; it is plain that St. Luke did not intend to write a regular history of the rise and progress of the Christian Church, for thirty years after the Ascension, but only what the French call *Mémoires pour servir à l'histoire.* The design of the writer seems to have been *two-fold;* 1st, to give an authentic account of the communication of the Holy Spirit on the day of Pentecost, and of the miraculous powers and supernatural gifts bestowed by the Spirit on the first preachers of the word and professors of the Gospel. Also, 2dly, to present such an authentic narrative of the early progress of the Gospel, as should establish the full claim of the Gentiles to be admitted into the Church of Christ — a claim even yet disputed by the Jews. And, in a general way, to afford matter of confirmation to the accounts in the Gospel, and supply irrefragable evidence of the Divine origin of the Christian religion. To advert to the Book itself — there is a manifest attention paid to chronological order; and some epochs being *fixed* by their combination with certain political events, there is little difficulty in determining the dates of almost all the events recorded in this book, with the exception, however, of those which took place between the years 33 and 34, and between 44 and 60, on which, and the chronology of the Book in general, see Bp. Marsh's Michaelis, vol. iii. P. 1. p. 336 — 338, and especially Hug's Introd. to the N. T. vol. ii. p. 312 — 334.

The *style* of this book is neat, and differs not materially from that of the later Greek writers in the Alexandrian and the *κοινὴ διάλεκτος.* On the *phraseology,* and the *peculiar terms, &c.,* see Schleiermacher's Essay on the Gospel of Luke, and the review of it in Brit. Crit., said to be by Dr. Burton. Of the *place* where the work was

μενος τοῖς ἀποστόλοις διὰ *Πνεύματος* ἁγίου, οὓς ἐξελέξατο, ἀνελήφθη.
3 Οἷς καὶ παρέστησεν ἑαυτὸν ζῶντα, μετὰ τὸ παθεῖν αὐτὸν, ἐν πολλοῖς
τεκμηρίοις, δι' ἡμερῶν τεσσαράκοντα ὀπτανόμενος αὐτοῖς καὶ λέγων τὰ
4 περὶ τῆς βασιλείας τοῦ Θεοῦ. [p] Καὶ συναλιζόμενος παρήγγειλεν αὐτοῖς p Luke 24. 49. John 14. 26. & 15. 26.
ἀπὸ Ἱεροσολύμων μὴ χωρίζεσθαι, ἀλλὰ περιμένειν τὴν ἐπαγγελίαν τοῦ
5 Πατρὸς, ἣν ἠκούσατέ μου. [q] ὅτι Ἰωάννης μὲν ἐβάπτισεν ὕδατι, ὑμεῖς q Matt. 3. 11. Mark 1. 8. Luke 3. 16.
δὲ βαπτισθήσεσθε ἐν *Πνεύματι* ἁγίῳ οὐ μετὰ πολλὰς ταύτας ἡμέρας. John 1. 33. infra 2. 4.
6 Οἱ μὲν οὖν συνελθόντες ἐπηρώτων αὐτὸν, λέγοντες· Κύριε, εἰ ἐν τῷ & 11. 16. & 19. 4.

written we have no certain information. It was probably *Achæa*, where, I conjecture, St. Luke chiefly resided after the year 58, and where Ecclesiastical tradition tells us that he died.

C. I. 1. Πρῶτον is for πρότερον; a use (as also that of the Latin *primus* for *prior*) frequent in the best writers. Λόγος, in the sense *narrative of words* or actions, *history*, occurs frequently in the Classical writers, and in the N. T. at Acts v. 24. John iv. 39. Hence historians were anciently called λογοποιοί; and λόγον ποιεῖσθαι signified to *compose a history*. This use of μὲν not followed by δὲ often occurs in the Classics, especially at the *beginning* of a work. By πάντων must be understood all things necessary to be revealed. See John xx. 30. sq.; xxi. 25. Ὧν for ἃ. by a common idiom, usually referred to the principal *Attraction*, on which see Alt's Gram. N. T. p. 89. The ἤρξατο is supposed by the Commentators, to be pleonastic, as in Mark vi. 7. Matt. xii. 1. and often elsewhere. But it is, properly speaking, never pleonastic. In several of those passages it signifies, "took in hand;" and in others, including the present, it has an *intensitive* force, intimating the great labour, difficulty, or importance of the work in question.

2. ἄχρι ἧς ἡμέρας — ἐξελέξατο.] Most of the later Commentators construe διὰ Πν. ἁγ. with ἐξελέξατο; the ancient and earlier moderns take them with ἐντειλάμενος; and rightly; for according to the former mode, there is some *violence* done to the construction. Διὰ πν. ἁγ. signifies "by means of the Holy Spirit." Here, as in some other passages, what our Lord taught and did is, with reference to his human nature, attributed to the Holy Spirit. Ἐντειλάμενος need not be confined to *any one direction*; but may be extended to *all* the injunctions given to them for the right discharge of their Apostolic office. See Matt. xxviii. 19. Mark xvi. 15—19.

3. παρέστησεν ἑ. ζ.] "proved or evidenced himself to be alive." This use of παριστάναι, which occurs also at xxiv. 13., is frequent in the Classical writers, and arises from that *physical* sense by which the word signifies to *place any thing down by another*. Τεκμηρίοις, "clear and evident proofs." Δι' ἡμερῶν τεσσ., i. e. at intervals during that period, and on no less than *eight* different occasions; 1. to Mary Magdalene and the other Mary; (Matt. xxviii. 1—9.) 2. to the two disciples on their way to Emmaus; (Luke xxiv. 15.) 3. to Peter; (Luke xxiv. 35.) 4. to ten of the Apostles; (Thomas being absent) (Luke xxiv. 36. John xx. 19.) 5 to the Eleven Apostles; (John xx. 26.) 6. to seven of the Apostles in Galilee, at the sea of Tiberias; (John xxi. 4.) 7. to James; (1 Cor. xv. 7.) 8. when the Apostles and Disciples were assembled together, and when he led them out as far as Bethany, (Luke xxiv. 50.) from whence he ascended to heaven in the presence of above 500 brethren at once, 1 Cor. xv. 6. On the present passage see Bp. Atterbury's Sermon, vol. i. p. 173, entitled, "Some Reasons assigned for our Saviour's appearing *chiefly* to his Apostles after his resurrection, and his manner of conversing with them represented."

"Our Lord (says Schoettg.) employed these 40 days in conversing with his disciples on all matters relating to the Constitution of the Christian Church to be planted and established among the Gentiles: 1. concerning *doctrines*, inculcating anew the instruction hitherto delivered to them, which, that it might be the more impressed on their memories, was afterwards *confirmed* at the effusion of the Holy Spirit. (See John xiv. 26.) 2. He gave them injunctions concerning the *rites* and *ceremonies* to be observed in the Church; as, for instance, in what manner the Sacraments were to be celebrated, the mode and time of assembling together," &c.

4. συναλιζόμενος.] Some MSS. have συναυλ., which is preferred by several Critics, but without reason; for its authority is very slender, and it is evidently a *gloss* on the received reading, which is rather difficult, and therefore variously interpreted. The ancients, and earlier moderns, in general explain it "*convescens*," by a derivation from ἅλς or ἅλας; the later Commentators, *conveniens* cum illis, deriving it from ἀλὴς *confertim*; taking it in a neuter sense. The former signification is of slender authority, and here unsuitable. The latter is greatly preferable, and is confirmed by many passages of the Classical writers adduced by the Commentators; e. gr. Herodot. i. 62. οὗτοι μὲν δὴ συνηλίζοντο. and v. 15. The construction is: ἁλιζόμενος σὺν αὐτοῖς, παρήγγειλεν (αὐτοῖς). Wakef. well renders: "During these communications with them." In χωρίζεσθαι we have another example of passive in a neuter sense.

— ἐπαγγελίαν τοῦ Πατρὸς] i. e. the promised gift of the Father, the Holy Spirit. See ii. 13. It was promised in the prophecies of the O. T. See Joel ii. 28. Ἣν ἠκούσατε, "which ye have lately heard of from me." Sub. ἐκ or παρά. See John xiv. 26. xv. 26. xvi. 7. Luke xxiv. 49. Here is a transition from the *oratio indirecta* to the *directa*; an idiom peculiar to the popular style in modern languages, though occasionally found in the best *ancient* writers.

5. Πνεύματι ἁγίῳ.] This must mean (especially as there is no Art.) the *influence* of the Holy Spirit. Βαπτισθ. suggests the *abundance* of the thing. q. d. "ye shall be plenteously imbued with the influences of the Holy Spirit."

6. εἰ.] Some of the Commentators explain *el num*; others, *annon*. The former is the more accurate version, and is supported by the Pesch. Syr. Version. This peculiar use of the particle seems to have arisen from a blending of the ora-

χρόνῳ τούτῳ ἀποκαθιστάνεις τὴν βασιλείαν τῷ Ἰσραήλ; Εἶπε δὲ πρὸς 7
αὐτούς· Οὐχ ὑμῶν ἐστι γνῶναι χρόνους ἢ καιροὺς, οὓς ὁ Πατὴρ ἔθετο
r Infra 2. 2. ἐν τῇ ἰδίᾳ ἐξουσίᾳ· ʳ ἀλλὰ λήψεσθε δύναμιν, ἐπελθόντος τοῦ ἁγίου 8
Πνεύματος ἐφ᾽ ὑμᾶς· καὶ ἔσεσθέ μοι μάρτυρες ἔν τε Ἱερουσαλὴμ καὶ
s Mark 16. 19. Luke 24. 51. [ἐν] πάσῃ τῇ Ἰουδαίᾳ καὶ Σαμαρείᾳ, καὶ ἕως ἐσχάτου τῆς γῆς. ˢ Καὶ 9
ταῦτα εἰπὼν, βλεπόντων αὐτῶν ἐπήρθη, καὶ νεφέλη ὑπέλαβεν αὐτὸν
ἀπὸ τῶν ὀφθαλμῶν αὐτῶν. Καὶ ὡς ἀτενίζοντες ἦσαν εἰς τὸν οὐρανὸν, 10
πορευομένου αὐτοῦ, καὶ ἰδοὺ, ἄνδρες δύο παρειστήκεισαν αὐτοῖς ἐν
ἐσθῆτι λευκῇ, οἳ καὶ εἶπον· Ἄνδρες Γαλιλαῖοι, τί ἑστήκατε ἐμβλέποντες 11
εἰς τὸν οὐρανόν; οὗτος ὁ Ἰησοῦς ὁ ἀναληφθεὶς ἀφ᾽ ὑμῶν εἰς τὸν
οὐρανὸν οὕτως ἐλεύσεται ὃν τρόπον ἐθεάσασθε αὐτὸν πορευόμενον εἰς
τὸν οὐρανόν. Τότε ὑπέστρεψαν εἰς Ἱερουσαλὴμ ἀπὸ ὄρους τοῦ καλου- 12
μένου Ἐλαιῶνος, ὅ ἐστιν ἐγγὺς Ἱερουσαλὴμ, σαββάτου ἔχον ὁδόν.

tio *directa* with the *indirecta*. According to the rules of regular composition, it would have been written *ἐπηρώτων εἰ ἀποκαθιστάνει*, or *ἀποκαθιστάνοι*. So Mark viii. 25. *ἐπηρώτα αὐτὸν, εἰ βλέπει τι*, and Acts xvii. 11. *ἀνακρίνοντες, εἰ ἔχοι ταῦτα*. There is another example of this idiom at vii. 1. *εἶπε δὲ ὁ ἀρχιερεύς· εἰ ἄρα ταῦτα οὕτως ἔχει*; and xxii. 27. *λέγε μοι, εἰ σὺ Ῥωμαῖος εἶ*.

Most Commentators either consider *ἐν τῷ χρόνῳ τ.* as pleonastic, or as serving to express anxiety or disapprobation. But the meaning intended seems to be simply this: "is the time now come for thy restoring," &c. Ἀποκαθιστάναι signifies properly to restore any thing, which has suffered change, to its former state; and it is not unfrequently used (as here and in Matt. xvii. 11. and Mark ix. 12.) of restoring a ruined kingdom or government to its ancient form, and there is usually implied some *improvement* upon that. Indeed, the Apostles seem to have thought that Christ would *then* restore the kingdom of Judæa to its former consequence, and would conjoin with it a spiritual kingdom, spoken of by the Prophets; (see Is. i. 26. ix. 7. Jer. xxiii. 6. xxxiii. 15—17. Dan. vii. 13. sq. Hos. iii. 4. sq. Am. ix. 11. Zach. ix. 9. sq.) and accordingly, that the Gentiles who expected salvation must first embrace Judaism. The answer to this question, though not direct, yet has reference to the words *ἐν τῷ χρόνῳ τ.* which shows that they ought by no means to have been regarded as *pleonastic*.

7. *οὐχ ὑμῶν ἐστι γνῶναι*, &c.] "it is not your business, it is not permitted you to know." Of the terms *χρόνους* and *καιροὺς*, the former denotes *tempus*; the latter, *tempus opportunum*. But with H. Steph., Valckn., and Wakef., they may be taken as put, per hendiadyn, for *opportunos temporum articulos*. But, strictly speaking, the latter term is put by an *epanorthosis* of the former. The whole has the air of a popular mode of speaking, properly used of *soldiers*, who as they know not the *τοὺς καιροὺς τῆς μάχης*, (of which their general alone can judge), ought not to pry into or criticise his plans.

—*ἔθετο ἐν τῇ ἰδίᾳ ἐξουσίᾳ*.] Most Commentators, since the time of Kypke, have assigned as the sense, "hath appointed [i. e. determined] by his own power." But this mode of interpretation is somewhat harsh; and there is no good ground to abandon the old one, "hath put in his own power," which seems to be a *popular* form of expression for "placed at," or "reserved in," "his own disposal;" which, however, cannot imply that Christ was *ignorant* of them, but that they were *secrets* reposed with the Father, which the Son was not authorized to disclose.

8. *δύναμιν*] here denotes the miraculous gifts of the Spirit; for (as Whitby truly observes) *δύναμις* in the N. T., when it relates to God the Father, Christ, or the Holy Ghost, imports some miraculous, or extraordinary power. Compare Luke xxiv. 50. Many Commentators, take *ἐπελθ. τοῦ ἁγ. Πν.* with *δύναμιν*, as in regimen with it. But I doubt whether the proprietas linguæ will permit this: and it is *forbidden* by *ἁγ. Πν.* being here plainly taken in the *personal* sense. Comp. Luke i. 35. The phrase *ἕως ἐσχάτου* (scil. *μέρους*) *τῆς γῆς* was probably understood by the Disciples that part of the East only — as Syria. But Christ, no doubt, meant it of the *whole world*, (as Ps. xix. 5. Is. xlix. 6.) agreeably to his Father's promise, Ps. ii. 8., of "giving Him the heathen for His inheritance, and the uttermost parts of the earth for his possession."

9. *καὶ νεφέλη ὑπέλ.*] "And [then] a cloud received him." Ὑπέλαβε is not, as some imagine, for *ἀνέλ.*; but there is a signif. prægn. for *ὑπῆλθε καὶ ἀπέλαβε*, *susceptum abstulit*.

10. *ἀτενίζοντες ἦσαν*] "were fixedly gazing." See Note on Luke xxii. 54. Ἀτενίζ. must be construed, not as Kuin. says, with *πορευομένου*, but with *εἰς τὸν οὐρ.*, as is plain from the other passages of the N. T. where the word occurs.

—*παρειστήκεισαν*] "came and stood by." They seem to have appeared suddenly and preternaturally (see Note on John xxi. 4.), and were, no doubt, angels in the form of men.

11. *ἑστήκατε ἐμβλέπ.*] as in amazement and awe. This sense is in some measure inherent in *ἑστηκέναι*; but is generally *expressed* by added words, as in a kindred passage of Aristoph. cited by Valckn. *τί πάσχετ᾽, ἄνδρες; ἕστατ᾽ ἐκπεπληγμένοι*.

—*οὗτος — ἐλεύσ.*] Namely, visibly and in the clouds. See Dan. vii. 13. Matt. xxiv. 30.

12. Ἐλαιῶνος.] These forms in —*ὼν* Bp. Blomfield (on Æschyl. Prom. 667.) thinks are derived from the Genit. plural of the primitive noun; and Valck. regards the form as having a *collective* force, and importing *plenty*.

—*σαββάτου ἔχον ὁδόν*.] Mr. Valpy pronounces that *ἔχον* is *not* for *ἀπέχον*; but that it signifies *being*, *consisting of*. That, however, yields a

13 *Καὶ ὅτε εἰσῆλθον, ἀνέβησαν εἰς τὸ ὑπερῷον οὗ ἦσαν καταμένοντες,
ὅ τε Πέτρος καὶ Ἰάκωβος, καὶ Ἰωάννης καὶ Ἀνδρέας, Φίλιππος καὶ
Θωμᾶς, Βαρθολομαῖος καὶ Ματθαῖος, Ἰάκωβος Ἀλφαίου καὶ Σίμων ὁ
14 Ζηλωτὴς, καὶ Ἰούδας Ἰακώβου. Οὗτοι πάντες ἦσαν προσκαρτεροῦντες
ὁμοθυμαδὸν τῇ προσευχῇ καὶ τῇ δεήσει, σὺν γυναιξὶ καὶ Μαρίᾳ τῇ μητρὶ
τοῦ Ἰησοῦ, καὶ σὺν τοῖς ἀδελφοῖς αὐτοῦ.*
15 *ΚΑΙ ἐν ταῖς ἡμέραις ταύταις ἀναστὰς Πέτρος ἐν μέσῳ τῶν μαθητῶν
16 εἶπεν· (ἦν τε ὄχλος ὀνομάτων ἐπὶ τὸ αὐτὸ ὡς ἑκατὸν εἴκοσιν·) [t] Ἄνδρες ἀδελφοὶ, ἔδει πληρωθῆναι τὴν γραφὴν ταύτην, ἣν προεῖπε τὸ
Πνεῦμα τὸ ἅγιον διὰ στόματος Δαυῒδ περὶ Ἰούδα τοῦ γενομένου ὁδη-*

[t] Psal. 41. 10. John 13. 18. & 18. 3.

sense quite foreign to the purpose. It is better, with many Commentators, from Chrys. to Kuin., to suppose ἔχον put for ἀπέχον. Of the examples of this idiom adduced by Kuin., the most apposite is a passage from Arrian's Periplus, p. 144, where the island of Orine is said to be τοῦ ἐσωτάτου κόλπου σταδίους ὡς ἐς πέλαγος ἔχουσα διακοσίους: and 171, two emporia are said to be ἀπὸ B. ἔχοντα ὁδὸν ἡμερῶν εἴκοσι. In the former passage we have the ἀπὸ *expressed;* in the latter it is left to be *supplied*. Indeed, in this kind of phrase, *distance*, being *suggested* by the context, is *understood*. A yet more elliptical expression occurs at John xi. 18. ἦν δὲ ἡ Βηθανία ἐγγὺς τῶν Ἰ. ὡς ἀπὸ σταδίων δεκ. where the complete expression would be ἔχουσα ὁδὸν σταδίων ὡς δεκ. ἀπὸ τῶν Ἰ. Also John xxi. 8. οὐ γὰρ ἦσαν μακρὰν ἀπὸ γῆς, ἀλλ' ὡς ἀπὸ πηχῶν διακοσίων, where the complete phrase would be: ἀλλ' εἶχον or ἦσαν for ἀπεῖχον ὁδὸν π. διακ. ἀπὸ τῆς γῆς. A Sabbath day's journey (as determined, not by the Mosaic Law, but by the Rabbies, from a calculation of the greatest distance of any part of the camp of Israel from the tabernacle) was 2,000 cubits, about 7 1-2 stadia.

13. τὸ ὑπερῷον.] This word is not a compound, but a simple, as Valck. observes, and is properly an adjective signifying *upper* with the ellips. of οἴκημα, which is sometimes *supplied*. The Commentators are not agreed whether we are to understand this of an upper apartment of the *Temple*, or of a room in a *private house*. The former view is supported by De Dieu, Hamm., Schoettg., Vitringa, and Krebs. But there is no one reason *for*, and many *against* that opinion. The words following, οὗ ἦσαν καταμένοντες, quite forbid it, and show the truth of the common opinion, that it was a large upper apartment of some *private house*, which served as a common lodging, or oratory, &c.; for all which purposes upper rooms in the Eastern countries have always been, for obvious reasons, preferred. Mede, in his Dissertation on the Churches of the Apostolic times, observes, that "the early Christians not having stately structures as the Church had after the Empire became Christian, were accustomed to assemble in some convenient upper room, set apart for the purpose, dedicated perhaps by the religious bounty of the owner to the use of the Church. Such were distinguished by the name Ἀνώγεον or Ὑπερῷον, and by the Latins *Cœnaculum*, and were generally the most capacious and the highest part of the dwelling, retired, and next to heaven, as having no other room above it."

If we may rely on early Ecclesiastical tradition, in a point where it can hardly be supposed to mislead us, the room in question was the one in which Christ celebrated the last Passover and instituted the Eucharist; also that in which the Holy Ghost descended; where Matthias was chosen the twelfth Apostle, where the seven Deacons were appointed, and where the first council of Jerusalem was held.

14. προσκαρτ. ὁμοθ. τῇ προσ.] Προσκαρτερεῖν is used with a Dative, both of *person*, in the sense to *wait upon* any one, and of *thing*, to *attend closely to* it; a signification found in the Scriptural and the Classical writers. Ὁμοθυμαδὸν is well explained by Suid. and Hesych. ὁμοψύχως. In the Classical writers it signifies ὁμοῦ. The words following καὶ δεήσει are *cancelled* by Griesb., Heinr., and Lachm.; but without sufficient reason. They are found in all the MSS. except six (and those abounding in all sorts of daring alterations): and *internal* evidence is quite in their favour; since it is far more probable that they should have been *struck out* by a few fastidious Alexandrian Critics, as appearing to be useless, (and thus they are considered by some recent Commentators as *pleonastic*,) than that they should have been *added* by *any* persons. For they are not required by the sense, though they serve to *strengthen* it; δέησις signifying supplicatory and earnest prayer. So Heb. v. 6. it is united with ἱκετήρια, and at Eph. vi. 18. with προσκαρτέρησις. Also at Phil. iv. 6. we have προσευχῇ καὶ δέησει, and at 1 Tim. v. 7. πρ. καὶ δ.

Γυναιξὶ must not be rendered (with some) "their wives," but "the women," many of whom, however, were the wives of the Apostles or disciples, and the rest those who had followed Christ out of Galilee, and ministered to him of their substance.

15. ἦν τε ὄχλος — εἴκοσιν.] Ὀνομ. may, with the best Commentators, be taken for *persons*, as in Rev. iii. 4, and often in the Classical writers. By ὄχλος, &c. is only meant the number then present; the disciples at large being far more numerous; about 600, as we have reason to think.

16. In this address Peter proposes to the disciples the choosing of another Apostle in the room of the traitor Judas, to complete the original number. He reminds them that the words, not so much of David, as of the Holy Spirit speaking by David, had been fulfilled. Of which fulfilment he adduces Ps. lxv. 25, and cix. 8. as *examples;* probably having in mind also Ps. xl. 1. 9, and lv. 12; and intimates, that as one Scripture has been fulfilled in the one case, so it now remained to be fulfilled in the *other*, by the business for which

γοῦ τοῖς συλλαβοῦσι τὸν Ἰησοῦν· ὅτι κατηριθμημένος ἦν σὺν ἡμῖν, 17
u Matt. 27. 5. *καὶ ἔλαχε τὸν κλῆρον τῆς διακονίας ταύτης.* (u *Οὗτος μὲν οὖν ἐκτήσατο* 18
χωρίον ἐκ [τοῦ] *μισθοῦ τῆς ἀδικίας, καὶ πρηνὴς γενόμενος ἐλάκησε*
μέσος, καὶ ἐξεχύθη πάντα τὰ σπλάγχνα αὐτοῦ· καὶ γνωστὸν ἐγένετο 19
πᾶσι τοῖς κατοικοῦσιν Ἱερουσαλὴμ, ὥστε κληθῆναι τὸ χωρίον ἐκεῖνο
x Psal. 69. 26. & 109. 8. *τῇ ἰδίᾳ διαλέκτῳ αὐτῶν Ἀκελδαμὰ, τουτέστι, χωρίον αἵματος.)* x *γέ-* 20
γραπται γὰρ ἐν βίβλῳ Ψαλμῶν· Γενηθήτω ἡ ἔπαυλις αὐτοῦ
ἔρημος, καὶ μὴ ἔστω ὁ κατοικῶν ἐν αὐτῇ. καί· Τὴν
ἐπισκοπὴν αὐτοῦ λάβοι ἕτερος. Δεῖ οὖν τῶν συνελθόντων 21
ἡμῖν ἀνδρῶν ἐν παντὶ χρόνῳ ἐν ᾧ εἰσῆλθε καὶ ἐξῆλθεν ἐφ᾿ ἡμᾶς ὁ
Κύριος Ἰησοῦς, ἀρξάμενος ἀπὸ τοῦ βαπτίσματος Ἰωάννου ἕως τῆς 22
ἡμέρας ἧς ἀνελήφθη ἀφ᾿ ἡμῶν, μάρτυρα τῆς ἀναστάσεως αὐτοῦ γενέσθαι
σὺν ἡμῖν ἕνα τούτων. Καὶ ἔστησαν δύο, Ἰωσὴφ τὸν καλούμενον Βαρ- 23
σαβᾶν, ὃς ἐπεκλήθη Ἰοῦστος, καὶ Ματθίαν. Καὶ προσευξάμενοι εἶπον· 24
*Σὺ, Κύριε, καρδιογνῶστα πάντων, ἀνάδειξον * ὃν ἐξελέξω ἐκ τούτων*

they were then assembled. The terms πληρωθ. and προεῖπε περὶ will not permit us to suppose, with most recent Commentators, that what is said by David of his treacherous companion, is here, on account of the coincidence of the cases, applied, by *accommodation*, to Judas: but we must suppose, that what was prophesied by the Holy Spirit was meant *primarily* of *David's* enemies and treacherous companions; but, secondarily and typically, of *Christ's* enemies and treacherous friends. See Doddr. The citations in question substantially agree with the Hebrew and Sept., except that the plural is changed to the singular, because it is applied to *Judas* only. The above principle of accommodation might, indeed, be admitted, if we could, with some recent Commentators, construe πληρωθῆναι with περὶ Ἰούδα. But that is forbidden by the construction; since περὶ Ἰ. plainly belongs to προεῖπε, not to πληρ.: and the term πληρ. is never used with περὶ to mean "in the case of," but with ἐπί. The first of the two passages presents a lively figure of *utter destruction*.

17. Λαγχάνειν signifies properly to *receive by lot*, have allotted to one. The κλῆρον is *not*, as Kuin. imagines, redundant, but signifies *appointment*. The meaning is, the appointment belonging to this ministry, or office.

18. The best Expositors are agreed that this and the next verse are parenthetical, and to be regarded as the words not of Peter but of Luke; who thus introduces some circumstances respecting this treachery; namely, what use he made of the wages of iniquity, and what was his fate. The obscurity of which the Commentators complain, has been chiefly occasioned by the sense at v. 17. being not sufficiently developed. For to assign (with Kuin.) the sense *although* to ὅτι is quite unauthorised. If the Apostle had subjoined the words ἐξ ἧς παρέβη πορευθῆναι εἰς τὸν ἴδιον τόπον, which he does afterwards at v. 25, all would have been plain. It is evident that he had them in *his mind*.

—ἐκτήσατο] i. e. was the means of its being purchased,—namely, by the chief priests. For the best Commentators are agreed, that this is to be referred to that idiom of Scripture by which an action is sometimes said to be *done* by a person who was the *occasion* of its being done. See examples in Recens. Synop. If that be thought harsh, it may be considered as a *figurative catachresis*, by which Judas might be said to have bought the field with the wages of iniquity, by receiving such wages as *would* have bought the field. So 2 Kings v. 26, "Was this a time to receive money and garments: and *olive-yards* and *vineyards*, and sheep and oxen, and men-servants and maid-servants?" On the seeming discrepancy between the account of Judas's manner of death here, and that at Matt. xxvii. 5. ἀπελθὼν ἀπήγξατο, see the Note there. To advert to the phraseology here, πρηνὴς signifies tumbling headlong,—and ἐλάκησε is for διεῤῥάγη or ἐσχίσθη. So Suidas: ἐλάκησε· διεῤῥάγη, and Schol. on Aristoph. Nub. 409. διαλακήσασα· διαῤῥαγεῖσα. Thus λακέω is synonymous with ψοφέω, *crepo*, to crack. So in a kindred passage of Joseph. Bell. vi. 1. 6. καὶ πταίσας πρός τινα πέτραν πρηνὴς ἐπ' αὐτῆς (read αὐτὴν with the best MSS.) μετὰ μεγίστου ψόφου κατέπεσεν. With ἐλάκησε μέσος comp. Plautus Curc. ii. 1. 7. Hoc metuo, ne *medius disrumpar*. On the difficulty in πρηνὴς—σπλάγχνα αὐτοῦ, see Note on Matt. xxvii. 5.

20. Ἐπισκοπὴ here signifies any office committed to one's charge.

21. τῶν συνελθ.] Sub. ἐκ. The sense is, "who have associated with us," formed part of the same society. In εἰσῆλθε καὶ ἐξῆλθε there is an idiom formed on the Heb. בוא וצאת, equivalent to *versatus est*. (See Acts ix. 28.) It has reference to conduct, manner of life, and administration of office, public and private.

23. ἔστησαν.] See Note infra vii. 59 & 6.

24. καρδιογνῶστα πάντων.] It is not agreed among Commentators whether this appellation be meant of *God*, or of *Christ*. That it is used of God in the O. T., Joseph., and Philo, is granted. But that it is equally applicable to Christ, appears from John xvi. 30, where see Note. See also John i. 48—50. ii. 24. vi. 69. xxi. 17. Apoc. ii. 23. Κύριος, too, was a common appellation of Christ, and, besides that the connection with ver. 21 seems to determine it to be meant of Christ, there would be peculiar propriety in addressing this prayer to Him, as the Head of the Church, and who originally appointed the other Apostles.

—ἀνάδειξον.] The term is often used of ap-

25 τῶν δύο ἕνα, λαβεῖν τὸν κλῆρον τῆς διακονίας ταύτης καὶ ἀποστολῆς,
26 ἐξ ἧς παρέβη Ἰούδας, πορευθῆναι εἰς τὸν τόπον τὸν ἴδιον. Καὶ
ἔδωκαν κλήρους αὐτῶν, καὶ ἔπεσεν ὁ κλῆρος ἐπὶ Ματθίαν, καὶ συγκατε-
ψηφίσθη μετὰ τῶν ἕνδεκα ἀποστόλων.
1 II. ΚΑΙ ἐν τῷ συμπληροῦσθαι τὴν ἡμέραν τῆς Πεντηκοστῆς, ἦσαν
2 ἅπαντες ὁμοθυμαδὸν ἐπὶ τὸ αὐτό. Καὶ ἐγένετο ἄφνω ἐκ τοῦ οὐρανοῦ
ἦχος, ὥσπερ φερομένης πνοῆς βιαίας, καὶ ἐπλήρωσεν ὅλον τὸν οἶκον
3 οὗ ἦσαν καθήμενοι. Καὶ ὤφθησαν αὐτοῖς διαμεριζόμεναι γλῶσσαι
4 ὡσεὶ πυρός, ἐκάθισέ τε ἐφ᾽ ἕνα ἕκαστον αὐτῶν. [y] Καὶ ἐπλήσθησαν y Supra 1. 5.
ἅπαντες Πνεύματος ἁγίου, καὶ ἤρξαντο λαλεῖν ἑτέραις γλώσσαις, καθὼς

pointment to office. The reading ὃν ἐξελέξω — ἕνα, for the common one ἐκ τούτων τῶν δύο ἕνα ὃν ἐξελέξω, is found in nearly all the MSS., Versions, and the Edd. up to Stephens, and is received by every Editor from Beng. to Scholz.

25. καὶ ἀποστολῆς.] This is exegetical of τῆς διακονίας just before. Παρέβη, abandoned, deserted; by a metaphor taken from a traveller who deserts the right road. Comp. 2. Pet. ii. 15. A very rare use, but of which I can adduce *one* example, namely, Joseph. Antiq. xiv. 9. 2. οὐδὲν πρὸς Ὑ. εὐνοίας καὶ πίστεως παρέβη.

— πορευθῆναι — ἴδιον.] On the sense of these words there have been many different opinions, which see detailed and reviewed in Recens. Syn. I still think the common interpretation (by which τὸν τόπον τὸν ἴδιον is taken to mean the place *suited* to him, — namely, the place of destruction) is alone the true one, as being recommended by its simplicity and suitableness to the usage of the Jewish writers, and confirmed by several passages of the Apostolic Fathers.

26. ἔδωκαν κλήρους.] The exact *mode* in which they cast the lots cannot be determined; various being the methods by which the ancients were wont to do it. They used to cast slips of parchment, or pieces of the *tabulæ scriptoriæ*, with the names inscribed, into an urn. And this kind of *sortitio* most Commentators here understand. Now the lots are said to be *theirs* on whom the lots are cast, and *fall* upon him who comes off successful in the *sortitio*. Συγκαταψηφίζειν properly denotes "to choose by common suffrages," and then "to number with or unto," συγκαταριθμεῖν. This deciding of a thing by casting lots was understood to be a mode of showing the will of the Almighty; and was, therefore, from the earliest times, resorted to in the creation of kings or the appointment of priests. See the numerous Classical citations in Recens. Synop., and compare Levit. xvi. 8. Numb. xxvi. 54. Josh. xiii. 6. On the appointment of Matthias, see a dissertation of Mr. Towns. Chr. Arr. ii. p. 9. sqq.

II. 1. συμπληροῦσθαι.] See Note on Luke ix. 51. At πεντηκοστῆς the Commentators suppose an ellip. of ἡμέρας, or ἑορτῆς. But there is perhaps no ellipse at all; πεντηκ. being a *substantive* and an appellative. This will afford a solution to several difficulties which perplexed Kuin.

— ἦσαν ἅπαντες.] The Commentators are not agreed *who* are here meant. Some say the *Apostles* only; others, the *disciples at large*, mentioned at i. 15. The *latter* is undoubtedly the true opinion. For (as Kuin. observes) the *subject* at i. 15. is the assembly of the 120 disciples whom Peter addressed, and from whom Matthias was taken into the Apostolic body; while the eleven Apostles are only mentioned *en passant* Now with the *predicate*, which is destitute of a subject, the subject immediately antecedent, and not that of which mention was made *en passant*, but *professedly*, ought to be taken. This, too, is clear from ἅπαντες, not οὗτοι, being used. Besides, the absence of the rest of the disciples on so solemn a festival cannot be supposed.

2. ὥσπερ φερομ. πνοῆς β.] Comp. the *luctantes venti tempestatesque sonoræ* of Virgil. This use of φέρεσθαι and its compounds, of the rushing of winds, and associated with πολλὸς, βίαιος, and other adjectives of similar signification, is frequent in the Classical writers.

— τὸν οἶκον] doubtless the ὑπερῷον supra i. 13., where see note.

3. διαμεριζόμεναι.] Not *cloven* (which sense would have required διασχιζόμεναι), but *distributed*, Vulg. *dispertitæ*, *divided*. As to the exact *mode* in which this took place there has been much said, but to little purpose. To refer it to *lightning*, or *electricity*, or to resolve all into Oriental metaphor, and Jewish notions, were alike unwarrantable.

— γλῶσσαι πυρὸς] i. e. pointed flames; the top of a flame of fire being called a *tongue*. So fire is sometimes in Hebrew said to *lick up* what it consumes. At ἐκάθισε some would supply πνεῦμα taken from πνεύματος. Kuin., however, with reason, objects that the phrase πνεῦμα ἅγ. ἐκάθισε is unexampled. He might have added, that πνεῦμα cannot be taken from πνεύματος afterwards, because that is not in the same sentence; for, notwithstanding what some think, a new one commences at καὶ ἐπλήσθ. Besides, *there* πν. ἁγ. signifies only the *influence* of the Spirit, not the Spirit *personally*. As to the true ellipse, Valckn. alone has seen that ἐκάθισε does *not* belong to γλῶσσαι, or to πυρός; but that we are to supply ἑκάστη, quod evolvendum ex ἕκαστον, as follows: ἐκάθισε (scil. ἑκάστη τῶν γλωσσῶν) ἐφ᾽ ἕνα ἕκαστον αὐτῶν. Thus the sense is: "And there were seen as it were *tongues* of fire, distributing themselves, and settling upon them, one on each." This symbol was meant to typify the gift of tongues, the first fruits of the Spirit.

4. Various are the hypotheses propounded by recent Commentators on the words ἤρξαντο — ἀποφθ. All, however, more or less liable to *insuperable objections*, being contort and far fetched, and such as no person of sober understanding and competent learning, who had no knowledge *except of the passage before him* would ever have thought of. Nor is there any phraseology in Pin-

τὸ *Πνεῦμα* ἐδίδου αὐτοῖς ἀποφθέγγεσθαι. Ἦσαν δὲ ἐν Ἱερουσαλὴμ 5
κατοικοῦντες Ἰουδαῖοι ἄνδρες εὐλαβεῖς ἀπὸ παντὸς ἔθνους τῶν ὑπὸ
τὸν οὐρανόν. Γενομένης δὲ τῆς φωνῆς ταύτης, συνῆλθε τὸ πλῆθος, 6
καὶ συνεχύθη· ὅτι ἤκουον εἷς ἕκαστος τῇ ἰδίᾳ διαλέκτῳ λαλούντων
αὐτῶν. Ἐξίσταντο δὲ πάντες καὶ ἐθαύμαζον, λέγοντες πρὸς ἀλλήλους· 7
Οὐκ ἰδοὺ πάντες οὗτοί εἰσιν οἱ λαλοῦντες Γαλιλαῖοι; καὶ πῶς ἡμεῖς 8
ἀκούομεν ἕκαστος τῇ ἰδίᾳ διαλέκτῳ ἡμῶν ἐν ᾗ ἐγεννήθημεν, — Πάρθοι 9
καὶ Μῆδοι καὶ Ἐλαμῖται, καὶ οἱ κατοικοῦντες τὴν Μεσοποταμίαν,
† Ἰουδαίαν τε καὶ Καππαδοκίαν, Πόντον καὶ τὴν Ἀσίαν, Φρυγίαν τε 10
καὶ Παμφυλίαν, Αἴγυπτον καὶ τὰ μέρη τῆς Λιβύης τῆς κατὰ Κυρήνην,

dar himself more lyrical than the high-wrought figure thus ascribed to a plain prose narration. Surely so magnificent and august a *preparation* as the preternatural appearance of the tongues of fire, and the ὤφθησαν αὐτοῖς διαμεριζόμεναι γλῶσσαι ὡσεὶ πυρὸς, *suggests the idea* of something *miraculous*, and not that they only *prayed* and *preached with unusual flow of language and fervour*. And indeed the conversion of the 3000 *supposes* something *miraculous* to have taken place.

The ancient and common interpretation, then, can alone be the true one, which assigns to ἑτέραις γλώσσαις the sense "languages *other than* those which they were acquainted with," i. e. "such as they were ignorant of." This is confirmed by the words following καθὼς, &c., where the supporters of the hypotheses above mentioned are compelled to assign to καθὼς the unauthorized sense *postquam, quoniam*, or *nam*. Ἀποφθέγγεσθαι (as the best Commentators have shown) is used of profound and sententious, and *also* of divinely inspired and prophetic, language.

5. κατοικοῦντες.] These were not, (as some imagine) *proselytes*, but *foreign Jews*; pious men, who had taken up their sojourn, or residence at Jerusalem, for the purpose of those greater facilities for religious duties which the place afforded, and because the advent of the Messiah was then expected. On this distinction between εὐσεβὴς and εὐλαβὴς, see Tittm. de Synon. p. 147. seq. The words ἀπὸ παντὸς, &c., are admitted to be hyperbolical; this being (as Mr. Scott observes) a general, not an universal proposition.

6. τῆς φονῆς ταύτης.] The Commentators are not agreed to what to refer this φωνή. Some think it has reference to the ἦχος at v. 2. But that is too remote, and the sense yielded is very unsuitable. It is *better*, with others, to suppose φωνῆς put for φήμης; a sense often occurring in the LXX. Thus ταύτης will be for περὶ τούτου. As, however, this is somewhat harsh, I prefer to take φωνῆς (with the ancient Versions, and Pisc., Menoch., Wakef., and Kuin.) of the noise produced by the multitude praying or conversing together, and, no doubt, in great commotion. This is confirmed by the words following.

— συνεχύθη] "was thrown into great perplexity." This was their *first* feeling. Their *second* was extreme amazement and astonishment. In ἐξίσταντο and ἐθαύμαζον the latter term is rather exegetical of the former.

7. Γαλιλαῖοι.] The sense is: "They were amazed at seeing persons nearly all of one country, (Galilee, as understood) and that a rustic and illiterate one, *all* speaking *foreign languages*, and addressing each of them in his own tongue."

8. ἐν ᾗ ἐγεννήθημεν.] This seems to be a *popular phrase*, for the adjective ἐγγενεῖ, *indigenous*, or *native*. The perplexity of construction in the words following, is best removed by the mode of punctuation which I have, with Knapp and Tittm., adopted. Sub. ὄντες. Render, "We, I say, who are Parthians." At ἀκούομεν there is a *repetition*, in order to clear the sense, long suspended by the interposed portion at vv. 9. and 10.

9. Ἰουδαίαν.] At this word Commentators and Critics, with reason, stumble; for what *Judæa* can here have to do, it is not easy to see. As to the defence set up for it by some Commentators, it proceeds on the *supposition* that the language of Judæa was a *different* one from the Galilæan; whereas there is great reason to think that the latter differed from the former only as the English of Middlesex differs from that of Somersetshire or Cornwall.

Besides, the air of the whole list is that of a list of *foreign* nations. Upon the whole, it is plain that Ἰουδαίαν cannot be accounted for in any satisfactory way; and must (as it is done by the most eminent Critics) be regarded as corrupt. Are we, then, to *cancel* it? In the first edition of this work I expressed it as my opinion that the word came from the *margin*. Yet, as it is difficult to *account* for it as a *gloss*; and as *such* a gloss was little likely to have crept into *all* the MSS., I must abandon that position; and am now fully persuaded, that the reading is simply *corrupt*, and probably to be emended from some hitherto uncollated MSS. In the mean time, I have little doubt but that the true reading is (according to the conjecture of Barthius, *which also occurred to myself*), Ἰδουμαίαν, which word bears a striking resemblance to the common reading: for Δ and M are perpetually confounded; and it is plain that part of the M being faded off, would leave a Λ; and the abbreviation for δου [δȣ] is very similar to ου. In fact, that the words Ἰουδαίαν and Ἰδουμαίαν are often confounded, I have already shown; and many instances could I adduce from Josephus. By *Idumæa* we may understand that tract of country situated on the other side of Jordan, and south-east of Judæa, which was sometimes called Arabia Petræa: and so the word is sometimes used in *Josephus*. And we know that Damascus was now in possession of Aretas, king of Arabia P. There is indeed the greatest reason to think, that the territory subject to him also extended to that part of Arabia which was N. E. from Judæa, and would thus be almost conterminous with Mesopotamia. And it is plain that the countries are mentioned in geographical order, *from East to West*.

10. κατὰ Κυρήνην] i. e. belonging to Cyrene.

11 καὶ οἱ ἐπιδημοῦντες Ῥωμαῖοι, (Ἰουδαῖοί τε καὶ προσήλυτοι), Κρῆτες
καὶ Ἄραβες,—ἀκούομεν λαλούντων αὐτῶν ταῖς ἡμετέραις γλώσσαις τὰ
12 μεγαλεῖα τοῦ Θεοῦ; Ἐξίσταντο δὲ πάντες καὶ διηπόρουν, ἄλλος πρὸς
13 ἄλλον λέγοντες· Τί ἂν θέλοι τοῦτο εἶναι; ἕτεροι δὲ ‡ χλευάζοντες
ἔλεγον· Ὅτι γλεύκους μεμεστωμένοι εἰσί.

14 Σταθεὶς δὲ Πέτρος σὺν τοῖς ἕνδεκα, ἐπῆρε τὴν φωνὴν αὐτοῦ, καὶ
ἀπεφθέγξατο αὐτοῖς· Ἄνδρες Ἰουδαῖοι καὶ οἱ κατοικοῦντες Ἱερουσαλὴμ
ἅπαντες, τοῦτο ὑμῖν γνωστὸν ἔστω, καὶ ἐνωτίσασθε τὰ ῥήματά μου.
15 Οὐ γάρ, ὡς ὑμεῖς ὑπολαμβάνετε, οὗτοι μεθύουσιν· ἔστι γὰρ ὥρα
16 τρίτη τῆς ἡμέρας. [a] ἀλλὰ τοῦτό ἐστι τὸ εἰρημένον διὰ τοῦ προφήτου [a] Joel 2. 28.
17 Ἰωήλ· Καὶ ἔσται ἐν ταῖς ἐσχάταις ἡμέραις [[λέγει ὁ
Θεός,]] ἐκχεῶ ἀπὸ τοῦ πνεύματός μου ἐπὶ πᾶσαν σάρ-

The Classical writers use the phrase, but with πρός; of which I have adduced examples in Recens. Synop.; as also one from Malchus with κατά. By οἱ ἐπιδημοῦντες Ῥ. are denoted those Jews who were settlers at Rome; which is rendered plain by the added words Ἰουδαῖοι, &c., indicating that they were Jews by descent, or by adoption and religious conversion. So Ἀντιοχεῖς occurs in Josephus for *Antiochian Jews*.

11. τὰ μεγαλεῖα.] See Note on Luke i. 49.

12. διηπόρουν.] Διαπορεῖν is a stronger term than ἀπορεῖν, and signifies "to be utterly at a loss what to do." By πάντες are meant the persons just mentioned, namely, the foreign Jews: to whom are, in the next verse, opposed the ἕτεροι, meaning those of Judæa. Τί ἂν θέλοι τοῦτο εἶναι, is a *popular* idiom (of which examples are adduced by Wets.) denoting, "what may this mean?" how has it arisen?

13. χλευάζοντες.] The word is best derived from χέλυς, synonymous with χεῖλος, *the lip*; and signifies to thrust out the lip, as in Ps. xxii. 7.

For χλευάζ. a few ancient MSS. and some Fathers have διαχλ., which is received by almost every Editor from Griesb., downwards, but without reason; for the *external* evidence for the new reading is very weak, and the *internal* evidence not strong. Simple verbs are not unfrequently changed into compounds, to communicate a stronger sense, or for greater elegance. Or the διά may have arisen from the δὲ preceding. Besides, χλευάζω occurs more than once elsewhere in this Book, and often in the LXX.; διαχλ., neither in the N. T. nor the LXX.

—γλεύκους.] Not, new-*made* wine, which is the *proper* signification of the word (for that is forbidden by the *time of year*); but *new*, i. e. sweet wine, which is very intoxicating. This was, as Markl. observes, a sneer on the meanness of their condition, since no person of respectability tapped the last year's γλεῦκος so early as June, unless compelled by necessity.

14. σὺν τοῖς ἕνδ.] Namely, to show their consent and concurrence in what Peter should say, who was to be spokesman. The force of the Article will be expressed by rendering: "the *other* eleven."

— ἄνδρες Ἰουδαῖοι.] Some recent Commentators maintain, that only the *substance* of the address is recorded, and that many things are omitted which were said by the Apostle. The *former* position *may* be true; but the *latter* is more than can safely be affirmed. At least an *inspired* writer cannot be supposed to omit any thing necessary to be recorded. Ἐνωτίσασθε, "receive into your ears," "hearken attentively to." An Hellenistic and Alexandrian word often occurring in the LXX. and the later Greek writers.

15. Ὥρα τρίτη.] Before that time none but debauchees took strong drink, and few took food or drink of *any kind*.

16. τοῦτό ἐστι.] The complete sense is: "this [state of things] is [a fulfilment of] what was predicted," &c.

17—21. A citation from Joel ii. 28—32., (in the Hebrew, iii. 1—5.) but with some slight difference. The chief difference is in ἐν ταῖς ἐσχάταις ἡμέραις being used for μετὰ ταῦτα, on which see further on. The words λέγει ὁ Θεός are not a part of the quotation; but are an *insertion by Luke*, to indicate the *person* who says this. I have expressed this by double brackets, thus distinguishing such insertions from words or clauses whose authenticity is doubtful. The two last clauses of v. 17. are *transposed*,—probably by citing from memory. At v. 18. γε is inserted, which strengthens the sense; for καί γε (which sometimes occurs in the Classical writers) signifies *quinetiam*. The words καὶ προφητεύσουσι are added (from the preceding context) by way of explanation. Finally, at v. 19. the words ἄνω and κάτω are added to strengthen the sense; accordingly, they are often found joined to ἐν οὐρανῷ and ἐπὶ τῆς γῆς, in the O. T. See Exod. xx. 4. Josh. ii. 11. The passage contains (as the Jewish Interpreters themselves admit) a highly figurative description of the state of things, which shall precede and accompany the coming of the Messiah; namely, by an extraordinary outpouring of the Spirit. But Peter himself did not *then* understand the full sense of the prophecy as regarded "all flesh," i. e. men of all nations, both Jews and Gentiles. אחרי־כן, rendered by the LXX. μετὰ ταῦτα, is admitted by Kimchi to be equivalent to the Hebrew words corresponding to ἐν ταῖς ἐσχάταις ἡμέραις in other passages of the LXX.; and that is universally granted by the *Jewish* Commentators to denote the times of the Messiah. Ἀπὸ τοῦ πνεύματος is said to be for πνεῦμα, as in the Hebrew. But it rather seems to be a slight *alteration* agreeably to the *sense* rather than the words, i. e. *a portion of my Spirit*. What kind of spiritual effects are meant, is clear from the following verses. Ἐκχεῶ is, like the correspondent terms in Greek and Latin, used to suggest the *exuberance* of the gifts

κα· καὶ προφητεύσουσιν οἱ υἱοὶ ὑμῶν καὶ αἱ θυγατέρες ὑμῶν· καὶ οἱ νεανίσκοι ὑμῶν ὁράσεις ὄψονται,
καὶ οἱ πρεσβύτεροι ὑμῶν ἐνύπνια ἐνυπνιασθήσονται.
Καί γε ἐπὶ τοὺς δούλους μου καὶ ἐπὶ τὰς δούλας μου, 18
ἐν ταῖς ἡμέραις ἐκείναις, ἐκχεῶ ἀπὸ τοῦ πνεύματός
μου, καὶ προφητεύσουσι. Καὶ δώσω τέρατα ἐν τῷ 19
οὐρανῷ ἄνω, καὶ σημεῖα ἐπὶ τῆς γῆς κάτω, αἷμα καὶ
πῦρ καὶ ἀτμίδα καπνοῦ. Ὁ ἥλιος μεταστραφήσεται 20
εἰς σκότος, καὶ ἡ σελήνη εἰς αἷμα, πρὶν ἢ ἐλθεῖν τὴν
a Rom. 10. 13. ἡμέραν Κυρίου τὴν μεγάλην καὶ ἐπιφανῆ. [a]Καὶ ἔσται, 21
πᾶς, ὃς ἂν ἐπικαλέσηται τὸ ὄνομα Κυρίου, σωθήσεται.
b Infra 10. 38. [b]Ἄνδρες Ἰυραηλῖται, ἀκούσατε τοὺς λόγους τούτους· Ἰησοῦν τὸν 22
Ναζωραῖον, ἄνδρα ἀπὸ τοῦ Θεοῦ ἀποδεδειγμένον εἰς ὑμᾶς δυνάμεσι
καὶ τέρασι καὶ σημείοις, (οἷς ἐποίησε δι' αὐτοῦ ὁ Θεὸς ἐν μέσῳ ὑμῶν,
καθὼς καὶ αὐτοὶ οἴδατε,) τοῦτον τῇ ὡρισμένῃ βουλῇ καὶ προγνώσει 23

imparted. Πᾶσαν σάρκα seems to mean some of all orders and ranks, and (in a secondary sense) of *all nations*. See Whitby.

— προφητ.] This must, in the full sense, denote *speaking under Divine inspiration*, whether by prophesying, (the strict sense), or otherwise. See xxi. 9. and Matt. vii. 22. This, of course, includes all the lower degrees of the προφητεία, (as in Rom. xii. 6. 1 Cor. xii. 10. xiii. 2.) to denote speaking and teaching the truths of the Gospel, exhorting, &c.; though even there *inspiration is implied*. The next clause denotes in general, that God would also reveal his will to both old and young, in a manner which partook of the προφ. just before mentioned, namely, by *visions* and *dreams*.

The terms προφητεία and ὅρασις are sometimes synonymous; but here ὅρασις is equivalent to ὀπτασία; in either of which an appearance is presented to the person, whether waking or by trance; whereas, ἐνύπνιον is always a dream. in which something is preternaturally suggested to the mind. Thus at 1 Sam. iii. 1. ὅρασις διαστέλλουσα denotes a *distinct revelation* by supernatural appearance, in opposition to the *less direct* revelation by dreams or otherwise. With respect to the present passage, the ὅρασις was fulfilled in the case of St. Paul; the ἐνύπνια in that of St. Peter. What is said at v. 19. was signally fulfilled by the communication of the Spiritual Gifts, mentioned in the Acts of the Apostles and Epistles.

19, 20. From these verses we are only to infer that the events here predicted will take place at *the times* of the Messiah. But whether they are to be referred to the *first* advent of our Lord at the destruction of Jerusalem, or his *second* at the day of judgment, Commentators are not agreed. They are exactly parallel to, and admit of, nay perhaps require, the same mode of explication as Matt. xxiv. 29. Luke xxi. 25., where see Notes. Αἷμα καὶ πῦρ are a formula exactly parallel to our *fire* and *sword*. The ἀτμίδα καπνοῦ is *graphic*, and completes the *picture* of devastation. Ἡμέραν ἐπιφανῆ denotes a day notable for the visitation of God's punishment on the guilty, and therefore *terrible*, as the Hebrew is rendered; though the former sense is assigned to the word נורא in *other* passages

21. πᾶς ὃς — σωθήσεται.] The best Commentators are agreed, that ἐπικ. τὸ ὄνομα here denotes religious invocation, as a disciple of Christ, by embracing his religion. Σωθ. denotes not temporal deliverance, (to which many recent Commentators confine it), but spiritual deliverance, by being received into the Gospel covenant, and thereby put into the way of salvation.

22. The Apostle, after having shown that a *Saviour* had been promised, who should save to the uttermost his faithful worshippers, proceeds to turn their attention to the grand subject of his discourse; showing that Jesus of Nazareth, whom they have crucified, is that personage, — that he was proved to be such by his resurrection to life; and pointing out the *purposes* for which he was raised from the dead. On this is engrafted a notice of the validity of the general *evidence* in favour of Jesus's Messiahship, and the nature of that evidence. Then is subjoined that this Jesus it is, thus raised and invested with supreme dignity, who hath procured this plenteous effusion of the Holy Spirit, as attested by the effects which they now see and hear. Of Him, too, the words of Ps. cx. 1. are meant; which their own Rabbis referred to the Messiah. Hence (the Apostle concludes) they may be assured that this Jesus, whom they have crucified, is the Lord and Christ appointed of God.

But to consider the passage in detail, the Apostle addresses them by the appellation *Israelites*, as the most conciliatory he could select. Ναζωραῖον is subjoined to Ἰησοῦν, because in mentioning his name thus formally, it was proper to add, what had indeed become a usual *appellative*. See Mark xvi. 6. Acts iii. 6. x. 38. and Note on John i. 45. xix. 19.

— ἄνδρα ἀπὸ — δυνάμεσι.] The construction is: ἄνδρα ἀποδ. εἰς ὑμᾶς ἀπὸ Θεοῦ, "a man approved to you on the part of God [to be a Divine Legate] by signs," &c. Of this sense of ἀποδ., by which it means to *demonstrate* or *evince*, examples are adduced from the Classical writers, by Kypke. Δυνάμεσι, τέρασι, and σημείοις, are nearly synonymous, but combined to *strengthen* the sense; as including every sort of *supernatural* work.

23. τῇ ὡρισμένῃ βουλῇ καὶ προγνώσει.] The best Commentators are agreed, that ὡρισμ. βουλῇ means

τοῦ Θεοῦ ἔκδοτον λαβόντες, διὰ χειρῶν ἀνόμων προσπήξαντες ἀνείλετε·
24 [c] ὃν ὁ Θεὸς ἀνέστησε, λύσας τὰς ὠδῖνας τοῦ θανάτου, καθότι οὐκ ἦν c Infra v. 32. & 3. 15.
25 δυνατὸν κρατεῖσθαι αὐτὸν ὑπ' αὐτοῦ. [d] Δαυὶδ γὰρ λέγει εἰς αὐτόν· & 4. 10. & 10. 40.
Προωρώμην τὸν Κύριον ἐνώπιόν μου διὰ παντὸς, ὅτι & 13. 30, 34. & 17. 31. Rom. 4. 24.
26 ἐκ δεξιῶν μου ἐστὶν, ἵνα μὴ σαλευθῶ· διὰ τοῦτο εὐ- & 8. 11. 1 Cor. 6. 14.
φράνθη ἡ καρδία μου, καὶ ἠγαλλιάσατο ἡ γλῶσσά & 15. 15. 2 Cor. 4. 14. Gal. 1. 1.
μου· ἔτι δὲ καὶ ἡ σάρξ μου κατασκηνώσει ἐπ' ἐλπίδι. Eph. 1. 20. Col. 2. 12.
27 Ὅτι οὐκ ἐγκαταλείψεις τὴν ψυχήν μου εἰς ᾅδου, οὐδὲ 1 Thess. 1. 10. Heb. 13. 20. d Psal. 16. 8.
28 δώσεις τὸν ὅσιόν σου ἰδεῖν διαφθοράν. Ἐγνώρισάς
μοι ὁδοὺς ζωῆς· πληρώσεις με εὐφροσύνης μετὰ τοῦ
29 προσώπου σου. [e] Ἄνδρες ἀδελφοὶ, ἐξὸν εἰπεῖν μετὰ παῤῥησίας πρὸς e 1 Kings 2. 10. infra 13. 36.
ὑμᾶς περὶ τοῦ πατριάρχου Δαυὶδ, ὅτι καὶ ἐτελεύτησε καὶ ἐτάφη, καὶ τὸ

the determinate, and consequently, immutable counsel of God; and that προγνώσει signifies *decree;* a signification common both to Hellenistic and Classical Greek. Ἔκδοτον δοῦναι or λαβεῖν denotes *to give up*, or *receive, at discretion, to treat at one's pleasure*. The expression διὰ χειρῶν ἀνόμων as conjoined with τῇ ὡρισμ. βουλῇ—Θεοῦ, is meant to suggest, that God's counsels and decrees did not absolve the Jews of guilt in putting Jesus to death, since they were still free agents. Some render "the hands of the sinners," i. e. the Gentiles. But that sense would require τῶν ἀνόμων. Προσπήξαντες scil. σταυρῷ is added to show that the putting to death was by the most cruel and ignominious mode.

24. λύσας τὰς ὠδῖνας τοῦ θαν.] The best Commentators, ancient and modern, are of opinion that ὠδῖνας denotes not *pains*, but *bonds;* a signification, indeed, scarcely known in the Classical writers, but occurring in the LXX. This interpretation, they say, is supported by the following λύσας, and especially by κρατεῖσθαι, and is confirmed by certain passages cited by Wets. But that λύσας may only mean *removed*, without any allusion to a *bond*, is clear from what I have annotated on the words λύσειν τῶν δειμάτων in Thucyd. ii. 101. Engl. Transl. It is best, therefore, to retain the common version *pains*, and merely suppose that in κρατεῖσθαι there is an *allusion* to the notion of *tight bands*, as in Ælian, H. A. 12. 5. τοὺς τῶν ὠδίνων λύσαι δεσμούς. The common version is, I find, retained and well defended by Tittm. de Syn. p. 196.

— οὐκ ἦν δυνατόν.] Inasmuch as He had life in Himself, John v. 26., and was the "Prince of life." For the δυν. is taken in a popular sense, to denote, as Scott explains, "impossible, consistently with the dignity of His Person, the nature of His undertaking, the perfecting of His work, the purpose of God, and the predictions of Scripture."

25. εἰς αὐτόν] "concerning," or "with reference to" him. Whether this reference be *primary* or *secondary*, Commentators are not agreed. The most eminent Interpreters have long been of opinion, that this 16th Psalm has in many of its parts a *double* sense, one *Historical*, of David, the other *mystical* and *allegorical*, of Christ. Be that as it may, the latter, if secondary in *order*, is primary in *importance*. It should seem that David spoke in the person of the Messiah.

— προωρώμην.] Προορᾶσθαι here signifies "to be so mindful of as to set always before us." The Aorist is expressive of what is perpetually and habitually done. By *the Lord* is meant his power to save. The words ὅτι ἐκ δεξιῶν μου ἐστὶν are intended to show in what light the Lord is considered,—namely, as *a helper*. Of these some think an allusion to those παράκλητοι, who stood as any one's supporters when he was brought to trial, we may compare the παρακελευστοὶ καθήμενοι mentioned in Thucyd. vi. 13. Ἵνα μὴ σαλ., "that I should not succumb or fall under calamity."

26. εὐφράνθη ἡ καρδία μου.] This and ἠγαλλ. ἡ γλῶσσά μου are meant to denote *extreme joy*, both heartfelt and expressed. Ἐπ' ἐλπ., namely, of being raised. See Rom. viii. 21.

27. εἰς ᾅδου] scil. δόμον, or οἶκον. See Notes on Matt. xvi. 18. Luke xviii. 23. v. 31. Οὐδὲ δώσεις, "nor wilt thou suffer." For διδόναι, like the Heb. נתן, denotes sometimes not a *physical*, but a *moral* giving. Τὸν ὅσιόν σου. This, by permission, is usually rendered "Thy pious worshipper;" a sense which may very well suit *David*, but not *Christ*, with reference to whom the sense must be, "me who am pre-eminently the *Holy one;* and *thine*, as united to Thee in the Godhead." Ἰδεῖν διαφθοράν, "to experience putrefaction," i. e. to lie so long as to be exposed thereto.

28. ἐγνώρισας—ζωῆς.] Render, "thou hast made known (i. e. opened for us) paths of life," i. e. the means of avoiding permanent death, and attaining unto life. The next clause adverts to the state of glory, and the fulness of joy which should succeed to that "earthly race which was set before him;" after which he should sit down at the right hand of God, and be blessed with his immediate presence.

29. The Apostle now proceeds to establish an argument (resting on the position that the *Messiah* is meant in the Psalm in question); and this he does by tacitly encountering an objection which might be made—q. d. These are the words of *David*, and are to be understood of *him*. In answering which the Apostle introduces the mention of David in very respectful language, calling him Patriarch. "I may be permitted (says he) freely to tell you concerning the Patriarch David, that he both died and was buried, and his sepulchre remains unto this day." And as David died, was buried, and his body experienced corruption, so it followed that, in the passage adverted to, he could not have spoken of *himself*.

f 2 Sam. 7. 12. 1 Chron. 22. 10. μνῆμα αὐτοῦ ἐστιν ἐν ἡμῖν ἄχρι τῆς ἡμέρας ταύτης. [f] Προφήτης οὖν 30
Ps. 132. 11. infra 13. 34. ὑπάρχων, καὶ εἰδὼς ὅτι ὅρκῳ ὤμοσεν αὐτῷ ὁ Θεὸς, ἐκ καρποῦ τῆς
ὀσφύος αὐτοῦ [τὸ κατὰ σάρκα ἀναστήσειν τὸν Χριστὸν,] καθίσαι ἐπὶ
g Psal. 16. 10. infra 13. 35. τοῦ θρόνου αὐτοῦ, [g] προϊδὼν ἐλάλησε περὶ τῆς ἀναστάσεως τοῦ Χριστοῦ, 31
ὅτι οὐ κατελείφθη ἡ ψυχὴ αὐτοῦ εἰς ᾅδου, οὐδὲ ἡ σὰρξ αὐτοῦ εἶδε
διαφθοράν. Τοῦτον τὸν Ἰησοῦν ἀνέστησεν ὁ Θεὸς, οὗ πάντες ἡμεῖς 32
ἐσμεν μάρτυρες. Τῇ δεξιᾷ οὖν τοῦ Θεοῦ ὑψωθεὶς, τήν τε ἐπαγγελίαν 33
τοῦ ἁγίου Πνεύματος λαβὼν παρὰ τοῦ Πατρὸς, ἐξέχεε τοῦτο ὃ νῦν
h Psal. 110. 1. ὑμεῖς βλέπετε καὶ ἀκούετε. [h] Οὐ γὰρ Δαυῒδ ἀνέβη εἰς τοὺς οὐρανοὺς, 34

30. In this and the next two verses the Apostle draws tight the argument. The sense may be thus expressed: "Now he being a Prophet (i. e. one endowed with a supernatural knowledge of future events), and, in that quality, knowing that God had sworn a solemn oath to him, that from the fruit of his loins (i. e. from his posterity) Christ should, as to his human nature, descend, in order to sit on his throne; he, foreseeing this event, spoke (in the passage in question) of the resurrection of *Christ*, when he said that his soul," &c. On this promise see 2 Sam. vii. 11—16, and the other passages adduced in the references. The expression ὅρκῳ ὤμοσε, as applied to God, denotes only "His fixed and immutable purpose," *sanctissimè promisit.*

The words τὸ κατὰ σάρκα — Χριστὸν were rejected by Mill and Beng., and cancelled by Griesb. and Knapp. But the authority for this omission is exceedingly small — only that of three MSS.; for the reading of the Cod. Cantab. is *ex emendatione.* And that the words were formerly in that MS. is plain, from their being found in the venerable *Latin Version* which accompanies the MS. Of the three MSS. which are said not to have the words, the Barb. 1. is of no authority. The other two (the Cod. Alex. and the Cod. Ephr.) are very ancient MSS., but bear perpetual marks of the liberties taken with them by some Biblical Critics of an early period. The words are found in *all* the *other* MSS. (not very far short of 200) including the most ancient of MSS., the *Cod. Vaticanus*, and (as we have seen) the *Cod. Cantab.* Thus the *external* evidence for the omission in question is exceedingly slight. As to the *internal*, it is far more probable that the words should have been omitted in two or three MSS. by accident, or perhaps removed designedly by Pelagians, than that they should have been foisted into *all the other* MSS. The evidence, indeed, of the *Versions* may seem more in favour of the omission. But let us examine. Those Versions are the printed Syriac (Peshito), the Vulg., Copt., Æthiop., Arm., and Arab. of Erpenius. Now though the *printed* Syriac has them not, yet the MSS., I am told, *have*. And, at all events, the authority of the Syriac in the *Acts* and *Epistles* is far inferior to that in the Gospels; it being supposed to be of a more modern date, and to have been sometimes altered from the Vulg. The authority of the *Vulg.* may *seem* weighty; but it is, in fact, not so in cases like the present, where it is unsupported by the ancient *Italic.* And that the words were in *that* Version, is plain from what is brought forward by Sabatier. See Matthæi and Nolan, p. 390. The authority of the *other* Versions is but slender. As to the *Fathers*, some of them, indeed, adduce the verse without the words in question. But others (as Theophyl., Theodoret, and especially Chrysost.) cite the verse *with* those words. And in the Fathers the evidence for *insertion* is much stronger than for *omission;* since citing, as they perpetually do, *from memory*, they often omit words, especially such as are not to their purpose. Heinrichs and Kuin., indeed, seek an argument for their omission, from the words being variously placed in the MSS. But the truth is, that in only some two or three MSS. is there a transposition, evidently from the carelessness of scribes; which, of course, *proves nothing.* As to their argument, that the omission of the words produces a *more difficult* reading, and therefore the more likely to be genuine, it is of greater weight, but by no means conclusive; for even *that* Critical Canon has its exceptions. It cannot, for instance, well apply to cases like the present, where the more difficult reading is found only in *two* or *three* MSS. out of a very great number; for then it is more probable that the reading in question arose from *alteration*, than that a false reading should have crept into all the other MSS. And if those *few* MSS. be such as abound in unauthorised and rash alterations of all sorts, the suspicion of alteration in such a case is greatly increased. However, I mean not to say that the words can *positively* be asserted to be genuine. We must be slow to impute *bad faith*, unless on the strongest evidence: and as the words, if removed by the Alexandrian Critics, must have been removed in order to suppress an evidence to the Divinity of Christ (a stigma which we are not enabled to fix on these persons), so I am induced to hesitate; and have therefore placed the words within *single* brackets. The *insertion* of the words may be accounted for without supposing any bad faith on the part of those who introduced them; since they might be brought in *gradually*, first Χριστὸν, then ἀναστήσειν, and lastly τὸ κατὰ σάρκα from the margin, where it had perhaps been noted from Rom. ix. 5. ὧν οἱ πατέρες καὶ ἐξ ὧν ὁ Χριστὸς τὸ κατὰ σάρκα. And indeed there is something to countenance this in the MSS.

32. τοῦτον τὸν Ἰ. &c. The *evidence* for this resurrection is now touched on, by adverting not only to the positive testimony of the Apostles, disciples, and other eye-witnesses (as contrasted with a *want* of evidence for the assertion of the Jews, that he *did* see corruption, and did *not* rise), but to that testimony of his resurrection (and consequent Messiahship) afforded by his exaltation to the right hand of God; by his having obtained (agreeably to the promise) the sending of the Holy Spirit and the copious effusion of his gifts; producing effects such as they now see and hear, and which, by their miraculous nature, attest the Messiahship of Him who procured them.

λέγει δὲ αὐτός· Εἶπεν ὁ Κύριος τῷ κυρίῳ μου, Κάθου
35 ἐκ δεξιῶν μου, ἕως ἂν θῶ τοὺς ἐχθρούς σου ὑποπό-
36 διον τῶν ποδῶν σου. Ἀσφαλῶς οὖν γινωσκέτω πᾶς οἶκος Ἰσραὴλ,
ὅτι Κύριον καὶ Χριστὸν αὐτὸν ὁ Θεὸς ἐποίησε τοῦτον τὸν Ἰησοῦν, ὃν
ὑμεῖς ἐσταυρώσατε.
37 Ἀκούσαντες δὲ κατενύγησαν τῇ καρδίᾳ, εἶπόν τε πρὸς τὸν Πέτρον
38 καὶ τοὺς λοιποὺς ἀποστόλους· Τί ποιήσομεν, ἄνδρες ἀδελφοί; Πέτρος
δὲ ἔφη πρὸς αὐτούς· Μετανοήσατε, καὶ βαπτισθήτω ἕκαστος ὑμῶν
ἐπὶ τῷ ὀνόματι Ἰησοῦ Χριστοῦ, εἰς ἄφεσιν ἁμαρτιῶν· καὶ λήψεσθε
39 τὴν δωρεὰν τοῦ ἁγίου Πνεύματος. Ὑμῖν γάρ ἐστιν ἡ ἐπαγγελία καὶ
τοῖς τέκνοις ὑμῶν, καὶ πᾶσι τοῖς εἰς μακρὰν, ὅσους ἂν προσκαλέσηται
40 Κύριος ὁ Θεὸς ἡμῶν. Ἑτέροις τε λόγοις πλείοσι διεμαρτύρετο καὶ
41 παρεκάλει, λέγων· Σώθητε ἀπὸ τῆς γενεᾶς τῆς σκολιᾶς ταύτης. Οἱ
μενοῦν ἀσμένως ἀποδεξάμενοι τὸν λόγον αὐτοῦ ἐβαπτίσθησαν· καὶ
προσετέθησαν τῇ ἡμέρᾳ ἐκείνῃ ψυχαὶ ὡσεὶ τρισχίλιαι.

34. *οὐ γὰρ Δαυῒδ, &c.*] *Δαυῒδ* is emphatical; and (as Mr. Holden observes) the Apostle's argument is this: That David speaketh concerning the *Messiah* (as cited ver. 25 et seq.) is clear from Ps. cx. 1, where he speaks of A LORD who was to be at God's right hand till all his enemies were subdued. For that patriarch is not raised from the dead, and "ascended into the heavens" to God's right hand, therefore he must have spoken this of some *other* person, namely, of Jesus Christ, "who hath shed forth this which ye now see and hear." The concluding words suggest the certainty of their own ruin, if they continued to reject Jesus Christ.

36. Here we have the *conclusion*,—that this same Jesus whom they had crucified was the divinely constituted Lord and Christ.

37. *κατενύγησαν τῇ καρδίᾳ*] "were pierced at the heart." *Κατανύσσεσθαι* signifies to be *pricked through*, and is used of the emotions of violent grief or remorse, whether *expressed* in words, or *silent*. See Ecclus. xii. 12. xx. 21. xlvii. 21. Susan. 11. Ps. iv. 5. Wets. and Kypke adduce several Classical examples; of which, however, two only are quite apposite,—namely, Simplicius on Epict. *ὡς τοὺς μὴ πάντως νενεκρωμένους νύττεσθαι ἐκ τῶν λόγων.* Plutarch. de Animi tranq. p. 476, where he says that the conscience of evil doers *τῇ ψυχῇ μεταμέλειαν αἱμάσσουσαν ἀεὶ καὶ νύσσουσαν ἐναπολείπει.* I would add from Liban. *τούτοις κεντοῦμαι τὴν ψυχήν.*

38. *μετανοήσατε.*] This repentance is supposed to include *reformation*, by an abandonment of their Jewish prejudices, and by acknowledging Jesus as the Messiah, and embracing his religion in baptism, and thereby engaging to observe all his injunctions, both of belief and practice. Comp. infra iii. 19. and Bp. Bull's Harm. Apost. p. 9.

—*τὴν δωρεὰν τοῦ ἁγίου Πνεύμ.*] By this seems to be here chiefly meant, not the *miraculous gifts* before adverted to, but, as appears from what follows, the ordinary aids and influences of the Spirit given to every man to profit withal.

39. *ὑμῖν—ἡ ἐπαγγ.*] "to you belongs the promise," namely, of sending the Spirit. *Πᾶσι τοῖς εἰς μακ.* must, notwithstanding the dissent of some, mean the *Gentiles*, as aliens from the commonwealth of Israel. See x. 45. xi. 15—18. xiv. 27. xv. 3. Eph. ii. 12. seq. These the Apostles *then* thought would be received into the Messiah's kingdom by becoming proselytes to the Jewish religion. See iii. 25. *Προσκαλ.*, "shall or may call," namely, by the preaching of the Gospel.

40. *διεμαρτύρετο καὶ παρ.*] "did he earnestly charge and exhort." See 1 Tim. v. 21.

—*σώθητε*] "save yourselves," suffer yourselves to be saved, or put into the way of salvation. *Σκολιᾶς* signifies *perverse* and generally *wicked*, by a metaphor taken from what is *crooked* as opposed to *straight*. The phrase is borrowed from Deut. xxxii. 5. *γενεὰ σκολιὰ καὶ διεστραμμένη.*

41. *ἀσμένως.*] This is omitted in a few ancient MSS. and Fathers, and is supposed spurious by some Biblical Critics; but without reason: for it was evidently either omitted by the scribes through inadvertence, or cancelled by the ancient Critics, because it *seems* not very necessary. That, however, is only by regarding the *οἱ* as a *relative;* which yet is not necessary, for *οἱ* is here the article, and is used with *μὲν* as the Classical writers use it with *δέ*. We *may*, then, render: "And they thereupon gladly receiving his word (or exhortation) were baptized;" which is confirmed by the Syriac and Arabic translators. After all, however, it may be best (with our authorized Version), to consider *οἱ* as closely connected with *ἀποδ.*, "those who accepted the offer were baptized." Yet this is passing over the *μὲν οὖν*, which may be rendered *whereupon;* it having a *transitive* and slightly *illative* sense; as ix. 31. xvi. 30. xvii. 30. In which case, and where it signifies *immo*, it should be written *μενοῦν*, to distinguish it from that use where the *μὲν* has *δὲ* corresponding to it. *Ἀποδέχεσθαι*, as used of *things*, signifies to approve, &c., and is often accompanied with *ἀσμένως*.

—*ἐβαπτίσθησαν.*] In the first age of Christianity, those who acknowledged Jesus to be the Messiah were received, by this solemn rite, into the Christian Church; so that a fuller instruction did not *precede*, but *follow* baptism. We need not, however, suppose that *all* were baptized; though 3000 must have formed a very considerable part of the multitude. *Προσετέθησαν*, "sese adjunxerunt?" Pass. for Middle, as often in this word. The use of *ψυχαὶ* for *persons* is common to the

Ἦσαν δὲ προσκαρτεροῦντες τῇ διδαχῇ τῶν ἀποστόλων, καὶ τῇ κοι- 42
νωνίᾳ καὶ τῇ κλάσει τοῦ ἄρτου, καὶ ταῖς προσευχαῖς. Ἐγένετο δὲ πάσῃ 43
ψυχῇ φόβος, πολλά τε τέρατα καὶ σημεῖα διὰ τῶν ἀποστόλων ἐγίνετο.
i Infra 4, 32. [i] Πάντες δὲ οἱ πιστεύοντες ἦσαν ἐπὶ τὸ αὐτὸ, καὶ εἶχον ἅπαντα κοινά· 44
καὶ τὰ κτήματα καὶ τὰς ὑπάρξεις ἐπίπρασκον, καὶ διεμέριζον αὐτὰ πᾶσι, 45

Classical as well as Scriptural writers (see examples in Recens. Synop.) as the Heb. איש נפש. Indeed the idiom is found in all languages.

42. Having recorded the amazing increase to the members of the visible Church, the Apostle takes occasion to notice their manner of living; and by προσκαρτ. τῇ διδαχῇ he intimates that they continued steadfastly to *adhere* to that profession which they so suddenly had taken up; though the words chiefly mean, "they were intently engaged on the Apostles' doctrine."

— ἦσαν προσκαρτ. τῇ διδαχῇ.] So προσκαρτ. τῇ προσευχῇ in Acts i. 14. vi. 4. Rom. xii. 12. Col. iv. 2. On the exact sense of the words following τῇ κοινωνίᾳ — προσευχαῖς considerable difference of opinion exists. Many eminent Expositors, ancient and modern, take κλάσει τοῦ ἄρτου of the *Eucharist;* which opinion may seem confirmed by the preceding τῇ κοινωνίᾳ; that term being frequently used of the Lord's Supper. Thus they in general take τῇ κοινωνίᾳ καὶ τῇ κλάσει, by a Hendiadys, for "the common participation of the Eucharistic bread broken and distributed." And so the Vulgate. Some, however (as the Pesch. Syriac Translator) understand κοιν. of *association for religious purposes:* while most of the recent Commentators understand by κοιν. *social intercourse;* and by τῇ κλάσει τοῦ ἄρτου, the exercise of mutual hospitality; which, they think, is supported by the expression κλῶν ἄρτον at ver. 46. But that sense is little agreeable to the context, which certainly requires something *more.* Nor is there any authority for such a sense of κοινωνία in Scripture; nor perhaps of τῇ κλάσει τοῦ ἄρτου; for ver. 46 (to which they appeal) may very well bear another sense. Some, again, join κοινωνίᾳ with the words *preceding*, namely, τῶν ἀποστόλων, q. d. "in intimate society with the Apostles." A construction most harsh, and a signification unauthorized. It must undoubtedly be taken with what *follows;* and τῇ κοιν. καὶ τῇ κλάσει seems put, by a *hysteron proteron*, for τῇ κλάσει καὶ κοιν.; or, by *hendiadys*, for "a common participation of bread broken." Now this *may* be understood of the *Eucharist:* yet as ver. 46. undoubtedly has reference to the same subject, but certainly *cannot* be so understood, as appears from the words following; so it should seem that in both *that* passage and *this* we are to understand the common participation of meals, taken in charitable communion and religious thankfulness, and followed by prayer. This view is confirmed by what is said at ver. 46. κλῶντές τε κατ' οἶκον ἄρτον, μετελάμβανον τροφῆς ἐν ἀγαλλιάσει καὶ ἀφελότητι καρδίας, αἰνοῦντες τὸν Θεόν. So St. Paul, 1 Tim. iv. 4, 5, says, (with reference, it may be supposed, to these *religious meals*), that every kind of food is good, if it be taken μετὰ εὐχαριστίας· for (he adds) ἁγιάζεται διὰ τοῦ λόγου καὶ ἐντεύξεως. By these religious meals I would not, however, with some, understand the *Agapæ*, or *Love-feasts*, which used to precede the Eucharist. For those, I apprehend, were not yet in being, having, it should seem, originated at a somewhat later period, when the custom of having all things in common, practicable only in a small society, was afterwards discontinued; and in the place of it was substituted a *formal communion*, at *certain stated* religious meals, which preceded the celebration of the Lord's Supper. See Rom. xiii. 6.

43. πάσῃ ψυχῇ] "every person," namely, of the multitude at large, the ὅλον τὸν λαὸν mentioned at ver. 46. Φόβος, "reverential awe."

44. ἦσαν ἐπὶ τὸ αὐτό.] This is generally taken by both ancient and modern Expositors of being collected together for divine worship. And although the great *number* (3120) of the disciples has been urged as an objection to that view; yet we need not suppose all to have been assembled at the same *time*, nor perhaps all at the *same place.* Still a certain degree of harshness attaches to that interpretation; and therefore it seems better (with Theophyl., Beza, Calvin, Pearce, Heumann, and Kuin.) to understand the expression of perfect *unanimity* and concord (as Ps. xxxiv. 4. and elsewhere in the Sept.); a view confirmed by iv. 34. and a passage of Thucyd. i. 79. What, however, is chiefly meant seems to be, that the believers all kept together as a distinct society; which is supported by the words following.

— εἶχον ἅπαντα κοινά.] The earlier Commentators in general understand by this a perfect community of goods; while many recent ones think that the words are to be taken only in a *popular* sense, nearly as the adage πάντα κοινά, as indicating great charity and beneficence. The next verse, however, excludes this latter view; yet it does not necessarily imply an absolute community by distribution. Some of the rich sold their property in part, in order to have more to give immediately to their poorer brethren; but the money accruing from thence did not cease to be at their own disposal. This is plain from iv. 32. v. 4. xii. 12. That *all* did not sell their property is evident from the fact that there were soon afterwards rich and poor among the Christians. See ix. 36. xi. 29. xx. 35. 1 Cor. xvi. 1. Eph. iv. 28. This intercommunity of goods was probably very limited; any sale of property for distribution being far from general, and the distribution itself varying; though the rich, we must suppose, for the most part (influenced by the admonitions of our Lord, as enforced by the Apostles) regarded their wealth as held in trust for the advantage of their fellow Christians. It is plain that this intercommunity of goods was voluntary, limited in operation, and produced by the peculiar circumstances of the infant Church at Jerusalem; composed as it was, in a great measure, of *foreign Jews* sojourning there, and detained by the natural wish of acquiring a thorough knowledge of the religion which they had adopted; and yet whose funds might, by their detention so much longer than they had expected, have fallen short, and thrown them on the charitable assistance of their richer brethren. As to the *native* Jews, the *poorer* converts were peculiarly objects of consideration to their richer brethren; since all charity from those who adhered to the Jewish religion would be denied them; and they would have

46 καθότι ἄν τις χρείαν εἶχε· [k] καθ᾽ ἡμέραν τε προσκαρτεροῦντες ὁμο- [k] Infra 20. 7.
θυμαδὸν ἐν τῷ ἱερῷ, κλῶντές τε κατ᾽ οἶκον ἄρτον, μετελάμβανον τροφῆς
47 ἐν ἀγαλλιάσει καὶ ἀφελότητι καρδίας, αἰνοῦντες τὸν Θεὸν, καὶ ἔχοντες
χάριν πρὸς ὅλον τὸν λαόν. Ὁ δὲ Κύριος προσετίθει τοὺς σωζομένους
καθ᾽ ἡμέραν τῇ ἐκκλησίᾳ.
1 III. ἘΠΙ τὸ αὐτὸ δὲ Πέτρος καὶ Ἰωάννης ἀνέβαινον εἰς τὸ ἱερὸν

scrupled to partake of the relics from the *Temple sacrifices* (which were distributed to the poor.) Nay, their means of supporting themselves might occasionally be taken from them by bigoted employers or customers. Under these circumstances, no relief or support could be expected, except from their Christian brethren; who therefore, it seems, were induced not only to contribute much of their *ready*-money, but, occasionally and in part, to sell their *possessions*. By which, however, we are not to suppose but that they had still a *property* both in the price of what was sold, and in the possessions yet unsold.

45. κτήματα.] This properly denotes possessions or property in general; but here it must be understood of the *bona immobilia* (lands and houses), as ὑπάρξεις of the *mobilia*.

46. προσκαρτ.] Προσκ. is put for προσκ. ταῖς προσευχαῖς, which occurred a little before. Render: "They persevered in attending the Temple service every day," i. e. (as is implied) at the stated hours of prayer.

— κλῶντές τε κατ᾽ οἶκον ἄρτον.] This is by many understood of the Eucharist, or at least of the *agapæ* which preceded the Eucharist: while others understand it of *common meals* taken by companies in certain houses in rotation. And certainly there is much to countenance this in what *follows*. Yet, if we consider the *preceding* words, it will seem more probable that the meals in question were the charitable and religious common meals treated of supra ver. 42. At κατ᾽ οἶκον supply ἕκαστον; an ellipsis frequent in adverbial phrases formed of a noun with κατά. The expressions ἐν ἀγαλλιάσει — καρδίας denote, I conceive, the *disposition of mind* in the partakers, rich and poor respectively. Thus ἀγαλλιάσει seems meant *chiefly*, though not entirely, of the poor; ἀφελότητι, principally, though not exclusively, of the rich. What is meant is, that the rich cordially rejoiced in the exercise of this liberality to the poor; and the poor were sincerely thankful for their liberality. Thus the rich were devoid of grudging or ostentation; the poor, of envy and ill-will.

47. αἰνοῦντες — λαόν.] This *may* signify, in a general way, "They were [in their mode of life] much occupied in prayer, and were in favour with the people." As, however, αἰνοῦντες is grammatically connected with μετελάμβανον, it seems better to suppose the sense to be: "And these common meals (namely those mentioned supra ver. 42.) they held with prayer to God; and by the use of these, and by their general conduct, they were in favour with the people at large," i. e. all except the Rulers, the Priests, and their party.

— προσετίθει τοὺς σωζομένους.] On the exact sense of these words considerable difference of opinion exists. Our authorized Version has "those that should be saved;" which rendering has been animadverted on as if it were *singular*; whereas the same sense is found, I believe, in all the early Versions which preceded it, supported by some Latin ones. But be that as it may, it is now almost universally agreed that this mode of rendering cannot be admitted, since it would require, not σωζομένους, but σωθησομένους. Thus even Calvin renders "qui salvi fierent," which yields a very different sense. The version in question must therefore be rejected, *not because it introduces a Calvinistic doctrine* (see Wets.), but because such a sense cannot be shown to be inherent in the words. The sense "*had* been saved," which some Anti-Calvinistic Commentators propose, is equally inadmissible. Others, as Grot., and Bp. Maltby, render "those who were being saved," namely, by being put into a state of salvation: an interpretation adopted by me in the first Edition of this work. But, on further consideration, I am induced to reject it; not that σώζεσθαι *might not* signify to be put into the way of salvation, if the context permitted or required it, but because such a sense would here be factitious. If we keep close to the *proprietas linguæ* (which, where a *doctrine* is concerned, must be considered the only right course), we cannot translate otherwise than "the saved," "those who were saved," as the expression is rendered by Doddr. and Mr. Wesley (see Horne's Introd. ii. 632.); which is also supported by the authority of the Pesch. Syr. Version. And if the sense be even yet thought *uncertain*, it is *determined* by the word σώθητε supra ver. 40; for the expression must denote those who *hearkened* to the earnest injunction, "Save yourselves from this perverse generation," namely, by abandoning their prejudices, renouncing Judaism, seeking admission into the Christian Church, and thus being saved from their sins by the washing of regeneration, and put into a *state* of salvation; whence, by the grace imparted under the Gospel, they might be *actually* saved both from the guilt and the power of sin. See Dr. A. Clarke, Dr. Hales, and Mr. Gilpin. Thus at 1 Cor. i. 18. and 2 Cor. xi. 15. τοῖς σωζομένοις, those who had received the Christian faith, are opposed, τοῖς ἀπολλυμένοις, to the Jews, who rejected it. Thus it comes to the same thing as their being *put into a state of* salvation. So at Luke xix. 9, our Lord says to Zacchæus: "This day is salvation come to this house." And at 1 Cor. xv. 2, we have δι᾽ οὗ (scil. τοῦ εὐαγγελίου) σώζεσθε. Tit. iii. 5. ἔσωσεν ἡμᾶς διὰ λουτροῦ παλιγγενεσίας, καὶ ἀνακαινώσεως Πνεύματος ἁγίου. also Revel. xxi. 24. καὶ τὰ ἔθνη τῶν σωζομένων ἐν τῷ φωτὶ αὐτῆς περιπατήσουσι.

III. 1. Ἐπὶ τὸ αὐτὸ must here mean *together*, *in company*, and be taken after ἀνέβαινον, "were going up." Sim. Joseph. cited by Krebs, μέχρι Ἀντιοχείας ἐπὶ τὸ αὐτὸ παρῆλθον. The use of ἐπὶ with an Accus. in the sense *to*, is found also in the Classical writers, and especially with nouns of *time*. Τὴν ἐνν. is in apposition with, and exegetical of ὥραν.

ἐπὶ τὴν ὥραν τῆς προσευχῆς, τὴν ἐννάτην. Καί τις ἀνὴρ χωλὸς ἐκ 2
κοιλίας μητρὸς αὐτοῦ ὑπάρχων ἐβαστάζετο· ὃν ἐτίθουν καθ᾽ ἡμέραν
πρὸς τὴν θύραν τοῦ ἱεροῦ τὴν λεγομένην Ὡραίαν, τοῦ αἰτεῖν ἐλεημοσύνην παρὰ τῶν εἰσπορευομένων εἰς τὸ ἱερόν. Ὃς ἰδὼν Πέτρον καὶ 3
Ἰωάννην μέλλοντας εἰσιέναι εἰς τὸ ἱερὸν, ἠρώτα ἐλεημοσύνην λαβεῖν.
Ἀτενίσας δὲ Πέτρος εἰς αὐτὸν σὺν τῷ Ἰωάννῃ, εἶπε· Βλέψον εἰς ἡμᾶς. 4
Ὁ δὲ ἐπεῖχεν αὐτοῖς, προσδοκῶν τὶ παρ᾽ αὐτῶν λαβεῖν. Εἶπε δὲ Πέ- 5
τρος· Ἀργύριον καὶ χρυσίον οὐχ ὑπάρχει μοι· ὃ δὲ ἔχω, τοῦτό σοι 6
δίδωμι. ἐν τῷ ὀνόματι Ἰησοῦ Χριστοῦ τοῦ Ναζωραίου ἔγειραι καὶ
περιπάτει. καὶ πιάσας αὐτὸν τῆς δεξιᾶς χειρὸς ἤγειρε. παραχρῆμα δὲ 7
ἐστερεώθησαν αὐτοῦ αἱ βάσεις καὶ τὰ σφυρά· καὶ ἐξαλλόμενος ἔστη, 8
καὶ περιεπάτει· καὶ εἰσῆλθε σὺν αὐτοῖς εἰς τὸ ἱερὸν, περιπατῶν καὶ
ἁλλόμενος καὶ αἰνῶν τὸν Θεόν. Καὶ εἶδεν αὐτὸν πᾶς ὁ λαὸς περιπα- 9
τοῦντα καὶ αἰνοῦντα τὸν Θεόν· ἐπεγίνωσκόν τε αὐτὸν ὅτι οὗτος ἦν ὁ 10
πρὸς τὴν ἐλεημοσύνην καθήμενος ἐπὶ τῇ Ὡραίᾳ πύλῃ τοῦ ἱεροῦ· καὶ
ἐπλήσθησαν θάμβους καὶ ἐκστάσεως ἐπὶ τῷ συμβεβηκότι αὐτῷ.

Κρατοῦντος δὲ τοῦ ἰαθέντος χωλοῦ τὸν Πέτρον καὶ Ἰωάννην, συνέ- 11
δραμε πρὸς αὐτοὺς πᾶς ὁ λαὸς ἐπὶ τῇ στοᾷ, τῇ καλουμένῃ Σολομῶνος
ἔκθαμβοι. Ἰδὼν δὲ Πέτρος ἀπεκρίνατο πρὸς τὸν λαόν· Ἄνδρες Ἰσ- 12
ραηλῖται, τί θαυμάζετε ἐπὶ τούτῳ, ἢ ἡμῖν τί ἀτενίζετε, ὡς ἰδίᾳ δυνάμει
ἢ εὐσεβείᾳ πεποιηκόσι τοῦ περιπατεῖν αὐτόν; [1] Ὁ Θεὸς Ἀβραὰμ καὶ 13

1 Infra 5. 30.

2. ἐκ κοιλίας μητρὸς] for ἐκ γενετῆς. See John ix. 1. Ἐκ γαστρὸς occurs in the Pseudo-Theogn. v. 307. Ἐβαστάζετο, "was being carried." Ἐτίθουν. The sick and poor were, both among Jews and Gentiles, usually laid, or placed themselves at the portals of the Temples, to ask charity of the worshippers; though sometimes at the gates or doors of rich men. See Luke xvj. 20. and Note.

— Ὡραίαν.] So I write with almost every Editor up to Wets. Those after him write ὡραίαν; but wrongly, I conceive; for Ὡρ. is a *proper name*, being one of that class which become such by an adjective with the Article having so defined some one of a class of things, that it is pointed out as single and apart from the rest. In *that* stage the adjective should be written with a *small* initial letter. But when the Article is *omitted*, it becomes a *proper name*, and consequently must have a capital. *Which* gate of the Temple is here meant, the Commentators are not agreed. It seems to have been either the Eastern gate, leading from the court of the women to that of the Israelites (overlaid with Corinthian brass wrought with consummate skill); or that called *Susan*. Schleusn. observes, that old Constantinople had a gate, which was also called, κατ᾽ ἐξοχὴν, ἡ ὡραία, as we find from Smith's Notitia Const. p. 121. I would add, that such names did not by any means *supersede* the *proper names*. Thus it appears from Spanh. on Julian, p. 75. that Constantinople was sometimes called by the name Καλλίπολις.

— ἐλεημ.] "alms," i. e. the *stips* or sum given; a signification only found in the later Greek writers.

4. ἀτενίσας εἰς αὐτόν.] See Note on Luke xxii. 56.

5. ἐπεῖχεν α.] Sub. ὀφθαλμούς.

6. ὃ δὲ ἔχω, τοῦτό σοι δίδ.] This has the air of a proverbial expression; with which I would compare Aristoph. Lysist. 671. ὅπερ οὖν ἔχω, δίδωμί σοι. Soph. Elect. 450. σμικρὰ μὲν τάδ᾽, ἀλλ᾽ ὅμως ἃ 'χω, δὸς αὐτῷ.

— ἐν τῷ ὀν.] "by the authority of Jesus [I say]."

7. βάσεις.] Some here render the word *planta pedis*; but others, better, *feet*; a signification not unfrequent in the later Greek writers, from whom many examples are adduced. The σφυρὰ are the *ankles* or *instep*.

8. ἐξαλλόμενος.] Not so much for *joy*, as many Commentators imagine; nor, as Œcumen. thinks, to try whether he could walk; but, it should seem, at first from ignorance how to walk, by which his essays would be rather *leaping* than walking; just as the imperfect glimmer of the newly acquired sight of the blind man at Mark viii. 24. made him first "see men as trees walking." Ἐξάλλεσθαι well describes the headlong eagerness of the incipient action, as ἔστη, καὶ περιεπ. the other stages of it: "he first leaped, then stood still, and [then] walked," i. e. in a regular manner. See Note on Acts xiii. 11.

11. κρατοῦντος.] Render, "keeping close to," as in Col. ii. 19. 2 Sam. iii. 6.

12. ἀπεκρ. πρὸς τὸν λ.] "addressed the people." Εὐσεβείᾳ, præ sanctitate.

— πεπ. τοῦ περιπ. α.] There is here an anomaly of construction; which some Commentators seek to remove by supposing an ellipsis of πρᾶγμα and ἕνεκα; others (as Markl. and Heinrichs), by resolving πεπ. into ποιηταῖς οὖσι; comparing Acts xxvii. 1. ὡς δὲ ἐκρίθη τοῦ ἀποπλεῖν ἡμᾶς, and xx. 3. But this principle of *resolution*, though often employed by Philologists, is seldom effectual, as

Ἰσαὰκ καὶ Ἰακὼβ, ὁ Θεὸς τῶν πατέρων ἡμῶν, ἐδόξασε τὸν παῖδα αὐτοῦ
Ἰησοῦν· ὃν ὑμεῖς παρεδώκατε, καὶ ἠρνήσασθε αὐτὸν κατὰ πρόσωπον
14 Πιλάτου, κρίναντος ἐκείνου ἀπολύειν. [m] Ὑμεῖς δὲ τὸν ἅγιον καὶ δίκαιον [m] Matt. 27. 20 Mark 15. 11.
15 ἠρνήσασθε, καὶ ᾐτήσασθε ἄνδρα φονέα χαρισθῆναι ὑμῖν· [n] τὸν δὲ Luke 23. 18. John 18. 40.
ἀρχηγὸν τῆς ζωῆς ἀπεκτείνατε· ὃν ὁ Θεὸς ἤγειρεν ἐκ νεκρῶν, οὗ [n] Supra 2. 24.
16 ἡμεῖς μάρτυρές ἐσμεν. Καὶ ἐπὶ τῇ πίστει τοῦ ὀνόματος αὐτοῦ, τοῦτον
ὃν θεωρεῖτε καὶ οἴδατε, ἐστερέωσε τὸ ὄνομα αὐτοῦ· καὶ ἡ πίστις ἡ
δι' αὐτοῦ ἔδωκεν αὐτῷ τὴν ὁλοκληρίαν ταύτην ἀπέναντι πάντων ὑμῶν.
17 Καὶ νῦν, ἀδελφοὶ, οἶδα ὅτι κατὰ ἄγνοιαν ἐπράξατε, ὥσπερ καὶ οἱ ἄρ-
18 χοντες ὑμῶν. [o] ὁ δὲ Θεὸς ἃ προκατήγγειλε διὰ στόματος πάντων τῶν [o] Luke 24. 44.
19 προφητῶν αὐτοῦ, παθεῖν τὸν Χριστὸν, ἐπλήρωσεν οὕτω. μετανοήσατε
οὖν καὶ ἐπιστρέψατε, εἰς τὸ ἐξαλειφθῆναι ὑμῶν τὰς ἁμαρτίας· ὅπως

being so hypothetical, and explaining nothing solidly. The *ellipses*, too, are liable to the same objection. It should seem that the present idiom proceeded originally from the employing of the Infinitive with ὥστε or εἰς τὸ denoting *end* or *aim*. This construction was afterwards changed to its *equivalent* τοῦ with an Infin., which is often found in the LXX. (see Win. Gr. Gr. § 38. 2. No. 3.), and was then changed in most cases to the *simple* Infinitive. The idiom formerly existed in our own language, and is still used by the vulgar; e. gr. "I should like for to know."

13. ὁ Θεὸς — ἡμῶν.] The repetition of ὁ Θεὸς is emphatical; and, as Doddr. observes, "the mention of the God of their Patriarchs was introduced to show that they taught no *new* Religion, which should alienate them from the God of Israel."

— ἐδόξασε] namely, by his resurrection and ascension. Ἠρνήσασθε, "renounced and denied him as Messiah." Κρίναντος, "when he had determined."

14. τὸν ἅγιον καὶ δίκ.] "the Holy and Just one." A cognomen of the Messiah, as in iv. 27. Rev. iii. 7. John x. 36. With ᾐτήσασθε — ὑμῖν I would compare Hesiod. Ἔργ. 190. μᾶλλον δὲ κακῶν ῥεκτῆρα καὶ ὕ β ρ ι ν ἀ ν έ ρ α τιμήσουσι. This sense of χαρ., "to be given up for pardon," is not unfrequent in the later writers.

15. τὸν ἀρχ. τῆς ζωῆς] "the author of life;" namely, as being the first to rise from the dead, he was thereby the cause of all men rising again. See John i. 4; v. 21; xiv. 6. and the Note. So Heb. ii. 10. ἀρχ. τῆς σωτηρίας. It is here observed by the very learned Valckn. that in these speeches of Peter (though not such pieces of finished composition as those of Demosthenes or the other Greek writers) there is a dignity in the historical and a grandeur in the didactic parts, to which it were impossible to add aught.

16. καὶ ἐπὶ — αὐτοῦ.] Render: "And his name (i. e. the power accompanying the invocation of his name) through faith in his name (i. e. him) hath made strong this man whom ye see and know." Ὁλοκληρίαν, complete soundness and health, as in Is. i. 6. and sometimes in the later Classical writers.

17. κατὰ ἄγνοιαν ἐπρ.] "It is somewhat difficult (says Mr. Townsend) to interpret these words in their literal sense, when we remember the numerous miracles of our Lord, and the abundant proofs the Jews received that he was their promised Messiah." Wolf and others (including Dr. Burton) indeed, attempt to get rid of the difficulty by adopting a different punctuation, and think the expression ὥσπερ καὶ οἱ ἀρχ. ὑμῶν belongs not to ἄγνοιαν, but to ἐπράξατε. And they assign the following sense: "I know that through ignorance you were induced to do as your rulers did." This, however, does violence to the construction. The difficulty may be best removed by not too rigorously interpreting either οἶδα ὅτι, (which has often but a faint sense) or ἄγνοιαν, but taking the whole as expressed *populariter*, q. d. "I am willing candidly to suppose that," &c. See Scott. Ἄγνοιαν may (as Whitby proposes) be taken of *error* or *prejudice*. At all events, Peter does not say that their ἄγνοια, whatever it might be, was blameless; for as it resulted from pride, prejudice, and worldly mindedness, and was co-existent with ample means of information, it was *criminal*. Nor was ignorance ever held as an excuse for *crime*, unless it were involuntary, when all the ancient moralists granted it was. See my Note on Thucyd. iii. 38 & 40; iv. 98. Thus Paul in 1 Tim. i. 13. urges *such* ignorance in extenuation of his guilt. Criminal, however, as was the ignorance in the present case, the Apostle hints that it admitted of *some* extenuation.

18. ὁ δὲ Θεὸς — ἐπλήρωσεν οὕτω] q. d. God hath used that ignorance *for good*, by permitting that you should commit this crime; *and moreover*, since thus would be fulfilled the declarations of the Prophets concerning the calamities with which the Messiah should be oppressed. The Rabbins themselves acknowledge that all the Prophets prophesied of the Messiah.

19. μετανοήσ. καὶ ἐπιστρ.] This is the *application* of the discourse, — in which ἐπιστ. is not (as many recent Commentators imagine) a mere synonyme of μεταν.; but, as the latter denotes a change of *mind*, so does the former a change of *conduct*; both necessary to real conversion. See Bp. Bull's Harmonia Apostolica, p. 9.

— εἰς τὸ ἐξαλ. ὑμῶν τὰς ἁμ.] Ἐξαλείφειν signifies properly *to wipe off oil from any thing*, and sometimes to wipe off characters chalked on a board, or traced on a slate; 3dly, to obliterate any writing, whether on waxed tablets, or written on parchment, either by *scratching* out, or *crossing* out. And, as crossing out accounts in a ledger implies that the sums are discharged, or the payment forgiven, so the word came to mean, in a figurative sense, to *forgive offences*, as in Is.

ἂν ἔλθωσι καιροὶ ἀναψύξεως ἀπὸ προσώπου τοῦ Κυρίου, καὶ ἀποστείλῃ 20
τὸν * προκεχειρισμένον ὑμῖν Ἰησοῦν Χριστόν· ὃν δεῖ οὐρανὸν μὲν 21
δέξασθαι ἄχρι χρόνων ἀποκαταστάσεως πάντων, ὧν ἐλάλησεν ὁ Θεὸς
p Deut. 18. 18. Infra 7. 37. διὰ στόματος πάντων τῶν ἁγίων αὐτοῦ προφητῶν ἀπ' αἰῶνος. p Μωϋ- 22
σῆς μὲν γὰρ πρὸς τοὺς πατέρας εἶπεν· Ὅτι προφήτην ὑμῖν
ἀναστήσει Κύριος ὁ Θεὸς ὑμῶν ἐκ τῶν ἀδελφῶν ὑμῶν,
ὡς ἐμέ· αὐτοῦ ἀκούσεσθε κατὰ πάντα ὅσα ἂν λαλήσῃ πρὸς
ὑμᾶς. Ἔσται δέ, πᾶσα ψυχὴ ἥτις ἂν μὴ ἀκούσῃ τοῦ 23
προφήτου ἐκείνου, ἐξολοθρευθήσεται ἐκ τοῦ λαοῦ.

xliii. 23. (which the Apostle has, no doubt, in mind) ἐγώ εἰμι ὁ ἐξαλείφων τὰς ἀνομίας σου. also 2 Macc. xii. 42. and Ecclus. xlvi. 20. This sense very rarely occurs in the Classical writers. One example, from Lysias, has been adduced by Wets: ὅπως ἐξαλειφθείη αὐτῶν τὰ ἁμαρτήματα. On the kindred notion of *expunging* and *consigning to oblivion*, see my note on Thucyd. iii. 57. To the examples there adduced may be added Æschyl. Ch. 496. and Theb. 15. Joseph. p. 787. 17. Huds.

—ὅπως ἂν ἔλθωσι, &c.] The Commentators are by no means agreed on the sense to be ascribed to ὅπως ἂν, which most modern Commentators suppose to be *when*, or *after that*, taking it for ἐπειδάν; others, *until*, i. e. waiting until. The latter, however, supposes a harsh ellipsis; and as to the former, though examples of ὅπως *in sensu* χρονικῷ are not rare, yet not with ἄν. Besides, turn it which way we will, it yields no satisfactory sense. See Scott. It is therefore better, with the Syr. Transl., and many eminent Commentators, from Luther downward, to take it in the sense *so that, in order that*, as Luke ii. 35. Matt. vi. 5. et alibi. Thus Tittm. de Syn. II. p. 63. (who adopts this sense) shows at large that ὅπως *never*, properly speaking, denotes time, unless it be time *past*, as in Hom. Od. xxii. 21. Herodo. ii. 13. In the present passage, he observes, it cannot have "notionem futuri exacti," *because* ἂν *is added.* And he renders, "ut hoc modo veniant dies ἀναψύξεως." The sense, then, is: "that so the times of refreshing may come from the *presence* of the Lord;" i. e. that ye may see with joy the time which the Lord hath appointed as the period of refreshing. Ἀνάψυξις properly denotes a regaining one's breath after it has been interrupted; 2. a breathing-time from some labour, a rest from trouble, or deliverance from evil generally; in which sense it occurs in the Sept. and Philo cited by the Commentators; to which examples I have in Rec. Synop. added others from the Classical writers. See Note on Heb. iii. 11. 3. It signifies (by *implication*) the happy state occasioned by such a change. What particular period is here designated, Expositors are not agreed. It must, of course, be at the *coming* of the Messiah: but some refer that to his coming at the *destruction of Jerusalem;* others, to his coming at the end of the world; and others, again, his coming in the Millenian reign. As to the *first* view, I see not how it can be maintained. The *third* has been ingeniously, but not satisfactorily defended. It seems safest to adopt the *second;* by which the ἀνάψυξις of the present passage will be the same with the ἄνεσις at 2 Thess. i. 7. ἐν τῇ ἀποκαλύψει τοῦ Κυρίου Ἰησοῦ ἀπ' οὐρανοῦ μετ' ἀγγέλων, the restitution of all things. In the expression ἀπὸ προσώπου we have a Hebrew periphrasis for ἀπὸ Κυρίου, which means, "by God's providence." Καὶ ἀποστείλῃ should be rendered, "and that he may send." Instead of the common reading προκεκηρυγμένον, some of the most ancient MSS., most of the ancient Versions, and all the early Edd., except the Erasmian, have προκεχειρισμένον, which is confirmed by several of the ancient Fathers, has been approved by most Commentators, and has been received by almost every Editor from Beng. and Wets. downwards: and justly; for the common reading seems to have been either a *paradiorthosis* of some Critics who did not understand προκεχειρ.; or a *gloss* on προκεχειρ.; for Suid. explains προχειρίζω by πᾶσι γνωριμὸν ποιῶ. Render: "him who was of old destined and appointed for you, (i. e. for your relief and salvation,) even Jesus Christ." Some would sink the προ, which, indeed, in Classical Greek is merged in the proper signification of the word; but this is not permitted by 1 Pet. i. 20. Χριστοῦ προεγνωσμένου πρὸ καταβολῆς κόσμου.

21. ὃν δεῖ οὐρανὸν μὲν δέξ.] The true sense of these words has been imperfectly understood by the Commentators, through their not perceiving their *scope*, which is to anticipate a possible objection,—that if Jesus had been the Messiah, he would have continued on earth, at least after his *resurrection*, and then founded his kingdom. To this the Apostle indirectly replies, that it was *necessary* (i. e. for the purposes mentioned at John xvi., xvii., and xviii.) for the present that he should abide in Heaven, there to remain till the time of restoration; literally, "that *heaven* should have him, and not *earth;*" for δέξ., as the best Commentators have seen, must mean *occupare*, not *accipere*.

Ἀποκατάστασις properly signifies a restoration of any thing to some former state; and, by implication, *for the better*, is capable of several interpretations, according to the view taken of the foregoing verse. According to the *second*, it will denote the consummation of all things at the end of the world. On the expression τῶν ἁγίων προφ. see Note at Luke i. 70; which passage will serve to confirm and illustrate the τῶν here inserted by the most eminent Editors, on weighty MS. authority.

22—24. One cannot imagine a more masterly address than this, to warn the Jews of the dreadful consequences of their infidelity, in the very words of *Moses*, out of a pretended zeal for whom they were rejecting Christianity, and attempting its destruction. (Doddr.) The Apostle means to say that they should hearken to Christ as the Prophet like unto Moses, of whom Moses predicted. For that the passage *has* reference to

24 Καὶ πάντες δὲ οἱ προφῆται ἀπὸ Σαμουὴλ καὶ τῶν καθεξῆς, ὅσοι
25 ἐλάλησαν, καὶ [προ] κατήγγειλαν τὰς ἡμέρας ταύτας. [q] Ὑμεῖς ἐστε [q Gen. 12. 3 & 22. 18. & 26. 4. Rom. 15. 8.]
υἱοὶ τῶν προφητῶν, καὶ τῆς διαθήκης ἧς διέθετο ὁ Θεὸς πρὸς τοὺς
πατέρας ἡμῶν, λέγων πρὸς Ἀβραάμ· Καὶ ἐν τῷ σπέρματί σου
26 ἐνευλογηθήσονται πᾶσαι αἱ πατριαὶ τῆς γῆς. [r] Ὑμῖν [r Infra 13. 46.]
πρῶτον ὁ Θεὸς, ἀναστήσας τὸν παῖδα αὐτοῦ Ἰησοῦν, ἀπέστειλεν αὐτὸν
εὐλογοῦντα ὑμᾶς ἐν τῷ ἀποστρέφειν ἕκαστον ἀπὸ τῶν πονηριῶν ὑμῶν.
1 IV. ΛΑΛΟΥΝΤΩΝ δὲ αὐτῶν πρὸς τὸν λαὸν, ἐπέστησαν αὐτοῖς οἱ

Christ, cannot be doubted, since the Apostle affirms it. Indeed, there will be no difficulty in so doing, if we consider the chief scope of the passage, in which (as Schoettg. has well pointed out) the peculiar points of resemblance are intimated at the ὡς αὐτὸν, "like unto himself;" namely, 1. in being the minister of a *new covenant*, as Moses was of the old, which the Prophets (especially Jeremiah) had distinctly announced should be done away. 2. in His close communication with God. And as Moses conferred much with God, so did Jesus Christ, who was in the bosom of God his Father. Though, after all, Moses may not have had directly in view this reference; and accordingly, this may be of the number of those passages of the O. T., "which (as Bp. Middleton says) are capable of a two-fold application; being *directly* applicable to circumstances then past, or present, or soon to be accomplished; and *indirectly* to others which Divine Providence was about to develope under a future dispensation."

The passage before us is not a literal *quotation;* and yet the variations that occur are not such as to affect its fidelity. In the first verse the words are put into another order, and σοὶ is altered to ὑμῖν, to make the case plainer. And so indeed Moses evidently meant it. After ἀκούσεσθε the words κατὰ — ὑμᾶς are added by Peter to show the *extent* of the injunction. In the next verse the variations are greater both from the Hebr. and the Sept. Yet (as Bp. Randolph observes) the general sense of both is expressed; for, to advert to the principal discrepancy, the אדרשׁ מעמו and ἐκδικήσω ἐξ αὐτοῦ mean, "I will require it at his hands, i. e. I will punish him for it" (namely, his disobedience.) Thus the words ἐξολ. ἐκ τοῦ λαοῦ are meant to *illustrate* a somewhat obscure phrase, and to point to the nature and extent of that punishment, the greatest known under the Jewish law. Ἐξολ. is a word found only in the Sept. and the later writers; signifying to "utterly exterminate."

24. πάντες] i. e. (in a restricted sense) a very considerable part; which, as Doddr. remarks, is quite sufficient for the purpose. Καὶ — δὲ, *quinetiam*. Ἐλάλησαν, "have spoken;" i. e. *prophetically;* for, as Kuin. observes, λαλεῖν is a vox sol. de hac re. Thus Acts xxvi. 22. Heb. i. 1. 2 Pet. i. 21. On the construction of the Genit. belonging to ὅσοι, but coming *before* it, I have, in Recens. Synop., adduced two examples; Aristoph. Plut. v. 1052. ἐν τῷ προσώπῳ τῶν ῥυτίδων ὅσας ἔχει, and Eurip. Med. v. 476. ὡς ἴσασιν, Ἑλλήνων ὅσοι Ταυτὸν συνεισέβησαν Ἀργῷον σκάφος. The αἱ ἡμέραι ταῦται are the καιροὶ ἀναψύξεως before mentioned.

25. υἱοὶ τῶν προφ.] i. e. as the best Commentators explain, "ye are the *disciples* of the prophets; those to whom the prophecies were addressed." Prophets and teachers were by the Jews styled *fathers*, and their disciples their *sons*. See Note on Matt. xii. 27.

— καὶ τῆς διαθήκης] "[ye are the] heirs by the covenant," i. e. to you these advantages pertain by the covenant, and therefore to you the offer of salvation is *first* made. The expression is formed on a Hebraic idiom of בן. The following citation is made with some small variation from the Hebrew and LXX. The Apostle means to affirm the same thing as St. Paul, Gal. iii. 16, — that by the Messiah, as the descendant of Abraham, shall all nations be blessed. Ἐν before τῷ σπέρμ. is found in all the early Edd., some Versions and Fathers, and has been received by almost every Editor from Beng. and Wets. downwards.

26 ὑμῖν πρῶτον.] The sense of these words will become clearer by supplying, what seems to be omitted (by an idiom frequent in the Scriptural writers), the particle οὖν. "Unto you, then," which very aptly introduces the *conclusion* from what has been said. Ὑμῖν *may* be taken (as some direct) for a *Dat. commodi*, and πρῶτον signify *especially;* but the usual sense is preferable, and is required by the preceding verse. Εὐλογοῦντα ὑμᾶς the Interpreters render, "in order to bless you." But this supposes a harsh idiom; and it is better to take εὐλογ. as in apposition, or for ὡς εὐλογ., "as a blesser of you," i. e. one who should bless and make you happy.

— ἐν τῷ ἀποστρ. ἕκαστον, &c.] There is here an ambiguity of interpretation, since ἀποστρ. may be taken either in a transitive or in an intransitive sense. The *former* is adopted by the generality of Translators and Commentators, and may be defended. But as it occasions some harshness of construction, and involves something objectionable in sense (unless action be taken for intention), the latter view (which is supported by the most eminent ancient and modern Interpreters) seems preferable. And ἐν τῷ *may* be taken for εἰς τὸν, denoting *purpose;* or for ἐπὶ q. d. "on every one of you turning from his iniquities," i. e. if every one of you shall turn. This is confirmed by the words of ver. 19. μετανοήσατε καὶ ἐπιστρέψατε; and by Is. i. 16. (which the Apostle seems to have had in mind) Παύσασθε ἀπὸ τῶν πονηριῶν ὑμῶν.

IV. 1. ἐπέστησαν αὐτοῖς] "*supervenerunt illis.*" Ἐφίστημι properly signifies "to be presented to the view of any one," in which is inherent some notion of *suddenness*, which occasionally (as here, Luke xx. 1., and elsewhere) implies some notion of *hostility*. On ὁ στρατηγὸς τοῦ ἱεροῦ, see Note on Luke xxii. 4.

ἱερεῖς καὶ ὁ στρατηγὸς τοῦ ἱεροῦ καὶ οἱ Σαδδουκαῖοι, διαπονούμενοι 2
διὰ τὸ διδάσκειν αὐτοὺς τὸν λαὸν, καὶ καταγγέλλειν ἐν τῷ Ἰησοῦ τὴν
ἀνάστασιν τὴν ἐκ νεκρῶν· καὶ ἐπέβαλον αὐτοῖς τὰς χεῖρας, καὶ ἔθεντο 3
εἰς τήρησιν εἰς τὴν αὔριον· ἦν γὰρ ἑσπέρα ἤδη. Πολλοὶ δὲ τῶν 4
ἀκουσάντων τὸν λόγον ἐπίστευσαν· καὶ ἐγενήθη ὁ ἀριθμὸς τῶν ἀνδρῶν ὡσεὶ χιλιάδες πέντε. Ἐγένετο δὲ ἐπὶ τὴν αὔριον συναχθῆναι 5
αὐτῶν τοὺς ἄρχοντας καὶ πρεσβυτέρους καὶ γραμματεῖς εἰς Ἱερουσαλὴμ, καὶ Ἄνναν τὸν ἀρχιερέα καὶ Καϊάφαν καὶ Ἰωάννην καὶ Ἀλέξαν- 6
δρον, καὶ ὅσοι ἦσαν ἐκ γένους ἀρχιερατικοῦ. Καὶ στήσαντες αὐτοὺς 7
ἐν [τῷ] μέσῳ, ἐπυνθάνοντο· Ἐν ποίᾳ δυνάμει ἢ ἐν ποίῳ ὀνόματι
ἐποιήσατε τοῦτο ὑμεῖς; Τότε Πέτρος πλησθεὶς Πνεύματος ἁγίου, 8
εἶπε πρὸς αὐτούς· Ἄρχοντες τοῦ λαοῦ καὶ πρεσβύτεροι τοῦ Ἰσραὴλ, εἰ 9
ἡμεῖς σήμερον ἀνακρινόμεθα ἐπὶ εὐεργεσίᾳ ἀνθρώπου ἀσθενοῦς, ἐν
s Supra 2. 24. τίνι οὗτος σέσωσται· [s] γνωστὸν ἔστω πᾶσιν ὑμῖν καὶ παντὶ τῷ λαῷ 10
t Psal. 118. 22. Isa. 28. 16. Matt. 21. 42. Mark 12. 10. Luke 20. 17. Rom. 9. 33. 1 Pet. 2. 7. Matt. 1. 21. Ἰσραὴλ, ὅτι ἐν τῷ ὀνόματι Ἰησοῦ Χριστοῦ τοῦ Ναζωραίου, ὃν ὑμεῖς
ἐσταυρώσατε, ὃν ὁ Θεὸς ἤγειρεν ἐκ νεκρῶν, ἐν τούτῳ οὗτος παρέστηκεν
ἐνώπιον ὑμῶν ὑγιής. [t] Οὗτός ἐστιν ὁ λίθος ὁ ἐξουθενηθεὶς ὑφ᾽ ὑμῶν 11
τῶν οἰκοδομούντων, ὁ γενόμενος εἰς κεφαλὴν γωνίας. Καὶ οὐκ ἔστιν 12

2. *διαπονούμενοι.*] *Διαπονεῖσθαι* signifies, 1. to be wearied out; 2. (as here) to feel aggrieved, be vexed, bear with impatience, a sense found in the LXX., but not in the Classical writers. *Διὰ τὸ διδάσκειν α. τὸν λαὸν* refers to the *Priests*; and *καταγγέλλειν — νεκρῶν* to the *Sadducees*. Ἐν τῷ Ἰησ. *by* or *in*, i. e. by the example of Jesus, as exemplified in Jesus.

3. *ἔθεντο εἰς τήρ.*] Some Expositors think that *τήρησις* here means the *custody* of *certain* persons to whose charge they were committed. But the common interpretation, a *prison*, is best founded, and is established beyond doubt by ver. 18. *ἔθεντο αὐτοὺς ἐν τηρήσει δημοσίᾳ*. This use is, however, confined to the later writers; for, in the passage cited by the Commentators from Thucyd. vii. 86, the sense is a *keeping in custody* (as, indeed, is evident by the use of the Article); which, indeed, is the primitive sense of the word (as also of the Latin custodia), but came in process of time to denote a place of custody, *carcer*.

4. *ἐγενήθη — χιλ. πέντε.*] The Commentators are not agreed whether this number is *inclusive* of the 3000 before converted, or *exclusive* of it. Yet no persons thoroughly conversant in the idiom of the Greek language can fail to perceive that the *former* is the sense intended. Ἐγενήθη signifies *was become*, a signification of *γίγνεσθαι* which often occurs in the N. T. and LXX. Ἀνδρῶν signifies, not *men*, but *persons* of both sexes; it being put for *ἀνθρώπων*, as Luke xi. 31. James i. 20. Acts vi. 11. et al.

5. *αὐτῶν*] scil. *τῶν Ἰουδαίων*, to be supplied from the context. By *τοὺς ἀρχ.*, &c. are denoted the Sanhedrim.

6. *ἐκ γένους ἀρχ.*] i. e. as some think, the *chiefs of the 24 Sarcedotal classes*; or, as others, the kindred of those who had lately served the office of High Priest.

7. *ἐν ποίᾳ δυνάμει — ὀνόματι.*] To determine the sense of this passage, we must ascertain the scope of the interrogation. Now *ἐποιήσατε τοῦτο* might refer, as some say it *does*, to the *general conduct* of the Apostles in their ministry. But from ver. 9. it is plain that it refers to the *miraculous cure* lately performed. Ἐν ποίῳ ὀνόματι further *illustrate the sense*. The *name* of a person is indeed often put for the *person* himself. See also iii. 16. Thus it may mean, by the *power* of such a person. But as it is certain that the Jews believed very wonderful works, even miracles, to be performed by magic arts and *incantation*, i. e. *invoking the names* of certain angels or illustrious Patriarchs, the full sense of *ὄνομα* may here be retained.

9. *εἰ ἡμεῖς σήμερον ἀνακρ.*] Render "Since we are called to examination this day." Ἀνακρίνεσθαι is a *forensic* term, signifying to be *examined by interrogation*. See Note on Luke xiii. 14. Εὐεργεσίᾳ ἀνθρώπου ἀσθ. is for *εὐεργ. εἰς ἄνθρωπον ἀσθενῆ*, on which use of the Genitive of object, see Winer's Gr. Gr. § 23. 1. At *ἐν τίνι* sub. *ὀνόματι*. Comp. v. 7 & 10.

11. See Note on Matt. xxi. 42.

— *οὐκ ἔστιν — ἡ σωτηρία.*] Many Commentators, from Whitby downwards, have argued from the context that *ἡ σωτηρία* means "this healing," and *σωθῆναι* "to be restored to health;" a sense, indeed, found *elsewhere*; but it cannot be admitted *here*, because it cannot have any sense varying from that of *ἡ σωτηρία* just before; and *ἡ σωτηρία*, notwithstanding what the first-mentioned Commentators may say, *cannot mean "the healing,"* because that signification of the word is found nowhere in the Scriptures, nor, I believe, in the Classical writers. And there is nothing to *compel* us to adopt it here. The use of the Article *does not*, because "the healing [in question]" yields an inapposite sense. Indeed there is no proof that the Article is here meant to exert any particular force, much less to be emphatic. I know of no passage in the N. T. where it has such a force, but several where the noun is used in its most abstract sense; in which case the force of the Article is merged in that of the noun. So John iv. 22. *ὅτι ἡ σωτηρία ἐκ τῶν Ἰουδαίων ἐστί*. Rom. xi. 11. *ἡ σωτηρία τοῖς ἔθνεσιν* [*ἐγένετο*]. Hebr.

ἐν ἄλλῳ οὐδενὶ ἡ σωτηρία· * οὐδὲ γάρ ὄνομά ἐστιν ἕτερον ὑπὸ τὸν
οὐρανὸν τὸ δεδομένον ἐν ἀνθρώποις, ἐν ᾧ δεῖ σωθῆναι ἡμᾶς.
13 Θεωροῦντες δὲ τὴν τοῦ Πέτρου παῤῥησίαν καὶ Ἰωάννου, καὶ κατα-
λαβόμενοι ὅτι ἄνθρωποι ἀγράμματοί εἰσι καὶ ἰδιῶται, ἐθαύμαζον, ἐπε-
14 γίνωσκόν τε αὐτοὺς ὅτι σὺν τῷ Ἰησοῦ ἦσαν· τὸν δὲ ἄνθρωπον βλέποντες σὺν αὐτοῖς ἑστῶτα τὸν τεθεραπευμένον, οὐδὲν εἶχον ἀντειπεῖν.
15 Κελεύσαντες δὲ αὐτοὺς ἔξω τοῦ συνεδρίου ἀπελθεῖν, συνέβαλον πρὸς
16 ἀλλήλους, λέγοντες· Τί ποιήσομεν τοῖς ἀνθρώποις τούτοις; ὅτι μὲν
γὰρ γνωστὸν σημεῖον γέγονε δι᾽ αὐτῶν, πᾶσι τοῖς κατοικοῦσιν Ἱερου-
17 σαλὴμ φανερὸν, καὶ οὐ δυνάμεθα ἀρνήσασθαι. Ἀλλ᾽, ἵνα μὴ ἐπὶ
πλεῖον διανεμηθῇ εἰς τὸν λαὸν, ἀπειλῇ ἀπειλησώμεθα αὐτοῖς μηκέτι
18 λαλεῖν ἐπὶ τῷ ὀνόματι τούτῳ μηδενὶ ἀνθρώπων. Καὶ καλέσαντες αὐτοὺς, παρήγγειλαν αὐτοῖς τὸ καθόλου μὴ φθέγγεσθαι μηδὲ διδάσκειν
19 ἐπὶ τῷ ὀνόματι τοῦ Ἰησοῦ. [u] ὁ δὲ Πέτρος καὶ Ἰωάννης ἀποκριθέντες [u] Infra 5. 29.
πρὸς αὐτοὺς εἶπον· Εἰ δίκαιόν ἐστιν ἐνώπιον τοῦ Θεοῦ ὑμῶν ἀκούειν

vi. 9. τὰ ἐχόμενα τῆς σωτηρίας. Rev. vii. 10. ἡ σωτηρία τῷ Θεῷ. and xix. 1. ἡ σωτηρία καὶ ἡ δόξα καὶ ἡ τιμὴ — τῷ Θεῷ. In short, it is plain that if there *were* even an emphasis in the Article, the sense would be "this mode of *salvation*" [namely, by the Gospel which we preach] not, "this *healing*." And there is something to countenance this in xiii. 26. That it must be understood of *salvation*, not of healing, is certain from the words following ἐν ᾧ δεῖ σωθῆναι ἡμᾶς; for (as Mr. Holden observes) "St. Peter takes it for granted that ALL must apply to Christ for this salvation. Now all are not afflicted with bodily maladies, but the salvation spoken of is that of which all stand in need; and consequently it must signify spiritual and eternal salvation."

12. οὐδέ.] This (instead of οὔτε), found in many MSS. and the Coptic Version, has been approved by Griesb., and received by Lachmann; being, as Fritz. (on Mark, p. 157) has shown, required by propriety of language. How little can be made of οὔτε, will appear from the paraphrase of the passage according to that reading offered by Dr. Burton. That οὐδὲ was read, too, in the MSS. from which the Edit. Princ. was formed, which has ο ὐ δ ὲ ν, I doubt not; for οὐδὲ was likely, in such a context, to be altered to οὐδὲν, especially as the γ following would easily be mistaken for a ν. The reading in question may, indeed, be suspected to have arisen from correction. But the MSS. are, with one exception, not of the *corrected* class: and when words like οὐδὲ and οὔτε are perpetually confounded in the MSS., grammatical propriety is of greater weight than external evidence.

— τὸ δεδομένον.] Said to be for ὃ δίδοται. But there is rather an ellipsis of κατὰ, *quod attinet ad*. Δεῖ here signifies *licet*, *permissum est*, as in Luke xiii. 14. (ἓξ ἡμέραι εἰσὶν ἐν αἷς δεῖ ἐργάζεσθαι.) and sometimes in the Classical writers.

13. τὴν παῤῥησίαν] "the freedom" or boldness of speech. So 1 Tim. iii. 13. περιποιοῦντα — πολλὴν παῤῥησίαν. and Joseph. Bell. i. 10. 7. τῶν πραγμάτων διδόντων παῤῥησίαν. On this παῤῥησία a learned Dissertation is written by Walch.

— καταλαβόμενοι] "having perceived," or learnt. This sense of the word occurs also at Acts x. 34. xxv. 25. Eph. iii. 18. Ἀγράμματοι, *unlettered*, i. e. ignorant of, or but slightly versed in that kind of knowledge which the Jews alone prized, namely, of the Scriptures as explained by their Rabbinical interpreters. (Comp. John vii. 15.) Such is the sense assigned to the expression by the best Commentators; who, however, I think, recede too far from the *Classical* use of the word, by which ἀγράμματοι denoted those who were devoid of learning or science, such as was imparted by the education which fell to the lot of the higher classes. So Athenæus, p. 176 (cited by Valckn.) ἰδιώτης καὶ ἀναλφάβητος. See Note on 1 Cor. xiv. 16. With respect to ἰδιῶται, it means *private* and *plebeian* persons, as opposed to those who hold any office Ecclesiastical or Civil. Ἐπεγίνωσκον, "recognised," as in Matt. xiv. 35. σὺν τῷ Ἰησοῦ ἦσαν, "that they had been Jesus' companions and adherents." So Mark xiv. 67. καὶ σὺ μετὰ τοῦ Ν. Ἰ. ἦσθα.

14. ἑστῶτα] "standing on his feet;" not, as before, a cripple without any use of them. See supra iii. 7, 8. and compare Mark v. 15. θεωροῦσι τὸν δαιμονιζόμενον καθήμενον, καὶ ἱματισμένον καὶ σωφρονοῦντα, where see Note.

15. κελεύσαντες — ἀπελθεῖν.] This bidding them withdraw was not meant by way of *insult*, but in order that they might consider in private what was best to be done. The expression often occurs in the Historians, where ambassadors, after delivering their message, are desired to withdraw, in order that the Council may deliberate upon it. See Thucyd. v. 112.

16. συνέβαλον.] Sub. γνώμην, or βουλεύματα, *expressed* in Eurip. Phœn. 700.

17. ἀλλ᾽] nevertheless. A sense not unfrequent, either in the Scriptural or Classical writers. Διανεμηθῇ. Supply τοῦτο scil. τὸ σημεῖον, the report of this miracle. Διανέμεσθαι signifies to be distributed among several, and, as used of a *report*, to be *spread abroad*. By λαὸν is meant the *people at large*, as opposed to the Priests, Pharisees, and higher classes. Ἐπὶ τῷ ὀνόματι τούτῳ signifies "in the name of this person," i. e. *Jesus*, the name being (as Kuin. observes) omitted through contempt.

18. παρήγγειλαν τὸ μὴ φθέγγ. may be rendered, "they interdicted to them the speaking." Διδάσκειν is exegetical of φθέγγ. Καθόλου is for παράπαν.

μᾶλλον ἢ τοῦ Θεοῦ, κρίνατε. οὐ δυνάμεθα γὰρ ἡμεῖς ἃ εἴδομεν καὶ 20
ἠκούσαμεν μὴ λαλεῖν. Οἱ δὲ προσαπειλησάμενοι ἀπέλυσαν αὐτούς, — 21
μηδὲν εὑρίσκοντες τὸ πῶς κολάσωνται αὐτούς, — διὰ τὸν λαόν· ὅτι
πάντες ἐδόξαζον τὸν Θεὸν ἐπὶ τῷ γεγονότι. Ἐτῶν γὰρ ἦν πλειόνων 22
τεσσαράκοντα ὁ ἄνθρωπος, ἐφ᾽ ὃν ἐγεγόνει τὸ σημεῖον τοῦτο τῆς
ἰάσεως.

Ἀπολυθέντες δὲ ἦλθον πρὸς τοὺς ἰδίους, καὶ ἀπήγγειλαν ὅσα πρὸς 23
αὐτοὺς οἱ ἀρχιερεῖς καὶ οἱ πρεσβύτεροι εἶπον. Οἱ δὲ ἀκούσαντες, ὁμο- 24
θυμαδὸν ἦραν φωνὴν πρὸς τὸν Θεὸν, καὶ εἶπον· Δέσποτα, σὺ ὁ Θεὸς
ὁ ποιήσας τὸν οὐρανὸν καὶ τὴν γῆν καὶ τὴν θάλασσαν, καὶ πάντα τὰ
x Psal. 2. 1. *ἐν αὐτοῖς· [x] ὁ διὰ στόματος Δαυῒδ τοῦ παιδός σου, εἰπών· Ἵνα τί* 25
ἐφρύαξαν ἔθνη, καὶ λαοὶ ἐμελέτησαν κενά; παρέ- 26
στησαν οἱ βασιλεῖς τῆς γῆς, καὶ οἱ ἄρχοντες συνή-
χθησαν ἐπὶ τὸ αὐτὸ, κατὰ τοῦ Κυρίου, καὶ κατὰ
τοῦ Χριστοῦ αὐτοῦ. Συνήχθησαν γὰρ ἐπ᾽ ἀληθείας ἐπὶ τὸν 27

19. *εἰ δίκαιον*, &c.] Of this sentiment see several examples from the Classical writers in Recens. Synop. *One* must here suffice, where Plato makes Socrates similarly address his judges: *πείσομαι τῷ Θεῷ μᾶλλον ἢ ὑμῖν*. On this subject see a learned dissertation in vol. ii. pp. 596—604. of the Novus Thesaurus Theologico-Criticus, (appended to the Critici Sacri), entitled "De limitibus obsequii humani;" in which is well traced out the true limits which bound the duty either way, and practical directions are given for the use of the maxim "to obey God rather than man."

20. *οὐ δυνάμεθα*] i. e. "We cannot [consistently with what is right and just;]" or, "we cannot bring ourselves to do it." So Papinian cited by Wets., "nam quæ facta lædunt pietatem, nec facere *nos posse* credendum est." This, it may be noticed, is one of those few passages in which two negatives do not strengthen the negation, but have an affirmative force. See Matth. Gr. Gr. § 601. Buttm. Gr. p. 261, and Win. Gr. p. 159, who account for it on the principle that the negatives *belong to two different verbs*. But, in a case like the present, that *explains* nothing. It is better to say that the two negatives belong, strictly speaking, to two different *clauses*, and are suspended on finite verbs, or Infinitives, either *expressed* or *understood*; as in *οὐδεὶς* (sub. *ἐστι*) *ὅστις οὐ ποιήσει*. In a case where an *Infinitive* occurs, the Infin. depends upon *ὥστε*, or *εἰς τὸ* understood. The ancient Syriac translator well *expresses* the two clauses by rendering, "We have not power, that we should not speak what we have seen and heard." The *ἡμεῖς* just before is emphatic, q. d. "*We*, for our parts," &c.

21. *μηδὲν εὑρίσκοντες τὸ πῶς*, &c.] There is here an anomaly of construction, in discussing which, the Commentators differ. Some think there is an ellipse of *αἴτιον*, which is *expressed* in Luke xxiii. 14. Others avoid the ellip. by taking *μηδὲν* for *μὴ*, and *πῶς* for *ὅπως*, regarding the *τὸ* as only indicating the following sentence, and consequently pleonastic. But it is better to admit the *ellip*. than admit such a harshness. So Prof. Dobree renders, "finding no witnesses." Thus the words following *τὸ πῶς*, &c., may be considered as exegetical and further evolving the sense. But the *πῶς* is *not* (as some suppose) *in apposition with μηδὲν*, but depends upon *κατὰ* or *εἰς* understood. Nor does the *τὸ* belong to the *πῶς*, but to the whole sentence following; for the words *τὸ πῶς — αὐτοὺς* form *grammatically* a separate clause. *Διὰ τὸν λαὸν* belong (there being a transposition) to *ἀπέλυσαν αὐτούς*. I have pointed accordingly.

23. *τοὺς ἰδίους*] i. e. "their associates," the other Apostles and the disciples at large; as Acts xxiv. 23. John xv. 19.

24—30. On this passage, Bp. Jebb (Sacr. Lit. p. 132. seqq.) truly remarks, "that this noble supplicatory hymn, poured forth at once by the whole Christian people, under the immediate influence of the Holy Spirit, is worthy of that inspiration from whence it flowed." The learned prelate well points out that vv. 27, 28. form a prophetical quotation of *ἵνα τί — αὐτοῦ*. And he rightly refers the *γὰρ* to a clause left to be understood: q. d. This prophecy is now fulfilled, *for* of a truth, &c. Thus the verses are not, as some imagine, *parenthetical*.

— *σὺ ὁ Θεὸς*, &c.] A sublime periphrasis for *the Lord of the universe*, with which Wets. compares Joseph. Ant. iv. 3, 2. *Δέσποτα τῶν ἐπ᾽ οὐρανοῦ τε καὶ γῆς καὶ θαλάσσης*. See also the prayer of Hezekiah, Is. xxxvii. 16—20. *Here εἰς* is to be supplied. In *ἐφρύαξαν* the metaphor is derived from the snorting and other sounds of impatience and rage, emitted by horses. Of *καὶ ἐμελέτ. κενὰ* the sense is, "and have formed vain plans." So a proverb cited by Wets. *κενὰ κενοὶ λογίζονται*.

26. *παρέστησαν*.] Not, as Kuin. imagines, for *ἀνθέστησαν*. The sense (as the parallelism requires) being "they stood side by side for mutual help," i. e. they banded together. Of this examples may be seen in Steph. Thes. 4599.

27. *συνήχθησαν γὰρ*, &c.] Here, as Bp. Jebb observes, the heathen, the peoples, the kings of the earth, and the rulers, (that is, all the rebellious personages of the second Psalm), are brought forward, as fulfilling whatsoever it was pre-appointed they should do. The equivalent terms in the prophecy and the declaration of its fulfilment correspond — the Rulers, to Herod — the kings of the earth, to Pontius Pilate — the heathen, to the heathen — the peoples, to the peoples of Israel — the Lord (Jehovah), to the

ἅγιον παῖδά σου Ἰησοῦν, ὃν ἔχρισας, Ἡρώδης τε καὶ Πόντιος Πιλάτος,
28 σὺν ἔθνεσι καὶ λαοῖς Ἰσραὴλ, ποιῆσαι ὅσα ἡ χείρ σου καὶ ἡ βουλή σου
29 προώρισε γενέσθαι. Καὶ τὰ νῦν, Κύριε, ἔπιδε ἐπὶ τὰς ἀπειλὰς αὐτῶν,
καὶ δὸς τοῖς δούλοις σου μετὰ παῤῥησίας πάσης λαλεῖν τὸν λόγον σου,
30 ἐν τῷ τὴν χεῖρά σου ἐκτείνειν σε εἰς ἴασιν, καὶ σημεῖα καὶ τέρατα γί-
31 νεσθαι, διὰ τοῦ ὀνόματος τοῦ ἁγίου παιδός σου Ἰησοῦ. Καὶ δεηθέν-
των αὐτῶν ἐσαλεύθη ὁ τόπος ἐν ᾧ ἦσαν συνηγμένοι· καὶ ἐπλήσθησαν
ἅπαντες Πνεύματος ἁγίου, καὶ ἐλάλουν τὸν λόγον τοῦ Θεοῦ μετὰ παῤῥησίας.
32 [y] ΤΟΥ δὲ πλήθους τῶν πιστευσάντων ἦν ἡ καρδία καὶ ἡ ψυχὴ μία· [y Supra 2. 44.]
καὶ οὐδὲ εἷς τι τῶν ὑπαρχόντων αὐτῷ ἔλεγεν ἴδιον εἶναι, ἀλλ' ἦν αὐ-
33 τοῖς ἅπαντα κοινά. Καὶ μεγάλῃ δυνάμει ἀπεδίδουν τὸ μαρτύριον οἱ
ἀπόστολοι τῆς ἀναστάσεως τοῦ Κυρίου Ἰησοῦ· χάρις τε μεγάλη ἦν
34 ἐπὶ πάντας αὐτούς. οὐδὲ γὰρ ἐνδεής τις ὑπῆρχεν ἐν αὐτοῖς· ὅσοι γὰρ
κτήτορες χωρίων ἢ οἰκιῶν ὑπῆρχον, πωλοῦντες ἔφερον τὰς τιμὰς τῶν

holy child Jesus — the Lord's anointed, to "Whom thou hast anointed." From this last parallel the learned Prelate elaborately proves that the holy child Jesus is identified with Jehovah of the second Psalm, and skilfully removes the objections which might occur on a superficial view of the passage, by referring to Psalm xlv. "Thy throne, O God, endureth for ever," and showing that the passages under consideration, and all such like, afford mutual light and support.

I have not ventured to follow several eminent Editors in introducing into the text (from many MSS., Versions, and Fathers) the words ἐν τῇ πόλει ταύτῃ, not so much because, as Bp. Jebb remarks, "they have no equivalent in the prophecy," as because it is very difficult to account for their *omission*, but very easy for their *addition*.

28. ποιῆσαι ὅσα, &c.] The sense is: "For the purpose of doing — what? why no other than what thy overruling power and predisposing wisdom pre-determined to be done."

29. The verse is well paraphrased by Bp. Jebb thus: "And, as thy wise counsel pre-determined that, through the confederacy of Jews and Gentiles, of kings and rulers, Christ should suffer; so let the same wise counsel be now made conspicuous, in the undaunted preaching of Christ crucified." At τὰ νῦν sub. κατὰ and ὄντα, also πράγματα. Ἔπιδε, i. e. so look upon their threats, as to ward off their execution.

30. ἐν τῷ τὴν χεῖρά σου ἐκτ.] "while thou art stretching forth thine hand, (i. e. exerting thy power) for healing, and while signs and wonders are performing;" for ἐν τῷ must be repeated.

31. Πνεύματος ἁγίου.] The interpretation of some recent Commentators "filled with sacred ardour," is a mere Unitarian gloss. Yet we need not, and, if the propriety of the Article be considered, we *must* not take Πν. in its personal sense, with Doddr. and Benson; but suppose, with Bp. Middlet., that it denotes the *influence* of the Holy Spirit, as communicating special and eminent gifts. Indeed, a *sensible illapse* is *implied*.

32. ἦν ἡ καρδία — μία.] A proverbial description of close amity, as in Plutarch: Δύο φίλοι, ψυχὴ μία. Οὐκ ἔλεγεν ἴδιον, "did not *call* them his own," or allege that as a reason why his poor brethren were not to be assisted therewith. This shows that their property was really *considered* as their own; and consequently that the expression κοινὰ in the words following must be taken with limitation; i. e. that they were common, not by *possession*, but by *use*. See Note supra ii. 45.

33. μεγάλῃ δυν.] Wolf, Heinr., and Kuin., think that the expression is to be understood only of the *power* of the Apostles' *eloquence*, &c. But, although I would not *exclude* the force of that inartificial, but impressive, eloquence, which, founded in conviction, and supported by the consciousness of Divine favour, would give their words an effect rarely to be found in the most polished oratory; yet I must maintain, that there is chiefly meant in the expression, an allusion to what would, above every thing else, enable them to speak with such effect, — namely, the *miracles* which they were occasionally enabled to work. In short, the term denotes *force* as regarded the *speakers*, and *efficacy* as respected the *hearers*.

— χάρις τε — αὐτούς.] Some Commentators understand χάρις of the favour of *God*. Others think, that it has reference to the *Jewish people*, q. d. "the favour of the people rested upon them." But though this be somewhat confirmed by ii. 47., yet there the interpretation first mentioned seems preferable; because if the αὐτοὺς be referred to the *Apostles*, it will give a *reason* for the force and efficacy of their preaching. I am, however, inclined to think that the αὐτοὺς is to be referred to the *people at large*; χάρις being understood of the grace of the Holy Spirit. So Luke ii. 40. καὶ χάρις Θεοῦ ἦν ἐπ' αὐτό. Indeed, thus alone can the γὰρ of the *following* clause be accounted for; which Translators and Commentators explain away to mean a mere καί. Calvin has alone seen that the γὰρ is, as usual, causæ redditio. Though by understanding χάρις of the favour of the people, he assigns a sense not a little frigid.

34. ὅσοι γὰρ κτήτορες — ὑπῆρχον.] Not, "as many as had;" for it is not πάντες ὅσοι, but "such as had," i. e. some of those who had: the ὅσοι being here, as often, put indefinitely. See Calvin and Heumann. Hence may be corrected an error into which Mr. Hinds has fallen in his valuable History of the Rise and Progress of Christianity, vol. i. p. 213. He understands that "*all* who had lands and houses sold them, and brought in the

πιπρασκομένων, καὶ ἐτίθουν παρὰ τοὺς πόδας τῶν ἀποστόλων· διεδί- 35
δοτο δὲ ἑκάστῳ καθότι ἄν τις χρείαν εἶχεν.
Ἰωσῆς δὲ, ὁ ἐπικληθεὶς Βαρνάβας ἀπὸ τῶν ἀποστόλων, (ὅ ἐστι με- 36
θερμηνευόμενον, υἱὸς παρακλήσεως) Λευΐτης, Κύπριος τῷ γένει, ὑπάρ- 37
χοντος αὐτῷ ἀγροῦ, πωλήσας ἤνεγκε τὸ χρῆμα, καὶ ἔθηκε παρὰ τοὺς
πόδας τῶν ἀποστόλων. V. Ἀνὴρ δέ τις, Ἀνανίας ὀνόματι, σὺν Σαπ- 1
φείρῃ τῇ γυναικὶ αὐτοῦ, ἐπώλησε κτῆμα, καὶ ἐνοσφίσατο ἀπὸ τῆς τι- 2
μῆς, συνειδυίας καὶ τῆς γυναικὸς αὐτοῦ, καὶ ἐνέγκας μέρος τὶ παρὰ
τοὺς πόδας τῶν ἀποστόλων ἔθηκεν. Εἶπε δὲ Πέτρος· Ἀνανία, διατί 3
ἐπλήρωσεν ὁ Σατανᾶς τὴν καρδίαν σου, ψεύσασθαί σε τὸ Πνεῦμα τὸ
ἅγιον, καὶ νοσφίσασθαι ἀπὸ τῆς τιμῆς τοῦ χωρίου; Οὐχὶ μένον, σοὶ 4
ἔμενε, καὶ πραθὲν, ἐν τῇ σῇ ἐξουσίᾳ ὑπῆρχε; Τί ὅτι ἔθου ἐν τῇ
καρδίᾳ σου τὸ πρᾶγμα τοῦτο; οὐκ ἐψεύσω ἀνθρώποις ἀλλὰ τῷ Θεῷ.

amount to the Apostles." And to remove the wonder and objection which this would involve, he supposes that the statement of their bringing in their money to the Apostles, by no means implies that it was in all instances *accepted*. This solution, however, is utterly inadmissible. The fact is, that we are not certain (for we are not told so), nor is it probable, that these proprietors sold *all* their possessions. They would benefit the poor more by holding part in reserve, and giving as need required.

Τιθέναι παρὰ is not merely a phrase signifying to commit to the care of, but, when joined with παρὰ πόδας, implies the *reverence* with which the deposit was made.

36. Λευΐτης.] Though the Levites had, *as a tribe*, no inheritance, yet they were allowed *individually* to hold landed property. Τὸ χρῆμα, the price, the money; a sense almost confined to the plural, though two examples of the singular are adduced, to which I have, in Recens. Synop., added another.

V. After the undissembled liberality of Barnabas, is recorded an example of the *contrary*, in the case of Ananias and Sapphira, and its termination in their sudden death. The nature of their crime has been by some misconceived, by others too much palliated, and by others again unreasonably exaggerated; but, at the most moderate estimate, it must be regarded, even on principles of natural religion, as a crime of no ordinary magnitude, and such as well merited the punishment with which it was visited; and which was more especially *necessary* in the then state of things, in order to prevent the Christian religion from being discredited by the hypocrisy of worldly-minded professors.

1. ἐνοσφίσατο ἀπὸ τῆς τ.] Sub. μέρος, "appropriated part to his own use." We may notice the force of the middle verb.

2. συνειδυίας.] Sub. τοῦτο. The ellipse is *supplied* in Thucyd. vol. ii. 92. 7. Bek. ξυνειδὼς τοῖς ἑτέροις τὸ ἐπιβούλευμα. The older Commentators esteem the crime *sacrilege*, which was punishable with death: but Mede well distinguishes between the *species facti*, and the *circumstantiæ* facti,—namely, *hypocrisy*, and *desire of vain glory*, &c., which was perhaps the chief motive which tempted them to the offence.

3. ἐπλήρωσεν—τὴν καρδίαν σου.] Many recent Commentators comparing this with that at v. 4. ἔθου ἐν τῇ καρδίᾳ σου τὸ πρᾶγμα τοῦτο, take it to mean no more than "why was thy heart filled with that diabolical plan?" But this is unjustifiably sinking the *personality* of Satan, and his *power* as well as will to suggest evil thoughts to the minds of men. The two expressions above mentioned are by no means inconsistent; for while the assaults of Satan *incite* men to sin, (and such the best Commentators are agreed is the sense of πληρ. τὴν καρδ.) their own natural corruption is sufficient of itself to *suggest* evil thoughts. Nor will there be any thing difficult in the interrogation διατί, &c., if we consider that the *full* force of πληροῦν τὴν καρδίαν τινὸς, which is πληροφορεῖσθαι, *implies* (as we know Satan's power is *limited*) such a *yielding* to the temptation as, while it argues the free agency of man, makes him at the same time strictly accountable. Ψεύσασθαι signifies to attempt to deceive by a lie; the *attempt* being, as often, put for the *performance*. This offence towards the Apostles involved the same crime towards the *Holy Spirit*, under whose inspiration they acted.

4. μένον] "remained unsold." The particip. is to be resolved into a verb and participle. Σοὶ, "at thy disposal." A dativus commodi. At τί ὅτι sub. γέγονε or ἐστι—for τί ἐστιν ὅτι. The Commentators compare in Aristophanes ὅτι τί δή; and in Plato ὅτι δὴ τί; Τιθέναι ἐν τῇ καρδίᾳ, or εἰς τὴν καρδίαν signifies to deliberately plan and determine on any thing.

—οὐκ ἐψεύσω—Θεῷ.] From a comparison of this verse with the preceding one [where Ananias is said to have lied against the *Holy Ghost*] as well as several other passages [John iii. 6. compared with 1 John v. 4. Matt. ix. 38. compared with Acts xiii. 4. 2 Tim. iii. 16. with 2 Pet. i. 21. John vi. 45. with 1 Cor. ii. 13. 1 Cor. iii. 16. seqq. with 1 Cor. vi. 19.] Theologians have in all ages inferred that the *Holy Ghost is* GOD. Wets., indeed, has remarked that ὁ Θεὸς with the Article is always confined to *God the Father*. But Bp. Middleton has shown that no such distinction is observed: ὁ Θεὸς and Θεὸς being used indiscriminately, except where grammatical rules interfere. See also the excellent note of Whitby.

The οὐκ—ἀλλὰ is by most recent Commentators rendered *non tam—quam*; which, however, is not very necessary. Perhaps, however, οὐκ may here be taken for οὐ μόνον, as in Thucyd. iii. 45. where see my Note, and also iv. 92. where

5 Ἀκούων δὲ Ἀνανίας τοὺς λόγους τούτους, πεσὼν ἐξέψυξε. καὶ ἐγένετο
6 φόβος μέγας ἐπὶ πάντας τοὺς ἀκούοντας ταῦτα. Ἀναστάντες δὲ οἱ νεώ-
7 τεροι συνέστειλαν αὐτὸν, καὶ ἐξενέγκαντες ἔθαψαν. Ἐγένετο δὲ ὡς
ὡρῶν τριῶν διάστημα, καὶ ἡ γυνὴ αὐτοῦ, μὴ εἰδυῖα τὸ γεγονὸς, εἰσῆλ-
8 θεν. Ἀπεκρίθη δὲ αὐτῇ ὁ Πέτρος· Εἰπέ μοι, εἰ τοσούτου τὸ χωρίον
9 ἀπέδοσθε; ἡ δὲ εἶπε· Ναὶ, τοσούτου. Ὁ δὲ Πέτρος εἶπε πρὸς αὐ-
τήν· Τί ὅτι συνεφωνήθη ὑμῖν πειράσαι τὸ Πνεῦμα Κυρίου; ἰδοὺ, οἱ
πόδες τῶν θαψάντων τὸν ἄνδρα σου, ἐπὶ τῇ θύρᾳ, καὶ ἐξοίσουσί σε.
10 Ἔπεσε δὲ παραχρῆμα παρὰ τοὺς πόδας αὐτοῦ, καὶ ἐξέψυξεν· εἰσελθόντες δὲ οἱ νεανίσκοι εὗρον αὐτὴν νεκρὰν, καὶ ἐξενέγκαντες ἔθαψαν
11 πρὸς τὸν ἄνδρα αὐτῆς. Καὶ ἐγένετο φόβος μέγας ἐφ᾿ ὅλην τὴν ἐκκλησίαν, καὶ ἐπὶ πάντας τοὺς ἀκούοντας ταῦτα.
12 Διὰ δὲ τῶν χειρῶν τῶν ἀποστόλων ἐγίνετο σημεῖα καὶ τέρατα ἐν τῷ

see Duker. As to the syntax of ἐψεύσω, Bp. Middl. thinks it strange that it should here be used with the *Dative*, while in the preceding verse it is used with the Accus. He seems to suppose, perhaps without reason, there is no other instance of the syntax with the Dative. The learned Prelate is, at all events, wrong in regarding the Dat. as put for the *Accus*. It is rather put for the *Genit*. with κατὰ, which yields a much *stronger* sense, and hence was used in a connexion which *required* something stronger. Examples of ψεύδεσθαι κατά τινος and καταψεύδ. τινος may be seen in Steph. Thes. and Wetstein's Note on 1 Cor. xv. 15.

5. ἐξέψυξε.] Supply πνεῦμα. On the atrociousness of Ananias's offence, see Wets. ap. Recens. Synop., and on the justice of his punishment, see Limborch, Biscoe, and Doddr. *ibidem*. The *Rationalists*, indeed, defend the Apostle from the charge of excessive severity — by maintaining (alas for the credulous incredulity of scepticism!) that Ananias and Sapphira died not by a Divine judgment, but of fright!! As if it were likely that so *very rare* an occurrence should have happened to *two* persons *at once*. And that the Apostle did not threaten, nor even allude to Ananias's *death*, is nothing to the purpose, and admits of being satisfactorily accounted for. See Recens. Synop.

6. οἱ νεώτεροι.] Called at v. 10. οἱ νεανίσκοι, and supposed by Hamm., Mosheim, Heinrichs, and Kuin., to have been Church officers (like our *Sacristans*) appointed to perform various duties; such as sweeping and cleaning the Church, preparing for the Lord's supper and the agapæ, &c. This is, they think, confirmed by νεανίσκοι denoting in Alexandrian Greek *servants*, and is countenanced by the use of the Article. They, however, adduce no *proofs* of the existence of such officers, at so very early a period; though we might have expected some *allusions* at least to them in the works of the Apostolical Fathers. There is, then, no sufficient reason to forsake the common interpretation, which supposes οἱ νεαν. to mean "the younger part of the men present." And thus the Article has great propriety. It seems to have been usual for the *younger* men of the Christian Church to perform, perhaps in rotation, the more laborious offices in the congregation; which were, at so early a period, not yet appropriated to *particular persons*, — and consequently the persons performing those offices were not likely to have any distinctive name of office. Συνέστειλαν, for περιέστειλαν, "wound him up;" namely, either in a winding-sheet laid up in the place, or perhaps, in the present emergency, only in a cloak. This sense of συστέλλειν is very rare, and the Commentators adduce only one example, to which I have added another in Recens. Synop. Burial on the same day was (and still is) usual in the East; and I have in Recens. Synop. shown that the custom was not unknown among the Greeks of the earliest ages, having probably been introduced by the Cadmo-Phœnician colonists.

7. ὡς ὡρῶν τριῶν διάστ.] Probably at the next Prayer-time.

8. ἀπεκρίθη δὲ αὐτῇ] "addressed her." Ἀποδόσθαι, to sell. There is not (as Kuin. imagines) in the use of the ἀπὸ any reference to the money to be received as the price, since ἀπὸ merely signifies *away*. Ἀποδίδωμι of itself only denotes to give *up* or *away*: just as does our *sell*, from the Anglo-Saxon *syllan*, to let go. Πωλέω signifies literally to *turn over to another* (from πολέω, *to turn*), and thus to *sell*. The Hebrew correspondent term properly denotes *to deliver up*. Thus the *capere* of the Latin, and the *caup-yan*, *caap-an*, and *koop-en* of the Northern languages, signify to *take to one's self*, to *buy*; and the German *ver-kaufen*, the *contrary*, namely to *give up to another*, to *sell*.

— τοσούτου] "for such a sum [as your husband says]."

9. πειράσαι τὸ Πνεῦμα Κ.] i. e. to try whether the Spirit of God would detect your hypocrisy and fraud.

— οἱ πόδες τῶν θαψ.] The Commentators regard this as a Hebraism, for οἱ θάψαντες; the Hebrews often expressing a *man* by some *member of his body* instrumental to some action in question. I have, however, shown in Recens. Synop. (by references to Eurip. Hipp. 657. Orest. 1205. Suppl. 90. and Herc. Fur.) that this idiom is found among the Greek Classical writers, though, I believe, confined to the *Poets*. See Note on Rom. x. 15.

— καὶ ἐξοίσουσί σε.] This does not contain a *threat*, much less (as Porphyry represents) an *imprecation*, but a *prediction*, i. e. "will carry thee out." The same Holy Spirit which revealed to Peter the *fraud*, made known the *punishment* which would follow it.

12. διὰ τῶν χειρῶν τῶν ἀπ.] i. e. by the Apostles.

λαῷ πολλά. καὶ ἦσαν ὁμοθυμαδὸν ἅπαντες ἐν τῇ στοᾷ Σολομῶνος·
τῶν δὲ λοιπῶν οὐδεὶς ἐτόλμα κολλᾶσθαι αὐτοῖς. ἀλλ' ἐμεγάλυνεν αὐ- 13
τοὺς ὁ λαός· (μᾶλλον δὲ προσετίθεντο πιστεύοντες τῷ Κυρίῳ, πλήθη 14
ἀνδρῶν τε καὶ γυναικῶν·) ὥστε κατὰ τὰς πλατείας ἐκφέρειν τοὺς ἀσθε- 15
νεῖς, καὶ τιθέναι ἐπὶ κλινῶν καὶ κραββάτων, ἵνα ἐρχομένου Πέτρου
κἂν ἡ σκιὰ ἐπισκιάσῃ τινὶ αὐτῶν. Συνήρχετο δὲ καὶ τὸ πλῆθος τῶν 16
πέριξ πόλεων εἰς Ἱερουσαλὴμ, φέροντες ἀσθενεῖς καὶ ὀχλουμένους ὑπὸ
πνευμάτων ἀκαθάρτων· οἵτινες ἐθεραπεύοντο ἅπαντες.
Ἀναστὰς δὲ ὁ ἀρχιερεὺς καὶ πάντες οἱ σὺν αὐτῷ, ἡ οὖσα αἵρεσις 17

12—14. *καὶ ἦσαν ὁμοθυμαδὸν, &c.*] In this passage there is an appearance of contradiction, or, at least, discrepancy in some things here said, and a seeming incoherence in the clauses respectively; to obviate which various methods have been adopted. Some, considering the passage as incurably *corrupt*, propose to *cancel the whole*. But before we resort to so desperate a course, let us consider whether it be absolutely *necessary*. Many Editors and Commentators place the latter part of ver. 12. *καὶ ἦσαν, &c.* and the whole of vv. 13 & 14 in a parenthesis. Yet that (as Zeigler and Beck have shown) is contrary to the *laws of parenthesis* observed by the ancients, and is of too violent and arbitrary a nature to be admitted. Others (as Bp. Sherlock, Dr. A. Clarke, and Mr. Townsend) attempt to remove the difficulty by *transposing* the verses and clauses thus: v. 14, v. 12. 2d clause; v. 13, v. 12. *first* clause, v. 15. But though "transposition of *words* is (as Porson observes) the safest of all modes of conjectural emendation," a transposition of *clauses* and *sentences* very remote from each other, is a sort of emendation the most licentious, being nearly the same as *re-writing* a passage. And as, in the present case, the transpositions are of the most violent kind, and wholly unsupported by any evidence, external or internal (for *how* could the passage have been so transposed, and the transposition been transmitted to all the MSS. and Versions?), the method in question must therefore by no means be thought of. Nor is there, I apprehend, any thing so inextricably confused in the passage as it now stands; which is of a similar kind to those at i. 11. ii. 1, 44. (see also xii. 20), in all of which the expression *εἶναι ὁμοθυμαδὸν* denotes the meeting together for public worship. And here the words *ἅπαντες* and *ἐν τῇ στοᾷ Σολ.* are added, because now that the believers were become so very numerous, they could no longer hold any *general* assemblies for divine worship in the *ὑπερῷον*, which they had before occupied, but were obliged to resort to the *portico of the Temple* here mentioned. Of course, by *ἅπαντες* are meant the *Christians at large*; not, as some have thought, the *Apostles*. And as *τῶν λοιπῶν* is opposed to *ἅπαντες*, it must denote (as Whitby and Doddr. explain) the rest of the worshippers, i. e. those who were *not Christians*. They, it is said, did not venture *κολλᾶσθαι*, i. e. (as the term, from the context, must mean) *προσέρχεσθαι*, to approach or come near them, whether for interference, or otherwise. This view of the sense is supported by the authority of the Pesch. Syr. Version, and that of Œcumenius, who explains the word by *προσεγγίζειν*. That *κολλᾶσθαι* and *προσέρχεσθαι* are synonymous terms, is plain from x. 28. *ἀθέμιτόν ἐστιν ἀνδρὶ Ἰουδαίῳ κολλᾶσθαι ἢ προσέρχεσθαι, &c.* where see Note. The *reason* for this may be explained from the *awe* which, we find from what precedes, had struck the people at the miracles that had been worked.

The next words *ἀλλ' ἐμεγάλ. αὐτοὺς ὁ λαὸς* may be rendered, "But the people at large (as opposed to the Rulers) held them in great reverence." Ver. 14 is (as Griesb., Knapp, and Gratz have seen) parenthetical, and meant to show that this awe or respect had, in some cases, induced them to join the Christian society. The sense is, "And believers in the Lord were more and more added." The *ὥστε*, of course, connects with *ἐμεγάλυνεν*, meaning that such was the reverence of the people, that, &c.

15. *ἐπὶ κλινῶν καὶ κρ.*] Since the latter term denotes a small and mean *couch*, the former a larger and better one, like our *sofa*; we see that persons of all classes alike resorted to the Apostles for aid.

— *ἵνα ἐρχομένου — αὐτῶν.*] The *approval* of this action, which was a *superstitious* one (as implying that the power of healing was *inherent* in the Apostles, and not, as it really was, *adventitious*, and procured at their prayers,) is not to be inferred, even if it were true (which, however, is disputed by most Commentators) that the persons in question *were* healed; for that would be procured by *their faith*, without the intervention of the Apostles. However, from what is said in the next verse and xix. 12, it seems (as Kuin. admits) highly probable that *many*, if not all the persons in question *were* healed, at least where the faith was strong enough to qualify them for that mercy. And in such a case the superstition would be forgiven, and the faith accepted.

16. *συνήρχετο τὸ πλῆθος τῶν πέριξ πόλεων.*] The common version cannot be tolerated, since it passes over the Article, and supposes a harsh ellipsis of *ἀπό*. Render: "The bulk of the population (or, as Wakef. renders, "the numerous inhabitants of") the surrounding cities flocked to Jerusalem." At *πέριξ* there is an ellipse of *κειμένων* or the like, common to all languages; though sometimes the *complete* expression occurs.

— *ὀχλ.*] See Note on the kindred phraseology at Luke vi. 18. It is plain that the *dæmoniacs* are distinguished from the *sick*.

17. *ἀναστάς.*] This is regarded by De Dieu and Kuin. as a Hebrew pleonasm; while Casaub. and Heum., more rightly, take it for *διεγερθεὶς*, i. e. *κινηθεὶς* scil. *ἐπὶ τοῖς γινομένοις*. In the words following it is *implied*, though not expressly said, that the High Priest was a Sadducee. And that some of the High Priests (as well as most persons of high rank) were such, we learn from Josephus. *Σὺν αὐτῷ* seems to be for *μετ' αὐτοῦ*, denoting to

18 τῶν Σαδδουκαίων, ἐπλήσθησαν ζήλου, καὶ ἐπέβαλον τὰς χεῖρας αὐτῶν
19 ἐπὶ τοὺς ἀποστόλους, καὶ ἔθεντο αὐτοὺς ἐν τηρήσει δημοσίᾳ. Ἄγγελος
δὲ Κυρίου διὰ τῆς νυκτὸς ἤνοιξε τὰς θύρας τῆς φυλακῆς, ἐξαγαγών
20 τε αὐτοὺς εἶπε· Πορεύεσθε καὶ σταθέντες λαλεῖτε ἐν τῷ ἱερῷ τῷ λαῷ
21 πάντα τὰ ῥήματα τῆς ζωῆς ταύτης. Ἀκούσαντες δὲ εἰσῆλθον ὑπὸ
τὸν ὄρθρον εἰς τὸ ἱερὸν, καὶ ἐδίδασκον. Παραγενόμενος δὲ ὁ ἀρχιερεὺς
καὶ οἱ σὺν αὐτῷ, συνεκάλεσαν τὸ συνέδριον καὶ πᾶσαν τὴν γερουσίαν
τῶν υἱῶν Ἰσραὴλ, καὶ ἀπέστειλαν εἰς τὸ δεσμωτήριον ἀχθῆναι αὐτούς.
22 Οἱ δὲ ὑπηρέται παραγενόμενοι οὐχ εὗρον αὐτοὺς ἐν τῇ φυλακῇ·
23 ἀναστρέψαντες δὲ ἀπήγγειλαν, λέγοντες· Ὅτι τὸ μὲν δεσμωτήριον
εὕρομεν κεκλεισμένον ἐν πάσῃ ἀσφαλείᾳ, καὶ τοὺς φύλακας [ἔξω]
24 ἑστῶτας πρὸ τῶν θυρῶν· ἀνοίξαντες δὲ, ἔσω οὐδένα εὕρομεν. Ὡς
δὲ ἤκουσαν τοὺς λόγους τούτους ὅ τε ἱερεὺς καὶ ὁ στρατηγὸς τοῦ ἱεροῦ
25 καὶ οἱ ἀρχιερεῖς, διηπόρουν περὶ αὐτῶν, τί ἂν γένοιτο τοῦτο. Παραγενόμενος δέ τις ἀπήγγειλεν αὐτοῖς [λέγων·] Ὅτι ἰδοὺ, οἱ ἄνδρες
οὓς ἔθεσθε ἐν τῇ φυλακῇ εἰσὶν ἐν τῷ ἱερῷ, ἑστῶτες καὶ διδάσκοντες
26 τὸν λαόν. Τότε ἀπελθὼν ὁ στρατηγὸς σὺν τοῖς ὑπηρέταις, ἤγαγεν
αὐτοὺς, οὐ μετὰ βίας, (ἐφοβοῦντο γὰρ τὸν λαὸν) ἵνα μὴ λιθασθῶσιν.

be of any one's party. See iv. 13. and Note. Some, however, take it to denote those who were his colleagues in his official duties, or of council with him. But as those could not be many, the πάντες seems to exclude that view. Αἵρεσις denotes properly a *taking up any thing*, as a *choice*, or an *opinion*; 2. the *opinion* so taken up; 3. as here, the *party maintaining it*, in which sense it often occurs in the later Classical writers, especially the Philosophers. Ζῆλος here denotes a combined feeling of *envy*, *malice*, and *wrath*, on the cause of which see iv. 2. and Note. Ζῆλος is *not* derived from ζέω and λίαν, as Mr. Valpy supposes: the λος is a mere *termination*, of which there are numerous examples. The η, as in βηλὸς, βέβηλος, and many other words, is formed by crasis from the vowel of the root and the ε of the termination; for the real termination is —ελος, as in ὕελος, μύελος, πύελος, &c. which seem to have been at first exclusively *adjectival*.

18. ἐν τηρήσει δημοσίᾳ is for εἰς τήρησιν δημ., as supra iv. 18., where see Note. Wakef. wrongly renders, "*a* common prison," not aware that the *absence* of the Article is no proof that τηρήσει is *not* taken κατ' ἐξοχὴν, such nouns being often, as Bp. Middlet. has shown, vi. 1., anarthrous. Though the learned Prelate does not say in *what cases*, or *why* they are so. It should seem that they are so when the substances designated are things of frequent use, and requiring often to be mentioned. In such a case the Article is *omitted*, because it may be *readily understood*, as in our own language perpetually.

19. ἄγγελος δὲ Κυρίου.] Render "*an* angel."

20. σταθέντες λαλ.] Beza and Kuin. regard σταθ. as a Hebrew pleonasm, and Grot. thinks it has reference to *constancy*. But it rather seems to be a forensic term, used of those who are *set up* to *speak*, either as orators and advocates, or as prisoners pleading their own cause. See Acts xvii. 22. xxv. 18.

— τῆς ζωῆς ταύτης] "of this doctrine or religion which leads to salvation." So John vi. 68. ῥήματα ζωῆς αἰωνίου. See vii. 38. There may, however as Kuin. thinks, be an *hypallage*, as in Acts xiii. 26. Compare Rom. vii. 24.

21. ὑπὸ τὸν ὄρθρον] "about day-break." So Thucyd. has ὑπὸ τὴν ἕω. On ὀρθ. see my Note on Thucyd. iii. 112. Τὴν γερουσίαν is supposed to have been added, to explain to foreigners the true meaning of τὸ συνέδριον. That word, however, was so commonly in use with the Greeks, that it could need no explanation. It should rather seem that γερουσίαν is added, because the term was *especially applied* to the Sanhedrim; and so it occurs in Philo and Josephus, though it is also used by Dionys. Hal. to express the Latin *Senatus*.

23. ἐν πάσῃ ἀσφ.] for σὺν πάσῃ ἀσφ.; an adverbial phrase for the adverb ἀσφαλεστάτως. Ἔξω is omitted in many MSS., Versions, and early Edd., and is cancelled by almost every Editor from Wets. downwards.

24. ὁ ἱερεύς.] Taken κατ' ἐξοχὴν for the *High* Priest, as in Heb. v. 6., and sometimes in the Sept. and Josephus. By οἱ ἀρχ. are meant the 24 Heads of the sacerdotal classes. See Note on Matth. ii. 4. On στρατηγὸς τοῦ ἱεροῦ see Note on iv. 1.

— τί ἂν γένοιτο τ.] On the sense of these words Commentators are not agreed. Many render "quonam hoc evasurum esset;" others, "quomodo hoc factum fuerit." But no proof has been adduced that such a sense is contained in the words; which are, I conceive, best rendered by Grot., Wets., and Valckn., "quid hoc esset rei," being a *popular* form of expression, importing, "did not know what to think of it," which is expressive of wonder at some circumstances connected with any thing; as, for instance, the *means*, *manner*, or *event* of it. So x. 17. διηπόρει τί ἂν εἴη τὸ ὅραμα.

26. ἵνα μὴ λιθ.] According to the punctuation and construction adopted by all the Editors and Commentators, ἵνα μὴ λιθ. is suspended on ἐφοβοῦντο. But that involves an unprecedented harshness of syntax; φοβεῖσθαι being often construed

Ἀγαγόντες δὲ αὐτοὺς ἔστησαν ἐν τῷ συνεδρίῳ· καὶ ἐπηρώτησεν αὐτοὺς 27
z Supra 4. 18. ὁ ἀρχιερεύς, [z] λέγων· Οὐ παραγγελίᾳ παρηγγείλαμεν ὑμῖν μὴ διδάσκειν 28
ἐπὶ τῷ ὀνόματι τούτῳ; καὶ ἰδοὺ, πεπληρώκατε τὴν Ἱερουσαλὴμ τῆς
διδαχῆς ὑμῶν, καὶ βούλεσθε ἐπαγαγεῖν ἐφ᾽ ἡμᾶς τὸ αἷμα τοῦ ἀνθρώ-
a Supra 4. 19. που τούτου. [a] Ἀποκριθεὶς δὲ ὁ Πέτρος καὶ οἱ ἀπόστολοι εἶπον· 29
b Supra 2. 24. & 3. 15. Πειθαρχεῖν δεῖ Θεῷ μᾶλλον ἢ ἀνθρώποις. [b] Ὁ Θεὸς τῶν πατέρων 30
ἡμῶν ἤγειρεν Ἰησοῦν, ὃν ὑμεῖς διεχειρίσασθε κρεμάσαντες ἐπὶ ξύλου·
c Heb. 2. 10. Luke 24. 47. [c] Τοῦτον ὁ Θεὸς ἀρχηγὸν καὶ σωτῆρα ὕψωσε τῇ δεξιᾷ αὐτοῦ, δοῦναι 31
d John 15. 26, 27. μετάνοιαν τῷ Ἰσραὴλ καὶ ἄφεσιν ἁμαρτιῶν· [d] καὶ ἡμεῖς ἐσμεν αὐτοῦ 32
μάρτυρες τῶν ῥημάτων τούτων, καὶ τὸ Πνεῦμα δὲ τὸ ἅγιον, ὃ ἔδωκεν
ὁ Θεὸς τοῖς πειθαρχοῦσιν αὐτῷ.

Οἱ δὲ ἀκούσαντες διεπρίοντο, καὶ ἐβουλεύοντο ἀνελεῖν αὐτούς. Ἀνα- 33
στὰς δέ τις ἐν τῷ συνεδρίῳ Φαρισαῖος, ὀνόματι Γαμαλιὴλ, νομοδιδά- 34

with μὴ, but never with ἵνα μή. And though some MSS. *omit* the ἵνα, that is but *cutting* the knot, which may be *untied* by simply placing ἐφοβ. γὰρ τὸν λαὸν in a parenthesis.

28. παρηγγείλαμεν.] See Note on iv. 17. Pearce, Rosenm., and Kuin. take ἐπὶ τῷ ὀνόματι to mean "respecting this person." But ἐπὶ has never that sense in the N. T., nor, I believe, in the Classical writers. It is plain from many similar passages of the N. T., that ἐπὶ must here denote "resting on the authority of," or "*by*," in which latter sense ἐν is more usual, and sometimes *no* preposition is found, as Matt. vii. 22. Mark ix. 38. The recent Commentators generally take ὀνόματι as here put *per periphrasin* for *person*. But though this may, in a popular view, be admitted, it is better to suppose the word to signify *authority*, &c. as often elsewhere; and τούτῳ to be put, by a common hypallage, for τούτου. This is required by a kindred passage at Acts iv. 7. ἐν ποίῳ ὀνόματι ἐποιήσατε τοῦτο; thus also in Matt. vii. 22. τῷ σῷ ὀνόματι προφητεύειν is put for the more usual τῷ ὀνόματί σου. The teaching ἐπὶ τῷ ὀνόματι τούτῳ implied, in the *Messiahship* of the person in question, his unjust condemnation, and the accountableness of the chief priests for his being put to death.

—πεπληρώκατε.] Of this figurative sense of πληρόω examples are adduced by Wets. Ἐπάγειν ἐπί τινα is a phrase denoting *to bring any thing* (always something evil) *upon a person*; and it is used in Demosth. and often in the later writers.

29. εἶπον] i. e. through the medium of Peter, as is suggested by the use of ἀποκριθεὶς, not ἀποκριθέντες. Thus Kuin. observes, that "in the *Gospels*, too, that is ascribed to many, which properly belongs only to one." See Matt. xv. 15. and Note. This, however, is not confined to the *Scriptures*, but occurs in the *Classical* writers. Thus in Thucyd. iii. 52, we have ἐπελθόντες ἔλεγον τοιάδε, though the speech was delivered by Astymachus alone.

—πειθαρχεῖν.] Used of implicit obedience to the orders of those who exercise authority of any kind. On the sentiment (with which the Commentators compare several from the Classical writers) see Note on iv. 19. The *reason* implied in the preference of the obedience is the same as in a kindred passage of Soph. Antig. 74. Ἐπεὶ πλείων χρόνος Ὃν δεῖ μ᾽ ἀρέσκειν τοῖς κάτω (scil. τοῖς Θεοῖς) τῶν ἐνθάδε. Ἐκεῖ γὰρ αἰεὶ κείσομαι.

30. διεχειρίσασθε.] Διαχειρίζεσθαι in the middle form, but used in a deponent sense, signifies, 1. to *take a business in hand, so as to despatch* it; 2. to despatch, *kill*. This use is only found in the later writers. The earlier ones use διαχρήσασθαι. Ξύλον denotes, not a *tree*, but a *post, gibbet, cross*, as x. 39. Gal. iii. 13. It properly signifies a hewn log. So Artemid. Onir. iv. 33. ἐπλήγη τὴν κεφαλὴν ξύλῳ.

31. ἀρχηγὸν καὶ σωτῆρα.] These words are in apposition with τοῦτον, and *may*, with Kuin. be regarded as put for εἰς ἀρχ. or εἰς τὸ εἶναι. But it is rather for ὡς ἀρχ.; for though apposition is *generally* employed to supply something for the completion of a definition, it often contains (as Matthiæ Gr. Gr. § 433 observes) not so much an *explanation*, or *fuller determination* of the former, as the *design* of it. See Thucyd. i. 1835.

—δοῦναι, &c.] "to be the means of producing repentance, [by his doctrine,] and effecting remission of sins by his all-atoning merits and blood." Comp. ix. 18.

32. τῶν ῥημάτων.] Many of the best Commentators take ῥημ. for πραγμάτων, by Hebraism, as referred to the *things* mentioned at vv. 30 & 31. Others take ῥημ. to denote the ῥήματα τῆς ζωῆς at v. 20; which is preferable, especially as the *doctrines* implied the *things*. Καὶ—δὲ, "quin imo, nay too." At τοῖς πειθαρχοῦσιν there is not (as Kuin. imagines) an ellipse of ἡμῖν, the ἡμῖν being suppressed through modesty.

33. διεπρίοντο.] Διαπρ. signifies properly *to be sawn through*. *Here* almost all the best Commentators are agreed that the sense is, "were filled with fury, and, as it were, gnashed their teeth;" a metaphor taken from gnashing the teeth, as one *draws a saw*. Indeed, from the more fully worded expression at vii. 54. διεπρίοντο ταῖς καρδίαις αὐτῶν, καὶ ἔβρυχον τοὺς ὀδόντας ἐπ᾽ αὐτόν, it is plain that there can only be a *metaphor*. After all, our common version, "were cut to the heart," may be tolerated, if it be understood to represent the combined effects of being *stung to the heart* with the just reproaches cast at them, and being *filled with rage and fury* at their accusers. So Plautus Bacch. cited by Steph. Thes. in v. "Heu *cor* meum *finditur*. Istius hominis ubi quoque fit mentio."

34. Γαμαλιήλ.] A frequent name among the Jews; though the Commentators are very much agreed, that this was the celebrated Gamaliel,

σκαλος, τίμιος παντὶ τῷ λαῷ, ἐκέλευσεν ἔξω βραχύ τι τοὺς ἀποστόλους
35 ποιῆσαι, εἰπέ τε πρὸς αὐτούς· Ἄνδρες Ἰσραηλῖται, προσέχετε ἑαυτοῖς
36 ἐπὶ τοῖς ἀνθρώποις τούτοις τί μέλλετε πράσσειν. Πρὸ γὰρ τούτων
τῶν ἡμερῶν ἀνέστη Θευδᾶς, λέγων εἶναί τινα ἑαυτὸν, ᾧ ‡ προσεκολλήθη
ἀριθμὸς ἀνδρῶν ὡσεὶ τετρακοσίων· ὃς ἀνῃρέθη, καὶ πάντες ὅσοι
37 ἐπείθοντο αὐτῷ διελύθησαν καὶ ἐγένοντο εἰς οὐδέν. Μετὰ τοῦτον
ἀνέστη Ἰούδας ὁ Γαλιλαῖος ἐν ταῖς ἡμέραις τῆς ἀπογραφῆς, καὶ ἀπέστησε λαὸν ἱκανὸν ὀπίσω αὐτοῦ· κἀκεῖνος ἀπώλετο, καὶ πάντες ὅσοι
38 ἐπείθοντο αὐτῷ διεσκορπίσθησαν. Καὶ τὰ νῦν λέγω ὑμῖν· ἀπόστητε
ἀπὸ τῶν ἀνθρώπων τούτων, καὶ ἐάσατε αὐτούς· ὅτι ἐὰν ᾖ ἐξ ἀνθρώ-
39 πων ἡ βουλὴ αὕτη ἢ τὸ ἔργον τοῦτο, καταλυθήσεται· εἰ δὲ ἐκ Θεοῦ

son of Simon and grandson of Hillel, and Paul's master.

— *ἐκέλευσεν — ἀποστόλους*.] Wakef. renders. "bade the Apostles to stay without a little while," — supposing, with Krebs, an ellipsis of *ἑαυτοὺς*, also, I find adopted lately by Dr. Burton. And indeed this may seem supported by iv. 15. But the ellipsis would be exceedingly harsh, the construction unprecedented, and the sense thence arising jejune. There is really no fault in our common version, except that the idiomatical *ἐκέλευσε*, which only means *counselled*, *exhorted*, is translated without any regard to, perhaps in forgetfulness of that idiom; which is the more excusable, since it did not occur to one so conversant with the Classics as was Wakefield, though it is frequent in Thucyd. and other of the best writers. Ἔξω ποιῆσαι, "to remove," is used according to that idiom by which *ποιεῖν* is employed with various adverbs of place, as *ἔσω*, *ἔξω*, *ἐντὸς*, *πόῤῥω*, by an ellipse of some verb of motion in the infinitive.

35. *προσέχετε — πράσσειν*.] The construction is, *προσέχετε ἑαυτοῖς, τί μέλλετε πράσσειν ἐπὶ τοῖς ἀνθρ. τ.* Examples of this use of *ἐπὶ* (concerning) *τινὸς* after *πράσσειν*, are adduced by Wets.

36. Θευδᾶς.] This cannot be the Theudas mentioned by Joseph. Ant. xx. 5, 1, as leader of an insurrection, and destroyed, with all his forces, by Fadius the Procurator; for that took place before the time of Gamaliel's speech. This difficulty some (as Abp. Usher, Capellus, Bp. Pearce, and Wets.) attempt to remove, by supposing the *Theudas* of St. Luke to be the same with the *Judas* of Josephus Ant. xvii. 12, 5, who raised an insurrection a little after the time of Herod the First, but was defeated and put to death. And they compare a similar interchange of the names *Judas* and *Thaddeus*. This, however, is wholly gratuitous, and by no means probable. It is better (with Scaliger, Casaubon, Camer., Lightfoot, Grot., Hamm., Krebs, Whitby, Doddr., Lardn., Rosenm., and Kuin.) to suppose, on the authority of Origen contra Cels. i. 6, p. 44, that there were *two persons of the name of Theudas*; though they are not quite agreed as to the period of the insurrection of the first Theudas. The *second* they suppose to have been son or grandson of the first, who again brought together his scattered adherents. Yet, as Dr. Lardner observes, there were several persons of the same name who were leaders of insurrections within no very long time: *four Simons* within 40 years, and *three Judas'* within 10. And as the references in Wets. show that the name Theudas was by no means an uncommon one, there is no occasion to suppose the second to have been a *son* of the first. Indeed, considering the case of the Simons and Judas', may we not suspect that some of the *succeeding* demagogues took the name of their *predecessors*, though not related to them? as knowing how efficient a *name*, in such cases, always is. From the small number of adherents mentioned (namely 400) it is plain that the insurrection of the first Theudas was not of any great consequence, and therefore was passed over by Josephus.

— *λέγων εἶναί τινα ἑ.*] Τινα for *μέγαν*, by an idiom common to both ancient and modern languages. Notwithstanding the custom of Editors, it should seem that *τις* in this sense is wrongly made an enclitic. It ought to retain its accent, being too insignificant to either *lose* or *incline* its accent. Instead of *προσεκολλήθη* some few good MSS. and Versions have *προσεκλίθη*, which is preferred by Mor., Hemsterh., Valckn., Schleus., and Kuin., as being too rare a word to have come from the scribes, and therefore changed into one more common. But the *scribes* rarely *changed* at all. The changes in the MSS. of the N. T. are chiefly from the ancient *Critics*, who frequently alter common words to more elegant ones, but *very rarely the reverse*. And when we consider that *προσκολλᾶσθαι* is of frequent occurrence both in the O. and N. T. (even in *this* Book), and that *προσκλίνεσθαι* occurs not once, there can be little doubt but that *προσεκλίθη* proceeded from the Alexandrian Critics, especially as it only occurs in *six* MSS. of the Alexandrian class. That the framers of the *Versions* read *προσεκλίθη* is by no means certain; for they may, as often, have translated *liberally*.

— *διελύθησαν*.] Διαλύεσθαι is often used of the *disbanding* of an army, or the *dispersion* of a multitude.

37. *τῆς ἀπογραφῆς*.] See Note on Luke ii. 1. Ἀπέστησε, "drew away into insurrection;" a signification frequent in the Classical writers from Herodot. downwards, but never, I believe, there used with *ὀπίσω αὐτοῦ* after it.

38. *τὰ νῦν*.] Sub. *ὄντα* and *πράγματα*. Ἀπόστητε ἀπὸ τῶν ἀνθρώπων is, as at Acts xxii. 29, a *euphemism* for "put them not to death, nor maltreat them." This signification of the word is said by Markl. to be peculiar to Luke. But something like it occurs in Thucyd. ii. 47. *αὐτῶν ἀπέστησαν*. With the present passage Pric. compares a very similar one in Diog. Laert. Μὴ ἀποκτείνετε τὸν ἄνθρωπον, ἀλλ', ἐμοὶ πεισθέντες, ἄφετε.

— *ὅτι ἐὰν ᾖ*.] With the sentiment see several kindred ones compared in Recens. Synop.

ἐστιν, οὐ δύνασθε καταλῦσαι αὐτό· μήποτε καὶ θεομάχοι εὑρεθῆτε.
Ἐπείσθησαν δὲ αὐτῷ· καὶ προσκαλεσάμενοι τοὺς ἀποστόλους, δείραντες 40
παρήγγειλαν μὴ λαλεῖν ἐπὶ τῷ ὀνόματι τοῦ Ἰησοῦ, καὶ ἀπέλυσαν αὐτούς.
ᵃ Οἱ μὲν οὖν ἐπορεύοντο χαίροντες ἀπὸ προσώπου τοῦ συνεδρίου, ὅτι 41
ὑπὲρ τοῦ ὀνόματος αὐτοῦ κατηξιώθησαν ἀτιμασθῆναι· πᾶσάν τε ἡμέραν 42
ἐν τῷ ἱερῷ καὶ κατ᾽ οἶκον οὐκ ἐπαύοντο διδάσκοντες καὶ εὐαγγελιζόμενοι
Ἰησοῦν τὸν Χριστόν.

ᵃ Matt. 5. 10, 11, 12. Rom. 5. 3. Phil. 1. 29. James 1. 2. 1 Pet. 4. 13.

VI. ἘΝ δὲ ταῖς ἡμέραις ταύταις πληθυνόντων τῶν μαθητῶν, ἐγέ- 1
νετο γογγυσμὸς τῶν Ἑλληνιστῶν πρὸς τοὺς Ἑβραίους, ὅτι παρεθεωροῦντο ἐν τῇ διακονίᾳ τῇ καθημερινῇ αἱ χῆραι αὐτῶν. Προσκαλεσάμενοι 2
δὲ οἱ δώδεκα τὸ πλῆθος τῶν μαθητῶν, εἶπον· Οὐκ ἀρεστόν ἐστιν
ἡμᾶς καταλείψαντας τὸν λόγον τοῦ Θεοῦ, διακονεῖν τραπέζαις. Ἐπι- 3
σκέψασθε οὖν, ἀδελφοί, ἄνδρας ἐξ ὑμῶν μαρτυρουμένους ἑπτὰ πλήρεις
Πνεύματος ἁγίου καὶ σοφίας, οὓς ᵇ καταστήσομεν ἐπὶ τῆς χρείας ταύτης.

39. *μήποτε καὶ θεομ. εὑρ.*] It is not agreed whether these words connect with *ἐάσατε*, &c., (as Pric., Hamm., Valckn., and Markl. maintain), or whether there be (as Camer., Beza, Grot., and Kuin. suppose) an ellipse of *ὁρᾶτε*. The latter is confirmed by a *plena locutio* at Luke xxi. 34. Yet the former is the more natural construction, and is espoused by Professor Dobree.

41. *χαίροντες.*] This is to be construed with *ὅτι ὑπὲρ*, &c. In *κατηξιώθησαν ἀτιμασθῆναι* Casaub. notices the elegant use of the figure *Oxymoron*, which arises when two ideas, repugnant to each other are so joined as not to be really repugnant; but only to *seem* so. Of this examples are adduced by Wets.

It must be remarked, that though flagellation was employed both among the Jews and Romans for even small delinquencies, yet it was considered a most ignominious punishment.

42. *κατ᾽ οἶκον.*]. This, as it is opposed to *ἐν τῷ ἱερῷ*, plainly signifies *in private houses*; *κατ᾽ οἶκον* being put in a generic sense, for *κατ᾽ οἴκους*, *from house to house*; since *κατὰ* here exerts a distributive force; though it is not perceptible in Acts xx. 20. *δημοσίᾳ καὶ κατ᾽ οἴκους*.

VI. 1. *τῶν Ἑλληνιστῶν.*] On the persons meant by these *Hellenists*, the Commentators are not agreed. Some think they were Greek *Proselytes to Judaism*, and now converted to Christianity. But that view is liable to many objections, which are stated in Recens. Synop. It is better, with the greater part and the more eminent of the Commentators, ancient and modern, to suppose that they were *foreign Jews*, whose *residence* was in Grecian cities, and who consequently ordinarily used the Greek language, but who were occasionally *sojourners* in Judæa. The Ἑβραῖοι were the Jews of Palestine, who spoke what was *then* called the Hebrew, namely, the Syro-Chaldee.

— *παρεθεωροῦντο.*] The word signifies, 1. to look aside of; 2. to overlook, neglect. *Παροράω* is the term used by the best Classical writers; and *παραθεωρέω* occurs, with one or two exceptions, entirely in the later ones. The fault of the neglect in question rested, of course, with the guardians of the poor; who, it is commonly supposed, were persons appointed by the Apostles to attend *in rotation*, or as it might otherwise be convenient, to superintend the distribution of the funds for the poor. The best Commentators, however, are of the opinion of Mosheim in his Comm. de rebus Christianorum ante Constant. p. 118 & 138, that they were certain persons *always the same*, and all Hebrews, who had hitherto been appointed by the Apostles, but were now to be elected by the people, and that to them were to be added seven persons of the Hellenists. Mosheim and Kuin. think that the whole body of the Jerusalemite Christians was divided into seven divisions, for which there were as many places of public worship; and that hence also *seven persons* were elected for the purpose of taking care of the poor and of strangers, each division choosing one. St. Luke does not, indeed, give a *particular account* of this office, but only touches on the chief heads of early Ecclesiastical history, leaving his readers a most ample field for enlargement, reflection, and conjecture on what is by him so succinctly narrated.

2. *οὐκ ἀρεστόν ἐστιν.*] "It is not meet or proper;" for by *ἀρεστόν* the LXX. express the Hebr. טוב and ישר of the Hebr. Our common Version, "it is not *reason*," is not so much improper as obsolete, (for reasonable,) though I find it used in Hobbes's Thucydides. *Τὸν λόγον τοῦ Θεοῦ*, "the preaching of the doctrines of the Gospel." By *διακονεῖν τραπέζαις* is meant, in general, the collection and distribution of the funds to be expended on the support of the poor.

3. *ἐπισκέψασθε.*] The word properly denotes to *look at, survey*, but here, from the adjunct, to look at *for choice*, to look *out*; a signification so rare, that not a single example has been adduced. *Μαρτυρουμένους*, scil. *εὖ*, "men of good repute."

— *πλήρεις Πνεύματος ἁγ. καὶ σοφ.*] The sense of *Πνεύμ. ἁγ.* is exceedingly lowered by many recent foreign Commentators, who take it to denote *a holy ardour*; though, on the other hand, it is raised too high by many old Commentators, who explain it of the *faculty of working miracles*. The maxim *in medio tutissimus ibis* will here, as often, hold good; for the expression must denote the being possessed of those gifts of the Holy Spirit, (some of them supernatural,) which were, in the Apostolic age, vouchsafed to many Christians, and of which St. Paul treats in his Epistles; including, of course, the *graces* of the Holy Spirit,

4 ἡμεῖς δὲ τῇ προσευχῇ καὶ τῇ διακονίᾳ τοῦ λόγου προσκαρτερήσομεν.
5 [f] Καὶ ἤρεσεν ὁ λόγος ἐνώπιον παντὸς τοῦ πλήθους· καὶ ἐξελέξαντο [f Infra 8. 5, 26. & 21. 8.]
Στέφανον, ἄνδρα πλήρη πίστεως καὶ Πνεύματος ἁγίου, καὶ Φίλιππον,
καὶ Πρόχορον, καὶ Νικάνορα, καὶ Τίμωνα, καὶ Παρμενᾶν, καὶ Νικό-
6 λαον προσήλυτον Ἀντιοχέα, οὓς ἔστησαν ἐνώπιον τῶν ἀποστόλων· καὶ
7 προσευξάμενοι ἐπέθηκαν αὐτοῖς τὰς χεῖρας. Καὶ ὁ λόγος τοῦ Θεοῦ
ηὔξανε, καὶ ἐπληθύνετο ὁ ἀριθμὸς τῶν μαθητῶν ἐν Ἱερουσαλὴμ σφόδρα,
πολύς τε ὄχλος τῶν ἱερέων ὑπήκουον τῇ πίστει.
8 ΣΤΕΦΑΝΟΣ δὲ πλήρης ‡ πίστεως καὶ δυνάμεως ἐποίει τέρατα καὶ
9 σημεῖα μεγάλα ἐν τῷ λαῷ. Ἀνέστησαν δέ τινες τῶν ἐκ τῆς συναγωγῆς
τῆς λεγομένης Λιβερτίνων, καὶ Κυρηναίων καὶ Ἀλεξανδρέων, καὶ τῶν

so suitable to the situation of the persons in question. By *σοφία* seems to be denoted not merely *divine* wisdom (or knowledge of the Scriptures), but *human* wisdom, which was equally necessary for the proper discharge of the office; namely, sound judgment, prudence, and knowledge of business. That the persons were called to exercise an *ecclesiastical* as well as a secular office, is clear, —1. from the expression Πνεύματος ἁγίου. 2. from their being ordained by the laying on of hands, which points at an *ecclesiastical* rather than secular office. 3. from the *fact*, that some of those who were appointed, exercised spiritual functions — as *Stephen*. Καταστήσομεν, instead of the common reading καταστήσωμεν, is found in many good MSS., some Fathers and Versions, and nearly all the early Edd.; and is received by almost every Editor from Wets. downwards. Χρείας simply means business — so *negotii* in the Vulg. and Syr. Versions. It is, however, implied to be of importance; and, therefore, Steph. Thes. renders it *necessario muneri*, of which sense there is an example in Joseph. Bell. i. 11. 4.

4. προσκαρτ.] See Note on i. 14. By προσευχῇ may be denoted not only *prayer*, but religious meditation, as preparatory to the discharge of the ministerial duties just afterwards mentioned.

5. ἤρεσεν — πλήθους.] This is a Hellenistic phrase, nowhere found in the Classical writers, but formed on the model of the Hebrew בְּעֵינֵי. So Deut. i. 23. 2 Sam. iii. 36. The Greeks would have said ἤρεσεν παντὶ τῷ πλήθει.

— προσήλυτον.] On the absence of the Article before this word see Prof. Stuart ap. Win. Gr. Gr. p. 60. I cannot, however, agree with him in thinking that προσήλυτος denotes *office*, *station*, or employment. In that case the *Article* would by no means be *requisite*: and *with* the Article, it would designate Nicolaus as *well known* from that circumstance; which is not likely to have been the case. Besides, the close connection of προσ. with Ἀντ. shows that the sense is "*a* proselyte of Antioch."

6. ἐπέθηκαν αὐτοῖς τὰς χεῖρας.] Selden and Wolf deduce the origin of laying on hands from the age of Moses, adverting to the seven *Seniores*, on whom Moses laid his hands (Num. xxvii. 18.). Hence the custom obtained in the Jewish Church, and was thence introduced into the Christian. As laying on of hands had always been used in praying for the good of any person present, in order to show, δεικτικῶς, *for whom* the benefit was entreated; so it was also, from the earliest ages, a rite of institution to office, which it conferred *by symbol*.

7. πολύς τε ὄχλος τῶν ἱερέων ὑπ. τ. π.] This statement has to some appeared so improbable, that they have either taken refuge in conjecture, or adopted the reading of a few MSS., Ἰουδαίων. But the former is unauthorized, and the latter is a mere error of the scribes, arising from ignorance of some abbreviation: besides that is so inapposite, that scarcely *any* authority could justify it. Many eminent Commentators, including Kuin., take ὄχλος to mean the *multitude* of the inferior priests as opposed to the *leaders* of the 24 classes. But that would require the *Article*, and then only *increase* the difficulty; which may best be removed by taking πολὺς ὄχλος in a restricted and popular sense, of a *considerable number*. This is confirmed by Chrysost., who interprets it by πολλοί. That a comparatively considerable number of the whole (which amounted to about 5000) should have become believers, is not strange, considering the miracles they had witnessed, both from Jesus and from the Apostles. The expression ὑπήκ. τ. π. is remarkable, and occurs nowhere else.

8. πίστεως.] Several MSS. and Versions, and some Fathers have χάριτος, which is preferred by most Commentators, and received by Griesb., Knapp, and Tittm.; but, I conceive, wrongly; for we may better account for the change of πίστεως into χάριτος than the reverse. Besides, the MSS. are chiefly such as abound in alterations; not to mention that the *number* of those MSS. is comparatively small, and the testimony of the Versions of no great weight. And although χάρ. is not unsuitable, yet πίστεως is more to the purpose.

9. Λιβερτίνων] *Who* are meant by these, is a question which will perhaps never be decided. The most probable opinion is that adopted by Wahl, that they were *Jews*, who had been taken captive by the Romans in war, and carried to Rome; and having there been manumitted, were accustomed to visit Jerusalem in such numbers as to erect a synagogue for their particular use; as was the case with Jews from other cities mentioned in the context. Others think them to have been the *posterity of Jews*, who had been carried into Egypt and Libya by the Ptolemies or Pompey, and afterwards made free citizens of the places where they dwelt. Others again suppose them to have been Jews who inhabited a city or tract called Libertum, somewhere in Africa Proconsularis. But there is no proof of the existence of any such city or region. By the Cyrenæans and Alexandrians, who seem to have had a synagogue to themselves, we are to understand Jews

ἀπὸ Κιλικίας καὶ Ἀσίας, συζητοῦντες τῷ Στεφάνῳ· καὶ οὐκ ἴσχυον 10
ἀντιστῆναι τῇ σοφίᾳ καὶ τῷ πνεύματι ᾧ ἐλάλει. Τότε ὑπέβαλον ἄνδρας 11
λέγοντας· Ὅτι ἀκηκόαμεν αὐτοῦ λαλοῦντος ῥήματα βλάσφημα εἰς
Μωϋσῆν καὶ τὸν Θεόν· συνεκίνησάν τε τὸν λαὸν καὶ τοὺς πρεσβυτέ- 12
ρους καὶ τοὺς γραμματεῖς. Καὶ ἐπιστάντες συνήρπασαν αὐτὸν, καὶ
ἤγαγον εἰς τὸ συνέδριον, ἔστησάν τε μάρτυρας ψευδεῖς λέγοντας· Ὁ 13
ἄνθρωπος οὗτος οὐ παύεται ῥήματα βλάσφημα λαλῶν κατὰ τοῦ τόπου
τοῦ ἁγίου τούτου καὶ τοῦ νόμου· ἀκηκόαμεν γὰρ αὐτοῦ λέγοντος· 14
Ὅτι Ἰησοῦς ὁ Ναζωραῖος οὗτος καταλύσει τὸν τόπον τοῦτον, καὶ ἀλλάξει
τὰ ἔθη ἃ παρέδωκεν ἡμῖν Μωϋσῆς. Καὶ ἀτενίσαντες εἰς αὐτὸν ἅπαντες 15
οἱ καθεζόμενοι ἐν τῷ συνεδρίῳ, εἶδον τὸ πρόσωπον αὐτοῦ ὡσεὶ πρόσωπον ἀγγέλου.

VII. Εἶπε δὲ ὁ ἀρχιερεὺς, εἰ ἄρα ταῦτα οὕτως ἔχει; ὁ δὲ ἔφη· 1

from Cyrene and Alexandria, in the latter of which places they were so numerous as to fill *two* of the four wards, and had a governor for themselves.

10. *σοφίᾳ καὶ τῷ πνεύματι.*] By the former is meant not merely human, but *divine* wisdom, as supplied by the Holy Spirit; for *πνεῦμ.* signifies the *influence* of the Spirit, under whose inspiration he spoke.

11. *ὑπέβαλον.*] Ὑποβ. signifies 1. to put under; 2. to introduce a supposititious child to any mother; 3. as here, to suborn, privily introduce an accuser. Examples occur in the *later* writers.

— *λαλ. ῥήματα βλάσφημα,* &c.] This constituted a capital offence; for, under the old Jewish Theocracy, it involved the crime of *treason* as well as blasphemy. This *blasphemy against* God has been shown by Bp. Horsley in his Answer to Priestley, p. 232, to be asserting the Deity of Christ — which Stephen died attesting.

12. *ἐπιστάντες.*] See Note on iv. 1. This must be referred to the people, elders, and scribes, not to the suborners; for the *subject* is changed, as often in Scripture and the best writers, especially Thucyd. In such a case, the Commentators take the *καὶ* for the relative; a bungling expedient, which *explains nothing*. We may render, "and they, having come upon him," &c.

13. *μάρτυρας ψευδεῖς.*] Namely. by intermingling falsehood with truth in their depositions, especially by perverting Stephen's words to a sense not intended by him, or exaggerating what he did say. How they did this, and on the language really held by him, see Recens. Synop.

14. *ἀλλάξει.*] This implies the notion of *abrogate*, i. e. by the introducing of some *other* law.

15. *εἶδον — ἀγγέλου.*] Some Commentators think that Stephen's face was made to shine supernaturally, by a visible glory like that of Moses (Exod. xxxiv. 29.). But the far greater number (and those the most eminent) are agreed in interpreting it as a popular form of expression, indicating majesty and divine grace, such as might inspire reverence and awe. And they appeal to Esth. v. 2. 2 Sam. xiv. 17. xix. 27. Gen. xxxiii. 10. This latter interpretation is preferable, since there is nothing said by St. Luke to lead us to suppose that this was a *supernatural glory*, like that of Moses; and as to the passage of Exod., the air and manner of it differ materially from that of the present. At the same time, the majesty and angelic innocence which shone forth in the countenance of this great protomartyr, can only be ascribed to the power of the Holy Spirit; and therefore the case of Moses may, not improperly, be *compared* with it.

VII. In this *Apologetical Speech* of St. Stephen (in reply to the High Priest's interrogation, whether the accusation of conspiring to destroy the Jewish religion, was true) there is much which to us appears obscure, though, no doubt, sufficiently intelligible to those to whom it was addressed. Various hypotheses have, indeed, been hazarded, to lessen the difficulty; but it is, after all, more *apparent* than *real*. And if we take into consideration the *scope of the address;* the *character of the composition*, and the *circumstances under which it was delivered*, no wonder is it that there should be found something which may seem abrupt, and even not quite apposite or coherent, or conclusive in the reasoning. To advert to the *scope*, this appears to have been to retort on his accusers the charge they were bringing forward against himself. He shows, by a brief review of the history of the Jews, and a detail of their various rebellions against God, that it was *themselves* rather who were guilty of contempt of their Law; and by their own disobedience and perversity had been the real occasion of the destruction of the *first* temple, as they might be of the *second*. In order to establish his position, he first reviews the early history of their nation, and points out the various instances of their disobedience to God: showing, moreover, that, though the rites of the Mosaic Law were appointed by the command of God himself, yet that the Israelites were not approved unto God solely by those observances. That their temple *might* be destroyed; and yet the true worship of God be carried on acceptably to him: that it even *would* be destroyed, unless they should repent.

To advert to the other particulars, — the *character* of the composition is at once unstudied and inartificial, and therein bears the strongest marks of authenticity. And if we consider the *peculiar circumstances* under which the address was delivered, we shall be at no loss to account for an occasional abruptness and want of coherence. As to the appositeness of the arguments

2 Ἄνδρες ἀδελφοὶ καὶ πατέρες, ἀκούσατε. Ὁ Θεὸς τῆς δόξης ὤφθη τῷ
πατρὶ ἡμῶν Ἀβραὰμ ὄντι ἐν τῇ Μεσοποταμίᾳ, πρὶν ἢ κατοικῆσαι αὐτὸν
3 ἐν Χαῤῥὰν, [g] καὶ εἶπε πρὸς αὐτόν· Ἔξελθε ἐκ τῆς γῆς σου [g] Gen. 12. 1.
καὶ ἐκ τῆς συγγενείας σου, καὶ δεῦρο εἰς γῆν ἣν ἄν
4 σοι δείξω. Τότε ἐξελθὼν ἐκ γῆς Χαλδαίων κατῴκησεν ἐν Χαῤῥάν·
κἀκεῖθεν, μετὰ τὸ ἀποθανεῖν τὸν πατέρα αὐτοῦ, μετῴκισεν αὐτὸν εἰς
5 τὴν γῆν ταύτην εἰς ἣν ὑμεῖς νῦν κατοικεῖτε. Καὶ οὐκ ἔδωκεν αὐτῷ

and illustrations, it must be observed that they were sufficiently apposite for the persons addressed, and quite according to the Jewish manner; the character of the composition being altogether Jewish. Finally, as to the *inconclusiveness* in argument objected to by some, it must be remembered that the course of argument was interrupted, and broken off in the middle by the infuriate multitude. Had it been brought to a conclusion, there would undoubtedly have been nothing left incomplete in that which was *intended* to be proved. The remainder of the address would doubtless have been occupied in *applying* the foregoing narration, to prove what was meant to be evinced. *How* this would have been done, it is by no means difficult to imagine. And the course of argument is here excellently pointed out by Schoettgen and others, whom see in Recens. Synop.

Before concluding the present sketch, it may be proper to advert to a charge somewhat more difficult to answer; — namely, that in detailing various particulars of the Jewish history, Stephen has here added some circumstances which seem contradictory to the accounts in the O. T. These will be briefly considered in the notes on the passages themselves, as they occur; in which it will, I trust, be shown, 1. that the discrepancies in question have been *greatly exaggerated;* 2dly that they are, in general, far from being *irreconcilable;* and, 3dly, that if, in one or two instances, they may be really such, yet if we consider that the speaker is arguing with the people, according to *Jewish ideas*, and on *Jewish principles*, and alleging facts which they themselves recognized, there is nothing which can reasonably impeach the veracity, or cast a slur on the inspiration of this great Protomartyr; for in those few particulars it is admitted that he spoke on the authority of those Rabbinical traditions, whose authority his hearers regarded as unquestionable. It is well observed in the Quarterly Review, for 1834, that if these discrepancies were far greater than they are, they need not perplex our faith; since the whole speech of Stephen — the whole view of the history of his forefathers, which it relates with such pregnant brevity, is obviously framed according to the accredited and received notions then prevalent among the Jews. For instance, the Egyptian learning of Moses, and the delivery of the law through the dispensation of angels, — a common tenet among the later Jews. It abounds in *traditional allusions*, which the more rigid Commentators have employed much unprofitable ingenuity in explaining away. It could not, indeed, in common sense or in real wisdom be otherwise. Had Stephen departed in the least particular from the established views of the early history, as taught by the wise men, the scribes and lawyers of the day, he would have given unnecessary offence; the solemn, all-important, all-absorbing question of the divine mission of Jesus, and the truth of Christianity, would have been in danger of degenerating into, or might have been interrupted by, idle and antiquarian disputes on the interpretation of the text of Genesis.

1. Εἰ — οὕτως ἔχει;] On the nature of this idiom, see Note supra i. 6.

2. ἄνδρες — πατέρες.] By ἄνδρες ἀδελφοὶ he means the multitude in general; and by πατέρες, the members of the Sanhedrim. The ἄνδρες is elegantly *pleonastic*.

— ὁ Θεὸς τῆς δόξης] "splendore et majestate insignis." See Ps. xxiv. 8. xxix. 1.

— πρὶν ἢ κατ., &c.] To remove a seeming discrepancy between what is here said and the account of Moses, the best Commentators are agreed that Stephen here followed the Jewish tradition, (adopted by Philo,) that God appeared *twice* to Abraham, — 1st, when living in Chaldea, and 2dly, when resident at Charran.

"This apparent discrepancy (observes the Quarterly Reviewer ubi supra), if it were still greater and more evident, it would not in the least perplex our faith. The statement of Stephen strictly harmonizes with the prevailing notions of the time, and, indeed, with no great difficulty, may be brought into accordance with the Scriptures, and this without removing Haran beyond the boundaries of Mesopotamia; though in fact, the situation of Haran is a question of very slight importance. The Jews supposed the first call of Abraham to have taken place, not in '*Haran*, but in *Ur, of the Chaldees*. They rested that belief on Gen. xv. 7. So in Neh. ix. 7.; and though the general course of the narrative in Genesis, would lead to the opinion, that no call took place till after the first migration to Charran and the death of Terah, yet the description of the call begins, in our version, with the words, 'Now, the Lord had said unto Abraham,' leaving the date of the transaction indefinite; and Rosenmuller observes on the Hebrew word — 'Dixitque. vel potius, dixerat autem, nempe quum esset in Chaldæâ, priusquam Carras venisset.' That this was the established opinion we have the authority of Philo de Abrahamo, vol. ii. p. 11; and of Joseph. Antiq. i. 7. 1. But the most remarkable evidence that the Jews of the later times, at least, drew a distinction between the land of the Chaldeans and Mesopotamia, though the former must have been comprehended within the latter, is to be found in the book of Judith."

3. δεῦρο.] Sub. ἐλθὲ which is *expressed* in Aristoph. Thesm. 324.

4. κἀκεῖθεν — μετῴκισεν.] Again, there is a trifling discrepancy between this account and that in Genesis, the most probable solution of which seems to be that which proceeds on the supposition, that here also Stephen followed the tradition of the Jews. See Rec. Syn.

5. οὐκ ἔδωκεν.] The best Commentators are agreed that ἔδωκεν is to be taken in a *pluperfect*

κληρονομίαν ἐν αὐτῇ, οὐδὲ βῆμα ποδός· καὶ ἐπηγγείλατο αὐτῷ δοῦναι
εἰς κατάσχεσιν αὐτὴν, καὶ τῷ σπέρματι αὐτοῦ μετ᾽ αὐτὸν, οὐκ ὄντος
h Gen. 15. 13. αὐτῷ τέκνου. [h] Ἐλάλησε δὲ οὕτως ὁ Θεός· ὅτι ἔσται τὸ σπέρμα 6
αὐτοῦ πάροικον ἐν γῇ ἀλλοτρίᾳ, καὶ δουλώσουσιν
αὐτὸ καὶ κακώσουσιν, ἔτη τετρακόσια. καὶ τὸ ἔθνος, 7
ᾧ ἐὰν δουλεύσωσι, κρινῶ ἐγὼ, (εἶπεν ὁ Θεός·) καὶ μετὰ
ταῦτα ἐξελεύσονται καὶ λατρεύσουσί μοι ἐν τῷ τόπῳ
i Gen. 17. 9. & 21. 2. & 25. 24. & 29. 32. & 30. 5. & 35. 23. k Gen. 37. 28. τούτῳ. [i] Καὶ ἔδωκεν αὐτῷ διαθήκην περιτομῆς. καὶ οὕτως ἐγέννησε 8
τὸν Ἰσαὰκ, καὶ περιέτεμεν αὐτὸν τῇ ἡμέρᾳ τῇ ὀγδόῃ· καὶ ὁ Ἰσαὰκ
τὸν Ἰακὼβ, καὶ ὁ Ἰακὼβ τοὺς δώδεκα πατριάρχας. [k] Καὶ οἱ πατριάρχαι 9
ζηλώσαντες τὸν Ἰωσὴφ ἀπέδοντο εἰς Αἴγυπτον. Καὶ ἦν ὁ Θεὸς μετ᾽
l Gen. 41. 37. αὐτοῦ, [l] καὶ ἐξείλετο αὐτὸν ἐκ πασῶν τῶν θλίψεων αὐτοῦ, καὶ ἔδωκεν 10

sense, and that the οὐ is for οὔπω. *Οὐδὲ βῆμα ποδὸς* is to be taken like our idiom, "not a *foot* of land," for, none at all. See Deut. ii. 5. Gen. viii. 1. and the examples of Wets. from the Classical writers. *Εἰς κατάσχεσιν.* Sub. αὐτῆς for ὥστε κατέχειν αὐτήν. Κατάσχεσις signifies *occupancy*, and, by the adjunct, *possession.*

6, 7. The passage is from Gen. xv. 13, 14. and as the Commentators remark, is cited from memory. There are several variations from the Sept., all, however, unimportant, except that, 1. καὶ ταπεινώσουσιν αὐτοὺς are added in the Sept. after κακ. Yet the words are not in the Hebrew, and seem to have come from the margin as a gloss, probably from Judith v. 11.; or perhaps were a different version of וְעִנּוּ. 2. The words Εἶπεν ὁ Θεὸς are found neither in the Hebrew nor LXX. But they form no part of the quotation, being a parenthetical remark, such as we often find interposed in citations from the O. T. As to the words ὧδε μετὰ ἀποσκευῆς πολλῆς being found in both the Hebrew and the LXX., but not in the N. T., this is no instance of *discrepancy;* because Stephen evidently did not mean to adduce *those* words, but stops at ἐξελεύσονται. There is a seeming discrepancy in the words καὶ λατρεύσουσί μοι ἐν τῷ τόπῳ τούτῳ, which are neither in the Hebrew nor the Sept. But though not there, something very similar occurs at v. 16. And Stephen does not adduce the words as *immediately following the preceding*. Surenh. too has proved that it was a custom with the Jewish doctors (and therefore sometimes adopted by the writers of the N. T.), when they cited any passages of the O. T., to occasionally *add* words *elsewhere* employed on the same subject, and occasionally with a slight variation of them *for adaptation*. And, besides, that the words are found *in substance* at v. 16., they seem to have been *suggested* by a kindred passage at Exod. iii. 12. ἐν τῷ ἐξαγαγεῖν σε τὸν λαόν μου ἐξ Αἰγύπτου, καὶ λατρεύσετε τῷ Θεῷ ἐν τῷ ὄρει τούτῳ. Thus there is, on the principles of Jewish writing, *no actual discrepancy.*

Πάροικον well expresses the Heb. גֵּר, because, as the latter is a participial noun, so is the former properly an *adjective*, as appears from Herodot. vii. 235. Thus, in the Heb. גֵּר יִהְיֶה. we may suppose a participial noun and the verb substantive as put for the finite verb, from which the participial noun is derived.

— τετρακόσια.] The Chronological difficulty here involved is not so much in the thirty years' difference between this estimate and that of Josephus (because τετρακ. may be taken as a round number; and even Josephus himself sometimes makes it 400), as how to reconcile this with the *fact*, that the Israelites were in Egypt *at the most* but 243 years. Nor can this difficulty be satisfactorily removed by the *parenthesis* which Markl. would introduce; besides, the construction of the Hebrew will not *permit* it. The difficulty may best be removed by bearing in mind that the *subject* of the verbs עֲבָדוּם and עִנּוּ, as also of δουλώσουσι and κακώσουσι, is to be sought in the noun אֶרֶץ γῇ, and thus it will be the *inhabitants of that land*. And if the truth of chronology limits the abode of the Israelites in Egypt to 243 years, and assigns 400 as the time which elapsed between Abraham's leaving Chaldea and the period when they were established in Canaan, I see not how we can suppose otherwise than that the verbs above-mentioned, though having a *common subject* in γῇ, yet have a *two-fold reference*, — in the former verb to the *Egyptians*, in the latter to the *inhabitants of the countries* wherein they sojourned *in affliction* from the time they left to the time they were settled in Canaan. Thus we may render, "And they (i. e. the Egyptians) shall enslave them, and they (i. e. the Edomites, Canaanites, &c.) shall afflict them." It is true that the Commentators, with our common Version, take עֲבָדוּם as a verb *neuter;* and this is maintained by Rosenm. Yet he is obliged to suppose, with great harshness. the suffix ם as put for the separate form לָהֶם. But that is surely *courting* a difficulty, since the verb may be taken in an *active* sense, as it was by the LXX., and is done by Montanus and Gesenius, who in his Lex. gives several examples, and *resolves* the suffix ם into בָּם; though *ellipsis* rather than *resolution* seems to be the principle here to be resorted to.

— κρινῶ] "I will *punish:*" a signification arising from the adjunct. See Pearce.

8. διαθήκην περιτομῆς] i. e. the covenant sealed by circumcision. The recent Commentators, for the most part, take it to mean "a precept or rite of circumcision." But the authority for that sense is but slender, and the necessity for it here not very urgent; for the objections raised by Kuin. to the *common* version do not apply to the *above.* This use of the Genit. is frequent.

— καὶ οὕτως] "and so," i. e. in virtue of that covenant. Πατριάρχας. So called as being the primogenitors and heads of the πατριαὶ or tribes.

9. ἀπέδοντο εἰς Αἰγ.] Here there is an ellip.

αὐτῷ χάριν καὶ σοφίαν ἐναντίον Φαραὼ βασιλέως Αἰγύπτου· καὶ
κατέστησεν αὐτὸν ἡγούμενον ἐπ' Αἴγυπτον καὶ ὅλον τὸν οἶκον αὐτοῦ.
11 Ἦλθε δὲ λιμὸς ἐφ' ὅλην τὴν γῆν Αἰγύπτου καὶ Χαναὰν, καὶ θλίψις
12 μεγάλη· καὶ οὐχ εὕρισκον χορτάσματα οἱ πατέρες ἡμῶν. [m] Ἀκούσας [m Gen. 42. 1.]
δὲ Ἰακὼβ ὄντα σῖτα ἐν Αἰγύπτῳ, ἐξαπέστειλε τοὺς πατέρας ἡμῶν
13 πρῶτον. [n] καὶ ἐν τῷ δευτέρῳ ἀνεγνωρίσθη Ἰωσὴφ τοῖς ἀδελφοῖς αὐτοῦ, [n Gen. 45. 3.]
14 καὶ φανερὸν ἐγένετο τῷ Φαραὼ τὸ γένος τοῦ Ἰωσήφ. [o] Ἀποστείλας δὲ [o Gen. 46. 27. Deut. 10. 22.]
Ἰωσὴφ μετεκαλέσατο τὸν πατέρα αὐτοῦ Ἰακὼβ καὶ πᾶσαν τὴν συγγένειαν
15 αὐτοῦ, ἐν ψυχαῖς ἑβδομήκοντα πέντε. [p] Κατέβη δὲ Ἰακὼβ εἰς Αἴγυπτον, [p Gen. 46. 5. & 49. 33.]
16 καὶ ἐτελεύτησεν αὐτὸς καὶ οἱ πατέρες ἡμῶν. [q] καὶ μετετέθησαν εἰς [q Gen. 47. 30. & 50. 13.]
Συχὲμ καὶ ἐτέθησαν ἐν τῷ μνήματι ὃ ὠνήσατο [Ἀβραὰμ] τιμῆς ἀργυ- [Gen. 23. 16. & 33. 19. Jos. 24. 32.]
17 ρίου παρὰ τῶν υἱῶν Ἐμμὸρ τοῦ Συχέμ. [r] Καθὼς δὲ ἤγγιζεν ὁ χρόνος [r Exod. 1. 7, 8.]
τῆς ἐπαγγελίας, ἧς ὤμοσεν ὁ Θεὸς τῷ Ἀβραὰμ, ηὔξησεν ὁ λαὸς καὶ
18 ἐπληθύνθη ἐν Αἰγύπτῳ, ἄχρις οὗ ἀνέστη βασιλεὺς ἕτερος, ὃς οὐκ ᾔδει
19 τὸν Ἰωσήφ. Οὗτος κατασοφισάμενος τὸ γένος ἡμῶν, ἐκάκωσε τοὺς
πατέρας ἡμῶν, τοῦ ποιεῖν ἔκθετα τὰ βρέφη αὐτῶν, εἰς τὸ μὴ ζωογο-

either of κομισθησόμενον, of which the Commentators adduce many examples, or of κατάγεσθαι, according to Bos. In saying ζηλώσαντες, Stephen means to hint at his own case; for Joseph, though the peculiar favourite of God, yet was hated by his brethren.

10. χάριν καὶ σοφίαν.] The best Commentators regard this as a Hendiadys, for χάριν σοφίας, "favour by his wisdom." But that is contrary to the nature of a Hendiadys. It would be *better* to suppose a *hysteron proteron*. Yet that will be unnecessary, if we take ἐναντίον as belonging to both χάριν and σοφίαν, with adaptation to each, q. d. "gave him favour in the sight of Pharaoh, and wisdom in his sight, so as to be also esteemed wise."

11. χορτάσματα.] The word is properly used of food for cattle; and (like χορτάζω in the N. T. and the later Greek writers frequently) is very rarely applied to food for *men* (see Valckn.); when it *is*, it is only to the coarser sorts, and such as are used from necessity.

12. σῖτα.] The plural is used to denote *generality* of kind, as we say *corn*, or *grain*.

13. ἀνεγνωρίσθη] "made himself known." This use of the Passive (like the Hebrew conjugation Hithpahel) answers to the *reflected* verbs of the modern languages.

14. ἐν ψυχαῖς ἑβδ.] The best Commentators would supply συνισταμένην. But that is too arbitrary an ellipse. In fact, there is here none at all; for in the passage of Deut. x. 22, on which the present is formed, the ἐν is for σὺν, and ב is for *with*, *accompanied by*. So Numb. xx. 20. בְּעַם כָּבֵד. The best mode of removing the seeming discrepancy in the number is that of Hamm., Wets., and others, who think that the LXX. numbered among the posterity of Jacob the five sons of Manasseh and Ephraim born in Egypt, and that these were omitted by *Moses*, because they were born after Jacob's departure, but by the LXX. at Gen. xlvi. 20. are expressly *added* from Paral. vii. 14.

16. As to the discrepancy between the present account and that in Gen. xlix. 30, the best Critics are of opinion, that Ἀβραὰμ is spurious, and that μετετέθησαν and ἐτέθησαν are to be referred to the words οἱ πατέρες ἡμῶν only, not to Ἰακὼβ also; and that at ὠνήσατο we must supply, from the preceding, Ἰακώβ. The reading of some very ancient MSS. ὁ πατὴρ ἡμῶν attests at least that, at an early period, Ἀβραὰμ was not here, and that something was thought to be wanting; which was, it seems, supplied in two ways. To understand Ἰακὼβ from the preceding, is not near so harsh, as in many examples which might be adduced from Thucyd. And indeed there is the less harshness here, since *Jacob* is the chief subject of these two sentences, that of the other is only incidental.

17. καθὼς] "when;" a very rare sense, but occurring in 2 Macc. i. 31. and formed on that of ὡς, *when*. It may best be rendered, *as soon as*.

18. οὐκ ᾔδει τὸν Ἰ.] "had no respect for Joseph, or his merits," was ill affected to him and his memory; as 1 Thess. iv. 4. v. 12. Matt. xxv. 13.

19. κατασοφισάμενος.] The sense is, "plotting our destruction by crafty devices;" a sentiment farther evolved in a kindred passage of Judith v. 11, which Stephen, no doubt, had in view: καὶ ἐπανέστη αὐτοῖς ὁ βασιλεὺς Αἰγύπτου, καὶ κατεσοφίσαντο αὐτοὺς ἐν πόνῳ καὶ ἐν πλίνθῳ, καὶ ἐταπείνωσαν αὐτοὺς, καὶ ἔθεντο αὐτοὺς εἰς δούλους. The passage, too, is formed on Exod. i. 10. Sept. Pharaoh's policy is called by Philo the using ἐπινοίας δυσσιούργους. In τοῦ ποιεῖν the Genit. expresses *scope* and *purpose*. Ποιεῖν ἔκθετα is for ἐκτιθέναι, a term appropriate to the abandonment of infants. It is strange that Hamm., Pearce, and Wakef. should understand this of the *Egyptians* causing or ordering the exposure, not of the *Israelites* themselves. The words will not bear that sense, and the context rejects it; for here we have an *illustration* of the crafty *policy* of Pharaoh, which was to reduce the Israelites to a state of such extreme misery, that the population might *at any rate* be kept down even by *infanticide*.

—εἰς τὸ μὴ ζωογ.] "that they might not be preserved," namely, to experience the miserable fate of their parents. On the same principle as that on which the N. American Indian women often destroy their female children. The verb ζωογ. is found also in the Sept.

s Exod. 2. 2. Heb. 11. 23. νεῖσθαι. s Ἐν ᾧ καιρῷ ἐγεννήθη Μωϋσῆς, καὶ ἦν ἀστεῖος τῷ Θεῷ· 20
t Exod. 2. 7. ὃς ἀνετράφη μῆνας τρεῖς ἐν τῷ οἴκῳ τοῦ πατρὸς αὐτοῦ. t Ἐκτεθέντα 21
δὲ αὐτὸν, ἀνείλετο αὐτὸν ἡ θυγάτηρ Φαραὼ, καὶ ἀνεθρέψατο αὐτὸν
ἑαυτῇ εἰς υἱόν. Καὶ ἐπαιδεύθη Μωϋσῆς πάσῃ σοφίᾳ Αἰγυπτίων· ἦν 22
δὲ δυνατὸς ἐν λόγοις καὶ ἐν ἔργοις. Ὡς δὲ ἐπληροῦτο αὐτῷ τεσσαρα- 23
κονταετὴς χρόνος, ἀνέβη ἐπὶ τὴν καρδίαν αὐτοῦ ἐπισκέψασθαι τοὺς
u Exod. 2. 11. ἀδελφοὺς αὐτοῦ τοὺς υἱοὺς Ἰσραήλ. u Καὶ ἰδών τινα ἀδικούμενον, 24
ἠμύνατο καὶ ἐποίησεν ἐκδίκησιν τῷ καταπονουμένῳ, πατάξας τὸν Αἰγύπτιον. Ἐνόμιζε δὲ συνιέναι τοὺς ἀδελφοὺς αὐτοῦ, ὅτι ὁ Θεὸς διὰ χειρὸς 25
x Exod. 2. 13. αὐτοῦ δίδωσιν αὐτοῖς σωτηρίαν· οἱ δὲ οὐ συνῆκαν. x Τῇ δὲ ἐπιούσῃ 26
ἡμέρᾳ, ὤφθη αὐτοῖς μαχομένοις, καὶ συνήλασεν αὐτοὺς εἰς εἰρήνην,
εἰπών· Ἄνδρες, ἀδελφοί ἐστε ὑμεῖς· ἱνατί ἀδικεῖτε ἀλλήλους; Ὁ δὲ 27
ἀδικῶν τὸν πλησίον ἀπώσατο αὐτὸν, εἰπών· Τίς σε κατέστησεν ἄρχοντα
καὶ δικαστὴν ἐφ᾽ ἡμᾶς; μὴ ἀνελεῖν με σὺ θέλεις, ὃν τρόπον ἀνεῖλες 28

20. *ἀστεῖος τῷ Θεῷ.*] Ἀστεῖος is from the dat. sing. of ἄστυ, and properly signifies (like the Latin *urbanus) polite* as opposed to ἀγροῖκος. And as the inhabitants of cities are supposed to exceed those of the country not only in politeness, but in comeliness, so ἀστεῖος came to mean *handsome.* Τῷ Θεῷ is by the Commentators referred to a Hebraism; by which, to express the excellence of any person or thing, the name of God, or those of the angels, are subjoined in the Genit. or Dat. to the Positive, which thus attains a Superlative sense. The *Greeks* effect this by an *adjective* derived from some name of God. Ὅς is to be resolved into "and he."

21. *ἐκτεθέντα δὲ αὐτόν.*] These words are commonly regarded as Accusatives absolute; though recent Commentators prefer supposing a pleonasm of αὐτόν; which, however, within so short a distance, can hardly be admitted. Perhaps it may better be referred to Matthiæ Gr. Gr. § 426. 3, by which, to a substantive expressing the leading idea of a proposition, and put at its beginning, is supplied *quod attinet ad;* where the old Philologists supposed an ellipse of κατὰ, but the recent ones suppose a breaking off of the construction; Ἀνελέσθαι properly signifies to *take up*, and is often used of raising up drowning men from the sea, or taking up corpses for burial; but sometimes, as here, of taking up exposed children. So Aristoph. Nub. 531. κἀγὼ Ἐξέθηκα, παῖς δ' ἑτέρα τις λαβοῦσ' ἀνείλετο. By the very nature of the sense there is an adjunct notion of *taking care of.*

22. *ἐπαιδεύθη*, &c.] In adverting to this circumstance, Stephen, as before, seems to follow the *tradition of the Jews;* for nothing to this purpose is found in *Scripture.*

— *πάσῃ σοφίᾳ Αἰγ.*] Of παιδεύεσθαι with the dative (ἐν being understood) examples are adduced by Wets., e. gr. Isocr. τοῖς νεωτέροις ἤθεσι π. With the expression παιδ. πάσῃ σοφίᾳ Αἰγ. Pricæus compares Lucian Philop. θαυμάσιος τὴν σοφίαν, καὶ τὴν παιδείαν πᾶσαν Αἰγυπτίων εἰδώς. This wisdom consisted (as we learn from Philo, in his life of Moses) of astronomy and astrology, the interpretation of dreams, magic, mathematics, medicine, &c. Nay, as Bp. Warburton (who in his Divine Legation everywhere extols the wisdom of the Egyptians) also avers, in the science of *Legislation* and *Civil Polity.* Indeed, all the greatest writers of antiquity agree in calling Egypt the mother of wisdom and science. See more in Rec. Syn.

— *δυνατὸς — ἔργοις.*] This may seem inconsistent with the impediment, which Moses is known to have had in his speech. Insomuch that at Exod. iv. 16. we find Aaron his *spokesman* to the people. But (as the best Commentators are agreed) δυνατὸς and ἐν λόγοις are applicable to *persuasive,* and therefore *powerful,* though not *eloquent,* oratory. And that Moses had *this* faculty, we learn from Joseph. Ant. iii. 1. 4. and may infer it from Scripture. I would here compare Thucyd. i. 139. λέγειν τε καὶ πράσσειν δυνατώτατος, where see Note.

23. *τεσσ. χρόνος.*] This circumstance, too, is founded solely on Jewish tradition, of which vestiges are found in the Rabbinical writings. On ἀνέβη, &c. see Note on Luke xxiv. 38.

24. *ἐποίησεν ἐκδίκ.*] An Hellenistic phrase for ἐξεδίκησεν. Πατάξας, i. e. unto death, as we find from what follows. Indeed ἐπάταξε should be rendered *slew,* which is supported by the Pesch. Syr. So also in Matt. xxvi. 31. Mark xiv. 27. and in the Sept., formed on the same use of the Heb. הכה which (at least in its form Kal.) gave birth to the Latin *nec*-are. τῷ καταπονουμένῳ means the aggrieved party. That Moses *intended* to slay the Egyptian, cannot be proved; though Grot. shows it was justifiable.

25. *συνιέναι — σωτηρίαν.*] They knew in general from tradition what God had promised to Abraham; and might imagine or hope that the time of their deliverance drew near. Hence from the proof given by Moses of his readiness to venture his very life to serve them, they might have concluded that he was appointed of God to be the means of their deliverance. And Moses might justly suppose that they would so conclude. Such appears to be the full sense intended.

26. *συνήλασεν — εἰρήνην.*] Συνελαύνειν signifies properly to compel a person to go anywhere by hedging him in, and leaving him no other course. It is, however, in the later writers used of *compulsion generally;* and sometimes, as here, the *moral* compulsion of *earnest persuasion* is meant.

27. *τίς σε κατέστησεν — ἡμᾶς.*] This has the air of a proverbial expression, and may be compared

29 χθὲς τὸν Αἰγύπτιον; Ἔφυγε δὲ Μωϋσῆς ἐν τῷ λόγῳ τούτῳ, καὶ
30 ἐγένετο πάροικος ἐν γῇ Μαδιάμ, οὗ ἐγέννησεν υἱοὺς δύο. ʸ Καὶ πλη- ʸ Exod. 3. 2.
ρωθέντων ἐτῶν τεσσαράκοντα, ὤφθη αὐτῷ ἐν τῇ ἐρήμῳ τοῦ ὄρους Σινᾶ
31 ἄγγελος Κυρίου ἐν φλογὶ πυρὸς βάτου. Ὁ δὲ Μωϋσῆς ἰδὼν ἐθαύμασε
τὸ ὅραμα· προσερχομένου δὲ αὐτοῦ κατανοῆσαι, ἐγένετο φωνὴ Κυρίου
32 πρὸς αὐτόν· Ἐγὼ ὁ Θεὸς τῶν πατέρων σου, ὁ Θεὸς Ἀβραὰμ καὶ ὁ
Θεὸς Ἰσαὰκ καὶ ὁ Θεὸς Ἰακώβ. Ἔντρομος δὲ γενόμενος Μωϋσῆς οὐκ
33 ἐτόλμα κατανοῆσαι. Εἶπε δὲ αὐτῷ ὁ Κύριος· Λῦσον τὸ ὑπόδημα
34 τῶν ποδῶν σου· ὁ γὰρ τόπος ἐν ᾧ ἕστηκας γῆ ἁγία ἐστίν. Ἰδὼν
εἶδον τὴν κάκωσιν τοῦ λαοῦ μου τοῦ ἐν Αἰγύπτῳ, καὶ τοῦ στεναγμοῦ
αὐτῶν ἤκουσα· καὶ κατέβην ἐξελέσθαι αὐτούς· καὶ νῦν δεῦρο, απο-
35 στελῶ σε εἰς Αἴγυπτον. Τοῦτον τὸν Μωϋσῆν ὃν ἠρνήσαντο, εἰπόντες·
Τίς σὲ κατέστησεν ἄρχοντα καὶ δικαστήν; τοῦτον ὁ Θεὸς ἄρχοντα
καὶ λυτρωτὴν ἀπέστειλεν ἐν χειρὶ ἀγγέλου τοῦ ὀφθέντος αὐτῷ ἐν τῇ
36 βάτῳ. ᶻ Οὗτος ἐξήγαγεν αὐτούς, ποιήσας τέρατα καὶ σημεῖα ἐν γῇ ᶻ Exod. 7. & 8. & 9. & 10. & 11. & 14. & 16. 1.
‡ Αἰγύπτου, καὶ ἐν Ἐρυθρᾷ θαλάσσῃ, καὶ ἐν τῇ ἐρήμῳ ἔτη τεσσαρά-

with what the Sodomites said to Lot, Gen. xix. 9. Compare also Luke xii. 14.

30. Σινᾶ.] Moses says *Horeb*. But the mountain had, like Parnassus, a double summit, forming two peaks, one Horeb, the other Sinai.

— ἐν φλογὶ πυρὸς β.] Literally, in a flame of a bush of fire, i. e. on fire, the Genit. πυρὸς being for an adjective. It is scarcely necessary to advert to the unhallowed speculations of some recent foreign Commentators on the nature of this circumstance, which they seek to lower to the level of a natural phænomenon, and endeavour to account for in various ways; but in vain; for the *preternatural* (and what *else* could have answered the purpose) cannot, after all, be got rid of. It were well if the persons in question would here learn a lesson from the *heathen sages*, the theme of their too indiscriminate admiration. Thus Pind. Pyth. x. 76. ἐμοὶ δὲ, θαυμάσια Θεῶν τελεσάντων, οὐδέν ποτε φαίνεται ἔμεν ἄπιστον. Such is, I conceive, the right reading and punctuation of this passage. The common reading θαυμάσαι might well perplex Heyne (who, indeed, confesses that he knows not what to make of it) since it is evidently *corrupt*. That the *metre* admits this reading, cannot be doubted; since the long syllable σαι has its equivalent in two short ones: and the two short ones may be pronounced as *one*, *per synizesin*. The term, too, is especially applicable to the works of the *Deity*. See Joel iii. 26. Is. xxv. 1. Hence in Num. xiv. 11. it is in the Alexandrian MS. used to denote *miracle*. With respect to the sentiment itself, it is a profound remark of Pausanias, x. 4, 4. ἐς τὰ παράδοξα ἀπίστους εἶναι τῶν ἀνθρώπων. οἷς ἂν μὴ παρὰ τὸν αὐτῶν γίνηται βίον θεάμασιν ἐπιτυχεῖν λόγου μείζοσιν.

31. Κατανοέω properly signifies, "to master any thing in thought," to "understand;" but here, by a usual interchange of the notions of internal and external sense, to *examine*; of which examples are adduced by the Commentators.

32. Ἔντρομος.] Of the same formation with ἔμφοβος, words *conjoined* in Heb. xii. 21. The tremor is, however, to be ascribed not so much to *fear*, as to *awe*.

33. λῦσον τὸ ὑπόδ. &c.] In order to secure a due cleanliness in the performances of any of the offices of religion, it was, from the earliest ages, directed that the worshipper should take off his sandals before he entered a temple. And the custom still continues in the East, where it, no doubt, originated. From thence it seems to have passed to Egypt, where it was noticed and borrowed by Pythagoras; who, among his other maxims, enjoins θύειν ἀνυπόδετον καὶ πρὸς ἱερὰ προσιέναι. That it passed early and was adopted universally in the West, is plain from the Greek and Latin citations in Wetstein and others.

34. ἰδὼν εἶδον] "planissimè cognovi." This idiom, (by which to a verb is subjoined a participle, either of the same verb or one of cognate signification), though by most Commentators esteemed a *Hebraism*, is yet pure Greek; though it occurs so rarely as scarcely to alter the case. The idiom was, no doubt, of Oriental origin, and the few examples found in the Classical writers are among the vestiges of the Oriental origin of the Greek language. Thus they are chiefly adduced from the most *ancient* writers, and in the most *antique* dialects.

— κάκωσιν.] A rare word, of which Wets. adduces only one example from Plutarch. Yet I have noted it also in Thucyd. vii. 4. and 82. ii. 43.

— κατέβην ἐξελέσθαι.] From this Kuin. takes occasion to observe, that the ancients supposed the Deity to act much after the manner of men. Yet expressions like the present κατ' ἀνθρωποπάθειαν, were rather resorted to from *necessity*, originated in *human ignorance*, and were used in condescension to *human weakness*.

35. τοῦτον — τοῦτον.] The construction is here κατ' ἀνανταπόδοτον, the τοῦτον being repeated after the parenthesis, for the sake both of clearness and strength. It is obvious that this is meant to bear upon the case of our Lord Jesus Christ, whom they had rejected, as their forefathers at first did Moses. See Doddr.

— λυτρωτήν.] The word properly means one who redeems another from captivity by paying his λύτρον or ransom.

36. Αἰγύπτου.] Αἰγύπτῳ is found in many MSS. and early Edd., and is preferred by several Editors

a Deut. 18. 15, 18. supra 3. 22. κοντα. [a] Οὗτός ἐστιν ὁ Μωϋσῆς ὁ εἰπὼν τοῖς υἱοῖς Ἰσραήλ· Προ- 37
φήτην ὑμῖν ἀναστήσει Κύριος ὁ Θεὸς ὑμῶν ἐκ τῶν
b Exod. 19. 3, 20. ἀδελφῶν ὑμῶν, ὡς ἐμέ· αὐτοῦ ἀκούσεσθε. [b] Οὗτός ἐστιν 38
ὁ γενόμενος ἐν τῇ ἐκκλησίᾳ ἐν τῇ ἐρήμῳ μετὰ τοῦ ἀγγέλου τοῦ λαλοῦντος αὐτῷ ἐν τῷ ὄρει Σινᾶ καὶ τῶν πατέρων ἡμῶν, ὃς ἐδέξατο
λόγια ζῶντα δοῦναι ἡμῖν. Ὧι οὐκ ἠθέλησαν ὑπήκοοι γενέσθαι οἱ 39
πατέρες ἡμῶν, ἀλλ᾽ ἀπώσαντο, καὶ ἐστράφησαν ταῖς καρδίαις αὐτῶν
c Exod. 32. 1. εἰς Αἴγυπτον, [c] εἰπόντες τῷ Ἀαρών· Ποίησον ἡμῖν θεοὺς οἳ προπορεύ- 40
σονται ἡμῶν· ὁ γὰρ Μωϋσῆς οὗτος, ὃς ἐξήγαγεν ἡμᾶς ἐκ γῆς Αἰγύ-
πτου —, οὐκ οἴδαμεν τί γέγονεν αὐτῷ. Καὶ ἐμοσχοποίησαν ἐν ταῖς 41
ἡμέραις ἐκείναις, καὶ ἀνήγαγον θυσίαν τῷ εἰδώλῳ, καὶ εὐφραίνοντο ἐν
d Jer. 19. 13. Amos 5. 25. τοῖς ἔργοις τῶν χειρῶν αὐτῶν. [d] Ἔστρεψε δὲ ὁ Θεός, καὶ παρέδωκεν 42
αὐτοὺς λατρεύειν τῇ στρατιᾷ τοῦ οὐρανοῦ· καθὼς γέγραπται ἐν βίβλῳ
τῶν προφητῶν· Μὴ σφάγια καὶ θυσίας προσηνέγκατέ μοι
ἔτη τεσσαράκοντα ἐν τῇ ἐρήμῳ, οἶκος Ἰσραήλ; Καὶ 43

and Commentators. The *οὗτος* is here emphatic, and very significant; q. d. vir ille magnus.

37. *ὡς ἐμέ.*] Sub. *ἀνέστησε* taken from *ἀναστήσει* preceding. See iii. 22. and Note

38. *ὁ γενόμενος — μετὰ*] "who communicated with the angel;" namely, by acting as mediating interpreter between God and the *ἐκκλησία*, i. e. the assembly of Israelites congregated on Mount Sinai, at the promulgation of the Law. The construction is *γενέσθαι μετὰ τοῦ ἀγγέλου καὶ (μετὰ) τῶν πατέρων ἡμ.* On the *ἀγγέλ.*, denoting the Angel-Jehovah, see Note on v. 53.

— *ζῶντα.*] *Ζῶντα* here means either *valid*, *efficacious*, or, taking it for *ζωοποιοῦντα*, as John vi. 51, and Heb. x. 20, (and so in Deut. xxxii. 47, the Law is said to be *ζωή*,) "most salutary;" namely, as regarded temporal life: or, again, conjoining both significations, "most efficacious and salutary." Thus the general sense of the passage is: "For even this Moses, who acted as the mediator between the Angel-Jehovah, and the congregation of the people, and who received these revelations of Divine will at the hand of God, even *he* could not secure their obedience to his authority. On the contrary, they rejected his authority, desired to return into Egypt, and seduced Aaron to make the golden calf, trampling on the authority both of Moses and God. See Note supra, v. 35.

39. *ἐστράφησαν — Αἴγυπτον.*] This is by some Commentators taken to mean, "they were bent on returning, their mind dwelt on returning thither." See Exod. xvi. 3; xvii. 3. Others interpret, "their affections reverted back to Egypt, its sensuality and idolatry." See Ezek. xx. 8. Both senses may be *included*.

40. *θεοὺς*] i. e. images of God. Of *προπορ. ἡμῶν.* It was customary with the Oriental nations of antiquity for the images of the gods to be borne before the people in journeys, or military expeditions, since they fancied they thus enjoyed their more effectual protection. See Numb. x. 33. compared with Deut. xxxi. 8. 1 Sam. iv. 3. (Heinr. and Kuin.)

— *ὁ γὰρ Μωϋσῆς*, &c.] An *anacoluthon*, to be filled up in translating by *quod attinet ad*.

41. *ἐμοσχοποίησαν.*] They had seen in Egypt Divinities worshipped under certain forms; and they were led to choose that of a *golden calf*, or ox, for a symbol of the true God, (though transgressing the Divine command, Exod. xx. 4,) because the Egyptians worshipped Osiris (a former monarch of Egypt, and the inventor or introducer of agriculture, &c.), under the form of a bull (Apis), as the symbol of agricultural labour. (Kuin.)

— *ἀνήγαγον θυσίαν.*] *Ἀνάγειν* signifies to *bring up*, and, from the adjunct, to *lay upon*; and is often used, especially in the later writers, of laying the victim on the altar. So the Hebr. הֶעֱלָה. *Εὐφραίνοντο ἐν.* The sense is, "celebrated sacrificial feastings to the honour of." See Exod. xxxii. 6.

42. *ἔστρεψε δὲ ὁ Θεός.*] This is variously explained by the Commentators; but the true interpretation is doubtless that of Beza, Pisc., Casaub., Grot., Hamm., Wets., Kuin., and others, *aversus est*, active for passive; or *se avertit*, act. for reflexive. *Παρέδωκεν*, "gave them up; i. e. *suffered them*, to serve," &c., as Chrys. and Theophyl. explain. *Στρατιᾷ τοῦ οὐρανοῦ*, צְבָא הַשָּׁמַיִם, the planets and stars. *Ἐν βίβλῳ τῶν προφ.*; i. e. the twelve minor (or shorter) Prophets.

— *μὴ σφάγια*, &c.] An interrogative sentence ushered in by *μὴ* (answering to the Hebr. הֲ) has generally the force of a negation. But as it appears from Scripture, that the Israelites *did* offer sacrifices to God in the desert, some other mode of explanation must be adopted. I am, therefore, still of opinion, (as in Rec. Syn.,) that the idiom has here the force of *assertion*: "Did ye indeed offer to me sacrifices for forty years in the wilderness? [yes;] and yet [*καὶ* for *καίτοι*] so little real was your piety, that [in conjunction with my worship] ye raised the tabernacle of Moloch." The above view is supported by a note of the learned Bornem. on Luke xvii. 9. "Rarissime *μὴ* interrogativum ita usurpatur, ut, qui loquitur, affirmari rem velit. Factum hoc memini Amos v. 35. indeque Acts vii. 42. *μὴ σφάγια καὶ θυσίας προσηνέγκατέ μοι* &c. (quo in loco multa frustra Kuinoelius tentavit) atque in iis exemplis, quæ hanc in rem laudavit Graser."

This citation is evidently from the *Sept.*, and in the main agrees with it exactly. The only variations are these, — that *οἶκος Ἰσραὴλ* is transposed, probably by citing from memory. For *Ῥεμφὰν* the Sept. has *Ῥαιφάν*; and for *Βαβυλῶνος*

ἀνελάβετε τὴν σκηνὴν τοῦ Μολὸχ, καὶ τὸ ἄστρον τοῦ Θεοῦ ὑμῶν Ῥεμφὰν, τοὺς τύπους οὓς ἐποιήσατε προσκυνεῖν αὐτοῖς· καὶ μετοικιῶ ὑμᾶς ἐπέκεινα † Βα-
44 βυλῶνος. [e] Ἡ σκηνὴ τοῦ μαρτυρίου ἦν ἐν τοῖς πατράσιν ἡμῶν ἐν τῇ ἐρήμῳ, καθὼς διετάξατο ὁ λαλῶν τῷ Μωϋσῇ, ποιῆσαι αὐτὴν κατὰ
45 τὸν τύπον ὃν ἑωράκει· [f] ἣν καὶ εἰσήγαγον διαδεξάμενοι οἱ πατέρες

e Exod. 25. 40. Heb. 8. 5.
f Josh. 3. 14.

has, together with the Hebrew, Δαμάσκου; which variations are discussed on the next verse.

43. τὴν σκηνὴν τοῦ Μολ.] On the subject *which* of the gods the Israelites worshipped under the name of Moloch (which signifies a *Sovereign Lord*) see Recens. Synop. Some suppose *Saturn*; others, *the Sun*, (the *King of* heaven) which is the more probable opinion, since Μολ. signifies *King*. Now all the nations of antiquity applied terms indicative of *royalty* to their gods. Thus, besides Moloch, *Bel* or *Baal*. Moloch was an image of immense size and hollow, brass gilt, (like several of the *Birman* idols,) with the face of a calf or bull, and the hands outstretched; very much like the *Mexican* idols described by Humboldt. This, however, only answers to the description of the idol in *after times*. At the period in question the idol was, no doubt, of small size, to admit of being easily hidden from the view of Moses and Aaron; and the σκηνὴ will thus denote a sort of *case* to inclose and convey it in; formed (it may be supposed) in imitation of a real *tabernacle*, and very much like those gilt *shrines*, or small *models* of the temple of Diana at Ephesus mentioned at Acts xix. 24, where see Note. Ἀνελάβετε refers to the bearing it on the shoulders, as in religious processions, or when raised and placed aloft at the celebration of religious worship.

— τὸ ἄστρον τοῦ Θεοῦ ὑμῶν] i. e. the image of him whom ye account as a God, and worship under the image of a star.

— Ῥεμφάν.] Mr. Townsend has diligently recounted the various hypotheses formed by the learned to reconcile the apparent discrepancy here between the Hebrew, the LXX., and N. T. As to the two last, it is plain that the same name is meant by both. The chief diversity is in the μ, which should seem not to be correct. The Ῥεφὰν of many MSS. of the N. T. or the Ῥαιφὰν of the LXX. seems to be the true spelling. Unless it be thought that the μ stands for another φ, of which, indeed, there is some vestige in the MSS. Be that as it may, all the most learned inquirers are agreed that by Ῥεφάν, or Ῥαιφὰν, was meant SATURN, of whom it was *one* of the names. And they are almost alike agreed in considering the CHIUN of the Hebrew as only *another name* of the same idol-deity. MOLOCH is also, with probability, supposed to be *another*: the compound idol (thinks Townsend) *originally* designed to represent the great Father, or *Noah*, but who was afterwards made the emblem of *the Sun*, the God of Zabaism. What is meant by the *star* is well explained by Faber ap. Townsend.

— καὶ] "and so," i. e. because of your idolatry and sinfulness, and that of your fore-fathers. Μετοικιῶ. The word generally imports no more than *to cause to emigrate*; but must here be understood of compulsory removal. Ἐπέκεινα is a compound expression, by an ellipse of μέρη, used for a preposition, and sometimes becomes a mere adverb. It governs the genitive, from the force of the noun μέρη, used in the *plena locutio*.

Instead of Βαβυλῶνος the Sept. has Δαμάσκου; a remarkable discrepancy, not easily reconciled. Some consider it as a slip of memory; which is little probable, and indeed cannot be admitted. It *may* possibly be (as Bp. Pearce supposes) an *alteration* of the speaker, accommodated to the fact; for, as the Israelites were carried so far into Media, (see 2 Kings xvii. 2,) which country lay not only *beyond Damascus*, but *beyond even Babylon*, Stephen, who knew that to be the fact, might justly say, as he does here, *beyond Babylon*; thereby fixing the place of their captivity more explicitly than the Prophet did, who spoke before the event had taken place. I am, however, rather inclined to suppose that the present reading is erroneous, and derived from the margin, where it was meant to state the *place* of the exile. And although the prophecy may be said to be *fulfilled*, as regards *Babylon* as well as Damascus, yet certainly there seems no reason why the speaker should have *exaggerated*. Nor are there wanting other instances of a gloss expelling the ancient reading.

44. Having dwelt on the ingratitude, impiety, and idolatry of the Israelites, Stephen adverts to the place of true Divine worship, — the τὴν σκηνὴν τοῦ μαρτυρίου by which the Sept. express the Hebr. אהל העדות at Numb. xvii. 8, and so called either with reference to the *tables of testimony* contained therein; or from its being the place where God gave witness of his glorious presence. See Exod. xxv. 40. Heb. viii. 5.

— καθὼς διετάξατο, &c.] The construction is elliptical, and the sense, when complete, is this: "[so built] as He who had conversed with Moses (i. e. Jehovah) had commanded him to build it, after the model shown to him." See Exod. xxv. 40. compared with Heb. viii. 5. The drift of the speaker in this and the three next verses is to moderate that self-complacent pride, which they entertained with respect to their Temple, by reminding them that, after the giving of the Law, their ancestors had worshipped God not in a magnificent temple, but in a moveable tabernacle. And therefore, that as the place for Divine worship *had been* changed at the pleasure of the Deity; so the worship of Him is not so bound to *one* place but that it might again be changed from the present Temple to some other place.

45. διαδεξάμενοι] scil. σκηνὴν, "having received it as handed down from their ancestors." The words μετὰ Ἰησοῦ are to be construed immediately after οἱ πατέρες. The best Interpreters are agreed that ἐν τῇ κατασχέσει is for εἰς τὴν κατάσχεσιν, as Numb. xxxii. 5. δοθήτω ἡμῖν ἡ γῆ ἐν κατασχέσει. and Deut. xxxii. 51, "into a land possessed by Gentiles." So supra v. 5. δοῦναι εἰς κατάσχεσιν αὐτὴν (τὴν γῆν). And so the LXX. render for [illegible]. I have, with Owen, Gratz, and Kuin., removed the comma after ἡμῶν, because ἕως τῶν ἡμ. Δ. cannot without great harshness be referred to εἰσήγαγον; whereas, when referred to ἐξῶσεν, &c., the construction is natural, and the sense arising excel-

ἡμῶν μετὰ Ἰησοῦ, ἐν τῇ κατασχέσει τῶν ἐθνῶν, ὧν ἐξῶσεν ὁ Θεὸς ἀπὸ
g 1 Sam. 16. 12, 13. προσώπου τῶν πατέρων ἡμῶν ἕως τῶν ἡμερῶν Δαυΐδ· [g] ὃς εὗρε χάριν 46
2 Sam. 7. 1. &c. 1 Chron. 17. 12. ἐνώπιον τοῦ Θεοῦ, καὶ ᾐτήσατο εὑρεῖν σκήνωμα τῷ Θεῷ Ἰακώβ.
Psal. 132. 5. h 1 Kings 6. 1. & 8. 27. [h] Σολομῶν δὲ ᾠκοδόμησεν αὐτῷ οἶκον. Ἀλλ᾽ οὐχ ὁ ὕψιστος ἐν χειρο- 47
infra 17. 24. i Isa. 66. 1. ποιήτοις [ναοῖς] κατοικεῖ, καθὼς ὁ προφήτης λέγει· [i] Ὁ οὐρανός 48
μοι θρόνος, ἡ δὲ γῆ ὑποπόδιον τῶν ποδῶν μου· ποῖον 49
οἶκον οἰκοδομήσετέ μοι, (λέγει Κύριος)· ἢ τίς τόπος τῆς
καταπαύσεώς μου; οὐχὶ ἡ χείρ μου ἐποίησε ταῦτα πάντα; 50
k Jer. 6. 10. & 9. 25, 26. Ezek. 44. 7. [k] Σκληροτράχηλοι, καὶ ἀπερίτμητοι τῇ καρδίᾳ καὶ τοῖς ὠσίν! ὑμεῖς 51
ἀεὶ τῷ Πνεύματι τῷ ἁγίῳ ἀντιπίπτετε· ὡς οἱ πατέρες ὑμῶν, καὶ

lent; for, as Bp. Pearce observes, those nations were not completely driven out till the days of David.

Bp. Newc. well represents the sense of ἐξῶσεν by "*continued* to drive out." Ἀπὸ τοῦ προσώπου is a Hebraism corresponding to מֵעַל פְּנֵי in the Hebrew Bible, and found in an ancient Punic inscription preserved by Procopius.

46. ᾐτήσατο] "asked for himself." De Dieu and Kuin. meet the difficulty involved in εὑρεῖν by a device of construction which is very harsh, and, indeed, unnecessary; for it may be effectually removed by a reference to Ps. cxxxii. 5, on which the expression here is founded, and where עַד־אֶמְצָא מִשְׁכָּנוֹת may be rendered, by supplying what is necessary to the sense from the preceding member (of which this is an exegetical parallelism), "Until I have found out a [*place for*; i. e. wherein I may *build* a] habitation," &c. For all the former member as far as לְ is to be *repeated* in the latter.

48. ναοῖς.] This is omitted in 7 MSS. and several Versions, and is cancelled by Griesb.; but, without sufficient reason, it being defended by Acts xvii. 24. Mark xiv. 58. Heb. ix. 11, 24; though, I grant, it *might* be introduced from the first of those passages. Nor is it very probable that the words should have been omitted from the *homeoteleuton*. Internal evidence is against it; but as the external evidence for it is very strong, it must be retained. Οὐ κατοικεῖ suggests the adjunct notion of "is not to be contained by." See Œcumen.

49, 50. The variations here from the LXX. will be in a manner none, if λέγει Κύριος be taken as *interposed* from what comes after. In the concluding words, indeed, instead of οὐχὶ — πάντα, we have in the LXX. πάντα γὰρ ἐποίησεν ἡ χείρ μου, which is countenanced by the Hebrew; where, if the present copies be correct, the sentence is expressed not interrogatively, but declaratively. I suspect, however, that the text is slightly corrupt, and needs the emendation which it may receive from the N. T. The corruption, if I mistake not, rests on וְאֶת, which seems not much to the purpose; for to take the וְ in the sense *for*, is *strained*. Some MSS. *omit* the וְ; but that is only *cutting* the knot. I suspect that the Prophet wrote הֲלֹא *nonne?* which occurs in Gen. iv. 7. and elsewhere. How easily וְ and הֲ and אֶת and לֹא might be confounded, it is scarcely necessary to remark.

I cannot but observe, that in the words immediately following, our common version, "and all these things have been," cannot be justified, as containing no suitable sense, nor such as the Hebrew words compel us to adopt. Still less can I approve Bp. Lowth's version, "and all these things are mine." He, indeed, supposes לִי (which he thinks absolutely necessary to the sense) *lost out of the text*, and to be *supplied from the LXX. and Syr.* But this is rash. The Syriac generally follows closely the LXX., and the Sept. Version is not by any means formed with such accuracy, as to enable us to be sure what was in the Hebrew at the time it was made. Not to say that לִי would not be good Hebrew. I suspect the ἐμὰ of the Sept. to have arisen from an attempt to *make out* the sense by the aid of the context. So far from the addition being indispensable, I see nothing wanting, if the passage be (as it ought to be) thus translated: "All these things did not my hand create? and [accordingly] they all of them were," i. e. brought into being. The passage, indeed, seems to have been in the mind of St. John, Revel. iv. 11. ὅτι σὺ ἔκτισας τὰ πάντα, καὶ διὰ τὸ θέλημά σου ἦσαν καὶ ἐκτίσθησαν.

51. There is here an abruptness of transition, which has led some Commentators to maintain that something was now said which has not been *recorded* by St. Luke. This, however, proceeds upon a most objectionable principle. The best Interpreters are agreed, that this change of manner, and transition from calm narration to sharp rebuke, was occasioned by some insult, or interruption on the part of the auditors. Yet that might not be, as they imagine, by open tumult, and clamours for the death of the prisoner, but rather (as Doddr. and Kuin. suppose) by low but deep murmurings, or hisses, and threatening gestures; which will account for, and justify the severity of what follows.

— σκληροτράχηλοι.] In most languages, obstinacy and perversity are expressed by terms derived from the notion of *stiffness*, or *hardness*. See Recens. Synop. In ἀπερίτμητοι τῇ καρδίᾳ, τῇ καρδίᾳ is added to show that the word is to be taken figuratively. For as circumcision was a symbol of moral purity, so περιτομὴ is, in the Old and New Testament, often applied to the mind and heart. See Jer. iv. 4. Thus by ἀπερίτ. τῇ καρδίᾳ are meant those whose vices are yet uncorrected (see Levit. xxvi. 41. Ezek. xliv. 7, 9.), and by ἀπερίτμ. τοῖς ὠσίν. those who turn a deaf ear to all calls to repentance and reformation, "whose ear (in the words of Jerem. vi. 10.) is uncircumcised, and they cannot hearken."

— ἀεὶ — ἀντιπίπτετε] "ye perpetually resist the Holy Spirit," i. e. the testimony of those who speak by the Holy Spirit; which is regarded as tantamount to resisting the Holy Spirit himself. See Matt. x. 40. and the parallel passages. Their

52 ὑμεῖς. Τίνα τῶν προφητῶν οὐκ ἐδίωξαν οἱ πατέρες ὑμῶν; καὶ ἀπέκτειναν τοὺς προκαταγγείλαντας περὶ τῆς ἐλεύσεως τοῦ Δικαίου, οὗ
53 νῦν ὑμεῖς προδόται καὶ φονεῖς γεγένησθε· [1] οἵτινες ἐλάβετε τὸν νόμον [1 Exod. 19. 3, et seqq. Gal. 3. 19.]
εἰς διαταγὰς ἀγγέλων, καὶ οὐκ ἐφυλάξατε· ......
54 Ἀκούοντες δὲ ταῦτα διεπρίοντο ταῖς καρδίαις αὐτῶν, καὶ ἔβρυχον
55 τοὺς ὀδόντας ἐπ᾽ αὐτόν. Ὑπάρχων δὲ πλήρης Πνεύματος ἁγίου, ἀτενίσας εἰς τὸν οὐρανὸν, εἶδε δόξαν Θεοῦ, καὶ Ἰησοῦν ἑστῶτα ἐκ δεξιῶν
56 τοῦ Θεοῦ, καὶ εἶπεν· Ἰδοὺ, θεωρῶ τοὺς οὐρανοὺς ἀνεῳγμένους, καὶ
57 τὸν Υἱὸν τοῦ ἀνθρώπου ἐκ δεξιῶν ἑστῶτα τοῦ Θεοῦ. Κράξαντες δὲ
φωνῇ μεγάλῃ, συνέσχον τὰ ὦτα αὐτῶν, καὶ ὥρμησαν ὁμοθυμαδὸν ἐπ᾽

forefathers had in like manner rejected the prophets sent from God, and inspired by the Holy Spirit. Ἀντιπίπτειν is *properly* used of one body falling foul of another, and figuratively signifies to *resist*. At καὶ there is an ellipse of οὕτω.

52. τοῦ Δικαίου] "the Messiah;" the term being (as Middl. observes) evidently used κατ' ἐξοχὴν to denote Christ. See iii. 14, 22. and Note on Luke xxiii. 47. In proof of the fact, that the name was used by the Jews to denote the expected Messiah, Bp. Middl. has adduced the strongest evidence, in a long extract from § 65. of the Dissert. Gener. subjoined to Kennicott's Hebrew Bible, to which he has added some additional proofs and illustrations.

— προδόται καὶ φονεῖς γεγέν.] The *former* by delivering him into the hands of Pilate, — the latter by requiring him to be put to death on false charges.

53. εἰς διαταγὰς ἀγγέλων.] This expression involves some difficulty, and consequently has been variously interpreted. Many eminent Commentators (as Schmid, Grotius, Glass, Heum., Doddr., Krebs, Loesn., and Morus) understand διαταγ. ἀγγ. to mean *troops or hosts of angels*; q. d. hosts of angels being present, as witnesses, at the promulgation thereof. But though that view seems much confirmed by Deut. xxxiii. 2. and Ps. lxviii. 17, yet we have no proof of διατ. ever having such a sense. And as what the above Expositors urge against the sense *promulgation*, — that to *God* alone, and not to angels, is the promulgation of the Law suited — the argument has in reality no force. It is truly observed by Calvin, that the best explanation of the present passage is one of St. Paul, Gal. iii. 19, where he says that the Law was διαταγεὶς δι' ἀγγέλων, as also at Heb. ii. 1. λαληθεὶς δι' ἀγγέλων. This may justly be thought to determine the interpretation here. I would therefore render, with Beza, Calvin, Hamm., Whitby, Wolf, Schoettg., Pearce, Kraus, Heinr., Koppe, Kuin., and Wahl: "Ye who have received the Law at the appointment of angels," i. e. angels being appointed as ministering instruments for its promulgation. Thus the expression is equivalent to ἐλάβετε τὸν νόμον διαταγέντα δι' ἀγγέλων. In this sense, too, the passage was taken by the ancients generally; and it is confirmed by a passage of Joseph. Ant. xv. 5. 3. ἡμῶν τὰ κάλλιστα τῶν δογμάτων καὶ τὰ ὁσιώτατα τῶν ἐν τοῖς νόμοις δι' ἀγγέλων τοῦ Θεοῦ μαθόντων. The plural διαταγὰς is put for the singular, with reference (as Bp. Pearce says) to the *several parts* of the Laws of Moses, which were given at different times, and were therefore several διαταγαί.

At ἐφυλάξατε the discourse seems to have been quite broken off, otherwise there would have been adduced the *inferences* and *application* from what had been said: on which see Note on ver. 1.

54. See Note supra v. 32, 33.

55. Πνεύματος ἁγ.] This must denote the *influence* of the Holy Spirit, animating and supporting him under the trial he had to encounter.

— εἶδε δόξαν Θεοῦ.] I can by no means approve of the view taken by many recent Interpreters, who regard the words as no more than a strongly figurative mode of expression, importing *full persuasion of what he did not see, as if he actually saw it*. But the words will not, without violence, admit of such a construction; and what follows, Ἰδοὺ θεωρῶ, quite *forbid* it, — being a positive assertion of something *really seen*. We *may* understand δόξαν Θεοῦ, with most Expositors, of the *Schechinah*, or symbol of the Divine presence, and suppose that the visual faculties of this illustrious Martyr were, miraculously, so strengthened, that the heavens and the throne of God were made visible to him; but I would rather, with some ancient and modern Commentators, suppose a *visionary representation*, — God miraculously operating on Stephen's imagination, as on Ezekiel's, when he sat in his house at Babylon among the Elders of Judah, and saw Jerusalem, and seemed to himself transported thither. See Ezek. viii. 1—4.

The best Commentators are agreed that Jesus was represented as sitting at the right hand of God, to suggest to Stephen the present help and support he might expect from the Divine power.

57. συνέσχον τὰ ὦτα.] Συνέχειν τὰ ὦτα signifies properly, not to *stop* the ears (Latin *occludere aures*), but to *close up* the ears by *drawing them together*, called in the Classical writers, ἐπιλαβεῖν, καταλαβεῖν, or ἐπέχεσθαι τὰ ὦτα. This they did, not so much to avoid hearing the fancied blasphemy, as it was a *symbolical action* expressive of detestation and abhorrence: this is plain from the passages of the Classical and Rabbinical writers adduced in Recens. Syn. So Plutarch, vol. ii. p. 1095. Τὰ ὦτα καταλήψῃ ταῖς χερσὶ, δυσχεραίνων καὶ βδελυττόμενος; That κράξαντες must be considered in the same light, and not be viewed as merely meant to drown the voice of Stephen, is plain from a passage of Irenæus ap. Euseb. Hist. Eccl. v. 20, cited by Wets.: εἴ τι τοιοῦτον ἀκήκοεν ἐκεῖνος ὁ μακάριος καὶ ἀποστολικὸς πρεσβύτερος, (Polycarp) ἀνακράξας καὶ ἐμφράξας τὰ ὦτα αὐτοῦ — πεφεύγοι ἂν τὸν τόπον, where Reading remarks: "Hic mos erat veterum Christianorum, ut si forte in familiari colloquio impium aliquem sermonem et à fidei Catholicæ regulâ dissentientem audiissent, protinus, obturatis auribus, sese in fugam darent."

m Infra 22. 20. αὐτόν. [m] καὶ ἐκβαλόντες ἔξω τῆς πόλεως, ἐλιθοβόλουν. καὶ οἱ μάρτυ- 58
ρες ἀπέθεντο τὰ ἱμάτια αὐτῶν παρὰ τοὺς πόδας νεανίου καλουμένου
n Matt. 5. 44. Luke 6. 28. & 23. 34. Σαύλου, [n] καὶ ἐλιθοβόλουν τὸν Στέφανον, ἐπικαλούμενον καὶ λέγοντα· 59
Κύριε Ἰησοῦ, δέξαι τὸ πνεῦμά μου! Θεὶς δὲ τὰ γόνατα, ἔκραξε φωνῇ 60
μεγάλῃ· Κύριε, μὴ στήσῃς αὐτοῖς τὴν ἁμαρτίαν ταύτην! καὶ τοῦτο
o Infra 22. 20. εἰπὼν ἐκοιμήθη. VIII. [o] Σαῦλος δὲ ἦν συνευδοκῶν τῇ ἀναιρέσει αὐ- 1
τοῦ. Ἐγένετο δὲ ἐν ἐκείνῃ τῇ ἡμέρᾳ διωγμὸς μέγας ἐπὶ τὴν ἐκκλη-
σίαν τὴν ἐν Ἱεροσολύμοις· πάντες τε διεσπάρησαν κατὰ τὰς χώρας τῆς
Ἰουδαίας καὶ Σαμαρείας, πλὴν τῶν ἀποστόλων. (συνεκόμισαν δὲ τὸν 2

58. ἐκβαλόντες] "having hurried him out of the city." Comp. Luke iv. 29.

— ἐλιθοβόλουν.] Since we have a little further on καὶ ἐλιθοβόλουν τὸν Στ., Markl. complains of an unnecessary repetition of the same thing. The difficulty, however (at which even Valckn. stumbled) may be removed by either, with Heinr., considering the first ἐλιθοβ. as denoting *preparation* for action; q. d. they set about stoning him; or (with Klotz, Pearce, Rosenm., and Kuin.) by taking the thing as expressed *more Historicorum generally:* and then (after an insertion respecting the keeping of the clothes by Saul) *particularly;* narrating by *whom* he was stoned, and describing some circumstances which attended the stoning.

— ἀπέθεντο.] A necessary preparation, since the stones destined for such a purpose were exceedingly large. This laying aside garments, in order to be lighter for any office, was usual with the long-vested inhabitants of Greece as well as of the East, and is alluded to by Aristoph. Vesp. 408. Ἀλλὰ θαἰμάτια βαλόντες, θεῖτε, καὶ βοᾶτε, καὶ — ἀγγέλλετε.

Though the whole proceeding was illegal and tumultuary, yet, (as Beza and Grot. observe), they conformed to the *letter* of the law; which directed that in cases of stoning, the witnesses should cast the first stone, — doubtless to denote their *responsibility* for what was done.

— νεανίου.] This term is used of men even in the flower of their age, and sometimes of those who have attained its maturity.

59. ἐπικαλούμενον, &c.] Bentley and Valckn. propose to insert Θεόν. The ΘΝ, they think, might easily have been absorbed by the preceding ON. But that this should have happened *in all* the MSS. is very improbable; not to say that the *Article* would be wanted. If, indeed, we were compelled to suppose invocation to *God* I see not how any thing short of the *express insertion* of the word could be admitted. That, however, is *not* the case; and why the Commentators should have been so anxious to make Stephen offer up invocation to *God*, I know not; since, as Markl. truly observes, "it were contrary to Stephen's intention; — which was to die a martyr to the *Divinity of Jesus Christ*. So that it is only *Him* he invokes." There is no reason why Κύριον Ἰησοῦν should not be *supplied* from the following words of the invocation Κύριε Ἰησοῦ. *Subauditions from the context* being, even in the Classics, sometimes taken from the words which *follow*. Or ἐπικαλούμενον may be taken in an *absolute* sense; (an idiom frequent in the best writers) and thus ἐπικ. and λέγ. may be rendered, "making invocation to this effect." It is quite plain that *Jesus* is the object of the invocation; which Kuin. fully admits, confirming this view from Rev. xxii. 20. where in the words ἔρχου, Κύριε Ἰησοῦ, it is certain that Jesus *is addressed in prayer* (as he is here) in terms which necessarily imply Divine power, and nothing short of *Deity*, even in language borrowed from his own holy example. See Luke xxiii. 34. How ill the Socinians digest this may be imagined; but one would scarcely suppose that even *they* could bring themselves to resort to the desperate expedient of supplying τὸν ὄχλον *ad libitum*. That, however, shows their conviction that τὸν Θεὸν cannot be supplied.

The best Commentators are agreed that δέξαι τὸ πνεῦμά μου must mean, "receive my soul to the mansions of the blessed." See Luke xvi. 9. John xiv. 3. and Notes, and consult Schoettg. ap. Recens. Synop.

60. μὴ στήσῃς α. τὴν ἁμ. τ.] Ἵστημι, as שׁקל, signifies, by an ellipse of ἐν ζυγῷ or σταθμῷ, (sometimes *supplied*) to *weigh*, and also (as the custom of remote antiquity was to weigh out, not number, money) to *pay*. And as God was by the Hebrews represented as weighing the actions of men, by placing the good and the evil ones in a pair of scales separately, (see Dan. v. 27. Ps. xc. 8.), so the best Expositors take the phrase to mean, "Do not examine their sin in the balance," and consequently visit it with punishment. But we may more simply consider the sense as "Do not put to the balance this their sin," i. e. do not put it into the scale which contains their sins, do not *impute* it to them, *lay it not to their charge;* as our authorized version renders.

— ἐκοιμήθη.] This is both an euphemism, and meant to suggest the composure with which this Protomartyr met so violent a death.

VIII. 1. Σαῦλος — αὐτοῦ.] These words are closely connected with the preceding, from which they ought not to have been disjoined by the division of Chapters. Συνευδ. signifies to approve of any thing with another. See Tittm. de Syn 191.

— πάντες.] This must be received with limitation, for *a very considerable number;* since there is little doubt but that many of the lower ranks were suffered to remain in Jerusalem.

— πλὴν τῶν ἀποστόλων.] *They remained* in order to support the courage of those who stayed, and the faith of those who had fled, being protected by the especial providence of God, in order to build the Church at Jerusalem, and, by their zeal and courage, to govern it by their wisdom.

2. συνεκόμισαν.] Συγκ. signifies properly to *bring together;* but is *specially* used as a funereal term, like the Latin *componere;* and sometimes denotes not only the laying out of the body, but other preparations for its interment. This sense is rare

Στέφανον ἄνδρες εὐλαβεῖς, καὶ ἐποιήσαντο κοπετὸν μέγαν ἐπ᾽ αὐτῷ.)
3 [p] Σαῦλος δὲ ἐλυμαίνετο τὴν ἐκκλησίαν, κατὰ τοὺς οἴκους εἰσπορευόμενος, p Infra 22. 4. & 26. 10, 11.
4 σύρων τε ἄνδρας καὶ γυναῖκας παρεδίδου εἰς φυλακήν. Οἱ μὲν οὖν
διασπαρέντες διῆλθον, εὐαγγελιζόμενοι τὸν λόγον.
5 Φίλιππος δὲ κατελθὼν εἰς πόλιν τῆς Σαμαρείας, ἐκήρυσσεν αὐτοῖς
6 τὸν Χριστόν. Προσεῖχόν τε οἱ ὄχλοι τοῖς λεγομένοις ὑπὸ τοῦ Φιλίππου ὁμοθυμαδὸν, ἐν τῷ ἀκούειν αὐτοὺς καὶ βλέπειν τὰ σημεῖα ἃ
7 ἐποίει. Πολλῶν γὰρ τῶν ἐχόντων πνεύματα ἀκάθαρτα, βοῶντα μεγάλῃ
φωνῇ ἐξήρχετο· πολλοὶ δὲ παραλελυμένοι καὶ χωλοὶ ἐθεραπεύθησαν.
8 Καὶ ἐγένετο χαρὰ μεγάλη ἐν τῇ πόλει ἐκείνῃ. Ἀνὴρ δέ τις ὀνόματι
9 Σίμων προϋπῆρχεν ἐν τῇ πόλει μαγεύων καὶ ἐξιστῶν τὸ ἔθνος τῆς

in the Classical writers; but it occurs in Soph. Aj. 1068.

— *εὐλαβεῖς*.] It is not agreed among Commentators whether these persons were *Christians*, or not. Most think they were religious Jews, or Hellenistic proselytes, and perhaps secret friends to Christianity. They probably consisted of religious men, both Christians and well-disposed Jews. So Luke ii. 25. such a one is called *δίκαιος καὶ εὐλαβής*.

— *ἐποιήσαντο κοπ.*, &c.] These words (formed perhaps on Gen. l. 10.) show, by example, the great honours shown him. On the point of Antiquities see Recens. Synop. and my Note on Thucyd. ii. 34. No. 12. Transl.

3. *ἐλυμαίνετο τὴν ἐκκλ.*] *Λυμαίνεσθαι* signifies properly to ravage and destroy, as a wild beast; but is often used of *men*, and signifies to waste or spoil, as said of *things*, or to destroy and persecute, as said of *persons*. Thus the sense here is equivalent to that in Gal. i. 13. where Paul says of himself *ἐδίωκον τὴν ἐκκλησίαν τοῦ Θεοῦ, καὶ ἐ π ό ρ θ ο υ ν αὐτήν*.

— *κατὰ τοὺς οἴκους εἰσπ.*] The full sense is, "entering into houses," "going from house to house." See v. 42. xx. 20. In the words following the sense is not quite developed; to complete which and rectify the construction an *οὓς* is required after *γυναῖκας*, the comma being cancelled after *εἰσπορευόμενος*.

4. *διῆλθον*.] The Commentators suppose an ellipse of *τὴν χώραν* or *τὰς χώρας*. But it is better to *repeat κατὰ τὰς χώρας*, or at least *τὰς χώρας* from the preceding.

5. *εἰς πόλιν τῆς Σαμ.*] It is not agreed whether by *Σαμ.* is meant the *country*, or its *metropolis* of the same name. The *latter* is the opinion of almost all the best Commentators; and with reason; since the former interpretation seems excluded by v. 14.; for to say that the *country* had received the Gospel, when it had been only preached at *one city*, would be an exaggeration. The *Article* (as Sychem) is not necessary, since in such a case it is usually omitted, being *implied*. That some of the most ancient MSS. *have* the Article will at least show the *antiquity* of this interpretation; and we may well suppose, that although the name of the city had been recently altered to *Sebaste* in honour of Augustus, it still retained popularly its original appellation.

— *ἐκήρυσσεν — Χριστόν*.] This does not necessarily import more than the *preaching the Gospel* publicly, and offering admonition or exhortation privately. See Hamm. on the distinction between *κηρύσσειν* and *εὐαγγελίζεσθαι*. Their *authority* to do this may very well be rested on their having the extraordinary and miraculous gifts of the Holy Spirit. Though indeed this question, so warmly debated by Whitby, as to their Clerical warrant, is frivolous; since the distinction between the Clergy and Laity was, no doubt, not yet made,—because it was not yet become *necessary*.

6. *προσεῖχον*.] The best Commentators are in general agreed, that this is for *ἐπίστευον*, "had faith in the Gospel." Comp. v. 14. Examples from Joseph., Philo, and the LXX., are adduced by the Commentators. *Ὁμοθυμαδὸν* must be construed with *προσεῖχον*. *Ἐν τῷ ἀκ. αὐτοὺς*, literally, "on their hearing," &c.

7. *πολλῶν — ἐξήρχετο*.] The construction (somewhat obscure by transposition) is thus laid down by Kuin.: *πνεύματα γὰρ ἀκάθαρτα (ἐκ) πολλῶν τῶν ἐχόντων (αὐτά), βοῶντα μεγάλῃ φωνῇ ἐξήρχετο*. Here again we may observe, that dæmoniacs and those merely affected with bodily disorders are carefully distinguished. *Ἐξήρχετο* is an example of the use of the neuter for the passive, the sense being "were expelled."

9. *Σίμων*.] Commentators are generally agreed that this is Simon the Cypriot, mentioned by Joseph. Ant. xx. 5, 2. as being a pretender to magic. *Προϋπῆρχεν* is by some Commentators taken by itself, in the sense, "had been staying;" but by others is joined with *μαγεύων*; and rightly, as appears from Lu. xxiii. 12. *προϋπῆρχον ἐν ἔχθρᾳ ὄντες*. where see Note. The sense is, "had been professing magic." *Μαγεύω* is a rare word, yet examples are adduced from Hippocr. and Plutarch. On the *μάγοι* in the *original* sense, see Note on Matt. ii. 1. "The appellation was, however, (observes Kuin.) then applied even to strolling mountebanks, pretending to a knowledge of medicine, natural philosophy, and astrology (which included fortune-telling by the stars), all of them being accompanied with the mummery of pretended incantations, and other devices, for evoking departed spirits and expelling dæmons." This Simon, however, was a person of a very superior order to the common run of such persons, being endued with much real knowledge of natural philosophy; though he, it seems, abused it to the purpose of working on the minds of the vulgar by pretended prodigies; throwing them into amazement, doubtless by the exhibition of certain phænomena known only to himself. See Sir Walter Scott's Essay on Demonology, and Dr. Hibbert's on Apparitions. Whether he actually used sorcery, or produced

Σαμαρείας, λέγων εἶναί τινα ἑαυτὸν μέγαν· ᾧ προσεῖχον πάντες ἀπὸ 10
μικροῦ ἕως μεγάλου, λέγοντες· Οὗτός ἐστιν ἡ δύναμις τοῦ Θεοῦ ἡ
μεγάλη. Προσεῖχον δὲ αὐτῷ, διὰ τὸ ἱκανῷ χρόνῳ ταῖς μαγείαις ἐξε- 11
στακέναι αὐτούς. Ὅτε δὲ ἐπίστευσαν τῷ Φιλίππῳ εὐαγγελιζομένῳ τὰ 12
περὶ τῆς βασιλείας τοῦ Θεοῦ καὶ τοῦ ὀνόματος τοῦ Ἰησοῦ Χριστοῦ,
ἐβαπτίζοντο ἄνδρες τε καὶ γυναῖκες. Ὁ δὲ Σίμων καὶ αὐτὸς ἐπίστευσε, 13
καὶ βαπτισθεὶς, ἦν προσκαρτερῶν τῷ Φιλίππῳ· θεωρῶν τε σημεῖα
καὶ δυνάμεις μεγάλας γινομένας ἐξίστατο. Ἀκούσαντες δὲ οἱ ἐν Ἱερο- 14
σολύμοις ἀπόστολοι, ὅτι δέδεκται ἡ Σαμάρεια τὸν λόγον τοῦ Θεοῦ, ἀπέστειλαν πρὸς αὐτοὺς τὸν Πέτρον καὶ Ἰωάννην. οἵτινες καταβάντες προσ- 15
ηύξαντο περὶ αὐτῶν, ὅπως λάβωσι Πνεῦμα ἅγιον. (οὔπω γὰρ ἦν ἐπ' 16
οὐδενὶ αὐτῶν ἐπιπεπτωκὸς, μόνον δὲ βεβαπτισμένοι ὑπῆρχον εἰς τὸ ὄνομα τοῦ Κυρίου Ἰησοῦ.) Τότε ἐπετίθουν τὰς χεῖρας ἐπ' αὐτοὺς, καὶ 17
ἐλάμβανον Πνεῦμα ἅγιον. Θεασάμενος δὲ ὁ Σίμων, ὅτι διὰ τῆς ἐπι- 18
θέσεως τῶν χειρῶν τῶν ἀποστόλων δίδοται τὸ Πνεῦμα τὸ ἅγιον, προσήνεγκεν αὐτοῖς χρήματα, λέγων· Δότε κἀμοὶ τὴν ἐξουσίαν ταύτην, ἵνα 19
ᾧ ἐὰν ἐπιθῶ τὰς χεῖρας, λαμβάνῃ Πνεῦμα ἅγιον. Πέτρος δὲ εἶπε 20
πρὸς αὐτόν· Τὸ ἀργύριόν σου σὺν σοὶ εἴη εἰς ἀπώλειαν, ὅτι τὴν δω-

extraordinary effects by Satanic influence, as some have supposed, may be doubted.

Some of the Ecclesiastical historians tell us that he pretended to be God the Father, others say the Messiah, or the Paraclete. He was no doubt willing to pass for whatever the multitude should please to account him. And they probably regarded him as the promised Messiah, or at least a divine legate.

— ἐξιστῶν.] See Matt. xii. 22. and Luke xxiv, 22. So Athen. cited by Wolf: ὃς πῦρ τε αὐτόματον ἐποίει ἀναφύεσθαι, καὶ ἄλλα πολλὰ φάσματα ἐτεχνᾶτο, ἀφ' ὧν ἐξίστα τῶν ἀνθρώπων τὴν διάνοιαν. And in Onosand. 93. ult. we have: ὄψις καὶ βοὴ καὶ πάταγος ὅπλων ἐξίστησι τὰς τῶν ἐναντίων διανοίας.

— λέγων εἶναί τινα ἑαυτὸν μέγαν] some extraordinary person. See Note supra v. 36. So also Herodot. iv. 198. δοκεῖ δέ μοι οὐδ' ἀρετὴν εἶναί τις ἡ Λιβύη σπουδαίη, ὥστε ἢ Ἀσίῃ ἢ Εὐρώπῃ παραβληθῆναι.

10. πάντες — μεγάλου.] The sense is, "all of every age and station." Ἐστιν ἡ δύν., &c. This may, with Kuin., be explained by hypallage, in the sense, "The mighty power of God energizes in him." See Rom. i. 16. 1 Cor. ii. 4.

13. ἦν προσκαρτερῶν τ. Φ.] "used to attend on Philip, viz. as a disciple." See x. 7. Most of the Commentators regard his embracing Christianity as a mere pretence; it is probable that he did not regard Jesus as the *Messiah*, and was guided by secular views.

14. ἀπέστειλαν πρὸς αὐτοὺς Π. καὶ Ἰ.] It is plain from what follows, that their primary purpose was to lay hands with prayer on the new converts, and thereby impart to them the gifts of the Holy Spirit. "The Apostles (says Kuin.) seem to have laid down a rule, that converts after being baptized and catechized, should have the imposition of hands, accompanied with prayer, in order to their receiving gifts of the Holy Spirit.

16. ἐπιπεπτωκός.] This word is used of what falls with abundance, as x. 44. xi. 15. The expression is formed on Ezek. xi. 5. ἐπέπεσεν ἐπ' ἐμὲ πνεῦμα Κυρίου.

20. τὸ ἀργύριον — εἰς ἀπώλειαν. On the exact nature of what is here said some difference of opinion exists. By many learned Expositors this is regarded as a *form of imprecation*; with which they compare similar Greek forms, such as ἀπόλοιο, or βάλλ' ἐς κόρακας or ἐς ὄλεθρον. But it is surely inconsistent with the Spirit of the Gospel to imprecate perdition on any man, however bad: and although the above forms were often used as little more than expressions of peevishness and ill humour, yet no such *diminution* of sense can be thought of in an Apostle of Christ. But, in fact, there is nothing in the passage before us, that can, properly speaking, be called *imprecation*. As to the words τὸ ἀργύριόν σου σὺν σοὶ εἴη, they *need* not, and, I think, *ought* not to be closely united in sense with εἰς ἀπώλειαν; since they merely import "may your money rest with *yourself*, i. e. (the *Optative* being often used for the *Imperative*) keep your money to *yourself* [I will have nothing to do with it]." Thus in a similar passage which I have noted in Joseph. Antiq. x. 11. 3. Δανιῆλος δὲ τὰς δωρεὰς ἠξίου αὐτὸν ἔχειν· τὸ σοφὸν γὰρ καὶ τὸ θεῖον ἀδωροδόκητον εἶναι. where, though the MSS. present no variation, I have no doubt that the true reading is, not αὐτὸν, but αὐτῷ, which, indeed, seems to have been in the copy of the ancient Latin Translator. This emendation indeed is placed beyond doubt by the passage of Dan. v. 17. which Josephus here followed, and which might also be in the mind of the Apostle: Καὶ εἶπε Δανιὴλ ἐνώπιον τοῦ βασιλέως, Τὰ δόματα σοὶ ἔστω, (or as the Alexandrian and other MSS. have, σὺν σοὶ) καὶ τὴν δωρεὰν τῆς οἰκίας σου ἑτέρῳ δός. Now the latter clause there *expresses* a sense which in the passage before us is left to be *understood*. Again, neither does the phrase εἰς ἀπώλειαν imply *imprecation*. By Whitby, Markl., Valpy, A Clarke, and Mr. Holden, it is taken to import *prediction*, namely, of what would befall him if he did not repent. Yet there is, I apprehend, nothing in the

21 ρεὰν τοῦ Θεοῦ ἐνόμισας διὰ χρημάτων κτᾶσθαι. οὐκ ἔστι σοι μερὶς
οὐδὲ κλῆρος ἐν τῷ λόγῳ τούτῳ· ἡ γὰρ καρδία σου οὐκ ἔστιν εὐθεῖα
22 ἐνώπιον τοῦ Θεοῦ. Μετανόησον οὖν ἀπὸ τῆς κακίας σου ταύτης, καὶ
δεήθητι τοῦ Θεοῦ, εἰ ἄρα ἀφεθήσεταί σοι ἡ ἐπίνοια τῆς καρδίας σου.
23 εἰς γὰρ χολὴν πικρίας καὶ σύνδεσμον ἀδικίας ὁρῶ σε ὄντα. Ἀποκρι-
24 θεὶς δὲ ὁ Σίμων εἶπε· Δεήθητε ὑμεῖς ὑπὲρ ἐμοῦ πρὸς τὸν Κύριον,
ὅπως μηδὲν ἐπέλθῃ ἐπ' ἐμὲ ὧν εἰρήκατε.
25 Οἱ μὲν οὖν διαμαρτυράμενοι καὶ λαλήσαντες τὸν λόγον τοῦ Κυρίου,
ὑπέστρεψαν εἰς Ἱερουσαλὴμ, πολλάς τε κώμας τῶν Σαμαρειτῶν εὐηγ-
γελίσαντο.
26 Ἄγγελος δὲ Κυρίου ἐλάλησε πρὸς Φίλιππον, λέγων· Ἀνάστηθι καὶ

words from which prediction can be directly elicited. The nature of the expression must depend upon the εἰς, which here seems to denote *tendency*; as at Rom. v. 16. εἰς κατάκριμα. and vi. 16. ἁμαρτίας (φερούσης) εἰς θάνατον. Thus it is intended to warn him of the consequences of so employing money, unless (as he gives him to understand at v. 22.) he averts it by timely repentance. As, however, prediction is almost *implied* in warning, both may here be included. Perhaps the term *denunciation* will best express the full import. The above view is, I find, supported by the authority of Calvin, who observes that St. Peter does not *imprecate*, but ustam vindictam Dei, incutiendi terroris causâ, *denuntiat* prope impendere. Thus the full sense is, "Keep your money to yourself—for your *own* perdition [not mine]."

21. οὐκ ἔστι—κλῆρος.] This seems to have been a common phrase, since it occurs in Deut. x. 9. ii. 12. 2 Sam. xx. 1. Job. xxii. 25. Τῷ λόγῳ τούτῳ, this *matter*; for λόγος and ῥῆμα, after the example of the Heb. דבר, often signify a *thing*.

—ἡ γὰρ καρδία—Θεοῦ.] Formed on 2 Kings x. 15. and denoting that his profession of Christianity was insincere and hypocritical, or corupted by pursuing bye-ends.

22. εἰ ἄρα ἀφεθήσεται, &c.] Εἰ ἄρα is by many learned Commentators taken in the sense *ut*, as εἴπως in Phil. iii. 11. and sometimes in the Classical writers. And so the Heb. אולי *si forte* is rendered ἵνα by the LXX. in Exod. xxxii. 30. But to so rare a signification we must not resort; especially as it weakens the sense. The phrase may be taken according to its ordinary use. In order, however, to fully understand the sense, it is to be observed that εἰ ἄρα when occurring any where except at the beginning of a sentence, is elliptical; and some participle, (usually πειρώμενος, or some equivalent term), is to be understood. So Mark xi. 13. εἰ ἄρα εὑρήσει τι. Acts xvii. 27. εἰ ἄρα γε ψηλαφήσειαν, and vii. 1. Sometimes, too, this is the case with the simple εἰ, as Eurip. Heracl. 640. πάλαι γὰρ ὠδίνουσα τῶν ἀφιγμένων, ψυχὴν ἐτήκον, νόστος εἰ γενήσεται. "Animo tabescebas, (dubitans)," &c. Thus the full sense is: "[trying] whether," &c.; and the doubt implied (as Grot., Doddr., and Holden observe) is not whether, on sincere repentance, Simon would be *forgiven*; but whether he would *sincerely repent*. This is clear from the words of the next verse, εἰς χολὴν, &c., which are illustrative of the matter, and show that the doubt rested on the state of Simon's heart towards God.

Ἐπίνοια signifies not so much *thought*, as *contrivance, device*; being usually taken in a bad sense. Perhaps it is here slightly emphatical—suggesting how heavy a guilt would have attended the *execution* of such a design.

23. εἰς γὰρ χολὴν—ὄντα.] These words are commonly taken as put for ἐν γὰρ χολῇ, &c., according to which, Castalio elegantly renders, "Nam te amaro felle præditum et injustitia constrictum esse video." The best Commentators, however, from Alberti and Wolf to Kuin., have been of opinion (comparing Deut. xxix. 18. with Heb. xii. 15.) that εἰς χολὴν is for χολὴν, as Acts xiii. 22. 47. vii. 21. Eph. ii. 15. And they assign the following sense: "I see thou art a most pernicious person, like to a bitter and poisonous plant, a pest to Christian society." So Anthol. Gr. ii. 11. πᾶσα γυνὴ χόλος ἐστίν. The σύνδεσμος they take to mean "a mere bundle of iniquity." But the soundness of this whole interpretation may be questionod; for in the passages adduced the εἰς is for ὥστε, and there is an ellipsis of εἶναι; which is not the case here. Besides, the style of unmeasured reproach involved in σύνδεσμον, if not in χολὴν, so interpreted, is not characteristic of the sacred writers; whose language, like that of our Lord, is sometimes severe, but never abusive. I must therefore acquiesce in the common interpretation, which yields a sense, though strictly just, little less severe, namely, "thou art immersed in wickedness of the vilest sort, and fast bound in the chains of sin and Satan." Εἰς may be taken for ἐν, as often in the N. T. and the Classical writers. In which case εἶναι is used in the sense to *come* (as here) or *become*; and the εἰς signifies *at* or *to*. χολὴν πικρίας is by Hebraism for χολὴν πικροτάτην.

24. δεήθητε ὑπὲρ ἐμοῦ.] Thus admitting his own unworthiness. See John ix. 31. By his using the *plural* number we may suppose that John was present. That his repentance, however, was not real, we have every reason to believe, from the circumstances of the case, as well as from his subsequent conduct, as recorded by early Ecclesiastical tradition.

25. διαμαρτυράμενοι.] Διαμαρτ. signifies to prove on good evidence, and, by implication, to teach.

26. ἄγγελος—ἐλάλησε.] Many recent Commentators suppose this communication to have been made by a *dream*. But there is nothing in the air of the passage to warrant this supposition; and, as Storr observes (Opusc. iii. 178), it is no wonder that Philip should have been admonished *sometimes* (as at 29 & 39) by the internal sugges-

πορεύου κατὰ μεσημβρίαν, ἐπὶ τὴν ὁδὸν τὴν καταβαίνουσαν ἀπὸ Ἱερουσαλὴμ εἰς Γάζαν. (αὕτη ἐστὶν ἔρημος.) Καὶ ἀναστὰς ἐπορεύθη· καὶ 27
ἰδοὺ, ἀνὴρ Αἰθίοψ, εὐνοῦχος, δυνάστης Κανδάκης τῆς βασιλίσσης Αἰ-
θιόπων, ὃς ἦν ἐπὶ πάσης τῆς γάζης αὐτῆς· ὃς ἐληλύθει προσκυνήσων
εἰς Ἱερουσαλὴμ, ἦν τε ὑποστρέφων· καὶ, καθήμενος ἐπὶ τοῦ ἅρματος 28
αὐτοῦ, [καὶ] ἀνεγίνωσκε τὸν προφήτην Ἡσαΐαν. εἶπε δὲ τὸ Πνεῦμα 29

tions of the Holy Spirit, and *sometimes* (as here) by the personal address of an angel; since, in a similar case, after he had been once and again internally admonished by a *vision* (see Acts xvi. 6. seqq.) he was at length externally admonished by a *messenger sent from God* (v. 10). See also Hammond.

26. αὕτη ἐστὶν ἔρημος.] With these words the Commentators are not a little perplexed; it being not agreed whether they are to be referred to Γάζαν, or to τὴν ὁδόν. So little satisfied, however, are some with either supposition, that Wessel., Valckn., Hein., and Kuin. suspect the words to be an *interpolation from the margin:* but of this there is not the slightest proof; and that is but *cutting* the knot, which may, I think, be very well untied. As to the two foregoing interpretations, that which refers the words to Γάζαν cannot be admitted; for, *taking for granted* that there *were* then two Gazas, *New* Gaza, and *Old* Gaza, destroyed by Alexander, and here thought to be meant; yet they were so near together, that it is not likely there were *two roads* leading from Jerusalem to each of them respectively. Besides, why a road should be carried to a place nearly uninhabited, it is not easy to see. That, indeed, would require, as Kuin. says, the Article to ἐρήμος. Or rather, Luke would have written εἰς τὴν Γάζαν ἥτις ἐστὶν ἔρ. The *latter* interpretation, which refers it to ὁδὸν, is adopted by the best Commentators, ancient and modern (supported by the Syriac Version), who suppose that there were two roads leading from Jerusalen to Gaza; one farther about and carried along the valley of the rivulet Eshcol, the other shorter, but traversing the rough tract of mount Casius, and therefore desert and unfrequented. But that there *were* two roads rests wholly on conjecture; and *thus* perspicuity, and even propriety, would require ἥτις ἐστὶν ἔρημος. Yet why embarrass ourselves unnecessarily? There is no reason why we should not, with Rosenm. and others, suppose the words to be those of *St. Luke*, not of the *Angel*, and (referring them, as we must do, tó τὴν ὁδὸν, &c.) regard them as a remark of the *Evangelist* similar to many such in the N. T. and (as I have elsewhere shown) in the Classical writers. See John vi. 10. and Note. St. Luke, I apprehend, means to intimate that it might seem strange that one so desirous to evangelize as Philip, should be sent upon so unfrequented a road as that from Jerusalem to Gaza. Reland, indeed, objects that there is no reason why *that* road should be called ἔρημος any more than any other road in Judæa. But that supposes far more knowledge of the ancient state of the country than we have, or is now attainable. Reland himself could not have proved that the road was *not* such. If it was carried in a straight course, it must have passed most of the way over a hilly and barren tract, through no city or town of any note. And therefore the epithet ἔρημος, which means uninhabited, i. e. very thinly peopled, would be suitable enough. So Arrian. Exp. Alex. iii. 21, 11. Οἱ δὲ εἰδέναι μὲν ἔφασαν (they said they knew a road), ἐρήμην δὲ εἶναι τὴν ὁδὸν δι' ἀνυδρίαν. and Thucyd. ii. 17. τὰ ἔρημα τῆς πόλεως.

27. I have placed a comma after Αἰθίοψ, because ἀνὴρ Αἰθ. stands for a substantive (the ἀνὴρ being almost redundant) and thus cannot well *qualify* εὐνοῦχος. Εὐνοῦχος signifies properly *cubicularius*, chamberlain, prefect of the bedchamber. And as such were generally *castrati*, so it came to mean *spado*, an eunuch. And such being, for their supposed fidelity, generally promoted to *other* confidential court offices, hence the term came to mean, in a general way, an officer of state (so here a *Treasurer*, as we find from what follows), whether an eunuch or not. Thus Potiphar, Gen. xxxix. 1, though called εὐνοῦχος Φαραώ, yet had a wife. Δυνάστης signifies properly one who has great power or influence. So μέγας εἶναί τινι in the ancient writers. The construction, however, here requires that it should be taken, not as an *adjective* (with almost all English Translators), but as a substantive, *magnas*, a *grandee*, as Doddr. renders. Wolf. and Wets. have proved from Pliny, Dio Cass., and Strabo, that *Candace* was a family name common to the Queens of Æthiopia Superior, or Meroe, like Pharaoh, to the kings of Egypt, which is well illustrated by Dr. Russell, in his account of Nubia, in the 12th vol. of the Edinburgh Cabinet Library.

This person was, no doubt, a Jewish proselyte: as appears, not so much by his reading the Prophet Isaiah, as by his coming to Jerusalem to worship there. That eunuchs were not admitted as proselytes, is no proof that he was not one; because εὐνοῦχος does not, we see, necessarily imply that he was an eunuch in the physical sense.

— ἐπὶ πάσης τ. γ.] Sub. τεταγμένος, which is sometimes *expressed*. Γάζα is a word of Persian origin, and signifies *treasure*.

28. καί, καθ. — ἀνεγίνωσκε.] I have in this passage adopted a punctuation somewhat varying from any former Edition; yet, I apprehend, demanded by propriety, and the nature of the context. Render, "who had gone to Jerusalem to worship there, and was returning; and, as he sat in his chariot, was also reading," &c. The second καί, however, is absent from many good MSS. (including the Alexandrian and Cod. Cantabr.), some Versions, as the Pesch. Syr. and Vulg.; and arose probably from the confusion occasioned by the true construction of the sentence being misunderstood. In thus reading the Scriptures, and, as it appears from the next verse, *aloud* on a journey, the proselyte was, probably, following the directions of the Jewish Rabbies, who (as we learn from Schoettg.) said, that "when any one was going on a journey, and had not a companion, he should study the Law." That students used to read aloud, appears also from several citations from the Rabbins adduced by Schoettg.

29. εἶπε τὸ Πνεῦμα.] Many ancient Commenta-

30 τῷ Φιλίππῳ· Πρόσελθε καὶ κολλήθητι τῷ ἅρματι τούτῳ. Προσδραμὼν δὲ ὁ Φίλιππος ἤκουσεν αὐτοῦ ἀναγινώσκοντος τὸν προφήτην
31 Ἡσαΐαν, καὶ εἶπεν· Ἆρά γε γινώσκεις ἃ ἀναγινώσκεις; Ὁ δὲ εἶπε·
Πῶς γὰρ ἂν δυναίμην, ἐὰν μή τις ὁδηγήσῃ με; παρεκάλεσέ τε τὸν
32 Φίλιππον ἀναβάντα καθίσαι σὺν αὐτῷ. [q] Ἡ δὲ περιοχὴ τῆς γραφῆς, [q Isa. 53. 7.]
ἣν ἀνεγίνωσκεν, ἦν αὕτη· Ὡς πρόβατον ἐπὶ σφαγὴν ἤχθη,
καὶ ὡς ἀμνὸς ἐναντίον τοῦ κείροντος αὐτὸν ἄφω-
33 νος· οὕτως οὐκ ἀνοίγει τὸ στόμα αὐτοῦ. ἐν τῇ ταπεινώσει αὐτοῦ ἡ κρίσις αὐτοῦ ἤρθη, τὴν δὲ γενεὰν
αὐτοῦ τίς διηγήσεται; ὅτι αἴρεται ἀπὸ τῆς γῆς ἡ
34 ζωὴ αὐτοῦ. Ἀποκριθεὶς δὲ ὁ εὐνοῦχος τῷ Φιλίππῳ εἶπε· Δέομαί
σου, περὶ τίνος ὁ προφήτης λέγει τοῦτο; περὶ ἑαυτοῦ, ἢ περὶ ἑτέρου

tors, and, of the modern ones, Bp. Pearce, take this to mean the *angel* mentioned at ver. 26. See Heb. i. 14. This, however, involves much harshness; and it is better, with the most eminent modern Commentators, to regard the words as a *popular* manner of expression, only denoting that such was the suggestion of the Holy Spirit; so communicated (like the *afflatus* of the Prophets) as that the inspired person could always distinguish such Divine suggestions from those of his own mind. And thus the Holy Spirit might, in a certain sense, be said to speak the words to him.

—κολλήθητι τῷ ἅρμ. τ.] Κολλᾶσθαι with a passive form has (like the Hebrew conjugation Hothpahel, which is at once passive and reflective) a reflective sense, and signifies to *attach one's self to, join company with.*" So the Heb. דבק in 2 Sam. xx. 2. 2 Kings xviii. 6. Ruth i. 14, where the LXX. use ἀκολουθεῖν. Thus at Ruth ii. 8. κολλήθητι μετὰ τῶν κορασίων, the sense is, "join company with my maidens." The *chariot* is here (by an usual popular idiom) for the *person in the chariot;* just as, in the Classical writers, *ships* are put for the sailors in them.

30. γινώσκεις — ἀναγινώσκεις.] Most Commentators from Grot. dowawards suppose a *paronomasia;* with which one might compare that of Julian in his laconic Epistle to Basil: Ἀνέγνων, ἔγνων, κατέγνων; to which the Father, with equal wit, and scarcely less brevity, replied: Ἀνέγνως, ἀλλ' οὐκ ἔγνως. εἰ γὰρ ἔγνως, οὐκ ἂν κατέγνως. But *paronomasia* in the *present* case would be frigid, and alike unsuitable to the gravity of the speaker, and the importance of the subject.

31. πῶς γὰρ ἂν δυν.] The γὰρ refers (as often) to a negative sentence omitted for brevity's sake. This omission of short clauses, both negative and affirmative, referred to by γὰρ, is frequent in the Classical writers, and several examples are adduced by Bp. Pearce. The words, we may observe, are a modest apology for ignorance. Ὁδηγ. is used in a figurative sense (*instruct*), as in John xvi. 13. and Ps. xxv. 5.

32. περιοχή.] This word usually signifies the *sum* of what is contained in any book, &c., but here it means a *passage* or *section*, of which sense Wets. and Valckn. adduce examples.

—ὡς πρόβατον ἐπὶ σφαγὴν — ζωὴ αὐτοῦ.] These words are taken from Is. liii. 7 & 8, and follow the Sept. Version exactly: the verbal discrepancies which occur not being found in the Alexandrian and other good MSS. of the Sept. Between the Sept., St. Luke, and the Hebrew, there is considerable difference, but not such as materially to affect the general sense. The various modes of reconciliation are fully detailed by Townsend, who laudably endeavours to remove the discrepancy without resorting to any conjectural emendation of the Hebrew. But to entirely reconcile the discrepancy is perhaps impracticable. It will, however, greatly contribute thereto, if we suppose that the LXX. read בעצרו משפטו לקח. The מ and ב are easily confounded. A מ might easily be lost before another מ, and ו might easily arise from the ל following. That the LXX. had ו after בעצר, we may infer from its being found in the N. T. in almost every MS. This, however, involves no real discrepancy from the Hebrew: for the ו may be taken with the *preceding*, quite as well as with the *following* word. And such, I suspect, is the true reading of the Hebrew. Whether the Hebrew had originally ב before עצר or מ, is a matter of more doubt, because מ may mean *at, under*, &c. See Gesen. Lex. in v. That there should be a full stop after בעצרו, cannot, I think, be doubted. Thus the Hebrew may be rendered, "So he opened not his mouth under his oppression. From judgment was he hurried off [to death]." Bp. Lowth, indeed, and Kuin. take בעצר with the words *following*, and render, "By an oppressive judgment was he cut off." But the *Hendiadys* thus involved is very harsh; and they are obliged to cancel the ו. If we were allowed to do *that*, the sentence would proceed better *without* the Hendiadys. But the LXX., I doubt not, had the ו, and attached to בעצר. And conjoining these words with what follows, they stumbled at ממשפט; and not knowing what to make of the first מ in the MSS., they passed it over, and either finding an ו after משפט in their MSS., or else supplying it, to make up the sense, rendered *as well as they could*, and thus gave a sense ["he was deprived of a just judgment"] very applicable to *Christ*, but not, I conceive, intended by the *Prophet*.

The words τὴν δὲ γενεὰν — αὐτοῦ are, like the correspondent Hebrew ones (of which they are a literal rendering), so obscure, that the true sense cannot be fully determined." Hamm., Doddr., Kuin., and most recent Commentators, take the

τινός; Ἀνοίξας δὲ ὁ Φίλιππος τὸ στόμα αὐτοῦ, καὶ ἀρξάμενος ἀπὸ 35
τῆς γραφῆς ταύτης, εὐηγγελίσατο αὐτῷ τὸν Ἰησοῦν. Ὡς δὲ ἐπορεύοντο 36
κατὰ τὴν ὁδὸν ἦλθον ἐπί τι ὕδωρ· καί φησιν ὁ εὐνοῦχος· Ἰδού, ὕδωρ·
τί κωλύει με βαπτισθῆναι; [εἶπε δὲ ὁ Φίλιππος· Εἰ πιστεύεις ἐξ 37
ὅλης τῆς καρδίας, ἔξεστιν. ἀποκριθεὶς δὲ εἶπε· Πιστεύω τὸν υἱὸν τοῦ
Θεοῦ εἶναι τὸν Ἰησοῦν Χριστόν.] καὶ ἐκέλευσε στῆναι τὸ ἅρμα· καὶ 38
κατέβησαν ἀμφότεροι εἰς τὸ ὕδωρ, ὅ τε Φίλιππος καὶ ὁ εὐνοῦχος· καὶ

sense to be, "who can describe the guilt of the men of his time [from whom he suffered such things]?" But this is negatived by what follows. Bp. Lowth renders, "and his manner who would declare?" i. e. bear witness in his favour? q. d. *No one.* This sense of דור has countenance in the Arabic. The *circumstance* was manifestly fulfilled in Christ: and the point of Hebrew Antiquities on which it depends is admirably illustrated by Dr. Kennicott and Bp. Lowth. The interpretation too, is much confirmed by the words following, and is probably the true one.

In the words ὅτι αἴρεται — αὐτοῦ the *sense* is the same as in the Hebrew; but the Sept. Translators either read otherwise, or translated freely.

35. ἀρξάμενος ἀπὸ τ. γ. τ.] Compare a kindred passage of Luke xxiv. 27. Γραφὴ as used of a single passage of Scripture, occurs in Mark xv. 58. and elsewhere. In εὐηγγελίσατο αὐτῷ 'I (which words signify, "he instructed him in the doctrine and principles of the religion of Jesus,") it is implied that he commenced by referring the words of the prophecy to Jesus, and from thence introduced whatever else he had to communicate. In Ἰησοῦν we have the *person* put for the *thing*, as Luke iii. 18. Acts xvi. 10. Gal. i. 9. 1 Pet. i. 12. An idiom frequent in the Classical writers, on which see Matth. Gr. Gr. § 409.

36. τι ὕδωρ.] Probably some fountain or pool, formed by a brook either running into the Eshcol rivulet, or formed at a bend of the Eshcol itself.

— ἰδού, ὕδωρ — βαπτισθῆναι.] From this we may infer, that Philip had fully instructed the Eunuch on the nature and necessity of baptism as an initiatory ordinance of Christianity; and that the Eunuch had professed his wish to receive, and Philip his willingness to administer it at a fit opportunity. In τι κωλύει the sense must not be *pressed upon;* for, from the examples of that phrase, and the *quid vetat* or *prohibet* of the Latin, it is probable that the sense meant to be expressed by the Eunuch was this: "Here is an opportunity for the thing to be done forthwith."

37. There has been no little debate as to the authenticity of this verse, which is not found in many of the best MSS. and most of the ancient Versions, including the Pesch. Syriac, and is omitted in several citations of the Fathers, as also in the Edit. Princ. Moreover, in some of the MSS. which *do* contain it, it is found with great diversity of reading. It is, therefore, cancelled or rejected by Grot., Mill, Wets., Pearce, Matth., Newc., Griesb., Tittm., Knapp, Kuin., Gratz, and Vat. It was, indeed, defended by Whitby and Wolf — strenuously, but not, I think, successfully. It is surely *not*, as Wolf contends, necessary to the context. The *external* evidence *against* it is certainly, if not equal to that *for* it, at least pretty strong. And *internal* is decidedly *against* it; for no good reason can be imagined why it should have been *thrown out*, or omitted inadvertently: whereas, for its *insertion* we may easily account, — namely, from the anxiety of well meaning, but misjudging persons to remove what they thought an abruptness; and to somewhat qualify what they deemed too favourable to haste in administering baptism; moreover to remove a stumbling-block from the rite not being described as performed in *due form*. As to Whitby's argument, on the ground that the verse was probably omitted in later times, because it opposed the delay of baptism which the catechumens experienced before they were admitted into the early Church, it has no force whatever. For surely if the verse be *removed*, the delay of baptism would seem to be still *more* opposed. The strongest argument brought forward *for* the authenticity of the passage is that it was read by Irenæus (see his work Adv. Hier. iii. 12. p. 196.), by Cyprian, nay, as Mill and others say, by *Tertullian*. But, upon referring to the passage (de Baptismo C. 18.), I find not a shadow of proof that the verse was read by him, but a probability that it was *not*. As to the authority of *Cyprian*, it is not great; for he generally follows the *Vulgate*, which *has* the verse. But indeed, had it been cited by Irenæus, it would only prove the great *antiquity* of the passage, not its *genuineness*. That, however, would show the caution of the primitive Church on this head, and prove that it required, previous to the administration of baptism to adults, an unhesitating avowal of belief in the *Divinity* as well as divine legation of Jesus Christ. See Doddr.

38. ἐκέλευσε στῆναι τὸ ἅρμα] "He gave orders for the carriage to be stopped."

— ἐβάπτισεν αὐτόν.] No doubt, with the use of the proper form; but whether by immersion, or by sprinkling is not clear. Doddr. maintains the *former;* but Lardner ap. Newc. the *latter* view; and, I conceive, more rightly. On both having descended into the water, Philip seems to have taken up water with his hands, and poured it copiously on the Eunuch's head. It is, indeed, plain, from various passages of the Gospels, that baptism was then administered by the baptizer, after having placed the person to be baptized in some river or brook. And that plenty of water was thought desirable, we learn from John iii. 23. But though this may seem to favour *immersion*, yet the other method might as well be adopted. Water *might*, indeed, be *fetched in a vessel* for the purpose of pouring it on the head of the person. Yet that it should *not*, may be accounted for by a reference to the climate, customs, and opinions of the people of Palestine, without rendering it necessary to suppose that nothing but a purpose of *immersion* could originate the custom for the baptizer and the baptized to both go into water of some depth. We learn from Euseb. Eccl. Hist. ii. 1, that the Eunuch afterwards preached the Gospel in Ethiopia.

39 ἐβάπτισεν αὐτόν. ὅτε δὲ ἀνέβησαν ἐκ τοῦ ὕδατος, *Πνεῦμα Κυρίου*
ἥρπασε τὸν Φίλιππον· καὶ οὐκ εἶδεν αὐτὸν οὐκέτι ὁ εὐνοῦχος, ἐπο-
40 ρεύετο γὰρ τὴν ὁδὸν αὐτοῦ χαίρων. Φίλιππος δὲ εὑρέθη εἰς Ἄζωτον·
καὶ διερχόμενος εὐηγγελίζετο τὰς πόλεις πάσας, ἕως τοῦ ἐλθεῖν αὐτὸν
εἰς Καισάρειαν.

1 IX. [r] Ὁ ΔΕ Σαῦλος ἔτι ἐμπνέων ἀπειλῆς καὶ φόνου εἰς τοὺς r Infra 26. 10. Gal. 1. 13.
2 μαθητὰς τοῦ Κυρίου, προσελθὼν τῷ ἀρχιερεῖ, ἠτήσατο παρ' αὐτοῦ 1 Tim. 1. 13.
ἐπιστολὰς εἰς Δαμασκὸν πρὸς τὰς συναγωγάς, ὅπως ἐάν τινας εὕρῃ
τῆς ὁδοῦ ὄντας, ἄνδρας τε καὶ γυναῖκας, δεδεμένους ἀγάγῃ εἰς Ἱερου- s Infra. 22. 6. & 26. 12.
3 σαλήμ. [s] Ἐν δὲ τῷ πορεύεσθαι ἐγένετο αὐτὸν ἐγγίζειν τῇ Δαμασκῷ, 1 Cor. 15. 8. 2 Cor. 12. 2.

39. Πνεῦμα Κυρίου ἥρπασε τὸν Φ.] In some ancient MSS. and late Versions are inserted between Πνεῦμα and Κυρίου the words *ἅγιον ἐπέπεσεν ἐπὶ* (or *εἰς*) *τὸν εὐνοῦχον, ἄγγελος δὲ*: which reading is approved by Hamm. and Towns.; but without reason; for it is a manifest interpolation of those who thought the *snatching up* of Philip more suitable to an angel than to the Holy Spirit. And there might be some ground for this, if we were to understand, with several Commentators (as Doddr. and Scott), that Philip *was caught up and carried through the air supernaturally*; for examples of which they refer to 1 Kings xviii. 12. 2 Kings ii. 16. Ezek. iii. 14. There is, however, no necessity to suppose that to be the case here. Nay, according to Bp. Middleton's Canon, the *personal* sense here in πνεῦμα is inadmissible; while, as Mr. Rose observes on Parkh. p. 700, if ἥρπασε be translated "caught away," it seems required. I quite agree with Parkh. and Mr. Rose, that nothing miraculous is here intended. Ἥρπασε may very well be understood of the *imperative suggestions* of the Holy Spirit; which Philip doubtless well knew how to distinguish from the motions of his own mind. The meaning, therefore, seems to be that assigned by Mr. Rose, as follows: "Philip went away quickly under the direction and influence of the Spirit." And I would compare Herodot. iv. 13. Ἔφη δὲ Ἀριστέης — ἀπικέσθαι ἐς Ἰσσηδόνας, φοιβόλαμπτος γενόμενος. The strong term ἥρπασε might, indeed, seem *selected* to suggest the *unwillingness* with which Philip must have torn himself away from this promising convert. Perhaps, however, no more may be meant than "hurried him away," as αἴρειν is sometimes used of the influence of the Holy Spirit in the LXX., so 1 Kings xviii. 12. καὶ πνεῦμα Κυρίου ἀρεῖ σε εἰς τὴν γῆν ἣν οὐκ οἶδα. and 2 Kings ii. 16. μή ποτε ἦρεν αὐτὸν πνεῦμα Κυρίου.

40. εὑρέθη εἰς Ἄζ.] The rendering *inventus est (was found)*, is so unsatisfactory, that most recent Commentators adopt that of Drusius, *fuit extitit (was*, or *abode)*. of which sense they adduce examples. But I prefer, with Beza, to suppose that the passive is used in a reciprocal or reflective sense, as in French *il se trouva* stands for *il fut trouvé*, made his appearance. There is an imitation of the Hebrew idiom, by which passive forms often have a reciprocal sense, as נִמְצָא. And so even in Greek. Thus in Herodot. iv. 4. we have the similar expression φανέντα αὐτὸν ἐς Προκόννησον. The air of the expression seems to refer to the *rapt feeling* with which Philip left the Eunuch and went to Azotus.

IX. 1. There is great reason to think (see Towns. Chr. Arr.) that what is now related took place before the baptism of the Eunuch, nay even before the journey of Peter and John into Samaria. See Dr. Burton, who thinks that Saul may have set out at the end of the feast of Tabernacles, and that his conversion took place at the same time as the conversions in Samaria.

— ἐμπνέων ἀπ.] Markl. sees not how ἐμπνέων, or even ἐκπνέων, can mean "breathing *out* threatening;" and he would conjecture ἐμπλέως. But no alteration is necessary. Ἐμπνεῖν signifies, 1. to inhale, and, by implication, exhale breath by the nostrils; 2. to breathe. Now to do this with quickness and vehemence, *implies* strong emotion, especially that of *anger*. In the later Greek writers, the word denoting the *kind* of passion is expressed in the *Genit.*, by an ellipse of ἀπὸ, signifying *origin*, *cause*, &c. In the earlier writers the Accus. is chiefly used. Examples are adduced in Rec. Syn. I shall here only adduce *one*, and that for emendation; since it is miserably corrupt, though the Editors pass it over sicco pede. It is in Nicephori Hist. Byz. p. 47. Ἔτι δὲ πνέων κατὰ τῆς ἀσεβείας, τὸ ἱερὸν τῶν Ναζωραίων σχῆμα καθύβριζεν. Read: ἔτι δ' ἐμπνέων κ. τ. εὐσεβείας, &c. It is evident that the historian had in mind the passage before us, otherwise πνέων might be tolerated, and then I should suspect that κακὰ had been lost, absorbed by the κατὰ following.

2. ἐπιστολὰς] i. e. letters credential. Article for Pron.

— τῆς ὁδοῦ.] For ταύτης τῆς ὁδοῦ, as John vii. 17. Ὁδὸς denotes not only a *way of life*, but a *way of thinking*, (as Judith v. 8. ἐξέβησαν ἐξ ὁδοῦ τῶν γονέων.) and hence a *sect*, either in *philosophy*, (as Suid. in v. Ἐμπεδοκλῆς, and Lucian Herm. p. 577.) or in *religion*, as here and in xxii. 4. ταύτην τὴν ὁδὸν ἐδίωξα. and xxiv. 14. From the populousness of Damascus, its constant communication with Jerusalem, and its being, probably, the place whither most of those who fled at the murder of Stephen took refuge, the number of Christians was likely to be considerable. So great was the authority of the Sanhedrim with the foreign Jews, that they readily submitted to its decrees in all matters spiritual; as for instance the suppression of what was esteemed heresy; especially as the then Ruler of Damascus, Aretas, king of Arabia, was either, according to some, a Jewish proselyte, or at least was well affected to the Jews, and permitted the exercise of this authority in things spiritual, on the part of the Sanhedrim.

3. On the subject of the conversion of St. Paul, now recorded by Luke, I cannot too strongly reprobate the hypothesis of certain foreign Theolo-

καὶ ἐξαίφνης περιήστραψεν αὐτὸν φῶς ἀπὸ τοῦ οὐρανοῦ· καὶ πεσὼν 4
ἐπὶ τὴν γῆν, ἤκουσε φωνὴν λέγουσαν αὐτῷ· Σαοὺλ, Σαοὺλ, τί με διώκεις; Εἶπε δέ· Τίς εἶ, κύριε; ὁ δὲ Κύριος εἶπεν· Ἐγώ εἰμι Ἰη- 5
σοῦς, ὃν σὺ διώκεις· [σκληρόν σοι πρὸς κέντρα λακτίζειν. τρέμων τε 6
καὶ θαμβῶν εἶπε· Κύριε, τί με θέλεις ποιῆσαι; καὶ ὁ Κύριος πρὸς
αὐτόν·] Ἀλλὰ ἀνάστηθι καὶ εἴσελθε εἰς τὴν πόλιν, καὶ λαληθήσεταί
t Infra 22. 9. & 26. 13. σοι τί σε δεῖ ποιεῖν. t Οἱ δὲ ἄνδρες οἱ συνοδεύοντες αὐτῷ εἱστήκεισαν 7
ἐννεοὶ, ἀκούοντες μὲν τῆς φωνῆς, μηδένα δὲ θεωροῦντες. Ἠγέρθη δὲ 8
ὁ Σαῦλος ἀπὸ τῆς γῆς· ἀνεῳγμένων δὲ τῶν ὀφθαλμῶν αὐτοῦ, οὐδένα

gians, who, building on the crude and half developed views of De Dieu, Elsn., and Hamm., regard the circumstances of the case as by no means miraculous; but as produced solely by certain terrific *natural phænomena;* which they suppose had such an effect on the high-wrought imagination, and so struck the alarmed conscience of Saul, as to make him regard as a reality, what was merely produced by fancy. I have at large considered, and, I trust, thoroughly confuted this unfounded notion in Recens. Synop. Suffice it here to say, that Paul, however ardent might be his temperament, and vivid his imagination, *could not* so far deceive himself, as to suppose that the *conversation* (related by him at large in his speech before Agrippa) really took place, if there had been no more than these Commentators tell us. And it were utterly inconsistent with truth and honesty to dress up *vivid fancies*, and manufacture into *dialogue*. Besides, he is so minute in his description as to say it was *in the Hebrew language;* and the address, as given most in detail at ch. 26., is a somewhat long one. Moreover, if *he* were so worked upon by his own high-wrought feelings, — *that* could not be the case with his *attendants:* and yet it is said that "they also, struck dumb with astonishment, *heard the voice*, though they saw no one."

Besides, if φωνὴ *could be* taken (though no *proof* of such a sense is established) to denote *thunder*, what would be more absurd than, "I heard a clap of thunder *saying?*" And his fellow travellers on hearing the — what? *the clap*, and seeing no one [whom could they have *expected* to see?] were mute with astonishment. Moreover, φῶς is nowhere used of *lightning;* nor is lightning anywhere said περιαστράπτειν. Finally, when we are told that this φῶς exceeded the brightness of the mid-day sun, how can it be understood of *lightning?* The light was doubtless, like the δόξα Θεοῦ presented to the view of St. Stephen, vii. 55., and meant to represent the *Schechinah*.

5. σκληρὸν — λακτ.] A proverbial form, common alike to the Hebrew, Greek, and Latin. The words σκληρὸν — πρὸς αὐτὸν are not found in a considerable number of the best MSS. and Versions, including the Syr. Peschito; nor in several citations of the Fathers, nor in the Ed. Pr.; and they are rejected by almost every Critic of eminence from Erasmus, Beza, and Grot., down to Tittm. and Vater. And rightly, for notwithstanding what Wolf urges in defence of the passage, there can be little doubt that it was introduced from the parallel passages at xxii. 10. xxvi. 14. It might well be expected that *the historian* should be less circumstantial than the *personal narrator* of facts. When the passage in question was brought in, the ἀλλὰ was sure to be ejected as worse than useless.

7. εἱστήκεισαν ἐννεοί.] As this seems at variance with the words πάντων καταπεσόντων ἡμῶν εἰς γῆν in the account of his conversion by St. Paul himself to Agrippa, Acts xxvi. 14. several expedients have been devised to remove the discrepancy. The most approved one is that of Valla and others, who suppose that they had first fallen down and then risen again. But though this is *preferable* to that of Beza and others, who remove the difficulty by almost silencing the εἱστήκεισαν, explaining it *were;* yet it is liable to several objections, which I have urged in Recens. Synop. The best solution may be, to suppose that Paul's companions at first *stood fixed* and mute with astonishment — and then, struck with awe at what they regarded as indicating the presence, however invisible, of a supernatural Being, fell with their faces to the ground, as Saul had done. Ἐννεοί, "mute," and, by implication, senseless. The word denotes not so much one who is destitute of the natural faculty of speech or hearing, as one in whom it is suspended, or accidentally lost.

— ἀκούοντες μὲν τῆς φωνῆς.] This seems at variance with the account at xxii. 9. τὸ μὲν φῶς ἐθεάσαντο, τὴν δὲ φωνὴν οὐκ ἤκουσαν τοῦ λαλοῦντός μοι. Of the various modes of removing the discrepancy (stated and discussed in Recens. Synop.) the most satisfactory one is to take ἤκουσαν, with Grot., Bowyer, Valck., Dobret, Kuin., and Schleus., in the sense *understood*, a signification of the word often occurring in the N. T. This signification, and also the construction, is found sometimes in the Classical writers, and often in the LXX. One *very apposite* example will suffice. Gen. xi. 7. συγχέωμεν αὐτῶν τὴν γλῶσσαν, ἵνα μὴ ἀκούσωσιν ἕκαστος τὴν φωνὴν τοῦ πλησίον.

They heard the sound of the voice which addressed Saul, — but did not, it seems, fully understand the *sense* of what they heard; either from imperfect acquaintance with the Hebrew language, or rather because the words would not to *them* carry their meaning so plainly, as to the conscience-stricken Saul. Possibly, too, the words might be pronounced in a low tone, as meant only for Saul.

8. οὐδένα ἔβλεπε.] i. e. neither *Jesus*, whom he opened his eyes to see, nor even his companions — in fact, he was *blind*. That on rising and opening his eyes, he had lost the power of seeing *any one*, whether Jesus or his companions, is also clear from xxii. 11. ὡς δὲ οὐκ ἐνέβλεπον ἀπὸ τῆς δόξης τοῦ φωτὸς ἐκείνου: where, from the context, it is obvious that the sense is: "having been blinded by that glorious light."

On the blindness of Saul the Commentators before mentioned again exert themselves to exclude all supernatural agency; but in vain. See

9 ἔβλεπε· χειραγωγοῦντες δὲ αὐτὸν εἰσήγαγον εἰς Δαμασκόν. Καὶ ἦν
10 ἡμέρας τρεῖς μὴ βλέπων, καὶ οὐκ ἔφαγεν οὐδὲ ἔπιεν. Ἦν δέ τις μαθητὴς ἐν Δαμασκῷ ὀνόματι Ἀνανίας· καὶ εἶπε πρὸς αὐτὸν ὁ Κύριος
11 ἐν ὁράματι· Ἀνανία. ὁ δὲ εἶπεν· Ἰδοὺ ἐγὼ, Κύριε. Ὁ δὲ Κύριος
πρὸς αὐτόν· Ἀναστὰς πορεύθητι ἐπὶ τὴν ῥύμην τὴν καλουμένην Εὐθεῖαν, καὶ ζήτησον ἐν οἰκίᾳ Ἰούδα Σαῦλον ὀνόματι, Ταρσέα· ἰδοὺ
12 γὰρ προσεύχεται, καὶ εἶδεν ἐν ὁράματι ἄνδρα ὀνόματι Ἀνανίαν εἰσελ-
13 θόντα καὶ ἐπιθέντα αὐτῷ χεῖρα, ὅπως ἀναβλέψῃ. Ἀπεκρίθη δὲ ὁ
Ἀνανίας· Κύριε, ἀκήκοα ἀπὸ πολλῶν περὶ τοῦ ἀνδρὸς τούτου, ὅσα
14 κακὰ ἐποίησε τοῖς ἁγίοις σου ἐν Ἱερουσαλήμ· καὶ ὧδε ἔχει ἐξουσίαν
παρὰ τῶν ἀρχιερέων, δῆσαι πάντας τοὺς ἐπικαλουμένους τὸ ὄνομά σου.
15 Εἶπε δὲ πρὸς αὐτὸν ὁ Κύριος· Πορεύου, ὅτι σκεῦος ἐκλογῆς μοι ἐστὶν
οὗτος, τοῦ βαστάσαι τὸ ὄνομά μου ἐνώπιον ἐθνῶν καὶ βασιλέων, υἱῶν
16 τε Ἰσραήλ. Ἐγὼ γὰρ ὑποδείξω αὐτῷ ὅσα δεῖ αὐτὸν ὑπὲρ τοῦ ὀνόματός
μου παθεῖν.

Recens. Synop. The most *plausible* view taken on that hypothesis, is to consider it as a temporary *amaurosis*, as the medical writers call it, such as is induced by excess of light. This, however, involves more difficulties than the common view, and leaves them unsolved. For 1. how is it consistent with what we read further on,—that *scales* had grown over the eyes? 2. This amaurosis is, as they themselves admit, an affection which lasts but a *very short* time; whereas Saul's blindness continued about *three days*. 3. How are we to account for a blindness, so complete as to be accompanied with *scales* over the eyes, leaving Saul *so soon*,—nay, immediately on Ananias's laying his hands on him. 4. How is it that *Saul alone*, and none of his companions, was struck with this *amaurosis*?

The *ζήτει χειραγωγοὺς* at Acts xiii. 11. may be compared with the *χειραγωγοῦντες αὐτὸν εἰσήγαγον* here; a circumstance introduced to show utter blindness, and which often occurs in the Classical writers. It should seem that in the case of Saul, as in that of Elymas, the blindness was not only *judicial*, but *typical* and emblematical. In the former case it was probably meant, by withdrawing his attention from external thoughts, and turning them inward, to favour reflection and self-examination, and thus lead to repentance.

9. *ἡμέρας τρεῖς.*] We need not understand three *complete* days, but suppose that among these three days is to be reckoned that on which Saul reached Damascus, and that on which Ananias came to him and removed his blindness. Thus when it is said that Christ was in the sepulchre *three* days, we know, it was, in fact, but one whole day and a part of two others.

—*οὐκ ἔφαγεν οὐδὲ ἔπιεν.*] We *might*, in any other case, understand this of extreme abstinence. But to suppose it *here* (with several recent Commentators) were an unwarrantable *lowering* of the sense; as indeed in most of the passages to which they appeal as examples of this hyperbole, as they term it. *Complete* fasting was very suitable under Saul's present awful visitation, which he could not know would ever be removed. Indeed the terror and remorse he felt, and the total absorption of his mind on a new and momentous subject, with the exercise of self-examination and earnest prayer for mercy and pardon, would leave him no inclination to eat and drink for *the time* mentioned, even had not his body been too disordered to admit of it.

11. Εὐθεῖαν.] I have so edited, with Beza, Wets., and others, for *εὐθ.*, because the word is evidently a substantive and a *proper* name.

—*Σαῦλον ὀν.*] Sub. *ἄνδρα*, and perhaps *καλούμενον*. The manner in which Saul is mentioned here and at ver. 13., quite discountenances the conjecture of many recent Foreign Commentators, that Saul and Ananias were acquainted with each other. I have, in Recens. Synop., shown how unfounded is this notion. Indeed how many difficulties are *created* by the attempt to reduce every thing to the level of common occurrence, or sometimes by even attempting to *intermix* the natural and the preternatural.

—*προσεύχεται*] is praying, namely, for pardon, and deliverance from the just judgment of God.

13. ὁ 'Αν.] A few ancient MSS. and early Edd. omit the Article, which is cancelled by almost all Editors from Matth. to Vater; but without reason. Its insertion is agreeable to strict propriety. See Middl. Gr. A Ch. iv. And it is far more likely that the Scribes should inadvertently *omit* than *insert* it.

—*τοῖς ἁγίοις σου.*] A periphrasis simply denoting *Christians*, as the Jews were styled קדושים. Both expressions denote what is *supposed to be* the case in persons so designated, and suggest what they *ought to be*.

14. ὧδε] "in this place." As Heb. xiii. 4.

15. *σκεῦος ἐκλογῆς.*] A Hebraism for *σκ. ἐκλεκτὸν*, a chosen *instrument* to work my purposes. For though *σκεῦος* (as also the Heb. כלי) properly denotes an *utensil*, or *piece of furniture*, yet, like כלי in Is. xiii. 5., it sometimes denotes *ὄργανον*, in both its literal and metaphorical sense, i. e. a person well adapted to the execution of any purpose. Thus Polyb. cited by Grot. *Δαμοκλῆς δὲ ἦν ὑπηρετικὸν σκεῦος, καὶ πολλὰς ἔχον ἀφορμὰς εἰς πραγμάτων οἰκονομίαν.*

—*βαστάσαι.*] There is a *significatio prægnans*, the word signifying to carry [forth] and make known.

16. Jesus does not actually bid Ananias to lay

Ἀπῆλθε δὲ Ἀνανίας καὶ εἰσῆλθεν εἰς τὴν οἰκίαν, καὶ ἐπιθεὶς ἐπ' 17
αὐτὸν τὰς χεῖρας εἶπε· Σαοὺλ ἀδελφὲ, ὁ Κύριος ἀπέσταλκέ με, (Ἰησοῦς
ὁ ὀφθείς σοι ἐν τῇ ὁδῷ ᾗ ἤρχου) ὅπως ἀναβλέψῃς καὶ πλησθῇς Πνεύματος ἁγίου. Καὶ εὐθέως ἀπέπεσον ἀπὸ τῶν ὀφθαλμῶν αὐτοῦ ὡσεὶ 18
λεπίδες, ἀνέβλεψέ τε παραχρῆμα· καὶ ἀναστὰς ἐβαπτίσθη· καὶ λαβὼν 19
τροφὴν ἐνίσχυσεν. Ἐγένετο δὲ ὁ Σαῦλος μετὰ τῶν ἐν Δαμασκῷ μαθητῶν ἡμέρας τινάς. Καὶ εὐθέως ἐν ταῖς συναγωγαῖς ἐκήρυσσε τὸν 20
‡ Χριστὸν, ὅτι οὗτός ἐστιν ὁ Υἱὸς τοῦ Θεοῦ. Ἐξίσταντο δὲ πάντες οἱ 21
ἀκούοντες, καὶ ἔλεγον· Οὐχ οὗτός ἐστιν ὁ πορθήσας ἐν Ἱερουσαλὴμ
τοὺς ἐπικαλουμένους τὸ ὄνομα τοῦτο· καὶ ὧδε εἰς τοῦτο ἐληλύθει ἵνα
δεδεμένους αὐτοὺς ἀγάγῃ ἐπὶ τοὺς ἀρχιερεῖς; Σαῦλος δὲ μᾶλλον ἐνεδυ- 22
ναμοῦτο, καὶ συνέχυνε τοὺς Ἰουδαίους τοὺς κατοικοῦντας ἐν Δαμασκῷ,
συμβιβάζων ὅτι οὗτός ἐστιν ὁ Χριστός. Ὡς δὲ ἐπληροῦντο ἡμέραι 23
u 2 Cor. 11. 32. ἱκαναὶ, συνεβουλεύσαντο οἱ Ἰουδαῖοι ἀνελεῖν αὐτόν· [u] ἐγνώσθη δὲ τῷ 24
Σαύλῳ ἡ ἐπιβουλὴ αὐτῶν· παρετήρουν τε τὰς πύλας ἡμέρας τε καὶ

his hands upon Saul: but that was *implied*, and Ananias could not but perceive that the affair was to take place in coincidence with the vision. Hence he tells Saul that the Lord hath sent him for that purpose.

17. ὅπως πλησθῇς Πν. ἁγ.] Jesus had not indeed told Ananias *this*, but he well knew it was impossible that Saul could be able to effect what he was to effect without a *copious effusion* of the Holy Spirit, which is implied in πλησθῇς.

18. εὐθέως ἀπέπεσον — λεπίδες.] What but *supernatural* power could produce this? It is pitiable to see the miserable straits to which those Commentators are reduced, who seek to accouut for this on *natural* principles. Nothing can be plainer, than that St. Luke *means* to represent the *removal* of the blindness, as he had done the *infliction* of it, as *supernatural*. It may not, however, be the less true that there is a disorder of the eyes, sometimes occurring in the East, called λεύκωμα, produced by certain humors in the eyes, which becoming *concrete*, form as it were scales. Thus Schleus. refers to Tob. ii. 9. and vi. 10., and cites Tob. xi. 13. καὶ ἐλεπίσθη ἀπὸ τῶν κανθῶν τῶν ὀφθαλμῶν αὐτοῦ τὰ λευκώματα. See Foes. Œcon. Hipp. p. 230. But this, as I learn, is a *lingering* disorder. And to bring it on suddenly and without a natural cause, and to remove it suddenly and alike without a natural cause, cannot but be *miraculous*.

19. ἡμέρας τινάς.] Not *certain* days, but *some* days. On the chronological difficulty supposed to be involved in this and the following verses, see Note on Gal. i. 17.

20. Χριστόν.] 13 MSS., most of the Versions, and Irenæus, have Ἰησοῦν, which is preferred by Grot., Mill, and Beng., and edited by Griesb., Knapp, and Tittm., with the approbation of Michaelis, Morus, Valckn., Rosenm., and Kuin. The preference, however, seems due to Χριστὸν, as being the more *difficult* reading: whereas the former bears the stamp of *emendation* upon it. The corruption may be attributed to those who stumbled at τὸν Χρ., taking it only to denote the same thing with Υἱὸν τοῦ Θεοῦ, and not being aware that τὸν Χρ. may be for τὸν Ἰησοῦν Χριστόν; and that that is sometimes only a *proper name*, even in the Gospels and Acts, as has been proved by Bp. Middl. See Note on Mark xi. 43., where he observes, that "the commonness of the name Jesus among the Jews both rendered an *addition* necessary, and also contributed to the gradual substitution of that addition for the real name." Thus all objection is removed, Χρ. being *equivalent* to Ἰησοῦν.

22. συμβιβάζων] "evincing," as in 1 Cor. ii. 16. Συμβιβάζειν properly signifies *to put together*, as carpenters' work. And since he who *proves* any thing does it by showing the connexion, and tracing the chain of facts or reasonings, so it comes to mean to *demonstrate*, a sense which occurs in 1 Cor. ii. 16. and sometimes in the LXX.; but rarely in the Classical writers. Ὁ Χριστὸς should be rendered "the Messiah;" for here it is plainly an *appellative*, descriptive of that office. See Note supra v. 20.

24. ἐγνώσθη — αὐτῶν.] This clause perturbs the construction, and is, therefore, removed by the Syr. Version and Wakef., and placed after παρετήρουν — ἀνέλωσι. That, however, is scarcely allowable, even in a *Translation*. In *preference* to supposing so very harsh a transposition, I would regard the clause with Abp. Newc., as parenthetical. But thus παρετήρουν is brought into the closest connexion with οἱ Ἰουδαῖοι as its Nominative. And the statement runs counter to that in 2 Cor. xi. 32. where St. Paul says not that *the Jews*, but that the *soldiers* of the Ethnarch of King Aretas occupied the gates, that he might not escape. Some Commentators, indeed, (as Kuin.), attempt to remove this discrepancy by supposing, either that the Jews may be said to have done *what they did*, by *another*, *they* having *suggested* the thing; or that the Jews by the authority of the Ethnarch, watched the gates in *conjunction with the soldiers*. Of these two solutions the *second* is preferable; but it may be doubted whether it be quite satisfactory. I would rather suppose that οἱ Ἰουδαῖοι is *not* the true Nomin. to παρετήρουν, but rather ἄνθρωποι understood, by a very common ellips. Thus the sense may be expressed as if the verb had been impersonal, "A watch was set at the gates, that he might be apprehended." Thus the discrepancy will be effectually removed. It was not *likely* that the Governor of the city should suffer a few

25 νυκτὸς, ὅπως αὐτὸν ἀνέλωσι· λαβόντες δὲ αὐτὸν οἱ μαθηταὶ νυκτὸς,
26 καθῆκαν διὰ τοῦ τείχους, χαλάσαντες ἐν σπυρίδι. Παραγενόμενος δὲ
ὁ Σαῦλος εἰς Ἱερουσαλὴμ, ἐπειρᾶτο κολλᾶσθαι τοῖς μαθηταῖς· καὶ
27 πάντες ἐφοβοῦντο αὐτὸν, μὴ πιστεύοντες ὅτι ἐστὶ μαθητής. Βαρνάβας
δὲ ἐπιλαβόμενος αὐτὸν, ἤγαγε πρὸς τοὺς ἀποστόλους· καὶ διηγήσατο
αὐτοῖς πῶς ἐν τῇ ὁδῷ εἶδε τὸν Κύριον, καὶ ὅτι ἐλάλησεν αὐτῷ, καὶ
28 πῶς ἐν Δαμασκῷ ἐπαῤῥησιάσατο ἐν τῷ ὀνόματι τοῦ Ἰησοῦ. Καὶ ἦν μετ'
αὐτῶν εἰσπορευόμενος καὶ ἐκπορευόμενος ἐν Ἱερουσαλὴμ, καὶ παῤῥησιαζό-
29 μενος ἐν τῷ ὀνόματι τοῦ Κυρίου Ἰησοῦ· ἐλάλει τε καὶ συνεζήτει πρὸς τοὺς
30 Ἑλληνιστάς· οἱ δὲ ἐπεχείρουν αὐτὸν ἀνελεῖν. Ἐπιγνόντες δὲ οἱ ἀδελφοὶ
κατήγαγον αὐτὸν εἰς Καισάρειαν, καὶ ἐξαπέστειλαν αὐτὸν εἰς Ταρσόν.

lawless foreigners φρουρεῖν τὴν πόλιν, i. e. τὰς πύλας.

25. καθῆκαν διὰ τοῦ τείχους.] Doddr. and Wakef. translate, "by the side of the wall," which is at least more perspicuous than our common version, "*by the* wall." It is not easy, however, to see how this could be done; and from a comparison with the parallel passage at 2 Cor. xi. 33. καὶ διὰ θυρίδος, it is plain that διὰ must here mean *through*, i. e. by an aperture. So Luke v. 19. διὰ τῶν κεράμων καθῆκαν αὐτὸν, and elsewhere. The Philological Commentators here fail us; but I have in Recens. Synop. supplied the deficiency by citations from Aristoph. Vesp. 354 and 379., Athen. p. 214., Palæphatus § 9. and Procop. p. 155., whence it appears this was often done. We are not, however, to understand by the θυρίδος above mentioned, a *window* in the wall itself (for the exceedingly thick city walls of the ancients scarcely admitted of windows), but in some turret on the wall, or perhaps a window of some house connected with the wall, so as to have part of the house *above* it. For it is certain that this was *sometimes* the case, as is clear from Thucyd. ii. 4, and the passages of the Classical writers cited by me in the Note there. It may be added, that this was an *Eastern* custom, exceedingly ancient, as appears from Josh. ii. 15. (of Rahab and the spies) where some of the Greek Translators render καὶ κατεχάλασεν αὐτοὺς διὰ τῆς θυρίδος ἐν σχοινίῳ, ὅτι ὁ οἶκος ἦν ἐν τῷ τείχει. So a Rabbinical writer cited by Wets. on 2 Cor. xi. 33. "Domus *in mœnibus exstructa*, cujus paries exterior est murus urbis."

26. παραγενόμενος — εἰς Ἱερ.] Not immediately, but after having gone (for the second time, it should seem) into Arabia. See Note on Gal. i. 17. This circumstance Luke omits, because he only meant to narrate such parts of St. Paul's history, and more public ministrations, as especially illustrated the providence of God over him, and the mode in which he was brought to devote himself to the conversion of the Gentiles. Chrysost. here remarks (p. 728.): Τί οὖν; τοιοῦτον κίνδυνον διαφυγὼν, ἆρα ἵσταται; οὐδαμῶς· ἀλλ' ἀπέρχεται ἔνθα μειζόνως ἂν αὐτοὺς ἐξάψοι. where for the confessedly corrupt ἵσταται Seville conjectures φεύγει; the true mode of emendation seems to be this: for ἆρα ἵσταται read ἆρ' ἀφίσταται. The verb ἀφίστασθαι is used in the sense *desert*, *abandon*, both in the Scriptural and Classical writers. But Chrys. seems to have had in view Luke viii. 13. καὶ ἐν καιρῷ πειρασμοῦ ἀφίστανται. See also 1 Tim. iv. 1 Heb. iii. 12.

27. Βαρνάβας δέ.] Paul is supposed to have been previously known to Barnabas; nay, to have been a fellow disciple with him under Gamaliel.

— ἐπιλαβόμενος.] The older Commentators interpret this "taking him;" by which it will be a mere pleonasm. And for the sense "received him into hospitality," assigned by Schleus. and others, there is no authority. It seems to denote (by an idiom common to our own language) "taking him by the hand," i. e. giving him his countenance, society, and aid. Thus the Syriac Version expresses it by "accepit;" better *suscepit*. This signification is rare; but there is an example in Ecclus. iv. 11. ἡ σοφία υἱοὺς αὐτῆς ἀνύψωσε, καὶ ἐπιλαμβάνεται τῶν ζητούντων αὐτῶν. The above interpretation I find supported by the authority of Tittmann de Syn. N. T. P. ii. p. 7., who also duces the passage of Ecclus. and besides the Scholiast on Æschyl. Pers. 739. ὁ Θεὸς ξυνάπτεται. who explains ξυνάπτ. by ἐπιλαμβάνεται. Συνεπιλ. is frequent in this sense. Ἤγαγε. Anglicè, *introduced*. Διηγήσατο must be referred to *Barnabas*. And the purport of what he says seems to be this: "If the Lord hath spoken to him, is it for us to shun him? if he has been bold in preaching the Gospel, is it for us to be timidly cautious in receiving him?"

28. εἰσπορευόμενος καὶ ἐκπ.] This is a phrase expressive of familiarity and intimacy. See i. 21. The construction here (not noticed by the Commentators) is as follows: καὶ ἦν μετ' αὐτῶν ἐν Ἱερ. εἰσπ. καὶ ἐκπορ. At καὶ παῤῥησ. repeat ἦν; for the sense is not, I conceive, (as Wakef. thought,) that Saul used much freedom of speech with the Apostles; though that is countenanced by the Vulgate. In fact, ἦν παῤῥησιαζόμενος is put for ἐπαῤῥησιάζετο, (as was well seen by the Pesch. Syriac translator) and thus connects well with ἐλάλει and συνεζήτει following, the sense being here, as at Eph. vi. 20. that he used freedom and boldness in the cause of Jesus, and the spread of the Gospel.

30. κατήγαγον.] This may have reference to the situation of Cæsarea on the sea-coast, as compared with the upland region of Damascus. So Plutarch Vit. Cic. (cited by Wets.) αὐτὸν οἵ τε δυνατοὶ πάντες ἀπὸ τῆς οἰκίας κατήγαγον εἰς τὸ πεδίον. But perhaps the sense is, "*conducted* him," as in Thucyd. iv. 78. οἱ ἀγωγοὶ — κατέστησαν αὐτὸν ἐς Δῖον. and Acts xvii. 15. καθιστῶντες τὸν Παῦλον ἤγαγεν ἕως Ἀθηνῶν. It is strange that Doddr. and Scott should take the Cæsarea here of *Cæsarea Philippi*, since (as Calmet well observes) when Cæsarea is mentioned without any addition, it means Cæsarea *of Palestine*. There is nothing in Gal. i. 21. to *compel* us (as Doddr. imagined)

Αἱ μὲν οὖν ἐκκλησίαι καθ᾽ ὅλης τῆς Ἰουδαίας καὶ Γαλιλαίας καὶ Σαμα- 31
ρείας εἶχον εἰρήνην, οἰκοδομούμεναι καὶ πορευόμεναι τῷ φόβῳ τοῦ
Κυρίου, καὶ τῇ παρακλήσει τοῦ ἁγίου Πνεύματος ἐπληθύνοντο.
ἘΓΕΝΕΤΟ δὲ Πέτρον, διερχόμενον διὰ πάντων, κατελθεῖν καὶ πρὸς 32
τοὺς ἁγίους τοὺς κατοικοῦντας Λύδδαν. Εὗρε δὲ ἐκεῖ ἄνθρωπόν τινα 33
Αἰνέαν ὀνόματι, ἐξ ἐτῶν ὀκτὼ κατακείμενον ἐπὶ κραββάτῳ, ὅς ἦν παρα-
λελυμένος. Καὶ εἶπεν αὐτῷ ὁ Πέτρος· Αἰνέα· ἰᾶταί σε Ἰησοῦς ὁ 34
Χριστός· ἀνάστηθι καὶ στρῶσον σεαυτῷ. Καὶ εὐθέως ἀνέστη· καὶ 35
εἶδον αὐτὸν πάντες οἱ κατοικοῦντες Λύδδαν καὶ τὸν Σαρωνᾶν· οἵτινες
ἐπέστρεψαν ἐπὶ τὸν Κύριον.
Ἐν Ἰόππῃ δέ τις ἦν μαθήτρια ὀνόματι Ταβιθὰ, ἣ διερμηνευομένη 36
λέγεται Δορκάς· αὕτη ἦν πλήρης ἀγαθῶν ἔργων καὶ ἐλεημοσυνῶν ὧν
ἐποίει. Ἐγένετο δὲ, ἐν ταῖς ἡμέραις ἐκείναις ἀσθενήσασαν αὐτὴν ἀπο- 37
θανεῖν. λούσαντες δὲ αὐτὴν ἔθηκαν ἐν ὑπερῴῳ. Ἐγγὺς δὲ οὔσης 38

to suppose the former; since εἰς there does *not* mean (when, indeed, does it?) *through*, but *unto*. And the expression εἰς τὰ κλίματα Συρίας would only induce us to suppose, that after having taken ship at Cæsarea, Saul did not go to Tarsus *by crossing the sea;* but as in his later voyages, by taking coasting vessels, and stopping at the principal maritime cities of Syria, (as Laodicea and Antioch), and perhaps proceeding from the latter place to Tarsus by land, through Upper Syria and Cilicia Campestris. He took this course, probably, in order to spread the Gospel over the flourishing and populous commercial places all along that coast, and especially among the Hellenists. Whereas, if he had gone *by land* from Cæsarea *Philippi*, he would have traversed a mountainous and thinly inhabited country, almost entirely peopled by heathens.

31. οἰκοδομούμεναι.] We have here an *architectural* metaphor; though the Commentators are not agreed whether it should be taken in the physical sense, of *increase in number* of persons, or metaphorically, of *increase in spiritual knowledge* and the grace of God. The *former* is mostly adopted by the older, the latter, by the recent Commentators; which is preferable, being supported by very many passages of the N. T., and far more agreeable to the construction. It is well observed by T. Sykes (ap. Doyly and Mant) that the term *edification* as applied to *individuals*, signifies sometimes advancement in knowledge of our duty, but generally an improvement in the *practice* of it. It is, however, usually, as here, applied to Christian communities, with reference to the duty of promoting peace, order, and unity, in the Church; to the duty of establishing and strengthening by the practice of all charity, that household of God which is built upon the foundation of the Apostles and Prophets; Jesus Christ himself being the chief corner stone, Eph. ii. 19.

32. From this verse to Ch. xi. 18. are related the journeys undertaken by *Peter* (who had hitherto confined his Evangelical labours to *Jerusalem*, with the exception of a short visit to Samaria, related at viii. 14.) for the purpose of visiting and confirming the churches founded in Palestine, and, by his preaching, increasing the numbers of their members.

33. Αἰνέαν.] From the name, he seems to have been an Hellenist; and, as the air of the passage seems to suggest, a Christian. Κατακείμενον ἐπὶ κραββ. Perhaps we need not suppose that he had been literally ten years laid on a bed; but that he had been ten years, as we say, *bedridden*.

34. στρῶσον σεαυτῷ.] This expression, like κοῖτον ποιεῖσθαι in Herodot. vii. 17, has reference not to such *portable couches* as cripples were laid upon, to excite charity, but to a bed of large size, and suited to Æneas's respectable station in life. Here Chrys., Calvin, and Doddr. remark on the different mode in which this miracle was performed, as compared with *Christ's*. "By thus speaking (says Calvin) Peter meant to openly declare, that he was only the *instrument*, while the miracle was performed by the virtue of Christ; that he might thus give the glory to Christ alone."

35. οἵτινες ἐπέστρεψαν.] Some Commentators (as Pearce, Wakef., Heinr., and Kuin.) take ἐπέστ. in a *pluperfect* sense, "*had* turned," rendering: "and all the inhabitants of Lydda and Saron who had turned to the Lord saw him." But that yields a very awkward sense; as if no *others* had seen the person when healed, *but the Christian converts*. Whereas *all* must have seen him. And that is what Luke seems to have meant to say; and after that, to describe the *effect* which the miracle had on the inhabitants of the place where it was worked, and its district. Comp. v. 42. The οἵτινες here has, in strictness, the force of a *relative;* but it may (as the relative ὅς often is) in translation be resolved into its equivalent καὶ and ἐκεῖνος. In fact, relatives in most languages are compounded of such; as, for instance, *qui* of *que* and *ille*, and *quis* of *qui* and *is*. As to the relative ὅς, it was formed from the old demonstrative ὅς, with the ellips. of the conjunction. The usage falls under the rule of Matth. Gr. Gr. § 477. "The relative sometimes serves, as in Latin, to connect propositions, instead of the demonstrative."

36. πλήρης ἀ. ἔ.] "abounding in, studious of good works." So John i. 14. πλήρης χάριτος.

37. λούσαντες δὲ αὐτήν.] As we cannot suppose that *men* would do such an office, (though there are passages in Herodotus which prove that it was in *Egypt* performed by men undertakers) we may, with Pearce and Markl., take λούσαντες

Λύδδης τῇ Ἰόππῃ, οἱ μαθηταὶ ἀκούσαντες ὅτι Πέτρος ἐστὶν ἐν αὐτῇ,
ἀπέστειλαν δύο ἄνδρας πρὸς αὐτὸν, παρακαλοῦντες μὴ ὀκνῆσαι διελ-
39 *θεῖν ἕως αὐτῶν. Ἀναστὰς δὲ Πέτρος συνῆλθεν αὐτοῖς· ὃν παραγε-*
νόμενον ἀνήγαγον εἰς τὸ ὑπερῷον, καὶ παρέστησαν αὐτῷ πᾶσαι αἱ
χῆραι κλαίουσαι καὶ ἐπιδεικνύμεναι χιτῶνας καὶ ἱμάτια, ὅσα ἐποίει μετ᾽
40 *αὐτῶν οὖσα ἡ Δορκάς. Ἐκβαλὼν δὲ ἔξω πάντας ὁ Πέτρος, θεὶς τὰ*
γόνατα προσηύξατο. καὶ ἐπιστρέψας πρὸς τὸ σῶμα, εἶπε· Ταβιθὰ,
ἀνάστηθι. Ἡ δὲ ἤνοιξε τοὺς ὀφθαλμοὺς αὐτῆς· καὶ ἰδοῦσα τὸν
41 *Πέτρον ἀνεκάθισε. Δοὺς δὲ αὐτῇ χεῖρα ἀνέστησεν αὐτήν· φωνήσας*
42 *δὲ τοὺς ἁγίους καὶ τὰς χήρας, παρέστησεν αὐτὴν ζῶσαν. Γνωστὸν δὲ*
ἐγένετο καθ᾽ ὅλης τῆς Ἰόππης· καὶ πολλοὶ ἐπίστευσαν ἐπὶ τὸν Κύριον.
43 *Ἐγένετο δὲ, ἡμέρας ἱκανὰς μεῖναι αὐτὸν ἐν Ἰόππῃ παρά τινι Σίμωνι*
βυρσεῖ.

1 X. *ἈΝΗΡ δέ τις ἦν ἐν Καισαρείᾳ ὀνόματι Κορνήλιος, ἑκατοντάρχης*
2 *ἐκ σπείρης τῆς καλουμένης Ἰταλικῆς, εὐσεβὴς καὶ φοβούμενος τὸν Θεὸν*
σὺν παντὶ τῷ οἴκῳ αὐτοῦ, ποιῶν τε ἐλεημοσύνας πολλὰς τῷ λαῷ, καὶ
3 *δεόμενος τοῦ Θεοῦ διαπαντός. Εἶδεν ἐν ὁράματι φανερῶς, ὡσεὶ ὥραν*
ἐννάτην τῆς ἡμέρας, ἄγγελον τοῦ Θεοῦ εἰσελθόντα πρὸς αὐτὸν, καὶ

as put for λούσασαι, by reference to ἄνθρωποι understood, that being a general term, and including females. Or it may be regarded as a popular mode of expression, in a *general* sense, merely denoting that she was washed and laid out. The masculine is here used for either sex, as being what the Grammarians call the worthier gender. That women are here meant, there is the more reason to think, since we learn both from the Scriptural and ancient writers in general, that *women* were employed on such offices, even towards men. So Ennius cited by Wets. Tarquinii corpus *bona femina* lavit et unxit. And Socrates (as we learn from Plato Phæd.) chose to take a bath just before he drank the fatal cup, ὥστε μὴ πράγματα ταῖς γυναιξὶν παρέχειν. Accordingly we cannot doubt that women always performed such offices to *women*.

38. μὴ ὀκνῆσαι] "not to delay." A sense rare in the earlier, but frequent in the later writers. We may hence clearly infer they had a hope of Peter's being able to bring the dead person to life.

39. ὑπερῷον.] See Note supra i. 13.

— ἐπιδεικνύμεναι — Δορκάς.] The sense is: "Showing coats and garments such as Dorcas used to make when she was with them." The use of the Imperfect to denote *custom* is not unfrequent. It is not certain whether the garments shown were, as the common opinion is, *stocks* of clothes provided for the poor; *or* (what is the opinion of some recent Commentators and of the ancients, Cyprian), such garments as the widows then had on. That, however, seems countenanced neither by the words themselves (for thus the *article* would be requisite at χιτῶνας and ἱμάτια; and ἃ, not ὅσα, would have been used), nor by the air of the context: not to say that there is something *frigid* and jejune in the latter view; while the former is perfectly natural and appropriate. The widows meant to justify, as it were, their grief, by showing Peter how industriously active Tabitha had been in her domestic duties, and how much she would be missed. That the women of ancient times, even those of the higher ranks, used to manufacture garments for the family use, is well known, and established by various proofs. There is no doubt, too, that these works were, by benevolent and charitable mistresses of families, carried on, not for the use of the family alone, but to give to the poor, and such as could not make them for themselves. And these widows had, doubtless, as we may infer from the air of the passage, partaken of Tabitha's bounty in that and other respects.

40, 41. ἐκβαλὼν ἔξω.] See Note on Matt. ix. 25. and compare 2 Kings iv. 33.

41. παρέστησεν αὐτὴν ζῶσαν.] There is great elegance in this use of παρίστημι, *exhibeo*, of which Wets. adduces an example from Sext. Emp. 254. ὅτε Ἀδμήτῳ ὁ Ἡρακλῆς τὴν Ἄλκηστιν γῆθεν ἀναγαγὼν παρέστησε.

43. παρά.] Not "with," but "in the house of," as the French say *chez soi*; there being an ellip. of ξενιζόμενος *expressed* at x. 6.

X. 1. σπείρης — Ἰταλ.] So called, as being chiefly formed of Italians; for most of the Roman corps in Syria and Palestine were composed of *provincials*. By this the older Commentators understand a *Legion* called the *Italian Legion*. And indeed such a Legion is mentioned in Tacitus, Dio Cass., and Josephus. But the expression σπεῖρα will not admit of such a sense: nay, there is (as Biscoe has shown) great reason to think that the Legion of that name was *not yet in existence*. Σπεῖρα can only mean a *cohort*; though, from what has been adduced by Biscoe, Valdem., and Kuin., it seems we are not to understand an ordinary *Legionary* cohort, but one similar to the *Prætorian* cohorts of the Roman Emperors, and forming the body-guard of the Roman President of Syria, and garrisoning Cæsarea. Of this Italian cohort mention is made by Arrian Tact. p. 73. (cited by Wets.) προσετετάχθησαν δὲ αὐτῶν οἱ τῆς σπείρης Ἰταλικῆς πεζοί. whence it appears

εἰπόντα αὐτῷ· Κορνήλιε. Ὁ δὲ ἀτενίσας αὐτῷ καὶ ἔμφοβος γενόμενος 4
εἶπε· Τί ἐστι, κύριε; εἶπε δὲ αὐτῷ· Αἱ προσευχαί σου καὶ αἱ ἐλεημοσύναι σου ἀνέβησαν εἰς μνημόσυνον ἐνώπιον τοῦ Θεοῦ. Καὶ νῦν 5
πέμψον εἰς Ἰόππην ἄνδρας, καὶ μετάπεμψαι Σίμωνα ὃς ἐπικαλεῖται
Πέτρος· οὗτος ξενίζεται παρά τινι Σίμωνι βυρσεῖ, ᾧ ἐστιν οἰκία παρὰ 6
θάλασσαν· [οὗτος λαλήσει σοι τί σε δεῖ ποιεῖν.] Ὡς δὲ ἀπῆλθεν 7
ὁ ἄγγελος ὁ λαλῶν ‡ τῷ Κορνηλίῳ, φωνήσας δύο τῶν οἰκετῶν αὐτοῦ,
καὶ στρατιώτην εὐσεβῆ τῶν προσκαρτερούντων αὐτῷ, καὶ ἐξηγησάμενος 8
αὐτοῖς ἅπαντα, ἀπέστειλεν αὐτοὺς εἰς τὴν Ἰόππην. Τῇ δὲ ἐπαύριον, 9
ὁδοιπορούντων ἐκείνων καὶ τῇ πόλει ἐγγιζόντων, ἀνέβη Πέτρος ἐπὶ τὸ
δῶμα προσεύξασθαι περὶ ὥραν ἕκτην. Ἐγένετο δὲ πρόσπεινος, καὶ 10
ἤθελε γεύσασθαι· παρασκευαζόντων δὲ ἐκείνων, ἐπέπεσεν ἐπ᾽ αὐτὸν
ἔκστασις. Καὶ θεωρεῖ τὸν οὐρανὸν ἀνεῳγμένον, καὶ καταβαῖνον ἐπ᾽ 11

that the cohort consisted both of infantry and cavalry.

With respect to Cornelius, it has been debated whether he was a Gentile or a Jewish Proselyte. Commentators are now generally agreed on the former (see Valckn. in Rec. Syn.); but though a Gentile, that he was a worshipper of the one true God, and probably the first-fruits of the conversion of the Gentiles to Christianity.

4. *τί ἐστι, κύριε.*] A *popular* form of respectful answer to the call of a superior, though sometimes to that of an inferior, varying according to the tone of voice with which it is pronounced. Kuin. aptly cites Esth. v. 1. *τί ἐστιν, Ἐσθήρ*; thus there is an ellips. of some such words as *αἴτημά σου* which is *supplied* at Esth. vii. 2.

— *ἀνέβησαν ἐνώπιον τοῦ Θεοῦ.*] This is only an Oriental and figurative way of expressing that any thing has come to the knowledge of God. Nor does it necessarily imply the Jewish notion, that men's prayers are carried up by angels to God in heaven. In *εἰς μνημ.* we have the Hellenistic use of *μνημόσυνον* for *μνημεῖον*, corresponding to the Heb. זכרון. The word almost always implies, as here, an *honourable* remembrance; and *εἰς μνημ.* here and at Matt. xxvi. 13. is put for *ὥστε μνησθῆναι*.

5. *καὶ νῦν.*] A hortatory form. See Elsner.

6. *ξενίζεται*] for *ξενοδοχεῖται*; a sense occurring elsewhere in the Acts, and in the Epistle to the Hebrews, and rarely found except in the later writers.

— *βυρσεῖ.*] The Attic writers used *βυρσοδέψης*, literally a skin-softener, corresponding to our *currier*. With them *βυρσεὺς* only denoted a *skinner*, though there can be little doubt but that, among the ancients, the two trades were often conjoined, as far as the rougher sorts of tanning were concerned: and both were proverbially mean occupations, and held in such contempt by the Jews, that various laws were in force regulating the exercise thereof. See Rec. Synop. Thus the house being *by the sea-side* (i. e. as opposed to the *harbour*, and consequently out of the city) was in conformity to a law, which obliged tanners to have their workshops outside of towns. They were always placed near rivers, or by the sea, for the convenience of water, so necessary for their trade.

— *οὗτος — ποιεῖν.*] These words do not appear in many of the best MSS., Versions, and Fathers, with the Edit. Princ., and are written so very differently in others, that almost all Critics and Editors are agreed that they are from the margin, introduced from ix. 6. xi. 14. xxii. 10.

7. *τῶν προσκαρτ. α.*] Pric., Schleus., and Kuin. take *προσκαρτ.* to mean "of those who stood sentry." But there is perhaps no sufficient reason to abandon the common version, "of those who *waited* upon him," namely, as *domestics*; for it seems that centurions were allowed to use some of their soldiers in that capacity. This sense is confirmed by the use of the word supra viii. 13, and is perhaps *required* by the *ἐκείνων* at ver. 10, where see Note.

10. *πρόσπεινος.*] A word said to occur nowhere else, though *κατάπεινος*, *ἔκπεινος*, and *ὀξύπεινος* are found. The *προς* has an intensive force, as derived from the signification *in addition to*. I know no other example of *προς with an adjective*, except it be *προσηνής*. At *γεύσασθαι* sub. *τῆς τροφῆς*. This idiom we should suppose would be used solely of taking a slight refreshment: but it is very often used of *taking a meal*, without reference to the quantity of food eaten. See my Note on Thucyd. ii. 70. The Classical writers rarely, if ever, use the word thus, *absolutely*; in which we may trace the force of the middle voice, by which the word means to *feed one's self*, and thence to *eat*.

— *ἐκείνων.*] Several MSS. and Origen have *αὐτῶν*, which *seems* to have greater propriety, since *ἐκεῖνος* is rarely found in this *absolute* use; but it is perhaps an emendation, especially as it comes from a quarter fruitful in such. Besides, *ἐκείνων* may even have greater propriety, if we consider it as having reference to the *τῶν προσκαρτερούντων αὐτῷ* supra v. 8.

— *ἔκστασις.*] The word properly signifies *a removal of any thing from any former situation* or state; but it is here applied to that removal of the *mind from the body*, by which, even though awake, we are insensible to external objects, and our senses are so far from conveying to us the impressions of those objects, that the mind seems, as it were, to have *retired* from the body, and to be wholly absorbed in the contemplation of internal and mental images. We may render "an *ecstasy*," or trance. Lightf. observes that there were seven ways in which God formerly revealed himself to men: 1. by dreams; 2. by apparitions while they were awake; 3. by visions while they

αὐτὸν σκεῦός τι ὡς ὀθόνην μεγάλην, τέσσαρσιν ἀρχαῖς δεδεμένον, καὶ
12 καθιέμενον ἐπὶ τῆς γῆς· ἐν ᾧ ὑπῆρχε πάντα τὰ τετράποδα τῆς γῆς καὶ
13 τὰ θηρία καὶ τὰ ἑρπετὰ, καὶ τὰ πετεινὰ τοῦ οὐρανοῦ. καὶ ἐγένετο φωνὴ

slept; 4. by a voice from heaven; 5. by the Urim and Thummim; 6. by inspiration, or auricular revelation; 7. by a sort of rapture or ecstasy (as here and Gen. ii. 21.), which was of all other modes the most excellent, and by which a man *was snatched into heaven* (2 Cor. xii. 2.), and *was in the Spirit* (Rev. i. 10.).

11. σκεῦος.] The word (derived from σκέω, or κέω, *tego*) signifies any article of furniture which is adapted to *contain* any thing, — a *vessel*. 'Οθόνην may mean either a sheet, or a *wrapper*, such as has ever been in use in the East to throw over any thing or person. So Aristoph. Vesp. 595. τῶν δ' αἱ μὲν λεπτὰς ὀθόνας ἔχον, οἱ δὲ χιτῶνας. Of this word the etymon is *given up* in despair by the Etymologists. But may it not come from ὄθω, cognate with ὄω and οἴω, to *bear* or carry? as our *sheet* comes from the Ang. Sax. ƿheꞇan, to cast or throw [over]. It is of the same form as σφενδόνη, ἀγχόνη, περόνη, βελόνη, &c.

On the typical intent of this and other parts of the vision, see a learned Dissertation by *B. Duysing*, in vol. ii. p. 610—20 of the Novus Thes. Theol. appended to the Dutch Edition of the Critici Sacri. In opposition to the view adopted by Hammond and others, he is of opinion that every thing included in the sheet (namely, four-footed and wild beasts, reptiles, and fowls of the air), were *unclean*; the whole object of the vision being to impress on the mind of the Apostle a *new doctrine*, relating to the *Gentiles only*, and not to the Jews and Gentiles together. "The sheet (says he) was a type of the *Christian Church*, separated from the world, which included every kind of people. It was *bound at the four corners*, to signify that the whole world should be received into the universal Church of God. It *descended from heaven*, in the same manner as the New Jerusalem is represented in the Apocalypse. And the *drawing back* of the sheet to heaven was meant to teach us that the Church, which has its origin from heaven, will return victorious to heaven." Thus the *four corners* have reference to the *four corners of the earth*, with allusion to the four cardinal points.

— ἀρχαῖς.] 'Αρχὴ signifies the *extremity* of any thing of an oblong form, — since each *end* may be considered as a beginning. See Galen ap. Rec. Syn. And, as in things of the form of a parallelogram, (as in a web of cloth) each end, having two angles, may be said to have *two* of these ἀρχαὶ; thus ἀρχαὶ might here be rendered *extremities*, or corners; though "*ends*" is the more accurate version. Wakef., indeed, renders "by four *strings*," referring, for an example of that signification, to a passage of Diod. Sic. And Bp. Middleton regards this as "a singularly happy criticism, and as probably worth all that remains in his New Testament." I can neither agree with the learned Prelate in his *commendation*, nor (low as I rate the value of Wakefield's labours on the N. T.) in the *censure* which it implies. After carefully examining all the authorities which have any bearing upon the point in question, I cannot discover any *proof* of the signification which Wakef. and Bp. Middl. adopt. The passages to which I allude are the following: Galen de Chirurg. ii. Exod. xxviii. 23. Diod. Sic. i. 109. ἀρχὴ σχοινίου. Lucian iii. 83. δεσμῶν ἀρχάς. Herodot. iv. 60. τὴν ἀρχὴν τοῦ στρόφου. Eurip. Hipp. 772. πλεκτὰς πεισμάτων ἀρχάς. Philo Jud. vol. ii. p. 117. δοκίδος τὰς ἀρχάς. But the first and second passages only prove that either or both *ends* of any oblong body may be called ἀρχαί. The rest show that it was not unfrequently used of the end of a *rope* or band. On which see Jacobs on Anthol. Gr. T. xi. p. 50. So far the proof only amounts to this, — that ἀρχὴ may denote the end of any thing, and, with the addition of a word signifying *band*, the *end of a rope*; but there is no proof that it ever meant a *rope*. Yet the passage of Diod. Sic. (T. i. 104. Edit. Bip.) was thought by Bp. Middl. to *supply* this proof. It respects the manner of harpooning the Hippopotamus, and the words are these: εἶθ' ἑνὶ τῶν ἐμπαγέντων ἐνάψαντες ἀρχὰς στυππίνας, ἀφιᾶσι μέχρις ἂν παραλυθῇ. But the very erudite Wesseling, in his Note, determines it to mean "hempen cable-*ends*." These were probably stronger than the rest of the cable; and they were, no doubt, fastened together, for the purpose of holding fast the Hippopotamus; hence the *plural* is used. Of this sense of ἀρχὴ, to denote *end*, Wessel. adduces two examples, from Plutarch and Philo Jud. And finally, he so explains the present passage of Acts. Bochart, indeed, most ingeniously, conjectures on the passage of Diod. σπάρτας or ἀρτάνας (which latter had also occurred to myself); but they are unnecessary, if the above mode of explanation be adopted. At all events, there is no proof made out that ἀρχὴ can *of itself*, denote a *rope*; which would involve an intolerable *catachresis*. The two learned Critics were deceived by not attending to the nature of the term δεδεμένον, which is often, as here, a *vox prægnans*, including the sense ἀπὸ or ἐκ σχοινίου. So Matt. xxi. 2. εὑρήσετε ὄνον δεδεμένον. Mark xi. 4. τὸν πῶλον δεδεμένον. In this case the ἀπὸ or ἐκ must be understood according as the sense be *suspension from* (as in the present passage), or *tying to*, as in the foregoing. Thus we may render "at the four ends." Bp. Middl., indeed, objects to the introduction of the *the*, because *there is no Article in the Greek*; forgetting that he thus falls into the very error for which he so often censures Wakef.; that of not bearing in mind those many cases where the *absence* of the Article affords no presumption of the noun's being indefinite. The present falls under the case of nouns used κατ' ἐξοχὴν; or rather nouns which, though by their very definite sense, they point only to certain individuals of a genus; yet that is so well understood, that the Article may be safely omitted. And this is still more frequently the case when the noun is accompanied with an adjective, and preceded by a preposition. Here ἐπὶ is understood.

12. καὶ τὰ θηρία.] These words are omitted in a few MSS., and some Versions and Fathers. And Griesb. and others are inclined to cancel them; but without reason; for the number of those MSS. is but *five*, and the omission of them may readily be accounted for from the two καὶ's. Or the *framers* of the text of those MSS. (*altered* ones) may have thought the words unnecessary, and better away. Either of these reasons, and especially the *latter*, may have occasioned their

πρὸς αὐτόν· Ἀναστὰς, Πέτρε, θῦσον καὶ φάγε. ὁ δὲ Πέτρος εἶπε· 14
Μηδαμῶς, Κύριε· ὅτι οὐδέποτε ἔφαγον πᾶν κοινὸν ἢ ἀκάθαρτον. Καὶ 15
φωνὴ πάλιν ἐκ δευτέρου πρὸς αὐτόν· Ἃ ὁ Θεὸς ἐκαθάρισε, σὺ μὴ
κοίνου. Τοῦτο δὲ ἐγένετο ἐπὶ τρίς· καὶ πάλιν ἀνελήφθη τὸ σκεῦος 16
εἰς τὸν οὐρανόν.

Ὡς δὲ ἐν ἑαυτῷ διηπόρει ὁ Πέτρος, τί ἂν εἴη τὸ ὅραμα ὃ εἶδε, καὶ 17
ἰδοὺ, οἱ ἄνδρες οἱ ἀπεσταλμένοι ἀπὸ τοῦ Κορνηλίου, διερωτήσαντες
τὴν οἰκίαν Σίμωνος, ἐπέστησαν ἐπὶ τὸν πυλῶνα· καὶ φωνήσαντες 18
ἐπυνθάνοντο, εἰ Σίμων ὁ ἐπικαλούμενος Πέτρος ἐνθάδε ξενίζεται. Τοῦ 19
δὲ Πέτρου * διενθυμουμένου περὶ τοῦ ὁράματος, εἶπεν αὐτῷ τὸ Πνεῦμα·
x Infra 15. 7. Ἰδοὺ, ἄνδρες τρεῖς ζητοῦσί σε· x ἀλλὰ ἀναστὰς κατάβηθι, καὶ πορεύου 20

omission in the *Versions* also, which, indeed, are not good evidence in matters of this kind. As to the evidence of the *Fathers*, it is but slender when it regards the *omission of words which seem not very necessary*. Besides, the common reading is placed beyond doubt by the recurrence of this passage verbatim infra xi. 6. without any Var. lect., except that *one Version* and Epiphanius omit καὶ τὰ θηρία. Some MSS., both there and here, place τῆς γῆς, not after τετράποδα, but either after τὰ ἑρπετὰ, or after τὰ θηρία. This, however, arose either (as Matth. supposes) "*ex pluralitate membrorum*," or rather from a desire to clear the *construction* of the clause, which the ancient Critics perceived (though the *Commentators* have not) to be as follows: ὑπῆρχε πάντα τὰ τετρ. καὶ τὰ θηρία καὶ τὰ ἑρπετὰ τῆς γῆς. Thus τῆς γῆς corresponds to τοῦ οὐρανοῦ, and is not to be regarded, with Vorst. and Kuin., as a Hebrew pleonasm. Τετράποδα denotes the tame beasts, בְּהֵמָה, as θηρία the wild ones, חַיָּה. Wet. compares Orpheus Argon. 73. κηλήσω δέ τε θῆρας, ἠδ' ἑρπετὰ καὶ πετεηνά. On the thing here typified (the removal of the distinction of clean and unclean meats, and the abrogation of the ceremonial law), even the Jewish Rabbies supposed that at the coming of the Messiah the distinction would be done away.

14. μηδαμῶς.] This and οὐδαμῶς (forms of denial and repugnance) are relics of the old word ἀμὸς, which in the ancient language signified *aliquis*. In the place of this formula is sometimes used μὴ γένοιτο· *Absit!* or μὴ δῆτα by the Tragedians. (Valckn.)

— κοινόν.] This term properly signifies what *belongs to all*, as in Sap. vii. 3. κοινὸς ἀήρ. But the Hellenists applied it (like the Heb. חֹל) to what was profane, i. e. *not holy*, and therefore of common and promiscuous use; as Ez. xlii., 20. (where it is opposed to ἅγιον), and Joseph. Ant. xii. 12, 13. τὰ θεῖα ἐκφέρειν ἐπὶ κοινοὺς ἀνθρώπους. They also applied the term to what was *impure*, whether *naturally*, or *legally*, (as in Mark vii. 2. compared with 1 Macc. i. 47, 62.); and finally, it was used of meats forbidden, or such as had been partaken of by idolaters, and which, as they rendered the eaters thereof impure, were themselves called κοινὰ and ἀκάθαρτα, terms also applied to the eaters. (Kuin.)

15. ἐκαθάρισε] i. e. hath *declared* pure, or made so by removing the law which forbade its use. Thus, by κοίνου is meant "account impure." So Scheoth Rabba, fol. 118, 3, it is said (on Job xxxi. 3.) "the stranger did not lodge in the street," Non enim Deus κοινοῖ, *profanum* judicat quemquam hominem, sed omnes recipit. It is well observed by Kuin. that in the Hebrew, Greek, and Latin, any one is said to *do* a thing who *declares* it to be done, as in Levit. xiii. 3. 13, and 17, μιαίνειν and καθαρίζειν are so used, and συγκλείειν in Gal. iii. 22. The Classical writers abound in examples. All this was (as Bp. Warburton has shown, vol. vi. p. 70.) equivalent to "saying, that the distinction between meats was abolished; and consequently that the *Gentiles* were to be admitted into the Church of Christ."

16. ἐπὶ τρίς.] There is not (as Kypke and Kuin. imagine) a redundancy in the ἐπὶ, which signifies *unto*, or *as far as*; it must always be *understood* in this phrase, and is generally *expressed*, or (at least εἰς) in the best writers. The vision was *thrice repeated*, for greater certainty, and to fix it more strongly on Peter's mind. So Genes. xli 32. "And for that the dream was doubled unto Pharaoh twice: it is because the thing is established by God, and God will shortly bring it to pass." The number *three*, too, was one in general use among the early Christians for such sort of repetition. So St. Paul besought the Lord *thrice* that the thorn in the flesh might be removed. Nor was it confined to Christians only, but the same was in use among the Heathens, as Bp. Pearce shows from Virg. Æn. p. 174. So also Horace Carm. iii. 22, 3. (of Diana) "Virgo quæ laborantes in utero puellas *ter vocata* audis."

17. τί ἂν εἴη] "what it might mean." Of this phrase Kypke adduces examples from the Classical writers; all of which have ποτε added, except one from Palæph. ἐθαύμασαν τί ἂν εἴη τὸ γεγονός. Peter's doubt was not whether the distinction of meats was abolished, but whether that implied a removal of the distinction between Jews and Gentiles; a doubt soon removed by the messengers.

19. διενθυμουμένου.] So almost all the Editors from Beng. and Wets. to Vat. edit, from many MSS., Versions, Fathers, and the Edit. Princ., instead of the common reading ἐνθυμουμένου, which is confirmed by those passages of Cyril and other Fathers cited by Boissonade ap. Steph. Thes. Indeed compounds are often changed to simples by the scribes. Were not the authority for διενθ. considerable, I should suspect that the δι arose from the δι a little before at διερωτήσαντες and διηπόρει. And this is countenanced by the fact that διενθυμεῖσθαι is nowhere else found. Many examples might be adduced of compound verbs which have no better origin than the mistakes of scribes; though they have been unwarily introduced into the new Edition of Steph. Thes.

— εἶπεν αὐτῷ τὸ Πν.] This must, notwithstand-

21 σὺν αὐτοῖς, μηδὲν διακρινόμενος, διότι ἐγὼ ἀπέσταλκα αὐτούς. Καταβὰς δὲ Πέτρος πρὸς τοὺς ἄνδρας [τοὺς ἀπεσταλμένους ἀπὸ τοῦ Κορνηλίου πρὸς αὐτὸν,] εἶπεν· Ἰδοὺ, ἐγώ εἰμι ὃν ζητεῖτε· τίς ἡ αἰτία
22 δι᾽ ἣν πάρεστε; οἱ δὲ εἶπον· Κορνήλιος ἑκατοντάρχης, ἀνὴρ δίκαιος καὶ φοβούμενος τὸν Θεὸν μαρτυρούμενός τε ὑπὸ ὅλου τοῦ ἔθνους τῶν Ἰουδαίων, ἐχρηματίσθη ὑπὸ ἀγγέλου ἁγίου, μεταπέμψασθαί σε εἰς τὸν
23 οἶκον αὐτοῦ, καὶ ἀκοῦσαι ῥήματα παρὰ σοῦ. εἰσκαλεσάμενος οὖν αὐτοὺς ἐξένισε. Τῇ δὲ ἐπαύριον ὁ Πέτρος ἐξῆλθε σὺν αὐτοῖς, καί τινες
24 τῶν ἀδελφῶν τῶν ἀπὸ [τῆς] Ἰόππης συνῆλθον αὐτῷ. Καὶ τῇ ἐπαύριον εἰσῆλθον εἰς τὴν Καισάρειαν· ὁ δὲ Κορνήλιος ἦν προσδοκῶν αὐτοὺς, συγκαλεσάμενος τοὺς συγγενεῖς αὐτοῦ καὶ τοὺς ἀναγκαίους φίλους.
25 Ὡς δὲ ἐγένετο εἰσελθεῖν τὸν Πέτρον, συναντήσας αὐτῷ ὁ Κορνήλιος,
26 πεσὼν ἐπὶ τοὺς πόδας προσεκύνησεν. Ὁ δὲ Πέτρος αὐτὸν ἤγειρε, λέ-
27 γων· Ἀνάστηθι· κἀγὼ αὐτὸς ἄνθρωπός εἰμι. Καὶ συνομιλῶν αὐτῷ
28 εἰσῆλθε, καὶ εὑρίσκει συνεληλυθότας πολλούς, [y] ἔφη τε πρὸς αὐτούς· [y John iv. 9.]
Ὑμεῖς ἐπίστασθε ὡς ἀθέμιτόν ἐστιν ἀνδρὶ Ἰουδαίῳ κολλᾶσθαι ἢ προσέρχεσθαι ἀλλοφύλῳ. καὶ ἐμοὶ ὁ Θεὸς ἔδειξε μηδένα κοινὸν ἢ ἀκά-
29 θαρτον λέγειν ἄνθρωπον. Διὸ καὶ ἀναντιῤῥήτως ἦλθον μεταπεμφθείς.
30 πυνθάνομαι οὖν, τίνι λόγῳ μετεπέμψασθέ με; Καὶ ὁ Κορνήλιος ἔφη·
Ἀπὸ τετάρτης ἡμέρας μέχρι ταύτης τῆς ὥρας ἤμην νηστεύων, καὶ τὴν

ing the dissent of Ros. and Kuin. be understood of the influence or inspiration of the Holy Spirit, as indeed Grot. explains it.

20. μηδὲν διακρ.] "making no scruple," namely, that thou art called to visit a *heathen*: On διακρ. see Note on Mark xi. 23.

21. τοὺς ἀπεσταλμένους — αὐτὸν] These words do not appear in very many MSS., Versions, and Fathers, and are with reason cancelled by almost every Editor of note.

— ἐγώ εἰμι ὃν ζητεῖτε.] So Eurip. Orest. 374. ὅδ᾽ εἰμ᾽ Ὀρέστης — ὃν ἱστορεῖς. See Virg. Æn. i. 593.

24. τῇ ἐπαύριον] on the morrow *after* the day he had set out; for the journey, being one of 15 *hours'* distance, was too great for *one* day.

— τοὺς ἀναγκαίους φίλους] Οἱ ἀνάγκαιοι, like *necessarii* in Latin, denotes 1. relations by consanguinity; 2. those by affinity; 3. persons connected by the bonds of friendship. When φίλοι is added, the sense is more determinate, and means confidential and intimate friends.

25. εἰσελθεῖν] Sub. τοῦ, as dependent on ἕνεκα understood, which is *expressed* in several MSS.

— προσεκύνησεν] This carried with it a prostration of the body to the earth, and was a mark of profound respect; which was rendered in the East not only to *monarchs*, but also to *other* persons of high dignity; though by the Romans it was rendered to the Deity alone. Certainly Cornelius, who was εὐσεβὴς καὶ φοβούμενος τὸν Θεὸν could not intend to offer any mark of respect inconsistent with his duty to God. He, no doubt, regarded Peter (as having been the subject of a preternatural communication) in the light of a Divine legate; and, as such, entitled to a mark of reverence like that offered to the Deity himself. Especially as he must have been aware, that Oriental custom allowed of such a mark of profound reverence being shown from *man to man*. Peter, on the other hand, bearing in mind the very different custom of the *Romans*, with unaffected religious humility declined it.

28. ἀθέμιτον] This is not well rendered *unlawful*; for that would require παράνομον. Whereas the sense here is ἀσεβὲς or ἀνόσιον. We may render *nefas est*. The phrase οὐ θέμ. ἐστι often occurs in the LXX., and sometimes in the Classical writers. Προσέρχεσθαι, to enter any one's house, is a further evolving of the sense contained in κολλᾶσθαι, on which see Note on v. 13.

— ἀλλοφύλῳ] The word properly means only *a foreigner*; but, as Kuin. observes, it is in the Sept., Philo, and Joseph. used (as here) in a *double* sense, so as to denote such as are *not Jews*, either by birth or by religion, and elsewhere styled ξένοι or ἀλλότριοι, Gentiles.

— καὶ ἐμοὶ] The καὶ is for καίτοι, *and yet*.

29. ἀναντιῤῥήτως] "without hesitation." The word occurs only in the later writers. Λόγῳ, *account*, *cause*, or *reason*; as 1 Cor. xv. 2. τίνι λόγῳ εὐηγγελισάμην ὑμῖν. So Eurip. Iph. Taur. 358. τίνι λόγῳ πορθμεύετε;

30. ἀπὸ τετάρτης — νηστεύων] Several eminent recent Interpreters take this to mean, that Cornelius had fasted from the time of his vision to the time when Peter arrived. And this would seem to be called for by the correspondence of ἀπὸ and μέχρι. But it involves a great improbability, and adverts to a circumstance which Cornelius would not have been likely to mention. Besides, it is liable to other and verbal objections, which are well stated by Kuin., who would take the ἀπὸ for πρὸ, as xv. 7. 2 Cor. viii. 10. ix. 2. and מ in Prov. viii. 23. and elsewhere. Yet ἀπὸ can never properly be said to be put for πρό. When it *seems* to be so used, there is an ellip., for τὴν

ἐννάτην ὥραν προσευχόμενος ἐν τῷ οἴκῳ μου· καὶ ἰδού, ἀνὴρ ἔστη
ἐνώπιόν μου ἐν ἐσθῆτι λαμπρᾷ, καί φησι· Κορνήλιε, εἰσηκούσθη σου 31
ἡ προσευχή, καὶ αἱ ἐλεημοσύναι σου ἐμνήσθησαν ἐνώπιον τοῦ Θεοῦ.
Πέμψον οὖν εἰς Ἰόππην, καὶ μετακάλεσαι Σίμωνα ὃς ἐπικαλεῖται Πέ- 32
τρος· οὗτος ξενίζεται ἐν οἰκίᾳ Σίμωνος βυρσέως παρὰ θάλασσαν· ὃς
παραγενόμενος λαλήσει σοι. Ἐξαυτῆς οὖν ἔπεμψα πρός σε· σύ τε 33
καλῶς ἐποίησας παραγενόμενος. Νῦν οὖν πάντες ἡμεῖς ἐνώπιον τοῦ
Θεοῦ πάρεσμεν ἀκοῦσαι πάντα τὰ προστεταγμένα σοι ὑπὸ τοῦ Θεοῦ.
a Deut. 10. 17. 2 Chron. 19. 7. Job 34. 19. Wisd. 6. 7. Eccl. 35. 16. Rom. 2. 11. Gal. 2. 6. Eph. 6. 9. Col. 3. 25. 1 Pet. 1. 17. a Luke 4. 14. [a] *Ἀνοίξας δὲ Πέτρος τὸ στόμα εἶπεν· Ἐπ' ἀληθείας καταλαμβάνο-* 34
μαι, ὅτι οὐκ ἔστι προσωπολήπτης ὁ Θεός· ἀλλ' ἐν παντὶ ἔθνει ὁ 35
φοβούμενος αὐτὸν καὶ ἐργαζόμενος δικαιοσύνην δεκτὸς αὐτῷ ἐστι. Τὸν 36
λόγον ὃν ἀπέστειλε τοῖς υἱοῖς Ἰσραὴλ, εὐαγγελιζόμενος εἰρήνην διὰ
Ἰησοῦ Χριστοῦ, (οὗτός ἐστι πάντων Κύριος) [a] *ὑμεῖς οἴδατε· τὸ γε-* 37
νόμενον ῥῆμα καθ' ὅλης τῆς Ἰουδαίας, ἀρξάμενον ἀπὸ τῆς Γαλιλαίας,
b Luke 4. 14. *μετὰ τὸ βάπτισμα ὃ ἐκήρυξεν Ἰωάννης·* [b] *Ἰησοῦν τὸν ἀπὸ Ναζαρέτ,* 38
ὡς ἔχρισεν αὐτὸν ὁ Θεὸς Πνεύματι ἁγίῳ καὶ δυνάμει, ὃς διῆλθεν
εὐεργετῶν καὶ ἰώμενος πάντας τοὺς καταδυναστευομένους ὑπὸ τοῦ Δια-
βόλου, ὅτι ὁ Θεὸς ἦν μετ' αὐτοῦ. Καὶ ἡμεῖς ἐσμεν μάρτυρες πάντων, 39
ὧν ἐποίησεν ἔν τε τῇ χώρᾳ τῶν Ἰουδαίων καὶ ἐν Ἱερουσαλήμ· ὃν καὶ
c Supra 2. 24. *ἀνεῖλον κρεμάσαντες ἐπὶ ξύλου.* [c] *Τοῦτον ὁ Θεὸς ἤγειρε τῇ τρίτῃ ἡμέρᾳ,* 40

τετάρτην ἡμέραν ἀπὸ ταύτης τῆς ἡμέρας. Thus the sense (as Beza, Grot., Pearce, and Kuin. have seen) is: "At the 4th day from to-day, i. e. four days ago, I was fasting up to this hour."

— *λαμπρᾷ*] not bright, but white; as in Luke xxiii. 11. *περιβαλὼν αὐτὸν ἐσθῆτα λαμπρὰν*, and sometimes in the later Classics. Some MSS. have here *λευκῇ*, of course a *gloss*, but a good one.

31. *προσευχὴ*] At ver. 4. we have *προσευχαί*: but the sense is the same, *προσευχὴ* being here, as very often, put in a *generic* sense, for a continued custom of prayer.

33. *καλῶς ἐποίησας παραγ.*] So Herodot. v. 24. *εὖ ἐποίησας ἀφικόμενος*.

34. *προσωπολήπτης*] i. e. one who is partial in his attentions, and shows his favours with preference to rank, dignity, or other grounds of external superiority, to the neglect of those who are destitute of these advantages. See Lu. xx. 21.

35. *ἀλλ' ἐν παντὶ ἔθνει — ἐστι*] This use of *ἐργάζεσθαι* like that of עָשָׂה or פָּעַל, with *δικαιοσύνην*, and other words expressive of actions or moral dispositions, involves a notion of *habit*. No examples are adduced by the Commentators from the Classical writers; and I can only instance one of the *verbal ἐργάτης*, in Lycoph. Cass. 128. *ἐργάτης δίκης*. In order to avoid the dangerous notion which has been grafted on these words, as if to fear God, and work righteousness, under *any* form of religious belief, were the only duties essential to salvation, see the excellent remarks of Dr. Hales, and especially of Mr. Townsend.

36. *τὸν λόγον — Κύριος*, &c.] There is here a perplexity of construction, which the Commentators seek in various ways to remove, either by making some slight alteration, or by taking the Accus. for a Nominat. But (as I have shown in Recens. Synop.) none of these modes is admissible, and the only satisfactory one is (with several of the older and some of the most eminent recent Commentators) to connect *τὸν λόγον* with *οἴδατε* in the next verse, and place *οὗτος — Κύριος* in a parenthesis, thus repeating *ῥῆμα*, as synonymous with *λόγον*, and in apposition with it. At *ἀπέστειλε* repeat *ὁ Θεὸς* from the context. *Λόγος* here signifies the *doctrine of Christ*, as xiii. 26. *Πάντων*, both Jews and Gentiles; for, as Lord of *all*, he must intend the salvation of all. *Κύριος* suggests that high dignity of the Redeemer, which is more distinctly expressed supra v. 31. Thus the passage may be rendered, with Prof. Scholefield, as follows: "The word which he sent to the children of Israel, preaching peace by Jesus Christ (he is the Lord of all), ye know: even the matter which took place throughout all Judæa, beginning from Galilee, after the baptism which John preached; concerning Jesus of Nazareth, how God anointed him," &c.

38. *Ἰησοῦν τὸν ἀπὸ N.*] This is suspended on the *οἴδατε* preceding; and in *οἴδατε Ἰησοῦν, ὡς ἔχρισεν αὐτὸν* there is a common Greek idiom. Thus there is no *transposition*, as Kuin. imagines. *Ἔχρισεν*, by a metaphor taken from the mode of inaugurating kings, signifies *invested*, and *endued*, namely, at his baptism. See iv. 27. and Luke iv. 18. And in *Πνεύματι ἁγίῳ καὶ δυνάμει* there is a Hendiadys. The sense is, "with the powerful influence of the Holy Spirit." See Bp. Middl. The *general* sense couched in *εὐεργετῶν* is *particularized* and *exemplified* in the words following *καὶ ἰώμενος — Διαβόλου*, where *καταδυν. ὑπὸ τοῦ Διαβόλου* seems to be a more explicit mode of speaking for *δαιμονιζομένους*.

39. *ὃν ἀνεῖλον κρεμ. ἐπὶ ξύλου*] Render, "whom they slew by hanging on a gibbet." See Note supra v. 30. Before *ἀνεῖλον*, *καὶ* is found in many of the best MSS., several Versions and Fathers, and in the Ed. Princ.; and is rightly admitted by

41 καὶ ἔδωκεν αὐτὸν ἐμφανῆ γενέσθαι· [d] οὐ παντὶ τῷ λαῷ, ἀλλὰ μάρτυσι d Infra 13. 31.
τοῖς προκεχειροτονημένοις ὑπὸ τοῦ Θεοῦ, ἡμῖν οἵτινες συνεφάγομεν καὶ
42 συνεπίομεν αὐτῷ μετὰ τὸ ἀναστῆναι αὐτὸν ἐκ νεκρῶν. [e] Καὶ παρήγ- e Infra 17. 31. Rom. 14. 10.
γειλεν ἡμῖν κηρύξαι τῷ λαῷ, καὶ διαμαρτύρασθαι, ὅτι αὐτός ἐστιν ὁ 2 Cor. 5. 10.
43 ὡρισμένος ὑπὸ τοῦ Θεοῦ κριτὴς ζώντων καὶ νεκρῶν. [f] Τούτῳ πάντες f Jer. 31. 34. Mich. 7. 18.
οἱ προφῆται μαρτυροῦσιν, ἄφεσιν ἁμαρτιῶν λαβεῖν διὰ τοῦ ὀνόματος infra 15. 9.
44 αὐτοῦ πάντα τὸν πιστεύοντα εἰς αὐτόν. Ἔτι λαλοῦντος τοῦ Πέτρου
τὰ ῥήματα ταῦτα, ἐπέπεσε τὸ Πνεῦμα τὸ ἅγιον ἐπὶ πάντας τοὺς ἀκού-
45 οντας τὸν λόγον. Καὶ ἐξέστησαν οἱ ἐκ περιτομῆς πιστοὶ, ὅσοι συνῆλθον
τῷ Πέτρῳ, ὅτι καὶ ἐπὶ τὰ ἔθνη ἡ δωρεὰ τοῦ ἁγίου Πνεύματος ἐκκέ-
46 χυται· ἤκουον γὰρ αὐτῶν λαλούντων γλώσσαις, καὶ μεγαλυνόντων
47 τὸν Θεόν. Τότε ἀπεκρίθη ὁ Πέτρος· [g] Μήτι τὸ ὕδωρ κωλῦσαι δύνα- g Infra 15. 8.
ταί τις, τοῦ μὴ βαπτισθῆναι τούτους, οἵτινες τὸ Πνεῦμα τὸ ἅγιον

Beng., Wets., Matth., Griesb., Titt., and Vat., since it is strongly supported by *internal* as well as external evidence.

41. οὐ παντὶ τῷ λαῷ, ἀλλὰ, &c.] Dr. Paley has ably pointed out a remarkable instance of the fairness of the sacred writers, in thus stating that Christ, after his resurrection, appeared to his *disciples alone*, when they might have asserted the appearance of Christ in general terms, so that it might have been supposed that he had appeared to his foes as well as his friends. This, if they had thought of any thing but the truth of the case, they would have done. As it is, their fairness is of more advantage to their testimony, than the difference in the circumstances of the account would have been to the nature of the evidence.

— προκεχειρον.] I would not, with Kuin., take this for the simple κεχειρ., since as the χειρ. imports *appointment*, so does the προ import *previous* destination. Μετὰ τὸ ἀναστῆναι ἐ. ν. some Editors and Commentators join with v. 40., placing the intermediate words οὐ παντὶ — συνεπίομεν αὐτῷ in a parenthesis. This they are induced to do because, they urge, we do not find that our Lord *drank*, however he might *eat*, with his disciples after his resurrection. Yet though that be not directly said, it seems *implied* at John xxi. 13. See Chrys. in loc.

43. ἄφεσιν ἁμαρτιῶν — αὐτὸν] From the anomalous nature of the construction here, several recent Editors write αὐτὸν...., to indicate that the sentence was left incomplete, namely by the falling of the Holy Spirit on the hearers, and their breaking out and speaking in new tongues. This method, however, is at once hypothetical and unnecessary; for the words in question contain a complete *sense*, though not a very regular *construction*, being intended, I conceive, to show the subject and *substance* of that testimony, namely that whosoever, &c., the construction being a *Latin* one. So the passage was understood by the Pesch. Syr. Translator, and by the authors of our common Version. The passages of the Prophets here meant are such as the following: Isa. xxviii. 16. "Behold I lay in Zion for a foundation a stone," &c., and "whosoever believeth in him shall not be confounded." Comp. viii. 14. Zech. xiii. 1., where he says that a fountain shall be opened for sin, &c. Thus from μαρτυροῦσιν we must take μαρτυροῦντες (to usher in the next clause), understanding it in the sense *declaring*, as John iv. 44. ἐμαρτύρησεν, ὅτι προφήτης ἐν τῇ ἰδίᾳ πατρίδι τιμὴν οὐκ ἔχει. Moreover, the πάντες, which the Commentators say must be taken *restrictedly*, for *very many*, may have its usual force; for all the prophets more or less testify of Christ. So Luke xxiv. 27. καὶ ἀρξάμενος ἀπὸ Μωϋσέως καὶ ἀπὸ πάντων τῶν προφητῶν, διηρμήνευεν αὐτοῖς ἐν πάσαις ταῖς γραφαῖς τὰ περὶ αὐτοῦ. And though *all* have not said that whosoever believeth, &c., yet πάντες need not be referred to the elliptical μαρτυροῦντες.

44. τὸ Πνεῦμα τὸ ἅγιον] i. e. the *influence* of the Holy Spirit, which has been before spoken of, (see Middl.) implying its *extraordinary gifts*, and especially, as we learn from v. 46, the speaking in languages foreign and before unknown to them. See supra ii. 4. and Notes; from a comparison of which passage with the present it is plain that by γλώσσαις is here meant (as there) ἑτέραις γλώσσαις, (and as is plain from the context) καθὼς τὸ Πνεῦμα ἐδίδου αὐτοῖς ἀποφθέγγεσθαι, as is there *expressed*. To have heard them speak the praises of God and Christ in their *own* language (Greek or Latin) would have conveyed no proof that they had received the gift of the Holy Spirit. Besides, compare v. 47. with xi. 16. The γὰρ, too, at v. 46. has reference to a clause omitted, q. d. "[And that it had been poured forth on these persons was certain] *for*" &c. I should not have thought it necessary to point out what is so plain, had not the sense been egregiously misstated by Noesselt, Heinr., and Kuin.

47. μήτι τὸ ὕδωρ κωλῦσαι] Wherever κωλύω takes (as here and in Luke vi. 29, and sometimes in the Classical writers) the *Accusative of a thing*, the verb may be supposed to have a *significatio praegnans*, including that of another verb, namely one of *taking* or *using*. The τοῦ μὴ βαπτ. is for ὥστε μὴ βαπτ. In this idiom the μὴ is said to be pleonastic; and this the grammarians tell us, extends to all verbs which involve a sense of denial, especially verbs of *hindering*. See Matth. Gr. Gr. § 533. Obs. 3. Thus the μὴ is sometimes omitted. But, in fact, there is no pleonasm, — since the μὴ belongs to *another sentence*, in which occasionally the verb in the preceding is to be repeated with some modification. As to the *omission* of the μὴ, *that* takes place chiefly when the verb of hindering is followed by another in the Infinitive without a τό; in which case the Infin. forms part of the preceding sentence, and therefore cannot

ἔλαβον, καθὼς καὶ ἡμεῖς; προσέταξέ τε αὐτοὺς βαπτισθῆναι ἐν τῷ 48
ὀνόματι τοῦ Κυρίου. τότε ἠρώτησαν αὐτὸν ἐπιμεῖναι ἡμέρας τινάς.
XI. ἬΚΟΥΣΑΝ δὲ οἱ ἀπόστολοι καὶ οἱ ἀδελφοὶ οἱ ὄντες κατὰ 1
τὴν Ἰουδαίαν, ὅτι καὶ τὰ ἔθνη ἐδέξαντο τὸν λόγον τοῦ Θεοῦ. Καὶ 2
ὅτε ἀνέβη Πέτρος εἰς Ἱεροσόλυμα, διεκρίνοντο πρὸς αὐτὸν οἱ ἐκ περιτομῆς, λέγοντες· Ὅτι πρὸς ἄνδρας ἀκροβυστίαν ἔχοντας εἰσῆλθες, καὶ 3
συνέφαγες αὐτοῖς. Ἀρξάμενος δὲ ὁ Πέτρος ἐξετίθετο αὐτοῖς καθεξῆς, 4
h Supra 10. 9. λέγων· [h] Ἐγὼ ἤμην ἐν πόλει Ἰόππῃ προσευχόμενος, καὶ εἶδον ἐν ἐκ- 5
στάσει ὅραμα, καταβαῖνον σκεῦός τι, ὡς ὀθόνην μεγάλην τέσσαρσιν
ἀρχαῖς, καθιεμένην ἐκ τοῦ οὐρανοῦ, καὶ ἦλθεν ἄχρις ἐμοῦ· εἰς ἣν 6
ἀτενίσας κατενόουν καὶ εἶδον τὰ τετράποδα τῆς γῆς, καὶ τὰ θηρία καὶ
τὰ ἑρπετά, καὶ τὰ πετεινὰ τοῦ οὐρανοῦ· ἤκουσα δὲ φωνῆς λεγούσης 7
μοι· Ἀναστάς, Πέτρε, θῦσον καὶ φάγε. εἶπον δέ· Μηδαμῶς, Κύριε· 8
ὅτι πᾶν κοινὸν ἢ ἀκάθαρτον οὐδέποτε εἰσῆλθεν εἰς τὸ στόμα μου.
Ἀπεκρίθη δέ μοι φωνὴ ἐκ δευτέρου ἐκ τοῦ οὐρανοῦ· Ἃ ὁ Θεὸς ἐκα- 9
θάρισε, σὺ μὴ κοίνου. Τοῦτο δὲ ἐγένετο ἐπὶ τρίς, καὶ πάλιν ἀνεσπά- 10
σθη ἅπαντα εἰς τὸν οὐρανόν. καὶ ἰδού, ἐξαυτῆς τρεῖς ἄνδρες ἐπέστησαν 11
ἐπὶ τὴν οἰκίαν ἐν ᾗ ἤμην, ἀπεσταλμένοι ἀπὸ Καισαρείας πρός με.
Εἶπε δέ μοι τὸ Πνεῦμα συνελθεῖν αὐτοῖς μηδὲν διακρινόμενον· ἦλθον 12
δὲ σὺν ἐμοὶ καὶ οἱ ἓξ ἀδελφοὶ οὗτοι, καὶ εἰσήλθομεν εἰς τὸν οἶκον
τοῦ ἀνδρός· ἀπήγγειλέ τε ἡμῖν πῶς εἶδε τὸν ἄγγελον ἐν τῷ οἴκῳ 13
αὐτοῦ σταθέντα καὶ εἰπόντα αὐτῷ· Ἀπόστειλον εἰς Ἰόππην ἄνδρας,
καὶ μετάπεμψαι Σίμωνα τὸν ἐπικαλούμενον Πέτρον, ὃς λαλήσει ῥήματα 14
i Supra 2. 4. πρός σε, ἐν οἷς σωθήσῃ σὺ καὶ πᾶς ὁ οἶκός σου. [i] Ἐν δὲ τῷ ἄρξα- 15
σθαί με λαλεῖν, ἐπέπεσε τὸ Πνεῦμα τὸ ἅγιον ἐπ᾽ αὐτούς, ὥσπερ καὶ
k Supra 1. 5. infra 19. 4. Matt. 3. 11. Mark 1. 8. Luke 3. 16. John 1. 26. ἐφ᾽ ἡμᾶς ἐν ἀρχῇ. [k] Ἐμνήσθην δὲ τοῦ ῥήματος Κυρίου, ὡς ἔλεγεν· 16
Ἰωάννης μὲν ἐβάπτισεν ὕδατι, ὑμεῖς δὲ βαπτισθήσεσθε ἐν Πνεύματι
ἁγίῳ. Εἰ οὖν τὴν ἴσην δωρεὰν ἔδωκεν αὐτοῖς ὁ Θεὸς ὡς καὶ ἡμῖν 17
πιστεύσασιν ἐπὶ τὸν Κύριον Ἰησοῦν Χριστόν, ἐγὼ δὲ τίς ἤμην, δυνατὸς
κωλῦσαι τὸν Θεόν; Ἀκούσαντες δὲ ταῦτα ἡσύχασαν, καὶ ἐδόξαζον τὸν 18
Θεόν, λέγοντες· Ἄραγε καὶ τοῖς ἔθνεσιν ὁ Θεὸς τὴν μετάνοιαν ἔδωκεν
εἰς ζωήν.

properly take a μὴ, though instances are found where it is used.

48. βαπτισθῆναι] It is not said by *whom* they were baptized; but there can be little doubt that (as the ancient and best modern Commentators supposed) the persons who baptized them were some of those whom Peter brought with him from Joppa. For it is to be observed, that the Apostles themselves rarely baptized. See John iv. 2. 1 Cor. i. 14. and notes.

XI. 2. διεκρίνοντο πρὸς αὐτὸν] "expostulated with him, litigating the question." The word answers to the Heb. ריב and שפט, and signifies properly to be *impleaded in a suit* with another—then to be opposed in argument.

3. ἀκροβ. ἔχοντας] Synonymous with ἐν ἀκροβυστίᾳ ὄντας, which is of frequent occurrence, "those who are uncircumcised."

5. τέσσαρσιν ἀρχαῖς] The true sense of this expression has been fully explained supra x. 11. It may suffice *here* to observe that the sense in the present passage cannot be made complete without *supplying* δεδεμένην, which is *expressed* in the parallel passages, and *here* by the Syriac Translators.

17. εἰ] "*siquidem*," "if [as was the case]."

— ἐγὼ δὲ τίς ἤμην, δυνατός.] The δὲ is omitted in many MSS. and Versions; but, I suspect, from the difficulty of explaining it. Yet it may very well be rendered *denique, then*. There is great spirit in this turn of expression, with which Wets. compares from Lucian, ἠρώτα τὸν Δ. τίς ὤν, χλευάζοι τὰ αὐτοῦ. The Commentators pass over the difficulty in construction as regards δυνατὸς, which is, by a harsh ellipsis, put for ὥστε δυνατὸς εἶναι. Thus the Syr. well renders *qui sufficerem ad*, &c.

18. μετάνοιαν.] It here means the grace of repentance.

19 [1]Οἱ μὲν οὖν διασπαρέντες ἀπὸ τῆς θλίψεως τῆς γενομένης ἐπὶ [1 Supra 8. 1.]
Στεφάνῳ διῆλθον ἕως Φοινίκης καὶ Κύπρου καὶ Ἀντιοχείας, μηδενὶ
20 λαλοῦντες τὸν λόγον, εἰ μὴ μόνον Ἰουδαίοις. Ἦσαν δέ τινες ἐξ αὐτῶν
ἄνδρες Κύπριοι καὶ Κυρηναῖοι, οἵτινες εἰσελθόντες εἰς Ἀντιόχειαν,
ἐλάλουν πρὸς τοὺς ‡ Ἑλληνιστὰς, εὐαγγελιζόμενοι τὸν Κύριον Ἰησοῦν·
21 καὶ ἦν χεὶρ Κυρίου μετ᾽ αὐτῶν· πολύς τε ἀριθμὸς πιστεύσας ἐπέ-

19. *οἱ μὲν οὖν διασπ.*] The particle *μὲν οὖν* is *resumptive*, reverting to what was said supra viii. 1. Ἀπὸ is here for ὑπὸ, as often both in the Scriptural and Classical writers. Commentators differ in their explanation of the force of ἐπὶ Στ., some rendering it *sub*, others *post*. The latter seems preferable.

20. Considerable difference of opinion here exists, both as to the *reading* and the interpretation. The reading of all the MSS. but two (A and D) is Ἑλληνιστάς. *These two* have Ἕλληνας, which is also thought to be supported by the Syr., Arabic, Copt., Æthiopic, and Vulg. Versions, and by Chrys., Theophyl., and Œcumen. This reading, too, has been preferred by almost every Critic and Commentator except Matthæi, and has been edited by Griesb., Knapp, Tittm., and Vater. Not, of course, upon the strength of *external* evidence, for that is next to none; the MSS. being very few, and *altered* ones; the testimony of Versions too in a case like this is of little weight; and that of the Fathers scarcely greater, especially as they sometimes cite Ἑλληνιστάς. Besides, of the two MSS. which here have Ἕλληνας, the principal one (namely, the Alexandrian) has this very reading in the place of Ἑλληνιστὰς, supra ix. 29, where it is by all Editors admitted to be a spurious reading. The same may be said of two of the Versions. And surely what was a παραδιόρθωσις in one case was likely to be so in the other. As, then, Ἕλληνας is thus deficient in *external* evidence, the preference must rest on *internal*. Let us therefore see whether that really exists. The chief ground consists in the *opposition* (denoted by μὲν and δὲ), which, it is alleged, exists between the persons addressed by these teachers respectively: those at ver. 19 addressing themselves to the *Jews* only; consequently those at ver. 20 to such as were *not Jews*. Thus Mr. Hinds (in his history of the rise and progress of Christianity, vol. i. p. 249) maintains that "the opposition expressed by the particles μὲν and δὲ indicates that the Cyprians and Cyrenæans were *not* doing what the dispersed *were* doing, namely, preaching to the *Jews alone*; but that they, on the contrary, were preaching — to whom? Not to the Hellenists, for they were *Jews* (and to them by the dispersed the Gospel had been preached, as in the case of Philip); but πρὸς τοὺς Ἕλληνας, the Gentiles, namely, the devout Gentiles." To this representation, however, several exceptions may be made. 1. The Cyprians and Cyrenæans (for so the name should be written) ought not to be *distinguished* from the *dispersed*, since in St. Luke's account they are considered as the *same persons*; the Cyprians and the Cyrenæans being said to be τινὲς ἐξ αὐτῶν — of *whom?* Of the *dispersed*. 2. As far as the arguments for Ἕλληνας depend upon there being an *opposition* intended, expressed by μὲν and δὲ, it is a very bad one; for in truth there is *no opposition* at all. Certainly the circumstance of the two verses being introduced respectively by μὲν and δὲ will not *prove* it: for here the μὲν is coupled with οὖν, and has, in the present case, that use which Hoogeven de Part. speaks of, No. viii. ἐν ἐπανόδοις, i. e. in transitions, when a writer goes back to something which had been begun to be treated on, but had been interrupted by some digression. Of this he adduces several examples, namely, Aristot. de Repub. i. 7. Thucyd. iv. 76, 77. Acts xxviii. 5; in *all* of which cases the sentence commencing with the resumptive μὲν οὖν is followed by another commencing (as here) with δὲ, which, however, is never an *adversative*, but always has a *continuative* force, and may be rendered *autem*.

Having, then, shown the fallacy of this opposition as depending on the μὲν and δὲ, let us see whether any opposition is intimated by the *context*. Those (it is said) who had been dispersed by the troubles which followed the martyrdom of Stephen, fled, and traversed the country, passing through Phœnice (for so I understand it) and proceeding some to Antioch. In their way thither (namely in Syria) they (i. e. both those who went to Antioch, and those who went to Cyprus) preached the Gospel to *none* but *Jews*. Those who went to *Antioch*, on their arrival thither, preached the word — to whom? To the Hellenists, i. e. foreign Jews, namely, such as spoke the Greek language; to whom, therefore, the Cyprians and Cyrenæans, who were Grecians, would be very fit preachers. The sacred writer, we may observe, could not very well say *Jews*, because Jews living in the foreign countries of Asia Minor and among Greeks, were called *Hellenists*. Now surely there is no such opposition as to compel us to suppose that St. Luke meant persons the opposite to Jews, namely *Gentiles*. *Had* there been any opposition intended, it might have been (as Matthæi supposes) between *Jews speaking Hebrew* and those *speaking Greek*. But there is, in fact, no opposition.

Having thus removed all objection to the reading Ἑλληνιστὰς, and shown that it *may be*, and, as far as external evidence can prove any thing, *is*, the true reading, I will now show that Ἕλληνας *cannot* be such, since, if external were in its favour, internal evidence would condemn it. If the nature of ver. 19 be considered, and if it be borne in mind that it is *resumptive* of what the writer had been relating at viii. 4, we shall see that the events recorded in vv. 19 & 20 of this Chapter must have taken place immediately after those at viii. 4, which immediately followed the martyrdom of Stephen, and consequently took place *before* the vision of Peter and the conversion of Cornelius; so that the Gospel could not have been preached to the *Gentiles*, because there had hitherto been no authority so to do. Indeed, had those Jews felt authorized to preach the Gospel to the *Gentiles*, they would have been far more likely to have first turned themselves to the *Jews* (i. e. the Hellenists) resident at Antioch, whose influence was, we may learn from Josephus Bell. vii. 3, 3, very great over the minds of the Anti-

στρεψεν ἐπὶ τὸν Κύριον. Ἠκούσθη δὲ ὁ λόγος εἰς τὰ ὦτα τῆς ἐκκλη- 22
σίας τῆς ἐν Ἱεροσολύμοις περὶ αὐτῶν· καὶ ἐξαπέστειλαν Βαρνάβαν
διελθεῖν ἕως Ἀντιοχείας. ὃς παραγενόμενος καὶ ἰδὼν τὴν χάριν τοῦ 23
Θεοῦ ἐχάρη, καὶ παρεκάλει πάντας τῇ προθέσει τῆς καρδίας προσμένειν
τῷ Κυρίῳ· ὅτι ἦν ἀνὴρ ἀγαθὸς καὶ πλήρης Πνεύματος ἁγίου καὶ 24
πίστεως. καὶ προσετέθη ὄχλος ἱκανὸς τῷ Κυρίῳ. Ἐξῆλθε δὲ εἰς 25
Ταρσὸν ὁ Βαρνάβας ἀναζητῆσαι Σαῦλον, καὶ εὑρὼν αὐτὸν ἤγαγεν αὐτὸν
εἰς Ἀντιόχειαν. Ἐγένετο δὲ αὐτοὺς ἐνιαυτὸν ὅλον συναχθῆναι ἐν τῇ 26
ἐκκλησίᾳ, καὶ διδάξαι ὄχλον ἱκανὸν, χρηματίσαι τε πρῶτον ἐν Ἀντιοχείᾳ
τοὺς μαθητὰς Χριστιανούς. Ἐν ταύταις δὲ ταῖς ἡμέραις κατῆλθον 27

ochians in religious matters. Dr. Burton, indeed (who supports the reading Ἕλληνας) thinks that what is mentioned at ver. 20, took place *a considerable time after* that in the preceding verse. That view, however, involves far too great a harshness and improbability to be admitted. Of course, equally objectionable as is the *reading* Ἕλληνας must be the *interpretation* by which Ἑλληνιστὰς is taken for Ἕλληνας. As to those who (like Salmasius) would take Ἑλλ. here to mean *proselytes of the gate*, there is no proof whatever that Ἑλληνισταὶ ever had that sense. Certainly the word is never so used in the N. T. Wherever St. Luke has occasion to express that idea, he uses the term προσήλυτος, as ii. 10. vi. 5. *Could* the word, indeed, have borne that signification, the sense arising would have been a good one; for we learn from Josephus Bell. viii. 3, 3, that there were great numbers of Jewish proselytes at Antioch. And to the conversion of such the Apostles and preachers of the word would have made no objection. But in the very same Chapter Josephus also notices the very great number of *Jews* who lived at Antioch above all other places of Syria.

22. ἠκούσθη εἰς τὰ ὦτα τῆς ἐκκλ.] This is accounted an Oriental redundancy. But it is better to consider it as a *stronger* expression than ἠκούσθη by itself, and formed by a blending of two expressions, i. e. "to come to the ears of," and "to be heard by."

23. τὴν χάριν τ. Θ.] "the favour and kindness of God," viz. in its *effects*, the admission of the Gentiles to the benefits of the Gospel.

— τῇ προθέσει τ. κ.] The Genit. of the noun in regimen has here, as often, the force of an *adjective*; and the sense must be, "with hearty and determined purpose and intent. This is, however, *not* (as it is usually esteemed) purely a *Hebrew* idiom, being occasionally found in the Classical writers. So Herodian cited by Wolf: ποθεῖν τινα ἀληθεῖ ψυχῆς διαθέσει. Προσμένειν signifies properly *to remain by*, and, with a Dat. of *thing*, signifies to *persevere in*, but with that of *person*, to *continue attached to*.

24. ὅτι ἦν ἀνὴρ ἀγαθός.] This may, as Heinr. says, be meant to give a *reason why* the Christians at Jerusalem chose Barnabas for the mission to Antioch. But I cannot agree with him that the words ὃς παραγενόμενος — τῷ Κυρίῳ are *parenthetical*. They ought rather to be referred chiefly to what immediately precedes in ver. 23. The sense of the expression ἀνὴρ ἀγαθὸς may be assimilated to an idiom of our own language, by which the expression *a good man* includes the notions of *virtue* or *integrity*, and *benignity* or *gentleness*. So Joseph. Antiq. xii. 9, 1. ὃς ἀγαθὸς ὢν ἀνήρ. The next words καὶ πλήρης Πνεύματος ἁγίου καὶ πίστεως must not be explained *away* as they are done by many recent Interpreters, but have assigned to them their full force.

26. συναχθῆναι ἐν τῇ ἐκκλησίᾳ.] This is usually rendered "assembled," or "assembled themselves, with the Church." And certainly this use of συνάγεσθαι to signify being assembled for religious worship is frequent. Here, however, it is unsuitable; and the true sense (though not pointed out by the Expositors (seems to be, "were associated [as colleagues] in the congregation." And this indeed seems to be what is meant by the *conversati sunt* of the Vulgate, and the expression of the Syriac, "they met upon equal terms in the congregation."

— χρηματίσαι — Χριστιανούς.] Χρηματίζειν signifies, 1. to despatch business; 2. to so despatch it as to obtain a name. Hence, 3. it came at length to mean "to be named or called." Of this sense (which occurs also in Rom. vii. 3.) several examples from Philo and Joseph. are adduced by the Commentators. It must, however, be allowed to involve a harsh catachresis. And this would be rather *increased*, were we (with Benson, Doddr., Bingham, and Towns.) to render "were called by *Divine appointment*;" and increased *unnecessarily*; for why should it not be thought as likely that the followers of Christ should have received the distinctive name, which they now *needed*, from *men*? Why call in *Divine* interposition so needlessly? Besides, the occurrence of πρῶτον seems to exclude that view. There is another and more difficult question connected with these words, — namely, whether the followers of Christ gave this appellation to *themselves*, or whether it was bestowed on them *by others*? The best Commentators are of the latter opinion, and Wets. and Kuin. adduce many arguments why the former view cannot be admitted; not all of them equally cogent, but, upon the whole, sufficient to establish their position. It was, indeed, the interest of the Christians to have some name which might not, like the Jewish ones (Nazarenes or Galilæans) imply reproach. And though the appellations *believers*, or saints, might suffice among *themselves*, yet the former was not sufficiently definite for an *appellation*; and the latter might be thought to savour of vanity. They would therefore be not disinclined to *adopt* one. Yet the necessity was not so great as to stimulate them to do this *very soon*: whereas the *people at large*, in having to speak of this new sect, would soon *need* some *distinctive* appellation; and what so distinctive as one formed from the *name of its founder*. Thus we find from Philostr. Vit. Ap.

28 ἀπὸ Ἱεροσολύμων προφῆται εἰς Ἀντιόχειαν. Ἀναστὰς δὲ εἷς ἐξ αὐτῶν
ὀνόματι Ἄγαβος, ἐσήμανε διὰ τοῦ Πνεύματος λιμὸν μέγαν μέλλειν ἔσεσθαι ἐφ᾽ ὅλην τὴν οἰκουμένην· ὅστις καὶ ἐγένετο ἐπὶ Κλαυδίου Καί-
29 σαρος. [m] τῶν δὲ μαθητῶν, καθὼς ηὐπορεῖτό τις, ὥρισαν ἕκαστος αὐτῶν
30 εἰς διακονίαν πέμψαι τοῖς κατοικοῦσιν ἐν τῇ Ἰουδαίᾳ ἀδελφοῖς· [n] ὃ καὶ
ἐποίησαν, ἀποστείλαντες πρὸς τοὺς πρεσβυτέρους διὰ χειρὸς Βαρνάβα
καὶ Σαύλου.

m Rom. 15. 26. 1 Cor. 16. 1. 2 Cor. 8. 1. Gal. 2. 10.
n Infra 12. 25.

1 XII. ΚΑΤ᾽ ἐκεῖνον δὲ τὸν καιρὸν ἐπέβαλεν Ἡρώδης ὁ βασιλεὺς
2 τὰς χεῖρας κακῶσαί τινας τῶν ἀπὸ τῆς ἐκκλησίας. Ἀνεῖλε δὲ Ἰάκωβον
3 τὸν ἀδελφὸν Ἰωάννου μαχαίρᾳ. Καὶ ἰδὼν ὅτι ἀρεστόν ἐστι τοῖς Ἰου-

viii. 21, that the disciples of Apollonius were called by the Greeks (it is not said by *themselves)* Ἀπολλώνιοι. And it was likely that the Gentiles should resort to such a sort of appellation,—since in that age those who were followers of any sect, or partizans of any leader, were usually called after their teacher or leader, by a term ending in —ιος or *anus*. There is no reason to think, with Wets. and Kuin., that the name Χριστιανοὶ was given in *derision*. When used by Agrippa (Acts xxvi. 28.) there is no proof that it was a term of reproach. Had he intended *derision*, he might have employed the term *Nazarene*, which was still in much use among the Jews, and what is remarkable, has continued in the East to the present day. Thus the followers of Christ would be the more likely to adopt the appellation Χριστιανοὶ, both for convenience, and to keep out a term of reproach. That they soon *did* adopt it, we find from 1 Pet. iv. 16. εἰ δὲ ὡς Χριστιανὸς (πάσχει,) μὴ αἰσχυνέσθω (scil. πάσχειν) where the appellation occurs as one applied by the followers of Christ to *themselves* as well as given by others.

27. προφῆται.] The term seems here to denote persons who, with more or less of the supernatural gifts of the Holy Spirit, applied themselves to teaching or preaching; and occasionally, under a more than usual influence of the Holy Spirit, foretold future events. This sense of the word is supposed to be confined to the Scriptures; but I have met with it in the Classical writers, e. gr. Herodian, v. 5, 21. ὑποδήμασι λίνου πεποιημένοις ἐχρῶντο, ὥσπερ οἱ κατ᾽ ἐκεῖνα τὰ χώρια προφητεύοντες. where Irmisch refers to Sext. Emp. p. 227. Lucian i. 391. Diod. Sic. 199. Herodot. 555—49.

28. ἐσήμανε] "he declared, or announced." The term was often applied to the uttering of predictions, &c. Ὅλην τὴν οἰκ. Bishop Pearce has adduced many solid reasons for supposing that this expression denotes not the *whole world*, not even the *Roman Empire*, but *Palestine alone*, as in Luke ii. 1, where see the Note. The same view is adopted, and ably supported by Walch, Doddridge, Krebs, Michaelis, Hales, and Kuin., who adduce statements of the *four* famines which history has recorded as happening in the reign of Claudius. As, however, all the countries put *together* would not make up a tenth even of the *Roman Empire*, they think it plain that we must understand the words of that famine which (as we learn from Josephus, Antiq. xx. 2, 6,), in the fourth year of Claudius, overspread Palestine; and for the relief of the *Christians* suffering under which, some money was being collected at Antioch. The poor Jews *in general* were, as we learn from Josephus, relieved by Helena

Queen of Adiabene, who sent to purchase corn in Egypt.

29. καθὼς ηὐπορεῖτό τις] "in proportion to the ability of each." Sub. χρημάτων, which is sometimes *expressed*. Εὐπορ. is a comparative term, and does not necessarily imply *wealth*, but only competence. So Muson. cited by Kypke: ἀλλ' εὔποροι χρημάτων ὄντες· τινὲς δὲ καὶ πλούσιοι. Ὥρισαν, "determined." The word signifies 1. *terminare*; 2. *determinare*; 3. *decernere*.

—εἰς διακονίαν.] Literally, "for a service," "for the relief of." So Heb. vi. 10. διακονήσαντες τοῖς ἁγίοις. This relief was the more necessary, since, independently of the present famine, the Christians at Jerusalem were generally poor. In sending this bounty they did but imitate the example of the foreign Jews; who (as Vitringa has proved) used to send contributions for the relief of their poor brethren at Jerusalem.

30. τοὺς πρεσβυτέρους.] Hamm. has here an able annotation on the origin and various uses of πρεσβύτεροι, showing that in the Christian Church of the Apostolic age (which was formed almost wholly on the model of the synagogue), the term πρεσβύτεροι (a term implying rather the *wisdom* of age, than age itself) was synonymous with ἐπίσκοποι. Their common office and duty (in the words of Forbiger ap. Schleus. Lex.), was in general to *govern* the Christian Church, not to *teach*; to preside over things sacred, to administer the sacraments, especially the Eucharist, to decide on Ecclesiastical matters, to compose and settle differences, and finally to set an example to all of rectitude of doctrine and sanctity of life. See xx. 17. 28. Phil. i. 1. 1 Tim. iii. 1. Tit. i. 5. 7. and consult an elaborate Note of Mr. Towns. on this subject, vol. ii. p. 151. sq.

XII. 1. ἐπέβαλεν—τὰς χεῖρας.] Literally, took in hand, set about. The Classical writers use the expression, but without χεῖρα or χεῖρας; though they more frequently use ἐπιχειρεῖν. It seems therefore to be Hellenistic Greek; which is confirmed by its occurring in Deut. xii. 7. εὐφρανθήσεσθε ἐπὶ πᾶσιν οἷα ἐὰν ἐπιβάλητε τὰς χεῖρας. The English translations are needlessly literal.

3. ἰδὼν ὅτι ἀρεστόν ἐστι τοῖς Ἰουδ.] By "the Jews" some understand the *Sanhedrim*. And, indeed the word has that meaning in the Gospel of *St. John*: but never, I apprehend, in St. Luke's writings. We may therefore understand it of the Jews generally, both rulers and people. And that Herod was fond of obliging the Jewish people, we learn from Joseph. Ant. xix. 7. 3. Yet he may have been *partly* induced to practise this harshness towards the Christians, from his being

δαίοις, προσέθετο συλλαβεῖν καὶ Πέτρον (ἦσαν δὲ ἡμέραι τῶν ἀζύμων)
ὃν καὶ πιάσας ἔθετο εἰς φυλακὴν, παραδοὺς τέσσαρσι τετραδίοις στρα- 4
τιωτῶν φυλάσσειν αὐτὸν, βουλόμενος μετὰ τὸ πάσχα ἀναγαγεῖν αὐτὸν
τῷ λαῷ. Ὁ μὲν οὖν Πέτρος ἐτηρεῖτο ἐν τῇ φυλακῇ· προσευχὴ δὲ ἦν 5
ἐκτενὴς γινομένη ὑπὸ τῆς ἐκκλησίας πρὸς τὸν Θεὸν ὑπὲρ αὐτοῦ. Ὅτε 6
δὲ ἔμελλεν αὐτὸν προάγειν ὁ Ἡρώδης, τῇ νυκτὶ ἐκείνῃ ἦν ὁ Πέτρος
κοιμώμενος μεταξὺ δύο στρατιωτῶν, δεδεμένος ἁλύσεσι δυσὶ, φύλακές τε
πρὸ τῆς θύρας ἐτήρουν τὴν φυλακήν. Καὶ ἰδοὺ, ἄγγελος Κυρίου 7
ἐπέστη, καὶ φῶς ἔλαμψεν ἐν τῷ οἰκήματι· πατάξας δὲ τὴν πλευρὰν
τοῦ Πέτρου ἤγειρεν αὐτὸν, λέγων· Ἀνάστα ἐν τάχει. Καὶ ἐξέπεσον
αὐτοῦ αἱ ἁλύσεις ἐκ τῶν χειρῶν. εἶπέ τε ὁ ἄγγελος πρὸς αὐτόν· Περί- 8
ζωσαι, καὶ ὑπόδησαι τὰ σανδάλιά σου· ἐποίησε δὲ οὕτω. καὶ λέγει
αὐτῷ· Περιβαλοῦ τὸ ἱμάτιόν σου, καὶ ἀκολούθει μοι. Καὶ ἐξελθὼν 9
ἠκολούθει αὐτῷ· καὶ οὐκ ᾔδει ὅτι ἀληθές ἐστι τὸ γινόμενον διὰ τοῦ
ἀγγέλου, ἐδόκει δὲ ὅραμα βλέπειν. Διελθόντες δὲ πρώτην φυλακὴν 10
καὶ δευτέραν, ἦλθον ἐπὶ τὴν πύλην τὴν σιδηρᾶν τὴν φέρουσαν εἰς τὴν
πόλιν, ἥτις αὐτομάτη ἠνοίχθη αὐτοῖς· καὶ ἐξελθόντες προῆλθον ῥύμην

a great zealot for the Jewish religion; for Josephus there says, τὰ πάτρια καθαρῶς ἐτήρει; and adds that he never omitted to attend on his religious duties at the Temple.

— προσέθετο συλλ.] "proceeded to apprehend." So Luke xx. 11, 12. προσέθετο πέμψαι. where see Note. This idiom occurs in the LXX. and is called a Hebraism, יסף being so used with an Infinitive following.

— ἡμέραι τῶν ἀζύμων] "the days of the paschal feast, during which they were ordered to have unleavened bread in their houses." See Deut. xvi. 6. Exod. xii. 18. Before ἡμέραι several MSS., some of them ancient, prefix the Article, which is admitted by Matth., Griesb., Knapp, and Tittm. But Bp. Middl. justifies the omission on the principle, that "in propositions which merely affirm or deny existence, the name of the person or thing whereof existence is affirmed or denied, is without the Article. So Matt. xiv. 6. γενεσίων ἀγομένων Ἡρώδου. and John v. 1." That principle, however, is, I apprehend, too refined and far-fetched. It is better in such a case to say, that the Article is omitted because unnecessary, the addition of the noun in the Genit. sufficing to establish the definiteness. Here there is also an *ellipsis*, the complete phraseology being ἦσαν δὲ αἱ ἡμέραι αἱ ἡμέραι τῶν ἀζύμων. This probably led to the αἱ being at first marked in the margin, which afterwards crept into the text.

4. τετραδίοις.] The τετράδιον was, as we learn from Polyb., the regular number for a guard, (as a file is with us), and four such quaternions were thought necessary to guard the cell and all the approaches to it, and for necessary relief of guard.

5. ἐκτενὴς] "intense, fervent." So Luke xxii. 44. ἐκτενέστερον προσηύχετο. The metaphor (which is taken from a rope at full tension) is found in the LXX. Judith iv. 7. 2 Macc. xiv. 38.

6. μεταξὺ — δυσί.] Prisoners, when thus carefully guarded, were usually, among the Romans, secured with a single chain; one end of which was attached to the right hand of the prisoner, and the other to the left hand of the person who guarded him. In the present instance, for better security, there were *two* chains, each fastened to a soldier. I would compare Eurip. Iph. Taur. 456. ἀλλ' οὐδὲ χέρας δεσμοῖς διδύμοις Συνερεισθέντες χωροῦσι.

7. ἄγγελος Κυρίου ἐπέστη.] The sceptical school in Germany deny the reality of this angelic appearance, and seek to account for Peter's release, from natural causes. But Mr. Towns. has shown that in their eagerness to do away angelic and miraculous interference, they suppose circumstances which involve even a *greater* miracle. Οἰκήματι, for δεσμωτηρίῳ, by a frequent euphemism or ὑποκορισμός. See my note on Thucyd. iv. 47. No. 3. (Transl.) On the *situation* of this prison there has been no little difference of opinion. Wolf thinks it was near to the judgment hall; De Dieu and Fessel that it was in the Court of Herod's palace, and was his *private* prison; while Walch supposes it to have been in one of the towers of the innermost of the three walls which surrounded the city, and the iron gate, he thinks, was at the entrance of the tower. This last opinion is the most probable, and is confirmed and illustrated by what I have said in my note on Thucyd. ii. 4.

— πατάξας τὴν πλευράν.] As is usual in rousing persons from sleep.

8. περίζωσαι.] See Note on Luke xii. 35.

— ὑπόδησαι τὰ σανδάλιά σ.] This is, as Chrys. remarks, a beautifully graphic circumstance: for, in the haste of his sudden departure, Peter would be likely to forget to bind on his sandals. The angel therefore tells him to do it; thereby intimating to him his perfect *security*.

10. πρώτην — σιδηρᾶν.] Φυλακὴ here means one of the *parties* on guard. We may suppose what is here called the *first* guard to have been the two soldiers stationed at the door of the cell: the *second*, those stationed at the door which led out of the building into a court yard: and the *third*, those at the iron gate which led out of the court into the city. Αὐτομάτη, literally, *self*-moved. The word is used both of persons and things, and must be rendered accordingly. Pric. and Wets. adduce several examples of the word in this sense,

11 μίαν· καὶ εὐθέως ἀπέστη ὁ ἄγγελος ἀπ᾽ αὐτοῦ. καὶ ὁ Πέτρος γενόμενος ἐν ἑαυτῷ, εἶπε· Νῦν οἶδα ἀληθῶς ὅτι ἐξαπέστειλε Κύριος τὸν
ἄγγελον αὐτοῦ, καὶ ἐξείλετό με ἐκ χειρὸς Ἡρώδου καὶ πάσης τῆς προσ-
12 δοκίας τοῦ λαοῦ τῶν Ἰουδαίων. Συνιδών τε ἦλθεν ἐπὶ τὴν οἰκίαν
Μαρίας τῆς μητρὸς Ἰωάννου τοῦ ἐπικαλουμένου Μάρκου, οὗ ἦσαν ἱκανοὶ
συνηθροισμένοι καὶ προσευχόμενοι.
13 Κρούσαντος δὲ τοῦ Πέτρου τὴν θύραν τοῦ πυλῶνος, προσῆλθε
14 παιδίσκη ὑπακοῦσαι, ὀνόματι Ῥόδη· καὶ ἐπιγνοῦσα τὴν φωνὴν τοῦ
Πέτρου, ἀπὸ τῆς χαρᾶς οὐκ ἤνοιξε τὸν πυλῶνα, εἰσδραμοῦσα δὲ ἀπήγ-
15 γειλεν ἑστάναι τὸν Πέτρον πρὸ τοῦ πυλῶνος. Οἱ δὲ πρὸς αὐτὴν εἶπον·
Μαίνῃ· ἡ δὲ διϊσχυρίζετο οὕτως ἔχειν. οἱ δὲ ἔλεγον· Ὁ ἄγγελος αὐτοῦ
16 ἐστιν. Ὁ δὲ Πέτρος ἐπέμενε κρούων· ἀνοίξαντες δὲ εἶδον αὐτὸν, καὶ

and as used of doors, from Homer (Il. ε. 749.) downwards. So the Latin writers (as Virgil Æn. vi. 82.) used the expression *suâ sponte*. The circumstance of a door self-moving was regarded by the ancients, both Jews and Gentiles, as a prodigy, attesting the presence of the Deity.

11. *γενόμενος ἐν ἑαυτῷ.*] "When, recovering from his surprise, he tranquilly exercised his understanding," and found it was not a *dream*, but reality.

— *πάσης τῆς προσδοκ.*] The best Interpreters are agreed, that *προσδοκίας* must be taken by metonymy, for the *thing* expected, i. e. his execution, as in Genesis xlix. 10. *ἕως ἂν ἔλθῃ καὶ αὐτὸς προσδοκία ἐθνῶν*. Thus the sense is, "from what was fully expected by," &c. The Syr. renders "ab omni *machinatione*." I suspect that he read *προλοχείας*, "lying in wait," and indeed *προλοχίζω* occurs in Thucyd. and other writers. *Λαοῦ* is added to Ἰουδ. because at the time of the Passover the whole nation, in a manner, was assembled.

12. *συνιδὼν*] "on considering," namely, his situation and the circumstances connected with it.

13. *κρούσαντος — τὴν θύραν.*] This phrase occurs also in Luke xiii. 25. and often in the later writers; the earlier ones use *κόπτειν*. The two words differ in sense as our *rap* and *knock*. *Τὴν θύραν τ. πυλῶνος*, the porch-door or outer-gate, as opposed to the inner door which led immediately to the court around which the apartment was built. By *παιδίσκη* many Commentators understand *the portress*. But though that office was often performed by females, it is improbable, considering the narrow circumstances of the Christians at Jerusalem, that there should have been one at this house. Besides, that would require the *Article*. The sense seems to be simply "a damsel," i. e. a maid-servant. Ὑπακοῦσαι signifies properly to *listen*; but when used of the office of a *Porter* (which it often is in the best writers), carries with it, by implication, other significations corresponding to the actions connected therewith; as, to inquire the *name* of the person knocking. So in Lucian. Icarom. p. 292, *ἔκοπτον προσελθὼν τὴν θύραν· ὑπακούσας δὲ ὁ Ἑρμῆς καὶ τοὔνομα ἐκπυθόμενος*. Xen. Symp. i. 11. *κρούσας τὴν θύραν, εἶπε τῷ ὑπακούσαντι εἰσαγγεῖλαι*, &c. No extraordinary caution (such as Bp. Pearce imagines) is implied.

15. *μαίνῃ.*] A popular form of expression, used of any one who utters what is incredible. *Διϊσχυρίζετο*, "positively asserted."

— *ὁ ἄγγελος αὐτοῦ ἐ.*] Many eminent Interpreters take this to mean "a messenger sent from him." But the word will not admit that sense; neither is it likely that Peter could have sent a messenger; still less that the maid should not have known the voice of a messenger from Peter's voice. The sense must be, "his angel," i. e. his tutelary angel, such as the Jews, and indeed the Gentiles, thought was appointed to every person, or at least every good person. They also supposed, that on the death of the person, this angel sometimes appeared in his exact form, and spake with his voice, to the friends or acquaintance of the deceased.

Thus there is nothing but what is plain and intelligible. Bp. Middl., however, taking exception to the employment of the *Article* here; (see Note on John viii. 44.) and yet finding no sufficient authority for its being cancelled, proposes to consider the *αὐτοῦ* as an *adverb*, and taking the Article for the pronoun possessive, would render "His angel is there;" which, however, renders *transposition* necessary, *ἐστὶν αὐτοῦ*. But for this there is no authority except that of *one* MS., and therefore in that it may very well be supposed to have been *accidental*, arising from the scribe's inadvertently *omitting αὐτοῦ*, and then *supplying* it, but not in its place; or from the Critic's fancying this would be a neater way of placing the words. If, however, we were to adopt that position of the words, and to take the *αὐτοῦ* as an adverb, yet, I apprehend, the Article could not stand for the pronoun possessive; since that idiom *has its limits*, and cannot be used where any *very great uncertainty* would arise. As to the *αὐτοῦ* being, as he thinks it *may, understood*, according to his Canon iii. 1. 4., that is the weakest part of Bp. Middleton's system. See Note supra v. 1. The learned Prelate, indeed, seems to have himself suspected his position to be untenable, by proposing to *read ὁ ἄγγελος αὐτοῦ ἐστιν αὐτοῦ*, which he would have us suppose is not a *Critical conjecture*, because it is *compounded* of *two readings*. But as there is next to no authority for the *αὐτοῦ* after *ἐστιν*, it can be viewed in no other light. Besides, when there *is* indeed MS. authority for two readings taken separately; and yet none for those readings taken *conjointly* — to *unite* them and form one reading, is neither more nor less than *Critical* conjecture. Nay, what is more, the second *αὐτοῦ* would be pleonastic and useless — quite unsuitable to the *brevity* of such exclamations, — and, in short, "*nive Sithoniâ frigidius*."

ἐξέστησαν. Κατασείσας δὲ αὐτοῖς τῇ χειρὶ σιγᾷν, διηγήσατο αὐτοῖς 17
πῶς ὁ Κύριος αὐτὸν ἐξήγαγεν ἐκ τῆς φυλακῆς. εἶπε δέ· Ἀπαγγείλατε
Ἰακώβῳ καὶ τοῖς ἀδελφοῖς ταῦτα. καὶ ἐξελθὼν ἐπορεύθη εἰς ἕτερον
τόπον. Γενομένης δὲ ἡμέρας, ἦν τάραχος οὐκ ὀλίγος ἐν τοῖς στρατιώ- 18
ταις, τί ἄρα ὁ Πέτρος ἐγένετο. Ἡρώδης δὲ ἐπιζητήσας αὐτὸν καὶ μὴ 19
εὑρὼν, ἀνακρίνας τοὺς φύλακας ἐκέλευσεν ἀπαχθῆναι. καὶ κατελθὼν
o 1 Kings 5. 9, 11. Ezek. 27. 17. ἀπὸ τῆς Ἰουδαίας εἰς τὴν Καισάρειαν διέτριβεν. [o] Ἦν δὲ ὁ Ἡρώδης 20
θυμομαχῶν Τυρίοις καὶ Σιδωνίοις· ὁμοθυμαδὸν δὲ παρῆσαν πρὸς
αὐτὸν, καὶ πείσαντες Βλάστον τὸν ἐπὶ τοῦ κοιτῶνος τοῦ βασιλέως,
ᾐτοῦντο εἰρήνην, διὰ τὸ τρέφεσθαι αὐτῶν τὴν χώραν ἀπὸ τῆς βασιλικῆς.
Τακτῇ δὲ ἡμέρᾳ ὁ Ἡρώδης ἐνδυσάμενος ἐσθῆτα βασιλικὴν, καὶ καθίσας 21
ἐπὶ τοῦ βήματος, ἐδημηγόρει πρὸς αὐτούς. Ὁ δὲ δῆμος ἐπεφώνει· 22
Θεοῦ φωνὴ καὶ οὐκ ἀνθρώπου! Παραχρῆμα δὲ ἐπάταξεν αὐτὸν ἄγγε- 23
λος Κυρίου, ἀνθ᾽ ὧν οὐκ ἔδωκε [τὴν] δόξαν τῷ Θεῷ· καὶ γενόμενος
p Isa. 55. 11. supra 6. 7. infra 19. 20. Col. 1. 6. σκωληκόβρωτος, ἐξέψυξεν. [p] Ὁ δὲ λόγος τοῦ Θεοῦ ηὔξανε καὶ ἐπλη- 24
q Supra 11. 29. θύνετο. [q] Βαρνάβας δὲ καὶ Σαῦλος ὑπέστρεψαν ἐξ Ἱερουσαλὴμ, πλη- 25
ρώσαντες τὴν διακονίαν, συμπαραλαβόντες καὶ Ἰωάννην τὸν ἐπικληθέντα
Μάρκον.

17. *κατασείσας τῇ χειρὶ σιγᾷν.*] Κατασείειν signifies to *wave the hand downwards*; a mode of enjoining silence. See xiii. 16. xix. 33. xxi. 40. It occurs also in the best writers, from whom examples are adduced by the Commentators.

— *ἐπορεύθη εἰς ἕτερον τόπον.*] *Where*, we are left to *conjecture*; the expression being quite indefinite. Some suppose *Cæsarea*; others, with more probability, *Antioch*; others, again, *Rome*; which last opinion, though long strenuously contended against by Protestant Commentators, has lately been ably maintained by Mr. Townsend, vol. ii. p. 140. seqq. in a Dissertation on St. Peter's visit to Rome and the writing of St. Mark's Gospel.

19. *ἀνακρίνας τοὺς φύλακας*, &c.] "after examining the keepers [and finding they offered nothing in justification] ordered them to be led away for execution." Ἀπάγειν is a vox sol. de hac re, *εἰς θάνατον* or *ἐπὶ θανάτῳ* being generally expressed, but sometimes left to be *understood*, for *death* is in this formula always implied. Thus there is no reason to suppose, with some, that their punishment was not unto death.

— *διέτριβεν*] scil. *ἐκεῖ*, which is implied in the preceding, as at xiv. 3. The word is generally *expressed*, as in John iii. 22. xi. 64.

20. *θυμομαχῶν Τυρίοις.*] Θυμομαχεῖν signifies "to have war at heart with," to be hostilely disposed towards, and sometimes to *be at war with*; which last signification is here adopted by some Commentators. But that involves such improbability, and is so destitute of Historical support, that it is better to interpret the expression *ᾐτοῦντο εἰρήνην*, on which the foregoing view is founded, in a *metaphorical* sense, i. e. they sought to be friends with, as *εἰρήνην ἔχουσι* elsewhere, and to take *θυμομ.* in the first mentioned and *general* sense. Kuin., with great probability, traces the origin of this misunderstanding to *commercial jealousies*, arising from Herod's having formed so admirable a port at Cæsarea. Ὁμοθυμαδὸν, conjointly, i. e. both Tyrians and Sidonians. Πείσαντες Βλάστον. The full sense is, "having prevailed on Bl. [to give them his aid in the business]." See Matt. xxviii. 14. Gal. i. 10.

21. *τακτῇ*] "appointed," as the day of public audience. It appears from Joseph. Ant. xix. 7, 2. to have been the second day of the Games then celebrating in honour of Cæsar. Βήματος signifies not *tribunal*, as in Matt. xxvii. 19., but a raised *suggestus*, presenting the appearance of a throne, in the theatre, where Herod viewed the games and delivered the oration.

— *πρὸς αὐτούς.*] Not the *people*, as some imagine, but the *ambassadors*; which is required by what precedes, and *δημηγορεῖν*, as often in the later writers, signifies simply to deliver a speech.

22. *ὁ δῆμος.*] Chiefly, if not exclusively, the *Gentiles*, (multitudes of whom inhabited Cæsarea), and set on by the courtiers and flatterers, as we find from Josephus; from whom we also learn, that the persons in question did really profess to regard him as *a God*; no doubt in that *qualified* sense in which the Roman Emperors were called *Divi*, not only after their death, but even in their lifetime; and in which the Greeks sometimes applied the term to great personages, (see Pind. Olymp. v. sub. init. Aristid. iii. 249, 250. Eunap. Prœr. p. 120. 163. Appian i. 635. Joseph. p. 533. ult.) but yet in such a sense as the *Jews* could not receive; and it clearly appears from Joseph. that the Jews were incensed with him for receiving this impious adulation.

23. *ἐπάταξε*] i. e. "struck him with disease." The expression *ἄγγελος Κυρίου ἐπάτ.* must at any rate mean that the disorder was inflicted by a Divine judgment, and not brought on by *dysentery* arising from a cold caught, as many recent Commentators pretend; whose arguments I have refuted in Recens. Synop. The circumstance of his being *σκωληκόβρωτος* will not prove that the disorder was of *human* origin, because the Deity often vouchsafes to act by second causes. Thus the seeming discrepancy between this account, and that of Josephus, is not really such. The

1 XIII. ʳ ῏ΗΣΑΝ δέ τινες ἐν Ἀντιοχείᾳ κατὰ τὴν οὖσαν ἐκκλησίαν r Infra 14. 26.
προφῆται καὶ διδάσκαλοι, ὅ τε Βαρνάβας καὶ Συμεὼν ὁ καλούμενος s Supra 9. 15. Infra 22. 21.
Νίγερ, καὶ Λούκιος ὁ Κυρηναῖος, Μαναήν τε Ἡρώδου τοῦ τετράρχου Rom. 1. 1. Gal. 1. 15.
2 σύντροφος, καὶ Σαῦλος. ˢ Λειτουργούντων δὲ αὐτῶν τῷ Κυρίῳ καὶ & 2. 8. Eph. 3. 8.
νηστευόντων, εἶπε τὸ Πνεῦμα τὸ ἅγιον· Ἀφορίσατε δή μοι τόν [τε] 1 Tim. 2. 7. 2 Tim. 1. 11. Matt. 9. 38.
3 Βαρνάβαν καὶ τὸν Σαῦλον εἰς τὸ ἔργον ὃ προσκέκλημαι αὐτούς. ᵗ Τότε Rom. 10. 15. t Supra 6. 6.
νηστεύσαντες καὶ προσευξάμενοι, καὶ ἐπιθέντες τὰς χεῖρας αὐτοῖς, ἀπέ- & 8. 15. & 14. 23.

historian narrates the *secondary* causes of Herod's death; the sacred writer considers the *primary* one, even the immediate interposition of Heaven. And this will hold good whether we take the ἄγγελος literally, or metaphorically; though it seems safer to take it (as does Doddr.) of the *real*, yet *invisible*, *agency of a celestial spirit*. See 2 Sam. xxiv. 16. 2 Kings xix. 35. Nor is there any discrepancy as to the *secondary* cause of his death, namely, the *disorder* of which he died. For although Josephus only mentions most violent pains in the bowels, and *dysentery*; yet that is very consistent with St. Luke's account; since the dysentery might very well be occasioned by *worms*; especially as, in such a case, the dysentery is preceded by violent pains in the bowels. See Thucyd. ii. 49. 6. However, Josephus may not have meant dysentery; for the terms he uses, ἀλγήματι τῆς γαστρὸς and ἄλγημα κοιλίας, may have only had reference to the violent pains occasioned by worms eating the bowels. Be that as it may, we may very well account for Josephus's making no mention of *worms*, from motives of *delicacy*, and especially as many tyrants, even in some measure the *first* Herod, had died of that (or a similar disorder, the morbus pedicularis); as for instance Antiochus Epiphanes. See 2 Macc. ix. 5. which passage St. Luke seems to have had in view. At the same time, it is plain from Josephus's manner, that he regarded Herod's death as brought on by *Divine interposition*. Thus he says that the exclamations of the adulators were οὐδὲ ἐκείνῳ πρὸς ἀγαθοῦ. And he represents Herod himself as avowing his persuasion that his death was brought on by Almighty Providence, to give the lie, as it were, to the impious assertions of the flattering multitude.

XIII. From this Chapter to the end of the Book, Luke narrates the various journeys of Paul, undertaken for the conversion of the Gentiles.

1. διδάσκαλοι.] i. e. publicly appointed teachers in the Church, mentioned also in 1 Cor. xii. 28. and Eph. iv. 11., where see Notes.

— Ἡρώδου.] That this is Herod Antipas, and not (as Grot. supposes) Agrippa the second, son of King Agrippa the first, whose death was recorded at xii. 23., has been proved by Walch in a Dissertation de Menachemo, of which the substance is given by Kuin., and may be seen translated in Recens. Synop.

— σύντροφος.] This is properly an *adjective*, signifying *brought up with*, (and in this sense only occurs in the earlier writers) but it is also used as a *substantive*, equivalent to our *foster-brother*, and is explained ὁμογάλακτος in the Glossaries. But the sense *foster-brother* sometimes implied also that of *table-fellow* and *school-fellow*. For it was not unusual in ancient times for children to be brought up with the sons of kings and great men. Examples are adduced by Raphel, Wets., and Munth., to which I add Joseph. Ant. xiv. 9, 5. and Bell. i. 10, 9. The custom continued even to modern times, as in the case of our James the first.

2. λειτουργούντων τ. Κ.] Λειτουργία denotes the discharge of some public office, whether *civil* or *religious*. In the Classical writers it is almost always used in the civil sense; but in the Scriptural, in the religious. In the O. T., and sometimes in the New, (as Heb. x. 11.), it denotes the ministration of the Priests and Levites. *Here* λειτουργεῖν *might* denote the discharge of all the duties of the ministerial office, both public and private, (praying, preaching, teaching, exhorting, &c.), but it seems only to denote the *public* duties. Καὶ νηστευόντων is meant to signify, that while they were thus engaged they were *fasting*: perhaps on an occasion of more than usual solemnity, when *fasting* had been *added* to prayer, &c., probably to ask a blessing on the means taken to spread the Gospel. The direction from the Holy Spirit was, it seems, communicated to them while thus engaged.

Of the difficulty which many have found, to reconcile the Apostolic commission of Paul by the *Holy Spirit*, with his having been set apart for the work of evangelizing the Heathen by Ecclesiastical officers, even of an inferior rank, the best solution is that of Mr. Townsend, — who supposes that the condescending of Paul to become the Apostle of the Church at Antioch, so far as it might be useful to the Catholic Church to act with their sanction, does not imply that their authority was superior to his. His object may have been to obtain in those places which were under the influence of Antioch, a better or an easier introduction than he would have otherwise experienced. There is some reason to think, with Hooker, Hales, and Mr. Townsend, that both Paul and Barnabas were now set apart for their Apostleship, to supply the vacancies in the original number; one having been killed by Herod, the other appointed bishop of Jerusalem.

— εἶπε τὸ Πνεῦμα τὸ ἅγιον.] Here and at ἐκπεμφθέντες ὑπὸ τοῦ Πνεύμ. τ. ἁγ. at v. 4. the Personality and Deity of the Holy Spirit is evidently implied.

— ἀφορίσατε δή μοι.] Ἀφορίζειν signifies 1. to *separate*; 2. (by implication) to *destine*; 3. to *appoint*, as here. The δὴ is *hortative*, and may be rendered *now*. The μοι seems to have the *imperative* force, highly suitable to the Divine dignity of the speaker. Of this idiom, (little known even to Critics), the following are examples. Ps. cxviii. 19. ἀνοίξατέ μοι πύλας. Thucyd. v. 10. τὰς πύλας ἀνοιγέτω ἐμοί. Eurip. Iph. Aul. 1340. διαχαλᾶτέ μοι μέλαθρα. Soph. Œd. Col. 1475. Lucian i. 718, 645. The προς in προσκέκλημαι is not pleonastic, but signifies *unto*, as if it were written πρὸς ὃ κέκλημαι.

3. νηστεύσαντες καὶ προσευξ.] The *fasting* seems

λυσαν. Οὗτοι μὲν οὖν, ἐκπεμφθέντες ὑπὸ τοῦ Πνεύματος τοῦ ἁγίου, 4
κατῆλθον εἰς τὴν Σελεύκειαν, ἐκεῖθέν τε ἀπέπλευσαν εἰς τὴν Κύπρον.
u Supra 12. 25. [u] Καὶ γενόμενοι ἐν Σαλαμῖνι, κατήγγελλον τὸν λόγον τοῦ Θεοῦ ἐν ταῖς 5
x Supra 8. 9. συναγωγαῖς τῶν Ἰουδαίων· εἶχον δὲ καὶ Ἰωάννην ὑπηρέτην. [x] Διελ- 6
θόντες δὲ τὴν νῆσον ἄχρι Πάφου, εὗρόν τινα μάγον, ψευδοπροφήτην,
Ἰουδαῖον, ᾧ ὄνομα Βαριησοῦς, ὃς ἦν σὺν τῷ ἀνθυπάτῳ Σεργίῳ Παύλῳ, 7
ἀνδρὶ συνετῷ. Οὗτος προσκαλεσάμενος Βαρνάβαν καὶ Σαῦλον, ἐπεζή-
y Exod. 7. 11. 2 Tim. 3. 8. τησεν ἀκοῦσαι τὸν λόγον τοῦ Θεοῦ. [y] Ἀνθίστατο δὲ αὐτοῖς Ἐλύμας 8
ὁ μάγος (οὕτω γὰρ μεθερμηνεύεται τὸ ὄνομα αὐτοῦ) ζητῶν διαστρέψαι
τὸν ἀνθύπατον ἀπὸ τῆς πίστεως. Σαῦλος δὲ (ὁ καὶ Παῦλος) πλησθεὶς 9

to be put first, because this solemnity (no doubt, performed some time after that on which the order of the Spirit was received) was ushered in *indicto jejunio.* So v. 2. λειτουργούντων καὶ νηστευόντων, where see Note and xiv. 23. προσευξάμενοι μετὰ νηστειῶν.

6. μάγον.] See Note supra viii. 9. Ψευδοπροφήτην. Pearce thinks it means *false teacher.* But the full sense must be one who falsely claims to speak under Divine inspiration, whether in foretelling future events, or in making known the will of God. Ὅλην is added before νῆσον by Griesb., Tittm., and Vater, from several MSS., Versions, and Fathers. But the evidence of the two last is here not material, and the word seems to have come from the margin.

7. ἀνθυπάτῳ.] Supposed by Grot. and Hamm. to be applied, by an error of title, for ἀντιστρατήγῳ. But Lardner and Kuin. have vindicated the accuracy of the expression; proving by reference to Dio Cass. and other writers, that those who presided over the provinces by the appointment of the Senate (and Cyprus was *then* of that number, though it had once been Prætorian), were *styled* Proconsuls, though they had never filled the chair. That the title did really belong to the Roman governors of Cyprus, has, indeed, been placed beyond all doubt by Bp. Marsh Lect. P. v. p. 85. sq., by reference to a coin (to be found in the Thesaurus Morell. p. 106.) struck in the very age in which Sergius Paulus was governor of that Island. It was coined in the reign of Claudius Cæsar, whose head and name are on the face of it; and in the reign of Claudius Cæsar St. Paul visited Cyprus. It was a coin belonging to the people of that island, as appears from the word ΚΥΠΡΙΩΝ on the reverse; and though not struck while Sergius Paulus himself was governor, it was struck, as appears from the inscription on the reverse, in the time of Proclus, who was *next* to Sergius Paulus in the government of that island. And on this coin the same title ἈΝΘΥΠΑΤΟΣ, is given to Proclus, which is given by St. Luke to Sergius Paulus. "That Cyprus (continues the learned Prelate) was a Proconsulate, is also evident from an ancient inscription, of Caligula's reign, (the predecessor of Claudius), in which Aquilius Scaurus is called the Proconsul of Cyprus."

— συνετῷ] "a man of ability." Literally, (as we say), a *clever* man; so Thucyd. i. 74. iii. 37. Galen, cited by Wets., speaks of him as a person excellently versed in philosophy; which will confirm the sense of μάγος above assigned. Sergius had, no doubt, been learning something of Philosophy and natural religion, if not the Jewish religion, from Elymas. Hence it was likely that he should send for those who taught a religion professing to be an *improvement* on the Jewish; and as likely that this should be opposed by Elymas, who was influenced only by worldly views.

8. Ἐλύμας.] From an Arabic word signifying *doctus*, or *sapiens.* So our wiz-ard from *wise.*

— διαστρέψαι.] At this some Commentators stumble, and Valckn. and Griesb. conjecture ἀποστρέψαι. But that is wholly destitute of authority, *Versions* having no weight. And if even it did occur in a few MSS., it must be rejected as a gloss. The common reading is confirmed by a similar construction in Exod. v. 4. ἱνατί διαστρέφετε τὸν λαὸν ἀπὸ τῶν ἔργων; The reason for the apparent anomaly in syntax is, that there is a significatio prægnans, namely, "to pervert and turn," i. e. to turn from the faith by a perversion and misrepresentation of it. So he is represented at v. 10. as διαστρέφων τὰς ὁδοὺς Κυρίου.

9. ὁ καὶ Παῦλος.] Sub. καλούμενος; for the Article is put for the Pron. relative, on which see Win. Gr. p. 57. fin. With respect to the name Παῦλος, it is well observed by Wets. that though Luke has before invariably called him Saul, now, no sooner has he mentioned the name of Paul, than Saul becomes so obliterated that we nowhere find it used again either by Luke, Peter, or Paul, in his Epistles. For this the Commentators are not a little perplexed to account. Some suppose that he had always had *both* names. But then why should Luke have hitherto invariably used Saul, and now as invariably Paul? Others are of opinion that Saul changed his name after his conversion. But that is refuted by his being called Saul by Luke *after* that time, and up to the present. Saul must have *himself* changed his name; not, however, as some imagine, out of humility, and deference to the Proconsul; but, it should seem (as Beza, Grot., Doddr., and Kuin. suppose), because he was now brought very much among Greeks and Romans, to whom the name *Saul* was unknown, but *Paul* familiar, especially as they would *pronounce* Saul like Paul. It may be added, that the name *Paul*, being a Roman one, would be so much the more suitable to a Roman citizen. And as the reason for the alteration, on taking the solemn charge he had now received, would be stronger than ever, — there can be no doubt that it was *now made.* It should seem by Luke's expression, that while he adopted this name, he yet did not absolutely *abandon* the other. Though as he was now the Apostle of the Gentiles, there was a propriety in Luke's henceforward giving him that name which he bore among Gentiles.

10 *Πνεύματος ἁγίου, καὶ ἀτενίσας εἰς αὐτὸν,* [z] *εἶπεν· Ὦ πλήρης παντὸς* z Matt. 13. 38.
δόλου καὶ πάσης ῥᾳδιουργίας, υἱὲ Διαβόλου, ἐχθρὲ πάσης δικαιοσύνης! John 8. 44.
11 *οὐ παύσῃ διαστρέφων τὰς ὁδοὺς Κυρίου τὰς εὐθείας; καὶ νῦν ἰδοὺ,* 1 John 3. 8.
χεὶρ [τοῦ] Κυρίου ἐπὶ σὲ, καὶ ἔσῃ τυφλὸς, μὴ βλέπων τὸν ἥλιον, ἄχρι
καιροῦ. Παραχρῆμα δὲ ἐπέπεσεν ἐπ' αὐτὸν ἀχλὺς καὶ σκότος· καὶ
12 *περιάγων ἐζήτει χειραγωγούς. Τότε ἰδὼν ὁ ἀνθύπατος τὸ γεγονὸς*
ἐπίστευσεν, ἐκπλησσόμενος ἐπὶ τῇ διδαχῇ τοῦ Κυρίου.

— *πλησθεὶς Πν. ἁγ.*] "filled with the influence and inspiration of the Holy Spirit," not under the impression of spleen or anger.

10. *ῥᾳδιουργίας.*] The word denotes 1. facility of action; 2. levity and carelessness, whether any action be good or evil; 3. villainy and wickedness in general, or rather what is designated by our *knavery* or *trickery*. Upon the whole, the word (which occurs chiefly in the later writers) corresponds to, and is indeed the *same with* our *roguery*, anciently written *ragerie*.

— *διαστρέφων τὰς ὁδοὺς Κ.*] Much learning has been employed to little purpose on this word *διαστρ.*, especially from pressing too much on the metaphor. It is also debated whether *τὰς ὁδοὺς Κ.* means the Lord's *religion*, or the *ways and purposes* of the Lord. Since the examples adduced of the former signification have only the *singular*, the latter is preferable, especially as it yields nearly the same sense. The words may be thus rendered: "misrepresenting the upright counsels and purposes of the Lord [for the salvation of men]." In this figurative diction there is, I conceive, an allusion to Is. xl. 4. "the crooked shall be made straight, and the rough ways plain," i. e. according to the LXX. (in the three principal MSS.) and the N. T. *ἡ τραχεῖα εἰς ὁδοὺς λείας*. And so ver. 3.

11. *ἰδοὺ*] As we say, *Mind!* take notice! *Χεὶρ τοῦ Κυρίου ἐπὶ σέ.* A Hebrew phrase, denoting that Divine punishment is suspended over a person. See Exod. ix. 3. Job. xix. 21. The *τοῦ* before *Κυρίου* is omitted in very many MSS., Fathers, and early Edd.; and perhaps is not genuine; though Bp. Middl. is of opinion that, if retained, it would not follow that *χεὶρ* would want the Article.

— *ἔσῃ τυφλὸς, μὴ βλ. τ. ἥ.*] This is thought to be a Hebrew mode of asserting the same thing, both by affirmation and by negation of the contrary. But the idiom occurs also in the *Greek* and *Latin* writers, and is only a relic of primitive simplicity of diction. It does not involve *pleonasm*, for the latter phrase serves to explain and strengthen the former; as in a kindred passage of Luke i. 20. *καὶ ἰδοὺ, ἔσῃ σιωπῶν, μὴ δυνάμενος λαλῆσαι.* *Here*, however, *μὴ βλέπων τὸν ἥλιον* is so much *stronger* an expression than *τυφλὸς*, (for all but persons *born* blind have some faint view of the sun) that there is a sort of *climax*, and we might render freely, "thou shalt be blind — yea *stone blind!*"

— *ἄχρι καιροῦ.*] The Latin Versions render it "usque ad tempus." And so the Syriac and some Oriental ones. Yet that would require *μέχρι*, as is proved by Tittm. de Synop. p. 37, who rightly observes: "*ἄχρι* non finem, sed ipsam durationem denotat, seu tempus totum, quo res quædam duravit, sed *μέχρι* finem designat, quo esse desiit, nisi addatur verbum, cujus notione ipsius termini s. finis tollatur cogitatio, ut in *μέχρι παντός*." He regards *ἄχρι καιροῦ* as equivalent to *ἕως τέλους*, i. e. *μέχρι τέλους*, *permanently*. But though right in the *rule*, he seems wrong in the *application*. The truth is, that the literal sense of *ἄχρι καιροῦ* is "during some time." Though as duration *for a certain time only*, necessarily *implies* termination *at the end of that time*, so *ἄχρι καιροῦ* may be *popularly* taken for *μέχρι καιροῦ*. The sense here is, I conceive, well expressed by our English Versions. But although the words of the Apostle *express* no more than this, — yet, as *καιροῦ* is used (which chiefly signifies a *point of time*), not *χρόνου*, he meant, I apprehend, to *hint* at that sense which might be more correctly phrased by *μέχρι καιροῦ*; meaning by *καιροῦ the time of his repentance and reformation*. Whether that time would ever arrive, the Apostle, it seems, knew not; the Holy Spirit not having informed him. And he felt so much doubt, — that he only just uses an expression which might fall short of driving the man into despair. Had he felt *hope*, he would perhaps have said (as at Heb. ix. 10.), *μέχρι καιροῦ διορθώσεως*.

— *ἐπέπεσεν ἐπ' αὐτὸν ἀχλὺς καὶ σκότος.*] Passing by the vain speculations of some Commentators on the *nature* of this blindness, and the unhallowed hypotheses of the sceptical school, by whom it is denied to have been produced supernaturally, I would only observe, that there is here *not* a hendiadys; but it should seem that the supervention of the blindness is *graphically* described, by various stages of the affection. See Note on Acts iii. 8. First a *cloud*, as it were, came over the eyes, which soon increased to *darkness*, and that terminated in that "*total eclipse*, in which the Sun is dark!"

12. There is something awkward in this verse, as regards *ἐπίστευσεν* and *ἐκπλησσόμενος*. Some various readings exist; though only such as show that the ancient Critics endeavoured to remove the difficulty by *emendation*; i. e. either by inserting *ἐθαύμασεν*, or making *ἐπίστ.* and *ἐκπλ.* change places. The *latter* mode is preferable; but it is supported by only one MS.: and no reason can be assigned why, if that were the true position of the words, the *verb ἐξεπλήσσετο* should not have been written. The Syriac Translator, indeed, renders as if he so read; but he, no doubt, rather gave what he conceived to be the *sense*, than followed the *words* of his original. Moreover, there is no example of *πιστεύειν* with *ἐπὶ* and a Dative of *thing*, unless where the thing is put for the person. Whereas examples of *ἐκπλήσσεσθαι* with *ἐπὶ* and a Dative of thing are frequent, and especially with *διδαχῇ*, e. gr. Matt. xxii. 33. Mark i. 22. xi. 18. Luke iv. 32, and very often elsewhere. The same syntax is found in the Classical writers. The words *ἐκπλησσόμενος — Κυρίου* are, I conceive, meant further to unfold the sense couched in *ἰδὼν τὸ γεγ.* with reference to the miracle, and may be freely rendered, "being amazed

a Infra 15. 38. [a]Ἀναχθέντες δὲ ἀπὸ τῆς Πάφου οἱ περὶ τὸν Παῦλον, ἦλθον εἰς 13
Πέργην τῆς Παμφυλίας. Ἰωάννης δὲ ἀποχωρήσας ἀπ' αὐτῶν ὑπέστρεψεν εἰς Ἱεροσόλυμα. Αὐτοὶ δὲ διελθόντες ἀπὸ τῆς Πέργης, παρε- 14
γένοντο εἰς Ἀντιόχειαν τῆς Πισιδίας, καὶ εἰσελθόντες εἰς τὴν συναγωγὴν
τῇ ἡμέρᾳ τῶν σαββάτων, ἐκάθισαν. Μετὰ δὲ τὴν ἀνάγνωσιν τοῦ νόμου 15
καὶ τῶν προφητῶν, ἀπέστειλαν οἱ ἀρχισυνάγωγοι πρὸς αὐτούς, λέγοντες·
Ἄνδρες ἀδελφοί, εἰ ἔστι λόγος ἐν ὑμῖν παρακλήσεως πρὸς τὸν λαόν,
b Supra 12. 17. & 19. 33. & 21. 40. λέγετε. [b]Ἀναστὰς δὲ Παῦλος, καὶ κατασείσας τῇ χειρί, εἶπεν· Ἄνδρες 16
c Exod. 1. 1. & 6. 6. & 12. 31. & 13. 14. Ἰσραηλῖται, καὶ οἱ φοβούμενοι τὸν Θεόν, ἀκούσατε. [c]ὁ Θεὸς τοῦ λαοῦ 17
τούτου [Ἰσραὴλ] ἐξελέξατο τοὺς πατέρας ἡμῶν· καὶ τὸν λαὸν ὕψωσεν
d Exod. 16. 2, 35. Num. 14. 34. Psal. 95. 10. ἐν τῇ παροικίᾳ ἐν γῇ Αἰγύπτῳ, καὶ μετὰ βραχίονος ὑψηλοῦ ἐξήγαγεν
αὐτοὺς ἐξ αὐτῆς· [d]καὶ ὡς τεσσαρακονταετῆ χρόνον * ἐτροφοφόρησεν αὐτοὺς 18

at this [authoritative] mode of teaching the Lord," i. e. his religion; i. e. "when he saw its truth confirmed by such power [of miracles]." For it is not the *internal* evidence of the truth (as Doddr. understands) which is here had in view, but its *external* evidence. This, indeed, is placed beyond doubt by the *authentic* interpretation of St. *Luke himself*, in his Gospel, iv. 32. καὶ ἐξεπλήσσοντο ἐπὶ τῇ διδαχῇ· ὅτι ἐν ἐξουσίᾳ ἦν ὁ λόγος αὐτοῦ.

13. οἱ περὶ τὸν Π.] This comes under *one* of the three divisions into which this idiomatical use of the Article masc. plur. with an Accusative of person is distributed; by which is meant "the person (as principal) and his company." But if we understand it of Paul and *Barnabas only*, it would seem harsh. May we not, then, suppose that some *other persons* had associated themselves with them, as subordinate helpers in the work of evangelization? That *Mark* had accompanied them is certain from the next Chapter. This idiom being used shows that Paul was already esteemed the principal, though Barnabas was, on many accounts, entitled to high consideration, and is mentioned first in the Divine appointment.

14. ἐκάθισαν] "took their seat," no doubt in the place where, as doctors, they had a right to sit. See Mr. Townsend's *Excursus* here, (formed from the elaborate researches of Grot., Lightf., Mede, and Vitringa,) "on the officers, and modes of worship in the synagogues."

15. εἰ ἔστι — λαόν, λέγετε.] The full sense seems to be "If either of you have any word [of exhortation] to address to the people, speak it." This instruction and exhortation was usually taken from the portions read of the Pentateuch or Prophets.

16. κατασείσας τῇ χειρί.] See note on xii. 17. In this address, which, as Doddr. observes, "seems chiefly intended to illustrate the Divine economy in opening the Gospel gradually, and preparing the Jews, by temporal mercies, for others of a higher nature," the Apostle (to use the words of Mr. Townsend) "reminds his hearers of the *former* mercies of God to the family of Abraham, and the prediction that their Messiah should be descended from David; and asserts that this Messiah was Jesus of Nazareth. He appeals to the well-known fact of the resurrection of Christ from the dead, as the principal evidence of the truth of his declaration, and concludes with enforcing that one important truth, in which the whole human race are so immediately interested, that forgiveness of sins is to be proclaimed through Him alone; and that Christ alone can justify the Christian, not only from those offences, from which they were typically purified by the ceremonial law, but from those sins also for which that law had made no provision."

— οἱ φοβ. τὸν Θεόν.] By these are meant the proselytes of the gate, — the οἱ σεβόμενοι προσήλυτοι. So Joseph. Ant. xiv. 7, 2, makes a similar distinction between Ἰουδαῖοι and σεβόμενοι. These persons were such as, having abandoned idolatry, *worshipped the true God*, and therefore, though they did not receive circumcision, were yet permitted to attend at the synagogues. Those Gentiles who *received* circumcision were reckoned *as Jews*. (Kuin.)

17. ἐξελέξατο] "chose as objects of his peculiar blessing." Ὕψωσεν is well explained by Elsn. and Doddr. "raised them out of a calamitous state," referring to several passages of the Psalms, to which I would add lxix. 14. μετὰ βραχ. ὑψηλοῦ, i. e. by the exertion of a mighty power.

18. ἐτροφοφόρησεν.] It is exceedingly difficult to determine which of the *two* readings here found (ἐτροποφόρησεν and ἐτροφοφόρησεν) is to be adopted. The *latter* has been preferred by H. Steph., Casaub., Mill, Pfaff, Hamm., Beng., Ernesti, Pearce, Wakef., Valckn., Morus, Schleus., Rosenm., Kuin., and Towns.; and has been edited by Griesb. and Knapp. The former, which is the common reading, however, has been ably supported by Grot., Gataker, Deyling, Whitby, Wolf, Wets., Doddr., Matth., and others. Many arguments are adduced by the disputants on *both* sides, which are either irrelevant, or inconclusive. What increases the perplexity is, that the words may easily be, and often are confounded by the scribes. Nay, in *certain senses* which the terms admit, the ideas noted by the two words merge into each other. Hence some advocates for the common reading have, in almost every passage, cited as authority for ἐτροφοφορέω, maintained that ἐτροποφ. is the true reading; but without reason. There can be no doubt but that *both* words were in use. For though we may doubt whether τροφοφορέω be analogically formed, yet we must bend to *use*, and the similar form διφροφορέω defends the seeming anomaly. That π and φ are interchanged in pronunciation, is an argument which draws *both ways*; while that the *words* are often confounded by scribes, is an argument which makes far more for the *new* than the *old* reading. Yet, upon the whole, *external*

19 ἐν τῇ ἐρήμῳ· ᵉ καὶ καθελὼν ἔθνη ἑπτὰ ἐν γῇ Χαναὰν, * κατεκληρονό- ᵉ Jos. 14. 1, 2. Jud. 2. 16. & 3. 9.
20 μησεν αὐτοῖς τὴν γῆν αὐτῶν. Καὶ μετὰ ταῦτα, ὡς ἔτεσι τετρακοσίοις
21 καὶ πεντήκοντα, ἔδωκε κριτὰς ἕως Σαμουὴλ τοῦ προφήτου· ᶠ κἀκεῖθεν ᶠ 1 Sam. 8. 5. & 9. 15.
ᾐτήσαντο βασιλέα· καὶ ἔδωκεν αὐτοῖς ὁ Θεὸς τὸν Σαοὺλ υἱὸν Κὶς, & 10. 1. Hos. 13. 11.
22 ἄνδρα ἐκ φυλῆς Βενιαμὶν, ἔτη τεσσαράκοντα· ᵍ καὶ μεταστήσας αὐτὸν, ᵍ 1 Sam. 13. 14. & 15. 28. & 16. 13.
ἤγειρεν αὐτοῖς τὸν Δαυῒδ εἰς βασιλέα, ᾧ καὶ εἶπε μαρτυρήσας· Εὗρον Psal. 89. 20. supra 7. 45.
Δαυῒδ τὸν τοῦ Ἰεσσαὶ, ἄνδρα κατὰ τὴν καρδίαν μου, ὃς ποιήσει πάντα ʰ 2 Sam. 7. 12. Isa. 11. 1.
23 τὰ θελήματά μου. ʰ Τούτου ὁ Θεὸς ἀπὸ τοῦ σπέρματος κατ' ἐπαγ- ⁱ Mal. 3. 1. Matt. 3. 1. Mark 1. 2.
24 γελίαν ‡ ἤγειρε τῷ Ἰσραὴλ σωτῆρα Ἰησοῦν, ⁱ προκηρύξαντος Ἰωάννου Luke 3. 3. John 3. 28.

testimony is so decidedly in favour of the latter (ἐτροφ. being found in very few MSS.), that if that were *all* we had to consider, it ought to be preferred. *Internal* evidence, however, is also to be taken into the account, and *that* is strongly in favour of the *new* reading. It is the less usual and more *difficult* term, and is far more suitable to the context; ἐτροφοφ. consorting better with ὕψωσεν, and ἐξήγαγεν before. Nay, as Kuin. observes, "the other can scarcely be borne out by facts; for it appears from Ps. xcv. 10. Heb. iii. 17. and other passages, that God did *not* very patiently bear their perversity." Finally, that τροφοφ. is *boni commatis*, is attested by its occurring also in Deut. i. 31, in 2 Macc. vii. 27, and in Macarius; also τροφόφορος in Eustathius. Thus the inferiority in *external* is compensated by the superiority in *internal* testimony; and, accordingly, this knotty point might be only decided "*ad Calendas Græcas*," were we not enabled to call in *another* principle, which may serve to turn the scale. No unprejudiced inquirer can doubt that the Apostle had in view Deut. i. 31; nay, Beng. and Kuin. with much probability, conjecture that Deut. i. and Is. i. were the two chapters of the O. T. which had been read that day. But, upon inspecting the passage, it will be obvious, that τροφοφορέω, and not τροποφορέω, is there the true reading. It is supported by 5-6ths of the MSS. (See Dr. Holmes' Sept.), and by Symm. and Aquila., and is required there by the context. Moreover, the great bulk of the MSS. and the Hebrew require that we should read not τροφοφορήσει, but ἐτροφόρησε, as the Apostle seems to have read. The words of the whole passage are, Εἴδετε — ὡς ἐτροφόρησέ σε Κύριος ὁ Θεός σου, ὡς εἴτις τροφοφορήσαι ἄνθρωπος τὸν υἱὸν αὐτοῦ, κατὰ πᾶσαν τὴν ὁδὸν εἰς ἣν ἐπορεύθητε, ἕως ἤλθετε εἰς τὸν τόπον τοῦτον. Ἐτροφοφόρησε is also confirmed by Numb. xi. 12. Λάβε αὐτὸν (scil. τὸν λαὸν τοῦτον) εἰς τὸν κόλπον σου, ὡσεὶ ἄραι τιθηνὸς τὸν θηλάζοντα, εἰς τὴν γῆν ἣν ὤμοσας τοῖς πατράσιν αὐτῶν; for it is probable that *this* passage *too* was in the mind of the Apostle, and that the two passages are respectively images of *a father carrying his little son over the rough places of a road*, and of a *nurse carrying an infant in her bosom*. *There*, I conceive the image *terminates*; and does not extend to *feeding*, which some ancient Interpreters seem to have thought; as we may infer from the Const. Apost. vii. 36, Hesych., and the Peschito Syriac, Arabic, Coptic, and Æthiopic, and two very ancient Latin Versions. Thus the question at issue has, I apprehend, been finally decided in favour of ἐτροφοφόρησε.

19. κατεκληρονόμησεν.] Such is the reading of many MSS., and several Fathers, and early Editions, which is adopted by almost every Critic and Editor of note, instead of the common reading κατεκληροδότησεν. And justly; for though κατακληροδοτέω is the less usual term, and therefore the other might seem a *gloss*, yet its authority is not very well established. It is found, indeed, in the LXX.; but the MSS. vary.

20. ὡς ἔτεσι τετρ. καὶ π.] As to the discrepancy between this number and that at 1 Kings vi. 1, we need not suppose an error either in one or the other, though the Apostle's number is confirmed by *Josephus*; but (with Mr. Towns.) take the words to mean: "and after these things, which lasted about the space of 450 years, he gave them judges, until Samuel the Prophet," i. e. from the time that God chose the fathers, (which some fix to the birth of Isaac) to the time the land was divided to them by lot, was nearly 450 years; and then God appointed judges in Israel. Or we may suppose (with Lightf. and Perizon.) that in *this* number are reckoned the years of the reigns of the *tyrants*, who occasionally held Israel in subjection during the dynasty of the Judges; and which, when added, make up exactly 450. Thus no error will attach to either passage, and only different modes of computation be supposed to be adopted.

21. ἐκεῖθεν.] This is properly used of *place*; but sometimes of *time*, as here and in Xen. cited by Kuin. Ἔτη τεσσαράκοντα. The truth of this is attested by Josephus. And the Apostle probably derived his information from the same source as the historian, — namely, the ancient records which were preserved in the Temple.

22. εὗρον — θελήματά μου.] The words are compounded of Ps. lxxxix. 20, and 1 Sam. xiii. 14, with some slight modification, on which mode of citing from the O. T. see Note on vii. 7.

— ἄνδρα κατὰ τὴν καρδίαν] viz. in his undeviating pursuit of the plans God would have carried into effect, and in accomplishing His purposes. For καρδία here signifies *will* or *purpose*. Nor is this use merely what the Commentators call it, a *Hebraism*; since similarly in Æschyl. Agam. 9. we have ὧδε γὰρ κρατεῖ γυναικὸς ἀνδρόβουλον, ἐλπίζον κέαρ, for so I would point the passage, which has been admirably emended by Bp. Blomfield; though, had the learned Editor recollected the force of κέαρ just mentioned, he would not have assigned to κρατεῖ the arbitrary and precarious sense of *jubet*, but would have perceived that it denotes simply "has prevailed;" i. e. has obtained its purpose, namely, that it should be so; a signification not unfrequent in Thucydides.

23. ἤγειρε — σωτῆρα Ἰ.] Griesb. and Matth. edit, from several MSS., and some Versions and Fathers, ἤγαγε, supposing the common reading to be a gloss. But though this may seem required by the Canon of preferring the more difficult reading, yet an exception is always allowed where

k John 1. 20, 26, 27. Matt. 3. 11. Mark 1. 7. Luke 3. 16. l Matt. 10. 6. supra 3. 26. & infr. v. 46. m John 16. 3. supra 3. 17. infra 15. 21. 1 Cor. 2. 8. 1 Tim. 1. 13. n Matt. 27. 20, 21, 22. Mark 15. 11, 12, 13. Luke 23. 18, 21, 22, 23. John 19. 6. o Matt. 27. 59. Mark 15. 46. Luke 23. 53. John 19. 38. p Supra 2. 24. q Matt. 28. 2, 16. Mark 16. 6, 14.

πρὸ προσώπου τῆς εἰσόδου αὐτοῦ βάπτισμα μετανοίας παντὶ τῷ λαῷ
Ἰσραήλ. [k] Ὡς δὲ ἐπλήρου ὁ Ἰωάννης τὸν δρόμον, ἔλεγε· Τίνα με 25
ὑπονοεῖτε εἶναι; οὐκ εἰμὶ ἐγώ· ἀλλ᾽ ἰδοὺ, ἔρχεται μετ᾽ ἐμὲ, οὗ οὐκ
εἰμὶ ἄξιος τὸ ὑπόδημα τῶν ποδῶν λῦσαι. [l] Ἄνδρες ἀδελφοὶ, υἱοὶ γένους 26
Ἀβραὰμ, καὶ οἱ ἐν ὑμῖν φοβούμενοι τὸν Θεὸν, ὑμῖν ὁ λόγος τῆς σωτηρίας ταύτης ἀπεστάλη. [m] Οἱ γὰρ κατοικοῦντες ἐν Ἱερουσαλὴμ, καὶ οἱ 27
ἄρχοντες αὐτῶν, τοῦτον ἀγνοήσαντες καὶ τὰς φωνὰς τῶν προφητῶν τὰς
κατὰ πᾶν σάββατον ἀναγινωσκομένας, κρίναντες ἐπλήρωσαν. [n] Καὶ 28
μηδεμίαν αἰτίαν θανάτου εὑρόντες, ᾐτήσαντο Πιλάτον ἀναιρεθῆναι αὐτόν.
[o] Ὡς δὲ ἐτέλεσαν * πάντα τὰ περὶ αὐτοῦ γεγραμμένα, καθελόντες ἀπὸ 29
τοῦ ξύλου, ἔθηκαν εἰς μνημεῖον. [p] Ὁ δὲ Θεὸς ἤγειρεν αὐτὸν ἐκ νεκρῶν· 30
[q] ὃς ὤφθη ἐπὶ ἡμέρας πλείους τοῖς συναναβᾶσιν αὐτῷ ἀπὸ τῆς Γαλι- 31

that reading is at variance with the *norma loquendi*. Now ἤγειν σωτῆρα, as Wets. observes, occurs nowhere; while ἐγείρειν is found in Judg. iii. 9 & 15. Besides, the MSS. in favor of ἤγαγε are comparatively few. And it has little support from Versions; while ἤγειρε is confirmed by the Pesch. Syr. It should seem that ἤγαγε arose merely from an error of the Scribes, who often confound ει (abbrev.) with α, and γ with ρ. It is truly observed by Wets.: "Ἐγείρειν σωτῆρα scribitur Jud. iii. 9. 15. ἄγειν σωτῆρα nusquam." Instead of σωτῆρα Ἰησοῦν Matthæi edits, from several MSS., σωτηρίαν; but rashly; for, as Mill long ago remarked, that reading arose from a mistake of the scribes, who mistook the abbreviation of σρα ιν for σριαν; i. e. the abbreviation of σωτηρίαν. And to this the learned and diligent collator of Biblical MSS., *Rinck*, assents. Σωτ. does *not*, as Matthæi thought, require the Article; because (as Bp. Middleton suggests) "nouns in *apposition*, not explanatory of the essence of the preceding noun, but of the *end* or object, are always anarthrous." See also Luke ii. 11.

24. πρὸ προσώπου.] This corresponds to the Hebr. לִפְנֵי, and simply signifies *before*. Εἰσόδου, "entrance upon his office;" in which sense the word is used in the Classical writers. On βάπτ. μετανοίας, see Note on Matt. iii. 2.

25. ὡς ἐπλήρου.] Render, "when he was finishing his course," i. e. towards the close of his course, or ministry. Τίνα is taken by many eminent Commentators for ὅντινα, in the sense "I am not he whom you suppose me to be." Of this they adduce examples; yet not one where the τις *commences a sentence*. It is therefore better to take the τίνα (according to the common interpretation) as interrogative, and then suppose, in the next sentence, an ellip. of οὗτος; which, when Christ is meant, is often, through reverence, suppressed. There is, besides, more of Pauline spirit in this construction.

27. οἱ γὰρ κατοικοῦντες.] The γὰρ is not *causal*, but has reference to some clause omitted, and may be rendered *etenim*.

— τοῦτον ἀγνοήσαντες — ἐπλήρωσαν.] There is here a difficulty of construction; to remove which several eminent Commentators suppose a *transposition*; and taking κρίναντες with τοῦτον, and ἀγνοήσαντες with τὰς φωνὰς, they assign the following sense: "They who dwelt at Jerusalem in condemning Him, not having known the voices of the prophets, which are read every sabbath day, have fulfilled [the prophecies]." But this does too much violence to the construction to be admitted. It is better (with Grot., Wolf, and Kuin.) to take ἀγνοήσαντες as belonging to both τοῦτον and (by adaptation of signification) to τὰς φωνὰς τ. π., in the sense, "not knowing Him to be the Messiah, and not understanding the words of the prophecy." At κρίναντες (for κατακρ.) sub. αὐτὸν taken from τοῦτον preceding, and render: "by condemning." Ἀγνοήσαντες cannot be again supplied at ἐπλήρωσαν, yet it is *implied*; the meaning being, that they unwittingly fulfilled the prophecies. So Joseph. Bell. iv. 6, 3. adverting to such prophecies, says of the Zelotæ: οἷς οὐκ ἀπιστήσαντες [I conjecture ἐπιστ.] διακόνους ἑαυτοὺς ἐπιδόσαν.

29. καθελόντες — μνημεῖον.] There has been a difficulty started, — that "the same persons who *condemned* Jesus did not *bury* him." To remove which, some Commentators would take the words καθελόντες — ἔθηκαν *impersonally*; and, indeed, active verbs are sometimes taken passively, or even impersonally. But the principle is here inapplicable, and savours too much of a device for the nonce; as does also the method of supplying Ἰουδαῖοι. Grot. and Rosenm. suppose the *Article omitted*; by which the sense will be, "those who took him down," meaning Joseph and his companions. But this is *forcing* a sense on the passage which could not be meant; for to express *that*, the Article must have been used; it being, as Bp. Middl. observes, in such instances *never omitted*. Nay, as he further remarks, even this would not remove the objection; for Joseph and his companions did not take down the body, but the *executioners*. He regards the wording as a trifling inaccuracy; which the Apostle, hastening to the grand subject of the Resurrection, cared not to avoid. It may, however, be doubted, whether there be any inaccuracy at all. It seems to be only a *popular form of expression*, by which any one is said to *do* what he *procures* or permits *to be done* by another. Those who brought about his crucifixion might be familiarly said to *bring him to his grave*, though they did not deposit him there. What the Apostle meant to say is this, — that when they had (unwittingly) done all that was predicted of him [up to his death], they had him taken down and buried [and thought there was then an end of him]. This last clause, though not *expressed*, is perhaps *alluded to* in the adversative δὲ, which commences the next sentence, "But *not so*; — God raised him," &c.

32 λαίας εἰς Ἱερουσαλήμ, οἵτινές εἰσι μάρτυρες αὐτοῦ πρὸς τὸν λαόν. [r] Καὶ
ἡμεῖς ὑμᾶς εὐαγγελιζόμεθα τὴν πρὸς τοὺς πατέρας ἐπαγγελίαν γενομέ-
νην· ὅτι ταύτην ὁ Θεὸς ἐκπεπλήρωκε τοῖς τέκνοις αὐτῶν ἡμῖν, ἀνα-
33 στήσας Ἰησοῦν· [s] ὡς καὶ ἐν τῷ ψαλμῷ τῷ δευτέρῳ γέγραπται· Υἱός
34 μου εἶ σύ, ἐγὼ σήμερον γεγέννηκά σε. [t] Ὅτι δὲ ἀνέστησεν
αὐτὸν ἐκ νεκρῶν, μηκέτι μέλλοντα ὑποστρέφειν εἰς διαφθοράν, οὕτως
35 εἴρηκεν· Ὅτι δώσω ὑμῖν τὰ ὅσια Δαυῒδ τὰ πιστά. [u] Διὸ
καὶ ἐν ἑτέρῳ λέγει· Οὐ δώσεις τὸν ὅσιόν σου ἰδεῖν δια-
36 φθοράν. [x] Δαυῒδ μὲν γὰρ ἰδίᾳ γενεᾷ ὑπηρετήσας τῇ τοῦ Θεοῦ βουλῇ,
ἐκοιμήθη, καὶ προσετέθη πρὸς τοὺς πατέρας αὐτοῦ, καὶ εἶδε διαφθο-
37 ράν· ὃν δὲ ὁ Θεὸς ἤγειρεν, οὐκ εἶδε διαφθοράν. [y] Γνωστὸν οὖν ἔστω

Luke 24. 36. John 20. 19. & 21. 1. supra 1. 3. 1 Cor. 15. 5, 6.
r Gen. 3. 15. & 22. 18. & 26. 4. & 49. 10. Deut. 18. 15. 2 Sam. 7. 12. Psal. 132. 11. Isa. 4. 2. & 7. 14. & 9. 6. & 40. 10. Jer. 23. 5. & 33. 14. Ezek. 34. 23. & 37. 24. Dan. 9. 24, 25.
s Psal. 2. 7. Heb. 1. 5. & 5. 5.
t Isa. 55. 3.
u Psal. 16. 10.

32. καὶ ἡμεῖς ὑμᾶς εὐαγγ. &c.] There is here a certain perplexity of construction, which some seek to remove by taking ἐπαγγελίαν for the *fulfilment* of the promise. But that is straining the interpretation. It is *better*, with Bengel, Heum., Heinr., and Kuin., to suppose a sort of Hebraic *synchysis*, by which the ταύτην just after is redundant, laying down the following construction: εὐαγγελιζόμεθα, ὅτι τὴν πρὸς τοὺς πατέρας γενομένην ἐπαγγελίαν ὁ Θεὸς ἐκπεπλήρωκε. To this method these Critics resort, because an Accus. of *thing* after that of *person* with εὐαγγ. is, they say, unexampled. A somewhat bold assertion, which seems contradicted by the *present passage*, and certainly is so by Rev. xiv. 6. εἶδον ἄλλον ἄγγελον — ἔχοντα εὐαγγέλιον αἰώνιον εὐαγγελίσαι τοὺς κατοικοῦντας ἐπὶ τῆς γῆς, in which construction the Accus. of person comes first. And indeed εὐαγγ. often occurs in the N. T. with the accus. of person. So Luke iii. 18. πολλὰ μὲν — εὐηγγελίζετο τὸν λαόν. The Accus. of *thing* may depend on some preposition understood; or rather on ἀγγέλλοντες to be fetched, *per synesin*, out of the verb. Here, at any rate, it must be supplied before ὅτι ταύτην, &c. Those who have any thing promised them, are in Scripture peculiarly said εὐαγγελίζεσθαι. So Heb. iv. 2. καὶ γάρ ἐσμεν εὐηγγελισμένοι, "to us pertains that promise." Thus it appears that the above *synchysis* need not be supposed to exist.

33. υἱός μου — σε.] "It is not (Mr. Holden observes) meant, that by raising up Jesus from the dead, God begat him in the relation of a Son; but that by raising him, God declared him to be the Messiah, according to the promise made to the fathers, ver. 32; and also, that by so raising him, he declared him to be his *only begotten Son*, according to what is written at Ps. ii. 7. Thus the Apostle states the resurrection as a *proof* that in Christ was fulfilled the *promise unto the fathers*, and the prophecy in Ps. xi.: for though the words had probably a primary reference to David, yet it bore a *secondary* and more important reference to *Christ*. So also, in the next verse, the Apostle proves that the Messiah promised to the fathers was to be raised from the dead without undergoing corruption."

34. ὅτι δὲ — εἴρηκεν.] The reasoning seems to be, that "it might be *inferred* that the resurrection in question would be *final and permanent*, from the words which God had spoken by his prophet (Is. lv. 4.) as follows: 'I will give,' &c." The Apostle does not *add*, *de suo*, ὅτι δώσω ὑμῖν, but he merely *introduces* δώσω, because in the clause in question it is to be *supplied* from the preceding one, διαθήσομαι, &c. And thus it *is* supplied in Bp. Lowth's version. Ὅσια is by most interpreters explained "*mercies*," by some "*benefits*," which latter sense is preferable. Yet Tittm. de Synon. p. 25. denies that ὅσια can mean this; and he (with Bp. Pearce) takes the sense of τὰ ὅσια to be "the sacred things of David," i. e. the *covenant made with David, and confirmed by an oath*; meaning the *performance* of it. And thus τὰ ὅσια πιστὰ will be equivalent to the ὅρκια πιστὰ of Homer. But there is surely a *greater* difficulty in regarding τὰ ὅσια as taken in so far-fetched a sense. And unless we suppose that the Sept. Translators entirely mistook the sense of the Hebrew חסדי, we can scarcely render otherwise than "the benefits mercifully promised;" as in 2 Chron. vi. 42. Schleus. in his Lex. adduces an example of this sense of τὸ ὅσιον (benefit) from Clemens. Ep. ad Corinth. Cap. 1. πόσα δὲ αὐτῷ (scil. Christo) ὀφείλομεν ὅσια. The Apostle argues, that these merciful promises have been proved to be *sure* and true by their *fulfilment* in the resurrection of Jesus; which resurrection (so accomplished as that, agreeably to the prophecy at Ps. xvi. 10, his body did not experience that corruption which results from permanent death) proved him to be the Messiah promised to the Fathers.

36. The Apostle here proceeds to show, that those words are not applicable to *David*; and then leaves it to be inferred that the person there meant must be *Jesus*, — the only one who had been so raised from the dead as not to *return* thither, or experience corruption. The construction has been thought doubtful; since ὑπηρετήσας may be construed either with ἰδίᾳ γενεᾷ, or with τῇ τοῦ Θεοῦ βουλῇ. The *former* method is adopted by some Interpreters and the E. V.; but the *latter* is the more natural construction, and yields a better sense; and such as is very applicable to one who was "the man after God's own heart," by accomplishing his purposes. See ver. 22. It is also confirmed by the ancient Versions, and by the use of the word in the Classical writers, — where ὑπηρετεῖν is often followed by a noun signifying *wishes*, *commands*, &c. Ἰδίᾳ γενεᾷ, "in his own generation," or age. See Luke xvi. 8.

— προσετέθη πρὸς τοὺς π.] An expression derived from the O. T. (as Gen. xlix. 29. xxv. 8. Judg. ii. 10.), in which there is an allusion to those vast *caves*, or *subterraneous vaults*, in which the Hebrews (as also the Egyptians, Babylonians, and other Oriental nations) used to deposit the dead of a whole family or race; sometimes arranged in recesses by the side of the vault, and sometimes

supra 2. 27, &c. x 1 Kings 2. 10. ὑμῖν, ἄνδρες ἀδελφοί, ὅτι διὰ τούτου ὑμῖν ἄφεσις ἁμαρτιῶν καταγγέλ- 38
supra 2. 29. y Luke 24. 47. λεται· ʸ καὶ ἀπὸ πάντων, ὧν οὐκ ἠδυνήθητε ἐν τῷ νόμῳ Μωϋσέως 39
1 John 2. 12. Rom. 3. 24, 28. δικαιωθῆναι, ἐν τούτῳ πᾶς ὁ πιστεύων δικαιοῦται. Βλέπετε οὖν, μὴ 40
& 8. 3. Gal. 2. 16. ἐπέλθῃ ἐφ᾽ ὑμᾶς τὸ εἰρημένον ἐν τοῖς προφήταις· ᵃ Ἴδετε, οἱ 41
Heb. 7. 19. & 9. 15. z Rom. 10. 4. a Habak. 1. 5. καταφρονηταί, καὶ θαυμάσατε, καὶ ἀφανίσθητε· ὅτι
ἔργον ἐγὼ ἐργάζομαι ἐν ταῖς ἡμέραις ὑμῶν, ἔργον ᾧ
οὐ μὴ πιστεύσητε, ἐάν τις ἐκδιηγῆται ὑμῖν.
Ἐξιόντων δὲ αὐτῶν [ἐκ τῆς συναγωγῆς τῶν Ἰουδαίων] παρεκάλουν 42
[τὰ ἔθνη] εἰς τὸ μεταξὺ σάββατον λαληθῆναι αὐτοῖς τὰ ῥήματα ταῦτα.

laid upon each other, until the place was quite full of bodies.

38, 39. The Apostle now *applies* the doctrine which he has already stated and proved, and proceeds, by inference, to show the *benefits* to be obtained by faith in the Messiahship of Jesus, and to point out the great superiority of the justification and remission of sins to be attained through him over that supplied by the Law of Moses. In short, here (as Dr. Hales observes) he states the doctrine of justification by *faith*, which forms the basis of the argument in his Epistles to the Romans, Galatians, and Hebrews. The *full sense* of the passage is thus ably traced and pointed out by Bp. Bull, Harm. Evang. p. 58, and Examen Censuræ, p. 89: "Duo videtur Apostolus affirmare, nempe, non tantùm per Jesum remissionem peccatorum, spiritualem sc. (quam Lex non omnino concessit) annunciari; sed et credentem justificari in ipso ab omnibus, à quibus nemo per Legem Mosis (ne carnaliter quidem) justificari poterat. Hinc infert Apostolus, non quærendam in Lege Mosaica Justificationem, sed confugiendum ad aliud plenioris misericordiæ Fœdus, nempe Fœdus illud in Christi Jesu Sanguine stabilitum." They could not be justified even *carnaliter*, since, as Mr. Scott observes, "the only effect of the sacrifices and purgations of the Mosaic law was admission into the congregation again, whence the breach of some positive ceremony had excluded a man: and some offences punishable with death admitted no sacrifice at all. Whereas this atonement of Christ reaches to the perfect and eternal forgiveness of every kind and degree of transgression in them that sincerely believe and obey him."

40. To this *encouragement to faith*, intended for the well-disposed, the Apostle subjoins a *warning*, meant for the refractory. Ἐν τοῖς προφ., i. e. that division of the O. T. called the Prophets. See Note on John vi. 45.

41. Ἴδετε, &c.] A citation from Habak. 1. 5. (though a similar apostrophe in Is. xxviii. 14. may have been in the mind of St. Paul) in which a word is omitted not necessary to the sense, and one or two supplied to make it clearer. Both the Apostle and the LXX. vary from the Hebrew, as regards οἱ καταφρονηταὶ and ἀφανίσθητε, in the former instance preserving the true reading, which seems to be not בגוים, but בגדים, which is read in some MSS., and confirmed by the Syriac and Arabic Versions. With ἀφαν. there is more of difficulty. The common version "Perish" is generally considered indefensible, as not even warranted by the Hebrew; and Beza, Doddr., Pearce, Wakef., Schleus., Wahl., and Kuin., render "*disappear*," viz. for *shame* and fear; a sense which Schleus. thinks reconcileable with the Hebrew, since שמם signifies both *vastari* and *stupere*. If so, the LXX. took the *worse* signification. But probably they read differently, namely, instead of תמהו, they read והשמו, *and be exceedingly amazed*. This I suspect to be the true reading in the Hebrew; for the letters might easily be confounded, and a ו lost after a ו. Thus there will be a *climax*; משם or השמם being a far stronger term (namely, to be destroyed, i. e. die, with amazement) than תמה. What idea St. Paul himself would have affixed to the word, as it respected the prophecy, we cannot know. But it should seem that he took occasion, from the ambiguity of signification, to hint to his unbelieving hearers a warning as to the consequences of their unbelief and rejection of the Messiah. The "*work*" was the *ruin of their country*, which certainly happened in *their time*, since it was done not many years afterwards.

42. There is in this verse much diversity of reading, and consequently variety of interpretations. Almost all the recent Editors are agreed in inserting αὐτῶν (for which there is great authority in MSS., Versions, Fathers, and early Edd.), and cancelling ἐκ τῆς — Ἰουδαίων and τὰ ἔθνη, with as great authority. Matth., however, retains τὰ ἔθνη, which may certainly be tolerated if the words be taken to denote the Jewish *proselytes*, mentioned in the next verse. But they are probably from the margin; as also, it should seem, are ἐκ τῆς — Ἰουδαίων, though the objection which Kuin. makes to τῶν Ἰ. (that of being useless and offensive) is refuted by xiv. 1. And after all, *both* the passages *may* be genuine, and have been excluded by the early Critics on the same grounds (some of them false) that they are objected to by Kuin. Or perhaps τῶν Ἰ. *only* may have come from the margin, as meant to denote the *subject* of the participle ἐξιόντων, as τὰ ἔθνη would seem to be meant to supply that of the verb παρεκάλουν. There is not a more frequent cause of marginal glosses (often *introduced into the text*) than when verbs or participles absolute are put without a subject. In the present instance, τῶν Ἰ. seems to have been supplied to αὐτῶν, and ἐκ τῆς συν. to ἐξιόντων, and finally τὰ ἔθνη to παρεκάλουν: introduced, I suspect, *after* τῶν Ἰ. The whole passage may be thus rendered: "As they (i. e. Paul and Barnabas) were departing from the synagogue, they (i. e. the congregation, or the Gentile proselytes) expressed a desire that these words might be spoken to them (i. e. that the same subject should be treated of) on the next sabbath day. And when the synagogue had broken up, many of the Jews and devout proselytes followed Paul and Barnabas." Paul and Barnabas did *not* go out, as Kuin. chooses to take for granted, *before the conclusion of the service*;

43 [b] λυθείσης δὲ τῆς συναγωγῆς, ἠκολούθησαν πολλοὶ τῶν Ἰουδαίων καὶ b Matt. 23. 15. supra 11. 23. infra 14. 22.
τῶν σεβομένων προσηλύτων τῷ Παύλῳ καὶ τῷ Βαρνάβᾳ· οἵτινες
προσλαλοῦντες αὐτοῖς, ἔπειθον αὐτοὺς ἐπιμένειν τῇ χάριτι τοῦ Θεοῦ.
44 Τῷ δὲ ἐρχομένῳ σαββάτῳ σχεδὸν πᾶσα ἡ πόλις συνήχθη ἀκοῦσαι τὸν
45 λόγον τοῦ Θεοῦ. Ἰδόντες δὲ οἱ Ἰουδαῖοι τοὺς ὄχλους, ἐπλήσθησαν c Matt. 10. 6.
ζήλου, καὶ ἀντέλεγον τοῖς ὑπὸ τοῦ Παύλου λεγομένοις, ἀντιλέγοντες supra 1. 8. & 3. 26, 26. & 13. 26.
46 καὶ βλασφημοῦντες. [c] Παῤῥησιασάμενοι δὲ ὁ Παῦλος καὶ ὁ Βαρνάβας infra 18. 6. & 28. 28.
εἶπον· Ὑμῖν ἦν ἀναγκαῖον πρῶτον λαληθῆναι τὸν λόγον τοῦ Θεοῦ· Exod. 32. 10. Deut. 32. 21.
ἐπειδὴ δὲ ἀπωθεῖσθε αὐτὸν, καὶ οὐκ ἀξίους κρίνετε ἑαυτοὺς τῆς αἰω- Isa. 55. 5. Matt. 8. 12. & 21. 43.
47 νίου ζωῆς, ἰδοὺ στρεφόμεθα εἰς τὰ ἔθνη. [d] οὕτω γὰρ ἐντέταλται ἡμῖν Rom. 10. 19. d Isa. 49. 6.
ὁ Κύριος· Τέθεικά σε εἰς φῶς ἐθνῶν, τοῦ εἶναί σε & 42. 6. Luke 2. 32.

for the service, except a brief concluding prayer, terminated with the *discourse;* but we are only to understand that they went out *first*, accompanied probably by the rulers of the synagogue; the people meanwhile reverently keeping their seats; and on their having left the place, the whole congregation broke up and departed.

The words *εἰς τὸ μεταξὺ σάββ.* are by many Commentators supposed to mean "on some intermediate week day." But that is refuted by v. 44., and the sense expressed in our common Version is, no doubt, the true one. It is adopted by the best recent Commentators, and confirmed by the ancient Versions. *Μεταξὺ* in the later writers has often the sense *post*. It is here put for *μετὰ τοῦτο*.

43. *ἐπιμένειν — Θεοῦ*] i. e. to perseverance in their belief of the Gospel, called also in 2 Cor. vi. 1. Phil. i. 7. Heb. xiii. 9. *κατ' ἐξοχὴν*, the *grace* of God, "as containing (says Doddr.) the richest display of his grace, i. e. the free pardon of our sins by Christ, and the provision he hath made for our sanctification and eternal happiness." See Rom. vi. 4. Col. i. 6.

44. *ἐρχομένῳ.*] Griesb., Knapp, and Tittm., edit, from 7 MSS., *ἐχομένῳ*, which Rinck approves, on the ground of its being the more learned and apt reading. And certainly this would hold good in an elegant *Classic:* but for that very reason *ἐχομ.* may be suspected to have come from the *ancient Critics*. Especially as the MSS. in which it is found are mostly such as have been *altered*. And as *τῇ δὲ ἐρχομένῃ* scil. *ἡμέρᾳ* is found not unfrequently in *Joseph.*, nay, *ἔτους ἐρχομένου* in Thucyd., who has not a few *archaisms*, we may suppose that this use of *ἐρχ.* for *ἐπερχ.* was an idiom of the popular dialect, derived from antique and perhaps Oriental use.

45. *ἀντιλέγοντες καὶ βλ.*] "both contradicting and reviling," i. e. adding insult to opposition. *Ἀντιλ. καὶ* are omitted in several MSS. and Versions, and marked as probably to be cancelled by Griesb. But they were manifestly thrown out by the early Critics, who, it seems, stumbled at the tautology. The reading *ἐναντιούμενοι* for *ἀντιλ.*, found in a few MSS. and preferred by Grot., Beza, and Beng., is only *another* mode of removing the tautology.

46. *ἀναγκαῖον*] i. e. by being so ordained in the counsels of God.

— *καὶ οὐκ ἀξίους — ζωῆς*] i. e. since you act as if ye judged yourselves unworthy of, &c. Whether it be a *metonymy*, as the Commentators regard it, or not, this is certainly a *delicate turn*, such as is found in the best writers, from whom examples are adduced by Wets.

— *στρεφόμεθα εἰς τὰ ἔθνη.*] We are not to understand by this, that Paul gave up the Jews, and became the Apostle of the Gentiles only; for he became such much later, and even then never to the *abandonment* of the *Jews*. In fact, the Jews of *Antioch* alone are meant; and by *τὰ ἔθνη* not the Gentiles at large, nor even the Gentiles of Antioch only, but chiefly the Gentile proselytes before mentioned; though the Gentiles at large may be *included*, since the Apostle would have been as ready to admit *them* as converts, as he had been to admit the Proconsul. That he deemed himself at full liberty to do this, is plain from the *application* which he gives to the words of Isaiah xlix. 6., which he now adduces as his authority.

47. *τέθεικά σε εἰς φῶς, &c.*] The words exactly correspond to the LXX., at least in the Alexandrian and other MSS., though the common text (formed on the Vatican MS.) has *δέδωκα* for *τέθεικα*, which is the more literal version of the Hebrew, of which *τεθ.* is a *free* rendering. In the common text are added *εἰς διαθήκην γένους*, of which the sense is, "as a bequest to the nation." But I suspect the words to have come from the margin. *Τέθεικα* should be rendered, "I have appointed," or "ordained." It is strange that Kuin. should consider this passage as properly applicable to *Isaiah* only, and his calling to the prophetical office, and merely *accommodated* by St. Paul to his own case. The words are scarcely applicable to the Prophet *at all*, and there are *many* parts of the Chapter, from whence this passage is taken, that *cannot possibly* apply to the *Prophet*, and have no propriety but as referred to the *Messiah*, "whose character and office (to use the words of Bp. Lowth) were exhibited in *general* terms at the beginning of Chap. xlii., but here is introduced *in person*, declaring the full extent of his commision; which is not only to restore the Israelites, and reconcile them to their Lord and Father, from whom they had so often revolted; but to be a light to lighten the Gentiles, to call them to the knowledge and obedience of the true God, and to bring them to be one church together with the Israelites, and to partake with them of the same common salvation procured for all by the great Redeemer and Reconciler of man to God." This passage of the Prophet might well be said to be *their warrant* for preaching to the Gentiles; and in some sense contains an *injunction*, since the Messiah could only be a light and salvation to the Gentiles by the means of those

εἰς σωτηρίαν ἕως ἐσχάτου τῆς γῆς. ἀκούοντα δὲ τὰ ἔθνη 48 ἔχαιρον, καὶ ἐδόξαζον τὸν λόγον τοῦ Κυρίου· καὶ ἐπίστευσαν ὅσοι

who should spread his Gospel. Paul, however, himself had received a sort of *positive* injunction, since (as we find from Acts xxii. 17—21.) on his first visit to Jerusalem after his conversion, Jesus appeared to him in a trance and said, "Depart, for I will send thee hence far off to the Gentiles."

48. ἐδόξαζον τὸν λόγον τοῦ Κ.] i. e. recognized the excellency of it, as worthy the impartiality of the God of the whole universe.

—καὶ ἐπίστευσαν ὅσοι —αἰώνιον.] There are few passages of which the interpretation has been more warmly debated than the present; and that from its being supposed to involve an important doctrine. Most Calvinistic Interpreters take τεταγμένοι εἰς to mean *fore-ordained*, or *predestinated unto*, by *God's decree;* the persons in question being represented as *believing under that decree*. In refutation of which, some Anti-Calvinistic Commentators rather apply themselves to show that the doctrines of Calvinism are untenable, than that they cannot be found here. But the only question before us is, what may be supposed to be the true sense of the words τεταγμένοι εἰς ζωὴν αἰώνιον, in their present position. Now there would seem to be no vestige of any thing savouring of an absolute decree, or predestination. The expression is not προτεταγμένοι, (much less, as invariable usage elsewhere would require, προωρισμένοι), but simply τεταγμένοι. There is neither προ nor any thing equivalent. We have besides, no mention of *God*, no such addition as ὑπὸ τοῦ Θεοῦ. Objections which are sufficiently obvious, and which have been strongly urged by Grot., Hamm., Wolf, Whitby, and A. Clarke. Though, indeed, were those *all* that could be urged against the interpretation in question, they might perhaps be deemed insufficient to disallow it. For τεταγμένοι *might* (though there is no *proof* of any such sense either in the Scriptural or Classical writers) mean *destined*. And if *destined* could be *supposed* to be the sense, the argument founded on the omission of ὑπὸ τοῦ Θεοῦ would not be of any great weight, since that might be thought *understood*, as in Eph. i. 11. προορισθέντες κατὰ πρόθεσιν, &c. Thus the sense which the above Commentators assign *might*, after all, be tolerated if *the context would permit it*. But that is by no means the case. There is assuredly nothing, either in the context, or in the language used by St. Luke, either in this Book or in his Gospel, that can lead us to suppose any such sense intended here: nay, there is not a little that utterly *excludes* it. This, however, is a field into which our limits will not permit us to enter. See Hamm. cited in Recens. Synop. Suffice it to say (confining ourselves to the *context*) that it is forbidden by the word ἐπίστευσαν, which, under the present circumstances, can mean no more than, that they "believed in the Lord Jesus, and received the religion which he came to promulgate." Yet it cannot be supposed that *all* who did so were predestined to eternal salvation. "There were, doubtless, (as Schoettg. observes), among those believers, many hypocrites and evil livers; who eagerly enough embraced the *theoretical truth*, but cared not for the *practice*. These, then, could not be predestined." And we do not find that those who believed at *other* times were *predestined;* some *falling away*, as is represented in the parable of the Sower. Nor is it likely that such as believed should come in all at once, but gradually. Ἐπίστευσαν, then, can have no reference to their *persevering* or not persevering. Besides, as the best Commentators are agreed (see Grot., Hamm., Whitby, Schoettg., Rosenm., and Kuin.) there is here an *opposition*, arising from a tacit comparison between the conduct of these Gentiles, on the one hand, and of the Jews, on the other. The Gentiles (τεταγμένοι εἰς ζωὴν αἰώνιον, and who accordingly received the Gospel) are contrasted with the Jews mentioned at ver. 46., who, by rejecting it, acted as if they thought themselves not worthy of eternal life. In short, ἀπωθεῖσθε τὸν λόγον τοῦ Θεοῦ is there opposed to ἐδόξαζον τὸν λόγον τοῦ Κυρίου; and οὐκ ἀξίους κρίνετε ἑαυτοὺς τῆς αἰωνίου ζωῆς, to ἦσαν τεταγμένοι εἰς ζωὴν αἰώνιον. See Krebs and Wets. And as no *absolute decree* can, by the words ὑμῖν ἦν ἀναγκαῖον — λόγον τοῦ Θεοῦ be supposed in the *latter* case, (see the able Note of Whitby) so none must be supposed in the *former*. The former act was voluntary, and so must the latter.

Having, then, seen what *cannot be* the meaning of the words, let us examine what *is* probably their sense. And in order to that, let us advert to their *construction*. Now here I would not adopt the construction laid down by many Interpreters of consideration, who would connect εἰς ζωὴν with ἐπίστευσαν. That is too violent a method, and requires an authorized sense to be assigned to ζωὴν αἰώνιον. The natural construction must be preserved, and such a sense assigned to τεταγ. as may be suitable to εἰς ζωὴν αἰώνιον, and is permitted by the usage of the Scriptural as well as the Classical writers. Many eminent Commentators trace in τεταγ. a *military* metaphor, and take the sense to be, "those who had arrayed themselves for salvation," namely, by hearing the word of God, and not resisting the work of the Holy Spirit on their hearts. Thus taking the passive here in a *reciprocal* sense; than which nothing is more common. Yet there is something so *far-fetched* in this *military* metaphor, that almost all the above Expositors are compelled to abandon it, when they descend to *full* explanation. It should seem best neither, on the one hand, to fancy any deeply recondite theological mystery, nor, on the other, to suppose any far-fetched allusion; but to take the words in their plain and popular acceptation. Now τάσσεσθαι εἰς sometimes signifies to be *thoroughly disposed for*, or *purposed for, bent on;* (like the expression εὔθετος εἶναι εἰς) where the *middle* or *reciprocal* force is very apparent, as often in Josephus. And this may justly be supposed the sense here intended. Of this signification examples are adduced by Krebs and Loesner; of which none, Bp. Middl. thinks, is so much to the purpose as that from Max. Tyr. Diss. x. p. 102. (Heins.) ἐπὶ σαρκῶν ἡδονὰς συντεταγμένος. Yet had the learned Prelate examined the passage in the best editions (namely, those of Davies and Reiske), he would have found that they have there edited, from some MSS., συντεταμένος, *immodice intentus*. In so editing, however, they were *wrong;* for though the context requires the sense *bent on, entirely disposed for*, yet that is no proof that συντεταμένος is the true reading. It may rather be suspected of being a *conjecture* suggested by the context. I have no doubt that τεταγμένος, the old reading, is the right one; and that the συν is not genuine, but arose from the ς preceding:

49 ἦσαν τεταγμένοι εἰς ζωὴν αἰώνιον. διεφέρετο δὲ ὁ λόγος τοῦ Κυρίου
50 δι' ὅλης τῆς χώρας. [e] οἱ δὲ Ἰουδαῖοι παρώτρυναν τὰς σεβομένας γυ- [e] 2 Tim. 3. 11.
ναῖκας καὶ τὰς εὐσχήμονας, καὶ τοὺς πρώτους τῆς πόλεως, καὶ ἐπήγειραν
διωγμὸν ἐπὶ τὸν Παῦλον καὶ τὸν Βαρνάβαν, καὶ ἐξέβαλον αὐτοὺς ἀπὸ
51 τῶν ὁρίων αὐτῶν. [f] Οἱ δὲ ἐκτιναξάμενοι τὸν κονιορτὸν τῶν ποδῶν [f] Matt. 10. 14. Mark 6. 11. Luke 9. 5. infra 14. 6, 11. & 18. 6.
52 αὐτῶν ἐπ' αὐτούς, ἦλθον εἰς Ἰκόνιον. οἱ δὲ μαθηταὶ ἐπληροῦντο χα-
ρᾶς καὶ Πνεύματος ἁγίου.
1 XIV. ἘΓΕΝΕΤΟ δὲ ἐν Ἰκονίῳ, κατὰ τὸ αὐτὸ εἰσελθεῖν αὐτοὺς
εἰς τὴν συναγωγὴν τῶν Ἰουδαίων, καὶ λαλῆσαι οὕτως ὥστε πιστεῦσαι

for it is well known that συν in composition was often written in MSS. σ. Thus the passage in question is even more apposite than Bp. Middl. considered it; τεταγμένος of itself giving the required sense. To the examples above mentioned I am enabled to add others from Plato de Legg. vi. p. 563. φύσις εἰς ἀρετὴν τεταγμένη. 2 Macc. vi. 21. οἱ δὲ πρὸς τῷ σπλαγχνισμῷ τεταγμένοι. Ps. lviii. 1. "Are your minds set upon righteousness?" In all which cases the *middle* sense is very apparent, and confirms the remark of Chrysost. that the expression τεταγμένοι is employed to show that the thing is not a matter of *necessity*, or what is *compulsory*. Thus, so far from favouring the system of *absolute election*, the words rather support the *opposite* doctrine, namely, that God, while "binding nature fast in fate, left free the human will."

The above, then, is very probably the true sense of the passage. Though even if the sense *ordained* were retained, it would not necessarily involve the doctrine of predestination. For in *this context* such would be (as has been seen) quite out of place. In that case we might, with the most eminent of the recent Commentators, as Morus, Schoettg. Rosenm., and Kuin., suppose the expression meant according to the usage of common life, without any reference to metaphysical subtilties, and not to the exclusion of all *conditions* or all means on the part of man for obtaining salvation; which would be opposed to Phil. ii. 13. seqq. It being in the expression τεταγμένος understood and *supposed* that the *cause* of their being so ordained or destined was *their faith*. This is confirmed by the Rabbinical citations adduced by Lightf., Schoettg., and Wets., from which it is plain that the expressions "to be ordained or destined to eternal life, or eternal destruction," were in frequent use among the Rabbis, but not with any reference to any *decree*, or to the exclusion of conditions; e. gr. Midrasch Mischle, 16. 4. Si non facit pœnitentiam, ordinatus est ad judicium gehennæ. In his Note on the present passage, Calvin, as may be supposed, strenuously maintains the sense of *predestination*; but with singular want of success. What Hamm. says of "the *no-reasons* produced that incline it that way," is entirely applicable to Calvin's note. The only attempt at argument he makes, is, that St. Luke does not say ordinati ad fidem, but ordinati ad vitam. But that is a most frivolous objection: for if *such* an expression had been employed, it would certainly have been one less pertinent than any other to be found elsewhere in the same writer. Whereas that of *ordinati ad vitam*, contains a sense at once profound and worthy of the Evangelist; the full meaning being — "whose minds were in a fit state to judge of the evidence for the truth of the Gospel, who were seriously concerned about their salvation, and were thoroughly *disposed* to make all sacrifices to obtain eternal life." Indeed, it argues little knowledge of human nature ("what is in man") not to see that the sacred writer has here reference, not to a mysterious theological doctrine, but (with a deep knowledge of human nature *as it is*) has respect to those powerful *moral motives* which induce the will and govern the man. "Hopes and fears (says the great Dr. South) govern all things. They are the two great handles by which the will of man is to be taken hold of, when we would either draw it *to* duty, or draw it off from sin. [Hence he who holds the *conscience*, holds the man.—Ed.] They are the most efficacious means to bring such things home to the will as are apt to work upon it. Every man, in all that concerns him, here stands influenced by his hopes and fears; and those by rewards and punishments, the proper objects thereof. And the *Divine law* is the grand adamantine ligament, tying both of them fast together, by assuring rewards to our hopes, and punishments to our fears. So that man being bound by the peremptory decree of heaven, must by virtue thereof, indispensably *obey* or *suffer*." At the same time, while we contend that the doctrine of predestination can by no means be found *here*, yet it is proper to bear in mind that the *dispositions* of the persons in question could not have been what they were, or have been originally such, from themselves; but must be ascribed to the *preventing grace* of God, to which it is owing that men are ever disposed to embrace or obey the Gospel of Christ.

50. τὰς εὐσχήμονας] "women of rank." See Note on Mark xv. 43.

— ἐξέβαλον ἀπὸ τῶν ὁρίων.] These may seem strong terms. But we need not suppose that *force* was employed in removing the Apostles; which, as no *resistance* was made, would have been unnecessary. This kind of *order for departure* used to be given in due form; and there were sometimes officers appointed to superintend the execution of it, by conducting the person over the borders. So Thucyd. ii. 12. καὶ ἐκέλευον ἐκτὸς ὅρων εἶναι αὐθημερὸν, ξυμπέμπουσί τε ἀγωγούς.

52. χαρᾶς] "the consolations of the Gospel." Πνεύμ. ἁγ. This must be explained of the gifts and graces of the Holy Spirit for *sanctification*, and not for *working miracles*, since hands had not been laid upon them for that purpose.

XIV. 1. κατὰ τὸ αὐτό.] The earlier Commentators suppose an ellip. of ἔθος. But it is better, with the later ones, to take it as equivalent to ἐπὶ τὸ αὐτό; Heysch. explaining it by ὁμοῦ, and both

Ἰουδαίων τε καὶ Ἑλλήνων πολὺ πλῆθος. Οἱ δὲ ἀπειθοῦντες Ἰουδαῖοι 2
ἐπήγειραν καὶ ἐκάκωσαν τὰς ψυχὰς τῶν ἐθνῶν κατὰ τῶν ἀδελφῶν.
g Mark 16. 20. infra 19. 11. Heb. 2. 4. [g] ἱκανὸν μὲν οὖν χρόνον διέτριψαν παῤῥησιαζόμενοι ἐπὶ τῷ Κυρίῳ τῷ 3
μαρτυροῦντι τῷ λόγῳ τῆς χάριτος αὐτοῦ, [καὶ] διδόντι σημεῖα καὶ
τέρατα γίνεσθαι διὰ τῶν χειρῶν αὐτῶν. Ἐσχίσθη δὲ τὸ πλῆθος τῆς 4
πόλεως· καὶ οἱ μὲν ἦσαν σὺν τοῖς Ἰουδαίοις, οἱ δὲ σὺν τοῖς ἀποστό-
h 2 Tim. 3. 11. λοις. [h] Ὡς δὲ ἐγένετο ὁρμὴ τῶν ἐθνῶν τε καὶ Ἰουδαίων σὺν τοῖς 5
i Matt. 10. 23. supra 8. 1. ἄρχουσιν αὐτῶν, ὑβρίσαι καὶ λιθοβολῆσαι αὐτοὺς, [i] συνιδόντες κατέφυ- 6
γον εἰς τὰς πόλεις τῆς Λυκαονίας, Λύστραν καὶ Δέρβην, καὶ τὴν περί-
χωρον, κἀκεῖ ἦσαν εὐαγγελιζόμενοι. 7
k Supra 3. 2. [k] Καί τις ἀνὴρ ἐν Λύστροις ἀδύνατος τοῖς ποσὶν ἐκάθητο, χωλὸς ἐκ 8
κοιλίας μητρὸς αὐτοῦ ὑπάρχων, ὃς οὐδέποτε περιεπεπατήκει. Οὗτος 9
ἤκουε τοῦ Παύλου λαλοῦντος· ὃς ἀτενίσας αὐτῷ, καὶ ἰδὼν ὅτι πίστιν

expressions being used by the LXX. to express the Hebr. ירע. By Ἑλλήνων are meant τῶν σεβομένων Ἑλλ. as they are called at xvii. 4.; equivalent, it should seem, to τῶν σεβομένων προσηλύτων at v. 43.

2. ἀπειθοῦντες] "refusing belief, unbelieving," μὴ πιστεύοντες. A sense occurring also at xvii. 5; xix. 9. John iii. 36. Heb. xi. 31, but rarely found in the Classical writers. Yet it occurs in Hom. Od. ν. 43. It generally means to refuse *obedience*.

— ἐπήγειραν — ἀδελφῶν.] Kypke and Krebs maintain that the true construction is, ἐπὶ τὰς ψυχὰς τῶν ἐθνῶν κατὰ τῶν ἀδ., καὶ ἐκάκωσαν. And it is true that τὰς ψυχὰς — τῶν ἀδ. are intended principally for ἐπήγειραν, as appears from xiii. 50. Yet perhaps those words are meant to be referred *also* to ἐκάκωσαν, two clauses being thus blended into one. Render, "instigated and embittered the minds of the Gentiles against the brethren;" of which sense of κακόω examples are adduced from Josephus. This verse is parenthetical; the μὲν οὖν at the beginning of the next verse has a *resumptive* force, and may be rendered *accordingly*.

3. παῤῥησιαζ. ἐπὶ τῷ K.] Most Commentators take this to mean "being bold in the profession of Jesus;" i. e. his doctrine and religion. But perhaps that would require ἐν τῷ K. It is better, with Grot., Pisc., Mor., Kuin., and Schleus., to render "speaking freely, in reliance on the Lord;" i. e. on Christ, as most Commentators explain, or, as Grot. and Kuin. understand, *God*. Similar uncertainties of interpretation often occur; but they, at least, strongly attest the grand doctrine of the *Deity of Christ*.

The καὶ before διδόντι is omitted in many of the best MSS. and Versions, and in almost all early Edd. It crept into the later Erasmian Editions, and was thence introduced into the third of Steph. It has been, very properly, cancelled by Matth., Griesb., Knapp, and Vater, both from *internal evidence* (since we may account for its omission, but not for its insertion) and from *propriety of language*; for (as Rinck observes) where a later participle is meant for the explication of a preceding one [and denoting *by what means*, i. e. how] the copulative is usually absent, as at vv. 17. & 22. See Note on ix. 28. Also Middl. Gr. A. iii. 3, 4. Wakef. has well rendered, "by granting."

4. ἐσχίσθη.] When σχίζεσθαι has the metaphorical sense to be divided in opinion, γνώμαις is generally added by way of explanation, though sometimes omitted, as here and in some passages cited by the Commentators.

5. ὁρμή.] This is by some rendered *impetus*, *assault*. But that sense is negatived by the συνιδόντες at v. 6. The best Commentators take it to denote *impulse*, of which sense Munthe adduces several examples. In those passages, however, the word is used with ἐνέπεσε, while here it rather seems to denote a set design, full purpose, ὁρμὴ ἐγένετο being for ὡρμῶντο scil. τὰ ἔθνη.

6. συνιδόντες.] The sense (mistaken by the Translators) is, "having taken consideration [respecting the matter, and what was best to be done]." So xii. 12. συνιδών τε ἦλθε.

— τὰς πόλεις τῆς Λ.] Here the Article is not without force, though it is not expressed by our Translators. Nor need the Commentators have supposed a transposition, thus: κατέφυγον εἰς Λ. καὶ Δ. τὰς πόλεις τῆς Λ.; for then the Article would have been improper, even in the Greek, *Iconium* being a city of consequence. The truth is, that Λύστραν and Δέρβην fall under the rule of *apposition for definition's sake*, (i. e. to determine the whole by specifying the parts. See Matth. Gr. Gr. § 431 & 432) and the use of the Article falls under that of *insertions in hypothesis*; moreover, the words τῆς Λυκαονίας are added by way of explication. If the Article, however, be allowed its force, it would appear that Luke did not reckon *Iconium* as being in Lycaonia. And yet Strabo, Pliny, and Steph. Byz. do. But Xenophon in his Cyrop. reckons it in *Phrygia*, though on the *borders* of Lycaonia. And probably so it continued till the Roman conquest; and even then was *popularly* regarded as in Lycaonia.

8. ἐκάθητο.] Wakef. and Kuin. scruple at the sense *sat*, and render "*was*," or dwelt; a frequent sense of κάθημαι, derived from the Hebr. ישב. And this interpretation is confirmed by the Pesch. Syr. Yet I prefer the common signification, — meant, it should seem, to express *graphically* the condition of this poor wretch, who *had never walked*. Ἀδύνατος signifies not *weak*, or *infirm*, or *disabled*, as some English Translators render; but *helpless in his feet*, or, as Wakef. expresses it, *who had no use of his feet*. Χωλὸς does not mean *lame*, as Newc. and Wakef. render, but a *cripple*; i. e. according to the true derivation of that word (not perceived by the Etymologists, which is suggested by the *old* spelling of the word) *creeple*,

10 ἔχει τοῦ σωθῆναι, [l] εἶπε μεγάλῃ τῇ φωνῇ· Ἀνάστηθι ἐπὶ τοὺς πόδας l Isa. 35. 6.
11 σου ὀρθός! καὶ ἥλλετο καὶ περιεπάτει. [m] Οἱ δὲ ὄχλοι ἰδόντες ὃ m Infra 28. 6.
ἐποίησεν ὁ Παῦλος, ἐπῆραν τὴν φωνὴν αὐτῶν, Λυκαονιστὶ λέγοντες·
12 Οἱ θεοὶ ὁμοιωθέντες ἀνθρώποις κατέβησαν πρὸς ἡμᾶς. ἐκάλουν τε
τὸν μὲν Βαρνάβαν Δία, τὸν δὲ Παῦλον Ἑρμῆν· ἐπειδὴ αὐτὸς ἦν ὁ
13 ἡγούμενος τοῦ λόγου. Ὁ δὲ ἱερεὺς τοῦ Διὸς, τοῦ ὄντος πρὸ τῆς πόλεως αὐτῶν, ταύρους καὶ στέμματα ἐπὶ τοὺς πυλῶνας ἐνέγκας, σὺν τοῖς
14 ὄχλοις ἤθελε θύειν. [n] Ἀκούσαντες δὲ οἱ ἀπόστολοι Βαρνάβας καὶ n Matt. 26. 65.
Παῦλος, διαῤῥήξαντες τὰ ἱμάτια αὐτῶν εἰσεπήδησαν εἰς τὸν ὄχλον, κρά-
15 ζοντες [o] καὶ λέγοντες· Ἄνδρες! τί ταῦτα ποιεῖτε; καὶ ἡμεῖς ὁμοιοπα- o Supra 10. 26. Gen. 1. 1.
θεῖς ἐσμεν ὑμῖν ἄνθρωποι, εὐαγγελιζόμενοι ὑμᾶς ἀπὸ τούτων τῶν Psal. 33. 6. & 124. 8.
ματαίων ἐπιστρέφειν ἐπὶ τὸν Θεὸν τὸν ζῶντα, ὃς ἐποίησε τὸν οὐρανὸν & 146. 6. Rev. 14. 7.
16 καὶ τὴν γῆν καὶ τὴν θάλασσαν, καὶ πάντα τὰ ἐν αὐτοῖς· [p] ὃς ἐν ταῖς p Psal. 81. 12. Infra 17. 30.

one who can only creep, and not walk [upright.] This is distinctly stated in the next clause.

10. ἥλλετο καὶ π.] See Note on Acts iii. 8.

11. Λυκαονιστί.] On the precise nature and character of this language the learned are not agreed. See the Dissertations on this subject by Jablonski, in vol. xiii. of the Critici Sacri, Ghuling's Tract referred to by Kuin., and the Mithridates, Vol. ii. p. 213. The most probable opinion is, that it was of Greek *origin*; but, by coalition with the languages of Asia Minor, peculiarity of pronunciation, and other causes, had become almost a distinct language from the Greek. St. Paul evidently did not understand what was spoken, otherwise he would have prevented the preparation for sacrifice.

12. ἐκάλουν — Ἑρμῆν.] From v. 13. it appears that Jupiter had a temple among them; nay, it is probable, from what is there said, that the city itself was sacred to him. And the ancients supposed the gods especially to frequent those cities which were sacred to them. It was not improbable, therefore, that he should appear; of course, in a human form; as also that he should be accompanied by *Mercury*, since Jupiter was supposed to be generally attended on such visits by Mercury. Not to say that, as Guhling thinks, there was likely to be *also* a temple of Mercury in so considerable a city of so commercial a part of the country. Though the *commerce* in question was confined to the coast, and consequently the *worship* also of that God. It is well observed, too, by Mr. Harrington (in his Works, p. 330.) that "the persuasion of their being Jupiter and Mercury, might gain the more easily on the minds of the Lycaonians, on account of the well known fable of Jupiter and Mercury, who were said to have descended from heaven in human shape, and to have been entertained by Lycaon, from whom the Lycaonians received their name." Of the opinions of the ancients as to the incarnations of their gods, see two Dissertations on the whole of the present interesting narrative, by Boerner and Pfizer, in Vol. xiii. of the Critici Sacri.

— ὁ ἡγούμενος τοῦ λόγου] "the leading speaker." Thus Mercury is called by Jambl. Θεὸς ὁ τῶν λόγων ἡγεμών.

13. ὁ ἱερεὺς] for ἀρχιερεύς. At τοῦ Διὸς Kuin. supposes an ellip. of ἱεροῦ, as in Aristoph. Plut. 358. ἥκεις παρὰ τοῦ Θεοῦ. and often. Perhaps, however, there is no ellip. at all, but only *Jupiter* is put for the *temple of Jupiter*, the god for the temple, by a common figure of speech; for Valckn. has shown that it cannot be understood of a *statue*, since *statues* had no Priests attached to them. The above view is, I find, supported by Bp. Middl., who adduces an apposite proof of this idiom from Pausan. iv. p. 337. Μάντικλος δὲ καὶ τὸ ἱερὸν Μεσσηνίοις τοῦ Ἡρακλέους ἐποίησε, καὶ ἔστιν ἐκτὸς τείχους ὁ Θεὸς ἱδρυμένος, which evidently means that the *Temple*, in which stood a statue of Hercules, was without the wall. The temple being situated in *front* of the city shows that Jupiter (thus πρόπολος) was accounted the πολιοῦχος or tutelary god of the place.

— στέμματα] "chaplets," to place around the horns of the bulls. It is not clear whether we are to understand πυλῶνας of the *gates* of the city, or the *portals of the temple*, or the *porch* of the house where the Apostles were.

14. διαῤῥήξαντες τὰ ἱμ.] See Matt. xxvi. 65. and Note.

15. ὁμοιοπαθεῖς.] This is not well rendered by Doddr. and Newc. "of like infirmities," nor by Wakef., "of like weaknesses." Still less by Pearce and Weston, "mortals subject to death." The term ὁμοιοπαθὴς is indeed too complex a one to be adequately represented by any such *special* expression. In fact ἄνθρωποι is *emphatic*, q. d. We are *men* only, not Gods. And ὁμοιοπ., as is plain from the Classical citations adduced by Wets., denotes the being subject to all those accidents which attach to mortality; namely, to the passions and affections, the wants and weaknesses, the liability to disease and death, to which flesh is heir; all involving the very reverse of the idea connected with the Godhead.

— τούτ. τῶν ματαίων.] Many Commentators take this in the masculine, and understand the *statues* of the God, δεικτικῶς; which, they think, is required by the antithetical Θεὸς ζῶν. But it is doubtful whether the words were pronounced at the Temple-*gate*; certainly not in the *temple*. It is better, with others, to refer the words to the *oxen and garlands*. Perhaps, however, the Apostle meant, in a general way, *the rites and ceremonies of idolatry*, as in 1 Kings xvi. 2. τοῦ παροργίσαι με ἐν τοῖς ματαίοις αὐτῶν. and Joseph. Ant. x. 4, 1. cited by Wets., on τὸν ζῶντα. See Note on Matt. xvi. 16.

παρῳχημέναις γενεαῖς εἴασε πάντα τὰ ἔθνη πορεύεσθαι ταῖς ὁδοῖς αὐτῶν. Καί τοι γε οὐκ ἀμάρτυρον ἑαυτὸν ἀφῆκεν, ἀγαθοποιῶν, οὐρανό- 17
θεν ‡ ἡμῖν ὑετοὺς διδοὺς καὶ καιροὺς καρποφόρους, ἐμπιπλῶν τροφῆς
καὶ εὐφροσύνης τὰς καρδίας ‡ ἡμῶν. Καὶ ταῦτα λέγοντες, μόλις κατέ- 18
παυσαν τοὺς ὄχλους τοῦ μὴ θύειν αὐτοῖς.

q 2 Cor. 11. 25. 2 Tim. 3. 11.

q Ἐπῆλθον δὲ ἀπὸ Ἀντιοχείας καὶ Ἰκονίου Ἰουδαῖοι, καὶ πείσαντες 19
τοὺς ὄχλους, καὶ λιθάσαντες τὸν Παῦλον, ἔσυρον ἔξω τῆς πόλεως, νομίσαντες αὐτὸν τεθνάναι. Κυκλωσάντων δὲ αὐτὸν τῶν μαθητῶν, ἀναστὰς 20

16. πάντα τὰ ἔθνη.] Not "all nations," (which would not be agreeable to facts) but all *the* nations, גוים, *the Gentiles*. (Pearce and Markl.) Πορεύεσθαι ταῖς ὁδ. α., to follow the course of their own imaginations respecting the Divine nature and worship; and to whom he had not given a revelation of his will either by Divine legates or by Revelation. The εἴασε, however, does not imply *allowance*, but *abandonment*. See Whitby.

17. οὐκ ἀμάρτυρον ἑαυτόν.] Ἀμάρτυρος unwitnessed as to existence, nature, attributes, &c. There is an elegant *meiosis* in οὐκ ἀμαρτ. for πολυμάρτυρον, of which I have adduced many examples on Thucyd. ii. 41. οὐ δή τοι ἀμάρτυρόν γε τὴν δύναμιν παρασχόμενοι.

— ἀγαθοποιῶν, &c.] There is a beautiful remark to this effect, in Synes. 192. A. ἐπεὶ δὲ οὐν ἅπαξ γίγονε τὰ κακὰ, τῆς θείας σοφίας καὶ ἀρετῆς καὶ δυνάμεως ἔργον ἐστὶν, οὐ μόνον τὸ ἀγαθοποιεῖν· φύσις γάρ, ὡς εἰπεῖν, αὕτη Θεοῦ, ὡς τοῦ πυρὸς τὸ θερμαίνειν, καὶ τοῦ φωτὸς τὸ φωτίζειν. Hence the name *God*, which means the Good Being, the Giver of all Good.

Instead of ἡμῖν many MSS., Versions, and Fathers have ὑμῖν; and, a little after, for ἡμῶν, ὑμῶν. Both these readings are received by Griesb., Knapp, and Tittm.; and I should have followed them, notwithstanding the insufficiency of external testimony. (for in words so similar MSS. have little authority) had I not suspected the readings to be *emendations* of the Alexandrian school. And though ὑμῖν and ὑμῶν would be more agreeable to strict propriety; yet ἡμῖν and ἡμῶν have more of nature and simplicity. The Apostle speaks (through delicacy) κοινῶς, q. d. "you as well as ourselves, both of us." There is in οὐρανόθεν ὑετοὺς διδοὺς something (blended with the simplicity of early times) almost poetic. So Aratus cited by Grot.: ὕδατος ἐρχομένοιο Διὸς παρά. which passage was probably in the mind of the Apostle; and if so, it will add another to the proofs (few in number) that he was not unacquainted with the Greek Classical writers; and it is remarkable that one of the passages alluded to is from the same Aratus. See xvii. 28. and Note.

— ὑετούς.] The Plural is used with reference to the two *periodical* rains, called in James v. 7. τὸν πρώϊμον καὶ τὸν ὄψιμον. and by Philo p. 390. καιροὺς ὑετίους. The plural is rare; yet Lucian i. 104. has ὑετοί τε ῥαγδαῖοι καὶ βίαιοι. Sir Isaac Newton, (as Dr. Hales observes, vol. iii. 511.) has in the *Scholium Generale* of his Principia, finely improved this argument of the Apostle — "From blind *metaphysical necessity*, which is always and everywhere the *same*, there arises no *variation* of things, p. 529.; or no *variety* of moist and *fruitful*, of dry and *barren* seasons, produced by God's Providence, only; in order to reward or punish his *rational* creatures."

— ἐμπιπλῶν — ἡμῶν.] Grot., Triller, and Schleus., attempt to remove the apparent harshness of this phraseology by taking εὐφροσύνης of *wine*, and τὰς καρδίας in the sense *stomachs*. A more ill-founded and tasteless criticism cannot well be imagined. Little better is that of Rosenm. and Kuin., who take τὰς καρδίας ἡμῶν, by Hebraism for ἡμᾶς. There need not be any perplexity. We have only to suppose a sort of *synchysis* or *brachylogia*. The sense, fully expressed, would be, "filling our stomachs with food, and our hearts with gladness."

"The Apostle (observes Dr. Hales) leaves *them* to draw the *conclusion* from these premises, that it must be the height of ingratitude [and impiety] to transfer to the *creature* the worship due only to the Creator."

19. καὶ πείσαντες — ἔσυρον.] The sense is here obscured by a blending of two sentences into one, and by a peculiar idiom in πειθ. (which word is here used as supra xii. 20. καὶ πείσαντες Βλ.) whereby it signifies to bring any one over to one's own views or wishes. Thus the full sense is, "And having prevailed on the multitude (to permit them to stone Paul) and having stoned him, they drew him out of the city." There may, however, be in πειθ. a sensus prægnans, for, "having persuaded the multitude that they were impostors and magicians, and prevailed upon them to," &c. It is here pithily remarked by Calvin: "In hâc historiâ graphicè nobis pingitur *mundi pravitas*," i. e. how much more easily they are persuaded to evil than to good, to superstition than to true religion.

The force of the words ἔσυρον ἔξω τῆς πόλεως is not well pointed out by Expositors. Σύρω, it may be observed, is a *vox solemnis de hac re*, having reference to the brutal insults offered to the dead bodies of executed malefactors, which were at last dragged by the heels out of the city-gates (according to the law which enjoined their removal) and if not interred, were cast as food for the dogs and birds of prey. So Herodian i. 13. 11. Σύροντες τὰ σώματα, καὶ πᾶσαν ὕβριν ἐνυβρίσαντες, ἔρριψαν, &c., and v. 18, 17. παρέδοσαν σύρειν καὶ ἐνυβρίζειν τοῖς βουλομένοις, namely, the bodies of Antoninus and Soæmis. Sometimes they used to be so dragged out of the city (or wherever the carcase was to be thrown) by a *hook*. So Ælius Lampr. tells us that the Roman people voted that the body of Commodus should "unco *trahi* et in cloacas conjici." This may serve to show the exceedingly miserable state to which the Apostle was reduced. Insomuch that it is doubtless to this he especially alludes at 2 Cor. xi. 23. ἐν θανάτοις πολλάκις. There is a similar construction at xii. 20. καὶ πείσαντες B. ᾐτοῦντο εἰρήνην.

— νομίσαντες αὐτὸν τεθνάναι.] There is no sort of foundation for the irreverent fancy of Pric. and Wets. that Paul *pretended* to be dead. He was, no doubt, in a swoon and senseless; and when we consider that he had been stoned at least *almost*

εἰσῆλθεν εἰς τὴν πόλιν· καὶ τῇ ἐπαύριον ἐξῆλθε σὺν τῷ Βαρνάβᾳ εἰς
21 *Δέρβην. Εὐαγγελισάμενοί τε τὴν πόλιν ἐκείνην, καὶ μαθητεύσαντες*
22 *ἱκανοὺς, ὑπέστρεψαν εἰς τὴν Λύστραν καὶ Ἰκόνιον καὶ Ἀντιόχειαν, ʳ ἐπι-* r Supra 11. 23. & 13. 43.
στηρίζοντες τὰς ψυχὰς τῶν μαθητῶν, παρακαλοῦντες ἐμμένειν τῇ πίστει, Matt. 10. 38. & 16. 24.
καὶ ὅτι διὰ πολλῶν θλίψεων δεῖ ἡμᾶς εἰσελθεῖν εἰς τὴν βασιλείαν τοῦ Luke 22. 28, 29. & 24. 26. 2 Tim. 3. 12.
23 *Θεοῦ. ˢ χειροτονήσαντες δὲ αὐτοῖς πρεσβυτέρους κατ᾽ ἐκκλησίαν, προσ-* Rom. 8. 17. s Supra 1. 28. & 11. 30.
ευξάμενοι μετὰ νηστειῶν, παρέθεντο αὐτοὺς τῷ Κυρίῳ εἰς ὃν πεπιστεύ- Titus 1. 5.
24 *κεισαν. Καὶ διελθόντες τὴν Πισιδίαν, ἦλθον εἰς Παμφυλίαν· καὶ*
25 *λαλήσαντες ἐν Πέργῃ τὸν λόγον, κατέβησαν εἰς Ἀττάλειαν· ᵗ κἀκεῖθεν* t Supra 13. 1, 3.
26 *ἀπέπλευσαν εἰς Ἀντιόχειαν, ὅθεν ἦσαν παραδεδομένοι τῇ χάριτι τοῦ*
27 *Θεοῦ εἰς τὸ ἔργον ὃ ἐπλήρωσαν. ᵘ Παραγενόμενοι δὲ καὶ συναγαγόν-* u Supra 15. 4. 1 Cor. 16. 9.
τες τὴν ἐκκλησίαν, ἀνήγγειλαν ὅσα ἐποίησεν ὁ Θεὸς μετ᾽ αὐτῶν, καὶ 2 Cor. 2. 12. Rev. 3. 8.
28 *ὅτι ἤνοιξε τοῖς ἔθνεσι θύραν πίστεως. διέτριβον δὲ ἐκεῖ χρόνον οὐκ*
ὀλίγον σὺν τοῖς μαθηταῖς.

to death, we shall see that his being enabled to walk home, and the next day to set out for Derbe, can be regarded in no other light than as involving the preternatural.

22. *παρακαλοῦντες.*] *And* is wrongly supplied in our common Version. The sense is, "by exhorting them." See Note supra v. 3. In *καὶ ὅτι διὰ*, &c., there is (as Krebs and Kuin. observe) an idiom, by which another word of cognate signification is to be supplied from one which has preceded; here *λέγοντες* from *παρακαλοῦντες*. The *διὰ πολλῶν — Θεοῦ* must not, with many recent Commentators, be confined to that time, but regarded as a general declaration intended for *every* age, that the working out of our salvation is not to be accomplished without numerous trials and tribulations.

23. *χειροτονήσαντες α.*] Erasm., Calvin, and Beza, and, more latterly, Knatchb., Raphel, Doddridge (indeed all the Presbyterian Commentators), take the sense to be, "having ordained their elders by the votes of the people." But the most learned Interpreters have long rejected this interpretation; which requires a very strained sense to be put on *χειροτον.*,—and one, moreover, which is forbidden by the *αὐτοῖς* following. There is, indeed, no point on which the most learned have been so much agreed as this, that *χειρ.* here simply denotes "having *selected, constituted, appointed.*" See Hammond, Whitby, Wolf, and especially Kuin. At the same time it is granted by some able maintainers of this interpretation, that the *appointment* in question is not the *same thing* with the formal *Ecclesiastical ordination* of a somewhat later period. And, on the other hand, the Presbyterians themselves admit, that *imposition of hands* accompanied this *χειροτονία*. But if it did *not* amount to the solemn ordination of a later period, there is the less reason to suppose, (as many do), that the *consent of the people* was previously obtained for these appointments. However, the *imposition of hands*, which both parties admit, taken in conjunction with the solemn fasting and prayer, which accompanied the appointment, seem to show that it *was*, in fact, *Ecclesiastical ordination;* while, at the same time, it seems probable that the situation of these *Elders* differed very much from the stated *Pastors* of a somewhat later age, when believers were divided into the two separate classes, of *Clergy*, and *Laity*. At the period now in question, the Presbyters probably exercised their ministry, in conjunction with the trades or professions to which they had been brought up. But when, in the next generation, it was thought expedient that Presbyters should be confined to their sacred duties, and kept apart from all secular occupations,—(*which* by the way, *occasioned* the two classes, of *Clergy* and *Laity*) then *ordination* would become a much more solemn affair, and the conferring of it such as not to be committed to any but to the highest *rulers of the Church*, who succeeded to the duties of the Apostles.

— *προσευξάμενοι μετὰ νηστ.*] i. e. "using prayer with fasting," *indicto jejunio*. See Note on xiii. 3.

— *παρέθεντο τῷ Κ.*] "committed them to the Divine protection." So xx. 32. *παρατίθεμαι ὑμᾶς τῷ Θεῷ, καὶ τῷ λόγῳ τῆς χάριτος αὐτοῦ.* and i. Pet. iv. 19.

26. *ὅθεν ἦσαν παραδ.*] *Παραδ.* is here synonymous with *παρατίθεσθαι* supra ver. 23. But though the general sense of the passage be clear, yet with *ὅθεν* the Commentators are not a little perplexed. Nay even those mighty Grecians, Hemster. and Valckn., thought the difficulty so great as to warrant Critical conjecture. They would read *ᾔεσαν* here, "whence they had gone." However, the MSS. afford no countenance; the *Greek* is questionable; and the form is not in use in the N. T. The common reading must be retained, and explained as it may. Now the best Commentators are of opinion that *ὅθεν* is to be taken for *ὅπου*; referring for examples to Matt. xxv. 24 & 26. Exod. xxx. 36. This, however, *explains* nothing, and in fact does but evade the difficulty. It is better to suppose a *significatio prægnans*, arising from a blending of two expressions; q. d. *whence they had been commended*, &c., and *from whence they had gone commended*, &c.; i. e. where, on their departing, they had been commended. Render, "whence they had set out, commended," &c. Ἐπλήρωσαν is well translated by Newcome and Wakefield "had fulfilled, or performed." When the Aorist is put for the Imperf., it is generally to be understood of action recently past, and is mostly used in *narration*.

27. *μετ᾽ αὐτῶν.*] The Commentators are not agreed whether the sense is "by their means,"

x Gen. 17. 10. Lev. 12. 3. Gal. 5. 1, 2. Phil. 3. 2. Col. 2. 8, 11, 16.
y Gal. 2 1. supra 11. 30.
z Supra 14. 27.

XV. [x] *ΚΑΙ τινες κατελθόντες ἀπὸ τῆς Ἰουδαίας, ἐδίδασκον τοὺς* 1
ἀδελφούς· Ὅτι ἐὰν μὴ περιτέμνησθε τῷ ἔθει Μωϋσέως, οὐ δύνασθε
σωθῆναι. [y] *Γενομένης οὖν στάσεως καὶ [συ]ζητήσεως οὐκ ὀλίγης τῷ* 2
Παύλῳ καὶ τῷ Βαρνάβᾳ πρὸς αὐτούς, ἔταξαν ἀναβαίνειν Παῦλον καὶ
Βαρνάβαν καί τινας ἄλλους ἐξ αὐτῶν πρὸς τοὺς ἀποστόλους καὶ πρεσ-
βυτέρους εἰς Ἱερουσαλὴμ, περὶ τοῦ ζητήματος τούτου. Οἱ μὲν οὖν, 3
προπεμφθέντες ὑπὸ τῆς ἐκκλησίας, διήρχοντο τὴν Φοινίκην καὶ Σαμά-
ρειαν, ἐκδιηγούμενοι τὴν ἐπιστροφὴν τῶν ἐθνῶν· καὶ ἐποίουν χαρὰν
μεγάλην πᾶσι τοῖς ἀδελφοῖς. [z] *Παραγενόμενοι δὲ εἰς Ἱερουσαλὴμ, ἀπε-* 4
δέχθησαν ὑπὸ τῆς ἐκκλησίας καὶ τῶν ἀποστόλων καὶ τῶν πρεσβυτέ-
ρων, ἀνήγγειλάν τε ὅσα ὁ Θεὸς ἐποίησε μετ' αὐτῶν. Ἐξανέστησαν δέ 5
τινες τῶν ἀπὸ τῆς αἱρέσεως τῶν Φαρισαίων πεπιστευκότες, λέγοντες
ὅτι δεῖ περιτέμνειν αὐτοὺς, παραγγέλλειν τε τηρεῖν τὸν νόμον Μωϋσέως.

(i. e. instrumentality) or, "to them," for *αὐτοῖς*. The latter mode of interpretation is adopted by the best Expositors, and is confirmed by several passages of the O. T.; but the former seems more agreeable to what follows. This may, however, have been a *popular* idiom comprehending *both* those senses.

XV. On the then situation of the Church at Jerusalem, and on the circumstances which led to the celebrated Apostolical decision of the question respecting the use of circumcision and the other forms of the Mosaic Law, as also on the nature and extent of that decree, I must refer my readers to Recens. Synop.

1. *τινες.*] These are thought to have been Antiochians, and Jewish converts, who had formerly been Pharisees, and still retained an attachment to the forms of the Mosaic Law. At *ἐδίδασκον τοὺς ἀδελφοὺς* must be understood *λέγοντες*.

— *περιτ.*] *Circumcision* is put for the whole of the ritual law of Moses, as being the principal ceremony, binding the person who underwent it to the observance of the rest. *Ἔθει*, "institution."

2. *στάσεως.*] Notwithstanding what Bp. Pearce objects, there is no reason why it should not be rendered *dissension*, or disputation; of which sense the Commentators adduce two or three examples, as Ælian V. H. ii. 34. cited by Wakef. *Ὦ βέλτιστοι, τί στασιάζετε καὶ διαφέρεσθε ὑπὲρ ὀλίγων ἡμερῶν*; to which I would add a most apposite one from Æschyl. Pers. 744. Blomf. *Λόγος κρατεῖ σαφηνὴς, τῇδέ γ' οὐκ ἔνι στάσις.* And so xxiii. 10. *πολλῆς δὲ γενομένης στάσεως, κ. τ. λ.*

— *συζητήσεως*] "mutual discussion," or controversy. This seems meant to explain and qualify *στάσεως*. Wets., Matth., Knapp, Griesb., and Vater edit *ζητήσ.*, from several MSS. and some Versions, and the Ed. Princ.; but without reason. The evidence of the Versions tends the contrary way. Nothing is more common than for compounds to be changed by the scribes into simples. Besides, *ζητ.* would here be a term not strong enough, and *συζητ.* is *required*, which occurs at ver. 7, whence the editors in question affirm the present reading to have been altered. But that is quite a gratuitous supposition. *Ἔταξαν*, scil. *οἱ ἀδελφοί*, the brethren at large, not the *Præpositi Ecclesiæ*, as Hamm. supposes.

3. *προπεμφθέντες.*] This is by some rendered "*præmissi, commissioned, delegated*;" by others, more rightly, *honorificè deducti*, "set forward on their way;" a mark of respect usually rendered to eminent persons among the ancients; and always shown to *Apostles*, and of which we have mention further on in this Book and in the Epistles. The *οἱ* is put for the pronoun demonstr., and consequently the punctuation should be that which I have adopted. *Ἐπιστροφὴν*, "conversion." Formed on the use of *ἐπιστρέφεσθαι*, as at xi. 21. xiv. 15. *Ἐποίουν χαρὰν μεγ.*, "occasioned great joy." So Aristid. cited by Wets.: *ὁ δὲ Θεὸς ἐποίησέ μοι χαρὰν ὑπερμεγέθη.*

4. *ἀπεδέχθησαν*] "were received with distinction," as xviii. 27.

5. *ἐξανέστησαν δέ τινες — λέγοντες.*] These words are so manifestly St. Luke's, that plain readers would be surprised to learn that any *other* opinion had ever been formed. And yet many eminent Commentators, stumbling at what they think the harshness of the *answer*, or *decision*, being given before the *question*, or difficulty, had been propounded, suppose the words to be those of the *Jewish party* at Antioch, reported by Paul and Barnabas. But although a transition from the oblique to the direct is occasionally found (as in i. 4. xvii. 7. and Luke v. 14), yet here it would be peculiarly harsh, and the ellip. of *ἔλεγον*, which they propose, is inadmissible. Besides, *ἐξανίστημι* would not be a suitable term. In fact, the difficulty is quite imaginary; for as the words *ἀνήγγειλαν — αὐτῶν* cannot but signify that *they gave an account of what had happened to them in the exercise of their mission*, so the *difficulty which brought them there* could not fail to be mentioned. See Kuin., who refers to a similar brevity at Acts xi. 3. Thus all difficulty vanishes, and *ἐξανέστησαν* has peculiar propriety, "then there started up," not "rose up," as in most versions. The word is often used in Thucyd., Xenoph., and the best writers, in the sense to *start forth from ambush*, or suddenly. The Judaizing party, on hearing the matter first propounded, suddenly and hastily started up, saying that it was proper to, &c. This opinion, it is plain, was given, not at a *public assembly*, called for the purpose of considering the matter in question, but probably at a private meeting to receive them on their return. The assembly denoted by *συνήχθησαν* was plainly *another*, called for the purpose of *deciding* on the ques-

6 Συνήχθησαν δὲ οἱ ἀπόστολοι καὶ οἱ πρεσβύτεροι ἰδεῖν περὶ τοῦ
7 λόγου τούτου. [a] Πολλῆς δὲ συζητήσεως γενομένης, ἀναστὰς Πέτρος εἶπε [a] Supra 10. 20. & 11. 1, 2.
πρὸς αὐτούς· Ἄνδρες ἀδελφοί, ὑμεῖς ἐπίστασθε ὅτι ἀφ᾽ ἡμερῶν ἀρ-
χαίων ὁ Θεὸς ἐν ἡμῖν ἐξελέξατο διὰ τοῦ στόματός μου ἀκοῦσαι τὰ
8 ἔθνη τὸν λόγον τοῦ εὐαγγελίου, καὶ πιστεῦσαι. [b] καὶ ὁ καρδιογνώστης [b] 1 Chron. 28. 9. & 29. 17.
Θεὸς ἐμαρτύρησεν αὐτοῖς, δοὺς αὐτοῖς τὸ Πνεῦμα τὸ ἅγιον, καθὼς καὶ Psal. 7. 9. Jer. 11. 20.
9 ἡμῖν· [c] καὶ οὐδὲν διέκρινε μεταξὺ ἡμῶν τε καὶ αὐτῶν, τῇ πίστει κα- & 17. 10. & 20. 12. supra 10. 43. &c.
10 θαρίσας τὰς καρδίας αὐτῶν. [d] Νῦν οὖν τί πειράζετε τὸν Θεόν, ἐπι- 1 Cor. 1. 2. [c] 1 Pet. 1. 22.
θεῖναι ζυγὸν ἐπὶ τὸν τράχηλον τῶν μαθητῶν, ὃν οὔτε οἱ πατέρες ἡμῶν [d] Gal. 5. 1.
11 οὔτε ἡμεῖς ἰσχύσαμεν βαστάσαι; [e] Ἀλλὰ διὰ τῆς χάριτος τοῦ Κυρίου [e] Eph. 2. 4, 8. Titus 3. 4.

tion after due deliberation. Πεπιστευκότες is Part., for Sub., and must be taken after τινες as determining the sense. The words ὅτι δεῖ — Μωϋσέως are, I think, not *in oratione directâ*, but *indirectâ*, as they are taken in our common version, and that of Doddr., confirmed by the Syr. Pesch.

6. συνήχθησαν δὲ οἱ ἀπ.] Thus was assembled what is called the *First Council* at Jerusalem, to counteract the baneful heresy which had sprung up from the bitter root of *Pharisaism*, and disturbed the harmony and concord of the infant Church. On the *time* of this council, see Towns. ii. 177—179; on its *nature*, see Vitring. de Syn. p. 598. seqq. and the writers referred to by Wolf. On the *circumstances* which led to it, and the rise and progress of the *heresy* it was meant to counteract, see Dr. Hales iii. 513. sq.

— ἰδεῖν περί.] This, by an idiom found both in Hebrew, Greek, and English, signifies, "*to consider about.*" See Cant. vi. 11.

— περὶ τοῦ λόγου] "concerning the matter spoken of," which, as Dr. Burton observes, involved *two questions*. 1. Whether the Gentiles should be circumcised. 2. Whether they should observe the customs of the Mosaic law. The former was answered decidedly in the *negative*; the latter partly in the *affirmative*. The συζητήσεως just after must be understood of disputation between the Apostles and presbyters, and those persons who had at the former private meeting given their opinion so positively.

7. ἀφ᾽ ἡμερῶν ἀρχαίων.] The Interpreters are not agreed on the sense of this expression. Several of them take it to mean *a principio*, "from the *beginning* of the *Gospel*." But the purpose in question was not made known till the conversion of Cornelius; for that is plainly alluded to in διὰ στόματος. And the expression will appear to be not inapplicable to that period (13 or 14 years before) if we consider that ἀρχαῖος is (as De Dieu and Grot. have shown) used simply of what has happened *heretofore*, — whether many ages before, or only a few years; of which examples are adduced.

There is more difficulty in ἐν ἡμῖν ἐξελέξατο, with which the Commentators are much perplexed. It is, however, pretty much agreed among the learned, that the expression is to be regarded as a Hebraism, בָּחַר in Hebrew taking after it בְּ, ἐν. And thus it will be equivalent to ἡμᾶς ἐξελ. That mode of solution, however, is precarious; and this occurrence of ἡμῖν and μου in the same clause would be harsh. As to ἐν ἡμῖν, it is, after all, best rendered in our common version (confirmed by the Syr. and De Dieu), "amongst us." Then ἐμὲ may be *supplied* (as in the Syr. and Bohem. Versions), which is *suppressed* through delicacy, as in very many passages which I could adduce from Thucyd. The Apostle, after uttering the word ἐξελ., does not add ἐμὲ and κηρύσσειν τὸν λόγον, &c., as he might have done, but omits them, and gives the sentence another turn, so as to avoid egotism.

8. καρδιογνώστης.] See Note on i. 24. By this the Apostle hints, that God can best determine *who* are worthy of being admitted as Christians, and who not; as also on the rites and ceremonies to be enjoined on them.

— ἐμαρτύρησεν αὐτοῖς.] The sense (unperceived by the Interpreters) seems to be, "hath borne testimony in their favour," "hath testified his approbation," namely, by giving them the Holy Spirit. Μαρτυρέω with a Dative also implies *favourable* testimony. This signification occurs in Luke xi. 48, and often in the Classical writers.

9. οὐδὲν διέκρινε] "made no distinction." A remarkable idiom, of which the Commentators adduce no apposite example. The following, however, which I have noted, will supply the deficiency. Thucyd. i. 49, 7. διεκέκριτο οὐδὲν ἔτι. Diod. Sinop. ap. Athen. p. 239. οὐχὶ διακρίνας τὴν πενιχρὰν ἢ πλουσίαν. By τὰς καρδίας are denoted, not their *minds*, but their *souls* and *consciences*: these were sanctified by the Holy Spirit, and purified by the great truths of the Gospel.

10. πειράζετε τὸν Θεὸν] i. e. "try the forbearance of God, by perversely resisting his will." So 1 Cor. x. 9. καθὼς καί τινες αὐτῶν ἐπείρασαν. Heb. iii. 9. and often in the O. T., as Exod. xvii. 2, 7. Such is the interpretation of Schleus. Lex.; which is, upon the whole, the best founded. Others may be seen in Recens. Synop. At ἐπιθεῖναι sub. ὥστε.

11. ἀλλὰ διὰ — κἀκεῖνοι.] There are few passages which, with the appearance of plainness, involve more difficulty than this; as may be imagined from the variety of senses assigned to the words by Commentators. And no wonder: since ἡμεῖς, though concealed in πιστεύομεν, and κἀκεῖνοι, are capable of being applied to different persons; and the ellip. at κἀκεῖνοι may be filled up in two ways. The *we* is by some referred to the *Apostles* Peter and James; by others to *Peter only*. *Neither* method, however, can be admitted. Again, κἀκεῖνοι is referred by some to οἱ πατέρες; by others, to *Paul* and *Barnabas*: both, I conceive, erroneously. It is, I think, plain that *we* and *those*, which are antithetical, must denote no other than the same persons as αὐτοῖς (i. e. the *Gentiles*) and ἡμῖν, similarly antithetical at ver. 8, and ἡμῶν and αὐτῶν at ver. 9, namely the *Jewish* and the *Gentile converts*. Again, there is, I apprehend, at διὰ τῆς χάρ. &c. the very common ellip. of μόνον

Ἰησοῦ Χριστοῦ πιστεύομεν σωθῆναι, καθ᾽ ὃν τρόπον κἀκεῖνοι. Ἐσι- 12
γησε δὲ πᾶν τὸ πλῆθος, καὶ ἤκουον Βαρνάβα καὶ Παύλου ἐξηγουμένων
ὅσα ἐποίησεν ὁ Θεὸς σημεῖα καὶ τέρατα ἐν τοῖς ἔθνεσι δι᾽ αὐτῶν.
f Supra 12. 17. [f] Μετὰ δὲ τὸ σιγῆσαι αὐτοὺς ἀπεκρίθη Ἰάκωβος, λέγων· Ἄνδρες ἀδελ- 13
g 2 Pet. 1. 1. φοί, ἀκούσατέ μου. [g] Συμεὼν ἐξηγήσατο, καθὼς πρῶτον ὁ Θεὸς ἐπε- 14
σκέψατο λαβεῖν ἐξ ἐθνῶν λαὸν ἐπὶ τῷ ὀνόματι αὐτοῦ. Καὶ τούτῳ 15
h Amos 9. 11, 12. συμφωνοῦσιν οἱ λόγοι τῶν προφητῶν, καθὼς γέγραπται· [h] Μετὰ 16
ταῦτα ἀναστρέψω καὶ ἀνοικοδομήσω τὴν σκηνὴν

See Luke xvii. 10. At κἀκεῖνοι the true grammatical ellip. would be πιστεύουσι. But, among the other peculiarities of the Hellenistic style, is that of *anomalous ellipsis*; as here of σωθήσονται. Finally, the ἀλλὰ is *adversative* (answering an objection), and signifies *imò, nay, yea*, as in 2 Cor. vii. 11. Thus we may render: "yea, by the grace of our Lord Jesus Christ alone do we trust we shall be saved — in which same way they too are alone to be saved." The *inference* is obvious, and therefore left to be *supplied*,—that a thing so unimportant to salvation as the observation of the ceremonies of the Mosaic Law ought not to be exacted from the Gentile converts. The true reference in *we* and *they* was alone perceived by Œcumenius, Hamm., Whitby, Doddr., A. Clarke, and Scott. The sentiment here is the very same as that in Galat. ii. 15, 16. Rom. iii. 30.

Here I must take occasion to notice the able discussion by Dr. Hales as to the time when the conduct of St. Peter, on another occasion, which drew forth such severe reprobation from St. Paul, really took place. He shows (after Basnage), in a most convincing manner, that his tergiversation at Antioch was *not* (according to common opinion) *after* the speech at the Council at Jerusalem, but *before* it, as much as four or five years, and so early as the time of Herod's persecution, when Peter first went to Antioch, A. D. 44, Acts xii. 17. and was then followed by Paul and Barnabas, Acts xii. 25; by which we may consider his speech on the present occasion as a public recantation of his former error. "It *must* (says Basnage) have taken place *before* this Council, otherwise Peter might have opposed the authority of their *Decree* as a shield against the attacks of the Judaizers. Indeed, nothing but the most undeniable evidence could induce us to suppose what would otherwise subject the noble-minded and straight-forward Apostle to the charge of the most glaring inconsistency of conduct with his own doctrine.

12. πλῆθος.] The word does not here signify *multitude*, but *assembly* (as Luke xxiii. 1. and elsewhere) consisting of persons convened for the special purpose of considering this question. The passage may be freely rendered, "Whereupon the assembly at large kept a reverential silence, and listened to Paul and Barnabas while recounting," &c. *That* was done for the purpose of *establishing* the facts on which the validity of Peter's reasoning rested.

13. ἀπεκρίθη] "addressed [the assembly]."

14. καθὼς] for ὡς, how. Πρῶτον is not well rendered *at the first*, because that might seem to mean at the Beginning of the Gospel. See Note on v. 7. Doddr. and Newc. well translate "*first*." Ἐπεσκέψατο λαβεῖν, &c. A blending of two clauses into one, for ἐπισκ. τὰ ἔθνη (ὥστε) λαβεῖν ἐξ αὐτῶν λαὸν κ. τ. ὀ. α. On ἐπισκ. see Note on Luke i. 68. Ἐπὶ τῷ ὀν. α., "in order to bear his name, and be called his peculiar people, by professing his Religion."

16—17. This quotation is taken from the LXX., with the following unimportant variations. Μετὰ ταῦτα is used for ἐν τῇ ἡμέρᾳ ἐκείνῃ, to give the *sense* more clearly. Ἀναστρέψω is supplied, though without any thing corresponding to it in the Hebrew, for the same cause. The next clause is *compressed*, by blending the two parts of a parallelism into one. The words καθὼς αἱ ἡμέραι τοῦ αἰῶνος are omitted; and with reason, since they make no sense. The Translators ought to have seen that there is an ellips. of ב at כִּימֵי. Though, indeed, כימי עולם (occurring in Mich. vii. 14. and Is. lxiii. 9.) may have been considered as a sort of adverb. Finally, the words τὸν Κύριον are not found in the LXX., at least in the Vatican text. Yet there is no real discrepancy, since it is impossible to suppose the above to be correct, the sense being left so miserably incomplete. The Alexandrian text supplies τὸν Κύριον, which is adopted by Abp. Newc. as representing the true reading of the Hebrew text. But rashly; for there can be little doubt that it is from the margin. And the conjecture of the learned Prelate that אֵת י׳ was changed into אֹתִי, however ingenious, must be pronounced unfounded, and is negatived by τὸν Κύριον not being brought in after ἐκζητ. I have no doubt that the reading of the *Aldine*, *Pachom*, and perhaps several other copies of the Sept., represents the true text; viz. ἐκζητήσωσί με. The μ. was changed into a μ, and the ι absorbed in οι: The τὸν Κύριον of St. James was a gloss on the με, and perhaps had at an early period expelled the textual reading in some MSS. At any rate it was *adopted* by St. James, as making the sense yet clearer. Still between the Sept. even thus emended, and the Hebrew, there is an important variation. Correspondent to ὅπως ἂν ἐκζητήσωσιν — ἀνθρώπων is למען יירשו את שארית אדום. "that they may possess the residue of Edom." But that makes such bad sense (even after all that Rosenm. has done with it) there can be no doubt that the words are corrupt. And this suspicion is countenanced by the remarkable varr. lectt., none of them, however, giving any aid. The corruption seems to be anterior to the Masoretic recension, and the true reading is, I doubt not, what Lightf. supposed, for יירשו את to read ידרשו אתי, and for אדום to read אדם.

But, to turn from words to things, it is not true, as some imagine, that the Apostle *accommodates* the passage to the propagation of the Gospel among the Gentiles. The Prophet himself doubtless so meant it,—at least, if he fully comprehended the sense of the prediction he was inspired to make. Nay, even the sceptical Rosenm. admits, "Quæ hic pollicetur vates *multo sunt ampliora* et *magnificentiora*, quam ut Hiskiæ tempore, aut post

Δαυῒδ τὴν πεπτωκυῖαν· καὶ τὰ κατεσκαμμένα αὐ-
17 τῆς ἀνοικοδομήσω, καὶ ἀνορθώσω αὐτήν· ὅπως ἂν
ἐκζητήσωσιν οἱ κατάλοιποι τῶν ἀνθρώπων τὸν Κύριον, καὶ πάντα τὰ ἔθνη, ἐφ' οὓς ἐπικέκληται τὸ
ὄνομά μου ἐπ' αὐτούς· λέγει Κύριος ὁ ποιῶν ταῦ-
18 τα πάντα. Γνωστὰ ἀπ' αἰῶνός ἐστι τῷ Θεῷ πάντα τὰ ἔργα αὐ- i Infr. ver. 29. Gen. 9. 4.
19 τοῦ. Διὸ ἐγὼ κρίνω μὴ παρενοχλεῖν τοῖς ἀπὸ τῶν ἐθνῶν ἐπιστρέφου- Lev. 3. 17. & 17. 14.
20 σιν ἐπὶ τὸν Θεόν. [i] ἀλλὰ ἐπιστεῖλαι αὐτοῖς τοῦ ἀπέχεσθαι ἀπὸ τῶν Deut. 12. 23. 1 Cor. 8. 1, 9, 10.
ἀλισγημάτων τῶν εἰδώλων, καὶ τῆς πορνείας, καὶ τοῦ πνικτοῦ, καὶ τοῦ & 10. 14, 20, 21. 1 Thess. 4. 8.

reditum e Babylonico exilio, aut Hyrcani tempore, impleta censeri possunt."

—σκηνήν.] The word properly signifies a *booth* or hut, but sometimes denoted a permanent *house*, and figuratively a *family;* and, when applied to a *royal* family, its reign or kingdom. Κατασκάπτω was often used of the utter destruction of houses or cities. See Bp. Blomf. on Æschyl. Theb. 46, who (as does also Kypke) adduces many examples; though not one that exactly suits the present use. The following may therefore prove acceptable. Ælian V. H. xii. 54. τὴν πατρίδα κατῴκισε κατεσκαμμένην ὑπὸ Φιλίππου.

—ἐκζητ. τὸν Κύριον.] This phrase here and at Rom. iii. 1. Heb. xi. 6. signifies, by an imitation of the Heb. בקש or דרש את יהוה, to earnestly seek, for the purpose of praying to, and serving him. The κατάλοιποι τῶν ἀνθρώπων is explained by the τὰ ἔθνη in the next clause. In ἐπ' αὐτοὺς there is a Heb. pleonasm.

18. γνωστὰ —αὐτοῦ.] There has to many Commentators appeared so much abruptness in the introduction of this remark, as to require much to be supplied, in order to unite the words in a chain of reasoning with the preceding. To remedy which, some propound novel interpretations; and others would cut out the words ἐστι —αὐτοῦ, and unite γνωστὰ ἀπ' αἰῶνος with the preceding. But there is very little authority for either *interpretation;* and the *cancelling* is negatived by both the Hebrew and Sept. Besides, *supposing* the words away, then *something is wanting;* and yet something which would never have been *thus* supplied. In fact, the verse seems necessary *as a link* in the chain of reasoning; and though it be introduced abruptly, yet it is in a manner very agreeable to the Hellenistic and Scriptural style, which deals much in such axiomatical sentences. Chrys. (as I have proved in Recens. Synop.) certainly read the words; and the sense they are meant to convey seems to be this: *God is immutable. He hath determined from all eternity (so that the thing is not a novelty) to found a spiritual kingdom into which not only Jews, but Gentiles shall be received.* Thus the scope of the verse is to ngraft on the correspondence of the conversion of the Gentiles with ancient prophecies a reflection on the prescience and providence of God.

19. ἐγὼ κρίνω.] The sense is, "My judgment or decided opinion [on the matter] is." So Thucyd. iv. 60. ὡς ἐγὼ κρίνω. and the Latin *Ita censeo.* Μὴ παρενοχλεῖν, "to give them no molestation." The παρὰ does *not*, as many fancy, import "*unnecessarily*," but coalesces with the ἐν and ὀχλ., to make up the sense. It seems to be a popular form of expression, and the only apposite example cited by the Commentators is Arrian. Epict. i. 9. Μηδὲ παρενοχλήσῃς τοῖς νέοις, μηδὲ τοῖς γέρουσι. See Heb. xii. 15.

20. ἐπιστεῖλαι αὐτοῖς] "to direct them by letter," as Acts xxi. 25. At τοῦ ἀπέχεσθαι the Genit. is dependent on ἕνεκα understood, equivalent to ἵνα ἀπέχωνται. But to advert to the *particulars* of the prohibition, τῶν ἀλισγημάτων, &c.; the term ἀλίσγημα is Hellenistic, and derived from ἀλισγεῖν, to pollute. *How* that signification arises the Lexicographers do not tell us. Perhaps it may be derived from ἀλίζω and ἀλίω, to roll, which in a neuter sense may mean to roll one's self, i. e. *to wallow*. And then, by an easy transition, (perhaps by a metaphor borrowed from *swine*, see 2 Pet. ii. 22.) it may denote to *suffer pollution*. Be that as it may, both it and the noun are used alike of physical and *moral* defilement, especially that of *idolatry*, as the greatest. See Dan. i. 8. Ecclus. xl. 33. Mal. i. 7, 12., where the subject is meat offered to idols. Here, however, to *determine* the sense, the words τῶν εἰδώλων are added. Now though the word might denote *any* participation in idolatry, yet the passages of Daniel and Malachi (which were probably in the mind of the Apostle), as well as the ancient glosses of Hesych. and Suid. (formed, no doubt, from the early Scholiasts), determine it to be *the eating of meat offered to idols*, not merely in the *temples*, but even the purchasing of it for use, when it was taken for sale into the *public market*. For, we learn from the passages cited by the Commentators, that among the Gentiles, after a victim had been sacrificed in the temple, and a portion had been given to the Priests, and sometimes another eaten by the offerer and his friends on the spot,—the residue was often taken home by the priests for domestic use, and sometimes was sent to the public shambles to be sold. The flesh, however, was, of course, held in abomination by the *Jews;* (see 1 Cor. x. 20.) and therefore the use of it was very properly forbidden, in order that no needless offence might be given to the Jewish Christians.

—καὶ τῆς πορνείας.] Most Commentators are much at a loss to account for *this* being inserted among things of themselves lawful, but from which the Gentiles were to abstain, lest they should offend the Jewish Christians: πορνεία, having never been accounted as a thing permitted; and no reason would appear why, if *greater* offences are mentioned with smaller ones, *this alone* should be taken; which, they think, would go far to put the things mentioned in this list on a level. To remove this difficulty, many methods have been devised, some proceeding on *Critical conjecture*. Thus Bentley proposed to read χοιρείας, *pork*. A conjecture, however, utterly unauthorized. Others seek to remove the difficulty by supposing some *unusual sense* of the word;

k Neh. 8. 1. supra 13. 27. αἵματος. [k] Μωϋσῆς γὰρ ἐκ γενεῶν ἀρχαίων κατὰ πόλιν τοὺς κηρύσσον- 21
τας αὐτὸν ἔχει, ἐν ταῖς συναγωγαῖς κατὰ πᾶν σάββατον ἀναγινωσκόμενος.
Τότε ἔδοξε τοῖς ἀποστόλοις καὶ τοῖς πρεσβυτέροις σὺν ὅλῃ τῇ ἐκκλη- 22
σίᾳ, ἐκλεξαμένους ἄνδρας ἐξ αὐτῶν πέμψαι εἰς Ἀντιόχειαν σὺν τῷ Παύλῳ
καὶ Βαρνάβᾳ· Ἰούδαν τὸν ἐπικαλούμενον Βαρσαβᾶν, καὶ Σίλαν, ἄνδρας
ἡγουμένους ἐν τοῖς ἀδελφοῖς, γράψαντες διὰ χειρὸς αὐτῶν τάδε· Οἱ 23
l Gal. 2. 4. supra ver. 1. 1 John 2. 19. ἀπόστολοι καὶ οἱ πρεσβύτεροι καὶ οἱ ἀδελφοὶ, τοῖς κατὰ τὴν Ἀντιόχειαν
καὶ Συρίαν καὶ Κιλικίαν ἀδελφοῖς τοῖς ἐξ ἐθνῶν, χαίρειν. [l] Ἐπειδὴ 24

some interpreting, *spiritual whoredom*, viz. idolatry: others, *marriage with idolaters*; others, again, *meat sold in the public shops*. Each of these is open to insuperable objections, (stated in Recens. Synop.) and in particular to *this* (which is applicable to *all* those interpretations) that no *recondite* or *uncommon* sense could be intended; since in public edicts words are supposed to be employed in their usual sense. And here there is no sufficient reason to abandon the common version, *fornication*; that having been well defended by Grot., Wets., Valckn., Schoettg., Pearce, Nitzch, Rosenm., Kuinöel, Scott, Wahl. and particularly Bp. Marsh, who satisfactorily removes the objections to the word being taken in its ordinary sense, — showing that there are *other* instances to be found of moral and positive precepts, duties of common and perpetual obligation, mingled with local and temporary ones, in the same list, — as in the Decalogue. "And since (continues he) it appears from the Acts of the Apostles, and the Epistles of Paul, that the precepts of the Pentateuch were abrogated only by degrees, it seems by no means extraordinary that the Decree of the Council in Jerusalem should contain a mixture of moral and positive commands." I would add, that it is not unimportant in this view, to remark, that in the words of the decision actually sent (v. 29.), we find the *two* kept *separate*, πορνείας being put apart from the rest, and placed *last*. As to the objection founded on πορνεία being never ἀδιάφορον, it might *not* in theory, or philosophical speculation, but was so considered *practically*. No one who is at all acquainted with the Classical writers can doubt, that simple fornication was, by the Heathens, considered as no crime at all. We find that even their *religion* permitted, nay encouraged, licensed fornication. Hence the recommendation of chastity of *this* kind (for that contained in abstaining from *adultery* could not need enforcing) was highly necessary, the main purpose (as Grot. observes) of this list being to specify from what practices, *besides known and flagrant sins*, the Gentile Christians ought to abstain, in order to coalesce with the Jewish Christians without offence. And there was the more occasion to give the injunction, since, for many reasons, (which are detailed in Recens. Synop.) fornication and idolatry were in the minds of the Jews inseparably connected, (compare 1 Cor. x. 7, 8. v. 11. Eph. v. 5. Col. iii. 5. Rev. ii. 14. 20.) and particularly since whoredom was especially committed at the heathen temples, and licensed by the idolatrous priests. See particularly Exod. xxxiv. 14—16.

— τοῦ πνικτοῦ] scil. κρέατος (*supplied* in Athen. L. ix.) meaning flesh of animals killed by strangling, which was very prevalent among the ancients, both Greeks, Romans, and Orientals. They used to enclose the carcase of the animal (so killed that the blood should remain in it) in an oven, or deep stewing vessel, and thus cook it in its own vapour or steam. As to the *blood* — the heathens, when butchering an animal, carefully preserved this, and mixing it up with flour and unguents, formed various sorts of dishes. Now as *both* the foregoing sorts of food were strictly forbidden by the Mosaic Law, there was ample reason to forbid them to the *Gentile Christians*, in order to avoid giving offence to their Jewish brethren. That an injunction so local in its nature, and of such temporary obligations, cannot be binding on Christians of *these* times, and must cease with the circumstances which gave occasion to it, has been convincingly shown by Schoettg. and Doddr., whom see in Recens. Synop.

21. Μωϋσῆς γὰρ, &c.] Here again, there has been imagined to be such abruptness of transition, and want of connexion between this subject and the preceding, that many have supposed something to have been lost out of the text. But the connexion, though obscure, may be traced as follows: "[And remember the breach of these will occasion not only private but *public* scandal,] *for* the Mosaic religion has for a very long period backward, had its professors in every city, and its Scriptures publicly read in the synagogues every sabbath-day."

22. ἔδοξε τοῖς ἀποστόλοις — πέμψαι.] The syntax in ἐκλεξαμένους is generally thought not agreeable to the *proprietas linguæ*; and γράψαντες deviates entirely from it. There ought, it is said, to have been written ἔδοξε τοῖς ἀπ. ἐκλέξασθαι ἄνδρας καὶ πέμψαι. Ἐκλεξαμένους, however, is as regular as ἐκλεξαμένοις, and is more frequent in the *later* writers, (as Josephus) the sense being "having chosen men from among themselves, to send [them]." Yet it is not exactly put (as Kypke and Rosenm. think) for ἵνα ἐκλεξάμενοι πέμψωσι, but is a *different* construction, in which the Accus. is closely associated with the Infin., and τὸ is understood. Thus it serves to explain what was meant by the "*it*" in "it seemed good." As to γράψαντες for γράψασι, that is merely an *anacoluthon*, such as in long sentences, especially containing parenthetical clauses, is not unusual. So Thucyd. iii. 36. αὐτοῖς — ἐπικαλοῦντες. iv. 42. τοῖς Συρακουσίοις — ὁρῶντες. and often; in which cases the participle in the Nomin. is used as if a verb in the third person plur. indic. had preceded. Ἄνδρας ἡγουμένους, denotes "*leading* men;" a Hellenistic idiom by which the Participle is used as an adjective or substantive. It occurs in the Participial form with an Article, put for a noun, in Luke xxii. 26.

23. χαίρειν.] Sub. λέγουσι or the like. The idiom frequently occurs in the later writers, and is said by the minor Greek Lexicographers to have originated with Cleon the demagogue, who

ἠκούσαμεν ὅτι τινὲς ἐξ ἡμῶν ἐξελθόντες ἐτάραξαν ὑμᾶς λόγοις, ἀνασκευάζοντες τὰς ψυχὰς ὑμῶν, λέγοντες περιτέμνεσθαι καὶ τηρεῖν τὸν
25 νόμον, οἷς οὐ διεστειλάμεθα· ἔδοξεν ἡμῖν γενομένοις ὁμοθυμαδὸν,
ἐκλεξαμένους ἄνδρας πέμψαι πρὸς ὑμᾶς, σὺν τοῖς ἀγαπητοῖς ἡμῶν
26 Βαρνάβᾳ καὶ Παύλῳ, [m] ἀνθρώποις παραδεδωκόσι τὰς ψυχὰς αὐτῶν [m Supra 13. 50. & 14. 19.]
27 ὑπὲρ τοῦ ὀνόματος τοῦ Κυρίου ἡμῶν Ἰησοῦ Χριστοῦ. ἀπεστάλκαμεν
οὖν Ἰούδαν καὶ Σίλαν, καὶ αὐτοὺς διὰ λόγου ἀπαγγέλλοντας τὰ αὐτά.
28 ἔδοξε γὰρ τῷ ἁγίῳ Πνεύματι καὶ ἡμῖν μηδὲν πλέον ἐπιτίθεσθαι ὑμῖν
29 βάρος, πλὴν τῶν ἐπάναγκες τούτων· [n] ἀπέχεσθαι εἰδωλοθύτων, καὶ [n Supra v. 20. Infra 16. 4. & 21. 25.]
αἵματος, καὶ πνικτοῦ, καὶ πορνείας· ἐξ ὧν διατηροῦντες ἑαυτοὺς εὖ
πράξετε. ἔῤῥωσθε.
30 Οἱ μὲν οὖν, ἀπολυθέντες, ἦλθον εἰς Ἀντιόχειαν· καὶ συναγαγόντες
31 τὸ πλῆθος, ἐπέδωκαν τὴν ἐπιστολήν. Ἀναγνόντες δὲ, ἐχάρησαν ἐπὶ τῇ
32 παρακλήσει. Ἰούδας δὲ καὶ Σίλας, καὶ αὐτοὶ προφῆται ὄντες, διὰ λόγου

prefixed it, in the place of εὖ πράσσειν, to his *distich*, announcing the victory at Pylum. Yet it was used a very short time after by one not likely to have imitated Cleon, namely, Xenophon. Cyr. iv. Κῦρος Κυαξάρει χαίρειν. In the Horatian "Celso *gaudere* et *bene rem gerere* refer" there is allusion to *both* forms.

24. ἐτάραξαν.] See Note on Matt. ii. 3. and comp. Gal. i. 7.

— ἀνασκευάζοντες.] Ἀνασκ. properly signifies to *pack up any thing* for removal; as in Thucyd. i. 18. and elsewhere; 2. to *remove*, as in Xenoph. An. vi. 2, 5.; 3dly, from this *packing up* and removal, easily arises the sense of *carrying off*, *plundering*. Thus the sense here seems to be, "removing and perverting your minds [from the truth]." Λέγοντες περιτ., "telling you to be circumcised," i. e. that you should be circumcised. Οἷς οὐ διεστ. Sub. οὐδὲν, "to whom we gave no direction or authority [so to act]." The οὐδὲν is necessary to be supplied, because οὐ διαστ. almost always signifies to *forbid*.

25. γενομένοις ὁμοθυμαδὸν.] Sub. ἐπὶ τὸ αὐτὸ, which is *expressed* at ii. 1. where see Note.

26. παραδ. τὰς ψυχὰς, &c.] i. e. "have jeoparded their lives," by a slight hyperbole, as the Commentators say. Though, considering that Paul was being stoned at Lystra, to use his own expression, ἐν θανάτῳ, the hyperbole is scarcely any. Ὑπὲρ τοῦ ὀν., on behalf of the religion.

27. καὶ αὐτοὺς διὰ λόγου ἀπαγγ. τὰ αὐτά.] I have on Thucyd. vii. 8. 10. (Transl.) treated on the subject of the bearers of public letters or despatches, being usually allowed to explain any obscurity therein. The truth is that such were, in the earlier ages, *always* sent, in the form of *verbal messages*, by trusty persons to deliver by word of mouth; and that had continued even up to the age of Thucyd. On the introduction, however, of *written* messages, or despatches, during the Peloponnesian war, still the custom was retained of permitting the messenger to explain any obscurity in the Epistle, or to give further *particulars* of matters only briefly adverted to in the letter; nay occasionally to act as a sort of *ambassador*, and treat on the business at issue. Sometimes, however, the messengers were *forbidden* to say any thing; and therefore the words καὶ αὐτοὺς διὰ λόγου, &c., here, may be considered as informing the persons addressed, that the messengers *were empowered* to deliver the same message by word of mouth, and of course more fully and explicitly, if desired. Ἀπαγγέλλοντας. Pres. for Fut.: or render "who are to tell you by message." So Fritsch. de Rev. not. Bibl. p. 81. says it may be rendered, "*qui nunc nuntient, or*, ut nuntient," i. e. as he adds "*permixtis temporibus dati* et *redditi* nuntii."

28. ἔδοξε γάρ.] I know not why all the English Translators should render the γὰρ "*for*." It is plainly *resumptive*, and put for οὖν, as often in the Sept. Ἔδοξε, "it hath seemed good," the term used in *decrees*. Τῷ ἁγ. Πνεύμ. καὶ ἡ., by Hendiadys, "to us who are deciding under the influence of the Holy Spirit."

— βάρος.] It was an early, and especially Oriental form of expression to apply the terms βάρος, ζυγὸς, &c., to all laws, orders, &c., *enjoined* on those subject to any one's authority, whether they were heavy or light. See Rev. ii. 4. Matt. xxiii. 4. and Note. Ἐπάναγκες (with which many Commentators are puzzled, and propose various conjectures, — all unnecessary), formed from the *phrase* ἐπ' ἀνάγκης, comes from the old adjective ἐπανάγκης, which is preserved only in the Nomin. or Accus. neuter. It is found in the best writers from Herodot. downwards, but only as an *adverb*. *Here* it may be an *adjective*, by the ellip. of ὄντων.

29. εὖ πράξετε.] This does not mean, "you will do right," as many Commentators suppose, but, "it will be happy for you," "it will tend to your salvation." Comp. Eccles. viii. 12. Is. iii. 10. Jerem. xlii. 6.

30. ἀπολυθέντες.] See Note v. 33. Ἐπέδωκαν τὴν ἐπ. A vox sol. de hac re.

31. ἐχάρησαν ἐπὶ τῇ παρακ.] I know not why so many eminent Commentators should have interpreted παρακλήσει *exhortation*, or *instruction*. The common interpretation, (confirmed by all the ancient Versions), *consolation* or *comfort*, is more suitable and natural. They rejoiced at the comfort which this Epistle gave them, by the assurance that they were delivered from whatever was burdensome in the Mosaic Law. See more in the able Note of Calvin. This use of the Article, however, as referring to something which may be supplied from the context or the subject matter, is rather uncommon.

32. προφῆται.] See xi. 27. and Note, Bp. Pearce in Rec. Syn., and especially Mr. Townsend's

πολλοῦ παρεκάλεσαν τοὺς ἀδελφοὺς καὶ ἐπεστήριξαν. Ποιήσαντες δὲ 33
χρόνον, ἀπελύθησαν μετ᾽ εἰρήνης ἀπὸ τῶν ἀδελφῶν πρὸς τοὺς ἀποστόλους. [ἔδοξε δὲ τῷ Σίλᾳ ἐπιμεῖναι αὐτοῦ.] Παῦλος δὲ καὶ Βαρνάβας 34
διέτριβον ἐν Ἀντιοχείᾳ, διδάσκοντες καὶ εὐαγγελιζόμενοι, μετὰ καὶ ἑτέρων 35
πολλῶν, τὸν λόγον τοῦ Κυρίου.

ΜΕΤΑ δέ τινας ἡμέρας εἶπε Παῦλος πρὸς Βαρνάβαν· Ἐπιστρέψαν- 36
τες δὴ ἐπισκεψώμεθα τοὺς ἀδελφοὺς ἡμῶν κατὰ πᾶσαν πόλιν, ἐν αἷς

o Supra 13. 13, 25. & 13. 5. Col. 4. 10. 2 Tim. 4. 11. Philem. 24. p Supra 13. 13. q Supra 14. 6. infra 17. 14. & 19. 22. & 20. 4. Rom. 16. 21. 1 Cor. 4. 17. Phil. 2. 19. 1 Thess. 3. 2. 1 Tim. 1. 2. 2 Tim. 1. 5.

κατηγγείλαμεν τὸν λόγον τοῦ Κυρίαν, πῶς ἔχουσι. ° Βαρνάβας δὲ 37
ἐβουλεύσατο συμπαραλαβεῖν τὸν Ἰωάννην τὸν καλούμενον Μάρκον·
ᵖ Παῦλος δὲ ἠξίου, τὸν ἀποστάντα ἀπ᾽ αὐτῶν ἀπὸ Παμφυλίας, καὶ μὴ 38
συνελθόντα αὐτοῖς εἰς τὸ ἔργον, μὴ συμπαραλαβεῖν τοῦτον. Ἐγένετο 39
οὖν παροξυσμὸς, ὥστε ἀποχωρισθῆναι αὐτοὺς ἀπ᾽ ἀλλήλων, τόν τε Βαρνάβαν παραλαβόντα τὸν Μάρκον ἐκπλεῦσαι εἰς Κύπρον· Παῦλος δὲ 40
ἐπιλεξάμενος Σίλαν ἐξῆλθε παραδοθεὶς τῇ χάριτι τοῦ Θεοῦ ὑπὸ τῶν
ἀδελφῶν. διήρχετο δὲ τὴν Συρίαν καὶ Κιλικίαν, ἐπιστηρίζων τὰς ἐκκλη- 41
σίας. XVI. ᑫ Κατήντησε δὲ εἰς Δέρβην καὶ Λύστραν. καὶ ἰδοὺ μα- 1

elaborate dissertation (here introduced) on the spiritual gifts, tithes and offices in the Church at Antioch. See also the Note on 1 Cor. xii. 10. Διὰ λόγου πολλοῦ, "in a discourse of considerable length." Παρεκάλ., "exhorted, admonished, and instructed them;" stating, we may suppose, the grounds and reasons on which the determination of the Synod was founded, showing why the *whole* ritual was not enjoined, and why a *part* was retained; and withal defining the cause, nature, and extent of the duty of abstaining, in certain cases, from things naturally lawful.

33. ποιήσαντες χρόνον] "having stayed some time." An idiom confined to the later and especially the Hellenistic writers. Μετ᾽ εἰρήνης, means, "with good wishes and prayers for their welfare," or whatever was included in the Heb. שלום.

34. ἔδοξε — αὐτοῦ.] This verse is omitted in several MSS. and Versions, and is rejected by Mill, Wets., Pearce, Newc., Kuin., and Griesb., bracketed by Vat., and cancelled by Matthæi. The reason which they assign for its having come to be *inserted*, is, that it was done to account for what might have seemed strange and inconsistent in Silas being said to have gone with Jude to Jerusalem; whereas, a few days after, he is said to have been chosen by Paul as his companion in his journey to visit the churches. Yet (say the Critics in question) "he may have gone to Jerusalem, and been sent for from thence, and the circumstance of his sending for, been omitted to be mentioned." I must own that there is nothing to negative this in the expression μετά τινας ἡμέρας, (especially if it be taken of the *first mention* of a *plan* which might not be carried into *execution* for some short time,) that being an indefinite term, which may, at least, mean after *not a very few* days. See xvi. 13. There is however, something very *hypothetical* in this way of accounting for the insertion. Instances of *insertions* for *such* a purpose, are very rare indeed, and not to be increased without urgent cause; as tending to lessen our confidence in the integrity of the Divine word. On the other hand, if we suppose the verse to be *genuine*, its *omission* may readily be accounted for; namely, to remove a seeming inconsistency, a person being here said to have *stayed*, who was just before said to have *gone*; in which case the readiest course, — and that on a level with the capacity of even the *scribes*, — would be to *cancel* the verse. And Critics and Commentators having felt the same difficulty, might resort to the same mode of removing it. Whereas it may satisfactorily be obviated by less violent means, namely, by taking ἀπελυθ. not in the sense *departed*, but in the usual one *dimissi sunt* (as in the Vulg.), meaning their dismissal and departure from the place where the brethren were assembled, not from Antioch itself. It should seem that between the time when they left the meeting, and that fixed on for their actual departure, Silas, from a desire to longer enjoy the society of Paul, resolved to stay longer at Antioch. One might, indeed, have expected that it should have been added, that *Jude* went on his journey. But this was not absolutely necessary, and such omissions are frequent. Words to that effect are, indeed, found in some MSS. and Versions; but it is so very difficult to account for their *omission*, and so easy for their *insertion* (from the margin) that they cannot be received. Thus *internal* evidence is decidedly in favour of the genuineness of the verse; and *external* evidence even more.

36. ἐπισκεψώμεθα τοὺς ἀδελφοὺς — πῶς ἔχουσι.] This may be a common Grecism for ἐπισκ. πῶς ἔχουσιν οἱ ἀδελφοί. Or at πῶς ἔχουσι we may supply σκεψόμενοι, from ἐπισκεψ. The ἐπισκ. must here denote inspection of their state as Christian professors. Hence was derived the use of the term ἐπίσκοπος in the sense *Bishop*, which not long afterwards arose.

38. ἠξίου] (which signifies, *wished* or *thought proper)* must be closely united with μὴ συμπαραλαβεῖν, as in several passages of Thucyd. cited in Recens. Synop.

XVI. 1. κατήντησε] Literally, "went down to." A sense often occurring in this Book, and found in the later Greek writers.

θητής τις ἦν ἐκεῖ, ὀνόματι Τιμόθεος, υἱὸς γυναικός τινος Ἰουδαίας
2 πιστῆς, πατρὸς δὲ Ἕλληνος· [r] ὃς ἐμαρτυρεῖτο ὑπὸ τῶν ἐν Λύστροις καὶ r Supra 6. 3.
3 Ἰκονίῳ ἀδελφῶν. [s] Τοῦτον ἠθέλησεν ὁ Παῦλος σὺν αὐτῷ ἐξελθεῖν, καὶ s 1 Cor. 9. 20. Gal. 2. 3.
λαβὼν περιέτεμεν αὐτὸν, διὰ τοὺς Ἰουδαίους τοὺς ὄντας ἐν τοῖς τόποις
ἐκείνοις· ᾔδεισαν γὰρ ἅπαντες τὸν πατέρα αὐτοῦ ὅτι Ἕλλην ὑπῆρχεν.
4 [t] Ὡς δὲ διεπορεύοντο τὰς πόλεις, παρεδίδουν αὐτοῖς φυλάσσειν τὰ δόγ- t Supra 15. 20, 29.
ματα τὰ κεκριμένα ὑπὸ τῶν ἀποστόλων καὶ τῶν πρεσβυτέρων τῶν ἐν
5 Ἱερουσαλήμ. Αἱ μὲν οὖν ἐκκλησίαι ἐστερεοῦντο τῇ πίστει, καὶ ἐπερίσ-
σευον τῷ ἀριθμῷ καθ᾽ ἡμέραν.
6 Διελθόντες δὲ τὴν Φρυγίαν καὶ τὴν Γαλατικὴν χώραν, κωλυθέντες
7 ὑπὸ τοῦ ἁγίου Πνεύματος λαλῆσαι τὸν λόγον ἐν τῇ Ἀσίᾳ, ἐλθόντες
κατὰ τὴν Μυσίαν ἐπείραζον ‡ κατὰ τὴν Βιθυνίαν πορεύεσθαι· καὶ
8 οὐκ εἴασεν αὐτοὺς τὸ Πνεῦμα. [u] Παρελθόντες δὲ τὴν Μυσίαν, κατέ- u Infra 20. 6. 2 Cor. 2. 12. 2 Tim. 4. 13.
9 βησαν εἰς Τρωάδα. καὶ ὅραμα διὰ τῆς νυκτὸς ὤφθη τῷ Παύλῳ·
ἀνήρ τις ἦν Μακεδὼν ἑστὼς, παρακαλῶν αὐτὸν καὶ λέγων· Διαβὰς εἰς

— ἦν ἐκεῖ] Whether this is to be understood of *Derbe*, or of *Lystra*, Commentators are not agreed. The present passage favours the opinion that he was of *Lystra*; while that at xx. 4. is thought by some to prove him to have been of *Derbe*. But the Δερβαῖος there must refer to *Gaius*, and Gaius only, otherwise St. Luke would have written καὶ Γάϊος καὶ Τιμόθεος, Δερβαῖοι. He does not add Λυστραῖος to Τιμ., because it was unnecessary, he having, he thought, expressed that *here*. And certainly the ἐκεῖ cannot well be understood of any other than *Lystra*, since that was the last mentioned place. From the position of the cities there can be no doubt that the Apostles went to Derbe first, and then to Lystra.

3. περιέτεμεν α.] He had not been circumcised, because (as we learn from the Rabbins) his mother had no right to do that without the father's consent. The reason why *Paul* circumcised him (which he might do without violation of Christian liberty, as being of *Jewish birth*, and because, though circumcision was not enjoined as *necessary* to the Gentile converts, it might be sometimes *expedient*) is just after suggested, namely, that he might not offend the Jews, who would conclude Timothy to be uncircumcised, because his father was a Gentile, and, consequently would not listen to his teaching; therefore the Apostle accommodated himself to the prejudices of weak brethren On the contrary, he did not permit *Titus*, who was of Gentile birth by *both* parents, to be circumcised, because it was demanded to be done by the false teachers as necessary to salvation. *There* conscience could not allow him to give way.

6. Ἀσίᾳ] This must here denote that part of Asia Minor which was peculiarly so called, i. e. *Proconsular* Asia, of which Ephesus was the capital. *How* this hindrance was imparted to them, whether by dream or otherwise, is uncertain.

7. κατὰ τ. Β.] Several MSS. have εἰς, which is adopted by Griesb. and other Editors; but without reason, since external evidence is decidedly in favour of κατὰ, and indeed internal too; for εἰς was doubtless only an alteration to remove a tautology. Versions ought not to have been appealed to by Griesb., since in a case like this they have no authority, and Fathers very little, because they often quoted from memory.

— Πνεῦμα] Nine MSS. add Ἰησοῦ, and others, with several Versions and some Fathers, τοῦ Ἰησοῦ, which is adopted by Mill and Wets., and received into the text by Griesb., Knapp, Tittm., and Vat., as had been long ago done by Beza. And it is expressed by Doddr., Newcome, and Wakef. Yet there seems no sufficient evidence of its genuineness to warrant its reception. The *external* evidence is weak, as far as regards *MSS.*; and Versions and Fathers are, in a matter of this kind, not quite unexceptionable testimony. But, to advert to *internal* evidence, it would at first sight seem that as Πνεῦμα Ἰησοῦ is a very rare expression, occurring nowhere else, but in Phil. i. 19. (and there in a different sense) we may far better account for the *omission* than for the *insertion* of Ἰησοῦ. And yet we do not elsewhere find that rare expressions are cancelled by the *scribes*. Besides, when any very rare forms of expression are connected with important *doctrinal* questions, we are to advert to the possibility, nay probability, that they may have been tampered with by the ancient *Theologians*, either by adding something to the text, or by removing something from it. Now, it appears from the Note of Wets. that the Romanists, a little after the printing of the Greek Text, maintained that Ἰησοῦ had been expunged by the *Nestorians*; which is incredible. They might rather have been expected to *add* than to *remove* it. The addition, however, I suspect, came from the *Arians*, who would have more reason to add it, in order to destroy so decided an example of τὸ Πνεῦμα in the *personal* sense. Thus it is caught up by all the Socinian interpreters. And when once introduced by the *Arians*, it would be likely to be admitted by the *Nestorians*, who would rather have it than not. From the *former* of these it was, I suspect, foisted into the *Vulgate*, and by the latter into the *Syriac* Version, and from thence it would be easily transmitted to the *Æthiopic*, *Coptic*, and *Armenian* Versions. Finally, the word is strongly discountenanced by the context. For, to use the words of Bp. Middl., "in the preceding verse we are told that the Apostles were forbidden of the Holy Ghost to preach the word in Asia; in the present,

Μακεδονίαν βοήθησον ἡμῖν· ὡς δὲ τὸ ὅραμα εἶδεν, εὐθέως ἐζητήσα- 10
μεν ἐξελθεῖν εἰς τὴν Μακεδονίαν, συμβιβάζοντες ὅτι προσκέκληται ἡμᾶς
ὁ Κύριος εὐαγγελίσασθαι αὐτούς. Ἀναχθέντες οὖν ἀπὸ τῆς Τρωάδος, 11
εὐθυδρομήσαμεν εἰς Σαμοθρᾴκην, τῇ τε ἐπιούσῃ εἰς Νεάπολιν, ἐκεῖθέν 12
τε εἰς Φιλίππους, ἥτις ἐστὶ πρώτη [τῆς] μερίδος τῆς Μακεδονίας πό-
λις, κολωνία. Ἦμεν δὲ ἐν ταύτῃ τῇ πόλει διατρίβοντες ἡμέρας τινάς·
τῇ τε ἡμέρᾳ τῶν σαββάτων ἐξήλθομεν τῆς πόλεως παρὰ ποταμὸν, οὗ 13

that on their attempting to go into Bithynia, the Spirit suffered them not." It is, therefore, highly unnatural that the τὸ Πνεῦμα of the latter verse should be meant of any other than the τὸ ἅγιον Πνεῦμα of the former.

10. ἐζητήσαμεν] As St. Luke here uses *we*, after having before all along used *they*, it is plain that he himself became the companion of Paul and Timothy in this journey.

— συμβ.] See Note on ix. 22.

12. πρώτη τῆς μερίδος τῆς Μακ. πόλις] No little perplexity here exists, from a difficulty to reconcile the present statement with the actual state of things then existing. According to the sense assigned by the Pesch. Syr. and some others, "which is the metropolis of the country of Macedonia," the words will involve an inaccuracy; *Thessalonica* being undoubtedly the capital. And if we take πρώτη for "most *considerable*," it will be equally irreconcileable with facts. Indeed, by so interpreting we overlook the force of μερίδος in such a connection, which can only be "*portion*," i. e. *district*. And that Macedonia had long been divided into four districts, we learn from the Historians. Indeed coins of the *Provincia prima* and *secunda* have been found. Hence it has been the opinion of many learned men that instead of πρώτη τῆς we should read πρώτης; by which the sense will be, "which is a city of the Provincia prima of Macedonia." But not a single MS. is found to support this conjecture; which, indeed is little supported by probability, as introducing a sort of minute circumstance not very likely to have been adverted to by the sacred writer. It is better, therefore, to retain the common reading; explaining it as we best may. Now the matter hinges on whether πρώτη may be supposed to mean "the principal," or "*a* principal." If we fix on the *former* sense, we encounter the objection, that Philippi was not even the capital of the *district*, but *Amphipolis*, as we learn from Livy and Diodorus. Hence Michaelis and Kuin. adopt the *latter* sense; and they appeal to the unexceptionable evidence of Eckel Doctr. Vet. Numm. P. I. Vol. 4. p. 282. in attestation of the fact, that πρώτη was sometimes so applied as to mean a principal, though not the principal city of a country. And certainly, this view being admitted, all objection on the score of geographical exactness will be removed. I am, however, inclined to think the word πρώτη was meant to have the sense "the principal." Nor is there any thing really formidable in the objection, that Amphipolis was the capital; for though Amphipolis had been originally the capital, yet it is very probable (as Wets. and Pearce suppose) that, after the battle of Philippi, *that* city was raised to the dignity of capital of the district, in the place of Amphipolis, which was then on the decline; especially since, we know, it was the policy of the Romans to make their *colonies* the *capitals* of the countries where they were situated. As, however, we have no historical proof of this transfer, it may be better (with Bp. Pearce) to understand πρώτη in the sense most considerable and important, in commerce, wealth, and population. And *such* the Romans would be especially anxious their colonies should be; and many causes would contribute to make them such. Still one difficulty yet remains. Whichever of the above senses be adopted, the τῆς before μερίδος is worse than useless: and has, I suspect, caused all the perplexity in question. Bp. Middl., indeed, places it in the least objectionable point of view by reading, "which is the chief city of its district, a city of Macedonia, a colony." But this is doing a manifest violence to the construction, and injury to the sense, which is thus very jejune. And Professor Scholefield acknowledges that he is by no means satisfied with that mode. I would therefore suppose a slight corruption to have crept into the text, occasioned by a mistake in placing the article τῆς. Now the first τῆς is not found in three ancient MSS., the Syriac Version, and Chrys.: nor does it appear to have been in the Copies read by the Pesch. Syr. and Vulgate Translators; nor in the originals of those MSS. which have μερίς, plainly by a confounding of the abbreviation of the termination δος with ς. And as *external* testimony is not wanting against this τῆς, so neither is *internal*; for it is *inexplicable* except on Bp. Middl.'s violent construction. I suspect, therefore, that it crept in by a mistake of the scribes; since those MSS. which have not the τῆς *here*, have it before Μακεδ.: and though it is there not found in ten MSS. (some of them of the highest antiquity) all of them *have* the τῆς before μερίδος. May we not, then, suppose that the article, which ought properly to be inserted but *once*, was first inserted in the *wrong* place, and afterwards (error gathering force like a snow-ball) both in the *right* place and the *wrong*. I have ventured to double bracket the τῆς, which is *cancelled* by Lachmann. Render "which is the most considerable city of a district of Macedonia." Mr. Arundell, in his Travels in Asia Minor, notices two medals, one bearing the inscription Εφεσιων . πρωτων . Ασιας . and another, Σμυρνα . Πρωτη . Ασιας . καλλει . και μεγεθει.

13. παρὰ ποταμὸν] "by the river side;" not "by a river," as our English Translators render, and the Article is omitted chiefly on account of the *notoriety* of the river, but partly by reason of a preposition being used. This ποταμὸς is a mere rivulet, formed by the *fountains*, from which Philippi derived its first name, *Crenides*, and running into the Strymon. A striking attestation to the truth of the narrative; for the river is so small as only to be found in the best recent maps on a large scale.

— οὗ ἐνομίζετο προσευχὴ ε.] The Commentators are not agreed on the sense of these words; which the earlier ones take to mean "where prayer was wont to be made;" while the later ones interpret,

ἐνομίζετο προσευχὴ εἶναι, καὶ καθίσαντες ἐλαλοῦμεν ταῖς συνελθούσαις
14 γυναιξί. Καί τις γυνὴ ὀνόματι Λυδία, πορφυρόπωλις πόλεως Θυατεί-
ρων, σεβομένη τὸν Θεὸν, ἤκουεν· ἧς ὁ Κύριος διήνοιξε τὴν καρδίαν,
15 προσέχειν τοῖς λαλουμένοις ὑπὸ τοῦ Παύλου. [x] Ὡς δὲ ἐβαπτίσθη, καὶ
ὁ οἶκος αὐτῆς, παρεκάλεσε λέγουσα· Εἰ κεκρίκατέ με πιστὴν τῷ Κυρίῳ εἶναι, εἰσελθόντες εἰς τὸν οἶκόν μου μείνατε. καὶ παρεβιάσατο

x Gen. 19. 3. & 33. 11. Jud. 19. 21. Luke 24. 29. Heb. 13. 2.

"where, according to [the Jewish] custom, there was a proseuche, or oratory." That such places (not *edifices*, but *groves*, like the ancient Druidical temples) were then frequent where no synagogue was found, is proved by the Commentators; as also that such were situated, for the convenience of purification, by a river-side. Yet I see not how οὗ ἐνομίζετο εἶναι can have the above sense, still less be taken for οὗ ἦν, with others. Neither do I see any force in the objections,—that the common interpretation yields too indefinite a sense, and is incorrect in phraseology. The former has not a shadow of reason; and the latter is overturned by one of the passages adduced to establish the *other* interpretation, namely, *Philo contra Flaccum*: Διὰ πολλῶν ἐκχυθέντες ἐπὶ τοὺς πλησίον αἰγιαλοὺς, τὰς προσευχὰς ἀφῄρηντο, οὗ ἐνομίζετο προσευχὴ εἶναι, where we have the very phrase, and in the very sense of the *common interpretation*. And although it is accompanied with the term προσευχὴ, *proseucha*; yet it is evident that Philo thought it necessary to add the words following, in order to *determine* the sense. It should therefore seem that, for a similar reason, *St. Luke* chose to use a *circumlocution*, in preference to a term which might require this very circumlocution to explain it. It is true that at ver. 16. the words πορευομένων εἰς προσευχὴν *seem* to require προσ. to be taken in the sense *proseucha*. But though I am not prepared to assert that the rendering "as we were going to prayer" is there to be justified (notwithstanding that in Joseph. Vit. § 57, I find ἡμῶν τὰ νόμιμα ποιούντων, καὶ εἰς προσευχὰς τετραμμένων), since that would make the *notice of the time* when the circumstance took place too indeterminate, and be not a little frigid, yet it may be observed that the sense *proseucha* would require the *Article*. Indeed, I know of no passage of any writer where it occurs in this sense *without* the Article. See Joseph. Vit. § 54. It seems pretty clear, however, that προσευχὴν there is used in the very same sense as the expression here at ver. 13, namely, by circumlocution, to denote the place οὗ ἐνομίζετο προσευχὴ εἶναι, the place where prayer was wont to be made; not indeed (as I would understand) a regular building, such as the *Proseuchæ* were, but a mere grove; as when Apion ap. Joseph. Contr. Ap. π. 2. says of Moses, αἰθρίους προσευχὰς ἀνῆγεν. Yet this sense, too, requires the *Article*; which, therefore, I have (with Griesb., Lachm., and Rinck) introduced, on the authority of many MSS. of the Western Class, and also of Origen and Theophyl.

With respect to the *time* when the circumstance mentioned at ver. 16 took place (which Commentators are so perplexed to determine), it should seem to have been on the *first* day that Paul and Silas went to the prayer-meeting. The δὲ there is *transitive* and *resumptive* (vv. 14 & 15 being in some degree parenthetical), and serves to introduce a narrative which, according to the order of time, ought to have come in at ver. 13 between προσευχὴ εἶναι and καθίσαντες. Though, indeed, there was some reason for mentioning it where it is, since, we find, the same occurrence took place several times afterwards on *other* days.

—ἐλαλοῦμεν.] Not "discoursed with," as Wakef. renders; for λαλεῖν must here be taken in the sense of *discourse to*, as a public teacher or preacher. Thus the preceding καθίσαντες alludes to the *posture* adopted, which was that of teaching. See Matt. v. 1. and Note. It is plain that the congregation consisted of women only, not, as is commonly supposed, a mixture of both sexes. To account for which, we may suppose that since that *separation of the sexes*, which always subsisted in regular buildings, such as synagogues, was impossible in places like *proseuchæ*, the same end was effected by the sexes attending at different times.

14. Λυδία.] Some take this as a name of country, and to be joined with γυνή. But the ὀνόματι associated with it shows it to be a *proper name*. The name was common both among the Greeks and Romans. Πορφυρόπωλις means a seller not of purple *dye*, as some suppose, but of purple *vests*, for the dying of which the Lydians were famous; who seem to have participated in, or succeeded to the reputation of the Tyrians. She seems to have been a resident of Thyatira in Lydia, where her vests were manufactured, but sojourning at Philippi, for the purposes of her business. By the expression just after σεβομένη τὸν Θεὸν is meant, that she was a devout Gentile, worshipping the one true God, or a proselyte of the gate.

—διήνοιξε τὴν καρδίαν.] The expression was probably derived from the Hebrew; for it occurs in the Jewish prayers, as also in 2 Macc. i. 14. δ. τὴν καρδίαν ἐν τῷ νόμῳ αὐτοῦ καὶ ἐν τοῖς προστάγμασι. The mind is said to be *closed* against admonition, when either from prejudice, it cannot discern the truth, or, from pride and perversity, will not admit it. Hence, to *open* the mind or heart denotes, to render it more intelligent,—to cause that any one shall better perceive the truth, and more readily yield assent to it. The opening in question was effected by the grace of God working by his Spirit with the concurrent good dispositions of Lydia.

15. πιστὴν τῷ Κυρίῳ] "a true believer in the Lord [and his religion]," so as to be fit to be admitted to baptism. The expression elsewhere occurs without the addition of τῷ K., and then denotes a *Christian*.

—παρεβιάσατο ἡμᾶς.] This term, like ἀναγκάζω, is used of the *moral* compulsion of urgent entreaty, such as, in a manner, compels the person to grant the request. St. Luke here, and in his Gospel xxiv. 29, seems to have had in mind Gen. xix. 3, where Lot, it is said, κατεβιάζετο (many good MSS. have παραβ., which is probably the true reading), the angel to enter; also 1 Sam. xxviii. 23, καὶ οὐκ ἐβουλήθη φαγεῖν, καὶ παρεβιάσαντο αὐτὸν οἱ παῖδες καὶ ἡ γυνή. The παρα signifies *præter* [scil. voluntatem], and thus παραβιάζειν is a stronger term than ἀναγκάζειν.

y 1 Sam. 28. 7. infra 19. 24. ἡμᾶς. [y] Ἐγένετο δὲ, πορευομένων ἡμῶν εἰς τὴν προσευχὴν, παιδίσκην 16
τινὰ ἔχουσαν πνεῦμα Πύθωνος ἀπαντῆσαι ἡμῖν, ἥτις ἐργασίαν πολλὴν
παρεῖχε τοῖς κυρίοις αὐτῆς μαντευομένη. Αὕτη κατακολουθήσασα τῷ 17
Παύλῳ καὶ ἡμῖν, ἔκραζε λέγουσα· Οὗτοι οἱ ἄνθρωποι δοῦλοι τοῦ
Θεοῦ τοῦ ὑψίστου εἰσὶν, οἵτινες καταγγέλλουσιν ἡμῖν ὁδὸν σωτηρίας!
z Mark 16. 17. [z] Τοῦτο δὲ ἐποίει ἐπὶ πολλὰς ἡμέρας. διαπονηθεὶς δὲ ὁ Παῦλος, καὶ 18
ἐπιστρέψας, τῷ πνεύματι εἶπε· Παραγγέλλω σοι ἐν τῷ ὀνόματι Ἰησοῦ
a 2 Cor. 6. 5. Χριστοῦ ἐξελθεῖν ἀπ' αὐτῆς. καὶ ἐξῆλθεν αὐτῇ τῇ ὥρᾳ. [a] Ἰδόντες δὲ 19
οἱ κύριοι αὐτῆς, ὅτι ἐξῆλθεν ἡ ἐλπὶς τῆς ἐργασίας αὐτῶν, ἐπιλαβόμενοι
τὸν Παῦλον καὶ τὸν Σίλαν, εἵλκυσαν εἰς τὴν ἀγορὰν ἐπὶ τοὺς ἄρχον-
b 1 Kings 18. 17. infra 17. 6. τας. [b] Καὶ προσαγαγόντες αὐτοὺς τοῖς στρατηγοῖς, εἶπον· Οὗτοι οἱ 20
ἄνθρωποι ἐκταράσσουσιν ἡμῶν τὴν πόλιν, Ἰουδαῖοι ὑπάρχοντες· καὶ 21
καταγγέλλουσιν ἔθη, ἃ οὐκ ἔξεστιν ἡμῖν παραδέχεσθαι οὐδὲ ποιεῖν,
c 2 Cor. 11. 25. 1 Thess. 2. 2. Phil. 1. 13. Ῥωμαίοις οὖσι. [c] Καὶ συνεπέστη ὁ ὄχλος κατ' αὐτῶν, καὶ οἱ στρατη- 22
γοὶ περιῤῥήξαντες αὐτῶν τὰ ἱμάτια, ἐκέλευον ῥαβδίζειν· πολλάς τε 23

16. παιδίσκην] i. e. a female servant or slave.

— ἔχουσαν πνεῦμα Πύθ.] Πύθων was properly an *appellation of Apollo*. But, as he was the God of Divination, it came to be applied to soothsayers, conjurors, and those who pretended to evoke spirits. Now as *ventriloquism* was a most useful art to persons of that profession, they generally acquired more or less of it; hence the word is sometimes explained to mean ventriloquist in the Greek Lexicographers. Now whether this girl was a ventriloquist, has been much debated; but the *negative* is the view adopted (and, I think, rightly) by the most eminent Commentators. See Deyling, Wolf, and Kuin. There is no sufficient reason to suppose so from the *name*, and still less from the *circumstances*. This is closely connected with another, and more important question, — *whether she was a pretender to the gift of divination*. This also has been by Deyling, Wolf, Walch, and Biscoe, decided in the *negative*. There is somewhat to countenance the opinion of certain eminent recent Commentators, that she was a *lunatic*, who (like Johanna Southcote) fancied that she was inspired to foretell future events. See Rec. Syn. and Townsend in loc., in his Dissertation on the nature of the Spirit of Divination in the Pythoness; whence it will appear that this notion involves insuperable difficulties, being inconsistent with the view taken by the Sacred writer; which requires us to suppose (as the ancient, and most modern Commentators have done) that the girl was *possessed with an evil Spirit*, which enabled her to occasionally foretell future events. So Hesychius explains Πύθωνα by δαιμόνιον μαντικόν. The expression, then, is a kindred one with that used by St. Luke in his Gospel, iv. 33. ἄνθρωπος ἔχων πνεῦμα δαιμονίου ἀκαθάρτου.

— ἐργασίαν.] This word, from ἐργάζεσθαι, to *make* money (as we say), signifies *gain*.

— τοῖς κυρίοις.] Fischer and Vater take this as plural for singular, as in Luke xix. 33. That passage, however, is of a different nature; and to call in *enallage* would be here entirely *unnecessary:* since Grotius and Wahl have fully proved, that the *common possession* of a slave, especially when exercising any gainful trade, was not unfrequent.

17. δοῦλοι τοῦ Θεοῦ — σωτ.] Though the expression δοῦλος Θεοῦ was in use among the Gentiles, to signify those devoted to any God as his Priests, yet as ὁδὸς σωτηρίας was one quite unknown to them, we might imagine that both expressions were derived from persons who had heard Paul and Timothy preach; but that it is best to suppose the words pronounced by *the dæmon* through the organs of the girl and thus bearing the same honourable testimony to the Apostles, as had been borne by the *dæmons* to our Lord.

19. ἐξῆλθεν.] There seems to be (as Valckn. remarks) a *paronomasia* with the preceding ἐξῆλθεν, since with the going out of the dæmon was gone their hope of gain. Ἐπιλαβόμενοι, "having [caused to be] apprehended;" as xviii. 17. xxi. 30. and Luke xxiii. 26. Ἕλκειν, like σύρειν and the Latin *rapere*, is often used of *impleading* any one, and consequently obliging him to go to judgment. Ἄρχοντας is a *general term;* in the place of which is, in the next verse, substituted the more *special* one στρατηγοί; for so, it seems, the magistrates at Philippi were called.

20. ἐκταράσσουσιν] "are causing great disturbance to." The ἐκ. is intensive. The charge made was two-fold: 1. that they were disturbers of the peace; and, 2. teachers of unlawful religious customs and rites: both charges alike falling under the cognizance of the magistracy. And though the Romans were not intolerant; — yet, in their permission to foreigners to worship God according to their consciences, it was understood that there should be no *public* attempts at proselytism. And whenever the *former* charge was connected with the latter, the magistrates were bound to punish. In Ἰουδαῖοι ὑπάρχοντες it is suggested that their offence is greater by the persons being, as foreigners and of a most despised nation, those who ought the less to have ventured to commit it.

22. περιῤῥήξαντες.] This use of the word is like that of the Latin *scindere*, and the corresponding words in Greek; and denotes a hasty, and, if done by another, a violent, stripping off of clothes. So Xenoph. p. 742. τὴν ἐσθῆτα περιῤῥήξαντες. and Diod. Sic. L. xvii. 35. αἱ τὰς ἐσθ. περιῤῥηγνῦνται. The scourging was probably ordered as a temporary punishment, to satisfy the people; the

ἐπιθέντες αὐτοῖς πληγὰς, ἔβαλον εἰς φυλακὴν, παραγγείλαντες τῷ δε-
24 σμοφύλακι, ἀσφαλῶς τηρεῖν αὐτούς· ὃς παραγγελίαν τοιαύτην εἰληφὼς,
ἔβαλεν αὐτοὺς εἰς τὴν ἐσωτέραν φυλακὴν, καὶ τοὺς πόδας αὐτῶν ἠσφα-
25 λίσατο εἰς τὸ ξύλον. [d] Κατὰ δὲ τὸ μεσονύκτιον Παῦλος καὶ Σίλας d Supra 4. 31.
προσευχόμενοι ὕμνουν τὸν Θεόν· ἐπηκροῶντο δὲ αὐτῶν οἱ δέσμιοι.
26 [e] Ἄφνω δὲ σεισμὸς ἐγένετο μέγας, ὥστε σαλευθῆναι τὰ θεμέλια τοῦ e Supra 5. 19. & 12. 7.
δεσμωτηρίου· ἀνεῴχθησάν τε παραχρῆμα αἱ θύραι πᾶσαι, καὶ πάντων
27 τὰ δεσμὰ ἀνέθη. Ἔξυπνος δὲ γενόμενος ὁ δεσμοφύλαξ, καὶ ἰδὼν ἀν-
εῳγμένας τὰς θύρας τῆς φυλακῆς, σπασάμενος μάχαιραν ἔμελλεν ἑαυτὸν
28 ἀναιρεῖν, νομίζων ἐκπεφευγέναι τοὺς δεσμίους. Ἐφώνησε δὲ φωνῇ μεγάλῃ ὁ Παῦλος, λέγων· Μηδὲν πράξῃς σεαυτῷ κακόν· ἅπαντες γάρ
29 ἐσμεν ἐνθάδε. Αἰτήσας δὲ φῶτα εἰσεπήδησε, καὶ ἔντρομος γενόμενος
30 προσέπεσε τῷ Παύλῳ καὶ τῷ Σίλᾳ· [f] καὶ προαγαγὼν αὐτοὺς ἔξω, ἔφη· f Luke 3. 10. supra 2. 37.
31 Κύριοι, τί με δεῖ ποιεῖν, ἵνα σωθῶ; Οἱ δὲ εἶπον· Πίστευσον ἐπὶ & 9. 6. John 3. 16, 36.
32 τὸν Κύριον Ἰησοῦν Χριστὸν, καὶ σωθήσῃ σὺ, καὶ ὁ οἶκός σου. Καὶ & 6. 47. 1 John 5. 10.
ἐλάλησαν αὐτῷ τὸν λόγον τοῦ Κυρίου, καὶ πᾶσι τοῖς ἐν τῇ οἰκίᾳ αὐτοῦ.
33 Καὶ παραλαβὼν αὐτοὺς, ἐν ἐκείνῃ τῇ ὥρᾳ τῆς νυκτὸς, ἔλουσεν ἀπὸ τῶν

final examination of the charge being reserved for another occasion.

24. τὴν ἐσωτέραν φυλ.] So Liv. Hist. xxxiv. 44. Pleminius in *inferiorem* demissus carcerem est. Jails were not so strongly built at the *outer* part as the *inner*; to which there was access by several gates, and where sometimes there were subterraneous dungeons. Chains, too, were then added (to secure the prisoners committed there), and a machine called ξύλον, of wood bound with iron, in which the arms and head were sometimes confined (as in our *pillory*), but more frequently the *legs* only; not, however, as in our *stocks*; for the machine was one in which the *feet* were constrained and bruised. Hence it was called ξυλοπέδη, ποδοκάκη, and ποδοστράβη (Heb. סַד, Job. xiii. 27.) Or, finally, one in which *all* the members were held, by being thrust through five holes. See more in Grot., Pric., Elsn., and Kuin.

25. ὕμνουν τὸν Θεὸν] i. e. returning thanks to God for the honour done them of suffering in his cause (see v. 41. and Matt. v. 11, 12.), and for the support He afforded them under affliction. The circumstance of the other prisoners "hearing them" is recorded, to intimate that they prayed aloud, doubtless in order to testify their conscience to be void of offence, and their joy in the Holy Ghost.

26. ἀνεῴχθησαν — πᾶσαι.] The opening of doors of themselves was always thought to attest the presence of God or an angel. See xii. 10.

— καὶ πάντων τὰ δεσμὰ ἀνέθη.] By this most Commentators understand, that the chains of the prisoners were relaxed, though not so much as to place them quite at liberty. This, however, is difficult to conceive; and, from the use of the word in the Classical writers (see the examples cited by Wets.), ἀνέθη τὰ δεσμὰ can only signify, "were *freed from their chains*." Yet, as the *doors* were, at the same time, *opened*, it would seem surprising that the prisoners should not have made their escape; which is by some Expositors attributed to their *extreme astonishment!* But that is surely a most frigid conceit: and the circumstance must undoubtedly be ascribed, with all the best Interpreters, to *Divine interposition*, so as to correspond to the rest of this supernatural transaction. The great intent of which seems to have been, to evince, in the most decided manner, the presence of the Deity. And as the opening of the prison doors might have been ascribed to *accident* and a *natural cause* (namely, the earthquake), therefore the prisoners were likewise *all of them* set free from their chains; yet held enchained by a secret influence, that they should not endeavour to make their escape. All which plainly bespoke the *miraculous*. Whether in this unbinding of the prisoners there was meant to be (as Dr. Clarke supposes) any symbolical allusion to the Gospel as "proclaiming deliverance to the captives, and the opening of the prison-doors to the bound," may be considered, to say the least, doubtful.

28. μηδὲν — κακόν.] An euphemism, like that of Xenophon, cited by Wets.: ἐδεδοίκει γὰρ μή τι ἑαυτὸν ἐργάσηται δεινόν.

29. ἔντρομος.] Various causes might produce this feeling; and among these, that of *awe*, as in the presence of Divine legates, attested to be such by the supernatural occurrence already witnessed.

30. ἔξω] i. e. out of the inner jail.

— τί με δεῖ — σωθῶ;] I have, in Recens. Synop., proved that this cannot mean (as Markl., Morus, Rosenm., and Stolz. suppose) "what must I do to be *safe?*" viz. from the punishment of the magistrates, or from the wrath of Heaven, for harshly treating such good persons; but, as the whole of the context requires, "by what means can I attain *eternal salvation?*" He knew they professed to show the means, — and their commission to do it was now established beyond doubt.

31. πίστευσον ἐπὶ — σου.] "Embrace the Christian religion, i. e. so as to obey it, and thou and all thy family shall attain salvation." See Doddr. It is *taken for granted* that his family became Christians as well as himself.

33. ἐν ἐκείνῃ τῇ ὥρᾳ τῆς ν.] "at that very hour

g Luke 5. 29. & 19. 6. πληγῶν, καὶ ἐβαπτίσθη αὐτὸς, καὶ οἱ αὐτοῦ πάντες παραχρῆμα· g ἀν- 34
αγαγών τε αὐτοὺς εἰς τὸν οἶκον αὐτοῦ, παρέθηκε τράπεζαν, καὶ ἠγαλ-
λιάσατο πανοικὶ πεπιστευκὼς τῷ Θεῷ.
Ἡμέρας δὲ γενομένης, ἀπέστειλαν οἱ στρατηγοὶ τοὺς ῥαβδούχους, λέ- 35
γοντες· Ἀπόλυσον τοὺς ἀνθρώπους ἐκείνους. Ἀπήγγειλε δὲ ὁ δεσμο- 36
φύλαξ τοὺς λόγους τούτους πρὸς τὸν Παῦλον· Ὅτι ἀπεστάλκασιν οἱ
στρατηγοὶ ἵνα ἀπολυθῆτε· νῦν οὖν ἐξελθόντες πορεύεσθε ἐν εἰρήνῃ.
h Infra 22. 25. h Ὁ δὲ Παῦλος ἔφη πρὸς αὐτούς· Δείραντες ἡμᾶς δημοσίᾳ ἀκατακρί- 37
τους, ἀνθρώπους Ῥωμαίους ὑπάρχοντας, ἔβαλον εἰς φυλακὴν, καὶ νῦν
λάθρα ἡμᾶς ἐκβάλλουσιν; οὐ γάρ· ἀλλὰ ἐλθόντες αὐτοὶ ἡμᾶς ἐξαγα-
γέτωσαν. Ἀνήγγειλαν δὲ τοῖς στρατηγοῖς οἱ ῥαβδοῦχοι τὰ ῥήματα 38
i Matt. 8. 34. ταῦτα· καὶ ἐφοβήθησαν ἀκούσαντες ὅτι Ῥωμαῖοί εἰσι, i καὶ ἐλθόντες 39
παρεκάλεσαν αὐτοὺς, καὶ ἐξαγαγόντες ἠρώτων ἐξελθεῖν τῆς πόλεως.
Ἐξελθόντες δὲ ἐκ τῆς φυλακῆς εἰσῆλθον εἰς τὴν Λυδίαν· καὶ ἰδόντες 40
τοὺς ἀδελφοὺς, παρεκάλεσαν αὐτοὺς, καὶ ἐξῆλθον.

XVII. ΔΙΟΔΕΥΣΑΝΤΕΣ δὲ τὴν Ἀμφίπολιν καὶ Ἀπολλωνίαν, 1
ἦλθον εἰς Θεσσαλονίκην, ὅπου ἦν ἡ συναγωγὴ τῶν Ἰουδαίων. Κατὰ δὲ 2

of the night," unseasonable as it was. Ἔλουσεν ἀπὸ τῶν πλ. It is not necessary to suppose ἔλουσε put for ἔλ. καθαρίζων, with Pisc., or, with Kypke, Kuin., and Campb., to take ἀπὸ in the sense *propter*, supplying *σώματα*. The true mode of taking the passage is to consider it as a blending of two forms of expression, — namely, ἔλουσεν αὐτοὺς, and ἀπέλουσεν αἷμα τῶν πληγῶν. So Hom. Il. Σ. 345. ὄφρα τάχιστα Πάτροκλον λούσειαν ἄπο βρότον αἱματόεντα. where λούσειαν — αἱματ. is for ἀπολούων β. αἱματ.

37. ἔφη πρὸς αὐτοὺς] i. e. to the beadles, by a message, it should seem, sent by the Jailor. In δείραντες — ἐκβάλλουσιν there is such spirit, brevity, and point (almost each word forming a head of complaint), as could not easily be paralleled, even in the writings of Demosthenes. Ἀκατακρίτους signifies, "not found guilty, on trial [of any wrong.]" On the Roman law on this point, and on the privileges of Roman citizens in foreign countries, the Commentators adduce numerous Classical illustrations and references. In *what sense* Paul was enabled to call himself a *Roman citizen*, is a point much debated. Some think it was on the ground that Tarsus was a Roman *colony*, or at least a *municipium*. Now the municipia were properly Italian towns, on which had been conferred the *jus civitatis*; whereby the citizens of those places had the public and private rights of *Quirites*; and moreover made their own laws, and elected their own magistrates. There were, however, some *municipia* which had *not* the right of suffrage; and so possessed not the full *jus civitatis*. Yet Tarsus (Paul's birth-place) was neither a colony nor a municipium, but an *urbs libera*. See Pliny v. 27. Now *these free cities* lived under their own laws, had their own magistrates, were independent of the jurisdiction of the Roman president, and were not occupied by Roman garrisons. With this freedom the Tarsæans had been presented by Augustus, as a compensation for the damages they had sustained in the cause of Julius Cæsar, in the course of the Civil War. That the *Tarsæans* had *not* the *jus civitatis Romanæ*, is also *hence* apparent, that the Roman Tribune, notwithstanding he knew Paul to be a Tarsæan (see xxi. 39.), ordered him to be scourged (xxii. 14.), though he desisted as soon as he understood that he was a *Roman* citizen. See xxii. 27. seq. It should therefore seem, as some suppose, that one of Paul's ancestors had had this freedom given him, for some service rendered to Cæsar in the civil wars.

When it is said ἡμᾶς Ῥωμαίους ὑπάρχ., the Commentators, supposing that *Silas* was not a Roman citizen, would take the singular as put for the *plural, dignitatis gratiâ*. But there is no necessity to resort to any such precarious device; for though, that "Silas is (as they say) nowhere else called a Roman citizen," be *true*, yet it is nowhere said, or even hinted, that he was *not* so. That he *was*, his very name Silas, for Sylvanus, renders probable. Nor was the *jus civitatis*, in its most limited sense, then so very difficult to be acquired.

— οὐ γάρ.] An elliptical formula, like many similar ones in Latin and English, in which the brevity (to be supplied by ποιεῖν ἔδει or the like) is very well suited to a feeling of indignation. Ἀλλὰ ἐλθόντες, &c., which would thus be a sort of symbolical action, expressive of their conviction of their innocence. It appears from the Commentators to have been not unfrequently resorted to.

39. παρεκάλεσαν αὐτοὺς] "appeased them."

40. εἰσῆλθον εἰς τὴν Λ.] Some stumble at this idiom, and would read Λυδίας. But the MSS. give no countenance; and it has been proved by Wolf, Alberti, Heumann, Kypke, and Valckn., that εἰσέρχεσθαι εἰς τινα is often used in the sense "to enter into any one's house." Several MSS. indeed, have πρὸς, which has been adopted by almost all the recent Editors. But without any good reason, for it seems to have originated in the *emendation* of the Alexandrian Critics.

— παρεκάλεσαν.] We may here unite the senses of *admonishing*, and *exhorting*, and perhaps comforting. See Note on 2 Cor. ii. 4.

XVII. 1. ἡ συναγωγὴ τῶν Ἰ.] Bp. Middl. ob-

τὸ εἰωθὸς τῷ *Παύλῳ* εἰσῆλθε πρὸς αὐτοὺς, καὶ ἐπὶ σάββατα τρία διε-
3 λέγετο αὐτοῖς ἀπὸ τῶν γραφῶν, [k] διανοίγων καὶ παρατιθέμενος, ὅτι k Psal. 22. 7. Isa. 53.
τὸν Χριστὸν ἔδει παθεῖν καὶ ἀναστῆναι ἐκ νεκρῶν, καὶ ὅτι οὗτός ἐστιν Matt. 16. 21. Luke 24. 26, 46. John 1. 42.
4 ὁ Χριστὸς Ἰησοῦς, ὃν ἐγὼ καταγγέλλω ὑμῖν. [l] Καί τινες ἐξ αὐτῶν l Infra ver. 17. & 28. 24.
ἐπείσθησαν, καὶ προσεκληρώθησαν τῷ *Παύλῳ* καὶ τῷ *Σίλᾳ*, τῶν τε
σεβομένων Ἑλλήνων πολὺ πλῆθος, γυναικῶν τε τῶν πρώτων οὐκ ὀλίγαι.
5 Ζηλώσαντες δὲ οἱ ἀπειθοῦντες Ἰουδαῖοι, καὶ προσλαβόμενοι τῶν ἀγοραίων τινὰς ἄνδρας πονηροὺς, καὶ ὀχλοποιήσαντες, ἐθορύβουν τὴν πόλιν·
ἐπιστάντες τε τῇ οἰκίᾳ Ἰάσονος, ἐζήτουν αὐτοὺς ἀγαγεῖν εἰς τὸν δῆμον·
6 [m] μὴ εὑρόντες δὲ αὐτοὺς, ἔσυρον τὸν Ἰάσονα καί τινας ἀδελφοὺς ἐπὶ m Supra 16. 20.
τοὺς πολιτάρχας, βοῶντες· Ὅτι οἱ τὴν οἰκουμένην ἀναστατώσαντες, οὗτοι
7 καὶ ἐνθάδε πάρεισιν! [n] οὓς ὑποδέδεκται Ἰάσων. Καὶ οὗτοι πάντες n Luke 23. 2. John 19. 12.
ἀπέναντι τῶν δογμάτων Καίσαρος πράσσουσι, βασιλέα λέγοντες ἕτερον
8 εἶναι, Ἰησοῦν. Ἐτάραξαν δὲ τὸν ὄχλον καὶ τοὺς πολιτάρχας ἀκούοντας
9 ταῦτα. Καὶ λαβόντες τὸ ἱκανὸν παρὰ τοῦ Ἰάσονος καὶ τῶν λοιπῶν,
10 ἀπέλυσαν αὐτούς. [o] Οἱ δὲ ἀδελφοὶ εὐθέως διὰ τῆς νυκτὸς ἐξέπεμψαν o Supra 9. 2.
τόν τε *Παῦλον* καὶ τὸν *Σίλαν* εἰς *Βέροιαν*. οἵτινες παραγενόμενοι, εἰς

jects to our English Version, "a synagogue of the Jews," and would render "the synagogue," as signifying merely that the Jews of the surrounding district had their synagogue there. That, however, is so little satisfactory (see xiv. 1. and Note, and compare xvii. 10.), that it is better to suppose the Article to have here crept in from the ἦν preceding. It is not found in *three* of the most ancient MSS., and perhaps others, such minute points escaping the most careful collators. To suppose that that was the *only synagogue* in Macedonia, though there might be many *proseuchæ*, is too hypothetical.

2, 3. διελέγετο — παρατιθ.] The full sense is, "he discoursed unto them out of the Scriptures," i. e. drawing from them his arguments, proofs, and illustrations. The two next words διανοίγων and παρατ. have reference to the two principal parts of the ratiocination. 1. *Opening out* and *bringing to light* truth (which was said to lie at the bottom of a well). 2. *Laying down* and *propounding* various truths, in order, from a collation of particulars, to deduce some general conclusion:— as here, ὅτι οὗτός ἐστι, &c. At ὅτι ὃν — ὑμῖν there is a transition from the oratio *obliqua* to the *directa*. See Acts i. 4.

4. προσεκληρώθησαν τῷ Π.] The verb has a reciprocal sense, "joined themselves to," "took their lot with."

— γυναικῶν τῶν πρώτων.] The τῶν εὐσχημόνων infra ver. 12 & xiii. 50, "honourable matrons," wives, or widows. Thus Apuleius speaks of *feminas primates*.

5. τῶν ἀγοραίων.] Ἀγοραῖος denotes "belonging to the forum, or market," and carries various significations according to the business done there, whether as applied to *things*, or *persons*. As regarded the *latter*, it denoted *market-people*; some of whom being *petty chapmen*, others acting as porters, nay, even *mere idlers*; (who, like the Lazzaroni at Naples, almost *lived* in the market). So Horace Ars. Poet. 245. *innati* triviis ac pene forenses. The term came at length to mean persons of the basest sort, — the dregs of society.

Πονηροὺς is wrongly rendered by Bp. Pearce, Abp. Newc., and others, "*wicked*." But as it is meant to qualify the τῶν ἀγοραίων, it is better to render τινὰς ἄνδρας πονηροὺς, "some mean fellows." This signification of πονηρὸς is indeed somewhat rare; but I could adduce several examples. The following will suffice: Thucyd. viii. 73. τινὰ μοχθηρὸν ἄνθρωπον (a beggarly fellow) ὠστρακισμένον — διὰ πονηρίαν, because of his meanness. Aristoph. Eq. 181, where to μέγας γίγνεσθαι is opposed πονηρὸς κἀξ ἀγορᾶς εἶναι. And in Xenophon the πολῖται πονηροὶ are often opposed to the οἱ χρηστοὶ, *the better sort*. See also Lucian i. 483. Hence may be understood Thucyd. vi. 53. διὰ πονηρῶν ἀνθρώπων πίστιν (by the credence of mean persons) πάνυ χρηστοὺς τῶν πολιτῶν κατέδουν. where all the Translators and Commentators have fallen into the same blunder as on this passage of the N. T. Possibly the framers of our common Version *meant* to express the above sense when they rendered "*lewd* fellows;" for in the passage of Thucyd. viii. 73, Hobbes renders μοχθηρὸν by *a lewd fellow*. Indeed the word may very well have such a sense, since in *that* signification it is derived from the A. S. læpb *gregarius*, "one of the mob," from leob, a mob.

— τὸν δῆμον.] Not "the people," as E. V.; much less "the mob," as Doddr. renders; but the *popular assembly*; a signification frequent in Thucyd., Xenoph., and the best writers.

6. ἔσυρον.] This is to be taken like εἵλκυσαν at xvi. 19, where see Note. Πολιτάρχας, "the city magistrates;" a later form, for πολιτάρχους, which is found in Æneas Poliorc. C. 26.

— τὴν οἰκ. ἀναστατώσαντες] This expression is to be taken in a *popular* sense, and not to be too rigorously interpreted. Ἀναστ. is a word only found elsewhere in the LXX. It is for ἀναστατὸν ποιήσαντες.

7. ὑποδέδεκται] "has received as guests and friends." So in Luke xix. 6. James ii. 25. and often in the Classical writers. It is for δέχεσθαι ὑπὸ τὸν οἶκον.

9. καὶ λαβ. τὸ ἱκανόν.] Τὸ ἱκανὸν λαβεῖν is a translation of the Latin law phrase *satisfactionem accipere*,

p Isa. 34. 16. Luke 16. 29. John 5. 39. τὴν συναγωγὴν τῶν Ἰουδαίων ἀπῄεσαν. p Οὗτοι δὲ ἦσαν εὐγενέστεροι 11
τῶν ἐν Θεσσαλονίκῃ· οἵτινες ἐδέξαντο τὸν λόγον μετὰ πάσης προθυ-
μίας, τὸ καθ᾽ ἡμέραν ἀνακρίνοντες τὰς γραφὰς, εἰ ἔχοι ταῦτα οὕτως.
Πολλοὶ μὲν οὖν ἐξ αὐτῶν ἐπίστευσαν, καὶ τῶν Ἑλληνίδων γυναικῶν τῶν 12
q 1 Thess. 2. 4. εὐσχημόνων, καὶ ἀνδρῶν οὐκ ὀλίγοι. q Ὡς δὲ ἔγνωσαν οἱ ἀπὸ τῆς 13
Θεσσαλονίκης Ἰουδαῖοι, ὅτι καὶ ἐν τῇ Βεροίᾳ κατηγγέλη ὑπὸ τοῦ Παύλου ὁ λόγος τοῦ Θεοῦ, ἦλθον κἀκεῖ σαλεύοντες τοὺς ὄχλους. Εὐθέως 14
δὲ τότε τὸν Παῦλον ἐξαπέστειλαν οἱ ἀδελφοὶ πορεύεσθαι ὡς ἐπὶ τὴν
r Infra 18. 5. θάλασσαν· ὑπέμενον δὲ ὅ τε Σίλας καὶ ὁ Τιμόθεος ἐκεῖ. r Οἱ δὲ 15
καθιστῶντες τὸν Παῦλον, ἤγαγον αὐτὸν ἕως Ἀθηνῶν· καὶ λαβόντες
ἐντολὴν πρὸς τὸν Σίλαν καὶ Τιμόθεον, ἵνα ὡς τάχιστα ἔλθωσι πρὸς
αὐτὸν, ἐξῄεσαν.

Ἐν δὲ ταῖς Ἀθήναις ἐκδεχομένου αὐτοὺς τοῦ Παύλου, παρωξύνετο 16
τὸ πνεῦμα αὐτοῦ ἐν αὐτῷ θεωροῦντι κατείδωλον οὖσαν τὴν πόλιν.

to take surety, the opposite of which is ἱκανὸν δοῦναι. The purport of the engagement probably was, that he would send away Paul and Silas forthwith, and would undertake to keep the peace.

11. εὐγενέστεροι.] Not more *noble* (for the men, we may suppose, were but tradesmen), but more ingenuous and well-disposed. So the best of the later Commentators take the word; and they adduce examples of this sense, which occurs chiefly in the later writers. So Philo de Nobil. p. 904. Ἐπειδὴ τοίνυν ἡ εὐγένεια κεκαθαρμένης διανοίας καὶ καθαροῖοις τελείοις κλῆρος οἰκεῖος, μόνους χρὴ λέγειν εὐγενεῖς τοὺς σώφρονας καὶ δικαίους. Perhaps, however, *both* significations may be included, viz. the *better sort of persons (more respectable), and better disposed.* And so Chrys. seems to have taken the word when he explains ἐπιεικέστεροι. Thus Thucyd. viii. 93. ἀνθρώπους ἐπιεικεῖς, where I have fully explained the idiom.

— τὸ καθ᾽ ἡμέραν.] The Article would seem to have no force, and is omitted in several MSS. It must, however, be retained; since we may better account for its omission than for its insertion. To account for its being used here, it is proper to bear in mind, that καθ᾽ ἡμέραν is often used with the Article for the adjective ἡμερινοί. The substantive is generally *expressed*, but sometimes *omitted*, and left to be supplied from the context, or the subject-matter. Here ἔθος may be supplied, and the common ellip. of κατὰ supposed. Thus the sense will be, "in their daily habits of life;" equivalent to the Thucydidean τὸν καθ᾽ ἡμέραν βίον, or the Æschinean τὴν καθ᾽ ἡμέραν δίαιταν. And so the best writers say τὸ κατ᾽ ἐμὲ, "*quantum ad me attinet.*"

— ἀνακρίνοντες.] This is well explained by Chrys. ἀνερευνῶντες. The ἀνα is intensive, and this sense of κρίνω springs from that primitive sense to separate, to *sift* the corn from the chaff, and, metaphorically, to sift out any thing, by separating truth from falsehood, or right from wrong.

12. τῶν εὐσχ.] See Note on xiii. 50. The word belongs both to γυναικῶν and to ἀνδρῶν.

13. σαλεύοντες] "agitating," from σάλος, *the surge of the sea.* The Classical writers have many passages where political turbulence is compared to the tossing of a tempestuous sea. See Soph. Œd. Tyr. 25.

14. πορ. ὡς ἐπὶ τὴν θάλασσαν.] Markl. asks to *what* sea? and would read Θεσσαλίαν. His query, however, may be satisfactorily answered. In the case of places situated, like Berœa, between two seas, to go to *the sea* must denote to the *nearest* sea; and if embarkation for a voyage be implied, the nearest sea-port may be supposed. *That*, in the present case, was *Pydna.* Thus in a kindred passage of Thucyd. i. 137, Admetus, to remove Themistocles out of the reach of those who were seeking his life, sends him ἐπὶ τὴν ἑ τ έ ρ α ν θάλασσαν, which must mean the *Ægean*; and, as we afterwards learn, to Pydna. But had τὴν θάλασσαν been written, the *Adriatic* must have been understood.

The ὡς ἐπὶ our English Translators render "as if," or "as it were;" which compels them to suppose that this going to the sea was only a *stratagem* to deceive his enemies; who might suppose he was taking ship, when he, in fact, meant to go to his destination by *land.* The ὡς, however, is but a slender foundation on which to erect such a notion. There can be no doubt but that the two words ὡς ἐπὶ are to be taken together, and understood, as in many passages of the Classical writers cited by the Commentators (e. gr. Pausan. καταβάντων ὡς ἐπὶ θάλασσαν. to which I could add others from Thucyd.) where the ὡς is pleonastic. Or the sense may be *unto*, i. e. down to. And so ἐπὶ τὴν θάλ. in Thucyd. vi. 66.

15. καθιστῶντες is not (as Kuin. imagines) for οἱ προπέμποντες, but for κατάγοντες, as in a kindred passage at ix. 39. κατήγαγον αὐτὸν εἰς Κ. The present term, however, is equally correct. So Thucyd. iv. 78. κατέστησαν (scil. οἱ ἄγοντες) αὐτὸν ἐς Δῖον. where I have adduced examples from Xenoph., Plutarch, and Jambl. The construction requires an εἰς, or ἐπὶ, or δὲ, as in the earliest example of this idiom, Hom. Od. γ. 274. ἀγ. Πύλονδε. Wets., however, cites an example of μέχρι from Arrian, which comes near to the ἕως of Luke.

16. ἐν αὐτῷ.] This is added, by a Hebraism, as in Dan. vii. 15. "I was grieved in my spirit in the midst of my body;" which passage was perhaps in St. Luke's mind.

— κατείδωλον] "full of idols." This force of κατὰ is found in many words, as κατάδενδρος, κατάμπελος, &c. With respect to the *fact*, it is fully established and copiously illustrated by Wets.; e. gr. Pausanias says, that Athens had more images than all the rest of Greece; and Petronius tells us, "it was easier to find there a God than a man."

17 [a] Διελέγετο μὲν οὖν ἐν τῇ συναγωγῇ τοῖς Ἰουδαίοις καὶ τοῖς σεβομένοις, [a Supra ver. 4.]
καὶ ἐν τῇ ἀγορᾷ κατὰ πᾶσαν ἡμέραν πρὸς τοὺς παρατυγχάνοντας.
18 Τινὲς δὲ τῶν Ἐπικουρείων καὶ τῶν Στωϊκῶν φιλοσόφων συνέβαλλον αὐτῷ· καὶ τινες ἔλεγον· Τί ἂν θέλοι ὁ σπερμολόγος οὗτος λέγειν; οἱ δέ· Ξένων δαιμονίων δοκεῖ καταγγελεὺς εἶναι. ὅτι τὸν Ἰησοῦν καὶ τὴν

To the passages of Pausan., Strabo, and Lucian, cited by Wets., I add Thucyd. ii. 38. θυσίαις διετησίοις νομίζοντες, where see my note.

17. διελέγετο — τοῖς Ἰ. κ.] See Mr. Townsend's remarks, in loco, *on St. Paul's plan of preaching*; in which he shows the Apostle's wisdom in varying his manner of address according to the persons to whom he spoke, and the circumstances in which he was placed, — and this with especial reference to his conduct at *Athens* — which was a model to all Christian missionaries to foreign lands. See also the learned dissertations by *Olearius* and *Schlosser, de Gestis* Pauli in Urbe Athen. in vol xiii. p. 661. seqq.

— τῇ ἀγορᾷ.] There were many market-places, but the most considerable were the Ceramicus, or *old*, and the Forum Eretriacum, or *New* Forum: the *former* of which is supposed to be the one here meant by Ikenius and Schleus., the *latter* by Kuin. and most Commentators. And that this was by far the most frequented, being in the most thickly inhabited part of the city, confirms the latter opinion.

— τοὺς παρατ.] "those whom he might happen to meet with." The *Forum* was best adapted to his purpose, because it was the place where people met for conversation. And from the citations of Wets. it appears, that that was the place where Socrates, and many other Philosophers, had been accustomed to hold their discussions.

18. Ἐπικουρείων καὶ τῶν Στ.] The *Epicureans* were practically *Atheists*, — since they held that the world was neither created by God, nor under the direction of his Providence. *Pleasure* they accounted the *summum bonum*, and *virtue* to be practised only for the sake of pleasure, not for its own sake. They maintained that the soul was material, like the body, and would perish with it, leaving nothing to be either hoped or feared after death. As to the *Stoics*, they did, indeed, believe in the *existence of a God*, but held such chimerical notions of his nature, attributes, and providence, as rendered that belief almost nugatory. They maintained, that both God and man were bound by *a necessitas fatalis*; that the wise man yielded in no respect to God; of whom they believed that his nature was *fire*, and diffused throughout the world. On the condition of the soul after death, and on the existence of a state of rewards and punishments, they varied in opinion; but all denied the *immortality* of a future state. Nay, some thought that, sooner or later, the soul merged in the celestial fire of the Deity. Thus while the former denied the existence, or at least providence, of God; the latter, though professing to believe both, — yet, by ascribing all human events to fate, destroyed the foundation of all religion as much as the former. It is obvious that *both* the above systems were as far as possible removed from the doctrines of Christianity; and therefore it is no wonder that the latter should have been both unaccountable and unacceptable to these Philosophers. There were, besides, two other sects, the *Platonists*, and the *Peripatetics*, the latter of whom probably came not near Paul, since their places of discussion were far removed. The opinions of the *former* made far nearer approaches than those of the other sects to the doctrines of Christianity; and these probably formed the far greater part of those who gave a qualified approbation of Paul's doctrines, by proposing to "hear him again" on the subject of the immortality of the soul.

— σπερμολόγος.] The word was used *properly* of those small birds (*sparrows*, &c.), which live by picking up scattered seeds; but *metaphorically*, to denote those *paupers*, who frequented the market-places, and lived by picking up any scattered or refuse produce; and generally, *persons of abject condition* without any certain means of support. Again, as the tribes of small birds which live by picking up seeds are especially garrulous, — the word came to denote a *prater*; and some Commentators think that is the sense *here*. But probably *both* senses may be intended, viz. "an *insignificant babbler*."

— ξένων δαιμ. καταγγ.] We are not here to understand *Gods* in the full sense of the term. It has been proved by the Commentators cited in Recens. Synop. (to whose matter I have subjoined much that is important from Max. Tyr., Jambl., Plutarch, Liban., Diog. Laert., Dion. Halic., Pindar, and others), that there was properly a *distinction* (though not always observed), between θεοὶ and δαίμονες, by which the former denoted Jupiter and the other Gods *by origin* — the latter those who had *become* so, though originally men. These, according to some, *included* the ἥρωες, as Hercules; though others made a *third class* of those. The above, then, were all the classes which, properly speaking, were reckoned as *Divinities*. But the Pagan Theology comprehended another order of beings, called δαιμόνια, holding the midway between *divinities* and *mere men*, who were supposed to act as *mediators* between God and men, by revealing the Divine will, and helping the imbecility of man. One of these was said by Socrates to visit him; on which, Xenoph. Mem. i. 1, 2. tells us, was founded the charge against him of introducing καινὰ δαιμόνια, almost the same expression as that used of St. Paul. Some eminent Commentators think that the Athenians meant by this to express that the place claimed by Paul for Jesus, was in this last class. But it is plain that what they heard the Apostle say of Jesus would give them a notion of a Being who was at least a δαίμων, and that one of the higher order. Nay there is great reason to believe that δαιμόνιον (and even Θεὸς, as is plain from the charge being elsewhere worded as τὸ περὶ Θεῶν καινοτομεῖν) was sometimes used in the sense of δαίμων, as in the above cited passage of Xenoph. and those of Diog. Laert., Dio Cass., Ælian, and Josephus, cited by Wets., where the expressions καινὰ δαιμόνια εἰσηγεῖσθαι, or εἰσφέρειν, and ξένους δαίμονας εἰσάγειν are equivalent.

— τὸν Ἰησοῦν καὶ τὴν ἀνάστ.] Many eminent Interpreters, ancient and modern, as Chrys., Œcumen.,

ἀνάστασιν αὐτοῖς εὐηγγελίζετο. ἐπιλαβόμενοί τε αὐτοῦ, ἐπὶ τὸν Ἄρειον 19
πάγον ἤγαγον λέγοντες· Δυνάμεθα γνῶναι, τίς ἡ καινὴ αὕτη ἡ ὑπὸ
σοῦ λαλουμένη διδαχή; ξενίζοντα γάρ τινα εἰσφέρεις εἰς τὰς ἀκοὰς 20
ἡμῶν· βουλόμεθα οὖν γνῶναι, τί ἂν θέλοι ταῦτα εἶναι. Ἀθηναῖοι δὲ 21
πάντες καὶ οἱ ἐπιδημοῦντες ξένοι εἰς οὐδὲν ἕτερον εὐκαίρουν, ἢ λέγειν
τὶ καὶ ἀκούειν καινότερον.

Selden, Hamm., Spencer, Cudworth, Warburton, Valckn., and Doddr., take ἀνάστ. (written Ἀνάστασιν) as the *name of a new Goddess.* And certainly there is not a little to urge in favour of that view, on which see Rec. Syn., and especially Cudworth's Intellectual Syst. B. I. ch. xxxiii., who shows at large, that the heathens were accustomed to deify not only virtues and vices, but many of the powers of nature. Yet the common interpretation, which is strenuously maintained by Bentley, bears in its simplicity the stamp of truth; the sense being, "preached Jesus, and the resurrection of the dead through Him;" He being the first fruits of those that slept. This, too, seems required by v. 31. ἀναστήσας αὐτὸν ἐκ νεκρῶν. and 32. ἀκούσαντες ἀνάστασιν τῶν νεκρῶν. As to the use just before of the *plural* δαιμόνια, it may readily be accounted for from an idiom of frequent occurrence in all languages, and mostly used when a *charge* is made against any one. Thus it may be considered as said *per hyperbolen.* It is not, however, improbable that they might so far mistake St. Paul, as to suppose that he preached two Gods, i. e. *God*, and *Jesus Christ.* The God (namely, *Jehovah*) preached by him, and avowedly different from the Jupiter of the Athenians, might very well be esteemed by them a new and *foreign God.*

19. ἐπιλαβόμενοι αὐτοῦ.] Commentators are not agreed whether this expression is to be regarded as importing *violence*, or *not.* There are examples in the N. T. of both uses. The former (which is supported by the ancient Versions, and is adopted by many Commentators), is most agreeable to the context. And it is countenanced by the *fact*, — that the Areopagus was a tribunal for the trial of impiety, such as the introducing of the worship of foreign deities. See a Dissertation of Scheidius de Areopago, and p. 674. seqq. of vol. xiii. of the Critici Sacri. Yet, after all, it may be doubted whether there was any thing of *apprehension*, properly so called, — since there is no appearance of any *regular trial* before the court of Areopagus. There is, indeed, reason to think, that this court retained but a shadow of its ancient consequence, — and (like the *Inquisition* in the present day) had abated much of its ancient severity in matters of religion, — otherwise foreign deities would not have been so worshipped as they then were at Athens. A stronger proof of which cannot be imagined than the following passage of Aristoph. Horæ, cited by Athen. L. ix. p. 372., where, after speaking of the abundance of every kind of produce supplied by the season, in such a manner that whatever was wanted could be had at any season, and one could scarcely tell what time of the year it was, this bounty of nature and the Gods is ascribed by a speaker (I imagine, the *Horæ* personified) to the piety of the Athenians; Τούτοις ὑπάρχει ταῦτ' ἐπειδὴ τοὺς Θεοὺς σέβουσιν· To this it is replied by one who stigmatizes the fondness of the Athenians for foreign superstitions, Ἀπέλαυσαν ἄρα σοῦ β ὄντες ὑμᾶς, ὡς σὺ φῄς· τί ἢ τί Αἴγυπτον αὐτῶν τὴν πόλιν πεποίηκας ἀντ' Ἀθηνῶν. (where the *confessed* corruption, which defied the endeavours of Brunck and others, may be easily removed, by simply, for τί ἢ τί, reading Τιητί; *Quid enim, what then?*) Αἴγυπτον αὐτῶν τὴν πόλιν πεποιήκασ' (for πεποιήκασι) ἀντ' Ἀθ. The form τιητίὴ often occurs in Aristophanes; and the error in question might easily arise. By saying that they had made an *Egypt* of Athens, it is meant, they had filled it as full of Gods. And of *Egypt* it was said, there one might sooner find a God than a man. But to return, — taken in conjunction with the preceding verse, the words, I conceive, suggest rather a *tumultuary* proceeding, on the part of the two classes of persons just before mentioned, than a *regular trial.* They, it should seem, thought proper to call Paul to a public *account;* and considered no place so proper as the hill of judgment called Areopagus. Thus the words just after, δυνάμεθα γνῶναι; (with which Wets. aptly compares from Plautus "possum scire, quo profectus, cujus sis, aut quid veneris?") as also βουλόμεθα γνῶναι. Paul, too, does not address them as *judges*, nor seek any justification of his conduct, but as *philosophers.* If, then, any of them were, as was Dionysius, *Areopagites*, they were there not sitting *ex officio*, but as private individuals. Perhaps this may account for the little seriousness or ceremony which the Apostle experienced.

— δυνάμεθα γνῶναι.] This is Hellenistic Greek; both in the use of δύνασθαι for "to be permitted," and in the not prefixing some particle of interrogation.

20. ξενίζοντα.] Literally, "things which strike us with surprise." The use of ἀκοὰς in the plural is thought to be rarely found out of the N. T. Yet I have in Recens. Synop. adduced examples from Euripides, Ælian, Herodian, Polyb., and Themist.

21. οἱ ἐπιδημοῦντες ξένοι.] The distinction between the ἀστοὶ and ξένοι was at Athens very marked. The ἀστοὶ considered themselves as alone possessing any rank; while all the rest were included indiscriminately under the name ξένοι. They called themselves the αὐτοχθόνες, or first inhabitants: the rest they styled ἐπήλυδες, or *new comers.* There was, however, a class *between* one and the other, called μέτοικοι, *sojourners*, who had a sort of *jus civitatis.* Now it has been debated whether by οἱ ἐπιδ. ξένοι are to be understood *all* the ξένοι, or only the μέτοικοι, or *both* of them. Kypke and Kuin. adopt the *second* view; and rightly; for though ξένων might include *both* (so Thucyd. ii. 36. τὸν ὅμιλον καὶ ἀστῶν καὶ ξένων), yet since ἐπιδημ. is here added; and as the difference between the μέτοικοι and the ξένοι was, that the *former* were regular *residents* of the city, and accordingly obliged to take the oath of allegiance, and participate in military service: the *latter* were merely *sojourners* drawn thither by business and pleasure.

— εἰς οὐδὲν ἕτερον εὐκαίρουν] nulli rei *magis vaca-*

22 Σταθεὶς δὲ ὁ Παῦλος ἐν μέσῳ τοῦ Ἀρείου πάγου, ἔφη· Ἄνδρες
23 Ἀθηναῖοι, κατὰ πάντα ὡς δεισιδαιμονεστέρους ὑμᾶς θεωρῶ. Διερχόμενος γὰρ καὶ ἀναθεωρῶν τὰ σεβάσματα ὑμῶν, εὗρον καὶ βωμὸν ἐν ᾧ
ἐπεγέγραπτο· ἈΓΝΩΣΤΩι ΘΕΩι. Ὃν οὖν ἀγνοοῦντες εὐσεβεῖτε, τοῦ-

bant. Εὐκαιρ. is for σχολάζειν, by a use confined to the later writers. The next words are graphic, and point at the chief traits of the Athenians' *garrulity* and *rage for novelty*, on which see many passages from the Classical writers in Recens. Synop. At Athens there were places called λεσχαί, appropriated to the reception of news-mongers.

22. In this brief but pithy address (which would doubtless have been longer, had it not been broken off by the scoffs of some, and the listlessness and abrupt departure of others) the Apostle wisely accommodates himself to the circumstances of his hearers. After a complimentary *exordium*, such as was usual in publicly addressing the Athenians, as also by a *praeoccupatio benevolentiae* frequent in the ancient Orators, he notices the *occasion* which led to his addressing them; and shows, that it is his desire to enable them to satisfy their wish of worshipping even *unknown gods*, by pointing out that *great Being* (to *them* hitherto unknown) who is *the* ONLY AND THE TRUE *GOD;* some of whose chief attributes, and the various benefits he hath wrought, Paul then proceeds to recount. From thence he infers the *duty* incumbent on God's creatures, of seeking, i. e. *worshipping* Him; at the same time noticing certain erroneous modes thereof, which had originated in utter ignorance of his true nature. This introduces an exhortation to *abandon* these errors, fortified by an announcement of a future day of judgment, and punishment for all wilful disobedience to the will of God. Now this implied a present state of accountableness, and the duty of guiding themselves by the light of that Gospel, which God had been pleased to reveal by Jesus Christ.

— δεισιδαιμονεστέρους.] This is commonly understood to mean "too superstitious." But that sense (formed on the Vulgate superstitiosiores) cannot by any means be defended. Neither, I apprehend, can that assigned by Dr. Hales, "too much addicted to the worship of dæmons." For, in either case, it were admitting (what surely could not be supposed) that there was a degree of superstition that was *good.* For the same reason, the sense ascribed by Calvin, Beza, Campb., and Newc., "somewhat too religious," cannot be admitted; for surely no one can be *too religious.* The most eminent Expositors for the last century have been of opinion that δεισιδ. is here employed in the *good* acceptation, to denote "very religious," i. e. attentive to religion [as far as they understood it]. That the expression will *bear* this sense, has been established by a multitude of proofs. And that the *Athenians* were very attentive to religious observances, has been proved on the testimonies of the ancient writers of every kind — Dramatists, Historians, and Philosophers; and has been evinced especially by Bishop Warburton in his Divine Legation, vol. ii. p. 6—8. See Note supra verse 19. That such is the sense intended in the present passage, is pretty evident from the *air of the context,* and will appear by a consideration of the *circumstances* in which the Apostle was then placed. To a people like the Athenians, so particularly observant of all the rules of courtesy on such occasions of public address, it was surely far more probable that the Apostle (with that discretion which ever attempered his zeal) should here choose to commence with the language of conciliation rather than *abrupt rebuke;* which, indeed, would have been the more pointed, considering that it was customary for foreigners who had to address the people, to begin with paying some compliment to the place; a respect *due* to this city, as being the mother of arts and sciences. Nevertheless, we shall, perhaps, not err, if we suppose that St. Paul purposely selected the ambiguous term δεισιδ., because he could not conscientiously use εὐσεβής; since the Gods whom they worshipped were, in *his* estimation, dæmons. So 1 Cor. x. 20. ὅτι ἃ θύει τὰ ἔθνη δαιμονίοις θύει, καὶ οὐ Θεῷ. He commends their *worshipping;* but shows that they "worship" they "know not what" (John iv. 22.), meaning, that they are very religious *in their way.* That the comparative here means *very,* and not *too,* is plain from the words following. And this view of the sense is supported by the authority of the Pesch. Syriac Version. The ὡς does not mean *quasi,* as some take it: and so far from its abating (as Campb. supposes) the import of the comparative, it is *intensitive;* as it always is, either when the comparative is put for the superlative, or when, as here, it notes a *high* degree of the positive.

23. τὰ σεβάσματα ὑ.] Not *devotions,* but (as Erasm., Koppe, Schleusn., and Kuin. render) the objects of your worship, as shown in temples, altars, images, sacrifices, &c.

— ἀγνώστῳ Θεῷ.] These words have occasioned no little perplexity to biblical interpreters. The difficulty hinges on *this* — that, although we find from Pausan. i. 1, v. 14, and Philostr. Vit. Ap. vi. 3, that there were at Athens altars inscribed "to unknown *Gods,*" yet no passage is adduced which makes mention of any altar "to *an* unknown *God.*" Now Jerome, Erasm., and others would remove this difficulty, by supposing, that the inscription in question was, Ἀγνώστοις Θεοῖς, or rather Θεοῖς Ἀσίας καὶ Εὐρώπης· καὶ Λιβύης Θεοῖς ἀγνώστοις καὶ ξένοις. But, as Bp. Middl. observes, "that is a most improbable supposition; and, indeed, the manner in which the inscription is introduced makes it incredible that St. Paul could intend merely a remote or vague allusion." Indeed *thus* (as Kuin. observes) the whole force of the Apostle's argument would be taken away, nay, his *assertion* would not be true. Therefore, "that the altar (as Middl. remarks) was inscribed simply Ἀγνώστῳ Θεῷ, must either be conceded, or all inquiry will be in vain." And, as Baronius and Wonna have observed, "though there might be *several* altars at Athens and elsewhere inscribed to *unknown Gods* generally, or to *the unknown Gods* of any particular part of the world, yet that there might occasionally be one inscribed to *one* of them, is extremely probable." Bp. Middl., indeed, thinks that the words of the author of the Philopatris (apud Lucian) νὴ τὸν Ἄγνωστον τὸν ἐν Ἀθήναις, are decisive, that Ἀγνώστῳ Θεῷ, in the singular, was a *well-known* inscription. Now this *would,* indeed, be the case, if the Philopatris stood in the same circumstances as almost

[1] Gen. 1. 1. 2 Chron. 6. 30. Psal. 33. 6. & 124. 8.

τον ἐγὼ καταγγέλλω ὑμῖν. [1] Ὁ Θεὸς ὁ ποιήσας τὸν κόσμον καὶ πάντα 24
τὰ ἐν αὐτῷ, οὗτος οὐρανοῦ καὶ γῆς κύριος ὑπάρχων, οὐκ ἐν χειροποιή-

every other work of the Classical writers preserved to us. But, in fact, that tract (which was written, as Gesner has proved, not by *Lucian*, but by an imitator of his style and manner, who lived 200 years after him, in the time of the Emperor Julian, and who bore the same name) contains (as I can attest, after having carefully examined the whole for the purpose of knowing) little short of *twenty* passages, written with manifest allusion to various parts of the Scriptures, chiefly of the N. T. There can be no doubt, then, that the writer had the present passage in view (the article having the use κατ' ἐξοχὴν, to denote the *well-known*), and consequently *his* testimony will only serve to prove, (what, however, is of some consequence) that the *singular* number *was* used by St. Paul. But though no other writer seems to have recorded the existence of any altar so inscribed, yet the thing has *probability* to support it: and no argument from the *silence* of authors can be drawn to the discredit of any writer of unimpeached integrity.

The question, however, as Bp Middl. observes, is, "was this inscription meant to be applied to *one* of a possible multitude, as if we should impute any kindness or any injury to an unknown benefactor, or enemy, — or was it meant to be significant of the *one true God?*" He maintains that the latter opinion (though the general one) is ungrounded. It involves, he thinks, a great improbability, that an inscription so offensive to a Polytheistical people could have been tolerated. Nay, he affirms that it is inconsistent with the propriety of the Article; and maintains that the *omission of the Article*, the *position of the words*, as also the rules of ordinary language and the custom of inscriptions, alike require that the words should be rendered "to an unknown God," or "to a God unknown." He asserts that the discourse of the Apostle is, even according to *that* way of taking ἀγνώστῳ, very pertinent; and that the mention *of any* unknown Deity gave him a sufficient handle for the purpose in question. But, on the supposition that the sense is, "to an unknown God," we are encountered with the difficulty, how it could happen that an altar should have been so inscribed. The best solution of which is, that it had been erected by the Athenian people, in acknowledgment of some signal benefit received by the city at large; which seemed attributable to *some* God, though to *whom* was uncertain. If this were the case, there would be little difficulty in supposing, (with Chrys., Theophyl., and Isidore, of the ancients, and several learned moderns), that the benefit in question was the removal of the Pestilence, which almost depopulated the city, so finely described by Thucydides. And this is thought to be proved by Diogenes Laert. i. 10. Yet (waiving the *fabulousness* of the story) we may observe that he says nothing about an *unknown* God, but represents the altars as erected Θεῷ προσήκοντι. And so far from being inscribed Θεῷ ἀγνώστῳ, he says they were ἀνώνυμοι, *without any inscription*. And to suppose that the one at Athens here meant had such an inscription, is far too hypothetical to be admitted. Not to say that, from the words of Diogenes, it seems very unlikely that there should have been one at Athens. That there were altars at Athens inscribed Θεοῖς ἀγνώστοις καὶ ξένοις, is nothing to the present purpose; since the union of ξένοις with ἀγνώστοις alters the allusion in ἀγν., and the passage merely attests that the Athenians were much attached to foreign superstitions. So Strabo L. x. p. 472. Falc. observes: Ἀθηναῖοι δ' ὥσπερ περὶ τὰ ἄλλα φιλοξενοῦντες διατελοῦσιν, οὕτως περὶ τοὺς Θεούς· πολλὰ γὰρ τῶν ξενικῶν ἱερῶν παρεδέξαντο. If it be asked, to *whom*, then, was the altar in question inscribed? I answer, doubtless, to the one true God, the Creator and Lord of all things: which, indeed, seems to be required by the *course of argument* in the passage, as thus stated by *Wonna*, in a Dissertation on the present subject, vol. ii. p. 464 of the Thesaurus Theolog. Philol.; "Quemcunque Deum Apostolus Atheniensibus annunciavit, is est verus Deus. Sed quem Deum Athenienses ignorantes coluerunt, eique aram inscripserunt, est is Deus, quem Apostolus Atheniensibus annunciavit. E. Is Deus, quem Athenienses ignorantes coluerunt, eique aram inscripserunt, est verus Deus. Major et Minor ex textu liquido constant." This, he shows, was also the opinion of Clemens Alex. and Augustine, of the ancient Commentators; and, of the modern ones, Baronius, Menochius, and Heinsius. To which names may be added, as instar omnium, *Cudworth*, Intell. System. i. 4, 18. From what he says, and especially from what is adduced by Bp. Warburton, in Sect. 4. L. ii. of his Divine Legation, it is plain that the ancient philosophers, both of Egypt, Greece, and Rome, were well acquainted with the doctrine of the *Unity* of the Godhead, to inculcate which was the grand end of the *Mysteries*, where (as he has shown) the errors of Polytheism were detected, and the doctrine of the Unity taught and explained.

With respect to the *term* here applied to the Deity, ἄγνωστος, it appears, from what is said by Cudworth and Warburton, to have been by no means unusual. So Damascius (See Cudworth, Intell. Syst. i. 4. 18), says, the Egyptian Philosophers of his time had found in the writings of the ancients that they held *one principle* of all things, and worshipped it under the name of the *Unknown Darkness*. So also in the celebrated Saitic inscription: *I am all that was, is, and shall be: and* MY VEIL HATH NO MAN UNCOVERED. And the Deity might well be so called, because He is not only *invisible* (hence the Egyptian appellation of the Deity, HAMMIM, *invisible*), but, in respect of his nature and essence, *incomprehensible*, being, as Josephus Contr. Ap. (cited by Cudworth) says, δυνάμει μόνον ἡμῖν γνώριμος, ὁποῖος δὲ κατὰ οὐσίαν ἄγνωστος. As to the objection urged by Bp. Middl., that thus Θεῷ ἀγνώστῳ would here have been written, it has very little force; and a mere question of *position* as respects one writing in a foreign language, involves too minute a criticism to stand in the way of a sense excellent in itself, and demanded by the context. Not to say, that the *inscription* might have Θεῷ ἀγνώστῳ, and St. Paul might thus alter it, whether inadvertently, or to give greater prominency to the word on which his argument was meant to rest. Or even St. Luke might alter its position. Moreover, in the Pesch. Syr. Version we have ܟܣܝܐ, *hidden*, from the Chaldee כסי, *to hide*. And, besides this, the Translator sub-

25 τοις ναοῖς κατοικεῖ, [u] οὐδὲ ὑπὸ χειρῶν ἀνθρώπων θεραπεύεται προσ- & 146. 6. Isa. 66. 1. supra 7. 48.
δεόμενός τινος, αὐτὸς διδοὺς πᾶσι ζωὴν καὶ πνοὴν καὶ τὰ πάντα· & 14. 15. Rev. 14. 7.
26 [x] ἐποίησέ τε ἐξ ἑνὸς αἵματος πᾶν ἔθνος ἀνθρώπων κατοικεῖν ἐπὶ πᾶν u Gen. 2. 7. Psal. 50. 8.
τὸ πρόσωπον τῆς γῆς, ὁρίσας * προστεταγμένους καιροὺς, καὶ τὰς ὁρο- x Deut. 32. 8.
27 θεσίας τῆς κατοικίας αὐτῶν· ζητεῖν τὸν Κύριον, εἰ ἄρα γε ψηλαφήσειαν αὐτὸν καὶ εὕροιεν· καίτοιγε οὐ μακρὰν ἀπὸ ἑνὸς ἑκάστου ἡμῶν
28 ὑπάρχοντα. ἐν αὐτῷ γὰρ ζῶμεν καὶ κινούμεθα καὶ ἐσμέν· ὡς καὶ

joins the ה emphatic (corresponding to the Greek article) to both words; which proves at least that he must have understood the expression of the *one* true God. As to the argument that the inscription would have been too offensive to Polytheists to be *allowed*, it is of no force; for it is well known how tolerant the people of Athens then were; and we may suppose that the inscription was worded by the same person or persons who erected the altar (doubtless, philosophers, who had been initiated in the greater Mysteries), and that with such discreet ambiguity, by the omission of the article, as to leave it uncertain whether it was meant to express *one* out of many, or *the one alone true God.*

— ὃν ἀγνοοῦντες εὐσ.] Render, "whom ye worship without knowing him."

24. The Apostle now proceeds to the *true nature* and *worship* of the Deity. It is justly observed that this seemingly plain statement of the truth is so skilfully managed, as to be directed against the irreligious scepticism of the philosophers and higher ranks, as well as the gross superstition of the common people. On the sentiment οὐκ ἐν χειροποιήτοις, &c. see vii. 48. and Note.

25. οὐ θεραπεύεται] "is not served or ministered unto by the hands of men;" i. e. by temples, sacrifices, &c. This is the primary sense of θεραπεύω. On which see my note on Thucyd. ii. 51. No. 5. At προσδεόμενος there may seem to be an ellip. of ὡς. But, in fact, the apposition *includes* that sense. Wets. notices the consummate prudence by which the Apostle so tempers his discourse, as, at one time, to contest on the side of the vulgar against the philosophers at large; and, at another time, with the philosophers against both. This he illustrates with references to the opinions of the Stoics and Epicureans (on which see Note supra v. 18), and of the common people respectively. With the *sentiment* Wets. and Kypke compare several similar ones from the Philosophers; chiefly the later ones, who may be supposed to have profited by the Scriptures. So Hierocles, p. 25. ὅστις τιμᾷ τὸν Θεὸν ὡς προσδεόμενον, &c. The Apostle here seems to have had in view 3 Macc. ii. 9.

For τὰ πάντα many MSS. have κατὰ τὰ πάντα, which was preferred by Wets. and edited by Matth., but without reason. For the authority of MSS. is very slender in so minute a variation. And it is very probable that the κατὰ arose, as often, from the juxta-position of καὶ and τά. Besides, the sense yielded by κατὰ τὰ πάντα is very unsatisfactory; whereas, that of καὶ τὰ πάντα is extremely apposite, viz. "all things necessary to the sustaining of life," and which are particularized in a similar passage at xiv. 17.

26. αἵματος] "race." See Note on John i. 13. Wets. compares Anthol. iii. 31, 6. Ἄστεα — ἑνὸς αἵματος. and Virg. *sanguine* ab uno. With respect to the *sentiment*, by thus tracing back the origin of mankind, the Apostle perhaps meant to check the vanity of the Athenians, who maintained that they were αὐτοχθόνες and γηγενεῖς. See my Note on Thucyd. i. 2. & ii. 36. The words ὁρίσας — κατοικίας αὐτῶν may be rendered, "having appointed certain determinate periods [for their inhabiting] and the boundaries of the regions they should inhabit." There seems a reference to the records of the early colonization and settling of the earth, in the Books of Moses. For Vulg. προσ. many MSS. and early Edd. have προστ., which is adopted by almost every Editor from Beng. and Wets. to Vater.

27. The Apostle now suggests the grand *design of man's creation*; namely, ζητεῖν τὸν Κύριον, to worship his Maker. See the noble Hymn of Cleanthes, given entire in Recens. Synop.

— εἰ ἄρα γε ψηλ. &c.] These words are exegetical of the foregoing; and the sense is, [to try] if indeed they could, by the glimmering light of reason, "feel out and find him." A Hendiadys for εἰ ψηλαφήσαντες εὕροιεν, if by investigating they could find out His attributes, will, &c. The Apostle may here have had in mind a passage of Plato Phæd. § 47, where he censures those who *feel* after God *in the dark*, by resting in second causes, without carrying up their inquiries to that *first cause*; and consequently worshipping the creature rather than the Creator. This passage of Plato is well rendered and illustrated by Dr. Hales, iii. 526. as follows: "They are unable to distinguish, that it is one thing to be the [*secondary* or *immediate*] cause of the existence of something, and another to be THAT [PRIMARY] CAUSE, without which the other could not be a cause at all. In this respect the many [rather *multitude*, Ed.] seem to be groping, as it were, in darkness (ψηλαφῶντες ὥσπερ ἐν σκότει), using others' eyes rather than their own; so as to denominate [the secondary] the CAUSE ITSELF." Here I would remark, that the version, "using others' eyes rather than their own," misrepresents the sense intended, being founded on the old and corrupt reading ὄμματι, instead of what is undoubtedly the true one, ὀνόματι, which has been restored by Fischer, and certainly is required in order to make the words following apposite. The last words, ὡς αἴτιον αὐτὸ προσαγορεύειν ought rather to have been rendered, "so as to call it a *cause* [whereas it is only that without which the real or actual cause τὸ αἴτιον τῷ ὄντι could not have existed]."

28. ἐν αὐτῷ — ἐσμέν.] Many here recognize a *climax*. But it rather seems to be a strong mode of expression, for "To Him we owe life and every faculty connected with it — by Him we are what we are." The link in the chain of reasoning which connects this verse with the last clause of the preceding, is well pointed out by Dr. Hales.

τινες τῶν καθ' ὑμᾶς ποιητῶν εἰρήκασι· *Τοῦ γὰρ καὶ γένος*
y Isa. 40. 18. *ἐσμέν.* ʸ Γένος οὖν ὑπάρχοντες τοῦ Θεοῦ, οὐκ ὀφείλομεν νομίζειν 29
χρυσῷ ἢ ἀργύρῳ ἢ λίθῳ, χαράγματι τέχνης καὶ ἐνθυμήσεως ἀνθρώ-
z Supra 14. 16. Luke 24. 47. πον, τὸ θεῖον εἶναι ὅμοιον. ᶻ Τοὺς μὲν οὖν χρόνους τῆς ἀγνοίας 30
ὑπεριδὼν ὁ Θεὸς, τανῦν παραγγέλλει τοῖς ἀνθρώποις πᾶσι πανταχοῦ
a Supra 2. 24. & 10. 42. μετανοεῖν· ᵃ διότι ἔστησεν ἡμέραν, ἐν ᾗ μέλλει κρίνειν τὴν οἰκουμένην 31
ἐν δικαιοσύνῃ, ἐν ἀνδρὶ ᾧ ὥρισε, πίστιν παρασχὼν πᾶσιν, ἀναστήσας
αὐτὸν ἐκ νεκρῶν. Ἀκούσαντες δὲ ἀνάστασιν νεκρῶν οἱ μὲν ἐχλεύαζον, 32
οἱ δὲ εἶπον· Ἀκουσόμεθά σου πάλιν περὶ τούτου. Καὶ οὕτως ὁ 33
Παῦλος ἐξῆλθεν ἐκ μέσου αὐτῶν. Τινὲς δὲ ἄνδρες κολληθέντες αὐτῷ 34
ἐπίστευσαν· ἐν οἷς καὶ Διονύσιος ὁ Ἀρεοπαγίτης, καὶ γυνὴ ὀνόματι
Δάμαρις, καὶ ἕτεροι σὺν αὐτοῖς.

XVIII. *ΜΕΤΑ* δὲ ταῦτα χωρισθεὶς ὁ Παῦλος ἐκ τῶν Ἀθηνῶν 1
b Rom. 16. 3. 1 Cor. 16. 19. 2 Tim. 4. 19. ἦλθεν εἰς Κόρινθον· ᵇ καὶ εὑρών τινα Ἰουδαῖον ὀνόματι Ἀκύλαν, 2

— *τῶν καθ' ὑμᾶς π.*] for *τῶν ὑμετέρων π.*, of which Wets. cites an example from Longinus. *Τοῦ γὰρ γένος ἐσμέν.* These words occur both in Arat. Phæn. 5, and in a Hymn of Cleanthes on Jove v. 5, given at length in Recens. Synop. Similar sentiments are adduced from several other writers by the Commentators; as Pind. Nem. Od. σ. *ἓν ἀνδρῶν, ἓν Θεῶν γένος,* to which I have added an interesting passage of Apollonius Epist. 44, no doubt fabricated by Philostratus, and formed on an imitation of this passage.

29. *γένος οὖν, &c.*] Here the Apostle adduces the *conclusion*, that mankind are bound to worship *God* THEIR FATHER; and that not with idolatrous, but *spiritual* worship, as being a Spiritual Being (see John iv. 23 & 24), and not like images made by human art.

30, 31. The Apostle now points out the *subject* of his preaching—JESUS AND THE RESURRECTION; to attend to which he excites them by *hope* and by *fear*. To call forth their *love* of God, and *hope* in Him, he tells them that their past ignorance of His true nature and worship God was pleased to overlook, and excuse their evil deeds; but had now sent His *Son* (that Divine Teacher so ardently wished and longed for by the wisest philosophers) to teach men *how* to worship God aright, and to save them, upon condition of repentance, for what was past, and reformation for the future. To work on their *fear* of the Divine Majesty, he apprises them that if they did not listen to the Lord Jesus and his Gospel, they would incur condign punishment, at the general resurrection and subsequent judgment held by him.

— *μετανοεῖν*] i. e. to cease to do evil and learn to do well; true repentance implying reformation. See Note on Matt. iii. 2. On the nature of true repentance, and how accepted in the Gospel system, see Bp. Warburton's Works, vol. vi. p. 307.

31. *διότι ἔστησεν, &c.*] q. d. "[And there is *need* that you should repent, and reform your lives] for you must give an account," &c. *Ἐν δικαιοσύνῃ*; i. e. in such strictness of justice as must exclude all mercy to the impenitent and unreformed. *Ἀνδρὶ* is (as Œcumenius observes) spoken *οἰκονομικῶς*, denoting, the *God-man* Jesus, &c.

— *πίστιν παρασχεῖν* here signifies (as often) "to produce faith in any thing, or confidence in any one's pretensions," by adducing sufficient proofs.

32. *οἱ μὲν ἐχλεύαζον.*] This feeling of contempt and ridicule of the doctrine in question will not appear so strange, when we consider how wholly unaccustomed were men's minds to the notion of a resurrection of the *body*, and consequently the *identity* of man in a future state. Of this their mythological accounts of Elysium had said nothing. And the thing, at first consideration, involved so much to stagger their faith, that the feeling was perhaps natural; but ought to have been suppressed by the consideration of the *omnipotence* of the great God who had pleased that life and immortality should be brought to light by the Gospel of Christ.

— *ἀκουσόμεθά σου π. κ. τ.*] I cannot accede to the opinion of those who here recognize a *wish to hear more*; for if so, why should they not hear it *then*, — for the Apostle had not wearied his gay fastidious hearers with obscure prolixity. The feeling seems to have been that of *indifference* and *distaste*; or rather we may consider this as a civil way of saying, We will hear no more of this at present. Some other time will do. See Doddr. and Scott. Thus the Apostle's reception was so very discouraging, that he, in disgust, terminates his discourse; which, therefore, may be said to have been as much interrupted and *cut short* as *Stephen's* was, and others recorded in this Book, nay, even some of our *Lord's* discourses to the Jews, in St. John's Gospel. Had that not been the case, St. Paul would doubtless have enlarged on the *nature* of that religion whose divine origin had been thus attested by God himself.

34. *κολληθέντες*] "having become his converts." See Note on v. 13. *Γυνὴ*, "a matron," no doubt, of some rank, as being here *mentioned*. The *glosses* (for they are no more) of the most ancient MSS. attest the early belief of this.

XVIII. 2. *Ἰουδαῖον.*] Whether Aquila was then a Christian is by the recent Commentators thought doubtful. But Luke often omits (as indeed do all ancient writers) minute circumstances, which may easily be supplied; and this probably is one of them; especially since the expression *προσῆλθεν αὐτοῖς* implies a sort of *connection*, which was probably that of identity of religion. Now there had been a congregation of Christians at Rome from the earliest period of the Gospel;

Ποντικὸν τῷ γένει, προσφάτως ἐληλυθότα ἀπὸ τῆς Ἰταλίας, καὶ Πρί-
σκιλλαν γυναῖκα αὐτοῦ (διὰ τὸ διατεταχέναι Κλαύδιον χωρίζεσθαι πάν-
3 *τας τοὺς Ἰουδαίους ἐκ τῆς Ῥώμης) προσῆλθεν αὐτοῖς·* [c] *καὶ διὰ τὸ* c Infra 20. 34. 1 Cor. 4. 12.
ὁμότεχνον εἶναι, ἔμενε παρ' αὐτοῖς καὶ εἰργάζετο· ἦσαν γὰρ σκηνο- 2 Cor. 11. 9. & 12. 13. 1 Thess. 2. 9.
4 *ποιοὶ τὴν τέχνην. Διελέγετο δὲ ἐν τῇ συναγωγῇ κατὰ πᾶν σάββατον,* 2 Thess. 3. 8.
5 *ἔπειθέ τε Ἰουδαίους καὶ Ἕλληνας.* [d] *Ὡς δὲ κατῆλθον ἀπὸ τῆς Μακε-* d Supra 17. 14, 15.
δονίας ὅ τε Σίλας καὶ ὁ Τιμόθεος, συνείχετο τῷ ‡ πνεύματι ὁ Παῦλος, e Lev. 20. 9, 12.
6 *διαμαρτυρόμενος τοῖς Ἰουδαίοις τὸν Χριστὸν Ἰησοῦν.* [e] *Ἀντιτασσομένων* 2 Sam. 1. 16. Ezek. 3. 18, 19. Matt. 10. 14.
δὲ αὐτῶν καὶ βλασφημούντων, ἐκτιναξάμενος τὰ ἱμάτια, εἶπε πρὸς αὐ- & 27. 25. supra 13. 45, 51.

which is supposed to have originated with some who had been present at the feast of Pentecost, when the Holy Ghost was imparted; and was doubtless increased by those Jewish Christians, who had occasion to repair to that city on commercial or other business.

— *προσφάτως*] for *πρόσφατος*, which, the Grammarians say, properly signifies *recently slain*, but is used, both in the Classical and Hellenistic writers, in the sense *recent*. So Pindar Pyth. iv. ult. *πρόσφατον Θήβᾳ ξενωθείς*.

— *διατεταχέναι*] "had issued a *διάταγμα*, or decree." This is noticed by Sueton. Claud. C. 23. thus, Judæos, impulsore Chresto assiduè tumultuantes, Româ expulit. This *Chrestus* is by most recent Commentators supposed to have been a Hellenistic Jew; but by the ancient and earlier modern ones taken to mean Jesus Christ, which is the best founded opinion. The tumults in question were dissensions between the Jews and Christians (whether Jewish or Gentile), and other political disturbances which so mighty a moral revolution was sure to produce; in which sense Christ might well say "he came not to send peace, but a sword." The change of Christus to Chrestus was likely to be made, and, in fact, we know *was* sometimes made. And Christ might, by means of his religion, be said to be the *impulsor*.

3. *σκηνοποιοί.*] Few terms so plain as this have given rise to more debate on the interpretation. The *general* opinion, both of ancients and moderns, is that it signifies *tent-makers*. Some Commentators, however (perhaps thinking it too mean a trade for the Apostle of the Gentiles), have devised other interpretations, e. gr. *weavers of tapestry — makers of mathematical instruments — saddlers*. But for any of these significations there is very slender authority; and St. Luke, writing in a plain style, must be supposed to use such a word as this in its *ordinary* sense; not to say that the two first mentioned trades would require far more exact skill and devoted attention than could be expected in one like Paul, the greater part probably of whose time was spent so very differently. There can be little doubt that St. Paul's trade was (as Chrysost. says) that of a maker of *tents*, formed of leather or thick cloth, both for military and domestic purposes; the latter sort having been, from the scarcity of inns, much used throughout the East in travelling; nay, in that warm climate, were, during the summer season, employed as *houses*.

4. *Ἔπειθε.*] This is strangely rendered by Kuin. and others *docebat*; for *πείθειν* must surely, *from the subject*, mean "swayed their minds, persuaded them [to embrace Christianity];" the *action* being here, as often, put for the *endeavour*. So 2 Cor. v. 11. *εἰδότες τὸν φόβον τοῦ Κυρίου ἀνθρώπους πείθομεν*. By Ἕλληνας we must understand *Proselytes of the gate*.

5. *τῷ πνεύμ.*] Some MSS., several Versions, and a few Fathers, have *τῷ λόγῳ*, which is preferred by Beng., Pearce, and Kuin., and edited by Griesbach, Knapp, and Tittm.; but without sufficient reason. The external authority for that reading is slender, and the internal by no means strong. The above Editors, indeed, urge that *λόγῳ* is to be preferred, as being the more *difficult* reading. But it must be observed, that that canon has its exceptions, and especially when the reading in question would do violence to the proprietas linguæ, or yield an absurd or unsuitable sense: which is the case here; for the sense "was *occupied* in preaching," is one surely most frigid, insomuch that Morus and Heinrichs render *συνείχετο cogebatur*, yet without assigning any tolerable sense to *τῷ λόγῳ*. But whence, then, it may be asked, *arose τῷ λόγῳ*? I answer, from a marginal or interlineary scholium, of some one who had in his copy, not *ἐνείχετο*, but *ἐνέκειτο*; and thus suggested that *λόγῳ* should be supplied, or substituted for *πνεύματι*, as required by *ἐνέκειτο*. That such must have been the reading in *Jerome's* copy, is plain from his (Vulgate) version *instabat verbo*. Indeed the common reading might seem to claim a preference on the score of being the more *difficult* reading; for Markland professes himself unable to *understand* it. Though, indeed, from a sort of mental *idio-syncrasy*, that Critic perpetually found or *made difficulties* where none but himself could see them. Here *συνείχετο τῷ πνεύματι* is capable of a very good sense; namely, as Beza, Luther, Calvin, and others explain, "intus et apud se æstuabat præ zeli ardore," "he was under the impulse of ardent zeal." So v. 25. *ζέων τῷ πνεύματι*. and xx. 22. *δεδεμένος τῷ πνεύματι*.

6. *ἀντιτασσομένων*] "contradicting and opposing by words:" a *military* metaphor, of which Elsn. and Markl. adduce two examples; but there is one more apposite in Thucyd. iii. 83. *τὸ δὲ ἀντιτετάχθαι ἀλλήλοις τῇ γνώμῃ ἀπίστως ἐπὶ πολὺ διήνεγκεν*.

— *ἐκτιναξάμενος τὰ ἱμάτια.*] A symbolical action (with which we may compare Nehem. v. 13.), like shaking the dust off one's shoes at any one, thereby signifying that we renounce all intercourse with him. See note on xiii. 51. At *τὸ αἷμα*, &c. sub. *τρέψεται*. By *αἷμα* is meant *destruction*; i. e. figuratively, perdition in the next world. This manner of speaking was common to the Hebrews (see 2 Sam. i. 16. Ezek. xxxiii. 4.) the Greeks and the Romans. See examples in Elsn. and Wets., who rightly derive it from the very ancient custom of putting hands on the heads of victims for sacrifice, and imprecating on them

τούς· Τὸ αἷμα ὑμῶν ἐπὶ τὴν κεφαλὴν ὑμῶν· καθαρὸς ἐγώ· ἀπὸ
τοῦ νῦν εἰς τὰ ἔθνη πορεύσομαι. Καὶ μεταβὰς ἐκεῖθεν ἦλθεν εἰς 7
οἰκίαν τινὸς ὀνόματι Ἰούστου, σεβομένου τὸν Θεὸν, οὗ ἡ οἰκία ἦν συν-
f 1 Cor. 1. 14. ομοροῦσα τῇ συναγωγῇ. [f] Κρίσπος δὲ ὁ ἀρχισυνάγωγος ἐπίστευσε τῷ 8
Κυρίῳ σὺν ὅλῳ τῷ οἴκῳ αὐτοῦ· καὶ πολλοὶ τῶν Κορινθίων ἀκούοντες
g Infra 23. 11. ἐπίστευον καὶ ἐβαπτίζοντο. [g] Εἶπε δὲ ὁ Κύριος δι' ὁράματος ἐν νυκτὶ 9
h John 10. 16. τῷ Παύλῳ· Μὴ φοβοῦ, ἀλλὰ λάλει, καὶ μὴ σιωπήσῃς· [h] διότι ἐγώ 10
εἰμι μετὰ σοῦ, καὶ οὐδεὶς ἐπιθήσεταί σοι τοῦ κακῶσαί σε· διότι λαός
ἐστί μοι πολὺς ἐν τῇ πόλει ταύτῃ. Ἐκάθισέ τε ἐνιαυτὸν καὶ μῆνας ἓξ, 11
διδάσκων ἐν αὐτοῖς τὸν λόγον τοῦ Θεοῦ.

Γαλλίωνος δὲ ἀνθυπατεύοντος τῆς Ἀχαΐας, κατεπέστησαν ὁμοθυμαδὸν 12
οἱ Ἰουδαῖοι τῷ Παύλῳ, καὶ ἤγαγον αὐτὸν ἐπὶ τὸ βῆμα, λέγοντες· Ὅτι 13
παρὰ τὸν νόμον οὗτος ἀναπείθει τοὺς ἀνθρώπους σέβεσθαι τὸν Θεόν.
i Infra 25. 11. [i] Μέλλοντος δὲ τοῦ Παύλου ἀνοίγειν τὸ στόμα, εἶπεν ὁ Γαλλίων πρὸς 14
τοὺς Ἰουδαίους· Εἰ μὲν οὖν ἦν ἀδίκημά τι ἢ ῥᾳδιούργημα πονηρὸν,
ὦ Ἰουδαῖοι, κατὰ λόγον ἂν ἠνεσχόμην ὑμῶν· εἰ δὲ ζήτημά ἐστι περὶ 15
λόγου καὶ ὀνομάτων καὶ νόμου τοῦ καθ' ὑμᾶς, ὄψεσθε αὐτοί· κριτὴς
γὰρ ἐγὼ τούτων οὐ βούλομαι εἶναι. καὶ ἀπήλασεν αὐτοὺς ἀπὸ τοῦ 16
k 1 Cor. 1. 1. βήματος. [k] Ἐπιλαβόμενοι δὲ πάντες οἱ Ἕλληνες Σωσθένην τὸν ἀρχι- 17

the evils which impended over the sacrificer, or the nation. *Εἰς τὰ ἔθνη πορεύσομαι* must not be understood as implying *abandonment* of the Jews, but an especial attention to the Gentiles.

7. *μεταβὰς ἐκεῖθεν.*] Not from the house of Aquila (thus *shifting his lodgings*), as most Commentators suppose; but from the *synagogue*, that being, no doubt, the place where the foregoing exhortations had been pronounced; as is plain from the words *διελέγετο ἐν τῇ συναγωγῇ*. Besides, if *συναγ.* be not taken as the substantive of place referred to, *there is no other*. Ἦλθεν *εἰς οἰκίαν* must be understood to mean "entered into," "entered upon, a house," for the purpose of teaching and preaching, perhaps in an upper apartment appropriated to that purpose. See a kindred passage at xix. 9.

— *συνομοροῦσα*] "conterminous, contiguous." The word occurs, I believe, nowhere else; though *συνόμορος*, from which it is derived, is found in the ancient glossaries. The *Classical* term is *συνορέω*, used by Polybius. And, indeed, some MSS. *here* have *συνοροῦσα*; though doubtless from emendation.

9. *λάλει καὶ μὴ σιωπήσῃς.*] This intermixture of the Imperat. with the Subjunct. is thought to be a Hebraism. Be that as it may, there is no *pleonasm*; for the Subjunct. form is more significant than the Imperative, there being an ellip. of *ὅρα*, q. d. Mind that ye be not silent!

10. *λαός ἐστι.*] The best Commentators remark, that the persons in question are called Christ's people by *anticipation*; just as the Gentiles, who should afterwards embrace the Christian religion, are in John x. 16. already called the *flock* of Christ.

11. *ἐκάθισε*] "took up his abode." A Hellenistic use of the word, as in Luke xxiv. 49.

12. *Γαλλ. ἀνθυπ. τῆς Ἀχ.*] The best Commentators are agreed that the sense is, "on Gallio becoming Proconsul." *Κατεφίστημι* is a very rare word, but may be compared with *κατεπιχειρέω* and others.

13. *παρὰ τὸν νόμον — Θεόν.*] As much as to say: "The Roman people permit us Jews in Greece to worship God after the rites of the Mosaic Law (See Joseph. Ant. xiv. 40; xvi. 2. and the Note on Acts xxiv. 6.); but this fellow teaches things *contrary* to our Law, and excites disturbances among us."

14. *ἀδίκ. ἢ ῥᾳδιούργημα π.*] The best Commentators regard *ἀδίκ.* as equivalent to *παρανόμημα*, any serious offence, and *ῥᾳδ.* they define *flagitium*. It should rather seem to correspond to the minor class of offences with us styled *larceny* (hence, indeed, the word *roguery* is derived. See Note on xiii. 10.), or even those petty breaches of the peace which with us are called *misdemeanours*. The *ῥᾳδ. πονηρὸν* perhaps had reference to those *mischievous frolics* often played off in Heathen countries in ridicule of the Jewish rites and ceremonies, like Alcibiades' defacing of the Hermæ, ridicule of the mysteries, &c., and such as that which Josephus tells us was committed by a Roman in ridicule of circumcision; and which were always severely punished, when the authors could be detected, by the Roman magistrates. *Ἂν ἠνεσχόμην.* "I should bear with you, lend a patient ear to you."

15. *λόγου καὶ ὀνομ.*] i. e. of doctrine and names [of the respective supporters, as of Moses and of Christ] and of the law which ye hold [as compared with another newly promulgated]. *Ὄψεσθε.* See Matt. xxvii. 4. *σὺ ὄψει.*

17. *ἐπιλαβόμενοι δέ.*] Render, "Whereupon the Greeks laying hold of," &c. There is no reason to suppose *Ἕλληνες* should be cancelled. By *πάντες οἱ Ἑλλ.* are denoted all the Greeks, namely, both Christians and heathens, of whom the latter as well as the former were incensed at the bitter spirit evinced by the Jews, and were glad to take this opportunity of insulting them. Sos-

συνάγωγον, ἔτυπτον ἔμπροσθεν τοῦ βήματος· καὶ οὐδὲν τούτων τῷ
Γαλλίωνι ἔμελεν.
18 [l] Ὁ ΔΕ Παῦλος ἔτι προσμείνας ἡμέρας ἱκανὰς, τοῖς ἀδελφοῖς ἀποτα- l Num. 6. 18. infra 21. 24.
ξάμενος, ἐξέπλει εἰς τὴν Συρίαν· καὶ σὺν αὐτῷ Πρίσκιλλα, καὶ Ἀκύ-
19 λας, κειράμενος τὴν κεφαλὴν ἐν Κεγχρεαῖς· εἶχε γὰρ εὐχήν. Κατήντησε
δὲ εἰς Ἔφεσον, κἀκείνους κατέλιπεν αὐτοῦ· αὐτὸς δὲ εἰσελθὼν εἰς τὴν
20 συναγωγὴν, διελέχθη τοῖς Ἰουδαίοις. Ἐρωτώντων δὲ αὐτῶν ἐπὶ πλείονα
21 χρόνον μεῖναι παρ' αὐτοῖς, οὐκ ἐπένευσεν· [m] ἀλλ' ἀπετάξατο αὐτοῖς, m 1 Cor. 4. 19. James 4. 15. Heb. 6. 3.
εἰπών· Δεῖ με πάντως τὴν ἑορτὴν τὴν ἐρχομένην ποιῆσαι εἰς Ἱεροσό-
λυμα· πάλιν δὲ ἀνακάμψω πρὸς ὑμᾶς, τοῦ Θεοῦ θέλοντος. Καὶ ἀν-
22 ήχθη ἀπὸ τῆς Ἐφέσου· καὶ κατελθὼν εἰς Καισάρειαν, ἀναβὰς καὶ
23 ἀσπασάμενος τὴν ἐκκλησίαν, κατέβη εἰς Ἀντιόχειαν. Καὶ ποιήσας χρόνον τινὰ, ἐξῆλθε, διερχόμενος καθεξῆς τὴν Γαλατικὴν χώραν καὶ Φρυγίαν, ἐπιστηρίζων πάντας τοὺς μαθητάς.
24 [n] Ἰουδαῖος δέ τις Ἀπολλὼς ὀνόματι, Ἀλεξανδρεὺς τῷ γένει, ἀνὴρ λό- n 1 Cor. 1. 12.
25 γιος, κατήντησεν εἰς Ἔφεσον, δυνατὸς ὢν ἐν ταῖς γραφαῖς. [o] Οὗτος o Infra 19. 3.
ἦν κατηχημένος τὴν ὁδὸν τοῦ Κυρίου, καὶ ζέων τῷ πνεύματι, ἐλάλει

thenes, who seems to have been successor to Crispus as Ruler of the synagogue, was thus treated, as being, no doubt, the spokesman, and perhaps the promoter of the persecution. By ἔτυπτον is merely to be understood beating him with their fists. probably as he passed through the crowd out of the Hall of justice; thus, as it were, running the gauntlet.

—οὐδὲν τούτων τῷ Γ. ἔμ.] "took no notice of these things;" not choosing to notice the assault, or interfere in the religious disputes of the parties. Οὐδὲν, for οὐ, as often after μέλει, which has a dative of *person* and a genitive of *thing*, either with or without a preposition.

18. κειράμενος τὴν κεφαλήν.] Commentators are not agreed whether this is to be referred to *Aquila* or to *Paul*. Yet all who were distinguished for knowledge of Greek (as Chrys., Œcum., Isid., Erasm., Beza, Calvin, Casaub., Salmas., Grot., Heinsius, Hamm., Whitby, Valckn., Wakef., Schleus., Heinr., Kuin.), and almost every *Editor* of the N. T., have adopted the former view, which is supported by the ancient Versions, and as it involves far more probability, and avoids the difficulties attendant on supposing *Paul* to be meant, it deserves the preference. The sense, then, is, "after having shorn his head at Cenchrea," which was the port where he embarked on his voyage. The Commentators are generally agreed that the vow was not one of *Nazarite*, but a *votum civile*, —such as was taken during or after recovery from sickness, or deliverance from any peril, or on obtaining any unexpected good, importing to consecrate and offer up the hair, the *shaving* of which denoted the *fulfilment* of the vow.

19. κἀκείνους κατέλ. αὐτοῦ, &c.] The sense is obscurely expressed, but there is no necessity to adopt the expedient proposed by Doddr., of transposing this clause, and placing it after θέλοντος, v. 21. The fact is that Paul had brought them with him, on his voyage to Cæsarea, as far as Ephesus, and there put them on shore; and, the ship stopping there a short time, *including a sabbath-day*, Paul took the opportunity of preaching to the Jews; to whom his discourse was so acceptable, that they pressed him to remain longer with them: which request, however, he was obliged to refuse, because if he permitted the ship to go without him, he should probably not be able to meet with another to convey him in time for the feast at Jerusalem.

21. ἑορτὴν ποιῆσαι.] A Hellenistic phrase. The sense is merely, "I must spend the feast time." Δεῖ με must be taken *populariter*, according to an idiom of our own language. The Apostle's purpose may be supposed to have been to promote the cause of conversion, and the communication between the Christians of Jerusalem and of other parts of the world. Hence we may suppose that this feast was the *Passover*.

22. ἀναβὰς] namely, to Jerusalem as some of the best Commentators are agreed. This may, indeed, *seem* a somewhat harsh omission; but as εἰς Ἱεροσόλυμα occurred only a little before, it is not so. To take ἀναβὰς, with some Commentators, of *Cæsarea*, involves far greater harshness, since it would exclude all mention of the going to Jerusalem, the great object of Paul's voyage into those parts. Κατέβη εἰς Ἀντ. would not be applicable to Cæsarea, whereas it *is* to Jerusalem; for Paul would, no doubt, go by sea, perhaps by Cæsarea.

24. Ἀπολλώς.] A name contracted from Ἀπολλώνιος, as *Epaphras* from *Epaphroditus*, and *Artemas* from *Artemonius*. A full account of every particular concerning Apollos may be seen in a learned dissertation of J. Pfeizer, at p. 691—701. vol. xiii. of the Critici Sacri.

—ἀνὴρ λόγιος.] An expression denoting, in the earlier writers, a *man of letters*, especially an historian; but in the later ones an *eloquent* man, which is probably the sense here (especially as the word is so used in Joseph. and Philo), though some Commentators adopt the first-mentioned signification. Δυνατὸς ἐν ταῖς γραφαῖς, "well versed in the interpretation of the Scriptures of the O. T."

25. κατηχημένος τὴν ὁδὸν τοῦ Κυρίου.] By the expression ὁδὸς τοῦ Κυρίου must (as appears from the words following) be meant that *part* of God's

καὶ ἐδίδασκεν ἀκριβῶς τὰ περὶ τοῦ Κυρίου, ἐπιστάμενος μόνον τὸ βάπτισμα Ἰωάννου· οὗτός τε ἤρξατο παῤῥησιάζεσθαι ἐν τῇ συναγωγῇ. 26
ἀκούσαντες δὲ αὐτοῦ Ἀκύλας καὶ Πρίσκιλλα, προσελάβοντο αὐτὸν, καὶ
p 1 Cor. 3. 6. ἀκριβέστερον αὐτῷ ἐξέθεντο τὴν τοῦ Θεοῦ ὁδόν. [p] Βουλομένου δὲ αὐτοῦ διελθεῖν εἰς τὴν Ἀχαΐαν, προτρεψάμενοι οἱ ἀδελφοὶ ἔγραψαν τοῖς 27
μαθηταῖς ἀποδέξασθαι αὐτόν· ὃς παραγενόμενος συνεβάλετο πολὺ
τοῖς πεπιστευκόσι διὰ τῆς χάριτος. εὐτόνως γὰρ τοῖς Ἰουδαίοις διακατ- 28
ηλέγχετο δημοσίᾳ, ἐπιδεικνὺς διὰ τῶν γραφῶν, εἶναι τὸν Χριστὸν
Ἰησοῦν.

q Supra 18. 24. 1 Cor. 1. 12. XIX. [q] ἘΓΕΝΕΤΟ δὲ, ἐν τῷ τὸν Ἀπολλὼ εἶναι ἐν Κορίνθῳ, 1
Παῦλον διελθόντα τὰ ἀνωτερικὰ μέρη, ἐλθεῖν εἰς Ἔφεσον· καὶ εὑρών
r John 7. 39. sup. 10. 44. &c. τινας μαθητὰς, [r] εἶπε πρὸς αὐτούς· Εἰ Πνεῦμα ἅγιον ἐλάβετε πιστεύ- 2

plan for the salvation of man by a Redeemer, as it regarded the doctrine and methods of John the Baptist, which enjoined repentance and reformation, and the being baptized unto the faith of the future Messiah. Or, taking Κύριος here to denote *Christ*, we may understand, "instructed in the doctrine of *a* Messiah," not, in the doctrine of *Jesus Christ;* for Apollos knew only the doctrine of *John*, who baptized εἰς τὸν ἐρχόμενον, preached repentance, and announced the coming of the Messiah: (see Matt. iii. 2. compared with Acts xix. 4.) while by the *more accurate instruction* which he received from Aquila and Priscilla, must be understood that of the Messiahship of *Jesus*, and what he had enjoined for faith and practice, in order to the attainment of everlasting salvation. By τὸ βάπτισμα is meant, per synecdochen, the doctrine of John the Baptist, of which baptism was a principal feature. Now it is *implied* that Apollos had received this baptism; and also by ἐπιστάμενος μόνον, that he had not received *Christian* baptism, though Mr. Scott supposes so. It is generally believed that he had been baptized by *John* himself, and had since that time obtained some knowledge of the Gospel; though he had not been baptized unto the faith of Christ. This, however, involves much improbability. It should rather seem that he had been baptized *not long before* by one of John's disciples; and, in short, was become one of the sect of the *Johannites*, which existed about this period, and on which see Tittmann's Introd. to the Gospel of St. John. Ἀκριβῶς has reference, not to the *doctrine*, but to the *manner of teaching it*, namely, as exactly as he knew how. Thus there will be no occasion to read, with Sherlock, Markl., and Wakef., οὐκ ἀκριβῶς. They adduce, indeed, a passage of Athenæus, p. 91. as an example of a similar omission of the negative particle, where the necks of shell-fish are said to be δυσκατέργαστοι· διὸ τοῖς ἀσθενοῦσι τὸν στόμαχον οἰκεῖοι. But there it is better to read ἀνοικεῖοι, since the αν might easily be absorbed by the ον preceding. The word occurs in good authors, especially *the later ones.*

26. παῤῥησιάζεσθαι.] This may have reference not only to his descanting on the necessity of repentance and reformation, but to his freely pointing out many errors in the usual mode of understanding the Scriptures, especially the Prophecies. This, from his great knowledge of the Scriptures, he would be qualified to do, and might speak authoritatively.

27. προτρεψάμενοι.] Exhorting him [to carry into effect his resolve].

— συνεβάλετο — χάριτος.] It is plain that συνεβ. must mean, "contributed [to the spiritual advantage of]." But on the sense and construction of διὰ τῆς χάριτος Commentators are not agreed; some, as Pisc. and Hamm., construing it with τοῖς πεπιστευκόσι; others, and indeed almost all the best Expositors, (together with the Pesch. Syriac), with συνεβάλετο. The latter method seems far preferable; for to construe it with τοῖς πεπιστευκόσι not a little embarrasses the sentence: and no such phrase as πιστεύειν διὰ τῆς χάρ. elsewhere occurs in Scripture. Not to mention that the sense thus arising would be *here* little suitable: whereas it might be expected that something should be said of the *especial grace of God* being afforded to one so zealous in preaching the Gospel. The transposition is by no means harsh; and, we may suppose, was here adopted because the words could not well have been introduced between συνεβάλετο and its dative, especially as πολὺ was also interposed. The omission of διὰ τῆς χάριτος in the Cod. Cant., the Vulg., and some Fathers, seems not to have been (as Dr. Clarke imagines) from *accident*, but from *design*, in order thus effectually to *remove* the harshness in question. The question, however, is, what is the *sense?* Beza, Camer., Raphel, Wets., Rosenm., and Heinr., take τῆς χάριτος to mean *grace of diction and manner*, as in Luke iv. 22. τοῖς λόγοις τῆς χάριτος. But that sense would *here* be not important enough, and *thus* τοῦ λόγου would be indispensable. There can be no doubt that τῆς χάρ. is for τῆς χάρ. τοῦ Θεοῦ, a phrase so frequent, that sometimes τοῦ Θεοῦ is dispensed with. So Rom. xii. 3. διὰ τῆς χάριτος τῆς δοθείσης. also xii. 6. xv. 15. and especially Rom. v. 17. οἱ τὴν περισσείαν τῆς χάριτος λαμβάνοντες. where τοῦ Θεοῦ must be supplied. And so at xix. 9. τὴν ὁδὸν is for τὴν ὁδὸν τοῦ Κυρίου.

XIX. 1. τὰ ἀνωτερικὰ μέρη] "the upper and inland regions," namely, Phrygia and Galatia. See my Note on Thucyd. i. 7.

— μαθητάς.] Many recent Commentators think that these persons were only believers in *a* Messiah, and followers of John the Baptist. But *thus* they could not have been *Christ's* disciples at all. Besides Paul addresses them as if *baptized* in the name of *Jesus;* which *at least* implies that they must have publicly professed faith in Jesus Christ.

σαντες; οἱ δὲ εἶπον πρὸς αὐτόν· Ἀλλ᾽ οὐδὲ εἰ Πνεῦμα ἅγιόν ἐστιν
3 ἠκούσαμεν. εἶπέ τε πρὸς αὐτούς· Εἰς τί οὖν ἐβαπτίσθητε; οἱ δὲ
4 εἶπον· Εἰς τὸ Ἰωάννου βάπτισμα. [s]Εἶπε δὲ Παῦλος· Ἰωάννης μὲν s Matt. 3. 11.
ἐβάπτισε βάπτισμα μετανοίας, τῷ λαῷ λέγων, εἰς τὸν ἐρχόμενον μετ᾽ Mark 1. 4, 8. Luke 3. 16. John 1. 26.
5 αὐτὸν ἵνα πιστεύσωσι· τουτέστιν εἰς τὸν Χριστὸν Ἰησοῦν. Ἀκούσαν- supra 1. 5. & 11. 16.
6 τες δὲ ἐβαπτίσθησαν εἰς τὸ ὄνομα τοῦ Κυρίου Ἰησοῦ. [t]καὶ, ἐπιθέν- t Supra 2. 4. & 6. 6.
τος αὐτοῖς τοῦ Παύλου τὰς χεῖρας, ἦλθε τὸ Πνεῦμα τὸ ἅγιον ἐπ᾽ & 8. 17. & 10. 46. & 11. 15.
7 αὐτοὺς, ἐλάλουν τε γλώσσαις καὶ προεφήτευον. Ἦσαν δὲ οἱ πάντες ἄν-
8 δρες ὡσεὶ δεκαδύο. Εἰσελθὼν δὲ εἰς τὴν συναγωγὴν, ἐπαῤῥησιάζετο,
ἐπὶ μῆνας τρεῖς διαλεγόμενος καὶ πείθων τὰ περὶ τῆς βασιλείας τοῦ
9 Θεοῦ. [u]Ὡς δέ τινες ἐσκληρύνοντο καὶ ἠπείθουν, κακολογοῦντες τὴν u 2 Tim. 1. 15.
ὁδὸν ἐνώπιον τοῦ πλήθους, ἀποστὰς ἀπ᾽ αὐτῶν ἀφώρισε τοὺς μαθητὰς,
10 καθ᾽ ἡμέραν διαλεγόμενος ἐν τῇ σχολῇ Τυράννου τινός. Τοῦτο δὲ
ἐγένετο ἐπὶ ἔτη δύο· ὥστε πάντας τοὺς κατοικοῦντας τὴν Ἀσίαν ἀκοῦ-
11 σαι τὸν λόγον τοῦ Κυρίου Ἰησοῦ, Ἰουδαίους τε καὶ Ἕλληνας. [x]Δυνά- x Mark 16. 20. supra 14. 3.
μεις τε οὐ τὰς τυχούσας ἐποίει ὁ Θεὸς διὰ τῶν χειρῶν Παύλου·
12 [y]ὥστε καὶ ἐπὶ τοὺς ἀσθενοῦντας ἐπιφέρεσθαι ἀπὸ τοῦ χρωτὸς αὐτοῦ y Supra 5. 15.
σουδάρια ἢ σιμικίνθια, καὶ ἀπαλλάσσεσθαι ἀπ᾽ αὐτῶν τὰς νόσους, τά

It should seem that the men had been, some time before, baptized by some of *John's disciples*, but had been not long at Ephesus; when, partly by means of Apollos, and partly of Aquila, they became convinced of the truth of the Christian religion (and were disciples of Aquila); though they were not yet thoroughly acquainted with its doctrines, nor had yet been formally baptized.

2. εἶπε πρὸς αὐτούς· Εἰ &c.] Here (as not unfrequently in interrogative sentences where the words of any speaker are recorded), there is a blending of the oratio directa and indirecta, q. d. He asked whether they had received,—and he asked them saying, have ye received?

— ἀλλ᾽ οὐδὲ — ἠκούσαμεν.] This, according to the sense assigned by our common Version, would imply such ignorance as, even on the supposition that the men were only *Johannites*, would be incredible. But indeed it is quite unnecessary to so interpret; for Grotius, Bp. Pearce, and others have proved, that διδόμενον, or λαμβανόμενον must be supplied at ἐστι· meaning that they had not heard whether the Holy Spirit was imparted—or, as Bornem. expresses, the full sense, Tantum abest, &c., so at John vii. 39. οὔπω γὰρ ἦν Πνεῦμα ἅγιον, where our Version very properly *expresses* the διδόμενον. In both passages the *extraordinary* influences of the Holy Spirit must be understood.

3. εἰς τί.] Sub. βάπτισμα. Εἰς here, and often, does not denote *purpose*, as most Commentators suppose; but εἰς with the Accus. is put for ἐν [by] with a Dative, as in forms of swearing, e. gr. Matt. v. 35. εἰς Ἱεροσόλυμα, which is just after followed by ὀμνύειν ἐν τῇ γῇ.

4. βάπτ. μετανοίας] meaning, "a baptism which bound those who underwent it to repentance, reformation, and purity of life." See xiii. 24. and Note. Τουτέστιν, εἰς τὸν Χ. Ἰ. are the words of the *Apostle*, briefly importing, "Now that Messiah whom John bound you to worship is *Jesus*." No doubt Paul proceeded to enlarge on the evidence for the Messiahship of Jesus, and to point out the benefits of his religion, and its doctrines.

6. ἐλάλουν — προεφ.] Contrary to the opinion of many recent Commentators, I must maintain the sense to be, "they spake with [foreign] tongues, and used their gift in the exercise of the προφητεία, or inspired teaching and preaching. It is plain that γλώσσαις here is for ἑτέραις γλώσσαις, as in the kindred passage of Acts ii. 4. ἤρξαντο λαλεῖν ἑτέραις γλώσσαις, where see Note. We may observe a *climax*; προφητεία being a higher gift than λαλεῖν γλώσσαις. So 1 Cor. xiv. 5. μείζων γὰρ ὁ προφητεύων ἢ ὁ λαλῶν γλώσσαις.

9. ἐσκληρ. καὶ ἠπείθουν.] A sort of Hendiadys; "obstinately refused to yield credence." So Ecclus. xxx. 11. μήποτε σκληρυνθεὶς ἀπειθήσῃ σοι. See also Ps. xciv. 8. and Heb. iii. 8. Ἀποστὰς must be understood of separation from the synagogue and church communion, and preaching elsewhere. See Note on xviii. 7.

— ἐν τῇ σχολῇ Τυράννου τ.] What *sort* of a school this was, biblical Critics are not quite agreed. Lightf., Vitringa, Hamm., Doddr., and Schoettg. suppose it to have been a kind of *Beth-Midrasch* or *Divinity Hall*, designed for reading theological lectures. Others, as Pearce, Rosenm., and Kuin., think it was a *philosophical lecture-room*, and that Tyrannus was a rhetorician, or sophist. If the former conjecture be correct, he was probably a converted Jew; if the latter, a converted Gentile. *Tyrannus* was a not uncommon name, answering to our *King*.

10. πάντας.] This *may* be taken, with many Commentators, in a qualified sense; but there was such a constant influx of persons to this emporium and capital of Asia Minor, that there could not be many individuals but had heard, at least by the report of others, of the doctrines of Christianity. By Ἀσίαν is meant the province of which Ephesus was more immediately the capital, and nearly corresponding to the ancient Ionia.

12. σουδάρια.] See Luke xix. 20. Σιμικίνθια, from the Latin *semicinctum*, a half-girdle, or garment, equivalent to our *apron*.

τε πνεύματα τὰ πονηρὰ ἐξέρχεσθαι ἀπ' αὐτῶν. Ἐπεχείρησαν δέ τινες 13
ἀπὸ τῶν περιερχομένων Ἰουδαίων ἐξορκιστῶν ὀνομάζειν ἐπὶ τοὺς ἔχοντας
τὰ πνεύματα τὰ πονηρὰ τὸ ὄνομα τοῦ Κυρίου Ἰησοῦ, λέγοντες· Ὁρ-
κίζομεν ὑμᾶς τὸν Ἰησοῦν ὃν ὁ Παῦλος κηρύσσει. Ἦσαν δέ τινες υἱοὶ 14
Σκευᾶ Ἰουδαίου ἀρχιερέως ἑπτὰ, οἱ τοῦτο ποιοῦντες. Ἀποκριθὲν δὲ τὸ 15
πνεῦμα τὸ πονηρὸν εἶπε· Τὸν Ἰησοῦν γινώσκω, καὶ τὸν Παῦλον ἐπί-
σταμαι· ὑμεῖς δὲ τίνες ἐστέ; Καὶ ἐφαλλόμενος ἐπ' αὐτοὺς ὁ ἄνθρω- 16
πος ἐν ᾧ ἦν τὸ πνεῦμα τὸ πονηρὸν, καὶ κατακυριεύσας αὐτῶν, ἴσχυσε
κατ' αὐτῶν, ὥστε γυμνοὺς καὶ τετραυματισμένους ἐκφυγεῖν ἐκ τοῦ
οἴκου ἐκείνου. Τοῦτο δὲ ἐγένετο γνωστὸν πᾶσιν, Ἰουδαίοις τε καὶ 17
Ἕλλησι, τοῖς κατοικοῦσι τὴν Ἔφεσον· καὶ ἐπέπεσε φόβος ἐπὶ πάντας
a Matt. 3. 6. αὐτοὺς, καὶ ἐμεγαλύνετο τὸ ὄνομα τοῦ Κυρίου Ἰησοῦ. [a] Πολλοί τε τῶν 18
πεπιστευκότων ἤρχοντο ἐξομολογούμενοι καὶ ἀναγγέλλοντες τὰς πράξεις
αὐτῶν. Ἱκανοὶ δὲ τῶν τὰ περίεργα πραξάντων, συνενέγκαντες τὰς βί- 19
βλους κατέκαιον ἐνώπιον πάντων· καὶ συνεψήφισαν τὰς τιμὰς αὐτῶν,
a Isa. 55. 11. supra 6. 7. & 12. 24. καὶ εὗρον ἀργυρίου μυριάδας πέντε. [a] Οὕτω κατὰ κράτος ὁ λόγος τοῦ 20
Κυρίου ηὔξανε καὶ ἴσχυεν.
b Supra 18. 21. Rom. 15. 25. Gal. 2. 1. [b] ὩΣ δὲ ἐπληρώθη ταῦτα, ἔθετο ὁ Παῦλος ἐν τῷ πνεύματι, διελ- 21
θὼν τὴν Μακεδονίαν καὶ Ἀχαΐαν πορεύεσθαι εἰς Ἱερουσαλὴμ, εἰπών·
c Supra 13. 5. Rom. 16. 23. 2 Tim. 4. 20. Ὅτι μετὰ τὸ γενέσθαι με ἐκεῖ, δεῖ με καὶ Ῥώμην ἰδεῖν. [c] Ἀποστείλας 22
δὲ εἰς τὴν Μακεδονίαν δύο τῶν διακονούντων αὐτῷ, Τιμόθεον καὶ
d 2 Cor. 1. 8. Ἔραστον, αὐτὸς ἐπέσχε χρόνον εἰς τὴν Ἀσίαν. [d] Ἐγένετο δὲ κατὰ τὸν 23

13. *περιερχ.*] See Note on iv. 7. Such persons were called by the Greeks *ἀγύρται*, and by the Latins *circulatores*. They were a kind of men who (like our travelling quacks, or mountebanks, or conjurors,) pretended to cure violent disorders beyond the skill of the physician, and even to cast out devils; and all this with the use of certain incantations, or charms made effective, partly by administering certain powerful medicines, and partly by strongly operating on the imagination.

14. *τινες.*] This must be construed with *ἑπτὰ*, "some seven persons, sons of Sceva." See xxxiii. 23. and Thucyd. iii. 11. vii. 87.

15. *τὸν Ἰησοῦν γινώσκω — τίνες ἐστέ;*] q. d. "I recognize the authority of Jesus and Paul, but yours I disavow." Wets. compares from Isæus *σὺ δὲ τίς εἶ; οὐ γινώσκω σε.*

16. *ἐφαλλόμενος.*] This use of the word (which is by a metaphor taken from wild animals) is rare, and not exemplified by the Commentators. I have, however, in Recens. Synop., adduced several examples from Homer.

— *κατακυρ. αὐτῶν, ἴσχ. κατ' α.*] Almost all Commentators for the last century are agreed in taking *ἴσχυσε κατ' αὐτῶν* to denote "exercised force over them by maltreating them," as in Wisd. xix. 20. But it may perhaps be regarded as a seemingly pleonastic, yet very significant expression, importing more than either term would mean alone. *Ἴσχυσε κατὰ* is for *κατίσχυσε*. *Γυμνοὺς* must be taken in a qualified sense, as in one of our own idioms.

18. *ἐξομολ. καὶ ἀναγγ.*] The expressions are nearly synonymous, and denote frank and open confession, with a narration of all circumstances. By the *πράξεις* are especially meant *magical* practices, though also including sins of every kind.

19. *τὰ περίεργα.*] Περίεργος, as applied to persons, signifies *nimis sedulus, male curiosus;* and hence, as applied to things, *supervacuus, vanus.* Thus it was used to denote the "*superstitious* vanities" of magic; a sense occurring both in the Scriptural and Classical writers. See Rec. Syn. The *books* here mentioned were, no doubt, treatises on magic; such as those of Artemidorus, and Astrampsychus on the interpretation of dreams. Ephesus was the chief resort of the professors of the black art, who drew up what are called in the Classical writers Ἐφέσια γράμματα; which were scrolls of parchment inscribed with certain formulæ, and bound to the body, being used as *amulets*. See more in a Dissertation of J. C. Ortlob, at p. 708. seqq. Vol. xiii. of the Critici Sacri. Of pernicious books being publicly burnt, several examples are adduced by Wets.

— *ἀργυρίου.*] What *kind* of silver coin is here meant — whether the silver shekel or the drachm — cannot be determined. The *latter* is the more probable opinion.

20. *κατὰ κράτος*] for *ἰσχυρῶς*, *extremely*. Ἰσχύειν is well explained by Schleus, *vim exseruit*.

21. *ἔθετο ἐν τῷ πν.*] "statuit apud se, resolved in his mind." The best Commentators have been long agreed in assigning this sense, in preference to referring the expression to the *Holy Spirit*.

22. *ἐπέσχε χρόνον.*] Ἐπέχειν signifies, 1. to *hold to any thing* (*ἐπὶ*), and 2. to *keep to, stay;* and has a reflected force by the ellip. of *ἑαυτόν*. In the sense of *stay*, it occurs either *without*, or (as here) *with* the addition of an Accusative (depending on *κατὰ*), denoting duration of time.

24 καιρὸν ἐκεῖνον τάραχος οὐκ ὀλίγος περὶ τῆς ὁδοῦ. [e] Δημήτριος γάρ τις [e] Supra 16. 16.
ὀνόματι, ἀργυροκόπος, ποιῶν ναοὺς ἀργυροῦς Ἀρτέμιδος, παρείχετο τοῖς
25 τεχνίταις ἐργασίαν οὐκ ὀλίγην· οὓς συναθροίσας, καὶ τοὺς περὶ τὰ
τοιαῦτα ἐργάτας, εἶπεν· Ἄνδρες, ἐπίστασθε ὅτι ἐκ ταύτης τῆς ἐργασίας
26 ἡ εὐπορία ἡμῶν ἐστι· [f] καὶ θεωρεῖτε καὶ ἀκούετε ὅτι οὐ μόνον Ἐφέ- [f] Psal. 115. 4. Jer. 10. 3.
σου, ἀλλὰ σχεδὸν πάσης τῆς Ἀσίας ὁ Παῦλος οὗτος πείσας μετέστησεν
27 ἱκανὸν ὄχλον, λέγων ὅτι οὐκ εἰσὶ θεοὶ οἱ διὰ χειρῶν γινόμενοι. Οὐ
μόνον δὲ τοῦτο κινδυνεύει ἡμῖν τὸ μέρος εἰς ἀπελεγμὸν ἐλθεῖν, ἀλλὰ
καὶ τὸ τῆς μεγάλης θεᾶς Ἀρτέμιδος ἱερὸν εἰς οὐδὲν λογισθῆναι, μέλλειν δὲ καὶ καθαιρεῖσθαι τὴν μεγαλειότητα αὐτῆς, ἣν ὅλη ἡ Ἀσία καὶ
28 ἡ οἰκουμένη σέβεται. Ἀκούσαντες δὲ, καὶ γενόμενοι πλήρεις θυμοῦ,
29 ἔκραζον, λέγοντες· Μεγάλη ἡ Ἄρτεμις Ἐφεσίων! [g] καὶ ἐπλήσθη ἡ [g] Infra 20. 4. & 27. 2. Col. 4. 10.
πόλις ὅλη συγχύσεως· ὥρμησάν τε ὁμοθυμαδὸν εἰς τὸ θέατρον, συν-
αρπάσαντες Γάϊον καὶ Ἀρίσταρχον Μακεδόνας, συνεκδήμους τοῦ Παύ-
30 λου. Τοῦ δὲ Παύλου βουλομένου εἰσελθεῖν εἰς τὸν δῆμον, οὐκ εἴων
31 αὐτὸν οἱ μαθηταί. Τινὲς δὲ καὶ τῶν Ἀσιαρχῶν, ὄντες αὐτῷ φίλοι,

24. *ἀργυροκόπος*.] The word signifies a *worker in silver*; but whether we are here to understand a *silversmith*, or a *manufacturer of small coins*, is uncertain. The former (which is the opinion of the best Commentators) is the more probable. The *ναοὶ ἀργυροῖ* 'Αρτ. are supposed to have been small silver models of the Temple of Diana at Ephesus (one of the wonders of the world), or at least of the *chapel*, which contained the famous statue of the goddess. These were much bought up, both for *curiosity* (being memorials of a building so matchless), and for *purposes of devotion* (as are the models of the Santa Croce at Loretto, in modern times), and were carried about by travellers or others, like the *moveable altars* in use among the Roman Catholics; the model being always provided with a small image of the goddess. There is little doubt, too, that the *ἀργυροκόποι also* executed large *coins* representing the temple, with the image of Diana, of which some have been preserved.

—*παρείχετο τοῖς τεχνίταις*, &c.] "produced much gain to," as Acts xvi. 16. *ἥτις ἐργασίαν πολλὴν παρεῖχε τοῖς*, &c. By the *τεχνῖται* are here denoted the *chief* workmen; and by the *ἐργάται*, the inferior citizens employed in manufacturing the rougher work of these portable chapels. *Τὰ τοιαῦτα*, i. e. statuary, painting, and such sort of matters connected with the Pagan religion.

25. *ἡ εὐπορία ἡμῶν*.] This is a term of middle signification, and is to be interpreted according to circumstances. See Note supra xi. 29.

26. *πείσας μετέστησεν*] "has by his persuasions drawn away." *Μεθιστάναι* signifies properly to *change the position* of any thing; to remove any one from any present station; and, figuratively, to alienate any one's attachment to another. Of all which senses examples are adduced by Kypke.

—*λέγων ὅτι οὐκ εἰσὶ θεοὶ οἱ διὰ χ. γιν.*] The heathens (at least the ignorant multitude) regarded the images of the gods as the *gods themselves*. Hence the makers of these were called *θεοποιοί*. And on the removal of the images, they supposed the *gods* themselves to be taken away. The better instructed, indeed, did not harbour so gross a fancy; yet they maintained that the gods *in illis* LATUISSE, and that hence they were *θεῖοι*, and filled with the presence of the Deity. They readily allowed that the gods did not *need* images; which, they said, were only invented in condescension to the weakness of men; and only meant as *helps, to raise the soul to heaven*, and as symbols and handmaids to Religion. They regarded the images as *representatives* of the gods; and as such entitled to every honour. Finally, they maintained that they did not adore the *images*, but only the *gods*, who, as it were, resided in them. In fact, the idolatries of the Romish Church have been ever defended by these and such like arguments; which were indignantly rejected by the great Christian Apologists (in their answers to Celsus, Porphyry, and Julian), who would, doubtless, were they alive now, be as strenuous opposers of *Romish* as they were once of *Pagan* idolatry.

27. *ἡμῖν τὸ μέρος*.] The sense seems to be, "this our part of the common employment, this our business." So the Syr. and Arab. Versions. The Dat. is for the Genit.

—*ἀπελεγμὸν*] *disgrace*, from *ἀπελέγχεσθαι*, to be utterly refuted or rejected. The word occurs in Symmachus, and *ἐλεγμὸς* in the Sept. The construction of this passage is somewhat anomalous; and it has therefore been treated as corrupt, and has been tampered with by both ancient and modern critics. But no change is necessary,—since the style is what is called *popular*, and the construction is: *κινδυνεύει τὸ ἱερὸν — λογισθῆναι, τήν τε μεγαλειότητα αὐτῆς μέλλειν καὶ καθαιρεῖσθαι*.

29. *θέατρον*] as being the place of public resort for every kind of business or pleasure. *Συνεκδήμους*, fellow travellers, or, as others explain, townsmen, those who had left their country together with Paul.

31. *Ἀσιαρχῶν*.] These *Asiarchs* were of the number of those annual magistrates, who, in the eastern part of the Roman Empire, were (like the Roman *Ædiles*) superintendents of things pertaining to religious worship, the celebration of the public games, &c. They were called, according to the *province* over which they presided, either Asiarchs, Lyciarchs, Bithynarchs, or Syriarchs,

πέμψαντες πρὸς αὐτὸν παρεκάλουν μὴ δοῦναι ἑαυτὸν εἰς τὸ θέατρον.
Ἄλλοι μὲν οὖν ἄλλο τι ἔκραζον· ἦν γὰρ ἡ ἐκκλησία συγκεχυμένη, καὶ 32
h Supra 12. 17. & 13. 16. infra 21. 40. οἱ πλείους οὐκ ᾔδεισαν τίνος ἕνεκεν συνεληλύθεισαν. h Ἐκ δὲ τοῦ 33
ὄχλου προεβίβασαν Ἀλέξανδρον, προβαλόντων αὐτὸν τῶν Ἰουδαίων· ὁ
δὲ Ἀλέξανδρος κατασείσας τὴν χεῖρα, ἤθελεν ἀπολογεῖσθαι τῷ δήμῳ.
Ἐπιγνόντες δὲ ὅτι Ἰουδαῖός ἐστι, φωνὴ ἐγένετο μία ἐκ πάντων ὡς ἐπὶ 34
ὥρας δύο κραζόντων· Μεγάλη ἡ Ἄρτεμις Ἐφεσίων! Καταστείλας δὲ 35

&c. The office was only for a year, and was elective; a certain number of persons (in Proconsular Asia, *ten*) being elected by the cities, and sent to form a common council at some principal city. Of these the Proconsul appointed *one* to be *the* Asiarch; the rest being his colleagues, and also styled Asiarchs: for those who had borne the office were afterwards called Asiarchs by courtesy. And hence Kuinoel thinks it *uncertain* whether the Asiarchs here mentioned were those actually in office (the Council being held at Ephesus) or those who *had been so*. But the air of the context evidently points to the *former*; and, indeed, the use of the *article* (which, in the latter case, was very unlikely to have been used) makes it certain.

—μὴ δοῦναι ἑαυτὸν εἰς τὸ θέατρον.] I cannot agree with Valckn. and Kypke, in regarding this as a *forensic* mode of expression, like εἰσελθεῖν εἰς δῆμον just before. For though they adduce examples of this use from Josephus, yet there εἰς κίνδυνον is added. It should rather seem to be a *popular* form of expression, denoting, "not to trust himself in the theatre." So Cicero C. Verr. iii. 19. Populo *se* ac coronæ *daturum*. This, therefore, may be considered one of the *Latinisms* in St. Luke.

33. This verse involves no little obscurity, partly from the words here occurring being used in a somewhat uncommon sense; but chiefly from the construction being left incomplete, and the circumstances of the transaction in question being rather to be *gathered* from what is said, than distinctly narrated. Hence considerable difference of opinion exists, both as to the *construction* and the *sense*. The construction commonly adopted is προεβίβασαν Ἀλέξανδρον ἐκ τοῦ ὄχλου· which, though involving a somewhat harsh transposition, might be admitted, if the *context* allowed of it. But this it *does not*; for thus no tolerable account can be given of the transaction in question. It must therefore be taken *before* προεβίβασαν (as was done by the Pesch. Syr. Translator, and is the method adopted by all the best Interpreters), and a nominative supplied,—either τινες, as referred to ἐκ τοῦ ὄχλου, or the common ellipsis ἄνθρωποι must be supposed at προεβίβασαν· the sense of which term will depend upon the view taken of the affair then going forward; which has been not a little misunderstood by some Expositors, as Hammond and Bp. Pearce. It should seem that certain well-disposed persons of the people present, with a view to quiet the tumult, were desirous to set up some one to address the multitude, and endeavour to appease their wrath, by showing that there was no good reason for it. Now the *Jews* present were sure to join them, because they saw that the anger of the multitude was directed against both the Christians and themselves: and they were anxious that the speaker should at least take the blame off *their* shoulders, and lay it,—where it ought, they thought, to be,—on the *Christians*. They therefore proposed, as a proper person to speak, one Alexander, who, it seems, had a talent for public speaking, and was a *Proselyte of the gate*; the same probably with Alexander the *coppersmith*. No other view but this can make any thing intelligible. Hence it appears that προβ. cannot mean (as our common Version renders) *drew* out, still less (as Prof. Scholef.) "*thrust forth*;" for the word has never that sense; and here the context would not permit it. It has not, I think, been sufficiently borne in mind by Expositors, that προβιβάζω and ἀναβιβάζω are very often used of *setting any one up to speak*, especially as an advocate for others: sometimes, however, only to *express their sentiments*. Examples in abundance are supplied by the Commentators and Steph. Thesaur. The above interpretation is supported by the authority of the Pesch. Syr. Version, which renders προεβίβασαν, by ܐܘܩܡܘܗܝ, *appointed*; literally, "*set him up*, made him get up [to speak];" this being of the Aphel Conjugation from ܩܘܡ, *to rise*.

Προβαλόντων just after may be taken in a metaphorical sense for *proposing* him, recommending him [as a fit person]. Of the sense *proponere*, Wets., Kypke, and Stephens in his Thesaur., furnish numerous examples. These words προβαλόντων αὐτὸν τῶν Ἰουδαίων are added, to point out the prominent part taken by the *Jews* in the transaction; who, indeed, had some cause to feel alarmed for their safety, since their hostility to all idol-worship was well known, and the bitter animosity felt towards them by the multitude is plain, from their refusing to hear the speaker because he was a *Jew*. Of ἀπολογεῖσθαι the sense is clearly that of *addressing* the people, to show them that no insult had been offered to the worship of Diana; or, at least, that the *Jews* were not the persons who had done the wrong.

34. ἐπιγνόντες.] This (for the common lection ἐπιγνόντων) is the reading of many of the best MSS., of almost all the early Edd., and of several Fathers; and it is adopted by almost every Editor from Wets. to Vat. And rightly; for besides the strong external evidence, *internal* evidence is quite in its favour, it being the more difficult reading. It is, however, not so much a Nominative absolute, as it involves an *anacoluthon*.

35. Καταστέλλω signifies properly to *put down*, as Ps. lxv. 8. καταστ. τὸ κῦτος τῆς θαλάσσης. But it is more frequently used in a metaphorical sense, of *quieting* a tumult.

—γραμματεύς.] It is easier to determine the *rank* and *duties* of this office, than to represent the term by any corresponding one of modern

ὁ γραμματεὺς τὸν ὄχλον, φησίν· Ἄνδρες Ἐφέσιοι, τίς γάρ ἐστιν ἄνθρωπος ὃς οὐ γινώσκει τὴν Ἐφεσίων πόλιν νεωκόρον οὖσαν τῆς μεγά-
36 λης [θεᾶς] Ἀρτέμιδος καὶ τοῦ Διοπετοῦς; Ἀναντιῤῥήτων οὖν ὄντων
τούτων, δέον ἐστὶν ὑμᾶς κατεσταλμένους ὑπάρχειν, καὶ μηδὲν προπετὲς
37 πράττειν. Ἠγάγετε γὰρ τοὺς ἄνδρας τούτους, οὔτε ἱεροσύλους οὔτε
38 βλασφημοῦντας τὴν * θεὸν ὑμῶν. Εἰ μὲν οὖν Δημήτριος καὶ οἱ σὺν
αὐτῷ τεχνῖται πρός τινα λόγον ἔχουσιν, ἀγόραιοι ἄγονται, καὶ ἀνθύ-

languages. From the passages of ancient writers adduced by Wets., it appears that he was *President of the Senate*, and that his duties embraced most of those of our *Chancellor, and Secretary of State*. It may be conjectured that this functionary (of different dignity in different cities) was so called, from being the keeper of the archives, containing all the *γράμματα* of the State; as public treaties, decrees, and documents of every kind.

—*τίς γάρ ἐστιν*, &c.] Pearce and Markl. observe that the *γὰρ* has reference to some clause omitted, and to be filled up thus: [There is no *need* of this clamorous repetition of "Great is Diana,"] for what man is there, &c. Of this elliptical use of *γὰρ* at the beginning of a speech, they adduce an example from Herodot. vi. 11. Ἐπὶ ξυροῦ γὰρ ἀκμῆς ἔχεται ἡμῖν τὰ πράγματα; q. d. I am now induced to address you; for our affairs are in the utmost danger.

—*νεωκόρον*.] The word at first denoted a *sweeper of the temple*. Afterwards, however, (when the humility of religious devotees made the office sought after even by persons of rank,) the term was employed to denote a *curator*, one whose office it was *to see* that the temple was kept clean and in good repair, and furnished with every thing proper for the celebration of public worship. Moreover, what was properly applicable only to a *person*, was transferred, by Prosopopœia, to *cities*; especially as it was *usual* to *personify* them. And thus, by an accommodation of the sense, the term came to signify *devoted, consecrated to*: in which acceptation it was used not only of *Ephesus*, but also of other cities of Greece and Asia Minor. Nay, sometimes one and the same city was called *νεωκόρος*, with respect to three or even four different gods. So great was this devotion of the Ephesians to Diana, that we find from Ælian Var. Hist. iii. 26. the city was styled an *ἀνάθημα*. And that it should have been thus attached to her service, we may easily imagine; since by devoting itself to the goddess, the city was said to have been formerly saved from destruction, when about to be stormed by Crœsus. (See Herodo. i. 26.) The dedication in question, we learn, was accomplished by a very significant action,—namely, that of fastening cords to the walls and gates, and tying the other end to the pillars of the temple: the very manner in which the Island of Rhenea was dedicated to Apollo by Polycrates. See Thucyd. iii. 94.—Θεᾶς before Ἀρτέμιδος (which is not found in several MSS. and Versions) is, perhaps rightly, cancelled by Griesb., Knapp, and Tittm.

—*τοῦ Διοπετοῦς*.] Sub. *ἀγάλματος*, which is supplied in the Syr. Version. It is remarkable that images of an antiquity so remote, as to ascend beyond all historical record, were feigned by the priests to have come "*from heaven*." And from heaven, in a certain sense, they might be said to have come, as far as regards the *material*; at least in the *first* rude images of the gods,—since *aerolites* of immense size, and most grotesque shapes, are known in all ages to have fallen from the skies. One or two of these might, in the infancy of society and the origin of idolatry (bearing, by a *lusus naturæ*, a rude resemblance to the human bust) have been regarded as images of gods, and (as coming from the skies) sent from heaven to be worshipped. Afterwards, similar aerolites, not *naturally* shaped like a bust, would be so formed by *art*. Of the latter kind were, I suspect, the far-famed *Palladia* of Troy and of Athens, both said to be διοπετῆ. Sometimes, however, in a rude condition of society, the aerolite was left in its natural state, without any attempt to form it into a bust. Of this we have at least *two* instances; *one* in the famous *black stone* in the *Kaaba* at Mecca,—which there is reason to think has been an object of worship from the earliest ages;—the other, in what we read in Herodian v. 5, where he mentions as existing in the Temple of the Sun (at Baalbec) a sort of image not *χειροποίητον*, but *ἀνεργαστὸν*, of black stone, and of a conical figure, bearing in form a resemblance to the sun, and said to be διοπετής. Probably, too, the image of Diana at Ephesus, though said to be of *ebony*, was, in fact, of black stone.

36. *κατεσταλμένους*] "quiet and orderly." Μηδὲν προπ. πράττειν, "to do nothing precipitate," is an *euphemism* not uncommon in the Classical writers. See Note on 2 Tim. iii. 2.

37. *ἠγάγετε γάρ*.] Here again the *γὰρ* refers to a sentence omitted, q. d. [And that you *have* been hasty and rash is certain,] *for* you have brought hither, &c.

—*θεόν*.] Such, for the common reading *θεὰν*, is found in many MSS., nearly all the early Edd., and some Fathers; and it is preferred by Mill, and adopted by Wets., Matth., Griesb., Tittm., and Vat. It is also confirmed by *internal* testimony; since the scribes were far more likely to change *θεὸν* into *θεὰν* than the contrary, as appears from this,—that some who had *θεὸν* in their originals changed *τὴν* into *τὸν*, which Griesb., by a grievous blunder, has *edited*.

38. *λόγον*.] Some take this to mean a *case at law*; but others, more agreeably to the simple style of Luke, interpret it a *complaint*, by an ellip. of *μομφῆς*, like the Heb. דבר in Exod. xviii. 16. So Col. iii. 13. ἐάν τις πρός τινα ἔχῃ μομφήν. At infra xxiv. 19. and Matt. v. 23. we have simply ἔχειν τι. Ἀγόραιοι scil. ἡμέραι, "court days [appointed for trying causes]." Hesych. explains ἀγοραῖαν by δικαιολογίαν. Ἄγονται, are [appointed to be] holden.

—*ἀνθύπατοι*.] The only satisfactory way of accounting for the *plural*, is to regard it not so much as an *hyperbole*, as a *popular* idiom,—by which the *plural* is put for the singular, in a *generic* sense, q. d. "It is for laws and proconsuls to de-

πατοί εἰσιν· ἐγκαλείτωσαν ἀλλήλοις. Εἰ δέ τι † περὶ ἑτέρων ἐπιζη- 39
τεῖτε, ἐν τῇ ἐννόμῳ ἐκκλησίᾳ ἐπιλυθήσεται. Καὶ γὰρ κινδυνεύομεν 40
ἐγκαλεῖσθαι στάσεως περὶ τῆς σήμερον, μηδενὸς αἰτίου ὑπάρχοντος
περὶ οὗ δυνησόμεθα ἀποδοῦναι λόγον τῆς συστροφῆς ταύτης. καὶ ταῦτα 41
εἰπὼν ἀπέλυσε τὴν ἐκκλησίαν.

i 1 Tim. 1. 3. XX. [i] ΜΕΤΑ δὲ τὸ παύσασθαι τὸν θόρυβον, προσκαλεσάμενος 1
ὁ Παῦλος τοὺς μαθητὰς καὶ ἀσπασάμενος, ἐξῆλθε πορευθῆναι εἰς τὴν
Μακεδονίαν. Διελθὼν δὲ τὰ μέρη ἐκεῖνα, καὶ παρακαλέσας αὐτοὺς 2
λόγῳ πολλῷ, ἦλθεν εἰς τὴν Ἑλλάδα· ποιήσας τε μῆνας τρεῖς, γενομέ- 3
νης αὐτῷ ἐπιβουλῆς ὑπὸ τῶν Ἰουδαίων μέλλοντι ἀνάγεσθαι εἰς τὴν
k Supra 16. 1. & 19. 29. Συρίαν, ἐγένετο γνώμη τοῦ ὑποστρέφειν διὰ Μακεδονίας. [k] Συνείπετο 4
infra 21. 29. & 27. 2. δὲ αὐτῷ ἄχρι τῆς Ἀσίας Σώπατρος Βεροιαῖος· Θεσσαλονικέων δὲ Ἀρί-
Col. 4. 7, 10. 1 Cor. 1. 14. σταρχος καὶ Σεκοῦνδος, καὶ Γάϊος Δερβαῖος, καὶ Τιμόθεος. Ἀσιανοὶ
Eph. 6. 21. 2 Tim. 4. 12, 20. δὲ, Τυχικὸς καὶ Τρόφιμος. Οὗτοι προελθόντες ἔμενον ἡμᾶς ἐν Τρω- 5
Titus 3. 12. άδι· ἡμεῖς δὲ ἐξεπλεύσαμεν μετὰ τὰς ἡμέρας τῶν ἀζύμων ἀπὸ Φιλίπ- 6
πων, καὶ ἤλθομεν πρὸς αὐτοὺς εἰς τὴν Τρωάδα ἄχρις ἡμερῶν πέντε,
l Supra 2. 42, 46. οὗ διετρίψαμεν ἡμέρας ἑπτά. [l] Ἐν δὲ τῇ μιᾷ τῶν σαββάτων, συνηγμέ- 7
1 Cor. 10. 16. & 11. 20. νων ‡ τῶν μαθητῶν [τοῦ] κλάσαι ἄρτον, ὁ Παῦλος διελέγετο αὐτοῖς,
μέλλων ἐξιέναι τῇ ἐπαύριον· παρέτεινέ τε τὸν λόγον μέχρι μεσονυκτίου.
Ἦσαν δὲ λαμπάδες ἱκαναὶ ἐν τῷ ὑπερῴῳ οὗ ἦσαν συνηγμένοι. καθή- 8
μενος δέ τις νεανίας ὀνόματι Εὔτυχος ἐπὶ τῆς θυρίδος, καταφερόμενος 9

cide such matters." I would compare Isæus p. 51, 3. οὔσων δικῶν, "though there was a power of seeking justice." Ἐγκαλείτωσαν ἀλλήλ. is for ἔγκλησιν εἰσαγέτωσαν, "let them go to law with each other."

39. ἑτέρων.] i. e. other matters of public concern, whether political or religious. For περὶ ἑτέρων 10 MSS. (some very ancient) have περαιτέρω, which was undoubtedly read by the Pesch. Syriac Translator. It is likewise found in the very ancient *Itala*, and was probably read by the Vulg.: for *alterius* there seems to be an error of the scribes for *ulterius*. So elegant a term as περαιτέρω was sure to be roughly handled by the scribes; especially as τι preceded, and ε and αι are, by Itacism, continually interchanged. In confirmation of this reading see the passages adduced in my Note on Thucyd. iii. 81. ex. gr. Æschyl. Prom. 255. Μήπου τι προὔβης τῶνδε καὶ περαιτέρω.

— τῇ ἐννόμῳ ἐκκλ.] Not "*a* lawful assembly," for the Art. is not pleonastic, but "*the* regular assembly:" τῇ κυρίᾳ, which is a pointed way of hinting that the present assembly was *not* such.

40. κινδυνεύομεν.] The second person is delicately used for the first, per κοίνωσιν. Στάσις, in the law sense, denoted not only *sedition*, but *tumult*, and is further explained by συστροφῆς following, which signifies a tumultuous assemblage, ξύστασις, as a Classical writer would have said.

XX. 3. ποιήσας.] A Nominat. absolute, or rather an anantapodoton. At αὐτῷ ἐπιβ. ὑπὸ, &c. ἐπιβουλὴ, as a verbal, takes the construction of the verb from which it is derived. On the plot in question Commentators variously speculate. It was probably one to contrive means to make away with Paul while on the voyage. At ἐγένετο γνώμη repeat αὐτῷ, from the preceding, "It was his purpose."

6. μετὰ τὰς ἡμ. τ. ἀζ.] "after Passover time;" for the Jews spoke of their festivals in the same way as we do, when we say *Christmas-time*, or *Michaelmas-time*. Ἄχρις ἡμέρας π., "within five days." This use of the word is Hellenistic, and found at Rom. viii. 22. xi. 25. See Tittm. de Syn. p. 35.

7. μιᾷ τῶν σαββ.] See Note on Matt. xxviii. 1.

— τῶν μαθ.] About 17 MSS. and several Versions have ἡμῶν, which is preferred by Grot., Mill, and Beng., and edited by Griesb., Knapp, Tittm., and Vat. But without sufficient reason. See Matth. The τοῦ is omitted in many MSS. and almost all the early Edd., and is cancelled by Matth. and Griesb. It probably came from the margin, especially as it is not found supra xv. 6. On the thing itself see ii. 42.

8. See Note on John vi. 10.

9. τῆς θυρίδος] "the window;" which, it seems, was a kind of lattice, or casement, admitting of being thrown back, so as to let air into the apartment, heated by so much company and so many lamps. The thing is well illustrated by Mr. Jowett, in the Missionary Reg., and Mr. Arundel in the 2d vol. of his interesting "Discoveries in Asia Minor." Καταφερόμενος ὕπνῳ, for εἰς or πρὸς ὕπνον, of which latter construction examples are adduced by the Commentators. The former is Hellenistic, but occurs in Parthen. Erot. 10. εἰς βαθὺν ὕπνον καταφέρεσθαι. The Commentators closely connect the καταφ. with ἔπεσεν, taking it to mean only ἔπεσεν κάτω. But the latter may denote the *completion* of the action described as in progress at καταφερ. Ἀπὸ is for ὑπό; or it may be rendered, "from the effects of sleep."

ὕπνῳ βαθεῖ, διαλεγομένου τοῦ Παύλου ἐπὶ πλεῖον, κατενεχθεὶς ἀπὸ τοῦ
10 ὕπνου, ἔπεσεν ἀπὸ τοῦ τριστέγου κάτω, καὶ ἤρθη νεκρός. [m] Καταβὰς m 1 Kings 17. 21.
δὲ ὁ Παῦλος ἐπέπεσεν αὐτῷ, καὶ συμπεριλαβὼν εἶπε· Μὴ θορυβεῖσθε· 2 Kings 4. 34.
11 ἡ γὰρ ψυχὴ αὐτοῦ ἐν αὐτῷ ἐστιν. Ἀναβὰς δὲ καὶ κλάσας ἄρτον καὶ
12 γευσάμενος, ἐφ' ἱκανόν τε ὁμιλήσας ἄχρις αὐγῆς, οὕτως ἐξῆλθεν. Ἤγα-
13 γον δὲ τὸν παῖδα ζῶντα, καὶ παρεκλήθησαν οὐ μετρίως. Ἡμεῖς δὲ
προελθόντες ἐπὶ τὸ πλοῖον, ἀνήχθημεν εἰς τὴν Ἄσσον, ἐκεῖθεν μέλλοντες ἀναλαμβάνειν τὸν Παῦλον· οὕτω γὰρ ἦν διατεταγμένος, μέλλων

— *τριστέγου*] "the third story;" for *στέγος* signifies not only a *roof*, but the *flooring* of an upper apartment, as being a roof to the apartment below. So the Latin *tristega tecta*, the third floor. And Juvenal iii. 199. Tabulata *tecta*.

— *ἤρθη νεκρός*.] Many recent Commentators from Bp. Pearce suppose the word to mean "was taken for dead." They urge that persons falling from a high place are often found in a swoon; and that there is nothing in the context that would lead us to think the lad was *dead*. Nay that Paul himself says, "he is *not* dead." The first argument, however, has no force against the plain words of St. Luke. And the second and third have next to none. There is no trait in the Apostles and Evangelists more remarkable, than their avoiding every thing like *setting off* any circumstance to the utmost. Again, it by no means follows from St. Paul's stretching himself upon the young man that he thought him alive, or meant to see whether he was so or not. The Apostle, by doing the very thing which Elijah in similar circumstances did, evidently regarded him as dead; and, no doubt, imitated the Prophet in offering up fervent prayers that he might be brought to life. And as to the expression of St. Paul, *ἡ ψυχὴ αὐτοῦ — ἐστιν*, we are no more to infer from *that*, that the young man was *not dead*, than, in the narration at Matt. ix. 14., from the words *οὐ γὰρ ἀπέθανε*, that the damsel was not dead. See the Note there.

10. *συμπεριλαβὼν*] "embracing." A sense very rare in the Classical writers, though *one* example, from Plutarch, is adduced by Wets.

11. *κλάσας ἄρτον καὶ γευσάμενος*.] Some difference of opinion here exists as to whether this is to be understood of the *Eucharist*, or of a *common meal*. The older Expositors adopt the *former* view; those from Grot. downwards, in general, the *latter*; and, I think, upon good grounds. For it may be observed. 1. that the expression *κλᾷν ἄρτον* is only applied to the *Apostle*. 2. Wherever that phrase is used of the *Eucharist*, it is used *simply*. never with the addition of *καὶ γευσάμενος*· especially since the term *γεύσασθαι* did not imply eating *little*, but (by an idiom found in our own language) denoted *taking food*, whether little or otherwise. 3. The following term *ὁμιλήσας* suggests the idea of a common *meal*, since wherever it occurs in Scripture it is used of *ordinary conversation*, not of *preaching*, as in the Ecclesiastical writers; for which *διαλέγεσθαι* is used, as just before. Not to mention, that as the Apostle had already so exceeded the usual time in his discourse, — he would not, at that unseasonable hour of the night, *resume* it, and continue it "a good while, till day-break;" nor would he then *celebrate the Eucharist*, which had doubtless been administered at an early period of the meeting. The meal in question was doubtless taken by St. Paul to strengthen him for his journey.

— *οὕτως ἐξῆλθεν*.] Render, "then he departed;" which is the sense expressed by the Syr. and the best modern Interpreters. Compare 1 Thess. iv. 17.

12. *ἤγαγον*] for *εἰσήγ*. The sense seems to be, "Now they had brought in," probably just before the Apostle departed. And so in the Cod. Cant. is added *ἀσπαζομένων αὐτῶν*, "as they were bidding each other farewell;" (see xx. 1. xxi. 6.) doubtless an insertion from the margin, but which serves to show the view of the sense adopted by the most ancient Interpreters. We may observe, that the introduction of this minute circumstance, though a little out of place, bears upon it the stamp of nature and truth.

— *ζῶντα*] "alive and well." That such is the sense, and not *alive* only, (as is alleged by those Commentators who deny the miracle), is clear from the context, especially the words following. Of this sense of *ζῆν* (but little known or borne in mind by Interpreters) examples occur in John iv. 50. *ὁ υἱός σου ζῇ*. (where see Note) 2 Kings i. 2. and Is. xxxviii. 9. (comparing the Heb. and Sept.) Soph. Trach. 235. *καὶ ζῶντα καὶ θάλλοντα κοὐ νόσῳ βαρύν*. Æschyl. Agam. 660. *καὶ ζῶντα καὶ βλέποντα*. Gen. xlviii. 27. *Ὑγιαίνει ὁ πατὴρ ὑμῶν ὁ πρεσβύτης*; to which the answer is *ὑγιαίνει ὁ πατὴρ ἡμῶν, ἔτι ζῇ*.

13. *προελθόντες ἐπὶ τὸ πλοῖον*.] No ship has been recently spoken of: but at v. 6. mention was made of one sailing from Philippi. Therefore Bp. Middl., with reason, supposes this to be the ship implied; in which, it seems, Luke and his party performed their coasting voyage from Philippi, touching at Troas and other places by the way, till they reached Patara, and there embarked on board another vessel bound to Phœnicia. There is, I think, little probability in the supposition of Doddr., Pearce, Michaelis, and Kuin., that the ship had been hired for the voyage; which would surely involve a cost disproportionate to the resources of the Apostle. The stay made by him may be accounted for by supposing, that the ship made occasionally a stop on account of commercial business. It should seem that Paul and his companions depended for their passage on such coasting vessels as they should meet with, and which would be likely to most forward them on their way to Jerusalem; embracing, at the same time, every opportunity (afforded by the occasional stoppage of those vessels for the purposes of trade) to salute and instruct their Christian brethren by the way.

— *μέλλων πεζεύειν*.] On the *reason* for this Commentators variously speculate. See Recens. Synop. I am still of opinion, that it was simply to avoid the tedious and (considering the want

αὐτὸς πεζεύειν. Ὡς δὲ συνέβαλεν ἡμῖν εἰς τὴν Ἄσσον, ἀναλαβόντες 14
αὐτὸν ἤλθομεν εἰς Μιτυλήνην· κἀκεῖθεν ἀποπλεύσαντες, τῇ ἐπιούσῃ 15
κατηντήσαμεν ἀντικρὺ Χίου. τῇ δὲ ἑτέρᾳ παρεβάλομεν εἰς Σάμον· καὶ
a Infra 21. 12. μείναντες ἐν Τρωγυλλίῳ, τῇ ἐχομένῃ ἤλθομεν εἰς Μίλητον. [a] Ἔκρινε 16
γὰρ ὁ Παῦλος παραπλεῦσαι τὴν Ἔφεσον, ὅπως μὴ γένηται αὐτῷ χρονοτριβῆσαι ἐν τῇ Ἀσίᾳ· ἔσπευδε γάρ, εἰ δυνατὸν ἦν αὐτῷ, τὴν ἡμέραν
τῆς Πεντηκοστῆς γενέσθαι εἰς Ἱεροσόλυμα.
Ἀπὸ δὲ τῆς Μιλήτου πέμψας εἰς Ἔφεσον, μετεκαλέσατο τοὺς πρεσ- 17
o Supra 19. 10. βυτέρους τῆς ἐκκλησίας. [o] ὡς δὲ παρεγένοντο πρὸς αὐτόν, εἶπεν αὐτοῖς· 18
Ὑμεῖς ἐπίστασθε, ἀπὸ πρώτης ἡμέρας ἀφ᾽ ἧς ἐπέβην εἰς τὴν Ἀσίαν,
πῶς μεθ᾽ ὑμῶν τὸν πάντα χρόνον ἐγενόμην, δουλεύων τῷ Κυρίῳ μετὰ 19
πάσης ταπεινοφροσύνης, καὶ [πολλῶν] δακρύων, καὶ πειρασμῶν τῶν
συμβάντων μοι ἐν ταῖς ἐπιβουλαῖς τῶν Ἰουδαίων· ὡς οὐδὲν ὑπεστειλά- 20
μην τῶν συμφερόντων, τοῦ μὴ ἀναγγεῖλαι ὑμῖν καὶ διδάξαι ὑμᾶς δη-
p Matt. 1. 15. Luke 24. 47. μοσίᾳ καὶ κατ᾽ οἴκους, [p] διαμαρτυρόμενος Ἰουδαίοις τε καὶ Ἕλλησι τὴν 21
εἰς τὸν Θεὸν μετάνοιαν, καὶ πίστιν τὴν εἰς τὸν Κύριον ἡμῶν Ἰησοῦν
Χριστόν. Καὶ νῦν ἰδού, ἐγὼ δεδεμένος τῷ πνεύματι πορεύομαι εἰς 22

of skill in the ancient navigators) *dangerous* circumnavigation of the promontory of Lectrum, which extends a long way into the sea; insomuch that the distance from Troas to Assos is about one-third shorter by land than by sea. And the Apostle's perils by sea had been so great, that he might well prefer going by land; especially when the distance was shorter.

15. Τρωγυλλίῳ.] The MSS. vary, Matthæi edits Τρωγιλλίῳ, which is certainly supported by several passages of Thucydides, in which we have Τρώγιλος mentioned as one of the ports of Syracuse; but never Τρώγυλος. It was so called from an adjacent village of that name. I suspect that Τρωγίλιον is merely *another form* (originally diminutive) of Τρώγιλος, and the primitive force of each was that of our *ness*.

17. τοὺς πρεσβυτέρους.] As these persons are at ver. 28 called ἐπισκόπους, and especially from a comparison of other passages (as 1 Tim. iii. 1.), the best Commentators, ancient and modern, have with reason inferred that the terms as yet denoted the same thing. Ἐπίσκοπος might denote either an *overlooker*, or *a care-taker;* and these senses would be very suitable to express the pastoral duties. But the word might also (correspondently to the Heb. פקיד) denote a *ruler*, or *governor*, an idea naturally arising out of the former. The term πρεσβύτεροι was borrowed from the Jewish Hierarchy, and corresponded to the זקנים, or Archisynagogi of the Jews. Now all πρεσβύτεροι were *officially* ἐπίσκοποι. Yet we are not therefore to infer that there was no *superintending supreme* authority in the primitive Church; for reason will show that no society can exist without some laws, and consequently persons to administer those laws. There can, then, be no doubt but that *one* of the presbyters (as there were *many* at Ephesus) was, in such a case, invested with authority over the others, and consequently was a *Bishop* in the modern sense of the term. And since, after Episcopacy, in that sense, was established, it became proper to have a *name* by which to designate the *ruling* Presbyter, none seemed so proper as ἐπίσκοπος, because it was far better fitted to denote the *Episcopal* than the *Pastoral* duties; while πρεσβ. had, no doubt, been always more in use to denote the *pastoral* or ministerial.

Markl. rightly infers from ver. 25, that Paul convoked not only the Presbyters of *Ephesus*, but of the *district;* no part of it being far from Ephesus (namely, *Asia proper*, the ancient Ionia), the *Christians* of all which constituted the *Church* of Ephesus.

18. πῶς μ. ὑ. ἐγενόμην] "How I have conducted myself among you."

19. δουλεύων — ταπεινοφ.] "discharging the ministry of the Lord with all humility and modesty." The μετὰ must be repeated at δακρύων, and rendered, with a small accommodation of the sense, *amidst*, or *amongst*. So the Heb. ב, *by*. Συμβ. ἐν, ב, "which happened through or by." See my Note on Thucyd. ii. 70. N. 3.

20. οὐδὲν ὑπεστ.] Ὑποστέλλεσθαι signifies, in the Middle form, "to withdraw one's self through fear;" and, in a deponent sense, "to withdraw, keep back any thing." In ἀναγγεῖλαι καὶ διδάξαι there seems to be a reference to the Gospel preached, being at once a *message* and an *instruction*. It is plain from the foregoing term δημοσίᾳ, which has reference to meetings of the *whole* congregation at once, that κατ᾽ οἴκους must mean, not "from house to house," but "in private houses," (the κατὰ only denoting *rotation*), namely, those where separate parts of the whole number of Christians met. So κατ᾽ οἶκον supra ii. 46. where see Note. Or we may (with Mosheim de rebus ante Const. i. 37.) suppose δημοσίᾳ to denote the place where the delegates from the different congregations, of which the Church of Ephesus was composed, met; and κατ᾽ οἴκους, the houses where the different congregations assembled.

22. δεδεμένος τῷ πνεύμ.] Many Commentators take πνεύμ. to mean the *Holy* Spirit. But thus δεδεμένος admits of no satisfactory sense, and the next clause discountenances this interpretation. It is better, with others, to take πνεύμ. of the

23 Ἱερουσαλὴμ τὰ ἐν αὐτῇ συναντήσοντά μοι μὴ εἰδώς· [q] πλὴν ὅτι τὸ [q] Infra 21. 4, 11.
Πνεῦμα τὸ ἅγιον κατὰ πόλιν διαμαρτύρεται λέγον, ὅτι δεσμά με καὶ
24 θλίψεις μένουσιν. [r] Ἀλλ' οὐδενὸς λόγον ποιοῦμαι, οὐδὲ ἔχω τὴν ψυ- [r] Infra 21. 13. Gal. 1. 1. Tit. 1. 3.
χήν μου τιμίαν ἐμαυτῷ, ὡς τελειῶσαι τὸν δρόμον μου μετὰ χαρᾶς, καὶ
τὴν διακονίαν ἣν ἔλαβον παρὰ τοῦ Κυρίου Ἰησοῦ, διαμαρτύρασθαι τὸ
25 εὐαγγέλιον τῆς χάριτος τοῦ Θεοῦ. Καὶ νῦν ἰδού, ἐγὼ οἶδα ὅτι οὐκέτι
ὄψεσθε τὸ πρόσωπόν μου ὑμεῖς πάντες, ἐν οἷς διῆλθον κηρύσσων τὴν [s] Luke 7. 30.
26 βασιλείαν τοῦ Θεοῦ. Διὸ μαρτύρομαι ὑμῖν ἐν τῇ σήμερον ἡμέρᾳ, ὅτι Eph. 1. 11.
27 καθαρὸς ἐγὼ ἀπὸ τοῦ αἵματος πάντων· [s] οὐ γὰρ ὑπεστειλάμην, τοῦ [t] 1 Pet. 5. 2. 1 Tim. 3. 1, 2. & 4. 16.
28 μὴ ἀναγγεῖλαι ὑμῖν πᾶσαν τὴν βουλὴν τοῦ Θεοῦ. [t] Προσέχετε οὖν Phil 1. 1. [3] Eph. 1. 7. Col. 1. 14.
ἑαυτοῖς καὶ παντὶ τῷ ποιμνίῳ, ἐν ᾧ ὑμᾶς τὸ Πνεῦμα τὸ ἅγιον ἔθετο 1 Pet. 1. 18. Rev. 5. 9.

mind of St. Paul; a very frequent sense of the word. Δεδεμένος is well explained by Rosenmuller, Kuin., and Middl., "under a strong impulse of my mind;" by a metaphor very similar to that in συνέχεσθαι τῷ πνεύματι at xviii. 5, where see Note.

23. πλὴν ὅτι.] Sub. ἓν and τοῦτο, "But this one thing [alone I know] that." So Soph. El. 426. πλείω δὲ τούτων οὐ κάτοιδα· πλὴν ὅτι πέμπει με, &c. The ἓν is supplied by Aristoph. Pac. 227. See Hoogev. de part. in voc. Τὸ Πνεῦμα τὸ ἅγιον is rightly taken by the best Commentators to denote *persons endued by the Holy Spirit.* The Holy Spirit in every city testified by the mouth of inspired prophets. See xxi. 4, 11. Μένουσι, "await me." This seems to be a Latinism.

24. οὐδενὸς λόγον ποιοῦμαι] "I make no account of," care not for any thing. An idiom occurring in the best writers. Not so the phraseology of the next clause, which is in the *popular* style; and ἔχω is employed according to the Latin use of *habeo.* Markl. and Kuin. think there is an ellip. of οὕτω, which is *expressed* in a similar passage of Liban. p. 407, cited by Wets. μήτ' οὕτω ποτὲ μέγα ἡγήσαιμι τὴν ψυχὴν, ὥστε πόθῳ τοῦ ζῇν βλάψαι τὴν ἐνέγκασαν. In τελειῶσαι τὸν δρόμον, there is an *agonistic* metaphor. Τελειῶσαι is employed in two senses, adapted to the two different clauses to which it belongs. Διαμαρτύρασθαι — Θεοῦ is exegetical of διακονίαν.

25. ἰδού.] The sense of the expression, (as at ver. 22,) is *Mind!* Οἶδα ὅτι οὐκέτι ὄψεσθε τ. π. μ. As it is next to certain that the Apostle did again visit Proconsular Asia, after his release from imprisonment at Rome, the Commentators are at a loss to reconcile what is here said to facts. They suppose, either that all the Presbyters now present were dead when St. Paul again visited Asia, or that he might mean, he should not see them *all* again. The former solution, however, is too much like a "device for the nonce," and the latter is far-fetched and unnecessary; since we have only to suppose that the Apostle here speaks ἐν πνεύματι, according to his human spirit or mind, and therefore (as he said just before) μὴ εἰδώς, not *certainly* knowing that it *would* be so, but *presaging* such from the threatening intimations he had received. Indeed the form οἶδ' ὅτι, or even εὖ οἶδ' ὅτι, is perpetually used in the best writers to denote something far short of certain knowledge, and only of *opinion*, or *present persuasion.* See my Note on Thucyd. iii. 34.

28 There is scarcely any passage of the N. T. on which the opinions of Critics and Expositors are more divided than the present. In examining what is the true *reading*, in order to ascertain the exact *sense*, we find the MSS. offering no less than *SIX* readings, namely, τοῦ Θεοῦ:—τοῦ Κυρίου:—τοῦ Χριστοῦ:—τοῦ Θεοῦ καὶ Κυρίου:—τοῦ Κυρίου Θεοῦ:—and τοῦ Κυρίου καὶ Θεοῦ: The relative merits of these are discussed by Wets., Griesb., Kuin., and Dr. Pye Smith, Scrip. Test. Vol. iii. p. 66. sq., who decide in favour of Κυρίου. On the contrary, other Critics of not less eminence, as Mill, Bengel, Wolf, Venema, Michaelis, Ernesti, Valckn., Wassenberg, Matth., Wakef., Tittm., Vater, Bp. Middl., Gratz, and Rinck, reject Κυρίου, and almost all read Θεοῦ: though some, as Matthæi and Middl., prefer τοῦ Κυρίου καὶ Θεοῦ. It is indeed a question of very difficult decision; in which the Critical arguments usually employed *draw two ways;* insomuch that a Critical Jury might most *prudently* return a verdict of NON LIQUET, and thus a positive determination of the exact reading might be deferred *ad Græcas Calendas.* In the former Edition of this work I decided in favour of the common reading τοῦ Θεοῦ. But I have been induced, by the remarks and suggestions offered, in an able Critique on this work in the Eclectic Review for Dec. 1832, to give the whole question a most attentive reconsideration, the result of which I shall proceed to lay before the reader.

And first let us examine the state of the evidence before us. Perplexing as it appears, yet it may be much cleared by the consideration, that *three* out of the above six Varr. Lectt. (namely τοῦ Χριστοῦ,—τοῦ Κυρίου Θεοῦ,—and τοῦ Θεοῦ καὶ Κυρίου), are scarcely entitled to the appellation of *varr. lectt.*, being partly formed on the others, and partly proceeding from an evident *alteration to avoid a difficulty;* and having scarcely any authority of MSS., they merit no attention, except as furnishing *data* to assist us in judging of the *remaining three* PRIMARY READINGS, namely, τοῦ Θεοῦ;—τοῦ Κυρίου;—and τοῦ Κυρίου καὶ Θεοῦ. Let us now examine these readings, as to the evidence *external* and *internal.* As to the *former*, Κυρίου is supported by 13 MSS. (five of them very ancient, and the rest neither ancient nor very valuable), by the Coptic, Sahidic, and Armenian Versions, and some Fathers, chiefly Latin. 2. Τοῦ Κυρίου καὶ Θεοῦ is supported by *one* very ancient MS. and 63 others, none of much antiquity or consequence, but of *different families;* also by the Sclavonic Version, the Edit. Princ., et Plantin. 3. Τοῦ Θεοῦ is supported by the most ancient of the MSS. (the Cod. Vat.) and 17 others; some of the 10th, 11th, or 12th centuries, but most of them more modern: also by the Pesch. Syr. in

ἐπισκόπους, ποιμαίνειν τὴν ἐκκλησίαν τοῦ Κυρίου καὶ Θεοῦ, ἣν περιεποι-
a 2 Pet. 2. 1. Matt. 7. 15. ήσατο διὰ τοῦ ἰδίου αἵματος. a Ἐγὼ γὰρ οἶδα τοῦτο, ὅτι εἰσελεύσον- 29
ται μετὰ τὴν ἄφιξίν μου λύκοι βαρεῖς εἰς ὑμᾶς, μὴ φειδόμενοι τοῦ

some MSS.; by the *Latin Vulgate*; and, according to some, the Æthiopic. Finally, it is quoted, or referred to, by Ignat., Tertull., Basil., Chrysost., Epiphan., Ambrose, Theophyl., Œcumen., and 12 other Fathers of the Greek and Latin Church. Now it is manifest, that τοῦ Κυρίου is greatly inferior in MS. authority to τοῦ Κυρίου καὶ Θεοῦ, and not superior to τοῦ Θεοῦ: and of the 4. valuable Venice MSS. lately collated by Rinck, *two* have τοῦ Κυρίου καὶ Θεοῦ, *one* τοῦ Κυρίου Θεοῦ, and *one* Θεοῦ. And as τοῦ Κυρίου was evidently formed on τοῦ Κυρίου καὶ Θεοῦ, that is decisive. Consequently the reading τοῦ Κυρίου καὶ Θεοῦ has an undoubted superiority as to *external* evidence. As to *internal*, the reading Θεοῦ has been contended for by eminent Critics (though with very different views) strenuously, but, I *now* think, not quite successfully; for while the phrase ἐκκλησία τοῦ Θεοῦ occurs 12 times in St. Paul's Epistles, ἐκκλησία τοῦ Κυρίου is found *nowhere* in the N. T.: consequently, it was far more probable that Κυρίου should be altered to Θεοῦ than Θεοῦ to Κυρίου. Besides, the former might be done without any evil intention, while the latter could only arise from sinister design; which ought surely never to be imputed without very strong reasons. Now if τοῦ Θεοῦ be the true reading, the sense will be that assigned by the above-mentioned learned Reviewer, "Feed the Church of Him who is God, which he hath purchased with his own blood;" implying an assertion at once of the *Deity* and the *Humanity* of our Lord, without confounding the "two natures." Yet this is somewhat harsh, and cannot fairly be elicited from the words; and therefore there is the less reason to impute the reading to any pious fraud on the part of the *Trinitarians*. And as little reason is there to impute the reading Κυρίου to an alteration of the *Arians*; for, not to say that they never had the *power* to foist in a reading, so as to introduce it into above two-thirds of the Copies, they were not driven to do so from necessity; having, as we see in the case of Mr. Wakefield, contrived such a sort of interpretation as to keep out any sense that might compromise their opinions. It may, indeed, be argued that τοῦ Θεοῦ, as being unquestionably the most *difficult* reading, ought to be preferred. And it is true that the readings may perhaps all of them be accounted for as so many various attempts to soften that harshness. Yet that is perhaps too hypothetical.

Let us now proceed to examine the comparative evidence, external and internal, for the readings τοῦ Κυρίου and τοῦ Κυρίου καὶ Θεοῦ. Now *external* evidence is decidedly in favour of the *latter*; but *internal* evidence is somewhat in favour of the former; for though Bp. Middl. (after Matth.) thinks it quite as probable that the readings τοῦ Θεοῦ and τοῦ Κυρίου may have arisen by *dividing* the reading τοῦ Κυρίου καὶ Θεοῦ, as that the reading τοῦ Κυρίου καὶ Θεοῦ was *compounded* of those readings; nevertheless, since the *former* circumstance so very rarely occurs, and the latter so frequently in all writers, I really cannot agree with the learned Prelate. I am quite disposed to assent to the observation of Dr. Pye Smith, that, "τοῦ Κυρίου being admitted to be the original reading, all the others may be accounted for by suppositions easy and probable in themselves, and known to have been realized in numerous instances." But, to advert to the evidence as regards the *secondary* readings,—the reading Χριστοῦ supports that of Κυρίου; and the reading τοῦ Κυρίου Θεοῦ supports τοῦ Κυρίου καὶ Θεοῦ; while τοῦ Θεοῦ καὶ Κυρίου, I think, supports τοῦ Θεοῦ: for it seems to have arisen from the alteration of some who, stumbling at the harshness of Θεοῦ, subjoined καὶ Κυρίου, in order to supply some word to which τοῦ ἰδίου αἵματος could be applied. Under all the circumstances, I have thought proper (with Matthæi and Vater), to *admit* the words Κυρίου καί; but, from the state of the comparative *internal* evidence, I have not chosen, with Vater, to *bracket* καὶ Θεοῦ; since, as all the other readings may be accounted for (though with less probability), on the supposition that τοῦ Θεοῦ is the true reading, it may, after all, be such; and it must be owned that the testimony of Versions and Fathers is strongly in its favour, and also that it is found in the most ancient of MSS. And certainly it is more likely to be the *original* reading than τοῦ Κυρίου καὶ Θεοῦ.

It is scarcely necessary to observe that if the reading τοῦ Κυρίου καὶ τοῦ Θεοῦ *be* authentic, it affords a strong proof of the Divinity of our Lord Jesus Christ; since (as Bp. Middl. has shown at large) the sense must be, "of Him being (i. e. who is) both Lord and God." And even if τοῦ Κυρίου be the true reading, yet the passage will still bear attestation to the same doctrine; for, (as the learned Reviewer above mentioned observes), the phrase "Church of the Lord" equally denotes the Divinity of the Proprietor and Redeemer of the Church, the Object of its worship, who has given himself for it, that he might sanctify it, and *present it to himself a glorious Church*, Eph. v. 27; where (as Dr. Burton remarks) we should rather have expected τῷ Θεῷ: but St. Paul uses ἑαυτῷ on account of the union of the Father and the Son.

— ἣν περιεποιήσατο.] Περιποιεῖσθαι signifies "to make one's own by purchase." See Dresig. de V. A. p. 378. and Winer's Gr. Gr. § 32. 2. The term was often used of acquiring a right to any one's services, by preserving or sparing his life in war. See Herodot. i. 110. Wets. compares Dionys. Hal. iv. 11. ἣν (scil. γῆν) ὑμεῖς δι' αἵματος ἐκτήσασθε.

29. St. Paul here adverts to the *reason* for this solemn admonition, namely, the *danger* which would shortly overtake the Church from *false teachers*, whose *rapacity* would be as great as their *hypocrisy*. We have here the same metaphor as at Matt. vii. 15, 16., where see Note. In the present instance, however, there is a tacit allusion to the case of the shepherd, or his watch-dogs appointed to guard the flock, gratifying their voracity by even preying on the flock itself. So Dio Cass. p. 389. ἐπὶ γὰρ τὰς ἀγέλας ὑμῶν φύλακες, οὐ κύνας οὐδὲ νομέας, ἀλλὰ λύκους πέμπετε. Themist. Orat. viii. οὐκοῦν οὐδὲ τὸν ποιμαίνειν παρά σου ταχθέντα, εἰ λύκος ἀντὶ ποιμένος ὀφθείη, κερδαίνειν τὴν προσήκουσαν δίκην ἐᾷς. So 2 Cor. xi. 20. the Apostle, with allusion to such teachers, says: ἀνέχεσθε τῶν ἀφρόνων, φρόνιμοι ὄντες· ἀνέχεσθε γάρ, εἴ τις ὑμᾶς καταδουλοῖ, εἴ τις κατεσθίει, &c. In ad-

30 ποιμνίου· [x] καὶ ἐξ ὑμῶν αὐτῶν ἀναστήσονται ἄνδρες λαλοῦντες διε- x Ps. 41. 9. Matt. 26. 21.
31 στραμμένα, τοῦ ἀποσπᾶν τοὺς μαθητὰς ὀπίσω αὐτῶν. [y] Διὸ γρηγορεῖτε, supra 1. 17. 1 John 2. 19. y Supra 19. 10.
μνημονεύοντες ὅτι τριετίαν, νύκτα καὶ ἡμέραν, οὐκ ἐπαυσάμην μετὰ
32 δακρύων νουθετῶν ἕνα ἕκαστον. [z] Καὶ τανῦν παρατίθεμαι ὑμᾶς, z Supra 9. 31. Eph. 1. 18.
ἀδελφοὶ, τῷ Θεῷ καὶ τῷ λόγῳ τῆς χάριτος αὐτοῦ, τῷ δυναμένῳ ἐποι-
κοδομῆσαι, καὶ δοῦναι ὑμῖν κληρονομίαν ἐν τοῖς ἡγιασμένοις πᾶσιν.
33 [a] Ἀργυρίου ἢ χρυσίου ἢ ἱματισμοῦ οὐδενὸς ἐπεθύμησα· [b] αὐτοὶ δὲ a 1 Sam. 12. 3. 1 Cor. 9. 12.
34 γινώσκετε ὅτι ταῖς χρείαις μου καὶ τοῖς οὖσι μετ' ἐμοῦ ὑπηρέτησαν αἱ 2 Cor. 11. 9. & 12. 13. b Sup. 18. 3.
35 χεῖρες αὗται. [c] Πάντα ὑπέδειξα ὑμῖν, ὅτι οὕτω κοπιῶντας δεῖ ἀντι- 1 Cor. 4. 12. 1 Thess. 2. 9.
λαμβάνεσθαι τῶν ἀσθενούντων, μνημονεύειν τε τῶν λόγων τοῦ Κυρίου 2 Thess. 3. 8. c 1 Cor. 9. 12.
Ἰησοῦ, ὅτι αὐτὸς εἶπε· Μακάριόν ἐστι διδόναι μᾶλλον ἢ λαμβάνειν.
36 [d] Καὶ ταῦτα εἰπὼν, θεὶς τὰ γόνατα αὐτοῦ, σὺν πᾶσιν αὐτοῖς προσηύ- d Infra 21. 5.
37 ξατο. Ἱκανὸς δὲ ἐγένετο κλαυθμὸς πάντων· καὶ ἐπιπεσόντες ἐπὶ τὸν
38 τράχηλον τοῦ Παύλου, κατεφίλουν αὐτόν· ὀδυνώμενοι μάλιστα ἐπὶ τῷ
λόγῳ ᾧ εἰρήκει, ὅτι οὐκέτι μέλλουσι τὸ πρόσωπον αὐτοῦ θεωρεῖν.
προέπεμπον δὲ αὐτὸν εἰς τὸ πλοῖον.
1 XXI. ὩΣ δὲ ἐγένετο ἀναχθῆναι ἡμᾶς ἀποσπασθέντας ἀπ' αὐτῶν,
εὐθυδρομήσαντες ἤλθομεν εἰς τὴν Κῶν, τῇ δὲ ἑξῆς εἰς τὴν Ῥόδον,

dition to *rapacity* and, it should seem, *hypocrisy*, the Apostle, in the next verse, subjoins the *sowing of heresies and schisms*, such as those of Phygellus and Hermogenes, and others, who afterwards promulged the Nicolaitan errors, against which some passages of St. John's Gospel seem directed.

30. *διεστραμμένα*] "erroneous." So Arrian opposes *δόγματα ὀρθὰ* and *διεστραμμένα καὶ στρεβλά*. The metaphor is the same as that in our adjective *wrong*, which comes from the Ang. Sax. ƿꞃinȝan to *twist*; and literally signifies [something] wrested from the right (i. e. straight) line or conduct.

31. *τριετίαν*] i. e. about the space of three years; for there is no occasion to suppose that the Apostle here speaks with arithmetical exactness. Though indeed, if to the *two* years he taught in the School of Tyrannus be added the three months he taught in the synagogue, and the time he taught privately with Aquila and Priscilla, we have something not far short of three years.

32. *καὶ τῷ λόγῳ τῆς χάριτος αὐτοῦ.*] *Λόγῳ τῆς χάρ.* *may* (with several eminent Interpreters, ancient and modern), be taken, by a Hebraism, for the *grace itself*, per Hendiadyn. And thus *δυναμένῳ* would be referred to *God*. But it is perhaps better taken (with Pisc., Wolf, Heinr., Kuin., the Syr., Arab., and our common Version) to mean the *Gospel and its doctrines*, which can alone edify men, &c. See 2 Tim. iii. 13. Eph. ii. 20. 1 Cor. iii. 10. The *ἐπ'* in *ἐποικοδομῆσαι* may refer to the *gradual* edification of the Gospel, as buildings are raised, *course by course*, by the architect. The metaphor in *κληρονομία* is meant to suggest the *certainty* of the rewards *laid up* in heaven for the righteous. *Τοῖς ἡγιασμένοις* does not (as most Commentators imagine) here and at xxvi. 18. and Heb. x. 14., denote simply *Christians*, but "those who have *walked worthy* of their high calling in baptism."

33. What is here said was evidently suggested by the conduct of the false teachers. By *ἱματισμὸς* is meant that handsome clothing which among the Hebrews was reckoned part of any one's wealth. See Matt. vi. 19. 2 Kings v. 26., and especially a passage of Thucyd. ii. 97., where, in reckoning up the revenues of the king of Thrace, one item consists of *δῶρα ὑφαντά τε καὶ λεῖα, καὶ ἡ ἄλλη κατασκευή*, stuffs, both embroidered and plain, and other household furniture. These it might have been supposed he had accepted as presents, especially since Ephesus was famous for the manufacture of stuffs. And we may infer from 1 Cor. xi. 21. that the teachers were paid partly in goods.

34. *αἱ χεῖρες αὗται*] "these hands," holding them up. There is a similar beauty in xxvi. 29. *παρεκτὸς τῶν δεσμῶν τούτων*. The Commentators compare several passages of the Classical writers, scarcely any much to the purpose. I have, however, in Recens. Synop., adduced a very apposite one from Philostrat. Vit. Ap. ii. 26. *πολλὰ δέ μοι καὶ ἀπὸ δένδρων φύεται, ὧν γεωργοὶ αἵδε αἱ χεῖρες.* Finally, *τοῖς οὖσι μετ' ἐμοῦ* may be regarded as a popular negligence of style, for *ταῖς τῶν ὄντων μετ' ἐμοῦ*.

35. *πάντα ὑπέδειξα ὑμῖν.*] Sub. *κατὰ*, and take *ὑπέδειξα* for *ὑποδείγματα ἔδωκα*, as in a kindred passage of John xiii. 15.

— *μακάριον — λαμβάνειν.*] This is one of the sayings of our Lord unrecorded in the Gospels, (see John xxi. fin.) such as, no doubt, there were then many circulated among the Christians, and some of which are recorded by the early Fathers; on which see Fabric. Cod. Apoc. N. T. i. 131., and especially the very scarce tract of *Koerner* de Sermonibus Christi *ἀγράφοις*, Lips. 1776. 8vo. With the *sentiment* the Commentators compare many from the Classical writers; and others may be seen in my Note on Thucyd. ii. 97. *νόμον — λαμβάνειν μᾶλλον ἢ διδόναι.* *Μακάριον* signifies "*magis juvat*," is attended with a greater blessing.

37. *ἐπιπεσόντες ἐπὶ τὸν τράχ.*] According to an Oriental custom, still retained in the East.

κἀκεῖθεν εἰς Πάταρα. Καὶ εὑρόντες πλοῖον διαπερῶν εἰς Φοινίκην, 2
ἐπιβάντες ἀνήχθημεν. ἀναφανέντες δὲ τὴν Κύπρον, καὶ καταλιπόντες 3
αὐτὴν εὐώνυμον, ἐπλέομεν εἰς Συρίαν, καὶ κατήχθημεν εἰς Τύρον·
e Supra 20. 28. infra ver. 12. ἐκεῖσε γὰρ ἦν τὸ πλοῖον ἀποφορτιζόμενον τὸν γόμον. [e] Καὶ ἀνευρόν- 4
τες τοὺς μαθητὰς, ἐπεμείναμεν αὐτοῦ ἡμέρας ἑπτά· οἵτινες τῷ Παύ-
f Supra 20. 36. λῳ ἔλεγον διὰ τοῦ Πνεύματος, μὴ ἀναβαίνειν εἰς Ἱερουσαλήμ. [f] Ὅτε 5
δὲ ἐγένετο ἡμᾶς ἐξαρτίσαι τὰς ἡμέρας, ἐξελθόντες ἐπορευόμεθα, προ-
πεμπόντων ἡμᾶς πάντων, σὺν γυναιξὶ καὶ τέκνοις, ἕως ἔξω τῆς πόλεως·
καὶ θέντες τὰ γόνατα ἐπὶ τὸν αἰγιαλὸν προσηυξάμεθα. Καὶ ἀσπασά- 6
μενοι ἀλλήλους, ἐπέβημεν εἰς τὸ πλοῖον, ἐκεῖνοι δὲ ὑπέστρεψαν εἰς τὰ
ἴδια. Ἡμεῖς δὲ τὸν πλοῦν διανύσαντες, ἀπὸ Τύρου κατηντήσαμεν εἰς 7
Πτολεμαΐδα· καὶ ἀσπασάμενοι τοὺς ἀδελφοὺς ἐμείναμεν ἡμέραν μίαν
g Supra 6. 5. & 8. 26, 40. Eph. 4. 11. παρ᾽ αὐτοῖς. [g] Τῇ δὲ ἐπαύριον ἐξελθόντες [οἱ περὶ τὸν Παῦλον] ἤλ- 8
θομεν εἰς Καισάρειαν· καὶ εἰσελθόντες εἰς τὸν οἶκον Φιλίππου τοῦ
h Joel 2. 28. supra 2. 17. εὐαγγελιστοῦ, [τοῦ] ὄντος ἐκ τῶν ἑπτὰ, ἐμείναμεν παρ᾽ αὐτῷ. [h] Τού- 9
i Supra 11. 28. τῳ δὲ ἦσαν θυγατέρες παρθένοι τέσσαρες προφητεύουσαι. Ἐπιμενόν- 10
των δὲ ἡμῶν ἡμέρας πλείους, κατῆλθέ τις ἀπὸ τῆς Ἰουδαίας προφήτης

XXI. 3. ἀναφανέντες τὴν Κ.] So the textus receptus, as well as the Ed. Princ., and almost all the MSS. The Stephanic reading ἀναφάναντες was taken from the Erasmian Editions, in which it was probably only a typographical error. Stephens and Beza conjectured ἀναφήναντες, which would make it correct in *Grammar*, and perhaps in *idiom*, since ἀποκρύπτειν τὴν γῆν is so used. See the examples adduced by me in Recens. Synop. and on Thucyd. v. 65. 7. And so the Latin idiom *aperire* terram, to *make* land, or a coast. Yet very different is the idiom here adopted, of which the Commentators cite examples, (as Theophan. p. 392. ἀναφανέντων δὲ αὐτῶν τὴν γῆν) and regard this as a *nautical idiom* for ἀναφανείσης τῆς Κύπρου. There is, indeed, a sort of *hypallage*, (ἀνεφάνην τὴν Κύπρον being equivalent to ἀνεφάνη μοι ἡ Κ.), and an ellip. of κατά. The sense is, "being brought into view of Cyprus." See the Vulg.

—καταλιπόντες αὐτὴν εὐών.] "leaving it on the left." Of this idiom examples are adduced by Wets. Perhaps there is an ellip. of κατά.

—ἦν ἀποφορτιζόμενον] for ἀπεφορτίζετο, literally "was unloading;" though in reality (by an interchange of past with present, to denote what is *intended* and *soon* to happen) it signifies "was soon to unload." See Win. Gr. Gr. § 396. C. This ship, and that mentioned at xxvi. 2. seem to have been in the carrying trade.

4. τοὺς μαθητὰς] "the disciples," i. e. such persons as were disciples. There is no necessity (as Bp. Middl. supposed) to omit the Article.

—ἔλεγον—μὴ ἀναβαίνειν.] There may seem something strange in these persons, under the impulse of the Spirit, bidding Paul not to go to Jerusalem, when it was doubtless the will of God that he should go. To remove this difficulty, some Commentators take διὰ τοῦ Πνεύμ. to mean "ex proprio spiritu." Such a phraseology, however, would be unprecedented. Still more objectionable are other methods adopted by foreign Commentators. See Recens. Synop. The expression must retain its force, and be rendered, "under the influence of the Holy Spirit." The difficulty, however, which that involves, will be removed by supposing in ἔλεγον—μὴ ἀναβαίνειν an idiom common in all the best writers, e. gr. Thucyd. vi. 29. ἔλεγον—πλεῖν: by which the words, being used *populariter*, may be understood as limited by some clause omitted; and thus the sense will be, "they counselled him [if he valued his safety] not to go to Jerusalem." The Spirit did not order them to bid him not go; but only enabled them to predict, that there would be *danger* in his going. It is plain that Chrysost. so took the words; for he explains them by προφητεύουσι τὰς θλίψεις. And that Paul so understood what they said, is certain; for if he had really regarded himself as *forbidden* by the Holy Spirit to go he would not have gone.

5. ἐξαρτίσαι] "had completed." This use of ἐξαρτίζειν ἡμ. is Hellenistic.

6. ἀσπασάμενοι ἀλλήλ.] "having bade adieu."

—εἰς τὰ ἴδια.] See John xvi. 32, and Note. Τὸ πλοῖον, i. e. the ship by which they had sailed from Patara to Tyre.

7. τὸν πλοῦν διαν.] The only mode of removing the difficulty involved in this expression is (with Markland and Kuin.) to take the Aorist as put for the Present, and render "thus accomplishing our *voyage*," i. e. the *sailing* part of our journey.

8. ἐξελθόντες—εἰς K.] It is not quite certain, whether they went by sea or by land; and Commentators are divided in opinion. Now ἐξελθ. can only mean *departing*, and that is more suitable to going by *land* than by sea. There can be little doubt but that they went by *land*; the ship, it seems, stopping at Ptolemais longer than *they* could conveniently stay. Besides, the land journey to Cæsarea was more convenient than that by sea; which must have been tedious and dangerous on account of doubling the formidable promontory of Mount Carmel. That they left their companions of the ship, is plain from the qualifying clause οἱ περὶ τὸν Παῦλον, which, however, recent Editors have unadvisedly cancelled, on the authority of some Manuscripts and Versions.

9. προφητεύουσαι] "endowed with the faculty of

11 ὀνόματι Ἄγαβος· [k] καὶ ἐλθὼν πρὸς ἡμᾶς, καὶ ἄρας τὴν ζώνην τοῦ [k Supra 20. 23. infra ver. 33.]
Παύλου, δήσας [τε] αὐτοῦ τὰς χεῖρας καὶ τοὺς πόδας, εἶπε· Τάδε
λέγει τὸ Πνεῦμα τὸ ἅγιον· Τὸν ἄνδρα, οὗ ἐστιν ἡ ζώνη αὕτη, οὕτω
δήσουσιν ἐν Ἱερουσαλὴμ οἱ Ἰουδαῖοι, καὶ παραδώσουσιν εἰς χεῖρας ἐθ-
12 νῶν. Ὡς δὲ ἠκούσαμεν ταῦτα, παρεκαλοῦμεν ἡμεῖς τε καὶ οἱ ἐντόπιοι,
13 τοῦ μὴ ἀναβαίνειν αὐτὸν εἰς Ἱερουσαλήμ. [l] Ἀπεκρίθη [δὲ] ὁ Παῦλος· [l Supra 20. 24.]
Τί ποιεῖτε κλαίοντες καὶ συνθρύπτοντές μου τὴν καρδίαν; ἐγὼ γὰρ οὐ
μόνον δεθῆναι, ἀλλὰ καὶ ἀποθανεῖν εἰς Ἱερουσαλὴμ ἑτοίμως ἔχω ὑπὲρ
14 τοῦ ὀνόματος τοῦ Κυρίου Ἰησοῦ. [m] Μὴ πειθομένου δὲ αὐτοῦ, ἡσυχά- [m Matt. 6. 10. Luke 11. 2. & 22. 42.]
σαμεν, εἰπόντες· Τὸ θέλημα τοῦ Κυρίου γενέσθω.
15 Μετὰ δὲ τὰς ἡμέρας ταύτας ‡ ἀποσκευασάμενοι ἀνεβαίνομεν εἰς Ἱε-
16 ρουσαλήμ. Συνῆλθον δὲ καὶ τῶν μαθητῶν ἀπὸ Καισαρείας σὺν
ἡμῖν, ἄγοντες παρ' ᾧ ξενισθῶμεν Μνάσωνί τινι Κυπρίῳ, ἀρχαίῳ
μαθητῇ.

speaking or preaching under divine inspiration." See ii. 18.

11. ἄρας τὴν ζώνην, &c. εἶπε.] Thus following the custom of the Prophets of the O. T., who, in order to impress more strongly on men's minds the things which they had to communicate (whether predictions or declarations), used to employ some corresponding *external* sign symbolical of the thing. See Jerem. xiii. 1; xxvii. 2. seqq.; xxxviii. 10 & 11. 1 Kings xxii. 11. Ez. iv. 1–13. See also vv. 11 & 12. Hos. i. 2. seqq. (Grot. and Wets.) It was not, however, confined to the *Prophets;* for the employment of *symbolical actions* was a custom generally prevalent in the early ages, both among the Jews and the Gentiles. See Note supra xix. 35.

12. οἱ ἐντόπιοι] "the inhabitants [of the place]," i. e. (with the limitation suggested by the circumstances of the case) the Christians of Cæsarea. Ἐντόπιος is properly synonymous with ἐγγενής, "a native of any place;" but it was, by the later writers used for ἐγχώριος, *an inhabitant of a place.* Yet the former signification is found in Soph. Œd. Col. 841.

13. τί ποιεῖτε.] This is regarded by Markl. as a popular form, for τί βούλεσθε; and Kuin. observes, that verbs denoting *action* often indicate, not the *effect* of the action, but only the intent and will. But τί ποιεῖτε is not, as he imagines, pleonastic. As to the idiom, it is found even in our own language. In συνθρύπτοντες the συν has an intensive force, as in συντρίβειν, συγκλᾷν, συντήκειν, &c., and denotes utter destruction of a thing by its being *crushed together*, and thus broken up. Pricæus compares numerous passages of the Classical writers. It is strange he should have forgotten to adduce the "Quid me querelis exanimas tuis?" of Horace. The sense of κλαίοντες καὶ συνθ. is "by weeping, and [thus] quite subduing my courage." Hence the γὰρ in the following sentence will have great propriety, q. d. For *courage* I *have*, being ready, &c. In ἑτοίμως ἔχω we have an example of that use of ἔχω by which it is so joined with an adverb, as to form a phrase equivalent to εἰμὶ and the *adjective* corresponding to that adverb. With this noble sentiment compare a similar one of St. Paul, 2 Cor. xii. 15.

15. ἀποσκευασάμενοι.] There has here been no little debate as to the *reading*. The MSS. fluctuate between ἀποσκ., ἐπισκ., παρασκ., and ἀποταξάμενοι, of which the last two are merely *glosses* on the preceding. Ἐπισκευασ. is found in several good MSS. and early Edd., as also in Chrysost., Theophyl., and Œcumen., is preferred by most Critics, and is edited by Beng., Matth., Tittm., and Vat. But without sufficient reason. They object, indeed, to ἀποσκ., that the word can only signify *to unpack luggage:* whereas the context requires the sense to *collect* one's baggage for a journey; which ἐπισκευάζεσθαι *does* express, being of frequent occurrence in the best writers. This is very true. But how then are we to account for the alteration of the ordinary term ἐπισκ. into what has been thought the anomalous term ἀποσκευασάμενοι? This, I conceive, will go far to prove, that the new reading is a mere *gloss*, and the old reading the true one. As to alleging that ἀποσκ. is not susceptible of the required sense, it were surely hypercritical to set limits to the significations of certain Greek words. And as ἀποσκευὴ both in the Sept. and the Classical writers often denotes *baggage* (see Steph. Thes. and Schleus. Lex. V. T.), why should not ἀποσκευάζεσθαι mean to *pack up one's baggage*, just as from ἀποσκευὴ in the sense *exoneratio alvi*, we have the verb ἀποσκευάσασθαι to signify *exonerare alvum.* In fact, an *example has* been adduced by Palairet from Dionys. Hal. ix. 23. οὐδὲ ἀποσκευάσασθαι δύναμιν ἔσχον οἱ φεύγοντες· ἀλλ' ἀγαπητῶς αὐτὰ τὰ σώματα διέσωσαν, οὐδὲ τὰ ὅπλα πολλοὶ φυλάττοντες. To which I add Polyb. iv. 81, 11. τὰ ἀπὸ τῆς χώρας ἀπεσκευάζοντο, where, though the sense is *removed*, yet that includes the *primary* idea, of *packing up*, previous to removal. Griesb. has here shown unusual discretion, by retaining the common reading; *perhaps because Matthæi rejects it.*

16. ἄγοντες — Κυπρίῳ.] The sense of the passage is plain: but not so the *construction*. Most Commentators from Grot. to Kuin. recognize here a *Hebraism*, the datives Μνάσωνί τινι Κυπρίῳ being put, like the Heb. ל, for accusatives with πρός. Yet, it may be observed, the two Apostles were not going to *call on* Mnason, but to *lodge at his house*. It is, therefore, better (with Beza, Byn., Wolf, Valckn., and Bornem.) to suppose here a frequent idiom, (usually called *Attic*, but in reality extending to the *common dialect)* by which a noun is attracted to the case of the relative, as in Matt. vii. 2. Lu. i. 4. Acts xxii. 24; xxiii. 28. Rom. vi. 17. ὑπηκούσατε ἐκ καρδίας εἰς ὃν παρεδόθητε

Γενομένων δὲ ἡμῶν εἰς Ἱεροσόλυμα, ἀσμένως ἐδέξαντο ἡμᾶς οἱ ἀδελ- 17
n Supra 15. 13. Gal. 1. 19. φοί. [n] τῇ δὲ ἐπιούσῃ εἰσῄει ὁ Παῦλος σὺν ἡμῖν πρὸς Ἰάκωβον, πάν- 18
τές τε παρεγένοντο οἱ πρεσβύτεροι. Καὶ ἀσπασάμενος αὐτοὺς, ἐξηγεῖτο 19
καθ᾿ ἓν ἕκαστον ὧν ἐποίησεν ὁ Θεὸς ἐν τοῖς ἔθνεσι διὰ τῆς διακονίας
o Rom. 10. 2. Gal. 1. 14. αὐτοῦ. [o] Οἱ δὲ ἀκούσαντες ἐδόξαζον τὸν Κύριον· εἶπόν τε αὐτῷ· 20
Θεωρεῖς, ἀδελφὲ, πόσαι μυριάδες εἰσὶν Ἰουδαίων τῶν πεπιστευκότων·
καὶ πάντες ζηλωταὶ τοῦ νόμου ὑπάρχουσι. Κατηχήθησαν δὲ περὶ σοῦ, 21
ὅτι ἀποστασίαν διδάσκεις ἀπὸ Μωϋσέως τοὺς κατὰ τὰ ἔθνη πάντας
Ἰουδαίους, λέγων μὴ περιτέμνειν αὐτοὺς τὰ τέκνα, μηδὲ τοῖς ἔθεσι
περιπατεῖν. Τί οὖν ἐστι; πάντως δεῖ πλῆθος συνελθεῖν· ἀκούσονται 22
p Supra 18. 18. Num. 6. 2, 13, 18. γὰρ ὅτι ἐλήλυθας. [p] Τοῦτο οὖν ποίησον, ὅ σοι λέγομεν. εἰσὶν ἡμῖν 23
ἄνδρες τέσσαρες εὐχὴν ἔχοντες ἐφ᾿ ἑαυτῶν· τούτους παραλαβὼν ἁγνί- 24
σθητι σὺν αὐτοῖς, καὶ δαπάνησον ἐπ᾿ αὐτοῖς, ἵνα ξυρήσωνται τὴν κε-
φαλήν· καὶ ‡ γνῶσι πάντες, ὅτι ὧν κατήχηνται περὶ σοῦ οὐδέν ἐστιν,
q Supra 15. 20, 29. ἀλλὰ στοιχεῖς καὶ αὐτὸς τὸν νόμον φυλάσσων. [q] Περὶ δὲ τῶν πεπιστευ- 25

τύπον διδαχῆς, for τῷ τύπῳ διδαχῆς, εἰς ὃν παρ. Thus in the present passage it is as if there had been written: ἄγοντας (ἡμᾶς, to be supplied from ἡμῶν preceding) παρὰ Μνάσωνά τινα, Κύπριον, ἀρχαῖον μαθ. παρ᾿ ᾧ ξενισθῶμεν. Examples of the phrase ἄγειν παρὰ are adduced by Bornem., who says it is pretty frequent in the Greek writers. Of the name *Mnason* several examples are adduced by Wets. It seems formed from the Future μνήσω of μνάω, to make any one remember; just as is μνήμων from μέμνημαι. It is *Doric* for *Mneson*. Of the same form are several words in Greek, as Σείσων, Καύσων, Δώσων, Φώσων, &c.

18. Ἰάκωβον.] Peter and John were, it seems, both absent; and James (son of Alphæus; see xv. 13.) is supposed to have presided, both in his Apostolical character and as Bishop of Jerusalem, at the meeting now held to consider of the business which regarded Paul.

21. κατηχήθησαν π. σ.] "they have been informed concerning thee." For Fab. on Sext. Emp. 285. 339. has shown κατηχεῖσθαι to mean "*auditione et famâ percipere.*" See Note on xviii. 25.

22. τί οὖν ἐστι;] This (as in 1 Cor. xiv. 15. 26.) seems to be a *popular* formula, similar to our "*what then!*" i. e. what then [is to be done]; Sub. πρακτέον. Markl. compares "quid ergo est?" and *quid igitur est?* in Cicero and Livy. So that it may be a *Latinism*; for I am not aware that it ever occurs in the Greek Classical writers. Though the formula τί οὖν (which sometimes occurs in the Philosophers, and of which Kypke cites examples from Arrian on Epict.), is somewhat *similar*.

— πάντως δεῖ πλῆθος συνελθ.] Pisc., Beza, and Grot. understand this of a *regular convocation* of the *people*, as contradistinguished from the *Presbyters*. But à Lapide and Pricæus, with all the best *recent* Commentators, seem right in determining the sense to be, "It is unavoidable, but that a multitude should flock together;" which is quite agreeable to what follows. Δεῖ like ἀνάγκη, often denotes only what *must and will* happen.

23. τοῦτο οὖν ποίησον.] The best Commentators are agreed that this is to be regarded as the language of *advice*, not of authoritative *command*. For a justification of the conduct of the Apostle, in thus conciliating the Jews (to the compromise, as some have thought, of the leading doctrines of the Gospel) see Witsius de Vitâ Pauli x., Dr. Hales iii. 536. sq., and Townsend. Suffice it to say, that though the Apostle taught that *Jewish* as well as Gentile Christians are freed from the observance of the Mosaic Law, yet he never forbade the *Jewish* converts to observe it, or any part of it, on the score of *expediency*. Since he occasionally did so, that he might "gain the more" to Christ. See 1 Cor. ix. 20. Acts xvi. 3. Whether εὐχὴν is to be understood of *votum civile*, undertaken on account of recovery from sickness, or deliverance from calamity, or *a vow of Naza-riteship*, is not agreed. The last is the more probable opinion, since the term ἁγνίζεσθαι which follows is appropriate thereto. See Numb. vi.

24. ἁγνίσθητι, &c.] i. e. "undertake the same abstinence and purity enjoined by the vow," and pay their expenses for them; namely, those of the sacrifice, on going to the temple, for the purpose of being released from the vow by shaving the head. From what has been adduced by Wets., Wits., and Lardner, it appears that this participation in the ἁγνεία did not necessarily make the person *himself* a *Nazarite*; and also, that to so participate with, and pay the expenses of Nazarites, was not unusual among the Jews, and was regarded as a mark of singular piety.

— ἵνα ξυρήσωνται.] Meaning, that they may end their vow by shaving their heads: which they could not do till the termination of their vow: and that could only be by offering sacrifice: but they not being able to provide the offering, could not shave their heads. Thus the phrases to *cause any Nazarite to be shorn*, and to *pay his expenses*, came to be convertible. So Maimonides says: "Mihi incumbit ut *radatur Naziræus per me.*"

— γνῶσι.] Many MSS. read γνώσονται, which is supported by some Versions, and edited by Griesb. and Tittm. But it seems to have arisen *ex emendatione*. Στοιχεῖς φυλάσσων τὸν νόμον signifies, "that thou livest in the habitual observance of the law;" Στοιχεῖν, like περιπατεῖν and the Heb. הלך, being used of habitual action.

25. περὶ δὲ τῶν πεπ., &c.] The δὲ is *adversative*, and the sense is, "But as to the *Gentiles*,

κότων ἐθνῶν ἡμεῖς ἐπεστείλαμεν, κρίναντες μηδὲν τοιοῦτον τηρεῖν αὐτοὺς, εἰ μὴ φυλάσσεσθαι αὐτοὺς τό τε εἰδωλόθυτον καὶ τὸ αἷμα, καὶ
26 πνικτὸν καὶ πορνείαν. [r] Τότε ὁ Παῦλος παραλαβὼν τοὺς ἄνδρας, τῇ [r Num. 6. 13. Infra 24. 18.]
ἐχομένῃ ἡμέρᾳ σὺν αὐτοῖς ἁγνισθεὶς εἰσῄει εἰς τὸ ἱερὸν, διαγγέλλων
τὴν ἐκπλήρωσιν τῶν ἡμερῶν τοῦ ἁγνισμοῦ, ἕως οὗ προσηνέχθη ὑπὲρ
27 ἑνὸς ἑκάστου αὐτῶν ἡ προσφορά. Ὡς δὲ ἔμελλον αἱ ἑπτὰ ἡμέραι συντελεῖσθαι, οἱ ἀπὸ τῆς Ἀσίας Ἰουδαῖοι θεασάμενοι αὐτὸν ἐν τῷ ἱερῷ,
συνέχεον πάντα τὸν ὄχλον, καὶ ἐπέβαλον τὰς χεῖρας ἐπ᾽ αὐτὸν, κράζον-
28 τες· Ἄνδρες Ἰσραηλῖται, βοηθεῖτε! οὗτός ἐστιν ὁ ἄνθρωπος ὁ κατὰ
τοῦ λαοῦ καὶ τοῦ νόμου καὶ τοῦ τόπου τούτου πάντας πανταχοῦ δι-
δάσκων· ἔτι τε καὶ Ἕλληνας εἰσήγαγεν εἰς τὸ ἱερὸν, καὶ κεκοίνωκε
29 τὸν ἅγιον τόπον τοῦτον. [s] ἦσαν γὰρ [προ]εωρακότες Τρόφιμον τὸν [s Supra 20. 4. 2 Tim. 4. 20.]
Ἐφέσιον ἐν τῇ πόλει σὺν αὐτῷ, ὃν ἐνόμιζον ὅτι εἰς τὸ ἱερὸν εἰσήγαγεν
30 ὁ Παῦλος. [t] Ἐκινήθη τε ἡ πόλις ὅλη, καὶ ἐγένετο συνδρομὴ τοῦ λαοῦ· [t Infra 26. 21.]
καὶ ἐπιλαβόμενοι τοῦ Παύλου, εἷλκον αὐτὸν ἔξω τοῦ ἱεροῦ· καὶ εὐ-
31 θέως ἐκλείσθησαν αἱ θύραι. Ζητούντων δὲ αὐτὸν ἀποκτεῖναι, ἀνέβη
32 φάσις τῷ χιλιάρχῳ τῆς σπείρης, ὅτι ὅλη συγκέχυται Ἱερουσαλήμ· ὃς
ἐξαυτῆς παραλαβὼν στρατιώτας καὶ ἑκατοντάρχους, κατέδραμεν ἐπ᾽ αὐτούς. Οἱ δὲ ἰδόντες τὸν χιλίαρχον καὶ τοὺς στρατιώτας, ἐπαύσαντο
33 τύπτοντες τὸν Παῦλον. [u] Τότε ἐγγίσας ὁ χιλίαρχος ἐπελάβετο αὐτοῦ, [u Supra ver. 11.]
καὶ ἐκέλευσε δεθῆναι ἁλύσεσι δυσί· καὶ ἐπυνθάνετο τίς ἂν εἴη, καὶ τί
34 ἐστι πεποιηκώς. Ἄλλοι δὲ ἄλλο τι ἐβόων ἐν τῷ ὄχλῳ. μὴ δυνάμενος δὲ
γνῶναι τὸ ἀσφαλὲς διὰ τὸν θόρυβον, ἐκέλευσεν ἄγεσθαι αὐτὸν εἰς τὴν
35 παρεμβολήν. Ὅτε δὲ ἐγένετο ἐπὶ τοὺς ἀναβαθμοὺς, συνέβη βαστάζε-

[the case is different, and] we have ordered [thus]; determining that," &c.

26. *ἁγνισθείς.*] See Note supra v. 24.

— *διαγγέλλων τὴν ἐκπλήρ.*, &c.] "giving notice [to the Priests] of the [period of the] completion of the days of purification;" which the persons themselves, it seems, had not been able to do, because they could not provide the offering. The period, as it appears from what follows, was *that day week*. Every one, it seems, was allowed to fix the period of his votive purification, either when he *commenced* it, or at any time during its course; so that the Priests had proper notice, in order to make the necessary arrangements as to the victims, &c. Ἕως οὗ, "at which;" as in Luke xv. 8. xxii. 16. 18. John ix. 18. Προσφορὰ is the *θυσία προσφερομένη*. See Eph. v. 2.

27. *αἱ ἑπτὰ ἡμέραι.*] As the number of days had not been before mentioned, this must be put for *αἱ ἡμέραι, ἑπτὰ οὖσαι*. Συνέχεον is for *συνεκίνουν*. So Demosth. cited by Schleus. Lex. *συγχεῖ ὅλην τὴν πολιτείαν*.

28. *βοηθεῖτε.*] The sense is, "Come to our aid [in apprehending this person]." A sense of the word very frequently occurring in Thucyd. and the best writers. Ἕλληνας is considered by Kuin. as an exaggeration for Ἕλληνα. But it is better to suppose an idiom, found in all languages, by which the plural is used instead of the singular, taken generically; a *single* action being spoken of as if it were *habitual*.

29. *προεωρακότες.*] The *προ* is not found in very many MSS., several Versions, and Fathers, and all the early Edd. except the Erasmian, and is cancelled by Beng. and Matth.

30. *συνδρομή.*] The word is often used of *riotous assemblage*. See Wets.

— *εἷλκον αὐτὸν ἔξω τοῦ ἱερ.*] i. e. in order (as Chrys. suggests) to avoid polluting the Temple with murder: and also, it should seem, to be more unrestrained, than the Priests and Levites could decently permit them to be; who appear to have themselves closed the doors, in order to preserve the Temple from pollution, and be thought to have no hand in whatever might ensue.

31. *φάσις* for *φήμη* is confined to the later writers.

33. *δεθ. ἁλ. δυσί.*] See Note supra xii. 6. Perhaps in the present case the feet also were bound with a chain. At least so we may suppose from supra v. 11.

34. *τὸ ἀσφαλές*] "what was assuredly the truth." So xxii. 30. xxv. 26. Παρεμβολὴ properly signifies a place where tents *παρεμβάλλονται*. But it here denotes the barracks in the castle of Antonia. And this is confirmed by the *ἀναβαθμοὺς* just after; for the castle of Antonia was situated on an eminence.

35. *τοὺς ἀναβ.*] This term is supposed to denote the flight of stairs leading from the portico of the Temple to the castle of Antonia, which nearly joined the Temple, being built (as we find from Joseph. B. v. 5, 3.) at an angle of it. In illustration of the present passage, I would adduce an apposite one of Joseph Bell. v. 5, 8. *ἐνδοτέρω*

x Luke 23. 18. John 19. 15. infra 22. 22.
σθαι αὐτὸν ὑπὸ τῶν στρατιωτῶν διὰ τὴν βίαν τοῦ ὄχλου. [x] ἠκολούθει 36
γὰρ τὸ πλῆθος τοῦ λαοῦ, ‡ κράζον· Αἶρε αὐτόν!

Μέλλων τε εἰσάγεσθαι εἰς τὴν παρεμβολὴν ὁ Παῦλος λέγει τῷ χιλι- 37
άρχῳ· Εἰ ἔξεστί μοι εἰπεῖν τι πρός σε; Ὁ δὲ ἔφη· Ἑλληνιστὶ γινώσκεις; οὐκ ἄρα σὺ εἶ ὁ Αἰγύπτιος ὁ πρὸ τούτων τῶν ἡμερῶν ἀνα- 38
στατώσας, καὶ ἐξαγαγὼν εἰς τὴν ἔρημον τοὺς τετρακισχιλίους ἄνδρας
y Supra 9. 11, 30. & 22. 3.
τῶν σικαρίων; [y] Εἶπε δὲ ὁ Παῦλος· Ἐγὼ ἄνθρωπος μέν εἰμι Ἰου- 39
δαῖος Ταρσεὺς τῆς Κιλικίας, οὐκ ἀσήμου πόλεως πολίτης· δέομαι δέ
σου, ἐπίτρεψόν μοι λαλῆσαι πρὸς τὸν λαόν.

z Supra 12. 17. & 13. 16. & 19. 33.
[z] Ἐπιτρέψαντος δὲ αὐτοῦ, ὁ Παῦλος ἑστὼς ἐπὶ τῶν ἀναβαθμῶν κατέ- 40
σεισε τῇ χειρὶ τῷ λαῷ· πολλῆς δὲ σιγῆς γενομένης, προσεφώνησε τῇ
Ἑβραΐδι διαλέκτῳ, λέγων· XXII. Ἄνδρες ἀδελφοὶ, καὶ πατέρες, ἀκού- 1
σατέ μου τῆς πρὸς ὑμᾶς νῦν ἀπολογίας. Ἀκούσαντες δὲ ὅτι τῇ Ἑβραΐδι 2
διαλέκτῳ προσεφώνει αὐτοῖς, μᾶλλον παρέσχον ἡσυχίαν. Καί φησιν·

δὲ τούτου (scil. ἦν) τὸ πᾶν διάστημα (I read from Cod. Bigot., *ἀνάστημα, ædificium, structura)*, τὸ δὲ ἔνδον βασιλείου εἶχε χώραν καὶ διάθεσιν. μεμέριστο γὰρ εἰς πᾶσαν οἴκων ἰδέαν τε καὶ χρῆσιν, περίστοά τε καὶ βαλανεῖα καὶ στρατοπέδων αὐλὰς πλατείας, ὡς τῷ μὲν πάντα ἔχειν τὰ χρειώδη, πόλεις εἶναι δοκεῖν, τῇ πολυτελείᾳ δὲ βασίλειον. where by the περίστοα are meant courts surrounded by columns. And by the στρατοπέδων αὐλαὶ πλατεῖαι, the *soldiers' barracks*, laid out, it should seem, in *quadrangles*. As to the words πόλεις εἶναι δοκεῖν, they are, perhaps, corrupt. If correct, they can only refer to *barracks*; and then βασίλειον must be wrong, and βασίλεια would be required. But *such* a description would not be suitable to the *barracks*, and is, no doubt, meant of the *whole of the citadel*, which formed a sort of *military city*. Now this sense (which is undoubtedly the true one) may be obtained by simply reading πόλις instead of πόλεις, and for δοκεῖν, δοκεῖ, or, from the Cod. Bigot., δοκοίη, which evidently requires πόλις.

— βαστάζεσθαι] "carried on their shoulders;" for security against the violence of the people. Pric. and Wets., however, think the term does not mean that he was literally *carried*, but was *borne* off his legs by the press. And they produce a passage of Dio Chrys. where one is described βαδίζοντα — ὑπὸ τοῦ ὄχλου. But there is here nothing said about a great *press*.

36. αἶρε αὐτόν] "away with him," viz. from the earth. So xxii. 22. αἶρε ἀπὸ τῆς γῆς.

37. εἰ ἔξεστι, &c.] On this idiom, which arises from a blending of the *oratio directa* with the *indirecta*, I have before treated.

— Ἑλληνιστὶ γινώσκεις.] Sub. λαλεῖν, supplied in Nehem. xiii. 24. This is not a Latinism, since we find in Xen. Cyr. vii. 5, 11. τοὺς Συριστὶ ἐπισταμένους. The *interrogation* here, as often, imports surprise.

38. Αἰγύπτιος, &c.] The story is related in Joseph. Ant. xx. 8, 6, and Bell. ii. 13, 5; between which, however, and what is here said, a considerable discrepancy exists; for Josephus, in the latter passage, reckons them at 30,000. Many methods have been adopted to remove the discrepancy. Of which most are mere devices for the nonce, and proceed wholly upon supposition. The only effectual mode is that supplied by the aid of *criticism*, applied to the texts of the two writers, in one of whom there must be some error, doubtless proceeding from the *scribes*. Now there is no reason to suppose any error in *St. Luke's* text, since the MSS. agree, and the number is a very probable one. The error, therefore, must rest with *Josephus*, as his Editor, Aldrich, has seen: though he has not succeeded in showing *where* it lies. That there is a corruption in Josephus is certain; the number 30,000 being incredibly large. And while in his *Antiq.* he says the number was 30,000, and of these πλεῖστοι, *very many*, were slain; yet in his *Wars*, though he does not mention the *total* number, he says that 400 were slain, and 200 taken prisoners. Now 400 cannot be considered *very many* out of 30,000. To remove this discrepancy, Aldrich would in the Antiq. read δισχιλίους instead of διακοσίους. A conjecture, however, little probable: and, indeed, it is not the number of the *prisoners* that we are concerned with, but that of the *slain*. I am persuaded that the error rests on τρισμυρίους. Yet I would not, with Aldrich, read in the Antiq. τετρακισχιλίους, *on purpose to make the* accounts of Josephus and St. Luke *exactly agree*. But for τρισμυρίους I would read τρισχιλίους, which will make Josephus consistent with himself; for certainly 600 may be considered *many* out of 3000. And the difference between the accounts in Josephus and that of the Chiliarch (not St. Luke) is of no consequence. It is scarcely necessary to observe how frequently χίλιοι and μύριοι in composition with δὶς, &c. are confounded, from the similarity of the contractions and single words to denote the numbers in question. Had indeed the real number been 30,000, Josephus would not have omitted in his Antiq. to advert to the *great multitude* of persons.

— σικαρίων.] The term seems to denote *banditti*, literally *cut-throats*; from *sica*, the short cutlass (of Oriental origin, in fact the *Kriese* of India and China), which was carried under the arm like the Italian *stiletto*. From being *private assassins*, the Sicarii at length became public murderers and rebels. The air of the question seems to imply, that the officer had been told, that Paul *was* that Egyptian.

39. οὐκ ἀσήμου πόλ.] An elegant litotes, to denote "a celebrated city." So Steph. Byz. calls it πόλις ἐπισημοτάτη.

3 [a] Ἐγὼ μέν εἰμι ἀνὴρ Ἰουδαῖος, γεγεννημένος ἐν Ταρσῷ τῆς Κιλικίας, a Supra 9. 11. & 21. 39.
ἀνατεθραμμένος δὲ ἐν τῇ πόλει ταύτῃ παρὰ τοὺς πόδας Γαμαλιὴλ, 2 Cor. 11. 22. supra 5. 34.
πεπαιδευμένος κατὰ ἀκρίβειαν τοῦ πατρῴου νόμου, ζηλωτὴς ὑπάρχων Gal. 1. 14. Rom. 10. 2.
4 τοῦ Θεοῦ, καθὼς πάντες ὑμεῖς ἐστε σήμερον· [b] ὃς ταύτην τὴν ὁδὸν b Supra 8. 3. & 9. 1.
ἐδίωξα ἄχρι θανάτου, δεσμεύων καὶ παραδιδοὺς εἰς φυλακὰς ἄνδρας τε infra 26. 9. 1 Cor. 15. 9.
5 καὶ γυναῖκας· [c] ὡς καὶ ὁ ἀρχιερεὺς μαρτυρεῖ μοι, καὶ πᾶν τὸ πρεσ- Gal. 1. 13. 1 Tim. 1. 13. c Supra 9. 2.
βυτέριον· παρ' ὧν καὶ ἐπιστολὰς δεξάμενος πρὸς τοὺς ἀδελφοὺς, εἰς infra 26. 12.
Δαμασκὸν ἐπορευόμην, ἄξων καὶ τοὺς ἐκεῖσε ὄντας δεδεμένους εἰς Ἱερου-
6 σαλὴμ, ἵνα τιμωρηθῶσιν. [d] Ἐγένετο δέ μοι πορευομένῳ καὶ ἐγγίζοντι d Supra 9. 3. infra 26. 12.
τῇ Δαμασκῷ, περὶ μεσημβρίαν, ἐξαίφνης ἐκ τοῦ οὐρανοῦ περιαστράψαι 1 Cor. 15. 8. 2 Cor. 12. 2.
7 φῶς ἱκανὸν περὶ ἐμέ. [e] Ἔπεσόν τε εἰς τὸ ἔδαφος, καὶ ἤκουσα φωνῆς e Infra 26. 14, 15.
8 λεγούσης μοι· Σαοὺλ Σαοὺλ, τί με διώκεις; Ἐγὼ δὲ ἀπεκρίθην·
Τίς εἶ, κύριε; εἶπέ τε πρός με· Ἐγώ εἰμι Ἰησοῦς ὁ Ναζωραῖος, ὃν
9 σὺ διώκεις. [f] Οἱ δὲ σὺν ἐμοὶ ὄντες τὸ μὲν φῶς ἐθεάσαντο, καὶ ἔμφο- f Supra 9. 7. Dan. 10. 7.
10 βοι ἐγένοντο· τὴν δὲ φωνὴν οὐκ ἤκουσαν τοῦ λαλοῦντός μοι. Εἶπον
δέ· Τί ποιήσω, Κύριε; ὁ δὲ Κύριος εἶπε πρός με· Ἀναστὰς πορεύου εἰς Δαμασκόν· κἀκεῖ σοι λαληθήσεται περὶ πάντων ὧν τέτακταί
11 σοι ποιῆσαι. Ὡς δὲ οὐκ ἐνέβλεπον, ἀπὸ τῆς δόξης τοῦ φωτὸς ἐκείνου,
12 χειραγωγούμενος ὑπὸ τῶν συνόντων μοι ἦλθον εἰς Δαμασκόν. [g] Ἀνα- g Supra 9. 17.
νίας δέ τις, ἀνὴρ εὐσεβὴς κατὰ τὸν νόμον, μαρτυρούμενος ὑπὸ πάντων
13 τῶν κατοικούντων Ἰουδαίων, ἐλθὼν πρός με καὶ ἐπιστὰς εἶπέ μοι·
Σαοὺλ ἀδελφὲ, ἀνάβλεψον· κἀγὼ αὐτῇ τῇ ὥρᾳ ἀνέβλεψα εἰς αὐτόν.
14 [h] Ὁ δὲ εἶπεν· Ὁ Θεὸς τῶν πατέρων ἡμῶν προεχειρίσατό σε γνῶναι τὸ h Supra 3. 14. & 7. 52.
θέλημα αὐτοῦ, καὶ ἰδεῖν τὸν δίκαιον, καὶ ἀκοῦσαι φωνὴν ἐκ τοῦ στό- infra 26. 16. 1 John 2. 1.
15 ματος αὐτοῦ· ὅτι ἔσῃ μάρτυς αὐτῷ πρὸς πάντας ἀνθρώπους, ὧν ἑώ-
16 ρακας καὶ ἤκουσας. [i] Καὶ νῦν τί μέλλεις; ἀναστὰς βάπτισαι καὶ i Matt. 3. 11. Mark 1. 4.
ἀπόλουσαι τὰς ἁμαρτίας σου, ἐπικαλεσάμενος τὸ ὄνομα τοῦ Κυρίου. Luke 3. 3.

XXII. 3. ἀνατεθραμμένος — πεπαιδ.] The Commentators are not agreed on the construction; some joining παρὰ τοὺς πόδας Γ. with the *preceding*, others with the *following* words. The former mode is generally adopted by the ancient and early modern Commentators, the latter by the more recent Interpreters. The former, however, seems preferable. As to the *regularity*, which the other construction would impart to the passage, that is not characteristic of the Scriptural style, nor indeed very much of the style of the ancients in general. And to the *tautology* of which they complain, we may oppose a harsh *transposition* in their own mode of construction.

The expression παρὰ τοὺς πόδας is an idiom importing no more than our being educated *under* such and such a master. Πεπαιδευμένος — νόμου, "trained [by him] to the most exact knowledge of the religion and laws of my country." Rosenm. thinks that ἀκρίβειαν has reference to the ceremonies and institutions of their ancestors. But Wets., Morus, Schleus., and Kuin. ascribe to it the signification *severity*, as in Acts xxvi. 5. and Sapient. xii. 21. And so Isocr. cited by Wets. νόμος μετὰ ἀκριβείας κείμενος. It is difficult to decide the preference, and there may be an *hypallage*. By νόμος (Kuin. observes) must be understood not merely the *patria lex*, but also the πατρικαὶ παραδόσεις mentioned in Gal. i. 14. Τοῦ Θεοῦ signifies "of God's [law]," i. e. what he *then* esteemed such. The Apostle speaks somewhat obscurely; intending by this use to delicately refute the charge of blaspheming the Law, by so speaking of it as to tacitly *admit its divine origin*.

4. ὅς.] The relative must be resolved, as often, into the demonstrative with a copula. Comp. Ezek. iii. 22.

13. ἀνάβλεψον.] Ἀναβλέπειν properly signifies to *look up*, and sometimes only to *look*; namely, when it is followed by εἴς τινα, *at* any person or thing. In the Classical writers τινι is used for εἴς τινα or τι. See Matth. Gr. Gr. p. 553, in which, among other passages, is cited Eurip. Ion. 1486. Ἄλλον δ' ἀναβλέπει λαμπάσι. Sometimes the ἀνα signifies *re*, and thus (βλέπειν signifying to *see*) ἀναβλέπειν has the sense to *recover sight*, or sometimes (as in John ix.) to receive, obtain the faculty of sight.

14. τὸν δίκαιον] "the Just one." See Note on Luke xxiii. 44–47.

16. ἀναστὰς βάπτισαι.] So supra ii. 38. βαπτισθήτω — εἰς ἄφεσιν ἁμαρτιῶν, reference being made, in each passage, to the method appointed by Christ for remitting the sins of those who *rightly*

k Supra 9. 26. [k] Ἐγένετο δέ μοι ὑποστρέψαντι εἰς Ἱερουσαλὴμ, καὶ προσευχομένου μου 17
ἐν τῷ ἱερῷ, γενέσθαι με ἐν ἐκστάσει, καὶ ἰδεῖν αὐτὸν λέγοντά μοι· 18
Σπεῦσον καὶ ἔξελθε ἐν τάχει ἐξ Ἱερουσαλήμ· διότι οὐ παραδέξονταί
l Supra ver. 4. σου τὴν μαρτυρίαν περὶ ἐμοῦ. [l] Κἀγὼ εἶπον· Κύριε, αὐτοὶ ἐπίσταν- 19
ται, ὅτι ἐγὼ ἤμην φυλακίζων καὶ δέρων κατὰ τὰς συναγωγὰς τοὺς
m Supra 7. 58. & 8. 1. πιστεύοντας ἐπὶ σέ· [m] καὶ ὅτε ἐξεχεῖτο τὸ αἷμα Στεφάνου τοῦ μάρτυ- 20
ρός σου, καὶ αὐτὸς ἤμην ἐφεστὼς καὶ συνευδοκῶν τῇ ἀναιρέσει αὐτοῦ,
n Supra 9. 15. & 13. 2. Gal. 1. 16. & 2. 8. Eph. 3. 8. 1 Tim. 2. 7. 2 Tim. 1. 11. καὶ φυλάσσων τὰ ἱμάτια τῶν ἀναιρούντων αὐτόν. [n] Καὶ εἶπε πρός με· 21
Πορεύου, ὅτι ἐγὼ εἰς ἔθνη μακρὰν ἐξαποστελῶ σε.
o Supra 21. 36. [o] Ἤκουον δὲ αὐτοῦ ἄχρι τούτου τοῦ λόγου, καὶ ἐπῆραν τὴν φωνὴν 22
αὐτῶν, λέγοντες· Αἶρε ἀπὸ τῆς γῆς τὸν τοιοῦτον· οὐ γὰρ * καθῆκεν
αὐτὸν ζῆν. Κραυγαζόντων δὲ αὐτῶν, καὶ ῥιπτούντων τὰ ἱμάτια, καὶ 23

receive this sacrament; for (as Doddr. observes) "God did not ordinarily give any particular person any public and visible token of pardon till he had submitted to *baptism*, which being a visible token of favourable regard, and a seal of pardon, might be said to wash away sins. See Calvin's Instit. iv. 15. 14."

17. *καὶ προσευχομένου μου.*] A change of construction, for *προσευχομένῳ μοι*. On *ἐν ἐκστάσει* (see Note at x. 10.), we must be content to see through a glass darkly. Mr. Hinds refers this not to the *first* visit to Jerusalem, but to that which immediately preceded his formal appointment by the Church at Antioch; which he thinks more agreeable to the chain of argument in the Epistle to the Galatians.

19, 20. Meaning to say, "Lord, as these (the Jews) well know how bitterly I persecuted those who believed in Thee, they must be convinced it is only on irresistible conviction, that I am become a preacher of the faith I once persecuted; and, accordingly, I may hope that they will hearken to my preaching." See Doddr. and Pyle.

19. *φυλακίζων*] "committing to prison," from *φυλακὴ*, a jail. The word is rare, but occurs in Sapient. xviii. 4.

20. On *συνευδοκῶν* see Note at viii. 1. And on *φυλ. τὰ ἱμάτια*, see Note on vii. 58. The persons employed in the office of stoning used to throw off their clothes like the *Athletæ*. So Macho ap. Athen. 348. F. where it is said that in the Gymnasia there were persons appointed *τὰ ἱμάτια τῶν εἰσιόντων λαμβάνοντας τηρεῖν*.

21. *πορεύου.*] The Lord overrules the plea by simply *repeating the order*: the only instance I believe in Scripture.

22. *καθῆκεν.*] This, for the common reading *καθῆκον*, is found in very many MSS., early Editions, and Fathers. And it has been received by almost every Editor from Wets. to Vater; to whose decision I have deferred, though it is by no means clear to me whether *καθῆκον* be not the true reading; for though *external* evidence be in favour of the other, yet, in so minute a matter as the difference between *ο* and *ε*, MSS., have little or no authority. *Internal* evidence seems decidedly in favour of *καθῆκον*; and that, as Rinck suggests, not only because it is the more recondite and difficult reading, but since the other readings *καθῆκεν* and *καθῆκαν* may the more readily be accounted for as *emendations* of this. And though a *present* sense be here required, yet *καθῆκον* is susceptible of this, by the ellipsis of *ἐστὶ* (as in a passage of Philo de Mundo, cited in Steph. Thes. 3147. D.), which is *supplied* infra xix. 36. *δέον ἐστὶ*, and 1 Pet. i. 6.

23. *ῥιπτούντων τὰ ἱμάτια.*] The Commentators are by no means agreed on the sense of this phrase. That it cannot mean, as some explain, "rending their garments," nor "shaking their garments," as if in rage, is plain. Many (as Pric., Wets., Rosenm., Schl., Heinr., Kuin., and Wahl) take it to mean, "*tossing up* their garments;" and suppose that this was done by those who were too distant to *otherwise* participate in the tumult. They also observe that this *tossing up* of garments, like *waving* of garments, was a mark of *approbation*. I see not, however, how *ῥίπτω* will bear the sense toss *up*, nor how it could be thought to import any thing but *disapprobation* and anger. After all, the true interpretation seems to be that of Grot., Tirinus, Parkh., and Bretschn., "tossing off, and casting down their garments," as a preparation for violence; (just as our pugilists *doff* their clothes to box) a *symbolical action* quite in unison with the *violent expressions* of such of their companions as stood near; the whole forming a lively picture of rabid fury.

There is, in fact, but a *union* of two senses, each separately occurring in both the Scriptural and Classical writers, viz. to *cast down*, and to *cast off*; one implied in the other. The above interpretation is indeed placed beyond doubt by a very similar passage of Plato de Rep. p. 665. *Ἡγοῦ ἐπὶ σὲ πάνυ πολλοὺς οἷον ῥίψαντας τὰ ἱμάτια. γυμνοὺς λαβόντας ὅ τι ἑκάστῳ παρέτυχεν ὅπλον, θεῖν διατεταγμένους.* For *ῥιπτούντων* here several ancient MSS., with Theophylact and Œcumen., and one of the early Editions, have *ῥιπτόντων*. I have, however, retained the former,—not only because *external* evidence is decidedly in its favour, but *internal* also; *ῥιπτούντων*, being a *stronger* expression, and therefore more suitable; if, at least, Hermann on Soph. Ag. 235. is right in saying that *ῥιπτεῖν* is a *frequentative* form of the simple verb *ῥίπτειν*.

In *κονιορτὸν βαλλόντων εἰς τὸν ἀέρα* we have *another symbolical action*, quite in unison with the preceding; for Grot., Wets., and Kuin., rightly take it of *kicking up*, or otherwise throwing up dust into the air; which, as appears from the Classical citations of Wets., and the accounts of modern travellers, was then, and still is, in the East, a frequent mode of raising a tumult: in our vulgar idiom "kicking up a dust."

24 κονιορτὸν βαλλόντων εἰς τὸν ἀέρα, ἐκέλευσεν αὐτὸν ὁ χιλίαρχος ἄγεσθαι
εἰς τὴν παρεμβολὴν, εἰπὼν μάστιξιν ἀνετάζεσθαι αὐτὸν, ἵνα ἐπιγνῷ δι᾽
25 ἣν αἰτίαν οὕτως ἐπεφώνουν αὐτῷ. p Ὡς δὲ ‡ προέτεινεν αὐτὸν τοῖς p Supra 16. 37.
ἱμᾶσιν εἶπε πρὸς τὸν ἑστῶτα ἑκατόνταρχον ὁ Παῦλος· Εἰ ἄνθρωπον
26 Ῥωμαῖον καὶ ἀκατάκριτον ἔξεστιν ὑμῖν μαστίζειν; Ἀκούσας δὲ ὁ ἑκατόνταρχος, προσελθὼν ἀπήγγειλε τῷ χιλιάρχῳ, λέγων· Ὅρα τί μέλλεις
27 ποιεῖν· ὁ γὰρ ἄνθρωπος οὗτος Ῥωμαῖός ἐστι. Προσελθὼν δὲ ὁ χιλίαρχος εἶπεν αὐτῷ· Λέγε μοι, εἰ σὺ Ῥωμαῖος εἶ; ὁ δὲ ἔφη· Ναί.
28 Ἀπεκρίθη τε ὁ χιλίαρχος· Ἐγὼ πολλοῦ κεφαλαίου τὴν πολιτείαν ταύ-
29 την ἐκτησάμην. ὁ δὲ Παῦλος ἔφη· Ἐγὼ δὲ καὶ γεγέννημαι. Εὐθέως
οὖν ἀπέστησαν ἀπ᾽ αὐτοῦ οἱ μέλλοντες αὐτὸν ἀνετάζειν. καὶ ὁ χιλίαρχος δὲ ἐφοβήθη, ἐπιγνοὺς ὅτι Ῥωμαῖός ἐστι, καὶ ὅτι ἦν αὐτὸν δε-
δεκώς.

24. μάστιξιν ἀνετ.] The *plural* is here used, with reference to the many things of which the μάστιξ was formed. Ἀνετάζειν signifies properly to examine carefully; but here *quæstionem habere*, denoting examination by torture. See Gen. xii. 17. xvi. 6. Wisd. ii. 19. 2 Macc. vii. 37. Sept.

— ἐπεφώνουν αὐτῷ.] The word signifies literally *to raise the voice* AT a person; and has therefore two senses, either *acclamo, applaud*, as in Acts xii. 22.; or *inclamo, exclaim against*, as here.

25. ὡς δὲ προέτεινεν αὐτὸν τοῖς ἱμᾶσιν.] There are few passages which, from variety of reading, and diversity of interpretation, are more perplexing than this. Not less than *six* or *seven* varr. lectt. exist; but the only material diversity is between the *singular* προέτεινεν, and the *plural* προέτειναν. For the *latter* there is considerable authority in MSS. and Versions; and it is adopted by Griesb. and Tittm. Yet the *singular* ought, by every principle of Criticism, to be retained, as being the more *difficult reading*; and the recent collations of Rinck confirm it. As to the *sense* of the passage, see the full details in Recens. Synop. Suffice it here to say, that one great error seems to run through most modern interpretations;—which is to take ἱμᾶσι in the sense *scourges*; q. d. "they stretched him up *for the scourges*." This is very harsh; and I know of no authority for that use of ἱμὰς in the *plural*. There is no doubt that the ancient and some modern Interpreters *rightly* take it in the ordinary sense *straps* or *thongs*; as Mark i. 7. Luke iii. 16. John i. 27. The *plural* is used because, it seems, the prisoner was fastened to the post, or block, with *two* straps. The employment of the *Article*, as Bp. Middl. suggests, shows that these thongs or belts were in *common use*. This view is exceedingly confirmed by a passage of an ancient Greek Martyrologist adduced by me in Rec. Syn. from a tract called *Martyrium Tarachi*: περιελόντες αὐτοῦ τὸ πάλλιον, καὶ περιζώσαντες, τείνατε, καὶ νεύροις ὠμοῖς τύψατε — δήσαντες αὐτὸν — τείνατε, καὶ νεύροις ὠμοῖς σχίσατε τὸ νῶτον αὐτοῦ — τείνατε αὐτὸν ἐν τοῖς πάλοις, καὶ νεύροις ὠμοῖς μαστίζετε. These *straps*, or *belts*, were, it should seem, fastened about the person something like the harness of our horses, at the same time confining his hands; and were then attached to the post by some ring or buckle there provided to receive them. In short, the mode was, I apprehend, exactly like that now adopted in Russia, in *applying* the punishment of the knout,—of which Captain Frankland, in his late Travels in Russia, vol. ii. gives the following description:—"It is a large solid piece of wood, about seven feet in height, thrust end-ways in the ground in an inclining posture. At the top is a groove cut for the reception of the neck of the sufferer; at the two sides are two other grooves for the arms. On the part fronting the spectators, opposite to the side on which the sufferer is placed, are three *iron rings*, to which the hands, neck, and feet of the criminal are made fast *by thongs*." Προέτ. must (though not one of the Commentators has seen it) be referred to the *Centurion*, who, also, is said to *do* what he *orders* to *be done*, and *sees* done. Thus the construction is as if Luke had written Ὡς δὲ προέτεινε αὐτὸν ὁ ἑκατόνταρχος [ἐν] τοῖς ἱμᾶσι, εἶπε πρὸς αὐτὸν ὁ Π. an *hypallage* common in the best writers. The sense is: "and now Paul said to the Centurion, as he was having him bent forward [to the block], and [bound round] with the belts," &c. The ellip. of ἐν is *supplied* in a kindred passage of Job xxxix. 10. δήσεις δὲ αὐτὸν ἐν ἱμᾶσι ζυγὸν σου.

— τὸν ἑστῶτα.] The Article has reference to the *custom* of the Romans, to have a centurion to stand by at the execution of any punishment.

28. ἐγὼ πολλοῦ — ἐκτησάμην.] These words imply *surprise* how a person of Paul's mean appearance could possess this. Perceiving which, the Apostle makes a rejoinder removing this difficulty: "*Aye, but I am even so by birth.*" Κεφαλαίου (at which supply χρῆμα) signifies properly the *total* arising from the addition of several small sums; but as that generally implies a tolerably large sum, so it came to mean *a considerable sum*. On the various modes whereby the freedom of Rome could be attained by foreigners; i. e. by *merit*, or *favour*, by *money*, or by *being freed from servitude*, and on the peculiar nature of the freedom claimed by the citizens of Tarsus, see Recens. Synop.

29. ἐφοβήθη — ὅτι ἦν αὐτὸν δεδ.] On the privilege of a Roman citizen under arrest, see the Notes of Kuin. and my own in Rec. Syn.; where I have proved that the term δεδ., here used, refers *only* to his having had the belts applied in order to scourging, not to his being put in irons, for Paul's citizenship was of a class which did not exempt him from *that*; and, in point of fact, we find the *bonds retained* after his liberation from the whipping-post, and he is afterwards called ὁ δέσμιος.

Τῇ δὲ ἐπαύριον βουλόμενος γνῶναι τὸ ἀσφαλὲς, τὸ τί κατηγορεῖται 30
παρὰ τῶν Ἰουδαίων, ἔλυσεν αὐτὸν ἀπὸ τῶν δεσμῶν, καὶ ἐκέλευσεν
ἐλθεῖν τοὺς ἀρχιερεῖς καὶ ὅλον τὸ συνέδριον αὐτῶν· καὶ καταγαγὼν
q Infra 24. 16. 2 Tim. 1. 3. τὸν Παῦλον ἔστησεν εἰς αὐτούς. XXIII. [q] Ἀτενίσας δὲ ὁ Παῦλος 1
τῷ συνεδρίῳ εἶπεν· Ἄνδρες ἀδελφοὶ, ἐγὼ πάσῃ συνειδήσει ἀγαθῇ
r 1 Kings 22. 24. Jer. 20. 2. John 18. 22. πεπολίτευμαι τῷ Θεῷ ἄχρι ταύτης τῆς ἡμέρας. [r] Ὁ δὲ ἀρχιερεὺς Ἀνα- 2
s Lev. 19. 35. Deut. 17. 4, 9. & 25. 12. νίας ἐπέταξε τοῖς παρεστῶσιν αὐτῷ τύπτειν αὐτοῦ τὸ στόμα. [s] Τότε 3
ὁ Παῦλος πρὸς αὐτὸν εἶπε· Τύπτειν σε μέλλει ὁ Θεὸς, τοῖχε κεκο-
νιαμένε! καὶ σὺ κάθῃ κρίνων με κατὰ τὸν νόμον, καὶ παρανομῶν
κελεύεις με τύπτεσθαι; οἱ δὲ παρεστῶτες εἶπον· Τὸν ἀρχιερέα τοῦ 4
t Exod. 22. 28. Θεοῦ λοιδορεῖς; [t] ἔφη τε ὁ Παῦλος· Οὐκ ᾔδειν, ἀδελφοὶ, ὅτι ἐστὶν 5
ἀρχιερεύς· γέγραπται γάρ· Ἄρχοντα τοῦ λαοῦ σου οὐκ ἐρεῖς
u Infra 24. 15, 21. & 26. 5, 6. Phil. 3. 5. κακῶς. [u] Γνοὺς δὲ ὁ Παῦλος, ὅτι τὸ ἓν μέρος ἐστὶ Σαδδουκαίων τὸ 6
δὲ ἕτερον Φαρισαίων, ἔκραξεν ἐν τῷ συνεδρίῳ· Ἄνδρες ἀδελφοὶ, ἐγὼ

30. *ἔστησεν εἰς αὐτούς.*] The full sense seems to be, "set him up to speak face to face, as to the charges they brought against him." On this use of *καθίστημι* see my Note on Thucyd. iv. 84. 1. The *παρὰ* just before is for *ἀπὸ* or *ὑπὸ*, "at the instance or accusation of." See Winer's Gr. Gr. p. 139. med. and 140. Note.

XXIII. 1. *πεπολίτευμαι.*] "I have conducted myself." The word properly signifies to *act as a citizen*, and sometimes to have the conduct of state affairs. See my Note on Thucyd. i. 84. 5. Hence it came to mean *conduct one's self, behave*, &c., in which sense the word frequently occurs in the later writers. *Ἐν πάσῃ συνειδήσει*, "according to the dictates of my conscience [whether, as at first, ill informed, or not]." See Whitby and Doddr.

2. The Ananias here meant, is undoubtedly Ananias, son of Nebidæus, (See Joseph. Ant. xx. 5, 3.), who had discharged the pontifical office under the procuratorship of Quadratus, predecessor of Felix. By Quadratus he was sent a prisoner to Rome, together with Annas, prefect of the temple, to give an account of his high-priesthood to Claudius Cæsar (see Joseph. Ant. xx. 6, 2.). But by the intercession of Agrippa, Junior, they were acquitted, and returned to Jerusalem. Ananias, however, was not reinstated in the pontifical office. For during the procuratorship of Felix it was filled by Jonathan, who (as Josephus tells us, Ant. xx. 10.) was successor to Ananias. This Jonathan was, afterwards, by the connivance, at least, of Felix, assassinated in the temple by some *sicarii*. See Joseph. Ant. xx. 8, 5. and the Note on Acts xxii. 4. The office then remained unoccupied until king Agrippa appointed Ishmael, son of Phabæus, Joseph. Ant. xx. 8, 8. Hence, at the period in question, Ananias was not High-Priest, but was usurping the dignity. (Krebs and Kuinoel.) See also Benson and Biscoe, Boyle Lectures. It should rather seem that Ananias was not *usurping* the office, but *holding it provisionally*. To this unjustifiable violence towards the Apostle he was induced, we may suppose, 1. by Paul's *solemn asseverations of innocence*, which gave the lie to the accusations of the Chief Priests. 2. By his addressing them as *Brethren*, not Fathers or Rulers of Israel. 3. From his having been liberated by Roman soldiers, and throwing himself on their protection, as a Roman citizen.

3. *τύπτειν — κεκονιαμένε.*] This is regarded by most Commentators as a *prediction*; while others (as Camer., Zeger, Limb., Wets., Heumann, and most of the recent Commentators), regard it as a *formula malè precantis*; q. d. God smite thee, as thou hast smitten me! There is, indeed, some reason to think that Ananias came to a violent death about six years after. Yet we are hardly warranted in recognising a *prediction*; for the words have not the *air* of a prediction. Nor is there any *proof* of the *fulfilment* of such a prediction; since, if Ananias *did* perish by violence, it would still be uncertain whether that was a judgment upon him for *this*, or for other bad actions in his life. We may rather consider the expression as the ebullition of a spirit impatient of injury: not, however, regarding the word as a *formula malè precantis*, but as merely the acrimoniously worded expression of a *persuasion*, that God would punish Ananias for this outrage. This view is confirmed by Chrysost., Jerome, and Augustine. See Dr. Graves in D'Oyly and Mant.

Τοῖχος κεκον. was a common metaphor to designate *hypocrisy*. See Note on Matt. xxiii. 37. How applicable this reproach was, we find from Josephus.

— *καὶ σὺ κάθῃ*, &c.] The *καὶ*, when prefixed to interrogative sentences implying admiration, is best rendered *itane? and so, so then?* See Kuin. *Παρανομῶν* for *παρὰ τὸν νόμον*. For *κρίνων* there is no occasion to read, with Valckn., *κρινῶν*; the Present being put for the Future.

5. *οὐκ ᾔδειν — ἀρχιερεύς.*] That the Apostle should have been ignorant of the presence of the High Priest, would seem strange; and has accordingly occasioned some difference of opinion. Of the various solutions of the difficulty offered by Commentators (See Recens. Synop.), *two* only seem to have any semblance of truth: 1. that of Chrysost., Dionys., Cajet., Gataker, Wolf, Michaelis, and Townsend, who prove, from the history of the times, as recorded in Josephus, that the office of the High Priest was then vacant, and that Ananias was only discharging its duties *pro tempore*; which Paul, having been in Jerusalem only a few days, might not be aware of. If this be thought not satisfactory, we may, with

Φαρισαῖός εἰμι, υἱὸς Φαρισαίου· περὶ ἐλπίδος καὶ ἀναστάσεως νεκρῶν
7 ἐγὼ κρίνομαι! Τοῦτο δὲ αὐτοῦ λαλήσαντος, ἐγένετο στάσις τῶν Φα-
8 ρισαίων καὶ τῶν Σαδδουκαίων, καὶ ἐσχίσθη τὸ πλῆθος. [x] Σαδδουκαῖοι [x] Matt. 22. 23. Mark 12. 18. Luke 20. 27.
μὲν γὰρ λέγουσι μὴ εἶναι ἀνάστασιν, μηδὲ ἄγγελον μήτε πνεῦμα·
9 Φαρισαῖοι δὲ ὁμολογοῦσι τὰ ἀμφότερα. [y] Ἐγένετο δὲ κραυγὴ μεγάλη· [y] Supra 5. 39. & 22. 7, 17, 18. Infra 25. 25. & 26. 31.
καὶ ἀναστάντες [οἱ] γραμματεῖς τοῦ μέρους τῶν Φαρισαίων διεμάχοντο,
λέγοντες· Οὐδὲν κακὸν εὑρίσκομεν ἐν τῷ ἀνθρώπῳ τούτῳ· εἰ δὲ
10 πνεῦμα ἐλάλησεν αὐτῷ ἢ ἄγγελος·—μὴ θεομαχῶμεν. Πολλῆς δὲ γενομένης στάσεως, εὐλαβηθεὶς ὁ χιλίαρχος μὴ διασπασθῇ ὁ Παῦλος ὑπ᾽
αὐτῶν, ἐκέλευσε τὸ στράτευμα καταβὰν ἁρπάσαι αὐτὸν ἐκ μέσου αὐτῶν,
ἄγειν τε εἰς τὴν παρεμβολήν.
11 [z] Τῇ δὲ ἐπιούσῃ νυκτὶ ἐπιστὰς αὐτῷ ὁ Κύριος εἶπε· Θάρσει, [z] Supra 18. 9.
Παῦλε· ὡς γὰρ διεμαρτύρω τὰ περὶ ἐμοῦ εἰς Ἱερουσαλὴμ, οὕτω σε δεῖ [a] Infra v. 20, 30.
12 καὶ εἰς Ῥώμην μαρτυρῆσαι. [a] Γενομένης δὲ ἡμέρας, ποιήσαντές τινες Matt. 26. 74.

Bps. Sanderson and Mann, Episcop., Bengel, Wets., Pearce, Valckn., Morus, Schott, and Kuin. (supported by the ancient Commentaries as found in the Catena) take the expression οὐκ ᾔδειν in the sense, "I did not reflect or consider" (as it were excusing a momentary impetuosity.) And they compare Eph. vi. 8. Col. iii. 24. and some passages from Classical writers. So in Acts vii. 18. for ᾔδει some MSS. have, by *gloss*, ἐμνήσθη. Bornem., indeed, denies that the word ever has that sense.

6. περὶ ἐλπίδος καὶ ἀναστ. νεκ.] The best Commentators here suppose a *Hendiadys*. Yet we may render, "for the hope of the dead and their resurrection." Comp. Ps. xvi. 5. 1 Thess. iv. 13.

8. ἀμφότερα.] Both the ancient and modern Interpreters stumble at this—since there seem to be *three* terms above mentioned, *resurrection*, *angel*, and *spirit*. To avoid this difficulty, some would cancel μηδὲ ἄγγελον. Others propose another (but most harsh) mode of punctuation. Others, again, remark that ἀμφότερα might, by a writer not very attentive to accuracy, be used of *more than two*. But of this they adduce no good proofs; and it involves a sort of imputation both unjust and irreverent. The sacred writer, I conceive, *meant* to advert to the *two* points of difference between the Pharisees and Sadducees; and the two things referred to are the *Resurrection*, and the *Existence of Immaterial Beings*; πνεῦμα and ἄγγελος being considered as falling under the same head. Ὁμολογοῦσι "profess [belief in]."

9. διεμάχοντο] "they contended [on behalf of Paul]." The word is also used by the Classical writers; not, however, followed by λέγοντες, but by an Infin. with an Accus., as in Thucyd. iii. 40 & 42, where see my Notes.

—εἰ δὲ πνεῦμα, &c.] Here we have only to suppose an *aposiopesis*,—such as is often found in the best writers, when something *which we do not care to directly mention* is omitted. Chrys. supplies ποῖον ἔγκλημα, and the Pesch. Syr. something similar. The words following, μὴ θεομαχῶμεν, are omitted in 7 MSS., 4 inferior Versions, and some Fathers, and cancelled by Griesb. and Knapp; but without reason. The *external* authority for so doing is very slender; and the *internal* is quite against the omission. Kuinoel acutely traces the origin of the omission to an ill founded *objection* to the words, as if too much favouring Christianity. To suppose them introduced from v. 39, is too hypothetical. All that can be said is, that the two passages are very similar. Besides, the aposiopesis before would be intolerably harsh without these words.

The *angel*, or *spirit*, is thought to have reference to the *two kinds of* appearance, which those who were inclined to think with Paul ascribed to the *Divine vision* narrated by the Apostle; for those appearances were always supposed to take place through the medium of an angel, or a *spirit*. Certain recent Commentators here attempt to *explain away* all idea of Divine appearance; considering the whole as a MERE *dream* produced by the workings of high wrought imagination, and the resolution previously taken by Paul to avail himself of *any* opportunity of appealing to Cæsar; and this from a desire to go to Rome, foreseeing that he should be able to accomplish much good there. "Hence (say they), as the event turned out *accordingly*, he, as usual, ascribed the dream to a Divine appearance!!" How little such a notion will bear examination (being no other than the same flimsy hypothesis advanced by these Commentators on various other occasions) it needs but little reflection to discover. So far from the resolution to make this appeal *giving occasion to the dream*, the appeal was most probably not thought of until *after the dream*; certainly not *carried into execution* till more than two years after; though many opportunities had, in the mean time, occurred for the Apostle to have appealed unto Cæsar; which he, however, did not. Nor is it probable that he would have done so *at last*, had he not been *compelled*, for his personal safety. I mean not to deny that the Apostle had thought of going to Rome: but surely he would be anxious not to go *as a criminal*. The vision then, was undoubtedly supernatural.

10. μὴ διασπασθῇ.] Pric., Kyp., and Wets. have proved by examples, that the term is often used of *great violence*, but *short of death*. Τὸ στράτευμα, "the forces." The word is a *vox mediæ significationis*, and signifies sometimes a whole *army*, sometimes, as here, a *small force*.

11. ἐπιστάς.] See Luke ii. 9. Acts xii. 7.

τῶν Ἰουδαίων συστροφὴν, ἀνεθεμάτισαν ἑαυτοὺς, λέγοντες μήτε φαγεῖν
μήτε πιεῖν, ἕως οὗ ἀποκτείνωσι τὸν Παῦλον. Ἦσαν δὲ πλείους τεσσα- 13
ράκοντα, οἱ ταύτην τὴν συνωμοσίαν πεποιηκότες· οἵτινες προσελθόντες 14
τοῖς ἀρχιερεῦσι καὶ τοῖς πρεσβυτέροις εἶπον· Ἀναθέματι ἀνεθεματίσα-
μεν ἑαυτοὺς μηδενὸς γεύσασθαι ἕως οὗ ἀποκτείνωμεν τὸν Παῦλον.
Νῦν οὖν ὑμεῖς ἐμφανίσατε τῷ χιλιάρχῳ σὺν τῷ συνεδρίῳ, ὅπως αὔριον 15
αὐτὸν καταγάγῃ πρὸς ὑμᾶς, ὡς μέλλοντας διαγινώσκειν ἀκριβέστερον τὰ
περὶ αὐτοῦ· ἡμεῖς δὲ, πρὸ τοῦ ἐγγίσαι αὐτὸν, ἕτοιμοί ἐσμεν τοῦ ἀνελεῖν αὐτόν. Ἀκούσας δὲ ὁ υἱὸς τῆς ἀδελφῆς Παύλου ‡ τὸ ἔνεδρον, 16
παραγενόμενος καὶ εἰσελθὼν εἰς τὴν παρεμβολὴν, ἀπήγγειλε τῷ Παύλῳ. Προσκαλεσάμενος δὲ ὁ Παῦλος ἕνα τῶν ἑκατοντάρχων, ἔφη· Τὸν 17
νεανίαν τοῦτον ἀπάγαγε πρὸς τὸν χιλίαρχον· ἔχει γάρ τι ἀπαγγεῖλαι
αὐτῷ. Ὁ μὲν οὖν παραλαβὼν αὐτὸν ἤγαγε πρὸς τὸν χιλίαρχον, καί 18
φησιν· Ὁ δέσμιος Παῦλος προσκαλεσάμενός με ἠρώτησε τοῦτον τὸν
νεανίαν ἀγαγεῖν πρός σε, ἔχοντά τι λαλῆσαί σοι. Ἐπιλαβόμενος δὲ τῆς 19
χειρὸς αὐτοῦ ὁ χιλίαρχος, καὶ ἀναχωρήσας κατ᾽ ἰδίαν ἐπυνθάνετο· Τί
b Supra v. 12. ἐστιν ὃ ἔχεις ἀπαγγεῖλαί μοι; [b] Εἶπε δέ· Ὅτι οἱ Ἰουδαῖοι συνέθεντο 20
τοῦ ἐρωτῆσαί σε, ὅπως αὔριον εἰς τὸ συνέδριον καταγάγῃς τὸν Παῦλον,
ὡς μέλλοντές τι ἀκριβέστερον πυνθάνεσθαι περὶ αὐτοῦ. Σὺ οὖν μὴ 21
πεισθῇς αὐτοῖς· ἐνεδρεύουσι γὰρ αὐτὸν ἐξ αὐτῶν ἄνδρες πλείους τεσσαράκοντα, οἵτινες ἀνεθεμάτισαν ἑαυτοὺς μήτε φαγεῖν μήτε πιεῖν ἕως
οὗ ἀνέλωσιν αὐτόν· καὶ νῦν ἕτοιμοί εἰσι, προσδεχόμενοι τὴν ἀπὸ σοῦ
ἐπαγγελίαν. Ὁ μὲν οὖν χιλίαρχος ἀπέλυσε τὸν νεανίαν, παραγγείλας 22
μηδενὶ ἐκλαλῆσαι, ὅτι ταῦτα ἐνεφάνισας πρός με. καὶ προσκαλεσάμενος 23
δύο τινὰς τῶν ἑκατοντάρχων εἶπεν· Ἑτοιμάσατε στρατιώτας διακοσίους,
ὅπως πορευθῶσιν ἕως Καισαρείας, καὶ ἱππεῖς ἑβδομήκοντα, καὶ ‡ δεξιο-

12. *συστροφὴν*] "a conspiracy." A signification of which I have produced examples from Dionys. Hal., Josephus, and Artemid., in Recens. Synop. These persons were probably *Zelotæ*, or *Sicarii*, set on by Ananias and his party.

— *ἀνεθεμάτισαν ἑ.*] This *ἀναθ.* implied the binding one's self under a curse to do any thing; and (as Selden and Wets. have shown) was sometimes, as in the present case, accompanied with a resolution not to eat or drink until the accomplishment of the thing vowed. Such execrable vows were, Doddr. observes, not unusual with the Jews; who claimed a right to punish those whom they considered transgressors of the law, even unto death.

15. *ἐμφανίσατε*] "give notice by letter." A forensic term. *Διαγινώσκω* has here the sense, also forensic, of *examine*, literally *determine* some point, of which examples are given by Wets. and Loesner. *Πρὸ τοῦ ἐγγίσαι αὐτόν*. Namely, that the Sanhedrim might not be thought to have any hand in the thing.

16. *Παύλου τὸ ἔνεδρον*] "the plot laid against Paul." Perhaps we should here read *ἐνέδραν*, as at xxv. 3, where all the MSS. have *ἐνέδρα*. The word is used here and in that passage simply for *ἐπιβουλὴ*, *a plot*, as in Ps. x. 8. Josh. viii. 9. Herodian iv. 5, 7; vii. 5, 8. Joseph. Bell. i. 5. 8. *ἐξελθεῖν εἰς τὴν ἐνέδραν*, "to go forth to carry into effect," &c.

19. *ἐπιλαβόμενος τῆς χειρὸς α.*] This is a *popular* form of expression, not to be pressed on, signifying little more than *taking aside*, as appears from the examples adduced by Pricæus, from Ach. Tat. and Herodian.

20. *ὡς μέλλοντές τι ἀκριβ. πυνθ.*] So Joseph. Vit. § 2. *συνιόντων — ὑπὲρ τοῦ παρ᾽ ἐμοῦ περὶ τῶν νομίμων ἀκριβέστερόν τι γνῶναι.*

21. *τὴν ἀπὸ σοῦ ἐπαγγελίαν.*] The Commentators are not agreed whether this should be explained *promise*, or *order*. There is much to be urged for either sense, but the context rather requires the latter. Render "the order to be given by you, for Paul to be brought up."

22. *παραγγείλας — πρός με.*] A blending of the *oratio directa* and indirecta, as sup. i. 4.

23. *δεξιολάβους.*] With this word the Commentators have been not a little perplexed. Some would read *δεξιοβόλους*, from one MS. and a few Versions. But that plainly arose from the *conjecture* of those who could not understand *δεξιολάβους*, which is generally supposed to denote *lictors*, like our *provost marshal* and his attendants. But although there is reason to think that the word came, in after ages, to bear that sense, yet it were absurd to suppose *so many* lictors to be attendant on the tribune's forces, as that 200

24 λάβους διακοσίους, ἀπὸ τρίτης ὥρας τῆς νυκτός· κτήνη τε παραστῆσαι, ἵνα ἐπιβιβάσαντες τὸν Παῦλον διασώσωσι πρὸς Φήλικα τὸν ἡγεμόνα·
25 γράψας ἐπιστολὴν περιέχουσαν τὸν τύπον τοῦτον. Κλαύδιος Λυσίας
26 τῷ κρατίστῳ ἡγεμόνι Φήλικι χαίρειν. [c] Τὸν ἄνδρα τοῦτον συλληφθέντα [c] Supra 21. 33.
27 ὑπὸ τῶν Ἰουδαίων, καὶ μέλλοντα ἀναιρεῖσθαι ὑπ᾽ αὐτῶν, ἐπιστὰς σὺν
28 τῷ στρατεύματι ἐξειλόμην αὐτὸν, μαθὼν ὅτι Ῥωμαῖός ἐστι. Βουλόμενος
δὲ γνῶναι τὴν αἰτίαν δι᾽ ἣν ἐνεκάλουν αὐτῷ, κατήγαγον αὐτὸν εἰς τὸ
29 συνέδριον αὐτῶν· ὃν εὗρον ἐγκαλούμενον περὶ ζητημάτων τοῦ νόμου
30 αὐτῶν, μηδὲν δὲ ἄξιον θανάτου ἢ δεσμῶν ἔγκλημα ἔχοντα. Μηνυθεί-
σης δέ μοι ἐπιβουλῆς εἰς τὸν ἄνδρα μέλλειν ἔσεσθαι ὑπὸ τῶν Ἰουδαίων,
ἐξαυτῆς ἔπεμψα πρός σε, παραγγείλας καὶ τοῖς κατηγόροις λέγειν τὰ
πρὸς αὐτὸν ἐπὶ σοῦ. ἔῤῥωσο.
31 Οἱ μὲν οὖν στρατιῶται, κατὰ τὸ διατεταγμένον αὐτοῖς, ἀναλαβόντες
32 τὸν Παῦλον, ἤγαγον διὰ τῆς νυκτὸς εἰς τὴν Ἀντιπατρίδα. Τῇ δὲ
ἐπαύριον ἐάσαντες τοὺς ἱππεῖς πορεύεσθαι σὺν αὐτῷ, ὑπέστρεψαν εἰς
33 τὴν παρεμβολήν· οἵτινες εἰσελθόντες εἰς τὴν Καισάρειαν, καὶ ἀναδόντες
34 τὴν ἐπιστολὴν τῷ ἡγεμόνι, παρέστησαν καὶ τὸν Παῦλον αὐτῷ. Ἀνα-
γνοὺς δὲ ὁ ἡγεμὼν, καὶ ἐπερωτήσας ἐκ ποίας ἐπαρχίας ἐστὶ, καὶ πυθό-

should be sent to guard one prisoner. One of the most probable opinions is that of Beza, Drus., Kuin., Schleus., and Wahl, that they were the Tribune's *body guards;* so called from taking the right side of any one (as being the *unguarded* side. See Thucyd. iii. 23. v. 10. 71.), and thus protecting him. I should rather think, however, that they were a kind of troops *attendant* on the heavy-armed and the cavalry, like the ἅμιπποι mentioned in Thucyd. v. 57. see my Note there. They were, it should seem, light-armed, and similar to the *lancearii*, who (as we find from Ammian. xxi. 13., cited by Wets.) covered in battle the right flank. They seem to have performed the duties both of *exploratores*, and of *attendant soldiers* on the heavy armed, and probably sometimes that of *body guards* on the principal officers, like our *sentinels*.

24. κτήνη.] There is no occasion to suppose (with Kuin.), that the beasts were for Paul and the two soldiers who held his chains. We may imagine them to have been for *Paul only;* for in so long and rapid a journey he would *require* more than one horse. The cavalry, we know, used (as the Tartars and other Oriental nations now do) often to take with them each a led horse; by which means they travelled very long distances without stopping.

25. περιέχ. τὸν τύπον τοῦτον.] There is no necessity (with Valckn., Heinr., and Kuin.), so to *press* on the primitive sense of the word, as to suppose that St. Luke has given us not *the* letter, but only the substance of it. It should rather seem that Luke wrote from a *copy* of the letter, preserved by himself or by Paul, from the persons who kept the public records. Paul, during his tedious captivity at Cæsarea, would be desirous of knowing the contents of the Epistle (which was of the sort called *elogia*), and probably preserved a copy, which Luke had the opportunity of using.

26. κρατίστῳ.] The usual and formal epithet employed in addressing a magistrate; as we say, your *Excellency*. On χαίρειν and ἔῤῥωσο, see Note on Acts xv. 23.

27. σὺν τῷ στρατεύματι.] Not "with an army," but "with the force [under my command]." So at Joseph. Bell. i. 7, 2. Πείσωνα εἰσπέμπει μετὰ στρατιᾶς I would render, "sends Piso with a body of troops."

— μαθὼν ὅτι Ῥωμ. ἐστι.] It is in vain to attempt to clear Lysias (as some Commentators do) of petty misrepresentation. He ventured to take a little more credit for zeal, in behalf of his fellow citizens, than he deserved.

31. ἤγαγον διὰ τῆς — Ἀ.] From the ancient itineraries brought to light by the researches of Reland, we are enabled pretty correctly to trace both the route and the different stages of it: namely, to Neapolis 22 miles; to Lydda (or Diospolis) 10; to Antipatris 10; to Cæsarea 6. But 42 miles would seem a distance too great for one night; even supposing all the rapidity of a forced march. And yet the words ἤγαγον εἰς τὴν Ἀ. seem to claim this sense; at least no other would be thought of in a *Classical* writer. Most Commentators (as Reland, Biscoe, Doddr., Schleus., and Kuin.) think it is not necessary to suppose that he was conveyed thither in *one* night; and they render *by night*, i. e. by the *next* night. But it could only mean *in the course* of the next night, which would be too *long* a time to allow. It therefore appears safer to understand διὰ τῆς νυκτὸς of the night on which they set out. And perhaps no more is meant by this expression (which seems a *popular* idiom) than that they conveyed Paul *all night long towards* Antipatris, and arrived there without halting. Now, as they might, by a forced march (the cavalry helping the infantry), arrive thither by ten or eleven o'clock in the morning; and as by far the *greater part* of the journey would be really accomplished by night, they might be said to have conveyed him thither διὰ τῆς νυκτός.

33. ἀναδόντες.] Vox solemnis de hac re.

μενος ὅτι ἀπὸ Κιλικίας· Διακούσομαί σου, ἔφη, ὅταν καὶ οἱ κατήγο- 35
ροί σου παραγένωνται. ἐκέλευσέ τε αὐτὸν ἐν τῷ πραιτωρίῳ τοῦ Ἡρώδου φυλάσσεσθαι.

d Supra 23. 2.

XXIV. [d] ΜΕΤΑ δὲ πέντε ἡμέρας κατέβη ὁ ἀρχιερεὺς Ἀνανίας μετὰ 1
τῶν πρεσβυτέρων καὶ ῥήτορος Τερτύλλου τινὸς, οἵτινες ἐνεφάνισαν τῷ
ἡγεμόνι κατὰ τοῦ Παύλου. Κληθέντος δὲ αὐτοῦ, ἤρξατο κατηγορεῖν ὁ 2
Τέρτυλλος, λέγων· Πολλῆς εἰρήνης τυγχάνοντες διὰ σοῦ, καὶ κατορθω- 3
μάτων γινομένων τῷ ἔθνει τούτῳ διὰ τῆς σῆς προνοίας πάντῃ τε καὶ
πανταχοῦ, ἀποδεχόμεθα, κράτιστε Φῆλιξ, μετὰ πάσης εὐχαριστίας. Ἵνα 4
δὲ μὴ ἐπὶ πλεῖόν σε ἐγκόπτω, παρακαλῶ ἀκοῦσαί σε ἡμῶν συντόμως,
τῇ σῇ ἐπιεικείᾳ. Εὑρόντες γὰρ τὸν ἄνδρα τοῦτον λοιμὸν, καὶ κινοῦντα 5

35. διακούσομαι.] This implies a diligent and thorough hearing. Τῷ πραιτωρίῳ τ. Ἡ. i. e. a palace formerly built by Herod, but then used as the residence of the provincial governor.

XXIV. 1. μετὰ δὲ πέντε ἡμ.] This is by some of the best Commentators explained, *from Paul's arrival at Cæsarea*; by others, *from the time of the notice given* to the High Priest by Lysias, which was on the day *before* Paul's arrival at Cæsarea.

— ἐνεφάνισαν.] Sub. ἑαυτούς. See John xiv. 22. and Note. Almost all the best Commentators are agreed in regarding this as a *forensic* term, equivalent to the Latin one *comparere in judicio*, or coram judice. It *may*, however, have the signification assigned by the Syr. Vers., Ammonius, Pric., Grot., and Wets., *gave information*.

— ῥήτορος.] The word properly denotes an *orator*. But as orators, who harangued on the public business before the public assembly, sometimes had the causes of private persons confided to them, — so it came to signify an *advocate*, and at length merely a *pleader*, or *barrister*, as here.

3. εἰρήνης.] The word here signifies public and political tranquillity; namely, from the troubles under which they had laboured, of rebels, brigands, robbers, and other disturbers of the peace. That Felix deserved this praise, appears from Joseph. Ant. xx. 8, 4. cited by Wets. And so at Bell. i. 10, 5. he says, that when Herod had put down the bands of robbers, the people celebrated his praises, saying ὡς εἰς εἰρήνην αὐτοῖς παρών, that he came to them for peace.

— κατορθωμάτων.] Κατορθόω is properly a term used in *bowling*, and signifies, primarily, to *take a straight course down to the end*; metaphorically, to *conduct an affair to a prosperous issue*; and, in the passive, to *be conducted*, &c.: as Thucyd. ii. 65, where κατορθούμενα (πράγματα) are opposed to σφαλέντα, *unsuccessful*. Thus κατόρθωμα denoted the *thing* thus brought to a *successful issue*.

— διὰ τῆς σῆς προν.] Elsn. observes that the *old* Romans used to ascribe national prosperity to the Gods; while, in after times, whatever happened prosperously was ascribed to the prudent counsels, and even the τύχη of their rulers, or generals, without any mention of Divine Providence.

— πάντῃ τε καὶ πανταχοῦ.] It is not agreed among Expositors whether these words should be taken with the *preceding*, or with the *following*. The *former* mode makes the better construction, and yields the better sense; namely, "in every respect (or, 'at all times'), and in every place." We may observe an elegance in this juxtaposition of terms commencing with the same syllable, something like *alliteration*. Many examples of which may be seen in Rec. Syn.

— ἀποδεχόμεθα.] The word signifies properly to *accept at any one's hands*, and, by implication, to *approve, commend*, and is used both of *persons* and *things*.

4. ἵνα μὴ — ἐγκόπτω.] The full sense is, "That I may not [longer than is necessary] detain you [from other business]." The term ἐγκόπτειν signifies properly to cut a ditch, as a separation between two plots of ground; and hence, to separate, detain from, &c.

— συντόμως.] The construction here is left imperfect; so that, as the words stand, we must supply λεξόντων from the subject-matter. Yet this involves such a harshness, that I am inclined to suspect some corruption in συντόμως, for which I would conjecture συντόνως (*vehementer. enixe*) to be construed with παρακαλῶ. Thus it will exactly correspond to the Latin phrase — "Te *vehementer* rogo," of frequent occurrence in the best writers, and probably employed, on the present occasion, by Tertullus; of which St. Luke has thus given a literal version. And although no MS. is adduced as having συντόνως, yet the two words are frequently confounded by the scribes; on which see Hemsterh. and Kuster on Aristoph. Plut. p. 71; Heyne's Homer v. 492; and Wessel. on Diodor. Sic. i. 279. λυπηθῆναι συντόμως, where συντόνως is evidently the true reading, though not found in any MS. And the expression may very well be explained to mean *earnestly*; since the adjective συντόνως is often opposed to ἀνειμένος, both in a *proper* and in a *metaphorical* acceptation. Thus the full sense is, "But that I may no longer hinder thee [I will cease this preface], and have earnestly to entreat thee, of thy benignity and condescension, to hear what we have to say." Τῇ σῇ ἐπιεικείᾳ is well rendered in the Vulg. "pro tuâ clementiâ:" the very expression, I imagine, used by Tertullus; the word *clementia* being in the ancient Latin Greek Glossaries explained by ἐπιείκεια.

5. εὑρόντες γὰρ, &c.] The γὰρ has the *inchoative* force, and may be rendered *nempe*. In εὑρόντες the Commentators suppose an ellip. of ἐσμὲν, so that εὑρόντες ἐσμὲν may be taken for εὕρομεν; of which they adduce examples. But in the passages they cite, no *other* principle could be resorted to: *here* there is no such compulsion; and it is better to regard the phraseology as falling

στάσιν πᾶσι τοῖς Ἰουδαίοις τοῖς κατὰ τὴν οἰκουμένην, πρωτοστάτην τε
6 τῆς τῶν Ναζωραίων αἱρέσεως· [e] ὃς καὶ τὸ ἱερὸν ἐπείρασε βεβηλῶσαι, [e] Supra 21. 28.
ὃν καὶ ἐκρατήσαμεν, καὶ κατὰ τὸν ἡμέτερον νόμον ἠθελήσαμεν κρίνειν.
7 Παρελθὼν δὲ Λυσίας ὁ χιλίαρχος μετὰ πολλῆς βίας, ἐκ τῶν χειρῶν
8 ἡμῶν ἀπήγαγε, κελεύσας τοὺς κατηγόρους αὐτοῦ ἔρχεσθαι ἐπὶ σέ·
παρ᾽ οὗ δυνήσῃ αὐτὸς ἀνακρίνας περὶ πάντων τούτων ἐπιγνῶναι, ὧν
9 ἡμεῖς κατηγοροῦμεν αὐτοῦ. * Συνεπέθεντο δὲ καὶ οἱ Ἰουδαῖοι, φάσκον-
τες ταῦτα οὕτως ἔχειν.
10 Ἀπεκρίθη δὲ ὁ Παῦλος, νεύσαντος αὐτῷ τοῦ ἡγεμόνος λέγειν· Ἐκ
πολλῶν ἐτῶν ὄντα σε κριτὴν τῷ ἔθνει τούτῳ ἐπιστάμενος, εὐθυμότερον
11 τὰ περὶ ἐμαυτοῦ ἀπολογοῦμαι· δυναμένου σου γνῶναι, ὅτι οὐ πλείους
εἰσί μοι ἡμέραι [ἢ] δεκαδύο, ἀφ᾽ ἧς ἀνέβην προσκυνήσων ἐν Ἱερου-
12 σαλήμ· [f] καὶ οὔτε ἐν τῷ ἱερῷ εὗρόν με πρός τινα διαλεγόμενον, ἢ ἐπι- [f] Infra 25. 8. & 28. 17.
σύστασιν ποιοῦντα ὄχλου, οὔτε ἐν ταῖς συναγωγαῖς οὔτε κατὰ τὴν πό-
13 λιν· οὔτε παραστῆσαί με δύνανται περὶ ὧν νῦν κατηγοροῦσί μου.
14 Ὁμολογῶ δὲ τοῦτό σοι, ὅτι κατὰ τὴν ὁδὸν, ἣν λέγουσιν αἵρεσιν, οὕτω

under the figure *anacoluthon*; especially as the sentence is long and involved: of which numerous examples might be adduced from Thucyd. See Note on xvi. 22.

—λοιμὸν] for λοιμικὸν, according to the usage of the best writers, from whom examples are adduced by Wets. and Kypke, almost entirely, however, from the later writers, as Ælian V. H. xiv. 11. δόξης φρόντιζε, ἀλλὰ μὴ ἔσο λοιμὸς, καὶ μὴ μεγάλη νόσος, ἀλλὰ ὑγιεία. Strictly speaking, the noun here is not put for the cognate adjective; but is used according to a frequent Greek idiom, by which a noun in its most abstract sense is, as it were, *personified* by taking the attribute inherent in the noun, and applying it to a person.

—πρωτοστάτην.] The word properly denoted the first man on the right in a line of troops. So Thucyd. v. 71. ὁ πρωτοστάτης τοῦ δεξιοῦ κέρως, where see my Note. But it is by the later writers used to denote a *front rank man*, and sometimes, figuratively, a principal person. On Ναζωρ. see Note at ii. 22.

8. παρ᾽ οὗ.] Namely, to *Paul*; though some ancient and modern Commentators refer it to *Lysias*. The ἀνακρίνας is supposed to refer to the examination by torture.

9. συνεπέθεντο.] So read many MSS., some Versions and Fathers, and the early Edd., with the exception of the Erasmian, for the vulg. συνέθεντο, and it has been adopted by almost every Editor from Wets. down to Vat.: and perhaps rightly. But the common reading may be defended, in the sense *assented*; and if ὧν just before be the true reading, this must likewise. Συνεπέθεντο signifies "acted in concert in the attack." So Thucyd. iii. 54. ξυνεπιτιθέμενοι ἐς ἐλευθερίαν, and Deut. xxxii. 27. Ps. iii. 6.

10. νεύσαντος] "nutu significavit." Or the sense may be, "gave him permission by a nod or beckoning;" on the nature of which expression, and the similar one νεύματι χρήσασθαι, &c., I have treated in my Note on Thucyd. i. 134.

—κριτήν.] This term is used, because the Procurator united the *judicial* functions to the civil and military ones. Τὰ περὶ ἐμαυτοῦ ἀπολ. Sub. πράγματα. Munthe aptly compares Diod. Sic. p. 351. τὰ καθ᾽ ἑαυτὸν ἀπολογησάμενος.

11. ἡμέραι δεκαδύο.] The chronology of this period may be adjusted as follows:—On the *first* day Paul arrives at Jerusalem. 2d. Attends the meeting of the Presbyters. 3d. Commences his week of votive abstinence, which he continues on the 4th, 5th, 6th, 7th, and 8th (for that seems required by the words at xxi. 27. ὡς δὲ ἔμελλον αἱ ἑπτὰ ἡμέραι συντελεῖσθαι). On the same day he is assaulted by the Jews, and committed to the castle. On the 9th day he is brought before the Sanhedrim. The 10th he spends in the castle (during which the plot against him is formed). On the night of the 10th he is removed to Antipatris, where he arrives early on the 11th day: and on the 12th he reaches Cæsarea. The *remaining* day is *not reckoned*, probably (as Kuin. suggests) because it is not in question, as he could *then* excite no tumult.

The Dative μοι may be accounted for on the principle mentioned by Matth. Gr. Gr. § 390.

The ἢ before δεκαδύο is not found in very many MSS. and some Fathers, and the early Edd., and is cancelled by Wets., Matth., Griesb., Tittm., and Vat.: and rightly; for it is far easier to account for its insertion than for its omission

12. ἐπισύστασιν.] The word is somewhat rare; but it is found in the Sept., Joseph., Sext., Emp., and others cited by the Commentators. Συνίστασθαι is found in the best Classical writers. See my Note on Thucyd. v. 34.

14. ὁμολογῶ, &c.] After having refuted the charge of sedition, the Apostle proceeds to answer that of taking up and maintaining a religion different from that of his countrymen. This he does by showing that the doctrines he professes are not *mere novelties* (or *sectarian*); but that he worships the same God with the Jews, receives the same sacred books, and has the same belief in the resurrection, both of the just and of the unjust; conformably to which he labours to preserve a conscience void of offence towards God and towards man.

Αἵρεσις properly denotes only the taking up of an opinion, whether well or ill founded; and sometimes it was applied to the *persons* who maintained the opinions. Hence many eminent Commentators here render it *sect*; a sense which the word does bear in other passages of Luke.

λατρεύω τῷ πατρῴῳ Θεῷ, πιστεύων πᾶσι τοῖς κατὰ τὸν νόμον καὶ τοῖς
g Dan. 12. 2. John 5. 29, 29. προφήταις γεγραμμένοις· [g] ἐλπίδα ἔχων εἰς τὸν Θεόν, — ἣν καὶ αὐτοὶ 15
οὗτοι προσδέχονται, — ἀνάστασιν μέλλειν ἔσεσθαι νεκρῶν, δικαίων τε
h Supra 23. 1. καὶ ἀδίκων. [h] Ἐν τούτῳ δὲ αὐτὸς ἀσκῶ, ἀπρόσκοπον συνείδησιν ἔχειν 16
i Supra 11. 29. Gal. 2. 10. Rom. 15. 25. πρὸς τὸν Θεὸν καὶ τοὺς ἀνθρώπους διαπαντός. [i] Δι᾽ ἐτῶν δὲ πλειό- 17
νων παρεγενόμην ἐλεημοσύνας ποιήσων εἰς τὸ ἔθνος μου καὶ προσ-
k Supra 21. 26, 27. φοράς· [k] ἐν αἷς εὗρόν με ἡγνισμένον ἐν τῷ ἱερῷ, οὐ μετὰ ὄχλου οὐδὲ 18
μετὰ θορύβου, τινὲς [δὲ] ἀπὸ τῆς Ἀσίας Ἰουδαῖοι· οὓς ‡ δεῖ ἐπὶ σοῦ 19
παρεῖναι καὶ κατηγορεῖν, εἴ τι ἔχοιεν πρός με. ἢ αὐτοὶ οὗτοι εἰπάτω- 20
σαν, [εἴ] τι εὗρον ἐν ἐμοὶ ἀδίκημα, στάντος μου ἐπὶ τοῦ συνεδρίου,
l Supra 23. 6. & 26. 20. [l] ἢ περὶ μιᾶς ταύτης φωνῆς, ἧς ἔκραξα ἑστὼς ἐν αὐτοῖς· Ὅτι περὶ 21
ἀναστάσεως νεκρῶν ἐγὼ κρίνομαι σήμερον ὑφ᾽ ὑμῶν!

Ἀκούσας δὲ ταῦτα ὁ Φῆλιξ ἀνεβάλετο αὐτούς, ἀκριβέστερον εἰδὼς 22
τὰ περὶ τῆς ὁδοῦ, εἰπών· Ὅταν Λυσίας ὁ χιλίαρχος καταβῇ, διαγνώ-

But the context will here scarcely permit it, and it should seem that Paul means to take exception at the *invidious* sense which the word admitted; and in which it was used by his opponents; just as in our word *new-fangled*, which properly denotes only *what is newly taken*. That Luke and Josephus sometimes use the word in a *good* sense is no proof that that was the general acceptation. *Paul* (with whose phraseology we have here to do) always uses it in a *bad* sense, of an opinion taken up on slight grounds: and so does Peter. And this is here required by the words ὁδὸν and ὡς λέγουσι.

Τῷ πατρῴῳ Θεῷ is for τῷ Θεῷ τῶν πατέρων, as in v. 30. Gen. xxxii. 9, 10, and elsewhere. Of the phrase πάτρῳοι Θεοὶ the Commentators adduce many examples from the Classical writers. But the sense, in almost all the passages cited, is not *the Gods of any one's ancestors*, but the *Gods worshipped at any place*. A more apposite example may be found in Thucyd. ii. 71, where see my Note. As the privilege of worshipping their Θεὸς πάτρῳος had been secured to the Jews by many Imperial charters, so Paul hereby throws himself under the protection of the Roman laws.

15. δικαίων τε καὶ ἀδίκων.] For that was the *general* opinion of the Pharisees; though some of them believed only in a resurrection of the *just*. The opinion, however, (as Drus. and Kuinoel show,) was new and not extensively held.

16. ἀσκῶ.] This is to be taken intransitively; of which use the Commentators adduce several examples; and others may be seen in Bp. Blomfield's Note on Æschyl. Prom. 1102.

— ἀπρόσκοπον συνείδησιν.] Ἀπρόσκ. is one of those adjectives which admit either an active or a passive sense. The *former* is here adopted. What is properly applicable only to the *person* acting, or to the *action*, is applied to the *conscience*, as being the regulator of the conduct.

17. Here the Apostle answers to the *third* point of accusation, *profanation of the Temple*. Δι᾽ ἐτῶν πλειόνων, "after very many years;" of which sense of διὰ I have cited several examples in Recens. Syn. Ποιεῖν ἐλεημοσύνας is an *Hellenistic* phrase signifying to *give* alms. Here, however, it must, from circumstances, be interpreted to *present* them. Paul hints that as his purpose was both benevolent and pious; he was unlikely to have been guilty of profanation of the Temple.

18. ἡγνισμένον] "living in votive sanctimony." Τινὲς δέ. So the Erasmian and Stephanic Edd. read. But the δὲ (which is not found in the Ed. Princ. and some other early Edd.) was cancelled by Beza, though recalled by Griesb., but, as I have proved at large in Recens. Synop., very uncritically.

19. δεῖ.] It is not easy to determine the true reading here. Several MSS. and most Editions from Beza downwards, have ἔδει, which is thought to be supported by some Fathers and Versions. If this were a matter wherein the proprietas linguæ could decide, there would, I think, be no hesitation in preferring ἔδει; notwithstanding what Matthæi says, that *one is as good Greek as the other*; which may be doubted. See Bornem.

20. αὐτοὶ οὗτοι] "these very persons." Εἰ before τι is not found in very many MSS., Versions, and early Edd., and is cancelled by most Editors from Wets. to Vat.; rightly, it should seem; for we can far better account for its insertion than for its omission. Ἀδίκημα may be rendered *misdemeanour* or *offence*. So xviii. 14. εἰ ἀδίκημά τι ἢ ῥᾳδιούργημα.

21. ἢ] "otherwise than." In περὶ μιᾶς ταύτης φωνῆς there is, as Beza remarks, a delicate irony, q. d. except for this one speech, [if they can make an offence of *that*]. See 2 Cor. xii. 13.

22. ἀνεβάλετο αὐτοὺς] "*ampliavit illos*," put off the decision of their causes. Ἀναβ. signifies to defer a thing (ανα) to another time, as ἀνατιθέναι τὸ ἔργον. It has almost always an Accusative of the *thing*, and is sometimes used *absolutely*. But when the business deferred is not our own, but another's, we may be said figuratively to put *him* off. And so here, and sometimes in the later Classical writers.

— ἀκριβέστερον εἰδὼς τ. π. τ. ὁ.] The best interpretation of these words is that of our common Version and Wets. "having become better acquainted with Christianity," namely from the account just given by St. Paul, as well as from what he had learnt during his residence at Cæsarea. Ἡ ὁδὸς seems to have been the name given to the sect of Christians by the Jews; though by the Gentiles they were generally called Χριστιανοί. Διαγνώσομαι τὰ καθ᾽ ὑμᾶς may be rendered, "I will

23 σομαι τὰ καθ᾽ ὑμᾶς· [m] διαταξάμενός τε τῷ ἑκατοντάρχῃ τηρεῖσθαι m Infra 27. 3. & 28. 16.
τὸν Παῦλον, ἔχειν τε ἄνεσιν· καὶ μηδένα κωλύειν τῶν ἰδίων αὐτοῦ
ὑπηρετεῖν ἢ προσέρχεσθαι αὐτῷ.
24 Μετὰ δὲ ἡμέρας τινὰς παραγενόμενος ὁ Φῆλιξ σὺν Δρουσίλλῃ τῇ
γυναικὶ [αὐτοῦ,] οὔσῃ Ἰουδαίᾳ, μετεπέμψατο τὸν Παῦλον, καὶ ἤκουσεν
25 αὐτοῦ περὶ τῆς εἰς Χριστὸν πίστεως. Διαλεγομένου δὲ αὐτοῦ περὶ
δικαιοσύνης καὶ ἐγκρατείας καὶ τοῦ κρίματος τοῦ μέλλοντος ἔσεσθαι,
ἔμφοβος γενόμενος ὁ Φῆλιξ ἀπεκρίθη· Τὸ νῦν ἔχον, πορεύου· καιρὸν

decide the [matter at issue] between you." See more in Rec. Syn. and Bp. Pearce.

23. τῷ ἑκατοντ.] Render, "the centurion," that one of the two centurions sent from Jerusalem with Paul; one of whom (xxiii. 31.) had left him at Antipatris; the other had gone with him to Cæsarea, there to remain in charge of him.

— τηρεῖσθαι and ἔχειν ἄνεσιν in this verse, are of such opposite senses, that it would seem they cannot be conjoined. Hence most recent Commentators place no stop after ἄνεσιν, but connect ἔχειν ἄνεσιν with the words *following*, which they suppose exegetical of these. See Kuin. This, however, is scarcely satisfactory; and the ἔχειν seems to have a signification more *special*. There can be little doubt but that the words are to be taken with the *preceding*, as they were by the ancients and the earlier modern Commentators. And if so, ἔχειν τε ἄνεσιν must be meant to *qualify* the τηρεῖσθαι: and the sense must be, "He ordered him to be kept in hold, and [at the same time] to enjoy some relaxation [of his confinement]; namely, as some Commentators think, by being kept ἐν φυλακῇ ἀδέσμῳ. But that is irreconcilable with xxvi. 25, and perhaps inconsistent with the due security of his person, as his friends were allowed to visit him. It should rather seem, that what is meant by the ἄνεσις is the changing the close custody of a *prison* into the milder durance of the *custodia militaris*, on which see Note supra xxii. 29. Of the phrase ἔχειν ἄνεσιν in this sense an example is cited by Loesner from Philo; and δοῦναι ἄνεσιν occurs in 2 Chron. xxiii. 15, and 3 Esdr. iv. 62. This view of the sense is supported by the authority of the Pesch. Syr. Version, in which the words are closely connected with the preceding; and Schaaf renders, "Præcepit Centurioni ut servarent Paulum in quiete." Rather it should be, "præcepit Centurioni ut *custodiret* Paulum cum *lenitate*;" for ܢܝܚܐ may very well bear that sense, since its *feminine* form ܢܝܚܘܬܐ has it at Eph. iv. 2. Col. iii. 12, and 2 Cor. x. 1. As to ܒ in this sense, that is almost its perpetual use. And moreover, the masculine form has a *similar* sense at 2 Cor. vii. 7, and 1 Tim. vi. 17. The words καὶ μηδένα — αὐτῷ are not meant to *explain* the preceding order, but to add *another* privilege, which did not belong to the *custodia militaris*, but solely appertained to the *custodia libera*, or the φυλακὴ ἄδεσμος.

I must not omit to state, that instead of τὸν Παῦλον ten MSS. and some inferior Versions have αὐτὸν, which was preferred by Mill and Beng., and has been edited by Griesb., Tittm., and Vat.; but rashly. For though it may *seem* countenanced by a Critical reason, yet it is, in fact, *not*; since if αὐτὸν were the original reading, we can scarcely conceive why such a marginal gloss as τὸν Παῦλον should have been so prevalent, as to eject the true reading in *all the* MSS. *but ten*. So very wide difference in MS. authority between the two readings should make us rather suspect that αὐτὸν came from the margin, where it was probably placed to express that it should be supplied *per ellipsin* at ἔχειν. The remark, it may be supposed, was made by those who did not perceive the true *connection* and *construction*.

— τῶν ἰδίων] i. e. "all persons in any way connected with him, whether as relations or friends." Of which sense Loesn. adduces some examples from Philo. Ὑπηρετεῖν is for διακονεῖν.

24. αὐτοῦ.] This is omitted in several MSS. and Theophyl., and is cancelled by Griesb. and others; perhaps rightly; for in several MSS. ἰδίᾳ is read; and in some both ἰδίᾳ and αὐτοῦ. Thus there is some reason to suspect *both* of them to be from the margin. The words οὔσῃ Ἰουδαίᾳ seem meant to assign the *reason* why Felix brought Drusilla with him. She, being a Jewess, would take some interest in the question as to the truth of the Christian religion. By ἤκουσεν αὐτοῦ περὶ is, I conceive, meant "heard what he had to say concerning."

25. δικαιοσύνης καὶ ἐγκρ.] These are especially mentioned, both as being the *principal* of the moral duties (which the Apostle, doubtless, treated on, with reference to their being necessary to prepare for the judgment to come) and because his auditors were especially *deficient* in those duties. For by ἐγκράτεια he meant not *temperance*, but *continence*, or *chastity*; of which use Kuin. adduces one example from Xenoph., and I have in Recens. Synop. added two others, from Joseph. and Sext. Emp. Of τοῦ κρίματος τοῦ μ. the sense is not well expressed, either in our common English Version, or that of Wakefield; the former not expressing the Article, and the latter rendering, "*a* judgment to come." The τοῦ seems to have reference to the doctrine, as being *well known* to Drusilla, and not unknown to Felix.

— ἔμφοβος γενόμενος.] On the *nature* and *extent* of this feeling, some difference of opinion exists. See Rec. Syn. Here it is well to avoid the *two extremes*, either of supposing Felix's feeling to have been that of *trembling terror* (as does Doddr.), or (as Bp. Pearce, and most of the recent foreign Commentators), simply an *uneasy feeling*. For the *former* view there is no warrant in the phraseology; since though the words ἔκφοβος and ἔντρομος are joined in Heb. xii. 21, yet ἔντρομος is a *stronger* term than ἔκφοβος, which is merely an *adjective* formed on the phrase ἐν φόβῳ εἶναι. And as little is to be found in the context for the *latter*; for considering the *subject*, (which could not fail to embrace the performance of the *moral duties* in their principal branches) of *justice* and

δὲ μεταλαβὼν, μετακαλέσομαί σε· ἅμα [δὲ] καὶ ἐλπίζων, ὅτι χρήματα 26
δοθήσεται αὐτῷ ὑπὸ τοῦ Παύλου, ὅπως λύσῃ αὐτόν· διὸ καὶ πυκνό-
a Infra 25. 14. *τερον αὐτὸν μεταπεμπόμενος ὡμίλει αὐτῷ.* [a] *Διετίας δὲ πληρωθείσης* 27
ἔλαβε διάδοχον ὁ Φῆλιξ Πόρκιον Φῆστον· θέλων τε χάριτας καταθέ-
σθαι τοῖς Ἰουδαίοις ὁ Φῆλιξ, κατέλιπε τὸν Παῦλον δεδεμένον.

XXV. *ΦΗΣΤΟΣ οὖν ἐπιβὰς τῇ ἐπαρχίᾳ, μετὰ τρεῖς ἡμέρας ἀνέβη* 1
εἰς Ἱεροσόλυμα ἀπὸ Καισαρείας. Ἐνεφάνισαν δὲ αὐτῷ ὁ ἀρχιερεὺς καὶ 2
οἱ πρῶτοι τῶν Ἰουδαίων κατὰ τοῦ Παύλου, καὶ παρεκάλουν αὐτὸν,
αἰτούμενοι χάριν κατ' αὐτοῦ, ὅπως μεταπέμψηται αὐτὸν εἰς Ἱερουσαλὴμ, 3
ἐνέδραν ποιοῦντες ἀνελεῖν αὐτὸν κατὰ τὴν ὁδόν. Ὁ μὲν οὖν Φῆστος 4
ἀπεκρίθη, τηρεῖσθαι τὸν Παῦλον ἐν Καισαρείᾳ, ἑαυτὸν δὲ μέλλειν ἐν

temperance, to make us fit for the mercy of God in Christ — and that with reference to the solemn period when we must give an account of the deeds done in the body. Whether, indeed, the Apostle made his observations personally applicable to Felix and Drusilla (who were both notorious for their breach of both justice and continence), may be doubted; it being little probable that he would choose so far to overlook the rules of good manners. And certainly Felix could not fail to apply to his *own* case what was put *generally*. Hence, I apprehend, it was *not* (as has been generally supposed) his discoursing of the *last judgment* only that raised this alarm in the breast of Felix, but the necessary connection of that doctrine with his own notorious breach of the moral duties. So Bp. Sanderson in his Sermons ad Populum, p. 147, says: "The thing that made Felix tremble was that Paul's discourse fell upon those *special* vices wherein he was notably faulty, and were then clapped in close upon him."

— *τὸ νῦν ἔχον.*] Sub. *μέρος χρόνου* and *κατά*. An Attic and elegant form, meaning "for the present," of which the Commentators adduce many examples. I have in Recens. Synop. compared a similar dismission, from nearly the same cause, received by Plato from Dionysius, the tyrant of Sicily. *Καιρὸν μεταλαβὼν* is regarded as a Hellenistic phrase for *καιρὸν λαβὼν*, or *καιροῦ μεταλ.* Yet Kypke has adduced *one* example from Polyb. ii. 16. On the difference between this and the Classical idiom see Rec. Syn.

26. *ἅμα δὲ καὶ ἐλπίζων.*] This is taken by the Commentators as a participle for the verb *ἤλπισε*. But it may, in construction, be suspended on the *ἀπεκρίθη* preceding; which has dependent on it *two* expressions, denoting the *two causes* which induced Felix to give Paul his dismission; 1. because he felt uneasiness and apprehension, and 2 because it was his *policy* to dismiss him and send for him again and again, in order to get a bribe to set him at liberty; for it appears from Joseph. Antiq. xx. 8, and Bell. ii. 141. that corruption of this kind was then common. And Felix might suppose that as Paul was one of the leaders of a sect disposed to raise money for any pious purpose, a considerable sum might be raised for his release. The *δὲ* is omitted in very many MSS. and some Versions, and early Edd., and is cancelled by Wets., Matth., Griesb., Knapp, and Tittm. It *may* have been a mere emendation on the *καὶ* following; but I cannot approve of its being *cancelled*, because of such passages as Thucyd. i. 25, 3. *ὑπεδέξαντο τὴν τιμωρίαν, νομίζοντες*, &c. *ἅμα δὲ καὶ μίσει*, &c.

27. *διετίας πληρωθ.*] Namely, from Paul's imprisonment by Lysias. It is truly observed by Lightf., that the sacred writers often number by tacit or unnamed epochs, as in 2 Sam. xvi. 7. 2 Chron. xxii. 2. Ez. i. 1.

— *χάριτας καταθέσθαι τοῖς Ἰ.*] An elegant phrase, by which favours are considered as a *deposit*, to be taken up afterwards. The Commentators adduce many examples; and others may be seen in my Note on Thucyd. i. 33.

It was usual for Roman governors to confer *some* favours upon the people on vacating their post; and *one* of these, as we learn from Joseph., was a general gaol-delivery; probably given here, but the benefit of which Paul was denied, that a *greater* favour might be done to the Jews.

XXV. 1. *ἐπιβὰς τῇ ἐπαρχίᾳ.*] This should be rendered, "after entering upon his government." It may be observed, that *ἐπαρχία* was the name applied to the *larger* provinces, to which were sent Proprætors or Proconsuls; while the *smaller* ones were termed *ἐπιτροπαί*, and their Governors *ἐπίτροποι*, *Procuratores*. These, indeed, were little more than *collectors* of the *revenues*; though in some provinces they exercised the *judicial* functions, and indeed most of those held by the *ἔπαρχοι*. Now Judæa, from particular circumstances, was one of these. Hence it might be called *ἐπαρχία*; and so Josephus sometimes terms the Governor *ἔπαρχος*. Ἐπιβ. is a vox sol. de hac re.

2. *ἐνεφάνισαν*] "laid a charge before him." See Note supra xxiv. 1.

3. *αἰτούμενοι χάριν κατ' αὐτοῦ.*] There seems a harshness in this expression; which is indeed not found in some MSS. and Versions, where is read *παρ' αὐτοῦ*. But that is evidently a mere emendation. It is *better* to take *κατὰ* (as I proposed in Recens. Synop.) in the sense *concerning*. Yet even that is unnecessary; for we may consider the expression as a *breviloquentia* for *αἰτούμενοι χάριν ἐν δίκῃ τῇ κατ' αὐτοῦ*. And this is confirmed by the words at v. 15. *αἰτούμενοι δίκην κατ' αὐτοῦ*. In *ἐνέδραν ποιοῦντες* we need not, with many of the best Commentators, take *ποιοῦντες* in a Future sense; for the difficulty alleged by them may be removed by taking *ἐνέδ. π.* *figuratively*, for "having laid a plot," as in xxiii. 16. *ἀκούσας τὴν ἐνέδραν*, and often both in the O. T. and the Classical writers.

4. *ἀπεκρίθη τηρεῖσθαι.*] I have in Recens. Synop. shown that the sense cannot be (as most Translators and Commentators suppose), "he answered, ordering that Paul should be kept;" but, that by reason of the clause following, it can admit of no other sense than "He answered, that Paul was in

5 τάχει ἐκπορεύεσθαι. οἱ οὖν δυνατοὶ ἐν ὑμῖν, φησὶ, συγκαταβάντες, εἴ
6 τι ἐστὶν ἐν τῷ ἀνδρὶ τούτῳ, κατηγορείτωσαν αὐτοῦ. Διατρίψας δὲ ἐν
αὐτοῖς ἡμέρας οὐ πλείους ὀκτὼ, [ἢ δέκα] καταβὰς εἰς Καισάρειαν, τῇ
ἐπαύριον καθίσας ἐπὶ τοῦ βήματος, ἐκέλευσε τὸν Παῦλον ἀχθῆναι.
7 Παραγενομένου δὲ αὐτοῦ, περιέστησαν οἱ ἀπὸ Ἱεροσολύμων καταβεβη-
κότες Ἰουδαῖοι πολλὰ καὶ βαρέα αἰτιάματα φέροντες κατὰ τοῦ Παύλου,
8 ἃ οὐκ ἴσχυον ἀποδεῖξαι· [o] ἀπολογουμένου αὐτοῦ· Ὅτι οὔτε εἰς τὸν [o] Supra 24. 12. infra 28. 17.
νόμον τῶν Ἰουδαίων, οὔτε εἰς τὸ ἱερὸν, οὔτε εἰς Καίσαρά τι ἥμαρτον.
9 Ὁ Φῆστος δὲ, τοῖς Ἰουδαίοις θέλων χάριν καταθέσθαι, ἀποκριθεὶς τῷ
Παύλῳ εἶπε· Θέλεις εἰς Ἱεροσόλυμα ἀναβὰς, ἐκεῖ περὶ τούτων κρίνε-
10 σθαι ἐπ᾽ ἐμοῦ; Εἶπε δὲ ὁ Παῦλος· Ἐπὶ τοῦ βήματος Καίσαρος
ἑστώς εἰμι, οὗ με δεῖ κρίνεσθαι. Ἰουδαίους οὐδὲν ἠδίκησα, ὡς καὶ σὺ
11 κάλλιον ἐπιγινώσκεις· [p] εἰ μὲν γὰρ ἀδικῶ καὶ ἄξιον θανάτου πέπραχά [p] Supra 18. 14.
τι, οὐ παραιτοῦμαι τὸ ἀποθανεῖν· εἰ δὲ οὐδέν ἐστιν ὧν οὗτοι κατηγο-

confinement at Cæsarea;" meaning, that where his place of confinement was, and where the residence of the Procurator was, there his trial ought to be. This mode of taking the words is confirmed by the Peschito Syr. and the Vulg. At *ἐκπορεύεσθαι* there is an ellip. of *ἐκεῖ*, as often in verbs of motion. The blending of the oratio directa et obliqua is frequent in Luke.

5. *οἱ δυνατοί.*] The sense is, "the persons of consequence among you," the *οἱ πρῶτοι* just before. So the Syr. and Arab., and most of the best modern Commentators, who adduce many examples from Philo and Josephus. I add Thucyd. iii. 27. ii. 65. iii. 47. viii. 63.

6. *ἡμέρας — δέκα.*] There are few passages more perplexed by variety of reading than this. The common reading *ἡμ. πλείους ἢ δέκα* cannot well be defended; for its *external* authority is not great, and its *internal* very slender. Beza, Beng., and Grot. have seen that the context requires that the *οὐ*, which is found in many of the best MSS. inserted before *πλείους*, should be adopted. And so Beza edited; though the word was afterwards thrown out by Schmid, or the Elzevir Editor. Are we, then, to read, with Griesb., Knapp., and Tittm., *ἡμέρας οὐ πλείους ὀκτὼ ἢ δέκα*? I think not; for there is no proof that the ancients used such an idiom of what was *past* and *certain*. Besides, it will be difficult to account how *ὀκτὼ* could have been omitted; for I *suspect* that the reading of Griesb. is compounded of *two* readings — *ὀκτὼ* and *δέκα* — each found in the MSS., of which the true one is *ὀκτώ*; for which there is great authority in MSS., Versions, and early Editions. The mistake, I appprehend, arose from *itacism*, which would produce a var. lect. upon *ή* (8), namely, *ί* (10). If, however, the first mentioned objection to Griesbach's reading could be removed, I would receive it; for in *οὐ πλείους ἢ ἢ ί*, *one ἢ* might easily absorb the other. At present, I have edited as Wets. directs should be read, except that, instead of cancelling the words in question, I have left them in within brackets.

7. *αἰτιάματα.*] Several MSS. and early Edd. have *αἰτιώματα*, which is adopted by Wets., and edited by Griesb., Knapp, Lachmann, and Valpy; but wrongly: for there is no proof that such a word as *αἰτίωμα* ever existed; and it is so contrary to analogy, that it scarcely *could*; especially as it was not *needed*, *αἰτίαμα* being in use, as I have, in Recens. Synop., proved by examples from Thucyd., Eurip., Dio Cass., and Plutarch.

9. *θέλεις*, &c.] It does not appear that Festus knew any thing of the intended assassination of Paul, on the road between Cæsarea and Jerusalem. He might say this, partly to gratify the Jews (who, he saw, were so earnestly desirous to get Paul to Jerusalem), and partly because he was at a loss, as he pretended (v. 20), how to proceed in the case, and willing to shift the matter from himself; otherwise he could not but know, that a person who was *innocent at Cæsarea* could not be found *guilty at Jerusalem*; and he plainly saw that Paul was *innocent*. Why, then, did he not *acquit* him? Because he durst not disoblige the Jews. But Paul was so well acquainted with their temper, that he chose to trust himself to *Heathens* rather than to those of his own religion; and he had *reason* to suspect that Festus would *give him up*, rather than incur the displeasure of the Jews; so that his safest way was to *appeal* to *the Emperor*, as a *Roman Citizen*. (Markland.) Paul, as being a Roman citizen, whose cause had been brought into the President's court, could not be *compelled* to have his cause shifted to Jerusalem, to be tried by the Sanhedrim.

10. *τοῦ βήματος Κ.*] "Cæsar's Court;" for it might be so called, as being held by the President on the authority of Cæsar, and in his name. At *με δεῖ κρίνεσθαι* there is an ellip. of *μόνον*, alluding to what he well knew was their design, to have him tried by the Sanhedrim, subject to the President's confirmation, who, he hints by the words further on, *οὐδείς με δύναται χαρίσασθαι*, would give him up to their fury. (See v. 16.)

11. *εἰ μὲν γὰρ — ἀποθανεῖν.*] The sentence is expressed *populariter*, and the *γὰρ* has reference to a clause omitted. The sense may be thus represented: "For tried I desire to be, so that it be but at a proper tribunal; and if I be found guilty of any offence which by the Roman laws is punished with death, I shall not decline even death." *Οὐ παραιτοῦμαι τὸ ἀποθανεῖν* is an elegant and not unusual formula, of which the Commentators adduce many examples.

ροῦσί μου, οὐδείς με δύναται αὐτοῖς χαρίσασθαι. Καίσαρα ἐπικαλοῦ-
μαι. Τότε ὁ Φῆστος συλλαλήσας μετὰ τοῦ συμβουλίου, ἀπεκρίθη· 12
Καίσαρα ἐπικέκλησαι; ἐπὶ Καίσαρα πορεύσῃ.
Ἡμερῶν δὲ διαγενομένων τινῶν, Ἀγρίππας ὁ Βασιλεὺς καὶ Βερνίκη 13
q Supra 24. 27. *κατήντησαν εἰς Καισάρειαν, ἀσπασόμενοι τὸν Φῆστον.* q *Ὡς δὲ πλείους* 14
ἡμέρας διέτριβον ἐκεῖ, ὁ Φῆστος τῷ βασιλεῖ ἀνέθετο τὰ κατὰ τὸν
Παῦλον, λέγων· Ἀνήρ τις ἐστὶ καταλελειμμένος ὑπὸ Φήλικος δέσμιος,
περὶ οὗ, γενομένου μου εἰς Ἱεροσόλυμα, ἐνεφάνισαν οἱ ἀρχιερεῖς καὶ οἱ 15
r Deut. 17. 4. *πρεσβύτεροι τῶν Ἰουδαίων, αἰτούμενοι κατ' αὐτοῦ δίκην·* r *πρὸς οὓς* 16
ἀπεκρίθην, ὅτι οὐκ ἔστιν ἔθος Ῥωμαίοις χαρίζεσθαί τινα ἄνθρωπον
εἰς ἀπώλειαν, πρὶν ἢ ὁ κατηγορούμενος κατὰ πρόσωπον ἔχοι τοὺς
κατηγόρους, τόπον τε ἀπολογίας λάβοι περὶ τοῦ ἐγκλήματος. Συνελ- 17
θόντων οὖν αὐτῶν ἐνθάδε, ἀναβολὴν μηδεμίαν ποιησάμενος, τῇ ἑξῆς
καθίσας ἐπὶ τοῦ βήματος, ἐκέλευσα ἀχθῆναι τὸν ἄνδρα· περὶ οὗ στα- 18
θέντες οἱ κατήγοροι οὐδεμίαν αἰτίαν ἐπέφερον ὧν ὑπενόουν ἐγώ· ζη- 19
τήματα δέ τινα περὶ τῆς ἰδίας δεισιδαιμονίας εἶχον πρὸς αὐτὸν, καὶ
περί τινος Ἰησοῦ τεθνηκότος, ὃν ἔφασκεν ὁ Παῦλος ζῆν. Ἀπορούμενος 20
δὲ ἐγὼ εἰς τὴν περὶ τούτου ζήτησιν, ἔλεγον, εἰ βούλοιτο πορεύεσθαι εἰς
Ἱερουσαλὴμ, κἀκεῖ κρίνεσθαι περὶ τούτων. Τοῦ δὲ Παύλου ἐπικαλε- 21
σαμένου τηρηθῆναι αὐτὸν εἰς τὴν τοῦ Σεβαστοῦ διάγνωσιν, ἐκέλευσα

— *οὐδείς — χαρίσασθαι.*] With this use of *χαρίσασθαι*, to signify "give up [for trial] (which was equivalent to condemnation and death; so infra v. 16. *χαρίζεσθαι εἰς ἀπώλειαν*) I would compare a similar one in Cicero's Oration pro Cœlio. v. 1. Here we have a delicate mode of censuring *Festus* for wishing to do a favour to the Jews at the Apostle's expense, and meant to hint to him that he has not the *power*. The expression *δύναται*, Grot. observes, refers to *lawful right*, as much as to say, "no one can, *salvo jure*."

— *Καίσαρα ἐπικαλοῦμαι.*] On the nature and extent of this privilege of a Roman citizen's appealing unto Cæsar in extreme cases, see Rec. Syn., where it is shown that the appeal in question was a *privilege*, which could not (as Grot. and Kuin. imagine) have been *disallowed* by Festus.

12. *τοῦ συμβουλίου.*] The *πάρεδροι*, or *assessores* of the President, something like the *σύμβουλοι* of the Lacedæmonian kings and generals mentioned in Thucyd. See Casaub. Exerc. Antibar. p. 137.

— *Καίσαρα ἐπικέκλησαι;*] Some Editors make the sentence *declarative*. But that, I think, weakens the spirit of the words, and the interrogation is confirmed by the Syriac and Vulg.

13. *ἀσπασόμενοι τ. Φ.*] "to congratulate and pay their respects to." See 2 Kings x. 13.

14. *ἀνέθετο τὰ κατὰ Π.*] "related the circumstances of Paul's case," thus referring it to his better judgment. With the *τὰ κατὰ τὸν Π.* I would compare Thucyd. iii. 68. *τὰ κατὰ Πλαταίαν.*

15. *δίκην*] for *καταδίκην*, judgment, i. e. condemnation and punishment; as in 2 Thess. i. 9. A signification occurring in the Classical writers, from whom Kuin. adduces several examples.

16. *χαρίζεσθαι — ἀπώλειαν.*] A brief manner of expression, of which the sense is, "to give up any one to condemnation and destruction (i. e. capital punishment) out of favour to another." So Seneca says damnare aliquem gratiâ scil. alicujus, and *ἀπώλεια* is so used in Hist. of Bel and Dr. v. 41. *τοὺς δὲ αἰτίους τῆς ἀπωλείας.* The sense of *τόπον ἀπολογίας λάβοι* is, "and shall have opportunity for exculpating himself." This sense of *τόπος* indeed often occurs with *διδόναι*, but very rarely with *λαμβάνειν*.

17. *ἀναβολὴν μ. ποιησάμενος*] "making no delay." An elegant phrase. So Thucyd. ii. 42, 4. *ἀναβολὴν τοῦ δεινοῦ ἐποιήσατο.*

18. *περὶ οὗ.*] This must be construed with *οὐδ' αἰτίαν ἐπέφερον*, and *ὧν ὑπενόουν* is for [*ἐκείνων*] ἃ ὑπεν. scil. *αἰτίαν ὑπενεχθῆναι.* Festus might think it was a charge of sedition. *Ἐπιφέρειν αἰτίαν* is a frequent phrase in the best Greek writers, corresponding to the *crimen inferre* of the Roman ones.

19. *ζητήματα*] "subjects for discussion and controversy." *Δεισιδαιμονίας* here denotes not *superstition*, but, as the best Commentators have been long agreed, *religion*. Indeed, the word is always used in a *good* sense in the N. T., as it often is in Josephus.

20. *ἀπορούμενος — ζήτησιν.*] The *τούτου* I would not (with some) refer, to the question about Jesus and his resurrection; but, by an ellipsis of *πράγματος*, to the whole matter in debate, the religion itself. By *τούτων* just after understand *ἐγκλημάτων*. "Here (observes Beza) Festus dissembles his offence, yet *convicts himself*: for why did he not acquit an accused person against whom nothing had been proved? For the same reason that he wished to have him removed for trial to Jerusalem; — namely, to *gratify the Jews*.

21. *ἐπικαλ. τηρηθῆναι.* At *τηρ.* sub. *εἰς τό.* Or *ἐπικαλ.* may be rendered "making his appeal;" which includes the sense "*claiming*." *Διάγνωσιν*, cognitionem, "determination." It has reference to the sense *cause* involved in *αὐτόν*.

— *Σεβαστοῦ*] Augustus. The surname borne

22 τηρεῖσθαι αὐτὸν, ἕως οὗ πέμψω αὐτὸν πρὸς Καίσαρα. Ἀγρίππας δὲ
πρὸς τὸν Φῆστον ἔφη· Ἐβουλόμην καὶ αὐτὸς τοῦ ἀνθρώπου ἀκοῦσαι.
ὁ δέ· Αὔριον, φησὶν, ἀκούσῃ αὐτοῦ.
23 Τῇ οὖν ἐπαύριον ἐλθόντος τοῦ Ἀγρίππα καὶ τῆς Βερνίκης μετὰ πολλῆς φαντασίας, καὶ εἰσελθόντων εἰς τὸ ἀκροατήριον, σύν τε τοῖς χιλιάρχοις καὶ ἀνδράσι τοῖς κατ᾽ ἐξοχὴν οὖσι τῆς πόλεως, καὶ κελεύσαντος
24 τοῦ Φήστου, ἤχθη ὁ Παῦλος. καί φησιν ὁ Φῆστος· Ἀγρίππα βασιλεῦ, καὶ πάντες οἱ συμπαρόντες ἡμῖν ἄνδρες, θεωρεῖτε τοῦτον, περὶ οὗ
πᾶν τὸ πλῆθος τῶν Ἰουδαίων ἐνέτυχόν μοι ἔν τε Ἱεροσολύμοις καὶ
25 ἐνθάδε, ἐπιβοῶντες μὴ δεῖν ζῇν αὐτὸν μηκέτι. [a] Ἐγὼ δὲ καταλαβόμενος [a] Supra 23. 9. infra 28. 31.
μηδὲν ἄξιον θανάτου αὐτὸν πεπραχέναι, καὶ αὐτοῦ δὲ τούτου ἐπικαλε-
26 σαμένου τὸν Σεβαστὸν, ἔκρινα πέμπειν αὐτόν. Περὶ οὗ ἀσφαλές τι
γράψαι τῷ Κυρίῳ οὐκ ἔχω· διὸ προήγαγον αὐτὸν ἐφ᾽ ὑμῶν, καὶ μάλιστα ἐπὶ σοῦ, βασιλεῦ Ἀγρίππα, ὅπως, τῆς ἀνακρίσεως γενομένης, σχῶ
27 τι γράψαι. Ἄλογον γάρ μοι δοκεῖ, πέμποντα δέσμιον μὴ καὶ τὰς κατ᾽
αὐτοῦ αἰτίας σημᾶναι.
1 XXVI. ἈΓΡΙΠΠΑΣ δὲ πρὸς τὸν Παῦλον ἔφη· Ἐπιτρέπεταί σοι
ὑπὲρ σεαυτοῦ λέγειν. Τότε ὁ Παῦλος ἀπελογεῖτο ἐκτείνας τὴν χεῖρα·
2 Περὶ πάντων ὧν ἐγκαλοῦμαι ὑπὸ Ἰουδαίων, βασιλεῦ Ἀγρίππα, ἥγημαι

by all the Emperors from Cæsar Octavianus, who first assumed it.

22. ἐβουλόμην — ἀκοῦσαι.] Abp. Newcome wrongly renders, "I desire to hear;" the Vulg. and Erasm. still worse, "volebam." The Syr. and almost all other Versions and Translations rightly render *vellem*, "I could wish." Yet there is *not*, as Camer. imagines, an ellip. of ἂν; for, as I have fully proved on Thucyd. iv. 54, 3. (Ed. and Transl.) Imperfects Indicative are often put for Pluperfects Subjunctive; of which I have adduced numerous examples. The sense therefore is, "I could have wished to have heard him myself;" a modest way of saying, "I could wish to hear him." Such a curiosity in Agrippa was very natural.

23. φαντασίας] "pomp," state; literally, *display*. Of the word and the sense several examples are adduced by the Commentators, as Hippocrat. ποιέειν μηδὲν περιέργως, μηδὲ μετὰ φαντασίας. Heliodor. φαντασίας τῶν δορυφόρων, καὶ κόμπου τῆς ἄλλης θεραπείας, which exactly represents the sort of pomp here meant. The word is, indeed, susceptible both of a good and bad sense; but there is no reason to here suppose the *latter*, with some Commentators. Ἀκροατήριον is explained *judgment-hall*, as *auditorium* is often used in the Latin. If such be the sense, it is a Latinism. As, however, there was no *trial*, it should rather seem to mean "a private examination room," where accused persons had a hearing before they were committed to prison. Τοῖς κατ᾽ ἐξοχὴν οὖσι is for ἐξόχοις, as ἡ ζωὴ ἡ κατ᾽ εὐσέβειαν for εὐσεβής.

24. οἱ συμπαρόντες ἡ. ἄ.] equivalent to ξυμπάρεδροι, for there is reference not only to the σύμβουλοι mentioned supra v. 12, but others; namely, persons of consideration and friends of the President, to whom he showed the courtesy of giving them a place on the bench, as Wets. shows; referring to Joseph. Ant. xvi. 11, 2. 4. τὸν βασιλεύοντα νῦν ἡμῶν καὶ σοὶ παρακαθεζόμενον. xvii. 5, 3.

— ἐνέτυχόν μοι] "have made urgent application to me." The word properly signifies "to address one's self to, hold converse with any one;" and it is usually *implied*, that the purpose is some request or petition. And this is sometimes, as here, expressed by a preposition, ex. gr. ὑπέρ. So also in Polyb. iv. 76. Theophr. Char. 1. 2. Wisd. viii. 21. xvi. 28. ἐνέτυχον τῷ Κυρίῳ καὶ ἐδεήθην αὐτοῦ. See Note on Heb. vii. 25.

26. τῷ Κυρίῳ.] Render, "to [my] Sovereign." A title of the Emperors, corresponding to the Roman *Dominus*, which is said to have been rejected as invidious by Augustus and Tiberius. It had afterwards, however, been used by succeeding Emperors, though instances of its use so early as this are very rare. Its being employed in *conversation* is much more than if it had occurred in any public writing. This force of Κύριος, by which it means Sovereign, is, I conceive, communicated by the *Article*, which is taken κατ᾽ ἐξοχὴν, to denote the Supreme Lord. So in an Inscription found at Smyrna: Καὶ ὅσα ἐπετύχομεν παρὰ τοῦ Κυρίου Καίσαρος Ἀδριανοῦ.

— ἀνακρίσεως.] This does not denote a regular trial, but a previous examination in order to trial; a sense often found in the Civilians, from whom Grot. adduces several examples; and Schleusn. refers to Taylor on Demosth. iii. 55. and cites 3 Macc. vii. 4. ἄνευ πάσης ἀνακρίσεως καὶ ἐξετάσεως.

XXVI. 1. ἀπελογεῖτο] In this is implied οὕτως, or λέγων. Ἐκτείνας τὴν χεῖρα is said *graphicè*, such being the attitude for a set speech.

2. ἥγημαι ἐμαυτὸν μακάριον, &c.] Here we have a beautiful προθεράπευσις (i. e. previous conciliation), as the ancient Rhetoricians called it, such as we find at xvii. 22. Pricæus compares a similar commencement of an oration before the Emperor

ἐμαυτὸν μακάριον μέλλων ἀπολογεῖσθαι ἐπὶ σοῦ σήμερον· μάλιστα 3
γνώστην ὄντα σε πάντων τῶν κατὰ Ἰουδαίους ἐθῶν τε καὶ ζητημάτων.
διὸ δέομαί σου, μακροθύμως ἀκοῦσαί μου.
Τὴν μὲν οὖν βίωσίν μου τὴν ἐκ νεότητος, τὴν ἀπ᾽ ἀρχῆς γενομένην 4
ἐν τῷ ἔθνει μου ἐν Ἱεροσολύμοις ἴσασι πάντες οἱ Ἰουδαῖοι, [t] προγινώ- 5
σκοντές με ἄνωθεν, (ἐὰν θέλωσι μαρτυρεῖν,) ὅτι κατὰ τὴν ἀκριβεστάτην
αἵρεσιν τῆς ἡμετέρας θρησκείας ἔζησα Φαρισαῖος. [u] Καὶ νῦν ἐπ᾽ ἐλ- 6
πίδι τῆς πρὸς τοὺς πατέρας ἐπαγγελίας γενομένης ὑπὸ τοῦ Θεοῦ
ἕστηκα κρινόμενος, εἰς ἣν τὸ δωδεκάφυλον ἡμῶν ἐν ἐκτενείᾳ νύκτα καὶ 7
ἡμέραν λατρεῦον ἐλπίζει καταντῆσαι· περὶ ἧς ἐλπίδος ἐγκαλοῦμαι,
βασιλεῦ Ἀγρίππα, ὑπὸ τῶν Ἰουδαίων. Τί; ἄπιστον κρίνεται παρ᾽ 8
ὑμῖν, εἰ ὁ Θεὸς νεκροὺς ἐγείρει; [x] Ἐγὼ μὲν οὖν ἔδοξα ἐμαυτῷ πρὸς 9

t Supra 23. 6. Phil. 3. 5. u Gen. 3. 15. & 22. 18. & 26. 4. & 49. 10. Deut. 18. 15. 2 Sam. 7. 12. Psal. 132. 11. Isa. 4. 2. & 7. 14. & 9. 6. & 40. 10. Jer. 23. 5. & 33. 14. Ezek. 34. 23. & 37. 24. Dan. 9. 24. Mich. 7. 20. supra 24. 15, 21. x Supra 8. 3. & 9. 1. & 22. 4. 1 Cor. 15. 9. Gal. 1. 13. 1 Tim. 1. 13.

Maximus, by Apuleius, "Gratulor quòd mihi copia et facultas, te Judice, obtigit, purgandæ apud imperitos Philosophiæ, et probandi mei." And Wets. compares Themist. Orat. p. 233. Ἐγὼ δὲ ἐμαυτὸν εὐδαίμονα ὑπολαμβάνω, ὅτι σε κηρύττειν ἔλαχον οἱ ἐμοὶ λόγοι.

3. *γνώστην*] for *ἐπιστάμενον* or *εἰδότα*, which are, indeed, found in some MSS. but are glosses. The Commentators regard *γνώστην ὄντα σε* as Accusatives absolute, of which they adduce examples. See also Elsm. on Eurip. Heracl. 693. It is however as well to account for them on the principle of *anacoluthon*. By the *ἔθη* are meant the *institutes*, *laws*, and *rites* of the Jews; and by the *ζητήματα*, the *questions*, which arose upon the *interpretation* of those laws, &c. That this compliment was not unmerited has been shown at large by Lardner.

— *μακροθύμως*] "patiently." See xxiv. 4. It is judiciously observed by Chrysost. that he says *δέομαί σου μακροθύμως ἀκοῦσαί μου*, since he was going to speak of *himself*, (which is always invidious), and was about to deliver a somewhat long speech.

4. *βίωσιν*] "mode of life." A word occurring nowhere else but in the Preface to Ecclus.: *διὰ τῆς ἐννόμου βιώσεως*. and in Ps. 38. 6. Symm.

5. *θρησκείας*] *religion*, as in James i. 27. The word, like *δεισιδαιμονία*, was, however, used by the Classical writers to denote *superstition*.

6. *ἐπ᾽ ἐλπίδι — τοῦ Θεοῦ.*] Commentators are not agreed on what is meant by *ἐλπίδι*. Chrysost. and most of the earlier *modern* Commentators understand *the hope of the resurrection of the dead*. So also Grot., Hammond, Whitby, Pearce, Doddr., Newc., and others, who appeal to Acts xxiii. 6. xxiv. 15. But almost all the later Commentators, as Michaelis, Wakef., Kuin., &c., think this refuted by v. 7. and explain it of the hope of the *Messiah*. Whitby, indeed, strenuously encounters this interpretation; but not, I conceive, successfully. At least this cannot be meant exclusively; for, as Mr. Scott says, "it is certain that the promise of a Redeemer was the most prominent part of the revelation made unto Abraham, Isaac, and Jacob, and the grand subject of prophecy; while the doctrine of the *resurrection* was not so fully revealed in the O. T. as in the New." "Thus the resurrection of Jesus (continues he) demonstrated that he was the promised Messiah, against all the unbelieving Jews; and the doctrine of the resurrection, against the Sadducees. The latter were instigated to persecute the Apostles, for "preaching through Jesus the resurrection of the dead;" (iv. 1—3. xxiii. 6—10.) the former, for preaching the very person whom they had crucified, as the Messiah, and as risen and 'exalted to be a Prince and Saviour.' Yet the whole nation expected a Messiah; and all, except the Sadducees, professed to believe the doctrine of the resurrection. In general, all that remained of the twelve tribes, wherever dispersed, hoped for the accomplishment of the promise concerning the Messiah, and a resurrection to eternal life through him." It may be added, that though the principal meaning of *ἐλπίδι* must be the promise of the *Messiah*, yet that *included* the promise of the *resurrection of the dead* by His means, as it was proved to have been fulfilled in Jesus Christ's rising from the grave: and as His resurrection was the pledge and proof of our own, it may here be admitted as a *secondary* sense; especially since St. Paul adds here (as at xxiii. 4.) *περὶ ἧς ἐλπίδος ἐγκαλοῦμαι ὑπὸ τῶν Ἰουδαίων*.

7. *δωδεκάφυλον.*] A periphrasis for "the Jewish nation," at which Sub. *ἔθνος*; I would compare *τὸ Ἑλληνικὸν* in Thucyd.

8. *τί; ἄπιστον — ἐγείρει;*] "What! is it considered by you as a thing incredible, that God is to raise the dead?" The older Commentators take the *τί* for *διὰ τί*, *why?* But the punctuation *τί* (found in the Greek Scholiasts), has been adopted by the best Commentators from Beza, downwards; and rightly; since it is far more spirited, and agreeable to Paul's style. See Rom. iii. 9. vi. 15. The *εἰ* may be rendered *siquidem*, "if [as is the case];" a sense often found both in the Classical and the Scriptural writers. The force of the argument is this: "You will not deny that God can raise the dead; why then deny that Jesus can have been raised, and thus be proved to be the Messiah."

9. *ἐγὼ μὲν οὖν ἔδοξα*, &c.] The transition is abrupt, and the connexion disputed. The sense seems to be this: "And remember, however positive you may be in your opinion, and however you may act according to the dictates of your conscience, you may be mistaken, and your conscience deceived. *I*, for instance, thought with myself (i. e. was self-persuaded), that I ought," &c. In *ἐμαυτῷ ἔδοξα* there is an idiom, (confined, however, to the *first* person, and almost always the *present* tense) of which many examples are adduced by Wets. *Δεῖν — πρᾶξαι*. The phraseology is idiomatical (of which many examples are adduced by Wets.) and may be rendered, "that

10 τὸ ὄνομα Ἰησοῦ τοῦ Ναζωραίου δεῖν πολλὰ ἐναντία πρᾶξαι. [y] ὃ καὶ [y Supra 8. 3.]
ἐποίησα ἐν Ἱεροσολύμοις· καὶ πολλοὺς τῶν ἁγίων ἐγὼ φυλακαῖς κατ-
έκλεισα, τὴν παρὰ τῶν ἀρχιερέων ἐξουσίαν λαβών· ἀναιρουμένων τε
11 αὐτῶν κατήνεγκα ψῆφον. Καὶ κατὰ πάσας τὰς συναγωγὰς πολλάκις
τιμωρῶν αὐτοὺς ἠνάγκαζον βλασφημεῖν· περισσῶς τε ἐμμαινόμενος
12 αὐτοῖς, ἐδίωκον ἕως καὶ εἰς τὰς ἔξω πόλεις. [z] Ἐν οἷς καὶ πορευόμενος [z Supra 9. 2. & 22. 6.]
εἰς τὴν Δαμασκὸν μετ᾽ ἐξουσίας καὶ ἐπιτροπῆς τῆς παρὰ τῶν ἀρχιε-
13 ρέων, [a] ἡμέρας μέσης κατὰ τὴν ὁδὸν εἶδον, βασιλεῦ, οὐρανόθεν ὑπὲρ [a Supra 9. 3.]
τὴν λαμπρότητα τοῦ ἡλίου, περιλάμψαν με φῶς καὶ τοὺς σὺν ἐμοὶ
14 πορευομένους. Πάντων δὲ καταπεσόντων ἡμῶν εἰς τὴν γῆν, ἤκουσα
φωνὴν λαλοῦσαν πρός με, καὶ λέγουσαν τῇ Ἑβραΐδι διαλέκτῳ· Σαοὺλ,
15 Σαοὺλ, τί με διώκεις; σκληρόν σοι πρὸς κέντρα λακτίζειν. Ἐγὼ δὲ
εἶπον· Τίς εἶ, κύριε; ὁ δὲ εἶπεν· Ἐγώ εἰμι Ἰησοῦς ὃν σὺ διώκεις.
16 ἀλλὰ ἀνάστηθι, καὶ στῆθι ἐπὶ τοὺς πόδας σου· εἰς τοῦτο γὰρ ὤφθην
σοι, προχειρίσασθαί σε ὑπηρέτην καὶ μάρτυρα ὧν τε εἶδες ὧν τε ὀφθή-

I was bound, in many ways, to oppose the doctrine of Jesus."

10. τῶν ἁγίων] "the Christians." The name the disciples then bore among *themselves*. Ἀναιρουμένων αὐτῶν. The sense is, "when they were being put to death;" for trial was, it seems, equivalent to execution. It is not necessary, (with many recent Commentators), to suppose this spoken with reference to *Stephen* only, and consequently a Rhetorical or Oratorical *amplification;* for though no other execution but Stephen's is *recorded* in the N. T., yet (as Doddr., Hasselaar, and Heinr. have shown), there is reason to think that many did occur; to which there are at least *allusions*. See viii. 1. ix. 31. xxii. 4. Κατήνεγκα ψῆφον is (as the best Commentators are agreed) to be taken, not in its *full* sense (for Paul was not a member of the Sanhedrim), but *metaphorically*, of *consenting* to and approving of what was done. Of this examples are adduced by the Commentators from the Classical writers.

11. κατὰ πάσας τὰς συν.] This is mentioned as being the *place* where the punishment was inflicted. Πολλάκις τιμωρῶν should be rendered "by chastising them continually." Βλασφημεῖν, i. e. the name of Christ, and thus to abandon the Christian religion and apostatize. That this was *then* done, we learn from this passage and Plin. Epist. xiii. 97. cited by Grot. And that it was still more practised *afterwards*, we find from Euseb. H. E. vi. 34. and a Homily of Hippolytus cited by Pricæus.

— τιμωρῶν αὐτοὺς ἠνάγκ. βλασφημεῖν.] The Christian converts were then, and still more afterwards, compelled by torture to pronounce certain forms expressive of abuse of Jesus, and consequently abandonment of his religion; as appears from Pliny's Epist. xiii. 97. Euseb. Hist. Eccl. vi. 34. and other passages cited in Recens. Synop. This was, however, but a repetition of the same cruelty that had been exercised by the Heathens towards the Jews, ἵνα βλασφημήσωσι τὸν νομοθέτην, ἢ φάγωσί τι τῶν ἀσυνήθων, as says Josephus Bell. ii. 8, 10.

— περισσῶς ἐμμαινόμενος.] A very strong expression, which may be rendered "and being exceedingly infuriate against them." Ἐμμαίνεσθαι is very rare; yet it is formed regularly from ἐμμανής. Εἰς τὰς ἔξω πόλεις, "to foreign cities;" referring to Damascus, though not, as we may imagine, to Damascus only.

13. ἡμέρας μέσης.] Sub. ἐπί. That the Attics used this expression occasionally (though more frequently μέσον ἡμέρας, or μεσούσης) is proved by Abresch. in loc. On this verse, and up to v. 15. see Note on ix. 5. seqq.

16. ἀνάστηθι.] Namely, as ready to execute my mandates.

— προχειρίσασθαι.] Sub. εἰς τό. Προχειρ. signifies to *select*, and, by implication, to appoint.

— ὑπηρέτην.] Since a person cannot be said to be a *minister* of what he has *seen*, though he may be a *witness*, Markl., with the Vulgate Translator, places a comma after ὑπηρέτην. The comma, however, is not quite essential to this sense; for it will only be necessary to keep ὑπηρέτ. distinct from ὧν τε εἶδες. Nay, as εἶναι must be understood both at ὑπηρ. and μάρτυρα, &c., propriety requires that there should be no comma. Ὑπηρέτην must be taken, by virtue of the context, to mean "my minister." So in Rom. xv. 16. Paul, adverting, as it seems, to this very circumstance, says it was done εἰς τὸ εἶναί με λειτουργὸν Ἰησοῦ X. εἰς τὰ ἔθνη.

— ὧν τε εἶδες — σοι.] The construction is rather unusual; but not such as to need the *conjectures* of Castalio and Markl. The first ὧν is for ἐκείνων ἅ. (see xxii. 15); and the second ὧν for ἐκείνων [καθ'] ἅ. Ὀφθήσομαι does *not* mean *revelabo tibi*, as Mor., Rosenm., Schleus., and Kuin. suppose. Nor is there any reason to abandon the common interpretation, "I shall be seen, or revealed;" i. e. will reveal myself to thee (see Isa. xxx. 2); which may be understood 1. of the *personal appearance* of Christ to Paul; 2. of the *revelations* which were vouchsafed to him. This view I find supported by the authority of the learned Thiele, in his Specimen Nov. Comm. in N. T. p. 8, where he shows that the general sense is, "eorum quæ et *vidisti* et *videbis* [me tibi monstrante]," meaning (he says) "et eorum in quibus tibi videbor," (i. e. conspiciendum me præbui) "et eorum quæ jam vidisti" (i. e. in quibus me tibi conspiciendum jam præbui.)

σομαί σοι, ἐξαιρούμενός σε ἐκ τοῦ λαοῦ καὶ τῶν ἐθνῶν, εἰς οὓς νῦν 17
b Isa. 35. 5. & 42. 7. & 60. 1. Eph. 1. 8. Col. 1. 13. 1 Pet. 2. 25. σε ἀποστέλλω, [b] ἀνοῖξαι ὀφθαλμοὺς αὐτῶν, τοῦ ἐπιστρέψαι ἀπὸ σκότους 18
εἰς φῶς καὶ τῆς ἐξουσίας τοῦ Σατανᾶ ἐπὶ τὸν Θεὸν, τοῦ λαβεῖν αὐτοὺς
ἄφεσιν ἁμαρτιῶν καὶ κλῆρον ἐν τοῖς ἡγιασμένοις, πίστει τῇ εἰς ἐμέ.
Ὅθεν, βασιλεῦ Ἀγρίππα, οὐκ ἐγενόμην ἀπειθὴς τῇ οὐρανίῳ ὀπτασίᾳ 19
c Supra 9. 20, 28. & 13. 14. & 22. 17, 21. Matt. 3. 8. [c] ἀλλὰ τοῖς ἐν Δαμασκῷ πρῶτον καὶ Ἱεροσολύμοις, εἰς πᾶσάν τε τὴν 20
χώραν τῆς Ἰουδαίας καὶ τοῖς ἔθνεσιν, ἀπήγγελλον μετανοεῖν, καὶ ἐπι-
d Supra 21. 30. στρέφειν ἐπὶ τὸν Θεὸν, ἄξια τῆς μετανοίας ἔργα πράσσοντας. [d] Ἕνεκα 21
τούτων με οἱ Ἰουδαῖοι συλλαβόμενοι ἐν τῷ ἱερῷ, ἐπειρῶντο διαχειρί-
σασθαι. Ἐπικουρίας οὖν τυχὼν τῆς παρὰ τοῦ Θεοῦ, ἄχρι τῆς ἡμέρας 22
ταύτης ἕστηκα μαρτυρόμενος μικρῷ τε καὶ μεγάλῳ, οὐδὲν ἐκτὸς λέγων
e Supra v. 18. 1 Cor. 15. 20. Col. 1. 18. Rev. 1. 5. Luke 2. 32. ὧν τε οἱ προφῆται ἐλάλησαν μελλόντων γίνεσθαι καὶ Μωϋσῆς, [e] εἰ 23
παθητὸς ὁ Χριστὸς, εἰ πρῶτος ἐξ ἀναστάσεως νεκρῶν φῶς μέλλει κατ-
αγγέλλειν τῷ λαῷ καὶ τοῖς ἔθνεσι. Ταῦτα δὲ αὐτοῦ ἀπολογουμένου, 24
ὁ Φῆστος μεγάλῃ τῇ φωνῇ ἔφη· Μαίνῃ, Παῦλε· τὰ πολλά σε γράμματα εἰς μανίαν περιτρέπει! Ὁ δέ· Οὐ μαίνομαι, φησι, κράτιστε 25
f John 18. 20. Φῆστε, ἀλλ' ἀληθείας καὶ σωφροσύνης ῥήματα ἀποφθέγγομαι. [f] Ἐπί- 26
σταται γὰρ περὶ τούτων ὁ βασιλεὺς, πρὸς ὃν καὶ παῤῥησιαζόμενος
λαλῶ· λανθάνειν γὰρ αὐτόν τι τούτων οὐ πείθομαι οὐδέν. οὐ γάρ
ἐστιν ἐν γωνίᾳ πεπραγμένον τοῦτο. Πιστεύεις, βασιλεῦ Ἀγρίππα, τοῖς 27

17. ἐξαιρούμενος.] The older Commentators explain this "delivering from," as vii. 34; xii. 11; xxiii. 27. Galat. i. 7. But that signification is scarcely permitted by the context, and, therefore, most of the later Interpreters rightly explain it "choosing," "separating for myself;" a signification occurring in Deut. xxxii. 8. Job xxxvi. 21; xlix. 7. and often in the Classical writers. This is very suitable to the context; for thus it would be a *further unfolding* of the sense at προχειρίσασθαί σε ὑπηρέτην. And it is confirmed by what was said by our Lord to Ananias: σκεῦος ἐκλογῆς μοί ἐστιν οὗτος τοῦ βαστάσαι, &c.

— εἰς οὓς.] This may be understood both of the Jews and the Gentiles: though the words which follow are more applicable to the *latter;* which interpretation is confirmed by the words νῦν ἀποστ.; for it appears that Paul was, for many years of the earlier part of his ministry, employed in Heathen countries. See Gal. i. 17, seqq.

18. πίστει τῇ εἰς ἐμέ.] The older Commentators (misled by the Vulg.) in general construe these words with ἡγιασμένοις. The best of the later Expositors, however, have seen that they must be taken with λαβεῖν. And this is confirmed by the Peschito Syr. Version, so also even Beza and Calvin; whom see. See also Bp. Bull's Examen Censuræ vii. 12. I have removed the comma after ἁμαρτιῶν because (as Bp. Bull has shown) λαβεῖν ἄφεσιν ἁμαρ. and λαβεῖν κλῆρον ἐ. τ. ἡγ. point out the *two* benefits from God through Christ, which denote what is elsewhere called being "justified by faith."

22. οὐδὲν ἐκτὸς — γίνεσθαι.] Constr. λέγων οὐδὲν ἐκτὸς [ἐκείνων] ἃ οἱ προφ. ἐλ. μελλόντων [for μέλλοντα] γίνεσθαι. The μελλόντων is drawn to μέλλοντα by the ὧν. I have, for μαρτυρούμενος, edited μαρτυρόμενος, with many MSS., early Edd., and editors; as also agreeably to the usage of the N. T., in which (as Rinck observes) μαρτυρεῖσθαι has always a *passive*, and μαρτύρεσθαι a *deponent* sense. And so also in the Classical writers, as Thucyd. vi. 80.

23. εἰ παθητὸς, &c.] The Interpreters are agreed, that εἰ is for ὅτι, *nempe quod.* But it may signify "seeing that [supply *by those writings*]." This is confirmed by the sense of παθητὸς, which is best rendered "must suffer." Schleus. acknowledges that it may be rendered "qui pati *debet.*" Ἐξ ἀναστ. νεκρῶν may be rendered either "after the resurrection from the dead," or, "by the resurrection;" but the latter is preferable, and is confirmed by i. 18.

24. μαίνῃ] The more recent Commentators are generally of opinion that this means no more than "Thou art a visionary enthusiast!" of which sense of μαίνεσθαι they adduce several examples from the Classical writers. But the words following, τὰ πολλὰ — περιτρέπει will not admit this sense; and, therefore, the common interpretation, "thou art mad," which is, with reason, defended by Kuin., must be retained. It has always been the common notion, that devoted attention to mental pursuits tends to madness; in illustration of which Wets. and Kypke adduce many passages from the Classical writers, as Lucian Solœc. σὺ δὲ ὑπὸ τῆς ἄγαν παιδείας διέφθορας. Petron. 48. Scimus te præ literis fatuum esse. Εἰς μανίαν περιτρέπει, "is driving thee to madness." These words of Festus seem to have interrupted the thread of the Apostle's reasoning; otherwise he would, probably, have proceeded to allege some particular proofs from the Prophets of what he had said.

27. πιστεύεις — προφήταις; οἶδα ὅτι πιστεύεις. Of this elegant use of the interrogation immediately followed by an answer on the part of the speaker himself, several examples are adduced by Grot.

28 προφήταις; οἶδα ὅτι πιστεύεις. Ὁ δὲ Ἀγρίππας πρὸς τὸν Παῦλον
29 ἔφη· Ἐν ὀλίγῳ με πείθεις Χριστιανὸν γενέσθαι. [g] Ὁ δὲ Παῦλος
εἶπεν· Εὐξαίμην ἂν τῷ Θεῷ, καὶ ἐν ὀλίγῳ καὶ ἐν πολλῷ, οὐ μόνον
σὲ, ἀλλὰ καὶ πάντας τοὺς ἀκούοντάς μου σήμερον γενέσθαι τοιούτους
30 ὁποῖος κἀγώ εἰμι, παρεκτὸς τῶν δεσμῶν τούτων. Καὶ [ταῦτα εἰπόντος
αὐτοῦ,] ἀνέστη ὁ βασιλεὺς, καὶ ὁ ἡγεμὼν, ἥ τε Βερνίκη, καὶ οἱ συγ-
31 καθήμενοι αὐτοῖς. [h] Καὶ ἀναχωρήσαντες ἐλάλουν πρὸς ἀλλήλους, λέγον- h Supra 23. 9. & 25. 25.
τες· Ὅτι οὐδὲν θανάτου ἄξιον ἢ δεσμῶν πράσσει ὁ ἄνθρωπος οὗτος.
32 Ἀγρίππας δὲ τῷ Φήστῳ ἔφη· Ἀπολελύσθαι ἠδύνατο ὁ ἄνθρωπος οὗτος,
εἰ μὴ ἐπεκέκλητο Καίσαρα.
1 XXVII. [i] ὩΣ δὲ ἐκρίθη τοῦ ἀποπλεῖν ἡμᾶς εἰς τὴν Ἰταλίαν, παρε- i Supra 25. 12.
δίδουν τόν τε Παῦλον καί τινας ἑτέρους δεσμώτας ἑκατοντάρχῃ, ὀνόματι
2 Ἰουλίῳ, σπείρης Σεβαστῆς. [k] Ἐπιβάντες δὲ πλοίῳ Ἀδραμυττηνῷ ‡ μέλ- k 2 Cor. 11. 25. supra 19. 29. & 20. 4. Col. 4. 10.
λοντες πλεῖν τοὺς κατὰ τὴν Ἀσίαν τόπους, ἀνήχθημεν, ὄντος σὺν ἡμῖν

and Pricæus, (so Lucian Dial. Meret. Τί φής; ποιήσεις ταῦτα; ποιήσεις, οἶδα,) yet none such as to equal in beauty the present passage. Insomuch that Longinus de Subl., who at § 18. treats of this as a component of *the Sublime*, as he had on another occasion adduced an example of the Sublime from the Mosaic: "Let there be light, and there was light:" so he might have adduced the present passage of St. Paul; especially as in his Frag. 1. Edit. Toupii, he reckons Παῦλος ὁ Ταρσεὺς among the celebrated Grecian orators.

28. ἐν ὀλίγῳ — γενέσθαι] If there be any ellip. at ἐν ὀλίγῳ (which may be doubted), it is διαστήματι or μέτρῳ. See Bos Ellips. p. 172. For the sense here must be "within a little," or *almost*, though the phrase usually signifies "in a short time." Yet *one* example of the other sense is adduced by Grotius from Plato, to which I would add Thucyd. i. 18. But was Agrippa *serious* in what he said? The earlier ones think he *was*, but the later ones generally that he was *not*, and they suppose the words to have been uttered sarcastically. For this last notion, however, there is no ground. Yet I am inclined to think, with Markl., that the words were merely a *civil speech*, pronounced in that complimentary insincerity into which good-natured, easy, and unscrupulous persons, like Agrippa (such as he is characterized by Josephus) are apt to run. Besides, it is unlikely that any strong impression could have been made *so soon*; or that, if made, Agrippa would have *interrupted* the Apostle; and then left him almost as abruptly as Felix had done, or Pilate did our Lord; — without waiting to hear the conclusion of his sentence. This, no doubt, arose from the Apostle's having become (as Markl. observes) more personal in his application to Agrippa concerning religion than he liked.

29. ἐν πολλῷ.] There has been some doubt as to the sense here; but the context determines it to be "*altogether;*" though it would be difficult to find another example of that signification. We may, however, account for it by supposing a paronomasia upon ἐν ὀλίγῳ. And this seizing on the words of another, and giving them a turn in favour of our own cause (which marks an able orator) often requires a slight distortion of the sense of a word or phrase. Παρεκτὸς τ. δ. τ. Spoken δεικτικῶς, holding out his chains. This proves that St. Paul was then *not* (as some imagine) ἐν φυλακῇ ἀδέσμῳ, but was *in custodia militari*, chained to the soldier who guarded him.

30. ταῦτα εἰπόντος αὐτοῦ.] These words are omitted in a few MSS. and Versions, and are cancelled by Griesb. But external evidence is so strongly in favour of the words, that notwithstanding internal is rather against them, they ought not to be cancelled.

32. εἰ μὴ ἐπεκέκλητο K.] For thus the power of the judge, whether for acquittal, or condemnation, had ceased, and the cognizance of the cause rested solely with the superior court.

XXVII. 1. ἐκρίθη] "was determined." Namely, by the decision of Agrippa and Festus, that Paul must be sent to Italy. At τοῦ ἀποπλεῖν there is not, as most suppose, an ellip. of περί; but τοῦ with the *infin.* is here, as supra xxvi. 18. and elsewhere, put for ἵνα and a *subjunctive*; only here the ἵνα is as often for ὅτι.

— παρεδίδουν.] Namely, οἱ δεσμοφύλακες.

— σπείρης Σεβ.] From the time of Augustus Octavianus, legions took the name *Augustan*. Thus in Claudian Bell. ix. 422. mention is made of a *legio Augusta*. Hence many Commentators are of opinion that, as in all the other legions, so in the five cohorts stationed at Cesarea, there was *one* cohort called the Augustan; or that the cohort here mentioned was a legionary cohort of an *Augustan legion* stationed in Syria and Judæa.

2. πλοίῳ Ἀδραμ.] As we say, "a London vessel," a "Liverpool vessel," &c. Adramyttium was in Mysia opposite to Lesbos; whither, it seems, the ship was bound. The Centurion, however, seems to have intended not to remain with the vessel to its place of final destination; but only to some point of Asia Minor, from which he might meet with a convenient passage to Italy, expecting to find some ship in the ports of Lycia or Caria, on board of which he might embark his soldiers and prisoners for Rome. The event answered his expectation: for at Myra in Lycia he found an Alexandrian vessel bound for Italy.

— μέλλοντες.] Several of the best MSS. and Versions have μέλλοντι, which is preferred by Mill, Beng., and Pearce, and edited by Griesb. and Knapp, with the approbation of Kuin., who thinks the change of μέλλοντι into μέλλοντες was made in accommodation to ἐπιβάντες preceding

1 Supra 24. 23. & 28. 16.

Ἀριστάρχου Μακεδόνος Θεσσαλονικέως. [1]τῇ τε ἑτέρᾳ κατήχθημεν εἰς 3
Σιδῶνα· φιλανθρώπως τε ὁ Ἰούλιος τῷ Παύλῳ χρησάμενος, ἐπέτρεψε
πρὸς τοὺς φίλους πορευθέντα ἐπιμελείας τυχεῖν. Κἀκεῖθεν ἀναχθέντες 4
ὑπεπλεύσαμεν τὴν Κύπρον, διὰ τὸ τοὺς ἀνέμους εἶναι ἐναντίους. τό τε 5
πέλαγος τὸ κατὰ τὴν Κιλικίαν καὶ Παμφυλίαν διαπλεύσαντες, κατήλθο-
μεν εἰς Μύρα της Λυκίας. Κἀκεῖ εὑρὼν ὁ ἑκατόνταρχος πλοῖον Ἀλεξ- 6
ανδρῖνον πλέον εἰς τὴν Ἰταλίαν, ἐνεβίβασεν ἡμᾶς εἰς αὐτό. Ἐν ἱκαναῖς 7
δὲ ἡμέραις βραδυπλοοῦντες, καὶ μόλις γενόμενοι κατὰ τὴν Κνίδον, μὴ
προσεῶντος ἡμᾶς τοῦ ἀνέμου, ὑπεπλεύσαμεν τὴν Κρήτην κατὰ Σαλμώ-
νην· μόλις τε παραλεγόμενοι αὐτὴν, ἤλθομεν εἰς τόπον τινὰ καλούμενον 8
Καλοὺς Λιμένας, ᾧ ἐγγὺς ἦν πόλις Λασαία. Ἱκανοῦ δὲ χρόνου διαγε- 9
νομένου, καὶ ὄντος ἤδη ἐπισφαλοῦς τοῦ πλοός, διὰ τὸ καὶ τὴν νηστείαν

and ἀνήχθημεν following. That, however, is too hypothetical; and the reading μέλλοντι looks like a mere *emendation*; to improve which others supplied εἰς or ἐπί. The reading of other MSS., μέλλοντος, confirms the common reading; since it is evidently a mere error of the scribes. No change is necessary; for the scope of the words μέλλοντες — τόπους seems to have been, to assign a reason why they went on board this Adramyttian vessel; namely, because they had to coast the [southern] part of Asia; for that is the sense of πλεῖν, &c. Μέλλοντες may very well be rendered intending, or *being bound*, as we say.

3. ἐπιμελείας τυχεῖν] "to receive their kind attention."

4. ὑπεπλεύσαμεν τὴν K. &c.] The Commentators have been not a little perplexed with these words and those at ver. 5. as far as διαπλεύσαντες. And that, chiefly from ignorance of the nautical term ὑποπλεῖν, but partly from inattention to the situation of the places mentioned. Now in sailing from Sidon to the coast of Lycia, it is probable that, had the weather been fair, they would have taken a course to the South of Cyprus, not, however, nearer its shores, except at the S. W. promontory, *Zephyrium*, and thence would have struck across to Rhodes, or the coast of Caria. As, however, we are told, the winds were contrary (viz. though varying, yet all more or less adverse), they changed that course, and ὑπεπλεύσ. τὴν K. Now, for the winds to be *contrary*, they must have been N. or N.E., or N.N.E., or such like. And then the best way to evade their force would be, to sail close under the coast of Cyprus, after having cut across to the promontory of Pedalium so as to reach the bay of *Catium*. That they coasted along *Palestine*, and then made for the *Eastern* promontory of Cyprus (as the best Commentators think), is improbable, because they would thus be brought more into the wind's eye (as the sailors say), and into tempestuous seas. At all events, it is plain that ὑποπλεῖν must mean *to sail under the lee of any high land* (such as is Cyprus), so as to get shelter from it. From Zephyrium it is plain they crossed over (διεπλεύσαντο) to Myra in Lycia; a port of great celebrity, and, (as appears from a passage of Porphyry cited by Wets.) was the one generally used in passing from Cyprus to Lycia or Caria, as also in the passage from Egypt to Lycia.

6. πλοῖον.] Here, as often in the Classical writers, the word donotes a ship of *burden*, as opposed to a ship of *war*. Such, it appears, the Alexandrian corn vessels were; and this was probably one (see v. 38). On these vessels, and the corn trade from Egypt to Italy, see Hasæus de navibus Alexandrinis, Crit. Sac., vol. xiii. p. 717, and Bryant's remarks on Euroclydon, in his Analysis of Myth., vol. iii. p. 343—9. Myra is indeed out of the track to Dicæarchia in Italy; but the winds had been contrary, and the ship had made for the Lycian coast for shelter.

7. μὴ προσεῶντος ἡμᾶς τοῦ ἀνέμου.] Προσεῶντος presents some difficulty, to remove which Markl. would read πρόσω ἰῶντος. But that is unnecessary; for the common reading may have the very same sense, πρὸς in composition being often used for πρόσω. See the passages of Soph., Eurip., and Diod., cited by me in Recens. Synop. Thus the sense is, "not letting us make any progress." I have, however, sometimes thought that the true reading might be προσωθοῦντος. So Hor. Od. iv. 12, 3. *Impellunt animæ* lintea Thraciæ. Ὑπεπλεύσαμεν. The sense is, "we ran under," i. e. made for Crete, at Salmone, and coasted along the island. This they did, thinking they should get more into the wind.

8. παραλεγόμενοι] "doubling it." The wind might be adverse; and doubling promontories was to the ancients a long and difficult affair; and usually effected (as we may infer from the term here employed) by *towing*.

— ἦν πόλις Λασαία.] Of this we find no mention in the Classical writers. Hence the Commentators either resort to conjectures, or suppose this one of the towns of the *hundred-citied isle* not mentioned by the geographers or other writers. This, however, is *cutting the knot*. I rather suspect that *Lasos* is meant, which occurs in Pliny's list of the *inland* towns; and Lasæa was, it is plain, such. The difference is trifling; since πόλις Λασαία means the city of Lasos. And this is confirmed by Hesych. Λασίων πόλις, ἢ χωρίον. where read Λασαίων. The situation of Fair-Havens is, by the modern term being discovered, fixed to a place a little to the N.E. of Cape Leon, the present C. Matala. Lasæa is supposed to be on the brow of the hills which rise about 4 miles from the shore.

9. διὰ τὸ τὴν νηστείαν ἤδη παρελ.] It is strange that νηστείαν should have so perplexed Markl., as to have led him to suppose it corrupt, and to propound various emendations, all unnecessary. Bp. Middl. notices the absurdity of Markland's reasoning, without being aware that it was borrowed at second hand from *Erasm.* and *Casaub.* The

10 ἤδη παρεληλυθέναι, παρῄνει ὁ Παῦλος λέγων αὐτοῖς· Ἄνδρες, θεωρῶ
ὅτι μετὰ ὕβρεως καὶ πολλῆς ζημίας οὐ μόνον τοῦ φόρτου καὶ τοῦ
11 πλοίου, ἀλλὰ καὶ τῶν ψυχῶν ἡμῶν μέλλειν ἔσεσθαι τὸν πλοῦν. Ὁ δὲ
ἑκατόνταρχος τῷ κυβερνήτῃ καὶ τῷ ναυκλήρῳ ἐπείθετο μᾶλλον, ἢ τοῖς
12 ὑπὸ τοῦ Παύλου λεγομένοις. Ἀνευθέτου δὲ τοῦ λιμένος ὑπάρχοντος
πρὸς παραχειμασίαν, οἱ πλείους ἔθεντο βουλὴν ἀναχθῆναι κἀκεῖθεν,
εἴπως δύναιντο καταντήσαντες εἰς Φοίνικα παραχειμάσαι, λιμένα τῆς
13 Κρήτης βλέποντα κατὰ Λίβα καὶ κατὰ Χῶρον. Ὑποπνεύσαντος δὲ
Νότου, δόξαντες τῆς προθέσεως κεκρατηκέναι, ἄραντες ἆσσον παρελέ-
14 γοντο τὴν Κρήτην. Μετ᾿ οὐ πολὺ δὲ ἔβαλε κατ᾿ αὐτῆς ἄνεμος τυφω-

true view seems to be that of Chrys. and Œcumen., adopted by Pisc., Beza, Rosenm., Mid., and Kuin., who observe that Luke designates the time, after the manner of the Jews; and means a certain *season of the year*, so called from the *great Fast* which fell at that time; just as we speak of *Christmas*, *Lady-day*, *Michaelmas*, &c., whether we be Protestants or Romanists. And this was usual with the Heathens. So Thucyd. ii. 78. περὶ Ἀρκτούρου ἐπιτολάς· (where see my Note), and Theophr. Ch. Eth. 3. τὴν θάλατταν ἐκ Διονυσίων πλώϊμον εἶναι. The *Article* here is used κατ᾿ ἐξοχήν. So Philo de Vit. Mos. (cited by Loesn.) calls it τὴν λεγομένην νηστείαν, meaning the day of expiation, the great Fast on the tenth of the month Tisri, about the tenth of October, answering to our *old Michaelmas*. Thus, even in our times, the Levantine sailors particularly dread what they call the *Michaelmas flows*.

10. ὕβρεως.] Grot., Wets., Kypke, and Kuin. rightly explain this *injury*; comparing Joseph. Ant. iii. 5. τῶν ὄμβρων ὕβρις. and Antholog. iii. 22, 56. θαλάττης ὕβριν. And so *injuria* in the Latin. Grot. observes that ὕβρις respects the *persons*, ζημία the *goods*; comparing Philo. ζημία χρημάτων.

11. τῷ κυβερνήτῃ καὶ τῷ ναυκλ.] These offices were properly distinct, on the nature and difference of whose duties I have copiously treated in Recens. Synop., adducing a great body of proofs and illustrations from the Classical writers. Suffice it here to say, that the former term denoted the *master*, the latter the *supercargo*. But it was only large merchant ships, like this, that had *both*. The smaller had but *one* person for both offices, who was then called ναύκληρος.

12. πρὸς παραχ.] Put for πρὸς τὸ παραχειμάζειν. The word occurs in Polyb. and Diod.

— εἰς Φοίνικα] "to Phœnix," (not Phœnice); the present port *Sphacia*. From its description (with which I would compare Pausan. v. 25, 2. ἄκραν τετραμμένην ἐπὶ Λιβύης καὶ Νότου) we may, (as Grot. and Schmid. think) infer that the port was formed by two jutting *horns*, which looked to seaward to the S. W. and N. W. respectively.

13. ἄραντες.] The Commentators generally supply ἄγκυραν, which is is often *expressed*, as in several passages cited by Wets. This term, however, may *also* allude to the raising the *masts*, which were usually *lowered* on shore. So in Thucyd. vii. 26. ἄρας ἐκ τῆς Αἰγίνης· where the Schol. supplies τὰ ἱστία. Yet, after all, from the expression ἔβαλε κατ᾿ αὐτῆς just after (on which see Note) it should seem that Luke intended τὴν ναῦν to be supplied; which is confirmed by Thucyd. i. 52. τὰς ναῦς ἄραντες ἀπὸ γῆς. where I have there shown that when ναῦν is expressed or understood, the phrase has respect to what we call *heaving* ship, or leaving a port where she had been drawn on shore.

— ἆσσον.] With this word the Commentators have been not a little perplexed. I have in Recens. Synop. fully proved that there is no need to resort to *conjectures*. The word is used by the best writers, not only poets, but prose writers; as Herodot. iv. 3; vii. 233. Joseph. Ant. i. 20, 1; xix. 2, 4. Hippocrates, Plutarch, &c. It signifies, not *nearer*, but *very near*, and here answers to our nautical term *in shore*, and (as sailors say) *to near* the shore. Thus the phrase ἆσσον παραλέγεσθαι signifies to *coast along close inshore*. The mariners were probably proceeding partly by their *oars* (for the wind was only a *side* wind, and of little use), and partly by being *towed*, which was called ῥυμουλκεῖσθαι, and has been copiously illustrated by me on Thucyd. iv. 25.

14. αὐτῆς.] It is not agreed to what this has reference. Some suppose to προθέσεως, others to πρώρας. But it is *better* (with most eminent Commentators) to refer it to Κρήτην. Yet that yields a frigid and inept sense. I would take it to mean the *ship itself*, with reference to ναῦν just before left to be supplied at ἄραντες. This is confirmed, and the force of ἔβαλε (which is wrongly rendered by Toup *disconcerted*) is illustrated by Pind. Pyth. xi. 60–62. Ὀρθὰν κέλευθον ἰὼν τὸ πρὶν ἤ μέ τις ἄνεμος ἔξω πλόου Ἔβαλεν, ὡς ὅτ᾿ ἄκατον εἰναλίαν.

— ἄνεμος τυφωνικὸς] i. e. a wind like a τυφών· the name then, and to the present day, given to a tempestuous wind prevailing in the Mediterranean, and blowing a sort of *hurricane*, in all directions from N. E. to S. E.; and perhaps meant by Homer Odyss. ε. 313. and Virg. Æn. i. 103–12. The word is, I think, wrongly derived by the Etymologists from τύφω, *fumo*; it rather comes from τύφω, cognate with τύπω and τύπτω, and properly signifies *the Striker*; which is confirmed and illustrated by Æschyl. Agam. 637. Blomf. Ναῦς γὰρ πρὸς ἀλλήλαισι Θρῄκιαι πνοαὶ Ἤρεικον· αἱ δὲ, κεροτυπούμεναι βίᾳ Χειμῶνι τυφῶ, σὺν ζάλῃ τ᾿ ὀμβροκτύπῳ, Ὤιχοντ᾿ ἄφαντοι, ποιμένος κακοῦ στρόβῳ.

It remains, however, to discuss the yet more difficult term Εὐροκλύδων, which has so perplexed Commentators and Critics, that they have anxiously sought a change of reading, either from MSS. or from the conjectures of the learned. Various objections have been made to the common reading; but of no great weight. As to the *chief* objection, the *incongruity of the compound*, — κλύδων may signify not only *a wave*, but a *rough wavy sea* (see the examples in Steph. Thes.); and must have been sometimes used as an *adjective* (which indeed, I suspect, was its *original form*),

νικός, ὁ καλούμενος ‡ Εὐροκλύδων. συναρπασθέντος δὲ τοῦ πλοίου, καὶ 15
μὴ δυναμένου ἀντοφθαλμεῖν τῷ ἀνέμῳ, ἐπιδόντες ἐφερόμεθα. Νησίον 16
δέ τι ὑποδραμόντες καλούμενον Κλαύδην, μόλις ἰσχύσαμεν περικρατεῖς
γενέσθαι τῆς σκάφης· ἣν ἄραντες, βοηθείαις ἐχρῶντο ὑποζωννύντες τὸ 17

as appears from the adjective 'Ερικλύδων, which is used by a later Greek writer ap. Steph. Thes. Of the conjectures which have been proposed, the only ones that merit attention are Εὐρυκλύδων and Εὐρακύλων. For the *former* (which has been propounded by Toup, Ernesti, Bryant, and Kuin.) there is no authority at all. Besides, the compound would be contrary to analogy; since there is no instance of εὐρυ with a *substantive;* and even those with *adjectives* are almost confined to the Poets; and moreover, the sense arising *(wide-wavy)* is too feeble. For the *latter*, (namely Εὐρακύλων, N. N. E. wind) which has been proposed by Grot., Mill, Le Clerc, Bentley, and Beng., there is *some*, though but very *slender*, authority in MSS. and Versions: while the objections against it are,—1. that it would not be formed analogically, but ought to be Εὐροακύλων. 2. That it would be heterogeneously compounded of *Greek* and *Latin.* And ἀκύλων could not well represent *aquilo.* Besides, the name was doubtless the same that had prevailed for centuries;—and was therefore not likely to be otherwise than *Greek throughout,* not Greek and Latin. 3. It would not at all correspond to the accurate descriptions of the τυφῶν, or *Tuffone,* given by ancients and moderns; who agree in representing it not as a *point-wind,*—but as shifting about, in all quarters from N. E. to S. E., *East prevailing.* Hence it is clear that both external and internal evidence unite in requiring the common reading to be retained; the sense of which may be thus expressed: "the wave-stirring Easter," or, literally, "*East-souser;*" which designation is confirmed and illustrated by the numerous passages of the Greek and Latin Classical writers adduced by me (chiefly from Wets.) in Recens. Synop.

15. συναρπασθέντος τοῦ πλοίου.] An expression often used of tempestuous winds; as is proved by the examples adduced by the Commentators: to which may be added Æschyl. Agam. 610. χεῖμα —ἥρπασε (scil. αὐτόν.) 'Αντοφθαλμεῖν, to bear up against the wind; *face* it. At ἐπιδόντες there is an ellip., either of πλοῖον, as many Commentators suppose; or, rather, of ἑαυτούς; which latter is confirmed by Lucian cited by Elsn.: ἐπιτρέψαντες οὖν τῷ πνεύματι, καὶ παραδόντες αὐτοὺς ἐχειμαζόμεθα. and Arrian. Epict. iv. 9. οἱ ἅπαξ ἐνδόντες εἰσάπαν ἐπέδωκαν ἑαυτοὺς, καὶ ὡς ὑπὸ ῥεύματος παρεσύρησαν. The sense of ἐφερόμεθα is "we were driven or drifted."

16. ὑποδραμόντες.] Not "running up to," but "running under;" i. e. close under shore. So Themist. p. 152, cited by Wets.: τὰ μὲν *(partly)* ὑποδραμοῦσαι, τὰ δὲ περιδραμοῦσαι.

—Κλαύδην.] The name given by Mela and Pliny countenances the reading Καύδην found in some Versions, &c. But the common reading is confirmed by Hierocl. ap. Ptolom. iii. 7. and Athenæus. Περικρατεῖς εἶναι, for περικρατεῖν, "to become masters of," "secure the boat;" which, it seems, whether it had been towed by a rope, or had hung fastened to the ship, or been on deck, had been washed away by the waves.

17. βοηθ. ἐχρῶντο, ὑποζ. τ. π.] This passage has occasioned no little perplexity to the Commentators, who are not agreed on the sense of βοηθ. and ὑποζ. Some take βοηθ. of the *aid* or *united help* of the mariners and the soldiers, or other passengers. But thus the sense would be very imperfectly expressed. Others take it of the *tackling*, ropes, hooks, chains, &c. by which assistance is rendered to a ship in rough weather. No *proof*, however, of this signification has been adduced. As to ὑποζ., *both* the above classes of Interpreters are agreed, that it must be taken of that *undergirding*, which, they say, was employed by the *ancients* as well as the moderns; whereby thick cables were drawn round a rickety ship, to keep the timbers tight together. In proof and illustration of this the Commentators adduce a great number of passages from the Classical writers. But, upon close examination, it will appear (as I have in some measure shown in Recens. Synop.) that scarcely any one of these is to the purpose; for the *sine funibus Vix durare carinæ* Possint imperiosius Æquor, of Horace, Od. i. 14. is uncertain; as may be imagined, since no Commentator, except Baxter, takes it to refer to the ungirding of a ship with ropes. And although in Hesych., in voc. ζωμεύματα, we have the gloss σχοινία κατὰ μέσον τὴν ναῦν δεσμευόμενα; yet that is known to refer to Aristoph. Eq. 279; and is only the opinion of a *Grammarian* on the sense of the word there; which is better explained by the *Scholiasts*, by *Suidas*, and even by another gloss of Hesych. himself, to mean ὑποζώματα· ξύλα τῶν νεῶν, which is far more agreeable to the context and the subject. And this is confirmed by the Schol. on Thucyd. i. 29. ζεύξαντες (ναῦς), where he speaks of these ξύλα (calling them ζυγώματα), as *stays* necessary to bind together a rickety ship's hull. And so Theogn. Adm. 513. νηός τοι πλευρῇσιν ὑπὸ ζυγὰ θήσομεν; i. e. ὑποθήσομεν ζυγά. In fact, *all* the passages that have been adduced in proof or illustration of the above *undergirding* belong to that operation, which is alluded to in the passages just cited, and which may be called *under* (or inner) *belting.* The passages, indeed, of *Appian*, are not quite decisive: but they are far better interpreted of *inner-belting* than *undergirding*, because the subject is *refitting for the purpose of war.* The passage of Polyb. admits of no other sense. Those of Plato, which are mere *allusions*, are far *better* so understood, because the term ὑποζώματα is employed. And however the ancients might sometimes apply their cables in the above way, yet they would scarcely have cables *made* for the purpose. The passage of Athen. p. 204, however, is quite decisive, where he says that the gigantic ship of Ptolemy Philopator had twelve ὑποζώματα, each 100 feet long. So also in the passage of *Plutarch*, which I have myself adduced in Rec. Syn., there is mention of these ὑποζώματα, which are said to be of *brass.* From what I have written on the passage of Thucyd. there can be no doubt but that the ζυγώματα, or ὑποζώματα, were pieces of strong *planking* to serve as *stays*, to bind the inner frame-work of a ship together; and were sometimes, in the case of an exceedingly large ship, put in at *first*, but usually after the ship had been some time in service, and had grown rickety. So Galen uses the term metaphorically, to denote

πλοῖον· φοβούμενοί τε μὴ εἰς τὴν Σύρτιν ἐκπέσωσι, χαλάσαντες τὸ
18 σκεῦος, οὕτως ἐφέροντο. Σφοδρῶς δὲ χειμαζομένων ἡμῶν, τῇ ἑξῆς ἐκ-
19 βολὴν ἐποιοῦντο· καὶ τῇ τρίτῃ αὐτόχειρες τὴν σκευὴν τοῦ πλοίου
20 ἐῤῥίψαμεν· μήτε δὲ ἡλίου μήτε ἄστρων ἐπιφαινόντων ἐπὶ πλείονας
ἡμέρας, χειμῶνός τε οὐκ ὀλίγου ἐπικειμένου, λοιπὸν περιῃρεῖτο πᾶσα
21 ἐλπὶς τοῦ σώζεσθαι ἡμᾶς. Πολλῆς δὲ ἀσιτίας ὑπαρχούσης, τότε σταθεὶς ὁ Παῦλος ἐν μέσῳ αὐτῶν εἶπεν· Ἔδει μὲν, ὦ ἄνδρες, πειθαρ-
χήσαντάς μοι μὴ ἀνάγεσθαι ἀπὸ τῆς Κρήτης, κερδῆσαί τε τὴν ὕβριν
22 ταύτην καὶ τὴν ζημίαν. Καὶ τανῦν παραινῶ ὑμᾶς εὐθυμεῖν· ἀποβολὴ
23 γὰρ ψυχῆς οὐδεμία ἔσται ἐξ ὑμῶν, πλὴν τοῦ πλοίου. Παρέστη γάρ
24 μοι τῇ νυκτὶ ταύτῃ ἄγγελος τοῦ Θεοῦ, οὗ εἰμὶ, ᾧ καὶ λατρεύω, λέγων·
Μὴ φοβοῦ, Παῦλε, Καίσαρί σε δεῖ παραστῆναι· καὶ ἰδοὺ, κεχάρισταί

the *midriff*, or *diaphragm*, which is the *inner belting* of the *human body*.

Another argument for the interpretation I propose, is this, — that, according to the *other* interpretation, βοηθείαις ἐχρῶντο, which occupies the most prominent place in the sentence, would be almost useless. At least we should expect ὑπεζώννυντο τὸ πλοῖον, βοηθείαις χρώμενοι. But to advert to βοηθείαις, in whichever of the two ways above detailed, the word be taken, it will be little suitable. I have no doubt but that the true sense is that, in which (as Wets. attests) it is used in the Greek writers on mechanics, namely, *props* or *stays*, viz. the ζυγὰ or ζυγώματα above mentioned. Thus the sense is, "they had recourse to props and *stays*, undergirding the ship [with them]." Those had been, no doubt, provided for any emergency; and there is reason to think that, in the largest class of merchant ships, *carpenters* were regularly employed. This was certainly the case in ships of *war*; for Xenoph. de Republ. Athen. 12, enumerating the various officers on board a trireme, reckons the ναυπηγοί.

— τὴν Σύρτιν] i. e. the Syrtis *major* on the coast of Africa, estimated at 4000 or 5000 stadia in circumference, and occupying the whole of what is now called the Gulf of Sidra.

— χαλάσαντες τὸ σκεῦος.] On what is meant by τὸ σκεῦος, the Commentators are not agreed. Some say the *sails*. But I have in Rec. Synop. shown that this sense cannot be admitted. Others take it to mean "*the anchor*," which was certainly *part* of the σκεύη. Yet the sailors were not in *soundings*; and if they had been, they would have let down *two* anchors, as v. 29. If we consider what *other* ὅπλον may deserve to be called *the* σκεῦος, we cannot doubt but that it must be the *mast*. And this signification is confirmed by the Syr. Ver. and adopted by Grot., Heraldus, Bolten, and Kuin. Χαλᾷν is used because the masts of the ancients were so formed as to go into a *socket*, and be raised or lowered at pleasure. The sense seems to be, that they lowered both masts and every sort of tackling which carried any canvass. If this be not admitted, we may, I think, suppose, that σκεῦος denotes the sail-yard at the poop, called ὁ ἀρτέμων at v. 40.

18. ἐκβολὴν ἐποιοῦντο] "heaved overboard," [the lading]; for of *that* the ἐκβολὴ, when used without any addition, is to be understood; since the order of the circumstances (as Grot. rightly observes) is, first, that the *lading* should be thrown overboard, as here; then the *tackling*, v. 19.; and lastly, the *provisions*, as v. 38. From the Classical citations of Wets. it appears that this ἐκβολὴ was not very unfrequent in ancient navigation: and, in violent storms, *necessary*, as the Classical citations of Wets. and Pric. prove; to which may be added, Jonas i. 5. ἐκβολὴν ἐποιήσαντο τῶν σκευῶν. Æschyl. Agam. 978. καὶ τὸ μὲν πρὸ χρημάτων κτησίων ὄκνος βαλὼν, Σφενδόνας ἀπ' εὐμέτρου, Οὐκ ἔδυ πρόπας δόμος. where for δόμος I would read γόμος. See also Theb. 767—9.

19. τὴν σκευήν.] Synonymous with the σκεύη at Jonas i. 5. and signifying all the *armamenta* navis, otherwise called ὅπλα, as masts and yards, sails, ropes, &c. (see Thucyd. vii. 24.), including the *luggage* of the passengers; for σκευὴ has sometimes that sense.

20. μήτε δὲ ἡλίου — ἡμᾶς.] This non-appearance of the sun and stars was to the ancients at all times perplexing, especially in tempestuous weather. Under such circumstances they were reduced to the utmost straits — not so much by want of practical skill in navigation, as by being destitute of what Lord Byron finely calls "The *feeling* Compass — Navigation's soul."

— χειμ. ἐπικειμένου.] Ἐπικ. is a very significant term; and Wets. cites an example of χειμῶνος ἐπικειμένου from Plato; and Wolf compares the Virgilian "tempestas *incubuit* silvis." See also Ps. lxxxviii. 7.

21. ἀσιτίας.] This is best rendered *inedia* a neglect of food, for which they could not, in their present state, have either appetite or relish. See Ps. cii. 4.

— κερδῆσαι — ὕβριν καὶ ζημίαν.] To explain this seemingly strange expression, we need not, with many of the older Commentators, extend the μὴ to κερδῆσαι, and render κερδ. *suffer*; but we may have recourse to a sense of κερδ. found in the best writers, on which I have fully treated in Recens. Synop. and on Thucyd. ii. 44. where I have shown that the literal sense is, "But it behoved you to have hearkened to me, and not to have loosed from Crete: and thus you would have been *gainers by* all this disgrace, (i. e. frustration) and this loss."

23. οὗ] scil. δοῦλος; as Exod. xxxii. 26. Who is the Lord's? and Levit. xx. 26. So also in Is. xlv. 14. where the LXX. render ולך יהיו by καὶ σοὶ ἔσονται δοῦλοι. Λατρεύω, as Kypke observes, implies *strenuous* and *active* service.

24. κεχάρισταί σοι — σοῦ.] Χαρίζεσθαί τινα or τινι sometimes signifies "to grant any one's life for

σοι ὁ Θεὸς πάντας τοὺς πλέοντας μετὰ σοῦ. Διὸ εὐθυμεῖτε, ἄνδρες· 25
πιστεύω γὰρ τῷ Θεῷ, ὅτι οὕτως ἔσται καθ᾽ ὃν τρόπον λελάληταί μοι.
m Infra 28. 1. [m] εἰς νῆσον δέ τινα δεῖ ἡμᾶς ἐκπεσεῖν. Ὡς δὲ τεσσαρεσκαιδεκάτη νὺξ 26
ἐγένετο, διαφερομένων ἡμῶν ἐν τῷ Ἀδρίᾳ, κατὰ μέσον τῆς νυκτὸς ὑπε- 27
νόουν οἱ ναῦται προσάγειν τινὰ αὐτοῖς χώραν. Καὶ βολίσαντες εὗρον 28
ὀργυιὰς εἴκοσι· βραχὺ δὲ διαστήσαντες, καὶ πάλιν βολίσαντες, εὗρον
ὀργυιὰς δεκαπέντε· φοβούμενοί τε μήπως εἰς τραχεῖς τόπους ἐκπέσωμεν, 29
ἐκ πρύμνης ῥίψαντες ἀγκύρας τέσσαρας, ηὔχοντο ἡμέραν γενέσθαι.
Τῶν δὲ ναυτῶν ζητούντων φυγεῖν ἐκ τοῦ πλοίου, καὶ χαλασάντων τὴν 30
σκάφην εἰς τὴν θάλασσαν, προφάσει ὡς ἐκ πρώρας μελλόντων ἀγκύρας
ἐκτείνειν, εἶπεν ὁ Παῦλος τῷ ἑκατοντάρχῃ καὶ τοῖς στρατιώταις· Ἐὰν 31
μὴ οὗτοι μείνωσιν ἐν τῷ πλοίῳ, ὑμεῖς σωθῆναι οὐ δύνασθε. Τότε οἱ 32
στρατιῶται ἀπέκοψαν τὰ σχοινία τῆς σκάφης, καὶ εἴασαν αὐτὴν ἐκπεσεῖν. Ἄχρι δὲ οὗ ἔμελλεν ἡμέρα γίνεσθαι, παρεκάλει ὁ Παῦλος ἅπαν- 33
τας μεταλαβεῖν τροφῆς, λέγων· Τεσσαρεσκαιδεκάτην σήμερον ἡμέραν
n Matt. 10. 30. Luke 12. 7. & 21. 18. προσδοκῶντες, ἄσιτοι διατελεῖτε, μηδὲν προσλαβόμενοι. [n] Διὸ παρακαλῶ 34
ὑμᾶς προσλαβεῖν τροφῆς· τοῦτο γὰρ πρὸς τῆς ὑμετέρας σωτηρίας
o 1 Sam. 9. 13. John 6. 11. 1 Tim. 4. 3. ὑπάρχει· οὐδενὸς γὰρ ὑμῶν θρὶξ ἐκ τῆς κεφαλῆς πεσεῖται. [o] Εἰπὼν 35
δὲ ταῦτα, καὶ λαβὼν ἄρτον, εὐχαρίστησε τῷ Θεῷ ἐνώπιον πάντων, καὶ
κλάσας ἤρξατο ἐσθίειν. Εὔθυμοι δὲ γενόμενοι πάντες, καὶ αὐτοὶ προσ- 36
p Supra 2. 41. & 7. 14. Rom. 13. 1. 1 Pet. 3. 20. ελάβοντο τροφῆς· [p] ἦμεν δὲ ἐν τῷ πλοίῳ αἱ πᾶσαι ψυχαὶ διακόσιαι 37
ἑβδομήκοντα ἕξ. Κορεσθέντες δὲ τροφῆς, ἐκούφιζον τὸ πλοῖον ἐκβαλ- 38
λόμενοι τὸν σῖτον εἰς τὴν θάλασσαν. Ὅτε δὲ ἡμέρα ἐγένετο, τὴν γῆν 39

another;" and examples are adduced by the Commentators. Here, however, it means, to spare any one's life on account of another.

27. *τεσσαρεσκ.*] Namely, from their having left Fair-havens. *Διαφερ. ἡμῶν*, "as we were tossed up and down." The sense is almost confined to the later writers.

—*Ἀδρίᾳ.*] By this is meant not what is now called the Adriatic gulf, but the Adriatic *sea*, which, as the Commentators have proved from Ptolemy, Strabo, &c., comprehended what had originally been called the *Ἰόνιον πέλαγος*, and denoted the sea between Greece, Italy, and Africa. See my Note on Thucyd. i. 24. *τὸν Ἰόνιον κόλπον.*

—*προσάγειν τινὰ αὐτοῖς χώραν.*] There is here a *nautical hypallage*, like *ἀναφανέντες τὴν* K. at xxi. 3. in either case originating in the optical deception, by which, on approaching a coast, the land seems to approach to the ship, not the ship to the land. Of this examples are adduced by the Commentators from both Greek and Latin writers. Nay, our own seamen have the same idiom, when they speak of *nearing* a coast, and *fetching* a port.

28. *ὀργυιάς.*] The word comes from *ὀρέγεσθαι*, and denotes the space that a man may compass by stretching out his arms to the farthest.

29. *τραχεῖς τόπους*] "rocky ground."

—*ἐκ πρύμνης.*] However unusual it may now be for anchors to be dropped from the *stern* of a ship, yet the passages adduced by Wets. and Pearce show that such was very usual in ancient times: nay, that even in modern times the same custom continues, in the ships plying between Alexandria and Constantinople: also that *four* anchors were thought necessary on occasions of great peril, and *two* ordinarily in a tempestuous night. *Ηὔχ. ἡμ. γεν.* This has the air of a proverbial expression, of which Wets. cites two examples from Longus, signifying "to anxiously wish for day."

30. At *μελλόντων* sub. *αὐτῶν*; an ellip. usual when the participle is accompanied with an *ὡς*.

31. *οὐ δύνασθε*] i. e. humanly speaking. For the promise of safety was conditional, and involved the obligation to use the ordinary means for preservation: to neglect which would have been tempting God. See Calvin.

33. *προσδοκῶντες.*] Namely, for the storm to cease. *Ἄσιτοι διατελεῖτε.* A popular form of speaking, which denotes "ye have taken little or no food," no regular meal. Examples are adduced by Kypke from Josephus.

34. *τροφῆς.*] Sub. *τι.* *Τοῦτο γὰρ*, &c. "this will be promotive of your safety." A sense of *πρὸς* frequent in the best writers, especially Thucyd. *Οὐδενὸς γὰρ*, &c. "little or nothing." An oriental and proverbial phrase, on which see Note at Matt. x. 30. and Luke xxi. 18.

37. The number 286 may seem large; but the Alexandrian vessels were very bulky, and fitted out for carrying a great number of passengers. Thus Joseph. in Vit. C. 3. (cited by Pearce) says the ship in which he sailed, and which was cast away in the Adriatic sea, had 600 persons on board.

38. *τὸν σῖτον.*] The best Commentators are agreed that this must signify the *provisions*, which

οὐκ ἐπεγίνωσκον· κόλπον δέ τινα κατενόουν ἔχοντα αἰγιαλὸν, εἰς ὃν
40 ἐβουλεύσαντο, εἰ δύναιντο, ἐξῶσαι τὸ πλοῖον. Καὶ τὰς ἀγκύρας περιελόντες εἴων εἰς τὴν θάλασσαν, ἅμα ἀνέντες τὰς ζευκτηρίας τῶν πηδα-
λίων· καὶ ἐπάραντες τὸν ἀρτέμονα τῇ πνεούσῃ κατεῖχον εἰς τὸν
41 αἰγιαλόν. [q] Περιπεσόντες δὲ εἰς τόπον διθάλασσον, ἐπώκειλαν τὴν [q] 2 Cor. 11. 25.
ναῦν. καὶ ἡ μὲν πρῷρα ἐρείσασα ἔμεινεν ἀσάλευτος, ἡ δὲ πρύμνα
42 ἐλύετο ὑπὸ τῆς βίας τῶν κυμάτων. Τῶν δὲ στρατιωτῶν βουλὴ ἐγένετο,
43 ἵνα τοὺς δεσμώτας ἀποκτείνωσι, μήτις ἐκκολυμβήσας διαφύγοι. Ὁ δὲ
ἑκατόνταρχος, βουλόμενος διασῶσαι τὸν Παῦλον, ἐκώλυσεν αὐτοὺς τοῦ
βουλήματος, ἐκέλευσέ τε τοὺς δυναμένους κολυμβᾷν, ἀποῤῥίψαντας πρώ-
44 τους ἐπὶ τὴν γῆν ἐξιέναι, καὶ τοὺς λοιποὺς, οὓς μὲν ἐπὶ σανίσιν, οὓς
δὲ ἐπί τινων τῶν ἀπὸ τοῦ πλοίου· καὶ οὕτως ἐγένετο πάντας διασω-
θῆναι ἐπὶ τὴν γῆν.

would be reserved till the last, the *lading* and *tackling* being before thrown overboard.

39. τὴν γῆν οὐκ ἐπεγ.] A brief mode of expression, denoting "they took a view of the country; but recognised it not." Κόλπον — ἔχοντα αἰγιαλόν. As all inlets have *shores*, Schmid. and Kuin. construe the words thus: κατενόουν αἰγιαλὸν ἔχοντα κόλπον τινὰ, "they perceived a shore having a certain creek." This, however, is doing violence to the construction. We must retain the natural one, and take αἰγ., with Grot., Matth., and Schleus., in a *popular* sense, to denote a *practicable* shore. And indeed the passages cited by those Commentators prove that αἰγιαλὸς signifies properly a *sandy* shore (as opposed to a rocky one) and consequently one convenient for landing. Κόλπος is taken in a sense which Theophyl. says is usual in the *common* dialect, viz. an *inlet*. This is on the N.W. side of the island, and now called La Cala di San Paolo. Ἐξῶσαι τὸ πλοῖον, "to strand the vessel." On this sense of ἐξωθεῖν see my Note on Thucyd. ii. 90.

40. περιελόντες.] This cannot mean, as several Commentators imagine, "having taken up the anchors;" for that sense would require ἀνελόντες, or ἀνελόμενοι; neither, as they were without boats, could they *weigh* the anchors; but the sense must be (as the best Interpreters, ancient and modern, are agreed) "removed the anchors," viz. by cutting the ropes and leaving them in the sea. And εἴων must (with De Dieu, Wets., Pearce, Markl., Schleus., Heinr., and Kuin.) be referred to the *anchors*, not to the *vessel*; still less to *themselves*.

— ἀνέντες τὰς ζευκτ. τῶν πηδ.] "having loosened the bands of the rudders." So Eurip. Hel. 1536. speaks of the rudder as fastened ζεύγλαισι. Some Commentators are not a little perplexed with the circumstance of *two* rudders being spoken of to one ship. But Grot., Bochart, Elsn., Scheffer, Lips, and Perizon. have proved, that among the ancients large ships of burden had *two rudders*. To the passages cited by them in proof I have in Recens. Synop. added a passage, yet more apposite than any, from Orpheus in Argonaut. 274. Καὶ οἱ ἐπ' ἄρτια θῆκαν ἀρηρότα τορεύοντες, Ἱστόν τ' ἠδ' ὀθόνας· ἐπὶ δ' αὐτ' οἤηκας ἔδησαν, Πρυμνόθεν ἀρτήσαντες, ἐπεσφίγξαντο δ' ἱμᾶσιν. From which passage it appears probable that the rudders were regularly taken off when the ship was in port, and were laid up in the docks. But the question is, *how* and *where* were they fixed on? Many (as Alberti, Bp. Pearce, and Kuin.) think that the rudders were one at the stern, and the other at the bow of the ship; while others suppose both to have been at the stern. I know not, however, of the numerous passages cited by the above Commentators, any one that *determines* this point; but that which I have adduced from Orpheus undoubtedly *does*: yet it decides the *contrary way*, namely, that they were both at the πρυμνή.

— ἐπάραντες τὸν ἀρτέμονα τῇ πν.] The term ἀρτέμων, it rarely occurs, is almost unnoticed by the ancients, and hence its sense is disputed. Luther took it to mean the *mast*; and Erasmus the *sail yard*: interpretations devoid alike of proof and probability. Bayf., Jun., Alberti, and Wolf, with more probability, explain it the *large sail of the poop*, answering to our *mizen sail*, and even yet called by the Venetians *artemon*. The best founded opinion, however, seems to be that of Grot., Voss, Heum., Wets., Mich., Rosenm., and Kuin., who understand by it a small sail near the prow, called by Pollux the *dolon*, which was used to keep the ship steady, and to prevent its working too much, when the larger and upper sails were set. See the passages of Papius and Juvenal Sat. xii. 68. cited from Wets. in Recens. Synop.

— κατεῖχον] scil. τὴν ναῦν; an ellipsis sometimes *supplied* in Homer and Herodot.

41. περιπεσόντες εἰς τόπον διθ.] Διθάλασσος has not here its usual signification an isthmus which divides seas, but denotes a peninsular promontory. The word, indeed, is usually applied to peninsulas of the largest size; but sometimes also to narrow *spits* of land jutting out into the sea; and sometimes to those *tæniæ*, partly above and partly under water, which guide the currents, and therefore make the place διθάλασσον, and consequently rough. So Clemens; cited by Wets. διθάλασσοι καὶ θηριώδεις τόποι. and Dio Chrys. Orat. v., who, speaking of the Syrtes, says it is surrounded by βράχεα καὶ διθάλαττα καὶ ταινίαι. The *spit* of sand in question was an elongation of a *ness*, represented in Cluverius's Map, and noticed by Dorville in his Sicula.

— ἐρείσασα] "having fixed itself." On this idiom, by which words with an active force, and generally active use, have sometimes a reflective sense, see my Note in Recens. Synop. With ἔμεινεν ἀσάλευτος, Pric. compares Virg. "Illisaque prora pependit."

44. οὓς μὲν — οὓς δὲ] for τοὺς μὲν — τοὺς δέ. On

r Supra 27. 26. XXVIII. [r] ΚΑΙ διασωθέντες, τότε ἐπέγνωσαν ὅτι Μελίτη ἡ νῆσος 1
s Rom. 1. 14. 1 Cor. 14. 11. Col. 3. 11. καλεῖται. [s] Οἱ δὲ βάρβαροι παρεῖχον οὐ τὴν τυχοῦσαν φιλανθρωπίαν 2
ἡμῖν· ἀνάψαντες γὰρ * πυρὰν, προσελάβοντο πάντας ἡμᾶς, διὰ τὸν ὑετὸν
τὸν ἐφεστῶτα, καὶ διὰ τὸ ψύχος. Συστρέψαντος δὲ τοῦ Παύλου φρυγά- 3
νων πλῆθος, καὶ ἐπιθέντος ἐπὶ τὴν πυρὰν, ἔχιδνα ἐκ τῆς θέρμης ἐξελθοῦσα καθῆψε τῆς χειρὸς αὐτοῦ. Ὡς δὲ εἶδον οἱ βάρβαροι κρεμάμενον 4
τὸ θηρίον ἐκ τῆς χειρὸς αὐτοῦ, ἔλεγον πρὸς ἀλλήλους· Πάντως φονεύς
ἐστιν ὁ ἄνθρωπος οὗτος, ὃν διασωθέντα ἐκ τῆς θαλάσσης ἡ δίκη ζῆν
t Mark 16. 18. Luke 10. 19. οὐκ εἴασεν. [t] Ὁ μὲν οὖν ἀποτινάξας τὸ θηρίον εἰς τὸ πῦρ, ἔπαθεν 5
u Supra 14. 11. οὐδὲν κακόν. [u] Οἱ δὲ προσεδόκων αὐτὸν μέλλειν πίμπρασθαι, ἢ κατα- 6
πίπτειν ἄφνω νεκρόν· ἐπὶ πολὺ δὲ αὐτῶν προσδοκώντων, καὶ θεω-

which idiom see Matth. Gr. Gr. Ἐπί τινων τῶν ἀπὸ τ. πλ., "some of the things which came out of the ship," i. e. barrels, boxes, &c.

XXVIII. 1. Μελίτη.] It was an old opinion, strenuously supported in the last century by *De Rhoer*, that this is not the *African* Melita, but *another*, on the coast of Illyricum; and has been of late revived, and ably defended by Mr. Bryant and others. Yet it is, I conceive, untenable, as had long ago been proved by Scaliger, Bochart, Cluv., Cellar., and Wendelin, de Melita Pauli.

2. οἱ δὲ βάρβαροι.] The pride of the Greeks and Romans accounted men of all other nations barbarians. The not being able to speak the languages of those countries involved the charge of *barbarism*; and indeed *that* is by many supposed to be the primitive sense of the word. See the Note on Rom. i. 14. But that is at variance with the *etymon*, rightly referred to an *Oriental* origin; though not from the Arabic *berber, to murmur*, but from the Punic *berber, a shepherd*. Now it was originally appropriated to the indigenous and pastoral inhabitants of Africa; who, to their more civilized fellow-men on the other side of the Mediterranean, appeared *rustics* and barbarians. Hence the term βάρβαρος came at length to mean a *rustic* or *clown*.

— οὐ τὴν τυχ. φιλανθ.] "no common benevolence, or kindness." An elegant *litotes*. Ἀνάψαντες πυράν. The best Commentators are agreed that this signifies "having set fire to a pyre [of wood];" a signification found both in the LXX. and the Classical writers. The common reading "lighting a fire" would require πῦρ. Προσελάβοντο, "took us into their protection and care." Ἐφεστῶτα. Qui *ingruerat*, as Grot. well renders. So Polyb. p. 1053. cited by Wets. ὥστε διὰ τὸν ἐφεστῶτα ζόφον μηδὲ τοὺς ἐν ποσὶ δύνασθαι βλέπειν.

3. συστρέψαντος] "when he had heaped together." There is something *graphic* in the term. Wets. compares Hesych. οἱ γναφεῖς ἀκανθῶν σωρὸν συστρέψαντες. By φρύγανα is meant dry brushwood, fit for fuel. So Xenoph. cited by Wets. φρύγανα συλλέγοντες ὡς ἐπὶ πῦρ.

— ἐκ τῆς θέρμης.] Our common version renders "out of the heat." But the best Interpreters, ancient and modern, are agreed that the sense is "præ calorem," "urged by the heat." For to take θέρμης for πυρὸς would be unprecedented. Καθῆψε is for καθήψατο, by a common Hellenistic idiom. Many eminent Commentators and Critics, indeed, maintain that it is not said the viper *bit* Paul; and that καθήπτετο, even were that *written*, could not have such a sense. I have, however, in Recens. Synop. shown that this position is untenable. Among other passages which I have cited in Cantic. i. 6. καθήπτετό μου ὁ ἥλιος, "laid hold on me" (as we say) tanned my skin. Upon the whole, it is undeniable that καθάπτεσθαι signifies *to lay fast hold of, fasten on*. But this, when used of a serpent, necessarily *implies biting*. As to the argument from the words ἔπαθεν οὐδὲν κακὸν at ver. 5, it is exceedingly weak; for, even in a *Classical* writer, the position of the clause, and the air of the narration, would exclude any such sense as that "the reptile had not hurt Paul." But in a *Hellenistic* writer the *popular* sense, which may be denoted by the words, namely, that "no harm came of it," must be preferred. Besides, such is so evidently the opinion of St. Luke (whom we cannot suppose to have been mistaken) that no other sense than the common one must be thought of. Besides, how, it may be asked, can a serpent *hang* by any part of a man's body (as at ver. 4.) but by his *teeth*?

4. τὸ θηρίον.] The word is used, not of *beasts*, properly so called, but of *serpents*; though it primarily means any *wild* creature; and Galen uses the word *Theriæ* to denote medicines to cure the bite of a serpent.

— φονεύς ἐστι — εἴασεν.] The words are to be taken in their plain and popular sense; and such refinements as those resorted to by Elsn., Heins., and others, are not to be thought of. The people seem to have meant to reason thus: "Die he surely will, and no doubt for some crime worthy of death; and considering that he has been thus rescued from the jaws of a watery grave, and brought here to suffer death, surely he must have been guilty of the greatest of crimes, — murder." From the passages of the Classical writers adduced by Grot., Pric., and Wets., it appears that the ancients thought Divine justice sometimes delivered criminals out of dangers, in order to reserve them for heavier calamities and severer punishments. Οὐκ εἴασεν, "has not suffered to live;" considering him as already dead; which proves that they must have been very sure the serpent had bitten Paul.

6. πίμπρασθαι, ἢ κατ. &c.] Here are accurately represented the *two classes* of symptoms which supervene on the bite of a poisonous serpent, according to the virulence of the poison, and the strength of the body to which it is communicated. The *first* represents the swelling, and *inflammation*, in the beginning local, then general, which brings on a burning fever, that quickly destroys the patient. The *second* is the effect of the *strongest* poison on the *weakest* body.

ϕρούντων μηδὲν ἄτοπον εἰς αὐτὸν γινόμενον, μεταβαλλόμενοι ἔλεγον θεὸν
7 αὐτὸν εἶναι. Ἐν δὲ τοῖς περὶ τὸν τόπον ἐκεῖνον ὑπῆρχε χωρία τῷ
πρώτῳ τῆς νήσου, ὀνόματι Ποπλίῳ, ὃς ἀναδεξάμενος ἡμᾶς τρεῖς ἡμέρας
8 φιλοφρόνως ἐξένισεν. [x] Ἐγένετο δὲ τὸν πατέρα τοῦ Ποπλίου πυρετοῖς x James 5. 14, 15.
καὶ δυσεντερίᾳ συνεχόμενον κατακεῖσθαι· πρὸς ὃν ὁ Παῦλος εἰσελθὼν,
9 καὶ προσευξάμενος, ἐπιθεὶς τὰς χεῖρας αὐτῷ, ἰάσατο αὐτόν. Τούτου
οὖν γενομένου, καὶ οἱ λοιποὶ, οἱ ἔχοντες ἀσθενείας ἐν τῇ νήσῳ, προσ-
10 ήρχοντο καὶ ἐθεραπεύοντο· οἳ καὶ πολλαῖς τιμαῖς ἐτίμησαν ἡμᾶς, καὶ
ἀναγομένοις ἐπέθεντο τὰ πρὸς τὴν χρείαν.
11 Μετὰ δὲ τρεῖς μῆνας ἀνήχθημεν ἐν πλοίῳ παρακεχειμακότι ἐν τῇ
12 νήσῳ, Ἀλεξανδρίνῳ, παρασήμῳ Διοσκούροις· καὶ καταχθέντες εἰς Συ-
13 ρακούσας, ἐπεμείναμεν ἡμέρας τρεῖς· ὅθεν περιελθόντες κατηντήσαμεν
εἰς Ῥήγιον, καὶ μετὰ μίαν ἡμέραν, ἐπιγενομένου νότου, δευτεραῖοι

—*μηδὲν ἄτοπον εἰς αὐτὸν γ.*] This phrase is Hellenistic in its manner, and corresponds to the *ἔπαθεν οὐδὲν κακὸν* just before, and confirms the common interpretation of that expression. Ἄτοπον is not unfrequent in the best writers in the sense *evil*. It here denotes *producing harm to the body*, in which sense it is often used in the best writers, especially the *Medical* ones.

—*θεόν*.] The Commentators are needlessly minute in debating *what* God; for the question is undeterminable; and, after all, the word might be used in that *lower sense* (to denote a *Divine person*) which is occasionally found in the later writers, especially *Philostratus* in his life of Apollonius.

7. *χωρία*] *estates*. See Note on Matt. xxvi. 36. Τῷ πρώτῳ. This *may* be interpreted, with most Commentators, "the *principal person* of the island:" a sense frequent in the N. T. As, however, the term is often found in Inscriptions and Coins, even of *Malta*, used in the sense *Governor*, —Grot., Bochart, and also the best *recent* Commentators are, with reason, of opinion that it signifies the *Prefect of the island;* yet ver. 27. defends the common interpretation.

—*ἀναδεξάμενος — ἐξένισεν*] "taking us to his house, kindly entertained us." Ἀναδ. is used for ὑποδ. Yet one example of this sense is adduced by Wets. from Ælian. Ξενίζειν and φιλ. are usual terms on this subject.

8. *πυρετοῖς — συνεχόμενον*.] There was no necessity for Dr. Owen to have conjectured πυρετῷ, since of the plural in a singular sense examples are adduced by Munthe. as also of *febres* in the Latin from Ammian by Wets. And several might be added from Hippocrates. Perhaps the plural may be used with reference to those *fits*, or paroxysms, by which fever makes its attacks. And possibly the θέρμαι ἰσχυραὶ of Thucyd. ii. 49. may be interpreted on the same principle. Συνέχεσθαι is a *vox sol. de hac re*, on which see Note on Mark i. 30. On οἱ ἔχοντες ἀσθενείας. see Luke xiii. 11. sq.

10. *πολλαῖς τιμαῖς ἐτίμησαν ἡμᾶς*]. Many of the best Commentators are of opinion, that τιμαῖς is here to be taken in a sense frequent in the Classical writers, and not unknown in the Scriptures, to denote *honorary rewards*. So Ecclus. xxxviii. 1. τίμα ἰατρὸν πρὸς τὰς χρείας τιμαῖς αὐτοῦ. 1 Tim. v. 17. οἱ καλῶς προεστῶτες πρεσβύτεροι διπλῆς τιμῆς ἀξιούσθωσαν: the former of which passages was probably in the mind of St. Luke. The sense seems to be "*honorary presents*." Not, however, of *money* (which Paul probably would refuse) but of *necessaries*. The words following seem meant to give an *example* of the *kind* of honorary presents made. Ἐπέθεντο is well explained by Wets., "onerarunt nos, et cumulata ingesserunt, et nec petentibus imposuerunt;" referring to Ruth iii. 15.

11. *παρασήμῳ Διοσκούροις*.] The τὸ παράσημον, or *insigne*, was that from which the ship derived its name. It was a painting or bas-relief on the prow, of some god or hero, or sometimes *animal;* nay, even *inanimate substance*, as *shield*, &c. See Ovid Trist. i. 10, 1., and Virg. Æn. v. 115. seqq. The *poop* bore the picture, or image, called the *tutela*, of some god, under whose protection the ship was supposed to be placed. Both the *tutela* and the *insigne* were of gold (or rather gilded metal), ivory, or other rich material. So Virg. Æn. x. 171. Et aurato fulgebat Apolline puppis. Thus, of the ship mentioned in the above cited passage of Ovid, the *numen tutelare* was *Minerva*, placed on the poop; but the *insigne*, or παράσημον, was a helmet of Minerva painted on the prow: and this *gave name* to the ship. Yet such was not the invariable custom. Sometimes the *tutela* and the παράσημον, were *the same;* as, for instance, whenever (as often happened) the effigies of the Deity himself, to whose protection the ship was committed, supplied the place of an insigne; then the ship was called by the name of that God who was painted or carved on the prow. Thus the Alexandrian ship in which Paul sailed had the *Dioscuri* for an *insigne* as well as a *tutela;* whence, too, it was called Διόσκουροι.

12. *ἐπεμείναμεν ἡμέρας τρεῖς*.] No doubt, in a great measure for commercial purposes.

13. *περιελθόντες*.] Not "fetching a compass," but "coasting about," as most Translators render; with reference, I imagine, to the promontories, especially that of Taurus, to be doubled in coasting the Sicilian shore; for, in the former sense, the term would not be justified by geographical truth; unless, indeed, it were to be understood of taking a course, by reason of a Westerly wind, very much to the East, and so getting to Rhegium by *tacking*. And from the ἐπιγενομένου νότου in the next verse, it is certain that the wind had shifted, and was not the same. But if so, they could not *coast* along Sicily.

—*ἐπιγ. νότου*] "the South wind having arisen."

ἤλθομεν εἰς Ποτιόλους· οὗ εὑρόντες ἀδελφοὺς, παρεκλήθημεν ἐπ' αὐ- 14
τοῖς ἐπιμεῖναι ἡμέρας ἑπτά· καὶ οὕτως εἰς τὴν Ῥώμην ἤλθομεν. Κἀ- 15
κεῖθεν οἱ ἀδελφοὶ ἀκούσαντες τὰ περὶ ἡμῶν, ἐξῆλθον εἰς ἀπάντησιν ἡμῖν
ἄχρις Ἀππίου φόρου καὶ τριῶν ταβερνῶν· οὓς ἰδὼν ὁ Παῦλος, εὐχαριστήσας τῷ Θεῷ, ἔλαβε θάρσος.
y Supra 24. 23. & 27. 3. [y] ὍΤΕ δὲ ἤλθομεν εἰς Ῥώμην, ὁ ἑκατόνταρχος παρέδωκε τοὺς δεσμί- 16
ους τῷ στρατοπεδάρχῃ· τῷ δὲ Παύλῳ ἐπετράπη μένειν καθ' ἑαυτὸν,
z Supra 21. 33. & 24. 12, 13, 14. & 25. 8. σὺν τῷ φυλάσσοντι αὐτὸν στρατιώτῃ. [z] Ἐγένετο δὲ μετὰ ἡμέρας τρεῖς 17
συγκαλέσασθαι τὸν Παῦλον τοὺς ὄντας τῶν Ἰουδαίων πρώτους· συνελ-
θόντων δὲ αὐτῶν, ἔλεγε πρὸς αὐτούς· Ἄνδρες ἀδελφοὶ, ἐγὼ οὐδὲν
ἐναντίον ποιήσας τῷ λαῷ ἢ τοῖς ἔθεσι τοῖς πατρῴοις, δέσμιος ἐξ Ἱερο-
a Supra 22. 24. & 24. 10. & 25. 8. & 26. 31. σολύμων παρεδόθην εἰς τὰς χεῖρας τῶν Ῥωμαίων· [a] οἵτινες ἀνακρίναν- 18
τές με ἐβούλοντο ἀπολῦσαι, διὰ τὸ μηδεμίαν αἰτίαν θανάτου ὑπάρχειν
b Supra 25. 11. ἐν ἐμοί. [b] Ἀντιλεγόντων δὲ τῶν Ἰουδαίων, ἠναγκάσθην ἐπικαλέσασθαι 19
c Supra 23. 6. & 24. 21. & 26. 6, 7, 29. Eph. 6. 20. 2 Tim. 1. 16. Καίσαρα, οὐχ ὡς τοῦ ἔθνους μου ἔχων τι κατηγορῆσαι. [c] Διὰ ταύτην 20
οὖν τὴν αἰτίαν παρεκάλεσα ὑμᾶς ἰδεῖν καὶ προσλαλῆσαι· ἕνεκεν γὰρ
τῆς ἐλπίδος τοῦ Ἰσραὴλ τὴν ἅλυσιν ταύτην περίκειμαι. Οἱ δὲ πρὸς 21
αὐτὸν εἶπον· Ἡμεῖς οὔτε γράμματα περὶ σοῦ ἐδεξάμεθα ἀπὸ τῆς Ἰουδαίας, οὔτε παραγενόμενός τις τῶν ἀδελφῶν ἀπήγγειλεν ἢ ἐλάλησέ τι

Of this idiom examples are given by Wets. and Munthe. On the idiom in δευτεραῖοι, see Note at John xi. 39. They were now in the regular track of vessels from Alexandria to Rome, as Wolf infers from Suet. Vesp. C. 5.

14. παρεκλήθημεν — ἑπτά] "we were entreated to stay seven days." It is probable that they had arrived there on the day after the Lord's day. Hence they were requested to stay the *next* Lord's day over, to give an opportunity to *all* the Christians of hearing Paul's preaching. See Note on Gal. i. 18.

15. ἐκεῖθεν — ἀκούσαντες] "having heard from thence," viz. from Puteoli, either by letter or by message. No doubt there was a constant communication between the two places.

— εἰς ἀπάντ. ἡμῖν ἄχρις Ἀ.] The distance (51 miles) marks the *profound respect* paid to Paul by the Roman Christians.

— τριῶν ταβερνῶν.] These are supposed to have been *inns*, for the refreshment of travellers passing to and from Rome; but they were probably rather *retail shops* for the sale of all sorts of eatables and drinkables. Thus Zosimus ii. 10. calls them the τρία καπηλεῖα: and indeed this was the usual sense of *taberna*, which word Donatus well derives from *Trabena*, such being at first *wooden houses* for *shops only*.

16. παρέδωκε, &c.] It was ordered by law that all those sent as prisoners to Rome should be delivered to the custody of the *Præfectus Prætorii*, and guarded in the Pretorian camp. Here Luke has expressed himself with extreme brevity; but his meaning seems to be this:—"The Centurion delivered his prisoners to the charge of the Prefect [by whom] it was permitted to Paul," &c. Καθ' ἑαυτὸν, i. e. "apart from the other prisoners," who were confined in the *carcer castrensis*. A great favour this; for even those, to whom the *libera custodia*, or φυλακὴ ἄδεσμος was granted, were yet usually confined in a part of the public prison, called the δεσμωτήριον ἐλευθέριον. So in Philostr. V. A. vii. 22. ἐκέλευσε τὸ ἐλευθέριον οἰκεῖν δεσμωτήριον.

— σὺν τῷ φυλ. α. σ.] And, as appears from v. 20., and according to the invariable custom of persons kept in such sort of durance, chained by the hand to the soldier. Nay, from Joseph. p. 814. 7. we find that even King Agrippa, when in confinement at Rome, was chained to a soldier.

17. ποιήσας] "though I had done;" a somewhat unusual sense of the participle. Ἐναντίον must be *accommodated* in sense to the two clauses to which it belongs, namely, "nothing injurious to the Jewish people, or at variance with the customs," &c.

19. οὐχ ὡς — κατηγορῆσαι.] Literally, "not as having aught to accuse my own nation of," i. e. not intending thereby to accuse.

20. ἕνεκεν γάρ.] The γὰρ refers to a clause omitted; q. d. [And I may justly claim to be free from all offence to my nation, nay, even to be *attached* to it] *for*, for the hope of Israel (i. e. the long expected Messiah), &c.

21, 22. The latter of these two verses shows that the former must, in interpretation, be qualified, and the sense contained in both may be thus expressed: "We have neither received any letters from Judæa [containing any bad account of thee] nor have any of the brethren come here and related or spoken aught of evil concerning thee. But we wish to hear from thee what thou thinkest, or hast to say, concerning this Sect [viz. in its justification]; for it has come to our knowledge that it is everywhere spoken of." There is something obscure and indefinite in the wording, which may partly be ascribed to the delicacy of the speakers. They say they have heard no evil of him, because they did not regard his professing Christianity as involving any thing πονηρόν· such rather respecting *actions* than opinions. Ἀξιοῦμεν — φρονεῖς is a delicate way of asking what he has to say in *defence* of Christianity.

22 περὶ σοῦ πονηρόν. [d] Ἀξιοῦμεν δὲ παρὰ σοῦ ἀκοῦσαι ἃ φρονεῖς· περὶ [d] Supra 24. 5, 14.
μὲν γὰρ τῆς αἱρέσεως ταύτης γνωστόν ἐστιν ἡμῖν ὅτι πανταχοῦ ἀντιλέ-
23 γεται. [e] Ταξάμενοι δὲ αὐτῷ ἡμέραν, ἧκον πρὸς αὐτὸν εἰς τὴν ξενίαν [e] Supra 28. 6.
πλείονες· οἷς ἐξετίθετο διαμαρτυρόμενος τὴν βασιλείαν τοῦ Θεοῦ,
πείθων τε αὐτοὺς τὰ περὶ τοῦ Ἰησοῦ, ἀπό τε τοῦ νόμου Μωϋσέως καὶ
24 τῶν προφητῶν, ἀπὸ πρωῒ ἕως ἑσπέρας. [f] Καὶ οἱ μὲν ἐπείθοντο τοῖς [f] Supra 17. 4.
25 λεγομένοις, οἱ δὲ ἠπίστουν. Ἀσύμφωνοι δὲ ὄντες πρὸς ἀλλήλους ἀπε-
λύοντο, εἰπόντος τοῦ Παύλου ῥῆμα ἕν· Ὅτι καλῶς τὸ Πνεῦμα τὸ ἅγιον
26 ἐλάλησε διὰ Ἡσαΐου τοῦ προφήτου πρὸς τοὺς πατέρας ἡμῶν, [g] λέγον· [g] Isa. 6. 9. Ezek. 12. 2.
Πορεύθητι πρὸς τὸν λαὸν τοῦτον καὶ εἰπέ· Ἀκοῇ Matt. 13. 14. Mark 4. 12.
ἀκούσετε, καὶ οὐ μὴ συνῆτε· καὶ βλέποντες βλέψετε, Luke 8. 10. John 12. 40. Rom. 11. 8.
27 καὶ οὐ μὴ ἴδητε. ἐπαχύνθη γὰρ ἡ καρδία τοῦ λαοῦ
τούτου, καὶ τοῖς ὠσὶ βαρέως ἤκουσαν, καὶ τοὺς ὀφθαλμοὺς αὐτῶν ἐκάμμυσαν· μήποτε ἴδωσι τοῖς ὀφθαλμοῖς, καὶ τοῖς ὠσὶν ἀκούσωσι, καὶ τῇ καρδίᾳ συν-
28 ῶσι καὶ ἐπιστρέψωσι, καὶ ἰάσωμαι αὐτούς. [h] Γνωστὸν [h] Supra 13. 46. & 18. 6.
οὖν ἔστω ὑμῖν, ὅτι τοῖς ἔθνεσιν ἀπεστάλη τὸ σωτήριον τοῦ Θεοῦ· Luke 24. 47.
29 αὐτοὶ καὶ ἀκούσονται. Καὶ ταῦτα αὐτοῦ εἰπόντος, ἀπῆλθον οἱ Ἰουδαῖοι, πολλὴν ἔχοντες ἐν ἑαυτοῖς συζήτησιν.
30 ἜΜΕΙΝΕ δὲ ὁ Παῦλος διετίαν ὅλην ἐν ἰδίῳ μισθώματι, καὶ ἀπε-
31 δέχετο πάντας τοὺς εἰσπορευομένους πρὸς αὐτὸν, κηρύσσων τὴν βασιλείαν τοῦ Θεοῦ, καὶ διδάσκων τὰ περὶ τοῦ Κυρίου Ἰησοῦ Χριστοῦ μετὰ
πάσης παῤῥησίας, ἀκωλύτως.

which they probably understood to be alluded to in the words ἕνεκεν τῆς ἐλπίδος τοῦ Ἰσραήλ.

23. ταξάμενοι, &c.] "having appointed," or as the sense rather seems to be, "having agreed with him for;" on which signification of the word, see my Note on Thucyd. i. 99. Ἐξετίθετο διαμ., "he earnestly set forth." See xviii. 26. Πείθων αὐτοὺς τὰ περὶ, &c. Sub. κατά.

26, 27. See Note on Matt. xiii. 14, 15. With this I would compare Soph. Aj. 85. where Minerva says to Ulysses, ἐγὼ σκοτώσω βλέφαρα καὶ δεδορκότα.

END OF THE FIRST VOLUME.

CPSIA information can be obtained
at www.ICGtesting.com
Printed in the USA
LVHW081409090922
727997LV00004B/172

9 781345 197051